CW01459817

THE COMMON LAW LIBRARY

NEGLIGENCE

OTHER VOLUMES IN THE COMMON LAW LIBRARY

THE COMMON LAW LIBRARY

CHARLESWORTH & PERCY
ON
NEGLIGENCE

TWELFTH EDITION

GENERAL EDITOR
CHRISTOPHER WALTON
A Circuit Judge on the North-Eastern Circuit

ASSOCIATE EDITORS

ROGER COOPER, BSc
A Barrister of Plowden Chambers, Newcastle upon Tyne

SIMON E. WOOD, LL.B
A Circuit Judge on the North-Eastern Circuit

STEPHEN TODD, LLM (SHEFF), LLD (CANT)
Of the Inner Temple, Barrister;
Professor of Common Law, University of Nottingham;
Professor of Law, University of Canterbury, New Zealand

SWEET & MAXWELL   **THOMSON REUTERS**

First Edition	(1938)	By J. Charlesworth
Second Edition	(1947)	" "
Third Edition	(1956)	" "
Second Impression	(1959)	" "
Fourth Edition	(1962)	By R.A. Percy
Fifth Edition	(1971)	" "
Sixth Edition	(1977)	" "
Seventh Edition	(1983)	" "
Eighth Edition	(1990)	" "
Second Impression	(1995)	" "
Ninth Edition	(1997)	" " and C. T. Walton
Tenth Edition	(2001)	By C. T. Walton
Eleventh Edition	(2006)	" "
Twelfth Edition	(2010)	" "

Published in 2010 by Sweet & Maxwell Limited of
100 Avenue Road, Swiss Cottage, London NW3 3PF
Typeset by Interactive Sciences Ltd, Gloucester
and Printed in the UK by CPI William Clowes Beccles NR34 7TL

No natural forests were destroyed to make this product; only farmed
timber was used and replanted

**A CIP catalogue record for this book is available from the
British Library**

ISBN 978–0 41404–015–1

FOREWORDS TO PREVIOUS EDITIONS

FOREWORD TO THE ELEVENTH EDITION

Dr John Charlesworth had chambers in Grainger Street, Newcastle upon Tyne. It was those chambers my father joined in 1947, and remained in until he took silk in 1954. When he moved, as the rules then required, to chambers in London, he took with him his set of law reports which, after his elevation to the Court of Appeal, he passed on to me. Many of the volumes contain Dr John Charlesworth's distinct signature. They were originally his set—a set I am doubly proud to maintain.

Dr John Charlesworth was a remarkable figure. It must have been an immense labour to write, from scratch, a book devoted to the tort of negligence, a book which quickly became regarded as authoritative. He would be proud that his book continues to command its place in the Common Law Library and proud that its connection with the North East survives.

Lord Justice Waller
2006

FOREWORD TO THE TENTH EDITION

One of the great attractions of a common lawyer's practice is its variety, but there is a price to pay. Having ascertained the facts the lawyer needs to identify the relevant law, and that is the point at which previous editions of this textbook have been invaluable. This is the first edition to be edited by Judge Walton, and it is clear that he and his fellow authors have done an excellent job. The lawyer who needs to discover quickly whether his client has a viable claim, or whether he can successfully resist the claim brought against him, will find reliable up-to-date guidance in these pages, and in a fast changing and fast developing area of the law such guidance is essential. Lord Denning, in his foreword to the eighth edition described it as "the standard work par excellence." The tenth edition clearly maintains that position.

Lord Justice Kennedy
2001

FOREWORD TO THE NINTH EDITION

This invaluable book has now entered its Ninth Edition, the last to be edited by Rodney Percy. He has once again produced a first-rate guide to the law of Negligence, dealing reliably and succinctly with the many changes and developments in the law which have taken place over the last five years. Throughout his period as Editor he has maintained the excellent standards of his predecessor, John Charlesworth, and of the North Eastern Circuit. I hope that there will be many more editions to continue this tradition far into the future.

Lord Taylor of Gosforth
1996

FOREWORD TO THE EIGHTH EDITION

In my time the law of Negligence has been transformed. It is a modern sky-scraper to which new storeys are added every year. Some by judges, others by Parliament. No-one can find his way up or down except with a knowledgeable guide. Rodney Percy is the very man. He has combined the experience of the practitioner with the research of the academic. He has produced a first-rate book. If you should take it into Court, the Judge will commend your choice. It is the standard work par excellence.

Lord Denning of Whitchurch
1990

PREFACE

In the four years since the last edition there have been a number of interesting and instructive decisions relevant to areas of law with which this book is concerned. In *Rothwell v Chemical & Insulating Co Ltd*, the House of Lords considered that basic requirement of the tort of negligence, the damage required to complete a cause of action. *Commisioners of Customs & Excise v Barclays Bank Plc, Mitchell v Glasgow City Council* and *Trent Strategic Health Authority v Jain* each raised the question whether it was fair, just and reasonable to impose a duty of care in factual situations which had potentially wide relevance by analogy. *Van Colle v Chief Constable of Hertfordshire* and *Smith v Chief Constable of Sussex Police* returned to the issue of the liability of the police to the victim of crime. *Stone & Rolls Ltd v Moore Stephens* dealt with the ambit of the defence of illegality in tort. *A v Hoare* involved clarification of the "knowledge" provisions of the Limitation Act 1980. In *Corr v IBC Vehicles* issues of remoteness and causation were examined where the victim of a breach of duty had committed suicide. And while they involved breach of statutuory duty rather than negligence, a trio of cases—*Robb v Salamis (M&I) Ltd, Spencer Franks v Brown & Root*, and *Smith v Northamptonshire County Council*—examined the provisions of the Work Equipment Regulations 1999.

So quite apart from the work of the Court of Appeal, particularly in the area of damages for very serious injury, there is more than enough material to justify a fresh assessment of the text.

For this edition the editiorial team has been joined by Stephen Todd who has undertaken the considerable task of rewriting that part of Chapter 2 which dealt with the duty of care. Stephen has also provided assistance with those sections of the work dealing with the accrual of a cause of action for limitation purposes, and remoteness of damage.

As a result of Stephen's work it seemed wise to give Parties and Vicarious Liability their own chapter, and that led to all subsequent chapters being renumbered. Hopefully this has caused more difficulty for the editors and the publishing staff at Sweet and Maxwell than it will cause the reader. The compensation for any sense of dislocation in not finding topics under chapter numbers they have occupied for a number of years, is a discussion of the duty of care which is both up to date, and with a frame of reference which extends over the several common law jurisdictions to an even greater degree than before.

Simon Wood and Roger Cooper have both revised the chapters for which they have previously taken responsibility; Simon, Chapters 11, 12, 14 and 15 and Roger Chapters 5, 10, 16, and 17. They shared Ch.13 and I have dealt with what remained.

We are grateful as ever for the efforts of the editorial staff at Sweet and Maxwell who have expertly shepherded us through the various stages of publication with a minimum of fuss, particularly Clare McMahon and Alexandra Hirst.

Sadly, as noted in the Second Supplement to the last edition, Rodney Percy died in April 2008. He had inherited responsibility for editing this book after his former master in the law, Dr Charlesworth, himself died suddenly in 1957. He then continued single handed until 1996 and remained actively involved up to the last edition. We work in Rodney's shadow but are committed to his vision of a text accessible and helpful to student and practising lawyer alike.

The law is stated at July 1, 2010.

Christopher Walton,
Gosforth,
Newcastle upon Tyne

CONTENTS

PART I
GENERAL PRINCIPLES

CONTENTS

PART II

STANDARD OF CARE

PART III
STATUTORY DUTY

PART IV

ABSOLUTE OR STRICT LIABILITY

PART V
DEATH

PART VI
MISCELLANEOUS MATTERS

TABLE OF ABBREVIATIONS

The dates denote the period covered by the reports or the latest editions of textbooks. Current series are marked with an asterisk (*).

A. & E.	Adolphus & Ellis's Reports, Q.B., 1834–40
A. & S.L.	Air and Space Law
A.C	Law Reports, Appeal Cases, 1875–90
[1891] A.C.	Law Reports, Appeal Cases, 1891–
ACOP	Approved Code of Practice
AIDS	acquired immune deficiency syndrome
A.L.J.R.	Australian Law Journal Reports
A.L.R.	Australian Law Reports, 1834–40
All E.R.	All England Reports
App.Cas.	Law Reports, Appeal Cases (1891 onwards)
ASHE	Annual Survey of Hours and Earnings
B. & S.	Best and Smith's Reports, Q.B. 1861–70
BRB	British Railways Board
BTC	British Transport Commission
B.W.C.C.	Butterworths Workmen's Compensation Reports
Bing. N.C.	Bingham's New Cases, C.P. 1834–40
Brownl.	Brownlow & Goldesborough's Common Pleas Reports
C.B.	Common Bench Reports, 1840–56
[1891] Ch.	Law Reports, Chancery
Ch.D.	Law Reports, Chancery Division, 1876–90
CICA	Criminal Injuries Compensation Authority
CICAP	Criminal Injuries Compensation Appeals Panel
CICB	Criminal Injuries Compensation Board
CIM	Uniform Rules Concerning the Contract of International Carriage of Goods by Rail
CIV	Uniform Rules Concerning the Contract of International Carriage of Passengers by Rail
C.L.	
Cl. & F.	Clark and Finelly's Reports, HL, 1831–46
C.L.C.	Current Law Consolidation
C.L.J.	Cambridge Law Journal
C.L.Y.	Current Law Year Book
C.M.L.R.	Common Market Law Reports
Cab. & El.	Cababe & Ellis' Queen's Bench Reports

Com. Cas.	Commercial Cases
Conv.	Conveyancer and Property Lawyer
COTIF	Convention concerning International Carriage by Rail
C.P.D.	Law Reports, Common Pleas Division, 1875–80
CPR	Civil Procedure Rules
Crim. L.R.	Criminal Law Review
Cro. Eliz.	Croke's King's Bench Reports
CRU	Compensation Recovery Unit
dB	decibel
D.L.R.	Dominion Law Reports
DSM-IV	*American Diagnostic and Statistical Manual of Mental Disorders*
Dunlop	Dunlop's Reports, Session Cases
DVT	deep vein thrombosis
DWP	Department for Work and Pensions
E. & E.	Ellis & Ellis, Q.B. Reports
Ed. C.R.	Education Case Reports
Ed. L.M.	Education Law Monitor
E.G.	Estates Gazette
Ex.	Exchequer Reports, 1848–56
EWCA Civ	Court of Appeal, England and Wales
EWHC	High Court, England and Wales
F. & C.L.	Finance and Credit Law [?]
F.C.R.	Family Court Reports
H. & C.	Hurlstone and Coltman's Exch. Reports, 1862–66
H. & N.	Hurlstone and Norman's Exch. Reports, 1856–62
HA	Health Authority
I.C.D.-10	*International Classification of Diseases and Related Health Problems*
I.C.R.	Industrial Cases Reports
I.F.L. Rev.	International Financial Law Review
IH	Inner House, Court of Session
J.P.I. Law	Journal of Personal Injury Law
[1901] K.B.	Law Reports, King's Bench (1901 onwards)
K.I.R.	Knight's Industrial Law Reports
L.J.C.P.	Law Journal Common Pleas, 1831–75
L.J.Ch.	Law Journal Chancery (1831–1946)

L.J.Ex.	Law Journal Reports, Exchequer (1831–75)
L.J.K.B.	Law Journal, King's Bench
L.J.Q.B.	Law Journal, Queen's Bench
L.Q.R.	Law Quarterly Review
L.R.A.&E.	Law Reports, Admiralty and Ecclesiastical, 1865–75
L.R.C.P.	Law Reports, Common Pleas, 1865–75
L.R.Ex.	Law Reports, Exchequer, 1865–75
L.R.H.L.	Law Reports, English and Irish Appeal Cases, 1865–75
L.R.Ir.	Law Reports, Ireland, 1867–93
L.S.Gaz.	Law Society's Gazette
L.T.	Law Times Reports, 1859–1947
Ld.Raym.	Lord Raymond's Reports, 1694–1732
Lloyd's Rep.	Lloyd's Law Reports
M. & W.	Meeson and Welsby's Exchequer Reports, 1836–47
Macq.	Macqueen's Reports, Session Cases
M.C.L.Q.	Lloyd's Maritime and Commercial Law Quarterly
ME	myalgic encephalomyelitis
MIB	Motor Insurers' Bureau
M.L.R.	Modern Law Review
MMR	measles, mumps and rubella vaccine
NCB	National Coal Board
NERC	National Environment Research Council
N.I.	Northern Irish Reports
N.L.J.	New Law Journal
New L.J.	[also used]
N.Z.L.R.	New Zealand Law Reports
OH	Outer House, Court of Session
O.J.L.S.	Oxford Journal of Legal Studies
P.	Probate Division
PD	Practice Direction
P.I.Q.R.	Personal Injury and Quantum Reports
P.N.	Professional Negligence Reports
P.N.L.R.	Professional Negligence and Liability Reports
Phillips	Phillips' Chancery Reports
PTSD	post-traumatic stress disorder
Q.B.	Law Reports, Queen's Bench, 1865–75
[1891] Q.B.	Law Reports, Queen's Bench (1891 onwards)
Q.B.D.	Law Reports, Queen's Bench Division
Q.L.R.	Queensland Law Reports

RSA	Returned Services Association
R.T.R.	Road Traffic Reports
S.A.	South African Law Reports
S.A.S.R.	South Australian State Reports
S.C.	Session Cases
S.C.L.R.	Scottish Civil Law Reports
SHA	Strategic Health Authority
S.J.	Solicitor's Journal
S.L.T.	Scots Law Times
SRN	state registered nurse
T.L.R.	Times Law Reports, 1885–1952
Tort L. Rev.	Tort Law Review
UKHL	House of Lords, United Kingdom
W.A.L.R.	Western Australian Law Reports
W.L.R.	Weekly Law Reports
W.N.	Weekly Notes, 1866–1952
W.W.R.	Western Weekly Reports

TABLE OF CASES

Att Gen of the British Virgin Islands v Hartwell [2004] UKPC 12; [2004]
 1 W.L.R. 1273; [2004] P.I.Q.R. P27; [2004] Po. L.R. 141; [2004]
 Inquest L.R. 89; (2004) 101(12) L.S.G. 37; (2004) 148 S.J.L.B. 267 ... 5–04,
 5–20
Att Gen of New South Wales v Perpetual Trustee Co [1955] A.C. 457;
 [1955] 2 W.L.R. 707; [1955] 1 All E.R. 846; (1955) 99 S.J. 233 PC
 (Australia) 3–111, 5–53
Att-Gen for Ontario v Fatchi [1984] 2 S.C.R. 536 SCC 2–107
— v Keller (1978) 86 D.L.R. (3d) 426 3–117
Austin v GW Ry (1867) L.R. 2 Q.B. 442 .... 10–85, 10–93, 10–96
Australian Racing Drivers Club v Metcalf (1961) 106 C.L.R. 177 8–87
Auto Scooters (Newcastle) v Chambers (1966) 197 E.G. 457; 116 N.L.J.
 388 CA 8–106, 8–164
Auty v National Coal Board [1985] 1 W.L.R. 784; [1985] 1 All E.R. 930;
 (1985) 82 L.S.G. 1782; (1985) 129 S.J. 249 CA (Civ Div) 5–61
Avery v London & North Eastern Railway Co (LNER) [1938] A.C. 606
 HL 16–26
— v Salie (1972) 25 D.L.R. (3d) 495 9–318
Avis v GE Ry (1892) 8 T.L.R. 693 10–113
Avondale Blouse Co Ltd v Williamson & Geo Town (1948) 81 Ll.L.Rep.
 492 9–180
Awoyomi v Radford [2007] EWHC 1671 (QB); [2008] Q.B. 793; [2008]
 3 W.L.R. 34; [2007] P.N.L.R. 34; (2007) 157 N.L.J. 1046 QBD 9–95
Axa Equity & Law v Goldsack & Freeman [1994] 23 E.G. 130; [1994]
 E.G. 34 (C.S.) QBD 9–316
Axa Insurance Ltd v Akther & Darby [2009] EWCA Civ 1166 .... 4–158b
Ayles v SE Ry (1868) L.R. 3 Ex. 146 .... 6–111, 10–101
Ayoub v Beaupre & Bense (1964) 45 D.L.R. (2d) 411 13–125
Azzopardi v State Transport Authority (1982) 30 S.A.S.R. 10–145
B v A County Council [2006] EWCA Civ 1388; [2007] 1 F.L.R. 1189;
 [2006] 3 F.C.R. 568; [2007] P.I.Q.R. P17; [2007] Fam. Law 292;
 (2006) 150 S.J.L.B. 1571 2–163
— v Att-Gen of New Zealand [2003] UKPC 61; [2003] 4 All E.R. 833;
 [2003] Lloyd's Rep. Med. 527 2–312
— v Camden LBC [2001] P.I.Q.R. P143 7–31
— v Murray (No.2); Whitton v Poor Sisters of Nazareth; sub nom S v
 Poor Sisters of Nazareth; Bowden v Poor Sisters of Nazareth [2008]
 UKHL 32; 2008 S.C. (H.L.) 146; 2008 S.L.T. 561; 2008 S.C.L.R.
 547; (2008) 152(22) S.J.L.B. 28 4–206
— v Thanet DC [1999] C.L.Y. 3965 6–15
B (A Child) v Camden LBC [2001] P.I.Q.R. P9 QBD 8–52
— v McDonald's Restaurants Ltd [2002] EWHC 490 (QB) 15–16
B Sunley & Co Ltd v Cunard White Star Ltd [1940] 1 K.B. 740; (1940)
 66 Ll. L. Rep. 134 CA 5–69
BFG Bank AG v Brown & Mumford Ltd [1997] P.N.L.R. 202; [1996]
 E.G. 169 (C.S.); [1996] N.P.C. 153 CA (Civ Div) 9–318, 9–325
BL Holdings Ltd v Roberts J Wood & Partners, 12 B.L.R. 1; (1979) 123
 S.J. 570 CA (Civ Div) 9–68

TABLE OF CASES

TABLE OF STATUTES

TABLE OF STATUTORY INSTRUMENTS

TABLE OF CIVIL PROCEDURE RULES

TABLE OF CIVIL PROCEDURE RULES: PRACTICE DIRECTIONS

TABLE OF EUROPEAN DIRECTIVES

TABLE OF EUROPEAN AND INTERNATIONAL CONVENTIONS AND TREATIES

Part I
GENERAL PRINCIPLES

CHAPTER 1

THE MEANING OF NEGLIGENCE

Three meanings of negligence. In forensic speech, "negligence" can have **1–01** three meanings: (1) in referring to a state of mind, when it is distinguished in particular from intention; (2) in describing conduct of a careless type; and (3) as the breach of a duty to take care imposed by either common law or statute. In some circumstances the three meanings can overlap.

1.—NEGLIGENCE AS A STATE OF MIND

The first meaning. Negligence as a state of mind can be contrasted with **1–02** intention. An act is intentional when it is purposeful and done with the desire or object of producing a particular result.[1] In contrast, negligence in the present sense arises where someone either fails to consider a risk of particular action, or having considered it, fails to give the risk appropriate weight. If a man thoughtlessly leaves open the gate of a field enclosing cattle, the likely inference is that he has failed to turn his mind to the risk they will escape. Alternatively, if he throws a stone over a wall, intending to do so but without intending anyone particular harm, the likely inference is that he has failed to give appropriate thought to the risk that someone may be on the other side.

A person's state of mind may be negligent even though there is an intention to **1–03** exercise some care. A motorist, in a hurry, who drives too quickly down a busy street and collides with a pedestrian may well intend to exercise as much care as possible, consistent with a desire to drive quickly; but indifference or reckless-ness[2] as to the risk to pedestrians amounts to a negligent state of mind.

Inevitably, when describing a state of mind, there are shades of meaning. A **1–04** variety of expressions have been used over time to characterise a "negligent"

---

[1] *Gollins v Gollins* [1964] A.C. 644 at 663–664, per Lord Reid. In *Imperial Chemical Industries Ltd v Shatwell* [1965] A.C. 656, Lord Reid referred at 672 to the "inaccurate habit of using the word 'negligence' to denote a deliberate act done with full knowledge of the risk".
[2] For the definition of recklessness in the criminal law, see *R. v G* [2004] 1 A.C. 1034: a person is reckless with respect to (i) a circumstance, where he is aware of a risk that exists or will exist, and (ii) a result, when he is aware of a risk that it will occur; and it is in the circumstances known to him unreasonable to take the risk.

state of mind. In some cases the words "indifferent" or "reckless" are used when it seems that the defendant turned his mind to the consequences of his act, but decided, inappropriately, to carry on anyway. "Inadvertance" appears appropriate where the suggestion is that the defendant has simply not turned his mind to a potential risk at all.[3] In one early case,[4] the defendant had been warned that he had stacked his hay so as to give rise to the risk of fire and advised to take down his rick. He said he would chance it, but unfortunately the chance materialised. In such a case you would say that the defendant was indifferent or reckless of the risk of fire, rather than inadvertent. Even if the risk of fire was not "obvious" it was one to which, in the circumstances, the defendant ought to have had regard.

1–05   References in the cases and statutes to "intention" and "negligence" as having opposed or contrasting meanings are legion.[5] Lord Denman used "negligence" as descriptive of a state of mind in *Filliter v Phippard*[6] when, referring to the way a fire might be started, he said:

> "In strictness the word 'accidental' may be employed in contradistinction to 'wilful,' and so the same fire might begin both accidentally and be the result of negligence. But it may equally mean a fire produced by mere chance or incapable of being traced to any cause."

Another judge was using it in the same sense where he said: "Fraud imports design and purpose; negligence imports that you are acting carelessly and without that design."[7] In the Civil Aviation Act 1949 s.40(2)[8] provided that damages should be recoverable from the owner of an aircraft "without proof of negligence or intention". The Bills of Exchange Act 1882[9] s.90 provided: "A thing is deemed to be done in good faith, within the meaning of this Act, where it is in fact done honestly, whether it is done negligently or not."[10]

2.—Negligence as Careless Conduct

1–06   **The second meaning.** "Negligence" can also be used as a way to characterise conduct, although such a use may lead to imprecision when considering negligence as a tort. Careless conduct does not necessarily give rise to breach of

---

[3] See e.g. per Eve J. in *Hudston v Viney* [1921] 1 Ch. 98 at 104: "an attitude of . . . mental indifference to obvious risks."

[4] *Vaughan v Menlove* (1837) 3 Bing. N.C. 468.

[5] In addition to the references in this paragraph see also the importance of the distinction in personal injury cases discussed at para.1–27 below.

[6] (1847) 11 Q.B. 347 at 357.

[7] Fry J. in *Kettlewell v Watson* (1882) 21 Ch.D. 685 at 706.

[8] See now the re-enactment of this provision in s.76(2) of the consolidating statute, the Civil Aviation Act 1982.

[9] An Act to be construed as one with the Cheques Act 1957 s.6(1).

[10] Before the Act, it had been well established that negligence, however gross in character, if it stopped short of fraud, could not affect the title of a bill: *Jones v Gordon* (1877) 2 App.Cas. 616.

a duty of care, the defining characteristic of the tort of negligence.[11] The extent of a duty of care and the standard of care required in performance of that duty are both relevant in considering whether, on any given facts, conduct which can be characterised as careless, is actionable in law. The distinction between conduct that is careless, and careless conduct which involves a breach of duty has not always been recognised, as for instance in the early definition of Alderson B.:

> "Negligence is the omission to do something which a reasonable man, guided upon those considerations which ordinarily regulate the conduct of human affairs, would do, or doing something which a prudent and reasonable man would not do."[12]

Such a form of words would now be insufficient, if intended as a comprehensive definition of actionable negligence, omitting as it does any reference to an antecedent duty of care, its extent, together with the standard of care which is appropriate in the circumstances.

"Negligence" has been used in the sense of careless conduct, without **1–07** reference to an antecedent duty of care, in many cases, of which the following are examples:

> "Although it may be true, that if a person keeps an animal of known dangerous propensities, or a dangerous instrument, he will be responsible to those who are thereby injured, independently of any negligence in the mode of dealing with the animal or using the instrument; yet when the legislature has sanctioned or authorised the use of a particular thing, and it is used for the purpose for which it is authorised, and every precaution has been observed to prevent injury, the sanction of the legislature carries with it this consequence, that if damage results from the use of such thing independently of negligence, the party using it is not responsible."[13]

> "Here the plaintiffs must be taken to have consented to this collection of the water, which was for their own benefit, and the defendant can only be liable if he was guilty of negligence."[14]

> "It is now thoroughly well established that no action will lie for doing that which the legislature has authorised, if it be done without negligence, although it does occasion damage to anyone; but an action does lie for doing that which the legislature has authorised, if it be done negligently."[15]

> "The way in which the case was tried was that it was put to the jury as a case of negligence, and the learned judge told the jury that unless the plaintiff proved that the

---

[11] Human error and the legal concept of negligence are not necessarily synonymous: *Flynn v Vange Scaffolding & Engineering Co, The Times*, March 26, 1987, CA (the fact that a power station employee operated switches in an incorrect order, which resulted in a turbine giving a shrill noise, causing a scaffolder, who was working on it, to jump with fright and sustain injury, did not by itself amount to negligence).
[12] *Blyth v Birmingham Waterworks Co* (1856) 11 Ex. 781 at 784.
[13] per Cockburn C.J. in *Vaughan v Taff Vale Ry* (1860) 5 H. & N. 679 at 685.
[14] per Bramwell B. in *Carstairs v Taylor* (1871) L.R. 6 Ex. 217 at 222.
[15] per Lord Blackburn in *Geddis v Proprietors of Bann Reservoir* (1878) 3 App.Cas. 430 at 455–456.

defendants had been guilty of negligence, he was out of court. That mode of putting the case was far too favourable to the defendants."[16]

"The foundation of the action was a claim based upon the familiar doctrine established by the case of *Fletcher v Rylands*,[17] which depends upon this—that even apart from negligence the use of land by one person in an exceptional manner that causes damage to another, and not necessarily an adjacent owner, is actionable."[18]

"A man is entitled to be as negligent as he pleases towards the whole world if he owes no duty to them."[19]

"It is common knowledge among lawyers that mere negligence in itself is not a cause of action. To give a cause of action there must be negligence which amounts to a breach of duty towards the person claiming. There are many cases where there has been clear negligence, in the absence of which damage would not have happened, and yet there is no liability under English law."[20]

"I treat it, therefore, as established that a public authority, whether doing an act which it is its duty to do, or doing an act which it is merely empowered to do, must in doing the act do it without negligence, or, as it is put in some of the cases, must not do it carelessly or improperly."[21]

1–08   **Negligence and "accident."** It is not surprising that "negligence" and "accident" are often used in close conjunction. Yet for similar reasons to those already discussed in relation to careless conduct, it cannot be assumed that all accidents are caused by negligence. For negligence liability to arise in tort there has to be a duty of care to avoid whatever result has arisen. Many examples could be found, throughout this volume, of an accident which happened without there being a duty of care to prevent it.

1–09   Further, the word "accident" can be used to describe happenings which arise without anyone being guilty of careless conduct. The phrase "pure accident" is often used to describe circumstances where no one can be regarded as having been to blame for what happened.[22]

1–10   In other cases there has been an accident and someone has clearly been to blame, although what happened would usually not be termed accidental. So, in *Chief Constable of Staffordshire v Lees*[23] the court held there was an accident where a motorist deliberately drove through a locked gate onto a parkland road. In *Chief Constable of West Midlands Police v Billingham*[24] it was thought the

---

[16] per Swinfen Eady M.R. in *Miles v Forest Rock Granite Co* (1918) 34 T.L.R. 500 at 501.
[17] (1866) L.R. 1 Ex. 265; (1868) L.R. 3 H.L. 330.
[18] per Lord Buckmaster in *Rainham Chemical Works v Belvedere Fish Guano Co* [1921] 2 A.C. 465 at 471.
[19] per Lord Esher M.R. in *Le Lievre v Gould* [1893] 1 Q.B. 491 at 497 (the ratio of this decision was, however, considered by the House of Lords to be wrong in *Hedley Byrne & Co Ltd v Heller & Partners Ltd* [1964] A.C. 465).
[20] per Greer L.J. in *Farr v Butters Bros & Co* [1932] 2 K.B. 606 at 618.
[21] per Lord Atkin in *East Suffolk Rivers Catchment Board v Kent* [1941] A.C. 74 at 90.
[22] See also the discussion of "act of God" in Ch.13, para.13–35.
[23] [1981] R.T.R. 506.
[24] [1979] 1 W.L.R. 747.

defendant had released the brake on a parked police car and steered it down a hill until it collided with a telegraph pole and careered down an embankment. Bridge L.J. said:

> "There have been many authorities dealing with the meaning of the word 'accident' in different statutory and contractual contexts. It is . . . a word which has a perfectly well understood meaning in ordinary parlance, but that meaning is an elastic one according to the context in which the word is used."[25]

He went on,

> " . . . it seems to me that 'accident' in this context is perfectly capable of applying to an untoward occurrence which has adverse physical results, notwithstanding that one event in the chain of events which led to the untoward consequence was a deliberate act on the part of some mischievous person."[26]

In everyday speech you would probably not describe what happened in the first of the two cases above as negligent; you probably would so describe what happened in the second. Each of them, however, might be seen as negligent in the technical sense with which this book is concerned, that is breach of a duty to take care.

Estoppel by negligence. Negligence is also referred to in its sense of careless   **1–11** conduct, without reference to a duty of care, in certain historic formulations of the rule of estoppel by negligence. In *Gregg v Wells*,[27] Lord Denman said that one who negligently or culpably stood by and allowed another to contract on the faith and understanding of a fact that he could contradict, could not afterwards dispute that fact in an action against the person whom he had himself assisted in deceiving. It can, however, be a very fine line between "standing by" on the one hand, and, on the other, leading another to sustain loss by words or conduct, in circumstances where a duty is imposed. By the time of *Swan v North British Australasian Co*,[28] Blackburn J. was summarising the position in the following terms:

> "It is pointed out by Parke B.[29] . . . that in the majority of cases in which an estoppel exists, 'the party must have induced the other so to alter his position that the former would be responsible to him in an action for it'; and he had before pointed out that 'negligence,' to have the effect of estopping the party, must be 'neglect of some duty

---

[25] ibid. at 752. See also *Hawley v Luminar Leisure Ltd* [2006] P.I.Q.R. P211, CA, (an insurance policy providing cover for "accidental bodily injury" applied to an incident in which a doorman deliberately punched a customer of a club so that he fell and suffered serious injury). For the meaning of "accident" in art.17 of the Montreal Convention 1999 (which gives passengers on aircraft the right to compensation in some circumstances) see Ch.10, para.10–180, below.

[26] ibid. at 753, quoted in *Charlton v Fisher* [2002] Q.B. 578 CA, Ch.17, para.17–05 below. See also the cases referred to in the first instance judgment in *Re Deep Vein Thrombosis and Air Travel Group Litigation* [2003] 1 All E.R. 935, (appeals dismissed, [2004] Q.B. 234, [2006] 1 A.C. 495 (a case about the meaning of the word "accident" in art.17 of the Warsaw Convention 1929, as set out in Sch.1, Pt I to the Carriage by Air Act 1961). See further Phillips and Coppinger, "International Top Trumps" 156 N.L.J. 260 and Ch.10, para.10–180, below.

[27] (1839) 10 A. & E. 90 at 98. See also *Pickard v Spears* (1837) 6 A. & E. 469 at 474.

[28] (1863) 2 H. & C. 175 at 181.

[29] In *Freeman v Cooke* (1848) 2 Ex. 654.

cast upon the person who is guilty of it.' And this, I apprehend, is a true and sound principle. A person who does not lock up his goods, which are consequently stolen, may be said to be negligent as regards himself, but inasmuch as he neglects no duty which the law casts upon him, he is not in consequence estopped from denying the title of those who may have, however innocently, purchased those goods from the thief, unless it be in market overt."

1–12   **Cheques.** The distinction had to be explored in interpreting the Bills of Exchange Act 1882 and its successors. Section 82 of the 1882 Act and subsequent legislation, protected bankers who "in good faith and without negligence" received payment for a customer of a crossed cheque: "without negligence" meant "without want of reasonable care in reference to the interests of the true owner."[30] As Scrutton L.J. put it:

> "A question at once arises, as there is no 'negligence' without a legal duty, what was the exact duty imposed on the bank, and to whom? . . . In my view, section 82 lessened the duty of the bank by limiting it to an obligation only to use reasonable case in dealing with the cheque, or by providing that if the bank proved that it had used reasonable care in discharging its obligation to the true owner not to convert his property, it was discharged from liability though it had converted that property."[31]

Although s.82 has now been repealed by the Cheques Act 1957, in effect its provisions, together with the subsequent amendments,[32] have been re-enacted by s.4 of the 1957 Act,[33] which has also extended the protection to uncrossed cheques.

1–13   **The Sale of Goods Act 1979.** The distinction was also considered in relation to s.21 of the Sale of Goods Act 1893 and its successor, the identical section of the Sale of Goods Act 1979, by which the buyer acquires no better title to goods than the seller had, unless the owner of the goods is "by his conduct precluded from denying the seller's authority to sell." In *Mercantile Credit Co v Hamblin*,[34] the defendant was persuaded by a rogue to sign blank hire purchase forms in relation to her own car in the belief that they were documents which provided security for a loan. Using the forms, the rogue then pretended the car was his and purported to sell it to the claimant finance company to support a hire purchase transaction between the company and the defendant. In the ensuing action, it was held that an estoppel by title under s.21, relying upon negligent conduct by an owner, could not arise unless:

---

[30] per Kennedy J. in *Hannan's Lake View Central v Armstrong & Co* (1900) 5 Com. Cas. 188 at 191.

[31] *Savory & Co v Lloyd's Bank Ltd* [1932] 2 K.B. 122 at 130.

[32] Revenue Act 1883 s.17, the Bills of Exchange (Crossed Cheques) Act 1906 and the Bills of Exchange Act (1882) Amendment Act 1932.

[33] As amended by the Cheques Act 1992. For an example where the bank did not have a defence under s.4 of the Cheques Act 1957, see *Architects of Wine Ltd v Barclays Bank Plc* [2007] 2 Lloyd's Rep. 471, CA (the bank failed to make sufficient enquiry about cheques paid into an account in the United Kingdom, none of which were payable to the company named on the account, all were in US dollars drawn on US banks, and some gave the payee's address in the Cayman Islands). See art.F. & C.L. 2007, April, 5–6.

[34] [1965] 2 Q.B. 242.

(a) the owner owed a duty of care to the buyer;

(b) there had been a breach of duty; and

(c) the negligence was the proximate or real cause of the buyer's loss.

In the instant case a duty of care was owed by the defendant but *absent* negligence on her part the claimants' claim failed.

Careless conduct and contributory negligence. Perhaps the best illustration **1-14** of the use of the word "negligence" in the sense of careless conduct is to be found in the phrase "contributory negligence". Here, the word does not mean breach of a duty to take care, but simply means careless conduct on the part of the person, usually the claimant, in failing to prevent or avoid the consequences of another person's breach of duty to take care.[35] A person who in broad daylight falls into an unfenced hole in the highway, as a result of not looking where he is going, may be unable to succeed fully in an action because of the degree of his contributory negligence. This is not because of any duty which he owes to the person who dug the hole and left it unfenced, but because of his failure to take reasonable care for his own safety.

Negligence in the performance of a contract is another typical example where "negligently" is used simply in its sense of the opposite of diligence.

Degrees of negligence. When used in the sense of careless conduct, degrees **1-15** of negligence are sometimes identified, such as "gross negligence",[36] "undue negligence",[37] "ordinary negligence", and "slight negligence". Strictly, such distinctions are inappropriate when considering negligence as breach of a duty to take care. When Rolfe B. said that he, "could see no difference between negligence and gross negligence, that it was the same thing with the addition of a vituperative epithet",[38] his criticism was justified in a context where he was using "negligence" in the sense of a breach of duty to take care.[39] That is not to say, however, that the expression "gross negligence" has always the same meaning as "negligence." It is an expression in regular use, and to deny it a meaning would be pedantic. It has some practical utility in describing a high degree of careless conduct, such as where a defendant did not intend a particular

---

[35] See Ch.4, below and Blackshaw, "Contributory Negligence and the Duty of Care" in 116 S.J. 577.
[36] For observations on the expression "gross negligence", see the judgment of Mance J. in *Red Sea Tankers Ltd v Papachristidis (The Hellespont Ardent)* [1997] 2 Lloyd's Rep. 547 (it was not gross negligence for a company which specialised in advice in shipping investment to fail to make certain enquiries in relation to a vessel they recommended the plaintiffs acquire).
[37] Where the phrase "undue negligence" appeared in a contract for the purchase of traveller's cheques, it meant "excessive negligence" and was a question of fact and degree to be decided in each case: *Fellus v National Westminster Bank, The Times*, June 28, 1983.
[38] *Wilson v Brett* (1843) 11 M. & W. 113, approved in *Grill v General Iron Screw Collier Co* (1866) L.R. 1 C.P. 600 at 612.
[39] See also, per Lynskey J. in *Pentecost v London District Auditor* [1951] 2 K.B. 759 at 764.

consequence to happen but nevertheless must have been able to foresee its occurrence.[40]

1–16   **Criminal negligence.** The degree of negligence shown by the accused is at the heart of criminal liability for manslaughter by gross negligence. The ordinary principles of negligence apply to determine whether an accused person is guilty of the offence.[41] It must be proved, to the criminal standard, that the conduct of the accused was, in the first instance, such as to amount to a breach of a duty of care towards the victim. The Crown must then show that the negligence in question caused the victim's death and should be characterised as gross negligence and therefore a crime. It is for the judge to direct the jury whether the facts are capable of giving rise to a duty of care and for the jury to decide, in light of the judge's directions, whether there was indeed such a duty on the particular facts.[42] The jury must then consider whether, having regard to the risk of death, the accused's conduct was so bad in all the circumstances as to amount to a criminal act or omission. Where the charge is brought against a professional person, care should be taken to direct the jury that, before they find gross negligence, they should be satisfied that there was a departure from the expected standard of professional practice so serious as to amount to a criminal act. These principles of criminal liability have been considered in light of the Human Rights Act 1998 and declared not so diffuse or unclear as to represent a breach of art.7. The offence of gross negligence manslaughter itself, is not incompatible with 1998 Act.[43]

1–17   Criminal liability based upon negligence has been further developed in the Corporate Homicide Act 2007.[44] The Act provides for the offence of corporate manslaughter (corporate homicide in Scotland). The offence is committed where the way in which a relevant organisation's activities are managed or organised by its senior management causes a person's death, and amounts to a gross breach of a relevant duty of care.[45] A gross breach arises where the conduct alleged to amount to a breach of duty falls far below that which could reasonably be expected in the circumstances.[46] Detailed provisions define the extent of the duty of care required for criminal liability under the Act, the exceptions, and the respective roles of judge and jury. In deciding whether a duty of care was owed to the deceased person, there falls to be disregarded (a) any common law rule that

---

[40] See *Red Sea Tankers Ltd v Papachristidis (The Hellespont Ardent)* [1997] 2 Lloyd's Rep. 547. In *Blake v Galloway* [2004] 1 W.L.R. 2844 CA, the court referred, in the context of personal injury resulting from horseplay between boys, to the need for "a very high degree of carelessness" before such a claim would be made out (see per Dyson L.J. at 2851).

[41] *R. v Adomako* [1995] A.C. 171.

[42] *R. v Khan and Khan* [1998] Crim. L.R. 830, CA.

[43] *R. v Misra (Amit) and Srivastava, The Times*, October 13, 2004, CA (Crim) (doctors concerned in the post operative care of the deceased, who died from toxic shock syndrome as a result of an untreated infection of the surgical wound). See Foster, "Killing by degrees" 148 S.J. 1226; Herring and Palser, "The duty of care in gross negligence manslaughter" Crim. L.R. 2007, Jan, 24.

[44] Which came into force on 6 April 2008. See further Harris, "Don't blame me" 158 N.L.J. 499; Ormerod and Taylor, "The Corporate Manslaughter and Corporate Homicide Act" 2007 Crim. L.R. 2008, 8, 589.

[45] s.1(1)(a) and (b) and (3).

[46] s.1(4)(b).

has the effect of preventing a duty of care from being owed by one person to another by reason of the fact that they are jointly engaged in unlawful conduct; (b) any such rule that has the effect of preventing a duty of care from being owed to a person by reason of his acceptance of a risk of harm.[47]

The degree of negligence required before the criminal offence can be made out   **1–18** was referred to in Lord Atkin's speech in *Andrews v Director of Public Prosecutions*.[48] He said:

> "The principle to be observed is that cases of manslaughter in driving motor cars are but instances of a general rule applicable to all charges of homicide by negligence. Simple lack of care such as will constitute civil liability is not enough: for purposes of the criminal law there are degrees of negligence: and a very high degree of negligence is required to be proved before the felony is established."[49]

The same meaning was given to the word by Lord Porter, when he said:

> "A higher degree of negligence has always been demanded in order to establish a criminal offence than is sufficient to create civil liability. An obvious illustration is the difference between the degree of negligence in accident cases required to prove the crime of manslaughter and that sufficient to create civil liability."[50]

3.—NEGLIGENCE AS THE BREACH OF A DUTY TO TAKE CARE

The third meaning. The third meaning of negligence, and the one with which   **1–19** this volume is principally concerned, is conduct which, objectively considered, amounts to breach of a duty to take care. Negligence as a breach of duty is "a specific tort in itself and not . . . simply . . . an element in some more complex relationship or in some specialised breach of duty".[51] In this sense, as a tort in its own right, negligence is a comparatively recent legal concept dating from about 1824.[52] From about the middle of the nineteenth century, the tort of negligence developed very rapidly and in the process swallowed up large portions of the law of nuisance and trespass to the person.[53] The distinctive feature of the tort, in its dependence upon proof of a breach of a duty of care owed by one party to the other, was identified and elaborated. In 1866, Wills J. referred to negligence as, " . . . the absence of such care as it was the duty of the defendant to use".[54] Later, Bowen L.J. described how the " . . . idea of

---

[47] s.2(6)(a) and (b). For the common law defence of illegality see Ch.4, para.4–248 below, and for "agreement to run the risk", Ch.4, para.4–73.
[48] [1937] A.C. 576.
[49] *Andrews v Director of Public Prosecutions* [1937] A.C. 576 at 583.
[50] *Riddell v Reid* [1943] A.C. 1 at 31.
[51] *Grant v Australian Knitting Mills* [1936] A.C. 85 at 103, per Lord Wright.
[52] See *Winfield* in 42 L.Q.R. 184.
[53] See, e.g. *Letang v Cooper* [1964] 2 Q.B. 53 (where the claimant was run over as she lay sunbathing in the grounds of an hotel, her action lay in negligence only, not in trespass). Compare *Williams v Humphrey, The Times*, February 20, 1975 (where the defendant pushed the claimant into the shallow end of a swimming pool he was guilty both of negligence and trespass to the person).
[54] *Grill v General Iron Screw Collier Co* (1866) L.R. 1 C.P. 600 at 612.

negligence and duty are strictly correlative, and there is no such thing as negligence in the abstract; negligence is simply neglect of some care which we are bound by law to exercise towards somebody".[55] His words found an echo in a speech of Lord Macmillan:

> "The law takes no cognisance of carelessness in the abstract. It concerns itself with carelessness only where there is a duty to take care and where failure in that duty has caused damage. In such circumstances carelessness assumes the legal quality of negligence and entails the consequences in law of negligence . . . The cardinal principle of liability is that the party complained of should owe to the party complaining a duty to take care, and that the party complaining should be able to prove that he has suffered damage in breach of that duty."[56]

1-20   **Breach of contractual duty to take care.** The central feature of the tort of negligence is accordingly breach of a duty to take care. It is distinct from a breach of contract.[57] While a contract may contain an obligation to take care in the performance of its terms, the obligation arises from the agreement or presumed agreement of the parties, whereas a tortious duty of care arises from an objective view of given facts, of which an agreement may be one. Accordingly, where a contract term imports a duty to take reasonable care in performance it can be concurrent with a duty to take care in tort,[58] but it is by no means the case that every breach of contract involves a breach of tortious duty as well. Where a duty of care arises between parties to a contract, wider obligations can be imposed in tort than those arising under the contract.[59] Conversely, there may be occasions where the remedy of damages is more attractive or generous if the claimant is able to establish a case in contract rather than tort.[60]

1-21   **Breach of fiduciary duty.** The tort of negligence is to be distinguished from a breach of fiduciary duty arising in equity. A duty of care can be imposed by courts of equity in situations where the parties are in a relationship characterised as imposing obligations of good faith. In *Bristol & West Building Society v Mothew*,[61] the characteristics of a fiduciary's duty were described as follows:

> "The distinguishing obligation of a fiduciary is the obligation of loyalty. The principal is entitled to the single-minded loyalty of his fiduciary. This core liability has several

---

[55] *Thomas v Quatermaine* (1887) 18 Q.B.D. 685 at 694.

[56] *Donoghue v Stevenson* [1932] A.C. 562 at 618–619.

[57] In *Brown v Boorman* (1844) 11 C.1. & F.1, the court treated breach of contract as negligence but as time passed such an approach could no longer be sustained.

[58] Examples are provided in the context of actions by employees against their employers for some lack of safety in the workplace; or by clients against professionals with whom they have contracted for loss occasioned by a failure to perform the work to a proper standard.

[59] See *Holt v Payne Skillington* [1996] 2 P.N.L.R. 179, CA. The danger of treating a breach of contract as simply co-extensive with a breach of duty in tort is well illustrated by *Berryman v London Borough of Hounslow* [1997] P.I.Q.R. P83, CA (the claimant suffered injury climbing stairs to her flat when the lift was out of order but her claim failed in circumstances where it was appropriate to apply the contractual rules as to remoteness of damage rather than those in tort).

[60] See, e.g. *Farley v Skinner* [2002] 2 A.C. 732, Ch.9, para.9–333, 334, below (circumstances in which a surveyor in breach of contractual duty to take reasonable care may be liable for damages for distress).

[61] [1998] Ch.1. In the context of negligence claims fiduciary relationships most often arise in cases concerning the breach of duty of solicitors.

facets. A fiduciary must act in good faith; he must not make a profit out of his trust; he must not place himself in a position where his duty and his interest may conflict; he may not act for his own benefit or the benefit of a third person without the informed consent of his principal."[62]

This list is not exhaustive, but is sufficient for present purposes. The fiduciary **1–22** duty may, as with contractual duties, run concurrently with any tortious duty of care the factual context also imposes, but in many cases will give rise to a potentially more extensive obligation.[63] The standard of care required for due performance of the fiduciary's duty can be more onerous. Likewise, the consequences of a breach of a fiduciary duty: assessment of damages is approached upon an indemnity principle more generous to the aggrieved party than the measure of damages in tort.[64]

Where solicitors acted for the claimants in their unsuccessful attempt to **1–23** purchase an inn, and then suggested that the claimants invest their funds in an already existing partnership with themselves and others, which ran a local hotel, it was held that a fiduciary duty continued between the solicitors and the claimants, even where the retainer relationship had come to an end. No duty of care in negligence was established because the solicitors were no longer acting as such at the time of the partnership transaction and there was no assumption of responsibility in relation to the partnership agreement sufficient to sustain a duty of care. But there was a breach of fiduciary duty in a failure to advise the claimants to seek independent advice before entering the transaction.[65]

Mortgagee's duty. A mortgagee owes a duty to the mortgagor. It is usually **1–24** expressed as a duty in equity but shares some characteristics of a common law duty. If powers become exercisable under the mortgage a duty is owed to exercise them with reasonable care, for instance to obtain a proper price if the property subject to the mortgage is to be sold.[66] The position is the same where powers are to be exercised by a receiver appointed under the mortgage. In *Medforth v Blake*[67] Lord Justice Scott said:

"I do not accept that there is any difference between the answer that would be given by the common law to the question what duties are owed by a receiver managing a mortgaged property to those interested in the equity of redemption and the answer that would be given by equity to that question. I do not, for my part, think it matters one jot whether the duty is expressed as a common law duty or as a duty in equity. The result

---

[62] ibid. at 17 per Millett L.J. See also Ch.9, para.9–215; also *Leeds & Holbeck Building Society v Arthur & Cole* [2002] P.N.L.R. 78 (per Morland J. at 83: the difference between negligence and breach of fiduciary duty in the context of solicitors' negligence is "conscious impropriety").
[63] See, e.g. *Meara v Fox* [2002] P.N.L.R. 93 (where the claimant and a professional advisor were essentially engaged in a business together so no special relationship arose as to give rise to a duty of care but allegations of breach of fiduciary duty could instead be considered).
[64] See, e.g. *Nationwide Building Society v Balmer Radmore* [1999] P.N.L.R. 606.
[65] *Longstaff v Birtles* [2002] 1 W.L.R. 470, CA. See Sprince, "The fiduciary liability of solicitors entering transactions with clients: searching for substance in the shadow of Caesar's wife" (2002) 2 P.N. 96.
[66] See the summary of Robert Walker L.J. in *Yorkshire Bank v Hall* [1999] 1 W.L.R. 1713 at 1728, CA. Also Ch.2, para.2–233, below.
[67] [2000] Ch. 86, CA (Civ Div).

is the same. The origin of the receiver's duty, like the mortgagee's duty, lies, however, in equity and we might as well continue to refer to it as a duty in equity."[68]

1–25   **Breach of statutory duty.** The tort of negligence is also to be distinguished from a breach of statutory duty. This topic is enlarged upon below[69] but it suffices here to point out that in modern society a multitude of situations in which one person's conduct may potentially harm another are the subject of regulation by Parliament. A certain standard of conduct is required if a breach of statutory duty is not to arise. It may or may not be the case that such conduct will be "careless" in the sense of failing to achieve the standard of care required for due performance of a common law duty of care. On the same facts a statutory duty may be co-extensive with a common law duty of care; it may be more extensive; or it may be less so. In some situations, the existence of a statutory duty may be part of the background facts against which a common law duty of care comes into being. It may be that in the past "negligence" was used to characterise conduct which resulted in a breach of statutory duty,[70] or for that matter a breach of contract or trust, but more recent usage tends to confine the term to its use as the name of the tort under present discussion.[71]

1–26   **Wilful negligence.** "Wilful" is a word in rather less common use now than formerly. Essentially it means intentional. The expression "wilful negligence" has been used in number of cases usually to characterise conduct which was intentional as well as careless. In *Emblen v Myers*,[72] the defendant had demolished his own house, adjacent to the plaintiff's stable, in such a reckless manner that the roof of the stable was damaged. A submission was made that because the demolition had been deliberate, the plaintiff could not succeed in negligence. Bramwell B. disagreed : "It is said that the act of the defendant was wilful, and therefore the plaintiff cannot recover on this declaration; but the act was negligent as well as wilful." So negligence may or may not arise where the damage complained of has arisen from some wilful or an intentional act.[73] The tort of negligence, as the breach of a duty to take care, is concerned with conduct and not with intention. It cannot be a defence to prove that the defendant intentionally inflicted damage, what is important is the nature of the act which gives rise to the claim. If the driver of a heavy lorry were to deliberately run into a bicycle and destroy it, he could be sued for negligence, just as if he had destroyed it by careless driving. If a trench is dug in the road and a lamp left to warn of its presence and the defendant, seeing the claimant approach, removes the lamp, intending the claimant to fall, there would be liability in negligence. Whatever the intention, the character of the act was, objectively, negligent.

---

[68] *Medforth v Blake* [2000] Ch. 86, CA (Civ Div) at 101.

[69] See Ch.12.

[70] See, e.g. per Fletcher Moulton L.J. in *David v Britannic Merthyr Coal Co* [1909] 2 K.B. 146 at 164; also, per Lord Atkin in *East Suffolk Rivers Catchment Board v Kent* [1941] A.C. 74 at 88.

[71] *L.P.T.B. v Upson* [1949] A.C. 155 at 168, per Lord Wright; *Riddell v Reid* [1943] A.C. 1 at 24–25.

[72] (1860) 6 H. & N. 54.

[73] Some confusion also arises from earlier decisions where "wilful" is not used as a term of art but is often used as meaning no more than a high degree of carelessness or recklessness: *Caswell v Powell Duffryn Associated Collieries Ltd* [1940] A.C. 152 at 176–177.

Intention, or at least recklessness, is required if the claimant is seeking to prove   **1–27**
the tort of trespass to the person or personal property. In relation to the former,
Lord Denning M.R. said in *Letang v Cooper*:

> "If he does not inflict injury intentionally, but only unintentionally, the plaintiff has no
> cause of action today in trespass. His only cause of action is in negligence, and then
> only on proof of want of reasonable care . . . If intentional, it is the tort of assault and
> battery. If negligent and causing damage, it is the tort of negligence."[74]

In *Imperial Chemical Industries Ltd v Shatwell*, Lord Reid was critical of the
use of the word "negligence" to denote a deliberate act done with full knowledge
of the risk, albeit he was speaking in the context of an issue of contributory
negligence.[75]

The borderline between negligently and intentionally inflicted harm was   **1–28**
explored in *Secretary of State for the Home Department v Wainwright*.[76] One of
the two claimants sought to recover damages for distress caused by a strip search
when she visited Armley Prison, Leeds. It was accepted that the manner of the
search was in breach of the Prison's rules and therefore unprotected by the statute
which authorised searches. The House of Lords rejected the claim. Policy
considerations limited the heads of recoverable damage in negligence, and
distress falling short of psychiatric injury was insufficient. While policy did not
limit the recoverable damage in the same way when the damage in question was
intended, it remained an open question whether the common law should provide
a remedy in circumstances such as those under consideration.[77] If it did, it would
be necessary to be careful in defining "intent":

> "The defendant must actually have acted in a way which he knew to be unjustifiable
> and intended to cause harm or at least acted without caring whether he caused harm or
> not."[78]

Intention in that sense was not established on the facts of the case.[79]

---

[74] [1965] 1 Q.B. 232 at 239–240.
[75] [1965] A.C. 656 at 672.
[76] [2004] 2 A.C. 406.
[77] In the leading speech Lord Hoffmann cast doubt on the role of *Wilkinson v Downton* [1897] 2 Q.B. 57 in modern tort law. Although in that case the claimant recovered damages for a shock received when a practical joker told her, falsely, that her husband had been seriously injured in an accident, he clearly felt the trial judge in *Wilkinson* had diluted the concept of intention to an unacceptable degree.
[78] ibid., per Lord Hoffmann at 426. He expressed reservations whether the common law should provide a remedy for conduct which, while ill mannered or boorish, was motivated only by an intention to humiliate or distress.
[79] The claimants in *Wainwright* were subsequently each awarded €3,000 in the ECHR for breach of their rights under art.8 of the European Convention on Human Rights. The requirement that they submit to a strip-search was an interference under art 8(1) and was required to be justified as being in accordance with the law and necessary in a democratic society for a legitimate aim, under art 8(2). The Court was satisfied that the manner of carrying out the searches to which the claimants were subjected was not proportionate to the legitimate aim relied upon, namely combating a drugs problem in the prison: *Wainwright v United Kingdom* App. No. 12350/04 European Court of Human Rights, 26 September 2006.

1–29   **Actionability.**[80] Breach of a duty of care only becomes actionable if accompanied by proof of actual damage.[81] There is no right of action for nominal damages.[82] As Lord Reading C.J. has said: "Negligence alone does not give a cause of action, damage alone does not give a cause of action; the two must co-exist."[83] Accordingly, a bare admission of negligence by a defendant is not necessarily an admission of liability. For instance, a claimant will presumably have to show that each element in his cause of action, including that he has suffered actual damage, is admitted, before being able to enter judgment under Pt 14.3 of the Civil Procedure Rules 1999.[84]

1–30   The need for damage can be illustrated in a number of different situations. In the context of claims for negligently inflicted personal injury there have been cases where the damage alleged has been regarded as too slight to be actionable. Pleural plaques, that is, areas of pleural thickening within the lungs, are thought to be a result of exposure to asbestos fibre. Save in rare cases they do not occasion any symptoms and, without more, their presence is insufficient to found a cause of action.[85] The chance that the claimant could develop more serious conditions such as asbestosis or mesothelioma, coupled with anxiety following diagnosis of an asbestos-related condition, is insufficient to amount to damage, where individually those elements are not in law capable of being damage so as to complete a cause of action in tort.[86]

1–31   Loss of use of a chattel, while being inspected as a result of a reasonable belief that it has sustained physical damage, is not itself damage so as to give rise to a claim in negligence.[87] Where a child was removed from his mother as a result of a mistaken belief that he had suffered non-accidental injury and placed with foster carers under the terms of an interim care order, there was no cause of action against the local authority whose social workers initiated the action, where any harm to the child was transient and non-justiciable.[88] Where the claimants were induced to take a lease of premises by a negligent misrepresentation of their estate agents that the net area was 948 square feet greater than it was, they failed to prove any damage where the evidence showed that the market value of the

---

[80] See further in relation to the need for proof of damage Ch.2, para.2–95, Ch.5, para.5–01, below.
[81] See *Rothwell v Chemical & Insulating Co Ltd* [2008] 1 A.C. 281 para.1–30, below.
[82] See further Ch.5, below, para.5–44.
[83] *J. R. Munday Ltd v London C.C.* [1916] 2 K.B. 331 at 334, a passage approved by Lord Simon in *East Suffolk Rivers Catchment Board v Kent* [1941] A.C. 74 at 86–87, and to which he added: "A third essential factor is the existence of the particular duty."
[84] For the position as it was under the former RSC, see *Fankine v Garton Sons & Co Ltd* [1979] 2 All E.R. 1185, CA, following *Blundell v Rimmer* [1971] 1 W.L.R. 123. See also *Parrott v Jackson*, *The Times*, February 14, 1996.
[85] *Rothwell v Chemical & Insulating Co Ltd*, n.81, above, at [68]. See further Ch.2 para.2–99, below.
[86] *Rothwell v Chemical & Insulating Co Ltd*, n.81, above, at [68]. The distinction should however be noted that *once* the claimant establishes some actionable physical injury then, in appropriate circumstances, compensation may reflect the risks of deterioration and any anxiety to which the physical injury has given rise. See further, Jones, "Liability for fear of future disease?" (2008) 1 P.N. 13.
[87] *European Gas Turbines Ltd (formerly Ruston Gas Turbines Ltd) v Msas Cargo International Inc* [2001] C.L.C. 880. See generally, Witting, "Physical damage in negligence" 61 C.L.J. 189.
[88] *D v Bury Metropolitan Borough Council* [2006] 1 W.L.R. 917, CA.

lease based on its actual area was in the range of £52,000–£60,000, and they had only paid £54,000.[89]

Damage to and loss of sperm provided by donors and stored by a hospital in **1–32** case they should become infertile, has been held not to constitute a personal injury. It was said it would be a fiction to to hold that damage to a substance generated by a person's body, inflicted after its removal for storage, amounted to a personal injury to that person. However, the claimants did retain rights of property in the sperm and the damage to those rights was sufficient to found a cause of action in negligence.[90]

The existence of damage and the time when it came into existence becomes an **1–33** issue in cases where the defendant raises an issue of limitation.[91] The claim will fail altogether if there is no proof that the claimant has suffered damage, let alone suffered it at a time within the period of limitation prescribed by law.[92] In a claim for negligent advice, as a result of which the claimant enters a voidable contract, damage is sustained, so as to give rise to a cause of action, once the claimant has acted upon the advice and entered the contract: so, for example, where a voidable insurance policy was taken out in consequence of negligent advice from an insurance broker, the cause of action accrued when a premium under the policy was paid, not later either when the insurer avoided the policy or when a fire occurred which gave rise to the claim for indemnity.[93]

The components of the modern tort of negligence. Many distinguished **1–34** judges have attempted the task of summarising the ingredients of the modern tort. Lord Wright said that in strict analysis: "negligence means more than heedless or careless conduct, whether in commission or omission: it properly connotes the complex concept of duty, breach, and damage thereby suffered by the person to whom the duty is owing."[94] Whatever form of words is adopted the essential components are recognised as three: "duty", "breach" and "resulting damage", i.e.:

1. the existence of a duty to take care, which is owed by the defendant to the complainant;

2. the failure to attain that standard of care, prescribed by the law, thereby committing a breach of such duty; and

---

[89] *Carreras v D. E. & J. Levy* (1970) 215 E.G. 707.
[90] *Yearmouth v North Bristol NHS Trust* [2009] 3 W.L.R. 118, CA.
[91] See further Ch.4, para.4–137, below.
[92] See, e.g. *Daniels v Thompson* [2004] P.N.L.R. 638, CA, where the allegation was that solicitors failed to advise the testatatrix about the effect of her continuing residence in a property, on the liability of her estate for inheritance tax. After her death proceedings were commenced by her executor, seeking to recover the loss to the estate which arose as a result of the liability to taxation. The Court of Appeal had to consider when, for limitation purposes, the cause of action accrued. It was concluded that in fact no cause of action had ever accrued to the testatrix because she would herself never be liable to pay the tax in question. Since she never suffered a loss sufficient to complete a cause of action, the action brought by her executor was bound to fail. See further, Tettenborn, "Professional negligence: can you owe a duty to the dead?" (2005) Conv. 288.
[93] *Knapp v Ecclesiastical Insurance Group plc* [1998] P.N.L.R. 172, CA.
[94] *Lochgelly Iron and Steel Co v M'Mullan* [1934] A.C. 1 at 25.

3. damage, which is both causally connected with such breach and recognised by the law,[95] has been suffered by the complainant.

Of this familiar analysis of the tort of negligence, Lord Pearson said it "is logically correct and often convenient for purposes of exposition, but it is only an analysis and should not eliminate consideration of the tort of negligence as a whole".[96]

1–35   If the claimant satisfies the court on the evidence that these three ingredients are made out, the defendant should be held liable in negligence. It will then be necessary to identify the extent of damage referable to the breach of duty, before assessing its value in money terms. The chapters which follow examine the various components in more detail.

---

[95] i.e. is not too remote: see Ch.5, below, paras 5–01 to 5–41.
[96] *Dorset Yacht Co Ltd v Home Office* [1970] A.C. 1004 at 1052.

CHAPTER 2

THE DUTY TO TAKE CARE

1.—CONCEPT OF A DUTY OF CARE

(A) Introduction

Generally. The word "duty" connotes a relationship by which an obligation   **2–01**
is imposed upon one person for the benefit of another to take reasonable care in
all the circumstances. Whether or not a duty of care exists on given facts is a
question of law.[1] Unless the existence of such a duty can be established, an action

---

[1] See *Black v Fife Coal Co Ltd* [1912] A.C. 149 at 159, per Lord Kinnear; *Deyong v Shenburn* [1946]
K.B. 227 at 233, per du Parcq L.J.; *Letang v Cooper* [1965] 1 Q.B. 232 at 241, per Lord Denning
M.R.

in negligence must fail. As Lord Wright put it in *Grant v Australian Knitting Mills Ltd*[2]:

> "All that is necessary as a step to establish the tort of actionable negligence is to define the precise relationship from which the duty to take care is deduced. It is, however, essential in English law that the duty should be established: the mere fact that a man is injured by another's act gives in itself no cause of action: if the act is deliberate, the party injured will have no claim in law even though the injury is intentional, so long as the other party is merely exercising a legal right: if the act involves lack of due care, again no case of actionable negligence will arise unless the duty to be careful exists."

Put in compendious form, so far as the law of tort is concerned, a man is entitled to be as negligent as he pleases towards the whole world, provided that he does not owe any particular person a duty to take care.[3]

2–02   The requirement for a duty exists because the potential scope of negligence as a basis for legal liability is virtually unlimited. On its face "negligence" looks only to the quality of the defendant's conduct and not to factors such as the likely or possible number of claimants, the likelihood that loss would be caused, the nature and extent of particular loss and the circumstances in which the loss came to be inflicted. Thus, principles have had to be devised to delimit the boundaries of liability. One solution is the requirement that the potential defendant must owe to the victim a legal duty to take care. The language of duty provides a formula for expressing how far the law ought to extend.

2–03   **Duty and other elements to liability.** This chapter deals only with the requirement in every negligence action that the defendant owes to the claimant a duty to take care. However, the role played by the other components of actionable negligence—breach of the duty, damage caused by the breach and damage which is not too remote—must always be taken into account, both in theoretical analysis and practice. Lord Pearson has recognised that "it may be artificial and unhelpful to consider the question as to the existence of a duty of care in isolation from the elements of breach of duty and damage".[4] It follows that it is always useful to consider for what purpose a duty of care is required, before going on to consider whether negligence can be established. Not every wrongful act can be compensated. Not every consequence of a compensable wrong can be the subject of an award of damages. The law has to draw a line[5]:

> "Sometimes it is done by limiting the range of the persons to whom duty is owed. Sometimes it is done by saying that there is a break in the chain of causation. At other times it is done by saying that the consequence is too remote to be a head of damage.

---

[2] [1936] 1 A.C. 85 at 103.

[3] *Le Lievre v Gould* [1893] 1 Q.B. 491 per Lord Esher M.R. at 497: "English law does not recognise a duty in the air, so to speak; that is, a duty to undertake that no one shall suffer from one's carelessness": *Bottomley v Bannister* [1932] 1 K.B. 458 at 476, per Greer L.J.

[4] *Dorset Yacht Co Ltd v Home Office* [1970] A.C. 1004 at 1052.

[5] See, e.g. *Compania Financiera "Soleada" SA v Hamoor Tanker Corporation Inc; The Borag* [1981] 1 W.L.R. 274 at 281, CA, per Lord Denning.

All these devices are useful in their way. But ultimately it is a question of policy for the judges to decide."[6]

The elements of liability are conceptually distinct, and it is helpful if they are **2–04** kept separate for the purposes of analysis. Whether a duty exists, whether a duty found to exist has been broken and whether the breach caused damage in fact are clearly different inquiries, even though they each control the question whether a defendant ought to be held liable for a claimant's loss. The distinction between the question of the duty owed to the claimant and the question as to the damage in respect of which the defendant is liable is harder to pin down. Both the Court of Appeal and the House of Lords have recognised the overlap between defining the scope of the defendant's duty, and the loss for which, whether by way of the rules of causation or remoteness, or both, he or she should be liable. These questions are discussed further below.[7] For the moment it can be said that, broadly speaking, the question of duty is concerned with putting claims into differing *categories* involving, for example, mental injury, or economic loss, or omissions, each requiring special treatment in accordance with relevant concerns of policy and principle. Whereas the existence or otherwise of a duty is determined by reference to policies of general import, the inquiry into the legal cause of harm and/or the remoteness of the damage takes account of the random and contingent features of the particular case at hand. It asks whether there was in the particular circumstances a sufficiently close or proximate connection between the defendant's initial negligent act and the damage suffered by the claimant. The element of foreseeability of harm plays a key role in this inquiry, just as it does in relation to whether a duty exists.

(B) Duty formulae

History. Liability for negligent conduct was first recognised in the 14th **2–05** century in actions against persons exercising "public" or "common" callings in carrying out services for their clients. The essential features of a common calling appear to have been that the services were generally available to the public and demanded skill on the part of the practitioner. Included were the carrier, innkeeper, apothecary, veterinary surgeon, smith and barber. Apart from common callings, other early examples of negligence liability included that of the bailee in performance of a bailment[8] and of a master to a servant.[9] It seems that in claims under these heads the cause of action could be founded indifferently on contract or on tort. With the advent of industrialisation came a substantial rise in the number of tort actions, prompting the courts to recognise various new categories of duty that were not necessarily coincident with contract. Thus, the owner of dangerous premises[10] or of an inherently dangerous chattel[11] was held to owe an obligation of care to certain visitors or users.

---

[6] *Lamb v Camden LBC* [1981] Q.B. 625 at 636, per Lord Denning.
[7] See Ch.5, para.5–01 (remoteness) and Ch.6, para.6–15 (causation), below.
[8] *Coggs v Bernard* (1702) 2 Ld Raym 917.
[9] *Wilson v Merry & Cunningham* (1868) L.R. 1 HL (Sc) 326.
[10] *Indermaur v Dames* (1866) L.R. 1 CP 274.
[11] *Langridge v Levy* (1837) 2 M & W 519; 150 E.R. 863 (liability was founded on the falsity of a representation that a gun was "good, safe and secure"); *George v Skivington* (1869) LR 5 Exch 1; *Clarke v Army & Navy Co-op Society Ltd* [1903] 1 K.B. 155.

2–06   By the late 19th century the burgeoning, although essentially ad hoc, developments in negligence liability led the courts to begin searching for a general statement of principle explaining when a duty would be imposed. The first major attempt at rationalisation was made in *Heaven v Pender.*[12] The plaintiff was employed by a ship's painter and was injured when staging, supplied by the dock owner, collapsed. The plaintiff's claim against the dock owner succeeded. Cotton and Bowen L.JJ. applied established rules relating to the obligation of care owed by an occupier of premises to his or her invitees,[13] but Sir Baliol Brett MR sought to identify a broad principle underlying the existing negligence cases[14]:

> "Whenever one person is by circumstances placed in such a position with regard to another that everyone of ordinary sense who did think would at once recognise that if he did not use ordinary care and skill in his own conduct with regard to those circumstances he would cause danger of injury to the person or property of the other, a duty arises to use ordinary care and skill to avoid such danger."

The other members of the court considered this statement too wide,[15] and it failed to gain acceptance in later cases.[16] Another fifty years were to pass before, in the landmark case of *Donoghue v Stevenson,*[17] the House of Lords set the law on a new and principled path of development.

2–07   **Donoghue v Stevenson.** In this case the pursuer alleged that she was made ill by drinking ginger beer manufactured by the defender which, it turned out, contained the decomposed remains of a snail. The question for their Lordships was whether the manufacturer owed a duty of care to the consumer of his product. In a majority judgment,[18] they held that he did, notwithstanding the absence of any contractual nexus. The duty was to take reasonable care that the ginger beer was free from defects that were likely to cause injury to the consumer's health. The implications of the decision in the particular field of products liability is examined in Chapter 15.[19] The present concern is with the impact of the decision on the general law of negligence.

2–08   Lord Atkin, delivering the leading judgment, recognised that there had to be some general conception of relations giving rise to a duty, of which the particular cases found in the books were but instances. He went on to state the principle to be applied in these words:

> "The rule that you are to love your neighbour becomes in law, you must not injure your neighbour; and the lawyer's question, Who is my neighbour? receives a restricted reply.

---

[12] (1883) 11 Q.B.D. 503 CA.
[13] *Indermaur v Dames* (1866) L.R. 1 CP 274.
[14] (1883) 11 Q.B.D. 503, 509 CA.
[15] Ibid, at 516–517.
[16] It was subsequently said to be too wide by Lord Esher M.R. himself (formerly Sir Baliol Brett M.R.) and Bowen and AL Smith L.JJ. in the Court of Appeal in *Le Lievre v Gould* [1893] 1 Q.B. 491, 497, 502, 504.
[17] [1932] A.C. 562.
[18] Lord Atkin, Lord Thankerton and Lord MacMillan, Lord Buckmaster and Lord Tomlin dissenting.
[19] See Ch.15, para.15–54 below.

You must take reasonable care to avoid acts or omissions which you can reasonably foresee would be likely to injure your neighbour. Who, then, in law is my neighbour? The answer seems to be—persons who are so closely and directly affected by my act that I ought reasonably to have them in contemplation as being so affected when I am directing my mind to the acts or omissions which are called in question."[20]

This statement of the law came to have wide acceptance as establishing the "general concept of reasonable foresight as the criterion of negligence,"[21] and it both provided a basis for, and encouraged, further elaboration. As Lord Macmillan said, also in *Donoghue v Stevenson*: "The criterion of judgment must adjust and adapt itself to the changing circumstances of life. The categories of negligence are never closed".[22]

As time passed it came to be doubted whether the existence of a duty of care **2–09** could be determined by a single general principle.[23] While cases involving physical injury caused by positive conduct, as in *Donoghue v Stevenson* itself, would usually be unproblematic, greater difficulty was likely where, say, the claimant suffered mental injury, or economic loss, or the damage was caused by a statement, or by an omission to act. It was necessary to consider whether or how far the neighbour principle might assist in these and other less straightforward cases.

Lord Reid, in *Dorset Yacht Co v Home Office* in 1970, pointed out the **2–10** continuing importance of *Donoghue* as it approached its fifty year anniversary, but at the same time added some cautionary words:

"In later years there has been a steady trend towards regarding the law of negligence as depending on principle so that, when a new point emerges, one should ask not whether it is covered by authority but whether recognised principles apply to it. *Donoghue v Stevenson* may be regarded as a milestone, and the well-known passage in Lord Atkin's speech should I think be regarded as a statement of principle. It is not to be treated as if it were a statutory definition. It will require qualification in new circumstances. But I think that the time has come when we can and should say that it ought to apply unless there is some justification or valid explanation for its exclusion."[24]

A few years later, Lord Simon appeared to endorse the idea that where the **2–11** neighbour principle was seen as fixing the defendant with responsibility for the claimant's damage, liability should follow, save where there was some good reason why it should not, and identified public policy as the qualifying factor:

[20] ibid, at 580.
[21] *Bourhill v Young* [1943] A.C. 92 at 107, per Lord Wright; *Davies v Swan Motor Co (Swansea) Ltd* [1949] 2 K.B. 291 at 307; *Denny v Supplies & Transport Co Ltd* [1950] 2 K.B. 374 at 377; *Candler v Crane, Christmas & Co* [1951] 2 K.B. 164 at 188; *Dutton v Bognor Regis UDC* [1972] 1 Q.B. 373 at 405. Ironically, Lord Atkin's statement was also criticised as being too wide, notably by Scrutton L.J. in *Farr v Butters Bros & Co* [1932] 2 K.B. 606 at 613–614; by Roche L.J. in *Hayes v Harwood* [1935] 1 K.B. 146 at 167–168; by Singleton J. in *Barnett v H & J Packer Co Ltd* [1940] 3 All E.R. 575 at 577, and by Lord Thankerton in *Bourhill v Young* [1943] A.C. 92 at 98.
[22] [1932] A.C. 532, at 619.
[23] See, for example, *Deyong v Shenburn* [1946] K.B. 227 at 233, per du Parc L.J.
[24] [1970] A.C. 1004 at 1027.

"where there is a duty to act with care with regard to another person and there is a breach of such duty causing damage to the other person, public policy in general demands that such damage should be made good to the party to whom the duty is owed by the person owing the duty. There may be a supervening and secondary public policy which demands, nevertheless, immunity from suit in the particular circumstances."[25]

2–12   So this approach recognised that policy concerns might operate to negate or to limit the acceptance of a duty of care, notwithstanding that harm might be reasonably foreseeable.

2–13   **Anns v Merton London Borough Council.** Shortly afterwards, in *Anns v Merton London Borough Council*,[26] Lord Wilberforce sought to explain how the neighbour principle could be reformulated as a two-stage test of duty, the first focusing on the relationship between the parties and the second on relevant policy concerns:

"Through the trilogy of cases in this House—*Donoghue v Stevenson, Hedley Byrne & Co Ltd v Heller & Partners Ltd*,[27] and *Dorset Yacht Co Ltd v Home Office*,[28] the position has now been reached that in order to establish that a duty of care arises in a particular situation, it is not necessary to bring the facts of that situation within those previous situations in which a duty of care has been held to exist. Rather the question has to be approached in two stages. First one has to ask whether, as between the alleged wrongdoer and the person who has suffered damage there is sufficient relationship of proximity or neighbourhood such that, in the reasonable contemplation of the former, carelessness on his party may be likely to cause damage to the latter—in which case a *prima facie* duty of care arises. Secondly, if the first question is answered affirmatively, it is necessary to consider whether there are any considerations which ought to negative, or to reduce or limit the scope of the duty or the class of person to whom it is owed or the damages to which a breach of it may give rise."[29]

2–14   A two-stage test was initially greeted with enthusiasm[30] and there appeared to be no area of the law of negligence which could resist its application. In particular, the House of Lords applied it when considering duties of care in the very troublesome areas of liability for nervous shock[31] and economic loss.[32] It was also widely accepted overseas, in particular by the Supreme Court of Canada[33] and the New Zealand Court of Appeal.[34] But there were reservations,

---

[25] *Arenson v Casson, Beckman, Rutley & Co* [1977] A.C. 405 at 419.
[26] [1978] A.C. 728.
[27] [1964] A.C. 465; see para.2–172, below.
[28] [1970] A.C. 1004; see para.2–88, below.
[29] [1978] A.C. 728, at 751–752.
[30] In *Paterson Zochonis & Co Ltd v Merfarken Packaging Ltd* [1986] 3 All E.R. 522 at 539, per Goff L.J.: "This statement (which was foreshadowed by more tentative remarks of Lord Reid in *Home Office v Dorset Yacht Co Ltd* [1970] A.C. 1004 at 1026) marked the coming of age of the law of negligence."
[31] *McLoughlin v O'Brian* [1983] 1 A.C. 410: see para.2–134, below.
[32] *Junior Books Ltd v Veitchi Co Ltd* [1983] 1 A.C. 520: see para.2–239, below.
[33] *City of Kamloops v Nielsen* [1984] 2 S.C.R. 2, at 10–11 SCC.
[34] *Scott Group Ltd v McFarlane* [1978] 1 N.Z.L.R. 553, at 565, 573–574, 583 NZCA; *Takaro Properties Ltd v Rowling* [1978] 2 N.Z.L.R. 318 at 323 NZCA; *Meates v Attorney General* [1983] N.Z.L.R. 308 at 334 NZCA.

and Lord Wilberforce's words came to be subject to an increasingly critical analysis.

Criticisms of Anns. The first check was in 1984. A number of cases had **2–15** arisen in which liability for a defective building was imposed upon the local authority responsible for supervising construction for purposes of building regulation. In *Governors of the Peabody Donation Fund v Sir Lindsay Parkinson & Co Ltd*,[35] Lord Keith pointed out that Lord Atkin's statement of general principle was not intended to afford a comprehensive definition. It could not be assumed that every situation which was capable of falling within its terms and which resulted in loss automatically afforded a remedy in damages. So his Lordship preferred to express the position in a different way:

> "The true question in each case is whether the particular defendant owed to the particular plaintiff a duty of care having the scope which is contended for, and whether he was in breach of that duty with consequent loss to the plaintiff. A relationship of proximity in Lord Atkin's sense must exist before any duty of care can arise, but the scope of the duty must depend on all the circumstances in the case."[36]

After quoting Lord Wilberforce's formula, Lord Keith cautioned that, "there has been a tendency in some recent cases to treat these passages as being themselves of a definitive character. This is a temptation which should be resisted".[37] Rather, it was appropriate to ask simply whether it was "just and reasonable" to impose a duty.

Yuen Kun Yeu v Attorney General of Hong Kong. Lord Keith returned to **2–16** the question in delivering the judgment of the Privy Council in *Yuen Kun Yeu v Attorney General of Hong Kong*.[38] He pointed out that there was potential ambiguity in the first stage of the two-stage test. Did Lord Wilberforce mean to test for proximity between the parties simply by the reasonable contemplation of likely harm? Or did he mean the expression, "proximity or neighbourhood" to reflect the necessary relationship between claimant and defendant in a wider sense? The implications of this ambiguity are significant. The first view entailed the notion that stage one raised a presumption of duty—a "prima facie" duty—whenever harm was foreseeable, which seemed to place an onus on the defendant at the second stage to adduce good reason for cutting down or negating the duty. From this perspective the test might open the way to a virtually unfettered potential liability as well as placing an unfair burden upon defendants. Indeed, shifting the onus to a defendant to disprove a duty would be wrong in principle, for ordinarily the claimant must carry the burden of proving all the elements to his or her claim.

Lord Keith accordingly favoured the second view. He said that the expression, **2–17** "proximity or neighbourhood" was intended to be a composite one, importing

---

[35] [1985] A.C. 210; and see also *Leigh & Sillavan Ltd v Aliakmon Shipping Co Ltd* [1986] A.C. 785, at 815.
[36] ibid, at 240.
[37] ibid.
[38] [1988] A.C. 175 at 191 PC.

the whole concept of the necessary relationship between plaintiff and defendant required to give rise to the duty. The trilogy of cases referred to by Lord Wilberforce each demonstrated particular sets of circumstances, differing in character, that were adjudged to have the effect of bringing into being a relationship apt to give rise to a duty of care. He observed that foreseeability of harm was a necessary ingredient of such a relationship, but it was not the only one.

2–18 Resolution of the stage one issue might, therefore, involve a wide-ranging inquiry into matters of policy and principle, which raised the question as to the function of stage-two. Lord Keith thought that a stage two issue would arise only in a limited category of case where, notwithstanding that a case of negligence is made out on a proximity basis, public policy required that there should be no liability.

2–19 **Caparo Industries Plc v Dickman.** Notwithstanding this clarification, Lord Wilberforce's two-stage test was at least misleading and at worst appeared to favour a wide and open-ended liability. A series of decisions[39] reflected a decline of judicial confidence and the two-stage test came to be abandoned. The process culminated in *Caparo Industries Plc v Dickman*,[40] where Lord Bridge emphasised the inability of any single general principle to provide a practical test that could be applied to every situation to determine whether a duty of care was owed and, if so, what was its scope. He continued:

> "What emerges is that, in addition to the foreseeability of damage, necessary ingredients in any situation giving rise to a duty of care are that there should exist between the party owing the duty and the party to whom it is owed a relationship characterised by the law as one of 'proximity' or 'neighbourhood' and that the situation should be one in which the court considers it fair, just and reasonable that the law should impose a duty of a given scope upon the one party for the benefit of the other."[41]

These concepts of proximity and fairness were not, he noted, susceptible of such precise definition as would give them utility as practical tests, but amounted, in effect, to little more than convenient labels to attach to the features of different specific situations which, on a detailed examination of all the circumstances, the law recognised pragmatically as giving rise to a duty of care of a given scope. His Lordship also quoted with approval the words of Brennan J. in the High Court of Australia in *Sutherland Shire Council v Heyman*,[42] that the law should develop novel categories of negligence incrementally and by analogy with established

---

[39] *Leigh and Sillavan Ltd v Aliakmon Shipping Co Ltd: The Aliakmon* [1986] A.C. 785; *Candlewood Navigation Corporation Ltd v Mitsui OSK Lines Ltd* [1986] A.C. 1 at 21, PC; *Curran v Northern Ireland Co-ownership HA Ltd* [1987] A.C. 718; *Yuen Kun Yeu v Attorney-General of Hong Kong* [1988] A.C. 175 PC; *Rowling v Takaro Properties Ltd* [1988] A.C. 473 PC; *CBS Songs Ltd v Amstrad Consumer Electronics Plc* [1988] A.C. 1013, 1059; *Hill v Chief Constable of West Yorkshire Police* [1989] A.C. 53; *Davis v Radcliffe* [1990] 1 W.L.R. 821 PC.
[40] [1990] 2 A.C. 605.
[41] ibid, at 617–618.
[42] (1985) 60 A.L.R. 1, approved in *Murphy v Brentwood DC* [1991] 1 A.C. 398.

categories, rather than by a massive extension of a prima facie duty of care restrained only by indefinable stage two considerations.

On a *Caparo* analysis, then, there is no question of a "prima facie" duty. **2–20** Rather, whether a duty of care should be recognised in a novel case depends on three criteria—the foreseeability of the harm, the proximity of the relationship between the parties, and considerations of fairness and reasonableness. However, whether these are in truth discrete criteria can be disputed. In *Caparo*, Lord Oliver drew specific attention to this point:

> "It is difficult to resist the conclusion that what have been treated as three separate requirements are, at least in most cases, in fact merely facets of the same thing, for in some cases the degree of foreseeability is such that it is from that alone the requisite proximity can be deduced, whilst in others the absence of the essential relationship can most rationally be attributed simply to the court's view that it would not be fair and reasonable to hold the defendant responsible."[43]

It is certainly true to say that in some cases the criteria may overlap or merge **2–21** with one another. Even so, the focus of each of the criteria is different and the *Caparo* approach is widely recognised as a helpful analysis.[44]

Other common law jurisdictions. Debate in overseas jurisdictions has **2–22** ranged over the same or similar issues. In Ireland the Supreme Court has accepted the *Caparo* formula,[45] whereas in Canada[46] and Singapore[47] the courts have retained the *Anns* two stage approach. In New Zealand the courts have restated the principles which should be applied in a way which combines the *Anns* and the *Caparo* analyses.[48] The ultimate question, it is accepted, is whether in the light of all the circumstances it is just and reasonable that a duty should be imposed, but in deciding this question the focus is on two broad fields of inquiry—first, the degree of proximity, and second, wider policy concerns. In Australia the initial view favoured in the High Court was to use the notion of proximity as an all-embracing touchstone to denote the circumstances giving rise

---

[43] [1990] 2 A.C. 605 at 633. See also the comments of Lord Bridge at 618 and Lord Roskill at 628.

[44] For general discussion of the duty issue, see McBride, "Duties of care—do they really exist?" (2004) 24 OJLS 417; Witting, "duty of care: an analytical approach" (2005) 25 OJLS 33; Morgan, "The rise and fall of the general duty of care" (2006) 22 P.N. 206; Hartshorne, "Confusion, contradiction and chaos within the House of Lords post *Caparo v Dickman*" (2008) 16 Tort L Rev 8.

[45] *Glencar Explorations Plc v Mayo CC (No 2)* [2002] 1 IR 84, 139, SC.

[46] *Cooper v Hobart* [2001] 3 S.C.R. 537; and see *Winnigeg Condominium Corp No. 36 v Bird Construction Co* [1995] 1 S.C.R. 85, at 113; *Hercules Managements Ltd Ltd v Ernst & Young* [1997] 2 S.C.R. 165 at 184; *Bow Valley Industries Ltd v St John Shipbuilding Ltd* [1997] 3 S.C.R. 1210. See generally Rafferty, "Pure economic loss in the Supreme Court of Canada—the final word?" (1999) 14 P.N. 13; Rafferty, "The test for the imposition of a duty of care: elucidation or obfuscation by the Supreme Court of Canada" (2002) 17 P.N. 218; Neyers, "Distilling duty: the Supreme Court of Canada amends *Anns*" (2002) 118 L.Q.R. 221.

[47] *Spandick Engineering Pte Ltd v Defence Science & Technology Agency* [2007] 4 S.L.R. 100; *Ngiam Kong Seng v Lim Chiew Hock* [2008] SGCA 23.

[48] *Rolls Royce New Zealand Ltd v Carter Holt Harvey Ltd* [2005] 1 N.Z.L.R. 324, at [58] NZCA; and see *Couch v Attorney-General* [2008] 3 N.Z.L.R. 725 at [48]–[52], [78]–[79], NZSC; *Te Mata Properties Ltd v Hastings DC* [2009] 1 N.Z.L.R. 460 at [32]–[35] NZCA.

to a duty,[49] but later cases recognised that proximity in this sense was a mere label and doubted its value.[50] However, the High Court also has rejected the approaches in both *Anns* and *Caparo*,[51] and some later decisions tend simply to revert to *Donoghue v Stevenson*.[52]

2–23   **Overview.** It may be that too much can be made of the difference between these approaches. The House of Lords has appeared on occasion to revert to something like a two-stage inquiry in resolving a disputed duty issue,[53] and Lord Hoffmann has remarked that provided the considerations of analogy, policy, fairness and justice are properly analysed it should not matter whether one adopts an *Anns* or an incremental analysis.[54] This is true provided the notion of a prima facie duty based upon foreseeability is abandoned. Elias C.J. in the Supreme Court of New Zealand noted a view in that jurisdiction that no substantial difference in result follows the change in emphasis from the *Anns* analysis to the *Peabody/Caparo* approach.[55]

2–24   **Other tests for duty.** The cases discussed so far may be regarded as the main current in the search for a test for the existence of a duty of care in novel situations. But there have been side currents, particularly in relation to liability for negligent misstatements. A line of authority from *Hedley Byrne Ltd v Heller and Partners Ltd*[56] based a duty upon an assumption of responsibility by the maker of a statement towards the recipient and reliance by the recipient upon the statement's accuracy. The cases are looked at in more detail below,[57] and we will consider then what exactly it means to say that a defendant "assumed responsibility" to the claimant, and whether this is a helpful or appropriate approach to the duty problem.

2–25   **Summary.** In broad summary, the leading cases indicate that the law favours an incremental approach to analysing allegedly negligent conduct in most new factual situations, that is, one which builds upon and proceeds from, past

---

[49] *Jaensch v Coffey* (1984) 155 C.L.R. 549 at 578–587, HCA; *Sutherland Shire Council v Heyman* (1985) 157 C.L.R. 424, at 495, HCA; *San Sebastian Pty Ltd v Minister Administering the Environmental Planning and Assessment Act* (1986) 162 C.L.R. 340 at 355 HCA; *Cook v Cook* (1986) 162 C.L.R. 376 at 381 HCA; *Gala v Preston* (1991) 172 C.L.R. 243 at 252 HCA; *Burnie Port Authority v General Jones Pty Ltd* (1994) 174 C.L.R. 520 at 543 HCA; *Bryan v Maloney* (1995) 182 C.L.R. 609, at 617–618, HCA.
[50] *Hill v Van Erp* (1997) 188 C.L.R. 159 at 175–179, 188–190, 210–211, 237–239 HCA; *Esanda Finance Corp Ltd v Peat Marwick Hungerfords* (1997) 188 C.L.R. 241 at 254–255, 263 HCA; *Pyrenees Shire Council v Day* (1998) 192 C.L.R. 330 at 360–361, 414–416 HCA; *Perre v Apand Pty Ltd* (1999) 164 A.L.R. 606 at 613–615, 623–629, 676–685, 697–699 HCA.
[51] *Sullivan v Moody* (2001) 207 C.L.R. 562 HCA.
[52] See, for example, *Tame v New South Wales: Annetts v Australian Stations Pty Ltd* (2003) 211 C.L.R. 317 HCA; *Graham Barclay Oysters Pty Ltd v Ryan* (2003) 211 C.L.R. 540 HCA; Witting, "The thee-stage test abandoned in Australia—or not?" (2002) 118 L.Q.R. 214; Derrington, "Theories of negligence advanced in the High Court of Australia" (2004) 78 ALJ 595.
[53] For example *Spring v Guardian Assurance plc* [1995] 2 A.C. 296; *Marc Rich & Co AG v Bishop Rock Marine Co Ltd* [1996] 1 A.C. 211.
[54] *Stovin v Wise* [1996] A.C. 923, 949.
[55] *Couch v Attorney-General* [2008] 3 N.Z.L.R. 725 at [52], NZSC.
[56] [1964] A.C. 465.
[57] See paras 2–180 to 2–184, below.

decisions. To the extent that a decision is required in a novel or borderline case, where the duty question is not clearly covered by authority, the usual analysis will be to ask whether the harm to the claimant was foreseeable, whether the parties were at the material time in a relationship of proximity or neighbourhood, and whether it is fair, just and reasonable, taking into account relevant policy concerns, that a duty of care should be recognised in all the circumstances of the case. However, in certain cases involving negligent misstatement, the defendant's assumption of responsibility for his or her words may be seen as the determining question. Furthermore, whatever test is applied, it is always necessary to ask not simply whether the defendant was under a duty of care but a duty of care in relation to what. It will become readily apparent in the discussion throughout much of the rest of this chapter that the question as to the existence of a duty of care may be intimately bound up with the kind of damage suffered by the claimant, its manner of infliction and, sometimes, its extent. In addition, the scope of the defendant's duty assists in identifying what harm can be legitimately regarded as arising as a result of a breach of duty, whether that particular link is expressed in terms of "causation" or "remoteness". Both of these are the subject of later chapters.

Value of duty formulae. In *Caparo* Lord Oliver doubted the value of looking   **2–26** for some over-arching principle:

> "I think that it has to be recognised that to search for any single formula which will serve as a general test of liability is to pursue a will-o'-the-wisp. The fact is that once one discards, as it is now clear that one must, the concept of foreseeability of harm as the single exclusive test—even a *prima facie* test—of the existence of the duty of care, the attempt to state some general principle which will determine liability in an infinite variety of circumstances serves not to clarify the law but merely to bedevil its development in a way which corresponds with practicality and common sense."[58]

But the criticism may be too harsh, for the *Caparo* formula (or something like   **2–27** it) does at least provide a helpful structure where there is a dispute whether a duty should be owed. The point is, its role should not be exaggerated. In the words of Cooke P in *South Pacific Manufacturing Co Ltd v New Zealand Security Consultants & Investigations Ltd*[59]:

> "A broad two-stage approach or any other approach is only a framework, a more or less methodical way of tackling a problem. How it is formulated should not matter in the end. Ultimately the exercise can only be a balancing one and the important object is that all relevant factors be weighed. There is no escape from the truth that, whatever formula be used, the outcome in a grey area case has to be determined by judicial judgment. Formulae can help organise thinking but they cannot provide answers."[60]

It is necessary therefore to consider the *content of* the component parts of the   **2–28** inquiry into duty. Our discussion must move beyond the formulae that can help organise thinking, to what the focus of that thinking should be.

---

[58] *Caparo Industries plc v Dickman* [1990] 2 A.C. 605 at 633.
[59] [1992] 2 N.Z.L.R. 282, NZCA.
[60] *South Pacific Manufacturing Co Ltd v New Zealand Security Consultants & Investigations Ltd* [1992] 2 N.Z.L.R. 282, NZCA, at 294.

(C) Application of the Caparo analysis

(i) *Foreseeability*

2–29   Foreseeability of damage. This is the starting point. The issue is whether the law imposes or ought to impose an obligation on the defendant to avoid conduct that exposes persons in the position of the claimant to unreasonable risks of harm.[61] Foreseeability of harm is a necessary, but not a sufficient, condition for a duty to be recognised.[62] In *McLoughlin v O'Brian*,[63] Lord Wilberforce explained its role in this way:

> "Foreseeability, which involves a hypothetical person, looking with hindsight at an event which had occurred, is a formula adopted by English law, nor merely for defining, but also for limiting, the persons to whom duty may be owed, and the consequences for which an actor may be held responsible."

Foreseeability is determined by an objective standard, albeit with reference to the person to whom it is to be applied.[64] Expert evidence may be adduced as to whether damage is foreseeable.[65]

ILLUSTRATIONS

2–30   The requirement of reasonable foreseeability of damage is usually not very demanding. Sometimes, however, a claim will fall at this first hurdle. In one instance, a drainage system installed by a water authority in a street had led to disease developing in the roots of the tree, and eventually the tree fell on a car, killing the plaintiff's husband. The High Court of Australia ruled the authority did not owe future road users in the area a duty of care, because when the drain was established the impact of disease-borne pathogens on trees, and the impact of trees on road users, was not reasonably foreseeable.[66]

2–31   Reasonable foreseeability tends to come to the fore in cases involving especially sensitive claimants. In *Hamilton v Papakura District Council*[67] the plaintiffs complained that toxic herbicide residues in the water supplied by the defendants had damaged their tomato plants and alleged, among other things, that the defendants had been negligent. The defendants contended that their obligation was to supply water to the current drinking standard, which permitted certain levels of impurities, and at no time did the water depart from that standard. The New Zealand Court of Appeal rejected the claim, holding that the damage was unforeseeable. Those with special needs for water of greater purity than

---

[61] *Tame v New South Wales: Annetts v Australian Stations Pty Ltd* (2003) 211 C.L.R. 317 at 103 HCA.
[62] *Yuen Kun Yeu v Attorney General of Hong Kong* [1988] A.C. 175 at 191 PC.
[63] [1983] 1 A.C. 410 at 420.
[64] *Surtees v Kingston-upon-Thames Borough Council* [1991] 2 F.L.R. 559 CA.
[65] See e.g. *Grieves v FT Everard & Sons* [2008] 1 A.C. 281 where the claim failed on this point: see further, para.2–128, below.
[66] *Sydney Water Corporation v Turano* [2009] HCA 42.
[67] [2000] 1 N.Z.L.R. 265, NZCA; [2002] 3 N.Z.L.R. 308 PC.

necessary to meet all reasonable public health requirements had to accept the water at a standard suitable for domestic purposes, and carry out their own treatment to meet more specific criteria. A further appeal to the Privy Council failed, because a duty to supply water beyond the existing standard would be wide-ranging, costly and burdensome, and because the finding of lack of reasonable foreseeability was firmly supported by the evidence.

The requirement of foreseeability of injury also can cause difficulty in mental   **2–32** injury claims, which are given separate treatment below.[68]

(ii) *Proximity*

Proximity or neighbourhood. Proximity involves an inquiry into a state of   **2–33** affairs, that is, whether or not the parties were so situated as to be close to each other, rather than into whether there was an antecedent *relationship*. The notion requires the isolation of factors that, in Lord Atkin's words in *Donoghue v Stevenson*, indicate that the defendant's act or omission closely and directly affected the plaintiff and that the parties are, in this sense, neighbours. The physical, circumstantial and causal connection between the parties are all brought into account. Finding a close connection of this kind, uncomplicated by significant intervening conduct or events, between particular conduct and subsequent damage serves to identify those persons who were most appropriately placed to take care in the avoidance of damage.[69]

There are many cases where the proximity between the parties is in issue. The   **2–34** question has arisen where, for instance, the defendant has failed to intervene to prevent the claimant from suffering harm inflicted by a third party or from some extraneous source[70]; in cases involving claims by secondary victims for mental injury caused by the death or injury of another person[71]; and in cases where the claimant has suffered financial loss by reason of the defendant's negligent statements or conduct.[72] But, as we shall see, all kinds of other situations can raise an issue of this kind.

So, in *Sutradhar v National Environment Research Council*[73] it was held that   **2–35** the NERC owed no duty of care to a citizen of Bangladesh by carrying out hydrochemical work in Bangladesh and issuing a report about the results, but failing to draw attention to the presence of arsenic in the water. The class of potential claimants was the entire population of Bangladesh, or at the very least that of the areas tested during the survey.

Duty to the claimant. The issue of proximity can arise in particular in cases   **2–36** where there has been a wrong to another and the question is whether the conduct is also a wrong to the claimant. A defendant may be under a duty to take care,

---

[68] See paras 2–124 to 2–129, below.
[69] Witting, "The three stage test abandoned in Australia—or not?" (2002) 118 L.Q.R. 214, 218–219.
[70] See paras 2–85 to 2–90, below.
[71] See paras 2–130 to 2–154, below.
[72] See paras 2–186 to 2–203, 2–223 to 2–237, below.
[73] [2006] 4 All E.R. 490 HL.

but that duty is not owed to the world at large. A claimant who happens to suffer harm as a result only of a breach of the defendant's duty to someone else cannot succeed: he or she must always be able to show that a duty was owed to him or to her, whether individually, as a member of a group or class, or more generally.

2–37   *Palsgraf v Long Island Railroad Co*[74] is a leading decision. Two employees of a railway company assisting a passenger to climb aboard a train, negligently knocked a parcel from his hands. The parcel contained fireworks, and these exploded, causing a weighing machine, some 25 feet away, to topple and fall upon the claimant. Her action failed, since what would have been an actionable wrong to the owner of the parcel was not actionable by herself, standing so far away. Cardozo C.J. said:

> "If no hazard was apparent to the eye of ordinary vigilance, an act innocent and harmless, at least to outward seeming, with reference to her, did not take to itself the quality of a tort because it happened to be a wrong, though apparently not one involving the risk of bodily insecurity, with reference to someone else. The plaintiff sues in her own right for a wrong personal to her, and not as the vicarious beneficiary of a breach of duty to another."

2–38   What is important is the proximity, in physical, temporal and other respects, between the happening of the relevant event and the damage it does to the claimant. In *Bourhill v Young*[75] the plaintiff, an Edinburgh fishwife, alighted from a tram and went to collect her fish-basket. On the other side of the tram a motorcyclist drove past at speed, collided with a car a short way further up the road, and suffered fatal injuries. The plaintiff sued the estate of the motorcyclist, alleging that she suffered nervous shock from hearing the noise of the accident and later seeing blood on the road. Lord Wright pointed out that it had to be determined not merely whether the act was negligent against someone else (that is, the car driver) but whether it was negligent vis-à-vis the plaintiff. If the plaintiff had a cause of action it was because of a wrong to herself. She could not build on a wrong to someone else. The claim failed because the plaintiff was outside the area of potential danger and the motorcyclist could not have foreseen damage to her bodily security when she was on the other side of the tram and at some distance from the accident.[76]

2–39   The question whether a duty was owed to the particular claimant bringing the action as well as a duty owed to another person can arise in all kinds of circumstances. It tends to have particular significance in claims for psychiatric injury by secondary victims[77] and in claims by rescuers seeking to assist endangered victims.[78] In a different type of case, where the legal title to land and facilities damaged by negligence was vested in one limited company, in which

---

[74] 162 NE 99 (1928).
[75] [1943] A.C. 92.
[76] See also *Kirkham v Boughey* [1958] 2 Q.B. 338, where Diplock J. held that the duty owed by the driver of a vehicle on a public highway is only to those persons or property that are in geographical proximity to the driver.
[77] See paras 2–138 to 2–149.
[78] See paras 2–259 to 2–265.

the claimant company had a beneficial interest, a duty of care was owed to the claimant, just as to the legal owner, in relation to damage that could reasonably be foreseen.[79]

(iii) *Fair, just and reasonable*

Fair, just and reasonable. Even if the defendant ought reasonably to have   **2–40**
foreseen harm to someone in the position of the claimant and the parties were in a relationship of proximity, a duty of care will not arise unless the third of the criteria identified by Lord Bridge in *Caparo*, is satisfied, namely that a duty to the claimant should in the circumstances be fair, just and reasonable. In *Barrett v Enfield London Borough Council*[80] Lord Browne-Wilkinson explained the test as follows:

> "In English law the decision as to whether it is fair, just and reasonable to impose a liability in negligence on a particular class of would-be defendants depends on weighing in the balance the total detriment to the public interest in all cases from holding such class liable in negligence as against the total loss to all would-be plaintiffs if they are not to have a cause of action in respect of the loss they have individually suffered."[81]

Ultimately it comes down to judicial conceptions of desirable policy. The   **2–41**
question of responsibility for negligence may be argued in an almost unlimited range of circumstances, and a court may take all kinds of considerations into account in deciding whether a duty ought to be owed. However, this does not mean that the question is entirely at large or that every new decision is no more than an ad hoc determination of policy. Certain core concerns of policy and principle can be identified to which the courts frequently refer and which provide guidance in making decisions.

Promoting autonomy. The common law draws a very significant distinction   **2–42**
between positive acts and failures to act. The distinction rests on a judicial policy which recognises and promotes individual autonomy. It is seen as important to avoid unduly restraining that autonomy when deciding whether a person should be under a duty to act to prevent harm being suffered by others. A duty will be imposed only where there are good and sufficient reasons for rejecting the general rule. Before a legal duty to act can arise there should be conduct by the defendant characterised by factors such as specifically induced reliance by the claimant that action would be taken, or the occupation of land creating a risk of harm, or the assumption of specific responsibility for or control over an activity or a particular danger or a particular person's behaviour.[82] Where these factors are present a duty is no longer seen as unjustifiably interfering with the defendant's freedom of action, and other concerns, like the fear of opening up a wide and uncertain area of responsibility, recede in significance.

---

[79] *Shell UK Ltd v Total UK Ltd, The Times*, March 30, 2010 CA.
[80] [2001] 2 A.C. 550.
[81] *Barrett v Enfield London Borough Council* [2001] 2 A.C. 550, at 558.
[82] See paras 2–60 to 2–95.

2-43 **Preventing indeterminate liability.** The extent of the consequences of a defendant's wrongdoing can vary widely according to the nature of the harm which the claimant has suffered and also the way in which the harm has been inflicted. There are profound objections to liability "in an indeterminate amount for an indeterminate time to an indeterminate class".[83] The justification is not simply one of practicality. Rather, it is the perception that the burden of liability would be a disproportionate response to the defendant's wrongdoing. It is a conclusion of policy that reflects a balancing of the claimant's moral claim to compensation for avoidable harm and the defendant's moral claim to be protected from an undue burden of legal responsibility.[84] Gleeson C.J. in the High Court of Australia has observed that the law is concerned not only with the compensation of injured plaintiffs but also with the imposition of liability upon defendants, and the effect of such liability upon the freedom and security with which people may conduct their ordinary affairs.[85] Examples of the so-called "floodgates" fear arise in a wide variety of contexts, for instance, claims for negligent misstatement,[86] for negligent conduct causing economic loss,[87] and for psychiatric injury.[88]

2-44 **Protecting the vulnerable.** The courts take into account whether, or the extent to which, a claimant should be entitled to legal protection. The principle has both a positive and a negative aspect. There is a concern to protect those at a disadvantage, who have no reasonably available means of protecting themselves. Decisions recognising a duty of care owed by a surveyor to the purchaser of a defective house,[89] and by a solicitor to the disappointed legatees of a will that the solicitor had failed to execute,[90] are examples. On the other hand, if a person is well positioned to look after him or herself, a duty may be thought to be unnecessary or inappropriate. The focus is on the steps a person reasonably could have taken to look after his or her own interests. So, accountants reporting on the state of a company's accounts were under no duty to prospective purchasers of the company, who it would be anticipated would consult with their own accountancy advisers.[91] And no duty was owed to buyers of goods that were damaged by the defendants when in transit and at a time before the buyers became the owners, partly because the buyers could have protected their interests in their contract with the sellers.[92]

---

[83] *Ultramares Corporation v Touche* 174 NE 441, 444 per Cardozo C.J. (NY 1931).
[84] *South Pacific Manufacturing Co Ltd v New Zealand Security Consultants & Investigations Ltd* [1992] 2 N.Z.L.R. 282 at 306 per Richardson J. NZCA
[85] *Tame v New South Wales: Annetts v Australian Stations Pty Ltd* (2003) 211 C.L.R. 317 HCA.
[86] See, e.g., *Caparo Industries Plc v Dickman* [1990] 2 A.C. 605, para.2–189, below.
[87] e.g., *Cattle v Stockton Waterworks Co* (1875) L.R. 10 Q.B. 453, para.2–209, below.
[88] See, e.g. *Alcock v Chief Constable of the South Yorkshire Police* [1992] 1 A.C. 310, para.2–136, below.
[89] *Smith v Eric S Bush* [1990] 1 A.C. 831; see para.2–199, below.
[90] *White v Jones* [1995] 2 A.C. 207; see para.2–222, below.
[91] *James McNaughton Paper Group Ltd v Hicks Anderson & Co* [1991] 2 Q.B. 113; see para.2–200, below; *Esanda Finance Corporation Ltd v Peat Marwick Hungerfords* (1997) 188 C.L.R. 241, 284 HCA.
[92] *Leigh and Sillavan Ltd v Aliakmon Shipping Co Ltd: The Aliakmon* [1986] A.C. 785; see para.2–213, below.

Maintaining coherence in the legal system. A duty of care should fit **2–45** coherently into an overall scheme of rights and responsibilities or, in other words, it should be consistent with other legal rules and principles. Imposing liability for negligence has the potential to undermine other principles of law imposing conflicting or inconsistent responsibilities on persons said to be under a duty to take care. Liability in negligence should not be imposed without a clear understanding of the implications. By admitting or excluding it in areas already governed by some legal regime the court seeks to strike an appropriate policy balance in the particular social context.

Examples are found in cases concerning the liability of public bodies for **2–46** alleged negligence in the exercise of a statutory power. A duty of care must at least be consistent with the provisions of any relevant statute, and if it is not then the duty will be denied.[93] Alternatively, the courts may require that the statute should have the purpose of protecting the claimant by way of an action for damages.[94]

A similar principle applies where the question is whether a duty of care in **2–47** negligence can co-exist with other rules of the common law. Expanding negligence liability into novel areas might tend to disrupt the policy balance struck by existing rules of tort which impose a stricter form of liability. For example, an action for negligence in bringing a criminal prosecution against a claimant has been rejected in circumstances where an action for malicious prosecution would lie.[95] In a different context, the argument that a duty of care would undermine the principle of privity of contract, while emphatically rejected in *Donoghue v Stevenson*,[96] carries greater weight in cases where loss is purely financial. This is a continuing source of tension in misstatement cases, where claimants sue in respect of negligent words without having given any contractual consideration in return. It has been called the "free rider" argument.[97] Another possibility is the impact of a duty on core principles of constitutional law. A distinction in public body cases between "policy" matters and "operational" matters is founded ultimately on the need for a proper separation of powers between courts and public bodies exercising discretionary functions. So a duty is owed only in respect of operational or "justiciable" matters, where the policy-making functions of the public body are not called in question.[98]

A case study. The conjoined appeals to the New Zealand Court of Appeal in **2–48** *South Pacific Manufacturing Co Ltd v New Zealand Security Consultants & Investigations Ltd* and *Mortensen v Laing*[99] illustrate the practical working out of a number of these concerns. The question for determination in *Mortensen* was whether an insurance investigator who allegedly negligently reported to an insurer that the insured had lit a fire on the insured property owed a duty of care

---

[93] See e.g., *Gorringe v Calderdale MBC* [2004] 1 W.L.R. 1057 HL, para.2–303, below.
[94] See e.g., *Jain v Trent Strategic Health Authority* [2009] 1 A.C. 853, para.2–322, below.
[95] See e.g., *Calveley v Chief Constable of Merseyside Police* [1989] A.C. 1228, 1238, para.2–317, below.
[96] [1932] A.C. 562.
[97] e.g., *Caparo Industries Plc v Dickman* [1990] 2 A.C. 605; see para.2–191, below.
[98] e.g. *Barrett v Enfield London Borough Council* [2001] 2 A.C. 550; see para.2–298, below.
[99] [1992] 2 N.Z.L.R. 282 NZCA.

to the insured. *South Pacific* was concerned with whether any such duty could extend to a creditor of the insured.

2–49   One factor telling in favour of a duty, applying only in *Mortensen*, was the close proximity between the parties. The investigator could easily foresee that negligence in the preparation of his report might cause injury to the insured. Another factor was the insured's vulnerability. The fate of the insured was very much in the hands of the investigator, and an adverse report was likely to have immediate and serious consequences. The statutory context also pointed in this direction. The provisions of a statute giving third parties affected by the activities of licensed private investigators the right to file a disciplinary complaint based on negligence was seen as a strong point in favour of recognition of a common law duty.

2–50   Opposing considerations, however, were decisive. One of these was the fear of opening the floodgates. Cooke P. remarked that even if investigators owed a duty of care to the insured, such duty would not extend to persons financially interested in the insured as in *South Pacific*. But in either case the recognition of any duty would be inherently expansive, in the sense that the duty could also apply to a vast range of similar everyday situations involving one person reporting about another. Next, there was the potential impact of negligence reasoning on the existing law of defamation. Cooke P. noted that the insurer's report might be defamatory of the plaintiff, yet the report would be protected by qualified privilege and this could be defeated only by proof of malice. The suggested cause of action in negligence would, therefore, impose a greater restriction on freedom of speech than existed under the law worked out over many years to cover freedom of speech and its limits.[100] The investigator might also be sued for malicious prosecution, so a negligence duty was similarly excluded. Other factors seen as militating against a duty included the possible undermining of a litigant's privilege from production and inspection of documents pertaining to expected court proceedings; possible conflict between the contractual duty of the investigator to the insured and any tort duty to the insured; and the existence of the insured's ordinary remedy in contract against the insurer.

(iv) *Conclusions*

2–51   **Overview.** The principles so far described are not exhaustive. Particular cases can always raise questions which cannot be covered by principles or policies of relatively general application. Uncertainty is inherent in the very concept of negligence. Even so, the principles are at least of broad predictive value, and assist in giving some content to what might be termed the duty inquiry.

2–52   **Structure of the duty inquiry.** Given a vast number of cases, raising all kinds of disparate issues, finding a structure that provides helpful guidance is no

---

[100] The High Court of Australia has taken a similar approach: see *Sullivan v Moody* (2001) 207 C.L.R. 562 HCA. Compare *Spring v Guardian Assurance Plc* [1995] 2 A.C. 296, which accepted that the decision in *South Pacific* was correct but declined to apply it in the context of a negligently written reference: see para.2–231, below.

straightforward task. The solution adopted in the rest of this chapter is to divide up the discussion under four heads : (a) the character of the wrongful conduct which is alleged to have caused harm, (b) the kind of harm alleged to have been caused, (c) the kind of person who is bringing the claim, and (d) the kind of person against whom the claim is brought. Although the four aspects are addressed separately, the facts of a case may of course raise issues under two or more of them.

2.—THE KIND OF CONDUCT

(A) Positive conduct

Positive acts. Where liability depends upon proof of some act of the defendant or a person for whom he or she is responsible,[101] as distinct from liability arising from an omission, the requirement of an act involves a bodily movement, resulting from an operation of the will.[102] The line between positive wrongdoing—misfeasance—and a mere failure to act—non-feasance—may sometimes be a fine one,[103] but this is not to throw doubt either on the existence or the significance of the distinction. Active, positive conduct more readily supports the existence of a duty of care than an omission to act. A person may be under a duty to take care not positively to injure another person in a road accident. It is quite another thing to say that a person who happens to be walking past the accident is under a duty to go to the victim's assistance. In the latter case the passer-by at least has not caused the initial harm, and a duty positively to intervene can be imposed only in limited kinds of circumstances.[104]

2–53

Acts and omissions. Sometimes the courts appear to have passed over the distinction between an act and an omission. In *Donoghue v Stevenson* itself Lord Atkin required that reasonable care be taken as regards both acts and omissions that might foreseeably injure one's neighbour.[105] Although he might be seen as treating misfeasance and non-feasance alike, what he clearly had in mind were negligent omissions in the course of some wider activity involving positive conduct. A failure to do something may amount to nothing more than negligently performing an act of commission and be indistinguishable in legal effect from that act.[106] So a motorist who fails to sound his horn at a blind crossing and/or to stop at a "Halt" sign, as a result of which some accident occurs, will be liable

2–54

---

[101] For vicarious liability see generally Ch.3 para.3–98, below.
[102] Holmes, *The Common Law*, p.54.
[103] *Cavanagh v Ulster Weaving Co Ltd* [1960] A.C. 145 at 165.
[104] See para.2–63 below.
[105] [1932] A.C. 562; and see *Read v J Lyons & Co* [1945] K.B. 216 at 228 per Scott L.J.: "It is the act of the defendant which entails liability on him for the harm happening to another, whether the act be one of commission or omission",
[106] See *Harnett v Bond* [1924] 2 K.B. 517 at 541 per Bankes L.J.: "A medical man who diagnoses a case of measles as a case of scarlet fever may be said to have omitted to make a correct diagnosis; he may equally well be said to have made an incorrect diagnosis." See also *Hawkins v Coulsdon & Purley UDC* [1954] 1 Q.B. 319 at 332, per Denning L.J.

for having performed a negligent but active operation in driving his vehicle.[107] Again, a contractor who digs a hole in a carriageway and leaves it unlit and uncovered is sued not simply for failing to put up a light but for the complex act[108]; and a failure to maintain a level crossing cannot be divorced from the positive operation of running trains.[109] Whether conduct should be characterised as misfeasance or non-feasance depends very much on the choice of the level of abstraction for describing it. Broadly, however, where the conduct that is alleged involves a composite of acts and omissions that cannot sensibly be disentangled, then it is treated as an instance of positive action, with the duty question being determined accordingly. But where the complaint is of harm being inflicted from a source initially unconnected with the defendant and to which he or she has not contributed, then the law concerning omissions comes into play.

2–55   **Creating a situation of danger.** It is apparent that creating a situation of peril or danger, even without negligence, engenders a duty to warn of or remove the danger. For example, a driver may be liable for failing to stop after an accident, leaving the victim at risk of further injury,[110] or for creating an obstruction in the road and failing to remove it.[111] In an arguably analogous case, a truck driver whose truck was hit by a rock owed a duty to check what damage had been done and to warn other road users about the danger caused by petrol leaking onto the road.[112] Again, a manufacturer is under a duty to give warning of any special risks involved in the use of its products. For example, the manufacturer of a crane was obliged to warn of the risk posed by a manufacturing defect,[113] and the manufacturer of breast implants to warn of the risk of rupture.[114]

2–56   These cases can be seen as nearer to misfeasance than non-feasance, for they depend on an innocent defendant having initially created the danger. And if the defendant is negligent in the first place, of course he or she must take reasonable care to prevent further damage occurring.

2–57   **Acts and statements.** A further distinction is that between acts and statements. Actions in respect of negligent words are treated differently according to whether the words cause financial or physical damage. Negligent misstatements causing financial damage tend to raise the fear of indeterminate liability, and a consequent need to impose strict limits on the existence or ambit of any duty. The relevant principles are considered later, in the context of the duty of care and

---

[107] See *Stovin v Wise* [1994] 1 W.L.R. 1124, 1138 CA (car driver cannot escape liability simply because his breach of duty consisted in a failure to apply the brakes); see also on appeal [1996] A.C. 923, 929–930, 945.
[108] *Newton v Ellis* (1855) 5 El & Bl 115; 119 E.R. 424.
[109] *Commissioner for Railways v McDermott* [1967] 1 A.C. 169, 189 PC.
[110] *Brook v Willig Transport Co* 255 P 2d 802 (1953).
[111] *McKinnon v Burtatowski* [1969] V.R. 899; and see *Johnson v Rea Ltd* [1961] 1 W.L.R. 1400 CA.
[112] *Sullivan v Stefanidi* [2009] NSWCA 313.
[113] *Rivtow Marine Ltd v Washington Ironworks Co* [1974] S.C.R. 1189 SCC.
[114] *Dow Corning Corporation v Hollis* [1995] 4 S.C.R. 634 SCC.

financial loss.[115] However, words are likely to be treated in the same way as positive conduct where reliance on the words leads to physical injury. The range of potential victims will usually be limited, and unless there is some other policy concern a duty can be imposed without difficulty.

Accordingly, an architect who assured a demolition contractor that a wall on   2–58
the demolition site could safely be left standing was liable when the wall later collapsed on a workman.[116] This was a case where liability could be founded upon ordinary *Donoghue v Stevenson* principles. In other examples, a doctor owed a duty to take care in warning a patient of the risks of undergoing an operation[117]; and a local authority was liable for giving negligent advice to a mother concerning the suitability of a registered child-minder.[118] Negligent advice leading to psychological or mental damage also may be actionable. The House of Lords has held that persons offering psychological or educational advice to members of the public are bound to exercise the skill and care reasonably to be expected of a reasonable psychologist or teacher.[119]

Exceptionally a court may deny a duty of care arising out of a negligent   2–59
statement resulting in physical injury or loss for special reasons of policy. In *Marc Rich & Co AG v Bishop Rock Marine Co Ltd*[120] a surveyor who classified a ship as seaworthy, after temporary repairs to a crack in the hull had been carried out, was held to owe no duty of care to cargo owners whose cargo was lost after the repairs proved inadequate and the ship sank. A major reason for the decision was that recognition of a duty would disturb the balance of rights and immunities between ship owners and those shipping goods under bills of lading governed by the Hague Rules and the Hague-Visby Rules.[121] The majority thought that exposure of classification societies to tort liability would lead to them obtaining liability risks insurance and passing on the cost to the ship owners or requiring indemnities from the ship owners. It would be unfair, unjust and unreasonable to make the ship owners bear the ultimate burden of liability and a duty should, therefore, be denied.

---

[115] See para.2–166 below.
[116] *Clay v A J Crump & Sons Ltd* [1964] 1 Q.B. 533. See also *Clayton v Woodman & Son (Builders) Ltd* [1962] 2 Q.B. 533, where at first instance an architect was held liable to a bricklayer for careless statements about how to carry on building work, which resulted in the bricklayer being hurt when a gable end collapsed. The decision was reversed on appeal ([1962] 2 Q.B. 546) on the ground that there was no evidence that the architect had been negligent.
[117] *Chester v Afshar* [2005] 1 A.C. 134. In this case the House of Lords imposed liability for a failure to warn of a risk even though the claimant could not show that she would not have undergone surgery at some time in the future, when the risk would have been the same. The majority held that the defendant was in breach of a duty to warn, and the injury suffered was within the scope of, and caused by, that breach of duty. See further Ch.6 para.6–54, below.
[118] *T v Surrey County Council* [1994] 4 All E.R. 577, CA.
[119] *Barrett v Enfield LBC* [2001] 2 A.C. 550; *Phelps v Hillingdon LBC* [2001] 2 A.C. 619.
[120] [1996] 1 A.C. 211; Mullender, "Negligence, the pursuit of justice and the House of Lords" (1996) 4 Tort L Rev 9; Tan Keng Feng, "Of duty" (1996) 112 L.Q.R. 209.
[121] The Hague and Hague-Visby Rules are in force in the UK: Carriage of Goods by Sea Act 1971.

(B) Omissions

(i) *Introduction*

2–60 **No general duty to act.** At least as a general rule, there is a duty to take care not positively to cause physical injury or damage to another. Conversely, where someone is put at risk from a source not connected in some way with the defendant, there is no general duty in tort requiring the defendant to intervene.[122] As Lord Diplock said in *Home Office v Dorset Yacht Co Ltd*[123]:

> "The very parable of the Good Samaritan (Luke 10, v 30) which was evoked by Lord Atkin in *Donoghue v Stevenson* illustrates, in the conduct of the priest and of the Levite who passed by on the other side, an omission which was likely to have as its reasonable and probable consequence damage to the health of the victim of the thieves, but for which the priest and Levite would have incurred no civil liability in English law."

2–61 A principle whereby citizens are under no general legal obligation to help or rescue others or to shout warnings or to provide a haven from danger might appear to be at odds with ordinary principles of common morality. The reasons for the principle and, importantly, the exceptions to it, require examination.

2–62 **Policy issues.** The general rule denying a duty to take care to act for the benefit of others is founded on a moral principle that seeks to promote individual autonomy. A person is not required to bear responsibility for a loss in circumstances where he or she chose to pass by or failed to help, because an enforceable legal duty is seen as an undesirable constraint upon individual freedom of action or of choice. This basic principle can be fleshed out by reference to political, moral and economic considerations identified by Lord Hoffmann in *Stovin v Wise*.[124] In political terms it was less of an invasion of an individual's freedom for the law to require him to consider the safety of others in his actions than to impose upon him a duty to rescue or protect. A moral version of this point might be called the "why pick on me?" argument. A duty to prevent harm to others or to render assistance to a person in danger or distress might apply to a large and indeterminate class of people who happened to be able to do something. Why should one be liable rather than another? In economic terms, the efficient allocation of resources usually required an activity should bear its own costs. If it benefited from being able to impose some of its costs on other people (what economists called "externalities") the market was distorted because the activity appeared cheaper than it really was. So liability to pay compensation for loss caused by negligent conduct acted as a deterrent against increasing the cost of the activity to the community and reduced externalities.

---

[122] McIvor, *Third Party Liability in Tort*, Oxford, Hart Publishing, 2006; Markesinis, "Negligence, nuisance and affirmative duties of action" (1989) 105 L.Q.R. 104; Fridman, "Non-vicarious liability for the acts of others" (1997) 5 Tort L Rev 102; Gray and Edelman, "Developing the law of omissions: a common law duty to rescue?" (1998) 6 T.L.J. 240; Bagshaw, "The duties of care of emergency providers" [1999] LMCLQ 71.

[123] [1970] A.C. 1004, 1060; and see *Zoernsch v Waldock* [1964] 1 W.L.R. 675, 685 per Willmer L.J., CA; *Pyrenees Shire Council v Day* (1998) 192 C.L.R. 330, 368 per McHugh J., HCA; *Brownie Wills v Shrimpton* [1998] 3 N.Z.L.R. 320, 327 per Tipping J., NZCA.

[124] [1996] A.C. 923.

But there was no similar justification for requiring a person who was not doing anything to spend money on behalf of someone else. Except in special cases English law did not reward someone who voluntarily conferred a benefit on another. So there should be some special reason why he should have to put a hand in his pocket.

Bases for a duty. These policies will not invariably come into play when a   **2–63** court is asked to impose liability for a mere omission. A legal obligation to act may arise in any particular case either because the omission in question should be viewed in the context of wider positive conduct, or because the case possesses certain features that reduce or outweigh their impact. Thus, a duty tends to be recognised in cases where the claimant reasonably relied on the defendant acting for his or her benefit or where the defendant exercised control over or assumed responsibility for the circumstances giving rise to the danger. Where these features are present it is no longer so convincing to argue that the defendant's freedom of action has been unjustifiably abridged, what is expected in fulfilment of the duty will be what is reasonable in the circumstances, taking into account the risks and costs of action. The duty is confined to the particular defendant and any potential there might otherwise be for a duty of indeterminate extent is kept in check. It will thus be seen that the elements of reliance, control and assumption of responsibility underlie the various categories of cases where there may be a positive duty to act.

Causal issues. How far a mere omission to prevent harm can be said to be a   **2–64** cause of the harm can be problematic. Where there is an existing risk or danger to which the defendant fails to respond, arguably the risk or danger alone is the cause of the harm which ensues. The defendant has not contributed to the risk, which simply continues to operate without interference on the part of the defendant or anyone else. For example, in *East Suffolk Rivers Catchment Board v Kent*[125] the defendant Board decided to exercise its statutory power to repair a sea wall, but did the work so negligently that the claimant's adjoining land remained flooded for far longer than would have been the case had the work been done properly. It was held that the Board was not liable, because the damage was due to natural causes. Lord Porter said that the loss which the respondents suffered was due to the original breach, and the appellants' failure to close it merely allowed the damage to continue.[126]

While *East Suffolk* appears to rest simply on the question of causation, it can   **2–65** also be seen as holding that the defendant was under no duty to act. Lord Romer said that if a statutory authority in the exercise of its discretion embarked upon an execution of its power, the only duty it owed to a member of the public was not thereby to add to the damages he would have suffered had it done nothing.[127] Certainly it may often be difficult in claims resting upon an omission to prevent harm to separate the issue of causation from that of duty. It is rather easier where

---

[125] [1941] A.C. 74.
[126] *East Suffolk Rivers Catchment Board v Kent* [1941] A.C. 74, at 105; and see at 85 per Lord Simon, at 96 per Lord Thankerton, at 99 per Lord Romer.
[127] *East Suffolk Rivers Catchment Board v Kent* [1941] A.C. 74, at 102.

the circumstances are such as to give rise to a positive duty to act, on one of the bases discussed below, because then a failure to act is treated as a cause if action would have prevented the harm. There would otherwise be little point in recognising the duty. In *Reeves v Commissioner of Police of the Metropolis*,[128] where the police were sued for not preventing a prisoner from committing suicide, Lord Hoffmann observed that a duty to protect a person of full understanding from causing harm to himself was rare indeed. But once it was admitted that a case was of a kind where a duty was owed, it seemed self-contradictory to say that the breach could not have been a cause of the harm because the victim caused it to himself.

2–66   Greater uncertainty surrounds the case where a basis for a duty to act exists but the circumstances are such that whether action by the defendant would have averted the claimant's loss is inherently unpredictable. One solution is for the court to evaluate the chance that the damage would have been avoided and give damages based on the value of that chance, provided that it was a real or more than minimal chance.[129]

2–67   **A case study.** *Mitchell v Glasgow CC*[130] concerned a claim against a local authority landlord. Mitchell (M) and Drummond (D) were tenants of Glasgow City Council. D frequently was abusive towards and made threats to kill M and was arrested on a number of occasions. The council warned D that they would take action to recover his house if he did not stop this conduct, but to no avail. Eventually the council summoned D to meeting and told him that he would be evicted if his anti-social behaviour continued. One hour later D attacked M, causing him injuries from which he died. The pursuers, M's widow and daughter, brought proceedings against the council, alleging, inter alia, that it was liable for negligence at common law.[131]

2–68   The House of Lords held unanimously that no duty of care was owed by the council to M. Lord Hope noted that it was clear that foreseeability of harm was not of itself enough for the imposition at common law of a positive duty to act. The law did not normally impose a duty on a person to protect others, and, in particular, there was no general duty on a person to protect others from being harmed by the criminal acts of a third party. However, a duty to intervene might exist where a defender (i) had created a source of danger, or (ii) had exercised control over another, or (iii) had assumed a responsibility to or induced reliance by the pursuer. But here there was nothing to show that the local authority had made itself responsible for protecting M from the criminal acts of D, and there was no duty on the authority to warn M of steps it was taking concerning D. And the implications of a duty to warn were complex and far-reaching. The defenders would have to determine, step by step at each stage, whether or not the actions

---

[128] [1999] 3 W.L.R. 363, 368 HL.

[129] *Davies v Taylor* [1974] A.C. 207; cp *Gregg v Scott* [2005] 2 A.C. 176. See further Ch.9 para.9–00.

[130] [2009] 1 A.C. 874; applied in *X v Hounslow London Borough Council* [2009] 2 F.L.R. 262 CA (no duty owed by council to vulnerable tenants to protect them from abuse by youths living on the same council estate).

[131] An alternative claim that the council was liable for breach of the Human Rights Act 1998 also failed: see para.2–336.

they proposed to take in fulfilment of their responsibilities as landlords required a warning to be given, and to whom. The more attentive they were to their ordinary duties as landlords, the more onerous the duty would become.

(ii) *Liability for property*

Generally. The occupation of premises carries with it a duty to act in relation   2–69
to dangers on the premises. An occupier exercises control over and has knowledge of the state of the premises and so it is seen as "natural and right" that he or she should have some degree of responsibility for the safety of persons and property on the premises.[132] As regards lawful visitors the Occupiers' Liability Act 1957, reflecting the common law, imposes on the occupier a "common duty of care" and this may require the occupier to abate dangers on the premises. Again, where damage is suffered by a trespasser, a duty may be imposed pursuant to the Occupiers' Liability Act 1984. The whole question of occupiers' liability to those who come on the land, lawfully or otherwise, can conveniently stand on its own and, accordingly, it is dealt with separately in Chapter 8. However, this still leaves the case where damage is caused by the state of land or premises to persons or property off the premises, where common law principles apply.

Of course, if an occupier actually creates a danger on premises that spreads   2–70
elsewhere he or she may be held liable in negligence the ordinary way. The present concern is with the case where the occupier does not create the danger but fails to prevent it from causing harm to another. The question here is whether the occupier comes under a duty of care to act positively to prevent the harm.

Known dangers. In the leading decision in *Goldman v Hargrave*[133] the Privy   2–71
Council held an occupier responsible in both negligence and nuisance for failing to take care to prevent a fire on his land, which had been started by a bolt of lightning, from encroaching onto nearby property. Liability was based upon the fact that the occupier knew of the fire but had failed to take reasonable steps to put it out. So also, an occupier was liable for allowing the slipping of earth and debris from his land on to adjoining property,[134] for letting variegated thistle seed proliferate on his land and failing to prevent it from spreading,[135] and for failing to pigeon-proof a bridge in order to prevent pigeons roosting in the bridge and fouling the pavement below.[136] In these various cases the harm was caused by the operation of natural forces or processes yet the occupier, being in the best position to obviate or contain the damage, nonetheless had an obligation to act. The danger having arisen without any personal fault, however, the content of the duty was essentially *subjective*, requiring the occupier to do what was reasonable in the light of his or her own resources and, it seems, the ability of the neighbour to take reasonable steps by way of self-protection. Again, on an analogous principle, an owner of inflammable goods was liable to a warehouse owner for having stored the goods in the warehouse in a way which made firefighting

---

[132] *Commissioner for Railways v McDermott* [1967] 1 A.C. 169, 186 PC.
[133] [1967] 1 A.C. 645 PC. See Ch.12 para.12–37, below.
[134] *Leakey v National Trust* [1980] Q.B. 485.
[135] *French v Auckland CC* [1974] 1 N.Z.L.R. 340.
[136] *Wandsworth London Borough Council v Railtrack Plc* [2002] 2 W.L.R. 512 CA.

difficult in the event of a fire, even though it could not be shown that the
defendant's conduct caused the fire which subsequently occurred to break
out.[137]

2–72   The *Goldman* principle can apply where an occupier allows intruders to create
a danger on his or her land which then causes damage to others. But the occupier
must know or have means of knowledge of the particular risk. So, in *Smith v
Littlewoods Organisation Ltd*,[138] Lord Goff held that the owners of a derelict
cinema owed no duty to an adjoining owner in circumstances where vandals
started a fire which damaged the adjoining property, because they had not known
of any previous acts of vandalism involving fire or a risk of fire. There are many
cases that illustrate the principle or something very similar. For example, an
occupier who did nothing to prevent unauthorised persons from gaining access to
his derelict property was not responsible when thieves broke through an interior
wall into the property next door and stole the claimant's goods[139]; and the
occupier of an unlit car park was not responsible for an assault on a person using
the park committed by unknown assailants.[140] By contrast, where known
trespassers on a vacant site started a fire, the defendant council was held liable
for leaving combustible material on the site and allowing the fire to spread.[141]

2–73   **Special sources of danger.** In *Smith*, Lord Goff also held that a duty could
arise where premises or a chattel were a special source of danger and it was
reasonably foreseeable that a third party might interfere and "spark off" the
danger. But he considered that an empty cinema could not be described as an
unusual danger in the nature of a fire hazard, and so on the facts this principle
could not apply either. However, a special danger principle can be seen as
underlying a number of cases involving third parties causing harm by using or
interfering with someone else's property. For example, a carter who left a horse-
drawn van unattended in a crowded street was liable to a policeman who was
injured in trying to stop the horse after a boy threw a stone at it, causing it to
bolt[142]; and the owner of a quarry was liable when the quarry safe was left in an
accessible place, some children retrieved detonators from it by driving the rod
out from the hinges, passed them on to a friend and one exploded when being
used as a plaything by the friend's small brother.[143] On the other hand, a motor
vehicle cannot be regarded as posing a special danger such that the owner is

---

[137] *Wilson & Horton Ltd v Attorney-General* [1997] 2 N.Z.L.R. 513 NZCA.
[138] [1987] A.C. 241.
[139] *P Perl (Exporters) Ltd v Camden LBC* [1984] Q.B. 342; and see *King v Liverpool CC* [1986] 1
W.L.R. 890 CA (any duty to secure property against thieves or vandals limited by impossibility of
taking effective steps to defeat their activities).
[140] *Modbury Triangle Shopping Centre Pty Ltd v Anzil* (2000) 205 C.L.R. 254 HCA; Dietrich,
"Liability in negligence for harm resulting from third parties' criminal acts: *Modbury Triangle
Shopping Centre Pty Ltd v Anzil*" (2001) 9 T.L.J. 152; Fordham, "Liability for the criminal acts of
third parties" (2001) 117 L.Q.R. 178.
[141] *Clark Fixing Ltd v Dudley MBC* [2001] EWCA Civ 1898 CA.
[142] *Haynes v Harwood* [1935] 1 K.B. 146.
[143] *McCarthy v Wellington CC* [1966] N.Z.L.R. 481 NZCA.

obliged to take care to prevent someone else from using it. So the owner of a car was not liable when a thief stole it and later ran down a pedestrian.[144]

Another approach to the problem, put forward by Lord Mackay in *Smith*, is to   **2–74** base the defendant's liability on proof of a high degree of likelihood of harm. However, in *Mitchell v Glasgow CC*,[145] Lord Hope said that it was not easy to reconcile an approach relying generally on the likelihood of harm with the rule that a person is under no general duty to protect another from harm. He favoured Lord Goff's approach, which depended on showing that the particular situation was one where it was readily understandable that the law should regard the defender as under a responsibility to take care.

Vendors and lessors. The question whether a duty to prevent harm can be   **2–75** imposed upon the owner or occupier of property also can arise where the property is sold or let to another. It is apparent that a vendor or lessor who has created a defect in the property can owe a duty of care to those who suffer physical harm caused by the defect. But the position where the vendor or lessor does not create the danger but fails to warn about it is controversial. A claim for economic loss made by a purchaser who has acquired already defective property is more controversial still, and this will be considered separately later on.[146]

Creating a danger. At common law, lessors and vendors who knew of a   **2–76** dangerous defect in premises and who let or sold the premises without warning were granted an immunity from suit. So, in *Robbins v Jones*,[147] a landlord who let a house in a dangerous state was not liable for injury to the tenant's customers or guests, for in the words of Erle C.J., fraud apart, "there is no law against letting a tumble-down house".[148] The immunity was held to apply even if the landlord had contracted with the tenant to do the repairs.[149] It is not clear whether the immunity as originally propounded was intended to benefit negligent builders, but the Court of Appeal subsequently applied it in favour of a landlord who had himself constructed the defect.[150] For a time the rule was maintained even after *Donoghue v Stevenson*,[151] but it came to be undermined by cases showing that a builder, architect or engineer who was not the owner could be liable for personal injuries caused by faulty work of construction or repair.[152] The immunity enjoyed by the builder/owner could not survive, and eventually it was

---

[144] *Topp v London Country Bus (South West) Ltd* [1993] 1 W.L.R. 976 CA.
[145] [2009] 1 A.C. 874; see para.2–67 above.
[146] See paras 2–238 to 2–248, also Ch.8 para.8–114, below.
[147] (1863) 15 CB (NS) 221; [1861–73] All E.R. Rep. 544. See further Ch.8, para.8–109 below.
[148] ibid, at p. 240, 547. The immunity did not apply in the case of a furnished letting: *Smith v Marrable* (1843) 11 M & W 5; (1843) 152 ER 693; *Wilson v Finch Hatton* (1877) 2 Ex D 336.
[149] *Cavalier v Pope* [1906] A.C. 428; *Cameron v Young* [1908] A.C. 176.
[150] *Bottomley v Bannister* [1932] 1 K.B. 458.
[151] *Otto v Bolton* [1936] 2 K.B. 46; *Davis v Foots* [1940] 1 K.B. 116 CA; *Travers v Gloucester Corporation* [1947] K.B. 71.
[152] *Clayton v Woodman & Son (Builders) Ltd* [1962] 2 Q.B. 533; *Sharpe v E T Sweeting & Son Ltd* [1963] 1 W.L.R. 665; *Clay v A J Crump & Sons Ltd* [1964] 1 Q.B. 533.

affirmed in the House of Lords that the same rules applied to all acts of a builder, whether he happened also to own the land or not.[153]

2–77   **Defective Premises Act 1972.**[154] The developments in the common law have been supported by legislative intervention. Section 3(1) of the Defective Premises Act 1972 provides:

> "Where work of construction, repair, maintenance or demolition or any other work is done on or in relation to premises, any duty of care owed because of the doing of the work, to persons who might reasonably be expected to be affected by defects in the state of the premises created by the doing of the work shall not be abated by the subsequent disposal of the premises."

Section 3 applies to both vendors and lessors. Certain further provisions also apply in the case of a lease. By s.4(1), where premises are let under a tenancy which puts on the landlord an obligation to the tenant for the maintenance or repair of the premises, the landlord owes to all persons who might reasonably be expected to be affected by defects in the state of the premises a duty to take such care as is reasonable in all the circumstances to see that they are reasonably safe from personal injury or damage to their property caused by a defect within the maintenance or repairing obligation. By s.4(4), a landlord who has the power to enter and repair is to be treated for the purposes of the section as if he were under an obligation to the tenant to repair. The persons who can sue under s.4 may include the tenant himself or herself,[155] family and friends, neighbours, visitors and even trespassers.

2–78   **Failing to warn.** Seemingly, it remains true that an owner who lets or sells premises containing a defect which he or she did not create owes no duty in tort to third persons who suffer harm caused by the defect. The immunity of the bare landlord or vendor has been seen as too deeply entrenched in the law for any court below the highest to question it.[156] However, different views were expressed in the High Court of Australia in *Northern Sandblasting Pty Ltd v Harris*.[157] The defendant landlord let a house to the parents of the infant plaintiff. Unknown to the landlord the earth wiring of the house was defective. Later, the landlord arranged for an independent contractor to repair the stove. The repair was carried out negligently and this, combined with the earth wiring defect, electrified a garden tap. The plaintiff was severely injured when she touched the tap. The court held by a four to three majority that the landlord was liable, but two different reasons were given and neither enjoyed majority support. Two majority judges (Brennan C.J. and Gaudron J.) held that the landlord was in breach of duty in letting out the premises in an unsafe condition which could

---

[153] *Anns v London Borough of Merton* [1978] A.C. 728, at 759 per Lord Wilberforce; and see *Rimmer v Liverpool CC* [1985] Q.B. 1; *Targett v Torfaen BC* [1992] 3 All E.R. 27 CA.

[154] See also Ch.8, para.8–123, below.

[155] *Sykes v Harry* [2001] Q.B. 1014. However, s.4(4) goes on to provide that the tenant is not owed any duty in respect of a defect arising from a failure to carry out an obligation expressly imposed on the tent by the tenancy.

[156] *Rimmer v Liverpool City Council* [1985] Q.B. 1.

[157] (1997) 188 C.L.R. 313 HCA; Handford "No consensus on landlord's liability" (1998) 6 Tort L Rev 105; Tan Keng Feng "Landlord's Liability" (1998) 114 L.Q.R. 193.

reasonably have been discovered. Four other members of the court rejected this reasoning. The other two majority judges (Toohey and McHugh JJ.) held that the landlord was under a non-delegable duty to ensure that the independent contractor took care in repairing the stove. All other members of the court disagreed.

(iii) *Inducing reliance*

Inducing reliance. The mere fact that a person is in a position to warn another   **2–79** of danger is no sufficient reason for imposing a legal duty to warn. In a much-cited example, Lord Keith maintained there could be no liability in negligence on the part of one who sees another about to walk over a cliff and fails to shout a warning.[158] So, insurers conducting pre-contractual negotiations with a bank who knew that the bank's insurance broker had been acting fraudulently were not obliged to give warning to the bank.[159] The silence of the insurers did not amount to an assurance that the broker was trustworthy and the bank did not rely on that silence. Again, lessors who had insured premises against loss or damage by fire, when under no legal obligation to do so, owed no duty to inform the lessees, who did have a duty to insure, that the insurance cover was not being renewed.[160] But there may be a duty to act if one has undertaken to do so or induced a person to rely upon one doing so.[161] The justice of imposing a duty in a case of this kind is readily apparent: the claimant may be deprived of the chance of assistance by third parties or the opportunity to take steps by way of self-protection, and may also be lulled into a false sense of security.

ILLUSTRATIONS

There are many examples. They include: a drainage board, contrary to   **2–80** previous practice, omitting to warn that land on which a house was to be built was subject to flooding[162]; an ambulance service which had undertaken to assist a patient delaying doing so, as a result of which other possible means of transporting the patient to hospital were abandoned[163]; a solicitor parting with control of a husband's passport after undertaking to retain it, leading the wife to refrain from taking precautions to keep out of her husband's way so as to prevent him from absconding overseas with the children of the marriage, all this causing psychiatric injury to the wife[164]; a rugby referee failing to enforce safety rules leading to the collapse of a scrummage and serious injury to the claimant[165]; tenants of factory premises failing to maintain a private alarm system in

---

[158] *Yuen Kun Yeu v Attorney General of Hong Kong* [1988] A.C. 175 at 192 PC; adopted by Lord Hope in *Mitchell v Glasgow City Council* [2009] 1 A.C. 874, at [15]; and see *The Majfrid* [1942] P 145 CA (no duty to preserve property put at risk by another).
[159] *Banque Keyser Ullman SA v Skandia (UK) Insurance Co Ltd* [1990] 1 Q.B. 665, affirmed [1991] 2 A.C. 249.
[160] *Argy Trading Development Co Ltd v Lapid Developments Ltd* [1977] 1 W.L.R. 444.
[161] *Stovin v Wise* [1996] A.C. 923 at 944.
[162] *Brown v Heathcote County Council* [1987] 1 N.Z.L.R. 720, PC.
[163] *Kent v Griffiths* [2000] 2 W.L.R. 1158 at 1162, CA.
[164] *Al-Kandari v J R Brown & Co* [1988] Q.B. 665; *Hamilton-Jones v David & Snape* [2004] 1 W.L.R. 924.
[165] *Vowles v Evans* [2003] 1 W.L.R. 1607, CA.

circumstances where they knew and accepted that the landlords were relying on the alarm to protect the premises from the activities of vandals[166]; a security firm inducing reliance by miners on it taking precautions to protect them from striking miners[167]; and a personnel officer inducing an employee to believe that he could rely on her in handling the financial arrangements in transferring to a new job but then failing to give proper advice.[168]

(iv) *Assuming responsibility for other persons*

2–81   **Duty to the other person.** A person may come under a legal duty to act because in one way or another he or she has taken on responsibility for the welfare of another. Sometimes this may induce reliance by the other, constituting an alternative reason for imposing a duty to act, but liability may arise independently of any question of reliance. So a parent or person in loco parentis, like a school authority, must take care to safeguard a child from danger on the road, or from dangerous premises, or from being assaulted or abused.[169] There are many examples where an assumed relationship of control over a person in a vulnerable or dependent position has led to a duty being imposed. For example, a prison authority was obliged to take care to protect a prisoner[170]; a police commissioner was required to protect a police officer from being victimised by fellow officers[171]; a doctor was obliged to treat a patient who had been admitted to hospital[172]; a competition organiser had to take reasonable care not to endanger an intoxicated competitor[173]; and an employer who deposited a drunken off-duty serviceman on his bunk to sober up was responsible when the serviceman later choked on his own vomit.[174]

---

[166] *Fry's Metals v Durastic* (1991) SLT 689, OH.
[167] *Fullowka v Pinkerton's of Canada Ltd* [2010] SCC 5.
[168] *Lennon v Metropolitan Police Commissioner* [2004] 1 W.L.R. 2594 CA.
[169] Parents: *McCallion v Dodd* [1966] N.Z.L.R. 710 CA; *Tweed Shire Council v Howarth* (2009) Aus Torts Reps 82–010, NSWCA; Local authority: *Barrett v Enfield LBC* [1999] 3 W.L.R. 79 HL. School: *Barnes v Hants CC* [1969] 1 W.L.R. 1563 HL; *Commonwealth v Introvigne* (1982) 150 C.L.R. 258 HCA; *Myers v Peel County Board of Education* [1981] 2 S.C.R. 21 SCC. Whether or how far a duty of this kind might extend to cover the promotion by parents of a child's general well-being was considered by the New Zealand Court of Appeal in *A v Roman Catholic Archdiocese of Wellington* [2008] 3 N.Z.L.R. 289. William Young P. explained that damages for bad parenting will not be entertained, for reasons associated with parental autonomy and a sense that the issues would not be practicably justiciable. But there could be a duty as to children's physical and psychiatric health and this would encompass emotional abuse. Provided it did not extend to anything approaching a duty to maximize or enhance the emotional well-being of children, it should be reasonably manageable.
[170] *Ellis v Home Office* [1953] 2 All E.R. 149; *Reeves v Commissioner of Police of the Metropolis* [2000] 1 A.C. 360; De Prez, "Liability for failure to prevent acts of self-destruction": the House of Lords decision in *Reeves v Commissioner of Police of the Metropolis* (2000) 16 P.N. 113; and see *Kirkham v Chief Constable of the Greater Manchester Police* [1990] 2 Q.B. 283; *Orange v Chief Constable of West Yorkshire Police* [2002] Q.B. 347 CA; *NSW v Budjiso* (2005) 227 C.L.R. 1 HCA.
[171] *Waters v Commissioner of Police of the Metropolis* [2000] 1 W.L.R. 1607 HL.
[172] *Barnett v Chelsea Hospital* [1969] 1 Q.B.D. 428; and see *Lowns v Woods* (1995) Aust Torts Reps 81–376 NSWCA.
[173] *Crocker v Sundance Northwest Resorts Ltd* [1988] 1 S.C.R. 1186 SCC.
[174] *Barrett v Ministry of Defence* [1995] 1 W.L.R. 1217 CA (but the damages were reduced by two thirds for contributory negligence); and see *Jebson v Ministry of Defence* [2000] 1 W.L.R. 2055 CA (duty founded on inadequate supervision of drunken servicemen in back of lorry).

On the other hand, a claim against the police for failing to prevent a person **2–82** from committing suicide failed, for while the police had the opportunity to prevent the suicide they had assumed no responsibility for the person concerned.[175] Again, the licensee of a club was not liable to a patron who became drunk and who suffered injury in a road accident, for the patron could make up his own mind in deciding whether or how much to drink.[176] In a somewhat similar case, a licensee who had, by agreement, taken control of a drunken patron's motorcycle and keys owed no duty to the patron to refuse to return them or to call his wife so she could drive him home.[177] The patron was an experienced drinker and was not vulnerable, his relationship with the licensee did not impair his autonomy, any duty to threaten or use force to prevent the patron from obtaining the keys clashed with the licensee's duty not to commit the torts of assault and battery, and the claimed duty also clashed with the duty of the licensee as sub-bailee to hand over the keys to the patron as bailee for his wife.

Proximity of relationship. Any assumption of responsibility must be in **2–83** relation to a particular person or class of persons, between whom there must be some form of close and direct relationship. So, members of the International Rugby Football Board owed no duty to rugby players to alter or amend rules to minimise the risk of injury to the players.[178] The members of the Board were not in a close and direct relationship with all rugby players, and to hold that a duty existed would diminish the autonomy of all who chose to engage voluntarily in playing the sport. But the British Boxing Board of Control owed and was in breach of a duty to a boxer to see that all reasonable steps were taken to ensure immediate medical attention was available should he be injured in a boxing match.[179] The Board exercised close control over every aspect of boxing, it had specifically assumed responsibility for safety matters, and boxers relied on it to take appropriate safety precautions.

Responsibility for another's economic welfare. In principle, a person may **2–84** also assume responsibility for another's economic welfare. However, an alleged duty on the part of a school to insure a pupil against the risk of accidental injury during school hours or to advise on the need for insurance was rejected,[180] as was a duty by an employer to insure his employee against the risk of injury while working abroad or to advise the employee to insure.[181] In neither case was there any basis for finding that the defendant had assumed any responsibility to insure or to advise or otherwise to safeguard the claimant's economic welfare. Again,

---

[175] *Stuart v Kirkland-Veenstra* (2009) 83 A.L.J.R. 623 HCA.
[176] *Cole v South Tweed Heads Rugby League Football Club Ltd* (2004) 78 A.L.J.R. 933 HCA; *Munro v Porthkerry Park Holiday Estates Ltd, The Times*, March 9, 1984; *Griffiths v Brown, The Times* October 23, 1198; *Joy v Newell* [2000] N.I. 91 CA; cf *Jordan House Ltd v Menow* [1974] S.C.R. 239, SCC.
[177] *CAL No 14 Pty Ltd v Motor Accidents Insurance Board* [2009] HCA 47.
[178] *Agar v Hyde* (2000) 74 A.L.J.R. 1219 HCA; cp *Vowles v Evans* [2003] 1 W.L.R. 1607 CA (referee owed duty to players in the game that was under his control).
[179] *Watson v British Boxing Board of Control* [2001] Q.B. 1134; George *"Watson v British Boxing Board of Control*: negligent rule-making in the Court of Appeal" (2002) 65 M.L.R. 106.
[180] *Van Oppen v Clerk to the Bedford Charity Trustees* [1990] 1 W.L.R. 235 CA.
[181] *Reid v Rush & Tompkins Group plc* [1990] 1 W.L.R. 212 CA.

the New South Wales Court of Appeal held that a club owed no duty of care to protect a member who was a problem gambler from financial loss caused by gambling.[182] By contrast, the Court of Appeal in England recognised a limited duty in circumstances where a problem gambler asked a book maker for specific help and was assured he would receive it.[183] The claim failed because the court decided he would in any event have gambled away his money with someone else. Further, in an unconvincing decision, it was held that a hospital holding a fair on its land, which hired an independent contractor to provide one of the fund-raising activities, owed a duty to a visitor injured by the contractor's negligence to see that the contractor was insured.[184] However, on the facts the duty had not been broken.

2–85   **Duty to a third party.** Where vicarious liability is imposed, the defendant is liable for someone else's conduct by reason of the particular relationship between the defendant and the other person and the connection between the relationship and the other person's tortious conduct. A defendant may also be *personally* liable for failing prevent tortious conduct by another where, once again, he or she has in some way assumed assumed responsibility for or control over the other. For example, parents or persons in loco parentis may be under a duty to take such precautionary measures as are appropriate to their supervisory position over their children. Accordingly, a school authority was held to be responsible for allowing a small child to go through an unlocked gate into the road and cause an accident resulting in the death of a driver who swerved to avoid him.[185] In Australia, a restaurant owed a duty to take reasonable care to prevent injury to patrons from the violent, quarrelsome or disorderly conduct of other patrons.[186] And in a New Zealand decision, a father was held liable for not preventing a 10-year-old son of known reckless disposition from taking a rifle out of the house and shooting the plaintiff.[187]

2–86   In *Fullowka v Pinkerton's of Canada Ltd*[188] the victims of a bomb blast at a mine set off by a striking miner sued P, a security firm, and the territorial government for failing to prevent the explosion. The Supreme Court of Canada held that both defendants owed a duty of care to the victims, and this was not negated by considerations of control and autonomy. While it was true that P and the government had no direct control over the instigator, they had a significant measure of control of the risk that his activities would kill miners. As for autonomy, the defendants were not mere bystanders who happened upon a dangerous situation and decided not to get involved. Given their contractual and

---

[182] *Reynolds v Katoomba RSL Club Ltd* (2001) 53 N.S.W.L.R. 41 NSWCA; *Politarhis v Westpac Banking Corporation* [2009] SASR 96.
[183] *Calvert v William Hill Credit Ltd* [2009] 2 W.L.R. 1065 CA.
[184] *Gwilliam v West Hertfordshire Hospitals NHS Trust* [2003] Q.B. 443; Stanton "A duty to provide insurance?" (2003) 11 Tort L Rev 65. ; cp *Glaister v Appleby-in-Westmoreland Town Council* [2009] EWCA Civ 1325 (no duty on council to secure placement of public liability insurance covering negligence by participants at a fair).
[185] *Carmarthen CC v Lewis* [1955] A.C. 549.
[186] *Adeels Palace Ltd v Moubarak* [2009] HCA 48. However, negligence found against the defendant was not shown to have been the cause of the plaintiffs' injuries.
[187] *Kenealy v Karaka* (1906) 26 N.Z.L.R. 1118 CA.
[188] [2010] SCC 5.

statutory obligations, it did not unduly interfere with their autonomy to impose a duty on them to take reasonable care for the miners' safety. The duty was to the finite group of miners working in the mine which the inspectors had inspected repeatedly. In all the circumstances, however, neither defendant had been shown to be in breach of the duty.

Intoxication cases. In principle, it is possible for those in supervisory or controlling positions to be held liable for drunken conduct by others. For example, it was held by the Supreme Court of Canada that a commercial vendor of alcohol owed a duty to persons who might foreseeably be injured by an intoxicated patron.[189] Clearly it is very relevant in this type of case that the defendant has actually contributed to the danger by supplying the alcohol. However, the Supreme Court declined to impose a similar duty on a social host in respect of injury caused by a drunken guest, but left open the possibility that the host might be liable if he or she continued to serve alcohol to a visibly inebriated guest who was known to be going to drive.[190] McLachlan C.J. thought that in this case the host might be sufficiently implicated in the creation of the risk posed by the guest as to owe a duty to third parties. **2–87**

Control over the wrongdoer. A duty to a third party cannot arise in the absence of at least a power of control over the person causing the harm. So, in *Hill v Chief Constable of West Yorkshire Police*,[191] a claim against the police by the mother of one of the victims of a multiple murderer, alleging negligence in failing to prevent the crime, was struck out as bound to fail. Further, in *Smith v Chief Constable of Sussex*[192] such a duty was rejected even where the police had been informed both of specific threats to the victim and the identity and whereabouts of the person making the threats. By contrast, in *Home Office v Dorset Yacht Co Ltd*[193] a prison authority owed a duty of care to the owner of a yacht when prisoners in the custody of the authority were negligently allowed to escape and cause damage to the yacht. Lord Morris and Lord Pearson both based their judgments squarely on the obligation of the prison officers to control the trainees. **2–88**

Where control or the right to control exists, there must also be a reasonably close and immediate link between the failure to exercise control and the damage which is suffered. A duty cannot be extended to remote victims of another's wrongdoing. So the duty in *Dorset Yacht* was owed to property owners in the vicinity of the escape: it could not be extended to anyone who suffered damage caused by the prisoners at some time in the future. In an Australian case, a prison authority was not liable to the owner of a newsagency who was held up and terrorised by an escaped prisoner two months after the escape.[194] **2–89**

---

[189] *Stewart v Pettie* [1995] 1 S.C.R. 131 SCC. In the circumstances there was no breach of the duty.
[190] *Childs v Desormeaux* [2006] 1 S.C.R. 643 SCC.
[191] [1989] A.C. 53.
[192] [2009] 1 A.C. 225.
[193] [1970] A.C. 1004.
[194] *State of New South Wales v Godfrey* [2004] NSWCA 113.

2–90   **Public bodies.** In each of the preceding examples the defendants were public bodies. The liability in negligence of public bodies is considered separately below,[195] and given their supervisory or controlling functions it is unsurprising that a duty to take care to protect people from wrongdoing by others is commonly asserted them. But while there are many claims, only rarely are the conditions for a duty—actual control over the wrongdoer coupled with close proximity between claimant and defendant—found to be satisfied.

(v) *Assuming responsibility by taking on a task*

2–91   **Generally.** The duty of a person taking on a responsibility for performing a task does not extend to a duty to protect the public at large. In a well known instance, a banking regulator was not liable to an investor who lost money after investing in an unsound company.[196] So also a Law Society with supervisory responsibilities over solicitors was not responsible for losses suffered by a client as a result of a fraud which the Society's inspector had not detected.[197] The New Zealand Court of Appeal noted that any duty necessarily would be to all clients of the firm and would require investigation of all matters that might bear upon their affairs. Such wide and indeterminate duties should not readily be imposed upon a regulatory (but not closely controlling) body, which received no fees from solicitors' clients, had limited resources, and had no links with solicitors' clients similar to those of professional service providers such as valuers, surveyors and auditors.

2–92   However, a duty of positive action may exist in certain exceptional cases where a person has taken on a particular task and in that way has assumed responsibility to carry out the task with due care. Merely assuming an office or status and having the ability to help is not usually seen as enough. But taking on or starting on a task can give rise to a duty to persons who are sufficiently closely and proximately affected by a failure properly to carry it out. There must be an assumed responsibility for a particular activity or task in relation to a particular person or class. In addition, the cases tend to indicate that the claimant should in some sense be dependent upon the defendant acting or intervening or otherwise vulnerable to the risk of harm.

2–93   **Assuming responsibility to perform professional services.** The decision of the House of Lords in *Henderson v Merrett Syndicates Ltd*[198] illustrates the principle in operation. Their Lordships held that where a person assumes responsibility to perform professional or quasi-professional services for another who relied on those services, then the relationship was sufficient to give rise to a duty on the part of the person providing the services to exercise skill and care in doing so. Applying the principle, managing agents at Lloyds had taken on responsibility for exercising care in advising and providing services for names

---

[195] See paras 2–300 to 2–313 below.
[196] *Yuen Kun Yeu v Attorney-General of Hong Kong* [1988] A.C. 175, PC.
[197] *Wellington District Law Society v Price Waterhouse* [2002] 2 N.Z.L.R. 767 NZCA; *Bank of New Zealand v Deloitte Touche Tohmatsu* [2009] 1 N.Z.L.R. 53, NZCA.
[198] [1995] 2 A.C. 145.

who were members of syndicates under the agents' management, and a duty accordingly arose.

Vulnerable claimants. The element of vulnerability can be seen in decisions   **2–94** involving disappointed legatees. In *White v Jones*[199] a testator instructed the defendant solicitors to prepare a will leaving certain legacies to the plaintiffs, yet two months later the testator died without a new will having been executed. A majority of the House of Lords held that the defendants owed a duty of care to the intended beneficiaries. Lord Browne-Wilkinson said that the defendants' assumption of responsibility for the task in hand created a special relationship with the plaintiff, in relation to which the law attached a duty to carry out carefully the task so assumed.[200] However, the courts have refused to apply a similar rule in cases where the claimant is not vulnerable. In *Brownie Wills v Shrimpton*,[201] a solicitor, in breach of contract with a client bank, failed to give advice to a non-client director of a company about the effect of signing a guarantee for a loan to the company, and was held to owe no duty to the director. The New Zealand Court of Appeal considered that the solicitor had not assumed any responsibility towards the director, who was not aware of the client's instruction and who could not expect that the solicitor would look after his interests without giving any indication of that to the solicitor. The claimant was not vulnerable and could have sought advice about the guarantee for himself.

Claims against public bodies. There have been many attempts to impose   **2–95** duties of positive action on public bodies, on the basis that by taking on their supervisory tasks they have assumed responsibility for acting to prevent harm. Usually such claims have failed, as with the claims alleging failure to control third parties, because no sufficiently proximate relationship between defendant and claimant can be shown. The cases are considered in more detail below.[202]

3.—THE KIND OF HARM

(A) Introduction

Lord Reid has pointed out that while a defender is not liable for a consequence   **2–96** of a kind which is not foreseeable, it does not follow that he is liable for every consequence which a reasonable man could foresee."[203] As already noted, not all kinds of damage can give rise to a successful action in negligence.

As a general rule at common law, in cases where personal injury of a physical   **2–97** nature has been sustained or where actual damage to or loss of a person's

---

[199] [1995] 2 A.C. 207. See Ch.9 para.9–220 below.
[200] *Gartside v Sheffield Young & Ellis* [1983] N.Z.L.R 37 NZCA is a similar decision in New Zealand but was explained simply in terms of the close proximity between the solicitor and the intended beneficiaries. See also *Hill v Van Erp* (1997) 188 C.L.R. 159, HCA.
[201] [1998] 2 N.Z.L.R. 320 CA.
[202] See paras 2–300 to 2–313, below.
[203] *McKew v Holland & Hannen & Cubitts (Scotland) Ltd* [1969] 3 All E.R. 1621 at 1623 HL.

property has been suffered, a duty to take care has readily been imposed. Where, however, the personal injury sustained consists of psychiatric illness, or where the loss is purely financial in nature, then the law has struggled to find a consistent approach, even though such losses are very real in human terms. It is proposed to consider the duty of care separately in relation to these different heads, considering first some marginal cases of physical damage to persons and to property, and then the rules relating to psychiatric injury and to economic loss.

(B) Physical

(i) *Damage to the person*

2–98　　**Physical damage to the person.** Deciding whether a person has suffered physical injury or harm will not normally give rise to special difficulty. An injury may be slight, like a bruise or a scratch, but, subject perhaps to the de minimis rule, be nonetheless real and actionable. However, questions as to the very nature of physical injury can sometimes arise.[204]

2–99　　**Phyisical change.** The decision in *Rothwell v Chemical & Insulating Co Ltd*[205] provides an example. The claimants were negligently exposed by their employers to asbestos dust, putting them at risk of developing one or more long-term asbestos-related diseases. While those risks had not materialised, their exposure had caused them to develop pleural plaques, that is, localised areas of pleural thickening in the lung. The plaques had no adverse effect on any bodily function and did not themselves have the propensity to develop into an asbestos-related disease, but the claimants argued that physical changes to the body, coupled with the risk of future injury from exposure to asbestos which caused consequent anxiety, could provide a cause of action in negligence. The House of Lords rejected their argument. Save in the most exceptional case, the plaques would never cause any symptoms, did not themselves increase the susceptibility of the claimants to other diseases and did not shorten their expectation of life. They had no effect on their health at all. So they were not damage.

2–100　　The question remained whether the plaques became damage when aggregated with the risk of other conditions or the anxiety which that risk caused. However, a risk of damage is not treated as actual damage,[206] and nor is fear or anxiety falling short of actual psychiatric illness.[207] So their Lordships held that, neither head being independently actionable, they could not be relied on to create a cause of action which would not otherwise exist. As pithily expressed by Lord Scott,

---

[204] See generally Witting, "Physical damage in negligence" [2002] C.L.J. 189; Nolan, "New Forms of damage in negligence" (2007) 70 M.L.R. 59.
[205] [2008] 1 A.C. 281; Jones, "Liability for fear of future disease" (2008) 24 P.N. 13; Turton, "Defining damage in the House of Lords" (2008) 71 M.L.R. 1009; Leczykiewicz, "Pleural plaques, the concept of damage and liability for psychiatric injury" (2008) 124 L.Q.R. 548.
[206] *Gregg v Scott* [2005] 2 A.C. 176.
[207] *Hicks v Chief Constable of the South Yorkshire Police* [1992] 2 All E.R. 65 HL.

"the aggregation of plaques, risk and anxiety could not sustain a tort action, because nought plus nought plus nought equals nought".[208]

Parts or products of a living human body. Suppose there is damage to a part **2–101** or product of a living human body which has been separated from that body. In *Yearworth v North Bristol NHS Trust*,[209] the six claimants had been diagnosed with cancer and had accepted advice to undergo a course of chemotherapy. Having been advised that the treatment might damage their fertility, they produced samples of semen which the defendant hospital agreed to freeze and store. The defendant negligently allowed the semen to thaw and the sperm contained in it to perish irretrievably. The claimants sought damages, alleging, inter alia, that they had suffered personal injury through destruction of a bodily product which was intended to be kept in a biologically active state in order to fertilise a human egg. The Court of Appeal rejected the argument, holding that to treat this as personal injury would be a fiction. It would generate paradoxes and lead to substantial uncertainty, for example in relation to the possible application of the principle in the case of damage to other bodily substances or parts, in an area of law which should be simple and clear. Had one of the men died prior to the loss of the sperm the suggested personal injury would have been inflicted upon all of the men save him; and had the loss occurred after the men had recovered their natural fertility, or the sperm had been lawfully destroyed,[210] the suggested personal injury would have been inflicted albeit damage would be absent and the injury would not be actionable.[211]

Impaired educational development. Another doubtful question has arisen in **2–102** the context of an action against an educational psychologist for failure to identify and treat a child's dyslexia. There was initially disagreement whether dyslexia could be an injury, but the question was eventually resolved in the House of Lords, which held that failure to ameliorate dyslexia was actionable damage.[212] Lord Slynn said that it would be wrong to adopt an over-legalistic view of what were personal injuries, and that a failure to mitigate the adverse consequences of a congenital defect could qualify.

Life with disabilities. An action for damages can lie at the suit of a child for **2–103** injuries received before its birth.[213] Quite different is a claim by a child who is born with a disability of some kind alleging negligence by the medical advisers of his or her mother or father in failing to diagnose or warn about the disability or risk of disability. Here, the damage is the child's loss in being born with an existing disability, not his or her loss in suffering a pre-natal injury which has

---

[208] [2008] 1 A.C. 181 at [73].
[209] [2009] 3 W.L.R. 118 CA; Hawes, "Property interests in body parts: *Yearworth v North Bristol NHS Trust*" (2010) 73 M.L.R. 130.
[210] The Human Fertilisation and Embryology Act 1990 s.14, imposes a maximum statutory storage period of 14 years.
[211] However, the defendants were held liable in their capacity as bailees of the sperm.
[212] *Phelps v Hillingdon LBC* [2001] 2 A.C. 619; *Robinson v St Helens MBC* [2002] EWCA Civ 1099; *Adams v Bracknell Forest BC* [2005] 1 A.C. 76, at [20], [68]; and see Ch.4 para.4–180, below. See also Simblet, "Dyslexia and negligence" 143 S.J. 484.
[213] *Burton v Islington HA* [1992] 3 W.L.R. 637 CA; Congenital Disabilities (Civil Liability) Act 1976 s.1; see para.2–268.

been caused by the defendant. For this reason it is usually called a claim for "wrongful life". Claims of this kind fail, for the courts refuse to accept that life itself can be treated as a loss. The relevant law will be discussed in more detail when considering claims for pre-natal injuries.[214]

2–104   **Unwanted pregnancy.** Unwanted pregnancy cases pose unique questions. A negligently performed sterilisation operation may fail to prevent the pregnancy of the patient or of the patient's partner and result in the birth of an unwanted child. Several questions arise. First, we must ask whether causing a woman to become pregnant and to bear a child against her will is a personal injury to the mother. The answer is not entirely clear but, broadly speaking, the physical effects of pregnancy are treated in the same way as physical injury.[215] Secondly, there may be a claim for the expenses of bringing up the child, and this is recognised as a claim for economic loss.[216] Thirdly, the mother's loss of autonomy in giving birth to an unplanned child has been recognised as a special head of damage, compensable by way of a conventional sum.[217] These heads of claim are discussed below[218] together with other forms of financial loss.

2–105   **Lost chance of avoiding injury.** Whether a lost chance of avoiding injury can amount to damage is controversial. The cases show that where there is a negligent failure to treat physical injury, and it cannot be established on the balance of probabilities that further injury would have been prevented had treatment been given, then the claim must fail: proof that a claimant has, by negligence, been denied the chance of a better outcome cannot be treated as proof of damage or of the outcome itself.[219] But the lost chance of a better financial outcome sometimes can be recognised as actionable damage.[220]

2–106   **Miscellaneous.** There are other borderline cases where the question whether a claimant has suffered actionable injury or damage has been a matter of dispute. The claim of a child made the subject of an interim care order in the mistaken belief that he had suffered non-accidental injury was dismissed where the damage relied upon was "transient and non-justiciable".[221] A claim by a convicted burglar whose previous convictions for sexual offences were negligently disclosed by prison staff was rejected, because the damage relied upon was simply his removal from association with other prisoners.[222] It is possible

---

[214] See para.2–272.
[215] *McFarlane v Tayside Health Board* [2000] 2 A.C. 59 ; *Mitchell v Glasgow City Council* [2009] 1 A.C. 874 at [75].
[216] *McFarlane v Tayside Health Board* n.215 above, at 75–76, 79, 89, 99–100, 109.
[217] *Rees v Darlington Memorial Hospital NHS Trust* [2004] 1 A.C. 309.
[218] para.2–249 et seq., below.
[219] *Hotson v East Berkshire Hay* [1987] A.C. 750; *Gregg v Scott* [2005] 2 A.C. 176; *Tabet v Gett* [2010] HCA 12.
[220] For example, *Chaplin v Hicks* [1911] 2 K.B. 786 CA; *Allied Maples Group Ltd v Simmons & Simmons* [1995] 1 W.L.R. 1602; see Ch.6, para.6–56 and Ch.9 para.9–295 below.
[221] *D v Bury Metropolitan Borough Council* [2006] 1 W.L.R. 917 CA.
[222] *H v Secretary of State for the Home Department* (1992) 136 S.J. 140 CA, following *R. v Deputy Governor of Parkhurst Prison Ex p Hague* [1992] 1 A.C. 58.

that a restriction on freedom of movement can qualify,[223] although it has been held that a claimant did not suffer damage for the purpose of an action for negligence on being trapped in a lift.[224] In *McLoughlin v Jones*[225] Hale L.J. suggested that depriving someone of physical liberty might amount to a form of actionable personal injury.

(ii) *Damage to property*

Physical damage to inanimate property. As with physical injury to the 2–107 person, there are borderline cases where the question whether there has been physical damage to property can be a matter of dispute. It is necessary that there should be some significant physical effect on, or a significant physical change to, the property concerned. Dust from building work is an example. While dust is an inevitable incident of urban life, building work causing excessive deposits leading to physical change to chattels and requiring remedial action could give rise to an action in negligence.[226] Again, a collision on the highway causing petrol to flow from both vehicles and broken glass and debris to be strewn around caused damage to the highway.[227] The Crown, as owner of the highway, had expended resources in clearing up after the accident in order to make whole its property, which had been significantly degraded by the actions of the defendant. In further examples, there was physical damage where a leak from drums of chemicals contaminated the ship in which they were stored, impairing its value and usefulness[228]; and where radioactive contamination altered the physical characteristics of soil and rendered it less useful.[229] On the other hand, property that is subject to electronic change seemingly is not actually damaged. Accordingly, the loss of computer data is only an economic loss.[230]

Abstraction of water. In *Stephens v Anglian Water Authority*,[231] the Court of 2–108 Appeal held that a landowner was entitled to abstract water percolating under his land, and owed no duty of care to a neighbour in respect of subsidence caused by the water abstraction to the neighbour's land. The decision does not suggest that

---

[223] See *De Freville v Dill* (1927) 96 L.J.K.B. 1056 (doctor negligently certified plaintiff to be of unsound mind, which led to her detention in a mental home); *W v Home Office* [1997] Imm. A.R. 302 CA (detention could be an actionable wrong); *Karagozlu v Commissioner of Police of the Metropolis* [2007] 1 W.L.R. 1881 CA (imprisonment recognised as damage in tort of misfeasance).
[224] *Reilly v Merseyside Regional Health Authority* (1995) 6 Med. L.R. 246.
[225] [2002] Q.B. 1312.
[226] *Hunter v Canary Wharf Ltd* [1997] A.C. 655, 676–677 (CA). The issue was not discussed in the appeal to the House of Lords.
[227] *Attorney-General for Ontario v Fatehi* [1984] 2 S.C.R. 536 (SCC).
[228] *Losinjska Plovidba v Transco Overseas Ltd (The "Orjula")* [1995] 2 Lloyd's Rep. 395.
[229] *Blue Circle Industries Plc v Ministry of Defence* [1999] Ch. 289 (CA) (radioactive contamination of soil had caused property damage for the purposes of the Nuclear Installations Act 1965.
[230] *Seaboard Life Insurance Co v Babich* (1995) 11 B.C.L.R. (3d) 385; *Rockport Pharmacy Inc v Digital Simplistics Inc* 53 F 3d 195 (1995).
[231] [1987] 3 All E.R. 379, following *Chasemore v Richards* (1859) 7 HL Cas 349 and *Bradford Corporation v Pickles* [1895] A.C. 587; and see *Langbrook Properties Ltd v Surrey County Council* [1970] 1 W.L.R. 161.

the neighbour did not suffer damage. Rather, it was a case of *damnum sine injuria*: while there was physical damage to the land, there was no legal injury and an action for negligence did not lie.

2–109   **Physical damage to animals.** Internal physical change in animals' bodies has been recognised as physical damage. So where crops were sprayed with an insecticide which led to the presence of inert chemical residues in the fat of cattle to which the crops had been fed, and which in turn postponed the saleability of the cattle, or reduced their price, or involved the owner in extra expenses, the cattle were treated as having been physically contaminated.[232]

2–110   A somewhat similar question has been raised in a number of decisions involving controls on the movement of cattle or other animals. In *Weller v Foot and Mouth Disease Research Institute*,[233] auctioneers who suffered financial loss on being unable to conduct their business following the escape of the foot and mouth disease virus from the defendant's premises were held to have suffered purely economic loss. The auctioneers did not own the affected cattle, and simply suffered a loss of business. However, in *D Pride & Partners v Institute for Animal Health*,[234] the loss suffered by the claimant farmers following an escape of the virus from the same premises was categorised differently. Farmers whose livestock were culled were paid statutory compensation, but here the claimants alleged loss because of the regulatory controls on the movement of livestock once infection was suspected or confirmed. The claimants argued that they had suffered physical damage to their property, in that the controls caused the animals to become older, or bigger, or fatter, or thinner, and accordingly less valuable in the market. Tugendhat J accepted that there was a real prospect of a court accepting that animal (and vegetable) produce passing the stage of its natural development at which it would be marketed was physical damage. However, the claimants could not show that they had a real prospect of establishing that a duty of care was owed to them in respect of this indirect loss. Such a duty could be owed to all farmers in Great Britain, and potentially auctioneers and many others. There was no uniquely prominent or even identifiable class that should have been within the defendants' contemplation, and the claims accordingly were dismissed.[235]

2–111   While the issue of indeterminate liability provided a policy reason for denying a duty, the reference to the damage being "indirect" is less easily explained. Whether or not damage is direct is usually seen as bearing upon issues of causation or remoteness of damage, and is not normally regarded as relevant to whether a duty exists. Perhaps the decision can best be explained by treating the imposition of controls on the movement and sale of cattle as an intervening cause of the harm, and in that way insulating the defendant from liability.

---

[232] *McMullin v ICI Australia Operations Pty Ltd* (1997) 72 FCR 1.
[233] [1966] 1 Q.B. 569; and see *Landcatch Ltd v International Oil Pollution Compensation Fund* [1999] 2 Lloyd's L.R. 216 (salmon farmers suffered economic loss when an oil spill in the sea resulted in the area where they grew smolt being statutorily designated an exclusion zone).
[234] [2009] EWHC 685.
[235] See further para.2–215, below.

(C) Psychiatric injury

(i) *Introduction*

General. Liability for psychiatric injury has evolved over the years as   **2–112**
understanding of the condition has itself grown.[236] In one of the leading cases,
Lord Wilberforce explained:

> "English law, and common understanding, have moved some distance since recognition
> was given to this symptom as a basis for liability. Whatever is unknown about the mind-
> body relationship . . . it is now accepted by medical science that recognisable and severe
> physical damage to the human body and system may be caused by the impact, through
> the senses, of external events on the mind. There may thus be produced what is as
> identifiable an illness as any that may be caused by direct physical impact."[237]

Unfortunately, while there is now no doubt that mental illness can be the   **2–113**
subject of an action for damages, there are a number of apparently arbitrary rules
limiting liability. In *Frost v Chief Constable of the South Yorkshire Police*[238] Lord
Steyn remarked that the law in England governing compensation for psychiatric
harm was a patchwork quilt of distinctions that were difficult to justify. Lord
Hoffmann agreed and pointed out that:

> "In order to give due weight to the earlier decisions, particularly at first instance, it is
> necessary to have regard to their historical context. They cannot be simply laid out flat
> and pieced together to form a timeless mosaic of legal rules. Some contained the
> embryonic forms of later developments; others are based upon theories of liability
> which had respectable support at the time but have since been left stranded by the
> shifting tides."[239]

Policy concerns. The unsatisfactory state of the law has emerged as result of   **2–114**
attempts to meet a number of special concerns of policy arising in cases of mental
injury. In *Frost*, Lord Steyn identified four possible reasons for caution. First, the
complexity and diagnostic uncertainty of mental injury claims, where the line
between compensatable psychiatric injury and other non compensatable psychiatric conditions would often be difficult to draw. Calling consultant psychiatrists on both sides was a costly and time consuming exercise and if claims were
to be treated as generally on a par with physical injury it would have implications
for the administration of justice. On its own, however, this factor might not be
entitled to great weight. Secondly, litigation was sometimes an unconscious

---

[236] See generally Mullany and Handford, *Tort Liability for Psychiatric Damage* (2nd ed), Sydney,
Law Book Co, 2006; Jones, "Liability for Psychiatric Damage: Searching for a path between
pragmatism and principle", in Neyers, Chamberlain, Pitel (eds), *Emerging Issues in Tort Law*,
Oxford, Hart Publishing, 2007, Ch.5; Law Commission, *Liability for Psychiatric Illness*, Report No.
249, 1998; Law Commission (Scot), *Damages for Psychiatric Injury*, Scot Law Com No. 196, 2004;
Woollard, "Liability for negligently inflicted psychiatric illness: where should we draw the line?"
(1998) 27 Anglo-Am L Rev 112; Teff, "Liability for negligently inflicted psychiatric harm:
justifications and boundatries" [1998] C.L.J. 91; Mullany, "English psychiatric injury law-
chronically depressing" (1999) 115 L.Q.R. 30; Wheat "Proximity and Nervous Shock" (2003) 32
C.L.W.R. 313.
[237] *McLoughlin v O'Brian* [1983] 1 A.C. 410 at 418.
[238] [1999] 2 A.C. 455 at 500.
[239] *Frost v Chief Constable of the South Yorkshire Police* [1999] 2 A.C. 455 at 502.

disincentive to rehabilitation. This factor was already present in cases of physical injury and concomitant mental suffering, but it might play a larger role in cases of pure psychiatric harm and could not be dismissed. Thirdly, the abolition or relaxation of special rules would greatly increase the class of persons who could succeed in recovering damages. The existing rules allowing routine recovery where the claimant had actually suffered or had apprehended physical injury involved in-built elements of immediacy. Cases of pure psychiatric harm lacked those elements. Fourthly, the imposition of liability in a wide range of situations might result in a burden of liability that was disproportionate to the tortious conduct involved.

2–115   Lord Steyn was exercised in particular by the third and fourth concerns—the danger of wide-ranging liability and of an unfair burden being placed on defendants. The Law Commission shared the "floodgates" fear and considered that special policy limitations over and above foreseeability were needed in some cases.[240] Whether or how far this kind of concern is justified has been contested,[241] and overseas authority might suggest that some at least of the special limitations applying in England should be abandoned.[242] Be that as it may, for the present a claim for mental injury must satisfy two general preconditions before it can succeed. First, it must be of a nature that is actionable. Secondly, in most cases[243] the claimant must be either a "primary" and "secondary" victim, with certain stringent conditions applying to claims made by those in the latter category.

(ii) *Actionable mental injury*

2–116   **Consequential injury.** Mental distress short of illness is compensable if it is consequential upon physical injury.[244] But if no such injury is suffered, the requirement that there be an actionable mental or psychiatric injury applies.

2–117   **Psychiatric illness.** Certain specialised types of claims in tort allow the recovery of damages for injury to feelings, upset, outrage and other mental consequences of wrongdoing.[245] But claims in negligence for mental injury must meet a more stringent test. Such claims traditionally have been known as claims for "nervous shock",[246] yet the expression is misleading, for the claimant seeks damages not for shock but for the damage caused by the shock. In *McLoughlin v O'Brian*,[247] the House of Lords held that in any claim for mental harm standing

---

[240] See above, fn 236, paras 6.5–6.9.

[241] See Mullany and Handford, above n.236.

[242] See especially *Tame v New South Wales: Annetts v Australian Stations Pty Ltd* (2003) 211 CLR 317, HCA; see para.2–152.

[243] For cases where the primary/secondary victim distinction does not apply see 2–161 below.

[244] *Rothwell v Chemical Insulating Co Ltd* [2008] 1 A.C. 281, where the claimant suffered only fear and no physical injury was shown: see para.2–99 above.

[245] For example, defamation, malicious prosecution, invasion of privacy.

[246] "As lawyers quaintly persist in calling" psychiatric illness: *McLoughlin v O'Brian* [1983] 1 A.C. 410 at 432, per Lord Bridge.

[247] [1983] 1 A.C. 410 at 418; and see *Hicks v Chief Constable of the South Yorkshire Police* [1992] 2 All E.R. 65; *Page v Smith* [1996] 1 A.C. 155 at 189; *Frost v Chief Constable of the South Yorkshire Police* [1999] 2 A.C. 455 at 469.

alone, the shock must cause the claimant to suffer either physical consequences, like a stroke or miscarriage, or some medically identifiable psychiatric illness or injury. Leading decisions overseas impose the same requirement.[248] References in the cases to damages for "nervous shock" must be understood in the sense used in these cases.[249]

Restricting claims arising from accidents to those in which the claimant can show psychiatric illness is one way of meeting the perceived need for the law to place limitations upon the extent of admissible claims. In *Tame v New South Wales: Annetts v Australian Stations Pty Ltd*,[250] Gummow and Kirby JJ. maintained that many of the concerns underlying recovery for psychiatric injury tended to recede if full force was given to the distinction between emotional distress and a recognisable psychiatric illness. It reduced the scope for indeterminate liability or increased litigation, restricted recovery to those disorders capable of objective determination, and posited a distinction grounded in principle rather than pragmatism that was illuminated by professional medical opinion rather than fixed by purely idiosyncratic judicial perception. **2–118**

Medical evidence. Whether mental harm amounts to a psychiatric illness or injury is a medical question usually resolved with the assistance of expert evidence. Diagnosis may be approached by reference to appropriate medical authority, in particular the *American Diagnostic and Statistical Manual of Mental Disorders* (DSM-IV)[251] and the *International Classification of Diseases and Related Health Problems* (ICD-10).[252] The Law Commission has given an overview of the medical background.[253] It recognised that the distinction between what constitutes mere mental distress and symptoms that amount to a recognisable psychiatric illness is not clear. So also, reliance on the diagnostic criteria contained in DSM-IV and ICD-10 was not always sufficient to distinguish those with the greatest impairment of functioning. There was seen to be an imperfect fit between questions of ultimate concern to the law and the information contained in a clinical diagnosis. Further, the clinical and scientific considerations involved in the categorisation of certain conditions as mental disorders might not be relevant to legal judgments, which had to take into **2–119**

---

[248] Australia: *Tame v New South Wales v Annetts v Australian Stations Pty Ltd* (2003) 211 C.L.R. 317 HCA; Canada: *Odhavji Estate v Woodhouse* [2003] 3 S.C.R. 263, [41], SCC; New Zealand: *van Soest v Residual Health Management Unit* [2000] 1 N.Z.L.R. 179, 197–199 NZCA.

[249] As Brennan J observed in *Jaensch v Coffey* (1984) 54 A.L.R. 417 at 425, despite its label of dubious medical acceptability, "the term 'nervous shock' is useful nevertheless as a term of art to indicate the aetiology of a psychiatric illness for which damages are recoverable in an action on the case when the other elements of the cause of action are present."

[250] (2003) 211 C.L.R. 317 HCA.

[251] (4th ed), 1994.

[252] 10th revision, vol 1, 1993.

[253] See generally the Law Commission's report No. 249, above, n.236; Mullany and Handford, above n.236, Ch.3; Sprince, "Negligently inflicted psychiatric damage: a medical diagnosis and prognosis" (1998) 18 LS 59; Butler, "Identifying the compensable damage in 'nervous shock' cases" (1997) 5 T.L.J. 67. The judgments in *Vernon v Bosley (No.1)* [1997] 1 All E.R. 577, CA, contain useful discussion of Post Traumatic Stress Disorder, some diagnostic criteria for which are set out at 584. See also the summary of Hale L.J. in *Hatton v Sutherland* [2002] 2 All E.R. 1, at [4]–[6], CA.

account such issues as individual responsibility, level of disability and competency. But, taking into account these caveats, it was accepted by psychiatrists and was an appropriate test for actionable damage.

ILLUSTRATIONS

2–120 It is apparent, then, that a claim where a mental injury of the requisite kind cannot be shown will fail at the outset. For example, a claimant could not recover damages for claustrophobia and fear where they did not form part of a psychiatric condition, such as post-traumatic stress disorder,[254] nor for concern and fear for the welfare of her children.[255] Indeed, fear of impending death, or fear of whatever degree, is insufficient.[256] Where a motorist suffered no physical injury but experienced only a nervous reaction, falling short of an identifiable psychological illness, it was held that he was not entitled to an award of damages.[257] A claim for damages for the normal emotions by way of grief, sorrow or distress attendant on the loss of a loved one, or for damages for "shattered family plans", were both rejected.[258] In a similar vein, there was no recovery for "shock, distress and emotional upset" at the discovery of the murdered body of a friend.[259]

2–121 **Physical injury caused by shock.** Sometimes shock can form part of the narrative which explains how a claimant came to sustain physical injury. The word is used in the sense of surprise and explains why the claimant acted as he or she did. The present discussion is not concerned with cases of this kind, which can be resolved by the application of ordinary principles governing claims for physical injury. So in a case where a railway shunter caused some wagons to collide with a force that produced an exceptionally loud bang, and this startled the claimant, who to the shunter's knowledge was examining the wagons, causing him to trip and fall, it was held that the defendant employer was vicariously liable for the shunter's negligence.[260] In contrast, where a claimant received a very great fright when a West African grass monkey suddenly appeared on top of her garden wall, causing her to turn away hurriedly and fall injuring her wrist, her action for damages failed. The court held that that her injury was unforeseeable, as it did not result from an attack of any sort by the animal.[261]

2–122 **Intentionally inflicted mental injury.** The question remains whether the rule requiring a recognisable mental disorder might be relaxed in the case of intentional harm. The rule in *Wilkinson v Downton*,[262] requiring conduct that is "calculated" to cause physical or mental harm, has largely been overtaken by developments in the law of negligence, but possibly it could give a remedy for mental upset falling short of actual injury where the upset is intentionally

---

[254] *Reilly v Merseyside Regional Health Authority* [1995] 6 Med. L.R. 246, CA.
[255] *De Franceschi v Storrier* (1989) 85 ACTR 1.
[256] *Hicks v Chief Constable of South Yorkshire Police* [1992] 2 All E.R. 65.
[257] *Nicholls v Rushton, The Times*, June 19, 1992, CA.
[258] *Kerby v Redbridge HA* (1993) 4 Med L.R. 178.
[259] *R v Criminal Injuries Board Ex p. Johnson* [1994] P.I.Q.R. P469.
[260] *Slatter v British Railways Board* (1966) 1 KIR 336.
[261] *Brook v Cook* (1961) 105 S.J. 684. For animals generally, see Ch.14, below.
[262] [1897] 2 Q.B. 57.

inflicted. However, in *Wainwright v Home Office*[263] Lord Hoffmann did not favour a relaxation in the law of this kind. His Lordship recognised that people constantly do and say things with the intention of causing distress and humiliation to others, but he was not sure that the right way to deal with it was always by litigation. The harassment legislation[264] showed that Parliament was conscious that it might not be in the public interest to allow the law to be set in motion for one boorish incident. It might be that any development in the common law should show similar caution. So also Lord Scott was satisfied that the infliction of humiliation and distress by conduct calculated to humiliate and cause distress was not without more, and should not be, tortious at common law.

(iii) *Primary victims*

Background. The unforgiving approach of nineteenth century courts to claims for mental injury can be seen in *Victorian Railways Commissioner v Coultas*.[265] The claimant, who had narrowly avoided being hit by a train, failed in her action for mental injury caused by the shock of the event. But there then began a gradual relaxation of the general rule. First, the rule was held not to apply where the defendant's conduct was calculated to cause harm.[266] Next, mental shock caused to a claimant who was put in fear for her own physical safety was held to be actionable.[267] A claim based on fear for others was then allowed,[268] and since that time the courts have been exercised in determining where exactly a line ought to be drawn.   **2–123**

In *King v Phillips*,[269] Denning L.J. maintained that the basis for liability for mental injury was foreseeability of injury by shock. For long this was recognised as a core requirement, applying in all mental injury cases. However, in *Page v Smith*[270] the House of Lords confined *King* to claims by secondary victims, and, accordingly, foreseeability will be left to be considered in that context.[271]   **2–124**

Page v Smith. The claimant was involved in a collision with the defendant while driving on the highway, resulting in damage to his car but no physical injury. For 20 years before the accident the claimant had suffered from myalgic encephalomyelitis ("ME"), and he alleged that the accident had caused his condition to become chronic and had rendered him permanently unfit for work. The Court of Appeal, applying the test of foreseeability of injury by shock, thought that there was no foreseeable risk of psychiatric injury to a person of   **2–125**

---

[263] [2004] 2 A.C. 406.
[264] Protection from Harassment Act 1977.
[265] (1883) 13 App Cas 221.
[266] *Wilkinson v Downton* [1897] 2 Q.B. 57.
[267] *Dulieu v White* [1902] 2 K.B. 669.
[268] *Hambrook v Stokes Bros* [1925] 1 K.B. 141.
[269] [1953] 1 Q.B. 429 at 441, approved in *The Wagon Mound (No. 1)* [1961] A.C. 388 at 426 PC.
[270] [1996] 1 A.C. 155; Rogers, "*Page v Smith*: shock, foresight and vulnerable personalities" (1995) 3 T.L.J. 149; Hopkins, "A new twist to nervous shock" [1995] C.L.J. 497; Sprince, "*Page v Smith*: being 'primary' colours House of Lords' judgment" (1996) 11 P.N. 124; Mullany, "Psychiatric damage in the House of Lords—fourth time unlucky" (1995) 3 JLM 112; Handford, "A new chapter in the foresight saga: psychiatric damage in the House of Lords" (1996) 4 Tort L Rev 5; Trindade, "Nervous shock and negligent conduct" (1996) 112 L.Q.R. 22.
[271] See para.2–132.

normal fortitude.[272] However, the House of Lords held in a majority decision that the claimant had been put at risk of physical injury and that he was, therefore, a "primary" victim to whom a duty to take care was owed. The essential question was whether some personal injury was reasonably foreseeable by the defendant and, if it was, it mattered not in relation to the claimant's ability to recover for psychiatric harm that no physical injury was suffered. In the words of Lord Lloyd:

> "It was enough to ask whether the defendant should have reasonably foreseen that the plaintiff might have suffered physical injury as a result of the defendant's negligence, so as to bring him within the range of the defendant's duty of care. It was unnecessary to ask, as a separate question, whether the defendant should reasonably have foreseen injury by shock; and it is irrelevant that the plaintiff did not, in fact, suffer any external physical injury."[273]

The defendant's duty to a primary victim was, therefore, the ordinary duty to take care not to cause personal injury. So in the instant case it was sufficient to ask whether the defendant should have foreseen that the plaintiff might suffer personal injury, whether physical or psychiatric, as a result of the defendant's negligence. Whether he or she should have foreseen psychiatric injury only had to be asked in secondary victim cases.

2–126   Their Lordships held further that once it was shown that there was a foreseeable risk of one form of personal injury, the rule that defendants take their victims as they find them applied. The claimant was not required to be a person of "ordinary phlegm". Accordingly, the defendant was liable even for unforeseeable shock. However, it had not been finally determined whether the claimant's condition had been caused by the accident, and the case was remitted to the Court of Appeal for a finding on this issue.[274]

Illustrations

2–127   Primary victims have succeeded in the following cases: the mother of a son born with severe and irreversible brain damage as a result of negligence in delivery who suffered trauma caused by her caesarian section, the first sight of her child and the conversation in which a doctor broke the news of her child's disabilities[275]; a police officer involved in a surveillance operation who on multiple occasions was required to attach a "tagging" device to a car, with increasing levels of fear and apprehension each time[276]; and a victim of relatively minor physical injury whose anger at an accident which he had warned his

---

[272] [1994] 4 All E.R. 522 CA.
[273] [1996] 1 A.C. 155, at 190.
[274] In *Page v Smith (No. 2)* [1996] 1 W.L.R. 855 the Court of Appeal held that the finding of the trial judge that a causal connection had been established was unassailable.
[275] *Farrell v Merton Sutton and Wandsworth Health Authority* (2001) BMLR 158.
[276] *Donachie v The Chief Constable of the Greater Manchester Police*, The Times, May 4, 2004 CA.

employers was possible contributed to the onset of a major depressive condition.[277]

Difficulties of classification. As will be seen, the requirements for the   **2–128** recovery of damages by a secondary victim are certainly harder to satisfy than those for a primary victim. It is crucial, therefore, to know who qualifies as a primary victim, yet the question cannot be determined with certainty.[278] In *Page* itself, and in the view of the majority in their Lordships' subsequent decision in *Frost v Chief Constable of the South Yorkshire Police*,[279] a primary victim was thought to be a person involved in an accident and within the range of physical injury. However, in the earlier decision of the House of Lords in *Alcock v Chief Constable of the South Yorkshire Police*,[280] Lord Oliver distinguished between cases in which the injured claimant was involved as a participant and those in which the claimant was no more than the passive and unwilling witness of injury caused to others. On this view a participant can be a primary victim without being put in danger. Again, quite how much risk or danger there must be (assuming this is necessary) may be a matter for debate, although, seemingly, a claimant's fear for his or her safety must at least be reasonable.[281] And not all forms of danger qualify. In *Grieves v F T Everard & Sons*,[282] where the claimant had developed a depressive illness on account of his fears from having been exposed to asbestos dust, the House of Lords decided that *Page* applied only to those within the zone of danger of physical impact, and could not be extended to cover the instant case. Lord Hope said that the category of primary victim should be confined to persons who suffered psychiatric injury caused by fear or distress resulting from involvement in an accident caused by the defendant. Here, the causal chain was stretched far beyond what was envisaged in *Page*.

It is also difficult to reconcile *Page* with various cases involving claimants   **2–129** who are not secondary victims fearing for another, but who have been owed a duty of care in respect of psychiatric harm even though they have not been physically endangered. Such persons include involuntary participants in shocking events, employees subjected to mental stress, and recipients of false information.[283] Clearly, a simple division between primary and secondary victims cannot cover the wide variety of ways in which a person may become a victim of psychiatric injury. The majority in *Page* thought that their approach had the advantage of simplicity, but in fact it has proved to be a source of

---

[277] *Simmons v British Steel Plc*, 2004 SLT 595, HL.

[278] Hilson, "Nervous shock and the categorisation of victims" (1998) 6 Tort L Rev 37; Hilson, "Liability for psychiatric injury: primary and secondary victims reconsidered" (2002) 18 P.N. 167.

[279] [1999] 2 A.C. 455; see para.2–155 below. Lord Goff, expressing a minority view, did not consider that Lord Lloyd intended to require foreseeability of physical injury as a necessary pre-condition of liability to a primary victim.

[280] [1992] 1 A.C. 310 at 407.

[281] *McFarlane v EE Caledonia Ltd* [1994] 2 All E.R. 1 CA; *Hegarty v E.E. Caledonia Ltd* [1997] P.N.L.R. 578 CA.

[282] [2008] 1 A.C. 281, sub nom *Rothwell v Chemical Insulating Co Ltd*.

[283] See further paras 2–155 to 2–165, below.

confusion.[284] So the decision should be seen as laying down a special rule for mental victims in immediate physical danger, with no wider role in classifying other kinds of cases. Secondary victims fall into a separate category as well, and other kinds of claim, where victims are neither primary nor secondary, have to be determined on their own particular merits.

(iv) *Secondary victims*

2-130   **Introduction.** Secondary victims are persons who are not personally in danger who suffer mental injury from perceiving or hearing about the death or injury to another or others. A claim by such a victim was first upheld in the decision of the Court of Appeal in *Hambrook v Stokes Bros*,[285] which involved a mother suing in respect of injury by shock caused by fear for her children. Then in 1942, in *Bourhill v Young*,[286] a case involving a claim for damages in respect of nervous shock reached the House of Lords. A motorcyclist rode his machine negligently at speed and was killed in a collision with a motor car. The sound of the happening of the accident was heard by the pursuer, an eight-months pregnant fishwife, standing about 45 feet away from the scene and she suffered a fright, resulting in severe nervous shock, which disabled her from working. About a month later she gave birth to a still-born child. Her action failed, because she was outside the area of those to whom injury was reasonably foreseeable. At no time had she had any reasonable fear of immediate bodily injury to herself.

2-131   What exactly *Bourhill* might be thought to have decided beyond the decision on the particular facts is not very clear. Accordingly, since *Bourhill*, the House of Lords and lower courts have sought to clarify the law and to identify the circumstances in which a claim by a secondary victim can succeed.

2-132   **Foreseeable mental injury.** A secondary victim must establish that the defendant should reasonably have foreseen as a consequence of his or her conduct that a person in the position of the claimant would or might suffer mental injury.[287] Some of their Lordships in *Bourhill* held that in deciding the question the defendant can assume that the claimant was a person of "customary phlegm", with the "normal standard of susceptibility.[288] However, in *Tame v NSW*[289] a majority of the members of the High Court of Australia did not see a "normal fortitude" test as having an independent existence of its own. Rather, they drew

---

[284] The primary/secondary distinction has failed to take root in Australia (*Tame v NSW: Annetts v Australian Stations Pty Ltd* (2003) 211 C.L.R. 317, HCA) and New Zealand (*van Soest v Residual Health Management Unit* [2000] 1 N.Z.L.R. 179, NZCA), and has been rejected in Canada (*Mustapha v Culligan of Canada Ltd* (2007) 275 D.L.R. 473, Ont CA) (appeal dismissed [2008] 2 S.C.R. 114, SCC, without discussion of the point). Some members of the House of Lords have questioned whether the distinction ought to be retained: see *Rothwell v Chemical Insulating Co* [2008] 1 A.C. 281, at [52] per Lord Hope, [104] per Lord Mance; *Corr v IBC Vehicles Ltd* [2008] 2 W.L.R. 499, at [54] per Lord Neuberger.
[285] [1925] 1 K.B. 141.
[286] [1943] A.C. 92.
[287] *Bourhill v Young* [1943] A.C. 92; *King v Phillips* [1953] 1 Q.B. 429; *Page v Smith* [1996] 1 A.C. 155 at 187.
[288] [1943] A.C. 92 at 117 per Lord Porter, 110 per Lord Wright; and see *Jaensch v Coffey* (1984) 155 C.L.R. 549 at 572 per Brennan J., HCA.
[289] (2003) 211 C.L.R. 317 HCA.

attention to the element of reasonableness in determining whether psychiatric injury could be said to be reasonably foreseeable. If the plaintiff has an "egg-shell personality" then his or her mental injury is unlikely to be reasonably foreseeable. In *Tame* itself the court held that it was not reasonably foreseeable that an erroneous report by a police officer after a traffic accident that the plaintiff (who was a teetotaller) had a high blood alcohol reading, which error was corrected shortly afterwards, would cause the plaintiff to suffer from a psychotic depressive illness.

ILLUSTRATIONS

Cases raising a question as to the foreseeability of mental injury are not limited to those involving especially sensitive claimants. In other examples, it was not foreseeable that an employee would suffer reactive depression as a result of his employer's disgraceful conduct in the manner of his investigating an unfounded suspicion that the employee was guilty of theft[290]; that psychiatric injury to a prisoner would result from a sexually inappropriate conversation between his wife and a prison officer[291]; and that psychiatric injury would be caused by misidentification of the body of an accident victim.[292] **2–133**

McLoughlin v O'Brian.[293] In *McLoughlin v O'Brian* the Law Lords once more had the opportunity to review the problems raised by claims by secondary victims. Mrs McLoughlin's husband and three of their children were involved in a dreadful road accident. At the time of the collision she was at home, and it was about an hour afterwards that she was informed of the accident by a friend and of the likelihood that her son was dying. She went to the hospital where her husband and children had been taken and was exposed to very distressing sights and sounds associated with their injuries. As a result she developed a severe psychiatric illness. **2–134**

Lord Wilberforce identified three factors as relevant in determining whether such a claim could succeed. It was necessary to consider (a) the class of persons whose claims ought to be recognised, (b) the proximity of such persons to the accident, and (c) the means by which the psychiatric illness was caused. **2–135**

As regards the class of persons, the possible range lay between ordinary bystanders and those with the closest of family ties, that is either parent and child or husband and wife. The claims of the latter were recognised by existing law. But the former were not so recognised, because either such a person had to be assumed to be possessed of fortitude, which was sufficient to enable him to withstand the calamities of modern life, or defendants could not be expected to compensate the world at large. As regards proximity to the accident, Lord Wilberforce considered that there should be some close connection in both time **2–136**

---

[290] *O'Leary v Oolong Aboriginal Corporation* [2004] NSWCA 7.
[291] *Duddin v Home Office* [2004] EWCA Civ 181.
[292] *Halech v State of South Australia* (2006) 93 SASR 427 [123] FC.
[293] [1983] A.C. 410.

and space between the happening of the traumatic event and it coming to the claimant's attention. However, to insist on direct and immediate sight or hearing would be impracticable and unjust. So under an "aftermath" doctrine, where a person came quickly upon the scene, a claim could be entertained. As regards communication, there was no case in which the law had compensated shock brought about by communication by a third party. The shock had to come about through sight or hearing of the event or its immediate aftermath.

2–137 Applying these factors, the claimant's shock had been the reasonably foreseeable result of the injuries to her family, she had directly perceived the aftermath of the accident, and she was entitled to recover damages.

2–138 **Alcock v Chief Constable of South Yorkshire Police.** In 1991, the House of Lords returned to the problem. *Alcock v Chief Constable of South Yorkshire Police*[294] was the lead case in a number of related appeals arising out of a major disaster at Sheffield Wednesday's football stadium at Hillsborough in Sheffield. An officer of the South Yorkshire Police negligently allowed the stadium to become overcrowded, as a result of which 95 spectators were crushed to death and more than 400 were injured. This horrifying spectacle was televised live as the fatal events were happening.[295] The claimants were relatives or friends of spectators caught up in the disaster. Some witnessed the unfolding tragedy from other parts of the stadium, some watched it live on television and some heard of it from friends or the radio and later saw recorded television pictures. They all claimed damages from the defendant police authority on the ground that the impact of what they had seen and heard caused them severe nervous shock.

2–139 Their Lordships held that in order to establish a claim for psychiatric injury arising from the incident, it was necessary to show, not only that psychiatric illness suffered by the particular claimant was reasonably foreseeable, but also, drawing upon Lord Wilberforce's judgment in *McLoughlin v O'Brian*, that there was a close tie or relationship between the claimant and the injured person, that the claimant was proximate to the accident in both time and space, and that the injury was caused by means of a sudden and unexpected shock. Each of these elements needs to be examined more closely.

2–140 **Class of claimants.** *Alcock* determined that the persons to whom a duty of care may be owed were not limited to those with a particular, familial, relationship with the primary victim, as in the case of husband and wife or parent and child. Rather, the relationship needed to be based on close ties of love and affection. There needed to be a case-by-case investigation of the relationship in order to determine whether the degree of love and affection felt by the claimant for the victim was such that the defendant ought to have foreseen that the

---

[294] [1992] 1 A.C. 310; Davie, "Negligently Inflicted Psychiatric Illness: the Hillsborough Case in the House of Lords" (1992) 43 N.I.L.Q. 237; Nasir, "Nervous shock and *Alcock*: the judicial buck stops here" (1992) 55 M.L.R. 705; Teff, "Liability for psychiatric illness after Hillsborough" (1992) 12 OJLS 440; Lynch, "A victory for pragmatism? Nervous shock reconsidered" (1992) 108 L.Q.R. 367.
[295] The occasion was the FA cup semi-final game between Liverpool and Nottingham Forest on April 15, 1989.

claimant might suffer psychiatric harm. However, there was some support for presuming the requisite relationship in the case of parents and children, spouses and perhaps engaged persons.[296]

Applying these principles, it was held that the claims by those at the ground **2–141** failed. The relationships of the claimants to the deceased victims included those of brother, brother-in-law, uncle and a particular friend, and none of them had proved a sufficiently close relationship of love and affection as to make his claim reasonably foreseeable by the defendant.

The need to show a relationship of this kind with the victim is likely to prevent **2–142** the recovery of damages by rescuers suing as secondary victims in relation to those they are seeking to rescue.[297] It may also prove to be a significant hurdle in the case of workplace accidents. For example, claims by two employees of the defenders, who both suffered psychiatric injury on witnessing the death of a third employee when he was suddenly blown from the bridge where they were working, were held to fail, because they were not bound by sufficiently close ties of affection with the deceased employee.[298]

Especially horrific accidents. Dicta in *Alcock* suggest that an action can **2–143** possibly lie where the circumstances of an accident are particularly horrific.[299] However, this was later rejected and emphasis given to the need for the claimant to show a close relationship with the primary victim.[300]

Proximity in time and space. The second element to liability identified in **2–144** *McLoughlin* and *Alcock* was the claimant's closeness in time and space to the happening of the accident or its immediate aftermath. This factor also was seen as relevant in their Lordships' earlier decision in *Bourhill v Young*,[301] where, as we have seen, the action failed on the general ground that injury to someone in the claimant's position could not have been foreseen by the negligent motorcyclist. But the decision might best be explained today on the basis that the claimant had no relationship of love and affection with the accident victim.

The need to show proximity in time and space means that claims for **2–145** psychiatric injury by those who hear about the death or injury of a loved one, but who do not witness the accident or its aftermath, will almost inevitably fail.[302] In *Alcock* itself the claims by those who watched the disaster on television were rejected, because the necessary proximity was lacking. The defendant could expect that the broadcaster would comply with the television code of ethics

---

[296] Per Lord Keith at 397, Lord Ackner at 403.
[297] *Frost v Chief Constable of South Yorkshire Police* [1999] 2 A.C. 455; see para.2–155, below.
[298] *Robertson v Forth Road Bridge Joint Board (No.2)* 1995 SLT 263; cp *Mt Isa Mines Ltd v Pusey* (1970) 125 C.L.R. 383 HCA.
[299] [1992] 1 A.C. 310, 397, 403, 416.
[300] *McFarlane v EE Caledonia Ltd* [1994] 2 All E.R. 1 CA.
[301] [1943] A.C. 92.
[302] *Taylor v Somerset Health Authority* [1993] P.I.Q.R. P262 (where a hospital doctor informed a wife of her husband's sudden death at work); *Abramzik v Brenner* (1967) 65 D.L.R. (2d) 651.

(which prohibited the transmission of scenes depicting the suffering of recognisable individuals), the edited pictures could not be seen as the equivalent of actual sight and hearing, and there was no sufficient degree of immediacy as to found a claim.[303] However, it was recognised that sometimes an action might lie, such as where parents might be expected to be watching live television pictures of their children going up in a balloon, which suddenly burst into flames. Here the impact might be as great or greater than actual sight of the accident.[304] Another question was whether viewing the bodies of relatives in a mortuary could be recognised as part of the aftermath of the accident. But it was held not, because this was not part of the immediate aftermath, or because the purpose of the visits was identification rather than rescue or comfort.[305] On the other hand, the Court of Appeal, in a decision that is difficult to reconcile with *Alcock*, upheld the claim of a mother who went to the scene of a road traffic accident in which her daughter had been fatally injured, arriving after the body had been removed, and then went then to the mortuary and saw her badly disfigured body. The visit to the mortuary was still part of the immediate aftermath, which "existed from the moment of the accident until the moment that [the mother] left the mortuary".[306]

2–146   **W v Essex County Council.** It is apparent that the answer to the question whether a claimant can be seen as sufficiently proximate to the happening of a shock-inducing event may turn on rather arbitrary drawing of lines. In *W v Essex County Council*.[307] the claimants agreed with the defendant council to become foster parents. After receiving assurances that no sexual abuser would be placed with them, and following a false representation by the council's social worker that a particular boy was not a known sex abuser, they agreed to foster the boy. A month later they discovered that the boy had sexually abused all four of their children. The claimants sought damages for psychiatric illness, partly based on their status as secondary victims,[308] and the House of Lords refused to strike out the claim. Lord Slynn thought that the concept of "immediate aftermath" of an incident had to be assessed in the particular factual situation. He was not persuaded that the parents had to come across the abuser or the abused "immediately" after the sexual incident had terminated. All the incidents happened in a period of 4 weeks, and it might be that the temporal and spatial limitations were satisfied.

2–147   **Shock-induced injury.** The third element which needs to be satisfied before a claim by a secondary victim can succeed focuses on the mechanism by which the psychiatric injury has been inflicted. The injury must be capable of being

---

[303] [1992] 1 A.C. 310, at pp.398, 405, 417, 423.

[304] ibid, at pp 405, 417.

[305] ibid, at 405 per Lord Ackner, at 424 per Lord Jauncey; and see *Devji v Burnaby (District)* (2000) 180 D.L.R. (4th) 205, BCCA; *Palmer v Tees Health Authority* [1999] Lloyd's Rep. Med. 351 CA.

[306] *Galli-Atkinson v Seghal* [2003] Lloyd's Rep. Med. 285 CA; Thomas, "Satisfying the nearness test" (2003) 153 N.L.J. 953.

[307] [2000] 2 W.L.R. 601 HL; Wightman "The limits of the rules on recovery for psychiatric damage in the United Kingdom" (2000) 8 Tort L Rev 169; and see *Lambert v Cardiff County Council* [2007] EWHC 869; cf *Palmer v Tees Health Authority* [1999] Lloyd's Rep. Med. 351 CA.

[308] For another basis to the claim see para.2–160, below.

described as caused by a "nervous shock" or, in other words, that it was shock-induced.[309] In *Alcock*, Lord Keith said that there must be "a sudden assault on the nervous system" and Lord Ackner spoke of a "sudden appreciation by sight or sound of a horrifying event, which violently agitates the mind." His Lordship added that it had yet to include psychiatric illness caused by the accumulation over a period of time of more gradual assaults on the nervous system."[310]

Suddenness. In a series of cases the courts have been exercised in determin- **2–148** ing whether shock has been suffered "suddenly" or as the result of the cumulative effect of events and a gradual realisation of the effect of the defendant's wrong. There was no actionable shock where a wife, having been informed of her husband's death, viewed his body in the mortuary to settle her disbelief about his death.[311] Again, parents of a 14-year-old boy who died three days after he was struck by a reversing vehicle did not suffer sudden shock, in circumstances where they did not see the accident but were told of it soon after, went to the hospital, and saw him in an ambulance and being taken into the Intensive Care Unit.[312] Their psychiatric illness, it was held, arose from understandable grief caused by the gradual deterioration in his condition. The claim of a father who stayed by his injured son's hospital bedside following an accident until his death two weeks later allegedly due to the defendant's misdiagnosis of his injuries similarly failed, since there had been no "shock" in the requisite sense.[313] And in a further example, a mother whose daughter was abducted and murdered suffered psychiatric illness only as a result of an "elongated process" which began with her receipt of the information that her daughter was missing and ended with her identification of the child's body six days later.[314]

On the other hand, there was "a sudden appreciation of a horrifying event" **2–149** where a mother suffered pathological grief reaction following a period of 36 hours starting with her seeing her child have a fit and ending with his death in her arms. It was impossible on the psychiatric evidence to isolate the causative effect of any particular incident in that time. It was a seamless tale and one drawn-out experience with an obvious beginning and an equally obvious end.[315] Again, a defendant's negligence in failing to deliver a child by caesarian section, causing the child to be born severely asphyxiated and to die two days later, was held to have caused actionable shock to the child's parents. The judge was satisfied that the period from onset of labour until the child's death was effectively one event, that there was no need to invoke the aftermath doctrine, and that the parents were victims of an experience sufficient to establish liability even though a full

---

[309] Teff "The requirement of 'sudden shock' in liability for negligently inflicted psychiatric damage" (1996) 4 Tort L Rev 44.
[310] [1992] 1 A.C. 310, at 398, 401.
[311] *Taylor v Somerset Health Authority* [1993] P.I.Q.R. P262.
[312] *Taylorson v Shieldness Produce Ltd* [1994] P.I.Q.R. P329 CA.
[313] *Sion v Hampstead Health Authority* [1994] 5 Med. L.R. 170.
[314] *Palmer v Tees Health Authority* [1999] Lloyd's Rep. Med. 351 CA; Mason and Laurie, "Misfeasance in public office: an emerging medical law tort?" (2003) 11 Med. L. Rev. 194.
[315] *Walters v North Glamorgan NHS Trust* [2003] P.I.Q.R. P232 CA.

appreciation of the gravity of that child's condition only developed in the 48 hours between birth and death.[316]

2-150   **Defendant as primary victim.** It is been held that a special rule applies in cases where the defendant is the immediate victim. A claimant who suffers psychiatric injury caused by injury to or fear for another cannot recover damages where that other was the defendant himself or herself.[317] So no duty of care was owed by a son to his father where it was alleged that the father developed psychiatric symptoms as a result of attending an accident caused by his son's negligent driving and seeing his son in an injured state.[318] The Law Commission has seen the justification for this exclusion as being based on a policy not to place an undesirably restrictive burden on a person's self-determination.[319]

2-151   **Damages.** It will be apparent that a strict application of the *Alcock* principles could cause difficulty in calculating the damages which ought to be awarded to those who qualify as secondary victims. Seemingly, it becomes necessary to separate the injury caused by perceiving the accident (compensable) from the injury caused by knowledge of its consequences (non-compensable). So a claimant whose husband was killed in an accident could recover for depression caused by shock from witnessing the accident, but not for depression caused by her grief and sorrow at losing her husband, anxiety about the welfare of her injured children, financial stress due to the loss of the family's bread-winner, and the need to adjust to a new life.[320] However, in a later decision the Court of Appeal declined to divide up damages in this way. Where mental illness was suffered by a father both from viewing an accident to his children and from an intense and abnormal grief reaction to his bereavement, the damages were not discounted for his grief and the "normal" consequences of bereavement even though his illness was partly so caused.[321] It was impossible as a matter of common sense to distinguish between the effect upon the claimants mind of seeing the accident and the effects of grief and bereavement that became inevitable when he knew his children had in fact been killed.

2-152   **Appraisal.** At the beginning of this discussion we noted a widespread recognition, both by judges and commentators, that the law applying to claims in negligence for mental injury is not at all in a satisfactory state. A possible solution—to base liability simply on foreseeability of psychiatric harm—has been seen as ruled out by precedent.[322] The High Court of Australia, not being similarly constrained, has taken this step. In *Tame v New South Wales: Annetts v*

---

[316] *Tredget v Bexley HA* (1994) 5 Med. L.R. 178.

[317] *Jaensch v Coffey* (1984) 155 C.L.R. 549, at 604 per Deane J. HCA; *Alcock v Chief Constable of the South Yorkshire Police* [1992] 1 A.C. 310, at 418 per Lord Oliver.

[318] *Greatorex v Greatorex* [2000] 1 W.L.R. 1970; Handford, "Psychiatric damage where the defendant is the immediate victim" (2001) 117 L.Q.R. 397.

[319] Report No. 249, above n.236, paras 2.66, 5.34–5.42.

[320] *Hinz v Berry* [1970] 2 Q.B. 40.

[321] *Vernon v Bosley (No.1)* [1997] 1 All E.R. 577 CA. See also *Dickens v O2 Plc* [2009] I.R.L.R. 58 CA, Ch.11 para.10–000 below (it is inappropriate to discount in cases of indivisible injury such as psychiatric injury for the effect of non-tortious factors).

[322] *Frost v Chief Constable of the South Yorkshire Police* [1999] 2 A.C. 455, at 500 per Lord Steyn.

Australian Stations Pty Ltd,[323] Gummow and Kirby J.J. recognised that a rule that rendered liability conditional on the geographic or temporal distance of the plaintiff from the distressing phenomenon, or on the means by which the plaintiff acquired knowledge of that phenomenon, was apt to produce arbitrary outcomes, to exclude meritorious claims and to mandate differential treatment of plaintiffs in substantially the same position. Pragmatic justifications for the rule—in particular the fear of indeterminate liability and of imposing a disproportionate burden on defendants—were unconvincing, and its harsh and arbitrary operation had attracted widespread criticism. They thought that the factual considerations contemplated by the rule might be relevant to assessing reasonable foreseeability, causation and remoteness, but were not themselves decisive of liability.

The claim in *Annetts* arose after the plaintiffs' 16-year-old son had become lost **2–153** and had died in the desert in Western Australia while working for the defendants in a remote area. The plaintiffs sought damages for mental injury, alleging that the defendants had assured them that their son would be properly looked after, but had failed to provide either supervision or company. Their claim succeeded notwithstanding that the harm came about from what they were told about the imperilment and death of their son, not from their actual perception of it. And similarly, in a later case,[324] the High Court held that an employer owed a duty of care to the children of an employee who was killed in an accident at work.

It is doubtful whether a similar reform in England would lead to an excessive **2–154** burden of liability. Nor would it necessarily make the law more uncertain. The boundaries of liability under the present law are already uncertain, and there would simply be a change in the focus of the debate away from the artifical proximity factors identified in *Alcock*.

(v) *Further categories of claimant*

Rescuers. In *Chadwick v British Transport Commission*,[325] a rescuer recov- **2–155** ered damages for psychiatric injury suffered as a result of ministering to the victims of a train crash, apparently on the straightforward basis that his injury was reasonably foreseeable. The "shock" was caused neither by fear for himself nor by fear or horror on account of the involvement of any near relative. However, in *Frost v Chief Constable of the South Yorkshire Police*,[326] where police officers who assisted in various ways at the scene of the Hillsborough disaster sued in respect of their consequential psychiatric injury, their Lordships

---

[323] (2003) 211 C.L.R. 317 HCA; Trindade, "Reformulation of the nervous shock rules" (2003) 119 L.Q.R. 204; Handford, "Psychiatric injury: the new era" (2003) 11 Tort L Rev 13; Dietrich, "Nervous shock: *Tame v New South Wales* and *Annetts v Australian Stations Pty Ltd*" (2003) 11 T.L.J. 11.
[324] *Gifford v Strang Patrick Stevedoring Pty Ltd* (2003) 214 C.L.R. 269 HCA; Handford "Psychiatric injury: duty to employees' children" (2003) 11 Tort L Rev 127.
[325] [1967] 1 W.L.R. 912.
[326] [1999] 2 A.C. 455; Todd, "Psychiatric injury and rescuers" (1999) 115 L.Q.R. 345; Rogers, "Psychiatric trauma: 'Thus far and no further'—In fact not quite so far as hitherto" (1999) 7 T.L.J. 23; Mullender and Speirs, "Negligence, psychiatric injury, and the altruism principle"(2000) 20 OJLS 645; Mendelson, "Quo iure? Defendants' liability to rescuers in the tort of negligence" (2001) 9 Tort L Rev 130; Cooke, "Primary victims: the end of the road?" (2004) 25 Liverpool L.R. 29.

held, in a majority decision, that the primary/secondary victim distinction applied and that none of the claimants could recover in their capacity as rescuers. Officers assisting at the scene who were within the range of foreseeable physical injury were primary victims who were owed a duty on the basis of the principle in *Page v Smith*, irrespective of whether psychiatric injury was foreseeable.[327] *Chadwick* was explained as a case where the rescuer was put in danger. Rescuers who had not been exposed to the risk of physical injury or who had not reasonably believed themselves to have been so exposed were to be classified as secondary victims who were required to satisfy the *Alcock* conditions. As they were unable to establish any relational proximity with the victims their claims had to fail. Lord Griffiths and Lord Goff dissented, taking the view that the test should be the foreseeability of psychiatric injury without any requirement of danger. In Lord Goff's view a rule limiting recovery by reference to personal danger was artificial and contrary to well-established authority.[328]

2–156   The danger requirement seems appropriate if a rescuer is seeking to recover for psychiatric injury suffered as a result of fear for his or her own safety. But if the injury is caused by fear for and perception of physical suffering by others it does indeed seem arbitrary, its sole purpose being to limit the ambit of liability.[329] A preferable approach might have been to move away from a rigid need to classify all claimants as "primary" or "secondary", but to identify deserving categories for recovery independently of that division. Claims by rescuers, as one such category, could be considered on their particular merits. This would be consistent with the kind of approach favoured by the Law Commission.[330]

2–157   **Employees.** An alternative basis for the claims in *Frost* was that founded upon the relationship of employer and employee. The Chief Constable could be liable, it was argued, in his capacity as the claimants' employer for negligently

---

[327] Lord Steyn (at 499) said that the rescuer must show that "he objectively exposed himself to danger or reasonably believed he was doing so". Lord Hoffmann (at 508) indicated that a rescuer claiming psychiatric injury would have to demonstrate foreseeability of physical injury and causation of psychiatric injury by witnessing or participating in the aftermath of accidents which caused death or injury to others.

[328] Their Lordships were agreed in rejecting a so-called "fireman's rule" applying in some of the states of the US, whereby a person is unable to recover for injury in circumstances in which he or she would normally be entitled to sue, merely because that person's occupation required him or her to run the risk of such injury. They regarded the matter as having been determined by *Ogwo v Taylor* [1988] A.C. 431, holding that a fireman could recover for scalding suffered while fighting a fire. But might there not be a distinction between physical and mental injury, in that mental injury suffered by a professional rescuer might well be seen as unforeseeable?

[329] See, for example, *Duncan v British Coal Corporation* [1997] 1 All E.R. 540 CA (claim of pit deputy who developed psychiatric injury after administering first aid at the scene of a colliery accident which had occurred 4 minutes before dismissed because, inter alia, he was not in danger); *Cullin v London Fire and Civil Defence Authority* [1999] P.I.Q.R. P314 CA (fireman's claim for psychiatric injury as rescuer arguable where he had made an unsuccessful attempt to recover two other firemen from a burning building and was present when their bodies were brought out and unsuccessful attempts made at resuscitation); *Keen v Tayside Contracts* 2003 SLT 500, OH (road worker and team foreman who was required by his employers to attend a road traffic accident in order to set up a road diversion and was exposed to the sight of dead and mutilated bodies at the scene not a primary victim).

[330] Report No. 249, above, n. 236.

exposing them to the risk of psychiatric harm. The argument was rejected; a majority in the House of Lords holding that the duty of an employer to safeguard employees from physical injury did not extend to a duty to protect them from psychiatric injury where there was no breach of the former duty. Lord Hoffmann noted that the relationship of employer and employee established the employee as a person to whom the employer owed a duty of care, but told one nothing about the circumstances in which he would be liable for a particular type of injury. For this, one had to look to the general law concerning the type of injury that had been suffered. The ordinary restrictions on the recovery of compensation for psychiatric harm should still apply, the claimants were secondary victims and their claims accordingly still failed.

Work-related stress. Claims for work-related stress where the background is   **2–158** the contract of employment between the parties are treated differently. In *Hatton v Sutherland*,[331] Hale L.J. said that liability was to be approached by way of the same principles that would apply in any claim by an employee against an employer. There were "no special control mechanisms applying to claims for psychiatric (or physical) injury or illness arising from the stress of doing the work which the employee is required to do".[332] In determining whether a duty was owed the crucial question was whether it was reasonably foreseeable that psychiatric harm would be suffered by the employee concerned. Few occupations were so inherently stressful that, without more, they put an employer on notice of the risk to his employee of psychiatric injury. For liability to attach, circumstances had to come to the attention of the employer from which the risk of injury ought to have been appreciated. Further, the claimant had to show as well that the employer was in breach of duty in failing to take proper steps to safeguard the employee, and that the cause of the harm was not just the work but the employer's breach in not dealing with the problem.[333]

---

[331] [2002] 2 All E.R. 1 CA (a composite judgment involving four appeals); Mullany, "Containing claims for workplace mental illness" (2002) 118 L.Q.R. 373; Teff, "Psychiatric illness caused by stress at work" (2002) 10 Tort L Rev 161. In *Barber v Somerset CC* [2004] 1 W.L.R. 1089 the House of Lords allowed an appeal in one of the other cases, on the basis that the evidence showed there had been a breach of the employer's duty, but nonetheless approved the statements of legal principle and practical guidance given by her Ladyship in the court below; Case, "Hues of foreseeability: employer liability for chronic stress and the impact of *Barber*" (2004) 20 P.N. 192. For further stress cases see *Walker v Northumberland CC* [1995] 1 All E.R. 737; *Pratley v Surrey CC* [2004] I.C.R. 159 CA; *Hartman v South Essex Mental Health NHS Trust* [2005] I.C.R. 782 CA; *Clark v Chief Constable of Essex* (2006) 103 LSG 32; *Daw v Intel Corporation UK Ltd* [2007] I.C.R. 318 CA; *Dickins v O2 Plc* [2009] I.R.L.R. 58, CA. See generally Elvin, "The legal response to occupational stress claims" (2008) 16 Tort L Rev 23; Barrett, "Psychological stress; an unacceptable cost to employers" [2008] JBL 64. See also Ch.11 para.11–84, below.
[332] ibid, at [22].
[333] In *Koehler v Cerebos (Australia) Ltd* (2005) 222 C.L.R. 44 the High Court of Australia pointed out (i) that an employer engaging an employee to perform stated duties normally is entitled to assume that the employee considers that he or she is able to do the job, (ii) that implying some qualification upon what otherwise is expressly stipulated would contradict basic principle, and (iii) that seeking to qualify the operation of the contract as a result of information the employer later acquires about the vulnerability of the employee to psychiatric harm would be no less contradictory of basic principle.

2–159   In one unusual variation a head teacher recovered damages for psychiatric injury caused by the local education authority's failure to exercise a statutory discretion to replace her school's governing body with an interim executive board under the provisions of the School Standards and Frameworks Act 1998. Acrimonious disputes had arisen in the governing body and unjustified complaints had been made against her. The authority's statutory duty had been to correct the position which had arisen at the school by the creation of an interim executive board and its common law duty of care towards her marched together with that statutory duty. The establishment of an inquiry to investigate the complaints where there was no public law imperative so to do and the failure to replace the governing body constituted a breach of the authority's duty of care and psychiatric injury to her was foreseeable as a result.[334] However, in *French v Sussex County Council*[335] a claim for work-induced psychiatric harm was seen as a step too far. The claimant police officers were involved at various levels of responsibility in connection with an armed raid on a suspect's home during which the suspect was fatally wounded. The claimants were then made subject to a variety of disciplinary and other proceedings, but these ultimately came to nothing. They sought damages from their employer, alleging psychiatric injury as a result of corporate failure and mismanagement in relation to these events, but their claims were struck out. Although it could be highly stressful to be the object of allegations such as they had faced, and it was arguably foreseeable that such stress was capable of causing psychiatric injury, allowing the claims would involve a significant and unjustified extension to the ambit of the duty of care not to cause psychiatric injury.

2–160   **Involuntary participants.** In *Alcock* Lord Oliver contemplated that there should be recovery in circumstances where the negligent act of the defendant had put the claimant in the position of being, or thinking that he or she was about to be or had been, the involuntary cause of another's death or injury.[336] In *Frost*, Lord Hoffmann thought there might be grounds for treating such a rare category of case as exceptional and exempt from the *Alcock* control mechanisms. For example, in an older decision, a crane driver could recover for mental injury caused by fear for his workmates after a defective rope snapped and the load from his crane fell into the hold of a ship where he knew they were working.[337] Again, in *W v Essex County Council*[338] the parents' psychiatric injury flowed from their feeling of responsibility in having brought the abuser into contact with their children, providing an alternative possible basis for recovery in that case. But where the claimant struck an improperly maintained protruding fire hydrant

---

[334] *Connor v Surrey County Council* [2010] EWCA Civ 286 CA.
[335] *The Times*, April 6, 2006 CA; and see *New South Wales v Paige* (2004) 60 N.S.W.L.R. 371 NSWCA (no duty owed by employer to provide safe system of investigation and decision making with respect to procedures for discipline and termination of employment so as to avoid psychiatric injury to employee).
[336] See Pickford, "Psychiatric harm and the involuntary participant: 'a story of the ebb and flow of tort liability'" (2005) 56 NILQ 602.
[337] *Dooley v Cammell Laird & Co Ltd* [1951] 1 Lloyd's Rep. 271.
[338] [2000] 2 W.L.R. 601, HL; see para.2–146, above.

while driving a vehicle at the defendant's mine and caused a fatal accident, his claim failed on the ground that he was not present at the scene of the accident but merely felt responsible when news of it was broken to him later.[339]

Miscellaneous cases. There are many cases involving claimants who have not 2–161
suffered a "shock" on account of a horrifying event of which they have been an observer or in which they have participated, where the distinction between primary and secondary victims is inapposite. Decisions involving fear of future harm are examples. In one, a duty to avoid psychiatric injury was owed to claimants who allegedly developed psychiatric injury after being injected with a human growth hormone product capable of infecting them with Creutzfeld-Jacob Disease, for the injury was reasonably foreseeable in light of the published risks and effects of that condition.[340] Again, it has already been seen that in *Grieves v F T Everard & Sons*[341] the House of Lords declined to treat a claimant who had developed a depressive illness from his fear from having been exposed to asbestos dust as being a primary victim, but seemingly the claim could have succeeded had such injury been held to be reasonably foreseeable.

A duty may be owed by a defendant who is responsible for communicating 2–162
false information. For example, a health authority conceded there was a duty to take care where the claimant was wrongly told her new-born baby had died.[342] It is possible that that there may be an obligation to take care in giving true bad news.[343] A duty was conceded in relation to the communication of information to former patients of a health worker about the remote risk of infection by AIDS.[344]

---

[339] *Hunter v British Coal Corporation* [1998] Q.B. 140; Teff, "Involuntary participation and survivor's guilt" (1998) 6 Tort L Rev 190. See also *Galt v British Railways Board* (1983) 133 N.L.J. 870 (a train driver succeeded in claim for nervous shock caused by thinking he had struck and killed two men on the track and which later brought on chest pains and a myocardial infarction to which he had had a pre-existing but symptomless predisposition); *Gregg v Ashbrae Ltd* [2006] N.I. 300, CA (a driver who drove digger past an unstable wall, causing it to collapse on another person, was not a primary victim and did not consider himself responsible for what had happened); *Monk v PC Harrington UK Ltd* [2009] P.I.Q.R. P3 (claimant's view that he had caused an accident at a building site was unreasonable, nor was he in danger in assisting the victims).
[340] *Group B Plaintiffs v Medical Research Council* (1998) 41 BMLR 157; O'Sullivan, "Liability for the fear of the onset of future medical conditions" (1999) 15 P.N. 96.
[341] [2008] 1 A.C. 281, sub nom *Rothwell v Chemical Insulating Co Ltd*; see para.2–128, above.
[342] *Allin v City & Hackney HA* (1996) 7 Med. L.R. 167; cp *Guay v Sun Publishing Co* [1953] 4 D.L.R. 577, where the Supreme Court of Canada held that the claimant had no right of recovery for nervous shock caused by a negligent misstatement in the defendant newspaper that members of the claimant's family had been killed.
[343] *Furniss v Fitchett* [1958] N.Z.L.R. 396 (doctor liable for negligently allowing a certificate stating his belief that a patient suffered from mental illness to come to the notice of the patient); *A B v Tameside & Glossop HA* (1997) 8 Med. L.R. 91 (duty conceded); Mullany, "Liability for careless communication of traumatic information" (1998) 114 L.Q.R. 380; see also *Powell v Boldaz* (1998) 6 Med. L.R. 112; cf *Mt Isa Mines Ltd v Pusey* (1970) 125 C.L.R. 383, 407 HCA.
[344] *A v Tameside and Glossop HA* [1997] P.N.L.R. 140 CA, where the proper formulation of the duty was in dispute as well as its application on the facts; Dzioborn and Tettenborn, "When the truth hurts—the incompetent transmission of distressing news" (1997) 13 P.N. 70; Jones, "Negligently inflicted psychiatric harm: is the word mightier than the deed?" (1997) 13 P.N. 111.

2–163   Recovery for psychiatric injury may be available in a number of other situations. These include: negligently damaging the claimant's property[345]; asking a voluntary worker to attend interviews with a multiple murderer and failing to provide counselling services afterwards[346]; failing to ensure that the identities of police informants were kept secret, thereby exposing them to threats of harm from a criminal[347]; putting a prisoner in a cell with another, suicidally inclined, prisoner, who later committed suicide.[348] To similar effect, claimants have sometimes been treated as primary victims although they have not been in any kind of danger and the requirements of *Page v Smith* have not been satisfied. So a father who developed psychiatric injury after mistakenly being told by nurses that his new-born son had died, and being given another baby's body to grieve over for twenty minutes, was regarded as a primary victim by virtue of his direct involvement in the traumatic incident.[349] Again, parents who claimed damages for psychiatric injury from clinicians who had carried out post-mortems on their deceased children and had removed, retained and disposed of bodily organs without consent were likewise seen as primary victims of the wrongdoing. There was a doctor-patient relationship, equivalent to contract, between the clinicians and the parents, and in the circumstances the clinicians owed the parents a duty of care.[350]

2–164   **Claims in contract.** In *McLoughlin v Jones*[351] the claimant sought damages for psychiatric injury resulting when he was convicted of and then imprisoned for a serious crime allegedly as a result of the negligence of solicitors instructed to conduct his defence. The trial judge dismissed the claim at a preliminary stage on the basis that the claimant's illness was not a reasonably foreseeable result of the breaches of duty of which he complained. He directed himself by reference to what a reasonable man would have foreseen in a person of normally robust constitution. It was held that he applied an incorrect test. The duty was owed to the claimant personally and the test was whether psychiatric illness had been reasonably forseeable to him. The standpoint from which this had to be decided was that of the ordinary reasonable man in the position of the defendants, not psychiatrists, but solicitors practising in criminal law.

2–165   Brooke L.J. indicated that the control mechanisms developed to determine the incidence of liability for psychiatric injury in accident cases were not appropriate "when the relationship between the parties is founded on contract, whether the

---

[345] *Attia v British Gas plc* [1998] 1 Q.B. 304, where the court refused to strike out a claim for mental injury suffered by the plaintiff as a result of seeing her house burned down.
[346] *Leach v Chief Constable of Gloucestershire Constabulary* [1999] 1 W.L.R. 1421 CA.
[347] *Swinney v Chief Constable of the Northumbria Police (No. 1)* [1997] Q.B. 464. In *Swinney v Chief Constable of the Northumbria Police (No. 2) The Times*, 25 May 1999 it was held that the police had not been shown to have been in breach of duty. See also *B & B v A County Council* [2007] 1 F.L.R. 1189 CA (local authority owed duty to an adopting family not to disclose their identity to the adoptive children's birth parents, although the claim failed on the facts).
[348] *Butchart v Home Office* [2006] 1 W.L.R. 1155 CA.
[349] *Farrell v Avon HA* [2001] Lloyd's Rep Med 458; Case, "Curiouser and curiouser: psychiatric damage caused by negligent misinformation" (2002) 18 P.N. 248.
[350] *In Re the Organ Retention Group Litigation* [2005] 2 W.L.R. 358 at [189]-[199]; Jones, "Retained organs: The legal fallout" (2004) 20 P.N. 182.
[351] [2002] Q.B. 312.

breach of duty relied upon is a breach of a contractual term, or a breach of a duty of care arising out of parties' contractual relationship which sounds in damages in tort".[352] Accordingly, rather than approach the case by reference to the distinction between primary and secondary victims, he discussed whether a duty was owed by reference to the various tests for the existence of a duty of care in new factual situations propounded in *Caparo Industries Plc v Dickman*[353] and other cases. Hale L.J. adopted a different approach but reached the same result. In her view the claimant was to be regarded as a primary victim, this by analogy with the position of those seeking damages in respect of work-related stress.

(D) Financial injury

Statements. Whilst the common law traditionally recognised a duty to take   **2–166** care to avoid causing physical injury to persons or property it was, at least until fairly recent times, much more cautious in recognising a duty to avoid causing non-physical or purely pecuniary loss, even when it was clearly foreseeable. The turning point was *Hedley Byrne & Co Ltd v Heller & Partners Ltd*,[354] in which the House of Lords held that a duty to take care could be owed by the maker of a statement to a person who suffered financial loss caused by relying on the statement. The decision provides the foundation for the present law concerning liability for negligent misstatements, and also opened the way for claims in negligence for financial loss caused in other ways.

Other cases. As regards misstatements the core principle of liability is well   **2–167** established, although the precise boundaries of the principle remain difficult to pin down. More intractable is the problem of defining how far a principle permitting the recovery of financial loss should extend. Claims for such loss can appear in a variety of forms, and whether they should succeed depends ultimately on policy. A major policy concern is once again the need for controls to prevent too wide a potential liability, and thereby uncertainty.[355] But a variety of other policy matters may be relevant and influential.

The distinction between careless statements causing detrimental reliance and   **2–168** careless acts may sometimes be difficult to draw, yet can have a critical bearing on whether there is a duty of care. So, on the one hand, a negligent representation as to the state of a building can give rise to a duty under the *Hedley Byrne* principle,[356] but, on the other, no duty of care is owed in respect of negligent work causing a building to be constructed with a latent defect.[357] Putting up a building with no visible signs of any defect might be seen as amounting to a representation that the building is sound, but it is not treated as such in this context. So what can amount to an actionable representation is an important

---

[352] *McLoughlin v Jones* [2002] Q.B. 312, at [22].
[353] [1990] 2 A.C. 605.
[354] [1964] A.C. 465.
[355] *Ultramares Corporation v Touche* (1931) 174 NE 441 per Cardozo J. at 444.
[356] See, for example, *Smith v Eric S Bush* [1990] 1 A.C. 831; see para.2–202, below.
[357] *Murphy v Brentwood DC* [1991] 1 A.C. 398; see para.2–241, below.

question where recovery for economic loss is concerned.[358] The discussion which follows starts by examining the principles governing liability for negligent statements, before turning to the more uncertain field where the cause is negligent conduct. The latter is subdivided into financial loss which is consequential upon physical damage to the claimant or to a third person, and financial loss standing alone, without physical damage to anyone. Next, and as a related topic, there are claims by owners or purchasers who suffer financial loss in acquiring defective property. And finally there is the very special case of a parent who suffers a failed sterilisation and who sues in respect of the cost of bringing up an unplanned child.

(E) Negligent statements causing financial injury

(i) *Introduction*

2–169   **Policy concerns.** Concerns about indeterminate liability have already been noted. In the nature of things, "words are more volatile than deeds, they travel fast and far afield, they are used without being expended".[359] Any duty of care must take account of this wide-ranging potential for causing loss. A second basic concern is the relationship between any duty in tort and well-established principles of contract. As a matter of contract a voluntary statement made to another without the support of any consideration is not actionable, yet an action in tort for negligence by an advisee who has not paid for the advice bypasses and arguably undermines this rule. In response to these objections the tendency has been to recognise only duties of specific focus and narrow ambit, countering the danger of indeterminate liability and minimising the scope for "free-riding" by those who have made commercial use of free advice.

2–170   **History.** Until relatively recent times, no action arose in respect of pecuniary damage from negligent misrepresentation save in two circumstances. If the parties were bound by contract there could of course be an action for breach of contract, and sometimes judges had to invent consideration in order to attach contractual force to an apparently gratuitous statement.[360] In the case of a fiduciary obligation, a failure by the fiduciary to take care in giving information or advice was seen as fraud in equity, such as could found a claim for an equitable indemnity rather than damages.[361] Otherwise the only remedy was an action in deceit, but fraud, in the sense of a false representation made knowingly or recklessly, was (and is) an essential element in such a claim and, without fraud, even statements made with "gross negligence" did not give rise to any cause of action.[362] There was no remedy for an expression of opinion given in good faith but without due care or skill by one person to another, where it was known the statement was likely to be acted upon by a third party, and where that person did

---

[358] See paras 2–176 to 2–179, below.
[359] *Hedley Byrne & Co Ltd v Heller & Partners Ltd* [1964] A.C. 465, per Lord Pearce at 534, per Lord Reid at 483.
[360] *De La Bere v Pearson* [1908] 1 K.B. 280.
[361] *Nocton v Lord Ashburton* [1914] A.C. 932.
[362] *Derry v Peek* (1889) 14 App Cas 337.

act upon it to his detriment. For example, in *Le Lièvre v Gould*[363] a surveyor
negligently issued progress certificates to a builder on the strength of which a
mortgagee advanced money to the builder and thereby suffered loss, and it was
held that the surveyor was not liable to the mortgagee. Bowen L.J. referred to
"the suggestion that a man is responsible for what he states in a certificate to any
person to whom he may have reason to suppose that the certificate may be
shown," and added that, "the law of England does not go to that extent: it does
not consider that what a man writes on paper is like a gun or other dangerous
instrument, and, unless he intended to deceive, the law does not, in the absence
of contract, hold him responsible for drawing his certificate carelessly".[364]

Denning L.J. criticised this state of affairs in a dissenting judgment in *Candler*   **2–171**
v Crane, Christmas & Co.[365] For his part he was prepared to recognise a duty to
take care, owed by accountants to any third person to whom they disclosed their
accounts in respect of transactions for which the accountants knew the accounts
were required. But the majority decision affirmed that there was no duty to take
care in the absence of either a contractual or fiduciary relationship between the
parties. It was not until *Hedley Byrne & Co Ltd v Heller & Partners Ltd*,[366] 13
years later, that the law changed. The House of Lords decided that a claim for
financial loss caused by negligent words could, in principle, be maintained. In
circumstances where a "special relationship" came into existence, there arose a
duty to take care in the making of statements, a breach of which would found
liability for either financial or physical harm, unless there was a disclaimer of
responsibility. *Le Lièvre* was disapproved, *Candler* was thought to be wrongly
decided, and Denning L.J.'s dissent was approved as laying down the foundation
for a duty.[367]

Hedley Byrne & Co Ltd v Heller & Partners Ltd. The decision in *Hedley*   **2–172**
Byrne arose from inquiries both by telephone and letter by one bank to another
about the financial position of a customer. The information was requested "in
confidence" and without responsibility on the part of the second bank. The
replies, given with a disclaimer of responsibility, were to the effect that the
customer was a respectably constituted company, considered to be good for its
normal business engagements. This information was duly passed on by the first
bank to the claimant advertising agents, and relying on it they entered into a
business transaction with the company. Shortly afterwards the company went
into liquidation, causing the claimants to suffer substantial financial loss. They
sued the second bank alleging both deceit and negligence, but later dropped the

---

[363] [1893] 1 Q.B. 491.
[364] ibid, at 502.
[365] [1951] 2 K.B. 164.
[366] [1964] A.C. 465.
[367] See generally Witting, *Liability for Negligent Misstatements*, New York, OUP, 2004; and see
Stevens, "*Hedley Byrne v Heller*: judicial creativity and doctrinal possibility" (1964) 27 M.L.R. 121;
Cane, "The metes and bounds of *Hedley Byrne*" (1981) 55 A.L.J. 862; Handley, "Some unsettled
aspects of the *Hedley Byrne* doctrine and Commonwealth perspectives" (2002) 31 CLWR 177;
O'Sullivan "Suing in tort where no contractual claim will lie—a bird's eye view" (2007) 23 P.N. 165;
Buxton, "How the common law gets made: *Hedley Byrne* and other cautionary tales" (2009) 125
L.Q.R. 60. For an economic analysis, see Bishop, "Negligent misrepresentation through economists'
eyes" (1980) 96 L.Q.R. 360

allegation of deceit and proceeded on the basis of negligence alone. The House of Lords held that the disclaimer of responsibility was sufficient to exclude the assumption by the bank of a legal duty of care, so for that reason the action failed. But all five of their Lordships went on to consider the legal position in the absence of any disclaimer, and all were agreed that in certain circumstances a duty of care in making statements was owed.

2–173   The speeches of their Lordships provided the bedrock for much subsequent development. But the basic proposition which they support is this: that if, in the ordinary course of business, a person seeks advice or information from another, who is not under any contractual or fiduciary obligation to give it, in circumstances in which a reasonable man so asked would know that he was being trusted or that his skill or judgment was being relied on, and such person, without clearly disclaiming responsibility for it, proceeds to give the advice or information sought, he accepts a legal duty to exercise such care as the circumstances require in making his reply. For a failure to exercise that care, an action in negligence will lie, if foreseeable loss or damage is the result.

2–174   **A duty in words.** The type of relationship giving rise to a duty of care in relation to words spoken or written was expressed in varying ways. First, let us take the approach of Lord Morris[368]:

> "It should now be regarded as settled that if someone possessed of a special skill undertakes, quite irrespective of contract, to apply that skill for the assistance of another person who relies upon such skill, a duty of care will arise. The fact that the service is to be given by means of or by the instrumentality of words can make no difference. Furthermore, if in a sphere in which a person is so placed that others could reasonably rely upon his judgment or his skill or upon his ability to make careful inquiry, a person takes it upon himself to give information or advice to, or allows his information or advice to be passed on to, another person who, as he knows or should know, will place reliance upon it, then a duty of care will arise."

Lord Devlin spoke in these terms[369]:

> "I shall . . . content myself with the proposition that wherever there is a relationship equivalent to contract, there is a duty of care. Such a relationship may be either general or particular. Examples of a general relationship are those of solicitor and client and of banker and customer . . . Where there is a general relationship of this sort, it is unnecessary to do more than prove its existence and the duty follows. Whereas in the present case what is relied on is a particular relationship created ad hoc, it will be necessary to examine the particular facts to see whether there is an express or implied undertaking of responsibility. I regard this proposition as an application of the general conception of proximity. Cases may arise in the future in which a new and wider proposition, quite independent of any notion of contract, will be needed."

2–175   In the discussion that follows, the starting point is the need for a statement upon which the claimant has relied. Next the summaries of Lord Morris and Lord Devlin direct attention to two rather different questions. One is concerned with

---

[368] [1964] A.C. 465 at 502–503.
[369] [1964] A.C. 465 at 530.

the notion of a person undertaking or assuming responsibility for his or her words, and the other with the nature of the relationship between the person giving advice and the person who acts upon that advice. Both of these possible bases for a duty of care will have to be addressed. Finally, there is the issue of disclaimers and the statutory controls on their effectiveness.

(ii) *The defendant's statement*

Statements of fact and opinion. A duty based on the *Hedley Byrne* principle   **2–176** can arise out of express statements of fact or of opinion. But a statement or representation can also sometimes be inferred from what a person has said or done, where there is a clear basis for so doing. A statement will not readily be inferred from what is essentially no more than an act or an omission to act. For example, inspecting and approving a house with a latent defect did not constitute a representation that the house was sound[370]; registering a finance company or allowing it to remain registered did not amount to a representation to potential investors that the company was credit-worthy[371]; and the public exhibition of a city redevelopment plan did not amount to an assurance that the plan would be continuously or inflexibly applied in the future or that it was feasible of implementation.[372]

Promises. This last example also demonstrates that there can be no duty of   **2–177** care to perform a promise and that negligence cannot be allowed to undermine basic principles of contract. However, in a borderline decision, the New Zealand Court of Appeal imposed liability on a government minister for negligently undertaking to give support to a fledgling industry in financial trouble, in reliance upon which the owner refrained from putting the company into liquidation and rescuing what he could from the venture.[373] Cooke J. maintained that a speaker who had promised to give assistance to another was bound to do what was reasonably within his power to bring about that result. This was not an absolute duty or guarantee, which belonged to the realm of contract. It depended simply on what a reasonable man would regard as his duty to his neighbour. Subsequently, however, Lord Oliver, delivering the judgment of the Privy Council in further litigation arising out of the same events, observed that their Lordships had considerable difficulty in grasping the concept of a duty in tort to take reasonable care to pay or procure payment of a sum that nobody was under any contractual obligation to pay.[374]

Negligent decision-making. There are examples where liability for negligent   **2–178** words has been imposed on public officials exercising decision-making powers. For example, an environmental health officer who required unnecessary work to

---

[370] See *Murphy v Brentwood DC* [1991] 1 A.C. 398, para.2–241 below, where there was no suggestion that a duty of care owed by a builder or an inspecting council could be founded on *Hedley Byrne*.
[371] *Yuen Kun Yeu v Attorney-General of Hong Kong* [1988] A.C. 175 PC.
[372] *San Sebastian Pty Ltd v Minister Administering the Environmental Planning and Assessment Act* (1986) 162 C.L.R. 340 HCA.
[373] *Meates v Attorney-General* [1983] N.Z.L.R. 308 NZCA.
[374] *Meates v Westpac Banking Corporation Ltd* [1991] 3 N.Z.L.R. 385, 403 PC.

be done to the claimant's guest house was held to be in breach of duty in giving negligent advice.[375] Arguably, however, any private law remedy in cases of this kind should be in the tort of misfeasance in a public office. Where the essential complaint is of misuse of public power, a duty of care has generally been denied.[376] The more stringent requirements of misfeasance—in particular, an intention to injure or deliberately unlawful conduct[377]—must be satisfied.

2–179   The position may be different where the claim does not seek to impugn a public officer's determination or the officer's power to make it. In *Davy v Spelthorne Borough Council*[378] the defendant local authority had agreed with the claimant, a landowner, that it would not enforce an enforcement notice, under the Town and Country Planning Act 1971, for a period of three years, provided no appeal against the notice itself was made. The claimant sued for damages, claiming that he had only entered into the agreement on the basis of the defendant's negligent advice. The defendants argued that there was a statutory bar on questioning the validity of the enforcement notice save by way of appeal under the 1971 Act,[379] but the House of Lords held that the statute was not engaged. Lord Keith pointed out that the claimant did not impugn or wish to overturn the enforcement notice. His whole case depended on the fact that he had lost the chance to impugn it. So an action in negligence could still lie. Their Lordships said nothing about liability for misfeasance, and indeed the claim was simply in respect of negligent advice, not in respect of an allegedly negligent decision.

(iii) *Assuming responsibility for words*

2–180   **Assuming responsibility.** There are many references in the cases to a duty of care in words being founded upon the speaker's assumption of responsibility for what he or she says. This important idea or test is found in the speeches in *Hedley Byrne* itself. Yet it is not always made clear what amounts to an assumption of responsibility and how it can be established.[380]

---

[375] *Welton v North Cornwall District Council* [1997] 1 W.L.R. 570 CA.
[376] For example, *Jones v Department of Employment* [1988] 2 W.L.R. 493 CA (a social security officer reaching a decision concerning a claim for unemployment benefit); *Bennett v Commissioner of Police for the Metropolis* [1995] 1 W.L.R. 488 (minister signing a public interest immunity certificate); *W v Home Office* [1997] Imm. AR 302 CA (immigration officer and Home Secretary deciding whether to end detention under the Immigration Act 1971); *Harris v Evans* [1998] 1 W.L.R. 1285 CA (environmental safety officer serving safety notice on bungee jump operator); *Rowley v Secretary of State for Work and Pensions* [2007] 1 W.L.R. 2861 (child support agency assessing, collecting and enforcing child support payments); *Bella Vista Resort Ltd v Western Bay of Plenty District Council* [2007] 3 N.Z.L.R. 429 NZCA (council granting non-notified application for variation of resource consent); *Jain v Trent Strategic HA* [2009] 1 A.C. 853 (registration authority seeking order for cancellation of registration of nursing home).
[377] See generally *Three Rivers District Council v Governor and Co of the Bank of England (No 3)* [2003] 2 A.C. 1.
[378] [1984] A.C. 262.
[379] Town and Country Planning Act 1971 s.243(1).
[380] Barker, "Unreliable assumptions in the modern law of negligence" (1993) 109 L.Q.R. 461; Whitaker, "The application of the 'braod principle of *Hedley Byrne*' as between parties to a contract" (1997) 17 LS 169; O'Sullivan, "Negligence liability of auditors to third parties and the role of assumption of responsibility" (1998) 14 P.N. 195; Coote, "Assumption of responsibility and pure economic loss in New Zealand" [2005] NZ Law Review 1.

Assumed duties are normally the province of contract. However, the notion of **2–181** an assumption of responsibility may have value in tort actions in deciding whether there is a duty to act or to speak. A person is under no general duty to speak or to act, but by undertaking to speak or to act or by inducing reliance in some way, responsibility is assumed, and the basis for a duty of care comes into existence.[381] In a number of leading decisions in the House of Lords, starting with *Hedley Byrne*, it has been recognised that assuming a responsibility means choosing or undertaking to speak or to act. A person owes a duty of care in tort because the law imposes the duty on the basis of what he or she has said or done or assumed to do, not because that person assumes or decides to assume legal responsibility.[382] Beyond this the notion seems to possess little substantial content. As Lord Slynn has said:

> "It is sometimes said that there has to be an assumption of responsibility by the person concerned. That phrase can be misleading in that it can suggest that the professional person must knowingly and deliberately accept responsibility. It is however clear that the test is an objective one . . . The phrase means simply that the law recognises a duty of care. It is not so much that responsibility is assumed as that it is recognised or imposed by the law."[383]

On this view the finding in any particular case that there was an assumption of responsibility simply amounts to a label, a shorthand statement that the circumstances were such as to give rise to a duty to take care.

ILLUSTRATIONS

Notwithstanding such reservations, the notion of an assumption of responsibil- **2–182** ity has been invoked as a test for duty, even where a person has acted positively in speaking or undertaking to speak, in order to decide whether that person has in some sense assumed legal responsibility for his or her words. In particular, in *Henderson v Merrett Syndicates Ltd*,[384] Lord Goff regarded the notion of assumption of responsibility as possessing objective content. He suggested that it provided an explanation for the recovery of economic loss in respect of the negligent performance of a service, and went on to say that in some circumstances there may be no assumption, as where the adviser disclaims responsibility. But while it can be agreed that as a matter of common law principle a person may disclaim responsibility,[385] the concept of no assumption of responsibility has on occasion been used to deny a duty *in the absence of* any disclaimer. Again, in

---

[381] See, for example, *Henderson v Merrett Syndicates Ltd* [1995] 2 A.C. 145; *White v Jones* [1995] 2 A.C. 207; *Lennon v Metropolitan Police Commissioner* [2004] 1 W.L.R. 2594 CA; compare, for example, *Argy Trading Development Co Ltd v Lapid Developments Ltd* [1977] 1 W.L.R. 444; and see further para.2–63, above.
[382] See, for example, *Hedley Byrne & Co Ltd v Heller & Partners Ltd* [1964] A.C. 465 at 486 per Lord Reid; *Smith v Eric S Bush* [1990] 1 A.C. 831 at 862 per Lord Griffiths; *Caparo Industries Plc v Dickman* [1990] 2 A.C. 605 at 628 per Lord Roskill, at 637 per Lord Oliver; *White v Jones* [1995] 2 A.C. 207 at 273–274 per Lord Browne-Wilkinson.
[383] *Phelps v London Borough of Hillingdon* [2001] 2 A.C. 619 at 654.
[384] [1995] 2 A.C. 145; and see *Noel v Poland* [2001] B.C.L.C. 645.
[385] See para.2–204, below.

Williams v Natural Life Health Foods Ltd,[386] Lord Steyn referred to the test being whether the claimant could reasonably rely on an assumption of personal responsibility by the individual upon whom it was submitted liability should attach. However, as shall be seen, he went on to consider factors bearing upon the closeness of the relationship between the parties, and these very arguably give a more helpful guide in determining the issue whether a duty arises than does the idea of a personal assumption of responsibility.

2–183   **Customs and Excise Commissioners v Barclays Bank Plc.** This view finds support in the important decision of the House of Lords in *Customs and Excise Commissioners v Barclays Bank Plc*.[387] Their Lordships agreed that the notion of a voluntary assumption of responsibility is or can be of some help in a *Hedley Byrne* action where the claimant sues in respect of his or her reliance on a negligent statement, but that the concept cannot be used as a general touchstone for liability in negligence for financial loss. However, even in a *Hedley Byrne* context it is difficult to pin down what exactly it means beyond the fact that the defendant chose to make the statement in question. Lord Bingham said that it was clear that the test was to be applied objectively: it was not answered by consideration of what the defendant thought or intended. Yet he recognised that the further it was removed from the actions and intentions of the actual defendant, the more notional the assumption of responsibility became and the less difference there was from the threefold test of *Caparo Industries Plc v Dickman*.[388]

2–184   In short, the speeches in *Barclays Bank* suggest that the law deems a defendant to have assumed responsibility where there is a proximate or special relationship between the parties in circumstances where policy supports a duty, as considered below. On this view, the *Hedley Byrne* inquiry does not stand apart from other duty questions although, as Lord Mance noted, it may sometimes subsume the elements of the *Caparo* inquiry.

(iv) *The special relationship*

2–185   **Reasonable reliance.** In order for there to be a duty in words, and in accordance with ordinary principle, the defendant must be able reasonably to foresee harm to the claimant. It follows that it must be reasonable for the claimant to rely on what the defendant has said, and certainly the courts have recognised that reasonable reliance causing foreseeable harm is a requirement in all cases.[389] So a statement made on a social or an informal occasion or in the course of a casual or perfunctory conversation may not be actionable.[390] But the statement of a solicitor acting as executor under a will gave rise to an action, even

---

[386] [1998] 1 W.L.R. 830, at 837 HL.

[387] [2007] 1 A.C. 181.

[388] [1990] 2 A.C. 605; see para.2–19, above.

[389] In *Berry Taylor v Coleman* [1997] P.N.L.R. 1 CA, it was pointed out that the speeches in *Hedley Byrne* did not specifically indicate that reliance upon the defendant's misstatement had to be reasonable before the claimant could recover, but Staughton L.J. accepted that reasonableness was an essential prerequisite to liability.

[390] *Hedley Byrne & Co Ltd v Heller & Partners Ltd* [1964] A.C. 465 at 482–483, 495, 510, 539; *Henderson v Merrett Syndicates Ltd* [1995] 2 A.C. 145 at 180–181.

though it was gratuitous.[391] Again, it may not be reasonable to rely on a response to an important business inquiry which is merely given over the phone rather than in writing.[392] And it was unreasonable for a solicitor to have relied upon the statement of an unnamed official of a local planning authority who, in a short telephone conversation, without notice, responded to an enquiry about a proposed development by saying, erroneously, that it would not be in breach of planning control.[393]

Proximity of relationship. Foreseeable and reasonable reliance is not enough **2–186** on its own. The ambit of any duty is limited in a number of additional respects, by requiring various indicators of closeness between the parties.[394] The kind of case where a duty is likely to be recognised is where a knowledgeable or skilled person acting in a strictly business context gives misleading information or advice directly to another person, knowing the specific purpose for which the information is wanted and that the other person attaches importance to, and will rely on, what he or she hears or reads. The relationship here is very close and proximate, not contractual in nature but somewhat akin to it.[395] But where these kinds of factors are not all present, and the relationship is less close in the relevant sense, the question whether a duty will be recognised is more controversial.

Special knowledge or skill. A duty of care will usually be confined to those **2–187** defendants who either have, or can properly be regarded as having, some special knowledge, arising from their skill, trade, business or profession. Indeed, in *Mutual Life & Citizens' Assurance Co Ltd v Evatt*[396] the Judicial Committee of the Privy Council seemed to treat a holding out by the defendant of special skill as an element of the claimant's cause of action. In this case the claimant, who was a policyholder in the defendant insurance company, had invested in a company associated with the defendant on the basis of careless advice from the defendant about its associate's financial stability. Lord Diplock, giving the majority opinion, observed that the defendant's business did not include giving advice on investments and it did not claim to have the required skill and competence to give advice and to exercise the necessary diligence to give reliable advice, and held that, accordingly, the only duty owed towards the claimant was to give him an honest answer to his inquiries. But Lord Reid and Lord Morris, in dissent, asserted that the "special relationship" was free from any requirement of particular skill. They thought that for present purposes the appropriate question was whether the advice was given on a business occasion or in the course of the company's business activities. They saw no ground for the distinction that a specially skilled person should exercise care but a less skilled person need not do so.

[391] See *Martin v Triggs Turner Bartons* [2010] P.N.L.R. 3, Ch.9, para.9–225, below.
[392] *Howard Marine & Dredging Co Ltd v A Ogden & Sons (Excavations) Ltd* [1978] Q.B. 574 per Lord Denning M.R. at 591–592 CA; but compare the views of Shaw L.J. at 600–601.
[393] *Fashion Brokers Ltd v Clarke Hayes* [2000] P.N.L.R. 473 CA.
[394] See generally Stanton "*Hedley Byrne v Heller*: the relationship factor" (2007) 23 P.N. 94.
[395] For example, see *Sutcliffe v Thackrah* [1974] A.C. 727 (architect and building owner); *Arenson v Casson Beckman Rutley & Co* [1977] A.C. 405 (valuer and share-holder); *Arthur JS Hall & Co v Simons* [2002] 1 A.C. 615 (barrister and client).
[396] [1971] A.C. 793 PC.

2–188   The majority view in *Evatt* has been rejected in the High Court of Australia[397] and in the Supreme Court of Canada,[398] and read down by the New Zealand Court of Appeal as being a case decided on its own particular facts.[399] It is not binding within the UK, and the Court of Appeal has also been unenthusiastic and preferred the minority approach.[400] Indeed, in one case a duty was imposed where the defendant, at the request of the claimant, had found a second-hand car for sale and had carelessly misled the claimant by advising her to buy it. The defendant was not in the used-car business, but he knew that the claimant was relying on his skill and judgment as someone who knew a great deal more about cars than she did.[401]

2–189   **Indicators of proximity.** In *Caparo Industries Plc v Dickman*,[402] the House of Lords gave close consideration to the nature and closeness of the relationship between the parties that needs to be shown in order for a duty of care to arise. Lord Oliver identified four key factors[403]:

> "What can be deduced from the *Hedley Byrne* case, therefore, is that the necessary relationship between the maker of a statement or giver of advice ("the adviser") and the recipient who acts in reliance upon it ("the advisee") may typically be held to exist where (1) the advice is required for a purpose, whether particularly specified or generally described, which is made known, either actually or inferentially, to the adviser at the time when the advice is given; (2) the adviser knows, either actually or inferentially, that his advice will be communicated to the advisee, either specifically or as a member of an ascertainable class, in order that it should be used by the advisee for that purpose; (3) it is known, either actually or inferentially, that the advice so communicated is likely to be acted upon by the advisee for that purpose without independent inquiry; and (4) it is so acted upon by the advisee to his detriment."

Although Lord Oliver disclaimed any suggestion that these conditions were either conclusive or exclusive, they nonetheless provide authoritative guidance in a wide range of cases where proximity between the parties is in dispute

2–190   **Company auditors.**[404] The question in issue in *Caparo* was whether company auditors owed a duty of care either to company shareholders or to third parties who relied on the company audit in purchasing shares in the company. Their Lordships held, applying the above principles, that the purpose of the statutory requirement for an audit of public companies was the making of a report to enable the body of shareholders as a whole to exercise informed control over

---

[397] *Shaddock & Associates Pty Ltd v Parramatta City Council (No 1)* (1981) 150 C.L.R. 225 HCA.
[398] *Queen v Cognos Inc* [1993] 1 S.C.R. 87, 117–118 SCC.
[399] *Meates v Attorney-General* [1983] N.Z.L.R. 308 at 333–334 NZCA.
[400] *Esso Petroleum Co Ltd v Mardon* [1976] Q.B. 801, 827; *Howard Marine & Dredging Co Ltd v A Ogden & Sons (Excavations) Ltd* [1978] Q.B. 574, 591, 600. In the House of Lords it has been observed that *Hedley Byrne* itself shows that the concept of "special skill" must be understood broadly, certainly broadly enough to include special knowledge: *Henderson v Merrett Syndicates Ltd* [1995] 2 A.C. 145, 180.
[401] *Chaudhry v Prabhakar* [1989] 1 W.L.R. 29 CA.
[402] [1990] 2 A.C. 605.
[403] ibid, at 638.
[404] For the liability of auditors generally, see Ch.9, para.9–23, below.

the company,[405] and not to enable existing shareholders or members of the public at large to buy shares with a view to profit. It followed that the auditors owed no duty of care to the respondents either as shareholders or as potential investors in the company.

Lord Bridge pointed to some key concerns of policy. He thought that to hold   **2–191**
the maker of a statement put into more or less general circulation, to be under a duty of care in respect of the accuracy of the statement to all and sundry for any purpose for which they may choose to rely on it, would not only raise an indeterminate liability, it would also confer on the world at large a quite unwarranted entitlement to appropriate for their own purposes the benefit of the professional expertise attributed to the maker. Furthermore, if a duty were owed to potential investors, it would be difficult to see why it should not also extend to all who relied on the accounts in relation to dealings with the company as lenders or merchants extending credit to the company.[406]

Decisions overseas. These arguments are compelling and their force is shown   **2–192**
by the fact that the courts in the USA,[407] Canada,[408] Australia[409] and New Zealand[410] have all taken the same or a similar approach to that adopted in *Caparo*.

Exceptions. While no duty can be owed to investors simply by reason of their   **2–193**
reliance on a statutory audit, the position may be different if auditors' reports are prepared specifically for the purpose of being used by investors or otherwise for a specific, known, purpose.[411] So accountants, who prepared financial statements in documents issued to shareholders in defence of a takeover bid, could owe a duty to the bidder if their purpose was to persuade the bidder to increase its bid.[412] Again, the purchasers of a business were owed a duty by its auditors in circumstances where the auditors knew the purchasers were "sizing up the company" with a view to acquiring it, they dealt directly with the purchasers, they were fully aware that the purchasers insisted on inspecting and would place reliance on the audited accounts, and they undertook an active role in effecting a sale based on those accounts.[413]

---

[405] See the Companies Act 1985 s.236.
[406] See further *Stone & Rolls Ltd v Moore Stephens* [2009] 3 W.L.R. 455 HL, Ch.4 para.4–252, below, where, against a background of fraud by a company's directing mind and will the House of Lords held in a majority decision that, assuming that the company auditors undertook a contractual duty of care, applying *Caparo* it was a duty owed to the company as a whole, not to individual or potential shareholders or current or prospective creditors.
[407] *Credit Alliance Corporation v Arthur Anderson & Co* 65 NY 2d 536 (1985).
[408] *Hercules Managements Ltd v Ernst & Young* [1997] 2 S.C.R. 165 SCC.
[409] *Esanda Finance Corporation Ltd v Peat Marwick Hungerfords* (1997) 188 C.L.R. 241 HCA.
[410] *Boyd Knight v Purdue* [1999] 2 N.Z.L.R. 278 NZCA.
[411] *Galoo Ltd v Bright Grahame Murray* [1994] 1 W.L.R. 1360 CA; *Royal Bank of Scotland plc v Bannerman Johnstone Maclay* [2005] 1 SC 437.
[412] *Morgan Crucible Co Plc v Hill Samuel & Co Ltd* [1991] Ch. 295; and see *Possfund Custodian Trustee Ltd v Diamond* [1996] 1 W.L.R. 1351.
[413] *Allison v KPMG Peat Marwick* [2000] 1 N.Z.L.R. 560 NZCA; and see *Dimond Manufacturing Co Ltd v Hamilton* [1969] N.Z.L.R. 609 NZCA.

2–194   **Company directors.** In *Williams v Natural Life Health Foods Ltd*,[414] the House of Lords held that a director of a company who prepared financial information about a franchise the company was selling, for the purpose of encouraging company clients to buy the franchise, owed no duty of care to a purchaser who relied on this information and lost his investment. Lord Steyn said that whether a principal was a company or a natural person, someone acting on his behalf might incur personal liability in tort as well as impose vicarious or attributed liability upon his principal. But in order to establish personal liability under the *Hedley Byrne* principle it was not sufficient that there should have been a special relationship with the principal. There must have been an assumption of responsibility such as to create a special relationship with the director or employee himself. His Lordship said that this posed an objective test, the focus being on things said or done by the defendant or on his behalf in dealings with the claimant. The inquiry was into whether the defendant conveyed to the claimant, directly or indirectly, that the defendant was assuming personal responsibility.

2–195   The point has already been made that defendants do not assume responsibility for torts in the sense of assuming legal liability for what they do. Liability is imposed where there is a sufficiently proximate relationship between claimant and defendant and the balance of policy concerns point in favour of a duty. Lord Steyn maintained that the test should be objective, yet seemed at times to focus on the defendant's subjective intention or recognition that he would be personally liable for negligence. Reasoning of that kind is not easy to reconcile with ordinary principle.

2–196   **Intentional torts.** The "assumption of responsibility" test for negligence can be compared with the approach taken to the question whether a director is personally liable for an intentional tort. In *Standard Chartered Bank v Pakistan National Shipping Corporation*[415] one of the questions at issue was the personal liability of a director of a company for fraudulent misrepresentations made by him on behalf of the company in obtaining payment under a false ante-dated letter of credit. The House of Lords held that the director was liable and that the *Williams* reasoning could not apply to fraud. Lord Hoffmann pointed out that no one can escape liability for his fraud by saying, "I wish to make it clear that I am committing this fraud on behalf of someone else and I am not to be personally liable". The director was not being sued for the company's tort. He was being sued for his own tort and all the elements of that tort were proved against him. Lord Hoffmann sought to distinguish *Williams*, on the ground that it was an application of the law of principal and agent to the requirement of assumption of responsibility under the *Hedley Byrne* principle. Yet it may be asked why exactly liability for an intentional tort ought to be treated differently to liability for negligence. It is certainly arguable that defendants no more "assume responsibility" for misstatements that are made negligently than for those that are made deceitfully. And if the notion of an assumption of responsibility is put aside and analysis proceeds by way of the core considerations identified by Lord Oliver in

---

[414] [1998] 1 W.L.R. 830 HL; and see *Trevor Ivory Ltd v Anderson* [1992] 2 N.Z.L.R. 517 NZCA.
[415] [2003] 1 A.C. 959.

Caparo, a clear basis for a duty becomes apparent. The defendant's words were given to a member of the intended class of recipients (prospective purchasers of the franchise) and were used for a known and intended purpose (purchasing the franchise).

Company employees. Another consequence of *Williams* is that directors may 2–197 be treated more favourably than employees who commit torts in the course of their employment. In the latter case both employer and employee are liable. In *Merrett v Babb*,[416] an employee of a firm of valuers and surveyors which had been instructed by a building society to report on the condition of a house was personally liable to a purchaser who relied on his negligently compiled report. The Court of Appeal recognised the difficulty in applying one rule for employees and another for directors, and sought to reconcile its decision with *Williams* by holding that the employee had assumed responsibility for the misrepresentation. For reasons already given, this is not a convincing way of resolving the problem. The policy justification for imposing liability in *Merrett* but denying it in *Williams* is obscure.

Pre-contract negotiations. A duty of care may attach to representations made 2–198 in the course of pre-contractual negotiations between the parties. For example, in *Esso Petroleum Co Ltd v Mardon*[417] the Court of Appeal held that a duty was owed by the lessor of a petrol station in giving an estimated annual throughput of petrol to the prospective lessee.

Misrepresentation Act 1967. The importance of the *Hedley Byrne* principle 2–199 in the context of pre-contractual negotiations is much reduced by s.2(1) of the Misrepresentation Act 1967. This provides that where a person has entered into a contract after a misrepresentation has been made to him by another party to the contract then, if the representor would have been liable in damages if the representation had been made fraudulently, he shall be so liable unless he proves that he had reasonable grounds to believe that the statement was true. Claimants may prefer to rely on this provision rather than the common law, for there is no issue of duty, the defendant bears the burden of proving the existence of the necessary reasonable grounds,[418] and there is authority that the measure of damages is the same as in an action for deceit.[419] However, s.2(1) does not apply if the person being sued is not a party to a contract made with the claimant, as where the action is against an agent who induces the representee to enter a contract with the principal.[420] In this case only the common law action is available.

Subverting contract. Section 2 also does not apply if no contract eventuates. 2–200 In this type of case, however, a common law duty of care may be denied for good

---

[416] [2001] 3 W.L.R. 1 CA.
[417] [1976] Q.B. 801.
[418] See *Howard Marine and Dredging Co v A Ogden and Sons* [1978] Q.B. 574.
[419] *Royscot Trust Ltd v Rogerson* [1991] 2 Q.B. 297. Whether *Royscot* was correctly decided has been left open in the House of Lords: *Smith New Court Securities Ltd v Scrimgeour Vickers (Asset Management) Ltd* [1997] A.C. 254, at 267, 283.
[420] *Resolute Maritime Inc v Nippon Kaiji Kyokai, The Skopas* [1983] 1 W.L.R. 857.

reasons of policy. In particular, a tort duty may tend to subvert the law of offer and acceptance, and this reasoning underlies decisions in the Supreme Court of Canada that there can be no duty to take care owed to the other party to failed commercial negotiations.[421] The New Zealand Court of Appeal has similarly held that an attempt to use the tort of negligence to make up for the lack of a process contract should be rebuffed on policy grounds.[422]

2–201   **Tenderers for contracts.** It has been held by the Supreme Court of Canada that an engineering firm which prepared specifications and construction drawings knowing that bidders for a construction contract would rely on it, owed a duty of care to one of those bidders.[423] The court explained that each bidder would otherwise be obliged to do its own engineering and to conduct a thorough professional review of the engineering design and information in a very limited time. The result would be considerable duplication of time and effort, higher bid prices and greater costs. The reasoning is convincing, but in a similar case in New Zealand the Court of Appeal held that the engineer owed no duty of care to the bidder.[424] The duty contended for would cut across and be inconsistent with the overall contractual structure which defined the relations of the various parties to the work. There was no justification for holding that the engineer should be regarded as having voluntarily assumed responsibility to the builder.

2–202   **Further illustrations.** There are many examples in the cases of a duty being recognised where the requirement of a close and proximate relationship, as explained in *Caparo*, is satisfied. They involve communication to a known individual or member of an identifiable class who would be likely to rely on the information specifically in connection with a particular transaction or kind of transaction for the purpose of deciding whether to enter into that transaction. Thus, a potato marketing business was responsible for the claimant's losses when it negligently gave inaccurate information about the creditworthiness of a third party with whom the claimant was being invited to contract[425]; surveyors instructed by a building society to value a house were liable to purchasers of the house who had applied to the building society for a loan and who the surveyors knew would rely on their report[426]; managing agents at Lloyds owed a duty to names who were members of syndicates under the agents' management[427]; accountants appointed by the directors of a company to value shares to be

---

[421] *Martel Building Ltd v Canada* [2000] 2 S.C.R. 860 SCC (alleged failure to pursue negotiations in a timely fashion and to provide timely and pertinent information, causing loss of an opportunity to negotiate renewal of a lease); Rafferty, "Tortious and contractual liability arising out of pre-contractual negotiations and the tendering process" (2001) 17 P.N. 179; *Design Services Ltd v Canada* (2008) 293 D.L.R. (4th) 437 SCC.

[422] *Prime Commercial Ltd v Wool Board Disestablishment Co Ltd* (2008) 14 N.Z.B.L.Q. 3 NZCA.

[423] *Edgeworth Construction Ltd v ND Lea & Associates Ltd* [1993] 3 S.C.R. 206 SCC.

[424] *RM Turton & Co Ltd v Kerslake* [2000] 3 N.Z.L.R. 406 NZCA.

[425] *WB Anderson & Sons Ltd v Rhodes (Liverpool) Ltd* [1967] 2 All E.R. 850; and see *Markappa Inc v NW Spratt & Son; The Arta* [1983] 2 Lloyd's Rep. 405.

[426] *Smith v Eric S Bush* [1990] 1 A.C. 831; Rogers, "Mortgage valuations, negligence and disclaimers" [1989] C.L.J. 366; Allen, "*Hedley Byrne* revalued" (1989) 105 L.Q.R. 511; *Yianni v Edwin Evans & Sons* [1982] Q.B. 438; *Roberts v J Hampson & Co* [1990] 1 W.L.R. 94.

[427] *Henderson v Merrett Syndicates Ltd* [1995] 2 A.C. 145; *BP Plc v Aon Ltd* [2006] 1 All E.R. (Comm) 789.

compulsorily acquired by the company owed a duty of care to the shareholder[428]; and an employer whose business was transferred to another company was liable for loss to former employees arising from negligent misstatements which led them to consent to and co-operate in the transfer.[429]

In other cases, involving less close relationships and/or lesser degrees of **2–203** knowledge about any contemplated transaction, a duty has been denied. For example, accountants who prepared company accounts knowing that they were likely to be used in takeover negotiations were held to owe no duty to the purchasers, because at the time the accounts were produced the future of the company was in the melting pot, the accounts were merely draft accounts, the accountants took no part in the negotiations and it was to be anticipated that the purchasers would consult with their own accountancy advisers[430]; directors who issued a prospectus specifically to enable shareholders to consider a rights offer owed no duty to those who relied on the prospectus for the purpose of buying shares in the market[431]; a Water Board that gave an estimate to a government minister of the likely cost of connecting a proposed subdivision of land with the water supply owed no duty to landowners who obtained the information and, without the Board's knowledge, passed it on to the bank that was financing the development[432]; the actuary of a company's pension fund did not owe a duty to the purchaser of the company, for he lacked specific knowledge of the plaintiff and of the transaction in which the work would be used[433]; and the proprietor of a trade website giving information about recommended swimming pool contractors did not owe a duty to claimants who relied on the website in engaging a contractor who subsequently became insolvent, because the website made it clear that potential customers would be expected to obtain an information pack and make further inquiries about tenderers for the work.[434]

(v) *Disclaimers*

Disclaimers. In *Hedley Byrne* the defendants expressly disclaimed any **2–204** responsibility on their part. All of their Lordships were agreed the defendants were not liable. Lord Morris maintained that the plaintiff could not accept a reply given with a stipulation and then reject the stipulation.[435] The reason is found in the principle of notice. The defendant must give reasonable notice of the disclaimer, but does not have to show that the claimant actually knew about it and voluntarily assumed the risk of harm.[436]

---

[428] *Killick v Pricewaterhouse Coopers* [2001] 1 B.C.L.C. 65.

[429] *Hagen v ICI Chemicals & Polymers Ltd* [2002] I.R.L.R. 31. The court considered that it was likely that if the group of staff to be transferred had been properly informed of the terms on offer they would have sought, as a body, to resist what was proposed, and that their resistance would in all likelihood have been successful and resulted in improved terms. So damages were assessed on that basis.

[430] *James McNaughton Paper Group Ltd v Hicks Anderson & Co* [1991] 2 Q.B. 113 CA; Percival, "After *Caparo*—Liability in business transactions revisited" (1991) 54 M.L.R. 739.

[431] *Al-Nakib Investments (Jersey) Ltd v Longcroft* [1990] 1 W.L.R. 1390.

[432] *Tepko Pty Ltd v Water Board* (2001) 206 C.L.R. 1 HCA.

[433] *Precis (521) Plc v William M Mercer Ltd* [2005] EWCA Civ 114.

[434] *Patchett v Swimming Pool and Allied Trades Association Ltd* [2009] EWCA Civ 717.

[435] [1964] A.C. 465 at 504.

[436] *Harris v Wyre Forest District Council* [1988] Q.B. 835 at 840 (on appeal [1990] 1 A.C. 831).

2–205 **Unfair Contract Terms Act 1977.** The impact of a disclaimer operates subject to the provisions of the Unfair Contract Terms Act 1977.[437] By s.2(1), a person cannot exclude or restrict his liability for death or personal injury resulting from negligence. By s.2(2), a person cannot by means of any contract term or notice restrict his liability for loss or damage other than personal injury caused by negligence in the course of a business, unless he shows that the term or notice is reasonable.[438] The Act provides guidelines for determining the question of reasonableness,[439] and while these are restricted in their scope, applying only to certain particular terms in certain specified types of contract, the courts have treated them both as being of general application and also as being non-exhaustive. Indeed, in *Smith v Eric S Bush*[440] the House of Lords recognised that it was impossible to draw up an exhaustive list of relevant factors, but some that have been taken into account, whether or not founded in statute, include the bargaining power of the parties, whether a disclaimer was freely negotiated and/or clearly explained, and the availability of insurance.

2–206 In *Smith* itself it was held that a notice purporting to exclude the liability for negligence by surveyors instructed by a building society to survey a house did not satisfy the reasonableness test. There was no equality of bargaining power between the purchasers and the surveyors, the houses were of modest value so it was not reasonable to expect the purchasers to commission their own survey, and the surveyors could have insured against liability. On the other hand, a disclaimer of liability by an estate agent to a prospective purchaser in respect of a representation as to the area of land being offered for sale, which land the purchaser subsequently contracted to buy for £875,000, was held to be reasonable: the purchaser could reasonably have been expected to make his own inquiries before entering the transaction.[441]

(F) Negligent conduct causing financial injury

(i) *Consequential economic loss*

2–207 **Consequential economic loss.** Where a careless act or omission has caused a claimant to sustain personal injury or suffer direct damage to property, the common law has always permitted the recovery of damages for resultant economic loss. In personal injury litigation, the successful claimant recovers damages not only for his or her pain, suffering and loss of amenity, but also in respect of medical expenses and any loss of earnings during a period of incapacity. These financial losses are consequential upon the claimant's physical injury and do not raise any special difficulty of principle.

---

[437] See generally Treitel *The Law of Contract* 12th edn 2007, Ch.7 ; also Ch.4, para.4–84, below.
[438] Section 13(1) of the 1977 Act extends the scope of s.2 to cover "terms and notices which exclude or restrict the relevant obligation or duty".
[439] See s.11 and Sch.2; and see Brown and Chandler, "Unreasonableness and the Unfair Contract terms Act" (1993) 109 L.Q.R. 41.
[440] [1990] 1 A.C. 831.
[441] *McCullagh v Lane Fox & Partners Ltd* [1996] 2 P.N.L.R. 205 CA.

Consequential loss in property damage cases is similarly recoverable. Two   **2–208**
decisions in the Court of Appeal will provide examples. In *SCM (UK) Ltd v WJ*
Whittall & Son Ltd,[442] contractors preparing to build a boundary wall negligently
pierced and damaged an 11,000–volt cable, running alongside the road, thereby
cutting off the electric power to the claimants' factory so that molten metal in
their machines solidified owing to lack of heat. The contractors were held liable
for the material damage and the loss of profit truly consequent on it but not for
any further economic loss,

Spartan Steel & Alloys Ltd v Martin & Co (Contractors) Ltd[443] is quite similar.   **2–209**
The defendants' employees negligently damaged an underground electricity
cable whilst digging up a road. As a result the power supply to the claimants'
factory was unexpectedly interrupted for more than half a day. During the time
it took to restore the power, the claimants had had to pour the molten metal out
of their furnace to prevent the metal solidifying and damaging it. They were held
entitled to the loss in value from metal that could not be kept hot enough to use
further, and their loss of profit on that metal, but not a further loss claimed from
the production that would have taken place while the power cut lasted. The losses
recovered resulted from the foreseeable physical damage, but not the loss in
production.

Inability to mitigate. A limit on recovery was formerly imposed as a result   **2–210**
of the decision of the House of Lords in *Liesbosch Dredger v SS Edison*.[444] The
defendants negligently sank the plaintiffs' dredger and were held liable, inter
alia, for the cost of a replacement but not for the cost of hiring a substitute until
the time damages were awarded. The latter expense was incurred because the
plaintiffs were unable to afford to buy a replacement any earlier, and in these
circumstances the cause of the loss was seen as the plaintiffs' own impecuniosity.
However, in *Lagden v O'Connor*[445] the House decided that *Liesbosch* should no
longer be followed. A wrongdoer had to take his or her victim as found, and bear
the consequences if it was reasonably foreseeable that the injured party's loss
would be augmented due to lack of the necessary funds to mitigate the damage

(ii) *Relational economic loss*

No recovery for relational loss. Financial loss that occurs only because of   **2–211**
the relationship between the immediate, physical, victim of a wrong and the
claimant is conveniently, and quite commonly, called relational financial loss.[446]
At common law this usually is irrecoverable. In the case of personal injury, there

---

[442] [1971] 1 Q.B. 337. In *British Celanese v A H Hunt (Capacitors) Ltd* [1969] 1 W.L.R. 959, strips
of metal foil were blown from the defendants' factory into contact with the bus-bars of an electricity
sub-station, causing a power failure which damaged the claimants' property and brought production
to a halt. It was held that the claimants could recover damages in respect of materials and time wasted
and production lost.
[443] [1973] Q.B. 27.
[444] (1933) 45 Lloyd's Rep 123. See also Ch.5, para.5–38, below.
[445] [2004] 1 A.C. 1067.
[446] See, for example, *Landcatch Ltd v International Oil Pollution Compensation Fund* [1998] 2
Lloyd's L.R. 552 at 570, per Lord Gill (OH).

is a long-standing refusal to recognise one person as having any legally compensable interest in the physical well-being of another person. Accordingly, in the case of fatal accidents involving the death of a breadwinner, the legislature had to step in to give the dependants a claim.[447] Claims by non-dependants suing in respect of injury to another person will fail. In a recent instance, it was held that a doctor owed no duty to the employer of the doctor's patient to take care in advising and treating the patient.[448]

2–212   In the case of damage to property, the equivalent rule denies recovery for financial loss stemming from damage to the property of another person. An early example can be found in *Cattle v Stockton Waterworks Co.*[449] The defendants had laid a defective water main under a turnpike road. The leakage of water delayed the contractor's work of tunnelling underneath the road causing him to suffer a loss of profit on his contract with the road owners. With some regret the court denied a remedy, because, said Blackburn J.:

> "If we did so we should establish an authority for saying that, in such a case as that of *Fletcher v Rylands* the defendant would be liable, not only to an action by the owner of the drowned mine, and by such of his workmen as had their tools or clothes destroyed but also to an action by every workman and person employed in the mine, who in consequence of its stoppage made less wages than he would otherwise have done. And many similar cases to which this would apply might be suggested. It may be said that it is just that all such persons should have compensation for such a loss, and that, if the law does not give them redress, it is imperfect. Perhaps it may be so."[450]

2–213   Shortly afterwards, in *Simpson & Co v Thomson*,[451] it was held by the House of Lords that an insurance underwriter had no direct right of action against a tortfeasor who damaged the underwriter's assured's property.[452] The decision affirmed that a person claiming damages in respect of loss of or damage to property must have had either the legal ownership of or possessory title to the property at the time when the damage occurred. It was not enough that he or she had merely contractual rights in relation to the property.

2–214   **Impact of Hedley Byrne.** The rule was applied thereafter in a number of decisions.[453] However, the decision in *Hedley Byrne & Co Ltd v Heller & Partners Ltd*[454] in 1963 pointed towards a possible change in the law. In that case, as we have seen, the door was opened to allow for the recovery in an action for negligence of financial loss standing alone. Lord Devlin considered the distinction between financial loss arising by the mechanism of physical injury or

---

[447] The first Fatal Accidents Act was passed in 1846. See now the Fatal Accidents Act 1976; see Ch.16, paras 16–05 to 16–70, below.
[448] *West Bromwich Albion Football Club Ltd v El-Safty* [2006] EWCA Civ 1299.
[449] (1875) L.R. 10 Q.B. 453.
[450] ibid, at 457.
[451] (1877) 3 App. Cas. 279.
[452] Of course the insurer is subrogated to the rights of the insured.
[453] For example, *Société Anonyme de Remorquage à Helice v Bennetts* [1911] 1 K.B. 243; *Chargeurs Reunis Compagnie Francaise de Navigation à Vapeur v English & American Shipping Co* (1921) 9 Lloyds L Rep 464 CA; *Brandon Electrical Engineering Co (Leeds) Ltd v William Press & Son Ltd* (1956) 106 L.J. 332.
[454] [1964] A.C. 465; see para.2–172, above.

being caused directly, and expressed the view that neither logic nor common sense was reflected in the proposition that the interposition of the physical injury made a difference of principle.[455]

Expectations that *Hedley Byrne* had brought about a more liberal approach **2–215** proved premature and in 1965 the traditional reluctance to allow a claim for recovery of relational economic loss surfaced in *Weller & Co v Foot & Mouth Disease Research Institute*.[456] The claimants' counsel had argued that *Hedley Byrne* had swept away any notion that direct injury to the person or property of the claimant was crucial to support an action in negligence for recovery of economic loss. The trial judge did not agree and upheld the defendants' contention, on a preliminary issue, that even if they were to admit the escape of the foot and mouth virus and/or the negligence, as well as foreseeability of the loss claimed, it did not constitute harm of the sort for which the law should grant a remedy.

The rule re-affirmed. The rule for non-owners has since been reaffirmed on **2–216** several occasions in the House of Lords and Privy Council.[457] In particular, in *Leigh and Sillavan Ltd v Aliakmon Shipping Co Ltd: The Aliakmon*,[458] it was held that buyers who were not owners of goods nor who had an immediate right to their possession had no right to sue ship owners in tort for damage done to the goods. Their Lordships refused to recognise a "transferred loss" exception, according to which a loss representing actual property damage which the owner would have suffered had the loss not been transferred by contract to another person could be recovered by that person. Such a rule would have covered the buyers' claim, but their Lordships considered that the general rule of non-recovery was conducive to certainty in the law, being simple to understand and easy to apply, and an exception to it in the case of a cif buyer of goods could not be justified.

Further illustrations. In other decisions, applying the general rule, a time **2–217** charterer could not recover for financial loss caused by damage to the chartered vessel[459]; defendants who caused siltation of a riverbed were not liable for the cost of dredging a channel to the claimants' wharf, because the claimants possessed no private rights over the riverbed that enabled them to insist on any

---

[455] ibid, at 517. See also, at 509, Lord Hodson's observation to the effect that it was difficult to see why liability as such should depend on "the nature of the damage" suffered.

[456] [1966] 1 Q.B. 569; cp *D Pride & Partners v Institute for Animal Health* [2009] EWHC 605, where similar claims made by farmers who could not move or sell their livestock during a foot and mouth disease outbreak were rejected, but for a different reason: see para.2–110, above.

[457] For a first instance decision, see *Electrochrome Ltd v Welsh Plastics Ltd* [1968] 2 All E.R. 205 (factory owners' claim for loss of production failed where the defendant had damaged a water authority's fire hydrant, causing the authority to turn off the water supply to the plaintiff's factory).

[458] [1986] A.C. 785. cp *Shell UK Ltd v Total UK Ltd* [2010] EWCA Civ 180, holding that a duty of care is owed to the beneficial owner of property by a defendant who can reasonably foresee that his negligent conduct will damage that property.

[459] *Candlewood Navigation Corporation Ltd v Mitsui OSK Lines Ltd (The Mineral Transporter)* [1986] A.C. 1 PC.

particular depth of water in connection with the operation of their business[460]; and an oil company that made voluntary payments to landowners whose foreshore had been polluted by oil after the tug towing the company's tanker caught fire, causing the tanker to crash into a jetty, could not recover the payments from the tug builders, because they were made only as a consequence of damage to the property of other persons.[461] But there is an exception where the claimant and the owner of damaged property are engaged in a joint venture, where the claimant's interest is regarded as sufficiently analogous to physical damage.[462]

2–218   The decision of the Court of Appeal in *Islington London Borough Council v University College London Hospital NHS Trust*[463] can also be understood in light of the relational loss principle. The local authority claimant sought to recover from the defendant the costs of care the authority was bound by statute to provide for someone injured as a result of negligence for which the defendant was responsible. The court found that loss was foreseeable, that there was a relationship of proximity between the parties, and that in a broad sense it was unfair to visit the loss in question on the claimant, but declined to find that a duty of care arose. The "fair, just and reasonable" requirement of *Caparo* was not to be read literally: it assumed that wider issues of policy might have to intervene. It was not appropriate that, in order to correct what seemed to be an inequitable distribution of liability between two public authorities, the common law of negligence be asked to do a job for which it was not qualified.

2–219   **Relational loss in Australia.** The High Court of Australia has taken a wider approach based on the close proximity between the parties. In *Caltex Oil Pty Ltd v The Dredge "Willemstad"*,[464] the defendant's dredger negligently damaged a third party's pipeline, which to the defendant's knowledge ran directly to the plaintiffs' oil terminal. The plaintiffs incurred extra expense in having to transport oil to their terminal by road. The High Court held that the expense was recoverable, because the harm was suffered by a particular known or identifiable plaintiff and it came about in a foreseeable kind of way. A later decision affirmed *Caltex* and reached a similar conclusion.[465]

2–220   **Relational loss in Canada.** In Canada, in *Bow Valley Husky (Bermuda) Ltd v St John Shipbuilding Ltd*,[466] the Supreme Court held that relational economic loss could be claimed only in exceptional cases. Those identified were cases of

---

[460] *Tate & Lyle Industries Ltd v Greater London Council* [1983] 2 A.C. 509; cf *Jan de Nul (UK) Ltd v AXA Royale Belge SA* [2002] 1 Lloyd's Rep 583 CA.

[461] *Esso Petroleum Co Ltd v Hall Russell & Co Ltd* [1989] A.C. 643.

[462] *Morrison Steamship Co Ltd v Greystoke Castle* [1947] A.C. 265; and see *Shell UK Ltd v Total UK Ltd* [2010] EWCA Civ 180 (a company having a beneficial interest in a second company which was the legal owner of land and facilities damaged by negligence could sue for economic loss).

[463] [2006] P.I.Q.R. P29 CA.

[464] (1976) 136 C.L.R. 529 HCA.

[465] *Perre v Apand Pty Ltd* (1999) 198 C.L.R. 180 HCA.

[466] [1997] 3 S.C.R. 1210; and see the dissenting judgment of La Forest J. in *Canadian National Railway Co v Norsk Pacific Steamship Co Ltd* [1992] 1 S.C.R. 1021, subsequently approved as representing the law in Canada in *Bow Valley*.

"transferred loss", cases where there was a common adventure between the plaintiff and the property owner, and shipping cases involving the law of general average. However, the instant case did not fall within one of these exceptional cases. The hirer of an oil rig sought to recover the hire rates and other expenses it had to pay during a period in which the rig was out of operation after it was damaged in a fire caused by the defendant's negligence. The hirer having suffered its losses by reason of damage to another's property and its contract with that other, this was a claim for contractual relational economic loss. The court held unanimously that the claim should fail.

The substantial difference between the law in the United Kingdom and in   **2–221** Canada is found primarily in the differing views that have been taken about transferred losses. However, as in the United Kingdom, the Supreme Court considered that it was desirable as a general rule to exclude claims for relational economic loss. The right of action of the property owner already put pressure on the defendant to act with care; an exclusionary rule channelled to the property owner both potential liability to the plaintiff and the right of recovery against the tortfeasor, encouraging the plaintiff to make appropriate contractual arrangements with the owner; and the ripple effects of property damage causing economic loss were such that perfect compensation was almost always impossible.

Relational loss in New Zealand. In New Zealand certain first instance   **2–222** decisions allow relational claims on a "proximity" analysis similar to that in Australia.[467] The Court of Appeal has not finally determined the question, but at least two decisions give some support to a transferred loss theory.[468]

(iii) *Pure financial loss*

Balancing policy concerns. Claims for pure financial loss come in a variety   **2–223** of forms which cannot easily be categorised. In each case any relevant concerns of policy and principle need to be weighed and assessed. *Customs and Excise Commissioners v Barclays Bank Plc*[469] is a good example of the balancing exercise. The Customs and Excise Commissioners, wishing to recover outstanding tax liabilities from two companies, obtained freezing injunctions in respect of their assets, which included funds held by the companies in accounts with Barclays Bank. The bank was notified of the injunctions but failed to prevent payments out of the accounts in breach of the injunctions. The question at issue was whether the bank owed a duty to the commissioners to take reasonable care to comply with the terms of the injunction. The judgments range over a number of issues, some pointing for and some against a duty, but ultimately their Lordships were unanimous in the conclusion that a duty ought to be denied.

---

[467] *NZ Forest Products Ltd v Attorney General* [1986] 1 N.Z.L.R. 14; *Mainguard Packaging Ltd v Hilton Haulage Ltd* [1990] 1 N.Z.L.R. 360.
[468] *Williams v Attorney-General* [1990] 1 N.Z.L.R. 646 NZCA; *Riddell v Porteous* [1999] 1 N.Z.L.R. 1 NZCA.
[469] [2007] 1 A.C. 181, para.2–183, above.

2–224   The considerations in favour of a duty were summarised by Lord Bingham. They were that the orders were made by the court and notified to the bank to protect their interests; that recognition of a duty would in practical terms impose no new or burdensome obligation on the bank; that the rule of public policy which has first claim on the loyalty of the law is that wrongs should be remedied; that there were no facts which would found a claim for effective redress for contempt and the commissioners would otherwise be left without any remedy; that a duty of care to the commissioners would not be inconsistent with the bank's duty to the court; and that there would be no indeterminacy as to those to whom the duty would be owed. Lord Bingham thought these were formidable arguments. But he rejected them, for the following reasons. First, the freezing jurisdiction had developed as one enforceable only by the court's power to punish those who break its orders. It made perfect sense on the assumption that the only duty owed by a notified party was to the court. Secondly, no duty was owed by the *customer* to that party. It would be a strange and anomalous outcome if an action in negligence lay against a notified party who allowed the horse to escape from the stable but not against the owner who rode it out. Thirdly, there was no authority holding that a non-consensual court order, without more, could give rise to a duty of care to the party obtaining the order: and one would have to ask whether a similar duty could be owed by the subject of a search order, or a witness summons, or other order where economic loss was a foreseeable consequence of breach. Fourthly, no comparative material had been adduced pointing to decisions elsewhere supporting recognition of a duty. And lastly, it would in the final analysis be unjust and unreasonable that the bank should, on being notified of an order which it had no opportunity to resist, become exposed to a liability which could be very large and for which exposure it had not been in any way rewarded.

2–225   The decision in the *Customs and Excise Commissioners* case illustrates the influence of policy concerns in the determination of the duty issue. In that case the relevant concerns pointed away from the imposition of a duty, and, speaking generally, claims in negligence seeking damages in respect of purely economic losses are treated with considerable caution. A duty of care has been recognised in only limited circumstances. Claims involving negligence in the execution of wills, other cases of professional negligence causing financial loss to third parties, and negligent preparation of reports and references, will illustrate where the line has been drawn.

2–226   **Disappointed legatees.** Recognition of a tort duty owed by a professional to a third person in carrying out a contract with a client has provoked controversy, due to its potential for undermining the privity rule ordinarily confining any action for negligence to the client. But a duty has been recognised in the "disappointed legatee" cases. In *White v Jones*,[470] a testator instructed solicitors to draw up a new will giving a benefit to the plaintiffs, but died before the solicitors had acted on the instructions. A majority in the House of Lords held that the solicitors were under a duty owed to the plaintiff legatees to carry out the instructions with care. Lord Goff thought that the *Hedley Byrne* principle could be extended to cover the case, and

---

[470] [1995] 2 A.C. 207. See para.2–94 above.

that the assumption of responsibility by a solicitor to his client should be held in law to extend to the intended beneficiary who may be deprived of his intended legacy in circumstances in which neither the testator nor his estate will have a remedy against the solicitor. He saw this conclusion as producing practical justice between the parties, as leading to no unacceptable circumvention of established principles of contract and as avoiding any problem by reason of the loss being of purely economic character. Lord Mustill, in a lengthy dissenting opinion, challenged the underlying moral imperatives of the majority approach. The absence of features identified in *Hedley Byrne*—mutuality, a special relationship, reliance and undertaking of responsibility—meant that imposing liability on the solicitor was not a principled extension of existing law, but an opening up of an extensive new area of potential liability.

Ambit of the duty. The same view as the majority has been taken in New   **2–227**
Zealand[471] and Australia[472] on similar facts. But the ambit of the principle involved is limited in a number of respects. First, the duty cannot normally be extended to cover an ineffective inter vivos transaction where the settlor remains capable of fulfilling his or her original intention.[473] Secondly, a solicitor is under no duty to potential beneficiaries to give positive advice to a testator as to who ought to be given a benefit under a proposed will.[474] Thirdly, a solicitor who was instructed to prepare a new will owed no duty to beneficiaries under an earlier will who incurred costs in successfully challenging the new will on the ground that the testator lacked testamentary capacity.[475] The solicitor was obliged to carry out the client's instructions, and the duty would lead to a conflict of interest between the beneficiaries and the client and between those beneficiaries and the intended beneficiaries under the proposed will. Fourthly, the duty owed to disappointed beneficiaries normally depends on there being no loss to the estate, which is not diminished merely because property passes to persons other than the testator's preferred beneficiaries. But if, exceptionally, there is a loss both to the estate and also to the beneficiary, then an action may lie.[476] Fifthly, where a solicitor is retained to administer an estate as opposed to prepare a will, and negligence by the solicitor causes a loss to the estate, an action may be brought by the executors and normally there is no need for an action by the beneficiaries.[477]

Other third party claimants.[478] The principle underlying *White v Jones* is   **2–228**
capable of application to other cases where a professional person promises to perform a service for a client and the client intends, and the professional person

---

[471] *Gartside v Sheffield, Young & Ellis* [1983] N.Z.L.R. 37 NZCA; *Ryan v Public Trustee* [2000] 1 N.Z.L.R. 700.
[472] *Hill v Van Erp* (1997) 188 C.L.R. 159 HCA; and see *Graham v Hall* [2006] NSWCA 208.
[473] *Hemmens v Wilson Browne* [1995] Ch. 223.
[474] *Clarke v Bruce Lance & Co* [1988] 1 W.L.R. 881 CA; *Sutherland v Public Trustee* [1980] 2 N.Z.L.R. 536; *Graham v Bonnycastle* (2004) 243 D.L.R. (4th) 617, Alta CA; but see *Hendriks v McGeoch* (2008) Aust Torts Reports 81–942 NSWCA.
[475] *Worby v Rosser* [1999] Lloyd's Rep P.N. 972 CA; *Knox v Till* [1999] 2 N.Z.L.R. 753 NZCA.
[476] *Carr-Glynn v Frearsons* [1999] 2 W.L.R. 1046 CA.
[477] *Chappell v Somers & Blake* [2003] 3 W.L.R. 1233; cf *Daniels v Thompson* [2004] EWCA Civ 307.
[478] See also Ch.9, para.9–222, below.

knows, that the service will confer a benefit on a third person if it is performed. Some third party claims of this kind have succeeded. Thus, an insurance company giving advice to a customer about pension and life insurance cover for the customer and his wife and children owed a duty to the wife and children as potential beneficiaries of the arrangements being made.[479] Again, a solicitor charged with effecting a valid security in favour of his client's lender owed a duty not simply to the client but also to the lender.[480] It is apparent, then, that a duty sometimes may be recognised where an intention to benefit the third party is clear and there is no possible conflict of interest between the client and the third party.

2–229   On the other hand, in a number of decisions a duty has been denied for various reasons of policy. The failure by a solicitor to give advice to the guarantor of a loan to a company, in breach of the instructions given to the solicitor by the client, was not actionable at the suit of the guarantor.[481] The client had no purpose of benefiting the guarantors, simply wanting enforceable securities, and the claimant was not dependent on the defendants and could easily have sought advice for himself. A failure by a bank to comply with an irrevocable payment instruction issued to it by its customer in favour of the claimant was not actionable, since recognising a duty of care would undermine well-established practices of the banking industry.[482] An employer's insurer owed no duty to an employee when considering and rejecting evidence of the employee's disability presented by the employer.[483] The employee was not party to the contract of insurance, the insurer's obligations were owed only to the employer, and the employee could sue the employer under his contract of employment. A lawyer conducting litigation or negotiating on behalf of a client normally owes no duty to his opponent, who should rely on his own lawyer.[484]

2–230   **Reports and references.** A similar question has been whether a person who writes a report about another owes a duty to that other. A particular concern in such cases is the effect of recognising a duty on existing principles of liability. In New Zealand, in *South Pacific Manufacturing Co Ltd v New Zealand Security Consultants and Investigations Ltd*,[485] the Court of Appeal held that an insurance assessor reporting to an insurer that the insured had started the fire which led to the destruction of the insured property owed no duty to the insured, partly because the suggested duty would cut across the rules governing liability for malicious prosecution and defamation. A duty in negligence would cover the same ground yet its elements would be less stringent and liability easier to establish. Likewise in Australia, in *Sullivan v Moodie*,[486] no duty was owed by

---

[479] *Gorham v British Telecommunications plc* [2000] 1 W.L.R. 2129 CA.
[480] *Dean v Allin & Watts* [2001] 2 Lloyd's Rep. 249 CA.
[481] *Brownie Wills v Shrimpton* [1998] 2 N.Z.L.R. 320 NZCA.
[482] *Wells v First National Commercial Bank* [1998] P.N.L.R. 14 CA.
[483] *Briscoe v Lubrizol Ltd* [2000] I.C.R. 694 CA.
[484] *Business Computers International v Registrar of Companies* [1988] Ch. 229; *Gran Gelato Ltd v Richcliff Ltd* [1992] 1 All E.R. 865; *Dean v Allin & Watts* [2001] 2 Lloyd's Rep 249; cp *Allied Finance & Investments Ltd v Haddow* [1983] N.Z.L.R. 22 NZCA; *Connell v Odlum* [1993] 2 N.Z.L.R. 257 NZCA.
[485] [1992] 2 N.Z.L.R. 282 NZCA.
[486] (2001) 207 C.L.R. 562 HCA; and see *Tame v New South Wales* (2002) 211 C.L.R. 317 HCA.

a social worker reporting about child abuse allegedly committed by the claimant.

In *Spring v Guardian Assurance Plc*,[487] a majority in the House of Lords   **2-231**
declined to apply the *South Pacific* reasoning, in deciding that an employer owed
a duty to his ex-employee when writing him a reference for a new employer, this
notwithstanding any overlap with defamation. Their Lordships considered that
defamation and negligence were not primarily directed at the same mischief, for
one was concerned with loss of reputation and the other with economic loss, so
the policy fear of undermining the law of defamation was overstated, and that
justice required that the employee should have an action. Also, in *Young v
Bella*,[488] the Supreme Court of Canada held that a social work student at
university could recover damages from her professor for negligently reporting to
a child protection service that she was suspected of being a child abuser.

It has been held that no duty was owed by a doctor retained by a company to   **2-232**
carry out a pre-employment medical assessment to the prospective employee
being assessed.[489] The duty of the doctor was owed to the company, not the
prospective employee. However, this last decision is not easy to reconcile with
either *White* or *Spring*. The claimant had no choice but to rely on the doctor, who
knew that she was dependent on her report.

Mortgages. A controversial question has been whether a mortgagee exercis-   **2-233**
ing a power of sale of land can owe a duty of care to subsequent encumbrancers
and the mortgagor to obtain the true market value of the property. It was held at
first that if a mortgagee decided to sell, he should take reasonable care to obtain
a proper price for the mortgaged property, namely the true market value, at that
time,[490] and Lord Denning MR later held that a like duty was owed to a guarantor
of the mortgagor's debt.[491] But there was then something of a retreat, it being
held that a mortgagee did not owe a person with a beneficial interest in the
property an independent duty over and above that which he owed to the
mortgagor to take reasonable care to obtain a proper price.[492] Nourse L.J.
recognised that the mortgagee's duty had long been seen as arising in equity, and
thought that it was unnecessary and confusing for the duties owed by a
mortgagee to the mortgagor and the surety, if there was one, to be expressed in

---

[487] [1995] 2 A.C. 296; and see *Bartholomew v Hackney LBCL* [1999] I.R.L.R. 246 CA; *Cox v Sun Alliance Life Ltd* [2001] I.R.L.R. 448 CA; cf *Kidd v Axa Equity & Law Life Assurance Society Plc* [2000] I.R.L.R. 301; *Legal & General Assurance Ltd v Kirk* [2002] I.R.L.R. 124 CA.
[488] [2006] 1 S.C.R. 108 SCC.
[489] *Kapfunde v Abbey National Plc* [1999] I.C.R. 1 CA.
[490] *Cuckmere Brick Co Ltd v Mutual Finance Ltd* [1971] Ch. 949. There is also a duty upon the mortgagee-in-possession to account to the mortgagor for any loss occurring through it or its agent's negligence in dealing with the mortgaged property between the date of taking possession and the date of sale : *Norwich General Trust v Grierson* [1984] C.L.Y. 2306 (the state of premises deteriorated seriously as a result of vandalism, because of the agent's failure to inspect from time to time whilst the premises lay empty and were unoccupied and to make sure they were locked and remained secure).
[491] *Standard Chartered Bank v Walker* [1982] 1 W.L.R. 1410 CA; and see *American Express International Banking Corporation v Hurley* [1985] 3 All E.R. 564.
[492] *Parker-Tweedale v Dunbar Bank Plc* [1991] Ch. 12.

terms of the tort of negligence. This approach was later confirmed in *Downsview Nominees Ltd v First City Corporation*[493] in the Privy Council. Lord Templeman said that a general duty of care owed by a mortgagee was inconsistent with the right of the mortgagee and the duties which the courts, applying equitable principles, had imposed on the mortgagee. The duties imposed by equity would be quite unnecessary if there existed a general duty in negligence to take reasonable care in the exercise of powers and to take reasonable care in dealing with the assets of the mortgagor.[494]

2-234   **Miscellaneous cases.** The question of recovery for negligently inflicted economic loss has arisen in a number of other situations whose resolution in terms of duty has turned ultimately on the application of policy concerns.

2-235   A duty may be found if the relationship between the parties is close and proximate and there are no other compelling policy concerns pointing the opposite way. For example, an insurance broker was liable to a person who he knew was to become an assignee of an insurance policy[495]; managing agents of an insurance syndicate were under a duty in respect of loss reinsurance cover that was owed to persons who were not members of the syndicate until after the reinsurance was effected[496]; and independent financial advisors to a building society involved in selling home income plans owed a duty to property owners with small incomes.[497] But a key factor is the risk of indeterminate liability. So no duty was owed by members of the Finance Board and Treasurer of the Isle of Man, who were responsible for licensing banks, to depositors in a failed bank[498]; nor by the Commissioner charged with regulatory functions in relation to deposit-taking business in Hong Kong to depositors who lost money invested with a deposit-taking company.[499]

2-236   A variety of policy concerns may point away from the existence of a duty. Parties who are not themselves joined by contract may nonetheless be part of an overall contractual matrix that renders inappropriate the imposition of a duty of care. So, an engineer who negligently prepared specifications for the heating system in a hospital owed no duty to the successful bidder for the contract to do the work.[500] Further limiting policies may apply where economic loss is caused by an omission. For example, no duty was owed by a finance company to a car dealer, where they were both members of HP Information Ltd, a trade association which maintained a register of hire purchase transactions, to register a particular

---

[493] [1993] A.C. 295 PC; and see *China and South Sea Bank Ltd v Tan Soon Gin* [1990] 1 A.C. 536 PC.
[494] In *Medforth v Blake* [2000] Ch. 86 the Court of Appeal held that it did not matter whether the duties owed by a receiver managing mortgaged property was expressed as a common law duty or a duty in equity and that their content was the same: see Ch.1 para.1–23 above.
[495] *Punjab National Bank v de Boinville* [1992] 1 W.L.R. 1138 CA.
[496] *Aiken v Stewart Wrightson Members' Agency Ltd* [1995] 3 All E.R. 449.
[497] *Investors Compensation Scheme Ltd v West Bromwich Building Society (No. 2)* [1999] Lloyd's Rep. P.N. 496.
[498] *Davis v Radcliffe* [1990] 1 W.L.R. 821 PC.
[499] *Yuen Kun Yeu v Attorney General of Hong Kong* [1988] A.C. 175 PC; and see *Fleming v Securities Commission* [1995] 2 N.Z.L.R. 514 NZCA.
[500] *RM Turton & Co Ltd v Kerslake* [2000] 3 N.Z.L.R. 406.

transaction with that association.[501] It was considered that an owner of property was entitled to be careless with his own property, and owed no duty to anyone else. Again, insurers negotiating with a bank were entitled to keep silent about a fraud being committed by the bank's own broker, for they had not assumed any responsibility to speak.[502]

Where an activity is governed by statute, the statutory purpose will be relevant.   **2–237** For example, a marine surveyor employed by the Department of Transport owed no duty to the purchaser of a ship in issuing a certificate of seaworthiness, for the relevant statutory purpose was to promote safety at sea, not to protect the financial interests of purchasers.[503] Again, Lloyd's Register of Shipping did not owe a duty to a vessel's prospective purchasers, even though the purchasers were likely to rely on the results of a classification survey conducted prior to the purchase, for the primary purpose of Lloyd's system of classification similarly was to enhance safety, not to safeguard property values.[504] But where personal injury is suffered the position is likely to be different. So, an inspector employed by a flying association authorised to grant certificates of fitness to fly owed a duty to a passenger injured in an accident caused by a defect in a duly certified aircraft.[505]

(G) Defective buildings

General. A builder owes an ordinary duty of care founded upon *Donoghue v*   **2–238** *Stevenson* with respect to negligent building work causing physical injury or physical damage to other property.[506] A different and much disputed question is whether the builder, or other person who has contributed to a defect in a building, like an architect or engineer, may be liable to the owner in the absence of any contract, in respect of the cost of putting right the property actually containing the defect.[507] In this case the owner's claim is for his or her disappointed expectations as to the true value of the property and, accordingly, is for a financial loss. This remains true irrespective of whether a defect has caused actual physical damage to the structure. Physical cracking or collapse may be a consequence of the defect, or the problem may be discovered before this happens.[508] In either case the owner seeks to recover the diminished value of the

---

[501] *Moorgate Mercantile Co Ltd v Twitchings* [1977] A.C. 890.
[502] *Banque Keyser Ullman SA v Skandia (UK) Insurance Co Ltd* [1991] 2 A.C. 249; see para.2–79, above.
[503] *Reeman v Department of Transport* [1997] 2 Lloyd's Rep 648 CA; *Philcox v Civil Aviation Authority, The Times,* June 8, 1995 CA; *Attorney General v Carter* [2003] 2 N.Z.L.R. 160 NZCA; cp *Rutherford v Attorney General* [1976] 1 N.Z.L.R. 403.
[504] *Mariola Marine Corporation v Lloyd's Register of Shipping "The Morning Watch"* [1990] 1 Lloyd's Rep. 547.
[505] *Perrett v Collins* [1998] 2 Lloyd's Rep. 255 CA.
[506] *Gallagher v N McDowell Ltd* [1961] N.I. 26 (CA); *Clayton v Woodman & Son (Builders) Ltd* [1962] 2 Q.B. 533; *Sharpe v E T Sweeting & Son Ltd* [1963] 1 W.L.R. 665; *Clay v A J Crump & Sons Ltd* [1964] 1 Q.B. 533. See further Ch.8, para.8–114, below.
[507] See generally Todd, "Policy issues in defective property cases", in Neyers, Chamberlain, Pitel (eds), *Emerging Issues in Tort Law,* Oxford, Hart Publishing, 2007, Ch.8.
[508] See, for example, *Batty v Metropolitan Property Realisations Ltd* [1978] Q.B. 554 (house built on land susceptible to slipping but at the time of the action it remained intact).

property or the cost of making good the defect together with, in the former case, its physical consequences.

2–239   **Dutton and Anns.** The Court of Appeal in *Dutton v Bognor Regis Urban District Council,*[509] and then the House of Lords in *Anns v Merton London Borough Council,*[510] originally permitted the recovery of damages in claims of this kind.[511] In *Anns* Lord Wilberforce thought that the damage sustained by the claimant was "material, physical damage". What was recoverable was the amount of expenditure necessary to restore the dwelling to a condition in which there was no longer a present or imminent danger to the health or safety of persons occupying it. Subsequently, in *Junior Books Ltd v Veitchi Co Ltd,*[512] the House of Lords extended the *Anns* principle, holding that subcontractors who had built a defective floor in the plaintiff's factory were liable for the cost of repairing the floor notwithstanding that the defect posed no injury to health. So here the damage was recognised as being for pure economic loss. But subsequently, in two key decisions, *Anns* was comprehensively rejected.

2–240   **D & F Estates v Church Commissioners.** In *D & F Estates Ltd v Church Commissioners for England,*[513] the House of Lords held that builders could not be liable to the lessees of a flat in respect of the financial loss incurred by the lessees in renewing plaster work incorrectly applied by subcontractors. To recognise a duty would be to impose on the builders for the benefit of those with whom they had no contractual relationship the obligation of one who warranted the quality of the plaster as regards materials, workmanship and fitness for purpose. A claim based on breach of a warranty of quality could only be maintained by one contracting party against the other. However, two lines of argument were left open. First, their Lordships did not decide whether there could still be recovery where a defect posed a danger to health. Secondly, they recognised the possibility that one element of a complex structure could be regarded as distinct from another element, so that damage to one part caused by a hidden defect in another part might qualify as physical damage to "other property". The recoverable damages might then include the cost of making good the defect, as essential to the repair of the property which had been damaged by it.

2–241   **Murphy v Brentwood District Council.** The House of Lords returned to the question in *Murphy v Brentwood District Council.*[514] The claimant purchased a newly-built house. Some 11 years later, signs began to appear that all was not well with the foundations and serious cracks developed in the internal walls. The gas pipe leading to the fireplace in the living room fractured, and so did the waste

---

[509] [1972] 1 Q.B. 373.
[510] [1978] A.C. 728.
[511] In both cases the claim was against the inspecting local authority, and this raises further issues arising out of the authority's status as a public body exercising public functions and the fact that it has not positively caused the harm but has merely failed to prevent it: see para.2–300.
[512] [1983] 1 A.C. 520.
[513] [1989] A.C. 177.
[514] [1991] 1 A.C. 398. See also *Department of the Environment v Thomas Bates & Son Ltd* [1991] 1 A.C. 499.

pipe leading to the main sewer, causing leakage of foul water into the foundations. The claimant decided to sell the house in its damaged state for £30,000, whereupon his insurers paid him £35,000, being the difference between the value of the undamaged house on the open market and the price received. The insurers then sought in the action to recover from the local authority, as sole defendants, that sum of £35,000 and further the costs incurred (a) in mending the fractured pipes, (b) in refitting carpets, and (c) in the sale. The trial judge held that in passing the building plans, the local authority, which relied on advice given negligently by a consulting engineer, had itself been negligent. The defects in the property, having become an imminent danger to the safety and health of the claimant whilst in occupation, gave the claimant a good cause of action against the defendants in tort.

An appeal by the defendants was dismissed by the Court of Appeal[515] but, on further appeal, was allowed by the House of Lords. A duty was owed by the builder of a house to take reasonable care to avoid injury or damage, caused by defects in its construction, to the person or property of those whom he ought to have in contemplation as likely to suffer such injury or damage. But once a defect was discovered and became patent, before any injury to person or health had resulted or any damage to property, other than the defective building itself, had been occasioned, any expense incurred by a subsequent purchaser in remedying the defect in question amounted to pure economic loss. The owner's claim, if allowed, would open up a very wide field involving the introduction of something in the nature of an indefinitely transmissible warranty of quality. And no distinction could be drawn between a mere defect of quality and a dangerous defect. In both cases the owner suffered a diminution in value of property, not injury to health. As for the "complex structure" theory, this was accepted in principle but held not to apply on the facts. Where inadequate foundations led to differential settlement and cracking, the structure as a whole was seen to be defective and as it deteriorated would only damage itself. So *Dutton* and *Anns* were thought to be wrongly decided and were overruled, and *Junior Books* was regarded as a case decided on its own special facts. In so deciding Lord Keith remarked, echoing Lord Bridge in *D & F Estates*, that in what was essentially the field of consumer protection, the precise extent and limits of the liabilities that in the public interest should be imposed on builders and local authorities were best left to be dealt with by the legislature.[516]

2–242

ILLUSTRATIONS

Since *Murphy* and sometimes before that decision, claims in respect of economic loss suffered by owners of defective buildings not in contractual privity with the defendant being sued have been held to fail. For example, where a sub-contractor negligently caused economic losses to the employer of a main

2–243

---

[515] *Murphy v Brentwood District Council* [1991] A.C. 398.
[516] As to which, see the Defective Premises Act 1972; see para.2–77.

contractor, which were unrelated to either actual or apprehended physical damage to other property, the employer's losses, albeit reasonably foreseeable, could not be recovered[517]; a builder was not liable to the lessees of a building for the cost of remedial work which was necessary for the purpose of rendering the building fit to support its design load[518]; and architects owed no duty to a company occupying newly-built garage premises as tenant of its holding company in respect of alleged lost profits arising as a result of structural and other defects in the building.[519] On the other hand, there is of course no objection to a claim of this kind being founded on contract, where no special difficulties of principle arising. Indeed, in *D & F Estates* and *Murphy* a claim in tort was denied precisely because it would intrude into the sphere of contract.

2–244 **Complex structures.** An action for negligence may still be maintained where defective building work damages separate property. In *Murphy* their Lordships accepted the complex structure argument in principle, although they declined to apply it on the facts. By this route, defective work done by a subcontractor in installing wiring that causes a fire, or a boiler that blows up, or a steel frame that collapses damaging property above it, can give rise to liability based on the damage to other property. For example, a builder who constructed an insufficient internal fire wall separating a storage area from the rest of a factory, allowing a subsequent fire to pass over the top, was liable for the damage to the owner's plant and equipment outside the storage area, but not for damage to the fabric of the building itself.[520] One possible consequence is that a subsequent owner, who has no action where a building is put up by one contractor, can sue where the work of one contractor damages that of another.[521]

2–245 **Decisions overseas.** Leading decisions overseas, in Australia,[522] Canada[523] and New Zealand,[524] have declined to follow *Murphy* and have upheld subsequent owners' claims. In particular, in *Bryan v Maloney*[525] in the High Court of Australia, their Lordships' opinions in *D & F Estates* and *Murphy* were dismissed as resting upon a narrower view of the scope of the modern law of negligence and a more rigid compartmentalisation of contract and tort than was acceptable in Australian law. However, in both Australia and New Zealand it has

[517] *Greater Nottingham Co-operative Society Ltd v Cementation Piling & Foundations Ltd* [1989] Q.B. 71.
[518] *Department of the Environment v Thomas Bates & Son* [1991] 1 A.C. 499.
[519] *Strathford East Kilbride Ltd v Film Design Ltd, The Times*, December 1, 1997 OH.
[520] *Bellefield Computer Services Ltd v E Turner & Sons Ltd* [2000] B.L.R. 97.
[521] In *Bryan v Maloney* (1995) 182 C.L.R. 609 at 623 HCA, it is suggested that this might be the effect of *Murphy*.
[522] *Bryan v Maloney* (1995) 182 C.L.R. 609 HCA.
[523] *City of Kamloops v Neilsen* [1984] 2 S.C.R. 2 SCC; *Rothfield v Manolakos* [1989] 2 S.C.R. 1259 SCC; *Winnipeg Condominium Corporation No. 36 v Bird Construction Co* [1995] 1 S.C.R. 85, where the Supreme Court of Canada imposed the duty specifically on the basis rejected in *Murphy*, that the defect posed a danger to health.
[524] *Bowen v Paramount Builders (Hamilton) Ltd* [1977] 1 N.Z.L.R. 394 NZCA; *Invercargill City Council v Hamlin* [1994] 3 N.Z.L.R. 513, NZCA, [1996] 1 N.Z.L.R. 513 PC.
[525] (1995) 182 C.L.R. 609 HCA.

been decided that the builder owes a duty only in respect of residential property. Purchasers of defective commercial property have no remedy in tort against the original builder, primarily because they are seen as well able to look after their own interests, either in the contractual matrix pursuant to which the building was erected or in contracting to buy the building.[526] Yet drawing a line between residential and commercial buildings poses very real difficulty. In *Woolcock St Investments Pty Ltd v CDG Pty Ltd*[527] the High Court of Australia thought that any such line would be far from bright, straight, clearly defined or even clearly definable. But while difficult, the line has nonetheless been maintained.

(H) Defective chattels

General. Claims in respect of defective chattels are governed by the same   **2–246** principles as apply to defective buildings. In *Murphy* one of the reasons for denying the claim by subsequent purchasers of defective buildings was that this would lead to similar claims by subsequent purchasers of defective chattels, which would undermine existing principles of products liability.

Damage to other property. Where a defect in a chattel causes damage to   **2–247** other property, a duty can be recognised in the ordinary way. For example, a manufacturer of electric motors which were used to power the oxygenation pumps for the claimant's lobster tank was liable for loss of the lobsters when the motors cut out.[528] This was physical damage to the lobsters. But where a defect simply damages the chattel itself, or reduces its value, the owner suffers an economic loss which is not recoverable. So, in the lobster case, the defendant manufacturer was not liable for other and separate economic losses, including the cost of the pumps and loss of profits on intended future sales; a supplier of glass under a building sub-contractor was not liable to the main contractor when the units were rejected as not complying with the contractual specification, in that they were not all the same shade of green, the colour of peace in Islam[529]; and the successors to a business which had manufactured an engine used in the claimant's vessel owed no duty to warn the claimants about the negligent design of the pistons (themselves manufactured by an independent contractor), for there

---

[526] In Australia, see *Woolcock St Investments Pty Ltd v CDG Pty Ltd* (2005) 216 C.L.R. 515 HCA. In New Zealand, see *Rolls Royce New Zealand Ltd v Carter Holt Harvey Ltd* [2005] 1 N.Z.L.R. 324 NZCA; *Te Mata Properties Ltd v Hastings District Council* [2009] 1 N.Z.L.R. 460 NZCA; *Queenstown Lakes District Council v Charterhall Trustees Ltd* [2009] 3 N.Z.L.R. 786 NZCA; *Sunset Terraces* [2010] NZCA 64. In Canada, in *Winnipeg Condominium Corporation No.36 v Bird Construction Co* [1995] 1 S.C.R. 85, the Supreme Court of Canada recognised a duty owed to the commercial owner of residential property.
[527] (2005) 216 C.L.R. 515 HCA ; *Sunset Terraces* [2010] NZCA 64.
[528] *Muirhead v Industrial Tank Specialities Ltd* [1986] Q.B. 507; and see *Aswan Engineering Establishment Co v Lupdine Ltd* [1987] 1 W.L.R. 1 CA.
[529] *Simaan General Contracting Co v Pilkington Glass Ltd (No. 2)* [1988] Q.B. 758. The assumed loss was the withholding of money, which the plaintiffs would have been entitled to receive otherwise from the building owners, Sheikh Al-Oteiba, and loss of interest on such a sum.

was no physical damage to person or property and the claimant's loss was entirely financial.[530]

2-248   **Dangerous property.** A simlar view has generally been taken overseas.[531] However, in Canada, such claims can succeed where the defect is dangerous.[532]

(I) Sterilisation cases

2-249   **Wrongful conception or birth.** A doctor or other medical professional may have negligently performed a sterilisation operation or given negligent advice as to its efficacy. If the patient later conceives an unplanned child, the question arises whether the doctor can be liable to the patient and his or her partner for the costs of bringing up the child. This can be called a claim for wrongful conception. So also, a claim may be brought if a patient is misinformed that she is not pregnant or if she is wrongly informed that her foetus is healthy, causing her to continue with the pregnancy and to lose the option of a lawful abortion and, again, to incur upbringing expenses. A claim of this kind can be called a claim for wrongful birth.[533] Both are claims for economic loss.[534]

2-250   **McFarlane v Tayside Health Board.** In *McFarlane v Tayside Health Board*,[535] the parents of a child born after a failed vasectomy brought an action against the surgeon, alleging negligence in advising them that the vasectomy had rendered the husband infertile, and claimed damages in respect of various losses associated with the birth of the child. The House of Lords held that the mother could claim general damages for the pain and suffering of pregnancy and childbirth and for certain associated expenses,[536] but that the parents could not recover

---

[530] *Hamble Fisheries Ltd v Gardner & Sons Ltd, The Times,* January 5, 1999, CA.

[531] *Minchillo v Ford Motor Co of Australia Ltd* [1995] 2 V.R. 594 (Australia); *New Zealand Food Group (1992) Ltd v Amcor Trading (NZ) Ltd* (1999) 9 T.C.L.R. 184 (New Zealand).

[532] *Privest Properties Ltd v Foundation Co of Canada* (1995) 128 D.L.R. (4th) 577 (appeal dismissed (1997) 143 D.L.R. (4th) 635); *Hughes v Sunbeam Corp* (2003) 219 D.L.R. 467.

[533] The terminology has been criticised: see Mason, "Wrongful pregnancy, wrongful birth and wrongful terminology" (2002) 6 Edinburgh L.R. 46.

[534] *McFarlane v Tayside Health Board* [2000] 2 A.C. 59, at 76, 79, 89, 99–100, 109.

[535] [2000] 2 A.C. 59. For commentary, see Weir, "The Unwanted Child" (2000) 59 C.L.J. 238; Norrie, "Failed sterilisation and economic loss: justice law and policy in *McFarlane v Tayside Health Board*" (2000) 16 P.N. 76; Booth, "A child is a blessing—heavily in disguise, right?" 151 N.L.J. 1738; Whitfield, "The fallout from *McFarlane*" (2002) 18 P.N. 234; Hoyano, "Misconceptions about wrongful conception" (2002) 65 M.L.R. 883; Dimopoulos and Bagaric, 'Why Wrongful Birth Actions Are Right' (2003) 11 JLM 230; Golder, "From *McFarlane* to *Melchior* and Beyond: Love, Sex, Money and Commodification in the Anglo-Australian Law of Torts" (2004) 12 T.L.J. 128; Mason, "The Reproductive Torts", in *Halsbury's Laws of England Centenary Essays*, London, Butterworths, 2007, 127.

[536] Lord Slynn (at 74) would have allowed a claim for associated special damages by way of extra medical expenses, clothes, equipment on birth and lost earnings; Lord Steyn (at 84) considered that a claim for the loss suffered by the wife giving up work in the later stages of pregnancy would be sustainable; Lord Hope (at 89) would have included any financial loss attributable to the pregnancy, including physical or emotional problems or loss of income after birth; and Lord Millett (at 115) would have allowed the replacement costs of baby equipment if the parents disposed of the items concerned in the belief that they would have no more children.

the costs of bringing up the child.[537] The policy considerations underlying the decision included an unwillingness to regard a normal, healthy child as a financial liability, or as more trouble and expense than it was worth, an acceptance that the rewards which parenthood may or may not bring cannot be quantified and, indeed, are incalculable, and, broadly, a recognition that while the birth of a child may be a mixed blessing, society must regard the balance as beneficial.[538]

Disability claims. Shortly after *McFarlane*, the question arose whether a   **2–251** claim might lie where the unplanned child suffered from a disability. In *Parkinson v St. James University and Seacroft Hospital NHS Trust*[539] the Court of Appeal held that the claimant mother was entitled to recover damages in respect of the costs of providing for her child's special needs and care relating to his disability, but, applying *McFarlane*, not for the basic costs of his maintenance. In so deciding, Hale L.J. did not wish to draw an invidious distinction between the "worth" of a healthy child and of a disabled child. As she observed, "this analysis treats a disabled child as having exactly the same worth as a non-disabled child. It affords him the same dignity and status. It simply acknowledges that he costs more."[540] However, in order to qualify for compensation the disability needed to be "significant". Brooke L.J. said that this would have to be decided on a case by case basis, that the expression would include disabilities of the mind and that it would not include minor defects or inconveniences.[541] Hale L.J. referred to the statutory definitions in welfare legislation identifying those whose special needs required special services,[542] and saw no difficulty in using the same definition in the present context.[543]

---

[537] Compare *Cattanach v Melchior* (2003) 215 C.L.R. 1, where the High Court of Australia, in a 4–3 decision, allowed a claim for the cost of raising an unplanned child; Vranken, "Damages for 'Wrongful Birth': Where To after *Cattanach?*" (2003) 24 Adelaide L Rev 243. The decision has been reversed by legislation in three states: see ss.49A, 49B Civil Liability Act 2003 (Qld); s.71 of the Civil Liability Act 2002 (NSW); s.67 of the Civil Liability Act 1936 (SA).

[538] In *Greenfield v Irwin* [2001] 1 W.L.R. 1279 of the CA, where the claimant alleged that a nurse's negligence resulted in her being unaware of her pregnancy and that she would have terminated had she known, no distinction was held to arise between cases involving the negligent supply of information and cases where the allegation was of negligent performance of the operation itself. The court also held that *McFarlane* applied both to a claim for the costs of rearing a child and to a claim for loss of earnings contingent upon the decision of the mother to leave work to care for her child.

[539] [2002] 2 Q.B. 266. See also *Rand v East Dorset HA* [2000] Lloyd's Rep. Med. 181 (failure to advise parents of Down Syndrome); *Hardman v Amin* [2000] Lloyd's Rep Med. 498 (failure to advise of risk of foetal abnormality due to maternal rubella); *Groom v Selby* [2002] P.I.Q.R. P201, CA (costs of bringing up a disabled child held recoverable following a negligent failure to detect pregnancy after sterilisation, and the baby developed meningitis with resulting brain damage as a rare but natural consequence of birth); *N v Warrington HA* [2003] Lloyd's Rep. Med. 356 CA (damages not limited to sums spent up to a handicapped child's eighteenth birthday); *Farraj v King's Healthcare NHS Trust* [2006] P.I.Q.R. P29 (duty owed by laboratory testing a sample of foetal material); and see *Farraj v King's Healthcare NHS Trust* [2009] EWCA Civ 1203 (no liability of hospital seeking a report on the material, laboratory solely liable).

[540] ibid. at [90].

[541] ibid. at [52].

[542] Hale L.J. referred in particular to the Children Act 1989 s.17(1), providing that a child is disabled if he is blind, deaf or dumb or suffers from mental disorder of any kind or is substantially and permanently handicapped by illness, injury or congenital deformity or such other disability as may be prescribed.

[543] [2002] Q.B. 206, at [91].

2–252   **Loss of autonomy.** In *Rees v Darlington Memorial Hospital NHS Trust*,[544] in another variation, the *mother* suffered from a disability. She had undergone a sterilisation operation because she feared that her significant visual disability would prevent her from properly looking after a child, but having later conceived and given birth to a healthy child she sought damages to cover the costs of providing for the child. In a majority decision, the House of Lords re-affirmed *McFarlane* and dismissed her claim for the additional costs of upkeep beyond those that would have arisen had she not suffered from the disability in question.[545] At the same time, however, their Lordships introduced a significant "gloss" on the earlier decision. Lord Bingham agreed that recovering the full cost of bringing up an unplanned child should be precluded, yet questioned the fairness of a rule which denied the victim of a legal wrong any recompense at all beyond the immediate expenses of pregnancy and birth. The real loss was that the parent, particularly the mother, had been denied by negligence the opportunity to live her life in the way that she wished and planned. His Lordship accordingly favoured the award of a conventional sum to mark the claimant's injury and lost autonomy.[546] This sum, fixed at £15,000, would not be the product of calculation but would be some measure of recognition for the wrong done. It would be in addition to any award for pregnancy and birth and would be applied without differentiation to all cases, including those in which either the child or the parent was disabled.

2–253   Lord Nicholls, Lord Millett and Lord Scott agreed that there should be a conventional award, but differed on whether disability expenses were recoverable as well. Lord Nicholls agreed with Lord Bingham, Lord Millett did not decide, and Lord Scott said that he might allow them if the purpose of the sterilisation was to avoid conception of a disabled child. Lord Steyn, Lord Hope and Lord Hutton, expressing a minority view, rejected a conventional award and would allow the disability costs where either the mother or the child was disabled. So *Parkinson* was not expressly overruled, and for the time being it would appear to remain good law.

2–254   **Doctor's duty to non-patient.** A further question, relevant in claims both for disability costs and for loss of autonomy, is whether or in what circumstances a

---

[544] [2004] 1 A.C. 309; Cane, "The Doctor, the Stork and the Court: A Modern Morality Play" (2004) 120 L.Q.R. 23; Pedain, "Unconventional justice in the House of Lords" (2004) 63 C.L.J. 19; Priaulx, "Parental disability and wrongful conception" [2003] Fam Law 117; Denyer, "Failed sterilisations and child costs" [2003] Fam Law 424; Dixon, "An unconventional gloss on unintended children" 153 N.L.J. 1732; Morris, "Another fine mess. The aftermath of *McFarlane* and the decision in *Rees v Darlington Memorial Hospital NHS Trust*" (2004) 20 P.N. 2.

[545] See also *AD v East Kent Community NHS Trust* [2003] P.I.Q.R. P34 CA, where the claimant, a patient under the Mental Health Act 1983, was unable herself to look after the child, who was placed with her grandmother under the terms of a residence order. The claimant claimed all the upbringing costs, arguing that the grandmother incurred them because of her own disability, but the court considered that there were no extra costs attributable to the mother's disability. Rather, they were the same costs but borne by the grandmother, and were not recoverable on the authority of *McFarlane*.

[546] Lord Millett had put forward this solution in *McFarlane*, n.535 above at 113–114, but on that occasion without support from the other members of the court.

doctor owes a duty of care to a person who is not his or her patient.[547] As regards mothers, the wife or partner of a male patient, who becomes pregnant after the patient's sterilisation fails as a result of the doctor's negligence, clearly has a cause of action against the doctor, as the mother's claim in *McFarlane* itself illustrates. But no duty is owed to the patient's future sexual partner.[548] As regards fathers, there is support in a number of decisions for allowing the claim, at least together with that of the mother.[549] Recently, in *Whitehead v Searle*,[550] Rix L.J. was prepared to recognise a duty owed to an estranged father who took on the responsibility for a disabled child after the mother committed suicide, but the question ultimately was left open.

4.—THE KIND OF CLAIMANT

(A) Introduction

A foreseeable claimant. Whether a defendant owes a duty of care to the person bringing the action depends ultimately on the application of the foreseeability principle to the facts of the particular case. Was the injured party either a foreseeable claimant whom the law will recognise, or an unforeseeable claimant whom it will not? As has been seen, a person owes no duty of care to the world at large. A duty can arise only as between a defendant and a claimant who is proximately affected by the defendant's conduct in all relevant physical, circumstantial and causal respects.[551] Speaking broadly, the duty is owed generally to everyone within the class of those who by reason of their proximity are likely to be injured if care is not taken. 2–255

Foreseeability has posed special problems in certain categories of case. Aspects of the issue have already been considered in relation to claims based on omissions to act, to claims for mental injury and to claims for financial loss. The focus now is on certain particular kinds of *claimant*. Claims by rescuers, by unborn children and by trespassers, each have certain special characteristics of their own.[552] 2–256

---

[547] *McFarlane* and subsequent decisions concerned claims in tort against National Health Service providers. An action in contract against a private provider arguably could be met by the same or similar concerns of policy, but there is no decision so holding. In *McFarlane* (n.535 above at 99) Lord Clyde recognised that actions in contract may give rise to different issues than those in tort. Lord Steyn (at 77) thought that the correctness of the assumption that it is immaterial whether an action is brought in contract or in delict might depend on whether the term amounted to a warranty of an outcome, but did not say whether it might depend simply on the cause of action which was asserted.

[548] *Goodwill v British Pregnancy Advisory Service* [1996] 2 All E.R. 161 CA.

[549] For example, *Salih v Enfield HA* [1991] 3 All E.R. 400 CA; *Rand v East Dorset HA* [2000] Lloyd's Rep. Med. 181; *Parkinson v St James and Seacroft University Hospital NHS Trust* [2002] Q.B. 206, at [93]; *Farraj v King's Healthcare NHS Trust* [2009] EWCA Civ 1203.

[550] [2009] 1 W.L.R. 549 CA.

[551] See paras 2–29–2–31.

[552] For special procedural features to claims by certain categories of claimant, see Ch.3, below.

2–257   Sometimes a defendant may be able to foresee damage to his or her neighbour in a general, Atkinian sense, yet the particular mechanism by which the harm was inflicted was unforeseeable or outside the defendant's sphere of contemplation. Cases of this kind[553] often are better explained in terms of the rules against remoteness of damage rather than in terms of the presence or absence of a duty of care.[554]

2–258   **Extra-sensitive claimants.** A claimant who is especially sensitive to injury may fail in showing a duty of care, on the simple ground that injury to him or her was unforeseeable. So a driver with an "egg-shell personality" who developed a psychotic illness after a police officer made a mistake in filling in a report following her involvement in a minor traffic accident failed on this ground.[555] Again, a person who is especially vulnerable to injury, because, say, he has an allergy to certain kinds of food, can reasonably be expected to take appropriate precautions for himself. But a claim did, exceptionally, succeed in *Bhamra v Dubb*.[556] A caterer for a Sikh wedding included egg in some of the dishes, when this was forbidden by the Sikh religion for cultural reasons. One of the guests who was allergic to egg ate a dish with egg in it, suffered an anaphylaxic reaction and died. The defendant caterer clearly owed a duty to the bride's father who employed him not to use eggs in the dishes, but the issue was whether he owed a duty to the claimant not to injure him by triggering the egg allergy. It was decided that the caterer was liable. It was said that, first, the caterer knew that some people were allergic to eggs and that any such person would suffer illness or more serious injury if he ate food containing eggs. He also knew that those who attended the wedding, including any guest who happened to suffer from egg allergy, would expect the food to be completely free of eggs and would therefore feel confident that no harm would come from eating it. Finally, the claimant, who knew himself to be allergic to eggs, had every reason to rely without inquiry on the caterer to supply food which did not contain egg, as would not have been the case if this had been anything other than an exclusively Sikh occasion. In the court's view, this "very unusual combination of circumstances" was sufficient to extend the scope of the caterer's duty of care to harm in the form of personal injury suffered as a result of eating food containing eggs.

(B) Rescuers

2–259   **An independent duty.** There are good reasons of policy in favour of supporting and encouraging those who seek to rescue another from danger.[557] One way in which the law does this is by recognising claims for compensation by rescuers who suffer injury in the course of their attempt at rescue. Accordingly, if a person by negligence creates a situation which puts other people

---

[553] See, for example, *Smith v London & South Western Railway Co* (1870) LR 6 CP 14; *Glasgow Corporation v Muir* [1943] A.C. 448; *Woods v Duncan* [1946] A.C. 401; *Thurogood v Van Den Berghs & Jurgens Ltd* [1951] 2 K.B. 537; *Margereson v Roberts* [1996] P.I.Q.R. P358 CA.
[554] See Ch.5, para.5–31, below.
[555] *Tame v NSW* (2003) 211 C.L.R. 317 HCA.
[556] [2010] EWCA Civ 13.
[557] See generally *Wagner v International Railroad Co* 133 NE 437 (1921).

in danger, he or she owes a duty of care to those whom he or she ought reasonably to foresee may hasten to the rescue at risk to their own safety.[558] If A negligently imperils B and then C tries to rescue B and is injured, A may be liable to both B and C. But the duty owed to a rescuer is quite independent of the duty, if any, which is owed to the actual person who has been endangered. It stands on its own.

In *Videan v British Transport Commission*[559] the infant son of a railway **2–260** station-master wandered unsupervised from the station house on to the railway track. His father was killed when he leaped on to the line in an attempt to save the child from being run down by an approaching motor trolley. Actions were subsequently brought by the child, who was badly injured, and by the wife of the deceased under the Fatal Accidents Act 1959, alleging negligence by the driver of the trolley. The child's claim failed because he was a trespasser and as such his presence was not foreseeable. The difficulty facing the widow was that if the presence of the child was not foreseeable, then logically neither was that of his rescuer. The answer found was that the rescuer's claim was not in any sense a derivative one. Lord Denning M.R. said that the defendants, having created a situation of peril, were obliged to answer for it to any person who sought to rescue the person in peril, a view which looks suspiciously like the recognition of a duty owed to the world at large. Pearson and Harman L.JJ. thought that the fact the child was the station-master's son obscured the issue. The plaintiff could recover on account of the defendant's breach of duty to the deceased in his capacity as station-master, having a general responsibility for any emergency that might arise and whose presence on the track was thus reasonably foreseeable.

ILLUSTRATIONS

Provided the rescuer has acted reasonably, in the sense that a reasonable person **2–261** would think there was a hope of success in the rescue attempt, his or her claim usually succeeds. In *Haynes v Harwood*[560] the defendants' two-horse cab was left unattended in a London street and the horses bolted. A policeman saw the horses and van coming and, fearful lest children be knocked down, he rushed out and stopped the horses but was injured in so doing. He was entitled to recover damages on the ground that, when horses are left unattended in such circum-stances, it should have been contemplated that they might bolt and that "if horses run away it must quite obviously be contemplated that people are likely to be knocked down. It must also, I think, be contemplated that persons will attempt to stop the horses and try to prevent injury to life or limb."[561]

There are many similar illustrations. Thus, it has been held that a duty was **2–262** owed by a boat owner to the rescuer of a guest who, through no fault of the

---

[558] Tiley, "The rescue principle" (1967) 30 M.L.R. 25; Linden, "Rescuers and Good Samaritans" (1971) 34 M.L.R. 241.
[559] [1963] 2 Q.B. 650.
[560] [1935] 1 K.B. 146; cp *Cutler v United Dairies* [1933] 2 K.B. 297, CA.
[561] ibid, per Findlay J., quoted with approval by Maugham L.J. at 163.

owner, had fallen off the boat[562]; by an employer to the rescuer of employees overcome by fumes at the bottom of a well[563]; and even by a doctor who had negligently removed a patient's kidney thinking it to be a cyst to the donor of a replacement kidney.[564]

2–263   **Rescue of property.** A duty also may be owed to the rescuer of property,[565] although it has been said that the need for intervention must necessarily be acute and the degree of risk in intervening must be weighed against the nature and value of property sought to be protected. In the case at hand it was held that a person who was responsible for lighting a tussock fire which got out of control owed a duty to a volunteer fire-fighter.[566] But a defendant who caused a roadside fire was not liable to a rescuer who injured his foot when running to the scene to assist, on the basis that the fire did not cause the accidental fall en route.[567]

2–264   **Action against the victim.** An action has even been brought against the endangered victim, on the basis that a person who negligently puts himself or herself in peril thereby creates a foreseeable risk that another person might be injured in coming to his or her assistance. In *Harrison v British Railways Board*,[568] the claimant was a guard on a passenger train, which the second defendant, a late-arriving passenger, attempted to board as it was pulling out of the station. The claimant, having failed in his attempt to signal the driver to stop the train, then tried to grab hold of the defendant in order to haul him aboard, but the latter lost his grip and fell, dragging the claimant off the train with him. Both men sustained severe injuries. It was held that a person who, through lack of care for his own safety, put himself into a dangerous situation and who, as a reasonable man, ought to have foreseen that some other person might endanger himself by attempting to rescue him, was liable to his rescuer for any injuries sustained by the latter during the rescue attempt.

2–265   **Psychiatric injury.** In *Chadwick v British Transport Commission*,[569] a serious railway accident had occurred and the claimant's late husband had gone immediately to the scene to take part in rescue operations. As a result of his horrific experiences he suffered psychiatric injury. Waller J. held that the defendants, having by their negligence put their passengers in peril, should reasonably have foreseen that someone would attempt a rescue and would suffer

---

[562] *Horsley v MacLaren* [1972] S.C.R. 441, where the Canadian Supreme Court confirmed that where someone embarked upon the task of rescuing a guest who had accidentally fallen overboard, then even though he was not under any duty to play "the good Samaritan," he could become liable in negligence, where the method of rescue or its abandonment left the person in danger worse off than otherwise would have been the case. See generally Spencer, "Rescuer as defendant—Reversal of roles reversed" [1971] C.L.J. 193; Alexander, "One rescuer's obligation to another: *The Ogopogo* lands in the Supreme Court of Canada" (1972) 22 Univ Tor L.J. 98.
[563] *Baker v Hopkins* [1959] 1 W.L.R. 966, CA.
[564] *Urbanski v Patel* (1978) 84 D.L.R. (3d) 650.
[565] *Hyett v GW Railway* [1948] 1 K.B. 345.
[566] *Russell v McCabe* [1962] N.Z.L.R. 392, NZCA; and see *Ogwo v Taylor* [1988] A.C. 431.
[567] *Crossley v Rawlinson* [1981] 1 W.L.R. 361.
[568] [1981] 3 All E.R. 679; and see *Chapman v Hearse* (1961) 106 C.L.R. 112, HCA; cf *Greatorex v Greatorex* [2000] 1 W.L.R. 1970, see para.2–150, above.
[569] [1967] 1 W.L.R. 912.

injury in the process and, accordingly, a duty was owed to the rescuer. However, this straightforward decision must now be understood in the light of the decision of the House of Lords in *Frost v Chief Constable of the South Yorkshire Police*,[570] applying the distinction between primary and secondary victims of shock-inducing events to claims by rescuers.[571] So *Chadwick* could be supported on the ground that the claimant was put in danger and was, therefore, a primary victim to whom a duty was owed based simply on foreseeability of personal injury; but rescuers who were secondary victims would have to meet the special conditions laid down in *Alcock v Chief Constable of the South Yorkshire Police*[572] before their claims could succeed.

(C) Unborn children

Background. Early decisions at common law held that claims by children 2–266
who were born alive but who had suffered injury prior to their birth should fail. For example, in the Irish decision in *Walker v Great Northern Railway of Ireland*,[573] the claimant's mother was injured in a railway collision caused by the defendants' negligence, and as a result the claimant, then within her mother's womb, was born with disabilities. The action failed on the ground that the defendants owed no duty to the claimant, as they were not aware of her existence, within her pregnant mother, let alone her presence on the train.

This reasoning was quite unconvincing—defendants in negligence claims 2–267
frequently know nothing about their victims before they injure them—and was a source of serious injustice. However, starting at around the middle of the twentieth century, the tide began to turn, and eventually the right of a child when born alive to sue for injuries caused by prenatal negligence became recognised by the courts in Australia,[574] South Africa,[575] Canada[576] and every state jurisdiction in the United States of America.[577] The same result was achieved by statute in Ireland.[578]

---

[570] [1999] 2 A.C. 455.
[571] See para.2–155 above.
[572] [1992] 1 A.C. 310.
[573] (1890) 28 L.R. Ir 69. For similar decisions in the United States, see, for example, *Dietrich v Inhabitants of Northampton* 138 Mass 14 (1884); *Drobner v Peters* 25 NY 220 (1921).
[574] *Watt v Rama* [1972] V.R. 353. In *X v Pal* (1991) 23 N.S.W.L.R. 26 the New South Wales Court of Appeal held that doctors who failed to screen and treat a mother for syphilis before she became pregnant owed a duty of care to a subsequently conceived child, on the basis that steps could have been taken to prevent the child from contracting it (although the evidence did not establish that the disease caused the child's disabilities). However, where a defendant negligently brings about the conception of a child who suffers from a disability which was not caused by, and could not have been prevented by , the defendant, the child's claim must face the objections to claims for so-called "wrongful life": see para.2–272.
[575] *Pinchin v Santam Insurance Co Ltd* [1963] 2 S.A. 254.
[576] *Duval v Sequin* (1972) 26 D.L.R. (3d) 418. The earlier decision of the Supreme Court of Canada in *Montreal Tramways v Leveille* [1933] S.C.R. 456 upheld a claim for pre-natal injury under the Civil Code of Quebec.
[577] The first successful claim seems to have been *Bonbrest v Kotz* 65 F Supp. 138 (1946). The change of view was complete by about 1972: see *Huskey v Smith* 265 So 2d 596 (1972). See Dobbs, *The Law of Torts* West Group, St Paul, Minn, 2000 p.781.
[578] Civil Liability Act 1961 s.58.

2–268   In England, Wales and Northern Ireland there was both statutory reform, with the passing of the Congenital Disabilities (Civil Liability) Act 1976, and also the recognition of a born-alive child's right of action at common law. In *Burton v Islington Health Authority: De Martell v Merton and Sutton Health Authority*,[579] where the injury to the child in both cases pre-dated the coming into force of the 1976 Act, the Court of Appeal accepted and applied the reasoning of the Supreme Court of Victoria in its influential decision in *Watt v Rama*.[580] In that case the claimant was injured in a road accident while still in her mother's womb. The defendant argued that at the time of the collision he owed no duty of care to the claimant and that the damages sought to be recovered were too remote. The court rejected both arguments. It considered that the defendant's duty of care initially was "contingent" or "potential" and that it would "crystallise" or "ripen into a relationship imposing a duty" when the claimant's identity as a legal person became defined by birth. At that point the defendant's conduct could be treated as a breach of duty, and the pre-natal injury simply as an evidential fact relevant to the issue of causation and damage. In brief, duty, breach, and damage remained potential until birth, at which point they became actual.

2–269   **Congenital Disabilities (Civil Liability) Act 1976.** Today, subject only to the highly unlikely possibility of there being further claims at common law, the Congenital Disabilities (Civil Liability) Act will apply. The key provisions are s.1(1) and s.1(2):

> (1) If a child is born disabled as the result of such an occurrence before its birth as is mentioned in subsection (2) below, and a person (other than the child's own mother) is under this section answerable to the child in respect of the occurrence, the child's disabilities are to be regarded as damage resulting from the wrongful act of that person and actionable accordingly at the suit of the child.
>
> (2) An occurrence to which this section applies is one which:
>
>> (a) affected either parent of the child in his or her ability to have a normal, healthy child; or
>> (b) affected the mother during her pregnancy, or affected her or the child in the course of its birth, so that the child is born with disabilities which would not otherwise have been present.

References in the Act to a child being born disabled or with disabilities are to the child being born with "any deformity, disease or abnormality, including predisposition (whether or not susceptible of immediate prognosis) to physical or mental defect in the future".[581] "Born" means "born alive (the moment of a

---

[579] [1993] Q.B. 204.
[580] [1972] V.R. 353.
[581] Congenital Disabilities (Civil Liability) Act 1976 s.4(1).

child's birth being when it first has a life separate from its mother)".[582]
Disabilities which result from certain infertility treatments are included.[583]

It is apparent that pre-conception occurrences are covered by s.1(2)(a) and **2–270**
post-conception occurrences by s.1(2)(b). In either case, the defendant will be
liable where it can be shown that the claimant's injuries were caused by the
defendant's negligence. However, s.1(1) excludes claims against a child's own
mother, subject to an exception, prompted by insurance considerations, where a
woman is driving a motor vehicle when she knows (or ought reasonably to know)
herself to be pregnant. Here the mother owes a duty to take care for the safety of
her unborn child.[584]

A derivative claim. The Act makes any liability of the defendant to the child **2–271**
derivative upon the liability of the defendant to the parent.[585] It thus avoids the
possibility that the defendant might owe two levels of duty in respect of one
incident, as for example might otherwise happen if the mother suffered injury at
a time when she was trespassing on the defendant's land. But it means that a
defence which would have been available in an action by the parent will also bar
or limit a claim by the child. So there is no liability for a pre-conception event
if, before conception, either or both of the parents knew of and accepted the risk
of their child being born disabled[586]; a contract term excluding or restricting
liability to the parent also excludes liability to the child[587]; and contributory
negligence by a parent is a good defence.[588]

Wrongful life. A claim for so-called "wrongful life" is a claim by a child **2–272**
who is born with a disability alleging negligence by the medical advisers of his
or her mother or father in failing to diagnose or warn about the disability or risk
of disability. Claims of this kind almost invariably fail at common law, because
the gist of the claim is that the child has a right not to be born disabled, meaning
in this context a right not to live or to be aborted before birth. So any duty
requires the court to say that life itself can constitute an injury in law and to
quantify the damage by comparing life with disabilities and non-existence, and
this the courts refuse to do.[589] The 1976 Act does not give a remedy either. In

---

[582] Congenital Disabilities (Civil Liability) Act 1976 s.4(2)(a).
[583] ibid s.1A(1)
[584] ibid s.2.
[585] ibid s.1(3).
[586] ibid s.1(4). If it is the child's father who is the defendant, this rule does not apply if he knew of
the risk and the mother did not. A similar rule to that in s.1(4) applies to claims arising out of
infertility treatment: see s.1A(3).
[587] Congenital Disabilities (Civil Liability) Act 1976, s.1(6); and see s.1A(4). But exclusion clauses
cannot exclude or restrict liability for death or personal injury resulting from negligence: see the
Unfair Contract Terms Act 1977, s.2(1); Consumer Protection Act 1987 ss.6(3)(c), 7.
[588] Congenital Disabilities (Civil Liability) Act 1976 s.1(7) s.1A(4).
[589] *McKay v Essex Area Health Authority* [1982] Q.B. 1166; *Harriton v Stephens* (2006) 226 C.L.R.
52, HCA; Teff, "The Action for 'Wrongful Life' in England and the United States" (1985) 34
I.C.L.Q. 423; Stolker, "The Limits of Liability and Beyond" (1994) 43 I.C.L.Q. 521; Morris and
Santier, "To Be or Not To Be: Is That the Question? Wrongful Life and Misconceptions" (2003) 11
Med. L. Rev 167; Dimopoulos and Bagaric, "The Moral Status of Wrongful Life Claims" (2003) 32
C.L.W.R. 35; Fordham, "A Life Less Ordinary—The Rejection of Actions for Wrongful Life" (2007)
15 T.L.J. 123; Ellis and McGivern, "The Wrongfulness or Rightfulness of Actions for Wrongful
Life" (2007) 15 Tort L Rev 135.

McKay v Essex AHA[590] the Court of Appeal interpreted s.1(2)(b) as being worded so as to import the assumption that, but for the occurrence giving rise to a disabled birth, the child would have been born normal and healthy, not that it would not have been born at all.

(D) Trespassers

2–273   **General.** Claims by trespassers have an eventful history. In early times trespassers, as a class, were not recognised as capable of suing occupiers of dangerous premises for injuries caused by negligence. They could sue only if their injuries were inflicted wilfully or with reckless disregard of their presence on the land.[591] By the time of *British Railways Board v Herrington*[592] this position was deemed unduly harsh. It was recognised that an occupier's relationship with a trespasser was forced on the occupier, and so it was inappropriate to impose upon the occupier a common or ordinary duty of care. Rather, the nature and extent of the occupier's duty had to be based on considerations of common humanity. Applying this principle, the defendants were liable to a child injured by touching an electrified rail. They had created a lethal danger, they knew that children played in the area and they could easily have taken steps to keep them off their land.

2–274   It was apparent from *Herrington* that the humanitarian duty differed from the duty of care in at least two respects. First, it was not enough that the presence of a trespasser was foreseeable: the occupier should know that there was a "substantial probability" of a trespasser coming on the land. Secondly, the humanitarian duty was essentially *subjective*. A duty of care could be broken regardless of the defendant's inability to prevent breach due to lack of skill or resources. Negligence lay in permitting the dangerous situation to occur in the first place. However, the capabilities and resources of the occupier were clearly of relevance as regards obligations to trespassers. As trespassers came uninvited then, in Lord Reid's words in *Herrington*, they had to take the occupier as they found him. The *Herrington* duty was applied by the Court of Appeal on a number of occasions without particular difficulty.[593] However, the Law Commission recommended further reform,[594] and this was achieved by the Occupiers' Liability Act 1984. The provisions of the Act and the cases considering it are discussed in Chapter 8.[595]

---

[590] [1982] Q.B. 1166.
[591] *Robert Addie & Sons Ltd v Dumbreck* [1929] A.C. 358. See further in rel to trespassers, Ch.8, para.8–140 et seq, below.
[592] [1972] A.C. 877; and see *Southern Portland Cement Ltd v Cooper* [1974] A.C. 623, PC.
[593] For example, *Pannett v P McGuiness & Co Ltd* [1072] 2 Q.B. 599; *Harris v Birkenhead Corporation* [1976] 2 W.L.R. 279, CA.
[594] *Report on liability for damage or injury to trespassers and related questions of occupiers' liability*, Law Comm. Rep. No. 75
[595] See paras 8–148 et seq, below.

5.—THE KIND OF DEFENDANT

(A) Introduction

General. Sometimes the function being carried out by particular kinds or categories of defendant can raise special problems of principle or of policy. In such cases it may be argued that the defendant owes a duty only of limited ambit or, indeed, enjoys an immunity from suit. A number of questions of this kind have already been examined in the context of wider issues. For example, we considered the scope for action against company auditors and company directors when looking at negligence liability for causing economic loss.[596] Other special categories are examined in later chapters.[597] The present focus is on a selection of discrete categories where the nature of the defendant's task or function may operate to limit or negate any duty which he or she may otherwise owe. 2–275

(B) Barristers[598]

Rondel v Worsley. In *Rondel v Worsley*,[599] the House of Lords determined that for reasons of policy a barrister (and a solicitor doing the work of a barrister) was entitled to an immunity from suit in respect of allegations by a former client that the barrister had been negligent in the conduct of the client's case in court and that, but for the negligence, there would have been a better outcome for the client. Arguments in favour of the immunity were that the barrister's duty to the court and to his or her client might sometimes come into conflict, that the "cab rank" principle obliged a barrister to accept any client, however difficult, that an action for negligence against a barrister could necessitate the retrial of the original action, and that the fear of action could cause a barrister to act defensively and unduly hamper the efficient administration of justice. Subsequently, in *Saif Ali v Sydney Mitchell & Co*,[600] the House of Lords expressed reservations about some of the justifications for the immunity, but the "retrial" argument was thought to be compelling. The immunity also was seen as part of the general privilege and immunity attaching to all persons in respect of their participation in proceedings before a court of justice. 2–276

Arthur J S Hall & Co v Simons. A complete reversal of view came with the decision in *Arthur J S Hall & Co v Simons*.[601] The House of Lords held that it was no longer in the public interest in England that the immunity should remain, this unanimously as regards the conduct of civil proceedings and by a 4–3 majority as regards the conduct of criminal proceedings. Lord Steyn considered 2–277

---

[596] See paras 2–190 to 2–195, above.
[597] E.g. occupiers (Ch.8), persons professing some special skill (Ch.9), highway authorities (Ch.10).
[598] See further Ch.9, para. 9–95, below.
[599] [1969] A.C. 191; adopted in *Rees v Sinclair* [1974] 1 N.Z.L.R. 180, NZCA; *Giannarelli v Wraith* (1988) 165 C.L.R. 543, HCA.
[600] [1980] A.C. 198.
[601] [2002] 1 A.C. 615. In *Lai v Chamberlains* [2007] 2 N.Z.L.R. 7 the New Zealand Court of Appeal followed *Hall* and removed the immunity from New Zealand law. In *D'Orta-Ekenaike v Victoria Legal Aid*, (2005) 223 C.L.R. 1, by contrast, the High Court of Australia upheld the principle of barristerial immunity in both civil and criminal cases, declining even to narrow its scope.

the various reasons for the immunity and rejected them all. First, the "cab rank" principle, while a valuable professional rule, could not justify depriving all clients of a remedy. Secondly, the immunities of witnesses and others involved in legal proceedings were founded on the public policy which seeks to encourage freedom of speech in court. This had little if anything to do with the alleged legal policy which requires immunity for negligent acts. Third, there was the public policy against relitigating the decision of a court of competent jurisdiction. This factor could not support an immunity if there was no verdict or decision. If there was, then it might be an abuse of process to initiate a collateral civil challenge by suing advocates in the earlier proceedings. The doctrine of abuse of process could cater for the retrial risk. Finally, there were substantial grounds for questioning whether an immunity was needed to ensure that advocates would respect their duty to the court. And the experience of other countries tended to demonstrate that fears that the public interest would be undermined were unnecessarily pessimistic.

2–278   Barristers and solicitors accordingly can no longer shelter behind an immunity from suit. However, bringing an action may still amount to an abuse of the process of the court. And even if it does not, the claimant must prove both that there was negligence and that this was this was a cause of his or her loss, which requirements may be difficult to satisfy.[602]

(C) Judges

2–279   **Judicial immunity.** Persons exercising judicial functions have a special immunity from suit, whether for negligence, false imprisonment, defamation or otherwise, for they are exempt from any personal civil liability for anything said or done by them in their judicial capacity.[603] Woodhouse J. in the New Zealand Court of Appeal has observed that such immunity is in no sense a private right, the judge being merely the repository of a public right designed to ensure that the administration of justice will be untrammelled by the collateral attacks of disappointed or disaffected litigants.[604] The extent of the immunity, and what amounts to a judicial act or function falling within its ambit, is considered below.[605]

(D) Sporting bodies and sportspeople[606]

2–280   **Sporting bodies.** The organisers of sporting events owe a duty to participants to ensure that the arrangements for an event do not give rise to a foreseeable risk

---

[602] See Ch.9 para.9–99.
[603] *Sirros v Moore* [1975] 1 Q.B. 118; *Nakhla v McCarthy* [1978] 1 N.Z.L.R. 291, NZCA; *Rajski v Powell* (1987) 11 N.S.W.L.R. 522, NSWCA; *Gallo v Dawson* (1989) 63 A.L.J.R. 121; *Harvey v Derrick* [1995] 1 N.Z.L.R. 314, NZCA; *Gazley v Lord Cooke of Thorndon* [1999] 2 N.Z.L.R. 668, NZCA; *Fingleton v The Queen* (2005) 227 C.L.R. 166, at [36]–[39], HCA.
[604] *Nakhla v McCarthy* [1978] 1 N.Z.L.R. 291, NZCA.
[605] See Ch.3 para.3–13, below.
[606] Opie, "Referees' liability in sport: negligent rule enforcement and *Smolden v Whitworth*" (1997) 5 T.L.J. 17; Pickford, "Playing dangerous games" (1998) 6 Tort L Rev 221; Yeo, "Accepting Inherent Risks among sporting participants" (2001) 9 Tort L Rev 114; Anderson, "Personal injury liability in sport: Emerging trends" (2008) 16 Tort L Rev 95.

of injury to those taking part. This is a straightforward duty category, founded ultimately on a simple application of the principles laid down in *Donoghue v Stevenson*. Disputes about liability in this area of activity sometimes take the form of debate about the existence or ambit of the defendant's duty,[607] but generally they involve issues about *breach* of the duty. For example, the organisers of an event at a racing circuit which was intended to allow motorcycle enthusiasts of all abilities to ride the circuit were in breach of duty in failing to ensure that slower riders were not allowed on the track at the same time as faster riders[608]; in light of the small risk, a football club was not liable when a player collided with a police officer supervising the crowd, and nor was the Chief Constable at fault in failing to issue an instruction that police officers facing the crowd for purposes of control should keep an eye on the pitch in the interests of their own safety[609]; the occupiers of a racing circuit were not liable for a fatal accident when, in the course of a race, a driver lost control on a bend and crashed into a tyre-fronted earth bank: the occupiers had reasonably relied upon independent expert advice in relation to the barrier design which was, in any event, reasonably safe[610]; and there was no duty owed by the owners of an activity centre to warn the claimant that safety matting below a "bouldering wall" could induce a false sense of safety, or to provide him with safety training before permitting him to climb on the wall.[611]

Participants. Those participating in a sporting event owe a duty of care to other participants.[612] There is no rule of law that in order to succeed in an action against a fellow competitor the claimant must prove the defendant guilty of some reckless disregard for his or her safety. The standard of care that is expected is reasonable care in relation to the activity in question, taking into account the risks of the activity, the exigencies of the moment and all the circumstances of the case.[613] In *Condon v Basi*,[614] the Court of Appeal held that if one player injured another, because either he had failed to exercise the degree of care which was appropriate in all the circumstances, or because he had acted in a way to which the other could not have been expected to consent, he would be liable for damages in an action in negligence brought by the injured player. "The standard 2–281

---

[607] For example, in *Watson v British Boxing Board of Control* [2001] Q.B. 1134, it was held that the BBBC had a positive duty to arrange for appropriate medical assistance for boxers at the ringside, this by reason of the BBBC's overall controlling position: see para.2–83.

[608] *Craven v Riches* [2002] P.I.Q.R. P320, CA.

[609] *Gillon v Chief Constable of Strathclyde Police, The Times*, November 22, 1996, OH.

[610] *Wattleworth v Goodwood Racing Co Ltd* [2004] P.I.Q.R. P369; and see *R and R (A Child) v Ski Llandudno Ltd* [2001] P.I.Q.R. P70, CA.

[611] *Poppleton v Trustees of the Portsmouth Youth Activities Committee* [2009] P.I.Q.R. P1, CA; and see *Harris v Perry* [2009] 1 W.L.R. 19, CA.

[612] *Rootes v Shelton* [1968] A.L.R. 33.

[613] *Wilks v Cheltenham Car Club* [1971] 1 W.L.R. 668, 673–674, CA; *Evans v Waitemata District Pony Club* [1972] N.Z.L.R. 773, 775–776; *McComiskey v McDermott* [1974] I.R. 75; *Condon v Basi* [1985] 1 W.L.R. 866, 868, CA; *Caldwell v Maguire* [2002] P.I.Q.R. 6, CA; *Blake v Galloway* [2004] 1 W.L.R. 2844, CA.

[614] [1985] 1 W.L.R. 866; *Watson v Gray, The Times*, November 26, 1998; *McCord v Swansea City AFC Ltd, The Times*, February 11, 1997; *Sharp v Highlands and Islands Fire Board* 2005 S.L.T. 855, OH; and see Khan & Wolfgarten, "Liability for Foul Play" 129 S.J. 859; McEwan, "Playing the Game: Negligence in Sport" 130 S.J. 581; Toczek, "A case of foul play" 152 N.L.J. 868; McArdle, "The enduring legacy of 'reckless disregard' " 34 CLWR 316.

is objective but objective in a different set of circumstances. Thus there will of course be a higher degree of care required of a player in a First Division football match than of a player in a local league football match."[615] In the instant case, a foul tackle by the defendant during a game of soccer resulted in the plaintiff sustaining a fractured leg and this, it was held, was a breach of the defendant's duty of care. But liability was not established where two fellow jockeys left insufficient room for a pursuing horse to come along the inside rail, as a result of which the horse fell and the claimant, on a following horse, sustained serious injury: there was no liability for errors of judgment, lapses or oversights of which any participant might be guilty in the context of a fast-moving contest.[616] Similar considerations have applied to injuries suffered while the victims were water-skiing,[617] playing golf,[618] playing games of tag,[619] and even ballroom dancing.[620]

2–282 Competitors in sporting events can also owe a duty of care to those watching them. So a competitor in a race, even though going all out to win, owes a duty of care towards a spectator watching the event.[621] But the question of breach once again must be assessed in light of all the circumstances. A performer who involves a member of the audience in the performance can owe a duty of care to preserve the subject from any reasonably foreseeable harm. However, there was no breach of the duty where a hypnotist had no reason to foresee a risk that his subject might suffer schizophrenia or other lasting physical effect from hypnosis.[622]

2–283 **Referees.** Those who referee or otherwise control sports can be liable for any failure to display reasonable competence which creates a reasonably foreseeable risk of injury to a participant, if that risk materialises and injury results.[623] But the circumstances in which liability arises will be rare. "Full account must be taken of the factual context in which a referee exercises his functions, and he could not

---

[615] *Condon Basi* [1985] 1 W.L.R. 866, at 868, per Sir John Donaldson M.R.
[616] *Caldwell v Maguire and Fitzgerald* [2002] P.I.Q.R. P28, CA; McArdle and James, "Are you experienced? 'Playing cultures', sporting rules and personal injury litigation after *Caldwell v Maguire*" (2005) 13 Tort L Rev 193.
[617] *Rootes v Shelton* [1968] A.L.R. 33, HCA.
[618] *Potter v Carlisle and Cliftonville Golf Club Ltd* [1939] N Ir 114; *Brewer v Delo* [1967] 1 Lloyd's Rep. 488; *Ellison v Rogers* [1968] 1 O.R. 501; *Clark v Welsh* [1975] (4) SA 484; see also Ch.3, para.00; *Feeney v Lyall* [1991] S.L.T. 156; *Lewis v Buckpool Golf Club* (1993) S.L.T. 43; *Pearson v Lightning, The Times,* April 30, 1998, CA. Golf in Australia has its own special hazards: see Mulheron, "Golf, kangaroos and negligence 'down under' " 144 S.J. 494, commenting on *Shorten v Grafton District Golf Club Ltd,* Unreported, March 23, 2000, NSWCA, (small boy not warned of danger from kangaroos feeding in the rough of a golf course where he was searching for his ball).
[619] *Orchard v Lee* [2009] P.I.Q.R. P16, CA; Weir, "Child's play" 159 N.L.J. 729.
[620] *Spry v Plowright, The Times,* March 14, 1988.
[621] *Wilks v Cheltenham Homeguard Motor Cycle & Light Car Club* [1971] 1 W.L.R. 668; applied in *Evans v Waitemata District Pony Club* [1972] N.Z.L.R. 773.
[622] *Gates v McKenna* [1998] Lloyd's Rep. Med. 405; and see *Howarth v Green* L.T.L.P.I. June 1, 2001.
[623] *Smolden v Whitworth* [1997] P.I.Q.R. P133, CA; *Allport v Wilbraham* [2004] EWCA Civ. 1668; Greenfield and Osborn, "The referees' fear of a penalty" (1996) 12 P.N. 63; Greenfield and Osborn, "Aesthetics, injury and liability in cricket" (1997) 13 P.N. 9; Trichardt and Cilliers, "Rugby administrators take note—a recent development in Antipodean law" (1999) 15 P.N. 153; Samuels, "Rugby injuries: liability of the college or school" (2003) 71 Med. Leg. J. 85.

properly be held liable for errors of judgment, oversights or lapses of which any referee might be guilty in the context of a fast-moving and vigorous contest."[624] Even so, in *Vowles v Evans*[625] the amateur referee of an amateur rugby union game was held negligent in failing to order non-contested scrummages, over the objections of the teams, where the loose-head prop of one team had to leave the field after injury and there was no experienced or trained front row forward to take his place in the scrum. A set scrum followed in which the claimant sustained permanent tetraplegia. The scrum itself was properly controlled and there was no shortcoming in the referee's general control of the game but his failure to require non-contested scrummages was a material cause of the claimant's injury and liability should follow.

(E) Public bodies

(i) *Introduction*

Generally. A public body which is alleged to have caused damage to the   **2–284** claimant frequently will have been purporting to exercise powers given to it by Parliament, and in that event an action for breach of statutory duty sometimes may lie. Liability for such a breach of duty does not depend on proving that the defendant has been careless or negligent. Rather, it must be shown that Parliament intended to confer a private right of action on a person who has suffered harm as a result of a breach of the duty, together with the further requirements that the duty on the defendant was owed to the claimant and that the damage was of a kind that the statute was designed to prevent. Breach of statutory duty is addressed in a later chapter, and, as will be seen, the courts are prepared to find the requisite intention and the other elements to liability only in limited circumstances.[626] However, quite apart from this cause of action, it is clear that negligent conduct by a public body may give rise to liability in negligence at common law.

The fact that a public body is engaged in exercising a statutory power is not   **2–285** of itself an answer to an allegation of negligence, but at the same time the careless performance of a statutory duty or power does not of itself create any liability for negligence. In *Gorringe v Calderdale Metropolitan Borough Council*,[627] Lord Scott maintained that where a statutory duty does not give rise to a private law right to sue for breach, the duty cannot create a duty of care that would not have been owed at common law if the statute were not there. Accordingly, the claimant has to show that the circumstances are such that there is a duty of care at common law. And the first question is the basis in principle for imposing this duty.

(ii) *Duty in public law*

Public law concepts. It is axiomatic that public bodies owe public law duties,   **2–286** enforceable by writs of certiorari, prohibition and mandamus, to give proper

---

[624] *Smolden v Whitworth* [1997] P.I.Q.R. P133, CA, at P139.
[625] [2003] 1 W.L.R. 1607, CA; Elvin, "Liability for negligent refereeing of a rugby match" (2003) 119 L.Q.R. 560.
[626] See Ch.12 para.12–04 et seq below.
[627] [2004] 1 W.L.R. 1057, at [71], HL.

consideration whether to act in any particular circumstances and, if action is decided, to act within power. On occasion these duties have been seen as providing the basis for imposing a duty of care in private law. On this view the conduct of a public body must be unlawful and outside the ambit of any statutory discretion before it can come under a duty, actionable in damages, to a victim of its conduct. In particular, in *X (Minors) v Bedfordshire County Council*,[628] Lord Browne-Wilkinson said that where Parliament has conferred a statutory discretion on a public authority, it is for that authority, not for the courts, to exercise the discretion; nothing which the authority does within the ambit of the discretion can be actionable at common law. But if the decision complained of falls outside the statutory discretion it *can* (but not necessarily will) give rise to common law liability, this depending on issues of justiciability.[629] So on this view the initial inquiry is into the question whether the conduct was within or outside power.

2–287   Again, in *Stovin v Wise*[630] Lord Hoffmann recognised that public bodies entrusted with statutory powers cannot simply ignore the existence and possible use of those powers. Rather they have a duty in public law, enforceable by mandamus, to consider their exercise in an appropriate case. In his view this duty was also the appropriate foundation for any duty in private law to act to prevent harm, giving rise to a claim for damages for failure to do so. Yet his Lordship recognised that a common law "ought" could not easily be derived from a statutory "may". He thought that there should be two minimum preconditions for basing a duty of care on the existence of a statutory power. These were, first, that it would in the circumstances have been irrational not to have exercised the power, so that there was in effect a public law duty to act, and secondly, that there were exceptional grounds for holding that the policy of the statute required compensation to be paid to persons who suffered loss because the power was not exercised.

2–288   **Distinction between public and private law.** The approach taken in *X (Minors)* and *Stovin* tends to conflate the two quite different questions of whether conduct is lawful and whether conduct is actionable in damages. In *Crimmins v Stevedoring Industry Finance Committee*,[631] a decision of the High Court of Australia, McHugh J. noted that public law concepts of duty and private law concepts of duty are informed by different rationales. He said that the negligent exercise of a statutory power is not immune from liability simply because it was within power, nor is it actionable in negligence simply because it is ultra vires.

2–289   The crucial point is that whether or not conduct is within power has no necessary connection with whether or not there is a private law remedy in damages. A public law remedy as applied to the holder of a statutory discretion does not impose a duty to do specific things; it simply requires the holder to act

---

[628] [1995] 2 A.C. 633; see also *Home Office v Dorset Yacht Co Ltd* [1970] A.C. 1004, 1031 per Lord Reid; *Anns v London Borough of Merton* [1978] A.C. 728, 755 per Lord Wilberforce.
[629] See para.2–296, below.
[630] [1996] A.C. 923; Harris "Powers into duties—a small breach in the *East Suffolk* wall" (1997) 113 L.Q.R. 398.
[631] (1999) 200 C.L.R. 1, [82]; and see also at [218] per Kirby J., HCA; and see *Attorney-General v Body Corporate No. 200200* [2007] 1 N.Z.L.R. 95, [48]-[49], NZCA.

reasonably or rationally in deciding whether to do those things.[632] But if damages are awarded, it is implicit that the authority should have acted to prevent the harm. So the court, not the authority, determines what, if anything, should have been done. This of course is what a court has to decide in any private law action for damages.

In the United Kingdom a public law analysis has not been rejected in explicit terms, but in a number of decisions of the House of Lords the question whether a decision was within power has not been treated as determinative. Rather, their Lordships have applied common law concepts of negligence, not public law concepts of irrationality.[633] So it has become tolerably clear that a duty on the part of public bodies to take care can be founded on ordinary principles of negligence liability.   2–290

Statutory discretion and breach of duty. While not determinative of the presence or absence of a duty of care, whether a public body has acted rationally or within the ambit of a statutory discretion is relevant in determining whether an authority is in *breach* of a duty which has been held to exist on the application of ordinary principle. Indeed, there is a direct analogy with the question whether a professional or skilled person took reasonable care in exercising his or her professional judgment.[634] The professional person is not bound to ensure that he or she has made the right decision or to guarantee success in any particular venture. Rather, his or her obligation is to speak or to act within the boundaries reasonably to be expected of a person claiming skill and competence in the particular area. Whether a public or a private defendant is involved, the same kind of question can be asked in relation to any acts or decisions involving the exercise of judgment. In the case of a public body the question is whether a decision was reasonably open to the defendant or, conversely, whether it was outside the range of decisions that a reasonable person charged with the activity concerned could have made.   2–291

Determining whether a duty has been discharged need not involve elaborate inquiry. It would seem to be sufficient for the defendant to point to the existence of relevant discretionary considerations and show that they had properly been taken into account. The question would be whether the particular exercise of discretion was reasonably open to the defendant, not whether it was in some sense right or wrong. And the degree of care expected of a public body in meeting the standard of reasonableness must be determined in the light of its obligation to carry out various statutory functions and its inability simply to desist from any exercise of its responsibilities.[635] So the funding and other resources which are available to meet the demands which are made upon the   2–292

---

[632] "Mandamus will compel proper consideration by the authority of its discretion, but that is all": *Sutherland Shire Council v Murphy* (1985) 157 C.L.R. 424, 465 per Mason J., HCA.
[633] *Barrett v Enfield LBC* [2001] 2 A.C. 550; *Phelps v Hillingdon LBC* [2001] 2 A.C. 619; *Gorringe v Calderdale MBC* [2004] 1 W.L.R. 1057, [4]–[5].
[634] See Ch.9, para.9–02, below.
[635] Dugdale, "Public authority liability: to what standard?" (1994) 2 Tort L Rev. 143.

public body are very relevant.[636] Whether the duty has been discharged has to be determined subjectively in relation to the particular defendant being sued.

2–293   On occasion a public body may owe a private law duty of care which requires it to exercise its public law discretion, although only if that can be done consistently with the full performance of its public law obligations. Such was the case where the claimant, a former head teacher of a multi-racial primary school, suffered psychiatric injury arising out of a campaign of harassment and intimidation by members of the school's board of governors, and sued her employer for failing to intervene to protect her and the school from this bullying conduct. The court held that there had been a serious breakdown in the way the school was governed, that the defendant's statutory duty was to correct that position, and that the duty of care owed by the defendant as the claimant's employer marched in step with its public law obligations. In the circumstances, the defendant's public law response was inadequate and was also in breach of its common law duty of care.[637]

(iii) *Duty in private law*

2–294   **Generally.** Special problems can arise when considering the liability of a public body when it has been alleged to have been negligent in its performance as a public authority, as opposed, say, to its status as an occupier or employer, which are subjects dealt with in subsequent chapters.[638] One concern is whether, in deciding a claim for negligence, a court risks overstepping its role in adjudicating between disputing parties and improperly trespasses into a non-justiciable or political sphere. Another, core, concern stems from the possible breadth of liability if a duty of care is imposed. Public bodies frequently have wide-ranging duties and powers which can impact on the community at large in all kinds of ways. They cannot be open to action by all who might be harmed in some way by the negligent exercise or non-exercise of their statutory responsibilities. Again, a court must be satisfied, for example, that any duty that it might recognise would operate coherently in relation to the statutory context, existing common law principles and the legal system as a whole. And no doubt many other concerns can arise on the facts of a particular case.[639]

2–295   Accordingly, just as in other contexts, the mere fact that a person, in this case a public officer or body, may have acted negligently in some general sense and

---

[636] See generally *Just v British Columbia* [1989] 2 S.C.R. 1228, 1243–1244, SCC; *Stovin v Wise* [1996] A.C. 923, 956–957; *Pyrenees Shire Council v Day* (1998) 192 C.L.R. 330, 371, 394, HCA; *Kent v Griffiths* [2000] 2 W.L.R. 1158, 1171, CA; *Hill v Hamilton-Wentworth Regional Police Services Board* [2007] 3 S.C.R. 129, [51]–[54], SCC; *Foley v Shamess* (2008) 297 D.L.R. (4th) 287, Ont CA; *Couch v Attorney-General* [2008] 3 N.Z.L.R. 725, [34]–[36], [58], NZSC.
[637] *Connor v Surrey CC* [2010] EWCA Civ. 286.
[638] Ch.8 and 11 respectively, below.
[639] In *W v Home Office* [1997] Imm. A.R. 302, CA, Lord Woolf M.R. said that relevant considerations included whether a potential conflict could arise between carrying out the public duty and acting defensively in fear that an action may be brought, whether it was necessary to reinforce the general sense of public duty by the imposition of liability, whether a substantial number of claims might ensue, thereby diverting attention from the demands of public service, and whether other private or public remedies were available.

caused loss is by no means sufficient for a duty to be imposed. Rather, applying the threefold test in *Caparo Industries Plc v Dickman*,[640] the claimant must show that the harm was foreseeable, that the relationship between the defendant and the claimant was sufficiently proximate, and that it would be fair, just and reasonable to impose a duty of care of the scope for which the claimant contends. In determining these questions the same techniques and controlling principles are used as have already been seen in operation in cases involving private defendants.

(iv) *Justiciability*

Policy matters and operational matters. Some leading decisions hold that it is necessary to distinguish between complaints against public bodies about the broad merits of a decision which is made in the exercise of a statutory power, and complaints about the manner in which a discretionary decision has been implemented in practice. A duty may be owed in respect of "operational" matters but not in respect of matters of "policy" or "discretion" which it is the function of the public body, not the court, to determine. The justification arises out of the proper relationship between judicial and executive power. Negligence actions should not be used to impugn a discretionary decision taken in the light of policy concerns, for the discretion is that of the public body, not the court. For a court to second guess the discretionary decision of a public body and to substitute its own discretion would be to usurp the legitimate functions of that body. However, the objection does not apply once a policy decision has actually been made, and the question is whether it has been put into effect with all due care. The court does not presume to question the policy, but simply decides whether the public body has been negligent in the manner in which it has brought that policy into effect. **2-296**

A distinction between policy matters and operational matters was initially developed in the House of Lords,[641] and was then taken up in Canada,[642] New Zealand,[643] and (to a limited extent) Australia.[644] But doubts also were expressed, with the distinction being described as "difficult" and "unhelpful".[645] The core **2-297**

---

[640] [1990] 2 A.C. 905: see further at para.2–19, above.

[641] *Dorset Yacht Co Ltd v Home Office* [1970] A.C. 1004, 1067; *Anns v London Borough of Merton* [1978] A.C. 728, 754; *X (Minors) v Bedfordshire County Council* [1995] 2 A.C. 633. Its origins are to be found in American jurisprudence: see, in particular, *Dalehite v US* 346 US 15 (1953); *Indian Towing Co Inc v US* 350 US 61 (1955).

[642] *Welbridge Holdings Ltd v Winnipeg (City)* [1971] S.C.R. 957, SCC; *City of Kamloops v Nielsen* [1984] 2 S.C.R. 2, SCC; *Just v British Columbia* [1989] 2 S.C.R. 1228, SCC; *Brown v British Columbia* [1994] 1 S.C.R. 420, SCC; *Swinamer v Nova Scotia (Attorney-General)* [1994] 1 S.C.R. 445, SCC; *Ingles v Tutkaluk Construction Ltd* [2000] 1 S.C.R. 298, SCC; *Cooper v Hobart* [2001] 3 S.C.R. 537, SCC; *Holland v Saskatchewan* [2008] 2 S.C.R. 551, SCC.

[643] *Takaro Properties Ltd v Rowling* [1978] 2 N.Z.L.R. 314, NZCA; [1986] 1 N.Z.L.R. 22, NZCA; [1987] 2 N.Z.L.R. 700, PC; and see *Gisborne District Council v Port Gisborne Ltd* [2007] N.Z.C.A. 344, NZCA.

[644] *Sutherland Shire Council v Heyman* (1985) 157 C.L.R. 424, 442, 468, 500, HCA; *Pyrenees Shire Council v Day* (1998) 192 C.L.R. 330, 357–358, 425–426, HCA; *Romeo v Conservation Commission of the Northern Territory* (1998) 192 C.L.R. 431, 484–485, HCA; *Crimmins v Stevedoring Industry Finance Committee* (1999) 200 C.L.R. 1, [87], [292], HCA.

[645] *Pyrenees Shire Council v Day* (1998) 192 C.L.R. 330, 491–492, HCA; *Romeo v Conservation Commission of the Northern Territory* (1998) 192 C.L.R. 431, 393–394, HCA.

objection, articulated by the US Supreme Court in *US v Gaubert*,[646] is that discretionary acts involving choice or judgment are not concerned exclusively with policy-making or planning functions, and that day-to-day decisions regularly require judgment as to which of a permissible range of courses is the wisest. As was pointed out by Lord Hoffmann in *Stovin v Wise*,[647] virtually any activity by a public body involves making decisions about priorities and resources. The policy/operational distinction did not provide a reliable guide as to where a dividing line ought to be drawn.

2–298   **Justiciability.** In *Rowling v Takaro Properties Ltd*,[648] Lord Keith formulated another test, asking whether or not the question before the court was suitable for judicial resolution, and in more recent cases this usually has been seen as the appropriate focus for the inquiry.[649] In *Barrett v Enfield London Borough Council*,[650] Lord Slynn and Lord Hutton both thought that the ultimate question is whether the particular issue is justiciable or whether the court should accept that it has no part to play. Whether an authority has acted within its discretion and the policy/operational distinction were guides in deciding that question. A similar approach was taken in *Phelps v Hillingdon LBC*.[651] Their Lordships recognised that a duty could be owed with respect to conduct carried out within the ambit of a statutory discretion. The policy/operational distinction and whether an issue was justiciable could provide a guide towards identifying cases where a duty might be thought to be inappropriate. At issue in this case was alleged negligence by a local education authority or its employees in the provision of educational services for children at school. It was held that the claim did not involve non-justiciable questions, and that it could be resolved by the application of ordinary principles relating to the duty of care owed by professional persons. Accordingly, an educational psychologist who failed to diagnose a child as dyslexic owed, and was in breach of, a duty to that child.[652]

2–299   **Political matters.** A further possible test is to ask whether a complaint involves political considerations. Decisions as to raising revenue and setting priorities in the allocation of public funds between competing claims on scarce resources, or about the extent of government regulation of private and commercial behaviour that was proper, may be regarded as essentially political and for that reason non-justiciable. An example is the decision of the High Court of

---

[646] 111 S Ct 1267 (1991).

[647] [1996] A.C. 923.

[648] [1988] A.C. 473, PC.

[649] *Rowling v Takaro* was applied in *Lonrho v Tebbit* [1992] 4 All E.R. 280, CA, Ch.3 para.3–13 below.

[650] [2001] 2 A.C. 550.

[651] [2001] 2 A.C. 619.

[652] Claims of this kind are likely to face considerable difficulties of proof in relation to causation and quantum of damage: see, for example, *Thurkettle v Suffolk CC* [1998] C.L.Y. 3944; *Jarvis v Hampshire CC*, *The Times*, November 23, 1999, CA; *DN v Greenwich LBC* [2004] EWCA Civ 1659; *Clarke v Devon CC* [2005] 2 F.L.R. 747, CA (sufficient that remedial teaching would have made "a real difference"). In *Carty v Croydon LBC* [2005] 1 W.L.R. 2312 at [43], CA, Dyson L.J. recognised that the difficulties in making decisions about children with special educational needs were such that a court would usually only hold that it was fair, just and reasonable to impose a duty of care to avoid decisions that were plainly and obviously wrong. See further Ch.9 para.9–185.

Australia in *Graham Barclay Oysters Pty Ltd v Ryan*.[653] The claimant was one of a large number of persons who had contracted the hepatitis A virus after consuming oysters which had been grown commercially in a lake in New South Wales. The oysters had been harvested from water polluted by human faeces following heavy rain in the catchment area surrounding the lake. The claimant alleged, inter alia, that the state of New South Wales was liable in negligence for failing to prevent the contamination or reduce the risk of it occurring. However, the High Court held unanimously that the state was under no private law duty of care, and Gleeson C.J. founded his judgment on the political nature of the complaint. The evidence showed that the extent of state government involvement in oyster quality control was a matter of policy, that it received attention at the highest level, that it had substantial budgetary implications and that it involved government concern to encourage an important primary industry. This demonstrated that the proposition that the state had a legal duty of care to exercise greater control could not be supported, for it took the debate into the area of political judgment.

(v) *Omissions to act*

Generally. Many of the cases concerning failure to prevent harm which were   **2–300** mentioned above in the discussion of omissions involved failures by public bodies. Certainly, the relevant principles can be seen in operation in a large number of decisions involving public or quasi-public bodies charged with exercising regulatory or supervisory responsibilities. It is clear that the mere assumption of a public office or position, coupled with a power to intervene, is no sufficient basis for a duty to take care in private law.[654] Rather, consistently with general principle, there needs to be conduct inducing reliance, or close control over, or a specific assumption of responsibility in relation to, the particular risk of harm or the person that caused the harm. And in all cases it is necessary to consider the proximity of the connection or relationship between the defendant public body and the claimant. There needs to be an assumed responsibility which brings about a special, proximate, relationship between the defendant body and the person affected by its failure to act. There follow some examples falling either side of the line.

The police. A Chief Constable may assume responsibility to take care to   **2–301** safeguard his officers, as in a case where an officer was negligently exposed to a foreseeable risk of injury in the course of a surveillance operation in which he was engaged.[655] Again, the Metropolitan Police Commissioner arguably owed a duty to an officer to take reasonable care to prevent acts of bullying or victimisation by other officers.[656] Responsibility also may be assumed by one police officer to another, as where an officer was attacked in the cells by a violent prisoner and another officer, in close attendance to assist if needed, did not

---

[653] (2003) 211 C.L.R. 540, HCA.
[654] See generally *Gorringe v Calderdale Metropolitan Borough Council* [2004] 1 W.L.R. 1057, HL especially at [17], [32], [70], [88], [102]–[103].
[655] *Donachie v The Chief Constable of the Greater Manchester Police*, *The Times*, May 4, 2004, CA.
[656] *W v Commissioner of Police of the Metropolis* [2000] 1 W.L.R. 1607, HL.

help.[657] But no duty was owed where a junior officer injured by rioters alleged that the police summoned to control them had been negligently deployed: to hold that a duty of care was owed in such circumstances would be significantly detrimental to the control of public order, in that critical decisions which often had to be made by senior officers with little or no time for considered thought would be prejudiced if they were affected by the fear of a potential negligence claim.[658]

2–302   **Hill and Smith.** In third party cases there can be no duty founded simply upon a failure by the police to protect members of the public at no special or particular risk of harm. In *Hill v West Yorkshire Police*,[659] the police did not owe a duty of care to protect members of the public from the attacks of a murderer. Further, in *Osman v Ferguson*,[660] the Court of Appeal held that the police owed no duty to protect even specifically identifiable persons foreseeably at risk from a known assailant, and this view was confirmed in the House of Lords in *Smith v Chief Constable of Sussex Police*.[661] The claimant had informed the police on several occasions of threats to kill made against him by telephone, text and internet by J, his estranged homosexual partner. After the police had taken some limited investigative, as opposed to protective, steps, J attacked the claimant with a hammer, causing very serious injury. The claimant brought an action in negligence against the defendant Chief Constable, but the majority view was that the core principle of *Hill*—that the police owed no common law duty to protect individuals against harm caused by criminals—ought to apply. Lord Hope said that this was justified by the interests of the whole community, the greater public good outweighing any individual hardship. A robust approach in assessing a person as a possible suspect or victim was needed, and making that judgment in any given case should be a matter for the police. But Lord Bingham, dissenting, said that if a member of the public (A) furnished a police officer (B) with apparently credible evidence that a third party whose identity and whereabouts were known presented a specific and imminent threat to his life or physical safety, B owed A a duty to take reasonable steps to assess such threat and, if appropriate, take reasonable steps to prevent it from being exercised.

2–303   The majority left open the possibility that there could be exceptional situations where a duty might be imposed. An example is where police were allegedly negligent in allowing publication of the names of informants, exposing them to threats of harm.[662] Another example, certainly at the limits of liability, may be seen in a Scottish case holding that police officers who coned off one side of a collapsed bridge, but who then left the scene without ensuring that a barrier was in place on the other side, had taken control of the hazard and, accordingly, owed

---

[657] *Costello v Chief Constable of the Northumbria Police* [1999] 1 All E.R. 550, CA.
[658] *Hughes v National Union of Mineworkers* [1991] 4 All E.R. 278.
[659] [1989] A.C. 53; and see *Brooks v Commissioner of Police for the Metropolis* [2005] 1 W.L.R. 1495, HL; see para.2–329, below.
[660] [1993] 4 All E.R. 344, CA; *Alexandrou v Oxford* [1993] 4 All E.R. 328, CA (no duty to member of the public whose burglar alarm system had been activated to take reasonable care to prevent a criminal from causing him to suffer loss).
[661] [2009] 1 A.C. 225.
[662] *Swinney v Chief Constable of Northumbria Police* [1997] Q.B. 464. In *Swinney v Chief Constable of Northumbria Police (No. 2)*, *The Times*, May 25, 1999, the claim failed on the facts, as no breach of duty was established.

a duty to road users likely to be immediately and directly affected by that hazard.[663] However, where the police have not actually created a new hazard a duty generally has been denied. So there was no liability where the police received information about malfunctioning traffic lights at a road junction, but did not act on that information,[664] nor where the police were made aware that a hazard, created by others, had appeared on the highway and they failed to give warnings to road users.[665]

Prison authorities. Those responsible for custodial establishments do not   **2–304** owe to the public at large any general duty of care to keep those in their custody in detention, but particular duties may arise where some act or omission gives rise to a foreseeable risk of damage or injury to some identifiable person or class of persons.[666] For example, in *Dorset Yacht Co Ltd v Home Office*[667] the House of Lords held that a prison authority, which had taken some youths to an island for the purpose of training, owed a duty of care to the owner of a yacht when the youths were negligently allowed to escape and cause damage to the yacht. The duty was based on the defendant's power of control over the youths, coupled with the close and immediate link between the failure to exercise control and the damage which was suffered. However, a duty cannot be extended to remote victims of another's wrongdoing. So the duty in *Dorset Yacht* was owed to property owners in the vicinity of the escape: it could not be extended to anyone who suffered damage caused by the prisoners at some time in the future. In an Australian case, a prison authority was not liable to the owner of a newsagency who was held up and terrorised by an escaped prisoner two months after the escape.[668]

A duty is also owed by a prison authority to take such care as is reasonable for   **2–305** the safety of its prisoners,[669] and this includes measures to preserve them safe from attack from fellow prisoners.[670] The duty arguably extends to protecting a prisoner from foreseeable psychiatric injury,[671] but not to preventing a prisoner from injuring himself when trying to escape.[672] A duty of care is also owed to those employed to control and supervise prisoners, not to expose them to foreseeable and avoidable risk. Plainly, employment in the prison service carries

---

[663] *Gibson v Orr* [1999] S.C.; Thomson, "The demise of *Donoghue* in Scotland" (2000) 8 Tort L Rev 23; and see *O'Rourke v Schacht* [1976] 1 S.C.R. 53, SCC.
[664] *Clough v Bussan (West Yorkshire Police Authority, Third Party)* [1990] 1 All E.R. 431.
[665] *Ancell v McDermott* [1993] 4 All E.R. 355, CA.
[666] *Dorset Yacht Co Ltd v Home Office* [1970] A.C. 1004.
[667] [1970] A.C. 1004.
[668] *State of NSW v Godfrey* [2004] NSWCA 113; and see *Palmer v Tees Health Authority* [2000] P.I.Q.R. P1, CA (no sufficient proximity between claimant and defendant where a patient negligently released from hospital attacked a victim who could not have been identified in advance); *K v Secretary of State for the Home Department, The Times*, July 22, 2002 (no proximity between the Secretary of State and the claimant where, after a deportation order had been made against M upon his conviction for serious offences of a sexual/violent character, he was released into the community and raped the claimant).
[669] *St George v Home Office* [2008] 4 All E.R. 1039, CA.
[670] *Ellis v Home Office* [1953] 2 All E.R. 149; *Porterfield v Home Office, The Times*, March 9, 1988.
[671] *Butchart v Home Office* [2006] 1 W.L.R. 1173, CA.
[672] *Vellino v Chief Constable of Greater Manchester Police* [2002] 1 W.L.R. 218, CA.

with it a high degree of personal risk, and the employer's duty is to take care to reduce such risk to the minimum, consistent with maintaining order and security in a custodial establishment.[673]

2-306   **The probation service.** It is possible that the probation service might owe a duty of care with respect to injury caused by a criminal. An example overseas is *Couch v Attorney-General*,[674] where the victim of a violent assault committed by a criminal while on parole sued the probation service, alleging grossly deficient supervision of the criminal. The assault on the plaintiff, and the murder of three colleagues, took place at the Returned Services Association premises where the victims worked. The criminal had been placed at the RSA for work experience, and he returned there to commit his crimes. It was recognised that the law had traditionally been cautious about imposing duties of care in cases of omission, in cases where a public authority was performing a role for the benefit of the community at large, and in cases where the actions of a third party were the immediate cause of loss. All three features were present. But there was a power of control over the wrongdoer and a relationship indicating a degree of proximity between the parties, suggesting that the claim was at least arguable. The criminal had a known alcohol addiction, he had been allowed to work at premises where significant cash was likely to be present, and he could find out about the security system. This might make the RSA a predictable target, so anyone present there was at greater risk than the general public, and would be particularly vulnerable because of the criminal's known tendency to random violence. The action was not be struck out and could proceed to trial.

2-307   **Local authorities.** A local authority may act in many different capacities in carrying out a variety of different activities. It may owe a duty of care in any such cases, but only where, on ordinary principles, the requirements for a duty are satisfied. So an authority may come under a duty as an occupier of premises[675]; or as landlord in relation to the safety of tenants[676]; or in providing a service[677]; or in giving advice.[678] In particular, where a complaint is of a failure to prevent harm, then there must be a proper foundation for imposing a duty of positive action. So in *Mitchell v Glasgow CC*,[679] as we have seen, a local authority landlord was not liable for failing to prevent one of its tenants from killing another tenant, for no such foundation could be shown. Again, local authority

---

[673] See, for example, *Connor v Secretary of State for Scotland* [2000] Rep. L.R. 18, OH; *Hendrie v Scottish Ministers* 2002 Rep. L.R. 46, OH; and see also *Briscoe v Secretary of State for Scotland* 1997 SC 14; *Grant v Chief Constable of Grampian Police* 2001 Rep. L.R. 74, OH; *Franklin v Chief Constable of Grampian Police* 2001 Rep. L.R. 79, OH.

[674] [2008] 3 N.Z.L.R. 725, NZSC.

[675] See e.g. *Harris v Birkenhead Corporation* [1975] 1 W.L.R. 379, CA; see Ch.7 below generally.

[676] See *Adams v Rhymney Valley District Council* [2000] Lloyd's Rep. P.N. 777, CA, (no breach).

[677] E.g *Ephraim v Newham London Borough Council* [1993] P.I.Q.R. P156, CA (no breach).

[678] See e.g. *W v Essex County Council* [2001] 2 A.C. 592; see para.2–146, above.

[679] [2009] 1 A.C. 874; see para.2–67, above; *X v Hounslow London Borough Council* [2009] 2 F.L.R. 262, CA.

building inspectors owe no duty of care to subsequent purchasers to prevent negligent builders putting up defective houses.[680]

Social welfare officers. A particular example of the duty issue as it applies to **2–308** failures to act by local authorities concerns social welfare officers. In *X v Bedfordshire CC*[681] the House of Lords considered whether a local authority could be liable in negligence for failing to exercise its statutory powers to protect children from parental abuse and neglect. "Policy" issues were not thought to be involved, but the actions were struck out. It was thought that a duty would cut across the whole statutory system for the protection of children at risk, would lead to almost impossible problems in disentangling the liability of the various persons and bodies involved in the process, and might make local authorities act defensively in dealing with children at risk.

Notwithstanding *X*, it is now clear, in a change of view prompted in part by the **2–309** passing of the Human Rights Act 1998,[682] that a duty may be recognised where a particular person or class is put at risk of harm. In *Barrett v Enfield LBC*[683] the House of Lords refused to strike out a claim by a child in care that the defendant local authority had been negligent in failing to protect him from physical, emotional and psychiatric injury while placed with foster parents and in care homes. And as noted above, in *Phelps v Hillingdon LBC*[684] their Lordships upheld a claim against a local authority's educational psychologist for negligence in failing to take reasonable care to diagnose and treat the claimant's learning difficulties and dyslexia. Again, in *D v East Berkshire Community Health NHS Trust*[685] the Court of Appeal held that social workers were obliged to take care to protect a child with whom it was dealing from suffering abuse. The case is also relevant in considering whether a duty could be owed to the suspected parents as well, and we shall return to this question when considering the impact of the statutory context on the duty issue.[686]

Highway authorities. A local authority, in its capacity as highway authority, **2–310** was not originally liable where an accident was caused by its failure to keep the roads in good repair, although it could be liable for acts of repair which had actually been carried out, albeit badly.[687] However, this immunity from liability for nonfeasance was abolished by the Highways (Miscellaneous Provisions) Act

---

[680] *Murphy v Brentwood District Council* [1991] 1 A.C. 398; see para.2–241, above.
[681] [1995] 2 A.C. 633. For subsequent proceedings before the European Court of Human Rights, see para.2–328, below.
[682] See para.2–323, below.
[683] [2001] 2 A.C. 550; *T v Surrey CC* [1994] 4 All E.R. 577, CA; *S v Gloucester CC* [2001] 2 W.L.R. 909, CA.
[684] [2001] 2 A.C. 619.
[685] [2004] Q.B. 558 (on appeal [2005] 2 A.C. 373); Wright, "'Immunity' no more: Child abuse cases and public authority liability in negligence after *D v East Berkshire Community Health NHS Trust*" (2004) 2 P.N. 58; and see *Pierce v Doncaster Metropolitan Borough Council* [2008] 1 F.C.R. 122 (local authority liable for abuse after returning the claimant to the care of his parents following a period in foster care without having first carried out a statutory review).
[686] See para.2–320 below.
[687] *Cowley v Newmarket Local Board* [1892] A.C. 345. See further Ch.10, para.10–01 et seq, below.

1961 which imposed a duty on highway authorities to maintain the highway, subject to a statutory defence.[688]

2–311　　As for the position at common law, in *Gorringe v Calderdale MBC*[689] it was held that a highway authority did not owe an individual user of the road a duty of care to prevent injury allegedly due to its failure to put up a "slow" sign warning of danger. But Lord Hoffmann indicated that an authority which acted so as to create a reasonable expectation about the state of the highway would be under a duty to ensure it did not create a trap for a motorist who drove in reliance upon such an expectation.

2–312　　**Fire services.** Fire authorities established under the Fire Services Act 1947 have statutory power to fight fires, but the existence of this power does not create a common law duty of care to answer a call for help, nor a duty to take care in doing so.[690] However, the fire service may incur liability if, by its actions at the scene, it creates a new or different danger, or if it causes additional damage beyond that which would otherwise have arisen. Accordingly, the fire service was liable for the negligence of an officer who ordered a sprinkler system in a building already alight to be turned off,[691] but not for negligence in failing to maintain fire hydrants in serviceable condition or to find them in good time,[692] or in leaving the scene of a fire which had been successfully extinguished without checking surrounding areas.[693] It has been held, similarly, that there is no duty on a coastguard responding to an emergency at sea.[694]

2–313　　**Ambulance services.** The position of the ambulance service is different. In *Kent v Griffiths*[695] the Court of Appeal held that an ambulance service was under a duty to respond promptly to a call for assistance, on the basis that it was part of the health service. Lord Woolf M.R. said that the ambulance service and its crews were under a duty to provide an ambulance. They were paid out of public

---

[688] The 1961 Act was then repealed and replaced by the Highways Act 1980. See, further, Ch.10 para.10–02 below.

[689] [2004] 1 W.L.R. 1057, HL; Morgan, "Slowing the expansion of public authorities' liability" (2005) 121 L.Q.R. 43; Howarth, "Public authority non-liability: spinning out of control?" (2004) 63 C.L.J. 546; *Sandhar v Department of Transport* [2005] 1 W.L.R. 1632, CA.

[690] *Capital & Counties plc v Hampshire CC* [1997] Q.B. 1007. Four appeals were consolidated, the others being *Digital Equipment Co v Hampshire CC, John Munroe (Acrylics) Ltd v London Fire and Civil Defence Authority* and *Church of Jesus Christ of Latter-Day Saints v Yorkshire Fire and Civil Defence Authority.* See Hartshorne, "The liability in negligence of the fire service—the Court of Appeal decides" (1997) 13 P.N. 53; Bagshaw, "The duties of care of emergency service providers" [1999] L.M.C.L.Q. 71; Harrison, "The emergency services, '999' calls and the duty of care" (2000) 16 P.N. 171; See also Ch.12, paras 12–20, 12–27, below. Compare *Burnett v Grampian Fire and Rescue Service* 2007 S.L.T. 61, OH. Compare also *Pyrenees SC v Day* (1998) 192 C.L.R. 330, where the High Court of Australia imposed a duty on a local authority which had failed to carry out its task of preventing the risk of a fire starting in a faulty fireplace.

[691] *Capital & Counties Plc v Hampshire CC*, n.690, above.

[692] *Church of Jesus Christ of Latter-Day Saints v Yorkshire Fire and Civil Defence Authority*, n.690, above.

[693] *John Munroe (Acrylics) Ltd v London Fire and Civil Defence Authority*, n.690, above.

[694] *OLL Ltd v Secretary of State for the Home Department* [1997] 3 All E.R. 897. See also *Skinner v Secretary of State for Transport, The Times*, January 3, 1995.

[695] [2001] 1 Q.B. 36; Williams, "Litigation against English NHS ambulance services and the rule in *Kent v Griffiths*" (2007) 15 Med. L. Rev. 153.

funds and should not be regarded as mere volunteers whose only obligation was not to add to the damage already suffered. The ambulance service should be regarded in the same way as the health service, where a duty of care normally existed. Its function was materially different from that of the police or fire service, where action in protecting victims of crime or of a fire was part of their general obligations to the public at large in, respectively, reducing crime or preventing fire spreading. And here the only member of the public who could be adversely affected was the claimant, for whom alone the ambulance had been called.

(vi) *Common law context*

Negligence and misfeasance. The common law context can have a sig- **2–314**
nificant influence on whether a public officer of body is under a duty of care. In *Takaro Properties Ltd v Rowling*,[696] the Privy Council considered that there was no duty on a minister to take care to act within power, and Lord Keith contemplated that it would be in the public interest for citizens to be confined to their remedy in those cases where the minister or public body had acted in bad faith. As already mentioned, an inquiry into the ambit of a public body's power is usually inappropriate in considering whether a duty of care is owed. By contrast, it is highly relevant to the question whether a public officer or body is liable in the tort of misfeasance in a public office. Misfeasance requires a deliberate and dishonest abuse of power by a public officer.[697] Mere negligence in acting outside power is not enough for liability. Recognising a duty of care would undercut the requirements for misfeasance. In *Northern Territory v Mengel*,[698] Brennan J. observed that the state of mind of a public officer which is a necessary element of misfeasance defines the legal balance between the officer's duty to ascertain the functions of the office which it is his or her duty to perform and the freedom of the individual from unauthorised interference with interests which the law protects. The balance that is struck is not to be undermined by applying a different standard of liability—namely liability in negligence—where a plaintiff's loss is purely economic and the loss is attributable solely to a public officer's failure to appreciate the absence of power required to authorise the act or omission which caused the loss.

Accordingly, in cases where a claimant alleges negligence by a public body in **2–315**
making a decision a duty of care is likely to be denied. The potential impact on misfeasance may not be clearly articulated as a reason, but nonetheless it may help explain the relevant decisions. Some examples of cases which can be explained on this ground include: a social security officer reaching a decision concerning a claim for unemployment benefit[699]; a minister signing a public

[696] [1988] A.C. 473, PC; and see *Comeau's Sea Foods Ltd v Canada (Minister of Fisheries and Oceans)* [1997] 1 S.C.R. 12, SCC.
[697] *Three Rivers DC v Governor of the Bank of England* [2003] 2 A.C. 1; *Akenzua v Home Office* [2003] 1 W.L.R. 741, CA.
[698] (1995) 185 C.L.R. 307, at 359, HCA.
[699] *Jones v Department of Employment* [1988] 2 W.L.R. 493, CA.

interest immunity certificate[700]; and a child support agency assessing, collecting and enforcing child support payments.[701]

2–316 **Planning and building regulation.** The activities of local authorities in relation to planning and building regulation can provide another example. As a general rule a local authority owes no duty of care in giving information about planning matters[702] or in granting planning permission,[703] or in deciding whether to exercise planning powers under highways legislation.[704] It is possible that a *Hedley Byrne* duty can arise when a local authority employee gives negligent advice in response to an inquiry about planning or building regulation,[705] but, seemingly, something more is required than the ordinary process of giving routine advice to an applicant seeking planning permission, particularly when the applicant is known to have the benefit of professional advice.[706]

2–317 **Negligence and malicious prosecution.** The common law context also can limit the ambit of a duty in fields covered by other torts. A clear example is provided by cases holding that there can be no duty to take care by police or prosecuting authorities in carrying out their investigative and prosecutorial functions.[707] This has been put broadly on the basis that a duty would have an inhibiting effect on the performance of these functions, would divert valuable resources in guarding against and defending civil actions, and would create tensions in the law and impair its coherence. Underlying these concerns is the

---

[700] *Bennett v Commissioner of Police for the Metropolis* [1995] 1 W.L.R. 488.

[701] *Rowley v Secretary of State for Work and Pensions* [2007] 1 W.L.R. 2861, CA.

[702] *Strable v Dartford Borough Council* [1984] J.P.L. 329, CA; *Tidman v Reading BC* [1994] N.P.C. 136; *King v North Cornwall DC* [1995] N.P.C. 21, CA.

[703] *Morrison v Upper Hutt CC* [1998] 2 N.Z.L.R. 331, NZCA; *Bella Vista Resort Ltd v Western Bay of Plenty District Council* [2007] 3 N.Z.L.R. 429, NZCA.

[704] *Stovin v Wise* [1996] A.C. 923; *Lam v Brennan and Borough of Torbay* [1997] P.I.Q.R. 488, CA; cp *Kane v New Forest DC* [2002] 1 W.L.R. 312, where the Court of Appeal considered that a duty could arise where an authority created a danger in the course of exercising its powers under the planning process.

[705] *Lambert v West Devon Borough Council, The Times*, March 27, 1997; cp *Fashion Brokers Ltd v Clarke Hayes* [2000] P.N.L.R. 473, CA. In *Welton v North Cornwall District Council* [1997] 1 W.L.R. 570, CA, an environmental health officer who required unnecessary work to be done to the plaintiff's guest house was held to be liable for giving negligent advice, but arguably any remedy should have been in misfeasance. See further Ch.8 para.8–119, below.

[706] *Haddow v Secretary of State for the Environment, Transport and the Regions* [2000] Env. L.R. 212, CA. In *Bella Vista Resort Ltd v Western Bay of Plenty District Council* [2007] 3 N.Z.L.R. 429, NZCA, Robertson J. thought that there could be no separate claim for misrepresentation arising out of advice given prior to the making of an impugned decision: but William Young P. thought such a claim might be possible.

[707] *Calveley v Chief Constable of Merseyside Police* [1989] A.C. 1228; *Elguzouli-Daf v Commissioner of Police of the Metropolis* [1995] Q.B. 335; *Jain v Trent Strategic Health Authority* [2009] 1 A.C. 853, at [29]-[35], discussed below; *M v Commissioner of Police of the Metropolis, The Times*, January 4, 2009; but see *Welsh v Chief Constable of the Merseyside Police* [1993] 1 All E.R. 692 (specific assumed responsibility). Compare *Odhavji Estate v Woodhouse* [2003] 3 S.C.R. 263, SCC (police chief liable for both misfeasance and negligence in failing to ensure police officers cooperated with inquiry into police shooting); *Hill v Hamilton-Wentworth Regional Police Services Board* (2007) 285 D.L.R. (4th) 620 (claim alleging negligence by the police in the investigation of a crime upheld); Rafferty, "The Canadian Supreme Court's approach to the duty question and the tort of negligent investigation" (2008) 24 P.N. 78; Chamberlain, "Negligent investigation: the end of malicious prosecution in Canada" (2008) 124 L.Q.R. 205.

proper role of the tort of malicious prosecution. The scope of this tort is deliberately limited, in order not to create a disincentive to the prosecution of offenders.[708] The expansion of negligence into the field would tend to undermine that general objective.

(vii) *Statutory context*

Purpose of statute. In developing the law of negligence the courts seek **2–318** consistency with any relevant statutes governing the activity of the public body. Sometimes courts have called in aid the purpose of the empowering statute in deciding whether an action will lie. For example, in *Gorringe v Calderdale MBC*[709] the House of Lords held that one purpose of a statutory provision imposing on local authorities a duty to carry out a programme of measures designed to promote road safety[710] was to ensure that authorities took road safety considerations into account when carrying out their highway functions. This was to be achieved by placing a wide public law duty, in the nature of a target duty, on the authorities concerned. The statute could not be read as intended to create specific duties owed to individuals.

Consistency with statute. In other cases the question has been whether a duty **2–319** of care is consistent with what the statute requires or empowers the public body to do. A duty may well be imposed if it would buttress and support the legislative policy, but denied if it would be likely to cut across or discourage performance of the statutory functions.

Child abuse cases. Certain child abuse cases provide clear examples of the **2–320** influence of the statutory setting. In *D v East Berkshire Community Health NHS Trust*[711] parents brought actions against healthcare authorities, and in one case a local authority, claiming damages for psychiatric harm caused by unfounded allegations that the parents had abused their children. The actions were dismissed at first instance, on appeal to the Court of Appeal and on further appeal to the House of Lords. Lord Nicholls maintained that health professionals should not be subject to potentially conflicting duties when deciding whether a child may have been abused, or when deciding whether their doubts should be communicated to others, or when deciding what further investigatory or protective steps should be taken. It would fundamentally alter the balance in this area of the law if those charged with protecting a child against criminal conduct owed suspected perpetrators the duty that was suggested. Rather, health and other professionals owed a suspected parent a duty to investigate alleged abuse in good faith. Such a parent was thereby afforded a similar level of protection to those suspected of committing crimes. In so deciding, his Lordship drew attention to the words of

---

[708] *South Pacific Manufacturing Co Ltd v New Zealand Security Consultants and Investigations Ltd* [1992] 2 N.Z.L.R. 282, NZCA.
[709] [2004] 1 W.L.R. 1057, HL.
[710] Road Traffic Act 1988 s.39(2).
[711] [2005] 2 A.C. 373; Case, "The accused strikes back: the negligence action and erroneous allegations of child abuse" (2005) 21 P.N. 214; and see *D v Bury Metropolitan MBC* [2006] 1 W.L.R. 917, CA; *L v Reading Borough Council* [2008] F.C.R. 295, CA.

Lord Bridge,[712] that "where no action for malicious prosecution would lie, it would be strange indeed if an acquitted defendant could recover damages for negligent investigation". Lord Nicholls was satisfied that this must be equally true of a person who has been suspected but not prosecuted. So while a duty was owed to a child known to be at risk (as determined by the Court of Appeal), both the common law and the statutory context pointed away from any duty owed to the parents.[713]

2–321   The same or a similar approach has been taken in decisions in other common law countries, claims of this kind failing in Australia,[714] Canada[715] and New Zealand.[716] As expressed by Lord Nicholls on appeal to the Privy Council in the New Zealand decision, in an inquiry into an abuse allegation the interests of the alleged perpetrator and of the children as the alleged victims are poles apart.

2–322   **Other protective powers.** Like reasoning was used by the House of Lords in *Jain v Trent Strategic HA*.[717] The defendant health authority obtained an ex parte order under the Registered Homes Act 1984 for the cancellation of the registration of the claimant's nursing home after presenting highly misleading information to the magistrate who made the order. The decision was overturned on appeal, but the claimants were unable to resuscitate their business and they became bankrupt. They then sued Trent for negligence in applying for the order of cancellation. It was held by the House of Lords, in a unanimous decision, that Trent owed no duty of care to the owners. Lord Scott said that where action is taken by a state authority under statutory powers designed for the benefit or protection of a particular class of persons, a tortious duty of care will not be held to be owed by the authority to others whose interests may be adversely affected by the statutory power. The reason was that the imposition of such a duty would or might inhibit the exercise of statutory powers and be potentially adverse to the interests of the class of persons the powers were designed to benefit or protect. And here the purpose of the powers under the 1984 Act was to protect the interests of residents in nursing homes, not the economic interests of owners. Again, no duty to an opposing party could arise in the conduct of, or the steps taken in preparation for, judicial proceedings before a court or tribunal. The protection of parties to litigation from damage caused to them by the litigation had to depend upon the control exercised by the court or tribunal and the rules

---

[712] *Calveley v Chief Constable of Merseyside Police* [1989] A.C. 1228, 1238.
[713] See also *A v Essex County Council* [2004] 1 W.L.R. 1881, CA, where the question was whether an adoption agency owed a duty to adoptive parents to warn them about the violent behaviour of the child they were about to adopt. Hale L.J. said that the agency owed no general duty in deciding what information was to be conveyed to prospective adopters. The statutory framework was very closely regulated with a view to ensuring best contemporary practice in a difficult and sensitive exercise in social engineering. A balance needed to be struck between the interests of the prospective adopters, the birth parents and the child, but the agency's first duty was to the child. But having taken a decision to give information, there was a duty to take care it was both given and received. On the facts there was a breach of this duty, although liability only extended up to the date of the adoption order. It would be contrary to the statutory scheme for liability to continue thereafter.
[714] *Sullivan v Moody* (2001) 207 C.L.R. 562, HCA.
[715] *D(B) v Halton Region Children's Aid Society* (2007) 284 D.L.R. (4th) 682, SCC.
[716] *B v Attorney-General* [2003] 4 All E.R. 833, PC.
[717] [2009] 1 A.C. 853.

and procedures under which the litigation was conducted. In the instant case the statutory requirements before an ex parte order could be made were sadly deficient, but the remedy lay in the formulation of appropriate safeguards, not in the creation of an inappropriate duty of care.

(viii) *Impact of European law*

General. Recent developments concerning the liability in negligence of public bodies have been heavily influenced by European law. The key development has been the passing of the Human Rights Act 1998, which gives the European Convention on Human Rights "further effect" in English law. 2-323

Certain provisions of the Act are concerned specifically with the liability of public bodies. It is unlawful for a public authority to act in a way which is incompatible with a Convention right, and the victim may bring proceedings in which a court may grant relief, which may include damages.[718] A court is a public authority for the purpose of the Act, yet the act of a court may not be subject to an award of damages.[719] Quite what the requirement that the court should not act incompatibly with the Convention means in this context is not entirely clear.[720] At least the courts must give effect to Convention rights by means of the mechanisms in the Human Rights Act. But what of the effect of the Convention on the common law? Seemingly a court is not required to declare and apply the common law in a way which is necessarily compatible with Convention rights. Otherwise the common law would be no more than a subsidiary regime shaped by the Convention. The two systems are in fact quite different. The European Convention is expressed in terms of very broad, general rights, but the common law builds up principle from case to case. Yet the Act has had more than procedural significance and certainly has had *some* impact on the substance of the common law. This is seen in particular in the cases involving police procedures and those involving social workers investigating child abuse. 2-324

Article 6. The question as to the relationship between the Convention and the common law has arisen in relation to the application of art.6 of the Convention. This provides that in the determination of civil rights and obligations, everyone is entitled to a fair and public hearing by an independent and impartial tribunal established by law. The right may be restricted or limited, yet the aim of the limitation must be legitimate, and the limitation must be proportionate to the aim. 2-325

Osman v UK. Article 6 on its face is procedural and does not guarantee any particular content to the rights in question, yet in *Osman v UK*[721] the European Court of Human Rights held that the decision of the Court of Appeal in applying 2-326

---

[718] Human Rights Act 1998 s.8(3).
[719] Human Rights Act 1998 s.9.
[720] See generally *Winfield and Jolowicz on Tort*, 17th edn 2006, paras 2.9–2.14.
[721] (1998) 29 E.H.R.R. 245, ECHR; de Prez, "Proportionality, symmetry and competing public policy arguments: the police force and civil immunity" (2000) 16 P.N. 217; Bowen, "A terrible misunderstanding? *Osman v UK* and the law of negligence" (2001) S.L.T. 7, 59.

the rule in *Hill v West Yorkshire Police*[722] and striking out the claim amounted to a violation of art.6. The court reasoned that the striking out deprived the claimant of effective access to the court in the determination of her civil right through the application of an exclusionary rule protecting the police from negligence actions in relation to the prevention and detection of crime. The Court of Appeal's decision had the effect of conferring a blanket immunity on the police, and this was excessive and disproportionate to the legitimate aim of preserving the efficiency of a vital sector of public service.

2–327   The decision caused some consternation in this jurisdiction and was attacked in the House of Lords. In *Barrett v Enfield LBC*,[723] Lord Browne-Wilkinson said that the European Court of Human Rights treated the claimant as having a substantive right in civil law which he was being prevented from asserting in a court. But in English law the existence of such a right was decided as a question of law, taking into account policy considerations. In striking out proceedings the claim did not proceed to trial if the court determined that the claimant could not succeed as a matter of law.

2–328   **Z v UK.** In *Z v UK*[724] (in further proceedings following the House of Lords decision in *X v Bedfordshire CC*[725]) the European Court accepted that its ruling in *Osman* was based on an understanding of the law of negligence "which has to be reviewed in the light of clarifications subsequently made by the domestic courts and notably the House of Lords." The Court was satisfied that the law as developed in *Caparo Industries Plc v Dickman*,[726] laying down the criterion of what was fair, just and reasonable, did not disclose the operation of an immunity and there was no restriction on access to a court. The claimant had had a hearing in which relevant policy concerns were weighed. Article 6 did not in itself guarantee any particular content for civil rights and obligations in national law, and to the extent that the claim was based on its breach the Court held that it should fail.[727]

2–329   **Brooks v MPC.** In *Brooks v Metropolitan Police Commissioner*[728] the claimant, who was present when his friend was murdered in a racially motivated attack, alleged negligence in the way in which he had been treated by the police following the murder and in the manner in which the investigation into the

---

[722] [1989] A.C. 53; see para.2–302 above.

[723] [2001] 2 A.C. 550 at 558–560.

[724] [2001] 2 F.L.R. 612. See also *TP v United Kingdom* [2001] E.C.H.R. 28945/95 (allegation of negligence in measures taken by local authority in receiving a child into care). See further Kingscote, "Have human rights principles eroded local authority immunity" 151 N.L.J. 844. In a different context see also *Reid v United Kingdom*, ECHR 33221/96, Unreported, June 26, 2001 (in relation to actions in negligence against the Crown Prosecution Service).

[725] As to which see para.2–308, above.

[726] [1990] 2 A.C. 605.

[727] However, although there was no breach of art.6 the ECHR found that there had been a violation of arts 3 and 13, the latter because the available remedies for the applicants, who had undoubtedly suffered inhuman and degrading treatment, were ineffective to give adequate redress. Given that the Human Rights Act 1998 now entitles claimants to bring free standing claims against public authorities for breach of Convention rights the art.13 point will presumably no longer apply.

[728] [2005] 1 W.L.R. 1495, HL.

murder had been conducted. The House of Lords took a similar approach as in *Hill*, holding that a duty to suspects or victims would impede the fearless and efficient performance of public functions and lead to an unduly defensive approach when combating crime. Lord Steyn further observed that the core principle of *Hill* remained unchallenged in domestic and European jurisprudence, although, in light of *Z v UK*, it would be best for the principle to be formulated in terms of the absence of a duty of care rather than blanket immunity. However, the reasoning denying a duty is not entirely satisfactory. *Hill* concerned injury done by the *criminal*. Here the allegation was of damage subsequently caused by the *police*.

Other articles. Other articles do create substantive rights. Article 3 imposes **2–330** a positive obligation on states to ensure that individuals within their jurisdiction are not subject to torture or inhuman or degrading treatment. In *Z v UK* the social services had had knowledge of the serious ill-treatment suffered by the children over a period of years, and despite means available to them had failed to take effective steps to bring the abuse to an end. Hence the state had failed in its positive obligation under art.3.

D v East Berkshire. More recently, the impact of the Human Rights Act on **2–331** domestic law was considered in *D v East Berkshire NHS Trust*.[729] The Court of Appeal was satisfied that, insofar as the position of a child was concerned, the decision in *X* could not survive the Act. In addition, in the context of suspected child abuse, breach of a duty of care would frequently also amount to a violation of art.3 (above) or art.8 (respect for family life). However, the court did not suggest that the common law duty of care would replicate the duty not to violate arts 3 and 8. Liability for breach of the latter duty and entitlement to compensation could arise in circumstances where the tort of negligence was not made out. The area of factual inquiry where breaches of the two duties were alleged was, however, likely to be the same.

In the House of Lords the issue was whether the wrongly suspected parents **2–332** had a remedy, and there was no appeal as regards the duty owed to the child. As we have seen, their Lordships held that the parents' claim should fail. In so deciding they said little about art.8, beyond indicating that the conflict of interest point was such as to prevail over any argument based on interference with family life.

The facts in *D v East Berks* predated the coming into force of the Human **2–333** Rights Act 1998. In *Lawrence v Pembrokeshire CC*[730] the Court of Appeal held that the common law should not be developed to recognise a duty owed to the parents following the advent of that Act and of art.8 of the Convention. Such a development would fundamentally distort the law of negligence in this area, putting at risk the protection for children which it provided in its present form. The provision of a discrete Convention remedy through the medium of the HRA

---

[729] [2004] Q.B. 558; [2005] 2 A.C. 373.
[730] [2007] 1 W.L.R. 2991, CA; Jones, "Child protection and duties to third parties" (2007) 23 P.N. 118.

did not necessitate change in the common law. The reasoning in *D v East Berks* stood, and it precluded the existence of a duty to the parent.

2–334 **Van Colle v Chief Constable of Herts.** In *Van Colle v Chief Constable of the Hertfordshire Police*,[731] which was taken to the House of Lords on a conjoined appeal with *Smith v Chief Constable of Sussex*, a witness who was due to give evidence for the prosecution at the trial of a person accused of theft was shot dead by the accused, who was convicted of his murder. The deceased's parents brought an action against the defendant Chief Constable for failing to protect the deceased, alleging that he was in breach of his duty to act compatibly with their son's right to life in art.2. The House of Lords recognised that under art.2 there was a positive duty on national authorities to protect an identified individual whose life was known or should have been known to be at real and immediate risk from the criminal acts of another, and that this obligation required the authorities to take measures within the scope of their powers which, judged reasonably, might well have been expected to avoid that risk. It was held that in light of the known facts and circumstances the police officer concerned could not reasonably have apprehended violence against the victim, and so a breach of this duty had not been established.

2–335 Accordingly, in *Van Colle* there was a cause of action under the ECHR whereas in *Smith* there was no cause of action at common law. Their Lordships did not see this as problematic, considering that the common law should be allowed to develop in its own way, side by side with the alternative remedy.

2–336 **Mitchell v Glasgow CC.** Breach of art.2 also was argued in *Mitchell v Glasgow CC*.[732] However, Lord Hope considered that there was no basis for saying that the council ought to have known that when D left the meeting there had been a real and immediate threat to M's life. Indeed, there was nothing to suggest that the deceased's life was really at risk at all, let alone that such risk was immediate. So this action too would be dismissed.

---

[731] [2009] 1 A.C. 225; McIvor, "The positive duty of the police to protect life" (2008) 24 P.N. 27.
[732] [2009] 1 A.C. 874; see para.2–67, above.

PARTIES AND VICARIOUS LIABILITY

1.—PARTIES

Introduction. The basic rule is that all persons are entitled to sue and are liable to be sued in negligence and/or breach of statutory duty, just as in most other actions in tort. There are, however, exceptions with which this part of the chapter deals. There are also some considerations relevant to particular classes of party which again it is convenient to deal with here.   **3–01**

Immunities from suit. One category of exception has already been referred to in the last chapter.[1] Historically certain defendants acquired what was said to be immunity from an action in negligence for reasons of public policy. The police and others involved in the administration of justice are examples. But after the Human Rights Act 1998[2] incorporated into domestic law the European Convention for the Protection of Human Rights and Fundamental Freedoms, any   **3–02**

---

[1] See Ch.2 para.2–302, above (the rule in *Hill v Chief Constable of West Yorkshire Police*).
[2] The relevant part of the Act came into force on October 2, 2000.

immunity from suit or other limitation upon a right of action had to be measured against the rights granted by the Convention and, in particular, art.6 (the right to a fair and public hearing). Existing immunities were re-examined and in some cases, such as barristers,[3] rejected. An alternative approach has been by way of the duty of care itself, examining whether on particular facts it was fair, just and reasonable to impose a duty upon, say, the police or social workers.[4] For the future, and save where Parliament itself has intervened, it is likely that claims in negligence against certain types of defendant will be scrutinised both from the aspect of a traditional immunity, where the facts of a claim are essentially irrelevant, and from the aspect whether, on the facts, policy reasons dictate that a duty of care should not be owed.

(A) The Crown

3–03   **At common law.** The position at common law was that the Crown could not be sued in tort either personally or by an action against one of its employees in a representative capacity, such as the head of the department or the superior officer of the wrongdoer.[5] An individual wrongdoer could be sued for a wrong which he had committed personally[6] or to which he was directly privy, such as by having ordered it,[7] but not otherwise. This was because the relationship of employer and employee did not lie between superior and subordinate officials,[8] they being all fellow employees of the Crown. Accordingly, the Postmaster-General was not liable for the negligence of a sectional engineer in the Post Office after the plaintiff was injured by falling on the pavement, it not having been relaid properly after the flagstones had been taken up to allow a telegraph cable to be repaired.[9] The only available procedure for seeking a remedy was by way of a petition of right.

3–04   **Crown Proceedings Act 1947.**[10] By virtue of the Crown Proceedings Act 1947, the Crown's immunity in tort was brought to an end and it may now be sued as of right, inter alia, in actions for negligence. Section 2(1) provides:

> "Subject to the provisions of this Act, the Crown shall be subject to all those liabilities in tort to which, if it were a private person of full age and capacity, it would be subject:
>
> (a) in respect of torts committed by its servants or agents[11];

---

[3] See Ch.2 para.2–276, 277. See also Ch.9, para.9–95, below.
[4] See Ch.2 para.2–308, above.
[5] *Raleigh v Goschen* [1898] 1 Ch. 73; *Hutton v Secretary of State for War* (1926) 43 T.L.R. 106; *Roper v Public Works Comrs* [1915] 1 K.B. 45; *Tobin v The Queen* (1864) 16 C.B.(N.S.) 310.
[6] See *Royster v Cavey* [1947] K.B. 204.
[7] *Mackenzie-Kennedy v Air Council* [1927] 2 K.B. 517 at 533.
[8] *Bainbridge v Postmaster-General* [1906] 1 K.B. 178.
[9] However, for the legal position of the Post Office today, see para.3–27, below.
[10] As regards proceedings in Eire against the state, see the Civil Liability Act 1961 s.57. Further, see *Byrne v Ireland* [1972] I.R. 241.
[11] Agent includes an independent contractor: Civil Liability Act 1961 s.38(2).

(b) in respect of any breach of those duties which a person owes to his servants or agents at common law by reason of being their employer[12]; and

(c) in respect of any breach of the duties attaching at common law to the ownership, occupation, possession or control of property.[13]

Provided that no proceedings shall lie against the Crown by virtue of paragraph (a) of this subsection in respect of any act or omission of a servant or agent of the Crown unless the act or omission would apart from the provisions of this Act have given rise to a cause of action in tort against that servant or agent or his estate."[14]

Such proceedings must be instituted against the appropriate government department,[15] a list of which is published by the Treasury, but, in the case of doubt, proceedings may be taken against the Attorney-General.[16]

Breach of statutory duty. The Crown is also liable for breach of statutory duty. By s.2(2): **3–05**

"Where the Crown is bound by a statutory duty which is binding also upon persons other than the Crown and its officers, then, subject to the provisions of this Act, the Crown shall, in respect of a failure to comply with that duty, be subject to all those liabilities in tort (if any) to which it would be so subject if it were a private person of full age and capacity."

Acts binding on the Crown. Sometimes a statute will say in terms that it **3–06** binds the Crown, as did the Factories Act 1961.[17] By ss.4(2) and (3) of the 1947 Act, the provisions relating to contribution and indemnity contained in s.6[18] of the Law Reform (Married Women and Tortfeasors) Act 1935, and those relating to contributory negligence contained in the Law Reform (Contributory Negligence) Act 1945, bind the Crown. In other cases the statute is silent as to its application to the Crown. The common law principle of construction, preserved by the 1947 Act is that the Crown is not bound by a statute in the absence of

---

[12] See Ch.11 generally.

[13] See now the common law as replaced by the Occupier's Liability Act 1957: Ch.8, below.

[14] Apart from the Act, the Crown still cannot be sued in tort; see *Trawnik v Lennox* [1985] 1 W.L.R. 532 (the plaintiffs could not bring an action against the Crown based on a threatened tort by its servants, the Ministry of Defence, in relation to the construction of a shooting range on an airfield in the British sector of Berlin, which would cause nuisance to the adjoining householders).

[15] e.g. *Roe v Minister of Health* [1954] 2 Q.B. 66; *Waldon v War Office* [1956] 1 W.L.R. 51; *Keatings v Secretary of State for Scotland* (1961) S.L.T. (Sh.Ct) 63; *Ready Mixed Concrete (South East) Ltd v Ministry of Pensions and National Insurance* [1968] 2 Q.B. 497; *Ministry of Housing and Local Government v Sharp* [1970] 2 Q.B. 223; *Bright v Ministry of Transport* (1970) 114 S.J. 475; *Becker v Home Office* [1972] 2 Q.B. 407; *Asher v Secretary of State for the Environment* [1974] Ch. 208.

[16] e.g. *Darling v Attorney-General* [1950] 2 All E.R. 793; *Blackburn v Attorney-General* [1971] 1 W.L.R. 1037; cf. *Attorney-General and Minister for Defence v Ryan's Car Hire* (1964) 101 I.L.T.R. 57.

[17] s.173. Other relevant Acts are the Law Reform (Personal Injuries) Act 1948 s.4; the Occupiers' Liability Act 1957 s.6; the Congenital Disabilities (Civil Liability) Act 1976 s.5; the Civil Liability (Contribution) Act 1978 s.5; the Limitation Act 1980 s.37; the Latent Damage Act 1986 s.3; the Consumer Protection Act 1987, ss.1–9.

[18] The Civil Liability (Contribution) Act 1978, ss.1 and 9(1) and Sch.2, repealed and replaced the provisions contained in s.6 of the Law Reform (Married Women and Tortfeasors) Act 1935.

express words or necessary implication. Having said that, the provisions of the Fatal Accidents Act 1976 and the Law Reform (Miscellaneous Provisions) Act 1934 s.1, are generally regarded as binding on the Crown.

3–07   **The sovereign.** The Act specifically provides by s.40(1) that nothing in it shall apply to proceedings by or against, or authorise proceedings in tort to be brought against, the sovereign in a private capacity.

3–08   **Torts committed by employees or agents.** It is clear from s.2(1) of the 1947 Act that the Crown is made vicariously liable[19] to injured third parties for torts committed by its employees in the course of their employment. It is also liable for torts committed by its independent contractors, where in the like circumstances a private employer would be liable.[20] There is an important proviso inasmuch as the Crown can avail itself of such defences as act of state[21] and the exercise of statutory or prerogative powers,[22] but the Crown is not protected from liability for either its servants' tortious acts, which are ultra vires the statute creating the powers purported to be exercised, or its servants' negligence in the exercise of such powers.[23] By s.2(3) of the Act where any functions are conferred or imposed upon an officer of the Crown by any rule of the common law or by statute, and that officer commits a tort while performing or purporting to perform those functions, he will be taken as acting by virtue of instructions lawfully given by the Crown.

3–09   The Crown's liability for the torts of its officers, including any employee or Minister of the Crown, is limited to those cases where the officer is appointed by it, directly or indirectly, and at the material time is paid wholly out of the Consolidated Fund, moneys provided by Parliament or a fund equivalent thereto in respect of his duties as its officer.[24] This provision has the effect of excluding liability for the police and other public officers who are either appointed or paid by local or other public authorities.[25] Section 2(4) gives the Crown the benefit of any statutory provisions which negate or limit the amount of the liability of a government department or Crown officer.

---

[19] For vicarious liability generally, see paras 3–98 to 3–206, below.

[20] Crown Proceedings Act 1947 s.40(2)(d).

[21] There is no principle in our law which permits the Crown in time of peace to act for the public good as it thinks best: *Entick v Carrington* (1765) 19 St.Tr. 1029. The Crown must be prepared to justify before the courts the legality of any act which interferes with the person or property of the subject. This does not apply when the plaintiff is a non-resident alien and the wrong is suffered elsewhere than in British territory. See *Burton v Denman* (1848) 2 Exch. 167; *R. v Bottrill* [1947] K.B. 41 at 57.

[22] See Crown Proceedings Act 1947 s.11. The Crown, nevertheless, incurs liability to pay compensation for any loss and damage caused by the exercise of its prerogative powers: *Burmah Oil Co Ltd v Lord Advocate* [1965] A.C. 75; *Nissan v Attorney-General* [1970] A.C. 179 at 227–228, per Lord Pearce.

[23] See *Dorset Yacht Co Ltd v Home Office* [1970] A.C. 1004. See further at para.3–10, below.

[24] ibid., s.2(6).

[25] *Stanbury v Exeter Corp* [1905] 2 K.B. 838 (agricultural inspector); *Fisher v Oldham Corp* [1930] 2 K.B. 364 and *Lewis v Cattle* [1938] 2 K.B. 454 (police officers).

Liability for negligence. *Dorset Yacht Club Ltd v Home Office* has already   **3–10**
been discussed as a leading case in relation to the liability of Government
Departments for negligence.[26] The issue whether a duty of care was owed for
damage caused by the escapees was tried as a preliminary issue and decided in
favour of the plaintiffs. In dismissing the appeal,[27] the House of Lords held that
the prison officers had owed the plaintiffs a duty to take such care as was
reasonable in all the circumstances. The duty extended to the due exercise of
discretion[28] in regard to Borstal training policy, with a view to preventing those
in custody from causing damage to the plaintiffs' property if that was a manifest
risk. Public policy did not require that the Home Office should have immunity
from such a claim.

In Scotland, it has been held that the prison service is not immune from suit
in relation to proceedings by prison officers for damages for personal injuries
sustained in the course of their employment in that behalf.[29]

The liability of Government departments is discussed in a number of contexts   **3–11**
throughout this work[30] and some examples will suffice here. So, the Ministry of
Transport was found to owe a duty of care in relation to the siting of road signs[31];
and the Export Credits Guarantee Department was liable for negligent advice as
a result of which the claimants suffered loss when those with whom they had
contracted abroad defaulted in payment.[32] In *Lonrho v Tebbit*,[33] it was held that
a private-law duty of care may exist, which required the Secretary of State to take
reasonable care in the exercise of his statutory powers. Similarly, in Australia, it

---

[26] [1970] A.C. 1004. See Ch.2 paras 2–297, 2–304 above. *Dorset Yacht Co Ltd v Home Office* was
approved by the Ontario Court of Appeal in *Schacht v The Queen in Right of the Province of Ontario*
(1972) 30 D.L.R. (3d) 641 (the police were required by statute to maintain a traffic petrol on highways
and to their knowledge a well-lit barrier marking a detour had been knocked down, leaving a
hazardous situation, but it was held that they had taken adequate steps to warn approaching motorists
of the danger).
[27] Above, affirming the Court of Appeal [1969] 2 Q.B. 412 but with Viscount Dilhorne dissenting.
[28] In the context of a claim by a prison officer who was attacked and injured by the brother of a
prisoner he was attempting to discipline, where both, unknown to him, had been allocated to the same
work group, it was said that the discretion extended to the appropriate disposition of prisoners, taking
into account the training of inmates, good order, the best use of resources and the safety of prison
officers: *Connor v Secretary of State for Scotland* [2000] Rep. L.R. 18, OH (the claim succeeded
because the claimant should have been informed that both potentially violent brothers were in the
group). See Ch.2, para.2–304, above for prison claims generally.
[29] *McCafferty v Secretary of State for Scotland* [1998] S.C.L.R. 379, OH.
[30] See particularly Ch.2, paras 2–284, 2–323, above.
[31] *Levine v Morris and Ministry of Transport* [1970] 1 W.L.R. 71 (where it is foreseeable that
motorists may inadvertently leave the road and collide with a road sign, the duty is to select the site
which combines visibility with the least hazard to the motorist). See further in relation to the siting
of road signs generally, Ch.10, para.10–10 below.
[32] *Culford Metal Industries Ltd v Export Credits Guarantee Department*, *The Times*, March 25,
1981.
[33] [1992] 4 All E.R. 280, CA (P gave certain undertakings not to acquire any more capital in a public
company, pending publication of the report after P's take-over bid had been referred to the
Monopolies Commission for consideration. It was held that, although the initial undertaking was
obtained as a matter of public interest, P had a private interest in having the undertaking released
promptly, when it was no longer required).

has been held that a duty of care could exist in a circumstance where a government minister makes a statement about future policy.[34]

3–12   **Nationalised bodies and hospitals.** Since the decision in *Mersey Docks Trustees v Gibbs*,[35] it is settled law that the mere fact that a body has been created by statute for public purposes does not mean that it is a servant or agent of the Crown. Accordingly, in *Tamlin v Hannaford*,[36] the Court of Appeal held that the nationalised railways' authority was not a servant or agent of the Crown, the proper inference being, at any rate in the case of a commercial corporation, that it acted on its own behalf, although it was subject to control by a government department. Hospital authorities are not servants or agents of the Crown.[37]

(B) Judges and quasi judges, prosecutors, the police

3–13   **Judicial acts.**[38] Section 2(5) of the Crown Proceedings Act 1947 excludes proceedings against the Crown "in respect of anything done or omitted to be done by any person while discharging or purporting to discharge any responsibilities of a judicial nature vested in him, or any responsibilities which he has in connection with the execution of judicial process". It follows that no vicarious liability attaches itself to the Crown for torts that may be committed by judges, magistrates and those others executing judgment who exceed the limits of the immunity which the law otherwise allows.

3–14   A judge acting within his jurisdiction is immune from suit, whether for defamation, false imprisonment or otherwise.[39] In *Sutcliffe v Thackrah*,[40] Lord Salmon referred to it being "well settled that judges, barristers, solicitors, jurors and witnesses[41] enjoy an absolute immunity from any civil action being brought against them in respect of anything they say or do in court during the course of a trial". While the position remains as he stated in relation to judges, jurors and

---

[34] *Unilan Holdings Pty v Kerin* [1992] A.L.M.D. 4561 (A claimed damages in negligence against a government minister in relation to a speech he had made at an international wool conference. Hill J. considered that the treatment of the duty of care in the context of misstatements is an application of general principle to which the relationship of proximity is integral and had no reason to assume that in other areas the government or its minister remained immune from judicial action).

[35] (1866) L.R. 1 H.L. 93. See also *Bank Voor Handel en Scheepvaart v Administrator of Hungarian Property* [1954] A.C. 584.

[36] [1950] 1 K.B. 18. See also *Glasgow Corp v Central Land Board* (1956) S.C.(HL) 1.

[37] *Bullard v Croydon Hospital Committee* [1953] 1 Q.B. 511 at 514.

[38] See Morgan, "Judicial Immunity" in 123 S.J. 398.

[39] See also Ch.2, para.2–279 above.

[40] [1974] A.C. 727 at 757.

[41] In *Evans v London Hospital Medical College* [1981] 1 W.L.R. 184, applying *Marrinan v Vibart* [1963] 1 Q.B. 528, it was held that the immunity from suit of a witness extended to any statement made prior to and in contemplation of the civil or criminal proceedings under consideration, as well as to the collection and analysis of material relevant to the investigation of the matter. See further, in relation to *expert* witnesses, Ch.9, para.9–05. Section 2(5) of the Crown Proceedings Act 1947 was applied in *Hinds v Liverpool County Court* [2008] 2 F.L.R. 63. The claim which was based on alleged negligence of judges and the court, in dealing with care proceedings which the claimant alleged had been wrongly decided, was struck out. The Act afforded immunity to judges and the court did not owe the claimant a duty of care in tort.

witnesses, the absolute immunity enjoyed by solicitors and barristers has disappeared.[42]

3–15 Where a judge, acting in his judicial capacity, does an act which is in fact outside his jurisdiction but which he believes, mistakenly, is within it, he, as well as police officers acting under his instructions, will be immune from any proceedings which may be taken against him in respect of that act.[43] Indeed, as the New Zealand Court of Appeal[44] has said, the absolute immunity of a judge from civil proceedings for acts done in the exercise of judicial office is given not as a private right but to ensure, in the public interest, that the administration of justice will be carried on without fear of the consequences, just as much as it must also be carried on without hope of favour.

3–16 Persons discharging quasi-judicial functions, such as arbitrators,[45] are similarly exempt. However, Buckley L.J. said four questions might arise:

"(1) Was the act non-judicial?

(2) If the act was, or purported to be, a judicial act, was it within the judge's jurisdiction?

(3) If the act purported to be a judicial act in the exercise of a jurisdiction which the judge possessed and about the extent of which he was under no misapprehension, did the judge act as he did upon an erroneous judgment that the circumstances were such as to bring the case within the ambit of that jurisdiction?

(4) If the act was not in truth within the judge's jurisdiction, did he act in conscientious belief that it was within his jurisdiction and, if so, (a) was this belief due to a justifiable ignorance of some relevant fact, or (b) due to a careless ignorance or disregard of some such facts, or (c) due to a mistake of law relating to the extent of this jurisdiction?

He will, in my opinion, be immune in cases (2), (3) and (4)(a), but not otherwise."[46]

3–17 Although a sequestrator appointed under a writ of sequestration is an officer of the court, he is not as such immune from liability in respect of any negligent act done or omission in the course of the sequestration, because he owes the ordinary duty of care to the owners of the sequestered property.[47] Likewise, a surveyor acting under a rent review clause is acting as an expert and not an arbitrator or quasi-arbitrator where he is entitled to rely on his own judgment and experience and is not obliged to decide the matter on the evidence and submissions of the parties, and thus is not immune from liability for negligence.[48]

---

[42] The immunity of advocates from actions for negligence, has been abolished: see Ch.2, para.2–276 above; Ch.9, para.9–95 below.
[43] *Sirros v Moore* [1975] Q.B. 118.
[44] *Nakhla v McCarthy* [1978] 1 N.Z.L.R. 291 (an allegedly improper determination of the plaintiff's appeal in criminal proceedings by the defendant, the former President of the Court).
[45] For the immunity of a valuer when acting as an arbitrator, see *Re Hopper* (1867) L.R. 2 Q.B. 367 and *Re Carus-Wilson and Greene* (1886) 18 Q.B.D. 7 but cf. the distinctions made in *Arenson v Arenson* [1977] A.C. 405, reversing the Court of Appeal [1973] Ch. 346.
[46] *Sirros v Moore*, n.43, above, at 140–141.
[47] *I.R.C. v Hoogstraten* [1985] Q.B. 1077.
[48] *Palacath v Flanagan* [1985] 2 All E.R. 161.

3–18   An expert witness has immunity from suit for negligence at the instance of a party for whom he provides advice extending to (i) evidence given in court; (ii) advice in a report prepared for trial where the expert did not in fact give evidence.[49] An official receiver is immune from suit when acting in the course of bankruptcy proceedings and within the scope of his powers and duties.[50] No immunity from suit arose in favour of the Crown Prosecution Service, which had assumed the responsibility, where, as a result of an administrative error, the claimant was arrested on a warrant not backed for bail after failing to appear for trial of offences already "taken into consideration" in the Crown Court.[51]

3–19   **Foreign judgments.** Section 18 of the State Immunity Act 1978[52] requires final judgments given against the United Kingdom by a court in another state which is party to the European Convention on State Immunity to be recognised in the courts of the United Kingdom. However, the courts in this country need not give effect to such requirements, either where to do so would be manifestly contrary to public policy or where the judgment was the result of proceedings which were unfair procedurally, or were in conflict with other earlier judgments, or were otherwise inadequate.[53]

3–20   **Police.**[54] Although a constable is not the employee or agent of the Crown, a chief officer of police, by virtue of the provisions of s.88(1) of the Police Act 1996, is liable in respect of torts committed by constables under his direction or control in the purported performance of their functions, in the like manner as a master is liable in respect of torts committed by his servants in the course of their employment.[55] The chief officer, usually the chief constable, will be a joint tortfeasor[56] with any police constable guilty of negligence but any damages and costs awarded against him are met out of the police fund. A chief constable can potentially be vicariously liable for injury to a subordinate officer caused by the negligence of officer holding a superior position to himself.[57] Police immunity from suit has already been discussed in relation to the duty of care generally and the topic is therefore not repeated here.[58]

---

[49] *Stanton v Callaghan* [1999] P.N.L.R. 116, CA (no liability in negligence where a consulting engineer retained to provide an expert report on subsidence in an action against insurers modified his views after a joint meeting of the experts on both sides). See Passmore, "Expert witness immunity" in 148 N.L.J. 1758. The immunity even extends to a case where the evidence given was allegedly dishonest: *Raiss v Palmano* [2001] P.N.L.R. 540 (claimant sued his former expert surveyor for breach of duty of care in that he wrongly claimed to be a member of the panel of arbitrators at the Royal Institution of Chartered Surveyors, conceding in cross examination at trial of the claimant's action that he was not) following *Palmer v Durnford Ford* [1992] 2 Q.B. 483.
[50] *Mond v Hyde* [1999] Q.B. 1097, CA. See Ch.9, below, para.9–45.
[51] *Welsh v Chief Constable of the Merseyside Police* [1993] 1 All E.R. 692 but cf. the situation in *Elguzouli-Daf v Commissioner of Police of the Metropolis* [1995] 2 W.L.R. 173, CA.
[52] Which came into force on November 22, 1978.
[53] See State Immunity Act 1978 s.19, which sets out the exceptions to recognition.
[54] For some decisions on the liability of police generally, see Ch.2, para.2–301 to 2–303.
[55] See para.3–112, below. See also, e.g. *N v Chief Constable of Merseyside Police* [2006] EWHC 3041 (QB), para.3–145, below (the chief constable was not liable for the actions of a police officer who used his uniform and position to create the opportunity to commit sexual assaults upon the claimant).
[56] See generally paras 3–99 to 3–159, below.
[57] *Hughes v National Union of Mineworkers* [1991] 4 All E.R. 278.
[58] See Ch.2 para.2–302.

(C) The armed forces

Generally.[59] Formerly, s.10(1) of the Crown Proceedings Act 1947 gave a   **3–21**
substantial immunity covering negligent acts by members of the armed forces on
duty causing injury. The section was repealed in 1987[60] but continues to have
some importance.[61] By its terms, no act or omission of a member of the armed
forces on duty should subject either himself or the Crown to liability in tort for
causing the death of another person, or for causing personal injury[62] to another
person, who was a member of the armed forces.[63] In order for the immunity to
attach the victim had (a) to be either on duty or be on any land, premises, ship
or vehicle being used for the purposes of the armed forces of the Crown[64]; and
(b) the Minister of Pensions[65] had to have certified that the death or injury would
be treated as attributable to service for pension purposes.[66] By virtue of the
proviso to the subsection, exemption from liability extended to the tortfeasor
personally, unless the court was satisfied that the act or omission complained of
was not connected with the performance and execution of his duties as a member
of those forces. Section 10(2) provided a similar exemption from liability in tort
where the death or personal injury had been sustained by a member of the armed
forces in consequence of the nature or condition of any land, premises, ship,

---

[59] Unlike the United Kingdom's Crown Proceedings Act 1947 s.10, and New Zealand's Crown
Proceedings Act 1950 s.9, which provide statutory schemes for compensation of servicemen and
exclude recourse to the common law, Australia has no equivalent legislation. Accordingly, in *Groves
v The Commonwealth* (1982) 150 C.L.R. 113 an airman who had suffered injuries as a result of the
negligence of a fellow member of the R.A.A.F. in the course of peace-time duty was held to be
entitled to maintain an action for damages.

[60] i.e. by the Crown Proceedings (Armed Forces) Act 1987 s.1.

[61] s.10 of the 1947 Act may be revived for all or some purposes by an order made under s.2. It
continues to apply in relation to injury suffered by a person in consequence of an act or omission
committed prior to May 15, 1987.

[62] But other losses caused by negligence were not excluded and the Crown's liability for other torts
remained.

[63] s.10(1) granted exemption in respect of "anything suffered" while a member of the armed forces.
In *Pearce v Secretary of State for Defence* [1988] A.C. 755, Lord Brandon of Oakbrook expressed
the view, obiter, that this was a reference to the casualty or other event caused by the act or omission
from which the personal injury or death resulted. In *Derry v Ministry of Defence, The Times*, June 8,
1998, a case of allegedly negligent failure to diagnose and treat a pre existing carcinoma, it was held
that the "thing suffered" was the progression of the claimant's condition, and the exemption
accordingly applied. (Appeal dismissed [1999] P.I.Q.R. P149, CA.). See also *Re Post Traumatic
Stress Disorder Group Litigation, Multiple Claimants v Ministry of Defence, The Times*, May 29,
2003 (in the context of claims by former members of the armed forces for alleged failures by the
defendant to take any or any adequate steps to prevent the development of psychiatric illness, and/or
to detect, diagnose or treat such illness, it was held that the "thing suffered" was either exposure to
traumatic events without the protection of the relevant preventative measures, or in relation to failures
after exposure to traumatic events, a state of greater vulnerability to the onset of psychiatric injury.
Both were continuing states of affairs, the overwhelming probability was that the claimants were
either on duty or on Crown property at the time that such a state of affairs arose, and they were thus
within the scope of s.10).

[64] e.g. *Bell v Secretary of State for Defence* [1986] Q.B. 322 (army medical officers and staff were
held immune from all tortious liability in respect of alleged negligence treatment of a member of the
armed forces as well as the failure to provide proper notes for a civilian hospital which had taken over
the treatment. However, the civilian hospital did not enjoy immunity).

[65] Subsequently, the Ministry of Social Security Act 1966 s.2(3) (now fully repealed), and SI
1968/1699, by which the Secretary of State for Social Services took over the functions.

[66] See *Adams v War Office* [1955] 1 W.L.R. 1116 (soldier killed during a gunnery exercise).

aircraft, or vehicle being used for the armed forces' purposes or in consequence of the nature or condition of any equipment or supplies used for those purposes.[67] While there remains, in battle conditions, a power, vested in the Secretary of State, to make an order reviving the effect of s.10 of the 1947 Act, it has been held that no duty of care is owed at common law in such conditions by one serviceman to another, nor any similar duty on the Ministry of Defence to maintain a safe system of work.[68]

3–22   The compatibility of s.10 with art.6 of the Convention on Human Rights was considered in a claim for injury arising from exposure to asbestos in the years 1955 to 1968 in the course of employment in the Royal Navy. It was successfully argued at first instance that the effect of the section was to prevent the claimant's access to a court and it was thereby incompatible with his rights under art.6, but the result was set aside on appeal. In the House of Lords, Lord Bingham rejected the suggestion that the claimant had a civil right to compensation with which art.6 could engage. It was not correct, as the claimant argued, that ss.2 and 10 of the 1947 Act gave him a right to recover damages in tort against the Crown only defeasible if and when the Secretary of State gave a certificate under s.10(1)(b) that the injury suffered had been, or would be, treated as attributable to his service for purposes of entitlement to a pension. The object of the certification procedure was to assist those denied a remedy by the absolute exclusion imposed by s.10(1), to obtain a pension under the Act if they otherwise qualified for it. Section 10 did not erect a procedural bar to enforcement of the civil right contended for, it denied the claimant any such right and art.6 did not accordingly apply.[69]

3–23   In *Pearce v Secretary of State for Defence*,[70] it was held that the defendant was not immune to actions in respect of alleged negligence by employees of the Atomic Energy Authority's weapons group. Not only is the Secretary of State

---

[67] An attempt to circumvent the exemption from liability in the case of a former member of the Royal Navy who had worked with asbestos during his service, failed in *Quinn v MOD* [1998] P.I.Q.R. P387, CA: the exemption applied even where the complaint was framed as failure to provide a safe system of work. See also *Re Post Traumatic Stress Disorder Group Litigation*, n.63 above (for employers' liability to be excluded from the section would have been anomalous and inconsistent with its wording).

[68] *Mulcahy v Ministry of Defence* [1997] 1 W.L.R. 20, CA (a soldier alleged that his hearing had been damaged by the negligent firing of a howitzer during the Gulf War; the court accepted that, on the facts, two preconditions for the existence of a duty of care were present namely foreseeability and proximity, but decided it would not be fair, just or reasonable to impose a duty in the circumstances). See also *Shaw Savill and Albion Co Ltd v The Commonwealth* (1940) 66 C.L.R. 344, and *Re Post Traumatic Stress Disorder Group Litigation*, n.63 above (combat includes all active operations against an enemy, including attack and resistance, advance and retreat, pursuit and avoidance, reconnaissance and engagement; it also includes anti-terrorist, policing and peacekeeping operations in which service personnel come under attack or the threat of attack. The saving from liability extends to the planning of and preparation for such operations, and includes decisions as to the deployment of resources). See Rowley, "Combat immunity and the duty of care" J.P.I. Law 2004, 4, 280.

[69] *Matthews v MOD* [2003] 1 A.C. 1163, 1171. See Weir, "The armed forces and Crown immunity" 152 N.L.J. 231.

[70] [1988] A.C. 755. The action was not barred, even though the Authority's liability had been transferred to the Secretary of State for Defence by the Atomic Energy Authority (Weapons Group) Act 1973 and an action against the Secretary of State in respect of such liability constituted proceedings against the Crown for the purposes of the 1947 Act.

merely an *officer* of the Crown (and not the Crown itself), but, in order to claim immunity under s.10(1), the loss had to arise from activities of a member of the armed forces on duty as such, which membership did not encompass employees of the Atomic Energy Authority.

The Ministry of Defence did not owe a duty of care and so was not liable in **3–24** negligence for failing to control excessive drinking, as a result of which a naval airman, known to be a heavy drinker, became so drunk during his birthday celebrations at the shore base in Bardufoss, Norway, that he fell into a coma and choked to death.[71] However, a duty did arise once an assumption of responsibility was made after his collapse, and the measures taken to take care of him having fallen short of the standard reasonably to be expected, negligence was established. Liability was also established for injury to an off duty soldier where a superior officer, also off duty, failed to order him not to engage in an obviously hazardous activity.[72]

Members of the armed forces have been held to owe duties of care to civilians **3–25** when conducting peace keeping operations under the auspices of the United Nations. So, the Ministry of Defence was liable for the negligence of soldiers who fired shots at two Kosovar Albanians in the course of such an operation, where one man was killed and another seriously wounded. The defence of self defence was rejected on the facts. For the defence to succeed, the soldiers' belief that they were going to be attacked had to be honest and reasonable. The witness and expert evidence suggested that the soldiers were not being threatened by the deceased when they fired their guns and there was no reasonable grounds for them to believe that they were being threatened.[73]

Ships and aircraft. By virtue of s.29 of the 1947 Act, no proceedings in rem **3–26** can be commenced against any of H.M. ships[74] or aircraft.[75]

(D) Post office and telecommunication services

History. The postal and telecommunications services have a complex legis- **3–27** lative history which it only possible to summarise here to the extent that it is relevant to the liability in tort of the service providers for the time being. By s.6

---

[71] *Barrett v MOD* [1995] 1 W.L.R. 1217, CA (the deceased was held two-thirds contributorily negligent). But in *Jebson v MOD* [2000] P.I.Q.R. P201, CA, liability was established, by analogy with the duty of care that would have been appropriate had the claimant been a civilian, where a drunken member of the Grenadier Guards fell from the back of an Army lorry through a gap between the tailgate and the canvas roof (claimant's contributory negligence assessed at 75 per cent). See Spicer, "Health and safety at work: war, disorder and public policy" 140 S.J. 452; Lyon, "Tommy this and Tommy that, and Tommy wait outside" in 149 N.L.J. 465; Gibson, "Duty of care in immunisation against biological warfare agents" 2002 Medical. L. Int. 5(3) 181.
[72] *Radclyffe v Ministry of Defence* [2009] EWCA Civ 635 (by his presence and by reason of his rank, the officer assumed responsibility to prevent subordinate soldiers from taking undue risks of which he was or should have been aware).
[73] *Bici v Ministry of Defence, The Times*, June 11, 2004.
[74] See s.38(2) of the Crown Proceedings Act 1947 for an extended definition of "ship."
[75] s.38(2) above also defines "aircraft".

of the Post Office Act 1969[76] the Post Office was given authority to administer all postal and telecommunication services. It operated as a commercial corporation independent of the Crown. Section 9 of the Crown Proceedings Act 1947 was repealed, although the exemptions from and conditions of the liability of the Post Office bore considerable similarity to those formerly governing the Crown's liability.

3–28   Subsequently, a decision was made to separate the postal services from those relating to telecommunication and data processing, which was achieved by the British Telecommunications Act 1981. As from October 1, 1981,[77] the British Telecommunications Corporation, had responsibility for these latter services. Then, following a decision to privatise the industry, the Telecommunications Act 1984[78] dissolved[79] the British Telecommunications Corporation after the transfer date[80] and transferred its operations to its successor limited liability company, British Telecommunications Plc.

3–29   **The Post Office.** The Post Office was converted from a statutory corporation to a public limited company owned by the Crown, by the Postal Services Act 2000.[81] The Act introduced a system of licensing and regulation for postal service operators and providers in the market previously reserved as a monopoly for the Post Office. On March 26, 2001, all the property, rights and liabilities to which the Post Office was entitled or subject became, immediately after that day, the property, rights and liabilities of Consignia Plc, as the company nominated to provide the service which the Post Office formerly provided.[82]

3–30   The civil liability of the provider of the postal service is dealt with by s.89 of the Act onwards.[83] By that section, the provider is permitted to make a scheme which determines the charges to be imposed for the service provided and other terms and conditions which are to be applicable. The scheme may not provide for limiting the liability of the provider for loss and damage or for amending the rules of law relating to evidence.

3–31   By s.90 of the Act no proceedings in tort shall lie, or in Scotland be competent, against a provider in respect of loss or damage suffered by any person in connection with the provision of a postal service because of:

> "(a) anything done or omitted to be done in relation to any postal packet in the course of transmission by post, or

---

[76] Which came into force on October 1, 1969.
[77] British Telecommunications Act 1981 (Appointed Day) Order No.1274.
[78] c.12.
[79] See s.79.
[80] Telecommunications Act 1984 (Appointed Day) (No.2) Order (SI 1984/876) appointed August 6, 1984, for the purposes of Pt V of the Act.
[81] For developments before the coming into force of the Postal Service Act 2000 which largely repealed earlier legislation, see the 10th edn of Charlesworth and Percy at Ch.2, para.2–170.
[82] See ss.62(1) and (4).
[83] These sections came into force on February 26, and March 26, 2001.

(b) any omission to carry out arrangements for the collection of anything to be conveyed by post"

Section 90(2) provides for the immunity from civil liability for (a) and (b) above, except at the instance of the postal service provider itself, of any of its officers, servants, employees agents or sub contractors; or any person engaged in the conveyance of postal packets or their officers, servants, employees agents or sub contractors.

However by s.91 of the Act proceedings *shall* lie or in Scotland be competent 3–32
against a service provider "under this section but not otherwise" in respect of relevant loss of or damage to an inland packet in respect of which the provider accepts liability pursuant to a scheme made under s.89. The reference to "relevant loss or damage" is " to loss or damage so far as it is due to any wrongful act of, or any neglect or default by, an officer, servant, employee, agent or sub contractor" of the provider "while performing or purporting to perform in that capacity his functions in relation to the receipt, conveyance, delivery or other dealing with the packet". The scheme may deal with the fees particular types of packet will attract and the conditions with which the consignor of the packet must comply at the time of posting.

British Telecommunications Plc. The powers and duties of the original 3–33
corporation were those set out in s.2(1) of the British Telecommunications Act 1981. As in relation to the Post Office, there was a general rule protecting the corporation from proceedings in tort.[84] A similar rule preserved the immunity of its employees from "any civil liability for any loss or damage" for which the corporation itself was not liable, except at the suit of the corporation itself.[85] By s.23(3), the immunity further extended to any person engaged in the receipt, collection or delivery in material form of its transmitted communications and to any servant, agent or sub-contractor of such person.

These provisions were repealed, without being specifically replaced, by the Telecommunications Act 1984, which was itself largely repealed by the Communications Act 2003, with the result that British Telecommunications Plc would appear to enjoy none of the immunities which formerly applied.

(E) Foreign sovereigns, other heads of state, ambassadors, public officials and visiting armed forces

Foreign sovereign or other head of state. At common law no action lies 3–34
against a foreign sovereign or other head of state, unless he submits to the jurisdiction, for any tort committed personally by him.[86] As Lord Atkin stated:

"The courts of a country will not implead a foreign sovereign, that is, they will not by their process make him against his will a party to legal proceedings whether the

---

[84] See s.23 of the British Telecommunications Act 1981.
[85] s.23(2) of the 1981 Act.
[86] cf. *Sultan of Johore v Abubakar* [1952] A.C. 318 where the Judicial Committee expressed the view that there had not been established any absolute rule that a foreign sovereign could not be impleaded in our courts.

proceedings involve process against his person or seek to recover from him specific property or damages."[87]

Section 20 of the State Immunity Act 1978 affirmed the immunity and extended, with any necessary modification, the Diplomatic Privileges Act 1964, so as to apply its provisions to those members of a foreign head of state's family who form part of his or her household or private servants, just as its provisions apply to heads of diplomatic missions, their household families and private servants.

Accordingly, the only remedy for injuries and damage caused by a foreign sovereign, and his or her connections as defined above, is diplomatic action on the part of the British Government. If the status of a foreign sovereign is in doubt the question may be resolved by the court seeking information from the Secretary of State on behalf of the Crown, whose certificate is conclusive.[88] However, the sovereign's immunity ceases upon the termination of sovereign status.[89]

3–35 **The State Immunity Act 1978.** Problems arose at common law, where a foreign state sought to rely on immunity from suit in relation to to an action otherwise within the jurisdiction of the courts in this country.[90] The essence of the proposed action might relate to some commercial venture undertaken by the state, or it might be that a tort had been committed in the United Kingdom, in circumstances which made it appropriate for the particular foreign state's obligation to be determined by UK courts. As a result, the State Immunity Act 1978 was passed in order to restrict the immunity of foreign states in some circumstances. The Act sought to achieve its objective by embodying the provisions of the European Convention on State Immunity 1972,[91] and permitting the ratification of the Brussels Convention 1926,[92] which relates to state-owned ships.

By s.1 of the Act, the general immunity of a foreign state is continued and the courts must give effect to it, even though the state does not put in an appearance in the proceedings. The Act then specifies, in ss.3 to 11, the only exceptions to the general rule. These include the provisions contained in s.5, relevant to actions in negligence, by which a foreign state is not immune in regard to proceedings in respect of death or personal injury or for damage to or loss of tangible property, caused by an act or omission in the United Kingdom. Further, by s.6, a foreign state is not immune as regards actions which relate to any interest in immovable property in the United Kingdom or which arise out of any obligation attached to its ownership, possession or use, except where such property is used for the purposes of a diplomatic mission.[93]

---

[87] *Compania Naviera Vascongado v S.S. "Cristina"* [1938] A.C. 485 at 490.

[88] See s.4 of the Diplomatic Privileges Act 1964.

[89] *Munden v Duke of Brunswick* (1847) 10 Q.B. 656 (abdication).

[90] In *Planmount v Republic of Zaire* [1981] 1 All E.R. 1110, it was held that a foreign sovereign state may only invoke sovereign immunity in respect of governmental acts, as opposed to transactions of commerce, in both actions in rem and in personam irrespective of the fact whether such took place before or after the coming into force of the State Immunity Act 1978. See Greenwood, "Sovereign Immunity and Commercial Contracts" in (1983) 4 B.L.R. 265.

[91] See Sinclair, "The European Convention on State Immunity" in (1973) 22 I.C.L.Q. 254.

[92] International Convention for the Unification of Certain Rules relating to the Immunity of State-Owned Vessels (Cmd. 5672) and Protocol (Cmd. 5763).

[93] See s.16(1)(b).

It follows that foreign states are potentially liable to actions for negligently   **3–36**
caused personal injury as well as, for example, under the Occupiers' Liability Act
1957.[94] However, since the Act does not apply retrospectively,[95] any claim
arising before November 22, 1978,[96] when its provisions came into force, falls to
be considered under the rules at common law.[97]

Ambassadors and public officials. The law regarding diplomatic immunity   **3–37**
is contained in the Diplomatic Privileges Act 1964[98] which gives the force of law
to the Vienna Convention on Diplomatic Relations of 1961, which is set out in
a Schedule to the Act. The main provisions of the Act and Convention bearing
upon actions in tort concern (a) the immunity of diplomatic agents, that is, the
head of a mission and members of its staff having diplomatic rank[99]; (b) the
duration of such immunity; and (c) the waiver of such immunity.[100]

Visiting forces. By virtue of the Visiting Forces Act 1952[101] the Secretary of   **3–38**
State for Defence has been authorised to make arrangements for the settlement of
claims against members of visiting forces from the Commonwealth and states
which are parties to the North Atlantic Treaty.[102] The scheme takes effect
whereby claims in respect of acts or omissions of members of visiting forces will
be satisfied by the Minister's making payment, out of moneys provided by
Parliament, of such amounts as may be either adjudged by any United Kingdom
court or agreed between the claimant and the Minister.[103] Such a scheme does not
appear to create any right of action against the Minister. Otherwise, the same
exemptions, privileges and immunities which apply to the Crown in respect of
the home forces apply similarly to visiting forces.[104]

---

[94] See, generally, Ch.8, below.
[95] See *Hispano Americano Mercantil SA v Central Bank of Nigeria* [1979] 2 Lloyd's Rep. 277, CA.
[96] SI 1978/1572, made under s.23(5) of the Act.
[97] As regards actions in rem, the Privy Council expressed the view in *The Philippine Admiral* [1977] A.C. 373 that immunity did not extend against foreign governments' vessels which were engaged in purely trading activities. For actions *in personam*, see *I Congreso Del Partido* [1983] 1 A.C. 244 and *Trendtex Trading Corporation Ltd v Central Bank of Nigeria* [1977] Q.B. 529.
[98] As regards representatives of the Member States of the Commonwealth and of Eire, see the Diplomatic Immunities (Commonwealth Countries and Republic of Ireland) Act 1952, substantial amendments to which have been made by those countries which have gained their independence since 1952.
[99] If a foreign state acts unilaterally in appointing a diplomatic agent, it does not confer diplomatic immunity on that representative until this country has accepted and received the intended representative as a persona grata: *R. v Governor of Pentonville Prison Governor, Ex p. Teja* [1971] 2 Q.B. 274.
[100] *Musurus Bey v Gadban* [1984] 1 Q.B. 533. For the retroactive effect of the 1964 Act in changing the law, see *Empson v Smith* [1966] 1 Q.B. 426.
[101] s.9.
[102] The Crown by Order in Council may designate a country as being one to which the provisions of the Act or any of them apply: Visiting Forces Act 1952 s.1(2).
[103] Visiting Forces Act 1952 s.9(1).
[104] Visiting Forces Act 1952 s.8. See Visiting Forces and International Headquarters (Application of Law) Order 1965 (SI 1965/1536) as amended (SI 1987/928).

(F) The European Economic Community

3–39   **Tortious liability of the Community.** By art.215(2) of the European Economic Community Treaty, the Community is liable, in relation to non-contractual
or tortious liability, to satisfy all claims brought against it for damage caused by
its institutions or by its servants in the performance of their duties, in accordance
with the general principles of law common to the Member States. Thus, by
art.178, any disputes that may arise in such matters are justiciable before the
European Court.

3–40   Some confusion arose as regards the right of individual persons, whether
natural or juristic, to proceed before the European Court against the Community
in respect of the acts or defaults of its institutions, where an annulment would be
the remedy, and the tortious liability of the Community for the acts or defaults of
its institutions or its employees, for which compensation for damage suffered
might be ordered. In *Compagnie d'Approvisionnement v E.C. Commission
(No.2)*,[105] the European Court pointed out that the action for compensation,
envisaged under arts 178 and 215 of the Treaty, touching tortious claims, was an
independent right, distinguishable from an action for annulment. The former was
appropriate where a claimant sought compensation for loss caused by a
Community institution in the exercise of its functions, while the latter was
appropriate where the remedy sought was quashing a Community measure.

3–41   Article 173 allows any natural or juristic person to institute legal action against
a decision, addressed to that person, or against a decision which is addressed to
another but concerns directly and individually that person, for the purpose of
asking the European Court to review the legality of such acts, decisions or
regulations of the E.C. Council or the E.C. Commission. If the European Court
considers the action well-founded, it is empowered to declare the matters
complained of to be void.[106]

3–42   In practice, it would seem that only pure administrative or executive acts on
the part of the E.C. Council or the E.C. Commission, which occasion damage or
injury to individuals, would render the Community liable to pay compensation.[107] On the other hand, there is no liability on the part of the Community for
damage or injury which individuals may have suffered by reason of any
legislative act involving choices of economic policy, unless there has been a
serious and flagrant infringement of a higher rule of law protecting the
individual.[108] Even so, the European Court has maintained that in the case of
normative acts which are measures of economic policy, the liability of the
Community for alleged losses suffered as a result of such acts can arise if there
has been a sufficiently recognisable breach of a superior rule of law protecting
individuals, in the light of the provision of art.215(2) of the Treaty.[109] The

---

[105] [1973] C.M.L.R. 529. In *Werhahn (Wilhelm) Hansamühle v E.C. Council* [1973] E.C.R. 1229, the
E.C. Council admitted its awareness of the distinction asserted by the Court.
[106] art.174(1).
[107] *Merkur-Aussenhandels GmbH v E.C. Commission* [1973] E.C.R. 1055.
[108] See *Werhahn* [1973] E.C.R. 1229 and *Merkur* [1973] E.C.R. 1055.
[109] *Compagnie d'Approvisionnement v E.C. Commission (No.2)* [1973] C.M.L.R. 529.

reluctance to render the Community liable for the acts or defaults of its institutions, when some individual may have suffered damage by reason of a legislative act involving choices of economic policy, reflects concerns of the "floodgates" type.

(G) Corporations and unincorporated associations

Corporations, directors and members. A corporation can sue and be sued in **3–43** an action for negligence[110] in the same way as an individual.[111] The directors of a limited company, however, are not liable personally for the torts of the company's employees by reason of their position as directors, unless they were responsible for ordering the acts to be done or the omissions to be made or had assumed a personal duty of care.[112] They may, though, be liable, if there are facts from which an inference can be drawn that the relationship of principal and agent has been established between the directors and the company, but the mere fact of their being the sole directors and shareholders is insufficient.[113] Similarly, the members of a corporation, are not, as such, liable for torts committed by the corporation.[114] As a body corporate, it has a personality which is distinct from its members. Nevertheless, it cannot be doubted that an employee or agent, by whom a corporation commits a tort, is personally liable to the same extent as would be any other employee or agent who commits a tort in the service or on behalf of a principal or employer. Moreover a director of a company owes a common law duty of care to the company which is the same as that set out in s.214 of the Insolvency Act 1986.[115]

Trade unions and employers' associations. In *Taff Vale Ry v Amalgamated* **3–44** *Society of Railway Servants*,[116] it was held by the House of Lords that a registered trade union, although not a corporate body, was a legal entity having sufficient of the characteristics of a juristic person to enable it to be sued in tort

---

[110] *Citizens Life Assurance Co v Brown* [1904] A.C. 423. Such an action may include breach of some statutory duty, e.g. as under the Factories Act 1961.
[111] *National Telephone Co Ltd v The Constables of St. Peter Port* [1900] A.C. 317, even if the corporation seemingly is engaged in an ultra vires undertaking (at 321).
[112] See *Williams v Natural Life Health Foods Ltd* [1998] 1 W.L.R. 830, HL; also *Hale v Guildarch Ltd* [1999] P.N.L.R. 44 (employees of a finance company not personally liable where they were taken not to have assumed personal responsibility for negligent advice which induced the claimants to enter a disastrous scheme, which involved their obtaining a loan secured on the equity of their home); also *Wragg v Partco Group Ltd, The Times*, May 10, 2002, CA (directors' liability for alleged misstatement in the context of a company takeover). See Henderson "Regulatory rules and duties of care" 146 S.J. 726, also Dugdale, "Director's negligence: new horizons" in (1997) 13 P.N. 106; Todd, "Liability of agents in tort" in (1998) 3 P.N. 136.
[113] *Rainham Chemical Works v Belvedere Fish Guano Co* [1921] 2 A.C. 465; *Performing Right Soc. v Ciryl Syndicate* [1924] 1 K.B. 1.
[114] See, e.g. *Sweeney v Duggan* [1991] 2 I.R. 275 (majority shareholder not liable to an employee of the company whose judgment against the company remained unsatisfied after it went into liquidation: in the absence of special circumstances, the relationship between the parties was not of itself sufficiently proximate to justify imposing a duty of care and further, the claim, if allowed, would offend the rule that the defendant and the company were separate and distinct persons in law).
[115] *Re D'Jan of London; Copp v D'Jan* [1994] 1 B.C.L.C. 561.
[116] [1901] A.C. 426.

for the wrongful acts or omissions of its officials. However, by virtue of s.4 of the Trade Disputes Act 1906 it was provided that:

> "an action against a trade union, whether of workmen or master, or against any members or officials thereof on behalf of themselves and all other members of the trade union, in respect of any tortious act[117] alleged to have been committed by or on behalf of the trade union, shall not be entertained by any court."

3–45   Whilst the protection given was not confined to torts which were committed in contemplation or furtherance of a trade dispute, the Act did not protect officials of a trade union from their personal liability for wrongful acts.[118] The Industrial Relations Act 1971 put an end to the general immunity from actions of tort by repealing the Trades Disputes Acts 1906–1965. The Act of 1971 was then itself repealed after a change of government. The present law is contained in the Trade Union and Labour Relations Consolidation Act 1992.[119]

3–46   A "trade union" is defined in the 1992 Act s.28(1). By s.2(1) it is provided, inter alia, that a trade union shall be capable of suing and being sued in its own name and by s.12(2) any judgment against it shall be enforced by way of execution against any property held in trust for it as if it was a body corporate. In all other respects, a trade union "shall not be, or be treated as if it were, a body corporate". An "employers' association" is defined in s.122 and by s.127 similar provisions are made as those cited above as regards such an association's capabilities of suing and being sued. Section 130 deals with restrictions on enforcement of any judgment against certain property. On the other hand, an employers' association may be either a body corporate or an incorporated association.

3–47   Subject to a number of exceptions, s.14 of the earlier 1974 Trade Union and Labour Relations Act had granted immunity for both trade unions and employers' associations in respect of actions in tort, whether or not the act complained of had been committed in contemplation or furtherance of a trade dispute. These special immunities were then abolished,[120] so that it is possible to sue a trade union or employers' association in negligence, inter alia, if it is responsible for unlawful acts, whether or not connected with industrial action.[121] It has been held that a duty of care is owed by a trade union advising or acting for a member, but the duty ceases once a solicitor is instructed on the member's behalf, provided that proper and complete instructions are given.[122]

---

[117] Breaches of contract are not protected: *Bonsor v Musicians' Union* [1956] A.C. 104.
[118] *Rookes v Barnard* [1964] A.C. 1129.
[119] c.52.
[120] See s.15(1) of the Employment Act 1982.
[121] See, e.g. *Dent v National Farmers Union, The Independent*, July 5, 1999 (union liable in contract and tort to both members and non members for negligent advice as to the procedure to be followed in seeking compensation for lost milk quota at the inception of a scheme in 1984).
[122] *Friend v Institution of Professional Managers and Specialists* [1999] I.R.L.R. 173.

Unincorporated associations. The principle in *Taff Vale* has been held to **3–48**
cover a registered Friendly Society[123]; a member's club incorporated under s.3 of
the Industrial and Provident Societies Act 1965[124] and a Trustee Savings Bank[125]
but not an ordinary members' club, which is neither incorporated nor proprietary.
Normally, an unincorporated association can only be sued by means of a
representative action under CPR Pt 19.6, provided that the members by or against
whom the claim is brought have the same interest as the body of club members,
i.e. they and all the other club members have a common interest in resisting the
claim.[126] In other cases a representative action will be unnecessary because the
wrongdoer was the servant or agent of a particular member or members, such as
the committee.[127]

Where the claimant is himself a member of the club which is sued, special **3–49**
considerations arise. Common membership of a club is on its own insufficient to
give rise to a duty of care. There is a rule against members suing each other, for
injury allegedly arising in the course of membership, since there is no distinction
between the members and the claimant would in effect be suing himself.[128] But
this rule does not afford a defence if a duty of care has arisen independently of
membership. So, the court can look to the circumstances, including the terms
upon which a club officer or other servant or agent of the club has been
appointed, or the club rules, to see whether some responsibility has been
conferred upon that individual which caused a duty of care to arise.[129] In such a
case the individual concerned may be deemed to owe the claimant a personal
duty of care, breach of which founds an action, notwithstanding that he is also a
member. If he is employed by the club, then he is appointed by all the members
and, additionally to any personal responsibility, may be deemed the agent of each
member to carry out with reasonable care those things he is required to do.[130]

These principles may be seen in action in *Vowles v Evans,*[131] a case already **3–50**
noted in relation to the liability of those who referee a game or sport. In rejecting
any liability on the part of the officers of an amateur rugby club for injury to the

---

[123] *Longdon-Griffiths v Smith* [1951] 1 K.B. 295.
[124] *Gesner v Wallingford and District Labour Party Supporters' Association Club Ltd, The Times,*
June 2, 1994, CA.
[125] *Knight & Searle v Dove* [1964] 2 Q.B. 631.
[126] *Campbell v Thompson* [1953] 1 Q.B. 445.
[127] *Brown v Lewis* (1896) 12 T.L.R. 455 (members of committee of Blackburn Rovers Football Club
personally liable for defective stand).
[128] *Prole v Allen* [1950] 1 All E.R. 476; *Shore v Ministry of Works* [1950] 2 All E.R. 228. This general
common law rule was not displaced by rules of a club which provided that the club's chairman and
secretary were responsible in law for the conduct of the club as a corporate body: *Robertson v Ridley*
[1989] 1 W.L.R. 872, CA; *Milne v Duguid* [1999] S.C.L.R. 512 (a member of a golf club who was
injured when the ball she had played struck a stone and flew into her eye could not sue other members
of the club who acted as greens committee and thereby undertook responsibilities in relation to the
playing areas of the course).
[129] *Jones v Northampton BC, The Independent,* May 25, 1990; *Grice v Stourport Tennis, Hockey and
Squash Club* [1997] C.L.Y. 3859, CA.
[130] *Prole v Allen* [1950] 1 All E.R. 476. See *Milne v Duguid* [1999] S.C.L.R. 51 (the claimant's action
was allowed to proceed against the club's greenkeeper).
[131] [2002] EWHC 2612. An appeal, on a different point, failed: [2003] 1 W.L.R. 1607, CA.

claimant in the course of a set scrum, the trial judge accepted a summary of the broad principles of liability in the following terms:

> "(i) At common law an unincorporated members club or its officers or committee members owe no duty to individual members except as provided by the Rules of the organisation;
>
> (ii) an individual member of a members club may assume a duty of care to another member or be found to owe such a duty according to ordinary principles of law and in those circumstances the fact of common membership of the association will not confer immunity from liability upon the member sued;
>
> (iii) whether or not such a duty is held to exist will depend upon all the circumstances of the case ... "

On the facts it was held that while the officers in question, who played in the game in which the claimant was injured, may have erred, along with other players, in declining the option of a non-contested scrummage when the referee offered it, that failure did not involve any breach of duty given the high threshold requisite for liability as between participants in sport. It was for the first defendant as referee, having regard to the interests of safety, to determine whether scrums should be non-contested.[132]

(H) Partners

3–51   **Generally.** The Partnership Act 1890 makes partners jointly and severally liable for the torts of any one of them where committed in the ordinary course of the business of the firm or with the authority of co-partners.[133] Where the giving of an undertaking lay within the normal ambit of a solicitor's function, by s.5 it bound his partners or principal, notwithstanding that the undertaking had been given fraudulently.[134] RSC Ord.81, rr.1 and 2[135] permit partners to sue and be sued in the name of their firm. Where a claimant sues one partner and accepts a sum in full discharge of all claims and disputes between them he cannot then sue

---

[132] The judge quoted from the judgment of Ralph Gibson L.J. in *Owen v Northampton BC* (1992) 156 L.G.Rev. 23: "It seems to me that it is open to the court to find that a duty of care existed where a club officer or a member of the committee takes upon himself some task which he is to perform for other members of the club in course of which he acquires actual knowledge of circumstances which he know gives rise to risk of injury to club members acting as he knows they will or maybe expected to act if not told of the cause of danger. I do not doubt that the nature of the relation between the members of a club may often be such that it will be impossible to find that one member has undertaken any responsibility to inspect, or to inquire, or to consider whether circumstances will or may give rise to a risk of injury. But there may be circumstances in which a member acquires knowledge both of an actual danger and of the fact, that if a warning is not given, the members upon whose behalf he is taken to perform a task will be exposed to the risk of injury. In such circumstances, and it is not necessary to inquire in which other circumstances, it is open to the court to find a duty of care existed and was broken."

[133] ss.10 and 12. See also *Hamlyn v Houston* [1903] 1 K.B. 81; *Mercantile Credit Co Ltd v Garrod* [1962] 3 All E.R. 1103; *Meekins v Henson* [1964] 1 Q.B. 472. See also Wenban-Smith, "Salaried Partners: on the notepaper but off the hook?" in (1999) 20 Co. Law 59.

[134] *United Bank of Kuwait Ltd v Hammoud* [1988] 1 W.L.R. 1051, CA.

[135] Re-enacted in Sch.1 to Pt 50 of the CPR 1998.

the other partner in respect of the same matter.[136] there is no statement in the Act of the duty of care which a partner owes the partnership and there are relatively few reported cases in which the question has been discussed. Even so it seems likely that a duty of care is owed by a partner to co-partners, the standard of care being reasonable care in the circumstances, although there is some authority that "culpable" or "gross" negligence is required.[137]

(I) Husband and wife[138]

Actions between spouses. At common law a husband could not sue his wife   3–52
in tort, whilst a wife's action in tort against her husband was limited to that "for the protection and security of her property."[139] A radical change was only effected by the Law Reform (Husband and Wife) Act 1962[140] whereby, following recommendations of the Law Reform Committee,[141] each of the parties to a marriage was given the like right of action against the other as if they were not married.[142] By way of qualification, where an action in tort is brought by one of the parties to the marriage against the other during the subsistence of the marriage, the court may stay the proceedings if it appears either that no substantial benefit will accrue to either party from the continuance of the action or that the question before the court could be more conveniently disposed of under s.17 of the Married Women's Property Act 1882. Commencing with the provisions of the Matrimonial Homes Act 1967 and then the Matrimonial Proceedings and Property Act 1970, which has been repealed in part and re-enacted in the Matrimonial Causes Act 1973, considerable changes have been brought about as regards property rights.

Law Reform (Married Women and Tortfeasors) Act 1935. At common law   3–53
a married woman could not sue or be sued unless her husband was joined in the action with her, either as the plaintiff or the defendant, as the case may be. Consequently, the husband, as a necessary if unwilling party to the proceedings for torts committed by his wife, was liable to pay damages for such wrongdoings by her. The Law Reform (Married Women and Tortfeasors) Act 1935 abolished both these rules. By s.1, a married woman may be sued for her torts and herself sue in all respects as if she were a *feme sole*; whilst by s.3 it is provided that a husband shall not, by reason only of his being her husband, be liable in respect of any tort committed by his wife, whether before or during the marriage.[143]

---

[136] *Howe v Oliver, Haynes, Third Party* (1908) 24 T.L.R. 781.
[137] See the discussion in *Tann v Herrington* [2009] P.N.L.R. 22 (partner who negligently failed to notify the firm's insurers of a substantial claim against the partnership failed to recover contribution from his co partner towards it).
[138] See generally paras 3–204 to 3–206, below, concerning those instances where one family member may be deemed to be the servant or agent of another.
[139] Married Women's Property Act 1882 s.12.
[140] Which came into force on August 1, 1962.
[141] Ninth Report (1961) Cmnd. 1268.
[142] *McLeod v McLeod* (1963) 113 L.J. 420.
[143] Which reverses *Edwards v Porter* [1925] A.C. 1; *Barber v Pigden* [1937] 1 K.B. 664.

(J) Children[144]

3–54   **Duty of care of parents.** Children are prone to all sorts of accidents and when something untoward happens, questions such as foreseeability, the extent of the duty of care owed and its breach, must be considered in the light of the context and whether what occurred was other than part of the daily domestic routine. The standard of care imposed on a mother is that of a careful parent in the circumstances. In *Surtees v Kingston-upon-Thames Royal Borough Council*,[145] the view was expressed that a court should be slow to characterise as negligent the care which ordinary loving and caring parents were able to give to children, given the rough and tumble of home life.

3–55   **Capacity to sue.** A child's capacity to sue is no different from that of an adult, although a litigation friend is required, who in practice is usually one of his parents.[146] In the event of a parent being sued by a child, for example, for personal injuries sustained whilst travelling in a vehicle driven negligently by the parent,[147] the litigation friend would be the other parent or a relative willing to undertake the responsibility on the child's behalf.

3–56   **Pre-natal injuries.** Any problem presented by the old rules of common law was resolved by the Congenital Disabilities (Civil Liability) Act 1976, as a result of which duties are owed to an unborn child. The topic is considered extensively in Chapter 2.[148]

3–57   **Injury to parent.** No duty of care is owed to a child not to cause injury to its parent. So, where the mother of a child was injured in a road traffic accident the child could not maintain an action against the negligent driver for the value of the care he had received from his grandparents during his mother's incapacity, travelling expenses incurred in visiting her and telephone calls to the hospital at which she was being treated.[149]

3–58   **Control by the court.** Where, in any proceedings, money is claimed by or on behalf of a child, no settlement, compromise or payment and no acceptance of money paid into court shall, so far as it relates to the child's claim, be valid without the approval of the court.[150] Whilst the court has no inherent jurisdiction to postpone a child's entitlement to damages beyond the age of majority, it may,

---

[144] The Family Law Reform Act 1969 Pt 1 of which reduced the age of majority from 21 years to 18 years, came into force on January 1, 1970 and thereafter persons under that age became known as "minors" instead of "infants" as before. The Civil Procedure Rules refer to persons under 18 as "children": see CPR 21.1(2)(b).

[145] [1992] P.I.Q.R. P101, CA. See also Wright, "Negligent Parenting—Can My Child Sue?" in (1994) 6 J.C.L. 104.

[146] CPR Pt 21, r.2(2).

[147] *McCallion v Dodd* [1966] N.Z.L.R. 710; *Kochel v Corley* [1971] 1 S.A.S.R. 73.

[148] See Ch.2 paras 2–266 to 2–272, above.

[149] *Buckley v Farrow & Buckley* [1997] P.I.Q.R. Q78, CA.

[150] See CPR 1998 Pt 21, r.10.

nevertheless, approve a compromise of an action to that effect, arrived at by the parties themselves.[151]

Capacity to be sued. The fact of infancy or minority is not a defence known **3–59** to the law of tort. Save that a child must appear by a litigation friend,[152] it may be sued in tort and found liable, just as if of full age.[153] Thus, where a boy of 15 had gone swimming with a neighbouring family and, acting out of playfulness, pushed his father into the swimming pool, he was held liable for the severe personal injury sustained.[154] It was considered that, whilst the boy was not yet an adult, he was not exactly a child and it would be inappropriate to judge his conduct by some lower standard of care than would be expected of an adult. Nevertheless, the age of a minor may be highly relevant,[155] since for liability to in negligence to be made out it must generally be proved that he failed to show that care reasonably to be expected of a child of that age.[156] Where relevant it would have to be established that the child was old enough to form an intent to do the act of which complaint is made.[157] It is insufficient for a claimant to prove that an adult, had he acted the same way in the like circumstances, would have been guilty of negligence.

The standard of care to be expected of a child has been considered by the High **3–60** Court of Australia, where Kitto J. said:

"The standard of care being objective, it is no answer for him, any more than it is for an adult to say that the harm he caused was due to his being abnormally slow-witted, quick-tempered, absent-minded or inexperienced. But it does not follow that he cannot rely in his defence upon a limitation upon the capacity for foresight or prudence, not as being personal to himself but as being characteristic of humanity at his stage of development and in that sense normal. By doing so he appeals to a standard of ordinariness to an objective and not a subjective standard."[158]

---

[151] *Allen v Distillers Co (Biochemicals) Ltd* [1974] Q.B. 384 (where the High Court approved 433 terms of settlement).

[152] CPR Pt 21, r.2(2).

[153] *Gorely v Codd* [1967] 1 W.L.R. 19.

[154] *Williams v Humphrey, The Times*, February 20, 1974.

[155] See, e.g. *Kerry v Carter* [1969] 1 W.L.R. 1372 at 1377, per Edmund Davies L.J.

[156] This seems to be implicit in decisions concerned with contributory negligence of children. See *Lynch v Nurdin* (1841) 1 Q.B. 29; *Harrold v Watney* [1898] 2 Q.B. 320; *Liddle v Yorkshire County Council* [1934] 2 K.B. 101 at 125, per Greer L.J.; *Yachuk v Oliver Blais Ltd* [1949] A.C. 386. On the other hand, where a child has been engaged in adult activities, such as driving a motor vehicle, no allowances will be given for his lack of experience and minority, and he will be held liable to the same extent as an adult would be in the same circumstances. See *Nettleship v Weston* [1971] 2 Q.B. 691.

[157] *Tillander v Gosselin* (1966) 60 D.L.R. (2d) 18 (a child who was not yet three years old was held not to be liable in negligence or trespass). As regards "fault", Lord Reid has said that a child aged four years was "not old enough to be responsible"; *Carmarthenshire County Council v Lewis* [1955] A.C. 549 at 563.

[158] *McHale v Watson* (1966) 115 C.L.R. 199 at 213 (a 12-year-old boy threw a sharpened piece of metal, shaped like a dart, at a post, but instead it struck and injured the plaintiff standing nearby). See also *O'Brien v McNamee* [1953] I.R. 86 (a seven-year-old child liable in trespass which resulted in the burning down of the plaintiff's hayrick).

3–61   Clearly a child of very tender age would not normally be expected to foresee injury,[159] even though liable if the tort were one of strict liability.[160]

3–62   In practice, consideration is usually given to whether it is worthwhile suing a child in tort, since there may well be no assets to satisfy a judgment. Sometimes the prospect of later wealth may be sufficient to justify a claim and a child may be sued on any judgment or else execution may be issued on it up to six years from its date or even at a later date, with prior leave of the court.[161] Where a judgment was obtained against a child, payable by instalments, it was said to be an abuse of process for him to file a petition in bankruptcy.[162]

3–63   **Liability of parent.** A parent's responsibility for a child's torts is discussed in Section 2, below.[163]

(K) Prisoners and bankrupts

3–64   **Prisoners.** A convicted person, serving a custodial sentence, is subject to no legal disability in taking or defending civil (or, for that matter, criminal) proceedings.[164] Article 6 of the European Convention on Human Rights guarantees a fair and public hearing, within a reasonable time, by an independent tribunal, in determining civil rights.[165] The Prisons Act 1952 does not confer powers to deny or interfere with the right of access to a court.[166] The Prison Rules provide for access to a prisoner by his lawyers and for examination of him by a registered medical practitioner in connection with any proceedings which have been instituted.[167] A prisoner, equally, may be made a defendant for the purpose of his being sued in tort.[168]

3–65   There is no special application of the civil burden and standard of proof in claims by prisoners based upon injury received while in custody. It is not the case that, as a consequence of the passing of the Human Rights Act 1998, the State, where an individual has suffered injury whilst in custody, has to provide a plausible explanation for those injuries or positively disprove its responsibility for the injuries. Necessarily however, where such an injury has arisen, there will be a powerful evidential burden on those responsible for a prisoner's management during incarceration to show that it came about without negligence on their part. It would almost inevitably be the case that in order to avoid liability

---

[159] *Tillander v Gosselin* (1966) 60 D.L.R. (2d) 11.
[160] *Carmarthenshire County Council v Lewis* [1955] A.C. 549; *McHale v Watson* (1966) 115 C.L.R. 199 at 205.
[161] RSC Ord.46, rr.2 and 4, re-enacted in Sch.1 to Pt 50 of the CPR 1998.
[162] *Re A Debtor* [1967] Ch. 590.
[163] See para.2–204, below.
[164] See Criminal Justice Act 1948 s.83(3), Sch.10, Pt 1, repealing the Forfeiture Act 1870.
[165] The Convention is incorporated into domestic law by the Human Rights Act 1998, which came into force on October 2, 2000.
[166] See *Raymond v Honey* [1983] 1 A.C. 1.
[167] Prison Rules 1999, rr.38(1) and 20(6) (SI 1999/728).
[168] See Ch.2, para.2–304, above, for actions against the Home Office in respect of damage caused by escaped prisoners.

attaching, a substantial positive case would have to be advanced by the defendant. Provided this is kept in mind, no special rule need be taken from decided cases in the European Court of Human Rights.[169]

Liability of bankrupt. Bankrupts may be sued in tort, whether such is alleged **3–66** to have been committed before or during bankruptcy, since they are in no special position in this respect. The Bankruptcy Act 1914[170] had provided that demands in the nature of unliquidated damages, arising otherwise than by reason of a contract, promise or breach of trust, were not provable against the trustee in bankruptcy. The Insolvency Act 1986[171] altered the situation by extending the definition of "bankruptcy debt" and liability to include tortious liability of the bankrupt.[172] Where a claimant has a right of action in tort against the estate of a deceased tortfeasor, under the Law Reform (Miscellaneous Provisions) Act 1934,[173] but the estate is insolvent, he may prove in the administration of the estate for unliquidated damages.

Bankrupt's capacity to sue. A distinction has to be drawn between a tort **3–67** committed against the bankrupt's person and his property. A right of action in respect of a tort which has resulted in personal injuries remains with the bankrupt and does not pass to the trustee,[174] whilst a right of action resulting in damage to the bankrupt's estate passes to the trustee. If the tort has resulted in damage both to the bankrupt's person and his estate, the right of action, insofar as it results in personal injuries, remains in him, whilst that damage to the estate will pass to the trustee.[175] In a case of this sort the trustee and the bankrupt can either bring separate actions or may join as claimants in the same action. In such an event the damages will have to be assessed separately under the two heads of damage.[176]

On a claimant's bankruptcy, any cause of action in negligence against former **3–68** solicitors and or counsel becomes vested in law in his trustee in bankruptcy without need for written notice of the bankruptcy being given to the potential defendants. Although the permission of the Department of Trade would be required for the assignment of the cause of action by his trustee back to the bankrupt, any failure to obtain such permission would not render a subsequent

---

[169] *Sheppard v Home Office*, Unreported, December 11, 2002, CA. See also Ch.2, para.2–305 above.
[170] s.30(1). This excluded claims for damages in tort generally: per Vinelott J. in *Re Berkeley Securities Ltd* [1980] 1 W.L.R. 1589 at 1610.
[171] c.45.
[172] By s.382(1) and (4) respectively, containing provisions formerly in the Insolvency Act 1985 (c.65), s.211(1) which in turn replaced the Bankruptcy Act 1914 s.30(1), above.
[173] s.1(6).
[174] *Beckham v Drake* (1849) 2 H.L.C. 579; *Ex p. Vine* (1878) 8 Ch.D. 364 (the bankrupt may spend damages he has recovered in the maintenance of himself and his family).
[175] *Rose v Buckett* [1901] 2 K.B. 449; *Wenlock v Moloney* [1965] 1 W.L.R. 1238.
[176] *Wilson v United Counties Bank* [1920] A.C. 102. See also *Mulkerrins v Pricewaterhouse Coopers* (2001) 98(5) L.S.Gaz. 36 (negligence that results in bankruptcy can lead to two kinds of loss: economic loss in loss future earnings that would have accrued but for bankruptcy and loss of status and reputation; the former vests in the trustee while the latter, being personal, vests in the bankrupt).

action commenced by the bankrupt a nullity. However, the action would be at risk of being stayed, and further, the bankrupt as an equitable assignee could not recover damages until the assignor had been joined in as co-plaintiff.[177]

(L) Persons suffering mental disorder

3–69   **Generally.** It might be expected that a similar approach would be taken to the liability of a person suffering mental disorder, as to, say, the liability of a child.[178] The defendant would escape liability if he exercised the degree of care reasonably to be expected of someone suffering from the mental disorder to which he was subject. Some inconsistency has emerged, however, as a result of the particular difficulty which arises in applying the usual rule that negligence is assessed by reference to objective standards, and without regard to the particular susceptibilities or qualities of the person alleged to be liable.[179] So, in *Roberts v Ramsbottom*[180] liability was established against a car driver, where he suffered a stroke and as a result became incapable of driving with proper care, so that he crashed into the claimant. He could not rely on his altered consciousness to excuse his failure to exercise the care and skill of a reasonably competent driver. By way of contrast, in *Mansfield v Weetabix Ltd*[181] a claim failed where the crash resulted from the defendant driver's suffering from hypoglycaemia. It was sought to distinguish *Roberts* on the basis that in the latter case the driver had been aware of his condition and carried on driving.

3–70   The test should in each case be what standard of care was reasonably to be expected of the defendant, given the nature of the activity being undertaken. So, in road traffic cases the standard, an objective one, is that of the reasonably careful driver. Care must be taken to avoid turning the test into a subjective one. It is not a question whether the claimant's personal characteristics limited the care which might reasonably have been expected of him; but whether the characteristics of the condition which he suffered had that effect. There will inevitably be cases where the distinction is not easily drawn. Although automatism is sometimes referred to as affording a defence, in the present context it is difficult to see that it adds more than providing a convenient label for those cases where the nature of the condition suffered by the defendant was at the time sufficient to deprive him of all control over his actions, so that he could not reasonably be expected to exercise appropriate care.[182]

3–71   Where the claimant, who had a history of mental illness requiring hospital treatment, killed a man in an unprovoked attack, it was held that the maxim *ex turpi causa non oritur actio* operated to prevent a court entertaining a cause of

---

[177] *Weddell v J. A. Pearce & Major* [1988] Ch.1.
[178] See paras 3–60 to 3–62, above.
[179] *White v White* [1950] P. 39 at 59, per Denning L.J.
[180] [1980] 1 W.L.R. 823. See also *Adamson v Motor Vehicle Trust* (1957) 58 W.A.L.R. 56 (a negligent motorist could not avoid liability by pleading in his defence that mental disorder was the cause of his failure to exercise the care of a reasonably competent driver).
[181] [1998] 1 W.L.R. 823.
[182] See further, Ch.4, para.4–133, below.

action based upon alleged negligence in treating his illness, where the damage he complained of was his own conviction of the offence of manslaughter.[183] For similar reasons the claim of an employee who suffered an electric shock in the course of his employment which, he alleged, altered his personality so as to cause him to commit serious criminal offences, was not allowed to proceed.[184]

Capacity to conduct legal proceedings. The Mental Capacity Act 2005[185] **3-72** and the Code of Practice that accompanies it determine the approach to capacity. In brief, the starting point are the five principles set out in ss.1(2) to (6) of the Act: a person must be assumed to have capacity unless it is established that he lacks capacity; a person is not to be teated as unable to make a decision unless all practicable steps to help him to do so have been taken without success; a person is not to be treated as unable to make a decision merely because he makes an unwise decision; an act done or decision made for and on behalf of a person who lacks capacity must be done or made in his best interests; before the act is done or the decision is made, regard must be had to whether the purpose for which it is needed can be effectively achieved in a way that is less restrictive of the person's rights and freedom of action.

Section 2 of the Act then provides a two stage test of capacity. By s.2(1) a **3-73** person lacks capacity in relation to a matter if at the material time he is unable to make a decision for himself in relation to it because of an impairment of or a disturbance in the functioning of the mind or brain. By subs.(2) it does not matter whether the impairment or disturbance is permanent or temporary. By subs.(4) any question whether a person lacks capacity is to be decided on a balance of probability. Section 3 sets out in detail what is meant by a person being unable to make a decision. By subs.(4) the information relevant to a decision includes information about the reasonably foreaseeable consequences of—(a) deciding one way or another, or (b) failing to make the decision.

The test of capacity under the Act is issue-specific.[186] It does not necessarily **3-74** follow that if a claimant lacks capacity for one purpose he lacks it for all purposes. A claimant over 16 who lacks capacity is not a "patient" but a "protected party" and the Civil Procedure Rules are amended both in that respect and to reflect the creation of a new Court of Protection, of wider jurisdiction than the old. A protected party must have a litigation friend to conduct proceedings on his behalf. Where money is recovered for a protected party, it will be dealt with as the Court directs, but consideration must first be given to whether the claimant

---

[183] *Clunis v Camden and Islington Health Authority* [1998] Q.B. 978, CA (distinguishing *Meah v McCreamer (No.1)* [1985] 1 All E.R. 367). See also Ch.4, para.4–248 below; also *Wilson v Coulson* [2002] P.I.Q.R. P300 (claimant unable to rely on damage allegedly flowing from his own unlawful and deliberate use of heroin after a road traffic accident in which he sustained brain damage and depression).

[184] *Worrall v British Railways Board* [1999] C.L.Y. 1413, CA. See further Ch.4, para.4–248.

[185] The Act came into force on October 1 2007 and replaced Pt 7 of the Mental Health Act 1983.

[186] Accordingly cases such as *Masterman–Lister v Bruton & Co* [2003] 1 W.L.R. 1511 in which an issue-specific approach was adopted under the old law, still provide helpful guidance. See also *Bailey v Warren* [2006] EWCA Civ 51 (a personal injuries claim in which it was held the claimant had capacity to make a decision to compromise the issue of liability, but not more complex issues which arose subsequently).

is also a "protected beneficiary", that is, someone who is not simply a protected party, but is also unable to manage and control any money recovered on his or her behalf. If the claimant is a protected beneficiary the Practice Direction to Pt 21 of the Rules as amended makes specific provision in relation to investment of such money.

(M) Assignees

3–75   **Assignees.** A right of action for damages in respect of a tort is not capable of assignment, on the grounds of public policy.[187] As Lord Abinger said:

> "It is a rule—not of our law alone, but of that of all countries, that the mere right of purchase shall not give a man a right to legal remedies. The contrary doctrine is nowhere tolerated, and is against good policy."[188]

On the other hand, an assignment of the damages to be recovered in an action in tort is capable of being made properly since it is an assignment not of a bare cause of action but of property, namely the fruits of an action, as and when recovered.[189] Provided that the assignee has given written notice of the assignment to the third party, in compliance with s.136 of the Law of Property Act 1925, the assignee can sue in his own name and, further, he can enforce his right of action against the third party.[190]

(N) Representation after death

3–76   What falls to be considered here is the question whether a cause of action survives the death of a person,[191] which is distinct from the question whether the act of causing the death of a person gives any, if so what, right of action for damages to his or her dependants.[192]

3–77   **Actio personalis moritur cum persona.** At common law a personal action died with the parties to the cause of action,[193] thus an action for negligence had to be begun during the joint lifetime of the person injured and the tortfeasor. Even after such an action had been so commenced, if either of the parties died before a verdict had been obtained, the action abated and could not be continued or recommenced by or against the deceased's personal representatives.

3–78   **Law Reform (Miscellaneous Provisions) Act 1934.** Before the passing of this Act, it was frequently commented that it was cheaper to kill a man than to

---

[187] *Defries v Milne* [1913] 1 Ch.98; cf. *Dawson v Great Northern and City Ry* [1905] 1 K.B. 260.
[188] *Prosser v Edmonds* (1835) 1 Y. & C. 481 at 497. See also, per Farwell L.J. in *Defries v Milne* [1913] 1 Ch.98 at 110; *Glegg v Bromley* [1912] 3 K.B. 474.
[189] *Glegg v Bromley* [1912] 3 K.B. 474.
[190] *Compania Colombiana de Seguros v Pacific Steam Navigation Co* [1965] 1 Q.B. 101.
[191] See Ch.16, below, para.16–75 et seq.
[192] See Ch.16, below, paras 16–05 et seq.
[193] Law Revision Committee's Interim Report 1934 (Cmnd. 4540).

maim him.[194] The growth of motor traffic and the increasing number of accidents on the roads highlighted the problem, since someone injured in a collision caused by the negligence of another driver could be without remedy, despite the existence of compulsory insurance[195] against third-party risks, if the negligent defendant subsequently died. Accordingly, the Act provided that on the death[196] of any person all causes of action subsisting against or vested in him should survive against, or, as the case may be, for the benefit of, his estate. A claim is brought by or against the executor or administrator of the deceased, pursuant to any procedural rules of the court.

(O) Joint claimants

Persons suffering joint loss and damage. The old rule at common law was **3–79** that all persons who suffered a joint injury must join in one action. This is no longer the case. The Civil Procedure Rules ("CPR") permit several claimants to use a single claim form to start claims against a single defendant, subject to a test of convenience.[197] But where a person claims a remedy to which some other person is jointly entitled with him, all persons jointly entitled to the remedy must be parties to the action unless the court otherwise orders.[198] If a person so entitled refuses to be a claimant in the action, he will be joined as a defendant, again unless the court otherwise orders.[199]

Of course, it may not always be necessary for each jointly injured person to be **3–80** a party to the action. Thus, a bailee in possession of a chattel can sue alone a defendant, whose negligence allegedly has damaged it, even if the bailee is not personally liable to its owner.[200]

Where two or more persons have suffered a joint but not a several loss or damage, a release granted by one such person, in the absence of fraud, will operate as a bar to an action by any of the others.[201]

(P) Joint and several tortfeasors

Joint and several torts. Three situations can arise where two or more **3–81** wrongdoers have committed torts which have caused damage to a claimant: (1) where the wrongdoers are joint tortfeasors; (2) where they are independent tortfeasors, causing the same damage; and (3) where they are independent tortfeasors, each causing different damage. In the last case each wrongdoer is

---

[194] For comment, see *H. West & Son Ltd v Shephard* [1964] A.C. 326 at 342, per Lord Reid.
[195] See Road Traffic Act 1930 and, subsequently, the Road Traffic Act 1988.
[196] Which includes subsequent suicide: *Pigney v Pointers Transport Services* [1957] 1 W.L.R. 1121.
[197] CPR 1998 Pt 7, r.3.
[198] CPR Pt 19, r.2(1). See *Shell UK Ltd v Total UK Ltd, The Times,* March 30, 2010, CA.
[199] CPR Pt 19, r.2(2).
[200] See *The Winkfield* [1902] P. 42. The bailee holds in trust for the true owners any excess he recovers over and above the full value of the damaged chattel from the tortfeasor. See also *A. Tomlinson (Hauliers) Ltd v Hepburn* [1966] A.C. 451.
[201] *Phillips v Clagett* (1843) 11 M. & W. 84.

liable only for that part of the damage caused by him, whilst if one of a number of joint tortfeasors or one of several tortfeasors causing the same damage is sued alone then, subject to any right he may have to contribution from the other tortfeasors, he is liable for the whole of the damage, even though he may have been responsible merely for just a small part of it.[202]

3-82   Prior to the passing of the Law Reform (Married Women and Tortfeasors) Act 1935, the distinction between situations (1) and (2) above was important. If a joint tort were committed, there could be only one action and one judgment obtained by the claimant for the whole of the amount of the damage suffered.[203] Accordingly, upon judgment being obtained against one joint wrongdoer, it acted as a bar to any further action against any of the others, despite the fact that the judgment may have remained unsatisfied.[204] This rule did not apply where there were several independent tortfeasors, each responsible for a distinctly separate tort. In those circumstances, successive actions could then be brought against them, even where the plaintiff's damage was incapable of being apportioned between them.[205]

3-83   **Abolition of the rule by statute.** A change was effected by the 1935 Act. Section 6 permitted the bringing of successive actions against joint as well as several tortfeasors, who were liable in respect of the same damage. In turn this section was repealed and replaced by the Civil Liability (Contribution) Act 1978[206] s.3 of which extends to cover all persons who are liable to the claimants in respect of the same damage. The section provides that the fact of a judgment recovered against any person liable in respect of any damage shall cease to be a bar to an action or to the continuance of an action[207] against any other person jointly liable with him, in respect of the same damage.[208] Thus, an unsatisfied judgment against one tortfeasor is not a bar any longer to recovery against other tortfeasors, whether such unsatisfied judgment arose out of either a single action

---

[202] *Clark v Newsham* (1847) 1 Ex. 131 at 140; *Longdon-Griffiths v Smith* [1951] 1 K.B. 295. For an exception to the usual rule, see *Barker v Corus (UK) Plc* [2006] 2 A.C. 572, Ch.6, para.6–52 below.

[203] *London Association for Protection of Trade v Greenlands* [1916] 2 A.C. 15.

[204] *Brinsmead v Harrison* (1872) L.R. 7 C.P. 547 (the tort became submerged in the judgment); *Parr v Snell* [1923] 1 K.B. 1; *Ash v Hutchinson & Co* [1936] Ch.489.

[205] *The Koursk* [1924] P. 140. In the absence of evidence upon which to apportion the damages, they are usually apportioned equally between the tortfeasors; *Bank View Mills v Nelson Corp* [1942] 2 All E.R. 477 at 483, which was reversed on other grounds [1943] 1 K.B. 337.

[206] A person shall not be entitled to recover contributions or be liable to make contribution in accordance with s.1 by reference to any liability based on breach of any obligation assumed by him before January 1, 1979, namely the date when this Act came into force: s.7(2).

[207] The significance of these words, relating to continuance, was to override the difficulties met in *Wah Tat Bank Ltd v Chan Cheng Kom* [1975] A.C. 507 and *Bryanston Finance Ltd v De Vries* [1975] Q.B. 703 in that s.6 of the Act of 1935 did not appear to apply to a single action against two joint tortfeasors, when judgment was recovered against one of them before completion of the proceedings against the other.

[208] If a judgment is satisfied against one of the tortfeasors such will be a bar to an action against the others, whether joint or several tortfeasors, as regards the same damage, except in the case of a foreign judgment: *Kohnke v Karger* [1951] 2 K.B. 670.

against the tortfeasors, which was concluded in separate judgments,[209] or out of successive separate actions against the tortfeasors.[210]

Where the claimant brings more than one action in respect of the same **3–84** damage, he will not be entitled to costs in the subsequent actions unless the court is of the opinion that there were reasonable grounds for his bringing such proceedings.[211] In that manner there is a safeguard against a multiplicity of actions against joint tortfeasors and others, who may be jointly or severally liable to the claimant.

The Civil Procedure Rules 1998 permit a single claim form to be used to start **3–85** all claims which can be conveniently disposed of in the same proceedings.[212] Moreover, the court has wide powers to add or substitute parties if it is thought desirable, with a view to ensuring that a claim is resolved between all affected parties.[213] Accordingly, there should be no difficulty in ensuring that all persons who are allegedly responsible for the damage suffered by the claimant are before the court, whether they are technically joint or several tortfeasors.

If judgment is obtained against one defendant only, the costs which the **3–86** claimant has to pay to the successful defendant, can be added to the costs which he can recover from the unsuccessful defendant, provided that the court decides that he had acted reasonably in joining the successful defendant as a party.[214] If judgment be obtained against more than one defendant, the claimant can recover the amount of his judgment from either or both of the defendants and he is not obliged to apportion the amount recovered between the various defendants. Among themselves, however, the defendants may recover contribution,[215] but this is a topic outside the scope of this work.

Joint tortfeasors. Wrongdoers are deemed to be joint tortfeasors, within the **3–87** meaning of the rule, where the cause of action against each of them is the same, namely that the same evidence would support an action against them, individually.[216] "There must be a concurrence in the act or acts causing damage not merely a coincidence of separate acts which by their conjoined effect cause damage."[217] Accordingly, they will be jointly liable for a tort which they both commit or for which they are responsible because the law imputes the commission of the same wrongful act to two or more persons at the same time.

---

[209] See, e.g. *Bryanston Finance Ltd v De Vries* [1975] Q.B. 703.
[210] See, e.g. *Wah Tat Bank Ltd v Chan Cheng Kom* [1975] A.C. 507.
[211] See s.4 of the Civil Liability (Contribution) Act 1978.
[212] CPR Pt 7, r.3.
[213] CPR Pt 19, rr.1 and 3. The court may add a party if it considers it right to do so; alternatively, one of the existing parties may make such an application.
[214] *Bullock v London General Omnibus Co* [1907] 1 K.B. 264; *Besterman v British Motor Cab Co* [1914] 3 K.B. 181. See also Pt 44, rr.3(4) and (6) of the Civil Procedure Rules 1998.
[215] In respect of which, see *Clerk & Lindsell on Torts* (19th edn, 2006), paras 4–24 et seq. for a detailed discussion.
[216] *Brunsden v Humphrey* (1884) 14 Q.B.D. 141 at 147, per Bowen L.J., quoting from older authorities.
[217] per Sargent L.J. in *The Koursk* [1924] P. 140 at 159.

This occurs in cases of (a) agency[218]; (b) vicarious liability[219]; and (c) where a tort is committed in the course of a joint act, whilst pursuing a common purpose agreed between them.

3–88   *Brooke v Bool*[220] is an example of both (a) and (c) above. The defendant landlord went to investigate the smell of gas in the claimant's lock-up shop, taking his lodger with him to assist. While the defendant examined the lower part of the gas pipe with a naked light, the lodger, a younger man, also carrying a light, climbed on top of the shop's counter. The lodger was examining the upper part of the gas pipe when a severe explosion occurred. The defendant was held liable to the claimant shopkeeper for the loss and damage suffered, even though actually caused by the negligent acts of his lodger.

3–89   **Concurrent tortfeasors.** Wrongdoers are not jointly liable for a tort where each is responsible for a different wrongful act, although the acts happen to produce the same damage,[221] but only where their wrongful acts and the resulting damage coincide.[222] However, there are many examples where the independent wrongful acts of separate persons, have operated concurrently to cause the same damage.[223] One relatively common situation is where a passenger in a car suffers a single injury as a result of a collision caused by the negligence of two or more drivers.[224] All drivers whose negligence caused the collision are liable to him. It would be otherwise if, for instance, there were a number of collisions causing separate injuries: there, on the face of it, each driver is responsible only for the injury which his negligence caused.[225]

3–90   **Several tortfeasors causing different damage.** Where two or more tortfeasors cause different damage to the same claimant, the causes of action against each wrongdoer are distinct. In *Dillingham Constructions v Steel Mains Pty,*[226] a workman, suffered shock and sustained personal injuries when a suspended load of steel fell from an overhead crane. His employer's negligence had caused the

---

[218] See generally, paras 3–360 to 3–171, below.

[219] See generally, paras 3–98 to 3–206, below.

[220] [1928] 2 K.B. 578, particularly at 585–586, per Salter J.

[221] *The Koursk* [1924] P. 140 at 156 where Scrutton L.J. adopted as correct, a passage in *Clerk & Lindsell on Torts* (see now the 19th edn, 2006, para.4–108): "but mere similarity of design on the part of independent actors, causing independent damage is not enough; there must be concerted action to a common end." Still less will persons be joint tortfeasors when there is not even similarity of design, but independent wrongful acts accidentally resulting in one damage.

[222] e.g. *King v Sadler* (1970) 114 S.J. 192 (the plaintiff was injured by carbon monoxide gas which escaped from the boiler room below the hotel room where he was staying. He claimed damages for negligence against the hotel owner and the gas board responsible for servicing the boiler. Sir Jocelyn Simon P. held that the board were in breach of their contract with the owner and in breach of their duty of care to the plaintiff; that the hotel owner was also in breach of duty to the plaintiff and that, on the facts, liability should be apportioned equally between the two defendants).

[223] *The Koursk* [1924] P. 140.

[224] *Drinkwater v Kimber* [1952] 2 Q.B. 281 at 292, per Morris L.J.

[225] However, by way of further refinement, the passenger injured in sequential collisions may be able to recover all his injury from the negligent author of the first where that caused the second to occur: *Ward v Palamarchuk and Pelech* [1977] 6 W.W.R. 193.

[226] (1975) 6 A.L.R. 171 (Law Reform (Miscellaneous Provisions) Act 1946 (N.S.W.) s.5(1)(c)), applying *Baker v Willoughby* [1970] A.C. 467.

accident, and he received damages. Two years later, the same individual, who by this time was employed by the defendants, suffered similar injuries in another accident, involving the fall of a steel pipe. When he sued the defendants for damages, they filed a cross-claim against his former employers, on the ground that the later injuries were an exacerbation of the earlier and amounted to the "same damage" within the meaning of the words of the comparable Act. On appeal the cross-claim failed: the injuries were not the "same damage" but arose from separate and completely unrelated acts. A claimant is able to recover from each tortfeasor only that part of his damage which is attributable to the negligence of the particular defendant concerned.[227]

In *Rahman v Arearose Ltd*,[228] the claimant's employers had been negligent in **3–91** failing to reduce the risk of assault upon him in the course of his employment at their fast food premises. He sustained an injury to an eye. Thereafter, as a result of negligence in the course of surgery to repair the injury, he sustained further injury causing blindness in the eye. The employers were held partly responsible for the claimant's losses, including those resulting from psychological symptoms, even though the negligent surgery had supervened. The case was not one of joint tortfeasors but each tortfeasor separately responsible for discrete parts of the claimant's loss and a proper apportionment between them was three-quarters—one-quarter against the second defendant.

Release. The release of one joint tortfeasor releases all the others, whether or **3–92** not that was what the parties had intended. Accordingly, where a claim, based upon the same facts, has been framed in alternative ways against several defendants and the claimant has decided to accept a sum paid into court by one of the defendants in satisfaction of one of the causes of action, the whole of the claim against all the defendants comes to an end if the damages recoverable upon all the claims are the same and the sum so accepted is sufficient to cover these damages.[229] This full release would seem to be effective even though this may not have been the intention of the parties. It was said to be:

> " . . . clear law, that a release granted to one joint tortfeasor, or to one joint debtor, operates as a discharge of the other joint tortfeasor or the other joint debtor, the reason being that the cause of action, which is one and indivisible, having been released, all persons otherwise liable thereto are consequently released."[230]

This rule applies equally where the release has been made under deed or by **3–93** way of accord and satisfaction.[231] On the other hand, a covenant or other agreement not to sue one joint tortfeasor does not operate as a release to the

---

[227] *Performance Cars Ltd v Abraham* [1962] 1 Q.B. 33; *Baker v Willoughby* [1970] A.C. 467.
[228] [2001] Q.B. 351 per Laws L.J. at 365 it is not a rule of law that later negligence always extinguishs the causative potency of an earlier tort: "The law is that every tortfeasor should compensate the injured claimant in respect of that loss and damage for which he should justly be held responsible. To make that principle good, it is important that the elusive conception of causation should not be frozen into constricting rules."
[229] *Beadon v Capital Syndicate* (1912) 28 T.L.R. 427; *Clark v Urquhart* [1930] A.C. 28 and see CPR Pt 36, r.17.
[230] *Duck v Mayeu* [1892] 2 Q.B. 511 per A.L. Smith L.J. at 513.
[231] *Thurman v Wild* (1840) 11 A. & E. 453.

others, the reason being that the joint action is still alive.[232] Such a contract merely prevents action against the particular tortfeasor, with whom the claimant entered into the agreement not to sue. In *Gardiner v Moore*,[233] it was held, inter alia, that while the release of one joint tortfeasor, whether by deed or by way of accord and satisfaction, released all others, the same principle did not apply to a case involving not joint but several independent tortfeasors. The form of release will be construed as being a mere agreement not to sue, if it contains an express or implied reservation of the right to proceed against the others, since otherwise the reservation would be wholly ineffective.

3-94　　Where settlement is achieved with one of a number of concurrent tortfeasors it will depend upon the terms of the agreement whether any action can survive against the others.[234] On the face of it, settlement "in full and final satisfaction of all causes of action" in a statement of claim against one concurrent tortfeasor discharged also the liability of the other tortfeasors even where they had not themselves been included in the claimant's suit. It was irrelevant that if the case had gone to trial the judge would have held a greater amount of damages to be due than were accepted. The critical questions were whether the claimant's claim was for the full amount of his loss and whether the sum accepted was in full settlement of that claim. If it was, then satisfaction of the claim extinguished the claim against other concurrent tortfeasors.[235] Even in a case where several tortfeasors have allegedly caused different damage the court will look, on the claimant's settlement with one, to see if the intention was to settle the claim in its entirety, and if that was the case, the claimant may be prevented from proceeding against the remaining defendants.[236]

3-95　　**Contribution between tortfeasors.** The complexities of this topic, which are now contained within the provisions of the Civil Liability (Contribution) Act 1978,[237] fall outside the scope of this work.[238] The right of contribution is a right sui generis and is not a cause of action in tort. As regards the limitation period which applies see the Limitation Act 1980 s.10.[239]

---

[232] *Duck v Mayeu* [1892] 11 A. & E. 453 at 513, per A. L. Smith L.J. The distinction is well established, even if it be a technical one; *Cutler v McPhail* [1962] 2 Q.B. 292. It has not been affected by the Civil Liability (Contribution) Act 1978, although criticised by Lord Denning M.R. in *Bryanston Finance Ltd v De Vries* [1975] Q.B. 703 at 723.

[233] [1969] 1 Q.B. 55.

[234] For concurrent tortfeasors see para.3–89, above.

[235] *Jameson v Central Electricity Generating Board* [2000] 1 A.C. 455, especially the speech of Lord Hope of Craighead at 472 et seq. See also *Heaton v Axa Equity and Law Life Assurance Society Plc* [2000] 3 W.L.R. 1347, where the claimant failed to distinguish *Jameson* on the basis that he had separate claims against the defendants arising under separate contracts with each. See also *Rawlinson v North Essex Health Authority* [2000] Lloyd's Rep. Med. 54 (claim struck out where the claimant had accepted compensation in an earlier group action against the company responsible for manufacturing a drug which the defendant's hospital used in his treatment). See also Ch.4, para.4–247.

[236] *Heaton v Axa Equity and Law Life Assurance Plc* [2002] 2 A.C. 329.

[237] Which came into force on January 1, 1979.

[238] See e.g. *Clerk & Lindsell on Torts* (19th edn, 2006), paras 4–12 et seq.

[239] See also Ch.4, para.4–230, below.

Employers and employees combined, as tortfeasors. It is an implied term   **3–96**
of an employee's contract of employment that he shall exercise reasonable care
in the performance of his duty to his employer. Accordingly, where employers
were held vicariously liable for their employee's negligence, it was held that they
were entitled to recover from him the damages they had been found liable to pay,
in an action brought against him for breach of contract.[240] An employer,
nevertheless, cannot rely upon an employee's or contractor's breach of contract
to recover an indemnity in respect of damages awarded against him, if he, either
by himself or by another employee, has also been guilty of negligence. In such
circumstances, his only remedy is to sue for contribution from the employee, as
a tortfeasor under the Act.[241]

In strict theory, while often spoken of in terms of vicarious liability, an   **3–97**
employer is jointly and severally liable for a tort which has been committed by
an employee acting in the course of employment.[242] It might be thought that the
concept of vicarious liability would be confined to those situations where a
person could be liable for the tort of another, even though he had neither
authorised nor ratified it.[243] However, it is to the scope of vicarious liability as it
has in fact developed that we should now turn.

2.—VICARIOUS LIABILITY

Introduction. Vicarious liability means that one person takes the place of   **3–98**
another so far as liability is concerned.[244] Lord Pearce has said, "the doctrine of
vicarious liability has not grown from any very clear, logical or legal principle

---

[240] *Lister v Romford Ice & Cold Storage Co* [1957] A.C. 555 (there was no implied term in the contract of service that the driver was entitled to be indemnified by the employer, whether the employer was insured, or was required by the Road Traffic Act to be insured, or if, as a reasonable and prudent person, he ought to have been insured). See also *Semtex v Gladstone* [1954] 1 W.L.R. 945; *Harvey v R.G. O'Dell (Galway, Third Party)* [1958] 2 Q.B. 78 (*Lister* had no application when an employee was not actually carrying out the duties, for which he was employed); and *Gregory v Ford* [1951] 1 All E.R. 121 (implied term in contract of service that employer would comply with the compulsory obligation to insure against third-party risks). cf. the like situation in *Paterson v Costain & Press (Overseas) Ltd* [1979] 2 Lloyd's Rep. 204, CA.

[241] i.e. the Civil Liability (Contribution) Act 1978: see *Jones v Manchester Corp* [1952] 2 Q.B. 852 at 870, per Denning L.J.; and *Daniel v Rickett, Cockerell & Co* [1938] 2 K.B. 322 (where it was held that the employer of an independent contractor was not entirely free from blame, so that the damage fell to be apportioned under the Act of 1935).

[242] In *Semtex Ltd v Gladstone* [1954] 1 W.L.R. 945 at 949, Finnemore J. said: "For some reason that I have never been quite able to understand, the master who is vicariously responsible for his servant is referred to as, and apparently treated as, a joint tortfeasor." See also *Treacy v Robinson & Son* [1937] I.R. 255 at 266.

[243] The legal concept of vicarious liability requires three parties: the injured party, a person whose act or default caused the injury and a person vicariously liable for the latter's act or default: *Boyle v Kodak* [1969] 1 W.L.R. 661, per Lord Diplock.

[244] See per Lord Denning M.R. quoting *The Shorter Oxford Dictionary* in *Launchbury v Morgans* [1971] 2 Q.B. 245 at 252 (although the decision of the Court of Appeal was reversed by the House of Lords [1973] A.C. 127). See generally, Case, "Developments in vicarious liability: shifting sands and slippery slopes" (2006) 3 P.N. 161.

[179]

but from social convenience and rough justice."[245] The rule has its roots in the early common law but it was not until the time of Sir John Holt (1642–1710) that it began to assume something of its modern aspect, being thereafter particularly advanced by the great judges of Queen Victoria's reign. It came to be established that the liability of an employer for the tort of his employee was based, not on a fiction that he had impliedly commanded his employee to act as he did, but on the ground that the employee had acted within the scope of, or during the course of, his employment or authority. Although the relationship of employer and employee is by far the most important, in terms of daily practice, of the various circumstances in which vicarious liability is recognised by the law, consideration must also be given to the rule as it applies in relation to agents, independent contractors and children.

(A) Employees

3–99   **Who is an employee?** An employee (or servant as the older authorities say), may be defined "as any person employed by another to do work for him on the terms that he, the servant, is to be subject to the control and directions of his employer in respect of the manner in which his work is to be done."[246] An employee is therefore one who is bound to obey any lawful orders given by the employer as to the manner in which his work shall be done. The employer retains the power of controlling him in his work, and may direct not only what he shall do, but how he shall do it.[247] Whether the employment is by the day or by the job, and whether the amount of wages or salary paid is great or small, is of little assistance in determining whether a contract of service exists.[248] "The test to be generally applied lies in the nature and degree of detailed control over the person alleged to be a servant."[249] In *Ferguson v Dawson*,[250] it was held that the claimant was an employee and not a sub-contractor, where he had no power to delegate his work to someone else to do for him. In ascertaining who is liable for the act of a wrongdoer, "you must look to the wrongdoer himself or to the first person in the ascending line who is the employer and has control over the work. You cannot go further back, and make the employer of that person liable."[251]

3–100   **Distinction between employees and independent contractors.** An independent contractor, as opposed to an employee, is one who carries on an independent business on his own account, in the course of which he contracts to

---

[245] *Imperial Chemical Industries Ltd v Shatwell* [1965] A.C. 656 at 685.
[246] See Salmond & Heuston on the Law of Torts, 20th edn (1992), p.448.
[247] *Sadler v Henlock* (1855) 4 E. & B. 570 at 578, per Crompton J.; *Simmons v Heath Laundry Co* [1910] 1 K.B. 543; *Yewens v Noakes* (1880) 6 Q.B.D. 530.
[248] *Sadler v Henlock* (1855) 4 E. & B. 570; *Performing Right Society Ltd v Mitchell and Booker (Palais de Danse) Ltd* [1924] 1 K.B. 762.
[249] per McCardie J. in the case last cited.
[250] [1976] 1 W.L.R. 1213. However it is questionable how far *Ferguson* can still be relied upon, bearing in mind the altered working environment: see *Lane v Shire Roofing Co (Oxford) Ltd, The Times*, February 22, 1995, CA, para.3–102, below.
[251] per Willes J. in *Murray v Currie* (1870) L.R. 6 C.P. 24 at 27.

do certain work.[252] He may, by the terms of his contract, be subject to the directions of his employer, but apart from the contract he is his own master as to the manner and time in which the work shall be done.[253] If, in order to carry out the work, he has to engage and pay workmen or other employees on his own behalf and not as agent for another, there is a strong presumption that he is an independent contractor even though his employer has reserved the right to dismiss any workman employed on his work.[254] It is sometimes said that an employee is employed under a contract of service, while an independent contractor is employed under a contract for services.[255] But this gives no assistance in determining whether a person is an employee or not, because in all contracts of service it is the services of the employee which the employer contracts to procure.

There was an important discussion of the topic in *Ready Mixed Concrete*   **3–101**
(South East) Ltd v Ministry of Pensions and National Insurance.[256] After a review of the authorities, including those outside England, MacKenna J. held that a contract of service existed if:

(i) the employee agreed that, in consideration of a wage or other remuneration, he would provide his own work and skill in the performance of some service for his employer;

(ii) he agreed, expressly or impliedly that, in the performance of that service, he would be subject to the other's control in a sufficient degree to make that other employer; and

(iii) the other provisions of the contract were consistent with its being a contract of service.[257]

Times move on and this analysis is no longer the last word. By the time of   **3–102**
Lane v Shire Roofing Co (Oxford) Ltd[258] it was noted that the employment background had altered. There were reasons for both employer and employees to avoid the "employment" label. It was said the court should look to the work being carried on and ask "whose business was it?" On the facts of the case, even

---

[252] *Allen v Hayward* (1845) 7 Q.B. 960, where the contractor was described as a "person carrying on an independent business, such as the commissioners were fully justified in employing to perform works which they could not execute for themselves, and who was known to all the world as performing them"; *Laugher v Pointer* (1826) 5 B. & C. 547; *Quarman v Burnett* (1840) 6 M. & W. 499.

[253] *Steel v S.E. Ry* (1855) 16 C.B. 550; *Hardaker v Idle District Council* [1896] 1 Q.B. 335.

[254] *Reedie v L. & N.W. Ry* (1849) 4 Ex. 244; cf. *Performing Right Society Ltd v Mitchell and Booker (Palais de Danse) Ltd* [1924] 1 K.B. 762, where the contract was made with the members of the band individually and they were held to be servants.

[255] See, e.g. *Stevenson Jordan & Harrison Ltd v MacDonald & Evans* [1952] 1 T.L.R. 101 at 111, per Denning L.J.; *Collins v Hertfordshire County Council* [1947] K.B. 598 at 615, per Hilbery J.

[256] [1968] 2 Q.B. 497, applied in *Davis v New England College of Arundel* [1977] I.C.R. 6 (where it was held that the relationship between the parties, when looked at objectively, was one of employee and employer and that neither the applicant's request to be treated as a self-employed freelance lecturer nor the fact that for advantageous fiscal purposes the college had treated him as self-employed altered their contractual position at all).

[257] [1968] 2 Q.B. 515.

[258] *The Times*, February 22, 1995, CA.

though the claimant had self-employed status from the fiscal point of view, and had provided his own tools and ladder, the business he was engaged in when he fell from a ladder and sustained serious head injury, was the defendants' and accordingly they stood in the relation to him of employer.[259]

3–103   In the result, despite a plethora of authorities, and precisely because social and employment conditions change, no single test has emerged that will conclusively point to the distinction in all cases. In the Privy Council, their Lordships approved[260] the summary of Cooke J. in *Market Investigations Ltd v Minister of Social Security* who said[261]:

> "The fundamental test to be applied is this: 'Is the person who has engaged himself to perform these services performing them as a person in business on his own account.' If the answer to that question is 'yes,' then the contract is a contract for services. If the answer is 'no,' then the contract is a contract of service. No exhaustive list has been compiled and perhaps no exhaustive list can be compiled of the considerations which are relevant in determining that question, nor can strict rules be laid down as to the relative weight which the various considerations should carry in particular cases. The most that can be said is that control will no doubt always have to be considered, although it can no longer be regarded as the sole determining factor[262]; and that factors which may be of importance are such matters as whether the man performing the services provides his own equipment, whether he hires his own helpers, what degree of financial risk he takes, what degree of responsibility for investment and management he has, and whether and how far he has an opportunity of profiting from sound management in the performance of his task."

3–104   Whatever formula is eventually thought to be appropriate in the particular case, a good starting point may well be the suggestion of Somervell L.J.: "one

---

[259] See *Wharf v Bildwell Insulations Ltd* [1999] C.L.Y. 2047, CA (although said to be self-employed the claimant worked for the defendant exclusively for six years, the defendant dictated payment terms and provided all necessary tools). See also *Stevedoring and Haulage Services Ltd v Fuller* [2001] I.R.L.R. 627, CA (workers were self-employed where their contracts expressly provided that they were to be engaged on a casual basis and there was no obligation on the employer to provide work or on the employee to accept it); and *Montgomery v Johnson Underwood* [2001] I.R.L.R. 296, CA (claimant not the employee of an employment agency with whom he was registered and who had assigned him to work with a client company: mutuality of obligations and control were minimum requirements of a contract of employment). For a similar approach in Australia, see e.g. *Sweeney v Boylan Nominees Pty Ltd* [2006] B.L.R. 440, HC (Aus)(a mechanic sent by the defendant company to repair its refrigerator on the premises of a third party, was an independent contractor: he invoiced the defendant for each job, provided his own liability insurance, supplied his own tools and equipment and was not presented to the public as the defendant's representative).
[260] *Lee Ting Sang v Chung Chi-Keung* [1990] 2 A.C. 374 at 382.
[261] [1969] 2 Q.B. 173 at 184–185.
[262] per Eveleigh J. in *Nottingham v Aldridge* [1971] 2 Q.B. 739 at 749: "In many cases the legal right of the employer to control the manner in which his servant works has little practical application in the days of highly trained specialists, and his protection, and, indeed, that of his victim, lies in his ability to control his insurance rather than to control his agent." Even if the employer has the necessary skill, he may not have the time nor the opportunity to give his servant technical directions as, e.g. in modern fast-moving traffic conditions: *Union S.S. Co v Colville* [1960] N.Z.L.R. 100 at 109, per North J. See also *Mersey Docks and Harbour Board v Coggins & Griffith (Liverpool) Ltd* [1947] A.C. 1 and para.3–152, below.

perhaps cannot get much beyond this: 'was his contract a contract of service within the meaning which an ordinary person would give to the words?'"[263]

Illustrations: unskilled occupations. A labourer, or other person carrying on   3–105
an unskilled occupation, if employed to do work himself will usually be an employee,[264] such as a person who is employed to clean out a drain on his employer's land.[265] On the other hand, if he is not obliged to do the work in person but may engage others to do it, as where he lets on hire to a local authority a vehicle and driver,[266] he will usually be an independent contractor, because he is carrying on a separate business of his own.

Illustrations: skilled occupations. As a general rule in a skilled occupation,   3–106
any self-employed person carrying on a separate business, is not an employee. Thus, a plumber employed to mend a cistern[267]; a licensed drover employed to drive cattle in a district where the employment of a licensed drover is compulsory[268]; an auctioneer conducting a sale on the premises of the person who employs him[269]; a music teacher who gives lessons to her pupils, whether or not at her own home[270]; a commercial traveller, paid by commission[271]; and a qualified licensed pilot,[272] all have been held not to be employees. Likewise, when the defendants, who had contracted with the owners of a theatre to produce a variety programme, made an agreement with certain artistes to appear in the programme, it was held that the artistes were not the defendants' employees.[273] Where the claimant had contracted with the defendant to construct stock fencing along a boundary, he was an independent contractor where, on standing back and asking whose business it had been, it had obviously been his business: he had been taking the financial risk, and had stood to gain or to lose according to the speed and efficiency with which the work was completed.[274] On the other hand, persons carrying on skilled occupations, who are not carrying on a separate

---

[263] *Cassidy v Ministry of Health* [1951] 2 K.B. 343 at 352–353 quoting a question posed by Buckley L.J. in *Simmons v Heath Laundry Co* [1910] 1 K.B. 543 at 553. See also, per Roskill J. in *Argent v Minister of Social Security* [1968] 1 W.L.R. 1749 at 1760; *Market Investigations Ltd v Minister of Social Security* [1969] 2 Q.B. 173.
[264] In *Ferguson v John Dawson & Partners (Contractors)* [1976] 1 W.L.R. 1213, the fact that a builder's labourer was employed as a "self-employed, labour-only subcontractor" (i.e. he was on "the lump," without cards and no deductions being made for income tax or national insurance contributions) did not affect the parties' true relationship which was one of employer and employee.
[265] *Sadler v Henlock* (1855) 4 E. & B. 570.
[266] *Jones v Liverpool Corporation* (1885) 14 Q.B.D. 890.
[267] *Blake v Woolf* [1898] 2 Q.B. 426.
[268] *Milligan v Wedge* (1840) 12 A. & E. 737. Otherwise in a district where it is not compulsory: *Turnbull v Wieland* (1916) 33 T.L.R. 143.
[269] *Walker v Crabb* (1916) 33 T.L.R. 119.
[270] *Simmons v Heath Laundry Co* [1910] 1 K.B. 543.
[271] *Egginton v Reader* (1936) 52 T.L.R. 212.
[272] *Esso Petroleum Co Ltd v Hall Russell & Co Ltd and Shetland Islands Council, The Times*, October 7, 1988. On the other hand, a shipowner was liable to third parties for negligent navigation by a pilot, both under common law and by statute.
[273] *Fraser-Wallas v Waters* [1939] 4 All E.R. 609.
[274] *Jennings v The Forestry Commission* [2008] EWCA Civ 581(the claimant suffered serious injuries when, in attempting to gain access to the site in his Land Rover, the vehicle overturned).

business, will be employees, such as a schoolmaster employed by a local education authority[275]; a freelance lecturer employed by a college[276]; a musician employed at a dance hall[277] and a doctor employed by a hospital whether he is full time or part time.[278]

3–107   **Inference of employment.** There is an inference to be drawn that a person is employed as an employee and not as an independent contractor where, despite any special skills required to fulfil his duties, he comes under the direct supervision or personal control of his employer and does not purport to exercise some independent employment.[279] Where a teacher is employed, paid and liable to be dismissed by a local education authority that authority, as employer, is vicariously liable for the teacher's acts and omissions in the course of his employment.[280] So, where a teacher punished a boy by striking his ear, thereby causing deafness, her employers were liable.[281] Doctors and other professional employees can come within the same category.[282]

3–108   At one time, it was considered that hospital authorities were not vicariously liable for the negligence of their medical staff. It was thought that the element of control over their methods of working was lacking, since such staff were employed to exercise their professional skills, according to their own discretion, without being bound to obey the authorities' directions.[283] The view to the contrary is now well established and radiographers,[284] house surgeons,[285] full-time assistant medical officers[286] and, probably, anaesthetists on the staff[287] have all been held to be employees for whose negligence a hospital authority can be vicariously liable.

3–109   By virtue of s.3 of the National Health Service Act 1946, it is the duty of the Minister to provide, inter alia, "medical, nursing and other services required at or for the purposes of hospitals" and "the services of specialists". Accordingly, because a hospital authority itself is under a primary duty to its patients, it cannot discharge that duty simply by delegating its performance to somebody else,

---

[275] *Smith v Martin and Hull Corporation* [1911] 2 K.B. 775.
[276] *Davis v New England College of Arundel* [1976] I.C.R. 6.
[277] *Performing Right Society Ltd v Mitchell and Booker (Palais de Danse) Ltd* [1924] 1 K.B. 762.
[278] *Bolam v Friern Hospital Management Committee* [1957] 1 W.L.R. 582. See generally Ch.9, paras 9–109 to 9–154, below.
[279] *Smith v Martin and Hull Corp* [1911] 2 K.B. 775; *Fryer v Salford Corp* [1937] 1 All E.R. 617.
[280] *Smith v Martin and Hull Corp*, above.
[281] *Ryan v Fildes* [1938] 3 All E.R. 517.
[282] But see *Davis v L.C.C.* (1914) 30 T.L.R. 275 (a local education authority which did not employ a doctor was not liable for negligent performance of an operation upon a pupil where an apparently competent doctor was engaged).
[283] *Hillyer v St. Bartholomew's Hospital* [1909] 2 K.B. 820 at 825, per Farwell L.J.
[284] *Gold v Essex County Council* [1942] 2 K.B. 293.
[285] *Collins v Hertfordshire* [1947] K.B. 598.
[286] *Cassidy v Ministry of Health* [1951] 2 K.B. 343.
[287] *Roe v Minister of Health* [1954] 2 Q.B. 66.

whether independent contractor or employee.[288] The hospital authority's statutory duty is not discharged, merely by the appointment of competent doctors, nurses and specialists.[289]

Persons held not to be employees. Nurses, when supplied by a nursing **3–110** association on terms that they were to obey the directions of the patient's doctor and were to be regarded as employed by the person engaging the nurse, were held not to be the employees of the nursing association, so as to make the association liable for the negligence of the nurse during an operation.[290] The resident medical staff and the nurses at a hospital were not the employees of the surgeon who was operating at the hospital.[291]

Persons appointed by a local authority to perform statutory or common law **3–111** duties have been held not to be employees of the local authority while performing those duties. So an inspector appointed under the Diseases of Animals Acts,[292] and a police constable appointed by the watch committee,[293] have each been held not to be employees of a local authority. Further, it has been held that the relationship of employer and employee did not exist between the state and a sergeant in one of the defence forces.[294] A scoutmaster and a cub mistress, who were in charge of schoolboys at an outing to Whipsnade Zoo, were not employees of the Boy Scouts Association.[295] Likewise, a schoolboy, aged 10 years, who was given the task of distributing milk to classrooms, was not an employee of the school authority.[296] Share fishermen who made up the crew of a fishing vessel were not employed under contracts of service, where they shared both profits and losses, paid tax as self-employed persons and were treated as self-employed under social security regulations.[297]

Negligence committed "in the course of employment."[298] An employer is **3–112** liable for the negligence of an employee if committed in the course of

---

[288] *Gold v Essex CC* [1942] 2 K.B. 293 at 301, per Lord Greene M.R. and at 309, per Goddard L.J.; *Cassidy v Ministry of Health* [1951] 2 K.B. 343 at 362–365, per Denning L.J.; *Roe v Minister of Health* [1954] 2 Q.B. 66, per Denning L.J.; *M v Calderdale and Kirklees HA* [1998] Lloyd's Rep. Med. 157 (health authority liable for negligent failure of an abortion performed by at a private hospital at which it had arranged for her to be treated). But see *Farraj v King's Healthcare NHS Trust* [2010] P.I.Q.R. P7, CA 1203 (the non-delegable rule depends upon the facts of the case: a hospital authority was not liable for the negligence of an apparently competent laboratory required to culture a sample of tissue for DNA analysis).
[289] *Razzel v Snowball* [1954] 1 W.L.R. 1382.
[290] *Hall v Lees* [1904] 2 K.B. 602. For the position of doctors and nurses at a hospital, see Ch.9, generally, below, paras 9–155 to 9–167.
[291] *Morris v Winsbury-White* [1937] 4 All E.R. 494.
[292] *Stanbury v Exeter Corp* [1905] 2 K.B. 838.
[293] *Fisher v Oldham Corp* [1930] 2 K.B. 364. See also *Attorney-General for New South Wales v Perpetual Trustee Co Ltd* [1955] A.C. 457. See the Police Act 1964 and para.3–20, above.
[294] *Attorney-General and Minister for Defence v Ryan's Car Hire* (1964) 101 I.L.T.R. 57. See also *Tozeland v West Ham Union* [1907] 1 K.B. 920. On the other hand, special constables employed by a railway company under powers conferred by a private Act of Parliament were held to be the servants of the company: *Lambert v G.E. Ry* [1909] 2 K.B. 776.
[295] *Murphy v Zoological Society of London, The Times*, November 14, 1962.
[296] *Watkins v Birmingham City Council, The Times*, August 1, 1975, CA.
[297] *Todd v Adams, The Times*, May 3, 2002, CA.
[298] Further, see Ch.11, para.11–40, below.

employment,[299] but not otherwise. The test, traditionally applied, was that an act was to be regarded as performed in the course of employment,

> "If it is either (1) a wrongful act authorised by the master, or (2) a wrongful and unauthorised mode of doing some act authorised by the master. It is clear that the master is responsible for acts actually authorised by him: for liability would exist in this case, even if the between the parties was merely one of agency, and not one of service at all. But a master, as opposed to the employer of an independent contractor, is liable even for acts which he has not authorised, provided that they are so connected with an act he has authorised that they may rightly be regarded as modes—although improper modes—of doing them."[300]

> "It is well settled law that a master is liable even for acts which he has not authorised provided that they are so connected with the acts which he has authorised that they may rightly be regarded as modes, although improper modes, of doing them.[301] On the other hand, if the unauthorised and wrongful act of the servant is not so connected with the authorised act as to be a mode of doing it but is an independent act, the master, is not responsible for, in such a case the servant is not acting in the course of the employment but has gone outside it."[302]

3–113   As the summaries indicate, an act is done in the course of the employment, not only when an employee is actually doing work which he is employed to do, but also when engaged in some activity incidental to what he is employed to do, and when he is about business which concerns the employer and the employee.[303] Another way of putting it is whether the employee is doing something which it is his duty to his employer to do,[304] pursuant to the terms of his contract of

---

[299] For a curious application of the principle see *James v Harrison* (1978) 18 A.C.T.R. 36 (the defendant, walking hurriedly in one direction, turned suddenly and began walking the other way, colliding with the plaintiff, who had been following behind, and knocking her down. The defendant was employed by a shopkeeper, whose premises the plaintiff had just left. The shopkeeper was vicariously liable to the plaintiff for the defendant's negligence).

[300] The formulation of Salmond, see, e.g. *Salmond & Heuston on the Law of Torts* (21st edn, 1996), p.443.

[301] See *Poland v John Parr & Sons* [1927] 1 K.B. 236 at 240; *Warren v Henlys Ltd* [1948] 2 All E.R. 935 at 937; *Ilkiw v Samuels* [1963] 1 W.L.R. 991 at 997, 1002, 1004.

[302] *Marsh v Moores* [1949] 2 K.B. 208 per Lynskey J. at 215. See *Lister v Hesley Hall Ltd* [2002] 1 A.C. 215, n.294, below.

[303] *Staton v N.C.B.* [1957] 1 W.L.R. 893 (an employer was vicariously liable for the negligence of an employee, who was involved in a collision when cycling on his employer's land to draw his pay at the pay office after he had finished work: the act of travelling to collect pay " was most clearly an act essentially incident to his employment". It was suggested that had the employee been on the highway and not on his employer's land vicarious liability could not have attached). Likewise, in *Compton v McClure* [1975] I.C.R. 378, where an employee had entered his employers' premises for the purpose of going to work, he was held to be acting in the course of his employment from the moment that he had passed through the employers' boundary gates. Further, see *O'Reilly v National Rail and Tramway Appliances Ltd* [1966] 1 All E.R. 499 and *Kay v I.T.W. Ltd* [1968] 1 Q.B. 140.

[304] *Paterson v Costain & Press (Overseas)* [1978] 1 Lloyd's Rep. 86 (on the facts it was held that it was part of the employee's employment to travel on the employer's vehicle on its journey from their offices at Abadan, Iran, to their construction site at Bid Boland). See also *Radclyffe v Ministry of Defence* [2009] EWCA Civ 635 (liability for the failure of an off duty military officer to prevent one of his men, also off duty, from jumping into water from a dangerous height where his responsibility extended to the safety of men under his command on such off duty occasions and included, the swimming expedition on which the claimant was injured).

employment.[305] In *Lister v Hesley Hall Ltd*[306] it was said in the House of Lords, that in a case of deliberate wrongdoing, the test was whether the employee's acts were "so closely connected with his employment that it would be fair and just to hold the employers vicariously liable for them."

An employee does not cease to act in the course of employment, unless he has **3–114** plainly gone beyond the bounds.[307] Of course, in one sense, it may be said that it is never within the scope of an employee's employment to commit an act of negligence.

"In all these cases it may be said, as it was said here, that the master has not authorised the act. It is true, he has not authorised the particular act, but he has put the agent in his place to do that class of acts, and he must be answerable for the manner in which the agent has conducted himself in doing the business which it was the act of his master to place him in."[308]

If the employee is doing negligently something, which he was employed to do carefully, the negligent act is in the course of his employment and the employer is liable.[309] But where no vicarious liability can be made out, employers are not liable for the fraudulent activities of an employee undertaken in a personal capacity even where his employment gave respectability to and may have facilitated the fraud if they were not on notice of his dishonesty.[310]

Course of employment a question of fact. In determining whether or not an **3–115** employee's wrongful act is done in the course of his employment, it is necessary that a broad view of all the surrounding circumstances should be taken as a whole and not restricted to the particular act which causes the damage.[311] There is no simple test which can be applied to cover every set of circumstances, so that it

[305] *Vandyke v Fender* [1970] 2 Q.B. 292 (approved by the House of Lords in *Smith v Stages and Darlington Insulation* [1989] A.C. 928) applying *St Helens Colliery Co Ltd v Hewitson* [1924] A.C. 59 and *Weaver v Tredegar Iron & Coal Co Ltd* [1940] A.C. 955, which established conclusively that when a workman was injured, while travelling to or from work in a form of transport provided by his employers either on a public road or elsewhere outside the work premises, he was not "in the course of his employment" unless his terms of employment obliged him to travel in that manner.
[306] [2002] 1 A.C. 215 (sexual abuse by a house-father in a children's home: the ground on which liability was established at first instance, that vicarious liability could attach for the offender's failure to report his activity to his employer, could not be sustained). See further para.3–142 below.
[307] *County Plant Hire v Jackson and Lane Bros (Builders) (Third Party)* (1970) 8 K.I.R. 989, CA.
[308] per Willes J. in *Barwick v English Joint Stock Bank* (1867) L.R. 2 Ex. 259 at 266.
[309] In 6 I.C.L.Q. 162 two tests are discussed: (1) "In Continental law at least one wide positive rule has been established: if there is a relation in time, space and as to the nature of the act between employment and act there will be liability"; (2) "this test asks the question whether the employment created or increased the opportunity for committing the tort; if the answer is positive, the tort will be regarded as being within the course of employment."
[310] *Hornsby v Clark Kenneth Leventhal* [1998] P.N.L.R. 635, CA (accountants owed no duty of care to supervise or investigate the activities of an employee who was permitted to undertake private work from his employer's premises during working hours). See Virgo and Ryley, "Employees' liability in financial services" in (1999) 11 C.M. 168.
[311] e.g. *Century Insurance Co v Northern Ireland Road Transport Board* [1942] A.C. 509. A further illustration of a broad approach to the problem can be found in *Duffy v Thanet District Council* (1984) 134 New L.J. 680. (two apprentices, A and B struggled for a chisel with which B was trying to damage A's work and the claimant was injured when the tool came into contact with his eye: A's employer was vicariously liable since A was trying to protect his work and what happened was a stupid mode of doing an authorised act, not something A had no reason to be doing at all. B's

remains essentially a question of fact for decision in each case.[312] Some common situations follow.

3–116   **Employer's vehicle entrusted to employee.** When an employer's vehicle is entrusted to the employee to be driven or used in some other way, the employer is liable if the employee is negligent while using the vehicle either wholly or partly on the employer's business or in the latter's interest. Conversely, the employer is not liable if the employee is negligent while using it for any other purposes, even though the employee has the employer's permission to use it for those purposes.[313] Diplock J. said:

> "I think that the true test can best be expressed in these words: was the [servant] doing something that he was employed to do? If so, however improper the manner in which he was doing it, whether negligent . . . or even fraudulently . . . or contrary to express orders . . . the master is liable. If, however, the servant is not doing what he is employed to do, the master does not become liable merely because the act of the servant is done with the master's knowledge, acquiescence, or permission."[314]

3–117   It is presumed that the vehicle is being used for the employer's purposes if the employee has authority to use it.[315] Thus, it has been held that, where a police officer was hurt as a result of his motor patrol car's going out of control and crashing, during a high-speed vehicle chase, the driver of which knew he was being pursued by the police and was trying to escape arrest, the injured policeman had a cause of action against both the employee driver and the vehicle's owner.[316]

3–118   Deviation from the employer's orders does not necessarily prevent the user from being for the employer's purposes; it is a question of degree. As Parke B. said:

> "If the servants, being on their master's business, took a detour to call upon a friend, the master will be responsible . . . The master is only liable where the servant is acting in the course of his employment. If he was going out of his way, against his master's implied commands, when driving on his master's business, he will make his master

---

employers were not vicariously liable because his provocation was not so connected with what he was authorised to do as to be a mode of doing it).

[312] per Finnemore J. in *Staton v N.C.B.* [1957] 1 W.L.R. 893 at 895. In *Hornsby v Clark Kenneth Leventhal* [1998] P.N.L.R. 635, CA, accountants were not vicariously liable for the fraudulent activities of an employee who was permitted to undertake private work in his own account, where his employment gave respectability to and may have facilitated the fraud but his employers were unaware of his activities.

[313] See *Launchbury v Morgans* [1973] A.C. 127, approving *Hewitt v Bonvin* [1940] 1 K.B. 188. In order to fix vicarious liability for the negligence of the driver of a motor car on the owner of the vehicle, it must be shown that the driver was using it for the owner's purposes under delegation of a task or duty. Mere permission to use it is insufficient to establish vicarious liability. In *Norwood v Nevan* [1981] R.T.R. 457, CA, mere knowledge of its use was not sufficient.

[314] *Hilton v Thomas Burton (Rhodes) Ltd* [1961] 1 W.L.R. 705 at 707.

[315] *Laycock v Grayson* (1939) 55 T.L.R. 698.

[316] *Attorney-General for Ontario v Keller* (1978) 86 D.L.R. (3d) 426.

liable; but if he was going on a frolic of his own,[317] without being at all on his masters' business, the master will not be liable."[318]

Where the employer, a wine merchant, sent his carman and a clerk with a horse and cart to deliver some wine and bring back some empty bottles, and the employees, on their return, when about a quarter of a mile from the office, drove in another direction on business of the clerk's and negligently ran over the plaintiff, it was held that the employer was not liable.[319] But:

"I am very far from saying, if the servant when going on his master's business took a somewhat longer road, that owing to this deviation he would cease to be in the employment of the master, so as to divest the latter of all liability; in such cases, it is a question of degree as to how far the deviation could be considered a separate journey."[320]

On modern roads, detours and deviations are not unexpected. A driver **3–119** deviating from a direct route would only be regarded as acting outside the scope of his employment if he departed altogether from his employers' business.[321] An employee, who, in the course of making a journey for his employer's purposes, goes off on a journey of his own so as to be outside the course of his employment, may return to the course of his employment when he has finished his own journey and has resumed the journey for his employer's purposes.[322]

If the employee is making a journey on the employer's business, the fact that **3–120** he is also doing business of his own on the same journey will not take him out of his employment.[323] But if he makes a journey on his own business, the fact that he does some small service for his employer on his return (for example by collecting two empty beer casks for which he received a penny each from his employer) does not render the journey one which was made in the course of his employment.[324]

Employee leaving vehicle unattended. It may still be possible to derive help, **3–121** by analogy, from some of the old examples. A carter, in charge of his employer's horse and cart for the day, was acting in the course of his employment where he left them unattended during the dinner hour, so that the horse ran away and an

---

[317] For the limits of the words: "a frolic of his own", see *Allen v Aeroplane & Motor Aluminium Castings Ltd* [1965] 1 W.L.R. 1244.
[318] *Joel v Morrison* (1834) 6 Car. & P. 501; *A. & W. Hemphill v Williams* (1966) 110 S.J. 549.
[319] *Storey v Ashton* (1869) L.R. 4 Q.B. 476. Similarly, see *Mitchell v Crassweller* (1835) 13 C.B. 237; *Hilton v Thomas Burton (Rhodes) Ltd* [1961] 1 W.L.R. 705. But in *Harvey v R.G. O'Dell Ltd* [1958] 2 Q.B. 78, on similar facts the employer was held liable.
[320] *Storey v Ashton* (1869) L.R. 4 Q.B. 476 at 479, per Cockburn C.J.
[321] *Angus v Glasgow Corporation* (1977) S.L.T. 206.
[322] *Creer v Brightside Foundry and Engineering Co* (1942) 35 B.W.C.C. 9.
[323] *Patten v Rea* (1857) 2 C.B.(N.S.) 606.
[324] *Rayner v Mitchell* (1877) 2 C.P.D. 357. See also *Hancock v Operating and Vending Machine Co Ltd* (1938) 31 B.W.C.C. 209 (the collector of money from automatic machines, who had a van which it was his duty to return to his employers' garage at night, was not in the course of his employment when after finishing collecting, he spent three hours in public-houses, and had an accident driving to the garage, albeit he had used his presence in the licensed premises as an occasion to obey an instruction to change copper coins into silver and notes).

accident occurred.[325] Similarly, where the horse and cart were left by the carter with a boy who helped deliver the parcels and the lad, contrary to his employer's orders, drove the cart and had an accident, the employer was liable for the damage.[326]

3–122 **Employee permitted to use employer's vehicle for his own purposes.** The fact that an employee is permitted to use his employer's vehicle does not make the employer liable for the employee's negligence in using that vehicle, unless it is being used for the employer's business.[327] So, where the employer lent his van driver his private motor car for the purpose of taking friends to the theatre and an accident occurred through the van driver's negligence, the employer was not liable because the motor car was not being used for the employer's purposes.[328] Again, where a boy was allowed to use a bicycle, belonging to his employers, to go home during his dinner break and he negligently ran into the plaintiff, it was held that the employers were not liable.[329]

3–123 If the employee does not have permission to use the vehicle, the case is even stronger. An employee, who, without his employer's knowledge or consent, takes his vehicle for purposes of his own and, by negligent driving, causes damage to a third party, does not render his employer liable.[330] On the other hand, if an employee instructs a subordinate to drive a vehicle for the higher-ranking employee's private business, and the subordinate is negligent, the employer is liable. The subordinate employee still remains in the course of his employment in obeying the orders of his superior.[331] Similarly, where an employee is given the use of his employers' vehicle on condition that, if he drives to work in it, he should also convey other employees free of charge, the employers are vicariously liable for the employee's negligent driving. He is driving the vehicle for their purposes and, accordingly, acting as their agent, whether or not he is actually driving in the course of his employment.[332]

3–124 **Employee permitted to use own vehicle.** The fact that an employee uses his own vehicle, instead of his employer's transport, does not preclude the employer being liable for the employee's negligent driving, if the employee was engaged on the employer's business at the time. Where an employer authorised an employee to use his own motorcycle combination to carry a fellow employee as

[325] *Whatman v Pearson* (1868) L.R. 3 C.P. 422. See also *Gayler & Pope v B. Davies & Son* [1924] 2 K.B. 75.
[326] *Engelhardt v Farrant & Co* [1897] 1 Q.B. 240.
[327] *Hilton v Thomas Burton (Rhodes) Ltd* [1961] 1 W.L.R. 705.
[328] *Britt v Galmoye* (1928) 44 T.L.R. 294.
[329] *Higbid v Hammett* (1932) 49 T.L.R. 104.
[330] *Sanderson v Collins* [1904] 1 K.B. 628 (the plaintiff and defendant were bailor and bailee, but this does not affect the law stated in the text. The bailee may be liable to the bailor for damage to the article bailed even though the bailee's servant was using it for his own purposes at the time it was damaged); *Aitchison v Page Motors* (1935) 154 L.T. 128.
[331] *Irwin v Waterloo Taxi-Cab Co Ltd* [1912] 3 K.B. 588.
[332] *Vandyke v Fender* [1970] 2 Q.B. 292 (applying *Ormrod v Crosville Motor Services Ltd* [1953] 1 W.L.R. 1120), which was distinguished in *Paterson v Costain & Press (Overseas)* [1979] 2 Lloyd's Rep. 204, CA, considered in *Buckley's Stores v National Employers Mutual General Association* [1978] I.R. 351, and approved in *Smith v Stages and Darlington Insulation* [1989] A.C. 928.

a passenger, whilst on the employer's business, the employer was liable for injury to the passenger, caused by the employee's negligent riding.[333] Where there is a special duty in a contract of employment to obey an emergency call at any hour, an employee has been held to be on duty whilst making his way to his place of work.[334] However, the employer is only vicariously liable for his employee's acts, if the latter was carrying out a task or duty delegated to him by the employer, and was not merely acting for the employer's benefit or at his request, such as by attending a residential training centre.[335]

Delegation of authority by employee in charge of vehicle. It has long been **3–125** established that unless express authority is given, a driver or other employee in charge of his employer's vehicle has no authority to delegate his control of the vehicle to another. As Parke B. said, "If you think the servants lent the cart to a person who was driving without the defendant's [the master's] knowledge, he will not be responsible."[336] Where the driver of the defendant's omnibus was ordered by the police to cease driving, on the ground that he was drunk, and, thereupon, a bystander was authorised by the driver and the conductor to drive home, it was held that the employer was not liable. Neither the driver nor the conductor had any actual authority to employ a substitute and they could not be agents of necessity, because they might first have communicated with the defendant.[337] Again, when the driver of a motor car, in order to discover the cause of a noise in the car, delegated the driving to a man who was not an employee of the defendant and an accident occurred, as a result of his negligent driving, it was held that the defendant was not liable because there was no necessity to keep the car moving while the driver examined the engine.[338]

Employee allows another to drive. It is evidence of negligence, for which an **3–126** employer will be vicariously liable, for an employee to permit an unauthorised person to drive the employer's vehicle. When the driver of a bus, at the end of the journey, allowed the conductor to turn the bus in readiness for the next

[333] *Harvey v R.G. O'Dell Ltd* [1958] 2 Q.B. 78. The vicarious liability of the employers was also established in *Elleanor v Cavendish Woodhouse Ltd* (1972) 117 S.J. 14 (two salesmen returning home together, after an evening's canvassing, when an accident happened involving their motor vehicle); and *Smith v Stages and Darlington Insulation* [1989] A.C. 928 (two workmen, each of whom was being paid eight hours' wages for sleeping time and a further eight hours' wages for travelling home from the distant place where they had been working, chose to travel without sleep in the car of one of them and a crash occurred as a result of fatigue of the one driving), applying *St Helens Colliery Co Ltd v Hewitson* [1924] A.C. 59.
[334] *Blee v L.N.E.R.* [1938] A.C. 126 (ganger called out to a derailment); *Stitt v Woolley* (1971) 115 S.J. 708 (fireman attending promptly at the fire station in response to an emergency call).
[335] *Nottingham v Aldridge and Another* [1971] 2 Q.B. 739, distinguishing *Harvey v R.G. O'Dell Ltd* [1958] 2 Q.B. 78 (the Post Office was not liable for the negligence of an employee who drove a fellow employee to a residential training centre, their detached duty place of work, in a car which was not owned by the Post Office, even though the employee who was driving received a mileage allowance and an additional allowance for his passenger).
[336] *Joel v Morison* (1834) 6 Car. & P. 501.
[337] *Gwilliam v Twist* [1895] 2 Q.B. 84.
[338] *Harris v Fiat Motors Ltd* (1906) 22 T.L.R. 556, reversed on other grounds, 23 T.L.R. 504.

journey and sat next to him while he was driving, it was held that there was evidence of negligence on the part of the driver when the conductor negligently killed a person on the footpath.[339] Although the employer was not liable for the negligence of the conductor, who had no authority to drive, he was liable for the negligence of the driver, who had allowed an unskilled man to drive. On the other hand, where the conductor drove his employer's bus negligently and caused damage during the absence of the driver, who was away for his dinner at the end of the journey, the employer was not liable because the driver had not been guilty of any negligence.[340]

3–127   If a driver negligently leaves his vehicle unattended in the highway, his employer will be liable for all damage which is a consequence of that negligence and not too remote. It has been held that, where a driver was drunk and a collision was caused by another drunken man who had taken over the driving from him, the damage was too remote.[341] When a horse and cart were left unattended on the highway and damage was caused by a third party's negligent driving of the vehicle, it was not too remote.[342] But in another case, where a motor vehicle, and not a horse and cart, had been so left, the damage was too remote.[343]

3–128   **Unauthorised invitees.** An employee who is in charge of a vehicle is not acting in the course of his employment if, without authority, he invites friends or other persons to enter it. Where such a person is injured while in the vehicle, the employer will not be liable for the driver's negligence. Conversely, where the driver's foreman, acting within the scope of his ostensible authority, consented to the driver's inviting someone into his vehicle, the invitation was not outside the course of the driver's employment and the employers were be liable for the driver's negligence.[344]

3–129   Where the claimant, at the request of the driver of the defendant's milk float, got into the float to help an injured boy, who was also an employee of the defendant, and, owing to the driver's negligence, was herself injured, the defendant was not liable. Even in an emergency, the driver had no authority to

---

[339] *Ricketts v Thomas Tilling Ltd* [1915] 1 K.B. 644; *Marsh v Moores* [1949] 2 K.B. 208.

[340] *Beard v London General Omnibus Co* [1900] 2 Q.B. 530; distinguished in *Kay v I.T.W. Ltd* [1968] 1 Q.B. 140 (employer vicariously liable for negligence of an employee who was attempting to remove a lorry obstructing access to the warehouse, so that he could bring his employer's vehicle inside). In *Iqbal v London Transport Executive, The Times*, June 7, 1973, CA, where a bus conductor had been prohibited on many occasions from driving buses but still attempted to drive one at a depot and injured a fellow employee, the employers were not liable for his negligence. Lord Denning M.R. in *Rose v Plenty* [1976] 1 W.L.R. 141 at 144 criticised this decision as seemingly "out of line" but Scarman L.J. (at 150) was able to distinguish it.

[341] *Mann v Ward* (1892) 8 T.L.R. 699. This case was criticised in *Engelhardt v Farrant* [1897] 1 Q.B. 240, but in relation to the issue of remoteness of damage it would appear to be sound.

[342] *Engelhardt v Farrant* [1897] 1 Q.B. 240 itself criticised by Lord Sumner in *Weld-Blundell v Stephens* [1920] A.C. 956 at 989.

[343] *Ruoff v Long & Co* [1916] 1 K.B. 148.

[344] *Young v Edward Box & Co Ltd* [1951] 1 T.L.R. 789 (consent given by a foreman even though he was not authorised so to do).

invite the claimant into the float.[345] When an employer expressly instructed a driver not to allow other persons to travel on his van, and notices to this effect were displayed in the van, he was not liable to a passenger who was injured by his driver's negligence. It was outside the scope of the driver's employment to carry the passenger, so the employer owed no duty to him.[346] When the driver of a tractor, which was unsafe for passengers and was not intended to carry them, gave a ride to a child, the employer was not liable for injuries sustained by the child after falling off while the driver was driving too fast round a bend.[347]

Disobedience of orders. The fact that an employee disobeys the orders of his   **3–130**
employer does not necessarily mean that he is acting outside the course of employment.[348] A distinction needs to be drawn between an order that limits the *scope* of the employment, disobedience to which means that the employee is not in the course of his employment, and an order that limits the *method* of performing the duties of the employee, disobedience to which does not mean that the employee is outside his employment. For example, an order that a van driver shall not allow any person to travel in his van, notice of which is displayed on the van, is an order limiting the scope of the employee's employment with the result that a breach of the order involves the employer in no liability.[349] By way of contrast, an order to employees not to use uninsured motor cars merely limits the way in which the work is to be performed, so that the liability of the employer is not excluded if damage is caused, when such order is disobeyed.[350]

---

[345] *Houghton v Pilkington* [1912] 3 K.B. 308; *Lygo v Newbold* (1854) 9 Ex. 302 (where a carrier contracted to carry the plaintiff's luggage in a cart and the plaintiff, with the permission of the carrier's employee but without any authority from the carrier, got into the cart, which subsequently broke down, the carrier was not liable). But see also *Rose v Plenty* [1976] 1 W.L.R. 141 (a milkman, contrary to his employer's instruction not to give lifts to children or let them assist in his duties, did so and the plaintiff, aged 13, fell off the milk float and was injured, owing to the milkman's negligent driving. It was held that since the instruction only affected the milkman's mode of conduct within the scope of his employment and did not limit or define the scope of the employment itself, the employer was vicariously liable).

[346] *Twine v Bean's Express Co* [1946] 1 All E.R. 202; affd. 175 L.T. 131. *Conway v George Wimpey & Co Ltd (No.2)* [1951] 2 K.B. 266 is a similar case, in which Asquith L.J. said, "taking men other than the defendants' employees on the vehicle was not merely a wrongful mode of performing an act of the class which the driver in the present case was employed to perform, but was the performance of an act of a class which he was not employed to perform at all". *Twine v Bean's Express Co* was followed and approved by the Court of Appeal in *Conway v George Wimpey & Co Ltd*. Both cases were distinguished by the Court of Appeal in *Rose v Plenty* [1976] 1 W.L.R. 140. See the provisions of s.149 of the Road Traffic Act 1988.

[347] *Nixon v Cairns* [1944] N.I. 21, following *Houghton v Pilkington* [1912] 3 K.B. 308.

[348] The New Zealand Court of Appeal in *Attorney-General v Hartley* [1964] N.Z.L.R. 785 held that it is not enough to decide whether what was done was a prohibited act, since prohibition may either limit the scope of the employment or merely regulate the conduct of the employee within its sphere.

[349] *Twine v Bean's Express Co* [1946] 1 All E.R. 202 and *Conway v George Wimpey & Co Ltd (No.2)* [1951] 2 K.B. 2. In both these cases a driver had given a lift to somebody else, contrary to a prohibition and not for the purposes of the employers; however, they include statements about trespassing which are no longer correct in light of subsequent developments, notably the Occupiers' Liability Act 1984. See Ch.8, paras 8–138 to 8–160, below, generally, on trespassers.

[350] *Canadian Pacific Ry. v Lockhart* [1942] A.C. 591.

3–131   In *Ilkiw v Samuels*,[351] the defendant was a transport company whose driver permitted another man, employed at a warehouse where he was picking up a load, to move his lorry before the load was sheeted, without first checking the man's competence to drive the vehicle. The man was incompetent and was unable to stop the vehicle which collided with the claimant. Even though they had forbidden their driver to allow anyone else to drive the vehicle, the defendants were held liable. Their driver was employed not only to drive but also to take charge and control of the lorry during the times when he was on duty, and he remained in charge of it, even when he was not actually sitting at the controls.[352]

3–132   In *Kay v I.T.W. Ltd*,[353] the driver of a fork-lift truck found that his sole means of access to his employers' warehouse was blocked by a visiting lorry. Without attempting to make any inquiry where the lorry driver was or what he should do, he entered the cab of the vehicle, started the motor and so negligently reversed the lorry that he crushed and injured the claimant storekeeper. Although, on the face of it, driving the lorry was unauthorised, his subsidiary purpose in wishing to to clear a passage and gain an entrance to the warehouse for the fork-lift truck brought the driving within the course of his employment.

3–133   There is no doubt that at times the distinction will be a narrow one. As Sachs L.J. pointed out:

> "there are instances in which the dividing line can be very thin between acts which constitute a wrong and indeed a very stupid mode of doing an authorised act and acts which involve doing something which the employee has no business at all to be doing. Whether the line ought to be drawn by examining the question in terms of degree or in terms of kind has been discussed. I do not propose to say more on that point save this, that in either case the line should be drawn fairly high in favour of the innocent sufferer injured by the act of somebody who was employed by the defendant employer and who was seeking to further that employer's interests."[354]

3–134   An order to an employee to make a journey in the employer's lorry, which is actually performed by using a private car, is not an order limiting the scope of the employment.[355]

In *Limpus v London General Omnibus Co*,[356] a bus driver drove his vehicle across the road in front of a rival bus, thereby causing it to overturn. His employers had issued written instructions that drivers were not to race or obstruct other buses but, despite the prohibition, they were held liable because the injury resulted from an act done by their driver in the course of his employment and for their purposes. The decisive point was that it was *not* done by the employee for his own purpose but was done for his employer's purposes.[357] Even fraud in the

---

[351] [1963] 1 W.L.R. 991. See also *Ricketts v Thos Tilling Ltd* [1915] 1 K.B. 644.
[352] *Ilkiw v Samuels* [1963] 1 W.L.R. at 998, per Willmer L.J. and at 1002, per Danckwerts L.J., but cf. the reasoning of Diplock L.J. at 1003–1006.
[353] [1968] 1 Q.B. 140; *East v Beavis Transport Ltd* [1969] 1 Lloyd's Rep. 302.
[354] *Kay v I.T.W. Ltd* [1968] 1 Q.B. 156.
[355] *McKean v Raynor Bros* [1942] 2 All E.R. 650.
[356] (1862) 1 H. & C. 526.
[357] *Limpus v London General Omnibus Co* (1862) 1 H. & C. 539, per Willes J.

method of carrying out his employment is an act done in the course of the employment, whether it was committed for the employer's benefit or not.[358]

Where a general garage hand, part of whose duties was to assist in moving cars **3–135** out of the way of other cars in the garage, had been forbidden to drive, since he had no driving licence, but had chosen to disobey such order, the garage proprietors were liable for the man's act in driving negligently a van into the highway in order to clear the access to the petrol pumps. He was doing an act within the scope of his employment, although he was doing it in an unauthorised way.[359]

Where an employee placed a loaded gun on a harvester, in disobedience to his **3–136** employer's instructions, and the gun fired accidentally, injuring the driver, it was held[360] that the employer was liable. Since the "scope" of employment must be construed liberally, the employer was vicariously liable for his employee's act in adding a further danger to the risk of the work.

Where a solicitor's clerk, contrary to his orders, used the lavatory in his principal's private room and negligently left the tap running, it was held that the employer was not liable, because "the prohibition is material as showing the local limit of the clerk's duties".[361] On the other hand, where a clerk used a lavatory, which he was allowed to use, his employer was held liable for his negligence in omitting to turn off the tap.[362]

Smoking at work. A number of cases have dealt with an employer's liability **3–137** for damage caused by an employee smoking at work. In *Williams v Jones,*[363] a carpenter was employed to make a signboard and, while engaged on his work, lit his pipe with a wood shaving, which he dropped among the other shavings thereby setting fire to a shed, which had been lent to his employer by the plaintiff. In a decision which may now be regarded as of dubious authority, it was held, by a majority, that the employer was not liable, on the ground that the act of smoking was not in any way connected with the making of the signboard.

In contrast, in *Jefferson v Derbyshire Farmers Ltd,*[364] employers were liable **3–138** where a youth drawing benzol from a drum in a garage, lit a cigarette and threw the match on the floor thereby lighting some petrol spillage. The flames set fire to the benzol in the drum and burnt the garage down. The youth was bound to use reasonable care in doing his work and "to smoke and throw a lighted match on

---

[358] *Lloyd v Grace, Smith & Co* [1912] A.C. 716. See also *Ward v L.G.O. Co* (1873) 42 L.J.C.P. 265 and *United Africa Co Ltd v Saka Owoade* [1955] A.C. 130.
[359] *L.C.C. v Cattermoles (Garages) Ltd* [1953] 1 W.L.R. 997. However, cf. *Rand Ltd v Craig* [1919] 1 Ch. 1 (where a contractor told his carters to tip rubbish at a particular place and nowhere else, and, in breach of their orders, they tipped it on the plaintiff's land, it was held that the act was outside the sphere of their employment and the contractor was not liable).
[360] *Spencer v Curtis Bros* (1962) 106 S.J. 390.
[361] *Stevens v Woodward* (1881) 6 Q.B.D. 318.
[362] *Ruddiman v Smith* (1889) 60 L.T. 708.
[363] (1865) 3 H. & C. 602.
[364] [1921] 2 K.B. 281.

the floor while doing this work was not to do the work with reasonable care".[365] The Court's approach was consistent with the dissenting judgment in *Williams v Jones* of Blackburn J. who said:

> "It is said that Davies, the servant, was not employed by his master to smoke or to light his pipe, and that is no doubt true; but the act of lighting a pipe was in itself a harmless act; it only became negligent and a breach of duty towards the plaintiff because it was done when using his shed and working there amongst inflammable materials . . . It seems to me, therefore, that it was negligence in the course of his employment."[366]

3–139   The view of the minority in *Williams v Jones* was preferred in *Century Insurance Co v Northern Ireland Road Transport Board*,[367] where employers were held liable for the act of the driver of a lorry containing petrol who lit a cigarette while petrol was being transferred from the lorry to a tank, and then threw the match away, causing a fire and an explosion. As Lord Wright pointed out, "I think what plausibility the contrary argument might seem to possess results from treating the act of lighting the cigarette in abstraction from the circumstances as a separate act".[368] On the other hand, where an explosion of firedamp in the National Coal Board's mine occurred as a result of a miner lighting a cigarette, which was an act prohibited by s.35 of the Coal Mines Act 1911, it was held that the miner who had caused the explosion was not acting in the course of his employment because he had no business to be in the waste, where he had gone in order to smoke.[369]

The rationale of these various examples appears to be that the employer will be liable if the employee's smoking is merely a negligent way of performing his employment. A prohibition against smoking, express or implied, affects the method in which the employee is to perform his duties, and does not limit the scope of the employment.

3–140   **Dishonesty, fraud or other criminal act.** At one time, it was considered that an employer could not be vicariously liable for a theft perpetrated by his employee, on the ground that such an act necessarily must have been committed for his own benefit and thereby outside the course of his employment.[370] However, the House of Lords, in *Lloyd v Grace, Smith & Co*,[371] decided that this was not so, and in effect the scope of an employee's employment could well be

---

[365] *Jefferson v Derbyshire Farmers Ltd* [1921] 2 K.B. 281 at 286, per Bankes L.J. *Williams v Jones* was distinguished on the ground that the negligent act of the carpenter in that case was unconnected with his work. The basis of the distinction may be a little strained: as the smoking was an act of negligence only because he was working in a place where shavings and other inflammable material were about, it is difficult to separate the negligence from the employment.

[366] (1865) 3 H. & C. 602 at 610.

[367] [1942] A.C. 509.

[368] *Century Insurance Co v Northern Ireland Road Transport* [1942] A.C. 519.

[369] *Kirby v N.C.B.* (1958) S.L.T. 47, IH. See also the Mines and Quarries Act 1954 ss.66 and 67.

[370] *Cheshire v Bailey* [1905] 1 K.B. 237; *Mintz v Silverton* (1920) 36 T.L.R. 399; cf. *Abraham v Bullock* (1902) 86 L.T. 796.

[371] [1912] A.C. 716 (a solicitors' managing clerk induced a client of his employers' firm to sell a property, call in the mortgage money and then, after he fraudulently misrepresented the nature of the deed of assignment, to transfer the money to him, which he misappropriated), distinguishing *Barwick v English Joint Stock Bank* (1867) L.R. 2 Ex. 259.

extended by his ostensible authority and not restricted merely to the correct performance of his duties.

In *Morris v C. W. Martin & Sons Ltd*,[372] the plaintiff sent her mink stole to a **3–141** furrier for cleaning and it was arranged with her permission that the fur would be delivered to the defendants, who specialised in such cleaning. Unfortunately, an employee of the defendants, whom they had no reason to suspect, stole the fur after it had been given into his custody.[373] The defendants were held liable to the owner for breach of their duty as bailees for reward. If they entrusted performance of their duty to protect the goods from theft to an employee they were responsible for the employee's breach of that duty. Two of the judgments resolved the case in terms of vicarious liability for conversion, rather than bailment. Emphasis was given to the fact that the employers had to discharge their obligation to clean the fur by giving it into the possession of their employees. The manner in which one of those employees chose to conduct himself in that aspect of his work was to steal the fur. It was thereby a dishonest act in the course of his employment for which his employers were liable.

When the House of Lords returned to the issue in *Lister v Hesley Hall Ltd*,[374] **3–142** a case of sexual assault by a teacher upon a pupil, it was emphasised that a central issue in deciding whether an employer is vicariously liable for the acts of an employee which have caused harm to a third party, is whether the employer himself owed some duty or responsibility towards the victim. If so, liability for the employee's actions cannot be avoided because responsibility for executing that duty was delegated to an employee who failed to comply with the employer's instructions. There was emphasis upon the closeness of the connection, on the facts, between the deliberate wrongdoing of the teacher and the duty which he had been employed to perform. The employer had assumed a relationship to the claimant which imposed specific duties in tort and the employee was the person to whom performance of those duties was entrusted.[375] Vicarious liability accordingly attached.

---

[372] [1966] 1 Q.B. 716, applied in *Fairline Shipping Corporation v Adamson* [1975] Q.B. 180 and *Nahhas v Pier House (Cheyne Walk) Management* (1984) 270 E.G. 328 (the defendants were liable in negligence for the actions of their employee, a man with a serious criminal record for dishonesty who they employed as a porter in a block of luxury flats, who took the opportunity to use the plaintiff's keys to enter her flat during her absence and steal jewellery). See further, para.3–196, below. See also *Mendelssohn v Normand Ltd* [1970] 1 Q.B. 177, CA.
[373] *Morris v C.W. Martin & Sons Ltd* [1966] 1 Q.B. 716 at 737, per Diplock L.J. and at 740, per Salmon L.J.
[374] [2002] 1 A.C. 215, overruling *Trotman v North Yorkshire County Council* [1999] L.G.R. 584, CA (another case of sexual abuse by a teacher). See also Collender, "Vicarious Liability: a position of trust" 2002 P.I.L.J. 1, 15; also Leng, "Vicarious Liability for intentional wrongdoing" (2002) 1 P.N. 1; Levinson, "Vicarious liability for intentional torts" J.P.I. Law 2005, 4, 34.
[375] *Lister v Hesley Hall Ltd* [2002] 1 A.C. 215 per Lord Hobhouse at 237. It is debatable whether the "close connection" test brings any greater precision than earlier tests. In *Dubai Aluminium Co Ltd v Salaam* [2003] 2 A.C. 366, Lord Nicholls aknowledged the shortcomings of the test as inevitable, given the range of circumstances which arose. He went on at [26], "Essentially the court makes an evaluative judgment in each case, having regard to all the circumstances, and, importantly, having regard also to the assistance provided by previous court decisions". It may be questioned whether decisions, arrived at by applying a different test, do provide the assistance to which he refers. In Scotland it has been said that it is difficult to see how *Lister* could be relevant to vicarious liability

3–143   Where a fraud is perpetrated by the employee for the benefit of his employers whilst doing their business, both principle and logic suggest that the employers ought to be liable. They have put the employee in their place to perform the duties which enable the fraud even though they have not authorised the particular act.[376] It was held otherwise, however, where a wrongful act was committed solely for an employee's own benefit[377] or where there was no authority for acts done by the employee outside the scope of his employment.[378]

3–144   In *Balfron Trustees Ltd v Peterson*[379] the claimants were trustees of a pension scheme set up for the benefit of former employees of a company. A large sum was misappropriated from the fund, paid to various off-shore entities and never recovered. The trustees sought to recover damages from a solicitor and or the firm which employed him on the basis that he had allegedly participated in the plan to misappropriate the scheme's assets in the knowledge that it involved a breach of trust by the then trustees. It was not suggested that his employers were themselves in any way dishonest. On an application to strike out, it was held to be at least arguable that, at the time the plan to misappropriate the pension scheme funds was implemented, the defendant firm of solicitors owed obligations to the members of the scheme and were therefore liable for the harm caused to the scheme and its members by the actions of their employee.

ILLUSTRATIONS

3–145   In other cases involving dishonesty or other criminal acts: the employers of a steward at a dance hall, who used force to eject a patron, were liable for a first assault, but not for subsequent violence which amounted to private retaliation[380]; the owners of a club were liable for the actions of doormen who attacked and injured the claimant after he had kicked in the glass of a door[381]; a railway company was liable for an assault upon a passenger by a ticket inspector which arose after an altercation about the claimant's entitlement to travel[382]; an employer was liable where the doorman of a club, in revenge for earlier violence inside the premises, went home, obtained a knife and stabbed the claimant in the street outside: the doorman's aggressive tendencies had been encouraged by his employer and the stabbing was the culmination of an incident within the club

arising from a case of agency properly so called (as opposed to employment): *M v Hedron* 2007 S.L.T. 467, IH (Ex Div).

[376] See, e.g. *Alliance and Leicester Building Society v Hamptons* [1994] N.P.C. 36 (the claimants had advanced monies for mortgage purposes in reliance on fraudulent valuations provided by an unqualified employee of a firm of estate agents).

[377] See *Heasmans v Clarity Cleaning Co, The Times*, January 23, 1987, CA (a cleaning contractor not liable for the tortious act of his employee, who, in the course of cleaning an office, dishonestly used a telephone for his own purposes).

[378] *Kooragang Investment Pty Ltd v Richardson & Wrench Ltd, The Times*, July 28, 1981 (employers not liable for an employee's negligent valuations, made solely for his own purposes and without their knowledge).

[379] [2001] I.R.L.R. 758.

[380] *Daniels v Whetstone Entertainments Ltd* [1962] 2 Lloyd's Rep. 1 at 10 (patron of a dance hall assaulted by steward who was ejecting him. *Held*, the employers were liable for a first assault by the steward, but were not liable for a subsequent assault which was one of private retaliation).

[381] *Vasey v Surrey Free Inns* [1996] P.I.Q.R. P373, CA.

[382] *Fennelly v Connex South Eastern Ltd* [2001] I.R.L.R. 390, CA.

where the doorman had been behaving in the violent and aggressive way his employer expected.[383] The Roman Catholic Church was liable for sexual abuse perpetrated by one its priests.[384] A chief constable was not liable for the actions of a police officer who, off duty, used his uniform and warrant card to gain the opportunity to commit sexual assaults upon the claimant.[385] A rugby club whose players were contracted on a semi professional basis, was vicariously liable for the deliberate action of a player in punching an opponent in the course of a match.[386] A local authority was not vicariously liable for the act of one its storekeepers in leaving a mineral water bottle containing paraquat weedkiller in a club where the deceased mistakenly drank it and died.[387]

Employee's other acts causing damage. Where an employee uses for his **3-146** own purposes goods which have been bailed to his employer, vicarious liability for his negligence can arise.[388] The fact that he acted out of revenge[389] or malice[390] makes no difference[391] and, provided that the act was within the scope of his employment,[392] his employer will be liable. The same applies to the employer's liability for employees, who cause injury as a result of horseplay, or practical jokes. It has been held that the test for determining vicarious liability in

---

[383] *Mattis v Pollock (t/a Flamingo's Nightclub)* [2004] P.I.Q.R. P21, CA. See Griffiths, "Vicarious liability revisited" 153 N.L.J. 721; Liebeck and Langleben, "Blameless . . . but liable" 151 S.J. 650.
[384] *Maga v Roman Catholic Archdiocese of Birmingham* [2010] 1 W.L.R. 1441, CA (the claimant had performed work for the priest such as cleaning his car or doing small jobs in the presbytery. He worked in the church itself on one occasion only. The priest did not involve him in the activities of the church and did not seek to engage with him on any religious level, but even so the priest's sexual abuse of him was so closely connected with his employment as a priest at the Church that it would be fair and just to hold the defendant vicariously liable).
[385] *N v Chief Constable of Merseyside Police* [2006] EWHC 3041 (QB). The trial judge applied the test whether the police officer's act was so closely connected with acts that he was authorised to do that, for the purposes of liability, his wrongful act might fairly and properly be regarded as performed whilst acting in the ordinary course of his employment. Whether he was acting apparently or ostensibly as a police officer at the time was an important factor to be considered, but was not in itself decisive; the misuse of a warrant card by a rogue police constable, whenever he formed the intention to assault, was not itself sufficient to impose vicarious liability.
[386] *Gravil v Redruth Rugby Club* [2008] EWCA Civ 689. The crucial question was whether the tort was so closely connected with the employment that it would be fair and just to hold the employers vicariously liable. The observations of McClachlin J. in *Bazley v Curry* (1999) 174 D.L.R. (4th) 45, at [41] were approved, to the effect that vicarious liability is generally appropriate where there is a significant connection between the creation or enhancement of a risk and the wrong that accrues therefrom, even if unrelated to the employer's desires. In such cases, vicarious liability serves the policy considerations of an adequate and just remedy and deterrence.
[387] *Vance v Bough* 2008 Rep. L.R. 90, OH.
[388] *Aitchison v Page Motors Ltd* (1935) 154 L.T. 128. See per Lord Denning M.R. in relation to this case in *Morris v C.W. Martin & Sons Ltd* [1966] 1 Q.B. 716 at 724–725.
[389] n.380 above.
[390] *Photo Production Ltd v Securicor Transport Ltd* [1980] A.C. 827 (the plaintiff's factory was destroyed by a fire started maliciously by one of the defendant's patrolmen on duty at the premises at night).
[391] *Warren v Henlys Ltd* [1948] 2 All E.R. 935 (after a business transaction was long over, the employee, who had transacted it, assaulted the plaintiff, *Held*, that the defendants were not liable).
[392] See, e.g. *Keppel Bus Co Ltd v Sa'ad Bin Ahmad* [1974] 1 W.L.R. 1082 (a bus conductor, who assaulted passenger, was held not to have been acting in the course of his employment).

such cases is whether a reasonable man would say either that the employee's act was part and parcel of his employment (in the sense of its being incidental to it), even though it was unauthorised or prohibited; or whether it was so divergent from his employment as to be wholly distinguishable from it.[393]

On the other hand, where firemen pursuing an industrial dispute, deliberately drove slowly to the scene of a fire, as a result of which delay the premises were totally destroyed, the local authority, as employer, was not vicariously liable, because its employees' action was not a mode of performing an authorised act.[394]

3–147   **Further examples of acts in the course of employment.** When a lighterman, under whose management the defendant's barge was sent to a wharf to be loaded, in order to get his barge alongside, moved the plaintiff's barge into such a position that it was damaged when the tide went down[395]; when iron was carted to a wharf, for loading into a ship by stevedores, and the stevedores' foreman, being dissatisfied with the unloading of the iron by the carters, began the work himself and threw out some iron negligently which injured the plaintiff[396]; when a coal merchant's carter, in order to deliver coals at a customer's premises, removed an iron plate in the footway, which covered the coal cellar's entrance, and the plaintiff fell down into the opening[397]; when a school teacher told a pupil to poke the fire and draw out the damper in a room which was used by the teachers for their own convenience, and the pupil's pinafore was set on fire[398]; when the defendant's employees, authorised by their employment to burn weeds, burnt them on land adjoining but not belonging to the defendant, so that the fire spread on to the adjoining land, causing damage[399]; when an off-duty employee saw a boy with his hand on a bag of sugar, which was being carried on one of the employer's wagons, and gave the boy a cuff over the back of the neck in the belief that he was about to steal it, causing him to be run over by the wagon[400]; where three employees were determined to play a practical joke on a schoolboy who was working during his holidays, and instructed him to put his hand up the spout of a mincer, which they then started up[401]; where a milkman had invited a

---

[393] *Harrison v Michelin Tyre Co Ltd* [1985] I.C.R. 696, per Comyn J. See further Ch.11, below, para.11–40, 11–41. See also *Smith v Crossley* (1951) 95 S.J. 655 (compressed air pipe forced up apprentice's rectum); *Hudson v Ridge Manufacturing Co* [1957] 2 Q.B. 348 (wrist fractured when seized from behind and thrown to the ground by a man, who was known to have an almost incurable habit of tripping people up); *Coddington v International Harvester Co of Great Britain Ltd* (1969) 6 K.I.R. 146 (lighted inflammable spirit in a tin kicked about, which spilled and burned the plaintiff).

[394] *General Engineering Services Ltd v Kingston & St Andrew Corporation* [1989] 1 W.L.R. 69 P.C.

[395] *Page v Defries* (1866) 7 B. & S. 137.

[396] *Burns v Poulson* (1873) L.R. 8 C.P. 563.

[397] *Whiteley v Pepper* (1876) 2 Q.B.D. 276.

[398] *Smith v Martin and Hull Corp* [1911] 2 K.B. 775.

[399] *Goh Choon Seng v Lee Kim Soo* [1925] A.C. 550.

[400] *Poland v Parr* [1927] 1 K.B. 236. But cf. *Keppel Bus Co v Sa'ad Bin Ahmad* [1974] 1 W.L.R. 1082.

[401] *Chapman v Oakleigh Animal Products* (1970) 114 S.J. 432 where it was held that, as the plaintiff was bound to obey his seniors' instructions, in the circumstances the employers owed him a duty of care and the argument that the fellow employees were not acting in the course of their employment could not avail them.

boy, contrary to the employer's orders, to ride on the milkfloat in order to assist him with his milk round[402]; where a shop assistant, who had left his employers' premises to go to the Post Office, was hurrying along the pavement and, suddenly realising that he had forgotten something, stopped abruptly, turned around and collided with the plaintiff pedestrian, who was walking behind him, whereby she was hurt.[403]

Although strictly outside the ambit of this volume, it may be noted that an employer can be vicariously liable for an employee's breach of s.1 of the Protection from Harrassment Act 1997, committed in the course of his employment.[404]

Examples of acts not in the course of employment. When a gas inspector, **3–148** who was not a repairer, attempted to remedy a defect in a gas meter by means of a pocket knife, and left the knife open when he went to get proper tools, whereupon the plaintiff's four-year-old son was able to get at the knife and cut himself[405]; when a house-maid, employed to light the fires but not to clean the chimney, finding the fire difficult to light, lit some straw to clean the chimney and set the house on fire[406]; when a lorry driver stopped at a wayside café and crossed one section of a dual carriageway on foot in order to get refreshment, but a collision occurred between him and a motorcyclist[407]; when a miner illegally lit a cigarette underground, in a place where he had no business to be at all, and caused an explosion of fire-damp[408]; where a bus conductor had struck a passenger after a quarrel between them[409]; where a barmaid threw a glass of beer at and severely injured a customer who had been rude to her[410]; where a Post Office worker wrote an offensive and racist remark on an envelope he was sorting[411]; where an off-duty police officer was playing in a football match as part of a force policy to foster good relations in the community.[412]

---

[402] *Rose v Plenty* [1976] 1 W.L.R. 140.

[403] *James v Harrison* (1978) 18 A.C.T.R. 36.

[404] *Majrowski v Guy's and St. Thomas's NHS Trust* [2005] Q.B. 848, appeal dismissed [2006] 3 W.L.R. 125, HL, Ch.11 para.11–100, below. See also *Banks v Ablex Ltd* [2005] I.C.R. 819, CA (it remains the case that for an employer to be liable for harrassment it must be shown that the particular type of injury suffered by the claimant was or should have been foreseen as a possible consequence of the conduct complained of. It was insufficient to prove no more than ill-tempered outbursts by one employee towards another and the employer was unaware of any vulnerability of the victim to psychiatric injury).

[405] *Forsyth v Manchester Corp* (1912) 29 T.L.R. 15.

[406] *M'Kenzie v M'Leod* (1834) 10 Bing. 385.

[407] *Crook v Derbyshire Stone Ltd* (1956) 1 W.L.R. 432 (on the ground that the lorry driver was not discharging any duty to his employer at the time when the accident occurred). See comment [1956] C.L.J. 156. The case was not followed in *Stewart's (Edinburgh) Holdings v Lord Advocate* [1966] S.L.T. 86 (on similar facts, army driver held not exclusively on his own business; accordingly, his employers were liable, applying *Harvey v O'Dell* [1958] 2 Q.B. 78).

[408] *Kirby v National Coal Board* (1958) S.L.T. 47. For smoking see further paras 3–137 to 3–139, above.

[409] *Keppel Bus Co v Sa'ad Bin Ahmad* [1974] 1 W.L.R. 1082. But cf. *Poland v Parr* [1927] 1 K.B. 236.

[410] *Deatons Pty Ltd v Flew* (1949) 79 C.L.R. 370.

[411] *Irving v Post Office, The Independent*, April 3, 1987.

[412] *Faulkner v The Chief Adjudication Officer* [1994] P.I.Q.R. P244, CA.

3–149   Employers were not liable where an employee, given to practical jokes, pushed a tin of burning spirit towards a man, who had kicked it away hastily, so that the tin overturned and burnt the plaintiff. Because the practical joker had never previously been guilty of any dangerous behaviour towards his colleagues, the employers were not negligent in continuing to employ him, although they knew of his propensity for "fooling about".[413] Similarly, the employer was not liable where the plaintiff was injured at work when another employee pushed an insecure washbasin up against her in order to startle her[414]; and where the plaintiff and a fellow worker were fooling about together playing on the trolleys used at their workplace, when the plaintiff's hand was crushed.[415]

3–150   **Employee lent to temporary employer.** An employee may be the general employee of one person, and yet his services may be for the time being put at the disposal of another, who may be described as the temporary (or sometimes, the particular) employer. In such a case, although the general employer may pay the employee, select him for the work in question and have the power of dismissing him, the temporary employer may in some circumstances be liable for employee's negligence.[416] Whether or not the employee has become *pro hac vice* the employee of the temporary employer is a question of fact in each case[417] and will depend largely on the construction of the contract, made between the general and the alleged temporary employer.[418] It was observed by Lord Dunedin that in this area the facts of one case can never rule another and are only useful to the extent that they aid and guide a decision,[419] although "it has been sought to find some general idea, or perhaps mere catchword, which may serve as a clue to solve the problem".[420]

---

[413] *Coddington v International Harvester Co of Great Britain* (1969) 113 S.J. 265. However, cf. the situation in *Chapman v Oakleigh Animal Products* (1970) 114 S.J. 432, where the employers were held to be vicariously liable. See Ch.11, below, para.11–40 et seq.

[414] *Alfred v Nacanco* [1987] I.R.L.R. 292, CA.

[415] *McCready v Securicor* [1991] N.I. 229, CA (NI), applying *Alfred v Nacanco* [1987] I.R.L.R. 292, CA.

[416] per Lord Watson in *Union Steamship Co Ltd v Claridge* [1894] A.C. 185 at 188: "That the servant of A may, on a particular occasion, and for a particular purpose, become the servant of B, notwithstanding that he continues in A's service and is paid by him, is a rule recognised by a series of decisions," and per Cockburn C.J. in *Rourke v White Moss Colliery* (1877) 2 C.P.D. 205 at 209: "When one person lends his servant to another for a particular employment, the servant for anything done in that particular employment must be dealt with as the servant of the man to whom he is lent, although he remains the general servant of the person who lent him."

[417] *M'Cartan v Belfast Harbour Commissioners* [1911] 2 I.R. 143, HL.

[418] *Arthur White (Contractors) Ltd v Tarmac Civil Engineering Ltd* [1967] 1 W.L.R. 1508, HL (where the written contract did transfer liability from the general to the particular employer).

[419] *M'Cartan v Belfast Harbour Commissioners* [1911] 2 Ir.R. 143 at 149. For examples see: *Donovan v Laing Construction* [1893] 1 Q.B. 629; *Bain v Central Vermont Ry* [1921] 2 A.C. 412; *Bull v West African Shipping Agency, etc., Co* [1927] A.C. 686; *Clelland v Edward Lloyd Ltd* [1938] 1 K.B. 272; *Mersey Docks & Harbour Board v Coggins & Griffith (Liverpool) Ltd* [1947] A.C. 1; *Herdman v Walker (Tooting) Ltd, City Plant Hirers (Third Party)* [1956] 1 W.L.R. 209; *Brogan v William Allan Smith & Co Ltd* (1965) S.L.T. 175; *McGregor v Duthie & Sons & Co Ltd* (1966) S.L.T. 133.

[420] per Lord Wright in *Century Insurance Co Ltd v Northern Ireland Road Transport Board* [1942] A.C. 509 at 515.

Given a high level of dependence on the facts of a case, authorities decided at **3–151** different times in the law's development can be difficult to reconcile. Latterly for instance, there has appeared to be an emphasis in favour of the employee remaining the responsibility of the general employer. So, in *J. Young & Co (Kelvinhaugh) v O'Donnell*,[421] the House of Lords held that the general employers of a hired crane driver, guilty of negligence, failed to shift the prima facie responsibility from themselves to the hirer, as temporary employer. Also, in *Morris v Breaveglen Ltd*,[422] the Court of Appeal held that an employer who, under a labour-only subcontract, sent his workman to work on site under the direction and control of the main contractor, remained liable to his employee if the system of work was unsafe.

The control test. One consistent theme has been the importance of the right **3–152** to control the employee. In *Donovan v Laing Syndicate*[423] Bowen L.J. said: "We have only to consider in whose employment the man was at the time when the acts complained of were done, in this sense, that by the employer is meant the person who has a right at the moment to control the doing of the act." So, too, Lord Dunedin said: "Payment is not everything; it is a circumstance pointing to who is the employer, but the real test is control."[424] Later, Lord Wright suggested[425] that control was not the test, but that the question was whether the employee himself, or only the use and benefit of his work, was transferred. In *Mersey Docks and Harbour Board v Coggins & Griffith (Liverpool) Ltd*,[426] the House of Lords re-emphasised the test of control by suggesting it was necessary to examine who had the right to control the way in which the negligent act was performed. However, the case can be interpreted as establishing no universal and conclusive test. Lord Porter stated: "Many factors have a bearing on the result.

---

[421] (1958) S.L.T. 46.

[422] [1993] P.I.Q.R. P294, CA (the claimant had volunteered to drive the main contractors' dumper truck, work for which he had not been trained and was injured when the truck fell over an edge at the site). It was pointed out that the position might be different where there was negligent supervision by the contractor to whom the workman had been "lent", for which see *Nelhams v Sandells Maintenance Ltd, The Times*, June 15, 1995, CA (where the claimant fell from an unfooted ladder as a result of negligent supervision, his employers were entitled to a complete indemnity from the contractor for whom he was temporarily performing work). See also *Crombie v McDermott Scotland* (1996) S.L.T. 1238, OH (the claimant could maintain an action against the agency which employed him even though his services were sub contracted to electrical contractors present on the site where he was injured).

[423] [1893] 1 Q.B. 629 at 633–634. Bowen L.J.'s judgment has been approved on a number of occasions, e.g. by the House of Lords in *M'Cartan v Belfast Harbour Commissioners* [1911] 2 Ir.R. 143, and *Century Insurance Co v N.I. Road Transport Board* [1942] A.C. 509, but was criticised in *Mersey Docks and Harbour Board v Coggins & Griffith (Liverpool) Ltd* [1947] A.C. 1.

[424] *Bain v Central Vermont Ry* [1921] 2 A.C. 412 at 416.

[425] In *Century Insurance Co v N.I. Road Transport Board* [1942] A.C. 509 at 516, following Bowen L.J. in *Moore v Palmer* (1886) 2 T.L.R. 781 at 782, where he had said: "The great test was this—whether the servant was transferred, or only the use and benefit of his work?" See also Lord Dunedin's approval in *M'Cartan v Belfast Harbour Commissioners* [1911] I.R. 143 at 152, and *Ready Mixed Concrete (East Midlands) Ltd v Yorkshire Traffic Area Licensing Authority* [1970] 2 Q.B. 397.

[426] [1947] A.C. 1 at 12, per Viscount Simon, at 17, per Lord Porter, at 23, per Lord Uthwatt.

Who is paymaster, who can dismiss,[427] how long the alternative service lasts, what machinery is employed, have all to be kept in mind."[428]

3–153   The control test was not satisfied in a claim for damage arising as a result of a fire on a construction site, caused by sparks from welding and grinding operations. The second defendant, as the party who had contracted with the company which employed the men responsible, was not vicariously liable for their negligence, given that they were skilled men, who had used their own welding equipment, their own gas cylinders and their own weld rods. Their foreman was present on site to supervise them, and there could be no question of the second defendant exercising control over the manner in which they welded.[429] The control test was also applied in *Colour Quest Ltd v Total Downstream UK Plc*,[430] which involved many claims arising from a series of explosions at the Buncefield Oil Storage Depot in Hemel Hempstead in December 2005. It was common ground that one of two companies, Total or HOSL, were responsible for the negligence of supervisors who failed to notice that a oil tank gauge was stuck, which resulted in the tank being overfilled and an accumulation of vapour which subsequently caught fire. Among the matters considered in deciding that Total were liable were the manner of selection of the supervisors, the method of payment, and who had the power of dismissal. The most telling indicator was the identity of the person who had the right to control the employee's method of work: not as to the nature of the work, but the manner in which it was to be undertaken.

3–154   **Dual control.** In *Viasystems (Tyneside) Ltd v Thermal Transfer (Northern) Limited*[431] the Court of Appeal questioned the assumption that only one employer could be vicariously liable for the negligence of an employee temporarily under the direction of another. The case arose from a dispute about which of two defendants was vicariously liable for the negligence of an apprentice, who crawled through ductwork within a building in which air conditioning was being installed, causing a fire protection sprinkler system to fracture and a flood to result. The apprentice was employed by the second defendant and was under the immediate control of a fitter also employed by them. The services of both men were provided under a labour only contract with the first defendant, which appointed another man as foreman, with responsibility for supervising their work. The Court decided that there was no reason in law to prevent a solution by which both defendants were vicariously liable for the apprentice's negligence. If in the particular circumstances the core question was who was entitled and, in theory, obliged, to control the employee's negligent act so as to prevent it, there

---

[427] Nevertheless, this was held not to be either the sole or a conclusive test by Parker J. in *Garrard v A.E. Southey & Co* [1952] 2 Q.B. 174 at 180.
[428] *Mersey Docks and Harbour Board v Coggins & Griffith (Liverpool) Ltd* [1947] A.C. 1 at 17 (the passage quoted was applied in *The Polartank* [1948] Lloyd's Rep. 108 and *The Panther and The Ericbank* [1957] P. 143).
[429] *Biffa Waste Services Ltd v Machinenfabrik Ernst Hese GmbH* [2009] P.N.L.R 12, CA. See also para.3–192, below. See also Warner, "Who's responsible?" 159 N.L.J. 1349.
[430] [2009] EWHC 540 (Comm), David Steel J.
[431] [2006] Q.B. 510.

would be cases in which the sensible answer would be each of two "employers".[432] The instant case was one such. The issue of apportionment of damages between the defendants, was resolved on the basis of equal division: "If the relationships (between employee and both employers) yield dual control, it is highly likely at least that the measure of control will be equal, for otherwise the court would be unlikely to find dual control."[433] That being so, "For dual vicarious liability, equal contribution may, on the facts, be close to a logical necessity."[434]

Hire of operator and plant. There are a number of cases dealing with the **3–155** hire of machinery and other plant with an operator in charge. In almost all of these cases, the hirer gives instructions to the driver or operator where he is to go and generally controls his actions in much the same way as if he were in the hirer's own employment. Nevertheless, the usual view is that the driver or operator remains the employee of the general employer,[435] unless there are quite exceptional circumstances pointing to the contrary. Such circumstances might arise where there was no intention to transfer the employee from the general employer to the particular employer, as where an apprentice was sent by his employers to work with some contractors, who were installing plant on his employers' premises, as an integral part of his training and not in response to any request for the loan of workmen by the contractors.[436] On the other hand, the courts will more readily find that a workman has become the employee of the particular employer where he has not been lent together with some complex piece of machinery or valuable plant, belonging to the general employer.[437]

---

[432] *Viasystems (Tyneside) Ltd v Thermal Transfer (Northern) Limited* [2006] Q.B. 510 para.[49].
[433] ibid. para.[52].
[434] ibid. See further, *Hawley v Luminar Leisure Ltd* [2006] P.I.Q.R. P211, CA (*Viasystems* not applied in circumstances where the first defendant contracted with the second defendant for the provision of doormen at a number of clubs and one of the men punched a customer so hard that he fell to the ground and suffered serious injury: on the facts the first defendant had exercised detailed control not only over what the door stewards were to do in supplying services but how they were to do it. The first defendant's control over the second defendant's employees was such as to make them temporary employees of the first defendant for the purposes of vicarious liability. Given an effective and substantial passing of control from the general employer to the temporary it was not appropriate for liability to be shared between them). See generally Cope, "Bouncing liability" 150 S.J. 1516.
[435] See, e.g. *Century Insurance Co v N.I. Road Transport Board* [1942] A.C. 509 (transport undertaking let on hire a tanker and driver to a petroleum company; there was a contract, relating to the service dealing with the question whose employee the driver was, but the HL attached no decisive importance to its terms); *Mersey Docks and Harbour Board v Coggins & Griffith (Liverpool) Ltd* [1947] A.C. 1 (owners of a crane hired out together with a crane-driver). A large number of other cases are also cited in the 11th edn of this work at Ch.2 para.2–303.
[436] *Clelland v Edward Lloyd Ltd* [1938] 1 K.B. 272.
[437] *Jones v Scullard* [1898] 2 Q.B. 565 (owner of a horse and carriage hired a driver to drive for him); *Bowie v Shenkin* (1934) S.C. 459 (owner of a motor car hired a chauffeur from a garage to drive the vehicle for him); *Perkins v Stead* (1907) 23 T.L.R. 433 (purchaser of a motor car agreed with its seller that the latter would supply a driver to drive the former to a particular destination); *Garrard v A.E. Southey & Co* [1952] 2 Q.B. 174 (electrician lent to a particular employer to work in the latter's factory). But to the contrary see *Chowdhary v Gillot* [1947] 2 All E.R. 541 (motor car left for repairs was then driven by an employee in the repairer's general employment to take the owner, i.e. the particular employer, to a railway station); *Johnson v A.H. Beaumont Ltd* [1953] 2 Q.B. 184 (trimmers, employed by contractors, working at unloading a ship, together with the workmen of the jetty owners in overall control of the operation.

Summary

3–156

1. The presumption is that the employee remains the employee of the general employer, the burden of proof being on those who assert the contrary. Usually this burden is a heavy one[438] but it can be discharged more readily in cases where the circumstances are exceptional.[439]

2. The employer at the material time is that employer who can exercise control, of the act or omission alleged to be negligent, in the sense of telling the employee not only what he has to do, but also the way in which he has to do it. If the employee, when doing the negligent act, is merely exercising the discretion vested in him by the general employer and not obeying the specific directions given by the particular employer, he remains the employee of the general employer.[440]

3. The contract between the employers may provide that the employee of one of them shall be the employee of the other. Such a contract is not conclusive.[441] It cannot be used "to contradict the fact, if it is the fact, that the complete dominion and control over the servant has not passed from one to the other."[442]

4. When the employee is employed to work with, drive or operate any machinery, plant, vehicle or animal, belonging to the general employer, he exercises the discretion in its management delegated to him by the general

---

[438] *Mersey Docks and Harbour Board v Coggins & Griffith (Liverpool) Ltd* [1947] A.C. 1; *Century Insurance Co v N.I. Road Transport Board* [1942] A.C. 509. The burden was discharged in *Gibb v United Steel Ltd* [1957] 1 W.L.R. 668, where a dock labourer, who was the general employee of a harbour board and was injured while working on premises of which they were the owners and occupiers, was held to be *pro hac vice* the employee of stevedores for whom he was working at the time of the accident. On the other hand, the burden was not discharged in *J. Young & Co (Kelvinhaugh) v O'Donnell* (1958) S.L.T. 46.

[439] In *McArdle v Andmac Roofing Co* [1967] 1 W.L.R. 356 at 361, Sellers L.J. said: "It should be remembered that *Mersey Docks & Harbour Board v Coggins & Griffith (Liverpool) Ltd* did not rule out the possibility that a man in the general permanent employment of one employer may be lent temporarily so as to be treated as the servant of the one whose work he was undertaking. The case only stated it to be a 'heavy burden of proof'. It may be that the decision did not sufficiently recognise the advantages where there is 'teamwork' where an employer's own servants and 'borrowed' labour work together in a joint effort or, as here, where labour alone is hired, in having responsibility placed on the employer undertaking the process of operation for which the borrowing takes place."

[440] *Mersey Docks and Harbour Board v Coggins & Griffith (Liverpool) Ltd* n.438, above. See also *Denham v Midland Employers' Mutual Assurance Ltd* [1955] 2 Q.B. 437 (unskilled labourer, lent by general employer to particular employer, injured by negligence of particular employer's employees was not "under a contract of service" with the particular employer within the meaning of an insurance policy).

[441] See, however, *Arthur White (Contractors) Ltd v Tarmac Civil Engineering Ltd* [1967] 1 W.L.R. 1508, HL.

[442] *Mersey Docks and Harbour Board v Coggins & Griffith (Liverpool) Ltd* n.438, above at 20, per Lord Simonds. As to the effect of the employee's consent to the transfer, see ibid. at 22, per Lord Uthwatt; *Century Insurance Co v N.I. Road Transport Board* [1942] A.C. 509 at 516, per Lord Wright. In both these cases there was a contract purporting to decide in whose employment the servant was, but little importance was attached to the contracts by the House of Lords. See also *Denham v Midland Employer's Mutual Assurance Ltd* [1955] 2 Q.B. 437 at 564, per Denning L.J. In *Bain v Central Vermont Ry* [1921] 2 A.C. 412, the contract was treated as decisive. See also *Poulson v Jarvis & Sons Ltd* (1919) 36 T.L.R. 160; *Malley v L.M.S. Ry*, 1944 S.C. 129 at 136.

employer, and remains the employee of the general employer, although there may be exceptions in special instances.

5. When the employee is not employed by the general employer, as in 4, above, it is easier to find that he has become the employee of the temporary employer.

6. In some cases where two employers are able to exert control over a negligent employee to an equal extent the proper result will be to find both vicariously liable to an equal extent.[443]

Temporary employer's interference. Even though the employee remains the **3–157** employee of the general employer, the temporary employer may make himself liable for the employee's negligence. This occurs when he removes control away from the general employer and instructs the employee to do a specific act which he would not have done without those instructions. As Lord Simon put it:

"If however the hirers intervene to give directions as to how to drive which they have no authority to give, and the driver *pro hac vice* complies with them, with the result that a third party, is negligently damaged, the hirers may be liable as joint tortfeasors."[444]

The liability of the temporary employer can only be based upon assumptions of control and not upon passive acquiescence in what is being done by the employee of the general employer.

Liability of general employer to temporary employer. If an employee in **3–158** the general employment of one person is temporarily in the employment of another, it follows that the temporary employer cannot claim from the general employer in respect of damage caused by the negligence of the employee, while in his temporary employment. In one case, a ship required repairs at Shanghai, and the engineer obtained the services of some of the dock company's workmen to do the necessary work. The engineer required the use of candles and, by the negligence of a workman, the ship caught fire. It was held that, as the workman committed his act of negligence at the time when he was employed by the shipowners, there was no liability upon his general employers, the dock company.[445]

Liability of temporary employer to general employer. Conversely, if the **3–159** employee, while in the service of the temporary employer, negligently causes damage to the general employer, the temporary employer is liable. So, where a lighter, manned by two lightermen, was let on hire to a ship for the purpose of loading it and, owing to the negligence of the lightermen in being absent during the night, the lighter got adrift and was damaged, it was held that the shipowners

---

[443] Para.3–154, above.
[444] *Mersey Docks and Harbour Board v Coggins & Griffith (Liverpool) Ltd* n.438, above at 12. See also per Parke B. in *Quarman v Burnett* (1840) 6 M. & W. 499 at 507 and, per Lush J. in *Poulson v Jarvis & Sons Ltd* (1919) 36 T.L.R. 160.
[445] *Société Maritime Française v Shanghai Dock and Engineering Co* (1921) 37 T.L.R. 379.

were liable for the damage to the lighter.[446] Similarly, where a motor-lorry with a driver was let on hire by the general employers, a firm of haulage contractors, to the temporary employers, and, owing to the negligence of the driver, the lorry was driven under a tunnel so that the load became jammed and the lorry was damaged, it was held that the temporary employers were liable for the damage to the lorry.[447]

(B) Agents

3–160   **Who is an agent?** An agent is one who is authorised to act on behalf of another. It is not necessary that there should be a background of some contractual relationship, as in the case of employer and employee. Friends, a spouse and the children of the principal have, on occasion, been found to be agents. However, neither scoutmaster nor cub mistress in charge of schoolboys at an outing to Whipsnade Zoo were agents of the Boy Scouts Association.[448] It was not contended that youths who escaped from custody and caused damage were agents for whom the Home Office was vicariously liable.[449] Where a child in the care of the local authority sustained personal injuries as a result of her foster parents' negligence, the local authority was held not to be liable vicariously for such negligence, because there was no relationship of principal and agent between them.[450]

3–161   Although a principal is liable for the negligence of an agent acting in the course of authority,[451] as joint tortfeasors they are jointly and severally liable[452]: a person who either authorises or procures another to commit a tort is equally responsible for the commission of that wrong, every bit as much as if he had committed it himself. In this way, if the principal gives the agent express or implied authority[453] to commit some tortious act, the former will be held liable, even although he may be the employer of an independent contractor.[454]

---

[446] *A.H. Bull & Co v West African Shipping Co* [1927] A.C. 686.

[447] *Leggott & Son v Normanton* (1928) 98 L.J.K.B. 145. The correctness of this decision is doubted on the question of "who the employer was?"

[448] *Murphy v Zoological Society of London, The Times*, November 14, 1962.

[449] *Dorset Yacht Co Ltd v Home Office* [1970] A.C. 1004 at 1057. It was conceded that the Home Office was vicariously responsible for the tortious acts of those officers and managers employed at the custodial institution in question.

[450] *S v Walsall Metropolitan Borough Council* [1985] 1 W.L.R. 1150, CA.

[451] "In each case the test to be applied is the same: was the servant or agent acting on behalf of, and within the scope of the authority conferred by, the master or principal?" per Lord Wilberforce in *Heatons Transport (St Helens) Ltd v Transport and General Workers' Union* [1973] A.C. 15 at 99. See also *Scarsbrook v Mason* [1961] 3 All E.R. 767, where the driver was the agent of all the passengers.

[452] See further, para.3–81, above.

[453] See, e.g. *Heatons Transport (St Helens) Ltd v T.G.W.U.* [1973] A.C. 15 (although certain shop stewards were not the servants of their Union, they had authority to take industrial action in accordance with Union policy, so that the Union itself was responsible for the results of the shop stewards' activities at the Liverpool and other dockyards).

[454] *Jolliffe v Willmett & Co* (1970) 114 S.J. 619. Also an employer would become liable if he knew or ought to have known of the existence of a danger created by his independent contractor: *Legacy v Chaleur Country Club* (1975) 53 D.L.R. (3d) 725, applying *Cushing v Peter Walker & Sons* [1941] 2 All E.R. 693. See further, paras 3–172 to 3–203, below.

A person may be the agent of another so as to make that other liable for his **3–162** negligence, even if a mere volunteer. Indeed, in most of the cases in which the principal has been held liable for the negligence of his agent, the agent has been a volunteer. The facts of *Brooke v Bool*[455] have already been referred to. One of the grounds on which the defendant was liable for the explosion was that the lodger was acting as his agent in trying to discover the escape of the gas.

Ratification. Liability of the principal may also be founded under the doctrine **3–163** of ratification. Thus, if one person commits a tort whilst acting on behalf of another person, albeit without his authority, and that other later ratifies the act, he becomes just as responsible for the wrong as if he had authorised it initially, before its commission.[456]

Driving motor car in presence of owner. The owner of a motor car who **3–164** allows someone to drive it in his presence makes such a person his agent and is liable for any negligent driving. In *Wheatley v Patrick*,[457] the defendant, having borrowed a horse and gig, went for a drive with a friend. During the excursion, he allowed the friend to drive and by the friend's negligence the plaintiff was injured. The defendant was liable. The same result followed where the defendant, in the course of attempting to sell his car, permitted the son of a prospective purchaser to drive the vehicle in his presence because he retained possession and control.[458] The owner of a car was also liable where he sat beside one of his friends, who drove, and by his negligent driving injured another passenger in the car.[459] Where the owner of a car's son negligently drove it, when accompanied by the owner's driver, it was held that the owner was liable for his son's negligence.[460]

When an employee, who is in control of a car for the purposes of his **3–165** employment, allows a third party to drive it and an accident occurs, as a result of the third party's negligence, the employer is liable, on the ground that the employee is in control of the car on the employer's behalf.[461] Lord Tucker said[462]: "It is now well settled that the person in control of a carriage or motor vehicle—though not actually driving—is liable for the negligence of the driver over whom he has the right to exercise control."

Owner not in car. Where the agent has authority to drive a motor car, on **3–166** behalf of or for the purposes of the owner (whether wholly or partly on the

---

[455] [1928] 2 K.B. 578, See further, para.3–88, above.
[456] *Wilson v Tumman* (1843) 6 M. & G. 236.
[457] (1837) 2 M. & W. 650.
[458] *Samson v Aitchison* [1912] A.C. 844.
[459] *Pratt v Patrick* [1924] 1 K.B. 488.
[460] *Reichardt v Shard* (1914) 31 T.I.R. 24. This case and those in nn.86–88, above, were followed in *Trust Co Ltd v De Silva* [1956] 1 W.L.R. 376. In contrast see, e.g. *Ansin v R. & D. Evans* [1982] 1 N.Z.L.R. 184 (the owner of the family car authorised her husband to drive but he became unwell to drive and a friend took over. The owner saw who was driving when she entered the car but did not comment and when an accident was caused by the friend's negligence she was held not liable since in the absence of any communication between them she had neither expressly nor impliedly authorised him to drive).
[461] *Trust Co Ltd v De Silva* [1956] 1 W.L.R. 376.
[462] ibid at 380.

owner's business or in the owner's interest), and negligently causes damage in the course of that authority, the owner of the car will be liable, as principal, even though he was not present in the car at the time.[463] On the other hand, where the owner has merely given his permission to another to use the car for his own purposes[464] or where the owner merely has the knowledge of the car's use for such purposes,[465] vicarious liability does not attach.

3–167   In *Launchbury v Morgans*,[466] the owner of a Jaguar motor car, with some prescience, gave her husband permission to get a sober friend to drive him, if ever he were to feel unfit to drive through drink. On one such occasion, while a friend was driving, there was a fatal head-on collision with a bus. The Court of Appeal held the owner liable, favouring the view that, as the law imposed vicarious liability for reasons of social policy, the owner of a family car should be liable for negligent driving by any member of the family household, or agent, permitted to drive it. The House of Lords[467] reversed that decision unanimously and said that it was not for the courts but for Parliament to make such a change in the basic concept of vicarious liability.

3–168   Where a third party was permitted to use a vehicle for the purpose of driving a child, whether the third party was acting as the parent's agent was held to depend on from whom the proposal emanated: if from the parent, then the driver was acting as his agent; but where from a 16-year-old child, then the driver was not acting as the parent's agent.[468] Where the owner of a car, who was unable to drive, had an arrangement with her son, whereby he drove her as a passenger in the car and kept it in a garage at his own house, and driving to the garage he had an accident, she was liable on the ground that the son was her agent.[469] When a parent owns and pays for the running expenses of a car, which children of the family are allowed to drive, they will usually be the parent's agents. However, where a child was refused permission to drive and did not have a driving licence, the child was not the parent's agent.[470]

3–169   In *Parker v Miller*,[471] the owner of a car went for a drive with a friend but, later, left the car and allowed the friend to drive on to his house. The friend parked the car there negligently, so that it ran down a hill and caused damage. The owner was liable on the ground that the friend was his agent and, although he was no longer in the car, he still had the right of control. Again, when a car

---

[463] *Thompson v Reynolds* [1926] N.I. 131 (brother of owner rides motorcycle from repairer's shop to owner's garage—agent); *Hewitt v Bonvin* [1940] 1 K.B. 188 at 191, per du Parcq L.J.
[464] *Launchbury v Morgans* [1973] A.C. 127; *Candler v Thomas* [1998] R.T.R. 214, CA (lender of car vicariously liable where driver was first delivering a package for the lender before using the car for his own purposes).
[465] *Norwood v Nevan* [1981] R.T.R. 457, CA.
[466] [1971] 2 Q.B. 245.
[467] [1973] A.C. 127.
[468] *Carberry v Davies* [1968] 1 W.L.R. 1103. In *Klein v Caluori* [1971] 1 W.L.R. 619 (the owner of a car was not liable when it was borrowed by a friend who, when ordered to return it, ran into a stationary car, as the friend was not his agent even though acting on his orders to return the car).
[469] *Smith v Moss* [1940] 1 K.B. 424.
[470] *Gibson v O'Keeney* [1928] N.I. 66.
[471] (1926) 42 T.L.R. 408.

was driven by a friend of the owner with the intention of reaching Monte Carlo, where the owner was to join him, so that they could use the car for a holiday together, the friend was held to be the owner's agent even before the owner had joined him.[472] "The owner is also liable if . . . the driver is, with the owner's consent, driving the car . . . partly for his own purposes and partly for the owner's purposes."[473]

A commercial traveller, who sells goods on commission for his principal but drives his own car, in respect of which he receives from his principal a weekly sum towards the running expenses, is not an agent so as to make his principal liable for his negligence in driving the car.[474]

Loan of a car. If the owner of a car lends it to a friend to be used for the **3–170** friend's purposes,[475] or allows his son[476] or his employee[477] to use his car for their own purposes, he does not make them his employees or agents so as to be liable for their negligence. The basic principle is that the bailor of a chattel is not liable for negligence of the bailee in using it. But where a car owner lent the vehicle for a few days to a prospective purchaser, he was vicariously liable for the latter's negligent driving. It was to the advantage of the owner, who had wanted to sell the vehicle, to allow the other to test-drive it, so that the other was driving it partly, if not wholly, on the owner's business or for the owner's purposes.[478]

Ownership of car is evidence of agency. The fact that the defendant is the **3–171** owner of the car in question is evidence that it was being driven by him or his servant or agent at the material time.[479] Alternatively, it can give rise to such an inference being drawn.[480] Nevertheless, evidence of ownership is not conclusive and may be rebutted by the circumstances in which the vehicle was actually being driven at the time.

(C) Independent contractors

Who is an independent contractor? An independent contractor is a person **3–172** who carries on a business independently on his own account and, in contracting for work, can decide for himself how it should be done.[481] Whilst he may be employed to perform certain work, he is not under any contract of service to, or under the control of the employer and he is free to perform the work on his own way.[482]

---

[472] *Ormrod v Crosville Motor Services Ltd* [1953] 1 W.L.R. 1120.
[473] *Ormrod v Crosville Motor Services Ltd* [1953] 1 W.L.R. 1120 at 1122, per Denning L.J.
[474] *Eggington v Reader* [1936] 1 All E.R. 7.
[475] *Monk v Warbey* [1935] 1 K.B. 75.
[476] *Daniels v Vaux* [1938] 2 K.B. 203; *Hewitt v Bonvin* [1940] 1 K.B. 188.
[477] *Britt v Gamoye* (1928) 44 T.L.R. 294.
[478] *Wong It Yorn v Lim Gaw Teong* [1969] 1 M.L.J. 79.
[479] *Barnard v Sally* (1931) 47 T.L.R. 557.
[480] *Rambarran v Gurrucharran* [1970] 1 W.L.R. 556.
[481] *Allen v Hayward* (1845) 7 Q.B. 960. See also, per Cooke J. in *Market Investigations Ltd v Minister of Social Security* [1969] 2 Q.B. 773 at 784–785.
[482] *Hardaker v Idle District Council* [1896] 1 Q.B. 335.

3-173   **The general rule.** Generally speaking, an employer is not vicariously liable for the negligence of an independent contractor, his workmen or agents in the execution of the work contracted for.

> "Unquestionably, no one can be made liable for an act or breach of duty, unless it be traceable to himself or his servant or servants in the course of his or their employment. Consequently, if an independent contractor is employed to do a lawful act, and in the course of the work he or his servants commit some casual act of wrong or negligence, the employer is not answerable."[483]

3-174   For example, if a man has his lorry repaired by competent motor repairers,[484] or his lift repaired by competent engineers[485] or his premises rewired by experienced electrical contractors[486] or has a large hawthorn tree cut down and removed from his front garden by an apparently competent tree felling contractor,[487] in each case he is not liable for damage caused by their negligent work. Likewise, where a building owner engages an architect, whom he reasonably believes to be competent, he will generally not be responsible for the architect's negligence, since he has no control over the manner, in which the architect does his work.[488] Further, where part of building works has been carried out by a sub-contractor, then, in relation to such works, the main contractor is not liable in tort either to the owner or the occupier of the building for the negligence of the sub-contractor.[489]

3-175   In other situations, it has been held that the duty imposed on a harbour authority by s.2 of the Pilotage Act 1987 was not to pilot ships but to to supply properly authorised pilots for ships, so that the authority was not vicariously liable for the negligence of the pilot on board the plaintiffs' ship.[490] Nor were English solicitors acting for clients who wished to purchase property in Spain, vicariously liable for the negligence of a Spanish lawyer who was instructed by them to perform the work necessary under Spanish law to effect the conveyance.[491]

3-176   **Exceptions.** An employer is liable for his own act or neglect. It follows that, if the defendant contracts with an independent contractor to do some act, which

---

[483] *Pickard v Smith* (1861) 10 C.B.(N.S.) 470, per Williams J. See also *Allen v Hayward* (1845) 7 Q.B. 960; *Steel v S.E. Ry* (1855) 16 C.B. 550; *Wilson v Hodgson's Kingston Brewery* (1915) 85 L.J.K.B. 270.

[484] *Phillips v Britannia Hygienic Laundry* [1923] 1 K.B. 539; affd. [1923] 2 K.B. 832; *Stennett v Hancock* [1939] 2 All E.R. 578.

[485] *Haseldine v Daw & Son Ltd* [1941] 1 K.B. 343.

[486] *Green v Fibreglass Ltd* [1958] 2 Q.B. 245. *Cook v Broderip* (1968) 112 S.J. 193 (nor was there a breach of the flat owner-occupier's duty under s.2 of the Occupiers' Liability Act 1957).

[487] *Salsbury v Woodland* [1970] 1 Q.B. 324.

[488] *Clayton v Woodman & Son (Builders) Ltd* [1962] 2 Q.B. 533. See 78 L.Q.R. 107.

[489] *D. & F. Estates Ltd v Church Commissioners for England* (1987) 11 Con.L.R. 12 (appeal dismissed [1989] A.C. 177).

[490] *Oceangas (Gibraltar) Ltd v Port of London Authority; The Cavendish* [1993] 2 Lloyd's Rep. 292.

[491] *Gregory v Shepherds* [2000] P.N.L.R. 44 (however, they were personally liable for their failure to check with the agent that he had performed a check for incumbrances upon the property: see the same case on appeal at [2000] P.N.L.R. 769, CA).

he, the defendant, is not entitled to do, or to perform some duty which is thrown upon himself to discharge, whether by statute or common law, he will be liable for the negligence of the contractor in the way in which he has performed the act or the duty. As Salmon J. said:

> "There are, of course, cases where, by virtue of a contract or by the operation of law,[492] an obligation may be imposed on a man to do an act or to ensure that it is done carefully. In such cases the defendant cannot shelter behind any independent contractor, whom he may have employed. If he breaches the obligation he is liable, not in negligence, but in contract . . . or by reason of some breach of duty other than a duty to take care . . . "[493]

In these instances, the contractor may be regarded as the agent of the employer **3–177** to perform the primary duty of the employer himself, whose liability cannot properly be called vicarious.[494] The employer is liable, not because he is liable for his contractor's negligence, but because he is himself in breach of his own, non-delegable, duty of care.[495] The principle was summarised by Denning L.J. as follows:

> "I take it to be clear law, as well as good sense, that, where a person is himself under a duty to care, he cannot get rid of his responsibility by delegating the performance of it to someone else, no matter whether the delegation be to a servant under a contract of service or to an independent contractor under a contract for services. Lord Blackburn laid that down on many occasions, see *Tarry v Ashton*[496]; *Dalton v Angus*[497]; and *Hughes v Percival*[498]; and so have other great judges . . . "[499]

A number of situations have arisen where liability is imposed on this basis, which it is proposed to consider separately.

Unlawful acts. If an employer has contracted with or has given express or **3–178** implied authority[500] to a contractor to do an act, which the employer is not entitled to do, such as to create a public nuisance, a private nuisance, or to trespass, the employer is liable for the resulting damage. Where a gas company, with no statutory powers for breaking up the highway, engaged a firm of contractors to dig trenches in the streets in order to lay gas pipes, and the contractors negligently left lying on the footway a heap of stones, over which the

---

[492] See for instance the non-delegable duty of a hospital authority under s.3 of the National Health Service Act 1946 para.3–109 above.

[493] *Green v Fibreglass Ltd* [1958] 2 Q.B. 245 at 250.

[494] *Daniel v Rickett, Cockerell & Co Ltd* [1938] 2 K.B. 322 at 325.

[495] See, e.g. *Rogers v Night Riders* [1983] R.T.R. 324, CA (a minicab firm, which undertook to the general public to convey passengers to their destination by means of a cab, owned, maintained and controlled by its driver, an independent contractor, owed such passengers a duty to take reasonable steps to ensure that the vehicle so provided was properly maintained and reasonably fit for that purpose).

[496] (1876) 1 Q.B.D. 314, 319.

[497] (1881) 6 App.Cas. 740 at 829.

[498] (1883) 8 App.Cas. 443 at 446.

[499] *Cassidy v Ministry of Health* [1951] 2 K.B. 343 at 363. The non-delegable principle does not impose liability where damage is caused by negligence of an independent contractor or his employees which can be described as casual or collateral: see para.3–199, below.

[500] *Jolliffe v Willmett & Co* (1970) 114 S.J. 619.

plaintiff fell and was injured, it was held that the gas company was liable. There was no power to instruct the contractors to do what they did and their actions were therby unlawful.[501]

> "Though it may be that if the workmen employed had been careful in the way in which they heaped up the earth and stones the plaintiff would have avoided them, still I think the nuisance which the defendants employed the contractors to commit was the primary cause of the accident."[502]

Similarly, if a contractor is employed to erect a building, which infringes the adjoining owner's ancient lights or is a trespass upon the land of another, the employer is liable.[503]

3–179   **Contractor performs duty imposed by law on employer.** If an employer, owing a duty to his employees imposed either by statute or at common law, engages an independent contractor to perform that duty, instead of performing it himself, he is liable for the negligence of the independent contractor in carrying it out. That liability does not exclude the contractors also being liable where they also owe a duty of care to the employer's employees and in such a case they will be jointly liable with the employers for any breach.[504] Where that arises, the employers may be entitled to recover such damages as are awarded against themselves, from the contractors, as the measure of loss for the latter's breach of contract.[505] The cases, in which a duty is thrown upon the employer, are: (i) in relation to dangerous things; (ii) dangers on the highway; (iii) duties imposed by statute; and (iv) where an act involves special risk of damage, each which requires separate discussion.

(i) *Dangerous things*[506]

3–180   A person who builds a reservoir is liable for damage caused by the escape of water, even though he employed a contractor to construct it.[507] The employer is under an absolute duty, which attaches to the ownership of dangerous things. The employer who employs a contractor to do an act involving the creation of or the interference with a dangerous thing (such as to burn brushwood on the employer's land,[508] or to take a photograph which can only be taken by a naked flashlight)[509] is liable for the negligence of the contractor in not preventing the dangerous thing from causing damage. Ship repairers, who used an oxyacetylene burner on the strength of a certificate issued by their consulting engineer that the vessel was "gas free", were liable for the damage caused by an explosion, which arose from the engineer's negligence in failing to make a proper inspection,

---

[501] *Ellis v Sheffield Gas Consumers Co* (1853) 2 E. & B. 767.
[502] per Wightman J.; cf. *Clarke v J. Sugrue & Sons Ltd*, The Times, May 29, 1959.
[503] *Upton v Townend* (1855) 17 C.B. 30.
[504] *Driver v William Willett (Contractors)* [1969] 1 All E.R. 665.
[505] *Sims v Foster Wheeler Ltd* [1966] 1 W.L.R. 769.
[506] See Ch.13, below.
[507] *Rylands v Fletcher* (1868) L.R. 3 H.L. 330; 37 L.J. Ex. 161. If the water is collected in a domestic cistern and escapes owing to the negligence of a plumber, an independent contractor, employed to mend the cistern, the employer is not liable: *Blake v Woolf* [1898] 2 Q.B. 426.
[508] *Black v Christchurch Finance Co* [1894] A.C. 48.
[509] *Honeywill & Stein Ltd v Larkin Bros Ltd* [1934] 1 K.B. 191.

before issuing his certificate.[510] A local authority, which employed a contractor to make a sewer, near to the mains of a gas company, was liable for the negligence of the contractor in interfering with the foundations of the gas main so as to cause an escape of gas.[511]

(ii) *Dangers on the highway*

When an employer engages a contractor to carry out work either upon or 3–181 adjoining the highway, which work is likely to involve danger to persons using the highway, a duty of care remains upon the employer. Where a local authority employed a contractor to make up a highway, upon which the contractor negligently left an unlit and unprotected heap of soil, and the plaintiff was injured by falling over it during the hours of darkness, the local authority was held liable.[512] There was approval on appeal for the statement of the trial judge, Bruce J., who had said:

"When a person employs a contractor to do work in a place where the public are in the habit of passing, which work will, unless precautions are taken, cause danger to the public, an obligation is thrown upon the person who orders the work to be done to see that the necessary precautions are taken, and that, if the necessary precautions are not taken, he cannot escape liability by seeking to throw the blame on the contractor."[513]

This duty at common law is recognised by the provisions of s.58(2) of the 3–182 Highways Act 1980,[514] which give a statutory defence to the highway authority in an action against it for damage, resulting from its failure to maintain a highway. The section provides that it shall not be relevant to prove that the highway authority had arranged for a competent person to carry out or supervise the maintenance of the part of the highway, to which the action relates, unless it is also proved that the authority had given him proper instructions with regard to the maintenance of the highway and that he had carried out the instructions.

Further illustrations are afforded by the following cases: where a telephone 3–183 company, which was engaged in laying telephone wires along a street, contracted

---

[510] *The Pass of Ballater* [1942] P. 112 at 117, per Langton J., it made no difference that the engineer was an independent contractor since where hazardous materials were involved the defendant's duty was to see that care was taken.

[511] *Hardaker v Idle District Council* [1896] 1 Q.B. 335.

[512] *Penny v Wimbledon Urban District Council* [1899] 2 Q.B. 72. Similar cases are *Burgess v Gray* (1845) 1 C.B. 578 (contractor employed to dig drain communicating with sewer in highway, leave heap of rubbish over which plaintiff falls—employer liable); *Gray v Pullen* (1864) 5 B. & S. 970 (trench improperly filled in by contractor); *Clements v Tyrone County Council* [1905] 2 Ir.R. 542 (contractor repairing road leaves of heap of stones); *The Snark* [1900] P. 105 (wreck in navigable river left unlighted by contractor); *Bright v Attorney-General* (1971) 115 S.J. 226 (white lines negligently removed from road's surface). But cf. the position where public works contractors were laying a drain and a length of rope was left on the highway by an independent contractor, over which rope the plaintiff tripped and fell. Lord Parker C.J. held that the defendants were not liable for this act of the independent contractor since they did not know that the rope was on the highway nor did they choose to leave it there: *Clarke v J. Sugrue & Sons Ltd, The Times*, May 29, 1959.

[513] [1898] 2 Q.B. 212 at 217.

[514] Which replaced s.1(3) of the Highways (Miscellaneous Provisions) Act 1961 as from January 1, 1981. See, further, Ch.10, below, para.10–02 et seq.

with a plumber for additional work, it was liable for his act in negligently dipping a defective lamp into a cauldron of melted solder, thereby causing an explosion, which injured a passer-by[515]; the occupier of a house, from which a lamp was suspended over the street, was liable for the negligence of an independent contractor in failing to repair the attachment, as a result of which the lamp fell and injured a person using the highway[516]; and where a contractor was employed to drive a heifer and calf along the highway, the employer was liable when the heifer tossed a dog and injured a passer-by, on the ground that a heifer with a calf might become dangerous on meeting a dog.[517]

3–184 There is a difference when a contractor is employed to deliver goods at premises of which the employer is not the occupier, since there is no liability on the employer if the contractor, in course of delivery, creates some danger in the highway and occasions injury to a passer-by. So, when a brewery company employed a contractor to deliver beer to a public-house, which was not in its occupation, and the contractor negligently left open the cellar flaps, causing the plaintiff to trip and fall as he was walking along the street, the brewery company were held not liable.[518] On the other hand, where the employer is the occupier of the premises, he will be liable if the work which he has employed the contractors to do involves their negligently leaving open a cellar flap or a man-hole plate or the creation of a heap of soil, coals or the like, being left in the highway.[519]

3–185 The principle is not confined to dangers created on a highway as such, but extends to dangers created in any place along which persons are lawfully passing. Accordingly, when the occupier of a refreshment room at a railway station employed a contractor to deliver coals down a coal hole in the platform, and the contractor negligently left the flap open, as a result of which a railway passenger was injured, it was held that the occupier was liable.[520]

3–186 The rule relates to work actually undertaken on the highway. Where an independent contractor was engaged to carry out work on land adjacent to the highway, which did not fall within the "inherently dangerous" category,[521] the exception imposing liability upon his employer did not apply.[522] In *Salsbury v*

[515] *Holliday v National Telephone Co* [1899] 2 Q.B. 392; cf. *Hardaker v Idle District Council* [1896] 1 Q.B. 335.
[516] *Tarry v Ashton* (1876) 1 Q.B.D. 314.
[517] *Pinn v Rew* (1916) 32 T.L.R. 451.
[518] *Wilson v Hodgson's Kingston Brewery Co* (1915) 85 L.J.K.B. 270.
[519] *Pickard v Smith* (1861) 10 C.B.(N.S.) 470; *Daniel v Rickett Cockerell & Co Ltd* [1938] 2 K.B. 322 (in this case the employer recovered substantial contribution from the independent contractor).
[520] *Pickard v Smith* (1861) 10 C.B.(N.S.) 470; cf. *Cunard v Antifyre Ltd* [1933] 1 K.B. 551 at 562, per Talbot J.; *Welfare v London & Brighton Ry* (1869) L.R. 4 Q.B. 693 (passenger in railway station injured by fall of zinc from roof which was being repaired by a contractor, railway company not liable) must be taken to have been wrongly decided. In *Pickard v Smith*, above, the railway company would have been liable because they were occupiers, see Ch.8. In spite of Williams J.'s opinion to the contrary (at 477) the contractor would have been liable; see *Whiteley v Pepper* (1876) 2 Q.B.D. 276.
[521] See para.3–192, below.
[522] *Rowe v Herman* [1997] 1 W.L.R. 1390, Can. (no liability upon the employer/occupier of premises adjacent to the highway when his building contractor laid metal plates across the pavement in order to protect it from the passage of heavy vehicles and the claimant tripped over the plate at night).

Woodland,[523] a house occupier employed an independent contractor, who was apparently competent to fell trees, to remove a large hawthorn tree which was standing in his front garden, adjoining the highway. Owing to the contractors' negligence in doing the work, some top branches of the falling tree brought down telephone wires, causing an obstruction to the highway. The plaintiff, who had been watching the operations out of curiosity, went forwards to try to remove the wires from the road but had to fling himself to the side to avoid a collision with a car, suffering serious injury. The occupier was not liable to the plaintiff for the negligence of the contractors, since the removal of the tree was neither work of an inherently dangerous nature nor was it work carried out on the highway itself.

(iii) *Statutory duty*

When an independent contractor is engaged to perform an absolute duty,   **3–187**
imposed by statute upon the employer himself, the employer is liable for a breach of the duty.[524] It makes no difference whether the duty is owed to the public at large or just to a section of it.[525] Where a railway company was authorised by statute to construct a bridge, which had to be capable of being opened so as to allow vessels to pass along the river, and its contractors, constructed a bridge, which would not open, the railway company was liable.[526] Again, where a local authority had undertaken the cleansing of cesspools under the Public Health Act 1875, and had employed contractors to do the work, it was liable for the act of the contractors in wrongfully depositing the sewage upon the plaintiff's land.[527]

Care must always be taken to distinguish those situations where, on analysis,   **3–188**
no delegation of the employer's duty arises. For example, where the police had fulfilled their statutory duty under the Removal and Disposal of Vehicles Regulations 1968,[528] which was a duty to take reasonable care in choosing a garage to remove a vehicle from a road, they were not liable for the subsequent negligence of the garage in removing the plaintiff's broken down motor car from the M1 motorway.[529]

---

[523] [1970] 1 Q.B. 324.
[524] *The Pass of Ballater* [1942] P. 112 at 117; *M v Calderdale and Kirklees Health Authority* [1998] Lloyd's Rep. Med. 157 (non-delegable duty of care owed in like terms to the statutory duty in s.1 of the National Health Service Act 1977 to provide or secure the effective provision of services; alternatively reasonable care not taken in the selection of an independent contractor to whom provision of the service in question, an abortion operation, was delegated).
[525] *Mulready v J.H. & W. Bell Ltd* [1953] 2 Q.B. 117.
[526] *Hole v Sittingbourne & Sheerness Ry* (1861) 6 H. & N. 488.
[527] *Robinson v Beaconsfield RDC* [1911] 2 Ch. 188 at 197–198, per Buckley L.J.: "They [the local authority] owed a duty to use all reasonable skill and care so to dispose of and deposit this sewage as not to injure or cause damage to any person. They were at liberty to employ a contractor to do the work, but if the contractor failed to do that which it was the duty of these defendants to do or get done, then these defendants are liable."
[528] SI 1968/43, which has been revoked and replaced. See now the Removal and Disposal of Vehicle Regulations 1986 (SI 1986/183). By reg.4 there is conferred on a constable both a power to remove the vehicle himself and a distinct and separate power to arrange for its removal by another, namely an independent contractor.
[529] *Rivers v Cutting* [1982] 1 W.L.R. 1146.

3–189 As a result of the Employer's Liability (Defective Equipment) Act 1969,[530] where an employee[531] is injured in consequence of a defect in equipment[532] provided by his employer, and such defect is attributable to the fault of a third party, the injury is to be deemed to be also attributable to the negligence of the employer. The Act does not, however, appear to create a situation of vicarious liability in the sense described above, because it covers all third parties, some of whom may have had no contractual relationship with the employer at all.

3–190 Similarly, where an employer was under a duty to fence dangerous[533] machinery under the Factories Act 1961 and to provide safe means of access,[534] he could not escape liability by delegating the performance of his statutory duty to an independent contractor. Further, it has been held that a carrier of goods by sea does not fulfill his statutory duty to use due diligence merely by employing a competent ship-repairer and, thereafter, having the repair work inspected in the usual way by a Lloyd's surveyor.[535]

3–191 In *Driver v William Willett (Contractors)*[536] it was held that an independent contractor, who contracts with employers to act as their consultant safety and inspecting engineer in connection with their business, also owes a duty of care to the latter's employees. Thus, where there had been breaches of the various building regulations and the employers had been held liable to an injured workman of theirs, the independent contractor was also held to be liable, since he had contractually undertaken the duties of a safety officer under the regulations.[537]

(iv) *Act involves special risk of damage*

3–192 An employer can be vicariously liable for the negligence of an independent contractor where the latter is engaged to perform work which, by its very nature, involves a special risk of danger to others. It has been said[538] that such a rule is justified because the extra hazardous or dangerous activities which gave rise to

---

[530] The Act, which came into force on October 25, 1969, binds the Crown and specifically preserves the right of the employer to contribution from the person at fault in supplying the defective equipment, whether he is the manufacturer or otherwise. This strict liability imposed cannot be limited or excluded by agreement.

[531] A self-employed person is *not* included.

[532] By s.1(3) this includes any plant, machinery, vehicle, aircraft and clothing, added to which there must be "a ship," whatever its size, if it has been provided by an employer for the purposes of his business: *Coltman v Bibby Tankers Ltd; The Derbyshire* [1988] A.C. 276. See further Ch.11, paras 11–55 to 11–61, below.

[533] *Groves v Lord Wimbourne* [1898] 2 Q.B. 402.

[534] *Hosking v De Havilland Aircraft Co Ltd* [1949] 1 All E.R. 540. But for the position under the building regulations, unless the employers had not divested themselves of the control of the work, see *Donaghey v Boulton & Paul Ltd* [1968] A.C. 1.

[535] *Riverstone Meat Co Pty Ltd v Lancashire Shipping Co Ltd* [1961] A.C. 807.

[536] [1969] 1 All E.R. 665.

[537] Applying *Sims v Foster Wheeler Ltd* [1966] 1 W.L.R. 769, the employers were entitled to recover that proportion of damages, awarded against themselves, from the independent contractor as damages for breach of contract.

[538] *Honeywill and Stein Ltd v Larkin Bros Ltd* [1934] 1 K.B. 191. The rule derived from the case has not been adopted in Australia: *Stevens v Brodribb Sawmilling Co Pty Ltd* (1985/6) 63 A.L.R. 513.

it are performed at the employer's peril.[539] However, the principle has been described as anomalous and it should be narrowly confined. It applies only to activities that are exceptionally dangerous whatever precautions are taken. Welding and grinding operations on a construction site, in the course of which sparks were generated, were incorrectly characterised as ultra-hazardous where insufficient account was taken of factors which were not the responsibility of the company which engaged the welding company to carry them out; and no account was taken of factors which would have rendered the operations safe.[540]

If a contractor is engaged to perform some work which involves special danger **3–193** of nuisance, the employer is liable for that nuisance.[541] Thus, where the owner of a house, from which the owner of the adjoining building has a right of support, employs a contractor to pull down his house, he is liable for any damage which is caused to the adjoining house by the failure of the contractor to provide proper support.[542] Where the owner of a building, the ground floor of which had been let to the plaintiff, employed a contractor to demolish the building above ground floor level, he was liable to the plaintiff for damage that had been caused by the dust and broken bricks entering his premises in the execution of the work.[543] Where the tenant of the first floor of a building employed an independent contractor to make structural alterations to that floor and caused a nuisance to the tenant of the second floor from the dust and noise set up by the alterations, the employer was held liable.[544] Likewise, where the owner of a house in a terraced row had employed a jobbing builder to carry out re-roofing work which involved some special risk of damage to the adjoining houses if such work were carried out incompetently, the employer was held liable for the failure to achieve a waterproof joint between the new roof and the old roof of the adjoining property, which suffered damage as a consequence.[545]

In these cases, there is a duty upon the employer not to do the damage in **3–194** question, and this duty is broken either by infringing some right of property, such as an easement of support, or by committing a nuisance.

Where the plaintiffs had agreed to allow a local authority to demolish a lean-to adjacent to their warehouse but, because of delay by contractors engaged by the authority, in making good the security of the premises, thieves successfully broke in and stole stocks of tobacco, it was held that the authority was liable. All the

---

[539] See [1934] 1 K.B. 191 per Slesser L.J. at 200.
[540] *Biffa Waste Services Ltd v Maschinenfabrik Ernst Hese GmbH* [2009] P.N.L.R 12, CA, para.2–301 above. After an analysis of the cases relied on in *Honeywill* it was observed that the decision has been heavily criticised.
[541] See *Balfour v Barty-King* [1957] 1 Q.B. 496; *Honeywill & Stein Ltd v Larkin Bros* [1934] 1 K.B. 191; *M.T.M. Construction Ltd v William Reid Engineering Ltd, The Times*, April 22, 1997, OH.
[542] *Bower v Peake* (1876) 1 Q.B.D. 321; *Dalton v Angus* (1881) 6 App.Cas. 740;. In *Hughes v Percival* (1883) 8 App.Cas. 443 Lord Blackburn said that the proposition of Cockburn C.J. in *Bower v Peake*, above, at 326, was too broadly stated.
[543] *Odell v Cleveland House Ltd* (1910) 26 T.L.R. 410.
[544] *Matania v National Provincial Bank Ltd* [1936] 2 All E.R. 633 at 646. per Slesser L.J.: "If the act done is one which in its very nature involves a special danger of nuisance being complained of, then it is one which falls within the exception for which the employer of the contractor will be responsible if there is a failure to take the necessary precautions that the nuisance shall not arise."
[545] *Alcock v Wraith*, 59 B.L.R. 20, CA.

parties knew of the warehouse's contents, and the loss had been occasioned by the neglect of the contractors, who were the authority's agents. The latter were held to be joint tortfeasors with the local authority.[546] Where a club employed contractors of little expertise to produce a pyrotechnic display on its property, it was liable to the claimant, whom the contractors had invited to help, when he was injured by an explosion as he placed gunpowder into a mortar tube.[547]

3–195   The rule imposing liability upon an employer for a contractor's negligence where work involves special risks has been said to have its basis in the employer's occupation or possession in land and his interest in the end product. For that reason it has been held not to apply as between the main contractor under a building contract and a subcontractor. So, where main contractors subcontracted contruction work and the subcontractors in turn contracted with others for dangerous welding operations which caused a fire, the main contractors were held unable to recover from the construction subcontractors: only the ultimate employer had any liability in tort co-existent with that of the party ultimately at fault.[548]

3–196   **Bailment.**[549] In the absence of an express term to the contrary, a bailee will be liable for loss or damage to goods in his possession under the terms of a bailment, where that loss or damage is caused by an independent contractor engaged by him. Thus, where the plaintiff's goods were damaged by sea water as a result of the unseaworthiness of the defendant's ship, and it had been proved that this state of affairs was caused solely by the negligence of a servant of a firm of ship-repairers, an independent contractor, the defendants were liable. It was no defence that their duty under the bill of lading contract was limited to exercising due diligence in making the ship seaworthy.[550] Again, a warehouseman, as a bailee for reward, would have been held liable for the negligence of a servant of the security guards, who were independent contractors, if it had been proved that it was his negligence in the discharge of his duties, which had been the cause of the theft of the plaintiff's valuable lorry-load of whisky.[551] There is no implied right to sub-contract, where the bailment is of valuable goods for carriage.[552]

3–197   **Lessor and lessee.** The lessor of land, which is let on a building lease, does not stand to his lessee in the relation of employer to independent contractor. So,

---

[546] *Stanners v High Wycombe Corporation* (1968) 67 L.G.R. 115. For joint tortfeasors see further para.3–87, above.
[547] *Bottomley v Todmorden Cricket Club* [2004] P.I.Q.R. P275, CA.
[548] *M.T.M. Construction Ltd v William Reid Engineering Ltd, The Times,* April 22, 1997, OH.
[549] Generally, see *Morris v C. W. Martin & Sons Ltd* [1966] 1 Q.B. 716 and the examples given by Lord Denning M.R. at 725–727. A person can be in the position of being a bailee, despite the fact that there is no contract between the owners of the goods and him. In *Fairline Shipping Corporation v Adamson* [1975] Q.B. 180 (applying *Morris v C. W. Martin & Sons Ltd,* above) Kerr J. added at 190, "I do not think that the refinements of the concepts of legal possession and bailment are or should be determinative of liability in the tort of negligence."
[550] *Riverstone Meat Co Pty Ltd v Lancashire Shipping Co Ltd* [1961] A.C. 807. But cf. *Leesh River Tea Co Ltd v British India Steam Navigation Co Ltd* [1967] 2 Q.B. 250.
[551] *British Road Services Ltd v Arthur v Crutchley & Co Ltd* [1968] 1 All E.R. 811 at 820, per Lord Pearson and at 824, per Sachs L.J.
[552] *Garnham, Harris & Elton Ltd v Alfred W. Ellis (Transport) Ltd* [1967] 1 W.L.R. 940.

if the lessee, in pursuance of the covenants contained in his lease, proceeds to erect buildings on the land demised, the lessor is not liable for damage caused by the negligence of the lessee or his contractor during the work.[553]

Occupiers' liability.[554] At common law, an occupier was not liable to a licensee injured by a danger of which the occupier had no knowledge, created by an independent contractor.[555] However, s.2(4) of the Occupiers' Liability Act 1957 provides that: **3–198**

"In determining whether the occupier of premises had discharged the common duty of care to a visitor, regard is to be had to all the circumstances, so that (for example) . . .

(b) where damage is caused to a visitor by a danger due to the faulty execution of any work of construction, maintenance or repair by an independent contractor employed by the occupier, the occupier is not to be treated without more as answerable for the danger, if in all the circumstances he had acted reasonably in entrusting the work to an independent contractor and had taken such steps (if any) as he reasonably ought in order to satisfy himself[556] that the contractor was competent and that the work had been properly done."

Casual or collateral negligence.[557] Even when an employer is under a non-delegable duty and thereby potentially liable for the negligence of an independent contractor, he will not be liable if the contractor's negligence is such that it does not involve the employer in a breach of his non-delegable duty. The employer is exempt from liability because the act done is outside the scope of the duty which is imposed on him and not so much because it could not have been foreseen and precautions taken against its occurrence. Lord Blackburn in *Dalton v Angus*[558] said: **3–199**

"Ever since *Quarman v Burnett*[559] it has been considered settled law that one employing another is not liable for his collateral negligence unless the relation of master and servant existed between them. So that a person employing a contractor to do work is not liable for the negligence of that contractor or his servants. On the other hand, a person causing something to be done, the doing of which casts on him a duty, cannot escape from the responsibility attaching on him of seeing that duty performed by delegating it to a contractor."

Commenting on this Lindley L.J. said: **3–200**

"Lord Blackburn in this passage contrasts a contractor's negligence, which he calls 'collateral,' with failure on the part of a contractor to perform the duty of his employer.

---

[553] *Hurlstone v London Electric Ry* (1914) 30 T.L.R. 398.
[554] See, in more detail, Ch.8, below.
[555] *Morgan v Girls' Friendly Society* [1936] 1 All E.R. 404; cf. an occupier was generally liable to his invitees, under the rule in *Indermaur v Dames* (1866) L.R. 1 C.P. 274 for the default of his independent contractor.
[556] In *A.M.F. International Ltd v Magnet Bowling Ltd* [1968] 1 W.L.R. 1028, the occupiers had failed to bring themselves within this subsection since they had taken insufficient steps to satisfy themselves that their independent contractor had done their work properly.
[557] The distinction between this and other negligence was criticised by Sachs L.J. in *Salsbury v Woodland* [1970] 1 Q.B. 324 at 348, CA, who said that he derived no assistance from it.
[558] (1881) 6 App.Cas. 740 at 829.
[559] (1840) 6 M. & W. 499.

For the first the employer is not liable; for the second he is, whether the failure is attributable to negligence or not."[560]

The following descriptions of casual or collateral negligence have been given:

"Where the act complained of is purely collateral, and arises incidentally in the course of the performance of the work, the employer is not liable, because he never authorised that act"[561];

"if the contractor performs their duty for them, it is performed by them through him, and they are not responsible for anything more. They are not responsible for his negligence in other respects, as they would be if he were their servant. Such negligence is sometimes called casual or collateral negligence"[562];

"when a person, through a contractor, does work which from its nature is likely to cause danger to others, there is a duty on his part to take all reasonable precautions against such danger, and he does not escape from liability for the discharge of that duty by employing the contractor if the latter does not take these precautions. I desire to point out that accidents arising from what is called casual or collateral negligence cannot be guarded against beforehand, and do not come within this rule"[563];

"before a superior employer could be held liable for the negligent act of a servant of a sub-contractor it must be shown that the work which the sub-contractor was employed to do was work the nature of which, and not merely the performance of which, cast on the superior employer the duty of taking precautions."[564]

3–201   The various statements appear to suggest that the distinction lies between negligence in fulfilling a duty which is cast upon the employer, resulting in the employer's being held liable; and negligence which is merely incidental to and does not arise directly out of the duty to be fulfilled.[565] Examples of the former are the cases cited above in connection with dangers in the highway.[566] On the other hand, if a workman, employed in road works, negligently leaves "a pickaxe, or suchlike, in the road",[567] or a length of rope on the highway, the negligence is collateral and the employer of the contractor is not liable. Similarly, where a sub-contractor was employed to put metal casements into the windows of a building and one of his servants left a tool on the sill of a window, which was blown shut by the wind, causing the tool to fall and strike a man who was passing along the highway,[568] the main contractor was not liable on the ground that the

---

[560] per *Hardaker v Idle District Council* [1896] 1 Q.B. 335 at 342.
[561] per Pollock C.B. in *Hole v Sittingbourne & Sheerness Ry* (1861) 6 H. & N. 488.
[562] per Lindley L.J. in *Hardaker v Idle District Council* [1896] 1 Q.B. 335 at 340.
[563] per Romer L.J. in *Penny v Wimbledon Urban District Council* [1899] 2 Q.B. 72 at 78.
[564] per Fletcher Moulton L.J. in *Padbury v Holliday & Greenwood Ltd* (1912) 28 T.L.R. 494.
[565] Collateral negligence raised as a specific defence succeeded in *Thompson v Anglo-Saxon Petroleum Co Ltd* [1955] 2 Lloyd's Rep. 363 (the plaintiff, a plumber employed by a sub-contractor of ship-repairers, was struck by a hatch cover which fell whilst he was descending a ladder. The hatch cover was normally perfectly safe when used properly, but fell as a result of the negligence of another sub-contractor's workmen. The ship-owners were held not liable).
[566] See para.3–183, above.
[567] per A. L. Smith in *Penny v Wimbledon Urban District Council* [1899] 2 Q.B. 72.
[568] *Clarke v J. Sugrue & Sons Ltd, The Times*, May 29, 1959.

injury was caused by an act of collateral negligence on the part of the sub-contractor's servant.[569]

In *Holliday v National Telephone Co*,[570] an explosion occurred as a result of   **3–202**
a plumber, employed as an independent contractor to carry out work on a public street, dipping his benzoline lamp into a cauldron of molten solder so that the plaintiff, a passer-by, was splashed by the molten metal. The employers of the plumber were sued and the Divisional Court[571] gave judgment in their favour on the ground that the negligence of the plumber was collateral, but the Court of Appeal disagreed, on the ground that the negligence arose out of the very act which he was employed to perform on the defendants' behalf.[572] When the Ministry of Fuel and Power, under statutory powers, entered a field to bore for coal, the act of its independent contractor in leaving a heap of timber in the field, which injured a horse grazing there, was held not to be collateral negligence. The Ministry owed to the occupier of the field a duty to take reasonable care, from which it could not absolve itself by employing an independent contractor.[573]

Insuring an independent contractor. In a number of cases, consideration   **3–203**
has been given to the circumstances in which an employer has to check whether an independent contractor, engaged to perform work for the employer's benefit, is insured.[574] A duty to check whether insurance cover was in place arose where a contractor was engaged to provide a "splat wall" amusement at a fair within the employer's grounds[575]; also where a club organised a fireworks display within its grounds.[576] The duty did not arise where the proprietors of a nightclub contracted with a firm providing the services of doormen to provide security at the club.[577]

(D) Children

Liability of parent. A parent, as such, is not liable for the negligence of a   **3–204**
child,[578] unless it happens that the child is also his or her employee or agent.[579] Parents, of course, are liable for their own negligence and they are under a duty

---

[569] *Padbury v Holliday & Greenwood Ltd* (1912) 28 T.L.R. 494; *Pearson v Cox* (1877) 2 C.P.D. 369 (plasterer's workman left a tool on window so that it fell into the street, employer of plasterer held not liable) is a similar case.
[570] [1899] 2 Q.B. 392.
[571] [1899] 1 Q.B. 221.
[572] [1899] 2 Q.B. 400, per A. L. Smith L.J.; *Darling v Attorney-General* [1950] 2 All E.R. 793. See further, per Denning L.J. in *Cassidy v Ministry of Health* [1951] 2 K.B. 343 at 365.
[573] *Darling v Attorney-General* [1950] 2 All E.R. 793.
[574] See also Ch.8, para.8–41, below.
[575] *Gwilliam v West Hertfordshire Hospital NHS Trust* [2003] Q.B. 443, CA.
[576] *Bottomley v Todmorden Cricket Club* [2004] P.I.Q.R. P275, CA.
[577] *Naylor v Payling* [2004] P.I.Q.R. P615, CA (the door staff were licensed under a scheme operated by the local authority and the police).
[578] *North v Wood* [1914] 1 K.B. 629; *Donaldson v McNiven* [1952] 2 All E.R. 691; *Gorely v Codd* [1967] 1 W.L.R. 19. Under the Children and Young Persons Act 1969, as amended by the Criminal Justice Act 1972, a parent may incur liability to pay a fine or to compensate those injured or those whose property has been damaged by the child.
[579] *Sullivan v Creed* [1904] 2 Ir.R. 317. But, as regards the doctrine of identification, see Ch.4, para.4–33, below.

to exercise such control over their children, as prudent parents would exercise. The age of the child is a material factor to be taken into account.[580] Thus, a father was liable where he gave his son, aged 15, an airgun, with which the boy broke a window, then, a few months later, shot the plaintiff in the eye.[581] A father of a 15-year-old boy, was liable for failing to take reasonable care to ensure that his son did not use an airgun in such a way as to injure other persons.[582] Similarly, where a father allowed his son, aged 12, to possess a .410 shotgun but did not instruct him how to handle it properly and safely when he was in the presence of others, the father was liable when a child was shot. It was no defence that he had forbidden his son to use the gun whilst he was accompanied by other children.[583] On the other hand, a father, who allowed his son, aged 13, to have an air rifle, on the condition he did not use it outside the house, was not liable when, in disobedience to his orders, his son fired the rifle in an alleyway, injuring a child. The precautions taken were suitable and would have been adequate, had it not been for the son's disobedience.[584] It has been held that where a parent knew that there were candles present in his house, he was under a duty to instruct his son, aged 14, as to the caution with which lighted candles should be treated and to supervise him with a view to preventing danger arising from their use by him.[585] However, in the case of normal 14-year-old boys, the duty of care owed by a parent must not be applied so over-cautiously and in such a manner as to stifle initiative and independence, both qualities in growing youngsters that ought to be encouraged.[586]

3–205   The duty of a parent to control his children would appear to be at least as stringent as that of a schoolmaster, which is said to be that of a "careful father".[587] If, therefore, a parent's children are playing with other children in the house or on land occupied by the parent, liability towards the other children for injuries inflicted by his or her own children will presumably be approached as that of a schoolmaster for injuries inflicted by one of his pupils on another.[588]

---

[580] The Family Law Reform Act 1969 Pt 1 of which reduced the age of majority from 21 years to 18 years, came into force on January 1, 1970.
[581] *Bebee v Sales* (1916) 32 T.L.R. 413. See also Ch.13, paras 13–183 to 13–191, below.
[582] *Court v Wyatt, The Times,* June 25, 1960, Donovan J. said that a parent's duty included giving instructions that a gun, loaded or unloaded, should never be pointed at other persons. A child should not be trusted with a gun at all when known to be unreliable in following instructions or paying heed to warnings. See article in 28 S.J. 166.
[583] *Newton v Edgerley* [1959] 1 W.L.R. 1031. See also note on this case in 76 L.Q.R. 15.
[584] *Donaldson v McNiven* [1952] 2 All E.R. 691; *Gorely v Codd* [1967] 1 W.L.R. 19.
[585] *Jauffur v Akhbar, The Times,* February 10, 1984.
[586] *Porter v Barking and Dagenham LBC, The Times,* April 9, 1990, in which Simon Brown J. emphasised that, in striking a balance, the boys, who were usually sensible and well-behaved, did not need wholly to be mollycoddled. There was no reason why a person would be regarded as imprudent in allowing two boys to practise "putting the shot" together, unsupervised, out of school hours on school property.
[587] per Lord Esher M.R. in *Williams v Eady* (1893) 10 T.L.R. 41. See Ch.9, para.9–185, below
[588] See *Williams v Eady* (1893) 10 T.L.R. 41 (phosphorus left where boys could get at it); *Jackson v L.C.C.* (1912) 28 T.L.R. 359 (heap of rubbish in playground); *Chilvers v L.C.C.* (1916) 32 T.L.R. 363 (children playing with toy soldiers); *Jones v L.C.C.* (1932) 48 T.L.R. 368; *Langham v Governors of Wellingborough School* (1932) 101 L.J.K.B. 513 (children injured in playing games). See Ch.9, paras 9–188 to 9–196, below.

The father of a four-year-old child was held to be guilty of negligence jointly **3–206** with the motorist, when the child was injured in a road accident. The father had failed to look after the child properly by letting him walk on the left-hand side of the highway, so that he had his back to oncoming traffic.[589] On the contrary, it was held that a grandfather did not owe a duty of care to his granddaughter, aged three, whom he had seen was unaccompanied and was attempting to cross over a road, when she was struck down by a passing motorist.[590]

---

[589] *McCallion v Dodd* [1966] N.Z.L.R. 710.
[590] *Hahn v Conley* (1971) 45 A.L.J.R. 631.

CHAPTER 4

PRINCIPAL DEFENCES AND DISCHARGES FROM LIABILITY

Introduction. Failure to prove any of the three essential ingredients of **4–01** actionable negligence[1] will always afford a complete defence to a claimant's claim. In the absence of proof either that a duty of care was owed, or that there was a breach of such duty, or that damage was suffered which is not too remote, or that such damage was caused by the breach, then a claim for damages will be dismissed.

Scope of chapter. In addition, there are certain specific defences available to **4–02** a defendant facing a claim in negligence which this chapter will address in more detail, notably:

(1) contributory negligence, which, although no longer a complete defence affects the measure of damages;

(2) agreement to run the risk of injury (traditionally known under the maxim "*volenti non fit injuria*");

(3) inevitable accident; and

(4) limitation of action.

There are also (5) a number of situations which it is convenient to group here in which an answer to a claim may arise in certain identifiable factual contexts. All other defences, for example, that the defendant has not caused the damage complained of[2] or the defendant's conduct was not wrongful[3] or where the

---

[1] Ch.1, para.1–34, above.
[2] e.g. novus actus: Ch.6, paras 6–62 to 6–84, below; act of God and defences to strict liability generally: Ch.13, paras 13–35 to 13–39, below
[3] e.g. the exceptions to liability under the Animals Act 1971: Ch.14, para.14–42, below.

defendant proves that some particular precaution was not reasonably practicable,[4] are dealt with in other chapters.

1.—Contributory Negligence[5]

4–03   **Meaning of "contributory negligence".** The phrase "contributory negligence" is probably now too firmly established to be disregarded, but unless properly understood is apt to be misleading. It applies solely to the conduct of a claimant.[6] It means that there has been some act or omission on the claimant's part which has materially contributed to the damage caused and is of such a nature that it may properly be described as negligence. For these purposes "negligence" is used in the sense of careless conduct rather than in its sense of breach of duty.[7] It means "negligence materially contributing to the injury,"[8] the word "contributory" being regarded "as expressing something which is a direct cause of the accident".[9] It connotes a failure by the claimant to use reasonable care for the safety of either himself or his property, so that to some extent, he becomes blameworthy as the "author of his own wrong".[10]

The difference in the meaning of "negligence,"[11] when applied to a claimant, on the one hand, and to a defendant, on the other, was pointed out by Lord Simon[12]:

> "When contributory negligence is set up as a defence, its existence does not depend on any duty owed by the injured party to the party sued, and all that is necessary to establish such a defence is to prove ... that the injured party did not in his own interest take reasonable care of himself and contributed, by this want of care, to his own injury. For when contributory negligence is set up as a shield against the obligation to satisfy the

---

[4] e.g. Ch.12, paras 12–109 to 12–116, below.
[5] See Spencer, "Widening Scope of Defence of Contributory Negligence" in 30 C.L.J. 27; Palmer, "Contributory negligence: percentage game" 2002 P.I.L.J. (9) 15, also Eklund, "Contribution and contributory negligence with particular reference to slowly developing conditions" J.P.I. Law 2004, 4, 270.
[6] It should be noted that the following paragraphs deal with contributory negligence in its application to claims themselves founded in negligence. Contributory negligence is not a defence, for instance, to a claim for fraud: *Alliance and Leicester BS v Edgestop* [1993] 1 W.L.R. 1462; *Nationwide BS v Thimblebly & Co* [1999] P.N.L.R. 733; or deceit: *Standard Chartered Bank v Pakistan National Shipping Corporation* [2000] 2 Lloyd's Rep. 511, CA.
[7] See Ch.1, para.1–06, above. See also, per du Parcq L.J. in *Lewis v Denye* [1939] 1 K.B. 540 at 554; also, per Atkin L.J. in *Ellerman Lines Ltd v Grayson Ltd* [1919] 2 K.B. 514 at 535–536, per Bucknill L.J. in *Davies v Swan Motor Co* [1949] 2 K.B. 291 at 309; and *Ross v McQueen* [1947] N.I. 81, per MacDermott J.
[8] per Lord Porter in *Caswell v Powell Duffryn Associated Collieries Ltd* [1940] A.C. 152 at 186.
[9] per Parke B. in *Bridge v Grand Junction Ry* (1838) 3 M. & W. 244. See also the judgment of Lord Maugham in *R v Southern Canada Power Co* [1937] 3 All E.R. 923 at 930.
[10] See Ch.1, para.1–14, above.
[11] See, per du Parcq L.J. in *Lewis v Denye* [1939] 1 K.B. 540 at 554; see also, per Atkin L.J. in *Ellerman Lines Ltd v Grayson Ltd* [1919] 2 K.B. 514 at 535–536, in a judgment affirmed in the House of Lords [1920] A.C. 466 at 477, per Lord Parmoor, per Bucknill L.J. in *Davies v Swan Motor Co* [1949] 2 K.B. 291 at 309, and *Ross v McQueen* [1947] N.I. 81, per MacDermott J.
[12] *Nance v British Columbia Electric Ry* [1951] A.C. 601 at 611.

whole of the plaintiff's claim, the principle involved is that, where a man is part author of his own injury, he cannot call on the other party to compensate him in full."[13]

Claimant can owe a duty of care. Although contributory negligence does not **4–04** necessarily mean that the claimant is in breach of some duty, this "is not to say that in all cases the claimant who is guilty of contributory negligence owes to the defendant no duty to act carefully".[14] In nearly all collision cases, each party owes to the other a duty to take reasonable care and, in many employer and employee cases, the workman owes a statutory duty to take some specified precaution. While such conduct is commonly described as "contributory negligence," it might be more accurate to omit the word "contributory" and express it just as "negligence" and "breach of statutory duty", respectively. Where a defendant has suffered damage as a result of the claimant's own breach of duty, a Pt 20 claim can be added to any defence filed in the proceedings. Irrespective of what happens to the claim, the defendant can pursue the Pt 20 claim to judgment.

Although it is right to draw attention to these distinctions, in practice they are **4–05** largely academic in view of the definition of "fault" in the Law Reform (Contributory Negligence) Act 1945. The Act refers to "fault" as including negligence, breach of statutory duty and contributory negligence. In the remainder of this discussion "contributory negligence" will be used in the sense of "fault" as defined in the 1945 Act, unless the contrary is indicated.

Taking a reasonable risk not contributory negligence. The fact that the **4–06** claimant has taken a risk does not amount to contributory negligence if the need to take the risk was created by the negligence or breach of statutory duty of the defendant and a reasonably prudent man in the claimant's position would have acted as he did. So, where a trench made at the only entrance to a mews was unfenced, leaving a narrow passage by which the plaintiff, a cabman, could get out his horse, and the horse while being led out slipped into the trench and was killed, a direction "whether the plaintiff acted as a man of ordinary prudence would have done, or rashly in defiance of warning" was upheld.[15]

Where a police officer used his patrol car as a roadblock against an escaping **4–07** motorist, who drove at high speed into it, there was no contributory negligence on the police officer's part, although public duty did not, of itself, relieve him of the obligation to take reasonable care for his own safety.[16] When the occupier of a requisitioned house reported a crack in the ceiling to the local authority but continued to use the kitchen until the ceiling fell and injured her, she did not fail

---

[13] Cases which refer to the need for there to be a breach of duty by the claimant, no longer represent the law. See, e.g. *Becker v Medd* (1897) 13 T.L.R. 313; *Compania Mexicana de Petroleo v Essex Transport Co* (1929) 141 L.T. 106; *Grayson Ltd v Ellerman Lines Ltd* [1920] A.C. 466; and *Vaile Bros v Hobson Ltd* (1933) 149 L.T. 283, considered in detail in early editions of this work, e.g. *Charlesworth on Negligence* (5th edn, 1971), paras 1006–1008.
[14] *Nance v British Columbia Electric Ry* [1951] A.C. 601 at 611.
[15] *Clayards v Dethick* (1848) 12 Q.B. 439. The jury found for the plaintiff. Lord Bramwell criticised this case in *Lax v Darlington Corp* (1879) 5 Ex.D. 28 at 35 and *MacMahon v Field* (1881) 7 Q.B.D. 591 at 594, but the direction to the jury was approved and followed by Cockburn C.J. in *Thompson v N.E. Ry* (1862) 2 B. & S. 119 and in *Billings & Sons Ltd v Riden* [1958] A.C. 240. See also *Baker v T.E. Hopkins & Sons Ltd* [1959] 1 W.L.R. 966.
[16] *Hambley v Shepley* (1967) 63 D.L.R. (2d) 94.

in her action, because "she was not free to avoid the danger. She had to stay there and live in her kitchen".[17] Where a tenant opened a window with one broken sash cord and was injured because the other cord snapped and the window fell, the landlord was liable for breach of statutory duty to keep the house fit for human habitation. Her conduct in attempting to open the window, although it involved a risk, was reasonable and did not render her blameworthy.[18]

4–08   **Dilemma created by another's negligence.** The "rescue" cases also serve to illustrate the approach where someone is placed in a position where they reasonably expose themselves to risk.[19] Where, negligently, one party places another in a situation of danger, it does not amount to contributory negligence if the other, in reacting, does something which with the benefit of hindsight, was a less than optimum solution. As Lord Hailsham put it[20]:

> "Mere failure to avoid the collision by taking some extraordinary precaution does not in itself constitute negligence: the plaintiff has no right to complain if in the agony of the collision the defendant fails to take some step which might have prevented a collision unless that step is one which a reasonably careful man would fairly be expected to take in the circumstances."

4–09   Clearly, the more agonising the dilemma in which a claimant is placed, the less critical anyone should be of the consequent reaction. The court will usually balance the risk taken against the consequences of the breach of duty. This could involve weighing the degree of inconvenience or danger to which a person had been subjected, with the risks incurred in an effort to do something about it. In *Sayers v Harlow Urban District Council*[21] the claimant, finding herself locked in a lavatory cubicle, attempted unsuccessfully to get out by climbing over the top. As she was trying to return to floor level she fell and injured herself. It was held that, whilst it was reasonable in the circumstances for her to explore the possibility of escape in the manner she did, she was careless in the process of climbing down by allowing her balance to depend on a rotating toilet roll.

4–10   **Standard of care in contributory negligence.** The standard of care when looking at contributory negligence is the same as that applied when considering negligence from the perspective of breach of duty.[22] If it were otherwise the anomalous position would be that the party who first started an action and thereby became the claimant, would have an advantage over the other, who, perforce, had to be the defendant.

> "Although contributory negligence does not depend on a duty of care, it does depend on foreseeability. Just as actionable negligence requires the foreseeability of harm to others, so contributory negligence requires the foreseeability of harm to oneself. A person is guilty of contributory negligence if he ought reasonably to have foreseen that,

---

[17] *Greene v Chelsea BC* [1954] 2 Q.B. 127 at 140, per Denning L.J. See also *Porter v Jones* [1942] 2 All E.R. 570.
[18] *Summers v Salford Corp* [1943] A.C. 283.
[19] See Ch.2, paras 2–259 to 2–262, above, as well as paras 4–51 and 4–114, below.
[20] *Swadling v Cooper* [1931] A.C. 1 at 9.
[21] [1958] 1 W.L.R. 623 (claimant's contributory negligence 25 per cent). See article at 21 M.L.R. 677.
[22] *A.C. Billings & Sons Ltd v Riden* [1958] A.C. 240.

if he did not act as a reasonably prudent man, he might hurt himself; and in his reckonings he must take into account the possibility of others being careless."[23]

It has been suggested that, "it is both in accordance with common sense and good morals to hold that a man need not pay as much attention to his own safety as he does to the safety of others". So: **4–11**

" . . . the inadvertence of a pedestrian who may step from the pavement into the road is not comparable to that of a driver who is proceeding at such a speed that he cannot stop within a reasonable distance. It is one thing to take a slight inadvertent risk with one's own life, even though one is not entitled to endanger it deliberately; it is an entirely different thing to risk the life of another by taking insufficient care."[24]

A pedestrian who steps onto the road from the pavement, owes a duty to exercise due care,[25] because a failure to do so may cause serious injury to person[26] and property. A person's duty to take reasonable care is enhanced by knowledge of the risks involved.[27]

Burden of proof. The burden of proving contributory negligence is on the defendant; it is not for the claimant to disprove it. "If the defendants' negligence or breach of duty is established as causing the [damage], the onus is on the defendants to establish that the claimant's contributory negligence was a substantial or material co-operating cause".[28] Moreover, **4–12**

"In order to establish the defence of contributory negligence, the defendant must prove first, that the plaintiff failed to take 'ordinary care of himself' or, in other words, such care as a reasonable man would take for his own safety, and, secondly, that his failure to take care was a contributory cause of the accident."[29]

The amount of care which a claimant may reasonably be expected to take necessarily varies with the circumstances. It is not necessary, in order to discharge the burden of proof, that the defendant give evidence, because contributory negligence can be inferred from the evidence adduced on the

---

[23] *Jones v Livox Quarries Ltd* [1952] 2 Q.B. 608 at 615, per Denning L.J. In commenting on these words, Lord Kilbrandon in *Westwood v Post Office* [1974] A.C. 1 at 17, said: "I suggest that the closing words of the passage from Denning L.J.'s judgment . . . while appropriate to a common law claim, which was there being considered, may be inapplicable in a case of statutory liability."
[24] 71 L.Q.R. 165.
[25] *Nance v British Columbia Electric Ry* [1951] A.C. 601 at 611, per Lord Simon, expressly disapproving a statement to the contrary by Denning L.J. in *Davies v Swan Motor Co (Swansea) Ltd* [1949] 2 K.B. 291.
[26] As in *Carmarthenshire CC v Lewis* [1955] A.C. 549, where a boy of four strayed on to the road and the driver of a lorry was killed in trying to avoid him.
[27] *Hicks v British Transport Commission* [1958] 1 W.L.R. 493.
[28] per Lord Wright in *Caswell v Powell Duffryn Associated Collieries Ltd* [1940] A.C. 152 at 172. See also *Wakelin v L. & S.W. Ry* (1886) 12 App.Cas. 41 at 47, per Lord Watson, and Lord Green M.R. in *Stimson v Standard Telephone & Cables Ltd* [1940] 1 K.B. 342, where, says Williams (*Joint Torts and Contributory Negligence*, p.387), the distinction between causation and contributory negligence "and the general effect of the distinction upon the burden of proof was beautifully explained".
[29] per Du Parcq L.J. in *Lewis v Denye* [1939] 1 K.B. 540 at 554.

claimant's behalf[30] or from the primary facts, as found by the court, on a balance of probabilities.[31]

4–13   **Contributory negligence must be pleaded.** If the defendant intends to rely upon averments of contributory negligence, the allegations must be specifically pleaded.[32] In the event of a failure to plead them, the trial judge is disentitled to apportion liability between the parties of his own motion[33] and is under no obligation to take contributory negligence into account.[34] If pleaded, there is no reason why contributory negligence cannot be raised at assessment of damages stage, after judgment has been entered, provided that the judgment does not itself settle the issues which the defendant wishes to raise.[35]

4–14   **Prior to 1945.** At common law, the effect of a finding of contributory negligence was originally that the defendant succeeded in the action. Thus, in *Butterfield v Forrester*[36] where the defendant had placed a pole across the highway with which the plaintiff collided when riding a horse at a fast speed, the claim failed, Lord Ellenborough C.J. saying:

> "A party is not to cast himself upon an obstruction which has been made by the fault of another, and avail himself of it, if he do not himself use common and ordinary caution to be in the right . . . One person being in fault will not dispense with another's using ordinary care for himself. Two things must concur to support this action, an obstruction in the road by the fault of the defendant, and no want of ordinary care to avoid it on the part of the plaintiff."

4–15   Historically therefore there had to be a judgment for one side or the other and there was no provision for apportioning the loss between them. When one of the parties alone was negligent, judgment had to be given for that party against the other. On the other hand, when both were negligent, the defendant could only be made liable if his negligence was the cause—what has been variously described as the "real cause", "effective cause", "direct cause", "substantial cause", "decisive cause", "proximate cause", and "immediate cause"—of the accident. As Lord Summer said[37]: "the inquiry is an investigation into responsibility."

---

[30] *Sharpe v S. Ry* [1925] 2 K.B. 311; *Baker v Longhurst & Sons Ltd* [1933] 2 K.B. 461 at 468; *Kerry v Keighley Electrical Engineering Co Ltd* [1940] 3 All E.R. 399.
[31] *Caswell v Powell Duffryn Associated Collieries Ltd* [1940] A.C. 152 at 169; *Gibby v East Grinstead Gas & Water Co* [1944] 1 All E.R. 358.
[32] *Fookes v Slaytor* [1978] 1 W.L.R. 1293. See Walker, "A Question of Contributory Negligence" in 129 New L.J. 674.
[33] *Christie v Bridgestone Australia Pty* (1984) 33 S.A.S.R. 377.
[34] *Taylor v Simon Carves*, 1958 S.L.T. (Sh.Ct) 23; *William J. Judge v William Reape* [1968] I.R. 226. See also 69 L.Q.R. 317 and Lord Asquith's comment upon a relevant incident during *Dann v Hamilton* [1939] 1 K.B. 509. Incidentally, contributory negligence was not raised in the latter case, only *volenti non fit injuria* (see Asquith J. at 512); cf. *Owens v Brimmell* [1977] Q.B. 859.
[35] *Maes Finance Ltd v A.L. Phillips & Co, The Times*, March 25, 1997 (a claim against solicitors who had acted for both sides in the course of a mortgage transaction; judgment was entered by consent but thereafter the defendants wished to argue that the lenders had been guilty of contributory fault).
[36] (1809) 11 East 60.
[37] *British Columbia Electric Ry v Loach* [1916] 1 A.C. 719 at 728.

Liability was a question of fact and the question was: Whose negligence was the real or substantial cause of the accident?[38]

After 1945. Section 1 the Law Reform (Contributory Negligence) Act 1945,[39]   **4–16**
provides:

> "1.—(1) Where any person suffers damage[40] as the result partly of his own fault[41] and partly of the fault of any other person or persons, a claim in respect of that damage shall not be defeated by reason of the fault of the person suffering the damage, but the damages recoverable in respect thereof shall be reduced to such extent as the court[42] thinks just and equitable[43] having regard to[44] the claimant's share in the responsibility for the damage: . . . "

The section "does not create a right of action; it removes an obstacle".[45] The   **4–17**
effect of the Act is that, in the cases to which it applies, the court must decide, (1) was the damage the result (a) of the claimant's fault or (b) of the defendant's fault or (c) partly of the claimant's fault and partly of the defendant's fault; (2) the total damages which would have been recoverable had the claimant not been at fault; and (3) when both parties are found to be at fault, the extent to which the claimant's damages are to be reduced.

Meaning of fault. "Fault" in the Act means "negligence, a breach of   **4–18**
statutory duty or other act or omission which gives rise to a liability in tort or would, apart from this Act give rise to the defence of contributory negligence".[46] It does not mean some fault which falls short of negligence.[47] A breach of

---

[38] *Swadling v Cooper* [1931] A.C. 1, where the direction of Humphries J., "Whose negligence was it that substantially caused the injury", was approved.

[39] In *Ginty v Belmont Building Supplies Ltd* [1959] 1 All E.R. 414, Pearson J. said at 424: "The Law Reform (Contributory Negligence) Act applies only in a case where the accident is caused partly by the fault of the plaintiff and partly by the fault of somebody else . . . the common law principle is still valid to this extent, that, if the accident is wholly caused by the plaintiff's own fault he is disentitled to recover." See also *Rushton v Turner Brothers Asbestos Co Ltd* [1960] 1 W.L.R. 96.

[40] "Includes loss of life and personal injury": s.4.

[41] See para.4–19, below.

[42] "Means, in relation to any claim, the court or arbitrator by or before whom the claim falls to be determined": s.4.

[43] The claimant's contention that his carelessness should be disregarded under these words ("thinks just and equitable") was rejected in *Boothman v British Northrop Ltd* (1972) 13 K.I.R. 112. See also *Hawkins v Ian Ross (Castings) Ltd* [1970] 1 All E.R. 180.

[44] "The words 'have regard to' call for the exercise of a broad judgment and any arithmetical conclusion is qualified by what is deemed to be fair and reasonable", per Lord Simon in *Palser v Grinling* [1948] A.C. 291 at 315. See also *Newport BC v Monmouthshire CC* [1947] A.C. 520 at 534.

[45] *Drinkwater v Kimber* [1952] 2 Q.B. 281 at 288, per Singleton L.J. (however the result in *Drinkwater* was overruled by the provisions of the Law Reform (Husband and Wife) Act 1962.

[46] s.4. "Fault" in s.4 of the Act is divided into two limbs, one relevant to defendants and the other to claimants. In the case of a defendant, fault means "negligence, breach of statutory duty or other act or omission" giving rise to a liability in tort; in the case of a claimant, it means that fault which formerly gave rise at common law to a defence of contributory negligence: see per Lord Hoffmann in *Standard Chartered Bank v Pakistan National Shipping Corporation (No.2)* [2003] 1 A.C. 959, at 964 (no common law defence of contributory negligence to an action for fraudulent mis-representation).

[47] *Jones v Price, The Guardian*, March 1, 1963.

contract does not amount to fault for purposes of the Act, if it is not co-extensive with breach of a duty to take care. In *Forsikringsaktielselskapet Vesta v Butcher (No.1)*,[48] the Court of Appeal distinguished situations where the defendant was liable only in contract from those where, because the duty was essentially the same, he was liable both in contract and in negligence. In the latter situation contributory negligence could be relied upon to reduce or extinguish the defendant's liability; in the former, it could not.[49] It has been held that where a claimant brings a claim in tort and the defendant counterclaims in contract alone, both claims being attributable to two concurrent causes operating contemporaneously, the problem of how liability ought to be apportioned cannot be solved by applying the Act. The solution is to assess the recoverable damages for each claim on the basis of causation, although the same result may well be reached as if the Act had applied.[50]

4–19   **Fault and causation.** The reference in subs.(1) to damage suffered, "as the result partly of . . . fault," means "caused partly by the fault of" the person concerned. The common law doctrine of contributory negligence was based on causation, and that was also the basis for apportioning fault under the Maritime Conventions Act 1911, with which no distinction in principle can be drawn. So, in every case it is necessary to consider not simply the claimant's fault (or blameworthiness) but also the causative potency or effect of that fault. It has been said that, "causation is the decisive factor in determining whether there should be a reduced amount payable to the plaintiff".[51]

4–20   Causation is considered generally in Chapter 6. The cause or causes of the damage suffered by the claimant is a question of fact. No one test of general application has emerged to assist in deciding the question. In the context of accidents caused by negligence it has been said that in considering what is the cause[52]:

"Causation is to be understood as the man in the street, and not as either the scientist or the metaphysician would understand it."[53]

"One may find that as a matter of history several people have been at fault and that if any one of them had acted properly the accident would not have happened, but that does not mean that the accident must be regarded as having been caused by the faults of all of them. One must discriminate between those faults which must be discarded as being

---

[48] [1989] A.C. 852 (insurers sued brokers who had failed to inform reinsurers that the insured could not comply with a term of the contract for reinsurance). See Smith "The Fish Farm Fiasco—Contributory Negligence, Contracts and Construction" in (1988) 4 Const.L.J. 75 at 47.
[49] The *Vesta* case was followed in *UCB Bank Plc v Hepherd, Winstanley and Pugh*, *The Times*, August 25, 1999, CA (apportionment performed under the Act where solicitors' breach of an implied term of their retainer amounted also to negligence at common law). It has not been followed in Australia: *Astley v Austrust Ltd* [1999] Lloyd's Rep. P.N. 758, HC (Aus).
[50] *Tennant Radiant Heat Ltd v Warrington Development Corp*, *The Times*, December 19, 1987, CA.
[51] per Denning L.J. in *Davies v Swan Motor Co (Swansea) Ltd* [1949] 2 K.B. 291 at 326.
[52] See further Ch.6, para.6–21, below.
[53] per Lord Wright in *Yorkshire Dale S.S. Co v Minister of War Transport* [1942] A.C. 691 at 706. See also *Sigurdson v British Columbia Electric Ry* [1953] A.C. 291 at 299; Wright, "Causation and Responsibility in English Law" in [1955] C.L.J. 163.

too remote and those which must not. Sometimes it is proper to discard all but one and to regard that as the sole cause, but in other cases it is proper to regard two or more as having jointly caused the accident. I doubt whether any test can be applied generally."[54]

Fault causing damage. In considering causation and fault for purposes of contributory negligence, the only relevant fault is that which is causative of the damage suffered. A distinction can arise between such fault and fault causative of an accident, even where the accident leads in turn to damage. In *Davies v Swan Motor Co*,[55] a collision had taken place between an omnibus and a dust-cart, owing to the negligence of each of the drivers, as a result of which the claimant's husband was killed. He had been standing on the dust-cart's steps, where he was forbidden to be, and was crushed. The accident, that is, the collision, was in no way caused or contributed to by his negligence in riding in a forbidden position, but his injuries were and the damages payable to his widow were reduced by one-fifth. Similarly, in *Jones v Livox Quarries Ltd*,[56] when the claimant, contrary to orders, was riding on the back of a traxcavator, it was run into from behind by a dumper that had been negligently driven by a fellow employee. The claimant was found guilty of contributory negligence, on the ground that he had unreasonably and improperly exposed himself to risk, even though his conduct was not a cause operating to produce this particular accident.

Further illustrations can be found in the class of cases where claimants either have not taken reasonable safety precautions or have failed to make use of available preventive measures provided specifically for the purpose.[57]

Suicide and other self harm. In *Reeves v Commissioner of Police of the Metropolis*,[58] the problem was whether the act of a prisoner in committing suicide could be regarded as contributory negligence, reducing the damages to which his estate was entitled for breach of a duty of care by the police to prevent his taking his life while in their custody. A majority of the House of Lords held that it could, rejecting the argument that it was inappropriate to regard the deceased as partly at fault, where the act relied upon was the very act which performance of the duty of care was designed to prevent. It was observed that in other common law jurisdictions the deliberate act of the claimant was regarded as capable of amounting to contributory negligence. "Fault" was wide enough to encompass deliberate acts. The deceased's responsibility for his own life meant that his act in bringing it to an end ought to be regarded as a cause of death jointly with the defendant's admitted breach of duty.[59] Liability was apportioned equally between the police and the deceased. In *Corr v IBC Vehicles*,[60] a majority of their Lordships again held that a finding of contributory negligence could arise after suicide, this time where the deceased's estate sought damages for his death after

4–21

4–22

---

[54] *Stapley v Gypsum Mines Ltd* [1953] A.C. 663 at 681, per Lord Reid.
[55] [1949] 2 K.B. 291.
[56] [1952] 2 Q.B. 608.
[57] See Ch.11, para.11–83, below.
[58] [2008] 2 W.L.R. 499, HL.
[59] [2001] A.C. 360. See in particular the speeches of Lord Jauncey and Lord Hope.
[60] [2008] A.C. 884. See further Ch.6 para.6–78, below.

he committed suicide in a state of depression induced by an accident for which the defendant was responsible.

4–23   **Apportionment of damages.** Section 1(1) of the Act provides that when both parties are at fault the claimant's damages are to be reduced "having regard to the claimant's share in the responsibility for the damage". The use of the word "responsibility" is intended to exclude the more remote causes of the damage and to concentrate on responsible causes. To quote Lord Wright in a case decided before the 1945 Act[61]:

> "The decision . . . must turn not simply on causation but on responsibility; the plaintiff's negligence may be what is often called *causa sine qua non*, yet as regards responsibility it becomes merely evidential or matter of narrative if the defendant acting reasonably could and ought to have avoided the collision."

For example, if a man lying drunk in the highway is run over in daylight by a motorist, the actions of both have caused the accident but they would not be equally responsible for what happened.[62] Where the claimant, who was emotionally disturbed, was struck by the offside of the defendant's car as she walked unsteadily down the central area of a dual carriageway, the driver, who had taken enough alcohol to impair his ability to drive, was at least as blameworthy as the pedestrian, but the causative potency of his fault was much greater and a 60:40 apportionment in favour of the pedestrian was appropriate.[63]

4–24   In *Brown v Thompson*,[64] the claimants were injured whilst travelling at night in their car. Although dipped headlights were in use, the car crashed into the back of a stationary lorry, which had been parked and left without rear lights on or reflectors. The Court of Appeal stressed that, in apportioning liability under the Act, the emphasis is on fault and not solely on the causative potency of the acts or omissions of either vehicle's driver and declined to interfere with the trial judge's apportionment that the lorry's owner was 80 per cent to blame.

4–25   **Share in responsibility for the damage.** The claimant's share in responsibility for the damage is approached by way of an overall appreciation of his blameworthiness, taken with the causative potency of his fault.

> "Whilst causation is the decisive factor is determining whether there should be a reduced amount payable to the plaintiff, nevertheless, the amount of the reduction does not depend solely on the degree of causation. The amount of the reduction . . . involves

---

[61] *M'Lean v Bell* (1932) 48 L.T.R. 467 at 469.
[62] See *Davies v Mann* (1842) 10 M. & W. 546, per Parke B.; *Paul v G.E. Ry* (1920) 36 T.L.R. 344. Nevertheless, the excuse of drunkenness has to be disregarded, when considering contributory negligence, see para.4–48, below.
[63] *Eagle v Chambers* [2004] R.T.R. 115, CA (the trial judge had attributed the greater share of responsibility to the claimant).
[64] [1968] 1 W.L.R. 1003.

a consideration, not only of the causative potency of a particular factor, but also of its blameworthiness."[65]

In *Stapley v Gypsum Mines Ltd*,[66] Lord Reid said:

"A court must deal broadly with the problem of apportionment and in considering what is just and equitable must have regard to the blameworthiness of each party, but 'the claimant's share in the responsibility for the damage' cannot, I think, be assessed without considering the relative importance of his acts in causing the damage apart from his blameworthiness."

Examples of apportionment. Both blameworthiness and causative potency   **4-26** were taken into consideration when assessing the contributory negligence of a claimant involved in a collision with a bus: so far as the former is concerned the claimant was 80 per cent to blame; considerations of causation suggested an equal contribution; taken together the two gave a result of 70 per cent contribution overall.[67] In a road accident case, where the claimant was an injured passenger, it was held that the respective faults of the parties ought not to be measured by taking percentages, attributable to different aspects of negligence, in an attempt at a mathematical computation. The facts should be looked at generally and justice done by a broad distribution of blame.[68]

Seat belts. Where a non-exempt[69] motorist failed to wear an available seat   **4-27** belt and damages for injuries sustained in an accident thereby fell to be reduced, it was said the appropriate deduction should be assessed by having regard to the extent to which the injuries were caused or contributed to by the failure to wear a belt. The court ought not to be invited to consider what the injuries might have been, if the motorist had worn the belt, because those circumstances had never arisen.[70]

Smoking. Blameworthiness and causative potency also arose for considera-   **4-28** tion in a fatal accident claim based on the deceased's exposure to asbestos, as a result of which he contracted lung cancer, which caused his death.[71] He had been a smoker throughout his adult life, smoking an average of twenty cigarettes a day. There was medical evidence that when combined with asbestosis, smoking cigarettes enhanced his risk of developing lung cancer beyond that of someone

---

[65] *Davies v Swan Motor Co Ltd* [1949] 2 K.B. 291 at 236. See also *Fitzgerald v Lane* [1989] A.C. 328 per Lord Ackner at 345.
[66] [1953] A.C. 663 at 682. See Hamson [1954] C.L.J. 40.
[67] *Cavanagh v London Transport Executive, The Times*, October 23, 1956.
[68] *Gregory v Kelly* [1978] R.T.R. 426.
[69] i.e. under the Motor Vehicles (Wearing of Seat Belts) Regulations 1993 (SI 1993/176) and see *Jones v Morgan* [1994] C.L.Y. 3344 (a taxi driver).
[70] *Patience v Andrews* [1983] R.T.R. 447, applying *Froom v Butcher* [1976] Q.B. 286.
[71] *Badger v Ministry of Defence, The Times*, 30 December 2005. See Kilminster, "Fire over smoking" 150 S.J. 242; McDonald, "Determining culpability for lung cancer" 2006 P.I.L.J. (Nov), 2. See also *St George v Home Office* [2009] 1 W.L.R. 1670, CA, para.4–48, below (abuse of drugs).

with asbestosis who had never smoked, or someone who had given up smoking at an earlier time than he did. Even before health warnings appeared on cigarette packets he had been advised that he was suffering symptoms attributable to smoking cigarettes. It was held that his widow's claim should be reduced by 20 per cent for his contributory negligence. By 1971 it was reasonably foreseeable by a reasonably prudent man that if he smoked he risked damaging his health. It must have been obvious to the deceased that there was a connection between his smoking and the health of his lungs. He could not be criticised for starting to smoke, since at that time the connection between smoking and serious ill-health was not widely accepted; his fault lay in not giving up. On the evidence, he could have given up smoking, and should have done so. A reasonably prudent person in his position and with his knowledge would have stopped smoking in the mid-1970s and had he done so, his risk of contracting lung cancer would have been significantly less.

4–29   **Degree of each party's fault unclear.** It is not uncommon for cases to arise where the court is unable to distinguish between the respective fault of each party. Where this arises, the practice under the 1945 Act, no doubt influenced by the rule in maritime cases,[72] has been to apportion blame equally. So, where the claimant was injured successively by two negligent motorists each acting independently, but was himself as much to blame as each of them, he recovered only 50 per cent of the appropriate damages,[73] the balance being divided between the two tortfeasors equally.[74] Also, where two drivers failed to see each other's respective vehicles when they should have done so and a collision ensued, it could be said that one was entirely to blame: on the facts one created the danger of collision and the other failed to avoid it and both were equally to blame.[75]

4–30   **Claimant's fault minor or peripheral.** In an unreported decision of the Court of Appeal[76] it was observed that very small percentages of apportionment ought not to be made, and the Act should not operate unless the degree of responsibility falling on one of the parties in the action was at least 10 per cent.[77] However, once the court has found contributory negligence on the part of the

---

[72] The court must apportion the liability in proportion to the degree of fault of each vessel unless it is impossible so to do: *The Anneliese* [1970] 2 All E.R. 29 at 131, per Davies L.J.; *The Linde* [1969] 2 Lloyd's Rep. 556.

[73] *Fitzgerald v Lane* [1987] Q.B. 781 (appeal dismissed, [1989] A.C. 328).

[74] i.e. one-quarter each defendant, above. Where a claimant successfully sues more than one defendant for damages for personal injuries and contributory negligence is established, the apportionment of the claimant's share in the responsibility for his injuries has to be kept separate from the apportionment of contribution between the defendants, *inter se.*

[75] *Jenkins v Holt, The Times,* May 27, 1999, CA.

[76] *Johnson v Tennant Bros Ltd,* Unreported, November 19, 1954, CA. See also per Ashworth J. in *Rushton v Turner Bros Asbestos Co Ltd* [1960] 1 W.L.R. 96 at 102.

[77] It follows that apportionments of 5 per cent contributory negligence, e.g. as in *Clifford v Challen & Son Ltd* [1951] 1 K.B. 495, should not now be made and that in *Pasternack v Poulton* [1973] 1 W.L.R. 476 (failure to wear a seat belt in a motor car) such a finding was made per incuriam. Likewise, an apportionment of one per cent, made against the defendant (although obiter), in *Johnson v Croggan Co Ltd* [1954] 1 W.L.R. 195 was wrong in principle.

claimant, it cannot then disregard the finding and refuse to reduce the award of damages.[78]

Finality of apportionment. Once a court has decided the apportionment of   **4–31** blame between drivers of motor vehicles involved in a collision in which a passenger was injured and had brought successfully an action for damages, it is no longer open to one of the drivers, relying on the same facts, to argue in a subsequent suit brought against the other driver that such apportionment ought to be varied.[79]

Appeal against finding of contributory negligence. Generally, if an appel-   **4–32** late court accepts the lower court's findings of fact, and there is no error of law, it will be reluctant to interfere with that court's apportionment under the 1945 Act. As a rule "an appellate body does not interfere with the discretion exercised by the judge who tried the case.[80] Only in the event of a successful attack on the fact-finding of the trial judge would the Court of Appeal reassess the apportionment,[81] that is, when satisfied that the assessment made by the judge was plainly incorrect[82]; or that some material aspects of the evidence of the claimant should have been rejected by the trial judge, having regard to his findings in relation to the credibility of the witness.[83]

Contributory negligence of non-party: the rule of identification. Instances   **4–33** can arise where a claimant's damages are reduced on account of the contributory negligence of someone who is not actually a party to the action. The individual guilty of contributory negligence may be the employee or agent of the claimant, for whom the claimant is vicariously responsible.[84] For example, if an employer's property is entrusted to his employee and is damaged, as a result of the negligence of both of them, the employer's claim should be reduced by apportionment, according to the extent of his employee's fault.[85] A further category of case arises in relation to claims under the Fatal Accidents Act 1976[86]

---

[78] *Boothman v British Northrop Ltd* (1972) 13 K.I.R. 112 where the claimant's contention that his own carelessness should be disregarded under the "just and equitable" provision contained in s.1(1) of the Act, was rejected. But, contra, see *Hawkins v Ian Ross (Castings) Ltd* [1970] 1 All E.R. 180.
[79] *Wall v Radford, The Times,* February 18, 1991. However the CA in *Talbot v Berkshire County Council* [1994] Q.B. 290 observed that if reliance had been placed on the doctrine of *res judicata,* as set out in *Henderson v Henderson* (1843) 3 Hare 100, it might well have afforded a complete answer to the claimant's claim. See further para.4–238, below.
[80] *NCB v England* [1954] A.C. 403 at 420, per Lord Porter. However the House of Lords altered the apportionment of the trial judge of one-half against the employee to one-quarter. The trial judge's apportionment was also altered in *Stapley v Gypsum Mines Ltd* [1953] A.C. 663.
[81] *Jennings v Norman Collinson (Contractors)* [1970] 1 All E.R. 1121. See also *Hodkinson v Henry Wallwork & Co Ltd* [1955] 3 All E.R. 236.
[82] *Hannam v Mann* [1984] R.T.R. 252, CA.
[83] *Braund v Henning* (1988) 79 A.L.R. 417, HC (Aus).
[84] For the vicarious liability of an employer for an employee or agent, see Ch.3, paras 3–99 to 3–171, above, generally.
[85] *Chaplin v Hawes* (1828) 3 Car. & P. 554; *Carberry v Davies* [1968] 1 W.L.R. 1103 (a parent gave the use of his vehicle to some other person to drive the farmer's child round as his agent).
[86] Which came into force on September 1, 1976.

for the benefit of a deceased person's dependants.[87] Their claims can be reduced to reflect a finding of contributory negligence against the deceased. A similar reduction in damages can arise under the Congenital Disabilities (Civil Liability) Act 1976 s.1(2) where a child who is born with disabilities, as a result of some pre-natal event, and the negligence of a parent was a contributory cause.

4–34   The bailor of a chattel is not precluded by the contributory negligence of the bailee from recovering damages from a third party at whose hands the chattel has been damaged or destroyed.[88] Where the claimant hired a car to a third party who was involved in a collision with another car, the negligence of the hired car's driver could not be imputed to the claimant in a claim against the driver of the other vehicle.[89]

The old rule of identification, by which an infant was disentitled from claiming damages if injured while in the care of an adult in charge of him, is no longer good law.[90] If a child is injured partly through the negligence of the defendant and partly through the negligence of an adult in charge of him,[91] the defendant is liable for the whole damage (albeit having a claim to contribution from the custodial parent).[92]

4–35   **Contributory negligence of children.**[93] In the old case of *Lynch v Nurdin*[94] the defendant negligently left his horse and cart unattended in the street, whereupon the plaintiff, aged seven, climbed on to the back of the cart to play. Another child led the horse on and the plaintiff was thrown down, sustaining injury. The defendant was held liable. It was contended that the plaintiff was guilty of contributory negligence, in that he could have prevented the accident by the exercise of ordinary care, but Lord Denman C.J. said: "Ordinarily care must

---

[87] The Law Reform (Contributory Negligence) Act 1945 s.1(4), which has been repealed but re-enacted by the Fatal Accidents Act 1976 s.5 for the provision of which see Ch.16, para.16–05, below. Where death results from negligence both of the defendant and one of the dependants of the deceased (and *absent* negligence of the deceased himself) the guilty dependant's proportion of the award will be reduced, although the claims of other dependants will not be: see *Mulholland v McCrea* [1961] N.I. 135.

[88] *Wellwood v A. King Ltd* [1921] 2 I.R. 274.

[89] *France v Parkinson* [1954] 1 W.L.R. 581.

[90] *Oliver v Birmingham and Midland Omnibus Co* [1933] 1 K.B. 35 (the claim of a child run over by a bus when crossing the road in in his grandfather's charge).

[91] For the vicarious liability of a parent and a parent's duty to his child, see Ch.3, para.3–204, above.

[92] A right to contribution arises under the Law Reform (Married Women and Tortfeasors) Act 1935. See, e.g. *Ducharme v Davies* [1984] 1 W.W.R. 699 (a motorist failed to ensure that her three-year-old daughter was secured by her seat belt but the parent's breach of duty could not be regarded as contributory negligence of the infant: the appropriate course for the defendant was to have claimed contribution against the child's parent as a joint tortfeasor). See also, e.g. *Hahn v Conley* (1971) 45 A.L.J.R. 631 where the Australian High Court held that a grandfather owed no duty of care to his three-year-old granddaughter whom he had seen was unaccompanied and was attempting to cross a road when she was struck down by a passing motorist. See Gibson-Watt, "Third-Partying the Parent" in 122 New L.J. 280 and Rowe, "Child v Parent" in 124 New L.J. 117.

[93] See Scott, "Children and Negligence" in 116 New L.J. 1394; Fridman in 117 New L.J. 35; "Children and Contributory Negligence" in 100 I.L.T. 425; "Contributory fault and minors" in (1997) 1 P.Injury (2), 8. The principles under which a young child may be guilty of contributory negligence were considered in *Speirs v Gorman* [1966] N.Z.L.R. 897, Sup. Ct.

[94] (1841) 1 Q.B. 29.

mean that degree of care which may reasonably be expected from a person in the plaintiff's situation; and this would evidently be very small indeed in so young a child."[95]

Children: degree of care expected. Accordingly, while the fact that the **4–36** claimant is a child does not prevent a finding of contributory negligence, the crucial points are the child's age and understanding. Infancy, as such, is not a "status conferring right"[96] so that the test of what is contributory negligence is the same in the case of a child as of an adult. However, that test is modified to the extent that the degree of care to be expected must be proportioned to the age of the child. The conduct of a child claimant cannot amount to contributory negligence if it was no more than could be expected of a child of that age.The degree of care it is appropriate to expect of a child is a matter of fact for decision on the evidence in the particular case.[97]

In *Jones v Lawrence*,[98] a seven-year-old boy, who was going to a fun-fair, ran **4–37** out from behind a parked van on the off-side of a road, without first looking to his right or left, and collided with a motor-cyclist travelling at about 50 mph in a 30 mph speed restricted area. The child was held not guilty of contributory negligence. It was accepted that children of that age were prone to forget what they had been taught about road safety, if their minds were engaged else-where.

There is no age below which, as a matter of law, it can be said that a child is **4–38** incapable of contributory negligence. Expressions can be found referring to children "too young to be capable of contributory negligence",[99] or "of such a tender age as to be regarded in law as incapable of contributory negligence"[100] but, these must be taken to refer to children found, on the facts of a particular case, to have been so young that contributory negligence could not be attributed to them. A recommendation has been made that the defence of contributory negligence should not be available in cases of motor vehicle injury where the claimant was under the age of 12 at the time of the injury.[101]

---

[95] The passage was approved in, e.g. *Harrold v Watney* [1898] 2 Q.B. 320 at 322, per A.L. Smith L.J.; *Glasgow Corp v Taylor* [1922] 1 A.C. 44; *Cooke v Mid. G.W. Ry of Ireland* [1909] A.C. 229; *Liddle v Yorkshire (North Riding) CC* [1934] 2 K.B. 101 at 129, per Slesser L.J. See also *Yackuk v Oliver Blais Co Ltd* [1949] A.C. 386. There, a boy of nine, with his brother aged seven, obtained petrol from the defendants by telling a lie about why he wanted it. He set fire to the petrol and was injured. The trial judge found contributory negligence on the child's part, but this finding was set aside by the appellate court. Per McRuer J.A. in the Ontario Court of Appeal [1945] O.R. 33: "if one gives to a child an explosive substance, and the child, with a limited knowledge in respect to the likely effect of the explosion, is tempted to meddle with it to his injury, it cannot be said in answer to a claim on behalf of the child that he did meddle to his own injury, or that he was tempted to do that which a child of his years might reasonably be expected to do."
[96] *Glasgow Corp v Taylor* [1922] 1 A.C. 44 at 67, per Lord Sumner.
[97] *Minter v D. & H. Contractors (Cambridge)*, *The Times*, June 30, 1983 (degree of case should be proportionate to age of child).
[98] [1969] 3 All E.R. 267.
[99] per Hamilton L.J. in *Latham v R. Johnson & Nephew Ltd* [1913] 1 K.B. 398 at 416.
[100] per Greer L.J. in *Liddle v Yorkshire (North Riding) CC* [1934] 2 K.B. 101 at 125. In *Phipps v Rochester Corp* [1955] 1 Q.B. 450, Devlin J. considered the meaning of "tender years".
[101] The Royal Commission on Civil Liability and Compensation for Personal Injury, Cmnd. 7054–I (1978) para.1077.

Illustrations

4–39   The defence of contributory negligence either failed[102] or was not raised: where a three-and-a-half-year-old child was run over in the street[103]; where a 13-year-old youngster emerged from behind a stationary lorry, the driver of which had stopped, had signalled to other traffic and had invited her to cross over the road, which she did without looking out and was struck by an overtaking vehicle[104]; where a four-year-old child, who had been sent on an errand, got on to a level crossing, in the absence of a gate or stile, and was injured by a passing train[105]; where a four-year-old child, whilst crossing a railway bridge, did not walk straight forward but slid along, his back pressed against the fencing of the bridge, and fell backwards through an opening in the fencing[106]; where a 10-year-old girl leant against a protecting bar, placed around the opening of an area, when it collapsed and she fell[107]; where a four-year-old child climbed on to a fence, adjoining the highway, and the fence broke[108]; where a girl aged nearly 14 was sent by her school-mistress to poke a fire in an adjoining room, and as she was doing so her pinafore caught fire[109]; where a 12-year-old boy, employed at a railway bookstall, was run over whilst crossing the railway lines instead of making use of the bridge[110]; where a seven-year-old child was poisoned by eating poisonous berries of attractive appearance on a shrub growing in a public park[111]; where a lorry laden with sugar dropped part of its load on the road and a seven-year-old child was injured trying to retrieve it[112]; where a seven-year-old boy fell off a high wall adjoining the highway[113]; where a 17-year-old girl, working a soda-water bottle filling machine, was injured by the bursting of a bottle, having failed to wear a mask provided to prevent such an injury[114]; where a 10-year-old boy kicked a bundle of straw into a threshing machine and his foot was caught in the moving machinery[115]; where a three-year-old child was not wearing a seat belt in a car, being driven by her mother.[116]

---

[102] Bearing in mind the purpose of the Law Reform (Contributory Negligence) Act 1945, it must not be assumed as a certainty that the decisions, which were made before the Act came into force, would necessarily be decided in the same way today.

[103] *Gardner v Grace* (1858) 1 F. & F. 359. "The doctrine of contributory negligence does not apply to an infant of tender age", per Channell B.

[104] *Gough v Thorne* [1966] 1 W.L.R. 1387.

[105] *Williams v G.W. Ry* (1874) L.R. 9 Ex. 157; *Thomas v B.R.B.* [1976] Q.B. 912 (a two-year-old child gained access to the defendant's railway lines through a defective stile, which had been ruined by vandals within a few days of its being erected in position). Further, cf. *Singleton v E.C. Ry* (1859) 7 C.B.(N.S.) 287 and *BRB v Herrington* [1972] A.C. 877.

[106] *Lay v Midland Ry* (1875) 34 L.T. 30.

[107] *Jewson v Gatti* (1886) 2 T.L.R. 441.

[108] *Harrold v Watney* [1898] 2 Q.B. 320.

[109] *Smith v Martin and Hull Corp* [1911] 2 K.B. 775.

[110] *Robinson v W.H. Smith & Son* (1901) 17 T.L.R. 423.

[111] *Glasgow Corp v Taylor* [1922] 1 A.C. 44.

[112] *Culkin v McFie & Sons Ltd* [1939] 3 All E.R. 613.

[113] *Liddle v Yorkshire (North Riding) CC* [1934] 2 K.B. 101, per Greer and Slesser L.JJ. on the assumption that there was negligence (which was not found) on the part of the defendants.

[114] *Crocker v Banks* (1888) 4 T.L.R. 324. See also *Grizzle v Frost* (1863) 3 F. & F. 622.

[115] *Holdman v Hamlyn* [1943] K.B. 664.

[116] *Ducharme v Davies* [1984] 1 W.W.R. 699, but see, further, on the doctrine of identification, para.4–34, above.

On the other hand, an 11-year-old boy was found 75 per cent to blame for a **4-40** motor accident when he had run out and tried to cross the road without first looking for moving traffic[117]; and a boy of the same age was one third to blame where, attempting to retrieve a ball he was injured in climbing a four foot high fence topped with spikes.[118] A boy of 13 was held 50 per cent to blame where he suffered burns as a result of interfering with flammable liquid in a container which the defendants left outside their factory in breach of duty under Environmental Protection Act 1990 s.76(3).[119] A boy of seven was held 60 per cent to blame when he sustained injury by punching a glass panel in a classroom door.[120]

For completeness, the following are examples in which contributory negli- **4-41** gence did not arise, since the child's claim failed: where a 17 and-a-half-year-old boy on a skiing trip to Austria organised by his school skied unsupervised, on piste that was partially closed as a result of insufficient snow[121]; where a three-year-old child strayed upon a railway line and was injured by a passing train[122]; where a four-year-old boy placed his fingers in a machine which was displayed for sale in a public place, and his fingers were crushed when its handle was turned by his brother, aged seven[123]; where a nine-year-old boy trapped his fingers in the shafts of a roller, which had been secured by a strong rope, when it was cut by another boy[124]; where a seven-year-old boy, who was playing with an unhorsed van that had been left in a street, fell off and was injured[125]; where a child, aged one year and nine months, who had been allowed to play on a piece of land which was used for tipping rubbish, strayed on to a railway line and was injured.[126]

There is a perception that Scottish courts have been readier to find contributory **4-42** negligence against children than their English counterparts. A finding against the child was made: where a four-and-a-half-year-old child did not look where he was going and was run over by a tram[127]; and where a five-year-old child ran

---

[117] *Morales v Eccleston* [1991] R.T.R. 151, CA.
[118] *Dawson v Scottish Power Plc* (1999) S.L.T. 672, OH.
[119] *C v Imperial Design Ltd* [2001] Env. L.R. 33, CA.
[120] *N v Newham LBC* [2007] C.L. 326 (the child knew the difference between right and wrong and knew he should not punch; even a seven-year-old child would have known that if he punched a pane of glass it was likely to break and cause him injury).
[121] *C v W School* [2003] P.I.Q.R. P81, CA, Ch.9, para.9–201, below.
[122] *Singleton v E.C. Ry* (1859) 7 C.B.(N.S.) 287;.but cf. as regards trespassers, e.g. *BRBoard v Herrington* [1972] A.C. 877 and, generally, Ch.8, paras 8–138 to 8–143, below.
[123] *Mangan v Atterton* (1866) L.R. 1 Ex. 239. This case was doubted in *Clark v Chambers* (1878) 3 Q.B.D. 327, and now would probably be decided otherwise.
[124] *Bailey v Neal* (1888) 5 T.L.R. 20.
[125] *Donovan v Union Cartage Co* [1933] 2 K.B. 71.
[126] *Schofield v Bolton Corp* (1910) 26 T.L.R. 230.
[127] *Cass v Edinburgh Tramways* (1909) S.C. 1068; *McKinnell v White* (1971) S.L.T. 61 (a five-year-old child, who ran across a main road and was struck by a motor car, was held to be equally to blame with the motor driver). See also *McCluskey v Wallace* (1998) S.C. 711, 2 Div. (four-year old child 20 per cent to blame where she ran into the path of a car she had not seen).

against an obstruction in the street.[128] It has been doubted whether English courts would have been quite so robust.[129]

4–43   **Physical or mental disability.** The duty of care is for the most part based upon what may reasonably be expected. Only when some special circumstance is known, or should be known, is the duty adjusted in the light of that knowledge. If someone is known to have only one eye, the duty of care owed to him will in certain respects be more onerous than the duty owed to a man with two eyes.[130]

> "A measure of care appropriate to the inability or disability of those who are immature or feeble in mind or body is due from others, who know of or ought to anticipate the presence of such persons within the scope and hazard of their own operations".[131]

4–44   However, a different question arises when contributory negligence is being considered. Someone with special characteristics owes the same duty of care to others as anyone else. The driver of a motor vehicle, who has run over a pedestrian, cannot set up as a defence that he suffered from defective eyesight or some other physical characteristic, which limited his ability to avoid the accident. If two vehicles collide, both drivers are judged by the same standards.[132] A driver cannot evade responsibility for negligent driving by proof of some physical, or psychological characteristic, which meant he was unable to drive with reasonable skill and care.[133] When the contributory negligence alleged involves a breach of duty, mental or physical infirmity has no effect on liability. A deaf motorist, whose infirmity has caused or contributed to a motor accident, is in no better position, when suing as claimant, than he would be when sued as defendant. Whichever party he is, his conduct is judged by an objective standard, without special consideration for his disability.

4–45   By way of contrast, when the contributory negligence does not consist of a breach of duty but concerns the failure of the claimant to take reasonable care for his own safety, ought physical characteristics to be taken into consideration? It

---

[128] *Plantza v Glasgow Corp* 1910 S.C. 786. Other cases where contributory negligence was found are: *Grant v Caledonian Ry* (1870) 9 Macph. 258 (six years); *Fraser v Edinburgh Tramways* (1882) 10 R. 264 (six years). But the Scottish court did not find contributory negligence in *Galbraith's Curator ad litem v Stewart (No.2)* (1998) Rep.L.R. 64, OH (child playing with unattended pipes).
[129] See, per Hamilton L.J. in *Latham v R. Johnson & Nephew Ltd* [1913] 1 K.B. 398 at 413. In *Andrews v Freeborough* [1967] 1 Q.B. 1 at 8, Willmer L.J. said of a child of eight years that even if she had stepped off the kerb into the path of the defendant's motor car, "I should have needed a good deal of persuasion before imputing contributory negligence to the child having regard to her tender age."
[130] *Paris v Stepney Borough Council* [1951] A.C. 367.
[131] *Glasgow Corp v Taylor* [1922] A.C. 44 at 67, per Lord Sumner. This dictum was applied in *Haley v London Electricity Board* [1965] A.C. 778.
[132] The learner driver is so included: *Nettleship v Weston* [1971] 2 Q.B. 691. See Ch.10, para.10–258, below.
[133] But see *Mansfield v Weetabix Ltd* [1998] 1 W.L.R. 1263, CA (where a driver was unaware that he suffered from a physical impairment which was likely to affect his driving, and he would not have driven had he known about it, liability was not established). See Ch.10, para.10–258, below.

comes back to fault. If the claimant is blameless, any damages recoverable cannot be reduced. So, there was no contributory negligence on the part of a pedestrian with impaired hearing who failed to avoid a vehicle which drove too close to him, the driver expecting he would hear its approach and get out of the way.[134] Likewise, where an elderly pedestrian failed to take avoiding action with sufficient speed.[135]

Where an operation is conducted which imposes a duty to give warning to persons "within the scope and hazard" of it, failure to heed the warning, where that failure arises as a result of some infirmity, does not usually amount to contributory negligence.[136] When a woman, who was almost blind, put her foot into an unguarded opening whilst walking along the footpath, because she failed to notice that a hydrant cover had been removed, it was held that her claim should succeed without deduction.[137] "On a question of contributory negligence you are entitled to take into account the defective eyesight or other infirmity of a person who meets with an accident."[138]   **4–46**

In *Haley v London Electricity Board*,[139] the House of Lords held that it was the duty of those engaged in operations on the highway to take reasonable care not to act in a way likely to endanger other persons who might reasonably be expected to walk along the pavement. Those with a disability were owed the same duty as those without, but the standard of care required in discharging the duty obliged the operators to take into account the infirmities of those who might be lawfully present in the highway. Extra precautions should be taken to safeguard blind pedestrians. Equally, the operators were entitled to assume that someone with impaired sight would take reasonable precautions for their own protection, such as using a stick. In the result a person under a disability can be guilty of contributory negligence if they fail to take reasonable care for their own safety, bearing in mind the limitations which that disability imposes.[140]   **4–47**

Intoxication. The excuse of drunkenness has to be disregarded when considering contributory negligence. It is no excuse for failing to take reasonable care that the person in question was unable to take proper care, as a result of voluntary intoxication. A person the worse for drink cannot demand a higher standard of care than a sober person or plead drunkenness as an excuse for not taking the same care when drunk, as would have been taken when sober.[141]   **4–48**

---

[134] *Gaffney v Dublin United Tramways* [1916] 2 Ir.R. 472; *Smith v Browne* (1891) 28 L.R.Ir. 1.
[135] *Daly v Liverpool Corporation* [1939] 2 All E.R. 142.
[136] See *Paul v G.E. Ry* (1920) 36 T.L.R. 344 (deaf man killed during shunting operations).
[137] *M'Kibbin v Glasgow Corp* (1920) S.C. 590.
[138] *M'Kibbin v Glasgow Corp* (1920) S.C. 597, per Lord Salvensen.
[139] [1965] A.C. 778.
[140] *Widdowson v Newgate Meat Corp* [1998] P.I.Q.R. 138, CA (a pedestrian suffering from serious mental disorder walking at night by the side of a dual carriageway was equally blameworthy with the driver of the van who failed to see him and knocked him down). See Ch.6, para.6–115, below.
[141] See *M'Cormick v Caledonian Ry* (1903) 5 F. 362 (drunken man killed on railway). See also Ch.2 para.2–87, above.

Where the Prison Service was to blame for an injury sustained by the claimant, a prisoner severely injured when he fell from the top bunk of a cell in the course of a seizure caused by withdrawal from illicit drugs, it was inappropriate to make a finding of contributory negligence on the basis that he was himself to blame as a result of his abuse of drugs and alcohol. To support such a finding it was necessary that there should be conduct that was both blameworthy and a potent cause of the ultimate injury. Causative potency was not made out since the claimant's addictions were too remote in time, place and circumstance and insufficiently connected with the negligence of the prison staff to be properly regarded as a cause of the injury.[142]

4-49 There can, however, be instances where a duty of care arises precisely because the defendant should have anticipated that the claimant would be the worse for drink and thereby less careful than otherwise. In any such case a finding of contributory negligence must reflect the blameworthiness of each party, rather than being confined to the claimant's own responsibility for the injuries sustained.[143]

4-50 Where an intoxicated pedestrian stepped into the roadway in front of a car at night and was killed in the ensuing collision, his responsibility for the accident was assessed at 35 per cent.[144] Likewise, a passenger in a car, so intoxicated as to be unable to perceive that the driver was unfit to drive through drink, was guilty of contributory negligence when a collision occurred, which caused him injury.[145]

4-51 **Rescuers.**[146] In rescue cases a rescuer, however brave, may yet be partially to blame if the action taken was unreasonable in all the circumstances. "If a rescuer acts with a wanton disregard of his own safety it might be that in some circumstances it might be held that any injury to him was not the result of the negligence that caused the situation of danger."[147] As this formulation suggests, the standard applied by a court is unlikely to be exacting. Proper allowance will have to be made for the circumstances in which a rescue is attempted. It would be difficult to find fault where, at the time, it would have appeared that the chances of success were diminishing with each second of delay.

4-52 **Sports.** The existence of a duty of care between competitors in sports is well established.[148] The duty is to take all reasonable care, bearing in mind the

---

[142] *St George v Home Office* [2009] 1 W.L.R. 1670, CA.

[143] *Brannan v Airtours Plc, The Times*, February 1, 1999, CA. See also Harvey and Marston, "Intoxication and claimants in negligence" 149 N.L.J. 1004.

[144] *Kilminster v Rule* (1983) 32 S.A.S.R. 39, Sup.Ct.

[145] *Owens v Brimmell* [1977] Q.B. 859. See further, paras 4–123 to 4–125, below, also Roberts and Richard, "Riding with a drunken driver and contributory negligence revisited" 2004 J.P.I.Law 1, 21.

[146] See Derwent, "Contributory Negligence in Rescue Cases" in 123 S.J. 383. See further in relation to rescuers Ch.2 para.2–259, para.4–08 et seq., above and paras 4–114 to 4–119, below.

[147] per Morris L.J. in *Baker v T. E. Hopkins & Son Ltd* [1959] 1 W.L.R. 966 at 977.

[148] See Ch.2, para.2–281, above.

particular circumstances in which the competing players were placed.[149] All the relevant circumstances of the individual case will need to be taken into consideration in order to determine whether or not there is a basis for a finding of contributory negligence against an injured sportsman. There may well be occasions where the claimant, as an ordinary prudent participant in a game and calling upon his experience in the sport concerned, ought to foresee danger, even to the extent of anticipating negligence of his fellow players. But just as in rescue cases, a court ought to make all proper allowances where the speed of the activity concerned reduces the time available to take stock of a situation and, hence, the opportunity to take evasive action, whether in avoiding the accident altogether or in reducing the degree of damage which results.

Playing a golf shot does not normally involve such pressure of time that **4–53** sensible precautions can be omitted. In *Feeney v Lyall*,[150] during a round of golf, the pursuer hooked his drive from the ninth tee on to the adjacent sixth fairway. He went to the ball in order to play his second shot and was struck and seriously injured by a ball driven off the sixth tee by another golfer, who had not appreciated he was there. Liability in negligence was not established but, if it had been, the opinion was expressed that the pursuer would have been held 25 per cent contributorily negligent.

Motor accidents.[151] It will be understood that any finding of contributory **4–54** negligence will depend upon the circumstances of each individual case. Whilst there is no general duty to foresee that another will be negligent,[152] instances can and do arise where it will be prudent to anticipate the negligence of others, especially where experience commonly has shown such negligence to be likely[153] or where resulting damage can be minimised.[154] So, it has been held to be contributory negligence for a foreman on a building project which involved restricting traffic to one lane of an adjacent road to step backwards into the path of an approaching car.[155] There was no contributory negligence where the claimant, cycling along the hard shoulder of a six-lane highway in Muscat, Oman, was struck by the opening door of a mini-bus which had stopped on the

---

[149] *Condon v Basi* [1985] 1 W.L.R. 866 (a foul tackle by the defendant player during a soccer game, which resulted in the plaintiff suffering a broken leg), applying *Rootes v Shelton* (1967) 116 C.L.R. 383, High Ct of Australia (an experienced water skier was performing "cross-overs" with other experienced men on the Macquarie River, travelling at about 35 mph behind a speedboat. Temporarily blinded by spray, he swung wider than intended and collided with a stationary boat).
[150] 1991 S.L.T. 156.
[151] See Ch.10, below for extended discussion. Examples of contributory negligence in road traffic cases also appear above variously at 4–26, 4–27, 4–29 and 4–30.
[152] *Compania Mexicana de Petroleo v Essex Transport Co* (1929) 141 L.T. 106 at 115. See similarly *Grayson Ltd v Ellerman Lines Ltd* [1920] A.C. 466.
[153] *Grant v Sun Shipping Co* [1948] A.C. 549 at 567; *L.P.T.B. v Upson* [1949] A.C. 155 at 173, where Lord Uthwatt said that whilst a driver need not anticipate folly in all its forms he is not "entitled to put out of consideration the teachings of experience as to the form these follies commonly take." See Ch.10, para.10–189, below. See also Braithwaite, "Cycling helmets and contributory negligence" in 143 S.J.1144.
[154] e.g. by wearing a safety helmet, when riding a motorcycle, or a safety belt, when travelling inside a motor vehicle. See Ch.10, para.10–156, 10–265, below.
[155] *Bryce v McKirdy* (1999) S.L.T. 988, OH (a driver travelling at some 10–20 mph was found 25 per cent to blame for not sounding her horn).

hard shoulder: it was unrealistic to suggest he should have stopped in case the door opened and moving into the road would have exposed him to even greater hazard).[156] The driver of a car which had been involved in a collision, and his passengers, were not negligent in failing to move away from the vehicle, which was stationary in the nearside lane of the carriageway, in the period of one or two minutes before a second car came on the scene and struck them.[157]

4-55 **Professional negligence.** A company whose directors had been guilty of a flawed commercial judgement in entering a joint venture agreement which adversely affected the value of its shares, was not thereby guilty of contributory negligence, reducing the liability of negligent solicitors who had failed to advise that approval of the members of the company was required, pursuant to s.320 of the Companies Act 1985, before the venture could proceed. It would be "wholly inconsistent with the statutory scheme" to attribute the undoubted negligence of the directors to the company.[158]

4-56 Solicitors have been held guilty of contributory negligence in a claim brought by them against an auditor whom they employed to complete consequential loss insurance certificates. They had failed themselves to notice a mistake in the figures, when they should have done. However, in *Henderson v Merrett Syndicates Ltd (No.2)*[159] auditors failed to establish that the claimants, certain names at Lloyd's, should be fixed with responsibility for the negligence of managing agents employed by them and were thereby guilty of contributory negligence. Apart from any other consideration, it appeared to be accepted that it would be unjust and inequitable to reduce the successful claimants' damages when the whole rationale of their having employed auditors was to obtain an independent evaluation of the managing agents' statements as to the financial consequences of their actions on the claimants' behalf.

> "It makes a nonsense of the purpose for which the auditors were employed if the names' claims against the auditors is defeated by reason of the very negligence to which the auditors were supposed to be alerting the names."[160]

4-57 Where solicitors have been found guilty of negligence in the context of mortgage transactions in which they acted both for borrower and lender, and failed to report the lender matters which cast doubt on the correctness of a valuation of the subject property or the good faith of the borrower, a number of

---

[156] *Burridge v Airwork Ltd* (2004) 148 S.J.L.B. 386, CA.

[157] *Lac v Clayton* [2009] EWCA Civ. 106 (given that the claimants had been shaken in the initial accident, and given also that there was not an obviously safe place to which they would have been drawn instinctively, it was right to hold that they had not been negligent to remain where they were by the car).

[158] *British Racing Driver's Club Ltd v Hextall Erskine & Co* [1996] 3 All E.R. 667 at 683, per Carnwath J. This decision has been criticised: see Bartlett Q.C. in "Attribution of contributory negligence: agents, company directors and fraudsters" in (1998) 114 L.Q.R. 460 which contains much useful analysis of other situations where questions of attributing contributory negligence arise; also Evans, "Attribution and professional negligence" (2003) 3 P.N. 470, Murdoch, "Client negligence: a lost cause?" (2004) 2 P.N. 97.

[159] [1996] 1 P.N.L.R. 32.

[160] *Henderson v Merrett Syndicates Ltd (No.2)* [1996] 1 P.N.L.R. 40, per Cresswell J., in summarising the claimant's contentions.

cases have identified contributory negligence on the lender's behalf which have reduced the damages recovered.[161] It was negligent of the lender, on the facts, to fail to obtain bank or credit references in the case of the purchase of a five bedroomed property by a youthful purchaser with no dependants[162]; to proceed with a loan where an employer's reference disclosed a lower income than that claimed and confusing, uncertain and inconsistent answers were given in interview[163]; not investigating the many credit searches against the borrower's name by financial institutions[164]; and in failing adequately to investigate the borrower's ability to pay.[165]

Where solicitors' are intentionally in breach of a fiduciary duty to the other **4–58** party, as opposed to a duty in contract or tort, no deduction from damages will be made for alleged contributory negligence of the innocent party. "To do otherwise ... risks subverting the fundamental principle of undivided and unremitting loyalty which is at the core's of the fiduciary's obligations."[166] However, that does not mean the claimant's conduct is irrelevant: it may be relevant to arguments of remoteness which limit the loss for which the defendant is liable or come into play as a factor determining the extent of loss for which recovery can be made.[167]

Where architects were negligent in failing to provide for adequate fireproofing **4–59** in a design of a factory in which ready meals were prepared for supermarkets and, as a result, a fire, caused by the negligence of the claimants' own employees, spread from the food preparation area to the rest of the factory, it was held that the claim should be reduced for contributory negligence by two thirds. The damage sustained by the claimants as a result of the spread of the fire throughout the factory had been the result partly of their own fault in causing the fire. There were, therefore, two effective causes of the spread of the fire and it was just and equitable to reduce the claimants' damages to reflect that conclusion.[168]

In a claim against auditors, arising from their failure to detect indications of **4–60** fraudulent trading by one of the claimant company's employees, it was argued that even if the management of the claimant had itself also been at fault, no contributory negligence should be found, given that it was the duty of auditors to

---

[161] See generally *Nationwide Building Society v Balmer Radmore* [1999] P.N.L.R. 606, and other cases in Ch.9, para.9–269, below.
[162] *Nationwide BS v J. R. Jones* [1999] Lloyd's Rep. P.N. 414 (40 per cent).
[163] *Nationwide BS v Archdeacons* [1999] Lloyd's Rep. P.N. 549 (90 per cent).
[164] *Nationwide BS v Vanderpump & Sykes* [1999] Lloyd's Rep. P.N. 422.
[165] *Nationwide BS v Littlestone & Cowan* [1999] Lloyd's Rep. P.N. 625.
[166] per Blackburne J. in *NB Society v Balmer Radmore* [1999] P.N.L.R. 606 at 677. It has been commented that in some cases the distinction between a breach of fiduciary duty and negligence can be a fine one, albeit, if Blackburne J.'s analysis is correct, having a major impact on quantum: see Dugdale, "Contributory negligence: continuing controversy" in (1999) 3 P.N. 164. See also *De Beer v Kanaar & Co* [2002] EWHC 688 (Ch) (the plea of contributory negligence has no application to liability for breach of fiduciary duty); also Mulheron, "Contributory negligence in equity: should fiduciaries accept all the blame?" (2003) 3 P.N. 422.
[167] *NB Society v Balmer Radmore* [1999] P.N.L.R. 677.
[168] *Sahib Foods Ltd v Paskin Kyriakides Sands* [2004] P.N.L.R. 403, CA (the judge at first instance erred in basing his finding of no contributory negligence in part upon a conclusion that the claimants owed no duty of care to the defendant).

protect the claimant from such errors. The argument found favour only in part. It did operate to prevent any finding of contributory negligence where the failure of the company to supervise its business and guard against fraud was excused by reliance on the audit report. The company could not rely on the argument in respect of wider failures to provide adequate supervision or initiate investigation.[169]

Contributory negligence has only rarely succeded as a defence to claims for clinical negligence.[170]

4–61   **Criminal enterprise.** Not surprisingly, a person who engages in criminal activities upon premises is open to a finding of contributory negligence in the event of his sustaining personal injuries during his venture.[171]

4–62   **Strict liability.** There are a number of situations in which strict liability for the claimant's damage can arise and contributory negligence is discussed in context in the chapters below where that particular form of liability is discussed.[172]

4–63   **Employees.**[173] As has been pointed out,[174] the standard of care in contributory negligence is the same as that in negligence. Some modification, however, occurs in the case of employees who suffer accidents in the course of their employment as a result of their employer's breach of statutory duty.[175] In order to understand why this exception to the general rule developed, it is necessary to compare the situations before and after the coming into effect of the Law Reform (Contributory Negligence) Act 1945.

4–64   **Prior to 1945.** Before the passing of the Act of 1945, the employee's contributory negligence afforded an employer a complete defence to an action based upon his own breach of duty. Against that background, the courts were reluctant to impose too rigorous a test when deciding whether a workman was guilty of contributory negligence. The view was taken that "some carelessness or inattention to his own safety" was not contributory negligence and that "the jury have to draw the line where mere thoughtlessness or inadvertence or forgetfulness ceases and where negligence begins".[176]

---

[169] *Barings Plc v Coopers & Lybrand (No.7)* [2003] P.N.L.R. 639.
[170] See Herring and Foster, "Blaming the patient: contributory negligence in medical malpractice litigation" (2009) 2 P.N. 76.
[171] *Revill v Newbery* [1996] 2 W.L.R. 239 (the claimant, who was shot by the occupier during a night-time attempted burglary of the latter's garden shed, was held two-thirds to blame for his wounds). See, further, para.4–250, below.
[172] See Ch.12, "Statutory Duty," Ch.13, "Dangerous Things," Ch.14, "Animals" and Ch.15 "Products Liability". Contributory negligence in fatal accident cases is discussed in Ch.16.
[173] See Fagelson, "The Last Bastion of Fault? Contributory Negligence in Actions for Employers' Liability" in (1979) 4 M.L.R. 646.
[174] See para.4–10, above.
[175] For a fuller discussion about the earlier development of the law on this subject, see *Charlesworth on Negligence* (6th edn, 1977), Ch.16, paras 1224–1228. See also Ch.12, para.12–69, below.
[176] per Lord Wright in *Caswell v Powell Duffryn Associated Collieries Ltd* [1940] A.C. 152 at 176.

"In considering whether an ordinary prudent workman would have taken more care than the injured man, the tribunal of fact has to take into account all the circumstances of work in a factory and . . . it is not for every risky thing which a workman in a factory may do in his familiarity with the machinery that a plaintiff ought to be held guilty of contributory negligence."[177]

In effect, a different standard of care was imposed than if the court had been considering the employee as someone for whose want of care towards a third party the employer was vicariously liable.

Post-1945. Similar thinking persisted after 1945, even when damages could   **4–65** be apportioned according to the degree of fault, and it might have been expected that any special consideration for employees might cease. Lord Tucker said that in cases under the Factories Act:

"the purpose of imposing the absolute obligation is to protect the workmen against those very acts of inattention which are sometimes relied upon as constituting contributory negligence so that too strict a standard would defeat the object of the statute."[178]

It was said that the courts must be careful not to emasculate the protection given by statutory regulations through the side wind of apportionment and that a workman must not be judged too harshly for a momentary error, where there was a continuing breach of the law by his employers.[179]

Nevertheless, there is no principle of law which requires that even when there   **4–66** has been a breach of statutory duty in circumstances where the intention of a statute is to give protection against folly on the part of an employee, there cannot be a finding of contributory negligence to the extent of 100 per cent against the claimant.[180] Also where both the claimant and the employer are in breach of their statutory duty, liability will not arise where the fault causing the accident is the claimant's, and there is no fault on the part of the employer, which goes beyond or is independent of the claimant's own omission.[181]

---

[177] per Lawrence J. in *Flower v Ebbw Vale Steel, Iron and Coal Co Ltd* [1934] 2 K.B. 132 at 139–140.

[178] *Staveley Iron & Chemical Co Ltd v Jones* [1956] A.C. 627 at 648. These words reflected an observation of Goddard L.J. in *Hutchinson v L.N.E.R.* [1942] 1 K.B. 481 at 488: "I always directed myself to be exceedingly chary of finding contributory negligence where the contributory negligence alleged was the very thing which the statutory duty of the employer was designed to prevent". See to the same effect, per Lord Greene M.R. in *Hopwood v Rolls-Royce Ltd* (1947) 176 L.T. 514 at 520.

[179] per Sachs L.J. in *Mullard v Ben Line Steamers Ltd* [1970] 1 W.L.R. 1414. See also *McGuiness v Key Markets Ltd* (1972) 13 K.I.R. 249, CA (a breach of s.14 of the Factories Act 1961); *Kansara v Osram (G.E.C.)* [1967] 3 All E.R. 230 (casual inadvertence of an employee is not necessarily negligence on his part); and *Ryan v Manbre Sugars* (1970) 114 S.J. 492 (employee failed to avoid stepping on a step which he knew to be slippery).

[180] *Jayes v I.M.I. (Kynoch) Ltd* [1985] I.C.R. 155, per curiam: "There comes a point in time where the degree of fault is so great that the court ceases to take fine distinctions and to hold that, in practical terms, the fault is entirely that of the workman" (applying the dicta of Sellers and Pearson L.JJ. in *Mitchell v W.S. Westin Ltd* [1965] 1 W.L.R. 297 at 305 and 309).

[181] *Ginty v Belmont Building Supplies Ltd* [1959] 1 All E.R. 414, CA.

4–67   It has been generally assumed that the same principles will apply in a case where the allegation against the employer is one of common law negligence. It will no doubt depend upon the facts whether they do. Doubt has been expressed whether in some situations they are appropriate:

> "I doubt very much whether they were ever intended or could properly be applied to a simple case of common law negligence such as the present where there was no evidence of workpeople performing repetitive work under strain or for long hours at dangerous machines."[182]

Illustrations

4–68   There was no contributory negligence found where: a crane driver failed to ensure that the crane properly took the strain of the load so that the load swung towards the claimant and injured him[183]; where a skilled rigger adopted a method of lifting that was obviously less safe than the method which he would have preferred to use had the employers provided the necessary and proper tackle[184]; where a workman operated a lathe in the manner he had been trained in and had used for five years, and sustained injury because this method was a dangerous one.[185] If a workman fails to choose the safer of two possible means of access, he is not necessarily guilty of contributory negligence.[186]

4–69   Nor was the employee guilty of contributory negligence where: a stevedore fell into the ship's hold, after the ship-repairers had removed both the hatch covers as well as the electric lights[187]; an electrician, carrying out maintenance work, caught his fingers in an electric fan[188]; a machine operative removed the lid from a box containing moving machinery, in order to effect an adjustment and his hand was trapped[189]; a fitter caught his finger in the drive belt, when rotating manually the transmission machinery[190]; a fitter's thumb was struck by a revolving grindstone,[191] an operator was injured whilst cleaning out a paddle mixing machine, the ongoing practice for which was to clean it still in motion with its fence removed[192]; a drunken cabin steward was scalded whilst taking a shower[193]; a steel erector's leg was broken, when a heavy piece of machinery fell, whilst it was being moved along planks laid across a trench,[194] a rigger used a less safe system for slinging and moving a half-ton section of pipe than he

---

[182] *Staveley Iron & Chemical Co Ltd v Jones* [1956] A.C. 627 at 647.
[183] *Staveley Iron & Chemical Co Ltd v Jones* [1956] A.C. 627 at 647.
[184] *Machray v Stewarts & Lloyd's Ltd* [1965] 1 W.L.R. 602.
[185] *Herton v Blaw Knox* (1968) 6 K.I.R. 35, applying *General Cleaning Contractors v Christmas* [1953] A.C. 180.
[186] *Fowler v B.R.B.* [1969] 1 Lloyd's Rep. 231.
[187] *Grant v Sun Shipping Co Ltd* [1948] A.C. 549; followed by Lord Kilbrandon in *Westwood v Post Office* [1974] A.C. 1, who (at 17) considered that it had lost none of its authority.
[188] *Thurogood v Van Den Berghs & Jurgens Ltd* [1951] 2 K.B. 537.
[189] *Charles v S. Smith & Sons (England) Ltd* [1954] W.L.R. 451.
[190] *Richard Thomas & Baldwins Ltd v Cummings* [1955] A.C. 321.
[191] *John Summers & Sons Ltd v Frost* [1955] A.C. 740.
[192] *Moffat v Atlas Hydraulic Loaders* [1992] S.L.T. 1123, Ct Sess. OH.
[193] *Foulder v Canadian Pacific Steamship Ltd* [1968] 2 Lloyd's Rep. 366.
[194] *Byers v Head Wrightson & Co Ltd* [1961] 1 W.L.R. 961.

would have preferred, as a result of which the pipe swung, hit him and fractured his ankle[195]; a machine operator put his hand under a fence and into contact with a guillotine knife[196]; a technical officer took an unauthorised short-cut through the lift machinery room, which he was forbidden to enter, in order to return to work, after taking a break on the flat roof of the building but fell to his death[197]; a workman fell from a ladder, after grasping and heaving himself up by means of a chain, which was attached to an object that moved.[198]

In many of these instances, had the context been otherwise than employment, a finding of contribution may well have resulted.

By way of contrast, the claimants in the following cases were found to have **4–70** been guilty of contributory negligence to the extent of:

90 per cent: where a workman climbed up to and interfered with unfenced transmission machinery[199];

80 per cent: where a quarryman failed to take down an unsafe roof and proceeded to work under it[200]; where a machinery attendant climbed up to unfenced transmission machinery in order to catch a pigeon, roosting behind it[201];

75 per cent: where a moulder failed to wear the protective spats provided by his employers and suffered severe burns to his ankle from molten metal splashes[202]; where a fitter had squeezed through an 18-inch gap in a handrail, guarding a ropeway, and was struck by a moving bucket[203]; where a miller, who was not authorised to use a particular saw for cutting metal, used it incompetently, without adjusting the guard, and part of his thumb was severed[204]; where a workman removed the guard of a paint-spraying machine, whilst carrying out repairs, and was trapped[205];

66.66 per cent: where a joiner/French-polisher used a circular saw, which was not securely fenced on some private work outside his employment hours and severely injured a hand[206]; where an experienced workman was injured when using unfenced machiner[207]; where an apprentice farmer, whilst using a circular saw to cut up logs, brought his hand across and into the path of the revolving

---

[195] *Machray v Stewarts & Lloyds Ltd* [1965] 1 W.L.R. 602.

[196] *Stocker v Norprint Ltd* (1971) 10 K.I.R. 10 (Cairns L.J. dissenting, thought 33-and-a-half per cent).

[197] *Westwood v Post Office* [1974] A.C. 1 (if liability had been decided in negligence rather than breach of statutory duty, the speeches in the House of Lords indicated a range of views on the extent of any finding of contributory negligence).

[198] *Sostman v Scruttons Maltby Ltd* [1974] 2 Lloyd's Rep. 379.

[199] *Hodkinson v Henry Wallwork & Co Ltd* [1955] 3 All E.R. 236.

[200] *Stapley v Gypsum Mines Ltd* [1953] A.C. 663.

[201] *Uddin v Associated Portland Cement Manufacturers Ltd* [1965] 2 Q.B. 15, approved in *Westwood v Post Office* [1974] A.C. 1 and followed by the CA in *Allen v Aeroplane & Motor Aluminium Castings Ltd* [1965] 1 W.L.R. 1244.

[202] *Haynes v Qualcast (Wolverhampton) Ltd* [1958] W.L.R. 225; reversed on other grounds [1959] A.C. 743.

[203] *Quintas v National Smelting Co Ltd* [1960] 1 W.L.R. 217.

[204] *Leach v Standard Telephones and Cables Ltd* [1966] 1 W.L.R. 1392.

[205] *Thornton v Swan Hunter (Shipbuilders) Ltd* [1972] 2 Lloyd's Rep. 112.

[206] *Napieralski v Curtis (Contractors) Ltd* [1959] 1 W.L.R. 835.

[207] *Tearle v Cheverton & Laidler Ltd* (1969) 7 K.I.R. 364.

blade, as he tried to catch a bit of falling wood[208]; where a building site foreman fell and was injured, whilst trying to shut a door by pulling on the key, which was inserted in the lock (varied on appeal from 80 per cent)[209]; where a trackman received fatal injuries, when he stepped into the path of an approaching train[210];

60 per cent: where a young bakery assistant put her fingers beneath the guard of a pastry-rolling machine, in order to push odd pieces of dough against the moving rollers[211]; where an experienced workman stood on the tarpaulin sheet covering a load on a trailer and pulled upon it in order to clear a ruck thereby losing his balance and falling.[212]

4–71   *50 per cent*: where a workman operated a circular saw, well knowing that the guard had not been lowered to its fullest extent[213]; where a trainee joiner, who knew of the danger of dermatitis arising from the use of synthetic glue and the need to use a barrier cream on the exposed surfaces of the skin of his hands, failed to take such precautions[214]; where a painter, who failed to disclose to his employers that he suffered from epileptic fits and had been instructed not to work at heights, disobeyed the warnings, fell and was injured[215]; where a coremaker in a foundry walked backwards, whilst helping others to carry a ladle of molten metal for the purpose of pouring it into a mould, failed to watch his feet and stumbled at the edge of a pit[216]; where a stevedore disobeyed instructions for unstowing sacks, forming the cargo of a barge, so that the stack collapsed and crushed him[217]; where a shunter rode on the bottom step of a locomotive and came into contact with a points' vertical lever[218]; where an experienced workman was injured when he fell from an unfixed and unfooted ladder[219]; where a workman was playing the fool with petrol, during the luncheon break at work[220]; where, in disobedience of instructions, a young employee attempted to clean the moving cylinders of a lithographic printing machine[221]; where a welder failed to ask for the assistance that was available, in turning over heavy stillages for painting[222]; where a joiner erected his own working platform less safely than he should, because of the lack of material required for its proper construction[223]; where a sales director of a company went upon the roof of the company's

---

[208] *Kerry v Carter* [1969] 1 W.L.R. 1372 but cf. *Hilton v F.H. Marshall & Co Ltd* [1951] W.N. 81 and *Smith v Supreme Woodpulp Co Ltd* [1968] 3 All E.R. 753, where contributory negligence in comparable circumstances was assessed as 25 per cent.

[209] *Jennings v Norman Collison (Contractors) Ltd* [1970] 1 All E.R. 1121.

[210] *Trotman v British Railways Board* [1975] K.I.R. 161.

[211] *Smith v Chesterfield & District Co-operative Society Ltd* [1953] 1 W.L.R. 370.

[212] *Blanchflower v Chamberlain* (1996) C.L.Y. 2997, CA.

[213] *Cakebread v Hopping Bros (Whetstone) Ltd* [1947] K.B. 641 (an accident which happened some three weeks after the passing of the 1945 Act).

[214] *Clifford v Charles H. Challen & Sons Ltd* [1951] K.B. 495.

[215] *Cork v Kirby Maclean Ltd* [1952] 2 All E.R. 402.

[216] *Harrison v Metropolitan-Vickers Electrical Co Ltd* [1954] 1 W.L.R. 324.

[217] *Williams v Port of Liverpool Stevedoring Co Ltd* [1956] 1 W.L.R. 551.

[218] *Hicks v British Transport Commission* [1958] 1 W.L.R. 493.

[219] *McMath v Rimmer Bros (Liverpool) Ltd* [1962] 1 W.L.R. 1.

[220] *Heffer v Rover Car Co, The Times*, November 26, 1964.

[221] *Denyer v Charles Skipper and East Ltd* [1970] 1 W.L.R. 1087.

[222] *Brown v Allied Ironfounders Ltd* [1974] 1 W.L.R. 527.

[223] *McIntyre v Strathclyde Regional Council* (1994) S.L.T. 933.

premises to investigate a wire thought to have been placed by vandals or burglars and fell through a skylight[224]; in falling from a suspended ladder giving access to the upper of two bunks on a semi-submersible production platform, stationary in the Moray Firth.[225]

40 per cent: where the appellant, who was employed as a director of the respondent company, together with two fellow directors had adopted a clearly unsafe system of work, devised by the others, in order to check the fixing of a banner to a flagpole[226];

33.33 per cent: where a farm assistant, a minor, helping in the operations of a threshing machine, whilst standing on the threshing platform took an incautious step on the way to the feeding box and his leg entered the moving drum, through the feeding mouth[227]; where a number of lengthmen, who were repairing a main railway line, ignored the signal that a train was approaching and were struck and killed[228]; where an experienced steel erector fell to his death from a ladder, which he had chosen to use instead of the much safer movable platform in order to reach the wire netting, suspended below an aerial ropeway[229]; where a riveter, carrying out repairs on a hatchcover, walked through the centre compartment of the ship, which was in complete darkness and fell down the open unfenced hatch[230]; where a worker failed to use a pusher when slicing frozen meat with a bandsaw[231]; where a tally clerk, acting as a banksman, was struck and injured when he stepped out into the path of an oncoming mobile crane[232]; where an inexperienced support worker employed by a health authority to take a patient on a camping holiday set fire to a tent and caused herself injury when changing the clinder of a gas cooker near to a lit candle[233]; where a kitchen fitter crashed his employer's van as a result of suffering an occasion of micro-sleep after being awake for 19 hours, a situation which arose from the circumstances of his employment, but the risk of which he must have been aware.[234]

25 per cent: where a mineworker was injured by a premature explosion of a   **4–72** shot whilst giving unauthorised assistance to the shot-firer by coupling up for him the cable to the detonator[235]; where a steel erector failed to use a crawling-board, whilst working on the roof of an aircraft hangar, laying asbestos sheets, and fell through the fragile roof[236]; where a burner, who was aware of the danger, stood too close to the sling of a crane taking the strain to pull an object away, as a result

---

[224] *Parker v PFC Flooring Supplies Ltd* [2001] EWCA Civ. 1533 affirming [2001] P.I.Q.R. P7.

[225] *Robb v Salamis (M&I) Ltd* [2007] 2 All E.R. 97, HL, Ch.12, para.12–224, below.

[226] *Nicol v Allyacht Spars Pty Ltd* (1987) 75 A.L.R. 1, High Ct of Australia (the system involved the use of an extension ladder, fixed to a trestle, and placed on the platform of a utility truck, when the foot of the trestle moved under the weight of the appellant at the top of the ladder and he fell to the ground).

[227] *Jones v Richards* [1955] 1 W.L.R. 444.

[228] *Reilly v B.T.C.* [1957] 1 W.L.R. 76.

[229] *Ross v Associated Portland Cement Manufacturers Ltd* [1964] 1 W.L.R. 768.

[230] *Mullard v Ben Line Steamers Ltd* [1970] 1 W.L.R. 1414.

[231] *McGuiness v Key Markets Ltd* [1972] 13 K.I.R. 249.

[232] *Rodway v P.D. Wharfage & Transport Ltd* [1973] 2 Lloyd's Rep. 511.

[233] *Fraser v Winchester HA*, The Times, July 12, 1999, CA. See Ch.11, para.11–46, below.

[234] *Eyres v Atkinsons Kitchens and Bedrooms Ltd*, The Times, May 21, 2007, CA.

[235] *National Coal Board v England* [1954] A.C. 403.

[236] *Donaghey v P. O'Brien & Co* [1966] 1 W.L.R. 1170.

of which he was struck in the face[237]; where a welder failed to look where he was going and tripped over the electric welding cable[238];

20 per cent: where a dustman was fatally injured in a collision between a bus and the refuse lorry on the outside steps of which he was taking a ride, contrary to authority, instead of walking[239]; where a quarryman, contrary to orders, was hitching a ride by standing on the towbar at the back of a traxcavator, a slow-moving tracked vehicle, and was severely injured when a dumper truck crashed into its rear end[240]; where the driver of a fork lift truck set the forks at too low a height so that they became stuck in the surface of an uneven road[241];

10 per cent: where a bricklayer, without looking properly at what he was doing, stepped on to the platform of a scaffold, that had been constructed badly, trod on the end of a board, which toppled and caused him to fall to the ground.[242]

2.—AGREEMENT TO RUN THE RISK: "VOLENTI NON FIT INJURIA"[243]

4–73   **Meaning of "volenti non fit injuria".** A person who makes an agreement, whether expressly or by implication, to run the risk of harm negligently inflicted by another, cannot recover in respect of damage suffered in consequence. The rule has traditionally been expressed by the maxim *volenti non fit injuria*. The defence, which must be pleaded specifically,[244] raises issues whether (a) the claimant agreed to the breach of a duty of care, owed him by the defendant; and (b) the claimant consented to waive his right of action against the defendant in respect of that breach. If the answer to each is in the affirmative then the wrongfulness of the defendant's conduct is excused and the claimant is precluded from recovering damages.

4–74   There has been uncertainty over the years whether the *volenti* doctrine can apply in cases of negligence. In the context of a road traffic case the view was expressed that it could, albeit depending upon the particular facts: " . . . it must depend upon the extent of the risk, the [claimant] passenger's knowledge of it and what can be inferred as to his acceptance of it".[245] In *Wooldridge v Sumner*,[246] Diplock L.J. took a different view and said that in his view in the

---

[237] *Ball v Richard Thomas & Baldwins Ltd* [1968] 1 W.L.R. 192.
[238] *Boothman v British Northrop Ltd* (1972) 13 K.I.R. 112.
[239] *Davies v Swan Motor Co (Swansea) Ltd* [1949] 2 K.B. 291.
[240] *Jones v Livox Quarries Ltd* [1952] 2 Q.B. 608.
[241] *Beggs v Motherwell Bridge Fabricators Ltd* (1997) Rep. L.R. 87, OH.
[242] *Simmons v Bovis Ltd* [1956] 1 W.L.R. 381.
[243] See generally Ingham, "A History of the Defence of *Volenti Non Fit Injuria*" in 1981 J.R. 1.
[244] *James v Wellington City* [1972] N.Z.L.R. 978.
[245] per Fox L.J. in *Morris v Murray* [1991] 2 Q.B. 6 at 15D; also, per Stocker L.J. at 26H.
[246] [1963] 2 Q.B. 43 at 69. His opinion was approved by Lord Denning M.R. in *Nettleship v Weston* [1971] 2 Q.B. 691 at 701. However, Stocker L.J. observed in *Morris v Murray* [1991] 2 Q.B. 6 that such comments were never intended to apply to the special relationship of driver/passenger in a motor vehicle.

absence of expressed contract the maxim had no application to negligence where the duty of care is based solely upon proximity or "neighbourship" in the Atkinian sense. It will certainly be a relatively rare case where the claimant consents both to harm and the negligent infliction of it.[247]

Contracting out of or limiting liability. In general,[248] there is no objection   **4–75** to contract terms which seek to limit or remove liability for negligence, whether personal or vicarious. In certain instances, however, contracting out of liability for negligence is prohibited, either at common law or by statute. A duty, which is imposed by common law or statute for the protection of a particular person or class of persons can, in general, be waived.[249] In the case of a statute, it is a question of construction of the particular statute whether contracting out is permissible.[250] In the case of a common law duty, contracting out is permissible unless it is against public policy. "Everyone may waive the advantage of a law made solely for the benefit or protection of him as an individual in his private capacity, but this cannot be done if the waiver would infringe a public right or public policy."[251] Perhaps the Occupiers' Liability Act 1957[252] provides the best illustration, not only because its main purpose was to provide new rules to replace the rules of the common law, but also because by s.2(1) it was specifically enacted that: "An occupier of premises owes the same duty, the common duty of care, to all his visitors, *except* insofar as he is free to and does extend, restrict, modify or exclude his duty to any visitor or visitors by agreement or otherwise."[253]

Examples of statutory restriction of agreements contracting out of liability are as follows:

(i) *Carriage of Goods by Sea Act 1971*

Article III(8) of the Hague Rules 1968 as amended is given the force of law   **4–76** by s.1(1) of the Carriage of Goods by Sea Act 1971, and provides, in relation to the carriage of goods by sea:

"Any clause, covenant, or agreement in a contract of carriage relieving the carrier or the ship from liability for loss or damage to, or in connection with, goods arising from negligence, fault, or failure in the duties and obligations provided in this article or lessening such liability otherwise than as provided in these Rules, shall be null and void and of no effect. A benefit of insurance in favour of the carrier or similar clause shall be deemed to be a clause relieving the carrier from liability."

---

[247] See below, para.4–120.

[248] For restrictions upon contracting out of liability for negligence in a business context see the provisions of the Unfair Contract Terms Act 1977, which are summarised in paras 4–84 to 4–88, below.

[249] "*Cuilibet licet renuntiare juri pro se introducto*" for those who still relish the old maxims.

[250] *Salford Guardians v Dewhurst* [1926] A.C. 619.

[251] *Bowmaker Ltd v Tabor* [1941] 2 K.B. 1 at 6, per Goddard L.J.

[252] See generally Ch.8.

[253] As to this section see Ch.8, para.8–36, below.

(ii) *Public Passenger Vehicles Act 1981*

4–77 The Public Passenger Vehicles Act 1981[254] s.29, provides that:

> "A contract for the conveyance of a passenger in a public service vehicle shall, so far as it purports to negative or to restrict the liability of a person in respect of a claim which may be made against him in respect of the death of, or bodily injury to, the passenger while being carried in, entering or alighting from the vehicle, or purports to impose any conditions with respect to the enforcement of any such liability, be void."

(iii) *Carriage by Air Act 1961*

4–78 The Carriage by Air Act 1961,[255] in relation to international carriage by air, by arts 17–30 in the First Schedule[256] provides for the liability of the carrier, and by art.23(1):

> "Any provision tending to relieve the carrier of liability or to fix a lower limit than that which is laid down in this Convention shall be null and void, but the nullity of any such provision does not involve the nullity of the whole contract, which shall remain subject to the provisions of this Convention."

(iv) *Companies Act 2006*

4–79 Section 532 of the Act contains provisions rendering void any provisions protecting a company's auditors from liability for negligence or other default, breach of duty or breach of trust in relation to the company occurring in the course of the audit of accounts; or by which a company directly or indirectly provides an indemnity (to any extent) for an auditor of the company, or of an associated company, against any liability attaching to him in connection with any negligence, default, breach of duty or breach of trust in relation to the company of which he is auditor occurring in the course of the audit of accounts. The section applies to any provision, whether contained in a company's articles or in any contract with the company or otherwise.[256a]

(v) *Building Societies Act 1986*

4–80 The Building Societies Act 1986 s.110 renders void any provision in the rules or in any contract exempting any director, other officer or person employed as auditor of a building society from any liability which, by virtue of any rule of law, would otherwise attach to him in respect of the negligence, default, breach

---

[254] This provision does not apply to a person who travels "on a free pass": *Wilkie v L.P.T.B.* [1947] 1 All E.R. 258. Nevertheless, a free pass cannot protect the negligent driver, because he is not one of the parties to the contract: *Genys v Matthews* [1966] 1 W.L.R. 758. See also *Gore v Van der Lann* [1967] 2 Q.B. 31 (likewise a bus conductor); Odgers, "Strange Case of Mrs Gore" in 86 L.Q.R. 69.

[255] Carriage by Air (Supplementary Provisions) Act 1962 (SI 1967/479, 480, 803–810); Carriage by Air Acts (Application of Provisions) Order 1967 (SI 1967/480), as amended by the Carriage by Air Acts (Application of Provisions) (Overseas Territories) (Amendment) Order 1984 (SI 1984/701). See the application of the Order in *Holmes v Bangladesh Biman Corp* [1988] F.T.L.R. 534, CA.

[256] In *Holmes v Bangladesh Biman Corp* [1989] 2 A.C. 1112, it was held that the Schedule did not have extra-territorial effect. See Nelson-Jones, "Injuries and Death on Domestic Flights" in 140 New L.J. 1652.

[256a] The Act provides for certain exceptions: see s.532(2).

of duty or breach of trust of which he may be guilty in relation to the society. It was held in relation to s.30 of the Building Societies Act 1962 that it did not operate to exclude any duty of care owed in respect of a mortgage valuation by a building society to an applicant for a mortgage as regards the condition or value of the property that is intended to be taken as security.[257] By s.110(4) of the 1986 Act the court may grant relief in cases of "negligence, default, breach of duty or breach of trust" as it can under s.1157 of the Companies Act 2006.

(vi) *Solicitors Act 1974*

A solicitor can make an agreement in writing with a client as to remuneration **4–81** for contentious business,[258] but by ss.60(5) and (6) of the Solicitors Act 1974,

"(5) A provision in a contentious business agreement that the solicitor shall not be liable for his negligence, or that of any employee of his, shall be void if the client is a natural person who, in entering that agreement, is acting for purposes which are outside his trade, business or profession.

(6) A provision in a contentious business agreement that the solicitor shall be relieved from any responsibility to which he would otherwise be subject as a solicitor shall be void "A provision in a contentious business agreement that the solicitor shall not be liable for negligence, or that he shall be relieved from any responsibility to which he would otherwise be subject as a solicitor, shall be void."

(vii) *Law Reform (Personal Injuries) Act 1948*

The Law Reform (Personal Injuries) Act 1948 provides: **4–82**

"1.—(3) Any provision contained in a contract of service or apprenticeship, or in an agreement collateral thereto, (including a contract or agreement entered into before the commencement of this Act)[259] shall be void in so far as it would have the effect of excluding or limiting any liability of the employer in respect of personal injuries caused to the person employed or apprenticed by the negligence of persons in common employment with him."

(viii) *Others*

Additionally, an agreement shall be void which purports to restrict the duty of **4–83** a carrier to insure against liability for death or bodily injury to passengers by any antecedent agreement or understanding (whether or not intended to be legally binding) made between the parties[260]; and to exclude liability to employees in

---

[257] *Beaton v Nationwide Anglia BS* [1991] 38 E.G. 218, applying *Smith v Eric S. Bush* [1990] 1 A.C. 831.
[258] As to the difference between contentious and non-contentious business, see *Re A Solicitor* [1956] 1 Q.B. 155.
[259] July 5, 1948.
[260] s.1(2) of the Motor Vehicles (Passenger Insurance) Act 1971, which was repealed by s.148(3) of the Road Traffic Act 1972, and is now re-enacted in the Road Traffic Act 1988 s.149, had overridden the decision in *Bennett v Tugwell* [1971] 2 Q.B. 267; *Birch v Thomas* [1972] 1 W.L.R. 294 and other similar decisions. See *Gregory v Kelly* [1978] R.T.R. 426.

respect of injuries sustained, as a result of defective equipment, manufactured by others but provided for their use by their employers.[261]

On the other hand, there are instances where Parliament has expressly provided that there is no liability in respect of some particular damage suffered by a person, where there has been a voluntary assumption of the risk, for example, strict liability for dangerous animals[262]; and the common duty of care owed to visitors to premises.[263]

(ix) *The Unfair Contract Terms Act 1977*

4–84   The Unfair Contract Terms Act 1977[264] restricts the ability of a person to exclude or otherwise limit liability by prior consent, after February 1, 1978, when the Act came into force.[265] The Act's principal purpose is to control the exclusion or restriction of liability both in contract and for negligence, arising in the course of business. Accordingly, those situations, *outside* the course of business,[266] remain unaffected. The Act does bite upon liability for breach of obligations or duties arising (a) from things done by a person in the course of a business (whether that person's own business or another's); or (b) from the occupation of premises used for the occupier's business purposes,[267] except insofar as it concerns access to land which has been granted for recreational or educational purposes that form no part of the occupier's business interests.[268] It is immaterial for any purposes of Pt 1 of the Act whether the breach alleged was inadvertent or intentional or whether liability for it arose directly or vicariously.[269]

Section 2 of the Act provides:

"(1) A person cannot by reference to any contract term or to a notice given to persons generally or to particular persons exclude or restrict his liability for death or personal injury resulting from negligence.

(2) In the case of other loss or damage, a person cannot so exclude or restrict his liability for negligence except insofar as the term or notice satisfies the requirement of reasonableness.

---

[261] The Employer's Liability (Defective Equipment) Act 1969 s.1(2) and see Ch.10, para.10–54, below.

[262] s.5(2) of the Animals Act 1971 and see Ch.14, para.14–44, below.

[263] See Ch.8, para.8–71, below, for the provisions of s.2(5) of the Occupiers' Liability Act 1957. But contrast the provisions of the Defective Premises Act 1972 s.6(3), in respect of which see Ch.8, paras 8–123 to 8–137, below.

[264] For articles on the Act, see Melville, "Fundamental Breach after the Unfair Contract Terms Act" in 128 New L.J. 127; Murdoch, "Misstatement and the Unfair Contract Terms Act 1977" in 129 New L.J. 4.

[265] Unfair Contract Terms Act 1977 s.31.

[266] The term "business" is defined by s.14 as including "a profession and the activities of any government department or local or public authority." See *Clerk & Lindsell on Torts* (19th edn 2006), paras 3–105 et seq. and 10–16 et seq. The definition is not exclusionary so what amounts to a business will be an issue of fact.

[267] Unfair Contract Terms Act 1977 s.1(3).

[268] This exception was added by the Occupier's Liability Act 1984 s.2, which enables an occupier to restrict his civil liability wherever access to premises is granted as a matter of goodwill but not where it is granted in the way of business.

[269] Occupier's Liability Act 1984 s.1(4).

(3) Where a contract term or notice purports to exclude or restrict liability for negligence a person's agreement to or awareness of it is not of itself to be taken as indicating his voluntary acceptance of any risk."

"Negligence" for the purposes of Pt 1 of the Act is defined in s.1(1) and means   **4–85**
the breach of:

(a) any obligation, arising from the express or implied terms of a contract, to take reasonable care or exercise reasonable skill in the performance of the contract;

(b) any common law duty to take reasonable care or exercise reasonable skill (but not any stricter duty); and

(c) the common duty of care imposed by the Occupiers' Liability Act 1957.

It follows that an exemption clause is not subject to control so far as it excludes or restricts liability under the rule in *Rylands v Fletcher*.[270] Nevertheless, where the facts which give rise to strict liability under the rule also connote negligence, the exemption clause will fall to be controlled under Pt 1 of the Act to the same extent that it is relied upon otherwise to exclude or restrict liability for negligence.

As will be seen from the summary, where the loss or damage concerned does   **4–86**
not involve death or personal injury, the exclusion or restriction of liability for negligence by some contract term or notice is subject to a test of reasonableness. Section 11 defines the requirements of "reasonableness" for the purposes of Pt 1 of the Act, both in relation to the contract term and a notice, and refers to Sch.2, which specifies matters for application of the test of reasonableness. The guidelines consist of any of the following matters which are relevant on the given facts:

"(a) the strength of the bargaining positions of the parties relative to each other, taking into account (among other things) alternative means by which the customers' requirements could have been met;

(b) whether the customer received an inducement to agree to the term, or in accepting it had an opportunity of entering into a similar contract with the other persons, but without having to accept a similar term;

(c) whether the customer knew or ought reasonably to have known of the existence and extent of the term (having regard, among other things, to any custom of the trade and any previous course of dealing between the parties);

(d) where the term excludes or restricts any relevant liability if some condition is not complied with, whether it was reasonable at the time of the contract to expect that compliance with that condition would be practicable;

---

[270] (1868) L.R. 3 H.L. 330, for which see Ch.13, generally.

(e) whether the goods were manufactured, processed or adapted to the special order of the customer."

4–87   **Burden of proof.** Whoever claims that a contract term or notice satisfies the requirement of reasonableness bears the burden of proving that it does.[271] In relation to a notice, not being a notice which has contractual effect, s.11(3) of the Act provides that the requirement of reasonableness "is that it should be fair and reasonable to allow reliance on it, having regard to all the circumstances obtaining when the liability arose or (but for the notice) would have arisen". The reference to "all the circumstances" is a wide one and means that even a disclaimer in a standard form, in use for many years, may not be efficacious in excluding liability in a particular case.[272]

4–88   Section 3 deals with liability arising in contract and applies as between contracting parties where one of them deals as consumer or on the other's written standard terms of business. By s.4, a person dealing as consumer cannot by reference to any contract term be made to indemnify another person (whether a party to the contract or not) in respect of liability that may be incurred by the other for negligence or breach of contract, except insofar as the contract term satisfies the requirement of reasonableness. The provisions of ss.2–4 of the Act do not extend to any contract of insurance (including a contract to pay an annuity on human life) inter alia, for which latter see Sch.1. In *George Mitchell (Chester Hall) Ltd v Finney Lock Seeds Ltd*,[273] Lord Denning, in his last judgment as Master of the Rolls, said that the multitude of cases on exemption clauses should be done away with. It is the test of reasonableness,[274] which should apply.

4–89   **Nature of the agreement.** Except in employer and employee cases,[275] the question whether or not the agreement must be a legally binding contract does not appear to have been considered prior to 1968. Then, in *Buckpitt v Oates*,[276] where the child claimant was travelling as a passenger in the defendant's motor car, knowing full well that he was not covered by insurance, and an accident happened, it was held that the defence of volenti succeeded, because in all the circumstances he had in fact consented to the risk of harm. Further, it was held that, since the arrangement between the parties to the car's journey was not one intended to create a legal relationship, there was no legal contract of carriage. It

---

[271] Section 11(5). See, e.g. *South Western General Property Co Ltd v Marton* (1982) 263 E.G. 1090 (general conditions of sale in an auction catalogue, which purported to exclude liability for misrepresentation, did not satisfy the test of reasonableness).

[272] *First National Commercial Bank Plc v Loxleys* [1997] P.N.L.R. 211, CA (which concerned a standard form used by solicitors to reply to inquiries about a mortgage agreement between their client and the proposed lender).

[273] [1983] Q.B. 284, affirmed [1983] 2 A.C. 803. See "The case of the Heartless Cabbage" in 268 E.G. 61; Khan, "Avoiding Limitation Clauses" in 127 S.J. 653.

[274] See para.4–86, above.

[275] For employer and employee cases, generally, in the context of this defence, see para.4–95, below.

[276] [1968] 1 All E.R. 1145, followed on this point in *Bennett v Tugwell* [1971] 2 Q.B. 267 at 273–274.

would appear, therefore, that the agreement need be neither a legally binding one, which would be enforceable at law,[277] nor one supported by consideration.[278]

Agreement express or implied. As already explained, no question of volenti **4–90** non fit injuria can arise, unless it is held that the defendant did owe the claimant a duty of care.[279] Where a duty of care exists and there is an express agreement to exempt the defendant from the legal consequences of negligence, no particular difficulty arises.[280] It should be noted that an exemption clause will be construed strictly against the party seeking to rely on it.[281]

Examples where consent can be implied include participants in sporting **4–91** activities[282] when properly organised and conducted.[283] In simple negligence cases, as a generality, implied consent will be rare.[284] As Diplock L.J. explained:

"the maxim in the absence of the expressed contract has no application to negligence simpliciter where the duty of care is based solely upon proximity or 'neighbourship' in the Atkinian sense. The maxim in English law presupposes a tortious act by the defendant. The consent that is relevant is not consent to the risk of injury but consent to the lack of reasonable care that may produce that risk . . . and requires on the part of the plaintiff at the time at which he gives his consent full knowledge of the nature and extent of the risk that he ran."[285]

His Lordship adopted the words of Morris L.J. in an earlier decision[286] to the effect that "the plaintiff could not have agreed to run the risk that the defendant might be negligent for the plaintiff would only play his part after the defendant had been negligent".[287]

In *Reeves v Commissioner of Police of the Metropolis,*[288] the defence of volenti did not operate to relieve the defendants from liability for the suicide of

---

[277] Williams, *Joint Torts and Contributory Negligence*, inclined to this view.

[278] *Buckpitt v Oates* [1968] 1 All E.R. 1145 at 1147 and *Bennett v Tugwell* [1971] 2 Q.B. 267 at 274. In the latter case, however, the provisions of the Road Traffic Act 1988 s.149 have nullified the effect of prior consent given in such circumstances.

[279] See *Ashton v Turner* [1981] Q.B. 137 (no duty of care owed by one burglar to another, in relation to an act done in the course of the commission of the crime, but even if such a duty were owed the driver of their get-away car could rely upon the maxim as a complete defence). See also para.4–248 below.

[280] In a business context, see the discussion of s.2 of the Unfair Contract Terms Act 1977 para.4–87, above.

[281] *Wooldridge v Sumner* [1963] 2 Q.B. 43 at 66; *Scruttons Ltd v Midland Silicones Ltd* [1962] A.C. 446.

[282] Which are considered in more detail at para.4–99, below.

[283] e.g. football players impliedly consent to force being used, which normally would be expected during the game, but not to unlawful incidents such as a "punch-up" in a game of rugby: see *R. v Billinghurst* [1978] Crim. L.R. 553.

[284] i.e. establishing consent by the claimant not only to his taking on the risk of harm but also the risk of the defendant's negligence.

[285] *Wooldridge v Sumner* [1963] 2 Q.B. 43 at 69.

[286] i.e. *Baker v T.E. Hopkins & Son Ltd* [1959] 1 W.L.R. 966 at 976.

[287] *Wooldridge v Sumner* [1963] 2 Q.B. 43 at 70.

[288] [1998] 2 W.L.R. 401, CA (a flap on the door of the cell where the deceased was held was not closed thereby giving him the opportunity to strangle himself); appeal dismissed [2000] 1 A.C. 360 at 363.

a prisoner in their custody where his act in causing his own death was the very act which the duty cast upon the defendants required them to prevent.

4–92   **Effect of knowledge.** Implied agreement will not be found unless the claimant had full knowledge of the nature and extent of the risk to be run.[289] Even with such knowledge the claimant will not be prevented from recovering unless the circumstances are such as to show that he incurred the risk on terms that the loss should fall on him and not on some other person.[290] Where two drivers raced each other along a country road for a bet, and during the race their vehicles touched, causing a crash, it was held that they were equally negligent. A claim by a passenger in one of the cars was not defeated by the volenti rule: he was regarded as consenting so far as mechanical hazards were concerned, over which the drivers would have had no reasonable or immediate control, but had not consented as regards their respective acts of negligent driving.[291] Knowledge of the risk is, therefore, only one of the elements, which, together with the other circumstances, has to be taken into account in deciding whether an inference that the claimant agreed to assume the risk can be drawn. "Evidence of knowledge may sometimes be evidence of assumption of risk, but in the nature of things this need not always be so. Each case must be judged on its own facts."[292]

4–93   **Consent freely given.** For purposes of the law of torts generally, any act or statement, from which an inference can properly be drawn that consent has been given freely, will suffice.[293] Where the court finds as a fact that the claimant has consented to the risk, it is immaterial that he is from a foreign country[294] or a child.[295] On the other hand, where the claimant has given an unambiguous indication that consent to assuming the risk is not given, for example by asking whether the defendant is insured against passenger risk before accepting a lift, the defence, if raised, cannot succeed.[296] Further, the fact that the defender was a learner rider of a motor scooter and, so, was not permitted by law to carry a pillion passenger was not of itself sufficient basis for a plea that such passenger, namely the pursuer, had voluntarily assumed the risk of harm.[297]

4–94   **General application of the maxim.** The maxim is general in its operation and has no special application to cases that arise out of the relation between

---

[289] *Osborne v L. & N.W. Ry* (1888) 21 Q.B.D. 22, followed by the Court of Appeal in *White v Blackmore* [1972] 2 Q.B. 651; *Wooldridge v Sumner* [1963] 2 Q.B. 43 at 69, per Diplock L.J.

[290] It has often been pointed out that the maxim is "*volenti non fit injuria*" and not "*scienti non fit injuria*": *Yarmouth v France* (1887) 19 Q.B.D. 647, per Lord Esher M.R.

[291] *Vorster v Santam Insurance Co Ltd* (1973) (2) S.A. 186.

[292] *Kelly v Farrans Ltd* [1954] N.I. 41 at 47; *Smith v Baker* [1891] A.C. 325 (the defendant's employee was drilling holes in rock near a crane used for lifting stones over his head. He knew of the danger but continued at work, and was eventually injured by a stone which fell from the crane. He was held entitled to succeed. Lord Watson said at 355: "The question which has most frequently to be considered is not whether he [the claimant] voluntarily and rashly exposed himself to injury, but whether he agreed that, if injury should befall him, the risk was to be his and not his master's.")

[293] *Wilson v Darling Island Stevedoring & Lighterage Co* (1955) 95 C.L.R. 43 at 82; *Morrison v Union Steamship Co Ltd* [1964] N.Z.L.R. 468.

[294] *Geier v Kujawa* [1970] 1 Lloyd's Rep. 364.

[295] *Buckpitt v Oates* [1968] 1 All E.R. 1145. Similarly, see *Birch v Thomas* [1972] 1 W.L.R. 294.

[296] *Nettleship v Weston* [1971] 2 Q.B. 691.

[297] *Fowler v Tierney* (1974) S.L.T. (Notes) 23.

employer and employee.[298] In *Osborne v L. & N.W. Ry*,[299] the plaintiff was injured by falling on steps leading to the platform of a railway station. The steps were covered with snow, which had been trodden down and frozen over, and the plaintiff admitted that he knew they were dangerous in that condition. Nonetheless he was not volens nor guilty of contributory negligence. Wills J. said:

> "If the defendants desire to succeed on the ground that the maxim '*volenti non fit injuria*' is applicable, they must obtain a finding of fact 'that the plaintiff freely and voluntarily, with full knowledge of the nature and extent of the risk he ran, impliedly agreed to incur it'."[300]

This statement was expressly approved by the Privy Council in *Letang v Ottawa Electric Ry*,[301] where the facts were very similar. In *Slater v Clay Cross Co Ltd*,[302] the plaintiff was injured, owing to the negligence of the defendants' engine driver, as she was walking along a narrow tunnel on a railway track despite her knowledge of the danger involved. Denning L.J. observed:

> "Although it may be said that she voluntarily took the risk of danger from the running of the railway in the ordinary and accustomed way, nevertheless she did not take the risk of negligence by the driver. Her knowledge of the danger is a factor in contributory negligence, but is not a bar to the action."[303]

Employer and employee. In employer and employee cases, based on common law negligence, the defence of volenti must be applied with particular caution[304]:   **4–95**

> "a real assent to the assumption of the risk without compensation must be shown by the circumstances . . . If, however, a man acts under the compulsion of a duty, such consent should rarely, if ever, be inferred, because a man cannot be said to be 'willing' unless he is in a position to choose freely."[305]

The defence failed. The defence failed: where a driver was kicked by a horse,   **4–96** which he knew to be savage and about which he had complained to his foreman[306]; where a workman, employed by one employer, was injured by a bolt, which had been dropped negligently by another employer's workman, who was working above him in the same building[307]; where a workman, in descending from an elevated tramway, from which no ladder or other safe means of descending had been provided, slipped and was killed[308]; where a dock labourer,

---

[298] *Smith v Baker* [1891] A.C. 325 at 337, per Lord Halsbury, and at 360, per Lord Herschell. See also para.4–95, below.
[299] (1888) 21 Q.B.D. 220, followed in *White v Blackmore* [1972] 2 Q.B. 651. See also Ch.8, para.8–72, below.
[300] ibid. at 233–224, following the words of Lord Esher M.R. in *Yarmouth v France* (1887) 19 Q.B.D. 647 at 657.
[301] [1926] A.C. 725 at 731.
[302] [1956] 2 Q.B. 264. See *Smith v Austin Lifts Ltd* [1959] 1 W.L.R. 100 at 119.
[303] *Slater v Clay Cross Co Ltd* [1956] 2 Q.B. 271.
[304] *Bowater v Rowley Regis Corp* [1944] K.B. 476 at 480, per Goddard L.J.
[305] *Merrington v Ironbridge Metal Works Ltd* [1952] 2 All E.R. 1101 at 1103, per Hallett J.
[306] *Yarmouth v France* (1887) 19 Q.B.D. 647.
[307] *Thrussell v Handyside* (1888) 20 Q.B.D. 359.
[308] *Williams v Birmingham Battery and Metal Co* [1899] 2 Q.B. 338.

who was engaged in loading a ship, was injured when he fell off a rope ladder which he had to use because the fixed ladder in the ship's hold had been obstructed[309]; where a schoolmaster was injured by the bursting of a heating apparatus, which he knew to be defective and about which he had complained to the school managers[310]; where a commercial traveller was injured whilst attempting to start a motor car, supplied by his employers, well knowing that the starting gear was defective, because he had already complained about it[311]; where a carter was injured by his horse running away, knowing that it had run away on previous occasions and that he had protested against driving the horse.[312]

4-97 **The defence succeeded.** The defence succeeded: where a workman employed in repairing a house, which he knew to be damaged by blast, was injured by the collapse of a floor[313]; where scaffolding was moved, contrary to the foreman's explicit orders, whilst the claimant deliberately had remained on top of the platform for the ride along[314]; where a claimant purposely struck an unexploded shell with a sledgehammer, although he had recognised what it was, because he had been dared to do it for amusement by his fellow employee[315]; where the claimant was a willing passenger, aware of the risk of journeying at night in a jeep over hilly and rough terrain in British Columbia, and actively participated in the ride.[316]

4-98 **Breach of statutory duty.** Normally, the maxim has no application to an action which is founded on a breach of statutory duty[317] but there is a limited exception that arises when there has been a breach of statutory duty imposed personally on a fellow workman.[318] The claimant's consent in such an instance may be deemed to be a waiver of a right of action.[319] The employers of the party, who has so consented, may take the benefit and rely upon that waiver as a complete defence to the claim made against them, provided they were not themselves at fault. *I.C.I. Ltd v Shatwell* provides an illustration.[320] Two brothers, both experienced shot-firers, combined deliberately to disobey a statutory requirement at the defendant's quarry. Despite each knowing of the risk of carrying out a continuity test on an electrical circuit connected to the detonators, without first taking cover in a proper shelter, they chose to proceed. As a result, there was an explosion, in which they were both severely injured, and, in due

---

[309] *Monaghan v Rhodes & Son* [1920] 1 K.B. 487.
[310] *Abbott v Isham* (1920) 90 L.J.K.B. 309.
[311] *Baker v James* [1921] 2 K.B. 674.
[312] *Bowater v Rowley Regis Corp* [1944] K.B. 476.
[313] *Taylor v Sims* [1942] 2 All E.R. 375 (another and, it is submitted, a better ground for the decision was that the employer owed no duty to see that the house was safe to work in).
[314] *Bolt v Wm Moss & Sons* (1966) 110 S.J. 385.
[315] *O'Reilly v National Rail & Tramway Appliances Ltd* [1966] 1 All E.R. 499.
[316] *Kinney v Havemann* (1977) 1 W.W.R. 405.
[317] *Baddeley v Earl of Granville* (1887) 19 Q.B.D. 423. See further Ch.12, para.12–68, below.
[318] *O'Hanlon v Electricity Supply Board* [1969] I.R. 75 at 90.
[319] *I.C.I. v Shatwell* [1965] A.C. 656. See also para.4–110, below.
[320] See above. See also articles founded on *I.C.I. Ltd v Shatwell*; Munkman, "Breach of Statutory Duty by Workmam: Acceptance of the Risk" in 114 L.J. 715; Goodman, "*Volenti Non Fit Injuria*—Detestable Maxim?" in 235 L.T. 607; "*Volenti Non Fit Injuria*" in 1965 S.L.T. 137; Atiyah, "Causation, Contributory Negligence and *Volenti Non Fit Injuria*" in 43 Can. B.R. 609.

course, one sued the employers on account of the other's breach of statutory duty. The employers could only be liable upon the basis of vicarious liability, the duty being imposed on the two shot-firers personally.[321] Liability was not made out. Lord Pearce observed:

> "On the facts it was an implied term (to the benefit of which the employers are vicariously entitled) that George would not sue James for any injury that he might suffer, if an accident occurred. Had an officious bystander raised the possibility, can one doubt that George would have ridiculed it?"[322]

Sport.[323] Where a spectator is injured in the course of a cricket or football **4–99** match or, indeed, at any sporting occasion, either by one of the players or by the ball or its equivalent, an action for damages cannot succeed in tort without proof of negligence.[324] Proving a breach of duty may in such cases be as much a difficulty for the claimant as a defence of consent.

In *Wooldridge v Sumner*[325] an experienced horseman, while taking part in a **4–100** competition for heavyweight hunters at a horse show, galloped his horse, "Work of Art", so fast around a corner of the arena that centrifugal force caused the animal to follow a wide arc, out towards the edge of the course, where it plunged down a line of potted shrubs bordering the arena, to a point where the claimant, a photographer, was standing. Having no experience of horses, the claimant was alarmed, stumbled into the animal's path, and was injured. Diplock L.J. summarised the relevant principles and went on:

> "The practical result of this analysis of the application of the common law of negligence to participant and spectator would, I think be expressed by the common man in some such terms as these: 'A person attending a game or competition takes the risk of any damage caused to him by any act of a participant done in the course of and for the purpose of the game or competition notwithstanding that such act may involve an error of judgment or a lapse of skill, unless the participant's conduct is such as to evince

---

[321] *I.C.I. v Shatwell* [1965] A.C. 656 at 674–675, per Lord Reid; at 682–683, per Lord Hodson; at 683–687, per Lord Pearce and at 692, per Lord Donovan, followed in *Hugh v National Coal Board* (1977) S.C. 252 (despite the defenders' persistant efforts to stop the practice, a number of miners, including the pursuer, all of whom where in breach of their statutory duty under the regulations, jumped off a moving train. The pursuer was knocked down and injured in the rush).
[322] *I.C.I. v Shatwell* [1965] A.C. 688. Further see at 693, per Lord Donovan.
[323] For the duty of care in sports cases, see Ch.2, para.2–280, above.
[324] *Hall v Brooklands Auto-Racing Club* [1933] 1 K.B. 205 (motor car at motor racing track left the final straight and injured the plaintiff spectator; no liability since no negligence); *Potter v Carlisle and Cliftonville Golf Club Ltd* [1939] N.I. 114; *Murray v Harringay Arena Ltd* [1951] 2 K.B. 529 (child spectator at ice hockey match injured by the puck leaving the arena; no negligence so no liability). See also *Miller v Jackson* [1977] Q.B. 966 (the claimant's house and garden adjoined a cricket ground, from which balls were struck whenever the batsman hit a six).
[325] [1963] 2 Q.B. 43. the decision was criticised, see, e.g. Goodhart in 78 L.Q.R. 490. See further: "Volunteers and Rescuers" in 234 L.T. 159; "Injuries to Spectators in the Course of Sporting Activities" in 25 M.L.R. 738; "The Sportsmen's Charter" in 78 L.Q.R. 490. The case was distinguished in *Quire v Coates* [1964] S.A.S.R. 294 and *Rootes v Shelton* (1947) 41 A.L.J.R. 172.

a reckless disregard of the spectator's safety.'[326] The spectator takes the risk because such an act involves no breach of the duty of care owed by the participant to him. He does not take the risk by virtue of the doctrine expressed or obscured by the maxim *volenti non fit injuria . . .* "[327]

4–101   So, where a competitor in a motorcycle scramble riding at between 25 and 30 mph suddenly left the track and collided with spectators lined up against the rope of the spectators' enclosure, it was held that even though he was going all out to win, he owed a duty to bystanders not to show a reckless disregard for their safety; or to cause injury by an error of judgment which a reasonable competitor would not have made and which could not, in the stress of circumstances, reasonably be regarded as excusable.[328] In a similar case the defence of *volenti* did not succeed where spectators were ignorant of the risk of injury arising from the failure of the organisers of a "jalopy" meeting properly to rope off enclosures.[329]

4–102   **Participants in sport.**[330] In *Rootes v Shelton*,[331] it was held that where a participant in a game or pastime is injured by an act or omission of another participant, the existence and extent of a duty of care are to be determined in the light of all the circumstances, including the risks, which may reasonably be inferred to have been accepted, by the very fact of participation. The rules of the game are a relevant but not a conclusive factor. Where, during a motorcycle race, a sidecar passenger was injured when the cycle crashed, that being caused partly by the failure of the rear brakes, as a result of a defect that ought to and could have been rectified by its rider before the race began, his action for damages succeeded. It was held that the rider owed his passenger the normal standard of care and not the modified one which usually applied to competitors in a sport, because the negligence had occurred in the relative calm of the workshop and not during the hazard and excitement of the race.[332]

4–103   **Implying consent.** Consent may *sometimes* be implied between persons engaged in sport,[333] As Lord Denning M.R. said:

---

[326] A competitor in a race "is expected to go as fast as he can, so long as he is not foolhardy", per Lord Denning M.R. in *Wilks v Cheltenham Homeguard Motor Cycle and Light Car Club* [1971] W.L.R. 668 at 670. This modified standard of care did not apply unless the circumstances were such that the acts complained of were done in the rush and excitement of the sport, as where a motorcycle rider missed a gear, when approaching a hairpin bend in a race and crashed: *Harrison v Vincent* [1982] R.T.R. 8, CA. See Kovats, "Sportsman's Charter Revoked" in 115 S.J. 824. But see in relation to "reckless disregard" Ch.2 para.2–281, above.
[327] *Wooldridge v Sumner* [1963] 2 Q.B. 43 at 68–69.
[328] *Wilks v Cheltenham Homeguard Motor Cycle & Light Car Club*, n.319, above; applied in *Evans v Waitemata District Pony Club* [1972] N.Z.L.R. 773. See Ch.2 para.2–282, also Ch.8, below, paras 8–86 to 8–88.
[329] *White v Blackmore* [1972] 2 Q.B. 652.
[330] See also Ch.2, para.2–281, above.
[331] (1967) 41 A.L.J.R. 172. A water skier brought an action against the driver of the towing speedboat, where he, one of a group of skiers which included the driver, was performing a complicated manoeuvre and was injured by a collision with a stationary obstruction of which the driver had given him no warning. It was held that the onus was on the driver to establish voluntary acceptance of a risk not inherent in the pastime.
[332] *Harrison v Vincent* [1982] R.T.R. 8, CA.
[333] *R. v Coney* (1882) 8 Q.B.D. 534.

"I agree that in an ordinary fight with fists there is no cause of action to either of them for any injury suffered. The reason is that each of the participants in a fight voluntarily takes upon himself the risk of incidental injuries to himself. *Volenti non fit injuria.* But he does not take on himself the risk of a savage blow out of all proportion to the occasion. The man who strikes a blow of such severity is liable in damages unless he can prove accident or self-defence."[334]

By analogy similar reasoning may apply to the minor violence that can be characterised as "horseplay". Consent may be implied between willing participants in horseplay, where what the defendant does is within what might be taken to be the tacit understanding of the parties or within the conventions of the game.[335]

In the context of golf, *volenti* did not avail the defendant where he caused   **4–104** injury to his caddy when swinging a golf club in demonstration.[336] The agreement to act as caddy did not extend to the risk of what happened.[337] Nor did the defence succeed where a ballet dancer enrolled in a judo class and in the course of the first lesson had his arm broken, the instructor having allowed what should have been practice to turn into dangerous competition.[338]

In *King v Redlich*[339] the claimant, who was not yet wearing his protective   **4–105** helmet, suffered a severe head injury during the warm-up prior to the start of an ice-hockey match. As he was skating out from behind the goal, the defendant, who had delayed momentarily to enable him to get clear, took a practice shot. The puck hit the post and ricocheted, striking the claimant. The Court of Appeal of British Columbia, held that the claimant should be deemed to have accepted the risk of injury, because practice shots at goal during warm-up were a normal part of the game. Further, although the defendant had seen the claimant and thereby realised there was some increased risk, he had responded appropriately by the delay in making his shot and could not be expected to have foreseen the ricochet. Accordingly, the claim failed.

Promoters of sport. The occupiers of sporting premises or the promoters of   **4–106** sport on such premises owe the same duty of care to lawful visitors, as any occupier namely the "common duty of care," which is examined in Chapter 8.[340] It is a question of fact in each case whether or not the spectator or participant who is present upon the premises in question has agreed to take upon himself the relevant risk.[341]

---

[334] *Lane v Holloway* [1968] 1 Q.B. 379 at 386–387.

[335] *Blake v Galloway* [2004] 1 W.L.R 2844, CA.

[336] *Cleghorn v Oldham* (1927) 43 T.L.R. 465, referred to in *Wooldridge v Sumner* [1963] 2 Q.B. 43 at 55–56. Also see *Ratcliffe v Whitehead* [1933] 3 W.W.R. 447 and *Hollerbone v Barnard* [1954] 2 D.L.R. 278.

[337] The judge spoke in terms only of express agreement but made the point that no authority had been cited to him.

[338] *Conrad v ILEA* (1966) 116 New L.J. 1630; on appeal the decision was reversed on the facts only and not on the principle involved: (1967) 111 S.J. 684.

[339] [1986] 4 W.W.R. 567.

[340] See especially Ch.8, paras 8–86 to 8–88, below.

[341] See Ch.8, paras 8–71 to 8–74, below.

Illustrations

4–107   A rugby footballer was held to have accepted willingly the risk of playing the game on the defendant's pitch which, although it complied with the byelaws of the Rugby Football League, had a concrete wall running at a distance of seven feet three inches away from and along the touchline.[342]

On the other hand, the defence was unsuccessful: where the driver of a racing car suffered injury in a crash caused by dangerous and inadequately protected flower bed running alongside the track, the driver being unaware of the nature and extent of the risk he was running[343]; also where claimant slipped on the highly polished floor of a hall in which physical training classes were being conducted, since he had not agreed to take upon himself the risk of slipping on a floor not reasonably fit for the purpose.[344]

4–108   **Other cases.** Although a fireman, who is attending a fire in the course of his duty, undertakes to bear the ordinary risks of fire, he does not undertake to accept without compensation the risk of being injured in an explosion caused by negligence of the occupier of a building on fire.[345] Where a lighterman, who was working for his employers but using the facilities of the defendant Board, was injured as a result of the latter's negligence, it was held that it could not properly be said that he had incurred the risk freely and voluntarily.[346] Likewise, a policeman, who used his vehicle as a road block to stop an escaping motorist, did not voluntarily assume the risk of injury resulting therefrom, when that motorist, driving at high speed, crashed into the car.[347] When the claimant delivered a valuable fur coat to the defendants' shop, where it was put on display in the shop window all day and night, and was stolen in a "smash and grab" raid, it was held that the defendants had been negligent in taking an unjustifiable risk and they could not rely upon the principle of *volenti*.[348]

4–109   **"Volenti" distinguished from contributory negligence.** Prior to 1945, the distinction between consent and contributory negligence was of no practical importance, because at common law each was a complete defence to the

---

[342] *Simms v Leigh RFC* [1969] 2 All E.R. 923.

[343] *Latchford v Spedeworth International, The Times*, October 11, 1983.

[344] *Gillmore v L.C.C.* [1938] 4 All E.R. 331.

[345] *Merrington v Ironbridge Metal Works Ltd* [1952] 2 All E.R. 1101. See further *Hartley v British Railways Board* (1981) 125 S.J. 169 (the defendants were liable for exposing a fireman to an unnecessary hazard by misinforming him as to the object of his going into the loft of premises on fire). Also, *Salmon v Seafarer Restaurants Ltd* [1983] 1 W.L.R. 1264 (a fireman attending the scene of a fire started negligently who sustained injuries in fighting the flames was able to sue the person who caused the fire: his own professional skills did not debar him from claiming damages). See, to the like effect: *Ogwo v Taylor* [1988] A.C. 431: the "rescue" principle in negligence (Ch.2, para.2–259, above) applies to the emergency services, as well as to ordinary members of the public. See Arnheim, "Playing with Fire" in 132 S.J. 1319; also Ch.2, paras 2–312, 2–313 (rescue services generally).

[346] *Burnett v British Waterways Board* [1972] 1 W.L.R. 1329.

[347] *Hambley v Shepley* (1967) 63 D.L.R. (2d) 94.

[348] *Saunders (Mayfair) Furs v Davies* (1965) 109 S.J. 922.

plaintiff's claim.[349] After 1945, however, it became necessary to be able to distinguish them, because consent continued to remain a total defence unlike contributory negligence, which operated chiefly to reduce damages in proportion to the degree of fault, by virtue of the provisions of the Law Reform (Contributory Negligence) Act 1945.[350] A number of points of distinction arise.

First, while contributory negligence has always been a defence to a breach of statutory duty, *volenti* was not,[351] at least until *I.C.I. Ltd v Shatwell*[352] when a limited exception emerged to the rule that a person cannot consent to dispense with a statutory duty imposed on the defendant. It arises where the facts are such that they amount to a waiver of the right of action by the claimant, provided always that this does not contravene public policy.[353] Secondly, a claimant may be consenting to a breach of duty while at the same time taking care for his own safety,[354] although for him to be guilty of contributory negligence he must have been careless for his own safety. Thirdly, a claimant may be guilty of contributory negligence where he ought to have known of a danger confronting him, whether or not he actually knew of it. He cannot be held to have been consenting to a breach of duty, unless it can be proved that he had full knowledge both of the nature as well as the extent of the risk involved.   **4–110**

Three different contexts. Assuming negligence on the part of the defendant, the defence of *volenti* can be considered in three types of circumstance: **4–111**

(i) where the claimant does not see a danger created by the negligence of the defendant, although he ought to have seen it;

(ii) where the claimant does see the danger and decides to run the risk of it; and

(iii) where the claimant sees the danger and agrees to exempt the defendant from liability.

(i) *Claimant does not see danger*

In this class of cases the claimant does not see a danger created by the defendant's negligence, although it should have been seen had reasonable care been taken. Such a failure is likely to be regarded as contributory negligence and the extent to which it reduces the damages which the claimant can recover will   **4–112**

---

[349] Indeed, it was common to find them both pleaded, each in the alternative, e.g. *Cutler v United Dairies* [1933] 2 K.B. 297; *Haynes v Harwood* [1935] 1 K.B. 146, but cf. *Dann v Hamilton* [1939] 1 K.B. 509. (Lord Asquith explained later in an article in (1953) 69 L.Q.R. 317 why the defence was not raised.)

[350] See para.4–03 et seq., above.

[351] *Baddeley v Earl of Granville* (1887) 19 Q.B.D. 423.

[352] [1965] A.C. 656, followed in *O'Reilly v National Rail and Tramway Appliances Ltd* [1966] 1 All E.R. 499 and *Hugh v N.C.B.* (1977) S.C. 252. Further see employer and employee cases, para.4–95, above.

[353] See para.4–96, above.

[354] *Prior v Kyle* (1965) 52 D.L.R. (2d) 272 at 281.

depend upon an application of the principles relevant to that defence.[355] *Volenti* has no application, because the claimant has simply not perceived there is a risk to be run.

(ii) *Claimant sees danger and decides to run the risk*

4–113   Here, the claimant does see a danger created by the defendant's negligence and decides to run the risk of it. Again, without more, the relevant principles are those of contributory negligence rather than *volenti*. To say that a person who negligently creates any risk or danger, however slight, thereby imposes upon those who decide to take the risk the burden of acting at their peril, is clearly wrong. So, railway undertakers were liable in negligence where the claimant, who had taken a friend's luggage to a compartment on a train, jumped from it as it moved off, no signal having been given of its impending departure.[356] The defence also failed in *Behrens v Bertram Mills Circus Ltd*,[357] Devlin J. saying:

> "If a man is on the highway and he sees elephants approaching in procession, the law does not require him to elect between turning down a side street or accepting the risk of their misbehaviour if he goes on; but if he sees them stampeding and remains where he is because he considers that he has as much right to the highway as they have, he might fail to recover [in his action for damages]."

4–114   Further illustrations can be found in the "rescue" cases where the claimant sustains injury after deliberately running the risk of a danger created by the defendant's negligence, in order to assist a third party. He has not consented to that risk which has been created by the defendant's breach of duty. In such a case the claimant will succeed in his action, *volenti* is not a defence, and the only question will be whether in some way the claimant has behaved unreasonably so as to give rise to a finding of contributory negligence.[358]

4–115   So, in *Haynes v Harwood*,[359] the claimant recovered damages because his injuries were the natural and probable consequences of the defendants' negligence, and the maxim *volenti non fit injuria* did not apply. There was discussion of a suggested legal or moral duty to save a life put in peril by another's negligence, but the principle remains that there is no legal duty to take active steps to prevent someone from being injured by the negligence of a third person.[360] The so-called moral duty, which depends on the relationship of the rescuer to the rescued and the imminence and gravity of the danger, is an element to be taken into account in deciding whether the act of the rescuer was the reasonable and probable consequence of the defendants' negligence. If the

---

[355] See para.4–72 et seq., above.
[356] *Caterson v Commissioner for Railways* (1972) 128 C.L.R. 99 (there was no finding of contributory negligence).
[357] [1957] 2 Q.B. 1 at 20.
[358] For contributory negligence in rescue cases see para.4–51, above.
[359] [1935] 1 K.B. 146 (the plaintiff was a policeman, who was injured in the course of stopping the defendants' horses that were bolting down a street, in which there was a large number of people, including children).
[360] per Swift J. in *Brandon v Osborne, Garrett & Co* [1924] 1 K.B. 548 at 554, per Maugham L.J. in *Haynes v Harwood* [1935] 1 K.B. 146 at 161.

person endangered is unable to save himself because of age, infirmity or ignorance of the impending danger, it is a natural and probable consequence of the negligence which has created the danger, that some other person will try to effect a rescue.

> "In deciding whether such a rescuer is justified in putting himself into a position of such great peril, the law has to measure the interests which he sought to protect and the other interests involved. We have all heard of the reasonable man who the law postulates in certain circumstances; the reasonable man here must be endowed with qualities of energy and courage, and he is not to be deprived of a remedy because he has in a marked degree a desire to save human life when in peril. So regarded, the present plaintiff was not acting unreasonably in the risks he took."[361]

The same result will follow whether or not the rescuer is a policeman.[362] Where a ship comes to the scene of a collision between other vessels, in order to rescue life, and is itself damaged through one of the other ships colliding with it, its owners' action for damages will not fail on the ground that it had voluntarily assumed the risk.[363]

A rescuer is not to be denied a remedy solely because the risk which is taken **4–116** is not of the same kind as that run by the person whom he is seeking to rescue. Hence, where a volunteer assisted in the rescue work at a serious rail disaster which had been caused by the defendants' negligence, it was held that he was entitled to recover damages for the nervous shock that he had suffered as a result of his frightful experience.[364] The rescuer, incidentally, owes a duty to carry out his rescue operations with reasonable care.[365]

The likelihood of the defence of *volenti* succeeding where the claimant has **4–117** been engaged in a rescue was considered by Morris L.J. in *Baker v T. E. Hopkins & Sons Ltd.*[366] He said[367] that if a man:

> " . . . actuated by an impulsive desire to save life acts bravely and promptly and subjugates any timorous over-concern for his own well-being or comfort, I cannot think that it would be either rational or seemly to say that he freely and voluntarily agreed to incur the risks of the situation which had been created by [another man's] negligence."

The fact is, it is logically inappropriate that *volenti* should be a defence in these **4–118** situations because to make the defence out the defendant will in effect be relying on the same circumstances which found the rescuer's claim. Those circumstances provide the basis for the rescuer/claimant to sue. The negligence of the defendant

---

[361] per Maugham L.J. in *Haynes v Harwood* [1935] 1 K.B. 146 at 162.
[362] *Morgan v Aylen* [1942] 1 All E.R. 489.
[363] *The Gusty and The Daniel M.* [1940] P. 159.
[364] *Chadwick v British Railways Board* [1967] 1 W.L.R. 912.
[365] *Horsley v Maclaren; The Ogopogo* [1971] 2 Lloyd's Rep. 410. See Ch.2, para.2–262, above.
[366] [1959] 1 W.L.R. 966, CA (a doctor attempted to rescue the lives of two men, who had been overcome by carbon monoxide poisoning, whilst working down a well, but himself became affected by the gas and died. It was held that his administrators were not prevented from recovering damages).
[367] *Baker v T.E. Hopkins & Sons Ltd* [1959] 1 W.L.R. 976.

in creating the emergency gives rise to an independent duty owed to any person reasonably attempting rescue. That duty is quite independent of the duty which the defendant owed the victim. In *Videan v British Transport Commission*,[368] Lord Denning M.R. stated:

> "the right of the rescuer is an independent right and is not derived from that of the victim. The victim may have been guilty of contributory negligence—or his right may be excluded by contractual stipulation—but still the rescuer can sue. So also the victim may, as here, be a trespasser and excluded on that ground, but still the rescuer can sue. Foreseeability is necessary, but not foreseeability of the particular emergency that arose."[369]

It might be added that the independent right of the rescuer may not be defeated by the suggestion that he willingly undertook the hazard, where that is the factual basis of the right which he asserts.

4-119   *Volenti* has not provided the defendant with a defence in cases of attempts to save property, whether belonging to a third party,[370] the rescuer himself[371] or, even, the defendant.[372] Consistent with the principles referred to above, the claimant who has made such an attempt will not have any award of damages reduced for contributory negligence unless he assumed an unreasonable risk in the circumstances. When a fire occurs, it is reasonable to foresee that volunteers will arrive at the premises and may be injured, whilst attempting to rescue either persons or property.[373] When a guard of a goods train was fatally injured, while trying to save his train from a collision with some wagons, which had run away owing to the defendants' negligence, his representatives were held entitled to recover damages on the finding that his attempt to save his employers' property was justifiable and a natural and probable consequence of the defendants' negligence.[374] Again, where a servant of some wagon repairers, on seeing that a railway company's wagon was on fire, went to try to extinguish the fire and was injured, he was held entitled to recover damages.[375]

However, even the rescuer of property can owe its owner a duty to take reasonable care.[376]

(iii) *Claimant sees the danger and exempts defendant from liability*

4-120   In this last of the three situations, the claimant sees the danger created by the defendant's negligence, and agrees, either expressly or by implication, to exempt the defendant from liability for any damage sustained as a result of that danger materialising. This is the only case in which the maxim *volenti non fit injuria* can afford a defence. If it applies, its effect is to prevent the claimant from succeeding

---

[368] [1963] 2 Q.B. 650.
[369] *Videan v British Transport Commission* [1963] 2 Q.B. 669.
[370] *Russell v McCabe* [1962] N.Z.L.R. 392.
[371] *Hutterley v Imperial Oil Co and Calder* (1956) 3 D.L.R. (2d) 719.
[372] *Hyett v G.W. Ry* [1948] 1 K.B. 345.
[373] *Russell v McCabe* [1962] N.Z.L.R. 396. See also *D'Urso v Sanson* [1939] 4 All E.R. 26.
[374] *Steel v Glasgow Iron and Steel Co* (1944) S.C. 237.
[375] *Hyett v G.W. Ry* [1948] 1 K.B. 345.
[376] *The Tojo Maru* [1972] A.C. 242.

in an action for damages. While it is sometimes said that the maxim applies if the claimant consents to run the risk, this is accurate only so long as it is understood that consent means an agreement[377] and the risk the claimant is agreeing to run is that of the defendant's negligence. It has been said that the maxim implies an election on the part of the claimant, rather than some legally binding contract.[378] Given these requirements, it must be a rare case in which agreement sufficient to found the defence can be established.

Volunteers and causation. In the three situations dealt with above, the   **4–121**
claimant is sometimes referred to as a "volunteer"in justifying a refusal to award damages. In strict usage however, and apart from a case in contract, the term should be used in this way only when the claimant has done something to break the chain of causation between the defendant's negligence and the damage. In such a case the claimant's action amounts to "a new intervening cause"[379] and the principles are the same whether the act in question was that of the claimant or a third party. In particular, there is no need to invoke the principles of *volenti*. The point may be illustrated by the facts of *Ilott v Wilkes*.[380] The claimant was a trespasser[381] who was shot by a spring-gun after entering the defendants' wood with the knowledge that spring-guns were set there. It was held that his action for damages could not succeed, because *volenti* applied and he had voluntarily exposed himself to the risk. But there was no need to invoke *volenti*. The claimant was a "volunteer", in the sense that his trespass was both wrongful and deliberate, and the injury he suffered was a consequence of his own breach of duty, not because he agreed to assume the risk of any breach of duty owed to him by the defendant.

Anticipating a breach of duty. In the cases already considered, the defendant   **4–122**
negligently created a danger before the claimant responded, so that the question arose whether by so responding the claimant had assumed an unreasonable risk. There may, also, be cases when the claimant acts first and the defendant's negligence follows afterwards, where the question will become whether the claimant should have forseen the possibility of negligence by the defendant and is thereby prevented from recovering damages.

In *Dann v Hamilton*,[382] the claimant knew that the defendant was drunk but   **4–123**
nevertheless chose to go as a passenger in a motor car driven by him and was injured in a collision caused by his drunk driving. In the absence of any allegations against her of contributory negligence, the claimant succeeded and it

---

[377] See para.4–73, above.
[378] See para.4–89, above.
[379] *Cutler v United Dairies* [1933] 2 K.B. 297 is an example of this.
[380] (1820) 3 B. & Ald. 304.
[381] For the duty owed to a trespasser, before and after the Occupiers' Liability Act 1984, see generally, Ch.2, para.2–273, also Ch.8, paras 8–138 to 8–160, below.
[382] [1939] 1 K.B. 509. In *Nettleship v Weston* [1971] 2 Q.B. 691, Salmon L.J. (at 704) considered that *Dann v Hamilton* was not correctly decided.

was held that *volenti* did not to apply.[383] She had not consented to negligent driving. Although it was suggested that extreme drunkenness might give a different result[384] it is difficult to see the logic in a distinction based on whether the driver was partially or completely drunk.[385]

4–124   One way of looking at such a situation is to ask the question whether the claimant is volens at the moment of the inebriated driver's negligent driving, which gives an obvious answer: no-one would consent to the driver's breach of duty at that moment. But in other jurisdictions it has been suggested that the time at which the test should be applied is when the claimant enters the vehicle, knowing of the defendant's condition. One suggested solution[386] has been that a drunken driver owes no duty to a passenger to drive safely, so the passenger has no claim.[387] Overall it would seem more satisfactory to approach these cases in terms of contributory negligence than willing assumption of risk.

4–125   *Volenti* did not apply where the defendant's mother-in-law, who knew very well that her daughter-in-law held no driving licence of any sort and had only minimal driving experience, persuaded her to drive the car on a short journey to some shops, in the course of which she lost control of the vehicle and crashed.[388] By way of contrast, the maxim did apply in the case of a passenger, who for amusement agreed voluntarily to go on a flight in a light aircraft flown by a friend with whom he had imbibed a very considerable amount of alcohol. It was held that he had been capable of appreciating the nature and extent of the risk of embarking on such a flight and, so, had engaged in an intrinsically and obvious dangerous activity. By accepting the risk of serious injury, he had impliedly

---

[383] In any event the defence of *volenti* has been abrogated in relation to passengers in motor vehicles which are covered by comprehensive insurance, by virtue of the Road Traffic Act 1988 s.149, re-enacting the earlier provisions of s.148(3) of the Road Traffic Act 1972.

[384] *Dann v Hamilton*, n.382, above.

[385] In the Australian case of *Insurance Commissioner v Joyce* (1948) 77 C.L.R. 39, noted in 65 L.Q.R. 20, *Dann v Hamilton* was dissented from and not followed, but the court in *Joyce* appear to have drawn no distinction between voluntarily running a known risk and voluntarily agreeing to relieve the other party from liability if the risk resulted in injury.

[386] In the Canadian case of *Miller v Decker* [1957] 9 D.L.R. (2d) 1, a majority of the Sup. Ct of Canada held that the time to test whether the appellant accepted the risk was when he and the defendant formulated a plan to "go beering", not when they both subsequently left a dance hall, drunk. The appellant was *volens* and could not recover. On the other hand, in *Stein v Lehnert* (1962) 31 D.L.R. (2d) 673, the claimant was not *volens* where she had gone with the defendant to a night club, he had drunk to excess and later, crashed his car, injuring her. The Manitoba Court of Appeal held that the test was whether the claimant had agreed to absolve the defendant from his duty to take care, not whether she willingly ran the risk of danger from his driving whilst intoxicated. She was, however, guilty of contributory negligence. In similar circumstances, in *Owens v Brimmell* [1977] Q.B. 859, the claimant passenger's share of the blame was assessed at 20 per cent.

[387] See, per Salmon L.J. in *Nettleship v Weston* [1971] 2 Q.B. 691 at 704. In *Pitts v Hunt* [1991] 1 Q.B. 24, no duty of care was found to be owed in the circumstances.

[388] *Cook v Cook* (1987) 41 S.A.S.R. 1 (a majority decision but the plaintiff's contributory negligence was assessed at 70 per cent as against the driver's 30 per cent); also *Donelan v Donelan and General Accident Fire and Life Assurance* [1993] P.I.Q.R. P205 (a passenger's contributory negligence was assessed at 75 per cent where he instigated the driving by his drunken girlfriend of a car, with which, to his knowledge, she was unfamiliar).

waived the right to claim damages for injuries caused by the pilot's negligence in crashing the aircraft.[389] Further, the maxim applied in the case of three young men, who spent the evening together drinking to an excess, then committed a burglary and sought to escape from the scene of the crime in a car, which crashed as a result of the driver's dangerous driving.[390]

Where a claimant walked along a narrow tunnel on a railway track over land,   **4–126** owned and occupied by the defendants, and was injured by a train driven by the defendants' employee, his claim succeeded, with a deduction for contributory negligence of 40 per cent. The driver had been negligent in failing to observe instructions to whistle and to slow down when entering the tunnel.[391] Of the defence of *volenti non fit injuria*, Denning L.J., following *Dann v Hamilton*,[392] said[393]:

> "Applying that decision to this case, it seems to me that when this lady walked into the tunnel, although it may be said that she voluntarily took the risk of danger from the running of the railway in the ordinary and accustomed way, nevertheless she did not take the risk of negligence in the driver. Her knowledge of the danger is a factor in contributory negligence, but is not a bar to the action."

A patient who submits to a surgical operation, agrees to accept the risk of the   **4–127** operation, but does not agree to accept the additional risk of the surgeon's negligence. However, surgical operations can be justified, according to the circumstances, both on the basis that consent nullifies wrongfulness and/or on necessity.[394] A man, who from drunkenness or any other cause, lies down in the middle of a busy street, does not agree to accept the risk of being run over but, if that happens, his failure to recover damages in full will be on the ground of contributory negligence.[395]

3.—INEVITABLE ACCIDENT[396]

Generally. In some cases the facts proved by the claimant raise a prima facie   **4–128** case of negligence, and an evidential burden is thrown upon the defendant to

---

[389] *Morris v Murray* [1991] 2 Q.B. 6.
[390] *Ashton v Turner* [1981] Q.B. 137. See Rowe, "Illegality as a Defence in Tort" in 131 New L.J. 570.
[391] *Slater v Clay Cross Co Ltd* [1956] 2 Q.B. 264.
[392] [1939] 1 K.B. 509.
[393] *Slater v Clay Cross Co Ltd*, n.391, above at 271.
[394] *Bravery v Bravery* [1954] 1 W.L.R. 1169 (consent to sterilisation). Where anaesthesia was administered against a patient's express wish, see *Beausoleil v La Communauté des Soeurs de la Charité de la Providence* (1964) 53 D.L.R. (2d) 65.
[395] For the distinction between volenti non fit injuria and contributory negligence, see para.4–109, above.
[396] See Bing, "Inevitable Accident in the Law of Negligence" in [1977] 1 M.L.J. 6.

establish facts negativing his liability.[397] One way in which this can be done is by proving inevitable accident.

4–129   **Meaning of inevitable accident.** Inevitable accident arises where a person performs some action, not in itself unlawful, which causes damage without negligence or intent. In a maritime case it was put as follows: "An inevitable accident in point of law is this: viz., that which the party charged with the offence could not possibly prevent by exercise of ordinary care, caution, and maritime skill."[398] The principle operates equally in cases on land.[399]

4–130   It should be said that the ambit of such a defence has been called into question. To quote the words of Lord Greene[400]:

> "I do not feel myself assisted by considering the meaning of the phrase 'inevitable accident.' I prefer to put the problem in a more simple way, namely, has it been established that the driver of the car was guilty of negligence?
> In such a case, loss lies where it falls, unless it can be shown that it was caused by a breach on the part of some other person of a duty to take care, or of some duty making it wrongful for him to have inflicted the loss upon the person who has suffered it."

4–131   In the result, while the defence may be said to be established,[401] there are only a few reported instances apart from Admiralty cases where it has succeeded. There can be no inevitable accident unless the court concludes that something happened over which the defendant had no control and the effect of which could not have been avoided by the exercise of care and skill[402]; indeed, the defence cannot be relied upon, where the risk is reasonably foreseeable.[403] In *Ritchie's Car Hire Ltd v Bailey*,[404] the defence did succeed where the defendant driver established that his collision with a kerbside tree, in the early hours of the morning, was caused by a swerve to avoid a cat which suddenly ran out into the road from his near side. There have been cases of inevitable accident where a collision between motor vehicles was caused by a latent defect in one of them.[405]

---

[397] In relation to an evidential burden, see Ch.6, para.6–02, below.
[398] *The Marpesia* (1872) L.R. 4 PC 212 at 220, citing Dr Lushington in *The Virgil* (1843) 2 W.Rob. 201.
[399] *The Schwan* [1892] P. 419 at 434.
[400] In *Browne v De Luxe Car Services* [1941] K.B. 549 at 552.
[401] *Fawkes v Poulson & Son* (1892) 8 T.L.R. 725. The test in *The Marpesia* (1872) L.R. 4 PC 212, was applied but it is not clear how the Court of Appeal felt itself able to set aside the verdict of the jury on the facts as reported.
[402] *The Albano* [1892] P. 419, per Lord Esher M.R.
[403] *Bell Telephone Co of Canada v The Ship Mar-Tirenno* (1974) 52 D.L.R. (3d) 702 (an underwater cable was damaged when a ship broke loose from its moorings at a pier, as a result of tidal ice, and an anchor had to be dropped. The ship's captain had been warned of the danger of ice and it was held that the onus was on him to establish that all reasonable precautions against the danger had been taken and there were no reasonable alternatives to securing the ship to the pier).
[404] (1958) 108 L.J. 348.
[405] *Winnipeg Electric Co v Geel* [1932] A.C. 690 at 694. However, for the high standard of care expected of vehicle owners, see *Henderson v Henry E. Jenkins & Sons* [1970] A.C. 282.

A defence to trespass. In addition to being a defence in actions of negligence, **4–132**
inevitable accident is a defence in trespass to the person, and in trespass to land
or goods on or adjoining the highway. In *Stanley v Powell*,[406] where a member
of a shooting party fired at a pheasant and one of the shotgun pellets glanced off
the bough of a tree and wounded the plaintiff, it was held that the defendant was
not negligent in firing as he did and the claim failed. The same result followed
in a claim in trespass where, without negligence on the part of the person in
control of the animals, horses bolted onto the claimant's land.[407]

Automatism, sudden illness or death. The sudden death of the driver of a **4–133**
motor vehicle from coronary thrombosis or a severe cerebral haemorrhage, as the
result of which there is an accident involving other vehicles, can amount to
inevitable accident.[408] The circumstances in which the illness develops must be
such as to found a defence of automatism, that is, amount to a situation where
what happened was wholly beyond the driver's control.[409] The driver must be
unaware of the condition which disables him.[410] However, even with awareness,
there may be a defence. In *Waugh v Allan*[411] it was accepted that a reasonable
man in the driver's position would have thought that preliminary symptoms
related merely to a gastric attack and not to coronary thrombosis, and he would
not have expected his driving ability to be impaired so as to cause danger to other
road users. But the defence did not succeed in *The Saint Angus*[412] when the
owners of a motor-ship, which collided with a steamship after the master had
fainted at the wheel, were liable because there was no other person on deck to
take over control from him.

Inevitable accident and act of God. Inevitable accident is not the same as **4–134**
"act of God." That term is appropriate where what happens is "due to natural
causes directly and exclusively without human intervention",[413] while inevitable
accident is not restricted in any such way.

---

[406] [1891] 1 Q.B. 86, approved in *NCB v Evans* [1951] 2 K.B. 861, notwithstanding some academic criticism.
[407] *Holmes v Mather* (1875) L.R. 10 Ex. 261; *Manzoni v Douglas* (1880) 6 Q.B.D. 145; *Hammack v White* (1862) 11 C.B.(N.S.) 588; *Gayler & Pope Ltd v Davies & Son* [1924] 2 K.B. 75. See also *Tillett v Ward* (1882) 10 Q.B.D. 17 (cattle being driven).
[408] *Ryan v Youngs* [1938] 1 All E.R. 522. But in *Boomer v Penn* (1965) 52 D.L.R. (2d) 673, the defendant, a diabetic, failed to prove that his driving was not a conscious act of will, and the defence of inevitable accident failed.
[409] *Roberts v Ramsbottom* [1980] 1 W.L.R. 823, applying *Hill v Baxter* [1958] 1 Q.B. 277. See also Smith, "Automatism—A Defence to Negligence?" in 130 New L.J. 1111; Wells and Morgan, "Sheer Heart Attack: the Queen of Defences?" in 140 New L.J. 1782. See further Ch.7, para.7–23, below.
[410] *Mansfield v Weetabix Ltd* [1997] P.I.Q.R. P526, CA (to the extent that *Roberts v Ramsbottom*, n.409 above, indicated that the driver's awareness of a disabling condition was irrelevant, it was disapproved).
[411] 1963 S.C. 175, affirmed 1964 S.C. (HL) 162 (lorry driver was held not to be liable when he lost control of his vehicle, as a result of a heart attack, mounted the pavement, struck and injured a pedestrian).
[412] [1938] P. 225.
[413] per Mellish L.J. in *Nugent v Smith* (1876) 1 C.P.D. 423 at 444. For the defence of "act of God" see further Ch.13, below, para.13–35.

4–135   **Burden of proof.** The burden of proof of inevitable accident is upon the party relying upon it.[414] Although *Stanley v Powell*[415] decided that inevitable accident was a good defence to an action of trespass, in *Fowler v Lanning*[416] Diplock J. stated that he regarded the decision as neutral on the question of onus of proof and went on to extend *Stanley v Powell* by holding that a plaintiff must always prove intention or negligence on the part of a defendant in such an action for the injuries sustained.

> "The onus of proving negligence, where the trespass is not intentional, lies on the plaintiff, whether the action be framed in trespass or in negligence. This has been unquestioned law in highway cases ever since *Holmes v Mather*[417] and there is no reason in principle . . . why it should be any different in other cases. It is, indeed, but an illustration of the rule that he who affirms must prove, which lies at the root of our law of evidence."[418]

4–136   It was formerly held that the defence of inevitable accident need not be specially pleaded in actions based on negligence, but the obligation under the present rules is to set out the nature of the defendant's case in response to the claimant's allegations and if a party wishes to rely on facts which, it is contended, excuse negligence, those facts should be set out.[419]

4.—Limitation of Action

4–137   **Introduction.**[420] Because there was no period of limitation within which an action had to be brought at common law, the Limitation Act 1623 was the first of many attempts to impose a limitation period by statute. As it provided, the expiry of the period of limitation did not extinguish the right of the claimant, but it did bar his remedy. Whilst certain alterations were made by subsequent statutes,[421] the real basis of the modern law emerged with the passing of the Limitation Act 1939.[422]

---

[414] *The Merchant Prince* [1892] P. 179, where in broad daylight the vessel of that name ran into a ship at anchor in the river Mersey. Fry L.J., at 189, said: "The burden rests on the defendants to show inevitable accident. To sustain that the defendants must do one or other of two things. They must either show what was the cause of the accident, and show that the result of that cause was inevitable; or they must show all the possible causes, one or other of which produced the effect, and must further show with regard to every one of these possible causes that the result could not have been avoided. Unless they do one or other of these two things, it does not appear to me that they have shown inevitable accident." See the discussion on this case in *Esso Petroleum Co Ltd v Southport Corp* [1956] A.C. 218; *Bell Telephone Co of Canada v The Ship Mar-Tirenno* (1974) 52 D.L.R. (3d) 702.
[415] [1891] 1 Q.B. 86.
[416] [1959] 1 Q.B. 426.
[417] (1875) L.R. 10 Ex. 261.
[418] *Fowler v Lanning* [1959] 1 Q.B. 426 at 439. To similar effect, see *Walmsley v Humenick* [1954] 2 D.L.R. 232, and *Beals v Hayward* [1960] N.Z.L.R. 131.
[419] See, generally, Pt 16.5 of the CPR 1998.
[420] See Turner, "Rewriting limitation?" 2001 N.L.J. 151, 574.
[421] For provisions extinguishing title to land, once the limitation period has expired, see s.15 onwards of the Limitation Act 1980 and so far as concerns personalty, s.3 of the same Act.
[422] The whole purpose of the Limitation Acts is that, from a common-sense point of view, "a plaintiff ought to know that he has a cause of action, before time starts to run against him" and, equally, "there should come a time when defendants can relax and know that actions against them are time-barred".

The Limitation Act 1939 imposed, in respect of all actions founded on tort, a   **4–138** time limit of six years, within which a claimant's action had to be brought.[423] The Law Reform (Limitation of Actions, etc.) Act 1954 s.2(1),[424] amended the period to three years in claims for personal injury. However, it came to be recognised that the brevity of the limitation period was capable of leading to a denial of justice in cases where the claimant's cause of action had become statute-barred before he realised that he even had one.[425]

This led first to the Limitation Act 1963, which provided for an extension of   **4–139** time in personal injury claims if certain conditions were satisfied, and then, following recommendations of the Law Reform Committee in its Twentieth Report,[426] to the Limitation Act 1975, which added four new sections[427] to the Limitation Act 1939.

In its Twenty-first Report,[428] the Committee considered limitation in cases of   **4–140** non personal injury, but although several recommendations were made, some of which were carried into effect by the Limitation (Amendment) Act 1980,[429] those relating to "latent damage" were not. The law as regards non-personal injury actions remained as it was, still governed by the principle in *Cartledge v E. Jopling & Sons Ltd*.[430] By this juncture the provisions relating to limitation were scattered so far and wide throughout the statute books that there was an urgent need for consolidation. This was sought to be achieved by the passing of the Limitation Act 1980,[431] which came into force on May 1, 1981.[432] Besides

---

See the succinct summary by Desmond Wright Q.C., leading counsel for the defendants, in his arguments before the House of Lords in *Pirelli General Cable Works Ltd v Oscar Faber & Partners* [1983] 2 A.C. 1 at 16.

[423] s.2(1). See Brown, "Limitation Periods in Negligence" in 2 Lit. 229.

[424] See now the provisions of the Limitation Act 1980 s.11(1).

[425] See, e.g. *Cartledge v E. Jopling & Sons Ltd* [1963] A.C. 758 (claimant ignorant of damage to his lungs which arose more than six years before proceedings were commenced). See also *Archer v Catton & Co Ltd* [1954] 1 W.L.R. 775; *Brazier v Ministry of Defence* [1965] 1 Lloyd's Rep. 26.

[426] i.e. *Interim Report on Limitation of Actions: In Personal Injury Claims*, Cmnd. 5630 (1974). The complex legislative history was considered in *Arnold v CEGB* [1988] A.C. 228 (the 1963 and 1975 Acts did not operate to overcome an accrued six year time bar) and again in *McDonnell v Congregation of Christian Brothers Trustees* [2003] 3 W.L.R. 1627, HL (a claim for sexual, emotional and physical abuse allegedly suffered between 1941 and 1951, where their Lordships declined to overrule *Arnold,* which had stood for 16 years and was not plainly wrong). See further McGee and Scanlon, "Judicial attitudes to limitation" 2005 C.J.Q. (Oct) 460.

[427] Which have been absorbed and re-enacted substantially in the provisions of the Limitation Act 1980, ss.11–14.

[428] i.e. *Final Report on Limitation of Actions*, Cmnd. 6923 (1977).

[429] c.24. By s.7, the Limitation Act 1939 s.26 was amended to provide in (b) that time was postponed where any fact relevant to the plaintiff's right of action has been deliberately concealed from him by the defendants.

[430] [1963] A.C. 758, which was applied in *London Congregational Union Inc v Harriss & Harriss* [1988] 1 All E.R. 15, CA, where it was held, inter alia, that the burden of proof was on the plaintiffs to show that the damage to the church hall, caused by the failure to damp-proof, had occurred within the period of six years previous to the issue of the writ.

[431] c.58.

[432] By s.41(2).

consolidation, the Act also included a new section[433] relating to new claims in pending actions, but no provision was made for "latent damage."

4–141 Whilst the Law Reform Committee was still considering the issue of "latent damage" its deliberations were overtaken by events. Late in 1982 the House of Lords heard the appeal in *Pirelli General Cable Works Ltd v Oscar Faber & Partners*.[434] As a result of that decision, a trend towards discoverability as the test in cases of latent damage to buildings was abruptly halted. Re-affirmed, instead, was the traditional approach that ordinarily[435] the claimant's cause of action accrued when the damage in fact occurred. It was also held that once time had begun to run against an owner of the building concerned, it continued to run against all subsequent owners.[436]

4–142 Following this unpopular[437] decision, the matter was referred once more to the Law Reform Committee, which completed its Twenty-fourth Report[438] after extensive consultations. It concluded that a significant change of approach was required to limitation in non personal injury cases. The Committee's recommendations centred on three main objectives, namely that (i) claimants must have a fair and sufficient opportunity to pursue their remedy; (ii) defendants should be protected against stale claims; and (iii) uncertainty in the operation of the rules of limitation should be removed, as far as it was possible.

In the result, the Latent Damage Act 1986[439] was passed, received the Royal Assent on July 18, 1986 and came into force on September 18, 1986.[440]

4–143 It will be appreciated that even in summary the history of legislative intervention is complex. It is proposed to approach the current law under the following headings:

---

[433] Namely s.35.

[434] [1983] 2 A.C. 1 (the claimants engaged the defendants, a firm of consulting engineers, to advise on and design an addition to their factory premises, including the provision of a chimney. The latter was built in June and July 1969 but the material used in its construction was unsuitable, so that by April 1970 cracking must have begun to develop at its top, albeit unobserved by the plaintiffs. Indeed, the damage was not discovered until November 1977 and no writ was issued until October 1978). For a discussion of the status of *Pirelli* after *Murphy v Brentwood DC* [1991] A.C. 398, see *New Islington and Hackney HA Ltd v Pollard Thomas & Edwards Ltd* [2001] P.N.L.R. 515. See also Murdoch, "A judicial roller coaster" E.G. 2005, 0513, 133; and *Abbott v Will Gannon Smith* [2005] P.N.L.R. 562, CA (*Pirelli* was not overruled in *Murph*, above, and contines to be applicable on appropriate facts). See further, Newman, "Sophistry damages law" Cons. Law 2005, 16(8), 23.

[435] As Lord Fraser pointed out: "There may perhaps be cases where the defect is so gross that the building is doomed from the start, and where the owner's cause of action will accrue as soon as it is built", although this would be an exceptional case: [1983] 2 A.C. 1 at 16.

[436] See now the Latent Damage Act 1986 para.4–219, below.

[437] See the observations of Lord Fraser, ibid. at 19: "the unsatisfactory state of the law on this subject", and of Lord Scarman, ibid. at 19, "harsh and absurd".

[438] Cmnd. 9390 (1984).

[439] s.37 which changes the law of limitations in a way that the House of Lords declined to do in *Pirelli General Cable Works Ltd v Oscar Faber & Partners* [1983] 2 A.C. 1 at 19, per Lord Fraser, the decision in which case had produced an unfair result for plaintiffs.

[440] By virtue of s.5(3). The provisions of ss.1 and 2 do not affect any action begun before this date (s.4(1)(b)) and no action may be brought, which was already statute-barred before September 19, 1986 (s.4(1)(a)) but, subject to these, the two sections shall have effect in relation to causes of action accruing, after the Act came into force.

A. General Principles;

B. Personal Injury Litigation;

C. Latent Damage in Cases other than Personal Injury; and

D. Miscellaneous Limitation Periods.

Except where otherwise stated, all references are to the relevant sections of the Limitation Act 1980.

(A) General Principles

Procedural rules. Because the 1980 Act is procedural in effect its operation   **4–144**
in practice needs to be reflected in the Rules. Those rules, the Civil Procedure Rules 1998[441] provide for various circumstances in which limitation is relevant, as identified in s.35 of the Act. Section 35(1) and (2) are concerned with establishing the date when proceedings are deemed to have been commenced for the purposes of the Act. Subsequent subsections deal with: adding an additional cause of action after limitation has expired (subss.35(4) and (5)(a)); adding additional parties (subss.35(4), (5)(b) and (6)); or capacities (subs.(7)); Part 20 proceedings (subs.(8)); and applications for extension of the limitation period under s.33.

Computation of time. When calculating limitation, the day on which the   **4–145**
cause of action arose is generally excluded, but the day when the action is begun is included.[442] After April 26, 1999, all civil proceedings are commenced by claim form. A personal injuries action was regarded as "brought" for purposes of s.11(3) of the Limitation Act 1980 when the claimant's request that a claim form be issued was brought to the correct court office within its opening hours, on the day before the limitation period was due to expire, rather than when it was actually issued by the court.[443] Although proceedings for negligence must be commenced within the period allowed by statute,[444] the claim form may be served up to four months after the date of issue.[445] There is a discretion, upon application, to extend the time for service.[446] As under the earlier Rules,[447] detailed provisions, outside the scope of this work, govern amendments of the type provided for by s.35 after the limitation period has expired, such as to a statement of case[448] or in particular the situation where it is desired to add or

---

[441] As from April 26, 1999, the Civil Procedure Rules 1998, provided a complete and unified code of rules for both High and County Court civil claims.
[442] *Marren v Dawson Bentley & Co Ltd* [1961] 2 Q.B. 135; cf. *Goldsmith's Co v West Metropolitan Ry* [1904] 1 K.B. 1 at 5, per Mathew L.J., which was applied in *Stewart v Chapman* [1951] 2 K.B. 792 but distinguished in *Hare v Gocher* [1962] 2 Q.B. 641.
[443] *Barnes v St Helens MBC* [2007] 1 W.L.R. 879, CA (the claimant had taken those steps which it was necessary for him to take to enable proceedings to be started within time).
[444] See paras 4–176, 4–178, below.
[445] CPR 1998, Pt 7, r.5.
[446] CPR 1998 Pt 7, r.6.
[447] The Rules of the Supreme Court (RSC), in particular Ord.20, as set out in the 9th edn of this work.
[448] CPR Pt 17, r.4.

substitute a party after that time.[449] There is a wide discretion,[450] subject to s.35 of the Act, to permit amendments even where the defendant may thereby be deprived of a defence.[451]

4–146   Once the period of limitation has begun to run in respect of a cause of action in tort, it is not broken if the claimant comes subsequently under a disability.[452] It makes no difference that at any one time over the material period there was nobody in existence capable of pursuing the action.[453] It follows that where a person, who has a completed cause of action, dies before proceedings are commenced and no personal representatives are appointed until the limitation period has expired, the action will be statute-barred.[454] It is an abuse of process, calling for striking out, for a claimant to commence a claim which he is not entitled to commence without an assignment of the cause of action to himself, simply to safeguard the position in relation to limitation.[455]

4–147   **Pleading the defence.** A defendant must plead specifically that the action is out of time if he desires to rely upon the defence of limitation to bar the action.[456] The Act does not confer any right on a defendant[457] other than to plead the defence, should he be so minded to do. It has been pointed out that:

> "the Act does not provide that after such period the plaintiff's remedy shall be extinguished or even wholly cease to be enforceable, and indeed the remedy is not extinguished, nor does it wholly cease to be enforceable; for if a defendant elects not to plead the Statute of Limitations, the remedy may be pursued after the period of limitation. Further than that, the benefit which a defendant derives from the Statute of Limitations is not, I think, properly described as a substantive benefit but really is

---

[449] CPR Pt 19, r.4. See, e.g. *H v Merck & Co Inc* [2002] P.I.Q.R. P17, sub nom. *Horne-Roberts v Smithkline Beecham* [2002] 1 W.L.R. 1662, CA, para.4–177 below (claim under the Consumer Protection Act 1987 for injury allegedly caused by vaccine where the claimant sought successfully to substitute the defendants after the ten-year-long stop period applicable under the Act after the batch number of the vaccine had been established but it had been incorrectly attributed to another manufacturer).

[450] Part 17, r.4 of the CPR 1998. Part 17, r.4(2) limits the discretion if "the new claim arises out the same facts or substantially the same facts as a claim in respect of which the party applying for permission has already claimed a remedy in the proceedings". But see *Goode v Martin* [2002] 1 W.L.R. 1828, CA, para.4–177, below, where the Court of Appeal found that on the particular facts, unless additional words were read into the rule, CPR 17.4(2) operated as an unfair limitation upon the claimant's right of access to a court in breach of art.6 of the European Convention for the Protection of Human Rights.

[451] Pre CPR, see, e.g. *Davies v Elsby Brothers* [1961] 1 W.L.R. 170 and the 9th edn of this work at Ch.3, para.3–142 et seq. See also *Charles Church Developments Ltd v Stent Foundations Ltd, The Times*, January 4, 2007 (the court has a discretion under CPR 17.4 (2) to permit the claimant to amend a claim to incorporate against a defendant after expiry of a relevant limitation period, allegations derived from the defence of another defendant to the same action).

[452] See paras 4–165 to 4–167, below, for greater detail of "disability".

[453] *Smith v Hill* (1746) 1 Wils. 134; *Homfray v Scroope* (1849) 13 Q.B. 509.

[454] *Penny v Brice* (1865) 18 C.B.(N.S.) 393; *Boatwright v Boatwright* (1873) L.R. 17 Eq. 71.

[455] *Pickthall v Hill Dickinson LLP* [2009] EWCA Civ 543.

[456] See para.17 of the Practice Direction to Pt 16 of the CPR 1998.

[457] *Mitchell v Harris Engineering Co Ltd* [1967] 2 Q.B. 703 at 718.

merely as a right to plead a defence if he chooses to do so that the plaintiff is barred from prosecuting his claim."[458]

In the absence of representations by the defendants or their insurers that either **4–148** they were admitting liability, or that the only issue between the parties was *quantum*, or that they would not rely on the Statute of Limitation, they were not stopped from raising the defence by pleading that the claimant's claim was statute-barred, merely because they had investigated the full circumstances of the accident and had had the claimant examined by their medical expert.[459]

The issue whether or not an action is statute-barred can be raiscd when interlocutory matters are being considered and tried as a preliminary issue. Otherwise, it will fall to be decided at the trial of the action itself.[460] Once the defendant raises the issue that a claim is not brought within time the onus is on the claimant to plead and prove a date which establishes that it is.

When time begins to run. In negligence actions the period of limitation starts **4–149** to run from the date on which the cause of action accrued.[461] However, there are two broad exceptions:

(i) those cases involving either personal injury or a fatal accident, where circumstances have arisen that may permit an alternative commencement date[462]; and

(ii) those cases involving neither personal injuries nor death but where facts relevant to the cause of action, are not known to the complainant at the date of accrual which may also permit an alternative commencement date.[463]

Accrual of a cause of action. The cause of action accrues when the claimant **4–150** suffers actual damage, whether or not that is also the date of the negligent act or omission.[464] Whether actual damage has happened is a question of fact in each case. If it has, then at common law the objection that the claimant does not know that he or she has suffered harm, or does not know that the defendant caused it, does not prevent time from starting to run. The principle has been modified by statute in claims for personal injury[465] and in claims involving latent damage,[466] but otherwise continues to apply in cases of damage to property and economic loss.

---

[458] per Nield J. in *Rodriguez v R.J. Parker* [1967] 1 Q.B. 116 at 136.

[459] *Doran v Thompson* (1978) 113 I.L.T.R. 93.

[460] The potential disadvantage of leaving the decision until trial was pointed out in *KR v Bryn Alyn Community (Holdings) Ltd* [2003] Q.B. 1441 albeit disapproved on a different point see: para.4–191, below.

[461] Limitation Act 1980 s.2: "An action founded on tort shall not be brought after the expiration of six years from the date on which the cause of action accrued."

[462] See further 4–178, below, and the Limitation Act 1980 ss.11 and 12.

[463] See further 4–219, below, and the Limitation Act 1980 s.14A, added by the Latent Damage Act 1986, as regards an action that was not already time-barred by September 18, 1986.

[464] *Nykredit Mortgage Bank Plc v Edward Erdman Group Ltd* [1997] 1 W.L.R. 1627, 1630, HL.

[465] See paras 4–178 and 4–182, below.

[466] See paras 4–220 to 4–225, below.

> "There is considerable case law concerning situations where a person's legal position has, through negligence, been altered to his immediate, measurable economic disadvantage, and it has been held that a cause of action accrued although the beneficiary neither knew nor had any reason to know about its existence."[467]

4–151   **Physical injury.** In cases of negligently inflicted personal injury, the cause of action is complete when the claimant suffers actionable damage. But what amounts to actionable damage may be a matter of dispute. In *Cartledge v E Jopling & Sons Ltd*,[468] Lord Reid referred to "personal injury beyond what can be regarded as negligible"[469] and Lord Evershed to "real damage as distinct from purely minimal damage".[470] Lord Pearce, in the leading judgment, said that evidence that physical changes in the claimant's body were not felt by him and might never be felt "tells in favour of the damage coming within the principle of *de minimis non curat lex*. On the other hand, evidence that in unusual exertion or at the onset of disease he may suffer from his hidden impairment tells in favour of the damage being substantial."[471] On the facts, a cause of action for injury by pneumoconiosis accrued when damage by scarring of the lung tissue from inhaling silica dust must have occurred, even though the claimant did not find out about the injury for a number of years.[472] On the other hand, in *Rothwell v Chemical & Insulating Co Ltd*,[473] the development of pleural plaques—localised areas of pleural thickening—caused by exposure to asbestos dust was not actionable damage, for the plaques had no adverse effect on any bodily function, did not increase the susceptibility of the claimants to other diseases and did not shorten their expectation of life. They had no effect on health at all.

4–152   **Property damage.** In similar vein, in cases involving loss of or physical damage to property, a cause of action accrues and the limitation period starts to run from the time when that loss or damage actually happens. This may be the time of the defendant's conduct or some later time. So where a security firm was negligent in the installation of a burglar alarm, allowing thieves to steal the plaintiff's property without activating the alarm, the cause of action accrued when the property was stolen, not when the faulty work was done.[474] Similarly, where a pipe in a chemicals factory which had cracked for an unknown reason was repaired, and later cracked again resulting in an explosion damaging the plant, it was held that the cause of action accrued at the time of the explosion rather than the initial cracking.[475]

4–153   **Economic loss.** The same principle applies in the case of claims for economic loss. But determining the date when economic loss was actually suffered may not be easy, for many of the cases involve a notional or potential loss, or a

---

[467] *Law Society v Sephton & Co* [2006] 2 A.C. 543, per Lord Mance at [67].
[468] [1963] A.C. 758.
[469] *Cartledge v E Jopling & Sons Ltd* [1963] A.C. 772.
[470] ibid. at 774.
[471] ibid. at 779.
[472] The decision provoked immediate legislative reform: see now Limitation Act 1980, ss.11, 14, below para 4–178.
[473] [2008] 1 A.C. 281; see further Ch.2, para.2–99, above.
[474] *Dove v Banham's Patent Locks Ltd* [1983] 1 W.L.R. 1436.
[475] *Nitrigin Eireann Teoranta v Inco Alloys Ltd* [1992] 1 W.L.R. 498; and see further para.4–156, below.

contingency which may or may not happen. Indeed, in Neil L.J.'s words, "the courts have been driven to draw narrow, some would say unconvincing, distinctions between transactions where it has been held that the loss was measurable when the relevant transaction was entered into and transactions where it has been held that the loss occasioned by the unsatisfactory bargain lay in the future".[476] Yet the difficulties are not impossible to surmount, and certain principles can be articulated which provide some practical assistance. On the one hand, there is actual loss if the claimant incurs an existing liability or suffers an existing diminution in value of land or personal property or a chose in action. A cause of action accrues at that date even though there has been no demand on the liability, or the loss has not crystallised, or there has been no out-of-pocket expenditure. On the other hand, there is only a potential loss where a right or liability is subject to a contingency which may or may not occur. A cause of action accrues only when it does occur and actual damage is suffered.

ILLUSTRATIONS

A client who acted on a solicitor's[477] allegedly negligent advice by executing   **4–154**
a mortgage as surety for her son's debts suffered economic loss and had a cause of action at that time, even though she was not required to pay the debts for another two years. The mortgage had the immediate effect of depressing the value of the mortgaged property.[478] Solicitors who prepared an agreement containing covenants protecting the claimants from competition by a former employee, which covenants turned out to be ineffectual, caused actual damage at the time the agreement was executed rather than when the error was discovered, since the claimants received at the outset a worthless covenant rather than a valuable chose in action.[479] Where the claimant, a member of a rock band, alleged negligence by solicitors in failing to verify that the terms of a recording contract reflected the members' intentions, or to advise him that he could be summarily expelled from the band without compensation, damage accrued when he entered the agreement, not later when he was actually expelled. The agreement he signed was commercially less favourable than it would have been

---

[476] *First National Commercial Bank Plc v Humberts* [1995] 2 All E.R. 673 at 680, per Neill L.J., CA.

[477] For further examples of accrual of a cause of action against solicitors see Ch.9, paras 9–275 to 9–277, below.

[478] *Forster v Outred & Co* [1982] 1 W.L.R. 86, CA. In *Tabarrok v EDC Lord & Co, The Times,* February 14, 1997, CA, it was said to be a question of fact in each case whether damage arose before the person whose debt was guaranteed actually defaulted: and see below, paras 4–159 and 4–160. See also *Bell v Peter Browne & Co* [1990] 2 Q.B. 495, CA (damage existed even at time when solicitor's negligent failure to act was remediable); *Daniels v Thompson* [2004] P.N.L.R. 638, CA (any possible cause of action against allegedly negligent solicitor, who failed to advise the deceased that if she continued to reside at a property which she wished to transfer to her son, there would be a risk on her death it would form part of her estate for tax purposes, arose when she relied upon the advice, not at her death); *Pegasus Management Holdings SCA v Ernst & Young* [2010] P.N.L.R. 23, CA (negligent advice from solicitor leading to the formation of a company in a way which had negative tax consequences caused damage at the time of the transaction, since the claimant did not have control of a company with characteristics that would be proof against those consequences).

[479] *DW Moore & Co Ltd v Ferrier* [1988] 1 W.L.R. 267; and see *Gordon v J B Wheatley & Co* [2000] Lloyd's Rep. P.N. 605, CA.

had the solicitors' duty been discharged, and that was sufficient damage to complete his cause of action.[480]

4-155   Claimants who acted on allegedly negligent advice from a solicitor to waive their right to completion of a building contract by a certain date, suffered loss at the time when the waiver was agreed, rather than when the building was in fact completed or after they obtained possession of the building and became aware of certain defects in the builder's work. The right to insist on completion by a certain date was an asset with measurable value. Its absence meant there was an immediate loss, albeit the loss became greater subsequently when the defects in the building were discovered.[481] Misrepresentation by an insurance broker inducing entry into a contract of insurance caused the contracting party to suffer damage when the contract was executed rather than when the insurer elected to avoid it, since at that earlier time the contract entered into was of less commercial value than the contract which he had engaged the broker to procure.[482] Where a voidable insurance policy was taken out in consequence of negligent advice from an insurance broker, the cause of action accrued when the claimant acted upon the advice to his detriment and entered the contract, thereby failing to obtain that to which he was entitled, and not when the insurer avoided the policy or when the fire occurred which gave rise to the claim for indemnity.[483] A negligent solicitor's client suffered immediate loss on his marriage to his wife without the protection of a valid agreement contracting out of a statutory regime for the sharing of matrimonial property. He did not get what he should have got, and his assets were diminished by an existing liability through the attachment of the matrimonial property regime.[484]

4-156   **Valuation of property.** Special difficulties arise where lenders rely on professional advice about the adequacy of a security, because the existence or amount of any loss may be uncertain and subject to variation. In *First National Commercial Bank Plc v Humberts*[485] the Court of Appeal held that the cause of action of a bank advancing monies on the basis of an allegedly negligent valuation accrued when its outlay, together with the cost of borrowing, or the profit that could notionally have arisen had the money been placed elsewhere, was less than the security held. Applying the principle, the defendant's valuation could not be said to have caused loss while there were means of recouping the loan, so a writ issued within six years of the end of that period, although more than six years from the date of the advance, was within time.

---

[480] *McCarroll v Statham Gill Davis* [2003] P.N.L.R. 509, CA.

[481] *Watkins v Jones Maidment Wilson* [2008] P.N.L.R. 23, CA; and see *Shore v Sedgwick Financial Services Ltd* [2008] P.N.L.R. 37, CA; Cathie and Schooling, "Stopping the clock" (2008) 152 SJ (19) 12; Preddy and Thomas, "Shore timings" 158 N.L.J. 1294.

[482] *Islander Trucking Ltd v Hogg Robinson & Gardner Mountain (Marine) Ltd* [1990] 1 All E.R. 826; *Iron Trade Mutual Insurance Co Ltd v J K Buckenham Ltd* [1990] 1 All E.R. 808.

[483] *Knapp v Ecclesiastical Insurance Group Plc* [1998] P.N.L.R. 172, CA.

[484] *Thom v Davys Burton* [2009] 1 N.Z.L.R. 437, NZSC.

[485] [1995] 2 All E.R. 673, CA; and see *UBAF Ltd v European American Banking Corporation* [1984] Q.B. 713.

The House of Lords gave further consideration to the question in *Nykredit*   **4–157**
Mortgage Bank Plc v Edward Erdman Group Ltd,[486] where Lord Nicholls
emphasised that the loss must be relevant loss. "To constitute actual damage for
the purpose of constituting a tort, the loss sustained must be loss falling within
the measure of damage attributable to the wrong in question".[487] He pointed out
that where as a result of negligent advice property was acquired as security, the
lender suffers a detriment in the sense that he parts with his money which he
would not have done if he was properly advised, but he may suffer no actual loss
at all, for instance if the borrower does not default. Lord Hoffmann, in similar
vein, maintained that the relevant damage in a negligent valuation case was that
attributable to the shortcomings in the valuation, and the lender's cause of action
accrued when he could show that he was actually worse off as a result.[488] So in
the instant case, where a borrower defaulted immediately and the amount lent at
all times exceeded the value of the property, the cause of action accrued at the
time of the transaction.

Delay in bringing action. A common class of case is that where solicitors are   **4–158**
alleged to have been negligent in allowing their client's claim to be struck out by
the court, for delay or some other reason. In such a case the question arises when
damage should be regarded as having accrued. Did it accrue at the moment of
strike out, or at some earlier time when by reason of the solicitor's negligence the
action was *liable* to be struck out? In one decision, involving a claim for medical
negligence which was struck out for want of prosecution, the Court of Appeal
favoured the former view, even though by then the value of the claim was much
reduced.[489] However, a differently constituted Court of Appeal later accepted that
that there can be damage in this type of case prior to the actual strike out, and
criticised the earlier decision as being inconsistent with the *Nykredit*.[490] In the
instant case, where solicitors had negligently failed to prosecute a client's claim
for personal injury, the court held that the negligence caused loss at the time
when the value of the claim was substantially diminished by the risk that it would
be struck out for want of prosecution.[491] Again, where solicitors only served a
claim form after obtaining an ex parte order to extend the period for service, on
an application unsupported by evidence, and the order was thereafter set aside,
damage was suffered by the claimant for the purposes of a claim against the

---

[486] [1997] 1 W.L.R. 1627, HL; Dugdale, "More than interest in *Nykredit*" (1998) 14 P.N. 118. See
also *Byrne v Hall Paine & Foster* [1999] 1 W.L.R. 1849, CA (purchaser's cause of action against
negligent valuer ran from exchange of contracts not completion).
[487] *Nykredit Mortgage Bank Plc v Edward Erdman Group Ltd* [1997] 1 W.L.R. 1627 at 1630.
[488] ibid. 1627 at 1639.
[489] *Hopkins v MacKenzie* [1995] P.I.Q.R. P43, CA.
[490] See para.4–157, above.
[491] *Khan v R M Falvey & Co* [2002] P.N.L.R. 28, CA. In *Hatton v Chafes* [2003] P.N.L.R. 489, CA,
Clarke L.J. said, at 494, "It seems to me that there are three possibilities as to when damage is caused
by negligence in such a case so that the claimant's cause of action has accrued and time begins to run
against him. The first is when the claimant has no arguable basis for avoiding the claim being struck
out, the second is when it is more probable than not that the claim will be struck out and the third
is when there is a real (as opposed to a minimal or fanciful) risk of the claim being struck out." He
went on to say that there was no need on the facts to determine which test was correct since the instant
case clearly fell within the first possibility, as had *Khan v Falvey*. See further *Jessup v Wetherell*
[2007] P.N.L.R. 10, where Silber J. discussed the limited circumstances in which *Hopkins v
Mackenzie* could still be relevant.

solicitors for negligence when the period for service had expired, not from the later date when the order extending service was set aside.[492]

4–159   **Contingent losses.** Exposure to a contingent loss is not actual damage before the contingency occurs. In *Law Society v Sephton & Co*,[493] the Law Society sued a fraudulent solicitor's negligent accountant in respect of money it had paid out of a compensation fund to the defrauded clients of the solicitor, and the question at issue was the date when the Society suffered damage and its cause of action accrued. It was argued for the accountants that the Society suffered damage whenever the solicitor misappropriated a client's money. The misappropriation gave the client a right to make a claim on the fund, and liability to such a claim was damage. The Society argued that it suffered damage only when such a claim was made. The misappropriation might have been repaid, from the solicitor's own money or from another client's account. The client might not have made a claim. All that could be said was that, after a misappropriation, a claim was likely. The House of Lords unanimously upheld the second argument. Lord Hoffmann said that the solicitor's misappropriations gave rise to the possibility of a liability to pay a grant out of the fund, contingent upon the misappropriation not being otherwise made good and a claim in proper form being made. But until a claim was actually made, no loss or damage was sustained by the fund. The existence of a contingent liability might depress the value of other property, or it might mean that a party to a bilateral transaction had received less than he should have done or was worse off than if he had not entered the transaction. But, standing alone as in the present case, the contingency was not damage.[494]

4–160   The distinction between a present liability on the one hand and a prospective or contingent liability on the other may be a fine one. Damage is contingent if it results from the claimant being exposed to a liability which is contingent on the occurrence of a future uncertain event. An example is the liability of a guarantor which is contingent on a default by the principal debtor. But if there is a present liability there is loss or damage when the liability is incurred, notwithstanding that it may not be dischargeable until a future date. So where a guarantee entered into by a client on the advice of his solicitor rendered the client a principal debtor, the liabilities assumed on signing were present rather than prospective and damage was suffered at that time.[495] Again, as we have seen, there may be a present loss if a contingent liability has the immediate effect of depressing the value of the claimant's property, as where the claimant has executed security over property, whether tangible or intangible.[496] The qualifications on the rule in *Sephton* are not to be construed as restricted to particular sorts of damage, such

---

[492] *Polley v Warner Goodman & Street* [2003] P.N.L.R. 784, CA.
[493] *Law Society v Sephton & Co* [2006] 2 A.C. 543; Evans, "Contingent liability and 'damage' " (2007) 23 PN 2; Butcher and Forsyth, "No contingent damage" (2006) 156 N.L.J. 1017; Heaton and Rouse, "No limits" (2006) 150 S.J. (29), 967.
[494] *Law Society v Sephton & Co* [2006] 2 A.C. 543 at [30].
[495] *Gilbert v Shanahan* [1998] 3 N.Z.L.R. 528, NZCA.
[496] See para.4–153 above.

as damage to a specific asset: they apply to additional loss, whatever its form.[497]

Defective property. Where an existing defect in property simply damages the   **4–161**
property itself, rather than other, separate property, a claim for the cost of
repairing or replacing the property is recognised as a claim for economic loss.
This loss occurs when the value of the property is diminished on the defect
becoming reasonably discoverable, not when there is undetected physical
damage,[498] but for various reasons of policy the loss is seen as irrecoverable.[499]

When time does not begin to run. Time does not begin to run, unless: (i) the   **4–162**
parties who are capable of suing and of being sued are in existence; (ii) the
person to whom a right of action accrues is not under a disability; and (iii) the
person's right of action has not been concealed from him by fraud. Each of these
situations requires separate discussion.

(i) *Parties in existence*

It has been emphasised that a "Statute of Limitations cannot begin to run   **4–163**
unless there are two things present—a party capable of suing and a party liable
to be sued".[500] If, therefore, the wrongdoer is entitled to diplomatic immunity[501]
at the time of the tort, time will not begin to run against the claimant until the
former's immunity ceases, there being no defendant capable of being sued at the
time when the cause of action arose.[502] Where all the ingredients of the cause of
action exist but the precise identity of the wrongdoer is unknown to the claimant,
time generally[503] continues to run. Thus, where a car was stolen by some
unknown thieves, the claimant's cause of action in conversion became statute-
barred six years later, although he never had the opportunity of suing any known
defendant.[504]

---

[497] *Axa Insurance Ltd v Akther & Darby* [2010] 1 W.L.R. 1662, CA (an insurance company's loss for allegedly negligent assessment of claims by solicitors under an ATE insurance shceme was contingent until a claim was made under the policy). See further Majumdar, "To have & have not" (2010) 160 N.L.J. 348; Evans and Harris, "The scope of *Sephton*: limitation where you don't get what you ought," (2009) 29 PN 15.
[498] *Invercargill City Council v Hamlin* [1996] 1 N.Z.L.R. 513, PC, disapproving *Pirelli General Cable Works Ltd v Oscar Faber & Partners* [1983] 2 A.C. 1.
[499] *Murphy v Brentwood DC* [1991] 1 A.C. 398; see further Ch.2, paras 2–238 to 2–247, above.
[500] per Vaughan Williams L.J. in *Thomson v Lord Clanmorris* [1900] 1 Ch. 718 at 728–729.
[501] See Ch.3, para.3–34, above.
[502] *Musurus Bey v Gadban* [1894] 1 Q.B. 533. See also *Awoyami v Radford* [2008] 3 W.L.R. 34 (Barristers who had represented the claimant in criminal proceedings in 1995 were not immune from suit at that time, even though the House of Lords decision declaring that immunity no longer existed was not handed down until 2000, since the basis of the majority speeches was that by 1991 the immunity could no longer be justified. It followed that a claim issued more than six years after 1995 was statute barred).
[503] For the special rule in actions for personal injury see para.4–183, below.
[504] *R.B. Policies at Lloyd's v Butler* [1950] 1 K.B. 76. See Goodman, "First Catch your Defendant—Limitation and Unknown Tortfeasor" in (1966) 29 M.L.R. 366. Also see *Clark v Forbes Stuart (Thames Street) Ltd* [1964] 1 W.L.R. 836.

4-164   On the death of a person who is liable to be sued for negligence, the cause of action survives against his estate.[505] No special time limit apples to the claim, other than those provided for in the Limitation Act 1980.[506] The position is the same where it is the claimant who has died and the cause of action has survived for the benefit of the estate.[507] Any claims by the dependants of the deceased, under the Fatal Accidents Acts, have a special time limit provided by s.12 of the Act.

(ii) *Person under disability*

4-165   The Limitation Act 1980, s.28 provides:

"(1) Subject to the following provisions of this section, if on the date when any right of action accrued for which a period of limitation is prescribed by this Act, the person to whom it accrued was under a disability, the action may be brought at any time before the expiration of six years from the date when he ceased to be under a disability or died (whichever first occurred) notwithstanding that the period of limitation has expired.
    (2) This section shall not affect any case where the right of action first accrued to some person (not under a disability) through whom the person under a disability claims.
    (3) When a right of action which has accrued to a person under a disability accrues, on the death of that person while still under a disability, to another person under a disability, no further extension of time shall be allowed by reason of the disability of the second person.
    (4) [. . .]
    (5) If the action is one to which s.10 of this Act applies subsection (1) above shall have effect as if for the words 'six years' there were substituted the words 'two years.'[508]
    (6) If the action is one to which s.11 or 12(2) of this Act applies, subsection (1) above shall have effect as if for the words 'six years' there were substituted the words 'three years' "[509]

4-166   The principal effect of this section was to abolish the rule whereby, in personal injury actions, time ran against a person under a disability who was in the custody of a parent at the time when the cause of action accrued. Accordingly, as a general rule, once such a person ceases to be under a disability, he or she has the same time within which to bring an action, whether for damages for personal injuries or otherwise, as a person not under a disability. A person is under a disability "while he is an infant,[510] or lacks capacity (within the meaning of the Mental Capacity Act 2005) to conduct legal proceedings".[511] A person who is not of full age may be described as a minor,[512] or child[513] instead of an infant.

---

[505] Law Reform (Miscellaneous Provisions) Act 1934 s.1(1).
[506] The procedure is governed by CPR 19.8.
[507] See again ss.2 and 11 and further paras 4–197 to 4–199, below.
[508] That is, where there is a claim for contribution between tortfeasors.
[509] That is, where there are claims for personal injuries or death or an action under the Fatal Accidents Act 1976.
[510] Since January 1, 1970, the age of 18 has been the age at which a person achieves their majority: Family Law Reform Act 1969 s.1(1).
[511] Limitation Act 1980 s.38(2).
[512] Family Law Reform Act 1969 s.12.
[513] The word "child" is used in CPR Pt 21.1.

Section 28 does not prevent a person under a disability from bringing an action **4–167** if otherwise he is able to do so. The section only extends the limit of time within which the action can be brought.[514] An child, for example, can bring an action by a litigation friend, as soon as the cause of action accrues,[515] and will usually be well advised to do so, since delay may affect the cogency of the evidence that can be produced.

(iii) *Fraudulent concealment*[516]

The Limitation Act 1980, s.32 provides: **4–168**

"(1) [. . .] where in the case of any action for which a period of limitation is prescribed by this Act, either—

(*a*) the action is based upon the fraud of the defendant; or
(*b*) any fact relevant to the plaintiff's right of action has been deliberately concealed from him by the defendant; or
(*c*) [. . .]

the period of limitation shall not begin to run until the plaintiff has discovered the fraud, concealment [. . .] (as the case may be) or could with reasonable diligence have discovered it.

References in this subsection to the defendant include references to the defendant's agent[517] and to any person through whom the defendant claims and his agent."

No degree of moral turpitude is necessary to establish fraud.[518] It is sufficient **4–169** that the defendant's conduct, having regard to the relationship of the parties, can be characterised as unconscionable.[519] Indeed, "deliberate commission of a

---

[514] *Forbes v Smith* (1855) 11 Ex. 161.
[515] See generally CPR Pt 21, and the Practice Direction thereto, also Ch.3, para.3–54, above.
[516] As Megarry V.C. said in *Tito v Waddell (No.2)* [1977] Ch. 106 at 245, "as the authorities stand, it can be said that in the ordinary use of language not only does 'fraud' not mean fraud but also 'concealed' does not mean 'concealed,' because any unconscionable failure to reveal is enough." See generally, Scott, "Postponement of limitation period in cases of concealment" (2001) C.J.Q. 20, 201.
[517] Which includes, in the context, an independent contractor. See, e.g. the building contractor in *Applegate v Moss* [1971] 1 Q.B. 406. It was also held to include the tenant for life, who had sold to the defendants an heirloom, unknown to the plaintiff trustees: *Eddis v Chichester Constable* [1969] 2 Ch. 345.
[518] *Beaman v A.R.T.S. Ltd* [1949] 1 K.B. 550 at 567.
[519] See per Lord Scott in *Cave v Robinson Jarvis & Rolf* [2003] 1 A.C. 384, n.521 below, at 403: most cases of a deliberate breach of duty will involve unconscionable behaviour but the statutory language does not require it and its addition as a criterion is unnecessary and unjustified. See Davidson Q.C., "An anxiety resolved" 146 S.J. 430; Prime, "Making 'deliberate concealment' concealment which is deliberate: policy and meaning in the House of Lords" 2002 C.J.Q. 21, 357. See also, *Tito v Waddell (No.2)* [1977] Ch. 106. See also *Clark v Woor* [1965] 1 W.L.R. 650 (inferior bricks); *Applegate v Moss,* n.503, above (defective unsafe foundations); *King v Victor Parsons* [1973] 1 W.L.R. 29 (foundations of house inadequate for the site which had previously been a rubbish dump and was liable to subside). See also Sophian, "Construction of House on Unsound Foundations: Liability for Damage: Concealed Fraud" in 70 L.S.Gaz. 1399.

breach of duty in circumstances in which it is unlikely to be discovered for some time amounts to deliberate concealment of the facts involved in that breach of duty".[520] In *Cave v Robinson Jarvis & Rolf*[521] it was said that, "deliberate commission of a breach of duty" is a phrase that requires no embellishment.[522] A breach which is not deliberate, but inadvertent, accidental or unintended is not included. Nor is a breach of duty which the defendant is unaware he is committing. Recklessness is likely to be insufficient.[523] Cases decided before this decision, which suggested that it was immaterial whether the defendant appreciated that he had been negligent, no longer provide useful guidance.[524]

4–170   It matters not whether the concealment occurs at the time of or after accrual of the cause of action, so that when after the cause of action accrued the defendant took steps to conceal relevant facts, the claimant had six years from the time he discovered the true state of affairs to bring his action.[525] But where there is one cause of action and a loss alleged to arise therefrom is deliberately concealed, and subsequently a further loss arises of which the claimant is aware, time starts to run from the latter and s.32 ceases to be relevant.[526]

ILLUSTRATIONS

4–171   Where solicitors failed to give a widow appropriate advice in a fatal accident claim, or inform her of a sum offered in settlement, their failure in the first respect did not of itself constitute a concealment of her right of action by fraud, but their failure in the second respect did, even though they were acquitted of any dishonest or oblique motive.[527] Failure by solicitors to advise a client of a possible claim against themselves or at least that other solicitors be consulted, can be deliberate concealment within s.32(1)(b).[528] Where a solicitor agreed to an order dismissing a personal injuries claim against a doctor and did not inform the claimant of that fact, he was guilty of deliberate concealment within the section: it had been his professional duty to inform the claimant of the order and he had deliberately decided not to do so.[529] The defendant was guilty of deliberate

---

[520] Limitation Act 1980 s.32(2).

[521] [2003] 1 A.C. 384, n.12 above (an allegation of negligent drafting of a contract in circumstances where the negligence was unlikely to be discovered for some time did not amount to a deliberate commission of a breach of duty and thereby prevent the running of time). For criticism of the position before this decision see Tompkinson, "Unconscious, unwitting and deliberate negligence—*Brocklesby* and section 32 of the Limitation Act 1980" (2002) 1 P.N. 27; also Dugdale, "Discoverability rules: *Cave* and the Law Commission Report" (2002) 3 P.N. 156.

[522] [2003] 1 A.C. 384 at 403.

[523] See per Ebsworth J. in *Companhia de Seguros Imperio v Heath (REBX) Ltd* [2001] 1 W.L.R. 112 at 124. In *R. v G* [2003] 3 W.L.R. 1060, HL the House of Lords reviewed the definition of recklessness in criminal cases. The speech of Lord Bingham of Cornhill summarises the various approaches to interpretation of the term over time.

[524] e.g. *Liverpool Roman Catholic Archdiocese Trustees Inc v Goldberg* [2001] 1 All E.R. 182.

[525] *Sheldon v R.H.M. Outhwaite (Underwriting Agencies) Ltd* [1996] 1 A.C. 102.

[526] *Williams v Sidwell, Lishman, Campbell & Price Ltd* [2010] EWCA Civ 418.

[527] *Kitchen v Royal Air Force Association* [1958] 1 W.L.R. 563.

[528] *Markes v Coodes* [1997] P.N.L.R. 252.

[529] *Williams v Fanshaw Porter & Hazelhurst* [2004] P.N.L.R. 544, CA (per Park J. at 554: it did not matter that the solicitor did not inform the claimant of the consent order out of embarrassment; what was relevant for purposes of s.32(1)(b) was the fact of concealment not the reason or motive for it).

concealment where, in the context of proceedings for breach of contract and negligence, it failed to disclose until after the proceedings had commenced, that a re-test of a quantity of gasoline had revealed it did not meet specification.[530]

There was no fraudulent concealment where the claimant was asked to sign a **4–172** form of disclaimer, which attempted to protect the defendants from a claim for damages in the event of injury, before he was admitted to their indoor go-karting track. The disclaimer could not be construed as a representation that, even if injured, the claimant would not have a cause of action. In any event, it was signed *before* the cause of action accrued and it was difficult to conceive of a case of concealment within the section unless the concealment took place at the time the cause of action was accruing or afterwards.[531]

Reasonable diligence. "Reasonable diligence" for purposes of subs.(1) **4–173** means not whether the claimant *should* have discovered the fraud sooner but whether he *could* with reasonable diligence have done so.[532] The burden of proof lies on him. He can succeed by showing that he could not have discovered the fraud without exceptional measures which he could not reasonably be expected to take. Reasonable diligence is not to be measured against a standard based upon the limitation period itself. It was suggested in the leading case that the test is "how a person carrying on a business of the relevant kind would act if he had adequate but not unlimited staff and resources . . . motivated by a reasonable but not excessive sense of urgency".[533]

In *Law Society v Sephton & Co*[534] claims in both negligence and fraud were **4–174** maintained against an accountant who had prepared annual reports for the Law Society in relation to a solicitor's practice and failed to discover that money was being fraudulently removed from client accounts. The Society had to pay compensation to those who lost money. The House of Lords ultimately gave a decision about when the cause of action in negligence arose. However, in the Court of Appeal there was also an issue in relation to the cause of action in fraud. In considering s.32(1) of the 1980 Act, the Court held that there had to be an assumption that a claimant desired to discover whether or not there had been a fraud. The concept of "reasonable diligence" carried with it the notion of a desire to know and indeed investigate. On the facts, the Society failed to prove that it

---

[530] *AIC Ltd v ITS Testing Services (UK) Ltd (The Kriti Palm), The Times*, December 21, 2006, CA.

[531] *Skerratt v Linfax Ltd* [2004] P.I.Q.R. P124, CA.

[532] *Paragon Finance Plc v D.B. Thakerar* [1999] 1 All E.R. 400, CA. See also *Ezekiel v Lehrer, The Times*, April 4, 2001, appeal dismissed [2002] Lloyd's Rep. P.N. 260, CA (the claimant could not avail himself of s.32(1)(b) where even though the defendant solicitor's conduct could amount to fraudulent concealment, the claimant could with reasonable diligence quickly have discovered he had been misled).

[533] *Paragon Finance Plc v D.B. Thakerar* [1999] 1 All E.R. 400, CA per May L.J. in the course of argument, quoted by Millett L.J. at 418. See also *Halifax Plc v Ringrose & Co* [2000] P.N.L.R. 483 (a building society could with reasonable diligence have discovered solicitors negligence in failing to disclose a back to back sale at such a time as to render the subsequent action statute barred).

[534] [2006] 2 A.C. 543, para.4–159, above.

could not with reasonable diligence have discovered the fraud in question within the relevant time frame.[535]

4–175   **No suspension once time is running.** Once the period of limitation in respect of a cause of action in tort has started to run, it is not broken either by any subsequent disability[536] which may have intervened, or by the fact that at some stage in the time there was no one who could sue,[537] or by any change of ownership,[538] or by any subsequent fraud,[539] or by an admission of liability.[540] Where a person has a vested cause of action but dies before he can begin his proceedings and no personal representative has been appointed until after the time limit has expired, the action is barred.[541] Further, a right of action for negligence once statute-barred cannot be revived by acknowledgment.[542] It should be noted, however, that under the principles which are applied in cases of insolvency, if a claim is not time-barred at the beginning of a bankruptcy or winding up, it does not become time-barred by the passage of further time thereafter.[543]

4–176   **Concurrent liability in contract and tort.** When there is in existence a contractual relationship between the parties, the question arises whether or not the claimant can also properly seek to establish the tortious liability of the defendant, in order to gain the advantage of a later commencement of the limitation period.[544] By ss.2 and 5, respectively, of the Limitation Act 1980 an action founded on tort, as well as one founded on simple contract, "shall not be brought after the expiration of six years from the date on which the cause of action accrued." A breach of contract is actionable per se, hence a cause of action accrues at the date of the breach and not, as generally in tort, when consequential damage results. Time runs against the claimant from the date of the breach, which

---

[535] See per Neuberger L.J. [2005] Q.B. 1013, at 1044, relying on *Paragon Finance Plc v D B Thakerar & Co*, n.518, above.

[536] See para.4–165, above, for "disability" in greater detail.

[537] *Smith v Hill* (1746) 1 Wils. 134; *Doe d. Duroure v Jones* (1791) 4 T.R. 300; *Homfray v Scoope* (1849) 13 Q.B. 509.

[538] *Pirelli General Cable Works Ltd v Oscar Faber & Partners* [1983] 2 A.C. 1.

[539] *Tito v Waddell (No.2)* [1977] Ch. 106.

[540] *Deerness v John R. Keeble & Son (Brantham) Ltd* (1982) 126 S.J. 729 (affd. by the House of Lord [1983] 2 Lloyd's Rep. 260) (an admission of liability did not operate to reset the limitation clock when the claim was for unliquidated damages: see s.29 of the Limitation Act 1980).

[541] *Rhodes v Smethurst* (1838) 4 M. & W. 42 and (1840) 6 M. & W. 351; *Penny v Brice* (1865) 18 C.B.(N.S.) 393; *Boatwright v Boatwright* (1873) L.R. 17 Eq. 71.

[542] *Hurst v Parker* (1817) 1 B. & Ald. 92; *Short v McCarthy* (1820) 3 B. & Ald. 626. See also Limitation Act 1980 s.29(7).

[543] See, e.g. *Financial Services Compensation Scheme Ltd v Larnell (Insurances) Ltd* [2006] P.N.L.R. 215, CA (claims against a company which was alleged to have given negligent advice about pensions, were not time barred where the company went into liquidation while the limitation clock was still running; it made no difference that the claims sought to take advantage of the Third Parties (Rights against Insurers) Act 1930, an asset not available to creditors of the company generally.

[544] See *Chesworth v Farrar* [1967] 1 Q.B. 407 at 416, and *Coupland v Arabian Gulf Oil Co* [1983] 1 W.L.R. 1136 at 1153, per Goff L.J. ("the plaintiff can advance his claim, as he wishes, either in contract or in tort; and no doubt he will, acting on advice, advance the claim on the basis which is most advantageous to him").

may on occasion be earlier than the date a cause of action in negligence accrues.[545]

Limitation and the Human Rights Act 1998. Section 3 of the 1998 Act   **4–177**
requires courts, so far as possible, to read and give effect to primary and subordinate legislation in a way which is compatible with rights guaranteed under the Convention. In the context of limitation this approach may afford a claimant some relief from technical provisions which would otherwise deny a remedy.[546] Even where the 1998 Act is not mentioned in terms, it may well be that the court's approach to technical arguments will be infused with its spirit: when considering whether it is necessary to add or substitute a new party to an action outside the limitation period, it has, for instance, been held that a restrictive interpretation should not be placed upon the word "mistake" in s.35(6)(a) of the 1980 Act.[547] Having said as much, by no means all limitation cases will be able to take advantage of art.6 arguments. The European Court of Human Rights has been prepared to allow individual States a margin of appreciation in relation to their limitation provisions, provided that the very essence of the right of access to the court is not impaired, and provided also that there is a reasonable relationship of proportionality between the limitation provision in question and the aim intended to be achieved.[548]

(B) Personal Injury Litigation

Limitation in personal injury claims: s.11. The Limitation Act 1980   **4–178**
provides for a special time limit applying to any action for damages for negligence, nuisance or breach of duty (whether the duty exists by virtue of a contract or of provision made by or under a statute or independently of a contract or any such provision) where the damages claimed consist of or include damages

---

[545] See, e.g. *F.G. Whitley & Sons v Bickerton* [1992] E.G.C.S. 25, where a site owner who had obtained conditional planning permission only for the intended extraction of silica, sued both his solicitors and his surveyors for alleged professional negligence in contract and tort, after the council had served an enforcement notice to prevent further extraction work taking place. See also para.3–149, above.

[546] *Cachia v Faluyi* [2001] 1 W.L.R. 1966, CA, Ch.16, para.16–22, below ("action" in s.2(3) of the Fatal Accidents Act 1976 Act read as "served process" so as to save the claims of children where at a stage within the limitation period proceedings had been issued but not served); also *Goode v Martin* [2002] 1 W.L.R. 1828, CA (personal injury claim where the claimant wished to add a new claim outside the limitation period, in effect adopting the defendant's case as an alternative mechanism of her accident: CPR 17.4(2) read so as to permit amendment).

[547] *H v Merck & Co Inc* [2002] P.I.Q.R. P17 (claim under the Consumer Protection Act 1987 for injury caused by a rubella and measles vaccine, where the claimant's solicitors mistakenly sued the wrong producer of the vaccine in question and only realised the mistake once the limitation period of 10 years had expired).

[548] See *Young v Western Power Distribution (South West) Plc* [2004] P.I.Q.R. P32, CA per Simon Brown L.J. at 47; also *Stubbings v UK* [1996] 23 E.H.R.R. 213 and *Dobbie v UK* (Unreported) 28477/95 E.C.H.R., as summarised in the judgment of Keene L.J. in *Rowe v Kingston upon Hull CC* [2004] P.I.Q.R. P238, CA, P245, para.4–181, below.

in in respect of personal injury to the claimant or any other person.[549] The claim may not be brought after the expiry of three years from the date the cause of action accrued[550] or the person injured's date of knowledge, whichever is the later.[551] Provision is made for claims on behalf of a deceased person's estate, where he or she has died before the expiry of the period referred to above.[552] or the claimant's date of knowledge (if later). The date of knowledge[553] is that time when the claimant knew: that the injuries in question were significant[554]; that they resulted from an act or omission, which was alleged to constitute negligence, nuisance or a breach of duty on the part of an identifiable defendant[555]; and, where it was alleged that the act or omission was that of a person other than the defendant, the identity of that person and the additional facts supporting the bringing of an action against the defendant.[556] Each of these requirements has provoked a good deal of comment and it is necessary to examine, in a broad way, the main areas of difficulty.

4–179   **"Personal injuries".** This expression is defined in s.38(1) and includes any disease and any impairment of a person's physical or mental condition. "Injury" and cognate expressions are to be construed accordingly. It has been held that a claim for the cost of bringing up a child, born after a failed sterilisation operation, was a claim for damages for "personal injuries" within s.11.[557] By way of contrast, an action by a member against his trade union for failing to pursue on his behalf his claim for damages for personal injury sustained in the course of his employment was not an action for personal injuries[558]; nor was a claim against insurance brokers who failed to carry out a claimant's instruction to obtain cover in respect of passengers travelling in his lorry and subsequently he was himself injured whilst a passenger in the vehicle: the action was for breach of contract, not personal injuries.[559] Depending upon the facts, an action against solicitors seeking damages for their negligence can be an action for "personal injuries" for

---

[549] s.11(1). When a claim for breach of contract in reality consists of or includes a claim for damages "in respect of personal injuries", the limitation period imposed by s.11 of the Act will apply: *Howe v David Brown Tractors (Retail) Ltd* [1991] 4 All E.R. 30, CA (the claimant bought an agricultural tractor and seven years later he was injured, by losing a leg, whilst operating it).

[550] See para.4–151, above.

[551] s.11(4).

[552] s. 11(5). See para.4–197, below.

[553] See para.4–182, below.

[554] See para.4–190, below.

[555] *Simpson v Norwest Holst Southern Ltd* [1980] 1 W.L.R. 968, although cf. *Walford v Richards* [1976] Lloyd's Rep. 526.

[556] See s.14(1)(b), (c) and (d).

[557] *Walkin v South Manchester HA, The Times,* July 3, 1995, CA (further, the Court of Appeal opined that an "unwanted pregnancy" constituted a single cause of action, howsoever pleaded, which arose at the time of conception and, thus, it was from that moment when the prescribed three-year limitation started to run). Also, see generally, *Godfrey v Gloucestershire Royal Infirmary NHS Trust* [2003] Lloyd's Rep. Med. 398 (a claim by a mother for the economic cost of bring up a severely brain damaged child on the basis that she had not been given accurate, appropriate or sufficient information upon which to make an informed decision about termination of the pregnancy).

[558] *McGahie v USDAW* (1966) S.L.T. 74.

[559] *Ackbar v C.F. Green & Co Ltd* [1975] Q.B. 582 followed in *Howe v David Brown Tractors (Retail) Ltd* [1991] 4 All E.R. 30 at 36. In *Clarke v Barber* [2002] C.L.Y. 464 a six-year limitation period was held appropriate to an action under s.2(2) of the Animals Act 1971 where the claimant sought damages for personal injury inflicted by the defendant's dog.

purposes of the Limitation Act 1980.[560] Where the claimant was injured by an allegedly uninsured driver, an action against the owner of the car for loss of the opportunity to be paid by insurers, on the basis that he permitted uninsured driving, was still an action for personal injuries with a three year limitation period.[561] Claims for personal injury which arise from a deliberate act, such as assault, can be claims for personal injury falling within s.11 and s.33 of the Act.[562]

There was, for a time, disagreement whether a failure to treat dyslexia could **4–180** amount to a claim for personal injury. However, in *Phelps v Hillingdon London Borough Council*,[563] Lord Slynn took the view that for purposes of the power to order discovery in a personal injuries claim:

> "psychological damage and a failure to diagnose a congenital condition and to take appropriate action as a result of which a child's level of achievement is reduced (which leads to loss of employment and wages) may constitute damage for the purpose of a claim. Accordingly, I consider that . . . a failure to mitigate the adverse consequences of a congenital defect is capable of being 'personal injuries to a person' within the meaning of the rules."[564]

One difficulty is how to reconcile the view that emotional and psychological **4–181** disturbance as a result of failing to diagnose and treat dyslexia can be the subject of an action for personal injury, with the general rule that there can be no recovery of damages in negligence for a psychological condition falling short of a recognised psychiatric injury. The difficulty was recognised in *Robinson v St Helens Metropolitan Borough Council*[565] but it was found that the weight of authority favoured a failure to treat dyslexia as capable of being an action for personal injury, where there was evidence of emotional or psychological impairment of the claimant, even if that impairment fell short of psychiatric injury strictly-so-called.[566] The House of Lords returned to the issue in *Adams v Bracknell Forest Borough Council*[567] and approved the *Robinson* approach.

---

[560] *Bennett v Greenland Houchen & Co* [1998] P.N.L.R. 458, CA (an action against solicitors based on alleged misconduct of earlier proceedings in relation to an employment contract, the plaintiff seeking damages for depression he had suffered as a result of the solicitors' conduct).

[561] *Norman v Ali* [2000] P.I.Q.R. P72, CA.

[562] See *A v Hoare* [2008] 1 A.C. 844, para.4–191 below.

[563] [2001] 2 A.C. 619.

[564] *Phelps v Hillingdon London Borough Council* [2001] 2 A.C. 664.

[565] [2003] P.I.Q.R. P128, CA.

[566] *Robinson* was followed in *Rowe v Kingston upon Hull CC* [2004] P.I.Q.R. P238, CA, para.4–185, below.

[567] [2005] 1 A.C. 76, para.4–187 below. Per Lord Hoffmann at 83, having accepted an analogy with negligent failure to treat a physical injury which the defendant did not itself cause, "It would be drawing too fine a distinction to say that the neglect caused no injury because nothing could be done to repair the congenital damage in the brain circuitry and the other parts of the brain which would have to be trained to compensate had never been injured. What matters is whether one has improved one's ability to read and write. Treating the inability to do so as an untreated injury originally proceeding from other causes produces a sensible practical result."

4–182   **Knowledge.**[568] Actual knowledge for purposes of s.14(1) is assessed on a subjective basis.[569] It should be noted that, once limitation is raised as an issue, the burden of proof is on the claimant to satisfy the court of the date upon which the cause of action accrued and, where relevant, when he first had knowledge of the facts in the sense identified in s.14 of the Act.[570] The claimant's belief or suspicion is not enough.[571] It has been held that "knowledge" within the meaning of s.14 arises where a claimant has sufficient confidence of the relevant facts to justify embarking on the preliminaries to the issue of a writ, such as submitting a claim to the proposed defendant, taking advice and collecting evidence: the availability of any particular remedy is an irrelevant consideration.[572]

4–183   In other words, time will run from the date when a claimant knows there is a possible case against the potential defendant. Knowledge of all the details necessary to prove the case is not required for time to start running.[573] In particular, it is unnecessary for a claimant to know that the act or omission upon which the action was based was arguably actionable in negligence to start time running.[574] However, it is an over-simplification to say that a claimant need only know that his damage has been caused by an act or omission of the defendant for time to run. What is required is knowledge in broad terms of the facts upon which a complaint is based.[575] It has been said that:

> "(1) The knowledge required to satisfy section 14(1)(b) is a broad knowledge of the essence of the casually relevant act or omission to which the injury is attributable;
> (2) 'Attributable' in this context means 'capable of being attributed to' in the sense of being a real possibility;
> (3) A plaintiff has the requisite knowledge when she knows enough to make it reasonable for her to investigate whether or not she has a case against the defendant. Another way of putting this is to say that she will have such knowledge if she firmly believes that her condition is capable of being attributed to an act or omission which she

---

[568] See para.4–221, below, for the similar considerations when knowledge is considered under s.14A of the Act. See also *Haward v Fawcetts* [2006] 1 W.L.R. 682, HL, and in particular the opinion of Lord Nicholls, for a summary of the relevant law.

[569] *Spargo v North Essex District HA* [1997] P.I.Q.R. P235, CA. For the interplay between actual and imputed knowledge, see further paras 4–186 and 4–191 below, and *A v Hoare* [2008] 1 A.C. 844.

[570] *Crocker v British Coal Corp, The Times,* July 5, 1995.

[571] *Stephen v Riverside HA, The Independent,* December 5, 1989 (the claimant had suspected that symptoms of erythema, the moist spots, and an increased risk of cancer were caused by over-exposure to radiation after a mammography. Because she was told repeatedly by medical experts that the mammography could not have caused the symptoms, it was held that she did not have knowledge of an injury attributable to negligence of the hospital's radiographer).

[572] *Halford v Brookes* [1991] 1 W.L.R. 428, CA.

[573] *Wilkinson v Ancliff (B.L.T.)* [1986] 1 W.L.R. 1352, CA.

[574] s.14(1): "knowledge that any acts or omissions did or did not, as a matter of law, involve negligence, nuisance or breach of duty is irrelevant." See also *Dobbie v Medway HA* [1994] 1 W.L.R. 1234, CA, where the claim was statute-barred, even though the claimant had not appreciated that the defendant's conduct might be actionable. For a critical view of this decision, see Care, "Limitations and Chemical Poisoning" in 139 S.J. 17.

[575] *Hallam-Eames v Merrett Syndicates* [2001] Lloyd's Rep. P.N. 178, CA, at 181, also *Nash v Eli Lilly & Co* [1993] 1 W.L.R. 782, at 799, per Purchas L.J.: knowledge of the "essence" of the act or omission to which injury was attributable; also *Whiston v London Strategic HA* [2010] EWCA Civ 195, para.4–184, below.

can identify (in broad terms) that she goes to a solicitor to seek advice about making a claim for compensation[576];

(4) On the other hand, she will not have the requisite knowledge if she thinks she knows the acts or omissions she should investigate but in fact is barking up the wrong tree: or if her knowledge of what the defendant did or did not do is so vague or general that she cannot fairly be expected to know what she should investigate; or if her state of mind is such that she thinks her condition is capable of being attributed to the act or omission alleged to constitute negligence, but she is not sure about this, and would need to check with an expert before she could be properly be said to know that it was."[577]

ILLUSTRATIONS

Where a child of eight was told that if a problem with her hip had been treated **4–184** earlier, she would not have required so many operations, time did not run against her since a mere statement that there had been a delay in treatment was insufficient to fix the claimant with knowledge that the delay was attributable to the defendant's negligence.[578] Time could not run against a claimant who was unaware he had suffered any injury at all.[579] The claimant did not have knowledge of the act or omission which was causally relevant where she became aware, shortly after the event, that she had received injury to her sphincter in the course of episiotomy, but did not know and was not told until much later that the injury should have been repaired immediately and that the failure to do so lessened her prospect of full recovery.[580] The claimant did not have actual knowledge sufficient to start the limitation clock running where she had been negligently advised that her injured shoulder would heal and required mobilisation since she did not know of a causative link between that treatment and the persistence of symptoms.[581] The claimant was not time-barred where he did not appreciate for some nine years that an operation should have been performed to reduce fractures of two fingers shortly after his original hospital admission, even though he had been aware for most of that time that in spite of a later operation, his disability was continuing.[582] The time bar did not operate against the claimant where, in a claim based on an accident at work, he mistakenly sued as his employer, the company whose name appeared on his payslips, rather than an

---

[576] See *Roberts v Winbow* [1999] P.I.Q.R. P77, CA (a medical negligence case in which the Court of Appeal considered the position where the claimant knows some, but not the main part of her injuries to be attributable to the act or ommission alleged to constitute negligence); also *Sniezek v Bundy (Letchworth) Ltd* [2000] P.I.Q.R. P213, CA (distinction between state of knowledge of a claimant whose belief that he has a condition attributable to his working conditions takes him to a solicitor; and someone who believes he may have or even probably does have such a condition, but is unsure and requires expert advice on the question).

[577] *Spargo v North Essex District HA* [1997] P.I.Q.R. P235 at P242, CA. See also *Sniezek v Bundy (Letchworth) Ltd* n.576, above (observations that the fourth *Spargo* principle should not be taken as contradicting the third: it deals with a situation antithetical to the third).

[578] *Colegrove v Smith* [1994] 5 Med. L.R. 111.

[579] *James v East Dorset HA, The Times*, December 7, 1999, CA (where the claimant was aware only that his condition after an operation had continued to deteriorate, and thereby that the operation had not been successful).

[580] *Hind v York Health Service NHS Trust* [1998] P.I.Q.R. P235.

[581] *Ostick v Wandsworth HA* [1996] 6 Med. L.R. 338.

[582] *Smith v West Lancashire HA* [1995] P.I.Q.R. P514, CA.

associated company which was actually his employer.[583] A claimant did not have knowledge of the essence of the act alleged to constitute negligence where he knew from an early age his cerebral palsy was caused by deprivation of oxygen during forceps delivery, but did not know of the elongated nature of the attempted delivery with inappropriate forceps.[584]

4–185   Time did run against a claimant who alleged shortcomings in medical treatment, not from the date of a medical report which identified the problems, but from a much earlier time when he had known the essential facts of his complaints as a result of a report from another consultant, which itself had not supported a claim for negligence.[585] The claimant did have such knowledge as caused time to run against him where by his eighteenth birthday he knew that he was dyslexic, that there were steps which could have been taken to help him, and that those steps had not been taken during his schooling.[586]

4–186   **Constructive knowledge.** A claimant who does not have actual knowledge may acquire constructive knowledge. By s.14(3), a person's knowledge:

> "includes knowledge which he might reasonably have been expected to acquire (a) from facts observable or ascertainable by him or (b) from facts ascertainable by him with the help of medical or other appropriate expert advice which it is reasonable for him to seek, but a person shall not be fixed under this subsection with knowledge of a fact ascertainable only with the help of expert advice so long as he has taken all reasonable steps to obtain (and, where appropriate to act on) that advice."

4–187   The test under the section contains only a limited subjective element. In *Adams v Bracknell Forest Borough Council,*[587] Lord Hoffmann indicated his approval of the general approach by the Court of Appeal in *Forbes v Wandsworth Health Authority,*[588] as opposed to the reasoning of the same court in *Nash v Eli Lilly & Co.*[589] Although the claimant had to be assumed to be a person who had suffered the injury in question and not some other person, his particular character or intelligence was not relevant. Section 14(3) required the court to assume that a person who was aware that he had suffered a personal injury, serious enough to be something about which he would go and see a solicitor if he knew he had a claim, would be sufficiently curious about the causes of the injury to seek

---

[583] *Cressey v E. Timm & Son Ltd* [2006] P.I.Q.R. P90, CA (the argument that time ran against the claimant because he knew that the accident was caused by his employer, even though he did not know who his employer was, failed: he had a reasonable time in which to make appropriate enquiries about the identity of his employer and could not have known the correct defendant until an insurers' letter identifying the correct employer was received; per Rix L.J. at 99: where there is a problem of identity "time could only be extended for the shortest period possible for objectively reasonable enquiries to be made. In the absence of a positively misleading response . . . it would be wise for a claimant to work on the basis that the three years had already started to run at the date of the accident").
[584] *Whiston v London Strategic HA* [2010] EWCA Civ 195.
[585] *Jones v Liverpool HA* [1996] P.I.Q.R. P251, CA.
[586] *Rowe v Kingston upon Hull City Council* [2004] P.I.Q.R. P238, CA.
[587] [2005] 1 A.C. 76, (a claim for an allegedly negligent failure to treat dyslexia where the claimant knew of his condition but there was no evidential basis for a finding at first instance that he had been too embarrassed to raise the problem with his GP).
[588] [1997] Q.B. 402.
[589] [1993] 1 W.L.R. 782.

whatever expert advice was appropriate.[590] Even if the claimant was dyslexic there was no reason why this assumption should not apply. If that were not the expectation, there would be no reason why the limitation period should not run indefinitely, until some contrary impulse led to the discovery which brought it to an end.[591] In agreeing with the majority, Lord Scott said:

" . . . The reference in s.14(3) to 'knowledge which he might reasonably have been expected to acquire' should, in my opinion, be taken to be a reference to knowledge which a person in the situation of the claimant, i.e. an adult who knows he is illiterate, could reasonably be expected to acquire. Personal characteristics such as shyness and embarrassment, which may have inhibited the claimant from seeking advice about his illiteracy problems but which would not be expected to have inhibited others with a like disability, should be left out of the equation. It is the norms of behaviour of persons in the situation of the claimant that should be the test."[592]

ILLUSTRATIONS

Where the claimant appreciated in general terms that a medical problem was **4–188** capable of being attributed to surgery although she did not know the precise nature of any error, she had knowledge for purposes of s.14(3).[593] Where an operation to cure partial deafness, which he had been assured would be successful, turned out instead to be a disaster, the claimant ought to have realised that something had gone badly wrong and was held to have constructive knowledge.[594] For the purpose of establishing his "date of knowledge" an injured claimant could rely on the fact that he had no resources and his solicitors had to work within the restrictions of a limited legal aid certificate.[595] Where in a claim alleging failure to protect from historic child abuse, the claimant delayed

---

[590] However, an "obligation of curiosity" does not to form part of the ratio of *Adams*: see per Dyson L.J. in *Whiston v London Strategic HA,* n.584, above at [54]. See further, Patten, "Constructing knowledge" 160 N.L.J. 486.

[591] [2005] 1 A.C. 76 at 89. Lord Hoffmann pointed out that this approach to the standard of reasonableness reflected the policy of the law. Since the Limitation Act 1975, and in particular s.33 thereof, the postponement of the commencement of the limitation period by reference to the date of knowledge was no longer the sole mechanism for avoiding injustice to a claimant who could not reasonably be expected to have known that he had a cause of action. It was therefore possible in intepreting s.14(3) to have greater regard to the potential injustice to defendants if the limitation period should be indefinitely extended.

[592] ibid. at 94. Lord Walker and Baroness Hale agreed in the result but were more cautions in entirely discarding the subjective element (see ibid. at 96, 100. *Adams* was applied in *Smith v Hampshire CC* [2007] E.L.R. 321, CA (untreated dyslexia was not itself a sufficient explanation for the claimant's failure to seek professional help sooner, since he had known ever since leaving school at the age of 15, that problems of reading and writing were capable of being attributed to his education, which had either failed to identify the problems or to do anything about them: the claimant did not need to be formally diagnosed as dyslexic before time ran against him). See also *Whiston v London Strategic HA,* n.584, above (the knowledge that a claimant might reasonably have been expected to acquire should be decided by reference to all the circumstances of the case).

[593] *Hendy v Milton Keynes HA* [1991] 3 Med. L.R. 114 approved in *Broadley v Guy Clapham & Co* [1994] 4 All E.R. 439, CA.

[594] *Baig v City and Hackney HA* [1994] 5 Med. L.R. 221. See also *Crocker v British Coal Corp* (1996) 29 B.M.L.R. 159 (where the claim for psychiatric injury was dismissed even though the plaintiff's obsessional neurosis had been formally diagnosed within three years of proceedings being commenced, since she had known for many years that she suffered from an abnormal affliction).

[595] *Khan v Ainslie* [1993] 4 Med. L.R. 319.

some 27 years in bringing proceedings, he had constructive knowledge of his cause of action from seven years before the claim was issued, being shortly after the time the defendant made an offer, which he did not take up, to permit him to view his file.[596]

4–189 **"Expert advice"**. The view has been expressed that the "expert advice" referred to in s.14(3)(b) is directed to experts in the sense of expert witnesses, so that a party's solicitor was not an expert within that meaning.[597] But the better view may well be otherwise: where her solicitors delayed in identifying the appropriate defendant for purposes of her claim, the claimant could not take refuge in the proviso to s.14(3) on the basis that she should not be fixed with knowledge of a fact ascertainable only with the help of expert advice so long as she had taken reasonable steps to obtain that advice[598]:

> "The proviso is not intended to give an extended period of limitation to a person whose solicitor acts dilatorily in acquiring information which is obtainable without particular expertise."[599]

Where knowledge as to whether deafness was noise-induced or age-induced could be gained only by means of expert medical advice, which the claimant had reasonably sought but not received, the proviso to s.14(3) applied and he did not have knowledge sufficient to cause the limitation period to run.[600]

4–190 **Significance.** Section 14(1)(a) of the Act provides that references to a person's date of knowledge are references to the date on which he first had knowledge of a number of facts, the first of which is that the injury in question was significant. In assessing significance, a preliminary issue will be to identify correctly what "the injury in question" is. It may be easy to identify the injury where the complaint is of a "one off" accident giving rise to physical injury, but cases in which the allegation is psychiatric injury whose onset may have been gradual, or delayed, the issue can be more difficult. The basic question will be "what is the action all about."[601]

4–191 Having identified the injury, s.14(2) provides an objective test. The injury is significant "if the person whose date of knowledge is in question would

---

[596] *Pierce v Doncaster MBC* [2008] EWCA Civ 1416.

[597] *Fowell v N.C.B.*, *The Times*, May 28, 1986.

[598] In *Henderson v Temple Pier Co Ltd* [1998] 3 All E.R. 324, CA, it was said that the opinions expressed on this point in *Fowell* were not part of the ratio decidendi. For knowledge of the plaintiff's expert, see *Marston v B.R.B.* [1976] I.C.R. 124.

[599] [1998] 3 All E.R. 324 at 329, per Bracewell J.

[600] *Ali v Courtaulds Textiles Ltd*, *The Times*, May 28, 1999, CA; also *Harrild v Ministry of Defence* [2001] Lloyd's Rep. Med. 117 (where the claimant suffered an acute heart attack while an in-patient and it was alleged that failure to carry out timely tests caused a condition which could have been avoided; he did not know of the possible attribution of his injury to the defendants' negligence until a later time when he spoke to his sister, a cardiac nurse).

[601] A phrase used by Croom-Johnson J. in *Ackbar v C.F. Green & Co* [1975] Q.B. 582, 587, in the slightly different context of whether a claim consisted of or included damages for personal injuries, see para.4–179, above.

reasonably have considered it sufficiently serious to justify instituting proceedings for damages against a defendant who did not dispute liability and was able to satisfy a judgment." The standard set by the subsection has been said to be impersonal: "not whether the claimant himself would have considered the injury sufficiently serious to justify proceedings but whether he would "reasonably" have done so."[602] The subsection sets a standard of seriousness by which to assess what the claimant knew or must be treated as having known. It is to be distinguished from s.14(3) which imputes knowledge by reference to what the claimant ought reasonably to have done.[603] Because the standard set by s.14(2) is objective the claimant's character and intelligence, and the effect of injury upon his ability to perceive and understand are all irrelevant to the question to be addressed. Subjective matters of that kind belong to the exercise of the court's discretion under s.33 of the Act if application is made to disapply the limitation period under that section.[604]

Looking at the approach to s.14 generally, the court should ask what the **4–192** claimant knew about the injury he had suffered; it adds any knowledge about the injury which may be imputed to him under s.14(3); and then asks whether a reasonable person with that knowledge would have considered the injury sufficiently serious to justify instituting proceedings for damages against a defendant who did not dispute liability and was able to satisfy a judgment.[605] In looking at the test of significance in relation to to both s.14(2) and (3) it is not the case that, as soon as a claimant is aware of symptoms that amount only to minor inconvenience, he is fixed with the knowledge that he would have acquired had he immediately taken expert advice. It is entirely natural that, when a person is suffering from minor symptoms, he will brush them to one side, with or without some private explanation to himself as to what is giving rise to the problem.[606]

ILLUSTRATIONS

A claimant who knew of significant harmful effects from the prescription of a **4–193** drug was fixed with knowledge of significant injury even though unaware that the side effects were disproportionate to the drug's therapeutic value.[607] An 18-year-

---

[602] *A v Hoare* [2008] 1 A.C. 844, per Lord Hoffmann at para.[34]. Observations in *McCafferty v Metropolitan Police District Receiver* [1977] 1 W.L.R. 1073, 1081, to the effect that the test was partially objective and partly subjective were disapproved, as was the similar approach taken in *KR v Bryn Alyn Community (Holdings) Ltd* [2003] Q.B. 1441. The approach taken in *Young v South Tyneside M.B.C.* [2007] Q.B. 932, was also flawed, in the suggestion that it was appropriate to consider under s.14 the effect an injury may have had upon the claimant's reasons for delay: such reasons were for consideration under s.33 of the Act (see para.4–200 below) not s.14. On this ground alone cases decided before the review of the law in *A v Hoare* will have to be treated with care since the court may not have been taking into account under s.33 that which it should. See further Keen, "Know your limits" 158 N.L.J. 360.
[603] *A v Hoare*, above, at [38].
[604] ibid. at [44].
[605] ibid. at [34].
[606] *Furniss v Firth Brown Tools Ltd* [2008] EWCA Civ 182 (an industrial deafness claim).
[607] *Briggs v Pitt-Payne* [1999] Lloyd's Rep. Med. 1, CA.

old soldier knew he had a significant injury where he had sustained an injury to his ear in a training exercise resulting in marked sensorineural hearing loss, although he only commenced proceedings seeking damages over 10 years later, after he had been told the injury was likely to exclude him permanently from active service.[608] Where the claimant did not have actual knowledge that he had suffered an injury to his hearing from exposure to noise at work, as opposed to knowledge of temporary and minor problems attributed to wax or infections, time did not run against his claim until tests diagnosed noise-induced hearing loss. It was reasonable for him not to seek further advice, especially when those who had carried out earlier tests had given him to understand that there was nothing much wrong with his hearing, and that he was fit to continue work.[609]

4-194   A claimant who was operated upon unsuccessfully in 1997 for a Hallux Valgus deformity of the left foot, was not out of time in commencing proceedings for negligence in 2006, where there had been many subsequent consulatations with doctors in the period after the operation and she had been left with the impression that it would take time for her condition to settle.[610] A dock worker knew he had a significant injury from the time when he had visited the practice nurse at his general practitioner's surgery and complained of hearing problems, although he did not pursue her suggestion that he make an appointment with the doctor, nor seek further medical advice in relation to the problem for seven years, until advised to do so by a legal advisor.[611]

4-195   **Different limitation periods arising from one incident.** Where injury to the person and damage to property arises in one incident, such as a to the driver of a car involved in a road traffic accident, there are, at least on the face of it, two relevant periods of limitation: three years for the personal injuries and six years for the damage to property.[612] But the doctrine of *res judicata* may operate to prevent a claim which could and should have been brought in earlier proceedings arising out of the same subject matter[613] and it may be that this rule would itself debar a claimant from bringing a claim for damage to property, otherwise within time, where earlier proceedings for the claimant's personal injury had been brought and decided.

4-196   **Limitation in negligence and assault compared.** In *Letang v Cooper*,[614] the claimant sued for injuries sustained when she was run over by a car as she lay on

---

[608] *McCoubrey v Ministry of Defence* [2007] 1 W.L.R. 1544, CA (significance has to be assessed by reference to the seriousness of the injury sustained, not, for instance, by reference to its effect, let alone its subjectively perceived effect, on the claimant's private life or career).
[609] *Field v British Coal Corporation* [2008] EWCA Civ 912.
[610] *Rogers v East Kent Hospital* [2009] EWHC 54 (Q.B.). It was accepted that her date of knowledge was in late 2003 when, having moved to a different area, she discussed the operation with a new consultant who told of her of other options that would have been available.
[611] *Teague v Mersey Docks & Harbour Company* [2008] EWCA Civ 1601.
[612] *Brunsden v Humphrey* (1884) 14 Q.B.D. 141.
[613] *Talbot v Berkshire County Council* [1994] Q.B. 290. See further at para.4–241, below.
[614] [1964] 2 Q.B. 53.

grass sun-bathing. A cause of action in negligence was time-barred since more than three years had passed when the proceedings were commenced. Instead, she pursued a claim based upon trespass to the person, that is, assault. The claim failed, it being found that what had happened was an accident, but it was said that had there been a cause of action in trespass, then the words "breach of duty" in the proviso added to s.2(1) of the Act of 1939[615] meant that the three-year limitation period applied. Subsequently, in *Stubbings v Webb*,[616] the House of Lords took a different view. It was decided that a six-year limitation period applied to actions arising from complaints of deliberate assault, including rape. However, some thirteen years later, there was a further change of direction and the House declared *Stubbings* wrongly decided. In *A v Hoare*,[617] it was held that the three-year period applied to assault cases and there was the opportunity for extension under s.33 of the Limitation Act 1980 where the court thought it just to do so. The law as laid down in *Letang* was reaffirmed.

Death of victim before limitation period expires: s.11(5). An action by the personal representative[618] of the deceased for damage to his estate under the Law Reform (Miscellaneous Provisions) Act 1934 is also governed by the Limitation Act 1980 s.11. If the person injured dies before the expiration of three years from either the date on which his cause of action accrued or the date of his knowledge[619] (if later) then by subs.(5) the period applicable as respects the cause of action surviving for the benefit of the estate of the deceased by virtue of the Law Reform (Miscellaneous Provisions) Act 1934 s.1 "shall be three years from—(a) the date of death; or (b) the date of the personal representative's knowledge, whichever is the later." If the action be begun before the grant of administration, a subsequent grant does not relate back so as to validate the proceedings.[620]   **4–197**

Limitation in fatal accidents claims. By s.12(1) of the Limitation Act 1980, no action under the Fatal Accidents Act 1976 can be brought where the death occurred after the injured person himself could no longer bring an action in respect of his injuries sustained, whether the reason for this was because of a time limit under the Limitation Act 1980 or under any other Act[621] or, indeed, for any other reason. Further, where any such action by the injured person before his death would have been barred by the time limit, contained in s.11 of the Act, no   **4–198**

---

[615] Now see s.11(1) of the Limitation Act 1980.
[616] *Stubbings v Webb* [1993] A.C. 498.
[617] [2008] 1 A.C. 844. In giving reasons for departing from *Stubbings* Lord Hoffmann referred to the words of Lord Reid in *R. v National Insurance Commisioners, ex p. Hudson* [1972] A.C. 944, at 966, that the House should overrule earlier decisions where they were "thought to be impeding the proper development of the law or to have led to results which were unjust or contrary to public policy."
[618] See s.11(6) and (7) of the Limitation Act 1980 regarding the persons included as a "personal representative" and their different "dates of knowledge".
[619] See paras 4–182 to 4–194, above.
[620] *Ingall v Moran* [1944] K.B. 160. See also *Hilton v Sutton Steam Laundry* [1946] K.B. 65; *Burns v Campbell* [1952] 1 K.B. 15.
[621] e.g. the Carriage by Air Act 1961, see para.4–233, below, and the Merchant Shipping Act 1995, see para.4–231, below.

account can be taken of the possibility of that time limit being overridden by the discretion of the court under s.33.

4–199 When the negligence, nuisance or breach of duty[622] of a person causes the death of another, an action by or on behalf of the dependants, under the Fatal Accidents Act 1976, must be brought within three years of either the date of death or the date of knowledge of the person for whose benefit the action is brought, whichever date is the later.[623] The provisions of s.14,[624] defining the date of knowledge, apply equally to fatal accidents claims as they do to those involving personal injury[625]; as do the provisions of s.33, which relates to the discretionary extension of time limits.[626] Where there is more than one person for whose benefit an action under the Fatal Accidents Act 1976 is brought then the provisions of s.12(2)(b), relating to the date of knowledge of the person for whose benefit the action is brought, "shall be applied separately to each of them".[627] If the action is brought outside the time limit as regards "one or more, but not all, of the persons for whose benefit it is brought, the court shall direct[628] that any person as regards whom the action would be outside that limit shall be excluded from those for whom the action is brought".[629]

Since time does not begin to run from the date of the wrongful act, neglect or default which is the subject of the complaint, but runs instead from the date of death, or the date of the dependant's knowledge, the action is dissimilar to an ordinary action for damages in tort.[630]

4–200 **Discretion to override time limits: s.33.** The court may allow an action to proceed, notwithstanding the expiry of the relevant period of limitation, by overriding the prescribed time limits, set out in either s.11 or s.12. The circumstances in which the court may exercise its discretion[631] are contained in s.33, which provides:

"(1) If it appears to the court that it would be equitable[632] to allow an action to proceed having regard to the degree to which—

---

[622] Namely "whether the duty exists by virtue of a contract or of provision made by or under a statute or independently of any contract or any such provision": s.11(1).

[623] ibid., s.12(2).

[624] Which has been discussed in more detail in paras 4–182 to 4–194, above.

[625] ibid., s.14(1).

[626] ibid., s.12(3). See para.4–200, below.

[627] See ibid., s.13(1).

[628] ibid., s.13(3), which contains the circumstances in which the court shall not give such a direction.

[629] ibid., s.13(2).

[630] *British Columbia Electric Ry v Gentile* [1914] A.C. 1034; *Venn v Tedesco* [1926] 2 K.B. 227.

[631] See Vickers, "Overriding the Time Bar in Personal Injuries Actions" in 130 New L.J. 380; Saunders, "Overriding the Time Bar in Personal Injuries Actions: An Unfettered Discretion?" in 131 New L.J. 346.

[632] s.33 asks not whether the claim itself was equitable but whether it would be equitable to allow the claim to proceed: *Ward v Foss, The Times*, November 29, 1993 (held, not inequitable to disapply the limitation period in respect of a claim for the "lost years" where that claim could have been made, if brought in time, but had become unavailable through a change in the law). See Ch.16, para.16–76, below.

    (a) the provisions of section 11 or 12 of this Act prejudice the plaintiff or any person whom he represents; and

    (b) any decision of the court under this subsection would prejudice the defendant[633] or any person whom he represents;

the court may direct that those provisions shall not apply to the action, or shall not apply to any specified cause of action to which the action relates.

(2) The court shall not under this section disapply section 12(1) except where the reason why the person injured could no longer maintain an action was because of the time limit in s.11.

    If, for example, the person injured could at his death no longer maintain an action under the Fatal Accidents Act 1976 because of the time limit in Article 29 in Schedule 1 to the Carriage by Air Act 1961, the court has no power to direct that section 12(1) shall not apply.

(3) In acting under this section the court shall have regard to all the circumstances of the case[634] and in particular to[635]—

    (a) the length of, and the reasons for, he delay on the part of the plaintiff;

    (b) the extent to which, having regard to the delay, the evidence adduced or likely to be adduced by the plaintiff or the defendant is or is likely to be less cogent than if the action had been brought within the time allowed by section 11 or (as the case may be) by section 12;

    (c) the conduct of the defendant after the cause of action arose, including the extent (if any) to which he responded to requests reasonably made by the plaintiff for information or inspection for the purpose of ascertaining facts which were or might be relevant to the plaintiff's cause of action against the defendant;

    (d) the duration of any disability of the plaintiff arising after the date of the accrual of the cause of action;

    (e) the extent to which the plaintiff acted promptly and reasonably once he knew whether or not the act or omission of the defendant, to which the injury was attributable, might be capable at that time of giving rise to an action for damages;

    (f) the steps, if any, taken by the plaintiff to obtain medical, legal or other expert advice and the nature of any such advice, he may have received.

(4) In a case where the person injured died when, because of section 11, he could no longer maintain an action and recover damages in respect of the injury, the court shall have regard in particular to the length of, and the reasons for, the delay on the part of the deceased.

(5) In a case under subsection (4) above, or any other case where the time limit, or one of the time limits, depends on the date of knowledge of a person other than the plaintiff, subsection (3) above shall have effect with appropriate modifications, and shall have effect in particular as if references to the plaintiff included

---

[633] See para.4–202, below.

[634] See, e.g. *Taylor v Taylor, The Times*, April 14, 1984, CA; *Lye v Marks & Spencer Plc, The Times*, February 15, 1988, CA (the court was entitled to have regard to the fact that a plaintiff was legally aided, as a result of which the defendant would have little prospect of recovering any of his costs, in the event of the plaintiff's action failing).

[635] For an analysis of the six sub-paras (*a*) to (*f*) that follow, characterised as "a curious hotchpotch" see, per Lord Diplock in *Thompson v Brown* [1981] 1 W.L.R. 744 at 751.

references to any person whose date of knowledge is or was relevant in determining a time limit.

(6) A direction by the court disapplying the provisions of section 12(1) shall operate to disapply the provisions to the same effect in section 1 of the Fatal Accidents Act 1976.

(7) In this section 'the court' means the court in which the action has been brought.

(8) References in this section to section 11 include references to that section as extended by any of the preceding provisions of this Part of this Act or any provision of Part III of this Act."

4–201   **Discretion is unfettered.** The exercise of the court's discretion to "disapply" the time limits prescribed by ss.11 and 12, is unfettered.[636] No distinction should arise between group actions, multi-party litigation and ordinary cases.[637] The section should not be read so as to confine its application to either a residual class of case or an otherwise exceptional one.[638] Since the statute confers on the court a discretion to be exercised with regard to all the circumstances of the case,[639] considerable difficulties will face any appellant seeking to challenge the exercise of discretion as wrongful.[640] An appellate court will only interfere if the first instance judge proceeded incorrectly by failing to direct himself to the matters set out in s.33.[641] Where the trial judge has not been invited to consider the application of s.33 at all, the appellate court may exercise the discretion which he would have exercised had he before him the material that was available at the hearing of the appeal.[642] A similar approach will be taken where an applicant has not complied with his duty to give full and frank disclosure of all relevant facts at the hearing of his application.[643]

---

[636] *Thompson v Brown* [1981] 1 W.L.R. 744, HL. The burden of proof in an application under s.33 rests upon the claimant: *Barrand v British Cellophane*, *The Times*, February 16, 1995, CA.

[637] *Nash v Eli Lilly* [1991] Med. L.R. 169, per Hidden J. For an example of the application of s.33 to group litigation see *KR v Bryn Alyn Community (Holdings) Ltd* [2003] Q.B. 1441 (para.4–191 above; it was observed that where various claimants were involved in one group action it was still necessary to consider this cases on limitation individually).

[638] *Firman v Ellis* [1978] Q.B. 886. Although the decision in *Firman* must be regarded as overruled by *Walkley v Precision Forgings Ltd* [1979] 1 W.L.R. 606, it was not overruled on this point, which was followed in *Simpson v Norwest Holst Southern Ltd* [1980] 1 W.L.R. 968. See also confirmation in *Thompson v Brown*, n.604, above. See Jones, "Solicitors Negligence—Discretionary Liability under the Limitation Act 1980" in (1985) 1 P.N. 159.

[639] Consideration should not be confined to the six matters in subs.(3)(a)–(f): see *Taylor v Taylor*, n.634, above.

[640] *Yates v Thakeham Tiles* [1995] P.I.Q.R. P135, CA.

[641] *Conry v Simpson* [1983] 3 All E.R. 369, CA.

[642] *McCafferty v Metropolitan Police District Receiver* [1977] 1 W.L.R. 1073, although the HL declined to do so in *Thompson v Brown*, above and remitted the matter to the trial judge.

[643] *Long v Tolchard and Sons Ltd* [2001] P.I.Q.R. P18, CA (long after liability had been resolved in the claimant's favour it was discovered that medical records contradicted his assertion, as to a limitation issue, that he had been unaware of a back problem before the relevant date: the Court of Appeal set aside the exercise of discretion under s.33 and declared the action statute barred).

Importance of prejudice.[644] Where the defendant has early notice of a claim, **4–202** the accrual of a limitation defence should be regarded as a windfall and the prospect of its loss, by the exercise of the s.33 discretion, should be regarded as either no prejudice or only minimal prejudice. What is at the heart of s.33 is whether it would be equitable to allow an action to proceed, and in fairness and justice, the obligation of a tortfeasor to pay damages should only be removed, if the passage of time has significantly diminished his opportunity to defend himself. Although on a literal construction section 33, it appears to be relevant to the exercise of the discretion that the defendant will suffer the financial prejudice of having to pay damages if the limitation period is disapplied, Parliament cannot have intended that such a prejudice should be taken into account. On the other hand, it could be relevant to take account of the fact that prejudice to the claimant in being prevented from proceeding with his claim will be greatly reduced, if he has a good claim against his solicitor. In a case where the defendant has suffered some forensic or procedural prejudice that diminishes his ability to defend himself, it will be proper to take into consideration that the claimant has another remedy.

The fact that the claimant has a possible claim against his solicitor will not **4–203** necessarily mean that the time limit should not be disapplied.[645] The basic question to be asked is whether it is fair and just in all the circumstances to expect the defendant to meet the claim on the merits, notwithstanding the delay in commencement. The length of the delay, of itself, is not a deciding factor. Although the delay referred to in s.33 is delay after the expiry of the limitation period, it will also be relevant to consider when the defendant knew that a claim was to be made against him and the opportunities he had to investigate the claim and collect evidence.[646] Even where the exercise is finely balanced, it is wrong for a judge to resolve the exercise of discretion under s.33 by considering whether the claimant acted reasonably, that not being a matter specifically identified in the Act.[647]

In *Thompson v Brown*,[648] the claimant had not issued his writ until some 37 **4–204** days after the expiry of the three-year limitation period but the defendants had no

---

[644] See *Cain v Francis* [2009] 3 W.L.R. 551, CA on which this para. is based (two appeals heard together, each a road traffic accident case: in the first the limitation period was disapplied where the claimant brought the claim one day out of time; in the second where the claim was brought one year late). See Wyles, "Limitation matters" 159 N.L.J. 252; Jefferson, "A lottery for litigants?" 159 N.L.J. 379.

[645] *Hartley v Birmingham City DC* [1992] 1 W.L.R. 968 (through no fault of her own, the plaintiff's writ was issued less than one day out of the limitation period). See also in relation to solicitors' negligence the comments of the Court of Appeal in *Das v Ganju* [1999] P.I.Q.R. P260; *Davis v Jacobs* [1999] Lloyd's Rep. Med. 72, CA, and para.4–208, below; *Corbin v Penfold Metallising Co Ltd, The Times*, May 2, 2000, CA.

[646] *Cain v Francis,* n.644, above.

[647] *McGhie v British Telecommunications Plc* [2005] EWCA Civ 48, CA, (a claim for injury at work where proceedings were commenced five years after the date of the accident and at its highest the claim was for acceleration of a pre-existing injury).

[648] [1981] 1 W.L.R. 744, HL. See Holgate, "The Time Limit in Personal Injury Claims" in 131 New L.J. 1124.

defence at all on the merits of the case. Lord Diplock pointed out that where "the time elapsed after the expiration of the primary limitation is very short, what the defendant loses in consequence of a direction might be regarded as being in the nature of a windfall".[649] In the event of proceedings, brought within the primary limitation period, being a nullity and so being discontinued, the claimant may bring himself still within the ambit of s.33 in respect of a second action.[650]

4–205   **Proportionality.** As with the exercise of any discretion after the introduction of the Civil Procedure Rules 1999, the question of proportionality ought to be kept in mind when considering whether to disapply the limitation period pursuant to s.33.[651] It was said in a claim based upon failure to identify or treat the claimant's dyslexia that courts "should be slow to exercise their discretion in favour of a claimant in the absence of of cogent medical evidence showing a serious effect on the claimant's health or enjoyment of life and employability". It was also relevant that such claims usually involved investigation, many years after the event, of decisions made at a school, and they would thereby be expensive and difficult to contest.

4–206   **A v Hoare.** Many of the general points referred to above were reflected in the speeches in *A v Hoare*,[652] a case in which the House of Lords considered the exercise of discretion under s.33 in the context of claims for assault, claims which it was thought could well become more frequent bearing in mind a change in the law which the House had itself made.[653] It was said that where the claimant alleged that delay had arisen as a result of psychological or other problems brought about by the very breach of duty of which complaint was made, it was appropriate to consider the issue under s.33 rather than under s.14 of the Act. The trial judge and Court of Appeal had approached the matter otherwise in one of the appeals before the House and that case was remitted for discretion to be exercised afresh.[654] It was pointed out that in exercising discretion the court would no doubt consider its ability to conduct a fair trial and the extent of the factual issues between the parties; likewise the ability of a defendant alleged to be vicariously

---

[649] *Thompson v Brown* [1981] 1 W.L.R. 744 at 750.

[650] *White v Glass, The Times*, February 18, 1989, CA; *McEvoy v A.A. Welding and Fabrication Ltd* [1998] P.I.Q.R. P266, CA, both distinguishing *Walkley v Precision Forgings Ltd* [1979] 1 W.L.R. 66. See further *Horton v Sadler* [2007] 1 A.C. 307, per Lord Bingham at [36] (*Walkley* overruled); also *Leeson v Marsden* (2008) 103 B.M.L.R. 49.

[651] *Robinson v St Helens MBC* [2003] P.I.Q.R. P128 at P140, CA. Similar considerations came into play in *Rowe v Kingston upon Hull CC* [2004] P.I.Q.R. P238, CA, para.3–185, above, and in *Adams v Bracknell Forest BC* [2005] 1 A.C. 76, para.4–187, above. In *Kew v Bettamix Limited* [2007] P.I.Q.R. P16, CA (a hand arm vibration syndrome claim) proportionality was described by Leveson L.J. at [41] as "not a specific financial hurdle which must be overcome for any claim of this nature to succeed, but rather a consideration both of the benefits to the claimant in terms of the strength and value of the claim and the potential cost both legal and in manpower or otherwise to the organisation of the proposed defendant."

[652] [2008] 1 A.C. 844.

[653] See above para.4–196.

[654] *Young v South Tyneside M.B.C.* [2007] Q.B. 932. *A v Hoare* was itself also remitted to the trial judge for an exercise of discretion under s. 33 for which see para.4–217, below.

liable for assaults committed by an employee, to investigate what happened, in some cases many years after the event.[655]

Subsection 33(3)(a). In investigating under s.33(1)(a) the reasons for the **4–207** claimant's delay, the inquiry is subjective, in the sense that the court is concerned with what the claimant knew and what reasons in fact operated upon his mind.[656] Having found out what the claimant's reason for delay was, the court has to decide if it was a good reason or not.[657] It may be a legitimate consideration under sub-para.(a) that a claimant has delayed: in ignorance of her legal rights as administratrix of the deceased's estate[658]; while attempting to identify the correct employers to be sued[659]; where he had decided initially that he did not want to sue in respect of something which he regarded merely as an "irritating nuisance"[660]; where he did not wish to be thought a "sponger" were he to have made a claim when he was able perfectly well to continue working[661]; where he had felt "pains" from time to time, following an accident at work in a butchery, when a carcass of beef, weighing 250lb, had fallen on top of him but he was unaware of the true extent of his injuries and had not sought legal advice, until six-and-a-half years later[662]; where he suffered from spastic cerebral palsy, allegedly as a result of negligent management of his birth, which caused severe physical and mental stress throughout the relevant period and where little additional prejudice had accrued to the defendant as a result of the delay[663]; where there is delay as a result of psychological problems brought about by the breach of duty of which complaint is made.[664]

Subsections 33(3)(b) and (c). Under sub-para.(b) account can be taken of **4–208** delay prior to the expiry of the period of limitation.[665] Account can also be taken, when considering prejudice to the defendant, of delay in giving notice of a claim and the late delivery of particulars of it so that it was virtually impossible for the

---

[655] [2008] 2 W.L.R. 311 at [81]–[82]. See also *Bowden v Poor Sisters of Nazareth* [2008] UKHL 32 (a Scottish case in which limitation was an issue in civil claim arising from alleged childhood abuse. The House of Lords upheld a decision not to disapply the limitation period under the Prescription and Limitation (Scotland) Act 1973 largely on the basis that prejudice arising from the lapse of time before the claims were brought was in itself a sufficient reason for not permitting the claim to proceed). See, Keen, "A matter of discretion" 158 N.L.J. 1059.
[656] See *Coad v Cornwall and Isles of Scilly HA* [1997] 1 W.L.R. 189, CA at 159.
[657] *Coad v Cornwall and Isles of Scilly HA* [1997] 1 W.L.R. 189, CA at ibid. In *Buckler v Sheffield CC* [2005] P.I.Q.R. P36, CA, Potter L.J. said at [26] this meant that, in effect, "having satisfied itself as to the genuineness of the claimant's reasons, in performing the overall exercise of deciding whether or not it is equitable to exercise the s.33 discretion in favour of the claimant, the court must consider whether or not, in all the circumstances, the reason or reasons advanced by the claimant are to be given real or decisive weight."
[658] *Halford v Brookes* [1991] 1 W.L.R. 428, CA.
[659] *Simpson v Norwest Holst Southern Ltd* [1980] 1 W.L.R. 968.
[660] *McCafferty v Metropolitan Police Receiver* [1977] 1 W.L.R. 1073.
[661] *Buck v English Electric Co Ltd* [1977] 1 W.L.R. 806.
[662] *Cornish v Kearley & Tonge* (1983) 133 New L.J. 870.
[663] *Pearse v Barnet Health Authority* [1998] P.I.Q.R. P39 (over two years delay).
[664] *A v Hoare*, para.4–206, above.
[665] *Donovan v Gwentoys* [1990] 1 W.L.R. 472, HL (on a correct assessment of the balance of prejudice, it would not be equitable to require the defendants to meet a claim, first made five years after the relevant event, when the claimant would suffer only the slightest prejudice if required to pursue an apparently unanswerable claim in negligence against her solicitor).

defendant to investigate it.[666] When considering prejudice, it is irrelevant that the defendant is insured, he and his insurer being treated as one when assessing the extent to which a proper defence of the claim has been prejudiced.[667] The "defendant" in sub-para.(c) includes, for instance, his agents, such as his solicitors.[668] The conduct which is relevant for purposes of subs.(c) is not confined to forensic tactics after intimation of a claim and could, for instance, include an employer's failure to provide the claimant with a health review suggested by its occupational health physician.[669]

4–209   **Section 33(3)(d)–(f).** "Disability", for purposes of sub-para.(d), refers to those claimants who are infants or patients within the Metal Health Act 1983, not those under physical disability, although the latter may be relevant when considering all the circumstances of the case.[670] In sub-para.(e) the test whether the claimant has acted reasonably in bringing his claim for damages late is an objective one, namely: "what would a reasonable man in the position of the plaintiff have done?"[671] In considering the "nature of any legal advice" received by the claimant for purposes of sub-para.(f), the court ought to inquire into the characteristics of such advice since it bears upon the question whether or not there has been unreasonable delay, once information has come to hand, which indicates there might be a cause of action against the defendant. The inquiry is not confined to such matters as whether advice was given by leading or junior counsel or whether it dealt with liability or quantum but should extend to whether that advice was favourable or unfavourable, even though the effect of this could be to encroach on the principle of legal privilege.[672]

4–210   **Very substantial delay.** Discretion can in an appropriate case be exercised in the claimant's favour even where the delay is substantial, but in such cases careful consideration will have to be given to the ability of the court to hold a fair trial. In *Buck v English Electric Co Ltd*,[673] a delay of nearly 16 years elapsed

---

[666] *Dale v British Coal Corp (No.2)* (1992) 136 S.J. (L.B.) 199. In *Buckler v Sheffield City Council*, n.657, above, (a case of alleged injury by exposure to asbestos) it was said by Potter L.J., at [33], that in considering prejudice to the defendant, the trial judge ought to have taken account of the difficulty, after a delay of nine years, in pursuing another potential defendant for contribution: "It is plain to me that the delay to which the judge should have had regard under para.(e) was a delay of nine years . . . in the context of a situation where, if two potential defendants were to be pursued and the full award of damages was to be justly apportioned between defendants, a full examination of the position of each defendant and the degree of the claimant's exposure while in their employment would be called for, on the basis of evidence of witnesses and such relevant documentary records as existed . . . "
[667] *Kelly v Bastible* [1997] P.N.L.R. 227, CA.
[668] *Thompson v Brown* [1981] 1 W.L.R. 744.
[669] *Kew v Bettamix Limited* [2007] P.I.Q.R. P16, CA, per Leveson L.J. at [36].
[670] *Yates v Thakeham Tiles Ltd* [1995] P.I.Q.R. P135, CA; *Thomas v Plaistow* [1997] P.I.Q.R. P540, CA.
[671] *Dale v British Coal Corp (No.2)* (1992) 136 S.J. (L.B.) 199. (A trade union member could be said usually to act reasonably if he followed union advice.) See also *Buckler v Sheffield CC*, n.657, above, (the claimant, whose work brought him into contact with asbestos, did not act reasonably where, having been told by his G.P. that he had developed pleural thickening, that there was a risk of lung cancer and that he could make a claim against his former employer, he delayed 8 years until an X ray revealed pleural plaques, before seeking legal advice: the heavy burden on a claimant to provide adequate reasons for a long delay had not been discharged).
[672] *Jones v G.D. Searle & Co Ltd* [1979] 1 W.L.R. 101.
[673] [1977] 1 W.L.R. 806.

between the time when the claimant, who subsequently died, discovered that he had contracted pneumoconiosis, and the time when proceedings were commenced. It was acknowledged that even five or six years' delay raised a presumption of prejudice to a defendant, but this presumption was rebuttable. The defendants had probably acquired sufficient relevant material as a result of a number of other similar claims made against them over the previous decade or more, so that the evidence was unlikely to be any the less cogent now than it had been in the past.[674]

As a general rule, the longer the delay after the occurrence of the matters **4–211** giving rise to the cause of action, the more likely it is that the balance of prejudice will swing against allowing the action to proceed by disapplying the limitation period. In cases of abuse of children, where issues of liability, causation and quantum are often difficult, with or without delay, the permissible delay in each case is likely to be highly sensitive to the prejudice it causes to the defence notwithstanding good reasons of the claimant for its length. Further, if the date of knowledge test in s.14 has been applied so as to provide a claimant with an extension of the period by reference to it, the weight to be given to his reasons for delay thereafter should, in normal circumstances, be limited.[675]

Walkley v Precision Forgings Ltd.[676] This case held that a court could **4–212** exercise its discretion under s.33, only if it was the provisions of ss.11 and 12 which prejudiced the claimant, not for instance, his own failure to prosecute an action correctly brought within the primary limitation period. The rule was applied for over a quarter of a century before, in *Horton v Sadler*,[677] the House of Lords took the rare step of reversing one of its own decisions. Lord Bingham of Cornhill pointed out the many fine distinctions that had arisen in attempting to avoid the consequences of *Walkley*.[678] Section 33 of the Act conferred a wide and unfettered discretion and it was inconsistent with the exercise of that discretion

[674] s.33(3)(b).
[675] See, e.g. *TCD v Harrow Council* [2009] 1 F.L.R. 719 (a claim based on several local authorities' failure to protect the claimant from historic child abuse where it was said that, in exercising the discretion under s.33, the court should never lose sight of the public policy considerations underlying the legislative regime. Public authorities, as well as commercial entities and individuals, should not remain exposed indefinitely to the threat of litigation based upon historic allegations. There was a public interest in certainty and finality, and such considerations could not be lightly discounted, especially not on the basis of sympathy for an individual litigant—even where there was, or might be, a strong case on liability and causation: see [35] of the judgment. See also, Garsden, "The test of time" 153 S.J. 15. Contrast *Raggett v Society of Jesus Trust 1929 for Roman Catholic Purposes* [2009] EWHC 909 (Q.B.) (discretion exercised in favour of the claimant in a case of sexual abuse even though he had delayed 28 years before commencing proceedings, there being no impairment of the ability of the defendant to defend on the issues of liability and causation).
[676] [1979] 1 W.L.R. 606 (claimant contracted Raynaud's disease, during his work as a grinder whilst employed by the defendants from 1966 to 1971, and issued proceedings in 1971. Inaction followed after he was advised that he did not have a good claim. Subsequently, after consulting new solicitors, a fresh claim was issued in 1976 asserting exactly the same cause of action but he was not allowed to proceed).
[677] [2007] 1 A.C. 307. Lord Brown referred to *Walkley* placing an "impossible and illogical construction" upon s.33. A list of the principal cases in which *Walkley* was applied is set out at [18] in the opinion of Lord Bingham. See also the 10th edn of *Charlesworth & Percy* at para.3–147.
[678] See [2007] 1 A.C. 307 at [24].

to have it confined by such a technical rule.[679] It was for the judge in each case to consider the various elements of s.33 and decide what was equitable or fair. If the decision was to permit an action brought out of time to proceed, and if an earlier action in relation to the same subject matter remained extant, the proper course would be to require the first to be discontinued.[680]

4-213   *Horton v Sadler* concerned a road traffic accident claim against an uninsured driver. The Motor Insurers' Bureau ("MIB")[681] nominated solicitors to act as its agent. Two days before expiry of the limitation period proceedings were issued, but the claimant's solicitor had failed within the time provided to comply with a condition precedent to the MIB's liability by giving notice that proceedings were to be commenced.[682] In order to avoid the difficulty a second claim was issued, albeit the limitation cut off date had passed. An application followed under s.33 to disapply the primary limitation period. The trial judge said that, although bound by *Walkley* to dismiss the second action, he would, if free to do so, have exercised discretion under s.33 in the claimant's favour. The delay involved was short and the evidential prejudice minimal. In the House of Lords it was accepted that the court could have regard to the parties' insurance rights, and the claimant's right of action against a negligent solicitor. However, even if he were able to sue his former solicitor, the claimant would suffer some prejudice. Although the balance was a fine one, the second action was permitted to proceed.[683]

4-214   **Limitation period not disapplied.** Section 33 did not avail the claimant: where there was a mistaken belief that she would cease to be under disability at the age of 21 and had until that age before the three-year period would commence[684]; where there was no explanation for delay after the instruction of solicitors, in circumstances where emergency legal aid could have been applied for and a protective writ served[685]; where in a claim for noise induced hearing loss, the relevant works had closed many years ago, records were destroyed, witnesses were dead or untraceable and some apportionment would have to be carried out between the defendants and other employers for whom the claimant had worked[686]; where he had received strong advice about his claim's negligible prospects of success and the passage of time meant that significant events could not now be established save by evidence of recollection[687]; where, even though

---

[679] See [2007] 1 A.C. 307 at [31].

[680] ibid. at [37].

[681] See generally Ch.17, below, for discussion of the agreements by which the MIB provides indemnity to the victims of uninsured or unidentified drivers.

[682] See Ch.17, paras 17–17, 17–18, below.

[683] See the discussion in *Horton v Sadler*, n.677, above, of the exercise of discretion under s.33, in the speeches of Lord Bingham at [32] and Lord Carswell at [52] et seq. In particular Lord Carswell touches on the effect of a legal representative's negligence, where that has resulted in a limitation date being missed: see para.4–216, below.

[684] *O'Driscoll v Dudley HA* [1998] Lloyd's Rep. Med. 210, CA.

[685] *Berry v Calderdale HA* [1998] Lloyd's Rep. Med. 179, CA.

[686] *Price v United Engineering Steels Ltd* [1998] P.I.Q.R. P407, CA (lack of evidence that particular records had been destroyed or witnesses memories impaired did not prevent judge drawing that inference from the facts).

[687] *Briggs v Pitt-Payne* [1999] Lloyd's Rep. Med. 1, CA.

liability had been established, the exercise of discretion under s.33 had been upon incorrect facts as a result of the claimant's failure to make frank disclosure.[688]

Further, the limitation period was not disapplied: where the claimant commenced proceedings six years after his eighteenth birthday against a local education authority for an alleged failure of teachers to identify his dyslexia and manage its effects, where it was clear on the evidence that the passage of time had significantly impaired the defendants' ability to defend themselves and that there was therefore little chance of a fair trial[689]; also where the claimant suffered dyslexia but there was no evidential basis for a finding that social embarrasment prevented him raising the problem with his G.P. and no special feature otherwise to balance the prejudice to the defendant if the action proceeded.[690] Discretion was not exercised in favour of a claimant who alleged negligence against counsel and solicitors who had represented him at a criminal trial nine years before proceedings were commenced, in failing to lead evidence of his good character: the claimant had been aware for many years of the mental health problems which he alleged were attributable to his conviction and the delay was largely unexplained.[691] **4–215**

Limitation period disapplied. The limitation period was disapplied: where the judge incorrectly considered financial prejudice to a Health Authority without also putting into account the financial prejudice to the claimant herself[692]; where the claimant was given misleading advice by her legal advisors which caused delay exceeding five years[693]; where the claimant suffered drug-induced hypomania and underwent brain surgery and radiotherapy, which were not conducive to the conduct of complex litigation[694]; where although there were evidential difficulties in relation to the state of medical notes from the time of the claimant's birth in 1971, they were common to both sides and expert evidence could deal **4–216**

---

[688] *Rowe v Kingston upon Hull City Council* [2004] P.I.Q.R. P238, CA, para.4–185, above.
[689] *Adams v Bracknell Forest BC* [2005] 1 A.C. 76; also *Smith v Hampshire CC* [2007] E.L.R. 321, CA (discretion under s.33 not exercised in favour of a dyslexic claimant who commenced proceedings against a local education authority alleging failure to diagnose his conditon in the course of his time at school, which had come to an end 8 years before proceedings were commenced).
[690] *Long v Tolchard and Sons Ltd* [2001] P.I.Q.R. P18, CA (the argument that the claimant had a cast iron case on liability generally did not avail).
[691] *Kamar v Nightingale* [2008] P.N.L.R. 15 (the claimant's conviction had been quashed in the Court of Criminal Appeal: the submission that the defendants were responsible for any evidential prejudice to their defence of the claim by failing to retain notes and papers from the time, was rejected).
[692] *Smith v Leicestershire HA* [1998] Lloyd's Rep. Med. 77, CA (it was said that he should have considered his power to restrict an award of interest upon any damages recovered).
[693] *Das v Ganju* [1999] P.I.Q.R. P260, CA (a claim for medical negligence. The Court of Appeal said that remarks in *Whitfield v North Durham HA* [1995] P.I.Q.R. P361, CA, quoted in the 9th ed. of this work should not be interpreted as meaning that anything done by the claimant's lawyers should be visited on their client). See also *Corbin v Penfold Metallising Co Ltd, The Times,* May 2, 2000, CA (delay in commencing proceedings arose not from any fault of the claimant, but as a result of delay by his solicitors: no rule of law that a solicitor's fault is to be visited on his client). However see also the speech of Lord Carswell in *Horton v Sadler,* n.677 above, at [52]. If it was being suggested in *Das v Ganju* that the court was not entitled to take into account against a party the failing of his solicitors, which resulted in a limitation date being missed, that was not a view which could be sustained.
[694] *Davis v Jacobs* [1999] Lloyd's Rep. Med. 72, CA (a claim based on claimant's treatment by defendant with an experimental drug for a pituitary gland problem).

with the state of medical knowledge at that time.[695] The discretion was also exercised in favour of a claimant who alleged exposure to hazardous chemicals at work causing bladder cancer, but at first knew of only two other cases of similar injury and delayed in bringing a claim until he had an expert's report which addressed the statistical probability of three people in the same employment over the same period developing the same disease[696]; also where proceedings were commenced seven years after the claimant was injured in an accident at work, but the facts were not substantially in dispute and the claimant was personally blameless so far as the delay was concerned.[697] The limitation period was disapplied where, before commencing proceedings arising from a road traffic accident against an uninsured driver, the claimant failed to give proper notice of the same to the Motor Insurers' Bureau, so that the claim had to be discontinued and started again.[698]

4-217   Section 33 was applied to disapply the limitation period in *A v Hoare* when that issue was remitted to the trial judge by the House of Lords.[699] The defendant had subjected the claimant to a serious and violent sexual assault in a public place. She alleged that as a result she suffered, inter alia, psychiatric illness in the form of post traumatic stress disorder. The defendant was convicted of attempted rape and sentenced to life imprisonment. Sixteen years later he won £7 million on a lottery while on day release. The judge noted that, as a result of the passage of time, there was some prejudice to the defendant in relation to expert evidence upon which he might wish to rely as to the extent of the claimant's injury, but decided that discretion be exercised in her favour bearing in mind in particular: (a) the nature and seriousness of the underlying tortious wrong; (b) the fact that the defendant had been impecunious as a result of that wrong (since being in custody he was unable to earn money by which he could otherwise have met a judgment for damages); (c) the fact that, prior to his lottery win, the defendant's impecuniosity meant that he was simply not worth pursuing in an action for damages; (d) the fact that the claimant acted promptly following the defendant's lottery win; and (e) the fact that the claimant's clinically significant PTSD in 2004 would be capable of being fully addressed by both parties at any trial.[700]

4-218   **Defendant company no longer in existence.** Where the claimant proposes to bring proceedings for personal injury against a company no longer in existence,

---

[695] *Appleby v Walsall HA* [1999] Lloyd's Rep. Med. 154 (a claim based upon negligent delivery at birth).
[696] *Fletcher v Containerbase (Manchester) Ltd* [2003] EWCA Civ 1635 CA, (the delay outside the limitation period was four-and-a-half years outside the three-year limitation period and the prejudice to the defendant was not significant).
[697] *Ashe Construction v Burke* [2004] P.I.Q.R. P136, CA.
[698] *Horton v Sadler* [2007] 1 A.C. 307, para.4–212 above. See also *Richardson v Watson* [2007] P.I.Q.R. P18, CA (similar facts to *Horton*, but with the feature that the claim was brought both on behalf of the estate of the deceased driver and his dependant children, where the children's claims were not statute barred and would continue in any event).
[699] *A v Hoare* [2008] EWHC 1573 (Q.B.), Coulson J. See above para.4–206.
[700] Although a case of assault many of these factors could equally apply to a negligence claim.

and to that end, seeks to restore it to the register of companies, an application may be made, pursuant to s.651 of the Companies Act 1985, for a direction that the dissolution of the company be declared void. On such application the court should not normally go on to direct that the period from dissolution to the date of the order is to be discounted for limitation purposes unless (a) notice of the application has first been given to all parties who may be expected to oppose the making of such a direction, including the company's insurers; and (b) the court is satisfied (i) that it has before it all the evidence that the parties would wish to adduce on an application by the prospective claimant under s.33 of the 1980 Act, and (ii) that an application under s.33 is bound to succeed. Where those conditions are not met, the applicant should seek relief under s.33.[701]

(C) Latent Damage

The Latent Damage Act 1986.[702] The 1986 Act altered the law by inserting **4–219** three new sections[703] into the Limitation Act 1980. It also made provision for the accrual of a cause of action to successive owners in respect of latent damage to property.[704] Its provisions are not confined to building and construction disputes but apply to all instances of latent damage,[705] other than cases of personal injury.[706] On a true construction of s.14A of the Act, its provisions are confined to actions for damages which arise out of tortious negligence only and do not apply to those claims which are framed in breach of a contractual duty.[707] The Act does not define precisely what constitutes "latent damage," but it presumably intended to be such damage as cannot be detected by reasonable care and skill.[708] By virtue of s.4(2), the provisions apply to causes of action, which have accrued both prior to the commencement of the Act[709] and afterwards, unless already statute-barred under an earlier Limitation Act.[710] To this latter

---

[701] *Smith v White Knight Laundry Ltd* [2002] 1 W.L.R. 616, CA.
[702] See the highly critical thesis by Phillip Capper in [1987] 3 P.N. 47.
[703] i.e. ss.14A, 14B, and 28A.
[704] See s.3, which gives effect to recommendations, set out in para.5.3(a) of the Law Reform Committee's 24th Report (Cmnd. 9390 (1984)), that the extended limitation period, in negligence cases, which involve latent damage, should run against an owner's successors in title, as well as the owner himself (see s.14A(4)(b)).
[705] e.g. negligent accountants, producing flawed accounts and negligent solicitors preparing defective deeds. See *Forster v Outred & Co* [1982] 1 W.L.R. 86 and *D. W. Moore & Co Ltd v Ferrier* [1988] 1 W.L.R. 267, both of which would be decided differently now under the Act.
[706] For which special provision is made already under s.11 of the Limitation Act 1980.
[707] *Société Commerciale de Réassurance v Eras (International) (Note)* [1992] 2 All E.R. 82, CA.
[708] This can be compared with the definition of latent defect, for which see *Readhead v Midland Ry* (1869) L.R. 4 Q.B. 379; *Ritchie v Western Scottish Motor Traction Co* (1935) S.L.T. 13 and *Marshall v Russian Oil Products* (1938) S.C. 773. See also *Abbey National Plc v Sayer, The Times*, August 30, 1999: where a mortgagee became aware of losses from mortgage fraud and took measures to protect itself in future but did not investigate past cases including the instant one in which the circumstances cried out for investigation, advantage could not be taken of any extension of time otherwise available under the 1980 Act as amended by s.1 of the 1986 Act.
[709] i.e. September 18, 1986.
[710] s.4(1)(a).

extent, therefore, the provisions of the Act do not operate to revive the claim of a claimant, who has been deprived of his remedy previously.

4–220 **Computation of time.** The rules which identify the date of accrual of a cause of action in negligence in cases involving latent damage to property and things were not changed by the Act. Thus, the six-year limitation period runs from the date when the damage occurred,[711] but the Act makes available an extension of three years.[712] Accordingly, an action may not be brought after the expiration of either six years from the date on which the cause of action accrued or three years from

> "the earliest date on which the plaintiff or any person in whom the cause of action was vested before him[713] first had both the knowledge[714] required for bringing an action for damages in respect of the relevant damage and a right to bring such an action,"[715]

whichever is the later.[716] In the result, where the period of six years has expired, before latent damage has become discoverable, a claimant will have a three-year extension period that starts to run against him from the discovery date, in which to commence his action.[717] There is no provision similar to that in personal injury cases[718] for any further extension of time in which to commence the action beyond the three-year period.[719]

4–221 **Knowledge.** Knowledge means:

> "knowledge both—
>
>   (a) of the material facts about the damage in respect of which damages are claimed; and

---

[711] *Pirelli General Cable Works Ltd v Oscar Faber & Partners* [1983] 2 A.C. 1; *Knapp v Ecclesiastical Insurance Group Plc, The Times*, November 17, 1997, CA (a case of negligent advice). See Ch.1, para.1–33, above. This basic limitation period is preserved by s.14A(4)(a). For a general discussion of damage and accrual of a cause of action, see para.4–150 and following, above.
[712] s.14A(4)(b).
[713] These words should be construed as extending to a claimant, whether suing in his own name, or in the name of another, by way of subrogation: *Graham v Entec Europe Ltd, The Times*, September 10, 2003, CA (the knowledge of a loss adjuster, investigating and advising on a claim on behalf of insurers, for the purpose of pursuing a subrogated claim by those insurers, was to be treated as knowledge of the insurers for the purposes of s.14A (5) of the Act).
[714] See para.4–222, below.
[715] s.14A(5).
[716] s.14A(3) and (4).
[717] If the damage became discoverable on the sixth anniversary this would give a total period of nine years from the date of the negligent act or omission of the defendant in completing the building; but the claimant could be caught by the "long stop" provisions of s.14B, para.4–226, below, if no action has been commenced within 15 years of the completion, even if no one was aware that a cause of action had accrued.
[718] i.e. ss.14 and 33. See further at paras 4–182 to 4–217, above.
[719] *Spencer-Ward v Humberts* [1994] N.P.C. 105, CA where the claim against a negligent valuer was held to be one day out of time and was therefore struck out.

(b) of the other facts relevant to the current action."[720]

For the purposes of sub-para.(a) the material facts about the damage are those that "would lead a reasonable person who had suffered such damage to consider it sufficiently serious to justify his instituting proceedings for damages against a defendant who did not dispute liability and was able to satisfy a judgment".[721] The "other facts" referred to in sub-para.(b) are:

(i) that the damage was attributable in whole or in part to the act or omission which is alleged to constitute negligence;

(ii) the identity of the defendant; and

(iii) if it is alleged that the act or omission was that of a person other than the defendant, the identity of that person and the additional facts supporting the bringing of an action against the defendant.[722]

The general approach to "knowledge" for purposes of s.14A is similar to that **4–222** in relation to the same issue where it arises under s.14(1).[723] Time does not begin to run until such time as the claimant has knowledge of the essence of the act or omission which is alleged to consitute negligence.[724] The claimant must have knowledge that the damage of which complaint is made was attributable in whole or in part to those acts or omissions. "Attributable" means a real posssibility, not

---

[720] s.14A(6). See also *H.F. Pensions Trustees v Ellison* [1999] P.N.L.R. 894 (knowledge of the law is not required to cause time to run against the claimant under s.14A of the Limitation Act, so where the claimant sought from the defendant solicitors, monies paid to Revenue as a result of advice that proved to be incorrect, the claim was out of time where he had known all material facts at the time the payment was made and only subsequently discovered that it was unlawful). But see further the criticism of Lord Walker in *Haward v Fawcetts* [2006] 1 W.L.R. 682, HL, n.725 below, at para.[60], of the concession made on behalf of the claimants which was decisive of the case.
[721] s.14A(7). See *Babicki v Rowlands* [2002] Lloyd's Rep. P.N. 121, CA (the receipt of an inaccurate fire certificate would not necessarily have suggested to the claimant that there was no adequate planning permission in place for his hotel or a failure to comply with building regulations). See also *3M United Kingdom Plc v Linklaters & Paines* [2006] P.N.L.R. 543, CA (at the relevant time the claimants did have knowledge that they had suffered serious damage as a result of their solicitors' negligence, since they had lost valuable rights in the form of break clauses: the remote posssibility that the damage might somehow be made good did not mean they did not have sufficient knowledge to satisfy subs.(7). It was emphasised that the subsection is directed to a narrow question. Per Moore-Bick L.J. at [33]: "It is not concerned with whether the claimant has such knowledge of the facts generally as would cause a reasonable person to commence proceedings there and then, or even such knowledge as would cause him to embark on the preliminaries to the issue of proceedings, but simply whether he has such knowledge of the material facts about the damage as would cause a reasonable person to consider it sufficiently serious to justify proceeding against a solvent defendant who did not dispute liability . . . by its own terms subsection (7) is concerned only with the claimant's knowledge of the seriousness of the damage."
[722] s.14A(8). The claimant had knowledge for purposes of s.14A(8) where she knew of a link between a solicitor's failure to explain a legal charge to her and the chargee's threat to enforce it even though she did not until later appreciate the solicitor's omission constituted a breach of duty: *Fennon v Anthony Hodari & Co* [2001] Lloyd's Rep. P.N. 183, CA; also where she knew that a solicitor had failed to explain a charge on the matrimonial home properly to her and that her home was at risk, even though she thought the solicitor was her husband's, rather than her own, and was not aware that he owed her a duty of care: *Bowie v Southorns* [2002] Lloyd's Rep. P.N. 564.
[723] See para.4–182, above.
[724] *Hallam-Eames v Merrett Syndicates* [2001] Lloyd's Rep. P.N. 178, CA, per Hoffmann L.J. at p.181.

a fanciful one. Once it is established that the cause of action accrued outside the the period of six years within which a claim ought to have been commenced, the burden rests on the claimant to establish that he lacked the knowledge necessary for time to run until a later date. In *Haward v Fawcetts*[725] that burden was not discharged, in a claim based on allegedly negligent investment advice given by accountants, where the claimant led evidence directed to when he first knew he might have a claim for damages: his evidence ought to have been directed to an earlier date, when he first knew enough to justify setting about investigating the possibility that the advice received was defective. *Haward* underlines the importance for a claimant, seeking to present an argument under s.14A, of anticipating the time-frame likely to concern the court, and leading evidence which addresses knowledge at that time.

Illustrations

4–223   Where the claimant sued on a negligent survey report, but had been aware at the time of some defects in the building not mentioned by the surveyor, it was held that so far as other defects were concerned, discovered several years later, he was not debarred from relying on the extended limitation period.[726] Nor did the defence succeed where consulting actuaries had failed to give adequate advice in relation to a client's purchase of a with-profits policy of annuity from the Equitable Life Assurance Society: annual statements from the Society which on a close reading were capable of informing the client of the correct position were insufficient to give knowledge for purposes of s.14A, where the defendant's advice had over the years conditioned him to consider that he did not need to read them closely.[727]

4–224   It has been held that a claimant cannot rely on s.14A where, although at the relevant time he did not know the identity of the potential defendant, he could have discovered it by making a simple enquiry.[728] In the context of negligent survey, the cause of action accrues when some damage is suffered, whether great or small, and time runs for purposes of s.14A of the Limitation Act from the date the plaintiff first acquires knowledge of some defect relevant to the cause of

---

[725] [2006] 1 W.L.R. 682, HL (the HL disagreed with the CA that time did not run where the failure of the company in which the claimant invested had a number of possible causes: the damage alleged was that the claimant had lost substantial sums invested in the company and per Lord Scott at [53] concentrating on the many reasons why the company may have failed was to look at the wrong event). See further *Shore v Sedgwick Financial Services Ltd* [2008] P.N.L.R. 10, applying *Haward v Fawcetts* in the context of a claim against a financial adviser, based on failure to advise the claimant to use accrued pension benefits to purchase an annuity. The claimant had knowledge sufficient for time to run against him when he became aware that there had been a substantial fall in annuity rates and that he had been taking the maximum permitted income from a personal pension scheme, not having been informed that no more than 75 per cent of the maximum should be withdrawn. See also Bird and Hassell, "Setting the limits" 150 S.J. 352.

[726] *Felton v Gaskill Osborne & Co* [1993] 43 E.G. 118.

[727] *Andrews v Barnett Waddingham* [2006] P.N.L.R. 15 (time ran from a later point when the defendant wrote to the client warning of the danger that the future profits of a with-profits annuity would be less than expected; appeal, on a different point, allowed [2006] P.N.L.R. 24, CA).

[728] *Heathcote & Heathcote v David Marks & Co* [1995] 6 C.L. 286.

action, even if it is minor in comparison with defects which only emerge later.[729] A claimant is not fixed with his solicitors' knowledge where in the circumstances they were not obliged to communicate their knowledge to the claimant nor were they authorised to receive the information on his behalf.[730] It has been said to be "too sweeping a proposition" that no aggregation of the knowledge of individual officers or employees of a company could lead to a company being imputed with knowledge for purposes of s.14A, if the result was to attribute to the company knowledge not enjoyed by any one individual. It was consistent with the content and purpose of the section for knowledge distributed among individuals to be aggregated, if in the particular context it was reasonable to suppose that the relevant information would have been aggregated within the organisation.[731]

A person's knowledge includes that which he might reasonably be expected to **4–225** acquire from facts observable or ascertainable by him, if necessary with the help of such expert advice as it is reasonable to seek.[732] Accordingly, a claimant was fixed with knowledge of a document in which a bank set out the effect of a charge securing further borrowing even though she had not read it.[733] It is not reasonable to defer seeking such advice because of well-founded fear of discovery in an unlawful activity[734]; nor where the claimant unreasonably delays in taking steps that would result in his learning of matters relevant to the proposed claim sooner than he does.[735] Where the defendant wishes to argue that it would have been reasonable for the claimant to obtain expert advice on or before a certain date, it

[729] *Hamlin v Edwin Evans* [1996] P.N.L.R. 398, CA (where the purchaser of a house found out about structural problems more than three years after he had first learnt of much less serious dry rot). See Catchpole, "Surveyors reports: one cherry, one bite" in 150 N.L.J. 197. *Hamlin* was followed in *McKillen v Russell* [2002] P.N.L.R. 653, CA (N.I.).
[730] *Lloyds Bank Plc v Crosse & Crosse* [2001] P.N.L.R. 830, CA (a claim against the defendant solicitors for failing to report to the lender of monies secured by mortgage that the land was subject to a restrictive covenant which greatly reduced its value: three years later the land was sold and other solicitors by then instructed, discovered the restrictive covenant but did not inform the claimant).
[731] *3M United Kingdom Plc v Linklaters and Paines* [2005] P.N.L.R. 903, per Hart J. at 915. The judge quoted the speech of Lord Hoffmann in *Meridien Global Funds Management Asia Ltd v Securities Commission* [1995] 2 A.C. 500 PC, at 507: the question whether the knowledge of an individual officer or employee of a company counts as knowledge of the company for the purpose of some substantive rule of law is to be answered by way of the usual canons of interpretation, "taking into account the language of the rule (if it is a statute) and its content and policy."
[732] s.14A(10). See generally McGee and Scanlan, "Constructive knowledge within the Limitation Act" 2003 C.J.Q. 22, 248; also O'Sullivan, "Limitation, latent damage and solicitors negligence" (2004) P.N. 20, 4, 218. In *Gravgaard v Aldridge & Brownlee* [2005] P.N.L.R. 319, CA it was held that time, for purposes of s.14A(10) of the Limitation Act 1980, ran against a claimant suing solicitors who acted for her when she charged property in favour of a bank in order to secure her husband's indebtedness, from the date when she ought reasonably to have taken legal advice in relation to her concerns about the propriety of the conduct of the bank in that transaction. She knew that the property was exposed to the risk of attachment for her husband's debts. In the circumstances it was reasonable to expect her to have sought legal advice as to her rights against the bank. The transactions with the bank had been so intimately bound up with the actions of the defendant solicitors that anyone advising in the first would have realised that the second had to be investigated as well.
[733] *Webster v Cooper & Burnett* [2000] P.N.L.R. 240, CA.
[734] *Coban v Allen, The Times*, October 14, 1996, CA (unlawful immigrant who delayed seeking advice in relation to a claim against solicitors because he feared discovery of his immigration status).
[735] *Finance for Mortgages Ltd v Farley & Co* [1996] E.G.C.S. 35.

will be for him to put evidence before the court to support the proposition for which he contends.[736]

4-226 **The "long stop" section.** The second new section to be inserted into the 1980 Act introduced a new 15-year period, which has been referred to as a "long stop".[737] Clearly the intention was to afford some protection to a defendant who could eventually relax in the knowledge that any action against him was statute-barred.[738] As a result of its provisions, after 15 years from the last date of the defendant's negligence, irrespective of whether damage had become manifest or had occurred only outside that period, a claimant is barred from commencing his action.[739]

(D) Miscellaneous Limitation Periods

4-227 **The Crown.** The period of limitation against the Crown in respect of actions founded on tort is the same as that in actions of tort against private persons.[740]

4-228 **Periods of limitation prescribed by other Acts.** The Limitation Act 1980 s.39, provides that it shall not apply to any action or arbitration for which a period of limitation is prescribed by any other enactment, or to any action or arbitration to which the Crown is a party and for which, if it were between subjects, a period of limitation would be prescribed by any such enactment. The following statutory provisions may arise for consideration.

(i) *Contributory negligence*

4-229 The Law Reform (Contributory Negligence) Act 1945 s.1(5), provides:

"Where, in any case to which subsection (1) of this section applies, one of the persons at fault avoids liability to any other such person or his personal representative by pleading the Limitation Act 1939 or any other enactment limiting the time within which proceedings may be taken, he shall not be entitled to recover any damages [or contributions][741] from that other person or representative by virtue of the said subsection."

---

[736] *Mortgage Corp v Lambert & Co* [2000] P.N.L.R. 820, CA (a mortgage valuation case where there was no evidence that it would have been reasonable for the mortgage lender to obtain a retrospective valuation of the property concerned, as opposed to waiting, as it did, to enter into possession).
[737] s.14B, the overriding time limit for negligence actions, not involving personal injuries.
[738] See para.4-200, above.
[739] s.14B(2). However, in the event of the claimant being under a disability or if there has been some some fraud, concealment or mistake it would be possible to pursue a remedy beyond the 15 year period: see s.28A, inserted into the 1980 Act and the consequential addition, by way of an amendment to s.32. See also *Financial Services Compensation Scheme Ltd v Larnell (Insurances) Ltd* [2006] P.N.L.R. 215, CA (the effect of a winding up order against a company is to stop the limitation clock running against a claimant, so the expiry of the 15 year period before proceedings are started is immaterial).
[740] Limitation Act 1980 s.37(1).
[741] These words in square brackets were repealed by the Civil Liability (Contribution) Act 1978, Sch.2, which came into force on January 1, 1979.

This subsection contemplates the case of one person at fault avoiding liability to another person at fault, but while it refers to the personal representative of the second-named person it does not refer to the personal representative of the first-named. If, therefore, the personal representative of one of the parties at fault avoids liability to the other party at fault by pleading the Limitation Act 1980, it is a possible construction of the subsection that the personal representative in such a case could still recover damages under the Law Reform (Contributory Negligence) Act 1945. Presumably, however, the ordinary rule will apply, by which a personal representative has no higher rights than the deceased, whom he represents, with the result that the personal representative avoiding liability would be unable to recover.

(ii) *Contribution between tortfeasors*[742]

Originally, the Law Reform (Married Women and Tortfeasors) Act 1935 s.6, **4–230** had provided for claims to contributions between tortfeasors but had made no provisions for the limitation of such claims. Since a claim for contribution under that Act was not a claim in tort,[743] before the Limitation Act 1963 was passed such claim had to be brought within six years of the accrual of the right. The 1963 Act then reduced the period to two years from the date when the right to recover contribution accrued, and made provision for ascertaining that date.[744]

Section 10 of the 1980 Limitation Act replaced these provisions. The two-year-period from accrual of the right to contribution was retained. The date upon which the right should be regarded as accruing where the tortfeasor was held liable for the relevant damage by a judgment in civil proceedings, or an award made on arbitration, should be the date on which the judgment is given, or the date of the award.[745] Where the tortfeasor makes or agrees to make in compensation payment for the damage, the relevant date is the earliest date the agreement between himself and the payee is made.

(iii) *Merchant Shipping Act 1995*[746]

Section 190 of the Merchant Shipping Act 1995 replaced s.8 of the Maritime **4–231** Conventions Act 1911 in its provision for a time limit for proceedings against the owners of a ship or or the ship itself. It provides for a time limit applicable to any proceedings to enforce any claim or lien against a ship or her owners:

    (a) in respect of damage or loss caused by the fault[747] of that ship to another ship, its cargo or freight or any property on board it; or

---

[742] In Eire the limitation periods are set out in s.31 of the Civil Liability Act 1961 but in England and Wales, see the provision of the Civil Liability (Contribution) Act 1978, which came into force on January 1, 1979 and repealed s.6 of the 1935 Act.

[743] *Post Office v Official Solicitor* [1951] 1 All E.R. 522; *Littlewood v George Wimpey & Co Ltd* [1953] 2 Q.B. 501; sub nom. *George Wimpey & Co Ltd v BOAC* [1955] A.C. 169; *Harvey v R. G. O'Dell Ltd* [1958] 2 Q.B. 78.

[744] s.4(2); cf. the like provisions in the Carriage by Air Act 1961 s.5(2).

[745] The two year period runs from any judgment which ascertains quantum, a judgment on liability alone does not start time running: *Aer Lingus v Gildacroft Ltd* [2006] 1 W.L.R. 1173, CA.

[746] Which came into force on January 1, 1996, see also Ch.10 para.10–160, below.

[747] By subs.(2) the extent of the fault is immaterial for purposes of the section.

(b) for damages for loss of life or personal injury caused by the fault of that ship to any person on board another ship.[748]

No proceedings to which the section applies shall be brought after the period of two years from the date when:

(a) the damage or loss was caused; or

(b) the loss of life or injury was suffered.[749]

No proceedings under any of ss.187 to 189 of the Act to enforce any contribution in respect of any overpaid proportion of any damages for loss of life or personal injury shall be brought after the period of one year from the date of payment.[750]

There is a saving in relation to all these provisions to the extent that any court having jurisdiction in the proceedings may, in accordance with rules of court, extend the period allowed for bringing proceedings to such extent and on such conditions as it thinks fit.[751] Further, any such court, if satisfied that there has not been during any period allowed for bringing proceedings any reasonable opportunity of arresting the defendant ship within:

(a) the jurisdiction of the court, or

(b) the territorial sea of the country to which the plaintiff's ship belongs or in which the plaintiff resides or has his principal place of business,

shall extend the period allowed for bringing proceedings to an extent sufficient to give a reasonable opportunity of so arresting the ship.[752]

4-232   It was held, in relation to s.8 of the 1911 Act that its provisions were not affected by, the alteration in the general law brought about by the Law Reform (Limitation of Actions, etc.) Act 1954. Accordingly, where the 1911 Act applied it was exclusive of other periods of limitation: the period which was appropriate to the case of a death on board one vessel, caused by the negligence of another ship, was two years and not three years as provided in normal fatal accident

---

[748] It was held, in relation to the s.8 of the Maritime Conventions Act 1911, that the word "vessel" as used there did not apply to a jet-ski, that not being a vessel used for navigation for the purposes of the Merchant Shipping Act 1894 s.742. Accordingly the two year limitation period under the 1911 Act did not apply: *Steedman v Schofield* [1992] 2 Lloyd's Rep. 163.

[749] Subs.(3), which reflects art.16 of the Athens Convention Relating to the Carriage of Passengers and their Luggage by Sea 1974. In *Higham v Stena Sealink Ltd* [1996] 1 W.L.R. 1107, CA, it was confirmed that such period of limitation could not be extended by virtue of the Limitation Act 1980 s.33. See also *Sweet v Owners of Blyth Lifeboat, The Times,* February 22, 2002 (the two-year period can run either from the time damage or loss is caused or from the date when loss of life or injury is suffered, so a claim for damages for psychiatric injury was started in time even though the injury arose more than two years after the vessels in question were in collision).

[750] Subs.(4).

[751] Subs.(5). For the principles held to be relevant to the exercsie of the similar discretion under the Maritime Conventions Act 1911 see *The Kashmir* [1923] P. 85; *The Arraiz* (1924) 132 L.T. 715; *The Vadne* [1959] 2 Lloyd's Rep. 480.

[752] Subs.(6).

cases. However, it was further held that where the defendant had been guilty of any culpable delay the two-year limitation would be extended in the court's discretion.[753] In *Navarro v Larrinaga Steamship Co Ltd*,[754] where the administratrix of the estate of a deceased mariner, who lost his life in a sea collision between the *Niceto de Larrinaga*, in which he was serving, and the *Sitala*, sued the owners of the former vessel for damages for loss of life, it was held that since s.8 of the Act only applied to actions against other vessels and not to actions against the vessel in which the damage, loss or injury had occurred, the normal three-year limitation period for actions under the Fatal Accidents Acts, as amended, applied.

(iv) Carriage by Air Act 1961[755]

Since the Act enacts that the provisions of the Warsaw Convention as amended **4–233** at The Hague, 1955 should have the force of law, s.5(1) provides that:

"No action against a carrier's servant or agent which arises out of damage to which the Convention relates shall, if he was acting within the scope of his employment, be brought after more than two years, reckoned from the date of arrival at the destination or from the date on which the aircraft ought to have arrived, or from the date on which the carriage stopped,"

which embodies art.29 of the Convention and certainly applies in all cases of non-fatal accidents. However, where the plaintiff was injured, whilst using the "moving pavement", after leaving the aircraft on landing at Heathrow airport, it was held that the Convention did not apply since she was no longer engaged upon the operation of disembarking at the time of her accident.[756]

Conversely, in cases of fatalities the position under the Act is the same as under the Fatal Accidents Act 1976 since by s.3:

"References in ... the Fatal Accidents Act [1976] as it applies in England and Wales, and in Northern Ireland, to a wrongful act, neglect or default shall include references to any occurrence which gives rise to a liability under Article 17 ... "

Hence, actions in respect of deaths caused by any such occurrence, being in effect ordinary actions under the Fatal Accidents Act, will be subject to those ordinary rules for limitation in such cases, namely three years. Where there is such an apparent divergence between the provisions of the Act and those of the Convention, the former must prevail over the latter, so that art.29 cannot have any bearing upon actions brought on behalf of dependants of deceased persons

---

[753] *The Alnwick* [1965] P. 357. The discretion was similar to that now available under s.190(5) of the Merchant Shipping Act 1995.
[754] [1966] P. 80.
[755] See further in relation to carriage by rail and road, Ch.10, paras 10–139 (rail) and 10–158 (road).
[756] *Adatia v Air Canada* [1992] P.I.Q.R. P238, CA.

who have been killed in some common flying disaster or another. If a person injured could at his death no longer maintain an action under the Fatal Accidents Act 1976, because of the time limit in art.29, the court has no power under s.33 of the Limitation Act 1980 to direct that s.12(1) of the same Act shall not apply.[757]

(v) *Nuclear Installations Act 1965*[758]

4–234   Section 15(1) enacts that: "notwithstanding anything in any other enactment", a claim under the Act shall not be entertained, "if made at any time after the expiration of thirty years from the relevant date", which date is that of the occurrence that gave rise to the claim and not of the infliction of damage. The limitation period begins to run from the date of the last occurrence, where it was either a continuing one or was one of a succession in the circumstances specified. Further, where a claim arises in respect of injury or damage, caused by an occurrence involving nuclear matter stolen from, or lost, jettisoned or abandoned by the person, whose breach of statutory duty under the Act gave rise to the claim, it is provided by s.15(2) that the limitation period in such circumstances is the period of 20 years. This period is to be a calculated "beginning with the day when the nuclear matter in question was so stolen lost, jettisoned or abandoned."

(vi) *Consumer Protection Act 1987*

4–235   Part 1[759] of the Act makes provision with respect to the liability of persons for damage[760] caused by defective products. Schedule 1 contains special time limits, which are inserted by way of amendment into the Limitation Act 1980 as s.11A,[761] and such time limits apply, to the exclusion of the Limitation Act's other provisions.[762]

By s.11A(4), in general, an action under the Act of 1987 shall not be brought after the expiration of the period of three years from whichever date is the later of: (i) when the cause of action accrued[763] and (ii) the injured person's acquisition of "knowledge"[764] or, in the case of loss of or damage to property, the like acquisition of knowledge of either the claimant or (if earlier) any person in whom his cause of action was previously vested. By s.11A(3), in general, an action under the Act of 1987 cannot be brought after the expiration of the period

---

[757] See the Limitation Act 1980 s.33(2).

[758] See generally Ch.13, paras 13–201 to 13–212, below.

[759] Which came into force in March 1, 1988, together with Sch.1, inter alia, by virtue of the Consumer Protection Act 1987 (Commencement No.1) Order (SI 1987/1680). See generally, Ch.15, below.

[760] i.e. "death or personal injury or any other loss of or damage to any property (including land)": s.5(1).

[761] By virtue of s.6(6).

[762] This method of amending the consolidating Act of 1980 follows the pattern of the Latent Damage Act 1986, with which it compares.

[763] See para.4–150, above.

[764] See para.4–182, (personal injuries), para.4–195 (fatal accidents) and para.4–219, (latent damage in non-personal injuries), above.

of 10 years from the date when the product was "supplied".[765] This period acts as a "long stop" provision,[766] which prevents a claimant from pursuing his remedy, irrespective of whether the cause of action had even accrued or time had begun to run before the expiration of that period. Exceptionally,[767] as this provision extinguishes the claimant's right and not merely bars his remedy, it cannot be waived by a willing defendant, who may wish to challenge the claim and have it decided on the merits.[768]

(vii) *Foreign Limitation Act 1984*

Where a negligence claim in England falls to be decided by the law of a **4–236** foreign country, the effect of the Foreign Limitation Act 1984 is to require the court to apply the limitation rules of the foreign country.[769] There is an exception where the application of the foreign limitation period would conflict with public policy and there is deemed to be such a conflict to the extent that its application would cause undue hardship to a party.[770] When professional divers commenced proceedings in England alleging that, while working in Saudi Arabia for the state-owned national oil company, they had been negligently exposed to toxic chemicals and suffered injury as a result, the question arose whether the claim was out of time. It was common ground that if Saudi labour law applied, the limitation period was one year calculated either from the date of the incident or alternatively, from the termination of the work relationship. However if shari'ah law applied there was no limitation period. On the defendant failing to prove which law would have been applied, the defence of limitation failed.[771]

Failure to implement European Directive. In a claim for damages against **4–237** the Government under the principle in *Francovich v Italian Republic*,[772] the limitation period is six years from accrual of the cause of action. It has been held that where the cause of action was failure to implement art.6(2) of Council Directive 89/391/EEC in the Management of Health and Safety at Work Regulations,[773] it accrued upon the claimant suffering the injury which was the subject matter of the claim, since at that time the claim for damages against, for

---

[765] For which, see s.4(2). See further Ch.15, para.15–32, below.

[766] For the similar "long stop" provisions contained in the Latent Damage Act 1986, see para.4–226, above.

[767] See further at para.4–147, above.

[768] But see *Horne-Roberts v Smithkline Beecham* [2002] 1 W.L.R. 1662, CA, para.4–145 above (no distinction, for purposes of the exercise of the power under r.19.5 of the CPR, to substitute a new party after the expiry of any period of limitation under the 1980 Act, between the ten-year period and any other period of limitation).

[769] Section 1(1) of the Foreign Limitation Act 1984. See further the summary in Halsbury's Laws of England, 4th Edn, Vol. 28, para.1136.

[770] Foreign Limitation Act 1984 ss.2(1) and 2 (2).

[771] *Harley v Smith* [2010] EWCA Civ 78; at first instance [2009] P.I.Q.R. P11 the judge said that had it been necessary he would have found undue hardship to the claimants, by the application of the twelve month rule, so as to bring them within the exception which the 1984 Act allowed.

[772] (Joined Cases C-6/90 and 9/90) [1995] I.C.R. 722).

[773] (SI 1992 No.2051). See further Ch.12, para.12–100, below.

instance, an employer, was less favourable than it would have been had the Directive been properly implemented.[774]

5.—Other Defences

(A) Henderson v Henderson[775]

4–238   A claim may fail if, in bringing it, the claimant is attempting to re-open litigation already decided; or if the claim could and should have been raised in the course of already-decided litigation:

> "where a given matter becomes the subject of litigation in, and of adjudication by, a court of competent jurisdiction, the court requires the parties to that litigation to bring forward their whole case, and will not (except under special circumstances) permit the same parties to open the same subject of litigation in respect of matters which might have been brought forward as part of the subject in contest but which was not brought forward . . . The plea of res judicata applies, except in special cases."[776]

4–239   **Purpose of the rule.** Although antique, the rule in *Henderson v Henderson* survives the introduction of the Civil Procedure Rules 1998.[777] The purpose of the rule is to achieve finality in litigation, a purpose at least consistent with the emphasis on efficiency and economy in the conduct of litigation in the interests of the parties and the public as a whole which underlies those Rules.

> "The rationale for the rule . . . that, in the absence of special circumstances, parties should bring their whole case before the court so that all aspects may be decided (subject to appeal) once and for all, is a rule of public policy based on the desirability, in the general interest as well as that of the parties themselves, that litigation should not drag on for ever, and that a defendant should not be oppressed by successive suits when one would do . . . "[778]

4–240   **Nature of the test.** It is too dogmatic an approach to proceed on the basis that simply because a matter could have been raised in earlier proceedings it should have been, so as to render the raising of it in later proceedings necessarily abusive. There should be a broad, merits-based judgment taking account of all the public and private interests involved and all the facts, focusing on the crucial question whether, in all the circumstances, a party is misusing or abusing the process of the court. Accordingly, it is preferable to ask whether in all the

---

[774] *Spencer v Secretary of State for Work and Pensions* [2008] P.I.Q.R. P21, CA. (In *Moore v Secretary of State for Transport*, considered on the same occasion, the Court of Appeal took a similar approach to a personal injuries' claim based upon failure to implement Council Directive 84/5/EEC into the Motor Insurers' Bureau Untraced Drivers Agreement of 1972: see Ch.17, para.17–19, below).

[775] (1843) 3 Hare 100 at 114.

[776] *Henderson v Henderson* (1843) 3 Hare 100 at 115, per Sir James Wigram V.C.

[777] Which came into force on April 26, 1999.

[778] *Woodhouse v Consignia Plc* [2002] 2 All E.R. 737, CA, per Brooke L.J. at 753.

circumstances a party's conduct is an abuse than to ask whether it is an abuse and, if it was, whether it was excused or justified by special circumstances.[779]

ILLUSTRATIONS

Where a motorist, who sustained injury in a road accident, brought a claim against a local highway authority, his claim was prevented because it could and ought to have been made in an earlier action by his front seat passenger[780]; likewise, where a claimant pursued to judgment an action arising from a road traffic accident where he sought and obtained damages for the value of a van, loss of use and incidental expenses and attempted thereafter to institute fresh proceedings for personal injuries[781]; and where there had been previous proceedings in Delaware, USA, in which the present claim could have been brought.[782]   **4–241**

The rule was not applied where the mother of a child brought an action arising from disrepair to a house and subsequently by separate proceedings her child sought damages for personal injury arising from the same incident, because it could not be said that there was such a nexus between the two claimants that they could be regarded as the same party[783]; nor where an unrepresented litigant had not been put on notice that, if he failed to make a Pt 20 claim, he risked being debarred from making a subsequent claim[784]; where one of two defendants failed to issue contribution proceedings in an action for personal injuries and after the claimant had recovered judgment against him commenced such proceedings against his co defendant[785]; where a shareholder took proceedings against solicitors for his personal loss from an allegedly negligent failure to exercise an option to purchase land in favour of the company, where that was not merely a reflection of the loss suffered by the company or too remote, he was not prevented from doing so, even though the company itself also instituted proceedings which were compromised[786]; where the parent of a deceased child wished to continue a claim for nervous shock alleged to arise as a result of negligent medical treatment of the child, after accepting a compromise of a   **4–242**

---

[779] *Johnson v Gore Wood & Co* [2002] 2 A.C. 1. See further the summary of May L.J. (which refers also to cause of action estoppel and issue estoppel) in *Specialist Group International v Deakin* [2001] EWCA Civ 777, paras [22] and [23], quoted in *Gribbon v Lutton* [2002] Q.B. 902 at 915. In *Woodhouse v Consignia Plc* n.68 above it was said that the rule in *Henderson v Henderson* should be applied less strictly in relation to successive pre-trial applications for the same relief than in relation to a final decision: per Brooke L.J. at 753. See generally Handley, "A closer look at *Henderson v Henderson*" (2002) L.Q.R. 118, 397.
[780] *Talbot v Berkshire CC* [1994] Q.B. 290. See also *Crawford v Dalley and Royal Marsden Hospital* [1995] 6 Med. L.R. 343.
[781] *Wain v F. Sherwood & Sons Transport Ltd* [1999] P.I.Q.R. P159, CA (it was said that the alleged negligence of legal advisors in the first case was an irrelevant consideration).
[782] *Fennoscandia Ltd v Clarke* [1999] 1 All E.R. (Comm) 365, CA. See also Ch.9, para.9–83, below.
[783] *C v Hackney LBC*, The Times, November 10, 1995, CA.
[784] *Sweetman v Shepherd*, The Times, March 29, 2000, CA.
[785] *Neasham v John Thompson* [1999] C.L.Y. 1376, CA.
[786] *Johnson v Gore Wood & Co* [2002] 2 A.C. 1.; applied in *Ellis v Property (Leeds) UK Ltd* [2002] 2 B.C.L.C. 175, CA (where a company had purchased a building site after an allegedly fraudulent valuation, a director of the company was not entitled to sue for personal, reflective loss).

second claim under the Fatal Accidents Acts[787]; where a shareholder sought to sue for loss arising from a wrong done to the company in which he held shares after the company had itself reached a compromise with the alleged wrongdoer.[788]

4–243   Nor was the rule applied: in complex reinsurance litigation where there were good tactical reasons for parties attempting to resolve a dispute by reference to a preliminary issue and accordingly claims were raised which, the dispute not having been resolved, were raised again in a subsequent action[789]; where director/shareholders first sued solicitors for negligently omitting to convey a parcel of land to the company whose shares they held, and subsequently commenced proceedings against a director/shareholder who had owned the land[790]; where the claimant alleged against a Citizens Advice Bureau case worker, negligence and lack of authority in settling his claim against a former employer, under the Disability Discrimination Act 1995. In earlier proceedings before an employment tribunal the chairman had ruled that the disability discrimination claim had been compromised, but that was no bar to the current claim continuing: the defendant was not being compelled to re-litigate an issue from an earlier decision to which he had been party, it was not manifestly unfair that the case proceed, and disclosure might reveal evidence different to that which had been before the tribunal.[791]

4–244   **Irrelevant factors.** It will be rare for the prospects of success for a second claim to be relevant to the question whether to strike it out as an abuse. If a case is hopeless it will always be possible to strike it out on that account. But, where the prospects for the second claim are uncertain, it is inappropriate to weigh the chances of success in the balance as part of the exercise of deciding whether it is an abuse. For similar reasons delay is also not relevant: if the claim is out of time there may be a limitation defence, but if it has been brought in time, the fact that the claimant has delayed is not relevant to the assessment whether it is an abuse. Nor is it right as a general proposition of law that where the claimant in current proceedings becomes aware, from information provided by the defendant, of a further cause of action different from the existing claim and one that

---

[787] *Toth v Ledger* [2002] P.I.Q.R. P1, CA (the parent had started the nervous shock claim himself, legal aid having been refused and the defendants had settled the Fatal Accidents Acts claim without reference to the other proceedings; per Laws L.J. "not a case of a claimant manipulating the procedures of the court … ").

[788] *Giles v Rhind* [2003] Ch. 618, CA (the company became insolvent as a result of the wrongdoer's breach of duty and was thereby disabled from pursuing its own cause of action).

[789] *Kennecott Utah Copper Corporation v Minet Ltd* [2004] P.N.L.R. 156, CA.

[790] *Perry v Day* [2005] B.C.C. 375.

[791] *Nesbitt v Holt* [2007] P.N.L.R. 24, CA. Smith L.J. at [23] quoted Sir Andrew Morritt in *Secretary of State for Trade and Industry v Bairstow* [2004] Ch. 1 at [38]: "If the parties to the later civil proceedings were not parties or privies of those who were parties to the earlier proceedings then it will only be an abuse of the process of the court to challenge the factual findings and conclusions of the judge or jury in the earlier action if (i) it would be manifestly unfair to a party to the later proceedings that the same issues should be relitigated or (ii) to permit such litigation would bring the administration of justice into disrepute."

could not reasonably be joined with it, he should be obliged to inform the defendant that he is contemplating bringing such a claim in the future.[792]

The fact that the defendants to the original action and the new action are **4–245** different, is a powerful, but not decisive, indication that a second action is not an abuse. No distinction should be drawn as a matter of law, between cases where the original action was settled, as opposed to those where it proceeded to judgment. The mere fact that claims could have been brought in an earlier action is not conclusive, where it cannot be said that the claimant has behaved in any way culpably or improperly.[793]

Where a party seeks to make a collateral attack on an earlier judgment in a **4–246** civil claim, that, too, is capable of attack as an abuse of process, with a similar underlying rationale to the *Henderson* rule, in preventing the administration of justice from being brought into disrepute.[794]

(B) "Full and final settlement"

Where the claimant in a negligence action reaches, on a proper construction of **4–247** an agreement, a full and final settlement of all claims arising from his cause of action, he cannot commence another action at some later date arising from the same matter even where some damage has arisen, for instance in an accident claim, some complication of injury, the possibility of which was not foreseen at the time of settlement.[795]

(C) Illegality[796]

Generally. A defence of illegality is available in tort as it is in contract.[797] The **4–248** old maxim was *ex turpi causa non oritur actio* but there has been uncertainty over the years as to the quality of the act liable to bring it into play. Was immorality sufficient, or some breach of the civil law, or was some act required which fulfilled the definition of a crime? One potential problem in arriving at a

---

[792] *Stuart v Goldberg Linde* [2008] 1 W.L.R. 823, CA.

[793] *Aldi Stores Ltd v WSP Group Plc.* [2008] P.N.L.R. 14, CA, per Thomas L.J. at [25] (the claimant alleged defective building work and in the first proceedings sued the builder, there being Pt 20 proceedings involving engineering and environmental consultants, against whom the claimant wished to proceed in the second claim). See further Bessey, "I'll get you later" Building (2008) (3), 59.

[794] See *Secretary of State for Trade and Industry v Bairstow (No.1)* [2004] Ch.1. See also Ch.9, para.9–249, below. See also *Great North Eastern Railway Limited v JLT Corporate Risks Limited* [2006] P.N.L.R. 34 (the claimant could sue its insurance brokers for losses not recovered in an earlier action against a tortfeasor).

[795] *Bristow v Grout*, The Times, November 9, 1987, CA. See also *David Yablon Minton v Kenburgh Investments (Northern) Ltd*, The Times, July 11, 2000, CA (settlement of an action by a liquidator against the directors of a company did not preclude a subsequent action against solicitors based upon their alleged negligent failure to protect the company's interests).

[796] See Murdie, "Compensation for criminals" 147 S.J. 252.

[797] *Clunis v Camden and Islington HA* [1998] Q.B. 978, 987. The leading contractual case is *Tinsley v Milligan* [1994] A.C. 340 which makes clear that once the illegality principle is engaged, the court has no discretion whether to apply it or not.

rule which will apply in all situations is understandable reluctance to reach a position where his own misconduct in effect makes the claimant an outlaw to whom no duty of care is owed. On the other hand cases do arise where it would not appear fair, just or reasonable to give a remedy to someone who suffers injury while engaged in some immoral or illegal act. A number of fine distinctions have resulted from attempts to reconcile these principles.

4–249 **Gray v Thames Trains Ltd.** It has been said that two strands of authority may be identified in which the illegality rule has been applied.[798] The wider rule is that a claimant cannot recover for loss which is the consequence of his own criminal act. The narrower principle is that he cannot recover for damage which is the consequence of a sentence imposed by a court for a criminal act. Both rules operated to defeat the claim in *Gray v Thames Trains Ltd.*[799] The claimant, who had been injured in an accident for which the defendant was responsible, developed post traumatic stress disorder. The symptoms included personality change and angry outbursts. While still receiving treatment he fell into an argument with a stranger, went home and obtained a knife with which he returned and stabbed the man to death. His plea of guilty to manslaughter was accepted on the grounds of diminished responsibility and he was sentenced to a hospital order of indefinite effect. It was held that he was unable to recover from the defendant as damages such earnings as he lost both before and after his conviction.[800] Most of his losses were caused by his arrest and sentence for manslaughter and were thereby irrecoverable as a result of the narrower rule. The wider rule covered other claims, such as a claim for general damages for feelings of guilt and remorse after the killing. The question was one of causation: while such damage would not have happened but for the tortious act of the defendant, the immediate cause of it was the claimant's own criminal act.[801]

4–250 **The wider rule.** It is in application of the wider of the two rules that questions of causation are likely to arise. Where, contrary to regulations, the claimant was injured when taking a ride on a builders' hoist, his claim could still succeed.[802]

---

[798] Per Lord Hoffmann in *Gray v Thames Trains* [2009] 1 A.C. 1339 at [32].

[799] [2009] 1 A.C. 1339 at [32]. See Warner, "Bad cause no action" 159 N.L.J. 1200. *Grey* was applied in *Nayyar v Denton Wilde Sapte* [2010] P.N.L.R. 15 (money paid as a bribe irrecoverable).

[800] The claim for financial losses was put as it was in *Gray* to avoid the difficulty created by the similar facts of *Clunis v Camden and Islington HA*, above, where illegality defeated the claim (the claimant was discharged from a hospital where he had been detained under the Mental Health Act, and then stabbed and killed a strangeris claim against the health authority, based upon his conviction and sentence for manslaughter, failed). Surprisingly illegality was not raised as a defence in *Meah v McCreamer* [1985] 1 All E.R. 367, (as a result of head injury and resulting change of personality in a road traffic accident caused by the defendants negligence the claimant raped three women and was imprisoned: he recovered damages for his loss of liberty).

[801] Per Sir Murray Stuart-Smith in *Vellino v Chief Constable of the Greater Manchester Police* [2002] 1 W.L.R. 218, CA at [70]: "The operation of the principle arises where the claimant's claim is founded upon his own criminal or immoral act. The facts which give rise to the claim must be inextricably linked with the criminal activity. It is not sufficient if the criminal activity merely gives occasion for tortious conduct of the defendant."

[802] *Progress and Properties Ltd v Craft* (1976) 12 A.L.R. 59.

A claim also succeeded where the defendant discharged his 12-bore shotgun through a hole in his garden shed in order to frighten off the claimant who intended burglary at the premises.[803] Where a 13 year old and his friend purchased petrol in order to sniff the fumes and, a match being lit, the claimant's clothes caught fire, the garage owner who sold the petrol in the first place was held liable for the injuries sustained: it was unlawful to sell petrol to someone of the claimant's age and a common law duty of care was owed to prevent the claimant having control of the petrol which was not extinguished by the claimant's own wrongdoing.[804] In these cases the illegality may be seen as as giving the occasion upon which the claimant's damage arose, but the defendant's breach of duty was the principal cause. Illegality may well not provide a defence to a claim where the claimant's action can be said to rest on a conceptual basis separate and distinct from an earlier fraud and cannot be said to rely on the fraud.[805]

The *ex turpi causa* maxim refers not so much to a principle as to a policy, **4–251** based upon reasons which can vary with the facts.[806] So, a motorist owes a duty of care to other road users, even if they are driving without due care and attention.[807] Further, a motorist owes a duty of care to a passenger, even if they are participating in a joint illegal venture, such as the commission of a driving offence.[808] However, a duty of care is not owed by one offender to another for acts done in the course of commission of a joint crime.[809] For similar reasons the claim failed where, following brain injury in a road traffic accident, the claimant developed an addiction to heroin which caused additional damage: it was contrary to public policy to allow compensation for injury which flowed from the

---

[803] *Revill v Newbery* [1996] 2 W.L.R. 239, CA, per Millett L.J.: "In my opinion . . . there is no place for the doctrine *ex turpi causa non oritur* in this context. If the doctrine applied, any claim by the assailant or trespasser would be barred no matter how excessive or unreasonable the force used against him."

[804] *Evans v Souls Garages Ltd, The Times*, January 23, 2001 (the claimant was guilty of contributory negligence to the extent of one third).

[805] *Sweetman v Nathan* [2004] P.N.L.R. 89, CA (the claimant was allowed to proceed with a claim against solicitors for negligence in the course of a property transaction in which he was admittedly guilty of fraud in obtaining a loan to fund the purchase).

[806] See per Lord Hoffmann in *Grey v Thames Trains*, n.798, above at [30]. Also, e.g. *Griffin v UHY Hacker Young & Partners* [2010] EWHC 146 (Ch) (arguably the ex turpi rule did not apply against a claimant convicted of an offence of strict liability where the element of personal fault was absent).

[807] *Rouse v Squires* [1973] Q.B. 889. It was said the duty would not be owed to those driving recklessly.

[808] *Jackson v Harrison* (1978) 19 A.L.R. 129 (the passenger, who was injured in a motor accident, was fully aware that his driver, whose negligence caused the accident, had been driving whilst disqualified). See also *Taylor v Leslie* 1998 Rep. L.R. 110, OH; *Currie v Clamp* 2001 S.C.L.R. 504, OH, and Ch.10, para.10–190, below.

[809] *Ashton v Turner* [1981] Q.B. 137 (the law did not recognise a duty of care owed by one burglar to another, in relation to an act done in the course of the commission of the crime, but even if such a duty were owed the driver of their get-away car could plead successfully the maxim as a complete defence). Further see Rowe, "Illegality as a Defence in Tort" in 131 New L.J. 570 and Swanton, "Plaintiff a Wrongdoer: Joint Complicity in an Illegal Enterprise as a Defence to Negligence" in 9 Sydney L.R. 304.

claimant's own deliberate and illegal act.[810] Where an arrested person escaped from police custody and thereafter, in order to elude capture, jumped through a window and injured himself, it was held that no duty of care was owed by the police, alternatively he was engaged in a criminal act and the maxim *ex turpi causa* applied by way of defence.[811] A defence that suicide is so morally offensive as to defeat a claim in negligence by the administratrix of a deceased person who took his own life while in police custody, failed in *Reeves v Commissioner of Police of the Metropolis.*[812]

4–252   **Stone & Rolls Ltd v Moore Stephens.** Where someone who represented the sole directing mind and will of a company, procured it to enter fraudulent transactions, the dishonesty of the company's human agent was attributed to the company itself. It became liable for the frauds and where it sought to bring a claim against its auditors for negligence in failing to carry out yearly audits with proper care, so as to discover the loss, the claim was rightly struck out by reason of the illegality rule. The company's answer to the illegality plea, that the auditors were seeking to rely on that which it had been their duty to detect and prevent, was rejected. There was no authority to support the proposition that if the very thing from which the defendant owed a duty to save the claimant harmless was or included the commission of a criminal offence, the ex turpi principle would be overridden.[813]

4–253   **Reducing the monetary award.** Even though the claimant may establish a right to the recovery of damages as a result of the defendant's negligent act, the award may be reduced in whole or in part if his monetary claim is based substantially, that is, not collaterally or insignificantly, on an unlawful act. So, where a claimant, a crane operator, suffered serious personal injuries as a result of admitted negligence, he was unable to recover future loss of earnings where, in order to keep his job at sea, he had failed to disclose that he had suffered from epilepsy. Ilegality prevented that part of the claim based upon his deception from being maintained.[814] But it is always necessary to analyse to what issue alleged illegality goes. A claimant was not disentitled from making a claim for future loss of earnings based on service in the RAF, by lies told on her application form for that employment, where she was not claiming lost RAF earnings as such, but was relying on them as evidence of what her future earnings would have been, had her accident not disabled her. In the circumstances, the fact that she had

---

[810] *Wilson v Coulson* [2002] P.I.Q.R. P300, Ch.3, para.3–71, above.

[811] *Vellino v Chief Constable of Greater Manchester* [2002] 1 W.L.R. 312, CA.

[812] [2000] 1 A.C. 360.

[813] *Stone & Rolls Ltd v Moore Stephens* [2009] 3 W.L.R. 455, HL (per Lord Walker and Lord Brown, it would be artificial not to fix the company with the knowledge and wrongdoing of its owner and also artifical to describe the company even as a secondary victim of the fraud; per Lord Phillips, those for whose benefit the claim was brought fell outside the scope of any duty owed by the auditors).

[814] *Hewison v Meridian Shipping PTE* [2003] P.I.Q.R. P252, CA (the argument that the failure to disclose epilepsy was wrong, but understandable, and thereby not offensive to public morality was rejected: the claimant had practised a deceit which was not collateral, but essential to establish the element of future loss of earnings and it could not possibly be described as insignificant in view of the risks involved to the claimant, those with whom he would work, and his employers).

obtained employment with the RAF by means of a lie was not relevant and did not affect her claim.[815]

(D) Striking out negligence claims

Basis of strike out. The ultimate weapon in the armoury of the defendant who **4–254** considers the claimant has no arguable case in negligence, is an application to strike out. The court is empowered by Pt 3.4 of the Civil Procedure Rules 1998[816] to strike out a statement of case if it appears that it discloses no reasonable grounds for bringing the claim. The associated Practice Direction indicates that two situations are contemplated by the rule: first, where the content of the statement of the statement of case is defective in that, even if every factual allegation in it were proved, the party relying on it could not succeed; and secondly where no matter how complete and apparently correct the statement of case may be, it would fail as a matter of law. Corresponding provisions appeared in the Rules of the Supreme Court[817] and the County Court Rules.[818]

Factual allegations to be assumed. It is a basic principle that on an **4–255** application to strike out on the ground that the claimant cannot succeed even if the facts he alleges are true, the court must accept at face value the proposition that those facts will be proved. In other words, the defendant must show that even upon the facts alleged and assumed for purposes of the application the claim could not succeed in law. The test is an onerous one and only if it is clear that grounds cannot reasonably be argued should the claim be dismissed.[819] There will be cases where until there has been a hearing to establish the facts, the court will not be able properly to assess the weight of the respective arguments in law.[820] The drawbacks of the pre-emptive strike were expressly referred to by Lord Browne-Wilkinson in *Barrett v Enfield London Borough Council*. He pointed out that unless it was possible

> "to give a *certain* answer to the question whether the plaintiff's claim would succeed, the case was inappropriate for striking out . . . in an area of the law which was uncertain and developing (such as the circumstances in which a person can be held liable in negligence for the exercise of a statutory duty or power) it is not normally appropriate

---

[815] *Major v Ministry of Defence* (2003) 147 S.J.L.B. 1206, CA. See McCaul, "Ill-gotten gains" 2003 P.I.L.J. 14, 8. See also *Ul-Haq v Shah* [2009] R.T.R. 27, CA (it was inappropriate to strike out the claimant's claim for personal injury as a result of a the road traffic accident because he participated in a fraudulent claim by someone who falsely alleged they were also present).

[816] See also the associated power under CPR 24.2 to enter summary judgment where the claimant has no realistic prospect of success; also Hall, "Strike out under the CPR" 145 S.J. 354.

[817] RSC Ord.18, r.19(a).

[818] CCR Ord.13, r.5(1)(a).

[819] See, e.g. *Palmer v Tees HA* [2000] P.I.Q.R. P1 at P6, CA; also, per Lord Slynn of Hadley in *W v Essex CC* [2001] 2 A.C. 592 at 599 (a claim for psychiatric injury by parents whose children had been sexually abused): " . . . it is not necessary to decide whether the parents' claim must or should succeed if the facts they allege are proved. The question is whether if the facts are proved they must fail." The House of Lords found it could not say on the facts that the parents could not be primary or secondary victims.

[820] See, e.g. *Farah v British Airways Plc, The Times*, January 26, 2000, CA (immigrants alleged a duty of care owed to them by the Home Office, one of whose immigration liason officers had advised an airline not to carry them to the United Kingdom).

to strike out. In my judgment it is of great importance that such development should be on the basis of actual facts found at trial not on hypothetical facts assumed (possibly wrongly) to be true for the purpose of the strike out."[821]

ILLUSTRATIONS

4-256   The claimant's action was not struck out: where it was alleged that a travel agent's accountants owed a duty of care to a company which provided the agent with a bond to cover obligations owed to customers[822]; where the claimants, child beneficiaries of a trust set up by their parents, sued the defendant, a chartered accountant, for negligence in connection with the setting up and monitoring of the trust, even though the defendant's retainer was with the parents and they had provided all funds[823]; and where a late application to amend would allow the claimant to plead a claim that was at least potentially viable.[824] A claim based upon alleged negligence by solicitors in pursuing a claim for damages arising from a road traffic accident, was struck out, where the court was entitled to conclude on the material before it that the claimant himself had been entirely to blame for the accident and his claim against the other driver was therefore valueless.[825]

4-257   **The human rights dimension.** In the context of a claim in negligence the claimant will have to allege facts which, if proved, will arguably meet the criteria by which the existence of a duty of care is tested.[826] He will have to allege damage of a type recognised as completing his cause of action. An application to strike out under Pt 3 of the Civil Procedure Rules can only succeed if it can be shown that one of these essential ingredients is missing. Given the approach of the European Court of Human Rights to art.6 of the Convention on Human Rights, in its application to striking out claims,[827] occasions when it will not be possible to show an arguable case on the third aspect of the *Caparo*[828] test will

---

[821] [2001] 2 A.C. 550 at 556. See also *Equitable Life Assurance Society v Ernst & Young, The Times,* September 10, 2003, CA (a court ought to be cautious in concluding, at the outset of a claim, that summary judgment should be given on the ground that even if successful on liability all issues of quantum would go against the claimant).

[822] *Independents' Advantage Insurance Company Ltd v Personal Representatives of Cook* [2004] P.N.L.R. 44, CA.

[823] *Hughes v Richards* [2004] P.N.L.R 35, CA.

[824] *Bluett v Suffolk County Council* [2005] 1 F.C.R. 89, CA.

[825] *Miller v Garton Shires* [2007] P.N.L.R. 11, CA.

[826] For which see Ch.2, above, generally. It has been said in relation to strike out under CPR 24.2 that the ordinary standard of proof on a balance of probabilities is inappropriate. The test is whether there is a realistic prospect of success, in the sense that the prospect is realistic rather than fanciful: *Royal Brompton Hospital NHS Trust v Hammond, The Times,* May 1, 2001, CA applying *Swain v Hillman* [2001] 1 All E.R. 91. In *Independents' Advantage Insurance Company Ltd v Personal Representatives of Cook,* n.822 above, it was said that where it is accepted that the claimant will be able to establish all the facts pleaded and where there are no additional facts on which the claimant seeks to rely, if the particulars of claim disclose no reasonable grounds for bringing the claim, the court has ample power to strike out the pleading and enter judgment for the defendant without recourse to summary judgment under CPR 24.2: ibid., per Chadwick L.J. at 50.

[827] *Osman v UK* [1999] F.L.R. 193, ECHR. See also Ch.2, para.2–326, above.

[828] [1990] 2 A.C. 605.

be rare[829]: it would be surprising if a claimant did not set out facts from which he could argue that it would be fair, just and reasonable to impose a duty of care.[830]

Having said that, the European Court has accepted that there will be occasions **4–258** when, consistently with art.6, a court could strike out on the ground of absence of proximity as between claimant and defendant and thereby exert control over claims which have no reasonable prospect of success.[831] Presumably the power could also be exercised if the damage alleged by the claimant was not recognised in law. In *Kent v Griffiths and the London Ambulance Service*,[832] Lord Woolf M.R. commented on the interplay between the striking out power and art.6 as follows:

" . . . it would be wrong for the *Osman* decision to be taken as a signal that, even when the legal position is clear and an investigation of the facts would provide no assistance, the courts should be reluctant to dismiss cases which have no real prospect of success. Court are now encouraged, where an issue or issues can be identified which will resolve or help to resolve litigation, to take that issue or those issues at an early stage of the proceedings so as to achieve expedition and save expense. There is no question of any contravention of Article 6 of the ECHR in so doing. Defendants as well as claimants are entitled to a fair trial and it is an important part of case management to bring proceedings to an end as expeditiously as possible. Although strike out may appear to be a summary remedy it is in fact indistinguishable from deciding a case on a preliminary point of law."[833]

Summary judgment and striking out compared. In *S v Gloucestershire* **4–259** *County Council* May L.J. considered what would be required for an application for summary judgment to succeed in a case where striking out would fail:

"the court will first need to be satisfied that all substantial facts relevant to the allegations of negligence, which are reasonably capable of being before the court, are before the court; that these facts are undisputed or that there is no real prospect of successfully disputing them; and that there is no real prospect of oral evidence affecting

[829] See the speech of Lord Browne-Wilkinson in *Barrett v London Borough of Enfield* [2001] 2 A.C. 550.
[830] For an example where the court felt compelled to let the claim proceed, see *L v Reading Borough Council and Chief Constable of the Thames Valley Police* [2001] P.I.Q.R. P387, CA, Ch.2, para.2–320, above (claim against police for allegedly misrepresenting the content of interviews of a parent so that Children Act proceedings were instituted).
[831] See, e.g. *DP and JC v UK*, *The Times*, October 23, 2002, ECHR (where children in care had claimed that a local authority was negligent in failing to protect them from sexual abuse the ECHR rejected the proposition that striking out where domestic law had decided there was no duty of care was a breach of art.6, but the claimants recovered compensation under art.13 for the failure of domestic law to give them a remedy). See also *Palmer v Tees HA* [2000] P.I.Q.R. P1, per Stuart-Smith L.J. at P8.
[832] [2000] P.I.Q.R. P57, CA.
[833] *Kent v Griffiths and the London Ambulance Service* [2000] P.I.Q.R. P67. So, there was no breach of Art.6 in striking out claims for negligence arising from false accusations of child abuse brought against the parents of children by child care professionals: *D v East Berkshire Community Health NHS Trust* [2005] 2 W.L.R. 993, HL. See further, Ch.2, para.2–331, above. The *East Berkshire* case was applied in *Lawrence v Pembrokeshire CC* [2007] 2 F.C.R. 329, CA, where the court struck out the negligence claim of a mother who alleged that her children had been incorrectly placed on the child protection register.

the court's assessment of the facts . . . Secondly, the court will need to be satisfied that, upon these facts, there is no real prospect of the claim in negligence succeeding and that there is no other reason why the case should be disposed of at a trial. If by this process the court does so conclude and gives summary judgment, there will, in my view, have been proper judicial scrutiny of the detailed facts of the particular case such as to constitute a fair hearing in accordance with art.6 of the convention."[834]

---

[834] [2000] 3 All E.R. 346 at 373.

CHAPTER 5

DAMAGES

1.—REMOTENESS OF DAMAGE

(A) Introduction

Generally. Three essential components of actionable negligence have been identified above: the existence of a duty to take care, breach of that duty, and damage suffered in consequence of that breach.[1] The focus now is on the third of these elements. Before a claimant can succeed in an action for negligence, the damage alleged must be damage which the law recognises and which, in the usual phrase, is not too remote.[2] The question whether such damage has in fact been caused by the defendant's breach of duty will be considered in Chapter 6.   **5–01**

Sometimes the consequences of a wrongdoer's negligence can go well beyond what reasonably could have been anticipated, or damage can occur in a manner that could not have been in contemplation. The rules of remoteness seek to provide a mechanism which helps to identify what may be recovered in terms of damage and what may not. They operate to draw a line between damage that in fact occurs as a result of negligence and that for which a defendant should actually be held liable. As Blackburn J. said, albeit in a duty case[3]:   **5–02**

---

[1] See Ch.1, para.1–34, above.
[2] See, generally, Sir Robin Cooke, "Remoteness of damage and judicial discretion" [1978] C.L.J. 288; Cartwright, "Remoteness of damage in contract and tort: a reconsideration" [1996] C.L.J. 488; Stauch, "Risk and remoteness of damage in negligence" (2001) 64 M.L.R. 191.
[3] *Cattle v Stockton Waterworks Co* (1875) L.R. 10 Q.B. 453 at 456, adopting the words of Coleridge J. in *Lumley v Gye* (1853) 2 E & B 216 at 252.

"Courts of justice should not 'allow themselves, in the pursuit of perfectly complete remedies for all wrongful acts, to transgress the bounds, which our law, in a wise consciousness as I conceive of its limited powers, has imposed on itself, of redressing only the proximate and direct consequences of wrongful acts.' "

Lord Wright, making a similar observation, explained why a line of this kind needs to be drawn[4]:

"the law cannot take account of everything that follows a wrongful act, it regards some subsequent matters as outside the scope of its selection, because 'it were infinite for the law to judge the cause of causes' or consequences of consequences .... In the varied web of affairs, the law must abstract some consequences as relevant, not perhaps on grounds of pure logic but simply for practical reasons."

There are many judicial references to the need to limit the extent of a defendant's liability simply on the grounds of practicality.[5] The argument in the cases has centred on just how this ought to be achieved.

5–03   **Duty, breach and damage.** Speaking very generally, the inquiry into the remoteness of damage seeks to ascertain whether there is a reasonably substantial link between the defendant's conduct and the damage that it has caused. Expressed in this way, it becomes apparent that the remoteness issue, like the duty issue, is a device for controlling or limiting the ambit of a person's liability for negligence. This overlap of function was noted at the beginning of Chapter 2, where the point was made that the inquiries are conceptually distinct.[6] Whether a defendant can be held to owe another person a duty to take care is determined by asking questions about the kind or nature of the defendant's conduct and of the damage sought to be compensated, together with, in some cases, the kind of claimant who is bringing the action and the kind of defendant against whom the action is being brought. These matters bring into account the special features of the various categories of claims or claimants which do not depend on the random and contingent circumstances in which the harm occurred in the particular case at hand. The remoteness inquiry, by contrast, brings into account precisely these circumstances. It asks whether there was a sufficiently close or proximate connection between the defendant's initial negligent act and the damage suffered by the claimant that it is reasonable as a matter of policy that the defendant should pay for that damage.

5–04   However, stating this distinction may be easier than applying it. Indeed, the question whether there is a duty to take care may be intimately bound up with questions about whether the duty has been broken and the damage in respect of which the duty is owed. The overlap is apparent from the decision of the Privy

---

[4] *Liesbosch Dredger (Owners) v SS Edison* [1933] A.C. 449 at 460, HL. In *Lagden v O'Connor* [2004] 1 A.C. 1067 it was decided that the actual decision in this case should no longer be followed: see para.5–88, below.
[5] See also *HMS London* [1914] P 72 at 78 per Sir Samuel Evans, CA; *Palsgraf v Long Island Railroad Co* 162 NE 99 (1928), at 104 per Andrews J.; *Weld-Blundell v Stephens* [1920] A.C. 956 per Lord Sumner at 986.
[6] See Ch.2, paras 2–03—2–04, above.

Council in *Attorney-General of the British Virgin Islands v Hartwell*,[7] where Lord Nicholls observed that the underlying principle was that reasonable foreseeability, as an ingredient of a duty of care, was a broad and flexible objective standard which is responsive to the infinitely variable circumstances of individual cases. The nature and gravity of the damage foreseeable, the likelihood of its occurrence, and the ease or difficulty of eliminating the risk were all matters to be taken into account in the round when deciding whether as a matter of legal policy a duty of care was owed by the defendant to the plaintiff in respect of the damage suffered by him.

Cause of damage. Questions of causation also may not be easily distinguish-   **5–05**
able from those relating to duty or to remoteness of damage. As Lord Hoffmann said in *Fairchild v Glenhaven Funeral Services Ltd*[8]:

" . . . the essential point is that the causal requirements are just as much part of the legal conditions for liability as the rules which prescribe the kind of conduct which attracts liability or the rules which limit the scope of that liability . . . one is never simply liable, one is always liable *for* something—to make compensation for damage, the nature and extent of which is delimited by the law. The rules which delimit what one is liable for may consist of causal requirements or may be rules unrelated to causation, such as the foreseebility requirements in the rule in *Hadley v Baxendale*[9] . . . But in either case they are rules of law, part and parcel of the conditions of liability. Once it is appreciated that the rules laying down causal requirements are not autonomous expressions of some form of logic or judicial instinct but creatures of the law, part of the conditions of liability, it is possible to explain their content on the grounds of fairness and justice in exactly the same way as the other conditions of liability."

Overview. However, and notwithstanding Lord Hoffmann's cautionary   **5–06**
words, it should be recognised that the inquiries into duty, into breach, into the cause of damage and into the remoteness of the damage are conceptually distinct, and also that in many decided cases it has usually been thought necessary or convenient to adopt an analysis which divides up the question of liability for negligence in the traditional way. Accordingly the emphasis in this chapter will be upon the evolution of the test for remoteness of damage as it has traditionally been perceived, and the next chapter will address causation. But this separate treatment should not obscure the overlap in function between the two.

(B) Development of the tests to be applied

Intended consequences. A consequence which is intended cannot be too   **5–07**
remote. "The intention to injure the plaintiff disposes of any question of remoteness."[10] So where the defendant, in pulling down his building, intention-ally caused materials to fall on the stable of the claimant, he was liable for the

---

[7] [2004] 1 W.L.R. 1273, PC.
[8] [2003] 1 A.C. 32, at 71.
[9] (1854) 9 Exch. 341. The decision is the starting point for considering the damages for which a defendant in breach of contract is liable.
[10] *Quinn v Leathem* [1901] A.C. 495 at 537 per Lord Lindley.

damage.[11] Reckless conduct is treated in the same way, so the consequences of such conduct, even though heedless, are compensatable as having been intended. In *Scott v Shepherd*,[12] for a joke, a person threw a lighted squib amongst a crowd of people in a covered market. In self defence the person nearest to it threw it towards someone else, who in turn picked it up and threw it away, whereupon it exploded and put out the claimant's eye. It was held that the person who started the incident by lighting and throwing the firework was liable to the claimant because he must have intended that it should explode somewhere in the crowd. Further, the risk of injury to somebody as a result of his action was at least foreseeable.

5–08   **Direct consequences.** In the case of unintended consequences of negligence, the classic case for many years was *Re Polemis*. The claimants were the owners of a ship, the *Thrasyvoulos*, which was being unloaded in Casablanca. Stevedores employed by the charterers of the ship negligently knocked a plank into the hold, where a quantity of benzine was stored. Leakage had caused benzine vapour to form, and a spark from the falling plank ignited the vapour and caused a fire which destroyed the ship. At trial it was held that the causing of the spark could not reasonably have been anticipated from the falling of the plank, although some small damage to the ship could have been contemplated. It was held by the Court of Appeal that the charterers of the vessel were liable to the owners for the loss of the ship, on the basis that this was the direct consequence of the stevedores' negligence.

5–09   Scrutton L.J. said that in determining whether an act was negligent, it was relevant to determine whether any reasonable person would foresee that the act would cause damage; if he would not, the act was not negligent. But if the act would or might probably cause damage, the fact that the damage it caused was not the exact kind of damage one would expect was immaterial, so long as the damage was directly traceable to the negligent act and not due to the operation of independent causes having no connection with the negligent act, except that they could not avoid its results. Once the act was negligent, the fact that its exact operation was not foreseen was immaterial. Applying these principles, he concluded that it was negligent in discharging cargo to knock down the plank, for it could easily cause some damage, either to workers, or cargo, or the ship. The fact that it did directly produce an unexpected result, a spark in an atmosphere of petrol vapour which caused a fire, did not relieve the person who was negligent from the damage which his negligent act directly caused.

5–10   **Foreseeable consequences.** The reasoning in *Re Polemis* was subsequently criticised on a number of grounds. First, it was said to be lacking in authority, on the basis that precedents cited by the Court of Appeal did not support the decision.[13] Secondly, the direct consequence test was seen as inherently uncertain and difficult to apply: it would provoke a "war of epithets" about what exactly

---

[11] *Emblen v Myers* (1860) 6 H & N 54.
[12] (1773) W B1 892.
[13] Pollock, "Liability for consequences" (1922) 38 L.Q.R. 165.

amounted to a "direct" consequence.[14] And thirdly, the very principle of the case was attacked as misconceived, on the ground that it was illogical and inconsistent to use the concept of foreseeability to create liability in negligence but to reject it when determining the ambit of recovery for that negligence. Rather, culpability and compensation should go hand in hand.[15]

The Wagon Mound (No.1). Criticisms such as these provide the background **5–11** to the decision of the Privy Council, on appeal from Australia, in *Overseas Tankship (UK) Ltd v Morts Dock & Engineering Co Ltd (The Wagon Mound (No.1)*.[16] The defendants carelessly discharged bunkering oil from a ship, the *Wagon Mound*, onto water about two hundred yards away from the claimants' wharf in Sydney harbour. The oil was carried by the tide to the claimants' wharf and fouled the slipways. Welding operations were being carried out by the claimants, and these caused the oil to ignite and the resulting fire to damage the wharf. At the trial it was found that damage to the wharf by fouling was reasonably foreseeable but damage by fire was not, and on this footing the Privy Council decided that the defendants were not liable. It was not enough that the negligence was the direct cause of the damage if that damage was not foreseeable, and *Re Polemis*, accordingly, should not be followed. Viscount Simonds explained why:

> "Enough has been said to show that the authority of *Polemis* has been severely shaken though lip service has from time to time been paid to it. In their Lordships' opinion it should no longer be regarded as good law. It is not probable that many cases will for that reason have a different result, though it is hoped that the law will be thereby simplified and that in some cases, at least, palpable injustice will be avoided. For it does not seem consonant with current ideas of justice or morality that for an act of negligence, however slight or venial, which result in some trivial foreseeable damage the actor should be liable for all consequences however unforeseeable and however grave, so long as they can be said to be 'direct'. It is a principle of civil liability, subject only to qualifications which have no present relevance, that a man must be considered to be responsible for the probable consequences of his act. To demand more of him is too harsh a rule, to demand less is to ignore that civilised order requires the observance of a minimum standard of behaviour."

In the result, following the decision in *The Wagon Mound (No.1)*, the test for **5–12** remoteness in actions for negligence is not directness but foreseeability: a tortfeasor is liable for damage of the kind that a reasonable person should have foreseen at the time of the negligent act or omission in question.

The Wagon Mound (No.2). The decision in *The Wagon Mound (No.1)* did **5–13** not bring all litigation resulting from the fire on Sydney harbour to an end. In *Overseas Tankship (UK) Ltd v The Miller Steamship Co Pty (The Wagon Mound*

---

[14] See especially Goodhart, "The imaginary necktie and the rule in *Re Polemis*" (1952) 68 L.Q.R. 514; Goodhart, "Liability and compensation" (1960) 76 L.Q.R. 567.
[15] ibid. Compare Davies, "The road from Morocco: *Polemis* through *Donoghue* to no-fault" (1982) 45 M.L.R. 534.
[16] [1961] A.C. 388, PC; Payne, "Foresight and remoteness of damage in negligence" (1962) 25 M.L.R. 1; Dias, "Remoteness of liability and legal policy" [1962] C.L.J. 178.

(No.2)[17] the claim was by the owners of two ships, the *Corrimal* and the *Audrey D*, which were tied up at the wharf at the time of the fire. The claimants adduced different evidence about the fire danger, leading the trial judge to conclude that: (i) reasonable people in the position of the officers of the *Wagon Mound* would regard the furnace oil as very difficult to ignite when on water; (ii) if they had given attention to the risk of fire, they would have regarded it as a possibility, but one which could become an actuality only in very exceptional circumstances; and (iii) they would have considered the chances of the required exceptional circumstances happening while the oil remained spread on the harbour waters as being remote. On these findings, the judge concluded that the damage was not reasonably foreseeable and that the claim in negligence failed. The Privy Council, however, reversed his decision. Lord Reid identified a foreseeable risk as a "real risk", being "one which would occur to the mind of a reasonable man in the position of the defendant's servant and which he would not brush aside as far-fetched".[18] The instant risk satisfied this test and the question then was what, if anything, the reasonable man would have done to counter it. There was no advantage in or justification for allowing the oil to escape, the damage could very easily have been prevented and in the circumstances, therefore, the risk was not one that could be neglected. The defendants accordingly were liable for the damage to the plaintiff's ships.

5–14   *The Wagon Mound (No.2)*, then, concerns the *degree* of foreseeability which can satisfy the test for remoteness of damage in *The Wagon Mound (No.1)*. The requirement that the risk be a "real risk" as explained by Lord Reid is not a demanding one, but sometimes a risk may be held to be unforeseeable in this sense and the damage too remote.

(C) Application of the foresight test

5–15   **General propositions.** Although uncertainty is inherent in the remoteness inquiry, some general propositions are possible. The defendant is liable for all damage of a kind that was reasonably foreseeable, given the scope of the duty of which he was in breach. And so long as the damage is of a kind that was reasonably foreseeable, it is not necessary that the precise mechanism by which the damage was caused was foreseeable. Again, the wrongdoer is liable for foreseeable damage even though its full extent may not have been capable of anticipation. In cases where the amount of the damage is exacerbated by the claimant's existing physical, mental or financial state, the defendant takes the claimant as he finds him and, once again, must pay the full amount of the damage.

---

[17] [1967] 1 A.C. 617, PC; Dias, "Trouble on oiled waters: problems of *The Wagon Mound (No 2)*" [1967] C.L.J. 62.
[18] *Overseas Tankship (UK) Ltd v The Miller Steamship Co Pty (The Wagon Mound (No.2))* [1967] 1 A.C. 617 at 643; The test also has been adopted in Australia: *Wyong Shire Council v Shirt* (1980) 146 C.L.R. 40, at 47–48, HCA; *New South Wales v Fahy* (2007) 81 A.L.J.R. 1021, at [7], [78], [133], [241], HCA; but see the criticisms of Callinan and Heydon JJ. at [216]–[227].

These propositions and their application in particular cases can be examined   **5–16**
under three heads: (i) personal injuries, (ii) damage to property, and (iii)
economic loss.

(i) *Personal injuries*

Mode of infliction of injury. As a general rule the courts have not sought to   **5–17**
distinguish between different kinds of injury to the human body. If personal
injury of some kind is foreseeable then the damage usually will not be regarded
as too remote, notwithstanding that the injury came about in some unforeseeable
way or that the particular form of personal injury was unexpected or unforeseeable.

Hughes v Lord Advocate. The general rule is seen in operation in the   **5–18**
decision of the House of Lords in *Hughes v Lord Advocate*.[19] Workers
maintaining telecommunications equipment in Edinburgh left an uncovered
manhole surrounded by a tent and guarded by red warning lamps lit by paraffin.
An eight-year-old boy entered the tent and caused one of the paraffin lamps to fall
down the hole. Some paraffin escaped and vaporised, creating an explosive
mixture which was detonated by the naked light of the lamp, and the boy was
severely injured in the explosion which followed. The defendants' employees
were found to be in breach of a duty of care to safeguard the boy against injury
from the lamp, containing as it did a highly inflammable substance. It was
reasonably foreseeable that if care was not taken he would be exposed to injury
from that source. The argument that the *way* that the damage resulted, by an
explosion, could not reasonably have been foreseen and that the damage was,
therefore, too remote was rejected. Given that injury from the lamp was
foreseeable, the accident in question "was but a variant of the foreseeable"[20] and
it mattered not that it may have arisen in an unforeseeable manner.

Doughty v Turner Manufacturing Co Ltd. *Hughes* may be contrasted with   **5–19**
Doughty v Turner Manufacturing Co Ltd.[21] The defendants had two cauldrons in
their factory's heat treatment room, in which they subjected metal parts to heat
by immersing them in a hot molten solution. They provided suitable covers for
the cauldrons, in order to conserve the heat, which had been made by reputable
manufacturers from asbestos cement. Nobody had supposed that, if one of these
covers were immersed in the cauldron, there would result any serious consequences. In fact, a cover was accidentally knocked into the cauldron, so that it
slid beneath the surface of the hot liquid, which erupted violently, causing the
claimant to sustain burns. It was accepted that there was a reasonably foreseeable
risk to the claimant from the splashing of hot liquid if a foreign body struck its
surface, but the claim nonetheless failed. The Court of Appeal held that, even if
the inadvertent immersion of the cover was negligent, the defendants were not
liable because the damage was not of such kind as could reasonably have been
foreseen. The duty was to safeguard from splashes, but not the kind of

---

[19] [1963] A.C. 837, HL.
[20] *Hughes v Lord Advocate* [1963] A.C. 837 at 858, per Lord Pearson.
[21] [1964] 1 Q.B. 518, CA.

unforeseeable explosion which actually occurred. Alternatively, the harm caused to the claimant was too remote.

5–20   On occasion the courts have taken a similarly restrictive view.[22] But it is not very easy to reconcile *Doughty* (or similar cases) with the decision in *Hughes*, for in both, foreseeable personal injury came about in an unforeseeable way. The Privy Council has raised the question whether the distinction that was taken in *Doughty* would commend itself to the courts today.[23]

5–21   **Jolley v Sutton London Borough Council.** The wider view is seen in the decision of the House of Lords in *Jolley v Sutton London Borough Council.*[24] A boat was left abandoned in the grounds of a block of flats of which the defendant was the occupier. The boat deteriorated and became rotten. The claimant, a boy of 14, and his friend jacked the boat up and attempted to repair it. While they were doing this the jack slipped and the boat fell on the claimant, causing very severe injury. At the trial the judge found that it was foreseeable that the boys would meddle with the boat in circumstances where they were at risk of physical injury, and imposed liability on the defendant. On appeal, it was conceded that the defendant had been negligent in failing to remove the boat and that the negligence had created a risk of injury from children climbing onto the boat and suffering injury from rotten planking giving way. However, the Court of Appeal allowed the appeal on the grounds that it was not reasonably foreseeable that the boys would decide to play by working under the boat whilst it was propped up. On further appeal to the House of Lords the decision of the trial judge was restored. Lord Hoffmann said that the defendant's duty was to take such care as was reasonable to see that the claimant was reasonably safe whilst he was on the defendant's premises, and the question here was whether the injury was of a description which was reasonably foreseeable so as to lie within the scope of that duty. The boys were likely to mimic behaviour of adults in the manner in which they played with the boat, and since it was reasonably foreseeable that the boys would suffer some injury from the negligent failure to remove the boat, the defendant was liable. The precise manner of the injury did not have to be foreseen. It was sufficient that there was a risk that children would meddle with the boat at the risk of some physical injury.

5–22   **Corr v IBC Vehicles Ltd.** The approach taken by the House of Lords in *Hughes* was confirmed once again in *Corr v IBC Vehicles Ltd.*[25] An employee of the defendant suffered serious head injuries in an accident at work, following which he underwent lengthy reconstructive surgery. He then began to suffer post-

---

[22] *Tremain v Pike* [1969] 1 W.L.R. 1556 (rare disease caused by exposure of the claimant to contact with rats' urine treated as different in kind from the effect of a rat bite or the consumption of food or drink contaminated by rats).

[23] *Attorney-General of the British Virgin Islands v Hartwell* [2004] 1 W.L.R. 1273, [29], PC.

[24] [2000] 1 W.L.R. 1082, HL; Williams, "Remoteness: some unexpected mischief" (2001) 117 L.Q.R. 30; Nolan, "Risks and wrongs—remoteness of damage in the House of Lords" (2001) 9 Tort L. Rev. 101; and see *Jebson v Ministry of Defence* [2000] 1 W.L.R. 2055, CA (defendants liable to drunken claimant who fell from the back of army lorry, because his conduct was within the general type that ought to have been foreseen, ie that, unsupervised, he and his fellows would encourage each other in foolish acts).

[25] [2008] 1 A.C. 884.

traumatic stress disorder, causing him to lapse into severe anxiety and depression, and eventually, some six years after the initial accident, he committed suicide. The issue requiring determination was whether the liability of the defendant extended to his suicide. Their Lordships held that the deceased's depressive illness had been the direct and foreseeable consequence of the accident for which the defendant was responsible, and that his suicide, although his own deliberate act, did not break the chain of causal consequences because it had been a direct result of that illness at a time when his capacity to make reasoned judgments about his future had been impaired. In so deciding, Lord Bingham recognised that it was not necessary, applying *Hughes*, that it be shown that the suicide was itself foreseeable where depression was a foreseeable consequence of the injuries and the suicide followed upon that depression. A tortfeasor who reasonably could foresee the occurrence of some damage did not have to foresee the precise form that that damage might take. Some consequences of depression might be so unusual or unpredictable as to be outside the bounds of what was reasonably foreseeable, but suicide was not.

Different kinds of injury. However, it may be that in some, rare, cases the **5–23** courts will differentiate between different kinds of personal injury. One obvious distinction already adverted to is that between physical and mental injury. At the duty stage, as we have seen, a claimant seeking damages for psychiatric injury who is a primary victim need show only that either form of injury was foreseeable, whereas in other cases the claimant must establish specifically that psychiatric injury was foreseeable.[26] In these latter cases the further question arises whether particular forms of psychiatric injury may be treated as different in kind. In *Pratley v Surrey County Council*[27] it was held that a foreseeable risk to an employee of psychiatric injury arising at some time in the future from a continuing work overload did not include a risk of an immediate mental collapse stemming from the employer's failure to introduce a new system of work. So here the court treated a particular form of mental injury as being different in kind and the mental collapse thus as too remote.

A court may also be prepared to distinguish between different kinds of **5–24** physical injury, but even then the defendant's conduct may be held to pose a risk of injury of more than one kind. In *Ogwo v Taylor*,[28] the defendant negligently started a fire in the roof of his house and the plaintiff, a fireman, was scalded by steam generated by water poured on to the fire. It was held that the defendant could foresee that the plaintiff would be subject to the risks inherent in fighting the fire, of which the risk of a scalding injury was certainly one.

Extent of injury. If personal injury of some kind is foreseeable, it is no **5–25** answer for the defendant to claim that he could not have foreseen its extent. So requiring an employee to drive an unheated van for 500 miles in freezing conditions exposed the employee to the risk of injury from cold and fatigue, and this included injury by frostbite even though this was an unusual consequence of

---

[26] See paras 2–116 to 2–154; and see further paras 5–31 to 5–33, below.
[27] [2004] I.C.R. 159, CA; and see *Rowe v McCartney* [1976] 2 N.S.W.L.R. 72, NSWCA.
[28] [1988] A.C. 431.

the cold in England.[29] Again, negligently controlling a rugby scrum rendered the referee liable for a serious injury to the player, notwithstanding that statistically it was very unlikely to occur.[30] The principle could indeed hardly be otherwise. It would be impossible to identify the extent of the consequences of an accident that might be treated as in some sense "average" or "normally to be expected".

5–26   **Eggshell skulls.** In a particular application of the preceding principle, a defendant has to take the victim of his or her tort as he or she finds that victim, so the defendant is liable for the whole damage even though its severity or extent has been increased because of the victim's pre-existing weakness or susceptibility to harm. Provided some personal injury was foreseeable, it is no answer that a "normal" person would not have suffered to the same extent. This is commonly known as the "eggshell skull" rule.[31]

> "[O]ne who is guilty of negligence to another must put up with idiosyncrasies of his victim that increase the likelihood or extent of damage to him: it is no answer to a claim for a fractured skull that its owner had an unusually fragile one."[32]

5–27   A much-cited decision is *Smith v Leech Brain & Co Ltd*.[33] A workman suffered a burn on his lip, which was a foreseeable happening, as a result of the defendant employer's negligent failure to provide adequate protection from the danger. The workman had a predisposition to cancer and a carcinoma developed on the site of the burn, which was not a foreseeable happening. The workman died from the disease three years later, and the defendant was held liable for his death. Lord Parker C.J. said that the test was not whether the employers could reasonably have foreseen that a burn would cause cancer and that the plaintiff would die, but whether the employers could reasonably foresee the type of injury suffered by the plaintiff, namely the burn. What was the amount of damage in the particular case depended on the characteristics and constitution of the victim.[34]

5–28   **Adverse consequences of medical treatment.** The rule can apply to cover the adverse consequences of medical treatment following an initial injury. In *Robinson v Post Office*,[35] the claimant sustained a minor wound as a consequence of the defendants' negligence, and visited his doctor to receive an anti-tetanus injection. He was allergic to the anti-tetanus serum and suffered the rare complication of encephalitis. The defendants sought to rely upon the doctor's action as a break in the chain of causation, and the trial judge agreed that the doctor had acted negligently in administering the injection, without applying properly the procedure for a test dose. However, this did not have causative

---

[29] *Bradford v Robinson Rentals Ltd* [1967] 1 All E.R. 267.
[30] *Smolden v Whitworth* [1997] P.I.Q.R. P133.
[31] See generally Rowe, "The Demise of the Thin Skull Rule?" (1977) 40 M.L.R. 377.
[32] *Owens v Liverpool Corp* [1939] 1 K.B. 394, at 400–401 per Mackinnon J.
[33] [1962] 2 Q.B. 405.
[34] Damages were, however, reduced because the husband might have developed cancer even if he had not suffered the burn.
[35] [1974] 1 W.L.R. 1176; and see *Winteringham v Rae* (1965) 55 D.L.R. (2d) 108 (claimant who was bitten by the defendant's dog received an anti-tetanus injection, to which he was abnormally susceptible: defendant liable for all the damage).

effect, since, even with proper precautions, the encephalitis would not have been prevented. The Court of Appeal, in dismissing the defendants' appeal, held that they could not rely on the doctor's negligence as a novus actus interveniens and were therefore liable for all of the claimant's disabilities.

Further illustrations. There are many further cases where the egg-shell skull **5–29** rule has been applied. They include: injury to a finger aggravating an existing eye injury[36]; an electric shock damaging nerve cells, allowing the poliomyelitis virus to attack those cells and bring about paralysis[37]; a leg injury leading to fat embolism, broncho-pneumonia and death[38]; a neck injury resulting in difficulty in wearing bifocal spectacles and a later fall.[39] Indeed, in the most obvious of examples, a number of claimants have suffered aggravated injury as a consequence of their particularly thin skulls.[40]

In *Stephenson v Waite Tileman Ltd*,[41] Richmond J. remarked that an inquiry **5–30** into the ability of a reasonable person to foresee compartmentalised risks of different kinds of harm would be both complex and unrealistic. His Honour recognised that it might be difficult to decide on an adequate theoretical reconciliation with the *Wagon Mound* principle, but was confident that for practical purposes it did not matter whether it be regarded as an exception or whether the unforeseeable consequences were regarded simply as going to the extent, rather than the kind, of the injury. And on the facts it was held that damage by way of an unknown virus infecting a wound and causing brain damage was covered.

Eggshell personalities. We have seen that in *Page v Smith*,[42] a vulnerable **5–31** claimant recovered damages for the recurrence of myalgic encephalomyelitis following a minor motor accident in which he was not physically injured, this notwithstanding the finding below that mental injury standing alone was unforeseeable. The House of Lords held that the claimant was a primary victim at risk of injury, that personal injury of some kind was reasonably foreseeable, and that the defendant was liable for all injury of that type, including psychiatric injury.[43] Their Lordships further held that it was no answer to the claim that the plaintiff was predisposed to psychiatric illness, nor that the illness took a rare form or was of unusual severity. The defendant had to take his victim as he found him. As Lord Lloyd said, "[t]here is no difference in principle . . . between an eggshell skull and an eggshell personality".[44]

---

[36] *Warren v Scruttons* [1962] 1 Lloyd's Rep. 497.
[37] *Sayers v Perrin* [1966] Q.L.R. 89.
[38] *Oman v McIntyre* [1962] S.L.T. 168.
[39] *Wieland v Cyril Lord Carpets Ltd* [1969] 3 All E.R. 1006.
[40] *Hole v Hocking* [1962] S.A.S.R. 128; *Wilson v Birt Pty Ltd* [1963] 2 SA 508; *Richards v State of Victoria* [1969] V.R. 136.
[41] [1973] 1 N.Z.L.R. 152, NZCA.
[42] [1996] 1 A.C. 155.
[43] See para.2–125.
[44] [1996] 1 A.C. 155, at 189, citing Geoffrey Lane J. in *Malcolm v Broadhurst* [1970] 3 All E.R. 508, at 511; and see *Mullins v Gray* [2004] EWCA Civ 1483 (claimant with vulnerable personality recovered compensation on the basis of her disproportionate perception of the pain, notwithstanding that she had no psychiatric illness strictly so-called).

5–32   In a more recent example,[45] the defendant employer negligently exposed a police officer to stress and fear, and this aggravated the officer's pre-existing hypertension, leading to a psychiatric condition which in turn caused a stroke. The Court of Appeal held that the claimant was a primary victim and, applying *Page v Smith*, so long as it was reasonably foreseeable that he would suffer some personal injury as a result of the negligence it did not matter that the injury was psychiatric rather than physical. The defendant had to take the claimant as it found him and, the stroke being a consequence of the defendant's breach of duty, the defendant was liable for that injury.

5–33   An unusual variation occurred in the Australian decision in *Kavanagh v Akhtar*.[46] The plaintiff suffered a shoulder injury as a result of negligence by the defendant. This meant that she could not properly care for her long hair, which she cut off. Her husband, a strict Muslim, was angered that she had done this without his consent and, as he saw it, contrary to the principles and customs of their religion. It led ultimately to the marriage breaking down and the plaintiff suffering psychiatric illness. The New South Wales Court of Appeal held that the defendant should take the plaintiff in her family and cultural setting and that she could recover for this loss.

(ii) *Damage to property*

5–34   **Foreseeability of the damage.** The question whether the damage following an accident is of a foreseeable kind tends to provoke a good deal more debate in the case of damage to property. Remoteness issues arise most commonly in this context. *Re Polemis*, *The Wagon Mound (No.1)* and *The Wagon Mound (No.2)* are of course examples.

5–35   Foreseeability issues can arise in relation to real property where an activity on land which was thought to be harmless at the time it was carried on later turns out to pose unforeseeable risks of harm to neighbouring landowners. In *Cambridge Water Co Ltd v Eastern Counties Leather Plc*,[47] the defendant leather manufacturers used a solvent called PCE in degreasing pelts at their tannery. Over the years spillages occurred, with the result that the PCE seeped into the ground and contaminated the plaintiff's borehole some 1.3 miles away. The water in the borehole became unfit for human consumption, and the plaintiff incurred expense in being forced to obtain its water from another source. The plaintiff thereupon sued to recover damages in respect of this loss in actions for negligence and nuisance and under the rule in *Rylands v Fletcher*,[48] but the claim failed. Foreseeability of harm of the relevant type was a prerequisite for the recovery of damages under all three heads, and at the time PCE was being used

---

[45] *Donachie v The Chief Constable of the Greater Manchester Police* [2004] EWCA Civ 405.
[46] (1998) 45 N.S.W.L.R. 588, NSWCA; cf. *Pritchard v J H Cobden Ltd* [1988] Fam. 22 (road accident victim who had sustained brain damage and whose marriage broke down as a result not entitled to damages to compensate for the financial consequences of his divorce).
[47] [1994] 2 A.C. 264; and see *Hamilton v Papakura District Council* [2002] 3 N.Z.L.R. 308, PC; see Ch.2 para.2–31, above.
[48] (1866) L.R. 1 Ex 265; (1868) L.R. 3 HL 330; see generally Ch.13, below.

it was not foreseeable that it would accumulate in the subsoil and be released into the aquifer or that it would thereafter pollute the plaintiff's water supply.

Different kinds of damage. In *Cambridge Water*, no damage was foresee- **5–36** able. But sometimes the defendant's conduct may expose the claimant to risks of different kinds, and the question is whether one or more is foreseeable. In *Polemis*, damage by impact was treated as of one kind, damage by explosion as of another. In *The Wagon Mound (No.1)* damage by fouling was foreseeable, but this was not damage of the same kind as damage by fire, which on the evidence was not. In *The Wagon Mound (No.2)*, however, the damage by fire was held to be foreseeable and hence recoverable. In a case in Canada,[49] it was held that exposing property to the risk of theft did not cover loss of the property by arson. And in a New Zealand example,[50] loss of profits consequent upon damage done by a lorry driver to the power cable supplying the plaintiffs' factory was held to be foreseeable, but a fire caused by a power surge leading to arcing in the factory telephone system was not.

Extent of the damage. Where damage is of a foreseeable kind, it is **5–37** immaterial that no-one could foresee the precise mechanism by which it was caused.[51] In a striking example from Australia, a driver towing a trailer with a worn wheel bearing should have foreseen that a wheel might fall off, that the axle might strike sparks, that a fire might start and thus that the plaintiff's building 12 km away might be burned down.[52] Damage foreseeable in kind but unforeseeable in extent similarly is recoverable. So, a manufacturer of electric motors, which were used to power the pumps which circulated and oxygenated the water in the plaintiff's lobster tank, was liable for the loss of the lobsters when the motors failed, and the fact that, by reason of the full stocking of the tank, the lobsters died more quickly or in greater quantities than might otherwise have happened was of no relevance.[53] Again, defendants who were negligent in failing to warn their customers that a chemical marketed by them was highly explosive when brought into contact with water, were liable for the full extent of the damage when a glass ampoule containing the chemical broke while the label was being washed off and an explosion occurred. The explosion and the type of damage being foreseeable, it was irrelevant that the magnitude of the former and the extent of the latter were not.[54] Furthermore, if extra damage to property occurs due to its weakness or fragility, the full extent of the damage also is recoverable. So where water and soil from the defendant's property damaged the claimant's wall, it was no answer that the wall would only have suffered minor damage if it had been better constructed.[55]

Claimant's financial state. Back in 1933, in *Liesbosch Dredger v SS Edison* **5–38** *(The Liesbosch)*,[56] the House of Lords decided that the impecunious owners of a

---

[49] *Trevison v Springman* (1996) 16 B.C.L.R. (3d) 138.
[50] *Mainguard Packaging Ltd v Hilton Haulage Ltd* [1990] 1 N.Z.L.R. 360.
[51] *Arscott v The Coal Authority* [2004] EWCA Civ 892, at [58].
[52] *Haileybury College v Emanuelli* [1983] 1 V.R. 323.
[53] *Muirhead v Industrial Tank Specialities Ltd* [1986] 1 Q.B. 507, CA.
[54] *Vacwell Engineering Ltd v BDH Chemicals Ltd* [1971] 1 Q.B. 88.
[55] *McColl v Dionisatos* (2002) Aust Torts Reports 81–652.
[56] [1933] A.C. 449.

dredger lost through the defendant's negligence could recover damages in respect of the value of the dredger and certain consequential losses, but could not recover the additional cost of hiring a replacement dredger until judgment was obtained, the plaintiffs having been unable to afford to buy one until then. That loss was attributable solely to the plaintiffs' impecuniosity. Lord Wright said that if the plaintiffs' financial embarrassment was to be regarded as the consequence of the tort, it was too remote, but he preferred to regard it as an "independent cause" or "extrinsic", though its operative effect was conditioned by the loss of the dredger. In a number of cases thereafter the decision was viewed with doubt or disfavour,[57] and eventually, in *Lagden v O'Connor*,[58] the House of Lords decided not to follow it. Lord Hope stated that it was not necessary to find that *The Liesbosch* was wrongly decided, but the law had moved on and the correct test of remoteness was reasonable foreseeability. He continued:

> "The wrongdoer must take his victim as he finds him . . . This rule applies to the economic state of the victim in the same way as it applies to his physical and mental vulnerability. It requires the wrongdoer to bear the consequences if it was reasonably foreseeable that the injured party would have to borrow money or incur some other kind of expenditure to mitigate his damages."[59]

It was held, accordingly, that a motorist whose car had been damaged by the negligence of the defendant could recover damages in respect of the additional costs of hiring a car under a credit hire agreement, and the fact that that agreement had been necessitated by the claimant's lack of financial means was immaterial.

5–39   A practical application of the approach taken in *Lagden* is seen in the rules governing the date by reference to which a claimant's damages should be assessed. If a claimant cannot afford to rectify the effects of a defendant's breach of duty, and acts reasonably in waiting until he recovers damages at the trial, then the quantum of damages will be assessed as at that date and will include any increase in costs which have been occasioned by the delay.[60]

5–40   **Scope of the relevant duty.** While the full extent of a foreseeable loss normally is recoverable, this may not be so where the defendant is held to owe a duty of limited scope. In *Holbeck Hall Hotel Ltd v Scarborough BC*[61] the claimant was the owner of a hotel situated at the top of a cliff overlooking the North Sea. The defendant was the occupier of land between the hotel and the sea and had knowledge that if remedial action was not taken, a landslip might at some future time affect the claimant's land. A massive land slip occurred which led to the hotel being demolished. The Court of Appeal recognised that in most cases where physical injury to the person or property of the claimant is

---

[57] *Martindale v Duncan* [1973] 2 All E.R. 355, CA; *Dodd Properties (Kent) Ltd v Canterbury City Council* [1980] 1 W.L.R. 433, CA; *Perry v Sidney Phillips & Son* [1982] 1 W.L.R. 1297, CA.
[58] [2004] 1 A.C. 1067.
[59] *Lagden v O'Connor* [2004] 1 A.C. 1067 at 1088.
[60] *Alcoa Minerals of Jamaica Inc v Broderick* [2002] 1 A.C. 371, PC; Jones, "The impecunious claimant" (2000) 16 P.N. 165.
[61] [2000] Q.B. 836; and see Ch.8, para.8–171, below.

reasonably foreseeable, the defendant will be liable for all damage of the type that was foreseeable, whether the actual extent was foreseeable or not. But the instant claim was a case of non-feasance. The defendant had done nothing to create the danger, which had arisen by the operation of nature. So the scope of the defendant's duty was limited to avoiding the infliction of foreseeable damage to the claimant's land. The scope of the duty being limited, the defendant should not be held liable for damage which, albeit of the same type, was vastly more extensive than that which had been foreseeable.

(iii) *Economic loss*

Claims for economic loss do not raise remoteness issues. A defendant who **5–41** causes foreseeable physical injury or damage is liable also for economic loss which is consequential upon that damage.[62] The court must simply quantify the amount of the loss. Whether there is a duty to take care to prevent economic loss standing alone of course can be a controversial question.[63] If a duty is upheld, any further question of remoteness is unlikely to arise. It is difficult to contemplate how foreseeable financial loss might be seen to be of an unforeseeable kind.

2.—DAMAGES GENERALLY

One action only for one cause of action. In an action for negligence, the **5–42** general rule[64] is that damages must be assessed once and for all at the trial, whether that is on the same occasion liability to compensate is found proved, or at a subsequent disposal hearing.[65] The quantum of loss reflects that damage or injury which arose at the date the cause of action accrued.[66] Even if it is found, after proceedings have come to an end, that the damage suffered was much greater than was originally supposed, no further action can be brought.[67] Again, "it is a well-settled rule of law that damages resulting from one and the same cause of action must be assessed and recovered once and for all".[68] Two actions

---

[62] See Ch.2, paras 2–98 to 2–111, above.

[63] See Ch.2, paras 2–166 to 2–206, above.

[64] The power to order provisional damages, or to make an order for periodical payments of damages, are exceptions to the "once for all" rule: see below paras 5–145 and 5–131 to 5–134 respectively.

[65] The court has power to order split trials under CPR Pt 3, r.1.

[66] See, e.g. *Amerena v Barling* [1993] N.P.C. 90, CA, following *British Westinghouse Electric & Manufacturing Ltd v Underground Electric Railways Co of London* [1912] A.C. 673 (negligent sale of shares: £1.7 million claimed, only £2 recovered!).

[67] See *Conquer v Boot* [1928] 2 K.B. 336; unless time for appeal has not expired so that leave can be obtained to adduce further evidence at the hearing of the appeal. However, if a claimant who has suffered personal injury, can take advantage of the provisions which permit an award of provisional damages (for which see para.5–145, below), or damages by periodical payment (for which see paras 5–131 to 5–134), the effects of some later deterioration in his medical condition may be mitigated.

[68] *Brunsden v Humphrey* (1884) 14 Q.B.D. 141 at 147, per Browen L.J. See too *Maden v Clifford Coppock & Carter (A Firm)* [2005] 2 All E.R. 43, CA in a professional negligence context, where there were two distinct acts of negligence and the damages did not overlap separate proceedings were permissible. For consideration of issue estoppel and the doctrine of res judicata see Ch.4, above, paras 4–238 to 4–246.

will not lie by one claimant against the same defendant for personal injuries, sustained in the same accident.

5-43   Where a passenger in a motor car, travelling in France, was injured in a collision between the car and a lorry, which was caused, as the French court had held, by the negligence of both drivers (two-thirds to the lorry and one-third to the car), after recovering damages in France against the lorry driver, she was held entitled to damages from the car driver. The amount of damages was not that fixed by the French court but had to be assessed by the English court. Since the claimant was willing to give credit for the damages recovered from the lorry driver, no decision was given whether or not she was bound to do so.[69]

5-44   **General principles.** The common law principle on which damages for negligence are assessed, is that they are to be regarded as compensation for an injury sustained and not as punishment for a wrong inflicted. That being the principle, a claimant ought not to recover more than in fact has been lost. Generally speaking in English law, subject to the qualification that the damages must not be too remote,[70] the governing rule is that of restitution,[71] whether the wrongful act arises out of breach of contract or tort.[72] However, in many instances "restitution" cannot be given its literal meaning. Where negligence has caused personal injury, a reasonable sum will be awarded for the pain and suffering sustained,[73] but the restitutionary principle may not be achieved, save in respect of those aspects of the claim where there has been an actual pecuniary loss, capable of a precise calculation.[74] Accordingly, in negligence actions the measure of damages is that, insofar as money *can* compensate for loss and damage, which is not too remote, the injured party is to be returned to the same position as he would have been in had it not been for the defendant's negligence. The court must only award "fair" compensation "yet not full"[75] and must not attempt to achieve a result which is "perfect".[76] Since the fact of damage having

---

[69] *Kohnke v Karger* [1951] 2 K.B. 670.

[70] See paras 5-01 to 5-41 above.

[71] Often referred to in law reports as *restitutio in integrum*.

[72] *The Argentino* (1888) 13 P.D. 191 at 200, per Bowen L.J., with which Lindley L.J. concurred. The decision itself was affirmed, (1889) 14 App.Cas. 519.

[73] *Livingstone v Rawyards Coal Co* (1880) 5 App.Cas. 25 at 39, per Lord Blackburn; *Phillips v L. & S.W. Ry* (1879) 5 Q.B.D. 78 at 87, per James L.J.; *The Mediana* [1900] A.C. 113 at 119; *Admiralty Commrs v S.S. Susquehanna* [1926] A.C. 655 at 661. In *Rushton v N.C.B.* [1953] 1 Q.B. 495 at 502, per Romer L.J.: "The principle has been adopted (and it is the only possible principle which can be adopted) of trying to compensate a man in the plight in which this plaintiff finds himself by awarding what may fairly be described as notional or theoretical compensation to take the place of that which is not possible, namely, actual compensation."

[74] *Admiralty Commissioners v S.S. Valeria* [1922] 2 A.C. 242 at 248, per Lord Dunedin; *British Transport Commission v Gourley* [1956] A.C. 185 at 208, per Lord Goddard. See also *Broome v Cassell & Co Ltd* [1972] A.C. 1027 at 1071, per Lord Hailsham L.C. (a defamation case).

[75] For a slight injury, see *Parry v English Electric Co Ltd* [1971] 1 W.L.R. 664. For the interpretation of what is meant by compensation that is fair and yet not full, see *H. West & Son Ltd v Shephard* [1964] A.C. 326 at 356–357, per Lord Devlin.

[76] *Rowley v L.N.W. Ry* (1873) L.R. 8 Ex. 221; *Phillips v L.S.W. Ry* (1879) 4 Q.B.D. 406; (1879) 5 Q.B.D. 78; *Fletcher v Autocar and Transporters Ltd* [1968] 2 Q.B. 322.

been suffered is an essential to an action for negligence,[77] no such action can lie for nominal damages.[78]

Mitigation of damage.[79] A claimant cannot recover damages in respect of **5–45**
losses which could reasonably have been avoided.[80] This so-called duty to mitigate is not a duty in sense of an obligation imposed. The claimant is free to act as he chooses, but if he fails to act reasonably and as a consequence his loss is greater than it would otherwise have been, he cannot look to the defendant to compensate him for the loss which could have been avoided.[81] Expenses incurred in attempting reasonably to mitigate loss can be recovered.[82] This is so even if the attempt at mitigation is unsuccessful and as a result the damage to the claimant is increased.[83] If the attempt at mitigation is successful then the defendant receives the benefit of the mitigation in having to pay reduced damages so far as the avoided loss is concerned. If, as a result of impecuniosity, the claimant has to borrow money in order to mitigate his loss, the cost of borrowing the money is recoverable.[84] The onus of proving that the claimant has failed to act reasonably in mitigating his loss lies on the defendant.[85] Whether a claimant has failed to act reasonably to minimise his damage is a question of fact not law.[86]

ILLUSTRATIONS

A failure to mitigate has been found: where a claimant who sustained personal **5–46**
injuries refused to undergo medical treatment,[87] where a claimant, who had been told that his psychosomatic symptoms would cease after the litigation had ended,

---

[77] See Ch.1, above, paras 1–29 to 1–33.

[78] *Munday Ltd v L.C.C.* [1916] 2 K.B. 331 (in an action for negligence payment into court admitting negligence but denying damage is a denial of liability, as damage is the gist of the action); *Hambrook v Stokes Bros* [1925] 1 K.B. 141 at 156, per Atkin L.J.; *The Amerika* [1917] A.C. 38 at 60, per Lord Sumner.

[79] For a more detailed consideration of this topic, see *McGregor on Damages* (18th edn, 2009), Ch.7.

[80] *British Westinghouse Co v Underground Ry* [1912] A.C. 673. Although *British Westinghouse* was a contractual claim the principle applies equally to tortious claims, see *Admiralty Commissioners v S.S. Chekiang* [1926] A.C. 637.

[81] See, per Sir John Donaldson M.R. in *The Soholt* [1983] 1 Lloyd's Rep. 605 at 608, CA.

[82] See, e.g. *Davies v Oswell* (1837) 7 C.&P. 804 (the cost of hiring a substitute for damaged property); *S v Distillers Company (Biochemicals)* [1970] 1 W.L.R. 114 (medical treatment for personal injuries); and *Spalding v Gamage* (1918) 35 R.P.C. 101, CA (cost of advertising to reduce the effect of an infringement of a trade mark).

[83] *Lloyds and Scottish Finance v Modern Cars and Caravans (Kingston)* [1966] 1 Q.B. 764.

[84] *Lagden v O'Connor* [2004] 1 A.C. 1067 above, para.5–38.

[85] *Roper v Johnson* (1873) L.R. 8 C. & P. 167; *Garnac Grain v Faure & Fairclough* [1968] A.C. 1130. Observations that the burden is on the claimant to prove he acted reasonably, contained in *Selvanayagam v University of the West Indies*, n.96 below, cannot be relied upon: see *Geest v Lansiiquot* [2003] 1 All E.R. 383, PC.

[86] *Payzu v Saunders* [1919] 2 K.B. 581; *The Solholt* [1983] 1 Lloyd's Rep. 605, CA. Although mitigation is a question of fact, an appellate court will interfere with a trial judge's finding where he fails to evaluate the claimant's reasons for refusing to embark on a particular course for, e.g. refusing to undergo a medical procedure: *Edmonds v Lloyds TSB Bank Plc* [2004] EWCA Civ 1526. See further, Thomas "Damage Limitation" 149 S.J. 10.

[87] *McAuley v London Transport Executive* [1957] 2 Lloyd's Rep. 500, CA; *Marcroft v Scruttons* [1954] 1 Lloyd's Rep. 395, CA; cf. *Savage v Wallis* [1966] 1 Lloyd's Rep. 357, CA.

failed to prosecute his claim expeditiously[88]; and where a claimant organised for his damaged car to be repaired at a cost in excess of the car's market value.[89]

5–47   In a professional negligence context, a mortgage lender claiming against a professional valuer, failed reasonably to mitigate by failing to bring a possession action in respect of the property which was the subject of the mortgage.[90] In *Patel v Hooper & Jackson*,[91] the claimants bought a house on the strength of a surveyor's valuation. The valuation was carried out negligently and the house was uninhabitable unless it was restored at a cost that the claimants could not afford. The claimants claimed for the cost of temporary accommodation for seven years up to the date of trial, but recovered damages only for five years' accommodation because by the end of five years they should have sold the house. Where a mortgage lender failed to effect a sale of re-possessed property at an early stage when the market was more favourable there was a failure reasonably to mitigate.[92] In *Walker v Medlicott & Son*,[93] a claim was brought by a beneficiary under a will against a solicitor for negligence in the preparation of the will. The claimant failed to mitigate by not pursuing a claim for rectification of the will.

5–48   Instances of reasonable mitigation include: where a claimant did not immediately replant land with trees, the original trees having been destroyed by weed killer negligently supplied by the defendants[94]; where the claimant's car was destroyed and a comparable car was hired until a new one could be obtained[95]; where a claimant refused to undergo a dangerous and risky surgical procedure[96]; refusing to undergo surgery where the prospects of success were evenly balanced[97]; where a claimant became pregnant after a failed sterilisation operation but refused to undergo an abortion[98]; in a professional negligence context, where the claimant did not pursue litigation, which would have been complicated and difficult, against a third party[99]; where a claimant refused to bring proceedings to seek a second default judgment in circumstances where the first default judgment was unenforceable because of the defendant's negligence in failing to serve the original proceedings properly[100]; where a purchaser of defective property did not obtain planning permission to sell the property at a

---

[88] *James v Woodall Duckham Construction Company* [1969] 1 W.L.R. 903, CA.
[89] *Darbishire v Warran* [1963] 1 W.L.R. 1067, CA.
[90] *Western Trust & Savings Ltd v Travers & Co* [1997] P.N.L.R. 295, CA.
[91] [1999] All E.R. 992, CA.
[92] *Bristol and West Building Society v Fancy & Jackson* [1997] 4 All E.R. 582.
[93] [1999] 1 W.L.R. 727, CA.
[94] *Dallinghoo Parochial Church Council v Fisons Ltd, The Times*, June 1, 1982.
[95] *Mattocks v Mann* [1983] R.T.R. 13, CA; see also *H.L. Motorworks v Alwabi* [1977] R.T.R. 276, CA; cf. *Watson Norrie v Shaw* (1967) 111 S.J. 117, CA. Damages in respect of hire costs are considered below at paras 5–63 to 5–70.
[96] *Selvnayagam v University of the West Indies* [1983] 1 W.L.R. 585, PC.
[97] *Savage v Wallis* [1966] 1 Lloyd's Rep. 357, CA.
[98] *Emeh v Kensington Area Health Authority* [1985] Q.B. 1012, CA. See generally Ch.2, para.2–104, above and *McFarlane v Tayside Health Board* [2000] 2 A.C. 59; also *Parkinson v St James and Seacroft University Hospital NHS Trust* [2001] EWCA Civ 530.
[99] *Pilkington v Wood* [1953] Ch. 770.
[100] *Olafsson v Foreign and Commonwealth Office* [2009] EWHC 2608 (Q.B.).

profit[101]; where a motor mechanic sustained serious knee injuries so that he could no longer work as a mechanic but instead trained as a less well paid taxi driver.[102]

In *Copley v Lawn*,[103] innocent motorists whose vehicles had been damaged in **5–49** road traffic accidents were offered replacement cars for use during the period of repair of the damaged cars by the negligent defendants' motor insurers. These vehicles were offered to the innocent motorists free of charge but the cost to defendants' motor insurers of supplying these vehicles was not communicated to the innocent motorists. It was held that the innocent motorists had not acted unreasonably in refusing to accept the offer of a free car from the defendants' motor insurers. Longmore L.J. explained:

"A claimant who has been deprived of the use of his car by the negligence of a tortfeasor only has to take reasonable steps to mitigate his claim for that loss of use and he cannot, in my judgment, be said to act unreasonably if he makes (or continues) his own arrangements with his own hire company, unless he is made aware that this commercial enterprise can be undertaken more cheaply by the defendant than by his own arrangements."

In *Morris v Richards*,[104] the claimant was compelled by injuries sustained in **5–50** a road traffic accident to give up her employment. She found another job from which, believing herself to have been discriminated against, she resigned after seven months. The defendant was liable to her in damages for lost earnings even after the time when she resigned. He was to blame for the injuries she had received and by reason of his negligence she had lost her original employment. The fact that she obtained another job and then lost it did not automatically disqualify her from recovering a further period of lost earnings. The crucial question was whether, in respect of that period, it was just that she should recover damages from the defendant. If she had been at fault in losing her new job then she would have faced difficulty, but bearing in mind that it been the defendant's wrongful act which had put her in the position of having to find a new job, she should not be judged too harshly and the monies were recoverable.

In *Limbu v the Ministry of Defence*,[105] an argument that an injured, former **5–51** Ghurkha soldier was acting unreasonably in returning to Nepal to work rather than remaining in the United Kingdom in order to find work at more remunerative rates was firmly rejected. In order for the claimant to have remained in the United Kingdom he would have had to move his family from Nepal and there was no evidence that but for the accident he would have contemplated such a measure.

Reflective loss. Where a claimant seeks to recover loss which is essentially **5–52** another's, the loss has been termed reflective loss. It has been considered

---

[101] *Hussey v Eels* [1990] 2 Q.B. 227, which was followed in *Gardner v Marsh & Parsons* [1997] 1 W.L.R. 489, CA.
[102] *Conner v Bradman & Co Ltd* [2007] EWHC 2789 (Q.B.).
[103] [2009] P.I.Q.R. P21.
[104] [2004] P.I.Q.R. Q30 CA.
[105] (2008) *Lawtel*, unreported elsewhere.

particularly in cases where shareholders have sought to recover loss which is reflective of damage actually sustained by the company whose shares are held. That was the situation in *Johnson v Gore Wood & Co.*[106] The claimant held a controlling interest in a property company whose solicitors were negligent in their service of an option to buy land. The company thereby suffered a considerable loss. The company's claim was settled and the claimant then sought, as an individual shareholder, to recover certain losses, which included the company's inability to contribute to his pension fund, and the diminished value of his shares. These claims were struck out, as reflecting loss which was essentially the company's and which must be deemed to have been included when the company reached its settlement, although other financial claims were allowed to continue.

5–53 **Reimbursement of a third party's losses.**[107] The basic principle is that the claimant can only recover damages in respect of his own losses. There are, however, cases where a service has been provided, or a payment made to the claimant by a third party. The question of gratuitously provided care is dealt with later.[108] Payments made by employers are also dealt with below.[109] At one time there was considerable support for the view that any person could sue, if he had necessarily incurred expense in consequence of the defendant's negligence. Hence, a parent could sue for expense, which he had incurred through injuries, caused to his child by the defendant's negligence.[110] The Receiver for the Metropolitan Police District, who had paid, under statutory powers, the pay and allowances of a member of the Metropolitan Police Force, who had been injured by the defendant's negligence, could recover from the defendant the sums he had so paid,[111] and the Crown could sue for wages paid to an airman who had been injured by the defendant's negligence.[112] However, in *Receiver for the Metropolitan Police District v Croydon Corporation*,[113] a police officer was injured, while on duty, by the defendant's negligence, as a result of which he was incapacitated for several months. During that period the police authority had had to pay the officer's full wages and allowances. In due course, the officer successfully sued for damages but made no claim for any loss of wages. Basing the claim on unjust benefit, the police authority then sued the defendants for the wages and allowances it had paid but the claim failed, since the police authority had not

---

[106] [2002] 2 A.C. 1, Ch.4, para.4–240, above. See also *Barings Plc v Coopers & Lybrand* [2002] P.N.L.R. 321; also Dugdale, "Audit liability and the protection of the public interest" (2003) 2 P.N. 350.

[107] See Samuels "Damages for Personal Injuries: Third Parties' Losses or Expenses" in 129 S.J. 645.

[108] See paras 5–103 to 5–107.

[109] See para.5–108, below.

[110] See *Barnes v Pooley* (1935) 51 T.L.R. 391 (stepchild) although this was decided on an admission of liability, there being no contention to the contrary. In *Cook v Wright* [1967] N.Z.L.R. 1034, where parents claimed for the expense of visiting their 15-year-old son in hospital, following an accident to him, it was held that the remedy is separate and distinct from that of the infant in respect of the original negligence and that the judgment on the infant's claim was not binding on either party, if the parents should later make a claim.

[111] *Receiver for Metropolitan Police v Tatum* [1948] 2 K.B. 68.

[112] *Attorney-General v Valle-Jones* [1935] 2 K.B. 209.

[113] [1957] 2 Q.B. 154; *Attorney-General for New South Wales v Perpetual Trustee Co Ltd* [1955] A.C. 457.

been called upon to pay anything which they would not otherwise have had to pay. The defendants had paid to the constable by way of damages all that they were in law liable to pay, which did not include loss of wages, because none had been incurred. Following this decision, the earlier view must be considered to be erroneous and those cases in support of it wrongly decided.

Knock-for-knock agreement. Payment by the claimant's insurance company **5–54** of the cost of repairs to the claimant's motor-car, under the terms of a "knock-for-knock" agreement with the defendant's insurance company, does not prevent the claimant, even if requested not to do so by his insurance company, from suing the defendant in negligence for damages, including the cost of such repairs.[114] That proportion of the damages recovered, as were attributable to the cost of the repairs, would be held by the claimant as trustee for his insurance company.

Nevertheless, where there is a "knock-for-knock" agreement in existence, it is a misuse of the process of the court for a claimant to recover from a defendant on an inflated claim for damages, part of which must in any event be repaid to him, merely as a peg to obtain an order for costs.[115]

Recovery of costs on behalf of medical providers. A registered medical **5–55** practitioner who gives emergency treatment to a person injured by a motor vehicle on a road can recover the fees which are laid down in the Road Traffic Act 1988 ss.157–159 from the person using the vehicle at the time. The injured person can then recover in respect of this liability from the person whose wrongful act had caused the injury.[116] In respect of accidents on or after January 29, 2007[117] the Health and Social Care (Community Health and Standards) Act 2003 introduced a scheme whereby the cost of treatment provided by an NHS hospital and/or the cost of the provision of an NHS ambulance is payable by the compensator. The scheme is administered by the Compensation Recovery Unit[118] (CRU), which is part of the Department for Work and Pensions (DWP). The scheme applies to all accidents including: road traffic accidents, accidents sustained in the course of employment, accidents sustained by members of the public and accidents arising out of the use of defective products but the scheme does not apply to disease cases.[119] The medical costs recoverable are calculated by reference to a tariff and are subject to a cap. The CRU will issue the compensator with a certificate setting out the recoverable costs. There is provision for review[120] of the certificates and for appeals.[121] The costs are

---

[114] *Morley v Moore* [1936] 2 K.B. 359.
[115] *Hobbs v Marlowe* [1978] A.C. 16.
[116] Road Traffic Act 1988 s.158.
[117] In respect of road traffic accidents before 29.1.2007 the Road Traffic (NHS Charges) Act 1999 applies whereby provision is made to recover the cost of NHS treatment from the defendant motorist.
[118] The address of the CRU is Durham House, Washington, Tyne and Wear, NE38 7SF and the website is at http://www.dwp.gov.uk/other-specialists/compensation-recovery-unit/
[119] The Health and Social Care (Community Health and Standards) Act 2003 s.150. Certain payments are exempt and these are listed in Sch.10 of the Act.
[120] s.156.
[121] s.157.

payable by the compensator to the DWP within 14 days of the making of a compensation payment if a valid certificate is held by the compensator.

5–56 In *Firth v Geo. Ackroyd Junior Ltd*,[122] the claimant was seriously injured by the fault of his employer. The claimant needed considerable care and was living in a residential home funded by his local authority. The local authority was joined to the action as a defendant and sought a declaration that it was entitled to charge the claimant for the care and thereby recover the cost of the care from the claimant's damages. The High Court held that any assessment of the claimant's capital to determine his liability to reimburse the local authority could not include any sum awarded for damages for personal injuries.

5–57 **Interim payments.**[123] The court has the power to make an order for payment on account by a defendant of any damages, debt or other sum (except costs) which the court may hold the defendant liable to pay.[124] Rules of court specify the procedure for making applications for interim payments.[125] In actions founded on negligence the court can only make an order for an interim payment if: the defendant has admitted liability[126]; or the claimant has obtained judgment with damages to be assessed[127]; or where it is satisfied that if the matter went to trial the claimant would obtain judgment for a substantial amount of money.[128] The court must not order an interim payment of more than a reasonable proportion of the likely amount of the final judgment.[129] Contributory negligence and any relevant set-off or counterclaim must be taken into account.[130]

3.—Heads of Damages and their Assessment

(A) General and special damages

5–58 **General damages.** Damages are divided into general and special damages. General damages are those which the law presumes to flow from the negligence alleged by the claimant. Although these damages must be averred to have been suffered[131] and, subsequently, need to be proved, it is not necessary to plead them in any detail in the statement of case. In claims for damages for personal injuries the particulars of claim must include brief details of the claimant's injuries[132] and the claimant must attach to the particulars of claim a report from a medical

---

[122] [2001] P.I.Q.R. Q27.
[123] For interim payments in claims for damages for personal injuries, see para.5–146, below.
[124] The statutory basis for the court's power to award interim payments is found in the Supreme Court Act 1981 s.32 and the County Courts Act 1984 s.50, respectively.
[125] CPR Pt 25.
[126] CPR Pt 25.7(1)(a).
[127] CPR Pt 25.7(1)(b).
[128] CPR Pt 25.7(1)(c).
[129] CPR Pt 25.7(4).
[130] CPR Pt 25.7(5).
[131] *Admiralty Commissioners v S.S. Susquehanna* [1926] A.C. 655 at 661, per Viscount Dunedin.
[132] CPR PD 16, r.4.1(2).

practitioner about the injuries.[133] It has been held that damages for loss of enjoyment of a holiday that has been spoiled, form part of the claim of general damages in a negligence action.[134]

Special damages. Special damage, in this context, means some specific item   **5–59**
of loss, which the claimant alleges to be the result of the defendant's negligence in the case, although it is not presumed by law to have flowed from it, as a matter of course.

> "If a plaintiff has suffered damage of a kind which is not the necessary and immediate consequence of the wrongful act, he must warn the defendant in the pleadings that the compensation claimed will extend to this damage, thus showing the defendant the case he has to meet and assisting him in computing a payment into court."[135]

Accordingly, the claimant must plead any item of damage, which represents out-of-pocket expenses incurred or earnings lost before the trial, since, probably, they are capable of an exact calculation. "Such damage is commonly referred to as special damage or special damages but is no more than an example of damage which is 'special' in the sense that fairness to the defendant requires that it be pleaded."[136]

Full particulars of all special damage must be given and, if not given, will be   **5–60**
ordered.[137] This obligation to give particulars arises not because the nature of the loss is necessarily unusual but because the claimant, who has been able to base his claim upon a precise calculation, ought to give the defendant access to those facts which have made that calculation possible. Clearly, by way of further example, an allegation of loss of profits is a claim of special damage and must be specifically pleaded, it being wholly insufficient in this connection merely to claim "damages".[138]

Additionally, there must be pleaded any particular circumstances, which   **5–61**
probably will lead the injured claimant to suffer financial losses in the future that may not in the ordinary way reasonably be expected to flow from the accident.

---

[133] CPR PD 16, r.4.3.
[134] *Ichard v Frangoulis* [1977] 1 W.L.R. 556, applying the comparable cases in contract, namely *Jarvis v Swan Tours Ltd* [1973] Q.B. 233 and *Jackson v Horizon Holidays Ltd* [1975] 1 W.L.R. 1468. See however, *Woodar Investments Developments Ltd v Wimpey Construction UK Ltd* [1980] 1 W.L.R. 277, in which the Law Lords disapproved Lord Denning's reasoning in *Jackson*, wherein he had purported to apply the dictum of Lush L.J. in *Lloyd's v Harper* (1880) 16 Ch.D. 290 at 321. See, further, Tettenborn, "Frustrated Holidaymakers and Frustrated Contracts" in 129 New L.J. 62; Picarda, "Professional Negligence: Damages for 'Aggro' " in 132 New L.J. 1175; Jacobs, "Damages for Distress" in 128 S.J. 75.
[135] *Perestrello e Companhia Ltda v United Paint Co Ltd* [1969] 1 W.L.R. 570 at 579. In a claim for damages for personal injuries the claimant must attach to the particulars of claim a schedule of details of any past and future expenses and losses pursuant to CPR PD 16, r.4.2. Accordingly the claimant must give details of estimated future losses, which strictly are a species of general damages, so, to that extent the rule that general damages need not be pleaded has been eroded by the Civil Procedure Rules 1998.
[136] *Perestrello e Companhia Ltda v United Paint Co Ltd* [1969] 1 W.L.R. 570 at 579, per Lord Donovan, who read the judgment of the Court of Appeal.
[137] *Watson v North Metropolitan Tramways Co* (1886) 3 T.L.R. 273.
[138] *Perestrello e Companhia Ltda v United Paint Co Ltd* [1969] 1 W.L.R. 570 at 579.

An example might be the lost chance of putting into effect an intention of setting up in some new business. The pleading would be necessary as introducing into the case an entirely new element, which would not otherwise be described in the statement of case.[139]

In any event, the size of all awards of damages must be determined by the value of money at the date of trial and not by its depreciation, during the interval of time before hearing the appeal.[140] Similarly, no account should be taken of the possibility of future inflation[141] or, even, the likelihood of continuing inflation, after the date of trial.[142]

The measure of damages in professional negligence claims is dealt with below.[143]

(B) Damage to chattels, land and buildings

(i) *Damage to chattels*

5–62   **Generally.** In the case of damage to chattels, the general rule is that the measure of damages is the difference between the value of the chattel, before the damage, and its value, as damaged. In the case of a partial loss, this will usually be the cost of repairing the chattel,[144] together with any depreciation in value,[145] that is the difference between the value of the chattel, when repaired, and the value before the damage, less any increase in value owing to the substitution of new for old material. It is irrelevant that the repairs have not in fact been carried out, before the trial of the action,[146] or that they can never be done, because, for example, the damaged goods have subsequently been lost.[147] In addition, consequential loss may be recovered, namely the cost of hiring another chattel, during the time taken to repair the damaged chattel[148]; loss of profits, during the time taken by the repairs; loss of a "no claim bonus" on a car insurance policy, together with the cost of paying the excess; and, in appropriate cases,[149] damages for loss of the use of the chattel prior to its replacement.[150]

---

[139] *Domsalla v Barr* [1969] 1 W.L.R. 630.
[140] *Taylor v Bristol Omnibus Co Ltd* [1975] 1 W.L.R. 1054.
[141] *Cookson v Knowles* [1979] A.C. 556.
[142] *Auty v N.C.B.* [1985] 1 W.L.R. 784, CA, applying *Cookson v Knowles* [1979] A.C. 556.
[143] See Ch.9, below in relation to particular areas of professional expertise.
[144] Such may consist of the cost of materials, necessary to repair the chattel and the cost of labour to carry out the repairs but not overheads, which were a constant factor of the claimants, because the work was done in their own repair shop, and remained unaffected by the need to repair the chattel: *Ulsterbus v Donnelly* [1982] 13 N.I.J.B.
[145] *Payton v Brooks* [1974] R.T.R. 169 (any loss of value proved, as a result of the chattel's being repaired, may be recovered).
[146] *The Kingsway* [1918] P. 344.
[147] *The York* [1929] P. 178 at 184–185, per Scrutton L.J.
[148] The *Greta Holme* [1897] A.C. 596; *Hughes v Quentin* (1838) 8 C. & P. 703 (damage to horse)—so far as this case decides that the plaintiff was not entitled to the cost of hiring another horse while his own was recovering from its injuries, it must be taken to be erroneous—see *Davis v Oswell* (1837) 7 C. & P. 804; *The Mediana* [1900] A.C. 113.
[149] *Ironfield v Eastern Gas Board* [1964] 1 W.L.R. 1125n.
[150] *Moore v D.E.R. Ltd* [1971] 1 W.L.R. 1476.

Hire of replacement chattel. Where an owner has had to hire a substitute 5–63
chattel for the damaged one, during the period taken for its repairs to be approved
and then completed, the cost of such a hiring will normally represent the damages
for loss of use.[151] On the other hand, the hiring must be reasonable in all the
circumstances.[152] The need for a hired chattel is not self-proving and the claimant
must demonstrate this need so if the owner of a damaged motor vehicle was due
to be overseas during the period over which repairs were scheduled and would
have no need for a replacement vehicle then there would be no loss. Where the
need for a replacement is demonstrated then the reasonable cost of hiring a
similar chattel is recoverable. In *Daily Office Cleaning Contractors v Shefford*,[153]
where a company's luxury American motor car was severely damaged in an
accident, it was held that the company had acted reasonably in hiring a substitute
prestige motor car at £75 per week over the period of 25 weeks, which was taken
to carry out the repairs, owing to the difficulties in obtaining spare parts in
England. Similarly, in *H.L. Motorworks v Alwahbi*,[154] the owner of a damaged
Rolls Royce motor car was under no duty to mitigate his loss by hiring a cheaper
even if adequate substitute vehicle, whilst the repairs were being carried out. If
the period of repair of the damaged chattel is very brief it may not be reasonable
to hire a replacement of equivalent prestige unless the need for such a specific
vehicle is plain.[155] Where, however the claimant hires a more modest car than
that which was damaged his loss is limited to the actual cost of hiring the modest
replacement rather than the notional cost of hiring a vehicle equivalent to that
which was damaged.[156]

The fact of the hiring must be pleaded in the statement of case and proved as 5–64
special damage, if it is intended to seek damages in that regard.[157] Where the cost
of hiring a replacement chattel is met by the claimant's own insurer the defendant
cannot take advantage of the claimant's insurance policy and the reasonable cost
of hire is recoverable against the defendant under the principle set out in
Bradburn v Great Western Railway.[158] The cost of transporting the chattel to the
repairers may also be recovered. However, where a motor car was damaged by
separate tortfeasors by successive torts, although each tort, if occurring alone,
would have rendered necessary the same work of repair, that is a paint respray,
it was held that the claimants were not entitled to recover the cost from the

---

[151] *Lord Citrine (Owners) v Hebridean Coast (Owners)* [1961] A.C. 545 at 560, per Devlin L.J.;
Moore v D.E.R. Ltd [1971] 1 W.L.R. 1476; *Martindale v Duncan* [1973] 1 W.L.R. 574; *Beechwood
Birmingham Ltd v Hoyer Group Ltd* [2010] EWCA Civ 647.
[152] *Dimond v Lovell* [2002] 1 A.C. 384; *Moore v D.E.R. Ltd*, above; *Martindale v Duncan*, above.
[153] [1977] R.T.R. 361.
[154] [1977] R.T.R. 276; see too *Brain v Yorkshire Rider Ltd* [2007] Lloyd's Rep. I.R. 564.
[155] See *Watson Norie v Shaw* [1967] 1 Lloyd's Rep. 515, CA.
[156] *Clark v Ardington* [2002] EWCA Civ 510 (this involved a several conjoined appeals one of which
was *Lagden v O'Connor* which was considered by the House of Lords on the issue of impecuniosity,
see para.5–38, above).
[157] *S.S. Strathfillan v S.S. Ikala* [1929] A.C. 196; *The Hebridean Coast* [1961] A.C. 545.
[158] (1874–1875) L.R. 10 Ex. 1 Ex Ct; so where an innocent motorist was supplied with a replacement
hire car under an arrangement made by his motor insurers the defendant, who had negligently
damaged the claimant's car was liable to pay the cost of the hire charges, including commission
which the insurers had received from the hire company, as damages: *Bee v Jensen* [2007] EWCA Civ
923.

subsequent tortfeasor, because this item of damage did not flow from his wrongful act.[159]

5–65   In *Macrae v Swindells*,[160] the claimant's Standard motor car was damaged, as a result of the defendant's negligence, whereupon the latter lent the claimant a Morris car, while the necessary repairs were being carried out. The Morris car was then itself damaged in a collision, caused by the negligence of the claimant, who hired a third car, until the repairs to the Standard were completed. He was entitled to recover from the defendant the cost of hire, because he was compelled to hire the car in consequence of the defendant's negligence and not as a result of his own negligence, in the course of driving the Morris. Indeed, he had mitigated his loss by using the Morris car, as long as it was available, and the reason for its ceasing to be available was irrelevant.

5–66   **Credit car hire.** In recent years a number of companies have conducted business offering replacement hire cars to innocent motorists whose vehicles have been damaged in road traffic collisions. These credit hire companies often charge an enhanced rate for the car hire over and above the open market or "spot" rate because the credit hire involves a number of additional services such as the supply of a vehicle on credit and assistance in conducting litigation.[161] In *Dimond v Lovell*,[162] an innocent motorist was supplied with a vehicle subject to a credit hire agreement, which had not been properly executed and thus was unenforceable as it did not comply with the provisions of the Consumer Credit Act 1974. She had incurred no liability to the credit hire company and accordingly the hire charges could not be recovered as damages against the negligent motorist who had damaged the claimant's car. The House of Lords nevertheless considered what the position would have been if the agreement had been enforceable: would the claimant have been entitled to recover the enhanced credit hire rates as damages or would she have been restricted to the spot rate? By a majority their Lordships indicated that the claimant would have been restricted to the spot rate because the credit hire rate included additional benefits which should be taken into account.[163] The situation is different, however, where the claimant is impecunious and without the benefit of a credit hire agreement he would not be in a position to obtain any hire car. Applying the principle that the defendant must take his victim as he finds him, it was held in *Lagden v O'Connor*[164] that the impecunious claimant is entitled to recover the credit hire costs and need not account for the additional benefits bestowed by the credit hire agreement, on the grounds that if the claimant wished to obtain a credit hire

---

[159] *Performance Cars Ltd v Abraham* [1962] 1 Q.B. 33.

[160] [1954] 1 W.L.R. 597.

[161] Such agreements are not champertous: *Giles v Thompson* [1994] 1 A.C. 142.

[162] [2002] 1. A.C. 384.

[163] Per Lord Hoffman at 401.

[164] [2004] 1 A.C. 1067 (observations were made to the effect that the rule in *Liesbosch Dredger (Owners of) v SS Edison (The Liesbosch)* [1933] A.C. 449, did not reflect the modern approach to questions of remoteness, the basic rule being whether the loss in question was foreseeable). See Heppinstall, "Sinking *The Liesbosch*" 148 S.J. 39; Tompkinson, "Thin skulls and thin wallets" 154 N.L.J. 424.

vehicle he had no alternative but to accept an agreement including additional benefits.

The burden of proving that the innocent motor vehicle owner has failed to 5–67 mitigate his loss by hiring a vehicle at a higher than market rate lies upon the tortfeasor.[165] Where innocent motorists whose vehicles had been damaged were offered replacement vehicles for the period during which their vehicles were being repaired, such offers having been made by the tortfeasors' insurers, they did not act unreasonably in failing to accept the offers and instead obtaining vehicles under credit hire agreements.[166] The tortfeasors' insurers had not informed the innocent motorists of the cost of supplying the vehicles and so the motorists had not been put in a position whereby they could judge if the credit hire cars could have been obtained more cheaply from the defendants' insurers.

Loss of profits during hire. Where a chattel is hired to replace a damaged 5–68 chattel during the period of repairs, there will, as a rule, be no basis for claiming loss of profits. However, if a profit-earning chattel is damaged and not replaced, the profits lost during the time of the repairs can be recovered.[167] Where the innocent owners of a vessel damaged in a collision caused by the defendant's negligence could show that but for the collision the vessel would have been profitably engaged on a pre-arranged fixture, the court was correct to make an assessment as to what profit would probably have been made and to award the same as damages; there was no place for a discount to reflect the chance that the vessel would not have been so engaged.[168] In circumstances where the hiring of a substitute has enabled the owner of the damaged chattel to succeed in making a larger profit than otherwise, the additional profit must be brought into account and set off against the amount of the owner's loss.[169] If there is no loss, because the chattel is already incapable of earning profit, as a result of some other independent cause, no damages for loss of use can be recovered.[170] Otherwise, the mere fact of the chattel's being non-profit making does not disentitle the owner to damages for loss of use.[171]

> "It is a sufficiently familiar head of damages between individuals that, if one person injures the property of another, damages may be recovered, not only for the amount

---

[165] For the principles applying to mitigation of damage generally see paras 5–45 to 5–51, above.

[166] *Copley v Lawn* [2009] P.I.Q.R. P21.

[167] *The Argentino* (1889) 14 App.Cas. 519; *Re Trent* (1868) L.R. 4 Ch. 112 at 117; cf. *The Soya* [1955] 1 W.L.R. 1246. In *Dixons (Scholars Green) v J. L. Cooper* (1970) 114 S.J. 319, the Court of Appeal held that where a valuable profit-earning articulated lorry, which had been in constant demand, had been put out of use for 11 weeks, because of the defendant's negligence, the court had a duty to award substantial damages and not merely £2 nominal damages, hence an award of £450.

[168] *Owners of the "Front Ace" v Owners of the "Vicky I"* [2008] EWCA Civ 101.

[169] *The World Beauty* [1969] P. 12 (reversed in part, on other grounds [1970] P. 144).

[170] *Carslogie S.S. Co v Royal Norwegian Government* [1952] A.C. 292.

[171] *The Greta Holme* [1897] A.C. 596; *The Mediana* [1900] A.C. 113; *The Marpessa* [1907] A.C. 241; *Admiralty Commissioners v S.S. Chekiang* [1926] A.C. 637; *Admiralty Commissioners v S.S. Susquehanna* [1926] A.C. 655; *Lord Citrine (Owners) v Hebridean Coast (Owners)* [1961] A.C. 545.

which it may be necessary to spend in repairs, but also for the loss of the use of the article injured during the period that the repairing may occupy."[172]

5–69 **Loss of use.** Even if there has been no loss of profits and no expense in replacing the chattel temporarily, damages may be recovered for loss of use.

"I take it to be clear law that in general a person who has been deprived of the use of a chattel through the wrongful act of another is entitled to recover damages in respect thereof, even though he cannot prove what has been called 'tangible pecuniary loss,' by which I understand is meant that he is a definite sum of money out of pocket owing to the wrong he has sustained."[173]

Damages for loss of use will normally be the total sum, which is made up of the depreciation of the chattel, the interest on the capital value, the cost of maintenance and the expenditure on wages "thrown away."[174]

5–70 In *Lord Citrine (Owners) v Hebridean Coast (Owners)*,[175] a collision occurred between a collier and another ship causing damage to the former, but the claimants had failed to show that they had chartered tonnage to replace the ship. Lord Reid said:

"With a non-profit-earning ship there is no direct financial loss and one must ask what harm was done to the owner by his being deprived of the use of his ship. Then comes what may be a very difficult task, to put a value in money on the harm which the owner has suffered. But you must first prove the harm. If no harm be proved beyond the mere fact that the owner is deprived of the services of his ship during the period of repairs, the opinion of Lord Herschell in *Steam Sand Pump Dredger No. 7 (Owners) v Greta Holme (Owners)*[176] appears to have given rise to the practice of awarding damages based on interest on the value of the ship."[177]

5–71 **Complete destruction of a chattel.** Where a chattel is completely destroyed or so damaged that it is not worth repairing, the measure of damages is the market value,[178] or the cost of replacement, together with any consequential loss arising out of the destruction.[179] Even if the replacement cost exceeds the market value of the chattel it can still be reasonable to claim the replacement cost as

---

[172] *The Greta Holme* [1897] A.C. 596 at 601, per Lord Halsbury; see also *The Argentino* (1889) 14 App.Cas. 519. See Naughton, "Damages for Loss of Use of Chattels and Inconvenience" in 121 S.J. 700.

[173] *The Greta Holme* [1897] A.C. 596 at 604, per Lord Herschell; see also *Admiralty Commissioners v S.S. Chekiang* [1926] A.C. 637.

[174] *Sunley & Co Ltd v Cunard White Star Ltd* [1940] 1 K.B. 740.

[175] [1961] A.C. 545.

[176] [1897] A.C. 596.

[177] *Sand Pump Dredger No.7 (Owners) v Greta Holme (Owners)* [1897] A.C. 596 at 577–578.

[178] Even where it cannot be shown that there was a market for negligently damaged goods intended for sale, it is necessary to establish their value if sound and the reduction in value caused by the negligence. *Derby Resources AG v Blue Corinth Marine Co Ltd (The Athenian Harmony)* [1998] 2 Lloyd's Rep. 410.

[179] e.g. *Moore v D.E.R. Ltd* [1971] 1 W.L.R. 1476. There may be circumstances where it would be reasonable for a plaintiff to replace a car, which has been so badly damaged as to be "written off," because of the defendant's negligence, with a new one, as opposed to a second-hand vehicle, comparable to the damaged one.

damages if the chattel has a particular quality, rarity or special character that warrants replacement and the owner intends to replace or reinstate the property. So where a rare collection of archive material was damaged by flooding, the proper measure of loss was the cost of reinstatement of the archive rather than the market value.[180] What is the market value is a matter of evidence.[181] If the chattel is profit earning, its value will take into account the profits which it was likely to earn in the future, and, thus, no additional damages can be recovered for loss of future profits, except such profits as were being earned when the chattel was destroyed.[182] Even if the chattel is non-profit earning, damages for loss of use are still recoverable.[183] It was once thought that where, as a result of impecuniosity, the injured party was unable to replace the damaged chattel, it was not possible to recover extra damage thereby arising, but that is no longer the case. The test of remoteness is what was reasonably foreseeable and the wrongdoer will "bear the consequences if it was reasonably foreseeable that the injured party would have to borrow money or incur some other kind of expenditure to mitigate his damages."[184]

When a motor car was so damaged as to be a constructive total loss, it was held **5–72** that the measure of damages was the market value of the car at the date of the loss and the cost of hiring a substitute, until such time as a substitute car could be procured and made fit for use, less the scrap value of the damaged car.[185]

Where a chattel has no market value for whatever reason, the courts tend to **5–73** award, as damages, the cost of its replacement.[186] Where a motor car owner had his damaged vehicle repaired at a cost exceeding its market value, instead of trying to purchase a comparable motor car at the market price, he could not recover the cost of such repairs. He had failed to mitigate his loss.[187] However, where the motor car involved was unique in character, for example a mechanised replica of the Lord Mayor's coach, and quite irreplaceable, the owner was held

---

[180] *Aerospace Publishing Ltd v Thames Water Utilities Ltd* [2007] EWCA Civ 3.
[181] *Southampton Container Terminals Ltd v Schiffahrts-Gesellschaft Hansa Australia MBH & Co, The Maersk Colombo* [2001] 2 Lloyd's Rep. 275. See also *Ali Reza-Delta Transport Company Ltd v United Arab Shipping Company* [2003] EWCA Civ 811 (where cargo handling equipment was destroyed in Saudi Arabia the market value was assessed by reference to the cost of buying second hand replacements in Europe, transporting them to Saudi Arabia and customising them for use there as the lowest cost option even though there was no evidence that the claimants actually intended to replace the equipment).
[182] *The Llanover* [1947] P. 80. See Jolowicz, "Negligence—Loss of profits—Economic loss" in [1973] C.L.J. 20.
[183] *Millar v Candy* (1981) 58 F.L.R. 145 (following *Berrill v Road Haulage Executive* [1952] 2 Lloyd's Rep. 490). For "loss of use" claims, when the damaged chattel is capable of being repaired and is undergoing such necessary repairs, see para.5–63, above.
[184] *Lagden v O'Connor* [2004] 1 A.C. 1067, disapproving *Liesbosch Dredger (Owners of) v SS Edison* [1933] A.C. 449 (see above, para.5–38).
[185] *Pomphrey v James A. Cuthbertson Ltd* 1951 S.C. 147.
[186] *Clyde Navigation Trustees v Bowring* (1929) 34 Ll.L.R. 319 but cf. *Ucktos v Mazzetta* [1956] 1 Lloyd's Rep. 209.
[187] *Darbishire v Warran* [1963] 1 W.L.R. 1067, distinguishing *O'Grady v Westminster Scaffolding* [1962] 2 Lloyd's Rep. 238. See also Ch.6, below, paras 6–79 to 6–81.

to be entitled to the cost of repairing it at a cost considerably in excess of its market value as a motor vehicle.[188]

5–74   In *Re-Source America International Ltd v Platt Site Services Ltd*,[189] the defendant's negligence caused a fire which destroyed certain spools which the claimant was contractually bound to refurbish. The measure of loss was the cost of replacing them with new spools, less the saved cost of refurbishment: it was not appropriate to award the full cost of replacement even where the new spools had to be purchased much earlier than would otherwise have been the case and second-hand or used spools were not readily available. Replacement value was not awarded where the claimants' crane was negligently damaged but replacement was not in fact contemplated and the cost of doing so would involve an extra £1.7m in shipping a replacement from the United States.[190]

(ii) *Damage to land and buildings*

5–75   **Generally.**[191] The measure of damages, when either land is damaged negligently or there has been a negligent failure to discover the existence of material defects in a building, is the same as in the case of chattels. So, if a building is damaged, the claimant can recover (1) the cost of repairs; (2) any depreciation in value,[192] namely, the difference in market value between the building as repaired and the building before the damage; and (3) the expense of obtaining equivalent accommodation, while the repairs are being carried out. Similarly, where a negligent survey[193] failed to reveal that the roof of a building was seriously defective, it was held that the true measure of damage was; (a) the difference between what figure the claimant had paid for the house and the market value in its defective condition, plus interest[194]; (b) the cost incurred in respect of taking emergency action to save the building from more harm, plus interest; (c) the cost of obtaining alternative accommodation; and (d) an appropriate sum in respect of vexation and inconvenience.

5–76   It is a fundamental principle that the measure of damages is the sum of money that puts the injured party in the same position as that in which he would have been, had he not suffered the loss and damage. Accordingly, although damages are normally assessed at the date on which the damage occurred, the rule may be

---

[188] *O'Grady v Westminster Scaffolding*, n.187, above. This remarkable vehicle was named "Hortensia" by its enthusiastic owner. "To the romantically-minded, this might seem a touching tale of loyalty and devotion. To be more prosaic, it is an action about a motor car": Edmund Davis J. at the start of his judgment.
[189] [2005] Lloyd's Rep. 50, CA.
[190] Only the resale value was awarded: *The Maersk Colombo, The Times*, June 13, 2001, CA (applying *Ruxley Electronics and Construction Ltd v Forsyth*). See also *Ali-Reza Delta Transport Ltd v United Arab Shipping Company, The Times*, May 27, 2003, CA, n.181, above.
[191] See Rogers, "Damages for Injury to a Building" in 124 S.J. 383.
[192] In cases involving a negligent survey, usually damages should be calculated by reference to the diminution in value. However, this is not an invariable rule and ought not to be followed if its application manifestly would not do justice to the case: *Hipkins v Jack Cotton Partnership* [1989] 45 E.G. 163 (but disapproved by the Court of Appeal in *Watts v Morrow* [1991] 1 W.L.R. 1421). See further, Ch.9, paras 9–327 to 9–329, below.
[193] *Treml v Ernest W. Gibson & Partners* (1984) 272 E.G. 68.
[194] Applying *Perry v Sidney Phillips & Son* [1982] 1 W.L.R. 1297.

relaxed in a case where either the damage could not reasonably be discovered then or some appreciable time may have to be taken in order to effect repairs.[195]

Consequential loss, such as loss of business or loss of production in a factory or the increased cost of carrying on business,[196] can also be recovered[197] but any financial loss which is not the direct result of physical damage is too remote and so cannot be recovered.[198] In the case of total destruction of a building, the measure of damages is more usually the value of the building destroyed and not the cost of replacement[199] but where such a building had been disused and would have had to be demolished in any event to clear the land for the proposed future redevelopment, the owners were only entitled to be compensated for the money expended on the immediate, necessary remedial and safety work.[200] By way of contrast, where the claimant had no option other than to rebuild a new factory, the proper measure of damages was the cost of replacement.[201] In such circumstances where claimants had acted reasonably to mitigate their loss, and there was no evidence called by the defendants to establish a case of betterment, the latter were not entitled to any allowance for a benefit accruing to the claimants from the fact of their having a new building, instead of their old premises.   5–77

In Ireland, it has been decided that the appropriate measure of damages should be that, which in the circumstances is best calculated to put the claimant fairly and reasonably in the position in which he was before the damage was occasioned. So, in *Munnelly v Calcon*,[202] it was held that only damages representing the diminished value of the premises ought to be awarded in a case   5–78

---

[195] *Dodd Properties (Kent) v Canterbury City Council* (1980) 1 W.L.R. 433, CA applied in *Jarvis v T. Richards & Co* (1980) 124 S.J. 793 (solicitors negligently advised client on ancillary relief matters in her divorce proceedings).
[196] *Caltrex Oil (Australia) Pty v The Dredge "Willemstad"* (1977) 51 A.L.J.R. 270.
[197] e.g. *S.C.M. (United Kingdom) Ltd v W.J. Whittall & Son Ltd* [1971] 1 Q.B. 337. See, however, per Lord Denning M.R. and Winn L.J. that economic loss without damage to person or property which arises from a negligent act is not recoverable as damages, except where such loss is the immediate consequence of the negligence, since such damage is otherwise too remote. *British Celanese v A.H. Hunt (Capacitors) Ltd* [1969] 1 W.L.R. 959. See further Ch.2, above, paras 2–207 to 2–237.
[198] *Spartan Steel & Alloys Ltd v Martin & Co (Contractors) Ltd* [1973] Q.B. 27.
[199] *Moss v Christchurch RDC* [1925] 2 K.B. 750. In *Farmer Giles Ltd v Wessex Water Authority* [1988] 42 E.G. 127, Peter Pain J. expressed the view that the loss of a building could be compensated adequately by an appropriate sum of money. But to achieve *restitutio in integrum* that sum was to be related to the use to which the claimant had intended to put the building. Accordingly, in the case of an old mill, already in a poor state of repair, damages were assessed both in contract and tort as the value of the original property, when refurbished, less the cost of such refurbishment.
[200] *C.R. Taylor (Wholesale) Ltd v Hepworths Ltd* [1977] 1 W.L.R. 659.
[201] *Harbutt's "Plasticine" Ltd v Wayne Tank & Pump Co Ltd* [1970] 1 Q.B. 447, which was applied in *Ward v Cannock Chase* [1985] 3 All E.R. 537 (the need for moderate repairs had become a need for complete rebuilding, as a result of the council's breaches of duty (a) to keep in a safe condition the adjoining property in a row of terraced cottages and (b) to repair the damages caused to the claimant's house, and, since it was reasonable for the claimant to wish to continue living in his house, he was entitled to damages on the basis of the cost of rebuilding, if he could obtain planning permission to rebuild). See, also *Hutchison v Davidson* (1945) S.C. 395 and *Cooper v Railway Executive* [1953] 1 W.L.R. 223, where straying cattle derailed a train, the cost of restoration of the permanent way, *inter alia*, was held to be the measure of damages.
[202] [1978] I.R. 387, applied in *Ward v Cannock Chase DC* [1985] 3 All E.R. 537, in the event of the necessary planning permission's being refused.

where it was held that reinstatement damages would have enriched excessively and unnecessarily the claimant and have punished the defendants unreasonably. Damages, reflecting the cost of remedying tortious damage to a building, may be assessed with reference to the cost at the date of trial, in a case where it was reasonable for the claimants to have postponed the carrying out of the repairs required.[203]

5–79   **Damage to land without buildings.** In this instance the measure of damages is the diminished value of the land. This usually means the cost of restoring the land to its original condition but there are cases in which this is not so, for example when a ditch was widened and, in doing so, a strip of a field was cut and carried away.[204] In *Rust v Victoria Graving Dock Co*,[205] the claimant's building estate was flooded as a result of the defendants' negligence. It was held that he could recover, as damages:

(1) the cost of repairing the damaged houses and the rent lost, during the period of repairs;

(2) in respect of houses in course of erection, on which the claimant was bound by contract to make and had made advances to builders by way of security, the amount by which the houses were a less sufficient security for the claimant's advances than they were before; and

(3) loss of estimated rent, caused through delay in letting the unbuilt-on land, owing to the flooding, However, it was held that he could not recover;

(4) loss arising from the prejudice against the neighbourhood, caused by the flood; or

(5) loss arising from the depreciation in the selling value of the ground rents, arising from leasing the houses to the builders, when it was found that there would be no flood-damage, which would last up to the end of the leases.

(C) Damages for personal injuries

5–80   **Definition of personal injury.** It is axiomatic that a cause of action in respect of negligence is only complete if it can be shown that the breach of duty has caused damage.[206] Personal injury is one kind of actionable damage and in the

---

[203] *Dodd Properties (Kent) v Canterbury City Council* [1980] 1 All E.R. 928, CA, applying *Birmingham Corp v West Midlands Baptist (Trust) Association* [1970] A.C. 874 and approving dictum of Oliver J. in *Radford v de Froberville* [1977] 1 W.L.R. 1262. See also *Alcoa Minerals of Jamaica Inc v Broderick* [2000] 3 W.L.R. 23, PC, where the claimant did not have the resources to pay for repairs to a roof damaged by noxious gases from the defendant's plant and they were reasonable in waiting until liability was established before undertaking repairs.
[204] *Jones v Gooday* (1841) 8 M. & W. 146.
[205] (1886) 36 Ch.D. 113. See also *Nitro-Phosphate and Odam's Chemical Manure Co v London and St Katharine Docks* (1878) 9 Ch.D. 503 at 520; *Workman v G.N. Ry* (1863) 32 L.J.Q.B. 279.
[206] See Ch.1, para.1–34, Ch.2, paras 2–96 to 2–254.

majority of cases the court will have little difficulty in recognising that an injury has been sustained. In the context of the Limitation Act 1980 the phrase "personal injuries" includes any disease and any impairment of a person's physical or mental condition.[207] It is necessary, however, to have regard to the degree to which any morphological change in the body gives rise to any impairment in the functioning of the body or any symptoms. An action for damages for personal injuries cannot be founded on a trivial injury and what is trivial is a question of fact and degree.[208]

Itemisation of awards by the courts.[209] In the majority of negligence   **5–81**
actions, the claimant has usually suffered damage of two separate kinds, namely pecuniary and non-pecuniary loss. In the past, the importance of the differences between these two kinds of damage had tended to become indistinct, because of the practice of the trial judge's awarding a global sum in respect of the proven heads of damage, without attempting either to itemise them or, indeed, to given any indication of the individual assessments, as a result of which no subsequent scrutiny was possible. The modern approach is to itemise awards, in some cases in great detail.[210] This was required in particular after *Jefford v Gee*,[211] held that it was necessary to apply different rates of interest to different heads of damages. It is also necessary for courts to distinguish between damages paid for past loss of earnings, the cost of care and loss of mobility so that the relevant DWP benefits can be deducted from awards pursuant to the Social Security (Recovery of Benefits) Act 1997 s.15.[212]

It is proposed to deal with the measure of damages separately in relation to: (i) non-pecuniary damage; (ii) past pecuniary loss; (iii) future pecuniary loss; (iv)the deduction of benefits; (v) provisional damages and interim payments; (vi)interest on awards; and (vii) consideration of other claims.

(i) *Non-pecuniary loss*

Generally. An injured person is likely to suffer loss in many ways in which   **5–82**
it is not possible to measure in financial terms, such as pain, disability and the reduced ability to derive pleasure from life. In order to attempt to achieve restitution,[213] which is the purpose of damages for personal injuries, the court must embark upon the wholly artificial exercise of placing a financial value upon such losses.

---

[207] The Limitation Act 1980 s.38.
[208] *Rothwell v Chemical and Insulating Co Ltd* [2008] A.C. 281, see further Ch.2 paras 2–99 to 2–100; Ch.4, para.4–151.
[209] Malaysian law allows the itemisation process in assessing general damages in personal injury claims: *Jamil Bin Harun v Yang Kamsiah Bte Moer Rasdi* [1984] A.C. 529 (applying *Lim Poh Choo v Camden and Islington Area Health Authority* [1980] A.C. 174).
[210] e.g. *Cassel v Riverside Health Authority* [1992] P.I.Q.R. Q1, CA. The approach was approved of by the Court of Appeal in *George v Pinnock* [1973] 1 W.L.R. 118, CA.
[211] [1970] 2 Q.B. 130, CA.
[212] See paras 5–140 to 5–142, below.
[213] Often referred to by the latin tag, *restitutio in integrum*.

5–83 Broadly speaking, the matters of a non-pecuniary nature which can arise in ascertaining damages, are: (a) pain and suffering, past, present and future; (b) loss of amenity, that is, inconvenience and loss of enjoyment of life, past, present and future; (c) the injury itself and any resultant harm to health and (d) any awareness of the shortening of the expectation of life.[214]

5–84 **Pain and suffering: symptoms.** In practice it is not often necessary to make a sharp distinction between the injury sustained and the symptomatic results, particularly where an injury is serious in nature or extent.[215] The most important aspect for a claimant is likely to be effects of an injury upon normal everyday life.[216] Less severe injuries, even if they leave a permanent reminder such as scarring,[217] usually result in only temporary effects upon earning capacity or activities. Clearly, in all cases where the body's integrity has been violated, resulting in either temporary or permanent impairment, the injury by itself properly attracts an award of damages. In an appropriate case, such damages will be substantial.

5–85 **Psychiatric injury.**[218] Where unaccompanied by any physical injury, damages are not recoverable in respect of the suffering associated with normal human emotions[219] such as grief,[220] distress or fear, since these conditions are not in themselves psychiatric injury. However, where physical injury has been suffered, the compensation for pain, suffering and loss of amenity can also reflect the worry and distress which the injury has caused.[221] If the claimant has a nervous personality and painful symptoms have thereby been exacerbated, compensation should be approached on the basis of the perceived level of pain. In such circumstances the threshold of psychiatric injury does not have to be achieved in order to attract compensation.[222] But if the claimant should suffer mental ill health sufficient to amount to psychiatric injury in addition to physical injury,

---

[214] See the summary of Cockburn C.J. in *Phillips v L. & S.W. Ry* (1879) 4 Q.B.D. 406, affd. 5 Q.B.D. 78.

[215] If it be alleged that the claimant is malingering, i.e. deliberately manufacturing symptoms for the purposes of gain, an allegation of dishonesty is involved and such a case should not be put to witnesses unless the defendant proposes to call positive evidence in support: *Stojalowski v Imperial Smelting Corp* (1976) 121 S.J. 118.

[216] *H. West & Son Ltd v Shephard* [1964] A.C. 326 at 341, per Lord Reid.

[217] See *Lampert v Eastern National Omnibus Co Ltd* [1954] 1 W.L.R. 1047.

[218] For discussion of the circumstances in which a duty of care arises in respect of psychiatric injuries, see Ch.2, above, paras 2–112 to 2–166.

[219] *Hicks v Chief Constable of South Yorkshire Police* [1992] 1 A.C. 310.

[220] An exception to this rule is in respect of fatal accidents whereby parents of an unmarried deceased child and surviving spouses can recover an award for their bereavement pursuant to s.1A of the Fatal Accidents Act 1976. See Ch.16, below, para.16–27.

[221] *Blake v Midland Ry* (1852) 18 Q.B. 93 at 111.

[222] *Mullins v Gray* [2004] EWCA Civ 1483, applying *Malcolm v Broadhurst* [1970] 3 All E.R. 508, para.5–31 above. In *Mullins* the claimant suffered an appalling history of pain after a whiplash injury. It was held unnecessary for her to establish by medical evidence that the anxiety trait which caused her enhanced perception of pain was a medically recognised psychiatric disorder. The tortfeasor took his victim as he found her and the fact that the claimant's pain and suffering had been heightened by her anxious personality did not make her claim any the less one in respect of physical injury.

then damages are recoverable in respect of both the physical and psychiatric injuries.[223]

Object of damages. Damages for pain and suffering are intended to provide   **5–86**
reasonable compensation for the claimant's actual and prospective bodily hurt,[224]
including that which results from necessary[225] medical care, surgery and
treatment. No perfect compensation can be given.[226] The court is not estimating
the price which the victim would have accepted as consideration for suffering the
injuries sustained.[227] Inevitably, monetary compensation will fall short of the
value placed by the victim upon the injury to his mental and physical health. The
assessment of damages under this head has throughout to be objectively fair and
so far as possible consistent as between cases with broadly similar facts.

The artificiality of the exercise required to translate an individual's pain and   **5–87**
suffering into an award of damages was recognised in *Heil v Rankin*,[228] one of
a number of appeals considered on the same occasion, when the court responded
to an invitation to increase the level of compensation for personal injuries in the
light of the changing value of money. It was pointed out that no simple formula
can convert a claimant's disability into monetary terms. Courts attempt to
achieve consistency, for instance, by applying guidelines as given in reported
cases, or as published by the Judicial Studies Board.[229] In individual claims, the
compensation must be fair and just to the claimant but not out of accord with
what society as a whole would perceive as reasonable.[230] If the value of money
alters it is usually enough to apply to a guideline the difference in the retail price

---

[223] See further as to psychiatric illness, Ch.2 paras 2–112 to 2–166, above. As to the level of damages, see the Judicial Studies Board Guidelines for the Assessment of General Damages. In *Coxon v Flintshire CC* [2001] P.I.Q.R. Q9, the CA doubted the application of the 5th edn of the Guidelines to cases of psychiatric injuries caused by the sexual abuse of children.

[224] *Heaps v Perrite Ltd* (1937) 81 S.J. 236, CA; *H. West & Son Ltd v Shephard* [1964] A.C. 326 (catastrophic injuries including reduced level of consciousness: in awarding damages court not concerned with use to which money would be put). See also *Briody v St Helens & Knowsley Health Authority* [2002] Q.B. 856, CA (the claim for pain, suffering and loss of amenity of an undischarged bankrupt is personal to the bankrupt and not vested in the trustee in bankruptcy).

[225] See *Cutler v Vauxhall Motors Ltd* [1971] 1 Q.B. 418.

[226] *Armsworth v S.E. Ry* (1847) 11 Jur. 758, per Parke B. In *Fowler v Grace, The Times*, February 20, 1970, Edmund Davies L.J. expressed misgivings about Baron Parke's words (a jury must not attempt to give damages to the full amount of a perfect compensation) since it was the manifest duty of the tribunal (whether judge alone or jury) to give as perfect a sum as was within its power. But the key is in what Parke B. added, namely, that the jury was: "to take a reasonable view of the case and give what you consider a fair compensation". See also, *Rowley v L. & N.W. Ry* (1873) L.R. 8 Ex. 221; *Phillips v L. & S.W. Ry* (1879) 5 C.P.D. 280.

[227] See *Owen v Sykes* [1936] 1 K.B. 192, per Greer L.J.

[228] [2001] Q.B. 272. A number of cases were considered. It was felt that modest increases in the level of some awards were justified. In the case of the most catastrophic injuries awards were increased by about one-third. No increase was considered appropriate for cases where, as at March 2000 (the time of the Court of Appeal's judgment) the award would not exceed £10,000. Between those two levels a range of adjustments were made. Tables are now available to allow practitioners to bring earlier awards up to date, see e.g. in *Facts and Figures* (Sweet and Maxwell).

[229] The current guidelines are in the 9th edition and reflect previous awards updated for inflation and, where appropriate, the effect of *Heil v Rankin* but they do not have the force of law and reference should always be made to examples such as those contained in *Kemp & Kemp, The Quantum of Damages* (Sweet & Maxwell).

[230] *Heil v Rankin*, n.228, above.

index at the date the guideline was laid down and the date of assessment.[231] Over time, this may be insufficient to keep awards abreast of what society considers reasonable and the Court of Appeal may intervene if there is real reason to think that the level of awards is significantly out of line with society's expectations.

5-88   **Appeals from awards of general damages.** Given the artificiality of the awards for pain, suffering and loss of amenity, appellate courts will only interfere with an assessment of the quantum of damages at first instance where the trial judge has acted on some wrong principle of law, has misapprehended the facts or the amount of the award is wholly erroneous. It is not sufficient that the members of the appellate court would have come to a different view to that of the trial judge.[232]

5-89   **Pain and suffering as distinct from loss of amenity.** In practice, pain and suffering is often aggregated with loss of amenities of life[233] for the purpose of awarding damages and a single sum is awarded. They are in fact two distinct heads of loss. The distinction has a material difference where the claimant is unaware of his injuries or their extent, e.g. where the claimant is in a persistent vegetative state. In relation to pain and suffering, a claimant can only recover damages to the extent that he actually endures pain or suffering so a claimant rendered immediately and permanently unconscious by the defendant's negligence would receive no damages for pain and suffering.[234] In contrast, damages for the loss of amenities of life are assessed on an objective basis for the fact of the deprivation irrespective of whether the claimant is aware of the loss.[235]

5-90   **Loss of amenity.** This head of damages takes into account the effect that the claimant's injuries have had on his ability to enjoy life. The emphasis is on any reduction in the claimant's ability to pursue enjoyable activities, as opposed to pain and suffering. The assessment is objective in the sense that the claimant is to be compensated in respect of the fact his inability to enjoy life as opposed to his perception of his inability to enjoy life.[236] But it is also subjective in the sense that the question is what a particular loss of amenity means to *this* claimant, not the generality.

5-91   Amongst the loss of the amenities[237] of life, there can be considered are: the inability of the injured person to engage in indoor or outdoor games[238]; their dependence, to a greater or lesser extent, on the help of others in their daily lives; inability to cope with looking after, caring for and rendering the accustomed

---

[231] *Heil v Rankin*, n.228, above.

[232] *Santos v Eaton Square Garage Ltd* [2007] EWCA Civ 225.

[233] See para.5–90, below.

[234] *Lim Poh Choo v Camden and Islington Health Authority* [1980] A.C. 174 at 188, per Lord Scarman.

[235] *H. West & Son Ltd v Shepard* [1964] A.C. 326; *Lim Poh Choo v Camden and Islington Health Authority* [1980] A.C. 174.

[236] *H. West & Son Ltd v Shepard*; *Lim Poh Choo v Camden and Islington Health Authority*, n.235 above.

[237] See Ogus, "Damages for Lost Amenities for a Foot, a Feeling or a Function" in 35 M.L.R. 1.

[238] *Rushton v NCB* [1953] 1 Q.B. 495 at 501, per Birkett L.J.; *Ward v Hertfordshire CC* [1969] 1 W.L.R. 790.

services to a dependent[239]; sexual impotence[240]; loss of happiness and satisfaction in bringing a pregnancy to a successful conclusion[241]; premature onset of menopause[242]; any prejudice to the prospects of marriage[243]; and restrictions upon a choice of life which injury brings in its wake.[244] In this connection, the age of the injured person must be taken into account, since an elderly person or a very young child[245] will not suffer the same loss in this respect as a young adult.[246] If the injury has resulted in disfigurement, this must be taken into account among the matters mentioned above.[247]

In assessing damages for physical injuries, it is an irrelevant consideration that **5–92** a victim may be unable to enjoy personally any award of damages and may be ignorant of the loss he has suffered, except that such ignorance will be an element

---

[239] *Rourke v Barton, The Times*, June 23, 1982 (the injured claimant could no longer give her devoted loving care to her husband, who was suffering from terminal cancer and depended heavily upon her for support, as well as for his daily requirements).

[240] *Cooke v J.L. Kier & Co Ltd* [1970] 1 W.L.R. 774. Because the claimant's wife had no claim in her own right for loss of consortium he could obtain damages not only for the loss to himself in this regard but also for "the effect on his family life which takes her into account" (per Lord Denning M.R. at 776).

[241] *Bagley v North Herts HA* (1986) 136 New L.J. 1014. In addition, it was held that whilst the claimant was not entitled to damages for the loss of the society of her still-born child, she was nevertheless entitled to be compensated for the loss associated with its physical loss. *Bagley* was not followed in *Kerby v Redbridge HA* [1994] P.I.Q.R. Q1. On a different point, see *Briody v St Helens and Knowsley HA* [2002] Q.B. 856, where the claimant could not recover the cost of obtaining a surrogate child through a commercial arrangement which was unlawful in the United Kingdom. The question of whether damages could be recovered in respect of a lawful surrogacy agreement was specifically reserved. In dismissing the appeal the Court of Appeal said it was unreasonable to award as damages the cost of "own egg" surrogacy where the chances of a successful pregnancy were extremely slight. The chances of success were greater with donor eggs but the proposal was in no way restorative of the claimants' position before the negligent act.

[242] *Sutton v Population Services Family Planning Programme Ltd, The Times*, November 7, 1981.

[243] *Harris v Harris* [1973] 1 Lloyd's Rep. 445; *Hughes v McKeown* [1985] 1 W.L.R. 963. See also *Moriarty v McCarthy* [1978] 1 W.L.R. 155 for the relationship between an award under this head and that in respect of future earning losses, in the case of a young woman.

[244] *Heaps v Perrite Ltd* [1937] 2 All E.R. 60. See also *Keating v Elvan Reinforced Concrete Co Ltd* [1967] 3 All E.R. 611 (an artist, who had chosen not to use his earning capacity doing such work but to do other non-lucrative work instead solely for the pleasure it gave him and his own satisfaction). (Appeal on a different point [1968] 1 W.L.R. 722). In rare instances such an inability could arise from the fact of his serving a subsequent term of imprisonment, e.g. *Meah v McCreamer* [1985] 1 All E.R. 367. For a comparable loss arising out of the permanent breakdown of a marriage, see *Jones v Jones* [1983] 1 W.L.R. 901 and, on appeal [1985] Q.B. 704.

[245] See, e.g. *Bird v Cocking & Sons Ltd* [1951] 2 T.L.R. 1260, CA (61 year old man suffering amputation of one hand with the other rendered useless); also *Nutbrown v Sheffield HA* [1993] 4 Med. L.R. 188, where Potts J. took the appropriate sum for a person in the prime of life and then reduced it to allow for the circumstances of the 72-year-old claimant, with his pre-accident condition and life expectancy.

[246] *Gray v Mid Herts Group Hospital Management Committee, The Times*, March 30, 1974 (child of one year old suffered cardiac arrest during surgery for an inguinal hernia, resulting in widespread brain damage, caused by negligence. The child survived two years and nine months before dying from his injuries, and during that period of time he had shown a slight reaction to familiar voices and friendly touch; his estate was awarded £5,000 for loss of amenities).

[247] See *Lampert v Eastern National Omnibus Co* [1954] 1 W.L.R. 1047; *McLaurin v N.B. Ry* (1892) 19 R. 346.

in the assessment of damages for pain and suffering.[248] So, where a 16-year-old, athletic, intelligent schoolboy sustained appalling injuries in a road accident, which had rendered him spastic, whereby he remained paralysed, mute and in a state of coma, its being unlikely that he would ever become aware of his plight, he was awarded substantial damages for loss of amenities.[249] In assessing damages, the court is not concerned to consider to what use the money will be put.[250]

5–93   **Loss of congenial employment.** Where a claimant has lost employment, which was a source of particular satisfaction or status, damages for loss of congenial employment may be recovered.[251] It is unclear whether this is an element of damages under the head of loss of the amenities of life or whether it is an element of damages for past pecuniary losses.[252] Many cases where damages for loss of congenial employment are awarded involve claimants who were formerly employed in the emergency services or as nurses, but awards are not confined to such occupations and extend to any case in which the employment which has been lost had, for the claimant, a special value.[253]

5–94   **Loss of expectation of life.** Injury to health, which has resulted in a shortening of the injured person's expectation of life,[254] used to be a matter that had to be taken into account.[255] This was because "a man [had] a legal right to his own life".[256] It was the House of Lords, in *Rose v Ford*,[257] which decided that a claim under this head of damage was available also in an action, brought under the Law Reform (Miscellaneous Provisions) Act 1934 on behalf of a deceased person's estate. This was so, even though the deceased had been killed instantaneously.[258]

5–95   As from January 1, 1983, the right to damages for loss of expectation of life[259] was abolished by s.1(1)(a) of the Administration of Justice Act 1982.[260]

---

[248] *Wise v Kaye* [1962] 1 Q.B. 638, approved by the Lords in *H. West & Son v Shephard* [1964] A.C. 326, where it was pointed out that the guidance in *Benham in Gambling* [1941] A.C. 157 concerning the award of moderate damages in fatal accident cases was intended to apply only to damages for loss of expectation of life and not to loss of amenities of life. See, further, *Croke v Wiseman* [1982] 1 W.L.R. 71.

[249] *Maxwell v Maxwell Scientific International (Distribution Services)*, The Times, June 28, 1963.

[250] *H. West & Son v Shephard* [1964] A.C. 326; *Andrews v Freeborough* [1967] 1 Q.B. 1.

[251] *Hale v London Underground Ltd* [1993] P.I.Q.R. Q30.

[252] In *Hale v London Underground Ltd*, above, Otton J. described loss of congenial employment as a "separate head of damage". *McGregor on Damages* (18th edn, 2009) discusses it as an element of damages for loss of amenity whereas *Kemp & Kemp, The Quantum of Damages* (Sweet & Maxwell) discusses it as an element of pecuniary losses.

[253] There is a table of previous awards for damages for loss of congenial employment in *Kemp & Kemp, The Quantum of Damages*. See also Martin, "Loss of congenial employment" 2002 J.P.I Law 3, 284.

[254] *Flint v Lovell* [1935] 1 K.B. 354 at 355, per Acton J.

[255] For the state of the law and the development of a "conventional figure" for damages, prior to January 1, 1983, see *Charlesworth on Negligence* (6th edn, 1977), paras 1428–1431.

[256] *Armsworth v S.E. Ry* (1847) 11 Jur. 758.

[257] [1937] A.C. 826, affirming *Flint v Lovell* [1935] 1 K.B. 354.

[258] *Morgan v Scoulding* [1938] 1 K.B. 786.

[259] It is to be noted that damages in respect of loss of income over the relevant period of loss of expectation of life remain unaffected by the abolition. See s.1(2) of the Administration of Justice Act 1982.

[260] s.1 was brought into effect on the date stated, by virtue of the provisions of s.76(11).

Nevertheless, by s.1(1)(b) of the Act, where injuries have reduced a victim's expectation of life, "the court, in assessing damages in respect of pain and suffering caused by the injuries, shall take account of any suffering caused or likely to be caused to him by awareness that his expectation of life has been so reduced".[261] Both the Law Commission of 1973[262] and the Royal Commission of 1978[263] had criticised loss of expectation of life as a separate head of damage and recommended that it ought to be abolished.

Future or potential events. In situations where either the prognosis for   **5–96** injuries is very obscure[264] or there is no readily available comparison, the result is likely to depend upon a good deal of judicial guesswork.[265] Not infrequently, in personal injury litigation, the trial judge has to try looking into the future, in order to fix a fair and proper figure, which necessarily has to take account of two conflicting possibilities, whether one the one hand that predicted complications will arise, and on the other that they will not. In such circumstances Widgery L.J. considered that:

> "there is only one practical method of approaching this kind of problem and that is to assess the kind of figure which would be appropriate in the extreme and serious case where the complications or future attacks were virtually certain. It then becomes possible to discount that figure according to the degree of optimism which is possible in the light of the medical reports,"

It can never be just a matter of simply arithmetic.[266]

In *Malec v J.C. Hutton Pty Ltd*,[267] the High Court of Australia held that the   **5–97** court must assess "the degree of probability that an event would have occurred, or might occur, and adjust its award of damages to reflect the degree of probability".[268] Unless the chance is either so low as to be regarded as speculative or so high as to be practically certain, the court will take that chance into account when assessing the damages.

---

[261] This is statutory confirmation of the important distinction, made by the House of Lords in *Rose v Ford* [1937] A.C. 826, between damages to be awarded to a claimant on his claim for loss of expectation of life and that to be awarded in respect of the mental anguish suffered in knowing that his life so had been shortened. See, per Lord Roche, ibid. at 859.

[262] No.56 (1973), paras 92–100.

[263] Cmnd. 7054 (1978), paras 363–372 (the "Pearson Commission").

[264] The discussion here does not concern *liability* for some future event, for which see Ch.6, paras 6–82 to 6–84, below, but assessment of *quantum* where liability is made out.

[265] *Hawkins v New Mendip Engineering Ltd* [1966] 1 W.L.R. 1341 at 1348, with Scarman J. in the Court of Appeal agreeing with the propriety of "guesswork" on the known facts; *Jones v Griffith* [1969] 1 W.L.R. 795 at 802, per Harman L.J.

[266] *Jones v Griffith* [1969] 1 W.L.R. 795 at 801.

[267] (1990) 92 A.L.R. 545.

[268] *Malec v J.C. Hutton Pty Ltd* (1990) 92 A.L.R. 545 at 549, per Deane, Guadron and McHugh JJ., approving and applying *Mallett v McMonagle* [1970] A.C. 166 and *Davies v Taylor* [1974] A.C. 207.

(ii) *Pecuniary loss*

5-98   **Generally.** An injured party is also entitled to damages for his financial loss, both actual and prospective.[269]

5-99   **Actual financial loss.** Actual financial loss may consist of: loss of earnings; medical[270] and nursing expenses[271]; additional cost of providing an invalid diet; damage to clothing, the employment of extra household or other assistance; residential care[272]; and any other loss which is the direct consequence of the injury,[273] including the cost of convalescence after an injury, necessitating a change of air in some place away from the injured party's home.[274] The fact that payment has not actually been made in respect of the liabilities, incurred under any of these heads of damage, is immaterial, as long as the liability which has actually been incurred is a genuine one. So, where a husband had incurred liability to a hospital for attendance upon his wife, it was held that he could claim the amount of the liability from the negligent defendant, although the money had not been paid and it was unlikely, or perhaps impossible owing to its being statute-barred, that the hospital would enforce payment from the husband.[275]

5-100   In considering loss to trial the likely course of events after an accident may be taken into account. Thus, in *Cutler v Vauxhall Motors*,[276] where the claimant suffered an injury at work, which necessitated an operation, and led to lost earnings which he claimed as special damage, the claim failed on proof that he had suffered from a pre-existing condition, which would have made the operation necessary in any event. When a decision had been made by parents, faced with the problems of bringing up a handicapped child, not to have another child, which otherwise they had planned to have but for the defendant's negligence, the court was entitled to take into account in assessing damages the saving of likely future expenditure consequent upon that decision.[277]

---

[269] In *Coates v Curry, The Times*, August 22, 1997, CA, it was stressed that separate assessments should be made under the respective heads of past and future loss of earnings.

[270] Medical expenses include the expenses of treatment incurred upon the advice of experts, even though the experts' diagnosis was mistaken and the treatment unnecessary; *Reubens v Walker* (1946) S.C. 215.

[271] See paras 5–103 to 5–107, below.

[272] See De Bono, "Who foots the bill?" 147 S.J. 1173.

[273] See *Liffen v Watson* [1940] 1 K.B. 556 (domestic servant whose injuries prevented her from following her employment entitled to damages for loss of board and lodging, in addition to loss of wages, although she was living with her father who provided her with free board and lodging); *Pitt v Jackson* [1939] 1 All E.R. 129 (injured schoolmistresses not allowed expenses for taxi fares in going to school).

[274] *Phillips v L. & S.W. Ry* (1879) 5 Q.B.D. 78 at 80; *Salmon v Newland, The Times*, May 16, 1983. A deduction may be made for board and lodging when the cost of staying at a nursing home is claimed; *Shearman v Folland* [1950] 2 K.B. 43; *Oliver v Ashman* [1962] 2 Q.B. 210; *Cutts v Chumley* [1967] 1 W.L.R. 742.

[275] *Allen v Waters & Co* [1935] 1 K.B. 200.

[276] [1971] 1 Q.B. 418.

[277] *Salih v Enfield Health Authority* [1991] 3 All E.R. 400, CA (allowing the appeal and holding that the damages would be limited to the extra cost of the upkeep of a handicapped child, applying *Cutler v Vauxhall Motors* [1971] 1 Q.B. 418. But *Salih* was not followed in *McLelland v Greater Glasgow Health Board, The Times*, October 14, 1998, OH, where, in addition to an award for shock and distress at learning that a child was affected by Down's syndrome and for the long-term stress in

Marital breakdown. A claimant may not recover damages to compensate for   **5–101**
any alteration to his financial situation, resulting from the irretrievable breakdown of his marriage, even where the divorce is a direct result of personal
injuries sustained in an accident for which the defendant was responsible. First,
such damages are too remote, and secondly, it is contrary to public policy to
import considerations of matrimonial breakdowns into personal injury litigation.[278]

The cost of investment advice. In *Eagle v Chambers (No.2)*,[279] a catastroph-   **5–102**
ically injured claimant, a patient within the Rules,[280] failed to recover the cost of
fees incurred by the Court of Protection when dealing with the investment of
funds on his behalf.[281] It was pointed out that in assessing the amount a defendant
had to pay, it was assumed that the return on the money would be by way of
investing in index linked government securities, even though in practice a higher
return could be gained by investing more widely. The investment of damages was
a matter for a claimant and if a particular decision involved incurring a fee then
that was a consequence of the investment decision and not the injury. The
position of a patient should be regarded as the same as any other claimant. The
fact that the Court of Protection chose to invest more widely than index linked
government securities was not a necessary consequence of the injury but a
consequence of the Court of Protection's own policy.

Gratuitously provided care and assistance. Where an injured claimant has   **5–103**
a need for nursing care and/or domestic assistance consequent upon the injuries
sustained, damages are recoverable for the value of those services even if the
services are rendered without charge. The principle has its origin in *Roach v
Yates*,[282] where the claimant recovered damages for the cost of nursing care
provided to him by relatives who had given up work to look after him. In
Cunningham v Harrison,[283] a wife provided unpaid assistance to her tetraplegic
husband. Damages were recoverable for that assistance. Lord Denning M.R.
expressed the view that the damages paid in respect of the assistance should be
held in trust for the carer.[284] At the same time as the Court of Appeal was
considering *Cunningham v Harrison*, a differently constituted court considered
Donnelly v Joyce[285] where a mother gave up her job to care for her injured child.

---

caring for such a child, the father recovered the costs of the child's basic maintenance even though
the parents would probably have gone on to have another child if the pregnancy had been terminated,
as they said it would have been if the doctor's duty of care had been properly discharged.

[278] *Pritchard v J.H. Cobden Ltd* [1988] Fam. 22. CA (not following *Jones v Jones* [1985] Q.B. 704,
wherein, it is to be observed, the matter of principle was *not* argued before the Court).

[279] [2004] 1 W.L.R. 3081, CA.

[280] The term is now "protected party," see CPR 21.1 A patient was "a person who by reason of
mental disorder within the meaning of the Mental Health Act 1983 is incapable of managing and
administering his property and affairs."

[281] Approving *Page v Plymouth Hospitals NHS Trust* [2004] P.I.Q.R. Q68. See Duckworth, "Clear
precedent" 148 S.J. 868; Hall and Norris, "Claims of the cost of investment management" J.P.I Law
(2004), 3, 214.

[282] [1938] 1 K.B. 256, CA.

[283] [1973] Q.B. 942, CA.

[284] *Cunningham v Harrison* [1973] Q.B. 942, CA at 952.

[285] [1974] Q.B. 454, CA.

The Court of Appeal held that the claimant could recover in respect of his mother's services and that the loss was the claimant's and not his mother's; the loss being the need for care.[286] In *Hunt v Severs*,[287] the House of Lords disapproved of the reasoning in *Donnelly v Joyce* and preferred the concept of holding the money in trust for the carer. Damages for gratuitously provided care and assistance are not recoverable in respect of care and assistance actually provided to the claimant by the tortfeasor.[288]

5–104   The decision in *Hunt v Severs*[289] causes practical problems in relation to claims for future care because there can be no certainty as to who would in fact provide the necessary care to any one claimant. In some cases claimants are cared for by elderly relatives who may be able to provide assistance for only a limited number of years and thereafter the claimant would have to seek paid assistance. There is also the question as to how the money would be applied if the claimant died unexpectedly before the damages had been exhausted. The Law Commission[290] has suggested an approach whereby in relation to past care the claimant should be under a legal obligation to account to the carer for the value of the care provided and that damages for the cost of future care should be recovered with no such legal obligation.

5–105   Awards of damages in respect of gratuitously provided care are not confined to cases involving serious injuries. In *Giambrone v JMC Holidays Ltd*,[291] a number of claims were brought on behalf of children who had contracted gastro-enteritis on holiday. In each case a significant claim was made for care provided by relatives attending on the children. The Court of Appeal dismissed a submission based on *Mills v British Rail Engingeering Ltd*[292] that such awards were reserved only for very serious cases.

5–106   Damages for gratuitously provided care and assistance are usually awarded with reference to the commercial rate for providing such care, with a discount. In *Housecroft v Burnett*,[293] a 20 per cent reduction from the commercial rate was applied; in *Nash v Southmead Health Authority*,[294] the reduction was one-third; and in *Fairhurst v St Helens and Knowslely Health Authority*,[295] one-quarter. In

---

[286] *Donnelly v Joyce* [1974] Q.B. 454, CA at 462, per Megaw L.J.
[287] [1994] 2 A.C. 350.
[288] *Hunt v Severs* [1994] 2 A.C. 350 at 363, per Lord Bridge.
[289] *Hunt v Severs* [1994] 2 A.C. 350.
[290] "Damages for Personal Injury: Medical, Nursing and Other Expenses; Collateral Benefits" in Law Com. No.262.
[291] [2004] 2 All E.R. 891, CA See Saggerson, "Personal injury and travel" E.P.I.S. (2005), 1(1); Imperato, "Cost of care" S.J. (2005), 149 (22), 659.
[292] [1992] P.I.Q.R. Q130, CA.
[293] [1986] 1 All E.R. 332, CA. In *Giambrone v JMC Holidays* n.291 above, it was suggested that damages for care relating to the care of a child with gastroenteritis should rarely exceed £50 per week. See Exall, "Compensation for gratutitous care" 2002 J.P.I. Law 1, 36; also Browne and Gardiner, "Damages for care: judges really do care" 2002 J.P.I. Law 4, 369; Kerai, "Care beyond the call of duty" 2005 P.I.L.J. 33, 23. See further *Ath v Ms* [2003] P.I.Q.R. Q1.
[294] [1993] P.I.Q.R. Q156.
[295] [1995] P.I.Q.R. Q1. See also *Hogg v Doyle*, unreported, March 6, 1991; *Kemp & Kemp, The Quantum of Damages*, Vol. 3, and *Fitzgerald v Ford* [1996] P.I.Q.R. Q72, CA.

substantial cases, experts with skills in providing nursing care and assistance to the disabled often provide reports which set out the relevant commercial rates. The court has control over the admission of such evidence.[296] In many cases, the first step is to order the parties to commission a jointly instructed expert. Where a substantial amount of money is at stake, if a party is concerned about the contents of the report, questions should be put to the expert. If there is still concern after the questions have been answered then consideration should be given to the commissioning of a second report.[297]

In *Lowe v Guise*[298] the claimant was injured in a road traffic accident and as   **5–107** a result of his injuries he was not able to provide the level of care to his disabled brother to the extent that he had before the road traffic accident. The Court of Appeal held that the claimant was entitled to recover damages from the defendant in respect of the loss of his ability to care for his brother.

Actual[299] **loss of earnings.**[300] Frequently, following an accident, the victim   **5–108** has been rendered unfit to work, either temporarily or, maybe, permanently, as a consequence of the personal injuries sustained. Where such losses have been suffered, and where they can be attributed to the defendant's negligence, it matters not from what sources they arose. Accordingly, an injured claimant is entitled to recover damages in respect of any resultant loss of wages, salaries or professional fees.[301] In addition, these may include certain other financial losses. For example, where an employee has lost the use of a company car[302] and where a director, who was also a substantial shareholder in a private company, was incapacitated from doing work for it, as a result of which its profits had slumped so that the amount distributed to him by way of dividends had been reduced, each such loss was held to be recoverable.[303] Where an injured claimant, in a one-man business, has suffered a loss of profits, in similar circumstances, it will probably be essential for him to produce satisfactory trading accounts, in order to substantiate his claim in respect of such a loss.[304] Where the claimant is in partnership with another he can only recover damages for loss of earnings to the extent of his interest in the partnership, notwithstanding that he can be described as the "head and heart" of the firm.[305] Wages lost can be recovered, even though

---

[296] CPR Pt 35.
[297] *D v Walker* [2000] 1 W.L.R. 1382, CA.
[298] [2002] Q.B. 1369.
[299] For future losses of earnings, see paras 5–118 to 5–129 below.
[300] See Bennett, "Claims for Loss of Earnings in Personal Injury Actions" in 2 Lit. 105. In *Stefanovic v Carter* [2001] P.I.Q.R. Q55, CA, the use of tables of comparable earnings found in the *Facts and Figures* (Sweet & Maxwell) was approved in relation to the calculation of loss of earnings.
[301] *Phillips v L. & S.W. Ry* (1879) 5 Q.B.D. 78 and, on a further appeal, after a new trial, (1879) 5 C.P.D. 280.
[302] e.g. *Kennedy v Bryan*, *The Times*, May 3, 1984.
[303] *Lee v Sheard* [1956] 1 Q.B. 192.
[304] *Ashcroft v Curtin* [1971] 1 W.L.R. 1731.
[305] *Neal v Jones* [2002] EWCA Civ 1731, applying *Kent v BRB* [1995] P.I.Q.R. Q42, and doubting *Ward v Newalls Insulation Co Ltd* [1998] 2 All E.R. 690.

they have been paid by the employers, if the claimant is under a moral obligation to repay them, in the event of his recovering such loss from the defendant.[306]

5–109   If the claimant's attempts to mitigate his loss produce some profit then it must be set off against the loss claimed, irrespective of whether the claim is based in contract or tort. This occurred in *Bellingham v Dhillon*[307] where the claimant, a driving school proprietor, was injured in an accident and, since he could not work for a while, he was unable to afford to complete the purchase of a driving simulator for £7,000. Later, he managed to acquire for £1,900 a second-hand machine, which he operated profitably. It was held that he must set off against his claim for loss of profit during the period he was without the machine, the extra profit he had made by operating successfully the simulator which he had bought so cheaply.

5–110   **Net Loss.** In assessing loss of earnings, the claimant's tax liability must be considered. It is the net amount of the disposable[308] earnings that can be awarded, since the applicable principle is restitution. For the purposes of calculating the claimant's relevant tax liability, the sums in question must be treated as those lying at the top layers of his earned income. So, the amounts of deductions to be taken into account will be based on the effective rates of tax, which are applicable to those slices of his earnings.[309] The assessment can be made on broad lines and it is not necessary to do it with mathematical accuracy.[310]

5–111   In addition to deductions in respect of tax liability, national insurance contributions also should be taken into account.[311] Similarly, where a claimant is compensated in damages for loss of pension rights, he cannot be awarded additionally a sum which represents earnings that would have been deducted compulsorily as contributions towards that pension, since such contributions would not have been at his disposal.[312] Likewise, where the claimant has received either statutory sickness pay[313] or a tax rebate, as a result of his loss of

---

[306] *Dennis v L.P.T.B.* [1948] 1 All E.R. 779 (claimant received equivalent of wages partly from the Ministry of Pensions and partly from sick pay from his employers—a direction was made by the court that the amounts so received should be repaid out of the damages recovered).

[307] [1973] Q.B. 304, applying the principle of *British Westinghouse Electric Co and Manufacturing Co v Underground Electric Rys of London Ltd* [1912] A.C. 673. See also *Port of Sheerness v Brachers* [1997] I.R.L.R. 214 (a company dismissed employees upon negligent advice from solicitors which did not advert to the possibility of claim for unfair dismissal: in calculating damages credit had to be given for the benefit of employing casual labour in place of the dismissed workers).

[308] See *Dews v N.C.B.* [1987] Q.B. 81 (appeal dismissed [1988] A.C. 1).

[309] *Lyndale Fashion Manufacturers v Rich* [1973] 1 W.L.R. 73. The court is entitled to take into account, in diminution of this prospective calculated tax liability, the probable amount of the allowable expenses, which the claimant would have incurred, in order to earn that additional income, and the appropriate proportion of what would then have been his earned income relief.

[310] *B.T.C. v Gourley* [1956] A.C. 185, overruling *Billingham v Hughes* [1949] 1 K.B. 643; *Jordan v The Limmer and Trinidad Lake Asphalt Co Ltd* [1946] K.B. 356. Where loss of earnings is pleaded as special damage by the claimant, the defendant is entitled to particulars of any assessments to income tax: *Phipps v Orthodox Unit Trusts Ltd* [1958] 1 Q.B. 314.

[311] *Cooper v Firth Brown Ltd* [1963] 1 W.L.R. 418 at 420.

[312] *Dews v N.C.B.* [1987] Q.B. 81.

[313] *Palfrey v G.L.C.* [1985] I.C.R. 437, DC.

earnings during his periods off work, he must give credit for that amount, since it is a direct consequence of his injury, for which he is being compensated.[314]

Where the claimant alleges a loss of earnings, between the date of an accident and trial, the loss must be pleaded with particularity, it being a part of special damage.[315] Since any such calculation depends upon an assumption that the claimant would have probably continued to work[316] and to earn at the same rate, had it not been for the intervention of the accident, some allowance will have to be made, if for any reason the assumption is doubtful.[317] Where a claimant's life expectancy has to be established for the purpose of calculating future loss, relevant statistical evidence, can and should be taken into account, in addition to the estimates of clinicians who have knowledge of particular clinical circumstances which may affect the claimant's life expectation.[318] In a typical personal injury claim, this loss is usually capable of a simple calculation and can be arrived at my multiplying the claimant's net pre-accident earnings by the total period of disability, before any return to work.[319] Where appropriate the loss may include the fact that the claimant has lost the opportunities of earning money, as in the case of an American golf club professional, who, following a relatively minor injury to his left hand, recovered substantial damages for the lost opportunity of competing in five tournaments. His inability to compete resulted both in the loss of experience and prestige, and the loss of the chance of winning prize money.[320] **5–112**

(iii) *Future pecuniary loss*

Generally. Future pecuniary loss is an estimate of the financial loss which is likely to be suffered by an injured party, after the date of trial, and can include such matters as prospective loss of earnings,[321] any loss of future earning capacity, and any extra expenses, including the cost of special accommodation.[322] Where past loss has to be established as a matter of probability, the calculation of future loss can take possibilities into account. In a case involving a protected party[323] the reasonable costs of a receiver are recoverable but the costs of **5–113**

---

[314] *Hartley v Sandholme Iron Co Ltd* [1975] Q.B. 600. *Brayson v Wilmot-Breedon* (1976) 12 C.L. 56 (income tax "holiday" after return to work—special damages reduced accordingly).

[315] See *Ilkiw v Samuels* [1963] 1 W.L.R. 991 (4 months loss of earnings pleaded but continuing loss sought at trial some eight years later: the CA said the claim could only be taken into account in considering general damages for future loss).

[316] The claimant's inability to work must have been caused by the defendant's negligence and not by his long delay in issuing proceedings and then in pursuing them to trial: *James v Woodall Duckham Construction Co Ltd* [1969] 1 W.L.R. 903.

[317] *Phillips v L. & S.W. Ry* (1879) 5 C.P.D. 280 at 291, per Brett L.J.

[318] *Royal Victoria Infirmary v B (A Child)* [2003] P.I.Q.R. Q10, CA.

[319] *Phillips v L. & S.W. Ry* (1879) 5 C.P.D. 280 at 287, per Bramwell L.J.

[320] *Mulvaine v Joseph* (1968) 112 S.J. 927.

[321] Also subsequent divorce where it is relevant in deciding whether, but for the accident, someone would have worked and, if so, their earnings: *Floyd v Dennis* (1983) 42 B.C.L.R. 282.

[322] See *Roberts v Johnstone* [1989] Q.B. 878.

[323] For which see CPR Pt. 21.1.

investment advice and broker's fees are not recoverable whether the claimant is a protected party or not.[324]

5–114   **Private care and publicly funded care.** When considering a claim for the future provision of care and accommodation for a severely injured claimant, a question often arises as to the availability of such care, free of charge from a public body such as a local authority, primary care trust or health authority. Local authorities have powers to provide residential care and domiciliary care pursuant to ss.21 and 29 of the National Assistance Act 1948 respectively.[325] Where such care is or will be provided by the state, is the claimant nevertheless entitled to recover as damages the cost of providing care privately? On the one hand the underlying principle is that damages are compensatory and if a claimant, as a consequence of the injury, receives benefits to which he would not otherwise have been entitled then they are to be set off against the damages recoverable.[326] Moreover, the court must be astute to avoiding double recovery. Conversely, if the burden of providing care to a tortiously injured claimant was to fall on the state then the wrongdoer would receive an undeserved windfall.

5–115   The issue was considered in *Peters v East Midlands Strategic Health Authority*[327] and the balance fell in favour of a claimant being entitled to recover damages in respect of the cost of the private provision of care, so long as double recovery could be avoided. It was trite law that the claimant could recover that compensation for his injuries which was reasonably required to meet his needs and there was no principle which should operate to require the use of any facilities provided at public expense. Although the issue of allowing a wrongdoer to benefit from state provision of care[328] was noted, the desire to avoid delivering such a windfall did not form part of the reasoning by which the court came to its conclusion.[329] Where, however, the court finds that in fact the care will be provided (or part provided) by the state then the value of such state provision must be set off against the damages recoverable for such care.[330]

5–116   It has been regarded as reasonable for a claimant to recover the cost of privately funded care and accommodation for a number of reasons: inadequacy of publicly funded care[331]; uncertainty as to the future provision of public care provided under primary legislation and ministerial guidance[332]; also the defendant's failure to prove that publicly funded care would meet the claimant's

---

[324] See *Eagle v Chambers (No.2)* [2004] 1 W.L.R. 3081, CA approving *Page v Plymouth Hospitals NHS Trust* [2004] P.I.Q.R. Q68 and see para.5–102, above. See Duckworth, "Clear precedent" 148 S.J. 868; Hall and Norris, "Claims of the cost of investment management" (2004) J.P.I Law 214.
[325] These statutory provisions are augmented by statutory instruments, ministerial guidance and policy documents. The effect is that the provisions are complex and labyrinthine.
[326] *Hodgson v Trapp* [1989] 1 A.C. 807, 891.
[327] [2010] Q.B., 48.
[328] Such as those expressed by Longmore L.J. in *Sowden v Lodge* [2005] 1 W.L.R. 2129, CA, by Leveson J. in *Tinsley v Sarkar* [2006] P.I.Q.R. Q1 and by Tomlinson J. in *Freeman v Lockett* [2006] P.I.Q.R. P23.
[329] n.327, above at [89].
[330] *Crofton v National Health Service Litigation Authority* [2007] 1 W.L.R. 923.
[331] *Crookdale v Drury* which was upheld on appeal in *Sowden v Lodge* n.334, below.
[332] *Godbold v Mahmood* [2005] EWHC 1005 (Q.B.).

needs.[333] The claimant should not be left in a state of uncertainty over funding of care when what is reasonably required can be assessed and provided privately. If there is a risk as to the certainty of the provision of publicly funded care then the claimant should not bear that risk.

In *Sowden v Lodge*,[334] it was observed that in determining whether a severely   **5–117**
disabled claimant could recover the cost of private residential care there was a difference between what a claimant might establish as reasonable in the circumstances and what a judge objectively concluded as in his or her best interests. The former represented the test: "in this context paternalism does not replace the right of a claimant, or those with responsibility for the claimant, making a reasonable choice."[335]

Loss of future earnings. Where a claimant's injuries prevent him from   **5–118**
carrying out his former employment, his loss of earnings are assessed as past losses to the date of the assessment of damages and from that date as future losses. The award for future loss of earnings is made by way of a lump sum arrived at by multiplying the claimant's annual net loss of earnings as at the date of trial ("the multiplicand") by a factor to reflect the number of years over which the claimant will be suffering the loss ("the multiplier").

The conventional approach. The conventional approach to assessing awards   **5–119**
for future loss of earnings was summarised by Potter L.J. in *Herring v MOD*[336]:

> "In any claim for injury to earning capacity based on long-term disability, the task of the court in assessing a fair figure for future earnings loss can only be effected by forming a view as to the most likely future working career ("the career model") of the claimant had he not been injured. Where, at the time of the accident, a claimant is in an established job of field of work in which he is likely to have remained but for the accident, the working assumption is that he would have done so and the conventional multiplier/multiplicand method of calculation is adopted, the court taking into account any reasonable prospects of promotion and/or movement to a higher salary scale or into a better remunerated field of work, by adjusting the multiplicand at an appropriate point along the scale of the multiplier. However, if a move of job or change of career at some stage is probable, it nee only be allowed for so far as it is likely to increase or decrease the level of the claimant's earnings at the stage of his career at which it is regarded as likely to happen. If such a move or change is unlikely significantly to affect the future level of earnings, it may be ignored in the multiplicand/multiplier exercise, save that it will generally be appropriate to make a (moderate) discount in the multiplier in respect of contingencies or the 'vicissitudes of life'."

Where the claimant is young and he has not yet set out on his career it may not   **5–120**
be possible to select a career model but instead by reference to the claimant's previous performance, intentions, ambitions and the steps taken to pursue a particular path it may be possible to establish a base line from which to calculate

---

[333] *Walton v Calderdale Healthcare NHS Trust* [2006] P.I.Q.R. Q3.
[334] [2005] 1 W.L.R. 2129, CA.
[335] Per Pill L.J.
[336] [2004] 1 All E.R. 44, CA at [23].

the future losses. The use of average earnings figures such as those contained in the Annual Survey of Hours and Earnings (ASHE)[337] can be of assistance in establishing such a baseline.

5–121   **The Ogden Tables.** In most cases multipliers in relation to to future loss are determined with reference to these actuarial tables.[338] The tables indicate the appropriate multipliers in various scenarios,[339] and give rates of return from 0 per cent to 5 per cent. The Lord Chancellor has the power to prescribe rates of return to be taken into account by the courts in assessing damages for future pecuniary loss and[340] a rate of 2.5 per cent has been set with effect from June 28, 2001.[341] In claims for future loss of earnings a further discount[342] has to be made from the multiplier derived from the Ogden Tables to reflect contingencies other than mortality. The sixth edition of the Odgen Tables contain a revised methodology for determining the discount factor for contingencies other than mortality to reflect academic studies[343] which identified three factors as having the greatest impact on an individual's employability: whether that person was in employment or not; disability and educational attainment. The reader is referred to the commentary to the Tables themselves for their detailed application.[344]

5–122   **Adjustments to the multiplier.** In appropriate cases, the multiplier can be split to reflect likely fluctuations in the claimant's future loss of earnings. This may occur, for instance, where a claimant with promising career prospects is

---

[337] Published by the Office of National Statistics.

[338] The tables are produced by H.M. Government's actuary's department. The tables have accompanying notes which explain how they are to be used and worked examples are provided. The tables are now in their 5th edition and were developed for use in personal injury litigation by a working party under the chairmanship of the late Sir Michael Ogden Q.C.

[339] For example, there are tables for pecuniary loss for life and for pecuniary loss to ages 55, 60, 65, 70 and 75. There are separate tables for males and females.

[340] The Damages Act 1996 s.1. Section 1(2) of the Act permits departure from the rate set by the Lord Chancellor where a different rate would be more appropriate in the case in question. In *Warriner v Warriner* [2002] 1 W.L.R. 1703, CA, it was said that such a departure would only be justifible where the case fell into a category which he had not taken into account and/or the case had special features which were material to the rate of return and had not been taken into account in the Lord Chancellor's reasons when the rate was set. See generally, Hermer and Pickering, "Future loss multipliers: the quantification of damages for catastrophic injuries" 2002 J.P.I. Law 377. See also *Cooke v United Bristol Health Care* [2004] 1 W.L.R. 251, CA (no departure from the principle in *Warriner* was justified where the claimant sought to argue that conventional assessment of the costs of future care of the claimant would result in under-compensation and sought in effect to apply a discount rate other than that fixed by the Lord Chancellor to a multiplicand arrived at by reference to the NHS Pay Cost Index).

[341] Damages (Personal Injury) Order 2001 (SI 2001/2301).

[342] In *Wells v Wells* [1999] 1 A.C. 345, Lord Lloyd impliedly approved the application of discounts to reflect contingencies other than mortality in relation to multipliers for damages for loss of future earnings; no such discounts should be made where the multiplier is in respect of damages for future nursing care and assistance.

[343] The research is referred to in extensive notes which accompany the 6th edition of the tables and was carried out by Professor Ricahard Verall, Professor Steven Haberman and Mr. Zoltan Butt of City University, London and by Dr. Victoria Wass of Cardiff University.

[344] See also, e.g. *Conner v Bradman* [2007] EWHC 2789 (Q.B.); *A v Powys Local Health Board* [2007] EWHC 2996 (Q.B.). See also Trusted, "The sixth edition of the Odgen Tables" 2007 J.P.I. Law 262; McManus, "Turning the tables?" 158 N.L.J. 1705.

incapacitated early in working life. For example, in *Brittain v Gardner*,[345] a multiplier of 14 was split into sections of four and ten years respectively. The claimant was a young solicitor who, on account of her injuries would never return to work. The first period of the multiplier reflected the period of time over which the claimant's earnings would be below equity partner level and the latter period reflected earnings at equity partner level.

Adjustments to the multiplicand. In *Leesmith v Evans*,[346] there was uncer-   **5–123** tainty as to the future career progression of a severely injured claimant who, at the time of the accident, was an apprentice lighting technician in the live music industry. It was held that, despite the uncertainties as to the career path that the claimant would have taken, there was a sufficient career model to approach the case on a multiplier/multiplicand basis. A single average or pro-rated multiplicand was chosen taking into account the earnings which could have been expected at the various stages in the career of a lighting technician. Having taken a single multiplicand no further adjustment was need to the multiplier to allow for uncertainties in the career path. The method suggested by the sixth edition of the Ogden was adopted as to the discounting of the multiplier for contingencies other than mortality.

Blamire[347] awards. Although the standard approach to a claim for future loss   **5–124** of earnings is by way of the Tables, in some cases, the future is too uncertain to approach the calculation of future loss in that way. Such instances include where the prognosis is uncertain or the claimant's employment situation is volatile or both. Where there are too many imponderables to apply a multiplier/multiplicand approach it is appropriate to adopt a broad approach which takes its name from one of the leading cases. Essentially the trial judge is permitted to come to a figure for future loss which taking into account the uncertainties and the benefit of accelerated receipt is fair. But the danger of under-compensation if this method is used should be kept in mind. It was not appropriate where the claimant was a young man in good health and the trial judge had accepted he was likely to be in employment throughout his working life.[348]

Loss of career prospects. In *Herring v Ministry of Defence*[349] the claimant,   **5–125** who suffered severe spinal injuries in an accident for which the defendant was liable, would otherwise probably have embarked upon a career with the police, and in course of time risen to the rank of sergeant. At first instance a deduction of 25 per cent was applied to the result of an arithmetical calculation of his loss based upon notional salary as a police officer and a multiplier drawn from the Ogden Tables, to take account of the possibility that he would not have pursued such a career at all. An appeal was allowed. It was inappropriate to make such a large deduction once it had been decided that the claimant's probable career would have been with the police. The assessment did not necessitate application

---

[345] *Kemp & Kemp, The Quantum of Damages.*
[346] [2008] EWHC 134 (Q.B.). See also *Housecroft v Burnett* [1986] 1 All E.R. 332, CA and *Chase International Express Ltd v McRae* [2004] P.I.Q.R. P314, CA.
[347] *Blamire v South Cumbria Health Authority* [1993] P.I.Q.R. Q1, CA.
[348] *Bullock v Atlas Ward Structures Limited* [2008] EWCA Civ 194.
[349] [2004] 1 All E.R. 44, CA, para.5–119, above.

of the technique of percentage assessment for "loss of a chance" based on the likely actions of third parties, set out in *Allied Maples v Simmons & Simmons*.[350] Rather, where a career model had been chosen because it was itself the appropriate baseline and/or was one of a number of alternatives likely to give more or less similar results, the multiplier or multiplicand within the career model would be adjusted as appropriate to the particular claimant. On the facts, a discount of no more than 10 per cent would have been appropriate.

5–126   In contrast, where the evidence suggests that, but for the accident, there may have been an unusual turn of events which would have had a significant impact upon the claimant's earning capacity, then the court must make an assessment of the chance of that turn of events arising and its financial consequences. So where a nineteen-year-old claimant contended that in the absence of the accident she would have embarked upon a career as a dance teacher the judge was correct to assess the chance of her becoming a drama teacher and to apply the percentage chance to the assessment of future loss of earnings.[351]

5–127   In *Brown v MOD*[352] a 24-year-old woman was only eight weeks into her career as a soldier when she suffered an injury which led to the end of her career in the Army. She claimed loss of pension rights based on a 22-year career in the Army. The Court of Appeal held that in such a case the court should look at the chances of the claimant's career developing in one way or another. In the instant case there was a negligible risk that she would have left the Army after only six years of service but after that point other factors such as changes in her personal and family situation could influence her approach to continuing in a full-time military career. So the percentage chances of the claimant reaching various temporal milestones in her career were assessed as were the chances of her achieving various ranks in the Army and the loss of pension was calculated by applying those percentages.

5–128   **Smith v Manchester awards.** Occasionally, the claimant has returned to gainful employment either at the same rate of remuneration as at the date of the injury or at a lower rate but continues to suffer from residual disability. It is recognised that in such a case, if that employment were to end for any reason the claimant would suffer a loss in the sense of being thrown on the labour market and thereby in competition with other able-bodies persons for work. The current practice is to meet this loss with a lump sum award named after the decision in *Smith v Manchester Corporation*.[353] The factors usually taken into account in assessing the size of the award are the degree of residual disability and the risk of the claimant being forced onto the labour market.[354] The court must bear in mind the risk of overlap between damages for future loss of earnings and

---

[350] [1995] 1 W.L.R. 1602, CA, Ch.9, para.9–295, below. See Kwiatkowsa, "Lost Chance" 147 S.J. 684.

[351] *Doyle v Wallace* [1998] P.I.Q.R. Q146, CA; see too *Langford v Hebran* [2001] P.I.Q.R. Q13, CA.

[352] [2006] P.I.Q.R. Q9, CA.

[353] (1974) 17 K.I.R. 1, CA. See Chippindall, "An alternative way of calculating *Smith v Manchester*" in 2001 J.P.I.L. 37.

[354] *Moeliker v A. Reyrolle & Co Ltd* [1976] I.C.R. 253, CA.

damages for loss of earning capacity or handicap on the labour market.[355] The claimant must demonstrate a substantial risk of being forced onto the labour market as opposed to a negligible risk.[356] The starting point usually bears some relation to the claimant's annual net earnings.[357] Given the enhanced methodology in the sixth edition of the Ogden tables[358] it may well be that separate awards for disadvantage on the labour market become less common.

A *Smith v Manchester* award should not be confused with a *Blamire* award.[359] **5–129** The latter is appropriate where there is a continuing loss of earnings, but the evidence is too uncertain to approach the assessment thereof on a conventional multiplier/multiplicand basis, whereas a *Smith v Manchester* award is contingent future loss dependent on the claimant losing his current employment and finding himself at a disadvantage in the labour market. The two may be combined but they are conceptually distinct.[360]

Lost years claims. A living claimant, whose injuries have reduced his life **5–130** expectancy, can bring a claim for damages for loss of earnings in respect of the "lost years" from his working life caused by that reduction in his life expectancy following the decisions of the House of Lords in *Pickett v British Rail Engineering Ltd*[361] and *Gammell v Wilson*.[362] Although there would clearly be difficulties as to proof and assessment, the is no reason in principle to prevent awards being made in such cases. Later in *Croke v Wiseman*,[363] the Court of Appeal decided that in the case of a young child with a reduced life expectancy no such award could be made and any damages for loss of earnings would be restricted to the period of time during which the claimant would live. In *Whipps Cross University Hospital NHS Trust v Iqbal*,[364] the view was expressed that *Croke v Wiseman* was inconsistent with the earlier House of Lords' decisions but that it was nevertheless binding and that any error, if there was an error, should be corrected by the House of Lords.

Periodical payments. In cases involving substantial damages in respect of **5–131** future pecuniary losses, especially in cases involving the need for substantial care, an award of damages as a lump sum at the date of the trial may well be unsatisfactory. There may be difficulties of calculating such a sum particularly given an uncertain life expectancy. There may be a risk that the money will be spent inappropriately and not used to meet the claimant's future needs. Even if

---

[355] *Clarke v Rotax Aircraft* [1975] 1 W.L.R. 132, CA.
[356] *Moeliker v A. Reyrolle & Co Ltd*, n.354 above.
[357] In *Dhaliwal v Personal Representatives of Hunt* [1995] P.I.Q.R. Q56, Auld L.J. indicated his agreement with a remark of Megaw L.J. in *Easton v Concrete (Northern) Ltd*, Unreported, CA, that the assessment of damages under this head involves "nothing more than a guess". Examples of awards for "*Smith v Manchester* damages" can be found in Kemp & Kemp, *The Quantum of Damages*.
[358] As to which see para.5–121, above.
[359] See para.5–128, above.
[360] *Ronan v Sainsbury's Supermarkets Ltd* [2006] EWCA Civ 1074.
[361] [1982] A.C. 136.
[362] [1982] A.C. 27.
[363] [1982] 1 W.L.R. 71, CA.
[364] [2008] P.I.Q.R. P9, CA

invested there may not be a sufficient return to allow the claimant's needs to be met throughout his or her life. From the defendant's perspective there is the risk that the claimant may die prematurely and damages will thus have been paid in respect of future needs which, in fact, never arose. These difficulties were initially met to an extent by the development of structured settlements[365] which were designed to provide regular payments from an annuity purchased from a life assurance company. Latterly, the court has been given power to impose an order for future periodical payments with the same ultimate purpose, that is, providing regaulr payments over the claimant's life to meet the costs of care.

5–132   Section 2(1) of the Damages Act 1996, which came into force on April 1, 2005, provides that in relation to claims for future financial loss, the court shall consider whether to make an order under which the damages are to take the form of periodical payments.[366] Power is given to make such an order in respect of heads of loss other than future financial loss, provided the parties consent.[367] An award under the section cannot be made unless the court is satisfied that continuity of payment is "reasonably secure".[368] Continuity of payment is to be regarded as reasonably secure if: (a) it is protected by a guarantee for a public sector settlement; (b) where payment is protected by a guarantee under the financial services compensation scheme; or (c) where the source of payments is a government or health service body.[369]

5–133   When deciding between a lump sum payment or periodical payments, the court is to consider "all the circumstances of the case and in particular the form of award which best meets the claimant's needs, having regard to the factors set out in the practice direction".[370] The reader is referred to the Rules for the detailed provisions. Model orders for use in periodical payments cases were approved by the High Court in *Thompstone v Tameside*[371] with the specific intention that they be used as the basis for periodical payments orders in future cases.

5–134   **Indexation of periodical payments.** One important issue is the index by reference to which future periodical payments are to be assessed. Although the default position under the Act is that they should very by reference to the Retail

---

[365] For consideration of structured settlements reference should be made to *Charlesworth and Percy on Negligence* 11th edn para.4–108.
[366] The procedural rules governing periodical payments are set out in CPR Pt 41.4.
[367] The Damages Act 1996 s.2(2).
[368] The Damages Act 1996 s.2(3).
[369] The Damages Act 1996 s.2(4).
[370] See CPR 41.7. The relevant Practice Direction is at PD 41B of the CPR. The PD says the factors to which the court shall have regard include the scale of the periodical payments, taking into account any finding of contributory negligence; the form of award preferred by the claimant (together with the reasons for that preference); and the form of award preferred by the defendant (together with the reasons). For an example of in which it was decided that periodical payments were appropriate to cover future care costs, see *Godbold v Mahmood* [2006] P.I.Q.R. Q70 at Q80. See also *Walton v Calderdale Healthcare NHS Trust* [2006] P.I.Q.R. Q3 (local authority failed to discharge the burden of showing that it would be contributing to the claimant's future care needs in a way that should have an impact on the calculation of future periodical payments).
[371] [2008] EWHC 2948 (Q.B.).

Prices Index, there is provision for the court to order otherwise. Awards for periodical payments are most likely to be made in cases where a severely injured claimant has ongoing care needs and the cost of meeting such needs has historically been greater than the changes in retail prices. On the appeal in *Thompstone*,[372] it was accepted that, rather than the RPI, the payments for the claimant's future care should be increased by reference to a sub-set of the Annual Survey of Hours and Earnings[373]: Waller L.J., giving the judgment of the court, said:

> "We hope that as a result of these proceedings the National Health Service, and other defendants in proceedings that involve catastrophic injury, will now accept that the appropriateness of indexation of the basis of ASHE 6115 has been established after an exhaustive review of all the possible objections to its use, both in itself and as applied to the recovery of costs of care and case management. It will not be appropriate to reopen that issue in any future proceedings unless the defendant can produce evidence and argument significantly different from, and more persuasive than, that which has been deployed in the present cases. Judges should not hesitate to strike out any defences that do not meet that requirement."

Although the above passage relates to periodical payments orders in respect of care, in *Sarwar v Ali and Motor Insurers' Bureau*,[374] the High Court ordered the indexation of a periodical payments order in respect of damages for future loss of earnings should be in relation to the ASHE aggregated earnings data for male full time employees. In a case involving a specific occupation a more specific sub-set of the ASHE data could no doubt be adopted as appropriate.

(iv) *Deduction of benefits.*

Generally. In Lord Reid's classic statement[375]:   **5–135**

> "Two questions can arise. First, what did the plaintiff lose as a result of the accident? What are the sums which he would have received but for the accident but which by reason of the accident he can no longer get? And, secondly, what are the sums which he did in fact receive as a result of the accident but which he would not have received if there had been no accident? And then the question arises whether the latter sums must be deducted from the former in assessing the damages."

Payments made under insurance policies. Where a claimant has purchased   **5–136**
accident insurance so that he receives a payment from a the insurance company after sustaining injuries, the payment made by the insurance company is not deducted from the damages payable by the defendant whose negligence caused the injuries. This principle was established in *Bradburn v G.W. Ry*[376] on the grounds that it was not the happening of the accident which caused the benefit to

---

[372] [2008] P.I.Q.R. Q2, CA. See also Leech and Sands, "The post-Thompstone landscape" P.I.L.J. (2009) No.72 and Piears and Potter "The Thompstone effect" 158 N.L.J. 1247.
[373] ASHE is compiled by the Office of National Statistics and provides information about the levels, distribution and make-up of earnings and hours paid for employees within industries, occupations and regions.
[374] [2007] EWHC 1255, (Q.B.).
[375] *Parry v Cleaver* [1970] A.C. 1 at 13.
[376] (1874) L.R. 10 Ex. 1.

the claimant but the purchasing of the insurance. The decision was endorsed by the House of Lords in *Parry v Cleaver*[377] where the principle was bolstered by the ruling that the tortfeasor should not benefit from the claimant's prudence. In *Page v Sheerness Steel*,[378] payments made under a permanent health insurance contract taken out by the claimant's employers, the defendant, as part of the claimant's employment package and in respect of which the claimant had not paid the premiums, were deducted against the damages for loss of earnings payable by the defendant. Similarly, in *Hussain v New Taplow Paper Mills Ltd*,[379] the claimant received payments under an insurance scheme to which he had not contributed. The payments were treated as sick pay and were deducted against the claim for loss of earnings.

5-137 **Payments from employers.** Where the claimant receives payment of wages as of right from his employer following injury, irrespective of whether the payment be described as sick pay or otherwise, the payments made fall to be deducted from any claim for loss of earnings.[380] It is common for employers to insert clauses into contracts of employment whereby in the event of an accident caused by a third party incapacitating the employee the amount of the employee's normal earnings will be advanced by way of a loan repayable in the event of the employee receiving damages from the tortfeasor. In *Dennis v London Passenger Transport Board*,[381] Denning J. awarded damages for loss of earnings where the claimant was under a moral obligation but not a legal obligation to repay money advanced by his employer. In *Williams v BOC Gases Ltd*,[382] an ex gratia payment made by the claimant's employer, the defendant, was deducted against the claimant's claim for damages for personal injuries.

5-138 **Gratuitous payments made by third parties.** On the grounds that the tortfeasor should not benefit from the benevolence of others, gratuitous payments made to claimants by charities and other third parties are not taken into account in assessing damages.[383] So, in *Redpath v Belfast & County Down Ry*,[384] payments to the victim of a railway disaster from a distress fund raised by public contribution were not deducted from the award of damages.

5-139 **Pensions.** The state retirement pension is not taken into account in assessing damages.[385] Disablement pensions, irrespective of whether they are contributory or non-contributory, are not taken into account in assessing damages.[386] The fact

---

[377] [1970] A.C. 1.
[378] [1996] P.I.Q.R. Q26. The decision at first instance was approved when the case reached the House of Lords [1999] A.C. 1; see too *Gaca v Pirelli General Plc* [2004] 1 W.L.R. 2683, CA.
[379] [1988] A.C. 514.
[380] *Hussain v New Taplow Paper Mills Ltd* [1988] A.C. 514 at 530, per Lord Bridge.
[381] [1948] 1 All E.R. 779.
[382] [2000] P.I.Q.R. Q253, CA. See also *Gaca v Pirelli General Plc* n.389 above.
[383] *Parry v Cleaver* [1970] A.C. 1 per Lord Reid at 14. In *Gaca v Pirelli General Plc* n.48 above, a distinction was drawn between payments made by an employer to an employee to compensate for the consequences of an injury and payments made by a third party out of sympathy for the injured person's plight.
[384] [1947] N.I. 167. See also *Liffen v Watson* [1940] 1 K.B. 556, CA and *Williams v BOC Gases Ltd* [2000] P.I.Q.R. Q253, CA.
[385] *Hewson v Downs* [1970] 1 Q.B. 73.
[386] *Parry v Cleaver* [1970] A.C. 1.

that the employer is also the defendant is irrelevant.[387] In *Longdon v British Coal Corporation*,[388] following *Parry v Cleaver*,[389] the House of Lords held that incapacity payments and disablement pension payments should not be taken into account in a claim for loss of earnings. In respect of a claim for loss of pension, however, such payments as were to be made after the normal date of retirement should be taken into account.

Social security benefits. The Social Security (Recovery of Benefits) Act   **5–140**
1997[390] governs the deduction of benefits paid by the Department for Work and Pensions (DWP) from damages recoverable in personal injury litigation. From October 6, 1997,[391] all compensation payments[392] made in consequence of an accident, injury[393] or disease by or on behalf of a person liable or alleged to be liable in respect of that accident, injury or disease are subject to deductions in respect of relevant benefits paid to the injured person by the DWP.

The relevant payments are those paid in the five years immediately following the accident or injury in question[394] or, in the case of a disease, five years beginning with the date on which the claimant first claimed a listed benefit in consequence of the disease.[395] If a compensation payment is made in final discharge of the claim before the end of the five year period then the period ends for the purpose of calculating recoverable benefits when that payment is made.[396]

Before a person makes a compensation payment he must apply to the Secretary   **5–141**
of State for a certificate of recoverable benefits.[397] The Compensation Recovery Unit is the section of the Department of Social Security responsible for issuing the certificates of recoverable benefits.[398] The certificate specifies the amount of each recoverable benefit paid or likely to be paid on or before a specified date and if the benefit is likely to be paid in the future the certificate specifies the rate and period for which the benefit is or is likely to be paid.[399]A person who makes a compensation payment is liable to pay to the Secretary of State an amount equal to the total amount of recoverable benefits.[400] The compensator can deduct from specific heads of damage the amount due to the Secretary of State in respect of

---

[387] *Smoker v London Fire Authority* [1991] 2 A.C. 502.
[388] [1998] A.C. 653.
[389] [1970] A.C. 1.
[390] See also the Social Security (Recovery of Benefits) Regulations 1997 (SI 1997/2205).
[391] The Social Security (Recovery of Benefits) Act 1997 (Commencement) Order 1997 (SI 1997/2085 (c.83)).
[392] Exempted payments are set out in Sch.1 of the 1997 Act, above and in reg.2 of the 1997 Regulations, above.
[393] In *Rand v East Dorset HA* [2001] P.I.Q.R. Q1 there was a negligent failure by a hospital to inform prospective parents that their child would be born with Down's Syndrome. Newman J. held that the DWP benefits paid were not paid as consequence of any injury and therefore fell outside the Social Security (Recovery of Benefits) Act 1997.
[394] 1997 Act s.3(1).
[395] 1997 Act s.3(2).
[396] 1997 Act s.3(4).
[397] 1997 Act s.4(1).
[398] The address of the Compensation Recovery Unit is Durham House, Washington, Tyne and Wear, NE38 7SF.
[399] 1997 Act s.5(1).
[400] 1997 Act s.6(1).

specific recoverable benefits.[401] The heads of loss in question and the corresponding benefits are set out in a table to Sch.2 of the Act.

5–142 The compensator is liable to pay the amount of the recoverable benefits even if there is no claim for damages under the heads of compensation set out in the table. There is no deduction of benefits against damages under heads of loss which are not specified in the table. Accordingly, there is no deduction of benefits against damages for pain, suffering and loss of amenity. As the benefits deducted are those paid in the relevant period[402] there can be no deductions against damages for future loss of earnings, the cost of future care or loss of pension rights. The Compensation Recovery Unit provides general guidance as to which elements of compensation fall under the heads of compensation specified in Sch.2 of the Act.[403] In assessing damages the amount of any listed benefits paid or likely to be paid is disregarded.[404] In calculating interest on awards of damages for loss of earnings, the calculation is to be made on the total amount of damages for past loss of earnings in the relevant period before the deduction of the relevant DWP benefits.[405] Where, however, the benefits to be deducted from a head of loss exceed the damages payable for that head of loss the excess of benefits can also be deducted from any interest payable under that head of loss.[406]

The Act and the Regulations[407] made thereunder contain provisions relating to the payment of monies into court,[408] complex cases[409] and periodical payments.[410] Applications can be made to the Compensation Recovery Unit to review[411] certificates of recoverable benefits and appeals[412] can be brought to the Medical Appeal Tribunal against the issuing of certificates of recoverable benefits.

---

[401] 1997 Act s.8(1). In *Chatwin v Lowther* [2003] P.I.Q.R. Q84, CA the claimant's business ran at a loss but was able to make a contribution towards five sevenths of the rent due for her business premises, the award of that amount made in her action for personal injuries against the defendant was "compensation for earnings lost" for the purposes of Sch.II of the Social Security (Recovery of Benefits) Act 1997.

[402] See para.5–140, above.

[403] The guidance is available from the Compensation Recovery Unit, n.398 above and on the Dept. For Work and Pensions website.

[404] 1997 Act, s.17. The language of s.17 precludes any insistence that any of the benefits should be used to mitigate loss: *Eagle v Chambers (No.2)* [2004] 1 W.L.R. 3081, CA.

[405] *Wadey v Surrey CC* [2001] 1 W.L.R. 820, HL. On the question of interest generally, see paras 5–147 to 5–150.

[406] *Griffiths v British Coal Corp* [2001] 1 W.L.R. 1493.

[407] The Social Security (Recovery of Benefits) Regulations 1997 (SI 1997/2205).

[408] 1997 Act s.16. In *Hilton International Hotels (UK) Ltd v Smith* [2001] P.I.Q.R. P201 the defendants paid into court £6,000 and in addition indicated in the notice of payment into court that they had withheld in excess of £40,000 in relation to DSS benefits. The defendant's valuation of the claim was therefore expressed to be a gross sum of in excess of £46,000. The claimant accepted the payment into court. The certificate of recoverable benefits was appealed by the claimant and a nil certificate was issued. The claimant applied successfully to the court to recover from the defendant the balance of the sum of more than £46,000, which had been expressed to be the gross amount of compensation.

[409] 1997 Act s.18.

[410] 1997 Act s.18.

[411] 1997 Act s.10.

[412] 1997 Act s.11.

Housing benefits. Although, unlike various other forms of benefits, Parlia- **5–143** ment has not expressly provided that housing benefit should be disregarded, or otherwise taken into account, when calculating an award of damages, there is no reason why, applying general principles of recoverability, any housing benefit received should not be set against lost earnings. So, where the claimant was seriously injured in a road traffic accident and consequently out of work and in receipt of housing benefit, that benefit was to be deducted from his claim for lost earnings. It had been paid to him because of circumstances in which he was in need which had arisen as a result of the tort. If he was to be entitled to recover for loss of earnings without housing benefit being taken into account, he would be overcompensated.[413]

Payments under the Pneumoconiosis, etc. (Workers' Compensation) Act **5–144** **1979.** In *Ballantine v Newalls Insulation Company Ltd*,[414] the Court of Appeal held that payments made under the Pneumoconiosis, etc. (Workers' Compensation) Act 1979 should be set off against both damages for pecuniary and non-pecuniary losses in claims brought in respect of the same injury for which payments were made under the Act.

(v) *Provisional damages and interim awards*

Provisional damages. In an action for damages for personal injuries where **5–145** there is proved or admitted to be a chance that at some time in the future the claimant will, as a result of the defendant's fault, develop some serious disease or suffer a serious deterioration[415] in his mental or physical condition the court can award provisional damages.[416] In such cases, the court awards damages on the assumption that the claimant will not develop the disease or suffer the deterioration in his mental or physical condition but the claimant is entitled to apply for further damages at a future date if he does develop the disease or deterioration in his physical or mental condition.[417] If an award of provisional damages is sought then a claim for provisional damages must be pleaded in the particulars of claim[418] and the disease or deterioration in respect of which an application for provisional damages may be made must be specified.[419]

Save in some special cases,[420] the rules do not at present permit an indefinite postponement of the assessment of damages where the claim cannot be brought

---

[413] *Clenshaw v Tanner* [2002] EWCA Civ 1848, considering *Hodgson v Trapp* [1989] A.C. 807.
[414] [2001] I.C.R. 25, CA.
[415] In *Willson v Ministry of Defence* [1991] All E.R. 638, Scott Baker J. held that serious deterioration is something beyond ordinary deterioration and depends on the effect of the deterioration upon the particular claimant. In that case, osteoarthritis of the ankle, which was likely to deteriorate to the point of necessitating surgery, did not qualify for an award of provisional damages. Again in *Davies v Wilkie* [2008] EWHC 740 (Q.B.).
[416] The Senior Court Act 1981 s.32A and the County Courts Act 1984 s.51, respectively.
[417] The Senior Court Act 1981 s.32A(2) and the County Courts Act 1984 s.51(2), respectively.
[418] CPR PD 16, r.4.4(1) and CPR Pt 41.
[419] CPR PD 16, r.4.4(3).
[420] See, e.g. *A v National Blood Authority* [2002] Lloyds Reports Med. 487, per Burton J. at 492 who suggests examples where the only issue is future care, or where particular items of special damages cannot be resolved immediately and "guesswork would be unfortunate and inadvisable".

within the statutory criteria set out in s.32A of the Supreme Court Act 1981.[421] What can be done, where the necessary preconditions are met, is to make a variable periodical payments order in addition to an order for provisional damages.[422]

5-146   **Interim payments in personal injury claims.**[423] In claims for damages for personal injuries, where the general conditions for obtaining an interim payment are satisfied, the court may only make an order for an interim payment if: the defendant is insured in respect of the claim[424]; or the defendant's liability will be met either by an insurer under s.151 of the Road Traffic Act 1988[425] or under one of the Motor Insurers Bureau's[426] agreements relating to uninsured motorists[427]; or the defendant is a public body.[428] In cases where there are two or more defendants, if the court is satisfied that if the claim went to trial the claimant would recover substantial damages against at least one defendant (even if the court has not yet determined which one is liable) and each defendant satisfies one of the above criteria, then the court can make an order for an interim payment.[429] It is not necessary for a claimant to prove, or for the judge to consider, any particular purpose for which the interim payment is intended to be used.[430]

(vi) *Interest on awards*

5-147   **Generally.** The court has the power to award simple interest at such rate as the court thinks fit or as rules of court may provide on all or part of the debt or damages in respect of which judgment is given or payment is made before judgment for all or part of the period between the date when the cause of action arose and (a) in the case of any sum paid before judgment, the date of payment; and (b) in the case of the sum for which judgment is given, the date of the judgment.[431] As Lord Denning M.R. had observed in *Jefford v Gee*[432]:

> "interest should not be awarded as compensation for the damage done. It should only be awarded to a plaintiff for being kept out of money, which ought to have been paid to him."

---

[421] In *Adan v Securicor Custodial Services Ltd* [2005] P.I.Q.R. 79 the claimant's application for damages to be assessed "as and when his condition and prognosis changed" was refused, since the principle of finality of litigation did not permit an indefinite postponement of the assessment of damages, when "the prospect of any significant improvement in the claimant's mental health is largely speculative" and it was not merely uncertainty in quantifying an established head of loss which arose.
[422] See the Damages (Variation of Periodical Payments) Order 2004.
[423] For the general principles in relating to interim payments see para.5–57, above.
[424] CPR Pt 25.7(2)(a).
[425] See Ch.17, paras 17–02 to 17–05, below.
[426] See Ch.17, below.
[427] CPR Pt 25.7(2)(b).
[428] CPR Pt 25.7(2)(c).
[429] CPR Pt 25.7(3).
[430] *Stringman v McArdle* [1994] 1 W.L.R. 1653, CA.
[431] The Senior Courts Act s.35A in the High Court and, in the county courts, the County Courts Act 1984 s.69.
[432] [1970] 2 Q.B. 130 at 146. See Mann "On Interest. Compound Interest and Damages" in 101 L.Q.R. 30; Nelson-Jones, "Personal Injury Interest Calculation" in 82 L.S. Gaz. 1553.

Although the time whence a claimant has been kept out of money, in some cases, could well be taken as the date of letter before action, at its earlier point, or the date upon which the writ was served, at its latest,[433] the court still has an unfettered discretion in the matter. Indeed, a later date than that, when the cause of action arose, has been chosen on an occasion by the House of Lords.[434] When a claimant had not been kept out of his money, for example where he had been indemnified by his insurers, and if any interest awarded would inure to the benefit of the assured, such interest ought not to be awarded, because it would result otherwise in the assured being overcompensated.[435] Nevertheless, where a claimant was insured in respect of his losses and had recovered the same from his own insurers, he ought not to be precluded from being awarded interest in respect of that period, running from the date of the insurer's payment until judgment, whenever they are entitled to reclaim such sum of interest from the claimant, their insured person.[436]

In relation to a judgment for damages for personal injuries,[437] which exceeds   **5–148**
£200, judgment for simple interest shall be included in the sum for which judgment is given on all or part of the damages unless the court is satisfied that there are special reasons to the contrary.[438] These provisions were previously enacted in the Administration of Justice Act 1969 and guidelines as to the principles were laid down by the Court of Appeal in *Jefford v Gee*.[439] The current guidelines may be stated as follows:

(a) interest on special damages between the accrual of the cause of action and trial should be awarded at half the special account rate[440];

---

[433] *Jefford v Gee* [1970] 2 Q.B. 130 at 147.
[434] *General Tire & Rubber Co v Firestone Tyre & Rubber Co* [1975] 1 W.L.R. 819 (damages for infringement of a patent).
[435] See *Harbutt's "Plasticine" Ltd v Wayne Tank & Pump Co Ltd* [1970] 1 Q.B. 447 and the effect of that decision, as to interest, as explained in *H. Cousins & Co Ltd v D. & C. Carriers Ltd* [1971] 2 Q.B. 230 at 243, per Davies L.J. See Leigh-Jones and Pickering, "Fundamental Breach and Exemption Clauses, Damages and Interest" in 86 L.Q.R. 513.
[436] *H. Cousins & Co Ltd v D. & C. Carriers Ltd* [1971] 2 Q.B. 230.
[437] Personal injuries includes any disease and any impairment of a person's physical or mental condition pursuant to the Senior Courts Act 1981 s.35A(7) in the High Court and, in the county courts, the County Courts Act 1984 s.69(6).
[438] The Senior Courts Act 1981 s.35A in the High Court and, in the county courts, the County Courts Act 1984 s.69.
[439] [1970] 2 Q.B. 130. The guidelines have evolved through a series of cases including: *Cookson v Knowles* [1977] Q.B. 913, CA; *Pickett v British Rail Engineering Ltd* [1980] A.C. 136; *Birkett v Hayes* [1982] 1 W.L.R. 816, CA; and *Wright v BR Board* [1983] 2 A.C. 773.
[440] In *Dexter v Courtaulds* [1984] 1 W.L.R. 372, the CA held that in the generality of cases the *Jefford v Gee* guidelines should not be departed from. Where there were special reasons to depart from the guidelines the facts supporting the reasons should be pleaded. The special account rate is prescribed by the Lord Chancellor and is currently 6 per cent. It was eight per cent from February 1, 1993 until August 1, 1999 when it was decreased to seven per cent. It was then decreased to 6 per cent on February 1, 2002. Tables for calculating interest on special damages are to be found in *Facts and Figures* (Sweet & Maxwell). In calculating interest on damages for loss of earnings relevant recoverable DSS benefits are not to be deducted, see *Wadey v Surrey CC* [2000] 1 W.L.R. 820, HL. Where, however, the benefits to be deducted from a specific head of loss exceeds the damages for that head of loss then the excess of benefits can also be deducted from the interest payable on that head of loss: *Griffiths v British Coal Corp* [2001] 1 W.L.R. 1493, CA. In relation to the deduction of DWP benefits generally, see paras 5–140 to 5–142, above.

(b) no interest is allowed on damages for future losses such as loss of future earnings or loss of earning capacity;

(c) in respect of damages for pain, suffering and loss of amenity interest is awarded at two per cent from the date of service of the proceedings.[441]

5–149 In exceptional cases, such as when one party had been guilty of gross delay, the court might depart from the above suggestions by diminishing or increasing the award of interest or altering the periods for which it was allowed.[442] This suggested approach has been confirmed by the Court of Appeal in *Birkett v Hayes*,[443] where Tasker Watkins L.J., whilst accepting the fact that interest usually would run from the date of service of the writ, added that:

"the court may in its discretion abridge this period when it thinks it is just so to do. Far too often there is unjustifiable delay in bringing an action to trial. It is, in my view, wrong that interest should run during a time which can properly be called unjustifiable delay after the date of the writ. During that time the plaintiff will have been kept out of the sum awarded to him by his own fault. The fact that the defendants have had the use of the sum during the time is no good reason for excusing that fault and allowing interest to run during that time."

5–150 By s.329[444] of the Income and Corporation Taxes Act 1988, the interest awarded on damages for personal injuries is exempt from being regarded as income for any tax purposes. Since such exemption is intended to be for the benefit of the claimant, the court ought not, in consequence, seek to award some lower rate of interest.[445] In commercial cases also, a party who is awarded damages is prima facie entitled to interest at a reasonable rate from the date when the sum should have been paid, unless there is some very good reason shown for there to be an exception to that rule.[446]

Where the appellate court has increased the award of damages, in awarding interest on that increase of damages, credit should be given for the interest automatically allowable under the Judgments Act 1838.[447] In the case of a split trial in actions for personal injuries the award of interest under the Judgments Act 1838[448] runs from the date of the judgment, which quantified or recorded the damages payable to the plaintiff, and not from the date of the judgment, which merely determined the issue of liability.[449]

---

[441] This guideline was introduced in *Birkett v Hayes* [1982] 1 W.L.R. 816. An attempt to increase the rate to 3 per cent following the judgment of the House of Lords in *Wells v Wells* [1999] 1 A.C. 345 was rejected by the Court of Appeal in *L v Chief Constable of Staffordshire* [2000] P.I.Q.R. Q349, CA.

[442] e.g. *Chadwick v Parsons* [1971] 2 Lloyd's Rep. 49 (on appeal, this point was not raised: [1971] 2 Lloyd's Rep. 322).

[443] [1982] 1 W.L.R. 816 at 825, which was immediately adopted by Lord Denning M.R. in an addendum to his judgment. The appropriate guideline was adjusted accordingly.

[444] Which has replaced the like provisions of s.375A of the Income and Corporation Taxes Act 1970, as amended by the Finance Act 1971 s.19.

[445] *Mason v Harman* [1972] R.T.R. 1.

[446] *Panchaud Frères SA v R. Pagnan & Fratelli* [1974] 1 Lloyd's Rep. 394.

[447] *Cook v J. L. Kier & Co* [1970] 1 W.L.R. 774.

[448] s.17.

[449] *Thomas v Bunn* [1991] 1 A.C. 362. It is to be noted that it was held to be immaterial whether or not the liability judgment had directed payment of the damages to be assessed.

Part 36 of the Civil Procedure Rules 1998. Part 36 permits a claimant to **5–151** make an offer to settle the whole of a claim, part of it or any issue that arises in the claim.[450] A Pt 36 offer is treated as "without prejudice save as to costs"[451] and so no reference to the offer can be made to the trial judge until judgment has been given and the issue of costs is being decided.

Where a judgment is at least as advantageous to the claimant as the proposals contained in a claimant's Pt 36 offer, the court may order interest on the whole or part of any sum of money (excluding interest) awarded to the claimant at a rate not exceeding 10 per cent over base rate for some or all of the period from the latest date on which the defendant could have accepted the offer without the court's permission.[452] In such cases, the court will make the order for enhanced interest unless it considers unjust to do so. In considering the justice of the case the circumstances generally will be considered together with certain specific matters set out in the rule. Where the court awards such interest and also awards interest under any other power the total rate of interest may not exceed 10 per cent over base rate.[453]

(vii) *Consideration of other claims*

Domestic employer's right of damages for injury to employee, and **5–152** **husband's right of damages for loss of consortium.**[454] As from January 1, 1983 each of these actions, in respect of any such loss suffered, was abolished by s.2 of the Administration of Justice Act 1982.[455]

Exemplary damages: aggravated damages. Exemplary damages, although **5–153** principally compensatory in their nature, do contain an element of punishment, which is intended for the defendant to suffer. They are awarded to teach the defendant a lesson, whenever necessary, "that tort does not pay",[456] as well as to be a deterrent both to him and others, similarly minded, against any future repetition. On the other hand, aggravated damages are, in essence, solely compensatory. If the manner of the commission of the tort were such as to injure the claimant's pride and feelings of dignity any resultant exacerbation of the damage suffered could well be reflected in the higher award of damages, than would otherwise be the case, perhaps.[457] Aggravated damages can be awarded in

---

[450] CPR Pt 36.2.
[451] CPR Pt 36.13.
[452] CPR Pt 36.14
[453] CPR Pt 36.14(5).
[454] For a review of the earlier law, prior to abolition, see *Charlesworth on Negligence* (6th edn, 1977), paras 1450–1452.
[455] Which was brought into effect on the date stated, by virtue of the provisions of s.76(11).
[456] *Rookes v Barnard* [1964] A.C. 1129 at 1227, per Lord Devlin.
[457] *Rookes v Barnard* [1964] A.C. 1129 at 1221. See also *Broome v Cassell & Co Ltd* [1972] A.C. 1027 at 1071 and 1073, per Lord Hailsham L.C., and at 1085–1086, per Lord Reid. In *Ansell v Thomas* [1974] Crim.L.R. 31, it was indicated that the court may take into account such matters as the claimant's sensitivity to humiliation, etc., as well as the defendant's conduct. In *Richardson v Howie* [2005] P.I.Q.R. Q3 it was suggested that in cases of assault damages for injuries to feelings should not be categorised as aggravated damages bus should be part of basic compensatory damages.

any class of action and are not restricted to torts, such as trespass or assault.[458] They may even be awarded in consequence of additional suffering, as a result of the conduct of the defendant or his counsel at the trial, by what is said there.[459]

5-154   Unfortunately, many older authorities had done little maintain the important distinctions between these two different kinds of damages, and, in practice, it was not always easy to keep them apart effectively. In *Rookes v Barnard*,[460] the House of Lords made the distinction very plain. Unless exemplary damages were expressly authorised by statute,[461] they should be awarded only in two classes of cases, namely (a) one, which involved behaviour amounting to "oppressive, arbitrary or unconstitutional action by the servants of the government," and (b) one, where "the defendant's conduct has been calculated by him to make a profit for himself, which may well exceed the compensation payable to the plaintiff."[462] In *Broome v Cassell & Co Ltd*,[463] the position was confirmed.

5-155   In the result, exemplary damages can theoretically be awarded in actions of negligence but they are virtually unknown. In the past, they were known to have been given in cases of "wilful negligence," that is when the negligence was accompanied with an element of contempt of the claimant's rights and convenience. In one such case the defendant was required by the police to pull down a dilapidated building, adjoining the claimant's stable, but did so in such a reckless manner that a large piece of timber fell on the stable, stove in the roof and damaged the claimant's horse and cart. On the claimant objecting the defendant told the workmen to "work anyhow", as a result of which great quantities of bricks and rubble were thrown down onto the stable.[464]

---

[458] e.g. *Pratt v British Medical Association* [1919] 1 K.B. 244 (conspiracy); and *Williams v Settle* [1960] 1 W.L.R. 1072 (infringement of copyright) but cf. *Fielding v Variety Incorporated* [1967] 2 Q.B. 841 at 850, where it was held that damages for injurious falsehood could not include compensation for injured feelings. In *Kralj v McGrath* [1986] 1 All E.R. 54, Woolf J. rejected the concept of aggravated damages applying to a claim in respect of clinical negligence; cf. *Appleton and others v Garrett* [1996] P.I.Q.R. P1, where in a dental negligence context aggravated damages were awarded because the treatment was carried out without the consent of the claimants and therefore amounted to trespass to the person.

[459] *Broome v Cassell & Co Ltd* [1972] A.C. 1027 at 1085, per Lord Reid.

[460] [1964] A.C. 1129.

[461] The Law Reform (Miscellaneous Provisions) Act 1934 s.1(2) makes a reference to exemplary damages in that they may not be recovered in proceedings brought for the benefit of a deceased person's estate. On the contrary, the Reserve and Auxiliary Forces (Protection of Civil Interests) Act 1951 s.13(2) expressly authorises an award of such damages.

[462] *Rookes v Barnard* [1964] A.C. 1129 at 1226, per Lord Devlin.

[463] [1972] A.C. 1027.

[464] *Emblen v Myers* (1860) 6 H. & N. 54. In the course of the trial, during the argument, Pollock C.B. said: "It is very improbable that the question of motive should arise in an action for negligence; but if it does, the judge is warranted in telling the jury that if the defendant did not intend any wrong, they should limit their verdict to the damage really sustained; but if the injury was committed in an insolent way, they might take into consideration the motive and give exemplary damages" and Wilde B. said: "Suppose a servant, while driving, was in the act of pulling up to prevent running against some person, and his master said: 'Never mind drive on' might not the jury take that into consideration?" It was followed in *Bell v Midland Ry* (1861) 10 C.B. (N.S.) 287; *Thompson v Hill* (1870) L.R. 5 C.P. 564.

In respect of an award of aggravated damages, any reprehensible behaviour[465] of the claimant may have a countervailing effect on its *quantum*, although there would be none on the award of damages in respect of any personal injuries.[466] In *Thompson v Commissioner of Police of the Metropolis*,[467] the Court of Appeal indicated the guidance which should be given to a jury in assessing damages in cases of unlawful imprisonment and malicious prosecution.

Parasitic damages.[468] In *Horton v Colwyn Bay and Colwyn Urban District Council*,[469] Buckley L.J. said: **5–156**

> "If an actionable wrong has been done to the claimant he is entitled to recover all the damage resulting from that wrong, and nonetheless because he would have had no right of action for some part of the damage if the wrong had not also created a damage which was actionable."

This is now too wide a statement and reference should be made to the discussion of remoteness of damage earlier in this chapter for the considerations which determine the extent of damage that may be recoverable.[470] Nonetheless, the statement illustrates what is meant by parasitic damage. It is damage, in respect of which no action could have been maintained, had it stood alone, but which attaches itself to some actionable item of damage, as it were as a host, in order for recovery to be permitted. The situation can be illustrated by the facts of *Malcolm v Broadhurst*,[471] although the question of parasitic damages was not actually considered there. The claimant, who had a vulnerable personality, and her husband were injured in a motor vehicle, which was caused by the defendant's negligence. As a consequence they each sustained personal injuries. Her injuries prevented her from following her full-time employment in a newspaper office, but because her husband could not work for the same reason, she was also denied the part-time secretarial work that she had been accustomed to do for him in his self-employed business. It was held that, whilst she could recover damages in respect of her injuries and loss of full-time wages, she could not do so in respect of her part-time wages. It was considered that, for her to have succeeded in such a claim, would have been "an unwarrantable extension of the present law."[472]

---

[465] *Broome v Cassell & Co Ltd* [1972] A.C. 1027 at 1071, per Lord Hailsham L.C.
[466] *Lane v Holloway* [1968] 1 Q.B. 379.
[467] [1997] 2 All E.R. 762, CA.
[468] See *McGregor on Damages* (17th edn 2003) Ch.6, para.6–110 for criticism of the term, and further discussion.
[469] [1908] 1 K.B. 327 at 341.
[470] para.5–01 et seq., above.
[471] [1970] 3 All E.R. 508. See Dobson, "Eggshell Reasoning" in 127 New L.J. 767; Rowe, "The Demise of the Thin Skull Rule?" in 40 M.L.R. 377.
[472] *Malcolm v Broadhurst* [1970] 3 All E.R. 508 at 512, Geoffrey Lane J. added: "It seems to me that the only way in which the defendant could be made liable under this head be by saying that he must take his victims as he finds them not only in relation to their physical infirmities but also in relation to their infirmities of employment. . . . To make the defendant liable for the unforeseeable effects of the accident on the special and unforeseeable circumstances of the wife's employment would be to go beyond the proper limits of compensation."

5–157   It must now be very doubtful that a doctrine of parasitic damage survives. The practical necessity for it is difficult to see when, in novel situations, the court has to consider the scope of the defendant's duty. Either there was a duty, the scope of which embraced the damage in question, or there was not. To return to *Malcom v Broadhurst*, it would now be said that the scope of the defendant's duty did not extend to compensate those who depended upon the husband's business for their own earnings. In *Spartan Steel and Alloys Ltd v Martin & Co (Contractors) Ltd*,[473] it was urged on the claimant's behalf that the economic damages suffered, which were not recoverable in themselves, could be so if they could be tacked on to a claim for physical damage and were foreseeable. Lord Denning M.R. expressed the view that there was no such doctrine at all but, even if there were, it did not apply to an action in negligence.[474]

---

[473] [1973] Q.B. 27.
[474] *Spartan Steel and Alloys Ltd v Martin & Co (Contractors) Ltd* [1973] Q.B. 27 at 35 and to the same effect see at 49, per Lawton L.J.

PROOF AND CAUSATION

1.—Proof: Generally

(A) The burden and standard of proof

Generally. In an action for negligence the burden of proof falls upon the **6–01** claimant[1] to establish each element of the tort.[2] The standard of proof is the usual standard of the balance of probabilities applied in all civil claims.[3] It is for the claimant to lead evidence of the facts on which the claim is based.[4] That evidence will consist in facts either proved or admitted, together with expert evidence[5] if appropriate and necessary. At the end of the evidence[6] questions will arise: (1)

---

[1] See *Donoghue v Stevenson* [1932] A.C. 562 at 622, per Lord Macmillan.

[2] In respect of which, see Ch.1, para.1–34, above.

[3] See, e.g. *Brown v Rolls-Royce Ltd* [1960] 1 W.L.R. 210 at 215, per Lord Denning; *Gardiner v Motherwell Machinery and Scrap Co Ltd* [1961] 1 W.L.R. 1424 (a decision by the HL about causation but the same degree of proof was held to be required). The standard of proof is not the balance of *improbability*: see para.6–17, below.

[4] In *Hughes v Liverpool City Council, The Times*, March 30, 1988, the CA held that where a claimant needs to prove that a defendant either knew or was on notice that equipment was defective, neither fact could be inferred from the failure of the defendant to call any evidence. In *Whalley v Montracon Ltd* [2005] EWCA Civ 1383, it was observed that the claimant does not have to make every piece of the evidential jigsaw fit. Even if an aspect of the evidence was without explanation the court could find that proof had achieved the civil standard. (A claim for damages for personal injury as a result of exposure to excessive vibration from work equipment, where one element in the claimant's description of symptoms was potentially inconsistent with a diagnosis of Hand Arm Vibration Syndrome).

[5] See Pt 35 of the Civil Procedure Rules and Ch.9, para.9–05, below, in relation to the admission of expert evidence generally.

[6] In relation to the end of the claimant's case and a submission of "no case to answer" see para.6–05, below.

whether, on that evidence, negligence may be reasonably inferred; (2) whether, assuming it may be reasonably inferred, negligence is in fact inferred[7]; and (3) whether a causative link is established between any proven negligence and the injury, loss or damage claimed.

6–02   These questions do not necessarily arise for decision at the same time. The first question usually arises at the end of the claimant's case, although it can also arise at the end of all the evidence, and is a question of law. The second question arises at the end of all the evidence and is a question of fact.[8] The third question is a question of mixed law and fact. During the course of a trial, whilst the state of the evidence as to some particular issue may impose a provisional burden of proof upon the defendant to rebut an inference or presumption to which the evidence gives rise, the legal burden of proof continues to rest throughout upon the claimant as the person alleging negligence.[9] By way of example, where an accident occured as a result of a spillage of yoghurt on a shop floor, there was a legal burden upon the claimant to prove the primary facts, but, that having been done, an evidential burden was imposed upon the defendant, as occupier of the shop, to show that the accident did not happen through any want of care on its part.[10] It has been said that in order to be able to draw an inference of negligence, the circumstances should be such that it could not be said that the type of accident was usual without negligence.[11]

6–03   **Applying the burden of proof.** The burden of proof does not require the claimant to eliminate each and every way in which what is complained of happened without fault on the part of the defendant, but the evidence led must allow the court to proceed beyond pure guesswork so as to reach an appropriate legal inference:

> "the dividing line between conjecture and inferences is often a very difficult one to draw. A conjecture may be plausible, but it is of no legal value, for its essence is that it is a mere guess. An inference in the legal sense, on the other hand, is a deduction from the evidence, and if it is a reasonable deduction it may have the validity of legal proof."[12]

---

[7] *Metropolitan Ry v Jackson* (1877) 3 App.Cas. 193 at 197, per Lord Cairns; *Bolton v Stone* [1951] A.C. 850 at 859 per Lord Porter; CPR 1998 Pt 35.

[8] *Ryder v Wombwell* (1868) L.R. 4 Ex. 32, per Willes J., quoted by Lord Blackburn in *Metropolitan Ry v Jackson*, above, at 207. "It has always been considered a question of law to be determined by the judge, subject, of course, to review, whether there is evidence which, if it is believed, and the counter evidence, if any, not believed, would establish the facts in controversy. It is for the jury to say whether and how far the evidence is to be believed."

[9] *Brown v Rolls-Royce Ltd* [1960] 1 W.L.R. 210 at 215, 216, per Lord Denning.

[10] *Ward v Tesco Stores Ltd* [1976] 1 W.L.R. 810, CA.

[11] *Brazier v Dolphin Fairway Ltd* [2005] EWCA Civ 1469 (no inference of negligence where an employee was injured lifting a stack of palletts, the factual evidence was limited and there was no expert evidence; *Sutton v Masters Performing Arts College Ltd* [2009] EWCA Civ 1440 (no inference of negligence where a dancer was injured when her teacher pressed her leg too far back in the course of cooling down); *Hall v Holker Estate Co Ltd* [2008] EWCA Civ 1422 (the evidence of an occupier's lack of care called for an answer when an unsecured portable goal frame tipped and fell on the claimant while he was keeping goal).

[12] per Lord Macmillan in *Jones v G.W. Ry* (1930) 144 L.T. 194 at 202. For an example of legal inference sometimes thought to fall near to the boundary of what is permitted, see *McGhee v National Coal Board* [1973] 1 W.L.R. 1, para.6–42, below.

Particular factual situations give rise to their own characteristic problems in **6–04** applying the burden of proof. These are perhaps best considered in detail when we turn later to the types of case in question. Suffice it to note here the problems that arise in cases of clinical negligence when the claimant contends that he has lost the chance of a better medical result[13]; or where the breach of duty alleged is an error of omission and the court has to decide what course of events would have followed had the error not occurred[14]; also the cases where it is alleged that solicitors' negligence has caused the claimant to lose the opportunity of some gain[15]; or exposed him to the risk of loss[16]; or where it is said other advice than was given would have led him,[17] or a third party,[18] to act differently. Similar problems can arise in claims against other professionals such as accountants,[19] and valuers.[20] It should be noted that while it is superficially attractive, when seeking to assess damages for loss of a chance as a result of tort, to compare the principles which apply upon a breach of contract, formidable difficulties lie in the way of the analogy.[21]

Submission of no case to answer. For many years a judge has had a **6–05** discretion, before ruling on a submission by the defence at the end of the claimant's case that there was no case to answer, to require the defendant to elect whether evidence will be called or not.[22] If the election is put and the defendant decides to call evidence the case continues and the submission can, if appropriate, be repeated once all the evidence is before the court.[23] The practice has been justified on the basis that if a ruling in favour of the defendant was reversed on appeal, the expense and delay of a new trial would be saved, because the defendant's evidence would be before the court.[24] If the judge does not put the defendant to an election and the submission fails, there is no bar to evidence

---

[13] See *Hotson v East Berkshire Area Health Authority* [1987] A.C. 750 (where the question was whether avascular necrosis to the hip joint of a 13-year-old would have occurred even if hospital treatment had been quicker); also *Gregg v Scott* [2005] 2 A.C. 176, para.6–56, below.
[14] See, in the context of clinical negligence, *Bolitho v City and Hackney Health Authority* [1998] A.C. 232 at Ch.9, para.9–143, below, also *Chester v Afshar* para.6–54, below.
[15] See, e.g. *Hartle v Lacys* [1997] C.L.Y. 3839, CA, at Ch.9, para.9–297, below.
[16] See, e.g. *Swindle v Harrison*, The Times, April 17, 1997, CA, at Ch.9, para.9–290, below.
[17] See, e.g. *Bristol and West Building Society v Mothew* [1997] 2 W.L.R. 436, CA, at Ch.9, para.9–289, below.
[18] *Allied Maples Group v Simmons & Simmons* [1995] 1 W.L.R. 1602, CA.
[19] See again, *Allied Maples Group v Simmons & Simmons* [1995] 1 W.L.R. 1602, CA, and see Ch.9, below, para.9–50.
[20] *South Australia Asset Management Corp v York Montague Ltd* [1997] A.C. 191, Ch.8, para.9–328, below.
[21] *Hotson v East Berkshire Health Authority* [1987] A.C. 750 at 782, per Lord Bridge. But see, e.g. per Arden L.J. in the CA in *Johnson v Gore Wood* [2003] EWCA Civ 1728, at para.[91], para.6–58, below.
[22] *Marbé v G. Edwardes (Daly's Theatre) Ltd* [1928] 1 K.B. 269; *Alexander v Rayson* [1936] 1 K.B. 169 at 178; *Young v Rank* [1950] 2 K.B. 510.
[23] *Parry v Aluminium Corp Ltd* [1940] W.N. 44; *Laurie v Raglan Building Co Ltd* [1942] 1 K.B. 152; *Alexander v Rayson* [1936] 1 K.B. 169 at 178. In *W.H. Müller & Co v Ebbw Vale Steel Co* (1936) 52 T.L.R. 655, the judge ruled that there was no case to answer, without requiring an undertaking from the defendants to refrain from calling evidence, but in view of later decisions this must be taken to be erroneous.
[24] See *Practice Direction (Submission of No Case)* [1962] 1 W.L.R. 227, per Parker L.C.J.

being led as if no submission has ever been made.[25] However, it should usually be the case that a defendant making a submission of no case should be put to an election whether to call evidence, although there may be rare cases in which an exception is justified.[26]

Illustrations

6–06   The circumstances were not sufficiently exceptional to justify ruling on a submission of no case, without putting the defendant to an election, where the trial judge considered that nothing in the defendant's evidence, whatever it might be, would affect the view he had formed of the claimant's case[27]; however, the judge was entitled not to put the defendant to an election in a clinical negligence claim, where the case turned on expert evidence and there was nothing in the defendant's evidence which could affect the decision whether the claimant had no prospect of success.[28] The test on a submission is whether there is a case to answer, that is whether realistically there is no basis upon which a jury, properly directed, could find in favour of the claimant on the evidence adduced.[29] If the defendant has elected to call no evidence the issue for the judge is not whether there is any real or reasonable prospect that the claimant's case will be made out, but the straightforward one whether or not the claimant has established the case on a balance of probabilities.[30]

(B) Proof by inference

6–07   **Facts more consistent with negligence than other causes.** There is evidence of negligence if the facts proved and the inferences to be drawn from them are more consistent with negligence on the part of the defendant than with other causes.[31] Negligence may be reasonably inferred from facts which make it more probable that it was negligence on the part of the defendant, that caused the damage in question, than any other cause.

---

[25] *Yuill v Yuill* [1945] P. 15.

[26] See *Karia v ICS Management Services Ltd* [2001] EWCA Civ 1025, (personal injury claim where at trial the claimant limited her case on liability to allegations of harassment and the judge at first instance allowed a submission of no case without putting the defendant to an election); also *Graham v Chorley Borough Council* [2006] P.I.Q.R. P367, CA.

[27] *Benham v Kythira Investments Ltd* (2004) 154 New L.J. 21, CA.

[28] *Nur Saed v Ealing Hospital NHS Trust* [2002] Lloyd's Rep. Med. 121. See also *Worsley v Tambrands* [2000] P.I.Q.R. P95 (submission of no case: no election required where there was a narrow issue determinative of the action which could properly be decided on the claimant's evidence alone).

[29] See *Bentley v Jones Harris & Co* [2001] EWCA Civ 1724.

[30] *Miller v Cawley, The Times*, September 6, 2002, CA.

[31] *Ellor v Selfridge & Co Ltd* (1930) 46 T.L.R. 236; *McCowan v Stott* (1923) 99 L.J.K.B. 357, per Atkin L.J. See also per Willes J. in *Daniel v Metropolitan Ry* (1868) L.R. 3 C.P. 216, reversed L.R. 5 H.L. 45: "It is necessary for the plaintiff to establish by evidence circumstances from which it may fairly be inferred that there is reasonable probability that the accident resulted from the want of some precaution which the defendants might and ought to have resorted to." See further the discussion of "unknown causes" at para.6–85, below.

ILLUSTRATIONS

Negligence has been inferred: where a ship under way ran into a ship at her **6–08** moorings in broad daylight[32]; where a vehicle mounts the footpath and collides with a pedestrian, or a structure, such as a lamp-post[33]; where a car in motion overturns for no apparent cause[34]; or strikes a pedestrian in the back when he is walking along the highway at night[35]; where a passenger in a train is injured by its sudden and violent stopping,[36] or starting[37]; where a tramcar, driven along a narrow road, crushed a man who had moved his truck to the side of the road in order to allow the tramcar to pass[38]; where a bus was so driven that one of its wheels was wrenched off by tramlines in the highway and it overturned.[39]

In a clinical negligence claim, it was held that where the claimants's left **6–09** testicle atrophied as a result of ischaemic orchitis, shortly after an operation to remove a hernia, the most probable cause of his condition was the surgeon's lack of care when removing the lipoma, even though expert evidence on both sides was to the effect that the operation was a standard one and the risk of atrophy much less than one per cent. The surgeon himself was unable to remember the details of the operation and could not explain why the atrophy should have occurred.[40]

An employee's claim for damages for breach of statutory duty, which **6–10** depended upon proof of a defect in a wrench, succeeded where, as between two possible but unlikely explanations for the accident, the employee's was the most probable.[41]

Disputing the inference. Of course, it is always open to the defendant to call **6–11** evidence contradicting or nullifying any inference which is sought to be drawn from the claimant's evidence. Moreover, if the claimant's evidence is only

---

[32] *The City of Peking* (1888) 14 App.Cas. 40; *The Annot Lyle* (1886) 11 P.D. 114; *The Merchant Prince* [1892] P. 179.
[33] *Walton (Isaac) & Co v Vanguard Motorbus Co* (1908) 25 T.L.R. 13; *Barnes Urban District Council v London General Omnibus Co* (1908) 100 L.T. 115; *Ellor v Selfridge & Co Ltd* (1930) 46 T.L.R. 236.
[34] *Halliwell v Venables* (1930) 99 L.J.K.B. 353.
[35] *Page v Richards and Draper* (Unreported) referred to in *Tart v Chitty* [1933] 2 K.B. 453 at 457.
[36] *Angus v London, Tilbury and Southend Ry* (1906) 22 T.L.R. 222.
[37] *Metropolitan Ry v Delaney* (1921) 90 L.J.K.B. 721.
[38] *Leaver v Pontypridd Urban District Council* (1911) 76 J.P. 31, HL.
[39] *Lilly v Tilling* (1912) 57 S.J. 59.
[40] *Betts v Berkshire Health Authority* [1997] 8 Med. L.R. 87. See also, in the context of a claim based on industrial disease, *Gardiner v Motherwell Machinery Co* [1961] 1 W.L.R. 1424 (when a man, who has not previously suffered from a disease, contracts such disease after being subjected to conditions likely to cause it, and when he shows that it starts in a way typical of disease caused by such conditions, there is a *prima facie* presumption that his disease was caused by those conditions).
[41] *Jakto Transport Ltd v Hall* [2006] EWCA Civ 1327 (although the appeal was dismissed the CA commented that the trial judge's process of reasoning was flawed, in that he had decided to accept the claimant's evidence without first considering the expert evidence as to the likelihood of the accident happening as the claimant described).

equally consistent with negligence on the part of the defendant, as against other causes, the claim cannot succeed:

> "The party seeking to recover compensation for damage must make out that the party against whom he complains was in the wrong. The burden of proof is clearly upon him, and he must show that the loss is to be attributed to the negligence of the opposite party. If at the end he leaves the case in even scales and does not satisfy the court that it was occasioned by the negligence or default of the other party, he cannot succeed."[42]

6–12   Consequently, where the claimant crossed in front of a bus in sight of the driver but then suddenly turned back while his attention was elsewhere and was run over by his vehicle when he set off, there was no evidence of negligence: the evidence was equally consistent with the existence or non-existence of negligence on the part of the driver.[43] Similarly, where the claimant, aged 13, could establish that he had been struck by the defendant's motorcar and that the defendant had not seen him, but other evidence suggested that the defendant had been driving normally prior to the accident, negligence was not established.[44]

6–13   In a negligence claim arising out of a collision between cars, the fact of ownership of a car is prima facie evidence that it was, at the material time, being driven by the owner or by someone on his behalf,[45] although the inference is rebuttable.[46] In collision claims it will usually be irrelevant that the driver was guilty of negligent driving on some earlier occasion since, even if that was the case, no inference arises that he was negligent later on. Questions can, however, be asked to test the driver's credibility as a witness or skill and competence as a driver, and they cannot be excluded merely because they show that the driver has been involved in previous accidents.[47]

2.—PROOF AND CAUSATION

(A) Evidence of causation

6–14   **Generally.** The claimant must lead either direct or circumstantial evidence[48] tending to establish both the facts necessary to establish a breach of duty and any additional facts required to establish causation of loss. To take a basic example, in an accident claim the evidence must demonstrate both how an accident

---

[42] per Lord Wensleydale in *Morgan v Sim* (1857) 11 Moo.P.C. 307 at 312. See also *Cotton v Wood* (1860) 8 C.B. (N.S.) 568, per Erle C.J.; *Hammack v White* (1862) 11 C.B. (N.S.) 588; *Wakelin v L. & S.W. Ry* (1886) 12 App.Cas. 14; *Brown v Rolls-Royce Ltd* [1960] 1 W.L.R. 210.

[43] *Cotton v Wood* (1860) 8 C.B. (N.S.) 568.

[44] *Carter v Sheath* [1990] R.T.R. 12, CA (applying the dictum of Lord Brandon in *Rhesa Shipping Co SA v Edmunds* [1985] 1 W.L.R. 948 at 955–956).

[45] *Barnard v Sully* (1931) 47 T.L.R. 557.

[46] *Rambarran v Gurrucharran* [1970] 1 W.L.R. 556.

[47] *James v Audigier* (1931) 48 T.L.R. 600; affirmed 49 T.L.R. 36.

[48] For a summary of the principles applicable where the defendant fails to call evidence, where evidence from him might reasonably have been expected and the claimant attempts to prove his claim by inference, see the judgment of Brook L.J. in *Wiszniewski v Central Manchester Health Authority* [1998] P.I.Q.R. P324, CA at P340.

happened and how, as a result, injury and other damage was sustained. The evidence must also be sufficient to show that, on a balance of probabilities, the most likely cause of both was the negligence or breach of statutory duty of the defendant, or some person for whose negligence the defendant is responsible in law.[49] If the claimant fails to establish that the defendant caused the harm of which complaint is made, or some part of it, then the action will fail.

ILLUSTRATIONS

Accident cases provide the clearest illustrations, although the principles are of general application. So, where the body of the claimant's husband was found at night on the defendant's railway line near a level crossing, the deceased having been killed by a train, it was held by the House of Lords, in the absence of evidence of the circumstances under which he had got on to the line, that even assuming there was evidence of negligence, there was still nothing to connect the happening of the accident with any negligent act[50]; where a van was overhauled and some two days later a stub axle broke and a wheel fell off, while it was in motion, it was held that there was no evidence of negligence against the repairers: although the facts suggested negligence on the part of someone, they did not point to the repairers as opposed to the driver of the van, the owner or somebody else[51]; where a lineman, working on an electrical installation, was electrocuted, without there having been any breach of the statutory regulations, the mere fact of his death was no evidence of any causal negligence on the part of his employers[52]; where there was no explanation for the claimant's fall from a ladder, his action for damages failed, even where the defendant, his employer, called no evidence, since the court was not bound to infer there had been a defect making his workplace unsafe[53]; also where a child stepped on a sharp object embedded in the sand of a beach but there was no evidence to identify what it was or its size, accordingly no assessment could be made whether the local authority had discharged its duty of care or not.[54] A tour operator's failure to position a representative at the end of a toboggan run in Austria was not causative of the claimant's injury after she lost control of her toboggan having remounted it at the end of the run. The purpose of so positioning the representative would only have been to repeat a warning already given not to get back on to the toboggan once the run was completed.[55]

6–15

---

[49] For a defendant's vicarious liability, see Ch.3, paras 3–98 to 3–206, above.

[50] *Wakelin v London and South Western Ry Co* (1886) 12 App.Cas. 41. See also, e.g. *Graham v East of Scotland Water Authority* 2002 S.C.L.R. 340, OH (cause of an accident at best speculative where a farmer wandered off a road in an intoxicated state at night and was later found drowned in a reservoir nearby, part of which was separated from the road by a wall only 30 cm in height).

[51] *Britannia Hygienic Laundry Co v Thornycroft* (1925) 95 L.J.K.B. 237 (in any event there was a finding of fact that the breakage was occasioned by metal fatigue, which could not have been discovered by reasonable inspection by the repairers). See also *Smith v Midland Ry* (1887) 57 L.T. 813; *Russell v L. & S.W. Ry* (1908) 24 T.L.R. 548; *Daniel v Metropolitan Ry* (1871) L.R. 5 H.L. 45.

[52] *Youngman v Pirelli General Cable Works* [1940] 1 K.B. 1.

[53] *Alderson v Piggott & Whitfield Ltd* (1996) 10 C.L. 224, CA (an unexplained fall from a step ladder). See also *Wiszniewski v Central Manchester Health Authority* [1998] P.I.Q.R. P324, CA.

[54] *B v Thanet District Council* [1999] C.L.Y. 3965.

[55] *Parker v TUI UK Ltd* [2009] EWCA Civ 1261.

6–16   Where both claimant and defendant call evidence of causation, the judge will no doubt start by deciding which account to prefer.[56] But that does not mean that, unless the defendants account is established as probably correct, the claimant will inevitably succeed. It can be sufficient if the defendant calls the claimant's case into question to such an extent as to prevent the judge accepting it. So, it was incorrect to approach a complex issue of medical causation from the aspect that, if the psychogenic explanation for the claimant's symptoms advanced by the defendant could not be accepted, it was illogical for him also to reject the claimant's case that her symptoms were organic in origin. The onus was upon the claimant to prove that her explanation was the right one and the defendant's failure to establish their suggested cause was simply a factor to be taken into account in deciding whether the burden of proof had been discharged.[57] A claim against a manufacturer of cigarettes failed where the claimant was unable to produce any expert epidemiological study concluding that there was a causal connection between cigarette smoking and cancer; or to prove that but for the deceased's smoking of cigarettes he would probably not have contracted cancer; or to show that any negligence of the defendant made at least a material contribution to his lung cancer.[58]

6–17   **The balance of probability.** It is not proper to reason that the least improbable of a number of possible causes of an event is *the* cause for purposes of satisfying the standard of proof.[59] However, where an issue of causation arises, and there are a number of competing explanations why an event occurred, which albeit uncommon are not improbable, it is a proper and logical train of reasoning, having eliminated all the causes of the loss but one, to ask whether, on the balance of probabilities, that one cause was the cause of the event. This is different to deciding which was the least improbable cause, and finding it therefore to be *the* cause. The point arose where the claimant alleged that a fall from his mountain bike was caused by a sudden and unexpected fracture of one of the handlebars, but the other explanation was that he had lost control of the bike and in the course of falling the handlebar fractured when it hit his body or

---

[56] It is incorrect to decide that the claimant is a credible witness and then analyse the expert evidence to see if it affects that conclusion. All relevant evidence should be considered before deciding a party's truthfulness: *Hall v Jakto Transport* [2006] EWCA Civ 1327 (an expert said he did not know how an accident happened but it could not happen as the claimant described).

[57] *Pickford v Imperial Chemical Industries Plc* [1998] 1 W.L.R. 1198, HL at 1200–1201.

[58] *McTear v Imperial Tobacco Ltd, The Times,* June 14, 2005, OH. See Pamplin, "Experts and a smoking statistic" 156 N.L.J. 314.

[59] In *Rhesa Shipping Co SA v Edmunds, The Popi M* [1985] 1 W.L.R. 948, HL, Lord Brandon observed, at 955, that the words of Mr. Sherlock Holmes to Dr Watson in "The Sign of Four": "How often have I said to You that, when You have eliminated the impossible, whatever remains, however improbable, must be the truth?" ought to be disregarded by a judge faced with complex issues of causation. He went on, at 956: " . . . the legal concept of proof of a case on a balance of probabilities must be applied with common sense. It requires a judge of first instance, before he finds that a particular event occurred, to be satisfied on the evidence that it is more likely to have occurred than not. If such a judge concludes, on a whole series of cogent grounds, that the occurrence of an event is extremely improbable, a finding by him that it is nevertheless more likely to have occurred than not, does not accord with common sense. This is especially so when it is open to the judge to say simply that the evidence leaves him in doubt whether the event occurred or not, and that the party on whom the burden of proving that the event occurred lies has therefore failed to discharge such burden."

the ground. The evidence disclosed only two explanations and once the defence expert's explanation was rejected as the most unlikely, all the evidence pointed to a defect in the handlebar as the probable cause of what happened.[60]

Similarly, where an issue arose as to which of three possible causes was **6–18** responsible for a fire which destroyed a Lexus car parked in the defendant's garage, that is, arson, a defect in the wiring in the garage, or a defect in the car, it was permissible to choose the last. The suggestion of arson was unlikely in the extreme. The remaining two possibilities were not both improbable, and one was more probable than the other. It was not a case where the decision turned on a finding of the least unlikely cause of the fire.[61] Where an allegation of professional negligence by solicitors was made and an issue arose in relation to the reason why a clause in a shareholders' agreement had been deleted, it was not permissible to find the reason advanced by the defendant "not improbable" but then to reject it. Once it was accepted that the explanation advanced by the defendant was plausible, it was for the claimant to satisfy the court that, nevertheless, that explanation ought to be rejected. The court was not compelled to choose between two theories, each of which were extremely improbable: if it was concluded that the occurrence of an event was extremely improbable, a finding that it was, nevertheless, more likely to have occurred than not, did not accord with common sense.[62]

Causation of damage. The claimant must also show that damage resulted **6–19** from the defendant's negligence, because negligence without proof of damage is not actionable.[63] It is a question of law, whether the evidence allows a reasonable finding of causation,[64] but it is a question of fact, whether any particular head of damage has been caused by a defendant's negligence or breach of statutory duty.[65]

(B) The causation tests

Introduction. Negligence cases arise in a wide variety of shapes and forms. **6–20** In terms of the courts' daily practice, personal injuries claims of one kind of another are, no doubt, the most heavily represented. Although less common, damage to property or to financial interests also forms the subject matter of negligence actions. In all these types of claim, the basic principles of proof and causation remain the same, but their application will reflect characteristics of the factual scenarios in which such claims arise. It is proposed therefore to look at

---

[60] *Ide v ATB Sales Ltd* [2008] P.I.Q.R. P13, CA.
[61] *Lexus Financial Services v Russell* [2008] P.I.Q.R. P13, CA.
[62] *Fulham Leisure Holdings Ltd v Nicholson Graham & Jones (a firm)* [2008] EWCA Civ 84.
[63] *Metropolitan Ry v Jackson* (1877) 3 App.Cas. 193. See further Ch.1, para.1–29 above. In *Sneddon v Scottish Ministers*, 2002 Rep. L.R. 52, OH the claim of a prison officer injured when pursuing an absconder across a field failed, where his employers were in breach of duty in failing to give instructions as to safety in the course of such pursuits, but even had such instructions been given, the chase would still have taken place.
[64] In *Re Pickles v N.C.B. (Intended Action)* [1968] 1 W.L.R. 997 at 1000, Lord Denning M.R. said: "In the ordinary way attributability or causation is regarded as a point of law."
[65] per McNair J. in *Mehmet Dogan Bey v G.G. Abdeni & Co Ltd* [1951] 2 K.B. 405 at 411.

causation in each of a number of individual areas of practice, highlighting the problems which, in that area, have come to prominence, starting with claims for personal injury.

In most personal injury cases, the cause of injury will have been an accident. But personal injury may be caused otherwise than by an accident and, in the context of causation, it will be necessary to look also at those cases where injury has been caused by, say, exposure to some harmful environment or substance; at clinical negligence cases; and at other cases of damage caused by the negligence of a professional person.

6–21   **Causation in personal injury claims: accident claims.** It is particularly in the context of accident cases that the higher courts have stressed the need for a robust and commonsense approach. As Lord Wright said:

> "Causation is to be understood as the man in the street, and not as either the scientist or the metaphysician, would understand it. Cause here means what a . . . man would take to be the cause without too microscopic analysis but on a broad view."[66]

6–22   In a later case, Lord Reid stressed his disinclination to lay down any one test as authoritative:

> "One may find that as a matter of history several people have been at fault and that if any one of them had acted properly the accident would not have happened, but that does not mean that the accident must be regarded as having been caused by the faults of all of them. One must discriminate between those faults which must be discarded as being too remote and those which must not. Sometimes it is proper to discard all but one and to regard that one as the sole cause, but in other cases it is proper to regard two or more as having jointly caused the accident. I doubt whether any test can be applied generally."[67]

6–23   Accordingly, the approach to causation in an accident case generally starts with the reasonable application of common sense. With this guide there is freedom to choose one or more causes out of a selection of factors which contribute towards the happening of the event in question.[68] However, given the number of potential causes on even straightforward facts, there is much room for disagreement about what should be regarded as decisive.

6–24   In *Stapley v Gypsum Mines Ltd*,[69] two men were ordered to take down an unsafe roof in a mine. After attempting it for a period of time, they gave up trying and Stapley returned to work under the unsafe roof, which then fell on top of him and killed him. Two members of the House of Lords thought that the sole cause

---

[66] *Yorkshire Dale S.S. Co v Minister of War Transport* [1942] A.C. 691 at 706. See also *Sigurdson v British Columbia Electric Railway* [1953] A.C. 291 at 299; Wright, "Causation and Responsibility in English Law" [1955] C.L.J. 163.

[67] *Stapley v Gypsum Mines Ltd* [1953] A.C. 663 at 681. In *Imperial Chemical Industries Ltd v Shatwell* [1965] A.C. 656 at 670, Lord Reid agreed that *Stapley* "gives authoritative guidance on the question of causation." See Hart and Honore in 72 L.Q.R. 260 and 398, also Williams, "Causation in the Law" [1961] C.L.J. 62.

[68] *Norris v W. Moss & Sons Ltd* [1954] 1 W.L.R. 346. See per Vaisey J. at 351 on this point.

[69] [1953] A.C. 663; followed, *Williams v Sykes & Harrison Ltd* [1955] 1 W.L.R. 1180; *Hodkinson v Henry Wallwork & Co* [1955] 1 W.L.R. 1195.

of the accident was the act of Stapley in returning to work under an unsupported roof, which he knew to be unsafe, but three members held that that was only partly the cause, the other part being the act of his fellow workmen in leaving the roof in such a state. Lord Asquith said:

> "I am persuaded that it is still part of the law of this country that two causes may both be necessary preconditions of a particular result—damage to X—yet the one may, if the facts justify that conclusion, be treated as the real, substantial, direct or effective cause and the other dismissed as at best a *causa sine qua non* and ignored for the purpose of legal liability. This is a doctrine affirmed by your Lordships' House and not, in my view, displaced by the Law Reform (Contributory Negligence) Act 1945."[70]

Formulating a test. While many of the older cases refer to a distinction between the *causa causans* and the *causa sine qua non*, enthusiasm for Latin tags has since gone into serious decline. It has been observed that: "The law has dug no deeper in the philosophical thickets of causation than to distinguish between a *causa sine qua non* and a *causa causans*. The latter is an empty tautology. The former proves everything, and therefore nothing."[71] In the absence of any one test, a variety of mechanisms have been used in order to identify that cause or combination of causes, which should be regarded as most probably responsible for what occurred. Depending on the circumstances reference may be made to facts "but for" which an accident would not have occurred[72]; or to facts which caused an accident as opposed to merely setting the scene for it. It will in all cases be important to identify the duty of which the defendant is said to be in breach, before going on to consider whether what occurred stood in some relevant causal relation to it.[73] **6–25**

ILLUSTRATIONS

In *Quinn v Burch Brothers (Builders) Ltd,*[74] where the claimant, an independent sub-contractor, fell from a trestle he borrowed and failed to have footed, it was held that the defendants, as the main contractors, were in breach of contract in failing to supply him with a step-ladder but that breach did not cause the accident, it merely gave him the opportunity to injure himself by his own negligent use of the equipment which he had selected.[75] Where employers were liable for an accident to their employee and then, some three weeks later, he suffered a second accident, allegedly as a result of a continuing weakness in the **6–26**

---

[70] *Stapley v Gypsum Mines Ltd* [1953] A.C. 663 at 687.
[71] per Laws L.J. in *Rahman v Arearose Ltd* [2001] Q.B. 351 at 367.
[72] See further, Jones, "Proving causation-beyond the 'but for' test" (2006) 4 P.N. 251.
[73] See, e.g. *Mountford v Newlands School* [2007] E.L.R. 256, CA (applying *Chester v Ashfar* [2005] 1 A.C. 134, para.6–54, below (the school played an over-age player in an under 15 rugby match and the claimant was injured in a lawful tackle by that player: held, that there had been a breach of duty since the greater maturity, weight and size of the older boy exposed the claimant to an increased risk of injury, and it was open to the trial judge to find that the increased risk materialised, in that those features contributed materially to the occurrence of injury). See further, article in Ed. L.M. 2007, May, 6.
[74] [1966] 2 Q.B. 370.
[75] To the like effect, see *Page v Read* (1984) 13 N.I.J.B., CA.

left leg, his action failed on the facts: the second accident amounted to an intervening act, which had broken the chain of causation.[76]

6–27   In contrast, where the claimant suffered a neck injury as a result of the defendants' negligence, and, because the movements of her neck were constricted by a cervical collar, she was unable to use her bifocal spectacles with her usual facility, the defendants were liable for a subsequent fall when she tripped and fell while going down stairs, the second fall also being attributable to the defendants' original negligence.[77]

6–28   Where the defendants' factory floor had become slippery, following the negligent spillage of some viscous fluid on it, the claimant was instructed to mop up, and, in order to do so satisfactorily, had first to remove a number of pallets, by fork lift truck. In fact, he chose to move even more pallets so as to expose a wider area of the floor. When he slipped and fell whilst standing on a slippery patch, it was held that there being no reasonably foreseeable risk when charged with such a simple task, he would injure himself in carrying it out, no causal connection was established between the negligent spillage and his subsequent fall.[78]

6–29   Where the claimant, an AA patrolman on duty at an AA service centre, saw a lorry on fire and grabbing a fire extinguisher, ran out to assist in putting out the flames, tripping as he did so in a concealed hole, again causation was not established because, although the fire had been created by the defendant's negligence,[79] the claimant's injury was caused by an accident which neither party could reasonably have foreseen.

6–30   Where the claimant suffered catastrophic injury after slipping from a wall into a swimming pool, it was not a correct to ask whether the absence of non-slip paint made a material contribution to the risk of a fall: in single incident cases the straightforward question was whether a suggested breach of duty caused the accident to occur and on the facts the court had not been satisfied, on a balance of probability, that the accident would have been avoided if non-slip paint had been used on the surface of the wall.[80]

6–31   **The "but for" test.** This rule is generally the starting point in proving a causative link with the damage suffered. The claimant seeks to show that but for the defendant's negligence the injury complained of would not have arisen. If he succeeds, that is enough to prove his loss and there is no additional requirement

---

[76] *McKew v Holland & Hannen & Cubitts (Scotland)* [1969] 3 All E.R. 1621, HL, *affirming* 1969 S.L.T. 101.

[77] *Wieland v Cyril Lord Carpets* [1969] 3 All E.R. 1006, followed in *Pyne v Wilkenfeld* (1981) 26 S.A.S.R. 441 on very similar facts.

[78] *Vinnyey v Star Paper Mills Ltd* [1965] 1 All E.R. 175, which is to be distinguished from the more usual situation to be found in cases, such as *Johnston v Caddies Wainwright* [1983] I.C.R. 407, CA, where different considerations apply. See, further, paras 12–139 to 12–147, below.

[79] *Crossley v Rawlinson* [1982] 1 W.L.R. 369. For 'Fire' generally see Ch.13 paras 13–102 to 13–128.

[80] *Clough v First Choice Holidays and Flights Ltd* [2006] P.I.Q.R. P325, CA. For cases where the "material cause" test *is* appropriate, see para.6–39, below.

to show that the defendant's negligence was the only, or the single, or even chronologically the last cause of injury.[81] So if some intervening event has occurred which has contributed to the claimant's ultimate harm, it is usually not permissible, if the but for test has been satisfied, to apportion the damages recoverable. The cases which allow for an apportionment based on the extent of the defendant's contribution to the claimant's injury, are an exception to the general rule. The exception is intended to do justice in particular situations, generally in the context of industrial disease or injury where the claimant has suffered successive exposure to harm, by a number of agencies, where the effect of the harm is divisible, and where it would be unjust for an individual defendant to bear the whole loss, when in common sense he is not responsible for all of it.[82]

Claimant's own negligence. Where the only effective cause of an accident is **6–32** the claimant's own negligence, the action should fail.[83] So, when a scaffold was erected in breach of the building regulations in that one of the uprights was not vertical and the claimant, a scaffolder, tried to remedy the defect in a manner described as "fantastically wrong", injuring himself when the scaffold collapsed, it was held there was no causal connection between the breach of statutory duty and his injury.[84] Further, where a factory worker put his hand deliberately into the moving parts of a crushing machine, in order to clean it, although the employers were in breach of a statutory duty to fence, they were not liable in damages because the actual cause of the accident, in the sense of the operative act and effective cause, was their employee's own fault.[85] In *McWilliams v Sir William Arrol & Co Ltd*,[86] an experienced steel erector, who was working on the erection of a steel lattice tower, fell some 70 feet from his place of work and was killed. His widow's claim, based on his employers' negligence in failing to provide a safety belt, failed, on it being accepted that he would not have worn a belt even if one had been provided. There was no obligation on the deceased's employers to force him to wear a safety belt.

Causation not precluded by joint breach. Two brothers, A and B, both **6–33** experienced shot firers, tested an electrical circuit connected to detonators without waiting for the proper equipment to be brought up to them and in plain

---

[81] *Ellis v Environment Agency* [2009] P.I.Q.R. P5, CA per May L.J. at [37] (the claimant's employers were responsible for an injury to his back but then, about a year later, he missed his footing on a ladder in an accident which was not their fault and suffered injuries which kept him away from work for some 5 months. Later again he fell on the staircase at his home as a result of his back giving way. While on the evidence the employers were liable for the effects of the fall on the staircase, it was not correct to discount 10 per cent from the damages for the effects of the fall from the ladder).
[82] *Ellis v Environment Agency* [2009] P.I.Q.R. P5, CA per May L.J. at [39]. For apportionment in disease cases see para.6–50 onwards, below. In effect the defendant in *Ellis* was attempting to introduce the apportionment rule applied in exposure cases, for which see para.6–52 below, into an accident case. See further *Dickins v O2 Plc* [2009] I.R.L.R. 58, CA, Ch.11, para.11–89, below: apportionment of damages inappropriate where the injury suffered by the claimant was a mental breakdown to which both negligent and non negligent causes contributed.
[83] *Canadian Pacific Ry v Fréchette* [1915] A.C. 871.
[84] *Norris v W. Moss & Sons Ltd* [1954] 1 W.L.R. 346.
[85] *Rushton v Turner Brothers Asbestos Co Ltd* [1960] 1 W.L.R. 96.
[86] [1962] 1 W.L.R. 295.

breach of the statutory regulations. An explosion occurred in which they were seriously injured. A sued their employer on the basis of a vicarious liability for the part taken by B. Application of the maxim volenti non fit injuria[87] was held to defeat the claim, but the alternative defence, that B's conduct had no causal connection with the accident, was specifically rejected. As a matter of law it was observed that an employee injured in the course of joint enterprise where both he and another employee are negligent or in breach of statutory duty, is not precluded from alleging that his injury was caused by the other's breach.[88]

6–34   **Causation and contributory negligence.** The importance of causation in relation to findings of contributory negligence has already been noted.[89] Some causative link between the claimant's contributory fault and the damage of which he complains is essential if a finding of contributory negligence is to be made.[90] Any question of contributory negligence has to be considered broadly and upon a common sense basis.[91]

Illustrations

6–35   Responsibility for injury following an accident was shared: when an epileptic, who failed to tell his employers that he had been warned by his doctor not to work at heights, had a fit when working from a 20-feet-high platform, fell to the ground and was killed: his conduct and the employers' breach of statutory duty, in not providing toe boards and handrails, were equal causes of the accident[92]; when a skilled workman who disliked working a circular saw with its guard brought to a height where it would comply with the woodworking regulations accidentally caught his hand on the blade: in fact the guard was not capable of adjustment so as to properly comply with the employers' statutory duty, but the accident would not have happened if the guard had been adjusted to its lowest possible position.[93] Where the claimant was found guilty of gross misconduct by his employers in relation to an accident in which he suffered injury, and he thereby suffered demotion and reduced earnings, he was able subsequently to recover the loss of earnings as a consequence of the accident where the court apportioned liability 85:15 in his favour. Had it been appreciated that his responsibility was limited to 15 per cent there would not have been any disciplinary proceedings at all, still less demotion and loss of pay. In the

---

[87] For which see Ch.4, para.4–73, above.
[88] *Imperial Chemical Industries Ltd v Shatwell* [1965] A.C. 656, per Lord Donovan at 691, commenting on *Stapley v Gypsum Mines Ltd* [1953] A.C. 663, para.6–24, above.
[89] See Ch.4, para.4–21, above. For the burden of proof of contributory negligence, see Ch.4, para.4–19.
[90] See per Lord Atkin in *Caswell v Powell Duffryn Collieries Ltd* [1940] A.C. 152 at 165 and Lord Asquith in *Stapley v Gypsum Mines Ltd* [1953] A.C. 663 at 687.
[91] See *The Volute* [1922] 1 A.C. 129 at 144, per Lord Birkenhead; *Stapley v Gypsum Mines Ltd*, above, per Lord Reid at 681. See Ch.4, generally, for this partial defence, which is considered at para.4–03 et seq., above.
[92] *Cork v Kirby Maclean Ltd* [1952] 2 All E.R. 402. Also *Laszczyk v N.C.B.* [1954] 1 W.L.R. 1426.
[93] *Cakebread v Hopping Bros* [1947] K.B. 641.

circumstances, his conduct could not be regarded as the predominant, real or effective cause of the disciplinary proceedings and his resulting loss.[94]

Cause of accident not the same as cause of damage. For purposes of **6–36** contributory negligence, what is relevant is fault causing the *damage*. This may not necessarily be the same as fault causing the *accident*, although that, in turn, causes the damage.[95] Situations can and do arise where the level of responsibility for causing an accident is not the same as that for causing damage suffered by a third person. An example might be a road traffic accident, where the passenger in one of two vehicles involved sustains injury by the combined negligence of both the drivers. In such a case, a driver is responsible for negligence causing the accident and for any further breach of duty towards a passenger, not to expose him or her to any foreseeable risk as a result of the manner in which he was being carried. Accordingly, in *Madden v Quirk*,[96] where two motorists were jointly liable for a collision caused by their negligence, the driver whose passenger had been injured was additionally liable for the extent to which the gravity of the passenger's injuries were increased because of the negligent way in which he had been carried in the vehicle.[97]

The test of "last opportunity". It was at one time suggested that the rule of **6–37** "last opportunity", could be applied to determine whose fault caused an accident. "When an accident happens through the combined negligence of two persons he alone is liable to the other who had the last opportunity of avoiding the accident by reasonable care."[98]

Although as a principle of law the rule of last opportunity (if it ever existed) is now defunct,[99] it may sometimes be a useful test to apply in deciding, as a matter of fact, whether an accident was caused by the fault of one or both of the parties. The determination of the chronological order of events can assume importance and may well be decisive.

Causation in claims for personal injury: "exposure" claims. Some claims **6–38** for personal injury arise from exposure to a harmful state of affairs rather than an

---

[94] *Casey v Morane Ltd* [2001] I.R.L.R. 166, CA.

[95] See Ch.4, para.4–21, above. The distinction has been emphasised in deciding contribution between tortfeasors. Facts which evidenced a defendant's blameworthiness, but which were not causative of the claimant's loss can be taken into account when deciding an apportionment between defendants for purposes of the the Civil Liability (Contribution) Act 1978: *Brian Warwicker Partnership Plc v HOK International Limited* [2006] P.N.L.R. 79, CA.

[96] [1989] 1 W.L.R. 702 (the first motorist, driving a pick-up truck with two friends riding in the open back, attempted an overtaking manouever and collided with the second, who was emerging from a side road into his path. The pick-up then crashed into a tree and the claimant, one of the passengers, was seriously injured. Responsibility for causing the accident was apportioned 80 per cent to the first driver and 20 per cent to the second, but the responsibility for the increased injury to the passenger was varied to the proportion 85 per cent to the first, and 15 per cent to the second.).

[97] As regards a passenger's own contributory negligence see Ch.10, para.10–263, below.

[98] *Service v Sundell* (1929) 99 L.J.K.B. 55, per Scrutton L.J., quoting *Salmond on Torts* (6th edn), p.59.

[99] See *Boy Andrew* [1948] A.C. 140 at 149, per Lord Simon; *Grant v Sun Shipping Co* [1948] A.C. 549 at 563, per Lord du Parcq; *Davies v Swan Motor Co Ltd* [1949] 2 K.B. 291 and *Harvey v Road Haulage Executive* [1952] 1 K.B. 120 at 126, per Denning L.J. Also *Lloyds Bank Ltd v Budd* [1982] R.T.R. 80 at 83 per Lord Denning M.R. "I would just like to say once more that the doctrine of last opportunity is gone for ever."

accident as such. In the absence of one clearly defined event as the alleged cause of injury, they can give rise to their own special problems so far as proof of causation is concerned.

6–39   **The "material cause" test.** It is particularly in the context of exposure claims that it has been held sufficient that a claimant prove, to the usual balance of probability standard, that the defendant's breach of duty was a material, rather than exclusive, cause of any injury sustained.[100] In *Bonnington Castings Ltd v Wardlaw*,[101] the pursuer complained that, in the course of his work over many years, he had inhaled minute particles of silica, which accumulated in his lungs and caused pneumoconiosis.[102] It was found that he had been exposed to two different sources of dust, against one of which no complaint could be made, and one arising from a breach of statutory duty. Such circumstances were sufficient to establish liability. It was not necessary to prove that the breach alleged was the whole or even the main cause of the accident. Liability would be established if the breach materially contributed to the damage. Lord Reid said:

> "The disease is caused by the whole of the noxious material inhaled and, if that material comes from two sources, it cannot be wholly attributed to material from one source or the other . . . and the real question is whether the dust from the swing grinders materially contributed to the disease . . . A contribution which comes within the exception *de minimis non curat lex* is not material, but I think that any contribution which does not fall within that exception must be material."[103]

6–40   Such an issue is principally one of fact, for the decision of the trial judge on the basis of medical or other evidence and the Court of Appeal will be slow to interfere.[104]

6–41   Where a parent whose child had died from leukaemia brought an action against British Nuclear Fuels alleging that pre-conception exposure to radiation from their Sellafield plant in Cumbria had damaged his spermatozoa and had thereby been a material cause of his child's cancer, but the state of medical knowledge did not establish that irradiation was indeed a material contributory cause of leukaemia, the claim failed.[105]

---

[100] But not exclusively, see paras 6–53 and 6–55, below.

[101] [1956] A.C. 613.

[102] A shortened version of Pneumonoultramicroscopicsilicovolcanoconiosis.

[103] *Bonnington Castings Ltd v Wardlaw* [1956] A.C. 613, per Lord Reid at 621. But other descriptions of what is material for these purposes are in more demanding terms: see, for instance, Lord Rodger in *Fairchild v Glenhaven Funeral Services* [2002] 1 A.C. 32, who considered that such a cause had to be substantial.

[104] *Page v Smith (No.2)* [1996] 3 All E.R. 272, CA. See Sprince, "*Page v Smith (No.2)*—the saga ends but the questions remain" (1996) 3 P.N. 80. The same test of causation is applied in cases of nuisance: *Loftus-Brigham v Ealing London Borough Council* (2004) 20 Const. L.J. 82, CA (where the claimant alleged both nuisance and negligence in a claim for subsidence caused by tree roots it was observed that the rules of causation were the same for each tort and it was sufficient if the claimant showed that the roots were an effective cause of damage or made a material contribution to it). See Brown and Lindsey, "Seeing the wood for the trees—Loftus-Brigham and apportionment of damage" 2005 Const. L.J. 21, 431.

[105] *Reay v British Nuclear Fuels* [1994] 5 Med L.R. 1.

Cause unknown. An approach based on commonsense, while appropriate in   **6–42**
an accident case, may prove unsatisfactory in some non-accident claims for
personal injury.[106] There may be a number of mechanisms by which a medical
condition could have arisen. Scientific knowledge may simply not extend to a
satisfactory explanation. Difficulties of this kind lay behind the reasoning in
McGhee v National Coal Board.[107] The claimant was employed to do hot, dusty
work. He cycled home each day caked with sweat and grime, since, in breach of
duty, the defendants failed to provide showers or proper washing facilities. The
evidence suggested that because of his exertions under such conditions the risk
of his contracting dermatitis had been appreciably increased and the defendants
were accordingly liable for the onset of that condition, even though the precise
mechanism by which the disease arose was not clearly understood.[108]

Fairchild v Glenhavon Funeral Services Ltd.[109] In *Fairchild*, the claimants   **6–43**
alleged injury from exposure to asbestos in the course of employment. They had
been employed by a number of employers who were made defendants to the
claim, but were unable to say which of the defendants had been responsible for
the particular exposure which caused their subsequent illness to develop. Given
that breach of duty had been conceded, the House of Lords was prepared,
exceptionally, to accept that conduct which exposed the claimants to the risk of
an injury, but which could not on the facts be shown probably to have caused it,
should nonetheless be regarded as sufficient to found a cause of action. Justice
required that the claimants should have a remedy against any defendant found to
be in breach of duty even if they could not show against a particular employer,
that on a balance of probability, his breach of duty had caused the damage

---

[106] *Fairchild v Glenhavon Funeral Services Ltd* [2003] 1 A.C. 32, n.109 below. Per Lord Hoffmann
at 71:" Of course the causal requirements for liability are normally framed in accordance with
common sense. But there is sometimes a tendency to appeal to common sense in order to avoid
having to explain one's reasons. It suggests that causal requirements are a matter of incommunicable
judicial instinct. I do not think that this is right. It should be possible to give reasons why one form
of causal relationship will do in one situation but not in another." That is not to say that the test of
commonsense is still not applied, even in the higher courts: in *Banque Bruxelles Lambert v John D.
Wood Commercial Ltd* [1996] P.N.L.R. P380, CA, at 382, Saville L.J. said that the question was
whether the negligence complained of was the effective cause of the loss and the test was "based
simply on common sense rather than philosophical or metaphysical considerations." See further
Ch.9, para.9–326, below. Contrast *Young v Purdy* [1997] P.N.L.R. 130, CA (a case of alleged breach
of duty by a solicitor in wrongfully terminating his retainer) where Leggatt L.J. said he found the test
of applying judicial common sense an unsure guide in seeking to ascertain whether a particular breach
of duty resulting in loss is to be regarded in law as having caused it.
[107] [1973] 1 W.L.R. 1.
[108] *McGhee* was described "difficult," per Sir Thomas Bingham M.R. in *Page v Smith (No.2)* [1996]
1 W.L.R. 855, CA (the claimant alleged that his pre-existing chronic fatigue syndrome had been
exacerbated by a road traffic accident for which the defendant was to blame); see also, however, Lord
Bingham's later remarks about the case in *Fairchild v Glenhavon Funeral Services Ltd* [2003] 1 A.C.
32, n.109 below. *McGhee* was applied in *Brown v Corus (UK) Ltd* [2004] EWCA Civ. 374 (a claim
for Hand/Arm Vibration Syndrome in which the claimants could prove a breach of duty by their
employer and thereby an increased risk of injury from the levels of vibration to which they had been
exposed but could not prove to what extent their injuries would have been avoided had levels of
vibration been reduced).
[109] [2003] 1 A.C. 32. See Parker, "A value judgment" 146 S.J. 606; Arnell, "Causation reassessed"
2002 S.L.T. 32, 265; Weir, "Making it more likely v making it happen" 61 C.L.J. 519; Stapleton,
"Cause-in-fact and the scope of liability for consequences" 2003 L.Q.R., (119) 388. See also the
further analysis of *McGhee* by the HL in *Barker v Corus (UK) Plc* [2006] 2 A.C. 572.

complained of.[110] Remarks of Lord Bridge in *Wilsher v Essex Area Health Authority*,[111] tending to diminish the significance of *McGhee*, were disapproved.[112]

6–44   Their Lordships expressed themselves variously in relation to the circumstances in which the *Fairchild* exception should apply. Lord Rodger identified six conditions:

> "First, the principle is designed to resolve the difficulty that arises where it is inherently impossible for the claimant to prove exactly how his injury was caused. It applies, therefore where the claimant has proved all that he possibly can, but the causal link could only ever be established by scientific investigation and the current state of the relevant science leaves it uncertain exactly how the injury was caused and, so, who caused it ... Secondly, part of the underlying rationale of the principle is that the defendant's wrongdoing has materially increased the risk that the claimant will suffer injury. It is therefore essential not just that the defendant's conduct created a material risk of injury to a class of persons but that it actually created a material risk of injury to the claimant himself. Thirdly, it follows that the defendant's conduct must have been capable of causing the claimant's injury. Fourthly, the claimant must prove that his injury was caused by the eventuation of the kind of risk created by the defendant's wrongdoing. . . . By contrast, the principle does not apply where the claimant has merely proved that his injury could have been caused by a number of different events, only one of which is the eventuation of the risk created by the defendant's wrongful act or omission. . . . Fifthly, this will usually mean that the claimant must prove that his injury was caused, if not by exactly the same agency as was involved in the defendant's wrongdoing, at least by an agency that operated in substantially the same way. . . . Sixthly, the principle applies where the other possible source of the claimant's injury is a similar, but lawful, act or omission of the same defendant. I reserve my opinion as to whether the principle applies where the other possible source of injury is a similar but lawful act or omission of someone else or a natural occurrence."[113]

6–45   Subsequently in *Barker v Corus (UK) Plc*,[114] Lord Rodger accepted that the sixth condition had been too narrowly formulated. The principle did apply where the other possible source of injury was a similar but lawful act or omission of the defendant or of someone else or a natural occurrence.[115] Lord Hoffmann agreed:

> "It should not therefore matter whether the person who caused the non-tortious exposure happened also to have caused a tortious exposure. The purpose of the *Fairchild* exception is to provide a cause of action against a defendant who has materially increased the risk that the claimant will suffer damage and may have caused that damage but cannot be proved to have done so because it is impossible to show, on a balance of probability, that some other exposure to the same risk may not have caused

---

[110] A similarly pragmatic approach in the context of clinical negligence was adopted in *Chester v Afshar* [2005] 1 A.C. 134. See para.6–54, below.

[111] [1988] A.C. 1074 at 1090.

[112] [2003] 1 A.C. 32 at 57.

[113] [2003] 1 A.C. 32 at [170]. In *Sanderson v Hull* [2009] P.I.Q.R. P7, CA, Smith L.J. described the conditions as a useful guide, provided that it was remembered the sixth had been modified (see below).

[114] [2006] 2 A.C. 572. See further para.6–52, below, n.127.

[115] *Barker v Corus (UK) Plc* [2006] 2 A.C. 572 at [97].

it instead. For this purpose it should be irrelevant whether the other exposure was tortious or non-tortious, by natural causes or human agency or by the claimant himself."[116]

ILLUSTRATIONS

Fairchild was applied where the deceased, a welder, had contracted mesothe-   **6–46**
lioma after working many years before for the defendant's predecessor, being then exposed to asbestos fibre, albeit not as extensively as in other employments. A finding was made that the breaches of duty by the defendant's predecessor had materially increased the risk to the deceased of his contracting the disease. It was not necessary for the claimant to establish the exact duration of the period over which exposure to asbestos took place in breach of duty. What was necessary was that the extent and duration of the exposure had constituted a material increase in the risk to the deceased of contracting mesothelioma. It would be sufficient if the exposure was more than de minimis.[117]

Fairchild was *not* applied where the claimant contracted campylobacter   **6–47**
enteritis as a result of her exposure to bacteria in the course of seasonal work as a plucker of turkeys for the Christmas market. There were both tortious and non tortious mechanisms by which the bacteria could have entered her body. It was not permissible to invoke the aid of *Fairchild* since the case was not one where the claimant was able to show that it was impossible for her, on the present state of scientific knowledge, to show which exposure caused the injury. With appropriate findings the case could have been resolved on the usual "but for" test.[118]

Nor was *Fairchild* of assistance to the claimant where it was alleged that, as   **6–48**
a result of a pharmacist negligently dispensing an incorrect contraceptive pill, the claimant conceived and gave birth. The wrong pill was taken on two successive nights before the claimant resumed the correct prescription. It was submitted on her behalf that because the state of scientific knowledge precluded her from establishing that but, for the taking the incorrect pill, she would not have conceived, she could invoke the *Fairchild* exception. The submission was rejected. On the facts the trial judge had been entitled to conclude that taking the wrong pill on two occasions had not led to any increased risk of pregnancy. *Fairchild* could not be used to overcome a factual finding to which the trial judge had been entitled to come.[119]

Although it is likely that the approach to causation in *Fairchild* is capable of   **6–49**
being invoked in many cases where scientific knowledge cannot provide a fully worked out link between the alleged breach of duty and the claimant's injury, it does not alter the burden of proof. That burden remains where it always was,

---

[116] *Barker v Corus (UK) Plc* [2006] 2 A.C. 572 at [17], per Lord Hoffmann.
[117] *Cox v Rolls Royce Industrial Power (India) Ltd* [2007] EWCA Civ 1189. See also *Sienkiewicz v Grief (UK) Ltd* [2009] EWCA Civ 1159 (material increase in risk of mesothelioma from occupational as opposed to environmental exposure to asbestos); *Willmore v Knowsley MBC* [2009] EWCA Civ 1211 (exposure to asbestos while a pupil at school).
[118] *Hull v Sanderson* [2009] P.I.Q.R. P7, CA.
[119] *Wootton v J Docter Ltd* [2008] EWCA Civ 1361.

upon the claimant, both in respect of proving a cause of action and also the damage alleged to have accrued as a result.[120]

6–50 **Apportionment between several defendants or several causes of harm.** In exposure cases a question can often arise as to the extent of the responsibility of a number of defendants who have, over time, employed the claimant and by their respective breaches of duty each made a material contribution to the condition of which he complains. If the question of apportionment between defendants is not raised in evidence, it will be sufficient in such a case for the claimant to prove against any one of them that his breach of duty was a material cause of his condition, for that defendant to be liable for the entire loss. But if, as it usually is, the issue of apportionment is raised, then strictly a defendant is liable only to the extent of his particular contribution and the court must determine what contribution is proved against him. In practice, such questions are most often resolved by taking into account the time of exposure to the circumstances which gave rise to the breach of duty, the relative extent of exposure, and, if necessary, the aetiology of the condition, which can determine the relative importance of exposure at particular times.[121]

6–51 Apportionment also arises for consideration where there are tortious and non-tortious causes of a condition for which compensation is sought. The defendant is only liable for the "culpable" damage, not that which would have arisen in any event, either from some constitutional cause, or from non-culpable exposure. These can be difficult questions where precise calculation on the evidence is not possible. In *Allen v British Rail Engineering Ltd*,[122] it was found that if the defendants had properly discharged their duty towards the claimant, he would probably have been moved to work requiring less use of vibrating equipment; and he would thereby have been exposed to an order of vibration in the region of one-half of that to which he was in fact exposed. On the basis that the defendants were liable to compensate only for that damage identified as caused by their negligence, it was right to discount from the award of damages to reflect symptoms that would have been experienced in any event. The Court of Appeal summarised the position as follows:

"The employee will establish liability if he can prove that the employer's tortious conduct made a material contribution to the employee's disability.

(i) There can be cases where the state of the evidence is such that it is just to recognise each of two separate tortfeasors as having caused the whole of the damage of which the claimant complains; for instance where a passenger is killed as a result of a head-on collision between two cars each of which was negligently driven and in one of which he was sitting.

---

[120] See *Page v Smith (No.2)* [1996] 1 W.L.R. 855, CA. See also *Dingley v Chief Constable of Strathclyde Police* (2000) 55 B.M.L.R. 1, HL (where there was insufficient evidence to establish whether, as a general proposition, multiple sclerosis could ever be caused by trauma, the claimant could not establish a connection between an accident and the subsequent onset of MS).
[121] *Holtby v Brigham and Cowan Ltd* [2000] P.I.Q.R. Q293, CA (the claimant suffered asbestosis, after being exposed for many years to asbestos dust in the course of various employments: the damages recovered reflected that proportion of the whole attributable to his employment by the defendant).
[122] [2001] P.I.Q.R. Q101, CA.

(ii) However, in principle the amount of the employer's liability will be limited to the extent of the contribution which his tortious conduct made to the employee's disability.

(iii) The court must do the best it can on the evidence to make an apportionment and should not be astute to deny the claimant relief on the basis that he cannot establish with demonstrable accuracy precisely what proportion of his injury is attributable to the defendants tortious conduct.

(iv) The amount of evidence which should be called to enable a judge to make a just apportionment must be proportionate to the amount at stake and the uncertainties which are inherent in making any award of damages for personal injury."[123]

Usually apportionment cannot arise where the injury which the claimant **6–52** suffers is not cumulative in effect, but indivisible. Asbestosis, pneumoconiosis, noise-induced hearing loss, may be described as cumulative conditions: the greater the period or intensity of exposure, the greater the resultant disease or disability. But mesothelioma, for example, is indivisible: current medical knowledge cannot identify whether, on a balance of probability, "any particular exposure to asbestos dust at any particular time contributed to the disease from which the claimant suffered."[124] The general rule in cases of indivisible injury is that "any tortfeasor whose act has been a proximate cause of the injury must compensate for the whole of it."[125] This general rule does not apply in cases that fall within the exception to the strict rule of causation created by *Fairchild v Glenhavon Funeral Services Ltd.*[126] Because the exception provides for joint and several liability in circumstances where the defendants' breach *may* only have caused the claimant's injury, it is regarded as fair and just that the extent of a particular defendant's liability should reflect his relative contribution to the chance of that injury being contracted.[127]

Psychiatric injury is usually indivisible and apportionment between negligent **6–53** and non negligent causes is inappropriate. So, where it appeared that the claimant had suffered a seriously damaged mental state following mental breakdown, but with more than one cause, there being causes for which the defendant was not responsible, the starting point was that she was entitled to recover damages in

---

[123] *Allen v British Rail Engineering Ltd* [2001] P.I.Q.R. Q101, CA at 109, per Schiemann L.J. For an example of the exercise of apportionment in a VWF claim in practice, see *Rugby Joinery UK Ltd v Whitfield* [2006] P.I.Q.R. Q40, CA. See generally in relation to VWF claims, Huckle, "Disease litigation: excitations in the Court of Appeal" 2005 P.I.L.J. 39, 5.
[124] *Fairchild v Glenhaven Funeral Services Ltd* [2002] 2 W.L.R. 1052, CA, per Brooke, L.J. at 1073 (this part of the analysis remains valid even though the Court of Appeal's decision was reversed on appeal, n.109 above).
[125] *Dingle v Associated Newspapers Ltd* [1961] 2 Q.B. 162, 188.
[126] [2003] 1 A.C. 32, n.109, above.
[127] *Barker v Corus (UK) Plc* [2006] 2 A.C. 572. It was swiftly perceived that the result in *Barker* could lead to injustice to employees who had contracted mesothelioma. Lengthy delays would ensue while an attempt was made to find and sue all relevant employers. Complex investigations could be required to establish the extent of each employer's contribution to the chance of the injury being contracted. If an employer could not be found or was not worth suing the claimant would be undercompensated for the consequences of a fatal condition. Parliament responded with s. 3 of the Compensation Act 2006 which in effect imposes a joint and several liability on any identified employer who exposed the claimant to asbestos in breach of duty. See further *Sienkiewicz v Greif (UK) Ltd* [2009] EWCA Civ 1159 (test of causation under s.3 is the "material cause" test).

full. While it was not possible to say that, but for the tort, she would probably not have suffered the breakdown, it was possible to say that the tort had made a material contribution to it, and that was sufficient. It was observed that, while a percentage deduction from damages, to take account of so-called constitutional causes of mental illness was not appropriate, it would always be important to bear in mind non tortious factors when considering particular items of damage, to reflect the risk that the claimant might in any event have suffered a breakdown at some time in the future and would then have suffered some loss of earnings or incurred some expense.[128]

6–54   **Causation in other claims for personal injury.** Clinical negligence cases are another area where particularly difficult questions of causation can arise.[129] In *Chester v Afshar*,[130] the House of Lords had to consider causation in the context of a claim based upon negligent failure by a medical professional to warn of the risks of surgery. Their Lordships declined to apply the "but for" approach to causation in circumstances where the defendant had been guilty of negligence, but the slight risk to which he failed to draw the claimant's attention would have existed wherever and whenever she had the surgery in question. In fact the risk materialised. It was said to be sufficient in the particular circumstances that the claimant could establish a breach of the duty to provide a warning and damage which it was within the scope of that duty to prevent.[131]

6–55   A modified version of the "but for" test can be relevant where a number of causes have contributed to a particular medical outcome, some the result of negligence, some not. There are three potential results. Where on the evidence, the outcome would probably have arisen anyway as a result of a non-tortious cause or causes, the claimant will have failed to prove that the negligent cause made an effective contribution. Conversely, if it is shown that "but for" the contribution of the tortious cause the injury would probably not have occurred, the burden of proof will have been discharged. In a case where medical science cannot establish the probability that "but for" an act of negligence the injury would not have happened but can establish that the contribution of the negligent cause was material, that is, more than negligible, the "but for" test is modified, and the claimant will succeed.[132]

---

[128] *Dickins v O2 Plc* [2009] I.R.L.R. 58, CA, per Smith L.J. at [43]. See the similar approach to non psychiatric injury in *Bailey v Ministry of Defence* [2009] 1 W.L.R. 1052, CA, n.132, below. But see also *Moore v Welwyn Components Ltd* [2005] P.I.Q.R. P19, CA, Ch.11, para.11–88, below.

[129] See further Ch.9, para.9–143, below.

[130] [2005] 1 A.C. 134. See further below Ch.9, para.9–147; also Shaw, "Sick pay" 148 S.J. 148, (41) 1228.

[131] *Chester v Afshar* has been applied in the non-clinical context, see *Mountford v Newlands School* [2007] E.L.R. 256, CA, para.6–25, above.

[132] *Bailey v Ministry of Defence* [2009] 1 W.L.R. 1052, CA, per Waller L.J. at [46] (after surgery, a patient aspirated her vomit, which led to a cardiac arrest and hypoxic brain damage: there were both negligent and non-negligent causes of the weakness which prevented her aspirating, but the negligent causes had contributed materially to that weakness and thus causation was made out). See also *Dickins v O2 Plc* [2009] I.R.L.R. 58, CA, n.128 above, also Ch.11, para.11–89, below (applying the approach in *Bailey*, it was inappropriate, in a case of indivisible psychiatric injury, to apportion damages between negligent and non-negligent causes).

Loss of a chance. In some professional negligence claims the claimant is able 6–56
to recover damages for loss of the chance that a third party would have acted in
a particular way, had the negligence not occurred.[133] Over the years, a number of
cases rejected the application of a "lost chance" approach to cases of clinical
negligence.[134] In *Gregg v Scott*,[135] the House of Lords was given the opportunity
to overrule that line of authority in order to permit a claimant, who could prove
that a doctor had acted negligently, to recover damages on the basis that the
chance of a better outcome for his condition had been reduced, even though proof
on a balance of probability that the outcome would be worse, was not available
to him. The House rejected the opportunity, by a majority. Lord Hoffmann
pointed out that the law regarded the world as bound by the laws of causality.[136]
In law everything is assumed to have a determinate cause. "There is no inherent
uncertainty about what caused something to happen in the past or about whether
something which happened in the past will cause something to happen in the
future . . . What we lack is knowledge and the law deals with lack of knowledge
by the concept of the burden of proof."[137]
Accordingly, in the context of clinical negligence, a claim would not be made
out in the absence of proof that the act or omission in question had, on a balance
of probability, caused particular injury or loss. In the view of the majority, to
abandon earlier authorities and adopt a rule whereby a claimant could recover for
possible as opposed to probable loss in a clinical negligence claim, was too great
a change safely to contemplate.

Causation in claims other than for personal injury. The preceding discus- 6–57
sion reflects the many negligence claims in which the court is required to identify
the cause of personal injury sustained by the claimant whether in an accident or
otherwise. But many negligence claims do not involve personal injury at all, as
opposed to damage to property or other financial interests. In such cases "but
for" or "common sense" tests can be positively misleading, since they can
misdirect the enquiry from its proper starting point, namely for what damage the
defendant ought to be responsible. In the words, again, of Lord Hoffmann[138]:

---

[133] See below, para.6–60 and, e.g. *Allied Maples Group Ltd v Simmons & Simmons* [1995] 1 W.L.R.
1602, CA, para.6–04 above and Ch.9, para.9–295, below.
[134] *Hotson v East Berkshire Health Authority* [1987] A.C. 750, and *Wilsher v Essex Health Authority*
[1998] A.C. 1074. See also *Bolitho v City and Hackney Health Authority* [1998] A.C. 232. See Start
and Bird, "Losing the way on lost chance" 156 N.L.J. 358.
[135] [2005] 2 A.C. 176, Ch.9, para.9–153, below (where the facts are summarised).
[136] *Gregg v Scott* [2005] 2 A.C. 176 at 195. Lord Hoffmann referred to the article of Helen Reece
"Losses of Chances in the Law" (1996) M.L.R. 188.
[137] *Gregg v Scott* [2005] 2 A.C. 176 at 196. Lord Hoffmann conceded that in cases of professional
negligence, outside the context of medical treatment, a different approach was adopted where the loss
contended for depended upon the chance that a third party would act in a particular way (see n.145
above), but said that, "The law treats human beings as having free will and the ability to choose
between different courses of action, however strong may be the reasons for them to choose one course
rather than another. This may provide part of the explanation for why in some cases damages are
awarded for the loss of a chance of gaining an advantage or avoiding a disadvantage which depends
upon the independent action of another person."
[138] *Kuwait Airways Corp v Iraqi Airways Co (No.3)* [2002] 3 All E.R. 209 at [128]. See also his
remarks in *Empress Car Co (Abertillery) Ltd v National Rivers Authority* [1999] 2 A.C. 22, 29.

"There is . . . no uniform causal requirement for liability in tort. Instead, there are varying causal requirements, depending upon the basis and purpose of liability. One cannot separate questions of liability from questions of causation. They are inextricably connected. One is never simply liable; one is always liable for something and the rules which determine what one is liable for are as much part of the substantive law as the rules which determine which acts give rise to liability."

So, in *Calvert v William Hill Credit Ltd*,[139] the claimant was unable to recover from bookmakers gambling losses alleged to follow from their failure to adhere to an agreement not to take bets from him over the telephone for a period of six months. The scope of the defendant's duty was limited to declining to receive telephone bets from the claimant and did not extend to losses which would probably have arisen even had the agreement been honoured.

6–58   **Professional negligence claims.**[140] It is particularly in this class of case that it is important to start by considering the scope of the defendant's duty of care before deciding whether the damage complained of can be regarded as having arisen from a breach of that duty. The approach has been described as follows[141]:

"Starting with *Caparo v Dickman* the courts have moved away from characterising questions as to the measure of damages for the tort of negligence as questions of causation and remoteness. The path that once led in that direction now leads in a new direction. The courts now analyse such duties by enquiring whether the duty which the tortfeasor owed was a duty in respect of the kind of loss of which the victim complains. Duty is no longer determined in abstraction from the consequences or vice-versa. The same test applies whether the duty of care is contractual or tortious. To determine the scope of the duty the court must examine carefully the purpose for which advice was being given and generally the surrounding circumstances. The determination of the scope of the duty thus involves an intensely fact-sensitive exercise. The final result turns on the facts, and it is likely to be only the general principles rather than the solution in any individual case that are of assistance in later cases."

6–59   In *Gorham v British Telecommunications Plc*[142] an insurance company were in breach of duty in selling Mr Gorham a personal pension policy which was unsuitable, when what he required would have been better served by an occupational pension scheme. But the defendant was not under a duty to advise him to join such a scheme. Accordingly when, on being informed by the defendant that an occupational pension scheme offered by his employers was indeed better than the personal pension, he did not check with his employers to see if he qualified, it was found that any causal link between the original breach of duty and a loss of lump sum death benefit was broken. After that time the earlier breach of duty ceased to have causative effect. In another pension case, consulting actuaries were not liable where the claimant relied upon a breach of

---

[139] [2009] 2 W.L.R. 1065, CA, Ch.2, para.2–84, above.
[140] See generally, Evans, "The scope of the duty revisited" (2001) 3 P.N. 146.
[141] per Arden L.J. in *Johnson v Gore Wood* [2003] EWCA Civ 1728 at para.91.
[142] [2000] 1 W.L.R. 2129, CA. Sir Murray Stuart-Smith dissented. He felt that Mr Gorham's failure could not be said to be the whole cause of his loss and the chain of causation was accordingly not broken. See Jones, "Practical justice, financial planning and the disappointed beneficiary" (2001) 3 P.N. 190.

duty in their failure to explain how the Policyholders' Protection Act 1975 would operate if their recommended pension provider, the Equitable Life Assurance Society, went into liquidation. The claimant made his investment, Equitable Life suffered serious financial problems, and the policy was as a result worth much less than anticipated, but the losses were outwith the breach of duty since the Society had not in fact gone into liquidation.[143] Other examples will be found in Chapter 8, below, when specific areas of professional expertise are considered.

One of the questions that frequently arises in claims against professionals for negligent advice, is what would have happened if the advice had been given correctly.[144] It has been emphasised that where a claimant alleges that, had certain advice been given which the defendant negligently failed to give, he would have done something which would have avoided his loss, the issue falls within the realm of causation and is to be decided on a balance of probability. But where proof of his loss also requires that a third party would or would not have acted in a certain way, the issue is one of quantification of damage and should be assessed by reference to loss of the chance that the third party would have acted as alleged. In some cases the lost chance will be a substantial one, in others speculative, depending upon the evidence.[145] **6–60**

Chester v Afshar[146] has already been mentioned in the context of personal injury claims, but in connection with the first alternative, that is whether the the claimant would have acted differently if proper advice had been given, may have wider application. While it was said to represent only a modest departure from principle, it is not difficult to imagine it being invoked, in other claims against professionals for failure to advise or warn, outside the medical context in which it arose. The extent to which such attempts will be successful is in doubt. In one of the first examples, the claimant complained of his former solicitors' negligence in advising him in a tenancy dispute with a housing association. He argued that the solicitors' advice had been incomplete, but he could not say how he would have reacted had the correct advice been given. As had the claimant in *Chester,* he invited the court to say that he should not be penalised for his honesty and that it was sufficient for him to show that he had been deprived of the opportunity to make up his mind how to act with the benefit of proper advice. **6–61**

---

[143] *Andrews v Barnett Waddingham* [2006] P.N.L.R. 24, CA.
[144] See *Prosser v Castle Sanderson Solicitors* [2002] B.P.I.R. 1163, CA (negligent advice that the claimant had no alternative but to agree to an immediate liquidation of a company in which he held shares not causative of loss, where different advice would have made no difference to the outcome). See also *Levicom International Holdings BV v Linklaters* [2010] EWCA Civ 494 (where a client consults top-tier solicitors the presumption is that he will follow any non-negligent advice that should have been given).
[145] *Allied Maples Group Ltd v Simmons & Simmons* [1995] 1 W.L.R. 1602, CA; approved in *Doyle v Wallace* [1998] P.I.Q.R. Q146, CA (where the court is concerned with quantification of future loss it can discount for the value of a chance). See further Ch.5, para.5–124, above; also Reid, "The hypothetical outcome in professional negligence claims: Part II" (2001) 4 P.N. 262 (a review of a number of cases); McGregor Q.C., "Loss of a chance: where has it come from and where is it going?" (2008) 1 P.N. 2. See also Ch.9, para.9–295, below.
[146] n.130 above. See also Ch.9, para.9–147 and *Thompson v Bradford* [2006] Lloyd's Rep. Med. 95, CA.

The argument failed: the finding at first instance had been that, even with complete advice, the defendant would have carried on in the same course and that was fatal to the claim. The defendant, even assuming negligence, was not liable if his wrongful conduct did not cause the loss alleged.[147]

3.—INTERVENING CAUSES

(A) The independent act of a third party

6–62   **Introduction.** On some facts it can be shown that the claimant's damage has resulted from the act of another person independent of the defendant. On the face of it, the defendant should not be held responsible for the independent act of a third party, even if his breach of duty has, as it were, given the third party the opportunity to intervene.[148] The chain of causation can be broken by[149] " . . . something . . . ultroneous, something unwarrantable, a new cause which disturbs the sequence of events, something which can be described as either unreasonable or extraneous or extrinsic".[150] As the very generality of these words suggests, finding a comprehensive test to assist in distinguishing situations where the intervening cause extinguishes the defendant's responsibility, from those where it does not, has been elusive. The traditional shorthand to describe what was required was novus actus interveniens.

> "Certain well-known formulae are invoked, such as that the chain of causation was broken and that there was a *novus actus interveniens*. These phrases, sanctified as they are by standing authority, only mean that there was not such a direct relationship between the act of negligence and the injury that the one can be treated as flowing directly from the other. Cases have been cited which show great difference of opinion

---

[147] *White v Paul Davidson Taylor* [2004] P.N.L.R. 245, CA (Arden L.J. emphasised that *Chester* established no new general rule of causation but applied *Fairchild v Glenhaven Funeral Services Ltd* [2003] 1 A.C. 32, para.6–43, above, in that the strict rules of causation may be modified in exceptional circumstances). See also *Beary v Pall Mall Investments* [2005] P.N.L.R. 35, CA (the application of *Chester v Afshar* was rejected in a claim for damages for negligent investment advice where the trial judge found that even if proper advice had been given the claimant's choice if investment would have been the same: it was observed that the policy considerations applicable to the duty to give proper financial advice and the duty to give proper medical advice were quite different).

[148] [1920] A.C. 956.

[149] [1920] A.C. 956 at 986. See, e.g. *Weld-Blundell v Stephens* [1920] A.C. 956, per Lord Sumner: "In general (apart from special contracts and relations and the maxim *respondeat superior*), even although A is in fault, he is not responsible for injury to C, which B, a stranger to him, deliberately chooses to do. Though A may have given the occasion for B's mischievous activity, B then becomes a new and independent cause." As was pointed out in *Stansbie v Troman* [1948] 2 K.B. 48, this dictum was not intended to apply to cases where the act of negligence itself consisted in the failure to take reasonable care to guard against the very thing that did in fact happen.

[150] *The Oropesa* [1943] P. 32 at 39. See also the discussion of novus actus interveniens in *Minister of Pensions v Chennell* [1947] K.B. 250.

on the true answer in the various circumstances to the question whether the damage was direct or too remote."[151]

Not surprisingly, it has been suggested that the intervening negligence of the defendant himself cannot operate to break the chain of causation between his own earlier breach of duty and the claimant's damage.[152]   **6–63**

Reasonableness as well as foreseeability. If the defendant's negligence creates a context in which a third party reasonably acts in some way which contributes to the claimant's damage, it is unlikely that the consequences of that fresh act will serve to break the chain of causation. But if there is some unreasonable intervention, it may so overwhelm the defendant's wrongdoing that it can be said to be a new intervening cause. It is a matter of judgment, based upon the facts of each case whether the intervening act is reasonable or not. Foreseeability comes into the equation too. If the defendant ought to have reasonably foreseen the third party's intervention as a result of his negligent act or omission, it will not open to him to suggest that the intervening act overtakes his own as the effective cause of loss.[153]   **6–64**

Examples of intervening causes. Where as a result of negligence, the defendant's railway engine negligently entered upon the claimant's garden and damage was caused, not only by the engine itself and by those who were engaged in removing it, but also by a crowd of persons who entered the garden to gratify their curiosity, that part of the damage attributable to the activities of the crowd could not be recovered.[154] Where a railway company negligently permitted a carriage to be over-crowded, in which the claimant was hustled and robbed, the action failed because the over-crowding did not conduce, directly or indirectly, to the robbery.[155]   **6–65**

Also, when one of three ships was sunk after a series of collisions between the vessels[156]; and where contractors, in replacing a sewer on behalf of a local authority, broke a water main causing subsidence damage, which rendered a nearby house unsafe, and, subsequently, squatters broke in during the owner's absence, causing substantial further damage, the defendants were not liable for   **6–66**

---

[151] *The Oropesa* [1943] P. 32.

[152] See *Normans Bay Ltd v Coudert Brothers* [2004] EWCA Civ 215, Ch.9, para.9–296, below. See also Braithwaite, "Cause and effect" 148 S.J. 964.

[153] per Hamilton L.J. in *Latham v R. Johnson & Nephew Ltd* [1913] 1 K.B. 398 at 413. See also *Iron and Steel Holdings and Realisation Agency v Compensation Appeal Tribunal* [1966] 1 W.L.R. 480, per Winn L.J. at 492: "In my opinion, wherever any intervening factor was itself foreseeable by the actor, the person responsible for the act which initiated the chain of causes leading to the final result, that intervening cause is not itself, in the legal sense, a novus actus interveniens breaking the chain of causation and isolating the initial act from the final result."

[154] *Scholes v North London Ry* (1870) 21 L.T. 835. cf. *Scott's Trustees v Moss* (1889) 17 R. 32, Ct. of Sess. (crowd gathered to watch an advertised parachute descent).

[155] *Cobb v G.W. Ry* [1894] A.C. 419.

[156] *S.S. Singleton Abbey v S.S. Paludina* [1927] A.C. 16.

the latter damage.[157] The claimant's employers were not liable for a breach of statutory regulation in relation to the safety of a tower scaffold not provided with stabilisers, where, while the claimant was working from it, a colleague with whom he had earlier had an argument, deliberately toppled it over: the wholly unpredictable, deliberate and violent action of the other man had been an event of such impact as to obliterate any responsibility the defendant might have had.[158]

6–67   Similar examples can be found in remoteness of damage cases. In one case the claimant developed an acute anxiety and litigation neurosis after an accident, because her doctor incorrectly informed her that she had sustained a fractured skull: it was held that the medical advice amounted to an effective novus actus interveniens.[159]

6–68   **Examples where there was no intervening cause.** A intervening cause was not found: where two vessels collided at sea and the captain of one put out in a lifeboat to consult with the captain of the other, but the boat capsized with loss of life[160]; where the captain of a damaged ship refused an offer of immediate towage by another ship, which was heavily laden, on the ground that it was impracticable, but his vessel sank within a short distance of a suitable place where she could have been beached: the refusal of towage was reasonable[161]; where the reverse engine of a ship failed to operate in a lock and a port operator was struck and injured by a rope being used in an attempt to arrest the vessel's forward progress[162]; where the defendant's vessel negligently collided with harbour installations and a jack-up barge, hired for the repair, was itself lost without negligence when the sea bed collapsed underneath it.[163]

6–69   No intervening cause was found where a lorry "jack-knifed" causing an obstruction on a motorway into which other vehicles crashed, one in particular, which killed the claimant's husband, because it was travelling at too fast a speed: it was held that if a driver negligently obstructed a highway, thereby creating a danger to other road users (including those driving too fast and not keeping a proper lookout, but not those who either deliberately or recklessly drove into such obstruction) then his negligence contributed to the causation of any subsequent accident, even though the immediate cause was the negligent driving

---

[157] *Lamb v Camden London Borough Council* [1981] Q.B. 625.

[158] *Horton v Taplin Contracts Ltd* [2003] P.I.Q.R. P180, CA, Ch.12, para.12–182 below.

[159] *Martin v Isbard* (1947) W.A.L.R. 52. See to the like effect *Hogan v Bentinck West Hartley Collieries (Owners) Ltd* [1949] 1 All E.R. 588 (miner, whose thumb was fractured, was ill-advised to have it amputated) but cf. *Malcolm v Broadhurst* [1970] 3 All E.R. 508; *Lucy v Mariehamns Rederi* [1971] 2 Lloyd's Rep. 314.

[160] *The Oropesa* [1943] P. 32. Since the captain's decision was a reasonable one in the circumstances, it did not constitute a novus actus interveniens. But cf. *The Empire Squire* (1943) 169 L.T. 252 where it was held that the master's action was unreasonable.

[161] *The Guildford* [1956] P. 364.

[162] *Binnie v Rederij Theodoro B.V.*, 1993 S.C. 1993.

[163] *Humber Oil Terminal Trustee Ltd v Owners of the ship "Sivand"* [1998] C.L.C. 751, CA (the defendant was liable for the value of the barge).

of another driver.[164] Where negligent loading caused an article to fall from the defendants' lorry and a following car braked successfully and stopped, only to be rammed into from behind by a second car, which had skidded on a large patch of fresh tar, the defendants were liable for the damage of the second car: the skid may well have contributed to the happening of the collision but it did not constitute an act of independent volition.[165] There was no intervening cause where, after a pharmacist negligently issued the claimant with medication in a dose eight times the strength she usually took, a doctor repeated the same prescription. It was reasonable for the doctor, who was seeing the claimant for the first time, to rely upon the information mistakenly recorded by the pharmacist on the label: it would not be right to say that the pharmacist's failure to question the prescription was so eclipsed by the doctors intervention, that it could properly be relegated to no more than a mere occurrence in that history.[166]

Again remoteness of damage cases afford similar examples: where the **6–70** claimant was seriously injured and her husband killed in a road traffic accident, and after she recovered consciousness, it was necessary to tell her of her husband's death, whereupon she suffered an additional shock, which produced further illness: the defendant was liable for the additional injury, since the fact of her being told of the death in those circumstances was a direct and reasonable result of his negligence[167]; also, where the claimant suffered a cut on his shin, as a result of the defendants' negligence, and attended for treatment by a doctor, who negligently injected him with an anti-tetanus serum, to which he was allergic and he thereby contracted encephalitis: even had a test been made in advance of the injection, the claimant probably would not have shown any reaction to it and since the doctor's negligence had not materially caused or contributed to the disease, the defendants were liable for it, as well as for the minor initial wound.[168] There was no intervening cause interrupting the chain of causation, where, after the claimant had been sterilised, a doctor negligently failed to take steps by which pregnancy would have been detected and the baby developed meningitis and consequential brain damage, as a rare but natural consequence of birth.[169]

---

[164] *Rouse v Squires* [1973] Q.B. 889 (C's driver held three-quarters to blame and A's driver held one-quarter). However cf. the situation in *Wright v Lodge* [1993] 4 All E.R. 299, CA, where it was held that the judge was entitled to conclude that the driver of a car, which had broken down on the nearside lane of a dual carriageway, was 10 per cent liable for the injuries caused to his passenger when a lorry, driven recklessly in the fog, crashed into the rear of the stationary vehicle. But the car driver was not liable at all for injuries caused to other road users when, after the collision, the lorry swerved across the central reservation and overturned on the opposite carriageway.

[165] *Goodyear Tyre & Rubber Co of Canada v MacDonald* (1974) 51 D.L.R. (3d) 623; *West v Hughes of Beaconsfield* [1971] R.T.R. 298 (a 15-year-old cyclist, who was negligently knocked down by one vehicle, foreseeably would be injured by another vehicle following on behind it and such an occurrence did not constitute a *novus actus interveniens* despite the fact that the second accident could have been avoided if the other driver had been keeping a proper lookout). See para.6–94, below.

[166] *Horton v Evans* [2007] P.N.L.R. 17, Ch.9, para.9–133, below.

[167] *Schneider v Eisovitch* [1960] 2 Q.B. 430.

[168] *Robinson v The Post Office* [1974] 1 W.L.R. 1176.

[169] *Groom v Selby* [2002] P.I.Q.R. P201, CA, Ch.2, para.2–251, above.

6–71   **Deliberate acts.** A deliberate unlawful act, such as burglary, will not necessarily exempt the defendant from liability for antecedent negligence, where such an act could be reasonably foreseen and ought to have been guarded against at the time. A painter/decorator, working in a house under contract with the occupier, knowing that he was alone in the home left the door unlocked whilst he went away for two hours to fetch more wallpaper. During that time, a thief entered the house and stole valuables and the decorator was held liable in damages.[170]

Where the claimant was thrown down as she was climbing on to a tramcar, because some unknown person had rung the starting bell whilst, in breach of duty, the conductor was upstairs rather than on the platform, the defendants were liable: the unauthorised or wrongful act of a third person did not break the chain of causation, when it might be reasonably foreseen[171]; when a barge was properly tied up at a wharf on the Thames, at a place where it was known that children and youths were wont to interfere with barges, and some unknown persons untied it, so that it collided with a ladies' rowing eight, the barge owners were liable for not fastening the barge more securely: it was not enough for them to prove that the cause of the damage was wrongful interference.[172]

6–72   Also, where the occupiers of a football ground failed properly to maintain the exit gates and an unruly crowd deliberately forced them open and surged into the ground, injuring the pursuer, a spectator who was knocked down, the crowd's behaviour did not amount to novus actus interveniens.[173] When a water board maintained in the street a metal cover for a valve box and some third party pulled it open so that the claimant, while crossing the road with reasonable care, tripped over it and fell, the water board was liable since they ought to have anticipated and provided against the damage.[174] Where a claimant's action became statute barred by reason of the negligence of his solicitors, it was not a fresh intervening act interrupting the chain of causation for his new solicitors to fail to pursue amendment of the proceedings in order to rely on s.14A of the Limitation Act 1980, where such an application was bound to fail at trial.[175]

6–73   The illustrations show that it is immaterial whether the act of the third party is wilful, negligent or even unlawful. The sole question is whether it ought

---

[170] *Stansbie v Troman* [1948] 2 K.B. 48. See also *Dorset Yacht Co Ltd v Home Office* [1970] A.C. 1004.

[171] *Davies v Liverpool Corporation* [1949] 2 All E.R. 175.

[172] *Newby v General Lighterage Co Ltd* [1955] 1 Lloyd's Rep. 273.

[173] *Hosie v Arbroath Football Club*, 1978 S.L.T. 122. See Stuart, "Bad Neighbours", 1984 S.L.T. 45.

[174] *Wells v Metropolitan Water Board* [1937] 4 All E.R. 639. But cf. *Simpson v Metropolitan Water Board* (1917) 15 L.G.R. 629. Further, in *McCarthy v Wellington City* [1966] N.Z.L.R. 481 and in *Purtill v Athlone Urban District Council* [1968] I.R. 205, where the occupiers of premises containing stored explosives failed to guard against the foreseeable mischievous acts of children, they were held liable. In a similar case, however, whilst it was held that the railways board were under a duty to use reasonable care to keep their detonators, which were dangerous things, safely, they could not have foreseen in the circumstances the theft of such detonators by trespassing boys: *Kingzett v British Railways Board* (1968) 112 S.J. 625. See also *Haynes v Harwood* [1935] 1 K.B. 146 (where a mischievous child frightened an unattended horse in the street).

[175] *Winston Cooper v Smith Llewellyn Partnership* [1999] P.N.L.R. 576.

reasonably to have been foreseen as likely to follow upon the defendant's negligence.[176]

(B) The intervening act of the claimant.

Generally.[177] Although typically the question of an intervening cause arises   **6–74**
in relation to the act of a third party independent of the defendant, it may also be that of the claimant himself or of some person for whom he is vicariously liable. As Lord Wright said: "the plaintiff's damage may still be the direct and natural consequence of the defendants' default, notwithstanding the co-operation of human conduct, whether of the plaintiff or of a third party."[178]

ILLUSTRATIONS

There was held to be an intervening cause, resulting from the claimant's own   **6–75**
act: where two vessels were in collision as a result of the defendant's vessel's negligence and the claimants' vessel, having tried to save the other by lashing her alongside and towing her inshore, grounded in fog and was further damaged[179]; where the defendants, as main contractors, were in breach of contract in failing to supply a step-ladder to the claimant, an independent sub-contractor, who borrowed a trestle, which he failed to have footed, and from which he fell[180]; where a claimant was gravely injured in a road traffic accident caused by the defendant's negligence but died after he was properly prescribed a drug which reacted with food he consumed to produce a stroke[181]; where the pursuer, who sought damages for a failed sterilisation, decided to have intercourse even though she knew the sterilisation had failed, thereby exposing herself to the risk of pregnancy[182]; where the deceased drowned while swimming in a pond on the defendant's land and the risks to competent swimmers were "perfectly obvious."[183] Where the claimant suffered brain damage and depression in a road traffic accident and began to use heroin to relieve headaches secondary to those conditions, the defendant was not liable for additional injury and loss arising

---

[176] *S.S. Singleton Abbey v S.S. Paludina* [1937] A.C. 16, per Lord Sumner at 28; "Cause and consequence in such a matter do not depend on the question, whether the first action which intervenes, is excusable or not, but on the question whether it is new and independent or not."
[177] See further, Ch.4, above, in relation to the defences of "*volenti non fit injuria*" or, "contributory negligence", which will usually also arise when considering some act of the claimant as contributing to the injury suffered.
[178] *Summers v Salford Corp* [1943] A.C. 283 at 296.
[179] *The San Onofre* [1922] P. 243.
[180] *Quinn v Burch Brothers (Builders) Ltd* [1966] 2 Q.B. 370. See also *Vacwell Engineering Co Ltd v B.D.H. Chemicals Ltd* [1971] 1 Q.B. 88; *McKew v Holland & Hannen & Cubitts (Scotland)* [1969] 3 All E.R. 1621, HL. But cf. the decision of Eveleigh J. in *Wieland v Cyril Lord Carpets* [1969] 3 All E.R. 1006.
[181] *Alston v Marine & Trade Insurance Co Ltd* 1964 (4) S.A. 112. The case provides a notable illustration both of a fresh independent act of the claimant himself and also that the test is not simply reasonableness, since the claimant's conduct in eating the food in question was not criticised.
[182] *Sabri-Tabrizi v Lothian Health Board* 1998 S.L.T. 607, OH.
[183] *Darby v National Trust* [2001] P.I.Q.R. P372, CA.

from his use of the drug which had been a voluntary, informed and unreasonable choice of his own.[184]

6–76   On the contrary, there was no intervening cause[185]: where the defendants mistakenly delivered five cases of scrap film to the claimants' premises, instead of to another address along the same street, and a typist intending to make "a small innocuous fire," touched a piece of the scrap with a lighted cigarette, causing an explosion: the typist's act was not a fresh cause relieving the defendants of liability, since although she knew that the scrap would burn, she had no idea it was so violently inflammable[186]; where the claimant cleaned a window of her home knowing that a sash had already broken, and the window fell and crushed her hand: her conduct was lawful, reasonable, and and in the ordinary course of things, so that the defendants could not avoid liability.[187]

6–77   Also, where the the defendant's negligence in carrying out repairs caused glass to fall from a skylight in the roof of a shop and the claimant, reasonably believing her husband to be in danger, instinctively clutched his arm and tried to pull him clear, straining herself in the process[188]; where the claimant, finding herself locked in a cubicle of the defendants' public lavatory, fell and was injured whilst returning to floor level after making an unsuccessful attempt to climb out over the top by standing on the toilet roll holder, which rotated under her foot: she had not taken any risk which was disproportionate to the necessities of her situation.[189] The conduct of the claimant, an experienced ship's electrical engineer, in loosening a nut on a defective thermosensor did not interrupt the chain of causation between the defendants' negligence and an accident on a ship in which he suffered burns from steam and hot water.[190] Likewise where the claimant, whose mobility was seriously impaired as a result of the defendant's negligence, chose not to call for help when trying to fill his car with petrol on a garage forecourt, or to use his sticks or prosthesis, and tripped over a raised manhole cover, aggravating his injuries.[191]

6–78   There is no intervening cause where a man, injured by the defendants' negligence, commits suicide, where that is ultimately a consequence of his injury[192]; likewise where the act of suicide is the very act which the duty cast

[184] *Wilson v Coulson* [2002] P.I.Q.R. P300, Ch.3, para.3–71, above.
[185] See the analysis of Lord Sumner in *Weld-Blundell v Stephens* [1920] A.C. 956. Lord Sumner at 984–985 set out a series of situation categories where this could happen.
[186] *Philco Radio and Television Corporation of Great Britain Ltd v J. Spurling Ltd* [1949] 2 K.B. 33.
[187] *Summers v Salford Corp* [1943] A.C. 283.
[188] *Brandon v Osborne, Garrett & Co Ltd* [1924] 1 K.B. 548.
[189] *Sayers v Harlow UDC* [1958] 1 W.L.R. 623 (the claimant was held one-quarter to blame for her accident).
[190] *Dziennik v CTO Gesellschaft Fur Containertransport MBH* [2006] EWCA Civ 1456 (negligence in failing to give the claimant clear direction how the job should be approached).
[191] *Spencer v Wincanton Holdings Ltd* [2009] EWCA Civ 1404 (the claimant was found guilty of contributory negligence to the extent of one third).
[192] *Corr v IBC Vehicles* [2008] A.C. 884 (suicide as a consequence of depression, itself caused by injuries received in an accident at work: held, employer liable).

upon the defendant requires it to prevent[193]; also generally, in the "rescue cases", where it is foreseeable that attempts at rescue will be made and reasonable in the circumstances to make such an attempt.[194]

Acts in mitigation of damage. Since it is the claimant's duty to mitigate **6–79** loss,[195] no act which is reasonably done to that end will break the chain of causation.[196] Conversely, such part of the claimed damage as can be attributed to a failure to mitigate, will not be recoverable.[197] The duty to mitigate has been long-established: "It is undoubted law that a plaintiff who sues for damages owes the duty of taking all reasonable steps to mitigate the loss consequent upon the breach and cannot claim as damages any sum which is due to his own neglect."[198] However, there is a distinction between failure to minimise damage already occasioned; and damage which probably would not have resulted at all had it not been for the claimant's failure, by act or omission, to prevent or mitigate loss.[199]

The claimant may not increase the damage for which claim is made by some **6–80** unnecessary act. Where a submarine sank as a result of the defendants' negligence with loss of the crew, the Commissioners unsuccessfully sought to claim the capitalised amount of the pensions payable by them to the crew's relatives: although the defendants' negligence had provided the occasion, it was not the cause of that item of loss, since the pensions were voluntary payments in the nature of compassionate allowances.[200] Where the pursuer's car was damaged by the defender's negligence and he recovered the cost from his own insurers but his policy thereby fell in and was cancelled, his claim for the loss of the unexpired portion of the premium was disallowed: he should first have exhausted his rights against the defender and, thereby, minimised his loss, which would have avoided the cancellation.[201]

The duty is to act reasonably.[202] Where the claimant refuses to accept medical **6–81** advice or treatment it will depend upon the circumstances whether that refusal is unreasonable. The medical advice received will, no doubt, be a major factor. The

---

[193] *Reeves v Commissioner of Police of the Metropolis* [2000] 1 A.C. 360, Ch.4, paras 4–22 and 4–91, above.
[194] See *Cutler v United Dairies (London) Ltd* [1933] 2 K.B. 297; *Haynes v Harwood* [1935] 1 K.B. 146; *The Gusty* [1940] P. 159; *Morgan v Aylen* [1942] 1 All E.R. 489; *Hyett v Great Western Railway* [1948] 1 K.B. 345; *Baker v T.E. Hopkins & Sons Ltd* [1959] 1 W.L.R. 966; *Videan v B.T.C.* [1963] 2 Q.B. 650; *Chadwick v B.R.B.* [1967] 1 W.L.R. 912. See also Ch.2, paras 2–259 to 2–265 above.
[195] See, further, Ch.5, paras 5–45 to 5–51, above.
[196] *Dee Conservancy Board v McConnell* [1928] 2 K.B. 159.
[197] *British Westinghouse Electric and Manufacturing Co Ltd v Underground Electric Ry Co of London Ltd* [1912] A.C. 673. Further, see *Macrae v H.G. Swindells* [1954] 1 W.L.R. 597; *Darbishire v Warran* [1963] 1 W.L.R. 1067; *Bellingham v Dhillon* [1973] Q.B. 304 (where it was held that the principle in *British Westinghouse*, above, was applicable and that there was no difference between actions in contract and tort in this respect).
[198] Lord Wrenbury in *Jamal v Moolla Dawood Sons & Co* [1916] 1 A.C. 175 at 179.
[199] See per Stamp L.J. in *Dutton v Bognor Regis UDC* [1972] 1 Q.B. 373 at 412, 413.
[200] *Admiralty Commissioners v S.S. Amerika* [1917] A.C. 38.
[201] *Alexander v Lang*, 1967 S.L.T. 64.
[202] *Watson Norie v Shaw* (1967) 111 S.J. 117; *Newland v Rye-Arc* [1971] 2 Lloyd's Rep. 64; *Moore v D.E.R. Ltd* [1971] 1 W.L.R. 1476; *Eley v Bedford* [1972] 1 Q.B. 155.

burden of proving that the claimant did *not* act reasonably rests upon the defendant.[203] Where the claimant is found to have acted unreasonably, damages should be assessed as they would have been had the treatment been received and been successful to the extent opined.[204] On the other hand, the defendant will be held liable in full if the original injury still subsists, but in aggravated form, despite the claimant undergoing an operation, prudently advised, which had been properly carried out.[205] If a damaged chattel was unique in character, its owner may be entitled to the cost of repairing it at a cost considerably exceeding its market value,[206] but not otherwise, since he has not taken reasonable steps to mitigate his loss.[207] What is reasonable mitigation of damage is not a question of law but one of fact in each case, and again the burden of proof is upon the defendant to show that the claimant has acted unreasonably.[208]

(C) Failure of an expected act to occur

6–82   **Generally.** We have already looked at cases where an intervening act may interrupt the chain of causation between a breach of duty and the claimant's loss. But intervening acts may also be relevant to whether a breach of duty arises at all. The defendant may reasonably anticipate some action which, if performed, would prevent any loss being occasioned. The situation is a common one in actions based on negligence against the manufacturers, retailers, repairers and transferors of goods, where some examination of the goods is anticipated before they are put to use. If no examination is to be anticipated, resulting damage will usually not be too remote.[209] On the other hand at common law,[210] if the manufacturer, retailer, repairer or transferor of goods could reasonably have expected an intermediate examination or that some important instruction would be carried out, before the goods were put to use, he could, and may still be able

---

[203] *Steele v Robert George & Co Ltd* [1942] A.C. 497; *Richardson v Redpath Brown & Co Ltd* [1944] A.C. 62. Statements to the contrary in *Selvanayagam v University of the West Indies* [1983] 1 W.L.R. 585 cannot safely be relied upon: *Geest Plc v Lansiiquot* [2003] 1 All E.R. 383, PC.

[204] *McAuley v London Transport Executive* [1957] 2 Lloyd's Rep. 500. In *Morgan v T. Wallis* [1974] 1 Lloyd's Rep. 165, the claimant, who had received back injuries at work, refused to submit to an operation which he genuinely feared, although the chances of achieving successful results were estimated by the surgeon to be about 90 per cent. Applying *Steele v Robert George & Co (1937) Ltd* [1942] A.C. 497, it was held that his refusal was unreasonable.

[205] *Hogan v Bentinck West Hartley Collieries (Owners) Ltd* [1949] 1 All E.R. 588.

[206] *O'Grady v Westminster Scaffolding Ltd* [1962] 2 Lloyd's Rep. 238 (a car which was originally a 1938 M.G. and had been converted into a unique article "like a mechanised replica of the Lord Mayor's coach," which its proud owner named "Hortensia." Harman L.J. described it in *Darbishire v Warren*, below (at 1072) as "a remarkable vehicle . . . the apple of the plaintiff's eye," but it was somewhat unkindly referred to as a "freak" by Pennycuick J. ibid. below (at 1079)). See Ch.5, para.5–46, above.

[207] *Darbishire v Warran* [1963] 1 W.L.R. 1067.

[208] *Roper v Johnson* (1873) L.R. 8 C.P. 167 at 181, per Brett J. For an example where the defendants failed to discharge the onus, see *Dallinghoo Parochial Church Council v Fisons Ltd, The Times*, June 1, 1982, CA (plantation destroyed by weedkiller but the defendants submitted that the owners ought to have replanted the land immediately, in order to have acted reasonably in mitigation of their loss).

[209] *Donoghue v Stevenson* [1932] A.C. 562; *Brown v Cotterill* (1934) 51 T.L.R. 21.

[210] A form of strict liability exists in relation to "defective products," by virtue of the Consumer Protection Act 1987. See further Ch.15, below.

to, avoid liability for damage arising from a defect which the examination would have disclosed, or for damage arising from failure to carry the instruction out.[211]

ILLUSTRATIONS

Where a noxious hair dye was manufactured and supplied without any **6–83** instruction for a skin test to be made before use, the defendant was in breach of duty and the claimant's loss was recoverable[212]; but not so where instructions were given but were disregarded.[213] Where damage resulted from the darkness in the passage of an air-raid shelter, the building contractor was not liable where it had been passed by the local authority as being in accordance with the contract.[214] A sub-contractor successfully avoided liability where a stop-cock had been carelessly painted over, but it was reasonably anticipated that the work would be inspected, and such a fault discovered and remedied.[215]

On the other hand, it was held that an architect, demolition contractors and the **6–84** claimant's employers were jointly liable, where a labourer was injured when a dangerous wall collapsed: no one involved had carried out a proper inspection of it. The architect and the demolition contractors could not escape liability unless they could show that examination by the building contractors was reasonably to be expected as a probability.[216]

4.—UNKNOWN CAUSES

Introduction. As already stated,[217] it is not necessary for the claimant to give **6–85** direct evidence of negligence. A case may be proved partly by direct and partly by indirect or circumstantial evidence. In some cases the facts of an accident are unknown and, in order to succeed, the claimant must then prove facts, from which an inference of negligence on the part of the defendant may be reasonably drawn. "It is a mistake to think that because an event is unseen its cause cannot be reasonably inferred."[218] The facts, however, must be such as to put the matter

---

[211] *Haseldine v Daw & Son* [1941] 2 K.B. 343, approving *Herschtal v Stewart & Ardern* [1940] 1 K.B. 155. Further, see Ch.15, para.15–88, below.
[212] *Parker v Oloxo Ltd* [1937] 3 All E.R. 524.
[213] *Holmes v Ashford* [1950] 2 All E.R. 76, which was distinguished in *Good-Wear Treaders v D. & B. Holdings* (1979) 98 D.L.R. (3d) 59 where it was held that the mere giving of a warning of the dangers of the product supplied was insufficient.
[214] *Buckner v Ashby & Horner* [1941] 1 K.B. 321.
[215] *Duncan v Cammell Laird* [1943] 2 All E.R. 621 (reversed on other grounds, sub nom. *Woods v Duncan* [1946] A.C. 401).
[216] *Clay v A.J. Crump & Sons Ltd* [1964] 1 Q.B. 533; followed in *Driver v W. Willett (Contractors) Ltd* [1969] 1 All E.R. 665.
[217] See para.6–14, above.
[218] Lord Buckmaster in *Jones v G.W. Ry* (1930) 47 T.L.R. 39, 41. See also *Lane v Shire Roofing Co (Oxford) Ltd* [1995] P.I.Q.R. P417, CA (where the claimant, who could remember nothing of the accident, had fallen from a roof); *Betts v Berkshire Health Authority* [1997] 8 Med. L.R. 87, para.6–09, above (where a surgeon had no recollection of an operation alleged to have been performed negligently).

beyond a mere surmise or conjecture and they must lead to an inference, which is a reasonable deduction from the facts actually observed and proved.[219] In a personal injuries action it has been held that where the evidence remained unclear as to the actual cause of the accident but it was established that it was normal for indisciplined behaviour to occur in circumstances which could have caused it, the judge was entitled to infer that such behaviour did account for the accident's happening.[220]

ILLUSTRATIONS

6–86   Factual inferences were drawn which permitted the claimant to succeed: after a bargeman was found drowned in a dock, where no chains or ladders were provided at the dock walls to help persons who accidentally fell into the water to get out and there had been earlier incidents of drowning in the dock and complaints of its dangerous condition[221]; where an explosion occurred at a cartridge factory, the cause being unknown, and it was found that appropriate machinery had not been supplied and proper precautions not taken to prevent an explosion[222]; after an employee was found dead between the buffers of two railway wagons on a siding, commonly used for access, where shunting operations had been performed[223]; after two motorcyclists collided on the highway and no one could give evidence as to what had happened, both cycles being interlocked on the claimant's proper side of the road.[224]

Where a helicopter suddenly lost height and crashed, it was accepted that some mechanical malfunction was to blame, although as a result of fire, there was insufficient evidence to identify the nature of the probable defect.[225]

6–87   On the other hand, negligence was not established: where an employee at docks left to go to the lavatory in dense fog and his body was subsequently found in a dock opposite a gap in chains placed about 12 feet from the water's edge[226]; where a man was killed by a train at a level crossing, at which there were the usual gates and a watchman and there was no evidence when or in what circumstances he had got on to the line[227]; where a prisoner was confined in a wooden lockup in a small rural municipality in British Columbia, a fire broke out

---

[219] *Jones v G.W. Ry* (1930) 47 T.L.R. 39 at 45, per Lord Macmillan. See, e.g. *Carroll v Fearon* [1998] P.I.Q.R. P416, CA, Ch.15, para.15–81, below, where a judge was entitled to draw the inference of negligence in the course of manufacture of a tyre even though no particular person or persons could be identified as to blame, or their negligent acts identified.

[220] *Clowes v N.C.B.*, The Times, April 23, 1987, CA (underground miner fell and was seriously injured when he was trodden on by his fellow miners in their stampede to get off the manriding train, in order to be the first to reach the lift at the end of their work shift).

[221] *Moore v Ransome's Dock Committee* (1898) 14 T.L.R. 539. Compare *Graham v East of Scotland Water Authority*, 2002 S.C.L.R. 340, OH, para.6–15, above.

[222] *McArthur v Dominion Cartridge Co* [1905] A.C. 72.

[223] *Jones v G.W. Ry* (1930) 47 T.L.R. 39.

[224] *Alexander v Anderson* [1933] N.I. 158.

[225] *Budden v Police Aviation Services Ltd* [2005] P.I.Q.R. P362.

[226] *Mersey Docks and Harbour Board v Procter* [1923] A.C. 253.

[227] *Wakelin v L. & S.W. Ry* (1886) 12 App.Cas. 41.

and he was burnt to death, there being no evidence as to its cause[228]; where two motorcars travelling in opposite directions collided, and the physical evidence was consistent with either car being at fault and there was no evidence that the defendant's car was ever on its wrong side of the white line.[229]

Identifying a cause. It has been emphasised that, where the evidence permits, **6–88** it is an essential part of the court's function to reach a definite conclusion and a claim may not be dismissed on the basis of inability to decide which party's negligence caused, for instance, an accident.[230] Where a collision occurred between two cars leaving the motorway in the same direction, there were no independent witnesses and both drivers were apparently truthful and credible witnesses, it was not a permissible conclusion that on the balance of probabilities neither had proved a case against the other. It would be rare for road traffic cases to fall into the exceptional category where it was possible for a judge to say "I just do not know"[231] in relation to an accident's cause.[232]

Particular difficulty can arise in identifying a cause where the acts of two or **6–89** more defendants are involved and it is uncertain who bore what responsibility. The examples are meat and drink to those who set examination papers in law, as for instance where two sportsmen together and carelessly discharged their shot-guns, the claimant being injured by a single pellet which could equally have come from either gun.[233] In such circumstances it has been held that where the careless act of each defendant has prevented the claimant from discovering the fact of whose negligence had caused him damage, then, on common-sense grounds and as a matter of policy, both defendants should be liable.[234] Doubtless a claim may be dismissed if there is no evidence from which to infer negligence on the part of one or other or both of the defendants, but, if the inference is that one or the other has, or both have, been negligent, then the claimant has made out a prima facie case against either one or both of them.

Accordingly, where two motor vehicles, travelling in opposite directions, **6–90** collided during the hours of darkness in the centre of the road, as a result of which both drivers were killed, it was held that the proper inference was that both

---

[228] *McKenzie v Chilliwack Corp* [1912] A.C. 888.
[229] *Hollington v F. Hewthorn & Co Ltd* [1943] 2 All E.R. 35.
[230] *Bray v Palmer* [1953] 1 W.L.R. 1455 (each vehicle swerved but collision still occurred in the centre of the road—new trial ordered). See, further, *Knight v Fellick* [1977] R.T.R. 316, CA.
[231] See per May L.J. in *Morris v London Iron and Steel Co Ltd* [1998] Q.B. 493, 504. See also para.6–90, and Ch.10, para.10–220 below.
[232] *Cooper v Floor Cleaning Machines Ltd*, *The Times*, October 24, 2003, CA (on analysis the defendant's version of the accident was to be preferred).
[233] e.g. *Oliver v Mills*, 144 Missouri 852 (1926); cf. *R. v Salmon* (1880) 6 Q.B.D. 7; *Mohan v R.* [1967] 2 A.C. 187.
[234] *Cook v Lewis* [1952] 1 D.L.R. 1 (two hunters one or other of whom fired the shot which wounded the claimant). See Hogan, "*Cook v Lewis* Re-examined" (1961) 24 M.L.R. 331. In *Power v Bedford Motor Co Ltd* [1959] I.R. 391 it was recognised that this principle could cause great hardship to the defendant, who was in fact innocent, where the damage must have been caused by one or other of them but not *both* defendants.

were equally to blame, there being no evidence pointing to one driver being any more blameworthy than the other.[235]

6–91   Similarly, where there has been a collision at a crossroads, both roads being of equal status, or on the brow of a hill: in the absence of some determining feature in the evidence, the inference to be drawn is that both drivers were equally negligent. A blameless passenger will have a prima facie case against both drivers or either of them.[236] Whilst this rule seems to apply even if it is perfectly feasible that neither had been negligent,[237] it certainly applies to instances of joint tortfeasors,[238] either as persons of whom one is vicariously liable for the negligence and breach of statutory duty of the other,[239] or as persons engaged on a concerted common design. In the case of manufacturers, where clearly someone has been at fault, the injured claimant "is not required to lay his finger on the exact person in all the chain who was responsible, or to specify what he did wrong. Negligence is found as a matter of inference from the existence of the defects taken in connection with all the known circumstances."[240]

5.—CONCURRENT AND SUCCESSIVE CAUSES

6–92   **Concurrent causes.** When separate and independent acts of negligence on the part of two or more persons together result in an accident, any one of which probably would have caused the like damage, then each tortfeasor will be liable for the full damage suffered. Each negligent act is a substantive cause in producing the end result.[241]

ILLUSTRATIONS

6–93   Where a gas company fitted a defective service pipe to convey gas to the claimant's shop, gas leaked, and an explosion was caused when an employee of the gas fitters approached the leak carrying a lighted candle, it was held that the

---

[235] *Baker v Market Harborough Industrial Co-operative Society Ltd* [1953] 1 W.L.R. 1472, per Denning L.J., that even assuming one of the vehicles was over the centre line, and thus to blame, the absence of any avoiding action by the other vehicle made that vehicle also to blame. Regarding the confines of this principle, however, see *Knight v Fellick*, above. The CA, in applying the dictum of Sachs L.J. in *Davison v Leggett* (1969) 113 S.J. 409, held that it was not necessary for the judge to conclude exactly what had happened in the accident. Thus, he was entitled to reach the opinion on the facts that no blame had attached to the defendant motorist, who had knocked down a pedestrian road-sweeper in an unlit street, during the hours of darkness, despite the fact that he had been driving on dipped headlights. See also *Cooper v Hatton* [2001] R.T.R. 36, CA, para.10–220, below (no witnesses to a collision in which one of two cars must have been on the wrong side of the road).
[236] *France v Parkinson* [1954] 1 W.L.R. 581.
[237] *Davison v Leggett* (1969) 113 S.J. 409. See also *Knight v Fellick* [1977] R.T.R. 316, CA.
[238] See, generally, Ch.3, paras 3–87, 3–88, above. Drivers involved in a collision are several and not joint tortfeasors.
[239] See *Cassidy v Ministry of Health* [1951] 2 K.B. 343, per Singleton L.J.; *Roe v Minister of Health* [1954] 2 Q.B. 66 at 80, 82, 88, per Somervell, Denning and Morris L.JJ.; *Walsh v Holst & Co Ltd* [1958] 1 W.L.R. 800 at 804, per Hodson L.J.
[240] *Grant v Australian Knitting Mills Ltd* [1936] A.C. 85 at 101. "Defective products" attract strict liability under the Consumer Protection Act 1987 Pt I. See further Ch.15, below.
[241] See, e.g. per Lord du Parcq in *Grant v Sun Shipping Co Ltd* [1948] A.C. 549 at 563.

gas company could be liable for the whole of the damage.[242] Where a local authority planted trees near the highway, the branches of which were allowed to overhang the road's surface, and the claimant, a passenger in the defendant's bus, which was negligently driven so close to the trees that a low branch struck the bus window, was blinded by broken glass, both the corporation and the bus company were liable for the injury.[243]

Where an electricity board carried out electrical wiring in a factory but **6-94** negligently transposed two wires, so that current remained on even after a switch had been turned off and the claimant's husband, a fireman called to fight a fire, was electrocuted, both the board and the occupiers of the factory were liable, the former because of their wiring error, the latter because they were unaware of the location of the main switch for the premises.[244] Where a 15-year-old claimant, was knocked from his bicycle by a van, without serious injury, but as he lay in the road was struck by a car and sustained very severe injury, he was entitled to judgment in full against both the van owners, as well as the car driver.[245]

Successive acts of negligence cause consecutive damage. In this class of **6-95** case remoteness of damage, which is discussed more fully elsewhere, can become an issue.[246] However, for immediate purposes, a distinction needs to be drawn between those cases where independently-acting wrongdoers concurrently cause the damage suffered by the claimant, and those cases where independently-acting wrongdoers successively cause consecutive damage.

ILLUSTRATIONS

The defendant negligently drove his car into collision with the claimants' Rolls **6-96** Royce, which was awaiting a paint respray as a result of an earlier similar collision. A judgment obtained in respect of the earlier collision being unsatisfied, the claimants sought unsuccessfully to recover from the defendant the cost of work which would have included the earlier damage: since the defendant damaged a car, which at the time, was already in need of respraying, that element in the claimants' loss did not flow from the defendant's wrongdoing and he was not liable.[247]

---

[242] *Burrows v March Gas and Coke Co* (1872) L.R. 7 Ex. 96.
[243] *Hale v Hants & Dorset Motor Services Ltd* [1947] 2 All E.R. 628 (although the apportionments made were different between the two defendants, each was negligent in failing to foresee the harm, which was likely to happen in combination with others' negligence).
[244] *Hartley v Mayoh & Co* [1954] 1 Q.B. 383.
[245] *West v Hughes of Beaconsfield* [1971] R.T.R. 298. (where a motorist, in a line of traffic on a busy road at night, negligently knocked down a cyclist, the plainly foreseeable consequence was that the latter might be injured by the next following vehicle. The fact that the driver of the next following car could have avoided a second impact, if he had been keeping a proper look-out, did not constitute a *novus actus interveniens*. However, since the first driver had the better opportunity to avoid the claimant, liability was apportioned as to 55 per cent against himself, and 45 per cent against the driver who followed).
[246] See Ch.5, paras 5–01 to 5–14, above.
[247] *Performance Cars Ltd v Abraham* [1962] 1 Q.B. 33.

6–97   In *Baker v Willoughby*,[248] the claimant sought damages for injury to his leg which had been was broken in an accident, for which he alleged the defendant was responsible. His claim included for the possibility of future degenerative change in the limb. Before trial, however, that same leg had to be amputated as a result of a gunshot wound, caused when he was a victim in an armed robbery, and this removed entirely the severe consequences of the first injury. The Court of Appeal held that the claimant's damages were limited to compensation for loss suffered up to the date of the shooting, on the basis that the court must not speculate when it knows the facts. The House of Lords[249] reversed the Court of Appeal's decision and restored the judgment of the trial judge, who had expressed the view[250] that a distinction should be made between a supervening event which prevented an anticipated loss from occurring, and a supervening event which caused a greater loss, whether or not of the same kind, resulting in the anticipated loss being either merged or submerged. It was incorrect in the latter instance, to consider the original loss as having been reduced. In the result, the claimant's actual and prospective loss had not been reduced by the subsequent loss of the leg.

6–98   By way of contrast, in *Jobling v Associated Dairies*,[251] where a claimant sustained injuries in an accident caused by the defendants' negligence, but it became known later that he was suffering from a debilitating illness, unconnected with the accident, it was held that the defendants were liable only to pay reduced damages, because the supervening event had not been caused by any further tort. While *Baker v Willoughby*[252] might be acceptable on its own facts, it had no application when, after the tort had been committed but before trial, the victim was overtaken by a wholly unconnected, permanently disabling, disease.

6–99   In *Rahman v Arearose Ltd*,[253] the court was concerned with causation where the claimant had suffered successive acts of negligence damaging his eye. It was said that it was it was not a rule of law that later negligence always extinguished the causative potency of an earlier tort:

---

[248] *Baker v Willoughby* [1970] A.C. 467. See Strachan, "Scope and Application of the 'but for' Causal Test", 33 M.L.R. 386; McGregor, "Variations on an Enigma: Successive Causes of Personal Injury", 33 M.L.R. 378.

[249] [1970] A.C. 467 at 494, per Lord Reid: "If the injury suffered before the date of the trial either reduces the disabilities from the injury for which the defendant is liable, or shortens the period during which they will be suffered by the plaintiff, then the defendant will have to pay less damages. But if the later injuries merely become a concurrent cause of the disabilities caused by the injury inflicted by the defendant, then in my view they cannot diminish the damages." For an example of the former, see *Hodgson v General Electricity Co* [1978] 2 Lloyd's Rep. 210 (heart disease was a supervening act, which rendered the claimant unfit for work).

[250] [1969] 1 Q.B. 38.

[251] [1982] A.C. 794. See Poole, "Pre-existing Medical Conditions and Awards of Damages", 131 New L.J. 696.

[252] [1970] A.C. 467.

[253] [2001] Q.B. 351, Ch.3, para.3–91, above (employers were negligent in failing to reduce the risk of assault upon the claimant, their employee, and thereby responsible for the consequences, including psychological symptoms, even though these were partially contributed to by negligent surgery which caused the claimant to lose the sight in his right eye).

"The law is that every tortfeasor should compensate the injured claimant in respect of that loss and damage for which he should justly be held responsible. To make that principle good, it is important that the elusive conception of causation should not be frozen into constricting rules."[254]

It was also observed that there was no inconsistency between *Baker* and *Jobling*:

"Once it is realised that every tortfeasor should compensate the injured claimant in respect of that loss and damage for which he should justly be held responsible, the metaphysics of causation can be kept in their proper place . . . in all these cases the real question is, what is the damage for which the defendant under consideration should be held responsible."[255]

6.—Res Ipsa Loquitur

Meaning. A special application of the principle that there is evidence of negligence if the facts proved are more consistent with negligence on the part of the defendant than with other causes, arises in those cases in which the maxim res ipsa loquitur is said to apply.[256] Although use of the maxim is periodically discouraged,[257] it is so well entrenched that it may take some time to dislodge entirely. However, it has never been correct to describe it in terms of doctrine: **6–100**

"I think that it is no more than an exotic although convenient, phrase to describe what is in essence no more than a common-sense approach, not limited by technical rules, to the assessment of the effect of evidence in certain circumstances."[258]

The question whether to apply the maxim has usually arisen where the claimant is able to prove the happening of an accident but little else. He might well be unable to prove the precise act or omission of the defendant which caused   **6–101**

---

[254] per Laws L.J. at 365.

[255] per Laws L.J. at 366.

[256] The maxim does not have to be pleaded if the facts both pleaded and proved showed that an accident was prima facie caused by some negligence on the part of the defendant: *Bennett v Chemical Construction* [1971] 1 W.L.R. 1571; *Love v Motherwell District Council*, 1994 S.C.L.R. 761.

[257] per Hobhouse L.J. in *Ratcliffe v Plymouth & Torbay HA* [1998] P.I.Q.R. P170, CA " . . . the expression *res ipsa loquitur* should be dropped from the litigator's vocabulary and replaced by the phrase 'a *prima facie* case'. Res ipsa loquitur is not a principle of law: it does not relate to or raise any presumption. It is merely a guide to help to identify when a prima facie case has been made out."

[258] per Megaw L.J. in *Lloyde v West Midlands Gas Board* [1971] 1 W.L.R. 749 at 755. Lord Denning M.R., in *Turner v Mansfield Corporation*, The Times, May 15, 1975, agreed that res ipsa loquitur was only a rule as to the weight of evidence, from which negligence could be inferred and could not accurately be described as a "doctrine" so that to that extent *Moore v R. Fox & Sons* [1956] 1 Q.B. 596 should be relegated to the background. See also *Fryer v Pearson*, The Times, April 4, 2000, CA (gas fitter injured by needle concealed in the pile of a carpet in a house at which he was working). Since it is a rule of evidence rather than substantive law, there seems no reason why it should not apply to a breach of statutory duty, although the circumstances in which it could be relied upon in that context are likely to be rare: see, e.g. *McDyer v Celtic Football and Athletic Co Ltd* 1997 Rep. L.R. 117, OH, Ch.8, para.8–37, n.111, below (an alleged breach of the Occupiers Liability (Scotland) Act 1960).

an accident to occur,[259] but if on the evidence it is more likely than not that its effective cause was some act or omission of the defendant, which would constitute a failure to take reasonable care for his safety, then in the absence of some plausible explanation consistent with an absence of negligence, the claim would succeed.[260]

6–102   **Not a rule of law.** The maxim is not a rule of law, it merely describes a state of the evidence from which it is possible to draw an inference of negligence.[261] It is based on common sense, its purpose being to enable justice to be done when the facts bearing on causation and the standard of care exercised are unknown to the claimant but ought to be within the knowledge of the defendant.[262] It cannot assist where there is no evidence to support an inference of negligence and a possible non-negligent cause of the injury exists.[263]

6–103   **A prima facie case.** It has been said that "a prima facie case" should be the preferred terminology. It means essentially a case which calls for some answer from the defendant and will arise upon proof of: (1) the happening of some unexplained occurrence; (2) which would not have happened in the ordinary course of things without negligence on the part of somebody other than the claimant; and (3) the circumstances point to the negligence in question being that of the defendant, rather than that of any other person.

6–104   The third requirement is usually fulfilled by showing that the instrument causing the damage was in the management and control of the defendant at the time of the occurrence, but this is not essential.[264] Where an object which causes an accident has, at all material times, been under the control of the defendants and there is no evidence to show how the accident happened, the presumption of negligence cannot be displaced by evidence of the general care that has been taken.[265] So, when a lorry's brakes had failed because of the sudden escape of brake fluid from a hole in a corroded part of a pipe in the hydraulic system,

---

[259] A claimant who tenders evidence directed to proving the defendant guilty of some particular negligence is not thereby precluded from relying upon the maxim: *Anchor Products v Hedges* (1966) 115 C.L.R. 493 (H. Ct. of Australia).

[260] See *Lloyde v West Midlands Gas Board*, above n.10, and *Widdowson v Newgate Meat Corp* [1998] P.I.Q.R. P138, CA at 141, para.6–115 below. In *Carroll v Fearon* [1998] P.I.Q.R. P416, CA the maxim was said to have no relevant application where a tyre burst many years after it had been manufactured and, given its use, there was a multitude of possible causes of its failure.

[261] *Ng Chun Pui v Lee Chuen Tat, The Times*, May 25, 1988.

[262] *Barkway v South Wales Transport Co Ltd* [1950] 1 All E.R. 392 at 399, per Lord Normand.

[263] *Howard v Wessex Regional Health Authority* [1994] 5 Med L.R. 57.

[264] See *McGowan v Stott* (1923), reported in note to *Halliwell v Venables* [1930] 99 L.J.K.B. 353 at 357, where the CA said that the dictum of Fletcher Moulton L.J. in *Wing v L.G.O.* [1909] 2 K.B. 652 that res ipsa loquitur only applied when "the direct cause of the accident and so much of the surrounding circumstances as was essential to its occurrence, were within the sole control and management of the defendants, or their servants," went too far. See, e.g. *Lloyde v West Midlands Gas Board* [1971] 1 W.L.R. 749 (liable for gas explosion where apparatus was not under the Board's exclusive control). However, in *Macleod v Glasgow Corporation*, 1971 S.L.T. 64, where the pursuer was injured when the lavatory pan broke as he sat down on it in a public toilet, owned and occupied by the defenders, it was held that, as the allegedly defective apparatus had been in regular use by members of the public to the exclusion of the defenders and its employees, the maxim did not apply.

[265] *Cox v Northwest Airlines Inc* [1967] 2 Lloyd's Rep. 45.

whereupon the vehicle ran out of control downhill and struck the deceased, the vehicle's owners were liable in negligence, despite the fact that they had regularly carried out a weekly routine examination of that length of the tube which was visible for inspection.[266]

When an object or an operation is under the control of two persons, who are **6–105** not in law responsible for the acts of each other, judicial opinions have differed whether it was appropriate to think in terms of res ipsa loquitur. In *Roe v Minister of Health*,[267] McNair J. expressed the opinion that in such a case the maxim did not apply, because the *res* did not speak of negligence against either person individually. Denning L.J. differed,[268] on the ground that in such a case the claimant can call on each of the persons for an explanation.

Cause must be unknown. This rule of evidence has never been thought to **6–106** apply where the cause of an accident is known. If "the facts are sufficiently known, the question ceases to be one where the facts speak for themselves, and the solution is to be found by determining whether on the facts as established, negligence is to be inferred or not."[269] For example, if a pedestrian is struck on the head by a cricket ball, driven out of the field by a batsman in the course of a cricket match, the facts of the occurrence are known and the court must decide whether or not those facts constitute negligence on the part of the defendant.[270]

Things falling from buildings or otherwise. In the leading case of *Scott v* **6–107** *London and St Katherine Docks Co*,[271] the claimant, an officer in the customs, was lawfully passing in front of a warehouse in a dock when six bags of sugar which were being lowered by the dock company's dockers fell and injured him. It was held that the accident was prima facie evidence of negligence against the dock company. The principle was stated long ago by Sir William Erle C.J., delivering the judgment of the Court of Exchequer Chamber, in these terms:

"There must be reasonable evidence of negligence. But where the thing is shown to be under the management of the defendant or his servants, and the accident is such as in the ordinary course of things does not happen if those who have the management use proper care, it affords reasonable evidence, in the absence of explanation by the defendants, that the accident arose from want of care."[272]

---

[266] *Henderson v H.E. Jenkins & Sons* [1970] A.C. 282. See also *Ludgate v Lovett* [1969] 1 W.L.R. 1016 (a hired van which suddenly swerved violently whilst being driven along at 65 mph).
[267] [1954] 2 Q.B. 66 at 70.
[268] *Roe v Minister of Health* [1954] 2 Q.B. 66 at 82. See also *Cook v Lewis* [1952] 1 D.L.R. 1.
[269] *Barkway v South Wales Transport Co Ltd* [1950] 1 All E.R. 392 at 395, per Lord Porter. See also to the same effect, *Bolton v Stone* [1951] A.C. 850 at 859.
[270] *Bolton v Stone*, above.
[271] (1865) 3 H. & C. 596.
[272] *Scott v London and St Katherine Docks Co* (1865) 3 H. & C. 596 at 601, applied in *Ward v Tesco Stores* [1976] 1 W.L.R. 810, CA (claimant slipped on some yoghurt spilt on the floor of the defendants' supermarket, in which she was shopping).

ILLUSTRATIONS

6–108   Where a man was walking in the highway and was passing the shop of the defendant flour-dealer, when a barrel of flour fell upon him, it was held that the accident was prima facie evidence of the defendant's negligence.[273] Similarly, the fall of a theatre ceiling, hitting a member of the audience, was prima facie evidence of negligence on the part of the occupiers of the theatre.[274] Where a packing-case, belonging to the defendant, was propped against the wall of the defendant's house and fell on a passer-by in the street,[275] or a brick fell out of a railway bridge and struck a person on the highway,[276] there was prima facie evidence of negligence, in the one case, against the owner of the packing-case and, in the other, against the railway company.

6–109   Likewise, a prima facie case arose where the claimant was standing nearby when electrical control panels were being moved, and was injured when he dashed forward to prevent one of the panels toppling over onto someone working in front of it.[277] Where a child of eight, who suffered from developmental delay, managed to leave his school unnoticed and strayed into a main road where he was struck by a car and seriously injured, the absence of proof as to precisely how he managed to leave was irrelevant, given findings that the defendants had been in breach of their duty to supervise him properly and had not adequately explained how he came to be where he was.[278]

6–110   **Contamination of manufactured goods.** Where an article which has been manufactured by the defendant is found to contain something which would not be present if due care in manufacture had been taken,[279] such as a stone in a Bath bun baked by the defendant,[280] and phenol in a bottle of scented toiletry,[281] there is evidence of negligence. This is so, even though the article is handled by others before it reaches the person injured, if it is more probable that the defect was the result of faulty manufacture than any other causes. An illustration is the case of certain woollen underwear which contained a chemical irritant which could not have got there except by negligence in manufacture.[282] On the other hand, where

---

[273] *Byrne v Boadle* (1863) 2 H. & C. 722 at 728, per Pollock C.B.: "So in the building or repairing a house, or putting pots on the chimneys, if a person passing along the road is injured by something falling upon him, I think the accident alone would be *prima facie* evidence of negligence." See also *Walsh v Holst & Co Ltd* [1958] 1 W.L.R. 800; *Hardy v Thames & General Lighterage* [1967] 1 Lloyd's Rep. 228.
[274] *Pope v St Helen's Theatre Ltd* [1947] K.B. 30.
[275] *Briggs v Oliver* (1866) 4 H. & C. 403.
[276] *Kearney v L.B. & S.C. Ry* (1871) L.R. 6 Q.B. 759. cf. *Palmer v Bateman* [1908] 2 Ir.R. 393, where the prima facie case was successfully rebutted by the defendant; *Welfare v London and Brighton Ry* (1869) L.R. 4 Q.B. 693 (claimant went to a railway station to inquire about trains when a roll of zinc fell through a hole in the roof and injured him—held no evidence of negligence) must be taken to be wrongly decided as the accident certainly called for an explanation from the railway company.
[277] *Bennett v Chemical Construction (GB) Ltd* [1971] 1 W.L.R. 1571 at 1575, per Davies L.J.
[278] *J v North Lincolnshire County Council* [2000] P.I.Q.R. P84, CA. Ch.9, para.9–193, below.
[279] For dangerous products, generally, strict liability under the Consumer Protection Act 1987 and, when appropriate, proof of negligence, see Ch.15, below.
[280] *Chapronière v Mason* (1905) 21 T.L.R. 633.
[281] *Lockhard v Barr*, 1943 S.C. 1.
[282] *Grant v Australian Knitting Mills* [1936] A.C. 85.

a glass windscreen on a motorcar broke without any apparent cause 12 months after the buyer had had the car, it was held that the fact of the breakage alone was not evidence of negligence against the maker of the windscreen.[283]

Railway cases. The mere happening of an accident was held to be evidence **6–111** of negligence against a railway company where a railway carriage broke down or ran off the rails[284]; also, where a collision occurred between two trains on the defendant company's line[285]; where a train ran into a station's buffers[286]; where the door of a carriage suddenly opened when a passenger looked out of the window[287] (but not where the door in a corridor-compartment containing numerous passengers suddenly opened)[288]; where a train stopped suddenly, with a jerk, and flung passengers across the carriage[289]; and where a railway embankment supporting the line subsided and the train was wrecked.[290]

Medical negligence cases. Cases of this type frequently raise difficult issues **6–112** of fact and expert opinion. It has, from time to time, been doubted whether the application of an evidential rule such as res ipsa loquitur could ever assist the claimant in a complex case of medical negligence where evidence has been led by both sides.[291] These doubts notwithstanding, its theoretical application is amply supported by authority,[292] provided it is understood that it does not raise any presumption but "is merely a guide to help to identify when a prima facie case is being made out."[293] If the position reached at the end of the case is that the evidence admits of an inference of negligence, but the defendant has provided

---

[283] *Evans v Triplex Glass Co* [1938] 1 All E.R. 283, but cf. *McIlveen v Charlesworth Developments* [1973] N.I. 216 (a folding push-chair had collapsed and injured the child sitting in it).
[284] *Dawson v Manchester, Sheffield and Lincolnshire Ry* (1862) 5 L.T. 682; *Flannery v Waterford, etc., Ry* (1877) Ir.R. 11 C.L. 30.
[285] *Skinner v L.B. & S.C. Ry* (1850) 5 Ex. 787; *Carpue v L. & B. Ry* (1844) 5 Q.B. 747, 751; *Ayles v S.E. Ry* (1868) L.R. 3 Ex. 146 (train belonging to company A collided with train belonging to company B, which had running powers over company A's line—held evidence of negligence against company A).
[286] *Burke v Manchester, Sheffield and Lincolnshire Ry* (1870) 22 L.T. 442.
[287] *Gee v Metropolitan Ry* (1873) L.R. 8 Q.B. 161; *Hamer v Cambrian Ry* (1886) 2 T.L.R. 508; *Dudman v North London Ry* (1886) 2 T.L.R. 365; *Adams v L. & Y. Ry* (1869) L.R. 4 C.P. 739; *Toal v N.B. Ry* [1908] A.C. 352 (passenger on platform struck by open carriage door); *Inglis v L.M.S. Ry*, 1941 S.C. 551.
[288] *Easson v L.N.E.R.* [1944] K.B. 421.
[289] *Angus v London, Tilbury and Southend Ry* (1906) 22 T.L.R. 222.
[290] *G.W. Ry of Canada v Braid* (1863) 1 Moo.P.C. (N.S.) 101; criticised in *Czech v General Steam Navigation Co* (1867) L.R. 3 C.P. 14, but followed in *City of Montreal v Watt and Scott* [1922] 2 A.C. 555.
[291] See, e.g. Stuart-Smith L.J. in *Delaney v Southmead Health Authority* [1995] 6 Med. L.R. 355, CA at 359. See also Jones, *"Res ipsa loquitur* in medical negligence actions: enough said" (1998) 3 P.N. 174.
[292] See the summary in the judgment of Brooke L.J. in *Ratcliffe v Plymouth & Torbay Health Authority* [1998] P.I.Q.R. P170, CA.
[293] *Ratcliffe v Plymouth & Torbay Health Authority* [1998] P.I.Q.R. P170, CA per Hobhouse L.J. at P189. See, e.g. *Richards v Swansea NHS Trust* (2006) 96 B.M.L.R. 180 (where a national standard prescribed a period of 30 minutes between making a decision to perform an emergency Caesarian section and delivery of the baby, and the claimant was born after 55 minutes, an evidential burden passed to the defendant to explain what, if anything, prevented earlier delivery, and in the absence of any such explanation, negligence was made out).

a plausible[294] explanation of what happened, consistent with the exercise of due care on his part, then the claim will fail. Likewise, the claim will fail where the defendant's evidence satisfies the judge that proper care was taken, even though the outcome itself cannot be explained in the current state of medical knowledge.[295]

> "At the end of the trial, after all the evidence relied upon by either side has been called and tested, the judge has simply to decide whether as a matter of inference or otherwise he concludes on the balance of probabilities that the defendant was negligent and that that negligence caused the plaintiff's injury. That is the long and short of it."[296]

6–113   **Highway cases.** It has been suggested that res ipsa loquitur does not apply to road traffic cases, because:

> "every vehicle has to adapt its own behaviour to the behaviour of other persons using the road, and over their actions those in charge of the vehicle have no control. Hence the fact that an accident has happened either to or through a particular vehicle is by itself no evidence that the fault, if any, which led to it was committed by those in charge of that vehicle."[297]

However, such a broad proposition is difficult to support, since there are many highway collisions, in which the accident itself suggests a reasonable probability of negligence in one of the parties rather than the other.

> "Where both parties are moving and have a right to move *prima facie* the mere fact that those moving bodies run into each other is not evidence of negligence . . . . When you get to the case of a man standing still in the highway in broad daylight and run into, I think myself that would be *prima facie* evidence of negligence of the driver of the vehicle that ran into him."[298]

6–114   Even in the case of moving vehicles which collide, the mere happening of the accident may be evidence of negligence against one of them. For instance, where one vehicle runs into another from behind in daylight, there can be no doubt that the very fact of the accident calls for an explanation from the overtaking vehicle.[299] A violent swerve,[300] a violent skid[301] and the sudden stopping[302] of a

---

[294] " . . . not a theoretically or remotely possible one . . . " *Richards v Swansea NHS Trust* (2006) 96 B.M.L.R. 180 per Brooke L.J. at P184.
[295] *Richards v Swansea NHS Trust* (2006) 96 B.M.L.R. 180 per Brooke L.J. at P184.
[296] ibid. per Hobhouse L.J. at P189.
[297] *Wing v London General Omnibus Co* [1909] 2 K.B. 652 at 664, per Fletcher Moulton L.J.; adversely commented on in *McGowan v Stott* (1923), reported in note to *Halliwell v Venables* [1930] 99 L.J.K.B. 353 at 357.
[298] *McGowan v Stott*, above, per Scrutton L.J.
[299] *Tart v Chitty & Co* [1933] 2 K.B. 453; *Baker v Longhurst & Sons Ltd* [1933] 2 K.B. 461 (in these cases, the question was whether the claimant in driving into a vehicle from behind was guilty of contributory negligence, and it was held that the fact of the collision alone was evidence of such negligence; it is not, of course, conclusive: *Tidy v Battman* [1934] 1 K.B. 319; *Morris v Luton Corp* [1946] 1 K.B. 114).
[300] *O'Hara v Scottish Motor Traction Co*, 1941 S.C. 363; *Doonan v S.M.T. Co Ltd*, 1950 S.C. 136; *Ludgate v Lovett* [1969] 1 W.L.R. 1016.
[301] *Richley v Faull* [1965] 1 W.L.R. 1454.
[302] *Parkinson v Liverpool Corp* [1950] 1 All E.R. 367; *Wooller v London Transport Board* [1976] R.T.R. 206, CA.

vehicle, causing injury to a passenger, have all been held to be prima facie evidence of negligence. On the other hand, accidental ejection of a passenger through an open door, while an omnibus was in motion, was not.[303]

When a motor vehicle, controlled by the defendant or his employee, over- **6–115** turned for no apparent cause while being driven along the highway, that fact alone was held to be evidence of negligence.[304] Likewise, the fact that a vehicle left the road and fell down an embankment.[305] The result was the same where a vehicle mounted the footpath and knocked down a lamp-post,[306] or a pedes- trian,[307] and where it projected over the footpath and knocked down a pedestrian.[308] Also where a pedestrian (who had a history of mental disorder but not of attempting suicide) was walking in clear view at the side of a dual carriageway at night.[309] Some of the older cases appear to suggest that if a horse came on to the footpath and collided with a pedestrian, there was no evidence of negligence against the person in charge, but it is doubtful whether they go as far as this.[310] In Eire, it had been held that the plaintiff's reliance on res ipsa loquitur was particularly appropriate where his motorvehicle was in collision with cattle straying on the highway.[311]

Unattended vehicles. Although it may have been negligent to leave a van **6–116** unattended on a level road, the mere fact that an accident had happened to a child, playing on the van, was not of itself evidence of negligence which caused injury to the child.[312] Similarly, although it may have been negligent to leave a lorry unattended in the street, a collision by that lorry with a shop front subsequently, when the lorry was being driven by trespassers, was not, by itself, evidence of negligence causing damage to the shop.[313] On the other hand, the fact that a motorcar had been left unattended and had run off down a hill, was itself evidence of negligence against the person in control of the car.[314]

Other cases (res ipsa applied). The maxim was held to apply, where the **6–117** trolley arm of a tram was plucked from a standard and struck a passenger on the head[315]; where a crane toppled over[316]; where a heavy electrical control panel

---

[303] *Johnstone v Western S.M.T. Co* (1955) 105 L.J. 762.
[304] *Halliwell v Venables* (1930) 99 L.J.K.B. 353; *Liffen v Watson* (1939) 161 L.T. 351.
[305] *Barkway v South Wales Transport Co Ltd* [1950] 1 All E.R. 392; *Elliott v Young's Bus Services Ltd,* 1945 S.C. 445.
[306] *Isaac Walton & Co v Vanguard Motorbus Co* (1908) 25 T.L.R. 13; see also *Barnes Urban District Council v L.G.O. Co* (1908) 100 L.T. 115.
[307] *Ellor v Selfridge & Co* (1930) 46 T.L.R. 236; *Hunter v Wright* [1938] 2 All E.R. 621 (defendant rebutted the presumption of negligence).
[308] *Laurie v Raglan Building Co Ltd* [1942] 1 K.B. 152.
[309] *Widdowson v Newgate Meat Corp* [1998] P.I.Q.R. P138, CA.
[310] For "horse cases," generally, in the context of these paragraphs, see editions of *Charlesworth on Negligence* earlier than the 8th edn.
[311] *O'Reilly v Lavelle* [1990] 2 I.R. 372.
[312] *Donovan v Union Cartage Co* [1933] 2 K.B. 71.
[313] *Ruoff v Long & Co* [1916] 1 K.B. 148.
[314] *Parker v Miller* (1926) 42 T.L.R. 408; *Martin v Stanborough* (1924) 41 T.L.R. 1.
[315] *Newberry v Bristol Tramways Co* (1912) 107 L.T. 801.
[316] *Swan v Salisbury Construction Co* [1966] 1 W.L.R. 204.

toppled over, just as another panel of lighter weight had begun to fall as well[317]; where a heavy piece fell off a machine in a factory, as a result of a bolt fracturing, it having been weakened by metal fatigue[318]; where a trawler was sent to be examined on the defendant's slipway and was put on to a cradle by the defendant's workmen, when it suddenly fell over and was damaged[319]; where a machine had been delivered to a railway company for transporting and afterwards was found to be damaged[320]; where a coupling on a railway train had parted[321]; where an aeroplane crashed to the ground just as it had become airborne, after taking off but before attaining the height at which the flight would be performed[322]; where an apparently airworthy aircraft, crashed on approaching its landing at Union Island in the Caribbean[323] where a barrel of petrol, supplied by the sellers, burst as it was rolling down a skid during unloading at the buyer's yard[324]; where a surgeon left a swab in the body of his patient after an operation.[325]

6–118   The maxim also applied where the healthy heart of a four-year-old child, undergoing surgery on her hip, stopped beating for a period of over half an hour[326] where a patient went into hospital, to be cured of two stiff fingers, and came out with four stiff fingers[327]; where a patient developed gangrene after receiving an injection in the arm[328]; when a plant, which was being managed by the defendants, exploded[329]; when an explosion in gas apparatus, which was not under the defendants' exclusive control, occurred in a private house[330]; when a rope broke at a haulage way[331] and at a hoist[332]; where moorings, let by the defendants for mooring the claimant's yacht, parted, which allowed the boat to

---

[317] *Bennett v Chemical Construction (GB) Ltd* [1971] 1 W.L.R. 1571.

[318] *Pearce v Round Oak Steel Works Ltd* [1969] 1 W.L.R. 595, following *Henderson v Henry E. Jenkins & Sons* [1970] A.C. 282.

[319] *Reynolds v Boston Deep Sea Fishing and Ice Co* (1921) 38 T.L.R. 22; affirmed 38 T.L.R. 429.

[320] *United Machine Tool Co v G.W. Ry* (1914) 30 T.L.R. 312.

[321] *Ballard v N.B. Ry*, 1923 S.C. 43.

[322] *Fosbroke-Hobbes v Airwork Ltd* [1937] 1 All E.R. 108; *Zerka, Romley and Alex v Lau-Goma Airways* (1960) 23 D.L.R. (2d) 145 (where the Ontario CA held that the doctrine applied in the case of an aeroplane, the engine of which had cut out shortly after it had become airborne).

[323] *George v Eagle Air Services Ltd* [2009] 1 W.L.R. 2133, PC (the burden was on the defendants as owners and operators on the aircraft, to explain how the crash came about; such crashes did not ordinarily occur in the absence of default by someone in connection with the design, manufacture or operation of the aircraft, and the defendants had failed to produce an explanation which was consistent with an absence of fault on their part). See further, Curley, "Hard to beat" 159 N.L.J. 1155.

[324] *Marshall v Russian Oil Products*, 1938 S.C. 773.

[325] *Mahon v Osborne* [1939] 2 K.B. 14.

[326] *Saunders v Leeds Western Health Authority* [1993] 4 Med.L.R. 355.

[327] *Cassidy v Ministry of Health* [1951] 2 K.B. 343.

[328] *Cavan v Wilcox* (1973) 44 D.L.R. (3d) 42.

[329] *Moore v R. Fox & Sons* [1956] 1 Q.B. 596.

[330] *Lloyde v West Midlands Gas Board* [1971] 1 W.L.R. 749.

[331] *Turner v National Coal Board* (1949) 65 T.L.R. 580 (the prima facie case was rebutted and the defendants succeeded).

[332] *Birchall v Bibby & Sons Ltd* [1953] 1 All E.R. 163 (on proof that the rope had been deliberately cut, it was held that the defendants had rebutted the *prima facie* case against them and were not bound to prove that it had not been cut by one of their servants).

break adrift[333]; where the defendant's barge left its moorings, drifted uncontrolled down the river and collided with a ladies' rowing eight.[334]

Other cases (res ipsa not applied). The maxim was held not to apply where **6–119** livestock was sent by railway and found damaged on arrival[335]; where a man, who was employed as a driver, was found dead in the employers' boiler house, having been asphyxiated by carbon monoxide[336]; where a schoolboy, during the morning "break", was in a corridor in the school building and was hit in the eye by a golf ball which had entered the corridor by the doorway, after it had been driven by another schoolboy in the playground,[337] where a cricket ball was driven by a batsman out of the ground and injured a pedestrian on a footpath.[338]

Also, where a tube was found in the bladder of a patient some weeks after an **6–120** operation was performed upon him by a surgeon, and doctors and nurses at a hospital, in addition to the surgeon himself, had been from time to time engaged in removing and replacing the tube[339]; where permanent tetraplegia occurred after a sagittal split osteotomy and the cause may have been either negligently-inflicted hypertension and shearing stress or fibro-cartilaginous embolism[340]; where there were two possible explanations for a failed sterilisation operation[341]; where a patient suffered neurological damage as a result of an injection of spinal anaesthetic, but the consultant anaesthetist had not been guilty of any want of care and the exact mechanism of injury was unclear[342]; where there were two defendants, who blamed each other for the damage, suffered by the claimant[343]; where the patient's jaw was broken and part of the root left in the jaw by a dentist, during the extraction of a tooth.[344]

Again, when, during a motorcycle scramble, a machine left the track, crossed **6–121** "no man's land", passed under a fence and ended up in the spectators' area[345]; where a lineman was electrocuted whilst working at an electrical installation, after coming into contact with an electrically charged wire[346]; where the lavatory pan in a public toilet broke, just as the claimant sat down on it[347]; where a fire was caused in a room by a spark, flying out from the domestic fire grate[348]; where a firework, manufactured with some latent defect, exploded in its launching tube

---

[333] *The Quercus* [1943] P. 96.
[334] *Newby v General Lighterage Co Ltd*, *The Times*, March 3, 1955.
[335] *Russell v L. & S.W. Ry* (1908) 24 T.L.R. 548.
[336] *Brophy v J.C. Bradfield & Co Ltd* [1955] 1 W.L.R. 1148.
[337] *Langham v Governors of Wellingborough School* (1932) 101 L.J.K.B. 513.
[338] *Bolton v Stone* [1951] A.C. 850.
[339] *Morris v Winsbury-White* [1937] 4 All E.R. 494.
[340] *Howard v Wessex Regional Health Authority* [1994] 5 Med L.R. 57.
[341] *Fallows v Randle* (1996) C.L.Y. 4469.
[342] *Ratcliffe v Plymouth & Torbay Health Authority* [1998] P.I.Q.R. P170, CA.
[343] *Hawkins v Dhawan and Mishiku* (1987) 19 H.L.R. 232, CA.
[344] *Fish v Kapur* [1948] 2 All E.R. 176.
[345] *Wilks v Cheltenham Home Guard Motor Cycle and Light Car Club* [1971] 1 W.L.R. 668.
[346] *Youngman v Pirelli General Cable Works* [1940] 1 K.B. 1.
[347] *Macleod v Glasgow Corporation*, 1971 S.L.T. 64.
[348] *Sochacki v Sas* [1947] 1 All E.R. 344 at 345; *Flannigan v British Dyewood Co*, 1969 S.L.T. 223, and on appeal 1970 S.L.T. 285.

in the course of a display[349]; and where the claimant averred only that, had premises been well maintained, a piece of timber would not have fallen on his hand.[350] There was no prima facie case against a local highway authority where the the claimant's car skidded on black ice and crashed, since there was no absolute duty upon the authority to prevent the formation of black ice and there were times when roads could be icy despite the exercise of reasonable care.[351]

6–122   **Rebuttal of negligence.** When a prima facie case of negligence against the defendant has been established, it is insufficient for the defendant merely to say that he had acted carefully, but he can rebut the case by proving that he was not negligent, even though he cannot prove how the accident happened.[352]

> "If the defenders can show a way in which the accident may have occurred without negligence, the cogency of the fact of the accident by itself disappears, and the pursuer is left as he began, namely, that he has to show negligence. I need scarcely add that the suggestion of how the accident may have occurred must be a reasonable suggestion."[353]

6–123   Where a barge, which was being towed by a tug, collided with the abutment of a bridge, it was held that the accident itself raised a prima facie case of negligence against the tug. However, upon the tug's owners showing that the collision might equally well have been caused by the negligence of men on the barge in not making a rope fast, judgment was given in favour of the tug's owners.

> "If they [the defendants] give a reasonable explanation, which is equally consistent with the accident happening without their negligence as with their negligence, they have again shifted the burden of proof back to the plaintiffs to show—as they always have to show from the beginning—that it was the negligence of the defendants that caused the accident."[354]

6–124   In *Colvilles Ltd v Devine*,[355] the defenders had installed a new system for the manufacture of steel by the injection of oxygen into converters, which involved bringing the gas from a source a mile away by means of a third party's pipe. At

---

[349] *McQueen v The Glasgow Garden Festival (1988)*, 1995 S.L.T. 211, OH.

[350] *McDyer v Celtic Football and Athletic Co Ltd*, 1997 Rep. L.R. 117, OH, Ch.8, para.8–37, below.

[351] *Morton v West Lothian Council* 2006 Rep. L.R. 7, OH.

[352] *Woods v Duncan* [1946] A.C. 401; *Barkway v South Wales Transport Co Ltd* [1948] 2 All E.R. 460 at 471, per Asquith L.J. (reversed by the HL on another point [1950] A.C. 185); *Esso Petroleum Co Ltd v Southport Corp* [1956] A.C. 218 at 242, 243, per Lord Radcliffe; *Walsh v Holst & Co Ltd* [1958] 1 W.L.R. 800; *Ludgate v Lovett* [1969] 1 W.L.R. 1016; *Henderson v H.E. Jenkins & Sons* [1970] A.C. 282.

[353] per Lord Dunedin in *Ballard v N.B. Ry*, 1923 S.C. 43 at 45, quoted with approval in *Langham v Wellingborough School* (1932) 101 L.J.K.B. 513. However, see also the formulation in *Moore v Fox & Sons* [1956] 1 Q.B. 596: it is not enough for the defendants merely to show that the accident could have happened without negligence on their part. They must show that they have taken all reasonable precautions to ensure that the accident did not happen. See *Esso Petroleum Co Ltd v Southport Corp* [1956] A.C. 218 at 243, per Lord Radcliffe.

[354] per Langton J. in *The Kite* [1933] P. 154 at 170. See also *The Mulbera* [1937] P. 82.

[355] [1969] 1 W.L.R. 475. But cf. *National Trust Co v Wong Aviation* [1969] 2 Lloyd's Rep. 340 (the explanation given was held to be consistent with no negligence).

the defenders' main intake there was a filter to remove foreign bodies from the oxygen and from that point a hose, belonging to the defenders, took the gas to a lance by means of which it was injected into the molten metal. Whilst the pursuer was working on a platform, some 75 yards away from the converter, a violent explosion occurred, which gave him a fright and caused him to jump down to the ground, hurting himself. Lord Guest expressed the opinion that the defenders:

"are absolved if they can give a reasonable explanation[356] of the accident and show this explanation was consistent with no lack of care on their part.... But this explanation only carries the [defenders] half way to success. The explanation to be available as a defence must be consistent with no negligence on their part."[357]

Lord Donovan said:

"It was for the [defenders] to show that the accident was just as consistent with their having exercised due diligence as with their having been negligent. In that way the scales which have been tipped in the pursuer's favour by the doctrine of *res ipsa loquitur* would be once more in balance, and the pursuer would have to begin again and prove negligence in the usual way."[358]

Reasonable explanation. Whether the circumstances raise a prima facie case **6–125** of negligence is a question of law. Whether negligence is indeed proved, is a question of fact. If a prima facie case of negligence is established against B it is still open to him to show that the facts equally establish a case against C, so that the inference of negligence on his part should not be drawn. In such a case, B would be entitled to succeed, unless B and C were sued in the same action jointly, severally and in the alternative, when B would not be entitled to judgment until C's case also was heard.[359] In a separate action against B, his explanation, if supported by the facts, would rebut the presumption which the evidence raised.

Where a surgeon performed a surgical procedure, without informing the **6–126** claimant of the one-in-a-thousand risk of paralysis, and that risk materialised, a claim in negligence, relying upon the fact of what had happened as raising a prima facie case, failed where the defendant relied at trial upon expert evidence which the claimant could not controvert. Res ipsa loquitur did not assist the claimant since the court had received an explanation which answered the prima facie case raised.[360]

An incomplete explanation is not enough. Where a bus overturned into a ditch **6–127** it was unsufficient to say that the accident was caused by a burst tyre, without

---

[356] i.e. "A plausible explanation," as spoken to by Lord Simonds in *Woods v Duncan* [1946] A.C. 401 at 441.
[357] *Woods v Duncan* [1946] A.C. 401 at 477, 478.
[358] ibid. at 479. See further *Ballard v North British Ry* 1923 S.C. (HL) 43 at 54, per Lord Dunedin; *Moore v R. Fox & Sons* [1956] 1 Q.B. 596 at 607, per Evershed M.R.
[359] *Hummerstone v Leary* [1921] 2 K.B. 664.
[360] *McLean v Weir, Goff and Royal Inland Hospital* (1977) 5 W.W.R. 609. See further *Jacobs v Great Yarmouth and Waveney Health Authority* [1995] 6 Med. L.R. 192 and para.6–130, below.

also leading evidence that the burst was not the result of the defendants' negligence.[361] Where a child left school without being noticed by teachers on duty, and there was no explanation as to how he came to be in a main road where he was knocked down, it was no answer for the defendants to say it had not been proved that their breach of duty caused his injury since they had failed to explain how he came to be where he should not have been.[362] Where the defendants were performing electrical work at the claimant's home while she was away and a fire broke out, there was an evidential burden upon them to show how the fire arose consistent with the exercise of due care on their part. They failed, the evidence disclosing no cause of the fire that was at least as likely as their failure to check that insulation was not unacceptably damaged, or that any existing damage had not been exacerbated by their activity in assembling light fittings onto a cable.[363]

6–128   **Latent defect.** Where the defendant relies upon a latent defect as explaining some event, there is an evidential burden to establish facts from which such a defect may be inferred.[364] A latent defect is a one which cannot be detected by reasonable care and skill.[365] It is not enough merely to establish that a latent defect was probably present; the defendant has to show that the event complained of would have occurred, despite all reasonable care having been taken.[366]

6–129   In *Henderson v Henry E. Jenkins & Sons,*[367] a sudden escape of brake fluid from a pipe in the hydraulic braking system of a lorry occurred after a hole developed as a result of some corrosion of that part of the pipe which could not have been seen on a visual inspection. The brakes failed as the lorry was descending a steep hill, so that it ran out of control and struck and killed the deceased. The House of Lords held that the lorry owners could not rely on the defence of latent defect unless they showed that they had taken all reasonable care in the circumstances. That was not made out where they failed to show that there were no special circumstances in the past use of the vehicle to indicate that it might have been subjected to a corrosive agent, causing corrosion of the pipe.

If the negligence alleged is the sudden swerve of a vehicle, the prima facie case of negligence, established by proof of the swerve, is not rebutted by the mere suggestion that a swerve may have been necessary to avoid a pedestrian in the highway. Full proof is required.[368]

---

[361] *Barkway v S. Wales Transport Co Ltd* [1950] 1 All E.R. 392.

[362] *J v North Lincolnshire CC* [2000] P.I.Q.R. P84, CA, para.6–109, above and Ch.9, para.9–193, below.

[363] *Drake v Harbour, The Times,* March 24, 2008, CA. See article, "Res ipsa loquitur and liability for fire damage" Build. L.M. 2008, Feb, 6.

[364] *Marshall v Russian Oil Products,* 1938 S.C. 773.

[365] *Readhead v Midland Ry* (1869) L.R. 4 Q.B. 379; *Marshall v Russian Oil Products,* 1938 S.C. 773; *Ritchie v Western Scottish Motor Traction Co,* 1935 S.L.T. 13. However, cf. *Henderson v H.E. Jenkins & Sons* [1970] A.C. 282.

[366] *Davie v New Merton Board Mills* [1959] A.C. 604; *Pearce v Round Oak Steel Works* [1969] 1 W.L.R. 595, CA.

[367] [1970] A.C. 282.

[368] *O'Hara v Scottish Motor Traction Co,* 1941 S.C. 363; *Ludgate v Lovett* [1969] 1 W.L.R. 1016.

Negligence need not be disproved. When res ipsa loquitur applies, it is not   **6–130** strictly necessary for the defendant to disprove negligence. It is sufficient for him to neutralise the effect of the presumption, raised by the res. In practice, the difference between neutralising the effect of the prima facie case and disproving the negligence may be so small as to be immaterial. The court has to judge, after all the evidence has been put before it, whether on balance the facts establish that the claimant has proved his case,[369] the burden of which remains at the end, as it was at the beginning, on him to discharge.[370] Where the claimant establishes a prima facie case by relying on the fact of an accident and the defendant adduces no evidence, the inference of negligence is not rebutted. But if evidence is adduced then it has to be evaluated to see if the inference of negligence is still one that should be drawn. If the defendant casts such doubt upon the claimant's account that the inference of negligence is regarded as unsafe, then the claim will fail.[371]

Finally. It is a generally encouraging thought that, in practice, causation in the   **6–131** vast majority of cases usually comes down to a question of fact. However, in novel factual situations, or where the facts are complex, it will always be important to bear in mind that,

> " . . . the real question is, what is the damage for which the defendant under consideration should be held responsible. The nature of his duty . . . is relevant; causation, certainly, will be relevant—but it will fall to be viewed, and in truth can only be understood, in light of the answer to the question: from what kind of harm was it the defendant's duty to guard the claimant. Novus actus interveniens, the eggshell skull, and (in the case of multiple torts) the concept of concurrent tortfeasors are all no more and no less than tools or mechanisms which the law has developed to articulate in practice the extent of any liable defendant's responsibility for the loss and damage which the claimant has suffered."[372]

Those words would be equally appropriate as a start to the discussion in Chapter 5 of remoteness of damage, as to a conclusion here.

---

[369] *Swan v Salisbury Construction Co* [1966] 1 W.L.R. 204.

[370] *Ng Chun Pui v Lee Chuen Tat* [1988] R.T.R. 298, PC.

[371] *Jacobs v Great Yarmouth and Waveney HA* [1995] 6 Med. L.R. 192 (the inference of negligence raised on the claimant's account that she had been conscious throughout a hysterectomy after an anaesthetist missed her vein when administering pre-operative anaesthetic, was rebutted by evidence that her memory was likely to have been affected by drugs she had received).

[372] per Laws L.J. in *Rahman v Arearose Ltd* [2001] Q.B. 351 at 367.

Part II
STANDARD OF CARE

CHAPTER 7

THE STANDARD OF CARE

1.—THE REASONABLE CARE STANDARD GENERALLY

A question of law. It is not enough to show that on particular facts a duty of care arose. The question is, given a duty, how much care was to be exercised. The standard of care is a question of law, although whether or not it was achieved is a question of fact[1] decided by reference to all the circumstances of the case.[2] Usually the standard will be proportionate to the gravity and imminence of the risk against which it was the defendant's duty to guard, so, the standard of care required from a motorist is to drive with reasonable care, but, on approaching a pedestrian crossing there is a greater chance of encountering pedestrians in the road, and more care than usual must be taken.[3]   **7–01**

Reasonableness. The ordinary standard of care applied is referred to as "reasonable care," namely the standard of care of a reasonable man. In Alderson B.'s classic statement,[4]   **7–02**

"Negligence is the omission to do something which a reasonable man, guided upon those considerations which ordinarily regulate the conduct of human affairs, would do: or doing something which a prudent and reasonable man would not do."

In the main the reasonable man standard is an impersonal test.   **7–03**

"It eliminates the personal equation and is independent of the idiosyncrasies of the particular person whose conduct is in question. Some persons are by nature unduly

---

[1] For comments on the undesirability of courts attempting to reduce to rules of law the question whether or not in any given case reasonable care has been taken: e.g. *Qualcast (Wolverhampton) Ltd v Haynes* [1959] A.C. 743, Lord Keith at 755 and Lord Somervell at 757–758; *Cavanagh v Ulster Weaving Co Ltd* [1960] A.C. 145, Lord Keith at 163–164; *Brown v Rolls Royce Ltd* [1960] 1 W.L.R. 210, Lord Keith at 214 and Lord Denning at 215.
[2] *Kite v Nolan* [1983] R.T.R. 253, CA.
[3] *Bailey v Geddes* [1938] 1 K.B. 156.
[4] *Blyth v Birmingham Waterworks* (1856) 11 Ex. 781 at 784.

timorous and imagine every path beset with lions. Others, of more robust temperament, fail to foresee or nonchalantly disregard even the most obvious dangers. The reasonable man is presumed to be free both from overapprehension and from over-confidence."[5]

7–04   The reasonable man is taken to know the standard of care which the law requires of him and to comply with it. If he owns a motorcar, he takes appropriate care to keep it in good repair. If he drives it, he does so with the skill and care of a reasonably competent driver with a comprehensive knowledge of the Highway Code and any statutory regulations which apply. But that is not to say that every breach of the Code or regulation evidences a failure to take the care which a reasonable driver would have taken. It may not, for instance, be unreasonable to exceed the speed limit if considerations of safety permit. While the standard is an impersonal one, it is by no means divorced from the circumstances in which it has to be applied. Circumstances do tend to repeat themselves, so that guidance as to what is or is not a reasonable standard of care can, in a novel case, often be derived by analogy from cases that have gone before.

7–05   The impersonality of the test is illustrated in those cases where the knowledge or experience of the defendant happens to be greater than the norm, but is nonetheless irrelevant in considering whether reasonable care was taken. Thus, no higher standard of care was required of a garage proprietor than of a prudent owner, in taking steps to immobilise his motor vehicle in some manner, to reduce the risk of it being stolen.[6]

7–06   However, although the standard is impersonal it does not wholly disregard the circumstances of the individual. When considering the standard of care required of a reasonable driver it may be irrelevant that the driver is male or female, a learner or experienced,[7] but it is not irrelevant if he is suffering from an illness of which he unaware which affects his ability to drive.[8] When considering the standard required of a reasonably competent medical practitioner, the specialism within which the individual practised must be taken into account, although not the extent of his experience in that specialism.[9] In *Arthur Guinness, Son & Co (Dublin) Ltd v The Freshfield (Owners)*,[10] a well-known brewing company was liable for failing properly to supervise the master of a vessel in their ownership which collided with another vessel in thick fog. Winn L.J. said that the law, "must apply a standard which is not relaxed to cater for their factual ignorance of all activities outside brewing: having become owners of ships, they must

---

[5] per Lord Macmillan in *Glasgow Corporation v Muir* [1943] A.C. 448 at 457. See other similar expressions, e.g. *A. C. Billings & Sons Ltd v Riden* [1958] A.C. 240 at 255, per Lord Reid, and *Carmarthenshire County Council v Lewis* [1955] A.C. 549 at 566; *Hawkins v Coulsdon and Purley Urban District Council* [1954] 1 Q.B. 319 at 341, per Romer L.J.; *Nettleship v Weston* [1971] 2 Q.B. 691 at 699, per Lord Denning M.R. See, generally, Mullender, "The reasonable person, the pursuit of justice, and negligence law" 2005 M.L.R. 68, 681.
[6] *Cowan v Blackwill Motor Caravan Conversions* [1978] R.T.R. 421.
[7] *Nettleship v Weston* [1971] 2 Q.B. 691, CA, Ch.10, para.10–258, below.
[8] *Mansfield v Weetabix Ltd* [1998] 1 W.L.R. 1263, CA.
[9] *Djemal v Bexley Health Authority* [1995] Med. L.R. 269, Ch.9, para.9–03, below.
[10] [1965] P. 294.

behave as reasonable shipowners."[11] Where the party alleged to have been culpable is a child it has been said that question is whether the child's conduct fell below a standard that should objectively be expected of a child of that age. For a child to be culpable it would have to be careless to a very high degree.[12]

Accordingly, to say that the standard of care is that of a reasonable man can be   **7–07** to beg the question. A tribunal of fact can only be directed to apply the standard of reasonable care if it is explained what amount of care the law regards as reasonable under the circumstances of the case being tried. If reasonable care alone were the only test, the following pages would be superfluous.

Lord Atkin made a similar point in connection with breach of statutory duty.   **7–08** He said:

"The employer is alleged to have committed a breach of a duty owed by him to his servant to take a particular precaution (namely, support of the roof) for his servant's safety whereby the servant was injured. . . . All that is necessary to show is a duty to take care to avoid injuring; and if the particular care to be taken is prescribed by statute, and the duty to the injured person to take care is likewise imposed by statute, and the breach is proved, all the essentials of negligence are present. I cannot think that the true position is, as appears to be suggested, that in such cases negligence only exists where the tribunal of fact agrees with the Legislature that the precaution is one that ought to be taken. The very object of the legislation is to put that particular precaution beyond controversy."[13]

The same result follows where the standard of care has been laid down by judicial decision. Where no particular standard has been identified, the tribunal of fact can apply the broad test of reasonable care, according to its own ideas of what is reasonable in the circumstances. In *Caswell v Powell Duffryn Associated Collieries Ltd*,[14] Lord Wright pointed out that the standard of care expected of a workman in a factory or mine who is subjected to long hours, fatigue, the slackening of attention which naturally comes from constant repetition of the same operation, noise and confusion generally, is not so high as that of a reasonable man in more serene circumstances.

The reasonable care standard is therefore flexible and should reflect the   **7–09** circumstances and evidence in the particular case. But while it is in this sense fact-sensitive, it is also important that a court should not lose sight of the implications of its decision for society generally. Reference is often made, on appeal, to the economic or social implications of a decision which appears to have set the standard of care at an unrealistic level. So, in claim for psychiatric injury arising from employment it was said in the Court of Appeal:

---

[11] *Arthur Guinness, Son & Co (Dublin) Ltd v The Freshfield (Owners)* [1964] P. 294 at 350.
[12] *Orchard v Lee* [2009] P.I.Q.R. P16, Ch.2, para.2–281 above (the claim of the employee of a school, required to supervise the children at lunchtime, who was injured when a 13-year-old boy collided with her as he played a game of tag, failed: no ordinarily prudent and reasonable 13-year-old boy playing tag in the relevant area of the school would reasonably have foreseen the risk of injury).
[13] *Lochgelly Iron and Coal Co v McMullan* [1934] A.C. 1, 9.
[14] [1940] A.C. 152 at 178.

"The law of tort has an important function in setting standards for employers as well as for drivers, manufacturers, health care professionals and many others whose carelessness may cause harm. But if the standard of care expected of employers is set too high, or the threshold of liability too low, there may also be unforeseen and unwelcome effects upon the employment market. In particular employers may be even more reluctant than they already are to take on people with a significant psychiatric history or an acknowledged vulnerability to stress-related disorders. If employers are expected to make searching enquiries of employees who have been off sick, then more employees may be vulnerable to dismissal or demotion on health grounds. If particular employments are singled out as ones in which special care is needed, then other benefits which are available to everyone in those employments, such as longer holidays, better pensions or earlier retirement, may be under threat."[15]

Many of the decisions which follow reflect similar considerations.

2.—MATTERS TAKEN INTO ACCOUNT

7–10   **Generally.** In *Morris v West Hartlepool Steam Navigation Co Ltd*,[16] in the context of a claim by an employee against his employer, Lord Reid said:

"It is the duty of an employer, in considering whether some precaution should be taken against a foreseeable risk, to weigh, on the one hand, the magnitude of the risk, the likelihood of an accident happening and the possible seriousness of the consequences if an accident does happen, and, on the other hand, the difficulty and expense and any other disadvantage of taking the precaution."

Although the four considerations which Lord Atkin identified concern the liability of an employer, as do many of the reported cases, they do have a wider application. It will be convenient to look at each in turn.

(A) Magnitude of the risk

7–11   The degree of care to be taken depends on the magnitude of the risk; the greater the risk the more care should be taken. In the words of Lord Macmillan:

"The degree of care for the safety of others which the law requires human beings to observe in the conduct of their affairs varies according to the circumstances. There is no absolute standard, but it may be said generally that the degree of care required varies directly with the risk involved. Those who engage in operations inherently dangerous must take precautions which are not required of persons engaged in the ordinary routine of daily life."[17]

As the same judge said in a later case: "the law in all cases exacts a degree of care commensurate with the risk created."[18] At one extreme, where dangerous

---

[15] per Hale L.J. in *Sutherland v Hatton* [2002] P.I.Q.R. P241 at P251, CA. See further para.7–36, below.
[16] [1956] A.C. 552 at 574.
[17] *Glasgow Corp v Muir* [1943] A.C. 448 at 456.
[18] *Read v J. Lyons & Co Ltd* [1947] A.C. 156 at 173.

things, such as explosives, are handled "the law exacts a degree of diligence so stringent as to amount practically to a guarantee of safety."[19] At the other extreme, the degree of risk may be so small that no care need be taken.[20]

ILLUSTRATIONS

In *Glasgow Corporation v Muir*,[21] the manageress of a tea room gave　**7–12** permission to two men to carry a hot tea urn to the tea room through a narrow passage, on one side of which was a counter, where some children were buying sweets. While carrying the urn, one of the men let go of the handle, so that the tea was spilled and scalded some of the children. It was held the operation of carrying a tea urn was a simple one and what happened was so unlikely that the manageress was not bound to anticipate it and, so, was not in breach of her duty of care.[22]

Bolton v Stone[23] is another well-known example. A cricket ball was driven out　**7–13** of the ground and injured a passer-by. While a duty to persons using the adjacent highway was accepted, there was no breach given the improbable character of what occurred.

> "It is therefore not enough for the plaintiff to say that the occupiers of the cricket ground could have foreseen the possibility that a ball might be hit out of the ground by a batsman and might injure people on the road; she must go further and say that they ought, as reasonable men, to have foreseen the probability of such an occurrence."[24]

So, where a golfer hooked his drive off the tee and the ball hit another player　**7–14** 200 yards away, the risk of such an accident happening was held to be either unforeseeable or was so slight that it could be ignored.[25] Likewise, where there was a very small risk of serious injury to participants in a team relay game which involved retrieving a piece of plastic fruit floating in a shallow inflatable pool.[26] However, golf course owners were held liable to a pedestrian, who was struck on the head by a golf ball, whilst walking along a narrow public lane: about 6,000

---

[19] *Donoghue v Stevenson* [1932] A.C. 562 at 612, per Lord Macmillan.

[20] In *Overseas Tankship (UK) Ltd v The Miller Steamship Co Pty* [1967] 1 A.C. 617 at 642 Lord Reid indicated: "But it does not follow that, no matter what the circumstances may be, it is justifiable to neglect a risk of such a small magnitude." The importance of reasonable foresight of risk was stressed in *Jones v Whippey* [2009] EWCA Civ 452, Ch.14, para.14–90, below (the owner of a Great Dane which was known as a placid and friendly dog, was not liable for an injury caused when it knocked over the claimant who was running in a public park).

[21] [1943] A.C. 448.

[22] *Glasgow Corporation v Muir* [1943] A.C. 448 per Lord Wright at 465. "It was a mere possibility, not a reasonable probability . . . the risk of negligence was a mere unlikely accident which no reasonable person in [the manageress's] position could naturally be expected to foresee."

[23] [1951] A.C. 850, the decision of which has been accepted and followed in Ireland, *Healy v Bray UDC* [1962–63] Ir.Jur.Rep. 9, 17, and in Australia, *Chapman v Hearse* (1961) 106 C.L.R. 112.

[24] *Bolton v Stone* [1951] A.C. 850 per Lord Normand at 861.

[25] *Brewer v Delo* [1967] 1 Lloyd's Rep. 488. See also *Gillon v Chief Constable of Strathclyde Police*, *The Times*, November 22, 1996, OH (Chief Constable not liable to police officer attending a football game to supervise the crowd, which he had been instructed to face, when he was struck and injured by a player whose momentum carried him from the pitch, since the risk was so minimal it could safely be ignored).

[26] *Uren v Corporate Leisure (UK) Ltd* [2010] EWHC 46 (Q.B.).

shots a year went over the fence on to the lane, so that, although there was no previous history of accident, it was nevertheless a foreseeable happening.[27] Also, where occupiers allowed children to play football on a piece of open grassland from which, from time to time, balls were kicked out on to the road, so that on one such occasion a passing motorcyclist was struck and killed as a result of his being knocked off his machine, they were held to have failed to take reasonable care.[28] The proximity of the road, the amount of traffic, the age of the children, the nature of their amusements and the frequency with which the green was used, were all matters which a reasonable man must have considered. The risk of damage to persons using the road as a result of the children's activities was not so small that it could be safely disregarded.

7–15   If a factory is damaged so that, to the knowledge of the employer, there is a risk of the roof falling or a wall collapsing, the degree of care to be taken may well require the building to be closed until such time as it is made safe.[29] By way of contrast, when part of the floor of a factory became slippery from floodwater and oil, it was held that "the degree of risk was too small to justify, let alone require, closing down"[30] and the employer was not liable to an employee, who was injured by slipping on the floor.[31]

7–16   **Absence of accidents.** When it comes to proof, the fact that under comparable circumstances for a significant period of time, there have been no, or infrequent, accidents of a similar type, is strong evidence that the standard of care is a proper one.[32] The force of the point will, no doubt, depend upon the extent to which any comparison of before and after is compelling. But an absence of accidents can, in an appropriate case, point to a low level of risk, although it is not conclusive.[33]

(B) Likelihood of injury

7–17   **Generally.** In many ways the considerations overlap those already discussed. However, here the question is not so much the magnitude of the risk of an accident in general terms, but the likelihood of that risk materialising so that injury occurs to the particular claimant at the particular time and place. For all that the test of reasonable foreseeability sets an objective standard, its application in terms of the standard of care required takes into account the circumstances and characteristics of the person or persons at risk. This emerges with particular

---

[27] *Lamond v Glasgow Corp*, 1968 S.L.T. 291.

[28] *Hilder v Associated Portland Cement Manufacturers Ltd* [1961] 1 W.L.R. 1434.

[29] *Latimer v A.E.C. Ltd* [1952] 2 Q.B. 701, per Singleton L.J. in a judgment approved in the HL, n. 30 below.

[30] *Latimer v A.E.C. Ltd* [1953] A.C. 643 at 662, per Lord Asquith.

[31] ibid. at 662, per Lord Asquith. It is doubted that the decision would be the same today, not the least because the statutory duty is different. cf. the Workplace (Health, Safety and Welfare) Regulations 1992 (SI 1992/3004), Ch.12, paras 12–117 to 12–152, below.

[32] See, e.g. *Wright v Cheshire County Council* [1952] 2 All E.R. 789 (schoolboy injured vaulting over an unattended "buck" in the gym).

[33] See, e.g. *Hurley v J. Sanders & Co Ltd* [1955] 1 W.L.R. 470 (shipyard painter slipping and falling on a route he had used many times).

clarity in the case of accidents to those with some vulnerability, such as physical or mental disability, or young age.

Illustrations

Where the defendant was felling a tree, knowing that he was being watched by **7–18** children, it was not enough for him just to warn them to stand well clear before the tree fell. Since young children could not be expected to appreciate the danger he ought to have taken active steps to make sure that they were out of harm's way.[34] But where a two-year-old child, being looked after by foster parents, scalded a foot when she came into contact with hot running water which she accidentally turned on while her foster mother was busy elsewhere, her injury was not reasonably foreseeable. To hold the foster parents liable would be to impose an impossibly high standard, which few parents could have matched.[35] Where an 11-year-old child was struck on the head by the heel of a larger boy aged 15, while they were both performing somersaults on a bouncy castle, the defendants, who had hired the equipment for a party to celebrate their triplets' tenth birthday, were not liable in negligence. The children were unsupervised when the accident happened because the second defendant had turned away to assist someone on another piece of equipment nearby. It was held that, given serious injury was not reasonably foreseeable from the childrens' use of the bouncy castle, there was no duty to maintain a constant watch on it. The standard of care required of the second defendant was that appropriate to protect children against a foreseeable risk of physical harm falling short of serious injury. It was reasonable for her to divide her attention between the two pieces of equipment.[36]

Where a blind man fell into an excavation in the pavement, which for sighted **7–19** persons only had been adequately protected by placing a long-handled hammer diagonally across its front, it was held that the defendants were liable since it was reasonably foreseeable that blind persons would pass along pavements.[37] On the other hand, taking one of the examples given by Lord Wright,[38] "a blind or deaf man who crosses the traffic on a busy street cannot complain if he is run over by a careful driver who does not know of and could not be expected to observe and

---

[34] *Mourton v Poulter* [1930] 2 K.B. 183; see also *Excelsior Wire Rope Co Ltd v Callan* [1930] A.C. 404 (setting machinery in motion without first warning children who were likely to be playing around about).

[35] *Surtees v Kingston-upon-Thames Borough Council* [1991] 2 F.L.R. 559, CA.

[36] *Harris v Perry* [2009] 1 W.L.R. 19, CA. It was observed at para.[34] that it was quite impractical for parents to keep children under constant surveillance and it would not be in the public interest to impose such a duty upon them. When the circumstances did involve an unacceptable risk unless a child was closely supervised the test was whether such supervision or surveillance had been provided as an adult knew, or ought to have known, was necessary to restrict the risk to an acceptable level. See McDonald, "Bouncing and bouldering" 158 N.L.J. 1209, Dobson, "Accidents do happen" 158 N.L.J. 1318.

[37] *Haley v London Electricity Board* [1965] A.C. 778 distinguishing *Pritchard v Post Office* [1950] W.N. 310 where the sole cause of the accident had been held to be the claimant's contributory negligence, a decision considered to be correct by Lord Reid (ibid. at 792).

[38] *Bourhill v Young* [1943] A.C. 92 at 109.

guard against the man's infirmity". Similar considerations ought to apply if the claimant is the worse for drink.[39]

7–20   Where the personal characteristics of an employee, such as a limited understanding of the English language, exposes him to an enhanced risk in the workplace, or exposes others to an enhanced risk from him, the employer must take such steps as are necessary to reduce or remove that risk.[40] The extent of any inquiry required to identify the enhanced risk before it arises will depend upon the facts, notably the likelihood of the risk arising and the gravity of the consequences, if it does.[41] Once an enhanced risk is perceived, the question will arise how properly it should be addressed.[42] Similarly where an indivudal has a known inexperience for a task or other activity in relation to to which a duty of care exists.[43]

(C) Gravity of the consequences

7–21   **Overlap.** Again there is some overlap with the preceding section. Here, the consideration is the seriousness of the potential outcome for an individual if due care is not taken. Just as in the discussion above the characteristics of the individual can be relevant. There is also the inherent risks of the activity in question. So the cases will be divided into two: those where the claim is by or against a person with a disability of some kind; and those involving the performance of some extra-hazardous act.

7–22   **Disability of body or mind.** If a defendant knows, or ought to know, that his actions or omissions may cause injury to persons with a disability, either individually or generally, the standard of care to be achieved reflects that knowledge. The care to be taken will be proportionate to the circumstances known.[44] It is not a question of taking more than reasonable care, but that, in the circumstances known, reasonable care requires precautions designed to protect the claimant from consequences aggravated by his disability. So, since a one-eyed man, working with hammer and chisel on metal, stands to suffer graver

---

[39] See the cases cited at Ch.4, paras 4–48 to 4–50, above, also *Griffiths v Brown* [1999] P.I.Q.R. P120, below, Ch.10, para.10–153.

[40] *Hawkins v Ian Ross (Castings) Ltd* [1970] 1 All E.R. 180 (an Indian labourer with an imperfect knowledge of English was employed to carry a ladle of molten metal with another labourer).

[41] *James v Hepworth & Grandage Ltd* [1968] 1 Q.B. 94 (a Jamaican immigrant who could neither read nor write was unable to read safety notices posted in the factory); also *Darvill v C. & J. Hampton* (1972) 13 K.I.R. 275 (contact with oil likely to cause dermatitis only to those with an individual susceptibility to it, where ample precautions were taken by the provision of gloves, barrier creams, washing facilities, etc.).

[42] See para.7–24 onwards.

[43] *Anderson v Lyotier* [2008] EWHC 2790 (Q.B.), where a skiing instructor was negligent in failing properly to assess the skiing ability of the claimant and thereafter supervise him sufficiently closely when taking him and others to ski off-piste: particular hazard was involved given the terrain, the quality of the snow and the presence of mature trees.

[44] See, e.g. Lord Wright in *Northwestern Utilities Ltd v London Guarantee & Accident Co Ltd* [1936] A.C. 108 at 126. See also Lord Macmillan, both in *Glasgow Corp v Muir* [1943] A.C. 448 at 456 and *Read v J. Lyons & Co Ltd* [1947] A.C. 156 at 173.

injury to his sight if he is struck in the face by a metal fragment than a man with two good eyes, he should be provided with goggles even where they would not otherwise be a necessary precaution.[45] In such a case, the possible consequences are obvious but it is not always so. It can be a matter of debate whether it would have been reasonable actively to investigate whether disability existed. Depending on the facts, employers may not have to take steps to discover whether their employee suffers disability.[46] Even if they discover he does, they may not be required to dismiss him because, for instance, no lighter work is available.[47]

The potential for grave consequences can also determine the standard of care   **7–23**
required of a person with a disability. If a driver knows that he is subject to sudden "black-outs" he may well be liable in negligence for an accident which occurs as a result since he has failed to acknowledge the grave consequences that could foreseeably arise if he had such an attack while driving.[48] However, in *Waugh v James K. Allen*,[49] a lorry driver, who was prone to suffer sudden gastric attacks from which he usually recovered quickly, was not guilty of negligence in continuing to drive after such an attack, when he subsequently died of a heart attack whilst still at the wheel of his vehicle: the first type of attack was foreseeable by him, the second, not.

Extra hazardous operations/activities. Other situations in which grave   **7–24**
consequences are relevant to the standard of care are those where something is being done which involves unusual hazard. So, where gas has been brought in containers on to a ship under construction, the degree of care to be exercised by those bringing it on board must be measured by the danger involved.[50] But it is the evidence adduced by the parties in a particular case which determines the view taken by the court of a hazardous operation and the result is not always that which at first blush might have been anticipated. Thus, while it might be thought that the risk of injury or death to a fisherman who fell overboard would be sufficient to justify the precaution of a life-jacket, against a background where there was no established practice of wearing such jackets, and a low incidence in the industry of injuries or death from falling overboard, it was not negligent for the employers of a trawlerman to fail to provide them.[51]

---

[45] *Paris v Stepney Borough Council* [1951] A.C. 367; *Porteous v N.C.B.*, 1967 S.L.T. 117.
[46] *Darvill v C. & J. Hampton* (1972) 13 K.I.R. 275 (contact with oil which was likely to cause dermatitis only to those who had an individual susceptibility to it, where ample precautions, including the provision of gloves, barrier creams and washing facilities, were provided).
[47] *Kosinski v Chrysler UK* (1974) 118 S.J. 97 ("tennis elbow" condition aggravated by claimant's continuing to work on car assembly line, operating a compressed air gun).
[48] See, e.g. *Hill v Baxter* [1958] 1 Q.B. 277 (the driver alleged that he had ignored an illuminated "HALT" sign by driving across the junction at a fast speed, because of his state of automatism); *Roberts v Ramsbottom* [1980] 1 W.L.R. 823.
[49] [1964] 2 Lloyd's Rep. 1.
[50] *Beckett v Newalls Insulation Co* [1953] 1 W.L.R. 8.
[51] *Gray v Stead* [1999] 2 Lloyd's Rep. 559, CA, para.7–38 and Ch.11, para.11–50, below. See also *Hopps v Mott MacDonald Ltd* [2009] EWHC 1881 (Q.B.) (defendant not required to provide its employee, an electrical engineer performing work to assist in the reconstruction of Iraq after war, with an armoured vehicle as protection against a roadside bomb.).

(D) Cost and practicability

7–25   Very few activities can be done without some risk. Crossing the street in a town exposes a pedestrian to risk but streets must be crossed. Cleaning the windows of a high building is a risk and, yet, the windows must be cleaned. Going to sea is a risky occupation but ships need sailors. The standard of reasonableness implies an evaluation in relation to the activity concerned, of the extent of any risk inherent to it, the justification for the risk being run, and the cost and practicablility of reducing or avoiding the risk.[52]

7–26   *Latimer v A.E.C. Ltd*, to which reference has already been made,[53] may also be taken as an illustration of the correlation between risk and the financial burden of remedying it is It was said in the Court of Appeal, by way of illustration, that if a factory was so damaged that there was a risk of the roof or the walls collapsing, the employer would no doubt have to close the premises until the danger was removed.[54] However, "in every case of foreseeable risk it is a matter of balancing the risk against the measure necessary to eliminate it".[55] On further appeal, the House of Lords found that the degree of risk was too small to justify closing down the factory and the claim failed.[56]

7–27   The problem was put in the following terms by Lord Reid in *Overseas Tankship (UK) Ltd v The Miller Steamship Co Pty*[57]:

> " . . . it does not follow that, no matter what the circumstances may be, it is justifiable to neglect a risk of such a small magnitude. A reasonable man would only neglect such a risk if he had some valid reason for doing so, e.g. that it would involve considerable expense to eliminate the risk. He would weigh the risk against the difficulty of eliminating it."

7–28   In some cases the cost of remedial measures will be a relatively unimportant consideration. In *Bolton v Stone*,[58] where a batsman hit a cricket ball out of the ground and struck a person on the highway, Lord Reid posed the question whether "a reasonable man in the position of the appellants, considering the matter from the point of view of safety, would have thought it right to refrain from taking steps to prevent the danger". He answered by saying, "I think that it would be right to take into account not only how remote is the chance that a

---

[52] *Briscoe v Secretary of State for Scotland*, 1997 S.C. 14, 2 Div. (prison officer, equipped with a helmet and body armour, sustained injury to his foot in the course of simulated riot which formed part of his training).

[53] [1952] 2 Q.B. 701, (appeal dismissed [1953] A.C. 643). See para.7–15, above; but cf. *Johnson v Rea* [1961] 1 W.L.R. 1400 (where soda ash seeped through the hessian sacks in which it was contained and spilled on to the floor of a shed, making it dangerously slippery, upon which the claimant fell: the defendants were liable since they had taken no steps to protect the claimant creating a danger, the mere giving of warning being insufficient).

[54] per Singleton L.J. in a judgment approved in the HL.

[55] ibid. per Denning L.J. at 710.

[56] [1953] A.C. 643, especially per Lord Asquith at 662. In view of the obligations contained in the Workplace (Health, Safety and Welfare) Regulations 1992 (SI 1992/3004) the decision on the facts would probably not be the same today.

[57] [1967] 1 A.C. 617 at 642.

[58] [1951] A.C. 850. See para.7–13, above.

person might be struck but also how serious the consequences are likely to be if a person is struck; but I do not think it would be right to take into account the difficulty of remedial measures."[59]

Importance of the end to be achieved. In assessing what can be done to   **7–29** meet an identified risk, the court will have regard to the end to be achieved, and its importance. In *Daborn v Bath Tramways Ltd*,[60] Asquith L.J. said:

> "In determining whether a party is negligent, the standard of reasonable care is that which is reasonably to be demanded in the circumstances. A relevant circumstance to take into account may be the importance of the end to be served by behaving in this way or in that. As has often been pointed out, if all the trains in this country were restricted to a speed of five miles an hour, there would be fewer accidents, but our national life would be intolerably slowed down. The purpose to be served, if sufficiently important, justifies the assumption of abnormal risk."

Acute risks may be part and parcel of the work of those employed in the   **7–30** emergency services, but a duty of care to them is still owed.[61] "Such public servants accept the risks which are inherent in their work, but not the risks which the exercise of reasonable care on the part of those who owe them a duty of care could avoid."[62] Where those working in the police, fire or ambulance services are exposed to a risk and where no reasonably practicable step could have been taken to avoid it, the employer will escape liability.[63]

Defendant's resources. Where the defendant is a public authority of some   **7–31** kind, account can be taken of any limitation in the financial resources available, as a result of the need to distribute available income between a number of demanding social or other functions.[64]

---

[59] *Bolton v Stone* [1951] A.C. 850 at 867.

[60] [1946] 2 All E.R. 333, at 336 (driver of ambulance with left-hand drive not negligent when, in wartime, she turned to the right without giving a signal). This passage was quoted with approval in *Watt v Hertfordshire County Council* [1954] 1 W.L.R. 835 at 838, and Denning L.J. added "It is well settled that in measuring due care you must balance the risk against the measures necessary to eliminate the risk. To that proposition there ought to be added this: you must balance the risk against the end to be achieved".

[61] *Ogwu v Taylor* [1988] 1 A.C. 43. See also in relation to the emergency services, Ch.2, paras 2–312, 2–313.

[62] per Hale L.J. in *King v Sussex Ambulance NHS Trust* (2002) 68 B.M.L.R. 177 at 182, CA.

[63] ibid. (employers not negligent in failing to instruct claimant to seek assistance of fire service, when in response to an urgent call-out he encountered difficulty in manouvering a patient down the stairs of his home).

[64] *East Suffolk Rivers Catchment Board v Kent* [1941] A.C. 74 at 95, 96 (where the Board took 164 days to repair a breach in the sea wall, work which could easily have been done in a fortnight). However, in *Haley v London Electricity Board* [1965] A.C. 778, the defendants, were held liable for failing to take precautions against a blind man falling down an inadequately guarded hole. A proper form of fencing, such as a light portable guard, could have been provided at a reasonable cost. See *Keating v Elvan Reinforced Concrete Co Ltd* [1968] 1 W.L.R. 722; also *B v Camden LBC* [2001] P.I.Q.R. P143 (defendants not liable for failing to lag central heating pipes against the risk that a baby might be trapped against them). See Craig, "Negligence in the Exercise of a Statutory Power", 94 L.Q.R. 428.

7–32   There is a question as to the extent to which in other cases limited resources should be taken into account. In *British Railways Board v Herrington*,[65] the court was considering the standard of care to be required of an occupier with considerable financial resources, who, it was suggested, by relatively small expense, could have reduced or prevented the possibility of a child trespasser coming into contact with a potentially lethal electrical installation. The House of Lords agreed that it was careless in the defendants not to take the steps suggested. But Lord Reid suggested that, " . . . an impecunious occupier with little assistance at hand would often be excused from doing something which a large organisation with ample staff would be expected to do".[66] Yet it cannot be that a *lower* standard of care is required of a large but impecunious organisation, than a similar concern with adequate resources. In most cases the objective cost and difficulty of remedial measures are relevant considerations, but the means of the particular defendant to meet those costs and difficulties should be disregarded. Once precautions designed to reduce the risk have been prescribed it will usually be negligent not to enforce them.[67]

7–33   **Discretion in a difficult field.** Reference has already been made to the cost considerations which can determine the standard of care appropriate to require from a public authority.[68] Such authorities are given by statute many responsibilities some of which can involve the exercise of difficult and sensitive discretions, one example arising in relation to the care of children. In *Barrett v Enfield London Borough Council*,[69] Lord Hutton drew attention to the fact that in assessing the standard of care in such cases, regard must be had to the circumstances in which the defendant had to exercise care and:

> " . . . when the decisions taken by a local authority in respect of a child in its care are alleged to constitute negligence at common law, the trial judge, bearing in mind the room for differences in opinion as to the best course to adopt in a difficult field and that the discretion is to be exercised by the authority and its social workers and not by the court, must be satisfied that the conduct complained of went beyond mere errors of judgment in the exercise of a discretion and constituted conduct which can be regarded as negligent."[70]

7–34   Elsewhere, reference has been made to the *circumstances* in which decisions with potentially grave consequences have had to be made. Medical experts may be required to decide upon a course of action where there is little time for reflection upon the choice to be made.[71] It has been said that setting too high a standard of care in such cases could encourage the practice of "defensive

---

[65] [1972] A.C. 877.

[66] *British Railways Board v Herrington* [1972] A.C. 877 at 899.

[67] See, e.g. *Hartshorn v Secretary of State for the Home Department* [1999] C.L.Y. 4012, CA (a prison rule which prohibited prisoners leaving the ground floor during a tea break was not enforced and the claimant was attacked by other inmates).

[68] At para.7–31, above.

[69] [2001] 2 A.C. 550, Ch.2, para.2–309, above.

[70] At 590. See also the similar observations of Lord Slynn at 571.

[71] Also, football referees: see the observations of Lord Woolf M.R. in *Smolden v Whitworth*, above, Ch.2, para.2–283.

medicine" in which the patient is given the safest treatment, rather than one in which the balance between risk and potential benefit is more finely drawn. In the *Barrett*[72] case, the judge at first instance, no doubt encouraged by observations in *X (Minors) v Bedfordshire County Council*,[73] had considered that imposing a duty of care upon the local authority and social workers involved might lead to an overly-defensive approach to the delicate task they had to perform in relation to children in care. But in the same case in the Court of Appeal and House of Lords this particular consideration was rejected: "If the conduct in question is of a kind which can be measured against the standards of the reasonable man, placed as the defendant was, then I do not see why the law in the public interest should not require those standards to be observed".[74] The suggestion was that the difficult circumstances in which a particular decision was made is a matter to be reflected in setting the appropriate standard of care, not in deciding whether to impose a duty of care at all. In a sport or game a participant may have only seconds, or divisions of a second, in which to make a decision with implications for the safety of others, whether competitors or spectators. The time available, the options open, the opportunity to assess the risks, are all matters which should be reflected in setting the appropriate standard of care.[75]

Considering the effects of prevention. In deciding the standard of care, a **7–35** court should be alert to the implications generally of a decision in the instant case. The price to be paid for complete safety can be unacceptable once wider social considerations are taken into account. Where a five-year-old child attending his primary school sports day, left his mother and went to play on some swings in the playground where he broke his arm, no liability attached to the school, even though the swings had been identified as a potential hazard. A reasonable level of supervision did not require that all access to the swings be prevented and if the standard was set so high events such as the sports day could not be held.[76] For similar reasons a local authority, which occupied a countryside park with a lake, was not liable when a young man suffered catastrophic injury diving into the water: the place was an amenity enjoyed by large numbers of people, usually without accident, and in deciding whether in effect access to the lake should be prevented, the court should take into account not simply considerations of cost, but also the social value of the activity which would be prohibited if protection was to be afforded.[77] Similarly, the Royal British Legion was not liable for an accident suffered when the claimant fell into a hole on a village green, left by a maypole, erected at a fete which the Legion had organised. One of the Legion's members had filled in the hole after the fete was over, but someone had removed the filling. It was said in the Court of Appeal that the

---

[72] n.69 above.
[73] [1995] 2 A.C. 633.
[74] per Evans L.J. in the Court of Appeal, quoted with approval by Lord Slynn of Hadley at 94.
[75] See, e.g. *Caldwell v Maguire and Fitzgerald* [2002] P.I.Q.R. P28, CA, para.2–281 above and *Smolden v Whitworth* n.71 above.
[76] *Simonds v Isle of Wight Council*, *The Times*, October 9, 2003.
[77] per Lord Hoffmann in *Tomlinson v Congleton Borough Council* [2004] 1 A.C. 46 at 82, Ch.8, para.8–152, below.

standard of care should not be set so high as to discourage or prevent maypole dancing or other traditional activities on a village green.[78]

7–36   **The Compensation Act 2006.** Concerns that valued or worthwhile activities were being adversely affected by judges' failure to consider the effects of a judgment in favour of a claimant with sufficient rigour, appear to lie behind s.1(1) of the Compensation Act 2006,[79] which provides:

> "A court considering a claim in negligence may, in determining whether the defendant should have taken particular steps to meet the standard of care (whether by taking precautions against a risk or otherwise), have regard to whether a requirement to take those steps might—
>
> (a) prevent a desirable activity from being undertaken at all, to a particular extent or in a particular way, or
> (b) discourage persons from undertaking functions in connection with a desirable activity."

7–37   It may be asked whether this is a necessary intrusion into an area of the common law with several hundred years of development and decided cases behind it. It must be assumed that the legislators are aware of the wide ranging judicial exercise involved in deciding what standard of care is reasonably to be required on given facts. That judges are able to take account of the consequences of a decision is illustrated by the cases referred to above. Some of the considerations, notably that those carrying out socially valuable activities may be unduly restricted if the standard of care is set at too high a level, were summarised in the context of a claim against an education authority, by Lord Clyde in *Phelps v London Borough of Hillingdon*, in a passage which appears to have general application[80]:

> "I am not persuaded that the recognition of a liability upon employees of the education authority for damages for negligence in education would lead to a flood of claims, or even vexatious claims, which would overwhelm the school authorities, nor that it would add burdens and distractions to the already intensive life of teachers. Nor should it inspire some peculiarly defensive attitude in the performance of their professional responsibilities. On the contrary it may have the healthy effect of securing that high standards are sought and secured. If it is thought that there would only be a few claims and for that reason the duty should not be recognised, the answer must be that if there are only a few claims there is the less reason to refuse to allow them to be entertained.

---

[78] *Cole v Davis-Gilbert, The Times*, April 5, 2007, CA (nor were the occupiers of the green liable: see Ch.8, para.8–39, below). See further, Pendlebury, "An outbreak of common sense" 157 N.L.J. 590. See also *Tysall Ltd v Snowdome* [2007] C.L. 434, Ch.8, para.8–38, below; *Uren v Corporate Leisure (UK) Ltd* [2010] EWHC 46 (Q.B.), para.7–14, above.

[79] c.29 of 2006. By s.2 an apology, an offer of treatment or other redress, shall not of itself amount to an admission of negligence or breach of statutory duty. See generally, Parker, "Changing the claims culture" 156 N.L.J. 702; Williams, "Politics, the media and refining the notion of fault: section 1 of the Compensation Act 2006" J.P.I. Law 2006, 4, 347; Herbert, "The Compensation Act 2006" J.P.I. Law 2006, 4, 337.

[80] [2001] 2 A.C. 619, 670. See further Williams, "Legislating in the echo chamber?" 155 N.L.J. 1938.

As regards the need for this remedy, even if there are alternative procedures by which some form of redress might be obtained, such as resort to judicial review, or to an ombudsman, or the adoption of such statutory procedures as are open to parents, which might achieve some correction of the situation for the future, it may only be through a claim for damages at common law that compensation for the damage done to the child may be secured for the past as well as the future. Any fear of a flood of claims may be countered by the consideration that in order to get off the ground the claimant must be able to demonstrate that the standard of care fell short of that set by the *Bolam* test[81] . . . That is deliberately and properly a high standard in recognition of the difficult nature of some decisions which those to whom the test applies require to make and of the room for genuine differences of view on the propriety of one course of action as against another."

(E) Other factors

Common practice. A court's assessment of the standard of care appropriate 7–38 in given circumstances will inevitably reflect the evidence received in the case. Where the evidence suggests that for a significant period of time a practice has been followed without untoward result, it will be regarded as a strong indication that to follow that practice is consistent with the exercise of reasonable care.[82] It will not be conclusive,[83] but, generally, "a defendant charged with negligence can clear [himself] if he shows that he has acted in accord with general and approved practice".[84] This is so, even if a body of opinion were to take a contrary view.[85] "A plaintiff who seeks to have condemned as unsafe a system of work which has been generally used for a long time in an important trade undertakes a heavy onus; if he is right it means that all, or practically all, the numerous employers in the trade have been habitually neglecting their duty to their men."[86] The weight to be given to a common practice is no less when considering an allegation of negligently-inflicted injury in a foreign country and it may well be

---

[81] *Bolam v Friern Hospital Management Committee* [1957] 1 W.L.R. 582. See below para.7–50 and Ch.9, generally.
[82] *Mahon v Osborne* [1939] 2 K.B. 14 at 43, per MacKinnon L.J.; *Whiteford v Hunter* [1950] W.N. 553; *Wright v Cheshire County Council* [1952] 2 All E.R. 789; *Simmons v Pennington & Son* [1955] 1 W.L.R. 183; *Morris v West Hartlepool Steam Navigation Co Ltd* [1956] A.C. 552; *Stokes v Guest, Keen and Nettlefold (Bolts and Nuts) Ltd* [1968] 1 W.L.R. 1776, 1783; *Henderson v H.E. Jenkins & Sons* [1969] 2 Q.B. 188 (reversed [1970] A.C. 282). *Gray v Stead* [1999] 2 Lloyd's Rep. 559, CA, Ch.11, para.11–50, below (fisherman not wearing life jacket: no liability where no practice to wear one).
[83] *Cavanagh v Ulster Weaving Co Ltd* [1960] A.C. 145.
[84] *Vancouver General Hospital v McDaniel* (1934) 152 L.T. 56 at 57, per Lord Alness. Lord MacDermott in *Whiteford v Hunter* [1950] W.N. 553 added that "such expressions beat the air and are meaningless unless used in relation to some particular condition or state of affairs."
[85] *Bolam v Friern Hospital Management Committee* [1957] 1 W.L.R. 582, per McNair J. at 587.
[86] *General Cleaning Contractors Ltd v Christmas* [1953] A.C. 180 at 192, per Lord Reid. However, in *King v Smith (t/a Clean Glo)* [1995] P.I.Q.R. P48, the CA opined that, over 40 years later, it ought not to be regarded as acceptable for a window cleaner to have to clean a window by standing on an outside sill without a safety harness. An employer should refuse to permit his employees to go onto a window sill where the customer has not provided anchor points for a harness and the window can be cleaned from inside.

relevant to consider the "local" standard of care in deciding whether a breach of duty was made out.[87]

7-39   When receiving evidence of what is alleged to have been a common and approved practice, the court must bear in mind its duty to assess the practice against considerations of logic and commonsense. It *may* simply be good fortune that an accident has not happened sooner. It may be that in the years since the practice was instigated, knowledge and standards have moved on. A "neglect of duty does not cease by repetition to be a neglect of duty".[88] In an employment context, once the employer knows, or should know, of the need to take some precaution, or the availability of some item of safety equipment, due discharge of his duty of care will require action on his part, and it will be no answer to say that his employees were pursuing some practice that had acquired the authority of time.[89]

7-40   It is always open to the court to hold that common practice does not make proper provision for a known risk.[90] The practice should looked at critically, to ensure that it merits the weight a defendant seeks to put upon it. In an employment case, in the context of negligence by omission, Lord Dunedin said that proof should be one of two kinds, "either to show that the thing which he did not do was a thing which was commonly done by other persons in like circumstances, or to show that it was a thing which was so obviously wanted that that it would be folly in anyone to neglect to provide it".[91] As often happens his words were thereafter overly emphasised and the balance had to be redressed. In *Cavanagh v Ulster Weaving Co Ltd*,[92] Lord Keith said:

> "Lord Dunedin cannot, in my opinion, have intended to depart from or modify the fundamental principle that an employer is bound to take reasonable care for the safety of his workmen, and in every case the question is whether the circumstances are such as to entitle judge or jury to say that there has or has not been a failure to exercise such reasonable care. It is immaterial, in my opinion, whether the alleged failure in duty is

---

[87] See, e.g. *Gouldbourn v Balkan Holidays Ltd* [2010] EWCA Civ. 372 (a claim for injury after an accident by a skiier under instruction where it was found that by Western standards, which reflected a "client-centred approach", the instructor "probably failed to assess the claimant properly", but, applying Eastern or "local" standards, which were more concerned with "procedure", the instructor had exercised the level of care and skill which was to be expected of him).

[88] *Carpenters' Co v British Mutual Banking Co Ltd* [1937] 3 All E.R. 811 at 820, per Slesser L.J. It does not mean, e.g. that an accident or a series of accidents has to happen before the general practice can be condemned as being unsafe: *Atkinson v Tyne-Tees Steam Shipping Co Ltd* [1956] 1 Lloyd's Rep. 244.

[89] See *Thompson v Smiths Ship Repairers (North Shields) Ltd* [1984] Q.B. 405 (employees in shipbuilding and ship-repairing work suffered from deafness as a result of excessive noise, the risk of which had been considered as an inescapable feature of the industry prior to 1963; thereafter the failure to take reasonable precautions, which were available, against the risk of deafness, amounted to negligence). See also Ch.11, paras 11–15 and 11–70, below.

[90] *Morris v W. Hartlepool S.N. Co* [1945] A.C. 552 where Lord Reid pointed out at 574 that evidence of general practice may not be worth very much unless it can be shown that it has been followed without mishap, over an appreciable period of time; *Bank of Montreal v Dominion Guarantee Co* [1930] A.C. 659; *Lloyds Bank Ltd v Savory & Co* [1933] A.C. 201; *Brown v John Mills & Co (Llanidloes)* (1970) 8 K.I.R. 702, CA.

[91] *Morton v William Dixon Ltd* 1909 S.C. 807 at 809.

[92] [1960] A.C. 145.

in respect of an act of omission or an act of commission. . . . Lord Dunedin was laying down, I think, no principle of law but stating the factual framework within which the law would fall to be applied".[93]

The fact that water undertakers for a district took standard precautions to **7-41** discover water escaping from their pipes, did not save them from a finding that they had failed to discharge their duty of care where the standard precautions were inadequate.[94] The fact that solicitors followed the then Hong Kong practice in conveyancing of handing over the purchase price of property to the vendor's solicitor in advance of the date of completion, on an undertaking to keep the money safely and repay it if the contract was not completed, did not prevent a finding in negligence where that practice was attended with obvious risk.[95] If the common practice is found to be a less than sufficient one, the defendant will be liable unless he can establish that no further precautions could have been taken which a reasonably prudent man would have taken to avoid or reduce the danger.[96]

It is necessary also to make the point that proof of a failure to comply with a **7-42** common practice is not itself conclusive of liability. One typical situation in the employment context, where so many of these examples arise, can be where precautions are habitually taken which would not have prevented the incident which is in question. Where an employer failed to supply a machine oiler with barrier cream, and he thereafter contracted dermatitis, the action failed even though other employers commonly supplied the cream, where it was not proved either that the cream was an effective precaution, or that it probably would have prevented the employee's injury. In the circumstances the employer had conformed to "the conduct and judgment of a reasonable and prudent man".[97]

These principles are not confined to employment cases, although many of the **7-43** examples come from that source. They arise, for instance, in relation to claims against professionals, such as solicitors,[98] and valuers.[99] In any set of circumstances, if there is a known danger, against which common practice makes no or no adequate provision, the proper standard of care is not attained unless it is proved that there are no further precautions which a reasonably prudent man would have taken to diminish the danger.[100]

---

[93] *Cavanagh v Ulster Weaving Co Ltd* [1960] A.C. 145 at 166.
[94] *Manchester Corp v Markland* [1936] A.C. 360. The point is brought out better in the CA [1934] 1 K.B. 566. See also *Shell-Mex Ltd v Belfast Corp* [1952] N.I. 72.
[95] *Edward Wong Finance Co v Johnson Stokes & Master* [1984] A.C. 1296.
[96] See *Mercer v The Commissioner for Road Transport and Tramways (N.S.W.)* (1936) 56 C.L.R. 580 at 593.
[97] *Brown v Rolls-Royce Ltd* [1960] 1 W.L.R. 210; the fact that it is proved that defendants have not followed a common practice of the trade does not necessarily raise a presumption of negligence, shifting an onus of proof to rebut it. The *legal* burden of proof is upon the claimant throughout, and it must be distinguished from a *provisional* (or evidential) burden which may be raised by the state of the evidence (per Lord Denning at 215).
[98] See n.95 above and Ch.9, para.9–235, below.
[99] See Ch.9, para.9–315.
[100] *General Cleaning Contractors Ltd v Christmas* [1953] A.C. 180; *Drummond v British Building Cleaners Ltd* [1954] 1 W.L.R. 1434; *Hurley v J. Sanders & Co Ltd* [1955] 1 All E.R. 833; *Barkway v S. Wales Transport Co* [1950] 1 All E.R. 392.

7–44   The existence of a common practice is a useful guide to the standard of care. It should not, however, be followed inflexibly to the conclusion that in every case where there is a common practice it is negligent to disregard it. The practice may itself carry danger and not therefore be encouraged.[101] It is no defence, in such circumstances, that many other employers permit the same method of work or that there have been no accidents over a considerable period of time.

7–45   **Guidance from statutory regulation or codes.** Compliance with statutory regulations applicable to a particular operation is evidence that reasonable care has been taken, although not conclusive.[102] An employer should be informed of the safety legislation relevant to the work undertaken, including, for example, the legislation of a foreign country when his employee is sent to work there.[103]

7–46   A recognised standard of conduct may be contained in statutory codes and official literature such as the Highway Code, Regulations for Preventing Collisions at Sea,[104] Stationery Office and Factory Department pamphlets, posters and notices, dealing with essential matters such as safety, handling loads, dust suppression and hygiene, particularly in regard to the avoidance of dermatitis, to which may be added the recommendations of the British Standards Institute.[105] All of these may be used as a practical guide to the standard of care to be aimed for, as well as the nature and extent of any particular danger which is likely to be encountered. Their use is admissible to establish the existence of known dangers and what practicable safety measures can be taken against them. The wide circulation of such information may be highly relevant when it comes to deciding what reasonably a prudent employer ought to know. Even so, neither do they have statutory force[106] nor do they supersede the common law duty. A code may appear to be exhaustive but there is always space left for discerning the common law duty of care.[107]

---

[101] *Brown v John Mills & Co (Llanidloes) Ltd* (1970) 8 K.I.R. 702, CA (the claimant, a skilled turner, used a common practice of polishing the outside of a brass nut, by securing it in a chuck revolving at high speed and holding against it a piece of emery cloth wrapped around his finger; he ought to have used a polishing stick but he had not been provided with one); applying *Blenkiron v Great Central Gas Consumers Co* (1860) 2 F. & F. 437.

[102] *Franklin v The Gramophone Co Ltd* [1948] 1 K.B. 542.

[103] See, e.g. *Executors of the Estate of O'Toole v Iarnrod Eireann Irishrail* [1999] 8 C.L. 354 (an employee of an Irish corporation was sent to work in England in 1950 and thereby exposed to asbestos dust, not at the time itself a known hazard in Ireland, although the employer ought to have been aware of UK legislation which sought to reduce exposure to workplace dust generally).

[104] *Thomas Stone Shipping Ltd v Admiralty (The Albion)* [1953] P. 117.

[105] As the CA has pointed out in *Ward v The Ritz Hotel (London)* [1992] P.I.Q.R. P315, the British Standards were not legally binding, but they were a guide which provided strong evidence as to the consensus of professional opinion and practical experience as to sensible safety precautions at their date of issue, to which the trial judge had failed to give appropriate weight. By way of contrast, in *Green v Building Scene Ltd* [1994] P.I.Q.R. P259, CA, failure to provide a handrail on a stairway in breach of the Building Regulations 1976 and the Code of Practice issued by the Institute, was held not to be unsafe and so the claim failed.

[106] *Clifford v Charles H. Challen & Son Ltd* [1951] 1 K.B. 495; *Dickson v Flack* [1953] 2 Q.B. 464.

[107] *Nicholls v NCB* (1952) 102 L.J. 357; *Matuszyczyk v NCB*, 1953 S.C. 8.

The effect of the Highway Code is set out in s.39 of the Road Traffic Act   **7–47**
1988,[108] and whilst a breach of the Code can be relied upon in an attempt to show
either negligence or contributory negligence, the Court of Appeal has emphasised that it is not to be elevated into a breach of statutory duty, which establishes
automatically either a separate cause of action or a partial defence.[109]

The provisions of s.16 of the Health and Safety at Work, etc. Act 1974[110]   **7–48**
authorise the issue of codes of practice for guidance on health and safety matters
which have been approved by the Health and Safety Commission. Any failure on
the part of any person to observe and comply with the approved code "shall not
of itself render him liable to any civil or criminal proceedings" but it is prima
facie evidence in criminal proceedings.[111] Although the Act is silent upon the
point, there can be little doubt that these codes of practice will be admissible in
an action for negligence for the same purpose and to the like effect as the various
other statutory codes, outlined above.

Being wise after the event. Either subsequent experience or hindsight may   **7–49**
show that some additional precaution was necessary but this fact by itself would
not prove that the defendants were guilty of negligence at the relevant date of the
accident.[112] Whilst it is always easy to be wise after the event,[113] there is nothing
which is so perfect that it cannot be improved by knowledge, experience and
understanding.[114]

Act requiring special skill. Where something is to be done which may give   **7–50**
rise to danger to the person or property of another, and can only be safely
performed by a person who has the requisite skill, the reasonable man would not
attempt it, unless he was competent to do it. The standard of care is adjusted to
take account of the fact that the task in question required special skill and that the
defendant attempted that task. The classic statement of the standard then to be
achieved was given by McNair J. in *Bolam v Friern Hospital Management
Committee*[115]:

> "In the ordinary case which does not involve any special skill, negligence in law means
> a failure to do some act which a reasonable man in the circumstances would do, or the
> doing of some act which a reasonable man in the circumstances would not do; and if
> the failure or the doing of that act results in injury, then there is a cause of action. How
> do you test whether this act or failure is negligent? In an ordinary case it is generally
> said you judge it by the action of the man in the street. He is the ordinary man. In one

---

[108] See further Ch.10, para.10–192, below.
[109] *Powell v Phillips* (1972) 116 S.J. 713 (perhaps surprisingly, the court refused to find the claimant
guilty of contributory negligence, when she had failed to walk on a pavement at night in a poorly lit
road, but had walked in the roadway with her back to oncoming traffic, wearing dark coloured clothes
and without carrying anything white in colour).
[110] Save for Pt III, the Act came into force on April 1, 1975, by SI 1974/1439. Pt III was later
substantially consolidated in the Building Act 1984.
[111] s.17.
[112] *Philpott v British Railways Board* [1968] 2 Lloyd's Rep. 495 at 502.
[113] *The Wagon Mound (No.1)* [1961] A.C. 388 at 424.
[114] *Pipe v Chambers Wharf and Cold Stores Ltd* [1952] 1 Lloyd's Rep. 194 at 195.
[115] [1957] 1 W.L.R. 582 at 586.

case it has been said you judge it by the conduct of the man on the top of a Clapham omnibus. He is the ordinary man. But where you get a situation which involves the use of some special skill or competence, then the test as to whether there has been negligence or not is not the test of the man on the top of a Clapham omnibus, because he has not got this special skill. The test is the standard of the ordinary skilled man exercising and professing to have that special skill. A man need not possess the highest expert skill; it is well established law that it is sufficient if he exercises the ordinary skill of an ordinary competent man exercising that particular art."[116]

7–51   **Degree of skill.** The *Bolam* test is of general application when assessing the standard of care appropriate from someone deploying some expertise and is not confined to the particular skill of medicine.[117] The standard is that of an ordinary competent person in the same calling. He or she should do "all that any skilful person could reasonably be expected to do in such a case".[118] A person driving a car on the public highway, for example, was bound to exercise the skill of a reasonably careful driver, even before the introduction of driving tests, and, if he failed to do so, was not excused by the fact that he was using such care and skill as he possessed. The standard of care is not affected or reduced merely because the driver happens to be a learner driver, since he must comply with the same objective and impersonal standard as must every other driver.[119]

7–52   The principle stated above is not engaged simply because a person holds himself out as having a special skill; it is based on the actual performance of an act which can only safely be done by a person with skill necessary to do it. For example, a surgical operation must be performed in the way that a skilled surgeon, who is accustomed to perform that operation, would perform it. With the likely exception of a sudden and serious emergency, it would be no defence, where damage ensued, as a result of unskilful performance, that the unskilfulness arose from the operator's lack of a surgical qualification or from any other cause.

7–53   In *Phillips v Whiteley Ltd*,[120] the claimant had her ears pierced for earrings by a jeweller, with the result that her ears became inflamed through infection. It was found that, whilst a surgeon would have sterilised his instruments, the jeweller would not have done, and that the operation was performed with the skill to be expected from a jeweller but not with the skill to be expected from a surgeon. Unlike the position in contract, where a different standard can be exacted from

---

[116] *Bolam v Friern Hospital Management Committee* [1957] 1 W.L.R. 582 at 586. Lord Diplock pointed out the long history behind the *Bolam* test in *Sidaway v Board of Governors of the Bethlem Royal Hospital and the Maudsley Hospital* [1985] A.C. 871 at 892: "The *Bolam* test is far from new, its value is that it brings up to date and re-expresses in the light of modern conditions in which the art of medicine is now practised, an ancient rule of common law. The original rule can be traced to the maxim *spondet peritiam artis et imperitia culpae admuneratur*. It goes back to the origin of *assumpsit*; it applied to all artificers and was firmly founded in 'case' (*moderniter negligence*) . . .".

[117] *Gold v Haringey Health Authority* [1988] Q.B. 481 at 489, per Lloyd L.J. (pet. dis. [1988] 1 W.L.R. 462).

[118] *Jones v Bird* (1822) 5 B. & Ald. 837 at 845, per Bayley J.

[119] *Nettleship v Weston* [1971] 2 Q.B. 691. See further, Ch.10, para.10–258, below.

[120] [1938] 1 All E.R. 566.

different persons, depending on the terms of the contract, it is submitted that, in tort, the degree of care to be expected from a person who performs a particular operation is the same for all. It may be that in the operation of ear-piercing the jeweller's standard of care is enough but, if that is so, then a surgeon, who merely attained the same degree, despite its falling appreciably short of the standard which might be exacted from him in contract, would not be liable, likewise, in tort.

In *Wells v Cooper*,[121] the Court of Appeal considered the standard of care to be exercised by a man having some experience as an amateur carpenter, who set about fitting a new door handle with three screws. Jenkins L.J. said: **7–54**

"We think the standard of care and skill to be demanded of the defendant in order to discharge his duty of care to the plaintiff in the fixing of a new handle ... must be the degree of care and skill to be expected of a reasonably competent carpenter doing the work in question. This does not mean that the degree of care and skill required is to be measured by reference to the contractual obligations as to the quality of his work assumed by a professional carpenter working for reward, which would, in our view, set the standard too high."[122]

Where someone executing a task requiring special skill has to devolve part of the task upon another, he will not achieve the standard of care required of him unless the agent or nominee selected is appropriately qualified for the job. In such a case the *Bolam* test will determine the appropriateness of the selection. The duty was discharged where patent agents were advising whether a product might infringe an existing United States patent, and they instructed a firm of American patent searchers to carry out a search to check whether the United States patent was still in force: since such a search was a straightforward task it was not negligent to fail to obtain the more sophisticated services of patent attorneys.[123] The decision of a professional body as to the standard of care deployed by the defendant in given circumstances may be taken into account by the judge at a later trial, but is not determinative of the issue and its weight will depend very much upon the precise issues which the professional body addressed and the evidence it heard.[124] **7–55**

Deciding the standard of care. It is for the judge at first instance to determine what, in all the circumstances of the case, is a reasonable standard of care.[125] An appellate court will not interfere with such a determination, unless it **7–56**

---

[121] [1958] 2 Q.B. 265. See note on this case, 74 L.Q.R. 474.
[122] *Wells v Cooper* [1958] 2 Q.B. 265 at 271.
[123] *Arbiter Group Plc v Gill Jennings & Every* [2000] P.N.L.R. 1, appeal dismissed [2000] P.N.L.R. 680, CA.
[124] See *Caldwell v Maguire and Fitzgerald* [2002] P.I.Q.R. P28, CA (a finding of careless riding by a stewards' inquiry after a horse race at Hexham, Northumberland was not determinative of negligence).
[125] [1965] A.C. 778. But cf. *Pritchard v Post Office* [1950] W.N. 310 where the blind claimant's own negligence was held to have been the cause of his accident. See further para.7–19, below.

can be demonstrated that the judge had erred.[126] In coming to a decision the overwhelming probability is that the trial judge will have regard to one, frequently more than one, of the general matters set out above. No doubt the weight to be attached to a particular circumstance will depend upon the evidence. But it will also depend upon the approach in similar circumstances taken in earlier cases. The chapters that follow seek to illustrate the standard of care that has been regarded as appropriate in the various general areas to which their heading refers.

---

[126] *Kite v Nolan* [1983] R.T.R. 253, CA (the minor claimant, aged five, ran out into the road from a line of parked cars, in order to get to an ice-cream van that was parked on the opposite side of the road. The defendant was driving his car along the road slowly, at about 15 mph but could not stop in time to avoid striking the child. It was held that, as the accident could have been avoided only if the defendant had been travelling at a crawling speed of around 5 mph, no negligence had been established against him and the CA declined to interfere with such a finding).

DANGEROUS PREMISES

Introduction. This chapter concentrates on the duty of care owed by an **8–01** occupier of premises to his visitors. It should, however, be kept in mind that the relationship of occupier and visitor is but one source of a duty of care in relation to the state of premises.[1] Different legal relationships between two persons may well exist side by side without being mutually exclusive. So, a claimant is not restricted to suing the defendant in his capacity as the occupier of dangerous premises, if he can also sue the same person in his capacity, for instance, as employer. As Lord Gardiner L.C. said, when delivering the judgment of the Privy Council in *Commissioner for Railway v McDermot*[2]:

"In their Lordships' opinion the basic principle for a case such as this is that occupation of premises is a ground of liability and is not a ground of exemption from liability. It is a ground of liability because it gives some control over and knowledge of the state of the premises, and it is natural and right that the occupier should have some degree of responsibility for the safety of persons entering his premises with his permission .... If there is no other relevant relationship, there is no further or other duty of care. But there is no exemption from any other duty of care which may arise from other

---

[1] See Allen and Holyoak, "Premises Liability: Recent Developments", 134 New L.J. 347; 369; 411; and 425. See generally, Lyons, "Occupiers' liability: back to basics" 2001 J.P.I. Law 4, 356.
[2] [1967] 1 A.C. 169 at 186, 187.

elements in the situation creating an additional relationship between the two persons concerned. Theoretically in such a situation there are two duties of care existing concurrently, neither displacing the other. A plaintiff could successfully sue for breaches of either or both of the duties if the defendant had committed such breaches, although for practical purposes the plaintiff could be content with establishing the general duty and would not gain anything by adding the special and limited duty."

8–02   An example of "other elements . . . creating an additional relationship" arose where, at a fireworks display, injury was caused to the agent of an independent contractor invited onto the occupier's land to provide the entertainment. The display involved hazard and the occupier made insufficient enquiry into the contractor's competence. In the circumstances a duty of care arose towards the contractor's agent, independently of the duty qua occupier, the requirements of foreseeability and proximity being satisfied and it being fair, just and reasonable to impose the duty.[3]

1. THE PREMISES

8–03   **Definition of premises.** For purposes of the occupier's duty, the "premises" in respect of which a duty is owed are not simply buildings, houses and other real property but include objects upon the land which the visitor has been invited or permitted to use. Grandstands,[4] electricity pylons,[5] seaside promenades[6] and diving boards at swimming pools have all been held to qualify as premises.[7] Further, the duty is not confined to premises that are fixed but extends to all moveable structures and conveyances, in or on which human beings are invited and permitted to entrust their safety. Accordingly, they include any aircraft,[8] railway carriages,[9] road carriages,[10] lorries,[11] trucks,[12] ships,[13] ladders,[14] lifts,[15] stagings[16] and scaffolds.[17] They also include wharves and berths to which ships are invited for the purpose of loading or unloading.[18] Liability does not arise as

---

[3] See *Bottomley v Todmordern Cricket Club* [2004] P.I.Q.R. P 275, CA.
[4] *Francis v Cockrell* (1870) L.R. 5 Q.B. 501.
[5] *Kenny v Electricity Supply Board* [1932] I.R. 73; *McLaughlin v Antrim Electricity Supply Co* [1941] N.I. 23.
[6] *Collier v Anglia Water Authority, The Times*, March 26, 1983, CA; *Harrison v Thanet District Council* [1998] C.L.Y. 3918.
[7] *Perkowski v Wellington Corp* [1959] A.C. 53; *Periscinotti v Brighton West Pier, The Times*, June 7, 1961.
[8] *Fosbroke-Hobbes v Airwork Ltd* [1937] 1 All E.R. 108.
[9] *Foulkes v Metropolitan Ry* (1880) 5 C.P.D. 157; *Readhead v Midland Ry* (1869) L.R. 4 Q.B. 379.
[10] *Moffatt v Bateman* (1869) L.R. 3 P.C. 115; *White v Steadman* [1913] 3 K.B. 340.
[11] *Lomas v M. Jones & Son* [1944] K.B. 4. See also *Phillips v Perry* [1997] 5 C.L. 486, CA (occupier not liable where delivery man straddled a 2ft 6in. gap between vehicles in loading a sack).
[12] *Elliott v Hall* (1885) 15 Q.B.D. 315.
[13] *Hillen v I.C.I. (Alkali) Ltd* [1936] A.C. 65; *London Graving Dock v Horton* [1951] A.C. 737.
[14] *Marney v Scott* [1899] 1 Q.B. 986.
[15] *Haseldine v Daw & Sons* [1941] 2 K.B. 343; *Sandford v Eugene* (1970) 115 S.J. 33.
[16] *Heaven v Pender* (1883) 11 Q.B.D. 503; *Kearney v Eric Waller Ltd* [1967] 1 Q.B. 29.
[17] *Woodman v Richardson* [1937] 3 All E.R. 866.
[18] *The Moorcock* (1889) 14 P.D. 64; *The Calliope* [1891] A.C. 11; *The Bearn* [1906] P. 48; *The Humorist* [1944] P. 28.

occupier where injury is caused by negligence on the part of a driver or other person operating or in charge of movable structures or conveyances, but only in so far as the damage has arisen from the dangerous structural condition of the object in question.

Liability for dangerous premises. Liability for dangerous premises must be   **8–04**
considered both in connection with persons who are injured while visiting the premises,[19] and persons who are injured when they are not on the premises, but whose injuries are caused by the dangerous state of the premises.[20]

Common law duty to visitors. Historically the extent of the occupier's duty   **8–05**
depended upon the circumstances under which the person to whom it was alleged a duty was owed came to be present on the premises. There were different categories of entrant upon land and the duty varied with the category. It was said that the least duty was owed a trespasser, then came a licensee and then an invitee.[21]

The three categories of invitee, licensee and trespasser were rigid and there   **8–06**
were no intermediate stages between them.[22] Accordingly, such expressions as "bare licensee," "licensee with an interest," "licensee for payment" were meaningless, except in so far as they could be referred to one of the three classes. It was, however, conceded that the law gave rise to distinctions which were "subtle and apt to be confused".[23]

The Occupiers' Liability Act 1957. From January 1, 1958, the common law   **8–07**
duties owed to lawful visitors were replaced by statutory provisions. The Occupiers' Liability Act 1957 provides[24] that the rules enacted by ss.2 and 3 "shall have effect, in place of the rules of the common law, to regulate the duty which an occupier of premises owes to his visitors in respect of dangers due to the state of the premises or to things done or omitted to be done on them". In so far as the duties owed to them were concerned, the three categories[25] of invitee, licensee and trespasser were merged into two, namely visitors and trespassers. Persons, who, up to that date, were treated as invitees or licensees became visitors[26] and the duty owed to them the "common duty of care".[27] The 1957 Act did not alter the law in relation to trespassers, which remained unchanged until

---

[19] Which is discussed in paras 8–06 to 8–160, below.
[20] See paras 8–161 to 8–171, below.
[21] per Hamilton L.J. in *Latham v R. Johnson & Nephew Ltd* [1913] 1 K.B. 398 at 410.
[22] *Robert Addie & Sons (Collieries) Ltd v Dumbreck* [1929] A.C. 358; *Liddle v Yorkshire (North Riding) County Council* [1934] 2 K.B. 101 at 119, per Greer L.J.; *Sutton v Bootle Corp* [1947] K.B. 359. For the old law, see *Charlesworth on Negligence* (3rd edn, 1956), Ch.9.
[23] per Atkin L.J. in *Coleshill v Manchester Corp* [1928] 1 K.B. 776 at 791.
[24] Which followed the Law Reform Committee's Third Report (Cmd. 9305) in 1954.
[25] These three categories still exist at common law. It is only the distinction between the duty owed to invitees and that owed to licensees which has been abolished and replaced by statute.
[26] s.1(2).
[27] s.2(1). This duty is defined in s.2(2) and is: "A duty to take such care as in all the circumstances of the case is reasonable to see that the visitor will be reasonably safe in using the premises for the purposes for which he is invited or permitted by the occupier to be there." See further para.8–36, below.

the intervention of the House of Lords in *Herrington v British Railways Board*.[28] Thereafter the Occupiers' Liability Act 1984[29] laid down the duty to trespassers in statutory form.

8–08   The common duty of care prescribed by ss.2 and 3 of the 1957 Act extends to regulate "the obligations of a person occupying or having control over any fixed or moveable structure, including any vessel, vehicle or aircraft". Although the common duty of care under the Act[30] has been restricted to the occupier or the notional occupier of premises[31] (since the Act does not apply to non-occupiers), nevertheless a duty to take care is owed by other persons, who are on the premises at the invitation or by the permission of the owner or occupier and even by trespassers.[32]

8–09   Section 1(1) provides that ss.2 and 3 (which set out the common duty of care) "regulate the duty which an occupier of premises owes to his visitors in respect of dangers due to the state of the premises or to things done or omitted to be done on them".[33] The same words also appear in the Occupiers Liability Act 1984, dealt with below. Both aspects, the state of the premises and use of them, merit separate consideration.

8–10   **The state of the premises.** At common law the occupier's duty to an invitee was confined to the physical condition of the premises. So, for instance, no special duty as occupier applied to the claim of a customer of public house when his motorcycle, which had been left in a covered yard at the premises, marked "garage," was stolen[34]:

> "There is no warrant . . . for holding that an invitor, where the invitation extends to the goods as well as the person of the invitee, thereby by implication of law assumes a liability to protect the invitee and his goods, not merely from physical dangers arising from defects in the premises, but from the risk of the goods being stolen by some third party."[35]

8–11   Likewise where injury was alleged as a result of some activity carried out upon the premises. A distinction was drawn before the 1957 Act between the liability of an occupier for the dangerous state of premises and liability in relation to dangerous activities carried out on the premises. Although now of only occasional significance, the distinction survives.[36] The Act replaced the common

---

[28] [1972] A.C. 877.
[29] Which came into force on May 13, 1984.
[30] See s.1(2) and (3).
[31] s.6 provides that the Act shall bind the Crown, but as regards the Crown's liability in tort shall not bind the Crown further than the Crown is made liable in tort by the Crown Proceedings Act 1947, and that Act and, in particular, s.2 of it shall apply in relation to duties under ss.2 to 4 of this Act as statutory duties.
[32] para.8–91, below.
[33] See para.8–14, below.
[34] *Tinsley v Dudley* [1951] 2 K.B. 18; cf. *Deyong v Shenburn* [1946] K.B. 227.
[35] *Tinsley v Dudley* [1951] 2 K.B. 18 per Jenkins L.J. at 31.
[36] *Fairchild v Glenhaven Funeral Services Ltd* [2002] 1 W.L.R. 1052 at 1083, CA (claims against the occupiers of premises based upon harmful exposure to asbestos dust while performing work there; appeal allowed on different grounds [2003] 1 A.C. 32); also *Bottomley v Todmordern Cricket Club*, n.3 above.

law rules in relation to an occupier's "occupancy duty," the duty which arose from the presence of some unusual[37] danger in or on the premises; the common law rules still govern liability for dangerous activities on the land.[38]

> "The 1957 Act imposed the new statutory common duty of care on an occupier towards all his visitors to take appropriate care to see that they would be reasonably safe in using his premises, . . . The Act does not provide an answer, however, when a question arises whether an occupier, without more, is liable to a visitor for an injury he suffers as a result of an activity conducted by a third party on his premises. For that purpose one has to go to the common law to see if a duty of care exists, and, if so, what is its scope, or to some other statutory provision such as the (now repealed) section 63(1) of the Factories Act 1961."[39]

In *Tomlinson v Congleton Borough Council*,[40] the claimant failed to establish **8–12** there was any risk to himself due to the state of the premises, where in throwing himself forward into the water of a lake to swim, he came into contact with the shallow bottom and suffered serious injury to his cervical spine. He had voluntarily engaged in an activity which involved a degree of risk and it was the activity, rather than the premises, which gave rise to that risk. There being no danger to him attributable to the state of the premises, no duty arose under either the 1957 or 1984 Acts to protect him from it. As Lord Phillips M.R. put it in *Donoghue v Folkestone Properties Ltd*[41]:

> "There are some features of land that are not inherently dangerous but which may tempt a person on the land to indulge in an activity which carries a risk of injury. Such activities include cliff-climbing, mountaineering, skiing, and hang-gliding by way of example. It does not seem to me that a person carrying on such an activity can ascribe to the 'state of the premises' an injury sustained as a result of a mishap in the course of carrying on the activity—provided of course that the mishap is not caused by an unusual or latent feature of the landscape."

Likewise, where the claim was for catastrophic injuries sustained when the **8–13** claimant dived into an hotel swimming pool that was too shallow for diving. It was said that the core of the reasoning in *Tomlinson* was that "people should accept responsibility for the risks they choose to run" and there was no duty to protect them against obvious risks (subject to qualification where there was no informed choice or some lack of capacity). The reasoning applied both to lawful visitors under the 1957 Act and trespassers under the 1984 Act and was also applicable to persons entering premises such as an hotel under a package holiday contract as in the instant case.[42]

---

[37] Attention was drawn by Brooke L.J.in *Fairchild*, above at 1084, to the list of "unusual" and "not unusual" dangers in *Charlesworth on Negligence*, 3rd edn (1956), pp.195–197.

[38] ibid. at 1085. The Court of Appeal in *Fairchild* drew support from the speech of Lord Goff in *Ferguson v Welsh* [1987] 1 W.L.R. 1553 HL.

[39] *Fairchild v Glenhaven Funeral Services Ltd*, n.36 above at 1088.

[40] [2004] 1 A.C. 46. See particularly the discussion in the speech of Lord Hoffmann at 78 onwards. See also Braithwaite Q.C., "Disastrous diving" 147 S.J. 984.

[41] [2003] Q.B. 1008 at [35]. The facts are summarised at para.8–149, below. *Donoghue* was decided before, but quoted with approval in, *Tomlinson* in the HL.

[42] *Evans v Kosmar Villa Holiday Plc* [2008] 1 W.L.R. 297, CA, especially per Richards L.J. at [39].

8–14   **Things done or omitted to be done.** The occupier owes the "common duty of care" not only in respect of dangers owing to the state of the premises, but also in respect of dangers arising out of "things done or omitted to be done on them".[43] This includes things done or omitted to be done by persons who are permitted by the occupier to make use of the premises, when reasonably using the premises for the purposes for which they are invited or permitted to be there. Where a firework party was held at a riverside bungalow, which was later set on fire as a result of a "jumping jack" accidentally finding its way into the lounge from the vicinity of the porch and there setting alight some other fireworks which had been stored in a cubby-hole made especially for the occasion, there was no breach of duty under the Act. The occupiers had done all that could reasonably be expected of them to store the fireworks safely.[44] By way of contrast, a football club was held liable for injuries sustained by police officers on duty at a football match, where they were the result of foreseeable acts of violence by hooligans who threw at them lumps of concrete torn up from the terraces.[45]

8–15   In the absence of evidence that the occupier of a camping site knew it was being used for the giving of driving lessons by one of the campers, it was held that the defendant was not in breach of duty in failing to provide a suitably marked-out area for such driving activities or to make or to draw attention to regulations which forbade vehicles to be driven in the vicinity of the tents erected on the site.[46]

8–16   **Damaging a visitor's property.** As to property brought by a visitor on to the premises, s.1(3) provides that the rules enacted by ss.2 and 3 apply to regulate "the obligations of a person occupying or having control over any premises or structure in respect of damage to property, including the property of persons who are not themselves his visitors".[47] Having regard to s.1(2) that the rules enacted in ss.2 and 3 "shall not alter the rules of the common law as to the persons on whom a duty is so imposed or to whom it is owed," the reference in s.1(3)(b) to the property of persons who are not themselves the occupier's visitors, must mean property not belonging to a visitor but which, nevertheless, he is invited or permitted to bring on to the premises. These are such things as articles in his possession under a hire-purchase agreement or otherwise, and articles of which he is bailee. Damages are not limited by s.1(3)(b) to compensation in respect of physical damage but may include damages in respect of consequential financial

---

[43] s.1(1). See *Honeybourne v Burgess* 2006 S.L.T. 585, OH (where the occupiers of a nightclub retained the services of a bouncer who had assaulted a patron some years before, that did not, for purposes of a claim for injuries received by the claimant when the bouncer threw him out of the club, amount to a danger due to "things done or omitted to be done on the premises" and the bouncer was not himself such a danger).

[44] *Horsenail v Kennedy, The Times*, April 30, 1964. See also, *Bottomley v Todmorden Cricket Club* [2004] P.I.Q.R. P275, CA (where the occupier was liable for an injury by fireworks to the servant or agent of an independent contractor the occupier had invited onto the land, see further para.8–81, below).

[45] *Cunningham v Reading Football Club Ltd* [1992] P.I.Q.R. P141.

[46] *Crickmar v Cleavers, The Times*, October 8, 1964.

[47] At common law the invitor's duty was to prevent not only personal injury but also damage to an invitee's goods. Section 1(3)(b) now affirms and extends the common law. Damage to property does not include the loss of property, see *Tinsley v Dudley* [1951] 2 K.B. 18 above.

loss.[48] An example has been suggested[49] of a visitor who brought on to the occupier's premises a car, which was used by him for hiring out. If it was damaged as a result of the dangerous state of the premises, the visitor could recover not only the cost of repairs to the vehicle but also any loss of profits from hiring it out over the period of repair.

As pointed out already, this section of the Act did not create any new liability (for example for the theft of goods) where none had existed at common law.[50]

2.—THE OCCUPIER

Definition of occupier. Liability for dangerous or defective premises is   **8–17** primarily on the occupier, whether he is the owner or not, and is based on the fact that he has control of the place in or on to which he has invited his lawful visitor.[51] The persons treated as occupiers under the Act[52] are the same as those who would be so described at common law. They do not include a landlord who has let premises by demise to a tenant, since he is regarded as having parted with control, even if he has undertaken to carry out repairs.[53] If a landlord does not demise all the premises but retains control of some parts, such as a common staircase or roof, he remains occupier of them.[54] The answer to the question who is an occupier, " . . . in each case depends on the particular facts of the case and especially upon the nature and extent of the occupation or control in fact enjoyed or exercised by the defendants over the premises."[55] An occupier is any person who is in actual occupation for the time being or having possession or physical control, the degree of which need neither be entire or exclusively his,[56] over the premises concerned or over any fixed or moveable structure including such things as a vessel, vehicle or aircraft.[57]

---

[48] *A.M.F. International v Magnet Bowling* [1968] 1 W.L.R. 1028.

[49] ibid. at 1050, per Mocatta J.

[50] Mocatta J. expressed this view also at 1050, *A.M.F. International v Magnet Bowling* [1968] 1 W.L.R. 1028.

[51] McMahon, "Conclusions on Judicial Behaviour from a Comparative Study of Occupiers' Liability", 38 M.L.R. 39.

[52] Occupiers' Liability Act 1957 s.1(2).

[53] Although he is not an occupier, he does owe duties qua landlord at common law. See also the provisions of the Defective Premises Act 1972 ss.3 and 4, which came into force on January 1, 1974, and para.8–123, below.

[54] *Wheat v E. Lacon & Co Ltd* [1966] A.C. 552 at 579, per Lord Denning. See also *Liverpool City Council v Irwin* [1976] Q.B. 319. Where the defendant landlord was occupier of the common staircase and passageway of a house which had been divided into flats, he continued to owe the relevant statutory and common law duties of care, notwithstanding that the local authority had taken over the payment of the electricity supply and was in receipt of the tenants' rents: *Jordan v Archara* (1988) 20 H.L.R. 607, CA.

[55] per Ashworth J. in *Creed v McGeoch & Sons Ltd* [1955] 1 W.L.R. 1005 at 1009.

[56] See, e.g. *Collier v Anglian Water Authority, The Times*, March 26, 1983, CA (a jointly shared promenade by the seaside).

[57] ibid. s.1(3)(a). In *Wheeler v Copas* [1981] 3 All E.R. 405, Chapman J. suggested that the subsection could apply to a ladder which belonged to the occupier provided that he had not ceased to be its occupier, after his having handed it over to his visitor to use.

8–18   **Illustrations of occupiers.** An owner in possession of premises; a tenant under a tenancy agreement of premises; a licensee of premises; a contractor, who is converting a vessel into a troopship[58]; various kinds of building contractors and their sub-contractors working on site[59]; a sideshow concessionaire in his stall on a show-ground[60]; a local authority, which had requisitioned houses[61]; a members club, incorporated under s.3 of the Industrial and Provident Societies Act 1965.[62] A wharfinger is the occupier of the quays or sea walls against which vessels moor when berthing in a tidal berth or layerage.[63]

8–19   **Illustrations of non-occupiers.** It has been held that a road contractor was not in occupation of land that flanked part of the road, where the edge of his workings finished[64]; a painting contractor of the roof of a house under construction[65]; an electricity company of land over which it had a wayleave agreement to erect poles or pylons and to pass across cables[66]; charterers of the hold of a ship, which had been loaded in Canada.[67] The mere fact that a local authority is liable to maintain a privately-owned footpath does not make it an occupier of that road for the purposes of the 1957 Act.[68] Householders whose premises overlooked the flat roof of another building on which they allowed their children to play had insufficient control over the roof to be deemed occupiers of it.[69]

8–20   **Multiple occupiers.** Occupation can be by more than one person, in which event each is under a duty of care to a visitor, dependent upon the degree of control exercisable by him. In *Wheat v E. Lacon & Co Ltd*,[70] the defendants, who were brewers, were the owners of a public house, the management of which they

---

[58] *Hartwell v Grayson Rollo and Clover Docks Ltd* [1947] K.B. 901.

[59] *Kearney v Eric Waller Ltd* [1967] Q.B. 29; *A.M.F. International Ltd v Magnet Bowling Ltd* [1968] W.L.R. 1028; *Bunker v Charles Brand & Son Ltd* [1969] 2 Q.B. 480; *Rannett v McGuinness & Co Ltd* [1972] 2 Q.B. 599.

[60] *Humphreys v Dreamland (Margate) Ltd* (1931) 100 L.J.K.B. 137.

[61] See *Hawkins v Coulsdon and Purley Urban District Council* [1954] 1 Q.B. 319. See also *Greene v Chelsea Borough Council* [1954] 2 Q.B. 127. In *Harris v Birkenhead Corp* [1975] 1 W.L.R. 379; affirmed [1976] 1 W.L.R. 279, CA, the defendants were held to have been the occupiers of the house, compulsorily purchased by them, from the moment that the previous tenant occupant had moved out of the premises.

[62] *Gesner v Wallingford and District Labour Party Supporters Association Club Ltd, The Times*, June 2, 1994, CA.

[63] *George v Coastal Marine 2004 Ltd* [2009] EWHC 816 (Admlty) (the claim failed on a finding that the owner of a vessel, damaged when it berthed over a sloping beach, had been warned that it would "ground hollow" when the tide went out).

[64] *Creed v J. McGeoch & Sons Ltd* [1955] 1 W.L.R. 1005.

[65] *Page v Read* (1984) 134 New L.J. 723.

[66] *Buckland v Guildford Gas Light & Coke Co* [1949] K.B. 410.

[67] *Ellis v Scruttons Maltby & Cunard Steamship Co Ltd* [1975] 1 Lloyd's Rep. 564 (the charter-party had provided, inter alia, that the charterers were to be responsible for all provisions and wages but the ship owners were to supervise the actual loading of the cargo of cheese).

[68] *Whiting v Hillingdon London Borough Council* (1970) 68 L.G.R. 437 (claimant tripped over a hidden tree stump, which protruded over the footpath, as she stepped to one side into the long grass and foliage in order to pass by some other pedestrians).

[69] *Bailey v Armes* (1999) 96 (7) L.S.G. 37, CA (reliance had been placed upon the fact that the defendants allowed access to the roof from a window of their home).

[70] [1966] A.C. 552.

entrusted to a manager employed under a service agreement. The first floor was used by the manager and his wife exclusively as their private dwelling, but the defendants allowed them, as a privilege, to take in paying guests. The claimant and her husband were paying guests of the manager's wife, staying on the first floor. At about 21.00 one evening the claimant's husband went to buy drinks from the bar downstairs. He was later found at the foot of the back staircase with severe injuries, from which he subsequently died. There was a handrail down one side of the staircase and an electric light at the top, although without a bulb. The manager's licence to occupy the private part of the premises gave him some control over them, but the brewery retained, inter alia, the right to carry out repairs.

Ultimately, the claim failed, because there was insufficient evidence that the **8–21** back staircase, although unlit, was dangerous to someone using it with proper care, but in arriving at that result it was held that both the manager and the brewery company were occupiers and each owed the common duty of care to their visitor, although the nature and extent of their respective duties were different. The brewers ought to have seen that the structure was reasonably safe, including the bannister rail, and the system of lighting was efficient, but not that the lights were switched on or the rugs laid safely on the floor, which day to day matters they were entitled to leave to the manager and his wife.[71]

Where more than one occupier is liable to the claimant for an accident the liability is joint and several and each occupier is liable for all the damage with a right to claim contribution from any other.[72]

Illustrations of multiple occupiers. In *A.M.F. International Ltd v Magnet* **8–22** *Bowling Ltd*,[73] the owners of a bowling centre and the builders were each occupiers of the premises. In *Fisher v C.H.T. Ltd*,[74] the proprietors of a club as well as the managers of a restaurant on the club premises were the occupiers of the restaurant for the purpose of the Act. Elsewhere a water authority and a local authority have been regarded as joint occupiers of a seaside promenade.[75] In *Stone v Taffe*,[76] it was conceded that the licensee manager of a public house was not an occupier but the brewery company which employed him, were, and thereby vicariously liable for his default. Under the comparable provisions of the Occupiers' Liability (Scotland) Act 1960 s.2(1), it has been held that where a child was injured as a result, inter alia, of the height of a service counter at a stall situated in an open air market, both the stall holder and the market's operators, from whom the former rented his pitch, were occupiers and in breach of their respective duties.[77] Where the claimant suffered injury in making her way across

---

[71] *Wheat v E. Lacon & Co Ltd* [1966] A.C. 552. See also *Bailey v Armes* (1999) 96(7) L.S.G. 37, CA, above.
[72] See Ch.3, above, paras 3–81 to 3–97.
[73] [1968] 1 W.L.R. 1028.
[74] [1966] 2 Q.B. 475.
[75] *Collier v Anglian Water Authority, The Times*, March 26, 1983, CA. See Samuels, "The Service Agreement and Occupiers' Liability", 110 S.J. 515.
[76] [1974] 1 W.L.R. 1575. See generally, Ch.3, paras 3–98 onwards, above.
[77] *Mallon v Spook Erections*, 1993 S.C.L.R. 845.

a track on land, the owners of the land were in occupation of the track, a notwithstanding that the claimant and her husband also exercised a degree of occupational control over it.[78]

3.—The Visitor

8–23   **Definition of visitor.** Those regarded as visitors under the Occupiers' Liability Act are the same as those who would have been treated as invitees or licensees at common law.[79] In this respect, the common law rules concerning the persons to whom the occupier owed a duty were not affected.

8–24   **Invitation or licence, express or implied.** An invitation or licence to a visitor to enter or use the occupier's premises can be either express or implied. Where to his knowledge, members of the public habitually visit the occupier's premises, but he takes no steps to prevent them, a licence can be readily inferred, depending upon the circumstances.[80]

8–25   **Illustrations of no implied licence.** Where the occupier frequently warned people to leave his premises, whenever he had seen them there[81]; where the occupier had erected a fence which, although broken from time to time, he continually replaced and kept in repair.[82]

8–26   **Illustrations of implied licence.** Where a road had been laid on a housing estate under construction, but the road had not yet been dedicated to the public[83]; where a field was habitually used by members of the public as a short cut, which fact was well known to the occupier.[84]

8–27   When a person has been given permission to enter the premises by the employee of the occupier, no particular problem arises, provided that the employee was acting within the scope of his actual authority. When a person was initially a lawful visitor on entry he will not become automatically a trespasser

---

[78] *Vodden v Gayton and Gayton* [2001] P.I.Q.R. P52.

[79] s.1(2). See *Maloney v Torfaen CBC* [2006] P.I.Q.R. P313, CA. n.82, below.

[80] See *Willey v Cambridge Leaseholds Ltd* (1976) 57 D.L.R. (3d) 550 where the Post Office was permitted to place a public letter box on a person's private land, adjoining a highway.

[81] *Hardy v Central London Ry* [1920] 3 K.B. 459; *Robert Addie & Sons (Collieries) Ltd v Dumbreck* [1929] A.C. 358 (although the rule in this case became obsolete following *Herrington v British Railways Board* [1972] A.C. 877, below).

[82] *Edwards v Railway Executive* [1952] A.C. 737; also *Maloney* n.79 above (no consent to use a sloping grass bank as access where it was clearly intended as landscape only. It did not answer the relevant questions that the defendant had done nothing to discourage use of the bank as access and very likely would not have objected to anyone so using it).

[83] *Coleshill v Manchester Corp* [1928] 1 K.B. 776.

[84] *Lowery v Walker* [1911] A.C. 10.

by remaining on the premises, if the employee were acting within his apparent authority, albeit in disobedience of his employer's orders.[85]

Licence confined to limited area. It can be important to define the geo-   **8–28**
graphical extent of a licence. Generally the area of invitation extends only to those places to which the visitor may reasonably be expected to go and where the visitor reasonably believes that he can go, within the purpose and scope of his visit.[86] In the words of Scrutton L.J., when " . . . you invite a person into your house to use the staircase, you do not invite him to slide down the bannisters. You invite him to use the staircase in the ordinary way in which it is used".[87] Controversy may then arise whether an invitation or permission to enter one part of the occupier's premises can be interpreted as an invitation or licence to enter other parts.

ILLUSTRATIONS

A guest who wandered about a hotel during the hours of darkness, and ended   **8–29**
up in a service room, had entered that part of the premises to which he had not been invited[88]; a customer was not invited into a shop, after the shutters had been placed in position but the door had not yet been locked[89]; the proprietor of an amusement park who had invited the public to enter, did not invite these members to enter that part of the land which had been let to a concessionaire for his use as a side-show.[90] Nevertheless, an involuntary encroachment outside the permitted or invited place, which is caused by the occupier's neglect, cannot convert a lawful visitor into a trespasser, merely because of his presence in that forbidden area.[91] Thus, when a customer in a public house is invited to use the lavatory, he remains a lawful visitor, despite his having strayed whilst making a reasonable search for it.[92] Where a person enters premises in order to call upon the occupier, whether for the purpose of canvassing business or begging or because he intends making a social call, any of which visits he reasonably believes to be acceptable, he will remain a lawful visitor only so long as he confines himself to that part of the premises which provides the normal access to the premises.[93] If such person has been forbidden to enter under any circum-stances at all either by express prohibitions or by the exhibition of a clear and

---

[85] e.g. see *Stone v Taffe* [1974] 1 W.L.R. 1575 (public house manager, although forbidden by the owners and occupiers to allow customers or friends to remain on the premises after licensing hours, permitted a social function to be held in an upstairs room beyond closing time). But cf. *Conway v George Wimpey & Co Ltd* [1951] 2 K.B. 266 (where the plaintiff in fact was a trespasser from the outset, when he accepted the offer of a lift by the defendant's driver, contrary to specific order not to give lifts, and climbed on to the defendant's lorry).
[86] *Mersey Docks & Harbour Board v Procter* [1923] A.C. 253 at 259, 260, per Lord Cave.
[87] *The Carlgarth; The Otarama* [1927] P. 93 at 110.
[88] *Lee v Luper* [1936] 3 All E.R. 817.
[89] *Mason v Langford* (1888) 4 T.L.R. 407; see also *Prole v Allen* [1950] 1 All E.R. 476.
[90] *Humphreys v Dreamland (Margate) Ltd* (1931) 100 L.J.K.B. 137.
[91] *Braithwaite v South Durham Steel Co* [1958] 1 W.L.R. 986.
[92] *Gould v McAuliffe* [1941] 2 All E.R. 527. See also *Pearson v Coleman Bros* [1948] 2 K.B. 359 (a similar situation at a circus).
[93] *Mersey Docks and Harbour Board v Procter* [1923] A.C. 253; *Hillen v I.C.I. (Alkali) Ltd* [1936] A.C. 65. cf. *Braithwaite v South Durham Steel Co* [1958] 1 W.L.R. 986.

general notice, then he is not even a visitor in using the access to the premises.[94]

8–30   **Licence limited in time.** An invitation or licence to a visitor to enter or use the occupier's premises may be subject to express or implied limitation of time. Accordingly, where permission, subsequently revoked, is given to enter premises, the visitor must be given a reasonable time to comply and leave by the most appropriate route. If he does so, he will not become a trespasser.[95] Similarly, if a customer stays behind deliberately in a shop after it has closed, or remains in the bar of a public house after licensing hours, knowing that the occupier objects, he will become a trespasser when his invitation or permission to be present expires. A distinction was drawn on the facts in *Stone v Taffe*,[96] where the manager of a public house, in breach of his instructions, permitted guests to remain on the premises after closing time and one of them was fatally injured, following a fall down some steep unlit stairs at about 01.00, as he was in the process of leaving. The deceased was not a trespasser, since the occupiers, through their manager, had not given any indication to him either that there was a clear limitation to the licence when first he had entered the premises, or that his licence to remain on the premises had been terminated at any precise time subsequently.

8–31   **Implied licence of children.** Whilst the same considerations apply in the case of a child[97] as in the case of an adult, the Law Reform Committee recognised that some circumstances, particular to children, may affect what on the face of it appears to be trespass:

> "The mere fact that the occupier has upon his premises a dangerous object alluring to children does not make him liable to a trespassing child who meddles with and is injured by it; but the presence of such an object in a place accessible to children may aid the inference of an implied licence."[98]

8–32   **Persons entering as of right.** At common law a question was often raised whether there was a class of persons that came within the description of persons entering "as of right" since they came on property, not because they were invited or permitted to do so but because the occupier had no power to prevent them from entering.[99] Section 2(6) of the Act resolved any such problem by providing that: "For the purposes of this section, persons who enter premises for any purpose in the exercise of a right conferred by law are to be treated as permitted by the occupier to be there for that purpose, whether they in fact have his permission or not." Accordingly, such persons are entitled to the benefit of the common duty of care, which the occupier owes to all his lawful visitors. Persons

---

[94] *Dunster v Abbott* [1954] 1 W.L.R. 58.
[95] *Robson v Hallett* [1967] 2 Q.B. 939. See per Diplock L.J. at 954.
[96] [1974] 1 W.L.R. 1575. It is to be noted that the occupiers' instruction to their manager not to permit visitors to remain on the premises after closing time was not a prohibition which limited the sphere of his employment but merely dealt with his conduct within the scope of his employment. See Ch.3, para.3–130, above.
[97] See para.8–48, below for a fuller discussion.
[98] In its Third Report, Cmd. 9305 (1954), para.30.
[99] More fully discussed in *Charlesworth on Negligence* (3rd edn, 1956) Ch.9, pp.220, 221.

entering as of right include employees of public utilities (for example, gas and electricity boards), police with search warrants, and numerous classes of enforcement officers and inspectors, all of whom have statutory rights to enter premises.[100] In addition, there are members of the public, who use premises provided for them, such as promenades,[101] public parks, playgrounds, libraries, shelters and conveniences.

The Act made no changes in the common law rules of liability relating to those **8–33** persons who exercise public rights of way. Therefore, since a highway is merely a public right of way over land, which remains throughout in the occupation of the owner of the land, the grantor of a public right of way owes no duty of care with regard to the condition of it.[102] It is only for acts of positive misfeasance, which result in obstruction or danger on the highway, that an occupier will be liable.[103] However an occupier will be liable if he allows property which adjoins a highway to become so dangerous that it becomes a nuisance.[104]

As a result of *Greenhalgh v British Railways Board*,[105] it seems equally clear **8–34** that a person exercising a private right of way is in no different position to a person exercising a public right of way in that he is not now a visitor on the premises within the meaning of the Act. Lord Denning M.R. said of the appellant, who had walked over the pot-holed surface of an accommodation bridge over a railway, tripped up and fallen, injuring herself:

> "It was said that she was a 'visitor.' But I do not think she was. Section 1(2) shows that, in order to determine whether a person is a 'visitor,' we must go back to the common law. A person is a 'visitor' if at common law he would be regarded as an invitee or licensee; or be treated as such, as for instance, a person lawfully using premises provided for the use of the public, e.g. a public park, or a person entering by lawful authority, e.g. a policeman with a search warrant. But a 'visitor' does not include a person who crosses land in pursuance of a public or private right of way. Such person was never regarded as an invitee or licensee, or treated as such."[106]

Then, after considering the words of s.2(6) of the Act, he continued:

> "The important words to notice are the opening words: 'For the purpose of this section,' i.e. for the purpose of section 2, which defines only the *extent* of the occupier's duty to

---

[100] Cmd. 9305, para.38. *Hartley v Mayoh & Co* [1954] 1 Q.B. 383 (firemen).

[101] *Collier v Anglian Water Authority, The Times*, March 26, 1983, CA.

[102] This, the so-called rule in *Gautret v Egerton* (1867) L.R. 2 C.P. 371, was re-affirmed in *McGeown v Northern Ireland Housing Executive* [1995] 1 A.C. 233. However, Lord Browne-Wilkinson reserved the question whether an owner of land may owe a duty of care to his invitees, as opposed to those exercising their right of way: ibid. at 247.

[103] Where an official path of the Forestry Commission led to a steep and dangerous unofficial path leading down to rocks above a river, no duty of care was owed to members of the public to take steps by fencing or otherwise to prevent them from straying on to the unofficial path: *McClusky v Lord Advocate, The Times*, August 18, 1993 (a decision under the comparable provisions of the Occupiers' Liability (Scotland) Act 1960 s.2(1)).

[104] See Ch.10, paras 10–52 to 10–58, below.

[105] [1969] 2 Q.B. 286; *Holden v White* [1982] Q.B. 679 (the owner of land over which there was a private right of way was not liable to a milkman for injuries sustained when he was using it to deliver milk to the person for whose benefit the right existed).

[106] *Greenhalgh v British Railways Board* [1969] 2 Q.B. 286 at 292, 293.

acknowledge visitors. It does not expand the range of persons who are to be treated as visitors."

8–35 Section 1(4) of the Act provides that: "A person entering any premises in exercise of rights conferred by virtue of an access agreement or order under the National Parks and Access to the Countryside Act 1949, is not, for the purposes of this Act, a visitor of the occupier of those premises." It is to be observed that where an access agreement or order is in force in respect of any land, a person who enters upon such land for the purpose of an open-air recreation, without breaking or damaging any wall, fence, hedge or gate or who is on such land for that purpose after having so entered thereon, shall neither be treated as a trespasser on that land nor incur any other liability by reason only of so entering or being on the land.[107]

4.—THE DUTY OWED

(A) The common duty of care

8–36 **Generally.** The duty owed in respect of dangerous premises is a single duty identified as the "common duty of care." Section 2 of the Act provides:

"(1) An occupier of premises owes the same duty, the 'common duty of care', to all his visitors, except in so far as he is free to and does extend, restrict, modify or exclude his duty to any visitor or visitors by agreement or otherwise.

(2) The common duty of care is a duty to take such care as in all the circumstances of the case is reasonable to see that the visitor will be reasonably safe in using[108] the premises for the purposes for which he is invited or permitted by the occupier to be there."

8–37 The Law Reform Committee had recommended "that the law can and should be simplified by the abolition of the existing categories of invitees and licensees, and the substitution of one uniform duty of care owed by the occupier of premises to all persons coming upon them at his invitation or by his permission, express or implied".[109] This was done, with the result that a number of irksome distinctions between unusual dangers and concealed traps, etc., disappeared and, as Lord Pearce said, "once the duty of care is imposed, the question whether a

---

[107] The National Parks and Access to the Countryside Act 1949 s.60(1); but s.66(2) provides that the operation of s.60(1) in relation to any land shall not increase the liability, under any enactment not contained in the Act or under any rule of law, of a person interested in that land or adjoining land in respect of the state thereof or of things done or omitted thereon.

[108] In *Ferguson v Welsh* [1987] 1 W.L.R. 1553, where the appellant, an independent contractor's workman, was injured during the course of a building's demolition and sued the occupiers, Lord Goff expressed the opinion that the Occupiers' Liability Act 1957 did not apply. The injury did not arise from any failure by the occupiers to take reasonable care that the premises would be reasonably safe for the appellant's use, but from the manner in which he had carried out his work on the premises (at 1563, 1564). The same distinction, based upon the common law before 1957, was adopted by the Court of Appeal in *Fairchild v Glenhaven Funeral Services Ltd* [2002] 1 W.L.R. 1052, para.8–11 above (claimants exposed to the peril of asbestos dust while working at the defendant's premises).

[109] Cmd. 9305 (1954), para.78.

defendant failed in that duty becomes a question of fact in all the circumstances.[110] Section 2(3) goes on to provide: "The circumstances relevant for the
present purposes include the degree of care, and of want of care, which would
ordinarily be looked for in such a visitor . . . "[111]

Illustrations of no liability. An occupier has been held not liable where a   **8–38**
stevedore allegedly injured himself by slipping on an oily patch on the deck of
a ship[112]; where a young schoolboy stumbled and fell, injuring himself on the
school's playground wall, built of brick and flint a century or more previously[113];
where a footballer probably came into contact with a wall near the touch-line and
sustained a broken leg[114]; where a safety net's guy-rope unforeseeably caused a
thrown discus which struck it to ricochet, so that it hit and injured another
athlete[115]; where a customer in a shop was struck and injured when part of the
ceiling, recently plastered by a firm of independent contractors, collapsed[116];
where an elderly lady slipped on the stairs of a block of flats when the lighting
over this access was turned off prematurely by the faulty adjustment of a time
switch, controlling the electricity supply[117]; where a customer in a shop fell over
some cartons stacked up in a gangway.[118]

Also: where an ambulance man carrying a patient tripped on a pile of books   **8–39**
lying on the floor in a poorly-lit house[119]; where a paying guest was found dying
at the foot of a staircase and there was no landing light at the top of the stairs,
because the electric bulb was missing, and the handrail allegedly was inadequate[120]; when a guest slipped on snow lying on the hotel's forecourt, where
nothing could have been done to render it less dangerous in the continuous
prevailing wintery weather conditions[121]; where a visitor to a club sat on a chair
which had been repaired negligently by another member, who was a skilled
craftsman, but it collapsed under the visitor's weight[122]; where a visitor to a
public house tripped over a dog in the bar, which had not been kept on a lead but

---

[110] *Wheat v E. Lacon & Co Ltd* [1966] A.C. 552, at 587.
[111] See para.8–75, below. In relation to the comparable provisions of the Occupiers' Liability
(Scotland) Act 1960, it has been held that since the occupier's duty is to take reasonable care it is
insufficient to say that an accident occurred as a result of the state of premises, without also alleging
some fault: *McDyer v Celtic Football and Athletic Co Ltd* 1997 Rep. L.R. 117, OH (a visitor to Celtic
Park attending the opening ceremony of the European Special Olympics who suffered injury when
a piece of timber fell onto his hand).
[112] *Lowther v H. Hogarth & Sons Ltd* [1959] 1 Lloyd's Rep. 171.
[113] *Ward v Hertfordshire County Council* [1970] 1 W.L.R. 356 (reversing on this point [1969] 1
W.L.R. 790). Contrast *Perry v Butlins Holiday World (t/a Butlins Ltd)* [1998] Ed. C.R. 39, CA,
para.8–41, below.
[114] *Simms v Leigh Rugby Football Club* [1969] 2 All E.R. 923. See further para.8–73, below.
[115] *Wilkins v Smith* (1976) 73 L.S.Gaz. 938.
[116] *O'Connor v Swan & Edgar* (1963) 107 S.J. 215; but see *Sharpe v E. T. Sweeting & Son Ltd* [1963]
1 W.L.R. 665 at 675.
[117] *Irving v London County Council* (1965) 109 S.J. 157.
[118] *Doherty v London Co-operative Society* (1966) 110 S.J. 74.
[119] *Neame v Johnson* [1993] P.I.Q.R. P100, CA.
[120] *Wheat v E. Lacon & Co Ltd* [1966] A.C. 552.
[121] *Wood v Morland & Co* (1971) 115 S.J. 569. See "Winter Hazards and Occupier's Liability", 122
New L.J. 99.
[122] *Carrol v Hibbert* (1967) 117 New L.J. 353.

was not making a nuisance of itself[123]; where a visitor to a public house slipped and fell, cutting himself on some glass which had been dropped by some other customer[124]; where a local authority failed to provide notices on a high path warning of dangerous cliffs[125]; where a firework exploded in its launching tube in the course of a display[126]; where no handrail was provided to steps, but no finding was made that the steps were unsafe[127]; where it would have placed an excessive burden upon the occupiers of a track over fields to require repair of potholes such as that which caused the claimant to fall from her moped[128]; where descending stairs the claimant slipped and his hand went through a glass door panel[129]; where a guest at an hotel fell through a fully opened sash window in a bedroom.[130] The occupiers of a village green were not liable for an accident suffered by the claimant, who fell into a hole left by a maypole used in a fete organised by the Royal British Legion[131]; the occupier of premises which provided a toboggan run was not liable where the claimant fell from her toboggan on a bend and was struck by another toboggan which had followed her down the slope.[132] Nor did liability attach where water accumulated on the floor in the vicinity of a defective jacuzzi in the period of five minutes before the claimant arrived on the scene and slipped.[133]

8-40   **Illustrations of liability.** On the other hand, an occupier has been held liable where a plasterer was redecorating a restaurant and came into contact with a live electric light wire, which had been carelessly switched on by the occupier's maintenance electrician[134]; where a cleaner slipped on a highly polished floor, which was dangerous in the circumstances[135]; where melted snow was not mopped up and no mats were laid temporarily in the entrance hall of a public library[136]; where, in the absence of a handrail, a visitor slipped and fell at a school on a steep pathway, despite the fact that its surface had been cleared of a heavy fall of snow and gritted before the accident[137]; where a passenger on the

---

[123] *Carroll v Garford* (1968) 112 S.J. 948.
[124] *Sawyer v H. & G. Simonds Ltd* (1966) 197 E.G. 877.
[125] *Cotton v Derbyshire Dales DC, The Times,* June 20, 1994. In Scotland it has been held, for purposes of the Occupiers' Liability (Scotland) Act 1960, that any duty on an occupier to fence off a danger does not apply to permanent, ordinary and familiar features of the landscape, whether natural, or man-made such as a reservoir: *Graham v East of Scotland Water Authority* 2002 S.C.L.R. 340, OH.
[126] *McQueen v The Glasgow Garden Festival (1988),* 1995, S.L.T. 211, Ct.Sess. OH.
[127] *Manning v Hope (t/a Priory), The Times,* February 18, 2000, CA.
[128] *Vodden v Gayton* [2001] P.I.Q.R. P4.
[129] *McGivney v Golderslea Ltd* (2001) 17 Const. L.J. 454, CA (the glass did not comply with current safety regulations, but did comply with regulations in force when it was installed and it was reasonable in the circumstances that it had not been replaced).
[130] *Lewis v Six Continents Plc, The Times,* January 20, 2006, CA.
[131] *Cole v Davis-Gilbert, The Times,* 5 April, 2007, CA, Ch.7, para.7–35, above.
[132] *Tysall Ltd v Snowdome* [2007] 7 C.L. 434.
[133] *Tedstone v Bourne Leisure Ltd* [2008] EWCA Civ 654,CA (the defendant could not reasonably have been expected to deal with the hazard in the very short time it had been present).
[134] *Fisher v C.H.T.* [1966] 2 Q.B. 475.
[135] *Adams v S. J. Watson & Co* (1967) 117 New L.J. 130.
[136] *Hopkins v Scunthorpe Corp* [1966] C.L.Y. 8112 (Judge Daly Lewis). But contrast *Thomas v Bristol Aeroplane Co Ltd* [1954] 1 W.L.R. 694; *Campbell v Royal Bank of Canada* (1963) 43 D.L.R. (2d) 341.
[137] *Murphy v City of Bradford Metropolitan Council* [1992] P.I.Q.R. P68, CA.

Thank you for purchasing **Charlesworth & Percy on Negligence**

☑ **Don't miss important updates**

So that you have all the latest information, **Charlesworth & Percy on Negligence** is supplemented regularly. Sign up today for a Standing Order to ensure you receive the updating supplements as soon as they publish. Setting up a Standing Order with Sweet & Maxwell is hassle-free, simply tick, complete and return this FREEPOST card and we'll do the rest.

You may cancel your Standing Order at any time by writing to us at Sweet & Maxwell, PO Box 2000, Andover, SP10 9AH stating the Standing Order you wish to cancel.

Alternatively, if you have purchased your copy of **Charlesworth & Percy on Negligence** from a bookshop or other trade supplier, please ask your supplier to ensure that you are registered to receive the new supplements.

All goods are subject to our 30 day Satisfaction Guarantee (applicable to EU customers only)

Yes, please send me new supplements and /or new editions of Charlesworth & Percy on Negligence to be invoiced on publication, until I cancel the standing order in writing.

☐ **All new supplements to the 12th edition**

☐ **All new supplements and editions**

Title	**Name**
Organisation	
Job title	
Address	
Postcode	
Telephone	
Email	
S&M account number (if known)	
PO number	

All orders are accepted subject to the terms of this order form and our Terms of Trading. (see www.sweetandmaxwell.co.uk). By submitting this order form I confirm that I accept these terms and I am authorised to sign on behalf of the customer.

Signed	**Job Title**
Print Name	**Date**

(LBU007) V7 (05.2010) JW / DA

SWEET & MAXWELL

THOMSON REUTERS

railway was walking along the platform and, finding himself hemmed in by goods trolleys, tried to step over a fallen bag, but tripped and fell[138]; where a shopper, mistaking a full length plate glass window situated next to the exit door in the defendant's supermarket for the open door, crashed into it[139]; where a visitor was electrocuted, because the occupiers had failed to warn him of the existence of a high voltage cable, some 22 feet above the exhibition site at an agricultural show, and he touched it accidentally with a metal flag pole that he was in the process of erecting.[140]

Liability was also established where there was a failure to light a steep narrow   **8–41** staircase in a public house, down which a visitor fell in the early hours of a morning, long after permitted hours[141]; where a holidaymaker struck his head on the bottom of the swimming pool, when diving off the diving board, which had been placed negligently over shallow water[142]; where a passenger on a liner slipped and fell on newly-laid, untreated linoleum over a sloping floor; where a deck passenger fell off an unstable chair during a heavy sea's running[143]; where a teenage girl's hand was injured after she had put it through the outer gate of a lift, in an attempt to close the inner gate and, unexpectedly, the lift moved[144]; where a fireman, called to premises to fight a fire, was exposed to unnecessary risks[145]; where a football spectator was knocked down and trampled underfoot by the sudden surge forward of a crowd of other spectators after some hooligans had forced their way into the ground[146]; where a local authority failed to assess and thereafter warn of the risk of injury to those diving into the sea from a promenade, where it was known that on occasion such activity took place[147]; where a three-year-old child at a holiday camp fell against a wall capped with a sharp engineering brick[148]; where an occupier engaged a contractor to provide a "splat wall" amusement at a fair in its grounds, but failed to check the content of the contractor's insurance policy[149]; where a club organised a fireworks display on its land and failed to ensure that the contractor providing the display

---

[138] *Blackett v B.R.B.*, *The Times*, December 19, 1967.

[139] *Vollans v Simco Supermarkets* [1982] 2 C.L. 129 and see Vollans, "Glass Fragmentation and the Duty of Care" 127 S.J. 385.

[140] *McDowell v F.M.C. (Meat)* (1968) 5 K.I.R. 456.

[141] *Stone v Taffe* [1974] 1 W.L.R. 1575.

[142] *Davies v Tenby Corp* [1974] 2 Lloyd's Rep. 469. Similarly, *Gerak v R.; In Right of British Columbia* (1984) 59 B.C.L.R. 273. See also *O'Shea v Royal Borough o'Kingston-upon-Thames* [1995] P.I.Q.R. P208, CA (given the depth of a swimming pool, diving should have been prohibited rather than merely discouraged by warning: 50 per cent contributory negligence on the claimant who dived nonetheless).

[143] *Appleton v Cunard Steamship Co* [1969] 1 Lloyd's Rep. 150.

[144] *Sandford v Eugene* (1970) 115 S.J. 33.

[145] *Hartley v British Railways Board* (1981) 125 S.J. 169; *Salmon v Seafarers Restaurants*, 132 New L.J. 882.

[146] *Hosie v Arbroath Football Club*, 1978 S.L.T. 122.

[147] *Harrison v Thanet District Council* [1998] C.L.Y. 3918 (the claimant was two-thirds to blame for diving into water of unknown depth).

[148] *Perry v Butlins Holiday World (t/a Butlins Ltd)* [1998] Ed. C.R. 39, CA (account was taken of measures which could have made the wall safer, its location and that children were likely to come into contact with it).

[149] *Gwilliam v West Hertfordshire Hospital NHS Trust* [2003] Q.B. 443, CA (the majority in the Court of Appeal decided, by different routes, that there was a duty to enquire of the contractor as to his insurance, but not a duty to investigate the terms of the policy).

had adequate public liability insurance cover and a safety plan.[150] The claimant succeeded in his claim where a portable tubular goal frame, provided by the occupier on a grassed area tipped and fell on him as he kept goal, the pegs to secure it to the ground being absent.[151]

(B) Extension, restriction, modification or exclusion of liability

8–42 **Generally.** The words of s.2(1),[152] "in so far as he is free to", would seem to be designed to ensure that an occupier's power to extend, restrict, modify or exclude his duty should not be any greater than the position was at common law. In *Burnett v British Waterways Board*,[153] it was considered that occupiers were not free to exclude themselves from liability in negligence, where their notice of conditions, exhibited on a board, was repugnant to s.10(1) of the Transport Act 1962 and, hence, of no effect in dealing with the claim made by the visitor against them. The words "by agreement or otherwise",[154] enable the occupier to exclude liability to his visitors not only by express or implied agreement but also by, for example, the provisions of any byelaws, rules or regulations which he may have power to make, whether or not the visitor has agreed to them or, of course, by the exhibition of a clear notice disclaiming liability for injury.

8–43 In *Ashdown v Samuel Williams & Sons Ltd*,[155] it was held that an occupier was not liable to a licensee because: (i) the conditions, which excluded liability, on which she was permitted to be on the land had been sufficiently brought to her attention by the posting of a notice, and, having read enough of the notice to know that she was on the land at her own risk, she was bound by the terms of the notice, although she had not read all of it; and (ii) the words of the notice were sufficient to exclude liability not only for dangers of the property in its static condition but also for activities carried on there negligently.

8–44 *Ashdown*, although decided before the passing of the Act, ought strictly to be unaffected by it, since the terms of the licence, held to be binding on the licensee, excluded the occupier's liability to take reasonable care. It was followed in *White*

---

[150] *Bottomley v Todmorden Cricket Club* [2004] P.I.Q.R. P275, CA (it made no difference that the contractor did not charge a fee). See further para.8–81, below. A duty to check an independent contractor's insurance cover did not arise in *Payling v Naylor (Trading as Mainstreet)* [2004] P.I.Q.R. P615, CA where the contractor provided door staff at a club who were licensed under a scheme operated by the local authority and the police.

[151] *Hall v Holker Estate Co Ltd* [2008] EWCA Civ 1422. The claimant succeeded notwithstanding that the defendant led evidence of a system of daily inspection of the structure (*Ward v Tesco Stores Ltd* [1976] 1 All E.R. 219, CA, Ch.6 para.6–02 above, considered).

[152] See para.8–35, above.

[153] [1973] 1 W.L.R. 700 at 706. Since there was no real freedom of choice given to the claimant, whether to enter the premises or not it was held that the defence of volenti non fit injuria did not apply. See further, para.8–71, below.

[154] In *White v Blackmore* [1972] 2 Q.B. 651.

[155] [1957] 1 Q.B. 409, applying *Parker v South Eastern Rail Co* (1877) 2 C.P.D. 416. See Bradbury, "Knowledge and Exemption in Occupiers' Liability", 119 New L.J. 520; Hodgin, "Exclusion and Warnings under the Occupiers' Liability Act", 25 N.I.L.Q. 105. For criticism of the decision see Gower (1956) 19 M.L.R. 532; 20 M.L.R. 181; Goodhart (1956) 72 L.Q.R. 470.

v Blackmore[156] where the deceased, a member of a "jalopy" club, went along to a meeting organised by the club but, whilst he was watching another race, was killed when the wheel of a car was caught up in a safety rope barrier and catapulted him a distance of about 20 feet. It was held that the organisers of this dangerous sport's meeting might, and did, effectively exclude their liability to spectators for accidents arising from their negligence at common law, as well as their breach of the common duty of care arising under the Act, by displaying notices warning the public of the dangers and stating that it was a condition of admission that they were absolved from all liabilities for accidents "howsoever caused".

Cases like *Ashdown* and *White* would now be argued quite differently, if they arose at all, in light of the Unfair Contract Terms Act 1977, the principal purpose of which was to control the exclusion or restriction of liability both in contract and for negligence arising in the course of business.[157] By s.2 of the Act the right of anyone to exclude or restrict his "business liability" for negligence was curtailed.[158] Section 1(3) defines business liability as being: **8–45**

" . . . liability for breach of obligations or duties arising—

    (a) from things done or to be done by a person in the course of a business (whether his own business or another's); or

    (b) from the occupation of premises used for business purposes of the occupier;

and references to liability are to be read accordingly [but liability of an occupier of premises for breach of an obligation or duty towards a person obtaining access to the premises for recreational or educational purposes, being liability for loss or damage suffered by reason of the dangerous state of the premises, is not a business liability of the occupier unless granting that person such access for the purposes concerned falls within the business purposes of the occupier]."[159]

Other than in an instance falling within the latter exception,[160] the test is not to inquire what purpose the visitor had in visiting the premises, but to discover the purpose of the occupier in his occupation of them. Whether or not any given **8–46**

---

[156] [1972] 2 Q.B. 651. Roskill L.J. considered that the persons bound by the notice were the members of the public watching the races and not, for example, ambulance drivers or the policeman on duty there (at 677). See Goodhart (1972) 88 L.Q.R. 453 and Clover, "Occupiers' Liability: Effects of Warning Notice", 123 New L.J. 938.

[157] For a fuller discussion of the provisions of the Act, see Ch.4, paras 4–84 to 4–88, above. See Mesher, "Occupiers, Trespassers and the Unfair Contract Terms Act 1977" [1979] Conv. 59.

[158] Which provides by s.2(1): "A person cannot by reference to any contract term or to a notice given to persons generally or to particular persons exclude or restrict his liability for death or personal injury resulting from negligence," and by s.2(2): "In the case of other loss or damage, a person cannot so exclude or restrict his liability for negligence except in so far as the term or notice satisfies the requirements of reasonableness." In turn, the concept of "reasonableness" is dealt with in s.11 but it is doubtful whether this will arise much for consideration in practice, because in the vast majority of cases involving occupiers' liability, the issue of damages will relate either to personal injury or death of the visitor.

[159] The bracketed words, which were added to s.1(3) by the Occupiers' Liability Act 1984 s.2, enable the occupier to allow access to his land for recreational or educational purposes on terms that do restrict his civil liability, wherever such access is granted simply as a matter of neighbourliness or goodwill but not where it is granted in the way of business.

[160] Which were added by way of amendment, above.

situation amounts to "a business" is a question of fact for the court to decide on the evidence but it seems likely that if *Ashdown* stood to be decided again today, the decision would have to be different. The first defendants, who owned the large dock estate near to the River Thames at Tilbury, including a coal-yard with all its railway sidings, were occupiers of premises "used for business purposes of the occupier".

8–47   Where the occupation is not for the occupiers' business[161] purposes, the provisions of the Unfair Contract Terms Act 1977 do not apply.

(C) Liability to children

8–48   **Introduction.** Section 2(3) of the 1957 Act also provides that: "an occupier must be prepared for children to be less careful than adults".[162] The decided cases at common law remain helpful, since the principles relating to the duty owed to invitees, licensees and trespassers applied to children as well as to adults.

8–49   **Liability differed at common law.** Although the principles of liability to children, who were upon premises either as licensees or invitees, were basically the same as applied in relation to adults, their application to the facts of any given case did produce differences. There were a number of reasons. In particular: (i) things which were not unusual dangers or traps to adults might well be such to children, so that steps were needed to be taken by lighting, guarding or otherwise to prevent them from being a danger to them; (ii) a notice or warning of the perceived danger, which might be adequate in the case of adults, might not be adequate necessarily in the case of children, so that if warning was relied upon as a defence, it had to be one that was capable of being understood by children; and (iii) there was a duty to guard children, who were on land lawfully, from things dangerous to a child, with which the child might be tempted to meddle. If there was no unusual danger or trap upon the premises, there was no liability to an infant licensee or invitee. So, where a child of between two and three years old, a licensee, hurt herself when playing on a heap of paving stones, the occupier was held not liable.[163]

8–50   **Traps for children at common law.** An unusual danger or trap might take the form of some object with which the child was not invited or licensed to meddle. In such a case, if the child was licensed or invited to be on the land, the occupier would be liable for injury sustained by the child in meddling with the object, if it were of such a nature that he ought to have anticipated what the child would

---

[161] The term "business" is defined by s.14 as *including* "a profession and the activities of any government department or local or public authority".
[162] As regards liability to children who are trespassers, see paras 8–144 to 8–160.
[163] *Latham v R. Johnson & Nephew Ltd* [1913] 1 K.B. 398 at 416, per Hamilton L.J. "a heap of paving stones in broad daylight in a private close cannot so combine the properties of temptation and retribution as to be properly called a trap."

do.[164] The object, though forbidden, might be an allurement[165] or temptation to a child.

> "The allurement may arise after he [the child] has entered with leave or as of right. Then the presence in a frequented place of some object of attraction, tempting him to meddle where he ought to abstain, may well constitute a trap, and in the case of a child too young to be capable of contributory negligence it may impose full liability on the owner or occupier, if he ought, as a reasonable man, to have anticipated the presence of the child and the attractiveness and peril of the object."[166]

Child's age with reference to traps. In *Phipps v Rochester Corporation*[167]   **8–51** Devlin J. distinguished between big children and little children, that is "children who know what they are about and children who do not".[168] He added that:

> " . . . a licensor who tacitly permits the public to use his land without discriminating between its members must assume that the public may include little children. But as a general rule he will have discharged his duty towards them if the dangers which they may encounter are only those which are obvious to a guardian or of which he has given a warning comprehensible by a guardian"

subject to the exception that the occupier

> "may have to take into account the social habits of the neighbourhood. No doubt there are places where little children go to play unaccompanied. If the licensor knows or ought to anticipate that, he may have to take steps accordingly."[169]

Where, therefore, the public was in the habit of going over land in the process   **8–52** of being developed as a building estate and a boy of five, whilst out blackberry-picking with his sister of seven, fell into an unguarded trench dug for the purpose of laying a sewer, the estate developers were not liable, there being no evidence to show that they should have anticipated the presence of unaccompanied little children. Devlin J. said[170]:

> " . . . the responsibility for the safety of little children must rest primarily upon the parents[171]; it is their duty to see that such children are not allowed to wander about by themselves, or at least to satisfy themselves that the places to which they do allow their children to go unaccompanied are safe for them to go to. It would not be socially desirable if parents were, as a matter of course, able to shift the burden of looking after their children from their own shoulders to those of persons who happen to have

---

[164] *Gough v N.C.B.* [1954] 1 Q.B. 191; *Holdman v Hamlyn* [1943] K.B. 664 at 668, per du Parcq L.J.

[165] See per Asquith L.J. in *Sutton v Bootle Corp* [1947] K.B. 359 at 369.

[166] per Hamilton L.J. in *Latham v R. Johnson & Nephew Ltd* [1913] 1 K.B. 398 at 416. See also *Jolley v Sutton London Borough Council* [2000] 1 W.L.R. 1082, HL, Ch.5 above, para.5–21 (an abandoned and decayed boat present on land owned by the defendant, in Lord Hoffmann's words, "for whatever use the rich fantasy life of children might suggest").

[167] [1955] 1 Q.B. 450, where the principal cases on this subject are well reviewed.

[168] *Phipps v Rochester Corporation* [1955] 1 Q.B. 450 at 458.

[169] ibid. at 472.

[170] *Phipps v Rochester Corporation* [1955] 1 Q.B. 450 at 472.

[171] See Williams "Parents' Duty or Occupier's Liability?", 127 S.J. 831.

accessible bits of land.[172] Different considerations may well apply to public parks or to recognised playing grounds where parents allow their children to go unaccompanied in the reasonable belief that they are safe."

So, where a very young child received serious burns by coming into contact accidentally with an unprotected hot water pipe of the central heating system in its parents' council-owned flat, the local authority was not liable. The defendants could reasonably rely on parents to devise means of safeguarding their children in their home from any risks posed by such pipes, and were justified in assuming that no particular precautions were necessary.[173]

8–53   **Illustrations of traps.** The following have been held *not* to be allurements or traps to children, so as to impose liability on the occupier: a pond[174]; a bluff on a mountainside[175]; a river[176]; a swing[177]; a chute[178]; an unhorsed van[179]; a tip-up lorry, in the charge of a competent driver[180]; a stack of steel latticework on a road[181]; a heap of soil at the foot of a wall adjoining the highway[182]; a scaffold with a rope coiled round a pulley 35 feet from the ground[183]; a trench on land in the process of being developed[184]; a hole in the ground[185]; a pile of mortar[186]; a heap of paving slabs.[187]

8–54   In contrast, the following *have* been held to be allurements and traps to children: a horse and cart, left unattended in the street[188]; a railway turntable[189]; a moving staircase at a railway station[190]; a shrub (*atropa belladonna*) growing

---

[172] Where there is a danger, such as a mountain with a steep bluff running down to a wall, abutting a highway, which is both familiar and obvious to adults, a local authority is entitled to assume that parents of children in the locality have taken the precaution of warning their children of such a danger. In this regard a local authority is under no higher duty than that of a prudent parent: *Simkiss v Rhondda Borough Council* (1983) 81 L.G.R. 460, CA.

[173] *Ryan v Camden London Borough* (1982) 13 Fam.Law 81, CA, applying words of Lord Shaw in *Glasgow Corp v Taylor* [1922] 1 A.C. 44 at 61. See also *B (A Child) v London Borough of Camden* [2001] P.I.Q.R. P143 (a similar case, the slight risk of contact between the child and hot pipes being insufficient to impose a duty to take protective measures).

[174] *Hastie v Edinburgh Magistrates*, 1907 S.C. 1102. See also *Marsden v Bourne Leisure* [2009] EWCA Civ 671.

[175] *Simkiss v Rhondda Borough Council*, (1983) 81 L.G.R. 460, CA.

[176] *Stevenson v Glasgow Corp*, 1908 S.C. 1034.

[177] *Purkis v Walthamstow Borough Council* (1934) 151 L.T. 30; *Sutton v Bootle Corp* [1947] K.B. 359.

[178] *Dyer v Ilfracombe Urban District Council* [1956] 1 W.L.R. 218.

[179] *Donovan v Union Cartage Co* [1933] 2 K.B. 71.

[180] *Rawsthorne v Ottley* [1937] 3 All E.R. 902.

[181] *Morley v Staffordshire County Council* [1939] 4 All E.R. 92.

[182] *Liddle v Yorkshire (North Riding) County Council* [1934] 2 K.B. 101.

[183] *Cuttress v Scaffolding (Great Britain) Ltd* [1953] 2 All E.R. 1075 at 1081.

[184] *Phipps v Rochester Corp* [1955] 1 Q.B. 450, applied in *Marsden v Bourne Leisure* [2009] EWCA Civ 671, para.8–57, below.

[185] *Perry v Thomas Wrigley Ltd* [1955] 1 W.L.R. 1164.

[186] *Prince v Gregory* [1959] 1 W.L.R. 177.

[187] *Latham v R. Johnson & Nephew Ltd* [1913] 1 K.B. 398.

[188] *Lynch v Nurdin* [1841] 1 Q.B. 29.

[189] *Cooke v M.G.W. Ry of Ireland* [1909] A.C. 229.

[190] *Hardy v Central London Ry* [1920] 3 K.B. 459. In this case the child was a trespasser but would have succeeded had he been a licensee—per Lord Dunedin in *Robert Addie & Sons (Collieries) Ltd v Dumbreck* [1929] A.C. 358 at 376.

a poisonous berry of attractive and appetising appearance[191]; an insecure wall, which might contain birds' nests[192]; a rope haulage system with a rope on which to swing[193] a lorry laden with sugar[194]; the opening on a threshing machine through which sheaves of grain were put to be threshed[195]; a chute in a children's playground[196]; broken glass on waste land, where children were allowed to play[197]; a paddling pool, which was provided by the local authority for the children to play in but which contained a broken piece of glass hidden in the sand[198]; a tree, close to a footpath, which could be easily climbed by children and above which there was stretched a live electricity cable[199]; slow-moving trams on an unguarded track, which people, including children, had been permitted to cross[200]; a bomb-damaged house in course of demolition[201]; an abandoned and rotten boat.[202]

Fences. If children were invited or permitted to come on premises, there was **8–55** no duty to erect a fence or otherwise to prevent them from wandering from the land, on which they were lawfully playing. So, where a railway company permitted children to play on a pile of sleepers adjoining a railway line, they were held to be under no liability to a two-and-a-half-year-old child, who had got onto the railway line and was injured by a train.[203] Again, where children were allowed to play in a sand pit and one of them, who was less than two years old, wandered from the sand pit onto a level crossing and was injured by a train, the local authority, which occupied the sand pit, was held to be under no liability.[204] When a child of four got through a gap in a fence of a public recreation ground, went onto a railway line and was injured by touching a live rail, the defendants, who had provided the recreation ground, were held not liable.[205]

Licence conditional on adult companion. It may be that an invitation or **8–56** licence to enter upon land is only given to young children when accompanied by an older person. In such a case, at common law, there was no liability to a young child not so accompanied. So, where a child of four in going up the steps leading to the defendant's front door, fell off, because the railings was defective, it was held that the occupier was not liable. "There was no invitation to the plaintiff if

---

[191] *Glasgow Corp v Taylor* [1922] 1 A.C. 44 (a shrub more commonly known as "deadly nightshade").
[192] *Boyd v Glasgow Iron and Steel Co*, 1923 S.C. 758.
[193] *Excelsior Wire Rope Co v Callan* [1930] A.C. 404.
[194] *Culkin v McFie & Sons Ltd* [1939] 3 All E.R. 613.
[195] *Holdman v Hamlyn* [1943] K.B. 664.
[196] *Bates v Stone Parish Council* [1954] 1 W.L.R. 1249; *Dyer v Ilfracombe Urban District Council* [1956] 1 W.L.R. 218.
[197] *Williams v Cardiff Corp* [1950] 1 K.B. 514.
[198] *Ellis v Fulham Borough Council* [1938] 1 K.B. 212.
[199] *Buckland v Guildford Gas Light & Coke Co* [1949] 1 K.B. 410.
[200] *Gough v N.C.B.* [1954] 1 Q.B. 191.
[201] *Davis v St Mary's Demolition and Excavation Co* [1954] 1 W.L.R. 592.
[202] *Jolley v Sutton London Borough Council* [2000] 1 W.L.R. 1058, HL, Ch.5, para.5–21, above. See Esam, "The perils of child's play" 2000 Comm. Law, 42, 87.
[203] *Jenkins v G.W. Ry* [1912] 1 K.B. 525; *Wade v Canadian National Ry* (1978) 80 D.L.R. (3d) 214.
[204] *Schofield v Bolton Corp* (1910) 26 T.L.R. 230.
[205] *Bint v Lewisham Borough Council* [1946] W.N. 12.

he was not guarded and, if guarded, then there was no trap".[206] It was held that a three-year-old child who was in the company of a boy of 14 was accompanied by a competent guardian,[207] but a boy of five who was accompanied by his sister of seven was not competently guarded.[208]

8-57   Where a child's hand was injured in a potato riddling machine on a farm, the Court of Appeal considered that a proper inference on the facts was that the occupier had taken on the child's mother to work and impliedly agreed that, when she came to work she would bring her children with her, but they were to remain her sole responsibility. On this basis the occupier was entitled to assume that the child would be kept reasonably safe from danger.[209] Similarly, where a child aged two was drowned in a pond at a leisure park where his parents were on holiday. The occupier was not obliged, in the exercise of reasonable care, to bring to the attention of parents the existence or precise location of the pond, when it was among many obvious dangers on the site to small unaccompanied children.[210]

(D) Duty to those engaged in work

8-58   **Special risks of work.** Section 2(3) continues further by providing that: "(b) an occupier may expect that a person, in the exercise of his calling, will appreciate and guard against any special risks ordinarily incident to it, so far as the occupier leaves him free to do so." This gives effect, therefore, to the recommendation of the Law Reform Committee that:

" . . . any redefinition of the occupier's duty should expressly provide that where a visitor enters premises for the purpose of carrying out any work of construction, maintenance, repair or other similar operation, the occupier should not merely in that capacity be held liable for damage arising to such visitor from any danger encountered in the course of such operation if the danger is not one which would have been encountered in the normal use of the premises. For example, if a window cleaner (not being a servant of the occupier) sustains injury through the insecurity of some part of the exterior of the premises which he uses as a foothold or handhold for the purpose of cleaning the outside of the windows, the occupier merely as such should not be liable.[211] *Aliter*, if the window cleaner is injured through some defect in the staircase

---

[206] per Lindley J. in *Burchell v Hickisson* (1880) 50 L.J.Q.B. 101. The passage from Lindley J.'s judgment was quoted with approval by Hamilton L.J. in *Latham v R. Johnson & Nephew Ltd* [1913] 1 K.B. 398 at 414, and, to the same effect by Farwell L.J. at 407. See further, *Schofield v Bolton Corp* (1910) 26 T.L.R. 230. the notion of a conditional licence was criticised by Devlin J. in *Phipps v Rochester Corporation*, para.8–51, above.
[207] *Coates v Rawstenstall Borough Council* [1937] 3 All E.R. 602.
[208] [1955] 1 Q.B. 450.
[209] *McCullie v Butler*, The Times, March 19, 1959.
[210] *Marsden v Bourne Leisure* [2009] EWCA Civ 671 (it was emphasised that it was a false dichotomy to suggest that either the parents or the occupier was to blame: on the facts, neither were).
[211] This subsection shows that *Christmas v General Cleaning Contractors Ltd* [1953] A.C. 180 is still good law under the Act.

when going upstairs in the ordinary way to reach the windows on an upper floor".[212]

In *Woollins v British Celanese Ltd*,[213] it was held that subsection (b) dealt with the special risks incident to work which being carried out on an occupiers' premises by a visitor, as where live wires are incidental to the work of an electrician, and did not apply to the ordinary risks incident to the premises themselves, such as the unsafe fragile roofing upon which a Post Office engineer put his foot when attempting to remove a cable from the occupiers' factory. **8–59**

ILLUSTRATIONS

A foreman boiler scaler established liability when he fell and hurt himself after having stepped on an empty bottle lying on a vessel's deck, because the risk of so treading on a bottle was not a special risk ordinarily incident to his work on boilers.[214] Where an independent contractor was employed by an occupier, and undertook to provide the necessary equipment, he was liable in negligence in failing to ensure that a ladder was suitable for his visitor's use.[215] The managers of a housing estate were liable to an experienced, self-employed joiner, contracted to replace the window of a house when, there being no lintel, bricks above the window frame fell on him as he worked.[216] A householder, carrying out construction works at his home was liable to a driver, delivering blocks for use in the work, who fell into an excavation.[217] An occupier was partially to blame where he admitted to his house the employees of a company who had contracted to provide a security system, and one of them fell from an unguarded landing upstairs: while the major share of responsibility fell on the employer of the injured man, the householder was also to blame in admitting the men to the house when it was unsafe.[218] **8–60**

On the other hand, an occupier was not liable where an experienced and skilled window-cleaner fell from a height, having lost balance when some ornamental trellis-work broke away[219]; where a clerk of works fell from a scaffold, not itself defective, there being no risk other than that ordinarily incident to the use of any **8–61**

---

[212] Cmnd. 9305, para.77(iii); *Bates v Parker* [1953] 2 Q.B. 231. The Committee added that in their view the provision of proper safeguards for window cleaners in factories, shops, offices and private houses was a matter which might usefully receive further attention. See also *Smith v Austin Lifts* [1959] 1 W.L.R. 100; *Heggie v Edinburgh & Leith Window Cleaning, etc., Co*, 1959 S.L.T. 30.
[213] (1966) 1 K.I.R. 438. See "The 'Occupier' and his 'Visitors,' " 130 J.P.J. 38; Bradbury, "Knowledge and Exemption in Occupiers' Liability", 119 New L.J. 520.
[214] *Bird v King Line* [1970] 2 Lloyd's Rep. 349 (although the claimant was held to have been guilty of contributory negligence to the extent of two-thirds, the defendants were one-third to blame, because the deck was more dangerous to work on than a normal deck of a vessel).
[215] *Wheeler v Copas* [1981] 3 All E.R. 405. Because the ladder's inadequacy ought to have been apparent to the claimant, an experienced builder, contributory negligence was found to the extent of 50 per cent.
[216] *Eden v West & Co* [2003] P.I.Q.R. Q16, CA (the claimant did not know, nor should he have been aware, of the possibility that the window lacked a lintel).
[217] *Moon v Garrett* [2007] P.I.Q.R. P3, CA.
[218] *Intruder Detection & Surveillance Fire & Security Ltd v Fulton* [2008] EWCA Civ 1009.
[219] *Caddis v Gettrup* (1967) 202 E.G. 517.

scaffold[220]; where an occupier had failed to design his premises in such a way that, in the event of a fire, it would be safe for the firemen, who were attending the scene of the blaze[221]; where two chimney-sweeps died by carbon monoxide poisoning, whilst they were engaged in sealing up a sweep-hole in a flue, which led from the occupier's boiler room[222]; where a farmer left a trailer on the road by his property to which cattle feed was to be delivered and while straddling a gap between the trailer and his own vehicle a delivery man fell and was injured[223]; where the lid of a skip into which a cleaner was emptying rubbish blew shut, injuring him, the occupiers of the premises where he was working were entitled to expect that his employers, who were on notice of the danger, had assessed the risk to their staff and provided accordingly.[224]

(E) Dangers

8–62   **Dangers: general matters.** The older cases are still of assistance in deciding whether or not an occupier has fulfilled the common duty of care. Regard may be had to such things as the purpose of the visit; the conduct to be expected of the visitor; the nature of the danger and whether it be obvious or not; what warnings, if any, should be given; what guarding, lighting and precautions should be taken; the state of knowledge of the occupier and the age of the visitor.

8–63   **Illustrations of dangers.** Drawn from the old common law decisions, dangers have been held to exist where a loose end of carpet was laid at the entrance to a room[225]; where a piece of vegetable matter on a shop floor, caused a customer to slip and fall[226]; where some steps leading from a club-house had been removed and re-erected in a different position but not lit so as to warn members of the alteration.[227]

On the other hand, no danger was held to exist: where a rug had been laid on top of a floor highly polished elsewhere but not under the rug[228]; where a window

---

[220] *Howitt v A. Bagnall & Sons* [1967] 2 Lloyd's Rep. 370.

[221] *Sibbald v Sher Bros*, The Times, February 1, 1980, HL, although cf. *Hartley v British Railways Board*, The Times, February 2, 1981, CA.

[222] *Roles v Nathan* [1963] 1 W.L.R. 1117 at 1123–1124, per Lord Denning M.R. "The occupier here was under no duty of care to these sweeps, at any rate in regard to the dangers which caused their deaths. If it had been a different danger, as for instance if the stairs leading to the cellar gave way, the occupier might no doubt be responsible, but not for these dangers which were special risks ordinarily incidental to their calling."

[223] *Phillips v Perry* [1997] 5 C.L. 486, CA.

[224] *Hannington v Mitie Cleaning (South East) Ltd* [2002] EWCA Civ 1847.

[225] *Kimber v Wm Willett Ltd* [1947] K.B. 570.

[226] *Turner v Arding & Hobbs Ltd* [1949] 2 All E.R. 911, approved in *Ward v Tesco Stores* [1976] 1 W.L.R. 810, CA (claimant slipped on some yoghurt spilled on the floor of the defendants' supermarket, in which she was shopping). To the contrary see *Dulhunty v J.B. Young Ltd* (1975) 7 A.L.R. 409 (grape in aisle of the defendants' store in Queensland, where no food was sold on the premises at all). See Bennett, "Slipping and Falling Accidents", 126 S.J. 600; Pawlowski, "Duty of care and slippery floors" L. Ex. 2007, Oct., 2.

[227] *Prole v Allen* [1950] 1 All E.R. 476.

[228] *Jennings v Cole* [1949] 2 All E.R. 191.

which was safe enough for ordinary purposes was not safe when held on to by a window cleaner.[229]

Warning and knowledge of dangers. It is implicit from the wording of s.2(4)   **8–64** of the Act that all relevant general matters, which have been noted above, can and ought to be taken into consideration by the court. It provides:

> "In determining whether the occupier of premises has discharged the common duty of care to a visitor, regard is to be had to all the circumstances, so that (for example)—
>
> (a) where damage is caused to a visitor by a danger of which he had been warned by the occupier, the warning is not to be treated without more as absolving the occupier from liability, unless in all the circumstances it was enough to enable the visitor to be reasonably safe . . . "

The effect of this subsection was to overrule the decision of the House of   **8–65** Lords in *London Graving Dock v Horton*.[230] A visitor's knowledge of danger is just one of the circumstances of the case to be taken into consideration in deciding whether or not reasonable care has been taken to see that he will be reasonably safe for the purposes for which he is invited or permitted to be present. If the danger was one which ought to have been obvious to visitors, exercising reasonable care for their own safety, an occupier will not be liable.[231] Depending on the facts of the particular case, a warning may or may not be sufficient to enable the visitor to be reasonably safe, such as where a verbal warning was not given seriously enough to impress,[232] or where a warning notice was exhibited in an unsuitable place,[233] or in too low a position to be seen.[234] A warning was held to have been insufficient where a deep pit was situated very close to the entrance of a dark shed, without any lighting, into which a visiting surveyor fell: a notice or barrier by way of an obstacle ought to have been put in

---

[229] *Christmas v General Cleaning Contractors* [1952] 1 K.B. 141 (affirmed on other grounds [1953] A.C. 180). Section 2(3)(b) shows that this case is still good law under the Act: *Bates v Parker* [1953] 2 Q.B. 231.

[230] [1951] A.C. 737, where it was held that notice to or knowledge by the visitor of the risk was sufficient to exonerate the occupier from liability, provided that it could be shown the visitor had recognised the full significance of the risk. Further, if the required degree of knowledge was brought home to the visitor, his claim would be equally defeated whether he freely and voluntarily undertook the risk or not.

[231] *Cotton v Derbyshire Dales District Council, The Times*, June 20, 1994, CA, applying a dictum of Lord Shaw in *Glasgow Corp v Taylor* [1992] 1 A.C. 44 at 60 (the absence of any notice warning visitors of dangerous cliffs on a high path on land much used by the public for walking at High Tor, Matlock was not a breach of the duty of care). See also *Staples v West Dorset District Council* [1995] P.I.Q.R. P 349, CA) (defendant not liable to visitor to the Cobb at Lyme Regis who slipped on algae on the stone surface of High Wall even though a warning notice was posted afterwards: the claimant had seen the algae before he slipped and the notice told him nothing he did not know already).

[232] *Bishop v J.S. Starnes & Son Ltd* [1971] 1 Lloyd's Rep. 162 (fitter was gassed in forepeak tank of ship; the warnings by the vessel's owners were held to be wholly insufficient).

[233] *Coupland v Eagle Bros* (1969) 210 E.G. 581; *Woollins v British Celanese Ltd* (1966) 1 K.I.R. 438. But contrast *Horton v Jackson* [1996] C.L.Y. 4475, CA (golf club gave players sufficient warning of danger from balls struck from the ninth tee when they provided a notice giving priority to players on an adjacent green).

[234] *Steward v Routhier* (1974) 45 D.L.R. (3d) 383 at 395.

position, because of the immediacy of the danger.[235] However, a warning was not required where a pond at Hardwick Hall presented an obvious, albeit slight, risk of danger from drowning. The widow's claim failed even though there was another danger which should have been the subject of warning, namely the risk of contracting Weil's disease from swimming in the pond and had such a warning been given the deceased would not have swum or been drowned.[236]

8–66   When *Horton* was before the Court of Appeal[237] Singleton L.J., in dealing with the sufficiency of a warning, said:

> "Whether the notice (or knowledge) is sufficient to absolve the occupier must depend on a variety of circumstances, including the nature of the risk and the position of the injured party. If a veterinary surgeon is called to a farm at night time to attend to a sick animal and the farmer tells him: 'Be careful how you go down the yard or you may fall into a tank,' and, in spite of every care, the veterinary surgeon meets with an accident through an unusual danger, though of the kind envisaged, he may be entitled to recover notwithstanding the warning or notice. On the other hand, if a shopkeeper says to a customer some such words as: 'Do not go to the far side of the shop; there is a hole there and it is dangerous,' and the customer disregards the warning and thereby meets with an accident, it is unlikely that he could recover even if he would be regarded as an invitee at that spot."[238]

8–67   When the same case was before the House of Lords, Lord MacDermott also proffered an example where, in his opinion, a warning would not be sufficient:

> "A, at the end of his day's work, repairs to the local railway station to get home. He goes to the ticket office by the usual and only means of approach. The roof overhead is in a dangerous state and bits of it are liable to fall at any moment. The railway company know of this and could readily avert the danger of those beneath by placing a temporary screen under the defective part. But all they do is to post a notice describing the danger in clear terms. A reads and understands this before he enters the perilous area, but hurries on in order to get his ticket and is hurt by a piece of falling glass. He was not *volens* or careless."[239]

8–68   In *Roles v Nathan*[240] two chimney-sweeps, in defiance of repeated warnings which had been given to them by the occupiers' agent concerning the dangers involved, nevertheless entered into the confined space of an alcove in order to obtain access to the sweep-hole, intent upon sealing it up. As a result, they suffered asphyxiation from carbon monoxide poisoning. The Court of Appeal held that by giving warnings the occupiers had discharged the common duty of care.

---

[235] *Rae v Mars UK Ltd* [1990] 03 E.G. 80; in contrast, in *Whyte v Redland Aggregates Ltd* [1998] 2 C.L. 485, CA, it was held unnecessary to warn specifically against swimming in a disused gravel pit where a sign "Danger, keep out" was provided.

[236] *Darby v National Trust* [2001] P.I.Q.R. P372, CA (a breach of duty to protect from Weil's disease did not support a claim attributable to another cause).

[237] [1950] 1 K.B. 421.

[238] [1950] 1 K.B. 421 at 428–429.

[239] [1951] A.C. 737 at 764–765.

[240] [1963] 1 W.L.R. 1117. cf. *Bishop v J.S. Starnes & Sons Ltd* [1971] 1 Lloyd's Rep. 162.

In contrast, in *Bunker v Charles Brand & Son Ltd*,[241] the claimant, an **8–69** employee of a constructional engineering firm, was engaged in work in a section of tunnel being cut by a machine hired by the defendants, the main contractors and occupiers of the site. As the machine advanced, the normal way to reach the front was to walk along a line of free-running rollers supported on angle irons. He was doing this when he missed his footing and fell. His claim succeeded because, although he was well aware of the risk involved in walking over the rollers, knowledge of the danger did not absolve the occupier from liability, unless in all the circumstances it was enough to enable a visitor to be reasonably safe, which, on the facts, it was not.

Clearly, the Act recognises the common law principle that a danger, if known **8–70** to a visitor, may cease to be a danger to him and it is a question of fact in each case whether or not such knowledge relieves the occupier from liability. As Denning L.J. said in *Slater v Clay Cross Co Ltd*:

"Even in cases which concern the condition of premises . . . knowledge of the danger is only a bar where the party is free to act on it, so that his injury can be said to be due solely to his own fault . . . Where knowledge of the danger is not such as to render the accident solely the fault of the injured party, then it is not a bar to the action but only a ground for reducing the damages."[242]

(F) Defences

Volenti non fit injuria. The Act specifically preserved the defence of **8–71** volenti.[243] Section 2(5) provides that:

"The common duty of care does not impose on an occupier any obligation to a visitor in respect of risks willingly accepted as his by the visitor (the question whether a risk was so accepted to be decided on the same principles as in other cases in which one person owes a duty of care to another)."

Illustrations of volenti. When the plaintiff was injured slipping on the **8–72** polished floor of a hall where physical training classes were conducted, it was held that he did not agree to take upon himself the risk of slipping upon a floor which was not reasonably fit for the purpose of physical training.[244] Where a member of a "jalopy" club went to compete at a race meeting, but was killed when watching a race from just outside the roped-off area of the spectators' enclosure, it was held that, because he did not know of the risk caused by the organisers' failure to take proper safety precautions, he could not consent to accept it.[245]

---

[241] [1969] 2 Q.B. 480.
[242] [1956] 2 Q.B. 264 at 271. See *A.C. Billings & Sons Ltd v Riden* [1958] A.C. 240, where (at 266) Lord Somervell thought that the words "free to act," used in the context by Denning L.J. may be ambiguous.
[243] The defence is discussed more fully in Ch.4, paras 4–73 to 4–172, above.
[244] *Gillmore v London County Council* [1938] 4 All E.R. 331. For the occupiers' or promoters' duty in respect of sports premises and sporting activities, see paras 8–86 to 8–80, below.
[245] *White v Blackmore* [1972] 2 Q.B. 651.

8–73   **Free choice.** Unless a visitor really does have freedom of choice whether or not to enter premises, the defence will not succeed, even if he were to have actual or constructive notice of the conditions, upon which he may so enter. Thus, where a lighterman, working on a barge being warped into dock, was injured when a defective rope snapped, the negligent occupiers were liable[246] even though the wording of a notice was apt to cover liability for the accident, because the plaintiff had neither expressly nor impliedly agreed to be bound by its terms and he had had no choice in the matter.

On the other hand, a rugby footballer was held willingly to have accepted the risk of playing the game on the defendant's ground, which, although it complied with the byelaws of the Rugby Football League, had a concrete wall running at a distance of 7ft 3in. away from and along the touchline.[247]

8–74   **Business liability.** The extent of the volenti defence is limited as regards "business liability"[248] by the Unfair Contract Terms Act 1977 s.2(3). The section provides that: "where a contract term or notice purports to exclude or restrict liability for negligence a person's agreement to or awareness of it is not of itself to be taken as indicating his voluntary acceptance of any risk." Since the Act invalidates exclusion clauses aimed at restricting an occupier's business liability for death or personal injury caused by negligence, the thrust of this section is to prevent volenti being used instead of an ineffective exemption. In any event, the application will probably be rare, because a finding of contributory negligence will be more likely[249] where the claimant is partially to blame.

8–75   **Contributory negligence.** Although the Act does not mention contributory negligence[250] in terms, the words of s.2(3) suggest apportionment of blame should be considered in an appropriate case: "the circumstances relevant for the present purposes include the degree of care, and of want of care, which would ordinarily be looked for in such a visitor . . . ". It is not uncommon for the successful claimant to be regarded as partially to blame for whatever misfortune has occurred.[251]

---

[246] *Burnett v British Waterways Board* [1973] 1 W.L.R. 700, affirming [1972] 1 W.L.R. 1329, Waller J.
[247] *Simms v Leigh Rugby Football Club* [1969] 2 All E.R. 923.
[248] See para.8–45. For further discussion see Ch.4, paras 4–84 to 4–88, above.
[249] See *Slater v Clay Cross Co Ltd* [1956] 2 Q.B. 264 at 271 per Denning L.J. but cf. *Cummings v Grainger* [1977] Q.B. 397 where the claimant's contributory negligence was equated with implied consent, hence she was held *volens* to the risk of being bitten by a fierce guard dog, whilst she was trespassing.
[250] The defence is discussed more fully in Ch.4, paras 4–03 to 4–72, above.
[251] *Wheat v E. Lacon & Co Ltd* [1966] A.C. 552 at 570, per Viscount Dilhorne. Then there have been findings of contributory negligence against the claimants in *Woollins v British Celanese Ltd* (1966) 1 K.I.R. 438 (one-half); *Blackett v B.R.B., The Times*, December 19, 1967 (one-third); *McDowell v F.M.C. (Meat)* (1968) 5 K.I.R. 456 (one-fifth); *Bunker v Charles Brand & Son Ltd* [1969] 2 Q.B. 480 (one-half); *Bird v King Line* [1970] 2 Lloyd's Rep. 349 (two-thirds); *Sole v W. J. Hallt Ltd* [1973] 1 Q.B. 574, (one-third); *Stone v Taffe* [1974] 1 W.L.R. 1575 (one-half).

(G) Effect of contract

Liability for independent contractors. Before the coming into force of the **8–76**
Act there was some doubt about the liability of an occupier for a danger known
to, or created by, an independent contractor employed by him.[252] However, s.2(4)
provides that: "In determining whether the occupier of premises has discharged
the common duty of care to a visitor, regard is to be had to all the circumstances",
and the Law Reform Committee's recommendations[253] have been reproduced by
the subsections as statutory examples. Thus, s.2(4)(b) provides that:

" . . . where damage is caused to a visitor by a danger due to the faulty execution of
any work of construction,[254] maintenance or repair by an independent contractor
employed by the occupier, the occupier is not to be treated without more as answerable
for the danger if in all the circumstances he had acted reasonably in entrusting the work
to an independent contractor[255] and had taken such steps (if any) as he reasonably ought
in order to satisfy himself that the contractor was competent[256] and that the work had
been properly done."

Section 2(4)(b) is by no means a carte blanche in favour of an occupier who **8–77**
entrusts work to an independent contractor. So, where claimants sought to
recover the value of equipment installed by them in a partially constructed
bowling centre, which extensively damaged when the building was flooded
after heavy rain, the occupiers claimed that they came within the protection of
s.2(4)(b) because they had arranged for the construction of their building by a
reputable contractor, who was under the supervision of a firm of qualified private
architects. Their argument failed. They had not taken steps before allowing the
claimants to commence work to satisfy themselves that the builders had done
their work properly, which included taking the necessary precautions against
flooding.[257]

By way of contrast, where the claimant, who was engaged in unloading a **8–78**
consignment of cheese from the hold of a ship, fell through an unsupported piece
of separation paper and was injured, the occupiers of the hold were not liable[258]:
the trap had been created when the vessel was loaded in Canada by independent
contractors and the occupiers could not have discovered the danger by reasonable
supervision during the loading operation.

Occupier effecting repairs. If an occupier undertakes to do work himself, **8–79**
which requires such a degree of highly specialised skill or knowledge that it

---

[252] See the discussion of *Haseldine v Daw* [1941] 2 K.B. 343 and *Thomson v Cremin* [1953] 2 All E.R. 1185 in the 10th edn of this work.
[253] Cmd. 9305, para.78(v).
[254] A broad and purposeful interpretation may properly lead to the conclusion that demolition is embraced by the word "construction": *Ferguson v Welsh* [1987] 1 W.L.R. 1553 at 1560, per Lord Keith.
[255] See *Christmas v Blue Star Line and Harland & Wolff Ltd* [1961] 1 Lloyd's Rep. 94.
[256] See *Gwilliam v West Hertfordshire Hospital NHS Trust* [2003] Q.B. 443, CA (an enquiry whether a contractor had insurance was a sufficient check without also checking the terms of the policy).
[257] *A.M.F. International Ltd v Magnet Bowling Ltd* [1968] 1 W.L.R. 1028.
[258] *Ellis v Scruttons Maltby Ltd* [1975] 1 Lloyd's Rep. 564.

should reasonably have been entrusted to competent experts, he may well find himself in breach of duty, but not if he undertakes some minor domestic repair work. Where a door handle came away in a visitor's hand, it was held that a man who had some experience as an amateur carpenter was justified in attempting the fitting of a new door handle with three screws. It was said that the standard of care required to discharge the defendant's duty to the claimant was that care and skill to be expected of a reasonably competent carpenter doing the work in question, but not measured by reference to the contractual obligations as to the quality of his work assumed by a professional carpenter working for reward.[259] It was stressed that the occupier's duty was no more than to take reasonable care. The standard required was not raised to anything higher than that by the circumstance that the occupier might choose to employ an independent contractor to do the work for him.[260]

8–80   Where the safety of the visitor is dependent on something being done, which an occupier can and should do personally, as not requiring technical skill or special knowledge, liability for failure to do what is necessary cannot be avoided by delegating it to an independent contractor who then negligently performs the work.[261] Even when the occupier has acted reasonably in entrusting work to an independent contractor and has satisfied himself that the contractor is competent, his duty may require him to check that the work is properly done by engaging expert supervision, where that is beyond his own capability.[262]

8–81   In many cases s.2(4)(b) will protect the occupier against liability to an employee or agent of an independent contractor who is present upon the premises as invitee. But there will be cases outside the section's strict terms and it is necessary to consider the circumstances in which liability to this class of persons may arise. One type of case has already been mentioned in another context. A liability to the independent contractor's employees or agents may arise if the contractor has been engaged to come onto the land for the purposes of performing some extra-hazardous activity, which he proceeds to perform negligently.[263] In that event, the occupier's liability will arise because, given the nature of the activity, he is personally responsible for having the work done in a competent manner, even if he selected a competent independent contractor.[264] Liability may also arise if, in all the circumstances, a duty of care is imposed, independent of the occupier's duty qua occupier. Such a duty arose where an occupier invited an independent contractor onto land to provide a fireworks display, and made no sufficient enquiries into his competence: injury to any of those attending was foreseeable as a result of the failure, there was a sufficient relationship of proximity between the occupier and the agents of the contractor

---

[259] *Wells v Cooper* [1958] 2 Q.B. 265, per Jenkins L.J. at 271.
[260] ibid., per Jenkins L.J. at 274.
[261] For example, cleaning up the garden path leading to the house; clearing away snow; and applying salt and grit to patches of ice.
[262] See Mocatta J. in *A.M.F. International Ltd v Magnet Bowling Ltd* [1968] 1 W.L.R. 1028 at 1044.
[263] See *Honeywill & Stein Ltd v Larkin Bros Ltd* [1934] 1 K.B. 191, Ch.3, para.3–192, above.
[264] *Salsbury v Woodland* [1970] 1 Q.B. 324, 347.

who were injured when fireworks exploded and it was fair, just and reasonable to impose a duty of care.[265]

Effect of contract on occupiers' liability to third party. Where there was a   **8–82** background of contract, the rule at common law was that the occupier owed the same duty to someone invited into the premises by the party with whom he had contracted, as he owed to the contracting party under the terms of the contract.[266] The Act provides by s.3(1):

> "Where an occupier of premises is bound by contract to permit persons who are strangers to the contract to enter or use the premises, the duty of care which he owes to them as his visitors cannot be restricted or excluded by that contract[267] but (subject to any provision of the contract to the contrary) shall include the duty to perform his obligations under the contract[268] whether undertaken for their protection or not, in so far as those obligations go beyond the obligations otherwise involved in that duty."

Section 3(3) defines "stranger to the contract" as "a person not for the time being entitled to the benefit of the contract as a party to it or as the successor by assignment or otherwise of a party to it, and accordingly includes a party to the contract who has ceased to be so entitled". In effect the duty owed by the occupier to such persons is the same common duty of care owed to all lawful visitors, unless the contract has imposed more onerous terms, in which event the visitors will be entitled to the benefit of any such additional obligations, in the absence of express exclusion. By way of illustration, if the lessor of a block of offices has retained control of the common staircase he cannot exclude or limit in the terms of the lease his common duty of care to the tenants' lawful visitors when using this means of access. Indeed, the tenants' visitors will be able to claim the benefit of any more onerous obligations undertaken in the lease, unless it contains terms contrary to the provision.[269]

Section 3(4) deals with persons admitted to the premises as a result of the   **8–83** terms of a tenancy:

> "Where by the terms or conditions governing any tenancy (including a statutory tenancy which does not in law amount to a tenancy) either the landlord or the tenant is bound, though not by contract, to permit persons to enter or use premises of which he is the occupier, this section shall apply as if the tenancy were a contract between the landlord and the tenant."

---

[265] *Bottomley v Todmorden Cricket Club* [2004] P.I.Q.R. P275.

[266] Cmd. 9305, para.55; see also *Fosbroke-Hobbes v Airwork Ltd* [1937] 1 All E.R. 108, 112.

[267] Normally the common duty of care can be restricted or excluded altogether, so that such visitors in this instance are in a privileged position (see s.2(1)). In any event, any attempt to exclude or limit liability would be defeated by the Unfair Contract Terms Act 1977 s.2(1) since the landlord would be incurring business liability. See further para.8–74, above.

[268] Provided an occupier has taken all reasonable care, he is not responsible for the default of an independent contractor unless the contract provides expressly that he should be (see s.3(2) of the Act).

[269] Cmd. 9305, paras 79 and 95(1)(ii).

8–84 **Contractual duty to persons entering the premises.** At common law,[270] when persons had entered premises under a contract for valuable consideration, some unsatisfactory distinctions had developed. In particular, much uncertainty had centred around the terms to be implied,[271] in the absence of express terms of the contract. The Act greatly simplified the law. In lieu of the terms implied at common law, s.5 provides:

> "(1) Where persons enter or use, or bring or send goods to, any premises in exercise of a right conferred by contract with a person occupying or having control of the premises, the duty he owes them in respect of dangers due to the state of the premises or to things done or omitted to be done on them, in so far as the duty depends on a term to be implied in the contract by reason of its conferring that right, shall be the common duty of care.
>
> (2) The foregoing subsection shall apply to fixed and movable structures as it applies to premises.
>
> (3) This section does not affect the obligations imposed on a person by or by virtue of any contract for the hire of, or for carriage for reward of persons or goods in, any vehicle, vessel, aircraft or other means of transport, or by or by virtue of any contract of bailment."

8–85 The purpose of the Act was to equate the duty owed by an occupier to a person who had entered by right of contract with that of a visitor. Accordingly, where someone has entered premises under a contract and has sustained injury, he can sue the occupier both in contract and tort unless he is bound by an agreement to restrict his claim to a contractual one. In *Sole v W.J. Hallt Ltd*,[272] where an experienced plasterer, who had entered a building under construction in order to fix ceilings, fell into an unguarded stair-well whilst he was walking backwards and looking up at the ceiling, and injured himself, it was held that he could sue for damages both in contract and tort. There was no implied term which restricted him to a claim only in contract. In *Maguire v Sefton Metropolitan Borough Council*,[273] where the claimant was injured while using a defective exercise machine in a leisure centre operated by the defendant, no wider duty was owed by the defendant, under an implied term of the contract by which the claimant was admitted to the premises, that the machine be reasonably fit for its purpose: ss.2 and 5 of the Act were intended to impose a single common duty of care, whether arising within or outside a contract, subject to contrary agreement.

8–86 **Persons entering premises for the purposes of sport or entertainment.** There is often a background of contract where persons enter premises in order to watch or participate in sport or entertainment.[274] Spectators and participants are also owed the common duty of care under the Act. Reasonable care must be taken therefore to make the premises safe, having regard to the

---

[270] For the position at common law, see *Charlesworth on Negligence* (3rd edn, 1956), paras 305–318.
[271] See the 9th and earlier editions of this work for examples of the distinctions which had arisen in the pre-1957 law.
[272] [1973] Q.B. 574.
[273] [2006] P.I.Q.R. P378, CA (the claim failed since the defendant council had discharged its common duty of care by arranging inspection of the machine by an apparently competent independent contractor some 6 weeks before the accident: see s.2(4)(b) of the 1957 Act para.8–76, above).
[274] See generally Ch.2, para.2–280, above.

nature of the sport or entertainment for which they provide a venue. At common law,[275] if the premises were to be used for the purpose of watching some sport, spectacle or theatrical entertainment, the contractual warranty was that they should be reasonably fit for that purpose, having regard to the normal risks of the activity in question. The person receiving payment was not "under any obligation to provide safety under all circumstances, but only to provide against damage to spectators which any reasonable occupier in their position would have anticipated as likely to happen".[276] The normal risks of the particular sport, spectacle or entertainment might, however, require that some additional safety device ought to have been added to the structure and, if this were not done, there would be a breach of duty.

> "The performance may be of such a kind as to render the structure an unsafe place to be in whilst the performance is going on, or it may be of such a kind as to render the structure unsafe unless some obvious precaution is taken. As an illustration under the latter head I would instance a case where a tightrope dancer performs on a rope stretched over the heads of the audience. In such a case the provision of a net under the rope to protect the audience in case the performer fell seems so obvious a precaution to take that in the absence of it the premises could not be said to be reasonably safe."[277]

ILLUSTRATIONS

Although defendants were not negligent in their organisation of a rally, they   **8–87** were nonetheless liable vicariously for the negligence of stewards who failed to advise spectators to move away from a vantage point on the outside of a dangerous bend on a slope.[278] Where a performer on a tightrope negligently dropped a chair, which struck a member of the audience because no net was provided, the proprietors of the hall were liable for breach of an implied contract that the seats were reasonably safe.[279] The organisers of a "jalopy" race meeting were found to be guilty of negligence in so arranging safety ropes that they were all tied to one master stake, so that when the wheel of a racing car became entangled in a rope it acted like a winch, which catapulted the deceased into the air and killed him.[280] The council which provided a leisure pool with defective

---

[275] For statutory provision, see the effect of the provisions of the Safety of Sports Grounds Act 1975. By s.13 no civil action lies in tort in respect of any breaches.

[276] per Greer L.J. in *Hall v Brooklands Auto-Racing Club* [1933] 1 K.B. 205 at 225.

[277] per Bankes L.J. in *Cox v Coulson* [1916] 2 K.B. 177 at 191–192.

[278] *Horne and Marlow v R.A.C. Motor Sports Association, Daily Telegraph,* June 19, 1989, CA. See further *Australian Racing Drivers Club v Metcalf* (1961) 106 C.L.R. 177 (organisers of a car race meeting contractually liable to a spectator injured by a car which left the track at a point where it was unfenced).

[279] *Welsh v Canterbury & Paragon Ltd* (1894) 10 T.L.R. 478. A plea that there was contributory negligence on the part of the claimant in sitting underneath the rope while the performance was going on was rejected. Of course, the provisions of s.2(4)(b) of the Occupiers' Liability Act 1957 would not apply (para.8–76, above), so that only if the court were to find that in the circumstances a net should have been provided to make the premises reasonably safe for use, would the claimant succeed against the occupiers.

[280] *White v Blackmore* [1972] 2 Q.B. 651, although the defendants avoided liability to the deceased's widow, because of the exclusion contained in the warning notices. See para.8–42.

means of access, namely an unsafe ledge at the side of the pool, were liable to the claimant who slipped on the ledge and was injured when he fell.[281]

8–88 A spectator at a motor race meeting at Brooklands who was injured by a car which came through the railing dividing the track from the space appropriated to the spectators, failed in his claim on proof that no similar accident had happened since the track was opened 20 years before.[282] Similarly, when a polo pony at Ranelagh ran through a hedge and injured a spectator, it was held that the spectator could not recover damages.[283] A visitor at a golf-club, who, while putting on a green, was struck by a ball which had been driven off by another player from an adjoining tee, failed in his claim against the club since his injury was a risk of the game and not the result of any lack of care in the design or construction of the course.[284] Nor were the club liable where an extension to a screen between the ninth tee and the sixth hole would not have prevented an accident in which a player was struck by a ball and lost the sight of an eye.[285] The claim for damages of a child spectator at an ice-hockey match, who was injured as a result of the puck leaving the arena and coming among the spectators, failed on its being proved that the rink was structurally safe and the risk was a risk of the game.[286] The claims of a father and son injured when the toboggan they were riding left the track of a purpose-built toboggan run, failed where a small degree of risk was an inherent part of the thrill of the entertainment and the run was not inherently dangerous.[287] The proprietors of a football club were not liable to a police officer, present to supervise the crowd, who was struck and injured by a player whose momentum carried him from the pitch while he attempted to control the ball, since the risk was so minimal it could safely be ignored.[288]

8–89 **Negligence of performer.** If there is negligence on the part of the performers, a claimant will establish liability against the occupier only if the circumstances are such that he is vicariously liable,[289] or if he knew or ought to have known that

---

[281] *Davies v Wyre Forest District Council* [1998] P.I.Q.R. 58.

[282] *Hall v Brooklands Auto-Racing Club* [1933] 1 K.B. 205; *Wilks v Cheltenham Homeguard Motor Cycle and Light Car Club* [1971] 1 W.L.R. 668 (a motorcycle scramble race where the CA allowed the competing rider's appeal). See also *White v Blackmore* [1972] 2 Q.B. 651.

[283] *Pidington v Hastings*, *The Times*, March 12, 1932.

[284] *Potter v Carlisle and Cliftonville Golf Club Ltd* [1939] N.I. 114. See also Ch.4, paras 4–99 to 4–107, above as regards spectators and participants, who are "taking risks" at sporting activities.

[285] *Horton v Jackson* [1950] 1 K.B. 421 (expert evidence was received from a former member of the Rules Committee of the Royal and Ancient Golf Club of St Andrews. Moreover, there had been only two accidents in over 800,000 rounds of golf).

[286] *Murray v Harringay Arena Ltd* [1951] 2 K.B. 529. The implied term in the contract did not become wider merely because one of the parties was a child. cf. *Klyne v Bellegarde* (1978) 6 W.W.R. 743 where the claimant, a spectator, was injured in the eye by an ice hockey stick, whilst standing in an aisle next to the side boards. Because the likelihood of a spectator being injured in this manner was foreseeable, the defendant occupiers were held liable in part to the claimant for their failure to provide protective guards above the side boards.

[287] *R and R v Ski Llandudno Ltd* [2001] P.I.Q.R. P70, CA. See also *Tysall Ltd v Snowdome* [2007] 7 C.L. 434, para.8–39, above.

[288] *Gillon v Chief Constable of Strathclyde Police*, *The Times*, November 22, 1996, OH.

[289] In *Wooldridge v Sumner and British Horse Society*, *The Times*, December 6 and 7, 1961, occupiers were said not to be vicariously liable for the negligence of a competitor. This was not the subject of any appeal at [1963] 2 Q.B. 43 but the appeal against the finding of negligence of the horseman was allowed. For the duty of care of competitors toward spectators, see Ch.2, para.2–281, above.

in the course of the performance a dangerous thing[290] would be employed. So, where the claimant paid for admission to the defendant's theatre, at which a travelling company, not the servants of the defendant, were performing a play, and she was injured when a blank cartridge pistol was fired by one of the actors, it was held that the defendant was bound to take reasonable care to see that such incidents as the firing of pistols were performed without risk to the audience.[291] Where when one player attacked another in the course of an ice hockey game and a spectator was injured, the occupier was not liable but the player was.[292] When the claimant entered a show-ground under a contract with the defendants, and went into a sideshow, where she was injured owing to the negligence of a person employed by a sideshow concessionaire, it was held that the defendants were not liable because the sideshow was not intrinsically dangerous.[293] When a member of the audience at a theatre was struck in the face by the heel from one of the performers' shoes during a performance which was not intrinsically dangerous, the claim failed.[294]

Exclusion or restriction of liability. As already noted,[295] the Unfair Contract **8–90** Terms Act 1977 s.1(3), controls the exclusion of restriction of liability both in contract and for negligence, arising in the course of business, after February 1, 1978. Section 1(3) was amended by s.2 of the Occupiers Liability Act 1984 Act, so as to enable occupiers to allow access to their premises for recreational or educational purposes on terms which restrict their civil liability. The ability to restrict liability was limited to those situations where access is granted as a matter of goodwill or neighbourliness: not to instances where access has been granted in the way of business.

5.—LIABILITY OF NON-OCCUPIERS

Liability of persons not in occupation. The duty to take care, when it is **8–91** known that a person is present upon land and is likely to be injured unless care is taken, is not confined to those who own or occupy the land. It is a duty owed by everybody about to do some act on the land which will cause injury unless care is taken, whether the doer of the act is the owner, the occupier, an invitee, a licensee or even a trespasser. In *Excelsior Wire Rope Co v Callan*,[296] the rope

---

[290] See Ch.13, below.
[291] *Cox v Coulson* [1916] 2 K.B. 177.
[292] See *Payne v Maple Leaf Gardens* [1949] 1 D.L.R. 369.
[293] *Sheehan v Dreamland (Margate) Ltd* (1923) 40 T.L.R. 155. Where no payment was made for entrance to the show-ground, but a sideshow was entered for payment which was made to a cashier who was employed by the show-ground, although under a contract made with the consessionaire, it was held that there was no contractual relation between the show-ground proprietors and the person entering the sideshow and also no relation of invitor and invitee between them. *Humphreys v Dreamland (Margate) Ltd* (1931) 100 L.J.K.B. 137.
[294] *Fraser-Wallas v Waters* [1939] 4 All E.R. 609 (the action was against the persons who engaged the artists at a variety entertainment and not against the occupiers of the theatre, but the liability of the occupiers could not be greater than that of the persons sued).
[295] See para.8–45, above.
[296] [1930] A.C. 404.

company were neither the owners nor the occupiers of the land but carried on their operations under a licence from the landowner. Their liability to trespassers, however, was the same as if they had been occupiers. In *Mourton v Poulter*,[297] the defendant was an independent contractor who had been engaged by the landowner to fell a tree, but it was not suggested that his liability was in any way affected by the lack of an interest in the property.

8-92   The duty of a person who is neither the owner nor the occupier of land may in some cases be greater than that of the owner or occupier.[298] If he is doing something on the land which he knows or ought to know will be a source of danger to persons on or likely to come on the land and meddle with the subject of his activity, he is under a duty to take precautions to prevent damage. Reasonable precautions will include such matters as giving warnings,[299] guarding, fencing off or otherwise taking steps to preserve the safety of the persons who come on the premises.

ILLUSTRATIONS

8-93   Electricity undertakers, who placed high voltage wires across a field near to a tree which could be easily climbed and the foliage of which prevented the wires from being seen easily, were held liable for the electrocution of a girl of 13 who climbed the tree and came in contact with the wires. It was held that, even if the girl were a trespasser on the tree, they should have contemplated that such an accident might occur and taken steps to prevent it.[300] Demolition contractors, who had demolished a house to the level of the first floor ceiling, were liable to a boy of 12 who trespassed on the premises and was injured by playing at a wall which was unsafe. They knew that children were in the habit of playing on a cleared site behind the house, and should have foreseen that children were likely to come to the building and interfere with the brickwork.[301] Contractors, who were engaged in road-making and had left a trailer, attractive to children, near to their work on some waste land which was not in their occupation, were liable to a young child who was injured when playing with the trailer.[302] On the other hand, contractors were not liable for injuries sustained by a child trespasser who had fallen through the skylight of a building which was waiting to be demolished.[303] Likewise, a householder could not reasonably be expected to

---

[297] [1930] 2 K.B. 183.
[298] The occupier has the authority to decide who does and who does not enter his premises, whilst the non-occupier has no choice in the matter. Nor does the non-occupier enjoy the right to exclude his liability to visitors by notice.
[299] Giving a warning only may be insufficient; a non-occupier may have to go further and make the premises safe. See *Johnson v Rea Ltd* [1962] 1 Q.B. 373.
[300] *Buckland v Guildford Gas Light & Coke Co* [1949] 1 K.B. 410. See also Ch.13, para.13–156, below.
[301] *Davis v St Mary's Demolition Co Ltd* [1954] 1 All E.R. 578. See the discussion of this case by Montrose, 17 M.L.R. 368.
[302] *Creed v McGeoch & Sons Ltd* [1955] 1 W.L.R. 1005. See 19 M.L.R. 79.
[303] *Aldrich v Henry Boyer Ltd, The Times*, January 16, 1960.

apprehend danger to children from lime mortar, which had been left in a heap in the gutter outside his house, prior to its use for repairs.[304]

The duty owed by a non-occupier. In *Miller v South of Scotland Electricity*   **8–94**
Board,[305] where the House of Lords held the defenders liable for negligently disconnecting their electricity supply to premises which were about to be demolished, so that a child trespasser received a serious electric shock, Lord Denning said:

> "We are concerned with the duty of care that is owed by a person doing work—or anything else—on land: and that duty is today best found by resort to the general principle enunciated by Lord Atkin in *Donoghue v Stevenson*.[306] Such a person—be he occupier, contractor, or anyone else—owes a duty to all persons who are so closely and directly affected by his work that he ought reasonably to have them in contemplation when he is directing his mind to the task".[307]

Further, the House of Lords in *A.C. Billings & Sons Ltd v Riden*,[308] held that a contractor who was working on premises owed a duty to take reasonable care to prevent damage to persons whom he may reasonably expect to be affected by his work of destroying the normal safe access to a building. The way was, thus, effectively cleared to extend the broad principle of *Donoghue v Stevenson*[309] to those cases where visitors, and even trespassers,[310] are injured on premises as a result of the negligence of non-occupiers. The Occupiers' Liability Act[311] has no application in the case of non-occupier.

Liability of owner. An owner who is not in occupation and has not contracted   **8–95**
to keep the premises in repair is under no liability at common law to the occupiers' visitors.[312] So, where a customer to a shop was injured because of the bad state of repair of the forecourt leading to the shop from the highway, the

---

[304] *Prince v Gregory* [1959] 1 W.L.R. 177.
[305] 1958 S.C. (H.L.) 20.
[306] [1932] A.C. 562 at 580.
[307] 1958 S.C. (H.L.) 20 at 37.
[308] [1968] A.C. 240, overruling both *Malone v Laskey* [1907] 2 K.B. 141 and *Ball v London County Council* [1949] 2 K.B. 159. There is also discussion in the case of how far the claimant's knowledge of a danger will either defeat his claim entirely or be a ground for a finding of contributory negligence: See Ch.4, para.4–03 et seq., above.
[309] [1932] A.C. 562.
[310] For both the common law and statute law relating to trespassers, after the decision of the HL in *Herrington v British Railways Board* [1972] A.C. 877, see paras 8–144 to 8–160, below and *Pannett v McGuinness & Co Ltd* [1972] 2 Q.B. 599.
[311] s.2(1). The common duty of care, which extended by virtue of s.1(3) of the Act of 1957 to persons occupying or having control of a structure, was not thereby imposed on the contractors, whose sub-contractors were in occupation and control of a particular working platform and scaffolding being erected amongst the roof members and trusses: *Kearny v Eric Waller* [1967] 1 Q.B. 29.
[312] *Lane v Cox* [1897] 1 Q.B. 415; *Bromley v Mercer* [1922] 2 K.B. 126. But see the provision of the Defective Premises Act 1972 ss.3 and 4, which came into force on January 1, 1974, Ch.2 para.2–77 above and paras 8–123 to 8–137, below.

owner, who was not in occupation, was not liable.[313] In *Jones v City of Calgary*,[314] a municipality owned an electric transformer on the premises of a supermarket shopping centre, which was not kept adequately locked or surrounded by a barrier, and a boy received an electric shock from it. It was held that the boy was not a trespasser, because the municipality could not be said to be the occupiers of the land on which the transformer stood. Further, it was held that the municipality could not succeed in its defence on the basis that the boy was a trespasser to the transformer itself, because it was an allurement and its attraction to children was foreseeable. The owners of the supermarket were held not to be under any duty of care in the matter, since the municipality had kept exclusive control of the transformer; hence only the latter was in breach of its common duty of care by reason of the lack of fencing and warning given.

8-96   **Occupier's liability for a visitor's acts.** As has been pointed out, the occupier owes the "common duty of care", not only in respect of dangers which arise from the state of the premises, but also in respect of dangers which are the results of "things done or omitted to be done on them".[315] Otherwise, the occupier is not liable for damage caused by one of his visitors to another, unless he could reasonably have foreseen that damage of that kind would be caused by that person when acting within the limits of his invitation or licence. Accordingly, the occupier of a shop, with a tea room annexed, was not liable when tea-room customers, who were carrying an urn of hot tea through the shop, negligently spilled the contents, scalding some of the customers.[316] The occupiers of a wharf, at which the claimant's barges were moored, were not liable when a ship, arriving at night at the wharf, moved the barges to an unsafe berth further up the wharf.[317]

8-97   **Liability of invitor or licensor not in occupation of premises.** A person not in occupation[318] of premises may give an invitation or licence to others to enter on the premises. This may occur, for example, in the case of a dance hall, where the hall is retained in the possession and control of the occupiers, but they authorise promoters of a dance or other entertainment to give visitors an invitation or licence to enter. In such a case both the occupiers and the promoters may well be liable to the visitor in the event of accident.

> "When a person invites another to a place where they both have business, the invitation creates a duty on the part of the invitor to take reasonable care that the place does not contain or to give warning of hidden dangers, no matter whether the place belongs to the invitor or is in his exclusive occupation".[319]

---

[313] *Howard v Walker* [1947] K.B. 860. The shopkeeper was held liable.
[314] (1969) 3 D.L.R. (3d) 455.
[315] Occupiers' Liability Act 1957 s.1(1).
[316] *Glasgow Corp v Muir* [1943] A.C. 448.
[317] *The Majfrid* [1942] P. 145.
[318] The Occupiers' Liability Act 1957 does not apply to non-occupiers. See paras 8–91 to 8–95, above.
[319] Lord Oaksey L.J. in *Hartwell v Grayson Rollo & Clover Docks Ltd* [1947] K.B. 901 at 913.

During the construction of a building, the head contractor is the invitor of the sub-contractors, including their workmen, but his duty as invitor ceases when he hands over exclusive control of any part of the premises to *any* of his subcontractors.[320]

Where a ship, at the invitation of a railway company who occupied a wharf **8–98** within a harbour under the control of harbour trustees, was damaged owing to the condition of the wharf, both the railway company and the trustees were held liable. The railway company were liable because, as invitors, they should either have taken reasonable care to see that the berth for the vessel was safe or to have given warning that they had not done so, and the trustees, as occupiers, were liable, because they should have taken reasonable care to keep the berth in a fit condition.[321] Similarly, a tenant of a flat, who has invited a visitor to see him on business, will be liable to his visitor for injury sustained as a result of an unusual danger in a staircase, retained by the landlord in his own possession, if he knew or ought to have known of the danger but has given no warning of it.[322] His liability would be independent of and unaffected by the provisions of the Occupiers' Liability Act 1957. The landlord, on the other hand, by reason of his occupation of the staircase, would owe the visitor the common duty of care.[323]

Liability of actual wrongdoer. In addition to the occupier, the non-occupier, **8–99** who actually creates a danger, will be liable if he has reason to expect that people will be present on the premises and thereby exposed to the danger which he has created.[324] His duty is to take that degree of care as is reasonable in all the circumstances,[325] which encompasses persons who are lawfully on the premises and can include a trespasser.[326]

---

[320] *Canter v Gardner & Co* [1940] 1 All E.R. 325 (an example of where one invitee may recover against another invitee); *Keegan v Owens* [1953] I.R. 267; *Whitehorn v Port of London Authority* [1955] 1 Lloyd's Rep. 54.

[321] *The Bearn* [1906] P. 48. See also *The Grit* [1924] P. 246; *The Calliope* [1891] A.C. 11; *The Moorcock* (1889) 14 P.D. 64; *The Empress* [1923] P. 96; *The Kate* [1935] P. 100; *The Unique* [1939] W.N. 60.

[322] *Fairman v Perpetual Building Society* [1923] A.C. 74 at 85, 95; *Howard v Walker* [1947] K.B. 860.

[323] See also the Defective Premises Act 1972 s.4 (landlord's liability towards others for defects in the state of the premises that he has let, where he has an obligation or the right to remedy such defects). See, further, paras 8–123 to 8–137, below.

[324] *Kimber v Gas Light & Coke Co* [1918] 1 K.B. 439 at 445, per Bankes L.J.: "If a person creates a dangerous condition of things (something in the nature of a concealed trap) whether in a public highway, or on his own premises, or on those of another, and he sees some other person who to his knowledge is unaware of the existence of the danger lawfully exposing himself or about to expose himself to the danger which he has created he is under a duty to give such a person a warning . . . the duty arises quite independently of the occupation of premises. It does not arise out of any invitation or licence."

[325] The broad principle of *Donoghue v Stevenson* [1932] A.C. 562 normally regulates the duty of care of non-occupiers.

[326] *Buckland v Guildford Gas Light & Coke Co* [1949] 1 K.B. 410 (schoolgirl of 13, who climbed an oak tree and was electrocuted upon touching the bare high-voltage wires, running concealed through the branches and foliage); *Miller v South of Scotland Electricity Board*, 1958 S.L.T. 227 (child trespasser received a severe electric shock from live cable left carelessly disconnected in a house about to be demolished).

Illustrations

8–100   Where a licensee used a private road and stumbled in the dark over a heap of slates which had been left by a builder with the permission of the owner, it was held that the builder was liable.[327] So also was a mason who negligently had erected in a churchyard a tombstone which toppled over on to the claimant and injured him.[328] Where the owner of a house employed builders to carry out repairs and the builders, in turn, employed a gas company to do the necessary work in connection with the gas fittings, the latter were liable to a prospective tenant who was injured whilst she was viewing the house and fell into their unfenced excavations.[329] The like duty of care is owed by one sub-contractor who is working on premises to the workmen of another.[330] A workman on a ship who fell down a hatchway which had been left open by stevedores employed by the shipowner to unload the ship, established liability against the stevedores on the ground that there is "a common law obligation upon one invitee working upon the premises to warn another invitee working there of any danger which he may have created, and for which he is responsible".[331]

8–101   Stevedores, knowing that they had created a slippery area on a shop floor by spilling soda ash, owed a duty to the claimant who was also a licensee of the premises, not merely to warn him of the danger but also to take such reasonable steps as could be taken to protect him from injury caused by the danger they had created.[332] Where the Ministry of Fuel and Power, under statutory authority, entered a field, which was not in their occupation, in order to bore for coal and their contractors left a heap of timber, which injured the occupier's horse, both the Ministry and their contractors were liable.[333] A contractor, who was employed to destroy the existing safe means of access to a building and construct a new one, was liable when he left the access unsafe during the course of the work, so that a person coming to visit the caretaker of the building suffered injury.[334]

8–102   **Belief that danger will be removed.** A person who creates a danger may not be liable for damage resulting from it, if there are reasonable grounds for believing that the danger will be removed or guarded against by someone else.

---

[327] *Corby v Hill* (1858) 4 C.B.(N.S.) 556 (an example where a licensee may recover against another licensee); *Waring v East Anglian Flying Services Ltd* [1951] W.N. 55.
[328] *Brown v Cotterill* (1934) 51 T.L.R. 21.
[329] *Kimber v Gas Light & Coke Co* [1918] 1 K.B. 439 at 447. Because the claimant was not invited or licensed by the gas company to be on the premises, Scrutton L.J. described the defendant's duty as follows: "It is A's [the gas company's] duty to carry on his work with due precautions for the safety of those whom he knows, or ought reasonably to know, may be lawfully in the vicinity of this work; and the most obvious precaution would be to warn B, [the claimant] who is going towards the hidden danger A has created."
[330] *Canter v Gardner & Co* [1940] 1 All E.R. 325 at 332.
[331] *Hawkins v Thames Stevedore Co* [1936] 2 All E.R. 472 at 476, per Atkinson J.
[332] *Johnson v Rea Ltd* [1962] 1 Q.B. 373.
[333] *Darling v Attorney-General* [1950] 2 All E.R. 793.
[334] *A.C. Billings & Sons Ltd v Riden* [1958] A.C. 240.

Thus, a contractor, working in a dark passage, may usually assume that the occupier will light it.[335] On the other hand, if a person who creates a danger has no reasonable grounds for believing that someone else will remove it, he will be liable. In *Grant v Sun Shipping Co*,[336] a stevedore working on a ship fell into the hold through the open hatch covers, which were unlit. The hatch covers had been removed by repairers, who ought to have replaced them, but did not. The shipowners were held to be under a duty to the stevedore to take care to see that the hatch covers were replaced but, as between the repairers and the shipowners, it was the repairers' duty to replace the covers. The repairers were held liable to the stevedore and were not excused by the subsequent negligence of the ship-owners.[337]

Where a sub-contractor working on a building under construction left his work **8–103** in a safe condition, he was not liable when another sub-contractor or some other person did something to make his work unsafe.[338] Where the owner of a building went around the incompleted building alone, examining its construction, it was held that the builder was not liable for an accident when the owner slipped on a loose plank.[339]

Reliance on inspection. A person working on a building may not be liable for **8–104** damage caused by his work, if it has been inspected and approved. When contractors roofed in a passage and left a sole plate near a pillar, over which the claimant tripped as he was walking along the passage, they were not liable. Their contract was to work to the satisfaction of the employers, and the work had been inspected and passed by the employers' works supervisor.[340] On the other hand, "in the case of a danger concealed from the occupiers of premises and their licensees", for instance in the case of a balcony which a builder has been employed to repair, the fact that the work had been approved would not exonerate the contractor if it were badly done, the defects not being apparent.[341] This was the situation in *Hartley v Mayoh & Co*,[342] where the work of installing electricity in a factory was done by an Area Electricity Board, which negligently transposed some wires. The work was accepted but the occupiers did not know and were not negligent in failing to discover this serious fault. Hence the Board was liable when a fireman was electrocuted as a result of its electrician's negligent work.

---

[335] *Buckner v Ashby & Horner Ltd* [1941] 1 K.B. 321; *Milne v Smith* (1814) 2 Dow 390; 3 E.R. 905.

[336] [1948] A.C. 549.

[337] The shipowners were also liable, and damages were apportioned 75 per cent to the repairers, and 25 per cent to the shipowners.

[338] *Canter v Gardner & Co* [1940] 1 All E.R. 325.

[339] *Nabarro v Cope* [1938] 4 All E.R. 565.

[340] *Buckner v Ashby & Horner Ltd* [1941] 1 K.B. 321.

[341] *Buckner v Ashby & Horner Ltd* [1941] 1 K.B. 321 at 338, per Lord Goddard L.J. See also *Brown v Cotterill* (1934) 51 T.L.R. 21.

[342] [1954] 1 Q.B. 383 (the Board was held 90 per cent to blame and the occupiers 10 per cent for failing to know about their own main switch, which consisted of two tumbler switches, both of which required to be operated before all current was cut off).

6.—Liability of Vendors, Lessors, Builders and Local Authorities

(A) Liability at common law

8–105   Traditionally, apart from contract or implied[343] warranty, neither a vendor nor a lessor of property[344] was under any tortious liability for its dangerous condition once possession was given over to a purchaser or lessee.[345] In the case of a vendor who is not the builder of the property this traditional rule remains; but the law has developed in relation to lessors and also vendors who build and sell.[346]

8–106   **The lessor.** The general rule was that, apart from any express or implied contract,[347] a landlord was under no duty to his tenant, or any other person who entered the demised premises during the tenancy, to take care that the premises were safe, whether at the commencement of the tenancy or during its continuance.

> "A landlord who lets a house in a dangerous state is not liable to the tenant's customers or guests for accidents happening during the term; for, fraud apart, there is no law against letting a tumble-down house; and the tenants' remedy is upon his contract, if any".[348]

8–107   Accordingly, unless a tenant had an express contract that the landlord would keep the demised premises in repair, he had no remedy against the landlord if he were injured by reason of their lack of repair. The rule was well settled, in the case of the letting of unfurnished houses or flats, that there was no implied term of the contract on the part of the landlord that either the premises were fit for

---

[343] See *Brown v Norton* [1954] I.R. 34 for a review of the authorities dealing with implication of such a warranty. Later the courts began to lean in favour of the purchaser as in *Billyack v Leyland Construction Co Ltd* [1968] 1 W.L.R. 471. As to implied warranties in building contracts see *Young & Marten Ltd v McManus Childs Ltd* [1969] 1 A.C. 454 and *Gloucester County Council v Richardson* [1969] 1 A.C. 480; and see *Lynch v Thorne* [1956] 1 W.L.R. 303 (where the contract is for the sale of a house "when completed" there is an implied contract that the house shall be completed in such a way that it is fit for human habitation). See further condition 12(3) of the National Conditions of Sale.

[344] The house did not have to be a completed house at the time of sale. See *Perry v Sharon Development Co Ltd* [1937] 4 All E.R. 390. The landlord's immunity was not restricted to buildings but extended to all sorts of dangers created or arising on other types of property, such as fields and trees growing in them: *Cheater v Cater* [1918] 1 K.B. 247; *Shirvell v Hackwood Estates Co* [1938] 2 K.B. 577.

[345] *Robbins v Jones* (1863) 15 C.B.(N.S.) 221. See Ch.2, para.2–76, above. See also para.8–122, below, for exceptions under the Landlord and Tenant Act 1985, also *Otto v Bolton* [1936] 2 K.B. 46; *Ball v London County Council* [1949] 2 K.B. 159; *Habinteg Housing Association v James* [1994] N.P.C. 132, CA (lessor not under a duty of care to prevent infestation by cockroaches after the demise had taken place).

[346] As to builders see para.8–114 below.

[347] e.g. see *Sleafer v Lambeth Borough Council* [1960] 1 Q.B. 43. There will not be implied any obligation to carry out repairs merely because there is a right reserved to the lessor to enter to effect such repairs.

[348] per Erle C.J. in *Robbins v Jones* (1863) 145 C.B.(N.S.) 221. Further, see *Autoscooters (Newcastle) Ltd v Chambers* (1966) 197 E.G. 457.

habitation at the commencement of the letting,[349] or would be maintained in repair during the tenancy.

The letting of a furnished house or rooms was an exception to the general rule, **8–108** such an agreement containing an implied condition that the premises and furniture within them were fit for immediate occupation or use at the beginning of the tenancy. Should they not be so fit, the tenant could terminate the tenancy or sue for damages in respect of any injuries sustained or loss and damage suffered.[350]

At common law, the lease transferred all obligations towards third parties from **8–109** the landlord to the tenant. As a result, the landlord, who could no longer be regarded as the occupier of the demised premises, was exempted from liability for any dangers existing on them. This remained the situation even where the landlord had taken upon himself contractually the obligation of keeping the premises in repair. *Cavalier v Pope*[351] established that such a contract, being *res inter alios acta*, did not confer upon strangers to it any rights against the landlord which they would not have had in any event. Thus, the landlord's immunity was at one time complete and covered not only non-feasance such as his omission negligently to carry out repair[352] but also malfeasance, such as his negligence in installing an unventilated gas geyser in a bathroom, putting the user at great risk of carbon monoxide poisoning.[353] His immunity even extended to give protection in respect of negligent acts or omissions which had taken place before or after the demise.[354]

One of the first steps in the erosion of the immunity of a lessor from actions **8–110** in negligence was taken in *A.C. Billings & Sons v Riden*,[355] where the House of Lords overruled those decisions which had held the landlord immune from liability in respect of dangers he had positively created after the demise. Today the immunity has largely disappeared, principally in consequence of the legislation discussed below,[356] but it should be noted that while the decision in *Cavalier v Pope*[357] has been reversed as regards situations falling within the Acts

---

[349] *Hart v Windsor* (1844) 12 M. & W. 68; *Cruse v Mount* [1933] Ch. 278; *Manchester Bonded Warehouse Co v Carr* (1880) 5 C.P.D. 507. But for furnished house see *Smith v Marrable* (1843) 11 M. & W. 5; *Collins v Hopkins* [1923] 2 K.B. 617.
[350] *Collins v Hopkins*, above, where the house had recently been occupied by a person suffering from pulmonary tuberculosis.
[351] [1906] A.C. 428. The important distinction between the situation of a "bare landlord" and that of a landlord who is also the designer, builder and owner of the premises, needs to be drawn: see *Rimmer v Liverpool City Council* [1985] Q.B. 1, since in the case of a bare landlord the doctrine of *Cavalier v Pope* is still binding on the court; see *McNerny v Lambeth London Borough Council, The Times,* December 10, 1988, CA, and *Targett v Torfaen Borough Council* [1992] 3 All E.R. 27, CA.
[352] *Lane v Cox* [1897] 1 Q.B. 415; *Cavalier v Pope* [1906] A.C. 428.
[353] *Davis v Foots* [1940] 1 K.B. 116; *Travers v Gloucester Corp* [1947] K.B. 71.
[354] *Malone v Laskey* [1907] 2 K.B. 141; *Ball v London County Council* [1949] 2 K.B. 159.
[355] [1958] A.C. 240.
[356] The Defective Premises Act 1972 s.3, which removes a landlord's immunity regarding dangers created by him before the letting commenced. See paras 8–123 to 8–137, below.
[357] [1906] A.C. 428.

of 1957 and 1972, it is still the law where the facts fall outside their scope. As was pointed out in *Rimmer v Liverpool City Council*[358]:

> "section 4(1) of the Occupiers Liability Act 1957, and section 4(1) of the Defective Premises Act 1972, which replaced and extended it, imposed a liability only on landlords who are under an obligation to repair and maintain the tenant's premises and only for defects in maintenance and repair. Section 4(1) of the Act of 1957 limited a landlord's liability to default in carrying out his obligations for maintenance and repair; section 4(1) of the Act of 1972, while it extends the ambit of the duty to all persons who might reasonably be expected to be affected by defects in the premises, retains the limitation by defining defects in section 4(3) as those arising from an act or omission which constitutes a failure by the landlord to carry out his obligations for maintenance or repair. Neither of these sections imposed on a landlord any duty in respect of the state of a tenant's premises at the date of the letting".[359]

8–111   The liability of the lessor under the Occupier's Liability Act 1957 where the claimant has suffered damage on premises retained by the lessor in his own occupation has already been considered above.[360] The case of a claimant who suffers damage while on adjoining premises, as a result of the defective condition of premises retained by the lessor in his occupation is considered at the end of the Chapter.[361]

8–112   **Sellers who build and sell or let.** It was formerly thought that the principle in *Donoghue v Stevenson*[362] applied only to the manufacturers of chattels and therefore that a builder owed no duty outside contract to those injured by defects in a building he had constructed and then sold. The harsh results sometimes produced by this rule led to much anxiety on the part of judges required to give it effect. But, in *Murphy v Brentwood District Council*,[363] the House of Lords confirmed indications in earlier cases[364] that the principle in *Donoghue* should apply equally to realty as it applies to chattels and accordingly a remedy is given, but subject to important limitations.

8–113   The facts of *Murphy* have already been set out in Chapter 2.[365] In brief at this stage, the claimant was the unfortunate purchaser of a semi-detached house bought from the builders who had constructed it. Eleven years on, cracks appeared and he discovered that the raft foundation was defective. He brought an

---

[358] *Cavalier v Pope* [1906] A.C. 428.
[359] *Cavalier v Pope* [1906] A.C. 428 at 10. See also *Habinteg Housing Association v James* [1994] N.P.C. 132, CA (lessor not under a duty of care to prevent infestation by cockroaches after the demise had taken place).
[360] See *Wheat v Lacon & Co Ltd* [1966] 1 Q.B. 335 at 366. See also *Liverpool City Council v Irwin* [1977] A.C. 239 (where the landlords of multi-storey dwellings retain control of the common parts of the buildings, there is by necessary implication an obligation on them to take reasonable care to maintain the common stairs and their lighting, the lifts and the communal rubbish chutes in reasonable repair and that obligation can only be excluded by express exclusion in the contract of letting) para.8–20, above.
[361] See paras 8–161 to 8–171, below.
[362] [1932] A.C. 562.
[363] [1991] 1 A.C. 398.
[364] e.g. *D & F Estates Ltd v Church Commissioners for England* [1989] A.C. 177.
[365] See Ch.2, para.2–236 above.

action against the local authority responsible for approving the raft design for purposes of building regulations and byelaws. The basis of his claim was the imminent threat to his health and safety said to arise from damage to gas and soil pipes. He succeeded in recovering his loss on a resale of the house at first instance and in the Court of Appeal.

The House of Lords allowed the council's appeal but in so doing first **8–114** considered the liability of the builder. Lord Keith pointed out that the latency of the defect in question was a vital feature of the liability imposed in *Donoghue v Stevenson*. Accordingly, the principle in that case was not apt to establish the builder's responsibility where an occupier came to know of the defect before injury to himself or his property had arisen: "if the defect becomes apparent before any danger or damage has been caused, the loss sustained by the building owner is purely economic".[366] Such loss is not recoverable in tort in the absence of a special relationship of proximity.[367] For these purposes, the defect itself was not "injury to property" entitling a subsequent occupier to sue since to hold otherwise would be to give a cause of action for the cost of rectifying a defect which *ex hypothesi* was no longer latent.

In the result, there is a duty of care on a builder not to construct a building **8–115** containing a latent defect which renders it dangerous to persons or property. If he does so and subsequently sells or lets the property his liability depends upon the time at which the defect is found. If it is discovered before damage to person or property arises, it is to be approached only as a defect in quality, giving a right of action in contract where the loser is the person with whom the builder contracted. Where the defect is only discovered after damage to person or property has arisen, the builder will be liable in tort for such damage, to persons whom he ought to have had in contemplation as likely to suffer injury from his default.

So far as economic loss is concerned, the scope of the builder's duty is far **8–116** more circumscribed. In *Department of the Environment v Thomas Bates & Son*,[368] Lord Keith said:

"It was the unanimous view that, while the builder would be liable under the principle in *Donoghue v Stevenson* in the event of the defect, before it has been discovered, causing physical injury to persons or damage to property other than the building itself,

---

[366] per Lord Bridge at 475.
[367] per Lord Bridge at 475, also *Abbott v Will Gannon Smith* [2005] P.N.L.R. 562, CA per Tuckey L.J. at 567. In the latter case the CA rejected the submission that the building owner's cause of action for defective design arose when the building work to implement the design was performed, albeit no defect was apparent for some years later. The facts of *Pirelli General Cable Works Ltd v Oscar Faber & Partners* [1983] 2 A.C. 1 were indistinguishable and the owner's loss arose when physical damage occurred. Tuckey L.J. reviewed *Pirelli, Murphy* and *Ketteman v Hansel Propoerties Ltd* [1987] A.C. 189 and expressed regret that with three House of Lords authorities to provide guidance, the state of the law was not clearer.
[368] [1991] 1 A.C. 499, at 519, a case heard before, but decided after, the speeches read in *Murphy*.

there was no sound basis on principle for holding him liable for the pure economic loss suffered by a purchaser who discovered the defect, however such discovery might come about, and required to expend money in order to make the building safe and suitable for its intended purpose."

The distinction between damage to property and economic loss rising from damage to the structure of the building itself, is a significant one. In *Bellefield Computer Services Ltd v E. Turner and Sons Ltd*,[369] the builder of a dairy was liable to a subsequent owner for damage to the contents of the building caused when a fire spread over a faulty wall, but not for damage to the structure itself.

8–117   **Local authorities.** It is convenient to consider at this point the liability of a local authority with regard to the exercise of its supervisory powers in relation to dangerous buildings. It was at one time thought that a duty of care was owed by the authority supervising work for purposes of the building regulations to avoid putting any future inhabitant of a building under threat of avoidable injury to person or health by reason of any defect. This duty was elaborated in *Anns v Merton London Borough Council*[370] and a number of subsequent decisions.[371] It was then rejected by the House of Lords in *Murphy v Brentwood District Council*[372] some 13 years after it had received their approval.

8–118   In *Anns* it had been suggested that the local authority's duty of care arose from a test of reasonable foreseeability of injury coupled with the absence of any policy consideration tending to negative, reduce or limit the scope of the duty. Such a test was rejected in *Murphy*. It was criticised for introducing "a new species of liability governed by a principle indeterminate in character but having the potentiality of governing a wide range of situations, involving chattels as well as real property, in which it had never hitherto been thought that the law of negligence had any proper place".[373] In the result, it was concluded that *Anns* was wrongly decided: the claimants in that case, who were claiming for the cost of rectification of defects which it was said the council ought by proper

---

[369] [2000] N.P.C. 9, CA. See James, "Tortious liability for defective buildings" (1996) 3 P.N. 94.

[370] [1978] A.C. 728. In *Anns'* case the claimants were long lessees of seven dwellings built in 1962 by the owner/builders. Prior to construction, the local authority approved the building plans. By February 1970 subsidence had started to occur, causing cracks in the walls and other problems. It was alleged that builders had been negligent in failing to sink foundations to the depth prescribed by regulation and that these defects ought to have been discovered by the local authority's building inspector. Writs were issued against the builder and the local authority. On a preliminary point it was held that the local authority did owe duties of care to the claimants to consider whether an inspection should be carried out and, if it was, to ensure that the builder had complied with the bye-laws or building regulations.

[371] Such as *Dutton v Bognor Regis UDC* [1972] 1 Q.B. 373 (overruled). In *Investors in Industry Commercial Properties Ltd v South Bedfordshire DC* [1986] Q.B. 1034 at 1062, Slade L.J. summarised the state of the law as it then stood. See the discussion in the 8th edn of this book at para.7–109, see also Ch.2, paras 2–238 to 2–245, above.

[372] [1991] 1 A.C. 398.

[373] *Murphy v Brentwood District Council* [1991] 1 A.C. 398 per Lord Keith at 471.

inspection to have discovered, had suffered purely economic loss which could not be recovered.[374]

Their Lordships tore down the principle in *Anns* but resisted any temptation to **8–119** reconstruct by way of some new and general rule. They were careful to identify the circumstances in which the local authority would not be liable, without identifying when it would. It should be borne in mind that the argument of the appellant local authority was only concerned with the scope of its duty of care; it did not seek to argue that in fact it owed no duty at all. Lord Keith said that, for himself:

> "Not having heard argument upon the matter, I prefer to reserve my opinion on the question whether any duty at all exists. So far as I am aware, there has not yet been any case of claims against a local authority based on injury to the person or health through a failure to secure compliance with building byelaws. If and when such a case arises, that question may require further consideration".[375]

Lord Mackay of Clashfern L.C. reserved the question whether a council charged with the duty of supervising compliance with building regulations would be liable to an occupier of defective premises if a latent defect caused personal injury.[376] Other of their Lordships mentioned—without specifically adopting—a suggestion that the council's duty was coextensive with that of the builder, which would indicate liability if injury to person or property arose before a defect was discovered.[377] But ultimately they favoured leaving protection of the "consumer" in the kinds of situation under discussion to Parliament. And it is to Parliament's earlier interventions in the realm of dangerous buildings that we should now turn.

(B) Statutory liability

Landlord and Tenant Act 1985. By 1936 an exception to the rule denying **8–120** the tenant remedy if he was injured as a result of the landlord's failure to keep the premises in good repair had been introduced in the case of small houses.[378]

---

[374] See also *Governors of the Peabody Donation Fund v Sir Lindsay Parkinson & Co Ltd* [1985] A.C. 210 (local authority not liable to building owners for failure of an inspector to report upon a departure from an agreed design of drains since it was not just and reasonable to impose a duty of care upon the authority where the owners were themselves in default as a result of their reliance upon advice from their architects, engineers and contractors. Further the authority had not been granted its powers of inspection for the purpose of avoiding economic loss to building owners and so owed no duty to exercise them to that effect); also the *Investors in Industry* case, n.371, above (local authority approved working drawings of the foundations of certain warehouses and approved the foundation bases, seen on site in the excavated trenches before they were filled in, although subsequently the foundations proved totally inadequate and the buildings had to be re-built). In Scotland it has been held that a local authority which inspected a negligently designed building in discharging duties under the building standards regulations, owed no duty of care to the proprietors of an adjacent building damaged by the defects: *Armstrong v Moore*, 1996 S.L.T. 690, OH.

[375] [1991] 1 A.C. 398 at 463G.

[376] [1991] 1 A.C. 398 at 457.

[377] See [1991] 1 A.C. 398, e.g. Lord Bridge at 479.

[378] Housing Act 1936 Pt 1.

The modern successor is the Landlord and Tenant Act 1985, a consolidating statute, s.8(1) of which provides:

> "In a contract to which this section applies for the letting of a house for human habitation there is implied, notwithstanding any stipulation to the contrary—
>
> (a) a condition that the house is fit for human habitation at the commencement of the tenancy, and
> (b) an undertaking that the house will be kept by the landlord fit for human habitation during the tenancy."

This does not apply to a letting for not less than three years without the option of determination during the term, where it is agreed that the house shall be put by the tenant into a condition reasonably fit for human habitation. It does however apply to a house which is occupied by an agricultural worker as part of his remuneration and not as tenant. In testing fitness for habitation,

> "regard shall be had to its condition in respect of repair, stability, freedom from damp, internal arrangement, natural lighting, ventilation, water supply, drainage and sanitary conveniences, facilities for preparation and cooking of food, and for the disposal of waste water."

The question is then whether a house is so far defective in one of these respects that it is not reasonably fit for occupation.

ILLUSTRATIONS

8–121   It has been held that there was no breach of the statutory condition: where a house was invaded from time to time by rats[379]; if a common staircase, not included in the letting, was in an unsafe condition[380]; when the hot water system was out of order but the house had alternative means of heating water, such as a gas cooker, and the gas and electricity systems were in working order.[381] A defective sash cord was a breach of the condition,[382] and so was a defective step leading from the kitchen to the back kitchen.[383] The landlord must have notice of the defect before he can be made liable.[384]

---

[379] *Stanton v Southwick* [1920] K.B. 642. Lord Wright in *Summers v Salford Corp* [1943] A.C. 283 at 295, disagreed with this decision.

[380] *Dunster v Hollis* [1918] 2 K.B. 795, which was based on *Miller v Hancock* [1893] 2 Q.B. 177. Whilst *Miller*, as a claim by a visitor, has been overruled in *Fairman v Perpetual Investment Building Society* [1923] A.C. 74, passages in the judgment of the CA, concerning the position as between landlord and tenant were approved by the HL in *Liverpool City Council v Irwin* [1977] A.C. 239. For the meaning of the expression "unfit for human habitation" see *Hall v Manchester Corp* (1915) 84 L.J.Ch. 732; *Estate and Trust Agencies Ltd v Singapore Improvement Trust* [1937] A.C. 898; *Bole v Huntsbuild Ltd* [2009] EWCA Civ 1146, para.8–126, below.

[381] *Daly v Elstree Rural District Council* [1948] 2 All E.R. 1.

[382] *Summers v Salford Corp* [1943] A.C. 283.

[383] *McCarrick v Liverpool Corp* [1947] A.C. 219; *O'Brien v Robinson* [1973] 1 All E.R. 583.

[384] *O'Brien v Robinson* [1973] 1 All E.R. 583.

Section 11 of the Act, which applies to most lettings of residential accom-   **8–122**
modation, implies a covenant to keep in repair the structure and exterior of the
dwelling-house including drains, gutters, and external pipes. Again a breach of
covenant can only be made out if the landlord has notice of the defect.[385] The
steps and path of a house can be part of the structure and exterior so as to render
a council liable to its tenant, who tripped when they were in a state of disrepair.[386]

The Defective Premises Act 1972. This Act, which came into force on   **8–123**
January 1, 1974, gave effect to recommendations of the Law Commission,[387] and
was intended to achieve four principal aims: (i) to impose a duty on anyone
taking on work in connection with the provision of a dwelling[388] as to the proper
carrying out of that work; (ii) to abolish the caveat emptor rule; (iii) to enlarge
the statutory duty of care imposed on a landlord by virtue of his obligation or
right to repair demised premises; and (iv) to render void any term of an
agreement, purporting to exclude or restrict the obligations imposed by the Act.
Each of these is considered separately below.

(i) *Duty to build dwellings*[389] *properly*

Section 1(1) of the Act provides that: **8–124**

"A person taking on work[390] for or on connection with[391] the provision of a dwelling
(whether the dwelling is provided by the erection or by the conversion or enlargement
of a building) owes a duty—

    (a) if the dwelling is provided to the order of any person, to that person; and
    (b) without prejudice to paragraph (a) above, to every person who acquires an
        interest (whether legal or equitable) in the dwelling;

to see that the work which he takes on is done in a workmanlike or, as the case may be,
professional manner, with proper materials and so that as regards that work the dwelling
will be fit for habitation when completed."

---

[385] *O'Brien v Robinson* [1973] 1 All E.R. 583.
[386] *Brown v Liverpool Corp* [1969] 3 All E.R. 1345.
[387] *The Civil Liability of Vendors and Lessors for Defective Premises* (No.40), 1970.
[388] The term dwelling, which is not defined in the Act, implies a building, used or capable of being
used as a residence by one or more families, that is provided with all necessary parts and appliances,
including things such as floors, windows, staircases, etc.
[389] In *Catlin Estates Ltd v Carter Jones* [2006] P.N.L.R. 273 a shooting lodge on the Burnhope and
Ousby moor, Co. Durham was regarded as a "dwelling" for purposes of s.1(1) of the 1972 Act, where
it was a building used or capable of being used as a dwellinghouse, and was not used predominantly
for commercial or industrial purposes.
[390] The words "taking on work" had their natural meaning and could not be construed as meaning
"doing work": *Alexander v Mercouris* [1979] 1 W.L.R. 1270; also *Mirza v Bhandal, The
Independent*, June 14, 1999 (a clear line has to be drawn between an owner who contracts for a house
to be provided and those who "take on work" in connection with the provision of a dwelling).
[391] See the comments of Lord Denning M.R. on these words in *Sparham-Souter v Town and Country
Developments (Essex) Ltd* [1976] Q.B. 858 at 870, which he thought would give rise to much
debate.

8–125   The duty applies to builders,[392] sub-contractors and professionals such as architects, surveyors and engineers, who take on work of the nature described, and upon developers, local authorities and others, who arrange for building contractors and other tradesmen to take on such work.[393] On the other hand, a valuer, acting simply within that capacity, would not be liable, assuming negligence, since a dwelling would not have been "provided" within the meaning of the subsection. The duty under s.1 does not apply to cases where the Secretary of State has approved a scheme which protects a purchaser.[394] Any person who takes on work to be done in accordance with instructions given him by another person is excluded from liability, provided that the particular work is done properly, in accordance with these instructions, and provided that he has discharged any duty he owes to that other to warn him of any relevant defects in the instructions.[395]

8–126   In *Alexander v Mercouris*,[396] it was held that the duty imposed by the statute arose at either the date of the agreement to take on the work or, at the latest, the date of commencement of such work. The quality to be achieved is not "fitness for purpose" but "fitness for habitation",[397] the meaning of which has already been discussed in relation to the provisions of the 1972 Act.[398]

8–127   Since there can be no difference between acts of commission and acts of omission in law, it has been held that s.1 of the Act applies equally to the failure to carry out remedial work, as well as to the carrying out of such work badly.[399]

(ii) *Abolition of caveat emptor rule*

8–128   Section 3 of the Act removed the special immunity from liability for negligent acts committed *before* the sale or letting, which was enjoyed at common law by vendors or lessors of land. Its effect is to provide that anyone who does work of

---

[392] The Act "is intended to apply not only to cases in which a contractual obligation to work exists, but also to cases in which the work may be done without contractual obligation but in circumstances in which he who does the work could claim reward on the basis of *quantum meruit*, to cases in which the work is done voluntarily without expectation of gain and, perhaps most importantly, to cases in which a building owner does the work himself": *Alexander v Mercouris* [1979] 1 W.L.R. 1270, per Buckley L.J. at 1273.

[393] s.1(4). It must follow that a main contractor may well be under a statutory duty to a purchaser or future tenant of the dwelling to see that a sub-contractor's work is carried out properly. See *D. & F. Estates Ltd v Church Commissioners for England* (1987) 3 P.N. 129 at 138 per Glidewell L.J., obiter. See also *Strathford East Kilbride Ltd v Film Design Ltd, The Times*, December 1, 1997, OH.

[394] s.2.

[395] s.1(2).

[396] [1979] 1 W.L.R. 1270, CA.

[397] *Bole v Huntsbuild Ltd* [2009] EWCA Civ 1146 (cracks in the foundations of a house: the necessity for the claimants to vacate the building for about twelve months was said to be a highly relevant indicator that the defects rendered the dwelling unfit for habitation).

[398] See para.8–121, above.

[399] *Andrews v Schooling* [1991] 1 W.L.R. 783, CA.

construction, repair, maintenance or demolition or other work to premises,[400] will have equivalent liability in negligence if the premises are later sold, let, or otherwise disposed of, to any builder or architect who was negligent in carrying out work on or in connection with a client or other persons' premises. At common law, a person who did such work was under a duty to take reasonable care to avoid injury to persons whom he might reasonably anticipate would be affected by defects in the state of the land or buildings, arising as a result of such work.[401] Accordingly, a vendor or lessor will continue to be under such a duty, after his occupation or control of the premises has ceased, and the duty will no longer cease once the premises have been sold or leased.[402]

It should be noted that the section abolished the lessor's or vendor's immunity **8–129** only in respect of malfeasance,[403] where the danger has been created on "premises"[404] by a work of "construction, repair, maintenance, or demolition or any other work".[405] Views to the contrary in *Dutton v Bognor Regis Council*[406] notwithstanding, it would appear that the immunity for non-feasance remains at common law.

(iii) *The enlargement of the lessors' duty of care*

Section 4 of the Act replaced s.4 of the Occupiers' Liability Act 1957.[407] The **8–130** section provides that a landlord's duty of care, where premises[408] are let under a tenancy,[409] which puts on him an obligation to the tenant for their maintenance or repair, extends not only to visitors, but to all persons who might reasonably be expected to be affected by defects in the state of the premises. The landlord's statutory duty of care, which is not the same as an occupiers' duty[410] under the 1957 Act, is "a duty to take such care as is reasonable in all the circumstances

---

[400] The term "premises" has not been defined in the Act. Although originally possessing a very limited meaning, i.e. the parts of a deed antecedent to the habendum, it is widely used today in the popular sense as including land, houses, buildings: *Metropolitan Water Board v Paine* [1907] 1 K.B. 285; *Whitley v Stumbles* [1930] A.C. 544 at 547; easements and other incorporeal hereditaments appurtenant to land. See further *Maunsell v Olins* [1975] A.C. 373 regarding the difficulties which arose in deciding whether a cottage formed part of the "premises" of a farm.
[401] *Clay v A.J. Crump & Sons Ltd* [1964] 1 Q.B. 533.
[402] *Otto v Bolton and Norris* [1936] 2 K.B. 46 has been overruled, as a result.
[403] i.e. a careless omission to carry out some essential repair is not included.
[404] See n.400, above.
[405] s.3(1).
[406] [1972] 1 Q.B. 373. See comments by the HL in *Anns v Merton London Borough Council* [1978] A.C. 728.
[407] Which latter section is duly repealed by s.6(4) of the 1972 Act.
[408] The word "premises" was wide enough to cover all of the letting and, thus, included the rear concrete yard, which was dignified by being called a "patio": *Smith v Bradford Metropolitan Council* (1982) 126 S.J. 624.
[409] Defined by s.6(1) as: "(a) a tenancy created either immediately or derivatively out of the freehold, whether by a lease or underlease, by an agreement for a lease or underlease or by a tenancy agreement, but not including a mortgage term or any interest arising in favour of a mortgagor by his attorning tenant to his mortgagee; or (b) a tenancy at will or a tenancy on sufferance; or (c) a tenancy, whether or not constituting a tenancy at common law, created by or in pursuance of any enactment; and cognate expressions shall be construed accordingly." In addition s.4, by its subs.(6), "applies to a right of occupation given by contract or any enactment and not amounting to a tenancy as if the right were a tenancy . . . ".
[410] Indeed, it is considerably more burdensome.

to see that such persons[411] are reasonably safe from personal injury[412] or from damage to their property caused by a relevant defect".[413] This duty cannot be excluded or restricted,[414] unlike the common duty of care under the 1957 Act, which, in certain circumstances, can be. It is extended to apply to cases where the landlord has a right, whether express or implied,[415] to enter premises to carry out any description of maintenance or repair but has no obligation to do so.[416]

8–131   Nevertheless, under these provisions, the landlord is only liable for damage *caused* by a relevant defect, which is defined by subs.(3) as meaning:

> "a defect in the state of the premises existing at or after the material time and arising from, or continuing because of, an act or omission by the landlord which constitutes or would if he had had notice of the defect, have constituted a failure by him to carry out his obligation to the tenant for the maintenance or repair of the premises; and for the purposes of the foregoing provision 'the material time' means:
>
> > (a) where the tenancy commenced before this Act, the commencement of this Act[417]; and
> > (b) in all other cases, the earliest of the following times, that is to say—
> >
> > > (i) the time when the tenancy commences;
> > > (ii) the time when the tenancy agreement is entered into;
> > > (iii) the time when possession is taken of the premises in contemplation of the letting."

8–132   The landlord's liability therefore depends upon his express or implied contractual "obligations" to repair. Importantly, the section did not reproduce subs.(4) of the 1957 Act, which confined a landlord's liability to those cases where default was actionable at the suit of the occupier,[418] thereby importing the requirement of actual notice of the defect given by the occupier to the landlord.[419] Indeed, the submission that s.4 does not impose any greater liability than s.11 of the Landlord and Tenant Act 1985, which requires notice of the defect before liability can be established, has been rejected. Liability follows if

---

[411] Who would include the passer-by on the public highway, as well as those exercising a private right of way, the neighbour in his garden, an entrant under the National Parks and Access to the Countryside Act 1949, and even trespassers, whose presence ought reasonably to be foreseen.

[412] Defined by s.6(1) as including: "any disease and any impairment of a person's physical or mental condition."

[413] s.4(1).

[414] s.6(3).

[415] For implication of terms see para.8–108, above. Where there was a defect which exposed the tenant to a significant risk of injury, in the absence of an express right to enter and carry out repairs, an implied right of the landlords to do so must be found in order to give business efficacy to the tenancy agreement: *McAuley v Bristol City Council* [1992] Q.B. 134, CA following *Mint v Good* [1951] 1 K.B. 517.

[416] s.4(4).

[417] Namely, January 1, 1974; s.7(2).

[418] This requirement was considered to have been too restrictive and was avoided deliberately, when the Law Commission drafted its proposals, which have been reproduced in s.4(2) of the Act, namely: "the said duty is owed if the landlord knows (whether as a result of being notified by the tenant or otherwise) or if he ought in all the circumstances to have known of the relevant defect."

[419] *West v R.C. Glaze (Properties) Ltd* (1970) 215 E.G. 921; *O'Brien v Robinson* [1973] A.C. 912.

there is a relevant defect and a landlord fails to take such care as reasonable in all the circumstances to see that the claimant is safe from personal injury.[420]

It must be noted that for there to be a "relevant defect" the landlord must be in breach of an "obligation to the tenant for the maintenance or repair of the premises".[421] For these purposes the meaning of "obligation" is extended by subs.(4), the effect of which is that, for the purposes of subss.(1) to (3) only, a landlord's powers of re-entry to carry out repairs are the equivalent of his obligation so to do; also by subs.(5), which provides: "for the purposes of this section obligations imposed or rights given by any enactment in virtue of a tenancy shall be treated as imposed or given by the tenancy." **8–133**

A duty to maintain and repair should not be equated with a duty to make safe. Moreover, a duty to keep in good condition, even if it encompasses a duty to put in good condition at the outset of the tenancy, does not encompass a duty to put in safe condition[422]

It was held that the owners of a Victorian house, built in or about 1896, and having a staircase which, by contemporary standards, would not conform with the Building Regulations, were not liable to their tenant, who fell on its steps. No accident or any significant injury had previously been reported and it was not reasonable to expect a prudent landlord to keep the house empty pending complete reconstruction of the stairs to comply with current requirements.[423] **8–134**

(iv) *The avoidance of exclusion or restriction*

Section 6(3) of the Act provides that: "any term of an agreement which purports to exclude or restrict, or has the effect of excluding or restricting, the operation of any of the provisions of this Act, or any liability arising by virtue of any such provision, shall be void." **8–135**

When a cause of action accrues. Section 1(5) of the Defective Premises Act 1972 provides that for the purpose of the Limitation Acts[424] any cause of action in respect of a breach of the duty imposed under that section, accrues[425]: **8–136**

" . . . at the time when the dwelling was completed but if after that time a person who has done work for or in connection with the provision of the dwelling does further work to rectify the work he has already done, any such cause of action in respect of that further work shall be deemed for those purposes to have accrued at the time when the further work was finished."

---

[420] *Sykes v Harry, The Times*, February 27, 2001, CA (a tenant suffered carbon monoxide poisoning from a defective gas fire).

[421] s.4(3).

[422] *Alker v Collingwood Housing Association* [2007] 1 W.L.R. 2230, CA (the tenant was injured when the annealed glass plane in her front door broke as she pushed upon it, but her claim under s.4 failed because, notwithstanding such glass had been regarded as unsafe since 1963, there was no want of maintenance or repair and the landlord was not under a duty to make the premises reasonably safe).

[423] *McDonagh v Kent Area Health Authority* (1984) 134 New L.J. 567.

[424] Now the Limitation Act 1980.

[425] For limitation of actions, generally, see Ch.4, paras 4–137 to 4–226, above.

8–137 The effect of these words was considered in *Alderson v Beetham Organisation Ltd.*[426] At the time a conversion of flats was completed in May 1994 the developer was in breach of duty in that no adequate damp proofing was provided. Work was carried out in May 1995 to rectify ensuing damp problems by relaying paving stones and providing new drainage pipes. Subsequently, a tenant suffered damage as a result of dampness and when proceedings were issued in January 2001 the developer argued that they were out of time, more than six years having elapsed since completion of the conversion work. In the result, s.1(5) was held to apply to all further work carried out to rectify the original work. It was right that the further work was not to the damp proofing, but it was dampness which had rendered the flats unfit for habitation and a fresh cause of action arose where the later work did not rectify the original work as intended.

7.—LIABILITY TO TRESPASSERS

(A) The common law before 1984

8–138 **Definition of trespasser.** A trespasser is one who wrongfully enters on land in the possession of another and has neither right nor permission to be there. He is one "who gets on the land without invitation of any sort and whose presence is either unknown to the proprietor or, if known, is practically objected to."[427] The term, "trespasser," although emotive, is comprehensive: it "covers the wicked and the innocent: the burglar,[428] the arrogant invader of another's land, the walker, blithely unaware that he is stepping where he has no right to walk or the wandering child . . . "[429]

8–139 A trespasser can be distinguished from a lawful visitor in two main respects. First, " . . . he has no right to enter on the land, or, having entered, to remain there". Secondly,

> " . . . so long as he is an unknown and merely possible trespasser, his presence and his movements are unpredictable. The lawful visitor, coming and remaining as of right, is expected to come and be there, also he is likely to come at a normal hour, and to enter by the proper entrance, and to go to, and normally to remain at, the part of the premises where he has business or with which he is concerned. By contrast, the unknown and merely possible trespasser may come at any time or may never come at all; if he does come, he may walk, break, creep or climb into the premises at any place and go by any route to any part of the premises and remain for any length of time."[430]

8–140 It may not always be easy to draw the necessary distinction between a person who enters lawfully, having at least tacit permission from the occupier, and a trespasser. When a householder lives in a dwelling-house to which there is

---

[426] *The Times*, April 19, 2003, CA.
[427] *Robert Addie & Sons (Collieries) Ltd v Dumbreck* [1929] A.C. 358 at 371, per Lord Dunedin.
[428] e.g. The Theft Act 1968 s.9. See *Revill v Newbery* [1996] 2 W.L.R. 239, CA and para.8–158, below.
[429] *Herrington v British Railways Board* [1972] A.C. 877 at 904, per Lord Morris.
[430] *Videan v British Transport Commission* [1963] 2 Q.B. 650 at 679, per Pearson L.J.

attached a garden and does not lock the garden gate, in the absence of any notice prohibiting entry, "it gives an implied licence to any member of the public who has lawful reason for doing so to proceed from the gate to the front door or back door, and to inquire whether he may be admitted and to conduct his lawful business."[431] Such members of the public will include police officers,[432] postmen, milkmen, commercial travellers, canvassers,[433] hawkers and beggars. It would seem, therefore, that a person does not become a trespasser if he were to enter premises for the purpose of holding some sort of communication with the occupier or other occupants,[434] unless he knows or has reason to believe that his entry is forbidden. However, any implied licence for a person to walk up the path to the doorstep does not give that person the right further to enter the house itself or other premises.[435]

The Occupiers' Liability Act 1957 did not alter the common law affecting **8–141** trespassers. The rules were long established, although the modern history might be said to begin in 1929[436] with the decision in *Robert Addie & Sons (Collieries) Ltd v Dumbreck*.[437] It was considered that since a trespasser came onto to the premises at his own risk, an occupier should be liable for injury to him, arising from the state of the premises, where that injury was due to a wilful act involving something more than the absence of reasonable care. There had to be some act done with the deliberate intention of doing harm to the trespasser, or at least with reckless disregard for his presence. This remained the position over the next 30 years.

In 1972, in *Herrington v British Railways Board*,[438] the House of Lords **8–142** departed from the earlier law. The plaintiff was a child aged six who had sustained serious burns after trespassing on an electrified railway line. There was evidence, of which the defendants were aware, that a gap in fencing was being used to give a short cut across the line. Nothing had been done to effect a repair. In deciding that the occupiers were liable their applied a test described in various terms: Lord Reid said the occupier's duty towards trespassers required him to do that which was humane or decent[439]; Lord Pearson that a trespasser should be treated with ordinary humanity[440]; and Lord Morris of Borth-y-Gest that such steps should be taken as ordinary thought and intelligence, exercising common sense would dictate.[441]

---

[431] *Robson v Hallett* [1967] 2 Q.B. 939 at 953, 954, per Diplock L.J.
[432] ibid.
[433] *Dunster v Abbott* [1954] 1 W.L.R. 58 (a canvasser, who called on the defendant, a builder, in order to sell him advertising space on the covers of telephone directories).
[434] *Christian v Johannesson* [1956] N.Z.L.R. 664.
[435] *Robson v Hallett* [1967] 2 Q.B. 939 at 954, per Diplock L.J.
[436] For a fuller account, see either the 5th (1971) or earlier editions of *Charlesworth on Negligence*. See also leading articles such as Hart, (1931) 47 L.Q.R. 92; Goodhart, (1963) 79 L.Q.R. 586; Goodhart, (1964) 80 L.Q.R. 559; Samuels, (1964) 27 M.L.R. 88 and 464; Atiyah, (1965) 81 L.Q.R. 186; Fleming (1966) 82 L.Q.R. 25.
[437] [1929] A.C. 358 per Lord Hailsham L.C. at 365.
[438] *Herrington v British Railways Board* [1972] A.C. 877.
[439] [1972] A.C. 877 at 899.
[440] ibid at 927.
[441] [1972] A.C. 877 at 909.

8–143   There was criticism of these tests as vague and uncertain in application. After further[442] reference to the Law Commission, a report was published in 1976,[443] which led eventually to the Occupiers' Liability Act 1984.[444]

(B) The Occupiers' Liability Act 1984

8–144   **Introduction.** The Occupiers' Liability Act 1984[445] came into force on May 13, 1984. Although its principal effect is in relation to trespassers, it is expressed as governing the relationship between an occupier of premises and "persons other than his visitors",[446] so its application is not simply to trespassers. It could apply, for instance, to people who enter land without consent but with lawful authority, for example in exercise of a private right of way,[447] or of a right of public access conferred by the National Parks and Access to the Countryside Act 1949.[448] On the other hand, the Act does not extend to persons using the highway, whether or not it is maintained at public expense.[449]

8–145   The meanings of "occupier of premises" and "visitor" are the same in both the 1957 and 1984 Acts.[450] There is also a similarity of wording, in that the duty imposed on the occupier is owed "in respect of any risk of their suffering injury on the premises by reason of any danger due to the state of the premises or to things done or omitted to be done on them".[451]

8–146   **The state of the premises.** These words have already been discussed in relation to the 1957 Act. A distinction is drawn between features of the land which are obvious and not in themselves dangerous, and dangerous activities carried out in or on them. In *Tomlinson v Congleton Borough Council*,[452] a

---

[442] The Law Reform Committee's Third Report (Law Com. No.52), Cmnd. 9305 (1954) recommended by a majority that there should be no change in the law as regards trespassers.

[443] *Report on Liability for Damage or Injury to Trespassers and Related Questions of Occupiers' Liability* (Law Com. No.75), Cmnd. 6428.

[444] Extracts from the Law Reform Committee's Report, summarising the options it saw, are set out in the 9th edn of this work at paras 7–155—7–156.

[445] c.3, s.4.

[446] Occupiers' Liability Act 1984 s.1(1)(a).

[447] *Greenhalgh v British Railways Board* [1969] 2 Q.B. 286; *Holden v White* [1982] Q.B. 679. See further para.8–32, above. See *Vodden v Gayton and Gayton* [2001] P.I.Q.R. P52, CA, for discussion of the alternative view that, having regard to his lack of control over the land, the owner of the servient tenement cannot be regarded as in control of land over which a right of way exists. On the facts of the case that view was rejected by the judge.

[448] c.97, s.60(1).

[449] Occupiers' Liability Act 1984 s.1(7).

[450] See s.1(2), which adopts and incorporates these same meanings from the 1957 Act. For "premises", see para.8–03; "occupier", see para.8–17; "visitor", see para.8–23 all above respectively.

[451] s.1(1)(a). These words compare with s.1(1) of the 1957 Act which provides that the "common duty of care" regulates the duty which an occupier of premises owes to his visitors "in respect of dangers due to the state of the premises or to things done or omitted to be done on them". See further para.8–10, above. Note that s.13 of the Countryside and Rights of Way Act 2000, in relation to land which is "access land" for purposes of the Act, modifies the duties contained in s.1 of the 1984 Act. See generally, Schaw Miller, "Access land and occupiers' liability" 2004 R.W.L.R. (11), 59.

[452] [2004] 1 A.C. 46. See particularly the discussion in the speech of Lord Hoffmann at 78 onwards. See also Braithwaite Q.C., "Disastrous diving" 147 S.J. 984.

shallow lake was not in itself dangerous, although diving into it created a risk. For similar reasons the occupiers of a building in hospital grounds were not liable to a trespassing child, aged almost 12, who climbed upon the underside of a fire ecape attached to the building and fell: the fire escape was a normal example of its type, and the danger arose from the claimant's activity in climbing on it, rather than from the state of the premises.[453] The reasoning in *Tomlinson* was applied in a claim for catastrophic injuries sustained when the claimant dived into an hotel swimming pool that was too shallow for that activity. It was observed that the core principle was that "people should accept responsibility for the risks they choose to run" and there was no duty to protect them against obvious risks (subject to qualification where there was no informed choice or some lack of capacity). It was applicable both to lawful visitors under the 1957 Act and trespassers under the 1984 Act and was also to persons entering premises such as an hotel under a package holiday contract of the type in the instant case.[454]

When the duty under the statute arises. An occupier owes a duty to **8–147** trespassers[455] and/or other uninvited entrants under the Act, if a number of conditions are satisfied. First, there must be in existence a risk of an entrant suffering injury on the premises, as described above.[456] The reference to "injury" in this context means "anything resulting in death or personal injury, including any disease and any impairment of physical or mental condition".[457] By s.1(3), the occupier owes a duty to uninvited entrants in respect of any such risk as aforesaid, only:

"if—(a) he is aware of the danger or has reasonable grounds to believe that it exists[458]; (b) he knows or has reasonable grounds to believe that the other is in the vicinity of the danger concerned or that he may come into the vicinity of the danger (in either case, whether the other has lawful authority for being in that vicinity or not); and (c) the risk is one against which, in all the circumstances of the case, he may reasonably be expected to offer the other some protection."

---

[453] *Keown v Coventry Healthcare NHS Trust* [2006] 1 W.L.R. 953, CA. See also *Siddorn v Patel* [2007] EWHC 1248 (Q.B.), Sir John Blofeld, (the claimant's fall through a skylight was as a result of her decision to engage in the activity of dancing on a flat roof in the vicinity of the skylight, at night, when not wholly sober, rather than the dangerous state of the premises). See Pawlowski, "Dizzy heights and occupiers' liability" L. Ex. 2007, Aug, 26.

[454] *Evans v Kosmar Villa Holiday Plc* [2008] 1 W.L.R. 297, CA, especially per Richards L.J. at [39].

[455] In *Donoghue v Folkestone Properties Ltd*, n.461, above, reservations were expressed whether someone who ignored a prohibition against swimming thereby became a trespasser where what was at issue was whether steps should have been taken to prevent his entering the lake, that is whether a duty was owed to him *before* he did the unauthorised act.

[456] i.e. "by reason of any danger due to the state of the premises or to things done or omitted to be done on them" s.1(1)(a), above. Per Stuart-Smith L.J. in *Ratcliff v McConnell* [1999] 1 W.L.R. 670 at 680, "it is important to identify the risk or danger concerned . . . "

[457] ibid. s.1(9). It is to be observed, therefore, that the trespasser or other uninvited entrant cannot maintain any claim for damages to property, unlike the lawful visitor under the 1957 Act's provisions, where there is no such restriction. However, a personal injury claim under the 1984 Act can, of course, include the normal claim for damages for consequential financial losses, past, present and future.

[458] See *Rhind v Astbury Water Park Ltd*, *The Independent*, June 25, 2004, CA (liability was not established where the claimant dived into a mere used for recreational purposes and hit his head on a fibreglass container, which, unknown to the defendant, was lying on the bottom covered in silt).

8–148   For purposes of s.1(3)(b) the occupiers' knowledge or grounds for belief are to be judged by reference to the state of affairs actually in existence at the time injury is sustained.[459] Actual knowledge of facts from which it may be inferred the defendant had reasonable grounds for belief must be shown for liability to attach.[460]

8–149   The operation of s.1(3)(b) of the Act was considered in *Donoghue v Folkestone Properties Ltd.*[461] The claimant, a professional diver, who had been drinking but was not drunk, dived from a slipway into Folkestone harbour shortly after midnight on December 27, 1997. He struck his head on an underwater obstruction, broke his neck, and was rendered tetraplegic. He sued the defendant, as owner and occupier of the harbour, relying upon a breach of duty owed to him under the Occupiers' Liability Act 1984. The judge at first instance held the defendant liable but an appeal was allowed.

8–150   It was pointed out that under s.1(3)(b) it was not necessary for an occupier to have personal knowledge of particular individuals who may come into the vicinity of the danger. It is enough for purposes of the subsection if the trespasser could show he was one of a class of persons whom the occupier had reason to believe might be in the vicinity of the danger. If that requirement was satisfied it was necessary to consider whether any duty was owed to the particular member of the class who had suffered injury. In determining the question regard must be had to the circumstances prevailing at the time it is alleged that the breach of duty resulted in injury to the claimant. In *Donoghue*, at the time the claimant suffered his injury, the defendant had no reason to believe that he or anyone else would be swimming in the slipway and the criterion in s.1(3)(b) was not satisfied.

8–151   **The standard of care.** Once a duty of care has arisen, then the standard of care is to "take such care as is reasonable in all the circumstances of the case to see that [the entrant] does not suffer injury on the premises by reason of the danger concerned".[462] This statutory definition substitutes a subjective test for the objective test which emerged in *Herrington*. Accordingly, matters such as an occupier's wealth, "ability and resources"[463] or impecuniosity are not relevant in determining liability. It is otherwise so far as the individual characteristics of the claimant are concerned. Since the occupier's duty is owed to the individual claimant, his or her characteristics should be considered. The question is what

---

[459] See *White v St Albans City & DC, The Times*, March 12, 1990, CA. See Sproull, "Trespass impasse" 148 S.J. 1136.

[460] *Swain v Puri* [1996] P.I.Q.R. P442, CA (claim of child injured while trespassing on a factory roof failed in the absence of evidence of previous trespass at the site). per Evans L.J. at P448: actual knowledge includes "shut-eye" knowledge, but not constructive knowledge. See also *Higgs v Foster* [2004] EWCA Civ 843 (simply because premises were easy to enter was insufficient basis for a finding under s.1(3)(b) in favour of a police officer, who fell into an uncovered inspection pit while trespassing within premises in the course of an investigation into a suspected stolen vehicle).

[461] [2003] 2 W.L.R. 1138, CA.

[462] s.1(4). per Lord Phillips in *Donoghue v Folkestone Properties Ltd*, n.461 above, at [54], the "other" in s.1(3) is the same person as "another" in s.1(4), namely the very individual who has sustained injury and in respect of whom the issue under consideration has arisen.

[463] *Herrington v British Railways Board* [1972] A.C. 877 at 899.

should reasonably have been done to protect *this particular claimant*, not trespassers generally.[464]

What amounts to "such care as in all the circumstances of the case is **8–152** reasonable" depends upon assessing, as with common law negligence, not only the likelihood that someone may be injured and the seriousness of the injury which may occur, but also the social value of the activity which gives rise to the risk and the cost of preventative measures. The various factors have to be balanced against each other.[465] In deciding what is reasonable it should be born in mind that where dangers are obvious, local authorities and other occupiers are under no duty to protect irresponsible visitors from them, where costs would thereby be incurred and access to land which provides an amenity to others prevented.[466] A balance has also to be struck between the risk inherent in some particular use of land and the individual's freedom to decide whether to incur that risk.[467]

In many claims brought against an occupier by an uninvited entrant on his **8–153** premises, there will be little distinction from a claim by a lawful visitor under the 1957 Act. But, where there is a difference, it is likely to lie in establishing foreseeability of the presence of the trespasser, which in practice may be more difficult for a claimant to prove than if he were a visitor.[468] Further, whilst the extent to which an occupier can be expected reasonably to take steps to protect, say, a child entrant, may well differ in the case of an adult, the extent will be less likely to differ between a child qua a visitor and one qua an uninvited entrant.

Discharges of duty and defences. By s.1(5) it is provided that where a duty **8–154** of care has arisen, the occupier may discharge it in an appropriate case by "taking such steps as are reasonable in all the circumstances of the case to give warning of the danger or to discourage persons from incurring the risk".[469] In addition, the defence of volenti non fit injuria is specifically made available by s.1(6) in that no duty under the Act is owed to any uninvited entrant "in respect of risks

---

[464] "It is ... of significance that the duty is a duty owed by the occupier to the individual visitor", per Kennedy L.J. in *Staples v West Dorset District Council* [1995] P.I.Q.R. 439, CA; "The duty, if any, is owed to the individual trespasser", per Stuart-Smith L.J. in *Ratcliff v McConnell* [1999] 1 W.L.R. 670 at 683, CA.
[465] per Lord Hoffmann in *Tomlinson v Congleton Borough Council* [2004] 1 A.C. 46 at 83.
[466] ibid. at 83. In fact the *economic* cost of remedial measures by the defendant council in *Tomlinson* was the modest sum of £5,000 and the council had already decided to spend that money before the claimant's accident. See Higgs, "Occupier's liability: a more onerous duty?" 2002 P.L.J. 101, 2; Ferguson, "Making a splash" 153 N.L.J. 1406; also Crowther, "A step back in the right direction—a review of the House of Lords decision in Tomlinson v Congleton Borough Council and others" 2003 H.&S.L. (3), 9.
[467] per Lord Hoffmann in *Tomlinson v Congleton Borough Council* [2004] 1 A.C. 46 at 83; also Lord Hobhouse at 96: "The pursuit of an unrestrained culture of blame and compensation has many evil consequences and one is certainly the interference with the liberty of the citizen."
[468] See, e.g. *White v St Albans City & District Council, The Times*, March 12, 1990, CA.
[469] cf. the similar provisions enacted by the Occupiers' Liability Act 1957 s.2(4)(a) as regards warnings to visitors. See further para.8–64, above; *Westwood v Post Office* [1974] A.C. 1; also *Tomlinson v Congleton Borough Council*, n.467 above, per Lord Hoffmann: there was no duty to warn a trespassing swimmer about the dangers of diving into a lake where the risk of shallow water was obvious and a warning would not have told him anything he did not know already.

willingly accepted as his by that person . . . ".[470] The subsection goes on to provide that the question whether a risk was so accepted by that person is one to be decided on the same principles as in other cases, in which one person owes a duty of care to another. However a trespasser is not an outlaw, even if engaged in criminal activity, and the maxim *ex turpi causa non oritur actio* does not provide a defence to his claim for negligently inflicted personal injury.[471]

8–155   Although no reference is made in the Act to the issue of contributory negligence, there can be no good reason for such allegations being excluded at the trial.[472] Likewise, a defence of limitation will be available where appropriate.[473]

ILLUSTRATIONS

8–156   The following serve to illustrate the standard of care required where the occupier either has been held liable to a trespasser or after the Act would probably be held liable: where there was kept on the land an unlocked railway engine turntable, upon which it was known that children were accustomed to play, having gained access to it through a gap in the fence separating the premises from the public road, and a child aged four was injured by it[474]; where a savage horse was placed in a field, without any warning to members of the public, accustomed to walk across it, as a short cut[475]; where a local authority planted and grew in a public park *atropa belladonna* ("deadly nightshade") shrubs, bearing poisonous berries of attractive and appetising appearance, some of which were fatally eaten by a boy aged seven[476]; when there was set in motion an unfenced wire rope haulage system on the land, without steps being taken to check that children, who were known to frequently play on the ropes, were safely out of the way of danger.[477]

8–157   Further, when an occupier felled a tree, knowing that a child was standing in the probable line of its fall, without having taken any steps such as by first

---

[470] cf. the similar provisions enacted by the 1957 Act, s.2(5), as regards the visitor's acceptance of risks. See also *Ratcliff v McConnell* [1999] 1 W.L.R. 670, CA (no duty owed to a 19-year-old man who dived into the shallow end of a swimming pool in the early hours of the morning, where he conceded he knew the risk he was running). See further para.8–71, above, as well as Ch.4, paras 4–73 to 4–127, generally.

[471] *Revill v Newbery* [1996] 2 W.L.R. 239, CA.

[472] In *Adams v Southern Electricity Board, The Times*, October 21, 1993, the CA reduced by two-thirds the damages of the claimant, "an intelligent teenage boy", because of his "substantial" contributory negligence in climbing up a pole-mounted high voltage electrical installation and passing over the attached anti-climbing devices; also *Revill v Newbery* [1996] 2 W.L.R. 239, CA (claim of burglar shot while attempting to break into the garden shed of the 76-year-old defendant at night reduced by two-thirds for contributory fault).

[473] See Ch.4, paras 4–137 to 4–226 generally.

[474] *Cooke v Midland Great Western Ry of Ireland* [1909] A.C. 229.

[475] *Lowery v Walker* [1911] A.C. 10.

[476] *Glasgow Corp v Taylor* [1922] 1 A.C. 44. A poisonous pool, as in *United Zinc & Chemical Co v Britt* (1922) 258 U.S. 268, may give rise to a special duty, per Lord Wilberforce in *Herrington v British Railways Board* [1972] A.C. 877 at 920.

[477] *Excelsior Wire Rope Co Ltd v Callan* [1930] A.C. 404 and the distinction in the facts making no difference now, *Robert Addie & Sons (Collieries) Ltd v Dumbreck* [1929] A.C. 358.

shouting a warning and seeing that the child was out of danger[478]; where boys entered a minefield, laid during wartime, on sand dunes to which the public had access in peacetime and were injured by a landmine explosion[479]; where ashes from railway engines' fire-boxes and furnaces were deposited to form banks which crusted over and, appearing cold and solid, a boy of 14 strayed on to them from the path alongside, and sustained extensive burns to his feet and ankles[480]; where an occupier of premises which contained stored explosives failed to guard against the foreseeable mischievous acts of trespassing children, who stole them and passed them on to other children who were injured as a result of an explosion.[481]

The occupier was liable: where the electricity authority maintained a highly **8–158** dangerous electrical transmission system over the land of another, to which people were accustomed to resort, and an 11-year-old boy climbed up a pole, which had been insufficiently cladded to prevent such access, and was burnt[482]; where the electricity authority erected a highly dangerous pole-mounted transformer but failed to maintain the anti-climbing devices, as a result of which a boy of 15 successfully climbed over them and touched the live conductors[483]; when workmen of contractors, demolishing a warehouse in a densely populated area near a park, lit a bonfire of rubbish, and, having chased away children, left the fire unattended, so that a five-year-old boy interfered with it and was injured[484]; where a local authority, warned in a telephone call by a member of the public of the danger on its land of a wall in an imminent state of collapse, failed to mend defective fencing surrounding it and, a child was injured, when part of the wall fell[485]; where a four-year-old child wandered from a playground, entered an empty house which the local authority had not bricked up in a slum clearance area extensively damaged by vandals, and fell out of an upstairs window[486]; where the elderly occupier of a brick shed armed himself with a shotgun and discharged it at the claimant, a burglar attempting to break in at night.[487]

Many pre-*Herrington* cases, in which the trespasser failed to establish liability **8–159** would probably be decided in the same way under the Act.[488] An occupier was not liable to an injured trespasser: when children were accustomed to break

---

[478] *Mourton v Poulter* [1930] 2 K.B. 183.
[479] *Adams v Naylor* [1944] K.B. 750, affirmed [1946] A.C. 543 on other grounds, where the claimant failed in his action but would now succeed on the facts, according to Lord Morris in *Herrington* [1972] A.C. 877 at 904.
[480] *Commissioner for Railways (N.S.W.) v Cardy* [1961] A.L.R. 16.
[481] *McCarthy v Wellington City* [1966] N.Z.L.R. 481; *Purtil v Athlone Urban District Council* [1968] I.R. 205, but cf. to the contrary *Kingzett v British Railways Board* (1968) 112 S.J. 625.
[482] *Munnings v Hydro-Electric Commission* (1971) 45 A.L.J.R. 378; similarly see *Jones v City of Calgary* (1969) 3 D.L.R. (3d) 455 and *Southern Portland Cement Ltd v Cooper* [1974] A.C. 623. See Poole, "Dangerous Power Cables and Trespassing Child", 119 S.J. 57.
[483] *Adams v Southern Electricity Board*, *The Times*, October 21, 1993, CA.
[484] *Pannett v McGuinness & Co* [1972] 2 Q.B. 599.
[485] *Melvin v Franklins (Builders) Ltd* (1972) 71 L.G.R. 142, CA (it was held that the local authority could not evade liability merely because the message had failed to find its way to the appropriate department).
[486] *Harris v Birkenhead Corp* [1975] 1 W.L.R. 379, affirmed [1976] 1 W.L.R. 279.
[487] *Revill v Newbery* [1996] Q.B. 567.
[488] For list of such cases, see *Charlesworth on Negligence* (5th edn, 1971), para.390.

through a well-maintained concrete post and wire fence, enclosing the defendants' electrified railway lines, and had made a toboggan slide down the embankment but the nine-year-old claimant climbed through the fence in order to retrieve a lost ball kicked out of the recreation ground, whereupon he tripped and fell against the "live" railway and was run over by a passing train[489]; and where a boy, aged 12, got onto a railway bank, stepped through a dilapidated fence separating it from the public footpath, climbed a high fence and squeezed through barbed wire surrounding a 2,500 volt transformer, all of which he well knew were obstacles intended to keep him out, and was injured by an electric shock.[490]

8–160   Further, where boys broke into a shed in the defendant's railway yard and stole detonators which were stored in an unlocked cupboard[491]; when a technician at the defendants' telephone exchange, in order to return to his place of work from the flat roof of the building upon which he had been taking his mid-morning break, climbed through a window into the lift motor room, despite knowing well that he was forbidden to enter it, and was injured by a trap door that collapsed[492]; where a nine-year-old child, playing on the defendants' rubbish tip, was injured when an aerosol container exploded when thrown onto the fire by another boy[493]; when a child gained entrance to a vacant property around which the landlord had erected an eight-foot fence, which could be negotiated only by climbing over it, or wriggling under it through an eight-inch gap[494]; where a 19-year-old man dived into the shallow end of a swimming pool in the early hours of the morning.[495]

8.—LIABILITY TO PERSONS ON ADJOINING PREMISES

8–161   **Generally.** There remains to be considered the question of an occupier's liability to persons who are not on the occupier's premises but sustain injury owing to their defective condition. Three types of situation can arise: damage

---

[489] *Edwards v Railway Executive* [1952] A.C. 737. The HL in *Herrington* did not fault this decision which their Lordships were able to distinguish on its facts. See [1972] A.C. 877 at 908, per Lord Morris of Borth-y-Gest: at 922, per Lord Wilberforce; at 923, per Lord Pearson (quoting Lord Porter) and at 925 (quoting Lord Goddard); at 934, per Lord Diplock.

[490] *McGlone v British Railways Board*, 1966 S.C. 1 (which was cited in *Herrington* [1972] A.C. 877, para.8–142, above, per Lord Wilberforce at 921 with approval and per Lord Pearson at 923 without criticism).

[491] *Kingzett v British Railways Board* (1968) 112 S.J. 625. cf. cases decided to the contrary: *McCarthy v Wellington City* [1966] N.Z.L.R. 481; *Purtil v Athlone Urban District Council* [1968] I.R. 205.

[492] *Westwood v Post Office* [1973] 1 Q.B. 591 (reversed by the HL [1974] A.C. 1 but only on a finding of breach of statutory duty under the Offices, Shops and Railway Premises Act 1963).

[493] *Penny v Northampton Borough Council* (1974) 72 L.G.R. 733. Although the presence of trespassers was known to the defendants, it would have been impracticable to have prevented such without incurring astronomical expense. This decision is clearly distinguishable on the facts from *Melvin v Franklin (Builders) Ltd* (1972) 71 L.G.R. 142, CA, where the danger could so easily have been eliminated by demolishing the peccant wall if it were not possible to have stopped the vandalism of the wooden fence surrounding it.

[494] *Platt v Liverpool City Council* [1997] C.L.Y. 4864, CA.

[495] *Ratcliff v McConnell* [1999] 1 W.L.R. 670, CA.

arising off the premises because they have been allowed to fall into disrepair; damage arising off the premises as a result of work carried out on them; and liability for the progressive deterioration of premises, where that exposes neighbouring premises to damage.

Premises falling into disrepair. There is a duty imposed on the occupier to **8–162** maintain his premises in such a condition that they do not become a nuisance.[496] Quite apart from any question of nuisance, an occupier of premises can be liable in negligence where some defect in them causes damage to the person or property of adjacent occupiers. In some cases, what can be characterised as a danger has arisen as a result of a failure to maintain the premises in good repair. In such a case, it is not sufficient for the occupier to say "I did not know" where his duty was to take reasonable care to ensure that a danger did not arise, and he has failed to take that care.

In *Cunard v Antifyre Ltd*,[497] the court spoke in terms of analogy with cases **8–163** where the state of land caused a danger to those lawfully using the highway. The defendants were lessees and occupiers of a building let out in flats, the main roof and guttering of which were vested in them as occupiers. The male claimant was a sub-tenant of a flat on the third floor and, whilst his wife was in the kitchen, a heavy piece of the guttering fell from the main roof, crashed through the glass roof of the kitchen and injured her. The guttering fell because it had never been properly supported, and the want of proper support was obvious to anyone looking at it. The defendants were held liable. "The plaintiffs' true cause of action (if they have one) is for negligence, for failure by an occupier of property to take reasonable care that his property does not get into such a state as to be dangerous to adjoining property or persons lawfully thereon".[498] The judge went on:

"There is no doubt that if this guttering had overhung the street in the condition proved in the case before us, and had fallen on someone passing below and injured him, that person would have had an action against the defendants on the principle of *Tarry v Ashton*.[499] What is that principle? It is in our opinion that anyone in occupation and control of something hung over a place, in which people may be expected lawfully to be, is bound to take reasonable care that it does not fall and injure them. This seems to us to be both law and justice; and, as we have already said, it is in our opinion immaterial whether in such a case the plaintiff is in the place where he is injured as one of the King's subjects entitled to use the highway, or in the exercise of any other legal right. A closely similar principle applies to work done or chattels kept or moved in the like dangerous situations: see such cases as *Byrne v Boadle*[500]; and it makes no difference whether the plaintiff was on the highway, as in that case, or in any other place

---

[496] *Brew Brothers Ltd v Snax (Ross) Ltd* [1970] 1 Q.B. 612 (the flank wall of the demised premises began to tilt towards the claimant's neighbouring premises and had to be shored up to prevent its fall into the latters' forecourt, causing an obstruction which continued for some 18 months).
[497] [1933] 1 K.B. 551.
[498] *Cunard v Antifyre Ltd* [1933] 1 K.B. 551 per Talbot J. at 557.
[499] (1876) 1 Q.B.D. 314. Also see Ch.10, paras 10–52 to 10–60.
[500] (1863) 2 H. & C. 722.

where he had a right to be, and where people might be expected to be: *Scott v London and St Katherine Docks Co.*"⁵⁰¹

8–164   Similarly, where three rooms in a house were let by the owners and the tenant's daughter was injured by a brick falling from a chimney stack, not included in the demise, the owners were liable:

"The landlord . . . who negligently allowed the brickwork to remain for a matter of five years in this dangerous state was equally liable at law whether the brick fell on his tenant, on his tenant's daughter or on a casual passer-by and whether the tenant or the daughter or the passer-by was in the yard or on the highway or on the property of an adjoining owner."⁵⁰²

8–165   In the examples above, the court may be seen to take a strict view of what the occupier *ought* to have known, which reflected the extent of the danger to others if he did not take steps to acquire knowledge. In other cases, where the defect does not have the same dangerous character, a different standard is applied and liability can be avoided if the defect was one of which the occupier was reasonably unaware. Where a washbasin's overflow pipe had become blocked, but the occupier was unaware of the fact and had no reason to suspect that anything was wrong, he was not liable in negligence for damage caused by the water escaping on to adjoining premises.⁵⁰³ However, there was liability where water leaked from one flat into another below, and the occupier of the upper flat took issue whether sufficient notice had been given: it was enough that he had been told that water was leaking through the ceiling, since that had put him on notice to investigate and to remedy a leak, if he found that it was his responsibility.⁵⁰⁴

8–166   The general rule as between landlord and tenant is that the tenant must take the premises as he finds them. Hence he has no right of action if yew trees, growing on the landlord's land and overhanging his land at the time of the demise, subsequently were eaten by and poisoned his cattle,⁵⁰⁵ or if a rotten overhanging branch of a beech tree fell and injured him or his employee.⁵⁰⁶

8–167   **Damage to adjoining premises from building works.** If the owner of property causes work to be done on his property either by way of repairs or rebuilding, he is under a duty to use reasonable care to see that the work does not

---

⁵⁰¹ (1865) 3 H. & C. 596; *Cunard v Antifyre Ltd* [1933] 1 K.B. 551 at 562.
⁵⁰² *Taylor v Liverpool Corp* [1939] 3 All E.R. 329. Similarly, see *Auto-Scooters (Newcastle Ltd v Chambers)* (1966) 197 E.G. 457, where a chimney-breast collapsed and damaged the tenants' property.
⁵⁰³ *Hawkins v Dhawan and Mishiku* (1987) 19 H.L.R. 232 in which the CA expressed the view that just as a dog was to be allowed its first bite, so a washbasin was to be allowed its first flood. An occupier was not under any duty regularly to inspect a washbasin's overflow pipe, if it had not previously become blocked and, thereby, alerted him to the danger.
⁵⁰⁴ *Irontrain Investments Ltd v Ansari* [2005] EWCA Civ 1681.
⁵⁰⁵ *Cheater v Cater* [1918] 1 K.B. 247. See *Lemmon v Webb* [1895] A.C. 1 for an abatement of such nuisance.
⁵⁰⁶ *Shirvell v Hackwood Estates* [1938] 2 K.B. 577. The CA cast doubts on *Cunard v Antifyre Ltd*, [1933] 1 K.B. 551, but Stable J. in *Taylor v Liverpool Corp* [1939] 3 All E.R. 329, reconciled it with *Cheater v Cater*, above.

cause damage to adjoining property. In *Hughes v Percival*,[507] there were three houses belonging to A, B and C respectively, B's house being separated from the houses of A and C by party walls. B's house was pulled down for the purpose of rebuilding, and the new building was tied into the party wall between A's house and B's house. The builder, employed by B, negligently cut into the party wall between B's house and C's house, as a result of which the new building, which was nearly finished, fell and dragged down A's house with it. B was held liable to A, because he owed to A a duty, as to which Lord Blackburn said:

> "I do not think that duty went so far as to require him absolutely to provide that no damage should come to the plaintiff's wall from the use he thus made of it, but I think that the duty went as far as to require him to see that reasonable skill and care were exercised in those operations which involved a use of the party wall, exposing it to this risk."

Also, where a house was pulled down negligently, so that damage was caused to a stable on the adjoining land and to a horse and cart in the stable, the person who had ordered the house to be pulled down was held liable.[508]

It has been said, in the context of a claim for damage caused by works carried **8–168** out to one side of a party wall, allegedly causing damage at the other, that a robust approach to causation of damage can sometimes be appropriate. In the case in question, a heavy duty hammer drill had been used to cut a channel to one side of the wall, and shortly after, damage became apparent to floor tiles adjacent to the other side. The judge at first instance accepted the evidence of an expert that the damage was coincidental. However, no notice of the proposed work had been served as required by the Party Walls etc. Act 1996 and it was said that a reasonably robust approach to causation was called for where the damage which subsequently arose was of a type that might have been expected to occur from the nature of the works, and the owner had been disabled from providing better proof of a causative link by the building owner's neglect of his statutory obligations.[509]

There is old authority for the proposition that an owner of property who pulls **8–169** down a wall under statutory powers is not liable to an adjoining owner for damage sustained, owing to his rooms being unprotected. It was held that the statute, authorises the wall to be pulled down, but does not oblige the person pulling it down to an independent act, such as putting up a hoarding.[510] However, more recently, where a house was demolished under a statutory demolition order served by a local authority, the owner of adjoining premises *did* succeed in establishing a common law duty upon the owner of the demolished premises to weatherproof the wall that had been exposed. The defendant should have known of the risk of damage likely to result from the demolition, if he failed to carry out

---

[507] (1883) 8 App.Cas. 443. See also *Keegan v Young* [1963] N.Z.L.R. 720.
[508] *Emblen v Myers* (1860) 6 M. & N. 54.
[509] *Roadrunner Properties Ltd v Dean* [2004]11 E.G. 140, CA.
[510] *Thompson v Hill* (1870) L.R. 5 C.P. 564.

weatherproofing, and the damage sought to be recovered would have been prevented by work it was reasonable for him to have carried out.[511]

8–170   Since the coming into force of s.4 of the Defective Premises Act 1972, a landlord has owed a statutory duty of care to persons who are off, as well as those who are on, the let premises.[512] The statutory duty is additional to any duties owed apart from the section.[513]

8–171   **Liability to adjoining occupiers for progressive deterioration.** Where a landowner knows, or ought to know, that there is a defect or some condition of his land which is likely to progress and thereby cause damage to his neighbour's land in the foreseeable future, a duty of care may arise. The scope of the duty will vary with the circumstances but might, for instance, involve warning his neighbour of the risk or sharing such information as has been acquired in relation to it. But where a council owned land forming the undercliff beneath a hotel on the north Yorkshire coast and knew that if remedial action was not taken, a landslip was likely to progress and at some indeterminate time in the future affect the claimant's land, it was not liable for the massive landslip which occurred, causing the hotel to collapse. The extent of the catastrophe was unforeseeable and it was not just, fair or reasonable to impose a duty of care extending to damage which could not have been foreseen without geological investigation. The scope of the duty was confined to avoiding damage to the claimant's land which ought to have been foreseen. It did not extend to carrying out extensive remedial work to prevent that damage.[514]

---

[511] *Rees v Skerret* [2001] 1 W.L.R. 1541, CA (the court was influenced by the *Holbeck Hall Hotel* case, n.514 below).
[512] See, generally, para.8–130, above.
[513] s.6(2).
[514] *Holbeck Hall Hotel Ltd v Scarborough Borough Council* [2000] Q.B. 836. See also *Goldman v Hargrave* [1967] 1 A.C. 645, and the cases referred to at Ch.13, para.13–33, below.

CHAPTER 9

PERSONS PROFESSING SOME SPECIAL SKILL

1.—ACTIONS AGAINST SKILLED PERSONS GENERALLY

(A) Introduction

The "Bolam" test. If a task requires special skill, a reasonable man will not **9–01** attempt it unless he possesses the skill in question. If he undertakes it, it is reasonable to expect that he display the same level of expertise as an ordinarily competent practitioner in the relevant specialty. The standard is reasonableness: "Every person who enters into a learned profession undertakes to bring to the exercise of it a reasonable degree of care and skill. He does not undertake, if he is an attorney, that at all events you shall gain your case, nor does a surgeon undertake that he will perform a cure; nor does he undertake to use the highest possible degree of skill. There may be persons who have higher education and greater advantages than he has, but he undertakes to bring a fair, reasonable and competent degree of skill."[1]

---

[1] *Lanphier v Phipos* (1838) 8 C. & P. 475, per Tindal C.J. See also *Harmer v Cornelius* (1858) 5 C.B.(N.S.) 236; *Greaves & Co (Contractors) Ltd v Baynham Meikle & Partners* [1975] 1 W.L.R. 1095 at 1100, per Lord Denning. In some cases the language of the contract may lead to the inference that the professional undertook to achieve a guaranteed result: see *Platform Funding Ltd v Bank of Scotland Plc* [2009] 2 W.L.R. 1016, CA, para.9–304, below.

9–02   The same rule applies to any man in a skilled trade or business. "If a smith prick my horse with a nail, etc., I shall have my action upon the case against him, without any warranty by the smith to do it well . . . for it is the duty of every artificer to exercise his art rightly and truly as he ought."[2] In *Bolam v Friern Hospital Management Committee*,[3] McNair J. said:

> "Where you get a situation which involves the use of some special skill or competence, then the test as to whether there has been negligence or not is not the test of the man on the top of a Clapham omnibus, because he has not got this special skill. The test is the standard of the ordinary skilled man exercising and professing to have that special skill . . . A man need not possess the highest expert skill; it is well established law that it is sufficient if he exercises the ordinary skill of an ordinary competent man exercising that particular art."

The *Bolam* test is of general application and is not confined to a defendant exercising or professing the particular skill of medicine.[4] It is sanctioned by long usage in determining issues of liability where breach of duty by professionals, or other persons applying professional skill,[5] is alleged.[6] It has no application when the court is addressing the task of making findings of fact[7]; or where the issues before the court do not raise something to which it is relevant.[8]

It follows that where a person holds himself out to be competent to do some special kind of job, an action for negligence will lie for damage which has been caused by any failure to exercise due care and skill, either by proving that the defendant did not possess the requisite skill or by showing that, although the skill may have been possessed, it was not exercised.

9–03   **The standard of care and skill.** In order to decide whether, on particular facts, the standard of care and skill of a person of ordinary competence in the relevant calling was achieved, it will be necessary to refer to professional

---

[2] F.N.B. 94D.

[3] [1957] 1 W.L.R. 582 at 586. See De Prez, "Something 'old', something 'new', something 'borrowed' . . . the continued evolution of *Bolam*" (2001) 2 P.N. 75.

[4] *Gold v Haringey Health Authority* [1988] Q.B. 481 at 489. See also Ch.7, para.7–51, above.

[5] *Adams v Rhymney Valley District Council* [2001] P.N.L.R. 68, CA, where there was disagreement whether the *Bolam* test applied to an allegation that the absence of window locks with push buttons was allegedly causative of a tragedy in which young children died in a fire: the majority rejected the view that it had no application because the defendant council never purported to exercise the relevant design skill; had professionals been asked to consider the matter, a responsible body of expert opinion would have supported the provision in fact made. per Sir Christopher Staughton at 79: "The *Bolam* test is not the monopoly of the expert."

[6] In *Phelps v London Borough of Hillingdon* [2001] 2 A.C. 619, Lord Slynn pointed out that the application of the *Bolam* test did not depend upon contract. It extended for instance to such groups of professionals as educational psychologists and teachers and also education officers performing the functions of local authorities in relation to children with special educational needs (at 653).

[7] *Penney v East Kent Health Authority* [2000] P.N.L.R. 323, CA.

[8] See *Michael Hyde Associates v J.D. Williams & Co Ltd* [2001] P.N.L.R. 233, CA, per Ward L.J. at 247, quoting Lloyd L.J. in *Ward v Haringey HA* [1988] 1 Q.B. 481, 490. Ward L.J. refers to other situations where the test cannot apply, as where there is no recognised body of professional opinion on the question and where whatever evidence of professional opinion is before the court, cannot withstand logical analysis.

practice or opinion in that expertise.[9] Inexperience cannot be a defence to a claim against a professional, so the same standard of care is required of a junior hospital doctor as of more senior colleagues.[10] In order to exercise care and skill to an appropriate standard, a professional should have a practical working knowledge of the law relating to his area of expertise.[11] Although the same standard is applied to both a specialist and a general practitioner,[12] the application of the standard will vary on the facts. It will be relevant whether the specialist claims knowledge, experience or excellence in an area outside the experience of a general practitioner. Such a specialist may have to take extra steps beyond those ordinarily required before the *Bolam* test is regarded as discharged.[13] It has been said that where a profession embraces a range of views as to what is an acceptable standard of conduct, the competence of the defendant is to be judged by the lowest standard that would be regarded as acceptable.[14] Where a professional has adopted a practice which any ordinary, reasonable and prudent person would foresee involved an inherent risk of loss to another, the practice is unlikely to be regarded as evidence of the taking of reasonable care.[15]

After a review of various authorities, Bingham L.J. summarised the *Bolam* test as follows: **9–04**

"From these general statements it follows that a professional man should command the corpus of knowledge which forms part of the professional equipment of the ordinary member of his profession. He should not lag behind other ordinary assiduous and intelligent members of his profession in knowledge of new advances, discoveries and developments in his field. He should have such an awareness as an ordinarily competent practitioner would have of the deficiencies in his knowledge and the limitations on his skill. He should be alert to the hazards and risks in any professional task he undertakes

---

[9] *A v Tameside and Glossop Health Authority* [1997] P.N.L.R. 140, CA, para.9–127, below.
[10] *Wilsher v Essex AHA* [1987] Q.B. 730 (appeal allowed on the issue of causation [1988] A.C. 1074). However, the standard of care expected of a prison hospital in relation to a mentally ill prisoner was not the same as that of a psychiatric hospital outside prison, since the two perform different functions and have different roles: *Knight v Home Office* [1990] 3 All E.R. 237 (a mentally ill detainee committed suicide in the remand prison's "special watch" cell before he could be transferred to a hospital wing). See also *Djemal v Bexley HA* (1995) 6 Med.L.R. 269, para.9–129, below; also *Brooks v Home Office, The Times*, February 17, 1999 (*Knight* did not support the proposition that a pregnant woman in custody was not entitled to the same standard of obstetric care and observation as if she was at liberty).
[11] *Jenkins v Betham* (1855) 15 C.B. 168; *Lee v Walker* (1872) L.R. 7 C.P. 121.
[12] *Wimpey Construction UK Ltd v Poole, The Times*, May 3, 1984.
[13] *Greaves & Co (Contractors) Ltd v Baynham Meikle & Partners* [1974] 1 W.L.R. 1261 (affirmed [1975] 1 W.L.R. 1095). See also *Seymour v Caroline Ockwell & Co* [2005] P.N.L.R. 758 (in the context of financial services, the standard of the reasonably competent professional could vary depending whether the individual concerned had specialist expertise).
[14] *Michael Hyde and Associates v J.D. Williams and Co Ltd* [2001] P.N.L.R. 233, CA, per Sedley L.J. at 254.
[15] *Edward Wong Finance Co v Johnson Stokes & Master* [1984] A.C. 1296 (the Hong Kong conveyancing practice of handing over the purchase price of property to the vendor's solicitor, in advance of the date of completion, on an undertaking to keep the money safely and repay it if the contract was not completed).

to the extent that other ordinarily competent members of the profession would be alert. He must bring to any professional task he undertakes no less expertise, skill and care than other ordinarily competent members of his profession would bring, but need bring no more. The standard is that of the reasonable average. The law does not require of a professional man that he be a paragon combining the qualities of polymath and prophet."[16]

9–05   **Expert evidence.** In deciding whether an appropriate standard of care and skill has been displayed, the opinions of experts, skilled in the calling in question, are admissible in evidence.[17] The court controls the reception of such evidence and has a duty to restrict it to that which is reasonably required to resolve the issues.[18] An expert witness enjoys a privileged position. He or she is entitled to give evidence not simply of the facts of a case, where they are within knowledge, but also to express an opinion as to the significance of the facts. But with privilege comes responsibility.[19] The expert must not usurp the position of the judge. Impartiality is essential even where it leads to conflict with the interests of the party giving instructions[20] In expressing an opinion, the expert must take into account the range of views which experts of like discipline could reasonably hold as to the facts.[21]

9–06   In receiving evidence as "reasonably required" to resolve a dispute about proper professional practice the court is not concerned to hear practising members of the profession in question say what they personally would or would

---

[16] *Eckersley v Binnie* [1988] 18 Con. L.R. 1 at 79.

[17] For the difficulties facing a party who has no appropriate expert evidence, or who attempts to rely on expert evidence from a professional outside the discipline of the defendant, see *Sansome v Metcalfe Hambleton & Co* [1998] P.N.L.R. 542, CA. See also Davies and Bergin, "Use of expert evidence in professional negligence cases" 140 S.J. 952; also Jones, "Using experts with expertise" (1998) 12 Lawyer, 20.

[18] See CPR 1998 Pt 35.1.

[19] The duties and responsibilities of expert witnesses were summarised by Cresswell J. in *National Justice Cia Naviera SA v Prudential Assurance Co Ltd, The Ikarian Reefer* [1993] 2 Lloyd's Rep. 68 at 81–82 (quoted with approval in *Vernon v Bosley (No.1)* [1997] 1 All E.R. 577, CA at 601). As to the need for an expert to be independent, see *Liverpool Roman Catholic Archdiocese Trustees Incorporated v Goldberg (No.2)* [2001] 4 All E.R. 950 (a claim for professional negligence against a barrister specialising in tax matters); per Evans-Lombe J.: "where it is demonstrated that there exists a relationship between the proposed expert and the party calling him which a reasonable observer might think was capable of affecting the views of the expert so as to make them unduly favourable to that party, his evidence should not be admitted however unbiased the conclusions of the expert might probably be."

[20] An expert witness has immunity from suit for negligence at the instance of a party for whom they provide advice: *Stanton v Callaghan* [1999] P.N.L.R. 116, CA. See Dye, "The immune system: liability and immunity of expert witnesses" 152 N.L.J. 1753 ; Carr Q.C. and Evans, "The future of immunity for expert witnesses" (2006) 3 P.N. 151 ; Carr Q.C. and Evans, "The future of immunity for expert witnesses: an update" (2007) 1 P.N. 27; Robertson Q.C., "Expert witnesses: professionally immune?" (2007) 2 P.N. 66.

[21] In summarising the court's approach to expert evidence Hoffmann L.J. in *Zubaida v Hargreaves* [1995] 1 E.G.L.R. 127 pointed out that it was " . . . not enough to show that another expert would have given a different answer . . . the issue . . . is whether [the defendant] has acted in accordance with practices which are regarded as acceptable by a respectable body of opinion in his profession." See Harpwood, "Bolam, expert evidence and the role of judges" Health Law 2001 (6)1.

not have done in the circumstances. As Oliver J. said in *Midland Bank Trust Co Ltd v Hett Stubbs & Kemp*[22]:

> "Clearly, if there is some practice in a profession, some accepted standard of conduct which is laid down by a professional institute or sanctioned by common usage, evidence of that can and ought to be received. But evidence which really amounts to no more than an expression of opinion by a particular practitioner of what he thinks that he would have done had he been placed, hypothetically and without the benefit of hindsight, in the position of the defendants, is of little assistance to the court . . . "

So, where the allegation was one of negligence by a medical practitioner, it was the duty of the expert witness to make clear whether the practice adopted by the defendant accorded with that regarded as proper by a responsible body of medical practitioners skilled in the area concerned, as opposed to whether the witness would, in the same circumstances, himself have acted in a different way.[23]

The duty of a court receiving evidence from experts on matters within their expertise is to examine it in a critical way to ensure it has a logical and defensible basis.[24] Where one expert opinion is preferred to another, a court should support its preference with reasons.[25] Such reasons may turn upon the court having taken a different view of the facts[26] to that taken by the witness, or upon a preference for the inherent likelihood of one view over another. The important point is that some reasoned basis for preferring one view to another must be given.[27] In an   **9–07**

---

[22] [1979] Ch. 384 at 402, quoted with approval in *McManus Developments Ltd v Barbridge Properties Ltd* [1996] P.N.L.R. 431, CA (a claim against a solicitor who was negligent in failing to investigate when a problem with a boundary fence surfaced in the course of a conveyancing transaction). See also *Bown v Gould & Swayne* [1996] P.N.L.R. 130, CA (again a case of alleged negligence by solicitors, where the claimant wished to call expert evidence to establish best conveyancing practice). *Bown* was distinguished in *May v Woolcombe Beer & Watts* [1999] P.N.L.R. 283 (the court would receive expert evidence of an experienced conveyancer as to an issue whether inquiries should have been made by a solicitor instructed in the purchase of property, who had learnt of an order of the Secretary of State modifying the status of certain rights of way nearby).

[23] *Sharpe v Southend Health Authority, The Times*, May 9, 1997.

[24] See Lord Browne-Wilkinson's observations about the *Bolam* test in *Bolitho v City and Hackney Health Authority* [1998] A.C. 232 at 240, 241. See further, Heywood, "The logic of Bolitho" (2006) 4 P.N. 225.

[25] See, e.g. *Flannery v Halifax Estate Agencies Ltd, The Times*, March 4, 1999, CA; also *Smith v Southampton University Hospital NHS Trust* [2007] EWCA Civ 387 (a clinical negligence claim in which there was an issue between expert witnesses whether surgery had been carried out negligently and, in rejecting a particular allegation the judge said only that the expert relied upon by the defendant was was highly reputable and that it had not been suggested that he did not represent the view of a responsible body of relevant medical opinion).

[26] For an example where it was permissible to reject the views of competent experts, genuinely held, about what was ultimately a question of fact, see *Penney v East Kent HA* [2000] P.N.L.R. 323, CA, below para.9–158. See in relation to medical experts, para.9–125, n.377, below.

[27] For a case in which the court was entitled to reject expert opinion see *Marriott v West Midlands Regional Health Authority* [1999] Lloyd's Rep. Med. 23, CA (claimant's G.P. negligent in failing to refer him to hospital after head injury even though an expert witness had said that keeping him at home under review was a reasonable course of action); also *D v South Tyneside Health Care NHS Trust* [2004] P.I.Q.R. P150, CA (a dispute between experts about the appropriate intervals between which a patient, detained in hospital in her own interests pursuant to the Mental Health Act 1983, should have been kept under observation). But in *Calver v Westwood Veterinary Group* [2001] P.I.Q.R. 168, CA it was not permissible to prefer one body of veterinary opinion to another where

appropriate case the court may receive expert evidence even if, in breach of the Code of Guidance on Expert Evidence annexed to the Civil Procedure Rules, most of the expert's work has been carried out on a contingency fee basis: one solution is to receive the evidence but assess the risk of bias in the light of cross examination.[28]

9–08 **Generality of the duty.** The duty to exercise reasonable care and skill is applicable generally to everyone whose calling involves professional expertise, including accountants and auditors,[29] agents,[30] architects, engineers and surveyors,[31] auctioneers,[32] barristers,[33] dentists,[34] directors of companies,[35] divers,[36] nurses,[37] patent and trade mark agents,[38] physicians and surgeons,[39] solicitors,[40] stockbrokers,[41] insurance brokers,[42] valuers[43] and veterinary practitioners.[44] Where, as they frequently are, professionals are in partnership, a duty of care can be owed by one partner to the others in relation to the conduct of a client's affairs,

---

there was nothing in the evidence to allow the conclusion that the opinion of the expert relied upon by the defendant was illogical (an allegation of negligent treatment of a horse after it had aborted a foal).

[28] *Davis v Stena Line Ltd* [2005] 2 Lloyd's Rep. 13. In a clinical negligence claim, a medical expert relied upon by the defendant was not automatically disqualified because he had been at a time before the trial a member of the cases committee of the Medical Defence Union. It was observed that when an expert provided a report he should produce his C.V., which should include details of any employment or activity which raised a possible conflict of interest: *Toth v Jarman* [2006] Lloyds Rep. Med. 397, CA. See Iller, "Conflicted experts" 2006 P.I.L.J. 50, 23.

[29] para.9–23, below.

[30] *Keppel v Wheeler* [1927] 1 K.B. 577; *Price v Metropolitan House Investment Agency* (1907) 23 T.L.R. 630; *Gokal v Ram* (1938) 55 T.L.R. 15.

[31] paras 9–50 and 9–304, below.

[32] *Parker v Farebrother* (1853) 1 C.L.R. 323; *Hibbert v Bayley* (1860) 2 F. & F. 48; *Cyril Andrade Ltd v Sotheby & Co* (1931) 47 T.L.R. 244; para.9–75, below.

[33] para.9–95, below.

[34] para.9–107, below.

[35] *Re City Equitable Fire Insurance Co* [1925] Ch.407. See also *Re D'Jan of London; Copp v D'Jan* [1993] B.C.C. 646. But in *Williams v Natural Life Health Foods Ltd* [1998] 1 W.L.R. 830, HL, para.9–20 below, there was no assumption of personal responsibility giving rise to a duty of care as between a director of a franchisor company and franchisees, for loss allegedly suffered as a result of negligent advice.

[36] *Wilton v Hampton*, The Times, November 10, 1959 (no negligence where a professional diver allowed his former pupil to dive in unfavourable conditions, the day after the latter qualified as a master diver).

[37] para.9–183, below.

[38] *Lee v Walker* (1872) L.R. 7 C.P. 121; *Halifax BS v Urquart-Dykes & Lord* [1997] R.P.C. 55 (the duty of a trade mark agent pursuing an application to register is to advise his client of all legal pitfalls reasonably connected with that application; there is no duty to give commercial advice but the client should be warned of commercial difficulty that may arise as a result of any legal problem).

[39] para.9–109, below.

[40] para.9–213, below.

[41] *Neilson v James* (1882) 9 Q.B.D. 546; para.9–301, below.

[42] *Chapman v Walton* (1833) 10 Bing. 57; 2 L.J.C.P. 210; *Coolee Ltd v Wing Heath & Co* (1930) 47 T.L.R. 78; *United Mills Agencies Ltd v R.E. Harvey Bray & Co* [1952] 1 All E.R. 225n; para.9–168, below.

[43] *Baxter v Gapp & Co* [1939] 2 K.B. 271; para.9–304, below.

[44] para.9–336, below.

although it should not be assumed that breach of duty to the one will necessarily import breach of duty to the others, since the two may not be co-extensive.[45]

Evolution of the duty. The liability of professionals evolved rapidly after   **9–09** *Hedley Byrne*,[46] although initially there was some reluctance to embrace the full implications of the decision. In *Mutual Life and Citizen's Assurance Co Ltd v Evatt*[47] the claimant sought damages from the defendant insurance company for loss suffered as a result of negligent advice given to him gratuitously. The Privy Council held, by a majority, that the duty of care was limited to persons who gave advice in the course of a profession or business. But subsequently this type of distinction was rejected. In *Esso Petroleum Co Ltd v Mardon*[48] both the trial judge and the Court of Appeal expressly stated their preference for the minority opinions of Lord Reid and Lord Morris of Borth-y-Gest. If some special relationship had arisen between the parties, the claimant had a remedy for advice negligently given, even if the defendant was not in the business of giving advice of that sort.[49]

Delegation of task. There is no reason why a professional cannot delegate the   **9–10** whole or part of a task, provided that the act of delegation is not itself a breach of duty (which is likely to be determined by the contract under which the task is performed) and provided that reasonable care is taken in what is done.

> "Whether he is entitled to delegate a particular task will depend upon the nature of the task. He is entitled to delegate some tasks to others but is not entitled to delegate others. It all depends upon the nature of the task involved. If he does delegate he must delegate to a suitably qualified and experienced person . . . "[50]

If there is a delegation to a suitable person the professional will not ordinarily be vicariously liable for any negligent failure of that individual, but there can be circumstances in which he continues to owe the claimant a personal duty of care, for instance to perform some check on what has been done.[51]

The burden and standard of proof. The burden of proving professional   **9–11** negligence normally rests on the claimant.[52] Where, however, there is a general

---

[45] *Ross Harper & Murphy v Banks, The Times*, May 30, 2000, OH (a firm of solicitors suing a former partner for liabilities incurred by the firm as a result of alleged negligence in handling a client's affairs). See further Schmitz, "Reviewing partners' liability principles" 152 S.J. 16.

[46] *Hedley Byrne & Co Ltd v Heller & Partners Ltd* [1964] A.C. 465. See Ch.2 para.2–172, above.

[47] [1971] A.C. 793.

[48] [1976] Q.B. 801, affirming on the question of liability [1975] Q.B. 819. See further, *Batty v Metropolitan Property Realisations Ltd* [1978] Q.B. 554.

[49] [1971] A.C. 793 at 810–813, both of whom were parties to the decision in *Hedley Byrne*, n.46, above.

[50] per Swinton Thomas L.J. in *Arbiter Group Plc v Gill Jennings & Every* [2000] P.N.L.R. 680, CA at 686.

[51] See, e.g. *Gregory v Shepherds* [2000] P.N.L.R. 769, CA (solicitors engaged to arrange a conveyance in Spain who passed the purchase price to the foreign vendor before obtaining a reply to their inquiry whether a search had disclosed any incumbrance on the property).

[52] In *Dwyer v Roderick, The Times*, November 12, 1983, the CA observed that, whilst there are no special rules about the burden or standard of proof in cases involving professional negligence, in reality it will be harder to prove a case on the balance of probabilities where it concerns the complicated and sophisticated professional activities of, say, a medical practitioner. In *Harrington v*

duty of care and failure to take a recognised precaution, followed by damage of the kind which that precaution was designed to prevent, an evidential burden shifts to the defendant to show either that there was no breach of duty or that the damage was not caused by the breach.[53] So far as the standard of proof is concerned, the civil standard applies. But that standard is not inflexible and it has been pointed out that a charge of professional negligence is a serious matter, requiring a standard of proof commensurate with the gravity of the allegation. As Lord Denning M.R. put it, the allegation of negligence against a professional person, " ... stood on a different footing to a charge of negligence against the driver of a motor car. The consequences were far more serious. It affected his professional status and reputation. The burden of proof was correspondingly greater. As the charge was so grave, so should the proof be clear."[54]

9–12   These words should not be taken to alter the balance of probabilities standard. How that standard may come to be applied to the facts was described by Lord Nicholls, albeit in a different context.[55]

> "The balance of probabilities standard means that a court is satisfied an event occurred if the court considers that, on the evidence, the occurrence of the event was more likely than not. When assessing the probabilities the court will have in mind as a factor, to whatever extent is appropriate in the particular case, that the more serious the allegation the less likely it is that the event occurred and hence the stronger should be the evidence before the court concludes that the event is established on the balance of probability. Fraud is usually less likely than negligence. Deliberate physical injury is usually less likely than accidental physical injury ... Built into the preponderance of probability standard is a generous degree of flexibility in respect of the seriousness of the allegation.
>
> Although the result is much the same, this does not mean that where a serious allegation is in issue the standard of proof required is higher. It means only that the inherent probability or improbability of an event is itself a matter to be taken into account when weighing the probabilities and deciding whether, on balance, an event occurred. The more improbable the event the stronger must be the evidence it did occur before, on the balance of probability, its occurrence will be established ... "

9–13   **Cause of action in both contract and tort.** The same circumstances may give rise to a cause of action against a professional both in tort and contract. In contract, the duty arises from the agreement of the parties; in tort, it is independent of agreement and is imposed upon the parties by law.

> "The distinction in the modern view, for this purpose, between contract and tort may be put thus: where the breach of duty alleged arises out of a liability independently of the personal obligation undertaken by contract, it is tort, and it may be tort even though

---

Essex Area Health Authority, The Times, November 14, 1984, the claimant failed to discharge the burden of proof in a case of clinical negligence, where there were two possible explanations for the occurrence of complications in his post-operative condition and the court was not prepared to select one of them. See further as to the burden of proof, Ch.6, paras 6–01 to 6–04, above; Lewis, "Medical Negligence: the Difficulties of Proof" 80 L.S.Gaz. 1647; Elsey, "Medical Negligence: Onus Proof on the Practitioner?" 2 Lit. 319.

[53] *Clark v MacLennan* [1983] 1 All E.R. 416.

[54] *Hucks v Cole, The Times,* May 9, 1968.

[55] *Re H and K* [1989] 2 F.L.R. 313, H.L. at 315.

there may happen to be a contract between the parties, if the duty in fact arises independently of that contract. Breach of contract occurs where that which is complained of is a breach of duty arising out of the obligations undertaken by the contract."[56]

It follows that an action in contract lies only between the parties to an agreement, whilst an action of tort has a much wider potential range.[57] Further, the measure of damages may well be quite different.   **9–14**

(i) Duty arising in contract

In most cases the legal relationship between a professional or other skilled person and a client, patient or customer, is based upon contract. In the event of some breach of duty, the cause of action is likely to be based on breach of that contract. Generally, in the absence of any express term, there is a term implied that the professional or other skilled person will exercise reasonable care and skill in rendering the service contracted for. There will also usually be at least an implied term as to payment of a reasonable fee for the work done. Indeed, as pointed out by Oliver J. in *Midland Bank Trust Co Ltd v Hett Stubbs & Kemp*,[58] there may be many more contractual obligations undertaken than these: **9–15**

> "The classical formulation of the claim in this sort of case as 'damages for negligence and breach of professional duty' tends to be a mesmeric phrase. It concentrates attention on the implied obligation to devote to the client's business that reasonable care and skill to be expected from a normally competent and careful practitioner as if that obligation were not only a compendious, but also an exhaustive, definition of all the duties assumed under the contract created by the retainer and its acceptance. But, of course, it is not. A contract gives rise to a complex of rights and duties of which the duty to exercise reasonable care and skill is but one."[59]

Among the terms of the contract both expressed and implied will be those which define the scope of the services to be rendered. As an example, where a solicitor has been instructed to effect the grant of an option, there is an implied term that he will register the estate contract before a third party has acquired an adverse   **9–16**

---

[56] See *Jarvis v Moy, Davies, Smith, Vandervell & Co* [1936] 1 K.B. 399 per Greer L.J. See also *Jackson v Mayfair Window Cleaning Co* [1952] 1 All E.R. 215 (a claim for damage to a chandelier caused by persons who had contracted to overhaul and clean it, is an action in tort. "If the defendants . . . interfere with [the claimant's] property whether with or without her permission and whether in pursuance of a contract or otherwise—they are under an obligation not to damage that property as a result of their negligence, or in other words, they are bound to take reasonable care to keep it safe").

[57] e.g. see *Holt v Payne Skillington* [1996] 2 P.N.L.R. 179, CA.

[58] [1979] Ch.384 at 434. The judge added as example: "If I employ a carpenter to supply and put up a good quality oak shelf for me, the acceptance by him of that employment involves the assumption of a number of contractual duties. He must supply wood of an adequate quality and it must be oak. He must fix the shelf. And he must carry out the fashioning and fixing with the reasonable care and skill which I am entitled to expect of a skilled craftsman. If he fixes the brackets but fails to supply the shelf or if he supplies and fixes a shelf of unseasoned pine, my complaint against him is not that he has failed to exercise reasonable care and skill in carrying out the work but that he has failed to supply what was contracted for."

[59] The decision was approved in *Henderson v Merrett Syndicates Ltd* [1995] 2 A.C. 145.

interest in the property concerned.[60] Similarly, where a surgeon has agreed to perform an operation on his patient in hospital, there may be implied a term that subsequently he will provide proper supervision of the patient's progress, including any further treatment which is required up until his discharge from care.[61] In the event of the defendant's being in breach of the contractual terms, he will be liable, despite the actual amount of care taken and the skill applied by him on behalf of the claimant.

9–17   The situation where a service is to be provided should be distinguished from one where a product has ultimately to be delivered. In the former case, only the duty of care described above is owed, whilst in the latter, there is also a warranty that the product will be reasonably fit for its purpose.[62] It has been argued cogently that this principle should apply in other professional contexts, for instance, as between consultant engineers or architects and their clients, where design work is undertaken in connection with a building project.[63]

(ii) *Duty arising in tort*

9–18   A tortious duty co extensive with a contractual duty towards a professional's client is well settled. But a duty in tort can also be owed to third parties and the formulae used in testing for the presence of such a duty have already been discussed in Chapter 2. It is the application of those formulae in the context of professional negligence that is the particular concern here.

9–19   **The duty formulae.** In *Henderson v Merrett Syndicates Ltd*,[64] it was important for limitation purposes that the claimants, certain Lloyd's Names, establish against the defendant underwriting agents a concurrent liability in contract and tort. They succeeded, their Lordships stressing that assumption of responsibility by a professional, coupled with reliance by the claimant was sufficient to raise a duty of care. Depending upon the facts, the tortious duty may be more extensive than that in contract.[65] In other important examples a solicitor has been held liable to an intended beneficiary on the basis of a deemed assumption of responsibility in spite of the absence of any reliance by the latter or any contractual relationship other than that between the solicitor and his own

---

[60] *Midland Bank Trust Co Ltd v Hett Stubbs & Kemp* [1979] Ch. 384, above.

[61] *Morris v Winsbury-White* [1937] 4 All E.R. 494 at 500 per Tucker J.

[62] For product liability generally see Ch.15. See also e.g., *Samuels v Davis* [1943] K.B. 526 (a dentist contracting to make a denture) per du Parcq J. at 530: "whether the contract be regarded as one for the sale of goods or one for work and labour done, the dentist is contracting to make a denture which will fit the patient's mouth."

[63] See *IBA v E.M.I. Electronics Ltd* (1980) 14 Build.L.R. 1 at 48, per Lord Scarman, who expressed the view, albeit obiter, that where a person contracts to design an article for a purpose that has been made known to him, he "undertakes that the design is reasonably fit for the purpose". For the facts, see, further, para.9–69, below. Also, see Stanton and Dugdale, "Design Responsibility in Civil Engineering Work" 131 New L.J. 583.

[64] [1995] 2 A.C. 145.

[65] *Holt v Payne Skillington* [1996] 2 P.N.L.R. 179, CA. Although for a contrary view see *Conway v Crowe Kelsey & Partners* (1995) 39 Con.L.R. 1.

client[66]; and it has been held that an employer can be liable to a former employee for a negligently written reference.[67]

In *Williams v Natural Life Health Foods Ltd*,[68] it was stressed that the test of   **9–20** assumption of responsibility was an objective one. The touchstone of liability was not the defendant's state of mind. Because the test is objective, the primary focus should be on those things that were said or done by the defendant or on his behalf in dealings with the claimant, their impact being judged in the light of the relevant contextual scene. The claimant must also prove reliance, since, if he failed to do so, it was not established that the assumption of responsibility had causative effect. Lord Steyn said[69]:

> "The test is not simply reliance in fact. The test is whether the plaintiff could reasonably rely on an assumption of personal responsibility by the individual who performed the services on behalf of the company."

It is recognised that in some complex contracts the very nature of the   **9–21** contractual arrangements may negative a corresponding duty of care in tort. In *Henderson v Merrett Syndicates*,[70] Lord Goff observed that a claimant who was owed a contractual duty of care might also be able to rely upon a duty of care in negligence, unless it would be "so inconsistent with the applicable contract that, in accordance with ordinary principle, the parties must be taken to have agreed that the tortious remedy is to be limited or excluded."[71] The existence of a contractual chain might militate against any assumption of responsibility because it would have the effect of short-circuiting the contractual arrangements which parties had been put into effect. Nevertheless, the basic question remains whether, in relation for instance to advice, an adviser has assumed responsibility to the claimant in light of all the circumstances including the contractual context. The speech of Lord Goff tends to support the approach that it was for the adviser to establish that the contractual arrangements negatived any assumption of responsibility; not for the claimant to show that an assumption of responsibility survived in spite of those arrangements.[72]

In the result a professional or other skilled person does owe a duty of care in   **9–22** tort to his client or customer concurrent with any contractual duty. Such duty can extend widely to third parties with whom no direct contact may have been

---

[66] *White v Jones* [1995] 2 A.C. 207.
[67] *Spring v Guardian Assurance Plc* [1995] 2 A.C. 296.
[68] [1998] 1 W.L.R. 830, HL, Ch.2, above, para.2–194 (the terms of a brochure issued by a company, which referred to the experience in the natural food trade of the managing director and principal shareholder and his particular experience in running a shop of that kind, were insufficient to give rise to a personal assumption of responsibility by that director to the claimant, a prospective franchisee).
[69] *Williams v Natural Life Health Foods Ltd* [1998] 1 W.L.R. 830 at 835.
[70] [1995] 2 A.C. 145.
[71] *Henderson v. Merrett Syndicates* [1995] 2 A.C. 145 at 186.
[72] See per Neuberger L.J. in *Riyad Bank v Ahli United Bank (UK) Plc* [2007] P.N.L.R. 1 at [43]–[48].

made.[73] It can be argued in terms either of an "assumption of responsibility" with or without reliance,[74] or the three-stage test of *Caparo*.[75] If the latter test is employed, the terms of any contract between the parties will doubtless be one of the matters considered in deciding whether it would be fair, just and reasonable also to impose a duty of care.[76] It has also been suggested that where the defendant's assumption of responsibility lies entirely within the context of the contract between the parties, the tortious and contractual duties are likely to be co-extensive: but not so where, against the background of a contractual relationship involving limited mutual obligations, the general law imposes a duty of care which exceeds the contractual duties in its scope.[77] The type of damage for which the defendant will be liable will vary with the circumstances, from physical injury in the cases of persons such as doctors, dentists, barbers, plumbers and similar occupations, to financial loss in the case of others, such as solicitors, accountants, surveyors, bankers and stockbrokers.[78] The claimant will have a choice of remedies and will adopt that most favourable, one frequently-cited advantage being that a claim in contract may well become statute-barred before its counterpart in tort.[79]

---

[73] Nasir, "Duties owed by professional advisors to third parties" (2002) 1 P.N. 12.

[74] See, e.g. *Brownie Wills v Ian Meredith Shrimpton* [1999] P.N.L.R. 552, CA (NZ) (no assumption of responsibility by solicitors acting for a bank towards the director of a company seeking an overdraft facility to be secured by personal guarantees from all directors, where the solicitors failed, contrary to instructions, to explain the nature of the transaction to the directors and the claimant then acted under a mistake as to the extent of his liability under the guarantee: he had not sought or received advice from the solicitors and was unaware at the time of the instruction the bank had given).

[75] In *Spring* [1995] 2 A.C. 296 above, only Lord Goff unequivocally approached the case by way of an extension to *Hedley Byrne*. Lords Slynn, Lowry and Woolf arrived at the same result after analysis in terms of the three stages of *Caparo*. See Smith, "The effect of contractual terms on the duty of care owed to a third party" (1998) 2 P.N. 83, which usefully compares Australian and English decisions; also Walford, "The evolution of liability of professionals to non-clients" (2002) 3 P.N. 177.

[76] See, e.g. *British Telecommunications Plc v James Thomson & Sons (Engineers) Ltd* [1999] 1 W.L.R. 9, HL, para.9–63 below (it was not unfair, unjust or unreasonable that a building sub-contractor, not nominated by the architect, should owe a duty of care to the employer and be liable in damages for causing to materialise a risk specified in the employer's building contract, in respect of which the employer was bound to provide insurance). The case has been applied in New Zealand, albeit on the facts no duty of care was imposed: see *R.M. Turton & Co Ltd (in liquidation) v Kerslake & Partners* [2000] Lloyd's Rep. P.N. 967, CA (NZ) (the engineer who was employed by architects to prepare a mechanical services specification for a building contract did not assume any responsibility to the head contractor so as to be liable for negligent misstatement). See generally, Stanton, "Professional negligence: duty of care methodology in the twenty first century" (2006) 3 P.N. 134.

[77] per Hirst L.J. in *Holt v Payne Skillington* [1996] 2 P.N.L.R. 179 at 194, 195, CA, distinguishing remarks of Lord Scarman in *Tai Hing Cotton Mill Ltd v Liu Chong Hing Bank Ltd* [1986] A.C. 80 at 107.

[78] For discussion of the recovery of damages for economic loss, see Ch.2, paras 2–169 to 2–237, above. Where the claim is for "loss of the chance" damages, see Ch.6, paras 6–04, 6–56, above, and the analysis of the CA in *Allied Maples Group Ltd v Simmons & Simmons* [1995] 1 W.L.R. 1602, particularly at 1623; also *First Interstate Bank of California v Cohen Arnold & Co* [1996] 1 P.N.L.R. 17, CA, para.9–48, n.168, below.

[79] See, e.g. *Lee v Thompson* [1989] 40 E.G. 89, CA (where both claims were statute-barred); *Power v Halley* (1978) 88 D.L.R. (3d) 381; *Holt v Payne Skillington* [1996] 2 P.N.L.R. 179, CA and para.9–275, below.

2.—Accountants and Auditors

The duty of care. The duties of an accountant or auditor[80] to a client arise: (i) **9–23** out of contract[81]; (ii) from any fiduciary relationship; (iii) under statute; and (iv) in tort, by way of the *Hedley Byrne*[82] principle as subsequently elaborated.[83] In addition, (v) a duty in tort can be owed to third parties such as shareholders,[84] potential investors including persons making takeover bids,[85] and creditors.[86]

The scope of the contractual duty. Although the standard of care and skill **9–24** required of an accountant is constant, the contract with a client defines the scope of the duties undertaken. Where, therefore, accountants were employed to certify a return which was made by a branch office of an insurance company to the head office, but not to make an audit of the branch books, they were not liable for failing to detect the fraud of one of the employees at the branch office.[87] Where accountants were employed to investigate the accounts of a business to which their client proposed to lend money, and they failed to discover that the stock sheets overvalued the stock by three per cent, they were not negligent. Their duty was to make a reasonable and proper investigation of the accounts and stock sheets, and if a reasonably prudent man would have concluded there was something wrong, to call their employer's attention to the fact.[88]

Where an accountant's task was to check books of account but not to make a **9–25** full audit, he was nonetheless negligent in drawing up a balance sheet where he did not check the cash, look at the bank pass book or obtain a certificate from the bank, but simply took the figures of cash at bank and cash in hand from the cash book, in which wrong figures had been entered by a dishonest clerk.[89] Even where a claimant informally employed a partner in a firm of accountants to advise him upon the sale of two businesses, it was held that a contractual relationship existed between the parties, which gave rise to liability for negligence in the accountant's failure to advise the claimant properly.[90]

Fiduciary duties. An accountant is under a duty to take reasonable care of **9–26** any documents entrusted to him by a client, and not to disclose confidential

---

[80] See Ch.2 para.2–190, above and also Kershaw, "Liability of professional advisers: *Caparo* and beyond" (1996) 7 P.L.C. (3), 42; Virgo and Ryley, "Setting the standards for advice" (1997) 11 Lawyer, 11.
[81] cf. *Nelson Guarantee Corporation Ltd v Hodgson* [1958] N.Z.L.R. 609.
[82] [1964] A.C. 465.
[83] See *Henderson v Merrett Syndicates Ltd* [1995] 2 A.C. 145, approving *Midland Bank Trust Co Ltd v Hett Stubbs & Kemp* [1979] Ch. 384.
[84] See *Caparo Industries Plc v Dickman* [1990] 2 A.C. 605.
[85] *Morgan Crucible Co Plc v Hill Samuel & Co Ltd* [1990] Ch. 259, but also see *Caparo Industries Plc v Dickman*, above.
[86] See para.9–40, below.
[87] *Maritime Insurance Co v Fortune & Son* (1931) 41 Ll.L.R. 16.
[88] *Henry Squire Cash Chemist Ltd v Ball, Baker & Co* (1911) 27 T.L.R. 269, affirmed on other grounds, 28 T.L.R. 81.
[89] *Fox v Morrish Grant & Co* (1918) 35 T.L.R. 126.
[90] *Bradford v Wright Stevens and Lloyd, The Guardian*, February 27, 1962.

information[91] where communicated,[92] or to make any secret profit.[93] Liability in damages will follow for breach of such duties.[94]

9–27   **Statutory duties under the Companies Acts.** When auditors of companies are appointed under the Companies Acts, their duties are governed by those Acts. Reference should be to the company law textbooks for a detailed statement of those duties. But, in brief statement, it has been held that the duty of an auditor is:

> "not to confine himself merely to the task of verifying the arithmetical accuracy of the balance sheet, but to inquire into its substantial accuracy, and to ascertain that it contained the particulars specified in the articles of association (and consequently a proper income and expenditure account), and was properly drawn up, so as to contain a true and correct representation of the state of the company's affairs."[95]

Accordingly, where audited accounts incorrectly showed that a company was entitled to "moneys lent" in a particular amount, and as a result of the erroneous statement dividends were paid out of capital, the auditor was held liable for negligence.[96]

9–28   The auditor's duty is to see that the accounts put before shareholders accurately state the company's financial position; it is not enough for him merely to indicate the means of ascertaining that position.[97] He fulfils this duty by examining books of the company, although he must also see that the books themselves show the company's true financial status.

> "An auditor, however, is not bound to do more than exercise reasonable care and skill in making inquiries and investigations. He is not an insurer; he does not guarantee that the books do correctly show the true position of the company's affairs; he does not even guarantee that his balance sheet is accurate according to the books of the company."[98]

9–29   An auditor is not bound to be suspicious, as opposed to reasonably careful.[99] So, where the money of a company has been misappropriated and the audited accounts are thereby inaccurate, the cause of action against the company's auditors will depend upon the manner in which any fraud has been committed and whether a reasonably competent auditor, exercising due skill, would have

---

[91] In *Morton v Arbuckle* [1919] V.L.R. 487 at 491, Irvine C.J. said the duty of an auditor was one of utmost good faith.

[92] See, e.g. *Fogg v Gaulter* (1960) 110 L.J. 718, which could equally have been decided on this basis.

[93] cf. *Boardman v Phipps* [1967] 2 A.C. 46 in the case of a solicitor. Breach of fiduciary duty does not require dishonesty.

[94] *Weld-Blundell v Stephens* [1920] A.C. 956.

[95] per Stirling J. in *Leeds Estate Co v Shepherd* (1887) 36 Ch. D. 787 at 802. The legal basis for a company audit is summarised by Lord Oliver in *Caparo Industries v Dickman* [1990] 2 A.C. 605 at 630.

[96] *Leeds Estate Co v Shepherd* (1887) 36 Ch. D. 787.

[97] *Re London and General Bank* [1895] 2 Ch. 673.

[98] ibid. per Lindley L.J. at 683.

[99] *Re Kingston Cotton Mill Co (No.2)* [1896] 2 Ch. 279, per Lindley L.J. at 284.

discovered the shortfall. Also, where a group of companies were the vehicle of a massive fraud which auditors did not detect, it was held they could be liable to the company for the payment of a dividend they had incorrectly approved and for failing to take appropriate action in relation to payments to a shadow director for which there was no apparent commercial justification.[100] But an auditor does not owe a general duty of care to safeguard the assets of a company for whom he acts, and so cannot be liable for trading losses alleged to arise as a result of his failure to report that the company is insolvent.[101] And where it was alleged that auditors caused a company to suffer loss, by failing to detect, in the course of an annual audit of its books, a fraud practised by the company's sole directing mind upon certain banks, they could rely upon the defence *ex turpi causa non oritur actio* to defeat the claim.[102]

Where the managing director of a large insurance company fraudulently **9–30** misappropriated a large part of the company's funds and, in order to conceal his fraud, for three successive years bought Treasury Bills just before the audit, thereby substantially improving the balance sheet, only to sell sold the bills immediately after the audit, the company's auditors were not negligent in failing to see what was going on: although the transactions, when isolated, should have led them to entertain suspicions, they formed only one item in a large audit.[103] However, where auditors, who had been put on inquiry by alteration of invoices, negligently failed to investigate, so that a falsely favourable picture of company profits was given, as a result of which dividends were declared, it was no defence that they had not been given enough time to do their job.[104] They should be liable to repay the dividends, and pay the costs of recovering the extra tax, and any of the extra tax not recoverable.

When audited accounts are incorrect, because of an overvaluation of assets, the **9–31** liability of the auditors depends on the circumstances. If they know that the assets are overvalued, they should report the matter to the shareholders. So, where

---

[100] *Sasea Finance Ltd (in liquidation) v KPMG, The Times*, August 25, 1998, appeal dismissed [2000] 1 All E.R. 676, CA (the CA also allowed the claimant's appeal against that part of the earlier judgment which struck out claims where the proceeds of sale of shares had been diverted to other companies in the group, distinguishing *Galoo v Bright Grahame Murray* [1994] 1 W.L.R. 1360, CA: in the instant case the losses alleged were within the scope of the duty of care for which the claimants contended, whereas in *Galoo* they were not and arose simply from the ordinary risks of carrying on business). See Maher, "The auditor's duty of care—*Caparo* test ten years on" (2000) 3 P.N. 150; Burbridge, "Liability of statutory auditors to third parties—is the European writing on the wall for *Caparo v Dickman?*" (2002) 1 P.N. 40; Dugdale, "Auditor's liability to the client: Ups and downs" (2003) 4 P.N. 536. Gwilliam, "Auditor liability: Law and myth" (2004) 3 P.N. 172; Heaton, "Duty calls" 2004 Lawyer 2004 (25) 41.

[101] *BCCI (Overseas) Ltd v Price Waterhouse (No.3), The Times*, April 2, 1998, applying *Banque Bruxelles Lambert SA v Eagle Star Insurance Co Ltd* [1997] A.C. 191. Compare, however, *Equitable Life Assurance Society v Ernst & Young* [2004] P.N.L.R.269, CA, where the court was prepared to regard as arguable the proposition that a company suing its auditors for negligence in the preparation of its statutory accounts could recover for loss of the chance of a sale of its business. See Westhead and White, "Are there claims to make against auditors?" 2005, Win. 27; also generally, Butcher Q.C., "Management fault, causation and scope of duty in auditor's negligence" (2004) P.N. 20, 4, 248.

[102] *Stone & Rolls Ltd v Moore Stephens* [2009] 3 W.L.R. 455, HL, Ch.4, para.4–252, above.

[103] *Re City Equitable Fire Insurance Co* [1925] Ch.407. It may be questioned whether, on similar facts, the result in this case would be the same today.

[104] *Re Thomas Gerrard & Son* [1968] Ch.455.

auditors reported to directors that they considered that the security for certain loans was insufficient and that there would be difficulty in realisation, but only reported to the shareholders that the value of the assets was dependent on realisation, they were liable for negligence.[105] On the other hand, auditors are entitled to accept the certificate of an appropriate official of the company relating to the value of stock, unless there are circumstances which ought to suggest to them, as reasonably competent auditors, that the certificate is incorrect. Where a manager certified the value of stock and this was accepted by auditors, although, if they had compared the amount of the stock at the beginning of the year with the purchases and sales during the year, they would have suspected that it was incorrect, it was held that they were not negligent.[106] Auditors are entitled to call for explanations of items in a stock sheet. Any failure to ask for an explanation of items which are apparently lumped together, may be negligence.[107]

9–32   Auditors should satisfy themselves that the company's securities are not only in existence but are in safe custody, either of the company itself or of some person, who, in the usual course of business, retains customers' securities. So, auditors acted negligently when they accepted a certificate of the company's stockbrokers, in which the company's managing director was the senior partner, that they held certain securities on behalf of the company and the securities were non-existent.[108] In *Dominion Free Holders Ltd v Aird*[109]; the company sued its auditors for damages for reporting incorrectly the accuracy of its balance sheet and profit and loss account. Thereupon the auditors joined in the company's accountant as a third party, claiming indemnity, alleging that he had, in turn, negligently misrepresented the accuracy of these two documents. It was held that where a statutory duty is cast upon a person to express his opinion and he relies upon and adopts as his opinion that of another, he has no cause of action in negligence against that other, should that other's opinion be wrong.

9–33   Further, where an auditor in New Zealand was under a duty imposed by the Securities Act 1978 to report to a trustee for the depositors of unsecured deposits, the Privy Council held that his duty was to report when he had actually formed his opinion that it was necessary to do so because of the company's insolvency[110]: since at common law there was no higher duty than that imposed by statute, there was no negligence in failing to report to the trustee when a prudent auditor might have reasonably formed such an opinion.[111]

9–34   **Duty to client in tort.** As already indicated,[112] accountants and auditors owe a duty of care to their clients, independently of any agreement between them.

---

[105] *Re London and General Bank* [1895] 2 Ch.673.
[106] *Re Kingston Cotton Mill Co (No.2)* [1896] 2 Ch.279.
[107] *Mead v Ball, Baker & Co* (1911) 28 T.L.R. 81.
[108] *Re City Equitable Fire Insurance Co* [1925] Ch. 407.
[109] [1966] 2 N.S.W.R. 293.
[110] *Deloitte Haskins & Sells v National Mutual Life Nominees Ltd* [1993] A.C. 774.
[111] *Deloitte Haskins & Sells v National Mutual Life Nominees Ltd* [1993] A.C. 774 applying *Hedley Byrne & Co Ltd v Heller & Partners Ltd* [1964] A.C. 465 and the dictum of Lord Keith in *Yuen Kun Yeu v Attorney-General of Hong Kong* [1988] A.C. 175 at 195, PC.
[112] para.9–23, above.

Well before *Hedley Byrne*,[113] this principle had been advanced by Denning L.J. in *Candler v Crane, Christmas & Co.*[114] In a dissenting judgment, he said that accountants, exercising a calling which required knowledge and skill, owed a duty to use care in the work which led to their accounts and reports, as well as in the rendering of such.

Duty to third parties in tort. In addition to the duty owed to a client Denning   **9–35** L.J. considered a duty was owed to any third person to whom accountants showed their accounts and reports or to whom they knew their clients were going to show them, when they knew that person would consider them with a view to the investment of money or taking other action to his gain or detriment.[115] A duty to third parties is no longer controversial in principle although defining its scope often will be. So, it has been held that auditors who prepare company accounts owe a duty of care to any person whom they ought reasonably to have foreseen would rely on them, for example in seeking to take over the company.[116] It was emphasised that they would be liable only where the information they provided played a real and substantial, although not necessarily decisive, part in the decision to purchase. In *Caparo Industries v Dickman*,[117] the House of Lords confirmed that while an auditor of a public company owed individual share-holders a duty of care in carrying out an audit and making a statutory report as required under the Companies Act 1985, the duty did not extend to providing information to assist anyone in making decisions as to future investment in, or to taking over, the company. It was a precondition of liability that the claimant establish some proximity between the defendant and himself, in the sense that:

"the defendant knew his statement would be communicated to the plaintiff, either as an individual or as a member of an identifiable class, specifically in connection with a particular transaction or transactions of a particular kind . . . and that the plaintiff would very likely rely on it for the purpose of deciding whether to enter upon that transaction or upon a transaction of that kind".[118]

---

[113] [1964] A.C. 465. See generally, Ch.2, para.2–172, above.
[114] [1951] 2 K.B. 164. There is little doubt but that the case would be decided differently today.
[115] *Candler v Crane, Christmas & Co* [1951] 2 K.B. 164 at 180. See per Denning L.J. at 180–181 and 182–184, described as a "masterly analysis" by Lord Bridge in *Caparo Industries v Dickman* [1990] A.C. 605 at 623.
[116] *JEB Fasteners Ltd v Marc Bloom & Co* [1981] 3 All E.R. 289 (appeal dismissed [1983] 1 All E.R. 583, CA).
[117] [1990] A.C. 605, applying *Hedley Byrne* [1964] A.C. 465, and *Smith v Eric S. Bush* [1990] A.C. 831 distinguishing *JEB Fasteners Ltd v Marc Bloom & Co*, above, and reversing in part that decision; [1989] Q.B. 653.
[118] *Caparo Industries v Dickman* [1990] A.C. 605 at 621. See also *H.I.T. Finance Ltd v Cohen Arnold & Co* [1998] 1 E.G.L.R. 140 (where, in supplying a statement of a third party's creditworthiness to a lender, auditors knew that a loan secured by his guarantee was to be advanced to him, or to a company of which he was principal shareholder, that was sufficient knowledge to satisfy the test in *Caparo* that in order to establish a breach of duty such a statement must be given specifically in connection with a particular transaction or transactions of a particular kind); also *Royal Bank of Scotland v Bannerman Johnstone MacLay* [2005] P.N.L.R. 883, CS (IH) (it was arguable that the proximity test was satisfied where, in addition to knowing that a bank lending money to a company might rely upon the audited accounts, auditors had been involved in the company's obtaining set-up finance and providing management accounts which were a condition of the bank's continued support). See Dugdale, "Audit liability and the protection of the public interest"(2003) 2 P.N. 350.

Such proximity between potential investors and the company's auditor was not established on the facts.

9-36   By way of example of the duty which can be owed by an auditor to a third party, where accounts were prepared for a subsidiary company in the knowledge that they would be placed before directors of the holding company, who, understandably, were interested in receiving a true and accurate view of the subsidiary's financial affairs, a duty of care was owed directly to the holding company itself. There was no reason in principle why it, as opposed to the subsidiary, could not sue for loss in the value of the subsidiary, where such loss arose in consequence of the auditor's negligence.[119] Also, it was arguable that a duty of care arose in relation to companies for whom accountants did not act as auditors, where those companies were part of a closely-knit group and the accountants acted for other companies in the group: this was the case even though it was not alleged that the accountants knew that the claimant companies would rely on the financial statements they had prepared, since the circumstances made it possible that the necessary proximity between the parties could be established.[120] A duty of care arose to shareholders where auditors were engaged by the directors of a company to perform a valuation of the company's shares thereby setting the price at which the shares were to be compulsorily acquired pursuant to the company's articles: there was an assumption of responsibility to the shareholders where it was known that the specific purpose of the valuation was to enable others to require them to sell their shares at the value which the auditors determined.[121]

9-37   In *James McNaughton Paper Group Ltd v Hicks Anderson & Co*,[122] it was held that a firm of accountants which had prepared at short notice draft accounts for the use of a company's chairman owed no duty of care to a bidder who had taken over the company after having inspected such accounts. In deciding whether a duty of care was owed to a third party in relation to a statement made by a professional, certain matters were of particular importance. They were: (1) the purpose for which the statement was made; (2) the purpose for which it was communicated; (3) the relationship between an adviser, the advisee and any relevant third party; (4) the size of any class to which the advisee belonged; (5) the state of knowledge of the adviser, and (6) reliance by the advisee.

9-38   In later cases the touchstone of liability has been whether, in relation to a particular statement, the maker assumed responsibility towards a category of

---

[119] *Barings Plc v Coopers & Lybrand* [1997] P.N.L.R. 179, CA (a claim arising out of an alleged failure by auditors to identify losses caused by the trading activities of Mr Nicholas Leeson, a manager of the claimant's subsidiary). See also *Chapman v Barclays Bank Plc* [1997] C.L.Y. 331, CA para.9–87, below.
[120] *BCCI (Overseas) Ltd v Price Waterhouse (No.2)* [1998] P.N.L.R. 564, CA.
[121] *Killick v Price Waterhouse Coopers* [2001] P.N.L.R. 1 (the judge was influenced by the fact that otherwise than by imposing a duty of care there would be no remedy and referred to the approach taken by the HL in such a situation in *White v Jones*, n.38, below).
[122] [1991] 2 Q.B. 113. See the judgment of Neill L.J. for discussion of the principles set out in the text.

persons which included the claimant.[123] It has been stressed that it requires exceptional circumstances before auditors can be found to owe a duty of care to anyone other than the company to which they are engaged.[124] A special relationship is required between the auditor and the third party in question before a duty will arise. In particular there must have been an intention (actual or to be inferred) on the part of auditors that a third party should rely upon their audit, together with actual reliance.[125] It has been said that it must be shown that some conscious[126] responsibility was assumed by the auditor, not so much for a statement made by him, but for the task in which he was engaged.[127] However, use of the word "conscious" should not be taken to imply a subjective test. The essential inquiry is, " . . . whether having regard to all the circumstances of the case and looking at the matter objectively it can be said that [the accountant] undertook responsibility to [the potential investor] for the substantial accuracy of the accounts."[128]

The law evolves, and it is always necessary to be aware of the historical **9–39** context of in which examples of the duty of care have arisen. However, it has been said that while an auditor owes no duty of care to potential takeover bidders in certifying company accounts, the directors, auditors and financial advisors of a target company might well owe a duty of care to such bidders not to mislead them.[129] A district auditor, employed by the Audit Commission to audit the accounts of a local authority in accordance with Pt III of the Local Government Finance Act 1982, owed a duty of care to the local authority itself rather than its officers because the purpose of the audit was directed primarily to the protection

---

[123] *Henderson v Merrett Syndicates Ltd* [1995] 2 A.C. 145, particularly per Lord Goff of Chieveley at 180.

[124] See Lightman J. in *Anthony v Wright* [1995] B.C.C. 768 at 770. But see also *Siddell v Smith Cooper & Partners* [1999] P.N.L.R. 511, CA (an auditor's duty of care is not necessarily limited to the company for whom he acts where he concurrently enters a contract to act as accountant to certain of its shareholders).

[125] *Anthony v Wright* [1995] B.C.C. 768, above.

[126] See, e.g. Carnwath J. in *Electra Private Equity Partners and others v KPMG Peat Marwick* [1998] P.N.L.R. 135 (no duty owed to potential investors for statements made at an informal meeting to the effect that a company's audited accounts were likely to meet the claimants' expectations). In the same case the judge drew attention to the dangers of extracting isolated statements of principle from earlier authorities where the law has been in a state of evolution. See also n.128, below.

[127] *White v Jones* [1995] 2 A.C. 207. For a review of the various tests, see *Bank of Credit & Commerce International (Overseas) Ltd (in liquidation) v Price Waterhouse (No.2)* [1998] P.N.L.R. 564, CA (whether the threefold *Caparo* test, the assumption of responsibility test of *White v Jones,* or an incremental approach was adopted, it was arguable, where the allegation was that two banks were operated as a single entity, that auditors of one bank owed a duty of care to the other). See also O'Sullivan, "Negligence liability of auditors to third parties and the role of assumption of responsibility" (1998) 4 P.N. 195.

[128] per Morritt L.J. in *Peach Publishing v Slater* [1998] P.N.L.R. 364, CA at 373 (no assumption of responsibility by accountants of a company towards a second company formed to acquire the first, in respect of a statement made to shareholders of the first that management accounts were substantially accurate). Contrast *ADT Ltd v BDO Binder Hamlyn* [1996] B.C.C. 808, CA, where, in a similar situation, auditors who said they "stood by" the audited accounts and attached no qualification to their statement were held to owe a duty of care. See also *Electra Private Equity Partners v KPMG Peat Marwick* [1999] Lloyd's Rep. P.N. 670, CA (it is too exacting a test to say that the assumption of responsibility must have been a conscious one). See generally, Arnull, "Auditors' reports, misconceptions and third party disclaimers" (2002) 3 P.N. 146.

[129] *Morgan Crucible Co Plc v Hill Samuel & Co Ltd* [1991] Ch.259.

of the authority, as well as local electors.[130] Accountants who prepared annual reports on solicitors' accounts for the latter to submit to the Law Society owed to the Society a duty of care in relation to the accuracy of their reports. The duty was not unreasonably open-ended where it was limited in time (until receipt of the following year's report) and where the potential liability was limited to payments to clients whose funds had been misappropriated.[131]

9–40   Although accountants may owe a duty of care to a third party, for instance in the preparation of accounts where the claimant intended to inject cash into a company that had run into difficulties, such duty did not free him from the need to take care to protect himself by making inquiries to obtain the customary warranties.[132] It is arguable that accountants who acted as a company's auditors, were under a common law duty of care to advise the directors of the company that loan payments to another company which had acquired the first company's issued shares contravened s.151 of the Companies Act 1985.[133] When an auditor's report on the finances of a company was prepared for and at the request of its bankers, it did not give rise to a duty of care owed either to the directors, whether or not they were guarantors of the company's debts, or the shareholders.[134] Similarly, no duty of care was owed to banks that were not existing creditors of a company at the date of its auditors' latest report which had not been made directly to the banks, or with the intention, or in the knowledge, that its contents would be communicated to them.[135] Accountants asked to provide a letter as to the worth of a client providing an unlimited personal guarantee as a condition of receiving a loan, owed a duty of care to the lender in formulating the letter.[136]

9–41   **The standard of care.** Accountants and auditors are liable for failing to exercise the skill and diligence of a reasonably competent and careful accountant or auditor.[137] The standard remains the same no matter upon what terms the

---

[130] *West Wiltshire District Council v Garland* [1993] Ch.409. But no duty of care was owed by auditors of a company to investors who were the beneficiaries of a trust where they did not rely on the audit and where in any event their relationship was not close enough to make such a duty appropriate: *Anthony v Wright* [1995] 1 B.C.L.C. 236. See also *Andrew v Kounis Freeman* [1999] 2 B.C.L.C. 641, CA (accountants who audited the accounts of an air travel organiser, knowing of a deadline which meant there would be no reasonable opportunity to check them, and also that the Civil Aviation Authority would rely on the information given when deciding whether to renew the organiser's licence, could owe a duty of care to the Authority, which suffered loss when the organiser ceased trading and its bookings had to be fulfilled at the Authority's expense).
[131] *Law Society v KPMG Peat Marwick* [2000] 1 W.L.R. 1921, CA.
[132] *Lloyd Cheynham & Co Ltd v Littlejohn & Co* [1986] P.C.C. 389.
[133] *Coulthard v Neville Russell, The Times*, December 18, 1997, CA.
[134] *Huxford v Stoy Hayward & Co* [1989] 5 B.C.C. 421.
[135] *Al Saudi Banque v Clarke Pixley* [1990] Ch.313, approved in *Caparo Industries Plc v Dickman* [1990] 2 A.C. 605.
[136] *H.I.T. Finance Ltd v Cohen Arnold & Co* [2000] 1 C.L. 315, CA (but no breach of duty was established where, on a proper construction, a statement as to the client's worth made in the letter was attributed to information provided by the client, the accuracy of which the accountants did not warrant).
[137] See *Re Kingston Cotton Mill Co Ltd (No.2)* [1896] 2 Ch.279, CA.

defendant has been engaged, although the steps required to achieve it may vary with the nature of the task given.[138] In determining whether the standard has been achieved regard can be paid to formal accounting and auditing standards set by professional bodies, such as the Accounting Standards Committee and the Auditing Practice Committee. Third parties reading accounts are entitled to assume that they have been drawn up in accordance with approved practice unless there is some clear indication to the contrary. Courts will attach considerable importance to formal standards in deciding whether auditors have been negligent in performing their work.[139] A minority shareholder's action failed where the company had appointed an auditor to value its shares, wishing to have the job done quickly and cheaply so as to enable the claimant to leave. It was held that the standards of a specialist valuer could not be applied to the auditor, who had not fallen short of the care required of a reasonably competent accountant acting as auditor.[140] Just as with other professional men, accountants and auditors are bound to have a knowledge of the practical rules of law which affect them in the exercise of their calling.[141] Where an accountant has accepted a retainer, and a particular matter is within the area within which he should have been competent to give advice, he will be liable for a failure to give that advice even where he tells his client to consult a specialist.[142]

Occasions will frequently arise when accountants have to give advice to a **9–42** client about the implications of a particular course as a matter of tax law. Where it is subsequently alleged that advice was given negligently the court may well have to decide whether it was right or wrong. It can be insufficient to approach the matter simply on the basis that there is a good chance that the advice was wrong.[143]

Acting as arbitrators. When auditors truly act as arbitrators, they do not owe **9–43** a duty of care, since they perform a quasi-judicial function.[144] However, in *Arenson v Arenson and Casson Beckman Rutley & Co*,[145] it was submitted that, since the auditors were acting as arbitrators in valuing shares on a contract of sale as between shareholders, they owed no duty of care in respect of such valuation, because they were performing a quasi-judicial function. In consequence, so the

---

[138] *Henry Squire, Cash Chemist Ltd v Ball Baker & Co*; *Mead v Ball Baker & Co* (1912) 106 L.T. 197 at 199–200.
[139] *Lloyd Cheynham & Co Ltd v Littlejohn & Co* [1986] P.C.C. 389.
[140] *Whiteoak v Walker* (1988) 4 B.C.C. 122.
[141] e.g. See *Thomas v Devonport Corp* [1900] 1 Q.B. 16; *Re Republic of Bolivia Exploration Syndicate Ltd* [1914] 1 Ch.139; *Frank H. Wright (Constructions) v Frodoor* [1967] 1 W.L.R. 506.
[142] *Sayers v Clarke Walker* [2002] B.C.L.C. 16 (a claim for allegedly avoidable tax liabilities and penalties against accountants, retained to advise in the purchase of a company, who failed to give appropriate advice about the structure of the sale agreement having told the claimant to consult specialist tax counsel).
[143] See e.g. *Grimm v Newman* [2003] 1 All E.R. 67, CA (an allegation of negligence on the basis of incorrect advice about the tax consequences of a gift where the court had to decide whether, against a complex background, the advice given was right).
[144] In *Re Hopper* (1867) L.R. 2 Q.B. 367. See, generally, Ch.3, paras 3–13 to 3–17, above.
[145] [1977] A.C. 405.

argument proceeded, they were immune from liability in an action for negligence, on the ground of public policy. Lord Salmon, in rejecting such submissions, expressed the opinion that they were discharging no function even remotely resembling a judicial function but were merely exercising a purely investigatory role.[146]

9–44   **Liquidators, receivers and sequestrators.** The liquidator of a company is liable for negligence in the discharge of his statutory duties. This renders him liable in damages to an injured creditor,[147] and to the creditors in general by means of a summons for misfeasance.[148] However, an administrator appointed under the Insolvency Act 1986 is in a position, as regard creditors, directly analogous to the position of the director of a company and its shareholders: *absent* special circumstances any duty of care is owed exclusively to the company and not to the shareholders themselves.[149]

Although sequestrators are officers of the court, they are not exempt from liability for professional negligence, based upon ordinary standards of care, in respect of the management of the property of a contemnor which comes into their possession.[150]

9–45   The position of official receivers is somewhat different. An official receiver has been held immune from suit on the grounds of public policy for an allegedly negligent statement made in the course of bankruptcy proceedings, and within the scope of his powers and duties in those proceedings.[151] However, where a receiver is appointed to manage the business of, for instance a mortgagee,[152] his duty is not limited to one of good faith. His main duty is to proceed so as to procure repayment of the debt and interest and if he is managing a business he has a duty to manage it with due diligence, which includes taking reasonable steps to carry it on profitably.[153] By way of example where a receiver appointed by mortgagees to manage several mortgaged properties let to different tenants,

---

[146] *Arenson v Arenson and Casson Beckman Rutley & Co* [1977] A.C. 405 at 840. The claimant held shares in a private company on terms that if his employment by the company ceased he would sell them back at "a fair value," defined as the value "..determined by the auditors for the time being of the company, whose valuation, acting as experts and not as arbitrators, shall be final and binding..". On the termination of his employment the auditors duly valued the shares but a dispute arose whether that valuation was negligent. The HL remitted the case for trial to determine whether the auditors had acted as arbitrators or not and, if so, were entitled to immunity or, if not, were in breach of duty.

[147] *Pulsford v Devenish* [1903] 2 Ch.625, followed in *James Smith & Sons (Norwood) Ltd v Goodman* [1936] Ch.216 where the CA in extending the principle, held the liquidator liable in negligence for disregarding even a contingent claim of a creditor.

[148] *Re Windsor Steam Coal Co* [1929] 1 Ch. 151; *Re Home and Colonial Insurance Co* [1930] 1 Ch.102.

[149] *Kyrris v Oldham* [2004] P.N.L.R. 317, CA.

[150] *I.R.C. v Hoogstraten* [1985] Q.B. 1077.

[151] *Mond v Hyde* [1999] Q.B. 1097, CA. per Beldam L.J. at 114, "to be afforded immunity from suit in respect of the statement made, the official receiver must be acting in the course of bankruptcy proceedings and within the scope of his powers and duties."

[152] i.e. not an official receiver.

[153] *Medforth v Blake* [2000] Ch.86. See Griffiths, "Receiver's duty of care" 143 S.J. 950.

failed to serve "trigger" notices to enable rent reviews to be initiated, it was held that he was in breach of a duty of care thereby owed to the mortgagors. As a result he was liable for the losses incurred by them when subsequently the properties were sold pursuant to the mortgagees' power of sale.[154]

Causation and damages. An accountant's liability in damages is assessed by   **9–46**
reference to the same principles as for professional persons generally. The claimant must establish a causative link between the loss he alleges and the particular act or omission upon which he relies.[155] Even where accountants had been negligent in failing to detect deficiencies in the accounts of their client, an ex-solicitor who had been struck off the Roll, liability was not established where the claimant's loss and damage were the consequences solely of his own dishonesty.[156]

It is always important, as in actions for professional negligence generally, to   **9–47**
identify the scope of the duty of care owed by the claimant to the defendant, before questions of causation can be properly addressed. So, a claim was struck out where auditors were alleged to have been negligent in failing to report that a company was insolvent and the damages that were sought were trading losses that had thereafter accrued. It was inappropriate to consider causation simply in terms of the traditional "but for" analysis and, on the facts, the losses arose from trading as opposed to the relevant breach of duty.[157] It may be otherwise where the the the claimant can demonstrate that in reliance upon figures represented to him as correct, he traded in a particular way that gave rise to loss.[158] Where, as a result of an auditor's negligence, company profits were overstated and a dividend to shareholders consequently paid, the argument was rejected that the proportion of the dividend paid out of capital was irrecoverable. The payment out of capital was a loss to the company because it was paid to the shareholders who were legally separate. It was not material, given the hypothetical nature of the point,

---

[154] *Knight v Lawrence* [1991] 01 E.G. 105, Browne-Wilkinson V.C. having concluded that the receiver had power to serve "trigger" notices under the Law of Property Act 1925 s.109, as amplified by the provisions of the legal charge.
[155] *Re City Equitable Fire Insurance Co* [1925] 1 Ch.407 at 482–483, para.9–30, above, also *J.E.B. Fasteners Ltd v Marc Bloom & Co* [1981] 3 All E.R. 289 (claimants would have acted no differently even had they known the true position).
[156] *Luscombe v Roberts and Pascho* 106 S.J. 373.
[157] *Bank of Credit and Commerce International (Overseas) Ltd v Price Waterhouse (No.3), The Times*, April 2, 1998, applying *Banque Bruxelles Lambert SA v Eagle Star Insurance Co Ltd* [1997] A.C. 191. The "but for" test had been applied in *Galoo v Bright Grahame Murray* [1994] 1 W.L.R. 1360, CA (where it was alleged that as a result of negligence in the preparation of auditors' accounts, companies continued to trade, when in fact they were insolvent and made losses which were claimed as damages: the claims were rejected on the basis that although it might be said that the losses would not have arisen but for the auditors' negligence, that test was not on its own determinative of liability and as a matter of common sense the negligence gave the occasion for such losses but did not itself cause them). *Galoo* was followed in *Sasea Finance Ltd v KPMG, The Times*, August 25, 1998, but criticised in *Aneco Reinsurance Underwriting Ltd v Johnson & Higgins Ltd* [2000] P.N.L.R. 152, Evans L.J. indicating his preference for a formula to the effect that "the risk was one which the claimant retained for himself." (ibid. at 161).
[158] *Temseel Holdings v Beaumonts Chartered Accountants* [2003] P.N.L.R. 532.

that the shareholders might benefit twice if the money was restored to the company.[159]

9–48   Where the accountant's negligence consists of some positive act or misfeasance, the question of causation is approached as one of historical fact, to be determined on a balance of probabilities. Where the negligence consists in an omission, as where there has been a failure properly to advise, causation depends upon an answer to the hypothetical question, what the claimant would have done had the defendant acted as he should, for instance in the giving of advice. If the claimant proves that, had the defendant acted properly, he would have so arranged his affairs as to avoid the loss he seeks to recover, then he will succed in recovering the full extent of that loss, without discount for the possibility he would have acted otherwise. A discount for chance will however be made where the loss depends, in addition to the acts of the claimant, upon the hypothetical actions of a third party. The claimant must then establish there was a real—as opposed to speculative—chance that his loss would have arisen but for the negligence in question. Once a real chance of loss is proved, he will recover, subject to a discount for the risk that the third party would not have acted as he claims.[160]

9–49   A negligent auditor's liability in damages can be reduced by the operation of s.1157 of the Companies Act 2006, which permits a court to relieve an auditor of liability for negligence, albeit only if the auditor has acted reasonably.[161] In a case where the auditors' negligence was technical, and minor in character, not "pervasive or compelling," and they had acted in good faith, a reduction in the damages for which their negligence rendered them liable was made.[162]

3.—ARCHITECTS, QUANTITY SURVEYORS, STRUCTURAL AND OTHER ENGINEERS, BUILDING CONTRACTORS

9–50   **The duty of care.** The duty of architects,[163] quantity surveyors,[164] engineers and building contractors is primarily determined by the contract under which

---

[159] *Segenhoe Ltd v Akins* [2002] Lloyd's Rep. P.N. 435, Sup. Ct (NSW). In contrast in *Floyd v John Fairhurst & Co* [2004] P.N.L.R. 41, CA it was said that in a case where the claimant was the sole shareholder in a company, principles of reflective loss applied by analogy, so that he should give credit for a gain that the company received as a result of the negligence on which he sued in his personal capacity.

[160] *Allied Maples Group v Simmons & Simmons* [1995] 1 W.L.R. 1602, CA; also *First Interstate Bank of California v Cohen Arnold & Co* [1996] 1 P.N.L.R. 17, CA (in assessing the damages recoverable for accountant's negligent misrepresentation of their client's ability to service a debt, it was necessary to decide whether the claimant, knowing the truth, would have sold its security sooner than it did and, if it had, whether there was a real, not merely speculative, chance of a sale at the value suggested). See also *Demarco v Bulley Davey* [2006] P.N.L.R. 512, CA. (loss of the chance, assessed at 85%, to obtain an IVA, had no market value or any intrinsic or inherent monetary value and only general damages could be awarded, to include the stigma of bankruptcy).

[161] Perhaps more usefully ss.534–536 of the Act, in force since April 2008, allow for agreements limiting the liability of an auditor for statutory audit work, subject to a number of conditons. See further, Butcher Q.C., "Auditors, Parliament and the courts: the development and limitation of auditors' liability" (2008) 2 P.N. 66.

[162] *Barings Plc v Coopers & Lybrand (No.7)* [2003] P.N.L.R. 639.

[163] See Leong and Chan, "Architect's design duties: a shift from *Bolam's* to the objective test", (1999) 1 P.N. 3.

[164] For the liability of surveyors other than quantity surveyors see para.9–304, below.

they are engaged.[165] In addition duties may be owed under statute[166] or in tort.[167] These duties may extend beyond the immediate client to third parties.

The extent and nature of the architect's duty is initially determined by his **9–51** instructions. Where instructions are ambiguous it is not necessarily incumbent on the architect to seek clarification.[168] The duty of care is the same whether the architect is fully qualified or not.[169] Where a specialist consultant is appointed for a particular aspect of building work, an architect owes no duty of care in relation to the consultant's work unless an ordinarily competent architect ought to be aware, and could reasonably be expected, to warn of a problem arising in connection with it.[170] Architects and engineers both owe a duty of care to the building owner to avoid economic loss, whether arising from delay in the execution of building works governed by the JCT form or from negligent extensions of time granted to the builder.[171] A structural engineer employed by the building owner can owe a duty to his client to point out obvious and apparent dangers in temporary works erected by the builder, even though those works are not within the engineer's sphere of responsibility.[172]

The Defective Premises Act 1972. A duty is imposed on anyone taking on **9–52** work in connection with the provision of a dwelling "to see that the work which he takes on is done in a workmanlike or, as the case may be, professional manner, with proper materials and so that as regards that work the dwelling will be fit for

---

[165] The Supply of Goods and Services Act will in many cases imply terms that the services of a building professional are performed with reasonable care. Where at the suggestion of the client a sub-contractor was employed by the main contractor under a building contract and thereafter the sub-contractor negligently damaged the client's goods, the liability of the main contractor was restricted to procuring the sub-contractor's services and did not extend to a parallel liability for the sub-contractor's tort: *Raflatac Ltd v Eade* [1999] 1 Lloyd's Rep. 506 (the sub-contractor failed to shut off the water supply when installing a sprinkler system).

[166] See the discussion of the Defective Premises Act 1972 below at Ch.8, para.8–123, below.

[167] See above at para.9–18 for a discussion of concurrent liability generally. See also *Wessex Regional Health Authority v HLM Design* (1994) 10 Const.L.J. 165 and *Conway v Crown Kelsey* (1994) 39 Const.L.R. 1 where the existence of concurrent duties upon architects and engineers was accepted; also *Storey v Charles Church Developments Ltd* (1996) 12 Const.L.J. 206 (where a builder designs as well as builds he is under concurrent duties in contract and tort not to cause economic loss); also Ndekugri, "Concurrent liability in contract and tort in the construction industry", (2000) 16 Const.L.J. 13; Newman, "Help—I do not have a contract" Cons. Law 2003, 14(6), 29.

[168] *Stormont Main Working Men's Club and Institute v J. Roscoe Milne Partnership* (1989) Con.L.R. 127 (failure to provide facilities for competitive snooker at a workingmens club not negligent where client had not indicated any clear desire for such facilities).

[169] *Cardy & Co v Taylor and Roberts* 38 Con.L.R. 79.

[170] *Investors in Industry Commercial Properties v South Bedfordshire DC* [1986] Q.B. 1034. But the status of this case is in doubt after *Murphy v Brentwood DC* [1991] 1 A.C. 398: see further Ch.8, paras 8–112 to 8–115.

[171] *Wessex Regional Health Authority v HLM Design* [1994] 10 Const.L.J. 165. In *Abbott v Will Gannon Smith* [2005] P.N.L.R. 562, CA (a claim against an allegedly negligent structural engineer) it was said that the building owner's claim arose when physical damage to the property came into existence not at an earlier time when a negligent design was implemented, thereby arguably giving rise to economic loss. See Ch.8, para.8–114, above.

[172] *Hart Investments Ltd v Fidler* [2007] P.N.L.R. 26 (the engineer had been employed in connection with underpinning of the basement of the property ; the builder's works left the façades of the properties dangerously unsupported so that they collapsed).

habitation when completed". The statutory duty[173] is imposed upon building contractors and sub-contractors, together with professional men such as architects, surveyors and engineers, who take on work of the kind described in the section.[174] The liability imposed cannot be excluded.[175]

9–53   **Duty to a third party in tort.** Attention has already been drawn to the basis upon which a professional may be liable in tort to a third party.[176] *Hedley Byrne & Co Ltd v Heller & Partners Ltd*[177] confirmed the potential for such a the duty, although its extent remains open to argument in each case. For instance, while a consulting engineer and an architect owed building contractors a duty of care in respect of supervision of the works, the duty did not extend to instructing them in the manner in which they were to carry out their work. The duty was limited by the assumption that the contractors would perform their obligations competently.[178] Similarly, the duty of a structural engineer who, together with an architect, was employed on the construction of an extension to an existing building, was held to be limited to notifying the architects of any defects of which he had knowledge. There was no obligation on the engineer to supervise the remedial work.[179] Where architects and consulting engineers each gave "duty of care" letters to a third party who intended to purchase a building they were engaged to construct, no duty of care arose under *Hedley Byrne* when a subsequent survey, after the purchase, revealed design and construction faults which led to a lower offer being made on a further attempted sale.[180] Engineers, appointed by employers to supervise extensive dredging and reclamation work off Dubai, owed no duty of care to the main contractors in the absence of contract between them.[181]

9–54   Employers under a building contract did not owe a duty of care, based upon assumption of responsibility, to a sub-contractor of the builder to whom their senior civil engineer gave directions expressing what would be satisfactory if carried out.[182] Nor was any duty owed, by way of the principles set out in *Caparo Industries Plc v Dickman*[183] where an architect provided a letter to the effect that works to that date had been satisfactorily completed, where the prospective purchaser of the property, to whom the seller supplied the letter, did not rely on the architect's advice and the latter was ignorant of the purpose for which the

---

[173] See Ch.2 para.2–77, Ch.8 para.8–123 above, for further consideration of the Act.
[174] Property developers and local authorities who arrange for other persons to take on such work, shall be treated as "included among the persons who have taken on the work": s.1(4).
[175] s.6(3).
[176] See para.9–18 above (general discussion); also para.9–35 above (accountants); para.9–217 below (solicitors); and para.9–304 (valuers).
[177] [1964] A.C. 465.
[178] *Oldschool v Gleeson (Construction)* (1976) 4 Build. L.R. 1053.
[179] *Kensington & Chelsea & Westminster Health Authority v Wettern Composites* [1985] 1 All E.R. 346.
[180] *Hill Samuel Bank v Frederick Brand Partnership* [1994] 10 Const.L.J. 72.
[181] *Pacific Associates Inc v Baxter, The Times*, December 28, 1988.
[182] *Plant Construction Plc v Clive Adam Associates*, 55 Con.L.R. 41.
[183] [1990] 2 A.C. 605.

letter was to be used.[184] No duty of care was owed by engineers retained by the building owner, who provided documents which formed the basis of the claimant builder's tender, in relation to to alleged misrepresentations in those documents.[185]

Aircraft maintenance engineers have been held to owe a duty to exercise **9–55** reasonable care to make accurate entries in log-books, since persons flying the aircraft to which the entries relate will rely on their accuracy, and if there is any want of care, personal injury or property damage may reasonably be expected to result.[186] In contrast, a marine classification society, engaged by ship-owners to carry out the task of surveying a vessel, were not liable to cargo-owners who suffered loss when it proved to be unseaworthy. It was not fair, just or reasonable to impose a duty of care which would have a substantial impact on international trade, where there was an existing system of protection in respect of such loss under the Hague Rules.[187]

Hedley Byrne was applied in *Clay v A.J. Crump & Sons Ltd*[188] where it was **9–56** held that an architect's duty was not confined to his contractual duty to the owners of a dangerous wall, which collapsed injuring a builder's workman, but extended to all those persons who would be so closely and directly affected by his acts or omissions that he ought reasonably to have had them in contemplation. Similarly, in *Voli v Inglewood Shire Council and Lockwood*,[189] the High Court of Australia concluded that an architect owes a duty of care to anyone entering a structure designed by him, when it could reasonably be expected that such person might be injured by a negligent design.

In *Murphy v Brentwood District Council*,[190] the House of Lords, considered **9–57** the scope of the duty of care owed by a builder to the purchaser of a house he had constructed He was liable under the principle in *Donoghue v Stevenson*[191] in the event of any defect, *prior* to its discovery, causing either physical injury to person

---

[184] *Machin v Adams*, 84 B.L.R. 79, CA; also *Strathford East Kilbride Ltd v Film Design Ltd, The Times*, December 1, 1997, OH (no duty owed to tenant by architects contracted to the landlord); also *Howes v Crombie* [2002] P.N.L.R. 60, OH (no forseeability of reliance sufficient to establish a duty of care where, not knowing that what he said would be relied upon to secure lending upon a property, a structural engineer wrote commending the structural integrity of a property he had inspected in the course of construction).

[185] *Galliford Try Infrastructure Ltd v Mott Macdonald* [2008] EWHC 1570 (TCC)(in the ordinary course of events, an architect or engineer engaged by a developer will not owe any duty of care, at least in relation to economic loss, to tendering contractors, even where the latter are supplied by the architect or engineer with tender information, drawings and specifications upon which to base their tenders).

[186] *Hawke v Waterloo-Wellington Flying Club Ltd* (1972) 22 D.L.R. (3d) 266.

[187] *Marc Rich & Co AG v Bishop Rock Marine Co Ltd* [1996] 1 A.C. 211, distinguished in *Perrett v Collins* [1999] P.N.L.R. 77, CA, Ch.10, below, para.10–172 on the basis that the reasoning of the HL was directed to claims for economic loss rather than claims for personal injury.

[188] [1964] 1 Q.B. 533; see "Negligent Architects—Falling Walls and Perils of Polling", 27 M.L.R. 216.

[189] [1963] A.L.R. 657.

[190] [1991] 1 A.C. 398, which overruled *Dutton v Bognor Regis UDC* [1972] 1 Q.B. 373 and held that *Anns v Merton LBC* [1978] A.C. 728 was wrongly decided. See Holtum, "Duties of care for latent damage in building cases" 151 N.L.J. 754. See also Ch.2, paras 2–238 to 2–245, above.

[191] [1932] A.C. 562.

or damage to property other than the building itself. On the other hand, where a purchaser who had discovered the defect, however such discovery had come about, spent money to make the building safe and suitable for its intended purpose, there was no sound basis in principle for holding the builder liable for the purchaser's pure economic loss.[192] The question was left open whether a negligent builder could be held responsible for the cost necessarily incurred by a building owner in protecting himself from potential liability to third parties, for example on the adjacent highway or the neighbouring land's boundary.[193]

9–58   *Murphy* does not operate to impose upon the builder liability to subsequent purchasers for defects that are patent, as opposed to latent. A patent defect is one which is discoverable with due diligence whether or not due diligence is exercised.

> "Where in the normal course of events, a surveyor would be engaged in a survey of a building for a purchaser, and, with the exercise of due diligence, that surveyor would have discovered a defect, that defect is patent whether or not a surveyor is engaged, and, if engaged, whether or not the surveyor performs his task competently."[194]

9–59   The principles set out in *Murphy* should apply equally to those advising in relation to building works, or structural engineers, as to builders.[195] Accordingly, where specialist engineering consultants had been instructed by a local authority to advise in relation to ground conditions and the requirements for adequate foundations for a proposed dwelling-house, upon which advice it relied, it was held that such specialists did not owe a duty of care to the subsequent purchaser from the local authority and or the owner occupier for the time being.[196]

9–60   An architect may, in appropriate circumstances, owe a duty of care in tort and be liable to a subsequent occupier of a building which he has designed, or the construction of which he has supervised, in respect of latent defects in the building of which there was no reasonable prospect of inspection. Conversely, he is not liable to a subsequent occupier of a building, in relation to a latent defect if, in the ordinary course of events a subsequent survey would have been expected, and would if carried out, have revealed the defect.[197] The question whether a particular defect in a building comes within the scope of his duty of care will depend upon the extent of his responsibility for the original design or the extent of any supervisory obligations he undertook. No duty of care would be

---

[192] To this effect, see per Lord Keith in *Department of the Environment v Thomas Bates & Sons Ltd* [1991] 1 A.C. 499, following *Murphy v Brentwood District Council*, [1991] 1 A.C. 398.

[193] [1991] 1 A.C. 398 at 475 (Lord Bridge) and 489 (Lord Oliver).

[194] *Baxall Securities v Sheard Walshaw* [2002] P.N.L.R. 564, CA, per Steel J. at 577.

[195] See, e.g. *Payne v John Setchell Ltd* [2002] P.N.L.R. 146. See Duncan, "Lucky architects: snail in an opaque bottle?" 2003 L.Q.R., (119) 17.

[196] *Preston v Torfaen Borough Council* [1993] N.P.C. 111, CA (the claimant buyers had alleged that Northwest Holst Soil Engineering owed a duty of care to the ultimate buyers of property, which was built on an infilled quarry, for further economic loss they would suffer if the expert's advice to the council had been negligent).

[197] *Pearson Education Ltd v The Charter Partnership Ltd* [2007] B.L.R. 324, CA.

owed in respect of defects for which he never had any design or supervisory responsibility in the first place.[198]

Where a number of persons acquire an interest in a property after a defect **9–61** arises, knowledge by one of them of the defect is not automatically acquired by successors in title: the defect remains latent so far as they are concerned until the circumstances in which it loses its "latent" quality, so far as they individually are concerned, arise. It will depend upon the facts whether the potential cause of action of a successor survives unaffected, or is lost because the defect is no longer latent. The successor's claim may also be defeated because the chain of causation was broken by the earlier discovery, or there may be a reduction in the damages awarded on account of contributory negligence. Finally, the claim may be defeated because it is no longer fair, just and reasonable for it to be maintained.[199] Applying these principles, architects were liable to lessees, with whom they had no contractual connection, where stock contained in a warehouse subject to the lease was damaged by a flood. The architects had designed a rainwater drainage system for the developer but negligently failed to provide it with appropriate capacity. Their argument that the under-capacity was a patent defect, failed. At the time the capacity of the system was specified, there was no reason to expect an inspection would reveal any error. There was no reason why the claimant should have carried out any investigation of the adequacy of the system for draining rainwater. The claimant was not fixed with knowledge of a flood which arose during an earlier tenancy.[200]

While it is possible for a sub-contractor to owe a duty of care to the employer **9–62** under a building contract the circumstances in which such a duty will be imposed are likely to be rare.[201] In *Henderson v Merrett Syndicates Ltd*,[202] Lord Goff of Chievely pointed out that:

---

[198] See, e.g. *Bellefield Computer Services v E Turner & Sons Ltd* [2003] Lloyd's Rep. P.N. 53, CA (a claim against architects based upon alleged faulty design of fire protection works for a dairy extension: no liability where the architects were not engaged to supervise the relevant work and a specialist sub contractor who did the work, failed to install the fire protection measures specified). See also *Sahib Foods Ltd v Paskin Kyriakides Sands* [2003] P.N.L.R. 585 (architects owed no duty of care to a freehold owner, in relation to the absence of proper fireproofing in factory premises, where there was no proof that the lack of fireproofing would not have been spotted by a reasonably competent surveyor engaged at the time the freehold was acquired); also the same case on appeal, [2004] P.N.L.R. 403, CA, para.9–65, below (a duty *was* owed to the tenant in occupation of the premises).

[199] *Pearson Education Ltd v The Charter Partnership Ltd,* n.197, above. See particularly per Lord Phillips M.R.: if an architect who had the primary responsibility for producing a safe design, produced a design that was defective, it was not obviously fair, just and reasonable that he should be absolved from liability in tort in respect of its consequences, on the ground that another professional could reasonably be expected to discover his shortcoming. See further, Minogue, "Here comes the rain again" 2007 Building, 12, 51; Murdoch, "After the flood has receded" 2007 E.G., 0721, 129 ; generally, Harder, "Is liability for defective buildings negated by a surveyor's intervening negligence" 2007 Conv., Sep/Oct, 417.

[200] *Pearson Education Ltd v The Charter Partnership Ltd,* n.199 above.

[201] A duty was imposed in *Junior Books Ltd v Veitchi Co Ltd* [1983] 1 A.C. 520, but that decision, while not formally overruled, has subsequently been said to be confined to its own special facts: see the summary in *Architype Properties Ltd v Dewhurst MacFarlane & Partners* [2004] P.N.L.R. 732 from 742.

[202] [1995] 2 A.C. 145.

"if the sub-contracted work or materials do not in the result conform to the required standard, it will not ordinarily be open to the building owner to sue the sub-contractor or supplier direct under the *Hedley Byrne* principle, claiming damages on the basis that he has been negligent in relation to the performance of his functions. For there is generally no assumption of responsibility by the sub-contractor or supplier direct to the building owner, the parties having so constructed their relationship that it is inconsistent with any such assumption of responsibility."[203]

9–63   In considering whether such a duty should be imposed it will no doubt be appropriate to consider the circumstances generally, but in particular, the terms of the contract between the employer and the main contractor. So, where that contract contained a term requiring the employer to insure against certain specified perils and that nominated sub-contractors should have the benefit of cover under the policy, it was fair, just and reasonable to impose a duty of care on a sub-contractor outside of the relevant provisions, in respect of physical damage which accrued as a result of his careless act.[204]

9–64   From a different perspective, both an independent contractor and the owner of a building can owe a duty of care to the employee of a sub-contractor. The question is one of mixed fact and law, and it is unnecessary and unhelpful to attempt to formulate a specific test for deciding when such a duty would arise.[205]

9–65   **The standard of care.** Architects have been held liable for not properly examining the foundations on which a bridge was to be built[206]; for not disclosing the risk of inflation and its likely effect on the costs of building work for which they had been asked to provide an approximate estimate[207]; for relying on second-hand information about the size of a site for which they had been asked to prepare plans[208]; for failing to perceive that as a result of fraud by the clerk of works,[209] floors had been laid contrary to specification so that dry rot arose; for not superintending properly actual construction of the building[210]; in

---

[203] *Henderson v Merrett Syndicates Ltd* [1995] 2 A.C.145 at 195.

[204] *British Telecommunications Plc v James Thomson & Sons (Engineering) Ltd* [1999] 1 W.L.R. 9, HL, para.9–24, n.85, above; also *R.M. Turton & Co Ltd v Kerslake & Partners* [2000] Lloyd's Rep.P.N. 967, CA (NZ); and *Norwich City Council v Harvey* [1989] 1 W.L.R. 828, CA.

[205] *Gray v Fire Alarm Fabrication Services Ltd, The Times,* November 22, 2006, CA (on the facts the deceased's employer was entirely to blame for an accident in which he fell to his death through a skylight while running cable for the fire alarm system through a cable tray fixed to the exterior wall of the building).

[206] *Moneypenny v Hartland* (1824) 1 C. & P. 352.

[207] *Lees v English & Partners* (1977) 242 E.G. 295. See Patterson, "Consultant's duty of care in the tender process" 2002 Cons. Law 13(4), 6.

[208] *Columbus Co v Clowes* [1903] 1 K.B. 244.

[209] *Leicester Guardians v Trollope* (1911) 75 J.P. 197.

[210] *Armstrong v Jones* (1869) 2 Hudson's B.C. 4th edn, 6; *Saunders and Collard v Broadstairs L.B.* (1890) 2 Hudson's B.C. 4th edn, 164; *Rogers v James* (1891) 8 T.L.R. 67; *Steljes v Ingram* (1903) 19 T.L.R. 534; *Florida Hotels Pty v Mayo* (1965) 113 C.L.R. 588. In *Kensington & Chelsea & Westminster Health Authority v Adams Holden & Partners* [1984] C.I.L.L. 91, the architects were held to be negligent where they became aware of poor workmanship but failed to react by increasing their supervision of the erection of an extension to a hospital. Supervision, in common parlance, means to keep an eye on and watch over, not a constant eye or continuous watch: *Summers v Congreve Horner & Co and Independent Insurance Co* [1992] 04 E.G. 144, CA.

approving drawings of a defectively designed building where, without authority, they had sub-contracted specialised design tasks[211]; in failing to terminate the builder's contract where he does not proceed regularly and diligently with the works as required by clause 25(1) of the JCT contract[212]; in failing to advise against employment of a builder known to have professional shortcomings.[213] In requiring a builder to remedy faults, an architect is entitled to take into account that a building is being erected at low cost.[214] Architects were negligent in failing, when planning to remodel a factory in which ready meals for supermarkets were prepared, to provide a high standard of fireproofing in food preparation rooms.[215]

An architect or surveyor will be liable for negligence in failing to measure   **9–66** accurately a builder's work or otherwise mistaking the amount due to the builder from his employer. In some circumstances an architect may be an arbitrator, with the benefit of an arbitrator's immunity, depending on the precise terms of his contract and whether, inter alia, he is called upon to exercise a judicial function.[216] Apart from special agreement an architect when issuing interim certificates does not normally act as an arbitrator between his client, the building owner, and the builder. Since he is under a duty to act fairly in making his valuation, an architect has been held liable at the suit of his client because he negligently over-certified sums claimed by the builder.[217] On the other hand, where an architect had issued interim certificates which included prime cost items which had been delivered to the site, but for which he knew the building owners and not the contractors would have to pay, it was held that, on construction of the contract, there was no negligence on the architect's part since all necessary financial adjustments could be made when the final certificate was issued.[218]

A clause in a contract providing that the decision of the architect as to the state   **9–67** of the works or in any wise relating to the execution of the works shall be final and binding only relates to disputes between the building owner and the

---

[211] *Moresk Cleaners v Hicks* [1966] 2 Lloyd's Rep. 338.

[212] *West Faulkner Associates v London Borough of Newham* [1995] Const.L.J. 15, CA.

[213] *Partridge v Morris* [1995] E.G.C.S. 158.

[214] *Cotton v Wallis* [1955] 1 W.L.R. 1168.

[215] *Sahib Foods Ltd v Paskin Kyriakides Sands* [2004] P.N.L.R. 403, CA, n.99 above (the fire started in the preparation room as a result of the negligence of the claimant's own employees, but spread to the rest of the factory as a result of the lack of proper fireproofing).

[216] *Arenson v Arenson* [1977] A.C. 405 (a case of auditors who had to value shares).

[217] *Sutcliffe v Thackrah* [1974] A.C. 727, overruling *Chambers v Goldthorpe* [1901] 1 K.B. 624. Lord Reid (at 738) said that many, probably most, of the earlier cases could be justified on their facts but there were borderline cases where it was far from easy to determine whether or not there was a sufficient judicial element to require an arbitrator's immunity to attach. Nevertheless "if that immunity is claimed, then it is for the person claiming it to show that the functions in the performance of which he was negligent were sufficiently judicial in character." See Poole, "Liability of Architects when Issuing an Interim Certificate", 124 New L.J. 603; *Tyrer v District Auditor for Monmouthshire* (1973) 230 E.G. 973.

[218] *Wisbech Rural District Council v Ward* [1928] 2 K.B. 1.

contractor. Thus a final certificate given under such a clause is no estoppel in an action by the owner against the architect in negligence.[219]

9–68 Architects, as with other professionals, are expected to have a working knowledge of the law as it relates to their discipline, sufficient to enable them to perform their duties adequately. However, where an experienced architect failed to warn his clients that a planning permission in their favour may be unlawful and thereby void, he was not negligent in circumstances where he believed the final and conclusive decision would be made by the planning committee: it mattered not whether he was right or wrong in law, because holding such an opinion did not amount to negligence.[220]

9–69 Building professionals do not guarantee the success of any project in which they are engaged but will be liable if, for instance, as engineering contractors they fail to design a building fit for the purpose for which they know it to be required. So in *Greaves & Co (Contractors) Ltd v Baynham Meikle & Partners*[221] consulting structural engineers employed to design a warehouse were liable for breach of implied warranty where the floor was not fit for its purpose. Likewise, engineers who negligently designed and constructed a 1,250ft-high cylindrical broadcasting mast at Enley Moor, Yorkshire were liable for its sudden collapse about two years after its completion: its fall was caused by a number of factors, principally a combination of heavy and uneven icing up of stay ropes, which had exerted pressures down the mast and the aerodynamic phenomenon known as "vortex shredding", which had produced additional stresses so that severe oscillations occurred, beyond the structure's endurance.[222]

9–70 Where architects' plans are so inaccurate on a matter such as ventilation as to make the building almost uninhabitable, a building contractor may be liable for breach of contract even where he has followed the plan and specification exactly. A builder's responsibility is not limited to matters of workmanship. Where a builder ought to recognise obvious defects in the design of a building, the obligation to carry out work which will perform its intended function overrides that of following the specification slavishly, particularly when he has agreed to "give efficient supervision . . . using his best skill and attention".[223]

9–71 The extent of a builder's duty to investigate and examine land before building on it is to be determined by what a careful and competent builder would have done in the circumstances. Such duty is not restricted merely to observable defects on land owned by the builder or to which he has a legal right of entry,

---

[219] *Rogers v James* (1891) 8 T.L.R. 67.
[220] *BL Holdings v Robert J. Wood & Partners* (1979) 123 S.J. 570, CA. See also *F.G. Whitley & Sons v Thomas Bickerton* [1993] E.G. 100 (surveyors acting for the owner of a site were liable both in contract and negligence where they failed to appeal a decision of the planning authority refusing planning permission).
[221] [1975] 1 W.L.R. 1095; Poole, "Liability of a Specialised Sub-Contractor", 125 New L.J. 31.
[222] *Independent Broadcasting Authority v E.M.I. Electronics and B.I.C.C. Construction Ltd* (1980) 14 Build. L.R. 1, HL. See Stantion and Dugdale, "Design Responsibility in Civil Engineering Work", 131 New L.J. 583.
[223] *Brunswick Construction v Nowlan* (1975) 49 D.L.R. (3d) 93.

where if he was careful and competent he would have observed defects on neighbouring land and would not have built until either there had been a further investigation of the site, or a satisfactory report had been received from an expert, for instance, on the condition of the subsoil.[224] Where damage was caused to houses by heave in the foundations, resulting from the removal of trees, both the builders and consulting engineers were liable in negligence as well as breach of contract.[225] A builder can be liable for the dust deposited during the building process, depending upon proof of physical damage.[226] As in other areas where the defendant holds himself out as having expertise, a builder is to be judged by the knowledge he ought, as a reasonably competent professional, to possess at the relevant time.[227]

Evidence of negligence. Failure of the works which he has been employed to   **9–72** design and superintend may be evidence of negligence on the part of the architect or engineer concerned, throwing upon him the burden of establishing that he has not been negligent. This will not be the case when he is required to engage in something of an experiment. Thus, where an architect was employed to design and superintend the erection of model lodging-houses, with instructions to include a newly-patented concrete roofing, less costly than lead or slate, negligence was not established when the roof admitted water.[228]

Equally, however, where substantial risks have to be incurred in a project   **9–73** involving novel design work close to or beyond the limit of existing knowledge or experience, a very high standard of care may be required. In a case where a 1,250ft-high cylindrical steel television broadcasting mast suddenly broke and collapsed in extremes of bad weather it was said that, while judgment with hindsight has to be avoided:

"justice requires that we seek to put ourselves in the position of B.I.C.C. when first confronted by their daunting task, lacking all empirical knowledge and adequate expert advice in dealing with the many problems awaiting solution. But those handicaps created a clear duty to identify and think through such problems, including those of dynamic and static stresses, so that the dimensions of the 'venture into the unknown'

---

[224] *Batty v Metropolitan Property Realisations Ltd* [1978] Q.B. 554 (although again this case is of uncertain status after *Murphy v Brentwood District Council* [1991] 1 A.C. 398).
[225] *Balcomb v Ward's Construction (Medway)* (1981) 259 E.G. 765.
[226] If he is sued by someone with an interest in the land affected: *Hunter v Canary Wharf Ltd* [1997] A.C. 655.
[227] See *Barclays Bank v Fairclough Building Ltd* [1995] 1 All E.R. 289, CA (contractors performing works involving asbestos ought by 1988 at the latest to have appreciated the dangers to health and safety associated therewith. Accordingly specialist roofing cleaners who undertook the cleaning of asbestos roofing with power hoses, which broke down the cement bonding of the roof and created a slurry, were liable in tort to those with whom they contracted for the work, there being a duty of care to avoid causing economic loss arising from their failure to prevent contamination of the building).
[228] *Turner v Garland* (1853) 2 Hudson's B.C. 4th edn, 1. In directing the jury, Erle J. said: "You should bear in mind that if the building is of ordinary description in which he [the defendant] had abundance of experience, and it proved a failure, this is evidence of want of skill or attention. But if out of ordinary course, and you employ him about a novel thing, about which he has little experience, if it has not had the test of experience, failure may be consistent with skill. The history of all great improvements shows failure of those who embark in them."

could be adequately assessed and the ultimate decision as to its practicability arrived at. And it is no answer to say, as did one witness regarding the conjunction of vortex shredding and ice loading, 'It wasn't obvious because it hadn't been considered'. The learned judge held that it should have been, and in my judgment he was right in saying so." [229]

In the absence of expert evidence as to standard practice, the omission of an architect to provide for downstairs toilets in the design of a range of mid-priced houses was not negligent. It was not self-evidently incompetent or so glaring an omission as spoke for itself. [230]

9–74   **Measure of damages.** The damages recoverable against an architect, quantity surveyor, engineer or building contractor fall to be determined on usual tortious principles. The measure of damages will depend upon the nature of the defendant's breach. The claimant should be restored, so far as he can by money, to the position he would have occupied had a breach of duty not occurred. [231] The starting point for claims will usually be the cost of rectification but in appropriate cases consequential loss may be recovered and also damages for physical inconvenience. [232]

4.—AUCTIONEERS

9–75   **The duty of care.** Auctioneers, [233] in common with others who profess to carry on a business which requires knowledge and skill, must exercise that care and skill reasonably to be expected from a competent auctioneer. Liability to a client, the seller, normally arises out of contract and it is their duty to sign a proper contract which is binding on the buyer. Any omission to do so will make them liable to the seller for the damage suffered as a result of their neglect. [234] They are under a duty to account for all moneys received on the seller's behalf and to pay over such moneys to him. [235] Auctioneers must follow the course of business that is ordinarily recognised by custom, [236] as well as that prescribed by

---

[229] per Lord Edmund Davies in *Independent Broadcasting Authority v E.M.I. Electronics and B.I.C.C. Construction Ltd* (1980) 14 Build. L.R. 1 at 31. The facts are more fully described at para.9–69, above.

[230] *Worboys v Acme Investments* (1969) 210 E.G. 335 (the houses were valued at about £8,000).

[231] In *Partridge v Morris* [1995] E.G.C.S. 158, where a negligent architect failed to warn against employment of a builder of doubtful "track record" whose work proved unsatisfactory, the claimant recovered losses arising because he had to engage two sets of builders, together with the cost of making good the defective work.

[232] *Watts v Morrow* [1991] 1 W.L.R. 1421, CA, where the trial judge's award of £4,000 to each claimant, a husband and wife whose marriage had broken down subsequently, was reduced to £750 each, assessed on the basis that the physical discomfort had extended for about eight months. But where an architect's contract is simply to design a house, and he fails to include agreed features of the design, no damages can be recovered for frustration or distress since the object of the contract was not the provision of pleasure or peace of mind: *Knott v Bolton* [1995] E.G.C.S. 59, CA.

[233] See "Auctioneer's Personal Liability", 267 E.G. 530; Jess, "Auctioneer's Negligence", 82 L.S.Gaz. 1915.

[234] *Peirce v Corf* (1894) L.R. 9 Q.B. 210.

[235] *Re Cotton Ex p. Cooke* (1913) 108 L.T. 310, CA.

[236] *Russell v Hankey* (1794) 6 Term Rep. 12.

statute.[237] It has been held that where an auctioneer, exercising his judgment, did not insist upon payment of a deposit by a buyer he had not acted negligently.[238] Indeed, auctioneers are under no general duty to sellers at all to get in the purchase price from buyers.[239] Although the point was put to one side in *Rainbow v Howkins*,[240] an action would lie in all probability against an auctioneer for failing to enter a memorandum of sale, binding his principal, in his books. [241] The auctioneer, as a bailee for reward, must exercise ordinary care and diligence in keeping the goods which have been entrusted to him by the seller.[242] On the facts, it was not negligent for an auctioneer to fail to procure the name and address of the buyer, upon whose bid the bargain had been struck, before the latter left the room hurriedly and disappeared.[243]

In considering the duty of a provincial auction house when valuing a painting **9–76** by an unknown hand, it was said in the Court of Appeal[244] that the valuation of pictures of which the artist was unknown would involve an exercise of opinion and judgment that by the very nature of things could well be fallible. Provided always that the valuer approached his job honestly, and with due diligence, a finding of negligence should be approach with caution; there was no blame merely in failure to spot a "sleeper" or the potentiality of such.[245]

The standard of care. It is not enough, in order to establish negligence on the **9–77** part of an auctioneer, to show that there is a body of competent professional opinion which considers his decision to have been wrong, where there also exists a body of equally competent professional opinion supporting the other point of view.[246]

Where the defendant auctioneers were not negligent in their catalogue **9–78** description of a pair of vases as "Louis XV porphyry and gilt-bronze two handled vases", they could not be in breach of duty to the claimant purchaser, even if the vases were worth much less than she paid, as a result of a risk that they were not Louis XV at all, but imitations made in the mid-19th century or later. There was no duty to advise the claimant of the difficulty of dating such objects and the risks which purchase entailed, despite the facts that she had been

---

[237] *Coppen v Moore (No.2)* [1898] 2 Q.B. 306; *Christie Manson & Woods Ltd v Cooper* [1900] 2 Q.B. 522.

[238] *Cyril Andrade Ltd v Sotheby & Co* (1931) 47 T.L.R. 244.

[239] *Fordham v Christie, Manson & Woods Ltd, The Times*, June 24, 1977. Whilst it is true that in *Chelmsford Auctions Ltd v Poole* [1973] 1 Q.B. 542 it was decided that auctioneers could sue in their own name for the whole of the purchase price, that entitlement did not impose an obligation to get in the money, but only an obligation to take reasonable care if and when they did so get it.

[240] [1904] 2 K.B. 322 at 326.

[241] To the contrary see *Richards v Phillips* [1967] 3 All E.R. 876 at 881.

[242] See Ch.3, para.3–196, above.

[243] *Hardial Singh v Hillyer & Hillyer* [1979] E.G. 951.

[244] *Luxmoore-May v Messenger May Baverstock* [1990] 1 W.L.R. 1009.

[245] In the esoteric world of antiques, an article which is unrecognised by the auctioneer.

[246] *Alchemy (International) Ltd v Tattersalls Ltd* (1985) 276 E.G. 675, applying *Maynard v West Midlands Regional Health Authority* [1984] 1 W.L.R. 634, HL, for which see para.9–125, below.

marked out as a special client, and provided with a "special client advisor" who was consulted about the lot.[247]

9–79   **Duty to third parties in tort.** There would appear to be no reason why a special relationship cannot arise, for reasons canvassed earlier in relation to other professionals, so as to expose an auctioneer to liability to a third party. Where an auctioneer, who had no qualifications in building construction, was employed by a housing authority to give a valuation of a house and in due course he reported the property to be in good repair and gave a valuation, no dispute arose that such auctioneer did owe a duty of care to a subsequent buyer of the property, albeit the buyer's claim failed in the absence of proof of carelessness.[248] A claim succeeded where an auctioneer's employee incorrectly represented that premises had been withdrawn from auction and the owner would sell the freehold. It was held he should have known his statement would be acted upon and a special relationship thereby arose.[249]

5.—BANKERS AND FINANCE COMPANIES

9–80   **The duty of care.** A banker must exercise due care and skill in the business of banking,[250] but the scope of the duty to a customer or a third party is highly sensitive to the particular factual background.[251] A number of broad categories of case can be distinguished.

9–81   **Giving advice or information.** Whilst it is no part of a banker's ordinary business to give a customer advice as to investments,[252] if advice is given, an obligation may be imposed to take reasonable care.[253] When a bank chooses to give preliminary advice to a customer about the nature and effect of a proposed mortgage in the bank's favour, it is under a duty not to misstate the effect of the mortgage. Further, the bank ought to explain to its customer, where that was the case, that a mortgage on a property, jointly owned by the customer and spouse,

---

[247] *Thomson v Christie Manson & Woods Ltd* [2005] P.N.L.R. 713, CA (the vases were bought for £1,957,388; if they were imitation they were worth some £25,000). See Stacey, "Under the hammer" 148 S.J. 778; Robins, "Urning their keep" Lawyer, 2005, 19(9), 20. Meisel, "Auctioneers and buyers: a special relationship?" (2005) 4 P.N. 250.

[248] *Ward v McMaster* [1985] I.R. 29 (other defendants were held liable instead).

[249] *McAnarney v Hanrahan* [1993] 3 I.R. 492.

[250] See Stanton and Dugdale, "Recent Developments in Professional Negligence—III: Bankers", 132 New L.J. 105; King, "The Receiving Bank's Role in Credit Transfer Transactions", 45 M.L.R. 369; Southern, "The liabilities and duties of banks to private customers", (1996) 11 B.J.I.B. & F.L.(5) 224; Tijio, "Duty of care and damages in banking cases", 1997 J.B.L., Jul. 350; Stanton, "Banks, negligence and the bankruptcy of theory", (1998) 14 P.N.(3), 131.

[251] See per Salmon J. in *Woods v Martins Bank Ltd* [1959] 1 Q.B. 55 at 70.

[252] See also *Lipkin Gorman v Karpnale* [1989] 1 W.L.R. 1340, CA (a bank's principal duty is to pay cheques signed in accordance with its mandate and there is no obligation imposed on it to inquire into the commercial wisdom of any transaction. A bank would be liable in such circumstances only if, on the facts found, any reasonable banker would have suspected fraud).

[253] *Woods v Martins Bank Ltd,* n.239a, above, per Salmon J. at 72.

specifically covered additional unlimited advances to the spouse.[254] A duty of care was owed where a bank manager was asked for and gave advice about the wisdom of purchasing a particular house as a business venture.[255]

However, where a customer, on the advice of his bank manager, advanced **9–82** money on mortgage to a company which was also a customer of the bank, and suffered loss when the company failed, it was held that the bank had owed no duty to advise him carefully or at all.[256] In the normal course of events a bank does not owe a duty of care, whether in tort or contract, to profer any explanation or to advise the taking of independent advice to a customer who comes to its premises in order to sign securities.[257] Where a wife had offered her interest in the matrimonial home as surety for her husband's loan from a bank, there was no duty to disclose matters such as the amount of the husband's debt or the purpose of the loan, even though they might have affected her view of the risk involved.[258]

When a bank is asked about the financial position of one of its customers it is **9–83** under a duty to answer honestly on the information which it has, but not to make inquiries elsewhere. If asked for an opinion whether a customer can be trusted for a specific sum of money, and an honest opinion is expressed, a bank will not be liable even if, on the facts available, other bankers might have expressed a different opinion.[259] Since *Hedley Byrne & Co Ltd v Heller & Partners Ltd*,[260] there is a clear distinction to be made between a duty to be honest and the duty to take reasonable care, which arises where a special relationship exists, quite independently of any contractual relationship between the parties.[261] No breach of duty arose where a bank was required by subpoena to produce a customer's statement of account in circumstances where no legal privilege against production could have been claimed.[262] A bank was under no duty to inform a customer who had personally guaranteed a loan to a company of which he was chief executive officer and chairman, of a boardroom plot against him.[263]

---

[254] *Cornish v Midland Bank Plc* [1985] 3 All E.R. 513.
[255] *Verity v Lloyds Bank Plc* [1995] N.P.C. 148.
[256] *Banbury v Bank of Montreal* [1918] A.C. 626.
[257] *Barclays Bank Plc v Khaira* [1992] 1 W.L.R. 623.
[258] *Midland Bank Plc v Kidwai, The Independent*, June 5, 1995, CA.
[259] *Parsons v Barclay & Co Ltd* (1910) 26 T.L.R. 628; (contrast the facts and the situation with those in *Hedley Byrne & Co Ltd v Heller & Partners Ltd*); *Batts Combe Quarry Co v Barclays Bank Ltd* (1931) 48 T.L.R. 4. In *Macken v Munster and Leinster Bank* (1960) 95 I.L.T.R. 17, Deale J. held that a bank manager was negligent when he failed to take reasonable care when supplying information to the claimant concerning the financial position of a certain Dutchman, as a result of which the claimant signed a promissory note, on which the Dutchman defaulted; *Commercial Banking Company of Sydney Ltd v R.H. Brown & Co* [1972] 2 Lloyd's Rep. 360 (the HC of Australia held that the bank's opinion was not honestly held by its manager concerning the business-worthiness of its customer, a wool buyer).
[260] [1964] A.C. 465. For the facts see Ch.2, para.2–172, above.
[261] See para.9–18, above.
[262] *Maurice Robertson v Canadian Imperial Bank of Commerce* [1994] 1 W.L.R. 1493, PC.
[263] *Fennoscandia Ltd v Clarke* [1999] 1 All E.R. (Comm) 365, CA.

9–84   **Cheques and credit.** A bank was under no duty to check the identity of a person in respect of whom it is being asked to provide a credit reference.[264] A paying bank does not normally owe a duty of care to a cheque's payee who is not its customer, but this was subject to qualification where the bank's conduct was calculated to deceive the payee in a manner which could result in financial loss to him. If the bank had refused payment of a cheque at once in an unqualified manner it would not have been liable, but by communicating a reason the bank had assumed responsibility to act honestly and carefully.[265] A bank which received a cheque drawn upon another bank upon the basis that it would be applied either to the purchase of shares or returned to the drawer, did not owe a duty of care to the drawer's bank not to lose it.[266]

9–85   Where a bank is acting as a clearing bank, that is, as agent for collection of a cheque on behalf of another bank or financial institution, it owes a duty of care to the true owner of the cheque, but is in general entitled to consider that the duty will be performed by its own customer, who should be in a far better position to know the circumstances in which the cheque was brought for collection and the identity of the person who submitted it. But the extent to which the clearing bank can rely on its customer will vary with the circumstances. Where the clearing bank acts for a foreign bank it does not, for instance, follow that it can assume that the foreign bank is aware of the effect in English law of an endorsement "a/c payee" by which a cheque becomes non-transferable and can only be paid to the named payee.[267]

9–86   **Assumption of responsibility.** A bank did not assume the responsibility of an insurance broker towards the claimant where its subsidiary company sent her a letter enclosing an insurance proposal form which she was subsequently pressed to complete and return, since on the facts the bank was simply trying to ensure that the claimant's preferred insurance cover was in place.[268]

9–87   **Duty to third parties.** So far as third parties generally are concerned, there is no reason why the ambit of a bank's duty of care should be approached otherwise than in the case of any other professional body. A claimant will have to demonstrate a relationship of proximity, with or without an assumption of responsibility, also foreseeability of damage and that it is fair, just and reasonable

---

[264] *Gold Coin Joailliers SA v United Bank of Kuwait Plc* [1997] P.N.L.R. 217, CA (a rogue assuming a false identity persuaded a bank to give a reference to the claimants who gave him watches as a result: the bank was not liable for the loss since they had not, on the facts, assumed a duty of care regarding the identity of the person in relation to whom the information was being provided).

[265] *Potterton v Northern Bank* [1993] 1 I.R. 413, following *Hedley Byrne & Co Ltd v Heller & Partners Ltd* [1964] A.C. 465 and, as regards the fact that a bank should either pay a cheque in legal form or refuse payment at once, *Bank of England v Vagliano Brothers* [1891] A.C. 107.

[266] *Yorkshire Bank Plc v Lloyds Bank Plc, The Times,* May 12, 1999 (a cheque for £90,000 which was stolen, fraudulently altered and negotiated after it came into the defendant's custody).

[267] *The Honourable Society of the Middle Temple v Lloyds Bank Plc* [1999] 1 All E.R. (Comm) 193 (Lloyds Bank did not have a defence under s.4 of the 1957 Act where it had not, as had other clearing banks, informed its foreign customer of the effect of the Cheques Act 1992 upon cheques marked "a/c payee" and was in breach of duty towards the true owner of a cheque presented at a foreign bank and sent by that bank to Lloyds for collection).

[268] *Frost v James Finlay Bank Ltd* [2002] Lloyd's Rep. I.R. 503, CA.

to impose a duty of care. The first of these requirements was not made out where a bank obtained a report upon the financial position of a company, its customer, and thereafter made formal demand for outstanding debts and went on to obtain administration orders, following which the company went into liquidation. No duty of care was owed to a director of the company, who had a right to acquire all its issued shares, and who alleged that the report was inaccurate and that as a result of the administration orders he had suffered loss, since he was not a customer of the bank and there were no circumstances from which it could be inferred that the bank had assumed any responsibility towards him.[269]

In relation to a person not actually its customer, no duty of care was owed by a bank whose customer had provided it with an irrevocable authority to pay that person a sum of money and the bank did not in fact pay the whole amount: there had been no communication between the bank and the payee and the court was not prepared to accept the general proposition that when foreseeability of financial loss is established to an individual it is fair, just and reasonable for the bank to owe a duty of care in addition to its contractual duty to its customer.[270]   **9–88**

No duty of care was owed by a bank to claimants who it was aware had obtained an asset freezing order from the court, which restrained payments out of the accounts of certain of its customers. While the foreseeability element in the threefold *Caparo* test was satisfied, the parties were proximate only in the sense that one served the order on the other, and the other appreciated the risk of loss if it was not obeyed. It was the third element in the test which gave difficulty: it was not fair just or reasonable that the bank should, on being notified of an order which it had not been able to resist, become exposed to a liability which principle could not limit. It was insufficient protection, besides being inconsistent with the existence of the duty of care contended for, that the claimant undertook to make good loss to the bank which the freezing order might cause.[271]   **9–89**

Customer's duty of care. It is appropriate to note for completeness that a customer has been held to owe a duty of care to a bank in connection with the operation of a current account. However, the duty was no wider than to use due care in drawing cheques, so as not to facilitate fraud or forgery and to notify the   **9–90**

---

[269] *Chapman v Barclays Bank Plc* [1998] P.N.L.R. 14, CA.

[270] *Wells v First National Commercial Bank* [1998] P.N.L.R. 552, CA. per Evans L.J. at 562, the duty contended for "would go a long way to revolutionise English Banking Law"; but he also said the position in the instant case might have been different if the third party had actually communicated with the bank, so as to establish some relationship between them. See also *O'Hara v Allied Irish Banks, The Times*, February 4, 1984 (no duty owed by bank to a guarantor, not one of its customers).

[271] *Commissioners of Customs and Excise v Barclays Bank Plc* [2007] 1 A.C. 181 (in error substantial sums were paid out of the accounts in question after the Bank received notice of the restraining order. The speech of Lord Bingham reviews the tests used to identify whether a duty of care should exist in novel circumstances). See Tinkler, "The bank, the thief, the freezing order—but whose duty?" 155 N.L.J. 82.

bank immediately of any unauthorised cheques of which the customer has become aware.[272]

9–91   **The standard of care.** The standard of care which the law requires of a bank with regard to the collection of a cheque is that shown in the ordinary practice of careful bankers. Where a bank did not fall short of that standard it was protected by s.4 of the Cheques Act 1957. It did not constitute any lack of reasonable care to refrain from making inquiries of a customer, which it was improbable would lead to detection of his purpose if he were dishonest, and which were calculated to offend him and maybe drive away his custom, if he were honest.[273]

9–92   Where there had been no failure to communicate information of sufficient importance to the claimants concerning a customer who had been refused a loan by the defendant bank, it was held that they were not liable to contribute towards the claimants' loss, when the customer defaulted in repayment of a loan.[274] A bank's duty of care to its customer does not extend to warning him that it was risky to pay into his account a generally endorsed cheque, crossed with the words "not negotiable—account payee only", because of the possibility of his liability should the person who had given him it not have had good title to the cheque.[275] The duty of care owed to a customer, when the bank acts as his agent, is the duty of an ordinary prudent banker. So, when a transfer was ordered by a person who had the requisite authority, and there were no obviously suspicious features of the transaction, the bank, which had not been put on inquiry was entitled or even obliged to execute the transfer, and was not negligent.[276] Bankers were not negligent where they processed a cheque forged with the signature of a solicitor who held the account on behalf of a client for whom he had power of attorney[277]; nor where they honoured a cheque for £20,000 drawn on an account with a nil balance where the cheque was validly signed and there were no other circumstances to put them on notice of fraud.[278] It was not negligent for a bank to allow withdrawals from an overdrawn joint account, where both parties to the account had signed a mandate authorising the bank to debit the account by cheques drawn by either of them, and there was no reason for the bank to suppose the mandate was being abused.[279]

9–93   The manager of a finance company owes a duty of care to prospective investors where he claims skill and competence in investment, especially when

---

[272] *Tai Hing Cotton Mill Ltd v Liu Chong Hing Bank Ltd* [1986] A.C. 80, PC; also *National Australia Bank Ltd v Hokit Pty Ltd* [1997] 6 Bank L.R. 177, CA (NSW) and see Marten, "Customer's duty to take care in the exercise of an account: a criticism of *Tai Hing Cotton Mills v Liu Chong Hing Bank Ltd*", (1986) 2 P.N. 17.
[273] *Marfani & Co v Midland Bank Ltd* [1968] 1 W.L.R. 956; *Thackwell v Barclays Bank Plc* [1986] 1 All E.R. 676 (a bank must take reasonable care to see that its customer has a proper title to a cheque presented for collection; however, a bank is entitled to assume that its customer is the true owner thereof, unless there are unusual facts or matters which would put a reasonable banker upon inquiry as to the true ownership).
[274] *Mutual Mortgage Corp v Bank of Montreal* (1965) 55 D.L.R. (2d) 164.
[275] *Redmond v Allied Irish Banks, The Times*, June 5, 1987.
[276] *Barclays Bank v Quincecare Ltd and Unichem Ltd* [1988] F.L.R. 166.
[277] *Weir v National Westminster Bank*, 1994 S.L.T. 1251.
[278] *Verjee v CIBC Bank* [2001] Lloyd's Rep. Bank. 279.
[279] *Royal Bank of Scotland Plc v Fielding, The Times*, February 26, 2004, CA.

he himself will benefit from brokerage. The standard of care is that of an ordinary prudent and skilful financial adviser.[280] In applying this standard, account can be taken of the extent to which the organisation in question specialises in transactions of the nature under review.[281] However, so far as the relationship between the Bank of England and any of the commercial banks in the United Kingdom is concerned, principles of common sense and reason indicate that no duty of care arises out of it.[282]

Proof of a causative link. Although a bank was in breach of its duty to investors in a fraudulent high yield investment scheme, where an employee negligently made representations about the bank's intention to deal with the invested monies in a particular way, it was not liable for the investors' losses when after the representation had been made they sought clarification from the bank, but before receiving it, proceeded with their investment relying on assurances from the fraudsters, who thereafter wrongfully appropriated the money.[283]   **9–94**

6.—BARRISTERS

The special immunity. For well over 150 years barristers enjoyed special immunity from actions in negligence.[284] The immunity was variously thought to arise from the absence of contractual obligation,[285] the difficult nature of the work,[286] and public policy.[287] As already mentioned in relation to other professional groups, after the decision in *Hedley Byrne & Co Ltd v Heller & Partners Ltd*,[288] it became clear that a duty to take reasonable care existed wherever a "special relationship" was created, independently of whether a contract was also in existence and it was only a matter of time before the barrister's immunity was tested. In *Rondel v Worsley*,[289] the House of Lords confirmed the advocate's immunity albeit in a limited way. Thereafter, in *Arthur J.S. Hall & Co v Simons*[290] their Lordships swept away those limitations and left   **9–95**

---

[280] *O'Leary and Short v Lamb and Lensworth Finance* (1973) 7 S.A.S.R. 159.
[281] See, e.g. *Investors Compensation Scheme Ltd v West Bromwich Building Society (No.2)* [1999] Lloyd's Rep. P.N. 496 (independent financial advisers selling home income plans to property owners with small incomes).
[282] *Minories Finance Ltd v Arthur Young, The Times,* July 27, 1988.
[283] *HSBC Bank Plc v 5th Avenue Partners Ltd* [2009] EWCA Cic 296.
[284] See *Fell v Brown* (1791) 1 Peake 131. A similar immunity covered a special pleader: *Perring v Rebutter* (1842) 2 M. & Rob. 429.
[285] per Pollock C.B. in *Swinfen v Lord Chelmsford* (1860) 5 H. & N. 890 at 920. Earlier decisions are cited in the 8th edn of this book. See also Ch.2 para.2–276, above.
[286] Suggested by Lord Campbell in *Purves v Landell* (1842) 12 C. & F. 91 at 102, 103; and Lord Pearson in *Rondel v Worlsey* [1969] A.C. 191 at 274.
[287] *Swinfen v Lord Chelmsford*, (1860) 5 H. & N. 890 at 921.
[288] [1964] A.C. 465.
[289] [1969] A.C. 191. See further Ch.2, para.2–276, above.
[290] [2002] 1 A.C. 615. For an account of the law as it stood before this decision, see the 9th edn of this work from para.8–68 onwards. See also, *Awoyami v Radford* [2008] 3 W.L.R. 34, Ch.4, para.4–163 above (the basis of the speeches in *Arthur J. S. Hall & Co v Simons* being that advocates' immunity could not be justified in civil proceedings in 1991, it was not available as a defence in relation to conduct in 1995, even though the decision in the House of Lords was handed down after that date).

it for argument in each case whether on the facts, the claim against the advocate should be struck out, for instance, as an abuse of process.[291]

9–96 **Abuse of process.** In removing the immunity it was anticipated that more cases would come before the courts in which the court would have to consider the rule in *Hunter v Chief Constable of West Midlands Police*,[292] preventing civil claims which are designed and intended to mount a collateral attack upon the final decision of a criminal court. It was emphasised that the rule is a flexible one, but in the usual case it would bring the administration of justice into disrepute if, having exhausted the process of appeal, a convicted person sought to reopen his conviction by way of initiating civil proceedings. Other than cases where the conviction was eventually set aside, subsequent civil proceedings would ordinarily amount to an abuse.

9–97 The position was seen as different where the claim for the barrister's negligence arises out of earlier civil proceedings, whether some form of general civil claim or matrimonial proceedings. There is not the same public interest in the result. One factor which might possibly give rise to an abuse of process argument would be manifest unfairness to some third party affected by the subsequent action.[293] But otherwise the likelihood of a second action amounting to an abuse would appear to be small and the factor limiting claims would more likely be the prospects of success for a second action, having regard to the way the first was resolved.[294]

9–98 **The duty of care.** In the result, a barrister, or solicitor advocate,[295] owes a duty of care to his clients, both lay and professional, for breach of which an action will lie when the act or default in question falls outside the abuse of process considerations discussed above.[296] Although formerly there was at least potential immunity in cases where the default relied upon occurred in court, or was closely connected with the advocate's work in court,[297] such limitations have disappeared. So far as a duty of care towards third parties is concerned, although authority is scant, it would appear logical that the advocate's duty should extend to third parties where that can be justified.[298] It has been held that, in the absence of any special assumption of responsibility, a barrister giving an undertaking to

---

[291] For striking out negligence claims, see Ch.4, para.4–254, above. See also, Evans, "*Hall v Simons* and abuse of process" (2001) 4 P.N. 218.

[292] [1982] A.C. 529.

[293] The example given by Lord Hoffmann was of a negligence claim arising from the conduct of an earlier defamation action, where the claimant attempted to justify an allegation for the second time.

[294] For striking out negligence claims, see n.291, above. See also CPR Pt 24.2 and the possibility of striking out a claim on a summary basis on the ground that there are no reasonable prospects of success.

[295] For these purposes there is no distinction between the two. See further para.9–258, below.

[296] para.9–96, above.

[297] See *Rondel v Worlsey* [1969] A.C. 191 and the cases which followed, notably *Saif Ali v Sydney Mitchell & Co* [1980] A.C. 198, *Somasundaram v M. Julius Melchior & Co* [1988] 1 W.L.R. 1394, CA, and the extensive review of authorities by Lord Bingham C.J. in *Arthur J.S. Hall & Co v Simons* in the CA, [1999] 3 W.L.R. 873.

[298] See para.9–18 above.

the court on his client's behalf owes no duty of care towards the opposing party.[299]

The standard of care. There is no reason why the standard of care should be **9–99** any different than for other professional persons. A barrister must exercise the care of an ordinarily skilled practitioner of his special skill.[300] The difficulty that may well arise is in relation to proof. It has been pointed out that a barrister is often asked for advice in situations that call for the exercise of judgment. It is easy to be wise after the event and simply because advice turns out to have been wrong does not mean that it was given negligently. An error of judgment,[301] if made in good faith and after care has been taken, is likely to be excusable.[302] Proof of negligence would require an error that goes beyond mere mistake.[303] In the words of one judge, negligence would be found only in the case of error that is "egregious".[304] Lord Diplock said there would have to be an error "such as no reasonably well-informed and competent member of that profession could have made".[305]

It is the duty of a barrister to give advice that is clear. A barrister may, and **9–100** should in some cases, be robust in advice, but should bear in mind the need for logical and sensible reasons to justify the conclusion reached.[306] Where advice is given orally in conference, in the presence of a solicitor and other professional advisers, it may not be necessary to ensure that the lay client follows all of the details. So, in one such case, where a barrister was asked to advise about a scheme to save estate duty on a millionaire's estate and the lay client was also advised by solicitors, it was held that the barrister was not under any professional

---

[299] *Connolly-Martin v Davis* [1999] P.N.L.R. 826, CA (an undertaking was given without instructions, and the barrister subsequently advised his client that it was no longer binding).

[300] The standard of care of a junior Chancery barrister is that of a reasonably competent practitioner in general Chancery practice: on the facts it was negligent not to advise that a gift of shares be effected by tax exempt trust, but not negligent to fail to recommend, for instance, share re-organisation: *Estill v Cowling Swift & Kitchin* [2000] Lloyd's Rep. P.N. 378.

[301] One exercise of judgment is deciding which points to plead. The proposition that a barrister would be negligent if he decided not to plead an unmeritorious point even though it could have been properly argued and might have led to an offer in settlement was strongly doubted in *McFarlane v Wilkinson* [1997] P.N.L.R. 578, CA, and those observations were not criticised in *Arthur J.S. Hall v Simons* in the CA, although reservations were expressed about the decision in *McFarlane* itself: see [1999] 3 W.L.R. 873.

[302] per Lord Wilberforce at 214.

[303] See Lawton J. in *Cook v S* [1966] 1 W.L.R. 635 at 641. See also, in the context of a complex tax avoidance scheme, and alleged negligence of a senior tax silk, the judgment of Lloyd J. in *Matrix Securities Ltd v Theodore Goddard* [1998] P.N.L.R. 290 at 321. The allegations failed.

[304] per Anderson J. in *Karpenko v Paroian Courey, Cohen & Houston* (1981) 117 D.L.R. (3d) 383 (Ont.H.C.) at 397–398.

[305] *Saif Ali v Mitchell* [1980] A.C. 198, 220 (failure by counsel to include an appropriate defendant in proceedings). See *Hickman v Blake Lapthorn* [2006] P.N.L.R. 20 (advice on settlement which did not take proper account of future loss of earnings) ; *Pritchard Joyce & Hind v Batcup* [2009] P.N.L.R. 28, CA (setting the standard of care too high should be avoided and counsel instructed in a claim based on a solicitor's negligence were not negligent in failing to notify their client and or instructing solicitors of a time limit in relation to commencing proceedings for negligence against yet another legal adviser).

[306] *Griffin v Kingsmill* [2001] Lloyd's Rep. P.N. 716, CA.

duty to ensure that the client understood fully all the implications of the advice given.[307]

ILLUSTRATIONS

9–101   It was potentially negligent for counsel specialising in an area such as family law, when advising in relation to proposals for settlement of a wife's financial claims, to fail to advise of a decision pending in the House of Lords which might benefit her financially, leaving to the client whether to seek a clean break or await the outcome of the decision.[308] On the facts, it was not negligent of counsel representing the claimant at the trial of a personal injuries action to say that she was hopeful the court would receive certain medical evidence for which permission had hitherto been refused, where she thought the chances of success for the application were somewhat over 50 per cent. Nor was it negligent to give advice that it was better to proceed with the application (which in the event failed) than to accept an offer of £150,000 in settlement. It was not necessary that in giving advice in such circumstances counsel should set out her process of reasoning in detail.[309]

9–102   It was not a negligent exercise of judgment for a barrister representing a claimant under the Sex Discrimination Act 1975 in the industrial tribunal, not to pursue allegations of victimisation as examples of direct discrimination, where she was given one lengthy statement and was not told of another very lengthy statement, provided to a firm of solicitors.[310] Nor was it negligent for defence counsel at a criminal trial to fail to remind the judge that he had not given an alibi direction, where she considered that an impression might thereby arise in the jurors' minds that the judge disbelieved the alibi evidence called.[311]

9–103   Counsel can reasonably be expected to be familiar with decisions reported in the Law Reports, the All England Law Reports, or the Weekly Law Reports, but " . . . the exercise of reasonable care has never extended to a command of unreported decisions of the Court of Appeal. It is only where some special feature of a case might reasonably be expected to have put a competent advocate on inquiry that he or she may be faulted for failing to carry out the necessary

---

[307] *Mathew v Maughold Life Assurance Co Ltd* (1985) 1 P.N. 142.

[308] *Williams v Thompson Leatherdale* [2008] 3 F.C.R. 613 (in the event no loss was suffered by the claimant because it was not clear that with the appropriate advice she would have rejected the clean break offer that had been made).

[309] *Moy v Pettman Smith* [2005] P.N.L.R. 426, HL, para.9–103 below, per Lord Carswell at [60]. per Baroness Hale of Richmond at [28] "the client pays for the advocate's opinion not her doubts." She stressed the absence of expert evidence to the effect that the terms of counsel's advice fell below the standard reasonably to be expected of counsel of her seniority and expertise. See Willis, "Advocates' duties" 149 S.J. 201; Phillips, "At the door of the court" 155 N.L.J. 352. See also *Luke v Wansbroughs* [2005] P.N.L.R. 2 (it was not negligent to advise in favour of settlement of an action for malicious falsehood and defamation in the sum of £10,000 albeit damages in excess of £200,000 were claimed, where there was every reason to suspect an application to strike out on grounds of delay and that, if made, the application would be successful).

[310] *Waters v Maguire* [1999] Lloyd's Rep. P.N. 855

[311] *Popat v Barnes* [2004] EWHC 741, *The Times,* July 5, 2004.

inquiry with reasonable diligence."[312] There was no liability where counsel advised his client that he should settle a claim for personal injuries arising from his employment by a company of which he was a director: the advice was within the range of responses of a reasonably competent member of the profession.[313] Nor was liability established where counsel's advice on a point in relation to the certification of completion of building works was within the reasonable range of options available, even though the Court of Appeal ultimately took a different view.[314] Liability was conceded where counsel gave negligent advice to a freehold owner in proceedings by a tenant for a new lease under the Leasehold Reform, Housing and Urban Development Act 1993, that resulted in the grant, by way of compromise, of long leases of two flats.[315] A barrister was not negligent where, shortly before trial, he advised that in his view there was a real risk that one of joint claimants whom he was instructed to represent, lacked capacity within the meaning of the Mental Health Act 1993, and that an application should be made to adjourn the hearing.[316]

Wasted costs. Barristers come into no special category when the court is considering its jurisdiction to make a wasted costs order.[317] The relevant principles are summarised below,[318] although more detailed guidance is given in Pt 44 of the Civil Procedure Rules and the Practice Direction thereto. The power to award wasted costs may be exercised both in relation to a barrister acting on behalf of the party making the application and the opposing party's advocate.[319] However, in considering whether to impose such a liability on any advocate, barrister or solicitor, no doubt the court will bear well in mind the following from the leading case: **9–104**

"Any judge who is invited to make or contemplates making an order arising out of an advocate's conduct of court proceedings must make full allowance for the fact that an advocate in court, like a commander in battle, often has to make decisions quickly and under pressure in the fog of war and ignorant of developments on the other side of the hill. Mistakes will inevitably be made, things done which the outcome shows to have been unwise. But advocacy is more an art than a science. It cannot be conducted according to formulae. It is only when, with all allowances made, an advocate's conduct

---

[312] *Moy v Pettman Smith* [2002] P.N.L.R. 961, CA per Brooke L.J. at 982 (appeal allowed, [2005] P.N.L.R. 426, HL, para.9–101 above).
[313] *McIlgorm v Bell Lamb & Joynson* [2001] P.N.L.R. 643.
[314] *First City Insurance Group v Orchard* [2002] Lloyd's Rep. P.N. 543.
[315] *Green v Alexander Johnson* [2005] EWCA Civ 775.
[316] *McFaddens v Platford* [2009] P.N.L.R. 26 (the judgment discusses inter alia the respective roles of a barrister and instructing solicitor).
[317] In *Ridehalgh v Horsfield* [1994] 3 W.L.R. 462, CA, the leading case on the topic, the court considered and specifically rejected the argument that s.62 of the Courts and Legal Services Act 1990 in effect gave an immunity to barristers where negligence could not be proved. For the like jurisdiction in New Zealand, see *Harley v McDonald* [2001] 2 A.C. 678, para.9–249, below.
[318] See below para.9–250 and, e.g. the notes to CPR Pt 44.14 in the *White Book* (Sweet and Maxwell 2010).
[319] *Medcalf v Mardell* [2003] 1 A.C. 120, n.321, below.

of court proceedings is quite plainly unjustifiable that it can be appropriate to make a wasted costs order against him."[320]

9–105 In *Medcalf v Mardell*,[321] it was indicated that the power to make a wasted costs order arises not only where an advocate is exercising a right of audience in court, but also where the matters complained of arose out of court but were immediately relevant to exercising a right of audience. The court could therefore properly consider an application for wasted costs which allegedly arose as a result of barristers making allegations of fraud in an amended notice of appeal and skeleton argument, where it was suggested that in drafting the allegations they could not have had before them "reasonably credible material"[322] in support of such a case. On the facts, the claim for wasted costs failed. It was not necessary for counsel making such allegations to have before them evidence in admissible form, provided that there was available material, in whatever form, capable of leading responsible counsel to conclude that serious allegations could properly be based upon it. Where a client did not waive his privilege and a barrister was thereby prevented from explaining what particular material was available at the time the allegations were made, the court should take extreme care and should not make a wasted costs order unless satisfied that there was nothing the barrister could say, if unconstrained by client privilege, to resist it and it was in all the circumstances fair to make the order. It has been emphasised that the basis of the wasted costs jurisdiction is breach of a duty owed to the court, not another party to the litigation.[323]

9–106 **Legal aid.** The Code of Conduct of the Bar of England and Wales contains guidelines[324] for use when a barrister is asked to represent a client in receipt of legal aid. There is a continuing duty to review the prospects of success in the case, whether or not instructions are before counsel for that particular purpose.[325] Guidance is given about the manner in which the prospects of success should be assessed.[326] However, the Code expressly provides that the statements made are essentially matters of good practice and its terms may not always be of assistance

---

[320] per Sir Thomas Bingham M.R. at 482. See also *Fryer v Royal Institution of Chartered Surveyors*, *The Times*, May 16, 2000, CA (for purposes of wasted costs, a barrister is not negligent if he fails to assess the prospects of success of particular points in percentage terms when advising on the merits for the purposes of legal aid: the guidelines in the Code of Conduct of the Bar of England and Wales, are essentially statements of good practice and should be used with care when considering whether counsel has been negligent). See further in relation to the Code para.9–106, below.

[321] [2003] 1 A.C. 120. See also *Brown v Bennett* [2002] 1 W.L.R. 713 (unsuccessful application for wasted costs against counsel made on the basis that the available evidence did not justify a pleading of negligence: per Neuberger J. at 750 "it would only be if the lawyer's conclusion that he could plead dishonesty was one which no reasonable lawyer, properly considering matters could have reached, that it can be criticised as being improper"). See Rees and Bell, "Giving lawyers a break" 146 S.J. 654.

[322] The phrase comes from para.5.8(c) of s.3 of the Code of Conduct of the Bar of England and Wales (8th edn, October 2004).

[323] *Persaud v Persaud* [2003] P.N.L.R. 519, CA. See also *Dempsey v Johnstone* [2004] P.N.L.R. 25, CA, para.9–254, below.

[324] See generally, Annex E of the Code (8th edn, October 2004).

[325] ibid. para.20 of Annex E.

[326] See in particular para.10 of Annex E.

in deciding whether a barrister has been negligent.[327] So, where a barrister failed to assess the prospects of success in a case in percentage terms, he was not negligent so as to be exposed to a wasted costs order, even though such an approach was suggested in the guidelines.[328] Nor was it necessary for counsel to identify the prospects of success of particular lines of argument or to suggest limitations on a legal aid certificate by reference to such lines of argument.[329]

7.—DENTISTS

The duty of care. The duty of a dentist[330] is to exercise due care and skill in treatment of his patients. The duty is the same as that owed by a surgeon or physician.[331] Liability is concurrent in both tort and contract.[332] Quite apart from negligence, a dentist will be liable for trespass to the person if he performs unnecessary treatment and deliberately conceals from the patient the fact that it is not required.[333] **9–107**

The standard of care. Where a tooth was extracted and, after the extraction, the jaw was found to be fractured, that of itself was held to be no evidence of negligence against the dentist, even if there were also part of the root of the tooth still left in the jaw.[334] It has been held that a dentist is entitled to rely upon a doctor's opinion as to the general response of a patient to antibiotic treatment, unless that opinion was quite clearly inconsistent with what the dentist observes on examination.[335] Whilst it was not evidence of negligence that a jaw had been dislocated during an extraction of teeth, it was negligent not to notice the existence of a dislocation during the dentist's further examinations over subsequent months of treatment.[336] In circumstances where a dentist performed surgery to remove wisdom teeth and caused damage to the lingual nerve, liability **9–108**

---

[327] See e.g. para.1 of Annex E and para.1 of s.3 of the Code. Also, see *Fryer v Royal Institution of Chartered Surveyors, The Times*, May 16, 2000, CA, and *Royal Institution of Chartered Surveyors v Wiseman Marshall* [2000] P.N.L.R. 649, CA.

[328] *Fryer v Royal Institution of Chartered Surveyors*, n.327, above.

[329] *Royal Institution of Chartered Surveyors v Wiseman Marshall*, n.327, above.

[330] Only a registered dentist is entitled to describe himself as: "dentist," "dental practitioner" or "dental surgeon" and to practise dentistry. Before a dentist can obtain registration with the General Dental Council's Registrar he must satisfy the requirements of the Dentists Act 1984. A dentist is subject to the discipline of the Council, the powers of which are derived from the 1984 Act.

[331] *Edwards v Mallon* [1908] 1 K.B. 1002.

[332] *Fish v Kapur* [1948] 2 All E.R. 176. See further para.9–18, above. In regard to a dentist's contractual liability where he has undertaken to make and supply dentures for a patient, see *Samuels v Davis* [1943] K.B. 526. See also para.9–22, above. See generally, Coleman, "Clinical negligence: dentists uncovered" 2006 P.I.L.J. 42 (Feb), 11.

[333] *Appleton v Garrett* [1996] P.I.Q.R. P1.

[334] *Fish v Kapur*. See also *O'Neill v Kelly, The Times*, December 15, 1961, and Ch.6, para.6–93 et seq., above.

[335] *Transwell v Nelson, The Times*, February 11, 1959, where a patient had had some teeth extracted by her dentist, who then referred her to a doctor, when her condition worsened. A doctor diagnosed an abscess and treated her with antibiotics, but later it was discovered that she was suffering from osteomyelitis. The patient could not succeed in an action against the dentist.

[336] *Lock v Scantlebury, The Times*, July 25, 1963.

was established on proof that the damage arose from negligent drilling rather than those surgical procedures from which, without negligence, such an injury could be caused.[337]

8.—Medical Practitioners

9–109   **The duty of care.**[338] The civil liability of medical practitioners[339] towards their patients was set out at length in *R. v Bateman*,[340] as follows:

"If a person holds himself out as possessing special skill and knowledge and he is consulted, as possessing such skill and knowledge, by or on behalf of a patient, he owes a duty to the patient to use due caution in undertaking the treatment. If he accepts the responsibility and undertakes the treatment and the patient submits to his direction and treatment accordingly, he owes a duty to the patient to use diligence, care, knowledge, skill and caution in administering the treatment. No contractual relation is necessary, nor is it necessary that the service be rendered for reward . . . The law requires a fair and reasonable standard of care and competence. This standard must be reached in all the matters above mentioned. If the patient's death has been caused by the defendant's indolence or carelessness, it will not avail to show that he had sufficient knowledge; nor will it avail to prove that he was diligent in attendance, if the patient has been killed by his gross ignorance and unskilfulness . . . As regards cases where incompetence is alleged, it is only necessary to say that the unqualified practitioner cannot claim to be measured by any lower standard than that which is applied to a qualified man. As regards cases of alleged recklessness, juries are likely to distinguish between the qualified and the unqualified man. There may be recklessness in undertaking the treatment and recklessness in the conduct of it. It is, no doubt, conceivable that a qualified man may be held liable for recklessly undertaking a case which he knew, or should have known, to be beyond his powers, or for making his patient the subject of reckless experiment. Such cases are likely to be rare. In the case of a quack, where the treatment has been proved to be incompetent and to have caused the patient's death, juries are not likely to hesitate in finding liability on the ground that the defendant

---

[337] *Heath v West Berkshire HAy* [1992] 3 Med.L.R. 57. The fact that the patient was not warned of the small risk of nerve damage was not evidence of negligence, because a respectable and responsible body of dentists would not have warned her of that risk but, in any event, even if she had been told, she would have consented to the treatment taking place.

[338] In New Zealand clinical negligence claims usually fall within the terms of the accident compensation scheme and are therefore not usually the subject of litigation, but there are exceptions, one such being claims for mental injury by secondary victims: see Todd, "Medical negligence in New Zealand" (2001) 4 P.N. 230. For a summary of the scheme see Todd, "Twenty years of professional negligence in New Zealand" (2005) 4 P.N. 257.

[339] Before a medical practitioner can obtain registration with the General Medical Council's Registrar, the requirements of the Medical Act 1983 must be satisfied, both as regards qualification and experience. Registration gives entitlement to practise as a registered medical practitioner, to apply for appointment as a medical officer in any hospital, whether inside or outside the National Health Service, and to give medical certificates required by any enactment. A registered medical practitioner is subject to the discipline of the Council, the powers of which are derived from the 1983 Act.

[340] (1925) 94 L.J.K.B. 791. See *Akerele v The King* [1943] A.C. 255.

undertook, and continued to treat, a case involving the gravest risk to his patient, when he knew he was not competent to deal with it or would have known if he had paid any proper regard to the life and safety of his patient."[341]

A single comprehensive duty of care. The doctor's relationship with his **9–110** patient gives rise to a duty of care to exercise skill and judgment in providing treatment. It is a single comprehensive duty. It covers all the ways in which a doctor is called upon to exercise his skill and judgment in treating the patient's physical or mental condition and in respect of which his services were engaged.

"This general duty is not subject to dissection into a number of component parts to which different criteria of what satisfy the duty of care apply, such as diagnosis, treatment, advice (including warning of any risks of something going wrong however skillfully the treatment advised is carried out)."[342]

The duty of a doctor is limited to the sphere of medicine. Accordingly, unless **9–111** specifically so instructed, the doctor is not concerned with the sphere of legal liability. In the absence of any special circumstances, a doctor is not required to contemplate or foresee any question which is connected with a third party's liability. So, where after negligent diagnosis by a hospital's casualty officer, the claimant sought damages to reflect the lower sum for which he alleged he had settled a personal injuries action, as against the value of his claim with a correct diagnosis, the action failed.[343]

Necessity of the patient's consent. A medical practitioner cannot examine, **9–112** treat or operate upon a patient, without the patient's consent, except by committing a trespass or assault.[344] This consent, which may be implied,[345]

---

[341] (1925) 94 L.J.K.B. 791 at 794, per Lord Hewart C.J.

[342] *Sidaway v Board of Governors of The Bethlem Royal Hospital and the Maudsley Hospital* [1985] A.C. 871 at 893, per Lord Diplock. See also *Gold v Haringey HA* [1988] Q.B. 481 at 489, per Lloyd L.J.: "a distinction between advice given in a therapeutic context and advice given in a non-therapeutic context would be a departure from the principle on which the *Bolam* test is itself grounded"; at 492, per Stephen Brown L.J.: "such a distinction is wholly unwarranted and artificial"; (pet. dis. [1988] 1 W.L.R. 462, HL(E)).

[343] *Stevens v Bermondsey and Southwark Group Hospital Management Committee* (1963) 107 S.J. 478.

[344] *Slater v Baker* (1767) 2 Wils. 359; *Beatty v Cullingworth* [1896] B.M.J., November 21; where a surgeon was alleged to have removed a woman's ovaries without her consent; *Appleton v Garrett* [1996] P.I.Q.R. P1 (dentist who carried out extensive treatment and deliberately concealed it was unnecessary committed a trespass to the person); also *Williamson v East London and City HA* [1998] Lloyd's Rep. Med. 6 (subcutaneous mastectomy performed although the patient had consented only to a replacement breast prosthesis).

[345] For implied consent see, e.g. *Abbas v Kenney* [1996] 7 Med.L.R. 47 (patient's consent implied where a surgeon, carrying out an exploratory operation, proceeded to total pelvic clearance where he reasonably but mistakenly concluded he had discovered a malignant lump: the patient was aware that more extensive surgery than that originally contemplated might become necessary if cancer was discovered and had been told that total pelvic clearance was the standard treatment for ovarian cancer).

amounts to an agreement on the part of the patient to permit the treatment in question and is sufficient consideration for an implied promise to exercise proper care and skill.[346]

9–113   In some circumstances an implied consent is insufficient and specific consent has to be obtained. So, in *Reibl v Hughes*,[347] it was negligent of a neurosurgeon not to explain the high degree of risk of an operation to a patient who subsequently suffered a stroke during the surgery and thereby became paralysed. Further, the absence of a consent based upon knowledge of the risks rendered the surgery a battery. In contrast, in *Male v Hopkins*[348] it was not negligent for a doctor, who had the claimant's consent to general treatment, to prescribe a particular drug known to have side effects, without first obtaining specific consent. It was a proper exercise of his discretion to prescribe the drug, even with the risk involved. However, negligence did arise in his failure to carry out recommended tests for the presence of the side effects, once prescription of the drug had commenced.

9–114   The duty of a medical practitioner is to give such explanation about intended treatment and the implications of it as would be given by a careful and responsible member of the specialty concerned, so that the claimant's consent to treatment is a real one.[349] The extent of the duty to disclose any risks involved must vary with the circumstances. It may be unnecessary, or even a positive disservice, to warn a patient of a minimal risk where an operation is essential to continued good health. Different considerations could well arise where the procedure was totally elective, for example a sterilisation operation.[350] It has been said that once the patient is informed in broad terms of the nature of the proposed treatment, and gives consent, that consent is real and no question of trespass to the person can arise. Accordingly, if it is alleged that there was a failure to give proper information about the risks, that is a matter of negligence,

---

[346] *Gladwell v Steggal* (1939) 5 Bing.N.C. 733; *Everett v Griffiths* [1920] 3 K.B. 163 at 193, per Scrutton L.J.

[347] (1977) 78 D.L.R. 35, following *Kelly v Hazlett* (1976) 75 D.L.R. 536.

[348] (1967) 64 D.L.R. (2d) 105.

[349] *Chatterton v Gerson* [1981] Q.B. 432; *Hills v Potter* [1984] 1 W.L.R. 641 (a doctor did not have to inform the patient of all the details of the proposed treatment or the likely outcome and the risk inherent in it but was merely required to act in accordance with a practice accepted as proper by a responsible body of skilled medical practitioners: what was required was for the patient to be supplied with sufficient information to enable him to decide whether or not to undergo the surgery proposed); *Makrose v Epsom & St. Helier NHS Trust* [2005] Lloyd's Rep. Med. 334 (where a surgeon forms the view that surgery is the right course it is not negligent to express that view firmly). See further n.351, below; also *Chester v Afshar* [2005] 1 A.C. 134, para.9–148, below, (neurosurgeon negligent in failing to warn of a slight risk of post-operative paralysis, the HL giving the claimant a remedy notwithstanding difficulties of proof, because to do otherwise would deprive of its content the right to a warning of the risks of surgery).

[350] *Videto v Kennedy* (1980) 107 D.L.R. (3d) 612. See also *Zamparo v Brisson* (1981) 120 D.L.R. (3d) 545. In *F v R* (1984) 33 S.A.S.R. 189, it was held that the defendant medical practitioner was not in breach of duty to the claimant, by reason of his failure to inform her of the risks before she submitted herself to a sterilisation operation by tubal tie.

rather than assault.[351] Circumstances may arise in which it is necessary to make the patient aware that fewer or no risks are associated with another available and alternative treatment.[352]

In *Sidaway v Board of Governors of the Bethlem Royal Hospital and the Maudsley Hospital*,[353] the Court of Appeal opined that there was no place in English law for the doctrine of "informed consent". The general duty of a medical practitioner to disclose information to his patient, before operating, was that such action by way of giving or withholding information should be taken, as was reasonable in all the circumstances which were known or ought to be known. The object was to place the patient in a position to make a rational choice whether or not to accept the medical recommendation. The duty was fulfilled where the medical practitioner acted in accordance with a practice accepted rightly as being a proper one by a body of skilled and experienced medical practitioners.

9–115

The House of Lords dismissed the further appeal, on the basis that the claimant had failed to prove that the surgeon had been in breach of any duty of care in failing to warn of the risk inherent in the proposed treatment.[354] In so doing, their Lordships recognised that the degree of disclosure required for a particular patient was an issue to be judged primarily on the basis of medical evidence. However, there could well be circumstances in which the proposed treatment involved such a substantial risk[355] of grave consequences that the court could conclude that the patient did have a right ultimately to decide, notwithstanding any practice to the contrary accepted as proper by a responsible body of medical opinion. As Lord Woolf M.R. put it:

9–116

"In a case where it is being alleged that a plaintiff has been deprived of the opportunity to make a proper decision as to what course he or she should take in relation to treatment, it seems to be the law that if there is a significant risk which would affect the judgment of a reasonable patient, then in the normal course it is the responsibility of a doctor to inform the patient of that significant risk, if the information is needed so that

---

[351] *Chatterton v Gerson* [1981] Q.B. 432. In *Videto v Kennedy*, n.350 above, it was held that the onus of showing informed consent or sufficient disclosure of the risks involved rested with the defendant. It is submitted that the better view is that of Bristow J. in *Chatterton* that the burden of proof rests upon the claimant throughout.

[352] *Birch v University College London Hospital NHS Foundation Trust* (2008)104 B.M.L.R. 168 (patient told of the risks of catheter angiography, the imaging procedure to which she consented, but not of the risks of MRI scan, the less invasive procedure originally recommended).

[353] [1984] Q.B. 493 (claimant suffered a recurrent pain in her neck, shoulder and arms and underwent a laminectomy of the fourth cervical vertebra, unaware of a material risk of damage both to the spinal column, which could severely disable her).

[354] [1985] A.C. 871. For an analysis of the speeches in the HL, see the judgment of Lord Woolf M.R. in *Pearce v United Bristol Healthcare NHS Trust* [1998] P.I.Q.R. P53, CA. See further, See "Surgeons side-line *Sidaway*" 142 Sol. J. 228 (the author points out that the Senate of Surgery of Great Britain and Ireland has published a code, "The Surgeon's Duty of Care", which gives guidance on proper standards of practice, e.g. in relation to the information which should be given about the nature of a patient's condition; its treatment; and the risks. The detail provided should be that required by a reasonable person to make a relevant and informed judgment whether to consent).

[355] The size of risk which will satisfy the test will vary from case to case and it is not possible to lay down any precise percentage: see *Pearce v United Bristol Healthcare NHS Trust* [1998] P.I.Q.R. P53, CA at P59.

the patient can determine for him or herself as to the course he or she should adopt."[356]

Liability can arise not simply as a result of failing to warn of risks when that should have been done, but also where negligence arises in a medical practitioner's omitting to inform himself of choices available to a patient so that, for instance, she is not taken to possible alternatives to surgery.[357]

9–117   Where treating a child, the duty of a medical practitioner is owed to the child itself, but discharged by taking reasonable care to give its parents such information and advice as will allow them to make an informed judgment of such treatment as is in the child's best interests. So, on the facts, no duty of care arose where it was not foreseeable by a doctor examining a child that failure to mention an alternative form of immunisation against measles would be likely to be regarded by her parents as definitive of, or would have a significant influence on, the question whether such immunisation should take place, where both he and they realised that another G.P. would be involved at the time of immunisation. Further, even if breach of such a duty had been shown, the chain of causation would have been broken where the parents subsequently received "proper" advice from other doctors, after the occasion upon which they alleged the defendant's breach of duty had arisen.[358]

9–118   Where a doctor is treating the mother of a child who has died, a duty will be owed to advise the mother about risks in future pregnancies. The outcome of any post mortem will be relevant to that issue and the duty will extend to giving some explanation of the post mortem procedures, of which the removal and retention of the child's organs is a relevant part. So, in circumstances where a mother has not been told that organs have been retained, and she has suffered psychiatric injury as a result of learning that the truth, a claim will lie for the doctor's breach of duty.[359]

9–119   **Liability in contract.** A distinction needs to be drawn between liability in contract and liability in tort.[360] In contract, liability depends on the express or implied terms of the contract and is based on what the medical man in question

---

[356] n.355 at P59. See also *Re Creutzfeldt-Jakob Disease Litigation (No.1)* (2000) 54 B.M.L.R. 1 (court did not permit amendment to a statement of claim to allege battery on the basis of a lack of informed consent, where the claimant allegedly developed CJD after treatment with contaminated batches of human growth hormone).

[357] *Webb v Barclays Bank Plc and Portsmouth Hospitals NHS Trust* [2002] P.I.Q.R. P61, CA (polio victim not advised to accept bracing or orthosis, rather than above-knee amputation).

[358] *Thompson v Blake-James* [1998] P.I.Q.R. P286, CA. See also *Poynter v Hillingdon HA* (1997) 37 B.M.L.R. 192 (although the claimant's parents were not warned of the risk of brain damage arising in the course of heart surgery, that risk was so low that, at the relevant time, a substantial body of medical opinion would not have disclosed it). See, Mahendra, "Consent and capacity in medical treatment" 151 N.L.J. 939.

[359] *AB v Leeds Teaching Hospital NHS Trust* (the Organ Retention Group Litigation) [2005] 2 W.L.R. 358. See Jones, "Retained organs: The legal fallout" (2004) 3 P.N. 182.

[360] For a general discussion of concurrent actions in contract or tort, see para.9–13 et seq., above.

contracts to do. If he holds himself out as a person who undertakes the cure or treatment of human ailments "there is on his part an implied warranty that he is of skill reasonably competent to the task he undertakes—*Spondes peritiam artis . . .* The public profession of an art is a representation and undertaking to all the world that the professor possesses the requisite ability and skill."[361] The amount of skill which must be displayed depends on the extent of the profession of the person employed. A specialist, for example, is one from whom, in a case of contract, more skill can be demanded than from a general practitioner. If an unqualified man is employed, then, unless he professes to be equal or more than equal in skill to a qualified practitioner, he is only liable for not employing such skill as he professes to have.[362]

The duty in contract is only owed to the parties to the contract, but it would **9–120** seem that there is in most cases a contract between patient and medical practitioner, even if the patient himself is not liable for payment of the services rendered, such payment being made by someone else.[363]

Concurrent liability in tort. In tort, no question of warranty, undertaking or **9–121** profession of skill can arise. The duty arises from the fact that the practitioner does something to a human being which is likely to cause physical damage unless it is done with proper care and skill. It is well settled that under such circumstances the practitioner owes a duty in tort to the patient.[364] There seems to be no good reason for thinking that the duty is in any respect different, if, in an emergency, an unqualified person renders medical or surgical aid to another. The officious aid of a well-meaning but unskilled person may cause greater damage than was suffered as a result of the original accident.[365] It must follow also that it is actionable negligence if such a person gives more treatment than is reasonably necessary in the special circumstances and the claimant suffers consequential loss.

Duty to third parties. There is scant authority on the question whether a **9–122** medical practitioner owes a duty of care to third parties. Although there is no

---

[361] per Willes J. in *Harmer v Cornelius* (1858) 5 C.B. (N.S.) 236.

[362] See *Shiells & Thorne v Blackburne* (1789) 1 H.Bl. 158, per Heath J. His opinion deals with the gratuitous rendering of services, but payment in these cases only goes to the amount and not to the existence of consideration.

[363] In *West Bromwich Football Club Ltd v El-Safty* (2006) 92 B.M.L.R. 179, the CA found that where a physiotherapist employed by a football club referred a player to a consultant surgeon, on an objective test, a contract arose between the player and the surgeon, even though the club was to pay his fees. It was unnecessary to imply a contract between the surgeon and the club. See further, Griffiths Q.C. and Whale, "Uneasy bedfellows?" 156 NLJ 1821 ; also Morgan and Purssell, "Negligence advice ending a career: calculatiing damages" 2007 W.S.L.R. (7) 3 ; O'Sullivan, "Negligent medical advice and financial loss: "sick as a parrot'?" 2007 C.L.J. (1), 14.

[364] *Pippin v Sheppard* (1822) 11 Price 400; *Edgar v Lamont*, 1941 S.C. 277. See, generally, Swaine, "Clinical negligence claims in tort" 151 N.L.J. 1076.

[365] *Gladwell v Steggal* (1839) 5 Bing.N.C. 733 (a clergyman who "also practised as a medical man", maltreated a child's painful knee, which resulted in her suffering dire consequences.

reason in principle why a duty should not be owed, the potential problems are illustrated by *Goodwill v British Pregnancy Advisory Service*.[366] A doctor advised a patient who had undergone vasectomy that the operation had been a success and that he no longer needed to use any method of contraception. The patient commenced a sexual relationship with the claimant. It was held that no duty of care was owed by the doctor to the claimant, who subsequently gave birth to a child, after the vasectomy underwent spontaneous reversal. There was insufficient proximity between the defendant, the doctor's employer and the claimant and it could not be said there had been any assumption of responsibility towards her when the advice was given. Such considerations will operate in many third party claims based upon allegedly negligent advice.[367] However, a feature of the case was the defendant's lack of awareness that the doctor's statement would be passed on to the claimant and it may be that a different view would prevail if that was otherwise.

9–123   One common situation is where a doctor is asked by a prospective employer to carry out a medical examination of an applicant for employment. A duty of care has been held not to arise. The position of the doctor was said to be analogous to that of the social workers in *X (Minors) v Bedfordshire County Council*[368] who, since they were advising their employer, the local authority, owed no duty of care to children examined and interviewed by them in relation to suspected child abuse. By similar reasoning a doctor did not owe any duty of care to an applicant for employment where she commented unfavourably to her employer on the applicant's medical questionnaire.[369] However, subsequently that aspect of the *Bedfordshire* case upon which reliance was placed has been called into question. It was said that the reasoning employed in the House of Lords could not survive the coming into force of the Human Rights Act 1998.[370] It remains to be seen whether the position of the doctor providing a reference will be re-examined.[371]

---

[366] [1996] 1 W.L.R. 1397, CA. See also *Powell v Boladz* [1997] 9 C.L. 472, CA (G.P. owes no duty of care to relatives of a patient to whom he has to relay bad news); Davies, "Reliance on medical advice by third parties: the limits of *Goodwill*" (1996) 2 P.N. 54.

[367] See e.g. *West Bromwich Albion Football Club Ltd v El-Safty* (2006) 92 B.M.L.R. 179, CA, n.84 above (a consultant surgeon negligently advised that a professional football player should have reconstructive surgery, which was unsuccessful causing the player to retire from the game: the player's club could not recover its economic loss, there being on the facts no assumption of responsibility to the club or sufficient proximity in the surgeon's relationship with the club, to give rise to a duty of care).

[368] [1995] 2 A.C. 633, Ch.12, para.12–12, below also Ch.2, para.2–308 above.

[369] *Kapfunde v Abbey National Plc*, *The Times*, April 6, 1998, CA (disapproving on this point *Baker v Kaye* (1997) I.R.L.R. 219). See further, Samuels, "The legal liability, if any, of the company doctor to the prospective employee or other examinee" (2001) 68 Med. Leg. J. 145.

[370] See *D v East Berkshire Community NHS Trust* [2004] Q.B. 558 (appeal dismissed [2005] A.C. 373) Ch.2, para.2–331, above.

[371] Although not a "reference" case, an example of the potential for third party liability is provided by *Farraj v King's Healthcare NHS Trust* [2009] EWCA Civ 1203, (a private laboratory required by a hospital to culture a sample for DNA analysis, owed a duty of care to the claimants, who were planning a family and provided the sample to the hospital in order to be screened for a hereditary blood disease).

Standard of care. The classic summary of McNair J. in *Bolam v Friern*   **9–124**
Hospital Management Committee has already been quoted.[372] In order to satisfy
the duty in tort, the standard of care and skill to be attained is that of the ordinary
competent medical practitioner, exercising an ordinary degree of professional
skill.[373] Although the standard is a high one, "a defendant charged with
negligence can clear himself if he shows that he acted in accord with general and
approved practice".[374] A medical practitioner:

> "is not guilty of negligence if he has acted in accordance with practice accepted as
> proper by a responsible body of medical men skilled in that particular art . . . merely
> because there was a body of opinion who would take a contrary view."[375]

Negligence in the diagnosis and treatment of a medical condition ought not to   **9–125**
be established by a judge's preference for one body of respectable professional
opinion before another.[376] Use of the words "responsible", "reasonable" and
"respectable", give the consequence that where, as often happens in cases of
alleged clinical negligence, a particular course of action is adopted after
weighing risks against benefits, a court considering expert evidence has to be
satisfied that in coming to their opinion the experts considered that particular
issue and reached a defensible conclusion about it.[377]

Applying current knowledge. The standard of care, when assessing a   **9–126**
medical practice or procedure, is judged in the light of knowledge available at the
time, not at the date of trial.[378] So, an anaesthetist was acquitted of negligence
where he administered an anaesthetic kept in a manner thought at the time to be

---

[372] para.9–02, above. See also *Gold v Haringey HA* [1988] Q.B. 481, 490, per Lloyd L.J.: "The standard is not that of the man on the top of the Clapham omnibus, as in other fields of negligence, but the higher standard of the man skilled in the particular profession or calling."

[373] *Rich v Pierpont* (1862) 3 F. & F. 35; *Chin Keow v Government of Malaysia* [1967] 1 W.L.R. 813. See also *Djemal v Bexley Health Authority* [1995] 6 Med.L.R. 269 (the standard of care required of a senior houseman at a hospital is that of a reasonably competent houseman, regardless of the individual's actual experience).

[374] *Marshall v Lindsey C.C.* [1935] 1 K.B. 516, 540, per Maughan L.J. and approved by the HL in *Whiteford v Hunter* [1950] W.N. 553. See further in relation to the relevance of general and approved practice, Ch.7, para.7–38, above.

[375] per McNair J. in *Bolam v Friern Hospital Management Committee*, above, at 587.

[376] *Maynard v West Midlands Regional HA* [1984] 1 W.L.R. 634, HL. What amounts to a responsible body of medical opinion cannot be determined by counting heads. It is open to a judge to decide that a small number of specialists constitute such a body; it is not necessary for the body to be substantial: *Defreitas v O'Brien* [1995] P.I.Q.R. P281, CA. See Khan and Roberts, "What is a responsible group of medical opinion?" [1995] P.N. 121.

[377] per Lord Browne-Wilkinson in *Bolitho v City and Hackney HA* [1998] A.C. 232, at 241, 242. For an example where the judge was said not to be entitled to reject the experts' opinions, see *Wiszniewski v Central Manchester HA* [1998] P.I.Q.R. P324, CA, Ch.6, para.6–15, above. However, provided a clear explanation of findings is given there are occasions where there is no need to explain in detail why the evidence of expert witnesses was unhelpful: *Lakey v Merton and Sutton HA, The Times*, March 11, 1999, CA. Where there are differences of expert opinion in relation to medical treatment, including the information which a patient should have been given in advance, but the opinions are genuinely held, competent and logically justifiable, the court should not choose between them: *Newbury v Bath District HA* (1999) 47 B.M.L.R. 138. See generally para.9–05, above.

[378] *Roe v Minister of Health* [1954] 2 Q.B. 66.

safe but which later experience proved to be dangerous.[379] By like reasoning it has been held: that a conservative approach to ultrasound scan was a tenable professional opinion in 1988[380]; and there could be no claim for negligent injury to a child's left foot arising after a leak from an intravenous line, albeit that the treatment given in 1991 was more conservative than would have been suggested by standards current at the date of trial.[381] But treatment with human growth hormone after July 1, 1977, where the claimants later developed CJD as a result, was negligent.[382] The same principle applies where the allegation is failure to use some particular item of equipment: the defendant will not be liable if the equipment was not generally available at the date it is suggested it should have been used.[383]

9-127   **The relevance of usual practice.** Deviation from normal professional practice is not necessarily evidence of negligence.[384] To be so it must be proved, (i) there is normal practice, which is applicable to the case; (ii) the defendant has not adopted it; and (iii) the course taken was one which no professional man of ordinary skill would have taken, had he been taking ordinary care.[385] In novel cases, where there is no recognised body of opinion to which to refer, the degree of care required is simply that reasonably to be expected in the circumstances.[386] Where a medical practitioner is called upon to advise partly on medical matters and partly on economic and administrative considerations, it is to the medical aspect only that the high standard of care is applied.[387]

9-128   **Clinical judgment.** Whether an error of clinical judgment amounts to negligence depends upon whether the error was one which a reasonably

---

[379] *Roe v Minister of Health* [1954] 2 Q.B. 66. For other cases involving the use of anaesthetics see *Williams v North Liverpool Hospital Management Committee, The Times*, January 17, 1959; and *Moore v Lewisham Group Hospital Management Committee, The Times*, February 5, 1959. But *cf. O'Donovan v Cork C.C.* [1967] I.R. 173.

[380] *C v Health Authority* [1999] C.L.Y. 4002 (and at that time there was a less than 50 per cent chance that foetal abnormalities would have been revealed).

[381] *Nawoor v Barking, Havering and Brentwood HA* [1998] Lloyd's Rep. Med. 313.

[382] *Newman v Medical Research Council, The Times*, December 20, 1997, CA.

[383] *Whiteford v Hunter* [1950] W.N. 553 (surgeon made error in diagnosis as a result of failing to use an instrument then very rarely to be found in England). See also *Chapman v Rix, The Times*, December 22, 1960; *McCormack v Redpath Brown & Co, The Times*, March 24, 1961.

[384] In *Holland v Devitt and Moore Nautical College, The Times*, March 4, 1960, Streatfield J. expressed the view that a doctor was entitled to use his common sense, experience and judgment in the treatment of each particular case, and a slight departure from the textbook would not of itself establish negligence.

[385] *Hunter v Hanley* 1955 S.C. 200; see also *Landau v Werner* 105 S.J. 1008.

[386] *A v Tameside and Glossop HA* [1997] P.N.L.R. 140, CA (the *Bolam* test was said to be inappropriate when considering the liability of a health authority for psychiatric illness alleged to arise as a result of the manner in which former patients of a trainee surgeon were informed of the remote risk that contact with him may have caused infection by AIDS. There was no well of professional experience on which the court could draw for comparison and it was sufficient to ask if the authority had fallen below the standard reasonably to be expected. On the facts, it was unnecessary for the distressing news to have been given by letter rather than in personal interview).

[387] per Swanwick J. in *Stokes v Guest Keen & Nettlefold (Bolts and Nuts) Ltd* [1968] 1 W.L.R. 1776, 1784 (a factory doctor).

competent medical practitioner professing to have the defendant's expertise would have made, if he had acted with ordinary skill.[388] It has been said that the question for the judge to decide is: "Did the surgeon in reaching his decision display such a lack of clinical judgment that no surgeon exercising proper care and skill could have reached the same decision as he did."[389] So, failure to intubate a patient was not negligent where the hospital authority had weighed up the risks and disadvantages which might occur as a result[390]; and the court would not criticise a clinical decision not to inform the claimant, who was 14 days beyond term, of the minor risk of stillbirth when advising her to wait a further time in the hope of a natural birth.[391]

Setting the standard of care. If the defendant specialises in some particular area of practice, he must be judged by the standard appropriate to that specialty.[392] Conversely, if he is in general practice, the standard to be applied is that of the ordinarily competent general practitioner with his qualifications.[393] The competent practitioner will know when a case is beyond his skill. It then becomes his duty either to call in a more skilful person or to order the removal of the patient to a hospital where skilled treatment is available. So, when a consultant has taken over responsibility for a patient's treatment, it is a defence to a competent medical practitioner that he acted on specific instructions which the consultant gave.[394] Whilst failure to use appropriate skill in diagnosis, as a result of which a wrong treatment is given, can amount to negligence[395] a wrong

9–129

---

[388] *Whitehouse v Jordan* [1981] 1 W.L.R. 246 (an obstetrician was not negligent where a baby sustained severe brain damage at birth allegedly caused by his pulling too hard and over too long a period during a difficult forceps delivery). See also *Early v Newham HA* [1994] 5 Med.L.R. (failure to intubate a patient not negligent where the hospital authority had weighed up the risks and disadvantages which might occur as a result); per Lord Denning M.R. in *Hucks v Cole, The Times,* May 9, 1968: "With the best will in the world, things sometimes went amiss in surgical operations or medical treatment. A doctor was not to be held negligent simply because something went wrong. He was not liable for mischance or misadventure, or for an error of judgment. He was not liable for taking one choice out of two or favouring one school rather than another. He was only liable when he fell below the standard of a reasonably competent practitioner in his field so much so that his conduct might be deserving of censure or inexcusable."

[389] *Hughes v Waltham Forest Health Authority, The Times,* November 9, 1990, CA.

[390] *Early v Newham Health Authority* [1994] 5 Med.L.R. 214.

[391] *Pearce v United Bristol Healthcare NHS Trust* [1999] P.I.Q.R. P53, CA.

[392] See, e.g. *Sidaway v Governors of Bethlem Royal Hospital* [1985] A.C. 871, per Lord Bridge at 897C.

[393] *Langley v Campbell, The Times,* November 6, 1975; in *Hucks v Cole,* above, Lord Denning M.R. said that the defendant "was to be judged as a general practitioner with a degree in obstetrics". The standard of care required of a senior houseman at a hospital is that of a reasonably competent houseman, regardless of the individual's actual experience: *Djemal v Bexley HA* [1995] 6 Med.L.R. 269.

[394] *Junor v McNichol, The Times,* March 26, 1959, where the HL held that a house surgeon was not liable for the treatment of a child who had to have an arm amputated because he was not given sufficient penicillin, since the prescribed treatment was being given under the instructions of a responsible consultant.

[395] See *Pudney v Union-Castle Mail S.S. Ltd* [1953] 1 Lloyd's Rep. 73; *Newton v Newton's Model Laundry, The Times,* November 3, 1959 (negligent failure to diagnose a broken patella after the plaintiff had fallen 12ft on to a concrete floor).

diagnosis in itself is not necessarily an unskilled or negligent diagnosis.[396] Negligence may consist of a failure to warn the patient of the dangers of certain treatment[397]; the unskilful or careless treatment of a complaint, properly diagnosed; and a failure to obey an urgent summons from a patient, seeking medical assistance.[398]

ILLUSTRATIONS

9–130   The following decisions illustrate the fine line between findings of negligence and cases where liability has not been established.

Liability was established: where a wad of gauze was left in the patient's body after an operation[399]; where, in giving treatment by injection, a needle was broken and left in the patient's body, and the patient not informed[400]; where a doctor gave his patient a hypodermic injection for malaria, as a result of which he pierced the sciatic nerve and caused foot drop[401]; where cocaine was injected instead of procaine[402]; where pentathol was injected while the patient was already under an anaesthetic, causing death[403]; where a doctor failed to administer penicillin for a condition of fulminating septicaemia of a finger, after the finish of a five-day course of tetracycline[404]; where, following surgery for removal of a swelling from the parotid gland under general anaesthetic, the claimant was taken to the recovery ward but suffered brain damage caused by hypoxia for a four-to-five-minute period, which the anaesthetist had failed to prevent[405]; where a consultant paediatrician failed to refer a hydrocephalic baby suffering symptoms consistent with blockage of its ventricular peritoneal shunt,

---

[396] See *Crivon v Barnet Group Hospital Management Committee, The Times*, November 18, 1958, CA (incorrect diagnosis of cancer by a pathologist leading to the wrong treatment); *Dale v Munthali* (1976) 78 D.L.R. 588 (no negligence in failing to distinguish symptoms of influenza and meningitis).

[397] *Bolam v Friern Hospital Management Committee* [1957] 1 W.L.R. 582, (electro-convulsive therapy leading to bilateral fractures of the acetabula as a result of the violent muscular contractions).

[398] In *Cavan v Wilcox* (1973) 44 D.L.R. (3d) 42 where a patient had developed gangrene after receiving an injection which had been administered by a nurse, it was held that since there was no effective treatment which could have been given to him, the failure of the physician to attend immediately was neither negligent nor had any causal connection with the eventual loss of his fingers.

[399] When the operation is a piece of team-work, it may be that the surgeon is entitled to leave part of the work, such as the counting of the swabs taken from the patient's body, to some other competent member of the team. Negligence was found in *Dryden v Surrey County Council and Stewart* [1936] 2 All E.R. 535; *Hocking v Bell* [1948] W.N. 21 (drainage tube left *in situ*), *Urry v Bierer, The Times*, July 15, 1955 and *Cooper v Nevill, The Times*, March 24, 1961 (abdominal swab not removed). On the other hand no negligence was found in *Mahon v Osborne* [1939] 2 K.B. 14, *Chasney v Anderson* [1950] 4 D.L.R. 223 and *White v Westminster Hospital Board of Governors, The Times*, October 26, 1961.

[400] *Gerber v Pines* (1933) 79 S.J. 13. Not followed, *Daniels v Heskin* [1954] I.R. 73.

[401] *Caldeira v Gray, The Times*, February 15, 1936.

[402] *Collins v Hertfordshire County Council* [1947] K.B. 598.

[403] *Jones v Manchester Corp* [1952] 2 K.B. 852.

[404] *Hucks v Cole* (1968) 118 New L.J. 469.

[405] *Coyne v Wigan Health Authority* [1991] 2 Med.L.R. 301.

for C.T. scan[406]; where the claimant developed a lump to the breast but no biopsy was undertaken to confirm a diagnosis of fibroadenoma, as opposed to carcinoma as in fact was the case and where chemotherapy was thereby unduly delayed.[407]

Negligence was also found: where a pregnant patient was admitted to hospital **9–131** for her confinement and was placed in the same ward as a woman suspected of and confirmed later to have been suffering from puerperal fever, where insufficient precautions to isolate her were taken[408]; where treating doctors did not proceed to delivery by Caesarean section after one of a series of cardiotoco-grams revealed gross abnormalities, although such a decision would have advanced delivery by two hours at most, and on balance did not contribute to the final state of an already damaged foetus[409]; where an abortion was performed which failed to terminate pregnancy, and the claimant was not informed that another such operation could have been performed until after it was too late, as a result of which she gave birth to a healthy child[410]; where a surgeon performed a sterilisation operation on the claimant but she subsequently became preg-nant[411]; where a surgeon failed to warn a vasectomy patient of a slight risk that the healing process after operation might render him fertile once more.[412] Any such warning must be clear and comprehensible and reasonable steps taken to ensure it is understood.[413]

A psychiatrist was negligent where he developed social contact with his **9–132** patient as a part of her treatment. She was in a vulnerable emotional state and, to his knowledge, already in love with him. There was no body of professional opinion which would have considered it desirable for a doctor to have such social contact with his patient in these circumstances.[414]

---

[406] *Robinson v Jacklin* [1996] 7 Med.L.R. 83; also *Rhodes v Spokes and Farbridge* [1996] 7 Med.L.R. 135, see n.41, below.

[407] *Taylor v West Kent HA* [1997] 8 Med.L.R. 251 (the claimant's death would have occurred in any event, but 18 months later, had the duty of care been properly discharged).

[408] *Heafield v Crane, The Times,* July 31, 1937.

[409] *Robertson v Nottingham Health Authority* (1997) 7 Med.L.R. 421.

[410] *Scuriaga v Powell* (1979) 123 S.J. 406 (the measure of damages consisted of her pain and suffering, loss of earnings and the diminution of her prospects of marriage). But see *McFarlane v Tayside Health Board* [2000] 2 A.C. 59, below.

[411] *Emeh v Kensington & Chelsea & Westminster HA* [1985] Q.B. 1012 (it was not a *novus actus interveniens*, nor a failure to mitigate loss, for the claimant to refuse to have a surgical abortion). As to heads of damage in such a case, see *McFarlane v Tayside Health Board,* n.410 above and Ch.2, para.2–250, above; In relation to warnings of the risk of pregnancy, see *Danns v Department of Health* [1998] P.I.Q.R. P226, CA, and Ch.12, para.12–29, below (the Department of Health was under no duty from 1984 onwards to warn the public of the risk of unwanted pregnancy after vasectomy).

[412] *Thake v Maurice* [1986] Q.B. 644. It was held that following the surgeon's failure to give such a warning, it must have been in the defendant's contemplation that the wife, relying on the fact of her husband's sterilisation, might not recognise the early stages of her unwanted pregnancy until it was too late for a lawful abortion. Hence it was reasonably foreseeable that a breach of duty, both contractual and tortious, would cause damage to each claimant. But as to the recoverable loss see *McFarlane v Tayside Health Board,* n.410 above.

[413] *Lybert v Warrington HA* [1996] P.I.Q.R. P45, CA.

[414] *Landau v Werner* (1961) 105 S.J. 257; affirmed 105 S.J. 1008.

9–133   Negligence may also consist of failing to make adequate arrangements for a patient[415]; failing to re-examine a patient within 24 hours where the initial diagnosis, although not negligent, could not be certain[416]; failing to write a prescription to a standard of legibility which would reduce the possibility of its being misread by a busy or careless pharmacist[417]; failing to prescribe an antibiotic to kill bacteria identified by a pathologist's report which ought to have alerted the doctor to the problem[418]; advising against measles vaccination where there was a history of convulsions[419]; failing to communicate findings to others responsible for continuing a patient's treatment[420]; failing to make proper inquiries to discover what treatment, if any, a patient has already received elsewhere[421]; failing to give warning to a patient who has a tendency towards phlebitis of the dangerous side-effects of an anti-coagulant drug, which has been prescribed[422]; and failing to consider the possibility that a patient, who had recently returned home to England from Uganda, could well be suffering from some tropical disease and not merely from influenza.[423] It was negligent for a pharmacy to fail to follow its own procedure by questioning the correctness of a prescription which was significantly stronger than the dosage the claimant had been previously prescribed.[424]

9–134   Liability was admitted where an obstetrician attempted to rotate internally a second twin by inserting his arm *per vaginam*, a procedure characterised as "horrific" and "totally unacceptable".[425] Further, it was negligent of an obstetrician to rely upon a midwife to make a clinical judgment for which she was unqualified, so that a Caesarean section was not carried out, as it would have been had he attended and himself observed signs of foetal distress[426]; for the claimant's medical attendants to permit her post partum haemorrhage to continue

---

[415] See *Corder v Banks*, *The Times*, April 9, 1960 (a plastic surgeon who allowed his patient to go home after an operation but failed to make proper arrangements for receiving telephone messages from that patient in the event of bleeding taking place during the first 48 hours after the operation).

[416] *Bova v Spring* [1994] 5 Med.L.R. 120.

[417] *Prendergast v Sam & Dee Ltd*, *The Times*, March 14, 1989, CA.

[418] *Hucks v Cole* [1993] 4 Med.L.R. 393, CA.

[419] *Thomson v James* (1996) 31 B.M.L.R. 1.

[420] *Rhodes v Spokes and Farbridge* [1996] 7 Med.L.R. 135 (G.P. failed to pass on crucial information to a consultant to whom he referred the claimant for investigation). See also *McCormack v Redpath*, *The Times*, March 24, 1961 (hospital casualty officer allowed claimant to leave after he complained of an accident at work in which he had been struck on the head by a falling spanner: in fact he had a depressed fracture of the skull).

[421] *Coles v Reading and District Hospital Management Committee* 107 S.J. 115.

[422] *Crichton v Hastings* (1972) 29 D.L.R. (3d) 692. But cf. *Smith v Auckland Hospital Board* [1964] N.Z.L.R. 241.

[423] *Langley v Campbell*, *The Times*, November 6, 1975.

[424] *Horton v Evans* [2007] P.N.L.R. 17 (the claimant had been given a long standing prescription of 0.5mg of dexamethasone, which was suddenly increased to 4mg and caused severe adverse effects: the pharmacist should have realised the prescription may be mistaken and questioned it with either the claimant or her G.P; had this been done a mistake would have been identified).

[425] *Kralj v McGrath* [1986] 1 All E.R. 54. See above Ch.5, para.5–153, above.

[426] *Wiszniewski v Central Manchester HA* [1996] 7 Med.L.R. 248, (appeal dismissed [1998] P.I.Q.R. P324, CA); also *Murphy v Wirral Health Authority* [1996] 7 Med.L.R. 99, para.9–144, n.463, below; *Hill v West Lancashire Health Authority* [1997] 8 Med.L.R. 196 (failure to perform earlier Caesarean section a material cause of claimant's cerebral palsy).

uncontrolled until hysterectomy became the only available treatment[427]; for a Professor of Obstetrics and Gynaecology to fail, when carrying out an ultrasound scan of a baby *in utero*, to appreciate that the scan showed abnormalities of the brain and to have advised accordingly[428]; for a gynaecologist not to warn the claimant at the time that if she was already pregnant a sterilisation operation would not be sufficient to abort the pregnancy[429]; where there was a negligent failure to deliver the claimant within forty five minutes of a decision to perform an emergency Caesarian section[430]; where there was a failure to diagnose pulmonary embolus in a patient after blood gas anomalies were indicated on ECG[431]; where anaesthetists should have responded to an episode of pre-operative hypotension sooner than they did[432]; where an anaesthetist failed to investigate the cause of a patient's bronchospasm some time after a muscle relaxant had been administered, and warn for future purposes that it was possibly an adverse reaction to the drug[433]; and failing in the course of a sterilisation operation to occlude the left fallopian tube.[434]

On the other hand, negligence was *not* found: where a child was born severely **9–135** handicapped with spina bifida and hydrocephalus, which conditions had not been diagnosed by doctors at the twenty-sixth week of the mother's pregnancy[435]; where an anaesthetist had adopted a technique during a Caesarean section generally accepted by a body of medical opinion, although it did carry with it some risk of slight awareness during the surgical procedure[436]; where a gynaecologist performed a sterilisation operation upon a patient who informed him in error that she was not pregnant[437]; where an operation for sterilisation had been carried out to protect a woman's health and the surgeon did not immediately

[427] *Le Page v Kingston and Richmond HA* [1997] 8 Med.L.R. 229.
[428] *Lillywhite v University College London Hospitals' NHS Trust* [2005] EWCA Civ 1466 (the case illustrates that there is not necessarily safety in numbers: two other experienced sonologists had effectively reached the same conclusion as the professor, but the CA commented upon the heavy burden upon him to reconcile his incorrect conclusion with the exercise of all reasonable care and skill, where he had purported to identify structures on the scan which were simply not there).
[429] *Crouchman v Burke* (1998) 40 B.M.L.R. 163, CA.
[430] *Richards v Swansea NHS Trust* (2006) 96 B.M.L.R. 180, Ch.6, para.6–112, above.
[431] *Hutton v East Dyfed HA* [1998] Lloyd's Rep. Med. 335 (another indicator was the patient's request for an oxygen mask).
[432] *Skelton v Lewisham & North Southwark HA* [1998] Lloyd's Rep. Med. 324 (in coming to its decision, the court would appear to have been influenced by the poor standard of the anaesthetic notes).
[433] *Eastwood v Wright* (2005) 84 B.M.L.R. 51, CA.
[434] *Taylor v Shropshire HA* [1998] Lloyd's Rep. Med. 395.
[435] *Rance v Mid-Downs HA* [1991] 1 Q.B. 587. Further, the mother's claim that, if only she had known, she would have arranged an abortion failed in any event on the grounds of public policy. Because the child was capable of being born alive at 26 weeks, within the meaning of the Infant Life (Preservation) Act 1929 s.1, and could continue to live without connection to the mother, such an abortion would have been illegal even where justified under the Abortion Act 1967 s.1(1)(b).
[436] *Taylor v Worcester and District HA* [1991] 2 Med.L.R. 215 (on the facts the patient failed to show that she had suffered awareness during the birth as opposed to after the operation when the anaesthetic was reversed).
[437] *Venner v North East Essex HA, The Times*, February 21, 1987 (it was neither necessary nor desirable for a dilatation and curettage operation, in addition, to be performed as a matter of course).

tell her that there was a slight risk of further pregnancy or advise her to use contraceptives[438]; where a consultant gynaecologist had advised initial conservative treatment of a patient who had suffered from cervical cancer and she developed intermittent vaginal bleeding some three years later[439]; where no evidence of diverticular disease was evident at the time of colostomy reversal, surgeons failed to perform a resection during that operation[440]; where hospital consultants treated endogenous candida endophthalmitis with an intravenous anti fungal drug, there being conflicting views on the appropriate treatment and no scientific comparisons of available treatments was in existence.[441]

9–136   It has been held that a general practitioner is not under a duty of care to make home visits to a patient over and above those requested[442]; and a doctor was not negligent in sending the practice nurses in response to concern about a baby's feeding and vomiting, when he himself was unable to attend.[443] It was not negligent: to fail to follow up a patient's change of address and to search for him, in the absence of any suggestion of his requiring urgent treatment[444]; to fail either to advise an elderly patient who was not suffering from any physical disability how to descend carefully from the examination table in his surgery, or assist her so to do[445]; to fail to report an incident of sexual abuse of a child to the authorities, when it was mentioned by the mother of a child in confidence and a credible assurance was provided that it would not recur.[446]

9–137   **Liability for negligence of others.** A medical practitioner can be liable for the negligence of an assistant or a *locum tenens* employed by him[447] but not for the negligence of nurses at a hospital, employed by a third party. Where two surgeons ordered that a patient in a hospital should have a hot bath and, owing to the negligence of nurses, the patient was injured, the surgeons were not themselves liable because the giving of a bath was properly left to the nurses and it was no part of the surgeons' duty to superintend the task.[448] Again, where a surgeon agreed to perform an operation upon the claimant and to give the case personal attention, but some three months later, after the claimant's discharge from hospital, a tube was found in his bladder, it was held that the surgeon was not liable: the patient's post-operative treatment had involved the frequent

---

[438] *Waters v Park, The Times*, July 15, 1961. In *Eyre v Measday* [1986] 1 All E.R. 497, CA, it was held that a contract for the sterilisation of a patient was not one for the result that she would never again fall pregnant.

[439] *Bancroft v Harrogate HA* [1997] 8 Med.L.R. 398.

[440] *McCafferty v Merton Sutton & Wandsworth HA* [1997] 8 Med.L.R. 387.

[441] *Bellarby v Worthing and Southlands Hospitals NHS Trust* (2005) 86 B.M.L.R.

[442] *Durrant v Burke* [1993] 4 Med.L.R. 258.

[443] *Stockdale v Nicholls* [1993] 4 Med.L.R. 191.

[444] *Kavanagh v Abrahamson* 108 S.J. 320.

[445] *Robertson v Smyth* [1979] S.A.S.R. 184.

[446] *C v Cairns* [2003] Lloyd's Rep. Med. 90 (it was accepted that in the mid 1970s the doctor's decision would have accorded with the practice of many responsible and caring colleagues).

[447] *Hancke v Hooper* (1835) 7 C. & P. 81.

[448] *Perionowsky v Freeman* (1866) 4 F. & F. 977.

insertion and replacement of tubes in his body and this had been carried out by surgeons and nurses resident at the hospital.[449]

Mentally disordered patients. Where an Act concerned with mental health **9–138**
provides for the giving of a certificate to enable something to be done under the statute, a medical practitioner who gives such a certificate is bound to exercise proper care and skill in that regard.

Section 3(3) of the Mental Health Act 1983[450] provides that an application for **9–139**
admission into hospital of a person suffering from a mental disorder for treatment must be founded on the written recommendations of two medical practitioners. Section 139(1) provides that no liability arises concerning acts done in pursuance of the Act unless done in "bad faith or without reasonable care".

The medical practitioner, in giving such a recommendation, owes a duty to the **9–140**
patient to exercise proper care and skill. A failure to perform that duty gives rise to liability in damages.[451] The duty "is not merely a duty to take reasonable care in making inquiries, that is, in ascertaining the necessary data, but includes a duty to exercise reasonable professional skill in forming a conclusion from such data".[452]
Before a civil action can be brought against a medical practitioner for negligently recommending a mentally disordered patient to undergo hospital treatment, leave must be obtained from the High Court.[453]

The medical superintendent of a mental hospital may be made liable if he **9–141**
negligently allows a mental patient to be at large. If the patient has been convicted of a criminal offence and assaults a member of the public during his period of freedom,[454] he may be liable. Such liability would be on the basis that he either knew or should have known that the patient, if not kept under control, was likely to commit an act of violence.[455] It is immaterial whether the violence is inflicted upon a third party or by the patient upon himself. Where a patient with a history of manic depression reported to a psychiatrist that he felt "like a volcano about to erupt", it was negligent not to question him further and there

---

[449] *Morris v Winsbury-White* [1937] 4 All E.R. 494 at 497, 498, per Tucker J.: "I think it is well established as a matter of law that the resident medical officers in a hospital of this kind, and the nursing staff, are not the agents of a specialist surgeon who comes and performs an operation of this kind, at any rate in so far as they are performing the ordinary routine duties which have to be carried out at a hospital of this kind."
[450] c.20, which repealed the Mental Health Act 1959.
[451] *De Freville v Dill* (1927) 96 L.J.K.B. 1056; decided under the Lunacy Act 1890 s.16, which provided for the signing of a medical certificate before an order could be made for the detention of a lunatic in an institution.
[452] *Everett v Griffiths* [1920] 3 K.B. 163 at 216, per Atkin L.J.
[453] Mental Health Act s.139(2). In *Winch v Jones* [1986] Q.B. 296, the CA expressed the view that on an application for such leave, the court need be satisfied only that, on the material immediately available, which includes any furnished by the intended defendant, the complaint is one that appears to deserve the fuller inquiry which a proper hearing would make possible.
[454] *Holgate v Lancashire Mental Hospitals Board* [1937] 4 All E.R. 19.
[455] *Ellis v Home Office* [1953] 2 All E.R. 149 (the report in [1953] 2 Q.B. 135 is only on the question of Crown privilege).

was a causative link with injuries the patient inflicted upon himself a few weeks later when he jumped from a balcony.[456]

9–142   Those with responsibility for the care of mentally disordered patients must take reasonable care for their safety while they are in their charge. So, where a patient attempted to commit suicide whilst under a regime of close observation instituted in a hospital to prevent this happening, the health authority was held liable when the patient made the attempt during a breakdown in the regime.[457]

9–143   **Damages.** Special problems of remoteness and causation arise in relation to damages in claims against negligent medical practitioners. In the context of unsuccessful medical treatment it can be problematic to identify precisely the injury flowing from a particular breach of duty. The burden rests upon the claimant to prove that the breach was a material cause of the adverse result of which he complains.[458] Having said as much, once a breach of duty is established and the claimant has thereby been exposed to the risk of an injury which in due course results, the exact mechanism by which that injury has arisen is immaterial and it matters not if, for instance, it was unforeseeable.[459] In all cases the primary question is one of fact: did the wrongful act cause the injury? But in cases where the breach of duty consists of an omission to do an act which ought to be done (such as the failure by a doctor to attend) that factual inquiry is, by definition, in the realms of hypothesis. The question is what would have happened if an event which by definition did not occur had occurred.[460] The *Bolam* test is not relevant when asking what as a matter of fact would have happened; but is when considering whether the medical attendant concerned would have acted properly in failing to take some particular action.[461] In the words of Hobhouse L.J.:

> "a plaintiff can discharge the burden of proof on causation by satisfying the court either that the relevant person would in fact have taken the requisite action (although she would not have been at fault if she had not) or that the proper discharge of the relevant person's duty towards the plaintiff required that she take that action. The former alternative calls for no explanation since it is simply the factual proof of the causative effect of the original fault. The latter is slightly more sophisticated: it involves the factual situation that the original fault did not itself cause the injury but that this was

---

[456] *Mahmood v Siggins* [1996] 7 Med.L.R. 76; also *Drake v Pontefract Health Authority* [1998] Lloyd's Rep. Med. 425 (failure to provide appropriate medication to a patient under treatment for depression and to ensure that she did not leave hospital unattended, as a result of which she jumped from a bridge in a suicide attempt and sustained injury).

[457] *Hay v Grampian Health Board*, *The Scotsman*, December 21, 1994; *G's Curator Bonis v Grampian Health Board* 1995 S.L.T. 652 Ct. Sess. OH. See paras 9–144, 9–145, below, for further examples; *Walsh v Gwynedd HA* [1998] C.L.Y. 3977.

[458] *Wilsher v Essex Area HA* [1988] A.C. 1074. See also, in the context of negligent failure to warn of risks, *Chester v Afshar* [2005] 1 A.C. 134, para.9–148, below.

[459] *Wiszniewski v Central Manchester HA* [1998] P.I.Q.R. P324, CA (the plaintiff developed hypoxia and thereby irreversible brain damage by reason of negligent management of his birth, and the defendant's neligence having exposed him to the risk of hypoxia, he succeeded even though the particular mechanism by which it resulted was not foreseeable).

[460] *Bolitho v City & Hackney HA* [1998] A.C. 232. See the discussion, of causation where the allegation is negligent failure to warn of the risks of treatment, at para.9–116, above.

[461] ibid. at 240. The claimant failed to discharge either burden in *Hallatt v North West Anglia HA* [1998] Lloyd's Rep.Med. 197, CA (alleged failure to take proper action after the pregnant claimant's urine sample disclosed glycosuria).

because there would have been some further fault on the part of the defendants; the plaintiff proves his case by proving that his injuries would have been avoided if proper care had continued to be taken."[462]

ILLUSTRATIONS

A causative link between the damage claimed and the breach of duty alleged **9–144** was established: where the claimant suffered cerebral palsy as a result of oxygen starvation at birth as a result of midwives' negligence in failing to carry out an examination that would have revealed a secondary arrest of labour[463]; where the claimant was passed fit for work after a negligently-conducted occupational health examination, which failed to identify an abnormality to the main pulmonary artery, and if the condition had been identified, it would have led to the claimant being referred to her own G.P. and thereafter to a consultant and she would have been advised of the possibly fatal consequences of pregnancy, and her baby not subsequently born[464]; where the claimant, who suffered various circulatory problems, presented at hospital with an ischemic left finger which was subsequently amputated, as later were the remaining digits of her left hand: she should have been referred to a specialist hospital and had that happened, appropriate surgery would have saved the fingers.[465]

No causative link was established: where a doctor in casualty failed to examine **9–145** three night-watchmen who complained of vomiting for three hours after drinking tea, but instead referred them to their own doctors, one of them subsequently dying from arsenic poisoning: the quantity of poison had been so large that probably the deceased would have died in any event, whether or not he had been examined properly and had received appropriate treatment[466]; where even if a vascular surgeon had been called shortly after an operation to assess whether an artery should be reopened it was unlikely he would have decided to operate given the risks: the claimant had to prove that he would in fact have reopened the artery or that it would have been negligent of him not to do so[467]; where the claimant failed to prove that the fatal result of an operation to correct an acoustic neuroma would have been different if the surgery had taken place earlier[468]; where a child suffering from respiratory difficulties collapsed owing to failure of his respiratory system and suffered a cardiac arrest and a doctor had been in breach of duty in failing to attend but even if she had attended she would not have arranged for the

---

[462] *Joyce v Merton, Sutton and Wandsworth HA* (1996) 27 B.M.L.R. 124 at 156 quoted with approval, at 240, in *Bolitho*, n.79, above ; applied in *Gouldsmith v Mid Staffordshire General Hospitals NHS Trust* [2007] EWCA Civ 397, n.465, below.

[463] *Murphy v Wirral HA* [1996] 7 Med.L.R. 99.

[464] *Roy v Croydon HA* [1997] P.I.Q.R. P445. An appeal on the proper *quantum* of loss was subsequently allowed: see [1998] P.I.Q.R. Q26, CA.

[465] *Gouldsmith v Mid Staffordshire General Hospitals NHS Trust* [2007] EWCA Civ 397 (the majority in the CA considered that it was sufficient to discharge the burden of proof to establish that had claimant been taken to a specialist hospital, most specialists in the expertise in question would have operated: she did not need to show which hospital, and what the practice of surgeons at that hospital would have been).

[466] *Barnett v Chelsea and Kensington Hospital Management Committee* [1969] 1 Q.B. 428.

[467] *Joyce v Merton, Sutton and Wandsworth HA* (1996) 27 B.M.L.R. 124.

[468] *Richardson v Kitching* [1995] 6 Med.L.R. 257.

child to be intubated, a procedure that would probably have prevented that which occurred.[469]

9–146   Where there were two competing causes of damage, namely an overdose of penicillin and the consequences of meningitis, the law could not presume in favour of the claimant that the tortious cause was responsible for the damage in the absence of proof that the tortious cause was capable of causing or aggravating such damage. Since, according to the expert evidence, an overdose of penicillin had never caused deafness, the appellant's son's deafness had to be regarded as resulting solely from meningitis.[470] When the claimant presented to her G.P. with bilateral sciatica and he failed to refer her immediately to a consultant, which could have led to earlier surgery and a better outcome, no causative link was made out: it could not be shown that, even if a same day referral had been made, a neurosurgeon would have operated sooner than in fact was the case, and so soon as to avoid the complications which actually ensued.[471]

9–147   **Failure to warn of risks.** Having proved that a warning of the risks of treatment ought to have been given but was not, it was traditionally thought the claimant must go on to establish that with such a warning the treatment would have taken a different course. In Australia it was held that the necessary causative link was established by a subjective test, that is, what would the claimant with his or her knowledge have chosen to do.[472] In this jurisdiction, it appeared that while the court would take a subjective starting point, objective criteria were also likely to be taken into account.[473]

---

[469] *Bolitho v City & Hackney HA* [1998] A.C. 232.

[470] *Kay v Ayrshire and Arran Health Board* [1987] 2 All E.R. 417, HL (distinguishing *McGhee v N.C.B.* [1973] 1 W.L.R. 1).

[471] *Zarb v Odetoyinbo* (2007) 93 B.M.L.R. 166.

[472] *Ellis v Wallsend District Hospital* [1990] 2 Med.L.R. 103, NSWCA (surgeon had failed to inform a patient suffering from severe neck pain that a surgical procedure proposed by way of treatment carried with it a risk of paraplegia which in the event materialised). In contrast, in British Columbia the test is objective: *Arndt v Smith* [1996] 7 Med.L.R. 35, SupCt. (BC) (an action on behalf of a child, injured before birth allegedly as a result of a doctor's failure to advise the mother of risks, was unsuccessful where the court found the mother would not have had an abortion even if proper advice had been given).

[473] *Smith v Barking, Havering and Brentwood HA* [1994] 5 Med.L.R. 285 (claimant facing likely onset of tetraplegia in nine months elected to have an operation which was attended with risk of immediate onset of the same condition. She was not warned of the risk. Her claim failed on a finding that even if she had been so informed she would have given consent: per Hutchinson J., at 288–289, while the question has to be decided on a subjective basis: "If everything points to the fact that a reasonable plaintiff properly informed, would have assented to the operation, the assertion from the witness box, made after the adverse outcome is known, in a wholly artificial situation and in the knowledge that the outcome of the case depends on that assertion being maintained, does not carry great weight unless there are extraneous or additional factors to substantiate it." Similar observations were made in *Webb v Barclays Bank Plc and Portsmouth Hospitals NHS Trust* [2002] P.I.Q.R. P61, CA (the Court of Appeal disagreed with the suggestion that where the basis of claim is failure to inform, the claimant must give evidence as to what would or would not have happened had the relevant information been given. By the date of trial it may well be difficult to attach particular weight to the claimant's own evidence on the question, conditioned as it must be by complex emotions reflecting, for instance, the legal proceedings themselves, as well as the extent to which the the claimant perceives the procedure in issue to have been successful or not and has adapted to resulting disability.

Traditional thinking was put aside in *Chester v Afshar*[474] where the House of **9–148**
Lords had to consider an unusual problem of causation in a claim based upon
negligent failure by a medical professional to warn of the risks of surgery. The
surgery in question involved a small (1 per cent–2 per cent) risk of serious
neurological damage which, sadly for the claimant, materialised. Ordinarily in
such a case the claimant would lead evidence upon which the court would be
invited to find, that if a warning of risks had been given, she would not have had
the surgery in question. That finding was not, could not, be made in *Chester* and
the trial judge confined himself to finding that the claimant would not have had
surgery on the day planned (when her injury in fact arose) but would have
explored other options. It was common ground that, on whatever occasion she
had the surgery, the same small risk would be present, and that, bearing in mind
the size of the risk, the probabilities were that it would not arise. In short, as Lord
Hope pointed out,[475] on the evidence,

> "the failure to warn [could not] be said in any way to have increased the risk of injury.
> The risk was inherent in the operation itself . . . it was also liable to occur at random,
> irrespective of the degree of care and skill with which the operation was conducted by
> the surgeon . . . the risk would have been the same whenever and at whoever's hands
> she had the operation."

On such facts it was difficult for the claimant to succeed on application of the **9–149**
conventional test of causation, that is, to show that the failure to warn was the
effective cause of injury. A majority in the House of Lords held that the claim
should nonetheless succeed. The view was expressed that where injury occurred,
which it was within the scope of the defendant's duty to prevent, the claimant
should have a remedy, even though unable to prove that had the duty been
performed the damage complained of would not have arisen. A very significant
factor was the patient's right to be informed of the risks. If on the present facts
the claimant was denied a remedy it would leave her with a right-the right to a
warning of the risks of surgery-but the right would be deprived of content.[476]
Policy and corrective justice therefore suggested "a narrow and modest departure
from traditional causation principles."[477] Bearing in mind the variety of
situations in which professional persons advise about risk, it remains to be seen
whether the "narrow and modest departure" is restrained within those confines.
The willingness of their Lordships to abandon traditional principles in favour of
providing what is seen as a just remedy to the claimant, bears comparison both
with *White v Jones*[478] and (another causation case) *Fairchild v Glenhaven*

---

[474] [2005] 1 A.C. 134. There was much reference in the speeches of their Lordships to *Chappel v Hart*
(1998) 195 C.L.R. 232 where, on similar facts, the High Court in Australia held that the claimant
could recover. See Jones, " 'But for' causation in actions for non-disclosure of risk" (2002) 3 P.N.
192; also Brahams, "Consent and the chain of causation and quantum" 2002 Med. Leg. J. 70,183;
O'Sullivan, "Causation and non-disclosure of medical risks-reflections on *Chester v Afshar*" (2003)
2 P.N. 370.
[475] [2005] 1 A.C. 134, per Lord Hope of Craighead at 154.
[476] [2005] 1 A.C. 134 per Lord Hope at 158: the position would be that a duty was owed, the duty
was breached and an injury was suffered that lay within the scope of the duty. Yet the patient to whom
the duty was owed would be left without a remedy.
[477] per Lord Steyn at 146.
[478] [1995] 2 A.C. 207.

Funeral Services Ltd.[479] It may not be fanciful to see the influence of the European Court of Human Rights, which in analysing Art.6 of the European Convention on Human Rights, has emphasised the importance of a legal system providing legitimate claims with a remedy.

9–150   **The scope of the duty.** A case with some similarity to *Chester* is illustrative of the close connection, in cases of negligent advice, between issues of causation and foreseeability. In *Thompson v Bradford*,[480] a doctor advised parents that immunisation of their baby could proceed notwithstanding that the child had a recurrent perianal abscess. Sadly, the procedure caused the baby to suffer a strain of polio caused by exposure to the vaccine used to immunise against that condition. The doctor was held to have been at fault in not informing the parents of the increased discomfort that would be caused if immunisation proceeded while the abscess was unresolved. It was accepted that, had that information been given, the parents would not have proceeded with immunisation at that time. But those facts did not render the doctor liable for the polio which developed. No reasonably competent G.P. could have foreseen that the presence of the abscess gave an increased risk of the contraction of vaccine-related polio. The development of that condition was not, therefore, within the scope of the duty of which the doctor was in breach. His liability extended only to the greater discomfort suffered by the child as a result of the vaccination being carried out when it was.

9–151   As Beldam L.J. said in *Brown v Lewisham and North Southwark Health Authority*[481]:

> "A doctor is obliged to exercise the care and skill of a competent doctor. He must take care in the examination, diagnosis and treatment of his patient's condition to prevent injury to his health from risks which a competent practitioner would foresee as likely to result from his failure to do so. He is not a clairvoyant nor if he tells his patient that he can find nothing wrong is he liable if his patient has a condition which is not discoverable by competent examination. The public policy of limiting the liability of tortfeasors by the control mechanism of foreseeability seems to me as necessary in cases of medical as in any other type of negligence. I do not see on what policy ground it would be fair or just to hold a doctor to be in breach of duty who failed to diagnose an asymptomatic and undetectable illness merely because he was at fault in the management of a correctly diagnosed but unrelated condition. In short it must be shown that the injury suffered by the patient is within the risk from which it was the doctor's duty to protect him. If it is not, the breach is not a relevant breach of duty."[482]

9–152   **Loss of a chance.** When considering the damages to which a claimant injured as a result of some clinical negligence is entitled, the usual starting point will be to identify the extent of injury that would have arisen in any event, that is, even if negligence had not occurred.[483] But while that might be regarded as the

---

[479] [2003] 1 A.C. 32.
[480] [2006] Lloyd's Rep. Med. 95, CA.
[481] [1999] Lloyd's Rep. Med. 110 at 117.
[482] Quoted by Waller L.J in *Thompson v Bradford,* n.367 above, at [18].
[483] See, e.g. *S v North Birmingham HA* (1998) 40 B.M.L.R. 103, CA, where the claim failed because although negligence was established, had it not occurred the claimant would not have been transferred any earlier to an Intensive Therapy Unit, and cardiac arrest would still have resulted.

standard approach, there are cases where the proof available to a claimant does not extend so far. In one situation experts are agreed that the defendant's negligence has probably reduced the chances of a better outcome, but are not able to indicate on a balance of probability what that outcome will be. These problems were considered in *Hotson v East Berkshire Health Authority*[484] and it was held that it was inappropriate to award a claimant damages for loss of the chance that treatment would have taken a more favourable course had the given breach of duty not happened.

An attempt to distinguish *Hotson* failed in *Gregg v Scott*.[485] The trial judge had **9–153** found that the defendant, a general practitioner, had been negligent in excluding the possibility that a growth under the claimant's arm might not be benign, and failing to refer him to hospital for examination. The claimant's case was that the failure to refer him reduced the prospect of a cure to less than 50 per cent. The judge found that the delay had not deprived the claimant of a cure because he would probably not have been cured anyway, but as part of the agreed factual background to the appeal it was suggested that the delay in treatment had, as a matter of statistics and expert medical judgment, reduced the claimant's prospects of survival for more than 10 years from 42 per cent to 25 per cent. The claimant contended that the court should provide a remedy where admittedly negligent medical advice or treatment led to a reduced chance of a favourable outcome, or increased the risk of an unfavourable outcome, even though a balance of probabilities test could not be satisfied.

The House of Lords concluded that the claim should fail. A majority was not **9–154** prepared to abandon the traditional balance of probability test applied in cases of clinical negligence. Lord Hoffmann emphasised the extent to which affording a remedy would involve abandoning an extensive and recently reviewed line of authority stretching through *Hotson*, to *Wilsher v Essex Area Health Authority*[486] and *Fairchild v Glenhaven Funeral Services Ltd.*[487] Further there was no adequate control mechanism to restrict the expansion of potential liability if it was established on the particular facts:

"a wholesale adoption of possible rather than probable causation as the criterion of liability would be so radical a change in our law as to amount to a legislative act. It would have enormous consequences for insurance companies and the National Health Service . . . I think that any such change should be left to Parliament."[488]

Lord Phillips' speech illustrated the problems that would arise if an approach to causation based on statistical analysis was adopted.

---

[484] [1987] A.C. 750. Scott, "Causation and damage in medico-legal practice" 149 N.L.J. 1152.
[485] [2005] 2 A.C. 176. See further, Jones, "Another lost opportunity?" (2003) 4 P.N. 542.
[486] [1988] A.C. 1074.
[487] [2003] 1 A.C. 32.
[488] [2005] 2 A.C. 176 at [90].

9.—HOSPITALS AND HEALTH AUTHORITIES

9–155 **Vicariously liability.** Prior to *Cassidy v Ministry of Health*[489] in 1951, it had been held that public hospitals were not liable for the negligence of physicians, surgeons and nurses at the hospital,[490] whilst acting in the discharge of their professional functions.[491] Today, it is well established that hospitals are liable vicariously for the negligence of members of staff,[492] including nurses[493] and doctors.[494] Someone with medical qualification employed part-time at a hospital, is a member of the staff, for whose negligence the hospital is responsible.[495] In a private hospital, the consulting physicians and surgeons are generally not employed by the hospital, so it is not liable for their negligence,[496] but, in the case of a hospital organised under the National Health Service Act 1946,[497] consultants or specialists are employed under the terms of the Act, and liability for their negligence follows.[498]

9–156 **The duty of care.** For most purposes the duty of care owed by a hospital authority is co-extensive with the duty owed by the medical staff for whom it is vicariously liable. However, independently-owed duties can arise, for instance under the Occupiers' Liability Act 1957 or as an employer.[499] In one unusual case,[500] it was held that a hospital owed no duty of care to the mother and son of a deceased patient who had died after having developed brain tumours, to preserve tissue from her brain so as to permit investigation with a view to a claim for damages. Doubt was expressed whether it would be right "to impose a duty on hospitals to retain tissue removed in a post mortem against the possibility that

---

[489] [1951] 2 K.B. 343.

[490] See Lee, "Hospital Admission—Duty of Care", 129 New L.J. 567. For the vicarious liability of health authorities, see Ch.3, para.3–108, above.

[491] For the reasoning behind the erroneous view, see the exposition by Denning L.J. in *Cassidy v Ministry of Health* [1951] 2 K.B. 343 at 360, 361.

[492] *Bullard v Croydon Hospital Group Management Committee* [1953] Q.B. 511, and is not protected by the National Health Service Act 1946, s.72.

[493] *Wardell v Kent County Council* [1938] 2 K.B. 768; *Voller v Portsmouth Corp* (1947) 203 L.T. 264 (nursing staff negligent in not disinfecting properly apparatus for the giving of injection); *Fox v Glasgow S.W. Hospitals Board*, 1955 S.L.T. 337.

[494] *Cassidy v Minister of Health*, [1951] 2 K.B. 343; *MacDonald v Glasgow Western Hospital Board of Management*, 1954 S.C. 453.

[495] *Roe v Minister of Health* [1954] 2 Q.B. 66.

[496] *Gold v Essex County Council* [1942] 2 K.B. 293; *Collins v Hertfordshire County Council* [1947] K.B. 598; *Cassidy v Ministry of Health* [1951] 2 K.B. 343 above. Denning L.J.'s view, which he repeated in *Roe v Ministry of Health*, above, was that the hospital was liable, if it provided the specialist but not if the patient obtained him.

[497] Now repealed and replaced by the National Health Service Act 1977.

[498] See *Razzel v Snowball* [1954] 3 All E.R. 429; *Higgins v N.W. Metropolitan Hospital Board* [1954] W.L.R. 411; *Hayward v Board of Management R.I. of Edinburgh*, 1954 S.L.T. 226. An NHS hospital was not liable for the negligence of an independent laboratory to whom it sent a sample of tissue for growth by culture: *Farraj v King's Healthcare NHS Trust* [2009] EWCA Civ 1203.

[499] See e.g., *Buck v Nottinghamshire Healthcare NHS Trust, The Times,* December 1, 2006, CA, Ch.11, para.11–81, below (hospital authority liable to nurses at a special hospital who were assaulted by a patient with a known personality disorder).

[500] *Dobson v North Tyneside HA* [1997] 1 W.L.R. 596, CA.

it might be material evidence in civil litigation commenced at some future time".[501] Where an NHS Trust was contracted to the Ministry of Defence to procure designated providers of healthcare services for Army personnel serving overseas and their dependants, and to manage the contracts it so procured, it was fair, just and reasonable to impose a duty upon the Trust, in relation to British patients, to take reasonable care in discharging the obligations concerned. However, the duty did not extend to ensuring that reasonable care was taken in the provision of treatment within a German hospital.[502]

The standard of care. The standard of care required of members of a **9–157** specialist hospital unit must be determined in the context of the particular posts held in the unit, rather than according to general rank or status.[503]

ILLUSTRATIONS

The hospital concerned has been held liable: where an in-patient was injured **9–158** by the negligence of the radiographer, a full-time employee of the hospital, in failing to provide adequate screening material during the use of X-rays[504]; when unqualified house surgeon negligently injected a patient with cocaine in mistake for procaine, a harmless drug[505]; when the medical staff were negligent in the post-operational treatment of a patient[506]; when an an aesthetic was negligently administered by a physician on the hospital staff[507]; when the casualty officer failed to discover a depressed fracture of the skull and penetration of the bone into the brain tissue[508]; where a nurse at a cottage hospital had failed to give an anti-tetanus injection to a man who had suffered a severe crush injury to a finger whilst shovelling coal, or had failed to take steps to communicate to others to ensure that the claimant got the proper treatment elsewhere[509]; in administering a contraceptive drug, without warning of possible side effects, despite a reasonable request by the claimant for detailed information, where she would not have agreed to its use had she been in possession of such information[510]; where a boy of seven, who was suffering from scarlet fever, was placed in a bed next to an open window in a ward on the ground floor and, during the absence of a nurse, he was injured when, somehow, he fell through the window[511]; where a patient, who was suffering from a form of epilepsy, characterised by a dangerous condition of post-epileptic automatism which was known to the staff, had been

---

[501] *Dobson v North Tyneside HA* [1997] 1 W.L.R. 596, CA per Peter Gibson L.J. at 602.

[502] *A (A Child) v The Ministry of Defence* [2005] Q.B. 183.

[503] *Wilsher v Essex Area HA* [1987] Q.B. 730 (appeal allowed on the issue of causation [1988] A.C. 1074). For the standard of care generally, see para.9–03, above.

[504] *Gold v Essex County Council* [1942] 2 K.B. 293.

[505] *Collins v Hertfordshire County Council* [1947] K.B. 598.

[506] *Cassidy v Ministry of Health* [1951] 2 K.B. 343.

[507] *Jones v Manchester Corp* [1952] 2 K.B. 852.

[508] *McCormack v Redpath Brown & Co, The Times*, March 24, 1961.

[509] *Coles v Reading and District Hospital Management Committee* (1963) 107 S.J. 115.

[510] *Blyth v Bloomsbury Health Authority, The Times*, May 24, 1985.

[511] *Newnham v Rochester and Chatham Joint Hospital Board, The Times*, February 28, 1936.

left unrestrained and unattended and jumped through an open window[512]; where a mother was incorrectly informed that her new baby had died, thereby causing her to suffer psychiatric injury[513]; where a screener failed to act upon apparent abnormalities in a cervical screen test, after which the claimant developed cervical cancer.[514] A hospital was liable for a systemic failure where, on booking in a patient in the advanced stages of pregnancy, no attempt was made to retrieve her past medical files, that not being usual unless she herself raised issues arising in an earlier pregnancy. Had the files been available the doctors would have been aware of the possibility of obstructed delivery and a caesarian section performed in case of emergency. In fact, the claimant suffered fetal asphyxia as a result of placental abruption shortly before birth and cerebral palsy resulted.[515]

9–159   In contrast, the hospital was held not liable : when a girl of nine, during the temporary absence of the ward orderly, injured herself by running along and crashing into the closed glass swing doors on the premises[516]; when a mental patient, who was receiving electro-convulsive therapy, a form of treatment given in accordance with a considerable body of medical opinion, sustained fractures of the pelvis on each side, which had been caused by the driving of the head of the femur through the acetabulum.[517] Although a greater degree of care and supervision was required in the case of a patient of known or suspected suicidal tendencies, there was no negligence found where a woman, having succeeded in eluding the nursing staff, returned to her home, there to commit suicide whilst mentally ill but not insane[518]; of where a patient at a prison hospital managed to commit suicide: such a hospital could not be expected to provide the same facilities as a psychiatric hospital in the community at large.[519]

9–160   In *Savage v South Essex Partnership NHS Foundation Trust*,[520] the House of Lords considered the nature of the duty owed by hospital authorities under art.2 of the European Convention on Human Rights, to potentially suicidal patients detained under the Mental Health Act 1983. It was said that in deciding what measures should be taken to protect the lives of patients in mental hospitals, or

---

[512] *Lepine v University Hospital Board* (1964) 50 D.L.R. (2d) 225, affirmed (1965) 54 D.L.R. (2d) 340. Likewise, in *Selfe v Ilford and District Hospital Management Committee* (1970) 114 S.J. 935 the hospital was guilty of negligence in failing to provide continuous supervision of a psychiatric patient and a known suicide risk, who left his bed by a ground floor window, climbed to a roof and threw himself off thereby sustaining severe personal injuries. See also *G's Curator Bonis v Grampian Health Board*, 1995 S.L.T. 652, OH, where the hospital were liable to the claimant, a known suicide risk on "close observation", who was found hanging from a shower fitment. The nurse was required to know at all times where the claimant was and had assumed on seeing her walk in the direction of the toilets and showers that she was going to the former.

[513] *Allin v City & Hackney HA* [1996] 7 Med.L.R. 167 (a duty of care was conceded).

[514] *Penney v East Kent HA* [2000] P.N.L.R. 323, CA.

[515] *Loraine v Wirral University Teaching Hospitals NHS Foundation Trust* [2008] LS Law Medical 573.

[516] *Gravestock v Lewisham Group Hospital Management Committee*, The Times, May 27, 1955. The hospital's duty, apart from the medical aspect, was said to be that of an ordinary prudent parent.

[517] *Bolam v Friern Hospital Management Committee* [1957] 1 W.L.R. 582.

[518] *Thorne v Northern Group Hospital Management Committee* (1964) 108 S.J. 484.

[519] *Knight v Home Office* [1990] 3 All E.R. 237. But see also *Brooks v Home Office*, The Times, February 17, 1999, para.9–03, n.10, above.

[520] [2009] 1 A.C.681 at [100].

of patients in general hospitals who were suffering from mental illness, the authorities should take account of the patients' vulnerability, including a heightened risk of suicide. In assessing what should reasonably be done in discharging their duty under art.2 to protect their patients' lives the importance of a range of considerations was aknowledged. The steps required were those that were proportionate. Developing a patient's capacity to make sensible choices and providing as good a quality of life as possible, were important components in protecting mental health. Keeping a patient absolutely safe from physical harm, by seclusion or restraint, might cause additional harm. In judging what could reasonably be expected, resources should come into account. The facilities available for looking after people with serious mental illnesses were not unlimited and health care professionals had to make the best of what they had.

A hospital was not liable where an out-patient, who had expressed threats **9–161** towards children, murdered the claimant's daughter: although the child's home was near to that of the patient that fact alone was insufficient to establish a sufficient proximity of relationship for purposes of the threefold test in *Caparo Industries Plc v Dickman*[521] in the absence of a specific class of person who could be described as being at risk; nor was it fair, just and reasonable to impose a duty of care where that would not lead to an improvement in standards and would divert hospital authorities from their primary functions.[522]

Duty as to hospital premises. Of the situation prior to 1958, it was said by **9–162** Lord MacMillan that a hospital authority must "take by themselves or by their officers all proper steps to keep the premises safe for the admission of the public, or if they have not done so either to exclude the public altogether, or at least to warn them of the danger".[523] Now the duty towards all lawful visitors is the "common duty of care".[524]

Hospital's duty to medical staff. A hospital owes no duty to a resident house **9–163** physician, living in a staff hostel adjoining the hospital, to safeguard his personal effects against theft by a third party who comes into the hospital.[525] Nor is a hospital authority negligent where it leaves to the judgment of a trained nurse the method by which a patient is lifted.[526]

---

[521] [1990] 2 A.C. 605. See Jones, "Liabilities for psychiatric patients: setting the boundaries" (2000) 1 P.N. 3.
[522] *Palmer v Tees HA* [2000] P.I.Q.R. P1, CA (it was conceded in the CA that in the light of observations in *Barrett v Enfield LBC* [2001] 2 A.C. 550 the court should not on a strike out application, where the facts have not been established, come to a conclusion on the question whether it was just, fair and reasonable to impose a duty of care).
[523] *Lindsey County Council v Marshall* [1937] A.C. 97, at 119.
[524] Occupiers' Liability Act 1957 ss.1(2) and 2(1) which came into force on January 1, 1958. Prior to that date, the duty was that owed to an invitee, see earlier decisions cited in in *Lindsey County Council v Marshall*, above per Lord Wright at 125, See, generally Ch.8, as regards dangerous premises.
[525] *Edwards v West Herts Group Hospital Management Committee* [1957] 1 W.L.R. 415. See also note, 73 L.Q.R. 313.
[526] *Woolger v West Surrey and North East Hampshire HA, The Times*, November 8, 1993, CA.

9–164   **Private nursing home.** In the case of a private nursing home, there will usually be a contractual duty. As to the duty in tort, it is difficult to see any principle on which the duty in such a home can differ from that in a public hospital.[527]

9–165   **Nursing association.** A nursing association which takes reasonable care to provide competent nurses is not liable for the negligence of the nurses it provides.[528]

9–166   **Health authorities.**[529] It has been held that an area health authority did not owe a duty of care in respect of an alleged careless investigation into a registered nursing home, leading to an urgent application under the Registered Homes Act 1989 s.30, for cancellation of registration.[530]

9–167   **Damages.** Identical questions to those already discussed in relation to medical practitioners generally arise in claims against hospitals or hospital authorities.[531] In one special case the Court of Appeal had to consider whether, assuming breach of duty, the claimant could recover damages by way of compensation for his own attempted suicide which had rendered him tetraplegic. The view was taken that on the facts the hospital were not negligent, but that even if negligence had been proved, the claimant's attempted suicide would have been too remote.[532] But the decision does not establish that such a claim could never succeed provided a sufficient causal connection was established between the breach and the claimant's resulting act of self harm, and the damage was not too remote.[533]

10.—Insurance Agents and Brokers

9–168   **Generally.** Most insurance business is transacted through intermediaries, who divide into insurance agents on the one hand, and insurance brokers on the other. An insurance agent is one who normally acts as an agent of particular insurers in regard to effecting any policy of insurance with them. The agent aims to attract insurance business for principals, rather than to extol the virtues of services

---

[527] See *Powell v Streatham Manor Nursing Home* [1935] A.C. 243; *Gold v Essex County Council* [1942] 2 K.B. 293.

[528] *Hall v Lees* [1904] 2 K.B. 602.

[529] See generally, Martin, "Public health and the scope of potential liability in tort" P.N. 2005, 21(1) 39 (discusses whether tortious liability can arise from the failure of public health authorities to protect health with particular reference to vaccination and screening programmes, blood donation and radiation services, and the failure to intervene when such threats to health arise as MRSA and CJD).

[530] *Martine v South East Kent Health Authority, The Times*, March 8, 1993, CA.

[531] For obvious reasons many of the claims against medical practitioners are brought against the health authorities or NHS Trusts which employ them and are vicariously liable for their negligence.

[532] *Hyde v Tameside Area Health Authority, The Times*, April 16, 1981, CA.

[533] See, e.g. *Selfe v Ilford and District Hospital Management Committee* (1970) 114 S.J. 935.

which may be on offer from their competitors.[534] Liability to the principal is determined by the law of agency, since the relationship is a contractual one.[535] Thus, if an insurance agent chooses to undertake to procure an insurance, a duty arises to use all due care and skill. The question in each case is whether the act or omission complained of is inconsistent with that reasonable degree of care and skill which persons of ordinary prudence and competence ought to show.[536]

It is a question of construction of the terms of the contract of agency whether the agent has contracted merely to use due care and skill to procure an effective insurance or has given an absolute undertaking that an effective insurance will be procured.[537]

An insurance broker is one who normally[538] acts as an agent of the insured **9–169** person and strives to find and arrange appropriate insurance for a client's requirements. The client's interests are his paramount conisderation.[539] Whilst it is perfectly true that an insurance broker is usually remunerated by commission, paid by the insurers with whom a client's business is placed, the broker's contractual relationship is with the client rather than the insurance company providing the cover.

One important exception to this general rule arises when the insurance broker **9–170** has been authorised by particular insurers to effect insurance on their behalf. In such instances, as between the insurance broker, the insurers and the insured, when involved in the field of non-marine insurance, there is a tripartite legal relationship and the broker's agency on behalf of the insurers is well established. Also, because brokers have the implied authority of road traffic insurers, for example, to effect interim motor insurance by the issue of cover notes, those members of the public dealing with them can regard them, for these purposes, as being the agents of the insurers and not of themselves, the insured.[540]

As the insurance market develops, other exceptions to the traditional distinc- **9–171** tion between brokers and agents may well arise. Where, for instance, there is reinsurance of an insured risk, the same broker may act both on behalf of the

---

[534] But an agent who places himself in the position of adviser to a prospective client of his principals will probably incur a liability, either individually and/or on their behalf, if he fails to describe the choices that can be made, for instance as between occupational and personal pension schemes: see, e.g. *Gorham v British Telecommunications Plc* [2001] P.N.L.R. 21, CA, para.9–171, below.

[535] The underwriting agents of Lloyd's Names owed a duty of care which could only be excluded by clear agreement: *Arbuthnott v Feltrim, Deeny v Gooda Walker, Henderson v Merrett Syndicates Ltd* [1995] A.C. 145. The duty was owed to future Names even though the members' agent was not acting for them at the time the negligence occurred. It did not extend to ensuring that care was taken by managing agents to whom work was delegated: *Aitken v Stewart Wrightson Members Agency Ltd* [1995] 1 W.L.R. 1281.

[536] *Chapman v Walton* (1833) 10 Bing. 57 at 63, per Tindal C.J.

[537] *Hood v West End Motor Car Parking Co* [1917] 2 K.B. 38.

[538] For an exception to this general rule, see n.540, below.

[539] See para.33 of the Code of Conduct, which has been drawn up, in pursuance of the obligation under the Insurance Brokers (Registration) Act 1977, s.10.

[540] *Stockton v Mason* [1978] 2 Lloyd's Rep. 430. See also *Woolcott v Excess Insurance Co Ltd* [1978] 1 Lloyd's Rep. 633; [1979] 1 Lloyd's Rep. 231, CA, and (re-trial) [1979] 2 Lloyd's Rep. 210 (brokers knew of claimant's serious criminal record, which they failed to disclose to the insurers, and later the claimant's house was destroyed by fire).

insured in placing the insurance and on behalf of the insurer in placing the reinsurance. Conflicts of interest may thereby arise.[541] In another variation, an insurance company can enter into a direct relationship of adviser/advisee with some actual or potential client and thereby owe a duty of care in the giving of advice. So, for instance, where advising an employee about appropriate insurance provision for himself and his dependants, the differences between any occupational pension scheme offered by employers and the personal scheme offered by the insurer itself ought to be described and the client given the opportunity to make an informed choice between the two.[542]

9–172   **The duty of care.** The legal relationship between insurance agents and brokers on the one hand and their clients on the other is primarily a matter of contract. A concurrent duty does, however, arise in tort.[543] Indeed it has been held for many years, that an insurance broker owed a client a duty of care in tort, whether or not there was a subsisting contractual relationship between them.[544] The tortious duty is owed not only to the party with whom the broker or agent has contracted, but also to third parties in appropriate circumstances.

9–173   The liability of an insurance agent to a third party, namely the assured, was examined in *Fine's Flowers Ltd v General Accident Assurance Co of Canada.*[545] The claimant, who owned an horticultural business, relied on the defendant insurance agent to secure insurance cover, which was obtained under a complex policy covering a number of business risks, although not damage to plants by freezing, which was exactly what occurred when a water pump broke down as a result of mechanical failure. It was held that the defendant had undertaken a contractual duty to keep the claimant covered for all foreseeable insurable and normal risks to the property and since the loss suffered was of that nature, the defendant was liable for breach of contract. In addition however, he was liable in tort for breach of a duty which arose by virtue of his special relationship with the claimant, in failing negligently to inform him of the gap in the insurance cover obtained. On the other hand, in *Veljkovic v Vrybergen,*[546] where a building subcontractor had instructed an insurance agent to obtain employer's liability insurance cover, which was done but did not include injury to the employer

---

[541] See e.g., *HH Casualty and General Insurance Ltd v JLT Risk Solutions Ltd* [2008] P.N.L.R. 3, CA, per Auld L.J. at [60]. He went on to observe that where an insurance broker had been at the centre of devising such a scheme for insurers and reinsurers there was a strong argument for imposing duties of care which would continue after the reinsurance was placed.

[542] *Gorham v British Telecommunications Plc* [2001] P.N.L.R. 21, CA.

[543] See McGee, "Negligence by an Insurance Broker—When Does the Cause of Action Accrue?" (1990) 6 P.N. 132. Also in the case of the managing agents of Lloyd's Names, *Arbuthnott v Feltrim, Deeny v Gooda Walker, Henderson v Merrett Syndicates Ltd* [1995] A.C. 145, above.

[544] e.g. *British Citizens Assurance Co v Woodland & Co* (1921) 8 Ll.L.Rep. 89 and *Strong & Pearl v Allison & Co Ltd* (1926) 25 Ll.L.Rep. 504. See also *London Borough of Bromley v Ellis* [1971] 1 Lloyd's Rep. 97 and *Cherry Ltd v Allied Insurance Brokers Ltd* [1978] 1 Lloyd's Rep. 274 (after termination of their appointment as brokers, the defendants led the claimants to believe that their original insurance policy would remain in force for a further four months whereas in fact it had been cancelled and they had no claim against insurers for losses from a fire).

[545] (1978) 81 D.L.R. (3d) 139.

[546] [1985] V.R. 419.

himself, it was held by the Supreme Court of Victoria that the agent had not been negligent in his interpretation of the claimant's particular instructions, namely to obtain the normal cover suitable for the employer's workmen.

Liability to third parties can also arise by way of analogy with *White v* **9–174** *Jones*,[547] in which prospective beneficiaries were held entitled to recover against solicitors charged with the task of preparing a will from which they would have benefited. Where the representative of an insurance company negligently failed to advise the company's customer of differences between a personal pension scheme and his employer's occupational scheme, so that, upon his death, his widow and dependent children received far less in pension rights than they otherwise would have done, they were entitled to recover the capitalised value of what they lost. The deceased had intended to make the best provision he could for his wife and children. That intention had been frustrated by the negligent failure to advise and in the circumstances a duty of care was owed to them as much as to the deceased himself.[548]

It is established that insurance brokers can owe a duty of care to such third **9–175** parties as the insurer, for example in a case where the broker has a contractual relationship with the insurer because a binding authority has been given to the broker by the insurer to effect insurance on his behalf.[549] In other cases it will depend on the circumstances whether a duty to third parties has arisen and may depend on whether the broker has acted beyond the basic function of conduit between insurer and assured.[550] It has been held that it would not be just and reasonable to impose liability to third party claimants on insurance brokers who insured other brokers who subsequently became insolvent.[551] Nor did brokers instructed on behalf of a limited company owe a duty to the company's directors, even where they were also its sole shareholders and carrying on business through the medium of the company in a form of partnership, since the duty contended for did not fit into any existing category and the extension contended for was unjustified.[552] Where insurance brokers instructed Lloyd's brokers to obtain from underwriters a quotation for insurance cover which their client agreed to take up,

---

[547] [1995] A.C. 207, below para.9–220.
[548] *Gorham v British Telecommunications Plc* [2001] P.N.L.R. 21, CA para.9–171, above.
[549] [1979] 1 Lloyd's Rep. 231, CA; [1979] 2 Lloyd's Rep. 210 (on retrial). See generally, Virgo and Riley, "Duties of insurance brokers" J.F.R.&C. 2004, 12 (2), 128.
[550] *Pryke v Gibbs Hartley Cooper Ltd* [1991] 1 Lloyd's Rep. 602; *Adams-Eden Furniture Ltd v Kansa General International Insurance Co Ltd* [1997] 6 Re L.R. 352, CA (Manitoba). See also *Punjab National Bank v De Boinville* [1992] 1 W.L.R. 1138 (a broker owed a duty of care to someone he knew was to be an assignee of the policy, particularly where that person had participated actively in giving instructions for the insurance); *Banque Paribas (Suisse) SA v Stolidi Shipping Co Ltd* [1997] C.L.Y. 3818 (duty of care owed by insurance broker to bank providing an advance to shipowners to finance the purchase of a vessel on security of hull and machinery insurance which the broker negligently and inaccurately led the bank to believe was in place). *Empress Assurance Corp Ltd v C.T. Bowring & Co Ltd* (1905) 11 Com. Cas. 107 and *Glasgow Assurance Corp Ltd v William Symondson & Co* (1911) 104 L.T. 254 cited to the contrary in earlier editions of this work should no longer be relied on.
[551] *Duncan Stevenson Macmillan v A.W. Knott Becker Scott and others* [1990] 1 Lloyd's Rep. 98.
[552] *Verderame v Commercial Union Assurance Plc* [1992] B.C.L.C. 793. Where an insurance broker arranged for an investor to raise money by mortgaging his property and thereafter to invest the proceeds in bonds managed by an insurance company, no duty of care was owed to the investor by

no duty of care was owed by the Lloyd's brokers to the client in the absence of any assumption of responsibility by them or reliance by the client on them, as opposed to reliance upon the client's own insurance brokers.[553]

9–176   **The standard of care.** Today, an insurance broker's business is regulated by the Financial Services and Markets Act 2000.[554] The Act established the Financial Services Authority for the purpose of regulating insurance companies and the carrying on of insurance business. The Authority is responsible for making rules and the preparation and issuing of codes under the Act, the giving of general guidance and the determination of the general policy and principles by reference to which it performs particular functions.[555] A person wishing to apply for permission to conduct the regulated activity of effecting or carrying out contracts of insurance, or to vary an existing permission, may make application to the Authority. The authorised person must be a body corporate (other than a limited liability partnership), a registered friendly society or a member of Lloyd's.[556] In giving or varying permission the F.S.A. must ensure that the person concerned satisfies certain conditions, which include being a fit and proper person.[557]

9–177   The usual scope of an insurance broker's business is to effect policies of insurance or reinsurance on behalf of a client; to give advice in connection with a client's likely requirements for the same[558]; and, in appropriate instances, to give all necessary assistance to a client to formulate and pursue claims against the insurers involved. So far as the standard of skill and care is concerned, what is required is that care which a reasonably competent insurance broker should bring to bear.[559] The broker is assumed to have knowledge of the ordinary, well-settled rules relating to insurance law[560] and other insurance matters, such as the details necessary to make the policy a legally valid instrument.[561] Whether an insurance broker has exercised reasonable care and skill in all the circumstances is a question of fact.[562] Evidence can be received from persons engaged in the same

---

the company to ensure that he was given proper advice or to manage the investment in a proper manner: *Searle v A.R. Hales and Co Ltd* [1996] I.R.L.R. 68.

[553] *Pangood Ltd v Barclay Brown & Co Ltd* [1999] P.N.L.R. 678, CA (premises insured against fire burned down and indemnity was refused for breach of a warranty in common form as to the disposal of smoking materials which the client alleged had not been brought to its attention).

[554] Which came into force on April 30, 2001.

[555] See s.2(4) of the Financial Services and Markets Act 2000.

[556] ss.40, 44 of the Act.

[557] See s.41(2) of the Act and Sch.6, para.5.

[558] See, e.g. *Fine's Flowers Ltd v General Accident Assurance Co of Canada* (1978) 81 D.L.R. (3d) 139 at 148, per Wilson J.A. with whom Blair J.A. concurred.

[559] See *Chapman v Walton* (1833) 10 Bing. 57 at 63, 64, per Tindal C.J. See also *O'Connor v B.D.B. Kirby & Co* [1972] 1 Q.B. 90 at 101, per Megaw L.J.

[560] *Lee v Walker* (1872) L.R. 7 C.P. 121.

[561] *Turpin v Bilton* (1843) 5 Man. & G. 455. However, if he decides to give legal advice himself or to attempt to deal with a problem himself, which is beyond his competence, he will do at his peril: see *Sarginson Bros v Keith Moulton & Co* (1942) 73 Ll.L.Rep. 104.

[562] *Hurrell v Bullard* (1863) 3 F. & F. 445.

business as proof of what would have been the conduct of a reasonably careful and skilful broker in the circumstances of the particular case.[563]

ILLUSTRATIONS

Brokers have been held liable for failing to give proper advice to a client on insurance matters, an important function of a broker's business[564]; failing to make proper inquiries of insurers to enable the broker to answer a client's queries whether a policy covered a risk, concerning which there was doubt[565]; failing to question a client sufficiently about his occupation in order to make sure that he came within the list of categories which were acceptable to an insurer providing motor insurance cover[566]; giving evasive answers to questions in the insurance proposal form, such as "Not known to brokers"[567]; failing to report to the client their inability to obtain the cover sought and to seek further instructions[568]; failing to carry out their client's instructions[569]; recommending motor insurance with a company which they ought to have known was in financial difficulty and failing to advise the client that he was no longer insured once the company became insolvent[570]; effecting an insurance which failed to cover all the risks against which a client had wished to be insured[571]; when instructed to arrange an extension of a client's motor insurance policy to include a named driver, making a misrepresentation to the insurers without first having checked properly the driving record of the additional driver[572]; failing to make certain that a risk to be reinsured was defined in precisely the same terms as the risk covered by the primary insurance policy[573]; failing to recognise "material" facts, which had to

9–178

---

[563] See per Tindal C.J. in *Chapman v Walton*, (1833) 10 Bing. 57, above.
[564] *M'Neill v Miller & Co* [1907] 2 I.R. 328; *Gomer v Pitt & Scott* (1922) 12 Ll.L.Rep. 115; *Sarginson Bros v Keith Moulton & Co* (1942) 73 Ll.L.Rep. 104.
[565] *Coles v Sir Frederick Young (Insurances) Ltd* (1933) 33 Ll.L.Rep. 83; *Melik & Co v Norwich Union* [1980] 1 Lloyd's Rep. 523.
[566] *McNealy v Pennine Insurance Co Ltd* [1978] R.T.R. 285 (the defendant brokers had caused the claimant, a part-time musician, to take out motor insurance with an insurance company which would not accept such persons as risks).
[567] *Ogden & Co Pty Ltd v Reliance Fire Sprinkler Co Pty Ltd* [1975] 1 Lloyd's Rep. 52.
[568] *Eagle Star Insurance Co Ltd v National Westminster Finance Australia Ltd* (1985) 58 Q.L.R. 165, PC.
[569] *Dickson & Co v Devitt* (1916) 86 L.J.K.B. 315 (the instructions to the brokers were to effect insurance for goods to be shipped on the "*Suwa Maru* and/or steamers," covering the claimants against both marine and war risks. The broker's clerk had omitted to include the words: "and/or steamers". The goods were shipped on a different ship to *Suwa Maru* and it was sunk by enemy action).
[570] *Osman v J. Ralph Moss Ltd* [1970] 1 Lloyd's Rep. 313, CA.
[571] *McCann v Western Farmers Mutual Insurance Co* (1978) 87 D.L.R. (3d) 135, Ont. H.Ct (brokers had arranged insurance on the claimant's premises which excluded any business use, although they knew the client used some part for his business purposes; *G.K.N. Keller Canada Ltd v Hartford Fire Insurance Co* (1983) 27 C.C.L.T. 61, Ont. H.Ct; *Mitor Investment Pty Ltd v General Accident Fire & Life Assurance Corp Ltd* [1984] W.A.R. 365, Sup. Ct of W. Aus.; *Ramwade Ltd v W.J. Emson & Co Ltd* (1986) 2 P.N. 197. See Jones, "Limits on Liability to the Impecunious Client" (1987) 3 P.N. 76.
[572] *Warren v Henry Sutton & Co* [1976] 2 Lloyd's Rep. 276, but cf. the situation if the client had misled the broker by approving expressly the information to be passed on to the insurers, e.g. *Commonwealth Insurance Co of Vancouver v Groupe Spinks SA* [1983] 1 Lloyd's Rep. 67 at 82 per Lloyd J. See further n.586, below.
[573] *British Citizens Assurance Co v Woolland & Co* (1921) 8 Ll.L.Rep. 89.

be disclosed to the insurers[574]; failing to give a client notice that his fire insurance policy was about to expire and to send him a renewal form to complete in ample time[575]; failing to inform a client as a matter of urgency that the insurers had cancelled his policy[576]; failing to inform the client of the incorporation in the current policy of the proposal form for a previous policy[577]; failing to bring to the client's attention a new and onerous clause that was being introduced to his existing insurance cover.[578]

9–179   Brokers have also been held liable: for failing to draw attention to the fact that a cheaper policy excluded certain risks, described as "extended theft", which in the event materialised[579]; in the context of building works, for failing to ensure that full insurance cover existed even for phases of the work where a completion certificate had been issued[580]; for failing to include a mortgage protection clause within an insurance policy under which property was insured in the joint names of the owner and mortgagee[581]; for failing to inform their client of a clause in their property insurance about maintenance and use of fire alarms.[582] Insurance brokers were negligent in failing to arrange insurance which met the requirements of a life assurance society, in that it provided an excess of £25m for each individual claim against the society, but in so doing, failed to recognise the risk of the society facing an aggregated claim, that is where numerous claims arising from the same basic cause, individually of modest value but collectively worth in excess of £100m, were aggregated together.[583] Brokers were also liable where,

---

[574] *Coolee Ltd v Wing Heath & Co* (1930) 47 T.L.R. 78 (the clients, in their sand quarrying operations, originally did not use explosives and were insured accordingly for employer's liability. When the policy came up for renewal they informed their brokers that explosives were now being used for their business but the latter failed to realise the significance, so that the renewal did not cover injury suffered by an employee as a result of the use of explosives).

[575] *Morash v Lockhart & Ritchie Ltd* (1979) 95 D.L.R. (3d) 647.

[576] *London Borough of Bromley v Ellis* [1971] 1 Lloyd's Rep. 97; *Cherry Ltd v Allied Insurance Brokers Ltd* [1978] 1 Lloyd's Rep. 274.

[577] *Mint Security Ltd v Blair* [1982] 1 Lloyd's Rep. 188.

[578] *Harvest Trucking Co Ltd v Davis* [1991] 2 Lloyd's Rep. 638 (the case involved an "insurance intermediary", a member of the British Association of Insurance Intermediaries, whose duty of care was held to be similar to that of an insurance broker).

[579] *George Barkes (London) Ltd v LFC (1988) Ltd (t/a LFC Life Insurance Group)* [2000] P.N.L.R. 21 (only nominal damages were recovered where, even if the claimants had been aware of the difference, they would have proceeded nonetheless).

[580] *Tudor Jones v Crawley Colosso*, Lloyd's List, August 1, 1996, (I.D.) (brokers who had placed the insurance with the defendant were themselves liable to contribute one-third of the loss for failing to make clear that full cover was required and to read the policy before approving it).

[581] *First National Commercial Bank Ltd v Barnet Devaney & Co (Harrow) Ltd* [2000] P.N.L.R. 248, CA.

[582] *J.W. Bollom & Co Ltd v Byas Moseley & Co Ltd* [1999] Lloyd's Rep. P.N. 598 (no contributory negligence in failing to guard against the broker's negligence).

[583] *Standard Life Assurance Ltd v Oak Dedicated Ltd* [2008] P.N.L.R. 26 (the claimant was seeking indemnity from its insurers in relation to some 97,000 claims arising from the mis-selling of mortgage endowment policies. Tomlinson J. referred at [102] to a body of authority establishing that "it is the duty of a broker to obtain, so far as it is possible, insurance coverage which clearly meets his client's requirements. Coverage is only clear in so far as it leaves no room for significant debate. The coverage will be unclear and the broker in breach of duty, if the form thereof exposes the client to an unnecessary risk of litigation.").

instructed to arrange insurance for certain stock held by the claimant companies on behalf of others, they arranged a policy covering damage to stock "held by the insured in trust for which the insured is responsible." Those words were not apt to cover property held by the claimants as bailees on terms which did not include liability for accidental loss. The brokers should have investigated the terms upon which the property was held and had that been done it ought to have been realised that the policy in fact recommended was inappropriate.[584]

In contrast, brokers have been held *not* to be negligent in failing to see that an   **9–180** assured read through an application for insurance before he signed it[585]; where a client had approved expressly and had confirmed, a communication, which to his knowledge contained a misrepresentation, passing from the brokers to the insurers[586]; where the assured's instructions were ambiguous, in interpreting them in a reasonable manner[587]; in failing to act expeditiously to effect insurance cover, where it did not amount to unreasonable delay in the circumstances[588]; where they had received instructions from a co-operative association of fishermen to arrange insurance for a member's vessel, which did not have the necessary current certificate of survey[589]; where they had received instructions to effect export insurance for their client's goods but had not pointed out that such insurance did not cover their goods whilst at the packers before export[590]; where they had forwarded a copy of a new policy to their client but had not drawn specific attention to a variation in one of its terms[591]; where they had effected a comprehensive insurance policy for a householder who failed to inform them of both his and his wife's history of previous claims[592]; in doing all that could be done by them in the circumstances to transfer insurance cover to new premises[593]; in failing to suggest a further valuation of premises damaged by fire

---

[584] *Ramco Ltd v Waller Russell & Laws Insurance Brokers Ltd* [2009] P.N.L.R. 14.

[585] *O'Connor v BDB Kirby & Co* [1972] 1 Q.B. 90 at 101, per Megaw L.J. "when the broker took it on himself to fill in the proposal form, the duty upon him was to use such care as was reasonable in all the circumstances towards ensuring that the answers recorded to the questions in the proposal form accurately represented the answers given to the broker by the assured. But the duty was not a duty to ensure that every answer was correct." Accordingly, the broker's inadvertence did not constitute negligence or breach of contractual duty, in fact he might reasonably rely on the assured to correct any error which had arisen because of any misunderstanding between him and the broker. However, cf. the situation in *Dunbar v A. & B. Painters Ltd* [1985] 2 Lloyd's Rep. 616 where the broker was well aware of the misstatement in the proposal form.

[586] *Commonwealth Insurance Co of Vancouver v Groupe Spinks SA* [1983] 1 Lloyd's Rep. 67 at 82, per Lloyd J., cf. *Warren v Henry Sutton & Co* [1976] 2 Lloyd's Rep. 276 and n.572, above.

[587] *Dixon v Hovill* (1828) 4 Bing. 665. On the question of interpretation generally, where there has been indistinctness of expression, see also *Ireland v Livingston* (1872) L.R. 5 HL 395.

[588] *Cock, Russell & Co v Bray, Gibb & Co Ltd* (1920) 3 Ll.L.Rep. 71.

[589] *Norwest Refrigeration Services Pty Ltd v Bain Dawes (WA) Pty Ltd* (1984) 55 A.L.R. 509 (H.Ct. of Australia).

[590] *United Mills Agencies Ltd v R.E. Harvey Bray & Co* [1951] 2 Lloyd's Rep. 631.

[591] *Michaels v Valentine* (1923) 16 Ll.L.Rep. 244.

[592] *Lyons v J.W. Bentley Ltd* (1944) 77 Ll.L.Rep. 335.

[593] *Avondale Blouse Co Ltd v Williamson & Geo. Town* (1948) 81 Ll.L.Rep. 492. (The fire insurance was transferred but the cover for burglary could not be so before a survey had been carried out and no such survey had been done).

where, in relation to buildings under construction, the valuation figure reflected the costs of construction coupled with design project fees.[594]

9–181   Where a Lloyd's Name had requested exposure only to low risk syndicates, but the underwriting agent exposed him to syndicates of high risk, it was held that the agent was liable in both contract and tort and, hence, for the foreseeable losses suffered by the Name. Such a policy was inherently risky and the Name was entitled to expect some warning of the risks irrespective of his sophistication as an investor.[595] The standard of care owed by an underwriting agent to a Lloyd's Name is that of a reasonably competent Lloyd's managing agent, specialising in the type of business written on behalf of the Name. Whether this standard has been achieved is to be assessed at the time of the alleged negligence and not with the benefit of hindsight.[596]

9–182   **Damage.** The tortious duty, in accordance with usual principles, becomes actionable only on proof of damage. In the case of an insurance broker who gives negligent advice as a result of which his client enters into an insurance contract which is voidable, damage arises when a premium is paid, not when the insurer elects to avoid the policy.[597] As with other professionals who advise or provide information on the basis of which a course of action is pursued, the first step in deciding the extent of loss for which a negligent insurance broker is liable is to define the scope of the duty of care owed in the particular case.[598] The usual principle is that the defendant will be liable only for the consequences of advice or information provided by him being wrong. Where, however, in an unusual case, insurance underwriters sought to recover substantial losses associated with what proved to be an imprudent venture and the defendant brokers' negligence had deprived them of the benefit of reinsurance cover, recovery was not limited to the value of the reinsurance which the claimant lost. Applying the usual rules did not give a fair result, since in reality reinsurance would not have been available at all had the brokers made proper disclosure and the claimants would not have proceeded had they been so informed, so that their extensive losses were a foreseeable consequence of the failure to pass that information on.[599]

---

[594] *William Jackson & Sons Ltd v Oughtred & Harrisson (Insurance) Ltd* [2002] Lloyd's Rep. I.R. 230.
[595] *Brown v K.M.R. Services Ltd* [1994] 4 All E.R. 385. In *Berriman v Rose Thomson Young (Underwriting) Ltd*, Lloyd's List, August 1, 1996, managing agents who employed a specialised Lloyd's underwriter were nonetheless vicariously liable for his negligence in failing to calculate his ultimate liability in the market, whereby loss was caused to a syndicate of Names.
[596] *Henderson v Merrett Syndicates (No.2)* [1996] 1 P.N.L.R. 32.
[597] *Knapp v Ecclesiastical Insurance Group Plc*, *The Times*, November 17, 1997, CA, above Ch.1, para.1–32.
[598] *South Australia Asset Management Corp v York Montagu Ltd* [1997] A.C. 191, para.9–279 below.
[599] *Aneco Reinsurance Underwriting Ltd v Johnson & Higgins Ltd* [2000] P.N.L.R. 152, CA.; appeal dismissed [2002] P.N.L.R. 201, HL (but there was not unanimity in the House of Lords as to how to characterise the transaction between the parties: an illustration, perhaps, of the difficulty of drawing a line, even on agreed facts, between a obligation to provide information and an obligation to provide advice). See Dugdale, "The House of Lords decision in *Aneco*: right result, wrong reasons?" (2002) 2 P.N. 129. See also *Moore v Zerfahs* [1999] Lloyd's Rep P.N. 144, CA (a claim based in part upon the negligent completion by a broker of an application for a loan, was struck out where the only damage shown was acceptance of the loan by the lender: the claimant would in any event have been unable to recover for losses of a company which the loan was used to finance, since they might have arisen from a number of reasons, including mismanagement or adverse trading conditions).

11.—NURSES

The duty and standard of care. As with any other professional providing   **9-183**
health care, nurses[600] owe a duty of care towards the patients who come within
their charge. The standard of care is that of a reasonably competent nurse
exercising proper care and skill. Thus it was held to be negligence: for a nurse
to misread a doctor's handwriting and as a result administer six ounces of
paraldehyde instead of the six drachms prescribed[601]; for a nurse to assume that
the claimant, a known suicide risk on "close observation", was going to use the
toilet when she saw her walking in that direction whereas she made an attempt
at suicide by hanging herself from a shower fitment[602]; for a midwife in
delivering a large baby to use force to an excessive degree and for longer than
was acceptable.[603]

12.—QUASI-ARBITRATORS

A quasi-arbitrator, such as one who is asked by a buyer and a seller of shares   **9-184**
to fix the value of the shares according to the method prescribed by the contract
made between them, is under no duty to exercise due care or skill. His only duty
is to act honestly.[604] "He is not liable to an action unless he is dishonest."[605]
Further, an expert who truly performs a quasi-judicial function as between two
parties, is immune from an action for negligence, brought by either party, on the
ground of public policy.[606]

13.—SCHOOLS AND SCHOOLTEACHERS

The duty of care. The duty of a schoolteacher has been said to be to take such   **9-185**
care of his pupils as would a reasonably careful parent of the children of the
family.[607] The duty does not require that a school either insure a pupil against

---

[600] For the vicarious liability of hospitals see para.9–155, above, and vicarious liability generally, see
Ch.3, para.3–98.
[601] *Strangways-Lesmere v Clayton* [1936] 2 K.B. 11. cf. *Dryden v Surrey County Council* [1936] 2
All E.R. 535 where the nurses were held not negligent.
[602] *G's Curator Bonis v Grampian Health Board*, 1995 S.L.T. 652, OH.
[603] *Gaughan v Bedfordshire HA* [1997] 8 Med.L.R. 182.
[604] *Finnegan v Allen* [1943] K.B. 425; *Boynton v Richardson* [1924] W.N. 262.
[605] *Dean v Prince* [1954] Ch. 409 at 427, per Lord Denning L.J. However for a "special relationship"
see *Hedley Byrne & Co Ltd v Heller and Partners Ltd* [1964] A.C. 465.
[606] See para.9–43, above, and Ch.3, above, para.3–13, but cf. *Arenson v Arenson and Casson,
Beckman Rutley & Co* [1977] A.C. 405.
[607] per Lord Esher M.R. in *Williams v Eady* (1893) 10 T.L.R. 41; *Jackson v London County Council
and Chappell* (1912) 28 T.L.R. 359; *Shepherd v Essex County Council* (1913) 29 T.L.R. 303, per
Darling J.; *Rawsthorne v Ottley* [1937] 3 All E.R. 902, per Hilbery J.; *Ricketts v Erith C.B.* [1943]
2 All E.R. 629; but see the criticism of this test without more, by Geoffrey Lane J. in *Beaumont v
Surrey County Council* (1968) 112 S.J. 704, although it was applied in *Sombach v Board of Trustees
Regina Roman Catholic Separate High School District of Saskatchewan* (1969) 9 D.L.R. (3d) 707.
For a school's vicarious liability for the deliberate wrongdoing of a teacher, see *Lister v Hesley Hall
Ltd* [2002] 1 A.C. 215, Ch.3, para.3–142, above.

accidental injury in order to protect the pupil's economic interests, or to advise a parent to obtain such insurance, because a duty of that scope would exceed the obligation a school undertook to educate and care for the child.[608]

9–186   It is a schoolteacher's duty to take all reasonable and proper steps, bearing in mind the known propensities of children, to prevent any pupil suffering injury, whether from inanimate objects, from the actions of fellow pupils[609] or from a combination of the two. Accordingly, a school-teacher ought not to leave lying about in a place to which the pupils have access, anything that would be likely to injure them or to cause injury to others, as a result of a temptation to interfere or play with it. So, for example when some phosphorus was left in a conservatory where the boys could get at it, a schoolmaster was held liable for the consequential injury caused to one of them.[610]

9–187   What things are likely to injure pupils is a question of degree, depending on the item in question and the age of the pupils. "To leave a knife about where a child of four could get at it would amount to negligence, but it would not if boys of 18 had access to it."[611] It would seem that the test is whether the thing is of a type which a child of the age concerned would, in the ordinary course of things, be supervised in using. For example, where a child at elementary school, with the consent of the teacher, brought some toy soldiers to play with, and another child, aged five, was injured by a sharp point on one of the toys piercing his eye, it was not negligent for the teacher to allow the children to play with them, since they were playthings in ordinary use in every nursery.[612] On the other hand, to allow children of tender years to have fireworks, without supervision on the part of the schoolteacher, has been held to amount to negligence.[613]

9–188   If something which is likely to injure a pupil is left lying about by a third party, the teacher is liable if it was known or ought to have be known that it was

---

[608] *Van Oppen v Clerk to the Trustees of the Bedford Charity* [1990] 1 W.L.R. 235. It would be neither fair nor reasonable to place a wider duty on the school, which stood in loco parentis, than was imposed upon a parent, who had no obligation to insure (schoolboy aged 16-and-a-half sustained severe personal injuries whilst attempting a head-on tackle on a forward-rushing opponent in the course of a rugby football game.)

[609] Thus, a school may be liable for injuries caused to a boy by the "horseplay" of other pupils: *Beaumont v Surrey CC* (1968) 112 S.J. 704; *Scott v Lothian R.C.*, 1999 Rep. L.R. 15, OH (the claimant's action failed where she alleged bullying had caused her to suffer psychiatric symptoms and miss time at school, but she failed to establish that the teachers' actions were such that no teacher of ordinary skill would have so acted if taking ordinary care); also *Bradford-Smart v West Sussex CC*, *The Times*, January 29, 2002, CA (school potentially liable for bullying even where it occurred off the premises, although on the facts the claim failed where a responsible body of professional opinion would have agreed that the school's protective measures were sufficient). See, Berman and Rabinowicz, "Bullying in schools claims" J.P.I. Law 2001, 3, 247; Warnock, "Negligence outside the gates" 2002 P.I.L.J. 5, 22.

[610] *Williams v Eady* (1893) 10 T.L.R. 41, per Kay L.J.: "Was it not evidence of negligence to have left the bottle of phosphorus lying about in a place to which the boys had access knowing what boys are?"

[611] per Cave J. in *Williams v Eady* (1893) 9 T.L.R. 637. Further, see *Clark v Monmouthshire County Council* (1954) 118 J.P. 244.

[612] *Chilvers v LCC* (1916) 32 T.L.R. 363; *Raven v Suffolk CC* (2002) CLY 3272 (no negligence in permitting a five-year-old child to be in possession of sharpened pencil).

[613] *King v Ford* (1816) 1 Stark.N.P. 421, per Lord Ellenborough.

accessible. So, a teacher was liable where one pupil threw a ball of builder's material, hitting another boy in the eye. The teacher was aware that the material had been left in a corner of the playground by a contractor carrying out repairs and thinking it would be dangerous had telephoned the contractor to remove it. The contractor was also liable for failing to remove the material within a reasonable time after receiving the teacher's message.[614] This case was distinguished in *Rich v London County Council*[615]: the school authority was not liable, where there had been an unfenced heap of coke in the school playground and a pupil threw a piece of coke at another, injuring him, despite there having been proper supervision.

It is no part of the duty of a teacher to foresee every act of stupidity that might take place.[616] It is necessary to strike a proper balance between too strict a supervision of children at every waking moment of their school life and the desirable object of encouraging sturdy independence as they grow up.[617] In *Camkin v Bishop*,[618] a 14-year-old schoolboy received injuries as a result of being struck by a flying clod of earth, thrown at him by another boy, after he had joined in some boistrous play. In exonerating the defendant from blame, Goddard L.J. said: "If every master is to take precautions to see that there is never ragging or horseplay among his pupils, his school would indeed be too awful a place to contemplate."   **9–189**

This is plainly right, but it may perhaps also be observed that standards change with the generations, and the law of negligence should reflect contemporary values. A level of violence between pupils may formerly have been tolerated which is no longer acceptable today.

It is not the case that an education authority owes no duty in law to take affirmative steps to obtain medical help for a pupil over the age of 16. The special relationship of teacher and pupil may in appropriate circumstances require a teacher to take positive steps to protect a pupil from harm, no matter what his or her age.[619]   **9–190**

Supervision in general. A schoolteacher is under a duty to exercise supervision over pupils, whilst they are on the school premises, whether in the   **9–191**

---

[614] *Jackson v LCC and Chappell* (1912) 28 T.L.R. 359, distinguished in *Prince v Gregory* [1959] 1 W.L.R. 177 (a pile of similar material left in the street).
[615] [1953] 2 All E.R. 376. The CA held that, when the supervision was adequate, there was no obligation to prevent the boys from having access to the coke by erecting some structure over which they could not climb. In a similar case, Lord Parker C.J. held that there was no obligation on the school authorities to provide sufficient supervisors to watch all parts of the playground all the time: *Newton v East Ham Corp, The Guardian*, July 11, 1963.
[616] *Perry v King Alfred School Society, The Guardian*, October 28, 1961. See also, e.g. *Ahmed v Glasgow City Council*, 2000 S.L.T. (Sh Ct) 153 (no liability where the claimant was struck in the eye by an eraser thrown by another pupil when a class was left unsupervised).
[617] *Jeffrey v London County Council* (1954) 52 L.G.R. 521.
[618] [1941] 2 All E.R. 713 at 716.
[619] *Hippolyte v London Borough of Bexley* [1995] P. 309, CA (the unfortunate claimant, a child of 16, suffered an attack of asthma at school which resulted in brain damage. The defendant was unsuccessful in its argument that no duty of care was owed to obtain medical help, but the action failed, since, on the facts, no blame attached for a failure to summon an ambulance earlier).

schoolroom or on the playground. A school's responsibility for the safety and welfare of the pupils may well begin before it opens in the morning for the day's work. Further, it does not necessarily end immediately that the schooling is over for the day and the premises close down. Whether or not a duty arises outside "ordinary school hours", depends upon the application of the general duty to take reasonable care to the particular circumstances. The duty of supervision also extends to those simple tasks that can be left reasonably to be performed by the children, which will result in the continuing safety of the school premises.[620]

9–192   **Supervision out of hours.** Where pupils were permitted to enter school early, and there was a risk of injury to children playing ball games in an overcrowded playground, a duty arose to provide adequate supervision.[621] However a school was not liable where an eight-year-old pupil arrived early and was seriously injured when he stumbled and fell while running a race with friends in the playground.[622] The absence of supervision was irrelevant, since a supervisor would not have prevented what, in essence, was an unfortunate accident with very severe consequences. A similar view was taken where, as a result of confrontation with another pupil, a nine-year-old boy suffered injury when making his way to the school gates.[623] When a child, aged five, fell through the glass roof of the children's lavatory in the playground, after school hours, the school authority was not liable. It was reasonable to have a rule that children under five were kept under supervision until collected by their mothers, but not those of five or over.[624]

9–193   **Supervision: dangers on the highway.** In the case of very young children, it is the duty of the school to take reasonable care to prevent them from getting out of the school and on to the highway.[625] The unexplained presence in the road of a child for whom at the time the school has responsibility is evidence of negligence, sufficient to found liability in the absence of explanation.[626] The school was liable when during a teacher's temporary absence, a four-year-old boy managed to get on to the road through a gate, which was either open or could possibly be opened by him and a driver, attempting to avoid the child, collided

---

[620] *Martin v Middlesborough Corp* (1965) 109 S.J. 576 (the children failed to remove crates of empty milk bottles so that some broke and a child sustained lacerations).

[621] *Geyer v Downs* (1977) 17 A.L.R. 408.

[622] *Ward v Hertfordshire County Council* [1970] 1 W.L.R. 356. In *Mays v Essex County Council, The Times*, October 11, 1975 it was held that there was no duty to provide supervision in the playground for early arrivals, unless the school voluntarily adopted responsibility for them. The school was not liable when an eight-year-old boy helped to construct a slide on an icy patch in the playground upon which he fell and fractured his skull: sliding on ice was an innocent and healthy amusement, which no average prudent parent would have thought necessary to prevent.

[623] *Wilson v Governors of Sacred Heart Roman Catholic Primary School, Carlton* [1998] P.I.Q.R. 145, CA. See also *Ahmed v Glasgow City Council*, 2000 S.L.T. (Sh Ct) 153, n.616 above.

[624] *Jeffrey v London County Council* (1954) 52 L.G.R. 521. Likewise, in *Good v Inner London Education Authority* (1980) 10 Fam.Law. 213, it was held that the teacher's "jurisdiction" had ended when the children left the school either to be collected by their parents or else to go to the play centre near at hand.

[625] *Carmarthenshire County Council v Lewis* [1955] A.C. 549.

[626] See *J v North Lincolnshire County Council* [2000] P.I.Q.R. P84, CA, Ch.6, para.6–109, above.

with a lamp-post and was killed[627]; also where a girl, aged five, was injured by a lorry as she was attempting to cross a busy main road, after she had been released from school five minutes early and before she had been met by a parent or other responsible person[628]; and again where a claimant aged eight who suffered from developmental delay left school by one of five gates unnoticed and was knocked down on a major road 1,000 metres away.[629] But an action on behalf of a child who ran out of the school playground and was struck by a car failed, where the school had a good safety record and the child was "determined to break the rules".[630]

Supervision in class. The amount of supervision which is required depends   9–194
on the age of the pupils and what they are doing at the material time, but no teacher can reasonably be expected to keep a close watch on each child every minute of the day,[631] unless there is some reason to be alerted or put on inquiry.[632] During hours of instruction, a greater degree of supervision is required than during hours of recreation. When a 15-year-old boy, who was in a chemistry class of 25 children, was struck in the face by a concentrated solution of caustic soda squirted at him through a pipette by another pupil, neither the teacher in charge of the class nor the education authority was liable where the standard of discipline maintained was sufficient from the safety point of view, even if it did not succeed in putting down all acts of impertinence and high spirits.[633] A teacher was not to be under a duty to require all work to cease in class while she attended to a particular child, during which time the claimant, a child of nearly 10, accidentally lost an eye as a result of her classmate waving in the air a pair of pointed scissors, when she was supposed to be cutting out some paper illustrations.[634] It was not negligent for a teacher to permit pupils unsupervised access to an empty classroom in order to retrieve study materials, where, once inside the room one of them added whiteboard cleaning fluid to another teacher's bottled water, causing subsequent injury.[635]

---

[627] *Carmarthenshire County Council v Lewis*, n.625, above.

[628] *Barnes v Hampshire County Council* [1969] 1 W.L.R. 1563.

[629] See *J v North Lincolnshire County Council* [2000] P.I.Q.R. P84, CA, above. See also *Toole v Sherbourne Pouffes Ltd)* [1971] R.T.R. 479 (school patrolman who failed to prevent a young pupil darting into a road).

[630] *Nwabudike v Southwark London Borough Council*, *The Times*, June 28, 1995.

[631] *Good v Inner London Education Authority* (1980) 10 Fam.Law. 213, CA (sand thrown during some spontaneous horseplay between two boys, aged about six-and-a-half, just after school hours and whilst they were waiting for a play centre to open).

[632] *Moore v Hampshire County Council*, 80 L.G.R. 481, CA (where a 12-year-old girl, who suffered from a congenital dislocation of the hip, wrongfully persuaded her teacher that she was allowed to participate in P.E. and, whilst attempting to handstand fell and broke her ankle, the defendants were liable for the failure of the teacher to observe the child's awkward movements and properly to supervise her as a child with a disability).

[633] *Crouch v Essex County Council* (1966) 64 L.G.R. 240.

[634] *Butt v Cambridgeshire and Isle of Ely County Council* (1969) 119 New L.J. 1118. However, cf. *Black v Kent County Council* (1983) 82 L.G.R. 39 CA, where the claimant's claim for damages succeeded after he had been jabbed in the eye, because it was foreseeable that the use of a pair of sharp-pointed scissors by a pupil, aged seven, in an art class, involved a greater risk than the use of a blunt-ended pair.

[635] *Alexis v Newham LBC* [2009] EWHC 1323 (Q.B.).

9–195   **Supervision of games or playing.** It is not necessary to provide continuous supervision in the playground of normally healthy children of school age,[636] even if some children are as young as six.[637] Where a boy was blinded in one eye as a result of being struck by a rounders bat whilst playing an unofficial game of rounders during the midday lunch break in the school playground, there was no failure of supervision.[638] On the other hand, where a pupil, during instruction in a gymnasium, vaulted over a horse, fell, and injured himself, it was held to be negligence for a teacher not to take reasonable care to prevent a fall. The games master had also not "acted with that promptitude which the law requires".[639] However, on somewhat similar facts, a boy of 12 who was injured in vaulting over a buck failed to prove liability. There were four classes in the gymnasium and the instructor was supervising another class at the time, but the level of supervision reflected approved practice and had been followed with safety for many years.[640]

9–196   **Supervision out of school.** The duty of care is not restricted to the school premises, but what ought reasonably done to discharge it will depend upon the circumstances. A local authority operating a school bus service did owe a duty to see that it was reasonably safe for children using it,[641] to include, where necessary, the provision of supervision. However, supervision was not required when boys were doing farm work during a half-term holiday and one boy injured another by throwing a clod of earth at him.[642]

9–197   **Breach of statutory duty.** No action for breach of statutory duty lies at the suit of an individual aggrieved by the alleged failure of the education authority to exercise carefully the statutory discretion conferred by the Education Acts 1944 and 1981 to provide sufficient and proper schools for all children, including those with special needs.[643] However, vicarious liability can at least potentially attach for the negligence of employees of the authority charged with the task of providing professional services in discharge of the authority's statutory duty.[644]

---

[636] *Rawsthorne v Ottley* [1937] 3 All E.R. 902; *Newton v East Ham Corp, The Guardian*, July 11, 1963. See also *Simonds v Isle of Wight Council, The Times*, October 9, 2003 (reasonable supervision did not require that all access to swings in a playground be prevented on the school sports day: if the standard was set so high such events would simply not be held).

[637] *Ricketts v Erith Borough Council* [1943] 2 All E.R. 629 (school not liable when boy of 10 injured girl of six during the break with a toy bow and arrow, in the teacher's absence).

[638] *Price v Caernarvonshire County Council, The Times*, February 11, 1960.

[639] *Gibbs v Barking Corp* [1936] 1 All E.R. 115, 116, per Slesser L.J. See also *Gillmore v London County Council* [1938] 4 All E.R. 331 (the claimant, who was performing an exercise which involved hopping about on one leg, making lunges at other participants, slipped on the highly polished floor of a dance hall provided by the defendants for adult physical training); *Thornton v Board of School Trustees of School District No.57* (1976) 57 D.L.R. (3d) 438 (a student of limited expertise in gymnastics fell on his neck and was severely injured whilst attempting a somersault from a springboard over a box-horse).

[640] *Wright v Cheshire County Council* [1952] 2 All E.R. 789.

[641] See further para.9–209, below.

[642] *Camkin v Bishop* [1941] 2 All E.R. 713. Further see *Trevor v Incorporated Froebel Educational Institute, The Times*, February 11, 1954 (where boy was hurt whilst on a picnic).

[643] *Phelps v Hillingdon LBCl* [2001] 2 A.C. 619 and see *X (Minors) v Bedfordshire CC* [1995] 2 A.C. 633.

[644] *Phelps v Hillingdon LBC*, n.643, above.

Such employees include, for instance, educational psychologists employed by a local authority to assess and determine the educational needs of a child.[645] Nevertheless, claims may well face formidable problems in practice. To succeed, it will be necessary to show, in relation to the particular child, that the employee was acting in a situation where the law recognised a duty of care.[646] Questions of causation and quantum of damage, long after the events, will doubtless be problematic. Bearing in mind the number of imponderables, a claimant could face difficulties in showing that an alternative approach to teaching would have led to a measurable difference.[647] The nature of the statutory function and the difficulty of decisions, such as an assessment of the needs of a child with special educational needs, are such that a court will usually hold that it is fair, just and reasonable to impose a duty of care only to avoid decisions that were plainly and obviously wrong.[648]

Standard of care. The standard of care required of a schoolteacher is that of **9–198** a parent with responsibility for the number[649] and type of children in the class,[650] but the standard of care must reflect the context of life at school rather than life at home.[651] Given the level of responsibility, the standard of care required is high, but is not expressed as any more than should be reasonably expected in the circumstances. It has been said to be higher than the common duty of care, owed under the Occupiers' Liability Act 1957.[652]

---

[645] *Phelps v Hillingdon LBC*, n.643, above. See also *X (Minors) v Bedfordshire CC* [1995] 2 A.C. 633 above, per Lord Browne-Wilkinson at 763, who said that such a claim could embrace the actions of a headmaster who gave negligent advice relating to the educational needs of a pupil. He went on to say that in giving advice the standard of care would be that of the reasonable head teacher, not for instance some other professional such as an educational psychologist. In *Gower v Bromley LBC, The Times*, October 28, 1999, CA, it was said to be arguable that teaching staff at a special school owed a duty of care to educate a particular individual with special needs according to those needs, where it was alleged that a failure to provide him with computer and other aids caused him to fail educationally and suffer emotionally and psychologically; appeal dismissed *The Times*, July 28, 2000. See Fowles and Winston, "Educational negligence: Learning difficulties" 2003 P.I.L.J. 19, 8.

[646] *Phelps v Hillingdon LBC*, n.643, above.

[647] *Phelps v Hillingdon LBC*, above. per Lord Slynn and see the judgment of Stuart Smith L.J. in the CA [1999] 1 W.L.R. 500, CA at 446. See also *Skipper v Calderdale M.B.C.* [2006] E.L.R. 322, CA (a claim for a school's failure to ameliorate the effects of the claimant's dyslexia in which the CA pointed out the difficulties which would arise in deciding whether and to what extent the claimant's earning capacity had been reduced, and opined that it would be wrong to strike out simply because the value of a claim was modest and the cost of pursuing it disproportionately high). Similar problems in relation to proof of causation were noted by the Court of Appeal in a child's claim for bullying out of school: *Bradford-Smart v West Sussex CC, The Times*, January 29, 2002, CA, n.609, above.

[648] *Carty v Croydon LBC* [2005] 2 All E.R. 517, CA (the claimant alleged, unsuccessfully, that an education authority had been negligent in failing to reassess and amend his statement of special educational needs after the breakdown of a school placement). See Hay, "A special case of negligence?" 155 N.L.J. 534 ; Ch.2 para.2–299, above.

[649] *Nicholson v Westmorland CC, The Times*, October 25, 1962, namely "a parent with a family of twenty children"; *Crouch v Essex CC* (1966) 64 L.G.R. 240. "It is unrealistic if not unhelpful, to say the standard of care owed by the headmaster of a school of 900 pupils is that of the reasonably careful and prudent father towards his own children", per Geoffrey Lane J. in *Beaumont v Surrey CC*, above. *Somerset CC v Kingscott* [1975] 1 W.L.R. 283.

[650] e.g. deaf and dumb children, *Ellis v Sayers Confectioners* (1963) 61 L.G.R. 299.

[651] i.e. where there was more skylarking to be expected as in *Lyes v Middlesex CC* (1962) 61 L.G.R. 443; applied in *Jacques v Oxfordshire CC* (1967) 66 L.G.R. 440.

[652] See *Reffell v Surrey County Council* [1964] 1 W.L.R. 358.

Illustrations

9–199   Negligence was found: where a teacher told a 14-year-old girl to go into the common room, to poke the fire and pull out the damper of a grate with which she was not familiar and in consequence her apron caught fire[653]; also where there was no guard for a gas stove in a cookery class for 11-year-olds.[654]

9–200   Negligence was not found: where a master told a 12-year-old boy to carry an oil can with a long spout from one classroom to another, and while he was doing that, another boy suddenly came around a corner in a passage and collided with the can, causing injury to his eye[655]; where a teacher allowed a 13-year-old boy to assist in moving a piano, which fell and crushed him[656]; where a 14-year-old girl carrying a teapot of hot tea down a school passageway was scalded when a boy, running along, collided with her[657]; where, during an unsupervised school period, the pursuer was injured by a pellet that had been shot from an air gun, used in contravention of school rules and the presence of which in the school was unknown[658]; where a girl at primary school was harrassed by boys who pulled her skirt open and the teacher who investigated failed to contact the child's parents to tell them of the incident.[659]

9–201   **Knowledge of dangerous games.** If a teacher knows or ought to know that pupils on the school premises are playing dangerous games or doing acts in such a manner or in such a place that they are likely to cause injury to one another, and does nothing to prevent it, he can be liable in negligence if an accident occurs.[660] But he is not liable for injury caused to a pupil playing a properly conducted game. For example, when a pupil at an instruction centre was playing a compulsory game of "riders and horses", during the ordinary course of which some of the players were thrown to the ground, and he was injured in falling, it was not negligent to have set the game going.[661] Also, when a boy of 14 took part in a relay race at a play centre and put his arm through a glass partition, there was no liability where the instruction had been to touch the teacher and run back, and specifically not to touch the glass partition.[662] When a boy in the school buildings

---

[653] *Smith v Martin and Hull Corp* [1911] 2 K.B. 775.

[654] *Fryer v Salford Corp* [1937] 1 All E.R. 617.

[655] *Wray v Essex CC* [1936] 3 All E.R. 97. Cf. *Crouch v Essex CC* (1966) 64 L.G.R. 240.

[656] *Moffatt v Dufferin County Board of Education* (1973) 31 D.L.R. (3d) 143.

[657] *Cooper v Manchester Corp, The Times,* February 13, 1959.

[658] *Colquohoun v Renfrew County Council,* 1973 S.L.T. 50.

[659] *Shaw v Redbridge London Borough Council* [2005] E.L.R. 320 (the teacher concluded the incident involved horseplay rather than indecent assault and the court accepted it was a proper exercise of professional judgment not to tell the parents).

[660] *Geyer v Downs* (1977) 17 A.L.R. 408. See also *Fowles v Bedfordshire CC* [1995] P.I.Q.R. P380, CA (local authority negligent where gymnastic activities were permitted at a youth centre without proper supervision or a proper system of instruction; the contributory negligence of the 21-year-old claimant was assessed at two-thirds for performing a forward somersault, assisted by a trampoline, when dangerously close to a wall). See also *Gillmore v London CC* [1938] 4 All E.R. 331 (county council liable for providing hall with a slippery floor for physical training classes).

[661] *Jones v London County Council* (1932) 48 T.L.R. 368.

[662] *Cahill v West Ham Corp* (1937) 81 S.J. 630. But in a similar case liability was established on the basis that the place at which the game in question was played was unsuitable: *Ralph v London County Council* (1947) 63 T.L.R. 546.

was hit in the eye by a golf ball, which had been struck by another boy from the playground, the schoolmaster was not liable, because there had been no previous example of such behaviour.[663] Nor was a school liable when, on a skiing trip in Austria, a pupil who had previously been reprimanded by the teacher in charge for skiing off-piste, chose to ski on a route partially closed as a result of insufficient snow, lost control and suffered serious injury.[664]

Liability *was* established where the teacher failed properly to organise a **9–202** "warm-up" exercise in a P.E. lesson in which girls were instructed to touch the four walls of the hall before returning to the teacher.[665] Also, a school was liable for a serious injury to a pupil's eye, when he was hit in the face in the schoolyard at 8.40 am by a full size leather football, even though such balls were banned at the school: reasonable spot checks should have been held to enforce the ban even before school itself started.[666] And where a schoolteacher decides to participate with his pupils in some organised sporting activity, such as a game of rugby, a duty of care arises to avoid making any physical contact with them that would be likely to result in any of the boys being injured.[667]

Accident not preventable. Even if there is a breach of the duty to exercise **9–203** supervision, a teacher is not liable for sudden occurrences, which simply could not have been prevented, as, where, in a school for blind children, one of the them, during the temporary absence of the person in charge, jumped on the back of another child and injured him,[668] or for accidents which could not be anticipated, such as an injury to a child at a swimming-bath, which was caused by one child suddenly releasing a springboard that she was clinging to, while the injured child was about to jump from it.[669] Where coke was delivered to a school in a tip-up lorry, which, unknown to the head teacher, arrived while the boys were in the playground, there was no liability for injury to one boy when others jumped on to the lorry and caused it to tip up. The employers of the driver were also not to blame, since he could not reasonably have anticipated such an

---

[663] *Langham v Governors of Wellingborough School* (1932) 101 L.J.K.B. 513, but the result would have been different if allegations that the teacher failed to exercise proper supervision over the pupils and knew or ought to have known that they were in the habit of hitting golf balls in a manner likely to be dangerous, had been proved).

[664] *Chittock v Woodbridge School* [2003] P.I.Q.R. P81, CA (a reprimand was within the range of reasonable responses which a teacher could have given after the first incident and even if was negligent to fail to remove the pupil's ski pass it would not necessarily follow that a causative link with the accident would have been established). See Stevens, "Duty of care: safety first" 2003 P.I.L.J. 15, 9.

[665] *A v Leeds City Council* [1999] C.L.Y. 3977 (two girls collided at speed, causing one to sustain injury).

[666] *Kearn-Price v Kent County Council* [2003] P.I.Q.R. P167, CA.

[667] *Affutu-Nartoy v Clarke, The Times*, February 9, 1984 (school liable where a 15-year-old player was injured by the teacher, as a result of a heavy tackle) ; also *Mountford v Newlands School* [2007] E.L.R. 256, CA, Ch.6, para.6–54, above (school liable where an over-age player was picked for a rugby team and injured a pupil from another school in a lawful tackle). See generally, Samuels, "Rugby injuries: liability of the college or school" 2003 Med. Leg. J. 71, 85.

[668] *Gow v Glasgow Education Authority*, 1922 S.C. 260; *Langham v Governors of Wellingborough School*, above per Scrutton L.J.

[669] *Clarke v Bethnal Green Borough Council* (1939) 55 T.L.R. 519.

interference with the lorry.[670] Where, before school began, an eight-year-old pupil was running a race with friends up and down the playground and stumbled forward, hitting his head against a jagged flint in the boundary wall of the playground, the school were not liable: even with supervision such an accident could not have been prevented.[671]

9–204   **Duty as to school premises.** Regulations under the Education Act 1996 provide for standards to which school premises maintained by local education authorities must be maintained.[672] The regulations provide, *inter alia* for the facilities which should be provided for staff and pupils,[673] and structural requirements such as load bearing[674] and weather protection.[675] Health, safety and welfare is also provided for.[676] Under earlier statutes, such an authority was bound to maintain and keep efficient all public elementary schools in its area,[677] and for breach of this duty it was liable in damages. When a boy who was playing in the playground caught his foot in a hole in the asphalt paving and injured his ankle, his claim for damages succeeded.[678]

9–205   The following examples reflect the application of the various statutory regimes which have been in place in relation to the design and maintainance of school buildings.[679] It was held that a local education authority's liability was not only to keep school premises in good repair, but to construct them so that they were not dangerous to children of the age intended to use them. Where a girl of seven, upon being told by the teacher to leave the room, had to open a heavy swing door fitted with a powerful spring, and trapped her hand in the door, it was held that the door was unsuitable as being dangerous to children of that age.[680] Where a 15-year-old schoolboy was injured when his hand broke through a glass-panelled door, the defendants were in breach of statutory duty, in that the glass panel was too thin and the door was, therefore, not "efficient".[681] Also, a girl aged 12 whose hand was injured when it crashed through the glass panel of a door upon it swinging back towards her, succeeded in a claim for damages for breach of

---

[670] *Rawsthorne v Ottley* [1937] 3 All E.R. 902.

[671] *Ward v Hertfordshire County Council* [1970] 1 W.L.R. 357, CA.

[672] See the Education Act 1996 s.542(1) as amended and the Education (School Premises) Regulations 1999 (SI 1999/2), which came into force on February 1, 1999. See generally, Palfreyman, "Suffer little children: the evolution of the standard reasonably expected in the duty of care to prevent personal injury on school premises" 2001 13(3) E. & L. 228.

[673] Education (School Premises) Regulations 1999 (SI 1999/2), regs 2–7.

[674] ibid., reg.15.

[675] Education (School Premises) Regulations 1999 (SI 1999/2), reg.16.

[676] ibid., reg.17: "Every part of a school building and of the land provided for a school shall be such that the health, safety and welfare of the occupants . . . are reasonably assured."

[677] Education Act 1921 s.17.

[678] *Ching v Surrey County Council* [1910] 1 K.B. 736 at 741, per Lord Halsbury: "Anyone charged with that duty [to keep the playground in proper condition] was bound to take care that the playground where boys were expected to play . . . should be in such a condition that they should not be exposed to unnecessary danger while playing there."

[679] i.e. before being replaced by the regulations under the 1996 Act, see n.672 above.

[680] *Morris v Caernarvon County Council* [1910] 1 K.B. 840, which was decided under the Education Act 1902.

[681] *Lyes v Middlesex County Council* (1962) 61 L.G.R. 443 (a breach of reg.5 of the Schools Grant Regulations 1951).

statutory duty[682] in that the "construction and properties of the materials", namely the glass panel, were not such that the "safety of the occupants shall be reasonably assured".[683]

Where a cleaner brushed loose snow from the step outside the church school, **9–206** but had failed to place ashes or grit on the icy surface beneath it, upon which the child claimant slipped and hurt himself, the local authority was liable.[684] There was no liability where a six-year-old child tripped in the school playground on a change of level where tarmac abutted upon a concrete edging.[685]

When a child of 11 was injured in the school playground, where she slipped, **9–207** fell and cut herself on a broken milk bottle, it was held that the defendants were negligent in failing to insist upon a safe system for storing and carrying away empty bottles and in failing to provide any proper supervision for these tasks.[686] A school was not liable in negligence where an eight-year-old pupil was injured when he fell from a bannister he intended to slide down, even though studs were afterwards put into position to discourage such activity: a pre-accident risk assessment had correctly concluded that the risk of a fall was insufficient to justify any special measure at that stage.[687]

Duty as occupier. The occupiers of school premises, usually the local **9–208** education authority or alternatively, the school's governors, owe the common duty of care towards lawful visitors to the school in relation to dangers due to the state of the premises or things done or omitted to be done on them, as prescribed by s.1(1) of the Occupier's Liability Act 1957. A duty is owed under the Occupier's Liability Act 1984 s.1, to persons other than lawful visitors (usually trespassers). The 1957 and 1984 Acts are discussed generally in Chapter 7.

Duty as to transport. Where an education authority decides to provide **9–209** transport for the purpose of taking children to and from school, it must be reasonably safe. Where a pupil, a girl aged 13, was injured by falling off the step at the rear of the vehicle provided, the authority was liable on the ground that, as it had provided a conveyance, it was its duty to provide for the safety of children using it. The jury found that the accident had been caused by the negligence of the driver and the non-provision of a conductor in order to help children on and off, and the House of Lords confirmed that a conductor ought to have been provided.[688] In *Jacques v Oxfordshire County Council*[689] the 14-year-old

---

[682] Reg.51 of the Standards for School Premises Regulations 1959 (SI 1959/890), subsequently revoked and now replaced by the Education (School Premises) Regulations 1999 (SI 1999/2).
[683] *Reffell v Surrey County Council* [1964] 1 W.L.R. 358. See also the similar obligation in reg.17 of the Education (School Premises) Regulations 1999 (SI 1999/2), n.676 above.
[684] *Woodward v Hastings Corp* [1945] K.B. 174.
[685] *B (A Child) v Cardiff City Council* [2002] E.L.R. 1, CA.
[686] *Martin v Middlesborough Corp* (1965) 63 L.G.R. 385.
[687] *Gough v Upshire Primary School* [2002] E.L.R. 169.
[688] *Shrimpton v Hertfordshire County Council* (1911) 104 L.T. 145.
[689] *Jacques v Oxfordshire County Council* (1967) 66 L.G.R. 440.

claimant, who was struck in the eye by a pellet, failed to establish liability where, as was the normal practice, the discipline over the 42 pupils in the bus was entrusted to two responsible prefects.

9–210   **Health and safety duties.** Statutory duties are imposed on employers by the Health and Safety at Work etc. Act 1974 which extend to schools and institutions providing higher education.[690] There is a general duty upon an employer or self employed person to conduct their undertaking in such a way as to ensure, so far as reasonably practicable, that members of the public who may be affected by them are not exposed to risks to their health and safety.[691] Concurrently with the Act a common law duty will arise to protect pupils from foreseeable risks to their health and safety. So, it was held that where pupils were invited or directed to use materials or equipment, there was a duty to see that they were reasonably fit for the intended use. However, a school authority could not be expected to analyse ordinary chemicals, such as manganese dioxide, supplied for use in schools, before they were in fact put into use.[692] Where equipment was potentially dangerous, for example a woodworking machine or a mechanical saw, the failure to ensure that a pupil received sufficient supervised training on them was negligent.[693] Although s.14 of the Factories Act 1961[694] did not impose a statutory duty on the school authority to fence a dangerous part of a machine, a similar duty was owed at common law to provide for the safety of pupils against such a recognised danger.[695] Where a girl of 11, who was attending a cookery school, was injured when her dress caught fire at a gas stove, the school authority was liable for not providing a guard for the stove.[696]

9–211   The statutory duties are owed both to pupils and teachers employed at a school. At common law, the same liability for the defective state of the premises exists towards teachers and other persons employed by the school as in other cases of employer and employee.[697] Knowledge of the defective condition of the school will not prevent the teacher or other employee from recovering damages, subject to contributory negligence. When a teacher was injured by the bursting of heating apparatus known by the managers of a school to be defective, they were liable for breach of their statutory duty to provide safe school premises.[698]

---

[690] See s.2(1).
[691] See Ch.12, para.12–85, below.
[692] *Kubach v Hollands* [1937] 3 All E.R. 907.
[693] See, e.g. *Hoar v Board of School Trustees, District 68 (Nanaimo)* [1984] 6 W.W.R. 133, British Columbia CA, (the claimant pupil was held 50 per cent contributorily negligent in respect of the accident to his fingers, which occurred when operating a wood-working machine, the safe operation of which had never been demonstrated).
[694] s.14 has been replaced by the provisions of the Provision and Use of Work Equipment Regulations 1998, for which see Ch.12, para.12–173, below.
[695] *Butt v Inner London Education Authority* (1968) 66 L.G.R. 379.
[696] *Fryer v Salford Corp* [1937] 1 All E.R. 617.
[697] See Ch.11, para.11–18, below.
[698] *Abbott v Isham* (1920) 90 L.J.K.B. 309.

Concurrent duties in contract and tort. Quite apart from liability in tort,   **9–212**
where pupils enter school premises under a contract,[699] there is presumably the
same implied warranty of safety as in the case of guests staying at an hotel.[700]

14.—Solicitors

(A) The duty of care

Introduction. The general duties of a solicitor[701] are to act on a clients' behalf   **9–213**
in all kinds of business which involve the law, and to give legal advice, in
accordance with the contract of retainer.[702] Where a solicitor is acting for a
number of clients with a similar interest, the retainer is with each individually
and any communication with one or more of them, as agent of the others, should
only occur with express authority, coming directly from them.[703] Solicitors are
bound to exercise a reasonable degree of care, skill and knowledge in all legal
business that they undertake. In common with most other professions, the duty of
a solicitor falls to be considered both in contract and tort. Although there is
authority to the contrary,[704] the preponderance in favour of concurrent liability is
overwhelming.[705] In addition, there is a fiduciary duty.

Contractual duty to client. The starting point when considering a solicitor's   **9–214**
liability to a client or another, whether in tort or contract, should always be the
precise ambit and nature of the instructions given.[706] Liability to a client arises

---

[699] See generally para.9–13, above.

[700] See Ch.8, above, para.8–84 and *Maclenan v Segar* [1917] 2 K.B. 325.

[701] See generally Jessel, "Solicitors' Professional Negligence" 145 New L.J. 498.

[702] See *Groom v Crocker* [1939] 1 K.B. 194 at 222, per Scott L.J., and *Midland Bank Trust Co Ltd v Hett, Stubbs & Kemp* [1979] Ch. 384 at 402, per Oliver J. See further paras 9–214 and 9–233 below.

[703] *Farrer v Copley Singletons* [1998] P.N.L.R. 22, CA. In contrast in *Berlevy v Blyth Dutton* [1997] E.G.C.S. 193, CA it was said that where a solicitor deals with a partner who has actual authority to give instructions on behalf of another partner, any advice given should be treated as given to both, and there was no requirement that the solicitor write directly to the other, even if the transaction in question was risky.

[704] *Groom v Crocker*, n.702, above: see the more extended treatment in the 8th edition of this work at para.8–153.

[705] See the observations of Lord Denning in *Esso Petroleum Co Ltd v Mardon* [1976] 1 Q.B. 801, applying *Hedley Byrne & Co Ltd v Heller & Partners Ltd* [1964] A.C. 465. Also Oliver J. in *Midland Bank Trust Co Ltd v Hett, Stubbs & Kemp* [1979] Ch.384, *Ross v Caunters* [1980] Ch.297 and *Forster v Outred & Co* [1982] 1 W.L.R. 86. In *Henderson v Merrett Syndicates Ltd* [1995] A.C. 145, Lord Goff specifically approved Oliver J.'s reasoning in the *Midland Bank* case, above.

[706] See *John Mowlem Construction Plc v Neil F. Jones & Co* [2004] P.N.L.R. 45, CA (solicitors acting for a subcontractor in dispute with the main contractor on a large building project, were not obliged to advise their client promptly to refer to its insurers a monetary claim made against it where the solicitors had not been engaged to give advice in relation to insurance and their client was perfectly competent to consider its own insurance position). See also *Football League Ltd v Edge Ellison* [2007] P.N.L.R. 2 (solicitors were not negligent in failing to advise their clients, in the course of work to licence media rights in relation to football matches, to secure a guarantee from third parties of the proposed licensee's financial obligations. It was neither an express or implied term of the solicitors' retainer to consider the solvency of the proposed licensee or advise that guarantees should be obtained). See further Horrocks and Brake, "Limitations of liability in solicitors retainers" (2007) 2 P.N. 108.

primarily out of contract[707] by virtue of the retainer, that is, the agreement under which the solicitor is engaged to act. The nature of a solicitor's duty was set out, in the course of a review of many earlier authorities, in *Midland Bank Trust Co Ltd v Hett, Stubbs & Kemp*.[708] In that case a solicitor was instructed to effect the grant of an option to purchase a farm at £75 per acre but had omitted to register it as an estate contract, under the Land Charges Act 1925, as a result of which failure a third party had acquired an adverse interest in the property. Oliver J. emphasised that "a contract gives rise to a complex of rights and duties of which the duty to exercise reasonable care and skill is but one".[709]

9–215   **Fiduciary duty to client.** In addition to a contractual duty, a solicitor owes a client a duty which arises from their confidential relationship. This fiduciary duty[710] requires the solicitor neither to abuse nor to take any secret advantage[711] of the special situation that has been created by their relationship. A breach of such duty will involve conscious impropriety,[712] although not necessarily dishonesty.[713] Since it is a separate and distinct duty from that owed by virtue of the contract of engagement, its breach will entitle the client to relief on that footing.[714] As Viscount Haldane L.C. pointed out:

> "when, as in the case before us, a solicitor has had financial transactions with his client, and has handled his money to the extent of using it to pay off a mortgage made to himself, or of getting the client to release from his mortgage a property over which the solicitor by such release has obtained further security for a mortgage of his own, a Court of Equity has always assumed jurisdiction to scrutinise his action. It did not matter that the client would have had a remedy in damages for breach of contract. Courts of Equity had jurisdiction to direct accounts to be taken, and in proper cases to order the solicitor to replace property improperly acquired from the client, or to make compensation if he has lost it by acting in breach of a duty which arose out of his confidential relationship to the man who had trusted him."[715]

---

[707] See paras 9–15 to 9–17 and para.9–22, above for fuller discussion.

[708] [1979] Ch.384.

[709] [1979] Ch.384 at 434. See further in relation to the scope of the retainer paras 9–233 and 9–266, below.

[710] As regards fiduciary relationships generally, see Ch.1, para.1–20, above. See further in relation to solicitors para.9–264, below. See also, Pratt, "All in a day's work." 157 N.L.J. 1688.

[711] Even after the fullest disclosure to his client, it may still be most unwise for a solicitor to act for a person in any transaction in which he is a party with an adverse interest to his client. See *Spector v Ageda* [1973] Ch.30.

[712] *Leeds & Holbeck Building Society v Arthur & Cole* [2002] P.N.L.R. 78, per Morland J. at 83 (the claimant failed to prove a deliberate and conscious breach of duty by solicitors in a conveyancing transaction and the action failed).

[713] See *Phipps v Boardman* [1967] 2 A.C. 46, also per Millett L.J. in *Bristol and West BS v Mothew* [1998] Ch.1 at 18, dealing with the common situation where solicitors act for both sides in a conveyancing transaction: conduct which is in breach of the duty of good faith "need not be dishonest, but it must be intentional. An unconscious omission which happens to benefit one principal at the expense of the other does not constitute a breach of fiduciary duty, though it may constitute a breach of the duty of skill and care. This is because the principle which is in play is that the fiduciary must not be inhibited by the existence of his other employment from serving the interests of his principal as faithfully and effectively as if he were the only employer."

[714] *Nocton v Lord Ashburton* [1914] A.C. 932.

[715] *Nocton v Lord Ashburton* [1914] A.C. 932 at 956, 957. To the like effect, see the opinion of Lord Dunedin, ibid. at 964–965.

The measure of damages flowing from a breach of fidcuiary duty is the same **9–216** whether or not the solicitor had a personal interest in the transaction which he failed to disclose. Hence, the client can recover damages amounting to the loss which has been suffered as a result of entering a transaction that would not otherwise have been entered, had the solicitor performed his duty.[716] So, where solicitors obtained mortgage moneys from a building society following a request based upon a warranty or representation which they knew, or ought to have known, was false, they were liable for breach of fiduciary duty and held such moneys on constructive trust for the building society. The fact that, even if properly informed, the society might have authorised the advance was irrelevant.[717]

Duty to third party in tort. Prior to 1963, except in cases where a solicitor **9–217** was liable as an officer of the court,[718] it was generally considered that no duty of care was owed to a person who was not a client.[719] Although not recognised at the time, the first erosion of this principle had actually taken place with the decision in *Donoghue v Stevenson*.[720] Then, in 1963, with *Hedley Byrne & Co Ltd v Heller & Partners Ltd*,[721] a wider principle emerged. A solicitor who, upon request, gave advice or information negligently, whether gratuitously or not, to a non-client, and had reason to believe that the advice or information would be acted upon, could well be liable, in the absence of clear disclaimer, for loss or damage suffered in consequence.

"Nowadays . . . it is clear that a professional man who gives guidance to others owes a duty of care, not only to the client who employs him, but also to another who he knows is relying on his skill to save him from harm. It is certain that a banker or accountant is under such a duty. And I see no reason why a solicitor is not likewise. The essence of this proposition, however, is the *reliance* . . . The professional man must know that the other is *relying* on his skill and the other must in fact rely on it."[722]

Although, in *Welburn v Mayberry*,[723] Lord Denning M.R. reiterated his **9–218** opinion that solicitors owed a duty in tort to a third party, it was not until *Ross*

---

[716] *Jacks v Davis* [1983] 1 W.W.R. 327, CA of British Columbia (on a property purchase, the loss is the difference between the net purchase cost to the client and the actual market value at the time of purchase).
[717] *Bristol & West Building Society v May, May & Merrimans* [1996] 2 P.N.L.R. 138.
[718] *Batten v Wedgwood Coal and Iron Co* (1886) 31 Ch.D. 346; *Re Dangar's Trusts* (1889) 41 Ch.D. 178.
[719] *Robertson v Flemming* (1861) 4 Macq. 167. The history is discussed in detail in early editions of *Charlesworth on Negligence*.
[720] [1932] A.C. 562.
[721] [1964] A.C. 465.
[722] per Lord Denning in *Dutton v Bognor Regis Urban District Council* [1972] 1 Q.B. 373 at 394, 395. The passage quoted remains apposite evewn though *Dutton* itself was overrruled. See further Ch.2, para.2–239, above.
[723] (1971) 115 S.J. 468, CA. The third parties concerned were dependent children whose mother had died in a road traffic accident caused by the negligent driving of her husband, also deceased. The fatal accident claim for damages, brought on the children's behalf had been dismissed for want of prosecution, as a result of the claimant's solicitors' admitted negligence, which had occasioned inordinate and inexcusable delay.

v Caunters[724] that the opportunity arose for a detailed consideration. Solicitors, who prepared a will, failed to warn the testator when they sent it to him for execution, that it must not be witnessed by the spouse of a beneficiary. The testator signed the will but one of his witnesses was the husband of a residuary beneficiary, which the solicitors failed to notice. Some two years later, the testator died without re-executing the will before different attesting witnesses, so that the gift to the beneficiary was rendered void. The solicitors' defence admitted that they had been guilty of negligence but only in respect of the duty, which they owed to their client, the testator. They denied that any duty of care at all was owed to the claimant, who was the thwarted beneficiary.

9–219   Sir Robert Megarry V.C. confirmed that not only was there no rule that a solicitor owed a duty in respect of professional work solely in contract, but a solicitor could also be liable in negligence to a client, as well as to a third party, where a prima facie duty of care to the latter could be established. In this instance the beneficiary was clearly somebody whom the solicitors ought to have had in their direct contemplation as being likely to be injured by their failure to carry out the testator's instructions. As the Vice-Chancellor explained:

> "to hold that the defendants were under a duty of care towards the plaintiff would raise no spectre of imposing on the defendants an uncertain and unlimited liability. The liability would be to one person alone, the plaintiff. The amount would be limited to the value of the share of residue intended for the plaintiff. There would be no question of widespread or repeated liability, as might arise from some published misstatement upon which large numbers might rely, to their detriment. There would be no possibility of the defendants being exposed, in the well-known expression of Cardozo C.J. 'To a liability in an indeterminate amount of an indeterminate time to an indeterminate class.'[725] Instead, there would be a finite obligation to a finite number of persons, in this case one."[726]

Liability to the beneficiary was made out.

9–220   *Ross v Caunters* was subsequently considered by the House of Lords in *White v Jones*.[727] The claim arose from the negligent failure of a testator's solicitors to prepare a fresh will in place of a previous will he had decided to revoke. He died before the new will was prepared and the claimants, who were not included in the

---

[724] [1980] Ch.297. In *Smith v Claremont Haynes & Co, The Times*, September 3, 1991, a solicitor was held liable in negligence where he had failed to act promptly in preparing the will of an intended testator in poor health, who had subsequently died, as a result of which failure intended beneficiaries were deprived of their expectation. See Baughan, "The Will That Never Was: *Ross v Caunters* extended" [1992] 8 P.N. 99. *Ross*'s case was distinguished in *Clark v Bruce Lance & Co* [1988] 1 W.L.R. 881 CA. See also *Kecskemeti v Robens Rubin & Co, The Times*, December 31, 1992, (where the solicitor failed to advise the testator about the effect of the rule of survivorship upon a joint tenancy).

[725] *Ultramares Corp v Touche* (1931) 174 N.E. 441 at 444.

[726] [1980] Ch.297 at 309.

[727] [1995] 2 A.C. 207. See Rich, "Errors in will drafting: the limits of a remedy in negligence" (2000) 1 P.N. 211. *White v Jones* has been followed in Scotland: *Davidson v The Governor and Company of the Bank of Scotland* [2002] P.N.L.R. 740, OH. See also Sprince, "Disappointed beneficiaries and disappearing principles" (2001) 2 P.N. 104; Jones, "Third party beneficiaries—disappointed again" (2001) 2 P.N. 113. See also Ch.2 para.2–226, above.

unrevoked original will, but were to be mentioned in the new one, were thereby disappointed. Conceptual problems associated with the earlier decision were acknowledged[728] but it was held that when a solicitor accepted instructions to prepare a will, his assumption of responsibility should be deemed in law to extend beyond his immediate client to the intended beneficiary, thereby giving[729] a remedy in the event of negligence under the *Hedley Byrne*[730] principle. An interesting feature of the decision is the absence of either any fiduciary duty owed to the beneficiary or reliance on his part on the solicitor discharging his task with due skill and care, features said elsewhere to be essential to the creation of the special relationship within that principle. The majority of their Lordships justified their approach in essentially pragmatic, although by no means identical,[731] terms, being concerned that not to provide the beneficiary with a remedy would leave a lacuna in the law.

Although one of the justifications for providing a remedy in *White v Jones* was **9–221** that, in the circumstances of the case, neither the testator or his estate would have other recourse against the negligent solicitor, it has been held subsequently, by "permissible incremental extension" that a remedy can be given even where the estate does have a cause of action.[732] In determining the recoverable loss where *White v Jones* applies, the scope of the solicitor's duty will have to be identified: the loss which the beneficiary can recover is that interest he would have had if effect had been given to the testator's intention.[733] It has also been emphasised that where a beneficiary complains that a will has not been drawn up in accordance with the testator's instructions, he will be expected, in reasonable mitigation of his loss, to seek rectification of the will before commencing an action for negligence against the person who drafted it.[734] But it is not necessary to take rectification proceedings where there is no evidence of clerical error or misunderstanding, so that such proceedings would have little prospect of success.

---

[728] See, e.g. Lord Goff at 255.

[729] It has been suggested that the duty of care cannot readily be extended to a beneficiary of whom the solicitor is unaware. As a minimum the solicitor will have to know what benefit the testator wished to confer and the person or class of persons for whom it was intended: *Gibbons v Nelsons* [2000] P.N.L.R. 734.

[730] [1964] A.C. 465. The remedy exists even where the will is drawn by a lay person, rather than solicitor: *Esterhuizen v Allied Dunbar Assurance Plc* [1998] Fam. Law 527 (defendant's representative failed to ensure that the will in question was properly executed, the claimants being the disappointed beneficiaries whose existence was known to the representative since he prepared the draft).

[731] per Chadwick L.J. in *Carr-Glynn v Frearsons* [1999] Ch.326 at 335 (discussing the speeches in *White v Jones*): "it is the reasoning in Lord Goff's speech—and only that reasoning—that can be said to have received the support of the majority in the House of Lords."

[732] *Carr-Glynn v Frearsons*, above (solicitors owed a duty of care to a beneficiary to ensure that property in which the testatrix intended her to share could indeed pass to her under the will and accordingly to advise the testatrix, who held the property as joint tenant immediately to serve notice severing the joint tenancy). The quotation is per Thorpe L.J. at 339.

[733] *Carr-Glynn v Frearsons*, above per Chadwick L.J. at 337.

[734] *Walker v Geo. H. Medlicott & Son* [1999] W.L.R. 727, CA (the beneficiary's action failed on the facts). In relation to the allied question of contributory negligence in this context see Reed, "Laying the blame on the testator" Tru. & E.L.J. 2002, 41, 15.

The question, even where such proceedings would probably have succeeded, is whether the claimant failed to act reasonably in failing to bring them.[735]

Illustrations

9–222   Solicitors were liable to a beneficiary under the principle in *White v Jones*[736] where they failed to satisfy themselves that delay in attending upon a client in hospital for whom they had drafted a will which had not been executed would not be disadvantageous to the proposed testator. It was emphasised that the duty to the beneficiary reflects that owed to the testator and is not altered by the circumstances of the beneficiary or the amount intended under the will to pass to him.[737] Solicitors were also liable where a will had been drafted by them on instructions of the deceased leaving his estate to his partner if he predeceased her, but the will was not properly executed, bearing a date and the signature of two witnesses but not his signature: as a result he died intestate and the estate passed to his parents.[738] It has been held that the *White v Jones* principle could also apply where the claimant, a beneficiary of his deceased mother's estate, alleged that solicitors who had been instructed by his mother to provide inheritance tax planning advice, had been negligent, in that certain assets remained part of her estate when with proper advice they should not have done.[739]

9–223   However, solicitors acting in the administration of a deceased person's estate have been held not to owe any duty of care to the beneficiaries.[740] Solicitors who negligently failed to arrange an effective gift inter vivos were not liable to the disappointed beneficiary because the settlor was still alive and could, if he chose, rectify the situation by instructing another firm.[741] No duty was owed to the beneficiaries under the earlier of two wills, to take care that the testator did not execute the later will in circumstances in which he lacked testamentary capacity

---

[735] *Horsfall v Haywards* [1999] P.N.L.R. 583, CA (on the facts such proceedings would not have mitigated the beneficiaries' loss where, inter alia, by the time they could have been brought, the major assets of the deceased had been disposed of so that there would have been no material recovery of the funds lost).

[736] n.727, above.

[737] *Hooper v Fynmores, The Times*, July 19, 2001. See Frost, "A risky business" 2002 Legal Bus. 127, 24.

[738] *Humblestone v Martin Tolhurst Partnership* [2004] P.N.L.R. 463.

[739] *Rind v Theodore Goddard* [2008] P.N.L.R. 24. The defendants argued that since the estate itself had a potential cause of action, there was no such lacuna in the remedies available as there had been in *White v Jones,* as to justify the extension of a duty of care to the claimant. However, *Daniels v Thompson*, (see Ch.1, para.1–33) suggested otherwise in that since the loss suffered by the testatrix arose only on her death, no completed cause of action accrued on death which would vest in her estate. See further, Blair and Shepherd, "Who can sue?" 158 N.L.J. 71. A cause of action in negligence for breach of a duty owed directly to the estate of a deceased person has been rejected in Scotland: *Matthews v Hunter & Robertson Ltd* [2008] P.N.L.R. 35, C.S. (OH).

[740] *Cancer Research Campaign v Ernest Brown* [1998] P.N.L.R., 592; *Chappell v Somers & Blake* [2004] Ch.19 (the judge also held that beneficiaries had no remedy against an executor for losses allegedly arising as a result of delay in obtaining probate: for criticism, see O'Sullivan, "Solicitors, executors and beneficiaries: Who can sue and who can be sued?" (2003) 4 P.N. 507).

[741] *Hemmens v Wilson Browne* [1995] Ch. 233, (although the claimant had proved foreseeability of damage and a sufficient degree of proximity between the defendant and himself, he failed to establish that it was fair, just and reasonable for a duty to be imposed in the circumstance).

and was subject to undue influence.[742] Executors of a will were held not to owe a duty of care to charities who were beneficiaries of the deceased's residuary estate, to advise the deceased about tax mitigation where she had herself inherited from her brother and died within the two-year period for executing a deed of variation of his will under the Inheritance Tax Act 1984.[743] No liability arose for failing to advise a testator about the effect of what he proposed, where he altered his will in a way that, should he predecease his wife, would render the devise to the claimant ineffective, since the effect of what was being done must have been clear to all concerned.[744] No liability arose where solicitors failed to act upon instructions to change her will given by the deceased five days before her death, where comments made to them by her and her medical notes justified the view that she would live at least another six weeks.[745] Nor did liability arise where personal representatives of the deceased sued for the costs of litigation in which they resisted the claims of beneficiaries disappointed when the defendant solicitors negligently executed an invalid will. The claim was ultimately for the benefit of would-be beneficiaries under an earlier will, the only effective one, and their loss was not within the scope of the solicitors' duty since, in light of the second ineffective will, the testator had no intention of benefiting those entitled under the earlier and they could accordingly not recover the sums in question.[746] No liability under the principle in *White v Jones* arose where the testator was erroneously advised by solicitors that he could not bequeath the tenancy of a croft jointly to the claimants and as a result instructed them to draft a will leaving it to a named individual instead.[747]

The extent to which the boundaries of a solicitor's liability will be enlarged to include additional classes of non-clients is still being worked out.[748] The starting point for any such extension should be the threefold requirements of *Caparo*   **9–224**

---

[742] *Worby v Rosser* [2000] P.N.L.R. 140, CA.

[743] *Cancer Research Campaign v Ernest Brown & Co* [1998] P.N.L.R. 592. See Murphy, "Probate solicitors, disappointed beneficiaries and the tortious duty to advise on tax avoidance" (1998) 2 P.N. 107; also, in the light of *Daniels v Thompson* [2004] P.N.L.R. 638, CA. Ch.1, para.1–33 above, Tettenborn, "Professional negligence: can you owe a duty to the dead?" Conv. 2005 Jul/Aug, 288.

[744] *Punford v Gilberts Accountants* [1998] P.N.L.R. 763, CA.

[745] *X (A Child) v Woollcombe Yonge* [2001] Lloyd's Rep. P.N. 274 (the judgment is critical of the reliance upon expert witnesses, called to deal with conveyancing practice, who did little more than say what they would themselves have done in the like situation, see para.9–06, n.22 above). See Jones, "Third party beneficiaries—disappointed again" (2001) 2 P.N. 113. Also, compare *Hooper v Fynmores, The Times*, July 19, 2001, n.44, above.

[746] *Corbett v Bond Pearce* [2001] P.N.L.R. 739, CA.

[747] *Fraser v McArthur Stewart* [2009] P.N.L.R 13, Ct of Sess. The remedy was not available where the solicitors carried out the testator's intentions at the time the will was drafted. It could not be extended to situations where the complaint was essentially that the solicitor had given the testator negligent advice.

[748] In New Zealand the view has been expressed that "will cases" including *White v Jones* are sui generis, so that in other factually distinct situations it may not be appropriate to consider their application by analogy: *Brownie Wills v Ian Meredith Shrimpton* [1999] P.N.L.R. 552, CA (N.Z.L.), at 559. For a discussion of the potential application of *White v Jones* in cases other than testamentary disposition, see O'Sullivan, "Professional liability to third parties for inter vivos transactions" (2005) 3 P.N. 142.

Industries v Dickman,[749] alternatively an assumption of responsibility[750] to the individual in question. Only if these tests fail to achieve a just result will it be necessary to approach the case by reference to *White v Jones.* However, any particular claim is approached, caution may well have to be exercised when considering whether a solicitor owes a duty to a third party, bearing in mind the paramount duty of a solicitor to protect a client's interests, even where some third party's interests must suffer thereby.[751]

ILLUSTRATIONS

9–225   Liability to a non-client was established, otherwise than by reference to *White v Jones*: where a moneylender agreed to make a loan and the borrower's solicitors gave incorrect details to his solicitors about the security being offered[752]; and where a solicitor, consulted by a motorist who never became a client about defending a charge of reckless driving, failed to explore the possibility of a defence funded by the motorist's insurers.[753] It was arguable that a solicitor owed a duty of care to one of two tenants in common, where the other instructed him to convey the property into her sole name thereby defrauding the first, who knew nothing of the transaction.[754] Also, where solicitors had given advice to the deceased about gifts of shares to various family members, which resulted in the setting up of a discretionary trust, they could be liable to the trustees when the settlement was not tax efficient and a heavy inheritance tax burden had to be paid.[755] Where a solicitor acted as executor of the claimant's deceased husbands' will and gave advice in relation to her in relation to her entitlement to a widow's pension, a duty of care arose given his assumption of responsibility, even though the advice was given gratuitously.[756]

9–226   In the context of a mortgage transaction, where the solicitor is acting for the party to whom the advance is being made, a duty of care can be owed to the mortgagee even though the latter is not strictly a client.[757] There are circumstances in which there may be an obligation to pass information to the mortgagee which would affect a decision whether to make an advance.[758] Where a conflict

---

[749] [1990] 2 A.C. 605.

[750] See para.9–19, above.

[751] In *Hemmens v Wilson Browne* [1995] Ch.223 (the claimant failed to surmount the "fair, just, and reasonable" hurdle): see n.741, above.

[752] *Allied Finance and Investments Ltd v Haddow & Co* [1980] 2 N.Z.L.R. 428.

[753] *Crossan v Ward Bracewell*, 136 New L.J. 849 (the motorist decided to plead guilty, without reference to his insurers, who later refused to indemnify him in respect of damage caused in the accident that had given rise to the criminal charge).

[754] *Harris v Nantes & Wilde* [1997] N.P.C. 7, CA.

[755] *Estill v Cowling Swift & Kitchin* [2000] Lloyd's Rep. P.N. 378.

[756] *Martin v Triggs Turner Bartons* [2010] P.N.L.R. 3 (the circumstances of the claimant's relationship with the defendant were such as to make it reasonable for her to have relied upon him).

[757] *Mortgage Express v Bowerman & Partners* [1996] 1 P.N.L.R. 62, CA (liability); [1995] 2 W.L.R. 607, CA (measure of damages). See para.9–268, below. See also *First National Commercial Bank Plc v Loxleys* [1997] P.N.L.R. 211, CA, Ch.4, above, para.4–87 (at least arguable that solicitors owed a duty of care to a lender proposing to advance moneys to their client upon security of a mortgage, when responding to inquiries in relation to the mortgage agreement upon a standard form).

[758] See the cases cited at para.9–268, n.970, below.

arises because information in the solicitor's possession is confidential, he or she must decline to act.[759] Where a company was the tenant of premises to which the Landlord and Tenant Act 1954 applied, solicitors owed a duty of care to the claimant, who with his wife held all the shares in the company and indeed was the company for all practical purposes, to inform him of the strict time limits under the Act for applying for a new tenancy.[760]

Liability to a third party was not established: on the part of a mortgagor's **9–227** solicitor, to the mortgagee, to disclose to him or his solicitors facts which were contrary to the interests of the mortgagor, where the mortgagee had solicitors of his own and had relied on their skill and judgment to ensure the propriety of the proposed transaction[761]; by the testator's step-children, where a solicitor took the testators instructions about the making of a will and he deliberately refused to nominate[762]; where a solicitor did not advise the purchaser of property of her obligations under a mortgage, his instructions having actually come from her father, the guarantor: a duty of care was owed to her, but extended only to the exercise of reasonable care and skill in putting her father's instructions into effect.[763] In normal conveyancing transactions solicitors who are acting as agents of the vendor do not in general owe the prospective purchaser a separate duty of care when answering inquiries before contract.[764]

Where non-client third parties in fact relied upon the expertise of the client of **9–228** solicitors, rather than on that of the solicitors themselves, no duty of care arose.[765] In the same case it was observed that even when an expert, such as a solicitor, offered advice which he knew others would or were likely to rely on, that fact on its own was insufficient to give rise to a duty of care, where the solicitor was not taking upon himself to advise the third party or allowing that advice to be passed to the third party.[766]

It has been held in New Zealand that while a solicitor can be liable towards a **9–229** third party for an omission to advise, it will also be necessary to establish in such a case an assumption of responsibility, express or implied, accompanied by

---

[759] *Hypo-Mortgage Services Ltd v David Parry & Co* [1996] E.G.C.S. 39 (where the mortgagee unsuccessfully argued that the solicitor should have passed on information that his client had two other mortgages); also *Nationwide Building Society v Balmer Radmore* [1999] P.N.L.R. 606, para.9–266, n.963, below.

[760] *R.P. Howard & Witchell v Woodham Matthews & Co* [1983] Com.L.R. 100.

[761] *Wynston v MacDonald* (1979) 105 D.L.R. (3d) 527.

[762] *Sutherland v Public Trustee* [1980] 2 N.Z.L.R. 536. See also *Trusted v Clifford Chance* (2000) 1 W.T.L.R. 1219 (on the evidence, the testator had been undecided whether to confer upon the claimant a particular benefit claimed and the position had not been reached where instructions could have been given as to dispositions under a proposed new will). See Reed, "The recalcitrant testator" Tru. & E.L.J. 2002, 39, 6.

[763] *Woodward v Wolferstans, The Times*, 8 April 1997.

[764] *Gran Gelato Ltd v Richcliff (Group) Ltd* [1992] Ch. 560. See also *Cemp Properties (UK) Ltd v Dentsply Research & Development Corp* [1989] 2 E.G.L.R. 205 at 207, per Morritt J.

[765] *A & J Fabrication (Batley) Ltd v Grant Thornton* [1999] P.N.L.R. 811 (the liquidator of a company was to advise the claimant creditors about possible claims against former directors of the company, but the claims became statute-barred when the solicitors instructed by him failed to advise him to bring proceedings in time).

[766] *A & J Fabrication (Batley) Ltd v Grant Thornton* [1999] P.N.L.R. 811 at 818.

reliance upon the absence of advice. There was no such reliance by the director of a company seeking an overdraft facility from a bank to be secured by a personal guarantee from all its directors, upon solicitors acting for the bank, who failed, although instructed, to explain the nature of the transaction to the directors and he then acted under a mistake as to the extent of his liability under the guarantee: he had not sought or received advice from the solicitors and was unaware at the time of the instruction the bank had given.[767]

9–230   **Duty to other party in litigation.** It has been said to be doubtful whether solicitors owe any duty to a party on the other side of litigation, such as to conduct the litigation with appropriate propriety.[768] But one instance may be where a solicitor gives an undertaking to the court for the benefit of a third party. By way of example, where in the course of contested custody proceedings between his client and the claimant, his client's former wife, a solicitor, gave an undertaking to the court to retain his client's passport, there being a perceived risk the client, a Kuwaiti citizen, would remove the children from the jurisdiction of the court, it was held that he owed the claimant a duty of care to inform her should the passport cease to remain under his control.[769] While a solicitor who starts, defends or continues proceedings warrants that the client has given authority to do so, the warranty does not extend to an implied statement that the client is named correctly.[770]

9–231   In other situations, where proceedings might well be in contemplation but have not actually been commenced, there has been reluctance to find a duty owed to a party on the opposite side.[771] There will be difficulty in establishing proximity where solicitors and the claimant were not "on the same side of the fence" so far as the transaction in question was concerned.[772] An assumption of responsibility towards an opposing party would be unusual. Having said all that, these are matters of proof and, in appropriate circumstances, there is no technical reason why a duty of care should not arise.[773]

---

[767] *Brownie Wills v Ian Meredith Shrimpton* [1999] P.N.L.R. 552, CA (NZL).

[768] *Orchard v South Eastern Electricity Board* [1987] Q.B. 565.

[769] *Al-Kandari v J.R. Brown & Co* [1988] Q.B. 665. Although public policy generally required that a solicitor should be protected from claims in negligence by his client's opponent, in agreeing voluntarily to hold the passport to the order of the court, he had gone outside his role as a solicitor acting for his client.

[770] *SEB Trygg Liv Holding Aktiebolag v Manches* [2006] 1 WLR 2276, CA. While the principle is one of agency law it is of some practical importance. The extent of the warranties given by solicitors conducting litigation are discussed in the judgment of Buxton L.J. The point is made that although no warranty is given as to name, if a solicitor mis-names a client, and that causes loss, issues of wasted costs and negligence may well arise.

[771] See, e.g. *BDG Roof-Bond Ltd v Douglas* [2000] P.N.L.R. 397 (no duty owed to a company where solicitors acted for a shareholder in a share re-purchase transaction); also *Dean v Allin & Watts* [2000] P.N.L.R. 690 (not fair, just, or reasonable to impose a duty of care where clients introduced to a solicitor the claimant, for purposes of the execution of a security which subsequently proved ineffective in law).

[772] ibid. at 420. The words quoted are per Sir Brian Neill in *BCCI (Overseas) Ltd v Price Waterhouse (No.2)* [1998] P.N.L.R. 564.

[773] A duty did arise in *Dean v Allin & Watts* [2001] P.N.L.R. 921, CA. (solicitors acting for borrowers in a loan transaction were liable to the lender for their failure to arrange effective security where they knew lender was unrepresented and their clients wished to provide an effective security for the transaction).

(B) The standard of care

Generally. The standard of care and skill which can be demanded from a **9–232**
solicitor is that of a reasonably competent and diligent solicitor.[774] Historically a
solicitor was said to be liable only for *crassa negligentia*,[775] which was otherwise
described as misconduct, fraudulent proceeding, gross negligence or gross
ignorance.[776] These old formulations should not now be taken to mean that any
different standard of care is imposed upon solicitors that other professional men.
In effect, they emphasise that it is not enough to prove that a solicitor has made
an error of judgment or shown ignorance of some particular part of the law: it
must be shown that the error or ignorance was such that an ordinarily competent
solicitor would not have made or shown it.

"It would be extremely difficult to define the exact limit by which the skill and
diligence which a solicitor undertakes to furnish in the conduct of a case is bounded, or
to trace precisely the dividing line between that reasonable skill and diligence which
appears to satisfy his undertaking, and that *crassa negligentia*, or *lata culpa* mentioned
in some of the cases, for which he is undoubtedly responsible. It is a question of degree
and there is a borderland within which it is difficult to say whether a breach of duty has
or has not been committed."[777]

Importance of the retainer. At the outset a solicitor should clarify with a **9–233**
client the precise problem for which he or she is being retained.[778] Although the
duty owed by a solicitor to a client is to exercise reasonable care and skill in
giving advice, discharging it requires a clear exposition of the legal position and
does not extend to advising on the commercial merits generally of a transaction.[779] Indeed, it has been held that a solicitor has no duty to offer unsought
advice on the wisdom of a particular course where the client is in full possession
of her faculties and apparently aware of what she is doing.[780] Further, it has been
held that whilst a solicitor's duty was to inform and advise the client and to
ensure that the client had understood the advice being given, there was no duty
to go further and compel the client to accept the advice.[781] Indeed, in an
appropriate case advice should be circumspect and a client should be warned of

---

[774] In *Duchess of Argyll v Beuselinck* [1972] 2 Lloyd's Rep. 172, Megarry J. appeared to favour the
view that a higher standard of care should be expected of solicitors who held themselves out to be
experts in a particular field, than of solicitors in general practice).
[775] *Baikie v Chandless* (1811) 3 Camp. 17, 20.
[776] *Purves v Landell* (1845) 12 Cl. F. 91 at 102. Lords Brougham and Lyndhurst expressed similar
opinions.
[777] Scrutton L.J. in *Fletcher & Son v Jubb Booth and Helliwell* [1920] 1 K.B. 275 at 281, following
Tindal C.J. in *Godefroy v Dalton* (1830) 6 Bing. 460. See also *Parker v Rolls* (1854) 14 C.B.
691.
[778] *Gray v Buss Murton* [1999] P.N.L.R. 882 (clients who wanted advice about the effectiveness of
a will to convey certain property absolutely who were instead given advice about the will's validity).
[779] *Reeves v Thring & Long* [1996] P.N.L.R. 265, CA (claimant bought a hotel but the conveyance
contained no right of way to reach the rear car park).
[780] *Clark Boyce v Mouat* [1994] 1 A.C. 428, PC.
[781] *Dutfield v Gilbert H. Stephens & Sons* (1988) 18 Fam. Law. 473, per Lincoln J.

the range of interpretations that may reasonably arise on given facts.[782] In a commercial context, the standard of care required to discharge a solicitor's duty will vary with the commercial sophistication of his client.[783]

9–234   Although the terms of the retainer are the starting point when determining both the scope of the solicitor's duty and the standard of care required, it behoves a solicitor to be wary and even where the retainer is capable of narrow definition a duty can arise, at least to warn of a problem of which there is actual or constructive knowledge, where it may prevent the ultimate object of a client being achieved.[784]

9–235   **General and approved practice.** Although the standard is a high one,[785] "a defendant charged with negligence can clear himself if he shows that he acted in accord with general and approved practice."[786] This is so, even if a body of opinion were to take a contrary view.[787] It follows that where a solicitor has acted within the general practice of the profession but has made some error, a finding of negligence will not be made,[788] save in rare circumstances.[789] On the contrary, where a solicitor has failed to adhere to the lines of the general practice and a mistake has occurred, a finding of negligence may be inevitable.[790]

9–236   No doubt problems can arise in situations where there are a number of different practices from which to choose and follow, each with its enthusiastic

---

[782] *Queen Elizabeth's School Blackburn Ltd v Banks Wilson Solicitors* [2002] P.N.L.R. 300, CA (an unusual case where the claimant succeeded because advice in relation to the meaning of a restrictive covenant was too robust as a result of which expense was incurred in altering the design of a new building). The decision has been the subject of adverse comment: see Gee Q.C., "The solicitor's duty to warn that the court might take a different view" (2003) 2 P.N. 362.

[783] *Commercial Bridging Plc v Nelsons* [1998] C.L.Y. 4018 (held unnecessary for a solicitor to explain the effect of a priority limit in a short Deed of Priority to a company specialising in providing bridging loan finance for commercial and residential land purchasers).

[784] See, e.g. *Mortgage Express v Bowerman & Partners* [1996] 1 P.N.L.R. 62, CA; also *Credit Lyonnais SA v Russell Jones & Walker, The Times,* October 9, 2002 (solicitors liable, where, having been instructed to act in relation to the exercise of a break option in a lease, they did not warn of the time for payment of a lump sum required as consideration for the exercise of the option and the opportunity to exercise it was lost).

[785] See Ch.7, para.7–51, above.

[786] *Vancouver General Hospital v McDaniel* (1934) 152 L.T. 56 at 57, PC, per Lord Alness, adopted in *Marshall v Lindsey County Council* [1935] 1 K.B. 516 at 540 by Maugham L.J. and approved by the HL in *Whiteford v Hunter* [1950] W.N. 533.

[787] *Bolam v Friern Hospital Management Committee* [1957] 1 W.L.R. 582, per McNair J. at 587.

[788] *Simmons v Pennington & Son* [1955] 1 W.L.R. 183 (the defendant solicitors, in answering the requisition, having acted in accordance with the general practice of conveyancers, which had been followed for many years without any dire consequences, were held not to have acted negligently, when by sheer ill-luck an error occurred: see per Denning L.J. at 186).

[789] Such as arose in *Edward Wong Finance Co Ltd v Johnson, Stokes & Master* [1984] A.C. 1296, where the buyer's solicitors were liable in negligence for participating in the Hong Kong style of completion, a well-known and accepted general practice which enables a speedier conveyance to take place in that the purchase price and the documents of title are exchanged simultaneously, but the seller's solicitors defaulted in their undertakings. In *Patel v Daybells* [2001] P.N.L.R. 43 the *Edward Wong* case was distinguished where time was so short that a solicitor had no alternative, if his client was not to forfeit a deposit, but to complete a purchase on an undertaking from the vendor's solicitor to redeem a pre-existing charge on the property to be transferred.

[790] *Stevenson v Rowand* (1830) 2 Dow & Cl. 104.

band of supporters.[791] The Law Society issues a Code of Conduct for Solicitors. Failure to follow the standards is not of itself negligent but is no doubt capable of supporting such a finding.[792]

Knowledge of the law. It may be negligence on the part of a solicitor to be **9–237** ignorant of the law applicable to the case, but, in the words of Abbott C.J.:

> "No attorney is bound to know all the law; God forbid that it should be imagined that an attorney, or a counsel, or even a judge is bound to know all the law; or that an attorney is to lose his fair recompense on account of an error, being such an error as a cautious man might fall into."[793]

The general duty in this respect is summed up by Tindal C.J.:

> "He is liable for the consequences of ignorance or non-observance of the rules of practice of this court; for the want of care in the preparation of the cause for trial; or of attendance thereon with his witnesses; and for the mismanagement of so much of the conduct of a cause as is usually and ordinarily allotted to his department of the profession. Whilst, on the other hand, he is not answerable for error in judgment upon points of new occurrence, or of nice or doubtful construction, or of such as are usually entrusted to men in the higher branch of the profession of the law."[794]

A solicitor is not bound to know the contents of every statute of the realm. The **9–238** test of what a solicitor ought to know is the standard of knowledge of a reasonably competent solicitor. The statutes of limitation ought to be known, and if a solicitor finds that the time of limitation is so near its end as to be likely to bar a client's right of action, the client must be warned. One of the earliest grounds of complaint against solicitors was failure to adhere to time-limits as a result of which a cause of action was lost.[795]

Where a solicitor is ignorant of the law on a point, the means of acquiring **9–239** knowledge of it should at least be known.[796] If the point is considered difficult or doubtful, the client should be informed and instructions taken whether or not to seek an opinion from counsel. If the client refuses to take counsel's opinion, the solicitor is only liable "where the law would presume him to have the knowledge himself".[797] If the solicitor decides to advise on a difficult or doubtful

---

[791] See, e.g. *G. & K. Ladenbau (UK) Ltd v Crawley & De Reya* [1978] 1 W.L.R. 266.
[792] *Johnson v Bingley, The Times*, February 28, 1995.
[793] *Montriou v Jeffreys* (1825) 2 C. & P. 113.
[794] *Godefroy v Dalton* (1830) 6 Bing. 460.
[795] *Fletcher & Son v Jubb Booth and Helliwell* [1920] 1 K.B. 275. cf. *Yardley v Coombes* (1963) 107 S.J. 575.
[796] *Parker v Rolls* (1854) 14 C.B. 691 (a personal injuries action against a defendant who admitted liability: the solicitor's client recovered the damages which the defendant to the action would have had to pay).
[797] per Tindal C.J. in *Godefroy v Dalton* (1830) 6 Bing. 460, suggesting that in matters which the law presumed a solicitor to know, he could not protect himself "by consulting another". See further in relation to the effect of taking counsel's opinion, para.9–240, below.

point without warning the client of the difficulty and without suggesting that counsel's opinion should be taken, there is a breach of duty.[798] Even where the area of law in question is a specialist one, it can be arguable that an ordinary high street solicitor should have appreciated that the client has no legal standing to bring a claim.[799] In a case where the law on a point is yet to be finally established, it may be the solicitor's duty to be informed of the state of debate in the legal profession and to act accordingly.[800]

9-240   **Effect of taking counsel's opinion.** Where counsel's opinion has been acted upon properly by a solicitor, negligence is unlikely to be established.[801] In order to obtain this protection all relevant facts should be laid before counsel,[802] included among which are all private Acts of Parliament and statutory regulations, known by the solicitor to be likely to be relevant.[803] In *Davy-Chiesman v Davy-Chiesman*,[804] May L.J., in agreeing that a solicitor was entitled generally to rely on the advice of properly instructed counsel, added:

> "However this does not operate so as to give a solicitor an immunity in every such case. A solicitor is highly trained and rightly expected to be experienced in his particular legal fields. He is under a duty at all times to exercise that degree of care, to both client and the court, that can be expected of a reasonably prudent solicitor. He is not entitled to rely blindly and with no mind of his own on counsel's views."

9-241   Although a solicitor may be justified in relying on counsel's advice, where it embodies a careful and sensible assessment of the legal and factual situation,[805] that may not, depending upon the facts, be a complete answer to a claim in negligence. A prudent solicitor is under a duty to exercise a reasonable degree of

---

[798] *Richards v Cox* [1943] K.B. 139 (advising on the construction of an insurance policy without counsel's opinion—liable for negligence).

[799] *Green v Hancocks, The Times*, August 15, 2000 (taking counsel's opinion was no protection where counsel did not address the relevant point); appeal dismissed [2001] Lloyd's Rep. P.N. 212, CA.

[800] *Dean v Allin & Watts* [2001] P.N.L.R. 921, CA, para.9–231 above (solicitor failed to recognise that a deposit of deeds as security without a memorandum in writing signed by each party to the contract, might be rendered ineffective by s.2 of the Law of Property (Miscellaneous Provisions) Act 1989).

[801] *Potts v Sparrow* (1834) 6 C. & P. 749; *Kemp v Burt* (1833) 4 B. & Ad. 424; *Andrews v Hawley* (1857) 26 L.J.Ex. 323; *Re Clark* (1851) 1 De G.M. & G. 43 at 49. See also *Francis v Francis & Dickinson* [1956] P. 87 at 96 per Sachs J.: "As a general rule a solicitor acting on the advice of properly instructed counsel can hardly be said to be acting unreasonably, save perhaps in a very exceptional set of circumstances." Where leading counsel with specialist experience has been instructed to give considered advice in conference it is a solicitor's duty to differ and give separate advice, or ask that his reservations be recorded, only if there is an important point on which he regards counsel's advice as being seriously wrong: *Matrix Securities Ltd v Theodore Goddard (A Firm)* [1998] P.N.L.R. 290, 323.

[802] *Ireson v Pearman* (1825) 3 B. & C. 799. See also *Locke v Camberwell Health Authority, The Times*, December 11, 1989(solicitor liable for costs thrown away where counsel was not provided with relevant information when asked to advise on the merits in a negligence action)

[803] *Glebe Sugar Refining Co v Greenock Harbour Trustees* (1921) 37 T.L.R. 436.

[804] [1984] Fam. 48 at 64.

[805] *Ward v Chief Constable of Avon and Somerset Constabulary, Daily Telegraph*, September 18, 1987, CA, applying *Orchard v South Eastern Electricity Board* [1987] Q.B. 565.

care to both the client and the court.[806] It is no defence to rely upon counsel's advice when a problem ought to be within the solicitor's own expertise.[807] Where solicitors instructed junior Chancery counsel to advise in connection with a proposed gift of shares, they were negligent in failing to review his advice before transmitting it to the donor; in failing to equip themselves with knowledge of basic inheritance tax principles; and in failing specifically to clarify the tax status of the transfer.[808]

Duty in contentious matters. In contentious matters,[809] a solicitor is under a   **9–242** duty, when instructions are first received, to consider whether a client may be eligible for public funding and it is wrong to incur substantial expenditure chargeable privately to the client, if public funding is available.[810] On taking instructions it is the solicitor's duty to ascertain the relevant facts in order that an opinion can be formed whether or not there is a right of action.[811] If the conclusion is that there is no cause of action, the client should be so advised.[812] If, notwithstanding that advice, the solicitor is instructed to proceed, no liability in negligence will arise.[813] There is no duty to compel a client to accept advice, provided that the solicitor has done that which is reasonably required to ensure that the client has understood precisely what has been advised.[814] The client must be told of any offer of compromise made by the other party. Such an offer should not be rejected without first taking instructions.[815] If advising a legally-aided claimant in relation to compromise, a solicitor has to be wary of incurring costs which may not be recovered from the defendant and the potential impact of the Legal Aid Board's statutory charge. Nevertheless, it was negligent to estimate a

---

[806] *Re A (A Minor) (Costs)* (1988) 18 Fam. Law 339 at 340, per May L.J. It was also observed that if solicitors become aware that counsel instructed by them is not competent to conduct the proceedings they have a duty to withdraw instructions and to instruct someone else in his place.

[807] *Bond v Livingstone & Co* [2001] P.N.L.R. 692 (solicitors ought to have appreciated that where claimant contracted for a hair implant and complained of injury thereby sustained, the claim was for personal injuries and therefore fell within s.11 of the Limitation Act 1980 even though contractually based). See *Hickman v Blake Lapthorn* [2006] P.N.L.R. 20 (solicitors were not protected by their reliance on counsel's advice on settlement where they were more familiar than he with the details of the claim and should have appreciated he was failing to take account of the possibility that the claimant might never work again). See also Bartle, "The defence of reasonable reliance on counsel" (2002) 2 P.N. 111.

[808] *Estill v Cowling Swift & Kitchin* [2000] Lloyd's Rep. P.N. 378, above para.9–99.

[809] Any agreement that a solicitor shall not be liable for negligence, in respect of contentious business, is void by virtue of the Solicitors Act 1974 s.60(5).

[810] *David Truex Solicitor v Kitchin* [2007] P.N.L.R. 34, CA (the solicitors' claim for fees was defeated by a finding that they had been negligent in failing properly to consider the financial position of their client in matrimonial proceedings: had they done so she would have been advised that she might be eligible for public funding and referred to a firm which undertook work of that type).

[811] *Gill v Lougher* (1830) 1 Cr. & J. 170; *Long v Orsi* (1856) 18 C.B. 610; *Thwaites v Mackerson* (1828) 3 C. & P. 341; *Ottley v Gilby* (1845) 8 Beav. 602; *Lawrence v Potts* (1834) 6 C. & P. 428.

[812] *Jacks v Bell* (1828) 3 C. & P. 316. Advice must be supported by analysis and highlight potential pitfalls, see *Levicom International Holdings BV v Linklaters* [2010] EWCA Civ 494.

[813] *Re Clark* (1851) 1 De G.M. & G. 43.

[814] *Dutfield v Gilbert H. Stephens & Sons* (1988) 18 Fam. Law 473, where the client had instructed her solicitors to obtain a speedy resolution to her divorce proceedings rather than embark on prolonged legal inquiry.

[815] *Sill v Thomas* (1839) 8 C. & P. 762.

claim for nuisance at less than £3,000 in value which the claimant subsequently pursued in his own right and compromised at £25,000.[816]

9–243   A solicitor has an implied authority to settle an action on behalf of a client. On the other hand, if the compromise was reached against the client's express instructions, the solicitor will be liable to an action for damages for breach of duty, even though the compromise was pursuant to an advice of counsel.[817]

> "It is within the scope of a solicitor's authority to compromise and if he uses all due diligence and acts bona fide and reasonably no action will lie against him; but if he has been expressly forbidden to compromise, and he does compromise, then, however beneficial that compromise may be, an action will lie against him for disregarding that express negative direction."[818]

If a solicitor advises a client not to defend an action, liability in negligence depends on the same principles.[819] On occasion the failure to appeal or cross appeal a judgment may be negligent, notwithstanding difficulty in estimating what a superior court hearing a case on appeal will do.[820]

9–244   It will usually be negligent for a solicitor to make a significant admission in a client's defence without express instructions. So, where an action for personal injuries sustained in a motor accident was brought against someone who put his defence into the hands of his insurers who, in turn, instructed a solicitor, it was held that the solicitor had to act in the interests of the lay client. It was not proper to subordinate the client's interests to those of the insurance company. Also, when a defence was delivered, admitting negligent driving without the client's instructions, the sole purpose being to give effect to a pooling arrangement among insurance companies and with the object of saving the insurance company money, the solicitor was held to be negligent.[821]

9–245   Even if the client is a slow, reluctant or non-payer of the solicitor's bills there is no excuse for failing to provide a proper service in litigation: the solicitor's remedy is to apply to come off the record.[822] While a solicitor acting for a claimant is obliged to use all due speed to bring the case promptly on for trial, that obligation does not require greater speed than would allow the defendant, with reasonable diligence, also to be ready.[823] So far as enforcement of judgment

---

[816] *Balamoan v Holden & Co, The Independent*, June 15, 1999, CA.
[817] *Fray v Voules* (1859) 1 E. & E. 839; *Butler v Knight* (1867) L.R. 2 Ex. 109.
[818] Farwell J. in *Re Newen* [1903] 1 Ch.812.
[819] *Hill v Finney* (1865) 4 F. & F. 616.
[820] *Dible v Morton Fraser Partnership* 2001 Fam. L.R. 84, OH (where the allegation was that solicitors had failed to take appropriate action following a court's misapplication of a binding decision in relation to financial provision in divorce proceedings).
[821] *Groom v Crocker* [1939] 1 K.B. 194.
[822] *F. & G. Reynolds (Whitchurch) v Joseph, The Times*, November 6, 1992.
[823] *The Flower Bowl v Hodges Menswear Ltd, The Times*, June 14, 1988.

is concerned, the duty to proceed with reasonable speed does not extend to enforcement of a judgment, unless there has been an assumption of responsibility for that aspect of the case, or sufficient notice of the defendant's impecuniosity to make it fair, just and reasonable to extend the duty to cover any loss arising from the inability of the claimant to enforce.[824]

Illustrations of liability. A solicitor has been liable in negligence for **9–246** proceeding under a wrong section of a statute[825]; deliberately allowing time to run out, without getting any instructions, in consequence of which an action for damages became statute-barred[826]; failing to bear in mind the period of limitation, as a result of which his client did not bring an action for personal injuries against the defendants within that limitation period[827]; bringing an action in a court which had no jurisdiction[828]; bringing an action, which might have been taken in the county court, in a superior court without first warning his client of the possible consequences as to cost[829]; not informing his client, the assignee of an insolvent debtor, that he was personally liable for the costs of an action, unless he obtained the consent of the creditors to bring the action[830]; not warning his client that unusual expense might have to be borne by the client himself, whatever the result of the action[831]; in advising a client involved in litigation to accept the other party's guarantee for costs, without making any inquiry as to the value of that party's equity in his house or the extent of his beneficial interest[832];

---

[824] *Pearson v Sanders Witherspoon* [2000] P.N.L.R. 110, CA; also *Thomson Snell & Passmore v Rose* [2000] P.N.L.R. 378, CA (no general duty to investigate the proposed defendant's financial standing before commencing proceedings).

[825] *Hart v Frame* (1836) 6 Cl. & F. 193.

[826] *Kitchen v Royal Air Force Association* [1958] 1 W.L.R. 563. It is not necessary that an omission by a solicitor to issue a writ in time be deliberate, since mere oversight to do so will be actionable. See also *Carlton v Fulchers* [1997] P.N.L.R.337, CA (solicitor instructed after the limitation period had expired was not negligent in failing to make application under s.33 of the Limitation Act 1980, to disapply the relevant period, during such time as he was in negotiation with insurers, although negligence did arise, once those negotiations had been broken off, in telling his client there was nothing further that could be done). In *Winston Cooper v Smith Llewellyn Partnership* [1999] P.N.L.R. 576, it was held not to be a fresh intervening act, interrupting the chain of causation, for the claimant's new solicitors to fail to pursue an application to amend proceedings which the original solicitors had allowed to become statute-barred; also *Hunter v Earnshaw* [2001] P.N.L.R. 42 (absence of instructions no defence to a claim for negligent conduct of proceedings for personal injury where the injury sustained was a head injury leaving the client with symptoms of short-term memory loss and lack of concentration: the solicitor should have been far more proactive and, had appropriate steps been taken, would have been able to remain in touch).

[827] *Fletcher & Son v Jubb, Booth and Helliwell* [1920] 1 K.B. 275, cf. *Glew v Krajewski* (1976) 120 S.J. 316, CA where, unusually, it was held that the solicitor had not been negligent in failing to serve the writ within 12 months of the date of its issue, during negotiations with the defendants' insurers.

[828] *Williams v Gibbs* (1836) 5 A. & E. 208; *Cox v Leech* (1857) 1 C.B.(N.S.) 617.

[829] *Lee v Dixon* (1863) 3 F. & F. 744. In *Barker v Fleetwood Improvement Comrs* (1890) 62 L.T. 833, it was not negligent to bring an action in the Lancaster Palatine Court which might have been brought in the county court.

[830] *Allison v Rayner* (1827) 7 B. & C. 441.

[831] *Re Blyth and Fanshawe* (1882) 10 Q.B.D. 207; *Re Roney & Co* [1914] 2 K.B. 529. In these cases the solicitor was disallowed the items on taxation as between solicitor and client.

[832] *Martin Boston & Co v Roberts* [1995] N.P.C. 28, CA.

being instructed to defend an action, allowing judgment to go by default of defence[833]; having received instructions to act for a tenant who had been served by his landlord with a notice under the Landlord and Tenant Act 1954 s.25, failing to take action by serving the necessary counter-notice because of some internal failure in the office to communicate those verbal instructions to the appropriate person in the firm[834]; failing to watch the court list, so that his client was unrepresented at the hearing[835]; where counsel was necessary, failing to instruct counsel[836]; or, in a criminal case, having instructed counsel, failing to follow his advice on evidence[837]; failing to see that the witnesses were at hand, when they were required at the trial[838]; failing to take proofs of the witnesses, before the trial[839]; where his personal attendance was necessary, failing to attend at the hearing[840]; whilst acting for the buyer of property, making no inquiry as to the standard rent[841]; making a mistake in the examination of a witness under the old Chancery practice[842]; making a mistake in drawing up a decree[843]; failing to deliver a pleading[844]; failing to take steps to set aside an irregular order[845]; failing to raise an issue in time to resist an application to strike out.[846]

9–247   Also: failing to take reasonable steps to ascertain the truth of a statement made to the court, because of which a wrong order was made[847]; neglecting to attend a summons, whereby the master was unable to proceed with an order of reference[848]; failing to issue execution[849]; failing to register a *lis pendens*[850]; bringing an appeal for his own purposes and not in the interests of his client[851];

---

[833] *Godefroy v Jay* (1831) 7 Bing. 413. See also *Laib v Aravindan, The Times,* November 13, 2003 (proceedings do not conclude with satisfaction of the claimant's claim and so it is possible, even after that has occurred, for the defendant to sue his then solicitors for negligence in failing to enter a defence or counterclaim).

[834] *Whelton Sinclair v Hyland* [1992] 41 E.G. 112, CA.

[835] *Burgoine v Taylor* (1878) 9 Ch.D. 1.

[836] *R. v Tew* (1752) Say. 50; *De Roufigny v Peale* (1811) 3 Taunt. 484; *Hawkins v Harwood* (1849) 4 Ex. 503; *Townley v Jones* (1860) 8 C.B.(N.S.) 289.

[837] *Acton v Graham Pearce & Co* [1997] 3 All E.R. 909.

[838] *Reece v Rigby* (1821) 4 B. & Ald. 202; *Price v Bullen* (1825) 3 L.J.(O.S.) K.B. 39; *Hawkins v Harwood,* above.

[839] *Manley v Palache* (1895) 73 L.T. 98.

[840] *Swannell v Ellis* (1823) 1 Bing. 347; *Nash v Swinburne* (1841) 3 M. & G. 630.

[841] *Goody v Baring* [1956] 1 W.L.R. 448. "It is still the duty of a purchaser's solicitor to make the appropriate requisitions and inquiries after the formal contract is signed, even if the preliminary inquiries have been so complete that it is only necessary to ask whether the answers thus received are still complete and accurate" (at 456).

[842] *Stokes v Trumper* (1855) 2 K. & J. 232.

[843] *Re Bolton* (1846) 9 Beav. 272.

[844] *Re Massey and Carey* (1884) 26 Ch.D. 459.

[845] *Frankland v Cole* (1832) 2 Cr. & J. 590.

[846] *Feakins v Burstow* [2006] P.N.L.R. 94 (in the context of a claim against his client by the Intervention Board for Agricultural Produce for clawback of certain premium payments on sheep, the solicitor failed to understand and investigate a counterclaim for "exempt sheep").

[847] *Re Spencer* (1870) 30 L.J. Ch. 841.

[848] *Ridley v Tiplady* (1855) 20 Beav. 44.

[849] *Harrington v Binns* (1863) 3 F. & F. 942.

[850] *Plant v Pearman* (1872) 41 L.J.Q.B. 169.

[851] *Harbin v Masterman* [1896] 1 Ch. 351.

failing to make an application on behalf of an injured child workman for a review, within six months of attaining his majority[852]; when, on his being instructed to draft wills for two clients, man and woman, who wished to confer benefits on each other, and his being told that they were likely to marry each other on some indefinite future date, failing to warn them that marriage would revoke the wills[853]; allowing a client's action to be dismissed for want of prosecution, as a result of the inexcusable delay in bringing the action to trial[854]; failing to ascertain his client's current address, so that she was not informed of the hearing of her husband's divorce petition, which she had desired to defend[855]; allowing the divorce suit of a client's husband to go undefended, so that she lost her right to an award of maintenance for herself and maintenance for her child[856]; when acting for the respondent wife in a divorce case which relied on the fact of separation for five years after a long marriage to the petitioner, a man in pensionable employment, failing to make an application under the Matrimonial Causes Act 1973 s.10, in order to protect her financial position before allowing the decree to be made absolute[857]; failing to prosecute effectively the legal proceedings, which had been taken on the client's instructions with the object of protecting her against the unwelcome attentions of and molestation by a former lover[858]; failing to make representations to the Legal Aid Board why legal aid should not be withdrawn and to advise their client that an appeal was available[859]; having been instructed by a mother in a dispute with a Tunisian father about custody of children, failing to renew or advise the renewal of an entry, in relation to the children, on the register of the Passport Agency, which would have had the effect of preventing the father from applying for a passport on which the children were named.[860]

Illustrations of no liability. Solicitors instructed in civil proceedings may not   **9–248** communicate to solicitors instructed by the same client in criminal proceedings, information they have acquired in the course of their retainer, without the knowledge or approval of their client. So, where the claimant had been convicted

---

[852] *Ashton v Philip Conway Thomas & Co* (1939) 32 B.W.C.C. 246.

[853] *Hall v Meyrick* [1957] 2 Q.B. 472, CA, in particular per Hodson L.J. at 475.

[854] *Fitzpatrick v Batger & Co Ltd* [1967] 1 W.L.R. 706; *Welburn v Mayberry* (1971) 115 S.J. 468; *Mainz v James and Charles Dodd* (1978) 122 S.J. 645 (it was said that if counsel was slow in dealing with instructions, in an action which was already stale as a result of delay, other counsel should be instructed). It is not a defence to an action for negligence, based upon the striking out of a case for want of prosecution, that a fresh action can be brought against the original tortfeasor and thereby no damage can be proved to have accrued, where a second action would be precluded by s.2(3) of the Fatal Accidents Act 1976 and in any event an abuse of process: *Croft v Shavin & Co* [1997] C.L.Y. 644.

[855] *D v D* [1963] 1 W.L.R. 194.

[856] *Cook v Swinfen* [1967] 1 W.L.R. 457.

[857] *Griffiths v Dawson & Co* [1993] F.L.R. 315.

[858] *Heywood v Wellers* [1976] Q.B. 446.

[859] *Casey v Hugh James Jones & Jenkins* [1999] Lloyd's Rep. P.N. 115 (but damages were nominal, since even if an appeal had been made there was no reasonable probability that legal aid would have been continued and even if it had, the claim enjoyed no realistic prospect of success).

[860] *Hamilton Jones v David & Snape* [2004] P.N.L.R. 381 (the father successfully removed the children from the jurisdiction: the mother recovered £20,000 for consequential mental distress).

of fraud and sentenced to a period of imprisonment, and subsequently commenced proceedings for damages, based on her loss of liberty, against solicitors who had represented her in contemporaneous civil proceedings, it was held that those legal representatives had owed her no duty to inform those representing her in the criminal case, of doubts or conclusions as to her mental capacity.[861] Solicitors were not in breach of duty in failing to advise a school compromising a claim made against it by the parents of pupils at the school, of the possibility that the pupils themselves, on attaining their majority, might also sue: the solicitors were justified in considering that a remote chance, which in any case it would not be possible to prevent.[862]

9–249 **The rule against re-litigating decided issues between different parties.**[863] A solicitor facing a civil claim based upon alleged negligence in earlier criminal proceedings in which the claimant was convicted, may well seek to defend on the basis that the claim is an abuse of the process of the court, as a collateral attack upon the final decision of a criminal court of competent jurisdiction. The rule prohibiting such attacks, as set out by the House of Lords in *Hunter v Chief Constable of the West Midlands Police*,[864] is of potential application where civil proceedings follow either earlier criminal or earlier civil proceedings, but was not intended to apply inflexibly to all cases which might arguably fall within it.[865] It is evident in civil cases particularly, that there may be occasions when a party may have lacked a proper opportunity to resist a hostile claim, as where judgment was entered for procedural fault or summary judgment given. Not all re-litigation will be manifestly unfair, or bring the administration of justice into disrepute.[866] It has been emphasised that the court has wide powers to strike out a civil claim following earlier civil proceedings both because there is no real prospect of success,[867] or because the re-litigation causes unfairness to a third party.[868] This power will be a sufficient control in many cases without recourse to the *Hunter* rule. In cases where the rule does apply the claimant will have to demonstrate that new and reliable evidence is available which substantially alters the aspect of the earlier criminal case, as a

---

[861] *Marsh v Sofaer* [2004] P.N.L.R. 443.

[862] *Gosfield School Ltd v Birkett Long* [2006] P.N.L.R. 19.

[863] How to prevent abuse of the procedures of the court by those with access to it, is of general relevance. In New Zealand have an inherent jurisdiction to make an order for costs personally against legal representatives in order to maintain appropriate levels of competence and to ensure public confidence: *Harley v McDonald* [2001] 2 W.L.R. 1749, PC (but pursuit of a hopeless case was insufficient to justify any penalty, nor was mistake or error of judgment enough; what was required was a serious default in the duty owed to the court).

[864] [1982] A.C. 529. See also para.9–96, above.

[865] See *Arthur J.S. Hall & Co v Simons* [2002] 1 A.C. 615, particularly the speech of Lord Hoffmann. He emphasised that the rule was of far more likely application after the final decision in a criminal case than after final judgment in a civil claim.

[866] *Arthur J.S. Hall & Co v Simons* [2002] 1 A.C. 615 per Lord Hoffmann at 703. See also *GNER Ltd v JLT Corporate Risks Ltd* [2006] P.N.L.R. 34, Ch.4, para.4–246, above.

[867] See CPR Pt 24.2, which empowers the court to give summary judgment in favour of the defendant where the claimant has no real prospect of success.

[868] The example given by Lord Hoffmann was a negligence claim following upon an earlier defamation action where, in effect, the claimant was seeking to justify a libel of a third party.

pre-condition of being permitted to proceed.[869] The claimant will also have to demonstrate why steps were not taken to set aside or challenge the relevant order or judgment in the original proceedings, for instance by way of appeal.[870]

ILLUSTRATIONS

Decisions before the House of Lords visited the topic in *Arthur J.S. Hall & Co v Simons*[871] have to be approached with care, but the following may at least illustrate the diverse circumstances which can arise. So, no abuse of process was found where the claimant mother sought to sue solicitors for alleged dilatoriness in pursuing a claim for increased contact with her child in care, where it was possible that prompter action may have permitted rehabilitation to her and avoided adoption, which was the eventual result after a contested hearing[872]; nor where solicitors attempted to strike out the claim of a former client in a matrimonial cause, who alleged that her consent to an agreed order for ancillary relief was given as the result of negligent advice: in making the order the judge would not have examined it in any purposeful way and the claim would not have been put fully before the court[873]; nor where the claimant alleged acts of negligence prior to a hearing of her claim for ancillary relief at which a consent order was made: in effect she was alleging that the solicitor's failure properly to investigate her husband's financial position meant the court was deprived of relevant facts so the judge granting the order was unable properly to exercise his discretion in approving the settlement[874]; where the civil court could avoid a rehearing of an earlier criminal case in which the claimant had been convicted by treating his claim for damages as a claim for loss of the chance that he would not have been prosecuted, or, if prosecuted, convicted, had the solicitor's breach of duty not occurred.[875] No collateral attack on an earlier decision arose where the claimant sued his former solicitors in respect of a failure to understand and timeously investigate an issue which, in the first proceedings, it was held was raised at too late a stage: since the issue itself had not been decided in those proceedings, the action against the solicitors did not involve an attack on the earlier courts' decisions.[876] It was not appropriate to strike out a claim against the Citizens Advice Bureau, based upon an alleged settlement by their representative of an employment tribunal claim without authority, even where the tribunal had itself refused to reinstate the original claim on the basis that the representative

9–250

---

[869] *Smith v Linskells*, *The Times*, February 7, 1996, CA (on the evidence it could not be said that the claimant had been deprived of a full opportunity to contest the criminal charge against him).

[870] [2002] 1 A.C. 615, n.71 above. The advocate's immunity remains in Scotland: see e.g. *Wright v Paton Farrell* [2003] P.N.L.R. 410, OH, on appeal, [2007] P.N.L.R. 7, CS (IH) (a claim against solicitors acting for the claimant in criminal proceedings in which he was convicted of theft and other offences, the conviction being set aside on appeal).

[871] n.865, above. See also the discussion in the judgment of Lord Bingham C.J. at [1999] 3 W.L.R. 873, CA in the same case.

[872] See, e.g. *R. (L) v Witherspoon* [1999] P.N.L.R. 776, CA.

[873] *B v Miller & Co* [1996] 2 F.L.R. 23.

[874] *Frazer Harris v Scholfield Roberts & Hill* [1998] Fam. Law 524, appeal dismissed [1999] P.N.L.R. 374, CA.

[875] *Acton v Graham Pearce & Co* [1997] 3 All E.R. 909 (the conviction had been quashed).

[876] *Feakins v Burstow* [2006] P.N.L.R. 94, n.846 above.

had ostensible authority to settle and the claimant had accepted the settlement terms.[877]

9–251   In contrast, the rule in *Hunter* was applied in the context of proceedings before the solicitor's disciplinary tribunal, where it was sought to challenge criminal convictions in the Crown Court for offences involving fraud against the Legal Aid Fund.[878] It was also applied where solicitors initiated interpleader proceedings in relation to a disputed deposit held by them, and then, in a subsequent negligence action, sought to challenge the interpleader ruling.[879] It did involve a collateral challenge to an earlier decision to bring proceedings in negligence against a firm of solicitors where the basis of the claim was an interpretation of a written agreement which had already been rejected by a judge in an earlier action.[880]

9–252   **Wasted costs.** Pursuant to s.51(6) of the Supreme Court Act 1981,[881] the court may disallow, or order any legal or other representative to meet, "the whole of any wasted costs or such part of them as may be determined in accordance with rules of court."[882] "Wasted costs" are defined as any costs incurred by a party "(a) as a result of any improper, unreasonable or negligent act or omission on the part of any legal or other representative or any employee of such a representative; or (b) which, in the light of any such act or omission occurring after they were incurred, the court considers it is unreasonable to expect that party to pay."[883]

9–253   The wasted costs jurisdiction exists in both civil[884] and criminal cases.[885] For a detailed treatment, the practitioner is referred elsewhere.[886] In brief, a three-stage test is to be applied before a wasted costs order is made. The court must

---

[877] *Nesbitt v Holt* [2007] P.N.L.R. 24, CA, Ch.4, para.4–243, above (it would not be unfair to let the action proceed, the CAB not having as yet disclosed its file, and the crucial issue, namely authority to commit the claimant to settlement, not having been tested in the Tribunal process). See Willis and Park, "Two bites at the cherry?" 147 N.L.J. 761.

[878] *Re A Solicitor, The Times*, March 18, 1996. Lord Taylor of Gosforth C.J. said that it would always be preferable to seek to have the conviction reviewed.

[879] *Gribbon v Lutton* [2002] 2 W.L.R. 842, CA (the solicitors were not party to the interpleader proceedings, so no issue estoppel arose, but it was still an abuse of process to attempt to go behind the result).

[880] *Laing v Taylor Walton* [2008] P.N.L.R. 11, CA.

[881] The present s.51 was substituted by s.4 of the Courts and Legal Services Act 1990.

[882] See CPR, Pt 48, r.7 and the Practice Direction thereto, formerly RSC Ord.62, r.10. It has been held that CPR Pt 48, r.7(3) is ultra vires having regard to the fact that legal professional privilege is a substantive legal right and not merely a rule of evidence: *General Mediterranean Holdings SA v Patel* [1999] P.N.L.R. 852 (the court refused to give a direction that solicitors, respondents to an application for wasted costs, disclose certain privileged documents to the court).

[883] Courts and Legal Services Act 1990 s.51(7).

[884] See *Ridehalgh v Horsfield* [1994] Ch.205.

[885] *Practice Note: Wasted Costs Order (No.1 of 1991)* [1992] 3 All E.R. 429. In *Re Sternberg Reed Taylor & Gill, The Times*, July 26, 1999, CA (Crim Div) it was said to be both negligent within the *Ridehalgh* test and an "unnecessary or improper act or omission" for purposes of reg.3C of the Costs in Criminal Cases (General) Regulations to take oral instructions from a client standing trial in a criminal case outside the courtroom and within the hearing of the jury.

[886] See, e.g. the notes to Pt 44.14 of the Civil Procedure Rules in the *White Book* (Sweet and Maxwell, 2010).

decide whether there has been some improper, unreasonable or negligent act or omission by the representative it is sought to condemn in costs; whether as a result unnecessary costs were incurred; and finally, whether in all the circumstances it would be just to order the representative to pay those costs or part of them.[887] It has been said that "improper" in this context suggests, but is not confined to, conduct which would ordinarily involve disbarrment, striking off or suspension. "Unreasonable" describes conduct which is vexatious or designed to harass the other party rather than advance the case. "Negligent" is not to be understood in a technical sense but describes a failure to act with the competence reasonably to be expected of an ordinary member of the profession and is no less a test than is applied in deciding whether an action for negligence against a legal practitioner is made out.[888] When considering wasted costs the first step is to identify the conduct which is improper, unreasonable or negligent, before assessing the costs wasted by that conduct. Provided the matter is approached in this way, a broad view may be taken and, for instance, in the context of delay, a solicitor may be ordered to pay the whole or part of the costs from a particular date.[889]

It is not an appropriate or useful exercise to analyse in depth into which category conduct which is plainly unacceptable falls. The words "improper," "unreasonable" and "negligent" are not to be regarded as having specific, self-contained meanings.[890] "Conduct which is unreasonable may also be improper, and conduct which is negligent will very frequently be (if it is not by definition) unreasonable." No sharp differentiation between these expressions is useful or necessary or intended.[891] Negligence in the context of wasted costs does not bear a special meaning, requiring, for instance, an additional element of abuse of process.[892] Where the complaint is pursuit of a hopeless case and there is *no* specific indication of negligence the court will no doubt consider whether the

---

[887] CPR 1998 Pt 48, P.D. para.48.7.2.4. It is not negligent for solicitors to rely upon the advice of counsel properly instructed, provided they also exercise their own independent judgment: *Reaveley v Safeway Stores Plc* [1998] P.N.L.R. 526, CA (solicitors relied upon advice from counsel about the likely quantum of a claim in a case where, in the result, the effect of the Compensation Recovery Scheme was that the claimant made no gain from the action beyond £2,500 already received by way of interim payment). Where solicitors have not acted in breach of the Civil Legal Aid (General) Regulations 1989, the court should not make a wasted costs order based on negligence or unreasonable conduct where to do so amounts to importing a more rigorous standard than that for which the Regulations provide: *Tate v Hart* [1999] P.N.L.R. 787, CA.

[888] per Sir Thomas Bingham M.R. in *Ridehalgh v Horsfield* [1994] Ch.205, 233. It is negligent for a solicitor's clerk to take instructions from a defendant in a criminal trial in a corridor of the court through which the jury hearing his trial might, and indeed, did, pass: *R. v Qadi* [2000] P.N.L.R. 137, CA. In *Re A (Costs)* (1988) 18 Fam. Law 339, the CA held that solicitors who become aware that counsel instructed by them was not competent to conduct proceedings have a duty to withdraw instructions from him and ensure that other competent counsel is instructed. See also *Locke v Camberwell Health Authority, The Times*, December 11, 1989.

[889] *Kilroy v Kilroy* [1997] P.N.L.R. 66, CA.

[890] *Dempsey v Johnstone* [2004] P.N.L.R. 25, CA (conceding a strike out in the course of a hearing did not on the facts establish that solicitors' prior evaluation of the case was negligent).

[891] *Dempsey v Johnstone* [2004] P.N.L.R. 25, CA per Latham L.J. at 34.

[892] The need for "something more than negligence . . . akin to abuse of process" was said to be required in *Persaud v Persaud* para.9–105, above, but it is suggested that this is to add to this part of the test an element not contemplated in *Ridehalgh v Horsfield*, above: see also per Buxton L.J. in *M (A Barrister) Re* [2004] P.N.L.R. 722, CA at 729.

conduct of the litigation has been an abuse of process. But even then the enquiry will often resolve into whether the legal representative has pursued a claim or defence which no reasonably competent practitioner could have done.[893]

9–255   The wasted costs procedure is intended to be a summary one.[894] "Hearings should be measured in hours, not in days or weeks."[895] Where such complex issues arise as to make an application for wasted costs not amenable to summary disposal, the jurisdiction should not be invoked.[896] Having said that, "it cannot be right that a legal representative can escape the consequences of the wasted costs jurisdiction by the mere fact that the litigation in which his conduct is challenged is complex."[897]

ILLUSTRATIONS

9–256   The commencement of proceedings against a party without having any or due regard to a basic precondition of that party's liability is capable of constituting negligence akin to an abuse of process, so as to expose solicitors to an order for wasted costs.[898] In normal circumstances a solicitor cannot be liable for wasted costs as a result of conduct before litigation has commenced, particularly if the conduct is no more than negligent and the solicitor never acts in the litigation subsequently commenced. The element of breach of a duty to the court is missing in such cases. But it can be otherwise if the conduct can be classed as unreasonable or improper and the solicitor does act once litigation is commenced.[899]

9–257   **Litigants in person.** While as a matter of courtesy and good practice, professional lawyers should, and frequently do, give litigants in person what

---

[893] See further *Morris v Roberts (Inspector of Taxes)* [2005] P.N.L.R. 835 at 847, per Lightman J.: "A legal representative will also be liable to a wasted costs order if, exercising the objective professional judgment of a reasonably competent solicitor, he ought reasonably to have appreciated that the litigation in which he was acting, constituted an abuse of process." (Solicitors were implicated in conduct designed to frustrate Revenue's enforcement of court orders against their client).

[894] See per Lord Woolf M.R. in *Wall v Lefever* [1998] 1 F.C.R. 605, 614.

[895] per Sir Thomas Bingham M.R. in *Ridelhalgh v Horsfield* [1994] Ch.205, 238.

[896] per Lord Woolf M.R. in *Manzanilla Ltd v Corton Property and Investments Ltd,* Unreported, Court of Appeal, April 23, 1997, quoted in *Wagstaff v Colls* [2003] P.N.L.R. 561, CA at 578.

[897] per Peter Gibson L.J. in *Medcalf v Mardell* [2001] L.L.R. (PN) 146, 159, CA ("remains good guidance" per Ward L.J. in *Wagstaff v Colls* above, even though the conclusion in *Medcalf* was reversed on the merits by the House of Lords at [2003] A.C. 120).

[898] *The Isaacs Partnership v Umm Al-Jawaby Oil Service Co Ltd* [2004] P.N.L.R. 136 (a contract claim in which solicitors acting for the claimant started proceedings without first obtaining a copy of the relevant document and continued the action in spite of the defendant's protestations—correct as it turned out—that it was not a party to the contract concerned). See also *Dempsey v Johnston,* n.94, above.

[899] *Radford & Co v Charles* [2004] P.N.L.R. 452 (solicitors who failed in time to issue an appeal against the decision of a local authority in a housing case, were not liable for the costs of their former client and the local authority when, their client having instructed a different firm, his application for permission to appeal out of time was dismissed).

assistance they can, consistent with their duty to their own client, it is unlikely that a failure to do so could amount to conduct justifying an order for wasted costs. "In the absence of some duty imposed by law, or direction of the court, a legal representative's duty is to his own client, not his client's opponent."[900]

Liability in acting as an advocate. There is no good reason in principle why the liability in negligence of solicitors acting as advocates should be any different than the liability of barristers. No point of distinction was referred to in the House of Lords in the leading case,[901] where the liability considered in the speeches was that of the advocate, rather than the member of a particular branch of the legal profession. Accordingly solicitor advocates are as liable for negligence both in the course of any hearing conducted by them and in their preparation before as would be a barrister, and cases in which immunity from suit was granted can no longer be taken as representing the law. **9–258**

Duty in non-contentious matters. In non-contentious matters[902] the duty of a solicitor depends upon the facts, and principally the nature of the transaction which is being carried out. **9–259**

Illustrations of liability. A solicitor has been held liable in negligence for not explaining to his client the documents which he is being asked to execute and the consequences to him of so executing them[903]; when acting for a buyer of property, not warning him that he was obtaining only a possessory title to the land[904]; not explaining the nature and terms of a composition deed to his client[905]; not making the usual searches[906]; by omitting to carry out any satisfactory independent check to establish that the whole of the land was included in the registered title, and failing to notice the true extent of the mortgaged property, on the strength of which inadequate security an advance was made by the client, a building society[907]; failing to search the commons register, set up under the Commons Registration Act 1965, when acting for buyers of unbuilt vacant land with which he was unfamiliar[908]; failing to register in time an estate contract, under the Land Charges Act 1925, so that a third party was able **9–260**

---

[900] per Carnwath L.J. in *Sherman v Fitzhugh Gates* [2003] P.N.L.R. 762, CA, quoting Brook L.J. in *Connolly-Martin v Davis* [1999] Lloyd's Rep. P.N. 790, 795, CA.
[901] See *Arthur J.S. Hall & Sons v Simons* [2002] 1 A.C. 615 and paras 9–95 and 9–249, above.
[902] See Williams, "Professional Negligence in Rent Review and Lease Renewal", 276 E.G. 146; Mitchell, "Ancillary Relief and professional negligence" 144 S.J., 756.
[903] *Stannard v Ulithorne* (1834) 10 Bing. 491. But cf. *Clark Boyce v Mouat* [1994] 1 A.C. 428, PC, and para.9–265, below.
[904] *Allen v Clark* (1863) 7 L.T. 781.
[905] *Watts v Hyde* (1846) 2 Coll. 368.
[906] *Cooper v Stephenson* (1852) 21 L.J.Q.B. 292. See also *Cottingham v Attey Bower & Jones, The Times*, April 19, 2000 (solicitors who failed to seek to obtain copies of building consents which the seller of property claimed, erroneously, to have obtained); *Asiansky Television Plc v Bayer-Rosin* [2003] N.P.C. 137, CA (failure to discover and advise a client of the existence and extent of compulsory purchase orders over a site which the client wished to acquire and develop).
[907] *Mercantile Building Society v J.W. Mitchell Dodds & Co* [1993] N.P.C. 99, CA.
[908] *G. & K. Ladenbau (UK) Ltd v Crawley & De Reya* [1978] 1 W.L.R. 226.

to acquire an adverse interest in the property[909]; not calling for the last receipt for rent when advising buyer of farming produce which was to be left growing in the ground[910]; mistakenly exchanging contracts before he had received the landlord's acceptance of the claimant as assignee, despite a clause in the lease which may well have made him unacceptable[911]; failing to give notice of new trustees of a reversionary interest to the trustees of the settlement fund[912]; failing to give notice so as to secure priority to his client[913]; where an option agreement was expressed to be exercisable "at a price to be agreed, by notice to the intending vendors", failing, when serving such a notice, to mention a price, as a result of which the option was held not to have been exercised validly[914]; failing to inform his clients that a club which they had formed had been refused registration by the magistrates' clerk[915]; failing to inform his client that a local search showed that plans of the building which had been erected on land his client had agreed to buy had not been approved by the local authority[916]; failing to inform lenders of facts that would cast doubt upon the accuracy of a valuation of premises, over which they would hold a first mortgage[917]; failing to point out to a bank a discrepancy in an insurance policy taken as part of the security for an overdraft.[918]

9–261   Also: failing to discover that a public footpath, which was believed by the vendor to have been abandoned, over land that was being sold at auction, was in fact registered on the County Definitive Map and to advise the purchaser that there was an existing public right of way across it[919]; advising a client that his interest in real estate was an absolute one, whereas in reality it was entailed, with the result that no disentailing assurance was executed and, on the client's death, the property did not form part of his estate[920]; when acting for the buyer of property, failing to discover that the seller had bought from the trustees of his father's will and that, himself being one of the trustees, his title was defective[921]; failing to advise on the effect of s.64 of the Landlord and Tenant Act 1954 and that no guarantee could be given that vacant possession would be obtained at any time for the purposes of the property deal concerned[922]; serving defective notices

---

[909] *Midland Bank Trust Co Ltd v Hett, Stubbs & Kemp* [1979] Ch.384. But, cf. *Stratton v Weston*, *Financial Times*, April 11, 1990, where it was held that a solicitor's negligent failure to register his client's agreement for a business lease, resulting in the landlord's receivers obtaining possession, did not give the client a right of action if the receivers could have sold free of the agreement in any event, because of their rights under a prior equitable mortgage.

[910] *Waine v Kempster* (1859) 1 F. & F. 695.

[911] *Transportation Agency v Jenkins* (1972) 223 E.G. 1101.

[912] *Bean v Wade* (1885) 2 T.L.R. 157.

[913] *Stevenson v Rowand* (1830) 2 Dow & Cl. 104; *Dondaldson v Haldane* (1840) 7 Cl. & Fin. 762.

[914] *Roberts v J.W. Ward & Son* (1982) 126 S.J. 120, CA.

[915] *Ashton v Wainwright* [1936] 1 All E.R. 805.

[916] *Lake v Bushby* [1949] 2 All E.R. 964.

[917] *Mortgage Express v Bowerman & Partners* [1995] 2 W.L.R. 607, CA (measure of damages); [1996] 1 P.N.L.R. 62, CA (liability).

[918] *County Natwest v Pinsent & Co* [1994] Bank L.R. 4 (however the bank's action failed on causation, the judge not accepting that it would have acted differently had the security not been given).

[919] *Trask v Clark & Sons* [1980] C.L.Y. 2588.

[920] *Otter v Church, Adams, Tatham & Co* [1953] Ch. 280.

[921] *Pilkington v Wood* [1953] Ch.770 (negligence was admitted).

[922] *Rumsey v Owen White & Catlin* (1976) 241 E.G. 611.

under the Landlord and Tenant Act 1954, with the result that on sale of the premises their client was unable to give vacant possession[923]; allowing a client, a prospective buyer of premises, to gain possession and spend money on repairs, pending execution of the contract, without first warning of the risk that the seller might change his mind and decide not to proceed with the sale[924]; when acting for both parties, failing to take proper instructions from one[925] and failing to advise as to the contents of a contract of sale or to explain the provisions so as to ensure that they provided adequate protection[926]; whilst acting for the buyer of a house unknown to him, accepting instructions from the seller and a competing buyer, between each of whom there were clear conflicts of interest.[927]

Further: failing to explain to a client, who was considering taking a lease, the **9–262** meaning of a clause in the proposed lease, which the solicitor knew or ought to have realised the client did not fully understand[928] and failing to alert a client to the existence, effect and risks involved in unusual clauses in the draft[929]; failing to take adequate instructions from a restaurateur about the plans for premises he proposed to lease and to ensure that the user covenants would permit his aims to be achieved[930]; failing to ascertain the expiry date of a planning permission, carried by land that was being purchased, and to advise that such permission would lapse shortly after the date of completion if no development had been begun[931]; failing to make inquiries of the planning authority that would have revealed the existence of a conditional planning consent affecting office premises which rendered them unsuitable for the client's purposes.[932]

Also : during negotiations for the purchase of land when a boundary fence was **9–263** moved, failing to press the seller's solicitors for a full explanation as to the intrusion onto the land, failing to ask their own clients upon which boundary they had relied, and failing to inspect the Land Registry site plan[933]; failing, when retained to advise in a planning appeal, to draw attention to the prospect of challenge to a local plan in the six period allowed after notice of its adoption had been given[934]; failing to obtain a deposit from a prospective buyer, before exchanging contracts for the sale of a flat, and failing to warn of the dangers of exchanging contracts for the purchase of a new house before obtaining an

---

[923] *Robins v Meadows & Moran* [1991] 2 E.G.L.R. 137.
[924] *Attard v Samson* (1966) 110 S.J. 249.
[925] *Treloar v Henderson* [1968] N.Z.L.R. 1085.
[926] *Fox v Everingham* (1983) 50 A.L.R. 337.
[927] *Nash v Phillips* (1974) 232 E.G. 1219.
[928] *Sykes v Midland Bank Executor and Trustee Co Ltd* [1969] 2 Q.B. 518 (reversed on the question of damages [1971] 1 Q.B. 113), distinguished in *Aslan v Clintons* (1984) 134 New L.J. 584. See Lewis, "Negligence and the Chance of Inquiry" 2 P.N. (1986) 119.
[929] *County Personnel (Employment Agency) Ltd v Alan R. Pulver & Co* [1987] 1 W.L.R. 916.
[930] *Le Roux v Pictons* [1994] E.G.C.S. 168.
[931] *Raintree v Holmes & Hills* (1984) 134 New L.J. 522.
[932] *G.P. & B. v Bulcraig & Davis* (1986) 280 E.G. 356 also, *Farragher v Gerber* [1994] E.G.C.S. 122 (solicitor failed to make inquiries which would have revealed proposal to build major new highway outside property to be purchased).
[933] *McManus Developments Ltd v Barbridge Properties Ltd* [1996] P.N.L.R. 431, CA.
[934] *Motor Crown Petroleum Ltd v Berwin & Co* [1998] C.L.Y. 4020, para.9–297, n.1066, below.

effective contract of sale of the flat being sold to finance the purchase[935]; failing to exchange contracts for the sale of a clients' former house simultaneously with the exchange of contracts for the purchase of their new one, so that they became homeless until obliged to buy another less suitable property[936]; failing to inform clients that contracts had been exchanged[937]; sending clients' cheques, made payable to the solicitors acting on behalf of builders, in respect of booking deposits but failing to make it clear that such were to be held by the solicitors as stakeholders and not as agents for the builders[938]; forwarding the whole of the purchase money to the buyer's solicitors in exchange for the latter's undertaking to forward the executed title documents within a reasonable time[939]; failing to complete conveyance[940]; advising a client to complete on the purchase of a house without first achieving the cancellation of a charge on the property imposed by the seller's spouse under the Matrimonial Homes Act 1976[941]; when acting in the sale of a farm and subsequent purchase of an agricultural tenancy, failing to advise that specific performance of the latter was not a foregone conclusion, when he knew that the agricultural tenant, who was serving a prison sentence, was challenging the authority of a surveyor to conclude any agreement on his behalf[942]; failing to supervise drafting of two parts of a commercial agreement entrusted to separate departments in the firm and to advise of the resulting document's actual effect[943]; failing to carry out instructions, when acting for the vendor of land, to obtain an enforceable agreement under which a deposit was forfeit, should the purchaser fail to complete[944]; failing to serve a completion notice, where the vendor was apparently delaying the completion of the transfer of a farm.[945]

9–264   **Illustrations of no liability.** A solicitor was *not* negligent when he had been engaged by the managing partner of a business in order to defend an action against the firm, and kept that partner informed of the progress of the action, but did not inform the other partners[946]; when a client, the wife of a licensed victualler, had lent money to her husband for the purpose of his business and the solicitor failed to advise the registration of a bill of sale or the necessity of the

---

[935] *Morris v Duke-Cohan* (1975) 119 S.J. 826; also *Law v Cunningham and Co* [1993] E.G.C.S. 126 (solicitor failed to identify for his client the risk of an agreement for the sale of property).

[936] *Buckley v Lane, Herdman & Co* [1977] C.L.Y. 3143.

[937] *Stinchcombe & Cooper v Addison, Cooper, Jessen & Co* (1971) 115 S.J. 368.

[938] *Desmond v Brophy* [1985] I.R. 449.

[939] In *Edward Wong Finance Co v Johnson Stokes & Master* [1984] A.C. 1296, the PC held that, because a conveyancing practice, known as a "Hong Kong style completion", involved a foreseeable risk of embezzlement by the recipient of the money, it was negligent in the circumstances. It was, of course, open to the buyers in such a situation to cover themselves by making all reasonable inquiries, before parting with the money. See Kenny, "Negligent Conveyancing—'Hong Kong' Style?" 134 New L.J. 309.

[940] *Dogma Properties v Gale* (1984) 134 New L.J. 453.

[941] *Holmes v H. Kennard & Son, The Times,* November 30, 1984, CA.

[942] *Warboys v Cartwright* [1992] N.P.C. 106.

[943] *Summit Financial Group Ltd v Slaughter & May, The Times,* April 2, 1999.

[944] *Gribbon v Lutton* [2002] Q.B. 902.

[945] *Williams v Gly Owen & Co* [2004] P.N.L.R. 367, CA.

[946] *Tomlinson v Broadsmith* [1896] 1 Q.B. 386.

transfer of the licence to the wife[947]; when instructed by an intending mortgagee, who had instructed valuers to value the proposed security, omitting to call the client's attention to the fact that the value, as assessed by the valuers, was considerably more than the price last paid for the property[948]; when misled by an auctioneer's mistake as to the amount of a tithe.[949]

Nor was a solicitor negligent: in advising Y that he could safely complete, **9–265** when the owner of the land, having contracted to sell to X, rescinded the contract, wrongfully as the court subsequently held, and sold to Y[950]; when acting for a seller of land, answering a requisition, made by the buyer in accordance with general conveyancing practice, although, as a result of the answer, the buyer was able to refuse to complete and recover his deposit[951]; in failing to advise an experienced property dealer that he exposed himself to a successful claim for damages, if subsequently he failed to give vacant possession in accordance with a clear term in the contract of sale, which he was about to sign[952]; in failing to prevent his client, a man with considerable experience in business of buying and selling leasehold reversions, who knew the significance of rent reviews, from taking the commercial risk of proceeding without knowledge of the figure under the rent review of a particular property[953]; in failing to advise experienced commercial clients of the VAT implications of payments under a sale and development agreement,[954] in failing to offer unsought advice on the wisdom of a transaction where the client was in full command of her faculties and apparently aware of what she was doing[955]; when acting for the lender and borrower in a remortgage transaction, failing to inform the lender of the borrower's bad record of repayment with a previous lender, where his instructions from the lender do not require him to report or advise such information[956]; when drawing deeds of cohabitation, and subsequently separation, for the claimant and a man with whom he had agreed to live in a relationship of "master" and "slave".[957] There is no invariable duty upon a solicitor to send out a reminder to a client when a draft will is not signed and returned.[958]

---

[947] *Faithfull v Kesteven* (1910) 103 L.T. 56.
[948] *Scholes v Brook* (1891) 63 L.T. 837 (the appeal, 64 L.T. 674, only deals with the valuers' liability).
[949] *Ellis v Sampson* (1927) 71 S.J. 621.
[950] *Bell v Strathern & Blair* (1954) 104 L.J. 618.
[951] *Simmons v Pennington & Son* [1955] 1 W.L.R. 183.
[952] *Aslan v Clintons* (1984) 134 New L.J. 584, distinguishing *Sykes v Midland Bank Executor & Trustee Co* [1969] 2 Q.B. 518.
[953] *Forbouys v Gadhavi* [1993] N.P.C. 122.
[954] *Virgin Management Ltd v De Morgan Group Plc* [1996] E.G.C.S. 16, CA.
[955] *Clark Boyce v Mouat* [1994] 1 A.C. 428, PC.
[956] *National Home Loans Corp Plc v Giffen Couch & Archer* [1997] 3 All E.R. 808, CA. See also the cases cited at para.9–267, below.
[957] *Sutton v Mishcon De Reya* [2004] Fam. Law 247.
[958] *Atkins v Dunn & Baker* [2004] W.T.L.R. 477, CA (a draft having been prepared and sent out to the testator, nothing further was done by the solicitor for some two years, save for a circular letter which gave information about the solicitor's move to another practice: the testator died intestate but the action of the claimant, who would have been entitled to a beneficial interest in the estate had the will been signed, failed). See "Professional negligence: wills and inheritance tax" S.P.C.L.R. 2004, 8 (Oct) 7.

9–266   **Acting for both sides.** There is no general rule of law that a solicitor should never act for both parties to a transaction where their interests may conflict; he may do so provided they give their informed consent.[959] The potential difficulty is that a fiduciary relationship[960] exists between the solicitor and both his clients, which, in some instances, can lead to a conflict of duties that cannot be reconciled. That was the position in *Hilton v Barker Booth & Eastwood*,[961] where solicitors acted for both vendor and purchaser in a property transaction and failed to disclose to the vendor that the purchaser had criminal convictions. The solicitors' difficulty was that they were under a duty to the purchaser not to disclose something which they ought to disclose to the vendor. The House of Lords rejected the solution adopted in the Court of Appeal, that a term should be implied in the contract between the solicitor and his client, excluding any duty to disclose that which they were bound in confidentiality to another client to conceal: "if a solicitor is unwise enough to undertake irreconcilable duties it is his own fault, and he cannot use his discomfiture as a reason why his duty to either client should be taken to have been modified."[962] The view taken was that since neither duty had a precedence over the other, the solicitor had to perform both as best he could, even if that involved performing one duty to the letter of the obligation and paying compensation for a failure to perform the other.

A fiduciary duty arises where a solicitor acts for both parties to a remortgage transaction and if a conflict arises, he must cease to act for one party if permission is not given to disclose otherwise confidential information which casts doubt upon the correctness of the valuation or the good faith of the borrower.[963]

9–267   **Duty when money is being lent.** When a solicitor is acting for a client who is lending money on security, there is a duty to see that the necessary legal steps are taken to make the security proper and sufficient in point of form. For example, the solicitor must make sure that there is no prior incumbrance of which a client was not aware when entering the transaction.[964] However, the solicitor is

---

[959] *Clark Boyce v Mouat* [1994] 1 A.C. 428, PC, applying the dictum in *Boulting v British Association of Cinematograph Television & Allied Technicians* [1963] 2 Q.B. 606. See also *Mortgage Express v Bowerman & Partners* [1995] 2 W.L.R. 607, CA (measure of damages); [1996] 1 P.N.L.R. 62, CA (liability). For the fiduciary duty which arises when a solicitor acts for both sides in a conveyancing transaction, see *Bristol and West B.S. v Mothew* [1998] Ch.1, para.1–21, above. See generally, Leech, "Acting for the insurer and the insured: dual retainers and conflicts of interest" (2009) 1 P.N. 231.
[960] See further para.9–215, above.
[961] [2005] 1 W.L.R. 567, HL per Lord Walker of Gestingthorpe at [29] "the relationship between a solicitor and his client is one in which the client reposes trust and confidence in the solicitor. It is a fiduciary relationship. But not every breach of duty by a fiduciary is a breach of fiduciary duty . . . If a solicitor is careless in investigating a title or drafting a lease, he may be liable to pay damages for breach of his professional duty, but that is not a breach of a fiduciary duty of loyalty; it is simply the breach of a duty to take care."
[962] *Hilton v Barker Booth & Eastwood* [2005] 1 W.L.R. 567, HL at [46].
[963] *Nationwide Building Society v Balmer Radmore* [1999] P.N.L.R. 606, para.9–268, n.973, below.
[964] *Whiteman v Hawkins* (1878) 4 C.P.D. 13.

not liable for any inadequacy in the value of the security,[965] unless instructed to advise on the value of it and such advice is given.[966] Nor is it a breach of duty towards a lender to fail, in the context of a loan secured upon property owned jointly by a husband and wife, to obtain written confirmation, signed by the borrowers' solicitor either that he acts for both parties to the marriage or has advised the wife to obtain independent legal advice.[967]

In *Mortgage Express v Bowerman & Partners*,[968] it was said [969] that if when **9–268** investigating title in the course of a mortgage transaction, "a solicitor discovers facts which a reasonably competent solicitor would realise might have a material bearing on the valuation of the lender's security or some other ingredient of the lending decision, then it is his duty to point it out." But the application of this general principle does depend upon the facts.[970] A solicitor is not normally bound to report to a mortgagee matters going simply to the borrower's creditworthiness.[971] There is an obligation to pass on information obtained in the course of investigating title or preparing for completion which it should be known may cause the mortgagee to doubt the correctness of the valuation or the bona fides of the borrower.[972] The starting point will be the solicitor's instructions and if no attempt is made to qualify them, they will be taken to have been accepted as they stand.[973] The lender's own contributory fault will operate to reduce the damages recoverable, save in those cases where the solicitors are guilty of a breach of

---

[965] *Brinsden v Williams* [1894] 3 Ch.185; *Scholes v Brook* (1891) 63 L.T. 837, affirmed 64 L.T. 674; *Howell v Young* (1826) 5 B. & C. 259; *Stewart v McLean*, 1915 S.C. 13. A solicitor, advising trustees, should advise them as to the rule of the court about the margin of safety between the value of the property and any sum lent on mortgage; *Stokes v Prance* [1898] 1 Ch.212.

[966] *Rae v Meek* (1889) 14 App.Cas. 558; *Morgan v Blyth* [1891] 1 Ch.337.

[967] *Mercantile Credit Co Ltd v Fenwick, The Times*, February 23, 1999, CA.

[968] [1996] 1 P.N.L.R. 62, CA (liability); [1995] Q.B. 375 (measure of damages).

[969] Sir Thomas Bingham M.R. at 69.

[970] *Halifax Mortgage Services Ltd v S & S* [1998] P.N.L.R. 616. See also *Bristol & West Building Society v May, May & Merrimans* [1996] 2 P.N.L.R. 138, *National Home Loans Corp Plc v Giffen Couch & Archer* [1998] 1 W.L.R. 207, CA, n.956 above, and *Nationwide Building Society v Balmer Radmore* [1999] P.N.L.R. 606. See also Halpern and Peacocke, "Are solicitors liable for damages resulting from a fall in the market?" 1996 12 P.N.(3) 77; Russell, "Negligent valuers and solicitors—what's the difference?" C.&F.L. 1997, 9(4), 99 (dealing in particular with the solicitor's duty in relation to secured loans and valuation); Holland, "Acting in mortgage transactions: the solicitor's duty of care" 141 S.J. 1048; Clarke, "A solicitor's duty to lenders" 1997 (9) C.&F.L., 147; Sprince, "The liability of solicitors to lenders on borrower default" (1998) 1 P.N. 3; Riossi, Haggett and Pestell, "Solicitor's duty to lender" 143 S.J. 386.

[971] See, e.g. *National Home Loans Corp Plc v Giffen Couch & Archer* [1998] 1 W.L.R. 207, CA, in which *Bowerman* above was distinguished. The basis of the distinction has been criticised: see, e.g. 141 S.J. 695; also *Halifax Mortgage Services Ltd v S & S* [1998] P.N.L.R. 616 (in which it was suggested that the judgments in the two leading cases could be reconciled only upon the basis that each new case has to be considered upon its merits). In *Nationwide Building Society v Balmer Radmore* [1999] P.N.L.R. 606, Blackburne J. expressed the view (at 634) that the *Bowerman* duty "is a species of obligation which the court will ordinarily imply or find present where a solicitor acts for a borrower in a mortgage transaction except . . . where to do so would be inconsistent with the express terms of the engagement or with the surrounding circumstances of the relationship".

[972] See the summary of many of the cases referred to above in *Nationwide Building Society v Balmer Radmore* [1999] P.N.L.R. 606.

[973] *Nationwide Building Society v Balmer Radmore* [1999] P.N.L.R. 606.

fiduciary duty in addition to their duty of care, in which event all losses are recoverable, subject to the duty to mitigate.[974]

ILLUSTRATIONS

9–269   In accordance with these principles, solicitors have been found negligent where they: failed to report a "back to back" sale and uplift in price[975]; failed to report a sale three months earlier in which the price was significantly less than the amount being lent in the current transaction[976]; failed to report ambiguity surrounding the purchase price and terms of payment[977]; in a remortgage transaction, failed to report not simply the price originally paid by the borrower but the date of his purchase and the reason for mentioning these facts, which would have cast doubt on the valuation[978]; failed to report transactions by the borrower in relation to the property which gave strong evidence of fraud[979]; failed to take heed of the direct payment of a deposit which ought to have alerted them to the suspicious nature of the transaction.[980]

9–270   A solicitor is liable if advice is given to a client about the value of a security, without full disclosure of all material facts known. When a solicitor advised a client to release a security mortgaged to him, representing that a sub-mortgagee had agreed to release it, but failing to point out the difference between the client's position and that of the sub-mortgagee, it was negligent.[981] Where a solicitor failed to tell the claimant widow, his client, about the borrower's untrustworthiness as regards money matters, which fact not only was known to him but made the claimant's loan unwise, it was held that he had been negligent: it was his duty either to advise the claimant of the material facts or, if he felt this would be in breach of professional confidence, to advise her to consult another solicitor.[982] Likewise, where a solicitor failed to make a bankruptcy search against a guarantor, when in possession of information about his financial ill health which the duty of confidentiality prevented being disclosed to the lender.[983] Where a solicitor had proceeded by letting a client sign a contract to purchase a house, whilst an application for a mortgage was still outstanding, in spite of warning of the risk that he might lose his deposit, the solicitor was not liable. His duty was sufficiently discharged by giving his client the warning of the risk, which he then decided to incur.[984]

---

[974] See further Ch.5, para.5–45, above.
[975] *Nationwide Building Society v ATM Abdullah & Co* [1999] Lloyd's Rep. P.N. 616. See also *Nationwide Building Society v JR Jones* [1999] Lloyd's Rep. P.N. 414 (again a "back to back" sale).
[976] *Nationwide Building Society v Archdeacons* [1999] Lloyd's Rep. P.N. 549.
[977] *Nationwide Building Society v Vanderpump & Sykes* [1999] Lloyd's Rep. P.N. 422.
[978] *Nationwide Building Society v Littlestone & Cowan* [1999] Lloyd's Rep. P.N. 625.
[979] *Nationwide Building Society v Goodwin Harte* [1999] Lloyd's Rep. P.N. 338 (also a breach of fiduciary duty).
[980] *Nationwide Building Society v Richard Grosse & Co* [1999] Lloyd's Rep. P.N. 348.
[981] *Nocton v Ashburton* [1914] A.C. 932.
[982] *Neushul v Mellish and Harkavy* (1967) 111 S.J. 399.
[983] *Omega Trust Co Ltd v Wright Son & Pepper (No.2)* [1998] P.N.L.R. 337.
[984] *Buckland v Mackesy* (1968), 112 S.J. 841.

Taking care of documents. A solicitor is under a duty to take reasonable care **9–271** of all documents provided by a client, and not to disclose any confidential information which the client has communicated. Breach of this duty will lead to liability for damage suffered by the client as a result.[985] When a will is retained by solicitors by whom it was drawn, they are under a duty to take reasonable steps to trace the executor and inform him of the contents of the will following the death of the testatrix.[986] Where a claimant sues his former solicitor for negligence, he thereby brings the confidential relationship that existed between them into the public arena and impliedly waives legal professional privilege in relation to any communication between them, so far as necessary to resolve the claim.[987]

Explaining the effect of documents. Where a solicitor is involved in a **9–272** negotiation on behalf of a client, there will usually be a duty to understand the import of documents upon which the negotiation depends and to correct any apparent misunderstanding of the client as to the documents' effect. So where, in the course of a meeting connected with the acquisition of property, the claimant made statements which ought to have alerted her solicitor to the fact that she did not understand the Green Belt procedure and the effect of an option was dependent upon that procedure being correctly understood, the solicitor was negligent.[988]

No duty to advise on business matters. A solicitor is under a duty to advise **9–273** his client on law but not, *absent* express agreement, on matters of business. There is no duty to remind a client of the approach of the date for giving notice to determine a lease[989] or, when retained to give general advice to a claimant, who was contemplating publishing her memoirs, to give advice which would allow her to avoid incurring a substantial tax liability by organising her affairs differently.[990] While it has been said that a solicitor is under no duty to advise an apparently competent client about the wisdom of a particular transaction,[991] a distinction has been drawn where it is alleged that the transaction is tainted by undue influence. So, solicitors were in breach of duty where in advising the claimant wife in relation to a mortgage transaction for the benefit of a business in which her husband had a controlling interest, they failed to ensure that she was

---

[985] *Weld-Blundell v Stephens* [1920] A.C. 956 (action against an accountant for negligently communicating confidential instructions).

[986] *Hawkins v Clayton* (1988) 78 A.L.R. 69. (In 1970 B made her will, appointing H as sole executor and leaving him the residue of her estate. The will was held by her solicitors for safe keeping. The testatrix died in 1975 and her solicitors, being aware of the death, took certain steps in the estate but did not try to locate H until 1981. By then the main asset of the deceased's estate, a house, had been lying empty for many years and had been allowed to fall into serious disrepair).

[987] *Paragon Finance Plc (formerly National Home Loans Corp Plc) v Freshfields, The Times*, March 22, 1999, CA.

[988] *Clarke v Iliffes Booth Bennett* [2004] EWHC 1731 (the claimant recovered only nominal damages because the court was not satisfied that, had her misunderstanding been corrected, the transaction would not have proceeded).

[989] *Yager v Fishman & Co* [1944] 1 All E.R. 552.

[990] *Duchess of Argyll v Beuselinck* [1972] 2 Lloyd's Rep. 172.

[991] *Clark Boyce v Mouat* [1994] 1 A.C. 428, PC.

acting free of any undue influence from him. If not satisfied that she was acting of her own free will, they should have declined to act further.[992]

9–274   It was not incumbent upon solicitors acting for the claimant in the sale of shares to a limited company, to advise him in respect of the wisdom of the transaction. An indemnity was provided by the company against any liability that might arise under a guarantee the claimant had given and from which he could not secure his release. It was said that the scope of a solicitor's duty towards his client, in a case not involving litigation, should reflect the instructions given. The transaction involved no hidden pitfalls, the claimant was an experienced businessman, and the possibility that the company might not at some subsequent time have the means to satisfy the indemnity was a commercial risk of which he could be expected to be aware.[993]

9–275   **Time-limit for action against negligent solicitor.** Although there is concurrent liability upon solicitors in contract and tort,[994] for purposes of limitation, time will not necessarily begin to run in each cause of action at the same moment. Generally in contract time runs from the date of breach, while in tort from the date damage is suffered.[995] So, where solicitors negligently exchanged contracts granting an option, the date at which damages fell to be assessed was the date the cause of action in tort accrued, namely upon the exchange, not when the option was exercised.[996] Where a negligent solicitor fails to bring proceedings within the limitation period, it has been held that the cause of action accrues once the relevant period of limitation has expired. It is then that the defendant to the client's claim acquires immunity from action and the client suffers measurable damage, in that the remedy which remains is of very different quality to that which existed prior to the expiry of limitation.[997] In contrast, where a solicitor gives negligent advice there is no presumption that damage occurs when such

---

[992] *Kenyon-Brown v Desmond Banks & Co* [2000] P.N.L.R. 266, CA (an earlier mortgage transaction should have put the solicitors on notice of the possibility of undue influence, and also the fact that the instant transaction was such as no client could be sensibly advised to undertake); see also *Royal Bank of Scotland Plc v Etridge (No.2)* [1998] 4 All E.R. 705, CA.

[993] *Pickersgill v Riley* [2004] P.N.L.R. 606, PC. See Clover and Robson, "*Pickersgill v Riley*—The extent of a solicitor's duty to advise"(2004) 3 P.N. 146. See also *John Mowlem Construction Plc v Neil F. Jones & Co* [2004] P.N.L.R. 48, CA, para.9–214 above (no duty to advise about insurance where the client was perfectly able to comprehend its own insurance position); also *Powell v Whitman Breed Abbot & Morgan* [2005] P.N.L.R. 1 (liability was established in a claim against a solicitor for negligent advice in relation to the acquisition by the claimant of a leasehold investment property using a company nominated by her, rather than by her personally).

[994] See para.9–214, above; also, Ch.4, paras 4–150 to 4–160, above.

[995] e.g. *Lee v Thompson* [1989] E.G. 89, CA. See, generally, Ch.4, para.4–150. In *Commissioner of Taxation v Zimmerlie* (1989) 91 F.L.R. 81 a solicitor who drafted an agreement for the sale of his client's share in a partnership failed negligently to provide for an indemnity in respect of liability for any amended assessment of tax: damage was identified as loss of the right to indemnity and not the liability to pay tax, and the client's remedy was time-barred. Loss of that right occurred when the client bound herself by a contract which did not contain an indemnity clause but ought to have contained one.

[996] *Amerena v Barling* [1993] E.G.C.S. 28. Similarly, if a solicitor negligently fails to warn his client that a lease he proposes to acquire has been extended under the Leasehold Reform Act 1967, time runs from the date of acquisition, the lease then not having the value assumed, not from the later date when he elects to exercise a right to buy: *Sullivan v Layton Lougher & Co* [1995] 49 E.G. 127, CA. Where damage is "latent" see Ch.4, para.4–219, above.

[997] *Doundoulakis v Sdrinis & Co* [1989] V.R. 791, Sup. Ct of Victoria.

advice is acted upon: it is a question of fact in each case whether actual damage has been established and when it occurred.[998] So long as actual damage arises, it matters not that it may be nominal, time runs all the same.[999]

ILLUSTRATIONS[1000]

Where a claim could be founded equally in contract and tort, a claimant, who   **9–276**
failed to obtain a good title to certain land because of his solicitors' negligence, could rely on whichever cause of action gave the more favourable position under a statute of limitations.[1001] Where solicitors were in breach of a continuing duty to register an estate contract up until the time that a third party's transaction rendered such registration ineffectual, neither of causes of action in contract or tort was statute-barred where the third party's action occurred within six years of commencement of the proceedings.[1002] Where a solicitors' failure to give proper advice resulted in the claimant's entering into a mortgage deed, charging her property as security for repayment of a loan, it was held that her cause of action in negligence accrued immediately she signed the deed. It was then that the damage crystallised, since it was quantifiable and, therefore, actual, irrespective of whether or not any subsequent demand was made upon her by the mortgagor. [1003] Where the claimant, who had been injured in a road accident, lost the chance to recover his losses, either from the driver or his own insurers, as a result of breach of their contractual duty by his professional advisers, it was held that because the measure of damages did not consist of or include damages for personal injuries, the proviso to s.2(1) of the Limitation Act 1939[1004] did not apply to reduce the six-year limitation period to one of three years.[1005] Where the claimant alleged that solicitors were negligent in failing to obtain security of tenure for her on the conveyance of a house to herself and another person as tenants in common, her cause of action arose at the time of the conveyance, when she did not obtain what she wanted, rather than later when a compromise agreement was reached giving her a tenancy of the first floor.[1006]

---

[998] *D.W. Moore & Co Ltd v Ferrier* [1981] 1 W.L.R. 267, CA (where solicitors gave negligent advice to insurance brokers about the effect of a trade restriction covenant with someone who sought to join their business and later branched out on his own, damage occurred at the time of executing the agreements because it was then the claimants received a worthless covenant) applying *Forster v Outred & Co* [1982] 1 W.L.R. 86, CA.

[999] See *Bell v Peter Browne & Co* [1990] 2 Q.B. 495. See also, *Law Society v Sephton & Co* [2006] 2 AC 543, Ch.4, para.4–159, above.

[1000] See also the examples at Ch.4, para.4–160, above.

[1001] *Power v Halley* (1978) 88 D.L.R. 381.

[1002] *Midland Bank Trust Co Ltd v Hett, Stubbs & Kemp* [1979] Ch.384.

[1003] *Forster v Outred & Co* [1982] 1 W.L.R. 86, applied in *D.W. Moore & Co Ltd v Ferrier* [1981] 1 W.L.R. 267, CA, above. See Dedman, "Professional Negligence—A Note on *Forster v Outred & Co*" 78 L.S.Gaz. 953; Hewitt, "Professional Negligence: Latent Economic Damage and Limitation" 81 L.S.Gaz. 3333.

[1004] See now the provisions of the Limitation Act 1980, s.11.

[1005] *Ackbar v C.F. Green & Co Ltd* [1975] Q.B. 582, following *McGahie v Union of Shop Distributive and Allied Workers*, 1966 S.L.T. 74 (the professional advisers were insurance brokers, who had failed to carry out the claimant's instructions to obtain passenger liability insurance for a lorry, in which he was injured but the principle should apply equally to actions against negligent solicitors)..

[1006] *Baker v Ollard & Bentley* (1982) 126 S.J. 593, CA (The fact that her loss could not be quantified until the later date was immaterial). See further, *Law Society v Sephton & Co*, n.999, above.

9-277   An action against a negligent solicitor in respect of his failure to prosecute a claim for personal injuries with due diligence is not itself "an action . . . where the damages claimed by the plaintiff . . . consist of or include damages in respect of personal injuries", so as to attract the three-year time-limit laid down by s.11(1) of the Limitation Act 1980.[1007]

(C) Causation and Damage

9-278   **Generally.** In many cases, particularly where a solicitor's negligence consists in giving or failing to give proper advice, there will be more than one cause of the loss that has arisen. There is a distinction between a breach of duty which merely gives the occasion for loss and one which is the substantial cause of that loss.[1008] The immediate cause of loss will probably be some risk or event which the claimant alleges ought to have been foreseen and of which he should have been warned. In deciding whether the solicitor's breach was the effective cause of the claimant's damage in such cases the question is "whether the particular loss was within the reasonable scope of the dangers against which it was the solicitor's duty to provide protection."[1009]

9-279   **Identifying the scope of the duty.** The importance of defining the scope of the duty has already been stated generally.[1010] Whether viewed from the perspective of causation, or from the perspective of remoteness of damage there must be a proper correlation between a breach of duty and the loss claimed. A proper emphasis on that correlation so far as claims against professionals are concerned is not always apparent from some of the cases decided before *South Australia Asset Management Corporation v York Montague Ltd*[1011] in 1996. While that group of appeals concerned, inter alia, the approach to causation of loss in the context of a valuer's negligence, there were also implications for the similar exercise that has to be carried out in some cases of negligence by a solicitor. In particular, in considering the scope of the duty of care a distinction was drawn between a professional person's giving of advice and the provision of information. A correct analysis should therefore include what type of duty was being undertaken and its scope.

[1007] See, e.g. *Hopkins v MacKenzie* [1995] P.I.Q.R. P43, CA, *Ackbar v C.F. Green & Co Ltd*, below.

[1008] See Glidewell L.J. in *Galoo Ltd v Bright Grahame Murray* [1994] 1 W.L.R. 1360, 1370 and 1374–1375.

[1009] per Carnwath J. in *British Racing Driver's Club Ltd v Hextall Erskine & Co* [1996] 3 All E.R. 667 at 681 (solicitors liable for a reduction in the value of the shares of a company where the immediate cause of the reduction was the flawed commercial judgment of the directors in approving the purchase of an interest in a motor retail business, but the solicitors had been negligent in failing to advise that, because of one director's interest in the business, prior approval of the transaction had to be sought from the members of the company, pursuant to s.320 of the Companies Act 1985). See further para.9–281 below.

[1010] See Ch.2, para.2–04, Ch.6, para.6–04, above.

[1011] [1997] A.C. 191. Sprince, "South Australia and solicitors: does the umbrella leak?" (2000) 3 P.N. 139; Kinskey, "SAAMCO 10 years on: causation and scope of duty in professional negligence cases" (2006) 2 P.N. 86.

"Wrong information" claims. In SAAMCO the basic principle was   **9–280**
expressed as follows:

> "a person under a duty to take reasonable care to provide information on which
> someone else will decide a course of action is, if negligent, not generally regarded as
> responsible for all the consequences of that course of action. He is responsible only for
> the consequences of the information being wrong."[1012]

By way of example, where solicitors' were negligent in failing to inform a lender
in a mortgage transaction that they did not have an official search certificate on
which it could rely for title, it was not enough for the claimant to establish that
the transaction would not have proceeded had it been informed of the true
position: in fact the title taken was a good one and the lender's loss arose because
the borrower did not have the means to meet the instalments due under the
mortgage, and that loss would have arisen in any event.[1013] It should be noted that
the distinction between allegations of negligent advice and allegations of failure
to provide information, may not always be apt to cases of solicitors' negligence,
where, depending upon the facts, a foreseeability test may be preferred.[1014]

"Bad advice" claims. When analysing causation in claims based upon a   **9–281**
solicitor's advice there is a difference between claims based on a failure to give
advice at all and those based upon the giving of incorrect advice. In the first the
claimant has to show what advice should have been given and, on a balance of
probability, that with such advice a particular transaction would not have been
entered or, if if it was entered, that it would not have been entered it upon
particular terms. In the second it is enough to prove reliance upon the incorrect
advice. It is not necessary for the claimant also to prove he would not have acted
as he did if proper advice had been given.[1015] The measure of loss for bad advice
is likely to depend upon the damage suffered as a result of the inaccuracy of the
advice given, or the failure to give advice. The solicitor is not responsible for all

---

[1012] *South Australia Asset Management Corporation v York Montague Ltd* [1997] A.C. 191 at 214. As
to the distinction between providing advice and information see further *Michael Gerson Investments
Ltd v Haines Watts* [2002] P.N.L.R. 761. The distinction has been criticised as a "false dichotomy":
see Jones, (2007) 1 P.N. 55, commenting on *Andrews v Barnett Waddingham* [2006] P.N.L.R. 24,
CA.
[1013] *Bristol and West Building Society v Fancy & Jackson* [1997] 4 All E.R. 582.
[1014] *Omega Trust Co Ltd v Wright Son & Pepper (No.2)* [1998] P.N.L.R. 337, at 359 (it was a
foreseeable consequence of solicitors' failure to provide correct information about a guarantor's
bankruptcy that a loan would be made and subsequently lost). See *Peterson v Personal Representatives of Rivlin* [2002] Lloyd's Rep. P.N. 386, CA, where the information/advice distinction *was*
applied (a property transaction where the solicitor negligently failed to make clear the amount of the
claimant's potential liability under an indemnity, but only nominal damages could be recovered).
[1015] *Bristol and West BS v Mothew* [1998] Ch.1 (where a solicitor acting for both the sellers and a
building society making a mortgage advance negligently failed to inform the society of a second
charge upon the property, but the defendant argued that even if the true facts had been known the loan
would still have been made). *Downs v Chappell* [1997] 1 W.L.R. 426, although overruled on a
different point by *Smith New Court Securities Ltd v Scrimgeour Vickers (Asset Management) Ltd*
[1997] A.C. 254 is an example of the second situation (once the buyer of a business established that
he had relied upon a negligent misrepresentation as to its profitability, it was unnecessary to examine
whether, had true figures been disclosed, he would have proceeded nonetheless). For criticism of the
reasoning in *Mothew* see O'Sullivan "Acts, omissions and negligent professionals: confusion over
counterfactuals" (2001) 4 P.N. 272.

the consequences of his bad advice, but only those caused by the inaccuracy. [1016] The loss actually incurred will have to be compared with that which would have been suffered if the transaction in question had not been entered into and the element of loss attributable to inaccurate advice identified.

9–282   **Measure of damages.** The broad and fundamental principle as to damages[1017] remains as stated over a century ago by Lord Blackburn, in *Livingstone v The Rawyards Coal Co*[1018]: the measure of damages is "that sum of money which will put the party who has been injured, or who has suffered, in the same position as he would have been in if he had not sustained the wrong for which he is now getting his compensation or reparation".[1019] The time at which damages are ordinarily assessed is the date of breach, but the rule is not invariably applied if, for instance, assessment at another date more fairly reflects the overriding compensatory principle.[1020] The damages awarded may encompass not merely pecuniary loss, but also damages for psychiatric injury where that is a foreseeable result of the solicitor's breach of duty.[1021] Physical inconvenience and distress may be recovered where foreseeable.[1022] But where the negligent solicitor was not instructed in some transaction which had as its object the provision of comfort or pleasure for the claimant, or the relief of discomfort, it is unlikely that damages for emotional distress falling short of a psychiatric illness can be awarded.[1023]

[1016] See above para.9–278, also the discussion at para.9–327, below. See also *Bristol and West BS v Mothew* [1998] Ch.1 and *Swindle v Harrison, The Times*, April 17, 1997, CA ; also *Roker House Investments Ltd v Saunders* [1997] E.G.C.S. 137 (negligent failure by solicitors to advise on the invalidity of a guarantee given by a lessee). See also Tomlinson and Grant, "Property finance negligence and damages after BBL" 140 S.J. 654; also Halpern and Peacocke, "Are solicitors liable for damages resulting from a fall in the market?" (1996) 3 P.N. 77.

[1017] See, further, Ch.5, above, generally.

[1018] (1880) 5 App.Cas. 25, applied in *Dodd Properties v Canterbury City Council* [1980] 1 W.L.R. 433.

[1019] *Livingstone v The Rawyards Coal Co* (1880) 5 App.Cas. 25 at 39.

[1020] *Portman BS v Bevan Ashford* [2000] P.N.L.R. 344, CA; also *Wapshot v Davies Donovan & Co* [1996] P.N.L.R. 361 (defective leases); *Kennedy v K.B. Van Emden* [1996] P.N.L.R. P409, CA (per Nourse L.J.: the mechanistic application of rules such as the diminution in value rule and the rule as to assessment of damages at the date of breach rather than the day of trial to give way, where appropriate, to the overriding compensatory principle in *Livingstone v Raywards Coal Co*). See also *Veitch v Avery* [2008] P.N.L.R. 7, CA (where negligent advice was given by a solicitor to consent to a suspended possession order on a property run as a country house hotel, the date for the assessment of loss was properly the date upon which the possession order became effective, at which time the net value of the business was less than the claimants' equity in it, entitling them only to nominal damages).

[1021] See, e.g. *Malyon v Lawrance, Messer & Co* [1968] 2 Lloyd's Rep. 539 (the solicitor's negligence extended the claimant's period of recovery from psychiatric injury after a road traffic accident).

[1022] *Wapshot v Davies Donovan & Co* [1996] P.N.L.R. 361 above (physical discomfort and distress arising from cramped living conditions).

[1023] *Hayes v Dodd* [1990] 2 All E.R. 815, CA; also *Bailey v Bullock* [1950] 2 All E.R. 1167 (after a negligent failure to serve a notice to quit, so that the claimant was unable to gain possession of a house, the cost of storing furniture, garage expenses and general damages for inconvenience and discomfort were recovered, although not for annoyance and mental distress); also *Channon v Lindley Johnstone* [2002] P.N.L.R. 884, CA, para.9–292, below (no award appropriate for inconvenience and distress arising from the negligent conduct of matrimonial property proceedings). See also in relation to mental distress, the cases at para.9–299, below.

Claims arising from the acquisition of property. In claims against solicitors 9–283
arising from defective investigation of title, or other negligence by which a
property is less valuable to the buyer than it should have been, the starting point
in assessing the measure of the claimants' loss is usually a diminution of value
test, that is, the difference between the market value of the property in question
and the price paid.[1024] Where a client loses the opportunity of acquiring property
at a particular price, the test is usually the difference between the market value
of the property and the price the client had agreed to pay.[1025] But these tests are
not invariably applied and will give way, where appropriate, to the overriding
compensatory principle.[1026]

ILLUSTRATIONS

Where a buyer wished to buy premises for £53,750 but, owing to his solicitors' **9–284**
negligence, they were sold elsewhere, which resulted in the buyer's eventually
having to pay £92,500 in order to buy the property, then of a market value of
£75,000, it was held that the amount recoverable was restricted to the difference
between £53,750 and £75,000 only.[1027] Where a solicitor gave negligent advice
that land his client was buying was free from a restriction to which it was in fact
subject, the measure of damages was the difference between the market value of
the land and the price paid, not the difference in market value with and without
the restriction.[1028] When a solicitor negligently failed to detect a flaw in the title
of the seller of land, it was said that the measure of damages was the difference
between the market value at the date of breach had a good title been given and
the market value with a defective title.[1029] The buyer was not required to mitigate
his loss by suing the seller on his covenant for title "in order to protect his
solicitor from his own carelessness". The cost of a valuation required by the
buyer's bankers and interest on an overdraft which remained undischarged
because the property could not be sold were not awarded, as being outside the
contemplation of the parties at the date of breach. Also, where solicitors were
negligent in failing to inform their client, a property development company, of a
defect in the title of a property which it would not otherwise have purchased, the
judge was entitled to take as the measure of loss, the difference in value of the
property with and without the defect.

[1024] *Piper v Daybell Court-Cooper* [1969] 210 E.G. 1047 (solicitor failed to inform his client, the
buyer of a house, of a right of way over the premises in favour of a neighbour); also *Wapshot v Davies
Donovan & Co* [1996] P.N.L.R. 361, above. But in *County Personnel (Employment Agency) Ltd v
Alan Pulver & Co* [1987] 1 W.L.R. 916, at 925, Bingham L.J. stressed that the rule was not an
invariable one. See also the summary of Lawrence Collins J. in *Greymalkin Ltd v Copleys* [2004]
P.N.L.R. 44, CA, n.1030 below, at [72] onwards.
[1025] See, e.g. *Nash v Phillips* (1974) 232 E.G. 1219.
[1026] For which see para.9–282, above.
[1027] *Simpson v Grove Tompkins & Co, The Times*, May 17, 1982, CA. See Brandler, 132 New L.J. 807
and Wise, 133 New L.J. 900.
[1028] *Ford v White* [1964] 1 W.L.R. 885; *Simple Simon Catering v Binstock Miller & Co* (1973) 117
S.J. 529; *Dent v Davis Blank Furniss* [2001] Lloyd's Rep. P.N. 534 (diminution in value test applied
where solicitors failed to search the commons register and after their client built a substantial property
on the land acquired, it emerged that part of the land was common land).
[1029] *Pilkington v Wood* [1953] Ch.770.

9–285   Claims for the cost of carrying out works to the property, and other costs involved in maintaining it before the defect was discovered, failed, where what had been done had actually enhanced the property's value.[1030] When, as a result of their solicitor's negligence, the claimants lost the protection of the Landlord and Tenant Act 1954 Pt II, and their lease of garage premises was determined, they were entitled to recover lost profits for such time as they might reasonably have been made, but account was not taken of the loss of other of the claimants' businesses which they had allowed to run down and be sold.[1031] Where solicitors gave negligent advice as to the effect of a sub lease when a commercial property investment company was contemplating the purchase of office premises, the appropriate date for assessment of the damages was the date of judgment, by which time it had been decided in an arbitration that the sub lease in fact operated as an assignment. The measure of damages was not the difference in value between the price paid and the value of the premises with vacant possession, but, given the solicitors knowledge of the purpose of the premises'acquisition, the reduction in income stream between that actually received and that which would have been received from another hypothetical property that may have been acquired had the transcation not taken place.[1032]

9–286   Where a solicitor negligently failed to advise a buyer that a premium sought by the seller was unlawful so that, as matter stood at the date of purchase, the buyer could not herself have effected a transfer of the property at such a premium, but the law was subsequently changed, it was held inappropriate to assess damages on the basis of the diminution in value at the date the property was acquired: by the date of trial the change in the law had restored her to the position she ought to have been in from the outset.[1033]

9–287   **Other claims arising from the negligent conduct of non-contentious business.** Where solicitors who were advancing a bridging loan to a client who had mortgaged her home to purchase another property, negligently failed to tell her that her son's bank was unwilling to provide a reference, which could mean he was unable to secure a loan to assist with the purchase, and failed to tell her that they themselves would profit from the bridging loan transaction, she failed to recover damages representing the value of the lost equity in her home. In the absence of fraud she was entitled only to be put in the position she would have been had the breaches of duty not occurred and in that event she would still have completed the loan and thereby suffered the same loss.[1034]

9–288   Where solicitors were guilty of negligent delay in carrying out instructions of the executrix of a deceased person's estate and as a result the beneficiaries were

---

[1030] *Greymalkin Ltd v Copleys* [2004] P.N.L.R. 44, CA.

[1031] *Matlock Green Garage Ltd v Potter Brooke Taylor & Wildgoose* [2000] Lloyd's Rep. P.N. 935.

[1032] *Keydon Estates Ltd v Eversheds LLP* [2005] P.N.L.R. 817.

[1033] *Kennedy v K.B. Van Emden & Co* [1996] P.N.L.R. P409, CA.

[1034] *Swindle v Harrison, The Times,* April 17, 1997, CA; also *Lloyds Bank Plc v Crosse & Crosse* [2001] P.N.L.R. 830, CA (solicitors acting in the purchase of land who failed to draw to their client's attention a restrictive covenant were liable only to the extent that the land acquired was less valuable than it would otherwise have been).

deprived of rental income from property forming part of the estate, the executrix was able to recover the loss. She was to be treated in law as the owner of the property and therefore entitled to recover damages, even though the loss had actually been sustained by the beneficiaries who would, had the solicitors acted promptly, have been in receipt of the rental income at an earlier time. The executrix would have to account to the beneficiaries for such sums as were recovered.[1035]

Negligence in the course of a contentious case. Here, the recoverable loss will again depend in the first instance on the scope of the solicitor's duty. Liability does not extend to all consequences flowing from, for instance, delay in bringing a case to trial, only those which are strictly referable to the duty to prosecute an action with reasonable expedition. So where such delay resulted in a case being heard at a time after the defendant had gone into liquidation and judgment could not be enforced, the court had to consider when the solicitors should have become aware of the defendant's financial difficulties and thereafter the earliest date that with due diligence the case could have been brought to trial.[1036]   **9–289**

Where the allegation is that as a result of a solicitor's negligence the claimant has lost the opportunity to pursue or defend a claim, there is a legal burden to show that what was lost had value, that is, there was a real and substantial as opposed to negligible prospect of success. Assuming that burden is discharged, the court will then have to evaluate the chance that has been lost, by making a realistic assessment of the prospects of success had the action been fought out.[1037] It is neither necessary nor proper to come to a definitive conclusion about how the original action would have been decided: the parties are different and the passage of time means that the evidence cannot be assumed to be in the second action as it would have been in the first. These principles will apply where, for instance, a solicitor fails to issue proceedings within the limitation period, or having issued them, fails to pursue them timeously so that they are struck out: if the claim enjoyed good prospects of success it may be that no, or only a small, deduction will be made from the damages recovered to take account of litigation risk.[1038] Should they have been very poor, the claim for damages may fail altogether, or only a nominal sum be recovered.[1039] In assessing prospects of success following a strike out, the starting point should be the earlier judge's conclusion that no fair trial is possible. It is not for the judge assessing those   **9–290**

[1035] *Chappell v Somers & Blake* [2004] Ch.19. See also *Westbury v Sampson* [2001] 2 F.C.R. 210 (no causative link was established where a solicitor admitted failure to advise a matrimonial client of the court's power to vary a lump sum instalment order, where in light of the changed circumstances, the paying party could have appealed the original order out of time).

[1036] *Pearson v Sanders Witherspoon*, *The Independent*, December 6, 1999, CA (where the CA made deductions from the recoverable claims both for the prospects of success and the chances of ultimate recovery).

[1037] *Mount v Baker Austin* [1998] P.N.L.R. 493, CA, per Simon Brown LJ at 510.

[1038] *Kitchen v Royal Air Force Association* [1958] 1 W.L.R. 563, per Lord Evershed M.R. at 574.

[1039] *Kitchen v Royal Air Force Association* [1958] 1 W.L.R. 563 and see the cases cited at n.292 below.

prospects to try issues of which a fair trial was at the earlier stage held impossible.[1040]

9–291   The prospects of success for a "lost" claim require an analysis of the contingencies which would have determined its success or failure.[1041] The assessment in favour of a successful claimant should be a generous one, given that it was the defendant's negligence which caused loss of the chance of succeeding in full or fuller measure.[1042] As part of the exercise, the court must decide when the original claim would have been heard, and assess damages as they would have been assessed at that date.[1043] However, the benefits of hindsight should not be ignored when assessing exactly what the claimant has lost.[1044] In Australia it has been held that where the negligence is in failing to prosecute the claim with due diligence, so that it is struck out, damages should be assessed as at the date of dismissal.[1045] In some cases it may be appropriate to take into account the possibility of compromise.[1046] Where the claim is for loss of the chance to settle earlier proceedings on favourable terms, and the court assessing damages does not hear from the other party to the original dispute, a discount for uncertainty should be made unless the court is certain or very close to certain as to what terms of settlement were available.[1047] The rate of interest to be awarded

---

[1040] *Sharif v Garret & Co* [2002] 1 W.L.R. 3118, CA, n.53 below, per Tuckey L.J. at 3125.

[1041] *Yardley v Coombes* (1963) 107 S.J. 575 (two thirds deduction for risks in personal injury claim with reasonable chances of success); *Gregory v Tarlow* (1964) 108 S.J. 219 (claimant recovered three-quarters of the damages it was thought it was likely he would have recovered against his employers).

[1042] *Sharif v Garret & Co*, n.998, above, per Brown L.J. at 3129.

[1043] *Charles v Hugh James Jones & Jenkins* [2000] P.I.Q.R. P1, CA (in an accident case, if an entirely new condition manifests itself for the first time after the trial date it may have to be ignored: but if the condition had appeared before the notional trial date but the prognosis was uncertain the court is entitled to take it into account).

[1044] *Dudarec v Andrews* [2006] 1 W.L.R. 3002, CA (a claim against solicitors after a personal injuries action was struck out as a result of their negligence: they alleged that the claimant's damages would have been reduced by reason of a failure to have surgery for a condition which was thought to have been caused by his accident; in fact it subsequently emerged that an operation was not required at all). See further Evans, "Lost litigation and later knowledge" 2007 P.N. (4), 204. See also *Whitehead v Searle* [2009] 1 W.L.R. 549, CA. (After she had commenced proceedings for negligence against a hospital authority, alleging negligence at and before the birth of her child, who was born suffering spina bifida, the mother committed suicide. The action was continued by her estate and compromised. A second action was then commenced on behalf of the estate against its former solicitors, alleging negligent failure to bring the first case to a successful outcome before the mother's death, thereby depriving her estate of damages calculated without reference to her actual life expectancy. The claim failed: events should not be ignored simply because they had happened after the notional original trial and were unknowable at that time. The law should not speculate when it knows. There had been no judgment so nothing upon which the need for finality should bite). See Counsell, "An unjustified windfall?" 158 N.L.J. 879.

[1045] *Johnson v Perez* (1988) 82 A.L.R. 587; *Nikolaou v Papasavas, Phillips & Co* (1988) 82 A.L.R. 587.

[1046] *Dickinson v James Alexander & Co* [1993] F.L.R. 521, above; also *Harrison v Bloom Camillin* [2001] P.N.L.R. 195 (Neuberger J. applied *Mount* above, adding that the court should be far readier to decide whether the claimant would have failed or succeeded on a point of law than on a point of fact or opinion).

[1047] *Maden v Clifford Coppock & Carter* [2005] P.N.L.R. 112, CA (on the facts, a discount of 20 per cent to take account of uncertainty was appropriate). See Braithwaite, "Chance calculation" 148 S.J. 838: also generally, Browne-Wilkinson, "Recent developments in the law of damages" 2004 P.N. (3), 152.

on the amount of damages against a negligent solicitor is that of a judgment debt.[1048]

Solicitors were liable to pay damages for the lost chance of success on appeal, **9–292** assessed at one-third when they failed to advise their client of the two-week time-limit for lodging an appeal following an arbitration[1049]; and where a solicitor, who represented a prisoner charged with the crime of robbery, failed to trace and to have available a witness to support an alibi, the accused, after conviction, was awarded nominal damages.[1050] Where solicitors gave negligent advice as to the appropriate sum to accept in settlement of a wife's financial claims against her husband, the measure of damages was held to be the difference between the amount she accepted and the value of her proper claim, subject to a one-third discount for litigation risk.[1051] In another matrimonial property case where the solicitors' preparation was negligent, the court valued the lost chance of a better result by discounting by 20 per cent the best result their client could have achieved.[1052] Although a solicitor acting for a wife in matrimonial proceedings for ancillary relief ought to have foreseen the risk of the husband's insolvency and advised in relation to it, her claim in negligence failed where the probability of some negotiated settlement before the bankruptcy materialised was fanciful.[1053] Where a pedestrian's accident claim failed because solicitors failed to give the appropriate notice to insurers under the Road Traffic Act 1988, it was not correct to say that she had lost nothing of value, where both the solicitors themselves and counsel had advised there were prospects of success.[1054]

A case study. The difficulties of assessing the prospects of success for **9–293** complex litigation, which has failed as a result of a solicitor's negligence, can be seen in *Hanif v Middleweeks*.[1055] The claim had been against insurers who had declined to indemnify the claimant after a fire. It was struck out for want of prosecution but not before the insurers had raised three main lines of defence. At

---

[1048] *Pinnock v Wilkins & Sons, The Times*, January 29, 1990. This is on the basis that the solicitor's negligence had prevented the claimant from obtaining a judgment which could have carried with it interest at such a rate.

[1049] *Corfield v D.S. Bosher & Co* [1992] 1 E.G.L.R. 163.

[1050] *Scudder v Prothero and Prothero* (1966) 110 S.J. 248. This decision was doubted by the HL in *Rondel v Worsley* [1969] 1 A.C. 191 at 231, per Lord Reid.

[1051] *McNamara v Martin Mears & Co* (1983) 127 S.J. 69. but cf. also *Dickinson v Jones Alexander & Co*, above where no discount was applied for the hazards of litigation. *Dickinson* was followed in *Sharples v Coole & Haddock* (1995) C.L.Y. 1832, CA (where solicitors failed to include an effective prayer for ancillary relief in a divorce petition, the correct measure of loss was the entitlement calculated by reference to ss.23–25 of the Matrimonial Causes Act 1973, not an informal agreement made between the parties without the benefit of legal advice). See also, *Browning v Brachers* [2005] EWCA Civ 753 (negligent preparation of a counterclaim based upon breach of a contract for the purchase of a herd of goats).

[1052] *Channon v Lindley Johnstone* [2002] P.N.L.R. 884, CA.

[1053] *Burke v Chapman and Chubb* [2008] B.P.I.R. 266.

[1054] *Sharpe v Addison (t/a Addison Lister)* [2004] P.N.L.R. 426, CA (the claimant recovered 10 per cent of the value of her claim, there being a 40 per cent chance that she would recover 75 per cent of the appropriate damages).

[1055] [2000] Lloyd's Rep. P.N. 920, CA.

the assessment of damages the judge identified the prospects for each argument in percentage terms: 25 per cent on the main issue and 80 per cent and 20 per cent respectively on subsidiary issues. He arrived at an overall chance of success of 25 per cent. The defendants' appeal succeeded in part. Their primary contention that mathematically the judge's findings suggested an overall chance of success of 12 per cent failed: but the Court of Appeal considered that, having come to a 25 per cent finding on the principal issue, the judge should then have reduced the overall figure to 20 per cent, to represent the chances on the subsidiary issues. It is to be hoped that, in cases of complexity, where many factual and legal findings may have gone one way or the other, a broad brush approach to the overall prospects of success would find at least as much favour on appeal as arithmetical assessment: the more complicated the original claim would have been to pursue, the more difficult for a court subsequently to arrive at a precise estimate of the result.[1056]

9–294   There is a significant evidential burden upon solicitors if they wish to show that in fact litigation which has failed through their negligence was of no value to their former client.[1057] Where claimants sought to recover damages from solicitors, who negligently allowed an action against insurance brokers for uninsured losses following a fire to be struck out, they were were not confined to recovering insurance premiums and legal costs.[1058] Where the claimant wished to sue his former solicitors for their failure to pursue an action for negligence against a G.P. it was accepted that, given in particular the absence of support for the case from medical records, the chances of success were properly assessed as nil.[1059] The measure of damages in a claim against solicitors for failing to bring a libel action within the one year limitation period, should reflect the probability that the claim, if issued in time, would have been settled on terms which took account of the publishers impecuniosity and the limited circulation of the libel.[1060]

9–295   **Loss of a chance.** It is important to distinguish between the need to prove causation, that is, what would have occurred if a solicitor's duty of care had been properly performed, and quantum of the resulting damage.[1061] The former has to be proved on a balance of probability. Usually the claimant will be required to give evidence that he would have acted in a particular way had the duty been properly discharged. However, in those instances (generally involving the

---

[1056] See e.g., *Philips & Co v Whatley* [2007] P.N.L.R. 27, PC where three different courts arrived at three different assessments of the claimant's chances of successfully recovering compensation after a solicitor's negligence caused a personal injury claim to be lost, where there was an issue whether the claimant's employers' insurers would have met the claim, due notice of it not having been given). It was said (per Lord Mance at [31] that in reckoning the chance of the insurers paying, the correct approach was to determine the prospects of a reputable insurer relying upon the breach of policy to repudiate liability, as to which the nature of the insured's breach of obligation and its effect upon the insurer's ability to handle the claim were particularly relevant.

[1057] *Mount v Barker Austin* [1998] P.N.L.R. 493, CA where, at 510, Simon Brown L.J. summarises the relevant principles.

[1058] *Sharif v Garret & Co*, n.1042 above

[1059] *Hatswell v Goldbergs* [2002] Lloyd's Rep. P.N. 359.

[1060] *Brinn v Russell Jones & Walker* [2003] P.N.L.R. 336.

[1061] For which see above, para.9–282.

negligent conduct of non contentious business) where a claim of loss involves the hypothetical actions not simply of the claimant, but also of a third party, it is not necessary that the claimant prove that the third party would probably have acted in a certain way: it suffices if it is shown that there was a substantial, rather than a speculative, chance that the third party would so have acted. Thereafter, the assessment of the value of that chance is a matter of quantification of damage.[1062]

There is an obvious tension between the basic rule that the claimant has to **9–296** prove on the balance of probabilities that the loss he claims has been suffered, and those instances where, being unable to establish that the full loss would have been suffered, he seeks to recover a percentage of that loss. At all times, however, the questions remain what damage the claimant has suffered, what damage the claimant seeks, and whether it can be established that the damage was caused by the defendant's breach of duty. Observations to this effect were made in a claim which arose after the defendant solicitors acted for the claimant in a tender for shares in a company, offered for sale under the Russian government's privatisation programme. A Russian court held the tender invalid for a number of technical reasons and it was alleged that the solicitors' failure to give proper advice contributed to that result. An issue arose whether the claimant was entitled to recover for loss of the chance that, had the tender been valid, the transaction would have succeeded. It was argued that the claimant should recover nothing because, on a balance of probability, a successful challenge to the transaction would have occurred in any event and at very least, the claimant could not establish the converse. This argument was rejected. The claim was rightly for loss of a chance bearing in mind first, that what the defendants had been contractually bound to supply, but did not, was the chance that the share transaction would not be defeated; and secondly, even that chance was dependant on the hypothetical acts of third parties in relation to the tender. But the value of the chance of success in the transaction could be put at no higher than 40 per cent and the damages were reduced accordingly.[1063]

[1062] *Allied Maples Group Ltd v Simmons & Simmons* [1995] 1 W.L.R. 1602, CA. See Reid, "The hypothetical outcome in professional negligence claims" (2001) 2 P.N. 129. See also *Boateng v Hughmans* [2002] P.N.L.R. 864, CA (the claimant's action failed because, having established that solicitors were negligent in failing to give advice, he was unable, in the context of a complex property transaction, to prove what he would have done had he been properly advised); *Clare v Buckle Mellows* [2005] EWCA Civ 1611 (a claim that solicitors were negligent in failing to advise the claimant to effect an immediate dissolution of a partnership to avoid or limit her future liability for its debts, and that she had thereby suffered additional loss as a result of having to enter an individual voluntary agreement (IVA) with creditors, failed, on a finding that even if the partnership had been dissolved earlier, the outcome would have been the same).

[1063] *Normans Bay Ltd v Coudert Brothers, The Times,* March 24, 2004, CA (the defendants' sought to rely upon their own separate breach of duty, not sued upon, in failing to seek anti-monopoly permission, as something which would have caused the claimant's plan to fail in any event: this was rejected and the view expressed that a person should not be able to take advantage of his own wrong to reduce the damages that would otherwise flow from his negligence. See generally Evans, "Lies, damn lies, and the loss of a chance" (2006) 2 P.N. 99 ; Neuberger, "Loss of a chance and causation" (2009) 1 P.N. 206.

ILLUSTRATIONS

9–297   It was not appropriate to discount 10 per cent from an award of damages where, as a result of a solicitor's failure to give proper advice, a client was deprived of the opportunity to disentail certain property before his death: the claim was made out as a matter of causation once it was proved that as a result of the negligence, the estate was not disentailed and, no third party being involved, it was unnecessary to take into account the chance that had proper advice been given the deceased would have not have acted on it.[1064] Where solicitors' negligence caused the claimant to lose the opportunity of a sale of property before a restrictive covenant was registered, the court assessed the chance that a sale would have been achieved before registration at 60 per cent and damages—being the price the seller lost the chance of achieving—were reduced by 40 per cent accordingly.[1065] Where solicitors were negligent in failing to challenge a planning notation within the correct time, the claimant recovered lost profits on the basis of a 40 per cent chance that such a challenge, if made, would have been successful and a petrol station would have been erected on the site.[1066]

9–298   In *Dixon v Clement Jones Solicitors*,[1067] the Court of Appeal had to consider a case where solicitors had negligently conducted a professional negligence claim against accountants, so that the claim was struck out for failure to serve particulars of claim. It was contended on behalf of the solicitors, that in the claim against themselves, the claimant had to prove on balance of probability, that the accountants' negligent advice made a difference, that is, that had it been otherwise the claimant would not have continued with a business project which she contemplated. The submission failed. The court had simply to consider the value of the chance which had been lost. In approaching that task, it was not necessary to conduct a trial within the trial to determine whether the claimant would have been successful in the original case. There was no requirement on the claimant to prove in her claim against the solicitors that she would not have proceeded with the business transaction had the accountants' advice been otherwise.

9–299   **Mental distress.** In contentious cases the damages recoverable for a solicitor's breach of duty may include compensation for distress, as where a solicitor negligently failed to secure a non-molestation injunction.[1068] Loss of reputation,

---

[1064] *Otter v Church, Adams, Tatham & Co* [1953] Ch. 280, but note the criticism in *Sykes v Midland Bank Executor and Trustee Co Ltd* [1970] 1 Q.B. 113 at 130, as supported by Stuart-Smith L.J. in *Allied Maples Group Ltd v Simmons & Simmons*, above, at 917.
[1065] *Hartle v Laceys* [1997] C.L.Y. 3839, CA. See also *First Interstate Bank of California v Cohen Arnold* [1996] 1 P.N.L.R. 17, CA and para.9–48 above (negligent misstatement by an accountant of a guarantor's financial worth).
[1066] *Motor Crown Petroleum Ltd v Berwin & Co* [1998] C.L.Y. 4020, para.9–263, n.934 above; appeal dismissed [2000] Lloyd's Rep. P.N. 438, CA.
[1067] [2005] P.N.L.R. 93, CA.
[1068] *Heywood v Wellers* [1976] Q.B. 446, applying *Jarvis v Swans Tours Ltd* [1973] Q.B. 233 and *Jackson v Horizon Holidays Ltd* [1975] 1 W.L.R. 1468 and see *Ichard v Frangoulis* [1977] 1 W.L.R. 556. See Marsh, "Mental distress: should lawyers pay more for their mistakes?" 140 S.J. 848.

which increased the claimant's mental distress, was taken into account in awarding damages against a solicitor whose negligence led to a wrongful conviction of assault.[1069] While compensation will not be given for mere disappointment at a solicitor's breach of contract, a distinction can be drawn when breach of the duty of care causes foreseeable physical discomfort and distress.[1070] Damages for mental distress were recovered where a solicitor gave negligent advice in the course of divorce proceedings, such distress being a direct and foreseeable result of the breach of duty.[1071] The court declined to discount from the sum awarded for the hazards of litigation. And where the solicitor's negligence consisted in failing to apply for adjournment of bankruptcy proceedings, damages for distress arising from the stigma of bankruptcy were awarded: a deduction was made to take account of the possibility that had an adjournment been applied for, it would have been refused.[1072] The claimant may recover compensation for a deterioration in a nervous condition over years of delay.[1073]

Payment made in settlement of negligence action. A payment made by a solicitor and accepted in "full and final" settlement of a negligence claim, brought against him by a client over a house sale transaction, protected him against subsequent contribution proceedings brought by the client upon her being sued by the dissatisfied buyer.[1074]   **9–300**

Contractual client has no duty to mitigate. Where a solicitor's liability lies in contract, rather than in tort, there is no duty on the client to mitigate his loss, because the degree of foreseeability is higher, both parties having participated. Accordingly, where a buyer of property had refused to abandon his original intention of making substantial improvements to it, after he had become aware of a defect in title, it was held that, since he was not in breach of any duty to mitigate his loss, he was entitled to the full measure of damages.[1075]   **9–301**

[1069] *McLeish v Amoo-Gottfried & Co, The Times,* October 13, 1993.

[1070] *Wapshot v Davis Donovan & Co* [1996] 2 P.N.L.R. 361 CA (a young couple who would have to start a family in the cramped condition of a flat to which, as a result of a solicitor's negligence, they had no valid leasehold title, recovered damages for the distress arising thereby).

[1071] *Dickinson v Jones Alexander & Co* [1993] 2 F.L.R. 521 (damages under this head assessed at £5,000, but cf. also *McAnarney v Hanrahan* [1993] 3 I.R. 492, where it was held that distress "could not be measured meaningfully"); also *Hamilton Jones v David & Snape* [2004] 1 W.L.R. 923 (£20,000 awarded for distress where a mother's children, which had been the subject of a custody dispute, were successfully removed from the jurisdiction by the father, as a result of a solicitor's negligence in failing to renew an entry in the records of the Passport Agency).

[1072] *Rey v Graham & Oldham* [2000] B.P.I.R. 354.

[1073] *Malyon v Lawrence Messer & Co* (1968) 112 S.J. 623.

[1074] *O'Boyle v Leiper, The Times,* January 26, 1990. The solicitor was not liable for further pecuniary loss suffered by the client after the settlement, when the buyers of the property sued for losses arising from failure to complete the sale in time.

[1075] *King v Hawkins & Co, The Times,* January 28, 1982 (the solicitors were well aware of the claimant's plans to modernise and extend a derelict cottage in the country, which he had purchased in order to convert it into a substantial family dwelling). See further Evans, "Solicitors' negligence and mitigation of loss" (2001) 2 P.N. 93.

15.—Stockbrokers

9–302   **General liability of stockbrokers.** A stockbroker's duty to a customer lies primarily in contract[1076] and stockbrokers are liable for failing to use that skill and diligence which a reasonably competent and careful stockbroker would exercise.[1077] The stockbroker's duty includes that of ascertaining with reasonable accuracy facts relating to any particular transaction, and transmitting them to the customer. If the latter suffers loss by the stockbroker's breach of duty, it matters not whether the stockbroker acted innocently or fraudulently.[1078] No duty was owed to a customer who had inquired only about the current market price of shares, to tell him that the shares in question were in primary distribution.[1079] A stockbroker was liable where, having been instructed to sell shares at a time when there was a market for them, he failed to do so. The measure of damages was the named price of the shares, less commission and taxes, the broker keeping the shares, which he had not been able to sell.[1080] Where stockbrokers relied upon informal arrangements with the market maker and casual exchanges of information with other dealers as a means of monitoring the performance of a bond, they were negligent not to have in place adequate market monitoring systems.[1081]

9–303   As with other professionals a stockbroker owes a duty to his customer in tort as well as contract. He can be liable to a third party with whom he has no contractual relationship, if, without a clear disclaimer of responsibility he negligently gives advice or material information on request to such a person, and has reason to believe that it will be acted upon. The mere fact of losses having been made on the commodities market cannot themselves provide evidence of negligence on the part of a broker, since the doctrine of res ipsa loquitur does not apply.[1082]

16.—Valuers, Estate Agents and Surveyors

9–304   **The duty of care.** As with, say, architects, the basis of the duty owed to a client by valuers, estate agents and surveyors is their contract.[1083] But they also owe a duty of care in tort[1084] and, in appropriate circumstances, that duty will

---

[1076] See *Jarvis v Moy, Davies, Smith, Vandervell & Co* [1936] 1 K.B. 399.

[1077] *Glennie v McD. & C. Holdings Ltd* [1935] 2 D.L.R. 561.

[1078] *Central B.C. Planers Ltd v Hocker* (1970) 72 W.W.R. 561.

[1079] *Laskin v Bache & Co Inc* (1972) 23 D.L.R. (3d) 385.

[1080] *Pankhurst v Gardner & Co* (1960) 25 D.L.R. (2d) 515.

[1081] *Voisin v Matheson Securities (CI) Ltd* (1999–2000) 2 I.T.E.L.R. 907, CA (Jer).

[1082] In *Merrill Lynch Futures Inc v York House Trading, The Times*, May 24, 1984, the view was expressed that compelling evidence from expert brokers in relation to individual transactions would be necessary if negligence was to be made out.

[1083] See Williams, "Professional Negligence in Rent Review and Lease Renewal", 276 E.G. 146. See also *Platform Funding Ltd v Bank of Scotland Plc* [2009] 2 W.L.R. 1016, CA (valuer liable for shortfall on a loan secured on property, where he was misled into valuing the wrong property: his contractual obligation was unqualified to value the address given in his instructions).

[1084] See *Smith v Eric S. Bush; Harris v Wyre Forest Urban District Council* [1990] 1 A.C. 831 at 870, per Lord Jauncey.

extend to third parties.[1085] This last is an area of the subject where there has been much development in recent years.

The essence of a third party claim will usually be bad advice. The principle in   **9–305**
Hedley Byrne & Co Ltd v Heller & Partners Ltd,[1086] as subsequently elaborated, will impose liability where there is reasonable foreseeability of damage, a relationship characterised in law as sufficiently proximate and where it is regarded as fair, just and reasonable that a duty of care should arise. An assumption of responsibility for the accuracy of advice may also suffice. So far as proximity is concerned, one crucial test is reliance: did the defendant know, or ought he to have known, that his advice would be relied upon, not simply by his client, but also by the claimant third party?[1087] If knowledge of reliance is proved, and in the absence of any clear and effective disclaimer of responsibility, liability will attach should a third party suffer loss and damage.[1088]

So where surveyors negligently represented the value of a dwelling-house in   **9–306**
a mortgage valuation prepared for a building society, and the prospective buyer in reliance upon the statement of its value, decided to buy the house and thereby suffered damage, the surveyors were liable to him even though there was no direct contractual nexus. A duty of care arose because it was in the reasonable contemplation of the defendants that carelessness on their part in valuation might be liable to cause damage to the buyer.[1089]

In the leading case[1090] the House of Lords was concerned to stress the limits   **9–307**
of the duty of care as much as its application. It was unlikely to extend to subsequent buyers and would rarely extend beyond the person for whose purposes it was given. Per Lord Jauncey:

> "I would certainly wish to stress that in cases where the advice has not been given for the specific purpose of the recipient acting upon it, it should only be in cases where the adviser knows that there is a high degree of probability that some other identifiable person will act upon the advice that a duty of care should be imposed. It would impose an intolerable burden upon those who give advice in a professional or commercial

---

[1085] See the discussion at paras 9–13, et seq., above.
[1086] [1964] A.C. 465.
[1087] per Lord Griffiths in *Smith v Eric S. Bush* [1990] 1 A.C. 831, at 865. See also *James McNaughton Paper Group Ltd v Hicks Anderson & Co* [1991] 2 W.L.R. 641. But for a case (in relation to solicitors) where the element of reliance was absent, see *White v Jones* [1995] 2 A.C. 207, para.9–220, above.
[1088] See para.9–311, below.
[1089] *Yianni v Edwin Evans & Sons* [1982] Q.B. 438, approved by the HL in *Smith v Bush*, above. See also *Civic Structures v Clark Quinney & Co* (1991) 47 E.G. 97, (a letter from an estate agent passing on to a prospective buyer information gained informally about the anticipated yield of the property was not to be regarded as giving such advice on yield as to give rise to a duty of care); *Merrett v Babb* [2001] Q.B. 1174 (valuer employed by a firm surveyors personally liable to mortgagor, where he knew that his valuation for mortgage purposes would be relied upon and he signed it in his personal capacity). See Murdoch, "Negligent advice: whose duty is it?" (2001) 2 P.N. 123.
[1090] *Smith v Eric S. Bush* [1990] 1 A.C. 831, above. See also *First National Commercial Bank Plc v Andrew S. Taylor (Commercial) Ltd* [1995] E.G.C.S. 200.

context if they were to owe a duty not only to those to whom they give the advice but to any other person who might choose to act upon it."[1091]

9–308   The vital element is proximity and if the claimant is unable to establish it no duty of care will be imposed. This was the problem in *Reeman v Department of Transport*[1092] where, in the context of a claim based upon the negligence of a surveyor employed by the defendant, Lord Bingham identified three conditions which, apart from any other considerations relevant to the test in *Caparo*,[1093] had to be met before a claim for financial loss arising from negligent misstatement could be established:

> "The statement (whether in the form of advice, an expression of opinion, a certificate or a factual statement) must be plaintiff-specific: that is, it must be given to the actual plaintiff or to an actual group, identifiable at the time the statement is made, to which the plaintiff belongs. Secondly, the statement must be purpose-specific: the statement must be made for the very purpose for which the actual plaintiff has used it. Thirdly, and perhaps overlapping with the second condition, the statement must be transaction-specific: the statement must be made with reference to the very transaction into which the plaintiff has entered in reliance on it."[1094]

To compound his difficulty the claimant also failed on the facts to persuade the Court that it would be fair, just and reasonable to impose a duty of care.[1095]

Illustrations

9–309   Estate agents acting in the capacity of the mortgagees' selling agents owed a duty of care to the mortgagor, a property developer, and were in breach of that duty in failing to prepare and distribute particulars of the property as well as advising upon its market value at a time when this was difficult to assess with precision.[1096] However, a marine surveyor did not owe a duty of care to a potential buyer where he had carried out a routine survey of a ship for Lloyd's, even though it was foreseeable that the latter buyer would rely on the report: Lloyd's are usually concerned with safety matters and not the protection of buyers, in the absence of factors giving rise to any sufficient proximity of

---

[1091] [1990] 1 A.C. 831, at 865. In *SecureAd Residential Funding Plc v Nationwide Building Society* [1997] E.G.C.S. 138 a valuer who prepared a mortgage valuation report did not owe any duty of care in relation to it to a lender of whose existence he was unaware (unknown to the valuer there were contractual arrangements between the apparent lender and the real one, by which the former was processing mortgage applications as agent for the latter). See Lawson, "Liability on a valuation" 141 S.J. 1108 and Coates and Evans-Tovey, "Duty of care of professional advisers" 142 S.J. 60.

[1092] [1997] P.N.L.R. 618, CA. A certificate had been granted indicating a vessel's compliance with regulations concerning seaworthiness, but the surveyor issuing it made an error in calculating the vessel's stability.

[1093] *Caparo Industries Plc v Dickman* [1990] 2 A.C. 605.

[1094] *Caparo Industries Plc v Dickman* [1990] 2 A.C. 605 at 639.

[1095] The case was analogous to *Marc Rich & Co AG v Bishop Rock Marine Co Ltd* [1996] 1 A.C. 211, para.9–55, n.187, above.

[1096] *Garland v Ralph Pay & Ransom* (1983) E.G. 106. But see *Huish v Ellis* [1995] N.P.C. 3, where it was held that in giving advice to a mortgagee in relation to the value of property being sold under a power of sale, an estate agent owed no duty of care to the mortgagor. A mortgagee exercising such a power owed a duty to the mortgagor to obtain a reasonable price and it was not necessary to impose upon the estate agent the further duty suggested.

relationship.[1097] Nor was a duty of care owed by valuers to mortgagees where borrowers executed a first legal charge on the relevant property in favour of one company but the charge was then assigned and the relevant funds provided by the mortgagees: the moment the loan was made, that is, when the first legal charge was executed, the liability of the valuers crystallised in favour of the person making the loan and their potential liability to any other party ceased.[1098]

Where receivers of a company entitled to exercise a power of sale over **9–310** properties owned by the claimant, appointed valuers to manage the sale, no duty of care was owed by the valuers to the claimant in relation to the price obtained. Any such duty would be limited by the scope of their instructions from the receivers, they had not assumed any responsibility towards the claimant and, in any event, the claimant had possible remedies against the receivers and the company for whom they acted in respect of any negligent undervaluation. In all these circumstances it was not fair, just, or reasonable to impose a duty of care on the defendants.[1099] A duty of care in making a valuation was not owed by a commercial surveyor advising a bank lending money to assist the purchase of property for development, to the developer: there was no established practice of passing valuation reports to the borrower in such cases and it was not foreseeable that the reliance would have been placed upon the surveyor's valuation.[1100]

Disclaimer. If a disclaimer is relied upon the Unfair Contract Terms Act will **9–311** apply,[1101] and it will be ineffective by virtue of s.2(2) unless it satisfies the test of reasonableness under s.11(3). Where the services of the valuer are paid for by the buyer it will not usually be fair or reasonable to allow liability to be excluded, whether the valuer acted as independent contractor,[1102] or as employee of a local authority.[1103] A building society may well not be liable for a valuer's negligence where its general conditions indicate that it assumes no responsibility for the accuracy of the valuation.[1104] A disclaimer in sales particulars was sufficient to negative proximity in *McCullagh v Lane Fox & Partners Ltd*,[1105] and it was not regarded as unreasonable for the defendant to rely upon it for purposes of the 1977 Act. The disclaimer also prevailed in *Omega Trust Co Ltd v Wright Son & Pepper*,[1106] the Court of Appeal saying that it was not unreasonable to rely upon it in a commercial context, where the parties were well able to look after

---

[1097] *Mariola Marine Corp v Lloyd's Register of Shipping, The Morning Watch* [1990] 1 Lloyd's Rep. 54, distinguishing *Smith v Eric S. Bush* [1990] A.C. 831.
[1098] *Barex Brokers Ltd v Morris Dean & Co* [1999] P.N.L.R. 344, CA.
[1099] *Raja v Austin Gray* [2003] E.G. 117, CA. See "Valuer's duty of care" 2002 P.L.C. (10) 76.
[1100] *Wilson v D.M. Hall & Sons* [2005] P.N.L.R. 22, OH.
[1101] See *Smith v Eric S. Bush*, [1990] A.C. 831 above, also *Cann v Willson* (1889) 39 Ch. D. 39.
[1102] As in *Smith v Bush*, above.
[1103] As in *Harris v Wyre Forest Urban District Council*, above n.1084.
[1104] *Tipton & Closeley Building Society v Collins* [1994] E.G.C.S. 120, CA.
[1105] [1996] 2 P.N.L.R. 205, CA.
[1106] [1997] P.N.L.R. 424, CA. See also *The Governor and Company of the Bank of Scotland v Fuller Peiser* [2002] P.N.L.R. 289, OH (in the context of negligent valuation by a surveyor, a disclaimer limiting liability to the surveyor's client was effective to protect the defendant and it was not unreasonable to allow reliance upon it for purposes of the Unfair Contract Terms Act where the pursuers were a large commercial banking entity and the transaction was entirely commercial in nature).

themselves and that valuers were entitled to know to whom their valuation may be shown (without their knowledge it had been disclosed to the lending bank). But it is always a matter of construction whether the disclaimer provides the defendant with a defence and it was insufficient where the defendant's knowledge of a third party's reliance on his statements as to the resale value of property, in circumstances where he knew the third party was not taking independent advice, was sufficient to bring into existence a duty of care.[1107]

9–312   **The standard of care.** The standard of care of these professionals has been described in the cases in similar terms to that of the other persons professing special skill described in this chapter. They are required to exercise the skill and care of a reasonably competent member of their profession.[1108] It is not a counsel of perfection, but neither is the level of care somehow reduced if the person concerned is unqualified,[1109] or making no charge,[1110] or performing a limited task.[1111]

9–313   **Valuers and estate agents.** Valuers must exercise the standard of care and skill possessed by a competent valuer.[1112] Their duty starts with the terms of their engagement. Where it is known that a report will be relied upon by a client and the valuer signs it in a personal capacity, a personal duty will arise, notwithstanding that the valuer is employed by a firm.[1113] When a valuer is employed to value a house, his duty to his client is to look with a practised eye for obvious defects that would affect significantly the value of the property.[1114] He is not required to undertake a structural survey or a survey in the detail called for in the standard form of the Royal Institution of Chartered Surveyors House Buyer's Report and Valuation Inspection, and to that extent the duty differs from that of a surveyor. Nor, in the absence of specific instructions, is the valuer required to go beyond advising on the price for the property and to express an opinion, for example, on its possible re-sale price.

9–314   It follows that a valuer is not obliged to warn his client of difficulties that might be met when attempting to re-sell the property.[1115] In *Bell Hotels (1935)*

[1107] *Duncan Investments Ltd v Underwoods* [1997] P.N.L.R. 521 (appeal on this aspect dismissed [1998] P.N.L.R. 754, CA, although allowed as to quantification of damage).

[1108] *Zubaida v Hargreaves* (1993) 43 E.G. 111 (the standard of care is that the valuer should act in accordance with practice accepted as proper by a substantial number of his profession).

[1109] *Freeman v Marshall & Co* (1966) 200 E.G. 777.

[1110] *Kenney v Hall Pain and Foster* (1976) 239 E.G. 355 at 429; per Goff J.

[1111] *Roberts v J. Hampson & Co* [1990] 1 W.L.R. 94. Although a building society's valuation of a property was only a limited appraisal, it was nevertheless undertaken by a skilled professional person who was aware that a copy of his valuation would be given to the buyer. Whilst the valuer could not be expected, in the course of inspection, to move furniture and lift up carpets as a matter of course, if there were some factor, such as a trail of rot, which ought to have put him on notice, it would be negligent of him not to investigate further. See also *Beresforde v Chesterfield BC* (1989) 39 E.G. 176, CA and *Henley v Cloke* (1991) 37 E.G. 145.

[1112] The following section addresses principally the negligence of estate agents and valuers and the section after, surveyors. The division is imposed for clarity but it will be appreciated that there is often considerable overlap in the tasks these professions perform. See generally in relation to property valuation Murdoch, "The nightmare zone" E.G. 2005, 0545, 164.

[1113] *Merrett v Babb* [2001] P.N.L.R. 660, CA.

[1114] See *Whalley v Roberts & Roberts* (1990) E.G. 104, above.

[1115] *Sutcliffe v Sayer* (1987) 281 E.G. 1452, CA.

Ltd v Motion,[1116] valuers had been instructed to advise whether a licensed hotel should be sold and further, since the hotel was the only free house in Melton Mowbray, whether brewery companies should be approached to see if they were interested. The valuers advised against such an approach and the hotel was sold privately. Within seven days it was re-sold at a profit to a brewery company and the valuers were held to have been negligent.

In order to establish liability in negligence against a valuer who has been **9–315** employed to give an independent determination of the proper rent, one or more of the following must be proved: (a) he has omitted to consider some matter which he ought to have considered; (b) he has taken into account some matter which he ought not to have done; (c) in some way or other he has failed to adopt the procedure and practices adopted as standard in his profession; and (d) has thereby failed to exercise the care and skill which, on accepting the appointment, he held himself out as possessing.[1117]

Where the complaint made is as to figures included in a valuation the court **9–316** must first consider whether the figure falls outside the range permitted to a non-negligent valuer.[1118] If there has been some error in the working process adopted by the valuer, that may be evidence that his figure contains an unacceptable degree of error.[1119] But if the court, notwithstanding such evidence, concludes that, by whatever means, the valuer has arrived at a result within the bracket, he cannot be characterised as negligent.[1120] A second stage is involved if the figure is outside the permissible bracket. The claimant should be regarded as having discharged an evidential burden and it is for the defendant to show that he nonetheless exercised the care and skill appropriate in the circumstances.[1121] At this stage the *Bolam*[1122] test comes into consideration. The fact that the figure is outside the bracket will no doubt militate strongly in favour of a finding that the valuer has fallen short of the appropriate standard. Before liability can be established the court must find both a figure outside the bracket and *Bolam*

[1116] [1952] C.P.L. 403.

[1117] *Belvedere Motors v King* (1981) 260 E.G. 81.

[1118] per Buxton L.J. in *Merivale Moore Plc v Strutt Parker* [2000] P.N.L.R. 498, CA at 515. The "permissible margin of error" was described by Watkins J. as the "bracket" in *Singer & Friedlander Ltd v John D. Wood* [1977] 2 E.G.L.R. 84. See also *McIntyre v Herring Son & Daw* (1988) E.G.L.R. 231 and *Beaumont v Humberts* (1990) 49 E.G. 46, CA; also Wilkinson, "Valuing within the 'Bracket' " 145 New L.J. 1267.

[1119] See *Merivale Moore Plc v Strutt Parker*, above; also *Mount Banking Corp v Brian Cooper & Co* (1992) 35 E.G. 123; *Axa Equity & Law v Goldsack & Freeman* (1994) 23 E.G. 130.

[1120] per Balcombe L.J. in *Craneheath Securities v York Montague* [1996] 1 E.G.L.R. 130, at 132: "It would not be enough for Craneheath to show that there have been errors at some stage of the valuation unless they can also show that the final valuation was wrong". See also *Legal & General Mortgage Services Ltd v HPC Professional Services* [1997] P.N.L.R. 567 (where although the valuation of the appropriately-named Wits End was "excessive" it was within the margin of error and accordingly it was said not to be open to the claimants to complain of an allegedly negligent method of arriving at it); *Goldstein v Levy Gee* [2003] P.N.L.R. 691. See Dugdale, "Process and outcome: the *Bolam* bracket" (2004) 1 P.N. 21.

[1121] per H.H. Judge Langan Q.C. in *Legal & General Mortgage Services v HPC Professional Services* [1997] P.N.L.R. 567 at 574, quoted with approval by Buxton L.J. in *Merivale Moore Plc v Strutt Parker* [2000] P.N.L.R. 498, CA.

[1122] *Bolam v Friern Hospital Management Committee* [1957] 1 W.L.R. 582.

negligence.[1123] It has been opined that a valuer could have a margin of error of 15 per cent before being held to have fallen short of the standard of care to be expected from an ordinary skilled valuer giving a site valuation against a falling market[1124] but it seems likely that the permissible margin of error is not a fixed quantity and will reflect the facts and evidence in each case.[1125] In many cases the evidence will disclose a bracket within which it is said the relevant value lies and in such cases having first decided the bracket, the court must go on to decide whether the valuation in question lies within it. However, it is worthwhile noting that not all cases can be decided by reference to a bracket, as where, for instance an ongoing business is being conducted from the premises,[1126] or where they are arguably so distinctive as to render comparison otiose.[1127]

9–317   When making a valuation of property, valuers must exercise care in ascertaining the date on which the valuation should be made, but are under no obligation to inquire into the financial position of the person to whom money is to be advanced, or as to title.[1128] They must have a knowledge of the general rules of law applicable to the subject of the valuation,[1129] and, where appropriate, the guidance notes prepared by the assets valuation standards committee of the RICS.[1130] When a landlord and tenant have agreed that a lease should be surrendered for a price to be determined by a valuer and, in due course, the lease is surrendered, the valuation is binding upon both parties. The court will not entertain a plea that the valuer must have been mistaken, unless the valuation is a manifestly erroneous "speaking" one. The remedy of an aggrieved party is to claim damages for the valuer's negligence.[1131]

[1123] *Merivale Moore Plc v Strutt Parker* [2000] P.N.L.R. 498, CA, at 516, per Buxton L.J. For criticism of this approach, see Murdoch, "Riding the market: 20 years of valuation negligence" (2005) 4 P.N. 233.

[1124] *Mount Banking Corp v Brian Cooper & Co* (1992) 35 E.G. 123, above, applying *Bolam v Friern Hospital Management Committee* [1957] 1 W.L.R. 582. The same margin was applied in *BNP Mortgages Ltd v Barton Cook & Sams* [1996] 1 E.G.L.R. 239 (no liability where the defendant's valuation was just under 13 per cent of the true value); see also Murdoch, "The margin of error approach to negligence in valuations" (1997) 3 P.N. 81; Wilkinson, "The permissible margin of error" 148 N.L.J. 481.

[1125] *Private Bank & Trust Co Ltd v S (U.K.) Ltd* (1993) 09 E.G. 112. See also *Allied Trust Bank v Edward Symmons & Partners* (1993) E.G.C.S. 163, and *Axa Equity & Law Home Loans v Goldsack & Freeman* (1994) 23 E.G. 130; *Credit Agricole Personal Finance v Murray* [1995] N.P.C. 33; *Birmingham Midshires Building Society v Richard Pamplin Co* [1996] E.G.C.S. 3 (on the facts, an 11 per cent margin of error was deemed permissible).

[1126] See *Legal & General Mortgage Services Ltd v HPC Professional Services* n.1120, above.

[1127] See Jacob J. in *Craneheath Securities Ltd v York Montague Ltd* [1994] 1 E.G.L.R. 159 at 162.

[1128] *Beck v Smirke* (1894) Hudson's B.C., 4th edn, Vol.2, p.259.

[1129] *Jenkins v Betham* (1855) 15 C.B. 168.

[1130] *Allied Trust Bank v Edward Symmons & Partners* (1994) 22 E.G. 116; *Crane Heath Securities v York Montague* (1994) 21 E.G. 124.

[1131] *Campbell v Edwards* [1976] 1 W.L.R. 403, applying *Arenson v Arenson* [1977] A.C. 405. There are observations upon the duties of valuers, particularly where valuing land against a volatile market in *Singer & Friedlander v John D. Wood & Co* (1977) 243 E.G. 212 at 295 (a case where the defendants made a negligent valuation in the strength of which the claimants advanced a loan of £1.5m. to developers whose company subsequently went into liquidation). Contrast *Predeth v Castle Phillips Finance Co* (1986) 279 E.G. 1355, CA (valuer instructed to carry out a "crash sale" valuation of a derelict bungalow not under a duty to advise as to its true market value since the requirement for a quick sale was crucial to his instructions). See Mulcahy, "Surveyors' Duties—Two Recent Cases" (1987) 3 P.N. 79.

Illustrations

Estate agents and valuers were liable in negligence to a client for whom they **9–318** were working gratuitously (their fee coming from the seller), where they failed to check on the length of an outstanding mortgage, in fact less than one week, the claimant having indicated that he wanted a house on which a long-term mortgage was available[1132]; where acting as house agents, they failed to obtain advance rent or deposit from an in-coming tenant[1133]; where in valuing land for purposes of assessing compensation for compulsory purchase, they failed to take into account a change in the law[1134]; where an employee with little knowledge or experience made a wholly erroneous valuation of property, which failed to sell as a result[1135]; where a valuer valued the rental value of a property without taking into account comparable rents paid in the locality[1136]; where a valuer failed to investigate thoroughly and give due consideration to the recent marketing history of the property including sales of similar properties[1137]; in failing to submit representations on behalf of a client, the tenant of a shop, to an independent expert appointed to determine a revised rent within the time specified in a rent review clause of an underlease[1138]; in misdescribing a garage, after carrying out a structural survey of a house, and then failing to give a warning that its roof was made of asbestos, through which the buyer fell on a later occasion while investigating a leak[1139]; where a surveyor failed to report a risk of subsidence which, two years later, was identified when the property was offered for sale again[1140]; where, in making a valuation report, he failed to comment upon a mis-positioned purlin in the roof space of a house when he ought to have been on notice of the kind of construction acceptable to a building society as security[1141]; in basing a valuation of land upon the prospect of planning permission being granted for development as a hotel when in fact that prospect was remote[1142]; in failing to inform prospective developers of leasehold land of the risks associated with their method of estimating its yield, whereby too high a price was paid for

---

[1132] *Avery v Salie* (1972) 25 D.L.R. (3d) 495.

[1133] *Brutton v Alfred, Savill, Curtis & Henson* (1970) 218 E.G. 1417.

[1134] *Weedon v Hindlewood Clarke & Esplin* (1974) 234 E.G. 121, following *West Midland Baptist (Trust) Association (Inc) v Birmingham Corp* [1968] 2 Q.B. 188.

[1135] *Kenney v Hall, Pain & Foster* (1976) 239 E.G. 355.

[1136] *United Bank of Kuwait v Prudential Property Services* (1994) 30 E.G. 103.

[1137] *Banque Bruxelles Lambert SA v Eagle Star Insurance Co* (1994) 31 E.G. 68; *Platform Home Loans Ltd v Oyston Shipways Ltd* [1996] 49 E.G. 112 (valuers failed to take account both of comparable properties and the original purchase price). For the subsequent appeals, on other grounds, see [1998] Ch.466 and [2002] 2 A.C. 190.

[1138] *Rajdev v Becketts* (1989) 35 E.G. 107.

[1139] *Allen v Ellis & Co* (1990) 11 E.G. 78, applying *JEB Fasteners v Marks Bloom & Co* [1983] 1 All E.R. 583, CA.

[1140] *Matto v Rodney Broom Associates* [1994] N.P.C. 40, CA.

[1141] *David and Margie Ezekiel v Ian McDade* [1994] E.G.C.S. 194, CA (surveyors preparing a mortgage valuation report failed to mention a gap of 40mm at the end of two roof purlins forming part of the roof structure).

[1142] *BFG Bank AG v Brown & Mumford Ltd* [1995] E.G.C.S. 21 (it was not contributory negligence for a bank to breach its own internal guidelines when extending a loan on the basis of the valuation since, on the facts, those rules were to be interpreted in a flexible manner); appeal dismissed [1996] E.G.C.S. 169, CA.

it.[1143] Land agents acting for the owner of a number of fields situated near to an airport, were negligent in negotiating leases of the fields for use as car parks at a fixed rent, with periodic reviews based on increases in car parking charges, rather than a rent based on turnover generated by the car parking charges.[1144]

9–319   On the other hand, there was no liability where the keys of café premises were handed over to prospective buyers, who went into occupation beneficially for a period of time pending a sale which did not ultimately proceed[1145]; where a prospective buyer of a house, the walls of which were showing signs of movement, was advised to obtain insurance against the risk of deterioration, rather than discouraging the purchase[1146]; where the buyer had not relied upon an estate agent's misrepresentation about the size of a garage of a dwelling-house but upon his own inspection of the premises[1147]; where a valuation included an element for the "hope" of planning permission[1148]; when the reinstatement value for insurance purposes of a 300-year-old village house was estimated, not on the basis of a replica, but of a new house having the same habitable floor space, style and general shape as the existing one, without certain idiosyncratic features[1149]; where estate agents had misled neither their client (the seller) not the potential buyer; but had acted throughout the transaction within their instructions[1150]; where false information was given in sales particulars but there was a written disclaimer and a reasonable person would have concluded that no responsibility for the accuracy of the information was assumed[1151]; where a valuation obtained for a building society that failed to warn of rusting to wall ties was within the range of valuations that could be expected from an ordinarily competent surveyor, given the limited nature of the inspection undertaken[1152]; where a valuer failed to detect that a building had been built some four inches out of level when there was no evidence of wall cracking and the defect was difficult to detect because it had been camouflaged so successfully by the builder that it had not been noticed even by the previous owner[1153]; where a valuer took legal advice about the proper method to employ in a valuation of business premises on a rent review, and adopted as a result a method which inappropriately conflicted with

---

[1143] *Merivale Moore Plc v Strutt & Parker* [1998] 2 E.G.L.R. 195; appeal dismissed [2000] P.N.L.R. 498, CA.
[1144] *Earl of Malmesbury v Strutt & Parker* [2007] P.N.L.R. 29. See Locke, "Don't be left scratching your head" E.G. 2007, 0723, 156.
[1145] *Edmonds v Andrew & Ashwell* (1982) 261 E.G. 53 (in any event there was little, if any, actionable damage arising from their occupation).
[1146] *Eley v King & Chasemore, The Independent,* April 24, 1989, CA.
[1147] *Hatfield v Sawyer & McClocklin Real Estate* [1977] 1 W.L.R. 481.
[1148] *Allied Trust Bank v Edward Symmonds & Partners* (1994) 22 E.G. 116.
[1149] *Beaumont v Humberts* (1990) 49 E.G. 46, CA.
[1150] *Watson v Lane Fox* (1991) 49 E.G. 71.
[1151] *McCullagh v Lane Fox & Partners* [1996] 2 P.N.L.R. 205, CA (oral misrepresentation that a garden extended to nearly an acre when in fact it was less than half an acre). A disclaimer in the same terms did not protect the defendant in *Duncan Investments Ltd v Underwoods* [1997] P.N.L.R. 521, since his negligent representation as to the value of property was not made in his capacity as agent of the seller. (Appeal on this aspect dismissed [1998] P.N.L.R. 754, CA, although allowed as to quantification of damage).
[1152] *Nash v Evens & Matta* (1988) 04 E.G. 131.
[1153] *Whalley v Roberts & Roberts* (1990) E.G. 104.

the presumption that the rent fixed on a review should bear as close a resemblance to reality as possible.[1154]

There was no assumption of responsibility and therefore no duty of care owed, **9–320** by a firm of actuaries who had prepared an actuarial valuation report in relation to the pension fund of a company, to the claimants, who made an offer for the shares of the company. The report negligently understated a deficit in the fund, but the actuaries had not assumed any responsibility for its accuracy so far as the claimants were concerned. It was observed in the Court of Appeal that reliance on the provision of information had to be viewed from the perspective of the provider of the information. There was no assumption of responsibility given that the parties had no pre-existing relationship, the information provided was historic, and the purpose for which the claimants wished to use the information was outside the purpose for which reliance was on the face of the document permitted. The claimants did not communicate directly with the defendants nor did they inform them why the information was requested. So far as the defendants were concerned, the claimants could be reasonably expected to have their own advisers.[1155]

Surveyors. A surveyor is not to be regarded as having the same expertise as **9–321** an architect or engineer. A surveyor's duties are usually confined to exercising reasonable skill and care in reporting reasonably discoverable faults.[1156] It has been said that in carrying out a mortgage valuation for an intended buyer the surveyor's inspection ought properly to include: (a) observing substantial defects that will require work to be done either at once, or soon, within a relatively small time against the life of the loan; and (b) putting the buyer on notice of inquiries that will have to be made in order to establish whether or not there are any substantial defects, all of which matters will have an effect on value.[1157]

ILLUSTRATIONS

Where a farm house had been built in 1880 and brickwork added in 1961 had **9–322** not been tied in properly, surveyors were negligent in failing to draw the buyers' attention to the defect even though serious cracks did not appear until after the survey had been carried out.[1158] Where an architect and a surveyor were instructed to inspect a farm and give a general opinion, not involving a detailed

---

[1154] *Lewisham Investment Partnership Ltd v Morgan, The Times*, November 25, 1997.

[1155] *Precis (521) Plc v William M. Mercer Ltd* [2005] P.N.L.R. 511, CA, applying *Henderson v Merrett Syndicates Ltd* [1995] 2 A.C. 145; *BCCI (Overseas) Ltd v Price Waterhouse* [1998] P.N.L.R. 564, CA and *Williams v Natural Life Health Foods Ltd* [1998] 1 W.L.R. 830, HL.

[1156] See *Eley v King & Chasemore, The Independent*, April 24, 1989, CA (no negligence where a surveyor had drawn attention to a structural defect and advised that insurance should be taken out to cover the cost of underpinning foundations that would become necessary in the future); also *Heatley v William H. Brown* [1992] 1 E.G.L.R. 289 (a surveyor failed to detect substantial defects in a property during a standard structural survey because it was not possible for him to gain access to the roof voids: he should have advised further investigation before reporting that the building was in "reasonable condition for its age").

[1157] *Lloyd v Butler* (1990) 47 E.G. 56.

[1158] *Lees v English & Partners* (1977) 242 E.G. 295.

survey, they were negligent in not discovering dry rot, woodworm and settlement.[1159] Where a surveyor, employed by a buyer to test a house for dampness, failed to find any even though serious damp was present, he was negligent: failure to discover dampness in one isolated spot might be excused, but not when it was so extensive that he could not have failed to detect it using reasonable care.[1160] A marine surveyor was liable where he reported negligently on the condition of a motor launch as a result of which it was purchased by his client[1161]; it was negligent for a surveyor, valuing a house for potential buyers, to fail to have regard to the type of construction likely to be acceptable to building societies as suitable security[1162]; further, to give an assurance to the claimant, who had paid an "introduction fee" for details of properties offered for sale by other firms, that floor areas were correctly stated when they were not[1163]; in carrying out a mortgage valuation survey, to infer from the absence of signs of distress that a chimney was properly supported, when the property had been recently refurbished.[1164] Surveyors employed to enter into leases with tenants were negligent in failing to notice that clauses providing for upwards only rent review had been removed by solicitors who prepared the leases in draft.[1165]

9–323   **Contributory negligence.** Even if a lender relies upon a negligent valuation he may himself be guilty of contributory negligence, for instance by failing to give clear instructions or failing to check the basis upon which the valuation is made. So, in *South Australian Asset Management v York Montague*,[1166] a bank was itself 25 per cent to blame where it advanced £11 million to assist the purchase of land subsequently valued at £2.5 million and it had made no proper check of the basis upon which the valuation was made, given unclear instructions and had not made an assessment of the risk classification as required by its own procedures.

9–324   In assessing what conduct may amount to contributory negligence in this context a number of different formulae have been adopted.[1167] It has been said that the lender was himself negligent if "the error was such as no reasonably

---

[1159] *Sincock v Bangs (Reading)* [1952] C.P.L. 562; *Philips v Ward* [1956] 1 All E.R. 874, which was applied in *Morgan v Perry* (1973) 229 E.G. 737 (where a house became almost valueless within five years of purchase as a result of slipping foundations. The surveyor instructed by the buyer was held liable because he had given the house a "clean bill of health" and valued it above the purchase price). In *Daisley v B.S. Hall & Co* (1972) 225 E.G. 1553 the surveyor was negligent in failing to report risks arising from the combination of poplar trees growing nearby and clay sub-soil, where shrinkage cracking was already visible in the house intended to be purchased. See also *Upstone v G.D.W. Carnegie & Co*, 1978 S.L.T. 4 (the presence of dry rot not mentioned in a surveyor's report, in reliance upon which the house was purchased).

[1160] *Fryer v Bunney* (1982) 263 E.G. 158.

[1161] *Gordon v Moen* [1971] N.Z.L.R. 526.

[1162] *David and Margie Ezekiel v Ian McDade* [1994] 10 Cons.L.J. 122.

[1163] *Hunt v Beasley Drake* [1995] N.P.C. 35.

[1164] *Sneesby v Goldings* [1994] E.G.C.S. 201 CA, (per Sir Thomas Bingham M.R.: "it should not be assumed that work to a property has been carried out properly, because it has been executed with the aid of a local authority improvement grant").

[1165] *Theodore Goddard v Fletcher King Services Ltd* [1997] 32 E.G. 90 (the surveyors were liable to contribute 20 per cent to the liability the solicitors incurred).

[1166] [1995] N.P.C. 66.

[1167] See Evans, "Contributory negligence by lenders" (1998) 1 P.N. 43 for a useful summary.

well-informed and competent member of that profession could have made"[1168]; or that he should be judged by the "standards of the reasonably competent merchant bank at the time"[1169]; or whether he conducted his business prudently[1170]; or whether a reasonably prudent person specialising in the relevant area would so have acted.[1171] It has been pointed out that a test based upon prudence may imply a more exacting standard than the *Bolam*[1172] test usually held to be the touchstone when considering the standard of care appropriate for a professional person.[1173]

It may, in any particular case, amount to contributory negligence for a lender   **9–325** to fail to take account of information which casts a significant and material doubt upon the accuracy of a valuation[1174]; or to fail to investigate the financial position of the borrower with sufficient thoroughness.[1175] It has been said that contributory negligence on the part of the lender in a surveyor's negligence case can arise either in relation to the surveyor's report itself, for instance, in failing to read it properly, or neglecting to investigate or follow up qualifications or other obscurities in it; or alternatively in relation to other extraneous matters such as failing properly to investigate the borrower or take proper care to protect the loan.[1176] In *Platform Home Loans Ltd v Oyston Shipways Ltd*,[1177] it was held to

---

[1168] See *Banque Bruxelles Lambert SA v Lewis & Tucker Ltd* [1995] 2 All E.R. 769, at 821.

[1169] *Banque Bruxelles Lambert SA v Lewis & Tucker Ltd* [1995] 2 All E.R. 769, at 821.

[1170] *Birmingham Midshires Ltd v Parry Jones* [1996] P.N.L.R. 431 at 442–443.

[1171] *United Bank of Kuwait v Prudential Property Services Ltd* [1995] E.G.C.S. 190.

[1172] *Bolam v Friern Hospital Management Committee* [1957] 1 W.L.R. 582.

[1173] (1998) 1 P.N. 43, n.1167, above.

[1174] *Banque Bruxelles Lambert SA v Eagle Star Insurance Co Ltd* [1994] 2 E.G.L.R. 108; *Nycklen Finance Co Ltd v Stumpbrook Continuation Ltd* [1994] 2 E.G.L.R. 143.

[1175] *Alliance & Leicester Building Society v Wheelers* (1997) 16 Commercial Lawyer 66. See also *Halifax Mortgage Services Ltd v Robert Holmes & Co* [1997] C.L.Y. 3846 (contributory negligence assessed at 25 per cent where the lender failed to seek the accounts of a property development company in which the mortgagor was joint shareholder, and failed to make further inquiries after the mortgagor omitted to disclose a second charge on the application form).

[1176] *First National Bank v Andrew S. Taylor Commercial Ltd* [1997] P.N.L.R. 37; see also *Chelsea Building Society v Goddard & Smith* [1996] E.G.C.S. 157: blame was apportioned equally between a valuer and a solicitor where, after negligent valuation, the latter failed to inform the lender of another sale which would have given grounds for questioning the valuation and negligently allowed mortgage funds to be used to fund the purchase. The judge also found 25 per cent contribution against the lender, inter alia, on the basis that accounts of the borrower were insufficiently investigated and the borrower was not interviewed and or an accountant's reference was vague but not clarified. In *Cavendish Funding Ltd v Henry Spencer & Sons Ltd* [1998] P.N.L.R. 122, CA, the failure of a bank specialising in short-term, high risk finance to query a difference of £0.5 million between two valuations of a property negligently undervalued by the defendants, did amount to contributory negligence partly causative of the claimants' loss (reversing [1996] E.G.C.S. on this point). See also *UCB Bank v David J. Pinder Plc* [1998] P.N.L.R. 398 (lender's contributory negligence assessed at one-third where up-to-date accounts, bank statements, or previous mortgage statements were not requested, or account taken of a refusal of mortgage indemnity insurance or the fact that the loan would do little more than pay off the borrower's existing indebtedness but no overdraft facility was insisted upon to provide working capital).

[1177] [1996] 49 E.G. 112; claimant's appeal on the point dismissed [1998] Ch.466. The CA's decision as to the method of calculating contributory negligence on such facts was then itself overturned on appeal: [2000] A.C. 190 (any deduction for the lender's own negligence should be made when his basic loss has been established, before making any further deduction required by the principles for

be contributory negligence for a lender to advance a non-status loan, that is, a loan made without investigation of the borrower's creditworthiness, of 70 per cent of a suggested value of £1.5 million. Such a loan provided insufficient cushion (or "loan to value ratio") given the inherent problems of valuing the more substantial type of property accurately. In so holding, the Court of Appeal appears to have resolved a number of conflicting decisions about the materiality of contributory negligence going only to creditworthiness or market risk.[1178] Quite apart from contributory negligence, there is the duty to mitigate loss which may involve attempting with reasonable expedition to realise the security by sale.[1179]

9–326   **Damages.** The assessment of damages in cases where negligence is proven against valuers, estate agents or quantity surveyors is a complex topic and the reader is referred to specialist works for a full treatment. In summary, as with any claim in tort, the claimant must establish a causal nexus between any breach of duty established and the damage he alleges has resulted.[1180] He must prove that his loss was a reasonably foreseeable result of the breach. Thereafter the court will consider the measure of damages appropriate for this loss.

9–327   **Measure of damages.** Although a distinction has been drawn in some cases between "successful transaction" and "no transaction" cases, it has been

---

assessing the measure of damages set out in the *Banque Bruxelles* and *Nykredit* decisions). For criticism of aspects of the first instance decision, see T. Dugdale, "Loss and liability: Platform Home Loans v Oyston Shipways" (1997) 1 P.N. 5.

[1178] See, e.g. *Interallianz Finance AG v Independent Insurance Company Ltd* [1997] E.G.C.S. 91. The basis of such cases was that, after SAAMCO, para.9–327, above, a valuer could be liable only for loss caused by breach of the duty to provide an accurate valuation and such loss would be limited to the difference between the actual and suggested value of the property: that being so, only negligence which contributed to that recoverable loss should be taken into account by way of contributory negligence and failure to assess the credit risk properly or take sufficient security should be outside consideration. It is doubtful whether this argument survives the *Platform Homes* decision where it was emphasised that "damage" for purposes of Law Reform (Contributory Negligence) Act 1945 s.1, meant the loss suffered by the claimant as a whole and not just that element in his loss attributable to the defendant's breach of duty. See also *Britannic Securities & Investments Ltd v Hirani Watson* [1995] E.G.C.S. 46 (no contributory negligence in failing to inquire into the borrower's ability to repay a loan for which the property valued had been offered as security) and *BFG Bank AG v Brown & Mumford Ltd* [1995] E.G.C.S. 21; also *Coventry Building Society v William Martin & Partners* [1997] 48 E.G. 159 (no deduction from damages where the lender's failure to inquire into the borrower's ability to service the loan was not causative of any loss); also Gascoigne, "Reducing a negligent valuer's liability" 141 S.J. 354; Hirst "The conduct of the lender" (1998) Lawyer 12(25) 18; Charlwood, "Deductions for contributory negligence" 143 S.J. 456.

[1179] *Alliance & Leicester Building Society v Wheelers* (1997) 16 Commercial Lawyer 66.

[1180] See, e.g. *Banque Bruxelles Lambert v John D. Wood Commercial Ltd* [1996] P.N.L.R. P380, CA (the bank, which had lent a substantial sum of money on security of a building negligently valued at £82 million, failed to establish a causative link between the valuation and its loss when the borrower defaulted on the loan, because the valuation itself had little causative potency when compared with other factors such as pressure to proceed with the loan from a special client and an expectation that property values would continue to rise); also *Brown v Cliff Roberts* [1996] C.L.Y. 4499, CA (no arguable claim for damages where buyers of a house would have proceeded with the transaction anyway even if they had known of a restrictive covenant against the erection of another building in the garden); also *Shankie-Williams v Heavey* [1986] 279 E.G. 316, CA (claimant had not seen the negligently-prepared report of a dry rot specialist and accordingly did not rely on its contents).

criticised as not resting upon any principles.[1181] It is of greater importance to establish the nature of the duty of which the defendant was in breach. So, where property was acquired in reliance upon a negligent surveyor's report, it was held in *Philips v Ward*[1182] that the appropriate measure of the claimant's loss was the difference between the price actually paid and the true value, assessed at the date of purchase. This decision was followed in *Morgan v Perry*[1183] where, five years after the claimant purchased in reliance upon the surveyor's report, it emerged that his property was substantially worthless because its foundations were slipping. The court held that it was entitled, in assessing the value at the date of purchase, to take into account knowledge acquired subsequently, up to the date of the hearing. In *Perry v Sidney Phillips & Son*,[1184] the Court of Appeal rejected the suggestion that the claimant should recover the difference between the value of the property at the date of trial as it had it been as described in the surveyor's report and its value at that date in its defective condition. Efforts to make the cost of repairs the appropriate measure of loss have likewise proved unsuccessful[1185]; although, as a matter of evidence, the cost of repairing the relevant defects may assist the court in determining the difference in value.[1186] One situation in which the cost of repairs can be a relevant consideration is where comparable properties do not exist to establish a value for a property, as it should have been described if the surveyor or valuer had done his job properly: it may become necessary in such a case to consider the price a theoretical buyer would have been willing to pay had he known of the likely costs of repair.[1187]

Where it is alleged that a loan would not have been made, or made on other **9–328** terms, had a correct valuation been given, the valuer is only responsible for the

---

[1181] *South Australia Asset Management Corp v York Montague Ltd* [1996] 3 All E.R. 365 at 376; per Lord Hoffmann.

[1182] [1956] 1 W.L.R. 471, CA; applied in *Ford v White* [1964] 1 W.L.R. 885, for which see further at para.8–284, above. It should be noted that the *Phillips v Ward* measure is not an absolute rule and can be departed from where a different sum is required properly to compensate the claimant. See *County Personnel (Employment Agency) Ltd v Alan R. Pulver & Co* [1987] 1 W.L.R. 916, 925 also *Devine v Jeffreys* [2001] P.N.L.R. 407 (claimants suffered no loss where their house was negligently undervalued but they subsequently transferred the freehold to a finance company in return for a settlement of their outstanding borrowing and a seven year tenancy).

[1183] [1973] 229 E.G. 1737, above; also *Shaw v Halifax (South West) Ltd* [1996] P.N.L.R. 451, CA (subsequent rise in the market value irrelevant). The difference between price and value can remain the measure of loss even where, for example, the claimant succeeds in having the defect repaired at a third party's expense: *Gardner v Marsh and Parsons* [1997] 1 W.L.R. 489, CA (where the claimant's landlord, pursuant to an obligation under the lease, rectified a defect missed by the negligent surveyor), but aliter if the repair was part of a continuous transaction of which the negligence was the inception. See Boxer, "Double Indemnity" 141 S.J. 1104; also Murdoch, "Value with hindsight" 2003 E.G. 0312, 126.

[1184] [1982] 1 W.L.R. 1297, CA.

[1185] See, e.g. *Watts v Morrow* [1991] 1 W.L.R. 14, 21, CA. See also *Smith v Peter North & Partners* [2002] P.N.L.R. 274, CA (difference in value remained the test in a case where the allegation was negligence in reporting that a property was in substantially good repair when it was not, the property being in fact worth more than claimants paid even if repairs taken into account).

[1186] *Watts v Morrow* [1991] 1 W.L.R. 14 per Ralph Gibson L.J., at 1435.

[1187] *Oswald v Countrywide Surveyors Ltd*, 47 Con L.R. 50 (where extensive repair was required to a newly-purchased property infested by deathwatch beetle). The case also suggests that where the cost of repairs is taken as the starting point for the calculation, it can be discounted for betterment.

foreseeable results of his mistake.[1188] It is necessary to identify what element in the foreseeable loss suffered is strictly attributable to the inaccuracy of the information from him. Where lenders advanced £11 million on a property valued at £15 million, the actual value of which was £5 million, and thereby had £10 million less security than they thought, they recovered their entire loss because, when credit was given for the proceeds of sale, it did not exceed the margin which the breach of duty lead them to believe they had.[1189] But where the loss was increased by the borrower's default, the lender was not able to recover from the negligent valuer the unpaid contractual interest which had accumulated: the valuers had not been asked to give advice on the risk of default and their liability should be confined to difference between the valuation and the correct value.[1190] This value, which fixes the limit of the negligent valuer's liability, should in principle be arrived at by taking the mean figure from a range of figures which reasonable valuers could have put forward; it should not, for example, be the maximum reasonable valuation which could have been made. The claimant will usually also be entitled to the reasonable cost of extricating himself from a purchase made in reliance upon a negligent report.[1191]

9–329   In the result, in order to establish the measure of loss, a comparison is required ("the basic comparison") between the amount lent, which the lender would have retained had the transaction not proceeded together with interest, and the value of the rights acquired under the loan, usually the borrower's covenant and the true value of the property. If this comparison reveals a loss, it is necessary to see what part of the loss is a consequence of a deficiency in the value of the security. Typically this will be the extent of the over-valuation. The time at which the basic comparison first reveals a measurable loss, and the lender's cause of action thereby arises, is an issue of fact.[1192]

[1188] *South Australia Asset Management Corp v York Montague Ltd* [1997] A.C. 191. Three appeals raising similar questions were consolidated, see n.1190, below. The decision of the Court of Appeal in *Banque Bruxelles Lambert SA v Eagle Star Insurance Co Ltd* [1995] Q.B. 375 was reversed. See also *Nykredit Mortgage Bank Plc v Edward Erdman Group (No.2)* [1998] 1 All E.R. 305, 309 HL, per Lord Nicholls. See further Cooke, "Remote Names and volatile markets" (1996) 2 P.N. 58; Dugdale, "*South Australia Asset Management*: Answers and Questions" (1996) 3 P.N. 71; Davidson Q.C., "BBL and damages—some problems in applying the *ratio decidendi*" (1997) 3 P.N. 89.

[1189] *South Australia Asset Management Corp v York Montague Ltd* [1997] A.C. 191.

[1190] *United Bank of Kuwait Plc v Prudential Property Services Ltd*, the second of the three cases determined by the HL, n.1188, above. The third case was *Nykredit Mortgage Bank Ltd v Edward Erdman Group Ltd*, in which again the claim for contractual interest was held to fail. See also *Swingcastle Ltd v Alastair Gibson* [1991] 2 A.C. 233 overruling in part *Baxter v Gapp & Co* [1939] 2 K.B. 271. See Hughes, "The Negligent Valuer after Swingcastle" [1992] 3 P.N. 103. In *Western Trust & Savings Ltd v Strutt & Parker* [1999] P.N.L.R. 154, CA, the valuer was liable even though the property for which a valuation was given was larger than the part of it taken as security: the valuation was still causative of the lender's loss as the difference in size of the properties was not such as to take the transaction outwith the scope of the valuer's duty.

[1191] *Patel v Hooper & Jackson* [1999] 1 W.L.R. 1792, CA (where the property was uninhabitable and the claimants were unable to move into it or sell it, they recovered the reasonable cost of selling it which included the cost of living elsewhere in the meantime).

[1192] *Nykredit Mortgage Bank Plc v Edward Erdman Group Ltd (No.2)* [1997] 1 W.L.R. 1627, HL (where the borrower's covenant was worthless because of immediate default, the cause of action arose shortly after the time the transaction took place). See also *Byrne v Hall Pain & Foster* [1999] P.N.L.R. 565, CA, Ch.4, above, para.4–157 (once claimants became irrevocably committed to acquiring a lease on exchange of contracts, which was worth less than they reasonably believed, and

Credit for the benefit of insurance. In many cases lenders insure—or require   **9–330**
borrowers to insure as a condition of the loan—against the risk of a shortfall in
the event that the security has to be realised. In the context of security taken after
a property has been negligently over-valued, the Court of Appeal has rejected the
argument that damages recoverable against a negligent surveyor should be
reduced to take account of recovery under such an insurance policy, to avoid the
risk of double recovery. The view was expressed that no such risk could arise
since, if the lender recovered damages before receiving indemnity under the
insurance, the amount recoverable under the indemnity would be reduced; if the
lender's recovery of damages occurred after indemnity was received it would
enure to the benefit of the insurers under their right of subrogation.[1193]

Contribution between tortfeasors. The negligent valuer may seek to reduce   **9–331**
his loss by attempting to obtain contribution from some other party alleged to be
liable. This may not be straightforward where the claim is against the defaulting
borrowers since, upon analysis, they are not liable in respect of the "same
damage" as required by the Civil Liability (Contribution) Act 1978 s.1(1).
Whereas the surveyor is liable for losses arising from a loan which would not
have been advanced if the valuation had been accurate, the defaulting borrower
is responsible for losses accruing from his non-payment of the original
debt.[1194]

In a different situation, the sponsors of a commercial property scheme, who   **9–332**
had admitted liability to the claimants for negligently misrepresenting the value
of a rental covenant which formed part of the scheme, sought contribution from
the surveyors who were the scheme's property advisers. It was accepted by the
surveyors that they had provided incorrect information in a prospectus for the
scheme, but they argued that the damage which the sponsors had admitted was
not the same as that for which they were liable since it arose from a different
error. The argument failed. "Damage" in the 1978 Act was to be given a broad
interpretation as the whole of the claimants' economic loss and both defendants
were liable for that damage albeit in different amounts.[1195]

Damages for distress. In general a contract breaker is not liable "for any   **9–333**
distress, frustration, anxiety, displeasure, vexation, tension or aggravation which
his breach of contract may cause to an innocent party."[1196] An exception arises
where it is an important object of the contract to provide the innocent party with

---

which they would not have committed themselves to but for the defendant valuer's negligence, they
suffered actual loss or damage sufficient for a cause of action to accrue).
[1193] *Arab Bank Plc v John D. Wood Commercial Ltd, The Times*, November 25, 1999, CA; *Bristol and
West Building Society v May, May & Merrimans (No.2)* [1998] 1 W.L.R. 336.
[1194] *Howkins & Harrison v Tyler, The Times*, August 8, 2000, CA.
[1195] *Ball v Banner* [2000] Lloyd's Rep. P.N. 569 (the Pt 20 defendants' liability was limited to the
difference between the amount which the claimant had invested and the amount that would have been
invested had accurate information been provided by them).
[1196] per Bingham L.J. in *Watts v Morrow* [1991] 1 W.L.R. 1421 at 1445, CA.

pleasure, relaxation or peace of mind.[1197] Ordinarily, this exception will not apply to a contract which requires a surveyor simply to investigate a property for defects. Another exception allows the recovery of damages for distress where it arises from physical inconvenience and discomfort caused by the breach.[1198] Awards should be "restrained and modest."[1199]

9–334   The principles referred to above would expose the negligent surveyor to liability for mental distress in situations where he performed his work under some contract with the claimant. Where there was no contract, on the ordinary principles applied in tort, a claimant cannot recover damages for distress unless it has caused psychiatric injury[1200] and it was reasonably foreseeable that physical or psychiatric injury would result from the defendant's breach of duty.[1201] In practice situations where a surveyor's negligence can give rise to such claims will be rare.

9–335   **Other cases.** Where a rent review clause provided that a revised rent was to be fixed in default of agreement by an independent expert, the surveyor acting for the lessee was negligent in failing to submit representations on his client's behalf within the time-limit specified and as a result a substantially higher rent was fixed. The measure of damages was held to be the difference in value between the rent as fixed and a more realistic market rent as decided by the judge.[1202] Where estate agents utterly failed to provide an acceptable level of service to the owner of a flat, as a result of which the tenant was able to put in other occupiers, commit dilapidations and act generally in default, it was held that the owner could recover the loss of rent arising from their failure to take rent in advance, other general arrears of rent, an unpaid telephone account, gas bills, the cost of dilapidations and for disturbance.[1203]

17.—VETERINARY SURGEONS AND PRACTITIONERS

9–336   **The duty and standard of care.** The civil liability of veterinary surgeons towards the owners of animals is similar in all respects to that of dental and

---

[1197] *Farley v Skinner* [2002] 2 A.C. 732 (where there was a specific contractual undertaking to investigate a matter important to the innocent party's peace of mind, namely whether a property would be affected by aircraft noise). See Lawson, "Inconvenient measures" 145 S.J. 1004; Turner, "Solicitors keep calm amid distress signals" L.S.G. 2003, 100(3), 37; Jones and Morris, "The distressing effects of professional incompetence" P.N. 2004, 20 (2) 118 ; Glover, "Distress signals" L.S.G. 2007, 104 (34), 30.

[1198] *Hobbs v London and South Western Railway* (1874) L.R. 10 Q.B. 111, per Mellor J. at 122, the physical element should at least a threshold where it can be described as "real and substantial".

[1199] per Lord Steyn in *Farley v Skinner*, n.1187 above, at 911 (£10,000 at the very top end of what was appropriate for distress caused by aircraft noise). See also *Watts v Morrow*, n.1 above (trial judge's award of £4,000 each to a couple whose marriage had allegedly broken down as a result of the surveyor's breach of duty, reduced to £750 since the proper basis of assessment was confined to their physical discomfort for about eight months).

[1200] What amounts to psychiatric illness is discussed in Ch.2, para.2–117, above.

[1201] See *Page v Smith* [1996] A.C.155 and Ch.2, paras 2–125 to 2–154, above.

[1202] *Rajdev v Becketts* [1989] 35 E.G. 107.

[1203] *Murray v Sturgis* (1981) 260 E.G. 61.

medical practitioners towards their patients.[1204] Their liability for any want of care will arise principally in contract[1205] but doubtless there is a concurrent duty in tort and they will be liable for any damage caused by their negligence. A veterinary practitioner impliedly warrants any drugs or substances used as being reasonably fit for the purpose for which they are required.[1206] The standard of care is that of the ordinarily competent veterinary practitioner displaying ordinary competence and skill.[1207]

ILLUSTRATIONS

In *Dodd and Dodd v Wilson and McWilliam*,[1208] the claimants, who were **9-337** farmers and cattle breeders, consulted the defendant, who was a veterinary surgeon, for advice concerning the use of corynebacterium toxoid, a serum which purported to reduce the incidence of summer mastitis among cattle. The defendant informed them that he had administered the toxoid to other herds and had obtained reasonably good results. Although he would not guarantee that the toxoid would prevent or cure the disease, it could do no harm. He was asked to inoculate the cattle but many of the beasts became seriously sick as a result of a defect in the serum used. The defendant was liable inter alia, for breach of an implied condition in the contract under which his services were supplied that the serum would be reasonably fit for the purpose for which it was required. In *Chute Farms Ltd v Curtis*[1209] the defendant, a veterinary surgeon, was called in to treat the claimants' thoroughbred yearling colt which had become lame. The treatment was carried out by an assistant, who merely applied a poultice to the animal's leg and the colt died soon afterwards. The defendant was held vicariously liable for his assistant's failure to use reasonable care and skill in treating the animal: proper treatment required injection with anti-tetanus serum. Experience had shown that a prophylactic dose, administered in time, was successful in the vast majority of such cases.

[1204] See para.9–107 and para.9–109, above. See also Foster, "The Price of Animal Suffering", 143 New L.J. 123.

[1205] *Glyn v McGarel-Groves, The Times,* August 22, 2006, CA (on the facts, a veterinary, instructed to attend while another veterinary carried out a drugs treatment to a horse, was under a contractual duty of care not simply to observe the treatment but also to satisfy himself that he knew precisely what the treatment was, so as to ensure that nothing remotely inappropriate occurred).

[1206] *Dodd and Dodd v Wilson and McWilliam* [1946] 2 All E.R. 691.

[1207] See para.9–124, above.

[1208] [1946] 2 All E.R. 691, above.

[1209] *The Times,* October 10, 1961.

CHAPTER 10

HIGHWAYS AND TRANSPORT

1. Highways

(A) Maintenance of the highway

Introduction. At common law no action lay if a highway, which was **10–01** repairable by the inhabitants at large, fell into a state of disrepair, resulting in damage to a person using it. Originally, liability to repair public highways rested upon the inhabitants of any parish through which the highway passed, each parish being responsible for that part of the highway within its own bounds. However the parishes had no collective fund from which damages could be recovered and it was impractical for a plaintiff to sue each individual member of the parish for a proportion of the damages.[1] That left an action by indictment as the only remedy for non-repair.[2] When the Highway Act 1835 transferred the duty of repairing highways to the surveyor of highways, it was held that he was entitled to the same immunity as the inhabitants of the parish.[3] In course of time various statutes, up to the Highways Act 1959, transferred the duty to maintain

---

[1] *Russell v Men of Devon* (1788) 2 T.R. 667.
[2] This procedure was abolished (though it had long fallen into disuse) by the Highways Act 1959. The procedure is now by way of service of a notice on the highway authority: see ss.56 and 322 of the Highways Act 1980, which consolidates the various previous Acts.
[3] *Young v Davis* (1862) 7 H. & N. 760; affirmed 2 H. & C. 197; *M'Kinnon v Penson* (1854) 9 Ex. 609.

the highway from the inhabitants of the parish to statutory highway authorities but it remained the position that no private law remedy was available to a person suffering loss as a result of non-repair.[4]

10–02   **The Highways Act 1980.** The position at common law was not consistent with modern requirements and after pressure to change the law[5] the Highways (Miscellaneous Provisions) Act 1961 was introduced which, inter alia, abrogated[6] the rule of law exempting the inhabitants at large from liability for non-repair of highways[7] and provided a defence of "due care" for a highway authority[8] sued for damage[9] arising from a failure to maintain the highway. This Act and the Highways Act 1959 were subsequently consolidated in the Highways Act 1980. It is important to recognise that the remedy in respect of a breach of the highway authority's duty to maintain the highway is founded upon a breach of statutory duty and not upon the tort of negligence.[10]

10–03   Section 41 of the Highways Act 1980 imposes a duty on highway authorities[11] to maintain the highway.[12] Maintenance includes repair.[13] The duty is to maintain the structure and fabric of the highway which includes not only the surface of the highway but the drains associated with it.[14] The duty is absolute,[15] but not in the sense that the highway has to be perfect.[16] A claimant cannot succeed in fixing the highway authority with liability for an accident unless it is proved that the

---

[4] See, e.g. the minority judgment of Lord Denning M.R. in *Haydon v Kent County Council* [1978] Q.B. 343, CA for a summary of the position at common law. Lord Denning's judgment was subsequently approved by the House of Lords in *Goodes v East Sussex County Council* [2000] 1 W.L.R. 1356, HL.

[5] Notably from the General Council of the Bar in 1960.

[6] The Highways (Miscellaneous Provisions) Act 1961 s.1(1).

[7] Any reference to a highway in s.1 included a reference to a bridge: The Highways (Miscellaneous Provisions) Act 1961 s.1(4).

[8] The Highways (Miscellaneous Provisions) Act 1961 s.1(4) provided that in the application of this section to highways in London repairable by the inhabitants at large, references to the highway authority were references to the council responsible for the maintenance of the highway.

[9] This section did not apply to damage resulting from breaking, opening, tunnelling or boring under a street by way of code-regulated works which occurred: (a) before the completion of the reinstatment or making good of the relevant part of the street (under the Public Utilities Street Works Act 1950 s.7(2)); or (b) where the relevant part of the street is the subject of an election (Public Utilities Street Works Act 1950 Sch.III); see subs.(7).

[10] *Gorringe v Calderdale MBC* [2004] 1 W.L.R. 1057, HL.

[11] See s.1, the highway authority is not always the Local Authority.

[12] Highway includes the whole or part of the highway and includes any bridge or tunnel (s.328 Highways Act 1980). The duty owed pursuant to s.41 can co-exist with duties owed by the providers of tramways where tram tracks are inserted into a road: *Roe v Sheffield City Council* [2003] EWCA Civ 01.

[13] s.329(1).

[14] *Burns v Emmerson* [1968] 1 Q.B. 374, also *The Department of Transport, Environment and the Regions v Mott Macdonald Ltd* [2006] EWCA Civ 1089. A failure to maintain road furniture, such as a bollard, does not give rise to a breach of s.41 although it may give rise to an action in negligence—see *Shine v London Borough of Tower Hamlets* [2006] EWCA Civ 852.

[15] *Griffiths v Liverpool Corp* [1967] 1 Q.B. 374.

[16] per Lord Hoffmann in *Goodes v East Sussex County Council* [2000] 1 W.L.R. 1356, HL.

highway was dangerous, in the sense that danger could reasonably be anticipated from its use.[17] For a claimant to succeed it must be proved that:

> "(a) the highway was in such a condition that it was dangerous to traffic or pedestrians in the sense that, in the ordinary course of human affairs, danger may reasonably have been anticipated from its continued use by the public;
> (b) the dangerous condition was created by the failure to maintain or repair the highway; and
> (c) the injury or damage resulted from such a failure."[18]

What amounts to a dangerous hazard depends on the circumstances of the case. It is no longer, if it ever was, simply a matter of measurement and attempts on that basis to make comparisons between cases have been deprecated. While a difference of level in a pavement of more than 25mm has been found to be a breach of s.41 of the 1980 Act, in some circumstances a smaller difference may be sufficient. The location of a potential hazard will generally be significant so that what may be acceptable on a quiet rural lane may not be on a busy city street, albeit the measurement is the same. Also, the type of traffic using the highway is likely to be relevant: a stretch of pavement outside a factory may be judged differently from pavement outside an old people's home.[19] The question is not whether the highway as a whole is in an unsatisfactory state, but whether the specific location where the accident occurred is dangerous.[20] The Local Authorities' Association publishes a code of good practice for highway maintenance. The code gives guidance as to the circumstances in which a particular defect is sufficiently hazardous as to justify repair having regard to its dimensions and location. Many highway authorities have adopted the code, which may be referred to by a court as a guide, in deciding if a defect was sufficiently dangerous to found a breach of s.41. **10–04**

ILLUSTRATIONS

A breach has been established where: a rocking flagstone protruded between half and three-quarters of one inch (12.7mm to 19.1mm) on a busy highway[21]; and where a manhole cover protruded 12mm above the pavement.[22] No breach was established where a paving stone had sunk to three-quarters of an inch (19.1mm) below an adjacent stone.[23] Erosion on a little used riverside path which had caused a depression to a depth of 0.6m but where there was ample room on the remainder of the path to pass in safety did not constitute a breach of **10–05**

---

[17] In *Burnside v Emmerson* [1968] 1 W.L.R. 1490, 1497 the duty was expressed to be a duty to keep the highway "in such good repair as it renders it reasonably passable for the ordinary traffic of the neighbourhood at all seasons of the year without danger caused by its physical condition." The highway authority in carrying out its duty must bear in mind that some users of the highway may be negligent or may make mistakes, see *Rider v Rider* [1973] Q.B. 343.
[18] See *Mills v Barnsley Metropolitan Borough Council* [1992] P.I.Q.R. P291, CA at 292.
[19] *Rider v Rider* [1973] Q.B. 505, CA, at 518.
[20] *James v Preselli Pembrokeshire District Council* [1993] P.I.Q.R. P114, CA.
[21] *Griffiths v Liverpool Corp* [1967] 1 Q.B. 374, CA.
[22] *Reid v British Telecommunications Plc, The Times*, June 27, 1987.
[23] *Meggs v Liverpool Corp* [1968] 1 W.L.R. 689, cf. [1968] 1 All E.R. 1137, CA.

10–05

s.41.[24] Where the verge of a narrow stretch of rural A road had sunk to depths of between four inches (10cm) and 12 inches (30cm) so that the driver of a car lost control of her car when the nearside wheel dropped onto the verge, a breach of s.41 was established.[25]

10–06   It has been held that a person who has suffered purely economic loss resulting from a highway authority's breach of its statutory duty to maintain a highway is not entitled to recover that loss from the authority.[26]

10–07   **Transient hazards.** In *Goodes v East Sussex County Council*[27] the House of Lords held that the duty to maintain the highway pursuant to s.41 of the Highways Act 1980, was the same duty as that described above as formerly imposed upon the inhabitants at large of a parish at common law.[28] Accordingly, there was no duty upon a highway authority to take measures to prevent the accumulation of snow and ice upon the highway by the application of salt or grit and there was no duty to take measures to remove snow and ice which had already accumulated. A modification of this common law rule is provided by s.111 of the Railway and Transport Safety Act 2003, which came into force on October 31, 2003, and amended s.41 of the Highways Act 1980 to place a duty upon a highway authority to ensure "so far as is reasonably practicable, safe passage along a highway is not endangered by snow and ice". It should be noted that this statutory amendment extends the duty only in relation to snow and ice. In respect of other transient hazards[29] the liability of the highway authority is limited to failures to maintain the physical fabric of the highway.

10–08   **Illustrations of liability for transient hazards.** Liability was established where floodwater collected on the side of the road after torrential rain: although the highway authority had established a proper system of maintenance, it was vicariously liable for a workman's failure to carry out the system properly.[30] But the mere fact that floodwater has collected on the side of the road after heavy rain is not itself evidence of lack of maintenance, so where a pedestrian was injured whilst trying to cross a flooded road, liability was not established.[31] Where the drainage system was not adequate or there was a failure to ensure that existing drains could cope, the highway authority was liable.[32] A local authority was

---

[24] *Jones v Rhondda Cynon Taff County Borough Council* [2008] EWCA Civ 1497.

[25] *West Sussex County Council v Russell* [2010] EWCA Civ 71.

[26] *Wentworth v Wiltshire County Council* [1993] Q.B. 654, (the survival of the claimant's dairy farm depended upon the ability of the Milk Marketing Board's road tanker to use the highway to collect the milk production but, owing to lack of repair, the road had become dangerous and no such collection could be made).

[27] [2000] 1 W.L.R. 1356, HL., overruling *Haydon v Kent County Council* [1978] Q.B. 343. In *Sandar v Dept of Transport, Environment and the Regions* [2005] 1 W.L.R. 1632, CA a common law duty of care owed to a motorist by a highway authority in respect of ice was rejected.

[28] para.10–01 above.

[29] In *Misell v Essex County Council, The Times,* December 16, 1994, a highway authority was held liable for failing to remove mud from the highway but the correctness of the decision must be in doubt following *Goodes v East Sussex County Council* [2000] 1 W.L.R. 1356, HL.

[30] *Burnside v Emmerson* [1968] 1 W.L.R. 1490, also *The Department of Transport, Environment and the Regions v Mott Macdonald Ltd* [2006] EWCA Civ 1089.

[31] *Pritchard v Clwyd County Council* [1993] P.I.Q.R. P21, CA.

[32] *Thoburn v Northumberland County Council* (1999) 1 L.G.L.R. 819.

liable where, after a request from the police, it removed "Keep Left" bollards before a protest march in order to prevent them being used as missiles and, before the road was closed, a motorcyclist collided with the plinth upon which the bollards had been positioned.[33]

Land adjacent to the highway. A highway authority's statutory duty to maintain the highway does not require it to carry out work on land adjacent to the highway but not forming part of it, and although there is power in the Act for notice to be served upon a landowner requiring the removal of an obstruction where it impedes the view of the highway's users,[34] it has been held that the existence of such a power does not provide a basis for imputing a common law duty of care to exercise it in an appropriate case.[35] **10–09**

Road marks.[36] In *Gorringe v Calderdale Metropolitan Borough Council*,[37] the claimant alleged that a collision between motor vehicles in which she was involved, was caused by the highway authority's failure to paint the word "slow" on the road at the crest of a hill where a driver's forward vision was limited. Her claim against the highway authority failed.[38] The failure to mark the road did not amount to a breach of s.41 of the Highways Act 1980. **10–10**

In *Thompson v Hampshire County Council*,[39] the claimant was walking in darkness along a beaten earth path beside a road. The path formed part of the highway and for a portion of its length it ran beside a ditch. The claimant fell into the ditch, sustaining injury. Her claim failed, because the existence of the ditch did not constitute a failure to maintain the highway itself and thus there had been no breach of s.41 of the 1980 Act. **10–11**

The statutory defence. If a breach of s.41 of the Highways Act 1980 is made out, liability will not follow if the highway authority if it can establish the statutory defence set out in s.58 of the Act. That section provides that it is a defence for a highway authority to prove that it had taken such care as in all the circumstances was reasonably required to secure that the part of the highway to which the action relates was not dangerous to traffic. In considering whether the defence is made out the court must have regard to the following factors: **10–12**

(a) the character of the highway and the traffic which was reasonably to be expected to use it;

---

[33] *Cassin v Bexley London Borough Council* [1999] L.G.R. 694, CA.
[34] s.79.
[35] *Stovin v Wise* [1996] A.C. 923. In *Yetkin v Newham Borough Council* [2010] EWCA Civ 776, a Highway Authority was liable for negligently placing and failing to cut bushes situated by a pedestrian crossing.
[36] See also para.10–15, below.
[37] [2004] 1 W.L.R. 1057, HL.
[38] In *Bird v Pearce and Somerset County Council* [1978] R.T.R. 290 white markings on a road at the mouth of a junction were obliterated. The highway authority's failure to display temporary warning signs was held to be negligent. In *Gorringe v Calderdale Metropolitan Borough Council*, this decision was considered and distinguished on the grounds that in *Bird* the highway authority had negligently introduced a new source of danger.
[39] [2004] EWCA Civ 1016.

(b) the standard of maintenance appropriate to a highway;

(c) the state of repair in which a reasonable person would have expected to find the highway;

(d) whether the highway authority knew, or might reasonably have been expected to know, that the condition of the part of the highway was likely to cause damage to the users of the highway; and

(e) where the highway authority could not reasonably have been expected to repair the highway before the cause of action arose, what warning notices of its condition had been displayed.

10–13   It is no defence for the highway authority to prove that it has arranged for a competent person to carry out the maintenance of the highway, unless it is also proved that it has given him proper instructions concerning the maintenance, and he has carried them out. The section binds the Crown and the Act applies where the claimant sues in negligence, breach of statutory duty or nuisance.

10–14   The defence may be established upon proof by a highway authority that it has a system of inspection whereby defects are recorded and those that require repair are subsequently repaired. In *Allen v Elmbridge Borough Council*,[40] a policy of inspecting access roads every 12 months was reasonable and provided a defence under s.58. Where in a residential area a highway authority inspected every six months and a missing stop cock cover was not noticed because it was covered by grass, the statutory defence was nevertheless made out.[41] In *Harrison v Derby City Council*[42] a six-monthly inspection system in an area where there were a lot of Victorian houses with cellars which were liable to drop, creating depressions in the surface of the footway, was held to sufficient.

10–15   **Statutory duty to monitor road accidents.** Pursuant to s.39 of the Highways Act 1980, as amended, highway authorities have a duty to carry out studies into road accidents within the area for which they have responsibility and, in the light of those studies, take such measures as appear to be appropriate to prevent accidents occurring. Although the section is expressed in mandatory terms there is a discretion how the duty is carried out. In *Larner v Solihull Metropolitan Borough Council*,[43] the claimant was injured when she drove from a minor road across a junction with a major road. She had passed two give way signs on her approach to the junction. The highway authority later placed an advanced warning sign indicating the need to give way at the junction. It was held that the authority had not acted outside the scope of its discretion and there was therefore no breach of duty. In any event the absence of the advance warning sign did not cause the accident. Thereafter in *Gorringe v Calderdale Metropolitan Borough Council*,[44] the House of Lords ruled that there was no private law remedy arising

---

[40] [1999] B.L.G.R. 65, Q.B.D.
[41] *Clark v London Borough of Havering* [2007] EWHC 3427. Although the Local Authority had the power to cut the grass verge where the stop cock was concealed, a failure to cut the grass regularly could not be founded upon as indicative of a failure to take reasonable measures for the purposes of the s.58 defence.
[42] [2008] EWCA Civ 583.
[43] (2001) R.T.R. 469, CA.
[44] [2004] 1 W.L.R. 1057, HL.

out of a breach of a highway authority's duties under s.39. No action in negligence can be maintained by an individual claiming that loss has been sustained by reason of a highway authority failing to implement the requirements of the section. Comments made by the Court of Appeal in *Larner*[45] that exceptionally a private law remedy might arise under s.39 were disapproved.

(B) Dangers on the Highway

Duties in respect of a highway. It is a public nuisance[46] to do any act on a **10–16** highway which hinders or obstructs the free passage of the public, and an action will lie for any damage suffered by an individual in consequence of such act, over and above the damage occasioned to the public at large.[47]

In many cases the facts which give rise to such an action by an individual member of the public will also provide the basis for an allegation that the defendant was in breach of a concurrent duty of care.

Illustrations of liability for obstructions. Where a local authority placed a **10–17** post in the middle of a footpath to prevent cattle straying and the claimant collided with the pole in darkness the authority was liable.[48] Liability was also established where a heap of rubbish from road repairs was left lawfully in the road but was left unlit.[49] Leaving an unguarded trench in the highway amounted to negligence.[50] Liability was established where a ridge was left in the highway which caused a vehicle to collide with a bridge.[51] There was a nuisance where a large crowd of people were permitted to gather outside the doors of a theatre.[52] Other examples of obstructions include: selling ice cream through the window of a shop instead of over the counter[53]; leaving horses and carts standing for an unreasonable length of time or in an unreasonable number[54]; leaving a large lorry in a town's main road[55]; parking two vehicles opposite each other[56]; a pool of acid on the highway[57]; a piece of fat from a butcher's shop on the pathway[58]; a

---

[45] (2001) R.T.R. 469, CA.

[46] For nuisance, generally, see *Clerk & Lindsell on Torts* 19th edn 2006 Ch.20.

[47] *Benjamin v Storr* (1874) L.R. 9 C.P. 400; *Fritz v Hobson* (1880) 14 Ch.D. 542; *Vanderpant v Mayfair Hotel Co* [1930] 1 Ch.138. As regards vehicles parked on the highway, see paras 10–253 to 10–257, below.

[48] *Lamley v E. Retford Corp* (1891) 55 J.P. 133.

[49] *Penny v Wimbledon Urban District Council* [1899] 2 Q.B. 72.

[50] *Gray v Pullen* (1864) 5 B.&S. 970.

[51] *Hill v Tottenham Urban District Council* (1898) 79 L.T. 495.

[52] *Barber v Penley* [1893] 2 Ch.447, but cf. *Dwyer v Mansfield* [1946] K.B. 437 (queuing for potatoes during wartime food shortages).

[53] *Fabbri v Morris* [1947] 1 All E.R. 315.

[54] *Fritz v Hobson* (1880) 14 Ch.D. 542.

[55] *Chesterfield Corp v A. Robinson (Transport) Ltd* (1955) 106 L.J. 61. See also *Dymond v Pearce* [1972] 1 Q.B. 496.

[56] *Stevens v Kelland* [1970] R.T.R. 445.

[57] *Pope v Fraser* (1939) 55 T.L.R. 324.

[58] *Dollman v Hillman* [1941] 1 All E.R. 355.

slick of mud on the road[59]; clouds of smoke and steam obscuring visibility[60]; and a group of people picketing an estate agency.[61]

10–18   Liability was established where the claimant was injured by a stream of water which had emerged in the highway without measures being taken to warn approaching traffic of its existence.[62] Where a heap of stones was lawfully left in the roadway but some of the stones had been spilled negligently on to the footpath, a pedestrian, who fell over them and was injured, successfully sued for damages.[63] A pedestrian may recover damages, even when the material in question is not on the footpath, if it is placed so close to it as to be a nuisance. Thus, when a man tripped over a pile of slates, lying in the highway near the kerb he succeeded in his action and was not guilty of contributory negligence "if he does not constantly look down to his feet".[64] A similar result followed where a carpet was put on the footpath, because "if a person puts anything across the pavement and a person stumbles over it, the owner is liable for the consequences. The passer-by is not bound to look for mats on the highway."[65] Likewise, where the defendant's workmen dug a hole in the pavement and left it unlit but covered over with a specially made steel plate which projected one-eighth of an inch, they were liable in negligence to the elderly claimant, who hurt herself by tripping and falling over it: they had introduced a new and unexpected addition to the surface of the roadway.[66]

10–19   On the other hand, during a drought, when a small hosepipe had been laid across the highway to enable water to be brought from a tank to the defendant's house, and the claimant, who was delivering milk, tripped over it, her action failed. The presence of the hosepipe on the highway was not a nuisance, because in the circumstances it was reasonable for the defendant to put it there.[67]

10–20   **Trees.** The occupier of land is not liable if a tree,[68] not known to be unsafe, falls on to the highway and injures someone passing by.[69] The duty is to act as a prudent landowner to prevent trees which adjoin the highway from being a danger to highway users, and there is no obligation to call in an expert to examine trees,[70] unless there is reason to believe that they may be unsafe. When a tree fell,

---

[59] *Alexander v Harrison* (1967) 63 D.L. R. (2d) 383.

[60] *Holling v Yorkshire Traction Co* [1948] 2 All E.R. 662, also *Funnell v C.P. Ry.* (1964) 45 D.L.R. (2d) 481.

[61] *Hubbard v Pitt* [1976] Q.B. 142.

[62] *Hill v New River Co* (1868) 9 B. & S 303.

[63] *Gould v Birkenhead Corp* (1910) 74 J.P. 105 (no contributory negligence was found).

[64] *Almeroth v Chivers Ltd* [1948] 1 All E.R. 53.

[65] *De Teyron v Waring* (1885) 1 T.L.R. 414, per Coleridge C.J.; *Watson v Ellis* (1885) 1 T.L.R. 317.

[66] *Pitman v Southern Electricity Board* (1978) 76 L.G.R. 579.

[67] *Trevett v Lee* [1955] 1 W.L.R. 113 applied in *Perkins v Glyn* [1976] R.T.R. ix Note (April) (visibility along a highway in daylight was obscured by smoke coming from burning stubble in an adjacent field and caused a collision); *Clarke v J. Sugrue & Sons, The Times,* May 29, 1959 (a piece of rope left on the highway by independent contractors).

[68] See Brown, "Trees: a Knotty Branch of the Law" 128 New L.J. 481.

[69] *Noble v Harrison* [1926] 2 K.B. 332; *Cunliffe v Banks* [1945] 1 All E.R. 459; cf. *Shirvell v Hackwood Estates Ltd* [1938] 2 K.B. 577. In Eire, see *Lynch v Hetherton* [1991] 2 I.R. 405.

[70] e.g. the situation in *Knight v Hext* (1979) 253 E.G. 1227, CA.

owing to a root disease which was not visible on an external examination, and caused damage, the owner was not liable.[71] When a motorcar on the highway was damaged by the fall of a 130-year-old elm tree, which had never been lopped, topped or pollarded, and the fall was caused by a long-standing disease of the roots, undetectable on external examination, the owner was not liable.[72] Conversely when a tree, which had been dying for some years and should have been known to be dangerous to an ordinary landowner, fell and caused damage, the owner was liable.[73]

10–21 A local authority which plants trees near the highway is under a duty to cut them back when they grow over the highway so as to interfere with traffic. When this was not done, liability followed when an overhanging branch broke a window in a bus and injured a passenger.[74] A local authority was also liable in negligence to the occupiers of property which suffered subsidence as a result of tree root dessication, caused by trees growing in the adjacent highway, where they were not the highway authority, nor owner or occupier of the land on which the trees grew, but provided an arboriculture service under an agency agreement with the highway authority which included inspecting and maintaining the trees in question.[75]

10–22 If, without negligence, a tree falls on to the highway, the occupier of the land is not bound to light it or give warning of it, so that, should a motorist collide with it, the occupier is under no liability.[76] By way of contrast, if a local authority in the course of road-widening operations leaves a tree, adjoining the highway, in such a danger of falling that it is both "patent and imminent", liability will be established for damage to users of the highway which is caused by its fall.[77]

10–23 **Trench improperly filled in.** If a trench is dug lawfully in the highway, for example to lay gas, sewer or water pipes, it must be filled in so as not to be dangerous to traffic, either by leaving a hollow[78] or a soft-filled trench[79] or by creating a raised mound in the highway.[80]

---

[71] *Cunliffe v Banks* [1945] 1 All E.R. 459.
[72] *Caminer v Northern and London Investment Trust* [1951] A.C. 88. The test as stated by Lord Normand therein was applied in *Quinn v Scott* [1965] 1 W.L.R. 1004 (the owner of a tree on a highway who has means of knowing that it is diseased and may fall is liable in negligence if it falls and causes an accident).
[73] *Brown v Harrison* [1947] W.N. 191.
[74] *Hale v Hants and Dorset Motor Service Ltd* [1947] 2 All E.R. 628. See too *Ponting v Noakes* [1894] 2 Q.B. 281; *Yetkin v Newham Borough Council* [2010] EWCA Civ 776.
[75] *L.E. Jones (Insurance Brokers) Ltd v Portsmouth City Council, The Times,* November 7, 2002, CA.
[76] *Hudson v Bray* [1917] 1 K.B. 520. Nor, apparently, to pay towards the costs of its removal, as was provided by the Highway (Miscellaneous Provisions) Act 1961 s.9, and, now re-enacted in the Highways Act 1980 s.150(4); *Williams v Devon County Council* (1966) 65 L.G.R. 119.
[77] *Mackie v Dumbartonshire County Council* [1927] W.N. 247.
[78] *Hartley v Rochdale Corp* [1908] 2 Q.B. 594.
[79] *Shoreditch Corp v Bull* (1904) 90 L.T. 210.
[80] *Peachey v Rowland* (1853) 13 C.B. 182. The decision that the employer was not liable for the negligence of his independent contractor in creating such a danger in the highway must be considered to be overruled by *Penny v Wimbledon Urban District Council* [1899] 2 Q.B. 72.

10–24   **Other hazards caused by excavation.** If a dangerous inequality in the highway is created, so as to cause a vehicle which is being driven along the highway to crash, the person creating the danger is liable.[81] Where a pavement is taken up and the paving stones are so laid as to give a false appearance of safety to pedestrians, the persons taking up the pavement will be liable for any injury thereby occasioned.[82] Again, when a telegraph pole was moved in order to allow the highway to be widened, and its hole was negligently filled in so that a wagon was damaged as a result of one of its wheels sinking into the hole, not only was the Post Office held liable for negligently filling in the hole, but the highway authority was also liable for throwing the road open for public use without first seeing that it was safe.[83] Where a local authority, which was both the highway and the sewer authority, employed a contractor to dig a trench and, afterwards, the trench was improperly filled in, so that the claimant's horse was injured in consequence of the surface giving way, the authority was liable.[84]

10–25   In contrast, a local authority was not liable where the owner of houses, pursuant to a notice served on him, dug a trench to connect his drains with the main sewer and improperly filled it in : he was not its agent for doing the work.[85] When a local authority, in the course of laying a new sewer, came across an old service pipe, which it knew was likely to become leaky, but neither carried out a repair nor laid down a new pipe, it was liable where, a few months later, the pipe did so leak that the earth subsided and caused a van to overturn.[86]

10–26   **Trench properly filled in but natural subsidence occurs later.** Where a trench has been dug in the highway and properly filled in but subsidence occurs later, owing to shrinkage of the materials, the person responsible for digging the trench may be held liable for damage thereby caused. In *Newsome v Darton Urban District Council*,[87] a local authority made a trench in the highway for the purpose of executing drainage work. The trench was filled in properly and the surface reinstated. A year after the work was finished, subsidence occurred, which caused a cyclist to be thrown from his bicycle. It was held that the local authority, having interfered with the surface of the road, was under a duty to restore it to its original condition, which could only be fulfilled by making good subsidence as and when it occurred. It was also negligent for the authority not to discover and rectify the danger.

---

[81] *Goodson v Sunbury Gas Co* (1896) 75 L.T. 251.
[82] *Drew v New River Co* (1834) 6 C. & P. 754.
[83] *Thompson v Bradford Corp and Tinsley* [1915] 3 K.B. 13.
[84] *Smith v West Derby Local Board* (1878) 3 C.P.D. 423.
[85] *Steel v Dartford L.B.* (1891) 60 L.J.Q.B. 256.
[86] *Cox v Paddington (Vestry)* (1891) 64 L.T. 566.
[87] [1938] 3 All E.R. 93. But cf. *Hyams v Webster* (1868) L.R. 4 Q.B. 138, which was not referred to in the judgment, where a contractor, employed by the Metropolitan Board of Works, dug a trench in the highway in connection with the laying of sewers and properly filled it in afterwards but it subsided later on during the winter months. The contractor was held not liable to the claimant for the injury to his horse, which had stepped in the subsided hole, on the ground that he was under no obligation to make good any subsequent subsidence, occurring after the trench had been properly filled in and the road reinstated.

Laying stopcocks, etc. in highway. When the highway is broken up to lay   **10–27**
sewers, gas or water pipes or the like, there is a duty to make good. A
reinstatement must be provided which will, in normal circumstances, be
serviceable for a reasonable length of time. When a local authority, which was
also the water authority, laid a stopcock in the footpath of an unmade highway at
the level at which the footpath would eventually have been made up but which,
at the time, projected above the surrounding pathway, and, in order to level it off,
rammed in earth, which the rain constantly eroded and washed away, it was liable
to a person who tripped over the projection.[88] On the contrary, where a stopcock
in the highway leaked and loosened some adjacent paving stones, as well as other
paving stones, some distance away, over which latter stones the claimant tripped
and fell, the Water Board, which had placed the stopcock in the highway, was not
liable: the leak was not the result of any negligence on the Board's part and there
was no evidence that the Board either knew or ought to have known that the stone
over which the claimant tripped was loose.[89]

Defective gratings, etc. in highway. A person who puts a grating, skylight,   **10–28**
coal plate or other structure in either the footpath or any other part of the highway
is bound to maintain it so that it does not become a source of danger. Thus, when
a man walked over a cellar cover set into the pavement, and it collapsed, his
claim for damages succeeded.[90] Such structures are usually part of a building and
so liability rests with the occupier although the owner may also be liable.[91] If the
structure in question is not part of a building but is part of the highway, the
highway authority and not the occupier is responsible for its maintenance.[92] If it
is neither part of a building nor part of the highway, then the person who placed
it in the highway is liable, unless it can be shown that the action was performed
under statutory or other authority exempting from liability in negligence.

Structure in existence before dedication of highway. At common law, if a   **10–29**
permanently fixed structure, such as a grating which formed part of the footpath,
was in existence before the dedication of the highway to the public, there was no
obligation on the occupier of premises adjoining the highway to repair it.
Accordingly, when a cellar flap projected above the street, so that a passer-by
stumbled over it and was injured at night, the occupier of the premises was held
not liable when it was proved that the flat was in existence before the highway.[93]

If the structure has been in existence as long as living memory, the inference   **10–30**
ought to be drawn that it was in existence at the time of the dedication, in the
absence of anything to suggest contrary inference.[94] The mere fact that it has
been pulled down and rebuilt, as where stone steps, leading from the street to the

---

[88] *Withington v Bolton Borough Council* [1937] 3 All E.R. 108; see also *Rider v Metropolitan Water Board* [1949] 2 K.B. 378.
[89] *Longhurst v Metropolitan Water Board* [1948] 2 All E.R. 834.
[90] *Heap v Ind Coope & Allsopp Ltd* [1940] 2 K.B. 476.
[91] See paras.10–37 et seq., below.
[92] *Robbins v Jones* (1863) C.A. (N.S.) 221.
[93] *Fisher v Prowse* (1862) 2 B. & S 770 at 779, 780.
[94] *Fisher v Prowse* (1862) 2 B. & S 770 at 779, 780.

door of a house, were removed and replaced by new steps to the street's newly altered level,[95] does not prevent the inference being drawn. Such structures become part of the highway and the highway authority is responsible for their maintenance and safety.

10–31   On the other hand, if a grating,[96] coal plate[97] or other movable structure is either under the control of the occupier, or is the property of the owner of the building to which it is appurtenant, it must be maintained in such a condition as not to be dangerous to the public. "The person who is in possession of the premises and who allows the coal-plate to be in a dangerous condition is the person responsible to the public for any injury resulting for its being out of repair."[98] Although described as nuisance, there is a concurrent duty of care. However, there is no absolute duty to make the structure safe, so that if, for example, a grating breaks because of some latent defect or for any other reason which is not the result of negligence, the occupier of the premises will not be liable.[99] Having said as much, this is an instance where the occupier can be liable for the negligence of his independent contractors.[100] Liability will also follow for failing to keep the structure in a proper state of repair, even if the occupier did not know that it was out of repair.[101]

10–32   When a structure in the highway does not form part of adjoining premises, an occupier or owner of those premises is not liable. Thus, where a highway authority formed a gutter in the highway, which was covered with removable iron carriage plates, and the cost of the works was paid by the frontagers, it was held that one of the latter was not liable to a person who caught her foot between two of the plates. It made no difference that the frontager had been in the habit of removing the plates for the purpose of cleaning the gutters.[102] Again, when there was a coal chute to the cellar of the defendant's house and, owing to the level of the pavement being raised, the local authority had left an access hole to it, the defendant was not liable to a person who had tripped in the hole so left: there was no duty on a frontager to maintain a highway which had been taken over by the local authority.[103] Likewise, where a local authority had raised a pavement and reset in it a metal slab, covering a cellar hole, which slab was in good condition before being reset but afterwards projected above the pavement, it was held that the frontager was not liable, under the Public Health Acts Amendment Act 1890 s.35(1),[104] to the claimant, who had tripped over the projection. He had not created the nuisance and had no power or duty to abate a nuisance created by the local authority.[105] By way of distinction the frontager was held liable under this

---

[95] *Cooper v Walker* (1862) 2 B. & S 770.
[96] *Gwinnell v Eamer* (1875) L.R. 10 C.P. 658.
[97] *Pretty v Bickmore* (1873) L.R. 8 C.P. 401.
[98] *Pretty v Bickmore* (1873) L.R. 8 C.P. 401 at 404, per Bovill C.J.
[99] See *Barker v Herbert* [1911] 2 K.B. 633; *Tarry v Ashton* (1876) 1 Q.B.D. 314; *Lambert v Lowestoft Corp* [1901] 1 K.B. 590.
[100] *Tarry v Ashton* (1876) 1 Q.B.D. 314.
[101] *Wringe v Cohen* [1940] 1 K.B. 229; *Heap v Ind Coope & Allsopp Ltd* [1940] 2 K.B. 476.
[102] *Jones v Rew* (1910) 79 L.J.K.B. 1030.
[103] *Horridge v Makinson* (1915) 83 L.J.K.B. 1294.
[104] This section is re-enacted in s.154 of the Highways Act 1980.
[105] *Penney v Berry* [1955] 1 W.L.R. 1021.

section where the purpose of the defective grating in the highway was to admit light to the cellar of the defendant's premises and the defendant knew of the defective condition of the grating.[106]

A statutory duty. The Highways Act 1980[107] s.180(6), imposes an obligation **10–33** on the owner or occupier or premises to keep every cellar-head, all gratings, lights, coal holes and the covers of surface openings in good condition, but the duty is not absolute. Someone alleging injury as a result of a breach of the section, must still prove either negligence or nuisance in order to recover damages. Hence, if a cover is broken, without the knowledge or fault of the owner or occupier, and very shortly afterwards an accident occurs, as a result of such breakage, liability may not be established.[108] For the purpose of this section, it does not matter whether the structure had been placed in the highway before or after dedication.[109]

Structures laid in highway under statutory powers. Many structures are **10–34** put upon the highway in connection with the supply of gas, water and electricity, and the provision of drains and sewers to adjoining properties. The work is performed under statutory authority, and accordingly, reference should always be made to the appropriate statute to see to what extent, if at all, the common law liability is affected.[110] Apart from any special statutory provisions, the duty is to take reasonable care to install and to maintain the structures, so that they are not dangerous to persons who use the highway with reasonable care.[111]

ILLUSTRATIONS

Where a water company laid a stopcock in the street, which was protected by **10–35** a guard box, a person who tripped over the lid of the box, which was out of repair, could recover from the water company, which alone had power to break up the street for the purpose of effecting repairs.[112] Where a water company was bound by statute to fix fire plugs into its mains and to keep them in proper order, it was liable when one of the caps to the plugs was broken and, thereby, the claimant's horse was injured.[113] Again, when a stopcock box was placed in the

---

[106] *Macfarlane v Gwalter* [1959] 2 Q.B. 332, distinguishing *Penney v Berry*, above.

[107] The Highways Act 1980 came into force on January 1, 1981, by virtue of s.345(2) and consolidated the Highways Acts 1959 to 1971 and related enactments.

[108] *Scott v Green & Sons* [1969] 1 W.L.R. 301, distinguishing *Macfarlane v Gwalter* [1959] 2 Q.B. 332, above.

[109] *Macfarlane v Gwalter* [1959] 2 Q.B. 332, distinguishing *Penney v Berry* [1955] 1 W.L.R. 1021.

[110] s.65 et seq. of the New Roads and Street Works Act 1991 set out general requirements as to standards and safety to be observed by any undertaker executing street works. There is unlikely to be a cause of action for breach of statutory duty where the Act imposes criminal sanctions, there being no such right under the comparable provisions of the Public Utilities Street Works Act 1950 which the 1991 Act replaced: see *Keating v Elvan Reinforced Concrete Co* [1968] 1 W.L.R. 722. The right to sue for negligence is, however, preserved by s.95(1).

[111] *Stockings v Lambeth Waterworks Co* (1891) 7 T.L.R. 460; *Hendra v Chelsea Waterworks Co* (1891) 8 T.L.R. 101; *Styles v East London Waterworks Co* (1887) 4 T.L.R. 190; *Strube v Southwark and Vauxhall Water Co* (1889) 5 T.L.R. 638.

[112] *Chapman v Fylde Waterworks Co* [1894] 2 Q.B. 599.

[113] *Bayley v Wolverhampton Waterworks* (1860) 6 H. & N. 241.

pavement, and, in order to make it level with the pavement, it was the practice of the water company to put in a wad to fill the hole caused by the box, a person who had caught her foot in the box, because no wad or an insufficient wad was put in, could recover.[114] In these cases, liability depended on the statutory duty to maintain. Thus, where the appropriate statute imposed the obligation to repair the box on the owner or occupier of the house and not upon the water company, the latter was not liable.[115]

10–36   It has been held that a statutory undertaker was not negligent in relying on a highway authority's six-monthly road inspection, rather than inspecting its manhole covers itself. But, it will be taken to have the same knowledge that it would have had, if it had inspected these covers at the time when the local authority had inspected its roads.[116]

10–37   If the work in question was properly maintained but became dangerous sometime later on, owing to the wearing away of the surrounding highway, the person whose duty it was to maintain the work was not liable.[117] On the other hand, if the highway has subsided owing to the negligent way in which the work was originally done, the person who did the work will be liable.[118] When a grating and framework were laid so as to cause a considerable depression in the road, but the work was done with due care and skill according to the usual method employed at the time, it was held that the claim of an injured cyclist failed, in the absence of evidence that either the road authority of the sewer authority knew, or could have known, by the exercise of reasonable care, of the existence of the defect.[119]

10–38   **Interference by third party.** If the lid of a valve-box or other cover which ought to be maintained level with the surface of the road, is pulled up by the act of a third party, the liability of the persons responsible for the maintenance of the lid or cover to persons falling over it, depends on whether the nature of the lid or cover is such that the act of the third party is one which ought reasonably to have been anticipated. Accordingly, where a large cover was pulled up, thereby causing a dangerous obstruction in the street, following "the malicious act of a third person against which precautions would have been inoperative", the Water Board which maintained the cover, was not liable.[120] Conversely, where the lid was a small one, which could be opened easily by a child, and the Water Board knew that children were apt to tamper which such lids, a person who had tripped

---

[114] *Osborn v Metropolitan Water Board* (1910) 102 L.T. 217; *Rosenbaum v Metropolitan Water Board* (1910) 103 L.T. 284 at 739.
[115] *Batt v Metropolitan Water Board* [1911] 2 K.B. 965; *Mist v Metropolitan Water Board* (1915) 84 L.J.K.B. 2041.
[116] *Reid v British Telecommunications, The Times*, June 27, 1987, CA.
[117] *Moore v Lambeth Waterworks Co* (1886) 17 Q.B.D. 462. cf. *Withington v Bolton Borough Council* [1937] 3 All E.R. 108.
[118] *Hartley v Rochdale Corp* [1908] 2 K.B. 594.
[119] *Papworth v Battersea Corp* [1916] 1 K.B. 583.
[120] *Simpson v Metropolitan Water Board* (1917) 15 L.G.R. 629.

over such on opened lid in the roadway succeeded in an action for damages.[121]

Liability of local authorities for street works. If a grid, covering the **10–39** entrance to a sewer, was defective, so as to injure persons who were passing along the highway, the sanitary authority was liable.[122] Similarly, where a local authority, to enable it to water the streets, had placed a box covered with an iron flap in the footway, so that a pedestrian slipped and was hurt because the flap had worn smooth, the authority was liable.[123] The same result followed with regard to a manhole.[124] Where a local authority had built a barrel drain under the highway, and the drain had fallen into disrepair, as a result of which a hole appeared in the road, it was liable to a person who was injured as a result of driving into the hole, which had been left open and unfenced.[125]

There is no liability, however, if reasonable care has been taken to erect or **10–40** maintain the work. Where a sewer was constructed with due care and of proper materials and, owing to the mortar in one of the joints having been worked away by rats, a cavity was formed below the surface of the road, which collapsed and injured a horse using the highway, the owner's action for damages failed. The existence of the cavity was not known to and could not by the exercise of reasonable care have been discovered by the sewer authority.[126]

Materials or equipment placed on highway. Even before the Highways **10–41** (Miscellaneous Provisions) Act 1961,[127] the old common law rule, namely that a highway authority was liable for misfeasance but not for nonfeasance, applied only to disrepair of the road qua road. It did not extend to something such as a grating[128] placed in the road, or ridges in the road surface, when they were left behind after the obliteration of the central white lines.[129] Accordingly, a local highway authority, which places and maintains traffic studs on a highway, must use reasonable care to maintain them in a safe condition. Where such a stud had become loose and dangerous, with the result that, some three weeks later, it shot across the road after a motorist had driven over it, and knocked down a cyclist, the authority was liable.[130]

A highway authority which became the owner of a tram track after it had been **10–42** abandoned by the undertakers, was liable to a cyclist who was injured owing to

---

[121] *Wells v Metropolitan Water Board* (1937) 54 T.L.R. 104.
[122] *White v Hindley Local Board* (1875) L.R. 10 Q.B. 219. This was so, even though in its capacity as highway authority, it was under no liability for nonfeasance at that time.
[123] *Blackmore v Vestry of Mile End Old Town* (1882) 9 Q.B.D. 451.
[124] *Winslowe v Bushey Urban District Council* (1908) 72 J.P. 259.
[125] *Borough of Bathurst v MacPherson* (1879) 5 App.Cas. 256 at 265. The decision was explained in *Municipal Council of Sydney v Bourke* [1895] A.C. 433.
[126] *Lambeth v Lowestoft Corp* [1901] 1 K.B. 590.
[127] The provisions of which were repealed and re-enacted in the consolidating Highways Act 1980, which came into force on January 1, 1981.
[128] *Connolly v Ministry of Transport* (1965) 63 L.G.R. 372, CA.
[129] *Bright v Ministry of Transport* [1971] R.T.R. 253. The dicta of Lord Denning M.R. (at 258D–E), however, was not followed by the CA in *Rider v Rider* [1973] Q.B. 505.
[130] *Skilton v Epsom Urban District Council* [1937] 1 K.B. 112.

the dangerous condition of the track, as a result of the failure to remove it and make good the road surface.[131] A private law remedy exists for a breach of statutory duty arising pursuant to s.25 of the Tramways Act 1870 whereby a the upper most surface of the tracks must be "on a level" with the adjacent road surface. [132]

10-43   Things which are placed temporarily in the highway, whilst necessary work on the highway is being carried out by the highway authority, do not give rise to liability if they are clearly visible. So, where a highway authority painted a white line in the highway and marked it with red flags, which had been set in tin cans to show that it was newly painted, no liability was incurred when, in daylight, a collision occurred because of a driver's failure to see and to avoid driving into them.[133]

10-44   If a drinking-fountain or similar structure is maintained in the highway, reasonable care must be taken to make it safe. Thus, where a stone on a drinking-fountain was loose so that, during a procession, it was dislodged by a person who had climbed on the fountain to gain a better view of the procession, and struck the claimant, the local authority was liable.[134] Where a nine-year-old boy attempted to leap-frog a bollard which was loose and wobbled causing the boy injury the local authority, who had placed the bollard on the highway, was liable in negligence for failing to maintain it.[135] It was reasonably foreseeable that a child would act as the claimant did.

10-45   If a local authority maintains a guard which is fitted with spikes to protect something erected in the highway, it must put them in such a position that they are not likely to be dangerous to persons using the highway with reasonable care. Accordingly, where trees which had been planted in the highway were guarded with iron spikes and the claimant collided with the spikes in the dark, during wartime lighting restrictions, his action for damages succeeded. The highway authority's duty was held to be not merely to make the guards reasonable safe at the date of their erection, but to continue to keep them reasonably safe.[136] Similarly, when a market was held in the public street, near to a statue which was surrounded by a spiked railing, on which the claimant's cow became impaled, liability was established on the ground that the place was not reasonably safe for the standing of cattle.[137]

---

[131] *Simon v Islington Borough Council* [1943] K.B. 188.

[132] *Roe v Sheffield City Council* [2003] EWCA Civ 01.

[133] *Hughes v Sheppard* (1940) 163 L.T. 177. But where a lamp-post became stranded near to the centre of a busy road, following road widening operations, liability was established against the highway authority, see *Davies v Carmarthenshire County Council* [1971] R.T.R. 112.

[134] *McLoughlin v Warrington Corp* (1910) 75 J.P. 57. cf. *O'Keefe v Edinburgh Corp*, 1911 S.C. 18.

[135] *Shine v London Borough of Tower Hamlets* [2006] EWCA Civ 852.

[136] *Morrison v Sheffield Corp* [1917] 2 K.B. 866.

[137] *Lax v Darlington Corp* (1879) 5 Ex.D. 28.

Lights on dangerous objects. Where a local authority, pursuant to statutory **10–46** powers, puts some structure in the highway, which is dangerous if unlit,[138] or where a road is constructed in such a position or manner that it is dangerous if unlit,[139] there is a duty to take reasonable steps to prevent such works from being a danger to the public.[140] Where, however, the highway authority merely kept an obstruction in the same state as when it took over responsibility for the highway, a failure to light it did not amount to negligence.[141] Lighting is an obvious means of discharging the duty during the hours of darkness.[142] So, where a post was put in the middle of a footpath in order to prevent cattle from straying, and, in the dark, a pedestrian collided with it, because it was not illuminated, an action against the local authority succeeded.[143] Again, when a local authority had made a road, ending in an unfenced ravine, so that it was dangerous to traffic unless sufficient lighting was maintained, it was liable for injuries sustained by a motorist who drove into the ravine during the dark.[144] Both the railway authority and the local authority were liable for not lighting a wall, which, under statutory powers, had been built across a road in a place where there had formerly been a level-crossing and a cyclist collided with it at night.[145]

The local authority was liable when it had erected a tram refuge in the middle **10–47** of the street, with a bollard at one end, which was illuminated at night, but the light failed, with the result that in the dark a motorist crashed into it.[146] Where an air raid shelter was usually lit by a red lamp, which became extinguished, and, as a result, a cyclist collided with the shelter in the dark, the local authority was liable, although the usual street lighting was illuminated. The existence of street lighting did not absolve them from their duty to take reasonable care to give warning to the public of the presence of the shelter, by lighting or otherwise.[147]

Where the presence of lighting is relied on by a highway authority, the duty is **10–48** to take reasonable care to maintain it. If a light is out at the material time, an evidential burden lies on the authority to show that it was not negligent in failing to maintain the light.[148] Failure to provide a sufficient number of night-watchmen to guard road works so as to prevent the extinguishing or stealing of warning lights by vandals may amount to negligence where vandalism is rife in the

---

[138] For the lighting of vehicles parked on the roadside and builders' skips, etc., see para.10–257, below.
[139] *McClelland v Manchester Corp* [1912] 1 K.B. 118.
[140] *Penny v Wimbledon Urban District Council* [1899] 2 Q.B. 72.
[141] *Baxter v Stockton-on-Tees Corp* [1959] 1 Q.B. 441.
[142] *Fisher v Ruislip-Northwood Urban District Council* [1945] K.B. 584 at 593, per Lord Greene M.R.
[143] *Lamley v Retford Corp* (1891) 55 J.P. 133.
[144] *McClelland v Manchester Corp* [1912] 1 K.B. 118.
[145] *Law v Railway Executive* [1949] W.N. 172.
[146] *Polkinghorn v Lambeth Borough Council* [1938] 1 All E.R. 339. cf. *Brown v Lambeth Borough Council* (1915) 32 T.L.R. 61, where on somewhat similar facts a finding of no negligence on the part of the defendants was upheld on appeal.
[147] *Whiting v Middlesex County Council* [1948] 1 K.B. 162.
[148] *Polkinghorn v Lambeth Borough Council* [1938] 1 All E.R. 339.

particular locality.[149] Conversely, where there has been no such vandalism previously, it was held that the defendants were under no duty to inspect their excavation periodically during the night, which they had left properly lighted and secured with barriers.[150]

10–49   The statutory provisions under which the works are maintained may provide for absolute immunity, even though no care is taken. When a railway company maintained gate posts at the entrance to one of their stations, under statutory powers, which were construed as not imposing any duty to light them or otherwise to obviate the danger that they caused, and a taxicab drove into them when they were unlighted in wartime, the railway company was not liable.[151]

10–50   **Statutory obligation to light.** If a local authority has not itself created a danger, by "putting posts in the highway without warning", by "placing traps and dangers in the streets and not lighting them at night", or by making a road "with a sudden drop into the adjoining land below",[152] its liability depends on the statutory obligation to light. If it is under a duty to light, such as was imposed by s.130 of the Metropolis Management Act 1855,[153] it is bound to see that every street is well and sufficiently lighted. Where there was a light some 70 feet from the entrance to an archway, which was dimmed owing to war restrictions then in force, and the driver of a van attempted to pass beneath the arch but was crushed between his van and the arch, the authority was liable for its breach of statutory duty in failing to light adequately.[154]

10–51   In contrast, where there is only a power and not an obligation to light, as under s.161 of the Public Health Act 1875, there is no obligation on the local authority to light any dangers, except those created by itself. So, the local authority was not liable where, at night, after a light had been extinguished, the claimant fell over a retaining wall into a street at a lower level.[155] Nevertheless, where an authority, with power to do so, exercises it by providing street lights to a certain standard, it assumes an obligation to exercise reasonable care to maintain the lights to that standard. In *Farrell v Northern Ireland Electricity Service*,[156] the failure to discharge such an obligation founded liability to a pedestrian who had fallen in the street and sustained injuries, because the street light provided by the defendants under statutory power, was not in working order.

(C) Dangers adjoining the highway

10–52   **Liability for dangerous buildings adjoining highway.** Buildings adjoining the highway must be maintained in such a condition that they are not dangerous

---

[149] *Murray v Southwark London Borough Council* (1966) 65 L.G.R. 145.
[150] *Lilley v British Insulated Callenders Construction Co* (1968) 67 L.G.R. 224.
[151] *Great Central Ry v Hewlett* [1916] 2 A.C. 511.
[152] Scrutton L.J. in *Sheppard v Glossop Corp* [1921] 3 K.B. 132 at 149.
[153] Repealed by the Local Law (Greater London Council and Inner London Boroughs) Order 1965 (SI 1965/540).
[154] *Carpenter v Finsbury Borough Council* [1920] 2 K.B. 195.
[155] *Sheppard v Glossop Corp* [1921] 3 K.B. 132.
[156] [1977] N.I. 39.

to users of the highway. Such buildings, if dangerous, constitute a public nuisance and liability is based on that tort, rather than on negligence. The occupier,[157] and sometimes the owner,[158] of the property is liable: (1) for creating the nuisance; and (2) for continuing the nuisance, after knowledge or presumed knowledge of its existence.[159] A nuisance is created if there has been negligence in maintaining buildings adjoining the highway, so that they get into a dangerous state of disrepair. The fact that their disrepair causes damage to a person in the highway, for example by a slate coming off a roof; or a brick dislodging from its structure[160]; or the collapse of a wall,[161] is itself evidence of negligence, which throws the burden of disproving it on the occupier or the owner.[162] Should that burden be discharged, so that there is no finding of negligence in maintaining the building, the question arises whether the owner or the occupier can be said to have created the nuisance. On this point, the authorities are conflicting. It is settled, however, that it is no defence to employ an independent contractor to keep the building in repair, the employer being vicariously liable for the independent contractor's negligence.[163]

There is no liability if the danger is the result of a latent defect which was not **10–53** discoverable by the exercise of reasonable care and skill on the part of anyone, or by "a secret and unobservable operation of nature, such as a subsidence under or near the foundations of the premises".[164] Again, it is a defence to show that the danger was caused by a trespasser and was not continued after knowledge or means of knowledge.[165] Where the blast from an enemy bomb loosened a slate which fell from the roof of a building in a high wind some 18 days later and injured a person using the highway, the occupier was not liable, on it being found that reasonable inspection of the roof did not disclose that the slate had been loosened by the blast.[166] On the other hand, liability is imposed for continuing a nuisance after it was or ought to have been known. When there was an accumulation of snow on the roof of a building and for four days the occupiers did not remove it, so that it fell on the claimant as she was walking on the

---

[157] See para.10–64, below. As regards an occupier's vicarious liability for the negligence of an independent contractor, see, generally, Ch.3, paras 3–172 to 3–203, above.
[158] See paras 10–65 to 10–67, below.
[159] *Sedleigh-Denfield v O'Callaghan* [1940] A.C. 880.
[160] *Kearney v London & Brighton Ry* (1871) L.R. 6 Q.B. 759 (brick fell from a pier of a recently constructed railway bridge).
[161] *Mullans v Forrester* [1921] 2 Ir.R. 412. In *Noble v Harrison* [1926] 2 K.B. 332 at 343, Wright J. said that he preferred the dissenting judgment of Moore J. that the liability of the occupier depended on knowledge.
[162] See, generally, Ch.6, paras 6–107 to 6–109, above. The burden of proof was discharged and the defendant was held not liable in *Palmer v Bateman* [1908] 2 Ir.R. 393 (piece of guttering fell from roof's edge). In *Wringe v Cohen* [1940] 1 K.B. 229 at 242, the Court of Appeal expressed the opinion that *Palmer* was wrongly decided.
[163] *Tarry v Ashton* (1876) 1 Q.B.D. 314 (lamp, fixed to side of a house, fell and struck the claimant, who was on the highway beneath).
[164] *Wringe v Cohen* [1940] 1 K.B. 229 at 233; *Lambert v Lowestoft Corp* [1901] 1 Q.B. 590.
[165] *Wringe v Cohen*, above; *Barker v Herbert* [1911] 2 K.B. 633.
[166] *Cushing v Peter Walker & Sons Ltd* [1941] 3 All E.R. 693.

footpath, the occupiers were liable.[167] Likewise, the occupier was liable when an air raid on a Friday night broke the windows of an empty house and the damage had remained unrepaired by the following Tuesday, when the claimant in the highway was injured by a fall of glass.[168]

10–54   **Dangerous fences and boundary walls.** The obligation to maintain premises adjoining the highway, so that they do not become dangerous to persons using it, extends also to fences and boundary walls. If a person, in the ordinary and reasonable use of the highway, leans upon or otherwise comes in contact with the fence or wall, so that it moves away or collapses, thereby injuring him, such person can recover damages from the occupier of the premises. So, where the defendants occupied a cellar in which scene-painting was going on and, in order to protect the area, a bar was put up, it was held that the claimant child, who had been leaning against it, was entitled to recover for injuries sustained through falling into the area when the bar gave way.[169] Again, when a fence was abutting the highway and a child of four, in order to play with some children on the other side, climbed on it, whereupon it collapsed and injured him, his action for damages succeeded.[170]

10–55   There is no liability, however, if the danger has been created by a trespasser, provided that the failure to remove it did not amount to negligence. Accordingly, when the defendant was the owner of a vacant house, the area railings of which had been broken by boys who had been playing football in the street, and the claimant, a boy aged four, while clambering along the railings fell into the area and was injured, his action failed. The defendant was held not liable on a finding of fact that he had used reasonable care to prevent the premises from becoming dangerous to persons using the highway, and that he neither knew nor would have known, by the exercise of reasonable care, of the break in the railings.[171]

10–56   A fence or a wall does not become dangerous merely because persons on the highway may climb up and fall off it. So, where a perfectly safe wall adjoined the highway, the presence of a heap of soil which enabled a boy of seven to climb on top of the wall from the highway imposed no liability on the owners and occupiers of the wall when the boy hurt himself by falling off it.[172]

10–57   *Great North Eastern Railway v Hart*[173] was a claim that arose from a catastrophic rail accident involving the collision of railway trains and a motor

---

[167] *Slater v Worthington's Cash Stores Ltd* [1941] 1 K.B. 488. See "Damage from Frost and Snow" 113 L.J. 179.
[168] *Leanse v Egerton* [1943] K.B. 323.
[169] *Jewson v Gatti* ((1886) 2 T.L.R. 441.
[170] *Harrold v Watney* [1898] 2 Q.B. 320 at 322. A. L. Smith L.J. said: "A rotten fence close to a highway is an obvious nuisance. If I were on the highway and wanted to tie up my boot, or got tired and leaned against the fence, should I not have been lawfully using the highway? The present case is a stronger one." Also see similar accident and decision in *Robertson's Tutor v Glasgow Corp*, 1950 S.C. 502 (wall adjacent to footpath collapsed, when the eight-year-old pursuer climbed up on to it).
[171] *Barker v Herbert* [1911] 2 K.B. 633. It was also held that even if the defendant were responsible for the nuisance, the injury was not the direct result of the nuisance.
[172] *Liddle v Yorkshire (North Riding) Councy Council* [1934] 2 K.B. 101.
[173] [2003] EWHC 2450.

vehicle. The defendant had been driving a motor vehicle on a motorway when he fell asleep. The vehicle drifted across the carriageway and went down an embankment onto a railway which ran beneath the motorway. There was a crash fence by the bridge which carried the motorway over the railway but it was not long enough to prevent the motor vehicle leaving the motorway and ending up on the railway. It was held that a duty of care was owed by the authority in relation to the design of the fence but, on the facts, negligence was not established.

Dangerous premises. If premises by the side of the highway are so   **10–58** constructed as to be dangerous[174] to users of the highway, they are a nuisance. In such a case, the state of repair is immaterial, because it is the very fact of their presence which constitutes the danger. So, where a barbed wire fence was maintained to fence off the defendant's premises from the highway, the claimant, who tore his coat upon it, was entitled to recover.[175] Where, in front of a shop window, there was an 18-inch-high wall, on the top of which was a row of spikes, and the claimant, a girl aged five, was found injured under circumstances consistent with her having fallen upon such spikes, it was held that they were a nuisance and the owners of the shop were liable.[176]

Dangerous excavations adjoining highway. The occupier of land is liable if   **10–59** he makes or continues an excavation on his own land, which is a danger to persons who are using the highway. Where an unfenced area within the curtilage of a house was at a lower level than adjacent footpath and the claimant, while walking along the street, fell in and was injured, the occupier was liable, despite the premises being in the same condition as they were when he went into possession.[177] Where a pedestrian fell into an unfenced hoist-hole, some 14 inches from the highway, the occupiers were liable on the ground that they "would be liable for a nuisance to the highway, if the excavation was so near to it that a person lawfully using the way, and using ordinary caution, accidentally slipping might fall into it".[178] It was no defence that the builder who made the hole might also be liable.

ILLUSTRATIONS

The occupier was under no liability: where cattle had strayed from the   **10–60** highway and fallen into a pit, about 36 feet from the highway[179]; where a man

---

[174] See further, Ch.8, paras 8–161 to 8–171, above.
[175] *Stewart v Wright* (1893) 9 T.L.R. 480.
[176] *Fenna v Clare & Co* [1895] 1 Q.B. 199. See also *Morrison v Sheffield Corp* [1917] 2 K.B. 866 (iron spiked guard placed around a tree). Conversely, where a horse spiked itself, see *Gibson v Plumstead Burial Board* (1897) 13 T.L.R. 273. Lopes L.J. said that "the law no doubt was that if a person erected on his own land anything calculated to interfere with the use of a highway, what he did was a nuisance." But he could not agree with the suggestion that "the erection of this iron fence, not with spikes jutting out into the road, but with perpendicular spikes, amounted to a nuisance". See also *Morton v Wheeler, The Times,* February 1, 1956.
[177] *Coupland v Hardingham* (1813) 3 Camp. 398. Similarly, see *Barnes v Ward* (1850) 9 C.B. 392, where Maule J. said: "The defendant, in having made that excavation, was guilty of a public nuisance, even though the danger consisted in the risk of accidentally deviating from the road."
[178] *Hadley v Taylor* (1865) L.R. 1 C.P. 53 at 55, per Erle C.J.
[179] *Blyth v Topham* (1607) Cro.Jac. 158.

wandered from the highway and fell into a reservoir, some little distance from the highway[180]; where a man walked off the towpath, adjoining a canal, went across a 24-foot-wide strip of land and fell into the canal, which was unfenced[181]; where a boy climbed up a height of three-and-a-half feet to an unfenced aperture in a wall and put his head through, when he was injured by the descent of a lift[182]; when a man at night and in a fog left the highway and fell into an unfenced dock 47 feet away[183]; when a man at night got on to a private road, from which he fell and was killed.[184]

10–61   Further, there is no liability on the ground of nuisance where a person suffers damage after leaving the highway.[185] Thus, where the defendants' shops were separated from the highway by a forecourt, in which there was a stopcock about two feet from the highway, projecting above the surface, and upon the claimant going to one of the shops, he tripped over the stopcock, the defendants were not liable, as the obstruction was not on the highway, so that it could not be a nuisance.[186] The claimant's remedy was to have sued the tenant of the shop, who was the occupier.[187]

10–62   **Natural dangers and builder's skips.** The occupier of land is under no duty to fence a natural danger, such as a stream, from the highway.[188] Further, where the surface of the highway has been raised above the level of the surrounding land, so that a dangerous drop has been left, the occupier of the land is under no obligation to erect a fence to prevent persons travelling along the highway from falling down it. However, the highway authority would be liable in such circumstances.[189] The provisions of the Highways Act 1980 Pt IX,[190] regulate any works carried out in or near the public highway, including the control of builder's skips.[191]

10–63   **Dangers caused by diversion of highway.** When a highway is diverted, protection must be provided at the point of diversion in order to prevent persons using the highway from going astray, since it may be implied otherwise that the original highway can be used safely.[192] So, where a railway company, in constructing their railway, diverted a footpath into a road but failed to indicate the point of the diversion, as a result of which a person left the footpath, got on to

---

[180] *Hardcastle v South Yorkshire Ry* (1859) 4 H. & N. 67, per Pollock C.B., *Carshalton Urban District Council v Burrage* [1911] 2 Ch.133.

[181] *Binks v South Yorkshire Ry* (1862) 3 B. & S 244.

[182] *Stiefsohn v Brook* (1889) 53 J.P. 790.

[183] *Casely v Bristol Corp* [1944] 1 All E.R. 14.

[184] *Melville v Renfrewshire County Council*, 1920 S.C. 61.

[185] A claimant cannot recover damages, even if the nuisance does substantially adjoin the highway, unless he was actually using the highway when his accident happened: *Bromley v Mercer* [1922] 2 K.B. 126.

[186] *Jacobs v London County Council*, above, overruling *Owens v Scott* [1939] 3 All E.R. 663.

[187] See Ch.8, generally.

[188] *Morrison v L.M.S. Ry*, 1929 S.C. 1.

[189] *Nicholson v Southern Ry* [1935] 1 K.B. 558.

[190] See also *Myers v Harrow Corp* [1962] 2 Q.B. 442.

[191] Highways Act 1980 Pt IX. by ss.139–140.

[192] *McClelland v Manchester Corp* [1912] 1 K.B. 118; *Coleshill v Manchester Corp* [1928] 1 K.B. 776.

the railway line and was injured, the railway company was liable.[193] Where a tunnel under an archway was substituted for a level crossing, so that a lad driving a van was crushed under the archway, the local authority which had built the tunnel, was liable.[194]

Liability of occupier. Liability for defective buildings and fences adjoining   **10–64** the highway, as well as all defective coal plates, gratings and other structures in the highway, is treated as if it were on the occupier. The rule is that the occupier is always liable,[195] apart from cases where the defect has been caused by the wilful act of a third person and there has been no negligence on the occupier's part in remedying the defect.[196] Indeed, the occupier is liable, even if the defect existed before occupation began. The occupier has continued the nuisance and it was his "fault to contract for an interest in land on which there was a nuisance".[197]

Liability of owner. The owner of the premises is liable if he has contracted[198]   **10–65** with the occupier to do the repairs. This was decided in *Payne v Rogers*,[199] where the claimant was injured by his leg slipping through a hole in the pavement into a vault or cellar, as a result of some plates or bars which went under the pavement, being out of repair. In such circumstances the owner is liable whether he has actual knowledge of the state of disrepair or not.[200]

Further, the owner is liable if he has let the premises, knowing them to be in   **10–66** a ruinous or dangerous condition without taking any steps to provide a remedy. Where, therefore, houses were demised with chimneys in a dangerous condition so that they fell upon the neighbouring building and damaged it, the lessor was held liable.[201] At one time it was held that a lessor could avoid liability by obtaining from his lessee a covenant to repair[202] but this proposition was criticised by the Court of Appeal in *Brew Bros Ltd v Snax (Ross) Ltd.*[203]

---

[193] *Hurst v Taylor* (1885) 14 Q.B.D. 918. See also *Evans v Rhymney Local Board* (1887) 4 T.L.R. 72.

[194] *Bedman v Tottenham Local Board* (1887) 4 T.L.R. 22. See also *Law v Railway Executive* [1949] W.N. 172, para.10–46, above.

[195] *Wilchick v Marks and Silverstone* [1934] 2 K.B. 56 at 68. See also para.10–33, above, in relation to the statutory duty.

[196] *Barker v Herbert* [1911] 2 K.B. 633.

[197] *Roswell v Prior* (1701) 12 Mod. 635.

[198] A landlord's covenant may be implied by statute, e.g. the Landlord and Tenant Act 1985 s.11, see further Ch.8, para.8–122, above.

[199] (1794) 2 H.Bl. 350. This case was approved in *R. v Pedly* (1834) 1 A. & E. 822; *Todd v Flight* (1860) 9 C.B.(N.S.) 377; *Nelson v Liverpool Brewery Co* (1877) 2 C.P.D. 311.

[200] *Wringe v Cohen* [1940] 1 K.B. 229, disapproving the opinion of Goddard J. in *Wilchick v Marks and Silverstone* [1934] 2 K.B. 56 at 66; *Heap v Ind Coope & Allsopp Ltd* [1940] 2 K.B. 476.

[201] *Todd v Flight* (1860) 9 C.B.(N.S.) 377. There is no reletting each week or month in a weekly or other periodic tenancy, and consequently a landlord is not liable, under this principle, for any damage through disrepair existing at the beginning of any week or month of the tenancy after the beginning of the letting. *Gandy v Jubber* (1864) 5 B. & S 78; *Bowen v Anderson* [1894] 1 Q.B. 164.

[202] *Pretty v Bickmore* (1873) L.R. 8 C.P. 401; *Gwinnell v Eamer* (1875) L.R. 10 C.P. 658.

[203] [1970] 1 Q.B. 612.

10-67 The owner is also liable where he reserves the right to enter the premises for the purpose of repair, without taking any covenant from the occupier to repair.[204] Where a claimant was injured by a window shutter, which fell while being closed by the tenant's son, both landlord and tenant were liable, in the absence of an agreement between them as to repairs: the landlord because he had power to repair and knowing of the disrepair did nothing; the tenant because he was under a duty to avoid injury to members of the public passing his house.[205] The position is the same when the owner, while not expressly reserving the right to enter and do repairs, in fact does them, there being in such a case an implied consent to entry for that purpose.[206]

10-68 **Actions of third parties.** There is no liability upon the owner of premises simply because there are features of the property, such as cellar flaps, plates or doors which are so close to the highway that if someone opens them up suddenly and carelessly, a user of the highway will be injured.[207] Where premises had a door which opened outwards and flush with the highway, the owner was not liable to a person who was injured by the door being opened suddenly, when there was no evidence that it was opened by him or anyone for whose acts he was responsible.[208] On the other hand, the occupier might very well have been liable if the door was opened by a lawful visitor.

10-69 In the event of cellar flaps or other structures in the highway being interfered with so as to render them dangerous, liability is primarily upon the person who interfered with them, although the occupier can also be liable in certain circumstances. If a cellar flap is opened so as to leave a hole in the highway or an obstruction, over which a pedestrian trips and falls, liability lies with the person who opened the flap or caused it to be opened. If someone employs an independent contractor to do work which necessarily involves the creation of such a danger, he is liable. So, where the lessee of refreshment rooms at a railway station employed an independent contractor to deliver coals through a hole into the coal cellar, he was held liable for damage caused to a passenger who had fallen into the cellar owing to its being insufficiently guarded.[209] Unsurprisingly there is concurrent liability upon the independent contractor.[210]

---

[204] *Wringe v Cohen* [1940] 1 K.B. 229.

[205] *Wilchick v Marks and Silverstone* [1934] 2 K.B. 56.

[206] *Heap v Ind Coope & Allsopp Ltd* [1940] 2 K.B. 476, followed in *Mint v Good* [1951] 1 K.B. 517, where a boy on the highway was injured by the fall of a wall separating the highway from the forecourt of a house let on a weekly tenancy. There was no right to enter to do repairs reserved to the landlord, who in fact did the repairs, but the landlord was held liable. *Pretty v Bickmore* (1873) L.R. 8 C.P. 401, was doubted by Denning L.J., but see 67 L.Q.R. 148 and 14 M.L.R. 348.

[207] *De Boos v Collard* (1892) 8 T.L.R. 338.

[208] *Evans v Edinburgh Corp* [1916] 2 A.C. 45.

[209] *Pickard v Smith* (1861) 10 C.B.(N.S.) 470. Although the accident happened in a railway station, "no sound distinction in this respect can be drawn between the case of a public highway and a road which may be and to the knowledge of the wrongdoer probably will in fact be used by persons lawfully entitled to do so."

[210] *Whiteley v Pepper* (1876) 2 Q.B.D. 276. Generally, see Ch.3, above, paras 3–172 to 3–203, above, and *Daniel v Rickett Cockerell & Co* [1938] 2 K.B. 322 (damages were apportioned as to ninety per cent to the coal merchant and ten per cent to the customer).

If work does not involve an interference with the highway, an employer is not **10–70** liable. Thus, where a brewery company employed a contractor to deliver beer to a public house and the occupier opened the cellar flaps on the highway, which were left unguarded, it was held that the occupier but not the brewery company was liable for damage suffered by the claimant who was passing by.[211] The ground of the decision was that the contractor was not employed to interfere with the highway. Nevertheless, this decision seems to be inconsistent with *Pickard v Smith*[212] and *Whiteley v Pepper*,[213] since liability on the part of the occupier does not prevent the employer of the independent contractor from being liable, too.

A canal company, with statutory authority to build a swivel bridge over a **10–71** canal, would be liable to persons falling into the canal when the bridge was open, if no fence or warning were provided. This is because they created a danger in the highway, by leaving an unfenced opening, whenever the bridge was swung open for canal traffic.[214]

Where a structure is interfered with by a third party, without the knowledge or **10–72** consent of the occupier, the occupier is not liable if he has made the structure reasonably secure, so that it will be safe unless intentionally, as opposed to accidentally, interfered with. Even where it has been intentionally interfered with, the occupier will be liable if it is the sort of interference which should have been anticipated as likely to occur.[215] A cellar plate, which was left so insecurely that any boy, poking about with a stick, could disturb it thereby making it loose, was held to be a danger, which imposed liability on the occupier where the user of the highway was injured as a result.[216]

A sun blind securely fixed in front of a shop does not give rise to liability on **10–73** the occupier if it is pulled down by persons jumping up at it while they are passing. The occupier is not bound to fasten it so securely as to bear the weight of two men, jumping up at it.[217] On the same principle, a water board was not liable for damage, caused through the act of a third person, in raising the lid of a water-box in the highway, in the absence of a finding that the occurrence could

---

[211] *Wilson v Hodgson's Kingston Brewery Co* (1915) 85 L.J.K.B. 270 at 272, per Avery J.: "Here the contractor was not employed in any sense to open the flap of this cellar. It was quite consistent with the contract of the contractor with the brewery company that the occupier of the house should himself have pushed back the flap, and if he did so and left it open, it was clearly his duty to see that it was not dangerous to the public using the highway."
[212] (1861) 10 C.B.(N.S.) 470.
[213] (1876) 2 Q.B.D. 276.
[214] *Manley v St Helens Canal Co* (1858) 2 H. & N. 840.
[215] *Daniels v Potter* (1830) 4 C. & P. 262 ; *Hughes v Macfie, Abbott v Macfie* (1863) 2 H. & C. 744.
[216] *Braithwaite v Watson* (1889) 5 T.L.R. 331. To the same effect is *Findlay v Angus* (1887) 14 R. 312 (shutter fastened by bolt fell when meddled with by children, occupier liable) and *Wells v Metropolitan Water Board* [1937] 4 All E.R. 639. See also para.10–38, above.
[217] *Wheeler v Morris* (1915) 84 L.J.K.B. 1435, 1437. Per Cozens-Hardy M.R.: "The liability in a case of this kind is not a liability of insurance or warranty that the blind will never come down. The utmost which can be put against the shopkeeper is that he, as occupant, is bound to take such reasonable precautions as a reasonable man would exercise to avoid the result of an accident which might be reasonably foreseen."

or ought to have been foreseen and provided against by taking reasonable precautions.[218]

10–74   **Occupier continuing a danger, created by third party.** Although a third party may have interfered with a structure in the highway for which an occupier is responsible, so as to create a danger, the occupier will be liable if the the danger is allowed to continue. Where, for example, a stranger opens cellar flaps, the occupier will not be liable unless he permits them to remain open after he knew or ought to have known that they were open. His duty is to shut or guard them within a reasonable time after knowledge which he actually has or ought to have under the circumstances.[219] Where a wall on the defendant's land was knocked down by trespassers, so that the bricks were, to his knowledge, scattered over the highway, the defendant was liable to the user for injury caused.[220]

(D) Miscellaneous dangers in the highway

10–75   **Dangerous machines left in highway.** Liability in respect of vehicles left unattended in the highway is discussed elsewhere.[221] In the case of adults, liability for other dangerous objects left in the highway depends upon the rules, already discussed, in relation to obstructions.[222] The duty towards a child is the same as where the child is a lawful visitor to premises.[223]

10–76   **Vehicles on premises adjoining highway.** When vehicles and machines are left on premises adjoining the highway, they must be left in such a position and in such a manner as not to be dangerous to highway users. If they are safe, the general rule is that the owner is under no liability when the acts of a third party make them unsafe. So, where boys trespassed on to a railway line and released the brakes of trucks parked on an incline in a siding, causing them to run on to the highway, injuring the claimant, his action against the railway company failed.[224] On the other hand, the owner of a vehicle will be liable if he knows there is a real and not just a possible risk of it being interfered with in the place

---

[218] *Mileham v Marylebone Corp* (1903) 67 J.P. 110; cf. *Wells v Metropolitan Water Board* [1937] 4 All E.R. 639.

[219] *Barker v Herbert* [1911] 2 K.B. 633 at 642, per Fletcher Moulton L.J.: "The gravamen is the continuance of the nuisance and not the original causing of it."

[220] *Silverton v Marriott* (1888) 52 J.P. 677, per Field J.: "If an owner of land becomes aware of something on his premises, though through the act of a stranger, which is a source of risk and danger, a duty arises on him to guard against that risk and danger. There is a duty on him to keep and maintain his premises in such a condition that they shall not be injurious to the public at large using them."

[221] paras 10–253 to 10–257, below.

[222] paras 10–17 to 10–19, above. Further, see *Clark v Chambers* (1878) 3 Q.B.D. 327 at 339, per Cockburn C.J.: "A man who leaves in a public place, along which persons, and amongst them children, have to pass, a dangerous machine which may be fatal to anyone who touches it, without any precaution against mischief, is not only guilty of negligence, but of negligence of a very reprehensible character, and not the less so because the imprudent and unauthorised act of another may be necessary to realise the mischief to which the unlawful act or negligence of the defendant has given occasion."

[223] See Ch.8, paras 8–48 to 8–57, above.

[224] *McDowall v G.W. Ry* [1903] 2 K.B. 331.

he has left it, unless he takes reasonable precautions to guard against that risk.[225]

Dangerous activities adjacent to the highway. The duty to take care to avoid   **10–77** doing anything which is likely to injure persons on the highway is only part of the wider duty to take reasonable care in doing, either on or adjoining the highway, anything likely to cause danger to persons who are passing along the highway. Where a telephone company was laying telephone wires in the street and had employed a contractor to help, the company was held liable when a lamp, used by one of the contractor's servants, exploded owing to the failure of the safety valve.[226] Similarly, where a person passing along the highway was injured by the defendants' blasting operations at their quarry nearby, liability was established. It was their duty to keep the effects of the blasting on their own land.[227] Also, where the claimant, who was using the pavement, slipped on fat from a butcher's shop, whether as a result of chopping done by the butcher or by it being carried on a customer's shoe, the butcher was liable, both in nuisance and in negligence. He should have foreseen the likelihood of fat from the shop getting on to the pavement.[228] When clouds of steam and smoke were emitted from coke ovens, on adjoining land, and engulfed the highway but no warning was given to approaching traffic, the person responsible was liable for a highway collision, caused by the resultant loss of visibility.[229] A local authority which failed to clear rubbish from a burning tip on land adjoining the highway, so as not to aggravate an industrial dispute with employees who were on strike, was not excused thereby from liability when the claimant was injured upon being struck by a fragment from an exploding aerosol can.[230]

Causing ice on highway.[231] When a van was washed in the street with the   **10–78** result that a sheet of ice formed, on which the claimant's horse slipped and was injured, it was held that, although the defendant's act in washing the van in the highway was wrongful, the damage was too remote.[232] Although this decision could not stand after *Polemis Re*[233] was decided, it was restored with approval by the Judicial Committee of the Privy Council in *The Wagon Mound (No.1)*.[234]

---

[225] See, per Vaughan Williams L.J. at 337.
[226] *Holliday v National Telephone Co* [1899] 2 Q.B. 392. At 399, Lord Halsbury said: "The telephone company, by whose authority alone these works were done, were, whether the works were done by the company's servants or by a contractor, under an obligation to the public to take care that persons passing along the highway were not injured by the negligent performance of the work."
[227] *Miles v Forest Rock Granite Co* (1918) 34 T.L.R. 500.
[228] *Dollman v Hillman Ltd* [1941] 1 All E.R. 355.
[229] *Holling v Yorkshire Traction Co* [1948] 2 All E.R. 662 which was followed in *Rollingston v Kerr & Co* [1958] C.L.Y. 2427. See also *Funnell v CPR & Bowden* (1964) 45 D.L.R. (2d) 481, where dense clouds of sand and dust blew across the highway as a result of the construction activities taking place on the adjoining land so that liability was established.
[230] *Woolfall v Knowsley Borough Council, The Times*, June 26, 1992, CA.
[231] For the duty of highway authorities regarding the formation of ice and snow on highways see para.10–07, above.
[232] *Sharp v Powell* (1872) L.R. 7 C.P. 253.
[233] [1921] 3 K.B. 560.
[234] [1961] A.C. 388, at 418: "The judgment of Bovill C.J. is particularly valuable and interesting." See Ch.5, paras 5–08 to 5–14, above, where the *Wagon Mound* and *Re Polemis* decisions are discussed.

10–79   However, in a somewhat similar case, when a pedestrian slipped on the pavement outside a garage yard, on ice formed as a result of the washing of motorvehicles in the garage on a November night, the garage proprietors were liable. They should have anticipated the possibility of the onset of a sudden frost and taken precautions to prevent the formation of ice on the pavement, despite the fact that it was not freezing when the vehicles were being washed.[235] Again, where water from a burst service pipe caused a pool of water to collect in the roadway, which lay unheeded for three days, before a frost occurred and formed ice upon which a motor car skidded, knocked down and killed a man, the water authority was negligent because it had failed to take prompt action to attend to the leak in order to prevent the road from becoming dangerous to traffic.[236]

10–80   **Acid on highway.** When a carboy of sulphuric acid fell off the back of a moving lorry and broke causing a pool of acid to be formed in the road and a motorcyclist, thinking it was water, attempted to ride through it, skidded and was burnt by the acid, the lorry driver was liable for allowing the acid to remain on the road for half an hour, after he knew that it was there, without giving warning of the danger.[237]

10–81   **Sport causing danger on the highway.** Where a hole on a golf course was placed adjoining the highway, and players regularly drove out of bounds on to the road, the club was liable in nuisance to a highway user who was injured.[238] A player who struck the golf ball would also be liable if he failed to take reasonable care in playing his ball.[239] The playing of cricket on a ground, from which cricket balls were hit out of the ground on rare occasions only, was not a nuisance and the club was not liable to a person who was injured by a ball in the highway.[240]

10–82   **Vehicles damaging the highway.** The use of a very heavy vehicle, for example a steamroller[241] or traction engine,[242] of such weight as to break gas or water pipes, which are laid properly and at sufficient depth in the highway, is actionable on the ground that "an action lies for an injury to property, unless such

---

[235] *Lambie v Western S.M.T. Co Ltd*, 1944 S.C. 415.
[236] *Manchester Corp v Markland* [1936] A.C. 360. See also *Shepherd v Midland Rail Co* (1872) 25 L.T. 879 (water trickled from a waste pipe at a railway station on to the platform and froze. The claimant, a passenger, stepped upon the ice, fell and was injured. The court held the defendant railway company liable for negligence in not removing the ice); *Osborne v London and North Western Rail Co* (1888) 21 Q.B.D. 220 (the claimant was injured by falling on steps leading to the defendant's railway station. The steps were worn and hollowed, and a light layer of snow which had been trodden down and formed ice had made them slippery).
[237] *Pope v Fraser* (1939) 55 T.L.R. 324.
[238] *Castle v St Augustine's Links* (1922) 38 T.L.R. 615.
[239] See *Cleghorn v Oldham* (1927) 43 T.L.R. 465. Compare *Potter v Carlisle and Cliftonville Golf Club Ltd* [1939] N.I. 114.
[240] *Bolton v Stone* [1951] A.C. 850. But see *Miller v Jackson* [1977] Q.B. 966 (cricket balls hit out of the grounds into the gardens of adjacent houses on fairly frequent occasions); *Hilder v Associated Portland Cement Manufacturers Ltd* [1961] 1 W.L.R. 1434 (footballs regularly kicked out of field).
[241] *Gas Light and Coke Co v St Mary Abbott's Kensington* (1885) 15 Q.B.D. 1; *Driscoll v Poplar Board of Works* (1897) 14 T.L.R. 99.
[242] *Chichester Corp v Foster* [1906] 1 K.B. 167.

injury is expressly authorised by statute, or is, physically speaking, the necessary consequence of what is so authorised".[243] When a vehicle on the highway dislodged a paving stone on the footpath, so that a pedestrian tripped over it, the driver of the vehicle was liable.[244]

2.—CARRIERS

(A) Generally

Introduction. A person, who undertakes, either for reward or gratuitously, to carry another person in a vehicle, is liable to that other for damage caused by negligence. The carrier's duty may be considered in connection with: (i) the carriage of a passenger; and (ii) the safety of the vehicle. Thereafter this section will consider negligence in its various forms as it has arisen in relation to particular modes of carriage. **10–83**

Duty as to carriage. The duty as to carriage is to use reasonable care and skill for the safety of passengers, during such carriage. The carrier is not an insurer of the safety of the passenger. The law was clear as long ago as 1825, having emerged with particular reference to the duty of stage-coach proprietors.[245] **10–84**

The duty extends to the luggage and belongings of the passenger[246] and the duty is the same, whether the carriage is undertaken for reward or gratuitously.[247] Liability is not limited to responsibility for gross negligence.[248] In *O'Connor v British Transport Commission*,[249] the defendants were not liable for the death of a young child, who had fallen out of a corridor-type guard's van, after he had opened the door with its handle specially provided on the inside for the guard's use. The claimant failed to prove that there was any failure on the part of the defendants to take all due care to carry their passengers safely. The Court of Appeal held that the defendants were entitled to assume that children of tender years would be accompanied by persons who would take due care in looking after them. **10–85**

Duty as to the safety of the vehicle. The primary duty as to the safety of a vehicle,[250] arises under any relevant contract, such as for the vehicle's hire, or for **10–86**

---

[243] *Gas Light and Coke Co v St Mary Abbott's Kensington* (1885) 15 Q.B.D. 1, per Lindley L.J. at 5.
[244] *Conelly v West Ham Borough Council* (1947) 62 T.L.R. 739.
[245] *Crofts v Waterhouse* (1825) 3 Bing. 319.
[246] *Vosper v G.W. Ry* [1928] 1 K.B. 340; *Houghland v R.R. Low (Luxury Coaches) Ltd* [1962] 1 Q.B. 694; *Mannix v N.M. Paterson & Sons* [1965] 2 Lloyd's Rep. 108.
[247] *Lygo v Newbold* (1854) 9 Ex. 302 at 305, per Parke B: "A person who undertakes to provide for the conveyance of another, although he does so gratuitously, is bound to exercise due and reasonable care." See also *Lewys v Burnett and Dunbar* [1945] 2 All E.R. 55; *Hyman v Nye* (1881) 6 Q.B.D. 685 at 687.
[248] *Austin v G.W. Ry* (1867) L.R. 2 Q.B. 442; *Harris v Perry & Co* [1903] 2 K.B. 219; *Karavias v Callinicos* [1917] W.N. 323. As to "gross negligence" see Ch.1, para.1–15, above.
[249] [1958] 1 W.L.R. 346.
[250] Which includes for these purposes, vehicles, vessels or aircraft.

the carriage for reward of persons or goods, or by virtue of any contract of bailment. The provisions of the contract, whether express or implied, are construed by reference to the common law. In many instances there will be a concurrent duty to similar effect in tort. It is specifically provided by the Occupiers' Liability Act 1957[251] that it does not affect the common law duty. In the absence of express agreement, the duty implied will be to take reasonable care to provide a safe vehicle. Carriers, for example, are not under an absolute obligation to provide a safe vehicle. They must take "a high degree of care" and are under "the duty of exercising all vigilance to see that whatever is required for the safe conveyance of their passengers is in fit and proper order"; but they are not liable for "a disaster arising from a latent defect in the machinery which they are obliged to use, which no human skill or care could either have prevented or detected."[252] Accordingly, where a railway carriage ran off the line owing to the breaking of the tyre of one of the wheels, arising from a latent defect not attributable to any fault of the manufacturer and not detectable before the breakdown, the railway company were not liable.[253] To rely on a defence of latent defect there must be proved: (1) the nature of the defect; and (2) that it could not have been detected with reasonable care and skill.[254]

10–87   The duty to exercise reasonable care involves the making of a reasonable examination of the vehicle from time to time, in accordance with the practice of a reasonably careful carrier.[255] A breakdown of the vehicle is evidence of negligence on the part of the carrier, throwing upon him an evidential burden to show that he exercised reasonable care and skill in detecting and remedying defects.[256] The onus is a heavy one, and rests upon the defendant to discharge. In *Henderson v H.E. Jenkins & Sons*[257] the defendant failed to discharge the evidential burden cast upon it by the happening of an accident as a result of mechanical defect, because no evidence was called to show the circumstances in which the vehicle had been used, with the object of establishing how the defect could have arisen, consistent with the exercise of reasonable care.

10–88   **Duty as occupier.** The main common law duty arises from the contract of carriage. The duty in tort is modified by the Occupiers' Liability Act 1957.[258] Section 1 provides that the rules enacted by ss.2 and 3 take effect in place of the common law. The duty owed pursuant to these sections is the "common duty of care" and it is owed by persons occupying or having control over any fixed or

---

[251] s.5(3).
[252] *Readhead v Midland Ry* (1869) L.R. 4 Q.B. 379, per Montague Smith J., at 393.
[253] *Readhead v Midland Ry*, above.
[254] *Ritchie v Western Scottish M.T. Co*, 1935 S.L.T. 13 (bus overturned owing to deflated tyre caused by a defect in metal of the flange under the tyre—company liable). In *Pearce v Round Oak Steel Works* [1969] 1 W.L.R. 595 and *Henderson v H.E. Jenkins & Sons* [1970] A.C. 282, the defendants failed to discharge the onus.
[255] *Bremner v Williams* (1824) 1 C. & P. 414.
[256] *Christie v Griggs* (1809) 2 Camp. 79.
[257] [1970] A.C. 282 (a failure of brakes occurred on a lorry because of the escape of brake fluid from a corroded hole in part of the pipe which was not accessible to the visual inspections conducted weekly). See further para.10–247.
[258] See generally Ch.8, above.

moveable structure, including any vessel, vehicle or aircraft, to his visitors.[259] The duty is to take such care as in all the circumstances of the case is reasonable to see that the visitor will be reasonably safe in using the premises (in this context: the vehicle) for the purposes for which he is invited or permitted to be there. The duty is owed to all visitors except in so far as the occupier is free to extend, restrict, modify or exclude his duty by agreement or otherwise.[260] The Unfair Contract Terms Act 1977 severely restricts the power of a carrier to limit or to exclude liability either by agreement or notice.

So far as the duty to warn a visitor of defects or dangers is concerned, it is **10–89** expressly provided that a warning by the "occupier" (that is, the carrier) of the existence of the danger or defect does not, in itself, absolve him from liability, unless, in all the circumstances, it was enough to enable the visitor to be reasonably safe.[261] Nevertheless, the defence of volenti non fit injuria is preserved, but only so far as it would have been available at common law.[262]

Where the claimant was alighting from the rear seat of the defendant's motor **10–90** car, with which she was familiar, and she tripped up, falling out on to the pavement and hurting herself, as a result of her foot having become entangled in the loop of a seat belt, it was held that the defendant was not liable.[263] There was no obligation upon the driver to make any visual check of the seat belts each time, upon getting in or out of the vehicle, to ensure that they were hooked up properly. Likewise, there was no obligation on him to issue a warning to his passengers to beware of this well-known hazard occasioned by the compulsory fitting of such belts, together with anchorages at ankle level.

Duty is owed to passengers. The common duty of care is owed to every **10–91** passenger who is a lawful visitor, but sometimes a difficulty arises in determining who is such a passenger. It is not necessary that the person in question should have a contract with the carrier. Where a train had been hired for an excursion from the railway authorities by a benefit society, from whom the claimant had bought a ticket, and there was a railway accident caused by the carrier's negligence, it was held that there was evidence on which a jury could find that the claimant was their passenger.[264] Where a valet was travelling on a railway, under a contract made between his employer and the railway company, and his portmanteau was lost, owing to the company's negligence, it was held that he could recover "not by reason of any contract between him and the company, but

---

[259] The Occupiers' Liability Act 1957 s.1(3)(a).
[260] The Occupiers' Liability Act 1957 s.2(1).
[261] The Occupiers' Liability Act 1957 s.2(4)(a).
[262] The Occupiers' Liability Act 1957 s.2(5).
[263] *Donn v Schacter* [1975] R.T.R. 238 (a passenger must take her own precautions and guard against such dangers), distinguished in *McCready v Miller* [1979] R.T.R. 186 (driver was liable to a passenger who caught her foot in a seat belt as she was getting out of the vehicle, fell and broke her ankle).
[264] *Skinner v L.B. & S.C. Ry* (1850) 5 Ex. 787.

by reason of a duty implied by law to carry him safely", which duty covered his luggage as well as himself.[265]

10–92   Where newspaper reporters were supplied with free tickets on a railway and the claimant used a ticket bearing the name of another reporter of the same newspaper, the question arose whether he was entitled to recover damages after he had been injured by the railway authorities' negligence. It was apparent that he had produced his ticket to a porter, whose business it was to examine tickets, and was shown into a carriage and in the circumstances he was lawfully in the carriage.[266] A passenger in an aeroplane, present as the guest of the hirer of the aeroplane, was held entitled to recover from the aircraft's owners for their pilot's negligence, since "the duty to him arose because he was carried in the aeroplane".[267] The duty was owed to a post office servant, travelling free of payment on the railway in order to accompany the mail[268]; and a passenger who had left the vehicle temporarily.[269]

10–93   **Non contractual passengers.** In the cases cited in the preceding paragraph, the claimant has been in the vehicle under a contract, although not one to which he was a party. It is not necessary, however, that there should be a contract, provided that the claimant is accepted as a passenger. Where the claimant, "a gentleman considerably advanced in years", signalled to the driver of an omnibus to stop, and the driver did so but, just as the claimant was putting his foot on the step, drove on and the claimant fell down and was injured, it was held that the claimant could recover, because there was evidence that he had been accepted as a passenger.[270] Where a child, just over three years old, was taken into a railway train by his mother, without any ticket having been taken for him, and was injured by the railway company's negligence, he was entitled to recover damages.[271]

10–94   **Passenger who has not paid the fare.** If the passenger has got on to the vehicle fraudulently, intending not to pay his fare or intending to pay only part of his fare or only a lower class fare, while travelling first class, he has still been accepted as a passenger. He is entitled to sue for injuries caused by negligence. "A third-class passenger is not an outlaw when he travels in a first-class carriage.

---

[265] *Marshall v York, Newcastle and Berwick Ry* (1851) 11 C.B. 655. The quotation is from the judgment of Jervis C.J. *Meux v G.E. Ry* [1895] 2 Q.B. 387 (servant contracted with railway company and lost his portmanteau, containing livery the property of his mistress, mistress entitled to recover). See also *Martin v G.I.P. Ry* (1867) L.R. 3 Ex. 9 (officer in India travelling on railway under contract between the Indian Government and the railway, lost luggage—was held to be entitled to recover).

[266] *Great Northern Ry v Harrison* (1854) 10 Ex. 376.

[267] *Fosbroke-Hobbes v Airwork Ltd* [1937] 1 All E.R. 108.

[268] *Collett v L. & N.W. Ry* (1851) 16 Q.B. 984.

[269] *Mitchell v Mason* (1966) 10 W.I.R. 26.

[270] *Brien v Bennett* (1839) 8 C. & P. 724. *Wilkie v L.P.T.B.* [1947] 1 All E.R. 258, is a similar case.

[271] *Austin v G.W. Ry* (1867) L.R. 2 Q.B. 442 at 445, 446, per Blackburn: "I think that what was said in the case of *Marshall v Newcastle and Berwick Ry* (1851) 11 C.B. 655 was quite correct. It was there laid down that the right which a passenger by railway has to be carried safely, does not depend on his having made a contract, but that the fact of his being a passenger casts a duty on the company to carry him safely."

When he does so the railway company are still under a duty to him person-ally."[272]

Trespassing passenger. A trespasser has been defined by Lord Dunedin as **10–95** one "who goes on the land without invitation of any sort and whose presence is either unknown to the proprietor or, if known, is practically objected to."[273]

The Occupiers' Liability Act 1984 provides for a duty to take reasonable care **10–96** that a trespasser does not suffer injury from some danger on the premises, which include vehicles.[274] The duty arises in respect of dangers of which the occupier is or ought to be aware.[275] Before he can be liable the occupier must know or have reasonable grounds to believe that the trespasser may be in, or come into, the vicinity of the danger concerned, and the risk must be one against which he may reasonably be expected to offer protection. It will matter not that the passenger is present on the vehicle, for instance, as a result of fraud.[276] What is important is the occupier's knowledge—of danger and the possible exposure of the trespasser to it—and the trespasser's own awareness that he should not be where he is will be relevant only to contribution.

Passenger riding with consent of employee. Where an employee of a carrier, **10–97** without his employer's authority and acting outside the scope of his employment, allowed a person to become a passenger in the vehicle, the employer was under no liability to him in respect of any damage suffered in an accident, caused by the employee's negligence: the person was a trespasser, whose presence was unforeseeable.[277] In a modern setting, however, the employer would probably be vicariously liable for such conduct, as in *Rose v Plenty*[278] where the defendant contracted to carry the claimant's goods in a cart and sent his employee with the cart, and the claimant, with the employee's permission but without the authority of the employer, rode in the cart, which broke down, the claimant could not recover damages.[279]

Injury caused by a stranger to the contract of carriage. Where a carrier **10–98** contracts to carry a passenger, partly on his own vehicle and partly on vehicles supplied by others he is liable not only for the negligence of himself and his employees but also for the negligence of those responsible for the other

[272] per Atkin L.J. in *Vosper v G.W. Ry* [1928] 1 K.B. 340 at 349 (passenger with third class ticket travels in a first class carriage and loses his luggage, held able to recover from the railway com-pany).
[273] *Robert Addie & Sons (Collieries) Ltd v Dumbreck* [1929] A.C. 358 at 371.
[274] See Ch.8, para.8–03, above (definition of "premises") and paras 8–144 to 8–160 (for discussion of the 1984 Act).
[275] Occupiers' Liability Act 1984 s.1(3).
[276] As in *Austin v G.W. Ry* (1867) L.R. 2 Q.B. 442.
[277] *Twine v Bean's Express Ltd* [1946] 1 All E.R. 202, affirmed 175 L.T. 131, which was distinguished in *Rose v Plenty* [1976] 1 W.L.R. 141, where the employer was held vicariously liable in the circumstances.
[278] [1976] 1 W.L.R. 141, CA (a milkman, who deliberately ignored an order not to employ children on his milk round, was not acting outside the scope of his employment).
[279] *Lygo v Newbold* (1854) 9 Ex. 302. See also *Houghton v Pilkington* [1912] 3 K.B. 308.

vehicles.[280] This is purely a contractual duty. Where there is no contract a carrier will still owe a duty of care in negligence, arising from acceptance of the passenger, as a passenger.[281] In *Dalyell v Tyrer*,[282] the lessee of a ferry hired such a vessel from the defendants, in order to assist him in carrying his passengers. The defendants provided their own tackle and crew. The claimant, who had contracted with the lessee to be carried across on the ferry, was injured on board by the breaking of some tackle, owing to the negligence of the crew. He was held entitled to recover, because "if the negligence in question had injured a mere stranger, not on board, but standing, for instance, on the pier at the time, they would have been liable".[283]

10–99   After the generality of the foregoing it will usually be the case that what amounts to negligence in the context of carriage depends on the nature of the the the carriage concerned and all the circumstances of the case. The appropriate duty and standard of care is considered below with reference to railways, road carriage, ships, aircraft, and hovercraft.

(B) Railways[284]

10–100   **General duty of railway authorities.** Railway authorities are under a duty to use reasonable care and skill in the provision and maintenance of their premises, including their carriages, the provision and maintenance of railway tracks, the provision of a proper system of signalling, and the carrying on of their activities[285] so as to prevent accidents. The standard of care is that of a reasonably careful and skilful body of persons, carrying on the work of such a transport undertaking.

10–101   **Illustrations of a prima facie case of negligence.** When either a collision between two trains occurs,[286] or a train runs off the lines,[287] or a train drives into the buffers,[288] or a train suddenly starts off without any warning,[289] which results in severe jolts being caused and injuries being sustained by someone, a prima facie case of negligence is established. This prima facie case, however, may be

---

[280] *G.W. Ry v Blake* (1872) 7 H. & N. 987; *Thomas v Rhymney Ry* (1871) L.R. 6 Q.B. 266. See also the analysis of Thesiger L.J. in *Foulkes v Metropolitan Ry* (1880) 5 C.P.D. 157 at 168, 169.

[281] *Foulkes v Metropolitan Ry* (1880) 5 C.P.D. 157; *Hooper v L. & N.W. Ry* (1880) 50 L.J.Q.B. 103; and see *Wright v Midland Ry* (1873) L.R. 8 Ex. 137.

[282] (1858) E.B. & E. 899. See also the similarity of decision in *Berringer v G.E. Ry* (1879) 4 C.P.D. 163.

[283] *Dalyell v Tyrer* (1858) E.B. & E. 899 per Erle J. at 905.

[284] For consideration of international carriage by rail see para.10–145, below.

[285] Indeed, the duty extends to passengers who are waiting on the platforms: *Public Transport Commission of N.S.W. v Perry* (1977) 14 A.L.R. 273 (claimant, whilst awaiting the arrival of a train, suffered a form of epileptic attack, fell unconscious on to the railway track and was struck by the approaching train).

[286] *Skinner v L.B. & S.C. Ry* (1850) L.R. 5 Ex. 787; *Ayles v S.E. Ry* (1868) L.R. 3 Ex. 146.

[287] *Carpue v London & Brighton Ry* (1844) 5 Q.B. 747; *Dawson v M.S. & L. Ry* (1862) 5 L.T. 682.

[288] *Burke v M.S. & L. Ry* (1879) 22 L.T. 442.

[289] *Caterson v Commissioner for Railways* (1972) 128 C.L.R. 99.

rebutted by proving a latent defect in the rolling stock[290] or by showing that the collision was caused by the wrongful act of a third person.[291] It is negligent to run a train over lines which were known to be defective and fractured.[292]

Overcrowding of carriages. Railway authorities are bound to provide reasonable accommodation for their passengers, and if too many people are put into the same carriage, they are liable for the damage resulting therefrom.[293] They are also bound to take reasonable steps to prevent people from getting into carriages already full.[294] It has been held that it is not the natural result of overcrowding that a passenger should have his hand trapped when the carriage door was shut,[295] or that he should be crushed by other passengers, who are hurrying to alight from the train,[296] or that he should be assaulted[297] or robbed[298] by other passengers. **10–102**

Injury caused to one passenger by another. Railway authorities are not liable if one passenger negligently or wilfully injures another. Where a passenger in a railway train brought into the carriage a parcel, which appeared to be harmless but actually contained bombs that exploded and injured a fellow-passenger, the railway authorities were not liable: they were not bound to search every parcel taken into the carriage, unless there was something to suggest danger.[299] If, however, the authorities know that a person, whether by reason of disease, drunkenness or avowed intention, is likely to be a danger to other passengers, they are under a duty to prevent him from entering the train.[300] They are also under a duty to take all reasonable steps to preserve order in their trains, which may require the removal of any disorderly persons. **10–103**

When a passenger in a train was robbed by a gang of men entering his compartment, and at the next station he asked the stationmaster to detain the train, so that the men could be given into custody and searched, a refusal to detain the train was not negligent because the railway authorities were not responsible for the robbery and under no duty to delay to enable the claimant to recover his property.[301] **10–104**

Shutting carriage doors. Railway authorities are under a duty to take reasonable care to see that the carriage doors are properly closed, before the train **10–105**

---

[290] *Readhead v Midland Ry* (1869) L.R. 4 Q.B. 379.

[291] *Latch v Rumner Ry* (1858) 27 L.J. Ex. 155.

[292] *Pym v G.N. Ry* (1861) 2 F. & F. 619.

[293] *Metropolitan Ry v Jackson* (1877) 3 App.Cas. 193 at 209, per Lord Blackburn.

[294] *Metropolitan Ry v Jackson* (1877) 3 App.Cas. 193 at 210.

[295] *Dublin, Wicklow and Wexford Ry v Slattery* (1878) 3 App.Cas. 1155 at 1166.

[296] *Machen v L. & Y. Ry* (1918) 88 L.J.K.B. 371.

[297] *Pounder v N.E. Ry* [1892] 1 Q.B. 385.

[298] *Cobb v G.W. Ry* [1894] A.C. 419. At 423 Lord Selborne doubted the correctness of the decision of the Divisional Court in *Pounder v N.E. Ry*, above, but contra Lord O'Hagan at 426.

[299] *East Indian Ry v Kalidas Mukerjee* [1901] A.C. 396.

[300] See per A. L. Smith J. in *Pounder v N.E. Ry* [1892] 1 Q.B. 385; *Murgatroyd v Blackburn Tramways* (1887) 3 T.L.R. 451.

[301] *Cobb v G.W. Ry* [1894] A.C. 419.

leaves the station.[302] Where the claimant got up and leant against the window while the train was in motion, but suddenly the door flew open and he fell out the railway authorities were liable.[303] In such circumstances, the fact of the carriage door opening could well be prima facie evidence of negligence.[304] On the other hand, it was held that the mere fact that a door which was not on the platform side of the train, came open on an express corridor train, did not give rise even to a prima facie case.[305] Such doors were not under the continuous control of the railway authorities throughout the train's journey. Where a four-year-old child fell out of a train, after he had opened the guard's van door by an internal handle, it was held that the carriers could not reasonably have foreseen that a mother, aware that such a door could be opened from the inside, would have let her child wander alone about the carriage. Accordingly, the defendants were not liable for the child's death.[306] Further, where a passenger was in a carriage, the door of which kept flying open, and, on his trying to close it for the fourth time, he fell out and was injured, it was held that his claim failed because he was doing something obviously dangerous, when he might have been sitting in the carriage in safety.[307]

10–106   Before the train is about to start its journey, the actual shutting of a door must be done with reasonable care. So, when a passenger is in the act of getting into, or out of a carriage, a warning should be given by the porter before he attempts to shut the door.[308] In such circumstances, any failure to give a warning is evidence of negligence.[309] When no warning has been given, the question arises: what would the person whose duty it was to shut the doors reasonably have supposed the position of the claimant to have been?[310] Obviously, there is no negligence in shutting a door, without warning, if the passengers are all seated in the carriage and not in the act of either getting out or in.[311] But it is equally obvious that to slam the door, without warning or giving a passenger reasonable opportunity first to alight and without taking reasonable care to see that it is safe to shut the door, is negligent.[312]

---

[302] *Thatcher v G.W. Ry* (1893) 10 T.L.R. 13; *Toal v N.B. Ry* [1908] A.C. 352; *Burns v N.B. Ry*, 1914 S.C. 754; *Hare v B.T.C.* [1956] 1 W.L.R. 250; *Brookes v L.P.T.B.* [1947] 1 All E.R. 506 (door left open when underground tube train started and passenger was precipitated out).

[303] *Gee v Metropolitan Ry* (1873) L.R. 8 Q.B. 1. See also *Warburton v Midland Ry* (1870) 21 L.T. 835; *Richards v G.E. Ry* (1873) 28 L.T. 711; *Dudman v N.L. Ry* (1886) 2 T.L.R. 365; *Hamer v Cambrian Ry* (1886) 2 T.L.R. 508; *Inglis v L.M.S. Ry*, 1941 S.C. 551.

[304] *Gee v Metropolitan Ry* (1873) L.R. 8 Q.B. 161; *Inglis v L.M.S.* 1941 S.C. 551.

[305] *Easson v L.N.E. Ry* [1944] K.B. 421.

[306] *O'Connor v British Transport Commission* [1958] 1 W.L.R. 346.

[307] *Adams v L. & Y. Ry* (1869) L.R. 4 C.P. 739. In *Gee v Metropolitan Ry* (1873) L.R. 8 Q.B. 161, Brett J., who was a party to the decision, said that the correct principle had been applied incorrectly to the facts in *Adams*. However today, it is much more likely that liability would be established in like circumstances, although the claimant would be guilty of a degree of contributory negligence.

[308] *Richardson v Metropolitan Ry* (1868) L.R. 3 C.P. 374n.

[309] *Fordham v L.B. & S.C. Ry* (1869) L.R. 4 C.P. 619; *Atkins v S.E. Ry* (1885) 2 T.L.R. 94.

[310] *Cohen v Metropolitan Ry* (1890) 6 T.L.R. 146.

[311] *Drury v N.E. Ry* [1901] 2 K.B. 322; *Benson v Furness Ry* (1903) 88 L.T. 268; see also *Metropolitan Ry v Jackson* (1877) 3 App.Cas. 193.

[312] *Bird v Railway Executive* [1949] W.N. 196.

If a carriage door has not been shut properly and, when the train starts, a **10–107** passenger, who has already alighted from the train, is struck by the door swinging open wide, there is evidence of negligence against the railway authorities.[313] Likewise, where a passenger entered an electric train and, before he had taken his seat, the train started off with a jerk, causing him to lose his balance, so that he put out his hand, which was caught by a sliding door.[314] The mere fall of a carriage door's window into its socket is not evidence of negligence against the railway company.[315] A passenger who, arriving late, dashed on to a moving train but left open the carriage door, was liable to the porter working on the platform whom the door struck and injured.[316]

Joining or leaving a train. Railway authorities are bound to provide **10–108** reasonable means for passengers to leave the train at all stations where it stops.[317] If the platform is too high or too low having regard to the height of the carriage, that is evidence of negligence.[318] Where the train was too long for the platform and a passenger was asked by a porter to leave the train beyond the end of the platform, the railway authorities were liable for an accident he sustained in so doing, since "the place and the means of descent provided were not reasonably convenient".[319]

The mere fact of a carriage overshooting[320] or failing to reach[321] the platform **10–109** is not evidence of negligence against the railway authorities. Where a passenger, in such circumstances, chooses to get off and in doing so is injured, he has no claim.[322] It is otherwise where a passenger is invited to alight, either expressly or by implication, and is injured in doing so as a result of the carriage not being opposite the platform.[323] It depends on the circumstances whether or not there has been an invitation to alight. Calling out the name of the station, as the train draws up, is not an invitation to get off immediately it stops.[324] But where the name of the station had been called out, the train had stopped, no warning had been given not to alight and some time had elapsed, there was sufficient evidence

---

[313] *Toal v N.B. Ry* [1908] A.C. 352; *Hare v B.T.C.* [1956] 1 W.L.R. 250.
[314] *Metropolitan Ry v Delaney* (1921) 90 L.J.K.B. 721.
[315] *Murray v Metropolitan Ry* (1873) 27 L.T. 762.
[316] *Booker v Wenborn* [1962] 1 W.L.R. 162.
[317] *Robson v N.E. Ry* (1876) 2 Q.B.D. 85, per Mellish L.J. at 88.
[318] *Foulkes v Metropolitan Ry* (1880) 5 C.P.D. 157; *Wharton v L. & Y. Ry* (1888) 5 T.L.R. 142; *Manning v L. & N.W. Ry* (1907) 23 T.L.R. 222.
[319] *Foy v L.B. & S.C. Ry* (1865) 18 C.B.(N.S.) 225.
[320] *Lewis v L.C. & D. Ry* (1873) L.R. 9 Q.B. 66; *Weller v L.B. & S.C. Ry* (1874) L.R. 9 C.P. 126.
[321] *Bridges v North London Ry* (1874) L.R. 7 H.L. 213.
[322] *Siner v G.W. Ry* (1869) L.R. 4 Ex. 117; *Harrold v G.W. Ry* (1866) 14 L.T. 440; *Owen v G.W. Ry* (1877) 46 L.J.Q.B. 486; *Abbott v N.B. Ry*, 1916 S.C. 306.
[323] *Struthers v British Railways Board* (1969) 113 S.J. 268 (the defendants were negligent in stopping their train short of the platform at a station, without any compelling reason and in siting the illuminated station sign where it was, which had prompted the claimant passenger to alight opposite it. The claimant was one-third to blame for failing to look where he was stepping); *Poole v State Transport Authority (Rail Division)* 31 S.A.S.R. 74, Sup. Ct. of South Australia (the defendants were liable in negligence where the train driver had overshot the station platform and had stopped so that a carriage doorway had opened out on to a sloping ramp at the platform's end. The claimant was guilty of contributory negligence to the extent of 25 per cent).
[324] *Lewis v L.C. & D. Ry* (1873) L.R. 9 Q.B. 66; *Plant v Midland Ry* (1870) 21 L.T. 836.

of an invitation to leave.[325] Similarly, when the train overshot the platform and porters called out to the passengers to keep their seats, but the claimant, who was in the front, did not hear and after a little time, got out and was injured, it was held that there was evidence of negligence against the railway authorities.[326]

10–110 Opening the door of the carriage is an invitation to alight.[327] Where, in darkness, the carriage in which the claimant was travelling drew up opposite a curved part of the platform, so that a gap appeared between the footboard and the platform, the claimant fell into it, liability was made out.[328] Conversely, where an intending passenger fell into the gap between an underground train and the curved edge of the platform, which was marked clearly with a white line and was illuminated adequately, the defendants were not negligent.[329] Even where an invitation to leave the train is made negligently a passenger must take reasonable care for his own safety, if he is to avoid a finding of contributory negligence.[330]

10–111 There is no invitation to alight where passengers are warned not to leave their seats. If a passenger disregards such a warning or gets off either before or immediately the train stops but before the railway staff have had time to give warning, his action for damages will probably fail.[331]

10–112 **Stopping and starting of trains.** Trains must be started and stopped with reasonable care. If a train is started with a sudden jerk, as a result of which a passenger is injured, for example, by a sliding door closing and trapping his hand,[332] there is evidence of negligence.[333] A violent and unusual stopping or starting of the train, which occasions injury to a passenger, is prima facie evidence of negligence. The railway authorities will have "to show both that they acted reasonably and properly in suddenly stopping the train, and also that the cause which led to the necessity of stopping the train was not brought about by any negligence upon their part".[334] Where the brakes of a train were suddenly applied, which threw the claimant off his seat, and it was proved that the train had stopped in that manner in order to avoid running over a passenger who was crossing the line, it was held, nevertheless, that the railway authority were liable. It had not been shown that the presence of the passenger on their line was not a consequence of their negligence.[335] Where a claimant boarded a long-distance train in order to help a passenger with his luggage, and the train suddenly started

---

[325] *Weller v L.B. & S.C. Ry* (1874) L.R. 9 C.P. 126. See also *Bridges v North London Ry* (1874) L.R. 7 H.L. 213 at 241, per Lord Hatherley; *Robson v N.E. Ry* (1876) 2 Q.B.D. 85.
[326] *Rose v N.E. Ry* (1876) 2 Ex.D. 248.
[327] *Praeger v Bristol and Exeter Ry* (1871) 24 L.T. 105.
[328] *Cockle v L. & S.E. Ry* (1872) L.R. 7 C.P. 321 at 326, per Cockburn C.J.
[329] *Stracstone v London Transport Board, The Times*, January 21, 1966.
[330] See, generally, Ch.4, paras 4–03 to 4–72, above.
[331] See, e.g. *Anthony v Midland Ry* (1908) 100 L.T. 117.
[332] *Metropolitan Ry v Delaney* (1921) 90 L.J.K.B. 721.
[333] *Langton v L. & Y. Ry* (1886) 3 T.L.R. 18; *L. & N.W. Ry v Hellawell* (1872) 26 L.T. 557; *Stockdale v L. & Y. Ry* (1863) 8 L.T. 289; *Goldberg v G. & S.W. Ry*, 1907 S.C. 1035, where the railway company succeeded in avoiding liability.
[334] Lord Loreburn L.C. in *Angus v London, Tilbury and Southend Ry* (1906) 22 T.L.R. 222.
[335] *Angus v L.T. & sRy* (1906) 22 T.L.R. 222.

to move off, without prior audible warning, the railway authorities were held liable to him when he jumped from the moving train, as it was gathering speed.[336] A guard has a duty to observe passengers on the platform in the moments before a train is about to depart. So where the guard failed to notice a drunken passenger, who was shouting and banging on the side of the train and who subsequently fell in a gap between the platform and the train so that he was injured when the train departed, the train company was liable for the guard's negligence.[337]

It is negligent for a passenger to: stand in a carriage by an open door, while the **10–113** train is in motion,[338] or attempt to board[339] or leave[340] a train in motion.

Duty to visitors. Persons resorting to railway premises, whether as intending **10–114** passengers, or as the senders or consignee of goods, are in the position of invitees[341] and, hence, "visitors" under the Occupiers' Liability Act 1957.[342] Similarly, a person seeing a friend off at a railway station or meeting a passenger arriving by train is a visitor.[343] It follows that the railway authorities are under a duty to take care that their premises are reasonably safe for persons using them in the ordinary and customary manner and with reasonable care. Quite apart from the duty in tort, a contractual duty is owed by railway authorities to ticket-holding passengers to use reasonable care to make their premises, including trains, safe for use by the passenger in the usual manner.[344]

Platforms. Platforms must be made and kept reasonably safe for their **10–115** purpose. They must be neither too high nor too low for the train's carriages.[345] The existence of an obstacle, projecting above the level of the platform, which someone might stumble over despite taking reasonable care, was evidence of negligence.[346] On the other hand, where there was a portable weighing machine on the platform, the foot of which projected six inches above the platform and the machine had been in the same position for five years, without causing an accident, the railway authority was not liable to a passenger who tripped over

---

[336] *Caterson v Commissioner for Railways (N.S.W.)* (1973) 47 A.L.J.R. 249.
[337] *Williamson v Silverlink Train Services Ltd* [2008] EWHC 2945 (QB) - the claimant was guilty of contributory negligence to the extent of one half.
[338] *Langton v L. & Y. Ry* (1886) 3 T.L.R. 18; *Folkes v North London Ry* (1892) 8 T.L.R. 269. Such evidence is not conclusive: *Hall v London Tramways Co* (1896) 12 T.L.R. 611.
[339] *Avis v G.E. Ry* (1892) 8 T.L.R. 693; *Booker v Wenborn* [1962] 1 W.L.R. 162.
[340] *Metropolitan Ry v Wright* (1886) 11 App.Cas. 152.
[341] *Norman v G.W. Ry* [1915] 1 K.B. 584. For the duty to visitors generally, see Ch.8, paras 8–23 to 8–35, above.
[342] s.1(2).
[343] *Watkins v G.W. Ry* (1877) 37 L.T. 193; *Stowell v Railway Executive* [1949] 2 K.B. 519 (father at station to meet his daughter arriving by train slipped on patch of oil on platform and succeeded in establishing liability); *Thatcher v G.W. Ry* (1893) 10 T.L.R. 13; *Hare v B.T.C.* [1956] 1 W.L.R. 250 (claimant, while standing on platform, after seeing her husband off in a train, was struck from behind by the open door of the guard's van). The issue of platform tickets will be affected by the terms of the Unfair Contract Terms Act 1977 as regards any attempt to restrict liability in negligence for personal injuries or death suffered by such a ticket holder.
[344] *Protheroe v Railway Executive* [1951] 1 K.B. 376 (where a contract ticket holder tripped in a crack between a paving stone and the coping stone at the edge of the platform and hurt herself).
[345] *Foulkes v Metropolitan Ry* (1880) 5 C.P.D. 157; *Wharton v L. & Y. Ry* (1888) 5 T.L.R. 142; *Manning v L. & N.W. Ry* (1907) 23 T.L.R. 222.
[346] *Sturges v G.W. Ry* (1892) 8 T.L.R. 231; *Bloomstein v Ry Executive* [1952] 2 All E.R. 418.

it.[347] If the platform is reasonably safe for persons using it in a reasonable way, the railway authorities are under no liability to persons using it in an unreasonable way. For example, where two passengers ran arm-in-arm along a platform, which was safe for one but too narrow for two abreast, and one of them fell on to the railway line and was injured, there was no liability.[348] Nor did liability attach where there were two doors close together on the platform, one marked "Gentlemen" and the other marked "Lamp Room", and the claimant, intending to go to the first mistakenly went through the second and fell down some steps.[349]

10–116   There may well be no liability on the railway authorities where they have taken reasonable care either to eliminate a source of danger or, if that is impracticable, to give reasonable warnings of its presence. Where, after snow, a porter at a station began to spread sand but had to attend to other work before he had finished and, shortly after a passenger alighting from a train slipped and was injured, there had been no failure of reasonable care and the claim failed.[350] Similarly, where the defendants' foreman at Paddington station saw a patch of oil lying on the surface and sent for sawdust, after calling out to stop passengers from walking in it, but the claimant did not hear his warnings, her action in negligence failed when fell after slipping on the oil.[351] Nevertheless, if slipping hazards are allowed to remain on the platform, after the station authority knew or or ought to be known of their presence, and an accident happens, there is evidence of negligence.[352] If the danger is obvious, there will be a potential finding of contributory negligence[353] on the part of the person who slips.[354]

10–117   Railway authorities must take reasonable care to provide and maintain such lighting on their platforms, as make them safe for persons ordinarily using them.[355] It may become essential in foggy conditions to take additional precautions in order to ensure that passengers are protected reasonably from dangers incidental to movement along a platform, such as from falling over the edge and on to the tracks.[356]

10–118   Railway authorities are under a duty to see that their platforms are not overcrowded, and to take reasonable care to control the crowd so as to prevent

---

[347] *Cornman v E.C. Ry* (1859) 4 H. & N. 781. See also to the same effect, *Blackman v L.B. & S.C. Ry* (1869) 17 W.R. 769.

[348] *Rigg v M.S. & L. Ry* (1866) 14 W.R. 834.

[349] *Toomey v L.B. & S.C. Ry* (1857) 3 C.B.(N.S.) 146. It is doubtful that this case would be decided the same way today. An obvious precaution would be to keep the lamp room locked, since the travelling public are not intended to have access to it.

[350] *Tomlinson v Railway Executive* [1953] 1 All E.R. 1.

[351] *Blackman v Railway Executive* [1953] 1 W.L.R. 2, affirmed [1954] 1 W.L.R. 220.

[352] *Shepherd v Midland Ry* (1872) 25 L.T. 879.

[353] For contributory negligence as a partial defence, see Ch.4, paras 4–03 to 4–72, above.

[354] *Osborne v L. & N.W. Ry* (1888) 21 Q.B.D. 220; *Brackley v Midland Ry* (1916) 85 L.J.K.B. 1596; *Letang v Ottawa Electric Ry* [1926] A.C. 725; *Stowell v Ry Executive* [1949] 2 K.B. 519.

[355] *Martin v G.N. Ry* (1855) 16 C.B. 179.

[356] *L.T. & sRy v Patterson* (1913) 29 T.L.R. 413. This decision can be criticised on the ground that there were no further precautions which the railway company could have taken in all the circumstances: *Schlarb v L.N.E. Ry* [1936] 1 All E.R. 71.

accidents. Thus, there was evidence of negligence where an excursion train was provided and more people were allowed on the platform than it could properly hold, as a result of which there was a rush when the train arrived, and the claimant was pushed on to the line.[357] It might be otherwise if adequate numbers of competent station staff were provided.[358]

The railway authorities are liable for the negligence of their employees. So, **10–119** they were liable when the claimant was struck by a portmanteau which fell from a luggage barrow, being pushed along the platform by a porter.[359] But they are not vicariously liable for the negligence of independent contractors,[360] or for the act of a stray dog, which bit a passenger on the platform, in the absence of negligence in allowing it on the platform.[361]

Approaches. The occupier's duty towards visitors is also owed in relation to **10–120** a footbridge or a staircase, either leading to a station or between one platform and another. Reasonable care must be taken to see that the premises are reasonably safe. So, railway authorities were liable where a passenger slipped on a worn flight of steps.[362] Likewise where the slip was on steps covered in snow. [363] When there is more than one approach to a platform, it is no defence for the railway authorities to show that the other route was safer, because a passenger is entitled to avail himself of any approach provided.[364]

The duty is not to keep everything in such a condition that nobody can, by any **10–121** possibility, be hurt. For example, where a woman tripped on an escalator, by catching her heel in the space between the bottom of the escalator and the platform, the railway authority was not liable in negligence, since the space's width was only half an inch (12.7mm).[365] On the other hand, a passenger, who tripped over a projecting nut and bolt, which was part of a weighing machine that was placed on a path leading from the platform to the street, succeeded in her claim.[366]

The mere fact that a passenger slips on some steps is not evidence of **10–122** negligence. Where a passenger slipped on steps which were used safely by hundreds of people daily, and it was proved that the nosing of the steps, which were made of brass, had become worn and slippery, negligence was not made out on proof that the accident would not have happened if lead had been used

---

[357] *Hogan v S.E. Ry* (1873) 28 L.T. 271; *McGregor v Glasgow District Subway Co* (1901) 3 F. 1131; *Fraser v Caledonian Ry* (1902) 5 F. 41.
[358] *M'Callum v N.B. Ry*, 1908 S.C. 415. See also *Cannon v M.G.W. Ry* (1876) 6 L.R.Ir. 199 (railway company not liable when passenger was pushed on to line from platform by a sudden rush of people on to platform without permission).
[359] *Tebbutt v Bristol and Exeter Ry* (1870) L.R. 6 Q.B. 73.
[360] See Ch.3, paras 3–172 to 3–203, above, for liability for acts of independent contractors.
[361] *Smith v G.E. Ry* (1866) L.R. 2 C.P. 4.
[362] *Osborne v L. & N.W. Ry* (1888) 21 Q.B.D. 220, 221. cf. a similar case on the facts, *Brackley v Midland Ry* (1916) 85 L.J.K.B. 1596, where the injured claimant failed to prove liability.
[363] *Letang v Ottawa Electric Ry* [1926] A.C. 725.
[364] *Longmore v G.W. Ry* (1865) 19 C.B.(N.S.) 183; *Letang v Ottawa Electric Ry*, above.
[365] *Alexander v City and South London Ry* (1928) 44 T.L.R. 450.
[366] *Bloomstein v Railway Executive* [1952] 2 All E.R. 418.

instead.[367] Where a consignee of goods sent a horse and cart to a goods yard to take delivery, and, on one side of the yard, there was an unfenced grass slope, down which the horse and cart fell while the carter was signing for the goods, the fact that the slope was unfenced did not give rise to liability.[368]

10–123   **Crossing between platforms or over the lines.** Suitable crossings must be provided to allow passengers to enter or leave the station or go from one platform to another. A crossing may take the form either of a bridge over the line or a level crossing. Where both are provided, a notice forbidding passengers to cross by means of the level crossing and directing them to use the bridge instead, will not provide a defence if they there has been acquiescence to passengers using the level crossing.[369] When a level crossing is used, a passenger must take reasonable care for his own safety.[370] Where a passenger could not see an approaching train, owing to darkness or to a curve in the line, and received no warning, either by way of a whistle from the engine or otherwise that a train was expected, there was evidence of negligence.[371]

10–124   **Embankments and bridges.** Embankments and bridges must be maintained in a reasonably safe condition. A collapse of an embankment or bridge is evidence of negligence and it is no defence to say that it was caused by exceptional weather conditions, because "the railway company ought to have constructed their works in such a manner as to be capable of resisting all the violence of weather which in the climate . . . might be expected, though perhaps rarely, to occur."[372] Even so, liability was not established where there was no evidence of negligence in construction or maintenance, it appeared that competent people had been employed in the work, and the best method and materials used.[373] When a highway is carried over the railway by a bridge, there is a statutory duty to maintain the bridge and its approaches.[374] When the road over such a bridge was in a bad state of repair, with several potholes and a large rut, as a result of which a cyclist was injured, the railway authorities were liable.[375]

10–125   **Level crossings over highways.** When a railway line crosses a highway,[376] by means of a level crossing, the railway authorities are under a duty to keep the

---

[367] *Crafter v Metropolitan Ry* (1866) L.R. 1 C.P. 300.

[368] *Norman v G.W. Ry* [1915] 1 K.B. 584.

[369] *Dublin, Wicklow and Wexford Ry v Slattery* (1878) 3 App.Cas. 1155; *Rogers v Rhymney Ry* (1872) 26 L.T. 879.

[370] See *Walker v Midland Ry* (1866) 14 L.T. 796 and *Davey v L. & S.W. Ry* (1883) 12 Q.B.D. 70, both of which would probably be decided differently today, although subject to findings of contributory negligence.

[371] See *Dublin, Wicklow and Wexford Ry v Slattery* (1878) 3 App.Cas. 1155, *Brown v G.W. Ry* (1885) 1 T.L.R. 614; *Wright v Midland Ry* (1885) 1 T.L.R. 406; *Crowther v L. & Y. Ry* (1889) 6 T.L.R. 18; *Dallas v G.W. Ry* (1893) 9 T.L.R. 344.

[372] *G.W. Ry of Canada v Braid* (1863) 1 Moo.P.C.(N.S.) 101, not following *Withers v North Kent Ry* (1858) 27 L.J. Ex. 417, where an unusually violent storm had washed away an embankment, which had stood for five years, the railway company was not liable.

[373] *Grote v Chester and Holyhead Ry* (1848) 2 Exch. 251.

[374] Railways Clauses Consolidation Act 1845 s.46.

[375] *Swain v Southern Ry* [1939] 2 K.B. 560.

[376] See James, "Railway Level Crossings and the Duty of Care", 145 J.P.N. 300.

crossing in a proper state for the passage of traffic. They must take reasonable care to reduce the danger created by the rails of their line to a minimum, although the precise nature of the measures to be taken will depend on the circumstances.[377] Thus, where rails were placed too high above the surface of a road, as a result of which the claimant's conveyance was caught by the rails and torn in two, the authorities were liable.[378] Further a crossing must be kept in proper repair,[379] which duty extends to any inclined approaches leading to it.[380] It is not however the case that they must reconstruct such approaches from time to time to meet modern traffic requirements.[381]

The Railway Clauses Consolidation Act 1845 s.47,[382] provides that if a **10–126** railway crosses a public carriage road on the level, the authorities must erect and maintain good and sufficient gates across the road, and must employ proper persons to open and shut them. Further, s.61 provides that if a railway crosses a highway other than a public carriageway on the level, the company must, if the highway is a bridleway, erect and maintain good and sufficient gates, and, if it is a footway, good and sufficient gates or stiles at each side of the railway where the highway communicates with it. For neglect to perform their statutory duty the railway authorities are liable. Where, therefore, a railway line crossed a footpath on the level and the company, in breach of their duty under s.61, had not erected a gate or stile, with the result that a child of four-and-a-half, who was out on an errand, got on to the crossing and was injured by a train, the authorities were liable.[383] Likewise where a good and sufficient stile had not been maintained, in that it had become ruined by vandals within about 10 days of its erection, as a result of which a two-year-old toddler got on to the railway lines and was severely injured.[384]

In the absence of a gatekeeper, as required by s.47, a member of the public ought not attempt to open the gate. There was no liability when someone did and

---

[377] *Smith v L.M.S. Ry*, 1948 S.C. 125. *Commissioner for Railways v Quinlan* [1964] A.C. 1054. In *Commissioner for Railways v McDermott* [1967] A.C. 169 it was held that in running trains through a level crossing there was imposed on the railway authority a general duty of care towards persons lawfully on the crossing, which extended not merely to positive operations but included keeping the crossing itself in a reasonably safe condition. See too *Clegg v* Rogerson [2005] CSOH 113. See Hall, "Occupiers' Liability towards Trespassers" 115 L.J. 87 (founded on this case); "Negligence at Level Crossings" 236 L.T. 101.
[378] *Oliver v N.E. Ry* (1874) L.R. 9 Q.B. 409.
[379] *Guilfoyle v Port of London Authority* [1932] 1 K.B. 336; *Swain v Southern Ry* [1939] 2 K.B. 560.
[380] *Hertfordshire County Council v G.E. Ry* [1909] 2 K.B. 403. The wide principle enunciated by Fletcher Moulton L.J. was said to be "too broadly expressed" in *Sharpness New Docks, etc., Co v Attorney-General* [1915] A.C. 654. The obligation under the Railways Clauses Consolidation Act 1845 s.16, does not extend to repairing the approaches: *West Lancashire Rural District Council v L. & Y. Ry* [1903] 2 K.B. 394.
[381] *Attorney-General v G.N. Ry* [1916] 2 A.C. 356.
[382] The Railways Clauses Act 1863 s.6, requires the company to erect a lodge at the point where the railway crosses a public carriage road. The Road and Rail Traffic Act 1933, s.42 the Transport Act 1968 ss.123–124, and the Local Government Act 1972 Sch.30, contain other provisions relating to level crossings, not affecting the text.
[383] *Williams v G.W. Ry* (1874) L.R. 9 Ex. 157, approved and followed by the CA in *Thomas v British Railways Board* [1976] Q.B. 912. For cases of injury to cattle through neglect of fencing, see also Ch.14, para.14–85, below.
[384] *Thomas v British Railways Board* [1976] Q.B. 912.

was injured[385] Apart from s.47, the railway authorities are under no obligation (except under a special Act) to employ a gatekeeper or a watchman at a level crossing.[386] The duty of a gatekeeper at a level crossing over a highway is not increased by the fact that there is an accommodation crossing near it.[387]

10–127 By the provisions of the Level Crossings Act 1983, the Secretary of State may by order provide for the protection of those using the level crossing. Such an order must be requested by the operator of the crossing. When it is in force, the duty is placed on the operator to comply with operational conditions and provide for use of protective equipment.

10–128 Railway authorities must take reasonable care to avoid injuring members of the public at level crossings. If their employees act in a way which would lead a reasonable person to believe that it is safe to cross the lines and a person attempts to cross and is injured by a train, then there is evidence of negligence.

ILLUSTRATIONS

10–129 Liability was established: where a railway gatekeeper indicated to a carman that the line was clear whereupon the carman entered the line and was hit by a train[388]; where the level crossing gates across a road were left open and a pedestrian, who assumed he could proceed in safety, attempted to cross the line and was run over[389]; where a man, after calling one night to inquire after his wife at the gatekeeper's lodge, proceeded to cross the line, not having been warned by the gatekeeper that a train was approaching, and was killed,[390] where a wicket gate, which was usually kept locked when a train was about to pass, was left unlocked and a pedestrian went through and was run over by a train.[391] In circumstances where there was no duty to whistle on the approach to a level crossing but it was a regular practice and the claimant assumed that it was safe to cross but was struck by a train, there was evidence of negligence.[392]

10–130 Apart from the provision of gates, reasonable precautions must be taken for the protection of persons using a crossing, such as by drawing attention to the need to look in both directions along the track before attempting to cross, whether on

---

[385] *Wyatt v G.W. Ry* (1865) 34 L.J.Q.B. 204.

[386] *Cliff v Midland Ry* (1870) L.R. 5 Q.B. 258; *Stubley v L. & N.W. Ry* (1865) L.R. 1 Ex. 13; *Newman v L. & S.W. Ry* (1890) 7 T.L.R. 138.

[387] *Liddiatt v G.W. Ry* [1946] K.B. 545 (level crossing 160 yards from accommodation crossing, south gate of which was visible to gatekeeper—gatekeeper opened level crossing when south gate open, and claimant's heifer was killed by a train—railway company were held not liable).

[388] *Lunt v L. & N.W. Ry* (1866) L.R. 1 Q.B. 277.

[389] *N.E. Ry v Wanless* (1874) L.R. 7 H.L. 12.

[390] *Smith v S.E. Ry* [1896] 1 Q.B. 178.

[391] *Mercer v S.E. & C. Ry* [1922] 2 K.B. 549; see also *North Eastern Ry v Wanless* (1874) L.R. 7 H.L. 12.

[392] *Dublin, Wicklow and Wexford Ry v Slattery* (1878) 3 App.Cas. 1155 at 1165, per Lord Cairns; *Smith v South Eastern Ry* [1896] 1 Q.B. 178 at 183, per Lord Esher.

foot or by vehicle.[393] An omission to whistle or otherwise to give warning of the approach of a train may be evidence of negligence, according to the circumstances,[394] but there is no obligation to whistle in every case.[395] But where a whistle board was placed so near to a crossing that it would only take 12-and-a-half seconds for the train to be on the crossing after blowing the whistle at the board, and there was a limited view of the track for qnyone using the crossing, there was evidence of negligence.[396]

Level crossings and the Highway Code. The driver or rider of a wheeled vehicle may be found negligent if he does not comply with the Highway Code,[397] which provides that a level crossing should be approached and crossed with care. A driver should never drive onto a crossing unless he can see the road is clear on the other side; drive too close to the vehicle in front; stop on or just after a crossing; or park too close to it.[398] Most modern level crossings have steady amber and twin flashing red traffic lights and an audible alarm which must always be obeyed.[399] The Highway Code paras 295–298, also covers crossings without traffic lights, user-operated crossings and open crossings . **10–131**

Contributory negligence on crossings. Not surprisingly, a person who crosses a railway line without first looking and listening to determine whether a train is approaching may be prevented from recovering in full on the ground of contributory negligence, particularly if the line is straight and he has an uninterrupted view along the line.[400] When the railway crossed a footpath and the plaintiff attempted to use the path by crawling under a standing train just before the train moved off, his claim failed altogether, even though no warning had been given that the train was about to start.[401] **10–132**

Private accommodation crossings. When a train is approaching an accommodation crossing,[402] reasonable care must be used, but there is no duty to drive **10–133**

---

[393] *Karamalis v South Australian Railways Commissioner* (1976) 14 S.A.S.R. 432 (held that the railway authority's share of the blame was 15 per cent, compared with the claimant cyclist's 85 per cent contributory negligence).

[394] *Dublin, Wicklow and Wexford Ry v Slattery* (1878) 3 App.Cas. 1155; *James v G.W. Ry* (1867) L.R. 2 C.P. 634n.; *Gray v N.E. Ry* (1883) 48 L.T. 904.

[395] *Ellis v G.W. Ry* (1874) L.R. 9 C.P. 551; *Newman v L. & S.W. Ry* (1890) 7 T.L.R. 138.

[396] *Jenner v S.E. Ry* (1911) 105 L.T. 131.

[397] Road Traffic Act 1988 s.38. The current edition was issued in 2007.

[398] At para.291.

[399] At para.293.

[400] See *Karamalis v South Australian Railways Commission* (1976) 14 S.A.S.R. 432. For some earlier English decisions on the point, when contributory negligence was a complete defence see: *Ellis v G.W. Ry* (1874) L.R. 9 C.P. 551; *Davey v L. & S.W. Ry* (1883) 12 Q.B.D. 70; *Skelton v L. & N.W. Ry* (1867) L.R. 2 C.P. 631; *Stubley v L. & N.W. Ry* (1865) L.R. 1 Ex. 13.

[401] *French v Hills Plymouth Co* (1908) 24 T.L.R. 644.

[402] These are sometimes referred to as "occupation crossings". If there is any significant distinction it seems to be that where there had been an existing private right of way before the railway was built the resulting level crossing made was to replace the roadway and was an "accommodation". When only the land without any right of way was severed by the advent of the railway, the level crossing provided was for the purpose of making a link between the severed parts of land under the same occupation and hence was an "occupation crossing".

so that it can be stopped within the limit of the driver's vision.[403] The degree of care to be exercised by a train driver approaching such a crossing is not as high as for a public level crossing. Further, where the driver of a tractor had sustained fatal injuries in a collision with a train at an accommodation level crossing on a foggy morning, it was held that the railway authorities were not bound to take any special precautions in foggy conditions.[404] They,

> "need not at common law go so far as to turn an accommodation crossing into a public level crossing, with all the statutory obligations incident thereto; but they must do all that could reasonably be required of them, in the way of warnings, whistles and so forth, to reduce the danger to people using the crossing."[405]

Also, when it is known that the public are using a private road crossing, there is a duty to take reasonable care to make the crossing safe. A notice, "Beware of the trains"[406] was held to be insufficient.

10–134 There is a duty not to expose users of the crossing to any perils, beyond those ordinarily inherent in the user of an accommodation crossing. Normally, if there is nothing in the layout of the crossing to call for special precautions,[407] the railway undertakers will not be liable, unless there can be established negligence on the part of the crew of the train. The duty of the engine driver is not the same as that of the driver of a motorcar. In particular, he is not bound to look out for either highway traffic, such as motor vehicles, approaching a crossing,[408] or for pedestrians, such as a railway employee, who was walking to his place of work along the line.[409]

10–135 When railway undertakers agreed with contractors to construct and maintain a temporary level crossing over a railway line, to enable timber to be carried across, their duty was to take reasonable precautions for the safety of persons who were using the crossing for such purposes. They were liable for the death of a lorry driver, who was killed by a railway train, when he was driving a load of timber over the crossing.[410]

---

[403] *Knight v G.W. Ry* [1943] K.B. 105 (the whistle was sounded where the whistle board was placed); *Short v British Railways Board* (1974) 118 S.J. 101.

[404] *Hazell v British Transport Commission* [1958] 1 W.L.R. 169. This followed *Kemshead v British Transport Commission* [1958] 1 W.L.R. 173, where a car, having reached the crossing, the gates of which had been left open, proceeded immediately over it in foggy conditions and was struck by a train.

[405] *Lloyds Bank Ltd v Railway Executive* [1952] 1 All E.R. 1248, per Denning L.J. (the defendants were liable both for breach of statutory duty, in failing to employ a gatekeeper, and in negligence, for failing to have a whistle board ; the deceased was guilty of contributory negligence to the extent of one-quarter.) See also *Smith v L.M.S.*, 1948 S.C. 125, both of which were distinguished in *Lloyds Bank Ltd v British Transport Commission* [1956] 1 W.L.R. 1279.

[406] *Smith v Smith and The Railway Executive* [1948] W.N. 276.

[407] Special precautions were held to have been necessary at an "extraordinarily dangerous" crossing near Hexham, Northumberland, on the Newcastle upon Tyne to Carlisle main line and the Board's failure to provide safety precautions within seven weeks of the matter having been brought to its notice, was held to be negligent: *Skeen v British Railways Board* [1976] R.T.R. 281.

[408] *Lloyds Bank v British Transport Commission* [1956] 1 W.L.R. 1279.

[409] *Trznadel v B.T.C.* [1957] 1 W.L.R. 1002 at 1006, per Morris L.J. See further n.414, below.

[410] *Anderson v John M. MacDonald Ltd* (1954) 104 L.J. 762.

Persons present on the track. Although a train driver's duty is different from **10–136**
that of a driver on a road,[411] nevertheless, he must still take reasonable care to
keep a look out along the track ahead, in order to avoid, if possible, persons who
may be in a position of danger either on or near the rails.[412] If there is a duty to
warn in the circumstances, then it must be to make the warning effective. Thus,
a train driver was found to be negligent in giving only a short blast on his whistle,
instead of a prolonged one, when driving along a dangerous part of the track
during a dark and stormy morning.[413] Where an employee of the railway
authorities was injured by a passing train whilst he was walking along the track,
however, the engine driver was not negligent in failing to see him.[414] A driver is
not under any duty to keep any special look out for animals which may have
strayed on to the track.[415]

Shunting. When shunting operations are taking place, railway authorities are **10–137**
under a duty to give warning to persons who are likely to be injured if no warning
were to be given. Failure to give such warning or to keep a look out for persons
whose presence on the line ought to be anticipated was held to be evidence of
negligence.[416] They are "under a duty to conduct their shunting operations with
due care for the safety of all persons lawfully going over the level-crossing on
business bent".[417] Railway authorities, which owned and worked lines in a
dockyard, were under no obligation, before carrying out shunting, to shut the
dock gates, which opened on to a public street.[418] Conducting noisy shunting
operations, so that a number of cattle were frightened whilst being driven on a
nearby siding, was evidence of negligence.[419]

Where a chargeman examiner was examining a stationary damaged wagon, **10–138**
which was suddenly shunted into so violently that he was startled and fell,
injuring himself, it was held that, as the claimant's injury was foreseeable, the
defendants were liable for their shunter's negligence in allowing abnormal
shunting, which had produced such an unnecessarily loud and violent crash.[420]

International carriage by railways. The Convention concerning Inter- **10–139**
national Carriage by Rail (COTIF) has the force of law in the United Kingdom
by the Railways (Convention on International Carriage by Rail) Regulations
2005. The Convention introduces a uniform rules governing international

[411] *Lloyds Bank v British Transport Commission* [1956] 1 W.L.R. 1279.
[412] *Conway v B.T.C.* (1962) 106 S.J. 78
[413] *Geddes v B.R.B.* [1957] 112 S.J. 194.
[414] *Trznadel v B.T.G.* [1957] 1 W.L.R. 1002. But where workmen are working on the maintenance of
the permanent way itself, see *Judson v B.T.C.* [1954] 1 W.L.R. 585; *Reilly v B.T.C.* [1957] 1 W.L.R.
76; *Hicks v B.T.C.* [1958] 1 W.L.R. 493; *Cade v B.T.C.* [1959] A.C. 256.
[415] *Beddie v B.T.C.* (1957) 74 Sh.Ct.Rep. 130.
[416] *Jones v G.W. Ry* (1930) 47 T.L.R. 39; *Paul v G.E. Ry* (1920) 36 T.L.R. 344; *Grant v G.W. Ry*
(1898) 14 T.L.R. 174.
[417] *Ross v Railway Executive*, 1948 S.C.(HL) 58, per Lord Uthwatt (deceased killed while crossing
railway line between wagons during shunting—he "walked into a danger which was obvious to an
ordinary man"—Railway Executive not liable).
[418] *Clark v N.B. Ry*, 1912 S.C. 1.
[419] *Sneesby v L. & Y. Ry* (1875) 1 Q.B.D. 42.
[420] *Slatter v British Railways Board* (1966) 110 S.J. 688 at 710.

carriage by rail: the Uniform Rules Concerning the Contract of International Carriage of Passengers by Rail (CIV) and the Uniform Rules Concerning the Contract of International Carriage of Goods by Rail (CIM).

(C) Road Carriage

10–140   **Duty generally.** The general principles of law, as set out above in relation to railways, apply to road carriage, with the necessary modifications. The carriers' liability as to the condition of the vehicle, which the intending passenger enters as a lawful visitor, is under the Occupiers' Liability Act 1957 and the duty owed is the common duty of care, which has already been explained.[421]

10–141   **Collisions.** Liability for a collision on the highway depends on proof of negligence of those in charge of the vehicles involved. As with any highway collision, an insured passenger in a public conveyance can sue the owners of the vehicles, including the one in which he is travelling, even though there may also have been fault on the part of some third party whose negligence contributed towards the happening of the accident.

10–142   **Passengers struck by external objects.** The fact of a collision between a passenger in a vehicle and a stationary object on the highway, is evidence of negligence against the person in charge of the vehicle. An evidential burden arises to show that the collision arose without negligence.[422] Thus, where a child was sitting with her elbow protruding through an open window of the defendant's bus and the bus pulled away from the kerb so close to a pole that her elbow was struck, it was held that the defendants' driver ought reasonably to have foreseen the possibility of such an accident happening and the defendant was liable.[423] Where a driver knows or ought to have realised that the trees were a potential source of danger and that they might overhang the highway, he should give them a wide berth.[424]

10–143   **Defective apparatus.** When a passenger in a tram was injured through a trolley arm becoming detached from the wire and striking him on the head, it was evidence of negligence against the owners of the vehicle. However, on proof the tram was in good order, was properly worked and every possible precaution had been taken to secure the safety of passengers, it was held that the prima facie case of negligence had been rebutted.[425] Where the wheel of a bus was wrenched off

---

[421] paras 10–88 to 10–90, above and, generally, Ch.8. For the obligatory road testing of motorvehicles, see the Road Traffic Act 1988 ss.46–53. Part II of the 1988 Act deals generally with the "Construction and Use of Vehicles and Equipment" and s.41 provides for the Secretary of State to make appropriate regulations, of which there are many in force.

[422] *Isaac Walton & Co v Vanguard Motorbus Co* (1908) 25 T.L.R. 13; *Barnes Urban District Council v London General Omnibus Co* (1908) 100 L.T. 115; *Ellor v Selfridge & Co Ltd* (1930) 46 T.L.R. 236; *Radley v L.P.T.B.* [1942] 1 All E.R. 433 (claimant succeeded where a bus collided with overhanging branch). See also *Simon v London General Omnibus Co* (1907) 23 T.L.R. 463; *Hase v London General Omnibus Co* (1907) 23 T.L.R. 616 and *Trinder v G.W. Ry* (1919) 35 T.L.R. 291.

[423] *Bohlen v Perdue* [1976] 1 W.W.R. 364, Alberta Sup. Ct.

[424] *Hale v Hants & Dorset Motor Services* [1947] 2 All E.R. 628 (the trees were planted by the Poole Corporation, which was held liable for allowing them to overhang the highway, the liability being apportioned two-thirds to the corporation and one-third to the motor company).

[425] *Newberry v Bristol Tramways Co* (1912) 107 L.T. 801.

by tramlines there was prima facie evidence of negligence against the bus company.[426] The fact of a breakdown of the vehicle is evidence of negligence on the part of carriers, throwing upon them the burden of showing that they had exercised reasonable care and skill in detecting and remedying defects but the onus is a very heavy one to discharge. This is well illustrated in *Henderson v H.E. Jenkins & Sons*,[427] where the House of Lords laid down that the standard of care is a high one, having regard to modern traffic conditions.

Injury caused by one passenger to another. It is the duty of those in charge **10–144** of public conveyances to take reasonable care to prevent them from being overcrowded[428] and, also, to take reasonable care to prevent persons who are likely to be dangerous to other passengers, by reason of disease, drunkenness, or a declared intention to use violence, to enter the vehicle. Where a drunk was allowed to enter a tram and he pushed a woman and her baby down from the top of the vehicle, so that she was injured and the baby was killed, the vehicle's owners were liable.[429]

Stopping and starting. There is a duty to exercise reasonable care in starting **10–145** and stopping. If a vehicle is started with such a jerk as to injure a passenger then that would indicate negligence on the part of the driver,[430] although absolute smoothness in starting and stopping cannot be expected.[431] There is no general duty upon the driver of a bus to wait until all boarding passengers have taken their seats before moving off, although if there is some particular risk, for example, in the case of the elderly or infirm, or a passenger encumbered with luggage or children then special care may have to be taken.[432] A driver may be required to take reasonable care to stop his passengers from acting negligently, in certain circumstances.[433] A taxi driver owes no special duty of care towards an inebriated passenger in choosing a place at which to set him down.[434]

---

[426] *Lilly v Tilling Ltd* (1912) 57 S.J. 59.
[427] [1970] A.C. 282 (a sudden failure of brakes owing to loss of brake fluid through a corroded hole in the pipe at a place beneath the vehicle which was inaccessible to routine weekly visual inspections).
[428] *Pickering v Belfast Corp* [1911] 2 Ir.R. 224, See also para.9–102, above, dealing with overcrowding on railways.
[429] *Murgatroyd v Blackburn Tramways* (1887) 3 T.L.R. 451.
[430] *Holland v North Metropolitan Tramways* (1886) 3 T.L.T. 245; *Geeves v London General Omnibus Co* (1901) 17 T.L.R. 249.
[431] *Manengela v Bay Passenger Transport Co Ltd* 1971 (4) S.A. 293.
[432] *Fletcher v United Counties Omnibus Co Ltd* [1998] P.I.Q.R. P154. cf. *Azzopardi v State Transport Authority* (1982) 30 S.A.S.R. Many of the older cases concern the behaviour of conductors (now something of a rarity) see: *Mottram v Lancashire Transport Co* [1942] 2 All E.R. 452 (giving the signal to move off when passengers are waiting to alight); *Wagner v West Ham Corp* (1920) 37 T.L.R. 86 (passenger giving the starting signal too soon: no liability); *Davies v Liverpool Corp* [1949] 2 All E.R. 175 (passenger giving starting signal when the conductor was absent from the platform for an appreciable time: liability established) cf. *Martin v Dublin United Tramways* [1908] 2 Ir.R. 13; *Prescott v Lancashire United Transport Co* [1953] 1 W.L.R. 232 (bus halted short of the authorised stop: conductor should have given a warning not to alight prematurely);
[433] *Curley v Mannion* [1965] I.R. 543.
[434] *Griffiths v Brown, The Times*, October 23, 1998 (alternatively it was said that even if a special duty existed it was not broken on the facts since the passenger's condition was not such as to make it obvious that he was incapable of taking care of his own safety in crossing the road).

10–146   It does not amount to contributory negligence on the part of a passenger to stand on the footboard, whilst waiting for a vehicle to stop, after a signal to stop has been given,[435] but if no signal to stop has been given, the passenger who stands on the step in anticipation of the tram stopping and sustains an injury, may find himself without a remedy.[436]

10–147   **Boarding and alighting from vehicle in motion.** If a passenger attempts to board a vehicle in motion, he does so at his own risk and the only duty of those in charge of the vehicle is not to act in reckless disregard of his safety. Where a drunk attempted to get on to a tram in motion and the conductor pushed him off, so that he fell and was injured, it was held, robustly, that he could not recover damages. He had wrongfully attempted to force himself on to the tram and had placed the conductor in a difficulty; the conductor, in the circumstances, had not acted with such want of care as to cause the accident.[437]

10–148   A passenger who attempts to leave a vehicle which is still in motion, may, at least, be guilty of contributory negligence.[438] Where the door through which a passenger was about to alight was opened by the driver or conductor and the passenger was forced out by the pressure of other passengers behind, his action in damages succeeded.[439] On the other hand, where a passenger on a double-decker bus was injured after he had lurched out and fallen through the open folded door of the vehicle from the platform, on which he was standing in order to alight, it was held by the House of Lords that the defendants were not liable. Since there were sufficient handholds, their failure to provide a central pillar in the doorway or else to institute a system whereby the door was kept closed until the vehicle had become stationary, was not negligent in the circumstances.[440]

10–149   **Operation of the doors.** A driver owes a duty to operate the doors of a bus so with reasonable care. In *Bollito v Arriva London*,[441] a bus driver allowed a passenger, who had run after the bus, to embark whilst the bus was stationary at some traffic lights. As the claimant stood on the platform by the doors, waiting for his companions to catch up the bus, the driver negligently closed the doors, trapping the claimant and causing him to fall from the bus.

10–150   **Statutory duties.** By reg.5 of the Public Service Vehicles (Conduct of Drivers, Inspectors, Conductors and Passengers) Regulations 1990,[442] a driver or

---

[435] *Hall v London Tramways* (1896) 12 T.L.R. 611; see also *Watt v Glasgow Corp*, 1919 S.C. 300 and *Anderson v Belfast Corp* [1943] N.I. 34.

[436] *Caldwell v Glasgow Corp*, 1936 S.C. 490; *Jude v Edinburgh Corp*, 1943 S.C. 399.

[437] *Delany v Dublin United Tramways* (1892) 30 L.R.Ir. 725, but cf. *Cullen v Dublin United Tramways* [1920] 2 I.R. 63, where it was held that there was evidence of negligence on the part of the conductor, who had refused to allow an intending passenger to climb aboard the slowly moving vehicle, which was full to capacity, at a stopping place whereupon the man had had to jump back off the step.

[438] *McSherry v Glasgow Corp*, 1917 S.C. 156. See, Ch.4, paras 4–03 to 4–72, above.

[439] *Pickering v Belfast Corp* [1911] 2 I.R. 224.

[440] *Wyngrove v Scottish Omnibuses*, 1966 S.C. (HL) 47.

[441] [2008] EWHC 48 (QB).

[442] SI 1990/1020, re-enacting with amendments the Public Service Vehicles (Conduct of Drivers, Inspectors, Conductors and Passengers) Regulations 1936 (S.R. and O. 1936/619).

a conductor is obliged to take all reasonable precautions for the safety of passengers who are on, or who are entering or leaving a public service vehicle. Where the conductor controls the door of a public service vehicle, he should not cause it to be opened before the vehicle stops.[443] Whilst this regulation imposes a duty of care with regard to passengers entitled to enter the vehicle, none is imposed with regard to a passenger who attempts to board the vehicle in motion.[444] Any intending passenger who attempts to board a bus which is not at a bus stop but either when it has stopped at traffic lights or has halted elsewhere, does so at his own risk.[445] The receipt of a signal to proceed, which has been given by the conductor, cannot absolve the driver of a bus from his duty to take reasonable care for an intending passenger's safety. Thus, where a driver moved off while a passenger was still in the act of climbing aboard, liability was established.[446]

Damage caused by driving. The driver owes a duty of care to passengers to   **10–151**
drive with reasonable care.[447] This duty is owed to both seated as well as standing passengers, whether the latter are holding on or not.[448] A sudden swerve causing injury to a passenger can be evidence of negligence[449]; in contrast the mere fact that a passenger was flung through the open door was not.[450] Usually, the sudden application of the brakes, which injures a passenger, is evidence of negligence, but where it was done to avoid running over a dog, the driver was not liable, since he had acted with reasonable care in an emergency.[451] Driving a bus at such a speed as to cause a passenger who suffers poor health to become ill, is not negligent: the driver is entitled to assume normal health in his passengers.[452]

Contracts restricting liability. A contract restricting liability in respect of the   **10–152**
death or bodily injury to a passenger either in a public service vehicle or any other vehicle[453] is void.

Hackney carriage passengers. A person who accepts another as a passenger   **10–153**
in a hackney carriage or other road vehicle is bound to exercise reasonable care for the safety of the passenger and of whatever he brings with him into the

---

[443] *Nicholson v Goddard* (1954) 118 J.P. 394.
[444] *Reid v MacNichol*, 1958 S.L.T. 42.
[445] *Police v Okoukwo* [1954] Crim.L.R. 869 but see *Bollito v Arriva London* [2008] EWHC 48 (Q.B.) para.10–149, above.
[446] *McLaughlin v Glasgow Corp* (1963) 79 Sh.Ct.Rep. 172.
[447] *Sutherland v Glasgow Corp*, 1951 S.C. 1; [1951] W.N. 111 (sudden braking to avoid a collision with a dog, shortly after the tram had been put in motion and while the pursuer was making her way to her seat).
[448] *Western Scottish M.T. Co v Allam* [1943] 2 All E.R. 742.
[449] *O'Hara v Scottish M.T. Co*, 1941 S.C. 363; *Doonan v S.M.T. Co*, 1950 S.C. 136.
[450] *Johnstone v Western S.M.T. Co* (1955) 105 L.J. 762.
[451] *Parkinson v Liverpool Corp* [1950] 1 All E.R. 367; *Wooller v London Transport Board* [1976] R.T.R. 206, CA.
[452] *Walker v Pitlochry Motor Co*, 1930 S.C. 565.
[453] See the provisions of the Unfair Contract Terms Act 1977, which are discussed in detail in Ch.4, paras 4–84 to 4–86, above, in connection with business liability.

vehicle. A taxi driver owes no special duty of care towards an inebriated passenger in choosing a place at which to set him down.[454]

10-154 Under the London Hackney Carriages Acts the registered proprietor of a hackney carriage is liable for the negligence of the driver, whether or not the relation of employer and employee exists between them.[455] So, if the passenger is injured or his luggage is lost owing to the negligence of the driver, the proprietor is liable.[456] Liability is imposed not only on the licensed proprietor but also on the actual proprietor, so that where a hackney carriage was owned by the defendant and her son, but the son alone was registered as proprietor, it was held that the defendant was liable.[457] Under the Town Police Clauses Act 1847 ss.37–68,[458] the registered proprietor of a hackney carriage is liable for the negligence of the driver while plying for hire.[459]

10-155 **Gratuitous rides.** A person who gratuitously gives another a ride in a vehicle is liable to the passenger for any damage, caused by the driver's negligence. It is the same whether he drives himself or another does so.[460] He is under a duty to warn his passenger of a danger which is known to him but unknown to his passenger, such as a low bridge, that is dangerous to persons inside the vehicle.[461]

10-156 **Seat belts.** The wearing of a seat belt is both a wise precaution for drivers and passengers and, save for exemptions, compulsory.[462] A driver or passenger who fails to wear a seat belt will be regarded as failing to take reasonable measures for their own safety. Since *Froom v Butcher*[463] it has been well settled that a passenger involved in an accident caused by the fault of another, is liable to a finding of contributory negligence to the extent that it can be shown that the wearing of a seat belt in the particular circumstances of the accident would have

---

[454] *Griffiths v Brown* [1999] P.I.Q.R. P131 (alternatively if a special duty existed on the facts it was not obvious that the passenger was not capable of taking care for his own safety).

[455] *Keen v Henry* [1894] 1 Q.B. 292; *King v London Improved Cab Co* (1889) 23 Q.B.D. 281; *Venables v Smith* (1877) 2 Q.B.D. 279.

[456] *Powles v Hider* (1856) 6 E. & B. 207.

[457] *Gates v Bill & Son* [1902] 2 K.B. 38.

[458] Repealed as to public service vehicles, Road Traffic Act 1930 Sch.V, in turn repealed by the Statute Law Revision Act 1950. The law as to hackney carriages applies to motorvehicles: Road Traffic Act 1988 s.191.

[459] *Bygraves v Dicker* [1923] 2 K.B. 585.

[460] *Pratt v Patrick* [1924] 1 K.B. 488; *Samson v Aitchison* [1912] A.C. 844; *Smith v Harris* [1939] 3 All E.R. 960; *Miller v Liverpool Co-operative Soc. Ltd* [1940] 4 All E.R. 367 (affirmed [1941] 1 All E.R. 379n.). For liability for acts of agents, see Ch.3, paras 3–160 to 3–171, above.

[461] *Lewys v Burnett & Dunbar* [1945] 2 All E.R. 555.

[462] A person of 14 years of age or more must wear a seat belt in the front seats of a motor vehicle and in the rear of a motor car, subject to various exemptions—the Road Traffic Act s.14 and the Motor Vehicles (Wearing of Seat Belts) Regulations 1993 (SI 1993/176) regs.5 & 6. Child restraints must be used for children of up to 12 years of age or 1.35m in height. Children of age 12 and 13 or over 1.35m in height must wear an adult seat belt—the Road Traffic Act s.15 and the Motor Vehicles (Wearing of Seat Belts by Children in Front Seats) Regulations 1993 (SI 1993/31) and the Motor Vehicles (Wearing of Seat Belts by Children in Front Seats) (Amendment) Regulations 2006 (SI 2006/2213).

[463] [1976] Q.B. 286.

prevented or reduced the injuries sustained. As usual where issues of contributory negligence arise, the court should consider both the causative potency and the blameworthiness of the relevant act of neglect. In road traffic accidents the principle negligence is that which caused the accident in the first place; the failure to wear a seat belt may cause the damage sustained to be more severe. In *Froom*, Lord Denning M.R. suggested that where the wearing of a seat belt would have prevented the damage from being sustained altogether the appropriate reduction for contributory negligence should be 25 per cent; where the wearing of the seat belt would have reduced the severity of the injury sustained to a considerable degree the appropriate reduction should be 15 per cent; and where the wearing of a seat belt would have made no difference to the outcome there should be no reduction.[464] The burden of proving that the wearing of a seat belt would have reduced or eliminated the injuries sustained lies on the defendant. The suggested deductions now have some weight of practice behind them and will generally be regarded as binding unless the facts of a case are exceptional.[465] Attempts to persuade courts at first instance to depart from the guidelines have been rejected.[466]

The driver's duty to exercise reasonable care and skill for the safety of his passengers does not require, in the absence of special circumstances, a request to wear a seat belt if one is provided. The driver of a car has a legal responsibility to ensure that a passenger under the age of 14 years uses a seat belt or child restraint if one is available.[467] **10–157**

International carriage by road. The Convention on the Contract for the International Carriage of Passengers and Luggage by Road of 1973 has never been ratified by the United Kingdom. The Carriage of Goods by Road Act 1965[468] gives effect in the United Kingdom to the Convention on the Contract for the International Carriage of Goods by Road, signed at Geneva which is known as the CMR Convention. Detailed consideration of this subject is outside the scope of this book. **10–158**

(D) Ships

Generally. The liabilities of ship owners towards passengers are governed by the Merchant Shipping Act 1995. The provisions of the Convention relating to the Carriage of Passengers and their Luggage by Sea (the Athens Convention) and the Convention on Limitation of Liability for Maritime Claims 1976 are **10–159**

---

[464] See, e.g. *Stanton v Collinson* [2010] EWCA Civ 81 (no seat belt worn by front seat passenger with another passenger on his lap where expert evidence not clear that his injuries would have been materially less had a belt been worn).
[465] *J v Wilkins* [2001] P.I.Q.R. P179, CA.
[466] See, e.g. *Gawler v Raettig* [2007] EWHC 373 (Q.B.) and *Stanton v Collinson*, above, at [2009] EWHC 342 (Q.B.).
[467] See n.462, above.
[468] Which came into operation on June 5, 1967, by virtue of the Carriage of Goods by Road Act 1965 (Commencement) Order 1967 (SI 1967/819).

given the force of law in the United Kingdom.[469] The time-limit for bringing proceedings regarding damage or loss caused by the fault of a ship to another ship, its cargo or freight or any property on board it or for damages for loss of life or personal injury caused by the fault of that ship to any person on board another ship, is two years.[470]

10–160   **The Athens Convention.** Under the Athens Convention[471] a carrier is liable for damage as a result of the death of or personal injury to a passenger and for the loss of or damage to luggage, if the incident which caused the damage occurred in the course of the carriage and was due to the fault or neglect of the carrier or of his employees acting within the scope of their employment.[472] Fault or neglect is presumed, unless the contrary is proved, if the death or personal injury or damage to cabin luggage arose in connection with the shipwreck, collision, stranding, explosion or fire, or defect in the ship.[473] In relation to passengers and their luggage carriage means the period during which the passenger is on board the ship or in the course of embarkation or disembarkation and includes transport by water from land to the ship or vice versa if the cost of such transport was included in the fare.[474] Death or personal injury or damage to luggage caused by negligence of the passenger can exonerate the carrier either wholly or partly.[475] The carrier's liability for death or personal injury cannot exceed 46,666 units of account[476] per case.[477] The carrier is not entitled to limit his liability if the damage resulted from an act or omission done with the intent to cause such damage or recklessly and with knowledge that damage would probably result.[478] No action can be brought otherwise than in accordance with the Convention.[479] Limitation periods are provided for in art.16, which is brought into effect in domestic law by s.190 of the Merchant Shipping Act 1995, as already discussed above.[480]

---

[469] The Merchant Shipping Act 1995 s.183(1) and s.185(1) respectively. See generally, Giddins, "Accidents do happen: boating PI claims" 153 N.L.J. 1879.

[470] The Merchant Shipping Act 1995 s.190.

[471] Formally known as the Convention Relating to the Carriage of Passengers and their Luggage by Sea 1974, a protocol to the convention was agreed on November 1, 2002. This protocol will come into force twelve months after the date on which ten states have ratified it.

[472] The Athens Convention art.3(1).

[473] The Athens Convention, art.3(3).

[474] The Athens Convention, art.1(8)(a).

[475] The Athens Convention, art.6.

[476] A unit of account is a Special Drawing Right as defined by the International Monetary Fund.

[477] The Athens Convention, art.7. The Convention states a limit of 300,000 units of account but in relation to carrier whose principal place of business is the UK the limit is set at 46,666 units by the Carriage of Passengers and their Luggage at Sea (United Kingdom Carriers) Order 1998. Pursuant to art.8 the limit of liability relating to luggage is: 833 units of account per passenger per carriage in the case of cabin luggage; 3,333 units of account per vehicle per carriage in the case of vehicles including all luggage carried in or on the vehicle; and 1,200 units of account per passenger per vehicle in the case of any other luggage.

[478] The Athens Convention, art.13(1). See *Goldman v Thai Airways* [1983] 1 W.L.R. 1186, CA, per Purchas L.J. at 1202; *Gurtner v Beaton* [1993] 2 Lloyd's Rep. 369; *Nugent v Michael Goss Aviation Ltd* [2000] P.I.Q.R. P175, CA and *MSC Mediterranean Shipping Co SA v Delumar BVBA* [2000] 2 Lloyds Rep 39.

[479] The Athens Convention art.14.

[480] See Ch.4, paras 4–231 to 4–232, above.

Safe access. A shipowner owes a duty to the passengers to take reasonable   **10–161**
care to provide safe access to the ship. Where, therefore, passengers were taken
to a hulk, from which they were to board a steamship, and the claimant, after
descending a ladder in the hulk, fell down an open hatchway that had been left
unguarded and imperfectly lighted, his action for damages succeeded.[481] On the
other hand, the claim for damages failed where a passenger, in embarking on a
ship, slipped from the gangway, which was three inches above the deck's level
and fractured her ankle. Although she claimed that the gangway was not properly
lighted and that there was no one to help her off the gangway, it was held that the
shipowners, who had embarked 30,000 passengers during the year, without more
precautions at night and in all states of the tide, were not liable.[482]

Safety on board. On board the ship itself, reasonable care must be taken for   **10–162**
the safety of passengers. Where there was no ladder provided to enable a female
passenger in an upper berth to descend, and the stewards had placed a chair for
the purpose but the passenger slipped, hurting herself, it was held that the
shipowners were liable. It was their duty "to provide means by which passengers
might get out of their berths without danger of falling."[483] Liability also attached
where the porthole glass in a cabin was not properly secured but was revolving
at a high speed, so that the passenger's hand was injured when he attempted to
draw the curtains aside.[484] Reasonable care must also be taken to provide
accommodation for passengers' luggage, so that where luggage was stowed in a
vacant lavatory, which became flooded as a result of an overflow of water from
an adjoining lavatory, the shipowners were liable.[485]

Where the floor of the passage outside a passenger's cabin had been made   **10–163**
slippery by washing, liability for the claimant's slip was not established where he
had seen what was done[486] although it was said that "wholly different
considerations would arise if the steward had gone away, leaving the floor wet
and slippery, without taking steps to warn perambulating passengers of its
condition".[487]

As with motor vehicles,[488] it is no answer to a claim in negligence against the   **10–164**
owner of a vessel to prove a system of inspection, maintenance and repair, if the
proof does not explain how a mechanical fault causative of injury could arise in
spite of the exercise of reasonable care. So, in *Binnie v Rederij Theodoro BV*[489]
where injury was caused to a port operator struck by a rope being used in an
attempt to arrest the forward progress of a ship, the reverse engine of which had
failed to operate in a lock, it was held that once on the evidence a prima facie

---

[481] *John v Bacon* (1870) L.R. 5 C.P. 437; this was so, in spite of the fact that the shipowner had only
the right to use the hulk on the ground that the claimant was invited to use it.
[482] *Cameron v L.M.S Ry* (1936) 54 Ll.L.R. 95.
[483] *Andrews v Little & Co* (1887) 3 T.L.R. 544.
[484] *Jones v Oceanic Steam Navigation Co* [1924] 2 K.B. 730 (the company was however absolved
from liability by the conditions of the contract).
[485] *Upperton v Union-Castle Mail Steamship Co* (1902) 19 T.L.R. 687.
[486] *Beaumont-Thomas v Blue Star Line Ltd* [1939] 3 All E.R. 127.
[487] *Beaumont-Thomas v Blue Star Line Ltd* [1939] 3 All E.R. 127 at 135, per Goddard L.J.
[488] See *Henderson v Henry E. Jenkins & Sons* [1970] A.C. 280, para.10–247, below.
[489] 1993 S.C. 1993.

case of negligence was raised, the burden passed to the defenders to explain how the accident could have occurred, consistent with the exercise of reasonable care. It was insufficient to lead evidence only of an engine inspection two months beforehand.

10–165   **Employees.** The health and safety of those working on board ships is protected by statutory duties similar to those applicable to onshore workers. It has been observed however that in framing such legislation, Parliament adopted a different approach as between fisherman and other workers at sea.[490] A system of certification was enacted to protect the former so that a fishing vessel could not go to sea without there being in force in respect of it a certificate issued by the Secretary of State after a survey to ensure that the vessel complied with the relevant rules.[491] In the case of other workers at sea they had a civil right of action for damages when a breach of statutory duty caused them to suffer injury.[492]

10–166   **The Carriage of Goods by Sea Act 1971.** The Act[493] gives effect to amendments to the Hague Rules, relating to the Carriage of Goods by Sea contained in the Protocol, agreed internationally in Brussels in 1968,[494] and repeals the Carriage of Goods by Sea Act 1924, which gave effect in the United Kingdom to the Hague Rules in their original form. The Brussels Protocol made two main amendments to the Rules,[495] the first of which increased the limits of liability under the Rules and made new provisions concerning the qualification of amounts, and the second extended the defences and limits of liability of the carrier[496] to his servants or agents, provided that they are not independent contractors.

10–167   Where a shipper discovered that cattle feed has become contaminated with lead during transportation, he discharged his duty of care by arranging for a reputable salvor to destroy it, and he was not liable in negligence when the salvor in fact sold it on.[497]

---

[490] See *Ziemniak v ETPM Deep Sea Ltd* [2003] EWCA Civ 636; *The Times*, May 15, 2003, CA.

[491] The system is described in *Todd v Adams* [2002] 2 Lloyd's Rep. 293.

[492] *Ziemniak v ETPM Deep Sea Ltd*, n.490, above (The claimant, a marine engineer, suffered serious injuries when testing the launching and recovery of lifeboats on board a merchant vessel and a suspension chain holding one of the lifeboats failed when he was sitting in it, causing the lifeboat to fall to the water below. It was held, distinguishing *Todd v Adams*, n.491 above, that he could rely upon the defendants' breach of reg.43(1) of, and Pt II(c) of Sch.16 to, the Merchant Shipping (Life Saving Appliances) Regulations 1980).

[493] It was passed on April 8, 1971 and came into force on June 23, 1977, by virtue of SI 1977/981. See article on the Act, Powles [1978] J.D.L. 141 and O'Hare, "The Duration of the Sea Carriers' Liability" 6 A.B.L.R. 65.

[494] Cmnd. 3743.

[495] Namely those contained in Arts IV(5) and IV *bis*. See, e.g. *Effort Shipping Co Ltd v Linden Management S.A.* [1998] A.C. 605, HL.

[496] Whenever loss or damage has resulted from unseaworthiness, the burden of proving the exercise of due diligence shall be on the carrier or other person claiming exemption under art.IV. Article IV(2)(c) precludes liability for perils of the sea. Foreseeability of bad weather does not prevent such immunity attaching: *Great China Metal Industries Co Ltd v Malaysian International Shipping Corp BHD (The Bungo Seroja)* [1999] 1 Lloyd's Rep. 512, H.C.(Aus).

[497] *Hanford Feeds Ltd v Alfred C. Toepfer International GmbH* (1996) C.L.Y. 5300, CA.

(E) Aircraft

(i) Common law liability

At common law, the liability of the owner of an aircraft does not differ from **10–168** that of the owner of a highway vehicle. An aircraft at rest is relatively harmless and even in motion is not an inherently dangerous thing or a thing dangerous in itself.[498] Accordingly, the principle of *Rylands v Fletcher*[499] does not apply to it. The result is that, apart from statutory provisions,[500] liability for aircraft is based on negligence. When negligence is in question, the principle res ipsa loquitur applies.[501] So, when an aircraft took off and crashed just outside the aerodrome "well before it had attained the height at which the journey would be performed", the doctrine was applied and the owners were held liable for the death of a passenger in the aircraft at the time of the crash.[502]

An aircraft company was held liable when a man who was seeing his wife and **10–169** daughter off was led to a position by one of the servants of the company and killed by one of the revolving propellers. The occupiers of the airfield were held not liable.[503]

The owners' liability as to the condition of the aircraft, which the intending **10–170** passenger enters as a lawful visitor, is under the Occupiers' Liability Act 1957 and, as already explained,[504] the duty owed is the common duty of care.

Liability of pilot. It is the duty of a pilot[505] to take reasonable care at all **10–171** material times, which must includes making all necessary and proper inquiries concerning the proposed flight, making sure of the availability of any items of equipment required during the flight, filing a flight plan, carrying out the proper preflight checks on the aircraft, keeping a proper lookout during the taxi-ing, take off and the flight, and carrying out the requisite checks before attempting to land at the airfield of destination. Where a light aircraft crashed on approaching the runway for landing, when it got caught in turbulence caused by a large jet aeroplane which had made a practice approach only to overshoot deliberately, it was held that the accident was the sole responsibility of the light aircraft's pilot. The air traffic controller at the airport was under no obligation either to warn of turbulence or to prescribe separation distance, prior to his giving the pilot landing clearance.[506] Likewise, the pilot was held entirely to blame for using an approach procedure that had been superseded, as a result of which he missed the runway and crashed into a nearby mountain. There was no responsibility resting on the

---

[498] See *Fosbroke-Hobbes v Airwork Ltd* [1937] 1 All E.R. 108 at 112, per Goddard J.
[499] (1866) L.R. 1 Ex. 265; 3 H.L. 330; 37 L.J. Ex. 161.
[500] Explained in para.10–173, below.
[501] See further Ch.6, paras 6–100 to 6–131, above.
[502] *Fosbroke-Hobbes v Airwork Ltd* [1937] 1 All E.R. 108. See also *George v Eagle Air Services Ltd, The Times,* May 15, 2009, PC, Ch.6, para.6–117, above (owners liable for unexplained crash arising as an apparently airworthy aircraft came in to land).
[503] *Waring v East Anglian Flying Services Ltd* [1951] W.N. 55.
[504] See para.10–88, above.
[505] See Abeyratne, "Negligence of the airline pilot" (1998) 4 P.N. 219.
[506] *Sexton v Boak* (1972) 27 D.L.R. (3d) 181.

air traffic controller to monitor the aircraft's descent to the runway and its course, after the pilot had accepted the clearance to land, unless it was for the purpose of providing separation between aircraft.[507] Both pilots were to blame where as a result of their failures to "see and avoid" two gliders collided in mid-air.[508]

10–172   **Duty to passengers during flight.** In *Chisholm v British European Airways*,[509] the captain of an aircraft received notice of an approaching storm, in consequence of which the passengers were told to remain seated and to fasten seat belts. The claimant however left her seat to go to the toilet and, as the aircraft encountered severe turbulence and plunged violently, fell sustaining injury. It was held that the warning given had been adequate and liability did not attach. By way of contrast the defendants were liable in *Goldman v Thai Airways International*,[510] where the pilot failed to light the sign to fasten seat belts, although he knew that moderate turbulence had been forecast and the aircraft struck severe turbulence, which resulted in the claimant being thrown from his seat and injuring his back. Where an inspector performed an inspection of an aircraft and certified its airworthy condition, he and his employer, an association empowered under s.3 of the Civil Aviation Act 1982 to issue a certificate of fitness for flight, owed a duty of care to a passenger, injured when the aircraft crashed during a test flight.[511]

(ii) Civil Aviation Act 1982

10–173   The Civil Aviation Act 1982,[512] s.76, provides:

> "(1) No action shall lie in respect of trespass[513] or in respect of nuisance, by reason only of the flight of an aircraft over any property at a height above the ground, which, having regard to wind, weather, and all the circumstances of the case is reasonable, or the ordinary incidents of such flight, so long as the provisions of any Air Navigation Order and any orders under section 62 above[514] have been duly complied with and there has been no breach of section 81 below.[515] (2) Subject to subsection (3) below, where

---

[507] *Churchill Falls (Labrador) Corp Ltd v The Queen* (1975) 53 D.L.R. 360. For the duties in controlling air traffic, see Gilchrist, "Air Traffic Control—The Operator's Liability" [1977] 2 Lloyd's M.C.L.Q. 204.

[508] *Curran v Derbyshire and Lancashire Gliding Club* [2004] EWHC 687 (the leading glider executed an 180 degree turn without being aware until too late of the presence of the glider following; liability was apportioned 60:40 in favour of the former).

[509] [1963] 1 Lloyd's Rep. 626.

[510] (1981) 125 S.J. 413.

[511] *Perrett v Collins* [1999] P.N.L.R. 77, CA. See also Ch.2, para.2–71.

[512] Which consolidates certain enactments relating to civil aviation and came into force on August 27, 1982 by virtue of s.110(2). See also the Regulations made under the Act, such as the Rules of the Air Regulations 1996 (SI 1996/1393), which came into force on June 19, 1996.

[513] In *Bernstein v Skyviews & General Ltd* [1978] Q.B. 479, it was held that the protection given by the subsection was not limited to a bare right of passage over land, analogous to the limited right of a member of the public to pass over the surface of a highway, but extended to all flights provided that they were at a reasonable height, complied with the statutory requirements, and did not constitute a harassment. (The defendants had taken aerial photographs of the claimant's country home, Coppings Farm, Kent).

[514] Which relates to control of civil aviation in time of war or emergency.

[515] Which relates to "dangerous flying," a criminal offence.

material loss or damage[516] is caused to any person or property on land or water by, or by a person in, or an article,[517] animal or person falling from, an aircraft while in flight,[518] taking off,[519] or landing, then unless the loss or damage was caused or contributed to by the negligence of the person by whom it was suffered, damages in respect of the loss or damage shall be recoverable without proof of negligence or intention or other cause of action, as if the loss or damage had been caused by the wilful act, neglect, or default of the owner of the aircraft. (3) Where material loss or damage is caused as aforesaid in circumstances in which—

(a) damages are recoverable in respect of the said loss or damage by virtue only of subsection (2) above, and
(b) a legal liability is created in some person other than the owner to pay damages in respect of the said loss or damage,

the owner shall be entitled to be indemnified by that other person against any claim in respect of the said loss or damage."
The burden of proving that the loss or damage was either caused by or contributed to by the negligence of the injured party is on the owner of the aircraft.[520]

Strict liability. The effect of s.76 is to impose a strict liability on the "owner" **10–174** of the aircraft, as defined in the Act, subject only to the qualified defence of contributory negligence. The Act clearly contemplates that the owner is liable, although the damage or loss has been caused by the wrongful act, neglect or default of a third party. Even if the damage or loss be caused by an "act of God,"[521] the reference to liability "without proof of negligence or intention or other cause of action" seems to indicate that the owner would still be liable.

The owner's liability, however, is confined to material loss or damage to any person or property on land or water,[522] and does not include loss or damage to person or property in the air. Liability for damage in the air will accordingly depend on proof of negligence.[523]

---

[516] The expression "loss or damage" includes, in relation to persons, loss of life and personal injury: s.105(1). Psychiatric damage is included provided that the claimant can satisfy the common law rules as to the categories of person entitled to recover for psychiatric injury: *Glen v Korean Airlines Company Ltd* [2003] 3 W.L.R. 273. (For the categories of person entitled to recover for such injuries where they arise in consequence of the defendant's negligence see Ch.10, paras 10–123 to 10–131, above).

[517] Which has been held to include a chemical liquid: *Weedair (N.Z.) Ltd v Walker* [1961] N.Z.L.R. 153, NZCA.

[518] *Greenfield v Law* [1955] 2 Lloyd's Rep. 696 (the claimant must prove that the damage was caused whilst the defendants' aircraft was in flight); see also *Piper v Darling* (1940) 67 Ll.L.R. 419 (the plaintiff's yacht lying in harbour was damaged by the accidental discharge of a torpedo from an aircraft—liability was admitted).

[519] As to the meaning of "taking off," see *Blankley v Godley* [1952] 1 All E.R. 436n.

[520] *Cubitt v Gower* (1933) 47 Ll.L.R. 65. In *Goldman v Thai Airways International* (1981) 125 S.J. 413 no contributory negligence was proved against the injured claimant for not wearing his seat belt, where the pilot had omitted to order, by illuminating the signs, the passengers to fasten their seat belts when he knew that the aircraft was likely to meet moderate clear air turbulence, forecast for the flight over Turkey. However, the trial judge's finding of common law liability against the defendants was reversed on appeal [1983] 1 W.L.R. 1186, CA.

[521] For the meaning of this expression, see Ch.13, paras 13–35 to 13–39, below.

[522] See s.76(2), quoted above.

[523] Regulations can be made for the prevention of collisions at sea between seaplanes and vessels on the surface of the water: s.97(1).

10–175   **Compulsory insurance.** A statutory code was enacted with a view to securing that air operators were compulsorily insured against third-party aviation risks,[524] which adopted that laid down by the Rome Convention 1933. The United Kingdom has neither ratified nor is bound by this Convention or the Rome Convention 1952, drawn up to supersede and improve the one of 1933. Indeed, the relevant sections of the Civil Aviation Act 1949 have been repealed.[525]

10–176   **Liability of hirer of aircraft.** Although the strict liability, set out above, is imposed on the owner of the aircraft, where any aircraft, "has been bona fide demised, let or hired out for any period exceeding fourteen days to any other person by the owner thereof, and no pilot, commander, navigator or operative member of the crew of the aircraft is in the employment of the owner," the owner of the aircraft is freed from liability. In such instance, the hirer then becomes subject to such liability, just as if he were the owner.[526]

(iii) Carriage by Air Conventions

10–177   **The Carriage by Air Conventions.** The starting point for the consideration of the liabilities of air carriers is the Warsaw Convention of 1929.[527] This was the first uniform international code governing the liability of air carriers regarding injury, loss and damage sustained in the course of and arising out of international air travel. Successive amendments were agreed and these were consolidated into the Montreal Convention 1999. These carriage by air conventions have the force of law in the United Kingdom by s.1 of the Carriage by Air Act 1961 (as amended).[528] All air carriers operating under a licence granted by an European Union member state are subject to the Montreal Convention as regards liability to passengers and baggage. The Convention came into force in the United Kingdom on June 28, 2004.

10–178   **The Montreal Convention.** The Montreal Convention applies to all international and non-international carriage of persons, baggage or cargo performed by aircraft for reward and includes carriage by the state or legally constituted public bodies. It also includes gratuitous carriage by an air transport undertaking. An aircraft includes a hot air balloon[529] but it does not include a tandem paraglider.[530]

---

[524] i.e. the Civil Aviation Act 1949. See s.43, which was the equivalent to the provisions of the Road Traffic Act 1972 s.143, in the case of motorvehicles used on the road.

[525] i.e. by the Companies Act 1967 s.128, which had repealed ss.43–46 and 49(1) of and Sch.6 to the Act of 1949, and the Civil Aviation Act 1968 s.26, which had repealed ss.42 and 48 of the 1949 Act. Now, the Civil Aviation Act 1968 s.26 has itself been repealed by the Civil Aviation Act 1982 Sch.16.

[526] Civil Aviation Act 1982 s.76(4). See also *Greenfield v Law* [1955] 2 Lloyd's Rep. 696 (low-flying aircraft over a road caused a horse to bolt—the pilot was not the owner of the aircraft).

[527] Formally entitled: the Convention for the Unification of Certain Rules Relating to International Carriage by Air.

[528] The carriage by air conventions only have the force of law in the UK to the extent that the Council Regulation (i.e. Council Regulation (EC) No. 2027/97 (as amended) does not. The EU has effectively adopted the provisions of the Montreal Convention by the amendments to Council Regulation (EC) No. 2027/97 by Regulation 889/2002.

[529] *Laroche v Spirit of Adventure (UK) Ltd* [2009] Q.B. 778.

[530] *Disley v Levine* [2002] 1 W.L.R. 785, CA.

Pursuant to Article 17:

"The carrier is liable for damage sustained in the case of death or bodily injury of a passenger upon condition only that the accident which caused the death or injury took place on board the aircraft or in the course of any of the operations of embarking or disembarking."

Bodily injury. In *King v Bristows Helicopters Ltd*,[531] two conjoined appeals **10–179** were heard where in both cases the claimant had suffered purely psychiatric injuries apart from that common element the facts of the two cases were starkly different. Mr. King was a passenger in a helicopter which had just taken off from a production platform in the North Sea. In poor weather the aircraft developed problems, it landed heavily on the platform engulfed in smoke. There was panic among the passengers and although Mr. King was not physically injured he developed moderate post traumatic stress disorder. In the conjoined appeal a fifteen year old girl fell asleep on a flight and awoke to discover the man in the seat next to her caressing her leg from the knee to the hip, she became distressed and subsequently developed a depressive reaction. The House of Lords held that these purely psychiatric injuries did not constituted bodily injuries for the purposes of art.17 of the Warsaw Convention and to hold otherwise would be inconsistent with a decision of the United States Supreme Court in *Eastern Airlines Inc v Floyd*.[532]

Accident. The word "accident" in the present context means an unexpected **10–180** or unusual event or happening that is external to the passenger; it does not include a passenger's own internal reaction to the usual, normal and expected operation of the aircraft.[533] In *Re Deep Vein Thrombosis and Air Travel Group Litigation*,[534] a culpable failure to warn a passenger of the risk of deep vein thrombosis (DVT), or to provide less cramped seating to minimise the risk of developing DVT, did not amount to an "accident"[535] for the purposes of art.17. An indecent assault by another passenger does constitute an accident.[536]

Fatal accident claims. Where an aircraft passenger dies as a result of an **10–181** accident the provisions of the Fatal Accidents Act 1976 (as amended) apply pursuant to s.3 of the Carriage by Air Act 1961 (as amended) and the damages would be assessed in accordance with that Act.[537]

---

[531] [2002] 2 A.C. 628.
[532] (1991) 499 US 530 (during flight the plane developed engine failure and the passengers were informed that the "plane would be ditched" the engine was restarted and the plane landed safely, some of the passengers suffered from emotional injury, which did not qualify as a bodily injury under art.17 of the Warsaw Convention.
[533] *Air France v Saks* 470 US 392.
[534] [2005] 3 W.L.R. 1320, HL. See also Tompkins, "Deep vein thrombosis (DVT) and air carrier legal liability: the myth and the law" A. & S.L. 2001 (26) 231; Meyer, "Deep vein thrombosis: blood flow v profit flow" A. & S.L. 2001 (26) 225; Gates, "Airline liability for DVT enters appellate arena; SARS poses no problem" (2003) I.F.L. Rev. 22 (7) 6; Panesar, "Air carriers' liability for deep vein thrombosis" J.P.I. Law 2004, 3, 192.
[535] See further as to "accident" Ch.1, paras 1–08 to 1–10, above.
[536] *Morris v KLM Royal Dutch Airlines* [2002] Q.B. 100.
[537] See Ch.16.

10–182   **Limitation of liability.** Under the Montreal Convention the air carrier cannot exclude or limit its liability in respect of claims for damages not exceeding 100,000 Special Drawing Rights[538] for each passenger.[539] To the extent that claims exceed 100,000 Special Drawing Rights for each passenger, the carrier is not liable beyond that extent if it proves that: (a) such damage was not due to negligence or other wrongful act or omission of the carrier its servants or agents; or (b) such damage was due solely to negligence or a wrongful act or omission of a third party.[540] The time limit for bringing claims is two years calculated from the date of arrival at the destination or the date on which the aircraft ought to have arrived or from the date on which the carriage stopped.[541]

10–183   **Baggage claims.** The carrier is liable for destruction of or loss or damage to checked baggage upon condition only that the event which caused the destruction, loss or damage took place on board the aircraft or whilst the baggage was in the charge of the carrier but it is not liable to the extent that the damage etc resulted from inherent defect in the quality of the baggage[542] Unless the passenger has made a special declaration as to the baggage and paid a supplementary sum, as necessary, the liability of the carrier in relation to destruction of or damage or loss to baggage is 1,000 Special Drawing Rights per passenger.[543]

10–184   In *Sidhu v British Airways*[544] the House of Lords considered whether the limitation against common law claims arose only in respect of the specific perils mentioned in art.17 of the Warsaw Convention or whether it was general, in the sense that only those perils mentioned in the Convention could be the subject of claim, and any such claim had to be brought under the Convention's terms. It was decided, using a purposive approach to construction, that the latter was the case:

> " . . . the purpose is to ensure that, in all questions relating to the carrier's liability, it is the provisions of the Convention which apply and that the passenger does not have access to any other remedies, whether under the common law or otherwise, which may be available within the particular country where he chooses to raise his action".[545]

---

[538] A unit of account as defined by the International Monetary Fund.
[539] The Montreal Convention art.21(1).
[540] The Montreal Convention art.21(2).
[541] The Montreal Convention art.35.
[542] The Montreal Convention art.17(2).
[543] The Montreal Convention art.22.2.
[544] [1997] A.C. 430. The claimant and others had been passengers on an international flight between London and Malaysia. Their aircraft landed in Kuwait to refuel several hours after Iraqi forces invaded and they were captured and detained in Baghdad. They sought damages for physical and psychological injury on the basis of alleged negligence in landing after the start of hostilities. The HL heard at the same time an appeal in *Abnett v British Airways Plc* originally reported at 1995 S.C.L.R. 654, Ct. Sess. OH which raised similar issues. See also Martin, "Airline legal liability—some developments?" [1995] T.L.J. 3.
[545] per Lord Hope at 41.

(F) Hovercraft

Generally. A hovercraft[546] is defined in s.4(1) of the Hovercraft Act 1968[547] **10–185**
as "a vehicle which is designed to be supported when in motion wholly or partly
by air expelled from the vehicle to form a cushion of which the boundaries
include the ground, water or other surface beneath the vehicle". The Act grants
wide powers for regulating hovercraft, particularly in relation to registration and
safety; liability for damage caused by or involving their use[548]; investigation of
accidents; the regulation of noise and vibration; the application of enactments
relating to other forms of transport and of general maritime law; and the
application of certain enactments limiting liability for damage. Certain enactments relating to Admiralty jurisdiction are applied to hovercraft by s.2, which
further enables provision to be made by Order in Council for modifying or
excluding the application of those enactments in prescribed cases.

Liability to passengers. In relation to damage to passengers and their **10–186**
baggage carried by hovercraft, the Carriage by Air Act 1961 and the Carriage by
Air (Supplementary Provisions) Act 1962 apply with modifications by virtue of
the Hovercraft (Civil Liability) Order 1986[549] as amended. Detailed consideration of these provisions is beyond the scope of this text. These statutory
provisions incorporate into United Kingdom law the rules relating to international carriage by air[550] and apply the rules to hovercraft. In summary, the
carrier is liable for damage sustained in the event of the death or wounding of a
passenger or any other bodily injury[551] suffered by a passenger if the accident
took place on board the hovercraft or in the course of any of the operations of
embarking or disembarking.[552] The carrier is liable for damage sustained in the
event of the destruction or loss of or damage to any baggage other than that
which the passenger takes charge of himself, if the occurrence which caused the
damage took place during the carriage by the hovercraft.[553] Where there is delay
in the carriage of passengers or baggage the carrier is liable.[554] The carrier is not
liable if he proves that he, his servants or agents, have taken all reasonable
measures to avoid the damage or that it was impossible for him or them to take
such measures.[555] If the damage was caused by the negligence of the injured
person then the carrier may be exonerated wholly or partly from liability.[556] In
relation to the carriage of persons, the carrier's liability is limited to £80,000 per

---

[546] For an historical introduction to this topic, see *Charlesworth & Percy on Negligence* (8th ed., 1990), Ch.9, para.9–182 et seq.
[547] Which came into force on August 26, 1968, with the exception of s.4(3), which came into operation on July 12, 1972, by virtue of the Hovercraft Act 1968 (Commencement) Order 1972 (SI 1972/979).
[548] See Hovercraft Civil Liability Order 1986 (SI 1986/1305).
[549] SI 1986/1305.
[550] See paras 10–177 to 10–184, above.
[551] "Bodily injury" will not usually include psychiatric symptoms: see *King v Bristow Helicopters Ltd, M v KLM Royal Dutch Airlines* [2002] 2 A.C. 628, n.531, above.
[552] art.17 of the Convention.
[553] art.18(1) of the Convention.
[554] art.19 of the Convention.
[555] art.20 of the Convention.
[556] art.21 of the Convention.

person.[557] In relation to baggage, liability is limited to £246 per passenger unless the passenger or consignor has made a special declaration of interest in the property.[558] The carrier cannot impose, by contract or otherwise, a lower limit on his liability.[559] The limits on the carrier's liability do not apply if the damage resulted from an act or omission of the carrier done with intent to cause damage or recklessly and with knowledge that damage would probably result.[560] Any action relating to personal injury or damage to baggage sustained during carriage by a hovercraft should be brought within two years from the date of arrival at the destination or the date upon which the hovercraft ought to have arrived.

3. HIGHWAY USERS AND COLLISIONS

10–187   **The duty of care generally.** As Lord du Parcq pointed out, "an underlying principle of the law of the highway is that all those lawfully using the highway . . . must show mutual respect and forbearance".[561] Hence, the duty of a person who either drives or rides a vehicle on the highway[562] is to use reasonable care to avoid causing damage to persons, vehicles or property of any kind on or adjoining the highway.[563] Reasonable care means the care which an ordinarily skilful driver or rider would have exercised, under all the circumstances, and connotes an "avoidance of excessive speed, keeping a good lookout, observing traffic rules and signals and so on".[564] It includes keeping reasonable control over passengers.[565] The steps that need to be taken in order to perform the duty have been considered in many situations of commonplace occurrence.[566] Since the duty is to drive with reasonable care and prudence a motorist will seldom be held liable for the outcome of a split second decision where a number of courses of action are open to him and each has potential disadvantages. Just because an accident could have been avoided by the taking

---

[557] art.22(1) of the Convention.
[558] art.22(2) of the Convention.
[559] art.23 of the Convention.
[560] ibid. Art.25. For the interpretation of this clause, see *Gurtner v Beaton* [1993] 2 Lloyd's Rep. 369 and *Nugent v Michael Goss Aviation Ltd* [2000] P.I.Q.R. P175, CA.
[561] *Searle v Wallbank* [1947] A.C. 341 at 361.
[562] per Potter L.J. in *Clarke v Kato* [1997] 1 W.L.R. 208, CA at 211: "The existence of a highway depends upon the establishment of a public right of passage whether on foot, on horseback or by vehicle, over the way concerned as a result of dedication or long usage."
[563] As regards a learner driver, see paras 10–258 to 10–261, below.
[564] *Bourhill v Young* [1943] A.C. 92 at 104, per Lord Macmillan.
[565] *Minister Van Polisie en Binnelandse Sake v Van Aswegan*, 1974 (2) S.A. 101 (police officers were held to be negligent in not keeping a prisoner under proper control inside their police car so that, with the object of gaining an opportunity to escape, the latter was able to grapple with the steering wheel, turn it and cause the vehicle to crash).
[566] In *Foskett v Mistry* [1984] R.T.R. 1, the CA applying the dictum of Lord Dunedin in *Fardon v Harcourt-Rivington* (1932) 146 L.T. 391 at 392, has reiterated that authorities seldom ought to be cited in simple running-down cases, where liability is dependent merely on whether or not the defendant can be shown to have failed to take reasonable care in all circumstances.

of a particular measure does not necessarily mean that taking of the measure which, in fact caused the accident was negligent. [567]

To whom the duty is owed. Primarily, the person who either drives or rides **10–188** a vehicle on the highway owes a duty of care to all other road users, as well as persons and their property on land adjacent to the highway. Likewise, a passenger[568] in a motorvehicle and a pedestrian[569] each owes a duty of care to other users of the highway.

A road user must not assume that others on the highway will themselves **10–189** behave with reasonable care, which common experience has shown to be a false assumption. Lord Uthwatt observed: "a driver is not, of course, bound to anticipate folly in all its forms, but he is not, in my opinion, entitled to put out of consideration the teachings of experience as to the form these follies commonly take".[570]

The duty of care is owed to "persons so placed that they may reasonably be **10–190** expected to be injured by the omission to take such care".[571] It is a separate and distinct duty, which is owed by one user of the highway to each other user,[572] so that, for example, an instructor driver and a learner driver owe duties to one another, as well as to other persons likely to be affected by the latter's driving.[573] A driver can still owe a duty of care to a passenger notwithstanding that they are jointly engaged in committing road traffic offences.[574]

Each decision turns on its facts. It is essential always to bear in mind, when **10–191** considering the following text, that each decision turns upon its own individual facts[575] and should be treated as a guide, rather than as a binding authority for a rule of law.

---

[567] *Lambert v Clayton* [2009] EWCA Civ 237 (no liability upon the defendant, who drove a pickup towing a cattle trailer in a right turn from a country road into a lane about 100m from a blind summit, for a collision with a motorcyclist who approached from behind the summit at very high speed : an argument that he should have decided in a split second to abort his manoeuvre was rejected.

[568] See para.10–262, below.

[569] See paras 10–268 to 10–278, below.

[570] *L.P.T.B. v Upson* [1949] A.C. 155 at 173.

[571] *Bourhill v Young* [1943] A.C. 92 at 104, with Lord Macmillan adding, "the duty is owed to those to whom injury may reasonably and probably be anticipated if the duty is not observed."

[572] *Randolph v Tuck* [1962] 1 Q.B. 175, 185.

[573] See para.10–258, below, and *Nettleship v Weston* [1971] 2 Q.B. 691. Where the owner of a car hands the keys to a learner driver, the correct test of negligence is whether or not a reasonable man in all the circumstances would have realised that there was a real risk of such learner driver driving it. *Setchell v Snowdon* [1974] R.T.R. 389.

[574] *Jackson v Harrison* (1978) 19 A.L.R. 129; *Taylor v Leslie*, 1998 Rep.L.R. 110, OH, *Currie v Clamp* 2001 S.C.L.R. 504, OH (passenger not disqualified from suing for injuries sustained in an accident by the criminal offence of being driven in a car taken without the owner's consent). See, on the general point of principle, Glofcheski, "Plaintiff's illegality as a bar to recovery of personal injury damages" (1999) 19 L.S., 6. See Ch.4, paras 2–248 to 2–253, above.

[575] *Scott v Warren* [1974] R.T.R. 104 (a motorist, who was driving in a line of moving traffic, was following a van, which made an emergency stop, and despite braking hard he was unable to stop in time and crashed into the van's rear): *Banfield v Scott and Ranzetta* (1984) 134 New L.J. 550; *Foskett v Mistry* [1984] R.T.R. 1.

10–192   **The Highway Code.** The Highway Code was originally established under s.45 of the Road Traffic Act 1930. The current, fifteenth, edition of the Highway Code was issued in 2007.[576] Its effect is set out in s.38(7)[577] of the Road Traffic Act 1988 as follows:

> "A failure on the part of a person to observe a provision of the Highway Code shall not of itself render a person liable to criminal proceedings of any kind, but any such failure may in any proceedings (whether civil or criminal, and including proceedings for an offence under the Traffic Acts, the Public Passenger Vehicles Act 1981 or sections 18 to 23 of the Transport Act 1985) be relied upon by any party to the proceedings as tending to establish or to negative any liability which is in question in those proceedings."

10–193   It follows that, usually, a failure to observe the provisions of the Code is prima facie evidence of negligence but the Code should not be treated as a statutory instrument and a breach of the Code does not necessarily indicate negligence:

> "it contains many propositions of goods sense, which may be taken into account in considering whether reasonable care had been taken, but it would be a mistake to elevate them into propositions of Law."[578]

For instance, it is unlikely that it would be regarded as evidence of negligence for a pedestrian on a footpath to walk next to the kerb with his back to the traffic (para.1). Also there is some reluctance to make findings of contributory negligence against pedestrians who walk on the "wrong" side of the road, thereby not facing oncoming traffic,[579] even when the only pavement was to the other side of the road[580]; or where the pedestrian was not wearing or carrying anything white, light-coloured or reflective.[581]

10–194   Compliance with the provisions of the Highway Code does not necessarily absolve a person from being guilty of negligence.[582] For example, although hand

---

[576] The resolutions of Parliament are required for any proposed revision: Road Traffic Act 1988 s.38(3).

[577] In order to rely on s.38(7) in a claim for damages, it is unnecessary to establish that the latest edition of the Code was available to the party who is alleged to have been in breach of its provisions, or that he had actually read it: *O'Connell v Jackson* [1972] 1 Q.B. 270.

[578] *Qualcast (Wolverhampton) Ltd v Haynes* [1959] A.C. 743 at 759 per Lord Denning. Regard must be paid to the circumstances in which the Code is invoked: *Rosser v Lindsay, The Times*, February 25, 1999, CA (the requirements of the Code as to the frequent use of a vehicle's mirrors could not be considered mandatory for a driver manoeuvring on a construction site).

[579] para.2 of the Code. See *Parkinson v Parkinson* (Note) [1973] R.T.R. 193, CA; but contrast the Australian case of *Evers v Bennett* (1983) 31 S.A.S.R. 228 (pedestrian 30 per cent to blame where he was struck by the motorist from behind while walking with his back to approaching traffic in bright sunlight).

[580] *Kerley v Downes* [1973] R.T.R. 189, CA.

[581] para.3 of the Code. See *Powell v Phillips* [1972] 3 All E.R. 864; but cf. *Jarvis v Fuller* [1974] R.T.R. 160 (collision with a pedal cyclist wearing dark clothing whose bicycle had no red light to the rear).

[582] *White v Broadbent and B.R.S.* [1958] Crim.L.R. 129. See also cases on traffic lights incidents, e.g. *Godsmark v Knight Bros (Brighton), The Times*, May 12, 1960 (approved and followed by the CA in *Radburn v Kemp*) [1971] 1 W.L.R. 1502 but cf. *Sudds v Hanscombe* [1971] R.T.R. 212; *Tingle Jacobs & Co v Kennedy* [1964] 1 W.L.R. 638n.

signals are seldom used nowadays, it can still be negligent not to give one when either an unusual or a hazardous manoeuvre is to be undertaken.[583]

Statutory regulations under Road Traffic Act 1988, etc. In addition to the Highway Code, there are various regulations, made under the earlier Road Traffic Acts, and the consolidating Act of 1988 s.41, regulating the use and construction of motorvehicles on roads.[584] Failure to comply with these regulations is a matter to be taken into account in deciding whether there is negligence. **10–195**

Many of these regulations impose a public duty upon road users and a breach will give rise to a criminal sanction, although not civil liability. Conversely, even where there has been full compliance with the Highway Code, and any relevant statutory provision, a finding of negligence may be made. **10–196**

Rule of the road. The rule of the road[585] is that when two vehicles are approaching each other from opposite directions, each must travel "on the left or near side of the road for the purpose of allowing" the other to pass.[586] Failure to observe this rule is prima facie evidence of negligence.[587] The Highway Code incorporates the rule of the road as to vehicles in para.160, and as to riders of horses in para.53. Even if a collision occurs on a driver's wrong side of the road it is not conclusive evidence of negligence against him. There may have been circumstances such as to make it reasonable for him to depart from the ordinary rule. But it does throw upon him the burden of proving what those circumstances were.[588] **10–197**

It has been said that "the rule as to the proper side of the road does not apply with respect to foot passengers; and as regards the foot passengers the carriages may go on whichever side of the road they please".[589] This misleading. The rule is, no doubt, primarily a rule regulating the course of vehicles, passing each other, but it leads to the result that all persons, including pedestrians, may reasonably expect that vehicles will be driving on or next to their near side of the road in anticipation of meeting approaching traffic, whose drivers will regulate their **10–198**

---

[583] *Goke v Willett* [1973] R.T.R. 422 (a misleading signal, using the right trafficator's flashing lights, was given by the driver, who not only pulled out to overtake traffic ahead but suddenly braked hard and attempted to execute a right turn, whereupon he was run into from behind by the following motorist, who mistakenly had believed that the intended manoeuvre being signalled was one of an *overtaking* movement only. The misleading signaller driver was held one-third to blame for the accident). See further, paras 10–233 to 10–234, below.

[584] See paras 10–245 to 10–249, above.

[585] For the effect of white lines, see para.10–203, below.

[586] Highway Act 1835 s.78, which imposes a penalty for breach of the section. The Act adopts the old common law rule of the road. There are no special precautions over and above the existence of reasonable care, which the owners of a large vehicle, using a narrow lane, necessarily ought to take: *Thrower v Thames Valley and Aldershot Bus Co Ltd* [1978] R.T.R. 271.

[587] *Chaplin v Hawes* (1828) 3 C. & P. 554.

[588] *Wayde v Lady Carr* (1823) 2 Dowl. & Ry 255; *Wallace v Bergius*, 1915 S.C. 205 (vehicles A and B approach each other from opposite directions on the same side of the road, A on its proper side and B on its wrong side, and when collision is imminent, A swerves to its wrong side, B at the same time swerving to its proper side causing a collision—B is liable to A).

[589] *Cotterill v Starkey* (1839) 8 C. & P. 691; see also *Lloyd v Ogleby* (1859) 5 C.B.(N.S.) 667.

actions accordingly. A pedestrian must keep a careful lookout, both before and during the crossing of a road,[590] but if a vehicle on its wrong side of the road collides with a pedestrian, the driver must explain how his position on the road is consistent with the exercise of reasonable care on his part.[591] When traffic is held up, no attempt should be made to gain a forward position by encroaching on the offside of the road.[592]

10–199   **Motorways.** These roads are designed to allow safe travel at high speed. Special rules apply to motorway travel and the Highway Code has a section devoted to motorways. Pedestrians, holders of provisional car or motorcycle driving licences, motorcycles under 50cc, cyclists and horse riders are prohibited from using motorways.[593] Agricultural vehicles and most invalid carriages are also prohibited.[594] Motorways have special signals situated in the central reservation and sometimes on overhead gantries.[595] These are used to warn drivers of the presence of hazards on the road ahead and to impose temporary speed restrictions. When red flashing lights are shown, drivers must not pass the signal.[596] The Highway Code advises that when joining a motorway drivers should: give priority to traffic already on the motorway; adjust their speed to fit safely into the traffic flow in the left-hand lane; not cross solid white lines separating lanes; remain on the slip road if it continues as an extra lane; and remain in the left-hand lane long enough to adjust to the speed of the traffic before overtaking.[597] The speed limit on motorways is 70 mph for cars, buses and coaches not exceeding 12 metres in length and goods vehicles not exceeding 7.5 tonnes maximum laden weight. For cars towing caravans or trailers, goods vehicles exceeding 7.5 tonnes maximum laden weight and lighter goods vehicles towing a trailer the speed limit is 60 mph.[598] Drivers on motorways must not reverse, cross the central reservation or drive against the flow of traffic.[599] Traffic must not stop on the carriageway, hard shoulder, central reservation slip road or verge except in emergencies or under the direction of a police officer or a

---

[590] See Highway Code, "The Green Cross Code" at para.7. *Hurt v Murphy* [1971] R.T.R. 186 (the deceased was held one-fifth to blame for not continuing to look to her left while crossing over the road).

[591] See *McKechnie v Couper* (1887) 14 R. 345; *Clerk v Petrie* (1879) 6 R. 1076; *Smith v Browne* (1891) 28 L.R.Ir. 1; *McKnight v General Motor Carrying Co*, 1936 S.C. 17.

[592] Highway Code para.151, advises drivers in slow moving traffic: to reduce the distance between their own vehicle and the vehicle in front to maintain traffic flow; never to get so close to the vehicle in front so as not to be able to stop safely; to leave enough space to be able to manoeuvre if the vehicle in front breaks down; not to change lanes to the left to overtake; and to allow access into and from side roads.

[593] Highways Act 1980 ss.16 and 17 and Sch.4, Motorways Traffic (England & Wales) Regulations 1982 (SI 1982/1163) and the Motorways Traffic (England & Wales) (Amendment) Regulations 1992 (SI 1992/1364).

[594] Motorways Traffic (England & Wales) Regulations 1982 (SI 1982/1163) reg.4.

[595] These are illustrated in the Highway Code.

[596] Road Traffic Act 1988 s.36 and Traffic Signs Regulations and General Directions 1994 (SI 1994/1519).

[597] para.233.

[598] Motorways Traffic (Speed Limit) Regulations 1974 (SI 1974/502).

[599] Motorways Traffic (England & Wales) Regulations 1982, (SI 1982/1163) regs 6 and 7.

signal.[600] Driving on the hard shoulder is prohibited.[601] Traffic must not overtake on the hard shoulder.[602]

Vehicles towing a trailer, goods vehicles with a maximum laden weight over **10–200** 7.5 tonnes and passenger vehicles with a maximum laden weight of over 7.5 tonnes constructed or adapted to carry more than eight passengers must not use the right-hand lane where there are three or more lanes.[603]

Paragraph 268 of the Highway Code advises drivers not to overtake on the left. **10–201** In congested conditions, however, where adjacent lanes of traffic are moving at similar speeds, it is permissible to keep up with traffic in the same lane even if that means passing traffic in a lane to the right, which is moving more slowly. In such conditions traffic should not weave in and out of lanes to overtake.

When leaving the motorway motorists should: watch for signs indicating the **10–202** position of their exit; move into the left-hand lane well before the exit; and signal left in good time.[604] On slip roads and link roads between motorways drivers should check their speedometers.[605]

Traffic signs and lines or marks on a road.[606] White or yellow lines or **10–203** marks[607] have been made specifically a "traffic sign," by s.64(1) of the Road Traffic Regulation Act 1984.[608] A double white line along the middle of the road is of particular significance, because if the nearer line is a continuous one, the vehicle must keep to its own side of it and is prohibited from crossing or straddling it. On the other hand, if the nearer line is a broken one, a vehicle may cross, in certain circumstances, although the mere presence of a broken line does not mean that it is safe for a vehicle to overtake. A failure to comply with the indication given by a "traffic sign" or with "traffic directions", is an offence under the 1988 Act.[609]

Overtaking and being overtaken. Overtaking must be done on the right- **10–204** hand or offside of the vehicle overtaken, save when the driver in front has signalled that he intends to turn right.[610] A driver must not overtake where his vehicle would have to cross or straddle double white lines with an unbroken line

---

[600] Motorways Traffic (England & Wales) Regulations 1982, (SI 1982/1163) regs 7(1), 9 and 10.
[601] Motorways Traffic (England & Wales) Regulations 1982, (SI 1982/1163) reg.5, save when an appropriate sign is displayed indicating that the hard shoulder is to be used as the nearside lane because of road works or other obstruction.
[602] Motorways Traffic (England & Wales) Regulations 1982, (SI 1982/1163) regs 5 and 9.
[603] Motorways Traffic (England & Wales) Regulations 1982, (SI 1982/1163) reg.12.
[604] Highway Code para.272.
[605] Highway Code para.273.
[606] For the liability of highway authorities regarding the provision of road signs see para.10–10, above.
[607] See Highway Code paras 106–111.
[608] Which has replaced s.54 of the Road Traffic Regulation Act 1967 that had overruled *Evans v Cross* [1938] 1 K.B. 694.
[609] ss.35 and 36.
[610] Highway code para.163. When traffic is moving slowly in queues, motorists should keep to their lane and may overtake traffic on their right-hand side in a queue which is moving more slowly.

nearest to him[611]; in the zig-zag area of a pedestrian crossing and after a "no overtaking" sign. A driver should not overtake approaching or at a corner or bend; a road junction[612]; a hump bridge, or the brow of a hill, or when he might come into conflict with other road users.[613] The driver or rider of the overtaking vehicle, before attempting to overtake, should see that it is safe to do so, and should be especially careful at night or in poor visibility, when it is more difficult to judge speed and distance.[614]

10–205   There will be occasions when a hand signal, in substitution for or in addition to a flashing indicator's signal, may become essential. For instance, it will be important to distinguish between the intention of overtaking, then either maintaining a constant speed or increasing it, and the intention of reducing speed, probably rapidly, then changing direction by turning to the right.[615] Failure so to give a clear indication, in such circumstances, could well confuse and mislead the drivers of following vehicles and cause a collision.[616]

10–206   In all cases it is the duty of the person who is overtaking to allow an adequate margin of safety between his vehicle and the vehicle overtaken,[617] and to overtake only when he can do so without causing danger to other traffic.[618] A driver, who overtook a stationary bus at some traffic lights just as they were changing to green, and struck the claimant, who was still in the process of crossing the road in front of the bus, was held liable. It was negligent to overtake the bus where he did, and in the circumstances, he should have waited until it was half-way across the crossroad before attempting to pass it.[619] Drivers should not assume that they can simply follow a vehicle in front which is overtaking because

---

[611] It is permissible to cross an unbroken white line if it is necessary to pass a stationary vehicle or to overtake a pedal cycle, horse, or road maintenance vehicle if they are travelling at 10 mph or less: Road Traffic Act s.36 and The Traffic Signs and General Directions 1994 (SI 1994/1519).

[612] *Joseph Eva Ltd v Reeves* [1938] 2 K.B. 393; *Goke v Willett* [1973] R.T.R. 422; *Joliffe v Hay*, 1991 S.L.T. 151. Different considerations may apply when approaching a side road: see *Tocci v Hankard (No.2)* (1966) 110 S.J. 835, but also the decisions referred to in n.621, below.

[613] Highway Code para.167. Examples of potential conflict with other road users include: on the approach to a junction on either side of the road; where the road narrows; when approaching a school crossing patrol; between the kerb and a bus or tram when it is at a stop; where traffic is queuing at junctions or road works; at a level crossing; and when a vehicle is indicating right.

[614] Highway Code paras 162 and 163. A driver is entitled to assume he can overtake without danger if what he is overtaking gives not the slightest sign of any unexpected manoeuvre: *Clark v Wakelin* (1965) 109 S.J. 295.

[615] *Joliffe v Hay*, 1991 S.L.T. 151 (the leading vehicle's driver had been approaching a junction with the intention of turning right and had commenced to do so, whilst the following vehicle's driver had moved out to overtake and had collided with the rear of the leading vehicle).

[616] *Goke v Willett* [1973] R.T.R. 422 (one-third responsibility on behalf of the driver giving the misleading signal). See *Joliffe v Hay*, 1991 S.L.T. 151 (30 per cent blame on the driver of the leading vehicle and 70 per cent blame on the following, overtaking vehicle's driver).

[617] *Henry v Santam Insurance Co Ltd*, 1971 (1) S.A. 468 (besides allowing for the normal clearance sufficient between the two vehicles when a two-wheeled machine is being overtaken due allowance must be given for some lateral movement on the part of the cycle rider, especially when the road's surface is rough).

[618] *Leaver v Pontypridd Urban District Council* (1911) 76 J.P. 31; *Umphray v Ganson Bros*, 1917 S.C. 371.

[619] *Shepherd v H. West & Son Ltd* (1962) 106 S.J. 391 ; [1964] A.C. 326 (damages only).

there may only be enough room for one vehicle to overtake.[620] A driver travelling in the outer lane on a main road and overtaking a queue of traffic which is stationary or moving very slowly or irregularly, must be prepared for the possibility that the inner lane's vehicles will give way to vehicles which are waiting to emerge from a side road and desiring to pass through a gap in the main road's traffic.[621] Having finished overtaking, a driver should not cut in, that is, pull sharply in front of the vehicle which has just been overtaken.[622] Animals should be passed slowly, be given plenty of room, and, if necessary, the driver should bring his vehicle to a stop.[623]

A driver should use reasonable care while being overtaken, and must not **10–207** swerve outwards, so as to get in the way of the vehicle overtaking him.[624] A driver should not accelerate while being overtaken,[625] but if he does, the driver of the overtaking vehicle should fall behind. The driver being overtaken should not impede an overtaking manoeuvre, but if a dangerous situation is created by the actions of the overtaking vehicle, the driver being overtaken is not negligent if he continues to drive at a proper speed upon a proper course.[626]

Drivers must show consideration for the safety of pedestrians. If a public **10–208** conveyance is either stationary or about to stop, the driver of an overtaking vehicle should anticipate that passengers are likely to be alighting and keep a good look out for them.[627]

Speed. It is the duty of the driver or rider of a vehicle to travel at a speed[628] **10–209** which is reasonable under the circumstances. In determining what is reasonable, the nature, condition, and use of the road in question, and the amount of traffic which is actually on it at the time, or which might reasonably be expected to be on it, are all important matters to be taken into consideration. The Highway Code provides:

> "125—The speed limit is the absolute maximum and does not mean it is safe to drive at that speed irrespective of conditions. Driving at speeds too fast for the road and traffic conditions can be dangerous. You should always reduce your speed when:
> the road layout or condition presents hazards, such as bends;
> sharing the road with pedestrians and cyclists, particularly children, and motorcyclists;

---

[620] Highway Code para.163.
[621] The "overtaker" was wholly to blame in *Clarke v Winchurch* [1969] 1 W.L.R. 69, explained by the CA in *Worsfold v Howe* [1980] 1 W.L.R. 1175, and to the extent of 80 per cent in *Powell v Moody* (1966) 110 S.J. 215, CA; two-thirds in *Garston Warehousing Co Ltd v O.F. Smart (Liverpool) Ltd* [1973] R.T.R. 377; and one-half in *Leeson v Bevis & Tolchard Ltd* [1972] R.T.R. 373.
[622] Highway Code para.163.
[623] See *Downing v Birmingham & Midland Trams* (1888) 5 T.L.R. 40.
[624] See *Milliken v Glasgow Corp*, 1918 S.C. 857.
[625] Highway Code para.168.
[626] *Smith v Cribben* [1994] P.I.Q.R. P218, CA.
[627] *Christie v Glasgow Corp*, 1927 S.C. 273; *Gambino v Di Leo* (1971) 7 D.L.R. (3d) 167 (children who emerged suddenly from behind an ice cream truck).
[628] For restrictions, generally, see the Road Traffic Regulation Act 1984 ss.81–88.

weather conditions[629] make it safer to do so;
driving at night as it is harder to see other road users."

If the driver of a vehicle sees a pedestrian in time to avoid a collision but does not slacken speed, because he thinks there will be no collision if the pedestrian moves normally, and the pedestrian, owing to age or infirmity, does not do so and a collision occurs, the driver will be liable.[630]

10–210　　A motorist should drive at a speed such that he can stop well within the distance that he can see to be safe.[631] So where a motorist approached the brow of a hill on a single track road at such a speed that she could not stop to avoid a stationary vehicle on the other side of the brow of the hill liability was established even though the defendant was only travelling at between 15 to 20 mph.[632] The maximum permitted speed of certain motor vehicles is regulated by statute[633] and, if that speed is exceeded, it is most probable that a case of negligence will be established against the driver.[634] Again, it is an offence to drive a vehicle at a speed exceeding 30 mph on a road in a built-up area, that is, a road where there are street lamps not more than 200 yards apart, or a road to which the speed limit has been applied by order of the Minister of Transport.[635] Obviously, it is *evidence* of negligence to exceed the speed limit in a built-up area, because other traffic and persons in the area may be assumed to regulate their conduct in the expectation that the law will be obeyed.[636] On the other hand, a driver may not necessarily be negligent if he fails to reduce his speed below 30 mph in a built-up area, or sound his horn along a residential street, although he is aware of the slight possibility that a child might suddenly dart out into the roadway from behind a parked car.[637]

10–211　　**Police.** A police oficer, like any other driver, owes a duty to drive with due care and attention and without exposing members of the public to unnecessary danger. So where a claimant was injured by a police motorcyclist, who was riding in pursuance of his duties at 60 mph on a road where the maximum permitted

---

[629] Failing to do so usually will result in the driver being found liable, either wholly or in part: *Harvey v Road Haulage Executive* [1952] 1 K.B. 120; *Rouse v Squires* [1973] Q.B. 889.

[630] *Daly v Liverpool Corp* [1939] 2 All E.R. 142. See generally, Cottrell, "Liability favours the pedestrian" 2004 P.I.L.J. (Oct) 10.

[631] Highway Code para.126.

[632] *Dawson v Angela* [2007] EWHC 3395 (Q.B.).

[633] Road Traffic Regulation Act 1984 s.86.

[634] *Kingman v Seagar* [1938] 1 K.B. 397; *Bracegirdle v Oxley* [1947] 1 All E.R. 126. See also the provisions of the Civil Evidence Act 1968 s.11, which places the burden on the defendant of disproving negligence where he has been convicted of an offence which is relevant to the issue.

[635] By the Road Traffic Regulation Act 1984 ss.81 and 82, certain roads, although provided with street lamps, may be and have been freed from the speed limit by Order. In such cases signs to that effect are fixed to the lamp-posts.

[636] See *Grealis v Opuni, The Times*, February 7, 2003, CA (driver of car travelling at 38mph in 30mph limit 20 per cent responsible for collision with moped driver who turned right, across his path). In *Puffett v Hayfield* [2005] EWCA Civ 1760 it was said that, as a matter of law, a finding that excessive speed at which a car had been driven was causative of an accident giving rise to personal injury could be made without the court actually specifying what was a safe speed.

[637] *Moore v Poyner* [1975] R.T.R. 127, applied in *Saleem v Drake* [1993] P.I.Q.R. P129, CA, but cf. the situation in *Armstrong v Cottrell* [1993] P.I.Q.R. P109, CA.

speed was 40 mph liability was established.[638] Where a police officer, in the execution of his duty, must necessarily exceed the speed limit, he must exercise a degree of care and skill proportionate to the speed and remember that the ordinary road user in a built-up area will not expect a motor vehicle being driven at a fast speed. It is desirable in such circumstances that particular care should be given to audible or other warning of approach.[639]

Braking, slowing, coming to a stop. The driver of a vehicle following   **10–212**
another ought to allow a sufficient space between the vehicles, in which to deal with the ordinary exigencies of traffic. It is evidence of negligence if a vehicle is too close to the rear of a vehicle ahead and so fails to pull up in time, when the other vehicle come to a sudden halt.[640] On the other hand, to say that a bus-driver, for example, must always preserve a gap in front of the bus, sufficient to enable it to come to a halt, is a counsel of perfection which ignores traffic conditions.[641]

The Highway Code suggests[642] that a safe rule is not to get closer to the   **10–213**
vehicle ahead than the overall stopping distance (as set out in the table of such distances); on roads carrying fast traffic a two-second gap should be left. On wet or icy roads the gap should be at least doubled. If the following driver allows proper space and the leading vehicle suddenly pulls up so that a collision cannot be avoided, the former may not be liable for the damage.[643]

The question of the leading vehicle driver's liability will depend on whether   **10–214**
the sudden stop was owing to that driver's negligence or to some other cause.[644] Where the defendant had applied her brakes violently in order to avoid hitting a pheasant running across the road in front of her car, so that the motorist following

---

[638] *Gaynor v Allen* [1959] 2 Q.B. 403. See further *Marshall v Osmond* [1983] Q.B. 1034 (police car, in hot pursuit of some youths, who had taken a motorcar without the owner's authority, injured one of them); *McLeod v Receiver of Metropolitan Police* [1971] Crim.L.R. 364 (a police car lost control at 70 mph, travelling in answer to an emergency call, and collided with another car); *Gilfillan v Barbour* 2003 S.L.T. 1127, OH (*Gaynor* doubted where a police officer responding to a call was approaching a junction on a damp surface at 60 mph and collided with a car whose driver, having heard the siren of the police car, nonetheless attempted to turn right).

[639] *Dyer v Bannell* (1965) 109 S.J. 216, applied in *Cox v Dixon* (1984) 134 New L.J. 236 and 451 (an unmarked police car was travelling at about 60 mph in a built-up area along a dual carriageway, which was subject to a 30 mph speed limit, in hot pursuit of a motorcyclist. Suddenly a motorist emerged on to the dual carriageway from a side turning and collided with the police car. Liability was apportioned, two-thirds to the police car driver, one-third to the motorist).

[640] *Thompson v Spedding* [1973] R.T.R. 312 (each driver held equally to blame).

[641] *Wooller v London Transport Board* [1976] R.T.R. 206, CA; applied in *Parnell v Metropolitan Police District Receiver* [1976] R.T.R. 201.

[642] Highway Code para.126.

[643] *Brown and Lynn v Western S.M.T. Co*, 1945 S.C. 31 at 36, *per* Lord Justice Clerk Cooper: "The following driver is, in my view, bound, so far as reasonably possible, to take up a position, and to drive in such a fashion, as will enable him to deal successfully with all traffic exigencies reasonably to be anticipated"; *Scott v Warren* [1974] R.T.R. 104.

[644] See *Smith v Harris* [1939] 3 All E.R. 960; *Sharp v Avery* [1938] 4 All E.R. 85 (leader of two motorcycles held liable for leading into a position of danger); *Goke v Willett* [1973] R.T.R. 422 (one-third responsibility held against the driver for giving a misleading signal to the traffic behind him).

her was unable to avoid a collision, the defendant was held liable.[645] Where a motorcyclist ran into the rear of a van which had braked suddenly, the view was expressed that, in such circumstances, the burden of proof lay on the van driver to explain why such braking was required.[646] On the other hand, where the leading vehicle had come to a gradual halt, as a result of a blockage in the fuel system, and was run into from behind, it was held that, because such a breakdown was a foreseeable emergency, the following vehicle's driver was negligent in failing to anticipate that it might have to slow down or stop.[647] Even so, a driver, who intends to slow down, albeit suddenly, whilst driving along a motorway, is under no duty to give any warning of his intention, because it is the duty of those following behind to keep clear.[648]

10–215   **Look out.** It is the duty of the driver or rider of a vehicle to keep a good look out. Indeed, a a failure to notice in time that the actions of another person have created a potential danger is negligent.[649] Attention must be paid to other traffic, which is or may be expected to be on the road, whether in front, behind, or alongside, especially at crossroads, junctions and bends.[650] A look out must be kept for traffic-light signals and traffic signs, including lines marked on the highway. Disregard of traffic signals[651] and failure to keep a proper look out are both evidence of negligence. When there are pedestrians about, the driver or rider must be ready in case they step from a street refuge or a footpath, or from behind a vehicle or other obstruction and, also, be prepared for children, knowing that they may be expected to run suddenly on to the road.[652] The mere fact of a motorist's failure to see a pedestrian in an unlit street during the hours of darkness, before a collision, does not necessarily mean that the defendant driver was negligent.[653] When passing a standing vehicle or other obstruction, which prevents a clear view of oncoming traffic or pedestrians, a good look out should be kept. It has been held that for a motorist to allow his wing mirror to strike a pedestrian, who either was standing on the kerb or had his back to traffic or, even, had gone an inch or two into the roadway, amounted to negligence and that the

---

[645] *Gussman v Gratton-Storey* (1968) 112 S.J. 884. Contrast *Welch v O'Leary* [1998] 11 C.L. 432 (motorcyclist 100 per cent to blame where the driver of the car he was following and about to overtake braked violently to avoid a collision with ducks); *Sharp v M.O.D.* [2007] EWCA Civ 1223 (seventh driver in military convoy colliding with the rear of the sixth vehicle—liability was not established even though the drivers of the fifth and sixth vehicles had been negligent in driving too close to vehicles ahead, because the effective cause of the accident was the claimant driving too close to the sixth vehicle). See also *Parkinson v Liverpool Corp* [1950] 1 All E.R. 367, para.10–285, below and *Ritchie's Car Hire v Bailey* (1958) 108 L.J. 348, para.10–250, below.

[646] *Elizabeth v Motor Insurers' Bureau* [1981] R.T.R. 405.

[647] *Rowlands v Street, The Times*, November 22, 1962.

[648] *Jungnickel v Laing* (1966) 111 S.J. 19.

[649] *Foskett v Mistry* [1984] R.T.R. 1, CA (motorist was driving at a reasonable speed in open parkland when claimant, aged 16, ran down a slope and out into the road into collision with the vehicle. Had the motorist seen the claimant he ought to have sounded his horn, in which event, on the balance of probabilities, the claimant's attention would have been alerted. Liability was apportioned the motorist one-quarter and the claimant three-quarters). See also *Rosser v Lindsay, The Times*, February 25, 1999, CA, para.10–201, above (frequent use of mirrors not a mandatory rule on a building site).

[650] *Springett v Ball* (1865) 4 F. & F. 472.

[651] See para.10–203, above.

[652] See Highway Code paras 204–209, and *Foskett v Mistry* [1984] R.T.R. 1, above.

[653] *Knight v Fellick* [1977] R.T.R. 316, CA; see too *Ahanonu v South East London & Kent Bus Company Ltd* [2008] EWCA Civ 274.

pedestrian was not guilty of contributory negligence.[654] Negligence was not established, however, where a bus driver saw a child running towards the bus on the kerb side of bollards lining the pavement and the child fell under the bus as it slowed down; the risk of injury was a remote one and not one which the driver should have recognised and reacted to.[655]

In broad daylight, a collision with a stationary vehicle on the highway is prima facie evidence of negligence. When a tractor came out of a field into a country lane, which was a highway, and collided with a stationary car that was facing the direction whence the tractor was coming, the tractor driver was liable.[656] The driver was caught in a bind: **10–216**

> "Either there was room to pass or there was not. If there was room to pass, then the fact that he damaged the plaintiff's vehicle in passing was *prima facie* evidence of negligence. If there was no room to pass, then he was negligent in attempting to do so when there was no room."[657]

Mobile telephones and in-car technology. The Highway Code advises motorists never to use a hand mobile phone or a microphone whilst driving.[658] Even a hands free telephone is likely to be a distraction to a motorist. Many vehicles now have route guidance and navigation systems and some have on board personal computers. The Highway Code advises drivers not to operate, adjust or view such equipment if it will cause a distraction.[659] **10–217**

Reversing. A motorist, before either reversing or turning around on the highway, should satisfy himself that it is safe to do so. The Highway Code stresses the importance of checking to the rear before reversing is commenced; being careful about the area that cannot be seen from the driver's seat; obtaining help if the view behind is obscured; and never reversing from a side into a main road.[660] **10–218**

When the driver of a bus was using his conductor, who was outside the vehicle, walking backwards and keeping level with the rear of it, as his "eyes", he was under a duty to make sure that those "eyes" were in a position to see what they were supposed to see, namely any person who was attempting to cross the street behind the back of the bus.[661] The duty being to take reasonable care, it is **10–219**

---

[654] *Chapman v Post Office* [1982] R.T.R. 165, CA; also *Ehrari v Curry* [2007] EWCA Civ 120 (driver 30 per cent to blame for wing mirror collision between lorry and a 13 year old child who had stepped into the road from behind a parked car and who was there to be seen for about 1 second before impact).

[655] *Chadli v Brooks* [2005] EWCA Civ 211.

[656] *Randall v Tarrant* [1955] 1 All E.R. 600.

[657] *Randall v Tarrant* [1955] 1 All E.R. 600 per Jenkins L.J. at 605.

[658] Highway Code para.149.

[659] Highway Code para.150.

[660] Highway Code paras 200–203; see also *McKnight v General Motor Carrying Co*, 1936 S.C. 17.

[661] *Liddon v Stringer*, The Times, April 15, 1967.

unrealistic to expect a bus driver to keep a constant eye on his nearside mirror when there would be other potential dangers to consider.[662]

It is an offence for a person to cause or permit a motor vehicle to travel backwards for a greater distance or time than may be requisite for the safety or reasonable convenience of the occupants of that vehicle or of other traffic on the road.[663]

10–220   **Collisions in centre of road.** When there is a collision between two motor vehicles in the highway and there is no evidence pointing to one driver being any more to blame than the other, the proper inference to be drawn is that they are both to blame.[664] So, when there had been a collision in the centre of crossroads of equal status and, after the accident, the defendant said to a policeman, "I was going along the road and we met in the middle", it was held there was a prima facie case that both drivers were to blame. The claimant was an innocent passenger and, as the defendant called no evidence, the claimant recovered in full against the defendant.[665] Each driver who was involved in an unwitnessed and inexplicable head-on collision between two vehicles is likely to be held equally to blame in negligence, even where there is some indication that one of them might have been on his wrong side of the road.[666]

10–221   Further, it is by no means conclusive evidence of negligence that a vehicle crossed over a dotted or single continuous white line in the middle of the road, although different considerations would arise if it were a double white line with a continuous line on the driver's side.[667] When a collision occurred, either through the gross negligence of a motorist or the gross negligence of a motorcyclist, but the judge, being unable to say which, dismissed both the claim and the counterclaim, it was held that he should have made up his mind either which one was to blame or have held both equally to blame.[668] On the other hand, it has been held, where there had been a head-on collision and each party had said that he was on his correct side of the road and that it was the other who had swerved, but the trial judge was unable to say that one account was more probably correct that the other, then both the claim and the counterclaim should be dismissed.[669]

---

[662] *Ahanonu v South East London & Kent Bus Company Ltd* [2008] EWCA Civ 274.

[663] reg.106 of the Road Vehicles (Construction and Use) Regulations 1986 (SI 1986/1078), except for a vehicle or road-roller engaged in work on the road.

[664] *Baker v Market Harborough Industrial Co-operative Soc.* [1953] 1 W.L.R. 1472 (two motor-vehicles, travelling in opposite directions, collided in the dark, in the centre of the road, both drivers being killed. There was no evidence pointing to one driver being more blameworthy than the other—held, both to blame); this decision was applied in *Howard v Bemrose* [1973] R.T.R. 32, CA also *Cooper v Hatton* [200] R.T.R. 36, CA (no adequate evidential basis for preferring the account of one driver over the other). See also *Cooper v Floor Cleaning Machines Ltd, The Times,* October 24, 2003, CA and the discussion at Ch.6, paras 6–88 to 6–91 above. That rule would seem to apply even if it be perfectly feasible that neither party was negligent: *Davison v Leggett* (1969) 113 S.J. 409; *Nettleship v Weston* [1971] 2 Q.B. 691.

[665] *France v Parkinson* [1954] 1 W.L.R. 581.

[666] *Howard v Bemrose* [1973] R.T.R. 32, CA.

[667] See para.10–203, above.

[668] *Bray v Palmer* [1953] 1 W.L.R. 1455.

[669] *Nesterczuk v Mortimore* (1965) 39 A.L.R. 288.

Traffic lights. It is an offence under s.36 of the Road Traffic Act 1988,[670] for   **10–222**
any driver or cyclist to disobey a traffic light signal.[671] Likewise, it is an offence
under s.37 of the Act for any pedestrian to disobey a uniformed police
constable's directions when he is engaged in regulating the vehicular traffic in the
road. Where a pedestrian starts to cross a road on a pedestrian crossing while the
lights are in his favour, he should be allowed free and uninterrupted passage over
the crossing, even though the lights change in the meantime. But, where there
was a central refuge in the road and the lights changed when the pedestrian
reached it, he was held to be at fault in stepping into the road without using due
care.[672]

The Highway Code instructs drivers to give way to pedestrians who are   **10–223**
already crossing a road into which they are turning.[673] Where the claimant had
begun to walk across the road at a junction, when the traffic lights were in his
favour, and the defendant's motor car emerged from a side road, turned to its
right and struck him as he had almost reached the central refuge, the defendant
was wholly liable, the claimant being under no duty to safeguard himself against
unforeseeably atrocious driving.[674] Similarly, where pedestrians were injured,
whilst crossing a road on a crossing marked by studs but with the traffic lights at
green in favour of vehicular traffic, it was held that the degree of blameworthiness to be attached to them was small, especially since the defendant's vehicle
was approaching at a very fast speed.[675]

Crossing a road in disobedience to a traffic light will amount to negligence. A   **10–224**
driver, who is crossing a junction when lights are in his favour, is under no duty
to look out for traffic which is crossing in disobedience to the lights. Even so, if
he sees such traffic, then he must use reasonable care to avoid a collision.[676] A
driver is under a duty not to enter a junction where traffic is already present prior

---

[670] See *Ryan v Smith* [1967] 2 Q.B. 893 (where the motorcar was already partially over the stop line
when the lights were at green before it had to stop but it proceeded farther after the signals changed
to red).
[671] Motorists must stop behind the white stop line unless a green light is showing in their favour.
Some junctions have advanced stop lines to allow cyclists to be positioned ahead of other road users.
Motorists must wait behind the first stop line and not encroach on the area marked for cyclists. See
the Traffic Signs Regulations and General Directions 2002 (SI 2002/3113).
[672] *Wilkinson v Chetham-Strode* [1940] 2 K.B. 310, which, today, would amount to contributory
negligence. See also the provisions of the Highway Code paras 7, 8 and 9. cf. where pedal cyclist
enters crossing on green light but the lights change: *Radburn v Kemp* [1971] 1 W.L.R. 1502.
[673] Highway Code para.170.
[674] *Frank v Cox* (1967) 111 S.J. 670.
[675] *Mulligan v Holmes* [1971] R.T.R. 179 (20 per cent contributory negligence).
[676] *Eva v Reeves* [1938] 2 K.B. 393; *Ward v London County Council* [1938] 2 All E.R. 341 (fire
engine not entitled to disregard traffic lights); *Knight v Cooper Supply Services* (1965) 109 S.J. 358
(the driver entering crossroads with the lights in his favour was not guilty of contributory negligence
if he collided with another vehicle entering the crossing against the lights); *Davis v Hassan* (1967)
117 New L.J. 72; *Butters v Fenner & Co* (1967) 117 New L.J. 213; *Ramoo S/O Erulapan v Gan Soo
Swee* [1971] 1 W.L.R. 1014; *Singh v Nixon and Costello* (1974) 21 W.I.R. 203, Guyana CA; *Horsman
v McGarvey* [1983] 3 W.W.R. 564, CA British Columbia but cf. Shepherd v Zilm (1976) 14 S.A.S.R.
257 (claimant drove through traffic lights set at red against him and collided with the defendant
motorist, who had taken no avoiding action, although he could have seen that the claimant was not
going to stop, it was held that the defendant was negligent and thereby liable for 25 per cent of the
claimant's damage).

to a change of lights, or which foreseeably may still be crossing it, until it is safe to do so.[677]

10–225   A driver who, in plain view, was turning to his right across a main road and into a side road at a junction, with traffic lights in his favour, was not negligent for failing to make allowance for an oncoming vehicle which did not stop at the lights against it.[678] Where a van driver executed such a right turn too early and collided with an approaching motorcyclist, who had also entered the crossroads with the traffic lights in his favour but was intent upon riding straight ahead, the van driver was wholly to blame.[679] A motorist, who failed to realise that traffic lights were not functioning properly could be guilty of negligence,[680] despite the presumption that traffic lights would be working properly.[681] Drivers of emergency vehicles[682] are, by reg.36 of the Traffic Signs Regulations and General Directions 2002, exempt from complying with traffic light signals in circumstances where the adherence to a red traffic light would hinder the purpose for which the vehicle was being used.[683] However a common law defence of necessity is not available should an accident occur. The essential effect of the regulation is that the driver must treat a red light as a "give way" sign and not enter upon the junction in a manner or at a time which would endanger another person or cause any motorist to change speed or course in order to avoid an accident.[684]

10–226   **Road junctions.** When coming from a side road into a main road, the driver or rider of a vehicle should select such a moment as will allow him to enter the main road with safety. There is no principle of law that a driver is entitled to emerge blind, from a minor road where his vision is obscured, by inching forwards beyond his line of vision.[685] At a junction with double broken white lines across the road a driver must let traffic on the major road go by first. When turning into a main road the obligation to give way is a continuing one and is owed even to vehicles which are themselves travelling at a speed in excess of the speed limit.[686] At junctions with a "Stop" sign and solid white line across the

---

[677] *Radburn v Kemp* [1971] 1 W.L.R. 1502 (pedal cyclist, who had entered a five-way road junction when the lights were at green in his favour and had crossed two-thirds of the junction before the lights changed in favour of the defendant, who then drove his car forwards and into collision with him).
[678] *Hopwood Homes v Kennerdine* [1975] R.T.R. 82, CA; applied in *Miller v Evans* [1975] R.T.R. 70, CA.
[679] *Smithers v H. & M. Transport (Oxford)* (1983) 133 New L.J. 558.
[680] *Ramoo S/O Erulapan v Gan Soo Swee* [1971] 1 W.L.R. 1014; *Sudds v Hanscombe* [1971] R.T.R. 212, CA.
[681] *Tingle Jacobs & Co v Kennedy* [1964] 1 W.L.R. 638n.
[682] In this context an emergency vehicle is one being used for fire brigade, ambulance, bomb or explosive disposal, national blood service or police purposes.
[683] SI 2002/3113.
[684] See *Griffin v Mersey Regional Ambulance Service* [1998] P.I.Q.R. P34, CA (claimant 60 per cent to blame after collision with ambulance crossing junction when lights on red since he failed to hear its klaxon, or to see it or to be alerted to the possibility of its presence by the movements of another vehicle).
[685] *Worsford v Howe* [1980] 1 W.L.R. 1175, CA.
[686] *Dolby v Milner* (1996) 10 C.L. 336, CA (driver of car turning right 75 per cent to blame; speeding motorcycle 25 per cent).

approach a driver must come to a halt at the line and wait before moving off.[687] A driver at a junction must not assume that a vehicle approaching from the right and signalling a left turn will in fact turn left: it is proper to wait to make sure. Where there is a doubt about priority at a junction there is a convention that the vehicle which has the other to its right is the give way vehicle.[688]

It is an offence to disobey a "Slow" or "Halt" sign.[689] However, although a vehicle on a minor road must give way,[690] it is the duty of a vehicle on the major road to approach with caution.[691] Should the possibility of danger be reasonably apparent, it would be negligent for a driver on the major road not to take precautions.[692] This does not involve keeping a foot over the brake pedal on the chance that a car, being driven dangerously, emerges suddenly from a side road without stopping,[693] unless it ought to have been apparent that the danger of a collision was more than just a mere possibility.[694]   **10–227**

Turning right. Paragraphs 179, 180 and 181 of the Highway Code deal with turning right. Motorists are advised: to use their mirrors to know the position of vehicles behind; to give a right-turn signal; to take up a position just left of the middle of the road or in a space marked for right turning traffic; and to leave room for other vehicles to pass on the left if possible. Before making the turn drivers should wait for a gap between themselves and any oncoming traffic and should check their mirrors and blind spot to be sure that they are not being overtaken.   **10–228**

Turning left. The Highway Code cautions left turning drivers not to overtake before turning left and to watch out for traffic coming up the nearside, especially cyclists and motorcyclists.[695] When turning left drivers should give way to any vehicles using a bus lane, cycle lane or tramway in either direction.   **10–229**

---

[687] See para.171 of the Highway Code; also *Macandrew v Tillard*, [1907] S.C. 78; *Campbell v Train*, 1910 S.C. 475.

[688] See Sellers L.J. in *McIntyre v Coles* [1966] 1 W.L.R. 831 at 834.

[689] Road Traffic Act 1988 s.36; *Tolhurst v Webster* (1936) 53 T.L.R. 174; *Anderson v Andrew's Ambulance Assn*, 1943 S.C. 248, where the effect of the "Slow, Major Road Ahead" sign is discussed. The sign "Slow" means proceed at such a speed that you can stop if, when you reach the crossing, you find someone in the process of crossing or about to cross: *Buffel v Cardox (Great Britain) Ltd* [1950] 2 All E.R. 878.

[690] In *Harding v Hinchcliffe, The Times*, April 8, 1964, it was held that the defendant, who was waiting to drive from a minor road, was negligent in doing so as a bus approached signalling a left turn: his vision was restricted and he could not see the motorcyclist with whom he collided, who had been overtaking the bus.

[691] See *Robertson v Wilson*, 1912 S.C. 398; *McNair v Glasgow Corp*, 1923 S.C. 398; *Hutchinson v Leslie*, 1927 S.C. 95; *Lang v London Transport Executive* [1959] 1 W.L.R. 1168; *Watkins v Moffatt* (1967) 111 S.J. 719.

[692] *Lang v London Transport Executive* [1959] 1 W.L.R. 1168. See also *Williams v Fullerton* (1961) 105 S.J. 208 where the CA held that a driver on a major road had a duty to look out for and guard against excessive speed by drivers on minor roads.

[693] *Humphrey v Leigh* [1971] R.T.R. 363 (doubting Ormrod L.J. in *Williams v Fullerton*, above).

[694] *Truscott v McLaren* [1982] R.T.R. 34, CA, applying the dictum of Lord Dunedin in *Fardon v Harcourt-Rivington* (1932) 146 L.T. 391, 392 (the driver on the major road was held to one-fifth and the driver on the minor road four-fifths to blame).

[695] paras 182 and 183.

10–230   **Roundabouts.** On approaching a roundabout a driver should decide as early as possible which exit to take and find the correct lane. Traffic from the right has priority unless road markings indicate otherwise. It is necessary to keep a watch for traffic, particularly cyclists and motorcyclists, already on the roundabout. At para.186 the Highway Code advises:

"When taking the first exit to the left, unless signs or markings indicate otherwise:

- signal left and approach in the left-hand lane
- keep to the left on the roundabout and continue signalling left to leave.

When taking an exit to the right of going full circle, unless signs or markings indicate otherwise

- signal right and approach in the right-hand lane
- keep to the right on the roundabout until you need to change lanes to exit the roundabout
- signal left after you have passed the exit before the one you want.

When taking any intermediate exit, unless signs or markings indicate otherwise

- select the appropriate lane on approach to the roundabout
- you should not normally need to signal on approach
- stay in this lane until you need to alter course to exit the roundabout
- signal left after you have passed the exit before the one you want.

When there are more than three lanes at the entrance to a roundabout, use the most appropriate lane on approach and through it."

10–231   A driver on a roundabout should bear in mind the likely movement of other traffic. Where a driver mistakenly passed the exit she wanted and believing it too late to turn, just carried on around the roundabout, thereby obstructing the path of the claimant motorcyclist who himself wished to use the exit and a collision ensued, liability was apportioned equally, even though the car had made no sudden or untoward movement in the road. The driver should have been aware that there might be somebody who wanted to leave the roundabout at that exit and taken care accordingly.[696]

10–232   **Mini-roundabouts.** Mini-roundabouts are much smaller than conventional roundabouts and usually have a painted disc in the centre rather than a physical island. The same rules apply to mini-roundabouts as to conventional ones.[697] All vehicles must pass round the central markings except large vehicles which are physically incapable of doing so.[698] At double mini-roundabouts drivers should treat each mini-roundabout as a separate roundabout.[699]

10–233   **Signals.** The driver or rider of a vehicle should give the proper signal before moving out or overtaking, before stopping, slowing down or changing his direction, and all signals should be given clearly and in good time to give an indication of intention to other users of the highway. Attention must be paid to

---

[696] *Grace v Tanner* [2003] EWCA Civ 354.
[697] Highway Code para.188.
[698] Road Traffic Act 1988 s.36.
[699] Highway Code para.189.

the signals of other drivers and prompt action taken in response. A driver should ensure that the indicator, if it is used, gives the signal intended, and is cancelled immediately after use.[700] Failure to do any of these is evidence of negligence.[701] A confusing or ambiguous signal which in turn causes an accident is likely to give rise to a finding of negligence.[702]

Whilst a driver must obey signals regulating traffic given by police officers, **10–234** traffic officers or traffic wardens,[703] but it is no defence to a claim based on an otherwise negligent manoeuvre that a signal to proceed was given by some person lacking such authority.[704]

Lights. During the period between sunrise and sunset and where there is **10–235** seriously reduced visibility is obligatory for the driver or rider of a vehicle to ensure that every front position lamp, rear position lamp and registration plate lamp is lit.[705] The Road Vehicles Lighting Regulations 1989 make provisions for the fitting of lamps, reflectors and rear markings, their use and maintenance.

Breach of the statutory duty to carry the lights prescribed by the regulations **10–236** does not of itself give a person, who has suffered damage in consequence thereof, any right to damages.[706] The duty is a public duty only, punishable by the penalties prescribed under the Road Traffic Offenders Act 1988, and is not enforceable by any individual aggrieved. Driving in the dark without proper lights, however, is evidence of negligence.[707]

Accordingly, failure to carry the usual lights, which misleads the driver of **10–237** another vehicle and causes a collision, is negligence.[708] The same applies if lights are used in a manner which is misleading. Where the defendant's lorry was

---

[700] Highway Code para.103.

[701] The duty of the driver of a vehicle with a left-hand drive is discussed in *Daborn v Bath Tramways Motor Co* [1946] 2 All E.R. 333.

[702] See *Coke v Willett* [1973] R.T.R. 422 (one-third responsibility on behalf of the driver giving the misleading signal); *Wadsworth v Gillespie* [1978] C.L.Y. 2534 (misleading trafficator signal was given by the claimant motorcyclist, driving along the major road, as a result of which the defendant motorist pulled out of a side road and across his path; claimant held one-third and defendant two-thirds to blame for the accident); *Winter v Cotton* [1985] 4 C.L. 339 (the defendant motorist, driving along the major road, was held wholly to blame for the collision). Compare *Soils Ltd v Bromwich* (1998) C.L.Y. 3913 (no liability upon driver indicating left where he intended to turn shortly after the junction from which the other vehicle emerged).

[703] Vehicle and Operator Services Agency (VOSA) officers have powers to stop vehicles on all roads in England and Wales. Highways Agency officers have powers to stop vehicles on motorways and some 'A' class roads in England.

[704] If such person, standing beside his parked motorvehicle, elects to give a signal to another motorist, although he is under no obligation to give any signs at all, as a result of which the latter overtakes the stationary vehicle, he owes a duty to him to give him an accurate signal, which will not result, for example, in his driving forward into head-on collision with another vehicle approaching from the opposite direction: *Grange Motors (Cwmbran) v Spencer* [1969] 1 W.L.R. 53.

[705] reg.24 of the Road Vehicles Lighting Regulations 1989 (SI 1989 no.1796).

[706] Currently the Road Vehicles Lighting Regulations 1989 (SI 1989/1796). See *Clarke v Brims* [1947] K.B. 497, approved by the CA in *Coote v Stone* [1971] 1 W.L.R. 279; see also *West v Lawson Ltd*, 1949 S.C. 430; *Moore v Maxwells of Emsworth Ltd* [1968] 1 W.L.R. 1077.

[707] *Baker v Longhurst & Sons Ltd* [1933] 2 K.B. 461 at 464, per Scrutton L.J.

[708] *Pressley v Burnett*, 1914 S.C. 874; *Wintle v Bristol Tramways and Carriage Co Ltd* (1917) 86 L.J.K.B. 24.

parked on the offside of the road at night with its headlamps on and the claimant drove into it, each party was equally to blame.[709] It was not negligent where, attending a fire, a fire engine was parked close to the kerb with only the blue, rather than the red, flashing warning lights illuminated. The fire brigade's first duty was owed to those in peril from the fire, and the blue lights were a sufficient warning to approaching traffic.[710]

10–238   Where the person responsible for a motor vehicle leaves it at night unlit on the road and it is involved in an accident, it is for that person to show that all reasonable steps have been taken to avoid creating or continuing the hazard.[711] When a lorry was properly provided with a rear light, which unknown to the driver and without negligence on his part, became extinguished, and a collision with an overtaking vehicle in the dark occurred, there was no liability on the lorry owner.[712] The presumption of negligence was also rebutted where a car, whose lighting system had failed without fault of the driver, was run into while stationary by a street light as it was towed away.[713] When a motorist stopped his car at night on a road in a position where it was only safe if it was exhibiting lights, it was negligent to use the "self-starter" for prolonged periods which had the effect or either dimming or extinguishing the compulsory lights.[714] It is negligent to drive a vehicle with inadequate lights so that the driver cannot see an obstruction or traffic on the road in front of him in sufficient time to stop or avoid it.[715]

10–239   A motorist must not use lights in a way which would dazzle or cause discomfort to other road users.[716] Where a vehicle's lights were so bright that they dazzled an approaching motorist, who, despite exercising reasonable care, collided with a pedestrian in front of him, liability was established.[717] Nevertheless, where a motorist drives on dipped headlights for the convenience of

---

[709] *Chisman v Electromation (Export)* (1969) 6 K.I.R. 456; *Watson v Heslop* [1971] R.T.R. 308.
[710] *Amos v Glamorgan County Council* (1967) 66 L.G.R. 166.
[711] In *Moore v Maxwells of Emsworth Ltd* [1968] 1 W.L.R. 1077 the CA held that the presumption of negligence arising from the presence of an unlit vehicle on a road after dark was rebutted by the evidence. For the exemption of certain vehicles, whilst standing or parked on roads, from the necessity to exhibit front and rear lights during the hours of darkness, see reg.24 of the Road Vehicles Lighting Regulations 1989 (SI 1989/1796). See also *Tompkins v Royal Mail Group Plc* [2006] R.T.R. 5 (where the claimant drove into an unlit trailer parked under a street light on its incorrect side of the road, he was himself principally to blame, however it was right to adjust the apportionment of responsibility as between himself and the owner of the trailer by 10 per cent to reflect the fact that the trailer had been deliberately and unnecessarily left in a location where it breached parking and lighting regulations: the final division was 65 per cent:35 per cent, the claimant bearing the greater share of blame). See further paras 10–253 to 10–257, below.
[712] *Maitland v Raisbeck* [1944] K.B. 689 (the driver of the overtaking vehicle, a bus, was not negligent, so that the injured passengers in the bus had no remedy).
[713] *Parish v Judd* [1960] 1 W.L.R. 867, considered in *Lee v Lever* [1974] R.T.R. 35, CA (where a car was left unlit because of lights failure on a clearway, which was well lit, the driver was negligent in failing to display a warning sign but similarly the other driver, who had driven into the stationary vehicle, was found to be equally negligent in failing to keep a proper look out).
[714] *Young v Chester* [1973] R.T.R. 319.
[715] *Pronek v Winnipeg, Selkirk and Lake Winnipeg Ry* [1933] A.C. 61.
[716] Highway Code para. 114.
[717] *Saville v Bache* (1969) 113 S.J. 228 (a driver is under a duty to dip his headlights unless there is some good reason for keeping them on at full beam).

oncoming traffic, he must travel at a speed which will enable him to deal with the ordinary problems of the highway.[718]

Flashing headlights. The Highway Code provides[719] that the flashing of **10–240** headlights means only one thing: it lets another road user know of a driver's presence. Headlights should not be flashed for any other reason and it must never be assumed as a result of such action that it is safe to proceed.[720] Although in some circumstances the flashing of headlights can mean "come along as far as I am concerned" it does not exonerate the driver who acts upon it from satisfying himself that his manoeuvre is safe.[721]

Hazard Warning Lights.[722] These days most motor vehicles are fitted with **10–241** hazard warning lights in the form of amber indicator lights which flash simultaneously. These may be used as a means of warning other road users that a stationary vehicle ahead may pose a hazard. They are not to be used as an excuse for dangerous or illegal parking. Hazard warning lights must not be used whilst the vehicle is being driven except where upon a motorway or unrestricted dual carriageway in circumstances where it is necessary to warn other road users of a hazard or obstruction ahead.

Sounding horns. Sounding a horn or a bell may be useful to warn other traffic **10–242** of the approach of a vehicle but does not absolve a driver or rider of the duty to take care or give a right of way.[723] The omission to sound a horn or a bell is "a collateral fact only, and not an independent act of negligence"[724]; by itself it is not evidence of negligence, although it may be taken into account, with other circumstances, in determining whether the driver or rider was negligent.[725]

Normally, there is no need to sound a horn when overtaking another vehicle **10–243** which is going straight ahead, but it may become necessary, if there is a

---

[718] *Young v Chester* [1973] R.T.R. 319. See also such cases as *Hill-Venning v Beszant* [1950] 2 All E.R. 1151 and *Harvey v Road Haulage Executive* [1952] 1 K.B. 120.

[719] para.110.

[720] Not as a salute or recognition between drivers, and certainly not as a warning of a police radar trap or check point ahead if the receiving driver is breaking the law when such a signal could possibly amount to an offence of obstructing police in the execution of their duty. See *Bastable v Little* [1907] 1 K.B. 59; *Betts v Stevens* [1910] 1 K.B. 1.

[721] *Clarke v Winchurch* [1969] 1 W.L.R. 69, which was explained by the CA in *Worsfold v Howe* [1980] 1 W.L.R. 1175; *Leeson v Bevis & Tolchard Ltd* [1972] R.T.R. 373.

[722] See Highway Code, para. 116.

[723] The Road Vehicles (Construction and Use) Regulations 1986 (SI 1986/1078) reg.37, requires the horn to be in working order. The horn must not be sounded at night (11.30 pm–7.00 am) in a built-up area. See Highway Code para.112.

[724] See *Wintle v Bristol Tramways and Carriage Co Ltd* (1917) 86 L.J.K.B. 240; *Smith v Co-operative Group Ltd* [2010] EWCA Civ 725.

[725] e.g. see *Foskett v Mistry* [1984] R.T.R. 1, CA, where it was held that if only the motorist had sounded his horn, on the balance of probabilities the claimant's attention would have been alerted, before running down a slope and thence out on to the roadway in open parkland, thus colliding with the vehicle. See also *Bryce v McKirdy*, 1999 S.L.T. OH, (driver 25 per cent to blame for collision with workman who stepped backwards into the path of her car when she realised he could do so and failed to sound her horn).

movement of the overtaken vehicle such as to put the overtaking driver on inquiry as to what it is going to do.[726]

10–244   It has been held that there is no duty on a motorist to sound a horn, on seeing a pedestrian standing on an adjoining pavement, whether or not that person is showing any signs of leaving the kerb and dashing across the road[727]; nor, on the facts, where a pedestrian was standing still in the middle of the road apparently intending to cross,[728] or when driving through a residential area, although the driver was aware of the slight possibility that a child might suddenly run out into the roadway from behind vehicles parked against the kerbside.[729]

10–245   **Defective vehicle.** The driver or rider of a vehicle has a duty to use reasonable care to keep the vehicle in a roadworthy condition, so that proper control over the vehicle can be exercised. There is no absolute duty in tort to keep the vehicle in proper condition.[730] So, where, owing to a defect in the axle of a lorry, a wheel came off while the lorry was being driven in the highway and damaged a van, there was no liability on proof that the lorry had been returned from the makers two days before, following repairs and an overhaul.[731]

10–246   The owner of a vehicle must take such steps as a prudent owner would take to keep a vehicle in a proper state of repair, maintenance and adjustment. If such care is not taken so that the vehicle is defective, for example, if the steering of a car becomes so worn that the driver's control is compromised,[732] or if the vehicle emits dense clouds of smoke from its exhaust pipe on the highway,[733] it is evidence of negligence. Thus, the driver of a vehicle known to be defective who nevertheless drove it on to the carriageway in foggy weather, where it broke down, bore a proportion of the responsibility for multiple collisions involving many following vehicles, each of which was being driven negligently.[734]

10–247   In *Henderson v Henry E. Jenkins & Sons*,[735] a fatal accident occurred where the brakes of a lorry failed. The brake failure was due to corrosion in a brake pipe

---

[726] *Holdack v Bullock Bros (Electrical) & Co* (1965) 109 S.J. 238.

[727] *Davies v Journeaux* [1976] R.T.R. 111, CA.

[728] *Liddell v Middleton* [1996] P.I.Q.R. P36, CA (where it was observed that it would be quite different if an emergency arose and a pedestrian started to cross the road at a time of danger: the motorist would then be under a duty to sound his horn even if he thereby committed a criminal offence under reg.99(1)(b) of the Road Vehicles (Construction and Use) Regulations 1986).

[729] *Moore v Poyner* [1975] R.T.R. 127, applied in *Saleem v Drake* [1993] P.I.Q.R. P129, CA, but cf. the situation in *Armstrong v Cottrell* [1993] P.I.Q.R. P109, CA. See also *Nolan v Marsh Motors Pty and Holzberger* [1965] Q.L.R. 490 (pedestrian walking out into road from behind vehicles travelling in the opposite direction to the driver).

[730] But as regards the criminal law, see the effect of the Road Vehicles (Construction and Use) Regulations 1986 (SI 1986/1078) and s.2A of the Road Traffic Act 1988.

[731] *Phillips v Britannia Hygienic Laundry Co* [1923] 1 K.B. 539, affirmed [1923] 2 K.B. 832. *Stennett v Hancock* [1939] 2 All E.R. 578 is a similar case.

[732] *Hutchins v Maunder* (1920) 37 T.L.R. 72, where the defendant was held liable, although he was not negligent in failing to discover the defect. In this respect, the case goes too far: see *Phillips v Britannia Hygienic Laundry Co* [1923] 1 K.B. 539, affirmed [1923] 2 K.B. 832.

[733] *Tysoe v Davies* [1984] R.T.R. 88.

[734] *Lloyds Bank Ltd v Budd* [1982] R.T.R. 80, CA.

[735] [1970] A.C. 282.

at a location where the corrosion could not be seen except by removing the pipe completely from the vehicle. The corrosion was unusual and no explanation was given by the defendants for its presence. The House of Lords held that the defendants had not discharged the burden of proving that they had taken all reasonable care. It was necessary for the defendants to prove that nothing unusual had occurred in the history of the lorry to account for the failure.

It has also been held that a purchaser, who buys a second-hand motor vehicle with a valid MOT certificate, is not necessarily relieved thereby of his duty of care in relation to the safety of the vehicle : the existence of the certificate is simply a factor which ought to be taken into account when deciding whether or not his duty has been discharged.[736]

Not only must proper care be taken to see that a vehicle is in a roadworthy condition before it is used on the road, but proper care must also be taken to see that it is properly loaded. When a vehicle was sent out with a load which was negligently secured, and was driven under a low bridge, so that the load was thrown off, injuring a passer-by, the lorry's owner was liable.[737] **10–248**

The fact that a vehicle overturns on the highway,[738] that a wheel comes off,[739] that a tyre bursts,[740] or that any part of the vehicle breaks and causes a collision,[741] is evidence on which, in the absence of a satisfactory explanation, a finding of negligence on the part of the owner can be made. **10–249**

Skidding and violent swerving. The fact that a vehicle, such as a motor-car, is liable to skid on the road in certain circumstances, does not make it a nuisance to use that vehicle on the road.[742] It does, however, make it incumbent on the driver to use additional care, proportional to the greater risk, both with regard to his driving and also to the condition of his tyres.[743] **10–250**

If a vehicle, driven in the roadway, collides with a fixed object or a pedestrian on the footpath,[744] the fact of the accident itself is evidence of negligence against **10–251**

---

[736] *Rees v Saville* [1983] R.T.R. 332, CA, distinguishing *Henderson v Henry E. Jenkins & Sons*, n.95, above. (On the facts, the defendant purchaser was not obliged, before he drove his used motorcar, to have it expertly examined, in the absence of any indication that it was defective ; nor to have the vehicle serviced within a month of its being purchased). See also *Worsley v Hollins* [1991] R.T.R. 252, CA (the existence of a valid Ministry of Transport certificate of roadworthiness was insufficient in itself to discharge the burden of showing that reasonable care had been taken in maintaining the defendant's vehicle).

[737] *Farrugia v G.W. Ry* [1947] 2 All E.R. 565.

[738] *Halliwell v Venables* (1930) 99 L.J.K.B. 353.

[739] *Phillips v Britannia Hygienic Laundry Co* [1923] 1 K.B. 539. It is not, by itself, evidence of negligence on the part of the repairers: *Britannia Hygienic Laundry Co v Thornycroft* (1926) 95 L.J.K.B. 237.

[740] *Barkway v South Wales Transport Co* [1950] 1 All E.R. 392 at 394, 395.

[741] *Templeman v Haydon* (1852) 12 C.B. 507; *Welsh v Lawrence* (1818) 2 Chit. 262; *Cotterill v Starkey* (1839) 8 C. & P. 691.

[742] *Wing v L.G.O. Co* [1909] 2 K.B. 652; *Parker v L.G.O. Co* (1909) 101 L.T. 623.

[743] *Ritchie's Car Hire Ltd v Bailey* (1958) 108 L.J. 348 (driver swerved violently and crashed into a tree on the kerb).

[744] *Chapman v Post Office* [1982] R.T.R. 165, CA (projecting wing mirror struck pedestrian on the pavement).

the driver, even if it is proved that the vehicle skidded into that position.[745] In the past, the mere fact of a skid was thought to be a neutral circumstance which assisted neither party. Hence, it was held to be no defence to the driver to prove that his vehicle skidded, and, equally, it was not held to be evidence of negligent driving on his part.[746] The fact of a skid may suggest, on the one hand, that the driver had been driving too fast or had applied his brakes too fiercely and suddenly, having regard to the road conditions prevailing at the time, so as to be evidence of negligence on his part. On the other hand, the skid may be consistent with the driver's having exercised proper caution but was caused by either the negligence of a third party or an inevitable accident.[747] Nevertheless, the modern approach has been to take an unexplained and violent skid as itself evidence of negligent driving.[748]

10–252   **Opening doors.** It is negligent to open the door of a vehicle,[749] without first taking reasonable care to see that it is safe. So, a passenger in a van was liable in negligence when he opened the nearside door to get out, without taking proper care, as a result of which a pedestrian on the pavement was struck and injured.[750]

10–253   **Obstructions: parking and leaving vehicles on highway.** Where a vehicle is left on the highway the person in charge of it owes a duty of care to leave it in such a place that it will not be a danger to other users of the highway.[751]

ILLUSTRATIONS

10–254   It has been held to be negligent: to park on a bend in a main road when the driver had overshot his turning[752]; to park near road works[753]; to leave a car

---

[745] *Isaac Walton & Co v Vanguard Motorbus Co* (1908) 25 T.L.R. 13; *Barnes Urban District Council v L.G.O. Co* (1908) 100 L.T. 115; *Ellor v Selfridge & Co Ltd* (1930) 46 T.L.R. 236; *Liffen v Watson* (1939) 161 L.T. 351 (the report in [1940] 1 K.B. 556 deals solely with damages); *Laurie v Raglan Building Co* [1942] 1 K.B. 152. The pavement should give security for those persons using it from vehicles using the road and if a pedestrian be injured by a vehicle overlapping the pavement, e.g. by a projecting door handle, then the driver may be liable in negligence: *Watson v Whitney & Co* [1966] 1 W.L.R. 57; *Ottley v L.T.B.*, *The Times*, January 21, 1966 (a pedestrian's foot was run over at a bus stop).
[746] *Laurie v Raglan Building Co* [1942] 1 K.B. 152.
[747] *Hunter v Wright* [1938] 2 All E.R. 621; *Ritchie's Car Hire Ltd v Bailey* (1958) 108 L.J. 348.
[748] *Richley v Faull* [1965] 1 W.L.R. 1454. cf. *Elizabeth v Motor Insurers' Bureau* [1981] R.T.R. 405 where a motorcyclist crashed into the back of a van, which had braked very suddenly, and the CA expressed the view that in these circumstances the burden of proof was on the van driver to explain why had braked in such a manner. See Simmonds, "A Skid as Evidence of Negligence" 130 J.P.J. 283.
[749] It is an offence under the Road Vehicles (Construction and Use) Regulations 1986 (SI 1986/1073) reg.105 to open a door of a motor vehicle on a road so as to cause injury or danger to any other person.
[750] *Brown v Roberts* [1963] 2 All E.R. 263.
[751] It is an offence to leave a vehicle on any road in such a position or in such circumstances as to be likely to cause danger to other persons using the road: Road Traffic Act 1988 s.42; Road Vehicles (Construction and Use Regulations) 1986 (SI 1986/1078), regs 101, 103; *Watson v Heslop* [1971] R.T.R. 308, CA. See also paras 214–226 of the Highway Code.
[752] *Waller v Levoi* (1968) 112 S.J. 865; *Stevens v Kelland* [1970] R.T.R. 445.
[753] *Stevens v Kelland* [1970] R.T.R. 445.

unattended on a slope when the handbrake was out of order and it was kept in position only by a block of wood underneath one of the wheels[754]; to leave a car unattended on a steep gradient, even though it remained at rest for half an hour and the cause of its starting downhill was unexplained[755]; to leave a lorry at the top of a steep and narrow street unattended with the engine running and without taking proper precautions to secure it[756]; to leave a car in such a position that it could be set in motion by a child.[757] There is no rule of law that a clumsily-parked motor vehicle can never give rise to liability in negligence.[758]

It raises a strong presumption of negligence to leave a vehicle unattended on **10–255** a dark road.[759] So, it was negligent to leave a vehicle parked on the right hand side of the carriageway at night[760]; to park at night in a busy main road where other traffic could not pass easily[761]; to stop at night on a road and exhaust the battery of the vehicle by repeatedly trying to start the engine so that compulsory lights were extinguished[762]; to leave a vehicle unlit because of an electrical fault, without displaying a warning sign, albeit on a well-lit clearway.[763] Where an unlit vehicle is left unattended at night and there is evidence of negligence, it is likely also to constitute a nuisance.[764]

Negligence was not established where a lorry broke down at night on a **10–256** clearway and when its rear lights were still illuminated, it was run into by the claimant from behind: it was immobile and the lorry driver had not been negligent in failing to take it into a side road or on to the verge. Nor was it negligent, in the absence of evidence of practice, to fail to provide a lorry driver with a torch or flashing warning light.[765] Where a motor-vehicle was left unattended on a level highway and trespassers moved it backwards into a shop window the owner was not liable.[766] Nor was an owner liable where an unhorsed van was left unattended and children climbed on to it and were hurt.[767]

---

[754] *Martin v Stanborough* (1924) 41 T.L.R. 1.
[755] *Parker v Miller* (1926) 42 T.L.R. 408.
[756] *Hambrook v Stokes Bros* [1925] 1 K.B. 141.
[757] *Martin v Stanborough* (1924) 41 T.L.R. 1.
[758] *Chop Seng Heng v Thevannasan S/O Sinnapan* [1976] R.T.R. 193.
[759] *Parish v Judd* [1960] 1 W.L.R. 867 at 870 and 871, per Edmund Davies J.; *Moore v Maxwells of Emsworth Ltd* [1968] 1 W.L.R. 1077; *Chisman v Electromation (Export)* (1969) 6 K.I.R. 456.
[760] *Abbot Kleysen's Cartage Co v Kasza and Ace Construction Co* [1976] 4 W.W.R. 20. To do so is an offence under reg.101 of the Road Vehicles (Construction and Use) Regulations 1986 (SI 1986/1078).
[761] *Watson v Heslop* [1971] R.T.R. 308; *Young v Chester* [1973] R.T.R. 319.
[762] *Young v Chester* [1973] R.T.R. 319.
[763] *Lee v Lever* [1974] R.T.R. 35; also *Campbell v Gillespie*, 1996 S.L.T. 503, OH (a mechanic extinguished the lights of a lorry parked at the side of a road, in the course of effecting a repair, but parked his own vehicle, which was displaying lights, to the front of the lorry rather than the rear; however, the motorist who collided with the lorry bore 60 per cent of the blame, since there was a police warning sign and other vehicles had seen and avoided the obstruction).
[764] *Maitland v Raisbeck* [1944] K.B. 689; applied in *Parish v Judd*, above.
[765] *Butland v Coxhead* (1968) 112 S.J. 465.
[766] *Ruoff v Long & Co* [1916] 1 K.B. 148.
[767] *Donovan v Union Cartage Co* [1933] 2 K.B. 71.

10–257   If an obstruction in the highway is caused and the claimant can prove some
particular damage over and above mere inconvenience, an action can be
maintained in nuisance, unless the obstruction is authorised by statute.[768] There
may well also be an action in negligence. While it may be a nuisance to leave a
large, wide lorry on the road overnight in a place where it was an obstruction,
albeit under a street light and with its own compulsory lights illuminated, a
claimant who collided with it would also have to establish it was a danger in
order to recover damages for his injuries.[769]

10–258   **Learner drivers, their passengers, instructors and examiners.** The duty of
care owed by a learner driver fell to be considered in *Nettleship v Weston.*[770] The
Court of Appeal held that the duty was the same objective and impersonal
standard as that owed by every driver to every passenger, including the person
teaching her, to the public at large and to the owners of property, both on and off
the highway, in the criminal and civil law.[771] Such a duty is to drive with that
degree of skill and care to be expected of a competent and experienced driver.
The standard of care was not affected or lowered in any way by reason of the
instructor's knowledge of the learner's lack of experience and skill[772] since
uncertainties, endless confusion and injustice would result if, in the law of
England, varying standards were applied according to one person's knowledge of
another's skill or lack of it or whether they were sound or unsound in mind and

---

[768] *Benjamin v Storr* (1874) L.R. 9 C.P. 400; *Fritz v Hobson* (1880) 14 Ch.D. 542; *Vanderpant v Mayfair Hotel Co* [1930] 1 Ch. 138.

[769] *Dymond v Pearce* [1972] 1 Q.B. 496; applied in *Wills v T.F. Martin (Roof Contractors) Ltd* [1972] R.T.R. 368 to a builder's skip, with lights, placed on the road. The meaning of the word "deposited" in the Highways Act 1980, s.139, includes the leaving of a skip on the highway and is not restricted to the act of placing it there: *Craddock v Green* (1983) 81 L.G.R. 235. For cases involving poorly-lit skips, see *Drury v Camden London Borough Council* [1972] R.T.R. 391 and *Saper v Hungate Builder Ltd* [1972] R.T.R. 380 (skip owners and those who collide with them may be liable in varying degrees of fault). See Poole, "Liability for Obstructing the Highway" 115 S.J. 940; Poole, "Skip on Highways" 124 New L.J. 1073; Poole, "Responsibility of Highway Authorities for Traffic Hazards" 125 New L.J. 1059; Williams "Skips on the Highway: Some Tips" 4 C.S.W. 281.

[770] [1971] 2 Q.B. 691 (the claimant, an experienced driver, agreed to give a friend's wife some driving lessons in her husband's own car, whereupon he took her out on the road, with her holding the steering wheel and controlling the pedals, whilst he moved the gear lever and handbrake. She made a mistake and took panic, as a result of which the car, moving slowly, mounted the kerb and struck a lamp standard, injuring the claimant); considered in *Lovelace v Fossum* (1972) 24 D.L.R. (3d) 561 where it was held that the duty of the pupil driver was to use the best skill he has and to obey the instructor in so far as he has acquired the necessary skill (the car got into a skid and the instructor was injured so that the blame was apportioned equally between himself and the pupil).

[771] See the comments about "fault" made by Megaw L.J. in *R. v Gosney* [1971] Q.B. 674 at 680.

[772] Salmon L.J., in disagreeing with the majority on this point, said that the learner could not, in the normal case, owe his instructor a duty to drive with a degree of skill which they both knew he did not possess. ibid. at 704B–C, 705A–B. See Weaver, "One Law for All" 121 New L.J. 634. It is to be noted that the HC of Australia in *Cook v Cook* (1986) 68 A.L.R. 353 took the same view as Salmon L.J. It accepted that in normal circumstances (i.e. in the absence of special and exceptional facts) the standard of care required is the degree of care which could reasonably be expected of an experienced and competent driver. Nonetheless, when the facts are such as to alter the ordinary relationship of driver and passenger, whereby it would be unreasonable for the usual standard of care to apply, these would constitute special and exceptional facts, e.g. the passenger well knew that the driver was unqualified and inexperienced.

limb, eyesight and hearing.[773] Further, it was held that, where the learner driver and the instructor were jointly controlling the driving, they were, prima facie, jointly responsible for the accident and, in the absence of evidence that one or other was to blame, both should be held equally to blame.[774]

A reasonably competent supervising driver may be justified in permitting a **10–259** learner driver to proceed without dual controls, since it is a perfectly natural progression in her training.[775] Further, it was held that whilst his failure to advise the learner on the advantages and disadvantages of wearing her seat belt[776] could amount to negligent instruction, it did not amount to negligence causative of the accident. The relevance of such negligence would only arise for consideration if the supervisory driver had been held liable to the injured learner driver and had alleged contributory negligence against her.

Where a learner driver is undergoing a driving test by an examiner appointed **10–260** by the Secretary of State, such a person does not have the same joint control of the vehicle as a driving instructor. The examiner's sole purpose is to assess the examinee's competence and that will not normally require any interference with the driving.[777] The learner driver owes to the examiner the same duty of care as to any other passenger. However, the examiner may be justified in interfering with the learner's driving if it became essential in the interests of safety.

The owner of a motorcycle was held to have been under a duty, before lending **10–261** it, to warn the rider, whom he knew was inexperienced, about the dangers and difficulties in handling the machine. But the rider, well knowing his inexperience, was equally blameworthy for an accident, in failing to ensure that he knew how to ride the machine properly, before setting off.[778] A breach of statutory duty on the part of a provisional licence holder in driving unaccompanied by a qualified driver, was insufficient in itself to give a cause of action.[779]

Passengers. Passengers, in common with their driver, owe a duty of care to **10–262** each other and to other users of the highway, such as for instance that already dealt with regarding the opening of doors, so as not to endanger other persons or things.[780] But it must surely be arguable that a passenger's duty is not limited to

---

[773] But see *Mansfield v Weetabix Ltd* [1998] 1 W.L.R. 1263, CA (no liability where a driver was unaware that he was suffering from a hypoglycaemic state which impaired his ability to drive, so that his lorry crashed into a shop, the standard of care to be expected being that of the reasonably careful driver unaware of a condition affecting his ability to drive). See also article "Negligent Driving" (1997) 9 Ins. L.M. (5), 5 (discusses liability in negligence where driver suffering from illness).
[774] Megaw L.J. dissented from the majority on this point and considered that nothing in the evidence justified a finding of any degree of contributory negligence of the claimant, the instructor driver. ibid. at 710–711. For the duty of the supervisor of the learner driver, see, e.g. *Rubie v Faulkner* [1940] 1 K.B. 571 at 575, per Hilbery J.
[775] *Gibbons v Priestly* [1979] R.T.R. 4.
[776] For "seat belts," generally, see paras 10–156 to 10–157, above.
[777] *British School of Motoring Ltd v Simms* [1971] 1 All E.R. 317.
[778] *Stermer v Lawson* (1979) 5 W.W.R. 628.
[779] *Verney v Wilkins* (1962) S.J. 879. Further, see generally Ch.12.
[780] See para.10–252, above.

such situations, but could properly be extended to include instances where he has assumed some responsibility to assist the driver, for instance, by warning of danger. Other similar situations might arise: where the passenger agrees to keep a look-out being better placed than the driver to do so; or where advice or directions are given; or where a passenger agrees to look and listen for approaching traffic, including trains at a level crossing[781]; or where the passenger has seen a danger developing, which the driver has apparently missed and fails of it. Nonetheless, the courts have been reluctant to make any findings of contributory negligence against a passenger,[782] even where his proper participation[783] might well have made up for the driver's incompetence[784] and, probably, have avoided an accident.

10–263   **Contributory negligence of passengers.** A passenger who accepts a lift in a car may be held guilty of contributory negligence if either he knew that the driver had consumed an excess amount of alcohol or, knowing that he would be given a lift afterwards, he had accompanied the driver on a bout of drinking[785]; or if he knew that the vehicle was in a defective condition, for example there was no effective foot-braking system[786]; or if he failed to take some precaution, such as wearing a seat belt.[787] Where a passenger travelled in the boot of a car knowing that the driver had consumed excess alcohol his damages were reduced by 30 per cent in respect of his contributory negligence.[788]

10–264   Where the driver and passenger are jointly engaged in some unlawful enterprise, which involves dangerous driving, the defence of ex turpi causa non oritur actio may apply to defeat the passenger's claim.[789] But the maxim volenti non fit injuria cannot be invoked to similar effect since, in the context of a road traffic accident, there is statutory provision which operates to prevent the driver relying upon it.[790] It is not appropriate to make a finding of 100 per cent contributory negligence against a passenger.[791]

---

[781] *Kemshead v British Transport Commission* [1958] 1 All E.R. 119 at 121A–B (per Lord Goddard C.J.) and at 122B (per Denning L.J.); *Skeen v British Railways Board and Scandle (Third Party)* [1976] R.T.R. 281.
[782] *Scandle v Skeen* [1976] R.T.R. 281 (Latey J.).
[783] See the development of this from the duty owed by the supervising driver in the case of a learner driver, referred to in the previous paragraph.
[784] *Rubie v Faulkner* [1940] 1 K.B. 571 at 575.
[785] *Owens v Brimmell* [1977] Q.B. 859. See, further, Ch.4, paras 4–03 to 4–72, above, and "Passengers with Drunken Drivers" 1977 S.L.T. 133; also Roberts and Richard "Riding with a drunken driver and contributory negligence revisited" J.P.I Law 2004, 1, 21.
[786] *Gregory v Kelly* [1978] R.T.R. 426 (such passenger, who had also failed to wear his safety belt, was held 40 per cent to blame for his damage).
[787] *Froom v Butcher* [1976] Q.B. 286. See also paras 10–156 to 10–157, above.
[788] *Gleeson v Court* [2008] EWHC 2397 (Q.B.).
[789] *Pitts v Hunt* [1991] Q.B. 24.
[790] *Pitts v Hunt* [1991] Q.B. 24. The current provision is s.149 of the Road Traffic Act 1998; see also *Morris v Murray* [1991] 2 Q.B. 6 where, in relation to a crash in a light aircraft, the maxim was successfully invoked.
[791] *Pitts v Hunt* [1991] Q.B. 24.

Motorcyclists. The rider and any pillion passenger on a motorcycle, scooter   **10–265**
or moped must wear a protective helmet which must be fastened securely.[792] The
Highway Code advises motorcyclists to wear eye protectors,[793] which, if worn,
must comply with the regulations.[794] Only one pillion passenger can be carried
and the passenger must sit astride the motorcycle on a proper seat and keep both
feet on the footrests.[795] During daylight riding motorcyclists are advised to make
themselves as visible as possible.[796] This involves wearing a light or brightly
coloured helmet and fluorescent clothing as well as displaying a dipped head-
light.[797]

Other cyclists. Much of the discussion above will apply to cyclists as it   **10–266**
applies to other road users. The Highway Code makes specific reference to the
duties of cyclists at paras 59–82. These duties include obligations as to
appropriate lights, and clothing; maintaining cycles in roadworthy condition;
wearing a helmet[798]; keeping a proper look out; and avoiding hazards such as
potholes. In *Smith v Finch*,[799] it was observed that a cyclist could be guilty of
contributory negligence in failing to wear a helmet, even though there was no
legal compulsion to do so, but on the facts the failure to wear a helmet had not
contributed to the extent of the injury suffered and so no reduction was
appropriate. The cyclist is directed not to use bus lanes other than those
displaying the symbol of a bicycle; to grip the handlebars with both hands save
where indicating a manoeuvre, not to carry a passenger unless the cycle has an
appropriate adaptation; and not to carry anything which may adversely affect
balance. For a full account, the reader is referred to the provisions of the Code
itself.

Cyclists may ride across special road crossings called "Toucan Crossings".   **10–267**
These are designed for use by both cyclists and pedestrians who receive an
illuminated signal together.[800]

Pedestrians. Pedestrians have a right to use the highway and may walk on the   **10–268**
carriageway of a road save that it is illegal to walk on a motorway or its slip roads
except in an emergency.[801] Pedestrians can expect motorists to take reasonable
care.[802] Paragraph 1 of the Highway Code advises pedestrians to use pavements

---

[792] Motorcycles (Protective Helmets) Regulations 1998 (SI 1998/1807).
[793] Highway Code para.84.
[794] Motorcycles (Protective Helmets) Regulations 1998 (SI 1998/1807).
[795] Road Traffic Act 1988 s.23.
[796] Highway Code para.86.
[797] For the use of lights generally, see paras 10–235 to 10–239, above.
[798] See generally, Fulbrook, "Cycle helmets and contributory negligence" J.P.I. Law 2004, 3, 171.
[799] [2009] EWHC 53 (QB). See generally, Stanley, "Head case" 150 S.J. 882; Porter Q.C., "Blame
the victim" 159 NLJ 337; Formby, "Wheels set in motion" 153 S.J. 3.
[800] See paras 10–273 to 10–274, above.
[801] Road Traffic Regulation Act 1984 s.17; Motorways Traffic (England & Wales) Regulations 1982
(SI 1982/1163).
[802] *Boss v Litton* (1832) 5 C. & P. 407.

and footpaths where available. It is likely that the failure to use a footpath would be considered to be contributory negligence under modern traffic conditions. Furthermore, a pedestrian is only entitled to expect other road users to exercise reasonable care. If, therefore, there is a footpath available then a motorist can expect a pedestrian, who is not crossing the road, to use the footpath. If under such circumstances a collision occurs a claim made by the pedestrian may fail on the ground that there was no negligence on the part of the motorist.[803] Where a pedestrian was found lying in the road at night having been struck by a van there was prima facie evidence of negligence on the part of the van driver.[804]

10–269   Where there is no footpath, the Highway Code advises pedestrians to walk on the right-hand side of the road,[805] however, it is not necessarily negligent to fail to do so.[806] A driver was negligent when his external wing mirror struck and injured a pedestrian who had been standing on the pavement's kerb.[807] Indeed, the Court of Appeal expressed the view that the pedestrian was not guilty of any contributory negligence, even if she had leaned outwards over the roadway or had had her back to the traffic, or, even, had gone an inch or two on to the roadway.

10–270   The Highway Code also advises pedestrians to wear or carry something light coloured, bright or fluorescent in poor light and to wear something reflective in darkness.[808] Young children should not be out alone on a pavement or road.[809] When walking with children adults are advised to walk between the traffic and the children and to hold their hands firmly.[810] Very young children should be strapped into pushchairs or restrained by reins.[811] The "Green Cross Code" is set out in para.7 of the Highway Code.[812] Although the Green Cross Code advises pedestrians to find a safe place to cross and to use a designated crossing if one is available, there is no legal duty upon a pedestrian to use such a crossing; a pedestrian can cross anywhere so long as he takes reasonable care for his own safety.[813] The Highway Code advises that where there are barriers, pedestrians should only cross at the gaps provided and should not climb over the barriers.[814] A failure to comply with the advice in the Green Cross Code to keep looking and

---

[803] See *Tidy v Battman* [1934] 1 K.B. 319; *Scott v McIntosh*, 1935 S.C. 1996.
[804] *Widdowson v Newgate Meat Corp* [1998] P.I.Q.R. P138, CA.
[805] para.2.
[806] *Kerley v Downes* [1972] R.T.R. 188; *Parkinson v Parkinson* [1973] R.T.R. 216, CA. See also *Powell v Phillips* [1972] 3 All E.R. 864.
[807] *Chapman v The Post Office* [1982] R.T.R. 165, CA.
[808] para.3.
[809] Highway Code para.4.
[810] Highway Code para.4.
[811] Highway Code para.4.
[812] The basic code reads as follows: "**a.** first find a safe place to cross, **b.** stop just before you get to the kerb, **c.** look all around for traffic and listen, **d.** if traffic is coming let it pass and **e.** when it is safe, go straight across the road—do not run." Further advice is given in relation to each section of the code in para.7 of the Highway Code.
[813] *Tremaine v Hill* [1987] R.T.R. 131, CA.
[814] para.9.

listening for traffic whilst crossing the road has resulted in a finding of contributory negligence on the part of the injured pedestrian.[815]

A pedestrian owes a duty to other highway users to move with proper care. **10–271** "When a man steps from the kerb into the roadway, he owes a duty to traffic which is approaching him with risk of collision to exercise due care."[816] Accordingly, where a pedestrian stepped out into the path of a motor scooter, so that the rider fell off his machine and was killed, the pedestrian was liable.[817] A pedestrian, who suffered from attacks of petit mal epilepsy was not negligent when she stepped off a pavement in a state of automatism and caused an accident, there being no evidence that she had received medical advice not to go out alone.[818] A pedestrian is obliged to comply with traffic directions given by a police constable in uniform.[819] It is unlawful for a pedestrian to hold on to a moving vehicle.[820]

On organised walks, if no path is available the group should keep to the left if **10–272** no footpath is available with lookouts stationed to the front and rear.[821] At night the lookout in front should carry a white light and the lookout to the rear should carry a red light.[822]

Pedestrian crossings. There are several types of designated pedestrian **10–273** crossings. "Zebra" crossings are provided for by the Zebra, Pelican and Puffin Pedestrian Crossings Regulations and General Directions 1997.[823] Any driver approaching a zebra crossing must proceed at such a speed so as to be able to stop if necessary. By virtue of reg.25 every pedestrian[824] within the limits of the crossing[825] has precedence over vehicular traffic. If by the exercise of reasonable care, the driver can see that there is a pedestrian on the crossing, it is no defence to prove that, before moving onto the crossing, the pedestrian did not look for the

---

[815] *Hurt v Murphy* [1971] R.T.R. 186 (20 per cent).
[816] *Nance v British Columbia Electric Ry* [1951] A.C. 601 at 611, per Lord Simon; see article "Liability of Pedestrians" 110 S.J. 934; also, *Gilmour's Curator Bonis v Wynn, The Times*, September 28, 1995, OH, Ct. Sess. (claim of pedestrian who suffered permanent brain damage in collision with car failed, where he had placed himself in the road to throw a stick at the car while it was swerving to avoid other similar attacks).
[817] *Barry v McDonald* (1966) 110 S.J. 56; *Nolan v Marsh Motors and Holzberger* [1965] Q.L.R. 490 (the driver of a motorcar does not have to drive in constant expectation that a pedestrian may at any moment project himself into the path of his car from behind a vehicle in a line of traffic on his right, which is moving in the opposite direction).
[818] *Green v Hills* (1966) 113 S.J. 385.
[819] Road Traffic Act 1988 s.37.
[820] Road Traffic Act 1988 s.26.
[821] Highway Code para.5.
[822] Highway Code para.5.
[823] SI 1997/2400.
[824] In *Crank v Brooks* [1980] R.T.R. 441 a person pushing a bicycle over a zebra crossing was a foot passenger within the meaning of the since revoked "Zebra" Pedestrian Crossing Regulations 1971 (SI 1971/1524).
[825] References to the limits of a crossing are to the striped area and not to the area bounded by the zig-zag lines: *Moulder v Neville* [1974] R.T.R. 53.

presence of traffic.[826] Where there is an island in the middle of a zebra crossing each section should be treated as a separate crossing.[827]

10-274 "Pelican" crossings[828] are crossings where the pedestrian can press a button to operate traffic lights. A driver is prohibited from driving on to the crossing when the lights are showing red.[829] A pedestrian also has precedence over vehicles while the light is flashing amber.[830] There are usually two illuminated figures to indicate to pedestrians when they should cross. When the red figure is illuminated it is a warning to pedestrians that in the interests of safety they should not cross the carriageway.[831] A steadily illuminated green figure indicates that pedestrians may begin to cross the carriageway and that vehicles may not enter the crossing.[832] A flashing illuminated green figure indicates to pedestrians, who are already crossing the carriageway, that they may continue to do so and would have precedence over any vehicle.[833] A flashing illuminated green figure indicates to pedestrians, who have not started to cross, that they should not, in the interests of safety, begin to cross.[834] A "puffin" crossing is similar to a pelican crossing except that there are no flashing amber and flashing green figure phases. A "toucan" crossing is similar to a puffin crossing except that there is a facility for cyclists to ride across together with pedestrians. At all crossings pedestrians should check that traffic has stopped before starting to cross.[835]

10-275 The duty created by the regulations is not absolute. In *Burns v Bidder*,[836] the Divisional Court held that there was no breach where the driver who failed to accord precedence to a pedestrian did so solely because his control of the vehicle was removed by the occurrence of an event beyond his possible or reasonable control and in respect of which he was in no way at fault. A latent defect in the vehicle's braking system may therefore be a good defence. If a pedestrian suddenly steps from the footpath on to a crossing, just as a vehicle is about to enter the same area, so that the driver is given no chance of avoiding a collision, there may be no breach of statutory duty, provided that all reasonable care has

---

[826] *Bailey v Geddes* [1938] 1 K.B. 156. But in so far as this case appeared to decide that when a pedestrian on a crossing was struck by a motor vehicle he could not be guilty of contributory negligence it has not been followed: see the cases cited at n.841, below.
[827] Highway Code para.20.
[828] See the Zebra, Pelican and Puffin Pedestrian Crossings Regulations and General Directions 1997 (SI 1997/2400).
[829] Zebra, Pelican and Puffin Pedestrian Crossings Regulations and General Directions 1997 (SI 1997/2400) reg.12.
[830] Zebra, Pelican and Puffin Pedestrian Crossings Regulations and General Directions 1997 (SI 1997/2400) reg.26.
[831] Zebra, Pelican and Puffin Pedestrian Crossings Regulations and General Directions 1997 (SI 1997/2400) reg.15(1)(a).
[832] Zebra, Pelican and Puffin Pedestrian Crossings Regulations and General Directions 1997 (SI 1997/2400) reg.15(1)(b).
[833] Zebra, Pelican and Puffin Pedestrian Crossings Regulations and General Directions 1997 (SI 1997/2400) reg.15(2)(a).
[834] Zebra, Pelican and Puffin Pedestrian Crossings Regulations and General Directions 1997 (SI 1997/2400) reg.15(2)(b).
[835] Highway Code para.18.
[836] [1967] 2 Q.B. 227; Megaw J. in *Kozimor v Adey* (1962) 106 S.J. 431 took a stricter view. See also *Maynard v Rogers* (1970) 114 S.J. 320.

been taken by the driver, having regard in particular to the fact that a crossing is present. In terms of civil liability, the driver could possibly avoid all responsibility,[837] although more usually it is shared.[838] Where a vehicle courteously stopped in front of a crossing for the purpose of giving way to a pedestrian who had not yet moved forward on to it, such vehicle was "stopped for the purpose of complying with regulation 8", within the meaning of reg.10(b), so that other drivers were at fault in trying to overtake it.[839]

The obligation to take care at a crossing does not fall entirely upon the driver. **10–276** The Highway Code reminds pedestrians to allow oncoming vehicles time both to see them and to react to their presence before they step into the road.[840] Where the view of the driver of a bus approaching a crossing was obscured by a taxi, so that he was unable to see a pedestrian upon it with whom he collided, it was held that the driver was in breach of the regulations and liable. However, the pedestrian was guilty of contributory negligence in crossing without first seeing that traffic lights were in her favour.[841]

Where a pedestrian seeks to cross a road either near to or at places other than **10–277** a pedestrian crossing, he or she has no specific precedence and the responsibility for causing an accident more often than not will be shared between the pedestrian and the vehicle driver.[842] Nevertheless, the court has held that a pedestrian may cross a road at any place, provided that reasonable care is taken. There is no obligation to cross the road only at an adjacent or nearby light-controlled crossing.[843]

Pedestrians are warned not to cross directly in front of or behind a bus and to **10–278** wait until it has moved off.[844] Tramways may run through pedestrian areas. Their

---

[837] *Chisholm v London Passenger Transport Board* [1939] 1 K.B. 426; *Sparks v Edward Ash Ltd* [1943] K.B. 223, followed in *Mignogna v Giaccio* (1975) 6 A.L.R. 502.
[838] e.g. *Maynard v Rogers* (1970) S.J. 320 (pedestrian two-thirds; motorist one-third); *Mulligan v Holmes* [1971] R.T.R. 179 and *Clifford v Drymond* [1976] R.T.R. 134, CA (pedestrians 20 per cent to blame). For the liability of a school crossing attendant who allowed a child to run into the road, see *Toole v Newport Corp (Third Party)* [1971] R.T.R. 479.
[839] *Gullen v Ford*; *Prowse v Clarke* [1975] 1 W.L.R. 335.
[840] See para.18–20.
[841] *L.P.T.B. v Upson* [1949] A.C. 155 (the driver and the pedestrian were held equally to blame). See also *Gibbons v Kahl* [1956] 1 Q.B. 59; *Levine v Morris* [1970] 1 W.L.R. 71 and *Goddard v Greenwood* [2003] R.T.R. 10, CA (joggers on a pedestrian crossing controlled by lights were 80 per cent to blame for an accident in which they were struck by the defendant's vehicle, which drove onto the crossing as the lights changed, although he was unable to see beyond a stationary lorry).
[842] In addition to examples involving the use of zebra crossings, there are *Hurt v Murphy* [1971] R.T.R. 186 (deceased, who failed to continue to look to her left whilst crossing over a straight but 30 mph speed restricted road, was held one-one fifth to blame); *Williams v Needham* [1972] R.T.R. 387 (pedestrian who stepped out and began to cross road, never having looked to her right, was held two-thirds to blame); *Powell v Phillips* [1972] 3 All E.R. 864 (no blame on pedestrian); *Moore v Poyner* [1975] R.T.R. 127 (no blame on motorist); *Liddell v Middleton* [1996] P.I.Q.R. P36, CA (motorist and pedestrian equally to blame).
[843] *Tremayne v Hill* [1987] R.T.R. 131, CA.
[844] *Tremayne v Hill* [1987] R.T.R. 131, CA, para.32.

path may be marked out by shallow kerbs, changes in the paving or other road surface, white lines or yellow dots. Pedestrians should cross at designated crossings where available.[845]

10–279   **Horses.** There is no absolute duty imposed on the rider of a horse to prevent it getting out of control, whilst it is being ridden properly along the highway. Where a horse shies, when a motorist was overtaking it, it is incumbent upon the rider to provide an explanation for the horse's sudden movement, sufficiently to negative any inferences of negligence.[846] Where a horse is being ridden along a narrow road, the driver of a vehicle must exercise great caution in passing it, his duty being to slow down and to give it a wide berth. Should this be impracticable, because of another vehicle's approach, then he should stop and wait, before attempting to pass the animal.[847]

10–280   At para.215, the Highway Code provides the following guidance:

> "Be particularly careful of horse riders and horse drawn vehicles, especially when overtaking, Always pass wide and slowly. Horse riders are often children, so take extra care and remember riders may ride in double file when escorting a young or inexperienced horse or rider. Look out for horse riders' and horse drivers' signals and heed a request to slow down or stop. Treat all horses as a potential hazard; they can be unpredictable, despite the efforts of their rider/driver."

10–281   **Led or herded animals.** The rule of the road in relation to horses or other animals, whether they are led, driven, or have a rider, is the same, that is, to keep to the left.[848] It is the duty of a person, leading or driving an animal or a number of animals along the highway, to take reasonable care that they do not cause damage either to other users of the highway or to property adjoining it.[849] If cattle are driven along the highway, it is the duty of the owner to keep them under proper control and to employ an adequate number of persons for that purpose.[850] Accordingly, where a drover failed to keep a heifer under proper control, so that it tossed a woman who was walking along the pavement, the owner was held liable.[851] Likewise where a car collided with a cow at night and the drover had not shown a light or shouted or otherwise given warning.[852] The Highway Code provides at para.58 that if animals are herded after dark, the herder should wear

---

[845] *Tremayne v Hill* [1987] R.T.R. 131, CA, para.33.

[846] *Haimes v Watson* [1981] R.T.R. 90.

[847] *Burns v Ellicot* (1969) 113 S.J. 490; *Carryfast v Hack* [1981] R.T.R. 464.

[848] For the old common law rule that the horse should be led along the right-hand or offside of the road, see early editions of *Charlesworth on Negligence*.

[849] *Deen v Davies* [1935] 2 K.B. 282.

[850] It was not negligent to fail to provide an extra drover on the crest of a rise in an undulating country road, along which livestock were being driven, in order to warn approaching traffic: *Graham v Crawford* [1964] N.Z.L.R. 668. See also para.58 of the Highway Code.

[851] *Pinn v Rew* (1916) 32 T.L.R. 451.

[852] *Turnbull v Wieland* (1916) 33 T.L.R. 143. Cf. *Ludlam v W. E. Peel & Son* (1939) 83 S.J. 832, where the owner succeeded.

reflective clothing and ensure that white lights are carried to the front and red lights to the rear of the herd.[853]

Motorists are recommended to travel slowly past animals in the highway, to **10–282** give plenty of room and be prepared to stop, if necessary. Care should be taken not to frighten animals by sounding the horn or revving up the engine. Motorists should look out for animals being led or ridden and take extra care at left-hand bends and on narrow country roads. If a road is blocked by a herd of animals a motorist is advised to stop and switch off the engine of the vehicle until the herd has left the road.[854]

Dogs on the highway. A collision with a dog in the highway imposes no **10–283** liability on the owner of the dog, unless the owner has been negligent in allowing the dog to be loose.[855] Even before the passing of the Animals Act 1971,[856] it was a general principle of English law (subject to the exception of immunity, when it arose) that a person was liable for injury or damage caused by his animal, as a result of his failure to take reasonable care. As Lord Atkin said:

"It is also true that, quite apart from the liability imposed upon the owner of animals or the person having control of them by reason of knowledge of their propensities, there is the ordinary duty of a person to take care either that his animal or his chattel is not put to such a use as is likely to injure his neighbour—the ordinary duty to take care in the cases put upon negligence."[857]

In *Gomberg v Smith*,[858] after dark, a shopkeeper came out of his shop, **10–284** adjoining a highway in a built-up area, with his St Bernard dog, which was not on a lead. Suddenly it ran across the road, hotly pursued by its owner, before turning back and colliding with a van, which was travelling slowly and on its correct side of the road. The dog owner was liable in negligence for the damage suffered, the rules applying to the escape of animals on to a highway,[859] being inapplicable where the dog was present on the highway as a result of deliberate

[853] In *Andrews v Watts* [1971] R.T.R. 484, a cattle owner, who had herded cattle on a road at night, was guilty of negligence in failing to equip his drovers with some form of lamp or a reflector, in accordance with the Highway Code. See too *Turner v Coates* [1917] 1 K.B. 670 (a colt allowed to travel loose with a mare at night running into the path of a cyclist; liability was established).
[854] Highway Code para. 214.
[855] For the position at common law, see *Gibb v Comerford* [1942] I.R. 295; *Milligan v Henderson*, 1915 S.C. 1030; *Hines v Tousley* (1926) 70 S.J. 732. Only in exceptional circumstances was there negligence in allowing a dog to be loose on the highway, as in *Pitcher v Martin* [1937] 2 All E.R. 918 (dog on lead broke away from person leading it and entangled pedestrians in the lead—owner liable). See also *Jones v Owen* (1871) 24 L.T.(N.S.) 587 (coupled greyhounds injured pedestrian—owner liable). In *Ellis v Johnstone* [1963] 2 Q.B. 80 at Donovan L.J. referred to the fact that if a dog were known to shoot out of a gate on to the highway more like a missile it would be negligent in allowing it so to do.
[856] See para.10–287, below.
[857] *Fardon v Harcourt-Rivington* (1932) 48 T.L.R. 215, 217. The position at common law has not been altered in this regard at all: *Draper v Hodder* [1972] 2 A.B. 556, CA (a pack of Jack Russell terrier puppies made a sudden dash to some adjacent premises, attacked and savaged the three-year-old claimant).
[858] [1963] 1 Q.B. 25.
[859] But, see now the provisions of the Animals Act 1971,s.8, para.10–287, below.

action by the owner. His failure to control the dog was a breach of the duty which he owed to other highway users.

10–285   Further, a person, who causes or permits a dog to be on a designated road, that is a road specified by an order made by the local authority in whose area the road is situated, without it being held on a lead commits an offence.[860] In the event of a motorist having to take sudden action to avoid hitting a dog which had run across his path, it was held that he was not liable for the injuries sustained by his passenger, since he had acted with reasonable care in the circumstances.[861] The Highway Code provides at para.42 that dogs should not be let out on their own and should be kept on a short lead when being walked on or near a road or a path shared with cyclists. Dogs and other animals should be suitably restrained when travelling in vehicles so that they cannot distract the driver and cannot cause injury if the vehicle is caused to stop quickly.[862] A dog should not be let out of a vehicle on to the road unless on a lead.

10–286   **Common law relating to straying livestock.** If cattle[863] which were being driven along the highway strayed from the highway into a shop or other property adjoining the highway, it was evidence of negligence that they were not being kept under proper control, whether because of an inadequate number of persons being employed to drive them or from carelessness on the part of those employed.[864] On the other hand, if there was no negligence on the part of the driver, there was no liability for the trespass of the animal in entering property adjoining the highway. So, where an ox was being driven through the streets of a country town and, without any negligence on the part of those in charge of it, entered a shop which adjoined the street and did damage, the owner was held not to be liable.[865]

10–287   **The Animals Act 1971.**[866] The Act is dealt with in Chapter 14, below. Briefly the common law rules, which excluded or restricted a person's duty to take care to avoid damage being caused by animals straying on the highway,[867] were abrogated by s.8(1). The effect of this section was to remove an exception to the common law, laid down in *Searle v Wallbank*,[868] namely that there was no duty, in the absence of special circumstances, relating to the behaviour of an animal

---

[860] Road Traffic Act 1988 s.27(1).

[861] *Parkinson v Liverpool Corp* [1950] 1 All E.R. 367, applied in *Wooller v London Transport Board* [1976] R.T.R. 206, CA.

[862] Highway Code para.43.

[863] For the state of the law after October 1, 1971, see the effect of the Animals Act 1971, para.10–292, below.

[864] See *Gayler and Pope Ltd v Davies & Son* [1924] 2 K.B. 75 at 87. See Highway Code, para.152 and para.10–281, above.

[865] *Tillett v Ward* (1882) 10 Q.B.D. 17. See now s.5(5) of the Animals Act 1971 and Ch.14, paras 14–84 to 14–85, below.

[866] This Act came into operation on October 1, 1971 by virtue of s.13(3), and gave effect with certain modifications to the recommendations contained in the Law Commission's report on Civil Liability for Animals. See generally Ch.14.

[867] For the common law rules which pre-date the Animals Act 1971, see *Charlesworth and Percy on Negligence* (9th edn, 1997; Ch.9, paras 9–282 to 9–285).

[868] [1947] A.C. 341.

known to the landowner, to fence or maintain existing fences on land adjoining highways, thus to prevent animals straying on to them. Following the Act damage which results from animals straying on to the highways renders their keeper liable to the extent that the damage was caused by his failure to take reasonable care. Section 8(2) makes special provision for the occupiers of unfenced land.

Defences. The general defences available in a negligence action are dealt with in Chapter 4, above. In the present section it will have been observed that on a number of occasions acts or omissions of a highway user have been described "as evidence of negligence". This is to indicate that on proof of the same the court *may* (not *must*) come to the conclusion that there is negligence on the part of the person responsible. Such negligence, if so found, is not necessarily conclusive of the issue of responsibility for the damage, because it may be shown that there was contributory negligence on the part of the claimant, in which event the damages have to be apportioned,[869] or that the negligence of a third party was the real cause of the damage. Evidence of negligence may also be rebutted, albeit rarely, by proving inevitable accident.[870] **10–288**

Suing more than one defendant. A collision may be the result of the negligence of more than one person, in which event an action can be brought against them all jointly, severally, and in the alternative. Judgment may then be given against either one or more but no more than the amount of damages awarded can be recovered by the successful claimant. If judgment has been obtained against one party whose negligence was responsible for the collision, he may obtain contribution from any other party whose negligence also was responsible.[871] If more than one defendant has been joined and judgment obtained against one of them only, the costs payable by the claimant to the successful defendants may be ordered to be included in the costs, which are payable by the unsuccessful defendant to the claimant. This is so, of course, provided that it was reasonable for the claimant to join the successful defendants in the first place.[872] If the defendants before or at the trial attempt to throw the responsibility for the collision upon each other, it will usually be held that the claimant was reasonable in joining them all in the one action. **10–289**

---

[869] Ch.4, paras 4–03 to 4–72, above.
[870] Ch.4, paras 4–128 to 4–136, above.
[871] See the provisions of the Civil Liability (Contribution) Act 1978. See also Ch.3, paras 3–81 to 3–97, above.
[872] *Bullock v L.G.O. Ltd* [1907] 1 K.B. 264.

CHAPTER 11

EMPLOYMENT AT COMMON LAW

1.—COMMON LAW DUTY OF EMPLOYER

(A) Introduction

Generally. At common law an employer may incur liability to an employee   **11–01**
sustaining injury in the course of employment in one of two ways:

(a) vicariously as a result of the negligence of another employee[1]; or

(b) where personally in default of some non-delegable duty of care.

In some circumstances, this liability is joint and several with other employees.[2]
In addition to liability at common law the employer will usually owe statutory
duties: historically by way of the Factories Acts and regulations made thereunder; increasingly since January 1, 1993, contained in regulations introduced
under the Health and Safety at Work, etc. Act 1974, the Framework Directive
89/391 and "daughter" directives which have sprung from the last.[3] These
remedies at common law and under statute are concurrent with, and without
prejudice to, an injured employee's rights to whatever compensation is available
under the Social Security Contributions and Benefits Act 1992. In this chapter,
only the common law duties are considered.[4]

Nature of the duty. The duty of an employer to employees, otherwise than as   **11–02**
imposed by statute, is to take reasonable care for their safety.[5] In the past, there
was no liability for damage suffered through the negligence of a fellow employee
in the course of his employment, when both the employee injured and the
employee who caused the injury, were engaged in a common employment. In

---

[1] See Ch.3, paras 3–98—3–206, above.
[2] See Ch.3, paras 3–99—3–159, above.
[3] See Ch.12, below.
[4] Statutory duties are considered in Ch.12, below.
[5] See Carby-Hall, "Common Law Duties of Employer Towards Employee" 114 S.J. 694 at 713 and
Poole, "Employers not Nursemaids" 118 S.J. 840.

Wilsons & Clyde Coal Co Ltd v English,[6] the general nature of the duty owed by an employer to an employee was described as follows:

"I think the whole course of authority consistently recognises a duty which rests on the employer and which is personal to the employer, to take reasonable care for the safety of his workmen, whether the employer be an individual, a firm, or a company, and whether or not the employer takes any share in the conduct of the operations. The obligation is threefold, as I have explained [i.e. 'the provision of a competent staff of men, adequate material, and a proper system and effective supervision']."[7]

The duty was described as threefold because the doctrine of common employment, abolished with effect from 1945,[8] was then still in existence.[9] It is necessary to have the doctrine in mind when looking at decisions made before it was abolished.

A later formulation of the employer's duty often cited is that of Swanwick J. in *Stokes v Guest, Keen and Nettlefold (Bolts and Nuts) Ltd*[10]:

"the overall test is still the conduct of the reasonable and prudent employer, taking positive thought for the safety of his workers in the light of what he knows and ought to know . . . [W]here he has in fact greater than average knowledge of the risks, he may be thereby obliged to take more than the average or standard precautions . . . He must weigh up the risks in terms of the likelihood of injury occurring and the potential consequences if it does; and he must balance against this the probable effectiveness of the precautions that can be taken to meet it and the expense and inconvenience they involve."[11]

11–03   **Nature of the duty: harm to health.** Whilst much of the jurisprudence relates to the protection of the employee from physical harm by taking measures for physical health and safety, [12] it also extends to the protection of mental health, in the form of a duty to protect an employee from suffering stress at work sufficient to cause psychiatric illness.[13] Other instances of liability for psychiatric injury may arise where an employee is a primary victim[14] or rescuer.[15] However, mere anxiety, for instance arising from physiological change to the lungs, secondary to asbestos exposure, has been held insufficient to found a cause of action. That remains the case whether considered on its own or in conjunction

---

[6] [1938] A.C. 57 at 84.

[7] per Lord Wright, *Wilsons & Clyde Coal Co Ltd v English* [1938] A.C. 57 at 78. There should be added: "a safe place of work".

[8] Law Reform (Personal Injuries) Act 1948 with effect from July 5, 1948.

[9] For a full account, see *Charlesworth on Negligence* (2nd edn, 1947), Ch.25.

[10] [1968] 1 W.L.R. 1776, cited with approval e.g. in *Barber v Somerset CC* [2004] 1 W.L.R. 1089, HL, para.11–86, below.

[11] *Stokes v Guest, Keen and Nettlefold (Bolts and Nuts) Ltd* [1968] 1 W.L.R. 1766 at 1883.

[12] For what physical injury is sufficient to found a cause of action, see Ch.4, para.4–151, above.

[13] *Sutherland v Hatton* [2002] P.I.Q.R. P241, CA, at para.20. See further para.11–84, below.

[14] For the distinction between primary and secondary victims, see Ch.2, paras 2–123—2–134, above. See particularly in relation to employees, para.2–157, 2–160 (involuntary participants); *Monk v PC Harrington* [2009] P.I.Q.R. P3, *Gregg v Ashbrae Ltd* [2006] NI 300, CA.

[15] For rescuers and recovery for psychiatric harm see Ch.2, para.2–155, above.

with physiological change not affecting function, or the risk of future disease.[16] It has been held that the duty of care does not extend to the pursuit and conduct of disciplinary proceedings which did not give rise to any foreseeable risk of injury of a kind capable of sustaining a cause of action in negligence.[17]

Economic harm. The extent to which the duty extends to the financial **11–04** concerns of the employee depends on a specific assumption of responsibility by the employer. Thus it has been held that an employer is not under a duty of care to arrange for suitable insurance for an employee working oversees[18] although a duty may arise if a carelessly researched reference for an employee results in the latter suffering economic loss.[19] An attempt to fix the director of a company employer with liability for failure to insure did not succeed, because there had been no voluntary assumption of risk or responsibility by the director.[20] Failure to advise an employee to join a pension scheme did not result in a breach of duty,[21] although an undertaking regarding housing allowances, did.[22] The Court of Appeal rejected the suggestion that an employer owed a general duty to take reasonable care of an employee's economic well-being where the employee, on medical advice, wrote a letter of resignation which, on acceptance by the employer, had the effect of disentitling him as of right to certain benefits under an employer's insurance scheme.[23]

Duty is personal and not delegable. The employer's duty to an employee is **11–05** a single, personal duty,[24] which is non-delegable,[25] so that the employer must not

---

[16] *Rothwell v Chemical and Insulating Co Ltd* [2008] 1 A.C. 281, Ch.1, para.1–30, above.
[17] *Calveley v Chief Constable of Merseyside Police* [1989] A.C. 1228, applied in *French v Sussex CC* [2005] P.I.Q.R. P243, Q.B.D., for the facts of which see Ch.2, para.2–159, above.
[18] *Reid v Rush & Tompkins Group Plc* [1990] 1 W.L.R. 212.
[19] *Spring v Guardian Assurance Plc* [1995] 2 A.C. 296.
[20] *Burns v Shuttlehurst Ltd* [1999] 1 W.L.R. 1449, CA. The claim additionally failed because it was one for economic loss and that the director's duty to insure was owed primarily to the company.
[21] *Outram v Academy Plastics Ltd* [2001] I.C.R. 367.
[22] *Lennon v Metropolitan Police Commissioner* [2004] 1 W.L.R. 2594, CA.
[23] *Crossley v Faithful & Gould Holdings Ltd, The Times,* March 29, 2004, CA.
[24] In *Wilson v Tyneside Window Cleaning Co* [1958] 2 Q.B. 110 at 123–124, Parker L.J. said: "I think that this case is a very good example of the difficulties that one gets into in treating the duty owed at common law by a master to his servant as a number of separate duties . . . It is no doubt convenient, when one is dealing with any particular case, to divide that duty into a number of categories; but for myself I prefer to consider the master's duty as one applicable in all the circumstances, namely, to take reasonable care for the safety of his men, or . . . to take reasonable care to so carry out his operation as not to subject those employed by him to unnecessary risk." See further the view to the same effect expressed by their Lordships in such cases as *Carroll v Andrew Barclay & Sons Ltd* [1948] A.C. 477; *Latimer v A.E.C. Ltd* [1953] A.C. 643; *General Cleaning Contractors Ltd v Christmas* [1953] A.C. 180; *Richard Thomas and Baldwins Ltd v Cummings* [1955] A.C. 321; *Davie v New Merton Board Mills Ltd* [1959] A.C. 604; *Qualcast (Wolverhampton) Ltd v Haynes* [1959] A.C. 743.
[25] As to the meaning of "personal or non-delegable", in *McDermid v Nash Dredging & Reclamation Co Ltd* [1987] A.C. 906 at 919, Lord Brandon said: "The essential characteristic of the duty is that, if it is not performed, it is no defence for the employer to show that he delegated its performance to a person, whether his servant or not his servant, whom he reasonably believed to be competent to perform it. Despite such delegation the employer is liable for the non-performance of the duty." See Arnheim, "Vicarious Liability and Employment" 132 S.J. 802.

simply take care, he must see that care is taken, by all those persons engaged by him. Judicial definitions have included: "The duty of an employer towards his servant is to take reasonable care for the servant's safety in all the circumstances of the case"[26] and "the duty of taking reasonable care . . . so to carry on his operations as not to subject those employed by him to unnecessary risk".[27] "The ruling principle is that an employer is bound to take reasonable care for the safety of his workmen, and all other rules or formulas must be taken subject to this principle."[28] It follows that the employer's duty is stricter than the duty to take reasonable care for oneself, and it exists whether or not the employment is inherently dangerous.[29]

11–06   An employer at sea is under the same liability as one on land and must have due regard, in the prevailing circumstances, to the reasonable safety of his men and the avoidance of anticipated perils.[30] This duty did not extend to the employer of a fisherman, to direct that a fisherman on watch alone should wear a single chamber inflatable life jacket,[31] because, notwithstanding the fact that such a buoyancy aid would probably have saved the man's life when he fell overboard, at the time responsible authorities had not sought to impose such a duty, nor was it custom and practice on other similar vessels. When a ship's master, armed with a Medical Guide, diagnosed insanity in a member of the crew, the correct test in judging what he should do in the circumstances and therefore his duty of care was: what would the hypothetical reasonably prudent employer, armed with the information in the Guide, have done in the like situation? When injury or death result from the employer's unreasonable failure to follow the recommendations in the Guide, the shipowners will be liable.[32]

11–07   **Statutory duty to insure.** The Employers' Liability (Compulsory Insurance) Act 1969 imposes on every employer carrying on business in Great Britain, a duty to insure and maintain insurance under one or more approved policies with an authorised insurer, against liability for bodily injury or disease sustained by

---

[26] per Lord Oaksey in *Paris v Stepney Borough Council* [1951] A.C. 367 at 384; see also Parker L.J. in *Davie v New Merton Board Mills Ltd* [1958] 1 Q.B. 210 at 237, 238; Lord Somervell in *Cavanagh v Ulster Weaving Co Ltd* [1960] A.C. 145 at 166, 167; Diplock L.J. in *Savory v Holland & Hannen & Cubitts (Southern) Ltd* [1964] 1 W.L.R. 1158 at 1164.

[27] Lord Herschell in *Smith v Baker* [1891] A.C. 325 at 362. This alternative form of expressing the duty is an older way of stating the law, but was used by Singleton L.J. in *Street v British Electricity Authority* [1952] 2 Q.B. 399 at 406.

[28] per Lord Keith in *Cavanagh v Ulster Weaving Co Ltd* [1960] A.C. 145 at 165. Lord Somervell added at 167: "Courts of first instance, whether judge and jury or judge alone, will proceed more satisfactorily if what I have called the normal formula—that is, reasonable care in all the circumstances—is applied whatever the circumstances."

[29] *Speed v Thomas Swift & Co Ltd* [1943] K.B. 557, per Goddard L.J.; *Colfar v Coggins & Griffith (Liverpool) Ltd* [1945] A.C. 197 at 202, per Viscount Simon L.C.

[30] *Saul v St. Andrews Steam Fishing Co* (1965) 109 S.J. 392.

[31] *Gray v Stead* [1999] 2 Lloyd's Rep. 559, CA, reversing [1999] 1 Lloyd's Rep. 377 which had held that such a buoyancy aid should have been provided notwithstanding the fact that such a custom and practice was not followed on similar vessels.

[32] *Ali v Furness Withy (Shipping)*, *Financial Times*, April 22, 1988.

employees and arising out of and in the course of their employment in Great Britain.[33] The Act creates only criminal liability for breach and not civil liability as well.[34]

Transfer of employment. Where a business is transferred to another the effect of reg.5(2)(a) of the Transfer of Undertakings (Protection of Employment) Regulations 1981[35] is to transfer liability for any antecedent negligence of the transferor, together with the benefit of insurance under which the transferor could have claimed indemnity.[36] **11–08**

Relevance of the contractual relationship. The employment relationship itself is based upon contract, but it has been the subject of some controversy in the past whether the common law duties regarding the employee's safety, are contractual, or lie in tort. There is now no doubt that a duty of care does arise under the general law of tort,[37] as expressed in *Donoghue v Stevenson*,[38] the scope of which will vary with the circumstances. In *Davie v New Merton Board Mills Ltd*,[39] Viscount Simonds considered that, although liability was to be regarded primarily as having arisen in tort, it could also be based on implied terms contained in the contract of employment.[40] **11–09**

In *Chesworth v Farrar*[41] Edmund Davies J. said that if the claimant's claim "could be said to be equally poised in contract and in tort, I should have held that the plaintiff could rely upon that aspect which put him in the more favourable

---

[33] The Employers' Liability (Compulsory Insurance) Act 1969 (Commencement) Order 1971 (SI 1971/1116) brought the Act into operation on January 1, 1972. See also the Employers' Liability (Compulsory Insurance) General Regulations 1971 (SI 1971/1117) which became operative on January 1, 1972, except for regs 6 and 7, which took effect on January 1, 1973, specifying exemptions additional to those contained in s.3 of the Act itself. See on the Act Blackshaw, 67 L.S.Gaz. 263 "The Employers' Liability (Compulsory Insurance) Act 1969"; Simpson, 35 M.L.R. 63 and Rowe, "Insurance and the Fault Principle: Some Recent Developments" 123 New L.J. 736.

[34] *Richardson v Pitt-Stanley* [1995] 2 W.L.R. 26, CA. See also *Burns v Shuttlehurst Ltd* [1999] 1 W.L.R. 1449, CA, para.11–04 and n.20, above.

[35] SI 1981/1794.

[36] *Martin v Lancashire County Council* [2000] 3 All E.R. 544, CA.

[37] See particularly those various decisions where there can be no other basis except tortious liability, namely in which an employer's duty of care has been held to extend to persons who are not employed by him, such as a doctor called to assist an injured workman: *Baker v T.E. Hopkins & Son Ltd* [1959] 1 W.L.R. 966, and a volunteer rescuer assisting at a railway disaster: *Chadwick v British Railways Board* [1967] 1 W.L.R. 912 (see Ch.2, paras 2–155–2–156, above); and to workmen who are unpaid by him and on loan from another employer: *Gibb v United Steel Companies Ltd* [1957] 1 W.L.R. 668. (See Ch.3, paras 3–150–3–156, above).

[38] [1932] A.C. 562. Further, see the speech of Lord Radcliffe in *Lister v Romford Ice and Cold Storage Co Ltd* [1957] A.C. 555 at 587 (quoted in the 8th edn of this work at Ch.10, para.10–07) and also *Matthews v Kuwait Bechtel Corporation* [1959] 2 Q.B. 57, per Sellers L.J. at 67 (claimant employed by foreign employer).

[39] [1959] A.C. 604 at 619.

[40] The summary in para.10–06 in the 8th edn of this work was quoted in the speech of Lord Woolf in *Spring v Guardian Assurance Plc* [1995] 2 A.C. 296 at 341, in relation to an employee's safety, to which he added: "It is equally applicable to duties owed in respect of a servant's welfare". See Njoya, "Employment, implicit contracts and the duty of care", [2005] 121 L.Q.R. 33.

[41] [1967] 1 Q.B. 407 at 416.

position."[42] Thus, in respect of a situation where it was appropriate to find that a duty of care had arisen in respect of an employee's economic losses, the Court of Appeal recognised an example of a tortious duty extending beyond the duty owed to the employee in contract.[43]

11–10   **Dismissal from employment and claims for injury.** The interplay of contract and tort in claims for injury in the course of employment, where the background has included the employee's dismissal, has been considered by the House of Lords. In *Johnson v Unisys Ltd*[44] an employee's claim that the manner of his dismissal had caused him psychiatric injury was rejected. The House held that it would not be proper to imply a contract term that the employer would not dismiss the employee in a way likely to cause him psychiatric injury, in circumstances where Parliament had provided a limited remedy for the conduct complained of in the Employments Rights Act 1996.[45] This outcome was perceived as giving rise to problems in those cases in which claimants wished to complain, for example, of injury caused by conduct of the employer which had preceded the decision to dismiss, but might be regarded as leading up to it. The difficulty of knowing where the line was to be drawn was addressed in *Eastwood v Magnox Electric Plc*[46] where Lord Nicholls, in the leading speech, suggested that identifying the boundary was comparatively straightforward: if before the date of dismissal, whether actual or constructive, an employee had acquired a cause of action for breach of contract or otherwise, that cause of action was unimpaired by any subsequent unfair dismissal and the statutory rights flowing therefrom.

It follows that if the claimant has suffered damage, whether financial loss or by way of psychiatric injury, or both, before dismissal, redress is available in the civil courts, without prejudice to the right to claim any entitlement to statutory compensation as a result of the dismissal in the Employment Tribunal.[47]

11–11   **Duty is not absolute.** Irrespective of whether the duty of the employer arises in tort or out of a contract of employment, it is not an absolute one. It can be performed by the exercise of due care and skill,[48] and while:

---

[42] Relevant considerations may be whether the defendant is a minor; remoteness of damage (e.g. *Cook v Swinfen* [1967] 1 W.L.R. 457); periods of limitation; obtaining leave to serve a writ out of the jurisdiction. However it has been said that a duty in tort is not to be imposed so as to increase the duties of the employer under the contract of employment: *Reid v Rush & Tompkins Group* [1990] 1 W.L.R. 212, CA (no duty of care on employer to arrange suitable insurance for an employee working abroad).

[43] *Lennon v Metropolitan Police Commissioner* [2004] 1 W.L.R. 2594, CA.

[44] [2003] 1 A.C. 518. See Morris, "The distressing effects of dismissal", (2004) 3 P.N. 161.

[45] Part X.

[46] [2005] 1 A.C. 503. The House also considered an appeal in *McCabe v Cornwall County Council* [2003] I.R.L.R. 87 but found that the Court of Appeal had been correct to allow the common law action to continue. See Lawson, "All stressed out?" H. & S.L. (2003), 3(2) 13. Hyams, "Bad Manners" 148 S.J. 930; Barnard, "Cherries: one bite or two?" (2006) C.L.J. 27.

[47] *Eastwood v Magnox Electric Plc* [2005] 1 A.C. 503 at 528.

[48] Lord Wright in *Wilsons & Clyde Coal Co v English* [1938] A.C. 57 at 78. See Williams, "Liability for Independent Contractors" (1956) C.L.J. 190, who points out that the duty of an employer to provide proper staff, premises, plant and system of work cannot be delegated to a contractor, although as he says (at 191): "it is not easy to see why the employer should be liable in tort where he has used every care to employ a responsible contractor." cf. Occupiers' Liability Act 1957 s.2(4)(b), which does not, however, apply to employer and employee cases.

"a high standard of care is exacted[49] [it is] desirable in these days, when there are in existence so many statutes and statutory regulations imposing absolute obligations upon employers, that the courts should be vigilant to see that the common law duty owed by a master to his servants should not be gradually enlarged until it is barely distinguishable from his absolute statutory obligations."[50]

Duty is owed to each employee individually. The duty is owed to each
employee as an individual.[51] This means an employer should take into account any peculiarity, weakness or special susceptibility of an employee, which is known or ought to be known. So, for example, where a man, known by the employer to be one-eyed, was employed in a garage, it was held that it was the employer's duty to provide him with goggles while he was employed on work which involved the risk of a fragment of metal entering his remaining eye, even though there might well be no similar duty towards a man with two eyes.[52] The employer's "liability in tort arises from his failure to take reasonable care in regard to the particular employee and it is clear that, if so, all the circumstances relevant to that employee must be taken into consideration."[53] In workplace stress claims, it was pointed out that, although by its nature pysychiatric injury may be more difficult to foresee than physical injury, an employer still owed a duty to individual employees. It might be easier to foresee such a condition in a known individual than in the population at large.[54] Where medical screening of employees revealed the development of hand/arm vibration syndrome, despite an exposure less than the recommended maximum exposure limit, it would be negligent thereafter to continue to expose an employee with that susceptibility to any further vibration.[55] Conversely, if the employer was unaware of his **11–12**

---

[49] Lord Porter in *Winter v Cardiff Rural District Council* [1950] 1 All E.R. 819 at 822. "The law exacts from employers a high standard of care; ignorance and inexperience which result in the creation of unnecessary risk cannot, in law, provide an excuse for departure from that standard": per Barry J. in *Baker v T.E. Hopkins & Sons Ltd* [1958] 1 W.L.R. 993 at 1001, affirmed [1959] 1 W.L.R. 966. See per Morris L.J. at 993.

[50] Lord Tucker in *Latimer v A.E.C. Ltd* [1953] A.C. 643 at 658; also *Chipchase v British Titan Products* [1956] 1 Q.B. 545. See also *Hopps v Mott MacDonald Ltd* [2009] EWHC 1881 (Q.B.): whilst an employer's duty of care required him to take reasonable care to devise and operate a safe system of work what was reasonable depended on the circumstances which here were highly unusual. (Claimant injured travelling in course of his employment in an unarmoured vehicle in Iraq when an improvised explosive device exploded. His claim that an armoured vehicle should have been provided or, alternatively, he should not have been permitted to travel if such a vehicle was not available, failed.) For further discussion see para.11–106, below.

[51] The fact that an employee is, for example, employed as a maintenance fitter, who may be called upon to put right defects that have occurred in the plant and apparatus on the employers' premises, does not alter the general duty owed him, although it might vary those precautions which the employers ought to take in the circumstances: *McPhee v General Motors* (1970) 8 K.I.R. 885.

[52] *Paris v Stepney Borough Council* [1951] A.C. 367; *Porteous v N.C.B.*, 1967 S.L.T. 117; in *Withers v Perry Chain Co* [1961] 1 W.L.R. 1314 it was held that the duty on employers merely was to take all reasonable care, having regard to the fact that the claimant had had dermatitis, which would be likely to recur. See also *Henderson v Wakefield Shirt Co Ltd* [1997] P.I.Q.R. P413, CA, where it was held that, on an employee developing symptoms said to be work-related, it was the duty of the employer to reconsider the equipment provided to her and the system of work even if this had been previously properly evaluated. If no criticism could be found of either, notwithstanding a finding that the claimant's constitutional symptoms were aggravated by the work, there was no obligation on the employer to provide a different type of work.

[53] Lord Simonds in *Paris v Stepney Borough Council* [1951] A.C. 367 at 375.

[54] *Sutherland v Hatton* [2002] P.I.Q.R. P241, CA at [23] and [43].

[55] *Doherty v Rugby Joinery (UK) Ltd* [2004] I.C.R. 1272, CA.

workman's individual circumstances and there were no reasons for holding that he ought to have known of any particular weakness or susceptibility, a finding of negligence on that ground at least, ought to be avoided.[56]

11–13   For similar reasons, a greater care has to be taken by an employer, where a workman is known to have limited experience of the job in hand and is unfamiliar with its dangers: adequate supervision and guidance will be required in order to protect him from the hazard of his own inexperience.[57] On the other hand, where an employee is a highly skilled and experienced, and is known to be aware of the dangers and can be trusted to be left to get on with his work with the minimum of outside direction or interference, the care required may be less.[58]

11–14   Where a job involves risks to health and safety, which are not common knowledge, but of which an employer knows or ought to know and against which it is not possible to guard, there is a duty to inform a prospective employee of them, if knowledge of the risks would be likely to affect the decision of a sensible level-headed workman, whether or not to accept the job in question.[59] Naturally, knowledge can increase with time, research or experience. It will be a matter of expert evidence in each case what knowledge of risks an employer ought to have had on the date the cause of action is alleged to have arisen, the information that should in consequence have been passed to the employee and the safety precautions that should have been taken. The shorthand often used is the "date of knowledge." In *Doherty v Rugby Joinery (UK) Ltd,*[60] Auld L.J. said:

> "Whilst the notion of a general 'date of knowledge' may provide a useful starting point for considering the date of knowledge in any particular case, that is all it is. Looking—as a court must—at each case on its facts, the relevant 'date of knowledge' will vary according, not only to the general nature of the industry in its widest sense . . . but also to the particular type of work within the industry that is under consideration, the tools used by the claimant, the nature and pattern of his use of them and the extent to which . . . the employer in those circumstances should have been put on notice that harm might ensue to the claimant if he, the employer, did not do something about it."[61]

ILLUSTRATIONS

11–15   Shipyards: negligent failure to take precautions to protect employees from noise and the risk of noise-induced hearing loss after 1963[62]; dangers from

---

[56] *James v Hepworth & Grandage Ltd* [1968] 1 Q.B. 94.

[57] *Byers v Head Wrightson & Co Ltd* [1961] 1 W.L.R. 961.

[58] *Qualcast (Wolverhampton) Ltd v Haynes* [1959] A.C. 743 but cf. the situation with that in *McCafferty v Metropolitan Police District Receiver* [1977] 1 W.L.R. 1073.

[59] *White v Holbrook Precision Castings* [1985] I.R.L.R. 215, CA (job involved grinding castings, which set up vibrations that were transmitted to the grinder's hands with to resultant risk of the employer developing hand/arm vibration syndrome.

[60] [2004] I.C.R. 1272, CA.

[61] *Doherty v Rugby Joinery (UK) Ltd* [2004] I.C.R. 1272, CA, at para.[57].

[62] *Thompson v Smiths Shiprepairers (North Shields) Ltd* [1984] 1 All E.R. 881. Where an employer in breach of duty fails to measure noise levels thus making it difficult or impossible for a claimant to prove that he was exposed to harmful levels of noise, the claimant's evidence should be viewed benevolently and that of the employer critically and the employer thereby exposes himself to the risk of being subject to adverse factual findings: *Keefe v Isle of Man Steam Packet Company Ltd* [2010] EWCA Civ 283.

exposure to asbestos.[63] Rubber-processing: risk of bladder cancer from substances used in the process.[64] Arc-welders: risk of contracting lung disease from fumes.[65] Keyboard operators: risk of contracting work-related upper limb disorder from repetitive use.[66] Coal industry: risk of hand/arm vibration syndrome from use of hand-held pneumatic tools foreseeable from January 1, 1973 such that warnings and job-rotation should have been provided from two and three years thereafter, respectively.[67] Motor fitter: an organisation of the size of the defendant should have had knowledge of the risk of harm from vibration at or shortly after the time of publication of BS6842 and made appropriate changes to their working practices within two years of it, and thus, on the particular facts, were negligent from 1989.[68] Train driver: British Rail should have had the knowledge necessary to appreciate the risk to hearing of noise levels in excess of 85dB(A) leq from 1973 at the latest.[69] Riveters, platers and welders in the rail industry should have been warned by British Rail Engineering of the risk of harm from vibration by the end of 1973 with a system of regular medical examination of exposed employees in place by the end of 1974.[70] From early

---

[63] *Smith v P. & O. Bulk Shipping Ltd* [1998] 2 Lloyd's Rep. 81: dangers from use of asbestos in shipyards. See also *Executors of the Estate of O'Toole (Deceased) v Eireann Irishrail* [1999] C.L.Y. 3961: exposure to asbestos dust between 1950 and 1955; *Shell Tankers UK Ltd v Jeromson* [2001] P.I.Q.R. P265, CA: risk to marine engineers from asbestos in ships in the 1950s; *Rice v Secretary of State for Trade and Industry* [2007] P.I.Q.R. P23, CA (dock workers unloading from ships hessian sacks filled with asbestos).The Court of Appeal has held that pleural plaques arising as a result of asbestos inhalation do not constitute an "injury": For the extent of harm to an individual as a result of exposure to asbestos necessary to found a cause of action in negligence, see *Rothwell v Chemical & Insulating Co Ltd* [2007] 3 W.L.R. 826, HL, Ch.1, para.1–30, above.
[64] *Wright v Dunlop Rubber Co Ltd and ICI Ltd* (1972) 13 K.I.R. 255.
[65] *Cartwright v GKN Sankey Ltd* (1973) 14 K.I.R. 349.
[66] *McSherry v British Telecommunications Plc* [1992] 3 Med.L.R. 129. See generally, Andoh, "Work-related upper limb disorders: employers beware" 2002 P. & M.I.L.L. 18(4), 2.
[67] *Armstrong v British Coal Corp, The Times*, December 6, 1996, CA. But compare *Heyes v Pilkington Glass Ltd* [1998] P.I.Q.R. P303, CA: risk of hand/arm vibration syndrome from electrically operated cranes not generally appreciated in the industry in the period up to 1987. See *Doherty v Rugby Joinery (UK) Ltd* n.55 above: the defendant, a door and window manufacturer, was in breach of a duty to monitor certain employees for the risk of hand/arm vibration syndrome from 1991–92. It was no defence that had the claimants' symptoms come to light, investigation would have shown that their use of vibratory tools did not exceed the recommended limits, since even if the employer had concluded that the symptoms had arisen in spite of exposure for less than the recommended maximum period, it would have been negligent to permit such employees to work with vibratory tools at all. See also *Brown v Corus (UK) Ltd* [2004] P.I.Q.R. P476, CA, where it was said that once it was proved that a claimant was subject to excessive vibration, the burden shifted to the defendant to justify why that situation was allowed to continue. See Ch.6, para.6–02, above. For a discussion of apportionment in a case of mixed non-guilty and guilty exposure, see *Rugby Joinery UK Ltd v Whitfield* [2006] P.I.Q.R. Q40, CA. See generally, Maddocks, "The British Coal vibration white finger litigation" J.P.I. Law 2006, 2, 199.
[68] *Brookes v South Yorkshire Passenger Transport Executive* [2005] EWCA Civ 452. The court stressed that the result was not a finding of general application that liability for hand/arm vibration syndrome in fitters in the transport industry arose in 1989: each case would depend on its facts. Contrast *Gray v Vesuvius Premier Refractories (Holdings) Ltd* [2006] 1 C.L. 309: former millman failed to establish that his employers should have foreseen that he was exposed to harmful vibration from the use of a jigger pick. See now the Control of Vibration at Work Regulations 2005 (SI 2005/1093) implementing the Vibration Directive 2002/44/EC with effect from July 6, 2005.
[69] *Harris v BRB Residuary Ltd* [2006] P.I.Q.R. P101, CA.
[70] *Allen v British Rail Engineering Limited* [2001] I.C.R. 942, CA.

1977 an employer of average size in the knitting industry, who had exposed his employees to 85dB(A)lepd or more without protection was in breach of its duty.[71]

On the other hand, where a typist alleged that she had been required to use a word-processor for long periods and thereby developed a strain injury to the hands, it was not necessary for her employers to warn her to take rest breaks from time to time where she had ample scope to interpose typing with non-typing work. It could reasonably be expected that a person of her intelligence and experience would break up the pattern of work without being told.[72]

11–16   **Duty to third party.** Where an employee had not himself been exposed to risk while driving lorry-loads of lead oxide waste from a site to a tip, it was held that no duty of care was owed by the employers to his wife, in spite of the fact that she had been exposed to a foreseeable and significant risk from inhaling dry dust of oxide during the handling, washing, and cleaning of her husband's work-clothes and had thereafter contracted lead poisoning.[73] However, where the deceased and another contracted mesothelioma as a result of exposure to asbestos dust emitted from a factory in the vicinity of his home, his widow established liability against the factory owners, on the basis that they ought to have known that dust emissions created conditions in the immediate vicinity of the factory approximating to those actually within it. Since those conditions raised a risk of personal injury that was notorious and the presence of children such as the deceased close to the factory was known to the owners, it was reasonably foreseeable that they would inhale asbestos dust and thereby be injured. The fact that the claimants were not employees of the owners did nothing to absolve the latter's liability.[74] On the other hand, where the wife of one of the defendant's employees developed mesothelioma as a result of exposure to asbestos dust brought home on her husband's workclothes, her claim for damages failed because, prior to 1965, it was unreasonable to expect a prudent employer to have appreciated the risk from asbestos dust to members of employees' families.[75]

---

[71] *Baker v Quantum Clothing Group* [2009] EWCA Civ 499 (on the facts, a reasonable time for the provision of ear protectors once the decision had been taken that they should have been provided would have been six to nine months and the defendant should therefore have taken that action by January 1978.

[72] *Pickford v Imperial Chemical Industries Plc* [1998] 1 W.L.R. 1189, HL. See also *Alexander v Midland Bank Plc* [1999] I.R.L.R. 723, CA: part-time encoders required to enter numerical data by means of a keyboard. For another example of an employer escaping liability where the employee ought to have used his common sense (for a task for which no instructions could appropriately have been given), see *Devizes Reclamation Co Ltd v Chalk*, *The Times*, April 2, 1999. Also *Wingrove v Employment Service* [2001] C.L.Y. 4471 (employee injured her neck sitting in draught due to defective air conditioning system: since she was a mature adult, it was not necessary for the employer to order her to sit out of the draught).

[73] *Hewett v Alf Brown's Transport Ltd* [1992] I.C.R. 530, CA, where it was also found that the defendants were not in breach of either common law or statutory duties owed to an employee, the claimant's husband, under the provisions of the Control of Lead at Work Regulations 1980 (SI 1980/1248) reg.8.

[74] *Margereson v J.W. Roberts Ltd* [1996] P.I.Q.R. P154, Holland J.

[75] *Maguire v Harland & Wolff Plc* [2005] P.I.Q.R. P243, CA.

(B) Elements of the duty

Introduction. Although a single, personal duty,[76] in order to understand **11–17**
properly its scope, the employer's duty needs to be considered under five
separate heads, which may frequently overlap[77]: (i) to provide a safe place of
work, including a safe means of access; (ii) to employ competent employees and
supervision; (iii) to provide and maintain adequate plant and appliances; (iv) to
provide a safe system of work; and (v) other cases. It is proposed to deal with
each in turn below.

(i) *Safe place of work*

The duty of employers to provide their workmen with a safe place of work was **11–18**
said by Goddard L.J. to be "not merely to warn against unusual dangers known
to them, . . . but also to make the place of employment . . . as safe as the exercise
of reasonable skill and care would permit."[78] The duty thus described is a higher
one than the rule in *Indermaur v Dames,* in which the origins of the law relating
to occupiers' liability are to be found.[79] The language used suggests that it was
intended to indicate the duty owed to persons entering premises under a
contract.[80] The employer's duty is to see that care is taken and he is liable even
if the failure to exercise reasonable care and skill is that of an independent
contractor. The employer is excused from liability only if the danger is due to a
latent defect, not discoverable by reasonable care and skill on the part of anyone.[81]

Generally, for the duty to be fulfilled, the place of work must have such **11–19**
protective devices as experience has shown to be desirable in other working
places of the same or a similar kind. Even where those other working places do
not have such devices provided, that will not necessarily absolve the employers
from liability.

---

[76] *Wilson v Tyneside Window Cleaning Co* [1958] 2 Q.B. 110 at 123–124, per Parker L.J. See
para.11–05, n.24, above.
[77] See *Winter v Cardiff Rural District Council* [1950] 1 All E.R. 819 at 823, per Lord MacDermott
that they "are not absolute in nature. They lie within and exemplify, the broader duty of taking
reasonable care for the safety of his workmen which rests on every employer."
[78] *Naismith v London Film Productions Ltd* [1939] 1 All E.R. 794 at 798; *Ebbs v James Whitson &
Co Ltd* [1952] 2 Q.B. 877; *Graham v Co-operative Wholesale Society Ltd* [1957] 1 W.L.R. 511;
Newland v Rye-Arc [1971] 2 Lloyd's Rep. 64. Further, an employer is under a duty to his employees
to take adequate precautions against risk from fire: *Nicholls v Reemer, Waugh & Reemer* (1957) 107
L.J. 378.
[79] (1866) L.R. 1 C.P. 274. The common law duties laid down in that case were, as from January 1,
1958, abolished as between occupiers of premises and their invitees and licensees. The common duty
of care laid down by ss.2 and 3 of the Occupiers' Liability Act 1957 was substituted.
[80] See Ch.8, "The duty of a master to his servant is higher than that of an invitor to an invitee", Lord
Porter in *London Graving Dock v Horton* [1951] A.C. 737; see also per Denning L.J. in *Christmas
v General Cleaning Contractors* [1952] 1 K.B. 141 at 148. The duty owed to persons entering
premises, when it is based on an implied term of the contract under which they enter, is now altered
by s.5 of the Occupiers' Liability Act 1957, but it does not affect the law stated in the text.
[81] But contrast the position under reg.5 of the Workplace (Health, Safety and Welfare) Regulations
1992, discussed at Ch.12, para.12–117 et seq., below.

ILLUSTRATIONS

11–20   The deceased, engaged in concreting the side of a dry dock working, slipped and fell to his death from an unfenced ledge, some 2 feet 6 inches wide, approximately 40 feet above the bottom of the dock. Despite the fact that such work had been going on for three years without complaint or mishap, the employers were found liable because the danger was such that some protection ought to have been provided.[82] A fitter's mate was electrocuted whilst working in a kiosk housing electricity transformers because there had been a failure to insulate the full length of the kiosk. The employers were held liable for their failure to provide a safe place of work.[83] It was said that this was a non-delegable duty and it was no answer to say that competent contractors had been engaged to provide a safe place or plant.[84] Further, the fact that the claimant was an experienced employee who had never complained about the safety of his workplace was equally no answer.[85] Where a fisherman on watch alone was lost and presumed drowned, the fact that the responsible authorities had not imposed a duty to wear a single chamber inflatable life jacket and, further, that custom and practice on other vessels did not include the wearing of such a life jacket absolved the employer from his failure to provide one in 1994.[86]

11–21   It has been suggested that the employer's duty as to the condition of the premises is less than that in respect of the plant and appliances,[87] but this is at variance with the authorities quoted above[88] and the probability is that the two responsibilities are very much alike. The duty to provide a safe place of work is fulfilled by providing a place as safe as care and skill can make it, having regard to the nature of the place. This may involve having to take competent advice about, for example, what precautions ought to be taken, such as the fitting of some form of sound-proofing materials.[89] If the workman is working on a scaffold or a roof, it must be a safe scaffold or roof. No complaint can be made that working there is not as safe as working on level ground. As long as the employer makes the working place as safe as it can reasonably be made, he has satisfied his obligation. Thus, situations often arise where there are possible dangers, the risk of which a prudent employer can foresee and yet the particular danger cannot be removed either easily or at all.

ILLUSTRATIONS

11–22   The employer's duty in such circumstances is to take reasonable precautions for his workmen's safety, which could involve the provision of fencing around a

---

[82] *Bath v British Transport Commission* [1954] 1 W.L.R. 1013.
[83] *Paine v Colne Valley Electricity Co* [1938] 4 All E.R. 803 at 807.
[84] per Goddard L.J. in *Paine v Colne Valley Electricity Co* [1938] 4 All E.R. 803 at 807. See especially *Riverstone Meat Co Proprietary Ltd v Lancashire Shipping Co Ltd* [1961] A.C. 807; *Sumner v William Henderson & Sons Ltd* [1963] 1 W.L.R. 823.
[85] *McCafferty v Metropolitan Police District Receiver* [1977] 1 W.L.R. 1073.
[86] *Gray v Stead* [1999] 2 Lloyd's Rep. 559, CA, reversing [1999] 1 Lloyd's Rep. 377.
[87] See para.11–44, below.
[88] In *Davison v Handley Page Ltd* [1945] 1 All E.R. 235, Lord Greene M.R. said at 237: "I very much doubt the correctness of that proposition."
[89] *McCafferty v Metropolitan Police District Receiver* [1977] 1 W.L.R. 1073.

tank at a sewage-pumping station[90]; adequate fencing to meet the risk of an employee falling off a narrow platform, whilst working with his back to a steep drop[91]; a handrail on a short but steep and irregular flight of steps[92]; a safety belt to save a ship's painter from falling whilst working from slippery steps in a dry dock[93]; a guard-rail round the open hatchway giving access to the 'tween deck of a ship out at sea[94]; a handhold on a crawling ladder used for carrying buckets of cement up on to a roof[95]; the fitting of some form of sound-proofing to a reverberant gun room where firearms were constantly being discharged for forensic purposes[96]; a thorough inspection of and not merely a cursory glance at the face of a quarry, before work was commenced beneath it, especially during or after inclement weather, which would loosen the stones[97]; a line of demarcation on a roof, over which a ropeway was operated[98]; a different type of engine so that the driver was not obliged to lean out of the cab to observe a signal placed near a bridge with an unusually narrow clearance[99]; the re-siting of a vertical points lever which had a clearance of only eight inches between it and a passing locomotive's steps, on which shunters habitually stood to ride[100]; a fence to divide the British Transport Commission's railway lines from a private line along which workmen were accustomed to walk[101]; a warning of the presence of shale from a colliery dirt stack which narrowed the route of a walking space alongside a railway track[102]; making inquiry into the safe level of exposure to fumes given off by X-ray chemicals and reducing an employee's exposure thereto[103]; a warning not to go upon a roof where there was a risk of slipping and falling through a skylight[104]; the opportunity to train drivers to wear ear protectors when driving noiser trains.[105]

On the other hand, it was held that the employer's duty to take reasonable **11–23** precaution for his workmen's safety did not include fencing the edge of a sloping roof.[106] It was not negligent to fail to provide a handrail to steps until after the claimant's accident because, on the facts, the steps were safe and the precaution taken after the event did not establish that they were unsafe prior to the

---

[90] *McIlhagger v Belfast Corp*, 1944 N.I. 37.
[91] *Bath v British Transport Commission* [1954] 1 W.L.R. 1013.
[92] *Kimpton v Steel Co of Wales Ltd* [1960] 2 All E.R. 274.
[93] *Hurley v J. Sanders & Co Ltd* [1955] 1 W.L.R. 470.
[94] *Morris v West Hartlepool Steam Navigation Co Ltd* [1956] A.C. 552.
[95] *Cavanagh v Ulster Weaving Co Ltd* [1960] A.C. 145.
[96] *McCafferty v Metropolitan Police District Receiver* [1977] 1 W.L.R. 1073.
[97] *Sanderson v Millom Hematite Ore & Iron Co Ltd* [1967] 3 All E.R. 1050.
[98] *Quintas v National Smelting Co Ltd* [1961] 1 All E.R. 630.
[99] *McArthur v British Railways Board* (1968) 6 K.I.R. 40 (alternatively the engine should have been re-routed).
[100] *Hicks v British Transport Commission* [1958] 1 W.L.R. 493. See note on this case, 74 L.Q.R. 337.
[101] *Braithwaite v South Durham Steel Co Ltd* [1958] 1 W.L.R. 986.
[102] *Westwood v N.C.B.* [1966] 1 W.L.R. 682 (sub nom. *Smith v N.C.B.* in the HL [1967] 1 W.L.R. 871).
[103] *Ogden v Airedale Health Authority* [1996] 7 Med. L.R. 153.
[104] *Parker v PFC Flooring Supplies Ltd* [2001] C.L.Y. 4491, CA, Ch.4, para.4–71, above: it was foreseeable that the claimant, a sales director of the defendant company, would go upon the roof to investigate a wire thought to have been placed by burglars or vandals.
[105] *Harris v BRB Residuary Ltd* [2006] P.I.Q.R. P101, CA.
[106] *Regan v G. & F. Asphalt Co Ltd* (1967) 2 K.I.R. 666.

installation of the handrail.[107] Nor was an employer obliged to provide a single chamber inflatable life jacket in the case of a fisherman on watch alone on a trawler together with a direction that it be worn in 1994 when the responsible authorities had imposed no such duty and it was not the custom and practice on other similar vessels.[108] It was not, on the facts, unreasonable for the claimant, who was injured when an improvised explosive device was detonated, to be carried around Basra in the aftermath of the Second Gulf War in an unarmoured vehicle.[109]

11–24   **Common law duty compared with statutory duty.** The employer's duty at common law is unlikely to be higher than that imposed by any relevant statutory duty. In the context of ss.28 and 29 of the Factories Act 1961,[110] Lord Tucker warned "that the courts should be vigilant to see that the common law duty owed by a master to his servant should not be gradually enlarged until it is barely distinguishable from his absolute statutory obligations."[111] More often than not, the statutory obligation will impose a higher duty on the employers than at common law,[112] absolute liability now being imposed with regard to a wide range of situations within and including the workplace.[113] So, where the claimant fell and hurt himself whilst trying to climb some ice-covered steps leading up to an office block at work, it was held that the defendant was liable, the court observing that it was a case where the statutory duty was higher than the common law duty and the claimant had failed to establish a breach of the latter.[114]

11–25   On the other hand, an employer can be found guilty at common law of a breach of his duty of care but is not necessarily in breach of his statutory duty thereby, in respect of the same matter.[115]

11–26   **Temporarily unsafe conditions.** Apart from the nature of its construction, a place of work may become unsafe owing to some temporary condition or some obstruction being created on it. In such a case, the test to be applied is whether or not a reasonably prudent employer would have caused or permitted the existence of that state of affairs of which the complaint is made. It follows that the question of what constitutes a breach of his duty in any given set of circumstances must be one of degree.

---

[107] *Coates v Jaguar Cars Ltd* [2004] EWCA Civ 337.

[108] *Gray v Stead* [1999] 2 Lloyd's Rep. 559, CA.

[109] *Hopps v Mott MacDonald Ltd* [2009] EWHC 1991 Q.B. See para.11–106, below.

[110] Which came into force on April 1, 1962, and repealed the Factories Acts 1937–59. Under the 1937 Act the relevant sections were s.25 and s.26. See the earlier decision of *Thomas v Bristol Aeroplane Co Ltd* [1954] 1 W.L.R. 694. This only dealt with s.26 but the observations of Somervell L.J. at 697 applied equally to s.25. For the duties imposed by these sections see Ch.11 of the 9th edn of this work. They are themselves repealed with regard to all workplaces as from January 1, 1996: The Workplace (Health, Safety and Welfare) Regulations 1992 (SI 1992/3004).

[111] *Latimer v A.E.C. Ltd* [1953] A.C. 643 at 658.

[112] See *Trott v Smith (Erectors) Ltd* [1957] 1 W.L.R. 1154 at 1158, per Jenkins L.J.

[113] See, e.g. *Malcolm v Commissioner of Police of the Metropolis* [1995] C.L.Y. 2880, Q.B.D.: reg.5 of the Workplace (Health, Safety and Welfare) Regulations 1992; *Stark v The Post Office* [2000] P.I.Q.R. P105, CA: reg.6 of the Provision and Use of Work Equipment Regulations 1992.

[114] *Powley v Bristol Siddeley Engines Ltd* [1966] 1 W.L.R. 729 at 732, per Megaw J.

[115] *Bath v British Transport Commission* [1954] 1 W.L.R. 1013, for the facts of which see para.11–20, above.

ILLUSTRATIONS

Where a place has become unsafe, because of some temporary or exceptional **11–27** danger (for example, an unexploded shell) and the only knowledge of the danger was that of fellow employees, who were neither foreman nor chargehands, it has been held that the employers were not in breach of their duty to provide a safe place of work, because such knowledge could not be imputed to them.[116] When a workman slipped on a patch of oil or water or both which had accumulated, possibly in a depression, on the concrete floor of a passage in a factory, it was said that it was impossible to say that the mere existence of these conditions "indicates any failure to take reasonable care to protect those employed from unnecessary risk".[117] When the entrance to a factory became slippery following a sudden fall of snow, which froze as it fell shortly before the factory opened, and a workman slipped on entering, the employers were held not liable, on the ground that there had been no failure to exercise reasonable care.[118] A fire authority was not negligent where a station officer slipped and hurt himself on a tiled floor after water, ubiquitous in the station, leaked from the valve of a fire appliance pump.[119]

In *Latimer v A.E.C. Ltd*,[120] as a result of an exceptionally heavy storm, the **11–28** floor of the factory became flooded. After the water had drained away, it left an oily film on the floor, which was slippery. Sawdust was put down but, because of the large area of floor involved, there was insufficient to cover it all and a workman slipped on a part of the floor that had not received any sawdust. It was said that the only question was, "Has it been proved that the floor was so slippery that, remedial steps not being possible, a reasonably prudent employer would have closed down the factory rather than allow his employees to run the risks involved in continuing work?"[121] As there was no evidence of any complaint or of any other person being in difficulty from the floor, the employers were held not liable, since they had taken all reasonable steps to deal with the conditions short of closing the factory or part of it, which would have been unreasonable in the circumstances.

Where a workman had been brought to the scene of a spillage of some slippery **11–29** substance, which had been allowed negligently to escape on to the floor, and charged expressly with the duty of cleaning up the mess with a squeegee, it was held that there was no reasonably foreseeable risk that he would slip and hurt

[116] *O'Reilly v National Rail and Tramway Appliances Ltd* [1966] 1 All E.R. 499.
[117] per Somervell L.J. in *Davies v De Havilland Aircraft Co* [1951] 1 K.B. 50 at 52.
[118] *Thomas v Bristol Aeroplane Co* [1954] 1 W.L.R. 694. No breach of the employers' common law duty was proved in *Powley v British Siddeley Engines* [1966] 1 W.L.R. 729 but Megaw J. held that there had been a breach of s.28 of the Factories Act 1961 in their failure to have the office steps cleared of ice, the statutory obligation being a higher duty than the common law duty in the circumstances. Similarly, see *Woodward v Renold* [1980] I.C.R. 387, where the employers had failed to grit in icy weather the area of the car park near to a footpath which was used extensively by their workmen walking up to the factory's entrance.
[119] *Dixon v London Fire and Civil Defence Authority*, [1993] 157 L.G.R. 1001.
[120] [1953] A.C. 643.
[121] *Latimer v A.E.C. Ltd* [1953] A.C. 643 per Lord Tucker at 659.

himself in the course of performing such a simple duty.[122] It may be sufficient to have a system whereby employees are themselves responsible for clearing away dangerous debris from the immediate vicinity of their work places.[123]

11–30   **Working in adverse conditions.** Where an employer required his employee to drive a van, which was not fitted with a heater in extreme wintry conditions on a long journey, so that he was exposed to considerable fatigue and a prolonged period of intense cold, thereby risking his health, the employer was held liable in respect of the injury sustained from frostbite.[124] It would not necessarily be negligent for the employer to require his employee to undertake such driving work for a long journey provided that he was supplied with sufficient warm clothing, suitable appliances or other such equipment adequately to protect him against the foreseeable risks of exposing him to the rigours of a hard winter.

11–31   **Employee gaining access to or working on another's premises or plant.** The general duty of an employer to his employee to take reasonable care for his safety does not come to an end merely because the workman has been sent to work at premises which are occupied by a third party and not by the employer. The duty remains throughout the whole of the course of his employment.[125] What will vary in each case is the degree of care to be taken by the employer: "The duty is there, whether the premises on which the workman is employed are in the occupation of the master or of a third party; but what reasonable care demands in each case will no doubt vary."[126] It was also said that:

> "The master's own premises are under his control: if they are dangerously in need of repair he can and must rectify the fault at once if he is to escape the censure of negligence. But if a master sends his plumber to mend a leak in a respectable private house, no one could hold him negligent for not visiting the house himself to see if the carpet in the hall creates a trap. Between these extremes are countless possible examples in which the Court have to decide the question of fact."[127]

11–32   Performance of the duty to provide a safe place of work will become more difficult where that place is in the occupation or control of another. Before sending men to work at a particular location the employer may[128] have to inspect

---

[122] *Vinnyey v Star Paper Mills* [1965] 1 All E.R. 175, per Cumming-Bruce J.

[123] *Stanley v Concentric (Pressed Products)* (1971) 11 K.I.R. 260, CA.

[124] *Bradford v Robinson Rentals Ltd* [1967] 1 W.L.R. 337.

[125] *General Cleaning Contractors Ltd v Christmas* [1953] A.C. 180 (window cleaners); *Thomson v Cremin* [1956] 1 W.L.R. 103, PC (stevedores); *Smith v Austin Lifts Ltd* [1959] 1 W.L.R. 100 (lift engineers); *McCloskey v Western Health and Social Services Board* [1983] 4 N.I.J.B., CA (visiting social workers).

[126] per Parker L.J. in *Wilson v Tyneside Window Cleaning Co* [1958] 2 Q.B. 110 at 124.

[127] *Wilson v Tyneside Window Cleaning Co* [1958] 2 Q.B. 110 per Holroyd Pearce L.J., at 121–122.

[128] See per Lord Wright in *Thomson v Cremin* [1956] 1 W.L.R. 103 at 111: "To hold a master stevedore in the absence of special circumstances of suspicion subject to a general duty towards his men to inspect the structure of the vessel, whether permanent or temporary, whether shifting-boards, stanchions or the like, would, I think, be contrary to practice and inconsistent with the exigencies of the case." Followed in *Szumczyk v Associated Tunnelling Co* [1956] 1 W.L.R. 98 (contractors down a coal mine may reasonably rely on the occupiers, namely the NCB, as regards providing proper support of the roof).

the place of work to establish that it is reasonably safe for the work proposed.[129] Indeed, as will be seen in Chapter 12, the current statutory framework is underpinned by the concept of "risk assessment". Regulation 3 of the Management of Health and Safety at Work Regulations 1999, which after October 31, 2003 imposes civil liability on employers,[130] requires employers, inter alia, to make a suitable and sufficient assessment of the risks to which their employees are exposed for the purpose of identifying the measures needed to be taken to comply with the relevant statutory duties. Since virtually every activity is covered by regulation, this obligation will arise in all work situations. Regardless of the remedy for breach, reg.3 is in practice taken as a starting point for determining whether an employer has complied not only with his statutory duties but, also, his common law duties as well. The following illustrations all pre-date these Regulations and would undoubtedly be decided by reference to the latter today.

ILLUSTRATIONS

Circumstances might dictate that, before sending an employee to a foreign site, **11-33** employers satisfy themselves that it is a safe place of work, but it will be unreasonable to hold them liable for every hazard, such as a defective tile in the floor of a control room.[131] Where a preliminary inspection reveals a danger outside the control of the employer to remedy, a warning to the employee of its existence may discharge the duty owed.[132] Where the risks at a site are too great, the prudent employer may have to require premises to be made safe before permitting his employees to commence work there.[133] Where reasonable steps can be taken to protect employees, they must be taken.[134] If such steps are not taken, the fact that the employee knowingly incurred the risk goes only to the question of contributory negligence.[135]

Usually in cases of this type, the workman will be a lawful visitor of the **11-34** occupier and, thus will be owed the common duty of care under the Occupiers' Liability Act 1957. But if the occupier is sued, he can plead in his defence that

---

[129] *McDowell v F.M.C. (Meat) Ltd* (1968) 3 K.I.R. 595 (workmen sent to work on a site in a showground in order to erect a flag-pole but were unaware of high voltage over-head cables). For a safe system of work, generally, see para.11-65, below.
[130] Reg.22(1), which formerly excluded civil liability, was amended by reg.6 of the Management of Health and Safety at Work and Fire Precautions (Workplace)(Amendment) Regulations 2003 (SI 2003/2457).
[131] *Cook v Square D. Ltd* [1992] P.I.Q.R. P33. See also, e.g. *Executors of the Estate of O'Toole v Iarnod Eireann Irishrail* [1999] C.L.Y. 3961, Ch.7, para.7-45, above: the defendant, an Irish corporation, was liable for injury to its employee, a carriage builder, sent to work at a site in England in 1950 where he was exposed to asbestos dust.
[132] *Smith v Austin Lifts Ltd* [1959] 1 W.L.R. 100.
[133] *Smith v Austin Lifts Ltd* [1959] 1 W.L.R. 100 at 117. See also *Smith v Vange Scaffolding & Engineering Co Ltd* [1970] 1 W.L.R. 733.
[134] *Smith v Austin Lifts Ltd* [1959] 1 W.L.R. 100 at 117: "by requiring the occupiers to make the [place] safe".
[135] *A.C. Billings & Sons Ltd v Riden* [1958] A.C. 240; *Bill v Short Bros & Harland, The Guardian*, May 22, 1962; *Baker v White's Window & General Cleaning Co, The Times*, March 1, 1962, where the claimant was held to be one-third to blame for trusting his weight to a sash window handle which gave way under the strain.

he is entitled to expect that a skilled workman will guard against the normal risks of his calling.[136] Where both employer and building owner are liable to the claimant, responsibility for his accident can be apportioned between them pursuant to s.2 of the Civil Liability (Contribution) Act 1978.[137]

ILLUSTRATIONS

11–35   Employers have been held liable where: a slaughterman, was sent to work at an abattoir belonging to the Corporation, and was injured when he was struck by a pig's carcass which had fallen from the conveyor because of unsuitable chains and shackle supplied by the occupiers[138]; a fitter, employed by a lift-repairing company, fell off the access ladder when he grasped hold of one of the machine house's access doors, which he knew to be defective from previous experience and gave way on this occasion[139]; a plasterer, employed by a plastering company, whilst working on the redecoration of a ceiling in the occupiers' restaurant, received an electric shock and fell after touching the exposed ends of an electrical cable which suddenly had become live when switched on by the occupiers' electrician[140]; an experienced manager, sent by his employers to work on a site at a show-ground occupied by another, failed to receive any warning about the presence of an overhead high-voltage electric cable, which was touched during the erection of a flag-pole[141]; a scaffolder, employed by scaffolding sub-contractors working on an excessively untidy building site occupied by the main contractors, tripped over a welding cable which had been suspended about nine inches above ground level, whilst walking back to the changing hut from his place of work at the end of the day's work.[142]

11–36   On the other hand liability was not established against the employer, albeit others may have been found liable, where: a plumber's mate, employed by a firm of building contractors, was electrocuted whilst gaining access to the loft in a private dwelling-house in order to attend to the water tank, when he touched a metal sheet which was live with electricity caused by a defective electrical

---

[136] For example, a householder is entitled to expect that a self-employed window cleaner will take his own precautions against all those risks which he must know are incidental to his work such as loose plywood: *Bates v Parker* [1953] 2 Q.B. 231; handles screwed into unsound woodwork: *Wilson v Tyneside Window Cleaning Co* [1958] 2 Q.B. 110.

[137] For the terms of s.2, see para.11–118, below. See also *Andrews v Initial Cleaning Services* [2000] I.C.R. 166, CA: employers of a cleaner injured by a defective sink in another's premises 75 per cent to blame, building owners 25 per cent to blame.

[138] *Gledhill v Liverpool Abattoir Utility Co Ltd* [1957] 1 W.L.R. 1028 (the employers alone were held liable).

[139] *Smith v Austin Lifts Ltd* [1959] 1 W.L.R. 100 (the employers were held 20 per cent and the occupiers 80 per cent to blame).

[140] *Fisher v C.H.T. Ltd* [1966] 2 Q.B. 475 (the employers were held three-quarters and the occupiers one-quarter to blame).

[141] *McDowell v F.M.C. (Meat) Ltd* (1968) 3 K.I.R. 595 (the claimant was found guilty of contributory negligence to the extent of one-fifth for his failure to spot the overhead obstruction).

[142] *Smith v Vange Scaffolding & Engineering Co Ltd* [1970] 1 W.L.R. 733 (although both defendants were held liable the main contractors proved a claim to be indemnified).

cable's conduit pipe[143]; a tunnel worker, employed by a specialist company which was constructing a tunnel in a coal mine, was injured by a roof-fall[144]; a labourer employed by a firm of stevedores, in discharging bulk grain in a ship's hold, was injured when he was struck by the fall of a "shore," which had been fixed by shipwrights in Australia in order to hold a shifting-board[145]; a window cleaner of wide experience, employed by a firm of window cleaning contractors fell whilst cleaning from the outside a window in a brewery, when the handle by which he had been supporting himself gave away from its rotten wooden frame[146]; a boilermaker, employed by the ship-repairers, fell whilst ascending a ship's ladder as a result of tripping over a rope which had been wound around one of its rungs.[147]

Employer making use of another's property. Where the employer intends **11–37** to use part of the premises for his own work, so as to put a greater strain upon that part than it usually bears, for example, if a builder is going to use a chimney stack as a support for his staging while he repairs the roof,[148] it would seem he is under a duty to take reasonable care to see that it is fit for that purpose, before putting it to that use.[149] Where demolition contractors were demolishing three blocks of gas retorts, housed in vertical columns, each of which was surrounded by brickwork, it was held that they were liable in negligence for failing to take reasonable precautions by shoring up unstable brickwork. It was the result of such failure that it collapsed, killing two employees, who were clearing away rubble nearby at the time.[150]

Including a safe means of access. An employer is under a duty to take **11–38** reasonable care to provide a reasonably safe means of access from a highway to the place of work. Where the place of work immediately adjoins the highway, his duty begins as soon as the workman leaves the highway and enters the place of work. Where the workplace does not adjoin the highway and can only be reached by crossing land occupied by a third party, the employer is under a duty to take reasonable care to see that the way is reasonably safe for his workman to use.

---

[143] *Cilia v H.M. James & Son* [1954] 1 W.L.R. 721 (in so far as it was decided that no duty was owed by the employer to safeguard his workman against dangers arising from the state of the premises of another this decision may not be relied upon in the light of the HL authorities cited in n.24, above.

[144] *Szumczyk v Associated Tunnelling Co Ltd* [1956] 1 W.L.R. 98 (but the NCB were held liable for breach of statutory duty in that the roof was insufficiently supported).

[145] *Thomson v Cremin* [1956] 1 W.L.R. 103 (but the shipowners were held liable).

[146] *Wilson v Tyneside Window Cleaning Co* [1958] 2 Q.B. 110 but cf. the facts of this case with the similar facts in *Baker v White's Window & General Cleaning Co Ltd, The Times*, March 1, 1962, where the employers' liability was established. The claimant was held to be one-third to blame. Also see *General Cleaning Contractors Ltd v Christmas* [1953] A.C. 180 (liability established).

[147] *Mace v R. & H. Green and Silley Weir Ltd* [1959] 2 Q.B. 14 (but the shipowners were held liable).

[148] See, per Goddard L.J. in *Bates v Parker* [1953] 2 Q.B. 231 at 236.

[149] On the other hand, it was not suggested in *General Cleaning Contractors Ltd v Christmas* [1953] A.C. 180 that a window-cleaning company were under a duty to see if the windows were safe to hold on to. Their duty was said to be to tell their men to test the windows and to provide them with apparatus to prevent their closing unexpectedly.

[150] *Knight v Demolition and Construction Co Ltd* [1953] 1 W.L.R. 981 (affirmed [1954] 1 W.L.R. 563).

Where access to the place of work was over land occupied by a third party and crossed by railway lines on which wagons were shunted occasionally, it was held at first instance[151] that there was a duty to warn of the danger although the appeal was allowed upon the basis that the employer's duty had been sufficiently discharged.[152]

The duty of employers to provide the employee with a safe place of work necessarily includes the provision of safe means of access to the workplace.

Illustrations

11–39   Liability was established: where an employee tripped and fell over a half-inch metal strip set in the tiled floor at the canteen entrance. This gave rise to a foreseeable risk of injury which could reasonably have been avoided by adopting alternative practicable measures to keep the floor dry[153]; where the employers knew that their circus ringmaster was of such vast bulk that he would have difficulty gaining access to and egress from a caravan supplied by them as a dressing room, they were held liable in negligence for their failure to provide steps to be used as a means of access, the absence of which caused the employee to fall and break his ankle[154]; where the employers, scaffolding sub-contractors, knew of the excessively untidy condition of a building site across which their employees had to walk to gain access to and from work, but failed to complain to the occupiers (the main contractors), their failure was held to be a contributory factor to the happening of an accident to one of their employees and, thus, they were held liable.[155]

(ii) *Competent employees and supervision*

11–40   The employer is under a duty to take reasonable care to employ competent workmen. This duty used to be of more importance, whilst the doctrine of common employment was relevant, on the ground that:

> "The servant, when he engages to run the risks of his service, including those arising from the negligence of fellow servants, has a right to understand that the master has taken reasonable care to protect him from such risk by associating him only with persons of ordinary skill and care."[156]

Following the abolition of the doctrine of common employment,[157] this duty is of less practical importance, although there have been instances where an employer has been held liable in negligence for failing to take measures to stop

---

[151] *Ashdown v Samuel Williams & Sons Ltd* [1956] 2 Q.B. 580 at 593.
[152] [1957] 1 Q.B. 409.
[153] *McMillan v Lord Advocate*, 1991 S.L.T. 150 (the contributory negligence of the pursuer in failing to keep a proper look out for the strip, which he knew to be there, was held to be one-third).
[154] *Emney v Chipperfields Circus & Zoo, The Times*, October 17, 1961. The claimant weighed 23 stones (146kg).
[155] *Smith v Vange Scaffolding & Engineering Co Ltd* [1970] 1 W.L.R. 733, per MacKenna J.
[156] Alderson B. in *Hutchinson v York, Newcastle and Berwick Ry* (1850) 5 Ex. 343 at 353.
[157] See the Law Reform (Personal Injuries) Act 1948 in cases where the cause of action accrued after July 5, 1948, and para.11–02, above. See also "The Rise and Fall of the Doctrine of Common Employment" [1978] J.R. 106.

bullying[158] and the playing of practical jokes in the workplace which have caused an employee injury. Such an instance arose, for example, where a workman had repeatedly made a nuisance of himself to his fellow workmen by "his almost incurable habit of tripping people up or otherwise engaging in horse-play and skylarking" and, had eventually caused injury to the claimant by grabbing him from behind and forcing him on to the ground. The employers were held liable for not taking proper steps to put an end to that workman's misconduct.[159]

In contrast, an employer was not liable for personal injuries sustained by an **11–41** employee as a result of the negligence of another employee in perpetrating an isolated act, such as a practical joke, that could not reasonably have been foreseen.[160] However, it does not necessarily follow that merely because the practical joke happens to have been an isolated incident, the employer automatically can avoid liability by arguing that its perpetrators were not acting in the course of their employment.[161] Such an argument would not avail an employer, where he owed a duty of care to the claimant, who was bound to obey the joker's instructions.[162]

If an employer has reason to anticipate misconduct from an employee which **11–42** puts other employees at risk, he is under a duty to those others to take reasonable steps to avoid the risk materialising, for example by a reprimand. Should a reprimand or a number of them be ignored, the duty could involve having to dismiss the employee in question.[163] An employer could be held liable for employing a workman who was known to be vicious and dangerous, if a fellow worker is injured in an attack.[164] In a different type of situation, where an

---

[158] *Veness v Dyston, Bell & Co* [1965] C.L.Y. 2691. See also, *Green v DB Group Services (UK) Ltd* [2006] I.R.L.R. 764 (employer liable for psychiatric harm caused to an employee with a pre-existing vulnerability, who was exposed to a campaign of bullying of which line managers either knew or ought to have known).

[159] *Hudson v Ridge Manufacturing Co* [1957] 2 Q.B. 348. See, further, Ch.3, para.3–146, above.

[160] *Smith v Crossley Bros Ltd* (1951) 95 S.J. 655 (a practical joke by two young apprentices in the misuse of a compressed air pipe which they shoved up another boy's rectum); *Coddington v International Harvester Co of Great Britain Ltd* (1969) 6 K.I.R. 146 (a tin containing "thinners" was set alight and another workman, passing by, as a joke flicked the tin with his foot in the direction of a fellow, who, in the agony of the moment, kicked the burning tin violently away so that it overturned and its highly inflammable contents spilled over the claimant, enveloping him in a sheet of flames); *Wood v Duttons Brewery* (1971) 115 S.J. 186. See also *Horton v Taplin Contracts* [2003] P.I.Q.R. P180, CA.

[161] In *Harrison v Michelin Tyre Co Ltd* [1985] I.C.R. 696, Comyn J. expressed the view that in a case which involved a frolic by an employee, the principle could be set out in two questions. First, was the incident part and parcel of the employment in the sense of its being incidental to it, albeit unauthorised and prohibited by the employer—if so, vicarious liability was established—or, else, was the incident so divergent from the employment as to be alien to and wholly distinguishable from the employment—if so, such vicarious liability was *not* proved. See Owles "Some Aspects of Negligence" 134 N.L.J. 737; Hodgkinson, "Vicarious Liability for the Practical Joker" 135 N.L.J. 1252.

[162] *Chapman v Oakleigh Animal Products* (1970) 8 K.I.R. 1063, CA.

[163] *Hudson v Ridge Manufacturing Co Ltd* [1957] 2 Q.B. 348 at 350, per Streatfield J.

[164] *Smith v Ocean S.S. Co Ltd* [1954] 2 Lloyd's Rep. 482 (a ship's officer was stabbed by a native labourer but his claim failed since the employers had no reason to expect any danger from employing native labour); *Walden v Court Line* (1965) 109 S.J. 151 (a ship's cook was injured by a crew member, who had previously assaulted others, but the employers were held not to be liable in the circumstances since they were not negligent in keeping the man on in their employment).

employer may have to bear in mind that an employee's lack of familiarity with the English language may give rise to an enhanced risk to his co-workers. So where the claimant and a 17-year-old labourer from India were required to carry a hand shank full of molten metal for pouring into moulds at the defendants' foundry, and, whilst pouring the metal, the claimant was burnt severely after losing his balance, because the other, whose knowledge of English was indifferent, had not responded to his shouts to stop pouring, it was held, inter alia, that a workman's imperfect knowledge of the English language imposed a higher standard of care on his employers.[165]

11–43   In addition to the provision of competent workmen, the employer owes a duty to give adequate supervision[166] and, where necessary, to give proper instruction.[167] In many instances, particularly in the cases of the less skilled or of younger employees, it is insufficient merely to supply adequate plant or appliances, then leave them to their own devices, either to try to find out how they work or how to use them properly.

(iii) *Adequate plant and appliance*

11–44   A reasonable employer must decide whether, and if so what, plant and appliances are required for a job, because the provision of proper plant is "especially within the province of the master rather than of his servants".[168] The employer's duty as to appliances has been stated to be one of "taking reasonable care to provide proper appliances, and to maintain them in a proper condition".[169] Also, "the obligation to provide and maintain proper plant and appliances is a continuing obligation".[170] Plant and appliances would consist of practically everything, including all such items as tools, equipment and machines, which the workman would need to use in order to do the required work. To qualify as adequate, equipment must be supplied in sufficient quantities.[171]

11–45   The obligation is not absolute[172]; it is to take reasonable care to provide and maintain adequate plant. In order to prove liability, fault must be established.

---

[165] *Hawkins v Ian Ross (Castings) Ltd* [1970] 1 All E.R. 180, per Fisher J.

[166] *Smith v Crossley Bros Ltd* (1951) 95 S.J. 655. See also *Jebson v Ministry of Defence* [2000] 1 W.L.R. 2055, CA, Ch.3, above, para.3–24: unsupervised soldier, the worse for drink, falling from the back of an army lorry. See further Elfield and Sharghy, "Win, lose or draw? Drunken misconduct and vicarious liability—the health and safety implications" H. & S.L. 2002, 1(2), 8.

[167] *General Cleaning Contractors Ltd v Christmas* [1953] A.C. 180.

[168] per Sir Arthur Channell in *Toronto Power Co Ltd v Paskwan* [1915] A.C. 734 at 738. There are instances, however, when the selection of equipment can be properly left to the experienced employee: *Richardson v Stephenson Clarke Ltd* [1969] 1 W.L.R. 1695.

[169] per Lord Herschell in *Smith v Baker* [1891] A.C. 325 at 362.

[170] per Lord Wright in *Wilsons & Clyde Coal Co v English* [1938] A.C. 57 at 84.

[171] *McGregor v A.A.H. Pharmaceuticals*, 1996 S.L.T. 1161: although stepladders were supplied in the warehouse at which the pursuer worked, there was no system to ensure that sufficient numbers of ladders were available when required to enable employees to reach high shelving.

[172] Contrast the position under reg.6 of the Provision and Use of Work Equipment Regulations 1992 and (now reg.5 of the Provision and Use of Work Equipment Regulations 1998) where strict liability applies to all "work equipment": *Stark v Post Office* [2000] P.I.Q.R. P105, CA, discussed in Ch.12, para.12–197, below.

Where a steel rope, which had been holding some trucks on a haulage way in a mine, broke so that the trucks ran away and injured a miner, the Coal Board was not liable on proof that a safe rope had been provided and that the system of inspection was proper, reasonable and customary.[173] Further, the obligation "is limited to reasonable exercise of care and skill to guard against danger which, as reasonable people, the employers ought to have anticipated".[174] Thus, where a circular saw, properly guarded in accordance with the Woodworking Machinery Regulations 1922, ejected a piece of wood which struck the operator, the employers were held not liable, because it was an accident "outside normal experience and such as could not reasonably have been anticipated".[175] But statutory regulations, defining an employer's duty concerning a particular machine, do not, per se, relieve him from the obligation to take reasonable care to make safe use of that machine.[176]

It is not necessary for an employer to tell an experienced, skilled workman **11–46** about matters of which he is well aware, or about precautions that ought to be adopted when using plant and appliances, unless there is reason to believe that he will not adopt them or the dangers are insidious. An employer is not obliged to give constant or repetitive reminders.[177] But where a young and inexperienced support worker employed by a health authority to accompany a patient on a week's camping holiday, suffered injury when changing the cylinder of a gas cooker near to a lighted candle, her employer was held liable for her injury notwithstanding the fact that she appreciated the risk: her employer was not thereby relieved from the consequences of providing her with equipment which was potentially dangerous and without instruction as to how to change the cylinder.[178]

Inspections and maintenance. The fulfilment of this duty may include the **11–47** carrying out of both regular inspections[179] of, and all necessary maintenance and repairs to, the plant and appliances, provided by the employer, as are reasonable

---

[173] *Turner v N.C.B.* (1949) 65 T.L.R. 580. See also to the same effect *Wilsons & Clyde Coal Co v English* [1938] A.C. 57 at 78.

[174] *Nicholls v F. Austin (Leyton) Ltd* [1946] A.C. 493 at 503, per Lord Wright.

[175] *Nicholls v F. Austin (Leyton) Ltd* [1946] A.C. 493 at 503.

[176] *Quinn v Horsfall & Bickham Ltd* [1956] 1 W.L.R. 264. Although the decision in this case has been reversed in the CA [1956] 1 W.L.R. 652, the statement in the text remains correct. Failure to fence a horizontal milling machine (assumed not to be required to be fenced by statute) was held to be a breach of the employers' common law duty "to take reasonable care so as not to subject their employees to unnecessary risks."

[177] *Baker v T. Clarke (Leeds)* [1992] P.I.Q.R. P262, CA (a very experienced electrician was injured when he fell from a mobile scaffold tower which toppled over after he had failed to lock its wheels and/or to use the outriggers that were available).

[178] *Fraser v Winchester Health Authority, The Times*, July 12, 1999, CA, Ch.4, para.4–71, above. The defendant's argument that the risk was so obvious that no instruction was required was rejected.

[179] Regarding the importance of carrying out examinations, see *Pearce v Round Oak Steel Works* [1969] 1 W.L.R. 595. If the apparatus is complicated, it may not be justifiable merely to rely upon the operator's inspecting it and reporting any faults that he can find: *Shotter v R. & H. Green & Silley Weir Ltd* [1951] 1 Lloyd's Rep. 329.

in the circumstances.[180] It may be necessary to follow up such an inspection with the preparation in writing of an appropriate defects report.[181]

ILLUSTRATIONS

11-48   The employer was held to be negligent: where a nurse sat on a chair weakened by wood-worm, which collapsed, there being no system of inspecting furniture[182]; when a screw on an electric drill loosened and, as a result, part of it flew off and injured the claimant, where the drill was only a year old and had recently been examined for an electrical fault, but the screw had never been checked for tightness.[183]

11-49   On the other hand, an employer will avoid a finding of liability where he can, with reasonable prudence, leave to his employee the task of selecting the right equipment for doing the job from those provided for him[184]; where such proper equipment has been provided but the employee puts it to improper use,[185] which may include an act of folly on the part of the workman in choosing the wrong tool for the job[186]; where a swivel chair was not, on the facts, inherently dangerous but had been misused by the claimant who had set it at its highest level despite having been warned in emphatic terms of the possible dangers of misuse.[187]

11-50   **Provision of protective device or clothing with or without advice, warnings or orders.** If the nature of work is such that a reasonable employer would provide an employee with some protective device or clothing, there is a duty to provide it and to take reasonable care to see that it is used.[188] The extent of the duty necessarily depends on a number of factors, which include: (i) the risk of injury[189]; (ii) the gravity of potential injury; (iii) the difficulty of providing

---

[180] An employer, besides being liable for the negligence of his employees, is also liable for the negligence of any independent contractors, to whom he had delegated the duty of maintaining the machine: *Rodgers v Dunsmuir Confectionery Co*, 1952 S.L.T. (Notes) 9.

[181] *Barkway v South Wales Transport Co Ltd* [1950] A.C. 185; *Franklin v Edmonton Corp* (1965) 109 S.J. 876; *Henderson v Henry E. Jenkins & Sons* [1907] A.C. 282.

[182] *Baxter v St Helena Group Hospital Management Committee*, *The Times*, February 15, 1972.

[183] *Bell v Arnott & Harrison Ltd* (1967) 2 K.I.R. 825.

[184] *Richardson v Stephenson Clarke Ltd* [1969] 1 W.L.R. 1695; *Smith v Shaw Savill & Albion Co Ltd* [1962] N.Z.L.R. 383; *Johnson v Croggon & Co Ltd* [1954] 1 W.L.R. 195; *Bristol Aeroplane Co v Franklin*, 92 S.J. 573.

[185] *Parkinson v Lyle Shipping Co* [1964] 2 Lloyd's Rep. 79.

[186] *Leach v British Oxygen Co Ltd* (1965) 109 S.J. 157.

[187] *Ismail v Bexley Health Authority* [1997] C.L.Y. 2615, CA.

[188] *James v Hepworth & Grandage Ltd* [1968] 1 Q.B. 94 (reasonable care did not require employers to check that employees could read notices advertising the availability of protective equipment) ; *Smith v Scot Bowyers Ltd* [1986] I.R.L.R. 315, CA (employers not required to instruct employees to replace worn-out boots when they had been told replacements were freely available, nor to check the boots'condition in use) ; *Crouch v British Rail Engineering* [1988] I.R.L.R. 404, CA (the provision of goggles where work involved foreseeable risks to the eyes). The position is now largely regulated by the Personal Protective Equipment at Work Regulations 1992: see Ch.12, para.12–232, below.

[189] See, e.g. *Gray v Stead* [1999] 2 Lloyd's Rep. 559, CA, reversing [1999] 1 Lloyd's Rep. 377, Ch.7, para.7–38, above (owner of trawler not obliged to provide life jackets and instructions to wear them at all times on deck where it was a recognised practice not to wear them and the incidence of injury or death in the industry from falling overboard was very low).

protection; (iv) the availability of protective clothing; (v) the distance which an employee may have to go to fetch such clothing; and (vi) the employee's skill and experience.[190]

ILLUSTRATIONS

Employers were negligent in submitting an employee to continuous very loud noise, without having tried to persuade him to wear protective ear muffs[191]; exposing a train driver to harmful levels of noise without providing the opportunity to wear hearing protection[192]; exposing him for many years to prolonged inhalation of noxious fumes emitted, during the employee's arc-welding work, which were injurious to his lungs, without proper ventilation or breathing apparatus.[193] If a one-eyed man is employed to loosen a bolt with a hammer, goggles must be provided.[194] Where it was reasonably foreseeable that a workman, who ordinarily wore glasses, would suffer a serious eye injury if a lens were to break during the performance of a potentially dangerous job, the failure to supply him with a pair of shatter-proof spectacles was held to amount to negligence.[195] A man, who was employed in a piano-fitting shop and contracted dermatitis after using synthetic glue established his employer's liability, because he was not required to use the protective cream which he ought to have used.[196] "When [an employer] asks his men to work with dangerous substances, he must provide proper appliances to safeguard them; he must set in force a proper system by which they use the appliances and take the necessary precautions; and he must do his best to see that they adhere to it."[197] Accordingly, where employers were under a duty to warn their cleaners of the dangers of handling chemical cleaning materials with unprotected hands and to instruct them as to the need to wear gloves at all material times, the mere provision of suitable gloves without giving instructions, was held to be insufficient to discharge the duty of care.[198] The failure to transport the claimant around Basra in the aftermath of the Second Gulf War in an armoured vehicle was not, on the facts and circumstances, a failure to take reasonable care to ensure his safety.[199]

11–51

---

[190] *Crouch v British Rail Engineering*, n.186, above.

[191] *Berry v Stone Manganese & Marine Ltd* (1971) 115 S.J. 966; *McCafferty v Metropolitan Police District Receiver* [1977] 1 W.L.R. 1073. *Thompson v Smith Shiprepairers (North Shields) Ltd* [1984] Q.B. 405. See now the Control of Noise at Work Regulations 2005, SI 2005/1643 implementing the Noise at Work Directive 2003/10/EC. See further, Handley, "Now hear this" 151 S.J. 753.

[192] *Harris v BRB Residuary Ltd* [2006] P.I.Q.R. P101, CA.

[193] *Cartwright v GKN Sankey* (1973) 14 K.I.R. 349.

[194] *Paris v Stepney Borough Council* [1951] A.C. 367. The HL did not decide whether a two-eyed man should have had goggles.

[195] *Pentney v Anglian Water Authority* [1983] I.C.R. 464.

[196] *Clifford v Charles Challen & Sons Ltd* [1951] 1 K.B. 495. See also *Crookall v Vickers-Armstrong Ltd* [1955] 1 W.L.R. 659, (silicosis); *Snell v Shelbourne & Co* (1965) 109 S.J. 270; *Voller v Schweppes (Home)* (1969) 7 K.I.R. 228.

[197] *Clifford v Charles Challen & Sons* [1951] 1 K.B. 495 at 497, 498, per Denning L.J.

[198] *Pape v Cumbria County Council* [1992] 1 All E.R. 211.

[199] *Hopps v Mott MacDonald Ltd* [2009] EWHC 1881 Q.B. See para.11–106, below.

11–52   There can be no liability where the employer supplies the necessary protective measure and instructs the employee how to use it.[200] Thus, where an experienced moulder was burnt whilst handling a ladle of molten metal which slipped, splashing metal on to his foot, his employers were not liable for failing to have ordered or advised him to wear the protective spats provided as a precaution against that very type of injury.[201] If the process were not known to be dangerous, the employer is not liable,[202] but failure to know of some consequence that is common knowledge may result in damage being found to be foreseeable, for example decompression, causing septic bone necrosis,[203] and the persistent use of vibrating tools, causing deterioration of the nerves in the hands, limbs or body.[204]

11–53   Where an employer has complied with his duty by providing his employee with appropriate clothing and has explained the reasons for using it, but the latter permits it to become worn out, it was held that the employer was not under any further obligation to inspect it, in order to decide whether or not it was time for it to be replaced.[205] The employer would become liable only if he had known or ought to have known that the workman was exposing himself to a significant risk of danger by failing to ask for and obtain a suitable replacement and had then failed to instruct him to obtain it.

11–54   **Employers' liability for defective equipment.** Prior to the Employer's Liability (Defective Equipment) Act 1969,[206] the employer was only liable on proof of negligence if equipment which he provided was defective and had caused injury to his employee. Although an employer was held not liable for a latent defect which could not have been detected on reasonable examination,[207] if equipment were known to be dangerous[208] and nothing were done about it, or where the employer retained it in use, knowing of its defects,[209] he would have been held liable. Further, an employer was held to be under no obligation to examine tools of a standard pattern bought from reputable manufacturers, before these were issued for use to his workmen. Thus, in the leading case of *Davie v*

---

[200] *Woods v Durable Suites Ltd* [1953] 1 W.L.R. 857. See *Berry v Stone Manganese & Marine Ltd* (1971) 115 S.J. 966.
[201] *Qualcast (Wolverhampton) Ltd v Haynes* [1959] A.C. 743. See the words of caution by Lord Radcliffe regarding the "much vaguer obligation of encouraging, exhorting or instructing" workmen to make regular use of the protective measures provided (at 753).
[202] *Ebbs v James Whitson & Co* [1952] 2 Q.B. 877; *Graham v Co-operative Wholesale Society Ltd* [1957] 1 W.L.R. 511 (West African hardwood dust causing dermatitis). See also the cases cited above at para.11–15.
[203] *Ransom v Sir Robert McAlpine and Sons* (1971) 115 S.J. 326.
[204] *Joseph v Ministry of Defence, The Times*, March 4, 1980, CA (negligence not found on the facts where a caulker-riveter developed hand/arm vibration syndrome). See also *Armstrong v British Coal Corp, The Times*, December 6, 1996, CA, above, para.11–15, n.67.
[205] *Smith v Scot Bowyers Ltd* [1986] I.R.L.R. 315, CA.
[206] See Ingman, 33 M.L.R. 70; Maggs, 67 L.S.Gaz. 262; J.A.K., 114 S.J. 895.
[207] *Toronto Power Co Ltd v Paskwan* [1915] A.C. 734 at 738; *Turner v N.C.B.* (1949) 65 T.L.R. 580.
[208] *Naismith v London Film Productions Ltd* [1939] 1 All E.R. 794 (inflammable material worn by actress caught fire).
[209] *Bissett v L. & G. Fire Appliance Co Ltd, Foamite, Shellmex and B.P. Ltd* [1965] 2 Lloyd's Rep. 93; *Taylor v Rover Co Ltd* [1966] 1 W.L.R. 1491.

New Merton Board Mills,[210] where a workman was using a drift to knock out a key, by striking it with a hammer, and the metal of the drift had been tempered dangerously too hard, as a result of which a chip of metal flew into the workman's eye, the employer was held not liable,[211] because the defect was not apparent.

Employers' Liability (Defective Equipment) Act 1969.[212] The broad approach of this Act is to protect the employee by providing him with a remedy against his employers which otherwise he would not have unless he first succeeded in establishing negligence against them. Thus, by s.1(1), where an employee[213] sustains personal injury[214] because of a defect in equipment[215] provided by his employer for the purposes of business[216] and the defect is attributable, either wholly or partly, to the fault of some third party (whether identified or not), the injury, nevertheless, is to be deemed to be attributable also to the "fault" of the employer.[217] As regards "fault," this is defined as "negligence, breach of statutory duty or other act or omission which gives rise to liability in tort in England and Wales or which is wrongful and gives rise to liability in damages in Scotland". **11–55**

The Act binds the Crown, and persons in the Crown's service are treated, for the purposes of the section, as being employees of the Crown even if they would not be so treated otherwise, apart from s.1(4). Any agreement purporting to exclude or limit the employer's liability under the Act is void by virtue of s.1(2), whilst the innocent employer's rights of contribution or indemnity are preserved, for what they may be worth in practice, by the remaining provisions of s.1(1). **11–56**

The effect of the Act was to reverse the decision in *Davie v New Merton Board Mills Ltd*.[218] It represented a landmark in the improvement of the rights of employees against employers in respect of defects in equipment due to the default of others. However, it conferred no benefit on an employee injured by a latent defect in work equipment where no fault could be directed at a third party, **11–57**

---

[210] [1959] A.C. 604.
[211] See also *Mason v Williams & Williams Ltd* [1955] 1 W.L.R. 549, *Sullivan v Gallagher and Craig*, 1959 S.C. 243.
[212] With effect from October 25, 1969.
[213] "employee" means any person who is employed under a contract of service or apprenticeship for the purposes of the employer's business.
[214] "personal injury" includes "loss of life, any impairment of a person's physical or mental condition and any disease".
[215] "equipment" includes "any plant and machinery, vehicle, aircraft and clothing". In *Knowles v Liverpool City Council*, [1993] 1 W.L.R. 1428, HL, it was held that a flagstone which broke and injured the employee as he was manhandling it, although strictly speaking "material", was nevertheless also "equipment" for the purposes of s.1(1) of the Act, affirming *Ralston v Greater Glasgow Health Board*, 1987 S.L.T. 38 and applying *Coltman v Bibby Tankers Ltd, The Derbyshire* [1988] A.C. 276 (where a ship was held to be "equipment" within the meaning of the Act).
[216] "Business" includes "the activities carried on by any public body".
[217] In *Clarkson v Wm Jackson & Sons Ltd, The Times*, November 21, 1984, the CA expressed the view that the Act did not give employees a new cause of action but prevented an employer from escaping liability, by claiming and relying on the fact that the faulty equipment was solely the responsibility of the supplier or manufacturer.
[218] [1959] A.C. 604.

a remedy for which had to await the Provision and Use of Work Equipment Regulations 1992.[219]

11–58   The Act does not appear to create a situation of vicarious liability in the ordinary sense,[220] because it covers all third parties, including those with whom the employer probably has had no contact whatsoever and who are as far removed from him as is possible to imagine. On the other hand, there will be several situations to which the Act does not apply. For instance, the personal injury suffered by the employee must have been "in consequence of a defect in equipment" provided by his employer. The mere fact of the unsuitability of equipment for the job will be insufficient to found liability.[221]

11–59   "Defect" is not defined in the Act, but in an old case it was said: "I take defect to include anything which renders the plant, etc., unfit for the use for which it is intended, when used in a reasonable way and with reasonable care".[222] The defect relied upon must be in "equipment provided" by the employer "for the purposes of the employer's business". Problems may arise as to what amounts to equipment's being "provided", but the usual meaning will be what has actually been provided. Possibly the provision will extend to equipment that has been borrowed, either with an employer's authority, or to his knowledge. Private use, which is not a business use, will not suffice. There must be third party "fault", as defined in the Act, which may not be easy to determine, given that the equipment may have been through the hands of a manufacturer, a supplier, an installer, a hirer, a repairer or whosoever. The employee must be employed under a contract of service, so the Act does not extend protection to a self-employed person. Where the Act does not apply, the common law will prevail, unless the claimant falls within the provisions of the Provision and Use of Work Equipment Regulations 1998.[223]

ILLUSTRATIONS

11–60   The employer was liable in the following instances: where a workman employed to hoist an iron cylinder, was killed when the tackle provided which was of insufficient strength, broke and the cylinder fell on him[224]; when a worker, employed to lubricate dangerous machinery, was injured as a result of the failure to maintain adequate fencing around it[225]; where a worker was injured owing to the collapse of a rotten scaffold pole, which the employer had failed to have inspected[226]; where a film actress had to cover her feet with some inflammable

---

[219] See Ch.12, para.12–173 et seq., below.
[220] See Ch.3, para.3–98 et seq., above.
[221] But see the duty imposed by reg.4 of the Provision and Use of Work Equipment Regulations 1998, Ch.12, para.12–190, below.
[222] per Lindley L.J. in *Yarmouth v France* (1887) 19 Q.B.D. 647 at 658. In *Tate v Latham & Son* [1897] 1 Q.B. 502 at 506, Bruce J. added that " 'Defect' means a lack or absence of something essential to completeness".
[223] See Ch.12, para.12–173 et seq., below.
[224] *Weems v Mathieson* (1861) 4 Macq. 215.
[225] *Clarke v Holmes* (1862) 7 H. & N. 937.
[226] *Webb v Rennie* (1865) 4 F. & F. 608.

material, which caught fire during the shooting of a film sequence[227]; where a workman was struck by the blades of a large electrically driven fan, which was revolving at high speed but was unguarded, during testing on the factory floor[228]; for failing to provide crawling boards for risky work on a roof and relying instead wholly on the claimant's skill as an experienced man[229]; where a stevedore was injured when a chain, which had been in use for seven years without any examination or testing, broke[230]; for failing to provide a ladder or other safe means of ascending to or descending from an elevated tramway, so that the workman fell to his death during his descent, when his foot slipped[231]; where an electrician, who needed a trestle and ladder, was told by his foreman to look around and find whatever equipment he required, which he did, but it had a defective rung that broke when he stood on it[232]; where a television engineer suffered frostbite, because of the absence of a car-heater, when he was required to travel a long distance in his employer's van during severe winter weather.[233]

Also; where no brush was available to sweep up loose ash lying on a platform,   **11–61**
which made the footing very unsafe[234]; where no fencing was provided on farm machinery[235]; where an electric drill was liable to throw out fragments of its bit, which shattered[236]; where a dock labourer was employed in loading a ship and was injured, whilst climbing an unsafe rope ladder, which had been provided by his employers in place of a fixed iron ladder[237]; where a commercial traveller was injured when trying to start his employers' motorcar, which had defective starting gear[238]; where a boilermaker was injured by the collapse of improvised staging, which had been erected by himself, after foraging for the bits and pieces, because of the employers' failure to supply him with proper materials[239]; where a ladder was provided, which was not in an efficient state and in good repair[240]; where a highly skilled rigger, who was faced with a matter of urgency, had to adopt a method of doing the job that was obviously less safe than the method he would have preferred to use if only the appropriate appliances had been provided[241];

---

[227] *Naismith v London Film Productions Ltd* [1939] 1 All E.R. 794.
[228] *Thurogood v Van den Berghs & Jurgens Ltd* [1951] 2 K.B. 537.
[229] *Jenner v Allen West & Co Ltd* [1959] 1 W.L.R. 554.
[230] *Murphy v Phillips* (1876) 35 L.T. 477.
[231] *Williams v Birmingham Battery and Metal Co* [1899] 2 Q.B. 338.
[232] *Garrard v A. E. Southey & Co and Standard Telephones and Cables Ltd* [1952] 2 Q.B. 174.
[233] *Bradford v Robinson Rentals Ltd* [1967] 1 W.L.R. 337.
[234] *Busby v R. Watson & Co (Constructional Engineers) Ltd* (1972) 13 K.I.R. 498.
[235] *Jones v Richards* [1955] 1 W.L.R. 444.
[236] *Close v Steel Co of Wales Ltd* [1962] A.C. 367 (not required to be fenced under Factories Act). For a similar situation, where there had been no regular inspection of the electric drill, see *Bell v Arnott & Harrison Ltd* (1967) 2 K.I.R. 825.
[237] *Monaghan v Rhodes & Co* [1920] 1 K.B. 487.
[238] *Baker v James* [1921] 2 K.B. 647, where McCardie J. refused to follow *Griffiths v London and St Katherine Docks* (1884) 13 Q.B.D. 259.
[239] *Lovell v Blundells and T. Albert Crompton & Co Ltd* [1944] K.B. 502.
[240] *Jones v Crosville Motor Services Ltd* [1956] 1 W.L.R. 1425.
[241] *Machray v Stewarts & Lloyd's Ltd* [1965] 1 W.L.R. 602.

where the corner of a flagstone broke off as a flagger was manhandling it into a shovel of a JCB causing it to fall and injure his finger.[242]

11–62 **The inclusion of other plant and appliances.** The duty of an employer to provide safe appliances covers appliances not only directly connected with the work, but also includes appliances used for purposes normally and reasonably incidental to it.

ILLUSTRATIONS

11–63 Negligence was established against the employer where a factory worker fell on a slippery duckboard, when going to wash a teacup for her own use[243]; where a waitress was injured in her bedroom, when she touched the electric fire provided, which was defective to the employers' knowledge.[244] An employer was negligent where more was not done to make safe a drinks dispensing machine prone to electrical fault, which emitted a flash in the direction of the claimant who was standing near, causing her to jump back and fall heavily to the floor.[245]

11–64 In contrast, the employer was held *not* to be liable where the workman failed to make proper use of the equipment provided[246]; where, as an act of folly on the workman's part, he chose the wrong tool to do the job[247]; where, in answering an emergency call, the fire service transported a heavy piece of lifting gear on a flat-platformed lorry, instead of on a vehicle which had been designed especially to carry it, and the gear (a mobile jack) moved forward, crushing the claimant's foot as the lorry braked hard and stopped[248]; where a skilled man, who was allowed to repair his own tools, selected for the purpose brittle materials which he had drawn from the stores[249]; where the claimant misused a swivel chair by positioning it at the highest setting possible despite warnings to the contrary.[250]

(iv) *Safe system of work*

11–65 If the employer[251] has instituted a defective system of work,[252] as a result of which an employee is injured, although there is no negligence in the actual working of the system, the employer is liable. This was laid down in the Scottish

---

[242] *Knowles v Liverpool City Council*, 90 L.G.R. 594, CA.

[243] *Davidson v Handley Page Ltd* [1945] 1 All E.R. 235.

[244] *McBrien v Arden & Cobden Hotels* (1963) 107 S.J. 791.

[245] *Given v James Watt College*, 2007 S.L.T. 39 OH.

[246] *Parkinson v Lyle Shipping Co* [1964] 2 Lloyd's Rep. 79.

[247] *Leach v British Oxygen Co* (1965) 109 S.J. 157; *Johnson v Croggan & Co Ltd* [1954] 1 W.L.R. 195 (chose an unsuitable ladder for the job).

[248] *Watt v Hertfordshire County Council* [1954] 1 W.L.R. 835.

[249] *Bristol Aeroplane Co v Franklin* [1948] W.N. 341.

[250] *Ismail v Bexley Health Authority* [1997] C.L.Y. 2615, CA.

[251] In Scotland it has been held that an employer's duty to devise and maintain a safe system of work extends to the master of a vessel: *MacIver v J & A Gardner Ltd*, 2001 S.L.T. 585, OH (accident to a safety officer who died when, during unloading of a ship's cargo, he was struck by a cage which fell from a deckside crane).

[252] Powell and Slater, "What is a safe system of work?" 1 I.L.J. 135.

case *Sword v Cameron*,[253] where the pursuer was employed at a stone quarry and was injured through blasting operations because the warning signal had not been given in sufficient time to enable him to put himself in a position of safety. Subsequently the House of Lords, in an English case, where it was not the main question before it,[254] held that "a negligent system or a negligent mode of using perfectly sound machinery may make the employer liable".[255] Despite this, the English courts were slow to recognise the principle that an employer could be held liable for an unsafe system of work, until the House of Lords' further decision in *Wilsons & Clyde Coal Co Ltd v English*[256] which firmly established the law in both jurisdictions. Thereafter the House added to these early decisions, the obligation to ensure the operation of the duly devised safe system of work.[257]

Meaning of "system of work". This is the term used to describe: (i) the **11–66** organisation of the work; (ii) the way in which it is intended the work shall be carried out; (iii) the giving of adequate instructions (especially to inexperienced workers); (iv) the sequence of events; (v) the taking of precautions for the safety of the workers and at what stages; (vi) the number of such persons required to do the job; (vii) the part to be taken by each of the various persons employed; and (viii) the moment at which they shall perform their respective tasks. Further:

> "it includes . . . or may include according to circumstances, such matters as the physical layout of the job—the setting of the stage, so to speak—the sequence in which the work is to be carried out, the provision in proper cases of warnings and notices, and the issue of special instructions. A system may be adequate for the whole course of the job or it may have to be modified or improved to meet circumstances which arise. Such modifications or improvements appear to me equally to fall under the head of system."[258]

Duty to prescribe a safe system of work. It is a question of fact whether or **11–67** not there is need for a system of work to be prescribed in any given circumstances. In deciding it, regard ought to be had to the nature of the work, that is whether properly it requires careful organisation and supervision, in the interests of safety of all those persons carrying it out; or it can be left by a prudent employer confidently to the care of the particular man on the spot to do it reasonably safely.[259] There was no failure to provide a safe system where an employee was faced with a "one-off" task requiring the exercise of common sense and it was difficult to see what relevant instruction could have been given

---

[253] (1839) 1 Dunlop 493, Ct. Sess. See also *Bartonshill Coal Co v Reid* (1858) 3 Macq. 266 at 290 where Lord Cranworth, referring to this case said: "The injury was evidently the result of a defective system not adequately protecting the workmen at the time of the explosions".
[254] *Smith v Baker* [1891] A.C. 325.
[255] per Lord Halsbury, *Smith v Baker* [1891] A.C. 325 at 339. See also *Bartonshill Coal Co v McGuire* (1858) 3 Macq. 300 and *C.P. Ry v Frechette* [1915] A.C. 871.
[256] [1938] A.C. 57.
[257] *McDermid v Nash Dredging and Reclamation Co Ltd* [1987] A.C. 906.
[258] Lord Greene M.R. in *Speed v Thomas Swift & Co Ltd* [1943] K.B. 557 at 563, 564. In *Colfar v Coggins and Griffith (Liverpool) Ltd* [1945] A.C. 197 at 202, Lord Simon said that the judgments in this case "carry the analysis of 'system of working' to the furthest point that can be reached."
[259] *Jenner v Allen West & Co Ltd* [1959] 1 W.L.R. 554.

to him.[260] But an employer is under a duty to prescribe a system of work, even where the operation is a single one, if it is necessary in the interests of safety.[261] Lord Reid said:

"A system of working normally implies that the work consists of a series of similar or somewhat similar operations, and the conception of a system of working is not easily applied to a case where only a single act of a particular kind is to be performed. Recently, however, this obligation has been extended to cover certain cases where only a single operation[262] is involved. I think that the justification for this is that, where the operation is of a complicated or unusual character, an employer, careful of the safety of his men, would organise it before it was begun and in that sense provide a safe system of working for it. Where such an organisation is called for, an employer must provide it . . . but cases in which such a duty has been found to exist are comparatively few, and it has never even been suggested that such an obligation arises in every case where a group of the employer's servants are doing some work which may involve danger if negligently performed."[263]

11–68 Accordingly, a system of work must be instituted when it is necessary in the interests of safety, even where the work consists of a regular and uniform kind, such as occurs in a mine, a factory or on a railway. The same applies when the danger arises in practice so constantly that it calls in advance for a system to meet it. In other cases, the need to prescribe a system only arises in the circumstances indicated by Lord Reid.[264]

11–69 **Nature of the duty.** The duty to prescribe a safe system of work is neither one to provide perfection[265] nor an absolute duty, so that where some commercial or other[266] necessity requires that an employer will expose a workman to some risks, he may be able to avoid liability for his failure to guard against such dangers.[267] It is a duty:

---

[260] *Devizes Reclamation Co v Chalk, The Times*, April 2, 1999, where a lump of lead had fallen from a lorry and the claimant attempted to move it by slewing it around.

[261] *Vernon v B.T.C.* (1963) 107 S.J. 113 (an employer should have made allowances for the fact that workmen do stumble sometimes); *Field v Jeavons & Co Ltd* [1965] 1 W.L.R. 996 (occupiers of a factory must be prepared for some degree of stupidity and forgetfulness on the part of those working in the factory); *McArthur v B.R.B.* (1968) 6 K.I.R. 40 (engine driver was killed when he was obliged to lean out of the cab to observe a signal placed near a bridge with an unusually narrow clearance); *McGhee v N.C.B.* [1973] 1 W.L.R. 1 (failure to provide adequate washing facilities which resulted in pursuer contracting dermatitis from the brick dust adhering to his skin).

[262] For a classic example of which, see *Nicol v Allyacht Spars Pty Ltd* (1987) 75 Q.L.R. 1, H.C. of Australia. See para.11–81, n.323, below for the facts.

[263] *Winter v Cardiff Rural District Council* [1950] 1 All E.R. 819 at 835.

[264] *Winter v Cardiff Rural District Council*, above. Note that this case was decided before the doctrine of common employment was abolished. Today, the employer would be liable: *Campion v Scruttons* [1968] 2 Lloyd's Rep. 469. But cf. *Roy v Co-ordinated Traffic Services* (1969) 113 S.J. 162.

[265] See *King v Smith (t/a Clean Glo)* [1995] P.I.Q.R. P48, CA; *Thomas v General Motors Holden* (1988) 49 S.A.S.R. 11.

[266] See, e.g. *Brisco v Secretary of State for Scotland*, 1997 S.C. 14, 2 Div: a prison officer, equipped with a helmet and body armour, sustained injury to his foot in the course of simulated riot forming part of his training.

[267] *Vickers v B.T.D.B.* [1964] 1 Lloyd's Rep. 275; also *Nilsson v Redditch Borough Council* [1995] P.I.Q.R. P199, CA (where it was held that the mere fact that the "black bag" system of collecting refuse was hazardous did not render it an unsafe system of work).

"to take reasonable steps to provide a system which will be reasonably safe, having regard to the dangers necessarily inherent in the operation. In deciding what is reasonable, long established practice in the trade, although not necessarily conclusive, is generally regarded as strong evidence in support of reasonableness."[268]

Long established practice will not avail an employer if he has failed to keep himself up to date. Knowledge moves on and an employer must keep reasonably abreast of developments which may afford greater protection against known risks, or alert him to risks which have not been identified. Considerations of this kind were discussed by Mustill J. in *Thompson v Smiths Shiprepairers (North Shields) Ltd.*[269] Having referred to the distinction between a recognised practice followed without mishap, and one which, in the light of common sense or increased knowledge is clearly bad, he went on: **11–70**

"Between the two extremes is a type of risk which is regarded at any given time (although not necessarily later) as an inescapable feature of the industry. The employer is not liable for the consequences of such risks, although subsequent changes in social awareness, or improvements in knowledge or technology, may transfer the risk into the category of those against which the employer can and should take care. It is unnecessary, and perhaps impossible, to give a comprehensive formula for identifying the line between the acceptable and the unacceptable. Nevertheless, the line does exist and was clearly recognised in the speeches in *Morris v West Hartlepool Steam Navigation Co Ltd.*[270] The speeches in that case show, not that one employer is exonerated simply by proving that other employers are just as negligent, but that the standard of what is negligent is influenced, although not decisively, by the practice in the industry as a whole. In my judgment, this principle applies not only where the breach of duty is said to consist of a failure to take precautions known to be available as a means of combating a known danger, but also where the omission involves an absence of initiative in seeking out knowledge of facts which are not in themselves obvious. The employer must keep up to date, but the court must be slow to blame him for ploughing a lone furrow."[271]

In some cases the court regards a danger as so obvious that a general practice to ignore it is clearly wrong.[272] By way of illustration, if window cleaners have to clean windows high above the ground by standing on a sill, approximately six inches wide, without any instructions either to ensure that the windows should be tested before cleaning or to use any apparatus, such as wedges, to prevent them from closing,[273] or, being provided with safety belts to attach them to available transoms,[274] there is a failure to provide a safe system of work: **11–71**

---

[268] *General Cleaning Contractors Ltd v Christmas* [1953] A.C. 180 at 195, per Lord Tucker.
[269] [1984] Q.B. 405.
[270] [1956] A.C. 552.
[271] [1984] Q.B. 405 at 415. Quoted by Smith L.J. in *Brookes v South Yorkshire Passenger Transport Executive* [2005] EWCA Civ 452, para.11–15, n.68, above.
[272] See generally Ch.7, para.7–38, above. Where a dangerous method of work used by a claimant had become a common practice amongst his fellow workmen, a fact which was known to the chief shift engineers but not to the works manager, the employers could not thereby avoid liability: *Bell v Greater London Council* (1969) 119 New L.J. 153.
[273] *General Cleaning Contractors Ltd v Christmas* [1953] A.C. 180; *Baker v White's Window & General Cleaning Co, The Times*, March 1, 1962.
[274] *Drummond v British Building Cleaners Ltd* [1954] 1 W.L.R. 1434. A further case concerning the provision of safety belts is *Roberts v Dorman Long & Co Ltd* [1953] 2 All E.R. 428, but see n.289, below. See, also, *King v Smith* [1995] P.I.Q.R. P48, CA.

"Where the negligence of the employer consists of what I may call a fault of omission, I think it is absolutely necessary that the proof of that fault of omission should be one of two kinds, either to show that the thing which he did not do was a thing which was commonly done by other persons in like circumstances, or to show that it was a thing which was so obviously wanted that it would be folly in anyone to neglect to provide it."[275]

11–72   Cases may well arise, where, at the outset, it will become essential for the employer to give adequate instructions to his workmen, especially when they are inexperienced. Such instructions would have to include not only the proper and safe method of doing the job but also the likely dangers to be met, if they were to depart from that prescribed method, by using some different or less safe way.

ILLUSTRATIONS

11–73   Liability was established: where an electrician was not instructed to remove a safety screen when carrying out some tests on some equipment[276]; where there was a failure to give an instruction to switch off a machine before removing a guard[277]; where there was a failure to prohibit the practice of oiling dangerous machines whilst they were in motion[278]; where a workman was not instructed to use a soft-headed hammer on brittle steel[279]; where there was a failure to warn an inexperienced labourer either to avoid striking a hard steel pin, which was likely to be brittle, or else to wear goggles[280]; where a fireman was required to use a type of ram with which he was unfamiliar, in stressful circumstances where he was trying to free a driver trapped in the cab of a lorry.[281]

A warning of the danger of standing on a box to gain access to the upper shelves in a warehouse was required, even though the risk was obvious.[282] Equally, there will be cases where no instructions or repetitions of warnings will be necessary at all. This applies particularly to experienced workmen.

11–74   It was unnecessary to give repeated warnings to experienced window cleaners about the dangers of loose and unreliable window handles which they knew they

---

[275] per Lord Dunedin in *Morton v William Dixon Ltd*, 1909 S.C. 807, quoted in *Paris v Stepney Borough Council* [1951] A.C. 367 at 382. See Ch.7, para.7–40, above, *Cavanagh v Ulster Weaving Co* [1960] A.C. 145, per Lord Somervell of Harrow: "Lord Dunedin's observation was, in its context, clearly only intended to apply where the practice proved was clearly proved and where the circumstances covered by the practice were precisely similar to those in which the accident happened. There may be many cases in which, although the circumstances are not precisely similar, evidence of practice should be given some though less weight." Further see *Graham v Co-operative Wholesale Society Ltd* [1957] 1 W.L.R. 511; *Riddick v Weir Housing Corporation*, 1970 S.L.T. 71.

[276] *Barcock v Brighton Corp* [1949] 1 K.B. 339.

[277] *Quinn v Horsfall & Bickham Ltd* [1956] 1 W.L.R. 652.

[278] *Lewis v High Duty Alloys Ltd* [1957] 1 W.L.R. 632.

[279] *Dimmock v British Railways Board*, The Times, July 1, 1965.

[280] *Payne v Peter Bennie Ltd* (1973) 14 K.I.R. 395.

[281] *Pennington v Surrey County Council* [2007] P.I.Q.R. P11 CA (the claimant had not been instructed in the use of the ram although he was familiar with a model which was substantially lighter).

[282] *Ammah v Kuehne & Nagel Logistics Ltd* [2009] EWCA Civ 11 (on the facts an appropriate warning was given and the claim failed). See Patten, "Do thy duty" 159 N.L.J. 579

would meet from time to time.[283] It was not necessary to tell cleaners how to wipe up slippery substances from a factory floor without slipping on the floor themselves.[284] It may not be necessary to warn where the risk is of a condition associated with a functional or psychogenic disorder and giving the warning might have the effect of bringing about the very condition it was desired to prevent.[285] In order to avoid liability, where a danger is known to exist, it may be insufficient for an employer merely to issue orders that something must not be done, without doing more to ensure that such prohibition is actually observed.[286]

The operation may be one dealt with specifically by statute or statutory   **11–75**
regulation, in which event compliance with the statutory requirements is evidence that the common law duty has been fulfilled.[287] This is illustrated in a case where a claimant, employed by a tunnelling company to work in a coal mine, was injured by a fall of stone from the roof. The mine was owned and occupied by the National Coal Board, which was under a statutory duty to secure the roof, and the system of working, so far as it concerned support for the roof, was that advocated by the Board. It was held that the tunnelling company had used reasonable care in following the advice of the Board and were not in breach of their common law duty to the claimant.[288] It is not, however, conclusive evidence, so that, either in exceptional circumstances or where some special peril is to be met, the common law duty is not restricted to the statutory requirements.[289]

Checking that the system is followed. The fact of prescribing a safe system   **11–76**
of work does not sufficiently discharge an employer's duty, unless it is also accompanied by steps reasonably to ensure it is followed, such as, for example, inspection and supervision. Where a tug captain properly directed that a signal be given before the vessel's engine was started, so as to ensure that a rope might be safely cast off, and then caused the vessel to move off before the signal was given, so that an employee was injured, the employers were held liable: the captain had abandoned a safe system of his own devising and substituted an

---

[283] *Wilson v Tyneside Window Cleaning Co* [1958] 2 Q.B. 110.
[284] *Vinnyey v Star Paper Mills Ltd* [1965] 1 All E.R. 175.
[285] *Pickford v Imperial Chemical Industries Plc* [1998] 1 W.L.R. 1189, HL, at 1206, above para.11–15, n.72.
[286] *Baker v T.E. Hopkins & Son Ltd* [1959] 1 W.L.R. 966.
[287] *Caulfield v Pickup Ltd* [1941] 2 All E.R. 510; *Franklin v Gramophone Co* [1948] 1 K.B. 542 at 558; *England v N.C.B.* [1953] 1 Q.B. 724 at 731, per Somervell L.J. (the case was reversed on other grounds [1954] A.C. 403); *Chipchase v British Titan Products Co Ltd* [1956] 1 Q.B. 545; *Smith v Austin Lifts Ltd* [1959] 1 W.L.R. 100.
[288] *Szumczyk v Associated Tunnelling Co Ltd* (1956), unreported in the CA, affirming [1956] 1 W.L.R. 98.
[289] *Roberts v Dorman Long & Co Ltd* [1953] 2 All E.R. 428 at 436, disapproved in *McWilliams v Sir William Arrol & Co* [1962] 1 W.L.R. 295, HL in so far as it purported to contradict the principle that a causal connection must be established between the damage suffered by an employee and a breach of common law or statutory duty.) Further, see *Harriman v Martin* [1962] 1 W.L.R. 739 and *Jones v N.C.B.* [1965] 1 W.L.R. 532 (where a breach of the common law duty was found but not a breach of statutory duty); also *Kelly v John Dale Ltd* [1965] 1 Q.B. 185 (vice versa).

unsafe system.[290] Supervision is particularly required when someone is given a task beyond their competence and initiative.[291] On the other hand, an experienced man does not need any warnings or advice about risks, with which he is thoroughly familiar.[292] Regulation 13 of the Management of Health and Safety at Work Regulations 1999 has effectively given this principle statutory force by providing that, as regards health and safety, an employer shall take into account his employees' capabilities in entrusting them with tasks. Merely giving written instructions, which set out and explain the system, and then telling the workman to comply with them, without doing more, was held to be insufficient to discharge the employer's duty.[293] An employer does not discharge his duty by establishing a system and turning a blind eye to its breach.[294] Likewise, the provision of necessary protective clothing, such as goggles or masks or barrier cream, may not be enough, unless reasonable steps also are taken to point out the risks of not using it and to explain its benefits in order to encourage men to use it.[295]

11-77   Although there are remarks in *Qualcast (Wolverhampton) Ltd v Haynes*[296] suggesting that the courts should be slow to extend the duty to provide safety equipment to include a duty to encourage the use of such equipment, they do not form part of the *ratio* of the decision of the House of Lords and are certainly at odds with later practice. The common law has largely been overtaken by statutory duty,[297] but in *Qualcast* itself, Lord Denning indicated that an employer should "advise and encourage" employees to wear the protective footwear available,[298] an approach also adopted in relation to work where the risk of injury

---

[290] per Lord Brandon in *McDermid v Nash Dredging & Reclamation Co Ltd* [1987] A.C. 906, at 919.

[291] *Byers v Head Wrightson & Co Ltd* [1961] 1 W.L.R. 961.

[292] *Qualcast (Wolverhampton) Ltd v Haynes* [1959] A.C. 743.

[293] *Barcock v Brighton Corp* [1949] 1 K.B. 339. But the HL queried in *Boyle v Kodak Ltd* [1969] 1 W.L.R. 661 whether there is any duty at common law to instruct workmen, when the statutory obligation is to do no more than a skilled man must know to be necessary.

[294] *McGregor v A.A.H. Pharmaceuticals*, 1996 S.L.T. 1161, OH: training and a booklet on good working practice was given but managers tacitly permitted warehouse operators to climb upon shelves whilst trying to retrieve boxes from a height of over 6ft.

[295] *Crookall v Vickers-Armstrong Ltd* [1955] 1 W.L.R. 659 (masks against breathing in harmful silica dust); *Clifford v Challen & Sons Ltd* [1951] K.B. 495 (barrier cream against contact with harmful synthetic glue); *Berry v Stone Manganese & Marine Ltd* (1971) 115 S.J. 966 (ear-muffs as a protection against noise). cf. *Woods v Durable Suites Ltd* [1953] 1 W.L.R. 857, where the duty was satisfied. In *Watson v Ready Mixed Concrete, The Times,* January 18, 1961, Edmund Davies J. held that the value of barrier cream was, on the then available scientific evidence, extremely questionable and that failure to provide such cream had not been proved to be a substantial causative factor by a claimant who had probably suffered from a constitutional skin disease.

[296] [1959] A.C. 743, per Lord Radcliffe at 753 and later approved by Viscount Simonds L.C. in *McWilliams v Sir William Arrol & Co Ltd* [1962] 1 W.L.R. 295 where it was held that there was no duty to require experienced steel erectors to wear safety belts when many such employees reasonably believed that there were disadvantages in wearing them.

[297] The Personal Protective Equipment at Work Regulations 1992 not only require the provision of suitable personal protective equipment but the provision of, inter alia, information, instruction and training as to the risks it is designed to avoid and the purpose and manner of its use: reg.9. See Ch.12, para.12–232, below.

[298] *Qualcast (Wolverhampton) Ltd v Haynes* [1959] A.C. 743 at 760.

was high.[299] So, more recently, it was held that, where the claimant's eyes were particularly at risk during the process of pouring molten aluminium alloy, the employer's duty of care extended to instructing, persuading and even insisting upon the use of protective equipment, it being insufficient simply to have provided him with goggles.[300] Likewise, where employees were exposed to detergents and chemical cleaning products capable of causing dermatitis, the employers were under a duty to warn their employees of the risk that the gloves were designed to protect and to instruct them in the need to wear them at all times.[301]

It has been held to be an answer to a claim for failing to provide the necessary   **11–78** protective clothing to say that the workmen would probably not have used it.[302] In *Qualcast* Lord Denning said:

> "it is often said that a person who omits to do his duty 'cannot be heard to say' that it would have made no difference even if he had done it . . . But this is an overstatement. The judge *may* infer the omission to be a cause, but he is not bound to do so. If at the end of the day he thinks that, whether the duty was omitted or fulfilled, the result would have been the same, he is at liberty to say so."[303]

Conversely, where it was probable that the workman would have used the safety equipment, had it been provided, the employers will be liable, once causation has been established.[304]

ILLUSTRATIONS

Systems held to be unsafe: when stones, likely to fall, were slung over the   **11–79** heads of men working below, without making any provision for warning the men, prior to the transference through the air[305]; where the employers' foreman had failed to instruct an employee not to stand beneath the overhead operation of the

---

[299] *Nolan v Dental Manufacturing Co Ltd* [1958] 1 W.L.R. 936 (wearing of goggles whilst grinding).

[300] *Bux v Slough Metals Ltd* [1973] 1 W.L.R. 1358: the claimant was nevertheless held 40 per cent to blame for his own failure to make "full and proper" use of the goggles provided for him to use.

[301] *Pape v Cumbria County Council* [1992] I.C.R. 132. See also *Campbell v Lothian Health Board*, 1987 S.L.T. 665. Quite apart from the statutory duty under the Personal Protective Equipment at Work Regulations 1992, it is doubtful whether *James v Hepworth and Grandage Ltd* [1968] 1 Q.B. 94 would be decided in the same way today: warning notices that spats were provided to guard against metal splashes constituted a sufficient discharge of the duty where, unknown to the employer, the claimant was illiterate. Contrast the view taken in *Tasci v Pekalp of London Ltd, The Times*, January 17, 2001, CA, discussed in Ch.12, para.12–202, n.673, below.

[302] *McWilliams v Sir William Arrol & Co Ltd* [1962] 1 W.L.R. 295, which was applied in *Wigley v British Vinegars Ltd* [1964] A.C. 307; see also *Nolan v Dental Manufacturing Co Ltd* [1958] 1 W.L.R. 936; *Percival v Leicester Corp* [1962] 2 Lloyd's Rep. 43, where a fireman had drowned practising aqualung swimming: he had received adequate instructions but had disregarded orders to use a safety line. Note that reg.10(2) of the Personal Protective Equipment at Work Regulations 1992, Ch.12, para.12–234, below, now places an obligation on the employee to use personal protective equipment provided to him in accordance with his instruction and training.

[303] [1959] A.C. 743 at 762.

[304] *Machray v Stewarts & Lloyds Ltd* [1965] 1 W.L.R. 602.

[305] *Smith v Baker & Sons* [1891] A.C. 325.

manual extension of a crane's jib and a part of it fell down and struck him[306]; where the haulage in a mine was continued during the period when it was known that men would be travelling along the road, at the end of their shift[307]; when, as a result of a misunderstanding, because of the method of teaching at a flying school, an aircraft's engine was started prematurely[308]; when lighting of great intensity was used in making a film, and neither was any warning given to the actors nor were precautions taken against injury to their eyes[309]; when a large quantity of highly combustible material was kept in immediate proximity to a boiler, from which sparks were likely to be emitted on it being fired[310]; when, in unloading a ship, no adequate barricade was placed on the deck to prevent cargo, which frequently slipped from the slings, from rolling over the ship's side and dropping on to a barge below[311]; when, in loading a ship, a rail was not removed, with the result that a hook caught it, which caused some timber to fall on to a barge alongside[312]; when a man was working in a ship on the 'tween deck under closed hatches next to an open hatchway, and no adequate light or fencing to the hatch was provided[313]; where the upper deck hatches were battened down but the 'tween deck hatch covers were not replaced, leaving the hatchway unfenced, so that a seaman, who was sent down to the 'tween deck, while the ship was at sea, fell into the hold and was injured[314]; in failing to depute one of the available men, engaged in lifting a heavy plate, to act as co-ordinator of the lifting operation as a whole.[315]

11–80   Also in requiring two dockers to lift and manhandle a load that necessitated their sharing equally a weight of 280lb, that is, 140lb each, which share was the maximum safe weight that either one man ought to have been asked to lift in the circumstances, when there was present a foreseeable risk of an uneven sharing of the load occurring between them[316]; when a man was required to wheel a heavy load on to a narrow ledge where it was likely to, and did, overbalance[317]; when a workshop contained a grinder, which created dust, and no exhaust appliance was provided[318]; where a workpiece, held in the rapidly revolving chuck of a lathe, was polished by a piece of emery cloth which was wrapped around the turner's finger and pressed up against it[319]; when men were working on the permanent way at the exit of a railway tunnel, without the lookout man so placed that he could warn the men in time to enable them to get to a place of safety, out

---

[306] *Kendis v State Transport Authority* (1984) 154 C.L.R. 672.
[307] *Wilsons and Clyde Coal Co v English* [1938] A.C. 57.
[308] *Olsen v Corry* [1936] 3 All E.R. 241.
[309] *Russell v Criterion Film Production Ltd* (1936) 53 T.L.R. 117.
[310] *D'Urso v Sanson* [1939] 4 All E.R. 26.
[311] *Grantham v New Zealand Shipping Co* [1940] 4 All E.R. 258.
[312] *Speed v Thomas Swift & Co Ltd* [1943] K.B. 557.
[313] *Garcia v Harland & Wolff Ltd* [1943] K.B. 731.
[314] *Morris v West Hartlepool Steam Navigation Co* [1956] A.C. 552.
[315] *Upson v Temple Engineering (Southend)* (1975) 1 K.I.R. 171.
[316] *Fricker v Benjamin Perry & Sons Ltd* (1974) 16 K.I.R. 356.
[317] *Rees v Cambrian Wagon Works* (1946) 62 T.L.R. 512 ("It was no answer to say that if the workman or the manager had looked about elsewhere proper materials could have been found").
[318] *Franklin v Gramophone Co* [1948] 1 K.B. 542.
[319] *Brown v John Mills & Co (Llanidloes) Ltd* (1970) 8 K.I.R. 702.

of the way of approaching trains[320]; when a workman was repairing a ship in dry dock, not taking any steps to prevent him from falling into the hold[321]; in failing to provide boards for men to stand on when they were working on a roof, from which they were likely to fall.[322]

Also, where an employee, in the course of removing a banner from a flag-pole, **11–81** located at a height of approximately 27 feet, fell from an extension ladder, which he had fixed to a trestle, standing on the platform of a utility truck[323]; where a workman died from scrotal cancer, which had been caused by regular contact over many years with mineral oil in the course of his employment, and there had been failure to warn him about the dangers to which he was being exposed, to advise him about the precautions he ought to be taking, and to institute six-monthly medical examinations in the circumstances[324]; in failing to warn an experienced cement labourer of the danger of his contracting dermatitis, to encourage him to take precautions and to provide adequate washing facilities, where his conditions of work with dry cement were exceptionally bad[325]; where a workman was required to handle detergents, likely to cause dermatitis, for use in cleaning work, but the employers supplied him with a pair of gloves which only extended a few inches up his forearms instead of up to the elbows, as a result of which his skin was contaminated and he developed the disease[326]; where a cleaner developed dermatitis from exposure to detergents and chemical cleaning products, the mere provision of protective rubber gloves without an accompanying warning of the danger of irritant dermatitis was an insufficient discharge of the duty to devise a safe system of work[327]; where a local authority failed to relieve the pressure of work on an employee who had suffered one nervous breakdown as a result of his work and thereafter suffered a second[328]; where pallets of bricks were so stacked as to obscure views by the side of a road through the premises of a builders' merchant[329]; where the owners of a tug, operating in a war zone, failed to give written instructions, identifying the type of risk to which the vessel was likely to be exposed and how such risk might be reduced or eliminated[330]; where employers of a cleaner, injured when a high

---

[320] *Dyer v Southern Ry* [1948] 1 K.B. 608.

[321] *Donovan v Cammell Laird & Co* [1949] 2 All E.R. 82.

[322] *Harris v Brights Contractors Co* [1953] 1 Q.B. 617.

[323] *Nicol v Allyacht Spars Pty Ltd* (1987) 75 A.L.R. 1 (the combined use of the ladder, trestle and utility had been arranged in consultation between the employee, who also happened to be a director of the employer, and other employees. But, this fact did not disentitle his claim concerning the unsafe system of work devised. His contributory negligence, on the other hand, did reduce his damages by 40 per cent).

[324] *Stokes v Guest Keen & Nettlefold (Bolts & Nuts)* [1968] 1 W.L.R. 1776. Similarly see *Wright v Dunlop Rubber Co* (1971) 11 K.I.R. 311, affirmed (1972) 13 K.I.R. 255, CA.

[325] *Snell v J. Shelbourne & Co* (1965) 109 S.J. 270. But cf. *Riddick v Weir Housing Corp*, 1970 S.L.T. 71.

[326] *Voller v Schweppes (Home)* (1969) 7 K.I.R. 228.

[327] *Pape v Cumbria County Council* [1992] I.C.R. 132, Waite J.

[328] *Walker v Northumberland County Council* [1995] 1 All E.R. 737. see further para.11–84, below.

[329] *Dew v Slocombe & Butcher Ltd* [1996] C.L.Y. 2998, CA.

[330] *Tarrant v Ramage, The Times*, July 31, 1997: there was no instruction, if there was risk from Exocet missiles, to move into the radar shadow of the damaged vessel being towed.

wind blew shut the lid of a skip into which rubbish was being emptied, failed to assess and act upon the foreseeable risk, although aware of the propensity of the lid to shut in that way.[331] A hospital authority was liable to nurses at a special hospital, injured in an attack by a patient with a personality disorder and a history of violence towards staff, where no assessment of the risk posed by the patient had been carried out ; and had such an assessment been performed it would have been unreasonable to conclude other than that the patient should have been confined at night in her room[332]; an employer was liable for causing or permitting an employee to drive who was too tired as a result of excessive working hours, as a result of which he fell asleep at the wheel of a van so that a road traffic accident occurred.[333]

11–82   Systems held not to be unsafe: when girls were put to work on mechanical mincers, after they were first employed for a week on general work and then, if thought suitable, were instructed to work the mincer by an experienced worker, supervising them[334]; when loading operations on a ship were resumed and the derrick arm, which was insecurely fastened, swung and caused some of the cargo being loaded to fall[335]; when a workman, who was insufficiently skilled for the purpose, was allowed to make a tool and was subsequently killed whilst using it, owed to it being inadequate[336]; where responsible employees were properly left with the tasks of clearing away any dangerous debris from the immediate vicinity of their workplace[337]; where a hospital authority left to the judgment of a trained nurse the method by which she lifted a patient[338]; where a meat inspector claimed repetitive strain injury because his job required him to examine the carcasses of pigs as they passed along a conveyor[339]; where, as a result of attempting to clear a jammed machine, the operator struck her wrist and thereby suffered disabling symptoms: although there was a known risk of minor injury it was not of such a character as to require her employers to instruct operators not to attempt to clear jams.[340]

11–83   Likewise, there was no negligence when a coachmaker used Monsonia wood, which caused dermatitis in a workman, and in the light of knowledge then available, it was not possible to say that a reasonable employer ought to have

---

[331] *Hannington v Mitie Cleaning (South East) Ltd* [2002] EWCA Civ 1847.

[332] *Buck v Nottinghamshire Healthcare NHS Trust, The Times,* December 1, 2006 CA (the court held that the defendant's duty to the patient herself was relevant to, but not determinative of, the duty to staff).

[333] *Eyres v Atkinsons Kitchens and Bedrooms Ltd, The Times,* May 21, 2007 CA.

[334] *Wood v London County Council* [1940] 4 All E.R. 149, reversed on another point [1941] 2 K.B. 232.

[335] *Colfar v Coggins and Griffith (Liverpool) Ltd* [1945] A.C. 197.

[336] *Franklin v Bristol Aeroplane Co* [1948] W.N. 341.

[337] *Stanley v Concentric (Pressed Products)* (1971) 11 K.I.R. 260, CA.

[338] *Woolger v West Surrey & North East Hampshire Health Authority, The Times,* November 8, 1993, CA; *Rozario v Post Office* [1997] P.I.Q.R. P15, CA: no duty to supervise lifting by an experienced employee, even though he had suffered previous back injury.

[339] *Wilebore v St Edmundsbury Borough Council* [1994] C.L.Y. 2282.

[340] *McErlean v J & B Scotland Ltd,* 1997 G.W.D. 6–253, OH.

anticipated that exposure to dust from the wood was likely to result in injury[341]; when employers provided an omnibus service to take their workmen from the working site and a workman was crushed in a disorganised rush by the waiting workmen to get into the bus[342]; when a workman in a shipyard had lifted up a cable, which was lying across a bogie track, in order to let the bogie pass along, but was struck and injured by it[343]; where a farm labourer, who had to clean out a loose box, in which was kept a fierce bull, was instructed first to secure the bull through a window and not to enter the loose box before the bull was properly secured[344]; when scaffolding, which had not been provided by the defendants but by other contractors working on the same building, had platform boards with spaces between them and no toe boards[345]; in cutting barbed wire by placing it on the metal head of a sledge hammer and striking it with a smaller hammer[346]; where an experienced workman knowingly used a wrong tool for the job and alleged that his employers ought either to have warned or have reminded him to use the correct tool, which they had supplied[347]; when, over a period of 10 years, the stevedore claimant had been carrying to the appropriate places in the holds of ships 2cwt cost bags of fertiliser, which had been lifted up to his shoulders, one bag at a time, by two other workmen.[348]

Stress at work.[349] The development of the law applicable to claims for **11–84** psychiatric injury caused by stress at work began with *Walker v Northumberland County Council.*[350] That case, in which the employer was held liable for psychiatric illness suffered by an employee who was of middle management status within its social services department, involved the allegations that the system of work was defective in the imposition of excessive stress upon the employee as well as the failure to identify and investigate stressful aspects of work as they arose. The court upheld his complaint that the employer had failed to respond to pleas for assistance despite the fact that it knew that he had previously suffered a breakdown attributable to stress caused by the volume of work and lack of assistance to carry out his duties. That earlier breakdown had rendered it reasonably foreseeable that he might suffer a further breakdown if appropriate precautions were not taken. However, the claim in respect of the first illness failed on the ground that it was not reasonably foreseeable that his workload would have given rise to a material risk of mental illness. Colman J. applied the following test in addressing the question of the magnitude of the risk to which the claimant was exposed:

---

[341] *Ebbs v James Whitson & Co Ltd* [1952] 2 Q.B. 877; *Graham v Co-operative Wholesale Society Ltd* [1957] 1 W.L.R. 511; cf. *Stokes v Guest Keen & Nettlefold (Bolts & Nuts)* [1968] 1 W.L.R. 1776.
[342] *Ramsay v Wimpey & Co*, 1952 S.L.T. 46.
[343] *Grace v Stephen & Sons*, 1952 S.L.T. 61.
[344] *Rands v McNeil* [1955] 1 Q.B. 253; *James v Wellington City* [1972] N.Z.L.R. 70 (chimpanzee bit off zoo-keeper's finger).
[345] *Hughes v McGoff & Vickers Ltd* [1955] 2 All E.R. 291.
[346] *Baker v Harvey Farms (Thorpe), The Times*, October 26, 1961.
[347] *Leach v British Oxygen Co* (1965) 109 S.J. 157.
[348] *Holmes v Tees & Hartlepool Port Authority* [1992] 48 E.G. 111.
[349] For claims for psychiatric injury generally, see Ch.2 paras 2–110–2–162, above.
[350] [1995] 1 All E.R. 737, Q.B.D.

"the question is whether it ought to have been foreseen that [the claimant] was exposed to a risk of mental illness materially higher than that which would ordinarily affect a social services manager in his position with a really heavy workload. For if the foreseeable risk were not materially greater than that there would not, as a matter of reasonable conduct, be any basis upon which the [defendant's] duty to act arose."[351]

11–85   Whilst *Walker's case* encouraged claims by others affected by mental illness which they attributed to their work, it did not have the effect of opening floodgates. Nearly a decade passed before the Court of Appeal had the opportunity to review the subject comprehensively. In *Sutherland v Hatton*,[352] Hale L.J. set out a series of practical propositions to be applied in such cases:

"1. There are no special control mechanisms applying to claims for psychiatric (or physical) injury arising from the stress of doing the work the employee is required to do. The ordinary principles of employer's liability apply.

2. The threshold question is whether this kind of harm to this particular employee was reasonably foreseeable: this has two components: (a) an injury to health (as distinct from occupational stress) which (b) is attributable to stress at work (as distinct from other factors).

3. Foreseeability depends upon what the employer knows (or ought reasonably to have known) about the individual employee.[353] Because of the nature of mental disorder, it is harder to foresee than physical injury, but may be easier to foresee in a known individual than in the population at large. An employer is usually entitled to assume that the employee can withstand the normal pressures of the job unless he knows of some particular problem or vulnerability.

4. The test is the same whatever the employment: there are no occupations which should be regarded as intrinsically dangerous to mental health.

5. Factors likely to be relevant in answering the threshold question include:

    (a) The nature and extent of the work done by the employee. Is the workload much more than is normal for the particular job? Is the work particularly intellectually or emotionally demanding for this employee? Are demands being made of this employee unreasonable when compared with the demands made of others in the same or comparable jobs? Or are there signs that others doing this job are suffering harmful levels of stress? Is there an abnormal level of sickness or absenteeism in the same job or the same department?

---

[351] *Walker v Northumberland County Council* [1995] All E.R. 737 Q.B.D. at 752e.

[352] [2002] P.I.Q.R. P241, CA. See also Mullany, "Containing claims for workplace mental illness" (2002) L.Q.R. 118, 372. Also *Young v Post Office* [2002] I.R.L.R. 660, CA (workshop manager who had a nervous breakdown as a result of work-related stress returned to work and broke down a second time. Arrangements to ease his return to work had not been adhered to and his employer was liable even though the claimant had not spoken up to say that his work was becoming too onerous again) ; *Bonser v UK Coal Mining Ltd, The Times*, June 30, 2003 (the claimant failed where the only sign visible to her employer that she was under stress was a single occasion where she was tearful and upset); *Pratley v Surrey CC* [2004] P.I.Q.R. P252, CA (a distinction can be drawn between a risk of illness arising from continuing work overload over a future period and a risk of immediate collapse. The fact that an employer can foresee continuing work overload does not mean that it can foresee an immediate collapse in the health of the employee).

[353] See, e.g. *Witham v Hastings and Rother NHS Trust* [2003] C.L.Y. 2967, Q.B.D. (SRN, who suffered post-natal depression and was intended to make a phased return to work, was left without management support and required to work far in excess of her contractual hours).

(b) Signs from the employee of impending harm to health. Has he a particular problem or vulnerability? Has he already suffered from illness attributable to stress at work? Have there been frequent or prolonged absences which are uncharacteristic of him? Is there reason to think that these are attributable to stress at work, for example because of complaints or warnings from him or others?[354]

6. The employer is generally entitled to take what he is told by his employee at face value, unless he has good reason to think to the contrary. He does not generally have to make searching enquiries of the employee or seek permission to make further enquiries of his medical advisers.

7. To trigger a duty to take steps, the indications of impending harm to health arising from stress at work must be plain enough for any reasonable employer to realise that he should do something about it.[355]

8. The employer is only in breach of duty if he has failed to take the steps which are reasonable in the circumstances, bearing in mind the magnitude of the risk of harm occurring, the gravity of the harm which may occur, the costs and practicability of preventing it, and the justifications for running the risk.

9. The size and scope of the employer's operation, its resources and the demands it faces are relevant in deciding what is reasonable; these include the interests of other employees and the need to treat them fairly, for example, in the redistribution of duties.

10. An employer can only be expected to take steps which are likely to do some good: the court is likely to need expert evidence on this point.[356]

11. An employer who offers a confidential advice service, with referral to appropriate counselling or treatment services, is unlikely to be found in breach of duty.[357]

12. If the only reasonable and effective step would have been to dismiss or demote the employee, the employer will not be in breach of duty in allowing a willing employee to continue in the job.[358]

---

[354] See, e.g. *Hone v Six Continents Retail Ltd* [2006] I.R.L.R. 49, CA: sufficient indicators of impending harm to health in employee who claimed to work in excess of 90 hours each week.

[355] Where there were no significantly plain indications to the defendant of impending harm to the health of the claimant to trigger the duty at a time when allegedly negligent corporate failings were active, the claim will be struck out: *French v Sussex CC* [2005] P.I.Q.R. P243, Q.B.D. See Ch.2, para.2–159 for the facts.

[356] The lack of expert evidence was not fatal to a successful claim in *Hone v Six Continents Retail Limited* [2007] I.R.L.R. 49, CA albeit it was nevertheless necessary to demonstrate that the workload in question gave rise to a foreseeable risk of psychiatric harm.

[357] For an example where there was an adequate policy of medical monitoring, see *Vahidi v Fairstead House School Trust Ltd* [2005] P.I.Q.R. P112. Compare *Daw v Intel Corporation (UK) Ltd* [2007] 2 All E.R. 126, CA (the availability of a counselling service is not a panacea by which employers will discharge their duty of care in all cases and on the facts it was open to the trial judge to find that the failure of the defendant to take urgent corrective action to reduce a totally unreasonable workload was causative of the severe depression suffered by the claimant, which would not have been avoided by the provision of counsellors). See also *Dickins v O2 Plc* [2009] I.R.L.R. 58, CA (an employer could still be in breach of duty, notwithstanding the availability of a counselling service, where the employee's problems could only be dealt with by management intervention). See further Marnham, "Stressed out" 157 N.L.J. 309; Case, "Occupational stress" P.N. 2007, 23(2), 123: Barrett, "Psychiatric stress—an unacceptable cost to employers" J.B.L. 2008,1, 64.

[358] For modern examples of where a duty to dismiss to protect an employee from physical danger see *Coxall v Goodyear Great Britain Ltd* [2003] 1 W.L.R. 536; *Lane Group Plc v Farmiloe* [2004] P.I.Q.R. P324, EAT.

13. In all cases, it is necessary to identify the steps which the employer both could and should have taken before finding him in breach of his duty of care.

14. The claimant must show that that breach of duty has caused or materially contributed to the harm suffered. It is not enough to show that occupational stress has caused the harm.

15. Where the harm suffered has more than one cause, the employer should only pay for that proportion suffered which is attributable to his wrongdoing, unless the harm is truly indivisible. It is for the defendant to raise the question of apportionment.[359]

16. The assessment of damages will take account of any pre-existing disorder or vulnerability and of the chance that the claimant would have succumbed to a stress related disorder in any event."[360]

11–86   In *Barber v Somerset County Council*,[361] the head of a school mathematics department established negligence against his employer where he fell off work for three weeks: sick notes and a sickness declaration form referred to stress and depression as the cause. On his return to work he was dealt with unsympathetically and his workload remained as heavy as before. It was said in the House of Lords that the managers of his school ought to have taken the initiative in making inquiries on his return to work and reduced his workload to ease his return. His condition should have been monitored and, if it did not improve, some more drastic action should have been taken.

11–87   Subsequently, in *Hartman v South Essex Mental Health and Community Care NHS Trust*,[362] the application of *Hatton* and *Barber* was considered in six appeals heard consecutively. Each case involved a claim for damages for psychiatric injury arising out of stress at work. Whilst the individual cases turned on their particular facts, the attention paid to the trial judges' findings of fact, as the basis upon which issues of foreseeability were determined, underlines the crucial importance of that aspect in establishing liability. In particular, it was emphasised that:

1. Liability for psychiatric injury caused by stress at work was in general no different in principle from liability for physical injury. It was foreseeable injury flowing from the employer's breach of duty which gave rise to the liability. It did not follow that because a claimant suffered stress at work and the employer was in some way in breach of duty in allowing that to occur, the claimant was able to establish a claim in negligence.

---

[359] This aspect of Hale L.J.'s judgment was described as *obiter* by Sedley L.J. in *Dickins v O2 Plc*, n.357 above. See further discussion of this issue at para.11–89 below.

[360] *Sutherland v Hatton* n.352, above at para.[43].

[361] [2004] 1 W.L.R. 1089, HL, one of the appeals heard in the CA with *Sutherland v Hatton* n.352, above. The general guidance given in *Sutherland v Hatton* was not disapproved in the HL, but it was emphasised that every case turns on its own facts. See Case, "Hues of foreseeability: Employer liability for chronic stress and the impact of *Barber*" (2004) 3 P.N. 192; Holgate, "Employers' liability for WRS" (2005) C.S.R., 28, 169.

[362] [2005] P.I.Q.R. P19, CA.

2. Great care had to be taken, in preparing for trial cases involving such claims to isolate the real issues between the parties and to ensure that expenditure on costs was proportionate to what was truly at stake.

3. Whilst the general principles relating to stress at work cases were to be found in *Hatton*, they needed care in their application to the facts of the case under consideration.[363]

Apportionment in work-place stress claims. Two of the cases considered in   **11–88**
Hartman raised issues of general application. In *Moore v Welwyn Components Ltd*, the court considered the approach to apportionment or reduction of damages, once a finding of liability has been made, where it is necessary to reflect non-negligent causes of the illness and/or take account of the fact that the claimant would have succumbed to a stress related disorder in any event. It was observed that where general damages fall to be assessed for breach of duty causing psychiatric injury, they ought to be reduced to reflect the fact that causes other than the breach of duty would, or might, in any event have caused a degree of injury. So far as loss of earnings are concerned, the court said that once it was shown that a breach of duty had caused a loss, it was for the employer to show that there were other causes as well. That would require clear medical evidence, not present in the case under consideration. The agreed medical evidence was equivocal and the oral evidence had not been primarily directed to issues of apportionment or assessment, but to the main issue at trial, namely whether a breach of duty had been established.[364]

However, in *Dickins v O2 Plc*,[365] reservations were expressed about the   **11–89**
correctness of apportionment in stress at work claims and it was suggested that remarks to that effect in *Hatton*[366] should be treated as obiter. It appeared that the claimant had suffered an indivisible injury (her seriously damaged mental state following mental breakdown) but with more than one cause. It was not possible to say that, but for the tort, she would probably not have suffered the breakdown, but it was possible to say that the tort had made a material contribution to it. If that was a correct analysis, the starting point should be that she was entitled to recover in full. Smith L.J. said[367]:

---

[363] See, e.g. *Deadman v. Bristol CC* [2008] P.I.Q.R. P2, CA (a claim for psychiatric injury as result of an employer's breach of the employee's contract of employment in failing to follow a harassment policy. The claimant was the subject of an allegation of harassment which the defendant, his employer, investigated, but in so doing failed to follow an agreed procedure in that the panel considering the matter had two rather than three members. Subsequently the claimant developed symptoms of depression and ceased work. It was held on appeal that the claim should fail where no finding could be made that injury to the claimant as a result of the breach of contract was reasonably foreseeable).

[364] Thus the CA did not criticise the trial judge's decision that this was not a case for apportionment.

[365] n.357 above. See also *Bailey v Ministry of Defence* [2009] 1 W.L.R. 1052, CA (a similar approach although the injury was not psychiatric); Ch.6, para.6–53, above.

[366] Proposition 14 at para.11–85, above.

[367] ibid at [43]. The logic of *Dickins* and *Bailey*, n.365, above, seems compelling. For the reasons given by Smtih L.J. an approach which deducts from general damages for non negligent causes should be avoided ; but that is not to say that the pre existing condition of a claimant is irrelevant when assessing general damages for pain suffering and loss of amenity. Perhaps the difference between these cases and *Moore* is in the end a matter of semantics?

"In *Hatton*, Hale LJ said that a claimant could establish causation by showing that the tort had made a material contribution to the injury. She was presupposing that there were other non-tortious factors in play and that it would not be possible for the claimant to succeed outright on causation by showing that, but for the tort, he would probably not have suffered the injury. That means that a claimant can succeed on causation even though he cannot demonstrate what the causative potency of the tort was, save to say that it had some effect which went beyond the minimal. It seems to me that, if in one breath the judge holds that all that can be said about the effect of the tort is that it made an unspecified material contribution, it is illogical for him, in the next breath, to attempt to assess the percentage effect of the tort as a basis for apportionment of the whole of the damages. That is not to say that it is not important to have in mind in assessing damages the condition of the claimant before any tortious act occurred. In particular it might be appropriate, where the judge holds that non-tortious factors have been in play, to discount particular heads of damage, for example, to reflect the risk that the claimant might in any event have suffered a breakdown at some time in the future and would then have suffered some loss of earnings or incurred some expense."

11–90   **Intrinsically shocking experiences.** In *Melville v The Home Office*,[368] the court considered foreseeability where an employee was exposed in the course of work to incidents of a particularly shocking kind. From time to time the claimant's duties as a prison officer had required him to participate in recovering the bodies of prisoners who had committed suicide in custody. There was documentary evidence that the Home Office had recognised a risk that persons who were called on to deal with such traumatic incidents might sustain injury to their health and that those persons should therefore receive support from the prison care team following such an incident. Liability for the claimant's psychiatric injury was established. It was not a precondition in all cases that the employer foresee the risk of harm to the particular individual who made the claim. Each case would turn on its facts but the court ended with words of caution[369]:

"The mere fact that an employer offers an occupational health service should not lead to the conclusion that the employer has foreseen risk of psychiatric injury due to stress at work to any individual or class of employee. And of course the availability of such a service will mean that the employer is unlikely to be found in breach even if harm is foreseeable.[370] Moreover in a case where a conscientious employer has assessed that there is a potential risk of psychiatric injury, it will still be open to him to argue that it was a mere possibility or so small that it was reasonable for him to neglect it.[371] Nor does it follow that if one employer has foreseen a particular risk, all others in the same field should have done so as well. If there is an issue as to whether a particular employer should have done so, it would fall to be decided in accordance with Swanwick J.'s statement of general principle in *Stokes v Guest Keen & Nettlefold (Bolts & Nuts) Ltd.*"[372]

11–91   **Pleading of "unsafe system".** There are differing views of the extent to which, if he raises the issue, the claimant must plead what the proper system was, and in what aspects it was not observed. In the view of one eminent judge he

---

[368] n.362, above.
[369] n.362, above at [137].
[370] See further, *Sutherland v Hatton*, n.352 above at [17] and [33].
[371] *The Wagon Mound No.2* [1967] A.C. 617 at 642–644. See further Ch.5, para.5–13, above.
[372] [1968] 1 W.L.R. 1776, para.11–02, above.

should set his case out with some particularity.[373] However, in *Dixon v Cementation Co Ltd*,[374] the court held that it was not necessary in every such case for the claimant to undertake the burden of pleading and proving an alternative system of work, which could have been adopted and would have been safe and Devlin L.J. stated:

> "There may be cases in which the plaintiff will not get very far with an allegation of unsafe system of work unless he can show some practicable alternative, but there are also cases—and I think this is one of them—in which a plaintiff can fairly say: 'If this is dangerous, then there must be some way of doing it that can be found by a prudent employer and it is not for me to devise that way or say what it is.' "[375]

An allegation was made by the claimant that the defendant employer had no system for clearing away leaves on which she fell and this was met with a simple denial. It was held that there was no principle of pleading which provided that, where the defence denies a negative averment, proof of which lies on the claimant, the defendant was to be treated as having admitted the averment, so as to deny the defendant the right to cross-examine or lead evidence to dispute it.[376]

Civil Procedure Rules 1998.[377] After April 26, 1999 whereas, unexception-   **11–92**
ally, CPR Pt 16.4 requires a claimant to include a concise statement of the facts relied on in the particulars of claim, CPR Pt 16.5 requires a defendant, who denies any allegation, to state reasons for such denial and, where an alternative version of events is to be advanced, to set that version out. So, where a claimant contends that certain precautionary steps should have been taken or considered by the employer in the face of some risk to which the employee was exposed, the Court of Appeal has said[378]:

> "it should normally be open at trial to the employer to raise a defence of impracticability or the like if it has been fairly and squarely raised on his behalf in the statement of case."[379]

(v) *Other cases*

Vicarious liability. In addition to the heads of liability already considered, an   **11–93**
employer is liable vicariously to an employee for damage caused through the

---

[373] Lord Simon in *Colfar v Coggins & Griffith (Liverpool) Ltd* [1945] A.C. 197 at 203. See the comment on this in *General Cleaning Contractors Ltd v Christmas* [1953] A.C. 180 at 190, per Lord Oaksey; at 195, per Lord Tucker.
[374] [1960] 1 W.L.R. 746.
[375] *Dixon v Cementation Co Ltd* [1960] 1 W.L.R. 746 at 748. But cf. *Gilfillan v N.C.B.*, 1972 S.L.T. 39; *Macdonald v Scottish Stamping & Engineering Co*, 1972 S.L.T. (Notes) 73. For the defendant's duty to answer the allegation so that the claimant knows the case he has to meet, see *Larner v British Steel Plc* [1993] 4 All E.R. 102.
[376] *Hockaday v South West Durham HA* [1994] P.I.Q.R. P275, CA, where the remedy for the claimant was said to be to seek particulars of the denial, failing which the implied affirmative case might be struck out.
[377] SI 1998/3132.
[378] *Harris v BRB Residuary Ltd* [2006] P.I.Q.R. P101, CA.
[379] *Harris v BRB Residuary Ltd* [2006] P.I.Q.R. P101, CA, per Neuberger L.J. at para.[28] applying *Larner v British Steel Plc* n.375 above.

negligence of a fellow employee acting in the course of employment, a topic dealt with in Chapter 3, above.[380]

11–94   **Running unnecessary risks.** As explained in the opening paragraphs of this chapter, the heads of liability discussed above are only a convenient method of grouping the most usual cases of the duty of an employer. The duty is to take reasonable care for the safety of an employee and the failure to perform this attracts liability, even where the facts do not fit conveniently into any of the categories. This is sometimes expressed by saying that the employer's duty is "so to carry on his operations as not to subject those employed by him to unnecessary risk".[381] An unnecessary risk is "any risk that the employer can reasonably foresee and which he can guard against by any measures, the convenience and expense of which are not entirely disproportionate to the risk involved".[382]

ILLUSTRATIONS

11–95   Where an electric fan was being tested in the factory's maintenance shop, by operating it at a high speed on the floor without any guard, and an electrician, in some unexplained way, had his hand caught in the revolving blades, the employers were held liable on the broad ground that, in the circumstances, it was reasonably foreseeable that some damage might result.[383] Where an employer knows that accidents to his workmen occasionally happen as a result of wire being ejected from a machine, it is his duty to take reasonable care to protect them from injury by such accidents, even though there is no breach of statutory duty[384] in relation to such machine.[385] Where a workman was employed in a factory in which were 500 machines, 12 of which were dangerous to lubricate during motion, and he was injured whilst so oiling one of the 12, the employers were held liable at common law.[386]

11–96   Where an employee suffered frostbite, following a long journey travelling in an unheated motorvan during freezing weather conditions, it was held that his employers were under a duty to take steps to protect him against reasonably foreseeable hazards. If, as a result of failure to take such steps, the workman

---

[380] See Ch.3, paras 3–98–3–159, above.

[381] *Smith v Baker* [1891] A.C. 325 at 362, per Lord Herschell. As to discovery of previous accidents, see *Edmiston v B.T.C.* [1956] 1 Q.B. 191. In *Houghton v Hackney BC* (1961) 3 K.I.R. 615 it was held that there had been no breach of duty to see that a rent collector was not exposed to unnecessary risks when he, in the course of his employment, had been robbed with violence of the money he had collected. The test was whether the employers had taken reasonable precautions in all the circumstances, and it was found that they had, by employing a uniformed porter to be about when rent was being collected. See generally at para.11–100, below.

[382] *Harris v Brights Asphalt Contractors Ltd* [1953] 1 W.L.R. 341 at 344.

[383] *Thurogood v Van den Berghs & Jurgens Ltd* [1951] 2 K.B. 537. See also *Sidor v N.C.B.* (1956) 106 L.J. 218.

[384] i.e. under s.14(1) of the appropriate Factories Act. See now reg.11 of the Provision and Use of Work Equipment Regulations 1998. Ch.12, paras 12–203–12–221, below.

[385] *Kilgollan v Williams Cooke & Co Ltd* [1956] 1 W.L.R. 527.

[386] *Lewis v High Duty Alloys Ltd* [1957] 1 W.L.R. 632. This was because: "(i) they failed to issue proper instructions to the plaintiff to ensure that he did not oil any of these 12 dangerous machines when in motion; and (ii) they took no effective step to ensure that instruction not to oil such machines when in motion were carried out." (The plaintiff was held one-third to blame.)

suffered injury of a kind that was reasonably foreseeable, even though its precise nature was not foreseen, the employer will be liable.[387] Where the driver of a skip lorry, some 12 feet high, was killed when he had attempted to drive the vehicle underneath an 11 feet 6 inches-high bridge, it was held that his employers had been negligent in failing to exhibit a written warning notice in the driver's cab, informing the driver of the lorry's exact height above the road's surface.[388]

A case study. *Radycliffe v Ministry of Defence*[389] was a claim by a second **11–97** lieutenant in the Army, who was injured whilst jumping from a bridge into a lake during a working break following a tour of duty in Iraq. On the day prior to the accident, some guardsmen had asked permission to jump into the lake and the captain in charge agreed they might, telling the claimant that it would be "bad form" for the officers not to join them. On the day of the accident, the claimant and some soldiers were at the same location and having regard to the captain's previous permission, the claimant agreed to the men jumping, but decided himself to go first in order to demonstrate how to do it properly. The jump was some 65 feet and he hit the surface water at such a speed that he sustained serious spinal injuries. It was found that, even though they were on a break, all of the men were acting under military discipline, evidenced by their having sought permission for the jump. That permission had been given by the captain in the course of his employment.[390] It was negligent given the absence of assessment of the consequences of a jump at that height and the likely speed generated.[391] The argument that the claimant had himself willingly assumed any risk in making the jump was rejected, this being an instance of the defendant, through its captain, assuming responsibility for the claimant's safety.[392]

On the other hand, when a workman, who was using a swab to clean a **11–98** stationary rotary press, cut his hand on one of the blades, there was no breach of duty on the part of his employers, given that the blades were not of razor-blade sharpness.[393] Where a cabinet maker contracted dermatitis through wood dust settling on his skin, and it was proved that the ventilation of the factory was adequate for ordinary purposes and that furniture manufacturers generally took no precautions to prevent dermatitis from West African hardwood dust, because it was not then thought likely to cause it, the defendants were held not liable.[394] Where the risk of infection from Weil's disease, contracted through contact with

---

[387] *Bradford v Robinson Rentals Ltd* [1967] 1 W.L.R. 337.
[388] *James v Durkin (Civil Engineering Contractors), The Times*, May 25, 1983 (deceased driver held 50 per cent to blame for the accident, because he had approached the low bridge much too fast).
[389] [2009] EWCA Civ 635.
[390] For course of employment generally, see Ch.3, paras 3–112–3–115, above.
[391] The claimant was found to be 40% to blame for having accepted, without question, his captain's flawed reasoning.
[392] The defendant relied upon *Tomlinson v Congleton Borough Council* [2004] 1 A.C. 46, Ch.8, para.8–146, above.
[393] *Buckingham v Daily News Ltd* [1956] 2 Q.B. 534 (the claimant and his witnesses said that a long-handled brush should have been used; the defendants called no evidence; the judge, at the parties' request, had a view before giving his decision, and the CA held he was entitled to follow his own impressions formed at the view).
[394] *Graham v Co-operative Wholesale Society Ltd* [1957] 1 W.L.R. 511; *Ebbs v James Whitson & Co Ltd* [1952] 2 Q.B. 877.

rat's urine, was not reasonably foreseeable and was entirely different from, for example, the effect of a rat's bite or food poisoning by the consumption of food or drink contaminated by rats, liability was not established.[395]

11–99   **No duty to employ.** There is no legal duty on an employer either to refuse to employ an adult to do work, or to prevent an adult employee doing work for which he is willing, merely because the employer considers it not in his best interests. In circumstances where a claimant had returned to work after an attack of dermatitis and had commenced other work which she knew was likely to exacerbate the condition, the employers were excused any blame for the injury which resulted, since their duty was limited to the taking of all reasonable care, having regard to the fact of her previous dermatitis.[396] It has been said that "the relationship between master and servant is not the same as that between nursemaid and invalid child."[397] There is no duty at common law, requiring an employer to offer a wholly different job or to dismiss an employee as an alternative to continuing to employ him, just because there is some risk which cannot be reasonably reduced.[398] In such a case, it is for the employee to weigh the risk against the desirability or necessity of the employment. Employers were not liable where they had failed to prevent a workman from exposing himself to danger, by letting him enter and remain in a tank that was being degreased by using trichloro-ethylene, to which the employers knew he was addicted, and, as a result he inhaled an overdose and died.[399]

11–100   **Duty regarding protection from crimes.** The employer's duty extends to taking reasonable steps to guard employees from criminal assaults or injury, in carrying out their tasks.[400] Where there had been a history of attacks on rent

---

[395] *Tremain v Pike* [1969] 1 W.L.R. 1556, Payne J. distinguishing *Bradford v Robinson Rentals* [1967] 1 W.L.R. 337, on the basis that the fact of risk of injury from extreme cold was foreseeable even if the degree of injury was not. See also *Smith v Leech Brain & Co Ltd* [1962] 2 Q.B. 405.

[396] *Withers v Perry Chain Co Ltd* [1961] 1 W.L.R. 1314.

[397] per Wright J. in *Ball v Post Office* [1995] P.I.Q.R. P5 (trigger finger syndrome). Contrast *Coxall v Goodyear Great Britain Ltd* [2003] 1 W.L.R. 536, CA: employer liable for exacerbation of an employee's constitutional asthma where, given the magnitude of the risk, it would have been proper to move him to other work or dismiss him; also *Lane Group Plc v Farmiloe* [2004] P.I.Q.R. P324, EAT: inability of employee to wear protective footwear necessary to ensure his safety due to constitutional condition.

[398] *Henderson v Wakefield Shirt Co Ltd* [1997] P.I.Q.R. P413, CA: claimant suffered discomfort whilst operating a garment press by reason of constitutional spondylosis.

[399] *Jones v Lionite Specialties (Cardiff)* (1961) 105 S.J. 1082. See also para.11–104, below for "ordinary risks of service".

[400] An employer may be vicariously liable under the Protection from Harassment Act 1997 for harassment of one employee by another : see *Majrowski v Guy's and St Thomas' NHS Trust* [2007] 1 A.C. 224. In *Majrowski* Lord Nicholls pointed out, at [30], the need for a claimant to establish the "close connection" test in order for vicarious liability to arise (see Ch.3, para.3–142, above). He went on: "Where the claim meets that requirement, and the quality of the conduct said to constitute harassment is being examined, courts will have in mind that irritations, annoyances, even a measure of upset, arise at times in everybody's day-to-day dealings with other people. Courts are well able to recognise the boundary between conduct which is unattractive, even unreasonable, and conduct which is oppressive and unacceptable. To cross the boundary from the regrettable to the unacceptable the gravity of the misconduct must be of an order which would sustain criminal liability under section 2." See also Hanning, "Employee harassment" 150 S.J. 1005 ; Belgrove, "Who's the bully?" 156 N.L.J. 1636 ; Brodie, "How prescient is parliament?" Edin. L.R. 2007, 11(1), 81.

collectors resulting in complaints by the claimant's union which asked for a secure rent collection point, the employer discharged its duty by requesting the police to keep an eye on the area at the time of collection, and by providing a porter together with a car and driver to collect the claimant.[401] A cricket club discharged its duty to its stewardess, who was robbed whilst carrying cash takings home, on the basis that, by ensuring that she was accompanied, there was no evidence that comparable establishments took any greater precaution.[402] Where an employee was robbed whilst he collected his employer's wages, it was held that the use of a security firm was not necessary, having regard to the amount involved.[403] The employer discharged its duty by giving proper instruction in the ways of reducing injury to himself in line with the practice of the majority of local firms.

The attitude of a workforce, while not determinative, can be a substantial **11–101** factor in considering whether a failure to provide a particular precaution amounts to a breach of duty. Thus, where experienced bus drivers in well organised trade unions had objected to the insertion of screens which might have reduced the risk of attacks by members of the public, such risk having been assessed as being of low order, it was not negligent to have failed to fit screens.[404] On the facts it was not negligent for an employer to abandon a double manning system when its employees attended properties in the Easterhouse area of Glasgow to carry out servicing work to electrical appliances. Nor was it established that, had the claimant attended the property in question with a colleague, the knife wounds he sustained in an attack would have been avoided.[405]

The position may be contrasted where there was a known risk of attacks on the **11–102** staff of a restaurant by gangs. Its owner was held liable to an injured employee on the basis of a failure to take care to reduce that risk.[406] Likewise, it has been held that it was the duty of a hospital to avoid risks to staff from psychiatric patients who were known to be dangerous.[407]

An employer owes no duty to employees to take care to protect their property **11–103** from the dishonesty of a third party. So where an actor's property was stolen from the theatre in which he was working, his claim against his employer failed.[408] Likewise, a resident house physician living in a staff hostel adjoining the hospital failed in his action against the hospital arising out of theft of his personal effects from the hostel.[409]

---

[401] *Houghton v Hackney Borough Council* (1961) 3 K.I.R. 615, per Diplock J.
[402] *Williams v Grimshaw* (1967) 112 S.J. 14.
[403] *Charlton v Forrest Printing Ink Co* [1980] I.R.L.R. 331, CA applying *The Wagon Mound No.2* [1967] 1 A.C. 617.
[404] *Yorkshire Traction Co Ltd v Searby* [2003] EWCA Civ 1856. It was also held that reg.5(3) of the Provision and Use of Work Equipment Regulations 1992 (now reg.4(3) of Provision and Use of Work Equipment Regulations 1998) afforded the claimant no remedy: see Ch.12, para.12–190, below.
[405] *McGinnes v Endeva Service Ltd* 2006 S.L.T. 638 OH.
[406] *Rahman v Arearose Ltd* [2001] Q.B. 351, CA.
[407] *Cook v Bradford Community Health NHS Trust* [2002] EWCA Civ 1616.
[408] *Deyong v Shenburn* [1946] K.B. 227.
[409] *Edwards v West Herts Group Hospital Management Committee* [1957] 1 W.L.R. 415. Note, however, the statutory requirement to provide employees with accommodation for clothing not worn in working hours: see Factories Act 1961 s.59; Offices, Shops and Railway Premises Act 1963 s.12,

11–104   **No liability for ordinary risks of service.** In instances where one employment happens to be more dangerous than another, a greater degree of care must be taken,[410] but, where the employer cannot eliminate the risk, he is required to take reasonable care to reduce it as far as is practicable.[411] However, an employer is not liable for damage arising out of the ordinary risks of the service, when there is no negligence on the part of either himself or his other employees. The death of a seaman drowned at sea, whether in a shipwreck or other disaster, gives no cause of action if the ship were properly manned and equipped and there was no other negligence on the part of the captain or the crew. This is because the risk of drowning is an ordinary risk of the seagoing service.[412] The underlying principle has been expressed as follows:[413] "A great deal of work which has to be done is dangerous, and if it is not reasonably practicable for the master to eliminate or diminish the danger, then the risk is a necessary incident of this employment, and a risk which the servant is paid to take." In relation to employment at sea it was said:

> "Sailors are, of course, necessarily exposed to many risks by the very nature of their calling, and no one would suggest that the courts should be ready to interfere with the practice based upon past experience with regard to such occupational risks."[414]

11–105   It will be a question of fact in each case whether an injury has arisen from an ordinary risk of the relevant service, or from some other special cause which ought to have been foreseen. The stress ordinarily incidental to his work was no defence to the claim of a social worker who suffered a nervous breakdown, where he had already suffered one such breakdown and it was reasonably foreseeable by the employer that, without assistance, he would suffer a second.[415] It has been observed that the balance of expert opinion does not support the proposition that some jobs are intrinsically dangerous to mental health: "it is the interaction between the individual and the job which causes the harm."[416]

11–106   An extreme example is afforded by *Hopps v Mott MacDonald Ltd.*[417] The claimant, a consultant electrical engineer, was injured when an unarmoured Land Rover in which he was travelling in the Basra area, in the aftermath of the Second

---

(repealed from January 1, 1996 for all workplaces and replaced by reg.23 of the Workplace (Health, Safety and Welfare) Regulations 1992); and *McCarthy v Daily Mirror Newspapers Ltd* [1949] 1 All E.R. 801, CA, where, in discharging this statutory duty the risk of theft was held to be a matter to be taken into account by the employer.

[410] See *Paris v Stepney BC* [1951] A.C. 367 at 385, per Lord Morton; *Read v J. Lyons & Co Ltd* [1947] A.C. 156 at 173, per Lord Macmillan and *Lloyds Bank Ltd v Railway Executive* [1952] 1 All E.R. 1248 at 1253, per Denning L.J.

[411] *General Cleaning Contractors Ltd v Christmas* [1953] A.C. 180.

[412] See also *Gray v Stead* [1999] 2 Lloyd's Rep. 559, CA, reversing [1999] 1 Lloyd's Rep. 377, para.11–06, above.

[413] per Glyn-Jones J. in *Hurley v J. Sanders & Co Ltd* [1955] 1 All E.R. 833 at 836.

[414] per Lord Tucker in *Morris v West Hartlepool Steam Navigation Co Ltd* [1956] A.C. 552 at 576. For a modern case to similar effect, see *Gray v Stead* [1999] 2 Lloyd's Rep. 559, CA, and above at para.11–06.

[415] *Walker v Northumberland CC* [1995] 1 All E.R. 737.

[416] per Hale L.J. in *Sutherland v Hatton* [2002] P.I.Q.R. P241, CA at P251 and P255.

[417] [2009] EWHC 1881 (QB). See also *Davies v Global Strategies Group (Hong Kong) Ltd* [2010] EWCA Civ 648 (failure to fit bullet proof windscreens on vehicles used by security patrols in Iraq not negligent).

Iraq War, was blown up by an improvised explosive device. His claim that he either should have been travelling in an armoured vehicle (there were contractual arrangements for the military to provide security), or confined to base until such a vehicle was available, was rejected. The employer's duty of care required him to take reasonable care to devise and operate a safe system of work but what was reasonable depended on all the circumstances. The nature of the risk had to be considered, also the likelihood of the risk materialising, the likelihood of harm and its extent if it did. It was relevant to take into account the nature and purpose of the work the claimant was there to perform, the priority of risks, the effectiveness of various protective measures that could be taken and the consequences of not taking them. If the claimant was to carry out his job, the risks he faced could not be eliminated: indeed the work to be carried out by him was an urgent and important work of reconstruction and was itself a measure to reduce risk. It was not established that the degree of risk from improvised explosive devices at the material date was such as to require the claimant to be confined to his base until an armoured vehicle became available.

ILLUSTRATIONS

No liability was established: where the defendants' skipper could not have **11–107** foreseen the risk of a sea breaking over the side of a trawler, which was fishing during bad weather and in heavy sea conditions, so as to cause any real danger to the claimant deck-hand[418]; where the skipper had kept the crew at work cleaning down the fish deck when very rough seas were running, and a seaman was injured by an exceptionally heavy wave;[419] where a workman slipped on the ice at the entrance to the defendant's factory, because "danger of finding surfaces icy is one of the incidents of winter in our country which everyone encounters";[420] where a fireman, responding to an emergency call, was injured by a heavy jack sliding along the platform of a lorry which was not specially fitted for carrying it, the risk to which he was exposed being incidental to the fire service;[421] where a nurse was attacked and injured by a patient who was suffering from some mental illness;[422] where a dangerous bull, which was untethered in a loose box, injured a farm labourer who entered the box to clean it out, without first having secured the beast in accordance with instructions;[423] where a night-watchman was injured when falling over a loose plank on a building site, because "one would expect that on a building site there would be obstructions and obstacles such as the plank in question, and a night-watchman must take the risk of them".[424] Where a fisherman acting as lone watchman on a trawler was lost at sea, his widow's claim failed because, in 1994, his employer could not be held

---

[418] *The Farnella* [1965] 2 Lloyd's Rep. 299.
[419] *The St Chad* [1965] 2 Lloyd's Rep. 1, CA.
[420] *Thomas v Bristol Aeroplane Co* [1954] 1 W.L.R. 694 at 696, per Somervell L.J. See Poole, "Winter Hazards and Occupiers' Liability" 122 New L.J. 99. See, however the distinctions made in *Woodward v Renold* [1980] I.C.R. 387, where a breach of s.29(1) of the Factories Act 1961 was established, and Ch.12, para.12–147, below.
[421] *Watt v Hertfordshire County Council* [1954] 1 W.L.R. 835.
[422] *Michie v Shenley, The Times*, March 19, 1952. But contrast *Cook v Bradford Community Health NHS Trust* [2002] EWCA Civ 1616, para.11–102 and n.407 above.
[423] *Rands v McNeil* [1955] 1 Q.B. 253.
[424] *Field v Perrys (Ealing) Ltd* [1950] W.N. 320, per Devlin J.

liable for failing to provide and direct that he wore a single chamber inflatable life-jacket when this was neither required by the responsible authorities nor the custom and practice on similar vessels.[425]

11–108   Liability was established: where a boy of 17 was left alone on the crew accommodation deck to clean out the scupper pipe on the port side and was never seen again, having fallen in shark-infested waters in the Indian Ocean, the shipowners having failed to provide him with an assistant. Hodson L.J. expressed the opinion that the case had to be approached with the knowledge that sailors had, by their calling, to perform dangerous tasks at sea and it was not always practicable to take effective steps to eliminate risk, but the duty of employers to safeguard their men from unnecessary risk applied equally at sea as on land.[426] Where a workman, in disobedience to his employer's instructions, placed a loaded gun on top of a harvester machine and it fired accidentally, injuring another employee, it was held that, because the "scope of employment" must be construed liberally, the employer was vicariously liable for his workman's act, in adding yet another danger to the ordinary risks of the work.[427]

11–109   **Employee placed with temporary employer.** The liability of an employer for an employee's tort where that person has been placed at the disposal of another temporary employer has already been discussed in Chapter 3.[428] The question considered here is who is liable to the employee for some breach of duty while that temporary placement subsists.

11–110   If the injury is caused by the negligence of a fellow employee vicarious liability will attach to the latter's employer. Where the injury is caused by unsafe premises, defective plant or materials or an unsafe system of work, different considerations may apply. It does not necessarily follow that someone, who is to be regarded as employer for the purpose of vicarious liability[429] will be the same as the person liable for breach of duty in one of these other respects.[430] If the injury is caused by unsafe premises, the person who is in occupation and control of the premises will be liable. If the injury is caused by defective plant or materials, the employer who has supplied them will generally be liable, subject to the provisions, when applicable, of the Employer's Liability (Defective Equipment) Act 1969.[431] Where an electrician, in the general employment of A, was lent to B to work in B's factory and, on his asking B's foreman for a trestle, was told to look round and find one, it was held that B was liable and not A, when the electrician was injured as a result of the trestle's defects.[432] If the injury is

---

[425] *Gray v Stead* [1999] 2 Lloyd's Rep. 599, CA, reversing [1999] 1 Lloyd's Rep. 377.
[426] *Ellis v Ocean Steamship Co Ltd* [1958] 2 Lloyd's Rep. 373.
[427] *Spencer v Curtis Bros* (1962) 106 S.J. 390.
[428] See Ch.3, paras 3–150–3–153, above.
[429] See Ch.3, para.3–155, above.
[430] *Garrard v Southey & Co* [1952] 2 Q.B. 174, per Parker J. See also 20 M.L.R. 189.
[431] For which, see para.11–55, above.
[432] *Garrard v Southey & Co* [1952] 2 Q.B. 174. The electrician was held to be, for the time being, in the employment of B.

caused by an unsafe system, the employer who prescribed and operated the system will be liable.[433]

There needs to be drawn a distinction between the loan of an employee, which **11–111** transfers the right of control to the temporary employer, and the making available of the benefit of an employee's services alone, where the essential control is retained by the permanent employer. Since the burden of proof of transfer is a heavy one to discharge,[434] it can only be in an exceptional case that the right of control over an employee is effectively transferred away from the general to the temporary employer. Particularly will this be so where the employee has been lent together with some valuable equipment or piece of machinery to be operated by him. But the inference that control has been transferred may be more readily drawn where only the labour of an unskilled employee has been lent.[435]

In *McGarvey v Eve NCI Ltd*,[436] the claimant, a labourer, was instructed by the **11–112** foreman of his employer, a specialist sub-contractor, to do what he was told by the foreman of the main contractor to whom his employer was sub-contracted. An instruction was given by the main contractor's foreman to use a particular set of ladders which were unsafe. The claimant did not secure the ladders and fell when they slipped. His employer had not give the claimant safety training. It was held that both the claimant's employer and the main-contractor were liable to him in damages. The employer was two thirds to blame for failing to fulfil non-delegable duties of care. The main contractor was liable for supplying an unsafe ladder and could not escape liability because it believed the claimant to have had the safety training which the employer did not give.

2.—LIABILITY BETWEEN FELLOW EMPLOYEES

Duty of employees to each other. Two or more employees, working for the **11–113** same employer, owe a duty to each other to take reasonable care and are liable to each other for damage caused by failure to perform that duty. Where one employee injured another through his breach of statutory duty, as a consequence of which the employer had to pay compensation to the injured man, it was held that the employer was entitled to an indemnity from the employee, who had caused the injury: the circumstances created a legal liability in that employee towards the injured man.[437] Further, where an actress on the stage negligently failed to hold on to a club securely, which slipped out of her hand and injured a

---

[433] See *Holt v Rhodes & Son Ltd* [1949] 1 All E.R. 478.
[434] *Mersey Docks and Harbour Board v Coggins & Griffith (Liverpool) Ltd* [1947] A.C. 1. See also *Morris v Breaveglen Ltd (t/a Anzac Construction Co)* [1994] P.I.Q.R. P294, CA (claimant working under labour-only sub-contract was injured while driving a dumper truck supplied by the temporary employer). See further the discussion at Ch.3, para.3–150, above.
[435] *Denham v Midland Employers' Mutual Assurance Ltd* [1955] 2 Q.B. 437 (a brick-field labourer was lent to contractors drilling on the site and was placed under orders from their foreman).
[436] [2002] EWCA Civ 374, CA.
[437] *Lees v Dunkerley Bros* [1911] A.C. 5. Workmen's Compensation Act 1925 s.30 (now repealed by the National Insurance (Industrial Injuries) Act 1946 s.89, Sch.IX which in turn was repealed by the Social Security (Consequential Provisions) Act 1975).

member of the orchestra, it was held that she was liable to the injured person.[438]

11–114   An employee owes to any fellow employee a duty to take care when they are working together in a joint operation. The claimant, one of a gang of six stevedores, was injured by the collapse of bags of sodium carbonate, which the gang were unloading from a barge. The collapse was caused by the unsafe method of unloading adopted by the gang, including the claimant, contrary to the express instructions of the foreman. The employers were held liable vicariously for the negligence of the other members of the gang, but the damages were reduced by 50 per cent because of the claimant's contributory negligence.

> "If a number of men engage in an occupation which is contrary to instructions, and which is also dangerous, there nevertheless is a duty owed by one to the other to use reasonable care, and that duty is not abrogated by joining together and carrying out a common operation. Even the assent to carrying out that operation might in certain circumstances amount to a breach of duty to a man who is also carrying it out; it is a breach of duty that one man owed to the other."[439]

3.—LIABILITY OF EMPLOYEE TO EMPLOYER

11–115   **Duty of employee to employer.** In *Century Insurance Co Ltd v Northern Ireland Transport Board*, Lord Wright expressed the view that:

> "the duty of the workman to his employer is to so conduct himself in doing his work as not negligently to cause damage either to the employer himself or his property or to third persons or their property and thus to impose the same liability on the employer as if he had been doing the work himself and committed the negligent act. This may seem too obvious as a matter of common sense to require either argument or authority."[440]

Accordingly, the employee owes a duty to take reasonable care as regards the employer but, unlike the similar duty in tort owed between fellow workers to one another,[441] it is deemed to be an implied contractual obligation, arising out of the employee's contract of service.[442] Should the employee be in breach of this duty,

---

[438] *Laubach v Co-optimists' Entertainment Syndicate* (1926) 43 T.L.R. 30.
[439] *Williams v Port of Liverpool Stevedoring Co Ltd* [1956] 1 W.L.R. 551 at 555, 556, per Lynskey J., cf. the situation that arose in *Imperial Chemical Industries Ltd v Shatwell* [1965] A.C. 656. See Ch.6, para.6–33, above.
[440] [1942] A.C. 509 at 519.
[441] paras 11–113–11–114, above.
[442] *Lister v Romford Ice & Cold Storage Co Ltd* [1957] A.C. 555. The Minister of Labour in 1957 appointed an inter-departmental committee to study the implication of this decision which made its report in 1959 [36–244]. No legislation was recommended because it was felt that insurers would not abuse the decision. In consequence of that report the members of the British Insurance Association adhered to their "gentleman's agreement" not to exploit their rights which might otherwise endanger good industrial relations. For a case which fell outside the scope of this "gentleman's agreement," see *Morris v Ford Motor Co Ltd* [1973] 1 Q.B. 792, where the CA held that when the risk of an employee's negligence is covered by insurance, his employer should not seek to make that employee liable for it; at any rate the court should not compel him to allow an indemnifier to use his name to do so by subrogation. See Ahmed, "*Quo Vadis*, Doctrine of Subrogation?", 124 New L.J. 26.

then the employer has a cause of action and may recover damages, unless they are too remote.

Employee liable to indemnify employer. A negligent employee is liable, therefore, to indemnify his employer against the damages which the latter is found liable to pay to any fellow employee because of his vicarious liability, as well as for any direct physical injury sustained by the employer himself.[443] In *Lister v Romford Ice and Cold Storage Co Ltd*,[444] the defendant, a lorry driver employed by the claimants, negligently ran into and injured his father, who also was employed by the claimants as a driver's mate. The father obtained judgment against the claimants on the ground of the defendant's negligence, for which they were vicariously liable. The House of Lords by a bare majority held that the claimants could recover from the defendant the amount of that judgment, on the ground that the defendant was in breach of an implied term in his contract of service that he would drive with reasonable care and skill. Lord Simons said, expressing what he believed to be the unanimous opinion: "The servant owes a contractual duty of care to his master and the breach of that duty founds an action for damages for breach of contract."[445]

11–116

In *Ryan v Fildes*,[446] a schoolboy was subjected to excessive physical chastisement by a teacher, and recovered damages against her and her employers, the school managers. The managers in turn obtained contribution from the teacher to the extent of a complete indemnity, and the question was discussed whether, instead of applying in tort for contribution, they could have recovered an indemnity in contract. The conclusion, though not expressed, seems to be that they could have done so.

11–117

Contribution between joint tortfeasors. As set out earlier,[447] where an employee and employers are joint tortfeasors, it is now settled law that the latter can claim contribution from the former. The amount of the contribution recoverable by the employer shall be that which the court considers "to be just and equitable having regard to the extent of that person's responsibility for the

11–118

---

[443] *Digby v General Accident Fire and Life Insurance Corp Ltd* [1943] A.C. 121 (the famous pre-war film actress Miss Merle Oberon sustained personal injuries whilst travelling as a passenger in her Buick motor car, which was being driven by her chauffeur, and she recovered £5,000 general damages for these injuries caused by his negligent driving).

[444] [1957] A.C. 555. See note on this case 74 L.Q.R. 169 and 20 M.L.R. 437. Distinguished in *Harvey v R.G. O'Dell Ltd* [1958] 2 Q.B. 78 (an employee used his own motorcycle to transport himself and a fellow employee and drove negligently, injuring his passenger. However, as he was employed as a storekeeper and not as a driver there was no implied term in his contract of employment that he would indemnify the employers for failure on his part to drive with care whilst using his vehicle on their business). See note on this case, 74 L.Q.R. 170.

[445] *Lister v Romford Ice and Cold Storage Co Ltd* [1957] A.C. 555 at 573. See also *Gregory v Ford* [1951] 1 All E.R. 121 at 124, per Byrne J. "A servant is, of course, liable at the suit of his master for damage which is the result of the servant's negligence."

[446] [1938] 3 All E.R. 517, which was expressly approved by Lord Simonds in *Lister v Romford Ice & Cold Storage Co Ltd* [1957] A.C. 555 at 580. Also see *Semtex Ltd v Gladstone* [1954] 1 W.L.R. 945.

[447] See Ch.3, paras 3–95–3–97, above

damage", under s.2 of the Civil Liability (Contribution) Act 1978.[448] Such contribution could amount, in an appropriate case, to an indemnity, but if an employer is himself negligent or is liable vicariously for the negligence of another employee,[449] he will not be entitled to an indemnity but only to contribution. In *Jones v Manchester Corporation*,[450] the widow of a deceased patient at a hospital recovered damages against the hospital authority and a doctor employed by them for the latter's negligence causing her husband's death. The hospital authority claimed an indemnity, alternatively a contribution, from the doctor but because it had also itself been negligent in a way which contributed to the loss, only contribution was recovered to the extent of one-fifth.

11–119   In *Semtex Ltd v Gladstone*,[451] the claimant's employee, a supervisor, was driving the company's vehicle back from work, giving a lift to a number of other employees. As a result of his negligent driving there was a serious accident in which one of the passengers was killed and several others were injured. In the subsequent actions both the employer and the driver were sued and each was held liable in negligence, the employer's only liability being vicarious for the driver's negligence. The employers having satisfied the claimant's claim, successfully sought, in the alternative, both an indemnity or 100 per cent contribution from their employee.

---

[448] Since January 1, 1979 repealing a similar provision in s.6 of the Law Reform (Married Women and Tortfeasors) Act 1935. See Williams, "Vicarious Liability and Master's Indemnity", 20 M.L.R. 220; Jolowicz, "Right of Indemnity between Master and Servant", 22 M.L.R. 71, 189.

[449] e.g. *Harvey v R.G. O'Dell Ltd* [1958] 2 Q.B. 78 (which was in fact 100 per cent in this case).

[450] [1952] 2 Q.B. 852. At 865 Singleton L.J., after quoting *Salmond on Torts*, 10th edn, p.78, said there was no right of indemnity from an employee where the employer had contributed to the loss. Denning L.J. expressed the view that the employee and employer were joint tortfeasors so that a contribution, but not an indemnity, could be obtained. Hodson L.J. thought that proof of negligence by the doctor amounted to a breach of his contract (the implied term to exercise reasonable skill) thus entitling the employer to an indemnity.

[451] [1954] 1 W.L.R. 945 at 949, per Finnemore J., where preference was expressed for the indemnity approach of Hodson L.J., which was expressly approved by Lord Simonds, but disapproved by Lord Somervell (dissenting) in *Lister v Romford Ice & Cold Storage Co Ltd* [1957] A.C. 555 at 570, 600.

Part III
STATUTORY DUTY

CHAPTER 12

LIABILITY FOR BREACH OF STATUTORY DUTY

1.—INTRODUCTION

General principle. A statutory duty frequently gives rise to a liability to a **12–01**
civil action. This liability is sui generis and independent of any other form of
tortious liability.[1] As Lord Wright said:

"The statutory right has its origin in the statute, but the particular remedy of an action
for damages is given by the common law in order to make effective, for the benefit of
the injured plaintiff, his right to the performance by the defendant of the defendant's
statutory duty ... It is not a claim in negligence in the strict or ordinary sense."[2]

And in an earlier decision[3]:

"I do not think that an action for breach of a statutory duty such as that in question[4] is
completely or accurately described as an action in negligence. It is a common law
action based on the purpose of the statute to protect the workman, and belongs to the
category often described as that of cases of strict or absolute liability. At the same time
it resembles actions in negligence in that the claim is based on a breach of a duty to take

---

[1] See *Bux v Slough Metals Ltd* [1973] 1 W.L.R. 1358 and Barrett, (1974) 37 M.L.R. 577.
[2] *London Passenger Transport Board v Upson* [1949] A.C. 155 at 168.
[3] *Caswell v Powell Duffryn Associated Collieries Ltd* [1940] A.C. 152 at 177, 178.
[4] Coal Mines Act 1911. See now the Mines and Quarries Act 1954.

care for the safety of the workman. The cause of action is sometimes described as statutory negligence[5] and it is said that negligence is conclusively presumed."

12–02   Historically, health, safety and similar regulatory legislation has been the dominant aspect of this tort in practice, and its interface with the law relating to employer's liability has justified it being included in a work concerned with negligence. Increasingly, however, litigation seeking to establish breaches of social welfare legislation, notably in the fields of child abuse[6] and education,[7] has occupied the House of Lords. Such litigation has brought mixed success for claimants. The trend appears to reflect a reluctance to hold that a private law right of action exists in respect of the more general, as opposed to specific, duties imposed on public authorities by statutes setting up broad schemes of social welfare. Athough this chapter will address general principles and the relationship between carelessness in this context and negligence, together with a survey of the most commonly encountered health and safety legislation, reference should be made to specialist texts for a more detailed survey of the law relating to breach of statutory duty.[8]

12–03   The existence of a statutory duty does not necessarily relieve an employer of his common law duty of care to employees although "in very many cases, it would be difficult, if not impossible, to maintain that an employer who had complied with regulations had been negligent at common law".[9] Indeed a statutory duty is likely to be higher than its common law equivalent: a claim based on a breach of statutory duty can succeed even though an employer is not liable in negligence.[10] Nevertheless, the existence of a statutory duty may indicate that a particular risk ought to have been foreseen and thus can be relied upon in order to establish negligence.[11] But this is not invariably the case. In

---

[5] The expression probably also derives from the fact that commonly in personal injury litigation allegations of "common law" negligence are made against the defendant which run parallel with and/or overlap the corresponding allegations of breaches of statutory duty. Many such examples may be found in *Bullen & Leake & Jacob's Precedents of Pleading* (16th edn, 2009) and *Personal Injury Pleadings*, Curran et al. (4th edn, 2008).

[6] e.g. *X (Minors) v Bedfordshire CC* [1995] 2 A.C. 633; *Barrett v Enfield LBC* [1999] 3 W.L.R. 79, HL.

[7] e.g. *M (A Minor) v Newham LBC; E (A Minor) v Dorset CC* [1995] 2 A.C. 633; *Phelps v Hillingdon LBC* [2000] 3 W.L.R. 776, HL.

[8] Stanton, Skidmore, Harris and Wright, *Statutory Torts* (2003) Sweet & Maxwell; *Clerk & Lindsell on Torts* (19th edn, 2006). See also Buckley, "Liability in Tort for Breach of Statutory Duty" (1984)100 L.Q.R. 204; Stanton, "New Forms of the Tort of Breach of Statutory Duty" (2004)120 L.Q.R. 324. In respect of health and safety legislation, see *Redgrave's Health and Safety* (6th edn 2008) Butterworths.

[9] *Franklin v Gramophone Co Ltd* [1948] 1 K.B. 542 at 558 per Somervell L.J. *N.C.B. v England* [1954] A.C. 403.

[10] *Hall v Edinburgh City Council*, 1999 S.L.T. 744, OH, in relation to the Manual Handling Operations Regulations 1992. See para.12–241, below.

[11] So, where a local authority's liability under the Housing Act 1985 s.365, was restricted to houses in multiple occupation that were three storeys in height or more, it was held not just and equitable to impose a duty of care in respect of the condition of two-storey houses: *Ephraim v Newham LBC* (1993) 91 L.G.R. 412, CA (claimant injured where no fire escape provided). A good example of a statutory duty, the breach of which did not give rise to a cause of action prior to October 31, 2003, and was regularly used by claimants to establish the standard that an employer ought to have achieved, is to be found in reg.3(1) of the Management of Health and Safety at Work Regulations 1999: see para.12–101, below.

Chipchase v British Titan Products Co Ltd,[12] it was argued unsuccessfully that, where the facts of the case lay just outside the protection of the statutory duty, the court ought to take the statutory provisions into account in deciding negligence.

The classes of breach of statutory duty must now be considered.

2.—CATEGORIES OF BREACH OF STATUTORY DUTY

Public and private law claims. By way of preliminary, it is important to draw a distinction between private law claims for damages and actions in public law by way of judicial review. Breach of a public law right itself gives rise to no action for damages and, thus, a claim for damages must be based on a private law cause of action. Public law rights are enforceable by judicial review. **12–04**

The modern[13] categories of liability arising out of breach of statutory duty in private law claims, were identified by Lord Browne-Wilkinson in *X (Minors) v Bedfordshire County Council* as follows[14]: **12–05**

(a) actions for breach of duty simpliciter (i.e. irrespective of carelessness);

(b) actions based solely on the careless performance of a statutory duty in the absence of any other common law right of action;

(c) actions based on a common law duty of care arising either from the imposition of the statutory duty or from the performance of it;

(d) misfeasance in public office,[15] i.e. the failure to exercise, or the exercise of, statutory powers either with the intention to injure the claimant or in the knowledge that the conduct was unlawful.

Breach of duty simpliciter. This comprises the case where the statement of case against the defendant alleges a statutory duty, breach of it and damage. The principles to be applied in determining whether such a cause of action exists are well established: **12–06**

"The basic proposition is that in the ordinary case a breach of statutory duty does not, by itself, give rise to any private law cause of action. However, a private law cause of action will arise if it can be shown, as a matter of construction of the statute, that the statutory duty was imposed for the protection of a limited class of the public and that Parliament intended to confer on members of that class a private right of action for breach of the duty. There is no general rule by reference to which it can be decided whether a statute does create such a right of action but there are a number of indicators. If the statute provides no other remedy for its breach and the Parliamentary intention to

---

[12] [1956] 1 Q.B. 545.
[13] For an early attempt at categorisation see *Wolverhampton New Waterworks Co v Hawkesford* (1859) 6 C.B.(N.S.) 336 per Willes J. at 356. See further Ch.2, above, paras 2–284–2–336 generally.
[14] [1995] 2 A.C. 633, at 730.
[15] For discussion of this tort, which is outside the scope of this work, see *Clerk & Lindsell on Torts* (19th edn, 2006) Ch.14 at para.14–56 onwards.

protect a limited class is shown, that indicates that there may be a private right of action since otherwise there is no method of securing the protection the statute was intended to confer. If the statute does provide some other means of enforcing the duty that will normally indicate that the statutory duty was intended to be enforceable by those means and not by private right of action: see *Cutler v Wandsworth Stadium Ltd*[16] and *Lonrho Ltd v Shell Petroleum Co Ltd.*[17] However, the mere existence of some other statutory remedy is not necessarily decisive. It is still possible to show that on the true construction of the statute the protected class was intended by Parliament to have a private remedy."[18]

An important example of the latter type of statutory duty is the protection afforded workers by duties imposed on employers, breach of which gives rise to an action for damages notwithstanding the imposition of criminal sanctions for breach.[19]

12–07   Accordingly, the question is always one of statutory construction. Lord Browne-Wilkinson went on to note that the cases where a private right of action for breach of statutory duty had been held to arise were both limited and specific in scope and did not extend to cases where a breach was alleged of a provision establishing a regulatory system or a scheme of social welfare for the benefit of the public at large.[20]

12–08   **Careless performance of a statutory duty.** This category includes the case where the statement of case alleges a statutory duty and a "negligent" breach of it but does not allege that the defendant was under a coterminous common law duty of care. This distinction with breach of duty simpliciter is important. It had formerly been argued that the careless performance of a statutory duty was in itself a sufficient cause of action without the need to show a concurrent common law duty. The House of Lords has concluded that this view is mistaken and that

---

[16] [1949] A.C. 398: breach of the Betting, and Lotteries Act 1934 s.11(2), intended to regulate the conduct of betting on racetracks, did not give a bookmaker thereby injured any right of action. See also *R. v Deputy Governor of Parkhurst Prison Ex p. Hague* [1992] 1 A.C. 58: per Lord Jauncey: "It must always be a matter for consideration whether the legislature intended that private law rights of action should be conferred upon individuals in respect of breaches of the relevant statutory provision. The fact that a particular provision was intended to protect certain individuals is not of itself sufficient to confer private law rights of action upon them, something more is required to show that the legislature intended such conferment."

[17] [1982] A.C. 173: breach of an Order in Council (which prohibited the supply of oil to Southern Rhodesia), intended to prevent trade with an unlawful regime, did not give the owners of a pipeline thus affected a cause of action against a rival who contravened the Order. The Order had not been imposed for the benefit or protection of a particular class of persons, namely those engaged in the supply of oil.

[18] per Lord Browne-Wilkinson in *X (Minors) v Bedfordshire County Council,* n.14 above, at 731.

[19] *Groves v Lord Wimborne* [1898] 2 Q.B. 402. See also *Roe v Sheffield CC* [2004] Q.B. 653, CA: in relation to the statutory duties imposed on tramway operators under ss.25 and 28 of the Tramways Act 1870, a private law cause of action could be maintained for breach of the duties to maintain tram rails on a level with the surface of the road and to maintain and keep in good repair the road between the rails. (On the facts, no breach was made out.)

[20] *X (Minors) v Bedfordshire CC,* n.14 above at 732.

carelessness in performing a statutory duty gives a good cause of action only if the circumstances are such as to raise a duty of care at common law.[21]

In *Carty v Croydon London Borough Council*,[22] it was held that education   **12–09** officers performing the statutory functions of local education authorities are professional persons for whose negligence education authorities might be held liable, albeit on the facts negligence was not made out. When considering the liability of a public authority in negligence for performance of a statutory function, Dyson L.J. quoted the summary of Hale L.J. in *A. v Essex County Council*[23]:

"Where the question of a common law duty of care arises in the context of the statutory functions of a public authority, there are three potential areas of inquiry: first, is whether the matter is justiciable at all or whether the statutory framework is such that Parliament must have intended to leave such decisions to the authorities, subject of course to the public law supervision of the courts; second, whether even if justiciable, it involves the exercise of a statutory discretion which only gives rise to liability in tort if it is so unreasonable that it falls outside the ambit of the discretion; third in any event whether it is fair, just and reasonable in all the circumstances to impose such a duty of care. The considerations relevant to each of these issues overlap and it is not always possible to draw hard and fast lines between them."

In commenting on the second question, Dyson L.J. pointed out that discretion,

"is a somewhat protean word. It connotes the exercise of judgment in making choices. In a sense, most decisions involve the exercise of discretion ... rather than focus on the elusive question of whether the decision at issue involved the exercise of discretion, it is preferable to look at the substance of the decision."

Thus, at one end of the spectrum, in the field of special education, were decisions which were heavily influenced by policy and came close to being non-justiciable. At the other were decisions involving pure professional judgment and expertise in relation to individual children, where the court would only find negligence on the part of the person who made the decision for which the authority may be vicariously liable, if he or she had failed to act in accordance with a practice accepted at the time as proper by a responsible body of persons of the same profession or skill. He saw much to be said for the view that there should only be two areas of potential enquiry where an issue arose whether a public authority was liable for negligence in the performance of its statutory function. The first

---

[21] *X (Minors) v Bedfordshire CC*, n.14 above. The leading speech was given by Lord Browne-Wilkinson whose analysis of the relationship between statutory and private law duties remains relevant, although the significance of the decision itself has been eroded: see Ch.2, para.2–286, above. For a case where no duty of care arose, see, e.g. *Blake and Brooks v London Borough of Barking & Dagenham* [1999] P.N.L.R. 171. See Bailey and Bowman, "Public Authority Negligence Revisited" [2000] C.L.J. 85 and Mullender, "Negligence, Public Authorities and Policy-Level Decisions" (2000) 116 L.Q.R. 40.
[22] [2005] 2 All E.R. 517, CA.
[23] [2004] F.C.R. 660 at [33].

was whether the decision was justiciable at all. The second was to apply the classic three stage test from *Caparo Industries v Dickman*.[24]

12–10   Early cases, which may appear to support an action for the careless exercise of a statutory power simpliciter, must be treated therefore with caution.[25] It is suggested that confusion originated from a dictum of Lord Blackburn in *Geddis v Proprietors of Bann Reservoir*[26] which, read in context, was dealing with the position where the defendant raised the exercise of statutory powers as a defence to a common law claim: no such defence arises where the powers have been carelessly exercised. In *Allen v Gulf Oil Refining Ltd*,[27] Lord Wilberforce treated *Geddis* as a decision that the careless exercise by a defendant of a statutory duty or power provides no defence to a claim by the claimant based on a free-standing common law cause of action:

> "It is now well settled that where Parliament by express direction or by necessary implication has authorised the construction and use of an undertaking or works, that carries with it an authority to do what is authorised with immunity from any action based on nuisance (see *Hammersmith and City Railway Co v Brand*[28]). To this there is made the qualification, or condition, that the statutory powers are exercised without 'negligence', that word here being used in a special sense so as to require the undertaker, as a condition of obtaining immunity from action, to carry out the work and conduct the operation with all reasonable regard and care for the interests of other persons."[29]

Thus whilst a statutory power can be invoked as a defence to an activity which would otherwise constitute a nuisance, if the activity authorised by the power has been carried out negligently, such a defence will not apply. Lord Browne-Wilkinson summarised the position as follows:

> "In my judgment the correct view is that in order to found a cause of action flowing from the careless exercise of statutory powers or duties, the plaintiff has to show that the circumstances are such as to raise a duty of care at common law. The mere assertion of the careless exercise of a statutory power or duty is not sufficient."[30]

12–11   **The common law duty of care.** A common law duty of care can arise as a result of the statutory duty in two ways: the statutory requirement upon the defendant to do or refrain from doing a particular act may itself gives rise to a common law obligation: alternatively, and perhaps more frequently, in carrying out the statutory duty, the defendant or the servants or agents for whom it is

---

[24] [1990] 2 A.C. 605.
[25] See the 8th edn of this work for a summary of the competing authorities, at Ch.11, para.11–43 et seq.
[26] (1878) 3 App.Cas. 430 at 455, 456.
[27] [1981] A.C. 1001.
[28] (1869) L.R. 4 H.L. 171.
[29] [1981] A.C. 1001 at 1011. See also *Sutherland Shire Council v Heyman* (1985) 157 C.L.R. 424 at 458 and Brennan, "Liability in Negligence of Public Authorities: The Divergent Views" (1990) 48 The Advocate 842 at 844.
[30] *X (Minors) v Bedfordshire County Council* [1995] 2 A.C. 633 at 734.

vicariously liable, may come into a relationship with the claimant that gives rise to a duty of care.[31]

In *X (Minors) v Bedfordshire County Council*,[32] in the context of claims **12–12** against public authorities arising from the discharge by them of statutory functions in the fields of child care and education, Lord Browne-Wilkinson distinguished between cases where it is alleged that the authority owes a duty of care in the manner in which it exercises a statutory discretion, and cases in which a duty of care is alleged to arise from the manner in which the statutory duty has been implemented in practice.[33] So far as the former was concerned it had to be borne in mind that the discretion had been conferred by Parliament upon the authority and it was not for the courts to exercise it: only if the exercise of the discretion fell outside the statutory ambit could it give rise to a common law duty, but even then no such duty could arise in relation to the taking of decisions involving matters of policy. So far as the latter group were concerned the existence of a duty of care at common law fell to be determined by reference to the tests in *Caparo Industries Plc v Dickman*.[34]

Caparo may not be a useful guide where the allegation is carelessness in the **12–13** purported exercise of a statutory *power*. In such a case the court is more likely to approach the existence of a duty of care by reference to the *Hedley Byrne* characteristics of responsibility and reliance.[35] So, arguably, a duty of care was owed to a child already in care to place him for adoption, find suitable foster homes and arrange his reintroduction to his mother.[36] This was so even though a claim in negligence in the taking of a decision to exercise a statutory discretion (the taking of a child into care) was likely to be not justiciable unless it was wholly unreasonable or involved the making of a policy decision involving the balancing of different public interests. In that latter case, acts done pursuant to the lawful exercise of the discretion could be found to be the subject of a duty of care, even if some element of discretion was involved.

---

[31] *X (Minors) v Bedfordshire County Council* [1995] 2 A.C. 633 at 735. See, in the case of public servants, the observations of Lord Woolf M.R. in *W v The Home Office, The Times*, March 14, 1997, CA, Ch.2, para.2–294, above. Also *S v Secretary of State for Health, The Times*, March 11, 2002. *A. v Essex CC* [2004] 1 W.L.R. 1881, Ch.2, para.2–000 above (duty of care to prospective adopters alongside statutory duty to provide information under the Adoption Agencies Regulations 1983). See also, in the case of dock workers working in the Liverpool Docks in the 1950s and 1960s, *Rice v Secretary of State for Trade and Industry* [2007] P.I.Q.R. P23, CA, para.12–16, below where the defendant was held potentially liable, as successor to the National Dock Labour Board, for injury resulting from the exposure of dock workers to asbestos.
[32] *X (Minors) v Bedfordshire CC* [1995] 2 A.C. 633 at 735, n.31, above.
[33] *X (Minors) v Bedfordshire CC* [1995] 2 A.C. 633 at 730.
[34] [1990] 2 A.C. 605.
[35] *Welton v North Cornwall DC* [1997] 1 W.L.R. 570, CA, (environmental health officer negligently purporting to exercise powers under the Food Safety Act 1990). See also *Gaisford v Ministry of Agriculture, Fisheries and Food, The Times*, July 19, 1996, CA. *Harris v Evans, The Times*, May 5, 1998, CA; also *Blake and Brooks v London Borough of Barking & Dagenham* [1999] P.N.L.R. 171 (not fair, just or reasonable to impose a duty of care upon a local authority when stating its opinion of the price of a property in a notice served under s.125 of the Housing Act 1985). See also Mullender, (2000) L.Q.R. 40.
[36] *Barrett v Enfield London Borough Council* [1999] 3 W.L.R. 79, HL.

12–14   In *Stovin v Wise*,[37] Lord Hoffmann said that, in making the determination as to whether the *Caparo* tests are satisfied, the policy of the statute will be crucial:

> "Whether a statutory duty gives rise to a private cause of action is a question of construction (see *R. v Deputy Governor of Parkhurst Prison Ex p. Hague*).[38] It requires an examination of the policy of the statute to decide whether it was intended to confer a right of compensation for the breach. Whether it can be relied upon to support the existence of a common law duty of care is not exactly a question of construction because the cause of action does not arise out of the statute itself. But the policy of the statute is nevertheless a crucial factor in the decision."[39]

Thus, a highway authority owed no private law duty to road users to take steps to improve visibility at a dangerous intersection where the claimant and defendant had collided. The minimum preconditions for basing a duty of care upon the existence of a statutory power in respect of an omission to exercise that power were that, in the circumstances, it would have been irrational not to have exercised it thus, in effect, creating a public law duty to act and, further, that there were exceptional grounds for holding that the policy of the statute conferred a right to compensation on those suffering a loss if the power was not exercised.[40]

12–15   Subsequently, by way of example, it has been held that it would not be fair, just or reasonable to impose a duty of care upon a district health authority or social services authority parallel to their statutory duty to provide aftercare services for any person previously detained in hospital under statutory powers and thereafter discharged into the community.[41] It was said:

> "We find it difficult to suppose that Parliament intended to create such an extensive and wide-ranging liability for breaches of responsibility under section 117 which would of its nature apply alike to those engaged as professionals as well as those in voluntary services in many disciplines."[42]

Thus no common law duty of care was owed to provide cot-sides for the bed of a claimant who, albeit unwell, lived at home and whose needs the local authority were obliged to assess pursuant to s.29 of the National Assistance Act 1948 and s.2 of the Chronically Sick and Disabled Persons Act 1970.[43] In *O'Rourke v Camden London Borough Council*,[44] a claim for damages, brought by a homeless person on the ground that the council had failed in its statutory

---

[37] [1996] A.C. 923.
[38] [1992] 1 A.C. 58 at 170; followed by Wright J. in *Danns v Department of Health* [1996] P.I.Q.R. P69 in the course of a judgment dismissing a claim against the Ministry advanced upon the basis of a breach of s.2 of the Ministry of Health Act 1919, the statute by which it was established: appeal dismissed, [1998] P.I.Q.R. P226, CA: see further para.12–46, below.
[39] *Stovin v Wise* [1996] A.C. 923 at 952.
[40] *Stovin v Wise* [1996] A.C. 923 at 953.
[41] *Clunis v Camden & Islington HA* [1998] Q.B. 978, concerned with s.117 of the Mental Health Act 1983. See also Hopkins, "Ex turpi causa and mental disorder" [1998] C.L.J. 444.
[42] per Beldam L.J., *Clunis v Camden & Islington HA* [1998] Q.B. 978 at 913. See Jones, "The violent mentally disordered patient: who cares?" (1998) P.N. 99.
[43] *Sandford v Waltham Forrest LBC* [2008] EWHC 1106, Q.B., para.12–25, below.
[44] [1998] A.C. 188.

duty to provide him with accommodation, was struck out because the statute did not create a private law right of action. In *Gorringe v Calderdale Metropolitan Borough Council*,[45] the House of Lords rejected a claim that s.39 of the Highways Act 1980 elevated a highway authority's duty of care to a sufficient standard to claim that an omission to provide signage constituted a breach of duty at common law. In so doing Lord Hoffmann adopted the concept of a "target duty",[46] namely one which did no more than require the authority to exercise its powers in the manner that it considers is appropriate, which could not be construed as owing specific duties to individuals. It formed part of the body of public law and, as such, could only be enforced by procedures and remedies available for enforcing public law duties.

On the other hand, in *Rice v Secretary of State for Trade and Industry*,[47] it was **12–16** held that a duty of care was owed by the National Dock Labour Board, a statutory body with some responsibility for the health and safety of dock workers from 1946 onwards, towards registered dock workers in relation to their health and safety. The workers alleged exposure to asbestos when unloading hessian sacks from certain vessels in the course of their employment in the Liverpool docks. It was held that, notwithstanding that the relationship between the Board and the dock workers was not strictly that of employer/employee it was fair, just and reasonable to impose the suggested duty. The Board knew or ought to have known of the risks associated with unloading asbestos. The policy of the statute which created the Board could only be seen as enabling such a relationship as would lead to the imposition of a common law duty of care. The duty was a specific one requiring the Board to protect individual employees from a known serious risk to their health. The scope of the duty was for later determination.[48]

Finally, in relation to the common law duty and its interaction with a public **12–17** bodies' statutory duties, there can be rare situations in which a private law duty arises which requires the performance of, say, a statutory discretion. Such situations are not likely to arise often precisely because a breach will arise only where it can be said that the discretion was not exercised, in circumstances where it could have been, consistently with full performance of the public law functions by the body which owed the duty.[49]

Vicarious liability. The issue of vicarious liability for the acts of others, **12–18** through whom a public authority discharges its statutory duty, also stands to be resolved on the usual principles. In the case of professional persons, such an authority would ordinarily be liable if the professional to whom performance of the statutory duty is delegated, or through whom it is performed, fails to exercise

---

[45] [2004] 1 W.L.R. 1057, HL. See Howarth, "Public authority non-liability: spinning out of control?", [2004] 63 C.L.J. 546; Morgan, "Slowing the expansion of public authorities' liability", [2005] 121 L.Q.R. 43.
[46] As described by Woolf L.C.J. in *Larner v Solihull MBC* [2001] P.I.Q.R. P17, CA, a decision on the facts disapproved in *Gorringe*.
[47] [2007] P.I.Q.R. P23, CA.
[48] See the judgment of May L.J. at [44].
[49] *Connor v Surrey CC* [2010] EWCA Civ 286, CA. See Ch.2, para.2–293, above.

the degree of care appropriate for one possessing the relevant qualification or expertise, a subject dealt with elsewhere in this work.[50]

3.—When an Action may be Brought

12–19   As already seen, the basic rule is that in the ordinary case breach of a statutory duty does not in itself give rise to a private law cause of action for damages. Such an action can arise if, as a matter of construction of the statute in question, it is shown "that the statutory duty was imposed for the protection of a limited class of the public and that Parliament intended to confer on members of that class a private right of action for breach of the duty".[51] No difficulty should arise where the statute under consideration, or indeed another statute,[52] indicates in terms that a civil remedy does[53] or does not,[54] arise for breach of the duty imposed.

12–20   More often, however, the statute is silent. Then, in the words of Lord Bingham C.J., " . . . regard must be paid to the object and scope of the provisions, the class (if any) intended to be protected by them, and the means of redress open to a member of such a class if the statutory duty is not performed."[55] No universal rule has been formulated which will answer the question whether in any given case an individual can sue for damages, but indicators include whether there is evidence of a Parliamentary intention to protect the class in question and whether the statute provides any other adequate remedy for its breach. It has been said that the "cases where a private right of action for breach of statutory duty have been held to arise are all cases in which the statutory duty has been very limited and specific as opposed to general administrative functions imposed on public bodies and involving the exercise of administrative functions".[56]

12–21   In *Lonrho Ltd v Shell Petroleum Co Ltd (No.2)*,[57] where damages were sought by the claimant for breach, by its rival, of sanctions imposed by an Order in

---

[50] See Ch.9, above.

[51] per Lord Browne-Wilkinson in *X (Minors) v Bedfordshire CC* [1995] 2 A.C. 633 at 731.

[52] e.g. the Health & Safety at Work, etc., Act 1974 s.71, which provides for civil liability for a breach of duty imposed by the building regulations made under the Public Health Acts 1936–1961 as amended by the 1974 Act.

[53] e.g. the Consumer Protection Act 1961 s.3, and see also the preamble of the Consumer Protection Act 1987; the Nuclear Installations Act 1965 and 1969; the Gas Act 1965 s.14; the Control of Pollution Act 1974 s.88; the Petroleum and Submarine Pipelines Act 1975 s.30.

[54] e.g. the Health & Safety at Work, etc., Act 1974 s.47(1)(a), which negatives the right of action in any civil proceedings in respect of any failure to comply with any duty imposed by ss.2–7 or any contravention of s.8 of the Act; the Safety of Sports Grounds Act 1975, s.13 which provides for the like effect as regards negligence actions; the Management of Health and Safety at Work Regulations 1999, reg.22 precluded a right of action in civil proceedings for any breach of a duty imposed by these regulations until the restriction was removed with effect from October 31, 2003 by the Management of Health and Safety at Work and Fire Precautions (Workplace) (Amendment) Regulations 2003 (SI 2003/2457).

[55] *Oloto v Home Office* [1997] 1 W.L.R. 328, CA.

[56] *X (Minors) v Bedfordshire CC*, n.51 above, at 732. See also Brodie, "Public authorities and the duty of care" (1996) 2 Jur. Rev. 127. For an example of the application of these principles in practice, see *Capital & Counties Plc v Hampshire CC* [1997] 3 W.L.R. 331, CA, in particular 362–363.

[57] [1982] A.C. 173.

Council which were enforceable by criminal prosecution, Lord Diplock stated the presumption,[58] namely that enforcement could only be by the manner prescribed, and identified two classes of exception to that presumption:

"The first is where on the true construction of the Act it is apparent that the obligation or prohibition was imposed for the benefit or protection of a particular class of individuals, as in the cases of the Factories Acts and similar legislation[59] . . . The second is where the statute creates a public right (i.e. a right to be enjoyed by all those of Her Majesty's subjects who wish to avail themselves of it) and a particular member suffers what Brett J. described[60] as 'particular, direct and substantial' damage 'other and different from that which was common to the rest of the public'."[61]

Parliamentary intention to protect. While the prima facie rule is that the special remedy provided by the statute is the only remedy, this rule yields to the proper construction of the statute: **12–22**

"When an Act imposes a duty of commission or omission, the question whether a person aggrieved by a breach of the duty has a right of action depends on the intention of the Act. Was it intended to make the duty one which was owed to the party aggrieved as well as to the State, or was in a public duty only? That depends on the construction of the Act and the circumstances in which it was made and to which it relates. One question to be considered is, Does the Act contain reference to a remedy for breach of it? *Prima facie* if it does that is the only remedy. But that is not conclusive. The intention as disclosed by its scope and wording must still be regarded, and it may still be that, though the statute creates the duty and provides a penalty, the duty is nevertheless owed to individuals."[62]

Phillips v Britannia Hygienic Laundry[63] provides a useful working illustration. For many years regulations have governed the construction and use of motor vehicles.[64] Detailed obligations are laid down as to weight and size of vehicles and the nature of their brakes, lamps and other fittings. But it has been held that   **12–23**

---

[58] By reference to *Doe d Bishop of Rochester v Bridges* (1831) 1 B. & Ad. 847 at 859, per Lord Tenterden C.J.: "When an Act creates an obligation and enforces the performance in a specified manner, we take it to be a general rule that performance cannot be enforced in any other manner."

[59] Lord Diplock went on to cite Lord Kinnear in *Black v Fife Coal Co Ltd* [1912] A.C. 149 at 165 where he said: "There is no reasonable ground for maintaining that a proceeding by way of penalty is the only remedy allowed by statute . . . We are to consider the scope and purpose of the statute and in particular for whose benefit it is intended. Now the object of the present statute is plain. It was intended to compel mine owners to make due provision for the safety of the men working in their mines, and the persons for whose benefit all these rules are to be enforced are the persons exposed to danger. But when a duty of this kind is imposed for the benefit of particular persons there arises at common law a correlative right in those persons who may be injured by its contravention."

[60] *Benjamin v Storr* (1874) L.R. 9 C.P. 400 at 407

[61] [1982] A.C. 173 at 186.

[62] per Atkin L.J. in *Phillips v Britannia Hygienic Laundry* [1923] 2 K.B. 832 at 841. The extent to which Atkin L.J.'s dictum survives *Lonrho Ltd v Shell Petroleum Co Ltd (No.2)* [1982] A.C. 173 and *X (Minors) v Bedfordshire CC* [1995] 2 A.C. 633 which appear to envisage a limited class enjoying a private law right of action, is open to question. See also *R. v Deputy Governor of Parkhurst Prison Ex p. Hague* [1992] 1 A.C. 58, n.38 above.

[63] [1923] 2 K.B. 832.

[64] Originally the Motor Car (Use and Construction) Order 1904 (SI 1904/315) currently the Road Vehicles (Construction and Use) Regulations 1986 (SI 1986/1078) as amended by the Road Vehicles (Construction and Use) (Amendment) (No.3) Regulations 1994 (SI 1994/3270).

no private right of action arises at the suit of a person injured by a failure of a vehicle to comply with such requirements. The regulations imposed penalties for breach. Further they imposed obligations of various different kinds, some relating to the maintenance of the highway and others dealing with the safety of the public, all of which were punishable by the same fine. Having regard to the existing remedies available against persons using vehicles on the highway, it was held that Parliament could not have intended to give an additional remedy to private individuals, where it did not expressly say so.[65] Some further examples of the way these principles have been put into practice follow.

12–24   **Illustrations: no intention to protect.** In the field of road traffic law, despite a penalty if a provisional licence holder fails to comply with conditions prescribed in regulations,[66] no cause of action for breach of statutory duty arose in favour of the passenger in a car injured when an unsupervised learner driver was involved in an accident[67]; the sale of a motor vehicle with defective brakes in breach of a statutory requirement[68] does not give the buyer a right of action against the seller, because the aim of this legislation is not to protect the buyer[69]; mere failure to carry a red rear-light on a car contrary to statute[70] gave no right of civil action to a person who collided with it[71]; similarly, statute[72] imposed no duty on an employer to his employee to see that the motor vehicle driven by the employee in the course of his employment was insured against third party risks[73]; where sheep were straying on the highway and their owner was subsequently fined for allowing them to stray contrary to statute,[74] it was held that this breach of statutory duty gave no right of action to a motorist whose car was overturned owing to the presence of the sheep on the road[75]; where a highway authority failed to remove an earth bank which obscured the view of a driver emerging from a junction who thereby caused an accident, notwithstanding the power so to do,[76] there was no intention to give rise to a private law claim for failure to

---

[65] *Phillips v Britannia Hygienic Laundry*, n.62 above; see especially Atkin L.J. at 842.

[66] Motor Vehicles (Driving Licences) Regulations 1950 (SI 1950/333).

[67] *Verney v Wilkins* (1962) 106 S.J. 879.

[68] Road Traffic Act 1988 s.75, (successor to the Road Traffic Act 1934 s.8) and Road Vehicles (Construction and Use) Regulations 1986 (SI 1986/1078).

[69] *Badham v Lambs Ltd* [1946] K.B. 45; *Vinall v Howard* [1954] 1 Q.B. 375. See now subs.(5), which is statutory affirmation of these two decisions.

[70] Road Transport Lighting Act 1927.

[71] *Clarke and Wife v Brims* [1947] K.B. 497 approved by the CA in *Coote v Stone* [1971] 1 W.L.R. 279, disapproving *Kelly v W.R.N. Contracting Ltd* [1968] 1 W.L.R. 921; *West v Lawson Ltd*, 1949 S.C. 430.

[72] Road Traffic Act 1930 s.35 amended by the Road Traffic Act 1956 s.29(1), which provided a defence to such employee for the offence thus committed if the vehicle was not so insured. See now Road Traffic Act 1988 s.143.

[73] *Gregory v Ford* [1951] 1 All E.R. 121. Followed in *Semtex Ltd v Gladstone* [1954] 2 All E.R. 206; *Lister v Romford Ice Co Ltd* [1957] A.C. 555. However, in each of these cases at common law an implied term was found in the contract of service that the employer will insure as required by s.35(1) of the Act of 1930.

[74] Highway Act 1864 s.25.

[75] *Heath's Garage Co v Hodges* [1916] 2 K.B. 370.

[76] Under the Highways Act 1980 s.41.

maintain the highway[77]; likewise the statutory duty to prepare and carry out a programme of measures designed to promote road safety,[78] being "typical public law duties expressed in the widest and most general terms,"[79] did not afford a claimant redress for her injuries allegedly caused by the absence of a sign to warn her of a hazardous crest in the road ahead.

In respect of claims against local authorities other than in the fields of welfare[80] and education,[81] a statutory duty to keep streets "properly swept and cleansed" and to remove "all street refuse," under penalty of a fine, did not render the authority liable to someone who fell as a result of a failure to remove snow. The definition of street refuse included snow but, on a proper construction, the statute did not disclose an intention to provide a private right of action in such a case.[82] Where a claimant injured his hand after falling on broken glass, it was held that there was no private law action in respect of legislation concerning litter[83]; local authorities responsible for sewers were not liable under s.22 of the Control of Pollution Act 1974 to a claimant who fell when wading in a flooded street.[84] Notwithstanding its important function in the public interest of controlling and regulating development and the discretionary nature of its powers, the policy of the Town and Country Planning Act 1971 is not such as to create a duty of care at common law which would render a local planning authority liable in negligence for foreseeable damage arising as a result of the exercise or non-exercise of the power to grant or refuse planning permission.[85] A byelaw prohibiting, under penalty of a fine, dogs being brought into a park unless they are under proper control is intended to protect the park, the plants growing in it and the comfort and convenience of those using the park, and gives no right of action to a member of the public when there is a breach. Thus, when an uncontrolled Alsatian dog jumped a fence and injured a claimant, an action for breach of statutory duty under the byelaw failed.[86] There was no arguable case where it was alleged that a local authority carelessly failed to exercise powers under the Housing Act to seek possession of the homes of certain secure tenants who, it was alleged, had been guilty of racial harassment causing the claimant injury.[87] No private law action for damages could be maintained against a local authority owing statutory duties to the deceased under the National Health

12–25

---

[77] *Stovin v Wise* [1996] A.C. 923.

[78] Highways Act 1980 s.39.

[79] per Lord Hoffmann in *Gorringe v Calderdale MBC* [2004] 1 W.L.R. 1057 at 1064.

[80] See Ch.2 at paras 2–308–2–309, above.

[81] See Ch.9 at paras 9–185–9–212, above.

[82] *Saunders v Holborn District Board of Works* [1895] 1 Q.B. 64. Mathew J. based his judgment solely on the ground of the intention of the statute, but Charles J. also relied on the ground that the local authority was not liable for nonfeasance. On this latter point, see the provisions of the Highways Act 1980.

[83] *M v Craigavon BC* [1998] N.I. 103 (art.7(1) of the Litter (Northern Ireland) Order 1994, SI 1994/1896).

[84] *Pritchard v Clwyd CC* [1993] P.I.Q.R. P21, CA.

[85] *Lam v Brennan and Borough of Torbay* [1997] P.I.Q.R. P488, CA, above Ch.2, para.2–316, n.704.

[86] *Newman v Francis* [1953] 1 W.L.R. 402.

[87] *Hussain v Lancaster CC* [2000] Q.B. 1.

Service and Community Care Act 1990 s.47(1) and the Chronically Sick and Disabled Persons Act 1970 s.2 where, after an assessment of her home-based needs, a recommendation was made for cot-sides to her bed and subsequently, the recommendation not having been implemented, she fell while getting out of the bed and sustained injury.[88]

12–26　So far as claims made against suppliers of public water[89] are concerned, where a water company was obliged by statute to supply water to the inhabitants of Newcastle and to keep their pipes, to which fire-plugs were fixed, charged with water at a certain pressure, under the penalty of a fine, it was held that they were not liable to a person whose premises were destroyed by fire in consequence of their failure to keep a sufficient pressure of water in the pipes to enable the fire to be extinguished. Lord Cairns said that if they were liable in the action "they would virtually become gratuitous insurers of the safety from fire, so far as water is capable of producing that safety, of all the houses within the district over which their powers were to extend," and held that the statute could not have intended any such result.[90] When water infected by typhoid bacillus caused the daughter of a rate-payer to contract typhoid fever, it was held that she had no right of action for breach of a statutory duty[91] owed to rate-payers to provide and keep in their pipes a supply of pure and wholesome water sufficient for the domestic use of the inhabitants of the district within their area of supply.[92]

12–27　The statutory obligation[93] on a fire authority to ensure the provision of an adequate supply of water and to secure its availability for use in fighting fire was not intended to give rise to a private law right of action, the duties imposed being in the nature of provisions to establish a regulatory system or scheme of social welfare for the benefit of the public at large.[94]

---

[88] *Sandford v London Borough of Waltham Forest* [2008] EWHC 1106 (Q.B.) (besides there being no private law action under the statutes in relation to the alleged breach of duty, no common law duty of care arose in the absence of a voluntary assumption of responsibility towards the deceased, independent of the statutory duty; and in any event on the facts it was not shown that injury would have been avoided had cot-sides been fitted).

[89] There is no private law action for breaches of the provisions of the Water Industry Act 1991 and the Water Resources Act 1991: *Bowden v South West Water Services Ltd* [1998] Env. L.R. 445, Q.B.D.

[90] *Atkinson v Newcastle Waterworks Co* (1877) 2 Ex.D. 441 at 446; *Johnston v Consumers' Gas Co of Toronto* [1898] A.C. 447 is a somewhat similar case but cf. *Dawson & Co v Bingley UDC* [1911] 2 K.B. 149. In *Clegg, Parkinson & Co v Earby Gas Co* [1896] 1 Q.B. 592, where an action was brought against a gas company for breach of their duty under the Gasworks Clauses Act 1871 to supply gas sufficient in amount and in purity to satisfy the requirements of the Act (the breach of which was enforced by a penalty), it was held that the only remedy of a consumer was to proceed for the penalty. *Stevens v Aldershot, etc., District Lighting Co* (1933) 102 L.J.K.B. 12 is another case to the same effect.

[91] Waterworks Clauses Act 1847 s.35.

[92] *Read v Croydon Corp* [1938] 4 All E.R. 631 (an action lay in common law negligence).

[93] Fire Services Act 1947 ss.1 and 13.

[94] per Stuart-Smith L.J. in *Capital & Counties Plc v Hampshire CC* [1997] 1 Q.B. 1004 quoting Lord Browne-Wilkinson in *X (Minors) v Bedfordshire CC* [1995] 2 A.C. 633. See further Ch.2, at para.2–286, above.

In Scotland it has been held that a breach of regs 24 and 25 of the Electricity **12–28** Supply Regulations 1988[95] could give rise to a private law action for damages against the electricity supplier at the suit of the owners of property allegedly damaged by fire arising from a fault in the electricity supply system.[96]

In respect of other public authorities generally, a breach of statutory provi- **12–29** sion[97] intended to regulate the conduct of betting on racetracks, did not give a bookmaker injured thereby any right of action[98]; nor did a breach of the duty requiring the Ministry of Health inter alia to "take all such steps as may be desirable to secure the preparation, effective carrying out and co-ordination of measures conducive to the health of people, including measures for the prevention and cure of diseases"[99]; when empowering the Secretary of State to set custody time-limits within which the Crown Prosecution Service had to bring an accused person before the Crown Court so that bail might be considered, Parliament did not intend to give a private law right of action to a person who spent longer in custody than should have been the case[100]; there is no right of action against the Legal Aid Board by a solicitor unlawfully suspended from the duty solicitor scheme: the intention of the scheme was to assist those requiring legal services, not those providing them[101]; the Health and Safety Executive did not owe a duty of care to the proprietor of a business in respect of information provided by one of its inspectors in respect of the safety requirements for that business because, having regard to the intention of the Health and Safety at Work, etc. Act 1974, which was to protect the public, the imposition of such a duty of care would be likely to engender untoward cautiousness which could be seriously detrimental to the proper discharge of the Executive's enforcement responsibilities[102]; no cause of action under the Human Tissue Act 1961 is available to parents whose deceased children's tissue was used for a research project despite the fact that such use would be unlawful and was carried out without the parents' knowledge or consent.[103] Patients in hospitals are not within the scope of the protection afforded by the Control of Substances Hazardous to

---

[95] S.I. 1988/1057.

[96] *Morrison Sports Ltd v Scottish Power Plc* 2007 S.L.T. 1103, OH.

[97] Betting and Lotteries Act 1934 s.11(2).

[98] *Cutler v Wandsworth Stadium Ltd* [1949] A.C. 398.

[99] *Danns v Department of Health* [1996] P.I.Q.R. P69 in respect of the Ministry of Health Act 1919 s.2: per Wright J., a powerful consideration leading to this conclusion was that Parliament had conferred on the minister a discretion to decide what steps he should or should not take in discharge of his ministerial function (a claim based upon alleged failure to discharge a duty to inform the public of the risk of unwanted pregnancy after vasectomy); appeal dismissed [1998] P.I.Q.R. P226, CA.

[100] *Olotu v Home Office* [1997] 1 All E.R. 385, CA. However, the L.C.J. commented that the court was not in full possession of the facts and it would be a matter of acute concern if the claimant had, through no fault of her own, spent an excessive length of time in custody without the right to compensation. The relevant statutory duty is contained in the Prosecution of Offences Act (Custody Time Limits) Regulations 1987 reg.6(1). Alternative remedies were available: *R. v Governor of Brockhill Prison Ex p. Evans (No.2)* [2001] 2 A.C. 19 (the tort of false imprisonment); *Clarke v Crew* (1999) 149 N.L.J. 899, CA (negligence). See also *Elguzouli-Daf v Commissioner of the Police of the Metropolis* [1995] 2 W.L.R. 173, CA, Ch.3, n.51, above.

[101] *R. v Legal Aid Board Ex p. Amoo-Gottfried, The Independent*, July 29, 1996.

[102] *Harris v Evans* [1998] I W.L.R. 1285, CA.

[103] *A. v Leeds Teaching Hospital NHS Trust* [2005] 1 Q.B. 506.

Health Regulations 1999.[104] No private law action in negligence could be maintained by a mother and her children for alleged negligence by the Child Support Agency in dealing with an application under the Child Support Act 1991 for child maintenance from a non-resident father.[105]

12–30   In the field of health and safety at work, the duty to fence under the Factories Acts did not give rise to liability if a part of the machine or some fragment of the material, upon which work was being done, flew out and hurt the operator, because the mischief at which the duty was directed was the protection of the operator from contact with the dangerous moving parts of the machine itself[106]; there was no remedy under the statutory provision requiring "sufficient and suitable sanitary conveniences"[107] for a workman who was injured using a lavatory, the seat of which was defective and came adrift from the lavatory pan, as the provision was concerned with health and the prevention of infection, and not with accidents causing injury[108]; and the widow of a fire officer, who was electrocuted whilst fighting a fire in a factory, had no cause of action for breach of the regulations involved because they were limited to the protection of "persons employed."[109] Main contractors have been held not liable under building safety regulations,[110] variously: to an independent contractor, namely a self-employed craftsman working for him, who was not by contract obliged to work on an operation to which the statutory regulations applied[111]; to the sub-

---

[104] S.I. 1999/437. See *Ndri v Moorfields Eye Hospital NHS Trust*, Q.B.D., November 24, 2006, Unreported (the claimant lost the sight of an eye as a result of receiving a corneal graft by way of donor tissue infected by bacteria).

[105] *Rowley v Secretary of State for the Department of Work and Pensions* [2007] 1 W.L.R. 2861, CA (Parliament had provided within the Act itself a rational scheme whose effect was that the victims of the CSA's incompetence would recover their losses in most cases and the fact that there would be some cases where those losses were not recovered, or not recovered in full, was not a sufficient reason for imputing to Parliament an intention that there should be a right of action for damages in negligence).

[106] *Close v Steel Company of Wales Ltd* [1962] A.C. 367, a decision under the 1937 Act which was replaced by the 1961 Act and which has now been repealed and replaced by reg.11 of the Provision and Use of Equipment Regulations 1998: see para.12–213, below. Regulation 12 now provides protection against, inter alia, articles being ejected from machines: see para.12–210, below. See further *Nicholls v F. Austin (Leyton) Ltd* [1946] A.C. 493; *Kilgollan v Wm Cooke & Co Ltd* [1956] 1 W.L.R. 527; *Rutherford v R.E. Glanville & Sons Ltd* [1958] 1 W.L.R. 415. Distinguished in *Littler v G.L. Moore (Contractors) Ltd* [1967] 1 W.L.R. 1241; *Millard v Serck Tubes Ltd* [1969] 1 W.L.R. 211; see Goodhart, (1969) 85 L.Q.R. 458 and Hendy, (1969) 32 M.L.R. 438.

[107] Factories Act 1961 s.7.

[108] *Hands v Rolls-Royce Ltd* (Unreported but noted in (1972) 69 L.S.Gaz. 504). He would now have an unanswerable claim under reg.5(1) of the Workplace (Health, Safety and Welfare) Regulations 1992. See *Malcolm v The Commissioner of Police of the Metropolis* [1999] C.L.Y. 2880, discussed at para.12–124, n.417, below.

[109] *Hartley v Mayoh & Co* [1954] 1 Q.B. 383. But cf. *Canadian Pacific Steamships Ltd v Bryers* [1958] A.C. 485. Further, under reg.2(1) of the Workplace (Health, Safety and Welfare) Regulations 1992, the outcome for the widow may have been different: if access is now made available to non-domestic premises to any person "while at work" such person is arguably afforded the protection of the regulations: see para.12–121, below.

[110] See generally these regulations, which are set out fully in the *Encyclopedia of Health and Safety at Work, Law and Practice* (Sweet & Maxwell), Vol.2. The cases which follow must now be regarded as being of limited assitance having regard to the scope of the regulations currently prevailing made pursuant to the Framework Directive: see paras 12–9–12–99, below.

[111] *Herbert v Harold Shaw Ltd* [1959] 2 Q.B. 138; *Kealey v Heard* [1983] 1 All E.R. 973

contractor in person[112]; to an employee of a sub-contractor[113]; to a labour-only sub-contractor working on "the lump"[114]; and to a clerk of works, employed by a local authority.[115] No civil liability is imposed upon the owner or master of a vessel operated in breach of regulations[116] in respect of fishing vessels in favour of those allegedly injured as a result of such breach.[117] No action for damages could be maintained in reliance on the Supply of Machinery (Safety) Regulations 1992, to recover damages for property and other damage when printing presses caught fire.[118]

Where a statute prohibited persons from sending to market diseased animals, **12–31** knowing that they were diseased, under penalty of a fine, and the defendant, in breach of the statute, sent to market pigs which were suffering from typhoid fever, as a result of which the claimant, who bought the pigs, suffered damage when his own pigs became infected with the disease, it was held that no action lay.[119] Although the statutes of forcible entry[120] make it unlawful, on pain of imprisonment, to enter upon land "with strong hand" or "with multitude of people", this gives no right of action to a person who is forcibly ejected.[121]

Further illustrations: intention to protect. In the field of road traffic law, the **12–32** precursor of s.143 of the Road Traffic Act 1988[122] did create a cause of action

---

[112] *Page v Read* (1984) 134 New L.J. 723.
[113] *Smith v George Wimpey & Co Ltd* [1972] 2 Q.B. 329 (alleged breaches under the Construction (Working Places) Regulations 1966. The purpose and effect of adding the words "him or" in reg.3(1)(a) was to bring the self-employed person or independent contractor within the scope of the regulations in order to make him responsible for his own safety and subject to penalties for breach). The CA specifically approved *Bunker v Charles Brand & Son Ltd* [1969] 2 Q.B. 480 and *Taylor v Sayers* [1971] 1 W.L.R. 561 but disapproved of *Upton v Hipgrave Bros* [1965] 1 W.L.R. 208 and *Baron v B. French Ltd* [1971] 3 All E.R. 1111. The 1966 Regulations were replaced, from September 2, 1996, by the Construction (Health, Safety and Welfare) Regulations 1996, SI 1996/1592, now repealed with effect from 6 April 2007 by the Construction (Design and Management) Regulations 2007, SI 2007/320: see paras 12–160–12–172, below.
[114] *Jones v Minton Construction Ltd* (1973) 15 K.I.R. 309 (alleged breaches under the Construction (General Provisions) Regulations 1961) which have been replaced by the Construction (Health, Safety and Welfare) Regulations 1996, now repealed with effect from April 6, 2007 by the Construction (Design and Management) Regulations 2007, SI 2007/320: see paras 12–160–12–172, below.
[115] *Wingrove v Prestige & Co* [1954] 1 W.L.R. 524.
[116] Fishing Vessel (Safety Provisions) Rules 1975 (SI 1975/330).
[117] *Todd v Adams* [2002] 2 All E.R. (Comm) 97, CA: the defendants' vessel capsized and sank while hauling her fishing gear and relatives of the claimants thereby lost their lives. But see *Ziemniak v ETPM Deep Sea Ltd* [2003] 2 Lloyd's Rep. 214, CA, Ch.10, para.10–165, n.490, above, where a distinction was drawn between fishermen and other workers at sea and the claimant, an engineer, recovered damages for a breach of reg.4(1) of, and Pt II(c) to, the Merchant Shipping (Life Saving Appliances) Regulations 1980.
[118] *Polestar Jowetts Ltd v Komori UK Ltd* [2006] P.I.Q.R. P134 (the Regulations (S.I. 1992/3073) did not confer a civil right of action for breach).
[119] *Ward v Hobbs* (1878) 4 App.Cas. 13: "The Act was passed for the benefit of the general public; it has nothing to do with the bargains of particular persons." Although the correctness of this decision was doubted by the HL in *Horley v Dyke* [1979] R.T.R. 265, an action in negligence would lie.
[120] 5 Ric. 2, st. 1, c. 8.
[121] *Hemmings v Stoke Poges Golf Club* [1920] 1 K.B. 720: any remedies he may have are limited to the common law actions of trespass and assault; *Harvey v Brydges* (1845) 14 M. & W. 437, per Parke B.; *Beddall v Maitland* (1881) 17 Ch.D. 174 at 188, per Fry J.
[122] Which has re-enacted and replaced the provisions of the Road Traffic Act 1972 s.143.

against the owner of a car who permitted it to be used by a friend who was uninsured for third party risks, on the basis that the section was enacted with the intention "of giving a remedy to third persons who might suffer injury by the negligence of the impecunious driver of a car".[123] A breach only arises if the owner, who alone is liable, causes or permits another to drive the vehicle[124] because he is the only person who can forbid another to use the vehicle.[125]

12–33   A public water supplier can be held liable to a pedestrian injured through its failure to reinstate pavements broken up pursuant to statutory powers,[126] despite provision for penalties on breach.[127]

12–34   In health and safety legislation, where a company hired out a crane and driver to a construction company for use on a building site, it was held to be an "employer of workmen . . . undertaking . . . operations or works" to which the regulations[128] applied, thus rendering it vicariously liable for the driver's breach[129]; the statutory duty to protect persons employed from electrically charged apparatus[130] was held to extend to the claimant employee who suffered psychiatric injury as a result of the shock of seeing his workmate electrocuted in circumstances in which he was fortunate to escape his own death because the duty was intended to protect and thereby give a remedy the claimant[131]; regulations concerned with asbestos processes[132] have been held not to be limited to the "asbestos industry" but to extend to any factory or workshop where a

---

[123] *Monk v Warbey* [1935] 1 K.B. 75; *Houston v Buchanan*, 1940 S.C. (HL) 17 (vehicle insured for commercial purposes, but not for private purposes; owner's brother given unrestricted permission to drive-owner liable when driven for private purposes, although he did not know it was being so used); *Martin v Dean* [1971] 2 Q.B. 208 (owner of a motorcycle was held liable after it had been involved in an accident, whilst it was being ridden by his friend, who was not covered by the insurance policy) but cf. *Daniels v Vaux* [1938] 2 K.B. 203 (mother allowed son to drive car, and on insurance policy lapsing told him to pay the premiums himself; not liable for damage caused when uninsured). In practice the Motor Insurers' Bureau usually meets such claims, see Ch.17, paras 17–08–17–26, below.

[124] Thus a breach did not arise where an auctioneer sold an unlicensed and uninsured car which the buyer drove away, thereafter negligently causing injury to another: *Watkins v O'Shaughnessey* [1939] 1 All E.R. 385.

[125] *Goodbarne v Buck* [1940] 1 K.B. 771. See also *Bretton v Hancock* [2006] P.I.Q.R. P1, Ch.16, para.17–02, n.5, below.

[126] Waterworks Clauses Act 1847, now the New Roads and Streetworks Act 1991.

[127] *Hartley v Rochdale Corp* [1908] 2 K.B. 594. Darling J. said: "I do not think that because there is the power to sue the defendants for penalties they are not liable to be sued for negligence in the doing of the work, provided it be proved that the negligence resulted in injury to a plaintiff." See also *Withington v Bolton Borough Council* [1937] 3 All E.R. 108.

[128] i.e. the Construction (Lifting Operations) Regulations 1961. From December 5, 1998, see the Lifting Operations and Lifting Equipment Regulations 1998 (SI 1998/2307). See paras 12–229–12–230, below.

[129] *Williams v West Wales Plant Hire Co* [1984] 1 W.L.R. 1311.

[130] Construction (General Provisions) Regulations 1961 (SI 1961/1580) reg.4(2) which provided: "Where any electrically charged overhead cable or apparatus is liable to be a source of danger to persons employed during the course of any operations or works to which these regulations apply . . . all practicable precautions shall be taken to prevent such danger . . . "

[131] *Young v Charles Church (Southern) Ltd, The Times*, May 1, 1997, CA. The defendant was also held liable in negligence.

[132] Asbestos Industry Regulations 1931.

defined process took place.[133] This enabled the widows of men,[134] who died as a result of their exposure to asbestos in the course of their employment, to succeed in claims for a breach of the duty to avoid the mixing of asbestos without prescribed precautions being taken.[135]

Claimant a member of a protected class. In *Phillips v Britannia Hygienic*   **12–35**
Laundry,[136] Atkin L.J. suggested that it was not an essential requirement that the claimant is a member of the class or group of persons the statute was designed to protect:

> "The question is not to be solved by considering whether or not the person aggrieved can bring himself within some special class of the community or whether he is some designated individual. The duty may be of such paramount importance that it is owed to all the public. It would be strange if a less important duty, which is owed to a section of the public, may be enforced by an action, while a more important duty owed to the public at large cannot. The right of action does not depend on whether a statutory commandment or prohibition is pronounced for the benefit of the public or for the benefit of a class."[137]

Phillips' case was not expressly considered by Lord Diplock in *Lonrho Ltd v*   **12–36**
Shell Petroleum Co Ltd (No.2)[138] nor, indeed, by the House of Lords in *X (Minors) v Bedfordshire County Council*[139] where Lord Browne-Wilkinson noted the absence of cases in which it had been held that statutory provisions establishing a regulatory system or a scheme of social welfare for the benefit of the public at large had been held to give rise to a private right of action.[140] It is suggested that if, on the construction of the statute, it appears that the statute was passed for the benefit of a particular section of the community, of which the claimant is one, strong ground is afforded for coming to the conclusion that the action will lie. Conversely, if the statutory duty appears to be for the protection of society as a whole, rather than a limited class, a private right of action may well not arise.[141]

---

[133] *Cherry Tree Machine Co Ltd & Shell Tankers UK Ltd v Dawson* [2001] P.I.Q.R. P265, CA disapproving *Watt v Fairfield Shipbuilding & Engineering Co Ltd*, 1999 S.L.T. 1084, OH, a Scottish decision which held that the 1931 Regulations related to the process of manufacturing asbetos and did not apply to those working in shipyards. Coincidentally *Watt's* case was supported by an unreported English decision, *Banks v Woodhall Duckham*, November 30, 1995, CA. This latter case was formally distinguished by the CA in *Cherry Tree Machine* but it was clear that the reasoning in both *Banks'* and *Watt's* cases was rejected by Hale L.J. and it is suggested that these cases should be regarded as decided per incuriam. Thus the decision in *Cherry Tree Machine* is to be preferred.
[134] An apprentice fitter exposed to asbestos in the course of manufacturing dry cleaners' presses and a marine engineer who had been exposed to asbestos in engine rooms of ships.
[135] Asbestos Industry Regulations 1931 reg.2.
[136] [1923] 2 K.B. 832.
[137] *Phillips v Britannia Hygienic Laundry* [1923] 2 K.B. 832 at 841.
[138] [1982] A.C. 173.
[139] [1995] 2 A.C. 633.
[140] *X (Minors) v Bedfordshire County Council* [1995] 2 A.C. 633 at 731.
[141] e.g. *KA & SBM Feakins Ltd v Dover Harbour Board*, *The Times*, September 9, 1998: an exporter of live animals, whose business was allegedly damaged when the port of Dover was closed to animal exports, had no private right of action for breach of the duty in s.33 of the Harbours, Docks and Piers Clauses Act 1847 to keep a port open to all persons.

12–37   In *Jain v Trent Strategic Health Authority*,[142] the principle was stated in the following terms:

> "where action is taken by a State authority under statutory powers designed for the benefit or protection of a particular class of persons, a tortious duty of care will not be held to be owed by the State authority to others whose interests may be adversely affected by an exercise of the statutory power. The reason is that the imposition of such a duty would or might inhibit the exercise of the statutory powers and be potentially adverse to the interests of the class of persons the powers were designed to benefit or protect, thereby putting at risk the achievement of their statutory purpose."[143]

Accordingly, no duty was owed by a local authority to the proprietors of a registered nursing home, in relation to economic loss flowing from a decision by the authority, which later proved unwarranted, to seek an ex parte order closing the home under s.30 of the Registered Homes Act 1984.[144]

12–38   Thus, a statutory duty[145] imposed to keep and maintain means of escape in case of fire is imposed principally for the benefit of a particular class, namely, persons in the building, and those persons have a right of action, although penalties are also imposed for breach of the duty.[146]

12–39   Duties imposed under the Factories Acts had long given rise to actions against factory occupiers at the suit of injured workers notwithstanding the provision for criminal penalties on breach[147]:

> "Where a statute provides for the performance by certain powers of a particular duty, and someone belonging to a class of persons for whose benefit and protection the statute imposes the duty is injured by failure to perform it, prima facie, and if there be nothing to the contrary, an action by the person so injured will lie against the person who has so failed to perform the duty."[148]

12–40   The expression "every person employed ... on the premises," contained in s.14 of the Factories Act 1961 included a person who was so employed but at the time of his accident was acting outside the scope of his employment.[149] The expression "any person" contained in s.29 included all those people who entered factory premises in order to work for the purposes of the occupier. Thus, a window cleaner, who was employed as an independent contractor by them, was held to be entitled to the protection of the statutory provisions.[150] Moreover, the expression requiring all floors "to be of sound construction and properly

---

[142] [2009] 2 W.L.R. 248, HL.
[143] *Jain v Trent Strategic Health Authority* [2009] 2 W.L.R. 248, HL per Lord Scott at [28].
[144] See also Ch.2, para.2–317, above.
[145] London Building Acts 1905 to 1939.
[146] *Solomons v Gertzenstein Ltd* [1954] 2 Q.B. 243.
[147] *Groves v Lord Wimborne* [1898] 2 Q.B. 402.
[148] *Groves v Lord Wimborne* [1898] 2 Q.B. 402 at 415, per Vaughan Williams L.J.
[149] *Uddin v Associated Portland Cement Manufacturing Ltd* [1965] 2 Q.B. 15 (workman, who left his allotted tasks and climbed up near an unfenced shaft to catch a pigeon), followed in *Allen v Aeroplane and Motor Aluminium Castings Ltd* [1965] 1 W.L.R. 1244 and approved in *Westwood v Post Office* [1974] A.C. 1.
[150] *Wigley v British Vinegars Ltd* [1964] A.C. 307, applied in *Howell v Caxton Printing Works Ltd* [1971] N.Z.L.R. 108.

maintained," contained in s.16 of the Offices, Shops and Railway Premises Act 1963, was held to afford protection to an employee who went to a place where he had no authority to be at all.[151]

Similarly, the failure of the occupier of a coal mine to comply with the **12–41** provisions of the Coal Mines Act,[152] as a result of which a miner is injured, renders the occupier liable to an action by the injured person.[153] Where an employee of the Ministry of Defence was injured on board a ship, when he caught his foot on a bolt projecting from the riser of a step, it was conceded that both the Merchant Shipping (Health and Safety: General Duties) Regulations[154] and the Merchant Shipping (Safe Movement on Board Ship) Regulations[155] applied and that breach would give rise to a civil cause of action.[156]

"Now the object of the present statute[157] is plain. It was intended to compel mine owners to make due provision for the safety of the men working in their mines, and the persons for whose benefit all these rules are to be enforced are the persons exposed to danger. But when a duty of this kind is imposed for the benefit of particular persons, there arises at common law a correlative right in those persons who may be injured by its contravention. Therefore I think it is quite impossible to hold that the penalty clause detracts in any way from the *prima facie* right of the persons for whose benefit the statutory enactment has been passed to enforce the civil liability."[158]

Under Regulations having their origin in the Framework Directive[159] duties **12–42** are generally owed by an employer to persons working in his undertaking.[160] The duties extend further than employees strictly so called and include, for instance, members of the public visiting premises to which the Workplace (Health, Safety and Welfare) Regulations 1992 applied even though the Directive refers only to workers.[161]

---

[151] *Westwood v Post Office* [1974] A.C. 1.
[152] See now the Mines and Quarries Act 1954 (the provisions of which are now modified by regulation: e.g. the Supply of Machinery (Safety) Regulations 1992 (SI 1992/3073), reg.33(2)(g) (disapplying s.83)).
[153] *Britannic Merthyr Coal Co v David* [1910] A.C. 74; *Black v Fife Coal Co* [1912] A.C. 149; *Watkins v Naval Colliery Co* [1912] A.C. 693. See now the Mines and Quarries Act 1954 to the same effect.
[154] SI 1994/408.
[155] SI 1988/1641.
[156] *Donovan v Ministry of Defence* [2001] 10 C.L. 280. See also *Ziemniak v ETPM Deep Sea Ltd* [2003] 2 Lloyd's Rep. 214, CA, para.12–30 above (breach of the Merchant Shipping (Life Saving Appliances) Regulations 1980).
[157] Coal Mines Regulation Act 1887.
[158] per Lord Kinnear in *Black v Fife Co* [1912] A.C. 149, at 165, 166.
[159] 89/391/EEC. See 12–91–12–99, below.
[160] See, e.g. the Management of Health and Safety at Work Regulations 1999, regs 3 and 12.
[161] *Banna v Delicato*, 1999 Rep. L.R. 89: customer in a shop tripped on a bread basket on the floor of the public area. Followed in *O'Brien v Duke of Argyll's Trustees* [1999] C.L.Y. 6222: visitor to hotel afforded protection by reg.12(3) because the locus was a workplace and Parliament had not seen fit to restrict the duty owed by employers to employees. See also *Mortimer v Safeway Plc*, 1998 S.C. 520, OH: duty would be owed to a person making a delivery to a shop even if not employed by the owner of those premises. *Banna's Case* was not followed in *Layden v Aldi GmbH & Co KG*, 2002 S.L.T. 71 (Sh. Ct.); also *Pickett v Forbouys Ltd* [2004] 1 C.L. 164 (customer in newsagent's shop tripped over pile of newspapers lying in aisle) and *McCondichie v Mains Medical Centre* 2004, Rep. L.R. 4, OH (visitor to a medical practice). But see para.12–138, below, for further discussion.

12–43   **Another remedy provided for the breach.** The availability of another remedy, emphasised in *Phillips v Britannia Hygienic Laundry*,[162] is confirmed as being an important indicator of whether the right to bring a private action law for damages exists by the House of Lords in *X (Minors) v Bedfordshire County Council*.[163] Lord Browne-Wilkinson said:

> "If the statute does provide some other means of enforcing the duty that will normally indicate that the statutory right was intended to be enforceable by those means and not by private right of action."[164]

12–44   It has been pointed out that the presence of another remedy is not decisive: the criminal penalties imposed upon employers in relation to the condition of factory premises were not fatal to the existence of a private law right to claim damages for breach because, it was held, the fact that the employer could be fined was not to be interpreted as Parliament intending to deprive the injured claimant of redress in the form of damages.[165] Indeed, a regime of criminal enforcement of the regulations implementing the Framework Directive[166] does not prevent private rights of action arising for breach despite the absence of any statutory defence of reasonable practicability[167] being afforded an employer, prosecuted for the breach of a strict duty. It has been held that this was insufficient a reason for not interpreting the regulation strictly in civil proceedings.[168]

12–45   Although the statute may provide a special remedy for breach of statutory duty, it may not be the only remedy provided. For example, in *Pickering v James*,[169] it was held that an action would lie on behalf of a person who had lost an election through the failure of the returning officer to perform his duty under the Ballot Act 1872 by disallowing votes for want of an official mark upon the ballot paper. The Act provided a penalty for breach of duty but it was expressly declared to be in addition to any other penalty.

12–46   **Statute creates a right but gives no remedy.** It was long suggested that where a statute imposed a duty, but provided no remedy by which the duty could

---

[162] [1923] 2 K.B. 832.

[163] [1995] 2 A.C. 633.

[164] *X (Minors) v Bedfordshire County Council* [1995] 2 A.C. 633 at 731. In *Lonrho Ltd v Shell Petroleum Co Ltd (No.2)* [1982] A.C. 173 Lord Diplock said: "Most of the authorities about this second exception deal not with public rights created by statute but with public rights existing at common law, particularly in respect of use of highways." See also Bailey & Bowman, "Public Authority Negligence Revisited" (2000) C.L.J. 270.

[165] *X (Minors) v Bedfordshire County Council* n.51, above. See also Lord Campbell in *Couch v Steel* (1854) 23 L.J.Q.B. 121 at 125 and Vaughan Williams L.J. in *Groves v Wimborne* [1898] 2 Q.B. 402 at 416.

[166] See para.12–91, below.

[167] For a discussion as to the meaning of reasonable practicability, e.g. as under reg.12(3) of the Workplace (Health, Safety and Welfare) Regulations 1992, paras 12–127–12–133, below and 12–109–12–116 et seq.

[168] *Stark v The Post Office* [2000] P.I.Q.R. P105 per Waller L.J. at P111–112.

[169] (1873) L.R. 8 C.P. 489. The duties of presiding officers and clerks at both parliamentary and local elections are now contained in the Representation of the People Act 1983.

be enforced, the general rule was that an action for damages could be brought, provided that the person suing was one of a class intended to be benefited by the duty.[170] "For, if it were not so, the statute would be but a pious aspiration."[171] Following a review of the authorities,[172] the House of Lords in *R. v Deputy Governor of Parkhurst Prison Ex p. Hague*[173] held that Parliamentary intention to protect, in the absence of any other remedy, was not sufficient alone to give rise to a private law claim. Lord Jauncey said:

> "It must always be a matter for consideration whether the legislature intended that private law rights of action should be conferred upon individuals in respect of breaches of the relevant statutory provision. The fact that a particular provision was intended to protect certain individuals is not of itself sufficient to confer private law rights of action upon them, something more is required to show that the legislature intended such conferment."[174]

Thus Hague, a prisoner, segregated in good faith but in breach of the procedures prescribed by rules made pursuant to legislation,[175] who sued inter alia for damages for false imprisonment, failed to demonstrate that the legislature intended to confer a right of action for breach of a preventative measure designed to give a necessary power to regulate the orderly conduct of the prison.

Accordingly, the fundamental test is always the Parliamentary intention. It has   **12–47** been held that the duties imposed on the Secretary of State by ss.1 and 3(1) of the National Health Service Act 1977 were probably not intended by Parliament to be enforceable by civil action, even though no other remedy was provided by

---

[170] In *Couch v Steel* (1854) 3 E. & B. 402 Lord Campbell said: "The Statute of Westminster the Second [13 Edw. 1, c.50], gives a remedy by action on the case to all who are aggrieved by the neglect of any duty created by statute: see 2 Inst. p.486, and in Com. Dig. tit. Action upon Statute, F, it is laid down that 'in every case where a statute enacts or prohibits a thing for the benefit of a person, he shall have remedy upon the same statute for the thing enacted for his advantage, or for the recompense of a wrong done to him contrary to the said law." See also to the same effect Kennedy L.J. in *Dawson v Bingley UDC* [1911] 2 K.B. 149 at 159.

[171] *Cutler v Wandsworth Stadium Ltd* [1949] A.C. 398 at 407, per Lord Simonds. To the like effect, see *Ministry of Housing and Local Government v Sharp* [1970] 2 Q.B. 223 at 267, per Lord Denning M.R. and at 274, per Salmon L.J.

[172] *Groves v Wimborne* [1898] 2 Q.B. 402, *Cutler v Wandsworth Stadium Ltd* [1949] A.C. 398, *Lonrho Ltd v Shell Petroleum Co Ltd* [1982] A.C. 173, *Pickering v Liverpool Daily Post and Echo Newspapers Plc* [1991] 2 W.L.R. 513 and *Calveley v Chief Constable of the Merseyside Police* [1989] A.C. 1228.

[173] [1992] 1 A.C. 58.

[174] *R. v Deputy Governor of Pankhurst Prison Ex p. Hague* [1992] 1 A.C. 58 at 170. See also *Olotu v Secretary of State for the Home Office* [1997] 1 W.L.R. 328, CA. Lord Bingham C.J. said: " . . . regard must be paid to the object and scope of the provisions, the class (if any) to be protected by them, and the means of redress open to a member of such a class if the statutory duty is not followed." The object of the Prosecution of Offences Act 1985 s.22 and the Prosecution of Offences (Custody Time Limits) Regulations 1987 reg.5(3)(a), breach of which was alleged, was to expedite the trial of remanded prisoners. An aggrieved defendant could apply for bail or habeas corpus and mandamus. Thus it could not have been the intention of Parliament to confer a private law right of action for damages.

[175] Prison Rules 1964 made pursuant to the Prison Act 1952.

statute for their breach.[176] An injunction can also be obtained at the suit of the Attorney-General, in a suitable case.

12–48   **Inadequacy of statutory remedy.** Where the statute creates a liability which does not exist at common law, and proceeds to provide a particular remedy for enforcing it, the question arises whether the particular remedy provided is the only remedy, or whether there is, in addition, a right of action for damages based on the breach of the statutory duty. As statutory duties deal with a great variety of matters of varying degrees of importance and are directed to a number of different objects, it is impossible to give a simple affirmative or negative answer to this general question. Everything depends on the object and intention of the statute.[177] As has been seen, the fact that the Factories Acts provided for employers to be fined for breach of statutory duties owed to their employees did not preclude an private law right of action for damages.[178] Likewise, the owner of a fishery was held to be entitled to sue for injury to fish from pollution despite the fact that breach of the statutory duty also gave rise to financial penalties for the same damage.[179] It has been held that a breach of reg.4 of the Working Time Regulations 1998 does not give a right of action for breach of statutory duty.[180]

12–49   On the other hand, in decisions all consistent with the need to consider the intention of Parliament, a person who contravened the Merchandise Marks Acts 1887 to 1953 was not liable in damages to a rival trader[181]; a person who sold impure milk was not liable to an action for damages in respect of his contravention of s.2(1) of the Food Act 1984[182]; a motorist could not sue for another motorist's contravention of the provisions of a statutory order making it illegal to park on a clearway[183]; a buyer of a motorvehicle had no right to sue

---

[176] In *Re HIV Haemophiliac Litigation* [1996] P.I.Q.R. P220, CA, it was said that it was at least strongly arguable that in law a claim could lie against the Department of Health for negligence in performing its functions under the Act. See also, *M v Calderdale & Kirklees HA* [1998] Lloyd's Rep. Med. 157, Ch.3, para.3–109, above, where it was held that the defendant owed a non-delegable duty of care in like terms to s.1 of the 1977 Act.

[177] *Black v Fife Coal Co Ltd* [1912] A.C. 149 at 165, per Lord Kinnear: "We are to consider the scope and purpose of the statute and in particular for whose benefit it is intended"; also *Atkinson v Newcastle Waterworks Co* (1877) 3 Ex. D. 411 at 448, per Lord Cairns L.C.: liability "must, to a great extent, depend on the purview of the legislature in the particular statute, and the language which they have there employed."

[178] See para.12–39, above.

[179] *Nicholls v Ely Beet Sugar Factory* [1936] Ch. 343. Under the Salmon and Freshwater Fisheries Act 1923.

[180] *Sayers v Cambridgeshire CC* [2007] I.R.L.R. 29 (a claim, which failed, based upon workplace stress caused by alleged overwork).

[181] *J. Bollinger v The Costa Brava Wine Co Ltd (No.3)* [1960] Ch. 262 at 287. The Merchandise Marks Acts were repealed by the Trade Descriptions Act 1968.

[182] *Square v Model Farm Dairies Bournemouth Ltd* [1939] 2 K.B. 365 (a decision under the earlier Act of 1928).

[183] *Coote v Stone* [1971] 1 W.L.R. 279 (a breach of the Various Trunk Roads (Prohibition of Waiting) (Clearways) Order 1963 (SI 1963/1172), approving *Clarke and Wife v Brims* [1947] K.B. 497, but overruling *Kelly v W.R.N. Contracting Ltd* [1968] 1 W.L.R. 921.

under s.75(1) of the Road Traffic Act 1988 and the Road Vehicles (Construction and Use) Regulations 1986, in respect of defective brakes.[184]

It was held that the rights and duties arising under the Housing Acts did not **12–50** give rise to a private law action for breach of statutory duty unless a decision made by the local authority was capable of being the subject of judicial review. In such circumstances, a claim for damages could be made at the same time as the application for judicial review to be determined if the public law remedy sought was granted. Thus, in *Cocks v Thanet District Council*,[185] Lord Bridge said[186]:

> "Once a decision has been reached by the housing authority which gives rise to the temporary, the limited or the full housing duty, rights and obligations are immediately created in the field of private law. Each of the duties referred to, once established, is capable of being enforced by injunction and breach of it will give rise to a liability in damages. But it is inherent in the scheme of the Act that an appropriate public law decision of the housing authority is a condition precedent to the establishment of the private law duty."

This passage was subsequently doubted by the House by reason of its failure to examine legislative intent.[187] The facts that the duty to provide accommodation to homeless persons was enforceable in public law and that the statute in question was part of a scheme of public welfare to confer benefits on society as a whole, as well as those who were homeless, all suggested that Parliament had not intended to create private rights of action. Accordingly, only public law remedies were available to an aggrieved claimant. Hence, an earlier decision that a disappointed claimant cannot seek damages for a local authority's failure to provide benefits under another scheme of social welfare, the Chronically Sick and Disabled Persons Act 1970, was approved.[188] The only available remedy lay with the default powers of the Minister on representation to him.[189] Likewise, the wording of s.117 of the Mental Health Act 1983 is not apposite to create a private law cause of action for failure to carry out the duty to provide after-care services for a person released after detention under s.3 of the Act.[190]

---

[184] *Badham v Lambs Ltd* [1946] K.B. 45; the subsection is statutory affirmation of this decision, while subs.(7) renders obsolete *Vinall v Howard* [1953] 1 W.L.R. 987, where the contract was held to be tainted with illegality and thereby unenforceable. cf. the position of the seller of unfenced machinery who was not liable to a workman for a breach of what was s.17 of the Factories Act 1961. *Biddle v Truvox Engineering Co Ltd* [1952] 1 K.B. 101. Section 17 was replaced, with effect from December 5, 1998 by reg.11 of the Provision and Use of Equipment Regulations 1998, (SI 1998/2306) as amended.
[185] [1983] A.C. 286 (a disputed finding of intentional homelessness under the Housing (Homeless Persons) Act 1977).
[186] *Cocks v Thanet District Council* [1983] A.C. 286 at 292, 293.
[187] *O'Rourke v Camden LBC* [1998] A.C. 188, per Lord Hoffmann at 196E.
[188] *O'Rourke v Camden LBC* [1998] A.C. 188 at 193: *Wyatt v Hillingdon London Borough Council* (1978) L.G.R. 727, CA, following *Southwark LBC v Williams* [1971] Ch. 734, applying the dicta of Lord Denning M.R. and the dicta of Veale J. in *Reffell v Surrey CC* [1964] 1 W.L.R. 358.
[189] National Assistance Act 1948 s.36.
[190] *Clunis v Camden & Islington HA* [1998] Q.B. 978. It was pointed out in the CA that the primary method of enforcement of the obligations under s.117 was complaint by the Secretary of State.

12–51   Notwithstanding the limited means of enforcement within the legislation, there is no private law right, either in negligence or breach of statutory duty, vested in children in the care of the local authority as regards the acts of the authority in the discharge of its statutory functions.[191] However, although a local authority's failure in discharging such functions[192] to cancel or suspend a child-minder's registration did not give rise to a private law right of action, it was held liable in negligence for misstatement.[193] As regards the statutory code, providing for the identification, assessment and assistance for children with special educational needs, prescribed by the Education Acts 1944 and 1981, inter alia, it has been held that such did not give rise to a private law right cause of action.[194] Similarly, the disclosure of restricted information in contravention of s.179 of the Financial Services Act 1986 was held not to have conferred any cause of action for breach of statutory duty.[195]

12–52   **Imperfect rather than inadequate remedy.** If the duty imposed by statute can be enforced by a statutory remedy, which is imperfect, as opposed to inadequate, an action for breach of duty may be brought. "If the statute creates such a duty which remains to be performed after the remedy provided by the statute has expired, the Court must infer that the continuing duty was not intended to become one of imperfect obligation, but must hold that an action at law will arise on the cesser of the statutory remedy."[196] By way of an example,[197] in *Attorney-General v St Ives Rural District Council*,[198] a farmer was able to recover damages for the resultant flooding of his land from the local authority, which was responsible under a statutory duty to maintain the drains on the highway, which it had neglected to do.

---

[191] i.e. under the Children and Young Persons Act 1969; Local Authority Social Services Act 1970; Child Care Act 1980 and the Children Act 1989 ss.17, 26, 37, 47, 84, Sch.2, Pt 1: *X (Minors) v Bedfordshire CC* [1995] 2 A.C. 633. But an authority can be vicariously liable for the negligence of members of its staff, and arguably where a child is already in care an action could lie for their failure to place a child for adoption or find him suitable foster homes: *Barrett v Enfield LBC* [2001] 2 A.C. 550 reversing [1997] 3 W.L.R. 628, CA, Ch.2, para.2–309, above. See also *Thurkettle v Suffolk CC* [1998] C.L.Y. 3944 (no duty of care arose under s.8 of the Education Act 1944 where the claimant was allegedly placed at an wholly unsuitable special school, over which the Education Authority had little control). See Bailey and Bowman, "Public Authority Negligence Revisited" (2000) C.L.J. 85 and Mullender, "Negligence, Public Authorities and Policy-Level Decisions" (2000) L.Q.R. 40.
[192] Nurseries and Child-Minders Regulation Act 1948.
[193] *T v Surrey CC* [1994] 4 All E.R. 577 (misstatement in saying there was no reason why a child should not go to a particular child-minder when there was an unresolved question of non-accidental injury to another child).
[194] *E (A Minor) v Dorset CC* [1995] 2 A.C. 633 in which it was held that the appropriate remedy lay through the appeal structure set out in the legislation and by way of judicial review; cf. also, *P v Harrow LBC* [1993] F.L.R. 723.
[195] *Melton Medes Ltd v Securities and Investments Board, The Times*, July 27, 1994.
[196] *Pulsford v Devenish* [1903] 2 Ch. 625 at 633, per Farwell J. (liquidator of company liable to creditor for non-performance of statutory duty).
[197] For other examples, see *Ching v Surrey CC* [1910] 1 K.B. 736 (a breach of statutory duty to maintain and keep efficient the school, injured pupil could sue education authority); *Blundy, Clark & Co v L.N.E.R.* [1931] 2 K.B. 334 (a railway company neglected to repair a canal); *Guilfoyle v Port of London Authority* [1932] 1 K.B. 336 (dock company failed to repair a road over a swing bridge).
[198] [1960] 1 Q.B. 312.

Damage as a result of the breach of duty. In *Bonnington Castings Ltd v*   **12–53**
Wardlaw,[199] the House of Lords laid down that unless a statute or regulation
provided to the contrary, the burden rested on the claimant to prove on a balance
of probabilities that the breach of statutory duty caused or materially contributed
to his damage.[200] Lord Reid stated:

> "It would seem obvious in principle that a pursuer or plaintiff must prove not only
> negligence or breach of duty but also that such fault caused or materially contributed to
> his injury, and there is ample authority for that proposition both in Scotland and in
> England. I can find neither reason nor authority for the rule being different where there
> is a breach of statutory duty. The fact that Parliament imposes a duty for the protection
> of employees has been held to entitle an employee to sue if he is injured as a result of
> a breach of that duty, but it would be going a great deal farther to hold that it can be
> inferred from the enactment of a duty that Parliament intended that any employee
> suffering injury can sue his employer merely because there was a breach of duty and it
> is shown to be possible that his injury may have been caused by it."[201]

To the like effect Viscount Simonds in *McWilliams v Sir William Arrol & Co*[202]   **12–54**
commented:

> "I do not doubt that it is part of the law of Scotland as it is part of the law of England
> that a causal connection must be established between a breach by an employer of his
> duty at common law or under a statute and the damage suffered by his employee: see,
> for example, *Bonnington Castings v Wardlaw*. If a contrary principle is thought to be
> established in *Roberts v Dorman Long & Co Ltd*[203] I cannot reconcile that case with
> *Wardlaw*."

Thus, where an experienced steel erector fell to his death, his widow's action   **12–55**
failed owing to her inability to establish a causal connection between his
employers' failure to provide the deceased with a safety belt and the happening
of the accident. On the evidence it was highly probable that the deceased would
not have worn the belt, even if it had been provided, and it was held that there
was no obligation on the employers to encourage and exhort him so to do.[204]
Similarly, a motorist's breach of a statutory duty to have a red light on the rear
of his motorcar would be no ground for an action for damages by a person who
collided with the front of it.[205] The claim for psychiatric injury of an employee
present on an oil rig some 550m from the exploding Piper Alpha platform failed

---

[199] [1956] A.C. 613; *Quinn v Cameron and Roberton Ltd* [1958] A.C. 9 at 23. See also *Nicholson v Atlas Steel Co Ltd* [1957] 1 W.L.R. 613; *Clarke v E. R. Wright & Son* [1957] 1 W.L.R. 1191; *Clarkson v Modern Foundries Ltd* [1957] 1 W.L.R. 1210; *Corn v Weir's (Glass) Ltd* [1960] 1 W.L.R. 577; *McGhee v N.C.B.* [1973] 1 W.L.R. 1; *Duyvelshaff v Cathcart & Ritchie Ltd* (1973) 1 A.L.R. 125.
[200] In *McGovern v British Steel Corp* [1986] I.C.R. 608, CA it was held that the claimant was entitled to an award of damages for an injury sustained whilst he was trying to remove an imminent danger, which had been caused by a breach of statutory duty. This was because the injury was directly caused in the first place by the breach of the regulations that he was seeking to remedy, hence the precise manner in which the injury had occurred was irrelevant (*Gorris v Scott* (1874) L.R. 9 Ex. 125 and *Grant v N.C.B.* [1956] C.L.Y. 5537 were applied).
[201] *McGovern v British Steel Corp* [1986] I.C.R. 608, CA, at 620.
[202] [1962] 1 W.L.R. 295 at 301, 302.
[203] [1953] 1 W.L.R. 942.
[204] *McWilliams v Sir William Arrol Co* [1962] 1 W.L.R. 295.
[205] See *Phillips v Britannia Hygienic Laundry* [1923] 2 K.B. 832 at 838, 840, per Bankes L.J.

where he could not establish that anything which occurred on the occasion in question was likely to endanger his own health and safety.[206]

12–56 It follows that where the effective cause of the accident is a deliberate act of folly by an employee, the employer may avoid liability altogether,[207] as was the case where an employee pushed over the scaffold tower on which the claimant was working.[208]

12–57 **Impact of the Human Rights Act 1998.** The policy considerations underlying the decision of the House of Lords in *X (Minors) v Bedfordshire County Council* and *M (Minor) v Newham London Borough Council*[209] to deny private law remedies in respect of alleged breaches of social welfare legislation, were overtaken by the coming into force of the Human Rights Act 1998. On complaint from the House, the European Court concluded that the failure of the authority to intervene to prevent the serious abuse of children, via the agency of its social services department, constituted a breach of art.3 of the European Convention on Human Rights, namely inhumane and degrading treatment. Further, the absence of an available remedy to the applicants constituted a breach of art.13: there was no appropriate means of determining their allegations of a failure to protect them from the treatment in question.[210] Additionally, in the *Newham* case, the failure to disclose to the mother of the child a video in the posession of the authority, which would have enabled her to demonstrate that her partner had wrongly been identified as the abuser, constituted a breach of art.8, the right to respect for family life.[211] The decision in *X (Minors)* has also been limited in scope by subsequent developments in domestic jurisprudence, already summarised.[212] The decision itself would appear now to be confined to its particular facts.

12–58 Following the decision in *D v East Berkshire Community Health NHS Trust*,[213] it has been said, in striking out a mother's claims in negligence and for breach of art.8 of the Convention concerning the investigation by a local authority of claims of abuse of her children by both of their parents, that, whilst there were clearly good policy reasons for declaring that no duty of care was owed by investigating professionals to parents suspected of such abuse, for acts and omissions alleged to have occurred after October 2, 2000, such a parent might

---

[206] *Hegarty v E. E. Caledonia Ltd* [1997] P.N.L.R. 578, CA. The plaintiff alleged breach of the Offshore Installations (Operational Safety, Health and Welfare) Regulations 1976, SI 1976/1019. See also Barrett, "Renaissance of civil liability for breach of statutory duty?" (1998) 27 I.L.J. 59.
[207] *Rushton v Turner Brothers Asbestos Co Ltd* [1960] 1 W.L.R. 96; *Horne v Lec Refrigeration Ltd* [1965] 2 All E.R. 898; *Homer v Sandwell Castings Ltd* [1995] P.I.Q.R. P318, CA (no breach of the Foundries (Protective Footwear and Gaiters) Regulations 1971 where the claimant, who suffered injury from an escape of molten metal from a mould, chose to wear the very boots of which he complained when other choices were available). Such employee may however succeed in proving negligence, e.g. *Nolan v Dental Manufacturing Co Ltd* [1958] 1 W.L.R. 936. For "causation in fact" and the burden of proof, generally, see Ch.6, above.
[208] *Horton v Taplin Contracts Ltd* [2003] P.I.Q.R P12, CA.
[209] [1995] 2 A.C. 633.
[210] See also *MAK and RK v UK, The Times*, April 19, 2010, ECHR where the absence of a common law duty of care (owed to parents in care proceedings) was unanimously held to violate art.13.
[211] *Z v UK* [2001] 2 F.L.R. 612.
[212] See Ch.2, paras 2–286–2–293, above.
[213] [2005] 2 A.C. 373, discussed at Ch.2, paras 2–331–2–333, above.

have a claim under art.8(2) and, were a remedy to be necessary, it should be restricted to the claim under the 1998 Act.[214]

4.—BURDEN AND STANDARD OF PROOF OF A BREACH OF STATUTORY DUTY

Burden of proof. The burden of proof,[215] in actions by employees against their employers for breach of statutory duty, is the same as that imposed on all other claimants but, as shown by the following, the question has sometimes given rise to difficulty.

12–59

The basic principle was stated by Lord Macmillan[216]:

12–60

"The mere fact that at the time of an accident to a [workman] his employers can be shown to have been in breach of a statutory duty is clearly not enough to itself to impose liability on the employers. It must be shown that the accident was causally associated with the breach of statutory duty."

It often happens, however, that the circumstances of an accident are unknown or only imperfectly known, so that it is a matter of inference whether a breach of statutory duty has caused it. In dealing with the problem, it was at one time suggested there was a rule that the claimant had only to establish that a breach of statutory duty had occurred and that his injury was one that could have been caused by such a breach, for the burden of proof to shift upon the employer to show that the breach was not the cause. Such a rule would, no doubt, have been of considerable assistance to claimants where the facts of an accident were open to some doubt, but it was attended by controversy, not least because the case in which the principle was enunciated did not strictly require its application.[217]

It was subsequently held by the House of Lords that no such rule exists.[218]

12–61

"No distinction can be drawn between actions for common law negligence and actions for breach of statutory duty in this respect. In both the plaintiff or pursuer must prove (a) breach of duty and (b) that such breach caused the injury complained of."[219]

"The employee must in all cases prove his case by the ordinary standard of proof in civil actions: he must make it appear at least that on a balance of probabilities the breach of duty caused or materially contributed to his injury."[220]

---

[214] *L v Pembrokeshire County Council* [2007] P.I.Q.R. P1 at [46].
[215] See further Ch.6, above.
[216] *Caswell v Powell Duffryn Associated Collieries Ltd* [1940] A.C. 152 at 168.
[217] The rule was suggested by Scott L.J. in *Vyner v Waldenberg Bros Ltd* [1946] K.B. 50 at 55. A somewhat similar view had been suggested by Goddard L.J. in *Lee v Nursery Furnishings Ltd* [1945] 1 All E.R. 387. See also *Stimson v Standard Telephones Cables Ltd* [1940] 1 K.B. 342; *Hughes v McGoff & Vickers Ltd* [1955] 1 W.L.R. 416.
[218] *Bonnington Castings Ltd v Wardlaw* [1956] A.C. 613, in which Lord Keith commented at 625, "I think most, if not all, of the cases which professed to lay down or to recognise some such rule could have been decided as they were on simple rules of evidence."
[219] *Bonnington Castings Ltd v Wardlaw* [1956] A.C. 613 at 624, per Lord Tucker. See generally Ch.1, paras 1–34–1–35.
[220] *Bonnington Castings Ltd v Wardlaw* [1956] A.C. 613 at 620, per Lord Reid.

12–62   Accordingly, where the evidence of causation is scant and a claimant fails to provide evidence of a defect which made a workplace unsafe, the court is not bound to draw an inference adverse to the employer, even though no evidence on the latter's behalf is led.[221] Where the factory's occupiers, in breach of their statutory duty,[222] failed to take all practicable measures to protect employees from inhaling dust and an employee became tuberculous, claiming that the disease may have been activated by the breach, it was held that he had not discharged the burden of proof.[223] The fact that the breach *might* have been a cause was not enough. It was for the claimant to prove that it probably was the cause. Again, when a workman, cutting off bolts from an engine, was not supplied with goggles, contrary to the regulations, and received an eye injury, which he claimed was caused by a flying bolt but which the judge refused to find was so caused, it was held that there was no presumption to induce the judge to find that it was.[224]

12–63   In *Cork v Kirby Maclean Ltd*,[225] the Court of Appeal overruled the trial judge who had held that breach of statutory duty to have a handrail and toe-boards to a platform, 20 feet above ground, threw a burden of proving that an epileptic who fell in a fit would have fallen even had those safeguards been provided. But, in *Allen v Aeroplane and Motor Aluminum Casting Ltd*,[226] where the facts showed that there had been a breach of statutory duty, because of which the accident had happened or without which it would not have done so, and that the employee was injured thereby, liability was established, notwithstanding that he had not given an acceptable version of how the accident occurred. Once employers are fixed with the knowledge that an irregular practice is taking place, such as, for example, using an squeezable bottle to squirt coolant liquid into the interior of a workpiece on a centre lathe, they must be taken to foresee the risk of injury.[227]

12–64   Where a helicopter crashed killing the husband of the claimant, it was held that, on a balance of probability, the accident had been caused by a mechanical defect, albeit the claimant was not able to say what that defect was. Evidence was led that the deceased had made an abrupt emergency turn away from his landing

---

[221] *Alderson v Piggott & Whitfield Ltd* [1996] C.L.Y. 3003, CA: an unexplained fall from a step-ladder.

[222] s.47(1) of the 1937 Act: subsequently s.63(1) of the Factories Act 1961.

[223] *Mist v Toleman & Sons* [1946] 1 All E.R. 139.

[224] *Watts v Enfield Rolling Mills Ltd* [1952] 1 All E.R. 1013. In *Nolan v Dental Manufacturing Co Ltd* [1958] 1 W.L.R. 936, the claimant had not established that the injury to his eye was caused by the defendants' breach of statutory duty, because he had not proved that he would have worn the goggles, if they have been provided; but the defendants were in breach of their common law duty not only to provide goggles, but also to give orders that they were to be worn, and to supervise the workmen to a reasonable extent to ensure that the others were obeyed. See *McWilliams v Sir William Arrol & Co* [1962] 1 W.L.R. 295, where a workman failed to prove that he would have worn a safety belt if one had been provided.

[225] [1952] 2 All E.R. 402.

[226] [1965] 1 W.L.R. 1244; Diplock L.J. observed at 1248, "Nor do I think that the expression 'a frolic of his own', which is relevant for the purpose of making a master vicariously liable for the torts of his servant, has any relevance to the question of whether a master is liable to his servant either for breach of statutory duty or at common law."

[227] *Johnson v F.E. Callow (Engineers) Ltd* [1970] 2 Q.B. 1 (affirmed [1971] A.C. 335).

path and descended sharply into a valley, where the helicopter had collided with power cables suspended from towers masked from the deceased by trees. The court applied the principle set out by Lord Brandon in *Rhesa Shipping Co SA v Edmunds (The Popi M)*[228] that a trial judge is not bound to find for a claimant where a defendant's explanation for an accident is rejected. In the absence of satisfactory evidence to show, on the balance of probabilities, how a calamity occurred then, however unpalatable and rare it may be, the judge must find for the defendant. In such a case a claimant will have failed to discharge the burden of proving the case. Causation was, however, made out where the court was able to infer the existence of a defect from the circumstances of the collision, a defect for which, by virtue of reg.6(1) of the Provision and Use of Work Equipment Regulations 1992, the defendant employer was strictly liable.[229]

Burden on defendant. Where a statutory duty is subject to a defence of reasonable practicability,[230] the defendant must demonstrate compliance with that proviso.[231] Furthermore, in order to avail himself of the defence that a particular safety measure is not reasonably practicable, not only must it be specifically pleaded,[232] but the burden of proving it lies on the defendant.[233] So, where a claimant had to allege and prove injury from working at a place which was not made or kept safe, the defendant had to plead and prove that it was not reasonably practicable to keep the premises safe if he was to escape liability.[234]   **12–65**

Standard of proof. The existence of a statutory duty does not necessarily relieve an employer of his common law duty of care to employees although "in very many cases, it would be difficult, if not impossible, to maintain that an employer who had complied with regulations had been negligent at common law."[235] On the other hand, it has recently been noted that a statutory duty is likely to be higher than its common law equivalent: a claim based on a breach of statutory duty can succeed even though the employer is held not to be liable in negligence.[236] Even so, the existence of a statutory duty may indicate that a particular risk ought to have been foreseen and can be relied upon in order to establish negligence.[237] But this is not invariably the case. In *Chipchase v British*   **12–66**

---

[228] [1985] 1 W.L.R. 1948, HL.

[229] *Budden v Police Aviation Services* [2005] P.I.Q.R. P362.

[230] See paras 12–109–12–116, below.

[231] *Johnson v F.E. Callow (Engineers) Ltd* [1970] 2 Q.B. 1 (affirmed [1971] A.C. 335).

[232] *Bowes v Sedgefield DC* [1981] I.C.R. 234, CA; *Moffat v Marconi Space and Defence Systems Ltd*, 1975 S.L.T. (Notes) 60.

[233] *Gibson v British Insulated Callender's Construction Co Ltd*, 1973 S.L.T. 2, HL see para.12–116, n.382, below.

[234] *Larner v British Steel Plc* [1993] I.C.R. 551.

[235] *Franklin v Gramophone Co Ltd* [1948] 1 K.B. 542 at 558 per Somervell L.J. *N.C.B. v England* [1954] A.C. 403.

[236] *Hall v Edinburgh CC*, 1999 S.L.T. 744, OH, in relation to the Manual Handling Operations Regulations 1992. See para.12–241, below.

[237] So, where a local authority's liability under the Housing Act 1985 s.365, was restricted to houses in multiple occupation that were three storeys in height or more, it was held not just and equitable to impose a duty of care in respect of the condition of two-storey houses: *Ephraim v Newham LBC* (1993) 91 L.G.R. 412, CA (claimant injured where no fire escape provided).

Titan Products Co Ltd[238] it was argued unsuccessfully that, where the facts of the case lay just outside the protection of the statutory duty, the court ought to take the statutory provisions into account in deciding negligence.

5.—DEFENCES TO ACTION FOR BREACH OF STATUTORY DUTY

12–67   **Statutory defences.** A statute may itself provide for a defence[239] to what would otherwise be a breach of its provisions. Whether or not a defendant can avail himself of such a defence will depend upon the precise wording of the statutory provision in question.[240] The defence most commonly encountered is that of reasonable practicability.[241]

12–68   **Voluntary assumption of risk.** In actions by employees against their employers for breach of statutory duty, the principle volenti non fit injuria will usually provide no defence.[242] It can only apply when there is an agreement between the parties, and it is not open to an employer to contract out of a statutory duty owed to employees. Nevertheless, the House of Lords held in *Imperial Chemical Industries Ltd v Shatwell*[243] that whilst the defence of "volenti" was not available to employers where they were in breach of their own statutory duty, there was nothing to prevent them relying on it where they were not in breach of a statutory duty, either themselves, or vicariously, as a result of the carelessness of someone the claimant was required to obey. There is also the point that in order to succeed in a claim, a claimant must prove causation and, if he has voluntarily assumed a particular risk, he will have difficulty in discharging the burden of proof, despite the defendant's being in breach of a statutory duty.[244] In claims other than those between employer and employee it will depend upon a construction of the statute in question whether it was, or was not, permissible to contract out of its terms.[245]

12–69   **Contributory negligence.** Subject to the provisions of the Law Reform (Contributory Negligence) Act 1945, the contributory negligence[246] of the claimant is a partial defence to an action for breach of statutory duty. Whilst this

---

[238] [1956] 1 Q.B. 545.
[239] See Ch.4 for defences, generally.
[240] For an example of a statutory defence, see para.12–113, below.
[241] See paras 12–109–12–116, below.
[242] *Baddeley v Granville* (1887) 19 Q.B.D. 423; *Davies v Thomas Owen & Co* [1919] 2 K.B. 39; *Wheeler v New Merton Board Mills* [1933] 2 K.B. 669. See further Ch.4, paras 4–73–4–127, above.
[243] [1965] A.C. 656 (distinguishing *Wheeler v New Merton Board Mills Ltd* [1933] 2 K.B. 669 and *Stapley v Gypsum Mines Ltd* [1953] A.C. 663) which was applied in *Bolt v William Moss & Sons Ltd* (1966) 110 S.J. 385, and in *McMullen v N.C.B.* [1982] I.C.R. 148 (claimant, who was well aware of the strict prohibition against miners jumping off the man-rider while it was in motion carrying them from the coal face to the cage, deliberately ignored it, jumped off and was crushed by a wheel). However, cf. *Hugh v N.C.B.*, 1972 S.C. 252 and, contra, *Progress and Properties Ltd v Craft* (1976) 12 A.L.R. 59.
[244] *Bonnington Castings Ltd v Wardlaw* [1956] A.C. 613; *Nolan v Dental Manufacturing Co Ltd* [1958] 1 W.L.R. 936; *Rushton v Turner Brothers Asbestos Co Ltd* [1960] 1 W.L.R. 96.
[245] See further Ch.4, para.4–75, above.
[246] See Ch.4, paras 4–03–4–72, above, where this subject is dealt with more fully.

applies in employer and employee cases[247] as well as in other cases,[248] Lord Wright in *Caswell v Powell Duffryn Collieries Ltd*[249] said that, in the case of employees, the courts should give:

> "due regard to the actual conditions under which men work in a factory or mine, to the long hours and the fatigue, to the slackening of attention which naturally comes from constant repetition of the same operation, to the noise and confusion in which the man works, to his preoccupation in what he is actually doing at the cost perhaps of some inattention to his own safety."

Momentary inattention or conscious acceptance of risk. It has long been **12–70** recognised that a purpose behind the imposition of statutory duties on employers "is to protect the workmen against those very acts of inattention which are sometimes relied on as constituting contributory negligence so that too strict a standard would defeat the object of the statute."[250] Accordingly a degree of carelessness on the workman's part may be overlooked by the court. In the context of this category of case, Buxton L.J. said: "It is not usual for there to be marked findings of contributory negligence in a breach of statutory duty case."[251]

A distinction has to be drawn between the situation where there has been **12–71** momentary inattention on the part of an injured employee and the conscious acceptance of a risk by an employee.[252] If the employee is skilled and the precaution which would have avoided the accident complained of is a simple one, it has been said that the claimant can properly be required to bear the greater responsibility,[253] but:

> "In each case it is a question of fact whether or not a breach of ... [statutory duty] ... by an employer through the fault of an employee gives rise to any claim by that employee. An employer can defeat such claim if he can say: 'I am in breach of the regulations because of, and only because of, your default. I, myself, have not failed in

---

[247] *Lewis v Denye* [1940] A.C. 921; *Dunn v Birds Eye Foods Ltd* [1959] 2 Q.B. 265.

[248] *Ellis v L. & S. W. Ry* (1857) 2 H. & N. 424; *Parkinson v Garstang & Knott End Ry* [1910] 1 K.B. 615. In *Bailey v Geddes* [1938] 1 K.B. 156, it was held that it was difficult, if not impossible, for contributory negligence to exist at a pedestrian crossing, but this was disapproved in *Sparks v Edward Ash Ltd* [1943] K.B. 223. See further e.g. *Mulligan v Holmes* [1971] R.T.R. 179 and *Clifford v Drymond* [1976] R.T.R. 134, CA. See further Ch.10, para.10–273, above.

[249] [1940] A.C. 152 at 178, 179. To the same effect, see per Lord Atkin at 166.

[250] per Lord Tucker in *Staveley Iron and Chemical Co Ltd v Jones* [1956] A.C. 627 at 648; see also *Quintas v National Smelting Co Ltd* [1961] 1 W.L.R. 401, per Sellers L.J. at 408. Both dicta were considered and applied by Sachs L.J. in *Mullard v Ben Line Steamers Ltd* [1970] 1 W.L.R. 1414 at 1418, who added that when a defendant's liability stemmed from a flagrant and continuing breach of statutory duty, "the courts must be careful not to emasculate those regulations by the side-wind of apportionment". Similarly, see *McGuiness v Key Markets* (1972) 13 K.I.R. 249, CA; *Payne v Peter Bennie* (1973) 14 K.I.R. 395; *Geddes v United Wires*, 1973 S.L.T. (Notes) 50.

[251] *Toole v Bolton MBC* [2002] EWCA Civ 588. See also, *McGowan v W & JR Watson Ltd* S.L.T. 169, Ex. Div. (no contributory negligence found where, as a result of a momentary lapse, a joiner's finger came into contact with the unguarded blade of a circular saw).

[252] *Sherlock v Chester City Council* [2004] EWCA Civ 201.

[253] *Sherlock v Chester City Council* [2004] EWCA Civ 201. A time-served joiner was held 60 per cent to blame in respect of an injury sustained using a portable bench saw on a building site, without a run-off bench or the assistance of a second man.

any respect (apart from my vicarious default through your wrongful act) and my breach is co-terminous with yours.' "[254]

12–72   It has also been stressed[255] that there is no principle of law which requires that even when there has been a breach of statutory duty, in circumstances where the intention of a statute is to give protection against folly on the part of employees, there cannot be a finding of 100 per cent contributory negligence. So, where the claimant's deliberate act of folly is held to be the sole operative and effective cause of injury, an action for damages will fail completely.[256] In another example, where a finding of 100 per cent contributory had been made, the better view was that there was no liability upon the defendant to be apportioned.[257] Where the deceased had no reason to foresee that disregard of an order to keep out of a lift motor room at work, to which premises the Offices, Shops and Railways Premises Act 1963 applied, would expose him to danger of a trapdoor collapsing underfoot, it was held by the House of Lords that the sole cause of the fatal accident was the employer's breach of statutory duty under the Act.[258] "Any fault on the part of the deceased was a fault of disobedience, not a fault of negligence" in such circumstances.[259]

12–73   Once it has been established that the claimant and the defendant have each been in breach of statutory duty, then "however venial the fault of each of them they must share between them the responsibility for the whole of the damage."[260] Where an unguarded circular saw was used by the claimant with the acquiescence of the employer, it was held that it was not open to the judge to conclude that it was the claimant's own act in using the saw in that fashion that caused the breach of statutory duty and the accident which resulted. The employer was one-quarter to blame.[261] In apportioning liability it is necessary to assess respectively

---

[254] per Pearce L.J. in *Jenner v Allen West & Co Ltd* [1959] 1 W.L.R. 554 at 561; Whincup, "Employees' Contributory Negligence", 118 New L.J. 972. See *Mullard v Ben Line Steamers* [1970] 1 W.L.R. 1414 and Ch.4, para.4–65, above.

[255] *Jayes v I.M.I. (Kynoch) Ltd* [1985] I.C.R. 155 (the claimant had admitted that his operation of a machine deliberately in breach of reg.15(d) of the Operations at Unfenced Machinery Regulations 1938 (S.R. & O. 1938/641), had been an act of utter foolishness on his part).

[256] *Ginty v Belmont Building Supplies Ltd* [1959] 1 All E.R. 414 (an experienced asbestos sheeter failed to use the boards provided for his use during roof work, and fell through the factory's roof); *Rushton v Turner Brothers Asbestos Co Ltd* [1960] 1 W.L.R. 96 (an experienced workman on a fibre-crushing machine, well knowing that it was forbidden to clear its grooves whilst it was in motion, attempted to do so deliberately without stopping the movement, whereupon his fingers were trapped); *Lineker v Raleigh Industries* [1980] I.C.R. 83, CA (the claimant who was unauthorised to do so, had changed the cutter on the horizontal milling machine but replaced the guard improperly whereupon an accident occurred to his fingers when he had resumed operating the machine again). It is does not follow that where there is a breach of statutory duty, coupled with the happening of an accident, liability inevitably will attach.

[257] *Anderson v Newham College of Further Education* [2003] I.C.R. 212, CA.

[258] *Westwood v Post Office* [1974] A.C. 1.

[259] *Westwood v Post Office* [1974] A.C. 1 at 17 per Lord Kilbrandon.

[260] per Lord Diplock in *Boyle v Kodak Ltd* [1969] 1 W.L.R. 661 at 674 (equal liability between the claimant and the defendants). See *Parker v PFC Flooring Supplies Ltd* [2001] P.I.Q.R. P115, Q.B.D., for an example of the application of this principle to the modern statutory regime; see also *Anderson v Newham College of Further Education*, n.257, above: both claimant and defendant equally responsible where the claimant, a school caretaker, tripped over a piece of classroom equipment and sustained an injury in breach of the Workplace (Health, Safety and Welfare) Regulations 1992.

[261] *McCreesh v Courtaulds Plc* [1997] P.I.Q.R. P421, CA.

the causative potency of the breach of statutory duty and the actions of the claimant. Where a defendant was in breach of duty in failing to provide the claimant with heavy duty gloves to protect against accidental contact with discarded hypodermic syringes, a finding that the claimant was guilty of contributory negligence in using rubber gloves for the task, these being the only gloves that he could find, was set aside because, even if he had used the gloves provided, they would not have afforded adequate protection from a needle.[262]

Act of God. Whether or not an act of God[263] is a defence to an action for   **12-74** breach of statutory duty is a question of construction of the statute in question[264]:

> "The really important part of the decision is that where a contract is made which does not either expressly or impliedly except the act of God, the Courts could not introduce that exception by intendment of law; and that makes strongly against the supposition that, in construing a statute where the Legislature might have expressed, but did not express, such an exception, the Court should introduce it. And there is no case cited, and as far as I can find no case exists, in which such a doctrine is laid down."[265]

Thus, an act of God was no defence on the construction of a statute imposing an obligation on a canal company to pay compensation for damage caused by an "accident".[266]

In a later case,[267] Lord Dunedin dissented from the view "that the exception   **12-75** of an act of God to a duty or liability cast on a person by the common law is equally true of a duty or liability cast on him by an Act of Parliament", but Lord Blanesburgh, on the analogy of *Rylands v Fletcher*,[268] said that liability was always subject "to the reservation that the damage is not attributable to an act of God".[269]

Independent act of a third party. Whether or not the independent act of a   **12-76** third party[270] is a defence is also not free from doubt. If an absolute statutory duty is the same as an absolute common law duty, it is clear that it is a defence.

---

[262] *Toole v Bolton MBC* [2002] EWCA Civ 588.
[263] For the meaning of the expression "act of God," see Ch.13, para.13–35, below.
[264] *Makin v L.N.E. Ry* [1943] K.B. 467; *Rothes v Kirkcaldy Waterworks Commrs* (1882) 7 App.Cas. 694; *Witham Outfall Board v Boston Corp* (1926) 136 L.T. 756 at 760.
[265] per Lord Blackburn, citing *Paradine v James* (1674) Alleyn K.B. 26 in *River Wear Commrs v Adamson* (1877) 2 App.Cas. 743 at 771. See also Lord Cairns, ibid. at 750. See also per Lord Gordon at 777.
[266] *Makin v L.N.E. Ry* [1943] K.B. 467.
[267] *G.W. Ry v Owners of S.S. Mostyn* [1928] A.C. 57 at 74. Lord Dunedin dissented, but this does not affect his opinion on the point set out.
[268] (1868) L.R. 3 H.L. 330.
[269] *G.W. Ry v Owners of S.S. Mostyn* [1928] A.C. 57 at 104. See also per McCardie J. in *R. v Marshland, Smeeth and Fen District Commrs* [1920] 1 K.B. 155 at 167; where, however, it is not clear that the duty was held to be absolute.
[270] For the meaning of this expression, see Ch.13, para.13–47, below.

12–77   In *Groves v Wimborne*,[271] Vaughan Williams L.J. said:

> "An obvious answer to an action against the master in such a case would be that the cause of the damage to the plaintiff was not the failure by the master to perform his statutory duty, but the particular action of someone else".

A similar view was expressed in *Horton v Taplin Contracts Ltd* where the third party's act was "wholly unpredictable, deliberate and violent . . . an event of such an impact as to obliterate the defendant employer's responsibility."[272] If, however, the "particular action of someone else" is one which the master ought to have foreseen and guarded against, the master, notwithstanding, will be liable.[273] Again, in *Cooper v Railway Executive*,[274] Devlin J. said that the Railways Clauses Consolidation Act 1845 s.68, imposes "an absolute obligation in this sense, that the Railway Executive is absolutely bound to maintain a fence, and it is no answer to say that some accident or act of a trespasser has made the fence defective."

12–78   In principle, it would seem that this defence rests on the same basis as the defence of act of God. If one is available then both must be available. It will be a question of construction in each case whether Parliament has regarded the duty enshrined in statute as one that should not depend upon proof of fault or blameworthiness, when it comes to providing a remedy to someone injured by its breach.

12–79   **Delegation of duty.** Lastly, it remains to be considered whether delegation of duty[275] can be a defence in the light of the general principle that, if a duty has been cast on a person to perform, he cannot escape responsibility for seeing to its performance by employing an independent contractor.[276] Obviously, if there is a breach of statutory duty, it will not be a defence that a contractor was employed to fulfil it, unless delegation itself can be regarded as a fulfilment of the obligation, which, in turn, depends upon the true construction of the statute concerned.[277]

12–80   Where the delegation by employers is to the claimant himself[278] the modern view is that such delegation of performance[279] is not in itself a defence but is a

---

[271] [1898] 2 Q.B. 402 at 418.

[272] [2003] P.I.Q.R. P180 at P185, CA: a scaffold tower on which the claimant was standing was deliberately pushed over by a fellow employee in the course of an altercation.

[273] *Northwestern Utilities Ltd v London Guarantee and Accident Co* [1936] A.C. 108.

[274] [1953] 1 W.L.R. 223 at 228.

[275] In relation to the considerations under the Factories Act 1961 and subsequent legislation, see para.12–96, below.

[276] *Dalton v Angus* (1881) 6 App.Cas. 740 at 829, per Lord Blackburn.

[277] *Gray v Pullen* (1864) 5 B. & S. 970; *Hole v Sittingbourne Ry* (1861) 30 L.J.Ex. 81. See *Mulready v J.H. & W. Bell Ltd* [1953] 2 Q.B. 117, although the CA reasoning was disapproved in *Donaghey v Boulton & Paul Ltd* [1968] A.C. 1; *Heard v Brymbo Steel Co* [1947] K.B. 692; *Jerred v Dent* [1948] 2 All E.R. 104.

[278] Namely where the statutory provisions expressly provide for the delegation of the duty, either in whole or in part, to the claimant such as in *Smith v Baveystock* [1945] 1 All E.R. 531, CA.

[279] The delegation has to be of a positive duty and not merely a negative one: *Gallagher v Dorman Long* [1947] 2 All E.R. 38.

material circumstance to be taken into consideration in deciding the question of whether the claimant has discharged the burden of proof of causation.[280] In *Ginty v Belmont Building Supplies Ltd*,[281] Pearson J. said, on this point, "In my view the important and fundamental question . . . is not whether there was a delegation, but simply the usual question: 'Whose fault was it?'"[282]

6.—EXAMPLES OF STATUTORY DUTY

Introduction. Although there are many areas of law in which examples of statutory duties arise, the field of employer's liability is that where they are encountered most commonly in practice. Although this is an area which strictly falls outside the scope of the present work, allegations of negligence and breach of statutory duty in the employment context are often made in tandem and at least an outline discussion of an employer's statutory duties is appropriate.   **12–81**

(A) The Health and Safety at Work, etc., Act 1974

Introduction. To a large extent[283] the provisions of this Act[284] are based on the work and recommendations of the Committee on Safety and Health at Work, which sat under the Chairmanship of Lord Robens and reported in 1972.[285] The Committee's first objective was the creation of a comprehensive, integrated system of law to increase the effectiveness of the State's contribution towards health and safety at work and the health and safety of the public, where it was   **12–82**

---

[280] *Bonnington Castings Ltd v Wardlaw* [1956] A.C. 613; *Ross v Associated Portland Cement Manufacturers Ltd* [1964] 1 W.L.R. 768 at 777.

[281] [1959] 1 All E.R. 414.

[282] *Ginty v Belmont Building Supplies Ltd* [1959] 1 All E.R. 414 at 423, 424. This view was approved by the CA in *McMath v Rimmer Bros (Liverpool) Ltd* [1962] 1 W.L.R. 1. Further, in *Ross v Associated Portland Cement Manufacturers Ltd* [1964] 1 W.L.R. 768 Lord Reid, at 777, said: "If the question is put in that way one must remember that fault is not necessarily equivalent in this context to blameworthiness. The question really is whose conduct caused the accident, because it is now well established that a breach of statutory duty does not give rise to civil liability unless there is proved a causal connection between the breach and the plaintiff's injury." See also *Boyle v Kodak Ltd* [1969] 1 W.L.R. 661.

[283] See Powell, 124 New L.J. 1085 at 1098; Carby-Hall, 118 S.J. 635 at 655; Holgate, "Standards of Care: Common Law and Statute Law", 133 New L.J. 549; Binchy and Byrne, "The Extension of the Scope of Breach of Statutory Duty for Accidents at Work: Pt 1" (1995) 13 I.L.T. 4. Also, on the impact on this area of the Human Rights Act 1998, Aldous, "Human Rights?" H. & S.L. 2002, 1(2), 18.

[284] Pts I, II and IV are brought into force by the Health and Safety at Work, etc. Act 1974 (Commencement No.1) Order 1974 (SI 1974/1349). Generally those sections relating to the establishment and functions of the Health and Safety Commission came into force first on October 1, 1974, whilst those relating to the establishment and functions of the Health and Safety Executive, to enforcement and to the Employment Medical Advisory Service came into force on January 1, 1975; the remaining provisions, relating to the general duties of employers and others did so on April 1, 1975. Pt III of the Act (ss.61–76) which provides for the extension of the scope and coverage of building regulations made under the Public Health Acts, inter alia, is not yet in force. See, on the Building Regulations 1972, as amended, Spencer, "When is a Law not a Law?", 131 New L.J. 644.

[285] Cmnd. 5034. See Simpson, 36 M.L.R. 192.

affected by working activities. The ultimate aim was to supersede all then existing industrial legislation and to replace it with regulations and approved codes of practice designed to maintain or improve standards of health and safety. Pending this, existing statutory provisions, such as the Mines and Quarries Act 1954, the Agriculture (Safety, Health and Welfare Provisions) Act 1956, the Factories Act 1961, the Offices, Shops and Railway Premises Act 1963 and the Nuclear Installations Act 1965 remained in force within the general framework of the Act.

12–83   The second objective of the Robens Report was the creation of conditions for more effective self-regulation. New legislation was proposed which should restate the common law duties of employers and employees in broad terms. That was achieved, by ss.2–8, which in the process carried the duties somewhat further than before.

12–84   **Section 2.** Under s.2, the employer's duty is to ensure so far as is reasonably practicable the health, safety and welfare at work of all his employees, particularly with regard to matters such as: (a) plant and systems of work; (b) the use, handling, storage and transport of articles and substances; (c) instruction, training and supervision; (d) the place of work and access routes to and from it, in so far as these are under his control; and (e) the provision of a safe working environment.[286] In *R. v Swan Hunter Shipbuilders*,[287] it was held that the duties of an employer, under s.2(2)(a) and (c) and s.3(1), were subject to the comprehensive duty, under s.2(1), to ensure, so far as was practicable, the health, safety and welfare at work of all his employees. The European Court of Justice has accepted that no infringement of European law arises by reason of the fact that the employer's duties under s.2 are imposed only "so far as reasonably practicable."[288]

12–85   **Section 3.** Section 3 of the Act states the general duty of employers and self-employed persons to conduct their undertakings in such a way as to ensure so far as is reasonably practicable that members of the public, who may be affected by them, are not exposed to risks to their health or safety. It has been held that a health and safety inspector who, in discharging his duties under the Act, gave

---

[286] By s.52(1)(b) an employee is not "at work" except only "when he is in the course of his employment."

[287] [1981] Crim.L.R. 833, CA. Because an employee of a third party had left the end of an oxygen hose in a badly ventilated compartment, a fire broke out, owing to the oxygen-enriched atmosphere. In order to satisfy their duty under s.2(1), it was necessary for the defendants, the ship-builders, to provide information and instruction regarding potential dangers to persons who were working on the vessel, other than their own workmen. Further, in *Bolton MBC v Malrod Insulations* [1993] I.C.R. 358, DC it was held that such duty was owed to all employees "at work" and was not restricted just to those working where the plant in question was used or available for use.

[288] *Commission of the European Communities v UK* [2007] I.C.R. 139, ECJ. The Commission argued that the proviso resulted in the United Kingdom failing to meet its obligations under Council Directive 89/391/EEC, i.e that an absolute duty on the employer should be imposed. However its position was somewhat undermined by concessions that an employer was not required to create a zero-risk environment; and that as a result of carrying out a risk assessment an employer might conclude that risks were so small that no preventative measures were needed. See Barnes, "Risky business" Building 2007, 13, 53.

advice to a local authority, which issued an enforcement or prohibition notice as a result, did not owe a duty of care not to cause economic loss to a business against which the notice was issued.[289] The statutory duty under s.3 is imposed on the employer himself and is not to be confused with the question whether he may bear vicarious liability for the acts of others.[290] Accordingly, if an employer engages an independent contractor to do work which is a part of the employer's undertaking he must require of his contractor such conditions as are necessary to avoid risks to health and safety, subject only to reasonable practicability.[291] The test of liability under the section is not whether the employer is in a position to control the activity of the contractor: if it forms part of his undertaking, it is his duty to control it.[292]

Sections 4 to 7. Section 4 of the Act imposes duties upon those having control **12–86** of non-domestic premises[293] for purposes of a trade, business or other undertaking, in relation to those who are not their employees, but use the premises as a place of work, or as a place where they use plant or substances provided for their use there. The duty is to ensure that the premises, the means of access or egress thereto, and any plant or substance in the premises are, so far as reasonably practicable, safe and without risks to health. By s.5, the person in control of premises must use "the best practicable means" for preventing the emission of noxious or offensive substances[294] into the atmosphere and, under s.6, there are laid down detailed duties for persons who design, manufacture, import, supply, erect or instal any article for use at work.

Section 7 sets out in general terms the duty of an employee, who must take reasonable care for his own safety whilst at work, as well as for others involved, and must co-operate with other persons to secure compliance with statutory duties imposed on them. Section 8 imposes a duty on persons neither intentionally nor recklessly to interfere with or misuse things which are provided in the interest of health, safety and welfare, in pursuance of any statutory provision.

Criminal liability. The failure to discharge any of the duties under Pt I of the **12–87** Act[295] is a criminal offence. Civil liability for breach of those duties is expressly excluded by s.47(1)(a). Section 47(4) preserves the common law, together with its defences, as well as the defences for breach of statutory duty.[296] Any

---

[289] *Harris v Evans* [1998] 1 W.L.R. 1285, CA, Ch.2 para.2–178, n.376, above.
[290] *R. v Associated Octel Co Ltd* [1996] 4 All E.R. 846, HL.
[291] *R. v Associated Octel Co Ltd* [1996] 4 All E.R. 846, HL at 850.
[292] *R. v Associated Octel Co Ltd* [1996] 4 All E.R. 846, HL at 852. *R.M.C. Roadstone Products Ltd v Jester* [1994] 4 All E.R. 1037 was described by Lord Hoffmann, in the leading speech, as a "difficult borderline case".
[293] Defined by s.53 to include "any place and, in particular . . . (a) any vehicle, vessel, aircraft or hovercraft, (b) any installation on land (including the foreshore and other land intermittently covered by water), any offshore installation and any other installation (whether floating, or resting on the seabed or the subsoil thereof, or resting on other land covered with water or the subsoil thereof) and (c) any tent or movable structure."
[294] Defined by s.53 as meaning "any natural or artificial substance, whether in solid or liquid form or in the form of a gas or vapour".
[295] i.e. ss.1–54.
[296] For such defences, see generally, Ch.4, and paras 12–67–12–80, above.

agreement purporting to exclude or limit civil liability for any contravention of health and safety regulations is void, unless expressly permitted.

12–88   **Regulations made under the Act.** Although employers' liability was dominated in the twentieth century by the Factories Acts 1937 and 1961 and their predecessors and, later, the Offices, Shops and Railway Premises Act 1963, those Acts have now been largely swept away and replaced by the Regulations made under s.15 to implement, in the United Kingdom, Directives from the European Commission.[297] The process of implementation began with seven sets of regulations taking effect from January 1, 1993 and others have followed. The existing statutory provisions have been repealed or modified under s.80 of the Act. Whilst accident claims will almost inevitably be decided under the new regulations, industrial disease cases will continue to arise where proof of breaches of the old legislation will be necessary.[298] Having regard to the operation of s.11 of the Limitation Act 1980 there will be very few accident claims commenced after January 1, 2000 the outcome of which does not depend on the new generation of regulations.

12–89   Accordingly, although it is not within the compass of this book to deal in detail with the "European Revolution", an introduction is given to and a general outline of the more important features of the current duties. Reference to earlier editions of this work will be necessary for detailed consideration of the Factories Act 1961 and the Offices, Shops and Railway Premises Act 1963 in particular.

12–90   **A difference in approach.** Whereas the old legislation was directed at specific places of work and categories of work, (e.g. factories or offices and the different types of work carried out in these premises) the intention of the new legislation is to cover all workplaces and all work thereby giving effect in domestic law to the European Directives. The scheme of the new legislation is to standardise the broad, general duties regarding health and safety applicable to all work, introducing the concept of risk assessment to all areas of work with health and safety implications regardless of where that work is to be carried out, thereby emphasising the question of prevention. These duties have gradually replaced duties specific to certain workplaces but, at the same time, do not affect the common law duties described in Chapter 10.

(B) The Framework Directive

12–91   The jurisprudential basis for the regulations made under the Act is the Framework Directive 89/391/EEC. It provides:

(1) for the introduction of "measures to encourage improvements in the safety and health of workers at work" to include "general principles

---

[297] See generally, Stranks, "A safe place to work" 140 S.J. 489.
[298] For an example, see *Baker v Quantum Clothing Group* [2009] P.I.Q.R. P19 (liability for industrial deafness under s.29 of the Factories Act 1961).

concerning the prevention of occupational risks, the protection of safety and health, the elimination of risk and accident factors"[299];

(2) for the employer to "have a duty to ensure the safety and health of workers in every aspect related to the work"[300];

(3) for the employer to "take the measures necessary for the safety and health protection of workers, including the prevention of occupational risks and provision of information and training, as well as provision of the necessary organisation and means",[301] such measures to be implemented on the basis of general principles of prevention to include:

(a) avoiding risks;
(b) evaluating the risks which cannot be avoided;
(c) combating risks at source;
(d) adapting the work to the individual;
(e) adapting to technical progress;
(f) replacing the dangerous with the non-dangerous or the less dangerous;
(g) developing a coherent overall prevention policy;
(h) giving collective protective measures priority over individual protective measures;
(i) giving appropriate instructions to the worker.[302]

(4) for the employer, in seeking to avoid risks altogether, to:

(a) evaluate the risks to his workers to include the risk to individuals to whom tasks are entrusted[303];
(b) ensure that this evaluation is in his possession[304];

(5) for workers to take care for their own safety and health and for others affected by their acts, there being a positive obligation to act in accordance with their training and instruction.[305]

Interpretation. Since the United Kingdom legislation is made pursuant to European Community Law, it is well established that "it is for a UK court to construe domestic legislation in any field covered by a Community Directive so **12-92**

---

[299] art.1. It has been held in Scotland that, in the light of contemporary documents, the European Commission did not at the time of the enactment of the Framework Directive contemplate the issue of the impact of stress at work on mental health: *Cross v Highlands and Islands Enterprise* [2002] I.R.L.R., OH (on the facts, liability was not established where there was only limited evidence to the employer that the claimant's job was injurious to his health).

[300] art.5. The fact that s.2 of the Health and Safety at Work Act 1974 imposes a duty upon an employer to ensure the safety and health of workers "so far as reasonably practicable," does not contravene art.5(1), which is not so qualified: *Commission of the European Communities v United Kingdom*, para.12–84, n.288, above (it was not shown that the Framework Directive was intended to impose no-fault liability).

[301] art.6 (1).

[302] art.6 (2). These general principles are now expressly incorporated into Sch.1 to the Management of Health & Safety at Work Regulations 1999, SI 1999/3242 discussed below at para.12–103.

[303] art.6(3).

[304] art.9.

[305] art.13.

as to accord with the interpretation of the Directive as laid down by the European Court of Justice, if that can be done without distorting the meaning of the domestic legislation".[306] With specific reference to this series of regulations, it was more recently said that it was important to interpret the Provision and Use of Work Equipment Regulations 1992 by reference to the E.C. Directive rather than the Factories Act 1961.[307] Having said that, in the same Regulations where the United Kingdom draftsman had used language with origins in the Factories Act 1937, it was held that it must have been used with the intention that it should bear its well-established sense providing that this was compatible with the Directive.[308] The fact that it went further than the Directive required was irrelevant because a Member State is entitled to set its own standard in accordance with art.1(3) of the Framework Directive which, with its various daughter directives, is to be taken as imposing minimum standards only.[309] It has been held that the Directive does not afford individuals rights for the purpose of the doctrine of direct effect.[310]

12–93 **Codes and guidance.** Most of the regulations with which we are here concerned are accompanied by either or both of Approved Codes of Practice (ACOP) or Guidance. Although admissible only in criminal proceedings[311] and having in the past been treated as advisory rather than directory, it is suggested that the Codes in many cases should be treated as representing good and current practice on the part of an employer. Thus a failure to consider the Code exposes an employer to the risk of criticism. Where a trial judge failed to consider the relevant Code of Practice when considering the extent of the duty under reg.12 of the Workplace (Health, Safety and Welfare) Regulations 1992, the Court of Appeal said:

> "It seems . . . . that a Code of Practice which is designed to give practical guidance to employers as to how to comply with their duties under statutory regulation can be taken as providing some assistance as to the meaning it was intended those regulations should have. However, it is always necessary to treat such guidance with caution. It may be wrong. It does not carry the authority of a decision of the courts."[312]

12–94 **Who is covered?** The individual Regulations make specific provisions. Whereas the domestic law definition of "employee" was formerly critical, the Framework Directive applies to workers (any person employed by an employer save for domestic servants) and employers (any person "who has an employment relationship with the worker and has responsibility for the undertaking and/or

---

[306] per Lord Templeman in *Duke v GEC Reliance Systems Ltd* [1988] I.C.R. 339 at 352G.
[307] *English v North Lanarkshire Council* 1999 S.C.L.R. 310, OH.
[308] *Stark v The Post Office* [2000] P.I.Q.R. P105, CA: "Maintained in an efficient state, in efficient working order and in good repair" taken from the Factories Act 1937 s.152(1) and later legislation.
[309] *Stark v The Post Office* [2000] P.I.Q.R. P105, CA per Waller L.J. at P112, P113.
[310] *Millward v Oxfordshire CC* [2004] EWHC 455, applying *Cross v Highlands and Islands Enterprise*, n.299, above.
[311] Health and Safety at Work, etc. Act 1974 s.17.
[312] per Smith L.J. in *Ellis v Bristol City Council* [2007] P.I.Q.R. P26, CA. Para. 93 of the Code of Practice issued by the Health and Safety Commission.

establishment").[313] Although this definition may appear to be restricted to those strictly having the status of "employee" it is suggested that, since the duty in the Directive is directed to workers "in every aspect related to work"[314] that this definition encompasses a wider class than hitherto protected and certainly no less a class than was contemplated by the Court of Appeal in *Lane v Shire Roofing Co (Oxford) Ltd.*[315] Where their peculiar characteristics inevitably conflict with the provisions of the Framework Directive, exceptions are provided in respect of public service and civil protection activities[316] but otherwise they extend a significant measure of statutory protection to, for example, the police who were largely left without statutory protection under the old legislation.[317]

Provision is made, additionally, in specific instances for the self-employed, **12–95** employers and those who control work.

Delegation. The duty imposed on a factory occupier under the Factories Act **12–96** 1961 could be fulfilled by delegating its performance to an official, foreman or other competent person.[318] In such a case, failure to perform on the part of the person to whom the duty had been properly delegated did not discharge the occupier from liability to third parties, but did relieve him from liability to the person to whom the duty had been delegated.[319] Whether or not there had been a breach of statutory duty by the employer was said to be a question of fact in each case.[320] It was said that the true test in each such case was not to ask whether there had been delegation but to ask "the usual question: 'whose fault was it?' "[321]

Delegation will now be considered in the context of the duty of an employer **12–97** to assess risk.[322] In practice it will not be possible to provide for every eventuality and decisions as to the detailed implementation of a task will still be delegated. Indeed it has been said that, despite an employer's duty to assess risk wherever a risk of injury arises out of a manual handling operation, a precise evaluation of each task where the risk of injury was of low order is beyond the

---

[313] Framework Directive art.3.

[314] art.5(1).

[315] [1995] P.I.Q.R. P417. See generally Ch.3, above, paras 3–99–3–159.

[316] Framework Directive art.2(2).

[317] By virtue of the Police (Health and Safety) Act 1997, with effect from July 1,1998 (SI 1998/1542 art.2), extending Pt 1 of the Health and Safety at Work, etc., Act 1974 to the police.

[318] *Vincent v Southern Ry* [1927] A.C. 430, per Lord Cave.

[319] *Smith v Baveystock & Co Ltd* [1945] 1 All E.R. 531 and see *Barcock v Brighton Corp* [1949] 1 K.B. 339.

[320] *Jenner v Allen West & Co Ltd* [1959] 1 W.L.R. 554 at 561 per Pearce L.J. See *McMath v Rimmer Bros (Liverpool)* [1962] 1 W.L.R. 1. See, further, para.12–70, above.

[321] *Ginty v Belmont Building Supplies Ltd* [1959] 1 All E.R. 414 at 423, 424 where Pearson J. added that "if the answer to that question is that in substance and reality the accident was solely due to the fault of the plaintiff, so that he was the sole author of his own wrong, he is disentitled to recover." This approach was affirmed by the HL in *Boyle v Kodak Ltd* [1969] 1 W.L.R. 661 and held to be equally applicable under the new statutory regime in *Parker v PFC Flooring Supplies Ltd* [2001] P.I.Q.R. P115, Q.B.D. For illustrations of the working of this principle under the Factories Act 1961 see the 9th Edition of this work at Ch.11, paras 11–81–11–82.

[322] See particularly the duty under reg.3(1) of the Management of Health and Safety at Work Regulations 1999, discussed below at para.12–102.

realms of practicality.[323] Nevertheless the duty has been held to be to investigate risks inherent in the operations of an employer, requiring the employer to take professional advice where necessary.[324]

12–98   **Burden of proof of delegation.** Nevertheless, the onus of establishing delegation lies on the employer and is a heavy one to discharge.[325] It is not sufficient to give instructions as to how to do the work in accordance with the statutory duty. It is necessary to make it clear that the statutory duty is being delegated.[326] Where the task of appraising what was necessary to enable a job to be done went beyond the workman's competence, the employer could not rely on the fact that he had delegated the task to the workman in the first instance.[327]

12–99   Where delegation is proved, it remains a matter of dispute as to whether it affords a complete defence, or whether it simply goes to the contributory negligence of the workman who has failed to comply with the duty in question. It was held that where a task was properly placed on a workman by an employer and the failure was that of the workman, there was no reason why the employer's proportion of responsibility "should be more than nominal".[328]

(C) The Management of Health and Safety at Work Regulations 1999 (The Management Regulations)

12–100   **Introduction.** The Management Regulations[329] were introduced pursuant to s.15 of the Health and Safety at Work etc. Act 1974 to give effect to the Framework Directive. They came into force on December 29, 1999 replacing similar Regulations which came into force on January 1, 1993.[330] They are accompanied by an Approved Code of Practice (ACOP). Their purpose is to provide for "preventative and protective measures"[331] in respect of all aspects of health and safety affecting work.

---

[323] *Koonjul v Thameslink Healthcare Services* [2000] P.I.Q.R. P123, CA, in relation to reg.4(1)(b) of the Manual Handling Operations Regulations 1992.

[324] *Allison v London Underground Ltd* [2008] P.I.Q.R. P10, CA (the context being the adequacy of training for the purposes of reg.9 of the Work Equipment Regulations).

[325] *Beal v E. Gomme Ltd* (1949) 65 T.L.R. 543: *Hilton v F.H. Marshall & Co Ltd* [1951] W.N. 81. See also *Rushton v Turner Bros Asbestos Co Ltd* [1960] 1 W.L.R. 96: *Boden v Moore*, 105 S.J. 510; *Stocker v Norprint* (1971) 10 K.I.R. 10.

[326] *Manwaring v Billington* [1952] 2 All E.R. 747. A vital distinction exists between the need to instruct a tradesman on how to avoid obvious dangers and the need to instruct him about the application of the regulations in situations where no danger is apparent. There is a duty to forestall, if the employers can, breaches of regulations: *Boyle v Kodak Ltd* [1969] 1 W.L.R. 661. See also *Parker v PFC Flooring Supplies Ltd* [2001] P.I.Q.R. P115 for the application of this principle to the modern statutory regime.

[327] *Byers v Head Wrightson* [1961] 1 W.L.R. 961.

[328] per Singleton L.J. in *Stapley v Gypsum Mines Ltd* [1952] 2 Q.B. 575 at 586 (reversed by the HL on other grounds: [1953] A.C. 663). See also *Cakebread v Hopping Bros* [1947] K.B. 641 and *Johnson v Croggan & Co Ltd* [1954] 1 W.L.R. 195.

[329] SI 1999/3242.

[330] The Management of Health and Safety at Work Regulations 1992 (SI 1992/2051) as amended.

[331] Management of Health and Safety at Work Regulations 1999 reg.5(1).

Civil liability. Whereas in their initial implementation breach of the Manage-   **12–101**
ment Regulations did not give rise to civil liability,[332] save in respect of persons
not in the employment of the employer, it is otherwise after October 31, 2003.[333]
However, the practical benefit of the additional statutory protection, given the
general nature of the obligations, will be of limited assistance to a claimant.
Usually it is wise to include in a statement of case reference to minimum
standards of health and safety embodied in reg.6 (risk assessment), reg.10
(provision of information to employees) and reg.13 (capability and training).
Employers are likely to invoke reg.14 (employees' duties).

Risk assessment. The concept of risk assessment underpins all of the   **12–102**
Regulations but the Management Regulations are likely to be the starting point
for any claim alleging an unsafe place or system of work. Indeed, increasingly,
the courts have identified the need to carry out a risk assessment as a duty of an
employer, breach of which is negligent.[334] Regulation 3(1) requires every
employer to make a suitable and sufficient assessment of the risks to the health
and safety of his employees to which they are exposed whilst they are at work
and the risks to other persons, not in his employment, arising out of that work.[335]
The assessment must identify measures that the employer needs to take to
comply with his other statutory duties.[336] The Regulations expressly incorporate
the general principles of prevention set out in art.6(2) of the Framework
Directive.[337] What is suitable and sufficient must also be considered in conjunction with the ACOP which, taken in conjunction with the general principles of
prevention, requires a complete assessment of the workplace and the hazards it
presents together with an assessment of the likelihood of the hazard materialising. Specific provision is made for reviewing the assessment in the light of
circumstances that lead an employer to suspect that it is no longer valid or where
there has been a significant change in the matters to which it relates.[338]
Competent persons must be appointed to assist in the process of risk assessment.[339] If the employer employs five or more employees, the findings of the
assessment must be recorded including the identifying of any group of employees
thought to be especially at risk.[340] Having identified the risks, an employer is then
required to make arrangements to plan, organise, control and monitor preventative and protective measures.[341] The employer must also provide health

---

[332] reg.22. In *Cross v Highlands and Islands Enterprises* [2001] I.R.L.R. the exclusion of civil
liability was held not to be incompatible with the Framework Directive.
[333] reg.22, as amended by the Management of Health and Safety at Work and Fire Precautions
(Workplace) (Amendment) Regulations 2003 (SI 2003/2457), reg.6. See Howes, "New civil action
against employers", 153 N.L.J., 1794.
[334] See, e.g. *Sherlock v Chester City Council* [2004] EWCA Civ 201, although Latham L.J. noted that
this need not always be a formal procedure but could, in certain circumstances, be an informal
assessment.
[335] reg.3(2) makes similar provision in respect of self-employed persons.
[336] The importance of the risk assessment was emphasised in *Allison v London Underground Ltd*
[2008] P.I.Q.R. P10, CA, n.351, below.
[337] Sch.1. Summarised in para.12–91, above.
[338] reg.3(3).
[339] reg.7.
[340] reg.3(6).
[341] reg.5(1). Where the employer employs five or more employees, such arrangements must also be
recorded: reg.5(2).

surveillance, as appropriate, for those employees who are exposed to risks identified in the risk assessment.[342] This is of obvious value in the case of processes, prolonged exposure to which can lead to the contraction of an industrial disease.

12–103   **Information for employees.** Following the Framework Directive, which requires extensive "worker information,"[343] the Management Regulations impose a positive obligation to provide employees with "comprehensible and relevant information" on the risks identified in the risk assessment and the preventative and protective measures implemented to minimise the chances of those risks materialising.[344] The duty to provide information extends to temporary workers[345] and others, who may not be employees but who happen to be working within his undertaking.[346] In either instance, the requirement that the information be comprehensible focuses on the individual to whom the information is imparted, thus requiring the employer to take the specific characteristics of that worker into account.[347]

12–104   **Capability and training.** An employer is required to take into account the capabilities of his employees regarding health and safety in entrusting tasks to them.[348] Adequate health and safety training must be provided not only on recruitment but at any exposure to a new or increased risk[349] with provision for periodic review.[350] It has been held that the test of the adequacy of training for the purposes reg.9 of the Equipment Regulations, to be considered in the light of the requirement of risk assessment under reg.3 of the Management Regulations 1999, is the training needed in the light of what an employer ought to know about the risks arising from the activities of its business. The duty requires more than that an employer deal with risks of which it actually knows. The statutory duty imposes on the employer a duty to investigate the risks inherent in its operations, taking professional advice where necessary. For these purposes the risk assessment under reg.3 is significant. An employer ought to have knowledge of those risks of which it would have been aware if it had carried out a suitable and sufficient risk assessment under that regulation. A risk assessment would provide the basis not only for the training which the employer had to give but also for other aspects of the employer's duty, such as, for example, whether the place of work was safe or whether work equipment was suitable.[351]

---

[342] reg.6. See, in relation to stress in the workplace, Ellison, "A weight on your mind" 2001 E.G. 01233, 74.
[343] Framework Directive art.10.
[344] Management Health and Safety at Work Regulations 1999 reg.10(1).
[345] reg.15.
[346] reg.12.
[347] See also the ACOP at para.54.
[348] Management of Health and Safety at Work Regulations 1999 reg.13(1).
[349] reg.13(2).
[350] reg.13(3).
[351] *Allison v London Underground Ltd* [2008] P.I.Q.R. P10, CA (a claim by a driver on the London Underground who developed tenosynovitis of the hand and wrist as a result of incorrectly gripping the traction brake controller on an underground train).

Employees' duties. Regulation 14 imposes a duty on all employees to use **12–105** equipment in accordance with their training and to inform the employer of any work representing a danger to health and safety or of any matter which they consider represents a shortcoming in the employer's protection arrangements for health and safety.

Serious danger. An additional provision is the need to establish procedures **12–106** for serious and imminent danger to include procedures for evacuation, the need to stop and not resume work and the nomination of competent persons to implement the procedures identified.[352] The provision of information both as to risks and steps to be taken is an integral part of the duty.

Protection of young persons. Regulation 19 provides much broader protec- **12–107** tion to young persons (those who have not attained the age of 18) than was formerly provided under s.20 of the Factories Act 1961 and s.18 of the Offices, Shops and Railway Premises Act 1963 which was restricted to the avoidance of exposure to the cleaning of machines that exposed them to the risk of injury. This Regulation was added to give effect to the Protection of Young People at Work Directive.[353] Regulation 19(1) requires employers to protect young persons from risks to their health or safety arising out of their lack of experience, their absence of awareness of risk or their immaturity. Thus, young persons may not be employed for certain types of work: work beyond their physical or psychological capacity[354]; work involving harmful exposure to dangerous agents (toxins, carcinogens or radiation)[355]; work involving the risk of accidents which young persons may not recognise due to their lack of attention to safety, lack of experience or training[356]; work where there is a risk to health from extreme cold or heat, noise or vibration.[357] In order to determine whether work involves harm or risk, regard must be had to the results of assessment. Regulation 19(3) enables a young person who is over compulsory school age to undertake any of the work prohibited by reg.19(2) where this is necessary for training or where there will be supervision by a competent person and, in each case where any risk will be reduced to the lowest level reasonably practicable.

Expectant and new mothers. Regulations 16 to 18 provide the measures to **12–108** be taken in respect of new or expectant mothers and these also include the need for risk assessment to determine the risks to both the mother and her baby from any processes or working conditions to which they may be exposed. These Regulations were included to give effect to provisions of the Pregnant Worker's Directive.[358]

"So far as is reasonably practicable"; "as soon as practicable"; "all **12–109** **practicable steps".** In many places in the Regulations (although not the Management Regulations themselves) there is a duty to take some safety measure

---

[352] reg.8.
[353] 94/33/EEC.
[354] reg.19(2)(a).
[355] reg.19(2)(b) and (c).
[356] reg.19(2)(d).
[357] reg.19(2)(e).
[358] 92/85/EEC.

"so far as is reasonably practicable", or to take some step "as soon as practicable" or to ensure that "all practicable steps" are taken.[359] "Practicable" is not the same as "possible" but involves some qualification of what is possible. The definition in the *Oxford English Dictionary*, "capable of being carried out in action", "feasible", has been adopted in two cases[360] and expresses a distinction between what it may be possible to do in exceptional conditions and in very favourable circumstances on rare occasions; and what can be done in practice by anyone with proper equipment, care and skill. It is possible, for example, for a man to run a stated distance in record time, because it has been done; but it is not practicable to run the distance in that time where no other person, including the record holder, has been able to do it either before or since. The definition in *Webster's Dictionary*, "possible to be accomplished with known means and known resources" has also been approved.[361]

12–110   In considering what is practicable, questions of cost are eliminated,[362] but regard must be had to the state of knowledge and invention current at the material time.[363] It is not "practicable" to take precautions against danger which at all material times was wholly unknown to the defendant.[364] Where a defendant is under a duty to take "all practical measures" to obviate some risk, this is likely to include a duty to supervise and, if necessary, enforce the use of protective equipment.[365]

12–111   In determining whether the taking of extra safety precautions would have been "reasonably practicable", regard should be had, inter alia, to the incidence of similar accidents, and the prevalence and convenience to employees of the system of work employed.[366]

12–112   Although the word "impracticable" is no longer used to give relief from a statutory obligation, it is to be noted that it was interpreted strictly and was held[367] to mean something more than just "not reasonably practicable", a phrase that is still used.[368] The fact that compliance with the obligation may involve unreasonable time or expense or both is quite irrelevant.[369] Nevertheless, there is a clear distinction between "impracticable" and "impossible": in the former,

---

[359] See, e.g. reg.12(3) of the Workplace (Health, Safety and Welfare) Regulations 1992 and regs. 4 and 6 of the Work at Height Regulations 2005, (SI 2005/735). See generally, Howard, "Professional negligence, employers' duties and the burden of proof" O.H.R. (2005), 113, 38.
[360] *Lee v Nursery Furnishings Ltd* [1945] 1 All E.R. 837 per Goddard LJ; *Adsett v K & L Steelfounders & Engineers Ltd* [1953] 1 W.L.R. 733, per Singleton L.J.
[361] *Adsett v K & L Steelfounders & Engineers Ltd* [1953] 1 W.L.R. 733 at 779; *Knight v Demolition & Construction Co Ltd* [1953] 1 W.L.R. 981 at 986: affirmed [1954] 1 W.L.R. 563.
[362] *Adsett v K & L Steelfounders & Engineers Ltd* [1953] 1 W.L.R. 773, per Parker J.
[363] *Adsett v K & L Steelfounders & Engineers Ltd* [1953] 1 W.L.R. 773 at 780, per Singleton L.J.; *Richards v Highways Ironfounders Ltd* [1957] 1 W.L.R. 781.
[364] *Adsett v K & L Steelfounders & Engineers Ltd* [1953] 1 W.L.R. 733; *Richards v Highway Ironfounders (West Bromwich) Ltd* [1955] 1 W.L.R. 1049; *Gregson v Hick Hargreaves & Co Ltd* [1955] 1 W.L.R. 1252.
[365] *Crookall v Vickers-Armstrong* [1955] 1 W.L.R. 659.
[366] *Thompson v Bowaters United Kingdom Paper Co* [1975] K.I.L.R. 47, CA.
[367] *Brown v N.C.B.* [1962] A.C. 574 at 598.
[368] In the Manual Handling Operations Regulations 1992 (SI 1992/2793) reg.4(1)(b).
[369] *Moorcroft v Thomas Powles & Sons Ltd* [1962] 3 All E.R. 741; *Cork v Kirby Maclean Ltd* [1952] 1 All E.R. 1064.

considerations of reasonableness arise and regard may be had to actual practice.[370]

If the regulation requires safety measures to be taken, as are "reasonably **12–113** practicable", the standard of care is lower than if the word "practicable" alone is used. The cost of any necessary safety measures can be weighed against the risk and the expected efficacy of the measures. Asquith L.J. put it[371]:

> " 'reasonably practicable' is a narrower term than 'physically possible' and seems to me to imply that a computation must be made by the owner, in which the *quantum* of risk is placed on one scale and the sacrifice involved in the measures necessary for averting the risk (whether in money, time or trouble) is placed in the other; and that if it be shown that there is a gross disproportion between them—the risk being insignificant in relation to the sacrifice—the defendants discharge the onus on them. Moreover, this computation falls to be made by the owner at a point of time anterior to the accident."

In considering what is reasonably practicable, an employer should take into **12–114** account the period of time over which a danger arises, and balance the time, trouble and expense[372] of the safeguards which are required. If the latter are disproportionate to the extent of the risk it will not be reasonably practicable to take them.[373] Accordingly, where a statutory duty is a duty of doing what is reasonably practicable, there may not be very much difference with the common law standard of taking reasonable care in all the circumstances,[374] although it has also been said that the statutory words give rise to a stricter obligation than the common law.[375] It has been held that to make a place as safe as is reasonably practicable is almost, if not quite, the same as the common law duty owed by an employer to his employee when working on his employer's premises.[376] The fact that the defendants were unaware of the existence of an obstruction on the factory floor did not mean that it was not reasonably practicable for them to keep such floor free of obstruction.[377]

---

[370] *Jayne v N.C.B.* [1968] 2 All E.R. 220 at 223.

[371] *Edwards v N.C.B.* [1949] 1 K.B. 704 at 712, quoted and amplified by Jenkins L.J. in *Marshall v Gotham Ltd* [1952] 2 All E.R. 1044, approved by Lord Reid in *Marshall v Gotham Ltd* [1954] A.C. 360 at 373 and applied in *Belhaven Brewery Co Ltd v McLean* [1975] I.R.L.R. 370. See also *Jenkins v Allied Ironfounders Ltd* [1970] 1 W.L.R. 304; *Wraith v N.C.B.* [1954] 1 W.L.R. 264 at 270; *Gregson v Hick Hargreaves & Co Ltd* [1955] 1 W.L.R. 1252; *Walsh v N.C.B.* [1956] 1 Q.B. 511; "whether or not some precaution is reasonably practicable" will depend on a number of considerations. "Cost is one and I think that any risk inherent in providing the precaution is another": Parker L.J. in *Trott v W.E. Smith (Erectors) Ltd* [1957] 1 W.L.R. 1154 at 1163. For a contemporary analysis see also *Mann v Northern Electric Distribution Ltd* [2010] EWCA Civ 141.

[372] See *Jordan v Norfolk County Council* [1994] 1 W.L.R. 1353, where Sir Donald Nicholls V.C. stated that what was "reasonably practicable" went beyond what was physically feasible and was apt to include financial consideration.

[373] *Coltness Iron Co v Sharp* [1938] A.C. 90; approved by Lord Oaksey in *Marshall v Gotham* [1954] A.C. 360.

[374] *Jones v N.C.B.* [1957] 2 Q.B. 55.

[375] *Trott v W.E. Smith (Erectors) Ltd* [1957] 1 W.L.R. 1154.

[376] *McCarthy v Coldair Ltd* [1951] W.N. 590, where the CA adopted, as being applicable equally to the Factories Act, the words of Tucker L.J. in *Edwards v N.C.B.* [1949] 1 K.B. 704 at 710: "in every case it is the risk that has to be weighed against the measures necessary to eliminate the risk." See also *McWilliams v Sir William Arrol & Co* [1962] 1 W.L.R. 295.

[377] *Bennett v Rylands Whitecross* [1978] I.C.R. 1031.

12–115   In *Dugmore v Swansea NHS Trust*,[378] consideration was given to reg.7(1) of Control of Substances Hazardous to Health Regulations 1988 and 1994.[379] The claimant, a nurse, developed an allergy as a result of exposure to latex in gloves with which she was supplied by her employers. The regulation was held to impose a strict liability to prevent the exposure of an employee to a substance hazardous to health, such as latex. The primary duty of the employer was to prevent any exposure at all, unless this was not reasonably practicable. Where prevention was not reasonably practicable, the secondary duty was adequately to control the exposure. In deciding whether the employer had complied with the primary duty, it was not necessary in a straightforward case to assess foreseeability of the degree of risk. In the instant case there was evidence from which an employer could have discovered what needed to be done:

> "To import into the defence of reasonable practicability the same approach to foreseeability of risk as is contained in the common law of negligence would be to reduce the absolute duty to something much closer to the common law, albeit with a different burden of proof."[380]

The Trust was held liable because it failed to show that it was not reasonably practicable to eliminate the risk to the claimant by replacing latex gloves with vinyl gloves before her attack occurred.

12–116   The statutory defence that a particular safety measure is not reasonably practicable cannot be relied upon by the defendants unless it has been pleaded in the defence[381] and the burden of proving such defence rests with the defendant to discharge.[382]

(D) The Workplace (Health, Safety and Welfare) Regulations 1992 (The Workplace Regulations)

12–117   **Introduction.** The Workplace Regulations[383] were introduced pursuant to s.15 of the Health and Safety at Work, etc. Act 1974 to give effect to the

---

[378] [2003] P.I.Q.R. P220, CA.

[379] See para.11–231, below. Regulation 7 provided that: "Every employer shall ensure that the exposure of employees to a substance hazardous to health is either prevented or, where this is not reasonably practicable, adequately controlled." Now superseded by the Control of Substances Hazardous to Health Regulations 2002 reg.7 drafted in identical terms.

[380] ibid., per Hale L.J. at P230. The judgment contains a review of authorities on the approach to what is or is not reasonably practicable.

[381] *Bowes v Sedgefield District Council* [1981] I.C.R. 234, CA; *Moffat v Marconi Space and Defence Systems Ltd*, 1975 S.L.T. (Notes) 60; *Larner v British Steel* [1993] 4 All E.R. 102, CA; *Mains v Uniroyal Engelbert Tyres, The Times*, September 29, 1995 IH Ct.Sess. See, generally paras 11–59–11–66, above.

[382] *Gibson v British Insulated Callender's Construction Co Ltd* 1973 S.L.T. 2, HL, resolved confusion caused by a series of earlier decisions and firmly established that the burden of proof to establish that he had taken all reasonably practicable steps rests on the employer to discharge. Should the employee attempt to establish the fact that a particular method is reasonably practicable but does not succeed, that does not discharge the general onus of proof on the employer at all.

[383] SI 1992/3004.

Workplace Directive.[384] They apply to all workplaces (see below) from January 1, 1996.[385] They are accompanied by an ACOP.[386] There have been remarkably few reported decisions concerning their interpretation and reference continues to be made, in practice, to decisions relating to earlier legislation despite there being, in certain instances, a strikingly different use of language. Breach of the Workplace Regulations is taken to give rise to civil liability.

The workplace. This is widely defined to include any non-domestic premises   **12–118**
or part of such premises which are made available to any person as a place of work.[387] So as to remove the difficulty caused by a person suffering an accident on work premises but not in a place where he "has to work"[388] the definition under the Workplace Regulations includes:

"(a) any place within the premises to which such person has access while at work;

(b) any room, lobby, corridor, staircase, road or other place used as a means of access to or egress from that place of work or where facilities are provided for use in connection with the place of work other than a public road."[389]

By s.4A, where a workplace is in a building, there is a requirement that the building have a stability and solidity appropriate to the nature of its use.[390]

This definition renders the former distinction between a workplace, and access   **12–119**
to and egress from a workplace, redundant.[391] A staircase in a police station has been held to fall within reg.2. It was further held that it would be artificial to distinguish between the carpet laid, which was loose, and the structure of the staircase itself.[392] The fact that a person had access to a warehouse roof has been held to render the roof a workplace within reg.2.[393] The definition makes even a temporary workplace a place made available to a person to work regardless of where it is.

---

[384] 89/654/EEC.

[385] Workplace Regulations reg.1. New workplaces or modifications, extensions or conversions of existing workplaces after December 31, 1992 were covered with effect from January 1, 1993.

[386] Made under s.16(1) of the Health and Safety at Work, etc. Act 1974 with effect from January 1, 1993.

[387] Workplace Regulations reg.2(1).

[388] Factories Act 1961 s.29.

[389] Workplace Regulations reg.2(1). The restriction excluding a "modification, extension or conversion" until the same is completed was removed by the Health and Safety (Miscellaneous) Amendment Regulations 2002 (SI 2002/2174) giving effect to art.2 of the Directive.

[390] Inserted by reg.6(c) the Health and Safety (Miscellaneous) Amendment Regulations 2002 (SI 2002/2174) giving effect to Annex I, para.1 of the Directive.

[391] See the 9th edn of this work at Ch.11, para.11–138 onwards.

[392] *Kirkham v Commisioner of Police of the Metropolis* [2005] P.I.Q.R. P147, Q.B.D. Contrast *Beck v United Closures and Plastics Plc* 2001 S.L.T. 1299, OH, where heavy doors to machinery were held not to be a "workplace". *Beck* was cited in *Kirkham* but did not form part of the decision.

[393] *Parker v PFC Flooring Supplies Ltd* [2001] P.I.Q.R. P115. Also, a hospital car park was held to be part of an administrative worker's workplace: *Pettie v Southampton University Hospitals NHS Trust* [2002] C.L.Y. 5377.

12–120   **Exclusions.** The Workplace Regulations do not apply[394] to workplaces which are or are on ships,[395] where the only activity is construction work,[396] mines,[397] workplaces which are or are on a vehicle,[398] workplaces in fields, woods or other agricultural or forestry land[399] or quarries.[400]

12–121   **Who is covered?** The duties imposed on employers are by reference to the workplace itself rather than those who work in it or the tasks they undertake. An employer who occupies a workplace is equally responsible towards self-employed workers and visitors[401] who are not "persons employed",[402] presumably including a self-employed contractor. Further, given concentration on the workplace itself, an employee who strays to a part of the workplace where he is not required to work or may not be authorised to visit is likely to be covered.

12–122   **Who is liable?** The duties are imposed on an employer who has a workplace under his control.[403] They also apply to every person who has to any extent control over a workplace in connection with the carrying on of a trade, business or other undertaking[404] in so far as any requirement of the Workplace Regulations relates to matters within that person's control.[405] By way of example, therefore, although the owner of premises at which the claimant was working as an employee of a cleaning contractor engaged by the owner, was a person with a degree of control over the claimant's workplace within reg.4(2), when the claimant slipped on ice that he was engaged in clearing in the course of his work, the owner was not liable to him under reg.12(3): the requirement to keep the workplace free from a substance which might cause a person to slip under that regulation related to matters within the employer's rather than the owner's control.[406] The Workplace Regulations do not apply to self-employed persons in respect of their own work or that of their partners.[407]

---

[394] Workplace Regulations reg.3.

[395] reg.3(1)(a).

[396] reg.3(1)(b), and see the Construction (Design and Management) Regulations 2007 (SI 2007/320) for parallel provisions for such workplaces. See paras 12–160–12–172, below. If construction work and non-construction work are carried out in tandem, both sets of regulations apply.

[397] reg.3(1)(c).

[398] reg.3(3) including aircraft, locomotives, trailers or any vehicle for which a licence is in force under the Vehicles (Excise) Act 1971. Note, however, that vehicles can and often will constitute "work equipment" for the purposes of the Provision and Use of Work Equipment Regulations 1998: see further below at para.12–180.

[399] reg.3(4).

[400] reg.3(5) save in respect of floors or traffic routes located within a building.

[401] Thus reversing the effect of *Hartley v Mayoh & Co* [1954] 1 Q.B. 383: see para.12–30, n.109, above.

[402] s.14 of the Factories Act 1961.

[403] Workplace Regulations reg.4(1).

[404] reg.4(2) and (3).

[405] reg.4(2)(c).

[406] *King v RCO Support Services Ltd* [2001] P.I.Q.R. P15, CA, at paras 34 to 36, Kay L.J.

[407] reg.4(5).

Maintenance of the workplace, equipment, devices and systems. Regula- **12–123**
tion 5 imposes a duty to maintain (including to clean) the workplace, and the
equipment, devices and systems within it to which the Regulations apply.[408]

The definition of "workplace" has already been discussed.[409] "Equipment, **12–124**
devices and systems", which, where appropriate, are required to be subject to a
suitable system of maintenance,[410] are defined by reg.5(3) as equipment and
devices a fault in which is liable to result in a failure to comply with the
Workplace Regulations,[411] mechanical ventilation systems[412] and equipment and
devices intended to prevent or reduce hazards.[413]

The duty is to maintain in an efficient state, in efficient working order and in
good repair. "Efficiency" is "efficient from the view point of health, safety and
welfare (not productivity or economy)".[414] The definition of "maintained" is
taken directly from the Factories Acts of 1937 and 1961[415] and imposes an
absolute obligation to achieve the required result: thus, where a breach of reg.5
was alleged where the claimant's arm was trapped in a defective lift door,
Galashiels Gas Co Ltd v O'Donnell[416] was applied in holding that the duty was
an absolute one not limited in any way by considerations of reasonable practicability.[417]

It has been held, adopting Lord Oaksey's words in *Latimer v AEC Ltd*,[418] that **12–125**
it will not necessarily follow that there will be a breach of this duty where
transient or temporary conditions result in the workplace not being in an efficient
state.[419] Where an employee slipped on floor which had flooded owing to the
burst of a concealed pipe, there was no breach of reg.5. The burst pipe did not
fall within the definition of a workplace within reg.2.[420] Although the pipe fell

---

[408] Heavy doors were neither a "workplace" nor a "device" within reg.5: *Beck v United Closures &
Plastics Plc*, 2001 S.L.T. 1299, OH.
[409] paras 12–118–12–120 above. The presence of redundant shelf bracket into which the claimant
walked injuring his eye did not constitute a breach of reg.5 as it could not be 'technically maintained'.
There was, however, a common law breach of duty because the bracket was a hazard: *McNaughton
v Michelin Tyre Plc* 2001 S.L.T. 67.
[410] reg.5(2).
[411] reg.5(3)(a).
[412] reg.5(3)(b).
[413] reg.5(3)(c) inserted by the Health and Safety (Miscellaneous) Amendment Regulations 2002 (SI
2002/2174).
[414] ACOP, clause 20.
[415] ss.151(1) and 176(1) respectively.
[416] [1949] A.C. 275.
[417] *Malcolm v Commissioner of Police for Metropolis* [1999] C.L.Y. 2880, Q.B.D. and *Lewis v Avidan
Ltd* [2006] P.I.Q.R. P69, CA, applying *Stark v The Post Office* [2000] P.I.Q.R. P105, a decision
concerned with the interpretation of identical words in reg.6 of Provision of Use and Work Equipment
Regulations 1992. Compare, however, *Fytche v Wincanton Logistics Plc* [2005] P.I.Q.R. P61, HL,
para.12–235, below, a decision under the similarly-worded reg.7(1) of the Personal Protective
Equipment at Work Regulations 1992 (the duty to maintain in repair has to be assessed in relation to
the risk which necessitates the protective equipment in question).
[418] [1953] A.C. 643 at 656 in relation to the construction of s.25(1) of the Factories Act 1937: "A
floor does not, in my opinion, cease to be in an efficient state because a piece of orange peel or a small
pool of some slippery material is on it."
[419] *Lewis v Avidan Ltd* [2006] P.I.Q.R. P69, CA. See Tomkins, [2005] J.P.I.L. 224.
[420] para.12–118, above.

within the definition of equipment and had failed, by itself that failure did not give rise to a breach of any of the Workplace Regulations.[421] In its proper context, the word "maintained" imported the concept of doing something to the floor itself, such as cleaning or repairing it, and the mere fact of a flood did not mean that the floor was not maintained in an efficient state.

12–126   The duty under reg.5 extends only to equipment already installed. Thus a failure to provide a handrail for steps which, it was held did not constitute a breach of reg.12(5), did not constitute a breach of the failure to maintain under reg.5 either.[422]

12–127   The relevant time for assessing compliance with reg.5 is the time of any incident or accident relied upon. Notwithstanding the provision of a suitable system of maintenance of equipment, devices and systems,[423] an employer will be liable, in the event that there was a failure on the occasion that caused an accident.

12–128   **Ventilation.** Regulation 6 provides for effective and suitable provision for the ventilation of every enclosed workplace by fresh or purified air with a visible or audible warning of the failure of any plant provided for this purpose.[424] Any such plant obviously constitutes equipment for the purposes of reg.5. Regulation 10 provides for workrooms to have sufficient floor area, height and unoccupied space for health, safety and welfare purposes.[425]

12–129   It was said, in relation to s.4 of the Factories Act 1961, that it dealt with "the circulation of fresh air which gets rid of impurities which come into the air, whereas section [47][426] is dealing with the methods of stopping impurities from ever getting into circulation at all"[427]; likewise that it was not concerned with the provisions of masks or respirators.[428] It seems likely that this regulation, which is general in effect and secondary to specific regulations dealing with dangerous fumes and dust, will be interpreted to similar effect. Whereas liability under s.4 of the 1961 Act was confined to those cases where the defendants had actual or constructive knowledge of the hazard,[429] including what they would have ascertained had they made the inquiries that a reasonably prudent and careful

---

[421] The flood did, however, give rise to a possible breach of reg.12(3) although not on the facts of *Lewis* because there was no evidence that there had been a failure to take reasonable steps by the employer to clear up the water.

[422] *Coates v Jaguar Cars Ltd* [2004] EWCA Civ 337.

[423] Workplace Regulations reg.5(2).

[424] reg.6(2) largely reproducing s.4 of the Factories Act 1961 and s.7 of the Offices, Shops and Railway Premises Act 1963. The former was confined to defects of ventilation and was aimed at requiring circulation of fresh air efficiently; *Ebbs v James Whitson & Co Ltd* [1952] 2 Q.B. 877; *Coote v Eastern Gas Board* [1953] 1 Q.B. 594.

[425] Reproducing s.2 of the Factories Act 1961 and s.5 of the Offices, Shops and Railway Premises Act 1963.

[426] Factories Act 1937 re-enacted by s.63 of the 1961 Act.

[427] *Graham v Co-operative Wholesale Society Ltd* [1957] 1 W.L.R. 511 at 522.

[428] *Ashwood v Steel Co of Scotland*, 1957 S.C. 17.

[429] *Cartwright v GKN Sankey Ltd* [1972] 2 Lloyd's Rep. 242.

employer would have made,[430] the emphasis under reg.3(1) of the Management Regulations[431] is upon an assessment of the risks for the purpose of identifying the measures needed to comply with the Regulations. The requirement is to seek the assistance of a competent person[432] which is in turn likely to fix the employer with actual or constructive knowledge of matters of which he ought to have been aware. Thus where it was established that the occupiers of a factory knew that cotton dust could cause byssinosis, they were liable under s.4 of the Act for failing to instal adequate ventilation, even though they had not realised that the dust, omitted from the particular machine, would be injurious to health.[433]

Lighting. Regulation 8 provides for every workplace to have suitable and   **12–130** sufficient lighting which, so far as is reasonably practicable, shall be by natural lighting. Suitable and sufficient emergency lighting must also be provided where persons at work are exposed to danger if artificial lighting fails.[434] Although former provision made no reference to a presumption that natural lighting should be provided, the duty here is likely to be just as strict as hitherto. Thus a breach of s.5 of the Factories Act 1961 was established where a light bulb failed immediately before the claimant's accident occurred because that section imposed an absolute duty on the factory occupier.[435] By contrast, no breach of s.5 arose when the claimant tripped over a tie bar lying in the shadow of a piece of machinery, as he crossed the floor to switch on more light to read his newspaper before work began, because the general standard of illumination at floor level was found to be adequate.[436] Whether a similar result would occur today is doubtful, particularly when reg.8 is interpreted in accordance with the Workplace Directive, which requires lighting to be "adequate for the protection of workers' safety" and requires lighting installations "to be placed in such a way that there is no risk of accident to workers as a result of the type of lighting fitted".[437] Although the similarity in wording suggests that the decisions under s.5 of the 1961 Act will continue to assist in the interpretation of reg.8, interpretation by reference to the Workplace Directive suggests that a higher standard now prevails.

Cleanliness. Regulation 9 provides that workplaces, furniture, furnishings   **12–131** and fittings shall be kept sufficiently clean with the surfaces of floors, walls and ceilings to be capable of being kept sufficiently clean.[438] Waste materials must not be allowed to accumulate in workplaces except in suitable receptacles so far

---

[430] *Wallhead v Ruston & Hornsby Ltd* (1973) 14 K.I.R. 285.
[431] See para.12–102, above.
[432] See reg.7 of the Management Regulations and para.12–102 above.
[433] *Brookes v J. & P. Coates (UK) Ltd* [1984] I.C.R. 158.
[434] Workplace Regulations reg.8(3).
[435] *Davies v Massey Ferguson Perkins* [1986] I.C.R. 580.
[436] *Lane v Gloucester Engineering Co* [1967] 1 W.L.R. 767. Section 5 of the 1961 Act also required suitable and sufficient lighting to be switched on whenever the natural light was insufficient: *Thornton v Fisher & Ludlow Ltd* [1968] 1 W.L.R. 655. See also *Rawding v London Brick Co* (1971) 10 K.I.R. 207, CA, and *Hillcoat v Swan Hunter Shipbuilders* [1976] C.L.Y. 305, CA.
[437] Annex I, paras 8.1 and 8.2. For an example of a claimant who succeeded in proving a breach of reg.8, see *Miller v Perth and Kinross Council* 2002 Rep. L.R. 22, OH (ill lit school path).
[438] Replacing s.1 of the Factories Act 1961 and s.4 of the Offices, Shops and Railway Premises Act 1963.

as is reasonably practicable. Along with other references to cleanliness[439] it is likely to remain the case that what is or is not a clean state will depend upon a finding of fact, which takes into account all the circumstances, including the nature of the workplace's operations and the work being performed.

12–132   **Workstations and seating.** Although "workstation"[440] is not defined, reg.11 provides that each workstation shall be so arranged that it is suitable both for any person at work in the workplace likely to use the workstation and for the work of the undertaking likely to be done there. A "workstation" has been held to connote a place where items of equipment are set up, for the purpose of enabling certain categories of work to be carried out there: a lavatory cubicle in which the claimant, a hospital outpatient assistant, was injured whilst helping a disabled patient, was not a workstation as a result simply of its containing apparatus for the performance of natural functions.[441] In so far as the work is to be carried out outdoors, protection from adverse weather must be provided within the limits of reasonable practicability together with the ability to leave the workstation swiftly in the event of an emergency.[442] The employer is also required to ensure that a person is not likely to slip or fall at the workstation.[443] Suitable seating must be provided for each person at a workplace whose work can or must be done sitting[444] and suitability relates to the person for whom the seat is provided as well as the operation to be performed, with a footrest to be made available where necessary.[445] Again, focus on the individual is emphasised, of considerable importance to those persons who perform, for example, prolonged and repetitive tasks in static seated positions.

12–133   **Floors and traffic routes.** Regulations 12 and 17 replace s.28 of the Factories Act 1961[446] and impose a requirement that every floor in a workplace and the surface of every traffic route[447] be of a construction suitable for its purpose. Suitability includes, but is not confined to, requirements that the surface in

---

[439] e.g. reg.5 and 20.

[440] Note that the Health and Safety (Display Screen Equipment) Regulations 1992 (SI 1992/2792) (implementing the Display Screen Equipment Directive, 90/270 EEC) provide detailed provision in respect of display screen equipment typically used at a workstation with effect from January 1, 1993. It is accompanied by Guidance which notes that, where there are both general and specific duties, the requirement is to comply with both: para.3.

[441] *Butler v Grampian University Hospitals NHS Trust* 2002 S.L.T. 985, OH.

[442] reg.11(2)(a) and (b).

[443] reg.11(2)(c).

[444] reg.11(4). Note that under s.14(2) of the Offices, Shops and Railway Premises Act 1963 there was absolute liability for breach of the duty to provide adequate and proper support for a seat while in use for the purpose for which it was provided: *Wray v Greater London Council* [1987] C.L.Y. 2560. A similar situation will now exist under reg.5(1) of the Workplace Regulations.

[445] reg.11(4). As regards the type of seat suitable for a supermarket cashier see *Tesco Stores v Edwards* [1977] I.R.L.R. 120 and for a data processing officer in an office, see *McSherry v British Telecommunications* [1992] 3 Med.L.R. 129.

[446] For a detailed discussion of the operation of ss.28 and 29 of the Factories Act 1961, see the 9th edn of this work at Ch.11, paras 11–128–11–149.

[447] Defined by reg.2(1) as "a route for pedestrian traffic, vehicles or both and includes any stairs, staircase, fixed ladder, doorway, gateway, loading bay or ramp;" Note that it does not have to lead to or from a place of work. In *Holtes v Aberdeenshire Council* 2006 S.L.T. 871, OH, reg.12(1) of The Workplace Regulations was applied to a staircase carpet which bulged in the area of the centre of the riser, causing the claimant to catch her heel and fall.

question be free from holes, slopes, unevenness[448] or slipperiness such as would expose any person to a risk to his health and safety, together with effective means of drainage.[449] Subject to the limit of reasonable practicability,[450] such surfaces must also be kept free from obstructions and from articles or substances which may cause a person to slip, trip or fall.[451] Handrails must be provided on all staircases save where this would obstruct a traffic route.[452]

"Floor" is not separately defined (although "traffic routes" are)[453] but it is **12–134** thought permissible to have regard to cases in which "floors, steps, stairs and gangways", mentioned in s.28 of the 1961 Act, were considered.

ILLUSTRATIONS

The following were held to be floors, etc. plant across a duct was a **12–135** gangway[454]; the floor of a gantry[455]; the base of a duct built on a factory floor was itself a floor[456] a duck board was a floor or, at least, a passage or a gangway[457]; the sand surface of a factory[458]; the storage place for large reels was part of a floor.[459]

The following were held not to be floors etc: planks on a gantry[460]; mother earth, along which a heavily laden truck on rails was being pushed[461]; the earth

---

[448] A difference in height between paving stones is more properly to be considered as an example of "unevenness" under reg.12(2)(a) than an "obstruction" under reg.12(3): *Craner v Dorset County Council* [2009] P.I.Q.R. P10, CA.

[449] reg.12(2), a regulation that imposes strict liability: *Drage v Grassroots Ltd* [2000] C.L.Y. 2967. It was no defence to a claim arising from an accident caused when a school caretaker pushed a trolley against a protruding paving slab, that it was a freak occurrence which could not have been guarded against: *Craner v Dorset County Council* [2009] P.I.Q.R. P10, CA.

[450] The onus of proving that it was not reasonably practicable to keep the workman's place of work safe lay firmly on the employer: *Nimmo v Alexander Cowan & Sons Ltd* [1968] A.C. 107: *Simmons v British Steel Plc*, 2001 Rep. L.R. 82, OH (tubes leading from a profile burner through which gas was supplied to the equipment).

[451] reg.12(3). See *McGhee v Strathclyde Fire Brigade* 2002 S.L.T. 680, OH (liability for a slip caused by the residue of recent polishing left on the floor). It was said in *Craner v Dorset CCl*, n.449 above, that an accident caused by a protruding flag in a paved area was more appropriately considered under regs 12(1) and (2) of the Workplace Regulations than reg.12(3) because the concept of "unevenness" in reg.12(2)(a) was more apt than the concept of "obstruction" in reg.12(3) to describe the difference in height: para.[11].

[452] reg.12(5). In *Coates v Jaguar Cars Ltd* [2004] EWCA Civ 337 no breach was proved where a handrail was provided only after the claimant's accident. The steps in question were not a "staircase" and posed no real risk to any person walking on them with all proper care and attention.

[453] reg.2(1) provides that " 'traffic route' means a route for pedestrian traffic, vehicles or both and includes any stairs, staircase, fixed ladder, doorway, gateway, loading bay or ramp;".

[454] *Hosking v De Havilland Aircraft Co Ltd* [1949] 1 All E.R. 540; *Hudson v Acme Flooring and Paving Co Ltd* (1904) (1963) 107 S.J. 234, CA.

[455] *Morris v Port of London Authority* (1950) 84 Lloyd's Rep. 564.

[456] *Devine v Costain Concrete Co Ltd* 1979 S.L.T. (Notes) 97.

[457] *Harper v Mander & Germain, The Times*, December 28, 1992, CA.

[458] *Harrison v Metro-Vickers Electrical Co Ltd* [1954] 1 W.L.R. 324.

[459] *Pengelley v Bell Punch Co Ltd* [1964] 1 W.L.R. 433.

[460] *Tate v Swan Hunter & Wigham Richardson Ltd* [1958] 1 W.L.R. 39.

[461] *Newberry v Joseph Westwood & Co* [1960] 2 Lloyd's Rep. 37.

and surface of an open air wood yard[462]; a 30ft wide roadway running through a factory was not a passage or gangway.[463]

12–136   In terms of suitability it has been held that the appropriate question to ask under regs. 12(1) and 12(2) is whether the floor has been constructed in such a way as to expose any person to a risk to his health and safety.[464] Regulations 12(1) and (2) were said by the Court to Appeal to:

> "require the court to consider suitability in the context of the circumstances of use, including circumstances which are temporary in nature, providing they arise with a sufficient degree of frequency and regularity. The paragraphs read together require that the surface of the floor or traffic route must not be slippery . . . . If a smooth floor is frequently and regularly slippery, because of a substance which lies upon it, albeit only temporarily, the surface of the floor may properly be said to be unsuitable, if the slipperiness is such as to give rise to a risk to the health and safety of those employees using it."[465]

12–137   Furthermore, the question is to be posed by reference to factors as they existed before the claimant's accident and not with any benefit of hindsight. It was formerly held that, in deciding whether or not a floor is of sound construction and is properly maintained, regard had to be had to the purposes for which the premises were intended to be used.[466] It is unlikely that a floor will ever need to be suitable for a purpose for which it was never intended.[467] The obligation to ensure that a floor surface is suitable is a continuing one, consistent with the requirement to review risk assessment pursuant to reg.3 of the Management Regulations.[468]

12–138   The reference to "person" in reg.12(2)(a) and (3)[469] has been the subject of much litigation, principally in Scotland, where it has been successfully argued that it extends beyond an employee or even a person working on premises who

---

[462] *Sullivan v Hall Russell & Co Ltd*, 1964 S.L.T. 192.

[463] *Thornton v Fisher & Ludlow Ltd* [1968] 1 W.L.R. 655; it would obviously be a traffic route within reg.12.

[464] *Palmer v Marks and Spencer Plc* [2001] EWCA Civ 1528: no breach in case of 8 to 9.5mm weather strip in floor of staff exit of shop over which employee tripped; *Lowles v Home Office* [2004] EWCA Civ 985: breach in case of 2 inch step in doorway of a portacabin over which employee tripped.

[465] per Smith L.J. at [44] in *Ellis v Bristol CC* [2007] P.I.Q.R. P26, CA applying *Palmer v Marks and Spencer Plc*, n.464 above. On the facts, the smooth floor of a care home for the elderly which was regularly made slippery by urine did not comply with the obligation in reg.12(2). See also *Craner v Dorset County Council* [2009] P.I.Q.R. P10 where a paving stone raised an inch or less was held to expose the claimant to a health and safety risk which materialised when he pushed a wheeled trolley against it causing the trolley to stop abruptly whereby the claimant suffered injury. The submission that the raised slab could not constitute a risk to health and safety was rejected.

[466] *Mayne v Johnstone & Cumbers* [1947] 2 All E.R. 159; *Fisher v Port of London Authority* [1962] 1 W.L.R. 234.

[467] *Beadsley v United Steel Co* [1951] 1 K.B. 408.

[468] *McGhee v Strathclyde Fire Brigade* 2002 S.L.T. 680, OH (firefighter slipping on recently polished floor in fire station).

[469] reg.12(2)(a) provides that the requirements of reg.12(1) include avoiding the exposure of "any person to a risk to his health and safety" and reg.12(3) is directed at obstructions etc., "which may cause a person to slip, trip or fall."

is not an employee.[470] Pending a definitive decision, more recent authority favours an interpretation whereby the duty is limited to persons employed in premises in accordance with the scheme of the Workplace Regulations as a whole.[471]

The requirement of reasonable practicability regarding obstructions, articles   **12–139**
and substances is not to be found in the Workplace Directive although it is possible that the Directive applies to the floor structure only.[472] Under both ss.28 and 29 of the Factories Act 1961, it was held that, in deciding whether a breach of duty was proved, the risk of injury had to be balanced against the steps required to eliminate that risk.[473] So, where an occupier allowed grease to drop on the factory floor from an overhead crane it was held that, in order to avoid liability for an accidental slip, he must establish that it was not possible to avoid the likelihood of slipping by any reasonably practicable measure, that is, one that was capable of being taken and which would not involve unreasonable expense or other effort or exertion in time and labour.[474] Where precautions to keep the floor of a corporation bus depot free from patches of oil were reasonably practicable, the failure to take such precautions amounted to a breach of the section.[475]

An illustration of the practical working of reg.12(3) is provided by *Burgess v*   **12–140**
Plymouth City Council.[476] A school dinner lady and cleaner tripped and fell on a lunch box left lying on a classroom floor. A breach of the regulation was upheld by the Court of Appeal because it was plainly practicable for the floor to have been kept clear of the obstruction. Indeed, there was a system in place which, if followed by the class teacher, would have ensured the obstruction's removal. That was so even though the claimant's own job included, in general terms, tidying items away. The fact that this was part of her responsibilities was not, however, determinative of the finding of breach of duty (although it went to the

---

[470] *Banna v Delicato* 1999 Rep. L.R. 89 (customer in a shop who tripped on a bread basket on the floor of the public area); *O'Brien v Duke of Argyll's Trustees* [1999] C.L.Y. 6222 (visitor in hotel protected because Parliament had not seen fit to restrict the duty owed by employers to employees); in *Mortimer v Safeway Plc* 1988 S.C. 520, OH the duty was extended to a person making a delivery to a shop even if not employed by the owner of those premises..
[471] *Layden v Aldi GmBH & Co*, 2002 S.L.T. 71; followed in *McCondichie v Mains Medical Centre* [2004] Rep. L.R. 4; *Donaldson v Hayes Distribution Services Ltd* [2005] CSIH 48. See further, McDonald, "To whom is a duty owed?" P.I.L.J. 2006, 180, 22.
[472] Annex 1, para.9.1. See Lawson, "Tripping and slipping at work; what precautions are 'reasonably practicable?'" (2002) H. & S.L. 1(2), 3; also Shetty, "Slipping and tripping in the workplace" (2003) H. & S.L. 3(3), 2.
[473] See para.12–102, above. See also *Vinnyey v Star Paper Mills Ltd* [1965] 1 All E.R. 175 where there was no breach of statutory duty where a slippery substance had been left on a factory floor for about 10 minutes and the slip occurred just as the cleaner was about to start mopping: the words of the section did not mean that the floor must be kept absolutely free at all times but all reasonable measures must be taken to keep it free: *Braham v J. Lyons & Co* [1962] 1 W.L.R. 1048 and *Ashdown v Jonas Woodhead & Sons Ltd* [1975] K.I.L.R. 27, CA.
[474] *Williams v Painter Bros* (1968) K.I.R. 487.
[475] *Fern v Dundee Corp* 1964 S.L.T. 294.
[476] [2006] I.C.R. 579, CA.

issue of contributory negligence[477]); rather, it was the fact that the floor had not been kept free of an article that might cause a person to fall.[478]

12–141   As regards the words "kept free" the House of Lords held in relation to s.28 of the 1961 Act that this required the defendants to keep a floor free, whether by preventing[479] things getting on it or by removing things which have got onto it.[480]

12–142   Although reg.12(3) refers to "obstructions", the words "any obstruction"[481] meant something which, though not forming part of the floor, is on the floor but is not normally there, since its presence there is not for any particular purpose.[482]

Illustrations

12–143   The following were held not to have been "an obstruction" within the meaning of s.28 in the circumstances, although each object in fact was a necessary and reasonable impediment to the gangway: where there was a vertical angle-iron projection, which was part of a machine fixed to the concrete floor in a foundry[483]; where a mould was placed on the gangway floor in a factory, it being a convenient and proper place for it,[484] where some heavy reels of paper were lying on the floor[485] and where a trolley, used to bring materials for lathes, was left at the edge of a gangway[486]; tubes through which gas was supplied to burning equipment used to cut metal plates.[487] Although found to be a breach of reg.12(3), uneven flagstones were more aptly considered to constitute an obstruction under reg.12(2)(a).[488]

12–144   On the other hand, the following *were* held to have been "an obstruction" under s.28: a number of steel plates, which were in fact pit covers that had been removed for the purpose of certain maintenance work, but had been laid temporarily on the factory floor at a slight angle[489]; where a "gate" was lying covered or partially covered by sand, which constituted the surface of the floor

---

[477] Assessed at 50 per cent.

[478] ibid. at para.[11].

[479] *Johnston v Caddies Wainwright* [1983] I.C.R. 407, CA.

[480] *Fairfield Shipbuilding & Engineering Co Ltd v Hall* [1964] 1 Lloyd's Rep. 73.

[481] Factories Act 1961 s.28(1).

[482] per Lord Denning in *Pengelley v Bell Punch Co Ltd* [1964] 1 W.L.R. 1055, 1058: "something on the floor that has no business to be there, and which is a source of risk to persons ordinarily using the floor." See however, *Lowles v The Home Office* [2004] EWCA Civ 985: defendant liable for claimant's trip over an unmarked 2 inch step between inner and outer doors leading to a portacabin subject to 50 per cent contributory negligence for failing to heed or act upon a sign warning of the step.

[483] *Drummond v Harland Engineering Co Ltd* 1963 S.C. 162.

[484] *Churchill v Louis Marx & Co* (1964) 108 S.J. 334, CA.

[485] *Pengelley v Bell Punch Co Ltd* [1964] 1 W.L.R. 1055.

[486] *Marshall v Ericsson Telephones Ltd* [1964] 1 W.L.R. 1367.

[487] *Simmons v British Steel Plc* (2001) Rep. L.R. 82, OH (the tubes were, however, "articles" for the purposes of reg.12).

[488] *Craner v Dorset County Council* [2009] P.I.Q.R. P10, CA.

[489] *Dorman Long (Steel) Ltd v Bell* [1964] 1 W.L.R. 333.

in the moulding shop of the respondent's foundry shop[490]; a discarded screw lying on the floor, which was struck by the wheel of a passing barrow[491] and a piece of wire was left inadvertently lying on the floor.[492] By way of examples under reg.12(3), it has been held that there was a breach where it was reasonably practicable to move a whiteboard[493] and a lunchbox[494] so that it did not consitute a tripping hazard.

The words "any substance likely to cause persons to slip", essentially **12–145** reproduced in reg.12(3), were held to include rain-water, lying on a passage floor, which caused a person to slip and fall.[495] Where an employee slipped on a small piece of metal rod lying on the floor, the employers argued that the duty of keeping the floor clear was limited not only by requirements of reasonable practicability but also by the words "likely to cause persons to slip". The court rejected this argument as too restrictive and held that the words qualified only the word "substance" and did not limit the area of floor that had to be kept free.[496] Where dust produced a slippery surface on two large heavy metal plates, which were lying on the floor and upon which anyone using the floor was likely to step, the fact that the dust was not in contact with the floor itself was immaterial.[497] It was also held that the statutory duty under s.28(1) of the 1961 Act was a higher duty than that at common law.[498]

The relationship between reg.12(3) and reg.5 has been held not to be mutually **12–146** exclusive, in that the specific obligations imposed by reg.12 do not prevent the operation of the obligations in reg.5.[499] Thus where the claimant tripped on raised carpet fitted to a staircase, the employers were found to be in breach of both.[500] This is to be contrasted with the position where a claimant slipped on an area of flooding, caused by an unforeseen escape of water from a concealed pipe which burst.[501] Despite being a duty of strict liability, there were limitations of the scope of reg.5 from a claimant's perspective.[502] She was unable to invoke reg.12(3) because the employer could show that it was not reasonably practicable, on the occasion in question, to have kept the floor free from water. Had the escape of

---

[490] *Jenkins v Allied Ironfounders Ltd* [1970] 1 W.L.R. 304, but it was held that it was not reasonably practicable to ensure that the floor was constantly kept free from such "gates".

[491] *Gillies v Glynwed Foundries*, 1977 S.L.T. 97 (liability under this section was avoided because the system of cleaning was satisfactory and it would not have been reasonably practicable to take any additional steps in the circumstances).

[492] *Bennett v Rylands Whitecross* [1978] I.C.R. 1031.

[493] *Anderson v Newham College of Further Education* [2003] I.C.R. 212, CA. A two inch step in a doorway has also been held to be an obstruction within the meaning of reg.12(3) as well as unsuitable in breach of reg.12(1): *Lowles v The Home Office* [2004] EWCA Civ 985.

[494] *Burgess v Plymouth City Council* [2006] I.C.R. 579, CA: see para.12–140, above.

[495] *Taylor v Gestetner* (1967) 2 K.I.R. 133.

[496] *Hall v Fairfield Shipbuilding & Engineering Co*, 1963 S.L.T. 37 but was reversed on another point by the HL: [1964] 1 Lloyds Rep. 73.

[497] *Dorman Long (Steel) Ltd v Bell* [1964] 1 W.L.R. 333.

[498] *Powley v Bristol Siddeley Engines Ltd* [1966] 1 W.L.R. 729.

[499] *Irvine v Metropolitan Police Commissioner* [2005] EWCA Civ 129.

[500] *Irvine v Metropolitan Police Commissioner*, n.499, above.

[501] *Lewis v Avidan Ltd* [2006] P.I.Q.R. P69, CA.

[502] In *Lewis v Avidan*, above n.501, May L.J. said,: "The construction I favour means that the pipe which burst, although it may have been equipment, was not equipment a fault in which was liable to result in a failure to comply with any of the regulations, in particular regulation 5(1)."

water from the concealed pipe been a recurrent problem, it is submitted that the claimant would have succeeded in respect of breaches of both reg.12(3) and reg.5.[503]

12–147 Accumulations of ice are a perennial source of accident.[504] The suggestion that s.28 of the 1961 Act was concerned with structural safety only, made in *Levesley v Firth &* Brown,[505] can be laid to rest, as the language of reg.12(3) makes it clear that the duty extends to transient conditions, subject always to the question of reasonable practicability. Cases concerned with ice under the Factories Act 1961 went both ways.[506] Since there is no doubt that ice can render a floor or traffic route into such condition as to cause a person to slip, avoidance of liability will turn on the provision of an adequate system for the taking of preventative measures in accordance with para.96 of the ACOP and proof that the system so devised operated as it should have done. Thus the reasoning in *Gitsham v CH Pearce & Sons Plc*[507] is likely to survive the new legislation, with a similar outcome for unsuccessful claimants where the employer discharges the duty thus described.[508]

12–148 Regulation 17 makes specific provision in respect of the layout of traffic routes[509] requiring workplaces to be organised in such a way that pedestrians and vehicles can circulate safely. Traffic routes have to be suitable for both persons and vehicles using them and will not be suitable unless they can be used by either pedestrians or vehicles without causing danger to the health and safety of the persons working near to them and unless there is sufficient separation between pedestrians and vehicles. Such routes must be marked where necessary for reasons of health and safety.

12–149 **Falls and falling objects.**[510] Prior to the implementation of the Work at Height Regulations 2005,[511] reg.13 of the Workplace Regulations provided that

---

[503] A repeated failure of the pipe was liable to cause a breach of reg.12(3) because it would not be open to the employer to argue that it was not reasonably practicable to avoid the flooding.
[504] For an interesting approach in a case where the claimant slipped on the ice which he was entrusted to remove in which the Manual Handling Operations Regulations 1992 were successfully invoked, see *King v RCO Support Services Ltd* [2001] P.I.Q.R. P15, CA.
[505] [1953] 1 W.L.R. 1206, CA.
[506] *Thomas v Bristol Aeroplanes* [1954] 1 W.L.R. 694, CA: claimant failed where surface was icy on a Monday morning; *Woodward v Renold Ltd* [1980] I.C.R. 387: claimant succeeded where icy car park ought to have been gritted; *Gitsham v C.H. Pearce & Sons Plc* [1992] P.I.Q.R. P57, CA: claimant failed where employer showed proper system for clearance properly executed.
[507] See n.506, above.
[508] For an example where a claimant succeeded following a car park slip: *Pettie v Southampton University Hospitals NHS Trust* [2003] C.L.Y 5377.
[509] See n.453 above. A breach was proved where an access gate in a fence was locked and the claimant was not provided with a key to open it: *Wallis v Balfour Beattie Rail Maintenance Ltd* (2003) S.J.L.B. 357, CA. The claim failed because the proximate cause of the accident was the claimant's decision to climb the fence.
[510] reg.13(1) to (4) of the Workplace Regulations has been repealed by the Work at Height Regulations 2005 (SI 2005/735), which came into force on April 6, 2005 and make provision for the organisation and planning of "work at height" (reg.4) and the avoidance of risks from work at height by risk assessment including avoidance where reasonably practicable (reg.6).
[511] S.I. 2005/735 as amended by S.I. 2007/114 and S.I. 2007/320. The Regulations were implemented on April 6, 2005: see further para.12–153, below.

suitable and effective measures be taken, so far as is reasonably practicable, to prevent a person falling a distance or a person being struck by a falling object, in either case likely to cause personal injury. The ACOP followed a like provision regarding persons falling in s.29(2) of the Factories Act 1961 in advising that fencing be provided where a fall is greater than 2m.[512] However, the former requirement that the fall has to be at a place where a person "has to work" had been removed. Thus, where the claimant, a sales director in a small family business, climbed on to its warehouse roof to investigate the activities of suspected prospective burglars, it was held that the roof was a workplace within the meaning of reg.2 and the provisions of reg.13 applied.[513] The roof had been made available to the claimant because he had not been prohibited from going on to it and the provision of a suitable ladder at the premises confirmed both availability and access.[514] Although the regulation was apparently limited by reasonable practicability (not to be found in the Workplace Directive[515]), it was further held that the regulation achieved strict liability and that the requirement of reasonable practicability affected the nature of the absolute duty rather than rendering it other than absolute.[516] Where an employee fell from the roof of a van with no guard rails whilst engaged in loading, a breach of reg.13 was established.[517] The measures to be taken were, so far as is reasonably practicable, to be other than the provision of personal protective equipment, information, instruction, training or supervision.[518] Thus, a prohibition or company rule would not constitute a suitable or effective measure within reg.13(1). A physical warning sign could constitute a discharge of the duty.[519] There is, however, a separate requirement as to the giving of warnings[520] and the secure covering or fencing of tanks and pits containing dangerous substances,[521] a more extensive duty than s.18 of the 1961 Act which it replaces.

Generally. Provision is also made with regard to the safety of windows and transparent doors, gates and walls,[522] the safe opening of windows and skylights,[523] the ability to clean windows and skylights safely,[524] the suitable construction of doors and gates[525] and safety regarding escalators.[526] In terms of personal comfort and hygiene the Workplace Regulations contain requirements   **12–150**

---

[512] para.108.
[513] *Parker v PFC Flooring Supplies Ltd* [2001] P.I.Q.R. P115, CA.
[514] *Parker v PFC Flooring Supplies Ltd* [2001] P.I.Q.R. P115, CA at P124. See Downey, "No signs? No wonder" H & S.L. 2002, 1(2), 15.
[515] Annex I, para.12.1.
[516] *Parker v PFC Flooring Supplies Ltd*, n.513, above at P126.
[517] *Wright v Romford Blinds and Shutters* [2003] EWHC 1165.
[518] Workplace Regulations reg.13(2).
[519] *Parker v PFC Flooring Supplies Ltd* n.513, above at P124.
[520] reg.13(4). Thus a failure to give a clear indication of the risk of a fall or falling objects itself constituted a breach of this duty: *Parker v PFC Flooring Supplies Ltd* n.513, above at P125.
[521] reg.13(5) to (7).
[522] reg.14.
[523] reg.15.
[524] reg.16.
[525] reg.18. For an example of doors which were not suitable: *Beck v United Closures & Plastics Plc* 2001 S.L.T. 1299, OH.
[526] reg.19.

with regard to working temperatures,[527] the provision and standard of sanitary conveniences,[528] washing facilities,[529] drinking water,[530] accommodation,[531] facilities for[532] changing clothing together with facilities for rest and eating meals,[533] and provision that all parts of workplaces used or occupied by disabled persons be organised to take account of their needs.[534]

12–151   **Safe.** Although "safe" may be the converse of "dangerous," the test of what is safe does not depend upon considerations of reasonable foreseeability, however relevant they may be when considering danger.[535] It has been said that "safe" is an ordinary English word and whether premises were safe had to be decided purely as a question of fact. To imply a requirement of foreseeability would be wrong, as the result frequently would be to limit success in a claim based on breach of statutory duty in circumstances where the workman would also succeed in a parallel claim for negligence, thereby reducing the utility of the section and the protection it afforded.[536] In a decision concerning s.29 of the Factories Act 1961, it was emphasised that the test of safety was an objective one rendering reasonable foreseeability irrelevant.[537]

12–152   There is no doubt that the approach has not always been consistent and there are examples in which the test of safety was by reference to what might

---

[527] reg.7.

[528] reg.20.

[529] reg.21. Presumably cases decided under s.58 of the Factories Act 1961, which this regulation replaces, will continue to be relevant in determining whether the obligation upon employers has been discharged. Thus, in a dermatitis case, the employer's contention that the allegation of such breach of a welfare provision was incapable of giving rise to an action for damages was rejected: *Reid v Westfield Paper Co*, 1957 S.C. 218. The provision of a cold water tap 70 yards away from the claimant's place of work where he was in constant contact with chemically impregnated sand was held to be sufficient compliance: *Wishart v Bradley & Craven Ltd* (1963) 107 S.J. 554; the contraction of dermatitis after subjection to conditions of work likely to cause it gave rise to a *prima facie* presumption that the disease was caused by such conditions: *Gardiner v Motherwell Machinery & Scrap Metal Co Ltd* [1961] 1 W.L.R. 1424, HL.

[530] reg.22.

[531] reg.23 following s.59 of the Factories Act 1961. Presumably consideration of whether accommodation was suitable involved taking into account the risk of theft as in *McCarthy v Daily Mirror Newspaper Ltd* [1949] 1 All E.R. 801.

[532] reg.24 as amended by the Health and Safety (Miscellaneous) Amendment Regulations 2002 (SI 2002/2174).

[533] reg.25 as amended by the Health and Safety (Miscellaneous) Amendment Regulations 2002 (SI 2002/2174) to include the making of arrangements to protect non-smokers from discomfort caused by tobacco smoke.

[534] Inserted by the Health and Safety (Miscellaneous) Amendment Regulations 2002 (SI 2002/174).

[535] *Larner v British Steel Plc* [1993] 4 All E.R. 102, CA, preferring the approach of Viscount Simonds in *John Summers & Sons Ltd v Frost* [1955] A.C. 740 at 753, and Lord Guest in *Nimmo v Alexander Cowan & Sons* [1968] A.C. 107 at 122, and *Robertson v R.B. Crowe & Co* 1970 S.L.T. 122. See also, *Mains v Engelbert Tyres*, *The Times*, September 29, 1995, Ct. Sess. IH: inappropriate to link "dangerous" in s.14 of the 1961 Act to "safe" in s.29(1) simply because the words are antonyms. The obligation imposed on the employer under the latter section was to prevent any risk of injury arising from the state or condition of the working place and not just those risks which are reasonably foreseeable.

[536] *Larner v British Steel Plc* [1993] 4 All E.R. 102, CA, per Gibson J.

[537] *Baker v Quantum Clothing Group* [2009] P.I.Q.R. P19, CA (industrial deafness claim). See also Weir, "Not aloud", N.L.J. 18 September 2009, 1279.

reasonably have been foreseen. So a means of access was not safe if it was a reasonably foreseeable cause of injury to anyone acting in a way that a human being may be reasonably expected to act, in circumstances which may reasonably be expected to occur.[538] For a means of access to be safe, it had to be safe for all contingencies that could reasonably be foreseen, likely as well as unlikely, possible as well as probable[539]; the fact that human beings may not exercise a high degree of care for their own safety is a relevant matter to be taken into account.[540]

(E) The Work at Height Regulations 2005

Generally. The Work at Height Regulations 2005, introduced pursuant to s.15(1) of the Health and Safety at Work, etc. Act 1974 to give effect to Council Directive 2001/45/EC,[541] revoke and replace many provisions of the Workplace (Health Safety and Welfare Regulations) 1992 and Construction (Health Safety and Welfare) Regulations 1996 as well as earlier legislation[542] and seek to bring under the umbrella of a single set of regulations the legal requirements relating to all forms of employment at height. Breach of these Regulations is taken to give rise to civil liability. A detailed consideration of these Regulations is outside the scope of this book but an overview of the salient features is given   **12–153**

Work at height. This is defined as including work in any place, which includes a place at or below ground level as well as the obtaining of access to or egress from such a place whilst at work other than by a staircase in a permanent workplace.[543]   **12–154**

Who is covered. Employees and self employed persons are protected.[544] Also protected are persons under the control of an employer to the extent of his control.[545] However, excluded from protection are the master and crew of a ship (or their employers) in respect of "the normal ship-board activities of a ship's crew",[546] places where persons are engaged in dock operations[547] or in fish   **12–155**

---

[538] cf. *Trott v W.E. Smith (Erectors) Ltd* [1957] 1 W.L.R. 1154, per Parker L.J. at 1162.

[539] *McCarthy v Coldair Ltd* [1951] 2 T.L.R. 1226: a ladder that slipped on a smooth surface was not a safe means of access. See also *Canning v Remington Rand Co* (1954) 104 L.J. 538, Ct. Sess; *Hill v J.O. Buchanan Ltd*, 1965 S.L.T. (Notes) 24; *Garner v John Thompson (Wolverhampton)* (1968) 112 S.J. 1006.

[540] *Sheppey v Matthew T. Shaw & Co Ltd* [1952] 1 T.L.R. 1272. A safe means of access, however, did not become unsafe because of some isolated and extraneous act of negligence of another person, such as where clouds of dust caused by a third party's activities obfuscated a gangway, which was otherwise perfectly safe.

[541] Minimum Safety and Health requirements of Work Equipment.

[542] The Shipbuilding and Ship-repairing Regulations 1960, the Docks, Shipbuilding etc (Metrication) Regulations 1983, the Docks Regulations 1988 and the Loading and Unloading of Fishing Vessels Regulations 1988.

[543] reg.2(1).

[544] reg.3(2) and (3).

[545] reg.3(2).

[546] reg.3(4)(a).

[547] As specified in reg.7(6) of the Docks Regulations 1988.

loading processes.[548] A special exemption is provided by reg.14A in respect of leaders or instructors of recreational caving or climbing.

12–156   **Who is liable.** Duties are imposed on every employer in relation to work done by their employees as well as others over whom they have control. The definition therefore extends to more than employees strictly so called and reinforces the importance of control, as recognised by the Court of Appeal in *Lane v Shire Roofing Co (Oxford) Ltd.*[549] In one example, a householder who imposed limits on a casual labourer's access to her property did not have the necessary control to bring her within the ambit of the Regulations. Even though the limits she imposed dictated that the means of access to a flat roof on which the claimant was required to work was by ladder rather than through a first floor window, the defendant was acting in her capacity as occupier in setting limits on the claimant's access to her property and not seeking to instruct or direct him in his work.[550]

It should be noted that a positive duty is also imposed on an employee carrying out construction work to comply with the Regulations and to report any defect of which he is aware to the person under whose control he is.[551] A failure to do so is, presumably, capable of amounting to a breach of statutory duty on the employee's part as well as contributory negligence.

12–157   **The scheme of the Regulations.** The Regulations provide a framework for ensuring safe working at height based on organisation and planning, the avoidance of risks from work at height and the selection of equipment for work at height. Thus reg.4 requires the employer to ensure that work at height is properly planned, appropriately supervised and carried out in a manner which is safe so far as is reasonably practicable. The planning must specifically include the selection of work equipment in accordance with reg.7 which provides a list of factors to take into account in giving collective protection measures priority over personal protection measures, an echo of the repealed reg.13(2) of the Workplace Regulations. However, before consideration of reg.7 arises, note that reg.6(2) imposes a duty on the employer to ensure that work is not carried out at height where it is reasonably practicable to carry out the work safely other than at height. Only if it is not so reasonably practicable does the duty to take sufficient and suitable measures to prevent, within the limits of reasonable practicability, any person falling a distance likely to cause personal injury arise.[552]

12–158   **Specific requirements.** Regulation 8 provides detailed requirements, in conjunction with a series of Schedules, in respect of particular work equipment such as guard-rails, toe-boards, barriers,[553] working platforms,[554] systems for

---

[548] As specified in reg.5(3) of the Loading and Unloading of Fishing Vessels Regulations 1988
[549] [1995] P.I.Q.R. P417. See Ch.3, paras 3–99–3–159.
[550] *Kmiecic v Isaacs* [2010] EWHC 381, Q.B.D.
[551] reg.14.
[552] reg.6(3)
[553] reg.8(a).
[554] reg.8(b).

arresting falls[555] and personal fall protection systems.[556] Ladders[557] are the subject of Sch.6, reflecting research of the Health and Safety Executive that a third of all reported fall-from-height incidents involve ladders and stepladders.[558] Thus, para.1 of Sch.6 requires an employer to ensure that a ladder is only used for work at height if risk assessment under the Management Regulations has demonstrated that the use of more suitable equipment is not justified because of the low level of risk and the short duration of use or existing features on site which cannot be altered. Schedule 6 goes on to provide detailed requirements as to the manner in which ladders are used in the event that their use can be justified. Note that, where work equipment is provided in connection with working at height, reg.14 provides a detailed inspection regime of that equipment. Likewise reg.9 provides detailed provision for working in the vicinity of fragile surfaces, another significant feature in accidents.[559]

Falling objects. Regulation 10 replaces, in part, reg.13 of the Workplace   **12–159** Regulations,[560] and provides for an employer, regardless of whether the work is work at height within the meaning of the Regulations, where necessary to prevent injury to any person, to take suitable and sufficient steps to prevent the fall of any material or object, so far as is reasonably practicable.[561] Where it is not reasonably practicable to comply with that requirement, suitable and sufficient steps have to be taken to prevent any person being struck by a falling object or material liable to cause injury.[562] Provision is made for the designation of danger areas[563] where there is a risk either of a fall of a distance or of a person being struck by a falling object, such areas being equipped with devices, so far as is reasonably practicable, to prevent unauthorised persons from entering such areas.

(F) The Construction (Design and Management) Regulations 2007 (The Construction Regulations)

Introduction. The Construction Regulations[564] revoked the Construction   **12–160** (Health, Safety and Welfare) Regulations 1996[565] along with the Construction (Design and Management) Regulations 1994,[566] and such parts of the Construction (Health and Welfare) Regulations 1966[567] and the Construction (Working Places) Regulations 1966[568] as remained in force. They are intended to give

---

[555] reg.8(c).
[556] reg.8(d).
[557] reg.8(e).
[558] HSE, Safe use of ladders and stepladders: an employers' guide. It is said that on average such falls account for 14 deaths and 1200 major injuries to workers each year.
[559] See also reg.13 which requires an employer to inspect places of work at height.
[560] Discussed at para.12–149, above.
[561] reg.10(1).
[562] reg.10(2).
[563] reg.11.
[564] SI 2007/320.
[565] SI 1996/1592.
[566] SI 1994/3140 as amended by SI 1996/1592.
[567] SI 1966/95 as amended by SI 1974/209 and SI 1981/917.
[568] SI 1966/94 and SI 1984/1593.

effect to the Temporary or Mobile Construction Site Directive[569] albeit some provisions in that Directive have been implemented by the Work at Height Regulations 2005. The Construction Regulations came into force on April 6, 2007. They are accompanied by an ACOP.[570] In broad outline, the duties under Pt 4 of the Construction Regulations, which relate to health and safety on constructions sites, give rise to civil liability generally. The duties under Pt 2 (general management duties applying to construction projects) and Pt 3 (additional duties in respect of notifiable projects), with minor exceptions, are actionable only by employees. A detailed consideration of Pts 2 and 3 of the Regulations is outside the scope of this book but a discussion of Pt 4 follows.[571]

12–161   **Construction work and construction sites.** Construction work is very broadly defined to mean the carrying out of any building, civil engineering or engineering construction work to include, amongst other things, alterations, conversion, fitting out, commissioning, renovation, repair, redecoration and maintenance.[572] Cleaning using substances under high pressure is also construction work. Work preparatory to construction (but not site surveys) is included, as is demolition. Any place where the principal work activity is construction work is a construction site. The exploration of sites for the extraction of mineral resources is excluded.

12–162   **Application.** Regulation 25, which applies to the duties under Pt 4, has widened the category of persons covedred by the revoked 1996 Regulations. The duty is placed on contractors carrying out construction work insofar as they affect him or any person carrying out construction work under his control or relate to matters within his control, contractors being any person (client, principal contractor or other person) who, in the course of business, carries out or manages construction work.[573] Employees are undoubtedly protected but so are persons in respect of whom another has control over the construction work they carry out.[574] This definition is therefore far wider than employees (strictly so called) and reinforces the question of control recognised by the Court of Appeal in *Lane v Shire Roofing Co (Oxford) Ltd*.[575] In *Moon v Garrett*,[576] it was said that persons at work, within the meaning of the 1996 Regulations, were not confined to persons carrying out construction work such that a person engaged in making a delivery to site or even carrying tea to workmates would be afforded the protection of those regulations. It is suggested that similar considerations apply under the 2007 Regulations. A positive duty also imposed on an employee

---

[569] 92/57/EEC.
[570] Managing Health and Safety in Construction.
[571] For an overview see Exall, "A positive development?" 151 S.J. (38), 1286.
[572] Construction Regulations reg.2(1).
[573] reg.2(1).
[574] reg.25. A defendant, at whose site the claimant's employer was working, did not acquire control over the construction work for the purposes of reg.4(2) of the 1996 Regulations by virtue of the obligation under reg.10 of the Construction (Design and Management) Regulations 1994 (to ensure that a health and safety plan was prepared for the work): *McCook v Lobo* [2003] I.C.R. 89, CA.
[575] [1995] P.I.Q.R. P417. See also *McCook v Lobo* n.574 above. See also Ch.3 paras 3–99–3–159, above.
[576] [2007] P.I.Q.R. P3, CA.

carrying out construction work to comply with the Regulations and to report any defect of which he is aware to the person under whose control he is.[577] A failure to do so is, presumably, capable of amounting to a breach of statutory duty on the employee's part as well as contributory negligence.

Safe places of work. Regulation 26(1) of the Construction Regulations imposes a duty, within the limits of reasonable practicability, to provide suitable and sufficient access to and egress from every place of work and to other places provided for the use of any person whilst at work, such access and egress to be properly maintained. Save in one respect,[578] this follows the form of the 1996 Regulations[579] and bears a striking similarity to s.29(1) of the Factories Act 1961 with important enlargements in two respects: it is the access that must be safe rather than the means of access and both every place of work (rather than the place at which a person has to work) and any other place provided for the worker must be provided to the standard required. Regulation 26(2) imposes a duty to make and keep places of work safe and without risks to health, again within the limits of reasonable practicability. There was no breach of its predecessor, reg.5(2) of the 1996 Regulations, when a tower scaffold, which was otherwise inherently safe, was deliberately pushed over by a fellow employee causing the claimant, who was working on it, to fall and suffer injury.[580] Note also the duty imposed by reg.27 to keep construction sites in good order and places of work in a reasonable state of cleanliness. **12–163**

Falls and falling objects. Regulation in respect of falls and falling objects has been removed, which appeared in the 1996 Regulations, has now been provided in the Work at Height Regulations 2005, para.12–159, above. **12–164**

Stability of structures. Regulation 28 of the Construction Regulations requires all practicable steps to be taken to ensure that any structure (new or existing), which is widely defined[581] to include, for example, formwork, falsework, scaffold or other structure designed or used to provide support or means of access during construction work. **12–165**

Demolition and dismantling. Regulation 29(1) of the Construction Regulations modifies its predecessor under reg.10 of the 1996 Regulations and ultimately replaces Pt X of the Construction (General Provisions) Regulations 1961 and imposes the requirement that any demolition[582] or dismantling of any structure (or part thereof) shall be planned and carried out in such a manner as to prevent danger or, where it is not reasonably practicable to prevent it, to reduce danger to as low a level as is reasonably practicable. Regulation 29(2) directs that the arrangements for carrying out demolition or dismantling be reduced to writing before work commences. **12–166**

---

[577] Workplace Regulations reg.25(3).
[578] The removal of the words "without risks to health".
[579] reg.5(1) of the Construction (Health, Safety and Welfare) Regulations 1996.
[580] *Horton v Taplin Contracts Ltd* [2003] P.I.Q.R. P180, CA.
[581] reg.2(1)
[582] See generally, Hughes, "Demolishing safely" (2004) H.& S.W. 26(2), 24.

12–167   **Specific hazards.** Risks from explosives,[583] excavations,[584] cofferdams and caissons,[585] drowning,[586] and fire[587] are all separately catered for.

12–168   **Traffic routes and vehicles.** Regulation 36 of the Construction Regulations is the counterpart to reg.17 of the Workplace Regulations[588] but note that the duty imposed is limited by reasonable practicability. Where there was a failure to construct a barrier or put up a sign to warn of the presence of studs set in concrete, a breach of the comparable provision in the 1996 Regulations[589] was made out.[590] Regulation 36 of the Construction Regulations is directed at eliminating the risk to persons from the movement of vehicles whether they are on them or near them so as to be likely to be affected by them.

12–169   **Emergencies.** Regulation 39 of the Construction Regulations requires the provision of emergency routes and exits where necessary and reg.40 requires the preparation and implementation of arrangements to deal with foreseeable emergencies to include procedures for evacuation where necessary. Provision is also made for fire detection and fire fighting in reg.41.

12–170   **Welfare provisions.** Whereas reg.22 of the 1996 Regulations provided detailed welfare provisions, regs 9(1)(b), 13(7) and 22(1)(c) Construction Regulations impose duties set out at length in Sch.2 for the provision of sanitary conveniences, washing facilities (to include showers where necessary) and a supply of drinking water together with accommodation for storing and changing clothing, thus mirroring regs 20 to 24 of the Workplace Regulations, now including facilities to eat meals as in reg.25 of the Workplace Regulations, a requirement omitted from the 1996 Regulations. There are also requirements as to the provision of fresh air[591] and a reasonable temperature when working indoors as well as protective clothing when working outdoors.[592]

12–171   **Lighting.** An absolute duty is imposed by reg.44 of the Construction Regulations in respect of the provision of suitable and sufficient lighting in every place of work which shall be by natural light so far as is reasonably practicable. Arguably it could have the effect of reversing the decision in favour of the employer who escaped liability to his night watchman who was injured when he fell over a loose plank on a building site.[593]

12–172   **Plant and equipment.** Regulation 27 of the 1996 Construction Regulations which required plant and equipment to be safe and without risk to health so far

---

[583] reg.30.
[584] reg.31.
[585] reg.32.
[586] reg.35.
[587] reg.38.
[588] para.12–133, above.
[589] reg.15 of the Construction (Health, Safety and Welfare) Regulations 1996.
[590] *Humpheryes v Nedcon UK Ltd* [2004] EWHC 2558.
[591] Workplace Regulations reg.42.
[592] reg.43.
[593] *Field v Perrys (Ealing) Ltd* [1950] W.N. 320, per Devlin J., discussed at Ch.11, para.11–107, above.

as is reasonably practicable was repealed by the Provision and Use of Work Equipment Regulations 1998[594] thus removing an anomaly whereby the requirement of maintenance was one within the limit of reasonable practicability in contrast to the strict nature of the duty under reg.5 of the Provision and Use of Work Equipment Regulations 1998.[595]

(G) The Provision and Use of Work Equipment Regulations 1998 (The Work Equipment Regulations 1998)

Introduction. The Work Equipment Regulations 1998[596] were introduced   **12–173**
pursuant to s.15 of the Health and Safety at Work, etc. Act 1974 to give effect to the Work Equipment Directive.[597] They came into force on December 5, 1998 replacing similar Regulations[598] which came partially into force on January 1, 1993, coming fully into force on January 1, 1997.[599] They revoke and replace many of the earlier important regulations relating to specific equipment such as, for example, the Woodworking Machines Regulations 1974.[600] The Provision and Use of Work Equipment Regulations 1992 were accompanied by a Guidance Note. It has been said that it is important to interpret the Workplace Regulations by reference to the Work Equipment Directive rather than the Factories Act 1961.[601] Breaches of the Work Equipment Regulations 1998 are taken to give rise to civil liability.

These are important regulations greatly increasing an employer's liability for   **12–174**
defective equipment and replacing many important earlier provisions such as s.14 of the Factories Act 1961 (fencing dangerous parts of machines).[602]

Who is covered. Employees are protected as against their employers in   **12–175**
respect of work equipment "provided for use or used at work . . . ".[603] This definition appears to be capable of covering an employee's own equipment which he happens to use at work. The duty extends beyond equipment owned by employers because any person who has control to any extent of work equipment or a person at work who uses, supervises or manages the use of work equipment or the way in which it is used at work is also liable.[604] Thus a wide category of

---

[594] Sch.4.
[595] SI 1998/2306 discussed in detail below at para.12–173.
[596] SI 1998/2306 as amended by SI 1999/860 and SI 1999/2001.
[597] 89/655/EEC.
[598] Provision and Use of Work Equipment Regulations 1992 (SI 1992/2932), as amended.
[599] Provision and Use of Work Equipment Regulations 1992 (SI 1992/2932) regs 11 to 24 and 27 and Sch.2 applied in respect of equipment first provided for use in the premises or undertaking before January 1, 1993 only after December 31, 1996. Care has to be taken to establish precisely what equipment is covered by which regulation.
[600] For a full list of revoked Regulations, see Sch.4 to the Provision and Use of Work Equipment Regulations 1998.
[601] *English v North Lanarkshire Council* 1999 S.C.L.R. 310, OH.
[602] See Goddard, "Work Equipment", J.P.I.L. 2000 4,220; also Carr, "The Provision and Use of Equipment Regulations 1992 and 1998—a decade on" 2003 A.B. 2(6), 7.
[603] Work Equipment Regulations 1998 reg.3(2).
[604] reg.3(3)(b). But see reg.3(5), n.58 below, regarding work equipment supplied by way of sale or hire-purchase agreement Such a person may have liability under the law of sale of goods: see Ch.15, below, generally.

persons will be afforded protection if they use work equipment subject to any of the controls mentioned.

12–176   The scope of the Regulations arose for decision in *Ball v Street*[605] where the claimant, a farmer, suffered severe injury to his eye whilst using a haybob machine belonging to another farmer, the defendant. The claimant had hired the services of the defendant together with the use of the machine. On the day of the accident the claimant was using it with the defendant's consent. The Regulations were held to apply. The defendant had control of the equipment and the way in which it was used for the purposes of reg.3(3)(b).[606] That control was in connection with the carrying on of his trade or business, namely the hiring out of services with equipment owned and maintained by himself.[607]

12–177   Furthermore, the exemption in reg.3(5)[608] did not assist the defendant as it did not extend to a person who hired equipment, or who lent it, in the sense that he simply handed over temporary physical control of the equipment for use by another in the circumstances where the opportunity and duty of maintaining it in safe working condition remained with him. The intention underlying the Regulations was no doubt that, so far as any commercial relationship was concerned, a line should be drawn between a sale or hire-purchase on the one hand, in which the obligation of maintenance and retention of any control unequivocally passed to the transferee, and short-term hire or loan of equipment in the course of business.

12–178   *Ball v Street* was distinguished in *Mason v Satelcom*.[609] There, the claimant suffered injury in the course of his employment when he fell from a ladder that was too short for the work on which he was engaged. His employer was liable to him under the Work Equipment Regulations but the issue was whether the owners of the building in which he was working should also be liable. They had afforded the claimant access to the room in which he was working and in which he had found the ladder. There was no evidence the ladder was the property of the building owners but it was argued that they had control of it for purposes of reg.3(3) sufficient for liability under the Regulations to attach. The argument was rejected. The building owners' control of the ladder was limited. They could have removed it from the room, or caused a notice to be fixed to it, but it was difficult to see how much further their control extended. It did not extend to ensuring, for

---

[605] [2005] P.I.Q.R. P22, CA.

[606] reg.3(3) provides, so far as is material: "The requirements imposed by these Regulations on an employer shall also apply . . . (b) subject to paragraph (5), to a person who has control to any extent of—(i) work equipment; (ii) a person at work who uses or supervises or manages the use of work equipment; or (iii) the way in which work equipment is used at work, and to the extent of his control."

[607] reg.3(4) provides: "Any reference in paragraph (3)(b) to a person having control in connection with the carrying on by him of a trade business or other undertaking (whether for profit or not)".

[608] reg.3(5) provides: "The requirements imposed by these Regulations shall not apply to a person in respect of work equipment supplied by him by way of sale, agreement for sale or hire-purchase agreement."

[609] [2008] I.C.R. 971, CA.

purposes of reg.4(1), that it was constructed or adapted so as to be suitable for the purpose for which the claimant used it.

Who is liable. As is apparent from the previous paragraphs, employers are **12–179** certainly liable but so are self-employed persons and persons who have control of work equipment or persons using work equipment. The word "employer" is used to cover all such persons.[610]

Work equipment. This is broadly defined as meaning any machinery, **12–180** appliance, apparatus, tool or installation for use at work. "Equipment" features in the Employer's Liability (Defective Equipment) Act 1969 and has been interpreted, in that context, as including a flagstone.[611] It is suggested that its potential application is wide, ranging from a needle being used by a seamstress, to a tanker being driven by a tanker driver (even though the latter would not constitute a workplace for the purposes of the Workplace Regulations[612]). A steel cabinet on which a nursery nurse cut her leg has been held to be work equipment.[613] There is no reason why a pen used by any worker in the course of his work should not constitute work equipment.[614]

The first occasion on which the House of Lords had the opportunity to consider **12–181** the scope of work equipment as envisaged by the Work Equipment Regulations was in *Spencer-Franks v Kellogg Brown & Root Ltd.*[615] An earlier decision of the Court of Appeal, *Hammond v Commissioner of Police for the Metropolis*[616] was disapproved and over-ruled.

In *Spencer-Franks*, the pursuer was required to inspect and repair the closing **12–182** mechanism on the door of the central control room on an oil rig in the North Sea. In the course of his inspection the linkage arm of the closer unexpectedly came free under tension and struck him in the face, causing injury. He sued both his employer, a supplier of services to the offshore industry, and the operators of the rig relying on breaches of the Work Equipment Regulations. The basic issues on appeal were whether the door closer was "work equipment" within the meaning of reg.2(1); and if it was, whether the pursuer was "using" it when injured. The underlying problems were whether the pursuer's employers could be liable for breach of regulation when he was working on a piece of apparatus which did not belong to them and whether the rig operators could be liable for any breach to a

---

[610] reg.3(3)(a) and (b). Thus the occupier of a school was held liable under reg.6 of Provision and Use of Work Equipment Regulations 1992 to the claimant, an employee of a contractor to whom it loaned a defective ladder to enable him to carry out work at its premises: *Donaldson v Brighton District Council* [2002] C.L.Y. 2241, the employers were also found liable for different reasons.
[611] *Knowles v Liverpool City Council* [1993] 1 W.L.R. 1428, HL.
[612] Workplace (Health, Safety & Welfare) Regulations 1992 reg.3(3), see para.12–120, above.
[613] *Duncanson v South Ayrshire Council*, 1999 S.L.T. 519, OH.
[614] See e.g. *Beck v United Closures & Plastics Plc* 2001 S.L.T. 1299, OH: heavy doors which had frequently to be opened to enable machinery to start up were "equipment" for the purposes of the Regulations; *Wright v Romford Blinds and Shutters* [2003] EWHC 1165: a van and roof rack were work equipment. Contrast *Wallis v Balfour Beatty Rail Maintenance Ltd* (2003) S.J.L.B. 357, CA, n.94 above, where it was not certain that a lock and key were work equipment.
[615] [2008] P.I.Q.R. P21, HL
[616] [2005] P.I.Q.R. P1, CA.

third party, not someone they employed. It was held unanimously that both basic issues should be answered in the pursuer's favour, although the routes taken by their Lordships in reaching this result were not identical.

12–183   In relation to the issue "work equipment or not", Lord Hoffmann pointed to the test as set out in reg.2: if the apparatus involved was for use at work it was work equipment. Since the door and its closer were used to enter and leave the control room they were for use at work. He rejected a suggestion that a door was not equipment because it forms part of the structure of the premises concerned; the distinction might be valid in relation to premises on land, but given the regulatory background the situation was otherwise offshore. The Court of Appeal, in *Hammond*, had been wrong to focus on reg.4 as defining the ambit of reg.2: it was the latter which defined what was work equipment and reg.4 then determined whether the Regulations applied to the particular item of work equipment in question. Lord Hoffmann went on to deal with the question discussed in *Hammond*, whether an employer could be in breach of the Regulations when his employees were repairing work equipment which was the property of a third party. He said not because the Regulations had to be construed by reference to the European Directive[617] which lay behind them: that made clear that the employer's duty was intended to arise in relation to work equipment provided for the undertaking in which the claimant was working. If it was provided for another, third party's, undertaking, liability would not arise. On the facts of *Spencer-Franks* the pursuer could succeed against the rig operator because the door closer was provided for use in its undertaking and the duties imposed by reg.3(3)(b) extended to a person having control of the relevant equipment. Whether he could also recover against his employer was academic and would depend whether the platform could be regarded as the site of an undertaking by the employers, which would depend on the arrangements between the employer and the operator, of which evidence was lacking.

12–184   Lord Rodger expressed the view that "work equipment" was any apparatus which performed a useful, practical purpose in an employer's undertaking. It followed that he, too, rejected the reasoning in *Hammond* and the distinction between that which an employee might be working on, as opposed to that which he was using for his work. He accepted that the door was work equipment because it was used as a means of access by employees to part of their place of work. The pursuer was using the work equipment in the course of his repair. The operators were at least potentially liable under reg.3(3)(b). Lord Mance, with whom Lord Neuberger agreed, considered that the pursuer could not recover against his employer: by reference to Lord Rodger's test, the door was not fulfilling a useful practical function in relation to the pursuer's employer's undertaking. He could, however, recover against the rig operator where the position was otherwise: given that the door closer was work equipment in the operator's business, its duty extended to employees of a third party such as the

---

[617] 89/655/EEC. See para.12–173, above.

pursuer. All had little difficulty with the proposition that the pursuer was using the door at the time of his accident.[618]

Equipment provided by the employee. In *Couzens v T McGee & Co Ltd*,[619]   **12–185**
the claimant driver was injured when his lorry overturned as a result of the excessive speed at which he had been driving it. He claimed that he had been unable to move his right foot from the accelerator to the brake as a piece of metal kept by him in the side pocket of the driver's door as a makeshift tool had caught in his trouser leg. It was held that the piece of metal was not work equipment where it was provided by the driver himself and his employer did not know of it. An item of equipment not supplied by an employer would not be "work equipment" for the purposes of the Regulations unless the employer expressly or impliedly permitted its use or must be deemed to have permitted its use.

Use. Regulation 3(2) provides that the requirements imposed by the Regula-   **12–186**
tions on an employer in relation to work equipment "shall apply to such equipment provided for use or used by an employee at work". Factors that may determine whether equipment was used "at work" were reviewed in a case where an employee suffered injury at the end of her working day when using a lift that was located in the common parts of a building occupied by her employers and others. Notwithstanding that the claimant had left her employers' offices before she used the lift, that it was outside her employers' control, and not for their employees' exclusive use, she was using the lift at work for purposes of reg.3(2). Among the factors idenitified as relevant in deciding whether equipment was being "used at work"were whether an employee was acting in the course of employment; also spatial or geographical limitation upon the places at which, and hence the equipment to which, the duty attached. The degree of control exercised over the equipment by the employer might also assist in the decision whether the equipment was being used at work within the meaning of the regulations.[620] Difficult questions may arise as an employee becomes more remote from their place of work or where there is no single, regular place of work.

In *Smith v Northamptonshire County Council*,[621] the House of Lords held, by   **12–187**
a majority, that a local authority was not liable under the Regulations when a

---

[618] See further, Clarke, "Work equipment is under control" 152 S.J. 16; Gold and Dixey, "PUWER to the people" 158 N.L.J. 1480. A faulty drinks dispensing machine which was held to be "work equipment" when it was available for use by employees such as the claimant, even though she was not herself actually using it at the time it emitted a flash, causing her to jump back and fall heavily: *Given v James Watt College*, 2007 S.L.T. 39, OH.
[619] [2009] P.I.Q.R. P14, CA.
[620] *Reid v PRP Architects (A Firm)* [2007] P.I.Q.R. P4, CA. In *Spencer-Franks v Kellogg Brown & Root Ltd*, n.579, above, Lord Hoffmann observed that there may be a good argument that the Work Equipment Regulations did not apply to equipment which actually formed part of land-based work premises, because duties in relation to the state of such premises were the subject of the Workplace (Health Safety and Welfare) Regulations 1992. It was otherwise in relation to an offshore oil platform to which the Workplace Regulations did not apply. The closing mechanism on an internal door on the platform could therefore be work equipment.
[621] [2009] P.I.Q.R. P17, HL. See also McDonald, "Making a connection", 159 N.L.J. 989; Patten, "Seizing control", 159 N.L.J. 773; Preston, "Debating the PUWER lines", 159 N.L.J. 883 and Dearden, "Slippery Slope" 153 S.J. 6.

ramp, installed by a third party at the home of someone whom the claimant, its employee, visited in the course of her work as a carer/driver, gave way causing her to fall. The issues were whether the ramp was "work equipment" as defined by reg.2(1); and whether it was "provided for use or [was] used by" the claimant at work so as to come within reg.3(2). The Regulations had to be interpreted to accord with the European Directive.[622] A specific nexus, beyond the mere fact of use, was required between the equipment and the employer's undertaking before the employer would come under the strict responsibilities imposed by the Regulations. They applied to equipment which was incorporated into, and adopted, as part of the employer's undertaking, and which was provided to the employee either by the employer or by someone else with the employer's consent. They were intended to impose absolute liability on an employer in a wide, but not infinitely wide, range of factual circumstances. The employer was not, on the facts of the instant case, liable where it had no control over the ramp, and it had no involvement in the way it was used or the management or supervision of its use and where it had not been incorporated into or adopted as part of the authority's undertaking.

12–188   In relation to work equipment, *use* "means any activity involving work equipment and includes starting, stopping, programming, setting, transporting, repairing, modifying, maintaining, servicing and cleaning".[623] This definition appears to be all encompassing.

12–189   **Exclusions.** Ships' work equipment is substantially excluded[624] from the Regulations on the basis that protection is provided elsewhere.[625]

12–190   **Suitability of work equipment.** Regulation 4 of the Work Equipment Regulations 1998 provides that employers shall ensure that work equipment is so constructed or adapted as to be suitable for the purpose for which it is used or provided. Regulation 4(2) provides assistance with regard to the question of "suitability" by charging an employer with having regard to the working conditions[626] and the risks to the health and safety of persons existing in premises or an undertaking in which the work equipment is to be used and any additional risk posed by the use of that equipment. Regulation 4(4)(a) defines "suitable" in this context as meaning "in any respect in which it is reasonably foreseeable will affect the health or safety of any person."[627] This is another example of the

---

[622] The Work Equipment Directive, 89/655/EEC, para.12–173, above.
[623] Work Equipment Regulations 1998 reg.2(1).
[624] reg.3(6).
[625] The Merchant Shipping (Guarding of Machinery and Safety of Electrical Equipment) Regulations 1988 and the Merchant Shipping (Hatches and Lifting Plant) Regulations 1988.
[626] *Yorkshire Traction Co Ltd v Searby* [2003] EWCA Civ 1856 where, in relation to the identically worded reg.5 of the Work Equipment Regulations 1992, it was held that "conditions" involved assessment of the degree of risk posed by the alleged shortcoming: in relation to a public service vehicle, consideration of the conditions in which it was used including the number and likely behaviour of passengers and other road users.
[627] A limited exclusion is provided in respect of offensive weapons and items used for arrest or restraint provided to the police and used in the execution of their duty: reg.4(4)(b). Such items have to be considered with regard to the health and safety of the policeman only.

requirement of an employer to undertake risk assessment, here specifically with regard to work equipment.[628]

ILLUSTRATIONS

A ladder which was too close to horizontal was unsuitable[629]; a tall vacuum cleaner was unsuitable for an employee of short and slight build[630]; a van roof on which an employee was expected to stand for loading purposes was unsuitable through want of guardrails[631]; a suspended ladder giving access to the upper of two bunks which was held in position by retaining bars was not suitable where there was a risk that, if not placed properly within the bars, it might come away in use.[632] **12–191**

Contrast a key which was suitable for its purpose when it operated one particular kind of lock on a fence even though it did not operate another kind.[633] Rescue equipment used by a firefighter, which included a ram, was not unsuitable by reason of the claimant being unfamiliar with it despite the fact it was thereby dangerous for him to use.[634]

The concepts of safety and risk involved in regs 4(1) and 4(2) have been held to require a court to reach a view as to what was reasonably foreseeable.[635] Thus, where the claimant was working from a scaffolding tower to whose base no stabilisers or outriggers had been fixed[636] and, in a fit of temper, his workmate pushed the tower over causing the claimant to suffer serious injury, it was held that it was not reasonably foreseeable that the workmate would have behaved as he did. **12–192**

It is to been held that reg.4 is concerned with the physical condition of work equipment on the basis that it is used by an employee properly trained to use it.[637] Thus, if injury results from a want of training in the use of otherwise perfectly suitable equipment, there is no breach of reg.4.[638] **12–193**

---

[628] The point was emphasised in *Yorkshire Traction Co Ltd v Searby*, n.626 above. Where there was no screen separating a public service vehicle driver from his passengers, thus protecting him from the risk of assault, which risk materialised, the court was unable to conclude that the bus driven by the claimant was unsuitable for use in the manner contemplated by the Regulations.

[629] *Wharf v Bildwell Insulations Ltd* [1999] C.L.Y. 2047.

[630] *Watson v Warwickshire CC* [2001] C.L.Y. 3302.

[631] *Wright v Romford Blinds and Shutters* [2003] EWHC 1165.

[632] *Robb v Salamis (M&I) Ltd* [2007] 2 All E.R. 97, HL, para.12–224, below.

[633] *Wallis v Balfour Beatty Rail Maintenance* (2003) S.J.L.B. 357, CA.

[634] *Pennington v Surrey CC and Surrey Fire and Rescue Service* [2007] P.I.Q.R. P11, CA. The defendants were thereby in breach of reg.11(2)(d), now repealed (the provision of information, instruction, training and supervision in relation to dangerous parts of machinery): see generally, para.12–202, below.

[635] *Horton v Taplin Contracts Ltd* [2003] P.I.Q.R. P180, CA where the identically worded reg.5(1) and (2) in the Work Equipment Regulations 1992 were under consideration. See also *Robb v Salamis (M&I)* n.632 above.

[636] *Horton v Taplin Contracts Ltd* [2003] P.I.Q.R. P180, CA. Held not to be a breach of reg.20 of Work Equipment Regulations 1992. Now reg.20 of the 1998 Regulations.

[637] *Griffiths v Vauxhall Motors* [2003] EWCA Civ 412: a torque gun was suitable in the hands of the correct operator.

[638] But breaches of regs 8 and 9 (information, instruction and training: see para.12–202, below) may be made out.

12–194   **Conditions.** Regulation 4(3) also imposes the duty on an employer to ensure that work equipment is only used for suitable operations and under suitable conditions.[639] Use of the word "ensure" in reg.4(3) does not impose an absolute duty upon an employer in the event that an accident occurs while work equipment is being used.[640]

12–195   **Maintenance.** Regulation 5(1) provides:

> "Every employer shall ensure that work equipment is maintained in an efficient state, in efficient working order and in good repair."

Efficiency, as under the old law,[641] relates to efficiency from the point of view of safety and not productivity or economy.[642]

12–196   The language of reg.5(1) is taken directly from s.151(1) of the Factories Act 1937. In *Galashiels Gas Co Ltd v O'Donnell*,[643] the House of Lords held that it imposed strict liability in respect of a lift which failed without warning, acknowledging the heavy burden on the employer that this imposed.[644] The obligation was to have the lift "in efficient working order" at the time of the accident as well as at other times.[645]

12–197   In *Stark v The Post Office*,[646] an attempt was made to argue that the words of reg.6(1) of the Provision and Use of Work Equipment Regulations 1992 (identical to reg.5(1) of the Work Equipment Regulations 1998) could not have been intended to have the same effect of imposing an absolute duty in respect of all work equipment. In the past, it was said, the words had been applied to dangerous equipment only (such as lifts and hoists) and the burden imposed on an employer would be intolerable if its application was extended to all work equipment. This argument was rejected by the Court of Appeal on the basis that the drafting was consistent with the Work Equipment Directive which imposed minimum standards only and that the language, in any event, must be taken as having been used in the sense that it had been construed since *Galashiels Gas Co*

---

[639] Where an employer failed to provide handholds in a van for prison officers who were transporting prisoners between prison and court, the van was either unsuitable work equipment or, alternatively, it was used in unsafe conditions: *Crane v Premier Prison Services Ltd* [2001] C.L.Y. 3298. It has been held that the word "suitable" is not an invitation to the court to consider all the circumstances, in particular what suitable equipment would have cost: *Skinner v Scottish Ambulance Service* [2004] S.L.T. 834, Ex. Div.

[640] *Reid v Sundolitt Ltd* 2007 Rep. L.R. 90, (Ex Div) (the claimant was injured when he climbed into a bin to compress scraps of plastic, a practice his employer had done its best to discourage).

[641] *Payne v Weldless Steel Tube Co Ltd* [1956] 1 Q.B. 196.

[642] See, e.g. the ACOP para.20, to the Workplace (Health, Safety & Welfare) Regulations 1992. See also *Atkins v Connex South Eastern Ltd* [2004] C.L.Y. 1812: a railway signalling system was not in an efficient state or efficient working order for the purposes of reg.5 when it went into fail-safe mode changing all signals to red.

[643] [1949] A.C. 275.

[644] *Galashiels Gas Co Ltd v O'Donnell* [1949] A.C. 275 per Lord Morton at 283.

[645] *Galashiels Gas Co Ltd v O'Donnell* [1949] A.C. 275 per Lord McDonald at 287, Lord Reid rejecting the employer's argument that such an interpretation made the employer an insurer as it was still necessary for the worker to show that he was injured as a result of the breach alleged: at 291.

[646] [2000] P.I.Q.R. P105, CA.

Ltd v O'Donnell.[647] Thus the claimant, who was injured when the stirrup of the brake of his Post Office issue cycle failed causing the cycle to stop abruptly with the result that he was catapulted over the handlebars, succeeded notwithstanding the fact that the defect was one never known to have occurred previously and could not have been detected by any reasonable inspection.

This decision therefore confirms that reg.5(1) imposes strict liability in respect of work equipment which fails, even if the part failing is an expendable part known to fail periodically without necessarily affecting the overall functioning of the machine.[648] Even where it is proved that an accident was caused by mechanical defect, but the exact defect cannot be identified, a breach is established with no burden resting on the claimant to prove by inference or otherwise what the precise problem was.[649] The Court of Appeal has further said that the focus of these Regulations is upon general considerations of safety, viewed against the broad risk of accidental injury inherent in the use of machinery which was not maintained in good repair and efficient working order, rather than on foreseeability of "identified risks". Thus, in appropriate circumstances, the fact that the type of accident which occurred was unforeseeable did not prevent reg.5 from biting.[650] The difficulties formerly facing claimants, who were met with the argument that the failure was due to a latent defect, no longer exist. Nor will an employer be helped by proving that he had as comprehensive a system of inspection and maintenance as could be imagined. On the other hand, a purely transitory condition, such as rainwater on the step of a public service vehicle, has been held not to amount to a failure to maintain either the step or the vehicle.[651] **12–198**

Regulation 3(5) of the Work Equipment Regulations 1998 does not impose the duties owed to workers contained in the Regulations on the seller or supplier of work equipment (unlike s.17 of the Factories Act 1961[652]). However, the Supply **12–199**

---

[647] [2000] P.I.Q.R. P105, CA per Waller L.J. at P112, P113.

[648] *Ball v Street* [2005] P.I.Q.R. P342, para.12–176 above.

[649] *Budden v Police Aviation Service Ltd* [2005] P.I.Q.R. P362,: it was proved on the balance of probabilities that a fatal helicopter crash had been caused by a mechanical defect which could not be identified; see also *Hislop v Lynx Express Parcels* 2003 S.L.T. 785: the spontaneous detachment of a radiator cap from a vehicle engine was a sufficient proof of breach of reg.6(1) of Provision and Use of Work Equipment Regulations 1992 (now reg.5(1) of the Work Equipment Regulations).

[650] *Hislop* n.649 above. The defendant was found liable to the claimant subject to 75 per cent contributory negligence for the latter's failure to wear safety goggles or note that the machinery was defective. The court rejected an argument based on *Fytche v Wincanton Logistics Plc* [2005] P.I.Q.R. P61, HL, a decision in relation to reg.7 of the Personal Protective Equipment at Work Regulations 1992, see paras 12–124, above and 12–235, below, where it was said that the words "efficient state, in efficient working order and in good repair" in that context did not create an absolute concept but had to be construed in relation to what made the equipment personal protective equipment, i.e. by reference to its purpose of protecting against the relevant risk. See Walsh, "Strict but fair" 148 S.J. (28) 842.

[651] *Green v Yorkshire Traction* [2001] EWCA Civ 1925.

[652] Which included the commission of an offence by the seller of new machinery which did not comply with the provisions of the Act, although such a seller was not liable as a joint tortfeasor to anyone injured as a result of the breach of duty: *Biddle v Truvox Engineering Co Ltd* [1952] 1 K.B. 101.

of Machinery (Safety) Regulations 1992[653] do impose duties on suppliers requiring them to satisfy the employer's health and safety requirements.[654] Although the Employer's Liability (Defective Equipment) Act 1969[655] enables an injured employee to bring an action directly against his employer in respect of equipment which is defective on supply, the employer will now be liable under reg.5(1) in any event thus rendering the usefulness of the 1969 Act otiose. The employer's right to seek redress from such a supplier will, of course, be preserved.

12–200   Regulation 5(2) also imposes a duty to ensure that any maintenance log for machinery is kept up to date. The Provision and Use of Work Equipment Regulations 1992 did not impose any duty to keep such a log but only to keep any maintenance log that existed up to date.[656] However, reg.6 of the Work Equipment Regulations 1998 imposes new duties with regard to inspection of work equipment where its safety depends on the installation conditions[657] or where work equipment is exposed to conditions causing deterioration liable to result in dangerous situations.[658] In either case the employer must record and keep (until the next inspection) a record of the inspection.[659] Inspection is defined as constituting such visual or more rigorous inspection by a competent person as is appropriate, to include testing.[660] Power presses, equipment for lifting loads, winding apparatus, work equipment required to be inspected by reg.29 of the Construction (Health, Safety & Welfare) Regulations 1996 and work equipment to which reg.12 of the Work at Height Regulations 2005[661] applies are excluded on the basis that other more detailed provision is made in those cases.[662] Regulation 6 of the Work Equipment Regulations 1998 appears, therefore, to go a significant, if not complete, way to cure the previous omission of any requirement to keep a log where none previously existed.

12–201   Regulation 22[663] requires employers to take appropriate measures, within the limits of reasonable practicability, to ensure that work equipment can be maintained without exposing the person concerned to a risk to his health and safety. If such risk cannot be avoided, protective measures must be taken against it. If work equipment is likely to involve a specific risk to health or safety, reg.7(1) requires the employer to restrict both its use and its maintenance to a

---

[653] SI 1992/3073 as amended by the Supply of Machinery (Safety) (Amendment) Regulations 1994, SI 1994/2063, 2004/693 and 2005/831. The amendments were operative from September 1, 1994 with the exception of reg.4 and Sch.2 which came into force on January 1, 1995 and, inter alia, insert a new definition of safety components and impose a general duty on any person supplying machinery to insure it is safe.

[654] It remains to be seen whether the rationale of *Biddle v Truvox Engineering Co Ltd* [1952] 1 K.B. 101 will continue to apply.

[655] See Ch.11, para.11–55, above.

[656] Repeated in the Provision and Use of Work Equipment Regulations 1998 reg.5(2).

[657] reg.6(1).

[658] reg.6(2).

[659] reg.6(3). Such equipment must not leave an employer's undertaking or be borrowed without physical evidence of the last inspection: reg.6(4).

[660] reg.2(1).

[661] SI 2005/735: inserted by reg.17.

[662] reg.6(5).

[663] Which replaces s.16 of the Factories Act 1961.

limited class of persons, namely those given the task of using it[664] and those designated maintenance duties[665] and, in the latter case, adequate training must have previously been given.[666]

Information, instructions and training. Regulations 8 and 9 of the Work   **12–202** Equipment Regulations 1998 can be read together imposing the responsibility on the employer to ensure that persons using work equipment have both adequate health and safety information[667] and have received training encompassing the risks involved in the use of the equipment and the precautions to take.[668] A primary breach of these regulations, of course, only gives rise to a claim for damages if the breach caused some damage.[669] Like provision is made in respect of those responsible for supervising or managing the use of work equipment.[670] "Information" is required to include the conditions in which, and the methods by which, the work equipment may be used together with "foreseeable abnormal situations" and how to react to them.[671] Such information must be readily comprehensible to those to whom it is imparted.[672] It has been held that the duty to train, imposed by reg.13(2) of the Woodworking Machines Regulations 1974, includes the duty to appraise whether the workman understood the instructions and the dangers of the machine.[673] For details of the matters to which an employer must have regard in making the assessment involved in discharging these duties, reference should be made to the Guidance.[674] Clarity of controls, markings and warnings is required by regs 17(1), 23 and 24.

Dangerous parts of machinery. Regulation 11 of the Work Equipment   **12–203** Regulations 1998 swept away ss.12 to 16 of the Factories Act 1961 and, with it, a huge body of case law.[675] Regulation 11 provides the measures which employers must take to prevent access to any dangerous part of machinery (or

---

[664] Work Equipment Regulations 1998 reg.7(1)(a).

[665] reg.7(1)(b).

[666] reg.7(2).

[667] reg.8(1). To include written instructions, where appropriate. A breach of reg.8 was found where the need to use a run-off table in conjunction with a bench saw could and should have been identified, with appropriate instruction given: *Sherlock v Chester CC* [2004] EWCA Civ 210.

[668] reg.9(1). For an example, see *Hamilton v Malcolm Group Ltd* [2007] 10 C.L. 197 (it was insufficient compliance with reg.9 for the claimant to be given a written risk assessment advising that operatives should stand back when trying to lock a bar under tension at the side of a trailer; the regulation created an absolute duty to provide adequate training and proper practical training in securing the bar was required).

[669] For a discussion of a similar duty under the Noise at Work Regulations 1989 (SI 1989/1790) as amended, see *Harris v BRB (Residuary) Ltd* [2005] I.C.R. 1680; [2006] P.I.Q.R. P101, CA: train driver would have asked for ear protection had he been given any "information, instruction or training".

[670] regs 8(2) and 9(2).

[671] reg.8(3).

[672] reg.8(4).

[673] *Tasci v Pekalp of London Ltd, The Times*, January 17, 2001, CA: Kurdish refugee with limited English of whose origin and status the employer was aware. It was likely that the workman had been economical with the truth about his previous experience and a prudent employer should have treated him as a complete novice.

[674] paras 84 and 85.

[675] For a full treatment of these repealed provisions, see the 8th edn of this work: Ch.11, paras 11–94–11–111.

rotating stock bar) or to stop the movement of such parts before the employee enters a danger zone. Fixed guards and other protection devices must be provided but subject to a requirement of practicability. This latter requirement represents a shortfall in the implementation of the Work Equipment Directive[676] and, further, the replacement of absolute duties without the qualification of practicability to be found in the 1961 Act.[677] All such guards must, inter alia, be suitable for their purpose, of good construction, sound material and adequate strength, and maintained in an efficient state, efficient working order and good repair.[678] "Danger zone" is defined as any zone in or around machinery in which a person is exposed to contact with a dangerous part.[679] "Machinery" is not defined in the Regulations and decisions under the Factories Act may continue to provide guidance.

Illustrations

12–204   A rope way consisting of an overhead travelling cable with large buckets attached at regular intervals, used for transporting materials was "plant" and not "machinery"[680]; a safety hook with its moving safety device was not a part of any machinery required to be fenced.[681]

On the other hand, a mobile crane was machinery[682]; a grinding machine with an 8ft-long flexible shaft connecting the 7-inch cutting wheel to a small portable electrical motor which could be plugged into any convenient electricity supply, was machinery and required to be fenced[683]; likewise the bit of an electric drill.[684]

12–205   **Whether machinery is dangerous.** There may still be some relevance in the cases under the 1961 Act which dealt with the concept of dangerousness in relation to machinery. What was a dangerous part of machinery was a question of degree and fact.[685] Wills J. suggested the following test:

"Machinery or parts of machinery is and are dangerous if in the ordinary course of human affairs danger may be reasonably be anticipated from the use of them without

---

[676] 89/655/EEC.

[677] Arguably, the failure to implement the Directive in full would enable an employee of the State or one of its emanations to enforce the Directive against the employer, rather than the Regulations as framed: see Redgrave's *Health and Safety* (6th edn, 2008). Furthermore, a UK court may be prepared to treat the duty imposed by the Directive as equivalent to a duty of common law, particularly where the legislation which the Regulations supersede impose a more exacting standard for that which they provide.

[678] See paras 12–124–12–127, above for a discussion of the meaning of this phrase.

[679] Work Equipment Regulations 1998 reg.11(5).

[680] *Quintas v National Smelting Co Ltd* [1961] 1 W.L.R. 401.

[681] *Mirza v Ford Motor Co Ltd* [1981] I.C.R. 757, CA.

[682] *Liptrot v British Railways Board* [1969] A.C. 136.

[683] *Lovelidge v Anselm Odling & Sons Ltd* [1967] 2 Q.B. 351.

[684] *Millard v Serck Tubes* [1969] 1 W.L.R. 211.

[685] *Carr v Mercantile Produce Ltd* [1949] 2 K.B. 601. In *Hindle v Birtwistle* [1987] 1 Q.B. 192 at 196, Wright J. said: "The mere fact that the shuttle will sometimes fly out, and that when it flies out it is dangerous, is not enough. It is a question of degree and fact in all cases whether the tendency to fly out is a tendency to fly out often enough to satisfy a reasonable interpretation of the word 'dangerous' ". Also see *Carr v Mercantile Produce Co* [1949] 2 K.B. 601 and *Close v Steel Company of Wales Ltd* [1962] A.C. 367.

protection. No doubt it would be impossible to say that because an accident had happened once therefore the machinery was dangerous. On the other hand, it is equally out of the question to say that machinery cannot be dangerous unless it is so in the course of careful working. In considering whether machinery is dangerous, the contingency of carelessness on the part of the workmen in charge of it, and the frequency with which that contingency is likely to arise, are matters that must be taken into consideration."[686]

In a later case this test was adopted and extended by du Parcq J. who said: **12–206**

"a part of machinery is dangerous if it is a possible cause of injury to anybody acting in a way in which a human being may be reasonably expected to act in circumstances which may be reasonably be expected to occur."[687]

Lord Cooper commented:

"The necessary and sufficient condition for the emergence of the duty to fence imposed by section [14] of the Factories Act is that some part of some machinery should be 'dangerous'. The question is not whether the occupiers of the factory knew that it was dangerous; nor whether a factory inspector had so reported; nor whether previous accidents had occurred; nor whether the victims of these accidents had, or had not, been contributorily negligent. The test is objective and impersonal. Is the part such in its character, and so circumstanced in its position, exposure, method of operation and the like, that in the ordinary course of human affairs danger may reasonably be anticipated from its use unfenced, not only to the prudent, alert and skilled operative intent upon his task, but also to the careless or inattentive worker whose inadvertent or indolent conduct may expose him to risk, injury or death from the unguarded part?"[688]

A machine is dangerous if danger should reasonably be anticipated from its use without protection.[689]

---

[686] *Hindle v Birtwistle* [1987] 1 Q.B. 192 at 195, approved by the HL in *Close v Steel Company of Wales Ltd* [1962] A.C. 367. See the comment on this by Slesser L.J. in *Higgins v Harrison* (1932) 25 B.W. C.C. 113 at 125. Also, *Stimpson v Standard Telephones and Cable* [1940] 1 K.B. 342 at 360.

[687] *Walker v Bletchley Flettons Ltd* [1937] 1 All E.R. 170 at 175. Later explained in *Stimpson v Standard Telephones and Cables Ltd.* Lord Reid in *John Summers & Sons Ltd v Frost* [1955] A.C. 740 suggested the substitution for "possible" or "reasonably foreseeable cause of injury". See also *Carey v Ocean Coal Co* [1938] 1 K.B. 365; *Williams v Sykes & Harrison Ltd* [1955] 1 W.L.R. 1180, *Crowe v James Scott & Sons Ltd*, 1965 S.L.T. 54 (applying the test laid down by Clauson L.J. in *Youngman v Pirelli General Cableworks Ltd* [1940] 1 K.B. 1 at 28).

[688] *Mitchell v N. British Rubber Co* 1945 S.C.(J) 69 at 73, quoted with approval by Lord Reid in *John Summers & Sons Ltd v Frost* [1955] A.C. 740 at 766.

[689] per Lord Caldecote C.J. in *Kinder v Camberwell Corp* [1944] 2 All E.R. 315 at 317: hand-operated pressing machine injured workman, owing to handle unexpectedly springing up-machines of that type were never fenced and had been used without accident for 20 years—evidence that handle might fly up if wiring improperly done, wire broke, or too much paper put into machine: breach of s.14 made out. There was a breach of reg.11(2)(d) of the Work Equipment Regulations where a fireman trapped his hand in a pinch point within moving parts of a ram which he was using to free a trapped driver from the cab of his lorry: *Pennington v Surrey County Council* [2007] P.I.Q.R. P11, CA.

12–207   Whether a machine could be held to be dangerous in connection with the material or article on it was considered by Pearce L.J. in *Eaves v Morris Motors*,[690] where he said:

> "Although *Bulloch v G. John Power (Agencies) Ltd*[691] does not allow us to equate dangers from the nature of the material (namely, the sharp edge of the bolts) to dangers from the machinery, it does not compel us when deciding whether machinery is dangerous to disregard the nature of the machine when it is doing its normal appointed task or from holding it to be dangerous if that task clearly involves danger from its juxtaposition with its normal material. If a moving arm of the machine does not project and is therefore safe when the machine is empty, but projects dangerously when the machine is supplied with its proper material, it can obviously be labelled as dangerous machinery. And if it creates a dangerous nip when supplied with its normal material and when working normally (or in a foreseeable manner) I see no reason in principle why the court cannot consider the machinery dangerous, even if that nip is only created by the juxtaposition of material and machinery. For in that case it is not the nature of the material and it is not the material itself which causes the danger. The danger is caused by the design of the machine itself working normally with harmless material."

12–208   In *Midland and Low Moor Iron & Steel Co v Cross*,[692] it was held that the question, whether a part of machinery was a dangerous part within the meaning of s.14(1), had to be determined on consideration of the machine when in normal operation doing the work which it was designed to do ordinarily. Accordingly, it was held that the leading-in rollers of a power-driven hand-fed bar-straightening machine, where there was created a dangerous nip between them and the moving metal bar that was being fed in, ought to have been fenced.

12–209   Machinery was dangerous where it was a reasonably foreseeable source of injury to a person,[693] even someone acting carelessly, if the carelessness was of a kind which may reasonably be expected to occur. If the claimant's carelessness was outside ordinary expectation, the fact that the machine had caused an injury was not conclusive proof that it was a dangerous machine.[694]

12–210   The obligation under s.14(1) to fence securely did not require that materials or articles should be fenced.[695] Regulation 12(1) of the Work Equipment Regulations 1998, however, requires an employer to take measures to ensure that a person using work equipment is prevented from being exposed to specified

---

[690] [1961] 2 Q.B. 385 at 395, 396, approved in *Midland & Low Moor Iron & Steel Co Ltd v Cross* [1965] A.C. 343 at 369.
[691] [1956] 1 W.L.R. 171.
[692] [1965] A.C. 343.
[693] In *John Summers & Sons Ltd v Frost* [1955] A.C. 740, the HL gave its general approval to this test of "reasonable foreseeability of injury". In *Close v Steel Company of Wales Ltd* [1962] A.C. 367 the "foreseeability" test was treated as the usual approach.
[694] e.g. see *Higgins v Harrison* (1932) 25 B.W.C.C. 113 (girl placed hand in moving machine having been told to pick up capsules from the floor. On it being established that there had been four similar unfenced machines in use for 16 years without incident or requirement from the factory inspector that they should be fenced, it was held that the machines were not dangerous machines); see also *Carr v Mercantile Produce Co* [1929] 2 Q.B. 601. These are both harsh cases of dubious contemporary authority.
[695] *Eaves v Morris Motors* [1961] 2 Q.B. 385 following *Nicholls v Austin (Leyton) Ltd* [1946] A.C. 493, and *Bullock v G. John Power (Agencies) Ltd* [1956] 1 W.L.R. 171.

hazards which, in the event of this not being reasonably practicable, must be adequately controlled. The hazards are specified by reg.12(3) and include the fall or rejection of articles from work equipment as well as the disintegration of parts of the equipment itself.

Nature of duty to fence. The duty to fence imposed by ss.12, 13 and 14 of the 1961 Act was an absolute one.[696] In comparison, as already mentioned, the 1998 Regulations impose a limit of practicability to the duty to take preventative measures and thereby appear to fall short of the Directive they are supposed to implement.[697]   **12–211**

Which machinery? The machinery referred to in ss.12, 13 and 14 meant machinery used[698] in the factory for the work carried on there and not, for instance, machinery made[699] or repaired for others in the course of the factory's ordinary work, unless it became part of the factory's installation.[700] Again by way of comparison, under the Work Equipment Regulations 1998 machinery falls to be considered as work equipment, as defined by reg.2(1).[701] Machinery under the Act was not "in use" if it was accidentally put in motion during repair,[702] but this eventuality would now be covered by reg.22 of the 1998 Regulations.[703]   **12–212**

To keep workmen out and not the machine in. The duty to fence under the 1961 Act was an obligation to screen or shield the machine so as to prevent the body of the operator from coming into contact with it, and did not include the duty of protecting the operator from being struck by any flying part of the machine itself or of the material on which the machine is working.[704] The distinction does not arise under the Regulations and many of the old cases would be decided differently. Thus, when transmission machinery was fenced but the fencing did not extend all the way up to the top of the overhead driving shaft and while the machine was being worked the belt broke, lashed out over the fence and struck the operator, there was held to be no breach of s.13.[705] It is probable that there would now be a breach of reg.12(1) of the Work Equipment Regulations 1998, subject to any defence of reasonable practicability and proof of adequate control measures. Likewise, where a workman was struck and   **12–213**

---

[696] *John Summers & Sons Ltd v Frost* [1955] A.C. 740; *Miller v William Boothman & Sons Ltd* [1944] K.B. 337; *Groves v Wimborne* [1898] 2 Q.B. 402; *Dunn v Birds Eye Foods Ltd* [1959] 2 Q.B. 265. The ambit of the duty to fence as interpreted by the courts was summarised by Lord Hailsham in *F.E. Callow (Engineers) Ltd v Johnson* [1971] A.C. 335 at 341–343.

[697] See para.12–203, above.

[698] See *Irwin v White, Tompkins & Courage Ltd* [1964] 1 W.L.R. 387 (sack hoist in use when installed but not in full commercial operation) applied in *Stanbrook v Waterlow Sons* [1964] 1 W.L.R. 825 and *Ballard v Ministry of Defence* [1976] I.C.R. 54.

[699] *Parvin v Morton Machine Co* [1952] A.C. 515.

[700] *Thurogood v Van den Berghs & Jurgens Ltd* [1951] 2 K.B. 537; *TBA Industrial Products Ltd v Laine* [1987] I.C.R. 75, DC.

[701] See para.12–180, above.

[702] *Horne v Lec Refrigeration* [1965] 2 All E.R. 898.

[703] See para.12–201, above.

[704] *Close v Steel Company of Wales Ltd* [1962] A.C. 367.

[705] *Carroll v Andrews Barclay & Sons Ltd* [1948] A.C. 477.

injured in the eye whilst operating an electric drill, the bit of which suddenly shattered and flung out its broken pieces, there was held to be no breach of the Factories Act.[706] These facts would now give rise to a breach of reg.5(1) of the 1998 Regulations, as already been discussed.[707]

12–214   **Good construction.** The Regulations use this phrase which appeared repeatedly in the Factories Acts. The question of safety was always one of degree in each case, which had to be decided on its own particular facts.[708]

12–215   "Construction" meant the original construction of whatever was in question as opposed to its subsequent maintenance.[709] "Sound construction" meant well made for what the article was and did not mean good or sound construction for some practicable purpose.[710] It did not include design.[711] It is doubtful whether any distinction can be drawn between the actual materials used in construction and the thing itself. There did not appear to be any difference between "good", "sound" and "substantial" construction, but "good mechanical construction" probably limited the construction, which had to be good, to such part of the product that could properly be described as mechanical.

12–216   **Sound material.** This phrase was not restricted to material that appeared to be sound on reasonable inspection.[712] There was an absolute duty to use material which was sound, even though it was unsound from a latent defect not discoverable on reasonable examination. The time at which material must be sound was the time of construction: its subsequent deterioration was not a breach of the duty to use sound material.

12–217   **Adequate strength.** This meant strength which was adequate for the work that the occupier of a factory required it to do. Failure of the appliance was prima facie but not conclusive evidence a breach of the requirement that something be of adequate strength: it was open to a factory occupier to prove that failure occurred due to some other cause.[713]

12–218   **Cases decided under the Factories Act.** Examples under the Act may still be of assistance in determining whether a dangerous part of machinery is adequately guarded. A machine was not securely fenced if the workman could get his hand

---

[706] *Close v Steel Company of Wales Ltd* [1962] A.C. 367.
[707] See paras 11–178–11–184, above.
[708] *Payne v Weldless Steel Tube Co Ltd* [1956] 1 Q.B. 196.
[709] *Cole v Blackstone & Co* [1943] K.B. 615.
[710] *Beadsley v United Steel Co* [1951] 1 K.B. 408; cf. *Mayne v Johnstone & Cumbers Ltd* [1947] 2 All E.R. 159. See also *Gledhill v Liverpool Abattoir* [1957] 1 W.L.R. 1028 at 1033: "Good construction" does not import suitability for some particular purpose.
[711] *Gibby v East Grinstead Gas Co* [1944] 1 All E.R. 358, CA; *Hawkins v Westinghouse Brake & Signal Co Ltd* (1959) 109 L.J. 89.
[712] *Whitehead v James Stott Ltd* [1949] 1 K.B. 358.
[713] *Reilly v Beardmore & Co* [1947] S.C. 275.

through the guard without any real difficulty.[714] Where a girl was working on a pastry rolling machine and deliberately put her hand beneath the guard to push some dough against the moving rollers, it was held that the machine was not securely fenced.[715] The words "securely fenced" meant fenced at the time of the accident. A machine fitted with a fence, which was raised at the time of the accident, was not fenced.[716] A guard, which can be lifted or removed, was not a secure fence if it were lifted or removed at the time of the accident.[717] On the other hand, a guard forced off or removed in some exceptional way which was inconsistent with a reasonable use of the machine was not a breach of the statute.

The duty to fence was not discharged by providing the necessary guards for **12–219** securely fencing the machinery and then putting the responsibility for using them upon the workmen.[718] When the guard was one which required adjustment, and the workman was injured because of inaccurate adjustment, the occupier was liable, although the workman was at fault in not making the necessary adjustment[719] but if the duty of making the adjustment were expressly and properly delegated to an experienced workman, who was injured because of his failure to make the necessary adjustment, the defendant was not liable.[720]

Further, a "fence must not merely guard against accident but must be such as **12–220** takes into account human weaknesses which include as well as forgetfulness and inadvertence, an inclination sometimes to run minor risks and to take short cuts. Some degree of recklessness (as well as carelessness) has to be foreseen. The fence need not be constructed so as to keep out a determined man, but I think it must be such as will deter a man who, in pursuit of a short cut, is willing to take a minor risk."[721] If a dangerous machine was securely fenced when working forwards, but remained dangerous when being worked backwards, the duty was not discharged.[722]

When machine cannot be fenced. Even when it is commercially impractica- **12–221** ble or mechanically impossible to fence the machine securely, it is still a breach of duty to leave it unfenced, and a workman who is injured in such circumstances

---

[714] *Wood v London County Council* [1940] 4 All E.R. 149, per Tucker J. the decision was reversed on other grounds [1941] 2 K.B. 232.
[715] *Smith v Chesterfield Co-operative Society* [1953] 1 W.L.R. 370 (60 per cent contributory negligence).
[716] *Smith v Morris Motors Ltd* [1950] 1 K.B. 194.
[717] *Charles v S. Smith & Sons (England) Ltd* [1954] 1 W.L.R. 451.
[718] *Thomas v Thomas Bolton & Sons Ltd* (1928) 139 L.T. 397.
[719] *Lay v D. & L. Studios Ltd* [1944] 1 All E.R. 322; *Vyner v Waldenberg Bros Ltd* [1946] K.B. 50; *Leach v Standard Telephones & Cables* [1966] 1 W.L.R. 1392 (workman set guard much too high on mechanical saw; his breach not wholly co-extensive with his employer's breach, since the guard would not have been fully effective even if set as low as possible. This failure to fence securely was not a duty which the employers could vicariously discharge only through the workman himself).
[720] *Smith v Baveystock & Co* [1945] 1 All E.R. 531.
[721] per Devlin J. in *Quintas v National Smelting Co Ltd* [1960] 1 W.L.R. 217 at 222, reversed on other grounds; [1961] 1 W.L.R. 401.
[722] *Pursell v Clement Talbot Ltd* (1914) 111 L.T. 827.

can recover damages, because "if a machine cannot be securely fenced while remaining commercially practicable or mechanically useful the statute in effect prohibits its use."[723]

12–222   **Defences.** In civil actions,[724] apart from the denial that there had been any breach of statutory duty at all, or, if so, such breach did not cause the claimant's accident,[725] or that the machine in question was one to which the particular section applied,[726] virtually the only remaining defence available is that the accident was caused entirely[727] or partly[728] by the workman's own fault.

12–223   **General safety provisions.** Regulations 14 to 18 of the Work Equipment Regulations 1998 impose duties with regard to controls. These include the requirement that controls are provided to start and control the speed or operating conditions of work equipment and that deliberate action on the control is necessary for any of these activities to occur.[729] Controls to stop work equipment safely must be provided, accessible and given priority over other controls.[730] Work equipment must be fitted with readily accessible emergency stop controls[731] and all controls must be clearly visible and identifiable, there being consequential provisions regarding positioning and warnings whenever equipment is about to start.[732] Regulation 18 provides for control systems to be safe: a control system is not safe unless its operation does not create any increased risk to health and safety. Where appropriate, work equipment must be provided with suitable means of isolation from energy sources with appropriate measures to ensure that the resumption of the energy supply does not expose any person to risk.[733]

---

[723] *Davies v Thomas Owen & Co Ltd* [1919] 2 K.B. 39 approved in *John Summers & Sons Ltd v Frost* [1955] A.C. 740.

[724] For defences generally see further paras 12–62–12–80, and Ch.4, above.

[725] See, e.g. *Fairfield Shipbuilding & Engineering Co Ltd v Hall* [1964] 1 Lloyd's Rep. 73.

[726] e.g. the situation in *TBA Industrial Products Ltd v Laine* [1987] I.C.R. 75, DC.

[727] For an example of a finding of 100 per cent contributory negligence made against a claimant in a breach of a s.14 claim for damages, see *Cope v Nickel Electro* [1980] C.L.Y. 1268, and *Humphries v Silent Channel Products* [1981] C.L.Y. 1209, namely, that they were the sole authors respectively of their injuries. See also *McCreesh v Courtaulds Plc* [1997] P.I.Q.R. P421, CA, where a 100 per cent finding against the worker was varied to 75 per cent on appeal on a basis of evidence that the employers had acquiesced in a dangerous practice.

[728] *Rushton v Turner Bros Asbestos Co* [1960] 1 W.L.R. 96. See also *McGuiness v Key Markets Ltd* (1972) 13 K.I.R. 249, CA (contributory negligence of two-thirds found). But in *Arbuckle v A.W. McIntosh & Co*, 1993 S.L.T. 857, Ct. Sess. OH it was held that the workman's own statutory duty under reg.14(1)(a) of the Woodworking Machines Regulations 1974 only arose once his employers had provided him with a mechanical circular saw with a properly adjusted guard. In *Scott v Kelvin Concrete (Ayrshire)*, 1993 S.L.T. 935 Ct. Sess. OH, no contributory negligence was established against the works manager who failed to operate an isolator button before entering an hydraulic press, in view of his employer's gross breaches of duty in by-passing other safety features on the machine.

[729] Work Equipment Regulations 1998 reg.14(2).

[730] Work Equipment Regulations 1998 reg.15.

[731] reg.16.

[732] reg.17.

[733] reg.19.

Stability. Regulation 20[734] provides that an employer "shall ensure" that **12–224** work equipment is stabilised. Whilst this wording may tend to imply strict liability, the use of the words "where necessary" have been held to import considerations of foreseeability, "since a step is realistically only 'necessary' when the mischief to be guarded against can be reasonably foreseen".[735] Thus, where it was not reasonably foreseeable that an angry workmate would push over the scaffolding tower on which the claimant was standing, the absence of stabilisers, on an otherwise stable tower, did not give rise to a breach of reg.20.[736] In *Robb v Salamis (M&I) Ltd*,[737] the House of Lords indicated that the same test should be applied to what was "necessary" for purposes of reg.20 as was applied to whether work equipment was "suitable" for purposes of reg.4. The obligation upon the employer under both regulations was to anticipate situations which might give rise to accidents. The employer was not permitted to wait for an accident to happen.

Regulation 21 requires suitable and sufficient lighting to be provided at places **12–225** where work equipment is used. It is not clear what reg.21 adds to reg.8 of the Workplace (Health, Safety and Welfare) Regulations 1992[738] but the duty is clearly a strict one.[739] Regulation 13 provides that both work equipment and articles or substances produced, used or stored at a high or very low temperature have protection so as to prevent injury to any persons.

Mobile work equipment. Regulations 25 to 30 provide measures to minimise **12–226** the risk of injury from mobile work equipment (not separately defined) in terms of suitability,[740] and the prevention of such equipment rolling over.[741] Provision is also made to secure the safety of self-propelled work equipment,[742] whether remote controlled or not,[743] and drive shafts where seizure may involve a risk to safety.[744]

Power presses. Regulations 31 to 35 replace the Power Press Regulations **12–227** 1965[745] and apply to power presses, namely presses or press brakes for the working of metal by means of tools, or for die proving, which are powered and

---

[734] reg.20 provides: "Every employer shall ensure that work equipment or any part of work equipment is stabilised by clamping or otherwise where necessary for purposes of health or safety."
[735] per Bodey J. in *Horton v Taplin Contracts Ltd* [2003] P.I.Q.R. P180, CA, at P182.
[736] per Bodey J. in *Horton v Taplin Contracts Ltd* [2003] P.I.Q.R. P180, CA at P182.
[737] [2007] 2 All E.R. 97, HL. The pursuer suffered injury after falling to the floor when descending a suspended ladder from a bunk bed: the ladder was not properly engaged within retaining bars and came away. The employer ought to have anticipated that moveable ladders could be misplaced in position, with the risk that they could become detached in use, but the pursuer was also 50% to blame.
[738] Discussed above at para.12–130.
[739] See *Davies v Massey Ferguson Perkins* [1986] I.C.R. 580 discussed at para.12–130, above.
[740] Work Equipment Regulations 1998 reg.25.
[741] Work Equipment Regulations 1998 reg.26: forklift trucks have a separate provision in reg.27.
[742] reg.28.
[743] reg.29.
[744] reg.30.
[745] SI 1965/1441 as amended which continued to apply up to December 4, 1998.

embody a flywheel and clutch.[746] Schedule 2 lists specific power presses to which regs 32 to 35 do not apply.[747]

12–228   Regulation 32 provides for thorough examination of power presses both on installation and periodically thereafter, Sch.3 providing very precise details as to what must be contained in the report of such examinations required by reg.34. Regulation 33 requires the inspection and testing of guards and protection devices after setting, resetting or adjustment and after every fourth hour of a working period, with the signing of a certificate as evidence of this having taken place. All information kept in such reports or certificates have to be kept available for inspection.[748]

(H) The Lifting Operations and Lifting Equipment Regulations 1998 (The Lifting Regulations)

12–229   **Generally.** The Lifting Regulations[749] were introduced pursuant to s.15 of the Health and Safety at Work, etc. Act 1974 and came into force on December 5, 1998. Sections 22, 23 and 25 to 27 of the Factories Act 1961 were thereby repealed.[750] They apply to lifting equipment (equipment for lifting or lowering loads: loads include a person)[751] and lifting operations (an operation concerned with the lifting or lowering of a load).[752] Regulation 4 requires lifting equipment to be of adequate strength[753] and stability for each load: this appears to fall short of the absolute obligation imposed by s.22 of the Factories Act 1961 which afforded a workman protection in the case of latent defect.[754]

12–230   Detailed reference to the provisions in respect of the organisation of lifting operations, examination and inspections, reporting and the keeping of reports is beyond the scope of this work.

(I) The Control of Substances Hazardous to Health Regulations 2002

12–231   These Regulations[755] replace the Control of Substances Hazardous to Health Regulations 1999[756] which in turn replaced regulations with the same name made

---

[746] Work Equipment Regulations 1998 reg.2(1).
[747] Those for the working of hot metal or not capable of a stroke greater than 6mm; guillotines; combination punching and shearing machines; machines for bending steel sections; straightening, upsetting, heading, riveting, eyeletting and press-stud attaching machines; zip fastener bottom stop attaching machines; stapling and wire stitching machines; power presses for compacting metal powders.
[748] Work Equipment Regulations reg.35.
[749] SI 1998/2307.
[750] Lifting Regulations reg.15.
[751] reg.2(1).
[752] reg.8(2).
[753] See para.12–217, above.
[754] *Galashiels Gas Co Ltd v O'Donnell* [1949] A.C. 275.
[755] SI 2002/2677 with effect from November 21, 2002. See Topping, "New COSHH approach to chemical control" (2004) O.H.R., 107, 9.
[756] SI 1999/437.

in 1994[757] and 1988.[758] The 1988 Regulations took effect from October 1, 1989, and repealed s.63 of the Factories Act 1961[759] replacing it with the detailed provisions therein set out. The 2002 Regulations came into force on November 21, 2002. The scheme of the regulations is to establish a code and procedures for virtually any substance which may be hazardous to health and impose duties in respect of the making of risk assessments with regard both to the risks to workers and the steps necessary to control exposure. They are accompanied by a series of ACOPs. Detailed discussion of these regulations is beyond the scope of this work.[760]

(J) The Personal Protective Equipment at Work Regulations 1992 (The Protective Equipment Regulations)

Introduction. The Protective Equipment Regulations[761] were introduced **12–232** pursuant to s.15 of the Health and Safety at Work, etc. Act 1974 to give effect to the Personal Protective Equipment Directive.[762] They came into force on January 1, 1993 replacing many earlier regulations.[763] They are accompanied by a Guidance Note. Breach of the Protective Equipment Regulations is taken to give rise to civil liability.

Regulation 4 created a new, general duty to provide suitable personal **12–233** protective equipment where there is a risk to health or safety. The presumption is that the risk identified will be controlled by other means and that personal protective equipment is provided as a course of last resort.[764] The duty to ensure the provision of suitable protective equipment has been held to be an absolute one such that, where this requirement cannot be complied with, the employer will be in breach of his common law duty by continuing to employ the employee in breach of the Protective Equipment Regulations.[765] In such circumstances, all

---

[757] SI 1994/3246.

[758] SI 1988/1657.

[759] Reference should be made to the 8th edn of this work, 1990, Ch.11, paras 11–48–11–51 for a discussion of this section.

[760] But see, e.g. *Dugmore v Swansea NHS Trust* [2003] P.I.Q.R. P220, CA, para.12–115 above: the duty under reg.7(1) of the 1994 Regulations (repeated in identical terms in the 1999 and 2002 Regulations) is an absolute one to prevent exposure to a hazardous substance. Thus foreseeability of risk is irrelevant and the defence of reasonable practicability qualifies only the duty of prevention.

[761] SI 1992/2966.

[762] 89/656/EEC.

[763] Such as the Protection of Eyes Regulations 1974 (SI 1974/1681), as amended. See Sch.3 to the Protective Equipment Regulations for a full list of revocations.

[764] See the Guidance Note at paras 20–22. For a specific example of this theme running through the Regulations, see reg.6(3)(d) of the Construction (Health, Safety and Welfare) Regulations 1996.

[765] *Lane Group Plc v Farmiloe* [2004] P.I.Q.R. P324, EAT: warehouseman, whose feet were at risk from falling items or being run over by fork lift trucks, was unable to wear protective footwear because it aggravated his constitutional psoriasis. There was no legal basis for the employers carrying out an individual risk assessment relieving the employers of the duty to provide such footwear. Nor did the employers have to balance the risk of injury with the detriment of potential dismissal.

other avenues having been properly explored, the employer will be obliged to dismiss the employee.[766] Personal protective equipment is defined as meaning all equipment including clothing which is intended to be worn or held by a person at work and which protects him against one or more risks to health and safety. Ordinary working clothes and uniforms are excluded[767] but the definition has been held to be wide enough to cover body armour.[768] These regulations give way to more detailed provision where such is provided elsewhere.[769]

12-234   Detailed provision is made with regard to suitability[770] and the need for risk assessment to be undertaken.[771] Regulation 5 requires compatibility as between several pieces of personal protective equipment used simultaneously. The employer must provide information, instruction and training regarding the risks the personal protective equipment is designed to avoid or limit,[772] the purpose for which and the manner in which it is to be used and the steps required to keep it in good repair.[773] As in other similar regulations, such information and instruction must be comprehensible to the worker.[774] Having provided the personal protective equipment, duties are imposed both on employer and employee to ensure that it is used in accordance with the regulations.[775] The employee is also under a duty to report its loss or any obvious defect.[776]

12-235   **Maintenance.** Once provided, personal protective equipment must be maintained and replaced where necessary[777] and accommodation must be provided for it.[778] Despite the absolute duty of the nature to maintain, in *Fytche v Wincanton Logistics Plc*,[779] the House of Lords held that a claim under reg.7(1) failed where the claimant sustained frostbite in extreme weather owing to the ingress of water through a tiny hole of the steel-capped boots provided to him by the defendant employer. No one knew of the presence of the hole and nor could it reasonably have been discovered by the employer. The boots were in otherwise satisfactory

---

[766] *Lane Group Plc v Farmiloe* [2004] P.I.Q.R. P324 at P335, para.43(b).

[767] Protective Equipment Regulations reg.3(2).

[768] *Henser-Leather v Securicor Cash Services Ltd* [2002] EWCA Civ 816 where, in the event of not being able to reduce the risk of attacks to a level comparable to that to which the public at large were exposed, the duty under reg.4 was engaged.

[769] reg.3(3): see, e.g. the Control of Substances Hazardous to Health Regulations 2002, the Control of Vibration at Work Regulations 2005 (SI 2005/1093) with effect from July 6, 2005 and the Control of Noise at Work Regulations 2005 (SI 2005/1643) repealing and replacing the Noise at Work Regulations 1989 with effect from April 6, 2006.

[770] reg.4(3).

[771] reg.6.

[772] In relation to analogous duties under Provision and Use of Work Equipment Regulations 1998 see para.12–202 and n.669 thereunder, above.

[773] reg.9(1).

[774] reg.9(2).

[775] reg.10.

[776] reg.11.

[777] reg.7: maintained in the sense discussed at paras 12–123–12–127, above, thus imposing an absolute duty.

[778] reg.8.

[779] [2005] P.I.Q.R. P61, HL. See also McCool "Danger at work" 149 S.J. 345.

condition and, in particular, the steel toecap gave the protection against the risks for which the protective equipment, namely boots of that type, had been provided. Lord Hoffmann said:

> " 'efficient state, in efficient working order and in good repair' is not an absolute concept but must be construed in relation to what makes the equipment personal protective equipment. What counts as being in an efficient state? Efficient for what purpose? In my opinion, for the purpose of protecting against the relevant risk. Regulation 7 extends in time the duty to provide suitable personal protective equipment under regulation 4. By virtue of regulation 7, it is not enough just to provide it and then leave the employee to his own devices. The employer has a duty to maintain it so that it continues to be suitable personal protective equipment. But he does not have a duty to do repairs and maintenance which have nothing to do with its function as personal protective equipment."[780]

(K) The Manual Handling Operations Regulations 1992

Introduction. The Manual Handling Operations Regulations 1992[781] were introduced pursuant to s.15 of the Health and Safety at Work, etc. Act 1974 to give effect to the Manual Handling Directive.[782] They came into force on January 1, 1993 and replaced s.72 of the Factories Act 1961 and s.23 of the Office, Shops and Railway Premises Act 1963 (the prohibition of the lifting of excessive weights). They are accompanied by a Guidance Note.[783] These are important regulations of widespread application. Whereas the former law (including regulations in respect of particular industries[784]) sought to concentrate on weights, the scheme of these regulations is to focus on lifting operations and the individuals who carry them out. Inevitably, therefore, the need to assess arises.   **12–236**

Who is covered. The Manual Handling Operations Regulations 1992 impose duties on employers in respect of their employees,[785] the definition being that set out in s.53(1) of the Health and Safety at Work, etc. Act 1974, namely an individual who works under a contract of employment. It is suggested that the   **12–237**

---

[780] *Fytche v Wincanton Logistics Plc* [2005] P.I.Q.R. P61, HL at P66, para.18. Lord Hope and Baroness Hale dissented. Lord Hope noted that the claimant had no choice but to wear the boots and, whilst suitability was to be determined by the risk which made it necessary for the PPE to be provided, that was not the only criterion. The employer must also ensure that the PPE was suitable for the conditions where the exposure to risk might occur and the obligation to maintain in good repair included keeping the PPE free from defects which may create risks to health and safety.

[781] SI 1992/2793. See Levy, "Manual handling cases—music to the ears" J.P.I. Law 2001, 2, 130; also, generally, Downey, "Work that body—a manual handling update" H. & S.L. 2002, 2(3), 8; Ritchie, "Recent developments in manual handling cases" H. & S.L. 2005, 336, 11.

[782] 90/269/EEC.

[783] A useful practical summary of which is contained within the publication "Getting to Grips with Manual Handling", H.S.E. IND(G) 143L, November 1993.

[784] e.g. the Woollen and Worsted Textiles (Lifting of Heavy Weights) Regulations 1926 and the Jute (Safety, Health and Welfare) Regulations 1948.

[785] Manual Handling Operations Regulations 1992 reg.4(1).

Court of Appeal's broad interpretation of employee in *Lane v Shire Roofing Co (Oxford) Ltd*[786] should apply. The regulations do not apply to the master or employers of a crew on a seagoing ship.[787] Their application does, however, extend to premises and activities outside Great Britain to which ss.1 to 59 and 80 to 82 of the Health and Safety at Work, etc. Act 1974 apply.

12–238   **Manual handling operations.** These are very broadly defined as including "any transporting or supporting of a load (including the lifting, putting down, pushing, pulling, carrying or moving thereof) by hand or bodily force", with load including a person or animal.[788]

12–239   **Injury.** Save for injury caused by the leakage or spillage of a toxic or corrosive substance being excluded, no restriction is placed on the type of injury which the regulations seek to avoid.[789] Despite their prevalence, the regulations are not restricted to back injuries. Thus, they have been held to cover a cut hand whilst an employee was supporting a sprung flap[790] and an injured foot suffered by a joiner who fell whilst carrying a door up a flight of stairs.[791] Consistent with this approach, it has been held that the regulations apply whenever there is a foreseeable risk of injury to an employee engaged in an activity which involves manual handling, even where the injury sustained is not in itself a strain injury.[792] A cleaning operative succeeded on appeal when he slipped on ice on which he inadvertently stepped in the course of spreading grit (itself held to be a manual handling operation) for the very purpose of removing the ice.[793] A claim based on the excessive use of a hand held spanner, however, was held not to constitute a manual handling operation because there was no allegation that the claimant's injury arose as a result of the transporting or supporting of a load.[794]

12–240   **The duty.** Within the limits of reasonable practicability,[795] the employer must avoid the need for an employee to undertake any manual handling operation at

---

[786] [1995] P.I.Q.R. P417. See further at para.12–100 above and generally. Ch.3, paras 3–99–3–159, above.

[787] Manual Handling Operations 1992 reg.3.

[788] reg.2(1). In *Hughes v Grampian Country Food Group Ltd* 2007 S.L.T.635, IH (1 Div) it was held that the trial judge had been entitled to conclude that the trussing of the wings and legs of chicken carcasses was not a manual handling operation. Although the language of the Regulations, if considered in isolation, was open to more than one interpretation, absurd results were to be avoided and the pursuer's interpretation would make every human activity, other than those purely cerebral, manual handling.

[789] reg.2(1).

[790] *Divit v British Telecommunications Plc*, 1997 G.W.D. 12–430, OH.

[791] *Hawkes v London Borough of Southwark*, Unreported, February 10, 1998, CA.

[792] *Cullen v North Lanarkshire Council*, 1998 S.L.T. 847, 2 Div.

[793] *King v RCO Support Services Ltd* [2001] P.I.Q.R. P15, CA.

[794] *King v Carron Phoenix Ltd*, 1999 Rep. L.R. 51, OH. Contrast the Guidance Notes which suggest that the turning of a starting handle would fall within the scope of the regs.

[795] See para.12–109, above generally and *Hawkes v London Borough of Southwark*, n.791, above, for specific application to reg.4. The onus rests on the employer to plead reasonable practicability by way of defence to an alleged breach and, in most cases, call evidence in support.

work which involves a risk of him being injured.[796] "Risk of being injured" is not more closely defined but the risk need not be a significant one. It has been held that a risk of injury arose if it was established that injury was a foreseeable possibility rather than a likelihood.[797] In making an assessment whether there is such a risk, an employer is not entitled to assume that all his employees will, on all occasions, behave with full and proper concern for their own safety but, at the same time, there should also be an element of realism. The question has to be context-based taking the operation, place of employment and individual employee all into account.[798] By reg.4(3), a list has been provided of the matters to which an employer should have regard in determining whether a manual handling operation at work involves a risk of injury.[799] Where the manual handling operation involved the distribution of grit in a yard affected by ice, taking the size of the yard and the duration of the task into account, it was held that there was a clear risk that an employee's foot might go on to a part of the yard that was not gritted. If it did, there was an obvious risk of injury.[800] On the other hand, in a small residential home for children, there were innumerable daily tasks, any one of which might be a manual handling operation. Where the level of risk involved was low, it was beyond the realms of practicality to meet each such risk with a precise evaluation of each task.[801] Nor is an employer liable under reg.4 if his employee acts in a way which is unforeseeably outwith the

---

[796] Manual Handling Operations Regulations 1992 reg.4(1)(a). Note that this duty removes the requirement (under s.72 of the Factories Act 1961 and s.23 of the Officers, Shops and Railway Premises Act 1963) that a person be "employed" or "required" to lift the item in question: see *Black v Carricks (Caterers) Ltd* [1980] I.R.L.R. 448, CA (the manageress of a baker's shop strained her back lifting trays of bread to reach a loaf for a customer when staff employed to do this task failed to turn in to work because of sickness. Her instructions left it to her own judgment as to whether she carried on and she was, thus, not "required" to perform the lift).

[797] *Anderson v Lothian Health Board*, 1996 S.C.L.R. 1068, OH (manual handling of laundry). *Koonjul v Thameslink Heathcare Services* [2000] P.I.Q.R. P123, CA; *Kerr v North Ayrshire Council* 2002 Rep. L.R. 35, OH (female caretaker moving a 13kg table); *Purdie v Glasgow CC* 2002 Rep. L.R. 26, OH (claimant slipped on a magazine whilst shovelling wet magazines into a JCB: held that there was a reasonably foreseeable possibility of injury as a result of slipping on magazines that were blown about by the wind).

[798] *O'Neill v DSG Retail Ltd* [2002] I.C.R. 222, CA: a claim by a warehouse manager. Generally on risk, see: *McIntosh v Edinburgh City Council*, 2003 S.L.T. 827, OH (one man handling a 50kg ladder was clearly exposed to a foreseeable risk of injury); *R. v East Sussex CC Ex p. A* [2003] EWHC 167, (the lifting of people with serious disabilities by care workers).

[799] Inserted by the Health and Safety (Miscellaneous) Amendment Regulations 2002 (SI 2002/2174) to give effect to Annex II of the Manual Handling Directive. It includes the physical suitability of the employee, the clothing and footwear worn, knowledge and training, risk assessment or health surveillance pursuant to regs 3 and 6 of the Management of Health and Safety at Work Regulations 1999.

[800] *King v RCO Support Services Ltd* [2001] P.I.Q.R. P15, CA. Note, however, that the defendant failed to advance any defence that it was not reasonably practicable to avoid this manual handling operation and so the CA assumed that it was reasonably practicable to avoid it, by the use of a mechanical gritter: see Kay L.J. at P15, para.24. The claimant was held to be 50% to blame, he being an experienced worker and the task not being a particularly difficult one.

[801] *Koonjul v Thameslink Healthcare Services* [2000] P.I.Q.R. P123, CA, at P127, P128, per Hale L.J. *Koonjul* was followed in *O'Neill v DSG Retail Ltd*, n.798 above: employer held liable to employee who, whilst carrying a microwave oven, twisted round instinctively in response to a call from a colleague. Training would have been an appropriate step to reduce the injury and, with such training, the employee would probably have paused before responding to the call.

procedures usually adopted in relation to the manual handling operation in question.[802]

Illustrations

12–241   Liability was established under this regulation where: a claimant tripped and fell from a vehicle which he was unloading thereby injuring his shoulder[803]; in the course of her employment by a hospital, the claimant was responsible for setting up a demonstration and, without knowing its weight, picked up from the floor a box of dummy arms weighing 50 to 60lbs, thereby causing her injury[804]; the lifting of a 50kg ladder by one man carried with it a foreseeable possibility of injury within in the ambit of reg.4(1).[805]

The duty here is likely to be higher than at common law[806] and it has been noted that it will not be unusual for a claim to succeed under reg.4 even though an employer is not in breach of his common law duty of care.[807] The duty owed is not restricted to the person engaged in the manual handling operation at the precise moment of injury. So a nurse struck by a trolley moved by another nurse was found to be within the ambit of the regulations.[808]

12–242   In the event that it is not reasonably practicable to avoid a manual handling operation involving a risk of injury, reg.4(1)(b) requires a risk assessment to be made. The assessment must be suitable and sufficient and made by reference to Schedule 1.[809] This sets out the factors to which the employer must have regard and the questions he must ask when carrying out the assessment. A comprehensive list, which can only be referred to in general terms here, concentrates upon the task and the circumstances in which it is to be carried out, rather than the weight involved, under four broad headings: the tasks, the loads, the working environment and individual capability. Focus on the individual again places the duty on the employer to take into account individual susceptibilities of which he is or ought to have been aware. Whilst an employer could not be criticised for being unaware of an asymptomatic constitutional condition, he must have regard for medical conditions about which he ought to have acquired knowledge if he had carried out a proper risk assessment.

---

[802] *Bennetts v Ministry of Defence* [2004] EWCA Civ 486: the claimant, a 64-year-old employee of the defendant, when removing items of post from a heavy post bag, contrary to usual practice, decided to lift the bag on to a trolley and, when the bag became snagged, continued to pull suffering injury to her back.

[803] *Cullen v North Lanarkshire Council*, 1998 S.L.T. 847, 2 Div.

[804] *Goodchild v Organon Laboratories Ltd* [2004] EWHC 2341: the box had been left on the floor by a co-worker and, in the circumstances, it was held that the defendant had failed to avoid, so far as was reasonably practicable, the need for her to undertake manual handling of the box, subject to 10 per cent contributory negligence on her part.

[805] *McIntosh v Edinburgh CC* 2003 S.L.T. 827, OH.

[806] See e.g. *Cullen v North Lanarkshire Council*, n.803 above, *Purdie v Glasgow CC*, n.797 above and *O'Neill v DSG Retail Ltd*, n.798 above.

[807] *Hall v Edinburgh City Council*, 1999 S.L.T. 744, OH (claimant and another lifting 50kg bag of cement).

[808] Although failed to establish a breach of duty on the facts: *Postle v Norfolk & Norwich NHS Healthcare Trust* [2000] 12 C.L. 280.

[809] Manual Handling Operations Regulations 1992 reg.4(1)(b)(i).

Having made the assessment, the employer must then take appropriate steps to   **12–243**
reduce the risk of injury arising out of the relevant operation to the lowest level
reasonably practicable.[810] The list in reg.4(3)[811] again applies in relation to the
matters to which an employer should have regard. The provision of information,
instruction and training will often be central to a decision as to whether
appropriate steps had been taken[812] although it should be the case that the mere
provision of information as to how to reduce risk will not usually be sufficient for
an employer to discharge the burden.

ILLUSTRATIONS

Insufficient steps were taken by employers where: although a system of   **12–244**
maximum loads was introduced in a laundry the employer failed, additionally, to
take reasonably practicable steps to ensure that the maximum was not
exceeded[813]; there was a lack of training on lifting[814]; there was a lack of detailed
guidance on how to lift and move school desks, with no practical training or risk
assessment[815]; there was insufficient provision of hoists for nurses involved in
lifting who resorted to the condemned "drag lift" as a consequence[816]; the
employer failed to provide a mechanical means of lifting bags of cement.[817]

The employer's duty was discharged where: training included a specific   **12–245**
instruction directed at preventing the employee from twisting whilst lifting[818]; in
a bus yard, the use of a mechanical gritter would have avoided the risk of injury
inherent in spreading grit by hand but the defendant failed to advance any
defence that it was not reasonably practicable to avoid that particular manual
handling operation.[819]

On the facts, it was inappropriate for the fire brigade to be called to assist
ambulancemen in manually handling an elderly patient down the stairs in his
home: relevant considerations were the difficulty of moving the patient, the
urgency of the case, and the actual or likely response of the patient or his
carers.[820]

Although there is no express requirement in the Regulations themselves for   **12–246**
training, it is implicit in the requirement to look at the individual carrying out the
manual handling operation and, by virtue of reg.4(3)(c), it is one of the matters
to which the employer must have regard when both assessing the risk of injury
and the steps taken to reduce injury. The Manual Handling Directive requires

---

[810] reg.4(1)(b)(ii). See e.g. *Skinner v Aberdeen CC*, 2001 Rep. L.R. 118, OH: employee lifting paving
slabs with a crow bar placed a hammer beneath the bar to improve leverage and the slab broke
causing him injury.
[811] See n.799, above.
[812] *Peck v Chief Constable of Avon and Somerset* [2000] C.L.Y. 2971.
[813] *Anderson v Lothian Health Board*, 1996 S.C.L.R. 1068, OH.
[814] *Peck v Chief Constable of Avon and Somerset*, n.812 above.
[815] *Eastgate v Oxfordshire County Council* [2005] 10 C.L. 192
[816] *Knott v Newham Healthcare NHS Trust* [2003] All E.R. (D) 164 (May), CA.
[817] *Hall v Edinburgh City Council*, n.807, above.
[818] *O'Neill v DSG Retail Ltd*, n.798, above.
[819] *King v RCO Support Services Ltd*, n.800 above.
[820] *King v Sussex Ambulance NHS Trust* [2002] I.C.R. 1413, CA.

proper training to be provided,[821] and reg.4(3)(d) requires regard to be had to risk assessments carried out pursuant to the Management of Health and Safety at Work Regulations 1999. Since reg.13 of the Management Regulations requires an employer to ensure the provision of appropriate training[822] it is clear that the requirement for training in this context is mandatory.

12–247   Finally, the duty also extends to taking steps to provide employees undertaking such manual handling operations with general indications, and where reasonably practicable, precise information on the weight of loads to be handled and the heaviest side of a load whose centre of gravity is not centrally positioned.[823]

12–248   The relationship between the three elements of the duty under reg.4(1)(b) was considered by the Court of Appeal in *Swain v Denson Marston Ltd*[824] and held to be disjunctive. Thus, an employer who failed to carry out a risk assessment under reg.4(1)(b)(i) (apparently because the job was an urgent maintenance job) was nevertheless held liable under reg.4(1)(b)(iii) for failing to give the claimant the weight of a roller (which turned out to be solid rather than hollow as was usual) and which took the claimant by surprise, trapping his hand.

12–249   The importance of reg.4(1)(b)(ii) was stressed in *Egan v Central Manchester and Manchester Children's University Hospitals NHS Trust*.[825] The claimant was a nurse who from time to time had to bathe a disabled patient, using a mobile hoist to transport the patient to and from the bath. She injured her back when the wheels of the hoist suddenly jammed, it was thought, as a result of coming into contact with a plinth upon which the bath stood. It was common ground that no risk assessment had been carried out, but the claim failed at first instance on the basis that an assessment would have made no difference: the claimant knew about the presence of the plinth and the need to avoid it. She succeeded on appeal on the basis that the employer had not shown that a risk of injury to her from a collision with the plinth had been reduced to the lowest level reasonably practicable. It was said that where no risk assessment had been carried out, the court should focus on the regulation which imposed the duty to take positive action to reduce risk, namely, reg.4(1)(b)(ii). Once it had been shown that the manual handling operation carried some risk of injury, the burden of proof was on the employer to plead and prove that it had taken appropriate steps to reduce that risk to the lowest level reasonably practicable.[826] There were steps which could have been taken to reduce the risk of a collision, such as moving and/or clearly marking the plinth and in the circumstances both parties were equally to blame.

12–250   The burden of proof was considered in *Davidson v Lothian and Borders Fire Board*.[827] A part-time fireman injured his back whilst participating in a drill on

---

[821] art.6(2).
[822] See para.12–104, above.
[823] Manual Handling Operations Regulations 1992 reg.4(1)(b)(iii).
[824] [2000] P.I.Q.R. P129.
[825] [2009] I.C.R. 585, CA.
[826] *Egan* n.825 above at [20]–[22] of the judgment.
[827] 2003 S.L.T. 939, Ex. Div.

a ladder which moved in a sudden gust of wind. It was held that once the claimant had established a prima facie breach of reg.4(1)(b)(ii), a burden was cast upon the defendant to establish that appropriate steps had been taken to reduce the risk of injury to the lowest level reasonably practicable. That burden had not been discharged where wind was a well known hazard and the defendant had not explained why it was not reasonably practicable to build appropriate precautions into the standard instructions for such drills.

Where the court found that a detailed risk assessment of a particular task had **12–251** been necessary, that none was carried out, and that guideline figures set by the Health and Safety Executive for the force required in the course of pushing and pulling operations had been exceeded, the claimant, who alleged injury as a result of his involvement in the work, was entitled to succeed. There was no evidence that the defendant had reduced the risks of the task to the lowest level reasonably practicable.[828]

Regulation 4(2) imposes the duty of reviewing risk assessments in the light of **12–252** changed circumstances. A duty is also imposed on employees to make full and proper use of any system of work provided by their employer in compliance with reg.4(1)(b)(ii).[829]

---

[828] *Parr v Gravatom Engineering Systems Ltd, The Times*, January 1, 2008, CA: claimant injured moving four very large and heavy machines from a delivery bay in the defendant's factory. per Keene L.J.: only if evidence showed both that a suitable and sufficient assessment of the operation in question had not been undertaken and that risks had not been reduced to the lowest level reasonably practicable could a claim for breach of duty under s.4 succeed.
[829] Manual Handling Operations Regulations 1992 reg.5.

Part IV

ABSOLUTE OR STRICT LIABILITY

CHAPTER 13

DANGEROUS THINGS: RYLANDS v FLETCHER

1.—PRINCIPLES OF LIABILITY

(A) Introduction

The rule in Rylands v Fletcher.[1] The origin of the rule of liability for the escape of dangerous things collected or accumulated upon land is the case of *Rylands v Fletcher*. The case arose as a result of an escape of water into the claimant's mine from a reservoir constructed by the defendant upon his land.   **13–01**

On appeal in the Court of Exchequer Chamber, the defendant was held liable by Blackburn J. In identifying the crux of the case, he said: **13–02**

"The question of law therefore arises, what is the obligation which the law casts on a person who, like the defendant, lawfully brings on his land something which though harmless whilst it remains there, will naturally do mischief if it escape out of his land. It is agreed on all hands that he must take care to keep in that which he has brought on the land and keeps there, in order that it may not escape and damage his neighbours, but the question arises whether the duty which the law casts upon him, under such circumstances, is an absolute duty to keep it in if at his peril, or is, as the majority of

---

[1] (1866) L.R. 1 Ex. 265 (first instance), (1868) L.R. 3 H.L. 330 (on appeal).

the Court of Exchequer have thought, merely a duty to take all reasonable and prudent precautions, in order to keep it in, but no more. If the first be the law, the person who has brought on his land and kept there something dangerous, and failed to keep it in, is responsible for all the natural consequences of its escape. If the second be the limit of his duty, he would not be answerable except on proof of negligence, and consequently would not be answerable for escape arising from any latent defect which ordinary prudence and skill could not detect."[2]

13–03   In words that have been quoted many times subsequently, Blackburn J. added:

"We think that the true rule of law is, that the person who for his own purposes brings on his lands and collects and keeps there anything likely to do mischief if it escapes, must keep it in at his peril, and, if he does not do so, is *prima facie* answerable for all the damage which is the natural consequence of its escape. He can excuse himself by showing that the escape was owing to the plaintiff's default; or perhaps that the escape was the consequence of *vis major*, or the act of God."[3]

After an appeal to the House of Lords, the decision was upheld.

(B) Principles of liability

13–04   **Relationship to nuisance.** It has been pointed out that the judges in *Rylands v Fletcher* probably did not regard themselves as enunciating any new principle. The tort of nuisance was already well developed, but generally such cases reflected a course of conduct rather than an isolated occurrence. What the *Rylands* case did was to set out the circumstances in which nuisance liability would attach for damage which arose to the claimant's land upon a single "escape".[4] Provided the damage arose from the accumulation by the defendant on his land of something which fulfilled a particular criterion of dangerousness, it mattered not that the escape could not have been prevented by the exercise of reasonable care. Thus the liability was described as absolute or strict.[5]

13–05   Given its relationship with nuisance, the *Rylands* rule shares a number of features with that tort. The object of both is to protect the claimant from and compensate for, injury to his enjoyment of land.[6] The extent of damage that may be recovered is the same in both: the defendant is liable for that which was

---

[2] (1866) L.R. 1 Ex. 265 at 279.

[3] (1866) L.R. 1 Ex. 265 at 279–280.

[4] See per Lord Bingham in *Transco Plc v Stockport MBC* [2004] 2 A.C. 1 at 7: "It seems likely, as persuasively contended by Professor Newark ("The Boundaries of Nuisance" (1949) 65 L.Q.R. 480 and 487–488), that those who decided the case regarded it as one of nuisance, novel only to the extent that it sanctioned recovery where the interference by one occupier of land with the right or enjoyment of another was isolated and not persistent."

[5] *Cambridge Water Co Ltd v Eastern Counties Leather Plc* [1994] 2 A.C. 264; also *Hamilton v Papakura District Council* [2004] UKPC 9, Ch.2, para.2–31, above (no foreseeability of damage from herbicide which contaminated water in a lake which was collected and sold to the claimants who used it in their business of growing tomatoes).

[6] See per Lord Hoffmann in *Transco* above n.4 at 19 "a remedy for damage to land or interests in land."

reasonably foreseeable as resulting from the escape complained of.[7] The distinguishing feature of *Rylands* liability is the absence of need to prove that the escape, classically a single unanticipated event, was itself reasonably foreseeable. That consideration does not usually arise when considering liability in nuisance for what is generally a course of conduct over time.[8]

Although it has attracted much interest and academic comment, the rule of **13-06** strict liability is successfully invoked in only rare cases in recent times.[9] In fact, the strictness of the liability has been mitigated by the emphasis given to the concept of reasonable forseeability in determining "dangerousness" and the extent of damage for which the defendant may be liable if a breach of duty is established. Because of the developing nature of the rules, what might be described as "historic" examples given in the discussion below, should be approached with discretion. The decided cases may not always be consistent with the way *Rylands v Fletcher* would be applied today.

Definition of dangerous things. Blackburn J. spoke in terms of a liability **13-07** which attached as a result of the accumulation upon land of anything "likely to do mischief" if it escaped. The shorthand came to be liability for "dangerous things", but the approach to what is dangerous, naturally enough, developed over time. Some things were always likely to be regarded as dangerous, such as fire, explosives, gas and electricity, but others might only be dangerous in particular times or circumstances; and the perception of dangerousness might also reflect advances in scientific knowledge, or increased technical expertise.

In *Transco Plc v Stockport Metropolitan Borough Council*[10] the difficulty in **13-08** formulating a comprehensive test of dangerousness was aknowledged but it was suggested that attention should be concentrated on foreseeability of danger:

"It must be shown that the defendant has done something which he recognised or judged by the standards appropriate at the relevant place and time, he ought reasonably to have recognised, as giving rise to an exceptionally high risk of danger or mischief if there should be an escape, however unlikely an escape may have been thought to be."[11]

---

[7] See e.g. *Arscott v The Coal Authority* [2005] Env. L.R. 6, para.13–69, below. See also Wright and Clarke, "Nuisance: Proteus begins to rise" 154 N.L.J. 1282.
[8] per Lord Hoffmann in *Transco*, above, at 15: "It is the single escape which raises the question of whether or not it was reasonably foreseeable and, if not, whether the defendant should nevertheless be liable. *Rylands v Fletcher* decided that he should." See also the speech of Lord Walker at 35 where he discusses the territories respectively of negligence, nuisance, and the *Rylands* principle.
[9] per Lord Hoffmann in *Transco*, above, at 19 (after summarising the exceptions and qualifications to the rule) "It is perhaps not surprising that counsel could not find a reported case since the second world war in which anyone had succeeded in a claim under the rule. It is hard to escape the conclusion that the intellectual effort devoted to the rule by judges and writers over many years has brought forth a mouse." However, the House of Lords declined to follow the Australian courts and subsume *Rylands v Fletcher* liability within the law of negligence.
[10] n.4 above.
[11] ibid. per Lord Bingham of Cornhill at 11. In *Rylands v Fletcher* itself, Lord Cranworth's formulation, in particular, had been generous: "anything which, if it should escape, may cause damage to his neighbour" (L.R. 3 H.L. 330, 340).

13-09   Given the considerations already mentioned, a list of things which have been categorised as dangerous in the past has its limitations, but is nonetheless given, since it may be of some value in analogous cases, to know what dangers have been regarded as within, and without, the rule.

ILLUSTRATIONS

13-10   The following have been held to be dangerous things for purposes of the strict liability rule: water, artificially accumulated[12]; sewage[13]; fire[14]; gas[15]; electricity[16]; poison[17]; explosives[18]; creosote-soaked wood blocks, which emitted harmful fumes[19]; a chemical giving off poisonous fumes[20]; jars containing sulphuric acid[21]; phosphorus[22]; poisonous paint, left in a field[23]; yew tree leaves[24]; poisonous berries, growing on a shrub in a public park[25]; a loaded gun[26]; underpants containing sulphites[27]; dangerous animals[28]; petrol[29]; oil[30]; paraffin[31]; airborne oily smuts, containing sulphur compounds[32]; a noxious hair dye[33]; a fairground roundabout, known as a chair-o-plane[34]; a cleaning fluid, which generated an explosive gas on coming into contact with cast-iron[35]; a

---

[12] *Rylands v Fletcher* (1866) L.R. 3 H.L. 330. *Charing Cross Electricity Supply Co v Hydraulic Power Co* [1914] 3 K.B. 442. Human ingenuity being what it is, the list of dangerous things is not closed. See e.g. "Legal liability for GM crops" Fam. Law 2003, 87, 23.

[13] *Humphries v Cousins* (1877) 2 C.P.D. 239; *Smeaton v Ilford Corp* [1954] Ch. 450.

[14] *Jones v Festiniog Ry* (1868) L.R. 3 Q.B. 733. This includes fire from a flame-bearing instrument such as an ignited blowlamp: *Balfour v Barty-King* [1956] 1 W.L.R. 779 (affirmed [1957] 1 Q.B. 496). See generally, Deacon, "Opening the floodgates to stop the fire?" 155 N.L.J. 1720.

[15] *Northwestern Utilities v London Guarantee and Accident Co* [1936] A.C. 108; *Hanson v Wearmouth Coal Co* [1939] 3 All E.R. 47; *Federic v Perpetual Investments* (1968) 2 D.L.R. (3d) 50.

[16] *National Telephone Co v Baker* [1893] 2 Ch. 186.

[17] *Dell v Chesham UDC* [1921] 3 K.B. 427.

[18] *Rainham Chemical Works v Belvedere Fish Guano Co* [1921] 2 A.C. 465.

[19] *West v Bristol Tramways* [1908] 2 K.B. 14.

[20] *Bamfield v Goole and Sheffield Transport Co* [1910] 2 K.B. 94.

[21] *Adelaide Chemical Co Ltd v Carlyle* (1940) 64 C.L.R. 514.

[22] *Williams v Eady* (1893) 10 T.L.R. 41.

[23] *Stewart v Adams*, 1920 S.C. 129.

[24] *Crowhurst v Amersham Burial Board* (1878) 4 Ex.D. 5.

[25] *Glasgow Corp v Taylor* [1922] 1 A.C. 44.

[26] *Sullivan v Creed* [1904] 2 Ir.R. 317.

[27] *Grant v Australian Knitting Mills Ltd* [1936] A.C. 85.

[28] *Filburn v People's Palace and Aquarium Co* (1890) 25 Q.B.D. 258.

[29] *Jefferson v Derbyshire Farmers* [1921] 2 K.B. 281 at 290, per Atkin L.J.; *Marshall v Russian Oil Products*, 1938 S.C. 773, 796. Also a motor vehicle with petrol in its tank, although the vehicle itself is not dangerous, *Musgrove v Pandelis* [1919] 2 K.B. 43; and petrol fumes in an otherwise empty tank of a vehicle, *Perry v Kendricks Transport Ltd* [1956] 1 W.L.R. 85.

[30] *Smith v G.W. Ry* (1926) 135 L.T. 112. See Ingram, "Oil Pollution—*Rylands v Fletcher*", 121 N.L.J. 183.

[31] *Mulholland & Tedd Ltd v Baker* [1939] 3 All E.R. 253.

[32] *Halsey v Esso Petroleum Co Ltd* [1961] 1 W.L.R. 683.

[33] *Parker v Oloxo Ltd* [1937] 3 All E.R. 524; *Watson v Buckley Osborne Garrett & Co* [1940] 1 All E.R. 174; *Holmes v Ashford* [1950] 2 All E.R. 76.

[34] *Hale v Jennings Bros* [1938] 1 All E.R. 579. It is difficult to see why this is a dangerous thing when an aeroplane is not, as in *Fosbroke-Hobbes v Airwork Ltd* [1937] 1 All E.R. 108, 110.

[35] *Anglo-Celtic Shipping Co Ltd v Elliott & Jeffrey* (1926) 42 T.L.R. 297.

chemical, which reacted violently on coming in contact with water[36]; an electric space heater[37]; a blowlamp.[38]

In other cases, vibrations from pile-driving operations, which caused damage **13–11** to a neighbouring building were held to fall within the *Rylands* principle[39]; as were caravan dwellers who left their site and trespassed on adjoining land[40]; also a rusted wire fence, a piece of which broke off and was eaten by a cow.[41] A flag-pole was held to be a dangerous thing where it was erected near a casualty tent in Hyde Park, London, for the day of a jubilee celebration[42]; also a mass of spoil tipped on to the side of a hill, in consequence of which a landslide occurred.[43]

The following have been held *not* to be dangerous things: a steam roller[44]; a **13–12** person who had recovered from scarlet fever and was discharged from hospital, whilst in an infectious condition[45]; an oil can[46]; a brazing lamp[47]; a tree with a branch, in a condition rendering it liable to fall, overhanging the highway[48]; a motorcar[49]; a stationary unhorsed van in a highway[50]; an aeroplane[51]; a domestic boiler without a safety valve[52]; an air rifle[53]; a catapult[54]; a cricket ball[55]; the operation of shooting "swarf" into barges.[56] The Court of Appeal has said that

---

[36] *Vacwell Engineering Co Ltd v B.D.H. Chemicals Ltd* [1971] 1 Q.B. 88.
[37] *Robinson v Technico Ltd* (1953), unreported decision of the Sup. Ct in Eire. See 70 L.Q.R. 170.
[38] *Balfour v Barty-King* [1957] 1 Q.B. 496.
[39] *Hoare & Co v McAlpine* [1923] 1 Ch. 167. Damage caused by vibrations would seem to be actionable as a nuisance or, possibly, as negligence, but to have no relation to *Rylands v Fletcher*. Further, see Sir F. Pollock's comment on this case (*Torts* (15th edn), p.377), which he described as a "fallacious extension" of the rule, and 39 L.Q.R. 145. Indeed, it was disapproved in *Barrette v Franki Compressed Pile Co of Canada* (1955) 2 D.L.R. 665.
[40] *Attorney General v Corke* [1933] Ch. 89. See the criticism by Holdsworth in 49 L.Q.R. 158. Pennycuick V.C. in *Smith v Scott* [1973] Ch. 314 at 321, 322 said that the case "could at least equally well have been decided on the basis that the landowner there was in possession of the property and was himself liable in nuisance for the acts of his licensees."
[41] *Firth v Bowling-Iron Co* (1878) 3 C.P.D. 254, which would seem to be a case of trespass or negligence.
[42] *Shiffman v Order of St John* [1936] 1 All E.R. 557. A tentative suggestion only: the basis of liability seems to be the same as that in respect of dangers adjoining the highway generally (i.e. negligence). See Ch.10, paras 10–52–10–74, above
[43] *Attorney General v Cory Bros* [1921] 1 A.C. 521: the company was liable both in negligence and under the rule of strict liability. The decision on the latter point was on the basis "of liability for not keeping under control an artificial structure in its character dangerous" (per Lord Haldane at 537).
[44] *Chichester Corp v Foster* [1906] 1 K.B. 167.
[45] *Evans v Liverpool Corp* [1906] 1 K.B. 160.
[46] *Wray v Essex CC* [1936] 3 All E.R. 97.
[47] *Blacker v Lake and Elliott Ltd* (1912) 106 L.T. 533.
[48] *Noble v Harrison* [1926] 2 K.B. 332.
[49] *Ruoff v Long & Co* [1916] 1 K.B. 148.
[50] *Donovan v Union Cartage Co Ltd* [1933] 2 K.B. 71.
[51] *Fosbroke-Hobbes v Airwork Ltd* [1937] 1 All E.R. 108 at 110.
[52] *Bail v London County Council* [1949] 2 K.B. 159 (overruled by *A.C. Billings v Riden* [1958] A.C. 240 in so far as it was based on *Malone v Laskey* [1907] 2 K.B. 141).
[53] *Donaldson v McNiven* [1952] 1 All E.R. 1213, affirmed [1952] 2 All E.R. 691.
[54] *Smith v Leurs* (1945) 70 C.L.R. 256.
[55] *Bolton v Stone* [1951] A.C. 850.
[56] *Burley v Stepney Corp* [1947] 1 All E.R. 507.

water, gas and electricity in domestic premises for ordinary domestic purposes are not to be regarded as dangerous things in the present context.[57]

13–13   **Escape.** Before liability can be established under the *Rylands* principle there must be an escape from a place under the defendant's control to some other place not under his control.[58] So, there was no liability, because there was no escape, where a horse reached across a fence and consumed the poisonous leaves of a tree on the other side of the boundary[59]; nor where a government inspector was injured in an explosion in the shell-finishing shop of the defendant's factory.[60] However, liability may well attach where the products of an explosion, such as shattered rock, are forcibly thrown from the defendant's land and cause damage elsewhere.[61]

13–14   **Natural and non natural user.** In *Rylands v Fletcher* it was said that the rule applied only to something on the land which was not naturally there.[62] Lord Cairns said that the defendant was only liable if, in bringing the danger on to the land, he was making a non-natural use of the land.[63] The latter test in particular has over time allowed courts to bring contemporary circumstances into account.[64] But the test has never been precise. It was said in one case that the distinction between natural and non-natural use of land was one which it was impossible to draw with any accuracy.[65] The test for distinguishing one from the other was said to await authoritative determination.[66]

13–15   Guidance on the nature of the use contemplated by the expression "non-natural" was given in *Cambridge Water Co Ltd v Eastern Counties Leather Plc*.[67] Whilst not attempting to create a new definition of natural or ordinary use, the

---

[57] *Collingwood v Home and Colonial Stores* [1936] 3 All E.R. 200. See para.13–100, below.

[58] *Read v J. Lyons & Co Ltd* [1947] A.C. 156 at 168, per Viscount Simon. See also *Howard v Furness Lines Ltd* [1936] 2 All E.R. 781. In *British Celanese Ltd v A.H. Hunt (Capacitors) Ltd* [1969] 1 W.L.R. 959 it was held that, once an escape had occurred and the damage complained of was a direct result of it, there was no need for the claimant to be the occupier of adjoining or any land for that matter, to maintain a cause of action. The authority of this aspect of the case must now be regarded as doubtful, see para.13–29, below.

[59] *Ponting v Noakes* [1894] 2 Q.B. 281.

[60] n.58, above.

[61] See *Miles v Forest Rock Granite Co* (1918) 34 T.L.R. 500 (man injured on the highway by rocks thrown there during blasting operations on the land nearby was entitled to recover damages).

[62] See Williams, "Non-Natural Use of Land" (1973) Camb. L.J. 310.

[63] (1866) L.R. 3 H.L. 330 at 339.

[64] *Read v J. Lyons & Co Ltd* [1947] A.C. 156 at 176 per Lord Porter. See *British Celanese Ltd v A.H. Hunt (Capacitors) Ltd* [1969] 1 W.L.R. 959 for an example of this in practice: metal foil used by defendant electrical component manufacturers blew from their land into neighbouring electricity sub-station causing a power cut. Defendant held not liable because it was not a "special use, bringing with it increased danger to others". In *LMS International Ltd v Styrene Packaging & Insulation Ltd* [2006] T.C.L.R. 6, a non natural use of land involving a foreseeable risk of harm was established where the process within the defendant's factory involved cutting flammable polystyrene blocks with a hot wire machine, which caused a fire, damaging adjacent premises and their contents.

[65] The creation of the distinction was characterised as "unconscious" and criticised by Salmond & Heuston, *Law of Torts*, (21st edn, 1996) p.312.

[66] Upjohn J. in *Smeaton v Ilford Corp* [1954] Ch. 450 at 474.

[67] [1994] 2 A.C. 264: chemical store in tanning business "an almost classic case of non-natural use".

House of Lords considered that the concept had been extended to an unreasonable extent in attempts to avoid the imposition of liability. Given that liability was restricted by the need to establish that harm of the relevant type was foreseeable, Lord Goff expressed the hope that, in future, courts would not feel obliged to extend the concept of natural use.[68]

In *Transco Plc v Stockport Metropolitan Borough Council*[69] the close **13–16** relationship between what is meant by non-natural use and the dangerous character of the accumulation by the defendant was stressed.[70] In *Transco*, without negligence, there was an escape from a pipe carrying water within a block of flats owned by the defendant authority. The water percolated into an embankment which supported the claimant's 16 inch high pressure gas main, causing the embankment to collapse and leaving the gas main exposed and unsupported. There was an immediate and serious risk that the main might crack and the claimant was put to expense in taking effective remedial measures. It was held that the cost could not be recovered under the rule in *Rylands v Fletcher*. In piping a water supply from the mains to the storage tanks in the flats the local authority was carrying out a routine function which did not raise any special hazard, and constituted a natural use of the land. The question of what was a natural use of land had to be judged by contemporary standards. The test was "whether the defendant has done something which he recognises or ought to recognise, as being quite out of the ordinary in the place and at the time when he does it."[71] The criterion of exceptional risk created a high threshold for a claimant to surmount. Lord Hoffmann, in particular, observed that a useful guide in deciding whether the risk had been created by a non-natural user of land was to ask whether the ultimate damage was something against which the occupier could reasonably be expected to have insured himself.[72] On the facts, there was no evidence that the local authority's use of the land had created a greater risk than was normally associated with domestic or commercial plumbing. Moreover, the risk of damage to property caused by leaking water was one against which most people could and did commonly insure.

Although the keeping of animals on land is likely to be a natural use of land, **13–17** the straying of livestock can attract strict liability by virtue of the provisions of s.4 of the Animals Act 1971.[73] Burning corn stubble in the normal course of agriculture has been held not to be a non-natural use of land and the emission of smoke therefrom was said not to be analogous to the escape of fire or sparks.[74]

Things naturally on the land. The rule in *Rylands v Fletcher* has tradition- **13–18** ally had no application to things, whether dangerous or not, naturally present on the land.

---

[68] *Cambridge Water Co Ltd v Eastern Counties Leather Plc* [1994] 2 A.C. 264 at 309.
[69] [2004] 2 A.C. 1. See Shilton, "Flooding-who bears the brunt?" P.L.J. 2003, 110, 13; also McIntosh, "*Ryands v Fletcher* re-stated" 147 S.J. 1413.
[70] n.69, above, at 11.
[71] per Lord Bingham of Cornhill in *Transco*, n.69, above, at 12.
[72] ibid., per Lord Hoffmann at 21, 22.
[73] See Ch.14, paras 14–58–14–83, below.
[74] *Perkins v Glyn* [1976] R.T.R. ix (Note in April issue).

ILLUSTRATIONS

13–19 Where previously cultivated land had been neglected, thistles sprang up and their seeds were blown onto the adjoining land, causing damage, but the landowner was held not liable for the natural growth of the soil.[75] Nor was the defendant liable where wild rabbits escaped from his land onto adjoining land and damaged crops, even where he had not done all that he could to control them.[76] Likewise, when an overhanging branch of a beech tree broke off and fell, damaging a vehicle on the highway beneath, the landowner was held not liable,[77] although if the branch had been in such a condition "that anyone could see that it might fall at any moment, and probably would fall very soon", there would probably have been be liability for negligence.[78] Similarly, where rocks overhanging a steep slope, broke away as a result of the action of the elements, and crashed into the claimant's house, the landowner was not liable.[79] Where a quarry filled with water as a result of both rain and percolation, the quarry owner was not liable for erosion of the adjoining land by the water, it being "impossible to say that the defendants . . . are responsible for water which they have not themselves brought on to the land, but which is there naturally".[80]

13–20 **Landowners interference with something naturally on the land.** While the defendant is not normally liable for the escape of something naturally on his land, he can become liable in ordinary negligence where he has interfered with a dangerous thing in a way that has contributed to its escape. He may have dug a ditch, altering the course of a stream or cut into an embankment, where it had served as a protection against the natural flow of flood-water on to adjacent land.[81]

13–21 There is a distinction, however, between taking some active step which causes an escape of existing water on to a neighbour's land, and taking protective measures against water that has yet to arrive. In the absence of some contractual obligation, grant or prescriptive right, an occupier is not bound to maintain on his

---

[75] *Giles v Walker* (1890) 24 Q.B.D. 656 a decision the correctness of which was questioned in *Davey v Harrow Corp* [1958] 1 Q.B. 60, CA. In *Morgan v Khyatt* [1964] 1 W.L.R. 475, PC, it was said that *Davey* had been correctly decided. For the possibility of criminal proceedings where damage is cased by injurious weeds, see the Weeds Act 1959.

[76] *Hall v Dart Valley Light Railway* [1998] C.L.Y. 3993.

[77] *Noble v Harrison* [1926] 2 K.B. 332.

[78] *Mackie v Dumbartonshire CC* [1927] W.N. 247. cf. *Bruce v Caulfield* (1918) 34 T.L.R. 204 (tree on defendant's land blown down on to claimant's stable—held, defendant not liable as no evidence that the tree was dangerous); *Shirvell v Hackwood Estates* [1938] 2 K.B. 577; *Cunliffe v Banks* [1945] 1 All E.R. 459 (in each of these cases damage was caused by the fall of a tree, but the defendant's negligence was not established). However, negligence was established in *Paterson v Humberside CC, The Times*, April 19, 1995, CA where damage to a house from the roots of trees caused by subsidence where the soil had dried out was held foreseeable.

[79] *Pontardawe RDC v Moore-Gwyn* [1929] 1 Ch. 656. On the other hand, if the fall of the rocks had been caused by the removal of their natural support so as to render their dangerous condition both patent and imminent, the landowner would have been liable on the ground of negligence.

[80] *Rouse v Gravelworks Ltd* [1940] 1 K.B. 489 at 505, per Goddard L.J. Similarly see *Bartlett v Tottenham* [1932] 1 Ch. 114 at 131, per Lawrence L.J. and per Goddard L.C.J. in *Neath RDC v Williams* [1951] 1 K.B. 115 at 123. See also *Ellison v Ministry of Defence*, 81 B.L.R. 101.

[81] *Whalley v L. & Y. Ry* (1884) 13 Q.B.D. 131.

land something which effectively gives protection to his neighbour against the entry of flood-water.[82] Further, an occupier is entitled to take preventive measures with impunity against something coming on to his land, even if the effect of such will be to cast that something upon his neighbour's land instead.[83] It follows that, in the case of some measure such as raising an embankment, where its purpose is to prevent the flow of flood-water entering his land, it makes no difference at all to the absence of liability, whether it is situated inside or on the boundary line between the land of the defendant and a neighbour.[84]

The wider application of the principle. As the *Rylands* rule developed, it **13–22** became clear that it was not confined simply to the rights of adjacent landowners as between themselves. Lord Sumner said:

> "I am satisfied that *Rylands v Fletcher* is not limited to the case of adjacent freeholders. I shall not attempt to show how far it extends. It extends as far as this case [which dealt with the position of an electricity supply company and a hydraulic power company both laying their mains in the streets], and that is enough for the present purpose,"

adding that in *Rylands v Fletcher*, "both courts however show that they have no intention of confining the principle to the case of adjacent freeholders."[85]

Who is liable for an escape? The positions separately of the owner of the **13–23** danger in question, the occupier of the land from which it escapes and the owner of that land, should be considered. So far as the owner of the danger is concerned, he or she is the person primarily liable, whether or not also having an interest in the land from which the escape occurs.[86] If the danger is brought on to another person's land, the owners of the danger are liable even though "they have no tenancy or independent occupation of the land, but use it thus by permission of the tenants or occupiers,"[87] and a fortiori, if they have no such permission. Under normal principles, the owner is vicariously liable for the actions of employees, agents and in some cases even independent contractors.[88] In the case of an explosion, liability attaches to the person who was carrying on the operations resulting in the explosion.[89]

The occupier of the land onto which the danger has been brought is liable if **13–24** the danger arrived with his knowledge and consent. Accordingly, when a company manufactured explosives on land, occupied by the defendants, and an

---

[82] *Mid-Rhondda Co-operative Society* [1941] 1 K.B. 381.
[83] *Greyvensteyn v Hattingh* [1911] A.C. 355 swarm of locusts; *Lagan Navigation Co v Lambeg Bleaching Co* [1927] A.C. 226, (the height of the river banks was raised against entry of flood water). See further, para.13–71, below.
[84] *Marriage v East Norfolk Rivers Catchment Board* [1949] 2 K.B. 456. See also *Arscott v The Coal Authority* [2005] Env. L.R. 6, CA, para.13–69, below.
[85] *Charing Cross Electricity Supply Co v Hydraulic Power Co* [1914] 3 K.B. 772 at 779, 780. See also per Atkinson J. in *Shiffman v Order of St John* [1936] 1 All E.R. 557 at 561.
[86] *Rainham Chemical Works v Belvedere Fish Guano Co* [1921] 2 A.C. 465 at 479.
[87] *Rainham Chemical Works v Belvedere Fish Guano Co* [1912] 2 A.C. 465 at 479, per Lord Sumner.
[88] *Black v Christchurch Finance Co* [1894] A.C. 48. See also Ch.3, above, paras 3–98–3–203.
[89] *Rainham Chemical Works v Belvedere Fish Guano Co* [1921] 2 A.C. 465.

explosion occurred, the defendants were liable on the ground that they had knowingly permitted the company to carry on its dangerous operations.[90] A little strangely, an occupier who gave a licence to caravan dwellers to park on his land, was liable when they caused damage in the neighbourhood.[91] Where oil leaked from an oil company's tank, which was standing in a railway siding, the railway company was not liable, but only because it could avail itself of a defence that the escape was the result of the wrongful act of third parties, the tank owners, who sent it out in a leaky condition.[92]

13–25   In *Rylands v Fletcher*, Blackburn J. spoke of a person who collected "for his own purposes" anything likely to do mischief if it escapes. Although these words were appropriate to the decision in which they were used, they have not been taken as limiting liability to those cases in which the defendant has obtained some financial or other advantage from collecting the dangerous thing. The purpose for which it is collected is immaterial.[93] When an owner/occupier is bound by contract or prescription or statutory duty to collect a dangerous thing on his land for the purposes of another, while he may be relieved from liability to that other if the dangerous thing were to escape and damage him, he is not thereby relieved from liability to third parties. Accordingly, a local authority which receives sewage into its sewers, in pursuance of its statutory obligations, may well be liable for any escape.[94] The occupier is liable because the dangerous thing was on his land with his knowledge and consent.

13–26   The owner of the land, who is not in occupation, is not the owner of or exercising control over the dangerous thing, and has not expressly or impliedly authorised its presence on the land, is under no liability for an escape. He is only liable, under the ordinary principles of the law of nuisance, if he has let the land for a purpose from which damage is bound to result, without negligence on the part of his tenant.[95] Where the landowner is also the owner of the dangerous thing, the question arises whether he is liable for damage done when the land and the dangerous thing is let to a tenant. Because an occupier of the land cannot escape liability by employing an independent contractor to perform his obligation,[96] in principle, it would seem that an owner is in the same position. This was the view of Atkin L.J. who, saying that the principle of *Pickard v Smith*[97] and *Penny v Wimbledon Urban District Council*[98] applied to persons who brought

---

[90] *Rainham Chemical Works v Belvedere Fish Guano Co* [1921] 2 A.C. 465 at 479 and 480.

[91] *Attorney General v Corke* [1933] Ch. 89.

[92] *Smith v G.W. Ry* (1926) 42 T.L.R. 391.

[93] "It scarcely seems accurate to hold that the nationalised gas industry collects and distributes gas for its 'own purposes'" within the rule in *Rylands v Fletcher*: per Sellers L.J. in *Dunne v North Western Gas Board* [1964] 2 Q.B. 806.

[94] *Smeaton v Ilford Corp* [1954] Ch. 450. See per Upjohn J. at 469, 472. cf. *Dunne v North Western Gas Board* [1964] 2 Q.B. 806.

[95] See *Harris v James* (1876) 45 L.J.Q.B. 545; *Jenkins v Jackson* (1888) 40 Ch.D. 71. In *St Anne's Well Brewery Co v Roberts* (1928) 140 L.T. 1, the CA expressed the opinion that a landowner not in occupation of the land was never liable under *Rylands v Fletcher*. This would require at least the limitation that he is not also the owner of the dangerous thing on the land.

[96] *Rainham Chemical Works v Belvedere Fish Guano Co* [1921] 2 A.C. 465, per Lord Sumner.

[97] (1861) 10 C.B.(N.S.) 470.

[98] [1899] 2 Q.B. 72.

dangerous materials onto land, added: "Can the person who has acquired a tiger, so long as he remains its owner, relieve himself of responsibility by contracting with a third person for its custody?"[99]

Who may sue. The older authorities speak in terms of anyone suffering   **13–27**
damage from an escape having the right to sue. It was not thought necessary that the claimant be the occupier of adjacent land, or indeed any land at all.[100] Blackburn J. himself commented that, on the facts of *Rylands v Fletcher*, the workmen in the drowned mine would have been entitled to recover the value of lost tools,[101] and in cases involving gas explosions[102] and escapes of water from mains,[103] members of the public who were passing along the highway at the time and suffered injury, have been held entitled to sue. It was said that the rule did not deal only with liability of landowners to each other, but made the owner of a dangerous thing liable "'for any mischief thereby occasioned,' that is to say, not mischief necessarily occasioned to the owner of the adjoining land, but any mischief thereby occasioned."[104] So where a claimant's motorcar, left out on the highway, and washing, hung out to dry, were damaged by sulphuric acid smuts or oily drops escaping from the defendant's chimneys at their oil distribution depot, the claimant was entitled to recover damages.[105]

More recently, the origins of the *Rylands* rule in nuisance have been   **13–28**
emphasised.[106] A claim for nuisance can only be maintained by someone having an interest in the land affected,[107] and logically the same should apply to a *Rylands* claim. In *Transco Plc v Stockport Metropolitan Borough Council*[108] it was said that the *Rylands* rule exists "as a remedy for damage to land or interests in land".[109] It would seem likely, given this approach, that earlier cases in which it was contemplated that the action might extend to groups without an interest in the land affected should no longer be regarded as authoritative.[110]

What damage may be recovered. In the leading case itself, Blackburn J. said   **13–29**
that the defendant was "*prima facie* answerable for all the damage which is the

[99] *Belvedere Fish Guano Co v Rainham Chemical Works* [1920] 2 K.B. 487 at 504. cf. Lord Wright in *Brackenborough v Spalding Urban District Council* [1942] A.C. 310 at 324: "In the case of dangerous animals, a transfer of actual possession and control would not necessarily terminate his [the owner's] responsibility."
[100] See *British Celanese v A.H. Hunt (Capacitors) Ltd* [1969] 1 W.L.R. 959.
[101] *Cattle v Stockton Waterworks Co* (1875) L.R. 10 Q.B. 453.
[102] *Price v South Metropolitan Gas Co* (1895) 65 L.J.Q.B. 126.
[103] *Markland v Manchester Corp* [1936] A.C. 360.
[104] *Charing Cross Electricity Supply Co v Hydraulic Power Co* [1914] 3 K.B. 772 at 785, per Bray J.
[105] *Halsey v Esso Petroleum Co Ltd* [1961] 1 W.L.R. 683. See "Wild Beasts in Fulham", 105 S.J. 579, cf. *Vaughn v Halifax-Dartmouth Bridge Commission* (1961) 29 D.L.R. (2d) 523: damage caused to a car by paint blown from painting process of bridge did not arise out of the use and occupation of land and the painting was a natural user of land.
[106] See above, para.13–04.
[107] *Hunter v Canary Wharf Ltd* [1997] A.C. 655.
[108] [2004] 2 A.C. 1.
[109] See per Lord Hoffmann at 19.
[110] In *McKenna v British Aluminium Ltd*, *The Times*, April 25, 2002 a judge at first instance refused an application to strike out claims by persons without an interest in land on the basis that it was arguable that such a restrictive rule should not survive the Human Rights Act 1998.

natural consequence" of the dangerous thing's escape.[111] In light of the House of Lords' decision in *Cambridge Water Co v Eastern Counties Leather Plc*[112] that is too wide a statement to represent the modern law. Foreseeability of damage of the relevant type is required.[113] Even then, not all types of damage are recoverable.

13–30   **Personal injury.** There were long-standing doubts whether the rule encompassed claims for personal injury,[114] but in *Cambridge Water* Lord Goff quoted with approval a passage from a "seminal article"[115] which described as "rash" the conclusion that a remedy for personal injury was given.[116] Thereafter, two members of the House of Lords indicated that damages for personal injuries should not be recoverable in *Rylands v Fletcher* although a contrary view was expressed by a dissenting member.[117] Taking into account further expressions of opinion in the House of Lords in *Transco*,[118] it had been felt that the balance of opinion was heavily against the rule having application to cases of personal injury.[119] Yet in an interlocutory appeal to the Court of Appeal against a refusal to strike out as an abuse of process a claim for personal injury arising out of an alleged public nuisance in *Group Claimants v Corby Borough Council*,[120] the submission that observations in *Hunter v Canary Wharf Ltd*[121] and *Transco Plc v Stockport MBC*[122] had the effect of overruling cases in which damages had been awarded for personal injury in cases of public nuisance was emphatically rejected. Dyson L.J. referred to the "long-established principle that damages for personal injury can be recovered in public nuisance"[123] and added:

> "In the circumstances, it is difficult to see why a person whose life, safety or health has been endangered and adversely affected by an unlawful act or omission and who suffers personal injuries as a result should not be able to recover damages. The purpose of the law which makes it a crime and a tort to do an unlawful act which endangers the life, safety or health of the public is surely to protect the public against the consequences of acts or omissions which do endanger their lives, safety or health. One obvious consequence of such an act or omission is personal injury. The purpose of this law is not to protect the property interest of the public. It is true that the same conduct can

---

[111] (1866) L.R. 1 Ex. 265 at 279.

[112] [1994] 2 A.C. 264.

[113] See per Lord Goff at 306.

[114] For cases on both sides of the question, see earlier editions of this work.

[115] Newark, "The Boundaries of Nuisance" (1949) 65 L.Q.R. 480.

[116] [1994] 2 A.C. 264 at 297, 298.

[117] *Hunter v Canary Wharf Ltd* [1997] A.C. 655 per Lord Goff at 692 and per Lord Lloyd at 696, but per Lord Cooke, dissenting, at 718.

[118] [2004] 2 A.C. 1.

[119] n.118, above e.g. per Lord Bingham of Cornhill at para.[9] and per Lord Hoffmann at para.[35].

[120] [2008] P.I.Q.R. P16 CA, claims by persons born with upper limb deformities who allege that their disabilities arose as a result of exposure of their mothers to toxic materials from a site controlled by the defendant during the embryonic stage of pregnancy. See also Pawlowski, "More than a nuisance: personal injury under Rylands", 153 S.J. 11 which suggests that *Rylands v Fletcher* may still give a remedy to someone claiming to have suffered personal injury as a result of a relevant escape.

[121] n.117, above.

[122] n.118, above.

[123] [2008] P.I.Q.R. P16 at para.[22].

amount to a private nuisance and a public nuisance. But the two torts are distinct and the rights protected by them are different."[124]

Loss[125] arising from damage to chattels has in the past been recovered under **13–31** the *Rylands* rule.[126] Indeed a claimant in nuisance may recover for consequential damage to chattels, provided always that land has also been affected in which he has an interest.[127] It seems likely however that purely economic loss will be regarded as too remote.[128] In *Weller v Foot and Mouth Disease Research Institute*[129] an action was brought by auctioneers, claiming the loss of business which arose when two markets at which cattle were sold by auction were closed after an outbreak of foot and mouth disease in the vicinity. On the assumption that the defendants had imported on their premises an African virus which had escaped and caused the outbreak of the disease it was held, inter alia, that the claimants were not entitled to recover their loss of profits under the *Rylands* rule. One basis of the judgment was expressed to be their lack of any proprietary interest in land on to which the virus could have escaped,[130] but the case is more satisfactorily regarded as an example of the type of loss which will be regarded as too remote.

Highway cases. The requirement that the dangerous thing must have escaped **13–32** from land in the defendants' occupation or control has one exception in the case of the user of a highway. The *Rylands v Fletcher* rule has been held to cover cases where the dangerous thing is brought or carried along the highway.[131] So, when a person brings on or interferes with any dangerous thing upon the highway, as a result of which adjoining property[132] suffers damage, he will be liable without proof of negligence.[133] Where a person sent on to the highway a traction engine and sparks emitted from it caused a fire, he was held liable.[134] Likewise, where an inflammable gas was created by the volatilisation of bitumen, surrounding the defendants' defective underground electricity cable laid in the street, whence it

---

[124] *Corby Group Litigation Claimants v Corby BC* n.123 above at para.[30]. The contrary view advanced by the defendant based on "The Boundaries of Nuisance", Newark, (1949) 65 L.Q.R. 480, was acknowledged by Dyson L.J. to be a "powerful argument", para.[31] but a matter for the House of Lords. The defendant, at the subsequent trial, accepted that it was bound by the decision of the CA but reserved its position for any further appeal: [2009] EWHC 1944 (TCC) para.[685].
[125] For economic loss generally, see Ch.2, paras 2–207–2–237.
[126] See para.13–27, above.
[127] *Hunter v Canary Wharf Ltd* [1997] A.C. 655 at 706.
[128] *Cattle v Stockton Waterworks* (1875) L.R. 10 Q.B. 453 (claimants failed to recover increased cost of constructing a tunnel after an escape of water from defendants' pipes).
[129] [1966] 1 Q.B. 569.
[130] *British Celanese v A.H. Hunt (Capacitors) Ltd* [1969] 1 W.L.R. 959.
[131] *Jones v Festiniog Ry* (1868) L.R. 3 Q.B. 733; *Powell and Fall* (1880) 5 Q.B.D. 597; *Halsey v Esso Petroleum Co* [1961] 1 W.L.R. 683 (where the dangerous thing escapes onto the public highway and damages a personal chattel such as a motorcar parked outside by the roadside).
[132] Which does not include other users of the highway. Such persons must still prove negligence: *Mitchell v Mason* (1966) 10 W.I.R. 26.
[133] "A tiger may neither trespass off the highway nor do damage on the highway without liability to the owner": per Atkin L.J. in *Manton v Brocklebank* [1923] 2 K.B. 212 at 231. Nevertheless, there would be defences open to him by proving either that the accident was the result of an act of God or of a stranger.
[134] *Powell v Fall* (1880) 5 Q.B.D. 597; *West v Bristol Tramways* [1908] 2 K.B. 14.

escaped into the claimant's dwelling-house and caused damage by an explosion and fire, the corporation was held liable.[135]

13–33   **Shipping cases.** The principle has been held not to be applicable where there was an escape from a ship.[136] However, it has been said that, given the extension of the *Rylands* principle to accumulations upon the highway, there are strong arguments to extend it to accumulations in or on a vessel in a navigable river.[137]

2.—DEFENCES

13–34   **Generally.** In giving judgment in *Rylands v Fletcher*,[138] Blackburn J. indicated that there were certain exceptions to the principle of strict liability and, because these will afford a defence to an action based on the rule, each should be considered. They fall under the heads of: (a) act of God; (b) default of the claimant; (c) consent of the claimant; (d) independent act of third party; and (e) statutory authority.

(A) Act of God

13–35   Although the question was reserved in *Rylands v Fletcher*, whether act of God might not have afforded a defence, this question was answered in the affirmative in *Nichols v Marsland*.[139] Strictly the position remains that it has not been established by any decisions of the House of Lords that act of God *is* a defence.[140] However, for an escape of a danger to fall within the description of "act of God" would be a very rare event.

13–36   It has been said that act of God arises as a defence in "circumstances which no human foresight can provide against, and of which human prudence is not bound to recognise the possibility... which when they do occur... are calamities that do not involve the obligation of paying for the consequences that may result from them."[141] Accordingly, to qualify, the occurrence in question must be the result of natural causes and not human agency.[142] If a ship on the high

---

[135] *Midwood v Manchester Corp* [1905] 2 K.B. 597; followed in *Charing Cross Electricity Supply Co v Hydraulic Power Co* [1914] 3 K.B. 772.

[136] *Miller Steamship Co v Overseas Tank Ship (UK) Ltd; The Wagon Mound (No.2)* [1963] 1 Lloyd's Rep. 402, which point did not fall to be considered by the PC [1967] 1 A.C. 617.

[137] per Potter J. in *Crown River Cruisers Ltd v Kimbolton Fireworks Ltd, The Times*, March 6, 1996.

[138] (1866) L.R. 1 Ex. 265, 279–280.

[139] (1876) 2 Ex.D. 1. It is to be observed that Lord Parker in *Greenock Corp v Caledonian Ry* [1917] A.C. 556 at 581 expressed doubts that the finding of fact was correct. See also Barrett, "Common Law Liability for Flood Damage Caused by Storms", 142 New L.J. 1608.

[140] *Greenock Corp v Caledonian Ry* [1917] A.C. 556; *Attorney General v Cory Bros* [1921] 1 A.C. 521.

[141] per Lord Westbury defining the Scottish equivalent (*damnum fatale*) in *Tennent v Earl of Glasgow* (1864) 2 M. (H.L.) 22, approved by the HL in *Greenock Corp v Caledonian Ry* [1917] A.C. 556.

[142] *Forward v Pittard* (1785) 1 T.R. 27, per Lord Mansfield: "Now what is the act of God? I consider it to mean something in opposition to the act of man."

seas were to be overwhelmed by some abnormal wave, this would be an act of God; but if it ran aground during a thick fog as a result of careless navigation, this would be an act of man.[143] To be an act of God an occurrence must be: (a) exclusively the consequence of natural causes; (b) of an extraordinary nature; and (c) such that it could not be anticipated or provided against by the defendant.

In some old cases there was debate whether an act of God was something **13–37** which could not be anticipated or guarded against (adopted by the House of Lords)[144]; or alternatively, something which could not *reasonably* be anticipated or guarded against.[145] The difference is of little practical significance. A man must anticipate as likely to occur, such natural phenomena as have already occurred in the United Kingdom and the margin of safety must be based not on the average but on the extreme. Even when extremes have been ascertained, it is not beyond contemplation that they may be exceeded. There is "no clear-cut choice in law" between the two views and the determination as to whether an occurrence was an act of God "always comes to a question of fact".[146]

Thus, it will be insufficient for the defendant merely to establish that it was not **13–38** reasonably possible either to anticipate the occurrence or to guard effectively against it. In order for the defence to succeed it must be proved that neither was possible. So, the defence was not established where there had been an exceptional storm[147]; a rainfall of extraordinary violence[148]; an exceptionally heavy snow storm[149]; a very high wind[150]; an extraordinarily high tide[151]; an action of a rat gnawing a hole, thereby allowing water to penetrate.[152]

While it is not possible to anticipate every natural catastrophe, it is suggested **13–39** that the only circumstances in which the defence would be likely to succeed in

---

[143] *Liver Alkali Co v Johnson* (1874) L.R. 9 Ex. 338.

[144] *Nugent v Smith* (1875) 1 C.P.D. 19 at 34, per Brett J.; *Hamilton v Pandorf* (1886) 17 Q.B.D. 670 at 675, per Lord Esher; *R. v Commrs of Sewers for Essex* (1885) 14 Q.B.D. 561 at 574, per Coleridge C.J. and Cave J. cf. *G.W. Ry v Owners of S.S. Mostyn* [1928] A.C. 57 at 105, where Lord Blanesburgh refers to an act of God as something which had taken a ship out of control "by an irresistible and unsearchable providence nullifying all human effort".

[145] *Nugent v Smith* (1876) 1 C.P.D. 423, per Cockburn C.J. (at 426) and James L.J. (at 444); *Nichols v Marsland* [1917] A.C. 556; *Nitro-Phosphate and Odam's Manure Co v London and St Katherine Docks* (1878) 9 Ch.D. 503, per Fry J.; *Baldwin's Ltd v Halifax Corp* (1916) 85 L.J.K.B. 1769, per Atkin J.

[146] per Lord Dunedin in *Greenock Corp v Caledonian Ry* [1917] A.C. 556 at 577.

[147] *Ruck v Williams* (1858) 3 H. & n.308. See per Bramwell B. at 318.

[148] *Greenock Corp v Caledonian Ry* [1917] A.C. 556 and criticising the finding of fact by the jury in *Nichols v Marsland* (1876) 2 Ex.D. 1; *G.W. Ry of Canada v Braid* (1863) 1 Moo. P.C. (N.S.) 101 at 121; *City of Montreal v Watt & Scott Ltd* [1922] 2 A.C. 555.

[149] *Fenwick v Schmalz* (1868) L.R. 3 C.P. 313 at 316; *Slater v Worthington's Cash Stores* [1941] 1 K.B. 488; *Makin v L.N.E.R.* [1943] K.B. 467 at 478, per Goddard L.J.

[150] *Cushing v Peter Walker & Son* [1941] 2 All E.R. 693 at 695, per Hallett J.; *Legacy v Chaleur Country Club* (1975) 53 D.L.R. (3d) 725.

[151] *R. v Commrs of Sewers for Essex* (1885) 14 Q.B.D. 561 at 574, affirmed (1886) 11 App.Cas. 449; *Greenwood Tileries Ltd v Clapson* [1937] 1 All E.R. 765.

[152] *Pandorf v Hamilton* (1887) 12 App.Cas. 518. cf. *Bishop v Consolidated London Properties* (1933) 102 L.J.K.B. 257 (a pigeon blocked an open gutter and caused an overflow but the landlord of the property was held liable. In any event the action of a rat both could be foreseen and guarded against by the defendant). Also see *Northwestern Utilities v London Guarantee and Accident Co* [1936] A.C. 108 (a comparable situation dealing with the act of a stranger).

the United Kingdom would be an event such as an earthquake, volcanic eruption or unusual tidal wave. Lightning is one of the more usual illustrations of an act of God,[153] although there is no decided case in England. But in Western Australia, where a fire was caused by lightning, it was held that it had not been caused by the defendant but "it came there from the skies".[154] The sudden death from heart failure of the driver of a motor vehicle while at the wheel, has been held to be an act of God.[155] It should be otherwise if a driver had reason to suspect that he was suffering from heart disease which was capable of affecting his ability to drive safely.

(B) Default of the claimant

13-40   In *Rylands v Fletcher*, Blackburn J. said that the defendant "can excuse himself by showing that the escape was due to the plaintiff's default".[156] In effect, if the sole cause of the damage is the act or default of the claimant himself, his action cannot succeed.[157] Thus, where the Postmaster-General negligently laid telegraph lines close to electric cables belonging to a local authority and the lines were thereby exposed to unnecessary danger, which it had been the duty of the person laying them to avoid, it was held that damages were not recoverable. This was in spite of the fact that under the Telegraph Act 1878 s.8, the local authority was made absolutely liable for damage to the lines caused by their cables.[158] An alternative solution to a similar claim was found in *Post Office v Hampshire County Council*,[159] where the claimant's action was dismissed on the grounds of circuity of action because, although the cause of the rupture to its underground cable was the voluntary act of the defendant council's workmen, the local authority had a good claim in damages, based on the negligence of the claimant for its misinformation, for whatever sum the defendant was held to be liable absolutely under the Act.

13-41   Where electricity leaked from the defendants' tram-lines circuit and damaged a very sensitive piece of apparatus on the claimants' premises, an action for

---

[153] See *Carstairs v Taylor* (1871) L.R. 6 Ex. 217; *Nichols v Marsland* (1875) L.R. 10 Ex. 255 at 260, per Bramwell B.; *Anon.* (1538) Dyer 33, Case (10).

[154] *Hargrave v Goldman* [1965] A.L.R. 377 at 386.

[155] *Ryan v Youngs* [1938] 1 All E.R. 522. See *J. Constantine S.S. Line Ltd v Imperial Smelting Corp Ltd* [1942] A.C. 154 at 202; also cf. *The Saint Angus* [1938] P. 225 (a case of illness).

[156] (1868) L.R. 1 Ex. 265 at 279–280.

[157] If the damage is only partly the result of the claimant's act or default, the damages will be apportioned under the Law Reform (Contributory Negligence) Act 1945, above, Ch.4, above, paras 4-03–4-72.

[158] *Postmaster-General v Liverpool Corp* [1923] A.C. 587, distinguished in *Post Office v Mears Construction Ltd* [1979] 2 All E.R. 813, where it was held that the Post Office was under a duty to do nothing more than supply a plan, indicating approximately where its cables lay, so that the contractors of the local authority were held liable for the damage caused to these cables by virtue of s.8 of the Telegraph Act 1878, irrespective of the disclaimer as to the plan's accuracy. See also *Postmaster-General v Beck and Pollitzer* [1924] 2 Q.B. 308. cf. *Bell Can v Cope (Sarnia)* [1980] 11 C.C.L.T. 170, where liability was apportioned one-third against the defendant contractors and two-thirds against the claimants, who were primarily to blame because of the carelessness in giving information about their cables so that the defendants had been lulled into a false sense of security, from which they had never extricated themselves.

[159] [1980] Q.B. 124.

damages failed, because it was held that a person cannot increase his neighbours' liabilities by applying some special use to his own property.[160] Likewise, where the claimants worked a mine beneath the defendants' canal, they failed in an action to recover for damage caused when water from the canal escaped into and flooded the mine.[161] Since a person is entitled to assume that others will perform that which is their legal duty, he may regulate his actions in that expectation, so that it is not usually negligence to omit to take precautions against the consequences of another's failure to perform his duty under *Rylands v Fletcher*.[162]

Persons who meddle with dangerous animals cannot recover damages if they are injured.[163]

(C) Consent of the claimant

If an injured person has agreed to run the risk of damage from a dangerous **13–42** thing, he cannot succeed in an action based upon its escape, unless it can be shown that the damage was caused by the omission to use reasonable care, that is, negligence, on the part of the defendant. So, when the owners of land gave permission to their lessees to tip colliery spoil on the side of the hill, they could not recover for damage caused by the spoil sliding down the hill into the valley below, except on proof of negligence on the part of the lessees.[164] Again, a person, who enters into occupation of premises, "takes the premises as they are, and, accordingly, consents to the presence there of the installed water system with all its advantages and disadvantages".[165]

The defence of consent to a claim based on *Rylands v Fletcher* was not **13–43** available to a negligent defendant in *Colour Quest Ltd v Total Downstream UK Plc*[166] which concerned a large number of claims arising out of explosions on December 11, 2005 at the Buncefield Oil Storage Depot at Hemel Hempstead, Hertfordshire. A large amount of petrol vapour accumulated after the failure of employees of one of the companies responsible for the storage of oil at the depot to notice that an oil tank gauge was stuck, as a result of which the amount of space within the tank for further oil to be added was incorrectly displayed. That and other systemic negligence defeated the defendants' contention that the

---

[160] *Eastern & South African Telegraph Co Ltd v Cape Town Tramways* [1902] A.C. 381.

[161] *Dunn v Birmingham Canal Co* (1872) L.R. 7 Q.B. 244.

[162] See *Miles v Forest Rock Granite Co Ltd* (1918) 34 T.L.R. 500, where the claimant, who was injured while passing along the highway, owing to the failure of the defendants to keep the results of their blasting operations on their own land, was not prevented from recovering by the fact that he disregarded the warnings of men and red flags posted by the defendants on the highway; also *Daniel v Metropolitan Ry* (1871) L.R. 5 H.L. 45.

[163] See Ch.14, paras 14–42–14–49, below.

[164] *Attorney General v Cory Bros* [1921] A.C. 521 at 539 per Lord Finlay: "A plaintiff who is himself a consenting party to the accumulation cannot rely simply upon the escape of the accumulated material; he must further establish that the escape was due to want of reasonable care on the part of the person who made the deposit."

[165] *Peters v Prince of Wales Theatre* [1943] K.B. 73 at 79, per Lord Goddard C.J.

[166] [2009] EWHC 540 (Comm), David Steel J., Ch.3, para.3–153, above.

claimants had consented to the bringing of oil product onto the site and its accumulation there.

13–44   Whether or not the claimant has agreed, expressly[167] or by implication, to take upon himself the risk of injury from the dangerous thing is a question of fact, but the mere fact that he occupies premises near to a gasworks or a munitions factory, does not mean that he has necessarily agreed to bear the risk of an explosion, except where he can prove negligence. It would be otherwise if he were the owner of the land and had let it to a tenant for that purpose.

13–45   **Common benefit.** If the dangerous thing has been brought upon premises for the common benefit of the claimant and the defendant, there is an implied agreement to run the risk of damage, unless negligence on the part of the defendant can be proved. A typical example of this is to be found in cases where water is collected from the spouts of a building, or a cistern is maintained for the common use of the occupiers of different floors in the same building.[168] These cases are considered in further detail, later.[169] There is no common benefit or common interest for this purpose between a statutory supplier of gas, water or electricity and the individual consumer.[170]

13–46   In addition to these cases, there is a tendency to hold that damage caused by the ordinary domestic installation of gas, water and electricity is never actionable except on proof of negligence.[171]

(D) Independent act of third party

13–47   The rule in *Rylands v Fletcher* does not apply where the damage has been caused by the independent act of a third party, which could not reasonably have been foreseen and guarded against. The basis for the exception[172] is that the defendant has fulfilled his duty of keeping the dangerous thing harmless and that the cause of the damage was "the conscious act of another volition".[173] In considering the escape of water from a reservoir, this question was posed[174]:

---

[167] Although an exemption clause is not subject to control so far as it excludes or restricts liability under the rule in *Rylands v Fletcher*, where the facts also give rise to liability in negligence, any such exemption clause then will fall to be controlled under Pt 1 of the Unfair Contract Terms Act 1977, which came into force on February 1, 1978. For a summary of its provisions see Ch.4, paras 4–84–4–86, above.

[168] *Carstairs v Taylor* (1871) L.R. 6 Ex. 217; *Rickards v Lothian* [1913] A.C. 263; *Anderson v Oppenheimer* (1880) 5 Q.B.D. 602; *Blake v Woolf* [1898] 2 Q.B. 426; *Kiddle v City Business Properties Ltd* [1942] 1 K.B. 269.

[169] paras 13–95–13–101, below (water).

[170] *Northwestern Utilities Ltd v London Guarantee and Accident Co* [1936] A.C. 108 at 120; *A. Prosser & Son Ltd v Levy* [1955] 1 W.L.R. 1224 (it was held that the claimant did not impliedly consent to the presence of a water pipe which, unknown to him, was defective).

[171] *Collingwood v Home and Colonial Stores* [1936] 3 All E.R. 200; *Tilley v Stevenson* [1939] 4 All E.R. 207.

[172] This exception was first recognised in *Box v Jubb* (1879) 4 Ex.D. 76 at 79, per Kelly C.B.

[173] Lord Dunedin in *Dominion Natural Gas Co v Collins* [1909] A.C. 640 at 647. See also *Northwestern Utilities v London Guarantee and Accident Co* [1936] A.C. 108 at 120.

[174] per Bramwell B. in *Nichols v Marsland* (1875) L.R. 10 Ex. 255 at 259, affirmed (1876) 2 Ex.D. 1.

"Suppose a stranger let it loose, would the defendant be liable? If so, then if a mischievous boy bored a hole in a cistern in any London house, and the water did mischief to a neighbour, the occupier of the house would be liable. That cannot be."

In a later case: "if the mischievous, deliberate and conscious act of a stranger causes the damage, the occupier can escape liability; he is absolved."[175]

13–48 Accordingly, when damage was caused to the occupier of the lower floor of a building by an overflow of water from the lavatory basin in the upper floor, and it was proved that the overflow was caused by the malicious act of a third person in turning the tap fully on and plugging the wastepipe, the occupier of the upper floor was held not liable.[176] The defendant could not be said "to have caused or allowed the water to escape if the malicious act of a third person was the real cause of its escaping without any fault on the part of the defendant".[177] Further, where a coach with an empty petrol tank was in a car park and some boys threw a lighted match into the petrol tank, which caused petrol fumes within to explode and injure the 10-year-old claimant, standing nearby, the owners of the coach were held not liable. The explosion was caused by the act of strangers, which could not reasonably have been anticipated and guarded against by the owners.[178] The exception does not apply in the case of damage caused by an animal in circumstances where liability attaches to the keeper under the Animals Act 1971.

13–49 **Meaning of "third party".** There has been no definition of "third party" (or the alternative expression "stranger") for these purposes, although the reported examples do provide a guide. Under the usual principles the defendant is liable for the acts of his employees or agents acting within the scope of their employment or authority.[179] Thereafter the starting point is control. Was the interfering third party one over whose activity the defendant had control?[180] He can be liable for the actions of an independent contractor where he has control over him, in the sense of having invited him upon the land and given a permission to work there which could at any time be withdrawn.[181] The liability goes beyond independent contractors to embrace anyone to whom he gives authority to interfere with the dangerous thing.[182] The defendant's licensee may or may not be a stranger depending upon whether his activities can be

---

[175] per Singleton L.J. in *Perry v Kendricks Transport Ltd* [1956] 1 W.L.R. 85 at 87.
[176] *Rickards v Lothian* [1913] A.C. 263; *A. Prosser & Son Ltd v Levy* [1955] 1 W.L.R. 1224.
[177] per Lord Moulton in *Rickards v Lothian* [1913] A.C. 263 at 278.
[178] *Perry v Kendricks Transport Ltd* [1956] 1 W.L.R. 85.
[179] *Baker v Snell* [1908] 2 K.B. 825 (CA ordered new trial to determine whether the defendant's employee was acting within the course of his employment when he incited a dog to attack a maid); *Stevens v Woodward* (1881) 6 Q.B.D. 318 at 321 (no liability for employee going where he was forbidden to go).
[180] *Perry v Kendricks Transport Ltd* [1956] 1 W.L.R. 85.
[181] *Rylands v Fletcher* (1866) L.R. 1 Ex. 265; *Balfour v Barty-King* [1957] 1 Q.B. 496 at 505.
[182] *Hardaker v Idle District Council* [1896] 1 Q.B. 335; *Black v Christchurch Finance Co* [1894] A.C. 48.

controlled.[183] There will be few cases in which a trespasser is not a stranger within the present meaning. A stranger is one over whom the defendant had no control and whose act was unforeseeable and without permission.[184]

13–50   **Test of negligence.** Even where the damage has been caused by the act of a third party, the owner of the dangerous thing is liable if there has been negligence on his part. Negligence, in this context, means failing to guard against that which the owner ought reasonably to have foreseen. For example, in *Box v Jubb*[185] the defendants were not liable, when the act of a stranger was one which they " . . . could not possibly have been expected to anticipate" and which they had no means of preventing. In a later case,[186] Lord Wright said: "Though the act of a third party may be relied on by way of defence in cases of this type, the defendant may still be held liable in negligence if he failed in foreseeing and guarding against the consequences to his works of that third party's act." Accordingly, where a gas main was broken, in consequence of the removal of support by a local authority constructing a sewer, it was held that, although the cause of the fracture was the act of a third party (that is, the local authority), the gas company was liable for the consequent explosion in failing to guard against possible damage to its mains from the local authority's excavation.[187]

13–51   The exception only applies when the act of the third party is a fresh, independent act.[188] In *Rickards v Lothian*,[189] the act of a third party was described as "malicious," later interpreted as meaning a deliberate or conscious act.[190] In *Philco v J. Spurling Ltd*,[191] carriers erroneously delivered highly inflammable film scrap to the wrong address. No proper warning of its dangerous character was given and when it was on the claimant's premises one of the claimant's typists set it on fire with her cigarette. An explosion occurred, causing serious damage. The defendants were held liable, because the evidence did not

---

[183] *Smith v G.W. Ry* (1926) 42 T.L.R. 391 (railway company not liable for leakage of oil from a truck into claimant's watercourse where the truck was owned by "third party" oil company); *Holderness v Goslin* [1975] 2 N.Z.L.R. 46 (defendant liable for fire damage to claimant's fences where the fire was started by the son of his farm manager, who burned gorse during the closed fire season).

[184] *Perry v Kendricks Transport Ltd* [1956] 1 W.L.R. 85, per Parker L.J. at 92 and applied in *H. & N. Emanuel v Greater London Council* [1971] 2 All E.R. 835, CA; see also *Hale v Jennings Bros* [1938] 1 All E.R. 579, CA.

[185] (1879) 4 Ex.D. 76. The same test was applied in *Smith v G.W. Ry* (1926) 42 T.L.R. 391. In *Rickards v Lothian* [1913] A.C. 263 at 274 it was held that the omission to ask the jury the question whether the defendant ought reasonably to have anticipated the act of the third party, was fatal to any attempt to render him liable, when the damage was in fact caused by the third party's act.

[186] *Northwestern Utilities v London Guarantee and Accident Co* [1936] A.C. 108 at 125. See also to the same effect, per Atkinson J. in *Shiffman v Order of St John* [1936] 1 All E.R. 557.

[187] *Northwestern Utilities Ltd v London Guarantee and Accident Co*, above. The failure to make proper inspections of a spillway so as to keep it clear of logs and boulders, even although such obstructions were caused partly by the act of another in diverting a small stream, amounted to negligence, since it ought to have been foreseen: *Lewis v District of North Vancouver* (1963) 40 D.L.R. (2d) 182.

[188] per Lord Dunedin in *Dominion Natural Gas Co v Collins* [1909] A.C. 640 at 646, quoted above at para.13–47.

[189] [1913] A.C. 263.

[190] per Lord Wright in *Northwestern Utilities Ltd v London Guarantee and Accident Co* n.186 above at 119.

[191] [1949] 2 All E.R. 882. See also *Prosser & Son Ltd v Levy* [1955] 1 W.L.R. 1224.

establish that the fire was caused by the deliberate act of the typist. Had it been so caused, the majority of the court would have held that the defendants were not liable.

Burden of proof. The burden of proving the defence of a third party's **13–52** independent act is on the defendant. On proof by the claimant that a dangerous thing, for which the defendant is responsible, caused the damage in question, the defendant is liable, unless it is shown: (a) that the damage was caused by the independent act of a third party; and (b) that the act could not reasonably have been anticipated and guarded against. These two elements, combined, form the defence. It is insufficient merely for the defendant to prove (a) and then to attempt to throw the burden of proving (b) on the claimant. So, in *Rylands v Fletcher*, Blackburn J. said: "He [the defendant] can excuse himself by showing that the escape was owing to the plaintiff's default; or perhaps that the escape was the consequence of *vis major*, or the act of God."[192] In a later case it was put as follows:

> "A person who brings a dangerous thing onto his land and allows it to escape, thereby causing damage to another, is liable to that other unless he can show that the escape was due to the conscious act of a third party, and without negligence on his own part. Obviously, the burden of showing that there was no negligence is not the defendants, and it is not for the plaintiff to prove negligence affirmatively."[193]

(E) Statutory Authority

If a danger has been created or maintained under statutory authority, there is **13–53** no liability under the rule in *Rylands v Fletcher*. Usually in such a case liability will only be established if negligence is proved. It "is now thoroughly well established that no action will lie for doing that which the legislature has authorised, if it be done without negligence, although it does occasion damage to anyone; but an action does lie for doing that which the legislature has authorised, if it be done negligently."[194] Accordingly, in actions against gas, water and electricity undertakings, which operate under statutory powers, the rule in *Rylands v Fletcher* is not applicable.[195] Of course, the statutory authorisation may preserve the liability of the statutory undertaker for nuisance[196] and, in such

---

[192] (1868) L.R. 1 Ex. 265 at 279, 280. See further per Lord Wright in *Northwestern Utilities Ltd v London Guarantee and Accident Co* [1936] A.C. 108, at 120.
[193] per Goddard L.J. in *Hanson v Wearmouth Coal Co* [1939] 3 All E.R. 47, 53.
[194] *Geddis v Proprietors of Bann Reservoir* (1878) 3 App.Cas. 430 at 455, per Lord Blackburn. See also *Dunne v North Western Gas Board* [1964] 2 Q.B. 806.
[195] *Green v Chelsea Waterworks Co* (1894) 70 L.T. 547; *Northwestern Utilities Ltd v London Guarantee and Accident Co* [1936] A.C. 108. See further para.13–129 (gas), 13–57 (water) and 13–153 (electricity), below.
[196] In *Department of Transport v North West Water Authority* [1984] A.C. 336, it was held that the Public Utilities Street Works Act 1950 s.18(2), did not alter the existing law that a body was not liable for a nuisance, which was attributable to its performance of a statutory duty, albeit the statute expressly preserved liability in nuisance (applying *Stretton's Derby Brewery Co v Mayor of Derby* [1894] 1 Ch. 431 and *Smeaton v Ilford Corp* [1954] Ch. 450).

a case, it is unnecessary to prove negligence.[197] To be a defence, the statute must authorise the creation or maintenance of the dangerous thing expressly or by necessary implication[198]; it is not enough merely to permit it to be used.[199] The exact position depends on the construction of the statute in question.

13–54   In considering whether the statutory authority has been exercised without negligence, the degree of care to be taken must be proportionate to the degree of risk involved.[200] When dealing with any dangerous things, a very high degree of care is required. The statutory undertakers must use all reasonable care in the erection and maintenance of their works. They are not bound "to ransack science in the hope of discovering some scientific specific against possible accident," but are bound "to use well-known scientific means".[201] This may involve their consulting outside experts in addition to the technical and scientific members of their own staffs.[202] Whilst they must use reasonable care to maintain their works in a state of efficiency, they are not liable solely because they have not "adopted the last inventions of ever-changing, ever-advancing scientific discovery."[203] At the same time,

" . . . the authority to erect and work the plant and the obligation in both respects to use reasonable care and precautions are correlative, and erection cannot be so severed from use and maintenance as to entitle the undertakers to go on permanently using a plant with all its original imperfections unremedied, merely on the ground that original faults in construction must be deemed to be irremediable in subsequent use. Reasonableness applies not merely to construction but to improvement."[204]

Inevitably what amounts to negligence will depend on the circumstances of the particular case.[205]

13–55   **Burden of proof.** The burden of proof is on the statutory undertaker to prove that it has statutory authority to create, maintain or use the dangerous thing, and that it is exercising its powers without negligence.[206]

13–56   **Statutes imposing strict liability.** Some statutes impose strict liability for the escape of a dangerous thing, for example, the Reservoirs Act 1975.[207] Likewise

---

[197] *Midwood v Manchester Corp* [1905] 2 K.B. 597; *Charing Cross Electricity Supply Co v Hydraulic Power Co* [1914] 3 K.B. 772.
[198] *West v Bristol Tramways* [1908] 2 K.B. 14.
[199] *Jones v Festiniog Ry* (1868) L.R. 3 Q.B. 733.
[200] *Northwestern Utilities Ltd v London Guarantee and Accident Co* n.195, above at 126, per Lord Wright.
[201] *Snook v Grand Junction Waterworks* (1886) 2 T.L.R. 308.
[202] *Manchester Corp v Farnworth* [1930] A.C. 171.
[203] *National Telephone Co v Baker* [1893] 2 Ch. 186 at 205.
[204] *Manchester Corp v Farnworth* [1930] A.C. 171, per Lord Sumner, at 202.
[205] In addition to the cases already quoted, the following may be referred to: *Midwood v Manchester Corp* [1905] 2 K.B. 597 at 608; *Quebec Ry v Vandry* [1920] A.C. 662; *Eastern and South African Telephone Co v Cape Town Tramways* [1902] A.C. 381.
[206] *Manchester Corp v Farnworth*, n.204, above.
[207] Which, by s.28 has repealed and re-enacted the Reservoirs (Safety Provisions) Act 1930. See para.13–84, below.

strict liability is imposed in relation to the escape of ionising radiations[208] oil pollution[209] and the dumping of very long-life toxic waste materials.[210]

3.—WATER

Liability for accumulating water. Someone who, as a non-natural user,   **13–57** accumulates water on land does so at their peril.[211] It matters not whether the water is accumulated in a reservoir,[212] a tank,[213] a mound of earth,[214] a cellar[215] or even a drain which has become blocked through neglect.[216]

On the other hand, if a person who is a natural user of land accumulates water   **13–58** on it, for example in a pond or a stream, there is no liability under *Rylands v Fletcher* for damage caused by its overflow.[217] The same applies where a landowner does something on his own land, such as digging a trench to lay a pipe,[218] which causes water naturally on the land to flow more quickly onto his neighbour's land, provided that he does not collect it in any way. But if he causes more water to be discharged from his land onto his neighbour's land than would normally be the case, or collects the drainage of his land into one place and discharges it onto his neighbour's land, he will be liable.[219]

Water on the highway. A highway authority is not entitled to discharge water   **13–59** from the highway onto the lands of adjoining occupiers, or to construct roads which are so inadequately drained that water is caused to flow onto the adjoining land. Where a local authority built a road on the side of a hill, so that it acted as a catch-water for rain-water from the upper slopes and also caught loose shale brought down by the rain, with the result that, in a heavy rain, vast quantities of

---

[208] Nuclear Installations Acts 1965–1969. See para.13–198, below, and Lloyd, "Liability for Radiation Injuries" [1959] C.L.P. 33.
[209] Prevention of Oil Pollution Act 1971. See paras 13–192–13–200, below.
[210] Deposit of Poisonous Waste Act 1972, which was repealed by the Control of Pollution Act 1974 Sch.4, and re-enacted in s.88.
[211] *Rylands v Fletcher* (1868) L.R. 3 H.L. 330.
[212] *Rylands v Fletcher* n.211, above.
[213] *Western Engraving Co v Film Laboratories Ltd* [1936] 1 All E.R. 106: closed apparatus, a boiler, a sink and other containers used in the cinematographic business.
[214] *Hurdman v North Eastern Ry* (1878) 3 C.P.D. 168. To the same effect is *Maberley v Peabody & Co* [1946] 2 All E.R. 192, and see *Broder v Saillard* (1876) 2 Ch.D. 692 (the defendant was liable where water from his broken soil pipe discharged into an artificial mound of earth made by him against the claimant's wall).
[215] *Snow v Whitehead* (1884) 27 Ch.D. 588.
[216] *Sedleigh-Denfield v O'Callaghan* [1940] A.C. 880.
[217] The decision that there had been a natural user of land in *Rouse v Gravelworks Ltd* [1940] 1 K.B. 489 where water had accumulated in a quarry was criticised in *Leakey v National Trust* [1980] Q.B. 485, the CA preferring *Davey v Harrow Corporation* [1958] 1 Q.B. 60 where the encroachment of roots and branches onto a neighbour's land causing damage gave the neighbour an action in nuisance.
[218] *Barlett v Tottenham* [1932] 1 Ch. 114: an underground spring was tapped with the result that water was discharged on to the claimant's land.
[219] *Hurdman v North Eastern Ry* (1878) 3 C.P.D. 168, *Whalley v L. & Y. Ry* (1884) 13 Q.B.D. 131.

water and shale were caught and overflowed onto property in the valley below, the authority was liable for failing to provide against what occurred.[220] A highway authority was also liable where it raised the level of a footpath, so that a wooden fence adjoining the path decayed, through the percolation of dampness from the adjoining soil.[221]

13-60   **Natural streams: diversions.** A person who diverts the course of a natural stream is liable for any reasonably foreseeable[222] damage caused by the water escaping from the channel, even if not negligent,[223] because:

> "it is the duty of any one who interferes with the course of a stream to see that the works which he substitutes for the channel provided by nature are adequate to carry off the water brought down even by extraordinary rainfall, and if damage results from the deficiency of the substitute which he has provided for the natural channel he will be liable."[224]

13-61   Other than the defences described above,[225] the defendant can escape liability by proving that a diversion has been established by prescription, in the sense that "the existence of a state of things for the period of the long prescription may serve to prevent any person alleging that another state of things was the true state of nature."[226] Notwithstanding prescription, where a culvert, built by the predecessor of the defendant highway authority to take a stream under the highway, ceased to be adequate for its purpose and caused flooding, it was held that there was a duty imposed on the defendant to do what was reasonable to abate what was causing or might become a nuisance.[227] There was a high obligation on the defendant to ensure that the stream continued to flow under the highway and the means existed to prevent flooding without great difficulty, albeit at some cost. A defendant may, of course, be able to establish that even if the diversion had not occurred the claimant's damage would have been the same.[228]

---

[220] *Baldwins Ltd v Halifax Corp* (1916) 85 L.J.K.B. 1769. See also *Thomas v Gower RDC* [1922] 2 K.B. 76 (highway authority held liable when it diverted two streams to one culvert and thereby flooded the claimant's land—s.67 of the Highway Act 1835 no defence.) But cf. *Ely Brewery Co v Pontypridd UDC* (1903) 68 J.P. 3 (retaining wall built across street—no interference with ordinary flow of surface water—diverted unusual flow caused by wrongful act of third parties onto claimant's land—highway authority not liable).
[221] *Rochford v Essex CC* (1915) 85 L.J. Ch. 281.
[222] *Cambridge Water Co v Eastern Counties Leather Plc* [1994] 2 A.C. 264 and para.13–15, above.
[223] See *R. v Southern Canada Power Co Ltd* [1937] 3 All E.R. 923.
[224] per Lord Finlay in *Greenock Corp v Caledonian Ry* [1917] A.C. 556 at 572, (the course of a natural stream was diverted to make a children's paddling pool which burst its banks during heavy rain and damaged railway property. See also *Fletcher v Smith* (1877) 2 App.Cas. 781 at 787, per Lord Penzance and *Workman v G.N. Ry* (1863) 32 L.J.Q.B. 279: diversion of a flood channel may be the quivalent of diverting the stream itself.
[225] paras 13–34–13–61, above.
[226] *Greenock Corp v Caledonian Ry* [1917] A.C. 556, per Lord Dunedin at 578.
[227] *Bybrook Barn Centre Ltd v Kent County Council, The Times*, January 5, 2001, CA.
[228] *Bybrook Barn Centre Ltd v Kent County Council, The Times*, January 5, 2001, CA. See further, *Nitro-Phosphate & Odam's Chemical Manure Co v London & St Katharine Docks* (1878) 9 Ch.D. 503; *Baldwins Ltd v Halifax Corp* (1916) 85 L.J.K.B. 1769 at 1774.

Natural streams: overflowing. In contrast to the above, an owner was not **13–62**
liable where there had been no diversion of a natural stream but it overflowed and
water accumulated against a wall, which failed to withstand the pressure and
burst, flooding adjacent land.[229]

Natural streams: damming. A dam built across a stream which gave way in **13–63**
a time of flood and caused damage to a neighbouring mill rendered the land
owner liable because his damming created the danger in the first place.[230]

Natural streams: bridging. If a bridge is built over a stream in such a way **13–64**
that it becomes choked in time of flood, the person responsible for building it is
liable for any damage which is caused by such flooding.[231]

Natural streams: culverting. If a stream is enclosed in a culvert and, owing **13–65**
either to its inadequacy to cope with the volume of water flowing at any one
time[232] or to its bad state of repair[233] it breaks through the culvert in time of flood
and damages neighbouring property, the owner of the culvert is liable on the
principle of *Rylands v Fletcher*.[234] Where an artificial watercourse was culverted
and became blocked, so that adjoining land was flooded, the occupier of the
watercourse was held liable in nuisance.[235]

Watercourse. A person who constructs a watercourse on his land will be **13–66**
liable, in the event of water escaping from it and doing damage, in the same
manner as was the owner of the reservoir in *Rylands v Fletcher*. Where a
landowner, in order to bring water from a river to his mill, made a watercourse
with a shuttle at its head to control the flow of the water from the river into the
watercourse, his successors in title were held liable for damage caused to
neighbouring owners by flooding owing to their failure to keep the shuttle in
repair.[236] Had a watercourse been constructed for the mutual benefit of the
claimant and the defendant, no liability for damage caused by an overflow would
arise unless there was negligence on the part of the defendant.[237]

Natural streams: silting up. While it was formerly held that the owner of the **13–67**
bed of a stream was not liable the growth of weeds caused the stream to silt up

---

[229] *Tennent v Earl of Glasgow* (1864) 2 M. 22, HL.
[230] *Kerr v Earl of Orkney* (1857) 20 D. 298, approved in *Greenock Corp v Caledonian Ry* [1917] A.C.
556. But cf. *Nichols v Marsland* (1876) 2 Ex.D. 1, where the defence of act of God succeeded,
although the finding was criticised in the *Greenock Corp* case.
[231] *Ferrand v Midland Ry* (1901) 17 T.L.R. 427.
[232] *Greenock Corp v Caledonian Ry* [1917] A.C. 556.
[233] *Booth v Thomas* [1926] Ch. 109, per Russell J.; affirmed on other grounds [1926] Ch. 397.
Pemberton v Bright and the Devon County Council [1960] 1 W.L.R. 436.
[234] (1866) L.R. 1 Ex. 265.
[235] *Sedleigh-Denfield v O'Callaghan* [1940] A.C. 880. See also *Bybrook Barn Centre Ltd v Kent
County Council, The Times*, January 5, 2001, CA.
[236] *R. H. Buckley & Sons Ltd v n.Buckle & Sons* [1898] 2 Q.B. 608 at 614.
[237] *Whitmores Ltd v Stanford* [1909] 1 Ch. 427.

so that flooding occurred,[238] it is doubtful after *Leakey v National Trust* whether that remains the position.[239] In extending the duty explained in *Goldman v Hargarve*,[240] Megaw L.J. recognised the potential for injustice to a neighbour who might be affected by an overflow due to flooding: "If the risk is one which can readily be overcome or lessened, for example by reasonable steps on the part of the landowner to keep the stream free from blockage by flotsam or silt carried down, he will be in breach of duty if he does nothing or does too little." The case would be largely[241] indistinguishable from a situation where the owners of a reservoir had power to discharge surplus water into a river, via a little stream, and, owing to the channel of the stream being silted up, the water overflowed the banks of the stream and caused damage. The owners were held liable because of their negligence in discharging water into a stream, a channel of which was silted up.[242]

13–68   **Discharging accumulated water onto land of another.** The proprietor of higher land has a natural right to have the water, which naturally falls on his land, discharge onto the contiguous lower land of another proprietor[243]; but if water has accumulated naturally on a person's land he must not interfere with it, so as to discharge it onto his neighbour's land. If the water goes onto his neighbour's land in the ordinary course of nature, without assistance from him, he is not liable for the resultant damage[244]; but, if he digs a drain or does any other act, which causes it to go into his neighbour's land, he is liable. Where a quantity of rainwater accumulated against a railway embankment and, to prevent the embankment from giving way, the railway company made cuttings which caused the water to go on to the neighbouring land, the company was liable.[245]

13–69   **Barriers against floods.** A landowner can erect a barrier to prevent flood water from coming onto his own land, although the natural consequence of his doing so is to cause more water to flow onto his neighbour's land.[246] It has been said that the application of such a rule would not give rise to a breach of art.8 of the European Convention on Human Rights as it met the balance between the demands of the general interest of the community and the need for the protection

---

[238] *Hodgson v York Corp* (1873) 28 L.T. 836; *Cracknell v Thetford Corp* (1869) L.R. 4 C.P. 629; *Mason v Shrewsbury and Hereford Ry* (1871) L.R. 6 Q.B. 578; *Neath Rural District Council v Williams* [1951] 1 K.B. 115 at 121, per Goddard L.J. who said: "I think that the common law of England has never imposed liabilities upon landowners for anything which happens to their land in the natural course of affairs if the land is used naturally."
[239] [1980] Q.B. 485, CA.
[240] *Goldman v Hargrave* [1967] 1 A.C. 645, PC.
[241] Megaw L.J. suggested that what was reasonable might turn on obvious discrepancies of financial resources.
[242] *Geddis v Proprietors of Bann Reservoir* (1878) 3 App.Cas. 430.
[243] *Gibbons v Lenfestey* (1915) 84 L.J.P.C. 158.
[244] *Rouse v Gravelworks Ltd* [1940] 1 K.B. 489.
[245] *Whalley v L. & Y. Ry* (1884) 13 Q.B.D. 131.
[246] *Nield v L. & N.W. Ry* (1874) L.R. 10 Ex. 4: canal owners placed planks in the canal to keep off flood water from a neighbouring river with the result that the claimant's land was damaged. The owners were acquitted of blame because they "had the right to protect themselves against it and the plaintiffs cannot complain although what the defendants did in so protecting themselves augmented the damage to them": at p.8, per Bramwell B. See also *Maxey Drainage Board v G.N. Ry* (1912) 106 L.T. 429.

of the fundamental rights of the individual.[247] In one catastrophic case, the defendant tipped spoil onto its land, raising its level by some ten feet and, thereafter, following exceptionally heavy rainfall the River Taff burst its banks and water, which would otherwise have flowed onto the defendant's land, flooded the homes of 32 claimants to a depth of one metre. The defendant was not liable for the damage. A landowner was permitted to erect defences, the effect of which would be to discharge elsewhere water which would otherwise have flowed onto his land, subject to two limitations: (i) interference with an established water-course was prohibited; and (ii) the landowner would not be permitted to take measures so as to cause water which had already or would in any event come onto his land to flow from it onto that of his neighbour. On the facts of the case, those two limitations had been met.[248]

Where, in order to carry out residential development, the occupier of lower **13–70** land filled in disused clay pits on his land in which the higher occupier's water accumulated, the latter had no cause of action against the former.[249] The words of Windeyer J. in an Australian case were adopted:

"Although he has no action against a higher proprietor because of a natural unconcentrated flow of water from his land, he is not bound to receive it. He may put up barriers and pen it back, notwithstanding that doing so damages the upper proprietor's land, at all events if he uses reasonable care and skill and does no more than is reasonably necessary to protect his enjoyment of his own land. But he must not act for the purpose of injuring his neighbour. It is not possible to define what is reasonable or unreasonable in the abstract. Each case depends upon its own circumstances."[250]

Thus, if the steps taken by the lower occupier to prevent water entering his land involve unreasonable user by that occupier, such that the land of the higher occupier is damaged, the lower occupier will be liable in nuisance. Accordingly, since in the same case the lower occupier also filled in an osier-bed into which water had accumulated and this had the effect of squeezing out temporarily, over a five-year period, the water that was already present in the bed, thereby causing reasonably foreseeable additional flooding, he was liable in nuisance or trespass for the damage foreseeably caused to the higher occupier's land, limited to the five-year period during which the water was squeezed out.[251]

A landowner is not obliged to erect on the boundary of his land a barrier to **13–71** keep off floods and, if he erects it some distance within the boundary, he is not responsible for so much of the flood-water as comes onto his land and is diverted by the barrier onto the adjoining land.[252] There seems to be no doubt that, as long as there is no defined course which flood-water was accustomed to take, a riparian owner can keep off flood-water by raising the height of the river

---

[247] *Arscott v The Coal Authority* [2005] Env. L.R. 6, CA.
[248] *Arscott v The Coal Authority* [2005] Env. L.R. 6, CA. See generally, Lamont, "As the flood water recedes who pays for the damage?" 152 S.J. 12
[249] *Home Brewery Plc v William Davis & Co (Loughborough) Ltd* [1987] 1 All E.R. 637.
[250] *Gartner v Kidman* (1962) 108 C.L.R. 12 at 49, applied in *Home Brewery Plc v William Davis & Co (Loughborough) Ltd* n.45, above.
[251] *Home Brewery Plc v William Davis & Co (Loughborough) Ltd* n.249, above.
[252] *Gerrard v Crowe* [1921] 1 A.C. 395.

banks.[253] A landowner is not obliged, apart from contract or statute, to maintain a barrier against floods for the benefit of neighbouring owners.[254] If, therefore, a riparian owner, who maintains a river wall for the protection of his own property, pulls down the wall, as a result of which his neighbour's land is flooded, he is not liable for the damage.[255]

13–72 **Erecting and maintaining barriers against sea and floods.** At common law a landowner is not bound to maintain on his own land a barrier against the sea for the benefit of inland owners[256] but is entitled to protect his land from the incursions of the sea by building a groyne or sea wall, even though the effect of his doing so is to cause the sea to flow with greater violence against adjoining land.[257]

13–73 **Removal or interference with natural barriers.** Nevertheless, a landowner cannot remove a natural barrier against the sea, even when it is on his own land, if the removal causes damage to the adjoining land.[258] The same applies if the removal will cause damage to a sea wall and drainage system maintained as protective works.[259]

13–74 **Interference with barriers erected against sea and floods.** If a wall is maintained by statutory authority to prevent flooding from the sea or a river, anyone who interferes with the wall is liable for damage by any flooding which results from such interference. Where a river wall was maintained along the side of the Thames and a dock company, acting under statutory powers, constructed a dock which communicated with the river by an artificial channel, it was held that they were under a common law duty to maintain the sides of their dock at the same height as that of the wall. As a result of their failure to do so they were liable for damage caused by an overflow from their dock.[260] Where a river bank was maintained under statutory powers and a landowner built a wall to replace a portion of the bank, but, during a particularly high tide, water broke through the wall, although not through the bank alongside, and flooded the neighbouring land, the landowner was held liable.[261]

---

[253] *Gerrard v Crowe* [1921] 1 A.C. 395. See also *Lagan Navigation Co v Lambeg Bleaching Co* [1927] A.C. 226.

[254] *Mason v Shrewsbury and Hereford Ry* (1871) L.R. 6 Q.B. 578; *Nield v L. & N.W. Ry* (1874) L.R. 10 Ex. 4.

[255] *Thomas & Evans Ltd v Mid-Rhondda Co-operative Society* [1941] 1 K.B. 381.

[256] *Hudson v Tabor* (1877) 2 Q.B.D. 290.

[257] *R. v Pagham Commrs* (1828) 8 B. & C. 355.

[258] *Crossman v Bristol and South Wales Union Ry* (1863) 11 W.R. 981; *Attorney General v Tomline* (1880) 14 Ch.D. 58.

[259] *Canvey Island Commissioners v Preedy* [1922] 1 Ch. 179.

[260] *Nitro-Phosphate and Odam's Chemical Manure Co v London and St Katherine Docks Co* (1878) 9 Ch.D. 503.

[261] *Greenwood Tileries Ltd v Clapson* [1937] 1 All E.R. 765 at 770, 771: Branson J. said of the defendant's case: "As soon as the wall fails it seems to me that their position is the same as the position of one who has cut through the bank and left a gap through which the sea enters. It seems to me that their position is really analogous to the position of the defendant in *Rylands v Fletcher*. They have created a danger which they must guard at all events."

Mining. In *Smith v Kenrick*,[262] it was held that if, in carrying on mining **13–75** operations in accordance with good mining practice and without negligence, a mine owner causes naturally accumulated water to penetrate by natural gravity into a neighbour's mine, the neighbour has no remedy against him. The working of a seam of coal caused the water to escape. In such a case, it was held, the claimant must protect himself by erecting a barrier in his own mine. However, whether the decision survives *Leakey v National Trust*[263] has been doubted.[264]

On the other hand, the mine owner will be liable "if he conducts the water **13–76** from his mine to the lower mine or mines by means of some opening made or other work executed with the express purpose of so conducting the water and not for the purpose of getting minerals".[265] Accordingly, if an artificial channel is made whereby water is conducted to a place in another mine, which it would not otherwise have reached, liability depends on the answer to the question: "Has the conducting of the water through the artificial channel increased the burden on the owner of the lower mine or not?" The material time for answering it is when the channel was made.[266] A mine owner must not pump water occurring naturally in his mine, into the mine of another.[267]

If the working of a mine causes a subsidence on the surface and, through the **13–77** resultant cracks, the surface water comes down into the mine, thence gravitating into an adjoining mine, the mine owner is under no greater liability than if the water had been naturally present in the mine all the time.[268] On the other hand, if the water which gravitates into the adjoining mine has come through holes in the surface, because of the diversion of a natural stream, the mine owner responsible for diverting the stream is liable.[269] If mine workings cause a subsidence in the bed of a natural stream, as a result of which water comes into a mine and gravitates into the adjoining mine, the liability of the mine owner depends on whether he is working his mine in an ordinary, reasonable and proper way. So it was held that defendants had no absolute right to work a mine where they could only do so by letting in river water thus flooding their own and their neighbour's mine. What was ordinary, reasonable or proper was a question of evidence.[270]

ILLUSTRATIONS

There is no liability on the part of a mine owner who stops up an opening **13–78** through which water had flowed into a neighbouring mine if, as a result of the consequent accumulation, the water then overflows via another opening into the

---

[262] (1849) 7 C.B. 515 at 566 per Cresswell J.
[263] [1980] Q.B. 485, CA.
[264] *Home Brewery Plc v William Davis & Co (Loughborough) Ltd* n.249, above.
[265] *Westhoughton Coal and Cannel Co v Wigan Coal Corp* [1939] Ch. 393 at 405, per Luxmoore L.J.
[266] *Westhoughton Coal and Channel Co v Wigan Coal Corp* [1939] Ch. 393 at 405 affirmed on other grounds [1939] Ch. 800.
[267] *Baird v Williamson* (1863) 15 C.B.(N.S.) 376, per Erle C.J. at 391, 392.
[268] *Wilson v Waddell* (1876) 2 App.Cas. 95.
[269] *Fletcher v Smith* (1877) 2 App.Cas. 781.
[270] *Crompton v Lea* (1874) L.R. 19 Eq. 115.

neighbour's mine.[271] However, the same mine owner would be liable if he used a pipe to send the water to his neighbour's mine.[272] There is no liability if the outcome of an altered system of working results in an increase in the amount of water flowing to a neighbour's mine.[273]

13–79 Liability will attach if a mine owner: conducts water in his mine to a weakness in his neighbour's boundary with the purpose of discharging it from his mine through that weakness into the neighbouring mine[274]; pumps up water from the lower part of his mine so that it flows into his neighbour's mine.[275] alters the natural flow of water within his mine so as to cause more water than would naturally do so to flow into the adjoining mine.[276] An alteration of the flow of water within his own mine, which does not increase the burden on the adjoining mine, is not actionable.[277]

13–80 **Canals.** Because canals are always constructed under statutory authority, canal companies are not liable for damage caused by an escape of water from their canals, unless it can be proved that they have acted negligently in the exercise of their powers. Thus, where a mine was worked and caused the surface of the land to crack, as a result of which water from the defendants' canal poured through the cracks into the claimant's mine, it was held that the defendants were not liable, since there was no negligence on their part.[278] On the other hand, where the defendants were liable to maintain a cut, to carry off water, but its banks were insufficient to cope, it was held that they were liable for an overflow caused by the stoppage of the outlet, which third parties had neglected to clear.[279]

13–81 Where a mill, built on the banks of a canal, was damaged by the leakage of water from the canal into the mill, as a result of mine-working by third parties, the owners of the canal were held liable in negligence for failing to prevent the damage.[280] But where, following exceptionally heavy rainfall, the sluices of a canal were opened with the result that the claimant's premises were flooded, on proof that the opening of the sluices had been necessary to prevent the failure of the canal banks, the canal company were held not liable.[281]

13–82 Since the owners of a canal are entitled to erect a barricade or to raise the banks of the canal in order to prevent its flooding, it has been held that no liability attaches to them if a secondary consequence is to cause damage by flooding

---

[271] *Lomax v Scott* (1870) 39 L.J. Ch. 834.
[272] *Lomax v Scott* (1870) 39 L.J. Ch. 834.
[273] *Scots Mines Co v Leadhills Mines Co* (1859) 34 L.T. (O.S.) 34.
[274] *Westminster Brymbo Coal and Coke Co v Clayton* (1867) 36 L.J.Ch. 476.
[275] *Baird v Williamson* (1863) 15 C.B.(N.S.) 376 at 391.
[276] *West Cumberland Iron and Steel Co v Kenyon* (1879) 11 Ch.D. 782.
[277] *West Cumberland Iron and Steel Co v Kenyon* (1879) 11 Ch.D. 782.
[278] *Dunn v Birmingham Canal Co* (1872) L.R. 8 A.B. 42.
[279] *Harrison v G.N. Ry* (1864) 3 H. & C. 231. Note that there was negligence both for failing to maintain the banks and for sending water through an outlet known to be blocked; also *Boughton v G.W. Ry of Ireland* (1873) I.R. 7 C.L. 178.
[280] *Evans v Manchester, Sheffield and Lincolnshire Ry* (1887) 36 Ch.D. 626.
[281] *Thomas v Birmingham Canal Co* (1879) 49 L.J.Q.B. 851.

elsewhere.[282] If they raise the banks of their canal causing flood-water to accumulate on the land of an adjoining owner, the latter is not entitled to cut through the banks of the canal in order to drain the floodwater from his own land.[283]

Where canal barges were frequently tied up against a wall abutting the **13–83** claimant's factory, despite the display by the defendants of a notice forbidding this practice, and, over the year, the banging of barges against this wall had caused water to seep through, as a result of which the wall's base collapsed and damaged the foundations of the factory, it was held that the defendants were liable because of their failure to take reasonable steps to prevent both heavy congestion at this point of the canal and collisions with the claimant's wall.[284]

Water undertakers' liability for reservoirs. Water undertakers operate **13–84** under statutory authority and are only liable on proof of negligence, unless the statute provides for the contrary.

"It is now thoroughly well established that no action will lie for doing that which the legislature has authorised, if it be done without negligence, although it does occasion damage to anyone; but an action does lie for doing that which the legislature has authorised, if it be done negligently."[285]

Having regard to the serious damage likely to result from a burst reservoir, the degree of care required is a very high one[286] and, in the case of a reservoir constructed after January 1, 1931, the fact that it was constructed under statutory authority does not exonerate the persons for the time being having its management and control from any legal action and liability.[287] Thus the full liability of *Rylands v Fletcher*, is imposed.

Water undertakers' liability for escapes from pipes. At common law the **13–85** liability of a statutory water undertaker for escapes of water from its pipes depended on whether or not there had been negligence.[288] However, by s.209 of the Water Industry Act 1991 strict liability is imposed where loss or damage[289] arises from an escape of water, however caused, from a pipe vested in a water undertaker.[290] There are defences that the escape was entirely the fault of the

---

[282] *Nield v L. & N.W. Ry* (1874) L.R. 10 Ex. 4; *Lagan Navigation Co v Lambeg Bleaching Co* [1927] A.C. 226.
[283] *Lagan Navigation Co v Lambeg Bleaching Co* [1927] A.C. 226.
[284] *Boxes v British Waterways Board* [1971] 2 Lloyd's Rep. 183.
[285] *Geddis v Proprietors of the Bann Reservoir* (1878) 3 App.Cas. 430 at 455, 456, per Lord Blackburn.
[286] See *Northwestern Utilities v London Guarantee and Accident Co* [1936] A.C. 108 (a gas case).
[287] Applying to reservoirs constructed pursuant to powers granted after August 1, 1930. See the Reservoirs Act 1975 s.28 and Sch.2, replacing s.7 of the Reservoirs (Safety Provisions) Act 1930. The Act still preserves strict liability for a reservoir's construction.
[288] For the position at common law, see earlier editions of *Charlesworth on Negligence*, e.g. 6th edn, 1977, paras 499, 500.
[289] Damage is defined in s.219(1) as including, in relation to individuals, death and any personal injury, including any disease or impairment of physical or mental condition.
[290] s.209(1). The Water Resources Act 1991 applies an identical liability to the National Rivers Authority.

claimant himself, or his employee, agent or contractor[291] and the right to raise contributory negligence is preserved[292]; but neither act of God nor independent act of a third party are available as defences. Thus, Parliament has created a liability even stricter than that attaching under *Rylands v Fletcher*.[293]

13–86   **Case study.** An example of a claim for such damage is provided by *Aerospace Publishing Ltd v Thames Water Utilities*[294] in which the defendant admitted liability for an escape of water into the premises of the claimant, a publishing company specialising in aviation matters, but denied the alleged quantum of loss. One argument was in relation to an archive of reference material which the claimant said it wished to reinstate: damages were awarded by reference to the cost of replacement rather than the market value. Another argument related to the value to be attributed to an alleged diversion of staff time to deal with the consequences of the flood. It was held that such a claim required proof that a diversion of staff had indeed caused significant disruption to business. Even though strictly the claim should be cast in terms of a loss of revenue attributable to the diversion of staff time, nevertheless in the ordinary case, and unless the defendant could establish the contrary, it was reasonable to infer that, had their time not been diverted, the staff would have applied it to activities which would, directly or indirectly, have generated revenue in an amount at least equal to the costs for employing them during that time.[295]

13–87   **Water undertakers breaking up streets.** The Water Industry Act 1991[296] empowers water undertakers to break up streets for laying and repairing their pipes. When they do break up a street, they are required by s.66 of the New Roads and Street Works Act 1991 to carry on and complete the works with such dispatch as is reasonably practicable, at penalty of a fine. General requirements as to the safety measures required not simply of water undertakers but all statutory undertakers executing street works are set out in s.65. Because the Act imposes a criminal sanction for breach of these provisions it is unlikely that any action would lie for breach of statutory duty on behalf of someone injured by a failure to carry out the work to the standards required.[297] Liability for common law negligence is, however, preserved.[298] The duty of care extends to the

---

[291] s.209(2).

[292] s.209(4). The Fatal Accidents Act 1976 and the Limitation Act 1980 also apply in relation to any loss or damage for which a statutory undertaker is liable under the section.

[293] s.209(5). The undertaker's rights under the Civil Liability (Contribution) Act 1978 are preserved. Nor does liability under the 1991 Act apply to loss or damage sustained by the National Rivers Authority or certain other statutory undertakers, public gas or electricity suppliers, highway authorities or persons with an entitlement to compensation under s.82 of the New Roads and Street Works Act 1991.

[294] (2007) 110 Con. L.R. 1, CA.

[295] See further, McIntosh, "Litigation: claiming it back" Legal Week, 2007, 9 (17), 12.

[296] s.158(1). There is a similar power for the National Rivers Authority in s.159(1) of the Water Resources Act 1991.

[297] See *Keating v Elvan Reinforced Concrete Co* [1968] 1 W.L.R. 722, where it was held, in relation to the similar duty under s.8 of the Public Utilities Street Works Act 1950, that no action for breach of statutory duty arose.

[298] s.95 of the Act states that any provision imposing criminal liability in respect of any matter is without prejudice to civil liability in respect of the same matter. See Ch.10, paras 10–23–10–25 for further examples.

apparatus of other statutory undertakers beneath the street, which for example must not be deprived of support so as to cause it to fracture.[299]

Quality of water supplied by water undertakers. Apart from liability for **13-88** the escape of water, a water undertaker must give notice to consumers of anything in the quality of water, which is likely to render it unfit for any ordinary use in the conditions that are likely to prevail in the consumer's premises. Where water was of such a quality that it was likely to become poisonous if it passed through lead pipes, the water supplier was held liable for its failure to warn consumers, whom it should have foreseen had lead pipes, of the necessary precautions to take.[300]

Water undertakers must take reasonable care to supply water fit for human **13-89** consumption. Thus, when they supplied water, which, as a result of their negligence, contained typhoid germs, they were held liable.[301] Likewise, there is a mandatory obligation for an employer to provide his workers with an adequate supply of wholesome drinking water at their workplace.[302]

Sewers and drains. Liability for sewage is the same as liability for water.[303] **13-90** Where a drain from the defendant's house, after receiving the drainage of several other houses, turned back under the defendant's house and, because such drain was in a rotten condition, sewage escaped and got into the claimant's cellar, the defendant was held liable[304] despite the fact that there was no negligence on his part, he being unaware of the existence of the return drain. Similarly, when a drain on the defendant's land became choked up causing adjoining land to be flooded, nuisance was established.[305]

Certain statutory undertakers are empowered to construct and maintain **13-91** drainage works for the benefit of a particular area. When damage is caused in consequence of those works, liability depends on the terms of the particular statutory provisions. As a general rule, they are only liable on proof of negligence[306] but the statute may impose a strict obligation upon them.[307] If

---

[299] *Huyton & Roby Gas Co v Liverpool Corp* [1926] 1 K.B. 146.

[300] *Barnes v Irwell Valley Water Board* [1938] 2 All E.R. 650.

[301] *Read v Croydon Corp* [1938] 4 All E.R. 631. The Water Industry Act 1991 s.68(1), imposes a duty upon a water undertaker to provide water for domestic or food production purposes which is wholesome at the time of supply. The duty is enforceable by the Secretary of State, pursuant to s.18 of the Act. A water undertaker who fails to supply water that is "wholesome" may also be strictly liable under the Consumer Protection Act 1987, for which generally see Ch.15.

[302] Workplace (Health, Safety and Welfare) Regulations 1992 reg.22(1).

[303] *Jones v Llanrwst-UDC* [1911] 1 Ch. 393 at 405, which was cited with approval in *Pride of Derby and Derbyshire Angling Association Ltd v British Celanese Ltd* [1953] Ch. 149 at 173, 174 by Evershed M.R.

[304] *Humphries v Cousins* (1877) 2 C.P.D. 239. He clearly must have known there was a drain, and so his knowledge of the precise course it took was immaterial. If he had had no reason to suppose there was a drain he would not have been liable: *Ilford Urban District Council v Beal* [1925] 1 K.B. 671, per Branson J.

[305] *Sedleigh-Denfield v O'Callaghan* [1940] A.C. 880; *Pemberton v Bright and the Devon County Council* [1960] 1 W.L.R. 436.

[306] *Collins v Middle Level Commrs* (1869) L.R. 4 C.P. 279; *Boynton v Ancholme Drainage and Navigation Commrs* [1921] 2 K.B. 213; *Sephton v Lancashire River Board* [1962] 1 All E.R. 183.

[307] *R. v Marshland Smeeth and Fen District Commrs* [1920] 1 K.B. 155.

flooding is caused because of the opening of water gates in a time of heavy rainfall, the defendants, although prima facie liable for the damage on the principle of *Rylands v Fletcher*, are protected by their statutory powers because the gates were constructed expressly to be opened in times of flood.[308] If a sewer is constructed in such a way that it causes adjoining land to subside, the person constructing it is liable for the resulting damage.[309]

13–92　　In a claim against a sanitary authority in respect of the death of one of their workmen from sewer gas, it was held that its only potential liability was in negligence. Since no sewerage authority was proved to have the knowledge necessary to anticipate such an occurrence, no negligence was established.[310]

13–93　　**Overflows from sewers.** An escape of sewage from a private sewer would, on the face of it, attract strict liability within the principle in *Rylands v Fletcher*,[311] although doubt has been expressed whether this would be correct of sewage on a domestic scale.[312] It is otherwise with public sewerage undertakers whose duties and standards of performance are governed by the Water Industry Act 1991.[313] They have a general duty to provide an adequate system of public sewers, enforceable under a statutory scheme.[314] There is no direct remedy under the scheme for a person who sustains loss or damage as a result of the statutory undertaker's failure to comply with its duties. It is unlikely that *Ryland v Fletcher* applies to cases where sewers have been constructed under statutory authority and then overflow, since the use of the land for drainage purposes is a use proper for the general benefit of the community.[315] But negligence liability can arise, for instance in relation to the original construction of the sewer or its maintenance thereafter,[316] or in diverting sewage from one sewer to another which is already overcharged.[317] Failure to enlarge a sewer to meet the growing demands of a district is not negligent, nor is there a claim in nuisance, in the event of an escape of sewage caused by the inadequacy of the system to meet the demands upon it.[318] One important purpose in Parliament providing a statutory scheme was to

---

[308] *Dixon v Metropolitan Board of Works* (1881) 7 Q.B.D. 418.
[309] *London General Omnibus Co v Tilbury Contracting Co* (1907) 71 J.P. 534.
[310] *Digby v West Ham Urban District Council* (1896) 13 T.L.R. 11.
[311] (1868) L.R. 3 H.L. 330; *Humphries v Cousins* (1877) 2 C.P.D. 239. See also Parker J. in *Jones v Llanrwst Urban District Council* [1911] 1 Ch. 393 at 405, quoted with approval by Evershed M.R. in *Pride of Derby and Derbyshire Angling Association Ltd v British Celanese Ltd* [1953] Ch. 149.
[312] See *Clerk & Lindsell on Torts* (19th edn 2006), p.1256, n.84.
[313] s.94(1).
[314] For a summary of the scheme see the speech of Lord Nicholls of Birkenhead in *Marcic v Thames Water Utilities Ltd* [2004] 2 A.C. 42 at 54.
[315] per Denning L.J. in *Pride of Derby* n.311, above.
[316] *Fleming v Manchester Corp* (1881) 44 L.T. 517; *Brown v Sargent* (1858) 1 F. & F. 112, *Dixon v Metropolitan Board of Works* (1881) 7 Q.B.D. 418.
[317] *Dent v Bournemouth Corp* (1897) 66 L.J.Q.B. 395.
[318] *Hesketh v Birmingham Corp* [1924] 1 K.B. 260; *Stretton's Derby Brewery Co v Derby Corp* [1894] 1 Ch. 431; *Robinson v Workington Corp* [1897] 1 Q.B. 619. For the criticism see Denning L.J. in *Pride of Derby* n.6, above at 190: the remedy of an aggrieved party is by way of complaint to the Minister by virtue of the provisions of s.322 of the Public Health Act 1936.

prevent individual householders who have suffered sewer flooding from bringing proceedings, in effect, in respect of the failure to build more sewers.[319]

Nuisance. The Water Industry Act 1991 specifically requires sewerage **13–94** undertakers so to carry out their functions under the Act as not to create a nuisance.[320] A nuisance is created if sewage is discharged upon, or caused to flow over, another's land,[321] although not where, as already said, the problem arises as a result of increased demands upon the sewerage system.[322]

Escape of water collected on roofs and in buildings. If water, which has **13–95** been collected on a roof to be conducted by gutters and pipes into drains, escapes onto adjoining premises this will fall within the principle in *Rylands v Fletcher*.[323] By contrast, if a claimant who suffers loss as a result of such an escape, is one of the persons for whose benefit the water has been collected, the defendant will only be held liable on proof of negligence because "a plaintiff who is himself a consenting party to the accumulation cannot rely simply upon the escape of the accumulated material; he must further establish that the escape was due to want of reasonable care on the part of the person,"[324] who had collected the material.

Thus, when water is collected with the consent of the claimant or in a situation where it is for the common benefit of the claimant and the defendant, it comes within the scope of one of the exceptions to liability under the rule in *Rylands v Fletcher*.[325] Common benefit is only evidence of consent and the principle is that when a person enters into occupation of premises, whether business or residential, he "takes the premises as they are, and, accordingly, consents to the presence there of the installed water system with all its advantages and disadvantages."[326]

ILLUSTRATIONS

The defendants' liability was not established in the following cases: where the **13–96** rainwater from the roof of a warehouse was collected by gutters into a box, from which it was normally discharged by a pipe into the drains, but due to a hole made by a rat, the water escaped into the ground floor where it damaged goods

---

[319] *Marcic v Thames Water Utilities Ltd* n.9, above, per Lord Nicholls at 58. While the case itself concerned a claim in nuisance, what he said should be equally applicable to a negligence claim. See also the similar remarks of Denning L.J. in *Pride of Derby* n.311, above at 190. See also Kimblin, "Intolerable nuisance" 148 S.J. 86.
[320] s.117 of the Water Industry Act 1991.
[321] *Glossop v Heston & Isleworth London Borough* (1879) 12 Ch.D. 102; *Attorney General v Dorking Union* (1882) 20 Ch.D. 595; *Smeaton v Ilford Corp* [1954] Ch. 450.
[322] See n.318, above. See also *Marcic v Thames Water Utilities Ltd* n.319, above.
[323] See *Cockburn v Smith* [1924] 2 K.B. 119 at 132, per Scrutton L.J. See *Transco Plc v Stockport MBC* [2004] 2 A.C. 1, para.13–97, below.
[324] per Lord Finlay in *Attorney General v Cory Bros & Co Ltd* [1921] 1 A.C. 521 at 539. See also *A. Prosser & Son Ltd v Levy* [1955] 1 W.L.R. 1224 at 1230 for remarks to like effect and a review of the authorities.
[325] See paras 13–42–13–56, above.
[326] *Peters v Prince of Wales Theatre (Birmingham) Ltd* [1943] K.B. 73 at 79, per Goddard L.J., criticising the passage at p.252 in the 1st edn of *Charlesworth's Law of Negligence*.

stored by the claimants[327]; where water from the roofs of both the claimants' and the defendants' buildings discharged via the defendants' flat roof through a gulley into drains and the gulley had unexpectedly become blocked, resulting a leakage into the claimants' premises[328]; where the goods of the tenant of a shop were damaged by an overflow of rainwater from a blocked gutter, which was under the control of his landlords[329]; where the water from the water closet of one tenant on the upper floor percolated to the lower floor of the same building, occupied by another tenant, and damaging his stock[330]; where some unknown person plugged the waste pipe of a wash basin and left the tap running on the top floor of a building, occupied by the defendant landlord, so that the water overflowed and damaged the claimant's goods on the floor below[331]; where the claimants occupied a shop, immediately above which was the defendant's flat, and, owing to a burst in the flat's rising main, the water escaped and flooded the shop.[332]

13–97   Also: where a landlord let a house, each tenant occupying a separate floor, and supplied the different floors with water from a cistern at the top of the house but the branch pipe supplying the first floor burst, with the result that the claimants' goods on the ground floor were damaged[333]; where the claimant occupied the ground floor of a building and the defendants were the owners of the house above and the defendants' cistern, which was not used to supply the claimant's premises, overflowed[334]; where the claimant had leased the shop part of a building, containing a theatre fitted with a sprinkler system and, during a severe

---

[327] *Carstairs v Taylor* (1971) L.R. 6 Ex. 217.

[328] *Gill v Edouin* (1895) 71 L.T. 762; 72 L.T. 579. cf. *Bishop v Consolidated London Properties* (1933) 102 L.J.K.B. 257 (dead pigeon blocked open gutter—an overflow occurred—landlord held liable for failure to clean gutter despite having had no notice of blockage); *Heintzmann & Co v Hashman Construction* (1973) 32 D.L.R. (3d) 622 (building debris fell on to claimant's flat roof—defendant failed to inspect and remove—defendant held liable in negligence, nuisance and *Rylands v Fletcher* for subsequent flooding).

[329] *Kiddle v City Business Properties Ltd* [1942] 1 K.B. 269. The contrary would be the case if there was no relationship of landlord and tenant, so that the adjoining owners were quite independent of one another, and the defendant owner of the blocked drawn would be liable.

[330] *Ross v Fedden* (1872) L.R. 7 Q.B. 611 (the claimant, in taking the ground floor, must be deemed to have accepted risk of such damage happening).

[331] *Rickards v Lothian* [1913] A.C. 263, Lord Moulton saying, at 281, 282: "The provision of a proper supply of water to the various parts of a house is not only reasonable, but has become, in accordance with modern sanitary views, an almost necessary feature of town life. It is recognised as being so desirable in the interests of the community that in some form or other it is usually made obligatory in civilised countries. Such a supply cannot be installed without causing some concurrent danger of leakage or overflow. It would be unreasonable for the law to regard those who install or maintain such a system of supply as doing so at their own peril, with an absolute liability for any damage resulting from its presence even when there has been no negligence."

[332] *Irish Linen Manufacturing Co v Lowe* (1956) 106 L.J. 828: (main embedded entirely in plaster—no duty to inspect in absence of warning that it was defective—as soon as burst discovered mains turned off—no duty to warn claimants in absence of indication of risk of water damage below).

[333] *Anderson v Oppenheimer* (1880) 5 Q.B.D. 602. N.B. Majority decision on basis that supply maintained for benefit of claimants and other tenants. Thesiger L.J. decided case on ground that, having taken a lease with the benefit of a water supply "they took the benefit and must take the burden".

[334] *Blake v Land and House Property Corp* (1887) 3 T.L.R. 667.

frost, it burst damaging the claimant's goods[335]; where the defendant's clerk went into his employer's private lavatory, which he was forbidden to use, and forgot to turn off the tap, flooding the claimant's premises on the floor[336]; where the owner of premises employed a plumber, who was an independent contractor, to mend a leaking cistern but the repairs were carried out negligently and water overflowed damaging the claimant's goods on the ground floor[337]; where the tenant did not go into occupation of an upper flat for some days and, meanwhile, a water pipe burst during a severe frost and damaged the property of the tenant in the flat beneath[338]; where, without negligence, there was an escape from a pipe carrying water within a block of local authority owned flats and the escaping water caused the collapse of an embankment which supported the claimant's gas main, the rule in *Rylands v Fletcher* did not apply. It was accepted that an immediate and serious risk had arisen which, at some expense, the claimant had to remedy but, judged by the prevailing standards of the day, there was no non-natural use of land.[339]

On the other hand, the defendant was liable in the following cases: where there **13–98** was a failure to replace the windows of the top storey of a multi-storey building blown out during an air raid and, as a result, a radiator pipe burst following a severe frost, flooding the claimant's floor below[340]; where the defendant's servant, in going to wash his hands, turned on the tap but, as no water flowed, forgot to turn it off again with the result that when the water came on it damaged the claimant's premises on the floor below[341]; similarly, when the defendant's servant had blocked up the waste pipe of a sink by emptying tea leaves into it[342]; where the ground floor building was let to the claimants, the first, second and third floors to the second defendants and the landlords, the first defendants, keeping the staircases and passages under their own control, and a tap on the second floor landing, which had been placed only three-and-a-half inches above floor level, was turned on by some unknown person[343]; where a rain-water gutter

---

[335] *Peters v Prince of Wales Theatre (Birmingham) Ltd* [1943] K.B. 73 (on the ground that he had impliedly consented to the presence of the sprinklers).
[336] *Stevens v Woodward* (1881) 6 Q.B.D. 318 (on the ground that the act of the clerk was outside the scope of his employment). But cf. *Abelson v Brockman* (1890) 54 J.P. 119 where the defendant was held liable for the negligence of his servant in blocking the waste pipe by emptying tea leaves into the sink.
[337] *Blake v Woolf* [1898] 2 Q.B. 426.
[338] *Tilley v Stevenson* [1939] 4 All E.R. 207 (unless it could be proved that he knew or ought to have known that the water had been turned on before his occupation had begun, liability could not be established).
[339] *Transco Plc v Stockport MBC* [2004] 2 A.C. 1.
[340] *George Frensham Ltd v Shorn & Sons Ltd* [1950] W.N. 406 (the landlords were liable for failing to keep the boiler fires lit or, if they could not keep them lit, for not warning the claimants).
[341] *Ruddiman v Smith* (1889) 60 L.T. 708.
[342] *Abelson v Brockman* (1890) 54 J.P. 119. But cf. *Stevens v Woodward* (1881) 6 Q.B.D. 318 see n.336 above.
[343] *A. Prosser & Son Ltd v Levy* [1955] 1 W.L.R. 1224 (it was held that the claimant did not impliedly consent to the presence of a water pipe, which, unknown to him, was defective; further, it was held that the landlords were liable, unless they could prove that it had been turned on by the deliberate and mischievous act of a third party, because the negligent act of a third party was no defence. The second defendants were not liable as they were not in possession or control of the tap).

in the roof, in the possession and control the defendants, remained blocked despite notice of the blockage having been given with the result that water penetrated part of the claimant's premises[344]; where the water was conducted from a building by means of open gutters through a box room, in which pigeons were in the habit of nesting, and one of the gutters was blocked by the body of a dead pigeon[345]; the cost of repairs to a common roof was equally divided where the freehold owner of the upper two floors of a property allowed the roof to fall into disrepair with the result that water leaked through her flat into premises on the ground floor which were damaged.[346]

13–99   **Water not collected for the common benefit.** In all the cases cited in the preceding paragraphs the parties either were the occupiers of different parts of the same building or else derived a common benefit, albeit they were in adjacent buildings. If the parties occupied different buildings and the water was not maintained for their common benefit, then the defence of consent would not apply.[347]

13–100   In contrast, the principle laid down in *Rickards v Lothian*[348] would cover damage done to adjoining premises by the escape of water from the domestic water supply and, in *Collingwood v Home and Colonial Stores*,[349] the Court of Appeal said that the doctrine of *Rylands v Fletcher* did not apply to the use of water, gas or electricity for ordinary domestic purposes, as distinguished from the handling of them in bulk in mains or reservoirs. Thus if water stored in a building for use in connection with the provision of meals and the supply of domestic sanitary ware in that building, escapes to another building, liability will only devolve on the owner or occupier on proof of negligence. By contrast, water stored in a building for manufacturing purposes which escapes to another building gives rise to *Rylands v Fletcher* liability, irrespective of negligence.[350]

13–101   Whether the mere escape of water from the defendant's premises is evidence of negligence has not been decided, but it would seem to be within the principle of res ipsa loquitur,[351] because it would be more consistent with negligence on the part of the defendant than with any other cause.

---

[344] *Hargroves, Aronson & Co v Hartopp* [1905] 1 K.B. 472; *Cockburn v Smith* [1942] 2 K.B. 119.
[345] *Bishop v Consolidated London Properties* (1933) 102 L.J.K.B. 257 see n.328 above. But cf. *Gill v Edouin* (1895) 71 L.T. 762.
[346] *Abbahall v Smee* [2003] 1 All E.R. 465, CA.
[347] *Anderson v Oppenheimer* (1880) 5 Q.B.D. 602 (water supply); *Humphries v Cousins* (1877) 2 C.P.D. 239 (domestic sewage): result dependent "simply on those principles of law which regulate the rights and duties of occupiers of adjacent pieces of land" per Denman J. at 246.
[348] [1913] A.C. 263 per Lord Moulton: see n.331, above.
[349] [1936] 3 All E.R. 200. See also to the same effect, *Miller v Robert Addie & Sons (Collieries) Ltd*, 1934 S.C. 150 (gas).
[350] *Western Engraving Co v Film Laboratories Ltd* [1936] 1 All E.R. 106; *Peters v Prince of Wales Theatre (Birmingham) Ltd* [1943] K.B. 73 at 79.
[351] Ch.6, above, para.6–100.

4.—Fire

Common law liability. Liability for fire is based on the rule of *Rylands v Fletcher*.[352] It follows that, save where the Fires Prevention (Metropolis) Act 1774 applies,[353] it is not necessary to prove negligence in an action for damage by fire.

13–102

The common law was stated long ago in Rolle's Abridgment: "If fire (I know nothing of it) suddenly break out in my house and burn my goods, and also the house of my neighbour he shall have an action on the case against me."[354] It matters not whether fire occurs in buildings or in fields.[355] Likewise, the defendants were held liable for sparks from a railway engine which ignited the claimant's haystack.[356]

13–103

The only defences available to a defendant were those falling within the exceptions to *Rylands v Fletcher*[357] namely fire started by an unforeseeable act of God[358] or an independent third party.[359] A guest in a house is not an independent third party for this purpose.[360] An occupier was held not be liable in

13–104

---

[352] *Jones v Festiniog Ry* (1868) L.R. 3 Q.B. 733; *Power v Fall* (1880) 5 Q.B.D. 597; *Gunter v James* (1908) 24 T.L.R. 868. See Ogus, "Vagaries in Liability for the Escape of Fire" 27 C.L.J. 104.
[353] para.13–102, below.
[354] Action sur Case (B) pur fewe, 2; *Beaulieu v Fingham* (1401) Y.B. 2 Hen. 4, 18, pl. 6, per Markham J: "But if a man outside my household against my will sets fire to the thatch of my house or does otherwise *per quod* my house is burned and also the houses of my neighbours, I shall not be held to answer to them, because this cannot be said to be ill on my part, but against my will." See also *Crogate v Morris* (1617) 1 Brownl. 197; *Anon.* (1582) Cro.Eliz. 10; and *Collingwood v Home and Colonial Stores* [1936] 3 All E.R. 200 per Lord Wright at 204: "Before [the Fires Prevention (Metropolis) Act 1774] if a fire spread from a man's premises and did damage to adjoining premises, he was liable in damage on the broad ground that it was his duty at his own peril to keep any fire that originated on his premises from spreading to and damaging his neighbour's premises."
[355] *Turberville v Stampe* (1697) 1 Ld.Raym. 264 where Holt C.J. said: "Every man must so use his own as not to injure another. The law is general; the fire which a man makes in his fields is as much his fire as his fire in his house; it is made on his ground, with his materials, and by his order; and he must at his peril take care that it does not, through his negligence, injure his neighbour; if he kindle it at a proper time and place, and the violence of the wind carry it into his neighbour's ground and prejudice him, this is fit to be given in evidence." See also *Canterbury v Attorney General* (1842) 1 Phillips 306; *Vaughan v Menlove* (1837) 3 Bing N.C. 468; *H. & N. Emanuel Ltd v G.L.C.* [1971] 2 All E.R. 835.
[356] *Jones v Festiniog Ry* (1868) L.R. 3 A.B. 733 at 736, Blackburn J., after stating the rule in *Rylands v Fletcher*, said: "Here the defendants were using a locomotive engine with no express parliamentary powers making lawful that use, and they are therefore at common law bound to keep the engines from doing injury, and if the sparks escape and cause damage, the defendants are liable for the consequences though no actual negligence be shewn on their part."
[357] See, further, paras 13–34–13–56, above. *Rylands v Fletcher* has been held not to apply to a fire in a domestic fireplace: *Johnson (t/a Johnson Butchers) v BJW Property Developments Ltd* [2002] 3 All E.R. 574. See paras 13–107 and 13–114, below.
[358] See generally paras 13–35–13–39, above. *Hargreave v Goldman* (1964) 110 C.L.R. 24 at 56, affirmed [1967] 1 A.C. 645.
[359] *Turberville v Stampe* n.355, above, per Holt C.J., "If a stranger set fire to my house, and it burns my neighbour's, no action will lie against me." See para.13–103, above.
[360] *Crogate v Morris* (1617) 1 Brownl. 197: "If my friend come and lie in my house and set my neighbour's house on fire, the action will lie against me." See *Allen v Stephenson* (1700) 1 Lut. 90, to the contrary.

the case of an employee who started a fire whilst cleaning his chimney because he was acting outside the scope of his employment.[361] Nor, in New Zealand, was an owner vicariously liable for fire caused by the son of his farm manager, left in charge of the farm whilst his father was on holiday, who burnt gorse in drought conditions.[362]

13–105   The burning of corn stubble during the normal course of agriculture is not a non-natural use of land, nor is the emission of smoke from it analogous to the escape of fire or sparks. So, there was no liability under *Rylands v Fletcher* where smoke from a field obscured visibility on an adjacent road and caused a collision.[363] On the other hand there is, at least potentially, liability for the act of an independent contractor[364] and so where owners of land gave instructions to their contractor to burn brushwood upon the land, they were liable when the wind carried the fire to adjoining land, where it did damage. Lighting the fire was an operation attended with so much danger that it imposed a duty on the person at whose behest it was undertaken to see that all proper precautions were taken.[365] Similar reasoning was applied where the owner of premises engaged a contractor to replace a fireplace in a party wall. The work was done negligently and when the fire was lit it caused damage to the adjoining property. The owner was vicariously liable for the negligence of the contractor in view of the hazardous nature of the work for which he had employed him.[366]

13–106   **Fires Prevention (Metropolis) Act 1774.** Common law liability for fire spreading from the defendant's land was modified by the Fires Prevention (Metropolis) Act 1774.[367] This provided: "No action, suit or process whatever, shall be had, maintained or prosecuted against any person in whose house, chamber, stable, barn or other building, or on whose estate any fire shall . . . accidentally begin." The operation of this enactment is not confined to the metropolis but extends to the whole of England.[368] Its effect is to protect the occupier of land from being liable for damage caused by fire accidentally[369] beginning on his land, the terms of the Act being comprehensive and the word "estate" applying "to land not built upon".[370]

---

[361] *M'Kenzie v M'Leod* (1834) 10 Bing. 385.

[362] *Holderness v Goslin* [1975] 2 N.Z.L.R. 46.

[363] *Perkins v Glyn* [1976] R.T.R. ix (note in April issue).

[364] *Balfour v Barty-King* [1957] 1 Q.B. 496 (independent contractor invited into house to thaw frozen pipes, did so negligently, and set the house on fire). See note on this case by T. Ellis Lewis in [1957] C.L.J. 132.

[365] *Black v Christchurch Finance Co* [1894] A.C. 48.

[366] *Johnson v BJW Property Developments Ltd* [2002] 3 All E.R. 574, Q.B.D.

[367] s.60, re-enacting Apprehension of Housebreakers Acts 1707, s.6, which only applied to a "house or chamber". For the effect of this, see Blackstone, *Commentaries* 1, 431.

[368] *Filliter v Phippard* (1847) 11 Q.B. 347; *Richards v Easto* (1846) 15 M. & W. 244, per Parke B., but not to Scotland: *Westminster Fire Officer v Glasgow Provident Society* (1888) 13 App.Cas. 699.

[369] "a term which has been construed to mean 'without negligence' " per Asquith J. in *Mulholland & Tedd Ltd v Baker* [1939] 3 All E.R. 253 at 255. See further Ch.1, para.1–08, above.

[370] per Denman C.J. in *Filliter v Phippard* (1847) 11 Q.B. 347, at 355.

The statute affords no protection in the case of fires which have been started **13–107** intentionally[371]; or caused or continued by negligence[372]; or caused by a nuisance.[373] Further, a defendant is liable not only in respect of his own acts or omissions, but those of his employees, agents and independent contractors, also.[374] It applies to fires "produced by mere chance or incapable of being traced to any cause",[375] and even to fires which can be traced to a cause if there was no negligence.[376]

ILLUSTRATIONS

Liability in negligence was established: when hay stacked in a damp condition **13–108** overheated, burst into flames and the fire spread to the adjoining property of the claimant[377]; where insufficient space was left between stacked bales of jute, which overheated and caught fire[378]; when, on a beam of wood igniting, an hotel caught fire due to a defective scheme for conveying smoke and burning soot from the kitchen chimney[379]; when paper was lit in a yard in order to smoke out a rat in a drain pipe and the fire spread to a packing case and exploded a drum of paraffin[380]; where highly combustible articles had been stored in conditions such that, should they catch fire, it would be likely to spread, which risk materialised and fire spread to the claimant's garden, causing damage[381]; when a fire was caused by the use of a blowlamp, during an attempt to thaw a frozen pipe in a roof.[382]

Liability in negligence was not established and it was held that the fire was **13–109** "accidental": when owing to an unknown electrical wiring defect a fire broke out in the basement of grocery store[383]; where an electrical short circuit caused a fire behind panelling near a ventilator on a landing on which materials were stored,[384] when a fire broke out from some unknown cause in a tip[385] and in a garage[386]; where a tractor, which was constructing a firebreak, emitted a spark and started a fire.[387]

---

[371] But for the effect of lighting a fire in a domestic fire grate, see *Johnson v BJW Property Developments Ltd* [2002] 3 All E.R. 574, and para.13–114, below.
[372] See paras 13–110 and 13–113, below.
[373] *Spicer v Smee* [1946] 1 All E.R. 489 (defective electric wiring caused fire, owner liable).
[374] *Black v Christchurch Finance Co* [1894] A.C. 48. See Ch.3, paras 3–98–3–203, above.
[375] *Filliter v Phippard* (1847) 11 Q.B. 347, per Denman C.J.
[376] For an example of this, see *Solomons v R. Gertzenstein Ltd* [1954] 1 Q.B. 565, reversed on other grounds [1954] 2 Q.B. 243.
[377] *Vaughan v Menlove* (1837) 3 Bing. N.C. 468.
[378] *H. & A. Scott v MacKenzie, J. Stewart & Co*, 1972 S.L.T. (notes) 69.
[379] *Maclenan v Segar* [1917] 2 K.B. 325.
[380] *Mulholland & Tedd Ltd v Baker* [1939] 3 All E.R. 253.
[381] *Mason v Levy Auto Parts of England* [1967] 2 Q.B. 530.
[382] *Balfour v Barty-King* [1957] 1 Q.B. 496.
[383] *Collingwood v Home and Colonial Stores* [1936] 3 All E.R. 200.
[384] *Solomons v R. Gertzenstein Ltd* [1954] 1 Q.B. 565.
[385] *Job Edwards Ltd v Birmingham Navigations* [1924] 1 K.B. 341.
[386] *Williams v Owen* [1955] 1 W.L.R. 1293.
[387] *Mackenzie v Sloss* [1959] N.Z.L.R. 533.

13–110   **Accidental fire continued by negligence.** A fire which started by accident, may be continued by negligence, thus depriving a defendant of the protection of the 1774 Act. In *Musgrove v Pandelis*,[388] the defendant occupied a garage beneath the claimant's rooms. Without negligence, the petrol in the carburettor of the defendant's motor car ignited. The defendant's chauffeur failed to turn off the tap from the petrol tank which permitted a spread of the fire, with the result that the claimant's rooms were burnt. The defendant was held liable for the destruction of the claimant's property because of the negligence of his employee in failing to turn off the tap.

13–111   **The duty to abate.** Subsequently, the Court of Appeal considered the duty which may arise where an owner becomes aware of a fire, accidentally begun, which he could, without difficulty, extinguish. Scrutton L.J. said[389]:

> "He is then aware of a dangerous thing on his land which may damage his neighbour, and which by reasonable care he can prevent from damaging his neighbour, and he does nothing. I agree he is not an absolute insurer of that dangerous thing, for he did not himself create it, but I think on principle he is bound to take reasonable care of a dangerous thing which he knows to exist."[390]

This view was approved and adopted by the Judicial Committee in *Goldman v Hargrave*.[391] So, when a fire broke out in a redgum tree on the defendant's land, after it had been struck by lightning, and, in due course, the fire spread to the claimant's properties causing damage, the defendant was liable in negligence for failing to extinguish it properly after felling the tree. He owed a duty of care, notwithstanding that the hazard initially had arisen accidentally, and failed to discharge it when the fire revived through his neglect and spread.

13–112   **Dangerous things.** An alternative ground for the decision in *Musgrove v Pandelis*[392] was that the 1774 Act was no defence when the fire originated from a dangerous thing.[393] This proposition has been criticised,[394] but it was adopted and followed in *Mulholland & Tedd Ltd v Baker*.[395] Since it is the fire which is the dangerous thing, whether it is caused by petrol, paraffin or anything else, and the object of the statute is to give protection against accidental fires, it is difficult to understand why the statute should not protect as much in one case as in the other. The presence of inflammable matter on premises is important when the

---

[388] [1919] 2 K.B. 43.

[389] *Job Edwards Ltd v Birmingham Navigations* [1924] 1 K.B. 341, at 361. Scrutton L.J. dissented, but his judgment was preferred by the HL in *Sedleigh-Denfield v O'Callaghan* [1940] A.C. 880. The effect of the statute was not discussed by the other members of the court.

[390] *Job Edwards Ltd v Birmingham Navigations* [1924] 1 K.B. 341 at 361. See also per Lush J. in *Musgrove v Pandelis* [1919] 1 K.B. 314 at 318.

[391] [1967] A.C. 645, see also *Leakey v National Trust* [1980] Q.B. 485, CA.

[392] [1919] 2 K.B. 43.

[393] "If this motorcar with the petrol in its tank was potentially dangerous, such as a man's own fire, then it was the defendant's duty to see that the potential danger did not become an actual danger causing damage to his neighbour. The Act [of 1774] is no protection against that liability." *Musgrove v Pandelis* [1919] 2 K.B. 43 at 49, per Warrington L.J. The other members of the court expressed themselves to the same effect.

[394] *Collingwood v Home and Colonial Stores* [1936] 3 All E.R. 200 at 209.

[395] [1939] 3 All E.R. 253.

question of negligence is being considered,[396] so that if there is no negligence and it is found that the fire is accidental, it is submitted that the statute is a defence to the occupier of the land on which it begins, whatever may be the origin of the fire.

Fire caused intentionally or negligently. If the fire has been started **13–113** intentionally or negligently[397] by the occupier, the statute affords him no protection. Accordingly, in *Filliter v Phippard*,[398] where the defendant lit a fire on his land to burn weeds and the fire spread so that it destroyed hedges and fences on the claimant's land, the statute did not provide a defence. This was not only because of the words of the Act itself but also because the fire had been lit deliberately.[399] Where the defendant occupier of a flat lit a paraffin-soaked rag and negligently applied it to a sparrow's nest built between a cornice and some wire netting, positioned to keep out house-martins and thus set alight to the roof, so that the whole house was burned down, he was liable both for the intentional lighting of the fire which escaped from his premises and for his negligent act in lighting the fire.[400] The rule in *Rylands v Fletcher* applies to the occupier, who intentionally kindles fires, which he is bound at his peril to keep from causing damage to other persons, subject to the exceptions.[401]

Ordinary domestic fire grate. Judicial differences of opinion as to the **13–114** application of the 1774 Act[402] to domestic fire grates were resolved in *Johnson v BJW Property Developments Ltd*.[403] It was held that, for the purposes of s.86 of the Act, the critical question was not whether the original fire started accidentally but whether the escape of fire was an accident. So, if the escape of fire from a grate is accidental, the Act affords the defendant from whose grate the fire had escaped a defence. By contrast, if the cause of the escape was negligence on the part of the defendant, the Act affords him no defence. The Act was of no relevance and was inapplicable to a fire started deliberately in a grate since the mere ignition of that fire gave rise to no liability either before or after the Act. Furthermore, the defendant was not provided with any defence under the Act to a claim based on the escape of fire as a result of negligence.

ILLUSTRATIONS

Liability was established against the defendant: where, owing to negligent **13–115** alterations to a fireplace, fire escaped from the grate causing damage to the

---

[396] See para.13–121, below.
[397] See Robertson, "Duty of Care and the Negligent Fire-raiser", 1980 S.L.T. 13.
[398] (1847) 11 Q.B. 347, decision approved by the Judicial Committee in *Goldman v Hargrave* [1967] 1 A.C. 645.
[399] *Filliter v Phippard* (1847) 11 Q.B. 347, at 358, per Lord Denman C.J.
[400] *Sturge v Hackett* [1962] 1 W.L.R. 1257.
[401] *Black v Christchurch Finance Co* [1894] A.C. 48, *Mulholland & Tedd Ltd v Baker* [1939] 3 All E.R. 253; *Emanual v G.L.C.*, *The Times*, July 21, 1970 (contractor lit bonfire—sparks spread to claimant's land damaging property). The exceptions to liability are set out paras 13–34–13–56, above.
[402] *Musgrove v Pandelis* [1919] 1 K.B. 314 per Duke L.J. at 51 and *Job Edwards Ltd v Birmingham Navigations* [1924] I K.B. 341 per Scrutton L.J. at 361.
[403] [2002] 3 All E.R. 574.

claimant's premises.[404] If a burning coal were accidentally to fall from the grate and ignite the carpet, a failure to take steps to extinguish the fire thus caused would be characterised as negligent thus depriving the defendant of a defence under the Act.[405]

13–116   Liability was not established against the defendant: where a lodger left unguarded, for two or three hours, the fire which he had lit and a spark set the room alight, with fire spreading to adjoining rooms, his landlady was afforded no remedy in the absence of evidence that the fire, thus left, had been excessive.[406]

13–117   **Where the Act provides no defence.** The statute has been held to afford no defence to contractual liability.[407] Further, the Act only affords protection to the occupier of the land on which the fire begins accidentally: a third party starting the fire would be exposed to *Rylands v Fletcher* liability and not protected by the statute. The statute affords no defence where the fire starts from the highway.[408]

13–118   **Burden of proof.** The burden of proving that the origin of the fire was caused by the negligence of the occupier, or his employees, agents or independent contractors, for whose acts or omissions he would be vicariously liable, rests firmly on the claimant.[409] It is not for the defendant to prove that the fire was either accidental in its origin[410] or, invoking the protection of the Act, to disprove negligence.[411] This is the reverse of the position where there is a bailment. In *Hyman (Sales) Ltd v Benedyke & Co Ltd*[412] it was held that, at common law, the onus of proof lay on the defendants, as bailees, to prove the absence of negligence on their part and that in those circumstances, even where they had pleaded the provisions of this Act, it was still for them to prove the defence relied upon, namely that the fire was accidental. This they had failed to do. It is to be observed that the Act expressly provides another exception, that is, the case of landlord and tenant.

---

[404] *Johnson v BJW Property Developments Ltd,* n.403 above.
[405] per Lush J. in *Musgrove v Pandelis* [1919] 1 K.B. 314 at 318; and per Scrutton L.J. in *Job Edwards Ltd v Birmingham Navigations* [1924] 1 K.B. 341 at 361.
[406] *Sochacki v Sas* [1947] 1 All E.R. 344. See also *Doltis v Braithwaite & Sons* [1957] 1 Lloyd's Rep. 522 (newspaper lit by defendant's employee to test chimney—unknown to the claimants and the defendant contractor, chimney inter-connected with another unused chimney. Sparks entered unused chimney causing damage to stored materials: held to be a natural use of the chimney).
[407] *Shaw & Co v Symmons & Sons* [1917] 1 K.B. 799: the claimant entrusted books to the defendant, a bookbinder, to be bound and he failed to deliver them within a reasonable time following which they were destroyed by accidental fire on his premises, rendering the defendant liable because "the breach of contract had been committed before the fire occurred".
[408] See para.13–120, below.
[409] See, in more detail, Ch.6, above.
[410] See *Becquet v MacCarthy* (1831) 2 B. & Ad. 951 at 958, per Tenterden C.J.; *Musgrove v Pandelis* [1919] 1 K.B. 314 at 317, per Lush J.; *Collingwood v Home and Colonial Stores* [1936] 3 All E.R. 200; *Williams v Owen* [1955] 1 W.L.R. 1293.
[411] *Mason v Levy Auto Parts of England Ltd* [1967] 2 Q.B. 530 at 539, per MacKenna J.
[412] [1957] 2 Lloyd's Rep. 601; *Smith v Taylor* [1966] 2 Lloyd's Rep. 231, where Blain J. held that although the claimant had not shown the probable cause of the fire, the onus was on the defendant, as a bailee, to prove that he was not negligent.

Other statututory provision. By way of example, the Fire Precautions Act   **13–119**
1971[413] and regulations made thereunder and pursuant to the Framework and
Workplace Directives[414] require factories to be provided with means of escape in
case of fire and also to have certain safety provisions in case of fire. Failure to
comply with these provisions, which results in injury to any person employed in
the factory, will render the owner liable in damages for breach of statutory duty,
despite the fire having been accidental in its origin.[415] A similar result would
follow where there has been a breach of the provisions of the London Building
Acts 1930 to 1939, dealing with the provision of fire escapes.[416] The byelaws of
local authorities usually require the provision of a fire escape for a building,
exceeding a certain height, used as a hotel, restaurant, hospital, boarding-house,
common lodging-house, or school, and in shops of the same height where
sleeping accommodation is provided for the persons employed. Any failure to
comply with the byelaws may be evidence of negligence against the occupier of
the building in an action by either a visitor to or a person employed in the
building.[417]

Sparks from railways or on the highway.[418] Special provision was also   **13–120**
made in respect of sparks from steam locomotives[419] and, in the absence of
statutory authority for the running of the railway, absolute liability at common
law remains.[420] Similarly, owners of steam powered vehicles who cause damage
by the emission of sparks on the highway are subject to *Rylands v Fletcher.*[421]

Doing acts likely to result in damage by fire. Persons who do acts which are   **13–121**
likely to cause a fire or to result in damage by fire, such as by handling objects
that are likely to burn persons or property, by placing combustible material where
it is likely to catch fire or by maintaining fires in stoves or braziers, are bound to
take a high degree of care to prevent damage. In this connection, they are liable
for the negligence not only of their employees or agents but also of their
independent contractors.[422]

---

[413] By virtue of the Health and Safety at Work, etc. Act 1974 s.78 and Sch.8, replacing the Factories
Act 1961 ss.40–47.
[414] Framework Directive 89/391/EEC, Workplace Directive 89/654/EEC, Management of Health and
Safety at Work Regulations 1999, Workplace (Health, Safety and Welfare) Regulations 1992 and the
Fire Precautions (Workplace) Regulations 1997.
[415] *Groves v Lord Wimborne* [1898] 2 Q.B. 402; *Solomon v R. Gertzenstein Ltd* [1954] 2 Q.B.
243.
[416] *Solomons v R. Gertzenstein Ltd* [1954] 2 Q.B. 243.
[417] In *Maclenan v Segar* [1917] 2 K.B. 325 the jury found no negligence on the part of the hotel
proprietor in omitting to provide a fire escape. It does not appear from the report whether the omission
was a breach of the byelaws.
[418] Detailed discussion is now beyond the scope of this work in view of the passing of steam
locomotion. The reader is referred to *Charlesworth on Negligence* (4th edn, 1962), paras
610–613.
[419] e.g. Railway Fires Acts 1905 and 1923.
[420] *Jones v Festiniog Ry* (1868) L.R. 3 Q.B. 733.
[421] *Powell v Fall* (1880) 5 Q.B.D. 597; *Gunter v James* (1908) 24 T.L.R. 868; *Mansell v Webb* (1918)
88 L.J.K.B. 323.
[422] *Honeywill & Stein Ltd v Larkin Bros Ltd* [1934] 1 K.B. 191; *Black v Christchurch Finance Co*
[1894] A.C. 48; *Brooke v Bool* [1928] 2 K.B. 578. See also Ch.3, paras 3–98–3–203, above.

Illustrations

13–122   Liability was established: where a ship repairer, who was working on a ship with red-hot rivets close to an open hatchway, dropped such a rivet into the hatch and ignited its cargo[423]; where an acetylene flame was being used to cut away a ventilator on a ship leading to a hold containing an inflammable cargo and there was a failure to plug the ventilator with the result that the cargo was set on fire[424]; where gas pipes were examined with a naked flame[425]; where large quantities of combustible materials were stored in a yard in connection with the defendant's business and were kept in such conditions that, were they to catch fire, it would be likely to spread to the claimant's land, which event materialised[426]; where an attempt was made to kill a rat, believed to be in a drain pipe, by burning paper in the pipe which, in turn, caused a 20 gallon drum of paraffin to ignite and explode[427]; where highly combustible material was placed near a boiler in circumstances where sparks on the boiler firing were liable to set the material alight[428]; where, mistakenly, highly inflammable celluloid scrap was delivered by carrier to the claimant's premises, without warning of its dangerous nature, where it was carelessly lit and fire spread rapidly destroying the premises, the carrier was held liable.[429]

13–123   **Risks to children from fire or fire-making materials.** School teachers must take particular care to prevent children under their charge from coming into contact with fire. Both teacher and education authority were held liable to a 14-year-old girl who was burnt whilst poking the fire in the teacher's room at the latter's request.[430] An education authority was held liable when a girl of 11 was injured on her apron catching fire during a cookery class due to contact with an unguarded gas cooker.[431]

13–124   **Highly combustible materials.** Highly combustible materials, including petrol, must not be placed in the control of a child too young to appreciate the nature of the danger it poses. Thus, when petrol was sold to a boy of nine, who was severely burnt while trying to light it in order to make a torch, the seller was

---

[423] *Ellerman Lines Ltd v H. & G. Grayson Ltd* [1920] A.C. 466, where Lord Birkenhead expressly approved the judgment of Atkin L.J. [1919] 2 K.B. 514 at 534: "anyone using such a dangerous element as fire is under an obligation to take special care, lest he injure his neighbour or his neighbour's property".
[424] *Nautilus S.S. Co v Henderson*, 1919 S.C. 605.
[425] *Brooke v Bool* [1928] 2 K.B. 578, per Talbot J. The position with regard to gas is now substantially regulated by statute: see the Gas Safety (Installation and Use) Regulations 1994, paras 13–129–13–152, below.
[426] *Mason v Levy Auto Parts of England* [1966] 2 Q.B. 530.
[427] *Mulholland & Tedd Ltd v Baker* [1939] 3 All E.R. 253. See also *Balfour v Barty-King* [1957] 1 Q.B. 496 (independent contractor employed to thaw frozen pipes in second defendant's loft—loft contained combustible material—application of blowlamp to lagged pipes caused fire which spread to claimant's neighbouring house).
[428] *D'Urso v Sanson* [1939] 4 All E.R. 26. See also *Honeywill & Stein Ltd v Larkin Bros Ltd* [1934] 1 K.B. 191 (where a photographer used the then usual method of igniting magnesium powder in a tray to take a flashlight photograph but, in addition, caused a fire).
[429] *Philco Radio Ltd v Spurling Ltd* [1949] 2 All E.R. 882.
[430] *Smith v Martin and Hull Corp* [1911] 2 K.B. 775.
[431] *Fryer v Salford Corp* [1937] 1 All E.R. 617.

held liable because "to put a highly inflammable substance into the hands of a small boy is to subject him to temptation and the risk of injury, and this is no less true if the boy has resorted to deceit in order to overcome the supplier's scruples".[432] This was equally so when the defendant sold petrol to two 13-year-old boys who purchased it to sniff it. One was seriously injured when petrol, spilled on his clothes, ignited after the other threw down a match whilst smoking cigarettes. The claimant was not proved to have done anything unlawful himself and, although his conduct was blameworthy, the defence of ex turpi causa did not succeed, still less volenti non fit injuria, because the claimant did not assent to the foolish conduct of his friend.[433] The defendant was in breach of his common law duty of care to prevent a person under 16 years from having control over petrol.

Handling petrol. The handling of petrol or other highly inflammable liquids   **13–125** is an act which requires special precautions to guard against fire. The occupier of a garage was held liable for a fire which was caused as a result of one of his employees lighting a cigarette and throwing the match on the garage floor, while drawing petrol from a drum into a tin.[434] Likewise, where petrol was being transferred from a lorry to a tank at a garage and while the petrol was flowing from the lorry to the tank, the lorry driver lit a cigarette and threw the lighted match away, as a result of which a fire was caused, resulting in an explosion. The driver's employers were held liable.[435] When petrol is being delivered through a pipe or other container, there is a duty to watch and control the flow of the petrol. Any failure to do this, which results in a fire or an explosion, renders the person in charge of the operation liable in damages.[436] When petrol is delivered in bulk in barrels or other containers, there is a duty to deliver it in containers which are fit to withstand the ordinary risks incident to delivery. Thus, where petrol was delivered in a barrel, which burst on being rolled down a skid in the buyer's yard, the sellers were held liable.[437]

The keeping and transport of petrol is governed by the Petroleum (Consolidation) Act 1928 and the regulations made thereunder.[438]

---

[432] *Yachuk v Oliver Blais Co Ltd* [1949] A.C. 386.
[433] *Evans v Souls Garages Ltd, The Times*, January 23, 2001. The claimant was found one-third to blame.
[434] *Jefferson v Derbyshire Farmers Ltd* [1921] 2 K.B. 281. See also *Ayoub v Beaupre & Bense* (1964) 45 D.L.R. (2d) 411, both mechanic and his employers found liable. In *Jefferson v Derbyshire Farmers Ltd*, above at 289, Atkin L.J. explained his duty as follows: "In dealing with these and like substances there is a special duty to take precautions that no damage shall accrue either to bystanders or to adjoining property by reason of explosion, fire, or other injury."
[435] *Century Insurance Co v Northern Ireland Road Transport Board* [1942] A.C. 509.
[436] *Kennedy v Nascar* [1941] 3 D.L.R. 755.
[437] *Marshall v Russian Oil Products Ltd*, 1938 S.C. 773.
[438] Although the claimant's employers were found guilty of negligence in *Heffer v Rover Car Co, The Times*, November 26, 1964, in permitting petrol to be kept in an open tin, the claimant was found equally to blame, because he had accidentally caused the lighting of the petrol by "larking about" during the lunch time at his place of employment. See Hardy Ivamy, "Petrol Delivery and Explosion Risks", 105 L.J. 163. The current regulations are the Dangerous Substances and Explosive Atmospheres Regulations 2002.

13–126   **Firemen.**[439] Where a fireman has been called to attend a fire at premises and has been injured in the performance of his duty, he does not thereby become entitled to recover damages from the occupier of the premises. The risk of injury, which is inherent in the work of fire fighting, must be taken as having been accepted by him.[440]

13–127   However, in *Salmon v Seafarer Restaurants Ltd*,[441] it was held that a fireman, who was attending the scene of a fire and was injured in the course of fighting the flames, was entitled to sue the person whose negligence started the fire. The fact of his having his own professional skills did not debar him from claiming damages. Further, a fireman may well become entitled to succeed in a claim against an occupier of premises, if it was known or ought to have been known that a serious risk of fire at the premises was being created or maintained. Where the occupiers of a factory had allowed the accumulation of thick deposits of dust, containing aluminium and carbon particles in combustible proportions, they knew or ought to have known of the exceptional risks of fire and explosion thereby arising. Accordingly, they were liable when a fireman, called with the fire brigade to put out a fire in the factory, was injured by a fire and explosion caused by that dust.[442] Similarly, the occupiers of a railway station, which caught fire as a result of negligence in leaving premises unattended with a lit but unguarded stove, were held liable for exposing a fireman to an unnecessary hazard when he was injured after entering the roof space in order to search for a supposed missing railway employee.[443] There is no duty on an occupier to provide an exit route, which would remain safe whenever firemen are dealing with a fire on the premises.[444] A fireman, who was seriously injured while fighting a fire in a factory, was held to be outside the ambit of the provisions of s.29(1) of the Factories Act 1961[445] in a claim for damages made against the occupiers.[446]

13–128   Where a volunteer intervenes in an attempt to rescue life or property of a third party endangered by a fire for which the defendant was responsible, he may be owed the duty of care already discussed in relation to the "rescue" cases,[447] and succeed in an action for breach of that duty.[448]

5.—GAS

13–129   **General rule of liability at common law.** Because gas is a dangerous thing anyone who makes, supplies or uses it is, on the face of it, subject to the rule in *Rylands v Fletcher*. As Lord Wright said:

---

[439] See further in relation to the fire service, Ch.2, para.2–312.
[440] See the Occupiers' Liability Act 1957 s.2(3) and, further, Ch.8, above.
[441] [1983] 1 W.L.R. 1264, approved in *Ogwo v Taylor* [1988] A.C. 431. Per curiam, "The American 'fireman's rule' has no place in English law." See Arnheim, "Playing with Fire", 132 S.J. 1319.
[442] *Merrington v Iron Bridge Metal Works Ltd* (1952) 117 J.P. 23.
[443] *Hartley v British Railways Board* (1981) 125 S.J. 169.
[444] *Sibbald v Sher Brothers*, The Times, February 1, 1980.
[445] See generally the 9th edn of this work, Ch.11, para.11–138, above.
[446] *Flannigan v British Dyewood Co*, 1969 S.L.T. (O.H.) 223.
[447] See, Ch.2, paras 2–60–2–94 and above, paras 2–254–2–260.
[448] *Russell v McCabe* [1962] N.Z.L.R. 392.

"That gas is a dangerous thing within the rules applicable to things dangerous in themselves is beyond question. Thus the appellants who are carrying in their mains the inflammable and explosive gas are *prima facie* within the principle of *Rylands v Fletcher*[449] affirming *Fletcher v Rylands*[450]; that is to say, that though they are doing nothing wrongful in carrying the dangerous thing so long as they keep it in their pipes, they come *prima facie* within the rule of strict liability if the gas escapes: the gas constituted an extraordinary danger created by the appellants for their own purposes, and the rule established by *Rylands v Fletcher* requires that they act at their peril and must pay for damage caused by the gas if it escapes, even without any negligence on their part."[451]

Public supply of gas. Gas undertakings were nationalised by the Gas Act **13–130** 1948, which established Area Gas Boards to provide and regulate the public supply of gas, and thus modified the rule of strict liability by the introduction of the defence that, save in a case of negligence, the supply was provided pursuant to statutory powers.[452] The burden of proving that there was no negligence in the exercise of the statutory powers lay on the Area Boards, and there was no obligation to the party suffering damage to prove negligence of their part.[453] Area Boards, accordingly, were held liable in negligence for the escape of gas from their pipes and they were also liable for nuisance.[454] By virtue of the provisions of the Gas Act 1972,[455] the Area Boards established under the 1948 Act were dissolved and replaced by the British Gas Corporation.[456]

By the provisions for re-privatisation of the industry contained in the Gas Act 1986, the British Gas Corporation was dissolved and its property, rights and liabilities were transferred, according to the statute, to British Gas Plc, an authorised "public gas supplier".[457]

The 1986 Act has, in turn, been amended by the Gas Act 1996[458] which provides for an altered licensing framework for the gas industry. The "public gas supplier" of the 1986 Act has been replaced by "public gas transporters", "gas suppliers" and "gas shippers".

---

[449] (1868) L.R. 3 H.L. 330.
[450] (1866) L.R. 1 Ex. 265.
[451] *Northwestern Utilities Ltd v London Guarantee and Accident Co* [1936] A.C. 108 at 118.
[452] [1936] A.C. 108 at 119. In *Price v South Metropolitan Gas Co* (1895) 65 L.J.Q.B. 126, Russell C.J. said: "Where a gas company such as this, having statutory powers to lay pipes does so in the exercise of its statutory powers, the 'wild beast' theory referred to in the well known case of *Rylands v Fletcher* is inapplicable"; *Dunne v North Western Gas Board* [1964] 2 Q.B. 806. However, see the doubts expressed about this decision by Rees J. in *Pearson v North Western Gas Board* [1968] 2 All E.R. 669 at 672.
[453] *Northwestern Utilities Ltd v London Guarantee & Accident Co* [1936] A.C. 108; *Manchester Corp v Farnworth* [1930] A.C. 171.
[454] para.13–138, below.
[455] Which came into force on August 9, 1972.
[456] Gas Act 1972 (Appointed Day) Order 1972 (SI 1972/1440 (c.35)) which came into force on January 1, 1973.
[457] Gas Act 1986 s.7. But a new s.7 has been substituted by the Gas Act 1995 s.5, for which see below. In addition to the framework legislation there is much detailed regulation by statutory instrument, e.g. the Gas Safety (Installation and Use) Regulations (SI 1994/1886); the Gas Safety (Installation and Use) (Amendment) Regulations (SI 1996/550); and the Gas Safety (Management) Regulations (SI 1996/551); the Gas Safety (Management) Regulations (SI 1996/51); and the Gas Safety (Installation and Use Regulations 1998 (SI 1998/2451). See Crowther, "Keep the pilot light lit: the dangers of carbon monoxide" (2003) H. & S.L. 3(1), 2.
[458] The 1995 Act came into force on March 1, 1996, by virtue of SI 1996/218.

Public gas transporters have the function of operating the pipeline system through which gas is delivered to consumers. Gas suppliers sell the piped gas to customers and gas shippers are responsible for making available appropriate amounts of gas for movement through the pipeline system. In the discussion which follows the "old" terminology is for the time being retained, but the new arrangements will have to be kept in mind if it is necessary to establish the responsibility of a licensee for a particular gas escape.[459]

13–131   **Liability in negligence of a public gas supplier for gas escapes.** Because public gas suppliers,[460] like their predecessors, keep gas under pressure in mains and pipes, a very high degree of care is exacted of them. In considering the examples which follow, it should be noted that many of the old common law decisions cannot stand, given the modern statutory regime governing gas.[461]

ILLUSTRATIONS

13–132   Liability was established against the gas undertaker: where an hotel was damaged by fire owing to an escape from the gas main operated under statutory authority. The main had fractured due to operations of the local authority constructing a storm sewer but the undertaker should have been vigilant to ensure that the local authority's work did not affect the main and, in particular, should not have assumed that the authority would fulfil its duty properly to support the pipe[462]; where a gas pipe laid ten and a half inches below the surface of a road cracked under the weight of traffic after a sewer authority had recently excavated the ground but failed to leave proper support for the pipe[463]; where an explosion occurred in a house due to escape of gas following a fracture of the main caused by colliery subsidence, there having been a failure to take precautions to guard against the known risk of subsidence[464]; where an explosion occurred on gas escaping from the main into a house where lights were burning.[465]

13–133   Liability was not established against the undertaker: following an escape and explosion where a gas pipe rusted owing to a leakage of water from an adjacent water pipe.[466]

---

[459] In the vast majority of cases it will be the public gas transporter which is responsible for an escape of gas: see n.470 below.

[460] See n.459, above.

[461] See n.457, above.

[462] *Northwestern Utilities Ltd v London Guarantee & Accident Co* [1936] A.C. 108, PC. Lord Wright said, at 126, that the undertakers owed: " . . . a duty to the respondents' [hotel] even though the case falls outside the rule of strict or absolute liability to exercise all care and skill that these [hotel] owners shall not be damaged. The degree of care which that duty involves must be proportioned to the degree of risk involved in that duty should not be fulfilled."

[463] *Price v South Metropolitan Gas Co* (1895) 65 L.J.Q.B. 126. Russell C.J. said that the gas company "should be vigilant in seeing that when any other body had reason to excavate near their pipes the pipes were left in a safe condition", and that they were negligent because they ought "to have known that the ground under the pipe had been disturbed and had not been properly replaced". See also to the like effect *Shell-Mex Ltd v Belfast Corp* [1952] N.I. 72.

[464] *Hanson v Wearmouth Coal Co* [1939] 3 All E.R. 47.

[465] *Blenkiron v Great Central Gas Consumer's Co* (1860) 2 F. & F. 437.

[466] *Stacey v Metropolitan Water Board* (1910) 9 L.G.R. 174.

Unexplained escape of gas. The unexplained escape of gas from the mains of   **13–134**
pipes is prima facie evidence of negligence on the part of the gas undertaker. If
the escape was through a crack in the pipe, it is for the undertaker to prove that
the crack was caused without any negligence on his part. Even if there is no
crack, but the pipe leaks in some way, the burden still rests on him to prove that
the leak is not a consequence of his negligence.

> "A person who brings a dangerous thing on his land,[467] and allows it to escape, thereby
> causing damage to another, is liable to that other unless he can show that the escape was
> due to the conscious act of a third party, and without negligence on his own part.
> Obviously the burden of proving that there was no negligence is on the defendants, and
> it is not for the plaintiff to prove negligence affirmatively."[468]

It follows that the law offers no remedy to a victim of a gas explosion if it
occurred without negligence on the part of the undertaker. Where an explosion
killed the claimant's husband, seriously injured her and destroyed their home, the
claim failed on proof that the gas had escaped from a main which had fractured
instantaneously in an exceptionally severe frost.[469]

Detection of gas escapes. A public gas company is bound to take all   **13–135**
reasonable precautions to detect escapes of gas[470] within the system and to deal
promptly with them. So, the gas company was liable where, having found the
source of an escape from the main, its employee left the scene to obtain repair
equipment only for an explosion to occur before he returned.[471] Liability also
followed where the combined effect of the removal of support below and the
weight of traffic above, caused a pipe to crack and escaped gas accumulated for
two or three days before an explosion occurred.[472]

Liability devolved on the occupier rather than the gas company where a visitor   **13–136**
to premises was injured by a gas explosion which was preceded by a strong smell

---

[467] The rule is not limited to cases where the defendant has been carrying or accumulating the
dangerous thing on his own land. "It applies equally . . . where the appellants were carrying gas in
mains laid in the property of the city (that is, in the subsoil) in the exercise of a franchise to do so":
Lord Wright in *Northwestern Utilities Ltd v London Guarantee & Accident Co* [1936] A.C. 108.
[468] *Hanson v Wearmouth Coal Co* [1939] 3 All E.R. 47 at 53 per Goddard L.J. See also *Lloyde v West
Midland Gas Board* [1971] 1 W.L.R. 749.
[469] *Pearson v North Western Gas Board* [1968] 2 All E.R. 669.
[470] By the Gas Act 1986 Sch.5, para.13, a public gas supplier was under a duty, immediately after
being informed of the escape, to prevent the gas from escaping, and should he fail to do such within
12 hours of being so informed, was liable to be fined. Sch.5 has been repealed by the Gas Act 1995,
for which see above para.13–130 and n.457. Duties where gas escapes from pipes are now set out in
para.20 et seq. of Sch.2 to the 1995 Act and fall upon the public gas transporter who owns them. The
transporter is under the like duties where gas escapes from a pipe or gas fitting used by a consumer
to whose premises he has conveyed gas. By the new s.9 to the 1986 Act the transporter is placed
under a general duty to maintain an efficient and economical pipeline system (see para.3 of Sch.3 to
the 1995 Act); and to carry out any necessary work of maintenance, repair or renewal of any gas
service pipe by which gas is conveyed by him to the consumer's premises (para.15 of Sch.2).
[471] *Mose v Hastings and St Leonards Gas Co* (1864) 4 F. & F. 324. See also *Manchester Corp v
Markland* [1936] A.C. 360, dealing with the detection of escapes from water mains, and para.13–85,
above, dealing with water companies.
[472] *Price v South Metropolitan Gas Co* (1895) 65 L.J.Q.B. 126; *Shell-Mex Ltd v Belfast Corp* [1952]
N.I. 72.

of gas for about eight hours without any report by the occupier to the gas company.[473] On the other hand, where, after a deliberate escape of gas by a suicide and following a report of a strong smell of gas to the gas company, an investigation occurred which found no fault, the company was held vicariously liable for an explosion which damaged three houses because its employee left the scene without taking any action.[474]

13–137   If the claimant himself causes the escape of gas, the gas supplier is not liable for damage arising, if there is no concurrent negligence on his part. No liability attached to the supplier where an explosion occurred after the claimant failed to turn off a gas stop-cock before leaving the house unoccupied.[475]

13–138   **Liability for nuisance.** The escape of gas is itself a nuisance[476] but, if it is caused by a public gas supplier,[477] it is not actionable without proof of negligence.[478] If an escape has not been caused by a public gas supplier but, rather, by the actions of another agency[479] or in any other case where the escape has been caused by another person, the public gas supplier is only liable for negligently allowing the gas to escape when the taking of prompt action could have prevented either the escape[480] or its continuance.[481] To be a nuisance it is not necessary that the escape of gas should have been going on for any prolonged period of time.[482]

13–139   **Strict liability for gas escapes from underground storage.** An exception to the need for proof of negligence, arises in the case of damage caused by gas in an underground gas storage or in the boreholes connected with an underground gas storage or by gas, which is escaping or has so escaped from any such storage or boreholes. By the Gas Act 1965[483] a gas authority, now the public gas transporter, is absolutely liable in civil proceedings for any such damage so

---

[473] *Glennister v Condon & Eastern Gas Board* [1951] 2 Lloyd's Rep. 115.
[474] *Smith v South Eastern Gas Board* (1964) 108 S.J. 337.
[475] *Holden v Liverpool New Gas & Coke Co* (1846) 3 C.B. 1.
[476] Preserved by the Gas Act 1972 Sch.4, para.33.
[477] This phrase is no longer used in the new licensing regime established by the Gas Act 1995: see para.13–130 and n.457, above.
[478] The CA has held that the gas board be liable either on a basis of strict liability under the *Rylands v Fletcher* rule or in nuisance, if the board had done what the statute had imposed upon it, without negligence, since it had been recognised that gas might escape as an incident of its statutory operations: *Dunne v North Western Gas Board* [1964] 2 Q.B. 806, distinguishing *Midwood v Manchester Corp* [1905] 2 K.B. 597 and *Charing Cross Electricity Supply Co v Hydraulic Power Co* [1914] 3 K.B. 772; *Manchester Corp v Farnworth* [1930] A.C. 171.
[479] e.g. *Stacey v Metropolitan Water Board* (1916) 9 L.G.R. 126 (a water pipe, for which the authority was not responsible, and a gas pipe were laid close together but, as a result of the water pipe leaking, the gas pipe rusted away and gas escaped; and *Pearson v North West Gas Board* [1968] 2 All E.R. 669 (a gas pipe was fractured by severe frost, a risk which could not have been "avoided by the exercise of reasonable care on the part of the defendants", at 672).
[480] *Hanson v Wearmouth Coal Co* [1939] 3 All E.R. 47, 55; *Smeaton v Ilford Corp* [1954] Ch. 450 at 472; approved in *Dunne v North Western Gas Board* [1964] 2 Q.B. 806.
[481] *Dunne v North Western Gas Board* [1964] 2 Q.B. 806.
[482] *Midwood v Manchester Corp* [1905] 2 K.B. 597.
[483] Which came into force on August 5, 1965.

caused[484] "Damage" includes loss of life, personal injury and damage to property.[485] The partial defence of contributory negligence is specifically retained.[486]

Breaking up streets, bridges, etc. The Gas Act 1986[487] contains provisions **13–140** which empower public gas suppliers to break up streets or bridges for the purpose of placing and from time to time repairing, altering, or removing pipes and other supply equipment. It imposes an obligation to do as little damage as possible and make compensation for any damage done in exercising these powers.[488]

Liability to highway users. When exercising their powers, they must take **13–141** reasonable care for the protection of people passing along the highway.

ILLUSTRATIONS

Gas companies were held liable to passers by: when, while laying pipes, their **13–142** workmen projected a piece of metal which struck and injured the claimant[489]; where, during a repair of a main, a fire pail with a ladle containing molten lead was placed on unenclosed land adjacent to the highway and a child was injured when a passer-by accidentally knocked over the pail, it being negligent to leave apparatus unattended and unguarded on land adjoining the highway without steps being taken to protect highway users.[490]

Gas meters. The Gas Act 1995[491] imposes duties as to the provision and **13–143** maintenance of any meters which public gas suppliers require their customers to use. If they are negligent in doing so, they are liable to any person injured.[492]

Installing or disconnecting gas in premises. In installing[493] or disconnecting **13–144** a supply of gas,[494] the person carrying out the work is only liable on proof of

---

[484] By s.14(1). Para.7(1) of Sch.4 to the Gas Act 1995 substitutes the words "public gas transporter" for the reference to a public gas supplier in s.14(1): see para.13–130, above.
[485] Defined in s.14(4).
[486] By s.14(3).
[487] Sch.4 as amended by para.57 of Sch.3 to the Gas Act 1995, which substitutes the words "public gas transporter" for the reference to a public gas supplier: see para.13–130 and n.457, above.
[488] *Goodson v Sunbury Gas Co* (1896) 75 L.T. 251; *Brame v Commercial Gas Co* [1914] 3 K.B. 1181.
[489] *Scott v Manchester Corp* (1857) 2 H. & n.204.
[490] *Crane v South Suburban Gas Co* [1916] 1 K.B. 33.
[491] Sch.2.
[492] *Clavett v Pontypridd Urban District Council* [1918] 1 K.B. 219. However, where an inspector left his open pen penknife in a house where he was investigating a defective meter and a four year old child picked it up and injured his eye, the gas company was held not liable: *Forsyth v Manchester Corp* (1912) 29 T.L.R. 15, on a jury finding that the inspector reasonably ought not to have anticipated danger arising from the knife left where it was.
[493] See also para.13–165, below, for the comparable position as regards the installation of electricity.
[494] For the provisions of the Defective Premises Act 1972, which are relevant as regards the duties owed where gas apparatus has been installed by an owner of a dwelling-house or its builders and, subsequently, the property is let or sold, see para.13–149, below.

negligence.[495] The degree of care and skill required is a very high one, because of the great danger which results from an escape of gas, and of the skill and experience which the statutory undertakers may be presumed to have in matters relating to the supply of gas.[496]

Illustrations

13–145   Liability was established against the gas company: where, following the disconnection of the gas supply to a meter, a long piece of pipe, properly stopped but still connected to the main, was left projecting in a cellar and third parties broke the pipe in attempting to take away the meter with the result that gas filled the cellar and caused an explosion[497]; where a defective pipe was supplied to convey gas from the main to the meter and, on gas escaping, the company's employee carried a lighted candle to find the source of the escape[498]; where the deceased died from carbon monoxide poisoning due to the escape of gas from a faulty and inadequately ventilated water heater. The company had negligently (i) failed to fit a larger airbrick following conversion to natural gas which required more oxygen to operate safely and (ii) advised the deceased that the heater was not dangerous to use[499]; where a safety valve, in a regulator fitted to apparatus designed to receive natural gas at very high pressure, was negligently installed so that it discharged gas indoors, instead of outdoors, resulting in a fatal explosion.[500]

13–146   **Liability of persons other than a public gas supplier.** The liability of persons, other than a public gas supplier or others, operating under statutory authority, who own, control or accumulate gas, is that laid down in *Rylands v Fletcher.* Where one municipality disposed of organic matter on the land of another, by way of a land-fill project, the resultant decomposition produced methane gas that escaped and seeped into adjoining lands upon which houses were built. On the claimant starting the engine of his motor car in the garage of his home, the gas exploded, destroying the building, damaging the vehicle and injuring him. Both municipalities were held strictly liable for the escaping methane gas, since land-fill with rubbish is a non-natural user of land in a heavily populated residential district. In addition, the defendants were negligent in that, inter alia, they knew or ought to have known that decomposition would produce appreciable quantities of a dangerous gas.[501] On the other hand, where gas escapes from an ordinary domestic supply, the owner is not liable except on proof

---

[495] But a claimant may well be able to argue that the facts speak for themselves, e.g. as in *Lloyde v West Midlands Gas Board* [1971] 1 W.L.R. 749. Further see Ch.6, para.6–100, above.

[496] See per Lopes J. in *Parry v Smith* (1879) 4 C.P.D. 325 at 327.

[497] *Paterson v Blackburn Corp* (1829) 9 T.L.R. 55.

[498] *Burrows v March Gas and Coke Co* (1870) L.R. 5 Ex. 67, affirmed (1872) L.R. 7 Ex. 96. The company was held liable both in negligence and for breach of contract.

[499] *Pusey v Peters*, The Times, October 26, 1974.

[500] *Dominion Natural Gas Co v Collins* [1909] A.C. 640. Lord Dunedin said:"In the case of articles dangerous in themselves, such as loaded firearms, poisons, explosives, and other things *ejusdem generis*, there is a peculiar duty to take precaution imposed upon those who send forth or instal such articles when it is necessarily the case that other parties will come within their proximity." See also *Parry v Smith* (1879) 4 C.P.D. 325.

[501] *Gertsen v Municipality of Metropolitan Toronto* (1973) 41 D.L.R. (3d) 646.

of negligence.[502] Thus, where gas escaped from an outside service pipe belonging to the owner of several houses and caused an explosion in the house of one of his tenants, it was held that, in the absence of negligence on the owner's part in the maintenance of the service pipe, there was no liability to the persons injured.[503]

Doing acts likely to cause gas to escape. A person doing an act likely to   **13–147** cause an escape of gas or a gas explosion is under a duty to take a very high degree of care to prevent damage from being caused. When gas pipes become cracked, owing to the removal of proper support by persons working near to the pipes, those responsible for removing the support are liable.[504] Where a local authority employed an independent contractor to construct a sewer in a street and, in doing so, the contractor left a gas main unsupported with the result that the main broke and an explosion ensued in an adjoining house, both contractor and local authority were held liable.[505] Where damage was caused to a gas undertaker's pipes due to the activities of water, sewer and other authorities, which had removed the support for its pipes in the course of fulfilling their statutory duties, the latter were held liable.[506]

Negligence of a third party. When a person would otherwise be liable for an   **13–148** escape of gas, it is no defence for him to show, for example, that the immediate cause of the explosion was the act of a third person using a naked light in an attempt to detect the place of the escape, because such an escape will almost inevitably cause an explosion and, thus, the precise circumstances in which it occurs are irrelevant. Accordingly, where a gas company was negligent in providing a defective service pipe, then supplying gas through it, and a gas fitter's employee caused an explosion negligently by using a naked light, it was held that the gas company was liable for the damage so suffered and that the negligence of the gas fitter's employee was no defence.[507] If necessary the gas fitter would also have been liable for the negligence of his employee.[508] Because the owner of a lock-up shop, which was let to a tenant, had suspected that gas was escaping in the premises after the tenant had left for the night, he entered the shop with a friend to investigate. With his approval, the friend examined the gas pipe, using a naked light for the purpose, whereupon an explosion occurred, which

---

[502] *Bleach v Blue Gate Products*, *The Times*, January 26, 1960 (defective tap on a gas cooker); *Collingwood v Home and Colonial Stores* [1936] 3 All E.R. 200, CA and para.13–100, above. See paras 13–95–13–101, above, dealing with the escape of water.
[503] *Miller v Robert Addie & Sons (Collieries)*, 1934 S.C. 150. Quaere whether this case does not go too far. cf. *Peters v Prince of Wales Theatre (Birmingham) Ltd* [1943] K.B. 73; *Tilley v Stevenson* [1939] 4 All E.R. 207; *Western Engraving Co v Film Laboratories Ltd* [1936] 1 All E.R. 106 (water cases).
[504] If the gas company has no right of support for its pipes, the person removing support will not be liable for any escape of gas: *Hanson v Wearmouth Coal Co* [1939] 3 All E.R. 47.
[505] *Hardaker v Idle District Council* [1896] 1 Q.B. 335. For cases where the gas main was fractured during road repairs and after it had been subjected to heavy pressures from the use of road rollers, see *Gas Light & Coke Co v St Mary Abbott's, Kensington* (1885) 15 Q.B.D. 1 and *Driscoll v Poplar Board of Works* (1897) 14 T.L.R. 99.
[506] *Ilford Gas Co v Ilford UDC* (1903) 67 J.P. 365; *Huyton & Roby Gas Co v Liverpool Corp* [1926] 1 K.B. 146.
[507] *Burrows v March Gas & Coke Co* (1872) L.R. 7 Ex. 96; *Parry v Smith* (1879) 4 C.P.D. 325.
[508] *Brooke v Bool* [1928] 2 K.B. 578.

damaged the goods in the shop. The owner was nevertheless held liable to the tenant.[509] The search for a gas escape was highly dangerous unless proper precautions were taken and a necessary precaution was to avoid the use of a naked light. Since the defendant had undertaken the examination he was under a duty to take reasonable care to avoid danger resulting from it. He was unable to escape the consequences of a failure to discharge this duty by getting another to make the examination, even if that other was a mere voluntary helper. A person dealing with a dangerous thing is liable not only for his own negligence, but also for the negligence of any independent contractor whom he may employ to deal with it.[510]

13–149   **Liability of landlord, seller or builder of real property.** At common law[511] there was no liability on the part of a landlord to a tenant or of a seller to a buyer for negligence in the installation of gas or any other dangerous thing[512] in the premises, either before or after the commencement of the tenancy[513] or before the completion of the purchase.[514] His immunity covered not only nonfeasance, for example his negligent failure to carry out necessary repairs, but also malfeasance, for example his negligent installation of an unventilated gas geyser in a bathroom[515] and his negligent removal of a gas fire from a bedroom,[516] each of which resulted in the death of an occupant from carbon monoxide poisoning. The landlord's immunity, in the absence of express contractual conditions, was abolished by s.3 of the Defective Premises Act 1972,[517] which imposes a duty of care. However, neither s.3 nor s.4 of the 1972 Act appears to cover the situation where a landlord lets business premises and has failed to carry out repairs. If such a tenant is injured as a result of some defect in the in defective premises, the immunity at common law could well apply still, because s.3 does not apply to work omitted to be done, only to work *done*, and under s.4, where the obligation to repair only exists if the landlord has expressly undertaken it.[518] A similar

---

[509] *Brooke v Bool* [1928] 2 K.B. 578.

[510] *Hardaker v Idle District Council* [1896] 1 Q.B. 335; *Honeywill & Stein Ltd v Larkin Bros Ltd* [1934] 1 K.B. 191; *Black v Christchurch Finance Co* [1894] A.C. 48; *Brooke v Bool* [1928] 2 K.B. 57; *Johnson (t/a Johnson Butchers) v BJW Property Developments Ltd* [2002] 3 All E.R. 574, Q.B.D. The rule imposing liability has been said not to apply to an intermediary in a contractual chain between the ultimate employer and the party at fault: *M.T.M. Construction Ltd v William Reid Engineering Ltd, The Times*, April 22, 1997, OH, above Ch.3, para.3–195.

[511] For the situation at common law in fuller detail, see *Charlesworth on Negligence* (5th edn, 1971), Ch.9.

[512] See para.13–07 et seq., above.

[513] *Malone v Laskey* [1907] 2 K.B. 141; *Ball v London County Council* [1949] 2 K.B. 159. However, it was suggested strongly in *A.C. Billings & Sons Ltd v Riden* [1958] A.C. 240 that a landlord would be liable in respect of things done *after* the commencement of the demise.

[514] *Bottomley v Bannister* [1932] 1 K.B. 458; *Otto v Bolton & Norris* [1936] 2 K.B. 46.

[515] *Travers v Gloucester Corp* [1947] K.B. 71.

[516] *Davis v Foots* [1940] 1 K.B. 116.

[517] Which came into force, by virtue of s.7(2), on January 1, 1974. See further Ch.8, above, paras 8–124–8–137.

[518] By the Landlord and Tenant Act 1985 ss.11–16, 32 and 36, there is imposed by law an obligation to repair in the case of short leases of dwelling-houses, which does extend similarly to business premises.

situation arises, probably, where the landlord has failed to warn of defects not created by him in business premises but of which he may have knowledge.

Different considerations apply if gas escapes from part of the premises **13–150** retained by the landlord into the tenant's part. In *Federic v Perpetual Invest-ments*,[519] a landlord, in operating on his own garage premises situated directly below a tenant's apartment, allowed gas to escape and penetrate the tenant's premises so that the tenant suffered chronic carbon monoxide poisoning. The landlord was held strictly liable under the rule in *Rylands v Fletcher*.

The duties of builders in relation to property which they have constructed have **13–151** been discussed already.[520] Duties can arise at common law by way of the principles set out in *Murphy v Brentwood District Council*,[521] alternatively under the Defective Premises Act 1972. By s.1 of the Act there is specifically imposed on builders, inter alia,[522] the duty of carrying out work in a workmanlike or professional manner and using proper materials, so that in respect of the contribution which that work makes to the dwelling, whether by erection, conversion, enlargement or otherwise, the dwelling is fit for habitation. The duty is owed not only to the first owner of the dwelling but also to his successors in title; but the usual periods for limitation of actions will apply and will begin to run, as a general rule, from the completion of the dwelling.

Gas contained in cylinders or otherwise. In *Beckett v Newalls Insulation* **13–152** *Co*,[523] a refrigeration company and an insulation company were working on a ship under construction. The refrigeration company was using Calor gas in a cylinder and left it in an outer chamber of the ship on a Friday, knowing that they would not be using it until the following Tuesday but that other men would be working on the ship in the meanwhile. On the Sunday, a man employed by the insulators, without any negligence, moved a gas cylinder from the outer to the inner chamber. On the Tuesday, the claimant, employed by the insulators, entered the inner chamber, struck a match and caused an explosion which injured him. The refrigeration company was held liable, because they had not taken the high degree of care imposed on them as the persons who had brought a dangerous thing on board the ship. Following the use of an oxyacetylene burner in the poop space of the claimant's oil tanker, an explosion occurred. The defendants, on whose floating pontoon the tanker was being repaired, were held liable for the negligence of their consulting engineer who, prior to burning commencing, had tested for gas and reported it to be free.[524]

---

[519] (1968) 2 D.L.R. (3d) 50.
[520] See Ch.2, para.2–233 and Ch.8, para.8–112, above.
[521] [1991] 1 A.C. 398.
[522] Including specialist sub-contractors and manufacturers of equipment made to order.
[523] [1953] 1 W.L.R. 8 (It was not proved how the gas had escaped.)
[524] *The Pass of Ballater* [1942] P. 112 at 117, per Langton J.: "Where the introduction of implements or substances dangerous in themselves, such as flame-bearing instruments or explosives, are necessarily incidental to the work to be performed, a contractor is equally bound by an inescapable duty. The point may perhaps be crystallised by saying that he has not merely a duty to take care but a duty to provide that care is taken."

6.—ELECTRICITY

13–153   **General rule of liability for electricity.** Electricity generated, stored or transmitted in a substantial quantity is clearly dangerous and the principle in *Rylands v Fletcher* applies.[525] Generators of electricity and those responsible for the transmission and supply of electricity would at common law be strictly liable for any escape of electricity causing damage to an interest in land.

13–154   **Statutory authority.** When electricity is generated, transmitted or supplied under statutory authority the rule of strict liability arising under *Rylands v Fletcher* will be displaced unless the statute authorising the activity preserves it.[526] If the statute is silent, the usual rule is that liability can only be established on proof of negligence. The generation, transmission and supply of electricity is now carried out by public electricity suppliers under licences[527] granted pursuant to the provisions of the Electricity Act 1989. The 1989 Act is silent as to the tortious liability of public electricity suppliers and thus it is likely that liability in respect of damage caused by the escape of electricity from apparatus operated by electricity companies will arise only on proof of negligence. The provisions of ss.77 and 81 of the Electric Lighting (Clauses) Act 1899, which specifically preserved the liability in nuisance of the old electricity boards were repealed by the 1989 Act and not replaced. Cases before 1989 where liability in nuisance was imposed without proof of negligence ought to be viewed with some caution.

13–155   **Liability in respect of negligence.** The standard of care required of a supplier of electricity is a high one, reflecting the intrinsically dangerous nature of electricity itself.[528] All reasonable known means of keeping electricity harmless should be used.[529] Where an electricity supply company erected two overhead cables carrying a high tension current and, in a wind, a tree branch snapped and brought them down, permitting current to escape along a low tension cable and cause a fire in the claimant's home, the company was liable. It had failed to earth the wires of transformers so that the electricity could pass harmlessly into the ground, instead of entering the neighbouring houses.[530] However, when a building contractors' workman was operating a derrick in the street to raise a stone and the derrick came into contact with the overhead wire, as a result of which electricity was conducted down the cable of the derrick, rendering the

---

[525] *National Telephone Co v Baker* [1893] 2 Ch. 186; *Eastern and South African Telephone Co v Cape Town Tramways* [1902] A.C. 381.
[526] *National Telephone Co v Baker* [1893] 2 Ch. 186.
[527] See the Electricity Act 1989 ss.4–6.
[528] See *Northwestern Utilities v London Guarantee and Accident Co* [1936] A.C. 108 (gas).
[529] per Collins M.R. in *Midwood v Manchester Corp* [1905] 2 K.B. 597 at 608.
[530] *Quebec Railway Light, Heat and Power Co v Vandry* [1920] A.C. 622. In dealing with the defence of statutory powers, Lord Sumner, at 679, said: "Such powers are not in themselves charters to commit torts and to damage third persons at large, but that which is necessarily incidental to the exercise of the statutory authority is held to have been authorised by implication, and therefore it is not the foundation of a cause of action in favour of strangers, since otherwise the application of the general law would defeat the purpose of the enactment."

workman unconscious and killing two men rushing to help him, the electricity company was not liable.[531]

When electricity is carried overhead by wires or cables, in addition to any **13–156** precautions required by statute, great care must be taken to see that it is not likely to become a source of danger. In *Buckland v Guildford Gas Light & Coke Co*,[532] high voltage electric wires were routed across a field, immediately over the top of a tree, part of which had been cut down to permit the passage of the wires. A girl of 13 climbed the tree, when it was in full leaf, came into contact with the wires and was electrocuted. The electricity undertakers were liable on the ground that they should have foreseen that someone might climb the tree and, being unable to see the wires obscured by the dense foliage, accidentally come into contact with them.[533] Nevertheless, a different result was reached in the somewhat similar case of *McLaughlin v Antrim Electricity Supply Co*.[534] There a boy of 12 had climbed a pylon, one leg of which was on public land and the other in a field used by children as a playground, and was injured when he came into contact with a wire conductor. He failed to recover damages on the ground that he was a trespasser on the pylon and had climbed at his own risk. It would seem, however, that the real question was not whether the boy was a trespasser but whether the electricity undertakers had fulfilled their duty to take care having regard to the situation and position of the wire and to the known circumstances generally.[535]

Where a high voltage underground cable had been laid at a depth of only 8 to **13–157** 10 inches beneath a pavement, instead of the normal depth of 18 inches, because of the presence of cellars below, the London Electricity Board decided to cover it with steel plates, in order to protect it as well as to prevent it becoming a trap to anyone working on the roadway. The Board, in such circumstances, was exonerated from all blame when a workman was electrocuted as a result of penetrating the cable with his employers' pneumatic drill.[536]

Limit of the electricity supplier's duty of care. Normally the supplier's **13–158** liability ends at the point when electricity is delivered to the consumer. So an electricity supplier was not liable where the claimant's wife was electrocuted as a result of a contractor's failure, when installing a new circuit for a boiler, to make a proper earth connection.[537] There was no duty to carry out any inspection or test of the new installation before supplying electricity.

---

[531] *Dumphy v Montreal Light, Heat and Power Co* [1907] A.C. 454.

[532] [1949] 1 K.B. 410. See also, Ch.8, para.8–93, above.

[533] The girl was found not to be a trespasser on the tree but, as the defendants did not own the tree or the field in which it was growing, this fact is irrelevant, except possibly on the question of foreseeability.

[534] [1941] N.I. 23. See also *Moyle v Southern Electricity Board* [1962] 1 Lloyd's Rep. 607 (where a kite being flown from a steel wire touched an overhead cable the accident could not have been foreseen).

[535] The trespasser point would now be determined by reference to the Occupiers' Liability Act 1984: see Ch.8, paras 8–144–8–160, above.

[536] *Lait v A.A. King (Contractors) Ltd, The Times*, April 11, 1975.

[537] *Sellars v Best* [1954] 2 All E.R. 389.

13–159   **Explosions.** Where an explosion occurred in the electric mains of a statutory undertaker owing to the ignition by the electric spark of an accumulation of gas which had leaked from a gas main, and there was evidence that a ventilator would have prevented the explosion, it was held that there was negligence on the part of the electricity undertakers.[538] An explosion, which has been created by an escape of electricity from the mains or wires of an electricity supplier, is prima facie evidence of negligence. Thus, where the claimant, who was walking along the street and passing a sunken chamber, was injured by an explosion, which caused a metal plate to open and a flash to emanate, it was held there was negligence on the part of the electricity undertakers.[539]

13–160   **Breaking up streets.** Those licensed to supply electricity are empowered under the Electricity Act 1989 to execute such street works as are required to inspect, maintain and keep their apparatus in repair.[540] The standard to which the work is performed and the safety measures to be adopted are governed by the New Roads and Street Works Act 1991, which has already been discussed above.[541]

13–161   **Liability of persons other than statutory suppliers.** The liability of persons who own or control electricity without any statutory authority[542] is that laid down in *Rylands v Fletcher*.[543] An exception, however, occurs in the case of "electric wiring which everybody, or most people, nowadays have in the houses which they occupy whether for domestic use, or for purposes of trade",[544] when negligence must be proved to establish liability. Thus, where there was some unknown defect in the electrical wiring in the basement of the defendant's grocery stores, causing a fire to break out, and the claimant's adjoining shop was damaged by the water used in extinguishing the fire, it was held that the defendant was not liable in the absence of evidence of negligence.[545] Again, when a fire was caused by a short circuit of the electric wiring, behind the panelling and near to a ventilator on the half landing of a building, where a stack of packing and wrapping material was stored, it was held there was no liability.[546]

---

[538] *Solomons v Stepney Borough Council* (1905) 69 J.P. 360. But, to the contrary, see *Goodbody v Poplar Borough Council* (1915) 84 L.J.K.B. 1230 (where there was a similar explosion and it was found that the chamber in which it occurred was constructed properly, the electricity undertakers were held not liable).

[539] *Farrell v Limerick Corp* (1911) 45 I.L.T. 169, per Palles C.B.: see also *Solomons v Stepney Borough Council* (1905) 69 J.P. 360, per Alverstone C.J.

[540] The powers are set out in the Fourth Schedule.

[541] para.13–87, above.

[542] See further, as in the case of gas, para.13–146, above, and the liability of landlord, seller or builder of real property, para.13–149, above.

[543] *National Telephone Co v Baker* [1893] 2 Ch. 186; *Eastern and South African Telephone Co v Cape Town Tramways* [1902] A.C. 381; *Hiller v Air Ministry, The Times*, December 8, 1962. Simultaneous electrocution of 19 cows in a field following an escape of electricity from an underground high voltage cable: the statutory power under which the cable was laid did not authorise such an escape.

[544] *Collingwood v Home and Colonial Stores* [1936] 3 All E.R. 200 at 208, per Lord Wright M.R.

[545] *Collingwood v Home and Colonial Stores* [1936] 3 All E.R. 200 at 208. Lord Wright said that the rule in *Rylands v Fletcher* did not apply "to the ordinary domestic installation of electric wiring for the ordinary comfort and convenience of life."

[546] *Solomons v R. Gertzenstein Ltd* [1954] 1 Q.B. 565, reversed on other grounds [1954] 2 Q.B. 243.

On somewhat similar facts, however, the defendant was held liable in nuisance in *Spicer v Smee*.[547] There, the claimant's house was destroyed by fire caused by a defect in the electric wiring of the adjoining house which was owned by the defendant. The condition of the wiring was found to be a nuisance, created by the defendant or those for whom he was responsible, and, as this nuisance had caused the fire, the defendant was held liable. In the particular circumstances, the defendant was also liable for negligence on the part of an independent contractor he had employed to instal the wiring.

In *Hartley v Mayoh*,[548] an electricity supplier's employees installed a new   **13–162**
meter on premises but did not test the circuits after completing the work. Negligently, they had crossed the leads, as a result of which a fireman, called to the scene to fight a fire on the premises, was electrocuted. They were held liable on the ground that they should have contemplated that their omission to make a test might cause damage to persons lawfully on the premises who came into contact with any part of the wiring system.

Again, an electrical contractor, who had installed at the claimant's house an   **13–163**
electric boiler, together with a new circuit, but negligently had failed to provide a fully efficient earthing system for it, was liable to the claimant for the death of his wife, who was electrocuted in consequence.[549] When two persons were using public baths but were electrocuted as a result of the negligence of the local authority in failing to earth the metal tubes employed in connection with the electric light system, liability was established against the local authority.[550]

Supply and installation of electrical equipment. This is tightly regulated by   **13–164**
statute. The Consumer Protection Act 1987[551] imposes strict liability in respect of defective products (which include electricity[552]) on the producer of products.[553] Regulations[554] provide detailed measures for safety and consumer protection with regard to electrical equipment. Recourse can also be had to the

---

[547] [1946] 1 All E.R. 489. *Collingwood v Home & Colonial Stores* [1936] 3 All E.R. 200, was distinguished on the ground that there had been no finding of fact that there was a nuisance or any negligence in the installation or maintenance. Obviously, it is unsatisfactory (if it is the law) that liability for damage which has been caused by the domestic installation of electric wiring should depend on whether the claimant sues in negligence or in nuisance. Possibly, the two cases may be reconciled on the ground that a person who instals electricity on his premises owes a duty to take care to instal and to maintain the installation in a safe condition and, if he fails to do this, whether by himself, his employees or agents or his independent contractors, he is liable for the resultant damage.
[548] [1953] 2 All E.R. 525, appeal on a different point dismissed [1954] 1 Q.B. 383. cf. *Green v Fibreglass* [1958] 2 Q.B. 245.
[549] *Sellars v Best* [1954] 2 All E.R. 389. See 70 L.Q.R. 170.
[550] See *Re Fulham Borough Council and National Electric Construction Co* (1905) 70 J.P. 55. (The local authority, however, failed to obtain an indemnity for breach of contract from the electrical contractors.)
[551] The Product Liability Directive 85/374/EEC, is thereby implemented. See Ch.15, below, for a detailed discussion of the Act.
[552] s.1(2).
[553] s.2 defines "producer" and it can include the person whose trademark appears on a product irrespective of the identity of the manufacturer or an importer.
[554] The Electrical Equipment (Safety) Regulations (SI 1994/3260) implementing Council Directive 73/23/EEC in respect of electrical equipment placed on the market on or after January 1, 1997.

Supply of Goods and Services Act 1982[555] with regard not only to the equipment itself but its installation.

7.—Explosions and Explosives

13–165 **Explosives Act 1875.** The manufacture, keeping, sale, importation and conveyance of explosives are regulated by the Explosives Act 1875.[556] It is provided by s.102 that:

> "This Act shall not, save as is herein expressly provided, exempt any person from any action or suit in record of any nuisance, tort, or otherwise, which might, but for the provisions of this Act, have been brought against him."

13–166 **Strict liability for explosives.** Persons who manufacture or store explosives are liable under the rule in *Rylands v Fletcher*[557] if an explosion occurs and causes damage, whether or not there is any negligence on their part. In *Rainham Chemical Works v Belvedere Fish Guano Co*,[558] a large quantity of dinitrophenol was stored in close proximity to sodium nitrate with the result that when a fire broke out there was a violent explosion which caused damage to adjoining property. Depite the defendant's ignorance of the risk of explosion from the storage of the two materials in close proximity, liability was established under the principles of *Rylands v Fletcher.*

13–167 Where a 20-gallon drum of paraffin exploded in a yard because of the spread of a negligently lit fire, the defendant was liable both in respect of negligence in starting the fire and under *Rylands v Fletcher* in respect of the storage of paraffin.[559] In *Read v J. Lyons and Co Ltd*,[560] the claimant was injured by the explosion of a high explosive shell inside a munitions factory. It was accepted that there had been no negligence. Liability was not established under *Rylands v Fletcher* because there had been no escape of a dangerous substance from the land. Lord Macmillan expressed doubt as to whether *Rylands v Fletcher* applied to cases of personal injuries,[561] similar doubts being expressed in *Transco Plc v Stockport MBC.*[562]

13–168 **Liability based on negligence.** A high standard of care is expected of persons who manufacture, store or use explosives given the potentially disastrous consequences of an explosion. Thus where a man was walking on a road adjacent

---

[555] See Ch.15, para.15–52, below.
[556] As amended by the Explosives Act 1923 and the Explosives Acts 1875 and 1923 etc. (Repeals and Modifications) Regulations 1974 (SI 1974/1885).
[557] para.13–10 et seq., above.
[558] [1921] 2 A.C. 465 at 479.
[559] *Mulholland & Tedd Ltd v Baker* [1939] 3 All E.R. 253.
[560] [1947] A.C. 156. See too *Howard v Furness Houlder Argentine Lines Ltd* [1936] 2 All E.R. 781 (welder injured by steam from exploding boiler—no liability under *Rylands v Fletcher* because no escape from the defendant's premises).
[561] *Read v J. Lyons and Co Ltd* [1947] A.C. 156 at 170.
[562] [2003] 3 W.L.R. 1487 per Lord Bingham at 1473 and per Lord Hoffmann at 1481. See further para.13–28, above.

to a quarry in contravention of a red warning flag and was injured when he was struck by a piece of stone thrown up by blasting operations, the quarry owner was liable for having provided an insufficient warning.[563]

A telephone company, which was engaged in laying telephone wires in a street, employed a plumber, who was an independent contractor. The plumber, in the course of soldering some tubes, dipped a lamp into a cauldron of melted solder. The safety valve on the lamp was defective; a fact that the plumber ought to have known and the lamp exploded injuring a passing pedestrian. The telephone company was held liable on the ground that "works were being executed in proximity to a highway in which in the ordinary course of things an explosion might take place", and that it was "under an obligation to the public to take care that persons passing along the highway were not injured by the negligent performance of the work".[564] The principle of this decision is not confined to work done in or near to the highway.[565] So, where some photographers, who were independent contractors, were engaged to take a flashlight photograph of the interior of a cinema, the persons employing them were held liable for the negligence of the photographers. The negligence had consisted in burning magnesium powder in a tray near a curtain, which was set alight by the naked flames. **13–169**

Similarly, a lock-up shop's owner, who entered the premises with a friend in order to try to locate an escape of gas, was held liable to the tenant of the shop for the goods damaged by an explosion, which was caused by a friend's act in using a naked light to discover the source of the gas escape.[566] Again, where a firm of ship-repairers, before using an oxyacetylene burner, had employed a consulting engineer to make a report and, on his reporting "gas free", had used the burner, when an explosion occurred, the ship-repairers were held liable for the negligence of the engineer in not making a proper inspection before giving his certificate. Their duty, when dangerous things were to be used, was not merely to take care but to ensure that care was taken.[567] **13–170**

In *Muir v Stewart*,[568] a customer in a chemist's shop produced an empty bottle and asked for some nitric acid. The chemist asked what the bottle had contained and, on being told nitric acid, filled it. An explosion occurred, injuring another person in the shop. The chemist was held not liable, because he had taken some **13–171**

---

[563] *Miles v Forest Rock Granite Co* (1918) 34 T.L.R. 500. Lord Swinfen Eady M.R. also stated obiter that liability could have been established pursuant to *Rylands v Fletcher* but this is inconsistent with dicta in *Read v J. Lyons & Co Ltd* [1947] A.C. 156 see para.12–167, above.
[564] *Holliday v National Telephone Co* [1899] 2 Q.B. 392 at 399, per Lord Halsbury L.C.
[565] *Honeywill & Stein Ltd v Larkin Bros Ltd* [1934] 1 K.B. 191 at 199, per Slesser L.J. who said that it "does not depend merely on the fact that the defendants were doing work on the highway, but primarily on its dangerous character, which imposes on the ultimate employers an obligation to take special precautions, and they cannot delegate this obligation by having the work carried out by the independent contractors. This is equally true when the work being done by the independent contractor for the ultimate employer is being done on another person's premises."
[566] *Brooke v Bool* [1928] 2 K.B. 578.
[567] *The Pass of Ballater* [1942] P. 112. See also para.13–152, above.
[568] 1938 S.C. 590.

care, and there was no evidence to show what was the practice of chemists in filling bottles.

13–172   The fact that either something belonging to the defendant explodes or an explosion occurs out of and in the course of some operation carried out by or under the control of the defendant, can be sufficient evidence of negligence on his part, so as to place an evidential burden on the defendant to demonstrate how the explosion occurred without negligence.[569] Where an explosion occurred at a cartridge factory, the cause of which was unknown, the owners were nevertheless found negligent in not supplying suitable machinery and in not taking sufficient precautions, to prevent an explosion. It was also held that exact proof of negligence was not necessary where the accident was the work of a moment, and its origin and cause were incapable of being detected.[570] Where two passengers carried fireworks onto a railway carriage and a passenger was killed when the fireworks exploded, the railway company was not liable because there was no evidence that it knew or ought to have known that that the fireworks had been carried on to the train.[571]

13–173   **Fireworks.** A person setting off fireworks is bound to take great care to prevent them from causing damage to others. In *Whitby v Brock & Co*,[572] where the claimant went to the Crystal Palace to see a firework display by the defendants but was struck by one and injured, it was held that the defendants were liable. Lord Esher M.R., in giving judgment, said that the defendants knew that fireworks were dangerous articles so that,

> "there was a duty to manage with care their dealings with the fireworks . . . The mere fact that the fireworks struck the plaintiff was sufficient prima facie evidence of negligence, because fireworks did not ordinarily strike the spectators and bystanders."

When a schoolboy was injured at a firework display at his school on November 5, Lord Ellenborough stated his opinion "that if the master of a school, knowing the fireworks would be used, were to be guilty of negligence in not preventing the use of them, he would be amenable for the consequence".[573] Where a boy, aged eight, bought from the defendant's shop a firework, which he later set off in such a manner that the explosion blinded him in one eye, Stable J. held that the shopkeeper had been negligent in allowing a firework to be sold to so young a child.[574] When the defendant threw a lighted squib into a crowded building and the person near whom it fell, picked it up and threw it away towards some other

---

[569] See *Solomons v Stepney Borough Council* (1905) 69 J.P. 360; *Farrell v Limerick Corp* (1911) 45 I.L.T. 169.

[570] *McArthur v Dominion Cartridge Co* [1905] A.C. 72.

[571] *East Indian Ry v Kalidas Mukerjee* [1901] A.C. 396.

[572] (1888) 4 T.L.R. 241. Further, Lopes L.J. said that he adhered to what he had said in *Parry v Smith* (1879) 4 C.P.D. 325, that under such circumstances the defendants were bound to use care and the fact that the claimant was struck was evidence of negligence.

[573] *King v Ford* (1816) 1 Stark.N.P. 421.

[574] *Beaver v Cohen, The Times*, May 14, 1960. The supply of a firework to a person who is apparently under the age of 18 is prohibited by reg.6 of the Fireworks (Safety) Regulations 1997 (SI 1997/2294).

man, who also hurled it away, whereupon it exploded and injured the claimant, the defendant was held liable.[575]

On the other hand, the claim failed where a firework party was held at a **13–174** riverside bungalow, and the house was set on fire as a result of a "jumping jack" accidentally finding its way into the lounge from the vicinity of the porch and there setting alight other fireworks stored in a cubby-hole especially made for the occasion.[576]

Petrol. When a vehicle is parked in a parking area occupied by its owner, and **13–175** the tank contains petrol fumes, the owner is not liable to a person who is injured by an explosion caused by the dropping of a lighted match into the petrol tank, whether by strangers[577] or by the injured person,[578] because such an act could not reasonably have been foreseen.

Explosive substances. The duty in the case of explosive materials is similar **13–176** to that in connection with firearms.[579] If they are delivered to a person competent to understand and profit by a warning, a warning should be given. When, for example, a carrier had delivered unexpectedly some celluloid scrap to a factory by mistake and had failed to give warning of its dangerous character, whereupon an employee in the factory, in ignorance of the explosive nature of the scrap, set it on fire by touching it with a lighted cigarette end, thereby causing an explosion, the carrier was held liable.[580] Explosive substances ought not to be delivered to a person who is not competent to understand a warning. In *Yachuk v Oliver Blais Co Ltd*,[581] a boy of nine obtained petrol from a filling station by falsely stating that it was needed for his mother's car, which "was stuck down the street". He then used the petrol to make a torch for a game which he was playing with his younger brother, and, on lighting the petrol, he was injured by its explosion. The owners of the filling station were held liable.

Similarly, explosive substances must be kept in a safe place, where they are not **13–177** likely to be interfered with by unauthorised persons. Where a bottle, containing a stick of phosphorus, was left by a schoolmaster in a conservatory, to which the boys had access, and one of the boys took the bottle, played with it and broke it as a result of which he was injured by coming into contact with the phosphorus, the schoolmaster was held liable. The Court of Appeal approved of the direction of Cave J. that, if a man kept dangerous things, he must keep them safely and

[575] *Scott v Shepherd* (1773) 2 W.Bl. 892.
[576] *Horsenail v Kennedy, The Times*, April 30, 1964. The occupiers, having done all that could be expected of them within reason to store the fireworks safely, were held not liable for the death of one of their visitors who had been caught in the inferno which resulted.
[577] *Perry v Kendricks Transport Ltd* [1956] 1 W.L.R. 85.
[578] *Adcock v Loveridge, The Times*, June 21, 1956.
[579] See paras 13–178–13–191, below.
[580] *Philco Radio Ltd v Spurling Ltd* [1949] 2 All E.R. 882.
[581] [1949] A.C. 386. It was held that the act of the claimant was one which he might be reasonably expected to do, so that there was no contributory negligence (at that time a complete defence) or new intervening act. See also *Evans v Soul Garages Ltd, The Times*, January 23, 2001: 13-year-old boy found one-third contributorily negligent.

must take such precautions as a prudent man would take, and that to leave such things about, in the way of boys, would not be reasonable care.[582]

8.—Firearms

13–178   **Firing guns.** Loaded firearms must be used with the greatest caution. "The law of England, in its care for human life, requires consummate caution in the person who deals with dangerous weapons."[583]

13–179   Before firing a gun, care must be taken to see that anyone whose presence is known or might reasonably be anticipated is not within the line of fire. Blackburn J. said[584]:

> "If a man fires a gun across a road where he may reasonably anticipate that persons will be passing, and hits some one, he is guilty of negligence and liable for the injury he has caused; but if he fires in his own wood, where he cannot reasonably anticipate that any one will be, he is not liable to any one whom he shoots, which shows that what a person may reasonably anticipate is important in considering whether he has been negligent."

Even a man who fires a gun in his own wood will be liable if he shoots a person who is visible to him without first looking to see whether that person is in the line of fire.[585]

13–180   In *Stanley v Powell*,[586] the defendant was a member of a shooting party and the claimant was employed to carry cartridges and the shot birds. The defendant fired at a pheasant and a shot from his gun struck the bough of a tree, glanced off, and struck the claimant. The distance between the claimant and the defendant was about 30 yards. The defendant was acquitted of negligence, but the case was not approached on the basis of the degree of care required in using a dangerous weapon, and the result can only be considered as based on a surprising finding of fact by a jury.

13–181   Despite the fact that a gun is only intended to be loaded with blank cartridges, there is still an obligation to take great care to see that only a blank is loaded, before it is fired. When a member of the audience at a theatre was injured by a "bullet", fired from a blank cartridge pistol by one of the actors, it was held that the proprietor of the theatre would be liable, although the actor was employed by

---

[582] *Williams v Eady* (1893) 10 T.L.R. 41; cf. *Shepherd v Essex CC* (1913) 29 T.L.R. 303, where a jury found no negligence on the facts.
[583] per Erle C.J. in *Potter v Faulkner* (1861) 1 B. & S. 800 at 805. See also the provisions of the Firearms Act 1968 as amended.
[584] *Smith v L. & S.W. Ry* (1870) L.R. 6 C.P. 14 at 22.
[585] *Chettle v Denton* (1951) 95 S.J. 802.
[586] [1891] 1 Q.B. 86. In *Fowler v Lanning* [1959] 1 Q.B. 426 at 438, Diplock J. expressed the view that the decision in *Stanley v Powell* was still good law. (See also 75 L.Q.R. 161.)

a theatrical company and not by the proprietor himself, if he failed to see that reasonable care was taken in the loading of the pistol.[587]

If a person shoots intentionally at another, the cause of action is in trespass to **13–182** the person but, if the injury sustained by the claimant was caused unintentionally, then proof of negligence is required before an action for damages can succeed. In *Fowler v Lanning*,[588] Diplock J. held that the onus of proving negligence, where the shooting injury was not intentional, lies upon the claimant, whether the action be framed in trespass or in negligence.

Entrusting firearms to incompetent persons.[589] The owner of a loaded gun **13–183** is under a duty not to entrust it to a person, who by reason of his youth, ignorance or lack of intelligence is incompetent to handle it. "Take the extreme instance of a loaded gun. This is so obviously dangerous when it gets into unknown hands that the law holds it to be negligence on the part of the owner to let the gun leave his possession in that state and be put in inexperienced hands."[590] It is a question of fact whether he is competent or not.[591]

Where a firearm is being entrusted to someone with competence in such **13–184** weapons, the duty is to give warning that the gun is loaded.[592] Conversely, there is a duty not to entrust a gun and ammunition for it, to a person who is not competent. A mere warning of the danger is not enough.[593] Where the father of a boy of 12 had allowed him to possess a .410 shotgun but had not instructed him properly in handling it while he was in the presence of other persons, the father

---

[587] *Cox v Coulson* [1916] 2 K.B. 177 at 187. Pickford L.J. put his duty as follows: "In this case it is obvious that firearms would be used, and it is common knowledge that unless proper care is taken in loading them they are dangerous, and I think there was an obligation on his part to take reasonable care that they were so loaded as not to be dangerous." The cause of action was breach of contract, but it was held that the duty owed by the defendant to the claimant was that of invitor to invitee.

[588] [1959] 1 Q.B. 426. Lord Denning M.R. in *Letang v Cooper* [1965] 1 Q.B. 232 at 240 added: "I would go this one step further: when the injury is not inflicted intentionally, but negligently, I would say that the only cause of action is negligence and not trespass. If it were trespass, it would be actionable without proof of damage; and that is not the law today . . ."

[589] By s.24(2) of the Firearms Act 1968 it is an offence to make a gift of or lend a firearm to a person under the age of 14.

[590] per Lord Dunedin in *Oliver v Saddler & Co* [1929] A.C. 584 at 599.

[591] *Dixon v Bell* (1816) 5 M. & S. 198 (defendant sent his servant, a girl of about 13 or 14, to a friend's house to fetch his gun, giving her a note asking the friend to remove the priming. The friend did so, as he thought, and the servant on her way home pointed the gun, as a joke, at a child and fired. The gun went off and the child was injured. The defendant was held liable).

[592] See per Scrutton L.J. in *Hodge & Sons v Anglo-American Oil Co* (1922) 12 Ll.L.R. 183 at 187.

[593] *A. & E. Kille* [1939] 2 K.B. 743. (the defendants sold a 12-year-old boy a "safety pistol" which was found to be dangerous by reason of its construction and the tendency of the barrel to become blocked. When the boy fired close to the claimant and a rim of the cartridge injured the latter's eye, the defendants were held liable for selling such a dangerous thing to a young boy). See also *Beaver v Cohen*, The Times, May 14, 1960 (firework to 8-year-old), *Yachuk v Oliver Blais Co Ltd* [1949] A.C. 386 (petrol to 9-year-old boy) and *Evans v Souls Garages Ltd*, The Times, January 23, 2001 (petrol to 13-year-old boy). But cf. *Ricketts v Erith B.C.* [1943] 2 All E.R. 629: seller of toy bow and arrow to 10-year-old boy not liable because it was not considered a danger in itself in the boy's hands.

was held liable when a child was shot accidentally. It was irrelevant that he had forbidden his son to use the gun in the company of such other children.[594]

13–185   **Not keeping loaded guns in a safe place.** In addition to the duty not to entrust firearms to the incompetent, there is a further duty to keep loaded firearms in a safe place, so that they cannot be used by anyone who is likely to use them carelessly. "You must not put anything dangerous in itself where the public may possibly have access to it, and the best known instance of that is the case of a loaded gun."[595] This was followed in *Sullivan v Creed*,[596] where the defendant left a gun loaded and at full cock inside a fence on his land, close to a path. His young teenage son picked it up and pointed it in play at the claimant, then pulled the trigger, causing the gun to fire and injure the claimant. The defendant was held liable, Fitzgibbon L.J. saying:

> "In the case of a gun loaded at full cock the measure of care is at its maximum. The scope of duty is the scope of danger, and it extends to every person into whose hands a prudent man might reasonably expect the gun to come, having regard to the place where he left it. The ground of liability here is not that the boy was the defendant's son, but the fact that the gun was left without warning, in a dangerous condition, within reach of persons using the pathway, and the boy was one of the very class of persons whom the defendant knew to be not only likely but certain to pass by, *viz.*, his own household."[597]

13–186   What amounts to a "safe place" for keeping a loaded firearm depends very much upon the circumstances, including what interference with it can reasonably be foreseen. The father of a family, which included a two-year-old boy, was held liable when he placed an air pistol, loaded with a dart, in a kitchen cupboard: even though it was well out of the reach of children, the mother, not knowing of the danger, brought it out and placed it within the boy's reach. The child quickly grabbed hold of it, playfully pointed it at a female visitor and discharged it, striking her in the eye with the dart.[598]

13–187   In the cases cited in the previous paragraphs, the gun concerned was fired by a child, but if it had been fired negligently, as opposed to intentionally, by an adult, a similar result would have followed. This is pointed out in *Sullivan v Creed* by Holmes L.J.:

---

[594] *Newton v Edgerley* [1959] 1 W.L.R. 1031.

[595] per Lord Dunedin in *Fardon v Harcourt-Rivington* (1932) 48 T.L.R. 215. To the same effect is the illustration given in *Lynch v Nurdin* (1841) 1 Q.B. 29 at 35, by Lord Denman C.J.: "If, for example, a gamekeeper, returning from his daily exercise, should rear his loaded gun against a wall in the playground of schoolboys whom he knew to be in the habit of pointing toys in the shape of guns at one another, and one of these should playfully fire it off at a school fellow and maim him, I think it will not be doubted that the gamekeeper must answer in damages to the wounded party." See also the Firearms (Amendment) Act 1988 s.14(1)(a), which imposes a duty on auctioneers, carriers and warehousemen to take reasonable precautions for the safe custody of firearms or ammunition in their possession without a certificate.

[596] [1904] 2 Ir.R. 317.

[597] *Sullivan v Creed* [1904] 2 Ir.R. 317.

[598] *Thomas v Bishop* [1976] C.L.Y. 1872 (Judge R.P. Smith Q.C., sitting as a deputy Judge of the High Court).

"I do not attach much importance to the age of the defendant's son. He was old enough to know that it was dangerous to handle the gun on full cock . . . Quite irrespective of the age of the persons who might use the path, I think that there was evidence from which the jury were at liberty to find that the defendant, when placing the gun against the fence, ought to have contemplated that it might fall into negligent hands . . . I hold that in a case of this kind there is a marked distinction between a negligent act and a wilful act. A man who negligently lays aside a loaded gun ought to contemplate that it may be taken up by a person who will handle or use it negligently. But I think that it would not be within reasonable contemplation that the finder of it would wilfully discharge it at another." [599]

Where an employee placed a loaded shotgun on top of a harvester machine in disobedience to his employer's instructions and the gun was accidentally discharged, injuring the driver, the employer was vicariously liable for the employee's negligence. [600]

Airweapons. [601] An airgun is not a thing dangerous in itself, [602] but it is **13-188** capable of causing injury to others if it is negligently used. It should not, therefore, be entrusted to a child, who is too young [603] to be likely to use it safely. Where it has been so entrusted and damage is caused, the parent or other person who either gave the airgun to the child or allowed the child to use it, will be liable. If the child is old enough to use it safely, provided that he has been warned and, where necessary, has been reminded of the dangers and provided that proper precautions, such as a reasonable and prudent parent would take, are taken, then the parent will avoid liability.

Where a boy was injured by an airgun pellet ricocheting when fired by a boy **13-189** of 12, who had been instructed properly in its use and had not been pointing the gun at him, it was held by Thesiger J. to have been purely accidental and not to have been caused by negligence of any person. [604] Further, where a father allowed his son, aged 13, to have an airgun, on condition that it was only used in the cellar of the house and not outside, but the boy, in breach of his promise to his father, used the airgun in the open and injured a child, the father was held not liable. [605]

Although, in *Gorely v Codd*, [606] the 14-year-old defendant was found to be **13-190** guilty of negligence, which caused the accident to the claimant, aged 16, when he was struck by an airgun pellet, whilst they were "larking about" together, the

---

[599] [1904] 2 Ir.R. 317 at 355, 356.

[600] *Spencer v Curtis Bros* (1962) 106 S.J. 390.

[601] A weapon is an air rifle, air gun or air pistol not of a type declared by the Secretary of State to be specially dangerous: s.1(3)(b) of the Firearms Act 1968. A weapon powered by compressed carbon dioxide is included in this definition: s.48 of the Firearms (Amendment) Act 1997.

[602] *Donaldson v McNiven* [1952] 1 All E.R. 1213, per Pearson J.

[603] By s.24 of the Firearms Act 1968 it is an offence to supply, which includes selling, letting and hire, lending or giving a gift, a firearm or ammunition to minors under certain specified ages. See also *Thomas v Bishop* [1976] C.L.Y. 1872.

[604] *Rogers v Wilkinson*, *The Times*, January 19, 1963.

[605] *Donaldson v McNiven* [1952] 2 All E.R. 691. (It was conceded that the father was not negligent in allowing his son to have the airgun).

[606] [1967] 1 W.L.R. 19.

defendant's father was held not to be negligent. This was because he had given his son proper and sufficient instruction in the use of the rifle and the defendant was found by the court normally to have been a responsible boy. The prohibition, in s.1(3) of the Air Guns and Shot Guns Act 1962,[607] against persons under 17 years of age possessing an air weapon, only extended to a public place and, as the shooting had taken place in a private place, it was of no application in the case. On the other hand, if experience had shown that the child could not safely be trusted to have the airgun, the parent will be liable. So, where a father gave an airgun to his son, aged 15, who had fired at and had broken a window in March, and then in June shot another boy in the eye, it was held that the father was liable, because "in leaving the air gun in his boy's hands the defendant had not exercised such reasonable care as a prudent person ought to exercise".[608] Also, the father of a boy of 15 was held liable for failing to take reasonable care to ensure that his son did not use an airgun in such a way as to injure other persons.[609] Donovan J. added that a parent's duty included giving instructions that the gun, whether loaded or unloaded, should never be pointed at other persons and, certainly, never be fired at anybody.

13–191   If, in breach of s.24 of the Firearms Act 1968,[610] which forbids inter alia the sale of firearms and ammunition by a seller when he knows or has reasonable grounds for believing that the buyer was under the age of 17, a person sells an air pistol to someone who is under that age, then prima facie such person has been negligent. Accordingly in *Hinds v Direct Supply Co (Clapham Junction) Ltd*[611] the sellers of an air pistol to an under-aged boy were held to be liable in negligence for the personal injuries sustained by the victim of the shooting by that boy.

9.—POISON AND POLLUTION

13–192   **Liability for poisons.** Poison,[612] when in liquid or gaseous form, imposes the same liability upon those who own or control it, as does water or gas, and reference should be made to the previous sections, which deal with those subject-matters.

13–193   **Rylands v Fletcher liability.** In *West v Bristol Tramways Co*[613] a tramway were authorised under statute to pave part of a road with wooden paving. The paving used had been coated in creosote, the fumes from which damaged plants belonging to a neighbouring market gardener. The tramway company was liable for the damage done by the escape of the fumes under the principle in *Rylands v Fletcher* nothwithstanding the absence of negligence on their part. The fact that

---

[607] Repealed by the Firearms Act 1968 s.59.
[608] *Bebee v Sales* (1916) 32 T.L.R. 413.
[609] *Court v Wyatt, The Times*, June 25, 1960.
[610] As amended by the Firearms (Amendment) Act 1988 s.23.
[611] *The Times*, January 29, 1966.
[612] The principal Act governing the control of poisons is the Poisons Act 1972.
[613] [1908] 2 K.B. 14.

the tramway company was authorised by statute to lay wooden paving did not afford a defence because the statutory authorisation did not extend to the laying of wooden paving coated with creosote.

The owner of yew trees must prevent the leaves, which are poisonous to cattle, **13–194** projecting over the boundary of his neighbour's land. If he fails to do this, whereupon his neighbour's cattle are poisoned by eating the leaves, on the principle of *Rylands v Fletcher* he is liable for the damage.[614] On the other hand, if he fulfils his duty, but his neighbour's cattle are poisoned by putting their heads over the boundary fence or otherwise trespassing on his land, he is not liable.[615] But, if the trespass occurred because of the defendant's failure to maintain a fence, which by contract, prescription or otherwise he is bound to maintain between his land and that of his neighbour, and his neighbour's cattle are poisoned on his land, he is liable.[616] Nevertheless, if a landlord lets land to a tenant and, at the time of the letting, there are yew trees upon other land belonging to the landlord which overhang the tenant's land, so that the tenant's cattle are poisoned from eating the yew trees, the landlord is not liable.[617]

Liability based on negligence. Where an oil company sent oil by rail in a **13–195** defective tank, from which the oil leaked and got into the watercourse, making the water unfit to be drunk by cattle, it was held that the company was liable for the resulting damage on the ground that it had consigned the tank in a condition in which oil was likely to escape from it.[618] Where the defendant delivered to the claimant's husband, the owner of a keel, a quantity of a chemical, ferro-silicon, which could give off dangerous fumes and the keel owner was killed as a result of inhaling the fumes, the defendant was liable for failing to provide such information as the defendant had as to the nature of ferro-silicon.[619]

Poisons, like explosives, must not be left in a place which is easily accessible **13–196** to third parties who may carelessly use them and so damage themselves or others.[620] A boat owner, who employed a joiner to repair his boats, was held liable for the act of the joiner in leaving scrapings of paint from the boats in a field, where they poisoned a cow, which ate them.[621] Where a local authority had planted in a public park shrubs with poisonous berries of attractive appearance, they were held liable for the death of a boy of seven, who ate some of the berries. Such liability was on the ground that "there was fault in having such a shrub where it was without definite warning of its danger and definite protection against the danger being incurred".[622] When the poison is in a place to which the public

---

[614] *Crowhurst v Amersham Burial Board* (1878) 4 Ex. D. 5; *Wilson v Newberry* (1871) L.R. 7 Q.B. 31.
[615] *Ponting v Noakes* [1894] 2 Q.B. 281.
[616] *Lawrence v Jenkins* (1873) L.R. 8 Q.B. 274.
[617] *Cheater v Cater* [1918] 1 K.B. 247; *Erskine v Adeane* (1873) L.R. 8 Ch. 756.
[618] *Smith v G.W. Ry* (1926) 42 T.L.R. 391.
[619] *Bamfield v Goole and Sheffield Transport Co Ltd* [1910] 2 K.B. 94. Liability was also established for a breach of an implied warranty that the goods were fit for carriage as an alternative to negligence.
[620] paras 13–165–13–177, above.
[621] *Stewart v Adams*, 1920 S.C. 129.
[622] *Glasgow Corp v Taylor* [1922] 1 A.C. 44 at 63.

has access, a mere giving of a warning of the danger is not enough. There must be some further precaution taken, either by removing the poisonous nature of the thing in question, if such a course is possible, or by putting it in such a position that it is not accessible. When the poison is not in a place to which the public has access, the duty is the same as that in respect of loaded guns[623] and explosive substances.[624]

13–197   **Animals poisoned on defendant's land.** A person who puts poisoned bait on his own land with the object of poisoning animals which are attracted by the food on his land, is liable to the owner of the animal.[625] However, if the poison is put down for another purpose, the person putting it down is not liable, unless he ought to have foreseen that it was likely to poison animals which were brought legitimately to his premises. Thus a confectioner, who had put some poisoned bait behind the counter of his shop with the object of poisoning rats and mice, was held not liable to the owner of a dog which was poisoned as a result of its going behind the counter and eating the bait.[626]

When the land of the claimant was separated from that of the defendant by a wire fence, which the defendant was bound by contract to maintain, but the wire decayed, so that a piece broke off and fell on the claimant's land, where it was swallowed by one of his cows, killing it, the defendant was held liable.[627]

13–198   **Statutory liability relating to environmental protection.** In addition to the common law principles discussed above civil liability is created in respect of certain types of pollution by the Environmental Protection Act 1990 as regards the deposition of waste on land and the Merchant Shipping Act 1995 as regards oil pollution at sea. Whilst a detailed analysis of these statutes is beyond the scope of this text, it is convenient to consider in outline the liabilities created.

(i) *The Environmental Protection Act 1990*

13–199   Pursuant to s.33(1) of this Act it is an offence: to deposit controlled waste[628] on land other than in accordance with a licence; to treat, keep or dispose of controlled waste other than in accordance with a licence; and to treat, keep or dispose of controlled waste in a manner likely to cause pollution of the environment or harm to human health. By s.73(6) where damage is caused by the deposition of waste in a manner so as to commit an offence under s.33(1) or an offence under s.63(2)[629] then the person who deposited it is liable for the damage. This strict liability arises without prejudice to liability arising otherwise than under this subsection and so liability pursuant to *Rylands v Fletcher* appears to be preserved by the Act. The liability under s.73(6) is subject to two exceptions namely: where the damage was due wholly to the fault of the person who

---

[623] See paras 13–178–13–191, above.
[624] See paras 13–165–13–177, above.
[625] *Townsend v Wathen* (1808) 9 East 277.
[626] *Stansfeld v Bolling* (1870) 22 L.T. 799.
[627] *Firth v Bowling Iron Co* (1878) 3 C.P.D. 254.
[628] Controlled waste is defined by s.75. The defintion is broad, encompassing household, industrial and commercial waste each of which is separately defined by s.75.
[629] s.63(2) creates an offence in relation to the deposition of waste other than controlled waste.

suffered it[630] and where the damage was suffered by a person who voluntarily accepted the risk of the damage being caused.[631] "Damage" is defined as including the death of or injury to any person (including any disease and any impairment of physical and mental condition).[632]

(ii) *The Merchant Shipping Act 1995*

In the case of ships constructed of adapted for carrying oil in bulk as cargo, liability for damage resulting from contamination caused by the discharge or escape of oil outside the ship in the territory of the United Kingdom is imposed upon the ship's owner by s.153(1) of the 1995 Act and in respect of other ships, liability is imposed in like circumstances by s.154(1). No liability is imposed under either section if the owner proves that that discharge or escape: resulted from an act of war, hostilities, civil war, insurrection or an exceptional and irresistible natural phenomenon[633]; or was due wholly to anything done or omitted to be done by another person not being a servant or agent of the owner, with intent to do damage[634]; or was due wholly to the negligence or wrongful act of a government or other authority in exercising its function of maintaining lights or other navigational aids for the maintenance of which it was responsible.[635] **13–200**

10.—NUCLEAR INSTALLATIONS

Generally. The harnessing of nuclear power, even for peaceful purposes, has become controversial. One aspect is the potential for widespread damage,[636] should there be any accidental release of even a single emission of ionising radiations. It being perceived that the common law would be an unsatisfactory basis for determining liability for such a disastrous "escape", whether by action in negligence, nuisance or based on the rule of absolute liability under *Rylands v Fletcher*, statutory intervention followed. **13–201**

Nuclear Installations Acts 1965 and 1969. By virtue of the provisions[637] of the Nuclear Installations Act 1965,[638] which is the principal Act, no person other **13–202**

---

[630] s.73(6)(a).
[631] s.73(6)(b).
[632] s.73(8).
[633] The Merchant Shipping Act s.155(a).
[634] s.155(b).
[635] s.155(c).
[636] We have the practical experience of the aftermath of the 1987 breakdown of a Russian nuclear power station at Chernobyl, contamination from which was borne by high easterly winds to the UK.
[637] The 1969 Act makes certain amendments to the 1965 Act, which were necessary in order to bring that Act into conformity with international agreements, and came into force on May 16, 1969. See also amendments brought by the Atomic Energy Act 1989, which come into force on September 1, 1989.
[638] Which consolidates with an exception (s.29(1)) the Nuclear Installations Acts 1959 and 1965, i.e. the Nuclear Installation (Licensing and Insurance) Act 1959 and the Nuclear Installation (Amendment) Act 1965. The Nuclear Installations Act 1965 (Commencement No.1) Order 1965 (SI 1965/1880) brought the Act into force on December 1, 1965, except for s.17(5) which bars enforcement in the UK of certain foreign judgments.

than the United Kingdom Atomic Energy Authority shall use any site for the operation of a nuclear plant, unless a licence to do so has been granted by the Health and Safety Executive[639] in respect of it. Such licences for nuclear sites are granted only to corporate bodies and are not transferable.[640] Liability can only arise in connection with any licensed nuclear site and it arises when a nuclear incident occurs at or in connection with certain nuclear installations, or in the course of carriage of nuclear matter. The Acts apply to occurrences outside the United Kingdom.[641]

13–203   **Who is liable?** The principle of the 1965 Act has restricted all liability to licensees only, which has also simplified the necessary insurance arrangements, since there is no need to extend the cover to such additional persons as the manufacturers, suppliers and contractors. Thus the Act confers on certain victims of exposure to the emission of ionising radiation a statutory right to compensation against the licensee, deemed responsible for the occurrence.[642] The United Kingdom Atomic Energy Authority and other Government Departments are likewise liable for emissions from their sites, by virtue of ss.8 and 9 respectively. Section 10 imposes duties on foreign operators and s.11 imposes duties on other persons causing nuclear material to be carried.

13–204   Further, s.12(1) provides that: "where any injury or damage has been caused in breach of a duty imposed" by the Act, then, subject to certain exceptions, "no other liability shall be incurred by any person in respect of that injury or damage". This effectively prevents the licensee from obtaining either an indemnity arising out of any contract[643] or contribution from any negligent third party[644] so that he alone still remains liable. Nevertheless, in order to meet a situation where two or more licensees are responsible in respect of the same injury incurred, s.17(3) expressly provides that both or all of those persons shall be treated as jointly and severally liable in respect of that injury or damage.

13–205   **The duty of the licensee.** It is enacted by s.7(1) of the 1965 Act:

"it shall be the duty of the licensee to secure that—

(a) no such occurrence involving nuclear matter as is mentioned in subsection (2) of this section causes injury to any person or damage to any property of any person other than the licensee, being injury or damage arising out of or resulting from the radioactive properties, or a combination of those and any toxic, explosive or other hazardous properties, of that nuclear matter; and

---

[639] See the Nuclear Installations Act 1965, etc. (Repeals and Modifications) Regulations 1974 (SI 1974/2056) reg. 2(1)(b), Sch.2, para.1.
[640] s.3(1).
[641] s.12(1).
[642] It is not actually necessary that the dangerous matter should "escape" as such from the site where it is kept on to other land, since by the very nature of radioactivity dangerous emissions occur constantly as do, for example, all the harmful rays of the sun.
[643] It should also prevent licensees from invoking the principle in *Lister v Romford Ice Co Ltd* [1957] A.C. 555 as a means of claiming an indemnity from the employee, whose negligence caused the nuclear occurrence.
[644] Contribution is only obtainable as between joint tortfeasors and for the purposes of the Act there can be only one tortfeasor, namely the licensee.

(b) no ionising radiations emitted during the period of the licensee's responsibility—

    (i) from anything caused or suffered by the licensee to be on the site which is not nuclear matter; or

    (ii) from any waste discharged (in whatever form) on or from the site, cause injury to any person or damage to any property of any person other than the licensee."

The duty is one of absolute or strict liability[645] and it is unnecessary to prove   **13–206** negligence on the part of anyone. There is one exception only, which is contained in s.13(4), to the strict nature of this liability, namely that it is a defence that the breach of statutory duty is attributable to hostile action in the course of any armed conflict, including any armed conflict within the United Kingdom. It is not, however, a defence which would be available otherwise under the rule in *Rylands v Fletcher*, that the breach is attributable to a natural disaster, notwithstanding that the disaster is of such an exceptional character that it could not reasonably have been foreseen.[646] By virtue of s.13(6) damages may be reduced by reason of the fault of the claimant if, but only if, and to the extent that, the causing of that injury or damage is attributable to any act of the claimant committed with the intention of causing harm to any person or property or with reckless disregard for the consequences of his act. This seems to be distinguishable from the provisions of the Law Reform (Contributory Negligence) Act 1945, where both the degree of blameworthiness and the causative potency of the claimant's act have to be taken into consideration in reducing damages. It would seem, therefore, that even if a trespasser on the site be hurt by a nuclear incident, provided that he is not guilty of any such intentional or reckless conduct, he is not precluded from recovering damages in full.[647]

The damage suffered. "Injury" for the purposes of the statutory obligation   **13–207** imposed by the Act means "personal injury and includes loss of life",[648] whilst "damage to any property" must be physical damage to the fabric or its contents and not, for example, the contamination of a dwelling-house with radioactive dust.[649] Losses which normally follow from such damage, namely loss of earnings, loss of profits, reduction of value and loss of use, etc., must also be recoverable but only in so far as they are consequential upon such injury or damage.[650] In the absence of any physical harm no remedy can lie.

The operation of these principles can be seen in *Blue Circle Industries Plc v*   **13–208** *The Ministry of Defence*[651] where a pond on an estate was contaminated by small

---

[645] For the nature of "absolute" or "strict" liability, see paras 13–04–13–06, above.

[646] s.13(4)(b).

[647] For the law relating to trespassers generally, see Ch.8, paras 8–144–8–160, above.

[648] s.26(1).

[649] *Merlin v British Nuclear Fuels Plc* [1990] 2 Q.B. 557. Contrast *Blue Circle Industries Plc v Ministry of Defence* [1999] Ch. 289, CA, n.52, below.

[650] *SCM (United Kingdom) v W.J. Whittall & Son Ltd* [1971] 1 Q.B. 337, affirming Thesiger J. [1970] 1 W.L.R. 1017. For the recover of damages for economic loss see Ch.2, paras 2–223–2–225.

[651] [1996] E.G.C.S. 190; appeal dismissed [1999] Ch. 289, CA.

quantities of radioactive material from the Aldermarston Weapons Establishment. Even though the level of contamination had been less than presented any risk to human or animal health, it could only be rectified by major engineering work, and was thereby held to involve a physical change to the area sufficient to qualify under s.7(1) of the 1965 Act. Further, it was said that the ordinary common law rules of causation, foreseeability and remoteness of damage applied. The claimants, who had lost a potential sale of the estate as a result of concern about the incident, were to be put into the position they would have been had the contamination not occurred, with a discount from the resulting figure to reflect any uncertainty about the sale proceedings.

13–209 **Special periods of limitation.** Section 15(1) enacts that "notwithstanding anything in any other enactment" a claim under the Act shall not be entertained "if made at any time after the expiration of thirty years from the relevant date", which date is that of the occurrence that gave rise to the claim and not of the infliction of damage. Where that occurrence was a continuing one or was one of a succession, all of which were attributable to a particular happening on a particular relevant site, or to the carrying out from time to time on a particular relevant site of a particular operation, the limitation period begins to run from the date of the last of those events.

13–210 Where a claim arises in respect of injury or damage, caused by an occurrence involving nuclear matter stolen from, or lost, jettisoned or abandoned by the person whose breach of statutory duty under the Act gave rise to the claim, it is provided by s.15(2) that the limitation period in such circumstances is the period of 20 years. This period is to be calculated "beginning with the day when the nuclear matter in question was so stolen, lost, jettisoned or abandoned".

13–211 **Limit of liability.** Section 16(1) provides:

"The liability of any person to pay compensation under this Act by virtue of a duty imposed on that person by section 7, 8 or 9 thereof shall not require him to make in respect of any one occurrence constituting a breach of that duty payments by way of compensation exceeding in the aggregate, apart from payments in respect of interest and costs, £140 million or, in the case of the licencees of such sites as may be prescribed, £10 million."

13–212 **Insurance arrangements.** Sections 17 and 18 make special arrangements for insurance cover of liabilities arising under ss.7 to 10 and provide for money to be made available to meet claims by Parliament in certain circumstances.

11.—AIRCRAFT AND SPACECRAFT

13–213 At common law the liability of the owner of an aircraft[652] does not differ from that of the owner of a highway vehicle in that, whilst at rest, it is quite harmless but, when in motion or flight, it becomes potentially very dangerous, because of

---

[652] See Ch.10, paras 10–168–10–170, above, where the subject is dealt with in more detail.

the fact of its movement. Nevertheless an aircraft in motion is neither an *inherently* dangerous thing nor a thing dangerous in itself,[653] hence the rule in *Rylands v Fletcher* does not apply to it. This situation has been altered by statute, namely the Civil Aviation Act 1982 s.76,[654] which provides:

"where material loss or damage is caused to any person or property on land or water by, or by a person in, or an article, animal or person falling from, an aircraft while in flight, taking off or landing, then unless the loss or damage was caused or contributed to by the negligence of the persons by whom it was suffered, damages in respect of the loss or damage shall be recoverable without proof of negligence or intention or other cause of action, as if the loss or damage had been caused by the wilful act, neglect or default of the owner of the aircraft."

The provisions of the Act only apply to civil aircraft and not to military aircraft, that is "belonging to or exclusively employed in the service of [Her] Majesty," unless by Order in Council.[655]

As regards liability for damage done by spacecraft, including the massive **13–214** ironmongery required to get it into space, it is probable that international law will recognise strict liability.[656] However, for the moment and until an accident happens, it must remain a case of "wait and see"![657]

---

[653] See *Fosbroke-Hobbs v Airwork Ltd* [1937] 1 All E.R. 108 at 112, per Goddard J.
[654] See Ch.10, para.10–173, above.
[655] s.101.
[656] See McMahon "Legal Aspects of Outer Space" (1962) 38 B.Y.I.L. 339, 384; Barrett "International Liability for Damages Caused by Space Objects", 76 L.S.Gaz. 646.
[657] The Outer Space Act 1986, which came into force on July 31, 1989 by virtue of SI 1989/1097 confers licensing and other powers on the Secretary of State to secure compliance with the international obligations of the UK as regards all activities in this field. The provisions of the Act do not concern civil liability, only criminal liability for breaches.

ANIMALS

1.—INTRODUCTION

Generally. Although there are certain similarities between liability for dan- **14–01**
gerous animals and the rule in *Rylands v Fletcher*,[1] since both are examples of
strict liability, they are nevertheless distinct and separate. This remained the case
after the Animals Act 1971, despite the fact that animals, just like other chattels,
are merely agents for causing damage. One obvious difference between the two
forms of liability is that no escape of an animal from the defendant's land is
required for liability to attach. Nor is natural use of the land a defence in the case
of a dangerous animal.[2]

Historic differences in liability. Prior to October 1, 1971, when the Animals **14–02**
Act 1971 came into force,[3] the law dealing with damage caused by animals had
become unduly complex.[4] From early days the owner had been liable for damage
caused by his animals, when trespassing on the land of another, but, apart from
cattle trespass, there was no liability at all for damage done by domestic animals.
In the course of time the owner became liable for some damage done by domestic
animals, but this was only for such damage as he knew the particular animal had
a propensity to commit. Liability was based on what was termed *scienter*,[5] for
convenience. In respect of damage done by wild animals the owner was

---

[1] (1868) L.R. 3 H.L. 330.
[2] *Rands v McNeil* [1955] 1 Q.B. 253. See observations of Denning L.J. at 258; *Behrens v Bertram
Mills Circus Ltd* [1957] 2 Q.B. 1 at 21, 22.
[3] As Lord Simonds observed in *Read v Lyons* [1947] A.C. 156 at 182; "The law of torts has grown
up historically in separate compartments and ... beasts have travelled in a compartment of their
own."
[4] See Williams, *Liability for Animals* (Cambridge, 1939) for a full account of the common law on this
subject, and Holdsworth, 55 L.Q.R. 588–591. As regards the law of Scotland, see Jackson, "Liability
for Animals in Scottish Legal Literature: From Stair to the Modern Law", 22 J.R. 139.
[5] A recognised foreshortening of words that were used in the form of the old writ, which ran: "*Quod
defendens quendam canem ad mordendum oves consuetum scienter retinuit*". See Jackson, "On the
Origins of Scienter", 94 L.Q.R. 85.

absolutely liable.[6] Then, very much later on, it was recognised that the ordinary duty to take care to prevent damage applied to animals, as well as to other things, but this was a modern creation which had to be fitted on to the earlier law. In short, there was considerable uncertainty. By way of an illustration, it was not settled whether damage included injury to human beings, in the absence of proof of *scienter*,[7] in actions for trespass and negligence.

14–03   It took a long time for change to be contemplated. In 1953 a report was produced on the law[8] but it was not until 1967 that the Law Commission resumed consideration of reform and reported to Parliament,[9] submitting a draft Bill to give effect to their recommendations. Finally, the Animals Act 1971 emerged, which, by s.13(3), came into operation on October 1, 1971.

14–04   **The Animals Act 1971.** For the most part the Act[10] rationalised existing rules, rather than replacing them. The old *scienter* action was abolished[11] and replaced by related provisions.[12] The basic distinction, however, between dangerous and non-dangerous animals was adapted and retained. One important change was to abolish the rule in *Searle v Wallbank*[13] relating to liability for animals which escaped on to the highway.[14] Nevertheless, it was not until 2003 that the House of Lords was finally presented with an opportunity to examine the Act's more difficult provisions, thus enabling a more certain interpretation of the liability attaching to non dangerous species.[15] In all other areas of tort, such as strict liability under the principle in *Rylands v Fletcher*,[16] trespass to the person,[17]

---

[6] Under the Dangerous Wild Animals Act 1976, a person acquiring a dangerous wild animal as a pet is required to obtain a local authority licence in respect of each such animal. Dangerous wild animals, as defined in this Act, include lions, tigers, poisonous snakes and certain monkeys and other unusual pets such as crocodiles, cassowaries and bears. The Act was introduced as a Private Member's Bill, following several incidents involving escapes of potentially dangerous animals kept as pets with little regard for public safety or the welfare of the animals. Circuses, zoos, pet shops and research laboratories are exempted under the Act, which creates criminal liability but does not affect civil liability as set out in this chapter.

[7] For a fuller discussion of the state of the law prior to the passing of the Animals Act 1971, see *Charlesworth on Negligence* (4th edn, 1962), Ch.17.

[8] Report of the Committee on the Law of Civil Liability for Damage done by Animals, Cmd. 8746 (1953), under the chairmanship of Lord Goddard.

[9] Law Com. No.13.

[10] See North, "The Modern Law of Animals", 1972. See articles on the Act: Powell-Smith, 112 New L.J. 584; Samuels, 115 S.J. 662 and 34 M.L.R. 550; Passingham, 66 L.S.Gaz. 397.

[11] s.1(1)(a).

[12] s.2.

[13] [1947] A.C. 341. The rule was that there was no duty, in the absence of special circumstances relating to the behaviour of an animal known to the landowner, to fence or maintain existing fences on land adjoining highways, thereby to prevent animals straying on to the highways. See Poole, "Fencing Against Cattle on Common Land" (1947) J.P.L. 587.

[14] Further see Ch.10, para.10–287, above.

[15] *Mirvahedy v Henley* [2003] 2 A.C. 491.

[16] See Ch.13, generally.

[17] Over 200 years ago, it was settled that trespass to the person could be committed through the agency of an animal, such as by the defendant deliberately setting his dog to attack the claimant: *Scott v Shepherd* (1773) 3 Wils. 403 at 408. Although clearly obiter on the facts under consideration, the Court of Appeal acknowledged that this remains the position today in *Gloster v Chief Constable of Greater Manchester Police* [2000] P.I.Q.R. P114 at P121.

trespass to chattels,[18] nuisance,[19] negligence[20] (except as mentioned above), including a lawful visitor's claim under the Occupiers' Liability Act 1957,[21] and a claim by an injured trespasser on premises (if his action is not barred by s.5(3)[22] of the Animals Act) the common law remains unaffected by its provisions.

It is proposed to follow the same order as the Act and discuss: (1) strict   **14–05** liability for damage done by dangerous animals, under s.2; (2) strict liability for injury done by dogs to livestock, under s.3; and (3) strict liability for damage done by straying livestock, under s.4.

2.—Strict Liability for Damage Done by Animals Generally

Liability for damage done by dangerous animals.[23] Section 2 of the 1971   **14–06** Act was described by Lord Denning M.R., who (correctly) anticipated "several difficulties in the future", as "very cumbrously worded."[24] It replaces the rules of the *scienter* action and provides that:

"(1) Where any damage is caused by an animal which belongs to a dangerous species, any person who is a keeper of the animal is liable for the damage, except as otherwise provided by this Act.
(2) Where damage is caused by an animal which does not belong to a dangerous species, a keeper of the animal is liable for the damage, except as otherwise provided by this Act if—

(a) the damage is of a kind which the animal, unless restrained, was likely to cause or which, if caused by the animal, was likely to be severe; and
(b) the likelihood of the damage or of its being severe was due to characteristics of the animal which are not normally found in animals of the same species[25] or are not normally so found except at particular times or in particular circumstances; and
(c) those characteristics were known to that keeper or were at any time known to a person who at that time had charge of the animal as that keeper's servant or, where that keeper is the head of a household, were known to another keeper of the animal who is a member of that household and under the age of 16."

---

[18] *Manton v Brocklebank* [1923] 2 K.B. 212. See further the example given by Atkin L.J. (at 229) of the owner who intentionally caused his dog to accomplish "an 'asportavit' of a golf ball".
[19] e.g. *Pitcher v Martin* [1937] 3 All E.R. 918 where a dog with a long loose leash escaped its owner's control and ran after a cat but in so doing the lead tripped up an elderly pedestrian, it was held to be a nuisance; and where herds of cattle in large numbers stray on to the highway and cause an obstruction such as occurred in *Cunningham v Whelan* (1917) 52 I.L.T.R. 67 and *Fleming v Atkinson* (1959) 18 D.L.R. (2d) 81.
[20] See further, paras 14–87–14–98, and *Cummings v Grainger* [1977] Q.B. 397.
[21] See Ch.8, generally.
[22] For the provisions of which, see para.14–46, below.
[23] See Begley, "Who let the dogs out?" 2002 H. & S.L., 2(2), 10.
[24] *Cummings v Grainger* [1977] Q.B. 397 at 404. Ormrod L.J. described s.2(2)(b) as "remarkably opaque" at 407 and similar criticism can be found in *Curtis v Betts* [1990] 1 W.L.R. 459, CA, para.14–11 below, and *Gloster v Chief Constable of Greater Manchester Police* [2000] P.I.Q.R. P114, CA, where Pill L.J. noted, at 117, that the Law Commission's draft, Law Com. No.13, had not been followed. See further para.14–11, below.
[25] See *Hunt v Wallis* [1994] P.I.Q.R. P128, para.14–12, n.42, below.

14–07   **Dangerous species.** It will be seen that a distinction is drawn between animals of a dangerous species and other animals. No attempt is made to define "animal" as such. By s.6(2) a "dangerous species" is defined as a species[26]—

> "(a) which is not commonly domesticated in the British Islands; and
>
> (b) whose fully grown animals normally have such characteristics that they are likely, unless restrained, to cause severe damage or that any damage they may cause is likely to be severe."

14–08   Whether or not a particular species of animals is dangerous is purely a question of law[27]:

> "the reason why this is a question of law and not a question of fact is because it is a matter of which judicial notice has to be taken. The doctrine has from its formulation proceeded upon the supposition that the knowledge of what kinds of animals are tame and what are savage is common knowledge. Evidence is receivable, if at all, only on the basis that the judge may wish to inform himself."[28]

14–09   Accordingly, in each case a decision must first be reached about the category, dangerous or non-dangerous, into which the animal falls. The answer is of considerable importance since, should s.2(1) apply, the keeper's state of knowledge of the animal's characteristics is irrelevant and proof of liability on behalf of an injured party ought to be a straightforward exercise. Under s.2(2) the claimant must establish each of the matters set out in subsections (a), (b) and (c).

14–10   Bears,[29] elephants,[30] and lions[31] have all been held to be dangerous species at common law. There was some doubt about bees.[32] Dogs, even a 50kg Rottweiler dog,[33] are not,[34] although the Dangerous Dogs Act 1991 imposes criminal penalties on those who fail to observe certain safeguards in relation to identified

---

[26] s.11 defines "species" as including "sub-species and variety."

[27] *Filburn v People's Palace and Aquarium Co* (1890) 25 Q.B.D. 258; *Mason v Keeling* (1699) 12 Mod. 332 at 355; *Besozzi v Harris* (1858) 1 F. & F. 92.

[28] per Devlin J. in *Behrens v Bertram Mills Circus Ltd* [1957] 2 Q.B. 1 at 15, 16. cf. the approach of Scrutton L.J. in *Glanville v Sutton* [1928] 1 K.B. 571, 575.

[29] *Besozzi v Harris* (1858) 1 F. & F. 92. See also *Wyatt v Rosherville Gardens* (1886) 2 T.L.R. 282; *Pearson v Coleman* [1948] 2 K.B. 359.

[30] *Filburn v People's Palace and Aquarium Co* (1890) 25 Q.B.D. 258. See also, *Behrens v Bertram Mills Circus Ltd* [1957] 2 Q.B. 1; per Lord Simonds in *Read v J. Lyons & Co Ltd* [1947] A.C. 156.

[31] *Murphy v Zoological Society of London, The Times,* November 14, 1962.

[32] At common law the responsibilities of an owner of hived bees were not entirely clear. The Irish case of *O'Gorman v O'Gorman* [1903] 2 I.R. 573, where a man was injured as a result of angered bees stinging his horse, was decided on a finding of negligence and is some authority for the proposition that bees are not *per se* "dangerous animals," but in a later Canadian case, *Lucas v Pettitt* (1906) 12 O.L.R. 448 where the beekeeper was also held liable, it was decided that the doctrine of *scienter* had no application. See also *Robins v Kennedy* [1931] N.Z.L.R. 1134. Bees are not included in the statutory definition of livestock in s.11 of the Act.

[33] *Chauhan v Paul* [1998] C.L.Y. 3990, CA.

[34] See, e.g. *Curtis v Betts* [1990] 1 W.L.R. 459; Peachey, "Dogs—Civil Liability for Damage and Injuries", 133 S.J. 1614. See also *Hunt v Wallis* [1994] P.I.Q.R. P128 and *Gloster v Chief Constable of Greater Manchester Police* [2000] P.I.Q.R. P114, CA, at P116.

breeds known for their aggressive qualities.[35] If the animal is of a dangerous species it is irrelevant that the keeper either did not know it was dangerous or believed the individual tame.[36] It is no defence that the damage resulted because the animal was suddenly frightened and not from any vicious propensity in its character.[37]

Non-dangerous species.[38] The effect of s.2(2) is that, in order to establish   **14–11** liability, an injured claimant must prove each of the three elements of the subsection as set out above. In *Curtis v Betts*,[39] it was emphasised that each part of the subsection should be examined in turn.

(a) *The damage is of a kind which the animal, unless restrained, was likely to*   **14–12** *cause or which, if caused by the animal, was likely to be severe.*[40] This requirement in s. 2(2)(a), along with s.2(2)(c), is relatively straightforward. There are two limbs to it. The former is illustrated by the facts of *Curtis v Betts*[41] where a young bull mastiff dog, which bit a 10-year-old boy, was found to be an animal of a kind which would satisfy s.2(2)(a) since the *damage was likely to be severe* if it did bite someone. *Hunt v Wallis*[42] is an example of the second limb. A border collie was not likely to cause physical injury but, since it ran into the claimant, given its size and speed, if it did *cause* damage *this was likely to be severe*, thus satisfying the second limb of s.2(2)(a). It should be noted that there is no requirement that the damage should in fact be severe: the test is one of foreseeability of damage.[43]

(b) *The likelihood of the damage or of its being severe was due to*   **14–13** *characteristics of the animal which are not normally found in animals of the same species or are not normally so found except at particular times or in particular circumstances.*[44] It is the requirements of s.2(2)(b) in particular, which have given rise to difficulty and led to two different lines of authority.[45] One would have expected the first limb of the subsection to be relatively un-contentious. Abnormal characteristics can, but do not necessarily, comprise a

---

[35] It is not as yet clear whether, in spite of the criminal sanctions contained in the Act, a civil remedy will also arise at the suit of someone injured as a result of a failure to heed the restrictions imposed.

[36] *Besozzi v Harris* (1858) 1 F. & F. 92.

[37] *Behrens v Bertram Mills Circus Ltd* [1957] 2 Q.B. 1 (the defendants were liable even though their Burmese elephants were normally obedient and well-behaved when on the way to the ring, being frightened by a small dog, they knocked over a booth in which two midgets were on show).

[38] "Species" is defined as including "sub-species and variety": s.11.

[39] [1990] 1 W.L.R. 459, applying *Cummings v Grainger* [1977] Q.B. 397.

[40] s.2(2)(a).

[41] n.39 above.

[42] [1994] P.I.Q.R. P128 Pill J. held that in the light of the definition of "species" in s.11, where an identifiable breed of dog existed such as "Border Collie", the relevant comparison ought to be made with that breed of dog and not dogs generally. See Exall, "Give a Dog a Bad Name", 135 S.J. 644.

[43] A child, who suffered a fractured humerus when thrown from a riding school pony, failed to establish that the damage caused was of a kind which a pony was likely to cause, or if it caused, was likely to be severe: *E v Townfoot Stables* [2004] C.L.Y. 169.

[44] s.2(2)(b).

[45] *Breeden v Lampart* March 21, 1985 and *Cummings v Granger* [1977] Q.B. 397.

vicious tendency based on past conduct[46] or simply unusual characteristics. Thus, in *Wallace v Newton*,[47] where the claimant, a groom in the defendant's training stables, was crushed and seriously injured, while attempting to lead a thorough-bred showjumper into a horse-box trailer, it was held that in order to succeed, it was not necessary that the horse had any vicious tendency to attack people, but only that it had particular characteristics of unpredictability and unreliability unusual in a horse, and that it was from those characteristics that injury arose. Similarly, where the claimant had been bitten by a dog, which was known to attack people carrying bags, it was held to possess a characteristic peculiar to itself within the meaning of para.(b).[48] By way of contrast, in *Fitzgerald v E.D. & A.D. Cooke Bourne (Farms) Ltd*, a pre-Act case, the claimant's claim failed where the court was satisfied that in knocking the claimant to the ground, a young unbroken thoroughbred filly was indulging in a natural propensity to be playful, rather than viciousness.[49]

14–14   More recently, it has been pointed out that before a claim on the basis of strict liability under the Act can attach, it has to be shown that the characteristic of an animal which is causative of damage to the claimant is a dangerous behavioural characteristic, even though only exhibited in particular times or circumstances. A claim under the Act for injury and damage caused by a cow, which escaped from a field on to a road, failed where the behavioural characteristic relied on by the claimants (agitation resulting from the cow's normal maternal instinct upon being separated from her calf) was itself neither dangerous nor causative.[50] The cow's behaviour, which included climbing a six bar livestock gate and crossing a 12 foot cattle grid, reflected exceptional and exaggerated agitation, so that she was in the state of an excited wild animal.

14–15   As is apparent from the previous paragraph, the interpretation and application of "characteristics" has continued to give rise to difficulty. Thus it has been held that a normally obedient horse which stepped into the road and collided with the claimant's car, contrary to the direction of its rider, did not have a characteristic or a characteristic only found at particular times and particular circumstances and the claimant failed.[51] Yet where an otherwise well behaved horse reared up causing the claimant rider to fall, it was held that the core meaning of "normal" in "characteristics . . . which are not normally found . . . ." was "conforming to type". Thus if a characteristic was usual then it would certainly be normal. The Court of Appeal said that it was difficult to see why Parliament should have intended to exclude from the ambit of s.2(2)(b) cases where the relevant characteristic was natural, although unusual, in the animal which caused the damage. If s.2(2)(b) was interpreted in that way, there was nothing unjust or

---

[46] e.g. *Parsons v King* (1891) 8 T.L.R. 114.
[47] [1982] 1 W.L.R. 375. The horse was called "Lord Justice".
[48] *Kite v Napp*, *The Times*, June 1, 1982; see also *Flack v Hudson* [2001] Q.B. 698: a horse liable to bolt when in the vicinity of agricultural machinery.
[49] [1964] 1 Q.B. 249. The decision was distinguished in *Morris v Bailey* (1970) 13 D.L.R. (3d) 150, where the defendant allowed his collie dog to run at large, knowing it had a propensity to run up to people barking furiously, although it stopped short of actually knocking them to the ground.
[50] *McKenny v Foster* [2008] EWCA Civ 173.
[51] *Clark v Bowlt* [2007] P.I.Q.R. P12, CA.

unreasonable, as between the keeper, who could decide whether to run the unavoidable risks involved in keeping horses, and whether or not to insure against those risks, and the victim of the horse's behaviour, in requiring the keeper to bear the loss.[52]

That reasoning was applied where a claimant fell from a horse which had a   **14–16**
habit of bucking when going into a canter.[53] The relevant characteristic for the purposes of s.2(2)(b) was said to be bucking, not bucking when going into a canter, as considerations of time and circumstances were only relevant elements in the second, alternative, limb of s.2(2)(b) and, thus the core meaning of "normal" was "conforming to type" and the judge had been entitled to find on the evidence that bucking was not a normal characteristic of horses generally. Under the second limb of s.2(2)(b), the relevant question was whether it was normal for horses generally to buck at particular times and in particular circumstances, including when beginning to canter. The words "at particular times or in particular circumstances" denoted times or circumstances that could be described and predicted. Since there was no evidence that horses generally bucked at particular times or in particular circumstances, the claim failed.

The second limb of the subsection is altogether more tortuous and gave rise to   **14–17**
a dispute as to whether a literal interpretation should prevail over an interpretation that did not treat as abnormal behaviour that is characteristic of the species in the circumstances in which the species found itself. More than 30 years after the passing of the Act, the House of Lords had an opportunity to resolve the difference in *Mirvahedy v Henley*.[54] The case arose from a collision on a road between a car and a horse, one of several that had panicked for some unknown reason and escaped from a field, pushing over an electric fence and travelling over a mile before they reached the road. It was agreed that while this behaviour was not normal for horses in normal circumstances, it was usual when such animals were alarmed or under threat. Thus, by a majority, it was held that the second limb of the subsection did indeed apply to temporary characteristics which were nevertheless normal for the animal in particular circumstances, even if those circumstances were unusual. Lord Hobhouse said:

> "It is true that there is an implicit assumption of fact in section 2(2) that domesticated animals are not normally dangerous. But the purpose of paragraph (b) is to make provision for those that are. It deals with two specific categories where that assumption of fact is falsified. The first is that of an animal which is possessed of a characteristic, not normally found in animals of the same species, which makes it dangerous. The second is an animal which, although belonging to a species which does not normally have dangerous characteristics, nevertheless had dangerous characteristics at particular times or in particular circumstances. The essence of those provisions is the falsification of the assumption, in the first because of the departure of the individual from the norm for its species, in the second because of the introduction of special factors."[55]

---

[52] *Welsh v Stokes* [2008] 1 W.L.R. 1224, CA.
[53] *Freeman v Higher Park Farm* [2009] P.I.Q.R. P6, CA.
[54] [2003] 2 A.C. 491. See Amirthalingham "Animal Liability—equine, canine and asinine" 119 L.Q.R. 563; Howarth "The House of Lords and the Animals Act: closing the stable door" 62 C.L.J. 548; Barker, "Animals: where should the loss lie?" E.P.S. 2006, 4(9), 9.
[55] *Mirvahedy v Henley* [2003] 2 A.C. 491 at 517, para.[71].

In reaching this decision, Lord Nicholls acknowledged public policy considerations:

> "Considered as a matter of social policy, there are arguments in favour of [imposing strict liability for damage caused by the animal when the animal's behaviour was not abnormal for an animal of the species in those circumstances]. It may be said that the loss should fall on the person who chooses to keep an animal which is known to be dangerous in some circumstances. He is aware of the risks involved, and he should bear the risk. On the other hand, it can be said, that negligence apart, everyone must take the risks associated with the ordinary characteristics of animals commonly kept in this country."[56]

14–18   It follows that, on establishing a pattern of behaviour capable of amounting to a "characteristic" in any given case, the characteristic so identified will either be abnormal, or normal: either way it will fall within one of the limbs of s.2(2)(b) and satisfy the requirement, leaving defendants to argue, if they can, over whether the requirements of s.2(2)(a) and (c) have been met.[57] Many earlier cases have now to be reconsidered in the light of *Mirvahedy*.[58] In relation to a relatively recent example, *Gloster v Chief Constable of Greater Manchester Police*,[59] discussed in the 10th edition of this work, the suggestion that a police dog which bit in accordance with its training was responding to that training, rather than an inculcated propensity to bite, was expressly disapproved.[60]

14–19   (c) *Those characteristics were known to that keeper or were at any time known to a person who at that time had charge of the animal as that keeper's servant or, where that keeper is the head of a household, were known to another keeper of the animal who is a member of that household and under the age of 16*.[61] The knowledge required to impose liability is the actual knowledge of the keeper or that to be imputed to him, through a particular employee or agent.[62] So, where only one of two keepers of a horse was aware that it had a propensity to be frightened of farm machinery and the keeper without such knowledge was killed when thrown from the horse, the keeper with knowledge was liable to the deceased's widower for her death. The Court of Appeal rejected the submission that the two keepers' knowledge of the horse's characteristics be treated as being the same.[63] It is not sufficient to prove that he ought to have known of the

---

[56] *Mirvahedy v Henley* [2003] 2 A.C. 491 at 503, para.[6].

[57] The Animals Act 1971 (Amendment) Bill, which proposed amending s.2 to limit the scope of *Mirvahedy* by affording keepers of animals a defence if they could show that there was no particular reason to expect an animal to react as it did, failed to attract sufficient Parliamentary support in March 2008.

[58] For example *Jaundrill v Gillett*, *The Times*, January 30, 1996, CA where an intruder maliciously opened a roadside field gate and, during the hours of darkness, drove out a number of horses which panicked and galloped along the highway and into collision with an oncoming car, and their keeper was held not liable.

[59] [2000] P.I.Q.R. P114.

[60] Thus Lord Scott said, at [126]: "If biting at its handler's command is a characteristic of German Shepherds only after they have been trained to do so, it is not a normal characteristic of the sub-species."

[61] s.2(2)(c).

[62] See s.2(2)(c).

[63] *Flack v Hudson* [2001] Q.B. 698.

propensity.[64] There is no definition of knowledge contained in the Act so that reference back to the common law must be made for assistance.[65] What is required is knowledge of characteristics of the animal that indicate a tendency to cause the damage or injury which in fact ensues.[66] In the light of the several provisions of the subsection, it will be necessary to consider this aspect by reference to the knowledge of: (i) the keeper himself; (ii) his servant in charge; and (iii) another keeper, who is a member of his household. Outside the confines of these categories, knowledge *cannot* be attributed to the keeper, under the Act.

(i) *Knowledge of the keeper*

Some guidance can still be gained from the common law principles, relating   **14–20** to proof of *scienter*,[67] perhaps now more appropriately called *knowledge of propensity*. Such proof is made by showing that the animal has a propensity to do the particular kind of damage in question and that the keeper knows of it. The best evidence is that the animal has, to the keeper's knowledge, done the same kind of damage before, but it is not essential to go as far as that. Proof of knowledge of unsuccessful attempts is enough.[68] In the case of a bull, evidence by one witness that the owner had said that the bull would run at anything in red, and by another witness that he had said that a bull would run at anything red, was held to be sufficient evidence on the ground that "either expression was some evidence to go to the jury that the defendant knew that this animal was a dangerous one".[69] In an action for damages for being bitten by a dog, where there was no evidence that the dog had ever bitten any person, but it was proved that, to the defendant's knowledge, the dog rushed out of his kennel when any stranger passed and barked and attempted to bite, it was held that that was sufficient to establish liability.[70] The fact that a dog was usually kept tied up was held to be

---

[64] *Mason v Keeling* (1699) 12 Mod. 332.

[65] See *Glanville v Sutton & Co Ltd* [1928] 1 K.B. 571 and *Brock v Richards* [1951] 1 K.B. 529.

[66] See *Smith v Ainger*, *The Times*, June 6, 1990, where it was held that the keeper of a dog with a known propensity to attack other dogs was liable to a claimant who was knocked over and hurt as it rushed to attack her own animal; it was incorrect to hold, as had the judge at first instance, that knowledge of his animal's aggressive tendencies towards other dogs was insufficient to fix the defendant with knowledge of a characteristic which caused the claimant's injury. See further *McKenny v Foster*, n.50 above, (cow separated from her calf: her behaviour in escaping from a field by climbing a six bar livestock gate and crossing a 12 foot cattle grid, reflected exceptional and exaggerated agitation, resulting from the animal's maternal instinct, so that she was in the state of an excited, wild animal. The potential for such behaviour had not been known to the defendants: neither the cow, nor the breed generally, were known to exhibit their maternal instinct with such excited and exaggerated anxiety as was shown, for whatever abnormal reason, on the relevant occasion).

[67] The Law Commission in para.18 reported: "The law at present achieves this imposition of strict liability by the *scienter* rules, but we think that this rule requires considerable modification and simplification. We would therefore abolish it in its common law form and substitute a new rule retaining what we conceive to be the essential rationale of the old law ... [i.e.] a propensity which is really likely to be dangerous," per Willmer L.J. and "a propensity to attack people," per Danckwerts L.J. in *Fitzgerald v E.D. & A.D. Cooke Bourne (Farms) Ltd* [1964] 1 Q.B. 249.

[68] See *Barnes v Lucille Ltd* (1907) 96 L.T. 680. See para.18(2) of the Law Commission's report.

[69] *Hudson v Roberts* (1851) 6 Ex. 697.

[70] *Worth v Gilling* (1866) L.R. 2 C.P. 1. See also to the same effect *Osborne v Chocqueel* [1896] 2 K.B. 109. The decision to the contrary of Lord Ellenborough in *Beck v Dyson* (1815) 4 Camp. 198, must be taken to be overruled. Thus the common suggestion that every dog is entitled to its first bite is scarcely accurate law. See further *Curtis v Betts* [1990] 1 W.L.R. 459.

insufficient evidence,[71] but a warning by the owner not to go near the dog was sufficient evidence.[72]

14–21   The evidence of one bite by a dog has been enough to establish proof and it has been held that it is not necessary that the dog should be generally prone to bite.[73] When the defendant went with his dog into a public house and his dog bit the potman, and half an hour afterwards, in the street, it again bit the potman, it was held, reversing the court below, that the defendant was liable, because "the action was not for the first bite, but for the second. Half an hour had intervened between them, and during that time it was the duty of the defendant, who knew his dog had just bitten a man, to secure him in some way so as to prevent him from biting again."[74] Interrogatories were not permitted to ascertain the names of the persons alleged by the claimant to have been previously bitten by the dog.[75] The scope of further information that can now be sought under the Civil Procedure Rules[76] is wider than under previous rules of court. However, whether this will extend to requiring the defendant to disclose the identity of a witness helpful to the claimant remains an open question.

14–22   It is not necessary to prove that the defendant's animal is always ferocious, as long as it is proved that, to his knowledge, it is fierce at certain times. So, when it was proved that a bitch which had bitten the claimant was, to the defendant's knowledge, fierce when she had pups, although harmless at other times, it was held that liability was established.[77] This principle is obviously enshrined in the second limb of s.2(2)(b) of the Act.[78]

14–23   It is a matter of evidence whether a keeper has been told about his animal's abnormal characteristics, whether by an employee (not in charge of it) or by anyone else, including any member of his family or household. In such event, it will not be necessary to consider paras (b) and (c), hereinafter, which are only concerned with the circumstances where knowledge will be *imputed*. Accordingly, a complaint made to the keeper's wife, who is living with him, was held to be evidence of her husband's knowledge.[79] But, on the other hand, a complaint made to the keeper's husband was held not to be evidence against her in an action

---

[71] *Beck v Dyson* (1815) 4 Camp. 198; *Hogan v Sharpe* (1837) 7 Car. & P. 755.

[72] *Judge v Cox* (1816) 1 Stark. 285. A "beware of dog" sign on the front gate did not imply knowledge that the dog was vicious: *Dolan v Bright, The Times*, November 17, 1962. It must today be doubted whether an offer of compromise would be capable of constituting evidence of knowledge of propensity, but see *Thomas v Morgan* (1835) 2 C.M. & R. 496. cf. *Sanders v Teape and Swan* (1884) 51 L.T. 263.

[73] *Charlwood v Greig* (1851) 3 Car. & Kir. 46; *Pacy v Field* (1937) 81 S.J. 160.

[74] *Parsons v King* (1891) 8 T.L.R. 114.

[75] *Knapp v Harvey* [1911] 2 K.B. 725. Interrogatories were the precursors of requests for further information under the present Rules.

[76] CPR Pt 18.

[77] *Barnes v Lucille Ltd* (1907) 96 L.T. 680 where Darling J. said: "I do not think, further, that in order to make the owner of the dog liable the dog must be always and invariably ferocious. If the owner knows that at certain periods the dog is ferocious, then he has knowledge that at those times the dog is of such a character that he ought to take care of it." cf. *Howard v Bergin O'Connor & Co* [1925] 2 Ir.R. 110 (bullock savage when being unloaded from railway).

[78] See para.14–17, above.

[79] *Gladman v Johnson* (1867) 36 L.J.C.P. 153.

brought by the claimant after the keeper's husband's death.[80] Where a young child, living with his parents, acquired knowledge of an animal's abnormal characteristics that fact alone did not, as a matter of law, pass on such knowledge to his parent, the keeper.[81]

(ii) Knowledge of keeper's servant

Section 2(2)(c) deals with the situation where the relevant knowledge will be **14–24** attributed to the keeper of an animal via the agency of another person. The words concerned are contained in s.2(2)(c). What has to be considered is whether: "those characteristics . . . were at any time known to a person who at that time had charge of the animal as that keeper's servant . . . ".[82]

It follows that the knowledge of the abnormal characteristics of the animal **14–25** need not be the personal knowledge of the keeper himself. It suffices if such knowledge is possessed by an employee, who had the care and control of the animal, such as a manager or agent of the keeper's business, in connection with which the animal is kept.

ILLUSTRATIONS

Owners were fixed with knowledge: where their coachman, who kept the dog **14–26** in the stable, knew it to be savage[83]; where barmen employees had received complaints that the dog had attacked customers of the bar even though there was no evidence of the complaints being communicated to the owner.[84] In contrast an education authority escaped liability for a dog kept on school premises by a school keeper with its knowledge and permission, where the dog was kept for pleasure rather than as a guard dog. The dog was acquired and kept by him in a personal capacity rather than as an employee.[85]

The words of the subsection restrict the category of the keeper's employee to **14–27** the one who had charge of the animal at the time of acquiring knowledge. Thus, if some other fellow employee had knowledge of its abnormal characteristics but he was not in charge of it, then such knowledge gained cannot be attributed to the keeper, his employer. This would appear to be so despite Lord Wheatley's strong comment that "if each is to be regarded in his own way as the *alter ego* of the employers it seems to produce a schizophrenic legal *persona*, and I cannot imagine the law leads to such a result."[86]

---

[80] *Miller v Kimbray* (1867) 16 L.T. 360.
[81] *Elliott v Longden* (1901) 17 T.L.R. 648.
[82] A "servant" is a person who is employed to perform services in connection with the affairs of his employer and over whom the latter has control in the performance of those services. For the distinction between servants and independent contractors see Ch.3, para.3–99, above.
[83] *Baldwin v Casella* (1872) L.R. 7 Ex. 325.
[84] *Applebee v Percy* (1874) L.R. 9 C.P. 647.
[85] *Knott v London County Council* [1934] 1 K.B. 126 at 134.
[86] *Maclean v The Forestry Commission*, 1970 S.L.T. 265, (the employee, actually in charge of a horse, did not know of its dangerous characteristic which was known to another employee who was not in charge of the animal at all).

14–28   So, complaints about a dog's ferocity to a domestic who did not have charge of the animal, in the absence of evidence that the fact of its ferocity had been communicated to the defendant or his wife, were insufficient to fix the defendant with knowledge.[87] Nor was knowledge acquired where it was proved that employees of a steamship company knew that a dog belonging to the company had previously bitten people but those employees had neither the control of the dog nor the management of the premises.[88]

(iii) *Knowledge of another keeper in this household*

14–29   Section 2(2)(c) also fixes the keeper with knowledge where the characteristics described in s.2(2)(b) "were known to another keeper of the animal who is a member of that household and under the age of sixteen." However, not every child within a household[89] will necessarily be another keeper of the animal in order to impute knowledge to the keeper, and problems may arise similar to those referred to in the previous paragraph, where one employee not in charge of the animal, has the appropriate knowledge but another who is in charge of it, lacks does not.[90]

14–30   **Liability of keeper.** Whether liability arises under s.2(1) or (2) of the Act, the keeper is the person liable for damage done by a dangerous animal. By section 6(3) a person is a keeper of an animal if (subject to subs.6(4)) either:

> "(a) he owns the animal or has it in his possession[91]; or (b) he is the head of a household of which a member under the age of sixteen owns the animal or has it in his possession."

14–31   At common law an owner who was in possession of an animal could not escape liability by abandoning ownership either before or after the damage was done.[92] Until he had transferred the ownership to another he was liable for not

---

[87] *Colget v Norrish* (1866) 2 T.L.R. 471.

[88] *Stiles v Cardiff Steam Navigation Co* (1864) 33 L.J.Q.B. 310.

[89] As to the meaning of "household" and the relationship of the members of the household to the head of the household, these were described by Rand J. in *Wawanesa Mutual Insurance Co v Bell* [1957] S.C.R. 581 at 584, as follows: "The 'household,' in the broad sense of a family, is a collective group living in a home, acknowledging the authority of a head, the members of which, with few exceptions, are bound by marriage, blood, affinity or other bond, between whom there is an intimacy and by whom there is felt a concern with and an interest in the life of all that gives it a unity. It may, for example, include such persons as domestic servants and distant relatives permanently residing within it. To some degree they are all admitted and submit to the collective body, its unity and its conditions, particularly that of the general discipline of the family head. They do not share fully in the more restricted family intimacy or interest or concern, but they participate to a substantial degree in the general life of the household and form part of it."

[90] But in respect of two keepers who were not members of the same household and their liability to each other, see *Flack v Hudson* [2001] Q.B. 698, para.14–19, above.

[91] Lord Wright in *Knott v London County Council* [1934] 1 K.B. 126 at 134, 141, stated the common law position: "The true test of liability, namely that of ownership or possession and control". Similarly, the "keeper" of animals, for the purposes of s.155 of the Highways Act 1980, is the person in whose possession the animals are, whether or not he derives any personal benefit from them. The fact that the straying cattle may also be in any other person's possession is irrelevant as regards committing an offence: *D.P.P. v Turton, The Guardian*, June 8, 1988, DC.

[92] *Brady v Warren* [1900] 2 I.R. 632; *Dee Conservancy Board v McConnell* [1928] 2 K.B. 159 at 163, per Scrutton L.J.

keeping it under control. His liability being based on strict liability, similar to the rule in *Rylands v Fletcher*,[93] he could not relieve himself from responsibility by delegating the performance of his duty to an independent contractor. In the words of Atkin L.J.: "Can the person who has acquired a tiger, so long as he remains its owner, relieve himself of responsibility by contracting with a third person for its custody?"[94] So, too, as Lord Wright observed: "In the case of dangerous animals, a transfer of actual possession and control would not necessarily terminate his [the owner's] responsibility."[95] Section 6(3) preserves and embodies the common law on the point by adding that:

> "if at any time an animal ceases to be owned by or to be in the possession of a person, any person who immediately before that time was a keeper thereof by virtue of the preceding provisions of this subsection continues to be a keeper of the animal until another person becomes a keeper thereof by virtue of those provisions."

In the light of the definition of a "a keeper", more than one person can be held   **14–32**
liable for the same animal, for example the owner, in addition to a person having its possession and control. Further, the there is nothing in the Act which limits those who can sue the keeper of an animal to third parties or strangers: hence one keeper was held liable to another keeper where the former had knowledge of a propensity of which the latter was in ignorance and where the latter was killed as a result of that propensity.[96]

ILLUSTRATIONS

A dog belonging to a former employee was permitted to live on the   **14–33**
defendant's premises. The defendant was found liable for the damage it caused on the basis that he was harbouring it.[97] In contrast, a father escaped liability for his 17-year-old daughter's savage dog on the basis that she was the owner and had control of the dog.[98] Likewise, an education authority escaped liability for a dog kept by its school keeper on its school premises with its knowledge and permission because the dog was kept by the keeper in a personal capacity and not as an employee.[99]

The mere fact of an animal's presence on the defendant's premises when it   **14–34**
does damage, imposes no liability on the defendant. So, where a dog made a sudden incursion at a railway station, bit the claimant and disappeared just as suddenly as it had appeared, the railway company was held not to be liable.[100]

---

[93] *Filburn v People's Palace and Aquarium Co* (1890) 25 Q.B.D. 258; *Knott v London County Council* [1934] 1 K.B. 126 at 139, per Lord Wright, and recognised in numerous cases.
[94] *Belvedere Fish Guano Co v Rainham Chemical Works* [1920] 2 K.B. 487 at 504; commented on by Lords Buckmaster and Parmoor [1921] 2 A.C. 465 at 477, 491.
[95] *Brackenborough v Spalding Urban District Council* [1942] A.C. 310 at 324.
[96] *Flack v Hudson* [2001] Q.B. 698.
[97] *M'Kone v Wood* (1831) 5 C. & P. 1.
[98] *North v Wood* [1914] K.B. 629.
[99] *Knott v London County Council* [1934] 1 K.B. 126.
[100] *Smith v Great Eastern Ry* (1866) L.R. 2 C.P. 4.

14–35   A person with the care and custody of the animal under contract with the owner, is under the same liability as the owner, since both are keepers under the Act. A trainer, who, under contract with the owner, had in his custody a horse, which he knew was accustomed to bite, was held liable when the horse, while being taken from the stables to a railway station, bit the claimant.[101]

14–36   The Act specifically provides that a person shall not be a keeper of an animal by virtue only of the fact of possession where he has taken it into and kept it in possession "for the purpose of preventing it from causing damage or of restoring it to its owner".[102]

14–37   **The damage for which the keeper is liable.** If the keeper is liable under either of the subsections of s.2, he will be responsible for "any damage" caused by his animal. "Damage" is defined in s.11 as including "the death of, or injury to, any person (including any disease and any impairment of physical or mental condition)" but the definition is clearly not exhaustive and the damage claimed may embrace any damage to the property or chattels of another, including an animal owned by him. There is no requirement that this damage be of a type the animal was likely to cause, because liability under the Act is independent of fault or any finding of negligence and the test of the damage recoverable is therefore directness of consequence not reasonable foresight.[103] "If a tiger is let loose at a funfair, it seems to me irrelevant whether a person is injured as a result of direct attack or because on seeing it he runs away and falls over."[104]

14–38   Even so, damage will not be recoverable if it is not strictly caused by the animal (for purposes of s.2(1)) or its abnormal characteristics (s.2(2)).[105]

14–39   The words of the two alternatives contained in s.2(2)(a), namely "the damage is of a kind which the animal, unless restrained, was likely to cause or which, if caused by the animal, was likely to be severe", are not intended as a restriction on the damage recoverable in an appropriate case, but merely set out the test of the likelihood of damage for the purposes of the subsection.[106] Certainly there is no requirement that the damage *has* to be severe in order to found an action.

14–40   **The keeper's defences: at common law.** Although a common law liability for damage caused by animals was regarded as similar to liability under *Rylands*

---

[101] *Walker v Hall* (1876) 40 J.P. 456.

[102] s.6(4).

[103] *Behrens v Bertram Mills Circus Ltd* [1957] 2 Q.B. 1 at 18. See generally Ch.5, para.5–41, and Ch.13, para.13–29, above.

[104] per Devlin J. in *Behrens v Bertram Mills Circus Ltd* [1957] 2 Q.B. 1 at 18.

[105] In *Jaundrill v Gillett, The Times*, January 30, 1996, the Court of Appeal held that damage to a car was not actionable against the keeper where it was caused by horses maliciously released on to the road by an unknown other. The animals had panicked and aimlessly galloped about but it was held that the "real and effective cause of the accident" was their release on to the highway, not any panicky characteristic. That approach was rejected by Hale L.J. in *Mirvahedy v Henley* [2002] 2 A.C. 491 whose remarks at para.[16] were expressly approved by Lord Walker of Gestingthorpe in the House of Lords: above para.[140]. On the facts, it is likely that the claimant would today succeed in *Jaundrill v Gillett* as he had done before the trial judge.

[106] See *Curtis v Betts* [1990] 1 W.L.R. 459.

v Fletcher, there was some doubt about the extent to which the same defences applied.[107] It was, however always a defence to prove that the injured person had brought the damage upon himself by either meddling with the animal or deliberately or rashly going too near the dangerous animal's cage,[108] well knowing that it was dangerous.[109]

ILLUSTRATIONS

The owner of some zebras was held not liable when he kept his animals secure **14-41** in a stable but the claimant entered the stable and, in stroking one of the animals, was kicked into the next stall where another zebra bit him.[110] Where, upon seeing a smouldering cigarette on some straw, an employee of the defendants, who was not employed to look after the animals, climbed over a barrier separating a leopard's cage from the part to which the public were admitted and was bitten, liability was not made out.[111] Where a child attempted to play with a dog of known mischievous propensity by and was bitten as a result, the claim failed.[112]

The keeper's defences: under the statute. Section 2 of the Animals Act **14-42** imposes liability "except as otherwise provided" and the statutory exceptions to liability are set out in s.5: (i) the fault of the claimant; (ii) voluntary acceptance of the risk; (iii) the claimant as trespasser. Other defences, at common law, are no longer available.

(i) *The fault and contributory negligence of the claimant*

Under s.5(1), "a person is not liable under section[s] . . . of this Act for any **14-43** damage which is due wholly to the fault of the person suffering it." In the light of the provisions of s.10[113] and the definition of fault, as having "the same meaning as in the Law Reform (Contributory Negligence) Act 1945" contained in s.11, the court may apportion damage where the claimant has been held partly to blame for the damage.

---

[107] See Bramwell B. in *Nicholls v Marsland* (1875) L.R. 10 Ex. 255 at 260 (act of God); see also *Rands v McNeil* [1955] 1 Q.B. 253 at 257, per Denning L.J. (no escape from control); *Fleeming v Orr* (1855) 2 Macq. 14; *Charlesworth on Negligence* (4th edn, 1962), p.744, *Baker v Snell* [1908] 2 K.B. 825 and Devlin J. in *Behrens v Bertram Mills Circus Ltd* [1957] 2 Q.B. 1, (independent act of third party).

[108] *Murphy v Zoological Society of London, The Times*, November 14, 1962 (a boy aged 10 who was a cub member of a scout group, visited a lion's cage, climbed between two fences, was mauled by the lion and died later. The deceased was held to be a trespasser at that place and as no animal had "escaped" the Zoological Society were not in breach of any duty owed him).

[109] In *Behrens v Bertram Mills Circus Ltd* [1957] 2 Q.B. 1 at 19, Devlin J. said of the defence (of the claimant's own fault): "I see no reason why the same sort of defence should not prevail where the fault of the plaintiff does not amount to recklessness . . . but is failure of due diligence to look after his own safety." See also *James v Wellington City* [1972] N.Z.L.R. 70 and para.14-45, n.19, below.

[110] *Marlor v Ball* (1900) 16 T.L.R. 239.

[111] *Sylvester v Chapman Ltd* (1935) 79 S.J. 777.

[112] *Lee v Walkers* (1940) 162 L.T. 89; see also *Sycamore v Ley* (1932) 147 L.T. 342.

[113] Which provides: "For the purposes of the Fatal Accidents Acts 1846 to 1959, [1976] the Law Reform (Contributory Negligence) Act 1945 and the Limitation Act[s] [1980] any damage for which a person is liable under ss.2 to 4 of this Act shall be treated as due to his fault."

(ii) *The claimant voluntarily accepting the risk*

14-44   Section 5(2) provides that: "a person is not liable under section 2 of this Act for any damage suffered by a person who has voluntarily accepted the risk thereof."[114] Accordingly, if a person intervened to separate his dog involved in a fight with another dog, he could well expect to have this defence raised against him.[115] Where a claimant deliberately trespassed in a scrap yard at night, although she was well aware that an Alsatian guard dog patrolled the premises unrestrained, she was held to have voluntarily accepted the risk and her action failed on appeal.[116] Where an experienced rider said she would continue to ride a horse after being thrown from it when it bucked on going into a canter, a characteristic of which she had been warned, she was to be taken as having accepted the risk of falling off when the horse behaved in that way again.[117] Presumably a suspect told by a pursuing police dog handler to "stand still or the dog will be sent" would be held to have voluntarily accepted the risk of being bitten if such clear warning was ignored.

14-45   An important change was made to the common law by s.6(5) of the Act which provides that "[W]here a person employed as a servant by a keeper of an animal incurs a risk incidental to his employment he shall not be treated as accepting it voluntarily". The defence of *volenti* formerly available[118] to an employer is thereby removed, even for a case where the claimant has been employed specifically for a purpose which includes coming into close proximity to a dangerous animal.[119]

(iii) *The claimant as trespasser*

14-46   By s.5(3):

"A person is not liable under section 2 of this Act for any damage caused by an animal kept on any premises or structure to a person trespassing there, if it is proved either—

(a) that the animal was not kept there for the protection of persons or property; or
(b) (if the animal was kept there for the protection of persons or property) that keeping it there for that purpose was not unreasonable."

14-47   In *Cummings v Grainger*,[120] Lord Denning M.R. considered that since the use of guard dogs had long been recognised as reasonable for the protection of property by the common law, it was not unreasonable for the defendants to have protected their scrap yard, which was enclosed by walls and wire fence, at night

---

[114] In *Cummings v Grainger* [1977] Q.B. 397 at 408, Ormrod L.J. urged that the words of s.5(2) should be given their ordinary English meaning not complicated with the old doctrine of volenti non fit injuria and the defence should not be whittled down by too fine distinctions of what they meant.
[115] *Smith v Shields* (1964) 108 S.J. 501.
[116] *Cummings v Grainger* [1977] Q.B. 397.
[117] *Freeman v Higher Park Farm* [2009] P.I.Q.R. P6, CA, para.14–16, above.
[118] *Rands v McNeil* [1955] 1 Q.B. 253.
[119] See, e.g. the circumstances in *James v Wellington City* [1972] N.Z.L.R. 70 (zookeeper bitten by chimpanzee).
[120] [1977] Q.B. 397.

by an Alsatian guard dog that was allowed to roam around loose within the confines of the premises.[121]

Although a trespasser cannot, therefore, generally rely upon strict liability   **14–48** under s.2, there may have the option of an action for damages in negligence.[122] Doubtless if the claim succeeds the damages recoverable will be reduced for contributory negligence.

If the presence of a trespasser were unforeseeable, the keeper of a tamed   **14–49** animal of a dangerous species, like a chimpanzee or a cheetah, would avoid liability both under the Act and in negligence should the trespasser be injured, as a result of an attack by the animal whilst still on the keeper's land.

Limitation of action. It has been held that the limitation period for a claim   **14–50** under s.2(2) of the Act is six years.[123]

3.—Strict Liability for Injury Caused to Livestock by Dogs

Basis of liability. Section 3 of the Animals Act provides: "where a dog causes   **14–51** damage by killing or injuring livestock, any person who is a keeper of the dog is liable for the damage, except as otherwise provided by this Act."[124] Just like the position under the provisions of s.2, the person responsible for damage caused by a dog is its keeper[125] but the only damage in respect of which he will be liable under the section must be restricted to that occasioned to "livestock". Livestock is defined as meaning: "cattle, horses, asses, mules, hinnies, sheep, pigs, goats and poultry, and also deer not in the wild state and . . . also while in captivity, pheasants, partridges and grouse". Poultry is defined as meaning the domestic varieties of "fowls, turkeys, geese, ducks, guinea-fowls, pigeons, peacocks and quails".[126]

---

[121] See now the Guard Dogs Act 1975, where a person commits an offence by keeping a guard dog on premises, unless there is a handler with it or unless it is securely chained. These provisions do not affect civil liability and, so far as reasonableness is concerned, the Act has no application. See Harper, "Guard Dogs to Legal Heel", 125 New L.J. 243; Although not strictly trespass, see, e.g. *Lowery v Walker* [1911] A.C. 10 (the occupier of a field who had given a tacit permission for it to be used as a short cut was held liable in negligence for injury caused by a savage horse). Roy, "Guard Dog Act 1975", 126 New L.J. 1001; Spencer, [1977] C.L.J. 39 at 42–43.

[122] See further Ch.8, generally, on Trespassers.

[123] *Clarke v Barber* [2002] C.L.Y. 464 (an action based upon personal injury caused by the defendant's dog) applying the reasoning in *Stubbing v Webbs* [1993] A.C. 498 now overruled in *A v Hoare* [2008] 2 W.L.R. 311, HL, Ch.4, para.4–196, above.

[124] As regards strict liability for damage done by dogs to livestock, the provisions of the 1971 Act repealed and replaced the Dogs Act 1906 and 1928. See also Samuels, "Dogs and the Law", 117 S.J. 238; Whalen, "Dog bites" (2003) H. & S.L.3(3), 4.

[125] See para.14–30, above. cf. the situation under the Dogs Act 1906 when the person liable was the owner of the dog or else the occupier of the place where the dog was kept. Under the Animals Act 1971 both the dog owner without possession of it and the possessor without ownership of it are "keepers".

[126] s.11. Rabbits are no longer included: *Tallents v Bell* [1944] 2 All E.R. 474; cats and dogs are not "cattle"; *Buckle v Holmes* [1926] 2 K.B. 125.

14–52   It can be seen that in an action under s.3 arising from injury to livestock by a dog, there is no need to prove either negligence or the application of the problematic s.2(2). As Goddard L.J. commented ironically, Parliament still thinks "that sheep require more protection than human beings"![127]

14–53   Where a number of dogs belonging to different keepers collect together and form, in effect, a hunting pack, the keeper of any one dog identified as part of the group can be sued for the entire damage caused, under the ordinary principles of liability of joint tortfeasors.[128]

14–54   Should a person kill or injure a dog, s.9 of the Act provides a defence if that person was acting or had reasonable grounds for believing he was acting for the protection of livestock, which was either being worried or was about to be worried by it and there was no other means in practice for preventing such an attack.[129]

14–55   **Exceptions from liability.** Section 3 of the Act clearly imposes strict liability, "except as otherwise provided" and these statutory exceptions to liability are contained in s.5. There are two only and they are respectively: (i) the fault of the claimant; and (ii) the livestock had strayed on to the land where the dog was kept. Any other defence at common law is not now available.[130]

(i) *The fault and contributory negligence of the claimant*

14–56   In common with actions under either s.2[131] or s.4,[132] the exception provided by s.5(1) can be relied upon, namely that the relevant damage was due to the fault of the person suffering it or else he contributed towards it.[133]

(ii) *The livestock had strayed*

14–57   By s.5(4), a new defence was made available to a keeper of a dog, namely "a person is not liable under section 3 of this Act if the livestock was killed or injured on land on to which it had strayed and either the dog belonged to the occupier or its presence on the land was authorised by the occupier". These latter words would obviously include the dog belonging to a visitor who happened to be staying with the occupier at the time. On the other hand, if the dog were trespassing at the material time, equally with the livestock that it subsequently injured or killed, the defence would no longer be available to its keeper.

---

[127] *Hughes v Williams* [1943] K.B. 574 at 580.
[128] *Arneil v Paterson* [1931] A.C. 560, which leaves the keeper to obtain whatever contribution that he can from the keeper of any other dog involved in the action or in third party proceedings.
[129] See para.14–66, below.
[130] See, generally, para.14–40, above.
[131] See further, para.14–42, above.
[132] See further, para.14–74, below.
[133] Which is the combined effect of ss.10 and 11 and enables the court to apportion damages.

4.—Strict Liability for Damage Done by Straying Livestock

Common law principles of liability. Quite apart from negligence, an **14–58**
owner[134] was strictly liable for damage caused by the trespass of his livestock.[135]
This was confined to trespass to land, as there was no liability for trespass to
person or goods by an animal in the absence of intention or negligence.[136] The
common law was stated by Williams J.:

> "If I am the owner of an animal in which by law the right of property can exist, I am
> bound to take care that it does not stray into the land of my neighbour; and I am liable
> for any trespass it may commit, and for the ordinary consequences of that trespass.
> Whether or not the escape of the animal is due to my negligence is altogether
> immaterial. I am clearly liable for the trespass, and for all the ordinary consequences of
> the trespass, subject to a distinction which is taken very early in the books, that the
> animal is such that the owner of it may have a property in it which is recognisable by
> law. For instance, if a man's cattle, or sheep, or poultry, stray into his neighbour's land
> or garden, and do such damage as might ordinarily be expected to be done by things of
> that sort, the owner is liable to his neighbour for the consequences."[137]

Illustrations

The defendant was liable when his mare strayed into the claimant's field and **14–59**
kicked a horse, the damage not being too remote[138]; where the defendant's horse
bit and kicked the claimant's mare through a wire fence, the protrusion of any
part of the horse over the boundary line was sufficient to found liability[139]; where
calves were penned on one side of a railway line and their dams on the other, the
fences between being erected and maintained by the railway authorities, and the
dams, by using exceptional force broke through the fence and got on to the line
where some of them were killed in a collision with a train, their owner was liable
for the damage caused by the derailment, on it being proved that the fence was
properly maintained in accordance with s.68 of the Railway Clauses Consolidation Act 1845[140]; when the defendant's cow entered the claimant's field where
there was a bull that broke its leg whilst chasing and attempting to mount the
cow, the claimant succeeded on the ground that the damage to his bull was the
natural consequence of the cow's trespass.[141]

Statutory liability for loss and damage caused by trespassing live- **14–60**
stock. The 1971 Act abolished and superseded the common law rules imposing

---

[134] For meaning of "owner" in this connection, see para.14–65, below.
[135] This is an ancient cause of action dating from the fourteenth century: *Wormald v Cole* [1954] 1
Q.B. 614, 620; Williams, *Liability for Animals*, pp.127, 135; Holdsworth, *A History of English Law*,
Vol. 8, pp.470–471. See also Blackstone, Comm., III, 211. See generally, Reid, "Go wild in the
country" 146 S.J. 748 (dealing with liability of landowner to a neighbour for damage caused by
wildlife or weed pests).
[136] *Manton v Brocklebank* [1923] 2 K.B. 212.
[137] *Cox v Burbidge* (1863) 13 C.B.(N.S.) 430.
[138] *Lee v Riley* (1865) 18 C.B.(N.S.) 722; *Holgate v Bleazard* [1917] 1 K.B. 443.
[139] *Ellis v Loftus Iron Co* (1874) L.R. 10 C.P. 10. Otherwise, where the horse was not trespassing:
Manton v Brocklebank [1923] 2 K.B. 212.
[140] *Cooper v Railway Executive* [1953] 1 W.L.R. 223.
[141] *Eustace v Ayre* (1947) 14 L.J.N.C.C.R. 106.

liability for cattle trespass and replaced them with a new, but similar, form of strict liability[142] Section 4 provides:

"(1) Where livestock[143] belonging to any person strays on to land in the ownership or occupation of another and—

    (a) damage is done by the livestock to the land or to any property on it which is in the ownership or possession of the other person; or

    (b) any expenses are reasonably incurred by that other person in keeping the livestock while it cannot be restored to the person to whom it belongs or while it is detained in pursuance of section 7 of this Act, or in ascertaining to whom it belongs;

the person to whom the livestock belongs[144] is liable for the damage or expenses, except as otherwise provided by this Act."

14–61   It follows that the straying of livestock is no longer actionable per se but is only actionable upon proof of actual damage, which includes those reasonable expenses incurred in detaining the animals, where there is a right to do so, or in finding the person to whom they belong, but which is otherwise limited to damage to land and chattels. In this respect the action under the statute is different to cattle trespass at common law.

14–62   **Damages for livestock trespass.** At common law when a trespass was committed by livestock, its owner was liable for the natural consequences of the trespass, although there was considerable uncertainty whether this included damage occasioned by an abnormal propensity, in the absence of *scienter*. In *Theyer v Purnell*,[145] where sheep suffering from disease trespassed upon the claimant's land and infected his sheep, it was held that the defendant was liable for that damage, whether or not he was aware of the condition of his sheep at the date of the trespass, on the ground that the doctrine of *scienter* had no application to an action founded on trespass.[146] Today, there can be little doubt that the same decision would be reached on the same facts, but on the ground that the damage suffered was that covered by s.4(1)(a) of the Act.

---

[142] The heading of s.4 is: "Liability for damage and expense due to trespassing livestock". Despite these words, there is no further reference to "trespass" included in the text. If, technically, a trespass need not be proved it would seem that *Ellis v Loftus Iron Co* (1874) L.R. 10 C.P. 10, is no longer the law. The word used in the section is "straying": see North, *op cit.*, p.107 for problems that may arise as to what could be important distinctions between "straying" and "trespassing". Some guidance relating to the meaning of "straying" can possibly be gained from *Wiseman v Booker* (1878) 3 C.P.D. 184.

[143] Livestock is defined in s.11: see para.14–51 above, and does not include wild animals which are not normally the object of ownership, e.g. rabbits, foxes nor such imported wild animals such as lions and tigers, whether captive or free.

[144] s.4(2) provides that "for the purposes of this section any livestock belongs to the person in whose possession it is".

[145] [1918] 2 K.B. 333 distinguishing *Cooke v Waring* (1863) 2 H. & C. 332, where the action was for negligence.

[146] On the other hand there were several opinions but not decisions expressing the contrary view, e.g. Blackburn J. in *Fletcher v Rylands* (1866) L.R. 1 Ex. 265 at 280; Lord Sterndale M.R. in *Manton v Brocklebank* [1923] 2 K.B. 212 at 223; and Atkin L.J. in *Buckle v Holmes* [1926] 2 K.B. 125 at 130.

Whilst the Act defines "damage" as including "any disease and any **14–63** impairment of physical or mental condition"[147] it is apparent from the wording of s.4 that the only actionable general damage done by straying livestock is either to land or any property on it, which is in the ownership or possession of the other person. It follows that a claim for damages in respect of personal injuries sustained by a claimant cannot be maintained in an action under s.4, as was possible at common law.[148] In addition, however, where any special damage has been suffered, namely expenses incurred in keeping the livestock until restored to the owner, such damage can be recovered under the section.

Section 7 abolished the ancient right to seize and detain any animal by way of **14–64** distress damage feasant replacing it with a more elaborate procedure for the detention and sale of trespassing livestock by way of remedy for the occupier of the injured land.

By and against whom the action is brought. An action for damage done by **14–65** straying livestock can be brought by anyone who has possession of the land or any part of it, and so the purchaser of a crop of growing turnips can sue for turnips eaten by trespassing sheep.[149] Anyone who can bring an action for trespass to the land can sue and this will include a person who has the exclusive right of pasture upon it.

At common law the owner of the animal was liable for its trespass. If, however, the animal was in possession of another under the contract of agistment when the trespass was committed, the owner was not liable, but the agister was.[150] This was on the principle that the person in possession and control of an animal was liable for the damage it caused, when there was any liability at all.[151] Section 4[152] of the Animals Act does not change the common law in this regard.

Trespass by dog. At common law there was no liability for trespass to land **14–66** committed by a straying dog[153] and this position remains unaltered under the Act, since the definition of "livestock" purposely has excluded a dog, hence its keeper will not be liable in respect of any action brought under s.4.[154] The reason for this was apparently:

"on account—first of the difficulty or impossibility of keeping the latter [dogs and cats] under restraint—secondly, the slightness of the damage which their wandering

---

[147] s.11.
[148] See *Wormald v Cole* [1954] 1 Q.B. 614, which has, accordingly, been overruled by the Act; Horrocks, "*Wormald v Cole* Lives?", 123 New L.J. 255.
[149] *Wellaway v Courtier* [1918] 1 K.B. 200.
[150] *Hammond v Mallinson* (1939) 6 L.J.C.C.R. 357.
[151] See now para.14–40 et seq. for the effect of the Animals Act 1971.
[152] In respect of which, see para.14–62, above.
[153] *Brown v Giles* (1823) 1 C. & P. 118; *Sanders v Teape & Swan* (1884) 51 L.T. 263; *Beckwith v Shordike* (1767) 4 Burr. 2092; *Mitten v Faudrye* (1626) Poph. 161. A dog is not included in the definition, contained in s.11 of the Animals Act 1971, of "livestock," for the trespassing of which the person to whom the livestock belongs is liable.
[154] This in no way affects the strict liability of a dog's keeper brought, appropriately, under ss.2(2) or 3.

ordinarily causes—thirdly, the common usage of mankind to allow them a wider liberty—and lastly, their not being considered in law so absolutely the chattels of the owner, as to be the subject of larceny."[155]

By way of contrast, an owner who incited his dog to enter the land of another was held liable for the intentional trespass thereby committed,[156] and he will still be so today.

14–67   Although the owner of a dog is not liable for damage it does when trespassing, he runs the risk of having it shot. At common law a trespassing dog which attacked livestock belonging to the occupier of the land might be killed if it were attacking the animals at the time, or there were a danger that it would renew any attack already made, should it have been left alone, and it was reasonable in all the circumstances for the protection of the animals to kill it.[157] Where by way of distinction, the animals chased were ferae naturae, in which the landowner had no property, such as pheasants, which were not in captivity, there was no right to shoot the trespassing dog.[158]

14–68   Section 9 of the Animals Act clarifies the precise circumstances in which a defendant may justifiably kill or injure dogs worrying livestock. The section provides—

"(1) In any civil proceedings against a person (in this section referred to as the defendant) for killing or causing injury to a dog it shall be a defence to prove—

(a) that the defendant acted for the protection of any livestock and was a person entitled to act for the protection of that livestock; and
(b) that within forty-eight hours of the killing or injury notice thereof was given by the defendant to the officer in charge of a police station.

(2) For the purpose of this section a person is entitled to act for the protection of any livestock if, and only if—

(a) the livestock or the land on which it is belongs to him or to any person under whose express or implied authority he is acting; and
(b) the circumstances are not such that liability for killing or causing injury to the livestock would be excluded by section 5(4) of this Act.

(3) Subject to subsection (4) of this section, a person killing or causing injury to a dog shall be deemed for the purposes of this section to act for the protection of any livestock if, and only if, either—

(a) the dog is worrying or is about to worry the livestock and there are no other reasonable means of ending or preventing the worrying; or

---

[155] *Read v Edwards* (1864) 17 C.B.(N.S.) 245, per Willes J. (where the dog had a known propensity to hunt and destroy game, the owner was held liable for the damage done, he being the owner of a mischievous dog, and the fact that the dog was trespassing when the damage was done did not affect his liability whatsoever). By way of contrast, see *Tallents v Bell and Goddard* [1944] 2 All E.R. 474 (where an owner was held not liable for his trespassing dog, which had killed rabbits kept for commercial purposes, in the absence of evidence of *scienter*).
[156] *R. v Pratt* (1855) 4 E. & B. 860.
[157] *Cresswell v Sirl* [1948] 1 K.B. 241; *Goodway v Becher* [1951] 2 All E.R. 349. See also Dogs (Protection of Livestock) Act 1953.
[158] *Gott v Measures* [1948] 1 K.B. 234.

(b) the dog has been worrying livestock, has not left the vicinity and is not under the control of any person and there are no practicable means of ascertaining to whom it belongs.

(4) For the purposes of this section the condition stated in either of the paragraphs of the preceding subsection shall be deemed to have been satisfied if the defendant believed that it was satisfied and had reasonable grounds for that belief.

(5) For the purposes of this section—

(a) an animal belongs to any person if he owns it or has it in his possession; and
(b) land belongs to any person if he is the occupier thereof."

Trespass by cat. A cat is in the same category as a dog when the liability of   **14–69**
the owner for its trespasses is in question. Accordingly, when a cat went onto the claimant's land and killed some of his pigeons and fowls, it was held that the owner was not liable.[159] However, if the cat did the same a second time, the keeper would be liable under the Act, not for trespass, but under s.2(2), for damage done by a cat with a known abnormal characteristic.[160]

Trespass by deer. At common law the owner of deer has been held liable for   **14–70**
trespass committed by them upon the neighbouring land.[161] In the case in question the deer had escaped from the owner's park some six years before, but were in the habit of returning. The defendant's keeper fed them in the park in the winter time, and a jury found that they were tame and kept by the defendant and under his control. Under the Act, the same result should probably follow. On the other hand, if the finding on the evidence was that the deer were "in the wild state," then they would not be livestock within the definition. In such an event there would be no liability, under s.4, in respect of their causing actionable damage, whilst straying.

Wild animals. There is no liability for wild animals,[162] breeding or living on   **14–71**
the land of one owner, which do damage on the land of another owner, although a landowner who brings game or other wild animals on to his land to an unreasonable extent, or causes them to multiply to an unreasonable extent, will be liable to his neighbours for any damage suffers as a result.[163]

ILLUSTRATIONS

It has been said that: "If a man makes coney-burrows in his own land, which   **14–72**
increase in so great a number that they destroy his neighbour's land next adjoining, his neighbours cannot have an action on the case against him who makes the said coney-burrows."[164] Where rabbits bred on the defendant's land and were trapped by the defendant for profit, he was not liable for damage done by their trespass on neighbouring land, although his predecessor had brought new

---

[159] *Buckle v Holmes* [1926] 2 K.B. 125.
[160] See para.14–13, above.
[161] *Brady v Warren* [1900] 2 I.R. 632.
[162] As regards bees, see para.14–10, n.32 above.
[163] *Farrer v Nelson* (1885) 15 Q.B.D. 258. See comment by Scrutton L.J. on this case in *Peech v Best* [1931] 1 K.B. 1 at 14.
[164] *Boulston's Case* (1597) 15 Rep. 104b; sub nom. *Boulston v Hardy*, Cro.Eliz. 547.

rabbits onto the land in order to improve the breed.[165] The presence of a large number of pheasants on the defendant's land, as a result of natural increase, does not render him liable for damage caused by the pheasants to crops on adjoining land.[166] Where rabbits that lived on a railway owner's land escaped onto the adjoining land of a farmer and ate his crop of swedes, the farmer's action in respect of his lost crop failed despite the fact that the rabbits came from the defendant's land and the defendant had not done all he could to control them, because the rabbits were naturally occurring wild animals and, as such, natural products of the soil.[167] A bone manure manufacturer whose business was on land close to a farmer's fields was not liable for damage done to the farmer's corn by rats attracted to the land by a heap of bones, on it not being proved that the bones kept were excessive or unusual in quantity.[168]

14–73   **Contrast with nuisance.** A landowner may, however, be guilty of nuisance where a substance is kept on his land in such circumstances as to attract animals or insects so as to create a nuisance. So, where a landowner had a heap of manure that was excessive in quantity so that its smell, as well as the number of flies it attracted and bred amounted to a nuisance, his neighbour was granted an injunction to prevent him from keeping it.[169]

14–74   **Exceptions from liability.** Section 4 of the Act imposes strict liability "except as otherwise provided" and statutory exceptions to liability are contained in s.5. There are two only and they are respectively: (i) the fault of the claimant, subject to certain special rules concerning fencing; and (ii) straying from the highway, when such livestock was present lawfully on the highway.

14–75   It follows that other defences, which could be relied upon at common law, namely an act of God, the independent act of a third party[170] and volenti non fit injuria are no longer available.

(i) *The fault and contributory negligence of the claimant*

14–76   At common law it was always a defence to an action for trespass by a person's livestock to show that the trespass was caused by breach of an obligation on the part of the claimant to fence, although the obligation to fence had to be enforceable by the defendant. Whilst it is the duty of the person to whom the

---

[165] *Birkbeck v Paget* (1862) 31 Beav. 403.
[166] *Seligman v Docker* [1949] Ch. 53, where Romer J. said, at 55: "The birds were ferae naturae and I am unable to see that the fact that the plaintiff had no right to shoot them imposed any duty in law upon the defendant to shoot them himself."
[167] *Hall v Dart Light Valley Railway* [1998] C.L.Y. 3933.
[168] *Stearn v Prentice Bros* [1919] 1 K.B. 394.
[169] *Bland v Yates* (1914) 58 S.J. 612.
[170] See Law Commission's recommendation in para.24: "We would abolish the defence of Act of God, which appears to be of little practical importance in this field and only to add an unnecessary complication to the law. We would also resolve any doubts which may remain in spite of the majority view in *Baker v Snell* [1908] 2 K.B. 825 as to the availability of the defence of the act of a third party, by a clear rule that this defence is not available. In view of the rationale of strict liability for special risks [see para.20] it is our view that the act of a third party is one of the circumstances against which the person creating the risk should take precautions."

animal belongs to prevent it from trespassing, if by statute or custom,[171] a right in the nature of an easement,[172] or some other agreement or prescription, that duty is imposed upon the claimant, then damages may not be recovered[173] if the duty has not been observed.

Section 5(1) of the Act preserves the common law defence by providing that **14–77** a person is not liable for the straying of his livestock causing damage, which is due wholly or in part[174] to the fault of the person suffering it. However, this defence needs to be considered in the light of subs.(6) which provides that:

"In determining whether any liability for damage under section 4 of this Act is excluded by subsection (1) of this section the damage shall not be treated as due to the fault of the person suffering it by reason only that he could have prevented it by fencing[175]; but a person is not liable under that section where it is proved that the straying of the livestock on to the land would not have occurred but for a breach by any other person being a person having an interest in the land, of a duty to fence."[176]

In these circumstances guidance may still be obtained from such authorities as the following.

ILLUSTRATIONS

Where a railway company was obliged by statute to fence its railway from the **14–78** land of adjoining occupiers and the claimant's sheep escaped from his land because his own fences were out of repair and got on to the land of a third party adjoining the railway and thence through the railway company's defective fence on to the track, where they were killed, the railway company was held not liable.[177] Where the claimant's cottage and the defendant's farm adjoined common land over which both parties enjoyed grazing rights but only the defendant exercised such right and his cattle strayed into the claimant's garden

---

[171] *Egerton v Harding* [1975] Q.B. 62 (where the defendants proved that the claimant, who occupied a country cottage, had a duty arising out of custom to fence against the common land, over which they both enjoyed grazing rights).

[172] *Crow v Wood* [1971] 1 Q.B. 77 (farms were let to individual farmers who had the right to "stray" a certain number of sheep on the moors, in Yorkshire, and who agreed to keep their fences and walls in repair).

[173] *Star v Rookesby* (1711) 1 Salk. 335 (prescription); *Singleton v Williamson* (1861) 7 H. & M. 410 (enclosure award); *Lawrence v Jenkins* (1873) L.R. 8 Q.B. 274. In *Wiseman v Booker* (1878) 3 C.P.D. 184, the liability to fence was imposed by statute on a railway company for the benefit of the defendant, and when the defendant's horses put their heads over the fence and ate the crops of the claimant, who was the tenant of the railway company, the defendant was held not liable on the grounds: (1) the claimant could not be in a better position than the railway company, (2) the damage was caused by the company's breach of the statutory duty owed to the defendant.

[174] Which is the combined effect of ss.10 and 11 and enables the court to apportion damages in an appropriate case.

[175] "Fencing" includes the construction of any obstacle designed to prevent animals from straying: s.11.

[176] This provision appears to be designed to overcome the difficulty caused by the decision and the circumstances prevailing in *Crow v Wood* [1971] 1 Q.B. 77.

[177] *Ricketts v East and West India Docks, etc., Ry* (1852) 12 C.B. 160. See also *Child v Hearn* (1874) L.R. 9 Ex. 176 (railway company bound to maintain fence—pigs got through and upset a railwayman riding a trolley—owner of pigs not liable).

through gaps in her hedge and caused damage, it was held that she was not entitled to recover damages: she had failed in her obligation to fence against the common, an obligation established by evidence of immemorial usage.[178]

14–79   In contrast, parties who occupied adjoining fields were both tenants of the same landlord and were each obliged to keep the fences on their holdings in repair under their respective tenancy agreements. Although the claimant was in breach of his obligation to fence, it was held that the defendant could not rely on the claimant's breach when some of the defendant's horses trespassed on the claimant's field and injured a colt.[179] Where a farm adjoined several allotments and shared a landlord with the allotment holders, who were bound to maintain a fence, and the farmer's cattle damaged crops in one allotment because the fence had been broken by the acts of the allotment holders, the farmer was held liable.[180] Where the defendant's sheep stayed from a moor on to the highway and thence on to the claimant's land as a result of a breach by a third party of their duty to fence, the defendant was held not liable. Although the third party's failure to fence was a wrongful act, it did not excuse the defendant as he was aware of the failure, a failure against which he could and should have guarded.[181]

14–80   **Defendant under an obligation to fence.** If the defendant was under a duty to fence, he was liable for consequential damage to his neighbour's cattle, if the duty was not discharged. So, where the claimant, the bailee of a horse, turned it into a field but, due to the dilapidated state of the fence, which the defendant was obliged to maintain, the animal fell into the defendant's field and was killed, the defendant was liable.[182] Liability also followed where the claimant's cows escaped through a gap in a fence which the defendant, by prescription, was obliged to maintain and ate yew leaves on the defendant's land, which caused them to be poisoned and die. The defendant was liable despite ignorance that the fence was broken before the cows escaped.[183] An occupier of land, under an obligation to fence against moorland cattle, including sheep, was held not bound to fence against sheep of a peculiarly wandering and active disposition, which jumped over his fence.[184]

(ii) *Straying from the highway*

14–81   At common law the occupier of premises, which adjoin a highway, was presumed to have accepted the risks that flowed from the passage of traffic along that highway.[185] So, where the defendant's ox, whilst being driven through the streets of a country town, entered the claimant's ironmonger's shop, which adjoined the highway, through its open doorway and damaged goods inside, it

---

[178] *Egerton v Harding* [1975] Q.B. 62.
[179] *Holgate v Bleazard* [1917] 1 K.B. 443.
[180] *Park v Jobson & Son* [1945] 1 All E.R. 222. A defence of leave and licence was rejected on the ground that there was no evidence that the cattle entered through any particular gap. If the claimant had broken down the fence and so let in the cattle, the defence would have succeeded.
[181] *Sutcliffe v Holmes* [1947] 1 K.B. 147.
[182] *Rooth v Wilson* (1817) 1 B. & Ald. 59.
[183] *Lawrence v Jenkins* (1873) L.R. 8 Q.B. 274.
[184] *Coaker v Willcocks* [1911] 1 K.B. 649.
[185] See further, Ch.10, para.10–287, above.

was held that the claimant was not entitled to recover damages since the escape was not the result of the defendant's negligence.[186]

Statutory recognition of this defence[187] is given by s.5(5) of the Act which **14–82** replaces the common law and provides that: "A person is not liable under section 4 of this Act where the livestock strayed from a highway and its presence there was a lawful use of the highway." The subsection is so worded that it is not restricted merely to land that adjoins the highway, from which the livestock has strayed,[188] but extends to apply to any land. Nonetheless, the "lawful use of the highway" is the right to pass and re-pass along it and not, for example, where an owner's livestock has been set to graze the verges or central reservations.

It should be noted that this statutory defence is only an exception to strict **14–83** liability under the Act and does not preclude an action succeeding based upon negligence. The common law still continues to recognise that a duty of care is owed to prevent animals straying from the highway.[189] As Lord Porter pointed out, in *Searle v Wallbank*, if animals lawfully are brought on the highway, "reasonable care must be exercised to control them".[190]

5.—Liability for Animals Straying on to Highways

Generally. Under the common law[191] there was an important exception to the **14–84** general principles of negligence. The rule in *Searle v Wallbank*[192] provided that, in the absence of special circumstances (relating to the behaviour of an animal which was known to the landowner), there was no duty to fence or maintain existing fences on land adjoining a highway so as to prevent an animal straying on to it.

The abolition of the rule in *Searle v Wallbank* represented the one radical **14–85** departure from the common law brought about by the Act. Section 8(1) provides that:

"So much of the rules of the common law relating to liability for negligence as excludes or restricts the duty which a person might owe to others to take such care as is reasonable to see that damage is not caused by animals straying on to a highway is hereby abolished."

---

[186] *Tillett v Ward* (1882) 10 Q.B.D. 17.
[187] In addition to *Tillett v Ward*, see *Gayler & Pope Ltd v B. Davies & Son Ltd* [1924] 2 K.B. 75, above.
[188] See Law Commission's recommendation, p.30, n.97.
[189] *Gayler & Pope Ltd v B. Davies & Son Ltd* [1924] 2 K.B. 75.
[190] [1947] A.C. 341 at 356. See Ch.10, para.10–283, above.
[191] See the 9th edn of this work, Ch.10, para.10–282 et seq., above for a fuller discussion of this topic. See also Harwood, "Raging Bull: Pt 2" 139 S.J. 628.
[192] [1947] A.C. 341.

As a result of the removal of this common law exception, injury or damage occasioned by an animal straying on to the highway renders its owner,[193] including the person having control of it, liable under the ordinary principles of negligence.[194] By way of example, where livestock strayed from the defendant's farm through an open gate, through which the public had a right of way, on to an abutting road and caused an accident, the defendant was found liable on the basis of a failure to assess the risk of livestock straying on to the highway. Had he done so, amongst the measures that could and should have been taken, was the installation of a self closing mechanism to the gate.[195] Section 8(2) of the Act reflects concerns that by custom or otherwise, including the question of sheer economics, many extensive parts of the country, especially the moorland areas, are completely or partially unfenced.[196]

6.—WIDER LIABILITIES AT COMMON LAW

14–86 **Other torts generally available.** Although the Animals Act 1971 abolished the old *scienter* and the even older cattle-trespass actions,[197] replacing them with strict liability, it left unaffected other areas of the law of torts relating to animals, save only for the exception, just discussed, in relation to animals straying on to the highway. As has been explained above, strict liability under the Act is independent of and distinct from strict liability under the rule in *Rylands v Fletcher*[198] as well as other torts such as trespass to the person and to chattels, nuisance[199] and negligence.[200] All of these give separate but potentially concurrent causes of action which may become necessary alternatives in a given case.[201] In many cases after the Act a keeper of an animal has been found to have been under a duty of care in negligence in relation to damage caused by it.[202] In

---

[193] In *Hoskin v Rogers, The Times*, January 25, 1985, the CA held that liability for the claimant's accident, which was caused by cattle straying on to the highway through inadequate fencing, attached itself to the cattle-owner rather than the landowner. At the time of the let of the land, the fencing had been adequate and the landowner was unaware that anything was wrong with the fencing prior to the happening of the accident.

[194] *Fardon v Harcourt-Rivington* (1932) 48 T.L.R. 215; *Pike v Wallis, The Times*, November 6, 1981. cf. the situation in *Jaundrill v Gillett, The Times*, January 30, 1996, CA for which see para.14–18, n.58, above.

[195] *Donaldson v Wilson* (2004) 148 S.J.L.B. 879, CA.

[196] For which, see Ch.10, para.10–287, above.

[197] s.1(1).

[198] See Ch.13, above, where the matter is fully discussed.

[199] para.14–04, above.

[200] In its report the Law Commission recommended that the general principles of the existing law of negligence, whereby the keeper of an animal is under a duty to prevent that animal causing injury or damage, should not be disturbed. See paras 26–28, which recommendation the Act has observed.

[201] Lord Atkin emphasised this in *Fardon v Harcourt-Rivington* (1932) 48 T.L.R. 215 when, at 217, he said: "Quite apart from the liability imposed upon the owner of animals or the persons having control of them by reason of knowledge of their propensities, there is the ordinary duty of a person to take care either that his animal or his chattel is not put to such a use as is likely to injure his neighbour—the ordinary duty to take care in the cases put upon negligence".

[202] See, e.g. *Draper v Hodder* [1972] 2 Q.B. 556, applying the dicta of Pearson L.J. in *Ellis v Johnstone* [1963] 2 Q.B. 8 at 29, as well as that of Lord Atkin in *Fardon v Harcourt-Rivington* (1932) 48 T.L.R. 215.

Scotland it has been held that the Occupiers' Liability (Scotland) Act 1960 can be invoked. Thus, where the claimant suffered injury when bitten by one of her employer's two dogs when she entered his garden to clean the windows, she succeeded both in a claim brought in employer's liability and under that Act.[203] In the latter cause of action the claim succeeded against the employer and his wife because the dogs were known to be "prone to nip" even though they had not previously attacked a stranger. Thus, just as liability can be established at common law, so should liability be established under the Occupiers' Liability Act 1957 where an occupier, by virtue of the presence of an animal which causes harm, fails to ensure that his premises are reasonably safe for lawful visitors.

Negligence as a concurrent cause of action. There is a duty to take **14-87** reasonable care to prevent damage from animals but, as a general rule there is no liability "where tame animals with no special individual mischievous propensity are lawfully let loose in the course of the ordinary use of them, and the only danger to be apprehended is from contact with other animals in places where they may all lawfully be".[204] The rule is the same as regards danger to human beings.[205] What is reasonable care depends essentially on the nature and habits of the kind of animal concerned, the circumstances of the case and the usual practice of mankind in dealing with that kind of animal. So, by way of example, a high standard of care must be required of those, such as the police, who use dogs for security purposes.[206] The facts of a case may show that the owner of an animal should have known that it was likely to cause damage, and taken reasonable steps to prevent it. If he has failed to do so and damage has resulted liability may well follow.

> "The root of this liability is negligence, and what is negligence depends on the facts with which you have to deal . . . If the possibility of danger emerging is only a mere possibility which would never occur to the mind of a reasonable man, then there is no negligence in not having taken extraordinary precautions."[207]

Lord MacMillan added:

> "In each case the question is whether there is any evidence of such carelessness in fact as amounts to negligence in law—that is, to breach of the duty to take care. To fulfil this duty the user of the road is not bound to guard against every conceivable eventuality but only against such eventualities as a reasonable man ought to foresee as being within the ordinary range of human experience."[208]

The differences between a cause of action under the Act and at common law **14-88** can be important in practice. There may be difficulties in establishing the

---

[203] *Hill v Lovett* 1992 S.L.T. 1991.
[204] *Manton v Brocklebank* [1923] 2 K.B. 212 at 232, per Atkin L.J.
[205] *Cox v Burbidge* (1863) 13 C.B.(N.S.) 430.
[206] *Gloster v Chief Constable of Greater Manchester Police* [2000] P.I.Q.R. P114 at P120, per Pill L.J.
[207] *Fardon v Harcourt-Rivington* (1932) 48 T.L.R. 215 at 216 per Lord Dunedin.
[208] *Fardon v Harcourt-Rivington* (1932) 48 T.L.R. 215 at 217.

requirements set out in s.2(2) of the Act, but not that a duty of care was owed.[209] The statutory keeper of the animal may not be covered by insurance, whereas others, who arguably owed the claimant a duty of care, are. On the other hand, if strict liability under the Act is made out, the test of remoteness of damage is more favourable than at common law.[210] It may often be wise for the claimant to protect his claim by pleading both sources of duty, in case one should fail.

ILLUSTRATIONS

14–89   In the following cases no negligence was proved: where an owner's Airedale dog, left shut up in his car parked by the kerb in a street, became so excited that it eventually smashed a window, a splinter of which struck and blinded a passing pedestrian in one eye[211]; where a dog was kept in a car confined by a leash, which prevented it from projecting its nose more than three inches over the rim of the door, and a child of five when leaning over the car was bitten[212]; when a large Newfoundland dog, roaming loose in a small garden, jumped over the garden wall, landed on the claimant's back and injured him, while he was digging a hole[213]; when a dog came out of the open gate of his owner's property, dashed across the road and, upon being frightened by an oncoming car, turned back into collision with the claimant's bicycle, knocking the claimant down[214]; when a racing greyhound, in the charge of two small boys, chased a cat, but then bit a woman who tried to rescue the cat[215]; where its owner had brought a dog into a public house, there being no duty to keep a constant watch upon it, unless there was reason to believe that it was making a nuisance of itself, which it did[216]; when a large, but well-behaved dog, owned by the tenant of an upper flat, came down the stairs unaccompanied and knocked against a woman who was coming up the stairs, and injured her.[217]

14–90   Likewise, negligence was not established: where a horse, which was being properly ridden on the highway, suddenly took fright, shied and caused an

---

[209] See, e.g. *Smith v Prendercast, The Times*, October 18, 1984, where the owner of a scrapyard had allowed a stray dog to establish its residence in his yard and had fed it but some three weeks later it had attacked a child passer-by. Having regard to the defendant's knowledge of the dog's background, his complete failure to attempt any systematic supervision and control, much less any training, of the dog amounted to negligence in all the circumstances.

[210] See para.14–37, above, and, generally, Ch.5, para.5–41, above.

[211] *Fardon v Harcourt-Rivington* (1932) 48 T.L.R. 215. The injured pedestrian's action in negligence against the dog's owner failed because the occurrence was such that "according to no reasonable standard could it be said that it ought to have been foreseen by the most careful owner of a motor with a dog in it on a highway" (per Lord Macmillan at 217). Further, whilst a person must guard against a reasonable probability of danger he was not bound to guard against a fantastic possibility. These circumstances, subject to the question of knowledge, would almost certainly now satisfy the "particular circumstances" requirement of s.2(2)(b) of the Animals Act 1971 following *Mirvahedy v Henley* [2003] 2 A.C. 491.

[212] *Sycamore v Ley* (1932) 147 L.T. 342.

[213] *Sanders v Teape & Swan* (1884) 51 L.T. 263.

[214] *Gibb v Comerford* [1942] Ir.R. 295, but cf. with the facts in *Gomberg v Smith* [1963] 1 Q.B. 25, where the owner was held to be negligent.

[215] *Toogood v Wright* [1940] 2 All E.R. 306.

[216] *Carroll v Garford* (1968) 112 S.J. 948.

[217] *Hines v Tousley* (1926) 95 L.J.K.B. 773, because there was no evidence to show how the dog had got out of the flat.

accident, whilst a motorist was in the process of overtaking it[218]; where a Limousin-cross cow placed in a field with her suckling calf attacked and injured a pedestrian using a public footpath through the field, there being a difference of expert opinion about the risk to passers-by[219]; where the claimant pedestrian was surrounded, jostled and knocked to the ground by horses whilst walking his dog, the horses being generally of good behaviour[220]; where a police dog handler in pursuit of a suspect slipped and fell as a result of which his trained police dog slipped its lead and mistakenly bit another officer. The judge described the incident as "an accident pure and simple"[221]; negligence was not made out where the claimant, an experienced runner, was running along a footpath by the side of a river when he was knocked off balance by the defendant's twelve and a half stone Great Dane, Hector, as a result of which he fell down a slope and broke his ankle. On the facts, given what was known of the dog, a reasonable man in the defendant's position would not have anticipated that physical injury to another adult park user such as the claimant would be caused by the dog coming into physical contact with him.[222]

On the other hand, in *Hines v Tousley*,[223] quoted above, Scrutton L.J. had   **14–91** occasion to add: "I reserve my opinion as to whether in other cases, where the owner of a dog is responsible for taking him into such a situation where the uncontrolled movements of the dog may cause damage, there may not be a liability on the owner of the dog." Indeed, such a case occurred when a dog, taken out into the street on a long lead, was held so loosely by its owner that it broke away from control to chase a cat, and in doing so the lead became entangled with the legs of the claimant, a woman of 73, who was thrown to the ground and injured.[224] Further, negligence was established when a three-year-old child, who was playing in the yard of his home, was savaged and severely bitten by a pack of about seven Jack Russell terrier puppies, which had escaped during their feeding time from the defendant's ungated land next door and had entered the claimant's premises, where they were accustomed to scavenge among the dustbins[225]; where an owner had been exercising two greyhounds, coupled together, in the highway near to a town at dusk so that the claimant was knocked down and injured[226]; where the defendant allowed his dog to run at large in the vicinity of a mink farm, during the whelping season, when he knew that there was a hostile reaction between mink and strange dogs.[227]

---

[218] *Haimes v Watson* [1981] R.T.R. 90, CA.
[219] *Ostle v Stapleton* [1996] 2 C.L.Y. 4443, Sachs J.
[220] *Miller v Duggan* [1996] 12 C.L.Y. 4444.
[221] *Gloster v Chief Constable of Greater Manchester Police* [2000] P.I.Q.R. P114, CA, at P120.
[222] *Jones v Whippey* [2009] EWCA Civ 452.
[223] (1926) 95 L.J.K.B. 773.
[224] *Pitcher v Martin* [1937] 3 All E.R. 918 (defendant was held liable in both nuisance and negligence).
[225] *Draper v Hodder* [1972] 2 Q.B. 556 (negligence was proved because the judge accepted expert evidence that dogs of that particular breed, when in groups, were highly dangerous and that no responsible dog breeder would allow such animals to be free to roam about uncontrolled. However, since there was no evidence that any of these puppies had ever before attacked a human being, no liability under a *scienter* action in addition could be established).
[226] *Jones v Owen* (1871) 24 L.T. 587.
[227] *Caine Fur Farms v Kokolsky* (1963) 39 D.L.R. (2d) 134.

14–92   Liability was also established: where the defendant permitted a stray dog to take up its residence in his scrapyard, without attempting any systematic supervision and control of it[228]; where he was driving a cow and calf on the highway, and the cow tossed a woman on the pavement[229]; where the defendant had tethered insecurely a pony in a stable, so that it broke loose, went into the streets of a town and caused the claimant to fall over and sustain injury[230]; for unloading from a train bullocks, excited by the journey, so that they escaped through an open gate into the streets of a town and did damage[231]; for keeping bees in unreasonable numbers, at an unreasonable place, smoking them out at an unreasonable time, so that they stung the claimant's horse which threw the claimant[232]; for supplying an unsuitable horse which bolted and threw the claimant, whom the riding stable's employee knew to be an inexperienced rider[233]; and for driving cattle four times a day along a road, bounded by the claimant's hedge, accompanied only by a boy incapable of controlling them, so that the cattle damaged the hedge, making it unsightly by pulling at and eating it.[234]

14–93   Further, where as a result of its suffering a fright when its rider had fallen off and its saddle had slipped underneath its belly, a pony in a gymkhana ran out of the ring and on to a road, thereby causing a motor collision, it was held that its straying was a foreseeable reaction by the animal in the circumstances. Hence the organisers were negligent.[235]

14–94   An attempt to fix a local authority with liability failed where a horse, whose owner was never identified, broke free from its tether at the Appleby Horse Fair and seriously injured the claimant: the suggestion that the local authority should have arranged public liability insurance to cover such a circumstance failed.[236] The defendant had no duty of care to organise the safe segregation and supervision of horses and, as such, there could be no duty of care to procure that a third party did so. Since the defendant had no duty to protect the claimant from the physical consequences of the unknown owner's negligence, it could not be just and reasonable to impose on it the more remote duty to protect the claimant against the economic consequences of not being able to enforce a judgment against the owner.

14–95   **Where the person having control is not the employee or agent of the owner.** In cases where liability is based on negligence, the owner is not liable for

---

[228] *Smith v Prendergast, The Times*, October 18, 1984, CA.
[229] *Pinn v Rew* (1916) 32 T.L.R. 451 (before meeting the claimant, the cow had met a dog, which she tossed. There was evidence that a cow with a calf might become dangerous on meeting a dog).
[230] *Deen v Davies* [1935] K.B. 282.
[231] *Howard v Bergin, O'Connor & Co* [1925] 2 I.R. 110.
[232] *O'Gorman v O'Gorman* [1903] 2 I.R. 573.
[233] *Collins v Richmond Rodeo Riding and Amundson* (1966) 56 D.L.R. (2d) 428. Similarly, *Carrera v Honey Church* (1983) 32 S.A.S.R. 511.
[234] *Allford v Maton* (1936) 3 L.J.C.C.R. 167.
[235] *Bativala v West* [1970] 1 Q.B. 716 (it was also held that the rule in *Searle v Wallbank* had no application, since the animal was under direct human control). For highway collision, involving animals, generally, see Ch.10, paras 10–281–10–286, above.
[236] *Glaister v Appleby-in-Westmorland Town Council* [2010] P.I.Q.R. P6, CA.

the negligence of someone who is not his employee or agent. So, where the defendant employed an auctioneer to hold a sale of horses in his yard and the claimant, attending the sale, was kicked by a horse, which was being run up and down, allegedly, in too narrow a space, it was held that the defendant was not liable for the negligence of the auctioneer, because he was not the defendant's employee.[237]

Liability in negligence may be independent of scienter. Where negligence   **14–96** is relied upon a question may arise whether or not the defendant is liable for damage caused by a mischievous propensity in his animal, not known to the defendant. The cases suggest that it is not necessary for the claimant to prove that the defendant had knowledge of propensity. The principle has been stated thus:

> "I agree that there may be cases in which a defendant may be liable for the bite of a dog even if the dog does not belong to the class of ferocious animals, if it be proved that the dog is put in such a position that a reasonable man would know that it was likely to cause danger and therefore he ought to regard himself as under an obligation to do something by way of precaution."[238]

ILLUSTRATIONS

Where a pony attached to a milk cart was left unattended for an hour-and-   **14–97** a-half, became restive and put its feet on the footpath attacking the claimant as she walked on the path, the owners were held liable in spite of a finding by the jury that the owners had no knowledge of any propensity on the part of the pony to attack human beings.[239] Where a bull attacked a cow in an auction yard, it was no answer to a claim in negligence to plead absence of knowledge of propensity.[240] Of course, where the defendant does have such knowledge, the claimant's task is rendered all the easier so, where a mare, known to be of an excitable and nervous disposition, was left unattended on a towpath, where it kicked a man leading a quiet horse pulling a barge, the owner was held liable.[241]

Damage may be too remote. Although negligence is proved, absence of   **14–98** knowledge of propensity may nevertheless result in the claimant failing on the ground that the damage sustained is too remote.[242] Where the defendants' horse, known to be of vicious temperament, was negligently left unattended in the claimant's yard and kicked and killed one of the claimant's employees as he passed behind it, the defendants were held not liable on the basis that the accident was not the natural result of the negligence.[243] The result would, no doubt, have been different if the defendants had done something to disturb the horse as the

---

[237] *Walker v Crabb* (1916) 33 T.L.R. 119.
[238] per Greer L.J. in *Sycamore v Ley* (1932) 147 L.T. 342 at 345. See also *Fardon v Harcourt-Rivington* (1932) 48 T.L.R. 215.
[239] *Rose v George Henry Collier Ltd* [1939] W.N. 19.
[240] *Aldham v United Dairies (London) Ltd* [1940] 1 K.B. 507.
[241] *Hinckes v Harris* (1921) 65 S.J. 781.
[242] For remoteness of damage see Ch.5, paras 5–01–5–41, above.
[243] *Bradley v Wallaces Ltd* [1913] 3 K.B. 629.

employee passed behind it.[244] Similarly, where a bullock, which was being unloaded at a butcher's premises, was negligently allowed to escape and, thereafter, attacked a cyclist, the defendant was held not liable. The damage was held not to flow naturally from the negligence in the absence of proof of a known mischievous propensity.[245] The owner of sheep was acquitted of blame when his sheep communicated disease to other sheep due to his negligence, since he did not know that his sheep were suffering from disease.[246]

---

[244] See *Abbott v Freeman* (1876) 35 L.T. (N.S.) 783, where the facts negatived negligence.
[245] *Lathall v Joyce & Son* [1939] 3 All E.R. 854.
[246] *Cooke v Waring* (1863) 2 H. & C. 332. Otherwise where the sheep were trespassing, see paras 14–60–14–64, above.

CHAPTER 15

PRODUCT LIABILITY

1.—CONSUMER PROTECTION

General introduction. Product liability[1] means civil liability for damage and **15–01** loss suffered or injury sustained, or both, caused by a defect or defects in a product consumed. The use of the word "product" is intended to refer to "goods", that is, to some material thing and not to a service, or other process provided as between one person and another. The subject-matter of the topic spreads right across the familiar traditional boundaries of the law of contract and the law of torts, as well as those of the criminal law.

Prior to 1893, there was little guidance available or protection offered by the **15–02** common law to the consumer. Indeed, the rule was *caveat emptor*—let the buyer beware—which placed the legal burden firmly on the buyer of goods to satisfy himself that whatever was purchased was neither unsafe for use nor of sub-standard quality, but was suitable for the purpose. If the buyer failed by contract to make alternative, adequate arrangements, which would protect in the event of the goods manifesting themselves to be defective, dangerous or otherwise useless, he was usually left without redress.

A significant change to the common law first appeared with the passing of the **15–03** Sale of Goods Act 1893,[2] whereby certain conditions were implied in the contract of sale of a product. Thus, where the buyer was injured or suffered loss

---

[1] "'Products Liability' has become an accepted term of art in this field", Royal Commission on Civil Liability and Compensation for Personal Injury, Vol.1, Ch.22, para.1193.
[2] The law relating to the sale of goods is consolidated in the Sale of Goods Act 1979, which replaced the whole of the Sale of Goods Act 1893, whilst retaining the basic structure of the earlier statute.

by a product, which he had bought, generally[3] he could rely upon a breach by the seller of an implied condition as to compliance with description, fitness for purpose, merchantable quality and/or conformity with the sample. In such an event, under the contract of sale, the seller was strictly liable if the goods did not reach the standard required under the statute. This was so despite the fact that the seller had not caused the defect, had not had the opportunity to discover it and had taken every reasonable precaution before the sale.[4] Clearly, the limitation of the 1893 Act was that, whilst it did provide a buyer in the course of a business with a sure remedy, it afforded no protection or relief to any other "non-business" buyer or any consumer who had not acquired a contractual interest in the defective product, for example, members of the buyer's family[5] and the buyer's donee.[6]

15–04   In 1932 a milestone was reached with the decision of the House of Lords in *Donoghue v Stevenson*.[7] By a majority of three to two, it was held that there are circumstances, quite apart from contract and without reference to any special rule concerning dangerous chattels, wherein a person owes a duty of care in tort in respect of defective products. Accordingly, where the ultimate consumer has sustained personal injury and/or has suffered loss and damage that was attributable to a defect in the thing consumed, an action lies in tort against its negligent manufacturer.

---

[3] Subject always to the inclusion in the contract of sale of any valid exemption clause. After the Unfair Contract Terms Act 1977 came into force on February 1, 1978 (s.31(1)), further limits were imposed on the extent to which civil liability for breach of contract, negligence or other breach of duty, each arising "in the course of a business," could be avoided by means of contract terms or otherwise.

[4] The seller, probably the retailer, if prudent would have provided for an indemnity under the contract of sale entered into between his supplier and himself. Likewise, similar indemnities would be contained in each of the transactions between the middlemen up the chain to the product's manufacturer. However all contractual terms which purport to exclude or limit the amount of liability are now subject to the provisions of the Unfair Contract Terms Act 1977.

[5] *Preist v Last* [1903] 2 K.B. 148, where an article, such as a hot-water bottle, is bought by one member of the family for general use by another member of the family, although cf. *Jackson v Horizon Holidays Ltd* [1975] 1 W.L.R. 1468. For criticisms of this decision of the CA which permitted the claimant, who had contracted for a disastrous family holiday in Ceylon, to recover damages both for his own discomfort and distress and that suffered by his wife and children, see *Woodar Investment Development Ltd v Wimpey Construction UK Ltd* [1980] 1 W.L.R. 277 (per Lord Wilberforce, at 283, 284 and per Lord Keith at 297).

[6] *Donoghue v Stevenson* [1932] A.C. 562. It should be borne in mind that even if the friend, who was the original buyer of the ginger beer, allegedly contaminated with the remains of a decomposed snail, had resold the bottled drink to the pursuer, there would have been no implied condition of merchantable quality or fitness for purpose in such contract, because the re-sale was not "in the course of a business". See now Sale of Goods Act 1979 s.14(2), (3).

[7] See above. See, further, paras 15–57–15–126, below and Ch.2, paras 2–07–2–28, above. Until this decision it was doubtful at common law whether the transferor of a product, in the absence of any contractual relationship with the ultimate transferee, owed him a duty of care unless, of course, the thing belonged to the class of "dangerous chattels" or was actually known to the transferor to be dangerous. By the 1950s this class of "dangerous chattels" had ceased to be of any significance, for which see *A.C. Billings & Sons Ltd v Riden* [1958] A.C. 240. The only relevance today of the old distinction between products "dangerous in themselves" and other products is that the greater the potential danger which is inherent in the product in question, the greater the need to match it with more stringent precautions to be taken in order to protect the consumer against that danger. See per Lord Macmillan in *Read v J. Lyons & Co Ltd* [1947] A.C. 156 at 172, 173.

Over the following half century, tortious liability in respect of defective   **15–05**
products continued to progress as public concern to protect consumers grew. In
order to keep up the pace of change and development, Parliament was active also
in strengthening the contractual rights of buyers,[8] or other transferees[9] of goods
and services[10] and in enhancing safety standards by use of the criminal law.[11]

In the meanwhile a number of proposals were put forward for a regime of strict   **15–06**
liability,[12] but negligence continued to remain as the basis of liability at common
law. The report of the Royal Commission, under Lord Pearson,[13] did not
recommend any replacement of negligence as the basis at large of tortious
liability. On the other hand, it did recommend that producers should become
strictly liable in tort[14] for death or personal injury, caused by defective
products,[15] "subject to a cut-off period of ten years from the circulation of the
product."[16]

In 1985[17] there was a further development when the Council of the European   **15–07**
Communities issued a Directive,[18] which required the Member States to
implement a regime of strict liability for defective products. In order to fulfil its

---

[8] i.e. the Sale of Goods Act 1979; see also n.2, above. See also the Supply of Goods to Consumers
Regulations 2002 (SI 2002/3045); Lawson,"Consumers acquire more rights" (2003) Bus. L.R. 24(5),
114.
[9] For all practical purposes the duties of a creditor under a contract of hire purchase are the same as
those of a seller; see the Supply of Goods (Implied Terms) Act 1973, as amended by the Consumer
Credit Act 1974.
[10] See the Supply of Goods and Services Act 1982, which implies similar stringent terms in other
forms of contract for the transfer of goods such as exchange and hire of goods.
[11] The Consumer Protection Act 1961 and the Consumer Safety Act 1978, both of which have been
repealed and replaced by the Consumer Protection Act 1987. It is to be observed that by s.41 of the
1987 Act, which came into force on October 1, 1987 (the Consumer Protection Act 1987
(Commencement No.1) Order 1987 (SI 1987/1680)) if an obligation imposed by safety regulations
is breached, an action for damages against the manufacturers can be brought, which can be based on
breach of statutory duty without the injured claimant having to establish negligence in order to
succeed.
[12] Notably the Strasbourg Convention on Products Liability, which was prepared by the Council of
Europe in January 1977, and the Third Draft Directive of the EEC, approved in September 1979. See,
further on this topic, Miller, *Product Liability and Safety Encyclopaedia* (Butterworths, 1979), as well
as the Report of the English and Scottish Law Commissions of Liability for Defective Products, Law
Com. No.82, Cmnd.6831 (1977).
[13] Cmnd. 7054 (1978). See n.1, above.
[14] The form of strict liability, which was preferred, was that one advanced by the Strasbourg
Convention, rather than the Third Draft Directive of the EEC, n.12, above.
[15] See n.1, above and, further, Vol.1, Ch.22, para.1236. See, generally, Giliker, "Strict liability for
defective products" (2003) Bus. L.R. 24(4) 87; Hunneyball, "The important distinction between
products that fail and the defective" L.L.I.D. 2004, December 24, 5.
[16] ibid. para.1269.
[17] July 25, 1985.
[18] 85/374/EEC. It was in the mid-1970s that the first draft was circulated but it was not until 1985,
after much debate and amendment, that a final compromise was reached between Member States. The
basis for agreement was to permit individual members to have a choice by means of derogation from
certain provisions, which involved "development risks" (see para.15–39 et seq., below), the financial
ceiling on quantum of damages and whether agricultural produce should be exempted. There is to be
a review of the derogations in 1995 to see if complete harmonisation can be achieved.

obligations under the Treaty of Rome, the United Kingdom responded by giving effect to this Directive in the form of the Consumer Protection Act 1987.[19]

15–08   It is important to bear in mind that neither the Act nor the Directive has deprived litigants of any of the other remedies at law open to them as regards product liability. In fact, such remedies remain untouched and are effective still, if and when chosen to be pursued.[20] What has been gained is the provision of a new additional remedy based upon strict liability,[21] which many an injured ultimate consumer may prefer to follow. Hence, although this a book on negligence, it is considered appropriate to deal first with the provisions of the Consumer Protection Act 1987 which, in most cases, is likely to be the remedy of choice. In turn, each other alternative or additional existing remedy will be considered below.

2.—GENERAL PRINCIPLES OF LIABILITY

(A) Under the Consumer Protection Act 1987: Part I "Product Liability"

15–09   **Generally.**[22] As has been pointed out above, the EEC Directive was designed to give uniformity with regard to liability for defective products throughout the Community.[23] By virtue of its treaty obligations the United Kingdom had to legislate to bring product liability law into alignment, thereby enhancing the rights given to compensate persons for damage caused by defective products. In the result, Parliament passed the Consumer Protection Act 1987, Pt 1 of which, inter alia, was implemented on March 1, 1988.[24]

15–10   **Interpretation.** Section 1(1) provides:

"This Part shall have effect for the purpose of making such provision as is necessary in order to comply with the product liability Directive and shall be construed accordingly".

---

[19] c.43, which received the Royal Assent on May 15, 1987.

[20] See, for example, the Employer's Liability (Defective Equipment) Act 1969 (compensation to employees injured by equipment which is defective other than by reason of the negligence of the employer) and the Vaccine Damage Payments Act 1979 (fixed-sum compensation payable to vaccine induced disablement of 80% or more).

[21] The emphasis is on *strict* liability, since it is by no means absolute. See further Ch.13, paras 13–01–13–03, above.

[22] See Macdonald, "Product Liability" L.Ex. 2001 Apr. 20; Lawson, "The Consumer Protection Act 1987-recent cases" J.P. 2006, 170 (29), 544; Mark, "Pitfalls in product liability" J.P.I. Law 2007, 2, 141. See also The General Product Safety Regulations 2005 which came into force on October 1st 2006 implementing European Parliament and Council Directive 2001/95. See Freeman and Birkinshaw, "Product safety: one year on" P.L.C. 2006, 17 (10), 15.

[23] See *Skov AEG v Bilka Lavprisvarehus A/S* [2006] 2 C.M.L.R. 16, ECJ (a preliminary ruling by the ECJ to the effect that the Directive was intended to bring about a total harmonisation of the laws of Member States and it was not thereby open to Denmark to apply earlier case law which went beyond the Directive by imposing no fault liability on the suppliers of defective goods as well as the producers of such goods).

[24] By the Consumer Protection Act 1987 (Commencement No.1) Order 1987 (SI 1987/1680).

Therefore, in the event of conflict arising concerning the interpretation of any provision of the Act, the court, for the purpose of deciding the point, is required to refer to the Directive itself, which sets out the guiding principles in the form of Articles.[25]

Definition of "product." "Product" is defined in s.1(2) as meaning: **15–11**

"any goods or electricity and . . . includes a product which is comprised in another product, whether by virtue of being a component part or raw material or otherwise."

In turn the word "goods" is defined as "including substances, growing crops and things comprised in land by virtue of being attached to it and any ship,[26] aircraft or vehicle."[27] The definition extends to primary agricultural produce and game.[28] But for liability to be established the defective product must be supplied[29] to another in the course of his business.[30]

In effect, all manufactured or processed goods which are supplied by way of business are included in the definition, as well as all the raw materials, movables and component parts built into the finished article or construction. Thus, all the materials put into a building or other structure[31] are covered, should the finished object either subside or collapse, as a result of some defect in the manufacture of an ingredient or component, and cause injury. The same must apply surely to individual pieces of equipment installed so as to become fixtures within both immovables, such as the hot-water supply and other forms of heating systems in a private dwelling-house, and movables, such as the engine of an aircraft or the hydraulics of a motor vehicle.[32] Water, gas and electricity are included, but as regards the latter the defect must exist at the time the energy is generated[33] and not some breakdown in the distribution system. Waste products will probably be covered, particularly if sold in the course of business as a by-product for

---

[25] The Act must be construed so as to be consistent with the Directive: *European Commission v United Kingdom (re Product Liability Directive)*, Case C–300/95 [1997] E.C.R. I–2649 although Directives, generally, only have a horizontal effect against emanations of the state: *Faccini Dori v Recreb S.r.l.* [1995] All E.R. (E.C.) 1. Nevertheless, it has been accepted without argument that, in the event of apparent inconsistency, the language of the Directive should be followed: *A v National Blood Authority* [2001] 3 All E.R. 289.
[26] A ship is also "equipment" within the meaning of the Employer's Liability (Defective Equipment) Act 1969, in respect of which see Ch.11, above, paras 11–55–11–64, and *Coltman v Bibby Tankers Ltd* [1988] A.C. 276.
[27] s.45(1).
[28] Since the repeal of s.2(4) by SI 2000/2771 passed to implement 1999/34/EC.
[29] For the extensive meaning of "supply", see s.46.
[30] For defences, see s.4 and paras 15–36–15–46, below.
[31] para.15-13 and n.43, below. The land, buildings and fixed structures in themselves are not products. Although the builder would not be liable strictly under the Act for shoddy workmanship, causing damage, he would be liable under the Defective Premises Act 1972 and the law of negligence, for which see Ch.8, paras 8–123–8–137, above.
[32] See art.2 of the Directive.
[33] See s.4(2). Of course, the industry is subject to certain duties to maintain electricity supplies, breach of which may become actionable under other statutes. See, generally, Ch.13, para.13–153, above.

recycling or other use.[34] It extends to transfused blood, the product which lead to the leading case on the Act.[35]

15–12   **Exclusions.** Prior to December 4, 2000[36] primary agricultural produce and game, defined[37] as meaning "any produce of the soil,[38] of stockfarming or of fisheries", did not fall within the definition of product if they had not gone through an industrial process.[39] Thus, the farmer who sold animals and produce which were defective because they were infected or contaminated would not be liable but once the animal or produce reached a processor and processed it into food, it would become a product within the meaning of the Act and a consumer suffering food poisoning thereby would be able to pursue a claim under s.2(1).[40]

15–13   Services are not products, hence the provision of information or advice,[41] simpliciter, in the absence of some physical product relevant to it, is outside the scope of the Act.[42] Similarly, land and fixtures on land do not fall within its provisions.[43]

15–14   Disruptions in the supply of electricity brought about through breakdowns in the system of distribution do not come within the scope of the Act,[44] because for the electricity to become a "product," there must be established a defect at the time of its generation.

---

[34] If the producer of the waste, instead of selling, has to pay others to dispose of it for him, such could still be included. On the other hand, in respect of the mere discharge of waste products, the producer will not be liable under Pt 1 of the Act for the simple reason that there is no "supply". Nevertheless, he is likely to be held liable for nuisance or under the strict liability doctrine of *Rylands v Fletcher*, for which see Ch.13, above. In addition he is certain to find himself incurring penalties for breach of the criminal provisions under the Control of Pollution Act 1974.

[35] *A v National Blood Authority* [2001] 3 All E.R. 289.

[36] art.2 of the Directive and ss.1 and 2(4) repealed by SI 2000/2771.

[37] s.1(2).

[38] "Soil" necessarily is associated with agriculture, as the usual growing medium, but produce nowadays can be and is grown sometimes by artificial methods which common sense dictates should be treated in the same manner.

[39] "Industrial process" was not defined: it is thought that the conversion into food by canning would obviously constitute a process but normal harvesting, washing, cleaning and packing would not.

[40] The thinking behind this approach seems to have been that neither farmers nor fishermen should be strictly liable for defects which are beyond their control, such as caused by the long-term dangers from the use of certain artificial fertilisers and pest-control chemicals, natural infestations and pollution. By way of contrast, the processor is at a distinct advantage in that he can carry out appropriate tests to discover defects at any stage of the processing procedure and, where necessary, can eliminate them before supplying to a consumer.

[41] Any redress for "bad advice" will lie instead under the rule in *Hedley Byrne & Co Ltd v Heller & Partners Ltd* [1964] A.C. 465. See Ch.2, paras 2–166–2–168, above.

[42] The giving of instructions in connection with the use of a product clearly is distinguishable and if it be misleading it could render the product defective when it would be perfectly safe otherwise. For a discussion of analogous issues in relation to "goods" under the Sale of Goods Act 1979, see *St Albans District Council v ICL* [1996] 4 All E.R. 481, C.A, Sir Iain Glidewell at 493. Note, however, Tettenborn [1986] C.L.J. 389 and Whittaker (1989) 105 L.Q.R. 125.

[43] However, see para.15–11, n.31, above, for the contrasts.

[44] See n.33, above.

Although the Pearson Report[45] recommended that human organs and blood   **15–15**
should be treated as "products", early drafts of the Directive expressly sought to
exclude them. In the final version no express reference to them is made. However
there is no reason, in an appropriate case, why human blood or tissue should not
be regarded as a product and blood was so regarded in *A v National Blood
Authority* where claimants sought damages after their infection with hepatitis C
contracted from blood and blood products used in blood transfusions.[46]

Definition of "defect." "Defect" is defined in s.3(1):   **15–16**

> "there is a defect in a product . . . if the safety of the product is not such as persons
> generally are entitled to expect: and for those purposes 'safety' in relation to a product,
> shall include safety with respect to products comprised in that product and safety in the
> context of risks of damage to property, as well as in the context of risks of death or
> personal injury."

Defects can exist in different guises. The product by its very nature may be
highly dangerous[47] or, if misused, may then become dangerous.[48] In either case
the failure to give adequate clear instructions as to careful use or the absence of
proper warnings against misuse or abuse of it will cause it to become defective,[49]
although if the risk is so notorious, such as the risk of scalding from piping hot
drinks in disposable cups, no such warning was necessary.[50] The product may
become defective, because it contains some foreign matter accidentally (or
deliberately)[51] introduced to it at some stage in the manufacturing process, which
includes the packaging in its sealed container. There may be defects in the
product's design, which cause the product to break down or otherwise to fail in
its operation when put to the intended use. No distinctions are drawn by the Act
between the different categories of defect. But, for the purposes of Pt 1, a product
is deemed to be defective when it fails to provide *safety* which "persons
generally are entitled to expect".[52] It must follow that the essence of strict
liability under the statute is whether the presence of any defect in the product
makes it unsafe. So, shoddy goods, which may well disappoint the consumer as

---

[45] See n.1, above, Vol.1, Ch.22, para.1276.
[46] [2001] 3 All E.R. 289. See below, para.15–17.
[47] Because of its poisonous, explosive or other hazardous dangerous characteristics. Concentrated
sulphuric acid would be an example of a product with all these traits.
[48] A bacon slicer, installed in a grocer's shop.
[49] See n.47, above, e.g. in order to dilute such an acid, the only safe way to do so is for the acid to
be added to the water and never the water to the acid.
[50] e.g. *B v McDonald's Restaurants Ltd* [2002] EWHC 490 applying *A v National Blood Authority*
[2001] 3 All E.R. 289 at 312.
[51] i.e. sabotage.
[52] s.3(1). See, e.g. *Abouzaid v Mothercare Ltd, The Times*, February 20, 2001, CA (where an
elasticated strap attached to one of the defendant's products recoiled striking the claimant in the eye,
the absence of a record of any comparable accident at the time of supply in 1990 excused the
defendant from a finding of negligence but the product was defective within the meaning of s.3 of the
1987 Act); however in *Richardson v LRC Products Ltd* [2000] P.I.Q.R. P164 (condom which failed
during sexual intercourse, leading to unwanted pregnancy) it was held that a consumer could not
expect a condom to be fail proof.

being hopelessly unfit for their purpose or, even, may be unmerchantable but are nonetheless "safe", cannot be brought within the ambit of s.3.[53]

15–17   **Expectation of consumers.** The test of safety must be interpreted in terms of the expectation of consumers. In *A v National Blood Authority*,[54] it was held that this was a reference to the legitimate expectation of the public (in that case uncontaminated blood) as opposed to its actual expectation (that despite all reasonable precautions being taken, some blood would be contaminated): "Their legitimate expectation is as to the safety of the product (or not)".[55] In order to decide what persons generally are entitled to expect in relation to a product, s.3(2) requires that the court shall take into account "all the circumstances" which are to include:

> "(a) the manner in which, and purposes for which, the product has been marketed, its get-up, the use of any mark in relation to the product and any instructions for, or warnings[56] with respect to doing or refraining from doing anything with or in relation to the product[57];
> (b) what might reasonably be expected to be done with or in relation to the product[58]; and
> (c) the time when the product was supplied by its producer to another[59];
>
> and nothing in this section shall require a defect to be inferred from the fact alone that the safety of a product which is supplied after that time is greater than the safety of the product in question."[60]

As technology grows and production standards improve doubtlessly public expectation will do the same, but a product must not be judged with hindsight

---

[53] But the buyer would have a remedy in contract in such circumstances under the Sale of Goods Act 1979. See further paras 15–50–15–56, below.

[54] [2001] 3 All E.R. 289, 334–339.

[55] *A v National Blood Authority* [2002] 3 All E.R. 289, 334 at 335.

[56] See *Worsley v Tambrands Ltd* [2000] P.I.Q.R. P95 (although the packaging on the defendant's tampons when sold in the US was of better design, a leaflet included in the packets sold in the UK did not fall below the standard which persons generally might expect and gave sufficient warning of possible adverse effects from the product's use).

[57] Marketing is the way in which the product is presented to the public and clearly has an effect as regards the impact on a person's expectations. In its widest concept marketing involves packaging and labelling together with all proper instructions and warnings, especially when any danger is not apparent on the face of the product. Any marks will disclose the standards attained and all service manuals, advertising material, brochures, etc., will add to expectations.

[58] This provision concentrates on what likely misuse of the product reasonably should be anticipated by the producer. This is wider than what the product was designed to fulfil. By itself improper use is not a defect in a product but where there is the likelihood of improper use of a product, which carried with it some hidden danger, either the hazard ought to be avoided by a change in design (e.g. child-proof stoppers on bottles to contain prescribed drugs) or, if this cannot be achieved, adequate warnings must be given as an alternative.

[59] The relevant time is the time of supply by the producer and not the time subsequently of supply to the ultimate consumer.

[60] Without this provision there would be no protection and it would become incumbent on producers to call in all their older products, in order to carry out modifications and improvements each time some new safety method was discovered or device was invented and adapted for fitting to new models.

and found to be defective, merely because the like products subsequently become even safer, as a result of such developments.

The working of the Act can be illustrated by *A v National Blood Authority*[61]   **15–18** where claimants sought damages after their infection with hepatitis C, contracted after receiving blood transfusions from infected blood products. It was decided that, in considering whether a product was defective, the first step must be to identify the harmful characteristic which allegedly caused the claimants' injury. Then the court would consider whether the product was standard or non-standard, which involved a comparison between it and other products of that type produced by the defendant: if the respect in which the offending product differed included the harmful characteristic then it was to be treated as non-standard. If it was non-standard, the primary issue was whether the public at large accepted it as such, that is accepted that a proportion of such products would be defective. Considerations appropriate to common law negligence, such as the avoidability of the harmful characteristic, the impracticability of precautions and the utility of the product to society were all irrelevant. Liability would ordinarily follow, subject to a defence under the Act being established, if the product was non-standard in a harmful way and the public did not accept that a proportion of such products would be defective. On the facts, the judge was satisfied that at the material time the public was entitled to expect that blood for transfusion was free from infection and it was not accepted that a proportion would be contaminated. It was irrelevant that avoiding the risk of infected blood was impossible of attainment. The defendants' contention that it was not legitimate for the public to expect the unattainable was rejected.[62]

Who can sue? Other than a reference in s.5(5), which is to a person with an   **15–19** interest in property, the Act is silent on this matter.[63] Since the whole topic concerns consumer protection and no class of persons has been excluded specifically, then, where a defect in a product either wholly or partly has caused

---

[61] [2001] 3 All E.R. 289. See also *X v Schering Health Care Ltd* [2002] EWHC 1420: after hearing detailed statistical evidence, the court concluded, on a balance of probabilities, that claims for damages for injury alleged to result from taking third generation oral contraceptive pills could not be sustained since it was not proved that the pills carried an increased risk of injury.

[62] For the alternative argument that there was a defence under art.7 of the Directive (the state of scientific or technical knowledge), see para.15–43, below. See further, *Pollard v Tesco Stores Ltd* [2006] EWCA Civ 393: a claim on behalf of a child who was just over a year old and became seriously ill after he apparently removed the cap of a plastic bottle containing dishwasher powder and thereby gained access to the contents. The trial judge found for the claimant on the basis that the cap had less resistance than required by the British Standard, but an appeal was allowed: it was held that there was no mandatory requirement for a child resistant top for such a container; further the manufacturer did not warrant that the container met all design standards and all that consumers would expect was that the bottle would be more difficult to open than if it had an ordinary screw top.

[63] For the reasons why relatively few people claim compensation under the Act for injury from defective products see article: Harriet Hall, "Unsafe Products" [1996] *Adviser*, 53. It is assumed that the abnormally sensitive claimant does not have a claim against a producer under the 1987 Act by analogy with the common law and the Sale of Goods Act 1979. Thus, where a defective garment caused dermatitis in a claimant with abnormally sensitive skin, the seller was afforded a defence: *Griffiths v Peter Conway Ltd* [1939] 1 All E.R. 685.

damage,[64] including personal injury or death, either the victim or his personal representative can sue under the Act. This is subject to two qualifications, namely that the product alleged to have been defective was supplied after March 1, 1988,[65] and in the course of a business.[66] Further, if the victim is a baby who had sustained pre-natal damage in its mother's womb, an action can be brought on its behalf after its live birth.[67]

A victim does not have to establish any proprietary interest in the defective product itself, provided the damage was of the type envisaged by the Act.

15–20   **Who can be held liable?** Article 3 of the Directive intended to give a very wide definition to the term "producer" by including those other persons who should be treated as if they were a producer, too. Doubtless the reasoning behind this was to provide the victim with an easily identifiable defendant or choice of defendants to sue in an appropriate case as being responsible to him for putting the defective product in question into circulation. This left to those persons who were involved in the chain that stretched from manufacture of the finished product to the supply, to work out between themselves where and upon whom the final liability should fall,[68] such matters being of no concern to the victim or the success of his action for damages.

15–21   This principle has been implemented by the Act but in a different form. It has been done first by restricting the provisions of strict liability to the product's manufacturer or processor and, then, by extending such liability to further classes of persons. These latter thus may be treated just as if they were producers, even though they were not involved actually in any manufacturing or processing at all.

It would seem that generally persons such as a retailer and those who carry out works of repair to or the installation of products of others, thereby providing services only, are outside the scope of the Act.[69]

15–22   **Producers.** By s.2(2)(a) liability primarily lies with the "producer of the product". Section 1(2) defines a "producer" as:

---

[64] Where a defect in a product results in damage to property, including land, compensation under the Act is only recoverable if the damage exceeds £275 in value and the property concerned is not used for business purposes, i.e. it is for private use or occupation: see s.5(3), (4).

[65] s.50(7). For the commencement date of Pt 1 of the Act, see para.15–09, n.24, above.

[66] See s.4(1)(c)(i) and "defences", paras 15–31–15–46, below.

[67] s.6(3).

[68] i.e. whether by way of indemnities or by sharing through contributions.

[69] See *Skov AEG v Bilka Lavprisvarehus A/S* [2006] 2 C.M.L.R. 16, ECJ, n. 23, above, in which the ECJ explained the reason for restricting no fault liability to the producer of defective goods, *i.e.* to avoid multiple actions where there was a chain of supply and thereby reduce costs. While Member States could not impose no fault liability other than on the producer (or a supplier where the producer could not be identified), they were not prevented from applying their own provisions where the liability was fault based. So, within our own jurisdiction, a supplier may be liable to another supplier or to a consumer where supply gave rise to a breach of a duty of care, or of contract. See ss.3 (paras 15–50–15–56) and 4 (paras 15–57–15–126) of this chapter, below, for alternative remedies, which are preserved by s.2(6). See, also, para.15–48, n.41, below.

"(a) the person[70] who manufactured it[71];

(b) in the case of a substance which has not been manufactured but has been won or abstracted, the person who won or abstracted it[72];

(c) in the case of a product which has not been manufactured, won or abstracted but essential characteristics of which are attributable to an industrial or other process having been carried out (for example, in relation to agricultural produce), the person who carried out that process".[73]

Persons holding themselves out as producers. By s.2(2)(b), liability additionally falls on: **15–23**

"any person who, by putting his name on the product or using a trade mark or other distinguishing mark in relation to the product, has held himself out to be the producer of the product".

This provision will apply to a manufacturer who causes another to manufacture a product which is then marketed under the exclusive name of the former. Whether the provision applies to the "own-brander", typically one of the national supermarket chains, remains controversial[74] and will depend on the construction of the words "had held himself out to be the producer". It may depend upon the impact on the reasonable consumer and his likely reaction to the product's presentation.[75]

Importers. By s.2(2)(c) liability also will fall on: **15–24**

"any person who has imported the product into a member State from a place outside the member States in order, in the course of any business of his, to supply it to another".

In the light of the enormous amount of consumer goods which are imported from abroad daily, relief becomes readily available to the victim who can sue the

---

[70] i.e. the manufacturer, including, vicariously, his employees. Ch.3, above, paras 3–98–3–206, for vicarious liability, generally.

[71] art.3(1) of the Directive refers, inter alia, to the "manufacturer of a finished product", as well as the "manufacturer of a component part". It must follow that the person who assembles together in order to create some finished product all its components, bought in from other sources, becomes a producer, too, equally with the other producers who have produced such components individually. The victim has the choice of being able to sue all such producers and, under s.2(5) he can rely upon the principle of their joint and several liability in respect of the finished product to satisfy his judgment.

[72] e.g. by mineral and coal mining; drilling for oil and gas; extracting clay, gravel or sand from beds and pits; or drawing up underground water.

[73] e.g. food processors producing frozen foods from agricultural products; refiners, whose industrial processes in working on extracted minerals produce changes in the essential characteristics and an end-product, such as petroleum spirits from the crude oil won.

[74] See e.g. *Clerk & Lindsell on Torts* (19th edn 2006), at para.11–75 where it is suggested that an "own-brander" may be subject to the more limited liability to name its source of supply.

[75] The ability to sue the "own-brander", of course, would afford the consumer added protection where the manufacturer, for whatever reason, was unable to satisfy a judgment.

importer of the defective product, so that he is spared the inconvenience of identifying and suing successfully the foreign manufacturer in the courts of his domicile with the risks of obtaining a barren judgment, too, at the end of the day.

15–25   **Suppliers.** The plain fact that a defective product has been supplied to another does not of itself bring a claim within the Act. So, normally, a supplier, which includes a distributor and a retailer, will not be liable under its provisions. However, by the nature of human affairs, there is always the possibility of a supplier not responding to inquiries directed to him by an injured consumer, who does not have to be the person to whom the supply was originally made, who is desirous of suing a producer which he is unable to identify. Thus, as long as a producer continues to remain anonymous, the victim's rightful claim would be frustrated. Since most products are perfectly capable of being traced back to their origins, the Act makes special provisions for this eventuality by making the supplier himself liable, in lieu of the unknown producer of the defective product.[76] In this way the victim's right to compensation is not denied him, because he can sue any supplier and not just the one which had supplied it directly to him, whenever there is a failure to identify along the chain of supply.

These provisions as to strict liability both in relation to each producer dealt with above and to the supplier, who is unable or unwilling to identify such producer, do not apply to a person in respect of any defect in any game or agricultural produce if the only supply of those latter goods by that person to another was at a time when they had not undergone an industrial process.[77]

15–26   **Liability of multiple producers.** For a consumer suffering relevant damage who is in a position, and elects, to sue more than one producer, s.2(5) provides that "their liability shall be joint and several" for the same damage.

15–27   **Damage.** Damage must have been occasioned[78] before liability to pay the victim any compensation can arise. Section 2(1) has not altered in any way the ordinary principle that the burden rests on the victim, as claimant, to prove that the defective product either wholly or in part caused his damage, before the producer will be held liable.[79]

---

[76] s.2(3).

[77] s.2(4).

[78] So long as damage has been caused to the claimant by the defective product that is sufficient for the purpose of s.2(1), unlike the comparable position in an ordinary negligence action, where vexed questions can arise involving foreseeability of damage, the kind of harm suffered and remoteness of damage issues. See Ch.2, above, paras 2–95–2–249, generally.

[79] See also art.4 of the Directive. See also *Richardson v LRC Products Ltd* [2000] P.I.Q.R. P164 (the claimant failed on the facts to prove that a defect in a condom was pre-existing as inexplicable failures of condoms did occur: thus it was not proved that an unwanted pregnancy resulting from the failure was *caused* by a defective product. It was nevertheless accepted that an unwanted pregnancy constituted "damage" within the section).

Causation. Causation is dealt with generally in Chapter 6. But in product **15–28** liability claims particular problems may arise. So, there may have been competing causes of the damage complained of, each of which may be uncommon but not improbable. In that event it is a permissible and logical train of reasoning, having eliminated all the possible causes bar one, to ask whether, on the balance of probabilities, that one cause was the cause of the event. It is not permissible to decide which competing cause was the least improbable and thus find that it was in fact the cause.[80] Since liability under the Act is strict, there is no need to go further and prove fault, as would be necessary in an ordinary negligence action.

Damage is defined in s.5(1) as meaning "death or personal injury or any loss **15–29** of or damage to any property (including land)", but s.5(2) draws the distinction that the producer will not be liable for loss or damage to the product itself and pure economic damage arising therefore.[81] By way of contrast, economic damage arising out of the victim's death or personal injury, as well as out of physical damage to property, other than to the defective product itself, will be recoverable.[82]

In the case of property damage there are two restraints. The first is to exclude **15–30** liability for damage, which has been occasioned to business property.[83] Section 5(3) provides that there shall be no liability if the property, which has been lost or damaged, is not: "(a) of a description of property ordinarily intended for private use, occupation or consumption; and (b) intended by the person suffering the loss or damage mainly for his own private use, occupation or consumption".[84] In *Société Moteurs Somer v Société Dalkia France*,[85] the European Court

---

[80] *Ide v ATB Sales Ltd, Lexus Financial Services t/a Toyota Financial Serⅴces UK Plc v Russell* [2008] P.I.Q.R. P13, CA: conjoined appeals: (1) the claimant was injured when the handlebar on his mountain cycle broke. The competing causes were a defect in the handlebar leading to catastrophic failure without warning *or* loss of control by the claimant and the failure of the handlebar as a consequence of the impact which then occurred. The judge's finding that it was a latent defect was upheld; (2) the defendant's cars were destroyed by fire, the defendant owing an outstanding sum in respect of one of them. The competing causes were arson, an electrical defect in either the garage *or* one of the cars. The judge's finding that it was a fault in the vehicle was upheld. In each case it was held that *Rhesa Shipping Co SA v Edmunds (The Popi M)* [1985] 1 W.L.R. 948, HL (where the competing causes were *either* virtually impossible *or* extremely improbable, the burden of proving the cause had not been discharged) did not apply.

[81] Although the Act has not included such a situation as that which occurred in *Junior Books Ltd v Veitchi Co Ltd* [1983] 1 A.C. 520, both in respect of economic damage, flowing from the defective product, and the fact that the premises were not for private use, the claimant may be able to pursue an alternative remedy at common law instead, particularly if he were the buyer.

[82] For economic losses, generally, see Ch.2, paras 2–163–2–165, above.

[83] So, where damage has happened to his business premises, it will be necessary for an alternative route to be taken at common law in order to recover damages in respect of it.

[84] The use of the word "mainly" must anticipate the fact that a claimant's intention was to include, with his own needs, the use, occupation or consumption by other members of his family. On the other hand, if he is the landlord who is not residing on the premises, which he has let to tenants, he cannot maintain an action under the Act, because he is not using the premises mainly for his private occupation.

[85] C-285/08, June 4, 2009. A generator installed in a hospital caught fire as a consequence of an alternator manufactured and put into circulation by Somer overheating. Dalkia was responsible for it maintenance and its insurers, Ace Europe, paid compensation to the hospital. Ace brought an action against Somer to recover its outlay. The Court of Appeal ordered Somer to pay sums to Dalkia and

of Justice held that damage to an item of property intended for professional use and employed for that purpose was not covered by the term "damage" for the purpose of the Directive and, consequently, could not give rise to liability on the part of the producer under art.1. Compensation for damage to an item of property intended and employed for such use was not covered by the scope of the application of the Directive. As the harmonisation brought about by the Directive did not cover compensation in such circumstances, however, the Directive did not preclude a member state from providing in that respect for a system of liability corresponding to that established by the Directive.[86] The second restriction is that unless the value of the claimant's total claim for property damage,[87] excluding interest, exceeds £275, his claim will not be entertained under the Act.[88]

15–31   **General defences.** Any one of a number of matters may bring the claimant's claim outside the scope of the Consumer Protection Act 1987. For the sake of convenience they can be summarised as:

(a) the claimant has failed to prove any one of the essential ingredients, which are necessary to establish strict liability, namely (i) he has suffered damage, (ii) caused by a defect, (iii) in a product, (iv) for which the defendant was responsible in his role as its producer or the equivalent[89];

(b) the product was supplied by its producer before March 1, 1988[90];

(c) the defective item falls outside the meaning of "product"[91];

Ace by reason of its obligation to ensure safety. The Court of Cassation referred to the ECJ Somer's contention that the safety obligation imposed on professional vendors did not cover damage caused to goods intended for professional use and employed by the injured person for professional purposes. By ordering it to pay compensation for purely material damage to the generator ordered and used by the hospital for its professional activities, the Court of Appeal had infringed the provisions of art.1603 of the Civil Code interpreted in the light of the Directive 85/374/EEC. Thus the question for the ECJ was whether arts. 9 and 13 of the Directive precluded the interpretation of domestic law or the application of settled domestic case law according to which an injured person could seek compensation for damage to an item of property intended for professional use and employed for that purpose where that injured person simply proved the damage, the defect in the product and the causal link between defect and damage.

[86] C-285/08, June 4, 2009, paras [17], [28] and [31].

[87] The fact that his claim, in excess of £275, may be reduced below the minimum figure, because of his contributory negligence, does not preclude him from suing under the Act.

[88] Instead, a claim below £275 would have to be brought in the county court and be based on breach of duty at common law in order to succeed.

[89] See also Ch.4, para.4–01, above.

[90] See s.50(7), the provisions of which apply to the time of supply of the product by its producer and not to importers or "own-branders". If the latter two supply their customers after March 1, 1988, with a defective product that causes damage they will be liable even though the actual producer had both manufactured and despatched it to them, before the material date, and, thus can avoid liability. Obviously, as time passes by and all old stocks of products become used up, this defence will become increasingly rare and will cease, ultimately.

[91] See paras 15–12–15–15, above.

(d) the defect in the product is not one which involves danger to safety[92];

(e) the only damage suffered by the victim was purely economic, which was not a consequence of his death or personal injury, caused by the defective product[93];

(f) as regards the claimant's property: (i) the only damage suffered by him was to the product itself[94]; (ii) the damage done was done to business property[95]; (iii) the amount of the damage suffered by it was less than £275, excluding interest.[96]

Limitation. A further general defence concerns limitation of action.[97] Deal-   **15–32** ing first with a case which includes personal injuries, the ordinary rules as to limitation apply, in effect, unaltered. An action must be brought within three years of the date either when the injury was sustained or of acquisition of the knowledge necessary to bring the proceedings, with the court having discretion whether or not to override such three-year period.[98] However, the addition of s.11A to the Limitation Act 1980,[99] created two exceptions to the general rules. First, as regards property damage, the normal period of six years[100] was reduced to three years, but with no discretionary powers to override that period.[101] Secondly, no action may be brought at all more than ten years from the date when the product in question was supplied by the producer of the product to another[102] although it has been said that art.11 does not provide an absolute period of 10 years after which rights are extinguished rather they were extinguished unless in the meantime the injured person had instituted proceedings against the producer.[103]

---

[92] See para.15–16, above.
[93] See paras 15–27–15–30, above, i.e. the expenditure wasted in acquiring what has turned out to be a useless product and/or the loss of profits resulting, because the defective produce had not performed its intended work, whether properly or at all.
[94] s.5(2) and see further, para.15–27, above.
[95] s.5(3).
[96] s.5(4).
[97] See Ch.4, above, paras 4–137–4–226, generally.
[98] Limitation Act 1980 s.33(1A)(b).
[99] By s.6(6) and Sch.1.
[100] See Ch.4, para.4–235, above.
[101] Limitation Act 1980 s.33(1A)(b).
[102] See s.11A of the Limitation Act 1980 and ss.2 and 4 of the Consumer Protection Act 1987, which implements the Directive on Liability for Defective Products, 85/374/EEC art.11. See also Ch.4, para.4–235, above. The provisions do not allow the court to exercise discretion in favour of a claimant under s.33 of the 1980 Act, a significant barrier, for example, to any proposed class litigation under the 1987 Act concerning pharmaceutical damage where the harmful effect of a drug only manifests itself long after supply. Other common law remedies would not, however, be affected by this restriction. In *Horne-Roberts v SmithKline Beecham Plc* [2001] EWCA Civ 2006, the CA permitted the substitution of the true producer for another company named in error even though the ten year longstop provision had expired. Likewise in *O'Byrne v Aventis Pasteur MSD Ltd* [2008] P.I.Q.R. P3, CA, a mistake as to the name of the party to be sued was held to be exactly the type of mistake contemplated by s.35 of the Limitation Act 1980 permitting the court to exercise its discretion in favour of the claimant.
[103] *O'Byrne v Aventis Pasteur MSD Ltd* [2008] P.I.Q.R. P3 at para.[43], CA.

15–33   A decision of the European Court of Justice illustrates the difficulty of deciding when a producer put an article into circulation.[104] A wholly owned distributing subsidiary of a manufacturer of a vaccine supplied it to a health authority which administered it to the claimant, who allegedly suffered brain injury as a result. On the issue of proceedings it was necessary to determine when the 10 year[105] period commenced. It was said that the question was when the product had left the producer's process and entered a marketing process in the format to be offered to the public for use or consumption. The issue was held to be fact-sensitive turning in part, in the instant case, on the relationship between production and distribution companies where the two were separate entities. In general, it was not important whether the product was sold directly to the consumer by the producer or through a distribution process involving others.[106] In a further reference,[106a] the European Court held that art.11 prevented a producer being sued after the expiry of 10 years unless proceedings were commenced against it within the 10 year period and that a national rule allowing the substitution of one defendant for another[106b] could not be applied in a way which allowed a producer to be sued after expiry. It might be permissible to substitute a producer for its wholly owned subsidiary sued within the period if it was found that the producer had determined the putting of the product into circulation: then it would be for the national court applying national rules to find whether it was proved that the putting into circulation had in fact been determined by the producer.[106c]

---

[104] *O'Byrne v Aventis Pasteur MSD Ltd* reported sub nom. *O'Byrne v Sanofi Pasteur MSD Ltd* [2006] 1 W.L.R. 1606, ECJ. The need for a second reference to the ECJ arose when the case proceeded through the domestic courts to the HL, the issue being whether it was consistent with art.11 for a domestic court to be able to find (as had the CA in *Horne v SmithKline Beecham Plc* [2002] 1 W.L.R. 1662, CA) that proceedings started against someone described as the producer should count as having been started against the real producer, where the claim mistakenly named as defendant someone who was not the producer. It was submitted that the ECJ's earlier answer was to be interpreted as meaning that no substitution was possible unless somebody deemed by art.3 of the Directive to be the producer had been named as defendant in the original proceedings. While Lord Hoffman doubted the correctness of this interpretation, he agreed a contrary view was no beyond reasonable argument and the matter should be re-referred: *O'Byrne v Aventis Pasteur MSD Ltd* [2008] UKHL 34. See Preston, "Product liability: a matter of time", P.I.L.J. 2005 39 (Oct), 12; same author, "Liable to change" 156 N.L.J. 538, "Product Liability", 150 S.J. 878.

[105] 85/374/EEC, art.11 provides: "Member states shall provide in their legislation that the rights conferred upon the injured person pursuant to this Directive shall be extinguished upon the expiry of a period of 10 years from the date on which the producer put into circulation the actual product which caused the damage . . . "

[106] The vaccine had been supplied by the French manufacturer to its UK distribution subsidiary, then sold to the Department of Health and hence put into circulation within the 10 year period. See Marsh, "Safety in numbers: Is your product immune from criticism?" Co L.J. 2006 (May/Jun) 9

[106a] [2010] All E.R. (EC) 522. See n.104, above.

[106b] In this instance, s.35(5)(b) and CPR r.19.5(3)(a).

[106c] On the facts, the claimant's argument that the supply of the vaccine to the producer's wholly owned subsidiary was an act by the producer determining that it should be put into circulation failed: [2010] UKSC 23. The Supreme Court, allowing an appeal from [2008] 1 W.L.R. 1188, CA, held that the ECJ had been contemplating a situation where, to outward appearances, a supplier had decided to put a product into circulation. Considering the matter in accordance with domestic rules of proof, there was nothing to suggest that the fact that the supplier was a wholly owned subsidiary of the producer could of itself be a reason for permitting substitution outside the limitation period: it was simply one factor to be taken into account by the domestic court in assessing how closely connected the subsidiary was involved in its parent's business as a producer.

Contributory negligence.[107] This can be raised, whether as a defence or, **15–34** more likely, a partial defence to the claimant's claim. Given that the producer is strictly liable, proof of fault is not required, but even so an apportionment of responsibility between claimant and defendant will depend upon a combination of blameworthiness and the causative potency.[108] By s.6(4), it is provided that where any damage is caused partly by a defect in a product and partly by the fault of the person suffering the damage, then, in order to give effect to the law relating to contributory negligence, the defect shall be treated as if it were the fault[109] of every person who would be liable for it under the provisions of the 1987 Act.

Exclusion of liability by contract. Section 7 prohibits any limitation or **15–35** exclusion of liability "by any contract term, by any notice or by any other provision". Such prohibition, being wider than the scope of the Unfair Contract Terms Act 1977, should be effective in achieving protection for someone who has suffered injury or other loss from a defective product. However, the 1977 Act does not apply as between suppliers or producers in relation to contribution or indemnity claims.[110]

Defences under the Act.[111] Section 4(1) provides defendants with six **15–36** defences, any of which will defeat a claim, always provided it has been raised and proved, the burden resting upon the defendant: (i) the product complied with legal requirements, (ii) there was no supply; (iii) there was no supply by way of business; (iv) the product was not defective when supplied; (v) "development risks" (alias "state of the art"); and (vi) there was no defect in a component part supplied by the defendant before it was included in a subsequent product of another. It is intended to deal with these defences separately below.

(i) *The product complied with legal requirements*

By s.4(1)(a) it is a defence to show that "the defect is attributable to **15–37** compliance with any requirement imposed by or under any enactment or with any Community obligation." Thus, in relation to the safety regulations under Pt II of the Act, the decisive factor is that the defendant had no choice in the matter because he was under a legal obligation to comply. Nevertheless the defendant must prove that the offending defect in his product was caused necessarily by his complying with the relevant regulations. It is unlikely to be a common defence, because it will involve the defendant establishing virtually that the legal

---

[107] Law Reform (Contributory Negligence) Act 1945. For which see Ch.4, paras 4–03–4–72, above.

[108] In *Richardson v LRC Products Ltd* [2000] P.I.Q.R. P172, although a breach of the duty under the 1987 Act was not established in respect of a failed condom, it was held that the claimant's failure to seek and obtain the "morning-after" pill would have acted as a complete defence and avoided the conception and consequences which followed.

[109] s.6(5) provides that "in subsection (4) above 'fault' has the same meaning as in the said Act of 1945".

[110] See *Thompson v T. Lohan (Plant Hire) Ltd* [1987] 1 W.L.R. 649, distinguishing *Phillips Products Ltd v Hyland (Note)* [1987] 1 W.L.R. 659 for an illustration of the working of s.2(1) of the Unfair Contract Terms Act 1977.

[111] art.7 of Directive 85/374 which the special defences reflect, is to be construed restrictively, setting out as it does exemptions from the basic principle in art.1: *Veedfield v Arhus Amstkommune, The Times*, June 4, 2001, ECJ.

requirement concerned was either so misconceived or outdated that it did not deal adequately with a potential danger, which a more modern research had revealed. The defendant, of course, as a producer cannot take the initiative by embodying such new ideas in his product in advance, if by doing so he finds himself to be in breach of the criminal law.

(ii) *There was no supply by the defendant*

15–38   By s.4(1)(b) it is a defence to show that "the person proceeded against did not at any time supply the product to another". The key word to this defence is the word "supply", which is defined widely[112] and it includes the selling, hiring, lending, exchanging and, even, the giving as a gift.[113] Supply can extend to goods not yet issued into the market place. It is not necessary for the defendant to show who did supply the claimant with the goods but, if he can, it is assumed that the burden will shift to the claimant to prove that the defendant was the supplier.

(iii) *There was no supply by way of business*

15–39   By s.4(1)(c) two different defences are provided for suppliers, on the one hand, and for producers and others falling within s.2(2)[114] on the other. In this regard, it should be noted that the whole thrust of Pt I of the Act is to protect the consumer by making strict liability fall upon commercial producers and not on some private individual, who is not engaged in any "business".[115] Thus suppliers of home made produce at a church bazaar escape liability if not acting in the course of a business but, for the producers of the same produce, they must go on to show that the supply was done otherwise than with a view to a profit, at least for themselves.

In the case of second-hand defective goods being sold by a private person he would succeed in avoiding the "tracing" liability under s.2(3),[116] since the provisions of s.2(2), aforesaid, would not apply to him, because he is not a "producer", within the meaning prescribed under the Act.

(iv) *The product was not defective when supplied*

15–40   Section 4(1)(d) affords a defence that "the defect did not exist in the product at the relevant time", which time is defined as being "when he supplied the product to another"[117] or, in the case of there being several producers liable

---

[112] By s.46. If the product is for consumption by the producer in his own business and his employees sustain injury or suffer damage thereby, their remedy will lie under some other appropriate legislation e.g. regulations made pursuant the Framework Directive 89/391/EEC or the Employer's Liability (Defective Equipment) Act 1969. See Ch.12, above, paras 12–91–12–99 and Ch.11, above, paras 11–55–11–64, respectively. It has been held that providing a medical product for use in publicly-funded hospital treatment was "putting the product into circulation" for purposes of the Danish law transposing Directive 85/374: *Veedfeld v Arhus Amstkommune, The Times*, June 4, 2001, ECJ.

[113] Such as free samples or other promotional gifts to induce the consumer to do business.

[114] Which is dealt with in some detail in paras 15–22–15–25, above.

[115] Assistance with this expression may be derived from cases under the Sale of Goods Act 1979 and the Supply of Goods and Services Act 1982. It has been held that the fact that a product was manufactured for use in the course of medical treatment of the claimant financed from public funds could not deprive from the business character of the manufacture: *Veedfeld v Arhus Amstkommune*, n.8, above.

[116] See paras 15–22–15–25, above.

[117] s.4(2)(a).

under the Act, the time "when the product was last supplied by a person" to whom s.2(2) applied in relation to the product, that is the own-brander or an importer into a Member State from overseas.[118]

This defence is the one most likely to be met in practice. Where the defendant proves that the product's defect had come into existence only after it had left his control, the injured person's claim under the Act will fail. Such circumstances as normal wear and tear, a lack of regular servicing, maybe misuse or some form of interference with the product's integrity, could all contribute to the development of a defect, for which the original producer would not be liable.[119]

The defence was successfully invoked in *Piper v JRI (Manufacturing) Ltd*,[120]   **15–41**
which concerned the supply of a prosthesis for use in a total hip replacement operation. Some time after implant the prosthesis failed, shearing in two beneath the femoral head. The claimant had to undergo a further operation, which resulted in significant loss of mobility. He sued the defendant as producer of the prosthesis. Experts agreed that the fracture was the result of a surface point defect, which led to fatigue failure in the titanium alloy from which the prosthesis was made. On the evidence the judge accepted that, when it had left the factory, the defect was not present. An appeal from the finding was dismissed: it was not necessary for the judge, having reached that conclusion, to identify when in fact the surface defect had arisen.

(v) *"Development risks" (alias "state of the art")*

Inclusion of this defence has provoked more debate and disagreement between   **15–42**
Member States than any of the other defences. For the consumer it is argued that, where a producer has put into circulation a product, which is discovered later to be defective and injury results, the victim deserves to be compensated by him come what may, even though his research, development and manufacturing techniques had been faultless. This would accord with the spirit of consumer protection, where a victim, almost certainly uninsured, could ill bear the loss compared with the producer who was in the business of making a profit and likely to be insured against such eventualities. By contrast, the producers argue that the proposed form of strict liability without the vital protection of this defence being available would discourage technical innovation for fear of provoking litigation. The result would be loss of technical advance, the prohibitive cost of insurance and ultimate benefit to foreign competition beyond the jurisdiction. It is further said that the imposition of liability in respect of defects incapable of being detected at the time of production, was unfair in principle and could not be justified.[121]

---

[118] s.4(2)(b).

[119] If the injured person is the purchaser of a "spiked" can of food, the shop-keeper who sold it to him would be liable for a breach of the Sale of Goods Act 1979 s.14, instead. See, paras 15–50–15–56, below.

[120] (2006) 92 B.M.L.R. 141, CA.

[121] See, e.g. Commission Green Paper, "Liability for Defective Products", Brussels, COM (1999) 396 final (July 28,1999), para.3.2: discussion of the liability of producers where danger is genuinely unforeseeable.

15–43   There can be little doubt that these strongly held opposing views made it extremely difficult to settle upon an acceptable formula. Accordingly, the Directive has left the adoption of this specific defence to the Member States individually,[122] safe-guarding the community's position by providing for a review after 1995, a review that is now long overdue. Hence, by art.7 it is laid down that:

> "the producer shall not be liable as a result of this Directive if he proves:
>
> . . . (e) that the state of scientific and technical knowledge at the time when he put the product into circulation was not such as to enable the existence of the defect to be discovered . . . "[123]

These words of the Article have not been adopted in the Act[124] and the provisions of s.4(1)(e) are noticeably different,[125] namely:

> " . . . that the state of scientific and technical knowledge at the relevant time was not such that a producer of products of the same description as the product in question might be expected to have discovered the defect if it had existed in his products while they were under his control."[126]

Thus the test provided by the statute was not what a defendant knew but what it could have known if it had consulted those who might be expected to know the state of research and all available literature sources.[127] This is similar to the traditional test in a negligence action of what reasonably could be expected from a producer in that particular line of business, but with the significant difference in that the onus rests on the defendant to prove his defence. However, since the Act is to be interpreted in a way consistent with the Directive,[128] it is questionable to what extent the statute may provide a wider defence than the Directive affords. It has been held that this defence was not available to a

---

[122] A number of countries have adopted the defence as per Directive but France, Belgium and Luxembourg have excluded the defence in its entirety. Germany, whilst accepting the defence in principle has excluded it from applying to pharmaceutical products. Britain does not include it in its Directive form.

[123] Since the test to be applied was whether the state of knowledge existed to enable the defect to be discovered it must have been envisaged in the Directive that if such knowledge did exist, embracing evidence from research carried out somewhere, but it was either too difficult or expensive for an individual producer to apply it, the test would not be satisfied and, accordingly, the defence would fail. Clearly, the Directive is providing an objective test by this approach.

[124] The Consumer's Association has requested the European Commission to express a view whether s.4(1)(e) of the Consumer Protection Act 1987 is compatible with the Directive and the Commission has issued a formal challenge (*Financial Times*, February 2, 1988) upon which the European Court of Justice may have to give a decision ultimately.

[125] Newdick, "The Development Risk Defence of the Consumer Protection Act 1987", [1988] 47 C.L.J. 455, argues that the form of s.4(1)(e) is a correct interpretation of art.7(1)(e).

[126] This suggests a subjective test as to what the actual state of scientific and technical knowledge was at the material time and whether or not in the light of such knowledge, as the producer, he might be expected to have discovered the defect. In *Abouzaid v Mothercare Ltd, The Times*, February 20, 2001, CA, para.15–16, n.52 above, where an elasticated strap attached to a product recoiled striking the claimant in the eye, doubt was expressed whether the absence of records of previous accidents amounted to "scientific and technical knowledge" not available in 1990.

[127] *Richardson v LRC Products Ltd* [2000] P.I.Q.R. P164.

[128] See above, para.15–09.

defendant unless the defect was one of which leading scientific knowledge was ignorant.[129]

In *A v National Blood Authority*,[130] the defendants argued unsuccessfully that **15–44** a defence under art.7 was established if knowledge of the existence of a defect at the material time was insufficient to allow the producer to identify its presence in any particular product. It was held to be inconsistent with the purpose of the Directive that a producer should be able to continue to supply products which to his knowledge were exposed to a particular risk, simply because he could not identify in which the defect would occur. Accordingly no defence was made out where the use of infected blood products for blood transfusion caused the claimants to contract hepatitis C, even where the defendants maintained that it was impossible for them in the state of medical knowledge at the time to test for the presence of the virus in a donor's blood.

When it comes to assessing the state of scientific and technical knowledge the **15–45** "relevant time" is the time of supply[131] which is not necessarily the same as when the product was manufactured or, even, when it was designed. Thus there a producer of a product who maintains large stocks of that product and who then becomes aware, following scientific or technical advances, of the possibility of being able to test the product for potential defects, may take unacceptable risks by continuing to supply the product from his stocks.

(vi) *There was no defect in a component part before it was included in a subsequent product of another*

Section 4(1)(f) affords the manufacturer of a component a defence if he can **15–46** show that the defect complained of is a defect is wholly attributable to the design of the finished product into which his component has been incorporated or to compliance with instructions given by the manufacturer of the finished product. Thus an otherwise "blameless" component manufacturer should not have to share either joint or several liability with the other producer or producers of the finished goods.

In order for the defence to be made out, it must be established that there would have been no failure of the component supplied, if only the end-product had been designed properly, in respect of which the manufacturer had not been consulted or involved, or it had been installed correctly by the subsequent producer.

(B) Under the Consumer Protection Act 1987: Part II "Consumer Safety"

Action for breach of statutory duty. From 1961 onwards liability for unsafe **15–47** products has been governed by a series of statutes,[132] all embodied today in the Consumer Protection Act 1987, Pt II, which have made provisions for preventive measures in furtherance of consumer protection, generally. Each statute has in

---

[129] *Richardson v LRC Products Ltd*, above.
[130] [2001] 3 All E.R. 289, and para.15–17, above.
[131] s.4.
[132] The Consumer Protection Act 1961 and its successor, the Consumer Safety Act 1978.

turn empowered[133] the Secretary of State to issue safety regulations, in order to prescribe detailed rules as regards particular goods.[134] These are intended, usually, to cover all aspects of product safety, including the design, construction, installation, testing and packaging, as well as the giving of proper warnings and adequate instructions or other essential information. Principally, the statutory regulations are enforceable by criminal process[135] but the 1987 Act, in keeping with the earlier Acts, by s.41(1) enables a person who has been injured[136] in consequence of a breach of some specific regulations to bring an action for damages founded on breach of statutory duty.[137]

15–48   A criminal prosecution is likely to be advantageous to those victims who have been injured but have suffered no property damage.[138] First, the evidence for the prosecution will have been assembled at public expense by the enforcement authority. A successful prosecution[139] may spare the victim the need to bring any action at all, because the criminal courts have a discretionary power to order a guilty defendant to pay compensation.[140] In the absence of any order for compensation, a successful prosecution will put the victim in a strong position to succeed in a civil claim. On the other hand, were the prosecution to fail, it would have done so at no expense to him and he will then be in a better position to assess the strength of his position, bearing in mind always the lower standard of proof in civil proceedings. A second advantage to a victim is identification of a further possible defendant to a civil action, such as a retailer.[141] If, by any chance, no producer or equivalent, liable under Pt I of the Act, exists or remains in business and/or is worth "powder and shot" for purposes of satisfying a

---

[133] This power is contained now in the Consumer Protection Act 1987 s.11.

[134] For details of the regulations, of which some 40 have been made, mostly under previous legislation, see Miller, *Product Liability and Safety Encyclopaedia* (Butterworths 1979), Division III. All are now subsumed under the 1987 Act and cover a wide range of hazardous and potentially hazardous products.

[135] s.12. The criminal proceedings are initiated by the Trading Standards Department of local authorities.

[136] Since safety regulations are concerned solely with personal safety and risks thereto, property damage is outside their scope.

[137] It is to be noted that it is only a breach of specific safety regulations under s.11 which give rise to the civil action concerned and not any infringement of the new general duty introduced by s.10. Such an action for damages is, of course, independent of proof of negligence. See further Ch.12, above, for actions for breach of statutory duty.

[138] Where the victim has suffered both kinds of damage from unsafe consumer goods which have contravened some safety regulation, there will be circumstances when he may sue under the Act both for the product's being "defective" under Pt I as well as for breach of the safety regulation under Pt II. This will occur where the breach of the regulation can be interpreted so as to come within the definition of the product being defective (see para.15–16, above, as to the meaning of "defect").

[139] For a discussion of the relevance and admissibility of the defendant's conviction, see Ch.5 of the 8th edn of this work and also the Civil Evidence Act 1968.

[140] Powers of Criminal Courts Act 1973 s.35, where the Crown Court may award summarily such amount of compensation as it considers appropriate, whilst under the Magistrates' Courts Act 1980 s.40 limits such an order to a maximum of £3,000.

[141] Retailers and others in the chain of distribution can be held liable for breach of statutory duty, in addition to the producers, since safety regulations apply, generally, to *any persons* who supply the goods in question. Although such persons as retailers would not normally be liable under Pt 1 of the Act, they could be made so under the "tracing" provisions, for which see para.15–25, above.

judgment, the prosecution may have identified at least one defendant who probably can pay!

A defendant prosecuted for breach of a safety regulation, has by s.39(1) a **15–49** defence if he shows that he took all reasonable steps and exercised all due diligence to avoid committing the offence.[142] No similar provision exists if the same defendant is then sued in a civil action under Pt II of the Act.[143] Section 41(1) does not state what is available by way of a defence. Liability will be subject to the usual defences which apply to actions for breach of statutory duty, generally.[144]

3.—LIABILITY IN CONTRACT

Strict liability. It will be recalled from the opening paragraph of this chapter **15–50** that it was only the law of contract which from the outset provided any form of protection to a consumer against faulty goods, a position reinforced by the enactment of the Sale of Goods Act 1893. Today, a manufacturer or other producer[145] of goods[146] is under a contractual duty to the buyer of them, and by virtue of the provisions of s.14 of the Sale of Goods Act 1979,[147] a number of implied terms are included.

In relation to contractual liability for quality and safety, it is provided by **15–51** s.14(3) that:

"Where the seller sells goods in the course of a business and the buyer, expressly or by implication, makes known—

(a) to the seller, or
(b) . . . any particular purpose for which the goods are being bought,

there is an implied [term] that the goods supplied under the contract are reasonably fit for that purpose, whether or not that is a purpose for which such goods are commonly

---

[142] The wording is such that this defence only applies to criminal liability. It has been held that it is an insufficient defence merely to show compliance with a British Standard: *Balding v Lew Ways Ltd, The Times*, March 9, 1995, DC. See Lawson, "Due diligence defence" 140 S.J. (25), 630 and (26), 666.

[143] It is to be noted that the defences specified in s.4 only apply in civil proceedings by virtue of Pt I of the Act and have no application in similar proceedings brought under Pt II.

[144] For defences in such actions, see Ch.12, paras 12–67–12–80, above.

[145] As to persons who now fall into the extended class of "manufacturers", see para.15–67, below. For the concurrent liability in tort of a retailer and other persons as transferors, see paras 15–90 and 15–94–15–97, below.

[146] Which includes the container of the goods: *Geddling v Marsh* [1920] 1 K.B. 668 (glass bottle containing the mineral water). See Miller, "Liability for Defective Products", 122 S.J. 631.

[147] The Act, which came into force on January 1, 1980, has re-enacted much of the 1893 Act as well as consolidating the law generally relating to the sale of goods.

supplied, except where the circumstances show that the buyer does not rely, or that it is unreasonable for him to rely, on the skill or judgment of the seller . . . "

Further, in the case of a seller who sells goods in the course of a business, s.14(2) provides that "there is an implied condition that the goods supplied under the contract are of merchantable quality",[148] save where the buyer examines the goods before the contract is made, as regards defects, which that examination ought to reveal, or as regards defects specifically drawn to the buyers' attention before the contract is made.

15–52　Since sale is not the only form of supply, statute also regulates contracts of hire and hire-purchase[149] as well as contracts for services in the course of which goods are supplied to the consumer. In the case of the last the Supply of Goods and Services Act 1982[150] provides for identical terms of quality and fitness as are implied in a contract for the sale of goods.

15–53　**The benefits and the limitations.** There are a number of benefits of the statutory regimes, as far as a buyer[151] is concerned. First, the liability is strict. The mere fact that a seller has taken every precaution, and is not to blame for the defective condition of goods in any way, or has had no opportunity to examine the goods, in order to discover if they are faulty, is irrelevant to liability. Secondly, the damages awarded for breach of contract are not limited to compensation for personal injury, physical damage to property and the consequential losses, which result. Pure economic loss can be recovered, that is, financial loss not accompanied by personal injury or physical damage to property. In turn a seller, held liable to the buyer, will have a claim against his supplier for the damages and costs he has had to pay to the claimant, together with the costs he incurred reasonably in defending the action brought by the buyer.[152] Such actions can theoretically continue down the line of supply until the manufacturer has been reached and held liable.

15–54　The limitations upon an action in contract spring from the rules of privity[153] which will inevitably exclude a wide a range of consumers. It is axiomatic that a person who is not a contracting party cannot enforce the terms of the contract made between others.[154] Attempts to circumvent the consequences, such as by claiming an agency on behalf of the injured consumer, have met with very

---

[148] Which is defined in s.14(6).

[149] The provisions of the various Hire Purchase Acts are now consolidated in the Consumer Credit Act 1974.

[150] See s.4.

[151] i.e. the buyer, hirer, person being supplied, etc., under his contract.

[152] *Kasler and Cohen v Slavouski* [1928] 1 K.B. 78.

[153] See *Chitty on Contracts* (30th edn), Vol.1, Ch.18.; Cheshire, Fifoot and Furmstone, *Law of Contract* (15th edn), Ch.14.

[154] In effect when he is not the buyer but is injured by the faulty goods, he cannot sue the seller; equally is he disadvantaged, when he is in fact the buyer, who is injured, but the seller has gone out of business, since he cannot then pursue his remedy against the wholesalers, which had supplied the seller in the first place, because there is no contractual relationship between them.

limited success.[155] Some assistance can be derived from the Contracts (Rights of Third Parties) Act 1999 which enables parties to a contract to agree that the seller's liability under a contract of sale should extend both to the purchaser and any other party whom the parties intend to benefit.

Accordingly, prior to the coming into force of Pt I of the Consumer Protection **15–55** Act 1987, the only remedy available to a person who had suffered loss from a defective product but was unable to establish any contractual relationship with the supplier that was in the course of his business, lay in negligence, together with its shortcomings. These are discussed below.

Claim under the Consumer Protection Act 1987 compared. A buyer's **15–56** preference will usually be to pursue a contractual remedy rather than a remedy under the 1987 Act. It will be necessary to do so where: (i) the "product"[156] is not one which is within the scope of the Act; (ii) the "defect"[157] is not one which is safety-related and, hence, does not come under the provisions of the Act; (iii) there is a potential defendant (that is, the retailer or someone else in the chain of distribution with whom the claimant has a contractual relationship) who does not qualify as a "producer"[158] under the Act; and (iv) the "damage"[159] is not of the kind which is recoverable under the Act.

4.—LIABILITY IN NEGLIGENCE

Emergence of the duty of care in tort. As mentioned in the opening **15–57** paragraph of this chapter,[160] prior to 1932 no general duty of care had been formulated as regards defective products. Indeed, it had remained dubious whether or not, in the absence of some contractual relationship between them, the transferor of a product owed the ultimate consumer any duty at all.[161] By providing for such a duty in *Donoghue v Stevenson*,[162] the House of Lords

---

[155] e.g. *Lockett v A. & M. Charles Ltd* [1938] 4 All E.R. 170 (in a café a husband and wife consumed together a meal which had been ordered and was paid for by him. The wife was taken seriously ill as a result of suffering food poisoning from the contaminated meal that she had eaten. It was held that because the husband in buying her meal had acted as his wife's agent, so he had contracted on her behalf enabling her to sue and recover damages).

[156] For what is not a product, see para.15–12, above.

[157] For the definition of defect, see para.15–16, above.

[158] For those who come within the meaning of producer, see paras 15–22–15–26, above.

[159] For the restriction on the kind of damage in respect of which an action can be brought under the Act, see para.15–27, above.

[160] And more particularly in Ch.2, paras 2–01–2–52, above.

[161] There were exceptional cases where it was decided on their particular facts that a duty of care did arise, notably in respect of: (a) goods "dangerous in themselves", such as a loaded gun where the owner was found to be under a duty not to put them "in a situation easily accessible to a third person who sustains damage" from them, (per Parke B. in *Longmeid v Holliday* (1851) 6 Exch. 761); (b) occupiers of premises who provided defective plant and appliances, such as staging with ropes in a dock, to be used by the workmen of their invitees (*Heaven v Pender*) (1883) 11 Q.B.D. 503); and (c) the failure by a supplier to give a consumer warning of known defects in a product, such as a tin of disinfectant powder, which was likely to cause injury when opened (*Clarke v Army & Navy Co-operative Society* [1903] 1 K.B. 155).

[162] [1932] A.C. 562.

created a new conceptual environment and the basis for the subsequent development of the tort.

It is proposed to consider the duty of care from two broad perspectives: (A) the manufacturer's duty; and (B)[163] the duty of other persons as transferors.

(A) The manufacturer's duty

15–58   **Donoghue v Stevenson: the "manufacturer's duty of care."** The appeal proceeded on the assumption that the facts alleged by the pursuer were true. She was a shop assistant, seeking to recover £500 damages from the respondent, who was a manufacturer of aerated waters, for sickness, loss of earnings, interest and expenses. She alleged that she had been injured by consuming part of the contents of a bottle of ginger beer, which had been manufactured by the respondent and had contained the decomposed remains of a snail. In her pleadings, she averred that the ginger beer had been purchased for her by a friend, whilst visiting the café occupied by Francis Minchella at Paisley; the bottle was made of dark opaque glass and she had no reason to suspect that it contained any foreign matter; Minchella poured out some of the drink into a tumbler of ice cream and she consumed part; her friend then proceeded to pour the rest of the bottle's contents into the tumbler, when a snail, in a state of decomposition, floated out of the bottle; and as a result of the nauseating sight and the consequential impurities in the drink, she suffered from shock and severe gastroenteritis. Upon these facts, the House of Lords decided by a majority[164] that subject to proof, there was a good cause of action.[165]

15–59   Lord Atkin, having dealt with the difficulties in finding some general principle underlying the law of negligence, proceeded to set out the concept of a duty to one's neighbour, which is the "broad rule" of this important decision.[166] Next, he went on to state the manufacturer's duty which is the "narrow rule" in his judgment in these terms:

> "My Lords, if your Lordships accept the view that this pleading discloses a relevant cause of action you will be affirming the proposition that by Scots and English law alike

---

[163] From paras 15–98–15–115, below.

[164] Lords Atkins, Thankerton and Macmillan with Lords Buckmaster and Tomlin dissenting.

[165] See article by Professor Heuston (1957) 20 M.L.R.1 at 2, n.5. Mrs Donoghue, who by this time was separated from her husband and was living with her mother in a tenement in Glasgow, did not in the end succeed in getting her £500. The issues of fact were never decided, since the defender died before proof and the pursuer, in consequence of difficulties facing her as regards evidence, compromised the action for £100. The assertion by Jenkins L.J. in *Alder v Dickson* [1954] 1 W.L.R. 1482 at 1483, therefore, is incorrect that when the trial was finally heard there was no snail in the bottle at all. See further 71 L.Q.R. 472 and 220 L.T. 291. As a postscript Mrs Donoghue's fortunes improved a long time after the case; she then lived her last years with her son in a neat house in Jameson Street, a respectable area of Glasgow, until 1958, when she died in a psychiatric hospital.

[166] Already discussed in Ch.2, paras 2–07–2–12, above.

a manufacturer of products, which he sells in such a form as to show that he intends them to reach the ultimate consumer in the form in which they left him, with no reasonable possibility of intermediate examination, and with the knowledge that the absence of reasonable care in the preparation or putting up of the products will result in an injury to the consumer's life or property, owes a duty to the consumer to take that reasonable care.

It is a proposition which I venture to say no one in Scotland or England who is not a lawyer would for one moment doubt. It will be an advantage to make it clear that the law in this matter, as in most others, is in accordance with sound common sense."[167]

Modifications of and extensions to the principle. The subsequent develop- **15–60** ments of the principle in *Donoghue's* case can be dealt with under the following headings: (i) intermediate examination; (ii) ultimate consumers; (iii) products; and (iv) manufacturers.

(i) *Intermediate examination*

The statement of duty contained in *Donoghue v Stevenson*[168] must be modified **15–61** in one respect. It is not essential that there should be no reasonable possibility[169] of intermediate examination, as long as the article is intended by the producer to reach the ultimate consumer or user in the state, in which it left him. In *Grant v Australian Knitting Mills*[170] it was held that:

"The decision in *Donoghue's* case did not depend on the bottle being stoppered and sealed: the essential point in this regard was that the article should reach the consumer or user subject to the same defect as it had when it left the manufacturer."

The claimant contracted dermatitis from a chemical irritant in underpants bought from a retailer. The defendants were held liable, in respect of their manufacture, in negligence. The possibility of intermediate examination was present, (handling by the retailer before sale or tampering after they left the manufacturer), but, since it was found there had been no such tampering in fact, the possibility of intermediate examination was held to be no defence. Likewise, the possibility of removal of the irritant by the claimant washing the pants before use was held to be no defence, because "it was not contemplated that they should be first

---

[167] ibid. at 599. This exposition of the obligation of a manufacturer, which is owed in respect of chattels, has never been questioned, but has been adopted, applied and even expanded in over 100 reported cases throughout the common law world, since 1932. See *English & Empire Digest* (1976, Reissue), Vol.36(1), pp.144–145, para.562.
[168] [1932] A.C. 562.
[169] Goddard L.J. suggested the substitution of "probability" for "possibility" in *Paine v Colne Valley Electricity Supply Co* [1938] 4 All E.R. 803, and in *Haseldine v Daw & Son* [1941] 2 K.B. 343 at 376.
[170] [1936] A.C. 85, per Lord Wright at 106, 107. When dermatitis has been caused by defective clothing, it is a defence to prove that the claimant has an abnormally sensitive skin; *Griffiths v Peter Conway Ltd* [1939] 1 All E.R. 685. When dermatitis has been contracted, after wearing a suit cleaned by the defendants, the burden is on the defendants to prove no negligence: *Mayne v Silvermere Cleaners Ltd* [1939] 1 All E.R. 693.

washed".[171] Thus the old case of *George v Skivington*,[172] after undergoing much criticism,[173] was expressly approved in *Donoghue v Stevenson*.[174]

ILLUSTRATIONS

15–62   A manufacturer of a sidecar, who had fitted it negligently to a motorcycle, was held liable to the sidecar's passenger who was injured when the cycle parted from the sidecar whilst climbing a hill. It was held that the manufacturer must have contemplated that the sidecar was to be used by third parties, without new tests.[175] The manufacturers of a defectively designed and dangerous towing coupling for a trailer, which subsequently had been fitted to a Land Rover supplied by certain retailers, were held liable to the extent of 75 per cent for putting such a coupling into circulation, which, together with the vehicle owner's negligence, had caused an accident.[176] When a reconditioned motorcar was let on hire-purchase, the suppliers knew it was to be used immediately, without any examination, although there was an opportunity of examining it. The suppliers, who were motor mechanics and engineers, were held liable, when, through their negligence, a wheel came off on the first morning that the car was used, whereby the driver was injured.[177] Similarly, a monumental mason, who had erected a tombstone, was held liable to a child on whom it fell as a result of its negligent erection, on the ground that he must have contemplated his work would be accepted, without any tests.[178]

15–63   A manufacturer of sweets who sold them to a wholesaler, from whom they were bought by a retailer, was liable to the retailer, whose hand was injured by a piece of wire in one of the sweets as he put them in his shop window, even although there he had been an opportunity to examine them.[179] Liability was also

---

[171] *Grant v Australian Knitting Mills* [1936] A.C. 85 at 105.

[172] (1869) L.R. 5 Ex. 1 (a chemist sold a hairwash, made by himself, to the claimant's husband knowing that it was to be used by the claimant. The hairwash was negligently compounded and was unfit for use, thereby injuring the claimant. The chemist was held liable on the ground that he knew that the claimant was to use his hairwash. Although the point was not made, it was obvious that the chemist contemplated that the hairwash would be used in the state in which he sold it, without further examination).

[173] "After a long and rough crossing has limped into port", per Asquith L.J. in *Candler v Crane, Christmas & Co* [1951] 2 K.B. 164 at 190. (The decision itself in *Candler v Crane, Christmas & Co*, however, was disapproved by the HL in *Hedley Byrne & Co Ltd v Heller & Partners Ltd* [1964] A.C. 465.) *Blacker v Lake and Elliott* (1912) 106 L.T. 533 (purchaser of brazing lamp, which exploded, owing to negligent manufacture, held not entitled to recover from manufacturer), in which *George v Skivington* was not followed, must be considered to be overruled by *Donoghue v Stevenson* (Lord Atkin at 594, Lord Macmillan at 616) on the ground that it did not give "sufficient attention to the general principle which governs the whole law of negligence in the duty owed to those who will be immediately injured by lack of care").

[174] [1932] A.C. 562.

[175] *Malfroot v Noxal Ltd* (1935) 51 T.L.R. 551.

[176] *Lambert v Lewis* [1979] R.T.R. 61 (not the subject of appeal [1982] A.C. 225, CA and HL(E)). See Leder, "*Lambert v Lewis*—A Hitch in the Chain of Causation", 78 L.S. Gaz. 597.

[177] *Herschtal v Stewart & Ardern Ltd* [1940] 1 K.B. 155. For other cases of wheels becoming detached, see *Stennett v Hancock* [1939] 2 All 578; *Power v Bedford Motor Co and Harris* [1959] I.R. 391; *Morrison v Leyenhorst* [1968] 2 O.R. 741.

[178] *Brown v Cotterill* (1934) 51 T.L.R. 21.

[179] *Barnett v Packer Ltd* [1940] 3 All E.R. 575.

established against the producers of a cold steel chisel, which had been made dangerously hard, where they had supplied it to the employers of a workman who was injured whilst using it properly, as a result of which a splinter of metal flew off and penetrated his eye. The employers were under no duty to examine the chisel, before issuing it to the workman to use or, thereafter, to institute frequent inspections, in the absence of anything to suggest that the chisel was defective.[180]

Where an intermediate examination is contemplated.   In a contrasting case   **15–64** where a chisel remained in use after it had initially splintered and went on to cause injury, the employers were held liable for their failure to withdraw the chisel in the face of known danger, but the manufacturers, who had contracted hardening to a reputable sub-contractor, were absolved from liability on the basis that there was no reasonable probability of them examining the chisel after that process but before supply to the employers.[180a] Where chemical manufacturers sold manganese dioxide contaminated with antimony sulphate to retailers who, in turn, sold it to a school where a pupil was injured as a result of the substance exploding in the course of an experiment, the manufacturers were held not liable on demonstrating that they had invoiced the retailers with a warning that it "must be examined and tested by the user before use". Despite such warning no such testing had been carried out. Since the retailers had failed to avail themselves of "ample and repeated opportunity of intermediate examination", which would have revealed the dangerous contamination, there was no liability on the manufacturers to indemnify the retailer and, it was said, on the same basis the injured pupil would not have been able to sue the manufacturers.[180b]

(ii) *Ultimate consumers*

The category of persons who may be deemed to be ultimate consumers has   **15–65** been extended to include both the user[181] of a defective product, as well as a person who comes into contact with it, whether accidentally[182] or deliberately.[183] Indeed, anybody who sustains personal injury thereby will have a cause of action in negligence against the manufacturer. The rule is not confined to persons

---

[180] *Mason v Williams & Williams Ltd* [1955] 1 All E.R. 808, which was referred to with approval by the HL in *Davie v New Merton Board Mills Ltd* [1959] A.C. 604, where a fitter had his eye injured because a tool, supplied by a reputable supplier, was negligently made in that it was excessively hard. Contrast the position in *Taylor v Rover Co Ltd* [1966] 1 W.L.R. 1499, para.15–64, below. Subsequently the common law underwent radical change, as a result first of the provisions of the Employer's Liability (Defective Equipment) Act 1969, which came into force on October 25, 1969 and, thereafter, the Provision and Use of Equipment Regulations 1992 which came into force on January 1, 2003 (now replaced by Provision and Use of Equipment Regulations 1998). See Ch.11, above, paras 11–55–11–64 and Ch.12, above, paras 12–173–12–228.
[180a] *Taylor v Rover Co Ltd* [1966] 1 W.L.R. 1499.
[180b] *Kubach v Hollands* [1937] 3 All E.R. 907, K.B.D.
[181] *Grant v Australian Knitting Mills Ltd* [1936] A.C. 85.
[182] See *Brown v Cotterill* [1934] 51 T.L.R. 21 (tombstone fell on a child); *Stennett v Hancock* [1939] 2 All E.R. 578 (flange of a lorry's wheel became detached, wheel came off, bowled down road, mounted pavement and struck a pedestrian); *Power v The Bedford Motor Co Ltd* [1959] I.R. 391 (track rods of a car were set incorrectly and caused a fatal accident through faulty steering).
[183] *Barnett v H. & J. Packer & Co Ltd* [1940] 3 All E.R. 575 (a piece of wire protruding from a sweet, pierced finger of a shop assistant picking it up).

involved in the sale of a defective product but applies equally to products on hire.[184]

(iii) *Products*

15–66   The rule has been extended to include, besides merely dangerous food and drink, any intrinsic part of the commodity itself[185] which inflicts harm, namely: bottles[186]; buildings[187]; chemicals[188]; designs[189]; hair dyes[190]; kiosks[191]; lifts[192]; motor vehicles[193]; tombstones[194]; undergarments[195]; wills.[196]

(iv) *Manufacturers*

15–67   The rule also has been extended by enlarging the category of persons who may be deemed to be "a manufacturer". Now there are included: assemblers[197]; bailors and donors[198]; builders[199]; erectors[200]; installers[201]; producers of careless statements[202] and defective documents[203]; repairers[204]; and suppliers.[205]

---

[184] See *Herschtal v Stewart & Ardern Ltd* [1940] 1 K.B. 155, where liability was based on the defective workmanship carried out by the defendant himself on the claimant's car which was subject to hire-purchase. In *Andrews v Hopkinson* [1957] 1 Q.B. 229 at 236, McNair J. held that the rule still applied even if the defendant had not done the work himself.

[185] *Tarling v Noble* [1966] A.L.R. 189 (chicken bone left in the meat in a sandwich).

[186] *Hart v Dominion Stores* [1968] 67 D.L.R. (2d) 675.

[187] *Murphy v Brentwood District Council* [1991] 1 A.C. 398.

[188] *Vacwell Engineering Co Ltd v BDH Chemicals Ltd* [1971] 1 Q.B. 88 and 111 (on appeal, which settled); *Wright v Dunlop Rubber Co* (1973) 13 K.I.R. 255.

[189] *Hindustan S.S. Co Ltd v Siemens Bros & Co Ltd* [1955] 1 Lloyd's Rep. 167 (defectively designed ships' telegraphs).

[190] *Parker v Oloxo Ltd* [1937] 3 All E.R. 524; *Watson v Buckley, Osborne, Garrett & Co Ltd* [1940] 1 All E.R. 174.

[191] *Paine v Colne Valley Electricity Supply Co Ltd* [1938] 4 All E.R. 803 (kiosks, housing electricity transformers).

[192] *Haseldine v Daw* [1941] 2 K.B. 343.

[193] *Herschtal v Stewart & Ardern Ltd* [1940] 1 K.B. 155.

[194] *Brown v Cotterill* (1934) 51 T.L.R. 21.

[195] *Grant v Australian Knitting Mills Ltd* [1936] A.C. 85.

[196] *Ross v Caunters* [1980] Ch. 297.

[197] *Howard v Furness Houlder Argentine Lines Ltd* [1936] 2 All E.R. 781 (steam valve assembled incorrectly). See, in further detail, para.15–95, below.

[198] See para.15–111, below.

[199] *Sharpe v E.T. Sweeting & Sons Ltd* [1963] 1 W.L.R. 665 (concrete canopy over front door of council house). See also the unanimous opinions in *Murphy v Brentwood District Council* [1991] 1 A.C. 398; and *Department of the Environment v Thomas Bates & Son Ltd* [1991] 1 A.C. 499.

[200] *Brown v Cotterill* (1934) 51 T.L.R. 21 (monumental mason erected a tombstone).

[201] *Hartley v Mayoh & Co* [1953] 2 All E.R. 525 (installation of faulty electricity meter). The appeal, which is reported [1954] 1 Q.B. 383, only concerned the matter of the occupiers' liability and not the installers'. See, in further detail, para.15–97, below.

[202] *Sharp v Avery* [1938] 4 All E.R. 85 (leading motorcyclist, who misled the following motorcyclist) which could today fall under the principle in *Hedley Byrne & Co v Heller & Partners* [1964] A.C. 465, as opined in *Smith v Auckland Hospital Board* [1965] N.Z.L.R. 191.

[203] *Ross v Caunters* [1980] Ch. 297 (a defective will, causing a bequest to fail to the beneficiary's disappointment).

[204] *Stennett v Hancock* [1939] 2 All E.R. 578 (flange of a lorry's wheel, which detached itself). See, in further detail, paras 15–93–15–115, below.

[205] *Barnes v Irwell Valley Water Board* [1939] 1 K.B. 21 (water supply became poisonous with lead); *Read v Croydon Corp* [1938] 4 All E.R. 631 (typhoid infected water supply). See Waddams, "Strict Liability of Suppliers of Goods", 37 M.L.R. 154.

The scope of the manufacturer's duty. The manufacturers' duty in relation **15–68**
to a product includes the following: (i) design and construction; (ii) the
component parts used in manufacture; (iii) any container; (iv) correct labelling;
and (v) the need to give proper instructions for safe use. It is proposed to deal
with each of these matters separately.

Design and construction. The manufacturer's duty is both to design and **15–69**
construct his product with a degree of care, appropriate to the dangers attendant
upon its use, so as to minimise the risk of injury, as well as to warn prospective
users of any dangerous quality. Even so, the duty of care imposed is not
tantamount to strict liability.[206]

The product's component parts. The manufacturer's duty is not restricted to **15–70**
those parts of a product which the producer makes. It includes all component
parts, supplied by sub-manufacturers or others, which are used in the manufacture of the products. Reasonable care must be taken, by inspection or
otherwise, to see that all such parts can properly be used to put the product in a
condition in which it can be safely used or consumed in the manner for which it
is designed.[207]

The product's container. The manufacturer's duty covers extends to any **15–71**
container in which the product is packed for the purpose of distribution or sale.[208]
If the container is produced by a third party, the manufacturer must exercise
reasonable care to see that it is fit for its purpose.[209] In *Elliott v Hall*,[210] a colliery
company, which supplied coal in a defective truck, hired from a wagon company,
was liable to an employee of the buyers of the coal for the injuries caused by the
defective condition of the truck, on the ground that, as they supplied their coal in
a truck, they were under a duty to use reasonable care to see that the truck was
safe for the purpose. In *Marshall v Russian Oil Products*,[211] petrol was delivered
in a barrel which burst when it was being rolled down a skid. The suppliers were
held liable for not taking reasonable care to see that the container was fit to
withstand the ordinary risks of delivery. If, however, the defect in the container
were a latent one, which could not be detected by reasonable care and skill on the
part of the producer, he would not be liable.[212] In such a case, the maker of the
container would be liable if the latent defect were the result of negligence in the
making. Where a bottler repeatedly used bottles for carbonated beverages,

---

[206] *Todman v Victa* [1982] V.R. 849 (claimant's action failed, where he had been struck in the eye by
some unidentified object, which had been propelled upwards by the blades of his lawn mower, whilst
he was cutting the grass).
[207] See *Macpherson v Buick Motor Co*, 217 N.Y. 282, referred to with approval by Lords Atkin and
Macmillan in *Donoghue v Stevenson*.
[208] See *Geddling v Marsh* [1920] 1 K.B. 668 (the glass bottle containing lime juice and soda burst and
seriously injured the claimant shopkeeper, who was in the act of serving her customer).
[209] See, e.g. *Barnes v Irwell Valley Water Board* [1939] 1 K.B. 21 (where pure and wholesome water
was provided in the defendants' main pipes but became contaminated with lead in a service pipe).
[210] (1885) 15 Q.B.D. 315. As Lord Atkin pointed out in *Donoghue v Stevenson* [1932] A.C. 562 at
585, this case was not decided on the ground that the truck was in the defendant's possession and that
the claimant was an invitee.
[211] 1938 S.C. 773.
[212] *Elliott v Hall* (1885) 15 Q.B.D. 315, per Grove J.

without having an adequate method of inspection to see whether or not the bottles had become weakened by previous rough handling, he was liable, when a bottle suddenly exploded while standing on the floor of a retail store, injuring the claimant.[213]

15–72   **The need to label the product.** The manufacturer's duty also involves the taking of care in properly labelling a product, when a failure to do so would be likely to cause danger to person or property. If, by negligent labelling, he causes damage to the ultimate consumer or user he will be liable.

> "If a person, for example, manufactures two different articles, one being a deadly poison and the other safe, and through a careless blunder labels as safe an article which he ought to have known was of the other category and sells it under that description, I should be slow to say that in such a case he would not be responsible to persons who he knew would use the article."[214]

Vacwell Engineering Co Ltd v BDH Chemicals Ltd[215] provides an illustration. The defendants supplied the claimants with boron tribromide to facilitate the claimants' manufacture of transistor devices. The chemical was manufactured and distributed by the defendants in glass ampoules each with a label bearing the warning "harmful vapour," because it was known that the chemical reacted by emitting toxic vapour on contact with water. Neither party knew that it reacted violently and exploded on such contact. Whilst two of the claimants' physicists were engaged on washing the labels off the ampoules in two adjacent sinks of water, the glass of one was broken and a violent explosion occurred, killing one of them and causing extensive damage to the claimant's premises. The defendants were held to be negligent for failing in their duty to take reasonable care to ascertain the major industrial hazards of chemicals marketed by them, and to give a more instructive warning of the hazards to their customer.[216]

15–73   Similarly in *Devilez v Boots Pure Drug Co*,[217] the defendants were liable for failing to give a warning of danger on the label of a bottle of their corn solvent, as well as for failing to secure the bottle in some better way than with a cork. So, where a purchaser dropped a bottle of the solvent, which contained a 12 per cent solution of salicylic acid, just as he was replacing it after use, and the cork came out, spilling some of the contents on to his genitals, the defendants were held liable for the injury he sustained.

15–74   **Proper instructions for safe use.** Products may be dangerous when used for a particular purpose unless certain precautions are taken. A drug, for example, may be perfectly safe if properly diluted, but may be dangerous if taken

---

[213] *Hart v Dominion Stores* (1968) 67 D.L.R. (2d) 675.
[214] Lush J. in *Blacker v Lake and Elliott* (1912) 106 L.T. 533 at 541.
[215] [1971] 1 Q.B. 88.
[216] The proper warning to have been placed upon labels ought to have been: "reacts violently with water and explodes".
[217] (1962) 106 S.J. 552 (the claimant was held one-third to blame for handling the bottle carelessly and in failing to call a doctor sooner).

undiluted. In such a case, it is the duty of the producer to deliver adequate instructions for use with his product.

ILLUSTRATIONS

Manufacturers of a cattle dip, who negligently labelled the product, so that, **15–75** when the instructions were carried out, the dip was insufficiently diluted and cattle were killed, were held liable in negligence to the buyers.[218] Likewise, manufacturers of a cleaning fluid, who sold their product to some ship-repairers, were held liable to the owners of a ship which was damaged by an explosion caused by the fluid. They had issued inadequate instructions for its use to the ship-repairers.[219] Where a warning concerning the use of weed killer was held to be an insufficient one, the manufacturers were held liable for the damage to plants caused by the invisible mist that was produced when the weed killer was being applied properly.[220]

Likewise, where the manufacturers of a herbicide issued instructions, giving **15–76** warnings of dangers, if certain crops were to be grown, but failed to include any reference to flax, they were held liable in negligence to the claimant, an experienced farmer, for the loss suffered by him, as a result of the reduction in yield of his crop, following his use of their product applied to his fields of flax.[221] Where the supplier of a product knew that the user intended to put it to a use that would endanger third persons, he owed a duty to such persons not to supply the product at all. The mere giving of a warning addressed to the user, of the dangers involved, was insufficient in the circumstances.[222]

Manufacturers of a hair dye knew that their product was dangerous if used on **15–77** a person without first conducting a skin test, but, nevertheless, sold it to a hairdresser without warning him of the necessity of a test before use. It was held that they were liable to one of the hairdresser's customers, who developed dermatitis as a result of the application of the dye.[223] However, in like circumstances when dye was supplied in labelled bottles, complete with a brochure of instructions, both of which contained a warning that a test ought to be made before use, and no test was made, the manufacturer was not liable to one of a hairdresser's customers who contracted dermatitis. A warning given to the hairdresser was enough.[224] "I think it would be unreasonable and impossible to expect that they [the manufacturers] should give warning in such a form that it must come to the knowledge of the particular customer who is to be treated."[225] If a test were made and the claimant passed it but still contracted dermatitis as a

---

[218] *British Chartered Co of S. Africa v Lennon* (1915) 31 T.L.R. 585. In this case the buyers brought direct from the manufacturers, but this does not affect the principle.
[219] *Anglo-Celtic Shipping Co v Elliott* (1926) 42 T.L.R. 297.
[220] *Ruegger v Shell Oil of Canada* (1963) 41 D.L.R. (2d) 183.
[221] *Labrecque v Saskatchewan Wheat Pool and Eli Lilley & Co (Canada) Ltd* [1977] 6 W.W.R. 122.
[222] *Good-Wear Treaders v D. & B. Holdings* (1979) 98 D.L.R. (3d) 59.
[223] *Parker v Oloxo Ltd* [1937] 3 All E.R. 524; cf. *Holmes v Ashford* [1950] 2 All E.R. 76, which was distinguished in *Good-Wear Treaders v DGB Holdings* (1979) 98 D.L.R. (3d) 59.
[224] *Holmes v Ashford* [1950] 2 All E.R. 76 (the hairdresser was held liable).
[225] *Holmes v Ashford* [1950] 2 All E.R. 76, per Tucker L.J. at 80.

result of being allergic to the form of dye used, it is possible that the manufacturer might be liable to the claimant for making a dangerous dye, if the retailer was not given adequate information about potential ill effects.[226]

15–78   **In conclusion.** Accordingly, the duty of the manufacturer may be said to be to take reasonable care in the manufacture of his product, and failure to take such care will render him liable to any consumer or user whose person or property is injured by his product, provided: (i) the product causing the injury has the same defect as it had when it left the manufacturer; and (ii) the manufacturer should have contemplated that the product would be consumed or used in the same condition as it was in when it left him.

15–79   **Proof of negligence.** Negligence on the part of the producer must be proved before liability can be established, and the proof is the same as in any other case of negligence.[227] In *Donoghue v Stevenson*, Lord Macmillan said[228]:

> "There is no presumption of negligence in such a case as the present, nor is there any justification for applying the maxim *res ipsa loquitur*. Negligence must be both averred and proved."

This may go too far.[229] Whilst it is true that there is no presumption of negligence, the maxim res ipsa loquitur, said to be "a common sense reasoning process",[230] applies to negligence in manufacture, when the circumstances are such as to call for its application, as with negligence in other instances. The extension of the law of negligence to product liability did not change any principle of evidence.[231] The mere fact of the presence of a snail in a stoppered and sealed bottle of ginger beer would appear to be within the maxim, because, owing to retention of effective control by the manufacturer until the ginger beer reached the consumer, there is a greater probability of negligence on the part of the manufacturer than on the part of any other person.

---

[226] See *Ingham v Emes* [1955] 2 Q.B. 366 (claimant, who was tested for the dye and passed the test but developed dermatitis, sued in contract on an implied warranty that the dye was fit to be used upon her. She knew she was allergic to that form of dye but did not tell the hairdresser. It was held that the warranty was only that the dye was fit to be used upon normal persons.)

[227] Ch.6, paras 6–100–6–131, above.

[228] [1932] A.C. 562 at 622. This dictum was applied in *Daniels v White & Sons* [1938] 4 All E.R. 258 (manufacturers held to have proved that the presence of carbolic acid in their lemonade was not the result of any negligence). However, the decision in *Daniels v White & Sons* cannot be reconciled with either *Chaproniere v Mason* (1905) 21 T.L.R. 633, or *Grant v Australian Knitting Mills* [1936] A.C. 85, which latter case appears not to have been cited. In *Hill v J. Crowe (Cases) Ltd*, *The Times*, May 17, 1971, MacKenna J. considered *Daniels v White & Sons*, above, to have been criticised justly and refused to follow it, since a manufacturer's liability in negligence did not depend on proving that either he had a bad system of work or his supervision was inadequate. The defendant was held liable in respect of the negligent manufacture of a wooden packing crate, which collapsed under the weight of the claimant lorry driver as he stood on it, whilst loading up his vehicle.

[229] If taken out of context Lord Macmillan's words can be misunderstood: per Judge L.J. in *Carroll v Fearon* [1998] P.I.Q.R. P416, CA.

[230] *Carroll v Fearon*, above n.229.

[231] *Carroll v Fearon*, above at P421.

In *Grant v Australian Knitting Mills*,[232] the court apparently proceeded on the **15–80** view that the presence of the chemical irritant in the garments was evidence of negligence:

"If excess sulphites were left in the garment, that could only be because someone was at fault. The appellant is not required to lay his finger on the exact person in all the chain who was responsible, or to specify what he did wrong. Negligence is found as a matter of inference from the existence of the defects taken in connection with all the known circumstances."[233]

Similarly, in the earlier case of *Chapronière v Mason*,[234] the presence of a stone in a bath bun produced by the defendant was held to be within the maxim res ipsa loquitur and to be evidence of negligence against the baker. When dermatitis was contracted in consequence of wearing a suit which had just been cleaned by the defendants, it was held that the burden was on the defendants to prove no negligence.[235] Where a person who is complaining of injury by a defective product brings an action against the manufacturers, he must show, on the balance of probabilities, that the product was defective when it left their hands. The claimant can show this by proving that, on the balance of probabilities, the defect complained of was not added after the product had left the manufacturer's control.[236]

Where it was proved, many years after a tyre left the factory where it was **15–81** manufactured, that it had from the beginning a latent flaw which lead to its failure while in use, and that the defect was the result of negligence in manufacture, liability followed, even though the individual or individuals responsible, and the precise act of negligence, could not be identified.[237]

It is not necessary to specify any particular act of negligence. When a **15–82** workman used a defective chisel which was excessively hard, and was injured as a result, it was held that on proving that the chisel came from the manufacturers and that the hardness had not been caused at his employer's factory, he had discharged the burden of proof.[238] When the issue is whether the product is dangerous or not, discovery may be obtained of complaints of personal injuries from users, not only before but after the date of the supply of the product.[239]

---

[232] [1936] A.C. 85 (Lord Macmillan was a member of this Judicial Committee, holding a contrary view to the dictum he expressed in *Donoghue*).
[233] See above, per Lord Wright at 101.
[234] (1905) 21 T.L.R. 633.
[235] *Mayne v Silvermere Cleaners Ltd* [1939] 1 All E.R. 693.
[236] *Smith v Inglis* (1978) 83 D.L.R. (3d) 215.
[237] *Carroll v Fearon* [1998] P.I.Q.R. P416, CA.
[238] *Mason v Williams & Williams Ltd* [1955] 1 All E.R. 808. See also *Davie v New Merton Board Mills Ltd* [1959] A.C. 604 (affirming the decision of the CA [1958] 1 Q.B. 210). In the American case of *Escola v Coca Cola Bottling Co of Fresno* (1944) 150 Pac. (2d) 436, the claimant was injured by a bottle of Coca-Cola, bought by her employer and bottled and sold by the defendant, exploding in her hand. It was held that res ipsa loquitur applied and she was entitled to recover, although there was no evidence of specific acts of negligence and the defendant proved he used approved methods of inspection.
[239] *Board v Thomas Hedley & Co Ltd* [1951] 2 All E.R. 431.

15–83   **Defences.** In negligence actions concerned with dangerous products, there are a number of defences[240] available, depending upon the user's knowledge of a defect; contributory negligence; whether a defect arose after the product left the manufacturer's possession or control; whether an inspection was contemplated before use.

15–84   **User's knowledge of defect.** The producer may not be liable, when the consumer or user knows of the defect:

> "The principle of *Donoghue's* case can only be applied where the defect is hidden and unknown to the consumer, otherwise the directness of cause and effect is absent: the man who consumes or uses a thing which he knows to be noxious cannot complain in respect of whatever mischief follows, because it follows from his own conscious volition in choosing to incur the risk or certainty of mischance."[241]

In *Farr v Butter Bros & Co*,[242] the manufacturers of a crane sent it out in parts, to enable it to be assembled by the buyers. The buyers' foreman, in assembling it, noticed that it was defective but continued to assemble and, regardless, to work the crane, before the defects were remedied. As a result, he was killed but the manufacturers were held not liable in respect of the death on the ground that the chain of causation was broken.

15–85   In *McTear v Imperial Tobacco Ltd*,[243] the claimant failed to establish liability against a cigarette manufacturer for the death of her husband as a result of lung cancer. Although proof of causation was held to be insufficient, the court also considered the manufacturer's duty of care towards someone who used its products between 1964 and 1992. It held that no duty of care arose where the person injured was well aware of the dangerous characteristics of the produce used. There was no defect in the product of which the deceased was not aware. Nor was there any duty to warn of risks of which the ordinary member of the relevant class of people might reasonably be assumed to be aware of. Presumably, similar considerations should apply to other commonly available products, for example, alcoholic drinks and medications commonly available for purchase without prescription, neither of which may contain any manufacturing defect but both of which are capable of being harmful if consumed inadvisedly.

15–86   Knowledge of a defect does not, as a matter of law, prevent the consumer or user from establishing liability. The manufacturer by negligently causing the defect has been guilty of a breach of duty. The question to be answered, namely whether any particular damage is causally connected with that breach, or the chain of causation between the breach and the damage broken, is essentially one of fact, depending on the circumstances. It is not a question of law. The circumstances may show that, even with knowledge of a defect, the consumer

---

[240] For defences and discharges from liability, generally, see Ch.4, above.
[241] Lord Wright in *Grant v Australian Knitting Mills Ltd* [1936] A.C. 85, 105.
[242] [1932] 2 K.B. 606. See the criticism of this decision in Williams, *Joint Torts and Contributory Negligence*, pub. 1951, p.324.
[243] *The Times*, June 14, 2005, OH. See also Ch.6, para.6–16, above.

may be justified in incurring the danger which it suggests. The test to is the old test, laid down in *Clayards v Dethick*,[244] "whether the plaintiff acted as a man of ordinary prudence would have done, or rashly and in defiance of warning". In other words, it is whether in the circumstances he has acted reasonably. This is illustrated by *Denny v Supplies & Transport Co Ltd*,[245] where a barge, containing timber, was so badly loaded by the defendants that it was dangerous to unload. The claimant, who was employed to unload it, had noticed that it was unsafe but proceeded to unload it, in consequence of which he was injured. It was held that he was entitled to recover damages on the ground that it was reasonable for him to unload, because the only alternative was to leave the barge loaded.

In *London Graving Dock v Horton*,[246] Lord Porter expressed the view that knowledge of the true position would be "a complete answer to the claim" against the manufacturer, but *Horton* was a decision on the principle of *Indermaur v Dames*[247] and it was held that *Donoghue v Stevenson*[248] could not have any application to the facts of that case. It is to be noted that *Denny* is not mentioned in any of the judgments. Nevertheless, in *Gledhill v Liverpool Abattoir Ltd*,[249] Lord Porter's view was followed and approved by the Court of Appeal. However, the facts of *Gledhill* do not appear to be in point. The claimant's employers, by arrangement with the Liverpool Corporation, used the Corporation's abattoir in which to slaughter pigs. The pigs, after being stunned, were fixed to an elevator by chains supplied by the Corporation. When the chains became worn the Corporation supplied new chains at the employers' request. The new chains were strong and properly made but were unsuitable because they were of a heavier type than was necessary, so that one of the pigs on being lifted slipped and fell on the claimant, injuring him. The new chains had been in use for about a year without complaint to the Corporation although the claimant and his employers both knew of their unsuitability for the work. The claimant's action against the Corporation failed.

15–87

> "The Corporation were entitled to assume that if the chains did not prove suitable or convenient they would not be used. They cannot be held responsible for their use by those who had full knowledge that some difficulties were in some cases and on some occasions presented."[250]

In this case there seems to have been no breach of duty on the part of the Corporation. The chains they supplied were not defective in any way and if they were not suitable for the purpose for which the claimant's employers required them that would not give rise to any liability in tort to a third party unless they were required for immediate use without any possibility of examination.

---

[244] (1848) 12 Q.B. 439.
[245] [1950] 2 K.B. 374.
[246] [1951] A.C. 737 at 750.
[247] (1866) L.R. 1 C.P. 274.
[248] [1932] A.C. 562. See ibid., the similar views expressed by Lord Normand and Lord MacDermott.
[249] [1957] 1 W.L.R. 1028.
[250] n.249, above.

15–88   **Contributory negligence.** Whether the producer is liable if the consumer, although ignorant of the defect, could have discovered its existence by the exercise of reasonable care, has not been decided. The consumer is presumably entitled to assume that the manufacturer has fulfilled properly his duty and is not bound to make an examination for defects.[251] On the other hand, if the defect would have become apparent to anyone consuming or using the article with reasonable care, the consumer or user may well be prevented from recovering in full, on the ground of his contributory negligence.

15–89   **Defect caused after the manufacturer has parted with the products.** The producer is not liable when the defect was not the result of his negligence but was caused by something which had happened after he had parted with the product. As Lord Macmillan said:

> "I can readily conceive that where a manufacturer has parted with his product and it has passed into other hands it may well be exposed to vicissitudes which may render it defective or noxious, for which the manufacturer could not in any view be held to blame."[252]

In considering whether the defect was owing to the producer's negligence, the lapse of time since he had parted with the article, the probability of damage from other causes, the speed with which articles of that kind deteriorate, and the necessity or otherwise of repair, are all matters to be taken into consideration.[253] So, where the windscreen of a car broke for no apparent cause after about a year's use, the producers were held not liable. After the lapse of time and the many opportunities for damage, including negligent fitting, it could not be said that the probable cause of the damage was negligence in manufacture.[254] Again, in the example suggested in *Grant v Australian Knitting Mills*[255] of a foundry which had cast a rudder to be fitted to a ship and after some years of use the rudder broke, owing to negligent casting, causing great loss of life and damage

---

[251] See *Mason v Williams & Williams* [1955] 1 All E.R. 808 where it was held that factory owners were not bound to examine tools supplied by reputable manufacturers for defects, before issuing them to their workmen to use. In *Davie v New Merton Board Mills Ltd* [1959] A.C. 604 at 630. The trial judge had held "that no intermediate examination of the drift between the time of the manufacture and the time of its actual use was reasonably to be expected. It seems to me wholly unreasonable to expect an employer to test a drift for hardness before issuing it to his employee, and no other examination would have revealed the danger existing in this particular drift.' Accordingly there was no negligence on the part of the employers. Contrast *Taylor v Rover Co* [1966] 1 W.L.R. 1491. See now the effects of the Employer's Liability (Defective Equipment) Act 1969, in the case of an employer and employee relationship, and, generally, Ch.11, paras 11–55–11–64, above.

[252] *Donoghue v Stevenson* [1932] A.C. 562 at 622.

[253] As an example, see *Gillespie v Grahame* (1956) 106 L.J. 458, where a joiner had erected a henhouse on land and, in a wind, the roof of the henhouse was blown on to the adjoining land, causing damage, the joiner was held not liable. Lord Hill Watson held that the joiner's liability depended on whether there was or was not a reasonable opportunity for inspection by an ordinary prudent owner who was doing his duty.

[254] *Evans v Triplex Safety Glass Co* [1936] 1 All E.R. 283.

[255] [1936] A.C. 85 at 107.

to property, the maker would not be held liable, because "so many contingencies must have intervened between the lack of care on the part of the makers and the casualty".

Where a product is intended for temporary use only, and the time for its use has expired, a manufacturer would be relieved from liability.[256]

Inspection contemplated before use. In *Donoghue v Stevenson*, the product **15–90** was delivered in a form which precluded the possibility of intermediate examination. However, the impossibility of examination is not essential for liability: it is sufficient that the producer contemplates that the product will be used immediately, without any previous examination or test, even though the possibility of examination is not precluded.

On the other hand, when it is contemplated that, in the ordinary course of **15–91** things, a product will not be used until after an examination or test is first made, a producer is not liable for defects which such an examination or test ought to have revealed.[257] On this principle, when contractors carried out work which was subject to the approval of the local authority, and their work was passed by the local authority's works supervisor, it was held that they were not liable to a person who tripped over a soleplate, which had been placed under an upright or pillar positioned on the floor in a passage.[258] If an examination or test is made, whether it was contemplated or not, the producer may not be liable for defects which that examination or test ought to have revealed. Liability depends on whether, in the circumstances of the case, the chain of causation is broken.[259] It has also been held that when a substantial period of time had elapsed between the delivery of the product and the occurrence of damage, during which period an examination might have been made, the producer was not liable.[260] It is submitted, however, that lapse of time between delivery and damage is only relevant to the question whether the products were in the same condition as when they left the manufacturer. If they were, then the manufacturer will be liable, notwithstanding that there was an opportunity, which was not taken, of examining the goods.[261] That will be so, unless, of course, he contemplated that his products would not be used, without first their being examined by the consumer.

---

[256] *Eccles v Cross & M'Ilwham*, 1938 S.C. 697 (electricians who installed a temporary electric lighting system were held not liable to builders' workman killed two months after).
[257] As in *Kubach v Hollands* [1937] 3 All E.R. 907, para.15–64, above.
[258] *Buckner v Ashby & Horner Ltd* [1941] 1 K.B. 321. See also *London Graving Dock v Horton* [1951] A.C. 737 at 750, per Lord Porter, "an examination by the retail vendor, if rightly expected, could be relied on by the manufacturer and would have been a complete answer to the claim".
[259] See para.15–89, above.
[260] *Paine v Colne Valley Electricity Supply Co* [1938] 4 All E.R. 803 (interval of two years between delivery of machinery and installation by buyers: manufacturers not liable).
[261] See *Mason v Williams & Williams Ltd* [1955] 1 All E.R. 808. This decision was approved by the HL in *Davie v New Merton Board Mills Ltd* [1959] A.C. 604, although the latter has now been reversed by the Employer's Liability (Defective Equipment) Act 1969 so far as concerned the duty between employer and employee.

15–92   If the producer sends out his products, accompanied by a warning that they are to be tested before use, he is under no liability for resultant damage caused by failure to observe the warning.[262]

(B) Duty of other transferors

15–93   **Extension of the principle.** It will be recalled that the "manufacturer's duty"[263] has been extended so that it covers other people besides the actual manufacturer of the product in question.[264] It extends for instance to those who install or erect products on premises, or who undertake to assemble or repair a product or other property and so negligently perform their work that physical damage is caused to the person or property of a third party. The duty in such cases is similar to that of a manufacturer in that care must be taken to do the work in question in such a way that a product is not a source of danger to those who might be injured if it was not to be installed, erected, assembled or repaired properly.

15–94   **Concurrent liability in contract and negligence.** It is quite clear that:

> "The fact that there is a contractual relationship between the parties which may give rise to an action for breach of contract, does not exclude the co-existence of a right of action founded on negligence as between the same parties, independently of the contract, though arising out of the relationship in fact brought about by the contract. Of this the best illustration is the right of the injured railway passenger to sue the railway company either for breach of the contract of safe carriage or for negligence in carrying him. And there is no reason why the same set of facts should not give one person a right of action in contract and another person a right of action in tort."[265]

But it is not the case that if one person commits a breach of contract with another, a third party, who is injured in consequence of the breach, must have a right of action in tort against the first party, by reason of such breach. In all cases the person suing in tort must show a breach of duty towards himself and cannot rely on a breach of duty towards any other person.

15–95   In addition to those cases[266] which have been discussed in the previous paragraphs, the following decisions are further illustrations of the applications of the rule. In *Swanson v Hanneson, Sterna and Henkel Enterprises Ltd*,[267] an owner of a racing car had carried out modifications negligently so that the accelerator mechanism jammed suddenly, as he was going at speed around a bend, causing the car to leave the race track and crashed into the spectators,

---

[262] *Kubach v Hollands* [1937] 3 All E.R. 907, para.15–64, above, and, likewise, *Holmes v Ashford* [1950] 2 All E.R. 76, which was distinguished in *Good-Wear Treaders v D. & B. Holdings* (1979) 98 D.L.R. (3d) 59, where it was held that the mere giving of a warning of the dangers of the product supplied was insufficient.

[263] See para.15–57, above.

[264] See para.15–67, above.

[265] Lord Macmillan in *Donoghue v Stevenson* [1932] A.C. 562 at 610.

[266] *Brown v Cotterill* (1934) 51 T.L.R. 21; *Malfroot v Noxal Ltd* (1935) 51 T.L.R. 551; *Herschtal v Stewart & Ardern Ltd* [1940] 1 K.B. 155, all in para.15–62, above.

[267] (1972) 26 D.L.R. (3d) 201; affirmed (1974) 42 D.L.R. (3d) 688.

killing two of them, for which he was held liable. In *Sharpe v E.T. Sweeting & Son Ltd*,[268] where the wife of the tenant of a council house was injured by the fall of a defective canopy which had been erected outside and above the front door, the builders were held liable. The basis of such a finding was that, as independent contractors of the Corporation, having erected the canopy in circumstances in which they did not and could not have reasonably anticipated that there would be any intermediate examination that would probably have revealed the defects, they owed her a duty of care. In *Howard v Furness Houlder Ltd*,[269] the claimant was injured by the negligent reassembling of a valve in a steamship. He was held entitled to recover, on the ground that the defendants by their negligence had converted an article not dangerous in itself into a dangerous article.

In *Haseldine v Daw & Son Ltd*,[270] a firm of lift repairers were held liable to **15–96** a passenger in the lift, who was injured in consequence of their negligent work:

> "Where the facts show that no intermediate inspection is practicable or is contemplated, a repairer of a chattel stands in no different position from that of a manufacturer, and does owe a duty to a person who, in the ordinary course, may be expected to make use of the thing repaired."[271]

In *Hartley v Mayoh & Co*,[272] the work of installing electricity in a factory was **15–97** carried out by an Area Electricity Board, which negligently transposed the leads at a meter on the premises. Thus, when the mains switch was thrown, it did not isolate entirely the supply of electricity, so that a fireman was electrocuted subsequently whilst assisting in fighting a fire, although the current supposedly had been switched off. The Board was held liable on the ground that they should have contemplated that their omission to test the circuit after the installation had been completed might cause damage to persons who were lawfully on the premises and who had occasion to come into contact with any part of the wiring system. Where burglars had effected entry to premises by means of forcing the security gate, which had been installed negligently by the defendants who were burglary prevention specialists, the latter were held liable to the owners, whose silver and valuables were stolen.[273]

(i) *Other transferors, the retailer*

The retailer. The position as regards a retailer calls for special attention since **15–98** his liability is likely to straddle both the law of contract and tort concurrently. Because the retailer of products is in a contractual relationship with the buyer, he will be held liable for breach of contract if he sells defective or dangerous

---

[268] [1963] 1 W.L.R. 665.
[269] [1936] 2 All E.R. 781.
[270] [1941] 2 K.B. 343.
[271] *Haseldine v Daw & Son Ltd* [1941] 2 K.B. 343, per Goddard L.J. at 379.
[272] [1953] 2 All E.R. 525. An appeal by the occupiers of the factory was reported in [1954] Q.B. 383, but such did not concern the liability of the electricity board.
[273] *Dove v Banhams Patent Locks Ltd, The Times*, March 5, 1983.

products.[274] The extent of his contractual liability has been dealt with already.[275] For breach of contract, the retailer is only liable in damages to the buyer. However, such damages may include the expense to which the buyer has been put, or the pecuniary loss which he has sustained through injury to those members of his family living with him that were caused by the breach of contract.[276] If there has been a breach of contract, it is immaterial whether or not the seller has been negligent; he is equally liable for latent defects in the articles which he sells, as for defects discoverable on reasonable examination.[277]

15–99   Where retailers had fitted to the rear of a Land Rover, supplied by them, a trailer's towing coupling, which was dangerously manufactured, owing to bad design, it was held that they were not in breach of any implied warranty under the Sale of Goods Act. The implied warranty, which related to the coupling as at the time of delivery, was a continuing one, namely that it would remain fit for its purpose for a reasonable length of time thereafter, provided that it was still in its same apparent state, fair wear and tear excluded. Thus, once it had become known to the vehicle's owner that the locking mechanism of the towing hitch was broken, the retailers' implied warranty ceased to take effect, because the coupling was no longer in the same apparent state as when it had been delivered.[278]

15–100   **Retailer's fraud.** A retailer is liable if he makes any fraudulent mis-representation in selling his products; his liability extends to any person who ought to have been in his contemplation as likely to be injured by his fraud. Accordingly, the seller of a gun, who warranted the gun to be safe, when he knew it was unsafe, was held liable to the buyer's son, who was injured as a result of the gun bursting.[279]

15–101   **Retailer's duty to warn.** Quite apart from any question of contract or fraud, a retailer owes a duty to the person to whom he supplies products, to warn him of any danger in them of which he knows and of which he could not reasonably expect the recipient to know. Likewise, he must warn him of any defect in the products which renders them unfit for the purpose for which he contemplates they will be used, provided that he knows of the defect. Failure to disclose the danger or defect will render him liable to the products' ultimate consumer, who suffers damage directly attributable to such danger or defect. When the claimant was supplied by the sellers with a tin of disinfectant powder, which, owing to the previous complaints they had received, the sellers knew would be likely to cause

---

[274] See paras 15–50–15–56, above.
[275] See above.
[276] *Preist v Last* [1903] 2 K.B. 148 (hot water bottle burst and injured buyer's wife); *Frost v Aylesbury Dairy Co* [1905] 1 K.B. 608 (milk contained germs of typhoid fever, whereby buyer's wife died); *Jackson v Watson & Sons* [1909] 2 K.B. 193 (tinned salmon poisoned buyer's wife). The contractual duty applies also to the container: *Geddling v Marsh* [1920] 1 K.B. 668 (lime juice and soda mineral water bottle).
[277] *Randall v Newson* (1877) 2 Q.B.D. 102 (carriage-pole); *Myers v Brent Cross Service Co* [1934] 1 K.B. 46 (connecting rod); *Grant v Australian Knitting Mills* [1936] A.C. 85 (underpants).
[278] *Lambert v Lewis* [1982] A.C. 225. See Leder, "*Lambert v Lewis*—A Hitch in the Chain of Causation", 78 L.S.Gaz. 579; Samuels, "Responsibility for Injury Caused by a Defective Coupling—1", 132 New L.J. 833.
[279] *Langridge v Levy* (1837) 2 M. & W. 519; affirmed 4 M. & W. 338.

injury unless the tins were opened with special care, and yet had given her no warning of the danger, the claimant was held entitled to recover damages for her injuries sustained.[280] Similarly, it would appear that a retailer who had negligently delivered products which he knew to be dangerous, in mistake for harmless ones that had been ordered by the buyer, would be liable to the consumer, who, believing that the retailer had delivered the correct articles, used them and, thereby, suffered damage.[281]

Duty to pass on the manufacturer's instructions. The retailer must also **15–102** pass on to the buyer any instructions for use or warnings which he has received from the producer. So, where a chemical was bought from a manufacturer, with a warning attached that it must be "examined and tested by user before use", and the retailer failed to hand on such warning to his customer, with the result that no examination was made and an explosion occurred, the retailer was held liable.[282] The retailer who has sold products that were dangerous by reason of a latent defect in them, may be able to escape liability for negligence to an injured consumer if it could be shown that he himself had purchased them from well-known and reputable suppliers. Such matter arose for consideration in *Fisher v Harrods*[283] where the retailers were held to be negligent in failing to make inquiries of the manufacturer of a cleaning liquid, which had exploded and injured a buyer, in failing to have it analysed and in marketing the product without giving a warning. If the retailers had made any inquiry they would have discovered that the manufacturer was a man of insufficient qualification for and experience in the manufacture of this type of cleaning product.

Retailer's duty not to damage product. When the retailer does not know **15–103** that the products are defective or dangerous and he sells them already packed or made up in a bottle, tin or other container, it is not reasonably possible for him to examine the goods without destroying the condition in which the manufacturer intended them to reach the consumer and in which the consumer would expect to receive them. In these circumstances he is under no liability in tort to a consumer or user who obtains the products with the same defects as they had when they left the manufacturer. In *Gordon v McHardy*,[284] where a consumer died after eating tinned salmon purchased at a grocery shop, it was held that, as the tin was only to be opened immediately before its use, it was not reasonable to expect the grocer to examine the product, hence he was not liable.

However, if the damage to the consumer is caused not by some defect which **15–104** the products had when they left the producer but by some other defect, the retailer will be liable if that defect was caused by his negligence. He should for instance take reasonable care to see that a product is apparently in the same

---

[280] *Clarke v Army and Navy Co-operative Society* [1903] 1 K.B. 155.
[281] cf. *Macdonald v Macbrayne Ltd*, 1915 S.C. 716; *British Chartered Co of S. Africa v Lennon* (1915) 31 T.L.R. 585; *Philco Radio v Spurling* [1949] 2 All E.R. 882.
[282] *Kubach v Hollands* [1937] 3 All E.R. 907. The trial of the issue between the claimant and the retailer is reported in *The Times*, June 17, 1937.
[283] (1966) 110 S.J. 133.
[284] (1903) 6 F. 210. Apparently approved in *Donoghue v Stevenson* [1932] A.C. 562; see at 604 (Lord Thankerton), and at 622 (Lord Macmillan).

condition as when it left the producer, and is free from external defect. If a tin or any other container has been damaged and the retailer knew or ought to have known of the defect, he would be liable if injury to the consumer arises as a result.[285] Also, if complaints have been received from consumers about a particular consignment of products, the retailer would be liable if he continued to sell them without taking precautions. The sale of a consignment of goods may have to be discontinued, or other precautions taken to eliminate any defect.[286]

15–105   **Retailer ignorant of damage.** If the form in which the producer makes his products does not preclude the retailer from making an examination of them before sale, the question then can arise, what is the liability of the retailer for damage which has been caused by the goods sold, when he did not know, although he could have known by the exercise of reasonable care, that the goods were dangerously defective?

15–106   First, the retailer is liable for damage which is the result of any dangerous defects that have developed in a product, caused by his own negligence. If, for example, he stores them in such a position or in such a manner that they are contaminated from external sources, such as rats, damp or dirt, the principle of *Donoghue v Stevenson* would render him liable to the ultimate consumer for his negligence. The same result would follow if he kept them in stock for so long a period that they became dangerous.

15–107   A retailer is under no duty to examine products for dangerous defects before resale, in the absence of circumstances suggesting that they might be defective, when he has obtained them from a manufacturer of repute.[287] If he obtains them from a dubious source, he may be under a duty to examine them, depending on the nature of the products and the probability or otherwise of danger to be expected from defects to which they are subject. Such a duty was held to exist in *Andrews v Hopkinson*,[288] where a second-hand motorcar, which had been selected by the claimant, was sold by the defendant, who was a dealer in second-hand cars, to a finance company, which then let it to the claimant on hire-purchase terms. The vehicle had a defect in the steering, which could have been discovered by a competent mechanic, though probably not by an ordinary owner-driver, and the defendant had no reason to suppose that the car would be examined, before use. The defendant was held liable, McNair J. stating[289]:

---

[285] See *Gordon v McHardy*, above, where the Lord Justice-Clerk said that an averment that the tin was dented so as to cut through the metal and cause injury to the contents, which the defender should have noticed, might have been ground for an action against him.

[286] See *Clarke v Army and Navy Co-operative Society* [1903] 1 K.B. 155, where the retailers knew of the dangerous condition of the goods, because of complaints they had received, and were liable for not giving warning, after knowledge of the danger.

[287] *Mason v Williams & Williams Ltd* [1955] 1 All E.R. 808, which was approved by the HL in *Davie v New Merton Board Mills Ltd* [1959] A.C. 604, although the latter decision has been reversed by the effect of the Employers' Liability (Defective Equipment) Act 1969, as regards employer and employee cases, for which see Ch.11, paras 11–55–11–64, above.

[288] [1957] 1 Q.B. 229. See note on this case, 73 L.Q.R. 147.

[289] *Andrews v Hopkinson* [1957] 1 Q.B. 229 at 237.

"Having regard to the extreme peril involved in allowing an old car with a defective steering mechanism to be used on the road, I have no hesitation in holding that the defendant in the circumstances was guilty of negligence in failing to make the necessary examination, or at least in failing to warn the plaintiff that no such examination had been carried out."

Similarly, in *Watson v Buckley, Osborne, Garrett & Co Ltd*,[290] a hair dye was distributed by a firm which was not the manufacturer to a hairdresser who proceeded to use it on the claimant, as a result of which the claimant contracted dermatitis. The reason was that the dye should have contained a four per cent solution of acid but in fact contained a 10 per cent solution. The distributors had obtained the dye from "a gentleman who had emerged quite unexpectedly from Spain", had advertised it as safe and fit for use, without the necessity for any preliminary test. Although they had given full directions for use, they had made no examination of the dye before distributing it. They were held to have been negligent, hence they were liable to the claimant. **15–108**

The duty in tort of a retailer, as stated above, applies to all sellers, who are not manufacturers, whether they sell by retail or wholesale, because a wholesaler, who distributes defective and dangerous products should be in precisely the same position as the retailer.[291] **15–109**

Where the producer is resident abroad. A foreign producer can be made answerable as a third party in an action in negligence, which has been commenced against the local distributors, where the damage was suffered within the jurisdiction,[292] thereby completing the tort.[293] However, liability, which is based on negligence, can be of no avail where the manufacturer is domiciled abroad and there is no local distributor.[294] **15–110**

(ii) *Miscellaneous other transferors*

A number of other persons may be involved in a trasnfer of a product amd it remains to consider the liability that may arise if damage is caused to the consumer or user.[295] The liability of these other transferors may arise either: out of contract or tort. They may be (1) the owner, including a bailee with the right to use the products, who transfers them by way of loan or gift or who lets them on hire; (2) the owner or bailee, who delivers them to a carrier for carriage; and (3) the carrier of products, who delivers them to a consignee. **15–111**

---

[290] [1940] 1 All E.R. 174.

[291] In *Goodchild v Vaclight, The Times*, May 22, 1965, it was held that as the defendants, the distributors in England of vacuum cleaners made in Germany, both serviced and guaranteed them in this country, they owed the same duty of care as the manufacturers.

[292] See *Charlesworth & Percy on Negligence* (7th edn, 1983) para.16–01, p.1023.

[293] *Castree v E.R. Squibb & Sons Ltd* [1980] 1 W.L.R. 1248 (a centrifuge machine, manufactured in Germany, was purchased by the claimant's employers from the manufacturers' sole distributors in England. The machine disintegrated, during use, and seriously injured the claimant).

[294] See, e.g. *Godley v Perry* [1960] 1 W.L.R. 9, where, if someone else had bought the defective plastic toy catapult and given it to the claimant, a child of six, the latter's remedy would have lain in tort only against the manufacturers, which were domiciled in Hong Kong.

[295] See "The Liability to Third Persons of the Transferor of Defective Chattels" (1951) 25 Austr. L.J. 2.

15–112   **Contractual liability.** In the case of hiring, it is an implied term of the contract that the article which is let on hire is as fit for the purpose as reasonable care and skill can make it.[296] There is some doubt whether this implied term covers latent defects.[297] However, the primary obligations to supply plant in good condition and provide a competent operator were not affected by the terms of standard conditions of hire.[298] In the case of carriage, there is an implied warranty on the part of the consignor that the goods are fit to be carried, and there arises no exception in the case of latent defects.[299] The carrier's duty, in the absence of any agreed term to the contrary, depends on whether or not he is a common carrier, and need not be considered here.

15–113   **Tortious duty: owner who lends, gives or hires.** The duty in tort of the owner of products, who delivers them by way of gift, loan or hire, is much the same as that of a retailer. In all these cases the liability of the transferor does not depend on any contract that he has entered into, and "no question of consideration between the parties is relevant."[300] Therefore, the fact that the retailer sells the products does not make his liability in tort any higher than if he donates them or lends them, with or without consideration being paid for their use. If the owner-transferor is also the manufacturer he owes the "manufacturer's duty".[301] Hence, in the supposition put forward by Denning L.J. in *Hawkins v Coulsdon & Purley Urban District Council*,[302] that where the manufacturer of a special soap sent out samples by way of gift to members of the public, and, owing to negligence in manufacturing, a user of the soap suffered from dermatitis, the manufacturer would still be liable, his manner of putting the soap in circulation, whether by gift or by sale, being totally irrelevant.

15–114   In the case of a gratuitous loan, the lender of familiar objects, such as a pair of step-ladders, an electric mincer, an electric drill, a lawn mower, power-driven hedge trimmers, etc., is bound to communicate any known defects in them with reference to the use to which they are to be put. If he does not know of them, although he might have discovered them by the exercise of reasonable care, he

[296] *Mowbray v Merryweather* [1895] 2 Q.B. 640, which was distinguished by Winn L.J. in *Hadley v Droitwich Construction Co* [1968] 1 W.L.R. 37, 43, where it was held that the implied warranty as to fitness of the crane, when handed over, was qualified by the hirer's undertakings to put a competent man in charge of it and to see that it was properly serviced but that this implied warranty could not survive the hirer's breach of those undertakings. It is to be observed that in *Lambert v Lewis* [1982] A.C. 225, 276, Lord Diplock opined that what Winn L.J. had said in *Hadley* was correct. See also *Vogan & Co v Oulton* (1889) 81 L.T. 435; *Hyman v Nye* (1881) 6 Q.B.D. 685.
[297] In *Hyman v Nye* n.296 above, Lindley J. said that a latent defect was a defence, but Mathew J. expressly reserved his opinion. In *Geddling v Marsh* [1920] 1 K.B. 668, a DC thought that *Hyman v Nye* decided that contract of hiring differed from a contract of sale of goods in this respect, *sed quaere*.
[298] *Edward McConkey v AMEC*, 27 Con. L.R. 88, CA.
[299] *Brass v Maitland* (1856) 6 E. & B. 470; *G.N. Ry v L.E.P. Transport Co* [1922] 2 K.B. 742; *Bamfield v Goole and Sheffield Transport Co* [1910] 2 K.B. 94.
[300] Lord Wright in *Grant v Australian Knitting Mills Co* [1936] A.C. 85, 103.
[301] See para.15–68, above.
[302] [1954] 1 Q.B. 319 at 333.

is not liable for damage caused by the defects.[303] As to gifts, it has been said[304]:

> "The principle of law as to gifts is, that the giver is not responsible for damage resulting from the insecurity of the thing, unless he knew its evil character at the time, and omitted to caution the donee. There must be something like fraud on the part of the giver before he can be made answerable."

15–115 Accordingly, an owner, who transfers products to another, whether by gift, loan or hire, is under a duty to warn the transferee of defects, which are actually known to him, if they render them unfit for the purpose for which he contemplates they will be used.[305] If he warns the transferee, he is under no further liability but, if he omits to warn the latter, he is liable to the consumer or user who suffers damage directly attributable to the defect in them.

No knowledge of defect. When the owner does not know that the products **15–116** are defective, the general rule is that he is under no liability. So, if factory owners give a general permission to contractors to use their plant, they do not contemplate that any particular piece of plant will be used for any particular work and are not liable to the contractors' workman who is injured through using one of their defective ladders.[306] The owner's position, as regards defects of which he ought to have known, is rather different from that of a retailer. A retailer of new as opposed to second-hand, products has not used them. He delivers them in the same condition as they were in when he received them, subject only to such deterioration either as they may have suffered in carriage, for which he should make some examination, depending on their nature, or as they have developed while in his custody, against which he ought to take reasonable steps to safeguard them. An owner, by way of contrast, either may have used the goods, whereupon they may have become worn or defective and in need of repair, or may not have used them, as a result of which they may have deteriorated by disuse and, as a reasonable man, he ought to know that they may have become unfit for the contemplated purpose. In such a case, an objective test will be applied and his knowledge of the facts, rendering the products defective could be considered to be knowledge of the defect.[307] Further, if he delivers the products for immediate use, there is some authority for the view that he must take reasonable care to examine them to see that they are fit for the contemplated use.[308]

---

[303] *Coughlin v Gillison* [1899] 1 Q.B. 145 (the defendants lent a donkey-engine to claimant. The engine's boiler, which was defective, exploded and injured the claimant. The defendants, however, avoided liability since they were unaware of the defect).

[304] per Willes J. in *Gautret v Egerton* (1867) L.R. 2 C.P. 371 at 375.

[305] *Clarke v Army and Navy Co-operative Society* [1903] 1 K.B. 155; *White v Steadman* [1913] 3 K.B. 340.

[306] *Marshall v Cellactite & British Uralite Ltd* (1947) 63 T.L.R. 456; *Johnson v Croggan & Co Ltd* [1954] 1 W.L.R. 195.

[307] See *Hawkins v Coulsdon & Purley Urban District Council* [1954] 1 Q.B. 319.

[308] See *Heaven v Pender* (1883) 11 Q.B.D. 503 at 511, per Brett M.R.; approved by Lord Atkin in *Donoghue v Stevenson* [1932] A.C. 562 at 581. In "The Liability of the Gratuitous Transferor" (1950) 66 L.Q.R. 39, Marsh argues that there is no difference between the liability in tort of the gratuitous transferor and a transferor for reward—a view which is clearly right. He then argues that a gratuitous transferor "must . . . use reasonable care if he chooses to put the chattel into circulation". If this means he must use reasonable care to discover defect it is too wide.

15–117   In *Heaven v Pender*,[309] a dock owner, as incident to the use of his dock, provided a shipowner with a staging to be used by workmen, who were engaged in repairing the ship. The claimant was a painter, whose employer was under contract with the shipowner to paint the ship. The ropes of the staging had been scorched and were unfit for use and were supplied without a reasonably careful attention to their condition, so that they broke, as a result of which the claimant fell into the dock and was injured. The dock owner was held liable to the claimant on the ground that, although he did not retain control of the staging, he had a duty to use:

> "reasonable care as to the state of the articles when delivered by him to the ship under repair for immediate use in relation to the repairers. For any neglect of those having control of the ship and the appliances he would not be liable, and to establish his liability it must be proved that the defect which caused the accident existed at the time when the article was supplied by the dock owner."[310]

15–118   In *Oliver v Saddler & Co*,[311] stevedores, in conjunction with porters, were unloading a ship. The cargo was hoisted in rope slings, provided by the stevedores, who gratuitously had permitted the porters to use the slings for transporting the cargo from the point where the stevedores' duty ended, to the dock. While a sling was being used by the porters it broke, killing one of them. The House of Lords held that because the stevedores owed a duty to the porters to use reasonable care to see that the sling was fit to take the weight loaded upon it, they were liable to the dependants of the deceased man.

15–119   Regarding an owner's duty to discover defects, it has been said:

> "I think that a person who has the means of knowledge and only does not know that the animal or chattel which he supplies is dangerous because he does not take ordinary care to avail himself of his opportunity of knowledge is in precisely the same position as the person who knows. A person who keeps for hire horses, some of which he knows may be dangerous, cannot shelter himself behind his own want of knowledge, if that arises from his indifference or carelessness. If he has the means of knowledge and shuts his

---

[309] (1883) 11 Q.B.D. 503.
[310] *Heaven v Pender* (1883) 11 Q.B.D. 503 at 515, per Cotton L.J. Also see *Elliott v Hall* (1885) 15 Q.B.D. 315 (coal sellers had hired a truck from a wagon company and had examined it before use but negligently had failed to discover that it was defective: they were held liable to an injured employee of the buyer, who had climbed into the truck to unload it and had fallen through the faulty trap-door); *Hawkins v Smith* (1896) 12 T.L.R. 532 (grain was loaded into sacks, which had been hired by consignees from the defendant, one which was defective and burst when it was hoisted up, causing injury to a dock labourer: the defendant was held liable, since he knew the purpose for which the sack was required and had delivered one which was unfit for that purpose). Both this case and *Elliott*, above, were mentioned with approval by Lord Atkin in *Donoghue v Stevenson* [1932] A.C. 562 at 585.
[311] [1929] A.C. 584. cf. *Gledhill v Liverpool Abattoir Ltd* [1957] W.L.R. 1028, where the distinction was made that the stevedores knew that the porters relied on them to take care that the slings were safe, since the porters had no prior opportunity of examination, but where ample opportunity for independent examination of the chains being used by slaughtermen existed before the accident, the suppliers of the chains were held not to be liable.

eyes to them, he does not thereby diminish or alter his duty towards those to whom he supplies a horse which is dangerous in fact."[312]

Hence, the lenders' duty is only to use reasonable care to see that the goods **15–120** lent for immediate use are reasonably fit for the intended purpose. Where a lorry driver was engaged in loading his lorry by means of some borrowed wire slings, which belonged to the quay's owners, and was injured by a frayed wire, it was held that, on proof that reasonable care was taken to keep the slings in good condition and that the sling in question was in good condition, when it had been taken out of the store, the owners were not liable.[313]

The mere fact that the article lent breaks while being used by the borrower is in itself no evidence of negligence against the lender.[314] For example, if the article lent is a sling, it may have been overloaded,[315] and in any case some affirmative evidence of negligence must be given.

In some of these cases last quoted, the products were intended to be used at **15–121** once, so that there was no reasonable opportunity of examination by or on behalf of the users before use. On the other hand, where there has been a reasonable opportunity of such an examination, the transferor would not be liable, because the transferee could see for himself whether the products were suitable for his purpose.[316]

Tortious duty: delivery to carrier. An owner or bailee of products, who **15–122** delivers them to a carrier for the purpose of carriage, is under a duty to take reasonable care to see that they can be carried without causing physical damage to the person or property of others with whom they are likely to come in contact, during such carriage. This would seem to follow from the statement of general principle above,[317] but the only cases on the subject are those dealing with dangerous goods. In *Farrant v Barnes*,[318] the defendant sent a carboy of nitric acid to a carrier for carriage, without giving any warning of its dangerous character. Whilst the claimant, an employee of the carrier, was carrying the carboy, suddenly it burst from some unexplained cause and injured him. The defendant was held liable on:

---

[312] per Lush J. in *White v Steadman* [1913] 3 K.B. 340 at 348 (an unsafe horse with landau, hired from a livery stable keeper).

[313] *Hardwood v Antwerp Quay* (1935) 51 Ll.L.R. 336.

[314] *Edwards v Newton* (1934) 48 Ll.L.R. 155 (workmen discharging cargo into lorry by means of ship's tackle—none of crew assisting—tackle breaks and workman is injured, no case of res ipsa loquitur).

[315] *McKinstry v Johannes (Owners)* (1935) 52 Ll.L.R. 339.

[316] See, e.g. *Caledonian Ry Co v Mulholland or Warwick* [1898] A.C. 216, which was distinguished by Lord Buckmaster in *Oliver v Saddler & Co* [1929] A.C. 584 at 591. See also Lord Atkin (with whom Lord Shaw concurred) at 597. As Lord Atkin pointed out, later, in *Donoghue v Stevenson* [1932] A.C. 562 at 597, "There was ample opportunity for inspection by the second railway company. The relations were not proximate."

[317] See para.15–113, above.

[318] (1862) 11 C.B.(N.S.) 553. When the goods are dangerous, the consignor is liable, even if he did not know they were dangerous and was not negligent in failing to discover that they were dangerous. *Bamfield v Goole and Sheffield Co* [1910] 2 K.B. 94.

"the general principle that, wherever a person employs another to carry an article which from its dangerous character requires more than ordinary care, he must give him reasonable notice of the nature of the article, and that, if he fails to do so, he is responsible for the probable consequences of his neglect."[319]

From the reference to goods, "which in the absence of extraordinary care are likely by escaping to damage other parts of the cargo", it seems clear that the damage, for which the consignor is liable, includes damage to other goods carried, as well as to individuals.[320] It would also seem to follow that for this purpose dangerous goods means products, which, by reason of defects or otherwise, are unfit to be carried in the manner contemplated.[321]

15–123   When a customer went to a chemist shop with a bottle, asked for nitric acid, and, in response to the chemist's inquiry about what the bottle had contained, replied that it had been nitric acid, the chemist was held not liable for the results of an explosion which occurred when he filled the bottle with acid. This was on the ground that he had, in the circumstances, taken enough care.[322]

15–124   **Tortious duty: delivery by carrier.** A carrier, who delivers the products in the same condition as they were in when he had received them for carriage, is not liable to the consumer for damage caused to them through their defects as he is a mere agent for the transmission of the goods, and not responsible for their inherent properties.

If, however, he delivers products which are not in the same condition as they were in when he received them different considerations will apply. Where there has been a change in condition, of which he ought to have been aware, whether or not it had been caused by his negligence, and the change is such as to render the products unfit for the contemplated use, in the absence of his giving warning, he will be liable to the consumer for the resultant damage.[323]

15–125   In *Taylor & Sons v Union Castle Steamship Co*,[324] the defendants, who were shipowners, delivered to the claimants some maize, which was mixed with castor seed. The castor seed was poisonous and poisoned some horses belonging to a person who had bought the maize from the claimants. The claimants sued to recover from the defendants the amount that they had paid to their buyer, as damages. In holding the defendants not liable, MacKinnon J. said:

"The question in each case must be whether the person delivering the article knew, or as a reasonable man ought to have known, that it was dangerous. Here the defendants

---

[319] (1862) 11 C.B.(N.S.) 553 at 564, per Willes J.

[320] See *G.N. Ry v L.E.P. Transport Co* [1922] 2 K.B. 742.

[321] *Losinjska Plovidba v Transco Overseas, The Times*, July 18, 1995 (distributors of dangerous chemicals which leaked from the drums in which they were contained were arguably liable to the charterer of the vessel in which they were being carried when the leak occurred, on the basis that steps should have been taken to neutralise the danger).

[322] *Muir v Stewart*, 1938 S.C. 590.

[323] See, e.g. *Cramb v Caledonian Ry* (1892) 19 R. 1054; *MacDonald v MacBrayne* 1915 S.C. 716.

[324] (1932) 48 T.L.R. 249.

were not dealers in grain and experts in that particular trade, but were shipowners carrying goods of every possible description."

Misdelivery. Where the defendant carrier had delivered by mistake and **15–126** without giving any warnings about the nature of the products, to the wrong consignees, some highly inflammable material, which caught fire as a result of the negligence of one of the latter's employees, he was held liable, because he should have contemplated what in fact happened.[325] However, the carrier is not necessarily liable for all the consequences of his misdelivery. It might well be that, as a reasonable man, the carrier ought to have contemplated that the products were unfit for use but not to have contemplated that the person to whom he had made the misdelivery would fail, before using them, to have made such examination, as would have discovered the defect.[326] An example is to be found in *Cunnington v Great Northern Ry*,[327] where the carriers, a railway company, knew that consignors were in the habit of sending empty casks to the consignees, who then filled them with ketchup and returned them. The carriers negligently delivered casks, which did not belong to the consignors and were unfit for filling with ketchup, because they had been used previously for the storage of turpentine. The consignees duly filled the casks with ketchup, which was spoilt, and, consequently, they suffered damage. The carriers were held to be under no liability to the consignees. It was not reasonable to suppose that the casks, which were to be filled with something edible, would not be examined, in order to discover whether there was anything deleterious inside them.

---

[325] *Philco Radio v Spurling* [1949] 2 All E.R. 882.
[326] In *Taylor & Sons v Union Castle Steamship Co* (1932) 48 T.L.R. 249, other buyers of the maize had discovered the presence of the castor seed, before delivery to the ultimate consumer, but it was unnecessary to decide whether the claimant's failure to discover the castor seed amounted to negligence.
[327] (1883) 49 L.T. 392. cf. *Muir v Stewart*, 1938 S.C. 590.

Part V
DEATH

CHAPTER 16

DEATH AND CAUSES OF ACTION

1.—The Common Law

The rules at common law. In 1808 Lord Ellenborough had said of the **16–01** position at common law that "in a civil court the death of a human being cannot be complained of as an injury".[1] The rule, known as the rule in *Baker v Bolton*, was affirmed by the House of Lords in *Admiralty Commissioners v S.S. Amerika*.[2] At common law it was not possible even for a husband to recover damages for the death of his wife,[3] a parent for the death of a child[4] or an employer for that of an employee.[5] A second rule[6] provided that all actions in tort, with a few exceptions[7] were extinguished at death. It mattered not whether it was the potential claimant or the potential defendant who had died.

The severity of these rules was subsequently alleviated by statute. Change **16–02** came first with the Fatal Accidents Act 1846, which was followed by a number of amending Acts,[8] which are now consolidated in the current provisions of the Fatal Accidents Act 1976[9] as amended by the Administration of Justice Act 1982,[10] and the Law Reform (Miscellaneous Provisions) Act 1934. As a result, there are now two separate and distinct causes of action maintainable following a person's death: a claim by any dependant of the deceased for financial loss suffered in consequence of the death; and a claim by the estate of the deceased

---

[1] *Baker v Bolton* (1808) 1 Camp. 493. An earlier illustration can be found in *Higgins v Butcher* (1606) Yelv. 89.

[2] [1917] A.C. 38.

[3] *Baker v Bolton* (1808) 1 Camp. 493; *Higgins v Butcher* (1606) Yelv. 89; *Burgess v Florence Nightingale Hospital for Gentlewomen* [1955] 1 Q.B. 349.

[4] *Clark v London General Omnibus Co* [1906] 2 K.B. 648.

[5] *Osborn v Gillett* (1873) L.R. 8 Ex. 88.

[6] The maxim was, *actio personalis moritur cum persona*.

[7] The main exception to the rule arose where property had been appropriated by a deceased person and added to his estate. An action could be sustained by the owner against the personal representatives of the deceased person.

[8] Principally by the Fatal Accidents Acts of 1864, 1908 and 1959.

[9] Which applies to a cause of action arising on a death occurring after September 1, 1976.

[10] See ss.3(1), (2) and 76(11), whereby such provisions came into operation on January 1, 1983.

for injury, loss or damage, which could have been claimed by him if he had lived.

16–03   It is necessary, therefore, to consider the subject in two parts: (1) the accrual of a cause of action, following the death of a person and (2) the survival of a cause of action, following the death of a person who was either the injured party or the wrongdoer, himself.

2.—THE ACCRUAL OF A CAUSE OF ACTION

16–04   **Generally.** There are a number of statutes under which a cause of action accrues as a result of death, but not all of them require proof of fault in order to establish liability. While the principal discussion will concentrate on the Fatal Accidents Act 1976, reference must also be made to the Coal Mining (Subsidence) Act 1991; the Carriage by Air Act 1961; and the Railways (Convention on International Carriage by Rail) Regulations 2005.

(A) The Fatal Accidents Act

16–05   **The Fatal Accidents Act 1976 (as amended).** In regard to any cause of action arising on a death, occurring after September 1, 1976,[11] the Fatal Accidents Act 1976 applies,[12] which repealed the relevant provisions of the Fatal Accidents Acts 1846 to 1959 and consolidated them in the one statute.[13] By s.1(1) it is provided that:

> "If death is caused by any wrongful act, neglect or default[14] which is such as would (if

---

[11] By virtue of s.3(1) of the Administration of Justice Act 1982, which section came into force on January 1, 1983 (s.76(11)), there have been substituted replacement sections for ss.1–4, both inclusive of the Fatal Accidents Act 1976.

[12] s.7(2).

[13] s.6(2).

[14] By virtue of the effect of the amendment contained in s.6(1) and Sch.1 the reference in this section to "wrongful act, neglect or default" includes: (i) any occurrence which gives rise to liability under the Carriage by Air Act 1961. Sch.1, art.17; (ii) any occurrence which gives rise to liability under the Gas Act 1965, s.14; (iii) any breach of duty which is actionable by virtue of the provisions of the Mineral Workings (Offshore Installations) Act 1971 s.11(2) as amended; (iv) any breach of duty which is actionable by virtue of the Deep Sea Mining (Temporary Provisions) Act 1987 s.15(1); (v) any damage which gives rise liability for defective products under the Consumer Protection Act 1987 s.2, see Ch.14; and (vi) any breach of duty which is actionable by virtue of regulations made under the Petroleum Act 1998 Pt III. Furthermore for the purposes of the Fatal Accidents Act 1976 the following damage is treated as due to a person's fault: (i) any damage for which a person is liable under the Animals Act 1971, see Ch.13; (ii) any damage for which a person is liable under the Control of Pollution Act 1974 s.88(1); (iii) any damage for which a person is liable under the Environmental Protection Act 1990 s.73(6); (iv) any loss or damage for which a water undertaker is liable under the Water Industry Act 1991 s.209; and (v) any loss or damage for which the Environmental Agency is liable under the Water Resources Act 1991 s.208.

death had not ensued) have entitled the person injured[15] to maintain an action and recover damages in respect thereof, the person who would have been liable if death had not ensued shall be liable to an action for damages, notwithstanding the death of the person injured."

As Lord Diplock pointed out,[16] the purpose of the Act is not to put dependants,   **16–06** especially widows, into the same economic position as they would have been, had the deceased lived. The court is forbidden to take into account the remarriage of the widow or her prospects of such[17] and also, in assessing damages, the court is required to disregard those benefits which have accrued or will or may accrue to any person from his estate or otherwise, as a result of the death.[18]

The nature of the action. To maintain an action under the Fatal Accidents   **16–07** Act 1976 it must be proved: (1) that the deceased person was injured by the wrongful act, neglect or default of the defendant; (2) that he died in consequence of such injury[19]; (3) that at the time he died he had a right to recover damages[20]; and (4) that the beneficiaries have suffered pecuniary loss from his death.[21] Failure to prove any one of these matters means that the cause of action cannot be made out.[22] A breach of contract, causing death, is an act, neglect or default within the meaning of the statute.[23]

The death. The action lies "notwithstanding the death of the person   **16–08** injured".[24] This will include a case of suicide, where it arises as a result of insanity caused by the defendant's negligence;[25] and suicide, even if someone is not insane according to the test of the M'Naughten Rules, where the death is

---

[15] See s.1(6), which provides that injury shall include "any disease and any impairment of a person's physical or mental condition".
[16] *Cookson v Knowles* [1979] A.C. 556 at 568.
[17] The Fatal Accidents Act 1976 s.3(3) and see para.16–45, below.
[18] The Fatal Accidents Act 1976 s.4. Further, see paras 16–47–16–52, below.
[19] For causation in this regard, see Ch.6, above.
[20] See *Jameson v C EGB* [2000] 1 A.C. 455 (concurrent tortfeasors liable in respect of the same injuries which led to the death of the deceased, the claim against one tortfeasor was settled in the deceased's lifetime, the claim on behalf of the dependent widow, under the Fatal Accidents Act 1976, was barred by the settlement of the first claim). See para.16–09, below.
[21] Crichton J. held that the widow and children of a deceased criminal were not entitled to maintain claims under the Fatal Accidents Act for loss of support from his "earnings", since such claims arose ex turpi causa: *Burns v Edman* [1970] 2 Q.B. 541. It is not certain that this is a correct approach to such a problem. See further the pertinent comments in Kemp & Kemp, *The Quantum of Damages* and in the article: "Damages—The Sins of the Fathers," 119 New L.J. 1083 and Fleming, "Wages of Sin—Fatal Accidents Act—Dependency—Proof—Damages" [1973] C.L.J. 17. Similar considerations arise in the "Fraud on the Revenue" type of case and in *Hunter v Butler*, [1996] R.T.R. 396, CA the CA held that there was no liability for a widow's loss of dependency in respect of her late husband's undeclared earnings, commonly referred to as "moonlighting".
[22] *Nunan v Southern Ry* [1923] 2 K.B. 703 at 712, per Swift J.; affirmed [1924] 1 K.B. 223.
[23] *Grein v Imperial Airways Ltd* [1937] 1 K.B. 50.
[24] Fatal Accidents Act 1976 s.1(1).
[25] See *Withers v L.B. & S.C. Ry* [1916] 2 K.B. 772 and *Dixon v Sutton Heath & Lee Green Colliery* (1930) 23 B.W.C.C. 135, decisions under the Workmen's Compensation Acts. For a discussion of the meaning of insanity in this connection, see Davis, 59 L.Q.R. 202.

directly traceable to the injuries sustained in an accident for which the defendants are responsible.[26]

16–09   **Effect of the death upon defences.** Because it must be shown that the deceased, had he not died, would have been able to maintain an action for damages, it follows that in resisting a claim a defendant can rely upon anything which would have negatived the right of the deceased himself to bring an action.[27] So, the dependants cannot sue: if the deceased in his lifetime compromised his claim for damages in respect of the act which later resulted in his death[28]; or if the deceased in his lifetime obtained judgment for damages in respect of his injuries or disease, from which subsequently he died[29]; or if the provisions of some statute have taken away any claim he would have had in his lifetime and substituted other rights[30]; or if the deceased's cause of action has already been barred by the statutes of limitation in his lifetime.[31] Whereas a claim cannot be brought if the deceased compromised his claim for damages during his lifetime, the situation is different if the personal injury claim is compromised after the death. The claim which continues on behalf of the estate is separate and distinct from the claim brought on behalf of the dependants pursuant to the 1976 Act. So where a solicitor negligently discontinued the personal injury claim after the death of the deceased such death having been caused by the original accident, the claims of the dependant family had not been extinguished and thus the solicitor was not liable in respect of the loss of those causes of action within the professional negligence action which ensued.[32]

"Once death occurs a dependency claim can arise and, logically, time for that claim begins to run. If before death a claim is settled or proceeds to judgment, the claim in respect of the personal injury claim is finally disposed of. Once death occurs, however, (provided that the personal injury claim is not finally concluded) a dependency claim can arise."[33]

---

[26] *Corr v IBC Vehicles Ltd* [2008] A.C. 884 (the claimant suffered severe, disfiguring injuries which caused post traumatic stress disorder and depression which in turn caused his suicide) see above Ch.5 para.5–22. See also *Pigney v Pointer's Transport Services Ltd* [1957] 2 All E.R. 807 (a man, injured through his employers' negligence, suffered from anxiety neurosis and depression and committed suicide 18 months later). Obviously, if a claimant fails to prove that the suicide of the deceased was attributable to the defendants' negligence, then different considerations apply, as e.g. in *Farmer v Rash* [1969] 1 W.L.R. 160 (causation not proved where the deceased who was normally of a naturally cheerful disposition became increasingly depressed after an accident and a year later killed himself). See too *Hyde v Tameside Area Health Authority, The Times*, April 16, 1981.
[27] See per Scrutton L.J. in *Nunan v Southern Ry* [1924] 1 K.B. 223 at 228.
[28] *Read v Great Eastern Ry* (1868) L.R. 3 Q.B. 555; *Mahon v Burke* [1991] 2 I.R. 495. In *Thompson v Arnold* [2007] EWHC 1875 (Q.B.) Langstaff J. rejected a potential argument that *Read v Great Eastern Ry* was wrongly decided and further held that there was no breaches of Articles 6 and 8 of the European Convention for the Protection of Human Rights.
[29] *McCann v Sheppard* [1973] 1 W.L.R. 540 at 545.
[30] *Walpole v Canadian Northern Ry* [1923] A.C. 113 (right barred by the Workmen's Compensation Act of British Columbia); *McColl v Canadian Pacific Ry* [1923] A.C. 126 (right barred by Railway Act of Canada).
[31] *Williams v Mersey Docks and Harbour Board* [1905] 1 K.B. 804; *British Columbia Electric Ry v Gentile* [1914] A.C. 1034 at 1042. Further, see para.16–18, below.
[32] *Reader v Molesworth, Bright Clegg* [2007] EWCA Civ 169.
[33] *Reader v Molesworth, Bright Clegg* [2007] EWCA Civ 169 per Longmore L.J. at para.52.

In *Jameson v Central Electricity Generating Board*,[34] the deceased died as a   **16–10**
result of occupational exposure to asbestos. The were two tortfeasors liable
namely: Babcock Energy Limited and the Central Electricity Generating Board.
During his lifetime the deceased brought an action against the first which was
settled "in full and final settlement" of the causes of action set out in the
statement of case. After his death the estate brought an action against the Central
Electricity Generating Board on behalf of the dependant, the widow of the
deceased, pursuant to the Fatal Accidents Act 1976. The Board then brought third
party proceedings for a contribution against Babcock Energy Limited. On appeal
from a ruling on a preliminary issue the House of Lords held that the payment in
satisfaction of the first claim extinguished any liability of the Board to the
deceased and therefore no action could be brought pursuant to s.1(1) of the Fatal
Accidents Act 1976. One concern was that if the claim under the Fatal Accidents
Act 1976 was allowed to proceed then the effect of s.4 would be that the payment
by Babcock Energy Limited to the estate under the first claim would not be set
off against any damages recoverable from the Board.

Contributory negligence. At one time both contributory negligence[35] and   **16–11**
common employment[36] were complete defences. Now, the contributory negligence of the deceased will not defeat the claim of the dependants but will cause
their damages to be reduced.[37] Available defences are discussed in greater detail
elsewhere,[38] but the partial defence of contributory negligence is dealt with
specifically in the Act itself. By the Fatal Accidents Act 1976, s.5,[39] as
amended[40]:

> "Where any person dies as the result partly of his own fault and partly of the fault of
> any other person or persons, and accordingly if an action were brought for the benefit
> of the estate under the Law Reform (Miscellaneous Provisions) Act 1934 the damages
> recoverable would be reduced under section 1(1) of the Law Reform (Contributory
> Negligence) Act 1945, any damages recoverable in an action brought for the benefit of
> the dependants of that person under this Act shall be reduced to a proportionate
> extent."

A similar result will follow where the negligence of a dependant itself contributes
towards the death of the deceased. That dependant's share of the damages for
loss of dependency will be reduced proportionately[41] but the shares of other
dependants will remain unaffected, even when the cause of the deceased's death
was solely the result of the negligence of one of them.[42]

---

[34] [2000] 1 A.C. 455, reversing [1998] Q.B. 323.
[35] *Senior v Ward* (1859) 1 E. & E. 385; *Nunan v Sourthern Ry* [1924] 1 K.B. 223.
[36] *Coldrick v Partridge, Jones & Co* [1910] A.C. 77. The defence was abolished by the Law Reform
(Personal Injuries) Act 1948.
[37] For a case where the deceased died as a result of his taking part in an affray, see *Murphy v Culhane*
[1977] Q.B. 94, CA.
[38] See Ch.4, above.
[39] Which repeals and re-enacts the Law Reform (Contributory Negligence) Act 1945 s.1(4) to the like
effect.
[40] By s.3(2) of the Administration of Justice Act 1982.
[41] *Mulholland v McCrea* [1961] N.I. 135.
[42] *Dodds v Dodds* [1978] Q.B. 543, following *Trueman v Hydro-Electric Power Commission of
Ontario* [1924] 1 D.L.R. 406 and *Mulholland v McCrea,* above.

16–12 **Volenti.** If, during his lifetime, the deceased agreed to take the risk of the accident on himself, in accordance with the maxim volenti non fit injuria, and thereby relieved the defendant from liability for his wrongful act, neglect or default, an action cannot be brought successfully under the statute.[43]

16–13 **Agreement to limit damages.** A contract made by the deceased limiting the amount of damages, payable on his death, is not binding on the dependants for the simple reason that the latters' cause of action is entirely different to and independent of the deceased's own personal injury claim, whatever the extent of those damages may have been.[44] Different considerations apply where an Act of Parliament provides that a person may so limit his liability to pay damages on the death of another.[45]

16–14 **Jurisdiction.** The dependants of a deceased alien can sue when the circumstances are such that they could have sued had he not been an alien,[46] or when the parties submit themselves to the jurisdiction of the English courts.[47]

16–15 **By whom action can be brought.** The Fatal Accidents Act 1976 s.2(1) provides: "The action shall be brought by and in the name of the executor or administrator[48] of the deceased." Subsection (2) goes on to provide that:

"If—

(a) there is no executor or administrator of the deceased, or
(b) no action is brought within six months after the death by and in the name of an executor or administrator of the deceased,

the action may be brought by and in the name of all or any of the persons for whose benefit an executor or administrator could have brought it."[49]

16–16 Thus, where there is no executor or administrator, one of the dependants[50] may bring an action within six months, without first waiting to see if a personal representative will be appointed.[51] In any event, the claimant, whosoever it is, is required to deliver to the defendant or his solicitor full particulars of the persons for whom and on whose behalf the action is brought and of the nature of the

---

[43] *Griffiths v Earl of Dudley* (1882) 9 Q.B.D. 357. For volenti generally see Ch.4, paras 4–73–4–127.
[44] *Nunan v Southern Ry* [1923] 2 K.B. 703; *Grein v Imperial Airways Ltd* (1935) 52 T.L.R. 28 (reversed on other grounds [1937] 1 K.B. 50).
[45] e.g. under the Carriage by Air Act 1961, which limits the liability of airlines in respect of death or injury to passengers, see paras 10–177–10–184, above and under the Merchant Shipping Act 1995 which limits the liability of ship owners and carriers to their passengers, see para.10–160, above.
[46] *Davidsson v Hill* [1901] 2 K.B. 606.
[47] *The Esso Malaysia* [1975] Q.B. 198.
[48] For a situation where the deceased person's administratrix herself subsequently dies, see *Voller v Dairy Produce Packers Ltd* [1962] 1 W.L.R. 960.
[49] In *Stebbings v Holst & Co Ltd* [1953] 1 W.L.R. 603, it was held that the words "as widow" added after the claimant's name on the endorsement on the writ were appropriate under this latter section and saved the action which had been brought by the deceased's widow prior to her having been appointed administratrix to his estate.
[50] See para.16–20, below.
[51] *Holleran v Bagnell* (1879) 4 L.R.Ir. 333.

claim in respect of which damages are sought to be recovered.[52] The particulars of claim must state: that the claim is brought pursuant to the Fatal Accidents Act 1976; the dependants on whose behalf the claim is brought; the date of birth of each dependant; and the details of the nature of the dependency claim.[53] If an administrator is subsequently appointed and brings an action, the court will not stay an action already brought in good faith by a dependant before the date of the appointment.[54]

It was formerly the case that if an action was brought by the claimant as administrator, before letters of administration were taken out, it was a nullity which could not be cured by a subsequent grant.[55] Now however, the court has power, by virtue of Pts 17.4(4) and 19.4 of the Civil Procedure Rules 1998 to alter the capacity in which a party sues, even after any relevant period of limitation has expired, if the new capacity is one which that party enjoyed at the commencement of proceedings, or has since acquired. Accordingly, if the claimant sues as administrator before the grant has been made, there is power to allow an amendment after the grant, even if the claim form has already been issued. **16–17**

When an action must be brought. The effect of s.12(2) of the Limitation Act **16–18**
1980 is that an action by or on behalf of the dependants under the Fatal Accidents Act 1976 must be brought within three years either of the date of the death or the date of knowledge of the person for whose benefit the action is brought, whichever date is the later. Unlike an ordinary action in tort, time does not begin to run from the date of the wrongful act, neglect or default, which is the subject of the complaint.[56] In order for a claimant to bring such an action, the deceased must have been able to bring an action at the date of his death,[57] so that if at that date his right of action were already time-barred the right of action under the Fatal Accidents Act 1976 is also barred.[58] However, if the deceased died before his right of action was barred, an action under the Fatal Accidents Act 1976 may still be brought, provided that three years have not elapsed since either the date of death of the deceased, even though his right of action would have become barred meanwhile, had he survived;[59] or the date of knowledge[60] of the person[61]

---

[52] Fatal Accidents Act 1976 s.2(4).
[53] CPR PD 16 5.1.
[54] *M'Cabe v G.N. Ry of Ireland* [1899] 2 Ir.R. 123.
[55] See cases cited in earlier editions of *Charlesworth and Percy on Negligence*. There was, and is, no comparable problem in the case of an executor, whose title to sue comes into existence by virtue of the terms of the will, when the deceased person dies.
[56] *British Columbia Electric Ry v Gentile* [1914] A.C. 1034; *Venn v Tedesco* [1926] 2 K.B. 227.
[57] Limitation Act 1980 s.12(1).
[58] *Williams v Mersey Docks and Harbour Board* [1905] 1 K.B. 804. It is further provided by s.12(1) that no account shall be taken of the possibility of that time-limit being overridden, under the provisions of s.33, where otherwise any such action by the injured person would have been barred by the time-limit in s.11.
[59] *Venn v Tedesco* [1926] 2 K.B. 227, following *British Columbia Electric Ry v Gentile* [1914] A.C. 1034.
[60] Which is defined in s.14.
[61] Where there is more than one such person, then, s.12(2)(b) shall be applied separately to each of them. See the provisions for such, which are contained in s.13(1).

for whose benefit the action is brought, whichever date is the later.[62] Under the provisions of s.33 of the 1980 Act, the court has power to override the time-limits prescribed in certain circumstances.[63]

16–19   Where appropriate, the court can order a trial to stand adjourned if the death of the claimant is anticipated, thereby allowing a new action to be commenced under the Fatal Accidents Acts 1976. This happened in *Murray v Shuter*,[64] where an action had been brought on behalf of an injured claimant, who had never emerged from a deep coma, which was the result of a motor accident caused by the defendants' negligence, but it was not expected that he could survive very much longer after the writ had been issued, just within the three-year limitation period.

16–20   **For whose benefit the action is brought.** The Fatal Accidents Act 1976 s.1 as amended by s.83 of the Civil Partnership Act,[65] further provides:

"(2) Subject to section 1A(2) below,[66] every such action shall be for the benefit of the dependants of the person ("the deceased") whose death has been so caused.
(3) In this Act "dependant" means—

(a)   the wife or husband or former wife[67] or husband of the deceased;
(aa)   the civil partner[68] or former civil partner of the deceased;
(b)   any person who—

(i)   was living with the deceased in the same household immediately before the date of the death; and
(ii)   had been living with the deceased in the same household for at least two years[69]; before that date; and
(iii)   was living during the whole of that period as the husband or wife or civil partner of the deceased;

(c)   any parent or other ascendant of the deceased;
(d)   any person who was treated by the deceased as his parent;

---

[62] s.12(2).
[63] Which circumstances are considered fully in Ch.4, paras 4–200–4–217, above.
[64] (1971) 115 S.J. 774. As was forecast, the deceased died within about four years of the accident and a fresh action was begun under the Fatal Accidents Act, which was consolidated with the original action that was ordered to be carried out for the benefit of the deceased's estate, as provided by the Law Reform (Miscellaneous Provisions) Act 1934. See too *Thompson v Arnold* [2007] EWHC 1875 (Q.B.) which illustrates the problem in compromising a claim before the impending death of the claimant.
[65] Which came into effect as from December 5, 2005: the Civil Partnership Act 2004 (Commencement No.2) Order 2005 (SI 2005/3175).
[66] Which concerns the claim for damages for bereavement that is available to certain dependants only. See para.16–27, below.
[67] Where the claimant had been divorced from the deceased, married again, and then left her husband after a short time to live once more with the deceased, she was still his "former wife" for purposes of s.1(3)(a) of the Act: *Shepherd v The Post Office*, *The Times*, June 15, 1995, CA.
[68] Defined as "a relationship between two people of the same sex which is formed when they register as civil partners of each other": the Civil Partnership Act 2004 s.1.
[69] It matters not that the two-year period is broken by brief periods of absence: *Pounder v London Underground Ltd* [1995] P.I.Q.R. P217.

(e) any child[70] or other descendant of the deceased;
(f) any person (not being a child of the deceased) who, in the case of any marriage to which the deceased was at any time a party, was treated by the deceased as a child of the family in relation to that marriage;
(fa) any person (not being a child of the deceased) who, in the case of any civil partnership in which the deceased was at any time a civil partner, was treated by the deceased as a child of the family in relation to that civil partnership;
(g) any person who is, or is the issue of, a brother, sister, uncle or aunt of the deceased.

(4) The reference to the former wife or husband of the deceased in subsection (3)(a) above includes a reference to a person whose marriage to the deceased has been annulled or declared void as well as a person whose marriage to the deceased has been dissolved.

(4A) The reference to the former civil partner of the deceased in subsection (3)(aa) above includes a reference to a person whose civil partnership with the deceased has been annulled as well as a person whose civil partnership with the deceased has been dissolved.

(5) In deducing any relationship for the purposes of subsection (3) above—

(a) any relationship by marriage or civil partnership shall be treated as a relationship by consanguinity, any relationship of the half blood as a relationship of the whole blood, and the stepchild of any person as his child, and
(b) an illegitimate person shall be treated as the legitimate child of his mother and reputed father."[71]

The claimant must deliver full particulars of the person or persons, on whose **16–21**
behalf the action is brought, and the nature of the claim made,[72] but he is not required in his statement of case to negative the existence of other dependants.[73]

Only one action may be brought in respect of the death. The Fatal **16–22**
Accidents Act 1976 s.2(3) provides that: "Not more than one action[74] shall lie for and in respect of the same subject matter of complaint."[75] This section has to be interpreted in a way which is compatible with the Human Rights Act 1998 and the rights contained in the European Convention for the Protection of Human Rights as scheduled to the Act. In *Cachia v Faluyi*,[76] three dependent children

---

[70] A posthumously born child is included: *The George and Richard* (1871) L.R. 3 A. & E. 466; *Lindley v Sharp* (1973) 4 Fam. 90, CA; and so is a child adopted, in pursuance of an adoption order, made under the Adoption Act 1976 or any previous enactment to the like effect: and so is an illegitimate child, in respect of which see para.15–58, below.
[71] These subsections replaced the provisions of the Fatal Accidents Act 1846 ss.2 and 5 and the Fatal Accidents Act 1959 s.1(1) and 2(b), (c) which were repealed accordingly. The Fatal Accidents Act 1959 s.2(a) had previously been repealed by the Children Act 1975 s.108(1), Sch.4, Pt 1.
[72] Fatal Accidents Act 1976 s.2(4). The particulars must be set out in the particulars of claim: CPR Pt 16 PD 16 5.1 to 5.3; *Stebbings v Holst & Co Ltd* [1953] 1 All E.R. 925; *Cooper v Williams* [1963] 2 Q.B. 567.
[73] *Barnes v Ward* (1850) 9 C.B. 392.
[74] CPR Pt 7.3 permits a claimant to use a single claim form to commence all claims which may conveniently be disposed of in the same proceedings, such as where, arising out of the same accident, a widow has a claim in her personal capacity for personal injuries and also claims as administratrix of her husband's estate under the Fatal Accidents Act 1976 and the Law Reform (Miscellaneous Provisions) Act 1934. See too CPR Pt 16 PD 5.3.
[75] Which corresponds to the provisions of the Fatal Accidents Act 1846 s.3.
[76] [2001] 1 W.L.R. 1966, CA.

wished to pursue a claim arising out of their mother's death. One claim had been issued but not served. A second claim was issued within the limitation period applicable for child dependants. It was held that "action" in s.2(3) should be read as "served process" so as not to present an artificial bar to the dependants' rights to bring a claim for compensation arising out of their dependency.

16–23   Section 2(3) of the Fatal Accidents Act 1976 does not prevent the personal representative, who has recovered damages for the benefit of the dependants from bringing in time a subsequent action for damage to the estate of the deceased.[77]

16–24   Since the advent of the Civil Procedure Rules 1998 the court has been granted extensive case management powers.[78] While previous editions of this work have stated that the effect of s.2(3)[79] of the Fatal Accidents Act 1976 is to preclude a person not named as a dependant from applying to be joined to an action for damages pursuant to the Fatal Accidents Act 1976, this no longer correctly states the position. Section 2(3) must be interpreted in line with the provisions of the Human Rights Act 1998. To prevent a dependant from being joined to an action for damages pursuant to the Fatal Accidents Act 1976 would deny that person's right to a determination of their civil rights as protected by art.6(1) of the European Convention for the Protection of Human Rights. Although such a dependant may have a cause of action against the original claimant, who brought the original action pursuant to the Fatal Accidents Act 1976, for breach of trust[80] or against the solicitor[81] who acted for the original claimant, the court would consider the overriding objective[82] and it is unlikely that further satellite litigation would be regarded as in the interests of justice.

16–25   **Apportionment of the damages.**[83] The damages recovered are to be apportioned among the dependants named in the particulars according to the degree of their pecuniary loss. By the Fatal Accidents Act 1976 s.3(1), "in the action such damages, other than damages for bereavement, may be awarded as are proportioned to the injury resulting from the death to the dependants respectively".

16–26   **Each dependant's claim to be considered separately.**[84] There is no question of there being any group compensation, with the amount of damages of any one

---

[77] *Leggott v G.N. Ry* (1876) 1 Q.B.D. 159.
[78] CPR Pts 3 and 19.
[79] See para.16–17, above.
[80] *Condiff v Condiff* (1874) 29 L.T. 831.
[81] *Ross v Caunters* [1980] Ch. 297.
[82] CPR Pt 1.1.
[83] Where a claim is made pursuant to the Fatal Accidents Act 1976 on behalf of more than one person and a sum of money is ordered or agreed to be paid in satisfaction or a sum is accepted in satisfaction of the claims the court shall apportion the sum between the dependants unless it has already been apportioned by the court or by agreement: CPR Pt 37.4(3). In a claim involving a child or a patient the court would have to approve any settlement or acceptance of money paid in court: CPR Pt 21.10.
[84] *Dietz v Lennig Chemicals Ltd* [1969] 1 A.C. 170 at 183, per Lord Morris, e.g. see *Williamson v John I. Thornycroft & Co Ltd* [1940] 2 K.B. 658; *Voller v Dairy Produce Packers Ltd* [1962] 1 W.L.R. 960; *Rawlinson v Babcock & Wilcox Ltd* [1967] 1 W.L.R. 481.

dependent member, whose claim is before the court, being regarded as a proportion of the limited whole sum.[85] Usually at the trial of a fatal accident claim, the practice is for the damages to be assessed for the whole of the dependants in one lump sum and then divided among the dependants as appropriate[86] in accordance with the pecuniary loss suffered by each individual.[87] When a defendant decides to make a Pt 36 offer, he need not apportion it among the dependants.[88] It is no concern of the defendant how the damages are apportioned among the dependants, and no appeal by him will lie against the apportionment.[89]

Bereavement. Section 1A of the Fatal Accidents Act 1976,[90] as amended by   **16–27**
s.83 of the Civil Partnership Act 2004, provides:[91]

"1A.—(1) An action under this Act may consist of or include a claim for damages for bereavement.

(2) A claim for damages for bereavement shall only be for the benefit—

(a) of the wife or husband or civil partner of the deceased; and
(b) where the deceased was a minor[92] who was never married or a civil partner—

    (i) of his parents, if he was legitimate: and
    (ii) of his mother, if he was illegitimate:

(3) Subject to subsection (5) below, the sum to be awarded as damages under this section shall be £11,800.[93]

(4) Where there is a claim for damages under this section for the benefit of both the parents of the deceased, the sum awarded shall be divided equally between them (subject to any deduction falling to be made in respect of costs not recovered from the defendant).

---

[85] *Avery v L. & N.E. Ry* [1938] A.C. 606 at 612, per Lord Atkin.
[86] See *Johnson v Hill* [1945] 2 All E.R. 272; *Bishop v Cunard White Star Ltd* [1950] P. 240 at 248, per Hodson J.; *Kassam v Kampala Aerated Water Co Ltd* [1965] 1 W.L.R. 668 at 672, per Lord Guest.
[87] *Pym v G.N. Ry* (1863) 4 B. & S. 396 at 407; *G.T. Ry of Canada v Jennings* (1888) 13 App.Cas. 800 at 803.
[88] Fatal Accidents Act 1976 s.3(6); this provision refers to payment into court which procedure no longer exists but it is likely that the provision would be interpreted as applying to Pt 36 offers.
[89] *Eifert v Holt's Transport Co* [1951] 2 All E.R. 665n. But cf. *Clay v Pooler* [1982] 3 All E.R. 570, where Hodgson J. held that where the deceased died intestate, the defendant had a direct interest not only in the computation of the two claims, i.e. those respectively under the Law Reform (Miscellaneous Provisions) Act 1934 and the Fatal Accidents Act 1976, but also in the distribution between dependants of the latter Act's fund.
[90] Which came into force on January 1, 1983.
[91] Which came into force on December 5, 2005: the Civil Partnership Act 2004 (Commencement No.2) Order 2005 (SI 2005/3175).
[92] Where, in an accident that happened before his 18th birthday, a bachelor sustained injuries which resulted in his death after he had attained his majority, the parents of the deceased were not entitled to damages for bereavement: *Doleman v Deakin, The Times,* January 30, 1990. No cause of action under the Act had accrued until the death, by which time the deceased was no longer a minor.
[93] The sum of £11,800 is recoverable in respect of causes of action accruing on or after January 1, 2008, by virtue of the Damages for Bereavement (Variation of Sum) (England and Wales) Order 2007 (SI 2007/3489) for causes of action arising after April 1, 2002 but before January 1, 2008 the sum is £10,000.

(5) The Lord Chancellor may by order made by statutory instrument, subject to annulment in pursuance of a resolution of either House of Parliament, amend this section by varying the sum for the time being specified in subsection (3) above."[94]

The section gives that which did not exist before,[95] namely a remedy for the mental suffering that any of the dependants has undergone, in consequence of the death, or for the pain and suffering of the deceased, prior to death.

16–28   **The measure of damages.** The measure of damages[96] is the pecuniary loss suffered by the dependants[97] as a result of the death. "What the court has to try to ascertain in these cases is: How much have the widow and family lost by the father's death?"[98] In determining such loss, Lord Wright said:

"The starting point is the amount of wages which the deceased was earning, the ascertainment of which to some extent may depend on the regularity of his employment. Then there is an estimate of how much was required or expended for his own personal and living expenses.[99] The balance will give a datum or basic figure[100] which will generally be turned into a lump sum by taking a certain number of years' purchase.[101] That sum, however, has to be taxed down by having due regard to uncertain-ties. . . . "[102]

---

[94] The sum was £3,500 until April 1, 1991 when it became £7,500 until April 1, 2002 when it became £10,000 until January 1, 2008 when it became £11,800 see n.93, above.

[95] See *Blake v Midland Ry* (1852) 18 Q.B. 93; *Davies v Powell Duffryn Associated Collieries Ltd* [1942] A.C. 601 at 607, per Lord Wright. For attempts to mitigate the rule, see *Hay v Hughes* [1975] Q.B. 790 at 802, 803, and *Regan v Williamson* [1976] 1 W.L.R. 305. See also *Kerby v Redbridge HA* [1994] P.I.Q.R. Q1 (damages for bereavement are recoverable only under statute; there is no common law right to damages for the normal emotions of grief, sorrow or distress on the death of a loved one).

[96] See Yell, "Assessing Damages in Fatal Accident Cases", 3 Lit 9.

[97] See para.16–20, above.

[98] *Heatley v Steel Company of Wales Ltd* [1953] 1 W.L.R. 405 at 408, per Lord Goddard C.J. but cf. *Cookson v Knowles* [1979] A.C. 556 at 568, per Lord Diplock.

[99] In *White v London Transport Executive* [1982] Q.B. 489 such expenses were described as the cost of maintaining himself and providing facilities appropriate to attain that standard of life. The CA in *Harris v Empress Motors Ltd* [1984] 1 W.L.R. 212, not only approved *White v London Transport Executive*, above, but held that the correct approach to the calculation of the deceased's living expenses, for the purposes of deciding a claim under the Law Reform (Miscellaneous Provisions) Act 1934, was to assess as a percentage the available surplus after deducting from the net earnings the cost of maintaining the deceased in his station of life. The approach of making an assessment of those expenses, as would be done for the purposes of calculating a dependency under the Fatal Accidents Act 1976, was an incorrect one. Further, in *Nutbrown v Rosier, The Times*, March 1, 1982 it was held that the phrase "living expenses" was to be construed as meaning expenses of living and was not confined to living expenses which were attributable solely to an individual's personal expenditure. Hence they included expenses that represented costs incurred on housing, food, clothing, necessary travelling, etc., which would enable him to have a reasonably satisfying and enjoyable life, having regard to his particular circumstances.

[100] i.e. the "multiplicand."

[101] i.e. the "multiplier," for which see, further paras 16–63–16–65, below. The multiplier to be applied in a fatal accidents claim, when assessing the number of years of the claimant's dependency, has to be selected once and for all as at the date of the deceased person's death: *Graham v Dodds* [1983] 1 W.L.R. 808 (a multiplier of 18 for a deceased breadwinner, aged 41, was held to be excessive). In *White v Esab Group (UK) Ltd* [2002] P.I.Q.R. Q76 the judge held that he was bound by authority to follow the rule whereby the multiplier is determined from the date of death.

[102] *Davies v Powell Duffryn Associated Collieries Ltd* [1942] A.C. 601 at 617. Further see para.16–64, below.

The pecuniary loss in question is the actual financial benefit of which the   **16–29**
dependants have in fact been deprived, whether that benefit was a result of a legal
obligation or of what may reasonably have been expected to take place in the
future.[103] It is that which it is reasonably probable the dependants would have
received if the deceased had remained alive.[104] "Legal liability alone is not the
test of injury in respect of which damages may be recovered under Lord
Campbell's Act . . . the reasonable expectation of pecuniary advantage to the
relation remaining alive may be taken into account . . . and damages may be
given in respect of that expectation being disappointed."[105] Accordingly, where
the deceased was a bachelor, aged 27, living away from his parents' home, and
he used to make gifts worth about £20 a year to his parents, the parents were each
held entitled to damages on his death.[106] In circumstances where the deceased
had managed and drawn income from a property portfolio and proof of actual
loss as a result of the death was attended with evidential difficulty, the dependents
were held entitled to claim a proportion of the cost of employing a manager to
replace the deceased: although the method of calculation was unusual the
assessment of dependency was a jury exercise and the court was entitled to draw
assistance from any of the materials put before it in coming to a fair conclusion
about the loss which had been sustained.[107]

Loss of a spouse's services. The pecuniary advantage, which has been lost,   **16–30**
need not have been received in the form of money or goods, but may have been
derived from services rendered by the deceased. So a workman was held entitled
to recover damages in respect of the death of his wife, because she used to do his
housekeeping and on her death he had to employ and pay a housekeeper, who
was not able to manage as economically as his wife used to do.[108] Similarly, in
the case of a disabled widow, who had lost the especial care and attendance that
the deceased, her husband, had furnished her, the quantum of damages was to be
assessed broadly on the evidence, taken as a whole.[109] This was so, even if the
quantum assessed in this manner exceeded the cost of employing a housekeeper
or nurse to provide instead what was needed by the dependant. Not every case
justifies an approach based on an arithmetical calculation by way of multiplier
and multiplicand. Where the deceased, aged 60, suffered from a number of
deteriorating ailments the future progress of which was unpredictable, the better
approach was to award a lump sum which reflected both the present value of the

---

[103] *Benson v Biggs Wall & Co* [1982] 3 All E.R. 300, Pain J. held that in assessing damages
attributable to a child under the Fatal Accidents Act 1976, regard must be had to his genuine
dependency and not to any notional "pocket money" figure.
[104] *Pym v G.N. Ry* (1863) 4 B. & S. 396, per Erle C.J. In *Preston v Hunting Air Transport* [1956] 1
Q.B. 454, in addition to financial loss, £400 was awarded for "damage possibly of a more intangible
character by reason of the loss of their mother".
[105] *Dalton v S.E. Ry* (1858) 4 C.B.(N.S.) 296, per Willes J.
[106] *Dalton v S.E. Ry* (1858) 4 C.B.(N.S.) 296, per Willes J.
[107] *Cape Distributions Ltd v O'Loughlin* [2001] P.I.Q.R. Q73, CA.
[108] *Berry v Humm & Co* [1915] 1 K.B. 627; *Feay v Barnwell* [1938] 1 All E.R. 31 (£625 awarded);
Burgess v Florence Nightingale Hospital [1955] 1 All E.R. 511 (£2,000 awarded).
[109] *Abrams v Cook, The Times*, November 26, 1987, CA.

services she performed and the uncertainty which surrounded her ability to carry on working.[110]

16–31   **Loss of a parent's services.** In determining the pecuniary value to be put on the services that used to be rendered by the deceased to her family, acknowledgment should be given to the fact of the constant attendance of a mother on her children. However, the level of dependency, as the children grow older and became more independent, must also be taken into account.[111] The value placed upon such services is not limited to a mere computation of the cost of the services of a housekeeper, less an estimate of the cost of maintaining the deceased wife.[112] Indeed, where on the death of his wife it was reasonable for the husband to give up his employment in order to look after the children, two of whom suffered from a rare blood disorder and required special attention, damages for loss of her housekeeping services were assessed by reference to his loss of wages and not to the cost of employing a housekeeper.[113]

16–32   By way of contrast, where a maternal grandmother voluntarily gave her services in looking after her deceased daughter's children, they were not services resulting from the deceased's death, within the meaning of the section, and, accordingly, could not be taken into account in assessing the pecuniary loss to the dependent children of their mother's services.[114] Where the services rendered by the deceased were paid for by the dependant at the ordinary rate of wages, there will be no pecuniary loss from the death, as the dependant will be able to employ another person to do the same work at the same cost. So, where a father employed his son as a bricklayer at the ordinary rate of wages he suffered no pecuniary loss on his son's death.[115] Further, a widow was not entitled to claim an increased dependency as a future loss, on the basis that she and the deceased

---

[110] *Thomas v Kwik-Save Stores Ltd, The Times,* June 27, 2000, CA (it was also inappropriate on the facts to use the cost of a housekeeper as the basis of the multiplicand where the services provided were bound to diminish).

[111] *Spittle v Bunney* [1988] 1 W.L.R. 847, CA.

[112] *Regan v Williamson* [1976] 1 W.L.R. 305. See Hodge, "When Another is Killed", 81 L.S.Gaz. 637.

[113] *Mehmet v Perry* [1977] 2 All E.R. 529, applying *George v Pinnock* [1973] 1 W.L.R. 118, *Donnelly v Joyce* [1974] Q.B. 454 and the dicta of Stephenson L.J. in *K. v JMP Co Ltd* [1976] Q.B. 85. Similarly, see *Bailey v Barking and Havering AHAy, The Times,* July 22, 1978, and *Cresswell v Eaton* [1991] 1 W.L.R. 1113, where the mother of three young children was killed in 1980 by a negligent motorist and, as a result, they went to live with their maternal grandmother until she died in 1983. Thereupon they went to live with their maternal aunt, who reasonably gave up her job as a traffic warden to look after them full time. The damages for loss of their mother's services were calculated, inter alia, by reference to the aunt's net earnings loss, projected over the remaining period of the dependency.

[114] *Hay v Hughes* [1975] Q.B. 790, which was followed in *Dodds v Dodds* [1978] Q.B. 543 and in *Hayden v Hayden* [1992] 1 W.L.R. 987, CA where it was held that the replacement services of a father did not result from the death of the claimant's mother, but the discharge of her father's parental duty. The claim was confined to loss of such services as the father had been unable to replace. The cost of a nanny was inappropriate measure of loss where one had not and never would be, employed.

[115] *Sykes v N.E. Ry* (1875) 44 L.J.C.P. 191.

had decided to have children, the event of which would necessarily have increased her dependency upon him.[116]

Nominal damages. No action can be maintained by the dependants for nominal damages.[117]   **16–33**

Dependency based on state benefits. A dependency can be established if the deceased and the dependant were before the death both in receipt of State social security benefits. The question is whether the claimant has suffered provable loss. While in many cases[118] benefits such as housing benefit and income support will continue to be received by the dependant after the death and there will therefore be no loss, the outcome is not inevitable and depends upon the facts.[119]   **16–34**

The pecuniary advantage must have arisen from relationship. The pecuniary benefit derived from the deceased must have arisen from the relationship and not from any other cause. Where a man and his wife were professional dancing partners, earning jointly more than the sum they would each have earned separately, and the wife died as a result of the defendant's negligence, it was held that the loss to the husband of the value of his wife as a dancing partner, could not be taken into account.[120] A different approach was taken where the claimant had been employed, at a salary of £600–£800 by her late husband's company, a "one man" enterprise which could not function without him. Her services to the company were valued at £200, which fell to be deducted, but the balance of her salary was a pecuniary benefit, derived from marital status, which she had lost and was entitled to recover.[121]   **16–35**

Dependants were held to have suffered a pecuniary loss, where, within seven years of his making gifts totalling £40,000 to his wife and son, the deceased was killed in a motor accident caused by the defendants' negligence. Because he had failed to survive the statutory seven-year period after making the gifts, their value at the date of his death had to be taken into account for the purposes of estate duty and additional duty paid. It was held that, because the benefit which had been lost to the two dependants by their having to pay the increased duty was one which arose from the relationship between themselves and the deceased of husband and wife and father and son respectively, it would have accrued to them if the deceased had survived. Accordingly, the payment of the duty represented the loss of an expectancy of future pecuniary benefit and, so, was an "injury", resulting   **16–36**

---

[116] *Malone v Rowan* [1984] 3 All E.R. 402.
[117] *Duckworth v Johnson* (1859) 4 H. & N. 653.
[118] *Hunter v Butler* [1996] R.T.R. 396, CA, being typical.
[119] *Cox v Hockenhull* [2000] 1 W.L.R. 750, CA (the claimant and his wife both received injuries in the same road traffic accident, hers being fatal: a distinctive feature of the case was that she had been disabled before the accident and the claimant had been her full time carer).
[120] *Burgess v Florence Nightingale Hospital* [1955] 1 All E.R. 511. See also *Grzelak v Harefield and Northwood Hospital Management Committee* (1968) 112 S.J. 195.
[121] *Malyon v Plummer* [1964] 1 Q.B. 330.

from the death of the deceased, within the meaning of the Fatal Accidents Act.[122]

16–37   When a husband and wife, each with separate incomes, are living together and sharing their expenses, so that their joint expenses are less than twice the expenses of each living separately, each confers a financial benefit on the other. It is in respect of the loss of such benefit that the husband is entitled to damages on the death of the wife.[123]

16–38   When the deceased covenanted to pay his mother an annuity during their joint lives, it was held that the tribunal of fact was entitled to take into account the probable duration of the lives of both the deceased and his mother and to award the present value of such an annuity. Such value was not to be assessed on the basis that it was as valuable as a government annuity or one secured by a good insurance company, but by having regard to the manner in which it was secured and the circumstances of the covenantor.[124]

16–39   **There must be a reasonable expectation of pecuniary benefit.** A reasonable expectation of pecuniary benefit can be established by showing that the deceased had in the past contributed to the support of the dependants, leading to the inference that the support would have been continued in the future. If the deceased had not attained a full earning capacity, damages can be given on the assumption that contributions would increase as earning capacity increased. So, where a father, who was old and becoming infirm, had been assisted by his son in doing some work, for which the father was paid a weekly wage, it was held that such parent was entitled to damages on the death of the son.[125] Also, where a young bachelor helped his elderly disabled father financially for about six months, during a period of unemployment some years previously, it was held that there was evidence of pecuniary loss suffered by the father upon the son's death.[126]

16–40   It is not necessary to show that the deceased must have been earning wages at the death, provided that it can be established that there was a reasonable expectation that money would have been earned in the future, which would have resulted in financial benefit accruing to his dependants. Accordingly, where the deceased was a girl of 16 who was nearing the completion of her apprenticeship as a dressmaker and would then have been likely to make substantial earnings in the near future, it was held that her parents were entitled to damages.[127] "The fact of past contribution may be important in strengthening the probability of future

---

[122] *Davies v Whiteways Cyder Co Ltd* [1975] Q.B. 262. A deduction was made to allow for the chance that the deceased might not have survived the three years remaining before the expiry of the statutory period. In fact the CA granted leave to the defendants to withdraw their appeal because the parties settled (at 274) and the effect was to leave intact the first instance judge's decision. In principle the same consideration would now apply to liability for inheritance tax.

[123] Since it is derived from their marital status; see *Malyon v Plummer* [1964] 1 Q.B. 330.

[124] *Rowley v L. & N.W. Ry* (1873) L.R. 8 Ex. 221.

[125] *Franklin v S.E. Ry* (1858) 3 H. & N. 211; see also *Duckworth v Johnson* (1859) 4 H. & N. 653.

[126] *Hetherington v N.E. Ry* (1882) 9 Q.B.D. 160.

[127] *Taff Vale Ry v Jenkins* [1913] A.C. 1. See, also, *Wathen v Vernon* [1970] R.T.R. 471.

pecuniary advantage, but it cannot be a condition precedent to the existence of such a probability."[128]

Further, it is not vital that the dependants prove some pecuniary benefit already **16–41** received from the deceased in his lifetime. Thus, when two young women, both qualified doctors, died in an air disaster, their elderly parents, who had intended escaping from Iraq to come to live with their daughters in England, where they would have been supported financially by them, were held entitled to recover such loss.[129] On the other hand, a mere speculative possibility of pecuniary benefit in the future is not enough. Where the deceased was a boy, aged four, and the father was in business, earning substantial wages, it was held that there was no reasonable expectation of pecuniary benefit.[130]

"The boy was subject to all the risks of illness, disease, accident and death. His education and upkeep would have been a substantial burden to the plaintiff for many years if he had lived. He might or might not have turned out a useful young man. He would have earned nothing till about 16 years of age. He might never have aided his father at all. He might have proved a mere expense. I cannot adequately speculate one way or the other."[131]

No presumption of pecuniary loss. The mere existence of the relationship of **16–42** either husband and wife or parent and child is not enough to show pecuniary loss and does not even raise a presumption of it.[132] Conversely, the fact that a husband and wife are living apart is not conclusive evidence that there is no pecuniary loss,[133] although where a wife is living in adultery it may be very difficult, if not impossible, to prove any such loss.[134] Since the test of a claim by a dependant, under the Acts, is whether or not there was a reasonable expectation of pecuniary benefit from the deceased, in the case of a deserting or adulterous spouse, it would have to be shown that there was some significant prospect, as opposed to a mere speculative possibility, of a reconciliation with the other partner, had he or she lived.[135] If a significant prospect of reconciliation was proved, any award would be made as a proportion of the full figure, had the marriage been stable. A wife may be partially dependent on her husband and suffer financial loss on his

---

[128] *Taff Vale Ry v Jenkins* [1913] A.C. 1, per Lord Moulton.
[129] *Kandalla v British European Airways Corporation* [1981] Q.B. 158.
[130] *Barnett v Cohen* [1921] 2 K.B. 461.
[131] *Barnett v Cohen* [1921] 2 K.B. 461, per McCardie J. at 472.
[132] *New Monckton Collieries v Keeling* [1911] A.C. 648; *Lee v S.S. Bessie* [1912] 1 K.B. 83. (These are cases under the Workmen's Compensation Act, but the principle is equally applicable to the Fatal Accidents Acts.) But where a mother lived with her son's family, doing all the housework and caring for the children whilst her son and daughter-in-law went out to work, in return for which services the mother received her board, lodging and pocket money, it was held, upon her death, that as there had been a benefit to the son during her lifetime which arose out of their relationship, he was entitled to recover damages for his loss under the Fatal Accidents Act: *Saikaley v Pelletier* (1966) 57 D.L.R. (2d) 394.
[133] *Harrison v L. & N.W. Ry* (1885) Cab. & El. 540.
[134] *Stimpson v Wood* (1888) 57 L.J.Q.B. 484.
[135] *Davies v Taylor* [1974] A.C. 207.

death, even though she has a substantial private fortune.[136] Further, on her husband's death, a widow may obtain employment and earn enough to support herself, but may still have been substantially dependent on him during his lifetime.

16–43   **Where marriage has been annulled or dissolved or parties are judicially separated.** In the light of the widened category of "dependants", contained in s.1(3)(a) of the Fatal Accidents Act 1976,[137] whereby the "former wife or husband"[138] of the deceased is included, any maintenance payments, which would have been made by the deceased to a former spouse, must be taken into account.

16–44   **Other considerations in ascertaining pecuniary loss.** In all cases the amount of the pecuniary loss suffered by a dependant is a question of fact. In ascertaining the pecuniary loss in cases where the deceased lived with the dependants, as in the case of a husband or a son, it is necessary to take into account, by way of a reduction, the cost of maintaining the deceased.[139] The court will take into account the risk that had the deceased lived the dependency may have been brought to an end on account of divorce.[140] In *Owen v Martin*[141] a widow, who had previously been divorced on grounds of adultery, committed adultery with the deceased's former professional partner after the death. The multiplier was reduced on the grounds that the marriage may not have lasted for the whole of the natural life of the deceased. Stuart-Smith L.J. said that he did not see why the court should shut its eyes to the fact that one in three marriages ends in divorce, although he recognised that where a marriage has lasted a substantial time and particularly where there are children the risk of divorce may be less.[142] Likewise, where the deceased had been committing adultery at the time of his death the prospect that the marriage may not have lasted was taken into account in assessing the multiplier.[143] There must also be taken into account the expectation of life of the deceased and of each of the persons claiming to be dependants.[144] If, before trial, one of the dependants has died, compensation can only be awarded for her actual loss and not for the loss she would have suffered had she continued to live throughout the period of her normal expectation of

---

[136] *Shiels v Cruickshank* [1953] 1 W.L.R. 533 (a Scottish case and not a decision on the Fatal Accidents Acts).
[137] Amended by s.3(1) of the Administration of Justice Act 1982. The category of dependants has been further widened to include civil partners by s.83 of The Civil Partnership Act 2004, see para.16–20, above.
[138] See s.1(4), also.
[139] *Duckworth v Johnson* (1859) 4 H. & N. 653; *Tamworth Colliery Co v Hall* [1911] A.C. 665, a case under the Workmen's Compensation Act 1906, where, on this point, the same principles are applicable.
[140] *Gray v Barr* [1971] 2 Q.B. 554; *Brown v Brockhouse Forgings* [1976] C.L.Y. 671.
[141] [1992] P.I.Q.R. Q151, CA.
[142] *Owen v Martin* [1992] P.I.Q.R. Q151 at Q162.
[143] *D and D v Donald* [2001] P.I.Q.R. Q44.
[144] *Price v Glynea and Castle Coal and Brick Co* (1915) 9 B.W.C.C. 188 at 198; *Barnett v Cohen* [1921] 2 K.B. 461. In *Hall v Wilson* [1939] 4 All E.R. 85 the possibility of the deceased being killed in war or in air-raids was taken into account, but in *Bishop v Cunard White Star Ltd* [1950] P. 240 no reduction was made on account of the hazards of life at sea during war.

life.[145] In determining the extent of the pecuniary loss, the dependant's future prospects, after the death of the deceased, must necessarily be taken into account. On the facts in *Howitt v Heads*,[146] it was held that no deduction should be made for the possibility of a widow finding work in the future, for example when her children would be grown up. Where a widow's expectation of life was held to be lower than average for her age, because of her chronic ill health, her period of dependency for the future was reduced proportionately.[147]

Prospects of remarriage. In assessing damages payable to a widow in **16–45** respect of her husband's death her remarriage or prospects of remarriage cannot be taken into account.[148] Nevertheless, a widow's remarriage or prospects of remarriage are still relevant considerations, when assessing the damages payable to dependent minor children.[149] No mention is made in the Act as to the position of a widower's remarriage or prospects of remarriage. In *Jeffrey v Smith*,[150] the prospects of a widower remarrying was taken into account. This was before the Fatal Accidents Act 1976 and, more importantly, before the 1976 Act was amended in 1982[151] whereby, pursuant to s.4,[152] benefits which accrue to the dependants from the estate of the deceased or otherwise as a result of the death are disregarded. It is at least arguable that the position of a widower is caught by this provision and remarriage or the prospects thereof should be disregarded.[153] Furthermore s.3(3) of the Fatal Accidents Act 1976 must be interpreted consistently with the provisions of the Human Rights Act 1998. To treat the position of a widower differently to the position of a widow in relation to a claim for damages may amount to a breach of art.14 of the European Convention for the Protection of Human Rights (prohibition from discrimination in relation to the rights protected by the Convention).

Subsequent events. Whilst it is clear that damages have to be assessed as at **16–46** the date of the deceased's death, the court, even so, must take cognisance of subsequent events which throw light upon the realities of the situation, since it

---

[145] *Williamson v John I. Thornycroft & Co Ltd* [1940] K.B. 658.
[146] [1973] 1 Q.B. 64, applying *Goodger v Knapman* (1924) S.A.S.R. 347 at 358, and *Usher v Williams* (1955) 60 W.A.L.R. 69 at 80, 81. Also *Carroll v Purcell* (1927) 35 A.L.J.R. 384 and *Jamieson v Green* [1957] N.Z.L.R. 1154. See Stanton, "Fatal Accidents: the Calculation of Awards", 128 New L.J. 81.
[147] *Whittome v Coates* [1965] 1 W.L.R. 1285. It has been held that, unless there are genuine and substantial reasons for so ordering her, a widow is not normally obliged to submit to a medical examination: *Baugh v Delta Water Fittings Ltd* [1971] 1 W.L.R. 1295.
[148] Fatal Accidents Act 1976 s.3(3). A widow's remarriage or prospects of remarriage were taken into account before August 1, 1971 when s.4(1) of the Law Reform (Miscellaneous Provisions) Act 1971 came into force; this provision was re-enacted in s.3(3) of the Fatal Accidents Act 1976.
[149] *Thompson v Price* [1973] Q.B. 838.
[150] [1970] R.T.R. 279, CA.
[151] Amended by s.3(1) of the Administration of Justice Act 1982.
[152] See paras 16–47–16–52, below.
[153] See *McGregor on Damages* (18th edn, 2009, para.36–066, Sweet & Maxwell). The Law Commission in its consultation paper "Claims for Wrongful Death" has recommended that the prospects of a person marrying, remarrying or entering into financially supporting cohabitation should be disregarded.

must not speculate when it knows.[154] So, where the claimant widow had died, 14 months, after the deceased's death but before her action was ready for trial, the court was obliged to award to her estate only a comparatively small sum, in the light of the known facts.[155] While the court will take account of events after the death of the deceased, which would affect the continuation of the dependency, that does not extend to actions of the dependants themselves, where they are said either to have increased or diminished it in amount. In *Welsh Ambulance Services NHS Trust v Williams*,[156] the deceased had been a successful entrepreneur, with three profitable enterprises: builders' merchant, property development and restoration of steam engines. During his life, the claimant and her three adult children received shares of the profits of the businesses which were substantially higher than the value of the work they did. After his death, they took over the businesses themselves increased the profits. The submission that, as a result of the success of their efforts there was no dependency failed. Nothing that a dependant did after the death could either increase or decrease the dependency, which was fixed at the moment of the death: dependency was what a dependant would probably have received as benefit from the deceased, had he not died. Decisions made by the dependants after the death were irrelevant.[157] The only post death events which were relevant were those which affected the continuance of the dependency.

16–47   **Pecuniary gains resulting from the death.** Historically, in respect of the assessment of claims for damages under the Fatal Accidents Acts, the rule was that there had to be taken into account any pecuniary benefit accruing to the dependant, by reason of the death of the deceased, and such had to be set against the pecuniary loss suffered.[158] A dependant's personal income was not a benefit arising in consequence of the death of the deceased, since it was a consequence either of the dependant's own work or his investment.[159] Likewise, the fact that her husband's death had enabled a widow to realise her own earning potential, were she to choose to work in the future, was not a pecuniary gain, accruing to her as a result of the death, so it did not fall to be taken into account to reduce her damages.[160] Savings, which had been set aside from a deceased husband's

---

[154] per Harman L.J. in *Curwen v James* [1963] 1 W.L.R. 748 at 753 and per Fenton Atkinson L.J. in *Baker v Willoughby* [1970] A.C. 467 at 481 (reversed on other grounds by the HL (at 489 *et seq.*). In *Curwen v James*, above the CA stated that when the exigencies of justice clearly outweigh the general undesirability of admitting evidence of matters which alter the effect of an order of the court below as to damages the appellate court has power in exceptional circumstances to hear it). The HL in *Murphy v Stone Wallwork (Charlton)* [1969] 1 W.L.R. 1023, approved of this statement.
[155] *Williamson v John I. Thornycroft & Co Ltd* [1940] 2 K.B. 658.
[156] [2008] EWCA Civ 81.
[157] A similar approach was taken in *Wolfe v Del' Innocenti* [2006] EWHC 2694 (Q.B.) (widow took up active role in garage business after the death of her husband; her earnings from the business were to be disregarded in assessing the dependency).
[158] *Grand Trunk Ry v Jennings* (1888) 13 App.Cas. 800 at 804, per Lord Watson; *Baker v Dalgleish S.S. Co Ltd* [1922] 1 K.B. 361. See too *Davies v Powell Duffryn Colleries* [1942] A.C. 601, per Lord Macmillan at 609.
[159] *Goodger v Knapman* (1924) S.A.S.R. 347 at 358, per Murray C.J.: "Any money she may earn would be the result of her labour, not his death".
[160] *Howitt v Heads* [1973] 1 Q.B. 64 at 69, 70.

income, were not regarded as the widow's capital asset but as income, part of which was to be spent for the husband's benefit.[161]

The onus of proving that the loss of some dependency had been reduced by a pecuniary gain lies with the defendant.[162]

Certain statutory exceptions to the rule at common law were first made in respect of contractual benefits by the Fatal Accidents (Damages) Act 1908 and later made in respect of national insurance benefits by the Law Reform (Personal Injuries) Act 1948. These provisions were replaced by the Fatal Accidents Act 1959 and, subsequently, were replaced by the Fatal Accidents Act 1976, which came into force on September 1, 1976, and applied only to a cause of action arising on a death occurring after that date. Now, s.4(1) of the Fatal Accidents Act 1976 provides: **16–48**

> "In assessing damages in respect of a person's death in an action under this Act, benefits[163] which have accrued or will or may accrue to any person from his estate or otherwise as a result of his death shall be disregarded."[164]

Substantial case law directed to the question of what benefits had or had not to be taken into account is now obsolete.[165]

Section 4 was considered in *Arnup v M.W. White Ltd*.[166] The deceased had been employed by a company who had set up a trust fund which purchased insurance from which a payment was made to the widow following the death. In addition the company operated a death in service benefit scheme which also made a payment to the widow. The deceased's employer was liable in respect of his death and sought to set off these two payments against the claim brought by the widow under the 1976 Act. It was held that all benefits[167] which came to the widow as a result of the death were to be disregarded.   **16–49**

In *Stanley v Saddique*,[168] a deceased mother's services to her son were replaced by a more caring stepmother, the benefit of the stepmother's services   **16–50**

---

[161] *Gavin v Wilmot Breeden Ltd* [1973] 1 W.L.R. 1117. See Glover, "Savings as a Factor in Fatal Accident Damages", 124 New L.J. 16.

[162] *Mead v Clarke Chapman & Co Ltd* [1956] 1 W.L.R. 76 at 84, per Jenkins and Parker L.JJ.: *Jenner v Allen West & Co* [1959] 1 W.L.R. 554 at 566, per Pearce L.J.

[163] As the word "benefits" has not been defined by the statute, it was apt to include an allowance, based on the deceased husband's pension and paid by his former employers to the widow, following his death in a road accident and, so had to be disregarded: *Pidduck v Eastern Scottish Omnibuses Ltd* [1990] 1 W.L.R. 993.

[164] It is to be observed that the words "shall be disregarded" supersede the original subsection's words "there shall not be taken into account".

[165] For historical interest see *Charlesworth on Negligence* (6th edn, 1977), paras 1370–1373.

[166] [2008] EWCA Civ 447.

[167] In *Cameron v Vintners Defence Systems Ltd* [2007] EWCA Civ 2267 (Q.B.) the High Court found that payments made under the Pneumoconiosis etc. (Workers Compensation) Act 1979 paid to a victim of mesothelioma were not benefits for the purposes of s.4 of the 1976 Act.

[168] [1992] Q.B. 1.

was not taken into account. The decision in *Stanley v Saddique*[169] is inconsistent with an earlier Court of Appeal decision in *Hayden v Hayden*,[170] where the deceased mother's services were replaced by the father, who was also the defendant, and the benefit of the father's services were taken into account in assessing the dependency. In *R. v Criminal Injuries Compensation Board Ex p. K*,[171] the Divisional Court applied *Stanley v Saddique*[172] in preference to *Hayden v Hayden*,[173] making no deduction where the services of an aunt and uncle replaced a murdered mother's services. *Hayden v Hayden* was distinguished on the basis that as it concerned services replaced by the father and tortfeasor. It is submitted that *Hayden* should be considered as confined to its own facts.[174]

16–51   *Hayden v Hayden* and *Stanley v Saddique* were further considered by the Court of Appeal in *Ath v Ms*.[175] There, at the time the mother of dependent children died in a road traffic accident, no financial support was received or was likely from their father who had earlier been convicted of attempting to murder her and after his release from the resulting sentence of imprisonment had found another partner. Even so, after mother's death he received the children into his care. It was held that father's support was a benefit which had accrued as a result of the death and must accordingly be disregarded in the assessment of loss and the calculation of damages.[176] Having said that, pursuant to *Hunt v Severs*,[177] such damages could only be awarded on the basis that they would be used to compensate the voluntary carer for services provided in the past, or to be provided in the future. They were to be held on trust "and if the terms of the trust seem unlikely to be fulfilled then the court awarding damages must take steps to avoid that outcome."[178]

16–52   In *Wood v Bentall Simplex Ltd*,[179] the profits derived from assets acquired by a widow because of her husband's death were benefits under s.4 of the Fatal Accidents Act 1976 and accordingly not taken into account when considering the widow's pecuniary loss arising from the death. It was observed in *McIntyre v Harland & Wolff Plc*[180] that it was no particular objection in a s.4 case that ignoring a benefit resulted in double recovery. That possibility was inherent in the statute itself, because the issue whether something should be disregarded

---

[169] *Stanley v Saddique* [1992] Q.B. 1.
[170] [1992] 1 W.L.R. 986, CA.
[171] [1999] Q.B. 1131, DC.
[172] [1992] Q.B. 1.
[173] [1992] 1 W.L.R. 986, CA.
[174] *Hayden v Hayden* was not referred to in the judgment of Smith L.J. in *Arnup v M.W. White Ltd* [2008] EWCA Civ 447 see para.16–49, above.
[175] [2003] P.I.Q.R. Q1. See Exall, "Fatal accident claims" 2003 J.P.I.Law, Jan. 51.
[176] *Ath v Ms*. [2003] P.I.Q.R. Q1 at Q11.
[177] [1994] 2 A.C. 350, Ch.5, para.5–104, above.
[178] [2003] P.I.Q.R. Q1 at Q12.
[179] [1992] 1 P.I.Q.R. P332, CA.
[180] [2006] EWCA Civ 287 (a case where a widow, as sole beneficiary of her deceased husband's estate, was entitled to receive monies which had already fallen due to him under his employer's provident health scheme, but also claimed dependency in respect of monies which would have been payable under the same scheme had he been able to put into effect a plan to retire).

could not arise, unless the money in question would, on a proper calculation, and without disregard, have to be taken into account as reducing the damages.

Funeral expenses. Prior to 1934, funeral expenses could neither be recovered   **16–53** in an action under the Fatal Accidents Acts nor at common law[181] but this unjust situation was rectified by the Law Reform (Miscellaneous Provisions) Act 1934. Accordingly the Act, by s.2(3), provided for the recovery of funeral expenses in respect of claims brought, not only on behalf of the deceased's estate, under s.1(2)(c) of the Act itself, but also on behalf of the dependants, under the Fatal Accidents Acts. These provisions have now been replaced by s.3(5) of the Fatal Accidents Act 1976, which provides:

> "if the dependants have incurred funeral expenses in respect of the deceased, damages may be awarded in respect of those expenses".

It is to be noted that there is no definition of "funeral expenses" contained in   **16–54** the Act of 1976 or, indeed, any of the earlier Acts. Further there is no precise judicial definition of the term so that the test appears to be whether or not the particular expense, which had been incurred in respect of the funeral and its arrangements, was reasonable in all the circumstances.

Funeral expenses, whilst not defined by the Act, include the cost of the   **16–55** provision of a headstone for a grave but they do not include the excessive cost of a monument.[182] The expenses of mourning[183] and other ceremonial expenses, incurred out of respect of the dead and his religion, cannot be recovered.[184] A claim was rejected that the funeral expenses included the cost of a return flight across the Atlantic to Scotland to enable the son of an American citizen, who had been killed whilst enjoying a Scottish holiday, to settle her affairs, including everything connected with the arrangements for and his attendance at his mother's funeral.[185] Likewise, neither the cost of flying back the body of a deceased student to the country of her birth for burial in Trinidad, nor the cost of the mother's return air fare to England was held to have been incurred

---

[181] See para.16–01, above.
[182] *Hart v Griffiths-Jones* [1948] 2 All E.R. 729. A tombstone has been held to be a funeral expense within the meaning of s.36 of the Assurance Companies Act 1909; *Goldstein v Salvation Army Ass. Socy* [1917] 2 K.B. 291. Funeral expenses must be reasonable having regard to the station in life of the deceased; *Re Walter* [1929] 1 Ch. 647 at 655. In *Stanton v Ewart F. Youlden Ltd* [1960] 1 W.L.R. 543 at 546, McNair J. said that a stone over a grave may properly be considered as part of the funeral expenses if it is a reasonable expenditure for the person in the station in life of the deceased and of the relatives who are responsible for the ordering of the stone; but in so far as it is merely a memorial set up as a sign of love and affection then it should not be included. In *Gammell v Wilson* [1982] A.C. 27 the CA declined to interfere with an award of £595, although as Sir David Cairns observed (at 55) it "was very near the boundary between a headstone and a memorial". In *Jones v Royal Devon & Exeter NHS Foundation Trust* [2008] EWHC 558 (Q.B.) the cost of the wake was not recoverable and only £2,000 was awarded for the cost of a specially commissioned headstone as against the expected cost of £4,000.
[183] *Dalton v S.E. Ry* (1858) 4 C.B.(N.S.) 296.
[184] *Barnett v Cohen* [1921] 2 K.B. 461.
[185] *Thomson v Neilly*, 1973 S.L.T. 53.

reasonably, in the absence of evidence that she had merely been making a sojourn in England and had had every intention of going back home to Trinidad.[186]

16–56   **Assessment of damages for dependent children.** Damages are recoverable in respect of the loss of a parent's services.[187] So, where an unwaged mother dies and leaves young children, the value of the dependency can be assessed by reference to the cost of replacing the mother's services with a paid housekeeper even if the services are, in fact, replaced gratuitously.[188] In assessing the value of the dependency, however, only pecuniary losses can be taken into account and this presents a particular difficulty in assessing the loss to a young child arising out of the death of a non earning parent. In *Regan v Williamson*,[189] the High Court recognised that in relation to the loss of a mother the services provided by a mother go beyond simple domestic activities such as cooking, housework, laundering clothes and so forth. In recognition of the constant attendance of a mother which cannot simply be replaced by the purchase of the services of a nanny or housekeeper an additional sum of damages was awarded. It is now common for such awards to be made.

16–57   The annual value of the services provided by a parent is often reduced as the children grow older and their need for care reduces.[190] Whilst a child's dependency may continue after the age of 16 years old, there had to be set off against that possibility the risks of accident, illness or unemployment, befalling the child, so that the appropriate multiplier usually ought not to be increased if the result is that the dependency is extended beyond normal school leaving age.[191] Where a wife and an infant daughter are both claimants under the Act but the wife dies soon after the husband from causes unconnected with the husband's fatal accident, the dependency of the daughter should be assessed separately.[192]

16–58   Illegitimate children are treated as dependants of their parents pursuant to s.1(3)(e) of the Fatal Accidents Act 1976 and an illegitimate person is treated as the legitimate child of his mother and reputed father.[193]

16–59   **Assessment of damages for the deceased's cohabitant (other than spouse).** Since a "dependant" under the Act has been widened to include:

"any person who—

---

[186] *Goodridge v During* [1976] 7 C.L. 59.
[187] See, e.g. *Spittle v Bunney* [1988] 1 W.L.R. 847, CA. There are many other examples set out in *Kemp & Kemp, The Quantum of Damages*.
[188] *Berry v Humm* [1915] 1 K.B. 627.
[189] [1976] 1 W.L.R. 305. To the extent that *Pevec v Brown* (1964) 108 S.J. 219 took a contrary view it may be now regarded as an outdated first instance decision.
[190] See *Spittle v Bunney* [1988] 1 W.L.R. 847, CA.
[191] *K. v JMP Co Ltd* [1976] Q.B. 85. The multiplier, however, should be calculated from the date of the deceased's death and not from the date of trial.
[192] *Moore v Babcock & Wilcox* [1966] 3 All E.R. 882 (on the facts, that assessment would be on the footing that if her father had lived but her mother had died, she would have stayed at home and would not have gone out to work for some years ahead).
[193] s.1(5)(b).

   (i) was living with the deceased in the same household immediately before the date of the death; and

   (ii) had been living with the deceased in the same household for at least two years before that date; and

   (iii) was living during the whole of that period as the husband or wife or civil partner[194] of the deceased".[195]

The only assistance given by the Act in relation to the assessment of damages in a claim by such a dependent is that contained in s.3(4), which provides that,

> "there shall be taken into account (together with any other matter that appears to the court to be relevant to the action) the fact that the dependant had no enforceable right to financial support by the deceased as a result of their living together."

General method of calculation. The general method of assessment is to   **16–60** determine the annual value of the dependency which is derived from the financial contribution which the deceased made from earnings together with the pecuniary value of the services which the deceased would have provided. The past losses can then be calculated to the date of the trial.[196] In order to calculate the future losses the annual value of the dependency or multiplicand is then multiplied by a multiplier to represent the number of years over which the deceased could have been expected to provide such pecuniary benefits to the dependants. The multiplier is calculated as from the date of death and so to calculate the future losses from the date of trial the number of years elapsed from death to trial must be deducted.

Calculation of the multiplicand. The starting point for the multiplicand is   **16–61** the net earnings of the deceased. From this a sum has to be deducted to represent the amount which would have been spent on the deceased's personal needs. The calculation of these sums is essentially a question of fact in any one case but the courts have evolved conventional methods of assessing figures. In *Harris v Empress Motors*,[197] it was recognised that the use of such percentages avoid the need for tedious inquiry as to the exact expenditure on specific items and that conventional percentages should be used unless there is striking evidence to the contrary. Where the family unit was a husband and wife and the husband has died the appropriate deduction from his annual earnings to represent his personal expenses is 33 per cent and where the family includes children the deduction should fall to 25 per cent. In *Owen v Martin*,[198] the use of conventional

---

[194] Inserted by s.83 of the Civil Partnership Act 2004 with effect from December 5, 2005.

[195] Fatal Accidents Act 1976 s.1(3)(b). *See Kotke v Saffarini* [2005] 1 F.C.R. 642, CA (cohabitation was not established for the relevant period where a couple shared shopping expenses when they were together in the claimant's house, but the deceased retained his own home, where he left his wardrobe and possessions, and was living out of an overnight bag at the claimant's house until such time as he could dispose of his house and buy a new house with her).

[196] Interest is recoverable on the past losses but not on the future losses: *A Train & Sons Ltd v Fletcher* [2008] EWCA Civ 413.

[197] [1984] 1 W.L.R. 212, CA.

[198] [1992] P.I.Q.R. Q151, CA.

percentages was rejected by the Court of Appeal where the claimant was a young childless widow whose husband had died within a year of the date of their marriage. Stuart-Smith L.J. held that it was plain that such a widow's dependency would not remain at two-thirds of the deceased's net earnings for the whole of his working life. Whilst conventional percentages were appropriate where a stable pattern had been established in a marriage and virtually all the earnings are spent in living expenses such an approach would not be appropriate where the deceased was a high earner with a higher proportion of personal expenses.

16–62   **The effect of the remaining spouse's earnings.** Most reported cases concern the death of a husband but the principles are likely to apply equally to cases concerning the death of an earning wife. Where the surviving spouse was earning at the date of the death and those earnings formed part of the family's pool of income then the surviving spouse's income must be taken into account in assessing the value of the dependency.[199] The situation may be different where at the date of the death the surviving spouse was not earning.[200] In *Coward v Comex Houlder Diving Ltd*,[201] where the deceased husband's earnings were more substantial than the widow's but where their earnings were pooled the dependency was calculated by taking 2/3 of the pooled earnings and deducting the widow's earnings. Such an approach was followed in *Crabtree v Wilson.*[202] Where, however, the particular circumstances do not permit a conventional approach the court will have to commence the assessment of the dependency with the net earnings of the deceased.[203]

16–63   **The multiplier.** The multiplier is determined by the judge having regard to the deceased's expectation of life and health,[204] the probable duration of earning capacity, together with the possibility of the earning capacity increasing[205] or decreasing, the expectation of life of the dependants[206] and the probable duration of the continuance of the deceased's assistance to the dependants, throughout

---

[199] *Cookson v Knowles* [1977] 1 Q.B. 913 (the case was considered by the House of Lords in respect of other issues); *Coward v Comex Houlder Diving Ltd* (1988) unreported, CA but to be found in *Kemp and Kemp, the Quantum of Damages*, Volume 4.

[200] In *Davies v Whiteways Cyder Co* [1975] 1 Q.B. 263 the High Court rejected a submission that the widow's post death increased earnings should be taken into account so as to reduce the value of the dependency.

[201] Note 199, above.

[202] [1993] P.I.Q.R. Q24.

[203] *H v S* [2002] EWCA Civ 792.

[204] e.g. *Gilbertson v Harland & Wolff Ltd* [1966] 2 Lloyd's Rep. 190. The deceased was an active healthy man of 70, who would have gone on working until the age of 75, although normally, it must be assumed in the absence of contrary evidence, a man would have retired at 65. See *Whittome v Coates* [1965] 1 W.L.R. 1285 at 1288, per Sellers L.J.

[205] *Brown v Brockhouse Forgings* [1976] C.L.Y. 671. Account should be taken of the chances of future increases in earnings from a promotion or improved standard of living but not to inflation. As regards "inflation", see para.15–60, below.

[206] *Grzelak v Harefield and Northwood Hospital Management Committee* (1968) 112 S.J. 195 where the dependants included the deceased's parents who were aged 77 and 80. Their multiplier was assessed as a three years' purchase.

their joint lives.[207] The starting point should be the Ogden Tables.[208] In the words of Lord Lloyd:[209]

> "I do not suggest that the judge should be a slave to the tables. There may well be special factors in particular cases. But the tables should now be regarded as the starting point, rather than a check. A judge should be slow to depart from the relevant actuarial multiplier on impressionistic grounds, or by reference to 'a spread of multipliers in comparable cases' especially when the multipliers were fixed before actuarial tables were widely used."

The sixth edition[210] of the Ogden Tables has tables specifically designed for   **16–64**
use in claims brought pursuant to the Fatal Accidents Act 1976. There are also explanatory notes and worked examples to which reference should be made. As explained by the late Sir Michael Ogden in the introduction to the fourth edition of the tables, the method suggested indicates that the multiplier should not be calculated from the date of death but from the date of trial. [211] This is inconsistent with the approach taken in *Cookson v Knowles*,[212] *Graham v Dodds*[213] and *Corbett v Barking, Havering & Brentwood Health Authority*,[214] where it was stated that the multiplier should be calculated from the date of death. In *White v ESAB Group (UK) Ltd*[215] at first instance Nelson J. indicated that whilst he would have preferred to assess the multiplier from the date of trial he was constrained by authority to assess it from the date of death. This was endorsed by the Court of Appeal in *H v S*.[216] If the multiplier is taken from the date of death then the approach suggested in the recent editions of the Ogden tables cannot be utilised, the tables can, however, be used as a guide to the appropriate multiplier to be selected as from the date of death.

Adjustments for future inflation. Now that multipliers are determined with   **16–65**
reference to the Ogden Tables the selection of the appropriate discount rate should take into account the risk of future inflation. The Lord Chancellor has the power to prescribe a rate of return to be taken into account by the courts in determining multipliers in claims under the Fatal Accidents Act 1976.[217]

---

[207] See *Grand Trunk Ry v Jennings* (1888) 13 App.Cas. 800; *Royal Trust Co v C.P. Ry* (1922) 38 T.L.R. 899; *Davies v Powell Duffryn Associated Collieries Ltd* [1942] A.C. 601 at 617; *Bishop v Cunard White Star Ltd* [1950] P. 240; *Nance v British Columbia Electric Ry* [1951] A.C. 601; *Heatley v Steel Company of Wales Ltd* [1953] 1 W.L.R. 405. The practical application of this method of calculation obviously must give results which vary according to the weight given to the different elements by the individual calculator.
[208] The sixth edition of the Ogden Tables includes tables designed for use in fatal accident claims.
[209] *Wells v Wells* [1999] 1 A.C. 345, at 379. See also *Barry v Ablerex Construction, The Times*, April 3, 2001, CA, in which it was observed by Judge L.J. that although guidelines were not tramlines and individual cases might require exceptional treatment, there would be little point in the HL giving guidance to lower courts if it was not followed.
[210] The Ogden Tables are available in the publication *Facts and Figures* (Sweet and Maxwell).
[211] This alternative approach was first suggested in the fifth edition of the tables.
[212] [1976] A.C. 556.
[213] [1983] 1 W.L.R. 808, HL.
[214] [1991] 2 Q.B. 408.
[215] [2002] P.I.Q.R. Q6.
[216] [2003] Q.B. 965.
[217] The Damages Act 1996 s.1(1). The rate has been set at 2.5 per cent with effect from June 28, 2001 by virtue of the Damages (Personal Injury) Order 2001 (SI 2001/2301).

16–66   **Summary judgment.** An action under the Fatal Accidents Act 1976 can be made the subject of an application for summary judgment, under Pt 24 of the Civil Procedure Rules 1998.[218] Indeed, it is rather surprising that this relatively inexpensive procedure, which is expeditious, is not made use of more often, especially in cases where there can be no real dispute as to liability, for example after the defendant's conviction of a criminal offence, which has arisen out of the happening of the accident, causing the deceased's injury and consequential death.[219]

16–67   **Interest on damages.** Up until January 1, 1970 the power of the courts to award interest in fatal accidents cases, inter alia, was purely discretionary[220] but, thereafter, the power has had to be exercised compulsorily, with very few exceptions.[221] As regards the development of the guidelines, advanced by the appellate courts, in order to assist in achieving some measure of conformity, see elsewhere in this work.[222]

16–68   However, in the normal run of "fatal" claims, the House of Lords, in *Cookson v Knowles*,[223] has indicated that, as a general rule, the damages ought to be split into two parts, namely (a) the pecuniary loss which it is estimated the dependants had already suffered from the date of death up to the date of trial ("the pre-trial loss"), and (b) the pecuniary loss which it was estimated they would suffer from the trial onwards ("the future loss"). Next, interest on the pre-trial loss ought to be awarded for a period between the date of death and the date of trial at one-half the special account rate[224] current during that period. On the other hand, no interest should be awarded at all on the future loss[225] and no other allowance should be made for the prospective continuing inflation after the date of trial.

16–69   **The ability to compromise a claim.** Because of the obvious convenience in practice, an action under the Fatal Accidents Act 1976 is usually brought by the personal representatives of the deceased in their name, as the claimants, at the same time as their claim on behalf of the estate of the deceased, under the Law Reform (Miscellaneous Provisions) Act 1934. Even so, they cannot make a binding agreement with the defendant to accept a lump sum settlement to cover all the dependants, unless (a) the court has sanctioned the agreement as being one

---

[218] *Dummer v Brown* [1953] 1 Q.B. 710.

[219] But a claimant wishing to rely upon s.11 of the Civil Evidence Act 1968 should note that by the words of subs.(2)(a) a defendant is given a clear mandate to attack any conviction relied upon on proof of the civil claim where he has good cause for doing so: *McCauley v Hope* [1999] P.I.Q.R. P185, CA.

[220] See s.3 of the Law Reform (Miscellaneous Provisions) Act 1934.

[221] The power to award interest is contained in the Supreme Court Act 1981 s.35A, in the High Court and, in the county courts, the County Courts Act 1984 s.69.

[222] See Ch.5, paras 5–147–5–150, above

[223] [1979] A.C. 556. An award of interest on future losses was not allowed in *A Train & Sons Ltd v Fletcher* [2008] EWCA Civ 413.

[224] The special account rate is prescribed by the Lord Chancellor. It was 8% from February 1, 1993 until August 1, 1999, when it was lowered to 7% It was lowered to 6% with effect from February 1, 2002.

[225] *A Train & Sons Ltd v Fletcher*, n.196, above.

for the benefit of each of the dependants, who are still minors at the time,[226] and (b) each of the dependants, who is sui juris and desirous of making a claim, has approved the agreement in so far as it affects him, individually.[227]

> "Where, however, the administrator has with the approval of any dependant who is *sui juris* entered into an agreement with the defendant should pay to that dependant (whom I shall call the settling dependant) a sum of money which is agreed to be sufficient as being proportionate to the injury suffered by the settling dependant, then the settling dependant is bound by the agreement as he would be if he personally entered into such agreement."[228]

In an applicable case, it is only after the court's approval has been given that **16–70** a binding agreement comes into existence.[229] Where a claim for damages under the Fatal Accidents Act 1976 is brought on behalf of more than one person any sum ordered or agreed to be paid in satisfaction of the claim must be apportioned by the court unless it has been apportioned by agreement.[230] If an agreement has been reached before proceedings have been issued and the sole purpose of an application to the court is approval of a settlement and apportionment of behalf of a child or a patient then the claim form can be issued under Pt 8 of the Civil Procedure Rules 1998.

(B) Other Statutory Provisions

(i) *The Coal Mining (Subsidence) Act 1991*

Coal mining subsidence. By s.32(1) of the Coal Mining (Subsidence) Act **16–71** 1991 liability is imposed on the British Coal Corporation in respect of deaths caused by coal mining subsidence where, apart from the subsection, no action to recover damages for the death is otherwise maintainable. In effect, it is enacted that the provisions of the Fatal Accidents Act 1976 shall apply in such cases but with the important distinction that the claimant is not required to prove that the death was caused by the British Coal Corporation's negligence, wrongful act or default.[231]

The British Coal Corporation is not liable if at the time of the injury causing **16–72** the death the deceased was a trespasser[232] or if the injury was wholly attributable

---

[226] No compromise on behalf of a child or patient is valid unless approved by the court, pursuant to CPR Pt 21.10.

[227] *Jeffrey v Kent County Council* [1958] 1 W.L.R. 927.

[228] *Jeffrey v Kent County Council* [1958] 1 W.L.R. 927 at 930.

[229] See *Dietz v Lennig Chemicals Ltd* [1969] 1 A.C. 170 (an agreement for the payment of a lump sum was reached between a widow with a young, dependant child and the defendant but a court order was not perfected and thus the court's approval of the agreement had not been obtained; the widow's circumstances materially changed and HL held that there had been no binding agreement without the court's approval).

[230] CPR Pt 37.4.

[231] The Coal Mining (Subsidence) Act 1991 s.32(2).

[232] The Coal Mining (Subsidence) Act 1991 s.4(a).

to the fault of the deceased.[233] If the deceased was partly at fault then the liability of the British Coal Corporation is reduced proportionately.[234]

(ii) *The Carriage by Air Act 1961*

16–73   **Carriage by air.** The principles applying to deaths of passengers on aircraft is considered in Chapter 10, paras 10–181 to 10–182.

(iii) *The Railways (Convention on International Carriage by Rail) Regulations 2005*

16–74   **International travel by rail.** The Convention concerning International Carriage by Rail (COTIF) has the force of law in the United Kingdom by the Railways (Convention on International Carriage by Rail) Regulations 2005. The Convention introduces uniform rules governing international carriage by rail: the Uniform Rules Concerning the Contract of International Carriage of Passengers by Rail (CIV) and the Uniform Rules Concerning the Contract of International Carriage of Goods by Rail (CIM). Regulation. Detailed consideration of this subject is outside the scope of this text. In summary, the CIV rules impose liability on rail carriers in respect of loss or damage resulting from the death or personal injury to a passenger caused by an accident arising out of the operation of the railway, subject to certain exceptions.[235] A claim must be notified to the carrier within twelve months of the accident.[236] The limitation period for bringing proceedings in relation to an accident under the rules is three years.[237] Regulation 5 of the 2005 Regulations makes provision for claims by dependants, and again the reader is referred to the regulation itself for the detail.

3.—THE SURVIVAL OF A CAUSE OF ACTION

16–75   **The Law Reform (Miscellaneous Provisions) Act 1934.** This Act made a substantial alteration in the law by providing that all causes of action, whether against or vested in a person at his death, should survive either against or for the benefit of his estate. The Act did not create any cause of action.[238]

16–76   The first result was to provide a remedy against the estate of a deceased person who had caused another person to sustain injury or suffer loss and damage, as a result of his negligence or other breach of duty. The second was to deal with the state of affairs, arising in such cases as *Pulling v G.E. Ry*,[239] where it was held that the administratrix of a person killed by the defendants' negligence could not recover either the loss of wages suffered or the expenses of receiving medical

---

[233] The Coal Mining (Subsidence) Act 1991 s.4(b).
[234] The Coal Mining (Subsidence) Act 1991 s.4.
[235] The CIV rules art.26.
[236] The CIV rules art.58.
[237] The CIV rules art.60.
[238] *Gammell v Wilson* [1982] A.C. 27 at 76, per Lord Scarman.
[239] (1882) 9 Q.B.D. 110.

attention and engaging nursing services, which had been incurred between the date of the accident and the subsequent death of the deceased.

The Act provides by its amended s.1:   **16–77**

"(1) Subject to the provisions of this section, on the death of any person after the commencement of this Act all causes of action subsisting against[240] or vested in him shall survive against, or as the case may be for the benefit, of his estate . . .

(1A) The right of a person to claim under section 1A of the Fatal Accidents Act 1976 (bereavement) shall not survive for the benefit of his estate on his death.[241]

(2) Where a cause of action survives as aforesaid for the benefit of the estate of a deceased person the damages recoverable for the benefit of the estate of that person—

(a) shall not include—

    (i) any exemplary damages;
    (ii) any damages for loss of income in respect of any period after that person's death[242];

(b) [. . .];

(c) where the death of that person has been caused by the act or omission which gives rise to the cause of action, shall be calculated without reference to any loss or gain in his estate consequent on his death,[243] except that a sum in respect of funeral expenses may be included.

(3) [. . .]

(4) Where damage has been suffered by reason of any act or omission in respect of which a cause of action would have subsisted against any person if that person had not

---

[240] If representation is not taken out, the court may appoint a person to defend the action under CPR Pt 19.4, or a grant may be made to the Official Solicitor: *In the Goods of Knight* [1939] 3 All E.R. 928.

[241] This subsection was added by the Administration of Justice Act 1982 s.4(1), which came into force on January 1, 1983 (s.76(11)). Bereavement, involving a claim which is restricted to certain dependants only, was first introduced as a head of damage by s.1A of the Fatal Accidents Act 1976 (see the Administration of Justice Act 1982 s.3(1)). See, further, para.16–27, above. Because bereavement is essentially personal to the sufferer, obviously there could be no justification at all why the beneficiaries of the late sufferer's estate should be entitled to such a windfall, to be added to it.

[242] Prior to this provision's being inserted in s.1(2)(a) of the Act, by virtue of the Administration of Justice Act 1982, s.4(2), the law had been that laid down and developed by the HL in *Pickett v British Rail Engineering Ltd* [1980] A.C. 136, as it was applied in *Gammell v Wilson* [1982] A.C. 27. In the latter case, each of the Law Lords had commented unfavourably on "the unhappy state into which this part of the law of England had fallen". As Lord Fraser said at 71, 72 it seemed difficult to justify a law "whereby the deceased's estate, which may pass to persons or institutions in no way dependent upon him for support, can recover damages for loss of earnings, or other income, which he would probably have received during the 'lost years'". Clearly, it was this absurdity and injustice to defendants that the legislation was intended to put to rights. See Cane and Harris, "Administration of Justice Act 1982, Section 4(2): a Lesson in How Not to Reform the Law", 46 M.L.R. 478.

[243] See *Gammell v Wilson* [1982] A.C. 27 at 78 where Lord Scarman expressed the opinion that in the context of the section the words "loss or gain to his estate consequent on his death" meant "a loss or gain *to the estate* consequent on death and do not cover a loss or gain capable of being suffered or collected by the deceased before his death". In *Kandalla v BEAC* [1981] 1 Q.B. 159, Griffiths J. said that the subsection must be construed as applying to those gains and losses to the estate that arose as a result of the death itself and independently of the fact that the death was caused by the defendant's wrongful act, e.g. annuities and insurance moneys (at 172).

died before or at the same time as the damage was suffered, there shall be deemed, for the purposes of this Act, to have been subsisting against him before his death such cause of action in respect of that act or omission as would have subsisted if he had died after the damage was suffered.

(5) The rights conferred by this Act for the benefit of the estates[244] of deceased persons shall be in addition to and not in derogation of any rights conferred on the dependants of deceased persons by the Fatal Accidents Act [1976],[245] and so much of this Act as relates to causes of action against the estates of deceased persons shall apply in relation to causes of action under the said Act[s] as it applies in relation to other causes of action not expressly excepted from the operation of subsection (1) of this section.

(6) In the event of the insolvency of an estate against which proceedings are maintainable by virtue of this section, any liability in respect of the cause of action in respect of which the proceedings are maintainable shall be deemed to be a debt provable in the administration of the estate, notwithstanding that it is a demand in the nature of unliquidated damages arising otherwise than by a contract, promise or breach of trust."

16–78   The object of s.1 "is to put a person, who has by his negligence caused damage to someone who has subsequently died, in the same position as regards liability (subject to certain qualifications . . .) as he would have been in, if the injured person had sued and recovered judgment while still alive."[246] Accordingly, there can be recovered for the benefit of the estate of the deceased not only any expense, to which the estate has been put, as was the case in *Pulling v G.E. Ry*,[247] but also damages for the pain and suffering experienced by the deceased and. Where unconsciousness and death occur in a short period of time after the injury no damages are recoverable by the estate for the deceased's pain and suffering.[248] In contrast where there is a substantial period of unconsciousness before death there can be a substantial claim for damages for loss of the amenities of life. The fact that the victim is unaware of his loss of amenity is not a ground for reducing the award.[249] Awards in relation to pain and suffering are, however, based on the victim's awareness of his injury.[250]

---

[244] As Lord Scarman indicated in *Gammell v Wilson* [1982] A.C. 27 at 76, if the deceased has made a will leaving his estate, or a substantial part of it, to others than his dependants, both the estate and the dependants will have a claim and added: "This element of advantage gained by beneficiaries of the estate who are not dependants of the deceased has been described by judges and others, as a 'windfall'. It arises because the estate's claim is additional to and not in derogation of the rights of the dependants." See also per Griffiths J. in *Kandalla v BEAC* [1981] 1 Q.B. 159 at 169, 170. See, however, *Jameson v CEGB* [2000] A.C. 455 (concurrent tortfeasors liable in respect of the same injuries which led to the death of the deceased, the claim against one tortfeasor was settled in the deceased's lifetime; the claim on behalf of the dependant widow under the Fatal Accidents Act 1976 was barred by the settlement of the first claim). See para.16–10, above.

[245] As consequentially amended by the Fatal Accidents Act 1976 s.6, Sch.1, and also see the provisions of the Carriage by Air Act 1961 para.16–73 and Ch.10, paras 10–181 to 10–182, above.

[246] *Rose v Ford* [1937] A.C. 826 at 838, per Lord Russell of Killowen.

[247] (1882) 9 Q.B.D. 110.

[248] *Hicks v Chief Constable of South Yorkshire Police* [1992] 2 All E.R. 65, HL.

[249] *H. West & Son Ltd v Shepard* [1964] A.C. 326. In *Andrews v Freeborough* [1967] 1 Q.B. 1, CA, an award of £2,000 was made where a child survived in a state of unconsciousness for a year.

[250] *Lim Poh Choo v Camden and Islington Health Authority* [1980] A.C. 174, per Lord Scarman. See Ch.5, para.5–89, above.

The damages include the costs of obtaining a grant of administration, if the   **16–79**
grant was obtained solely to enable an action to be brought, but not the additional
costs incurred by the personal representatives in consequence of the action, such
as the cost of filing a corrective affidavit.[251] Also they will include compensation
for loss of the probability of an inheritance but not for loss of income from capital
owned by the deceased at the time of his death.[252] Situations can arise where all
the damages will be apportioned under the Act and none under the Fatal
Accidents Act at all.[253]

It is to be presumed that the provisions of subs.(4) are intended to deal with   **16–80**
cases in which damage is essential to the cause of action. For example, a
negligent manufacturer might manufacture noxious ginger beer, which is not
consumed for some months. If, after the manufacturer's death, the consumer
suffered damage from drinking it, he would have a right of action against the
manufacturer's estate, as if the latter had died immediately after the consumer's
damage, and his right of action would not be barred by the manufacturer's
subsequent death. So, the effect of the subsection is that, in cases of negligence
on the part of the deceased, which, some time after his death, results in damage
to another, the right of that injured party to obtain damages from his estate is
preserved subject, of course, to the provisions of the Limitation Act 1980.[254] For
example, a claim for contribution under the Civil Liability (Contribution) Act
1978[255] can be brought by virtue of this subsection against the personal
representatives of a deceased wrongdoer, regardless of the fact that the claimant's
cause of action for contribution did not begin to exist until the injured party had
proved liability against him and hence did not subsist against the deceased at the
time of his death.[256]

Joinder of causes of action. The cause of action which an estate may bring   **16–81**
pursuant to the Law Reform (Miscellaneous Provisions) Act 1934 is additional to
the cause of action on behalf of the dependants pursuant to the Fatal Accidents
Act 1976. In practice the claims are often brought in the same proceedings by the
personal representatives of the estate on behalf of the estate and on behalf of the
dependants. In many cases the beneficiaries of the estate are the same as the
dependants. The fact that an action has been brought under the Fatal Accidents
Act 1976 is not a bar to an action being brought under the Law Reform
(Miscellaneous Provisions) Act 1934.[257]

---

[251] *Thomas v Cunard White Star* [1951] P. 153.
[252] *Adsett v West* [1983] Q.B. 826.
[253] *Farmer v Rash* [1969] 1 W.L.R. 160 (the claimant widow had been living separate and apart from
the deceased, her husband, who committed suicide a year after he had sustained severe personal
injuries in a motor accident); *Kandalla v BEAC* [1981] Q.B. 158 (the parents, living in straitened
circumstances, were the parents of two spinster daughters, each of whom was a medical practitioner,
and they inherited the entire estates, as well as their being the sole dependants).
[254] For the provisions of which, see Ch.4, paras 4–178–4–218, above.
[255] Which came into force on January 1, 1979, and repealed s.6 of the Law Reform (Married Women
and Tortfeasors) Act 1935.
[256] *Harvey v R. G. O'Dell Ltd* [1958] 2 Q.B. 78.
[257] *May v Sir Robert McAlpine & Sons Ltd* [1983] 3 All E.R. 85.

16–82   **Contributory negligence of the deceased.** Damages awarded to the estate must be reduced to a proportionate extent, where there had been on the part of the deceased negligence which contributed either to the cause of the accident or the extent of his injuries, loss or damage.[258]

16–83   **When an action must be brought.** The Limitation Act 1980 s.11(5), governs an action[259] by the personal representatives of a deceased person for damage to his estate, under the Law Reform (Miscellaneous Provisions) Act 1934, so that, if the deceased died before the expiration of three years from either the date on which his cause of action accrued, or the date, if later, of his knowledge,[260] the period as respects the cause of action surviving for the benefit of the estate of the deceased "shall be three years from—(a) the date of death, or (b) the date of the personal representative's knowledge; whichever is the later." The special rules for the limitation of actions, which were contained in the Law Reform (Miscellaneous Provisions) Act 1934 s.1(3) and applied to proceedings brought against the deceased tortfeasor's estate, were abolished by the Proceedings Against Estates Act 1970.[261] Thereafter, the limitation period, as stated above, has remained unaffected by the fact of the defendant's death.

16–84   **Another person's special damage arising out of death.** When the injured party has died as a result of the injuries inflicted by the negligence of the defendant, no action at all can be brought by a person, whether husband, parent or employer, who has sustained *special* damage thereby. This was decided in *Baker v Bolton*,[262] where the claimant and his wife were injured by the negligence of the proprietors of a stagecoach, and the wife died of her injuries. It was held that the husband could only recover damages for his own injuries and not for the loss of his wife's help in his business or for his grief and distress of mind. Lord Ellenborough said: "In a civil court, the death of a human being could not be complained of as an injury." This was followed in *Osborn v Gillett*,[263] where it was held that a father was not entitled to damages for injuries caused to his "daughter and servant" by the negligence of the defendant, resulting in his daughter's death, either in respect of the loss of her services or of the expense to which he had been put in burying her.[264]

16–85   On the same principle, the Admiralty Commissioners could not recover the amount of the pensions payable by them to the relatives of an officer and seamen who were crew members of a submarine and were drowned, following a collision

---

[258] Law Reform (Contributory Negligence) Act 1945 s.1. For the adoption of its provisions and enactment under the Fatal Accidents Act 1976, see s.5, as amended by the Administration of Justice Act 1982 s.3(2). Also, see Ch.4, paras 4–03–4–72, above.

[259] See Ch.4, paras 4–178–4–218, above, for limitation of actions, generally.

[260] For the definition of date of knowledge for the purpose of s.11 of the Limitation Act 1980, see the provisions of s.14, and Ch.4, paras 4–182–4–194, above.

[261] Which in turn was abolished by the Statute Law (Repeals) Act 1986.

[262] (1808) 1 Camp. 493.

[263] (1873) L.R. 8 Ex. 88, followed and approved by the CA in *Clark v L.G.O.* [1906] 2 K.B. 648.

[264] By virtue of s.1(2)(c) of the Law Reform (Miscellaneous Provisions) Act 1934, the cost of the funeral expenses can now be recovered by the personal representative on behalf of the deceased's estate.

caused by the negligence of the defendants.[265] The law, as stated above, is not affected by the provisions of the Law Reform (Miscellaneous Provisions) Act 1934,[266] so that the result is that *special* damage suffered by a third party in respect of the death of another, caused by the defendant's negligence, is irrecoverable. Of course, different considerations may apply if the negligence also constitutes a breach of contract.[267]

The principle stated above is comparable with that which applies where a   **16–86** person has been injured and not killed, since a third party's losses, resulting from such injury, similarly cannot be reimbursed, unless it can be deemed to be a part of the injured person's own losses.[268]

---

[265] *The Amerika* [1917] A.C. 38.
[266] *Rose v Ford* [1937] A.C. 826; per Lord Russell of Killowen at 839, per Lord Roche at 854.
[267] *Jackson v Watson & Sons* [1909] 2 K.B. 193.
[268] See Ch.5, para.5–53, above.

Part VI
MISCELLANEOUS MATTERS

INSURANCE AND OTHER COMPENSATION SCHEMES

1.—COMPULSORY INSURANCE

17–01 Normally whether or not to take insurance cover is a matter of individual choice, but in certain instances this is not the case and failure to do so is an offence punishable by the criminal law.

(A) Motor insurance

17–02 **Motor insurance.** Pursuant to s.143 of the Road Traffic Act 1988 a person must not use a motor vehicle on a road[1] or other public place[2] unless there is in force in relation to that use a policy of insurance in respect of any liability in respect of death or bodily injury or damage to property[3] caused by, or arising out of, the use of that vehicle. The owner of a vehicle who, in contravention of the above provisions, allows someone, who is not insured against third party liabilities, to drive the vehicle is himself liable to any person injured by the negligence of the driver.[4] Thus, where such a driver is impecunious, an action can be brought against the vehicle's owner for breach of statutory duty. This does not permit one of two drivers to recover contribution from the vehicle's owner towards damages for injuries which she herself sustained in the relevant

---

[1] Road is defined in s.192 as any highway and any other road to which the public has access.
[2] The words "or other place" were inserted into s.143 by the Motor Vehicles (Compulsory Insurance) Regulations 2000 (SI 2000/726) which came into force on April 3, 2000.
[3] The limit for insurance for damage to property is £200,000: s.145(4)(b).
[4] *Monk v Warbey* [1935] 1 K.B. 75. The various agreements involving the Motor Insurers' Bureau covering uninsured drivers do not provide a defence to such a claim, see paras 17–08–17–18, above.

collision: the claim was for pure economic loss and the owner's duty to insure was owed to the public at large but not to herself.[5]

17–03 Pursuant to s.145(3) of the Road Traffic Act 1988, motor insurance policies must insure the driver of a motor vehicle in relation to any liability which may be incurred by the driver in respect of the death of or bodily injury to any person or damage to property caused by, or arising out of, the use of the vehicle on a road or other public place.[6] Motor insurers must satisfy judgments obtained against drivers arising out of the use of a motor vehicle where there was in force at the time of the use a policy of insurance in respect of the use of that vehicle[7] and the liability was incurred in circumstances whereby it was compulsory for the liability to be covered by a policy of insurance[8] in respect of the use of that vehicle. This provision covers the use of the vehicle by any person and not just those insured to drive the vehicle under the policy.[9] Where, however, the vehicle has been stolen or unlawfully taken the motor insurers do not have to meet any judgment obtained in respect of the death of or bodily injury to a person, who, at the time, was allowing himself to be carried when he knew or had reason to believe[10] that the vehicle had been stolen or unlawfully taken.[11] Where such a person did not know and had no reason to believe that the vehicle had been unlawfully taken at the commencement of the journey and could not reasonably have been expected to alight during the journey the exception does not apply.[12]

---

[5] *Bretton v Hancock* [2006] P.I.Q.R. P1 (B was injured in a collision between a car registered in her name but driven by her fiance and a van driven by H, in circumstances where H was 75 per cent to blame. The fiance was killed and his estate was impecunious. B was held to be in breach of the duty to insure against third party risks, but that did not entitle H to claim from her the 25% contribution towards her own damages which could not, as a result of her breach of duty be recovered from the estate).

[6] The words "or other public place" were inserted into s.145(3) by the Motor Vehicles (Compulsory Insurance) Regulations 2000 (SI 2000/726) which came into force on April 3, 2000.

[7] See *Keeley v Pashen, The Times*, November 17, 2004, CA (insurers failed to avoid liability under s.151, on the basis that the use of a vehicle at the material time had been outside the terms of the policy, where, having deposited his fares, a taxi driver reversed his car with the intention of frightening them and collided with one of them, killing him: since the fares' journey was over, the car was not being used for hire or reward and an exclusion under the policy in those terms did not apply; after the driver deposited his last fare the vehicle was being used for social, domestic and pleasure purposes, and the essential character of the journey was not altered by the deviation in reversing towards the former passengers).

[8] The Road Traffic Act s.151(2).

[9] The Road Traffic Act s.151(2). Pursuant to s.151(8) the insurer has a right of recovery against the uninsured driver who caused the accident whom the insurer is obliged to indemnify and any person who: (a) was is insured by the policy and (b) caused or permitted the use of the vehicle which gave rise to the liability, as to the interpretation of this legislative provision and its compatibility with the Second Council Directive on the approximation of the laws of the Member States relating to insurance against civil liability in respect of the use of motor vehicles these issues have been referred by the C.A. to the Court of Justice of the European Union—*Churchill Insurance Co Ltd v Wilkinson* [2010] EWCA Civ 556.

[10] The words "or had reason to believe" mean that the injured passenger had the information which would have afforded him good reasons for believing that the vehicle had been stolen or unlawfully taken had he applied his mind to the matter : *McMinn v McMinn* [2006] EWHC 827 (QB).

[11] The Road Traffic Act s.151(4).

[12] The Road Traffic Act s.151(4)(a) and (b).

Reference to a person being carried includes references to a person entering, getting onto or alighting from the vehicle.[13]

Section 152 notice. Notice of the commencement of proceedings must be   **17-04**
served upon the insurers, either before proceedings are commenced, or within seven days after they commenced.[14] There is a summary of the authroties relating to the service of such notices in *Wake v Page*.[15] A notice can be oral but it must have a degree of formality and not just be a mere piece of a casual conversation.[16] Whether or not it is shown that the insurer had notice is a matter of fact and degree. Kennedy L.J. provided the following salutary advice:

> "a prudent solicitor would be well advised to ensure that the insurer received written notice within seven days after the commencement of proceedings. There can then be no room for argument."[17]

Roads as distinct from other public places. Before it became compulsory to   **17-05**
insure liabilities in respect of the use of a motor vehicle in public places[18] other than roads, motor insurers were only obliged to meet judgments in relation to liabilities arising out of the use of motor vehicles on a road.[19] Thus, in *Clarke v Kato, Cutter v Eagle Star Insurance Company Ltd*,[20] motor insurers were not obliged to meet judgments arising out of injuries sustained by the use of motor vehicles in car parks because a car park fell outside the definition of a road.[21] This meant that the innocent victims of negligent motorists went without compensation merely because they had the misfortune to be injured on a car park rather than on a road. In order to remedy the mischief the Road Traffic Act 1988 was amended by the Motor Vehicles (Compulsory Insurance) Regulations 2000, which came into force on April 3, 2000. The regulations are not retrospective in effect. Thus, in *Inman v Kenny*,[22] a person injured in 1995 by the use of a motorcycle in a public park had no means of enforcing the judgment obtained.[23] In *Charlton v Fisher*,[24] the victim of an incident in an hotel car park in which the driver of a car deliberately collided with the vehicle in which she was a passenger had to argue that the driver should be indemnified under the terms of his own insurance policy: unsuccessfully, because public policy would not allow the

---

[13] The Road Traffic Act s.151(4).
[14] The Road Traffic Act s.152(1).
[15] [2001] R.T.R. 20, CA.
[16] In *Nawaz and Another v Crowe Insurance Group* [2003] R.T.R. 29, CA a conversation between a trainee solicitor acting for the claimant and a legal secretary employed by the insurer's solicitors did amount to sufficient notice.
[17] *Wake v Page* [2001] R.T.R. 20, at 302.
[18] Before April 3, 2000 see para.17-02, above.
[19] See para.17-03, above.
[20] [1998] 4 All E.R. 417, HL.
[21] Defined in the Road Traffic Act s.192 as any highway and any other road to which the public has access.
[22] [2001] P.I.Q.R. P256, CA.
[23] In fact the motorcyclist was uninsured but the Motor Insurers Bureau would have had to meet the judgment only in circumstances where motor insurance would have been compulsory. See paras 17-08–17-18, below.
[24] [2002] Q.B. 578, CA.

driver to recover indemnity against a liability arising from his own intentional criminal act.

(B) Employers' liability insurance

17–06   **Employers' liability insurance.** The Employers' Liability (Compulsory Insurance) Act 1969 imposes a duty on every employer to insure against liability for bodily injury or disease sustained by employees arising out of and in the course of their employment.[25]

(C) Other compulsory insurance

17–07   **Nuclear installations.** Licensees under the Nuclear Installations Acts of 1965 and 1969 must have insurance to cover their statutory liabilities.[26]

2.—The Motor Insurers' Bureau

17–08   Notwithstanding the provision for compulsory Road Traffic Act insurance, problems could still arise if a driver ignored the criminal law and drove without insurance, or for some reason his insurance was ineffective to provide indemnity, or he could not be traced. To meet this problem, by agreement between the Government Minister responsible for Transport, and insurers transacting compulsory motor insurance cover, the Motor Insurers' Bureau[27] was incorporated.[28] Further the United Kingdom now has duties to provide compensation schemes to ensure that victims of uninsured drivers receive compensation pursuant to the five EU directives on motor insurance[29] The arrangements made in order to implement these obligations must be equivalent to and as effective as the protection available under national law in cases involving insured drivers.[30]

17–09   **The current agreements.** The current MIB agreements provide for compensation of the victims of: (i) uninsured drivers; and (ii) untraced drivers. Although the agreement is with the Secretary of State, the " . . . practice is for the M.I.B. never to take the point that the agreement is with the Secretary of State rather than the injured person: everyone proceeds on the basis that the agreement is with the latter. The M.I.B. has, however, always felt free to take against an

---

[25] See Ch.11, para.11–07, above.
[26] See Ch.13, above, paras 13–201–13–212.
[27] See Tennant, "The Motor Insurers' Bureau", 1 Lit. 281; *Gurtner v Circuit* [1968] 2 Q.B. 587.
[28] It is not clear if the MIB is an emanation of the state. In *McCall v Poulton, Helphire (UK) Ltd. intervening* [2008] EWCA Civ 1263 the Court of Appeal upheld the decision of the judge to refer the question to the ECJ.
[29] Namely: 72/166 EEC; 84/5/EEC; 90/232/EEC; 2000/26/EEC and 2005/14/EEC. In *European Commission v Ireland* (C-211/07), February 21,2008 ECJ and in *Farrell v Whitty* (C-356/05 ECJ) the European Court of Justice found that the Irish MIB uninsured drivers agreement failed to comply with the relevant directives.
[30] *Evans v Sec. of State for Environment, Transport and the Regions* (C-63/01) ECJ.

applicant any point that it would be free to take against the Secretary of State."[31]

(A) Uninsured drivers' agreement 1999

The most recent agreement is dated August 13, 1999 and took effect in relation   **17–10**
to accidents on or after October 1, 1999.[32] The Motor Insurers' Bureau
(Compensation of Victims of Uninsured Drivers) Agreement of December 21,
1988 operates in relation to accidents occurring on or after December 31, 1988
up to and including September 30, 1999.[33]

Obligation to meet unsatisfied judgments. The principal obligation under   **17–11**
the agreement is for the Bureau to meet unsatisfied judgments where the liability
arose in circumstances where it was mandatory for there to have been a policy of
motor insurance in force.[34] The obligation to meet unsatisfied judgments applies
whether or not the person liable to satisfy the judgment was in fact covered by
a contract of insurance and whatever the cause of that person's failure to satisfy
the judgment. The Bureau is thus an insurer of last resort.[35]

Exceptions. There are various substantive exceptions to the Bureau's obliga-   **17–12**
tion to meet unsatisfied judgments. These are set out in Clause 6. The Bureau is
not liable to meet an unsatisfied judgment where the injury, loss or damage was
caused by the use of a vehicle owned by or in the possession of the Crown unless
either the responsibility for insuring the vehicle had been undertaken by someone
else or the vehicle was in fact insured.[36] Where the claim is against a person who
by virtue of s.144 of the Road Traffic Act 1988[37] was not required to hold motor
insurance the Bureau is not liable to meet an unsatisfied judgment.[38] There is no

---

[31] per Schiemann L.J. in *Mighell v Reading and the Motor Insurers' Bureau* [1999] P.I.Q.R. P101, CA.

[32] This agreement is amended by a Supplementary agreement dated November 7, 2008.

[33] For details of the 1988 agreement see *Charlesworth and Percy on Negligence* 10th edn. Copies of the 1999 agreement together with notes on the agreement and application forms can be obtained from the Bureau at *www.mib.org.uk.*

[34] cl.5.1. For the circumstances in which a policy of motor insurance is mandatory see para.16–03, above.

[35] The 1999 Uninsured Drivers' Agreement complies with E.U. Council Directive 84/5 on the approximation of the laws of the Member States relating to insurance against civil liability in respect of the use of motor vehicles. See *Evans v Secretary of State for the Environment, Transport and the Regions* (C63/01) *The Times*, December 9, 2003, ECJ (5th Chamber).

[36] cl.6.1(a).

[37] s.144 provides that motor insurance is not compulsory in respect of vehicles owned by certain classes of person such as local authorities and police authorities.

[38] cl.6.1(b). Exceptions to the liability of the MIB under the Uninsured Drivers Agreement include the payment of compensation for hire charges where the innocent party has hired a vehicle to replace his own while it is repaired. In *McCall v Poulton* [2008] EWCA Civ 1263, para.17–08, above, it was held that a judge was right to refer to the European Court issues: (i) whether the Agreement was a contract made for the purposes of discharging the UK's obligations under Council Directive 84/5 EEC; (ii) whether there should accordingly be applied to it the principle in *Marleasing SA v La Comercial Internacional de Alimentacion SA* [1993] B.C. C. 421 EC, by which laws enacted by Member States to bring into effect obligations imposed by Community law have to be interpreted and applied so as to give such a Directive full effect; (iii) whether the MIB was an emanation of the State, with the result that the claimant, who had incurred hire charges after an accident caused by the negligence of an uninsured driver, had a direct claim against it under the Directive.

liability to meet unsatisfied judgments arising out of claims for damage to vehicles where the damaged vehicle was not itself covered by a contract of insurance.[39] The Bureau has no obligation to meet subrogated claims.[40]

17–13   Pursuant to Clause 6(1)(e) where the claim is made by a claimant who, at the time of the use giving rise to the relevant liability of a vehicle was voluntarily allowing himself to be carried in the vehicle and, either before the commencement of the journey or after such commencement if he could reasonably be expected to have alighted from it, he knew or ought to have known that—

(i) the vehicle had been stolen or unlawfully taken,

(ii) the vehicle was being used without there being in force in relation to its use such a contract of insurance as would comply with Pt VI of the 1988 Act,[41]

(iii) the vehicle was being used in the course or furtherance of a crime, or

(iv) the vehicle was being used as a means of escape from, or avoidance of, lawful apprehension,

then the Bureau has no obligation to meet the claim. In *Phillips v Rafiq*,[42] the claimant was the widow of a passenger, who had been killed by the negligence of the driver of a motor car the use of which was uninsured and where the deceased knew or ought to have known that the use was uninsured. The Court of Appeal, noting the stark change of wording from the 1988 Agreement, held that the exception in Clause 6(1)(e) should be given its literal meaning and that as the reference there was to the knowledge of the "claimant," the widow, as dependant under the Fatal Accidents Act 1976, was entitled to enforce her judgment against the MIB as she herself did not have knowledge of the defendant's uninsured status.

17–14   **Knowledge.** Knowledge in these circumstances includes knowledge of matters which the injured person could reasonably have been expected to have been aware had he not been under the self-induced influence of drink or drugs.[43] The burden of proof rests on the Bureau, but in Clause 6(3) there are presumptions to the effect that where any of certain facts[44] are proved it is assumed, in the absence of evidence to the contrary, that the claimant knew that the driver was

---

[39] cl.6.1(d).

[40] cl.6.1(c).

[41] See above paras 17–02–17–05.

[42] [2007] EWCA Civ 74.

[43] cl.6.4.

[44] The relevant facts are: (a) that the claimant was the owner or registered keeper of the vehicle or had caused or permitted its use; (b) that the claimant knew the vehicle was being used by a person who was below the minimum age at which he could be granted a licence authorising the driving of a vehicle of that class; (c) that the claimant knew that the person driving the vehicle was disqualified from holding or obtaining a driving licence; (d) that the claimant knew that the user of the vehicle was neither its owner nor registered keeper nor an employee of the owner or registered keeper nor the owner or registered keeper nor the owner or registered keeper of any other vehicle: cl.6.3(a)–(d).

uninsured. In *White v White*,[45] the House of Lords held, in relation to the corresponding exception in the 1988 Uninsured Drivers' Agreement, that the phrase "ought to have known" should be interpreted restrictively. The phrase does not encompass a passenger who, through carelessness or negligence, failed to make enquiries of the driver the answers to which would have given him actual knowledge that the driver was uninsured.[46] The phrase would, however, cover a passenger who deliberately closed his mind to the issue of insurance.[47] The 1988 Agreement does not contain the presumptions set out in Clause 6(3) of the 1999 Agreement.

In *Pickett v Motor Insurers' Bureau*,[48] the claimant travelled as a passenger in **17–15** a car driven by her boyfriend. The car was registered in the claimant's name and she knew that it was not insured. During the excursion the boyfriend started to carry out a series of handbrake turns on a gravel path. The claimant became concerned for her own safety and exhorted the driver to stop the car. The driver lost control of the car whilst carrying out another handbrake turn and the claimant sustained serious injuries. At first instance the trial judge held that the Bureau were entitled to rely upon the exception in the 1988 agreement which is in similar terms to the exception in Clause 6(1)(e)(ii) of the 1999 agreement. It was held that the point in time at which the claimant's consent to being carried in an uninsured vehicle had to be judged was the time of the accident and not the time of the commencement of the journey. Thus it would have been possible for the claimant to have withdrawn her consent by an unequivocal request to the driver that the car be stopped so that she could alight. On the facts the court drew the inference that the exhortation to the driver to stop was insufficient to withdraw consent. The claimant had not demanded to be allowed to alight from the car so as to dissociate herself from its use.[49]

Procedural hurdles. The 1999 agreement contains a number of procedural **17–16** hurdles for the claimant to surmount before liability will be accepted. Application must be made in such form, accompanied by such documents, and giving such information about the relevant proceedings and other relevant matters, as the Bureau may require.[50] Notices will only be sufficient if transmitted by fax or recorded delivery to the Bureau's registered office. Delivery shall be proved by the production of a fax transmission report from the sender's fax machine or an appropriate postal receipt.[51]

The Bureau shall not incur liability unless proper notice is given within 14 **17–17** days of the commencement of proceedings.[52] Notice must be in writing and

---

[45] [2001] 1 W.L.R. 481, HL.
[46] *White v White* [2001] W.L.R. 481, HL per Lord Nicholls at [17].
[47] See also *Akers v Motor Insurers' Bureau* [2003] Lloyd's Rep. I.R. 427, CA (the deceased "knew or ought to have known" that the driver was uninsured where there was evidence that, before the fatal journey, there had been a discussion in a group, containing himself, a companion and the uninsured driver, about the fact that the first defendant was uninsured).
[48] [2004] 1 W.L.R. 2450, CA.
[49] *Pickett v Motor Insurers' Bureau* [2004] 1 W.L.R. 2450, CA per May L.J. at [50].
[50] cl.7.
[51] cl.8.
[52] cl.9.1.

accompanied by a copy of the sealed claim form, writ or other official document providing evidence of the commencement of proceedings, together with a considerable list of other documentation.[53] The obligation is to give notice both of issue of proceedings and their service. It is not, however, an abuse of process to issue fresh proceedings outside the limitation period where the notice requirements had not been complied with in the original proceedings.[54] There are also provisions whereby notice must be given of: the filing of a defence; any amendment of the particulars of claim or any schedule served along with the particulars of claim and either the setting down of the case for trial or the court setting a date for trial. In the above situations notice must be given within seven days.[55]

17–18   Wherever the Agreement places an obligation upon the claimant the obligation is deemed to include solicitors instructed to act on his behalf.[56] So, where the Agreement requires, as a condition precedent to liability, that the claimant shall furnish such information and documents in support of the claim as the Bureau shall reasonably require,[57] the obligation is imposed equally upon his solicitor as the claimant himself. No liability will be incurred by the Bureau unless the claimant has, after commencement of proceedings and not less than 35 days before the appropriate date, given notice in writing of his intention to apply for judgment.[58] Nor will the Motor Insurers' Bureau be liable unless the claimant, as soon as reasonably practicable, has demanded the information specified in s.154(1) of the Road Traffic Act 1988 (i.e. particulars of the other party's insurance).[59] If the person of whom demand is made fails to comply there must be formal complaint to a police office and the claimant must obtain the name and address of the registered keeper of the vehicle and use all reasonable endeavours to obtain the name and address of the registered keeper.[60] The Bureau incurs no liability unless the claimant has, if so required, taken all reasonable steps to obtain judgment against every person who may be liable (or vicariously liable) in respect of the claim.[61] If so requested, the claimant must consent to the Motor Insurers' Bureau being joined as a defendant.[62]

(B) Untraced drivers

17–19   Prior to 1969, the Bureau would not, in terms, accept liability to compensate victims for death or personal injury, arising out of accidents on roads in Great Britain, which had been caused by "hit-and-run" drivers, namely those persons or the owners of the vehicles involved, whose identities could not be established,

---

[53] cl.9.1.
[54] *Richardson v Watson* [2006] EWCA Civ 1662.
[55] cl.11.1.
[56] cl.2.5(a).
[57] cl.11.1(c).
[58] cl.12.1.
[59] cl.13.1(a).
[60] cl.13.2.
[61] cl.14.
[62] cl.14.

even after extensive inquiries.[63] In spite of this approach, it would and did make ex gratia payments to such victims, in many instances. The uncertainty of the situation, however, was met by the provisions of a second and different agreement with the Minister of Transport, dated April 21, 1969.[64] This put on a formal basis the previous arrangements, as regards those payments that had been made hitherto without admission of liability.

There have since been several agreements, the most recent agreement is dated   **17–20** February 7, 2003 and it applies in relation to accidents occurring on or after February 14, 2003. The preceding agreement is dated June 14, 1996 and it applies in relation to accidents which occurred on or after July 1, 1996. As in the case of uninsured motorists the United Kingdom now has obligations to make arrangements to ensure that victims of the negligence of untraced drivers receive adequate compensation under the relevant EU directives.[65]

The 2003 Agreement.[66] The agreement applies where the death or bodily   **17–21** injury to a person or damage to any property was caused by or arising out of the use of a motor vehicle on a road or other public place in Great Britain where the applicant is unable to trace the person responsible or one of the persons responsible and the event giving rise to the liability occurred on or after February 14, 2003. The use of the phrase "bodily injury" is noteworthy; in the context of injuries sustained during carriage by air the term "bodily injury" does not include psychiatric injuries.[67] Generally in relation to road traffic accidents the courts do not distinguish between physical and psychiatric injuries as foreseeable consequences of an accident.[68] Since the purpose of the agreement is to provide compensation for victims of unidentified drivers on the same basis as if the driver had been identified it would defeat the purpose of the scheme if victims suffering psychiatric injuries cannot obtain benefit under the agreement.

In cases involving death or bodily injury the application must be made no later   **17–22** than three years after the date of the event which is the subject of the application.[69] In *Byrne v Motor Insurers Bureau*,[70] this three year time limit was held to be in breach of Directive 84/5/EEC. A child claimant whose claim was not presented to the MIB within three years of the accident was denied

---

[63] Kerse, "Victims of Untraced Drivers: Suing Motor Insurers' Bureau", 119 S.J. 279.
[64] For the text of the 1969 Agreement see *White v London Transport* [1971] 2 Q.B. 721 at 729–739 together with its published notes.
[65] Namely: 72/166 EEC; 84/5/EEC; 90/232/EEC; 2000/26/EEC and 2005/14/EEC. In *Moore v Sec. State for Transport* [2008] EWCA Civ 750 the claimant brought a *Francovich* action against the Sec. of State for Transport alleging that the relevant uninsured drivers agreement failure to implement adequately Directive 84/5/EEC. It was held that once the victim had sustained injuries then his cause of action was complete and that his claim had been brought more than six years after the accident his claim was statute barred.
[66] See Crefield, "Untraced drivers: the new rules" (2003) N.L.J. (7076) 586. The full text of the agreement and application forms are available at the Bureau's website: *www.mib.org.uk*.
[67] *King v Bristow Helicopters Ltd, M v KLM Royal Dutch Airlines* [2002] 2 A.C. 628, see Ch.10, para.10–179.
[68] See e.g. *Page v Smith* [1996] A.C. 155.
[69] cl.4(3)(a)(i).
[70] [2009] Q.B. 66.

compensation by the MIB under the Untraced Drivers Agreement whereas at common law a claim against a traced motorist could have been issued at any time up to the victims twenty first birthday. Where the applicant could not reasonably have been expected to have become aware of the existence of the bodily injury the three-year time limit does not apply and instead the applicant must apply as soon as practicable after he did become aware and no later than 15 years after the accident.[71] The time limits for fatal accident and bodily injury cases apply irrespective of whether there was property damage caused by the same event. In relation to property cases the time limit for applying is nine months after the date of the event giving rise to the application irrespective of whether death or bodily injury was caused by the same event.[72] This limit does not apply where the applicant could not reasonably have been expected to have become aware of the property damage in which case the application must must be made as soon as practicable after he did become aware and no later than two years after the event giving rise to the application.[73]

17–23   The agreement does not apply where at the time of the accident the person suffering death or injury was allowing himself to be carried in a vehicle and before the journey or during the journey, if he could reasonably be expected to have alighted, he knew or ought to have known that the vehicle:

   (i) had been stolen or unlawfully taken; or

   (ii) was being used without third party insurance; or

   (iii) was being used in the course or furtherance of crime; or

   (iv) was being used as a means of escape from lawful apprehension.[74]

The agreement does not apply in relation to vehicles owned by the Crown or in the possession of the Crown. There are other exclusions set out in Clause 5 of the agreement including cases where the death, bodily injury or damage was caused by terrorism.[75]

17–24   Where an applicant qualifies for an award, the Bureau makes a payment which is assessed in the same way as a Court in England or Wales would have assessed the damages if a successful claim had been brought against the untraced driver, except where the event occurred in Scotland in which case Scottish principles as to the assessment of damages would apply.[76] No payments for loss of earnings are made where the applicant has in fact been paid in lieu of wages or salary even if the advancement of wages or salary is repayable.[77] There are detailed

---

[71] cl.4(3)(b)(i).
[72] cl.4(3)(a)(ii).
[73] cl.4(3)(b)(ii).
[74] cl.5(1)(c). For the interpretation of knowledge for the purposes of these exceptions see *White v White* [2001] 1 W.L.R. 481, HL and para.17–14, above.
[75] cl.5(1)(d).
[76] cl.8(1).
[77] cl.6(2).

provisions in the agreement dealing with situations where some person other than the untraced driver is liable for the death or injury.[78] Essentially the applicant is required to obtain a judgment against the other tortfeasor and the Bureau will meet the proportion of the liability of the unidentified driver.

An applicant must give all reasonable assistance to the Motor Insurers'   **17–25** Bureau[79] and the Bureau can require an applicant to take proceedings against any person who may be liable for the death or injury subject to the Bureau providing an indemnity in relation to the costs of such proceedings.[80] An application may be refused by the Bureau after a preliminary investigation if the agreement does not apply to the case or after a full investigation make a report on the claim.[81] There is an accelerated procedure[82] whereby if after a preliminary investigation the Bureau is satisfied that the agreement applies to the case, rather than carrying out a full investigation, the Bureau can make a offer to the applicant to settle his application. Acceptance of such an offer discharges the Bureau for all further liability to the applicant in respect of the death or injury for which the payment is made.

There is a right of appeal to an arbitrator against a decision that an award   **17–26** should not be made or against the amount of any award.[83] Arbitrators are Queen's Counsel selected by the Secretary of State from a panel chosen by the Lord Chancellor.[84] Notice of appeal must be given to the Bureau within six weeks of the notice of the decision from against which the appeal is brought.[85] There is provision for the payment of legal costs to be met by the Bureau.[86]

3.—CRIMINAL INJURIES COMPENSATION

Development of the Scheme. In June 1964, a scheme was first promulgated   **17–27** under prerogative powers for the purpose of compensating victims of crimes of violence by way of ex gratia payments out of funds, provided through a grant-in-aid.[87] In order to administer the scheme, the Criminal Injuries Compensation Board was set up. The scheme came into effect in its original form on August 1,

---

[78] cl.11, 12 and 13.
[79] cl.11(1).
[80] cl.11(4).
[81] cl.7(1).
[82] cll.26 et seq.
[83] cl.18.
[84] cl.21.
[85] cl.19.
[86] cl.10 the amount of legal costs payable are assessed in accordance with a formula set out in a Schedule to the agreement.
[87] The net expenditure of compensation awarded falls on the funds of the Ministry of Justice in England and Wales and the Scottish Home and Health Department.

1964, but was amended and, later, revised with effect from October 1, 1979 (the "Revised 1979 Scheme"). A 1990 revision (the "1990 Scheme") applied to all applications received by the Board on or after February 1, 1990. From April 1, 2000 the Criminal Injuries Compensation Board ceased to exist. Claims are still proceeding under the 1990 Scheme but they are being administered by the Criminal Injuries Compensation Authority.[88]

17-28   In 1994 an attempt was made to replace these arrangements with a new, "tariff-based" scheme, but it had to be withdrawn after the House of Lords ruled that its introduction, while ss.108–117 of and Schs 6 and 7 to the Criminal Justice Act 1988 remained unrepealed, was unlawful. All claims which from April 1, 1994, had been made under the tariff scheme had to be reassessed.

17-29   **The new scheme.** The Criminal Injuries Compensation Act 1995[89] repealed the provisions of the 1988 Act referred to above.[90] It provided for a new scheme which came into force on April 1, 1996, after Parliamentary approval was given.[91] This current scheme is the Criminal Injuries Compensation Scheme 2008 which applies in relation to applications for compensation made on or after November 3, 2008.[92] The scheme is administered by the Criminal Injuries Compensation Authority (CICA).

17-30   Applications for compensation may be made in respect of criminal injuries sustained on or after August 1, 1964. Criminal injury means one or more personal injuries sustained in Great Britain and directly attributable to:

    (a) a crime of violence[93] (including arson, fire-raising or an act of poisoning); or

    (b) an offence of trespass on a railway[94]; or

---

[88] All inquiries should be addressed to: The Criminal Injuries Compensation Authority, Tay House, 300 Bath Street, Glasgow, G2 4JR.
[89] The Act came into force on November 8, 1995.
[90] The Criminal Injuries Compensation Act s.12(1).
[91] The Criminal Injuries Compensation Act s.11(1).
[92] This replaced the eponymous 2001 scheme.
[93] Like the 1990 scheme there is no definition of crime of violence in the new schemes. This was criticised by the Divisional Court of the Queen's Bench Division of the High Court in *R. v CICB Ex p. Webb* [1986] Q.B. 184. In *R. v CICAP Ex p. August, The Times*, January 4, 2001, the Court of Appeal upheld the Panel's finding in two separate cases that where the applicants had taken part in consensual homosexual activity no crime of violence had been committed within the scheme. See also *R. (E) v CICAP, The Times*, March 17, 2003, CA (in relation to a claim based upon alleged indecent assaults by a prisoner upon another, the basic question was whether the claimant was a victim of a crime of violence, and the ability of a vulnerable individual to give real consent to such acts was but a part of the decision whether he was in truth a victim).
[94] See *R. (on the application of Mair) v CICB* [2002] P.I.Q.R. P28 (no injury attributable to the commission of an offence of trespass on a railway for the purposes of the Scheme where the claimant sustained post-traumatic stress disorder as a result of giving help to a young boy who had fallen under a train and suffered the loss of his arm as he attempted to board without a ticket).

(c) the apprehension or attempted apprehension[95] of an offender or a suspected offender, the prevention or attempted prevention[96] of an offence or the giving of help to any constable who is engaged in any such activity.[97]

Where an injury is sustained accidentally during any of the law enforcement activities set out in (c), above or during any other activity directed to containing, limiting or remedying the consequences of a crime,[98] compensation is not payable unless the injured person was, at the time, taking an exceptional risk which was justified in the circumstances.[99]

It is not necessary for the assailant to have been convicted for an applicant to qualify for an award. Violent acts for which the assailant cannot be convicted by reason of age, insanity or diplomatic immunity are still treated as criminal acts.[100] Injuries attributable to the use of motor vehicles do not qualify unless the vehicle was used so as deliberately to inflict injury or attempt to inflict injury.[101] Where the driver of a stolen car rammed a police car with the motive of disabling the car with the result that the passenger in the police car was injured a crime of violence was established.[102]   **17–31**

Compensation may be reduced or withheld where: **17–32**

(a) the applicant has failed without delay to take all reasonable steps to inform the police (or other appropriate authority) of the circumstances giving rise to the injury; or

(b) the applicant has failed to co-operate with the police or other authority in bringing the assailant to justice; or

(c) the applicant has failed to give all reasonable assistance to the CICA; or

---

[95] The completion of the application for a person's detention in hospital gave a fresh and independent right to the police to detain him under the Mental Health Act 1959 and in no way deprived them of the right to detain him as a person suspected of theft. So, where a person, suspected of theft, had been arrested and was awaiting transport to hospital under a detention order but escaped, whereupon he was pursued by the applicant who sustained an injury, it was held that the latter came within the Scheme because he was "attempting to arrest an offender" when his accident happened: *R. v CICB Ex p. Lawton* [1972] 1 W.L.R. 1589.
[96] Where the driver of a police car was injured and killed whilst driving through some traffic lights at red shortly after midnight when answering an emergency radio call, it was held that he was hurt in an "attempted prevention of an offence" because he had driven as he had done acting on information which gave him reasonable cause for believing that an offence of burglary was either imminent or actually being committed at the place he was trying to reach: *R. v CICB Ex p Ince* [1973] 1 W.L.R. 1334 (the fact that there was no such offence taking place at all was an irrelevant consideration).
[97] The Criminal Injuries Compensation Scheme 2008 para.8.
[98] In this respect the CICA schemes differ from the 1990 scheme. This provision allows claims by paramedics, ambulance personnel and fire fighters to be considered alongside those of police officers.
[99] para.12.
[100] para.10.
[101] para.11.
[102] *R (on the application of Tait) v CICAP* [2010] R.T.R. 6.

(d) the conduct of the applicant before, during or after the incident makes in inappropriate that a full award or any award be made; or

(e) the applicant's character as shown by his convictions (excluding spent convictions) or otherwise makes it inappropriate that a full award or any award be made.[103]

In considering the issue of conduct, where excessive consumption of alcohol or the use of illicit drugs by the applicant contributed to the circumstances which gave rise to the injury it may be appropriate to withhold an award or to make a reduced award.[104] No award will be made if there is a likelihood that the assailant could benefit from the award.[105]

17–33   **The basis of the assessment of compensation.** The compensation payable is a standard amount based on a tariff, which sets out fixed levels of compensation and the amount payable in respect of each description of injury.[106] Multiple injuries are compensated for by applying the tariff amount for the most serious injury plus 30 per cent of the tariff amount for the next most serious injury and 15 per cent of the tariff amount for the third most serious injury.[107] Minor multiple injuries only qualify where the applicant has sustained three separate injuries of the following types:

(a) grazing, cuts, lacerations;

(b) severe and widespread bruising;

(c) severe soft tissue injury;

(d) black eye(s);

(e) bloody nose;

(f) hair pulled from scalp;

(g) loss of fingernail.

In addition, the residual effects of one of the injuries must have lasted six weeks after the incident and the injuries must have necessitated two visits to or by a medical practitioner within the six week period.[108] Payments for loss of earnings or loss of earning capacity are only made where, as a direct consequence of the

---

[103] para.13. In *R (on the application of Andronati) v CICAP* [2007] P.I.Q.R. P2 no award was made because the applicant was unlawfully present in the UK at the time of the criminal injury.
[104] para.14(2).
[105] para.16(a).
[106] para.23. Examples of descriptions contained in the Tariff include, "upper limbs: fractured humerus—full recovery" and "upper limbs: fractured humerus—continuing disability". In *R. v CICAP Ex p. Embling* [2000] P.I.Q.R. Q361, the High Court indicated that the phrases "full recovery" and "continuing disability" related to the limb or organ in question and not to the applicant. Where there was observable and measurable loss of function or faculty, which could sensibly be described as continuing rather than temporary such that the ordinary person adopting a sensible view of life would not be prepared to agree that there had been a full recovery, the case would be one of "continuing disability".
[107] para.27.
[108] para.27 and note 12.

injury, the applicant has suffered a loss of earnings or loss of earning capacity for a period of more than 28 weeks from the date of the incapacity.[109] Where an applicant qualifies for an award for loss of earnings or loss of earning capacity an award for special expenses may also be made. Special expenses include: loss of or damage to property; costs associated with National Health Service treatment; the private cost of medical treatment (where the private treatment and its cost are considered reasonable); the cost of special equipment; the cost of adaptations to the applicant's accommodation; the cost of care (where care is not provided or available free of charge); fees payable to the Public Guardian or the Court of Protection; other costs associated with administering the applicant's affairs due to a lack of capacity and the reasonable costs of setting up a trust.[110] Future loss of earnings and future loss of earning capacity are compensated for on a multiplier/multiplicand[111] basis and if that approach is impracticable then a lump sum can be awarded.[112] All awards are subject to a maximum value of £500,000.[113]

Claims involving the death of the victim. Where the victim has died as a   **17–34** consequence of the injury the estate can recover only the reasonable funeral expenses.[114] Other claims in cases where the victim has died since sustaining the injury can be brought by qualifying claimants. A qualifying claimant is defined as:

"(a) ... the partner of the deceased, being only, for these purposes:

    (i) a person who was living with the deceased as husband and wife or as a same sex partner in the same household (or a person who would have been so living but for infirmity or ill health preventing physical proximity in the same house) immediately before the date of death and who, unless married to that person or a civil partner of that person, had been so living throughout the two years before that date; or

    (ii) a spouse or civil partner or former spouse of the deceased who was financially supported by him immediately before the date of death; or

(b) a natural parent of the deceased, or a person who was not the natural parent but was accepted by the deceased as a parent within the deceased's family; or

(c) a natural child of the deceased, or a person who was not the natural child but was accepted by the deceased as a child within the deceased's family or was dependant on the deceased"[115]

A claim brought by a qualifying claimant can be refused or reduced on the grounds of the deceased's conduct and character or the conduct and character of the qualifying claimant.[116] Where the victim has died as a consequence of the injury and there is only one qualifying claimant (other than a former spouse), a standard amount of compensation at Level 13 of the scheme is awarded as a

---

[109] para.30.
[110] para.35.
[111] paras 31.
[112] para.33.
[113] para.24.
[114] para.37.
[115] para.38(2).
[116] para.15.

bereavement award.[117] Where the victim has died as a consequence of the injury and there is more than one qualifying claimant (other than a former spouse) then each qualifying claimant receives a standard amount at Level 10 on the tariff.[118] Where a qualifying claimant can establish a financial or physical dependency upon the deceased, additional compensation is awarded.[119] A financial dependency cannot be established where the deceased's normal income was based solely upon social security benefits. Where the deceased was living in the same household as a qualifying claimant, the multiplicand is reduced to reflect the proportion of the deceased's income which he would have spent on his own personal and living expenses. In assessing the dependency no account is taken of a widow(er)'s prospects of remarriage. Where a qualifying claimant was under 18 years of age at the date of the death and was dependent upon the deceased for parental services, additional compensation can be paid for the loss of parental services at an annual rate assessed at Level 5 of the tariff together with other resultant losses. Such annual losses are multiplied by a figure to reflect the time until the qualifying claimant reaches the age of 18, taking into account any relevant contingencies.[120] Where the victim has died other than in consequence of the relevant criminal injury and would have qualified for additional compensation for loss of earnings or special expenses, then a qualifying claimant who can establish a financial dependency, can claim compensation for loss of earnings and special expenses for a period after 28 weeks from the date of the deceased's incapacity.[121] The total amount payable cannot exceed £500,000.[122]

17–35 **Deduction of benefits.** Social security payments relating to the same contingency as the compensation claim are deducted from all awards except tariff based awards.[123] In certain circumstances awards are reduced to take into account payments made under insurance contracts the victim or his parents had personally effected.[124] The value of any compensation awarded by criminal courts and received by the victim is deducted from any award under the scheme.[125] Payments made in respect of civil claims arising out of the incident giving rise to the claim are also deducted from awards.[126] The value of any pension accruing as a result of the injury is taken into account.[127] Where the pension is taxable, one-half of the value of the pension is deducted from any award for loss of earnings; where the pension is not taxable, it is deducted in full from any award for loss of earnings. Similarly if the victim has died pensions are deducted from the claim for financial dependency. Pensions accruing solely as a result of payments made by the victim or a dependant are disregarded.

---

[117] para.39.
[118] para.39.
[119] para.40.
[120] para.42.
[121] para.44.
[122] para.44.
[123] These deductions are made against awards in relation to private medical treatment, costs for special equipment, adaptations to the applicant's accommodation and the cost of paid care.
[124] para.45.
[125] para.48(1)(d).
[126] para.48(1)(c).
[127] para.46.

Procedure for making applications. Applications must be made in writing   **17–36**
on a form obtainable from the Authority.[128] The application should be made as
soon as possible after the incident giving rise to the application and within two
years of the incident.[129] In the first instance applications are considered by claims
officers, who are civil servants, engaged by the Authority. Claims officers have
the power to waive the time-limit for the presentation of applications where: (a)
it is practicable for the application to be considered and it would not have been
reasonable to expect the applicant to present the application within the two-year
period.[130] When a claims officer has determined an application written notice of
the determination is sent to the applicant or his representative.[131] At any time
before a payment of a final award is made a claims officer may reconsider the
decision.[132] Once a final award is accepted the decision is usually regarded as
final but where the victim's medical condition has changed materially so that to
allow the original decision to stand would amount to an injustice, the matter may
be re-opened.

Reviews and appeals. Applicants can apply for a review of a claim officer's   **17–37**
decision or determination of the application.[133] Applications for review must be
made in writing and must be received by the Authority within 90 days of the
decision to be reviewed.[134] An applicant, who is dissatisfied with the decision
taken on review, can apply to appeal to the First-tier Tribunal.[135] On an appeal the
First-tier Tribunal may make such direction as it thinks fit appropriate as to the
decision to be made by a claims officer but any such direction must be in
accordance with the relevant provisions of the Scheme.[136] In addition the First-
tier Tribunal has the power to direct that an interim payment be made or where
it is found that the appeal is frivolous or vexatious it may direct that the
compensation be reduced by such amount as it considers appropriate.[137]

Criminal injury outside United Kingdom. On June 1, 1990, the United   **17–38**
Kingdom ratified the European Convention on the Compensation of Victims of
Violent Crimes. Accordingly it is now possible for British people who sustain
injury as a result of violent crimes on the Continent, or the dependants of such
visitors if they have been injured fatally, to claim compensation from the country
where the crime was committed.

---

[128] para.18.
[129] para.18.
[130] para.18.
[131] para.50.
[132] para.53 and see *R. v CICB Ex p. Williams* [2000] P.I.Q.R. Q339, CA (re-opening a case after an
exacerbation of a back injury under the 1990 scheme).
[133] para.59.
[134] para.59 (both schemes). The time-limit can be varied where a claims officer more senior than the
one who took the original decision considers that an application to waive the time-limit made within
the 90-day period was based on good reasons, or that it would be in the interests of justice to waive
the time-limit.
[135] Formerly known as the Criminal Injuries Compensation Appeals Panel.
[136] para.64.
[137] para.65.

INDEX

LEGAL TAXONOMY
FROM SWEET & MAXWELL

This index has been prepared using Sweet and Maxwell's Legal Taxonomy. Main index entries conform to keywords provided by the Legal Taxonomy except where references to specific documents or non-standard terms (denoted by quotation marks) have been included. These keywords provide a means of identifying similar concepts in other Sweet & Maxwell publications and online services to which keywords from the Legal Taxonomy have been applied. Readers may find some minor differences between terms used in the text and those which appear in the index. Suggestions to *taxonomy@sweetandmaxwell .co.uk*.

(All references are to paragraph number)

Abatement
Rylands v Fletcher liability, 13–111
Absolute liability
See **Strict liability**
Abstraction of water
duty of care, 2–108
Abuse of process
barristers, 9–96—9–97
Acids
dangers on the highway, 10–80
Accident prevention
standard of care, 7–35—7–37
Accidents
carelessness, 1–08—1–10
causation
'but for' test, 6–31
cause of accident not same as cause of damage, 6–36
claimant's own negligence, 6–32
contributory negligence, 6–34—6–36
generally, 6–21—6–30
introduction, 6–14—6–15
joint breach of duty of care, 6–33
'last opportunity' test, 6–37
Accountants
arbitrators, as, 9–43
confidentiality, 9–26
contractual liability, 9–24—9–25
damages, 9–46—9–49
duty of care, 9–23—9–40
fiduciary duty, 9–26
liquidators, as, 9–44—9–45
receivers, as, 9–44—9–45

Accountants—*cont.*
sequestrators, as, 9–44—9–45
standard of care, 9–41—9–42
statutory duties, 9–27—9–33
tortious liability to client, 9–34
tortious liability to third parties, 9–35—9–40
Accrual of cause of action
damages, 5–42
death
carriage by air, 16–73
carriage by rail, 16–74
coal mining subsidence, 16–71—16–72
dependency claims, 16–05—16–70
generally, 16–04
defective premises, 8–136—8–137
limitation periods, 4–150—4–161
Accumulations
Rylands v Fletcher liability, 13–57—13–58
Acquisition of property
solicitors, 9–283—9–286
Act of God
breach of statutory duty, 12–74—12–75
inevitable accident, 4–134
Rylands v Fletcher liability, 13–35—13–39
Acts of commission
See **Wrongful acts**
Acts of omission
See **Wrongful acts**

INDEX

INDEX

Highways—*cont.*
  dangers on the highway—*cont.*
    trees, 10–20—10–22
    trenches, 10–23—10–25
  defective vehicles, 10–245—10–249
  defences, 10–288
  diversion of highway, 10–63
  dogs, 10–283—10–285
  drinking fountain, 10–44
  duty of care, 10–187—10–191
  falling trees, 10–20—10–22
  fixed structures
    barrel drains, 10–39
    existence before dedication of
      highway, 10–30—10–32
    generally, 10–28
    grids, 10–39
    laid by statutory undertakings,
      10–34—10–37
    manholes, 10–39
    raised lids, 10–38
    statutory duty, 10–33
  gratings, 10–28
  Green Cross Code, 10–270
  flashing headlights, 10–240
  guards, 10–45
  hazard warning lights, 10–241
  headlights, 10–239—10–240
  herded animals, 10–281—10–282
  highway authorities
    maintenance, 10–01—10–15
  Highway Code
    braking, slowing and stopping,
      10–213
    cyclists, 10–266
    dogs, 10–285
    flashing headlights, 10–240
    herded animals, 10–281
    horses, 10–280
    introduction, 10–192—10–194
    mobile telephones, 10–217
    motorcyclists, 10–265
    motorways, 10–199—10–202
    pedestrian crossings, 10–276
    pedestrians, 10–268—10–272
    reversing, 10–218
    roundabouts, 10–230
    rule of the road, 10–197
    speed, 10–209
    traffic lights, 10–223
    turning left, 10–229
    turning right, 10–228
  highway maintenance
    common law, at, 10–01

Highways—*cont.*
  highway maintenance—*cont.*
    introduction, 10–01
    land adjacent to highway, 10–09
    reasonable care defence,
      10–12—10–14
    road marks, 10–10—10–11
    siting of road signs, 10–15
    statute, under, 10–02—10–06
    transient hazards, 10–07—10–08
  highway users
    animals, 10–279—10–287
    braking, slowing and stopping,
      10–212—10–214
    children, 10–270
    codefendants, 10–289
    collisions in the road,
      10–220—10–221
    contributory negligence, 10–288
    cyclists, 10–266—10–267
    defective vehicles, 10–245—10–249
    defences, 10–288
    dogs, 10–283—10–285
    duty of care, 10–187—10–191
    Green Cross Code, 10–270
    flashing headlights, 10–240
    hazard warning lights, 10–241
    headlights, 10–239—10–240
    Highway Code, 10–192—10–194
    herded animals, 10–281—10–282
    horns, 10–242—10–244
    horses, 10–279—10–280
    joint and several liability, 10–289
    junctions, 10–226—10–227
    learner drivers, 10–258—10–261
    leaving vehicle on highway,
      10–253—10–257
    led animals, 10–281—10–282
    lights, 10–235—10–238
    look out, 10–215—10–216
    mini-roundabouts, 10–232
    mobile telephones, 10–217
    motorcyclists, 10–265
    motorways, 10–199—10–202
    obstructions, 10–253—10–257
    opening doors, 10–252
    overtaking, 10–204—10–208
    parking on highway,
      10–253—10–257
    passengers, 10–262—10–264
    pedestrian crossings,
      10–273—10–278
    pedestrians, 10–268—10–272
    police, 10–211

[1242]

Personal injury claims—*cont.*
future loss—*cont.*
generally, 5–113
loss of career prospects,
5–125—5–127
loss of earning capacity, 5–113
loss of future earnings,
5–118—5–129
lost years claims, 5–130
multiplicand, 5–118—5–120
multiplier, 5–118—5–121
Ogden tables, 5–121
periodical payments 5–131—5–134
Smith v Manchester damages,
5–128—5–129
gratuitous payments, 5–138
gratuitous services, 5–103—5–107
housing benefits, 5–143
insurance monies, 5–136
interest
Civil Procedure Rules, under, 5–151
generally, 5–147—5–149
taxation, 5–150
interim payments, 5–146
investment advice, 5–102
limitation periods
company no longer in existence,
4–218
constructive knowledge,
4–186—4–188
damage to property, and, 4–195
death, 4–197—4–199
discretion of court, 4–200—4–217
expert advice, 4–189
generally, 4–177
knowledge, 4–182—4–194
'personal injuries', 4–178—4–181
substantial delay, 4–210—4–211
loss of amenity, 5–90—5–92
loss of congenial employment, 5–93
loss of consortium, 5–152
loss of earning capacity, 5–113
loss of earnings
generally, 5–108—5–109
net loss, 5–110—5–112
loss of enjoyment, 5–90
loss of expectation of life, 5–130
loss of future earnings
adjustments, 5–122—5–123
Blamire awards, 5–124
generally, 5–118—5–102
loss of career prospects,
5–125—5–127
multiplicand, 5–118—5–120

Personal injury claims—*cont.*
loss of future earnings—*cont.*
multiplier, 5–118—5–121
Ogden tables, 5–121
Smith v Manchester damages,
5–128—5–129
lost years claims, 5–130
medical expenses, 5–99
multiplicand
adjustment, 5–123
generally, 5–118—5–120
multiplier
adjustment, 5–122
generally, 5–118—5–121
non-pecuniary loss
future events, 5–96—5–97
generally, 5–82—5–83
loss of amenity, 5–90—5–92
loss of congenial employment, 5–93
loss of enjoyment, 5–90
loss of expectation of life,
5–94—5–95
pain and suffering, 5–84—5–89
potential events, 5–96—5–97
psychiatric injury, 5–85
nursing expenses, 5–99
Ogden tables, 5–121
pain and suffering
appeals from awards, 5–88
loss of amenity, and, 5–89
object of damages, 5–86—5–87
psychiatric injury, 5–85
symptoms, 5–84
parasitic damages, 5–156—5–157
Part 36 offers, 5–151
pecuniary loss
actual financial loss, 5–99—5–112
benefits received, 5–135—5–144
Blamire awards, 5–124
care expenses, 5–97
clothes, 5–99
divorce, 5–101
future loss, 5–113—5–134
future probabilities, 5–100
generally, 5–98
gratuitously provided care and
assistance, 5–103—5–107
investment advice, 5–102
loss of career prospects,
5–125—5–127
loss of earning capacity, 5–113
loss of earnings, 5–108—5–112
loss of future earnings,
5–118—5–129